The
MVR Access
and
Decoder Digest

2013 Edition

The Complete National Reference to
State Motor Vehicle Records – Including Access, Content,
and State Conviction Code Tables

Also Includes Content From the U.S. Motor Vehicle Reference Book

©2013 By BRB Publications, Inc.
www.brbpublications.com
www.mvrdecoder.com

POWERED BY
BRB PUBLICATIONS

The MVR Access and Decoder Digest

©2013 By BRB Publications, Inc.
PO Box 27869
Tempe, AZ 85285-7869
800 929-3811 • Fax 800 929-4981
www.brbpublications.com

Editor: Michael L. Sankey
Cover Design: Robin Fox & Associates
ISBN: 978-0-9885636-1-2

Cataloging-in-Publication Data
    (Provided by Quality Books, Inc.)

    Sankey, Michael L., 1949-
        The MVR access and decoder digest : the complete
    national reference to state motor vehicle records,
    including access, content, and state conviction code
    tables / [author, Michael L. Sankey]. -- 2013 ed.
        p. cm.
        ISBN 978-0-9885636-1-2

        1. Automobile drivers' records--United States--States
    --Information services--Directories. 2. Drivers'
    licenses--United States--States--Information services--
    Directories. 3. Traffic violations--United States--
    States--Information services--Directories.   I. BRB
    Publications. II. Title.

    HE5614.2.M88 2013   364.1'47
                               QBI13-600003

Table of Contents

Acknowledgements

The objective of this publication is to help you access and understand motor vehicle records and decipher the information found on driving records. Keeping this content accurate and up-to-date involves many, many hours of research and fact-checking.

With this in mind ... I wish to acknowledge and sincerely thank certain people who continually play a major role in the publication of this book—

The Various State Motor Vehicle Agency Administrators and their staffs
Every year certain individual state administrators assist with the compilation and verification of the detailed facts within this book that pertain to their state. They insure the information is accurate and timely.
I wish to sincerely thank each of you for not only your time, but also because you genuinely care. It is indeed a pleasure to work with you. This publication would not exist without your help and ongoing support over the years.

The American Association of Motor Vehicle Administrators (AAMVA)
The good people at AAMVA provide to this book their copyrighted AAMVA Code Dictionary (ACD). Many of the programs and agreements mentioned in this book are administered to a large degree by AAMVA.
I sincerely wish to thank the AAMVA for not only the permission to reprint, but also for the ongoing guidance they have provided over the past24 years.

Sincerely,

Michael Sankey
January 2013

Introduction

The MVR Access and Decoder Digest Book is an all-authoritative resource used to find accurate information about state and federal regulations affecting the access and the content of motor vehicle records. Information about each state's policies and procedures regarding driver licensing issuance, suspensions and revocations, financial responsibility issues, and vehicle or vessel title and registration record access is crucial to many industries. *The Decoder* is an extremely valuable reference for those needs as well.

Although specifically designed for the insurance and trucking industries, employers of drivers, attorneys, and state administrators, this jurisdictional guide is useful to any business or individual working with motor vehicle records.

New for 2013: All MVR Content is Now in One Book

If you have been a past purchaser of our motor vehicle books you are probably aware there have always been two books about motor vehicle data. Actually, we have been printing two different books annually since 1989.

In an effort to make a more affordable product and to save paper, this year we have combined the *U.S. Motor Vehicle Reference Book* (formerly known as *The MVR Book*) and *The MVR Access and Decoder Digest* into one complete title using the latter's name.

We feel the new book and its new format will be much easier to use. If you have any questions or comments, feel free to pass them along to us, please send to brb@brbpublications.com.

How to Navigate and Use This Book

To give you a better understanding of the content provided herein, below is an overview of each section in the book.

A Guide to Motor Vehicle Records

This short but informative section provides a detailed blueprint on what you need to know about obtaining motor vehicle records. Each type of motor vehicle record is analyzed including driving records, accident reports, status reports on drivers; and title, ownership and lien records on vehicle and vessels. Other topics include and overview of access methods, the type of data that may or may not appear on records, searching tips, and the affect that certain federal laws have made on record content and access.

The State Chapters

All states and the District of Columbia are examined within individual chapters. Within each state chapter there are ten sections presented in this order—

1. Driver's License Format, Issuance and Renewal
2. Vehicle Insurance, Title and Registration Facts
3. Alcohol and Drug Testing, and Withdrawal Disqualifications
4. Record Access: Laws, Rules, and Forms
5. Access to Driver-Related Records
6. Access to Vehicle-Related Records
7. Access to Vessel-Related Records
8. Driving Record Content and Reciprocity
9. Codes for License Classes, Restrictions, and Endorsements (and Other Codes or Abbreviations in use)
10. The State Conviction Table (with ACD, Points, Statute, Full Descriptions When Available)

We suggest you take a few minutes and review a state chapter to become familiar with the format. Later, this will help you quickly find the information you need.

For example, Access to Driver-Related Records embraces not only the various access methods to obtain records, but also special programs a state might provide such as a free or low cost *Status Check* of a driver's license or a vehicle registration. Plus there is a detailed description for those states that offer a monitoring or notification program to employers or insurance companies to track driver incidents. In the Driving Record Content and Reciprocity portion, look for the *What's On or Not On the Driving Record* section for details about convictions or actions that are reported, or not reported. You may be surprised by the lack of consistency from state to state.

The AAMVA Code Dictionary (ACD)

The ACD Table is the coding tool used to exchange conviction and withdrawal information among the states' driving record repositories and to several national indices. Many states show the corresponding ACD with a conviction on their driving records, especially for out-of-state violations. Knowing what a specific ACD Code means can be a very helpful indication of the meaning of a questionable violation.

The ACD Code Table is owned and administered by the AAMVA which stands for the American Association of Motor Vehicle Administrators. They have graciously permitted us to reprint their copyrighted code table in this publication.

The SMS Motor Carrier Violation Tables

The U.S. Department of Transportation's Federal Motor Carrier Safety Administration (FMCSA) administers a Comprehensive Safety Analysis (CSA) program known as the Motor Carrier Safety Measurement System (SMS). The SMS quantifies the on-road safety performance of carriers and drivers to identify candidates for interventions, determine the specific safety problems that a carrier or driver exhibits, and to monitor whether safety problems are improving or worsening.

SMS uses a motor carrier's data from roadside inspections, including all safety-based violations, State-reported crashes, and the Federal motor carrier census to quantify performance in the seven Behavior Analysis and Safety Improvement Categories (BASICs).

This section presents an overview of SMS, how to obtain motor carrier assessment ratings, and the BASICs violation tables including the severity weighting for each violation.

The Importance of the Appendix

Quite simply, the Appendix can answer a lot of questions.

- **Appendix 1 CDL and Federal Regulations** is an extremely useful section. Beside a review of past and **current legislation**, this section spells out many of the **federal regulations** affecting commercial drivers including licensing, testing, data retention, and mandatory CDL disqualifications.

- Appendix 2 is a copy of the text from the **Driver's Privacy Protection Act (DPPA)**

- Appendix 3 provides an overview of **significant organizations agreements and programs** that affect the access of motor vehicle records. The knowledge of how these agencies and agreements affect the states' driving and vehicle record practices and procedures is very useful.

- Appendix 4 is the **License Format and Driving Record Fees Table**. This useful tool is a quick reference showing the makeup of the numbering formation used by each state's driver's license document PLUS a list of the fees states' charge for a driving records, per access method.

- Appendix 5 is the **State Reciprocity of Conviction Information for Non-CDL Drivers.** Using data found in the state profiles, this tool provides a quick, at-a-glance synopsis of what data transfers on a non-CDL driving record when a driver moves from one state to another, and what shows on a home state record if a driver receives a ticket/conviction when "out-of-state."

We strongly urge readers to review and refer to these pages.

A Guide to Motor Vehicle Records

What Does the Term MVR Mean?

The acronym MVR is most often known as the slang term used for "driving record." But MVR is actually taken from the phrase "Moving Violation Record" or "Motor Vehicle Record." Hence, the term may often also refer to a vehicle registration or title record.

The key fact to keep in mind here is that when communicating with someone at a state motor vehicle department (DMV) about records, be sure you are clear on exactly what record you have in mind. For example, a state motor vehicle official could hear the words motor vehicle record or MVR and may think you are referring to a vehicle title or registration record or a status record, yet you may be referring to a driving record.

There are Inconsistencies and Idiosyncrasies Between the States Regarding Record Access and Data Reported

Who is legally permitted to access driving or vehicle records? What degree of authority is needed to obtain a full history record? What data is found on a record? What information is masked from the public's view?

The answer to many of the above questions is subject to the individual state statutes, state administrative rules and regulations, and compliance with federal laws. The type of data that appears on one state's driving record may not appear on record provided by a bordering state. Who may access a record and to what degree can and does vary from state to state. In addition, the manner in which states communicate internally or externally and their policies of reciprocity reflect the diversity that contributes to making each state unique.

All of the facts contribute to the need for a centralized resource of these state idiosyncrasies – hence this book.

Keep in mind each state maintains its own separate, unique database(s) of licensed drivers, vehicle registrations, vehicle ownership, accident reports, and other associated records. There is not a national, all-inclusive database of motor vehicle records. However, there are several national indices of records, as explained in the Appendix.

One of the most instrumental laws affecting motor vehicle records is the federal Driver's Privacy Protection Act (DPPA).

The Affect of DPPA on Record Access

The Driver's Privacy Protection Act (DPPA) is a 1996 federal law that had an important influence on motor vehicle records. It mandated the states to pass laws or administrative rules to differentiate between permissible and non-permissible use requests to determine if personal information can be released on motor vehicle records. DPPA designates fourteen permissible uses. Personal Information is defined as "...information that identifies an individual, including an individual's photograph, social security number, driver identification number, name, address (but not the 5-digit zip code), telephone number, and medical or disability information." Records with personal information are only given to those with a listed permissible use OR with the written consent of the driver.

All states are in compliance with the DPPA standards. However, these standards while extensive are only minimal. States can be more restrictive than DPPA. For example some states refuse to disclose the personal information contained on the records to anyone from the public sector, even with consent of the subject. On the other hand nearly half of the states sell sanitized records (with personal information redacted) to casual requesters (requesters without a permissible use). In some states, sanitized records can be viewed or purchased online.

A copy of DPPA including the permissible uses can be found in the Appendix. A copy of DPPA is online at www.mvrdecoder.com and at http://uscode.house.gov/download/pls/18C123.txt.

The rest of this chapter examines aspects and searching tips on the various types of motor vehicle records and closes with a discussion on using a record vendor.

Driving Records

Accessing driving records is big business. An estimated 700,000+ driving record requests are processed daily in the U.S. With the average fee for an individual state driving record over $8.00, the states receive well over $5,000,000 daily in revenue from driving record sales.

Key Data Found on Driving Records

A driving record provides a historical index of a driver's moving violation convictions, accidents, and license sanctions. Depending on the state's record reporting procedure, the record may show activity from three years to a lifetime.

Nationally the information found on each state's record is standardized to a point, but not all states provide the same information and certainly not in the same format.

Traffic Violations and Accidents

At the core of the driving record is a list of traffic tickets of moving violations which result in a conviction.

Typical information on a driving record will often include date of violation, date of conviction, location of incident, points assessed, and description or descriptive code of the violation. Other possible pieces of information include the state statute related to the violation, the type of court, and court location. Accident involvement is also reported, but reporting who is at fault is spotty at best. Generally, the driver at fault will have a citation on the same date appearing on the record.

The only time a *pending* conviction will appear on a record is if the incident involves a situation that triggers an immediate suspension — such as if alcohol-related — or if an alleged violator fails to appear in court.

Withdrawals and Administrative Actions

Motor vehicle officials often use the term *withdrawal actions* when referring to restrictive action taken against an individual's privilege to drive. These actions include suspensions, revocations, disqualifications, and denials. Sometimes a withdrawal may be triggered by a statue per a specific violation or series of violations. Or perhaps the withdrawal and level of action taken may be administered by a judge or DMV official.

The information listed on a driving record typically includes the history of withdrawals with effective dates or when the driver is eligible to be reinstated. Some states cloak information of prior withdrawals, depending on who is the requester.

Personal Information about the Driver

As previously mentioned, the release of personal information on motor vehicle records is governed by the DPPA. To be clear, DPPA does not determine who can obtain a motor vehicle record. Instead DPPA regulates who can receive records with personal information by limiting record release to only those with a listed permissible use, or with the written consent of the driver.

Thus the disclosure of personal information is a record reporting aspect that is inconsistent from state-to-state. Nationally, Social Security Numbers and medical information are redacted and not released to record requesters. But in practice, the personal information found on a driving record may or may not include the licensee's address, height, weight, date of birth or medical information. The words *may include* are important because as mentioned above some states will not release personal information regardless if the requester has a DPPA permissible use or if consent of the subject is given.

The Appendix contains a copy of the DPPA which lists the fourteen listed permissible uses.

Record Reporting and Data Retention

How far back information is reported on records and what is actually reported are other common variables that change from state to state. The exception is record reporting on commercially licensed drivers, which is more precise.

In most states, the standard reporting period generally coincides with insurance purpose requests. This standard is at least three years of moving violations and five to ten years for administrative actions. However, a number of states provide a longer time period on their standard records, and many states offer additional options for more in-depth records. For example, besides the standard three-year record Georgia also provides a seven-year record, Vermont an eight-year record, and Pennsylvania a complete (lifetime) record. Extra fees are often involved.

What is reported can also vary widely. Some states do not report certain low-level moving violations, especially to insurance companies. Accident reporting is not consistent, neither is the length of time shown for previous suspensions or major convictions such as alcohol-related incidents.

How long the states keep record data varies also. But, there are federally mandated data retention and reporting standards for commercial drivers per Federal regulations, most recently updated by provision in the Motor Carrier Safety Improvement Act (MCSIA). This Act and the mandated standards are examined in the Appendix.

The Different Types of Driving Records

The data found on a driving record may vary by the record type. Depending on the state, driving records sometimes can be requested by a category type. These include—

- Employment (as a commercially-licensed driver)
- Non-Employment
- Insurance
- Certified

An employment record usually will only report actions occurring when an individual with a commercial driver's license (CDL) is driving a commercial motor vehicle (CMV). A non-employment record usually excludes CMV-related incidents. An insurance record may be filtered so not to include certain low-impact moving violations (such as a speeding ticket less than 10 mph over the limit) or even accident involvement. Certified records are paper records with a state seal affixed. Sometimes records can be a combination of insurance and employment, or for a specific type employment. For example, the state of Washington offers eight different types of driving records.

Record Access Methods

Access methods fall into two overall categories: manual and electronic. Typically, a request for an individual's driving record must include the full name with middle initial, driver license number, and/or date of birth. Similarly, vehicle record requests require the name and plate number and/or VIN. States do not perform a *name only* search for the public.

Manual Access

Manual access request methods include mail, in person, fax, and telephone. Every state does not offer every access method. Most do not offer access records by telephone or fax, but some do for approved, ongoing accounts (MO, NV, and OR for example). There are at least four states that do NOT provide a centralized counter service to the general public (CA, ID, MI, and WI). In some states, the county or local licensing agencies provide record access services, but often this service is only available to the record holders.

Electronic Access

All states offer electronic access. The methods can vary by the way orders are grouped or submitted, and by the media type. In general, there are two types of electronic access: batch and interactive.

Batch processing is when a large group of record requests — with the specific names and necessary identifiers — are submitted at once. Results are "picked up" hours later. The means of access is usually the web, but a couple of states use a private dial-up system, and some process requests by cartridge when asked. Batch processing should not be confused with **bulk access**, which is the purchase of a partial or complete database of records and not a request of records using a list of specified names.

Interactive processing occurs when individual requests are sent and results are returned immediately, often in rapid succession. This method is popular when a quick decision needs to be made about hiring or about the issuance of a new insurance policy.

Over 50% of the states provide a **monitoring service** for designated entities such as employers or insurance companies. The participating party submits a list of driver names to the state agency. The state agency will then inform the requester when there is activity on a submitted person's record. Descriptions of these programs are found in the individual state chapters.

Another progressive trend is allowing license holders to view their records online, with a PIN or coded password.

Driving Record Fees

The fees that states charge to access their motor vehicle records vary widely. There is no consistency. For example, the state fee for an electronic driving record ranges from $2.00 in California to $27.50 in Oklahoma. A similar range exists for manually processed records. Overall the average fee for electronic access is just over $8.40.

A state's fee structure may vary by the type of access method. At least seventeen states charge more per record for electronic access than for manual, and six states charge more for manual processing than electronic. For example, Louisiana charges $15.00 for a manual record and $6.00 for an electronic record, while Montana charges $7.24 for an electronic record and $4.00 for a manual record.

If access is online, states may also charge set-up fees or annual fees to be an online subscriber. Generally, these fees are under $100 per year. Also, some states (see California) require extensive deposits or even performance bonds to be placed as collateral.

The License Status Check

Another useful motor vehicle record is the license status report. Taken from portions of a driving record, the license status indicates three important pieces of information—

1. The type or class of license issued, which indicates what types of vehicles (commercial, non-commercial, etc.) can be operated. The various commercial license classes further indicate the size and/or weight of the vehicle licensed to be driven.

2. Any special conditions placed on the license holder. These permissions and limitations are known as endorsements and

restrictions. A typical restriction is a requirement to use "corrective lenses" when driving. Another example is a commercial license may have an endorsement that regulates if hazardous material can be hauled.

3. If the license is valid or under suspension or revocation.

A number of states offer status checks online and the list is growing. Some checks are accessible for free and some for a fee, as indicated within the state chapters.

Regulations on Commercial Drivers

Since April 1, 1992, persons who drive a commercial motor vehicle (CMV) involving interstate, intrastate, or foreign commerce drivers are required to have a commercial driver's license (CDL). Derek Hinton, President of DOTJOBHistory.com, estimates there are over 3.5 million licensed commercial drivers operating in the U.S.

The Federal Motor Carrier Safety Administration (FMSCA) has developed and issued standards for testing and licensing CMV drivers. As part of these standards, states are required to issue CDLs to CMV drivers only after the drivers have passed knowledge and skills tests administered by the state, related to the type of vehicle to be operated. The Code of Federal Regulations Title 49, Part 383 (49 CFR § 383) designates specific CDL license classifications depending upon the type of commercial vehicle operated.

CDL drivers must pass additional tests to obtain an endorsement from a state in order to operate specialty vehicles such as tankers, double or triple trailers, or to operate vehicles that haul hazardous materials. Each state chapter provides a complete list of commercial (and non-commercial) license classes, endorsements, and other state-imposed license restrictions.

The Code of Federal Regulations Title 49, Part 383 (49 CFR § 383.51) also provides standards for maintaining and checking conviction records of commercial drivers, and provides penalties for traffic convictions by commercial drivers.

Additional information about the regulations placed on commercial drivers and CDLs, including specific penalties and record keeping procedures, is found in Appendix 1.

The ACD Codes — A Key Component to State Reciprocity

As shown in this book, each state has unique conviction reporting language and codes inherent to their motor vehicle statutes and specific violation language. Per compliance with the programs and compacts described in the Appendix, each state must communicate with one another or with a centralized index regarding commercial drivers, problem drivers, out-of state actions, and license disqualifications. These questions then surface—*How do states know what the conviction codes from other states mean and how do they translate this information into their own language and code set?*

The answer is the states utilize the AAMVA Code Dictionary (ACD) as a translation table. The primary function of the ACD Codes is to enable the Commercial Driver's License Information System (CDLIS) to exchange convictions and withdrawals. Other applications, such as the Problem Driver Pointer System (PDPS), use the codes as well.

So in practice, the ACD Code System is used to exchange conviction and withdrawal information between the states' driver licensing authorities. A number of states have incorporated the ACD Codes within their own conviction and action tables. For example, Alaska, has converted their conviction table to the ACD Code system as their primary conviction code table. Many states use the ACD to indicate out-of-state convictions on driving records.

Therefore, the knowledge of what a specific ACD Code means can be a helpful indication when deciphering the meaning of a conviction or withdrawal action.

The ACD Codes appear as a chapter in the book. Both CDLIS and PDPS are reviewed in depth in Appendix 3.

Accident Reports

Many states (Texas and Missouri, for example) prefer to use the term *crash reports* rather than *accident reports*. For the sake of clarity, we will refer to these incidents as *accidents* here. An accident report is created when a either there is an injury or death, or a designated threshold of property damage is reached. There are two different accident records filed; 1) by the citizens involved and 2) by the investigating officers. Copies of citizens' accident reports are not usually available to the public. In the state chapter when text refers to obtaining accident reports, this is generally discussing how to obtain the report from the investigating officer.

A good rule of thumb is that accident records must be obtained from the agency that investigated the incident. When accident records are maintained by the same agency that holds driving records, the DPPA guidelines are followed with regards to honoring record requests. There is no overall national database of historical accident information maintained by either a government agency or by private enterprise.

Typical information found on a state accident report includes drivers' addresses and license numbers as well as a description of the incident. Only a handful of states offer online access to accident reports.

Vehicle Records

Vehicle records include detailed information about two categories of records: ownership including titles and liens; and registration of the vehicles. Generally, vehicle ownership and title records can be ordered either as a record of current ownership, or as a historical record showing all previous owners. Title data can also indicate if a vehicle was at one time a junk vehicle or if the vehicle was once a subject of title washing (previously branded as a salvage or flood-damaged vehicle), or perhaps previously a government vehicle. Information found on records can include vehicle identification numbers (VINs), license plate or tag numbers, and address information of owners and lienholders. Registration records are issued annually and will also provide personal information regarding whom the vehicle is registered to. Certain entities are entitled to search for registration information by the license plate number.

Never assume the same state agency that administers driving records also administers vehicle records, such as in Arizona or Florida. In a number of states vehicle records are controlled by an entirely different state government department or division, such as in Texas and Oklahoma. Finding lien records can also vary from state-to-state. In some states, liens on vehicles are recorded at the county level and in some states at the Secretary of State's Office where UCCs are filed.

If vehicle records are administered by the same agency that handles driver records, then there will be similarities between accessing driving records and vehicle records, especially in regard to fees and forms. Regardless of which state agency oversees the record-keeping, the data found on records is regulated by the federal DPPA.

Vehicle record data that includes personal identifiers is never sold for marketing purposes, per DPPA.

The Importance of the VIN

VIN stands for *Vehicle identification Number*. This number is internationally recognized as the way to identify an individual vehicle. When buying a used vehicle, many consumers and dealers check the history of a VIN with a private vendor to help make an informed decision about the quality and value of the vehicle. Vehicles have a metal plate stamped with unique VIN located somewhere on the dashboard or door. The VIN may also be found attached to other locations on the vehicle.

A VIN consists of 17 characters (vehicles manufactured before 1981 may have fewer characters) in a highly coded but strict format structure based on the manufacturers and vehicle models. A code table showing all the possible meanings for each position is a very extensive document, and this list is added to frequently. Several excellent Web resources to decode a VIN include—

- www.autocheck.com
- www.cardetective.com
- www.carfax.com
- www.decodethis.com

Watercraft Records

Often the state agency that administers vehicle records also administers vessel records, but that is not always the case. In some states vessel records are controlled by an entirely different state government department or division. Examples include the Department of Wildlife and Parks in Kansas and the Department of Natural Resources in Minnesota.

An important fact to keep in mind is not all states title watercraft. Those that do generally only require titles if the vessel is over a certain length or if motorized. Requirements similar to motor vehicles maybe imposed on vessels when registration is mandatory.

When watercraft and watercraft records are governed by a different government agency, the agency's access policies are usually not governed by DPPA. In these states, access is governed by administrative rules or by statute and the policy can be stricter or less restrictive than DPPA.

Similar to liens on vehicles, liens on watercraft can be recorded locally or at the Secretary of State's Office. The state chapters provide details about each state's access procedures to watercraft records.

About Large Commercial Vessels

Vessels weighing more than five tons are registered with the U.S. Coast Guard, www.st.nmfs.noaa.gov/st1/CoastGuard/. Another handy resource to search for larger vessels, or to search by lien or title, is the Coast Guard's National Vessel Documentation Center found at www.uscg.mil/hq/cg5/nvdc/.

Using a Driving Record Vendor

The vast majority of permissible use requesters who have high volume needs for driving records (such as the insurance and trucking industries) use the services of record vendors. Driving record vendors are sophisticated service bureaus providing access to records for a small service fee per record. There are many advantages of using a driving record —

- One-Stop Shopping for All States
- Speed of Access - Often Instantaneously
- Experts on State Compliance Issues
- Help with Reading or Deciphering Records
- Technical Communication Experts
- Aware of State Changes
- Provide Uniform Record Format
- Provide Customized Match Back Data Fields
- Thrive in a "How Fast - How Much" Environment

But not all driving record vendors are alike. Nor do they all work with every *type* of record requesters. Some vendors specialize in the occasional users; others specialize in servicing users with high demands. Do a Google search on *driving records* or *driving record check* and you will find many service companies, but you will not going to find the industry icons. The fact is there are very few driving record vendors who offer deep volume pricing with true national coverage. And many of these large vendors limit their services to specific high volume clientele, such as to only the insurance industry or motor carrier industry. In fact only a few of the larger vendors will work with pre-employment screening companies. You won't often find Google ads posted by these vendors.

Where to Find a Driving Record Vendor

If you are looking for a driving record vendor for a one-time or limited situation, then certainly use one of the consumer services found when doing a Google search. But be careful and be cognizant of the compliance issues that we have taken great pains to explain throughout this book.

If you are in a business that heavily uses driving records and you are in search of a vendor or new vendor, here is an idea. Check with a trade association that your company may or should belong to. Vendors like to support their clients and often join an association to stay better connected. For example, if you are a pre-employment screening company, check the membership list for the National Association of Professional Background Screeners at www.napbs.com.

Another way to find the names of some of the nation's leading driving record vendors is to go to the BRB Publications' web page at www.brbpublications.com and follow the menu options to find a list of companies that provide motor vehicle related record searches.

The bottom line about a record vendor is there is no doubt they provide excellent services with a minimal fees — providing you find the right vendor to match your particular needs.

Alabama

Administration	Important Telephone and Web Contacts
Major Terry Chapman, Division Chief Driver License Division 301 S Ripley St, Montgomery AL 36104 334-353-1470 http://dps.alabama.gov Brenda Coone, Director - Motor Vehicle Division Department of Revenue 50 N Ripley St, 1202 Gordon Persons Bldg Montgomery AL 36104 334-242-9000 www.revenue.alabama.gov/motorvehicle/index.html	Driver Licensing....................................334-242-4400 Safety Responsibility..............................334-242-4222 Commercial Driver License ....334-242-3427 General Registration............... 334-242-9006 or 9007 Vehicle Records ....334-353-1604 IRP ....334-242-2999 State Dept of Insurance ....334-269-3550 Highway Patrol, DPS ....334-242-4393 State statutes look-up at: www.legislature.state.al.us Motor Vehicle Rulebook is found at: www.revenue.alabama.gov/motorvehicle/mvrules/mvrulebook.html

Driver's License Format, Issuance and Renewal

Classes, Restrictions and Endorsements Appear After the Driving Record Content Section

License Format

Seven numbers; there is no code or sequential arrangement which determines the characters making the license number.

Document Appearance

In late 2011, the DPS began issuing a new Real-ID compliant driver license and ID card known as the Star ID. This is optional for new licensees and renewals. The appearance of this card varies slightly from the Digitized Document (see below) issued since 2005. STAR ID documents have a gold star in the upper left corner to make them easily recognizable as Real-ID compliant.

Current Digitized Documents

This digitized license has been issued since late 2005 and most recently was upgraded to be issued also as a Star ID document.

Security Characteristics: The new cards have a laminate coating. Features include a 2-D barcode, magnetic stripe, digitized portrait image, signature and various security features including a optically variable image of the state outline text that changes color as license is tilted. The new card design includes the state capital and state seal.

Position of Photo: Bottom left, for under 18/21 bottom middle.

Minor Age Driver Locator: The "Under 18/21" driver licenses and identification cards are issued in a vertical format. Cards display the words "UNDER 18 UNTIL" or "UNDER 21 UNTIL" followed by the date the cardholder will turn 18 or 21 in bold red text. This text is positioned vertically next to the portrait.

CDL Indicator: The words "Commercial Driver License" appear on the card.

Older Documents - pre 2005

Security Characteristics: A red state seal appears.

Position of Photo: Bottom left.

Minor Age Driver Locator: A heat embossed star.

CDL Indicator: "CDL" is bordered w/ broken lines and right of DOB.

Issuance

Location of Requirements for Proof of Identity:

http://dps.alabama.gov/Home/wfContent.aspx?ID=80&PLH1=plhDriverLicense-StarIDDocumentList

Age Requirements

A Learner's License is required at age fifteen and valid for four years or until driving test is passed. The minimum age for an operator's permit is sixteen; eighteen for intra-state CDL; twenty-one for CDL; fourteen for motor driven cycle; and twelve for a vessel. The Graduated Driver License Plan went through changes effective July 2010. See http://dps.alabama.gov/Documents/Documents/DriverLicense-GraduatedDLProgram.pdf.

Residency

New residents must apply within thirty days of establishing residency.

Renewal

Four years from date of issue, driver keeps same number when renewing. Military personnel, their dependents, students or other licensed drivers who are temporarily out-of-state due to job requirements may be eligible to apply if they have obtained an AL driver license with photo and signature within past 4 years. The license must be renewed every four years. An Alabama driver license may be renewed without examination within a three-year period after it has expired. A license may be renewed in person by a Probate Judge or at a DPS Licensing Examine Office, one is found in each county. Renewal is not available online.

Note the new STAR ID DL is issued only at the DPS Driver License examining offices.

Elderly-Related Restrictions

None are indicated by the DPS.

Vehicle Insurance, Title and Registration Facts

See the Motor Vehicle Rulebook at: www.revenue.alabama.gov/motorvehicle/mvrules/mvrulebook.html

Insurance and Financial Responsibility

Self-propelled vehicles registered in Alabama are required to have liability insurance coverage and proof of coverage must be carried in the vehicle. The mandatory insurance provisions are in the amounts of $25,000/$50,000/$25,000, or must be covered by a motor vehicle liability bond or cash deposit of $50,000. Proof of coverage must be presented at all traffic stops and accidents or the vehicle's tag registration will be suspended. Proof is required with an SR-22 if convicted of having no insurance, if judgment is rendered following an accident and for revocation actions. Violations of the state's mandatory insurance laws are punishable with a fine of up to $500 for the first conviction and $1,000 and/or suspension of the driver's license for up to 6 months for each subsequent conviction.

Registration

Motor vehicles are registered through the offices of county license plate issuing officials. Trucks and truck tractors operating to points outside the State of Alabama are registered through the Department of Revenue, Motor Vehicle Division, Motor Carrier Services Unit. Motor vehicles owned by the state, county, municipality, public utility departments, or volunteer fire departments are registered through the Department of Revenue, Motor Vehicle Division, Registration Section.

Alabama law does not require registrants to show proof of insurance prior to registering a vehicle. Registrants are required, however, to maintain liability insurance by a company licensed to conduct business in Alabama. Registrants affirm, by signing the registration receipt, that the vehicle being registered is insured.

Renewal

Alabama registers vehicles under a staggered registration system, January through November, based on the first letter of the owner's last name. For example, someone whose last name begins with the letters F, G, or N is required to re-register his/her vehicle in the month of **April**, with the previous registration expiring on **April 30**. Leased vehicles, commercial, and fleet vehicles are subject to renewal in the months of October and November.

Since January 1, 2005, the expiration date for motor vehicle is the last day of the renewal month. Prior to that date, Alabama law provided that registrations expire on the last day of the month prior to the renewal month. Forty-four of the sixty-seven Alabama counties offer online vehicle registration.

For New Residents

Section 40-12-262, Code of Alabama provides that the owner of a non-commercial vehicle with a **valid registration** from another jurisdiction has thirty days from the date entered the state to register the vehicle. Also, the vehicle owner has twenty calendar days from the date of vehicle purchase or acquisition to register the vehicle without penalty.

Inspections and Emissions Testing

Alabama has no state-required annual inspection or emissions test; however, a prerequisite to titling is a mandatory Identification Inspection. Also, cities have the right to impose either type of test.

Passenger Plate Facts

There is one plate with two decals (MO) (YR). The first number(s) of the plate designates the county. The coding runs as follows: 1 is Jefferson, 2 is Mobile, 3 is Montgomery; numbers 4 through 67 correspond to an alphabetical listing of the remaining counties, thus 4 is Autauga and 67 is Winston. There is no city code. The tags follow the owner when sold.

Withdrawal Sanctions, and Alcohol and Drug Testing

Alcohol and Chemical Testing

Alabama has provisions for urine, blood, and breath testing. The intoxication limit level is .08 BAC, .04 for drivers of a CMV, .02 for school bus and day care drivers, and .02 for persons under 21 years of age. The state also has an implied-consent violation. Riding a horse or bicycle under the influence is also considered illegal.

Suspensions and Revocations

See the Appendix for a list of the federally mandated disqualifications for offenses occurring in a CMV per MCSIA.

Driving Under the Influence

No Previous Convictions ....Ninety-days minimum suspension.
One Previous Conviction within 5 years...............................One-year revocation.
Two Previous Convictions within 5 years ....Three-year revocation.
More Than Three Previous Convictions (Class C felony) ....Five-year revocation.
CDL - No Previous Convictions not Carrying Hazardous Material......One-year disqualification.
CDL - No Previous Convictions Carrying Hazardous Material............Three-year disqualification.
CDL - Previous Convictions not Carrying Hazardous Material ....Lifetime disqualification.
CDL - Previous Convictions Carrying Hazardous Material.................Lifetime disqualification

Violations by a holder of a GDL may be suspended 60 days for conviction of the following:

- Driving on the wrong side of the road
- Fleeing or attempting to elude a law enforcement officer
- Failure to give information or render aid
- Illegal passing
- Racing
- Reckless driving
- Second moving traffic violation
- Or any other offense where four or more points are assessed.

Other Violations Which May Result in Suspension

- DUI-Drugs
- Altering or Mutilating License
- Attempting to Elude a Peace Officer
- Racing on Highway
- Failure to Appear or Pay
- Failure to Pay Child Support Payments
- Points Accumulation (see last page in this chapter)
- DUI-Combined Alcohol and Other Controlled Substances
- DUI-Under Influence of any Substance Which Impairs Mental or Physical Faculties
- Refusal to Submit to Chemical Test

- 2 Convictions of License Restriction Violation
- Minor in Possession of Alcohol Beverage

Other Violations Which May Result in Mandatory Revocation

- Hit-and-Run/Leaving the Scene
- Manslaughter; Second-Degree Murder with Vehicle
- Commission of Felony Involving Operation of Vehicle
- Homicide by Vehicle
- Unauthorized use of Motor Vehicle Belonging to Another
- Perjury/False Statement Relating to Ownership or DL Laws
- Three Reckless-Driving Convictions in Twelve Months
- Two Convictions for Driving While License Suspended, Revoked, or Cancelled

Violations Which May Result in CDL Disqualification

- Accident Resulting in a Fatality in a CMV
- CDL Used in Commission of a Felony
- Two or More Serious Violations in a CMV (3 yr period)
- Railroad Violations in a CMV DUI .04 or More in CMV
- DUI Any Substance in CMV
- Refusing the Chemical Test in a CMV
- Admin Per Se .04 or More in CMV

Reinstatement Requirements

Suspension $100 reinstatement fee and time lapse.

Revocations $175 reinstatement fee; time lapse; proof of financial responsibility; and re-examination.

Extra   Fee is $275 if alcohol involved and $25 additional fee if drug-related. Other reinstatement fees include $50.00 for non-payment of child support; $50.00 fee if failed to surrender license within thirty days. Vessel reinstatements are $50.00.

Record Access: Laws, Rules, and Forms

Note: This Section Applies to Both Driver and Vehicle Records.

Governing Statutes and Rules

State Statutes: www.legislature.state.al.us

Motor Vehicle Rulebook:

www.revenue.alabama.gov/motorvehicle/mvrules/mvrulebook.html
The state adopted Rule 810-5-1-.485 to implement and adopt the provisions and permissible uses per DPPA (Public Law 103-322). Note *personal information* is defined as "information that identifies a person, including an individual's social security number, name, address (but not the 5-digit zip code), telephone number, and medical or disability information.

Driving Records: Personal information is released to those entities qualified per DPPA and approved by the DPS, but records with personal information are only available via the online access mode. The DPS does not release personal information to mail or walk-in requesters.

Vehicle Records: Private investigators must disclose their PI license number when requesting information. The state determined that non-disclosure of personal information is applicable for individuals only, and not "...to motor vehicle records of proprietorships, partnerships, corporations, associations, estates, trusts or limited liability partnerships."

Request and Consent Forms

Driving Records: No special forms are required for mail or walk-in requesters. Third parties should use the *Request for Motor Vehicle Record Containing Personal Information* form. Drivers wanting their own record copy should use the *Driver Record Request* form. Both forms are found at:
http://dps.alabama.gov/Home/wfContentTableColumned.aspx?ID=30&

PLH1=DLFORMS.
Online requesters must be pre-approved and sign a contractual agreement.

Vehicle Records: Form MV-DPPA1 *Request for Motor Vehicle Records* is required. This form can be downloaded at www.revenue.alabama.gov/motorvehicle/forms.html. The form must be signed by the requester if the reason for the request is a permissible use then personal information is released.

Vendor and Third Party Access Policy

Driving Records: Certain end users (employers) may obtain electronic records from an approved employment screening company via an authorized vendor. Otherwise, vendors cannot obtain records for other vendors.

Vehicle Records: Vendors must ensure that those receiving requested records are authorized under the DPPA to receive such information. Vendors that resell or re-disclose personal information must keep for a period of five years, records identifying each person or entity that receives such information and the permitted purpose for which the information will be used.

Records Ordered For Non-permissible Uses

Driving Records: Consent is not required for in-person or mail requests since no personal information is released for these requests.

Vehicle Records: Casual requesters can only obtain records with personal information with the consent of the subject using Form MV-DPPA1 as described above. This form requires the subject's signature be notarized. Otherwise records are available, without personal information.

Access to Driver-Related Records

Driving Records

General Information and Fees

Driver Record Request, Driver License Division, PO Box 1471, Montgomery AL 36102-1471, 334-242-4400 or 4241, fax: 334-353-8477 http://dps.alabama.gov
The current fee is $5.75, $7.75 if accessed online, and no increases are planned. No personal checks are accepted. The license number, the full name and date of birth are needed when ordering.

In-Person – Individual requests may be made over-the-counter from the Public Safety Department in Montgomery at 301 S Ripley St and are processed while you wait. Also, walk-in requests are processed at Driver License District Offices in Birmingham, Dothan, Foley, Huntsville, Jacksonville, Mobile, Opelika, Sheffield, and Tuscaloosa.

Mail – Mail-in requests are processed within three-to-five days. Use the address listed above. A self-addressed stamped envelope is suggested.

Electronic – OnlineAlabama.gov, 104 N. Jackson St, Montgomery AL, 36104, 866-353-3468
www.alabama.gov/portal/secondary.jsp?id=subscriptionServices.
Alabama.gov is the state's designated online agent to purchase the three-year record online. Both Alabama.gov and the DPS must approve all subscribers.   For access to this service, users MUST complete the following 1) Alabama Interactive Subscription Agreement, 2) Agreement for Official Drivers License Data Processing, and 3)

Alabama Department of Public Safety Driver or Vehicle Data Information Request.   There is a $75.00 annual administrative fee for new accounts and the search fee is $7.75 per record. The driver license number is needed to search. The Web-based system is open 24 hours daily. Records may be accessed on an interactive, batch, or on a "point-to-point" basis in real time.   The driver's address is not provided as part of the record. Billing is monthly. Visit the web page (click on Online Service then click on Subscribe to Online Services) above or call 866-353-3468.

Bulk – The state does not sell its license database, or portions there of.

By Person of Record – AL drivers may obtain their own driving record by mail or walk-in as described above. At present, there is no program for drivers to order or view their own record online. However, individuals are urged to download the Driver Record Request form at the web page listed above.

Verification of Licensee or ID Card

ALVerify provides the ability to verify an Alabama driver license or non-driver identification card at https://alverify.mvtrip.alabama.gov. The site purpose is for demonstrating U.S. citizenship and/or lawful presence in the U.S.

Notification/Monitoring Program

At present, Alabama does not offer a monitoring system or notification program to allow employers or insurance companies to track incidents of their drivers.

Crash Reports

Reporting – Crashes resulting in injury, death, or damage in excess of $250.00 must be reported immediately to the local or state police, and a written report (Form SR-13) must be filed within 30 days with the Safety Responsibility Unit, PO Box 1471, Montgomery 36102. For questions, call 334-242-4222. The form can be downloaded from http://dps.alabama.gov/Documents/Forms/SafetyResponsibilityAccident Report-SR-13.pdf.

Record Access – Crash reports may be obtained from the Alabama Department of Public Safety, Accident Reports, P.O. Box 1471, Montgomery 36102-1471, 334-242-4241 or 242-4371. Also, walk-in requests can be processed at Driver License District Offices in Birmingham, Dothan, Foley, Huntsville, Jacksonville, Mobile, Opelika, Sheffield, and Tuscaloosa. The cost is $15.00 per report. Only certified funds are accepted; no personal checks. Please include the names, license number (if possible), date, and county. A self-addressed stamped envelope is strongly suggested. Turnaround time is normally 10 to 12 days. SSNs are not released. Records may not be requested by telephone, but one may call to see if a report is ready. Records are available for past 10 years.

Use of the Crash Report Request form is suggested – go to www.dps.alabama.gov/driverlicense/forms.aspx.

Electronic Request: One may purchase a PDF copy of an accident report for $17.00, using a major credit card. The report is accessible online for seven days from the date of purchase. See https://www.alabamainteractive.org/dps_crash_report/welcome.action.

Access to Vehicle-Related Records

General Information and Fees

Dept. of Revenue, Motor Vehicle Division, Records Unit, 50 North Ripley Street, Ste 1223, Montgomery, AL 36140, 334-353-1604 and 334-242-9006, Fax is 334-353-2221 titles@revenue.alabama.gov www.revenue.alabama.gov/motorvehicle/index.html. A printout of the current title record including owner and lien holder information is $5.00 per vehicle. A complete title history is $15.00; however title records are not available pre-1975 vehicles. A year must be included as part of the request or a printout of the registration record for each year to be searched is $5.00 per year. An abandoned motor vehicle record request is $10.00. Personal checks are not accepted.

Registration records are retained for 10 years maximum.   But certificates of title are not issued by the Department of Revenue for ATVs, snowmobiles, and travel trailers, mobile homes and utility trailers that are designated as 1989 or older. Email vehicle-related questions to mvrecords@revenue.alabama.gov, email title-related questions to titles@revenue.alabama.gov.

In-Person – Immediate service is usually available, but extensive requests may take overnight to complete.

Mail – Mail requests are accepted as follows: Records Unit, PO Box 327680, Montgomery, AL 36132-7630; Title, PO Box 327640, Montgomery, AL 36132-7640. If the person requested lives in a city, an address must be submitted with the name for registration checks. Mail requests will take 1 to 2 weeks

Electronic – There are four search services available at www.revenue.alabama.gov/motorvehicle/mvinfo.html. All four may be accessed by subscribers of Alabamainteractive.org. Also, one of the services is available to the public - the **Vehicle Information Check** (also called VIN Check) which provides year, make, model, odometer, and vehicle brands. The fee is $6.00. The three services which require a subscription are the **Current Registration Record** search which includes current owner/operator, address, year, make and model, for $6.00; the **Current Title Record** search which lienholder plus current owner/operator, address, year, make and model, for $6.00; and the **Abandoned Motor Vehicle Notification Information** which is $12.00. Subscribers may be eligible to use other premium services.

Bulk – The MVD will only sell the complete database of vehicle registration and title information to vendors if the records are for permissible use. A signed contract is required. Contact the Motor Vehicle Division, Title Section at the address listed above

Access to Vessel-Related Records

General Information, Access and Fees

Department of Conservation and Natural Resources, PO Box 301451, Montgomery 36130, 334-242-3673, dcnr.boatreg@dcnr.alabama.gov. www.outdooralabama.com/boating/.

Operators must be licensed and at least 14 years of age to operate a boat alone, or 12 years old with an adult present. The vessel class "V" is required to operate a motorized vessel A written examination is required for applicants, except those who have successfully completed boating courses given by the U.S. Coast Guard Auxiliary, the U.S. Power Squadron or the Alabama Marine Police "Boating Basics" course, or have an age exemption.

All mechanically propelled, sail or rental boats must be registered, except vessels that have been commercially documented by the Coast Guard are not required to register in Alabama. Boat trailers do not need to be licensed and vessels do not need to be titled.

The owner's name, boat hull number (decal) or registration number is required to do a search. There is no fee unless large lists are presented, then the fee is $1.00 per search. Also, requests can be faxed to 334-242-0366. Requests can be emailed (call first). Turnaround time is usually 1-2 days, but can be longer in the summer. It can take as long as 6 months before new records are available for inquiry. Liens are not recorded here, but at the central state location for UCC filings, call 334-242-5324 or visit www.sos.alabama.gov/BusinessServices/UCC.aspx.

Driving Record Content and Reciprocity

What's On or Not On the Driving Record

- Alabama reports all convictions going back the past three years, regardless of type of conviction or status.
- Accident involvement is reported, but fault is not shown.
- The driver's address and personal information are not included as part of the record, even if the requester has a permissible use.
- Will not permit driver school attendance in lieu of conviction.

Data Retention

CDL driver records are purged based on the timetable per the MCSIA as shown in the Appendix.

Court to Repository

Law mandates that violation information must be submitted to the state within ten days. Convictions are transmitted through a computerized system by many courts, others follow as time and funds permit. Courts submitting convictions by paper (within the ten-day time frame) are entered onto the record within two weeks of the date received.

State Reciprocity for Non-CDL Drivers

- Will suspend license of driver for unpaid out-of-state convictions.
- Record of new incoming driver is not shown on MVR.
- Out-of-state convictions are shown on MVR.

- Out-of-state accidents are not shown on MVR.
- Convictions of out-of-state drivers are sent to home state.
- Record is not forwarded to new state upon surrender of license.

License Classes, Restrictions, and Endorsements

License Classes— Commercial

Alabama began issuing the CDL in October 1990. "CDL" shows as an extra imprint on the Driver License

Class A   This classification applies only to "combination" vehicles with a Gross Combination Weight Rating (GCWR) exceeding 26,000 pounds, provided the Gross Vehicle Weight Rating (GVWR) of the vehicle being towed exceeds 10,000 pounds. The holder of a Class A license, which includes any appropriate endorsements, may operate all vehicles included in Class B, C, and D.

Class B   This class includes single or combination vehicles where the GVWR of the single vehicle exceeds 26,000 pounds. The vehicle in tow must not exceed 10,000 pounds. Class B licensees, with appropriate endorsements, may drive all vehicles in Class C or D.

Class C   Vehicles designed to transport 16 or more passengers, including the driver, and vehicles placarded for hazardous materials, that do not meet the criteria for Class A or B above fall under this classification and may drive all vehicles in Class D.

License Classes— Non-Commercial

Class D   Operator (if Learner's License, then must have Y restriction)
Class M   Motorcycle (motor driven cycle only with B restriction)
Class V   Vessel (4-year license for all boat operators)

Restrictions

A	Corrective Lenses	H	Outside Mirror-Right	L	Power Steering	S	School Bus or Class D
B	Motor-Driven Cycle	I	Outside Mirror-Right and	M	Power Brakes	V	Boating Daylight Only
D	Outside Mirror-Left		Left	N	Built-Up Pedals	W	Intrastate Commerce Only
E	Daylight Only	J	Hearing Impaired	O	Built-Up Seat	Y	Learner's License
F	Hand Controls	K	Commercial Vehicle	P	Left-Foot Accelerator		
G	Automatic Transmission		Without Air-Brakes	R	Mechanical Signals		

Endorsements

H	Hazardous Material	P	Passenger	S	School Bus
N	Tank Vehicle	T	Double/Triple	X	Hazardous/Tank

Conviction Table with ACD, Points, and State Code

- The State Code does not appear on driving records and is for internal use only.

Description	ACD	Points	Actions	State Code
Adm Action Rescinded		0		127
Adm Action/DUI	A98	0		123
Adm Action/DUI < .08 CDLl	A94	0		143
Adm Action/Refusal	A12	0		122
Admin Perse .10	A90	6		186
Admin Perse Specific BAC	A91	6		365
Allow Minor Oper Mv-Veh		0		48
Allow Other Use License		0	SUSP	15
Assault	U06	0	REV	66
Attempt To Elude Police	U01	0	SUSP	57
Auto-Commission Of Felny	U03	0	REV	54
Brakes Required	E31	2		101
Brakes Used Improper	E71	0		211
Careless Driving	M81	2		67
CDL Not in Possession	B57			366
CDL W/O Being Licensed	B56	0		145
Child Restraint Viol.	F02	0		61
Child Support Clearance		0		130
CMV W/O Proper Documents		0		116
Coasting	N80	2		278
Comm Felony/Contr/Cv	A50	0		317
Commiss Of Felony/Cv	U03	0	REV	316
Confidential		0	SUSP	79
Confidential		0	SUSP	84
Confidential		0	SUSP	85
Confidential		0	SUSP	99
Confidential	A60	0		120
Consum Possess Alc/Drug	A31	2		118
Criminally Negligent Hom	U07	0	REV	65
Defective Haz Mat Dev	E33	0		204

Description	ACD	Points	Actions	State Code
Defective Lights	E34	0		205
Defective Sb Equip	E36	0		206
Disreguard-Safety/Cv	M80	6		319
Dr Lic(Mutilated,Alterd)	B41	0	SUSP	34
Dr Thru Barcde/Closed Rd	M02	2		18
Drink Alc Driving	A26	2		184
Drive 12 Am To 6 Am GDL		0		140
Drive While Barred	B21	0		196
Drive While Denied	B23	0		197
Drive While Withdrawn	B20	0		195
Driver Out Of Service		0		105
Driver's Vision Obscured	D70	2		17
Driving Impaired	A25	6		182
Driving While Canc/Cv	B22	0		115
Driving While Cancelled	B22	0		9
Driving While Disqu/Cv	B24	0		112
Driving While Rev/Cv	B25	0		114
Driving While Revoked	B25	0		7
Driving While Susp/Cv	B26	0		113
Driving While Suspended	B26	0		8
Driving Wrong Way	N60	2		310
Drug Law Act 93-352		0	SUSP	98
Drvng Under Influ Missip		6		52
DUI - Alcohol And Drugs	A23	0		71
DUI - Any Substance	A20	0		72
DUI - Drugs	A22	0		5
DUI - Liquors	A21	0		4
DUI .08 Or More	A08	6		178
DUI .10 Or More	A10	6		179
DUI BAC Over Limit	A11	6		180
DUI Meds Not Intend	A24	6		181
DUI Sb/Day Care	A21	0		121
DUI-.04 Above/Comm Veh	A04	0		311
DUI-Drugs/Comm Veh	A22	6		314
DUI-Liquors/Comm Veh	A21	0		312
Equip Used Imp/Obst	E70	0		210
Erratic Sudden Chg Speed	S97	2		175
Excessive Spd/Comm Veh	S15	2		318
Fail Cancel Signal	N41	0		265
Fail Check RR Tracks CDLl	M20	2	DISQ	133
Fail Clear RR Tracks CDL	M21	2	DISQ	134
Fail File Fin Resp	B63	0		198
Fail Heed Siren Blu Lite	N04	2		20
Fail Leave Dist Pass	M31	2		223
Fail Negotiate A RR CDL	M24	2	DISQ	138
Fail Notify Parked Vehicle	B08	2		360
Fail Obey RR Traf Devcdl	M10	3	DISQ	137
Fail Pay Damages Or Pymt	D37	0		306
Fail Signal Lane/Turn	N43	2		267
Fail Signal To Pass	N42	2		266
Fail Space RR Cross CDL	M23	2	DISQ	136
Fail Stop RR Track CDL	M22	2	DISQ	135
Fail Surrender Haz Endor	W09	0		330
Fail To Appear/Pay Fine	D56	0		150
Fail To Comply Fin Resp	D35	0		305
Fail To File Ins	B64	0		199
Fail To File Med Cert	B65	0		200
Fail To Keep Proper Lane	M41	2		160
Fail To Obey Flagger	M04	3		215
Fail To Obey Traffic Sgn	M17	3		159
Fail To Obey Yield Sign	M19	3		158
Fail To Pay Child Support	D51	0	SUSP	129
Fail To Post Security	D38	0		307
Fail to Render Aid	B05	2		359
Fail To Stop As Reqd	M25	2		309
Fail To Use Brakes	E51	0		208

Description	ACD	Points	Actions	State Code
Fail To Use Equip Rqd	E50	0		207
Fail To Use Haz Mat Reqd	E53	0		284
Fail To Use Lgt As Reqd	E55	0		156
Fail To Yield Emergency	N04	4		347
Fail To Yield Rht-Of-Way	N01	5		6
Fail Use Of Sb Safety Eq	E56	0		149
Fail Use Snow Tires	E57	0		209
Failed Show Non-Comm DL	B78	0		354
Failed to Show Insurance Cert	B74	0		357
Fail-Stop At Rr Crossing	M09	3		62
Fail-Stop At Stop Sign	M15	3		12
Failure To Appear	D45	0		51
Failure To Dim Lights	E54	2		19
Failure To Pay	D53	0		73
Failure To Report Acc	B61	0		21
Failure To Signal	N40	2		22
Felony DUI	A08	0	REV	340
Flaglight Projected Load		2		102
Follow Emgy Veh Unl	M32	2		224
Follow Fire Veh Unl	M33	2		225
Follow Too Close/Com V	M34	3		322
Following Improperly	M30	3		222
Following Too Close	M34	3		23
Fta Clearance		0		94
FTO Constr/Maint Marker	M03	3		214
FTO Lane Marks/Signal	M05	3		216
FTO Officer/Device Rr	M10	0		177
FTO Police/Peace Offr	M08	3		217
FTO Restricted Lane	M11	3		218
FTO Safety Zone	M12	3		219
FTO School Cross Grd	M13	3		220
FTO Traffic Signal/Lgt	M16	3		285
FTO Warn Light/Flash	M18	3		221
Ftp Clearance		0		74
Ftr Identity Ftl/Inj	B14	0		194
FTY Animal/Animal Driven	N02	5		288
FTY Crosswalk	N20	5		256
FTY Funeral/Parade	N05	5		251
FTY Overtaking Vehicle	N07	2		253
FTY Pedestrian/Blind/Dis	N08	5		254
FTY Right Of Way Cycle	N03	5		250
FTY Rotary	N21	5		257
FTY School Bus	N09	5		255
FTY Stop Sign	N22	5		258
FTY To Other Vehicle	N06	5		252
FTY Traffic Sign	N23	5		259
FTY Traffic Signal	N24	5		260
FTY Unsigned Inters	N25	5		261
FTY Warn On Oth Veh	N30	5		263
FTY When Turning	N31	5		264
FTY Yield Sign	N26	5		262
Gun Law Act 94-820		0	SUSP	78
Hit N Run Fatal	B02	0	REV	188
Hit N Run Per Inj	B03	0	REV	189
Hit N Run Prop Dmg	B04	0	REV	190
Hit N Run Stop Aid	B01	0		187
Hiway Loading From Ramp		0		32
Homicide By Vehicle	U07	0	REV	59
Homicide By Vehicle	U07	0	REV	323
Hours Of Service		2		104
Ignition Interlock	A41	0		183
Illegal Oper Emgy Veh	U21	2		282
Illegal Possess Alcohol	A31	0		343
Illegal Possess Of Drugs	A33	0		283
Illegal Towing		0		25
Imminent Hazard	W70	0		331

Description	ACD	Points	Actions	State Code
Imp Lane Loc Str Ctr Ln	M61	2		240
Imp Lane Or Location	M40	2		286
Imp Lane/Loc Bic Lane	M47	2		230
Imp Lane/Loc Crossovr	M44	2		227
Imp Lane/Loc Crosswlk	M45	2		228
Imp Lane/Loc Dtch/Shd	M58	2		238
Imp Lane/Loc Fire Hose	M56	2		236
Imp Lane/Loc Lmt Hwy	M50	2		233
Imp Lane/Loc Median	M51	2		234
Imp Lane/Loc Occ Lane	M48	2		231
Imp Lane/Loc Onc Trf	M57	4		237
Imp Lane/Loc Rail	M55	2		235
Imp Lane/Loc Ramp	M46	2		229
Imp Lane/Loc Slow Lane	M60	2		239
Imp Lane/Loc Turn Lane	M62	2		241
Imp Load(Shift/Spill)		2		26
Imp Oper/Ride Mcyle	F06	2		212
Imp Or Err Lane Chg	M42	2		342
Imp Use Siren/Blue Light		0		30
Imp-Err-Lane Chg/Com V	M42	2		321
Improper Backing	N82	2		16
Improper Class/Endo Lic	B91	0		148
Improper Equipment	E70	2		13
Improper Lane Changing	M42	2		47
Improper Lane Usage	M41	2		63
Improper Left Turn	N53	2		270
Improper Method Turn	N51	2		268
Improper Parking		0		27
Improper Passing	M70	4		14
Improper Pos For Turn	N52	2		269
Improper Right Turn	N54	2		271
Improper Routing Hazmat		0		110
Improper Ship Document		0		111
Improper Starting	N83	0		300
Improper Tag		0		28
Improper Turn	N50	2		29
Improper Turn Around	N55	2		272
Improper U Turn	N56	2		273
Improper Window Tint		0		75
In Restricted Lane	M49	2		232
Inability To Control Veh	D72	2		151
Inattentive Driving	M82	0		248
Juvenile		0		95
Leave Scene Fatal Acc	B06	0	REV	191
Leave Scene Per Inj	B07	0	REV	192
Leave Scene Prop Dmg	B08	0	REV	193
Left Acc-Scene/Com Veh	B05	0	DISQ	315
Left Scene Of Accident	B05	0	REV	24
LSA Private Property		2		364
Mandatory Insurance	D36	0		131
Manslaughter	U08	0	REV	33
Manufacture False Lic	D10	0		304
Minor/Possession Alcohol		0	SUSP	82
Misrepresent Buy Alcohol	D06	0		344
Misrepresent On Appl	D02	0		303
Move Over Emerg Vehicle		2		350
Mtr Carrier (No Points)		0		70
Mtr Carrier (Points)		2		69
Murder	U07	0	REV	64
Negligent Driving	M83	2		249
Negligent Hom Oper Cmv	U09	0		281
Negligent Oper Cmv Ftl	U10	0		147
No Driver's License	B51	0		3
No Flags Or Flares		0		35
No Hdlgt When Raining	E55	2		81
No Helmet/Shoes-Mtrcycl	F03	2		37

Description	ACD	Points	Actions	State Code
No Medical Card		0		108
No Points In CMV		0		107
No Tag		0		117
No Tag Regis In Vehicle		0		128
Not Obey Traf Cntrl/Sign	M14	3		68
O/S Adm Perse Haz Mat/CMV	A98	0		325
O/S Fail To Appear/CMV	D45	0		328
O/S Failure To Pay/CMV	D53	0		329
O/S Refusal Haz Mat/CMV	A12	0		327
Obstruct/Impede Traffic	F34	0		346
Obstruction Of Traff Way	F34	2		38
Off Truck Route		2		50
One-Way Street	N63	2		31
Open Container	A35	0		139
Oper Improer Mtl/Phy Dis	D75	2		153
Oper Improper Drowsiness	D74	2		152
Oper Veh No Owner Consnt		0		49
Oper W/O Haz Mat As Reqd	E08	0		157
Oper W/O Lights Reqd	E05	0		154
Oper W/O Sb Equip Reqd	E06	0		155
Operat W/O Equip	E01	0		341
Operate W/O Brakes Reqd	E02	0		345
Operating Unsafe Cmv	F66	0		109
Other St Dwi/DUI Reduced		6		55
Other-Moving And Traffic		2		96
Other-Not Move Nor Traff		0		97
Out Of Serv W/Pass	B19	0	DISQ	142
Out Of Service Violation	B27	0	DISQ	124
Out-Of-State Adm Perse/C	A98	0		324
Out-Of-State Refusal	A12	0		326
Over 4 Passengers Gdl		0		141
Overheight Truck		0		40
Overlength Truck/Trailer		0		41
Overweight Truck		0		42
Overwidth Truck		0		43
Pass In Viol Opp Dir Rst	M72	4		243
Pass In Viol Sign/Marker	M71	4		242
Pass On Hill/Curve	M74	4		245
Pass W/Insuff Dist/Visb	M77	4		247
Pass Where Prohibited	M76	4		246
Passed Stopped Schol Bus	M75	5		44
Passing On Wrong Side	M73	4		244
Perjury Oper Motor Veh	D78	0	REV	146
Placarding	E04	2		100
Possess Mult Lic	D07	0		203
Prima Facia/Too Fast Cnd	S94	2		173
Racing On Highway	S95	0	SUSP	58
Radar Detector In A Cmv	E23	0		119
Ran Off Road	M43	2		226
Reckless Carless Neg Dr	M80	6		287
Reckless Driving	M84	6		2
Reckless Driving/Com V	M84	6		320
Reckless Endangerment	M80	6		126
Refusal Fatal Accident	A12	0	SUSP	351
Refuse Chem Test/Cv	A12	0	DISQ	313
Refused Chemical Test	A12	0	SUSP	90
Rescind Refusal Accident				363
Resisting Arrest	U02	0		302
Reveal Identity Acc	B14	0		144
Running Red Light	M16	3		10
Seat Belt Violation	F04	0		77
Show Or Use Lic Imp	D16	0		201
Speed < Minimum	S96	2		174
Speed 1-10 Over Limit	S51	2		170
Speed 11-14 Over Limit	S14	2		358
Speed 16-20 Over Limit	S16	2		164

Description	ACD	Points	Actions	State Code
Speed 21-25 Over Limit	S21	2		165
Speed 21-3- Over Limit	S71	2		171
Speed 26-30 Over Limit	S26	5		166
Speed 31-35 Over Limit	S31	5		167
Speed 31-40 Over Limit	S81	5		172
Speed 36-40 Over Limit	S36	5		168
Speed 41 Or More Over	S41	5		169
Speed 6-10 Over Limit	S06	2		163
Speed On Freeway	S98	2		176
Speeding	S93	2		1
Speeding 1-5 Over Limit	S01	2		162
Speeding 26 Or More Over	S92	5		353
Speeding Over 79 Mph		2		80
Speeding Over 85 Mph		2		125
Strike Fixed Object - Accident	B08	2		361
Texting While Driving	M85			367
Theft Of Gas		0		132
Tires	E37	2		103
Transport Illegal Whisky		0		45
Unauthorized Use Vehicle		0	REV	352
Under Age Perse	A61	6		185
Unlaw Blood Alchl Lvl-Fl		6		56
Unsafe Operation	N84	2		301
Unsatisfied Judgment	D39	0		308
Use Communication Dev				362
Use Mobile Device	M86			368
Use Of Anothers License	D16	0	SUSP	76
Use Of Dl/Minor/Alcohol	D06	0	SUSP	83
Use Veh Aid/Abet Felon	U05	0		280
Use Veh In Misdemeanor	U04	0		279
Usecured Pass Open Area	F05	0		213
Veh Feticide 1st Degree	U27	0		355
Veh Feticide 2nd Degree	U28	0		356
Vehicle Out Of Service		0		106
Violate Lmt Lic Cnd	D27	0		202
Violating Restrictions	D29	2		46
Violation Result Fatal Acc	U31	0		161
Write Send Read Text Message		2		369
Wrong Side Divide Hwy	N71	4		276
Wrong Side Of Road	N70	4		11
Wrong Side Undivided	N72	4		277
Wrong Signal	N44	2		299
Wrong Way Divide Hwy	N62	4		275
Wrong Way Rotary	N61	3		274

Point System Summary

Points are assessed for various violations summarized as follows:

Any conviction which resulted from a charge that involved the drinking of alcoholic beverages and the driving of a motor vehicle but did not require mandatory revocation of the driver license	6 points
Admin per se	6 points
Reckless driving or reckless endangerment involving operating a motor vehicle	6 points
Speeding (85 mph or above)	5 points
Failure to yield right-of-way	5 points
Passing stopped school bus	5 points
Speeding 26 or more MPH over the posted limit	5 points
Wrong side of road	4 points
Illegal passing	4 points
Following too closely	3 points
Disregarding traffic control device (stop sign, traffic light, etc.)	3 points
Fail to obey construction/maintenance zone markers/flagman/police officer/restricted lane	3 points
Speeding in excess of posted limits	2 points
All other moving violations	2 points

Suspensions and Revocations Due to Point Accumulation

12-14 points in 2 years	60-day suspension	24 or more points in 2 years 365-day suspension
15-17 points in 2 years	90-day suspension	After a traffic conviction is 2 years old, it loses its point count for
18-20 points in 2 years	120-day suspension	suspension purposes but remains on a driver's record.
21-23 points in 2 years	180-day suspension	

Alaska

Administration	Important Telephone and Web Contacts

Shelly Mellott, Acting Director and Division Operation Manager
 	
Division of Motor Vehicles
1300 W. Benson Boulevard, STE 900
Anchorage, AK 99503-3696
907-269-5559
 	
Research and Correspondence
1300 W. Benson Boulevard, STE 200
Anchorage, AK 99503-3600
http://doa.alaska.gov/dmv/
	Driving and Vehicle Record Information 907-269-5551
	Driver Licensing..907-269-3770
	Financial Responsibility and SR-22 907-465-4361
	State Division of Insurance.............................907-465-2515
	State Trooper Headquarters 907-269-5511
	
	Email: MIL@alaska.gov or
	          DOA.DMV.WebMaster@Alaska.gov
	An excellent topic index is found at:
	          http://doa.alaska.gov/dmv/general/index.htm
	Statutes www.legis.state.ak.us/basis/folio.asp
	Topic-Regulation List: http://doa.alaska.gov/dmv/faq/regs.htm

Driver's License Format, Issuance and Renewal

License Classes, Restrictions and Endorsements Appear After the Driving Record Content Section

License Format
There are seven numbers. Normally, low numbered licenses are started with zeros, i.e. 0000001, 0000002, etc. There is no code for license format; numbers are assigned by computer in a numerical order.

Document Appearance
The appropriate section of the application card is photographed with the driver. Since 2004, Alaska has issued a digitized license document. The replacement of older documents will take at least six years, both types are described below. If the courts have prohibited the driver from purchasing alcohol, the words "Alcohol Restricted" appear in a red banner.

Note that Alaska is **not** participating in the Enhanced Driver License Program for border crossings.

Newer Format
 Security Characteristics: License is a plastic card, laminated on both sides, 2D bar code on back. Also, includes ghost image, optical outline of ALASKA followed by outline of state flag alternates in two horizontal rows on front. ALASKA is printed on left and right edges and is visible under UV light.
 Position of Photo: Top right corner.
 Minor Age Driver: Card in vertical format, photo at lower left. "Under 21" in white in red on right bar above photo.
 CDL Indicator: "COMMERCIAL DRIVER LICENSE" on blue print in yellow bar.

Older Format
 Security Characteristics: Location number and state seal overlap the photo and licensing information. Licenses issued prior to August 2000 may include hologram on license pouch. Since 2001, the state name is center of license in optical reflective lettering that changes color when license is tilted.
 Position of Photo: Top left corner.
 Minor Age Driver: "Under 21" is printed in red on right side and left of

license. All print is in red (not blue).
 CDL Indicator: None, other than classification.

Issuance
Location of Requirements for Proof of Identity:
See http://doa.alaska.gov/dmv/akol/original.htm
Age Requirements
An applicant must be at least 16 and have held a valid driving permit for at least six months. A 14 year-old may apply for an Instructional Permit. Applicants under 18 with parental consent may apply for a Provisional License. New drivers under 18 must have had an Instruction Permit for 6 months before the driver is issued a license. During the first year after a license is issued to a person under 18, the license is considered a Provisional License. There are stringent guidelines regarding such items as who can be in the vehicle and time of day driven. For more information, visit the web page.
Residency
New residents must obtain license within 90 days, if CDL then within 30 days.

Renewal
Birth day and month of fifth year, driver keeps same number when renewing. Active duty military personnel non-commercial licenses expire 90 days after discharge from military or 90 days after return to the state of Alaska, whichever comes first. If an Alaska resident is temporarily out of state and discovers that the license is expired, an extension letter can be mailed or faxed to extend the expiration date. CDL extensions are limited to 30 days. Some drivers may renew by mail after first registering online.
Elderly-Related Restrictions
None indicated other than person may not renew by mail if 69 years of age or older on the expiration date of the driver's license being renewed.

Vehicle Insurance, Title and Registration Facts

Insurance and Financial Responsibility
Alaska has both financial responsibility and mandatory Insurance laws. Proof must be shown after any reportable accident. Minimum financial responsibility limits are $50,000/100,000/25,000. An SR-22 insurance policy is normally required for reinstatement after a driver's privileges

to drive have been suspended or revoked. For DWI and refusal convictions an SR-22 is required for 5 years from the ending date on a first offense, 10 years from the ending date on a second offense, and 20 years from the ending date on a third offense. SR-22 must be carried for the **life** of the driver for a fourth conviction for a DUI or Refusal, and for an unsatisfied judgment.

In Alaska, insurance is not required in areas where registration is not required, with the exception of a driver who has received a ticket for a violation of 6 points or more within the last 5 years and must have liability insurance. A list of these locations is shown at http://doa.alaska.gov/dmv/dealer/sop_reg/R002_Exempt_Areas.htm. Effective 01/01/2012 vehicles driven in Kotzebue are no longer exempt.

Registration

The Division of Motor issues titles to passenger vehicles, trucks, buses, vans, motorhomes, mobile homes, motorcycles and trailers. Registration is biennial.

Renewal

Renewal is available by mail, in person or online. There are some *Registration Only Station* locations. Online registration renewal is found at www.alaska.gov/dmv/faq/renewal.htm. Address changes may also be made online.

For New Residents

Non-residents must register vehicles after sixty days or within ten days of accepting employment or intention of establishing residency.

Inspections and Emissions Testing

Although there is no annual required safety inspection, Alaska State Troopers may inspect—at their discretion—when it is believed a vehicle is unsafe.

There is no provision for emissions testing statewide. The municipality of Anchorage required an emissions inspection at one time, but this was discontinued as of March 1, 2012.

Note About Studded Tires

It is unlawful to operate a motor vehicle with studded tires on a paved highway or road from May 1st through September 15th, inclusive, north of 60 North Latitude (all communities north of Ninilchik) and from April 15th through September 30th, inclusive, south of 60 North Latitude (Anchor Point, Homer, Kodiak and cities and towns in Southeast Alaska), except that at any latitude on a paved portion of the Sterling Highway a person may not operate a motor vehicle with studded tires from May 1st through September 15th, inclusive

Passenger Plate Facts

Alaska law requires motor vehicles to display **two** license plates. A month tab and a current year tab must be displayed on the back plate, only. Motorcycles and trailers have **one** license plate with month and year tabs. There is no coding on the plate to indicate the city or borough of issuance. Plates remain with vehicle is when sold, unless they are specialized plates.

Withdrawal Sanctions, and Alcohol and Drug Testing

Alcohol and Chemical Testing

Alaska's under-the-influence laws and the administrative license revocation law take effect at a .08 percent level and .04 percent level for those operating a commercial vehicle. The state has an implied-consent law. There is a zero (.00) tolerance for those under 21 years of age. Breath, blood, or urine testing may be used.

Suspensions and Revocations

See the Appendix for a list of the federally mandated disqualifications for offenses occurring in a CMV per MCSIA.

Note: A revocation may result for refusal to submit to a breath, blood, or urine test for the purpose of determining alcohol content or the presence of controlled substances.

Defaulting on Promissory Note .... Indefinite suspension.
Driving Under the Influence
  No Previous Convictions .... Ninety-days minimum revocation.
  One Previous Conviction... One-year revocation.
  Two Previous Convictions... Three-year revocation.
  More Than Two Previous Convictions .... Five-year revocation.
Driving Under the Influence, Minor
  No Previous Convictions .... Thirty-days minimum revocation.
  One Previous Conviction... Sixty-days revocation.
  Two Previous Convictions... Ninety-days revocation.
  Three or More Previous Convictions .... One-year revocation.
Failure to Appear for Driver Improvement Interview......... Waives the right to hearing, action becomes final.
Failure to Pay Child Support .... Indefinite Suspension.
Failure to Show Proof of Insurance .... Ninety-days to one-year suspension.
Fraudulent Use of License Document -
  Under 21, 1st Offense... Sixty-day suspension.
  2nd or Subsequent Offense... One-year suspension.
Non-Compliance with Recommendations
  of DI Specialist... Suspension of one year or until compliance, whichever is first.
Point Accumulation
  Twelve or more points in twelve months...................... One-month suspension.
  Eighteen or more points in twenty-four months .... One-month suspension.
  Second point suspension in twenty-four months .... Three-month suspension.
  Third point suspension in twenty-four months .... One-year revocation.

Note: Drivers receiving traffic citations which total 6 or more points in a 12 month period or 9 or more points in a 24- month period, must take a nationally certified defensive driving course. Otherwise, the DMV may suspend the privilege to drive.

Other Mandatory Suspensions
  Operating or owning an uninsured vehicle involved in a crash.
  Repeated violations of the motor vehicle laws (accumulation of points).
  Driving in violation of license restrictions.
Other Mandatory Revocations
  Driving while under the influence, or refusal to take a chemical test.

Driving while license is cancelled, suspended, or revoked.

Reckless driving.

Failure to stop and render aid at the scene when involved in a personal injury crash.

Perjury (giving untrue information relating to motor vehicles to the department).

Unlawful flight by motor vehicle to avoid arrest.

Felony in connection with a motor vehicle causing injury or death such as Manslaughter, Negligent Homicide, or Assault with a vehicle.

Reinstatement Requirements

Suspension $100 reinstatement fee if only one license action is in effect within the past 10 years; $250 if more than one action in past ten years; SR-22.

Revocation $200 reinstatement fee if only one license action is in effect within the past 10 years; $500 if more than one action in past ten years; SR-22; knowledge test. Road test may be required. Alcohol treatment verification is required following a conviction of DWI or Refusal or for an administrative revocation for "Minor in Possession." 1st offenders must submit proof of compliance with an alcohol education or rehabilitation program, 2nd or more offenders must submit proof of completion and payment for said program.

Record Access: Laws, Rules, and Forms

Note: **This Section Applies to Both Driver and Vehicle Records.**

Governing Statutes and Rules

AK Admin. Code: www.legis.state.ak.us/cgi-bin/folioisa.dll/aac ?
Statutes and Rules: www.legis.state.ak.us/basis/folio.asp
§28.10.505 and §28.15.151 govern the release of driver information and are substantially similar to DPPA. The numbering of the exceptions is a somewhat different. Additionally, Alaska combines 18 USCA §2721(b)(11) and (13). Sec. 28.10.505 provides for the exceptions (permissible uses) as follows:

(a) Notwithstanding AS 40.25.300 and except as provided in this section, the department may not disclose personal information contained in motor vehicle records maintained by the department under this chapter.

(b) Personal information shall be disclosed for use in connection with matters of motor vehicle or driver safety or theft; motor vehicle emissions; motor vehicle product alterations, recalls, or advisories; performance monitoring of motor vehicles and dealers by motor vehicle manufacturers; and removal of non-owner records from the original owner records of motor vehicle manufacturers as required by federal law.

(c) Personal information may be disclosed if the requesting person demonstrates, in a form and manner the department prescribes, that the requesting person has obtained the written consent of the person who is the subject of the information.

(d) Personal information may be disclosed by the department upon proof of the identity of the person requesting a record and representation by the requesting person that the use of the personal information is strictly limited to one or more of the following uses:

(1) for use by a government agency, including a court or law enforcement agency, in carrying out its functions, or a private person or entity acting on behalf of a government agency in carrying out its functions;

(2) for use in the normal course of business by a legitimate business or an agent, employee, or contractor of the business, but only (A) to verify the accuracy of personal information submitted by an individual to the business or an agent, employee, or contractor of the business; and (B) if the information submitted is not correct, to obtain the correct information, but only for the purposes of preventing fraud by pursuing legal remedies against, or recovering on a debt or security interest against, an individual;

(3) for use in connection with a civil, criminal, administrative, or arbitration proceeding in a court or government agency or before a self-regulatory body, including service of process and the execution or enforcement of a judgment or court order;

(4) for use in research activities, or in producing statistical reports, if the personal information is not published, redisclosed, or used to contact an individual;

(5) for use by an insurer or insurance support organization, or by a self-insured entity, or an agent, employee, or contractor of an

insurer, in connection with claims investigation activities, anti-fraud activities, rating, or underwriting;

(6) for use in providing notice to the owners of towed or impounded vehicles;

(7) for use by an employer or an agent or insurer of an employer to obtain or verify information relating to a holder of a commercial driver's license that is required under 49 U.S.C. 31101 - 31162 (Commercial Motor Vehicle Safety Act);

(8) for use in connection with the operation of private toll transportation facilities;

(9) for use in connection with a legitimate business operating under a contract with the department;

(10) for bulk distribution for surveys, marketing, or solicitations if the person who is the subject of the information has provided written consent to the release; and

(11) any other purpose specifically authorized by law that is related to the operation of a motor vehicle or related to public safety.

(e) Personal information contained in an individual record may be disclosed, without regard to the intended use of the personal information, if the person who is the subject of the information has provided written consent to the release.

Alaska does not have the equivalent of 18 USCA §2721(b)(8), which allows disclosure to any licensed private investigative agency. Alaska added a provision to the exceptions for use in connection with a legitimate business operating under a contract with the department. AK ST §28.10.505(d)(9). The state does not distinguish between permissible and casual requesters. The state considers driver's license records and records of conviction as confidential. The records may not be released to anyone other than the licensee or duly appointed agent for the licensee (with written authorization).

More about Vehicle Records

Record requests are honored for: lien holders if a business (individual lien holder must have consent); employment screening purposes; insurance related purposes; to provide notice to impounded, towed or abandoned vehicles; in connection with a court or government agency matter; or if a signed release by the vehicle owner is attached. The agency follows the permissible user guidelines of the DPPA with the exception that private investigators are not exempt

Request and Consent Forms

Driving Records: There are three useful forms, all are available at http://doa.alaska.gov/dmv/forms/forms.htm. The state requires a *419 Release* form to be signed by the licensee for access by a third party. These requesters can maintain the signed release forms in-house rather than send individual forms with electronic request files. A third form can be used by drivers to obtain their own records.

A Special Form - *Company Release For Multiple Driving Records* - is available at http://doa.alaska.gov/dmv/forms/pdfs/co_release.pdf. On the form the listed drivers provide signed authorization for the company to check records. The form is valid for 90 days. These requesters can maintain the signed release forms in-house rather than send individual forms with electronic request files. The third form can be used by drivers to obtain their own records.

Vehicle Records: Use of *Form 851 Request for Vehicle Record* is required. This form requires signature and statement of purpose from the requester, but not from the subject, for the purposes stated above. Otherwise, consent is needed. This form and other vehicle-related forms are available at http://doa.alaska.gov/dmv/forms/forms.htm.

Vendor and Third Party Access Policy

Driving Records: The records can only be used for the purpose stated (i.e., insurance purposes). Driver record data cannot be stored and resold. Approved online vendors may not access records for other vendors (who are not online, etc.) who will then sell to a permissible end

user without prior approval.

Vehicle Records: Commercial vendors must be approved by the Director and declare or show that usage is of a legal nature. Permissible users purchase in bulk or database format. Resale of data to other permissible users is subject to the following restrictions—

a.   Other vendor (reseller) must be registered with the state
b.   End user must be registered with the state
c.   Contract between original vendor and reseller must contain same language as contract between the state and the original vendor

Contract between reseller and end user must contain same language as contract between the state and the original vendor.

Non-permissible Use Requests

No records are released without consent. This also applies to individual lien holders of vehicles - written consent must be given by the subject.

Access to Driver-Related Records

Driving Records

General Information and Fees

Division of Motor Vehicles, Attn: Research, 1300 W Benson Blvd. Ste 200, Anchorage, AK 99503-3600, 907-269-5551.

The fee for a driving record is $10.00 per request. The last fee increase was July 2006. Alaska gives a credit for "no record found" request. As mentioned above, the DMV requires a release form signed by the licensee to access a driving record. Approved, volume requesters can maintain the signed release forms on file rather than forward with requests. The driver's full name, license number, and date of birth must be submitted.

In-Person – Individual requests may be processed within minutes at any Division of Motor Vehicles field office. Credit cards are accepted for payment.

Mail – Turnaround time can be as long as 30 days, especially of a large list is presented. The fee must accompany the request.

Fax – Provided the person of record signs the request form and gives valid reason for a request, a driving record can be faxed or mailed to a given address. Requests must be faxed to 907-269-5202. Use of credit card is required for the $10.00 fee. The request form is located at http://doa.alaska.gov/dmv/forms/pdfs/faxdh.pdf.   Records can be returned by fax or mail. Records are normally returned within 30 days or less.

Electronic – The online system is a commercial dial access program and is not web-based. The program is only open to pre-approved entities in compliance with DPPA. Inquiries may be made at any time, twenty-four hours a day; batch inquiries may call back within thirty minutes for responses. Generally, the first four letters of the driver's last name, the license number, and date of birth are required to receive a record. Access is limited only to those involved with insurance underwriting or to those that submit the signed release with the request. The fee is $10.00 per record, but some data vendors are grandfathered into a fee for $5.00.

Bulk – This is not available.

By Person of Record – Alaska residents and former residents have three options obtain a copy of their driving record. One may request the record by mail, or by fax (as explained above), or by going to any DMV office and showing proper identification. The form is found at http://doa.alaska.gov/dmv/forms/pdfs/faxdh.pdf. At present, there is no program for drivers to order or view their own record online. Note Alaska gives drivers the ability to order either a 5-year insurance record or a full lifetime record. A Point Review form is found at http://doa.alaska.gov/dmv/forms/pdfs/510.pdf.

Notification/Monitoring Program

Alaska does not offer a monitoring system or notification program to employers or insurance companies to track incidents of drivers.

Accident Reports

Reporting –Accidents involving property damage in excess of $501, injury, or death must be reported to the local police or state troopers plus any driver involved in the collision, regardless of fault, is required to show proof of motor vehicle liability insurance. Use of an Accident (Crash) Report form is required when there is a crash resulting in either an injury or total property damage of $2,000 or more. This report is not required if the crash was investigated by a peace officer. This report must be filed within ten days with the Department of Administration, Division of Motor Vehicles, PO Box 110221, Juneau, AK 99811-0221. The report can be made directly via the Web; go to http://www.dot.state.ak.us/stwdplng/accreptapp/index.shtml. There are no special reporting requirements for commercial drivers.

Record Access – Reports filed by authorities are public. Copies of accident reports filed by participants are considered private and confidential. The cost of obtaining an accident report is $10.00 per record, credit cards are accepted. A request does not need to be notarized, but must be in writing with a proper explanation. New records are available for inquiry in 30 days or less. Records are stored for 7 years. Written requests should be submitted to: Division of Motor Vehicles, Juneau Driver Licensing, PO Box 110221, Juneau, AK 99811-0221.

Access to Vehicle-Related Records

General Information and Fees

Division of Motor Vehicles, Attention: Research, 1300 W Benson Boulevard #200, Anchorage AK 99503-3600, 907-269-5551. Fax is 907-269-5202. Email is doa.dmv.research@alaska.gov.

The Division of Motor issues titles to passenger vehicles, trucks, buses, vans, motorhomes, mobile homes, motorcycles and trailers.   Only registration is issued for boats, ATV's and snowmachines. Motorized snow machines are not required to be registered if only ridden on private property.

As previously mentioned, personal information is firmly integrated into the vehicle record so the record cannot be released unless the person,

business, or organization requesting the record qualifies under one of the authorized exceptions shown on *Form 851-Request for Vehicle Record.* For purposes of the law *personal information* includes name and both mailing and residence addresses of any individual on the record. The definition of "individual" includes a person, an organization, or an entity. This is broad enough to include people, businesses, trusts, organizations, and lienholder, if the lienholder is an individual. If the lienholder is a business or institution, the release is not required.

There is a $10.00 fee for all vehicle records. Personal checks are accepted only if in-state. The search includes a computer printout and any copies of documents retained in the microfilm files, if requested.

Mail, Fax, or In-Person – Turnaround time for mailed requests depends on workload, but typically is 2 business days. In-person requests are generally limited to three searches if records can be printed from computer, rest are mailed. Lists or historical requests take longer.

Electronic – Alaska does not offer online access to businesses or to the public at this time.

Bulk – The entire master tape file of registration information is available to approved requesters per accepted permissible use. Call the Director's office at 907-269-5559 for more information.

Access to Vessel-Related Records

General Information, Access and Fees
www.doa.alaska.gov/dmv/reg/boat.htm

Alaska is not a "title" state for vessels; only vessel registration is required. Boats are registered by hull number, AK number and by name. Non-powered boats are not required to be registered unless by choice of owner. State law requires the following to be registered:

• All powered boats used on any water in the state. This includes all rivers, streams, and lakes, regardless of size, and all salt water within 3 miles of land.
• All boats used by registered Sport Fishing Guides (including non-powered boats).

There is a $10.00 fee per search from the same agency described above that handles vehicle record requests.

Effective January 1st, 2001, the Division of Motor Vehicles assumed the boat registration program from the U.S. Coast Guard. Prior to January 1st, 2001, the Coast Guard registered powered boats that are used on navigable waterways of the state. Now, only large commercial vessels are registered with the U.S. Coast Guard (call 800-799-8362).

Liens on vessels can be recorded by either of two locations (two databases) maintained by the Recorder's Office at the Department of Natural Resources (DNR). One DB is for UCC filings, the other for recorded documents. One may search the index free on the web, by if asking the for a document search by mail or in person. Each database must be searched. The UCC search fee is $15.00 or $25.00 for a search with copies. The Recorder' Office search is $25.00. See http://dnr.alaska.gov/ssd/recoff/searchRO.cfm.

Driving Record Content and Reciprocity

What's On or Not On the Record
• Records contain the residence, mailing address, height, weight and DOB, but not the SSN.
• Alaska reports all convictions except parking violations.
• Accidents are not reported unless action is taken, and then only specific action taken on the license is shown on the record.
• Alaska does not permit driver school attendance in lieu of conviction.
• The minimum length of time non-CDL convictions are listed on a public record is three years for minor moving violations; five years for major offenses (reckless driving, hit-and-run, etc.).
• Suspensions are shown three years from ending date.
• Drivers may order their own "lifetime" record

Data Retention
CDL records are purged based on the timetable per MCSIA, see the Appendix for this timetable. No statement was issued by the DMV regarding data retention of non-CDL records.

Court to Repository
Input of convictions is done online by the arresting agency, convicting court, and/or by the Division of Motor Vehicles. The state mandates that the court must report all convictions to the Department of Motor Vehicles, but indicates no time constraints.

State Reciprocity for Non-CDL Drivers
• Will cancel (not suspend) for unpaid out-of-state convictions.
• Only major convictions of new incoming driver shown on MVR.
• Out-of-state convictions are shown on MVR.
• Out-of-state accidents are not shown on MVR.
• Only major convictions of out-of-state drivers are sent to home state upon request to new state when driver moves

License Classes, Restrictions, and Endorsements

License Classes– Commercial
Alaska began issuing the CDL in January 1991

Class A   Any combination of vehicles (excluding motorcycles) with a GCWR of 26,001 or more pounds, provided the GVWR of the vehicle(s) being towed is in excess of 10,000 pounds (e.g., eighteen-wheelers, log trucks, etc.).

Class B   Any single vehicle (excluding motorcycles) with a GVWR of 26,001 or more pounds, or any such vehicle towing a vehicle not in excess of 10,000 pounds GVWR (e.g., dump trucks, cement-mixer trucks, box trucks, motor coaches).

Class C   A motor vehicle or a combination of a motor vehicle and one or more vehicles (except motorcycles) in which:
  1. The GCWR is greater than 26,000 pounds while the GVWR of the towing vehicle is 26,000 pounds or less, and the combined GVWR of the vehicle or vehicles being towed is 10,000 or less; or
  2. Does not meet the definition of Class A/CDL or Class B/CDL and
     a. is designed to transport more than sixteen passengers (including the driver); or
     b. is used in the transportation of materials which require the motor vehicle to be placarded under the Federal Hazardous Materials Regulations. Holders of a Class C/CDL may also operate a Class D vehicle.

Instruction Permits for Commercial Drivers
Alaska issues instruction permits for commercial drivers. The permits are known as IA, IB, and IC. IC is used for the C Class vehicles only, IA is for A Class and IB for B Class.

The commercial instruction permit allows a beginning driver to practice driving skills to qualify for the road test for a commercial vehicle. An IA is required to practice in a Class A, B or C vehicle, an IB is required to practice in a Class B or C vehicle, and an IC is required to practice in a Class C vehicle. The intent of these permits is not to legalize the operation of a commercial vehicle by underage persons during the period when they are waiting to become old enough for the issuance of a commercial license

License Classes– Non-Commercial

Class D   Single vehicle less than 26,001 pounds or combination of towed vehicle which is less than 10,000 pounds (except motorcycle).
Class M1   Motorcycle.
Class M2   Motorscooter (under sixteen years of age).
Class IP   Instruction Permit.
Class IE   Driver Training Permit (good for six months while under supervision).

Off-Highway License and Class R License

To serve Alaska residents in rural communities, the DMV issues an "Off-Highway" license that allows an individual to drive in specific Alaskan communities. An Off-Systems license allows an individual to drive on roads that are not connected to the State highway system and on roads that are not connected to a highway or vehicular way with an average daily traffic volume greater than 499. To obtain an "Off-Highway" license, the applicant must complete all licensing requirements except for the skills (road) test and photograph.

In Kotzebue and other communities there may be municipal ordinances that allow the operation of snowmachines and ATVs on public roads. Normally, a valid driver license (A, B, C, or D) covers the operation of a snowmachine or ATV. But if the driver does not have a driver license, the driver must obtain a Class R license in order to drive a snowmachine or ATV on the public roadways when allowed by ordinance. A Class R license holder must be 16 years or older.

Restrictions

1 Corrective Lenses Required
2 Outside Mirrors Required
3 Automatic Transmission Only
4 Daylight Driving Only
5 Other
6 Off Systems (for those who live and drive in remote areas, can only drive in such areas and not on main highways)
7 CDL Valid in Alaska Only
C Interlock Device Required
J No Alcohol Purchase (can apply to all permits, licenses or ID cards)

CDL Only Restrictions

K Intrastate Only (usually associated with a commercial driver who is either under 21 or has a vision or SPE waiver)

L Vehicles Without Air-Brakes Only
M Road Tests in Class B Bus
N Road Tests in Class C Bus
O Road Tests in Class A Vehicle, But Not Tractor-Trailer

Endorsements

Non-CDL Endorsement

S School Bus (separate permit renewed annually in September)

CDL Only Endorsements

T Double-/Triple-Trailers
N Tanks
P Passengers (sixteen or more, including driver)
H Hazardous Materials
X Combination Tank/HazMat
S School Bus

Conviction Table with ACD and Full Description

- The Alaska Conviction Table is presented in the order of the Code field. Alaska provides a "code" and an abbreviated text field on their driving records. Also presented in this table are the translating ACD Codes when appropriate and the full description of the conviction.
- Note that the Code column is very similar to the ACD Code Set. When the Code matches an ACD code that is no longer used (perhaps removed in October 2005) or there is no ACD, then this Code could be obsolete and may no longer be issued. These Codes are included because they may appear on some older driving records.
- A summary of the Alaska Point System follows this table.

MVR Code	ACD	MVR Text	Full Description
011		SR22 OLD CODE FORFIX	SR-22 old code for fix
094		POINT SYSTEM SUSPEND	Point system suspend
096		POINT SYS WARNING	Point sys warning
098		LIMITED LICENSE	Limited license
A04	A04	DUI .04 OR MORE	Driving under the influence of alcohol with BAC at or over .04
A08	A08	DUI .08 OR MORE	Driving under the influence of alcohol with BAC at or over .08
A10	A10	DUI .10 OR MORE	Driving under the influence of alcohol with BAC at or over .10
A11	A11	FAILED BAC .___	Driving under the influence of alcohol with BAC at or over ___ (detail field required)
A12	A12	REFUSAL/IMP CONSENT	Refused to submit to test for alcohol - Implied Consent Law
A20	A20	DUI ALCOHOL OR DRUG	Driving under the influence of alcohol or drugs
A21	A21	DUI ALCOHOL	Driving under the influence of alcohol
A22	A22	DUI CONTROLED SUBST	Driving under the influence of drugs
A23	A23	DUI ALCOHOL & DRUG	Driving under the influence of alcohol and drugs
A24	A24	DUI MEDICATION	Driving under the influence of medication not intended to intoxicate
A25	A25	DRIVE WHILE IMPAIRED	Driving while impaired - ability definitely impaired
A26	A26	DRINK WHILE OPERATE	Drinking alcohol while operating a vehicle
A27	A21	DRIVE AFTER DRINKING	Driving after drinking - level of intoxication or impairment not known
A30	A31	ILLEGAL POSSESSION	Possession
A31	A31	POSSESS ALCOHOL	Illegal possession of alcohol
A32	A33	ILLEGAL POSS OF DRUGS	Illegal possession of alcohol or drugs
A33	A33	POSSESS DRUG	Illegal possession of drugs (controlled substances)
A34		POSS FIREARM	Illegal possession of weapon including firearm
A35	A35	OPEN CONTAINER	Possession of open alcohol container
A40	A41	INTRLOCK/AID IN VIOL	Aiding in violation of ignition interlock or immobilization device
A41	A41	VIOLATE INTERLOCK	Driver violation of ignition interlock or immobilization device

MVR Code	ACD	MVR Text	Full Description
A50	A50	MANU/DIST/DISP DRUGS	Motor vehicle used in manufacturing, distributing, or dispensing a controlled substance
A51	A50	TRANSP ALCOHOL ILLEG	Transporting liquor illegally
A52	A50	TRANSPT ALC TO MINOR	Transporting liquor to a minor
A60	A60	UNAGE DRNK/DRV CONV	Underage Convicted of Drinking and Driving at .02 or higher BAC
A61	A61	UNAGE DRNK/DRV ADMIN	Underage Administrative Per Se - Drinking and Driving at .02 or higher BAC
A90	A90	ADMIN PER SE .10	Administrative per Se for .10 BAC
A91	A91	ADMINPERSE FOR BAC	Administrative Per Se for BAC at _ _ (detail field required)
A94	A94	ADMIN PER SE .04	Administrative per Se for .04 BAC
A98	A98	ADMIN PER SE .08	Administrative per Se for .08 BAC
B01	B01	HIT & RUN	Hit and run - failure to stop and render aid after accident
B02	B02	HIT & RUN FATALITY	Hit and run - failure to stop and render aid after accident - Fatal accident
B03	B03	HIT & RUN INJURY	Hit and run - failure to stop and render aid after accident - Personal injury accident
B04	B04	HIT & RUN PROPERTY	Hit and run - failure to stop and render aid after accident - Property damage accident
B05	B05	LV SCENE OF ACCIDENT	Leaving accident scene before police arrive
B06	B06	LV SCENE FATAL ACC	Leaving accident scene before police arrive - Fatal accident
B07	B07	LV SCENE INJURY ACC	Leaving accident scene before police arrive - Personal injury accident
B08	B08	LV SCENE PROPERT ACC	Leaving accident scene before police arrive - Property damage accident
B09	B14	CONCEAL ID AFTER ACC	Refusal to reveal identity after accident
B10	B14	CONCEAL ID FATAL ACC	Refusal to reveal identity after accident - Fatal accident
B11	B14	CONCEAL ID INJUR ACC	Refusal to reveal identity after accident - Personal injury accident
B12	B14	CONCEAL ID PROP ACC	Refusal to reveal identity after accident - Property damage accident
B13	B14	DMG UNAT PROP/ANIMAL	Failure of duties upon damaging unattended vehicle or injuring animal
B14	B14	FAIL ID/FATAL/INJ AC	Failure to reveal identity after fatal or personal injury accident
B19	B19	DAW/TRANSP 16PP/HAZM	Driving while out of service order is in effect and transporting 16 or more passengers, including the driver and/or transporting hazardous materials that require a placard
B20	B20	DRV W LIC WITHDRAWN	Driving while license withdrawn
B21	B21	DRV W LIC BARRED	Driving while license barred
B22	B22	DRV W LIC CANCELED	Driving while license cancelled
B23	B23	DRV W LIC DENIED	Driving while license denied
B24	B24	DRV W LIC DISQUALIFY	Driving while license disqualified
B25	B25	DRV W LIC REVOKED	Driving while license revoked
B26	B26	DRV W LIC SUSPENDED	Driving while license suspended
B27	B27	DRIVE/OUT OF SERVICE	Driving while out of service order is in effect
B28	B51	DRV W/REGSTR CANCEL	Driving while registration cancelled
B29	B51	DRV W/REGSTR SUSPEND	Driving while registration suspended
B30	B51	ALLOW UNLIC DR TO DR	Permit unlicensed person to drive
B40	B41	POSS ALTERD/FALS DOC	Possess or provide counterfeit or altered document
B41	B41	POSS ALTERD/FALS LIC	Possess or provide counterfeit or altered driver license (includes DL, CDL, and Instruction Permit) or ID
B42	B41	DISPLAY REG/TIT INVA	Possess or provide counterfeit or altered registration or title
B43	B41	OP MISS/OBS/DEF PLAT	Missing, defaced, or obscured license plates
B44	B41	MUTILATED DOCUMENT	Mutilated document
B45	B41	MUTILATED DL/ID	Mutilated driver license (includes DL, CDL, and Instruction Permit) or ID
B46	B41	MUTILATED REG/TITLE	Mutilated registration card or title
B50	B51	EXP/NO REQUIRED DOC	Expired or no document (or item) which is required
B51	B51	OPER W/O PROPER LIC	Expired or no driver license (includes DL, CDL, and Instruction Permit)
B52	B41	EXP/NO EMISSION INSP	Expired or no emissions inspection
B53	B41	EXP/NO PLATE	Expired or no license plates or decal/sticker
B54	B41	OPER VEH W/O REGIST	Expired or no registration or title
B55	B41	EXP/NO VEH SAFE INSP	Expired or no vehicle safety inspection
B56	B56	CMV W/OUT CDL	Driving a CMV without obtaining a CDL
B57	B57	CMV NO CDL P	Driving a CMV without a CDL on their person
B60	B51	FT FILE DOC/REPORT	Failed to file document or report as required
B61	B61	FAIL FILE ACCID REPT	Failed to file accident report
B62	B51	FT FILE NM/ADD CHANG	Failed to file change of address or name
B63	B63	FT FILE FTR FIN RESP	Failed to file future proof of financial responsibility
B64	B64	FT FILE INSURAN CERT	Failed to file insurance certification
B65	B65	FT FILE MEDICAL CERT	Failed to file medical certification/disability information
B70	B41	FT SHOW REQUIRED DOC	Failed to show document as required
B71	B41	FT SHOW WEIGHT CERT	Failed to show certificate of weight
B72	B41	FT SHOW OPERATOR LIC	Failed to show driver license (includes DL, CDL, and Instruction Permit)
B73	B41	FT SHOW EMISS/SAFETY	Failed to show emissions or vehicle (safety) inspection
B74	B74	FT SHOW INSURAN CERT	Failed to show insurance certification
B75	B41	FT SHOW OPERATOR LOG	Failed to show operator's (driver's) log
B76	B41	FT SHOW REGISTRATION	Failed to show registration

MVR Code	ACD	MVR Text	Full Description
B77	B41	FT SHOW REG/DL/TITLE	Failed to show registration, title or driver license (includes DL, CDL, and Instruction Permit)
B78	B78	FT SHOW NON-CDL	Failed to show non-commercial driver license (includes Instruction Permit)
B80		FT SURR DRIVER LIC	Failed to surrender driver license (includes DL, CDL, and Instruction Permit)
B81		FAIL SURR LIC/REG/TI	Failed to surrender driver license, registration, plates, or title
B82		FT SURR REG/TI/PLATE	Failed to surrender registration, plates, or title
B83		FALSE REPORT	False report
B84		FALSE RPT OF ACC	False report of accident
B85		FALSE RPT EMIS INSP	False report of emissions inspection
B86		FALSE RPT ODOMETER	False report of odometer reading or disclosure
B87		FALSE RPT OPERAT LOG	False report of Operator's (driver's) log
B88		FALSE RPT VEH THEFT	False report of theft
B89		FALS RPT VEH SAF INS	False report of vehicle (safety) inspection
B90		FT SHOW TITLE TRANSF	Failed to provide or submit title transfer documents
B91	B91	IMPROPER DL CLASSIFI	Improper classification or endorsement on driver license (includes DL, CDL, and Instruction Permit)
B92		LOANING A DL	Loan driver license (includes DL, CDL, and Instruction Permit) to another person
B93		LOAN REG/PLATES	Loan registration or plates to another person
D01	D02	MISREP ID/FACTS	Misrepresentation of identity or other facts
D02	D02	MISREP ID/FACT DL	Misrepresentation of identity or other facts on application for driver license (includes DL, CDL, and Instruction Permit)
D03	D02	MISREP HANDICAP PERM	Misrepresentation of identity or other facts on application for handicap permit/plates
D04	D02	MISREP IDENT/REG/TIT	Misrepresentation of identity or other facts on application for registration or title
D05	D02	MIS REP EVADE ARREST	Misrepresentation of identity or other facts to avoid arrest or prosecution
D06	D06	C93MISREP TO OBTAIN ALC	Misrepresentation of identity or other facts to obtain alcohol
D07	D07	POSS MULTIPLE DL	Possess multiple driver licenses (includes DL, CDL, and Instruction Permit)
D10	D10	MAKE FAKE DL	Manufacture or make false driver license (includes DL, CDL, and Instruction Permit)
D11		MAKE FAKE EMIS/SAFE	Manufacture or make false emissions or vehicle (safety) inspection certificates
D12	B41	MAKE FAKE REG/TITLE	Manufacture or make false registration or title
D15	D16	USE DOC IMPROPERLY	Show or use improperly - Document (or item) not specified
D16	D16	USE DL IMPROPERLY	Show or use improperly - Driver license (includes DL, CDL, and Instruction Permit)
D17	B41	USE EMIS/SAFE IMPROP	Show or use improperly - Emissions or vehicle (safety) inspection
D18	B41	USE INSUR CERT IMPRO	Show or use improperly - Insurance certification
D19	B41	USE OPER LOG IMPROP	Show or use improperly - Operator's (driver's) log
D20	B41	USE REG/PLATE IMPROP	Show or use improperly - Registration, plates, or decal/sticker
D21		USE REC/TITLE IMPROP	Show or use improperly - Registration or title
D25	D16	DISPLAY OTHER'S DL	Use another's driver license (includes DL, CDL, and Instruction Permit)
D26	B41	USE OTHERS REG/TI/PL	Use another's registration, plates, or title
D27	D27	VIOLATE LIMITED LIC	Violate limited license conditions
D28	B41	VIO REG RESTRICTIONS	Violate limits of registration (manufacturer, transporter, dealer, farm, antique, etc.)
D29	D29	VIO DL RESTRICTIONS	Violate restrictions of driver license (includes DL, CDL, and Instruction Permit)
D35	D35	FT COMPLY FIN RESP	Failure to comply with financial responsibility law
D36	D36	FT MAINT LIABILI INS	Failure to maintain required liability insurance
D37	D37	FTP DAMAGE/INSTALMEN	Failure to pay for damages or make installment payment
D38	D38	FT POST SECUR/RELEAS	Failure to post security or obtain release from liability
D39	D39	UNSATISFIED JUDGMENT	Unsatisfied judgment
D40	D56	FTA: GENERAL	Failure to appear
D41	D56	FTA: HEARING	Failure to appear for hearing or mandatory appearance
D42	D56	FTA DEPT INVESTIGA	Failure to appear – Dept investigation
D43	D56	FTA EXAM/RE-EXAM	Failure to appear – exam or a re-exam
D44	D56	FTA DEPT INVESTIGAT	Failure to appear for or complete required courses
D45	D45	FTA FOR HEAR/TRIAL	Failure to appear for trial or court appearance
D50	D56	FTP:GENERAL	Failure to make required payment
D51	D51	FTP CHILD SUPPORT	Failure to make required payment of child support
D52	D56	FTP REQUIRED FEE	Failure to make required payment of fee
D53	D53	FTP FINE/COSTS	Failure to make required payment of fine and costs
D54		FTP REQUIRED TAX	Failure to make required payment of tax
D55	D56	FTP REQUIRED TOLL	Failure to make required payment of toll
D56	D56	FTA/FTP: GENERAL	Failure to answer a citation, pay fines, penalties and/or costs related to the original violation
D65	E70	LIT/HAZ/BURNING SUBS	Depositing harmful (including injurious and burning) substance on traffic way
D66		FT REMOVE HARMFUL SUBST	Failure to remove harmful substance on traffic way
D67	E70	LITTERING FROM MV	Littering from a motor vehicle
D68		THROW MV BURN SUBST	Throwing from vehicle any harmful substance
D70	D70	DRIVER VIEW OBSTRUCT	Driver's view obstructed

MVR Code	ACD	MVR Text	Full Description
D71	D74	EXCEED HR DUTY LIMIT	Exceeding hours on duty limitations
D72	D72	NO CONTROL OF VEH	Inability to control vehicle
D73	D72	TAMPERING WITH SIGNS	Obscuring, tampering with, or illegally displaying traffic control devices, warning, or instructions
D74	D74	OPERATE WHILE DROWSY	Operating a motor vehicle improperly because of drowsiness
D75	D75	OPER MV W/DISABLED	Operating a motor vehicle improperly due to physical or mental disability
D76	D78	PERJURY/MV RELATED	Perjury
D77		SEX OFFENSE IN VEH	Sex offense in a motor vehicle
D78	D78	PERJ/OPERATE MV	Perjury about the operation of a motor vehicle
DT1		DRIVER IMPRVE COURSE	Driver improvement course
DT2		DRIVER IMPRVE COURSE	Driver improvement course
E01	E01	OPERATE W/OUT EQUIP	Operating without equipment as required by law
E02	E02	OPER W/OUT BRAKES	Operating without brakes as required by law
E03	E03	OP W/OUT HZMT SAFETY	Operating without HAZMAT safety equipment as required by law
E04	E04	OP W/OUT HZMT PLACAR	Operating without HAZMAT placards/markings as required by law
E05	E05	OPER W/OUT LIGHTS	Operating without lights as required by law
E06	E06	OP W/OUT SCH BUS EQU	Operating without school bus equipment as required by law
E20		EQUIP PROHIB BY LAW	Use of equipment prohibited by law
E21		LIGHTS/SIREN PROHIB	Use of colored lights and/or siren prohibited by law
E22		EMERVEH EMBLEMS PROH	Use of emergency vehicle markings prohibited by law
E23	E23	RADAR/LASER DET PROH	Use of radar or laser detector prohibited by law
E24	E55	VEH LIGHTS PROHIB	Use of vehicle lights prohibited by law
E30	E70	DEFECTIVE EQUIPMENT	Defective equipment
E31	E31	DEFECTIVE BRAKES	Defective brakes
E32		DEFCT EMISS CONTROL	Defective emissions control device
E33	E33	DEFCT HZMT SAFETY	Defective HAZMAT safety devices
E34	E34	DEFECTIVE LIGHTS	Defective lights
E35		DEFECTIVE EXHAUST	Defective or noisy exhaust system or muffler
E36	E36	DEFCT SCH BUS EQUIP	Defective school bus equipment
E37	E37	DEFECTIVE TIRES	Defective tires
E50	E50	FT USE REQUIRE EQUIP	Failure to use equipment as required
E51	E51	FT USE BRAKES	Failure to use brakes
E52	E50	FT USE LIGHTS/FLARES	Failure to use disabled vehicle lights, reflectors, or flares as required
E53	E53	FT USE HZMT SAFTY EQ	Failure to use HAZMAT safety devices as required
E54	E54	FAIL TO DIM LIGHTS	Failure to use headlight dimmer as required
E55	E55	FT USE LIGHTS	Failure to use lights as required
E56	E56	FT USE SCHBUS SAF EQ	Failure to use school bus safety equipment as required
E57	E57	FT USE SNWTIRE/CHAIN	Failure to use snow tires or chains as required
E70	E70	EQUIPMENT MISUSE	Equipment used improperly or obstructed
E71	E71	IMP USE BRAKES	Brakes used improperly
E72		IMP USE EMISS CNTR	Emissions control device used improperly or obstructed
E73	E70	IMP/EQUIP EXCES NOIS	Equipment used improperly - making excessive noise
E74	E70	IMP EXHAUST SYSTEM	Exhaust system used improperly or obstructed
E80	E70	DISREGRD REPAIR NOTI	Failure to correct defects after inspection failure or notice
F01	F04	FT USE SAFETY EQUIP	Safety equipment not used properly as required
F02	F02	IMP/NO CHILD RESTRAI	Child or youth restraint not used properly as required
F03	F03	IMP/NO MC SAFETY EQU	Motorcycle safety equipment not used properly as required
F04	F04	IMP/NO SAFETY BELT	Seat belt not used properly as required
F05	F05	UNSECURED PASSENGERS	Carrying unsecured passengers in open area of vehicle
F06	F06	RIDE/OP MC IMPROPER	Improper operation of or riding on a motorcycle
F10	F66	OVERLD SIZ/LG/HT/PAS	Exceeding or violating size, weight, or passenger/cargo limits
F11	F66	VIO PASS/CARGO LIMIT	Exceeding or violating passenger or cargo limits of vehicle/truck
F12	F66	VIO VEH SIZE LIMIT	Exceeding or violating size limits of vehicle/truck
F13	F66	VIO VEH WEIGHT LIMIT	Exceeding or violating weight limits of vehicle/truck
F14	F66	VIO MC PAS/CARGO	Exceeding or violating passenger or cargo limits of motorcycle
F15	F66	RD/BRDG/TUN SIZE LIM	Exceeding or violating size limits of road/bridge/tunnel
F16	F66	RD/BRDG/TUN WGT LIM	Exceeding or violating weight limits of road/bridge/tunnel
F20	F66	FT STOP @ WGT STATIO	Failure to weigh vehicle or stop at weigh station
F21	F66	IMP/NO TRIP PERMIT	No or improper trip permit
F22	F66	NO PROJ LOAD WARNING	No warning for projecting load
F23	F66	SPIL/DRAG UNSE LOAD	Spilling, dragging, unsecured or unsafe load
F24	F66	VIO EXCES/SZ/WGT/PER	Violation of excess size/weight permit
F30	F66	FT USE REDFLG/FLARES	Failure to place red flags or flares
F31	F66	FT SET BRAKE	Failure to set brake(s)
F32	F66	NON EMERGENCY STOP	Non emergency stop
F33	F66	PARK HANDICAP ZON	Parking in a handicap zone

MVR Code	ACD	MVR Text	Full Description
F34	F34	OBSTRUCT TRAFFIC	Stopping, standing, or parking: obstructing or impeding traffic
F35	F66	IMP STOP/STAND/PARK	Stopping, standing, or parking where prohibited or improper
F40	F66	IMP VEH ON ROADWAY	Improper vehicle used on roadway
F41	F66	VEH WHERE PROHIBITED	Operate or permit vehicle where prohibited or not authorized
F60	F66	ABANDONED VEH	Abandoned vehicle
F61	F66	ALTERED EMISS CNTRL	Alteration of emissions control device
F62		FAIL TO GET VIN	Failed to get VIN
F63	F66	UNATTEND RUNNING VEH	Leaving vehicle unattended with engine running
F64	F66	OPEN DOOR INTO TRAFI	Opening vehicle door into moving traffic or while vehicle is in motion
F65	F66	IMPROPER TOW OR PUSH	Towing or pushing vehicle improperly
F66	F66	UNSAFE VEHICLE	Unsafe condition of vehicle (no specified component)
M01	M08	FAILURE TO OBEY	Failure to obey
M02	M02	FTO BARRIER	Failure to obey barrier
M03	M03	FTO CONSTRUC MARKER	Failure to obey construction or maintenance zone markers
M04	M04	FTO FLAGGER	Failure to obey flagger
M05	M05	FTO LANE MARK/SIGNAL	Failure to obey lane markings or signal
M06	M08	FTO MOTORCARRIER REG	Failure to obey motor carrier rules/regulations
M07	M02	FTO PED CNTR DEVICE	Failure to obey pedestrian control device
M08	M08	FTO POLICE/PEACE OFF	Failure to obey police or peace officer
M09	M09	FTO RR CROSSING REST	For all drivers, failure to obey railroad-highway crossing restrictions not specifically noted in other railroad-highway grade crossing related codes
M10	M10	FTO RR GATES/SIGNS	For all drivers, failure to obey a traffic control device or the directions of an enforcement official at a railroad-highway grade crossing
M11	M11	FTO RESTRICTED LANE	Failure to obey restricted lane
M12	M12	FTO SAFETY ZONE	Failure to obey safety zone
M13	M13	FTO SCH XING GUARD	Failure to obey school crossing guard
M14	M14	FTO SIGN/TRAF CNTRL	Failure to obey sign or traffic control device
M15	M15	FTO STOP SIGN	Failure to obey stop sign
M16	M16	FTO TRF SIG/LIGHT	Failure to obey traffic signal or light
M17	M17	FTO TRAFFIC SIGN	Failure to obey traffic sign
M18	M18	FTO WARNING LIGHT	Failure to obey warning light or flasher
M19	M19	FTO YIELD SIGN	Failure to obey yield sign
M20	M20	FT SLOW:RR CROSSING	For drivers not required to always stop, failure to slow at a RR highway grade x-ing and check tracks are clear of approaching train
M21	M21	FT STOP:RR CROSSING	For drivers not required to always stop, failure to stop before reaching tracks at RR-highway grade x-ing when tracks are not clear
M22	M22	FT STOP:B4 ENT RRXG	For drivers who are always required to stop, failure to stop as required before driving onto railroad-highway grade crossing
M23	M23	INSUFF SPACE: RRXG	For all drivers, failing to have sufficient space to drive completely through the railroad-highway grade crossing without stopping
M24	M24	INSUF CLR/UNDER:RRXG	For all drivers, failing to negotiate a railroad-highway grade crossing because of insufficient undercarriage clearance
M25	M25	STOP B4 ENTER RD WAY	Failure to stop - basic rule at unsigned intersection or when entering roadway from private driveway, alley, etc.
M30	M30	FOLLOW IMPROPERLY	Following improperly
M31	M31	FT LEAVE PASS SPACE	Failure to leave sufficient distance for overtaking by other vehicles
M32	M32	FOLLOW EMERGENCY VEH	Following emergency vehicle unlawfully
M33	M33	FOLLOW FIRE EQUIP	Following fire equipment unlawfully
M34	M34	FOLLOW TOO CLOSE	Following too closely
M40	M40	IMP LANE/LOCATION	Improper lane or location
M41	M41	FT KEEP IN LANE	Failure to keep in proper lane
M42	M42	IMP LANE CHANGE	Improper or erratic (unsafe) lane changes
M43	M43	RAN OFF ROAD	Ran off road
M44	M44	IMP LOC/CROSSOVER	Improper lane or location - crossover
M45	M45	IMP LOC/CROSSWALK	Improper lane or location - crosswalk
M46	M46	IMP ENTRY/EXIT RAMP	Improper lane or location - entrance/exit ramp or way
M47	M47	IMP LOC/BICYCLE LANE	Improper lane or location - in bicycle lane
M48	M48	IMP LOC/OCCUPIED LAN	Improper lane or location - in occupied lane
M49	M49	IMP LOC/HOV RES LANE	Improper lane or location - in HOV or restricted lane
M50	M50	IMP LOC/LIMTD ACCESS	Improper lane or location - limited access highway
M51	M51	IMP LOC/MEDIAN	Improper lane or location - median
M52		IMP LOC/NOT NTL NTWK	Improper lane or location - not on National Network
M53	M40	IMP LOC/UNAUTH ROUTE	Improper lane or location - not on route authorized by permit
M54	M40	MP LOC/NOT TRUCK RT	Improper lane or location - not on truck route
M55	M55	IMP LOC/RAIL/ST CAR	Improper lane or location - on rail or streetcar tracks
M56	M56	CROSS FIRE HOSE	Improper lane or location - on fire hose

MVR Code	ACD	MVR Text	Full Description
M57	M57	IMP LOC/ONCOMING LAN	Improper lane or location - oncoming traffic lane
M58	M58	IMP LOC/SHOULDER	Improper lane or location - road shoulder, ditch or sidewalk
M60	M60	IMP LOC/SLOW LANE	Improper lane or location - slower vehicle lane
M61	M61	IMP LOC/CENTER LINE	Improper lane or location - straddling center line(s)
M62	M62	IMP LOC/TURN LANE	Improper lane or location - traveling in turn (or center) lane
M63	M09	INSUFF SPACE: RRXG	Railroad grade crossing, insufficient space; failure to obey railroad-highway grade crossing restrictions
M70	M70	IMPROPER PASSING	Improper passing
M71	M71	IMP PASS/VIO SIGN	Passing in violation of posted sign or pavement marking
M72	M72	IMP PASS/OPOSITE DIR	Passing in violation of opposite directions restriction
M73	M73	IMP PASS/WRONG SIDE	Passing on wrong side
M74	M74	IMP PASS/HILL CURVE	Passing on hill or curve
M75	M75	PASS SCH BUS W/RED	Passing school bus displaying warning not to pass
M76	M76	IMP PASS/PROHIBITED	Passing where prohibited
M77	M77	PASS W/O PROP SPACE	Passing with insufficient distance or visibility
M80	M84	RECKLES/CARELES/NEG	Reckless, careless, or negligent driving (Per updated ACD Codes, this is now defined as Inattentive, careless, or negligent driving)
M81	M81	CARELESS DRIVING	Careless driving
M82	M82	INATTENTIVE DRIVING	Inattentive driving
M83	M83	NEGLIGENT DRIVING	Negligent driving
M84	M84	RECKLESS DRIVING	Reckless driving
M85		WILLFULL DISREGARD	Willful disregard
M86	M86	HHMT WH DRIV	Handheld text while driving
N01	N01	FT YIELD RIGHT OF WY	Failure to yield right of way (FTY ROW)
N02	N02	FTYROW/ANIMAL/RIDER	FTY ROW to animal rider or animal-drawn vehicle
N03	N03	FTYROW/CYCLIST	FTY ROW to cyclist
N04	N04	FTYROW EMERGENCY VEH	FTY ROW to emergency vehicle (i.e ambulance, fire equipment, police, etc.)
N05	N05	FTYROW/FUNERAL/PARAD	FTY ROW to funeral procession, procession or parade
N06	N06	FTYROW/OTHER VEHICLE	FTY ROW to other vehicle
N07	N07	FTYROW/OVRTAKING VEH	FTY ROW to overtaking vehicle
N08	N08	FTYROW/PEDESTRIAN	FTY ROW to pedestrian (includes handicapped or blind)
N09	N09	FTYROW/SCHOOL BUS	FTY ROW to school bus
N20	N20	FTYROW/CROSSWALK	FTY ROW at crosswalk
N21	N21	FTYROW/ROTARY INTERS	FTY ROW at rotary
N22	N22	FTYROW/STOP SIGN	FTY ROW at stop sign
N23	N23	FTYROW/TRAFFIC SIGN	FTY ROW at traffic sign
N24	N24	FTYROW/TRAFIC SIGNAL	FTY ROW at traffic signal
N25	N25	FTYROW/UNSIGNED INTR	FTY ROW at unsigned intersection
N26	N26	FTYROW/YIELD SIGN	FTY ROW at yield sign
N30	N30	FTYROW/OTHR VEH WARN	FTY ROW when warning displayed on other vehicle
N31	N31	FTYROW/WHEN TURNING	FTY ROW when turning
N40	N40	IMP SIGNAL OR FT USE	Failure to use or improper signal
N41	N41	FT CANCEL DIR SIGNAL	Failure to cancel directional signals
N42	N42	FT SIGNAL B4 PASSING	Failure to signal intention to pass
N43	N43	FT SIGNAL LANE CHANG	Failure to signal lane change or turn
N44	N44	GIVE WRONG SIGNAL	Giving wrong signal
N50	N50	IMPROPER TURN	Improper turn
N51	N51	IMP TURN/METHOD OF	Improper method of turning
N52	N52	IMP TURN/POSITION	Improper position for turning
N53	N53	MAKE IMP LEFT TURN	Making improper left turn
N54	N54	MAKE IMP RIGHT TURN	Making improper right turn
N55	N55	MAKE IMP TURN AROUND	Making improper turn around (not U turn)
N56	N56	MAKE IMP U TURN	Making improper U turn
N60	N60	DRIVE WRONG WAY	Driving wrong way
N61	N61	WRONG WY @ROTARY INT	Driving wrong way at rotary intersection
N62	N62	WRONG WAY/DIVIDE HWY	Driving wrong way on divided highway
N63	N63	WRONG WAY ON ONE WAY	Driving wrong way on one way street or road
N70	N70	DR/WRONG SIDE OF RD	Driving on wrong side
N71	N71	WRONG SIDE/DIVID HWY	Driving on wrong side of divided highway
N72	N72	WRONG SIDE/UNDIV HWY	Driving on wrong side of undivided street or road
N80	N80	COASTING	Coasting (operating with gears disengaged)
N81	N84	CLING TO VEHICLES	Clinging to other vehicles
N82	N82	IMPROPER BACKING	Improper backing
N83	N83	IMPROPER START	Improper starting from a parked position
N84	N84	UNSAFE OPERATE MV	Unsafe operation
S00	S93	SPEED OVER POST MAX	Speeding (detail given)

MVR Code	ACD	MVR Text	Full Description
S01	S01	SP XS: 01-05	Speeding 01-05 > Speed limit
S02-05	S01	SPEED 2-5MPH OVER	Speeding 02-05 >Speed limit
S06	S06	SP XS: 06-10	Speeding 06-10 > Speed limit
S07-10	S06	SPEED 7-10MPH OVER	Speeding 07-10 >Speed limit
S11-14	S93	SPEED 11-14MPH OVER	Speeding 11-15 > Speed limit
S15	S15	SP XS: 15&GR	Speeding 15 mph or more above speed limit
S16	S16	SP XS: 16-20	Speeding 16-20 > Speed limit
S17-20	S16	SPEED 17-20MPH OVER	Speeding 17-20 >Speed limit
S21	S21	SP XS: 21-25	Speeding 21-25 > Speed limit
S22-25	S21	SPEED 22-25MPH OVER	Speeding 22-25 >Speed limit
S26	S26	SP XS: 26-30	Speeding 26-30 > Speed limit
S27-30	S26	SPEED 27-30MPH OVER	Speeding 27-35 >Speed limit
S31	S31	SP XS: 31-35	Speeding 31-35 > Speed limit
S32-35	S31	SPEED 32-35MPH OVER	Speeding 32-35 >Speed limit
S36	S36	SP XS: 36-40	Speeding 36-40 > Speed limit
S37-40	S36	SPEED 37-40MPH OVER	Speeding 37-40 >Speed limit
S41	S41	SP XS: 41&GR	Speeding 41+ > Speed limit
S42-49	S41	SPEED 42MPH OR MORE	Speeding 42-49 >Speed limit
S50	S92	SPEED-SCHOOL ZONE	Speeding in a school zone
S51	S51	SP XS: 01-10	Speeding 01-10 > Speed limit
S61	S51	SP XS: 11-20	Speeding 11-20 > Speed limit
S71	S71	SP XS: 21-30	Speeding 21-30 > Speed limit
S81	S81	SP XS: 31-40	Speeding 31-40 > Speed limit
S91	S91	SP XS: 41&GR	Speeding 41+ > Speed limit
S92	S92	SPEED DTAIL:	Speeding - Speed limit and actual speed detailed
S93	S93	SPEEDING****	Speeding
S94	S94	PRIMA FACIE*	*Prima Facie* speed violation or driving too fast for conditions
S95	S95	RACING/SPEED CONTEST	Speed contest (racing) on road open to traffic
S96	S96	INSUFFICIENT SPEED	Speed less than minimum
S97	S97	ERRATIC SPEED	Operating at erratic or suddenly changing speeds
S98	S98	WASTING FUEL	Speeding on freeway ("wasting fuel")
S99	S92	SPEED/SCHL ZONE	Speeding in school zone
U01	U01	FLEE/ELUDE POLICE	Fleeing or evading police or roadblock
U02	U02	RESIST ARREST IN MV	Resisting arrest
U03	U03	USE MV IN FELONY	Using a motor vehicle in connection with a felony (not traffic offense)
U04	U04	USE MV IN MISDEMEANO	Using a motor vehicle in connection with a misdemeanor (not traffic offense)
U05	U05	USE MV TO AID FELON	Using a motor vehicle to aid and abet a felon
U06	U06	ASSAULT 4TH IN MV	Vehicular assault
U07	U07	NEG HOMICIDE WITH MV	Vehicular homicide
U08	U08	MANSLAUGHTER WITH MV	Vehicular manslaughter
U09	U09	NEG HOMICIDE W/CMV	Negligent homicide while operating a CMV
U10	U10	FATALITY/NEG OPS CMV	Causing a fatality through the negligent operation of a CMV
U20	E50	DAMG/TAMP W/VEH	Damaging or tampering with vehicle
U21	U21	ILEGAL OP EMERG VEH	Illegal operation of emergency vehicle
U22	E50	ODOMETER TAMPERING	Odometer tampering
U23	E50	REC/DISP STOLEN VEH	Receiving or disposing of stolen vehicle or its parts
U24	B51	FALS/STOLEN VIN/PLAT	Removal, falsification, or unauthorized use of VIN or registration plate
U25	E70	OPER MV W/O OWN CONS	Unauthorized use of a vehicle or taking a vehicle without owner consent
U26	E70	VEHICLE THEFT	Vehicle theft
U27	U27	VEH FETIC 1	Vehicular feticide (1st degree)
U28	U28	VEH FETIC 2	Vehicular feticide (1st degree)
U30		VIO RESULT ACC	Violation resulting in accident
U31	U10	VIO RESULT FATALITY	Violation resulting in fatal accident
U32	M80	VIO RESULT/INJURY	Violation resulting in personal injury accident
U33		VIO RESULT PROP DAMG	Violation resulting in property damage accident
W00	W00	WITHDRAWAL/NON ACD	Withdrawal, Non-ACD violation
W01	W01	ACCUM PTS/HAB OFFEND	Accumulation of convictions (including point systems and/or being judged a habitual offender or violator)
W09	W09	FTS HAZMAT ENDORSMNT	Failure to surrender HAZMAT endorsement as required by the US PATRIOT Act
W10		WITHDRAWAL	Withdrawal (reason not specified)
W11		FAMILY REPRT	Family report recommended
W12		IMMIGRAT LAW	Immigration law offender
W13	W13	WITHDR PARENT CONSEN	Parental consent withdrawn
W14	W14	PHYS/MENT DISABLED	Physical or mental disability
W15	W15	PHYSICIAN REPORT	Physicians' or specialists' report recommended
W20	W20	FAIL DL TEST/QUALIFI	Unable to pass DL test(s) or meet qualifications

MVR Code	ACD	MVR Text	Full Description
W21	W20	FAIL TO RE-EXAM	Unable to pass re-examination
W22	W20	UNDERAGE FOR DL/IP	Under age for license
W23		UNDERAGE/TABACCO	Under age possession of tobacco
W24		SCHL DROPOUT	Under age school dropout
W25		DISOBEY PROBATION	Disobeying terms of probation
W26		INSUFFICIENT FUNDS	Insufficient funds
W30	W30	TWO SERIOUS VIO/3YRS	Two serious violations within three years
W31	W31	3 SERIOUS VIO/3 YRS	Three serious violations within three years
W40	W40	2 OR MORE MAJOR OFF	Two or more major offenses
W41	W41	MAJ OFF AFTER REINST	An additional major offense after reinstatement
W45	W45	PR DISQ CMV	Suspended for driving a CMV while disqualified for previous violations in a CMV
W50	W50	2 OOS VIOL W/IN 10YR	The accumulation of two out-of-service order general violations (violations not covered by W51) within ten years
W51	W51	2 VIOL 10YR/16PP/HAZ	The second out-of-service order violations within ten years while transporting 16 or more passengers, including the driver and/or transporting hazardous materials that require a placard
W52	W52	3+ OOS VIOL W/IN 10Y	The accumulation of three or more out-of-service order violations within ten years
W60	W60	2 RRGC VIOL W/IN 3YR	The accumulation of two RRGC violations within three years.
W61	W61	3+RRGC VIOL W/IN 3YR	The accumulation of three or more RRGC violations within three years.
W70	W70	IMMINENT HAZARD CMV	Imminent hazard - in a CMV
W72	W72	PEND FINAL	Suspended pending final disposition
W80	W80	FAIL DRUG	Failed employer-directed drug test
W81	W81	REFUSE DRUG	Refusal to submit to an employer-directed drug test

Point System Summary

Alaska employs a point system with points ranging from 2 to 10 points. A driver can be suspended with 12 or more points in a 12- month period or 18 points in 24 months.

Assault with a motor vehicle	10 points
Careless driving	4 points
Driving while intoxicated	10 points
Failure to obey official traffic control devices in school zone, playground crosswalk, or park	6 points
Failure to show insurance certificate	6 points
Failure to stop for school bus while bus is loading or unloading	6 points
Failure to stop or yield	4 points
Failure to yield to authorized emergency vehicle	6 points
Fleeing or attempting to elude police officer	10 points
Following too close	4 points
Leaving the scene of an accident	9 points
Manslaughter with a motor vehicle	10 points
Negligent driving	6 points
Negligent homicide with a motor vehicle	10 points
Operating a motor vehicle when license is suspended or revoked	10 points
Operating a motor vehicle in violation of a limited license	10 points
Reckless driving	10 points
Refusal to consent to alcohol/drug testing	10 points
Resisting arrest in a motor vehicle	10 points
Speed contest - racing	10 points
Speeding:	
In school zone or playground crosswalk	6 points
3 to 9 mph over limit	2 points
10 to 19 mph over limit	4 points
20 mph or more over the limit	6 points
Underage drinking/driving conviction	6 points
Violation of oversize or overweight permits pertaining to restriction on hours of operation	3 points
Violation of oversize or overweight permits pertaining to restriction of speed:	
3 to 9 mph over limit	2 points
10 to 19 mph over limit	4 points
20 mph or more over the limit	6 points
All other moving violations	2 points

Arizona

Administration	Important Telephone and Web Contacts
Stacey K Stanton, Division Director Motor Vehicle Division Department of Transportation PO Box 2100, Mail Drop 500M Phoenix 85001-2100 602-712-8152 www.azdot.gov/mvd/index.asp	Driver Licensing and Vehicle Information ....602-255-0072 Financial Responsibility & SR-22 ....602-255-0072 Commercial Driver License.............................623-932-7731 State Department of Insurance..........................602-364-3100 Department of Public Safety............................602-223-2000 General Email: mvdinfo@azdot.gov Statutes and Rules www.azdot.gov/mvd/mvdrules/index.asp

Driver's License Format, Issuance and Renewal

License Classes, Restrictions and Endorsements Appear After the Driving Record Content Section

License Format

Licenses are issued as one letter plus eight numbers. However, in the past some licenses were issued using the Social Security Number as the DL# and some of these licenses are still active. Current military licenses remain valid until out of service, some duplicates are issued without photo.

Document Appearance

The license is printed on standard plastic credit card stock.

Security Characteristics: Hologram overlay, bar code, magnetic strip, secondary "ghost" signature and digital signature.

Since February 7, 2001, the Motor Vehicle Division uses these security enhancements:

- Background image of the Grand Canyon
- Horizontally printed license for drivers age 21 and over.
- Vertically printed license for drivers under age 21. Displays date when licensee will be age 21.
- Magnetic "MAG" stripe contains license information, including endorsements and restrictions.
- Barcode moved to back of license. Secures credential information.
- Optically Variable Ink (OVI) technology used to provide security and reduce fraud.

Position of Photo: Lower right.

Minor Age Driver Locator: "UNDER 21 UNTIL..." is printed in red.

CDL Indicator: "COMMERCIAL DRIVER'S LICENSE" is printed on heading.

Issuance

Location of Requirements for Proof of Identity:
http://mvd.azdot.gov/mvd/formsandpub/mvd.asp?txtNumber=96-0155

Age Requirements

The minimum age for an operator's permit is 18. The current Graduated Licensing Program was been in operation since July 2008. A Graduated Instruction Permit is issued to an applicant who is at least 15 years and 6 months old. The teen must have a licensed driver at least 21 years of age seated in front seat at all times. The Graduated Driver License is issuable to those at least 16 years of age. For at least 6 months a variety of requirements are in place, including supervised driving practice and requirements on who can be in the car. A driver can apply for the Class D driver license at age 18. Exact requirements are indicated on the web.

Residency

Non-residents must obtain license upon establishing residency, accepting employment, enrolling children in public school, or remaining in the state for seven months or more.

Renewal

Extended licenses expire at age 65 with mandatory photo update every twelve years. Limited licenses expire on the birth date of the fifth year. The driver keeps same number when renewing. Driver's license reinstatement and address changes can be done online at servicearizona.com, but not renewal.

Elderly-Related Restrictions

When driver is over 65, renewal licenses are issued every 5 years.

Vehicle Insurance, Title and Registration Facts

Registration

A five-year registration is available to any vehicle not subject to emissions testing requirement for the entire five-year registration cycle.

Renewal

Renewal is annual, biennial, or five-year (depending on emissions testing) and is not otherwise systemically tied to last names or location. The MVD offers renewal of vehicle registration and address changes online at www.servicearizona.com.

For New Residents

A new resident is required to immediately obtain AZ plates for his/her vehicle. A resident is generally defined as someone employed or with children in school.

Inspections and Emissions Testing

Arizona has no provisions for statewide emission testing or annual safety inspections. However, Maricopa, Pima and portions of Yavapai and Pinal counties require an annual emissions test for vehicles manufactured in 1967 or later, but exempt most vehicles of the newest models of five years.

Passenger Plate Facts

One plate and one tab issued. The tab displays the licensed number of the vehicle and the month and year of expiration. Arizona does not use a code on a plate designating the county of issuance. Plate does not remain with vehicle if sold, it goes with the original owner.

Insurance and Financial Responsibility

Arizona minimum limits are $15,000/30,000/10,000. Proof is not required at the time of annual vehicle renewal or registration. Law enforcement officers will ask for proof of insurance at the time of traffic stops or accidents. Insurance companies notify the MVD of all policy cancellations, non-renewals, and new policies. SR-22 forms are used in this state. **De-insurance** is a method of temporarily not maintaining the required insurance on a vehicle until it is ready to be driven or placed on the road again. A de-insured vehicle will not be suspended due to lack of insurance unless driven on the roadways of this state. Mandatory

Financial Responsibility also includes coverage on golf carts, motorcycles, and mopeds.

Withdrawal Sanctions, and Alcohol and Drug Testing

Alcohol and Chemical Testing

Arizona's illegal intoxication level is .08 % and above for ages 21 and older; .00 % for ages 16 to 21; and .04 % for commercial vehicle drivers. Urine, blood, and breath testing are authorized. Extreme DCCI is .15 % and above. Arizona has both an implied-consent violation and a provision for an administrative suspension. Operating a bicycle under the influence is also considered illegal.

Suspensions and Revocations

See the Appendix for a list of the federally mandated disqualifications for offenses occurring in a CMV per MCSIA.

The State Shall Revoke the License of a Driver for Any of the Following Offenses—
- Any Felony Committed While Using a Motor Vehicle
- Any Homicide Resulting From the Operation of a Motor Vehicle
- Conviction or Forfeiture of Bail Not Vacated, Upon Second or Subsequent Charge of Reckless Driving, Racing or Any of the Above in Combination With DUI Driving
- Driving Under the Influence of Drugs or Alcohol-Multiple Offenses Within 60 Months
- Failure to Stop and Give Aid When Involved in an Accident Resulting in Personal Injury or Death
- Perjury or Making a False Affidavit Under Oath to the Department, Including Related to Ownership of Vehicle
- Second or Subsequent Conviction for DUI Within Sixty Months
- Violation of Railroad Crossing Law or Regulation

The State May Suspend the License of a Driver for Any of the Following Offenses—
- Committing or Permitting Unlawful or Fraudulent Use of a License
- Conviction of Driving or Being in Actual Physical Control of a Motor Vehicle, While Under the Influence of Liquor or Drugs
- Failure to Pay Child Support
- Failure to Complete Traffic Survival School (TSS)
- Habitual Offender, Disrespect for Traffic Laws and the Safety of Others
- Incompetence
- Involvement in an Accident Resulting in Death, Personal Injury or Serious Property Damage
- Providing or purchasing spirituous liquor for an individual under 21
- Reckless Driving Conviction or Being Habitually Reckless or Negligent

The Following Suspensions are Mandated—

Drag Racing ....One year revocation
DUI for Minors Under 21 years of age ....Two-year suspension
Extreme DUI, 2nd Offense ....One year revocation
Failure to Complete TSS for a Red Light Violation ....Indefinite suspension
Failure to Stop and Give Aid When Involved in an Accident Resulting in Personal Injury or Death:
    Revoked for 5 years if involving death or serious physical injury
    Revoked for 3 years if involving injury other than death or serious physical injury
    Suspended for 1 year if involving only damage to a vehicle
Moving Violations for Minors under 18 years of age (first violation not cited if subject attends driving school; however Class G is extended for 60 days):
    2nd Violation (1st conviction) ....No susp, attend Traffic Survival School, extend Class G restriction 60 days
    3rd Violation (2nd conviction) ....Three-month suspension
    4th Violation (3rd conviction) ....Six-month suspension
    Refusal to Submit to a Chemical Test...One-year suspension.

The Following May Require Attendance at a Traffic Survival School:
- For convictions causing the accumulation of at least 8 points, but not more than 12 points, within a 12-month period, providing no Traffic Survival School was completed in the previous 24 months.
- For a conviction of one of the following violations: Aggressive Driving, Moving Violation Resulting In An Accident Causing Serious Physical Injury, Moving Violation Resulting In An Accident Causing Death.
- For the first moving violation of a driver under 18 years of age
- For a conviction for Red Light Running

Reinstatement Requirements

Suspension $10.00 fee, plus re-application fee according to age; SR-22 required in some cases. $50.00 fee for DUI or "Admin Per Se."
Revocation $20.00 fee, plus re-application fee according to age; SR-22 may be required for three years; time lapse of at least one year.
Note: Disqualification for a BAC .04 in CMV requires a $10.00 fee, plus re-application fee according to age; no SR-22 required

Record Access: Laws, Rules, and Forms

Note: **This Section Applies to Both Driver and Vehicle Records.**

Governing Statutes and Rules

Statutes and Rules: www.azdot.gov/mvd/mvdrules/index.asp
The release of records is governed by Title 28, Chapter 2, Article 5, and

specifically ARS 28-449 and 28-447. Although the state is in compliance with DPPA, Arizona's statute is substantially different from the federal statute. The only provisions the they have in common are 18

USCA §2721(b)(4), (6), (8), and (11).

Arizona added the following to its state statutes:

2) A financial institution or enterprise under the jurisdiction of the state banking department or a federal monetary authority.

4) An attorney who is admitted to practice in this state and who alleges that the information is relevant to a pending or potential court proceeding.

5) A motor vehicle dealer who is licensed and bonded by the department or a state organization of licensed and bonded motor vehicle dealers.

6) The release of any of the following information to a person who is involved in an accident or to the owner of a vehicle involved in an accident if the person who requests the information submits proof to the department of involvement in the accident:

(a) The driving record of a person who operates a motor vehicle involved in the accident.

(b) The vehicle title or registration record of a vehicle involved in the accident.

9) The release of a title and registration record if all of the following conditions exist:

(a) The requester verifies to the satisfaction of the director that the vehicle on which the requester is requesting the record is in the requester's possession.

(b) The record is requested in order for the requester to notify the registered owner of the requester's intent to apply to the department for a bonded title.

(c) The requester provides a verification of a vehicle inspection that was performed by an authorized department employee or agent.

10) An operator of a self-service storage facility located in this state who alleges all of the following:

(a) That the vehicle on which the operator is requesting the record is in the operator's possession.

(b) That the record is requested to allow the operator to notify the registered owner and any lien-holders of record of the operator's intent to foreclose its lien and to sell the vehicle.

(c) That the operator obtained a verification of a vehicle inspection that was performed by an authorized department employee or agent.

Policy Regarding Insurance Uses

Insurance companies under the jurisdiction of the Arizona Department of Insurance may receive records by meeting only two of the three record-criteria requirements (below). This exemption is not applicable to processing companies unless they are the authorized agent (as defined in ARS 28-450.C) of an Arizona vehicle insurer. ARS 28-450 prescribes other requirements for insurer-authorized agents. Persons involved in an accident with an Arizona-licensed driver and/or Arizona-licensed vehicle may request record information without meeting the full criteria. They must, however, provide proof of the accident.

Use of Consent Forms

Use of a *Motor Vehicle Records Request Form 46-4416* is required for non-electronic access. For both driver and vehicle records, forms are located at http://mvd.azdot.gov/mvd/formsandpub/mvd.asp. At this screen enter "46-4416."

Records are released if the subject gives written consent or has opted-in. There is another way to obtain records, which assumes consent. The state will release information concerning a motor vehicle record if the requester provides ALL of the following:

1. the name of the licensee (as it appears on the state database);

2. the driver's license number or a statement that the license is suspended or revoked; and

3. the date of birth of the licensee or the license expiration date.

This requester must provide identification—usually the driver's license—and state the reason for making the request. Then, the Division will verify the name and address of the requester and release the record. If the request is mailed in, the requester's signature must be notarized. Exemptions to this requirement are listed in ARS 28-450.B.

Vendor and Third Party Access Policy

Approved online vendors can access records for other vendors (who are not online, etc.) who will then sell to an end user provided—

a. If contract between original vendor and reseller contains same language as contract between the state and the original vendor

b. If contract between reseller and end user contains same language as contract between the state and the original vendor

Records Ordered For Non-permissible Uses

No records, even without personal information, are released without consent or as described above.

Access to Driver-Related Records

Driving Records

General Information and Fees

Record Services Section, PO Box 2100, Mail Drop 504M, Phoenix 85001-2100, 602-255-0072.

Arizona provides both a thirty-nine-month (insurance) record and a five-year record. Employers and individuals may request a five-year record. Fees are listed below by request method. It takes a minimum of two weeks before new records are available for inquiry.

To order, submit: 1) full name; 2) the driver's license number or statement of fact that license is suspended or revoked, full name; 3) and date of birth, or license expiration date are required when ordering a manual search. "Exempt" requesters are not required to provide full criteria, but must supply sufficient information to enable location of the correct record. Insurance companies, who are exempt, can only receive the 39-month record.

Mail – The record fee for a 39-month record is $3.00, and $5.00 for a certified 5-year record. The state charges full price for a no record found search. Mail requests *for casual requesters with consent* must be notarized for the requester's signature. Mail requests are processed within one week of receipt. This may increase to 10 days during peak months (November to February). The driver's mailing address is provided as part of the record to permissible use requesters.

In-Person – The counter is at Customer Records Services, 1801 West Jefferson, Lobby, Phoenix AZ 85007, 602-255-0072. Records may be requested at this office as well as any MVD field office. The fee for an uncertified 39-month record is $3.00 if accessed immediately (limit of 4 only) or $2.00 if picked up the next day. The fee is $5.00 for a certified 5-year record. Casual requester signatures must be notarized. There is a limit of two requests per trip to the window. If more records are needed, the requester must go to the end of the line and wait for another turn.

Electronic – The Motor Vehicle Record Request System (MVRRS) is a web-based application used by commercial and government entities contracted with MVD to electronically request records. Certified and uncertified driver license records and/or title and registration records can be obtained in the interactive or batch mode. Interactive requests are returned in seconds, batch requests are processed within two hours. Interactive records have a fee of $6.00 (39-month) and $8.00 (5-year). The fee for batch records is $5.00 (39-month) and $6.00 (5-year). A NRF is $5.00. All fees include the $3.00 portal fee surcharge. For more information about MVRRS, contact the Electronic Data Services Unit by email at eds@azdot.gov or call 602-712-7235. There is no information displayed on the web about this service beyond the contact information.

Note there is a separate online access system for drivers to obtain their own records, see below.

CDL holders and/or persons applying for a CDL who submitted their medical certification may review the status of their certification at www.azdot.gov/mvd/medicalreview/cdlstatus.asp.

Bulk Sales – The state does not make its driver license file available to private or commercial vendors for marketing purposes. However Arizona will sell driver history or status in bulk if the purpose is DPPA related.

By Person of Record – Arizona drivers may obtain their driving record by mail or walk-in as described above. Driver license offices throughout the state will provide records if the request is for the applicant's own record. Also one may ask what tickets are on their own record by calling a Customer Service Representative.

In addition, the MVD allows customers to request, view, and print their own 39-month uncertified driving record via an electronic service provider at www.servicearizona.com. There is a $3.00 fee and a credit card is required. For all methods, the licensee must provide the full name, date of birth, driver license number, and last four digits of the SSN. This information is confirmed before the record is released.

Notification/Monitoring Program

A standalone Notification Program is not offered; however, a vendor may purchase data in bulk and technically establish a monitoring system. Also, reportedly, at least one vendor is obtaining court record data (tickets) to monitor drivers.

Accident Reports

Reporting – Reports must be filed immediately with the local police within the municipality for accidents involving injury, death or damage over $1,000; accidents outside the municipality should be reported to the county sheriff or the nearest state police patrol. Accident reports completed by law enforcement must be filed in the same way. Commercial drivers must report convictions to employers within ten days of conviction and must report to their home state within thirty days of conviction. No special form is required; a letter with information is sufficient.

Record Access – The Department of Public Safety provides access to accident reports unless the accident occurred on a city or county road; in that case contact the law enforcement agency that investigated the accident. The fee is $9.00 per record for up to first 9 pages, then $1.00 for each additional page. Photographic contact sheets are $10.00 each. Individual photos (either 8 X 10 or 4 X 6) are $4.00 each. Personal checks are not accepted. A request form is available on the web. The requester must state his/her connection to the incident (the reports are not available for commercial retrieval purposes). A written request should include: the date; time; location; drivers' names; officer's name and report number; case number; and a self-addressed, stamped envelope. Mail to: Department of Public Safety, Accident Reports, PO Box 6638, Mail Drop 1110, Phoenix, 85005, 602-223-2230, fax: 602-223-2915. Turnaround time is 1 to 2 weeks. New records are available for inquiry within a minimum of 2 weeks after the incident. See www.azdps.gov/Services/Records/Department_Records/.

Access to Vehicle-Related Records

General Information and Fees

Record Services Section, PO Box 2100, Mail Drop 504M Phoenix AZ 85001, 602-712-8866.

The Record Services Section handles search requests for vehicles and both attached and unattached mobile homes. The $3.00 search fee is for a legal document which is defined as one page, both sides. Vehicle liens are filed with the MVD. A title history will show liens. A separate lienholder record is sold for $1.50.

When ordering a vehicle record, the vehicle owner's name, VIN number, and Arizona license plate number are required. (If record is your own, only name, VIN, or Arizona license plate is required.) Credit cards are accepted for payment. A statement of purpose for request is required. Exempt requesters do not have to meet full criteria, but must provide sufficient information to enable location of the correct record.

In-Person or Mail – The courier address is 1801 W Jefferson, Lobby, Phoenix 85007. Registration information is available upon providing the vehicle owner's full name, the Arizona license plate number, and VIN. The applicant must state the purpose for the request, have the signature notarized, and enclose $3.00 for each copy (if request is made by mail). Walk-ins are $3.00; overnight $2.00; and certified requests are $5.00.

By Person of Record – Auto license offices throughout the state will provide a record, if it is the requester's own vehicle record. In addition, the MVD allows customers to electronically request, view and print *their*

own uncertified title and registration records at www.servicearizona.com. The fee is $3.00 and use of a credit card is required. If there is more than one record, the user is given a selection list displaying multiple records available. The licensee must provide the full name, date of birth, VIN, and last four digits of the SSN. This information is confirmed before the record is released. Liens are indicated.

Fax – Only ongoing permissible use requesters may have records returned by fax, usually next-day, for an additional fee of $4.00 per record

Electronic – The Motor Vehicle Record Request System (MVRRS) is the single access point for electronically accessing all Motor Vehicle Records including driver records as well as title and registration records. This is only for authorized users. The system is open 24 hours a day, 7 days a week and is set up for both interactive and batch. There is a $3.00 portal fee added to the $3.00 record fee charge. For more information contact the Electronic Data Services Units at 602-712-7235 or eds@azdot.gov.

Bulk – There is a program established to receive registration information electronically with a minimum of 100 inquiries. The fee is $2.00 per inquiry. Additionally, Arizona will provide license name and address, or vehicle owner name and address, for specific commercial-mailing purposes. However, information is only released on those subjects who have opted in.

Access to Vessel-Related Records

General Information, Access and Fees

Game & Fish Department, 5000 West Carefree Highway, Phoenix 85086, 602-942-3000, fax: 623-236-7919.

http://www.azgfd.gov/outdoor_recreation/boating.shtml.

All watercraft must be registered unless they are non-motorized. Titles are not required in this state. Records are available from 1977 to present but only indexed on computer the past 5 years. Anyone can search in-person or by mail but only if the hull ID, or owner's name, or registration # is presented. Otherwise, record release with personal information follows DPPA guidelines. Commercial records are sold, if requester is eligible, in bulk list, CD or Excel table. Use *Public Record*

Request Form 15.12 Form #430. Record access is governed by AZ Revised Statutes, Title 5-324 and is considered public record providing the requester states reason for request and gives proper identification. However a name search is not done unless if for a DPPA use. Access requires notarized signature of requester. Minimum fees range from $20 to $100 or $04 to $.10 per name. Also, the department is selective as to who can receive record information by phone or fax: these requesters are limited to law enforcement, private investigators, insurance companies (as of 8-2-2012) and attorneys. Mail requests are returned within 30 days. There is no fee. Lien records are not maintained here and must be researched at the county recorder offices.

Driving Record Content and Reciprocity

What's On or Not On the Driving Record

- The records released to permissible users contain address, height, weight, and DOB.
- Violations disposed by the court are not reported on the driving record. Parking violations are not listed either, but may be in the near future.
- Accidents are not required to be reported by police to the Motor Vehicle Division.
- A citation for "Speed Greater Than Reasonable and Prudent" allows the police officer to cite for speed due to conditions rather than specific miles per hour over limit. This cite is frequently used with accidents.
- The length of time moving violations, DWIs and suspensions are listed on the non-CDL public driving record is either thirty-nine months or five years depending on type of record ordered. For CDL can be ten years to fifty-five years.
- Points stay on a record for five years from the date of conviction, if for major violations (6-8 points) ten years. By special request, the licensee may obtain this record. Arizona permits defensive driver school attendance in lieu of conviction for certain violations, if the driver has not attended a defensive driver school within the last two years (prior attendance is tracked by the Superior Court). Additional criteria are established by the individual courts.

Data Retention

The state keeps an in-house record for five years after application, suspension, revocation or abstract of a court record of conviction or judgment has become inactive. Surrendered licenses are kept on the system for five years (if record is clean) or five years after the last conviction date. Arizona abides by the federal mandates for record retention when driver is a CDL holder (generally 55 years). See the timetable per the MCSIA in the Appendix.

Court to Repository

Violation data must be submitted within varying time periods depending on the type of court. Phoenix, Tempe, Tucson, Pima County, and Scottsdale City transfer violation and conviction data by tape; Mesa city courts transfer information online and on paper; the rest are submitted on paper. Conviction information transferred to the state via paper is usually entered onto the state system within approximately two weeks.

State Reciprocity for Non-CDL Drivers

- Will suspend driver for unpaid out-of-state convictions.
- Record of new incoming driver is not shown on MVR.
- Out-of-state convictions are shown on MVR
- Out-of-state accidents shown on MVR only when a conviction occurs.
- Convictions of out-of-state drivers are sent to home state.
- Record is forwarded to new state upon surrender of license

License Classes, Restrictions, and Endorsements

License Classes– Commercial

Arizona began issuing the CDL in January 1990.

Class A	Any combination of vehicles with a GVWR of 26,001 or more pounds—provided the GVWR of the vehicle(s) being towed is in excess of 10,000 pounds (holders of A, B, C, and D license categories)
Class B	Any single vehicle with a GVWR of 26,001 or more pounds, or any such vehicle towing a vehicle not in excess of 10,000 pounds GVWR (holders of a B license may also operate all vehicles within the C and D license categories)
Class C	Any single vehicle less than 26,001 pounds GVWR; or any such vehicle towing a vehicle not in excess of 10,000 pounds GVWR; or any such vehicle towing a vehicle which is in excess of 10,000 pounds GVWR—provided the GCWR is less than 26,000 pounds, or is: placarded for hazardous materials; designed to transport sixteen or more persons (including the operator); and to operate a school bus with at least ten passengers (including the operator). Holders of a C license may also operate all vehicles within the D license category.

License Classes– Non-Commercial

Class D	Any single vehicle less than 26,001 pounds GVWR, and such vehicle towing a vehicle not in excess of 10,000 pounds GVWR, and any such vehicle towing a vehicle which is in excess of 10,000 pounds GVWR—provided the GCWR does not exceed 26,000 pounds.
Class M	A motorcycle or motor-driven cycle.
Class G	Graduated Driver License, between the ages of 16 to 18. Must have regular driver with either Class A, B, C, or D when operating vehicle. Effective 07/18/00, an instructional permit must be held for 5 months or until age 18. The applicant is not required to hold the Instruction permit past his/her 18th birthday. However, this does not preclude the applicant from obtaining a permit for 4 months or less.
Class I	Not a license to drive, but an Identification License. No age requirements.

The following license classes are no longer issued, but remain valid until expiration date.

Class 1	Motorcycle	Class 4	Chauffeur
Class 2	Operator Class 8 Instruction permit	Class 5	Chauffeur and motorcycle
Class 3	Operator and motorcycle	Class 9	Restricted instruction permit

Restrictions

A	Corrective Lenses	F	Full Hand Controls	L	Non-Air-Brake Vehicles Only
B	Outside Left Rear-View Mirror	G	Mechanical Signals	M	Moped/Motorized Cart Only
C	Automatic Transmission Only	I	Right, Left, and Inside Mirrors	O	Other
D	Daylight Hours	J	Motorcycle 100cc or Less Only	P	Instruction Permit
E	Golf Cart Only	K	Intrastate Operation Only	R	Restricted Instruction Permit

Endorsements

H	Hazardous Materials	S	School Bus (new)	D	Class D Vehicles
N	Tank Vehicle	T	Double-/Triple-Trailers	M	Motorcycle
P	Bus/School Bus	X	Combination Tank Carrying HazMat		

Important Abbreviations Shown on Driving Records

A series of Abbreviations and the codes used for Action and Withdrawals are followed by the Conviction Code Table with ACD and statute.

Abbreviation Glossary

AAC	Alcohol classes required	EXPUNGEMENT	Setting aside judgment of guilt
ACC	Accident	FR & F/R & F.R.	Financial responsibility action
VIOL DTE	Action or violation date	FTA	Failed to appear
ADMIN PER SE	Administrative "Per Se"	FTP	Failed to pay
AGCY	Agency	MI & M/I & M.I.	Mandatory insurance
AF/SF	Location	MVD	Motor Vehicle Division
AP/SP	Lawful speed/approximate speed	MVR	Moving violation record
APX	Approximate	NRVC	Non-Resident Violator Compact Action
CDL	Commercial Driver License	R	Revocation
CDL Q	Commercial driving privilege withdrawn	REIN	Reinstatement of privilege
CNCL	Cancelled/cancellation	R & P	Reasonable and prudent
CRT or C	Court	RX	Re-examination
CS	Failure to pay civil sanction	SR22	Proof of future financial responsibility
CA Action	Civil Sanction Action	SUSP	Suspension
DI	Driver improvement	TSS	Traffic survival school action
DISP	Disposition	WAR	Warrant
DL	Driver license	TCS	Traffic Complaint Suspension
EFF	Effective		

Notification Status

A	Acknowledged	R	Remailed
M	Mailed	S	Served by officer
N	Not applicable	U	Unclaimed

Action Status

A	Amended Action	R	Rehearing Scheduled
B	Hearing Requested	S	Summary Review
C	Action Completed	T	Terminated
D	(no longer used)	U	Sustained (upheld)
E	Expunged	V	Voided
H	Hearing Scheduled	W	Hearing waived
O	Stay Order	X	Rescinded
P	Appeal	Z	Due process stopped due to dismissal or not guilty
Q	Rehearing Requested		

Action and Withdrawal Codes

A	Probation	PA	Pending Action
4AE	Admin Per Se Suspension Extended	R	Revocation
AP	Admin Per Se Suspension	RA	Revocation Apply
C	Cancellation	RE	Revocation Extended
Q	CDL Disqualification	RP	Revocation Pending
D	Denied	RS	Revocation Status
I	Implied-Consent Suspension	RX	Re-examination Scheduled
ID	Interview Date	S	Suspension
IE	Implied-Consent Suspension Extended	SE	Suspension Extended
IP	Implied-Consent Suspension Pending	SP	Suspension Pending
JC	Juvenile Court Suspension	T	Traffic-Survival School Referral
N	No Action	W	Warning Letter

Conviction Table with Statute and ACD

This table is presented in order of the Statute, which appears on the driving record. A **Summary of the Point System** follows this table.

The **type** of **citation** is indicated by the beginning number in the statute column. For example, if starting with:

- 28 – indicates Transportation citations (see www.azleg.gov/ArizonaRevisedStatutes.asp?Title=28)
- 4 – indicates Alcoholic Beverages citations (see www.azleg.gov/ArizonaRevisedStatutes.asp?Title=4)
- 13 – indicates Criminal Code citations (see www.azleg.gov/ArizonaRevisedStatutes.asp?Title=13)

If the Violation Description is not found in this table, please refer to the ACD Code Table at the back of this book or visit one of the web pages listed above.

Certain administrative actions and out-of-state convictions that appear on the driving record will not be associated with a statute. Withdrawal action related to out of state conviction mat be shown as an ACD Code. See this code list at the back of the book.

Statute	ACD	Description
13-1102,A	U07	Vehicular Homicide

Statute	ACD	Description
13-1103,A	U08	Vehicular Manslaughter
13-1103A1	U08	Manslaughter Reckless Causing Death
13-1104,A	U07	Vehicular Homicide/2nd Degree Murder
13-1105,A	U07	Vehicular Homicide/1st Degree Murder
13-1201,A	U03	Substantial Endangerment To Life Involving A Vehicle
13-1204,A	U06	Aggravated Assault
13-1209,A	U03	Drive By Shooting
13-1602,A	U03	Criminal Damage With Use Of Motor Vehicle
13-1602A1,A5	U03	Criminal Damage
13-1604A		Aggravated Criminal Damage
13-1802,A	U03	Auto Theft
13-1803,A	U03	Unlawful Use Of Vehicle
13-1803A1	U03	Unlawful Use Of Means/Takes Unauth Control
13-1803A2	U03	Unlawful Use Of Means/Transpt & Phys Located In Veh
13-1806,A	U03	Unlawful Failure To Return Rented Vehicle
13-1814	U03	Theft Of Means Of Transportation
13-1814A1	U03	Theft Of Means/Control Another W/Intent
13-1814A2	U03	Theft Of Means/Entrusted To Indiv Possession
13-1814A3	U03	Theft Of Means/By Material Misrepresentation
13-1814A4	U03	Theft Of Means/Control Of Anothers Lost Or Misdelivered
13-1814A5	U03	Theft Of Means/Controls Knowingly
13-1902	U03	Robbery
13-1904	U03	Armed Robbery
13-2307	U03	Trafficking In Stolen Property; Vehicle
13-2508,A	U02	Resisting Arrest With A Motor Vehicle
13-2508A1	U02	Resisting Arrest Use Of Force With Motor Vehicle Only
13-2508A2	U02	Resisting Arrest Substantial Risk With Motor Vehicle Only
13-2509,A	U04	Resisting An Order With A Motor Vehicle
13-2702,A		Perjury By Making A False Sworn Statement
13-2703,A		False Swearing
13-2705		Perjury By Inconsistent Statements
13-2906,A		Obstructing The Highway
13-3111A	U03	Minor Prohibited From Carrying Or Possessing Firearms
13-3402,A	A33	Possession And Sale Of Peyote
13-3403,A1	A33	Possession And Sale Of Vapor Releasing Substance
13-3403.02C		Minor Misrepresenting Age - Nitrous Oxide
13-3403A2	A33	Sell/Transfer A Vapor-Releasing Substance To Person Under 1
13-3403A3	A33	Sell/Transfer A Vapor-Releasing Subst Not In Course Of Emplment
13-3403B1	A33	Failure To Keep Proper Record Including Name Of Glue
13-3403B2	A33	Failure To Keep Proper Record Including Date And Hour Of De
13-3403B3	A33	Failure To Keep Proper Record Including Intended Use Of Glu
13-3403B4	A33	Failure To Keep Proper Record/Signature And Address Of Purchaser
13-3403B5	A33	Failure To Keep Proper Record/With Signature Of Seller
13-3403C	A33	Failure To Keep Vapor Releasing Glue Unavailable To Customer
13-3403D	A33	Failure To Display Sing Indicating Dangers Of Inhalation Of
13-3404	A33	Failure To Submit Report Of Sale/Transfer Precursor Chemical
13-3404.01,A	A33	Violation To Knowingly Sell/Transfer Prec Chem Ii For Unlaw
13-3404A	A33	Failure To Submit Report Of Sale/Transfer Precursor Chemica
13-3404D	A33	Failure To Submit Rept Of Transaction Within 21 Days Before
13-3404E	A33	Failure To Submt Rept For Recpt Of Precursor Chem From Outs
13-3404G	A33	Failure To Submit Theft/Lost Report Of Any Precursor Chemic
13-3405	A33	Possession/Use/Production/Sale/Transportation Of Marijuana
13-3405A1	A33	Possession Or Use Of Marijuana
13-3405A2	A33	Possess Marijuana For Sale
13-3405A3	A33	Produce Marijuana
13-3405A4	A33	Transport/Import Into State/Offer To Sell Marijuana
13-3406	A33	Possession/Use/Admin Of Prescription-Only Drugs
13-3406A1	A33	Possession/Unlawful Use Of Prescription-Only Drugs
13-3406A2	A33	Possession Of Prescription-Only Drug For Sale
13-3406A3	A33	Possess Equipment & Chemicals For Purpose Of Manuf/Prescrpt Only
13-3406A4	A33	Manuf Of Prescription Only Drug
13-3406A5	A33	Administering Prescription Only Drug
13-3406A6	A33	Obtain Or Procure The Administ. Of Prescript Drug By Fraud
13-3406A7	A33	Transport For Sale, Import Into State Prescription Only Drug
13-3407	A33	Possession/Use/Admin/Of Dangerous Drugs
13-3407A1	A33	Possession Or Use Of A Dangerous Drugs

Statute	ACD	Description
13-3407A2	A33	Possess Dangerous Drugs For Sale
13-3407A3	A33	Possess Equipment For Purpose Of Manuf. Dangerous Drug
13-3407A4	A33	Manufacturing A Dangerous Drug
13-3407A5	A33	Administering A Dangerous Drug To Another Person
13-3407A6	A33	Administ Of Dangerous Drug By Fraud/Misrepresentation
13-3407A7	A33	Transpt/Import/Sell Transfr Or Offer To Sell A Dangerous Dr
13-3408	A33	Possession/Use/Admin/Of Narcotic Drugs
13-3408A1	A33	Possession Or Use Of Narcotic Drugs
13-3408A2	A33	Possess Narcotic Drug For Sale
13-3408A3	A33	Possess Equipmt For Purpose Of Manuf Of Narcotic Drug
13-3408A4	A33	Manufacturing A Narcotic Drug
13-3408A5	A33	Administrer A Narcotic Drug To Another Person
13-3408A6	A33	Administering Narcotic Drug By Fraud/Misrepresentation
13-3408A7	A33	Transport/Import/Sell,Transfer Or Offer To Sell Narcotic Dr
13-3409	A33	Involving Or Using Minors In Drug Offenses
13-3409A1	A33	Hire/Employ Minor In Drug Offenses
13-3409A2	A33	Sell,Transfer Or Offer To Sell To Minor Any Illegal Substance
13-3411	A33	Possession/Use/Sale Of Drugs In School Zone
13-3411A1	A33	Unlawful To Intentionally Be Present In School Zone To Sell
13-3411A2	A33	Unlawful To Possess Or Use Drugs In A School Zone
13-3411F	A33	School Personnel Failure To Rept Violation Of This Section
13-3415,A		Possession/Manuf/Of Drug Paraphernalia
13-3415B	A33	Deliver,Manuf/Of Drug Paraphernalia Knowingly Used For Viol
13-3415C	A33	Placement Of Advertisement To Promote Sale/Drug Paraphernalia
13-3417A	U03	Use Of Wire Communication In Drug Transactions
13-3421,A	U03	Building Use For Sale/Manufacture Of Drugs
13-3421B	U03	Intent To Suppress Law Enforcement Entry/Sale/Manf Of Drugs
13-3453,A	A50	Manufact/Distribution Of Imitation Controlled Substance
13-3454,A	A50	Manufact/Distribution Of Imitation Prescription Only Drug
13-3455,A	A50	Manufact/Distribution Of Imitation Over The Counter Drug
13-3824		Failure To Comply W/Requirements Of Sex Offender
13-4702	U03	Conducting A Chop Shop
13-4702A1		Chop Shop Own Or Operate
13-4702A2		Chop Shop Transport Motor Vehicle Or Part To Or From
13-4702A3		Chop Shop Sell Transfer Or Purchase A Motor Vehicle Or Part
13-4702A4		Chop Shop Remove Destroy Or Deface A Motor Vehicle Vin
13-4702A5		Chop Shop Buy Sell Or Transfer Vehicle Or Part Knowing Vin
13-902	U03	Robbery
13-904	U03	Armed Robbery
19-102		Improper U Turn
19-103		Backing Into An Intersection Or Crosswalk
19-107		Driving On Closed Roadway Or Traffic Lane
19-110		Driving Above 15 Mph In An Alley
19-151		Crossing A Railroad
19-152		Railroad Gates
19-16		Obedience To Police And Fire Department Officials
19-166	N84	Board/Exit Moving Vehicle
19-167	N84	Tracking Rubbish On Roadway
19-17		Traffic Regulations By Persons On Animals Or Pushcarts
19-18		Toy Veh/Go-Cart Restrictions
19-188		Avoiding Stop Via Private Property
19-33	E01	Signs Prohibiting The Movement Of Trucks
19-42		Enter Intersection Restrictions
19-43	N05	Parades And Motorcades
19-44	E70	Overweight Or Oversize Vehicle Regulations
19-48		Driving Across Traffic Marking Or Barricade
19-49		Driving Upon Certain Real Property
19-50		Hauling Waste Prohibitions
19-51		Sound Amplification Systems In Vehicles
19-52	N84	Cruising Prohibited
19-53	N56	Unsafe U-Turn
19-62		Limits In Through Alleys
19-63		Speed Limits Enumerated
19-96		Driving On Sidewalk
19-97		Following Or Parked Too Close To Emergency Vehicles
19-98		Driving Over Fire Hose

Statute	ACD	Description
20-111		Obedience Required
20-112		Avoiding Stop Via Private Property
20-113		Underage Misrepresentation Affidavit
20-115, 20-117		Improper Turn
20-136 thru 146		Speed Zones
20-148		Following Or Parked Too Close To Emergency Vehicles
20-149		Crossing Fire Hose
20-151		Driving Through Procession
20-152		Method Of Driving In Processions
20-153		Driving On Sidewalk
20-156		Obstructing Intersection Or Side Walk
20-178	N01	Failure To Yield The Right Of Way
20-179		Wrong Way On One Way Street Or Alley
23-37		Operation Of Motor Vehicles Or Horses
28-1091,A		Vehicle Size Or Weight Or Load Requirements
28-1093,A		Violation Of Vehicle Width Regulations
28-1093B1		Vehicle Exceeds Allowed Width
28-1093B2		Load W/Pneumatic Tires Exceeds Allowed Width
28-1094,A		Vehicle Exceeds Height Limit W/O Permit
28-1095A		Vehicle Exceeds Length Limit
28-1095B		Exceed Allowed Number Of Towed Vehicles/Trailers
28-1095C1		Semitrailer Combo Exceeds Allowed Length
28-1095C2		Semi/Trailer Combination Exceeds Allowed Length
28-1095C3		Trailer Exceeds Maximum Length In Combo
28-1095C4		Semi Or Combo Exceeds Allowed Length For Road
28-1095C5		Vehicle Transporter And Semi Exceed Allowed Length
28-1095F		Vehicle Combo W/Permit Exceeds Max Length
28-1095G1		Improper Vehicle Towing
28-1095G2		Vehicle Combo Exceeds Maximum Length
28-1095G3		Recreational Vehicle Exceeds Tow Limits
28-1096		Projecting Loads On Passenger Vehicles
28-1097		Violation Of Load Extensions And Length Limits For Pole Tra
28-1097A1		Front Load Projection Exceeds Limits
28-1097A2		Rear Load Projection Exceeds Limits
28-1097C		Pole Trailer Load Greater Than 80feet W/O Permit
28-1098		Violation Of Vehicle Load Requirements
28-1098A		Spilling Load On Highway
28-1098B		Load Or Cover On Load Insecure
28-1099,A		Single-Axle Load Exceeds 20,000 Lbs
28-1100		Maximum Gross Weight For Vehicle/Load Exceeded
28-1100A1		Single Axle Weight Over Limit
28-1100A2		Tandem Axle Weight Over Limit
28-1100A3		Vehicle Combo Weight Over Limit
28-1100A4		Consecutive Axles; Weight Violation
28-1100E		Exceed Allowed Number Of Axles
28-1100F		Variable Load Axle Violation
28-1102		Failure To Weigh Vehicle Or Remove Excess Load
28-1102		Failure To Submit To Weighting
28-1102C1		Failure To Stop Or Submit To Weighting
28-1102C2		Failure To Unload If Overweight
28-1102D		Failure To Allow Weighing Of Commercial Vehicle
28-1104		Violation Of Permit For Excess Size/Weight
28-1104C		Failure To Carry/Display Excess Weight/Size Permit
28-1108		Violation Of Vehicle Towing Regulations
28-1108A		Space Between Towed Vehicles Exceeds Limit
28-1108B		Violation Of Vehicle Towing Regulations/White Flag
28-1108D		Violation Of Vehicle Towing Regulations/Unregistered Truck
28-1110C4	W00	Minimum 4 Hours Training
28-1142,A		Failure To Have Envelope Permit Required
28-1144		Issuing Envelope Permits; Restriction Requirements
28-1144C		Failure To Have Envelope Permit In Possession/Supply On Dem
28-1149,A		Failure To Keep Records
28-1149C		Failure To Allow Inspection Of Envelope Permit Records
28-1151		Operation On Violation Of Envelope Permit
28-1174	M80	Reckless Driving/Off Highway Vehicle
28-1174A1	W00	Off Hwy Vehicle: Reckless Driving

Statute	ACD	Description
28-1174A2	W00	Off Hwy Vehicle: Damage To Habitat
28-1174A3	W00	Off Hwy Vehicle: Drive Closed Area
28-1174A4	W00	Off Hwy Vehicle: Drive Unimproved Road
28-1174B	W00	Off Hwy Vehicle: Non Open Area
28-1174C	W00	Off Hwy Vehicle: Damage Environment
28-1174D	W00	Off Hwy Vehicle: Removal Of Sign
28-1177A	W00	Off Hwy Vehicle: Without User Indicia
28-1179A1	W00	Off Hwy Vehicle: Inadequate Brakes
28-1179A2	W00	Off Hwy Vehicle: Inadequate Lights
28-1179A3	W00	Off Hwy Vehicle: Inadequate Muffler
28-1179A4	W00	Off Hwy Vehicle: No Spark Arrestor
28-1179A5	W00	Off Hwy Vehicle: Safety Flag Violation
28-1179B	W00	Off Hwy Vehicle: Headgear Violation
28-1321	A12	Implied Consent Affidavit
28-1321A	A12	Implied Consent/Gives Consent To Tests
28-1321D	A12	Implied Consent/Refuses To Submit To Test
28-1381A1	A20	Dui Of Liquor, Drugs Or Vapors Or Combination
28-1381A2	A08	Dui With Alcohol Concentration Of .08 Or More
28-1381A3	A22	Driving Under The Influence Of Drugs
28-1381A4	A04	Dui With Alcohol Concentration Of .04 Or More In A CMV
28-1382A1	A21	Dui Extreme BAC .15 To .20
28-1382A2	A21	Dui Extreme BAC Over .20
28-1383A1	A20	Aggravated Dui; Dui While Suspended
28-1383A2	A20	Aggravated Dui Of Liquor Or Drugs
28-1383A3	A20	Driving Under The Influence While Minor Present
28-1383A3A	A20	Aggravated Dui W/Passenger Under 15yr
28-1383A3B	A20	Aggravated Extreme Dui W/Passenger Under 15 Yr
28-1383A4A	A20	Refusal To Submit To Any Test While Required To Have A CIID
28-1383A4B	A20	Aggravated DUI, DUI Or Extreme DUI With CIID Requirement
28-1385	A98	Admin Per Se Affidavit
28-1385A2	A20	Admin Per Se No BAC Available
28-1464A	A41	Ignition Interlock/Failure To Carry Proof Of Employer Notif
28-1464B		Ignition Interlock/Knowingly Rents, Leases Or Lends Vehicle
28-1464C		Ignition Interlock/Fail To Notify IID Req When Rent/Lease/L
28-1464D	A41	Ignition Interlock/Permits Another To Breathe Into IID
28-1464E		Ignition Interlock/Breathing Into IID For Another
28-1464F	A41	Ignition Interlock/Limited Driver Tampering With IID
28-1464G		Ignition Interlock/Operating Vehicle W/O IID
28-1464G		Unauth Person Tampering With Ignition Interlock Device
28-1464H	A41	Driving W/O Required Ignition Interlock Device
28-1464H	A41	Operating Vehicle Without Ignition Interlock Device
28-1522		Damaging Or Preventing Operation Of A Vehicle
28-1522A1		Damages Vehicle W/O Consent Of Owner
28-1522A2		Malicious Interference With Vehicle Operation
28-1522A3		Damage Vehicle With Intent To Commit Crime
28-1522A4A		Operate Mechanism While Vehicle Unattended
28-1522A4B		Set Vehicle In Motion While Unattended
28-1523		Improper Transport Of Hazardous Material
28-1524		Improper Operation By Owner Or Controller Of A Vehicle
28-1551		Party To A Crime
28-1551A		Aid Or Abet A Violation Of Chapter 3 Or 4
28-1551B		Induce/Cause/Direct/Permit Violation; Chapters 3/5
28-1560,A		Illegal Cancellation Of Traffic Citation
28-1595,A		Failure To Stop Vehicle Upon Police Command
28-1595B		Refusal To Show Identification Or Driver License
28-1595C		Refusal To Show Identification Or Driver License/Non-Driver
28-2008		Failure To Obtain Duplicate Plate
28-2058		Failure To Register Transfer Of Title
28-2058A2B		Failure To Notify MVD On Transfer Of Title
28-2060,A		Failure To Obtain Transfer Of Registration
28-2060B		Failure To Obtain New Certificate Of Title
28-2060C		Failure To Obtain Transfer Of Reg After Purch Of Forfeited
28-2060E		Improper Movement Of Repossessed Vehicle
28-2091		Violation Of Salvage Certificate Of Title
28-2091I		Failure To Disclose Salvage Title Before Sale
28-2091M		Failure To Disclose Deployment/Removal Of Airbag Before Sal

Statute	ACD	Description
28-2091O	W00	Fail To Disclose Vehicle As Salvage
28-2091R		Failure To Notify Owner Of Replacement Part With Vin
28-2095		Salvage Title Violation
28-2095A		Failure To Obtain Restored Salvage Title
28-2095H		Failure To Disclose Vehicle Is Salvage
28-2152,A		Regist In A County Other Than Residence/Intent To Evade Emi
28-2152C		Vehicle Registration In A County Other Than Residence
28-2153		Violation Of Registration Laws
28-2153A		Violation Of Registration Laws/No Current Registration
28-2153B1		Violation Of Registration Laws/Owned By Nonresident
28-2153B2		Violation Of Registration Laws/Leased By Resident
28-2153E		Violation Of Registration Laws/Failure To Notify County Ass
28-2154.01C	W00	90 Day Permit Not Visible From Outside Vehicle
28-2155D	W00	3 Day Permit Not Visible From Outside Vehicle
28-2156D	W00	30 Day Permit Not Visible From Outside Vehicle
28-2158,C		Failure To Carry Vehicle Registration Card
28-2164,.3		Failure To Obtain Commercial Registration
28-2165,A		Failure To Request Special Serial Or Id #
28-2166,G		Violation Of Registration For Rented Vehicles
28-2203		Failure To Display Or Carry Regist Card Or Sticker For Flee
28-2266,C		Failure To Carry Registration Card In Vehicle
28-2269,D		Violation Of License Plate Display
28-2295,A		Display Of Indicia Violation
28-2295B		Failure To Carry Commuter ID Card
28-2321,A		Failure To Regist Foreign Vehicle Used By Business
28-2322		Violation Of License Plate Requirement For Nonresident
28-2324D		Limited Registration/Display Of Certificate
28-2354		License Plate Violation
28-2354A1		Rear License Plate Required
28-2354A2		Rear Or Front And Rear Plate Required
28-2354B		Display Legible Plates
28-2354B1		Swinging Plate Improper
28-2354B2		Improper Placement Of License Plate
28-2354B3		License Plate Not In Visible Position
28-2354C	W00	License Plate State Obstruction
28-2403		Special Plate Violation
28-2403D1		Improper Transfer Of Special Plates
28-2403D2		Gives False Information To Receive Special Plates
28-2403D3		Commit Fraud To Receive Special Plates
28-2416.01E	W00	HOV Lane False Marked As Low Emissions
28-2416F	W00	HOV Lane False Marked As Alt.Fuel
28-2451		Violation Of Honored Military Plate
28-2451B		Display Of Honored Military Plate On Unauth Vehicle
28-2451D2		Gives False Info To Obtain Honored Military Plate
28-2451D3		Commits Fraud In Application For Honored Military Plate
28-2453A,A1		Former Prisoner Of War Recipient Violation
28-2511		Official Vehicle Registration Exemption
28-2511A		Failure To Display Exempt Plates
28-2511E		Failure To Display Alternate Fuel Plate
28-2512		Violation Off-Road Recreational Vehicle Lic Plate
28-2512D1		Violation Off-Road Recreational Vehicle Lic Plate Attached
28-2512D2		Viol Off-Road Recreational Vehicle Lic Plate Securely Fastened
28-2513		Moped Violation
28-2513.2		Moped W/O Permanently Affixed Registration
28-2513.8	M47	Operating Moped On Bike Path/Lane
28-2531		Title And Registration Violation
28-2531A1		Intentional Removal Of Manufacturer's Serial Number
28-2531A2		Knowingly In Possession Of Vehicle With Altered Id #
28-2531A3		Plate Issued Without Full Payment Of Fees
28-2531B1		Display/Possession Of Fictitious Regist Card/License Plate
28-2531B10	D27	Alter/Forge Permanently Disabled Placard
28-2531B2		Lending Of Regist Card Or License Plate
28-2531B3		Refusal To Surrender To Dept License Plate
28-2531B4		Use Of False Or Fictitious Name
28-2531B5		False State/Fraud In Application For Registration
28-2531B6		Knowingly Issues Regist Card Not Containing All Information

Statute	ACD	Description
28-2531B7		Placement Of Info On Regist Card Not On Title
28-2531B8		Operating Vehicle Without An Emissions Control Device
28-2531B9	D27	Regist Card/License Plate On Vehicle Certif Nonoperational
28-2532,A		Operation Of Vehicle Without Current Registration
28-2533,A		Failure To Register Vehicle For First Time In AZ
28-3151,A	B51	Driving Without License And Proper Endorsements
28-3154		Violation Of Instruction Permit
28-3154B1		Instruction Permit/Not In Possession
28-3154B2		Instruction Permit/Permittee Not Accompanied
28-3155		Violation Of Restricted Permit
28-3155B1		Restricted Permit/Permit Not In Possession
28-3155B2		Restricted Permit/Failure To Drive Within Designated Area
28-3155B3		Restricted Permit/Permittee Not Accompanied
28-3156		Violation Of Motorcycle Permit
28-3156B		Motorcycle Permit/Not In Possession
28-3156C1		Motorcycle Permit/Operation Of Cycle On Controlled Access H
28-3156C2		Motorcycle Permit/Operation Of Cycle While Insufficient Lig
28-3157		Violation Of Temp Driver Permit
28-3157B		Violation Of Temp Driver Permit/ Not In Possession
28-3169,A	B51	License Exhibited On Demand/No Legible License In Possession
28-3174D	W00	Class G Restricted Curfew Violation
28-3174E	W00	Class G Restricted Under Age 18 Passenger Violation
28-3222	B51	Commercial Driver/Failure To Make Domicile Change
28-3225		Viol Of Commercial Driver Instruction Permit
28-3225B1		Viol Of Commercial Driver Instruction Permit/Not In Possess
28-3225B2		Viol Of Commercial Driver Instruction Permit/Not Accompanied
28-3225B3		Viol Of Commercial Driver Instruction Permit/Under 21-Inter
28-3227	D02	CMV Driver;Conviction;Notification Requirements;Violations
28-3227A	D02	CMV Driver-Failure To Report Traffic Conviction
28-3227B		CMV Driver-Failure To Notify Employer Of Conv. Of Violation
28-3227C		CMV Driver-Failure To Notify Employer Of CMV Disqualificatin
28-3227D		CMV Driver-Failure To Give Employer Information
28-3228,A		Operating School Bus Without Proper License
28-3310,A	D16	Improper Use Of License
28-3316	B20	Operation Of Vehicle While License Is Suspended Or Revoked
28-3472,A		Renting Vehicle To Unauthorized Person
28-3472B		Renting Vehicle To Unauthorized Person/Failure To Inspect L
28-3472C		Renting Vehicle To Unauthorized Person/Failure To Keep Reco
28-3472D		Renting Motorcycle To Unauth Person/Failure To Equipped W/G
28-3473A	B20	Driving While License Suspended/Revoked/Canceled
28-3473B	B20	Driving While License Suspend/Revoked/Cancel/For DUI, Admin
28-3473C	B26	Driving While License Suspend/Revoked/Cancel/For FTP Or FTA
28-3474		Permitting Unauthorized Minor To Drive
28-3475		Permitting Unauthorized Person To Drive
28-3476,A	D02	Falsification Of A Driver Or Identification License
28-3477		False Certification Of Renewal By Mail Application
28-3478	B41	Unlawful Use Of License
28-3478.1	B41	Knowingly Display Unlawful License
28-3478.2		Knowingly Permit/Lend Driver License
28-3478.3	D16	Knowingly Display/Unlawful Use Of License
28-3478.4A	D02	Unlawful Use Of License/Fictitious Name Used In Application
28-3478.4B	D02	Unlawful Use Of License/False Statement Used In Application
28-3478.4C	D02	Unlawful Use Of License/Conceal Fact In Application
28-3478.4D	D02	Unlawful Use Of License/Commit Fraud In Application
28-3478.5	D16	To Permit An Unlawful Use Of Driver License
28-3478.6		Knowingly Falsify Nonoperating ID Application
28-3479		False Affidavit/Perjury
28-3480	D27	Operation Of Vehicle In Violation Of Restriction
28-3481	B56	Driving Without Commercial License
28-3481A	B51	Driving Without Commercial License
28-3512E	W00	Fail To Retain Required Information
28-3512J	W00	Violation Of Impoundment Agreement
28-369E		Failure To Stop At A Port Of Entry
28-4036,.1		CMV Failure To Meet Financial Responsibility Requirements
28-4036.2		CMV Failure To Meet Financial Responsibility/Involved In Ac
28-4135,A	D35	Motor Vehicle Financial Responsibility Requirement

Statute	ACD	Description
28-4135B,C	D35	Motor Vehicle Financial Responsibility-Failure To Produce Ev
28-4136	D35	Failure To Provide Proof Of Financial Responsibility
28-4136A		Evidence Of Financial Responsibility
28-4136B	D36	Failure To Produce Evidence Of Financial Responsibility
28-4139,A		Displaying Suspended Number Plates
28-4142		Failure To Certify Financial Responsibility Compliance
28-4142E1		Falsification Of Proof Of Financial Responsibility
28-4142E2		Falsification Of Proof Of Financial Responsibility/W/O Auth
28-4142E3		Falsification Of Proof Of Financial Responsibility/Knowingly
28-4153		False Certification Of Financial Responsibility
28-4153A		False Certification Of Financial Responsibility/Vehicle Not
28-4363		Violation Of Franchises Filing Agreement
28-4363F		Franchises; Filing Agreement Failure To Notify
28-4404		Failure To Maintain Required Dealer Records
28-4404F		Business Records Required/Failure To Display Records
28-448,A		Failure To Report Change Of Address
28-450		Release Of Information Prohibited
28-450E.1		Give False Information/Record Released
28-4544		Violation Of Laden Vehicle Test Plate Requirements
28-4544C		Improper Use Of Laden Test Plates
28-4544C		Violation Of Laden Vehicle Test Plate Requirements
28-4544D		Violation Of Laden Vehicle Test Plate/Personal Use
28-4545		Violation Of Permit To Move Vehicle Without Plates
28-4550		Violation Of Temporary Registration Requirements
28-4551,B		Expiration Of Temporary Registration
28-4553,B		Violation Of Temporary Registration Requirements
28-457A		Records No Disclosure Of Personal Information
28-457B		Records No Disclosure Of MVD Information
28-457C		Records False Disclosure To Obtain MVD Information
28-4593,A		Altering A Serial Or Identification Number
28-4593B		Altering A Serial Or Identification Number/Removes With Intent
28-4625		Violation Of Transporters Plate Requirements
28-4625A		Violation Of Transporters Plate Requirements/Failure To Display
28-4625B		Viol Of Transporters Plates/Failure To Display Proper Plate
28-4626,A		Failure To Maintain Required Transporter Records
28-4626C		Failure To File Copy With The Director
28-4663		Violation Of Transporters Plate Requirements
28-4663A1		No Valid Transporter Plate
28-4663A2		No Vehicle Service Plate Shown
28-4663A3		Transporter Improper Vehicle Movement
28-4663B		Operation Of Vehicles Bearing Transporter Plate
28-4664,A		Failure To Maintain Required Transporter Records
28-4831		Abandoned Vehicle
28-4836,A		Failure To Report Towed Vehicles
28-4838,A		Failure To Report Abandoned Vehicle
28-4839,A		Failure To Report Abandoned Vehicle Storage
28-4846,F		Refusal To Permit Inspection For Stolen Vehicle
28-5204		Dept Administration/Enforcement Of Rules/Motor Carrier Safe
28-5231,A		Failure To Maintain Motor Carrier Records
28-5236		Violation Of Operating A Vehicle Transporting Haz Material
28-5236A		Operation Of Vehicle Transport Haz Material W/O Inspection
28-5236B		Failure To Contain Hazardous Material When Transporting
28-5241	B27	Out Of Service Orders
28-5241A1	B27	Carrier Violated Out Of Service Order
28-5241A2	B27	Operating Vehicle W/Out Of Service Order
28-5241B1	B27	Operation Of Commercial Veh While Out Of Service Order
28-5241B2	B27	Driver Subject To Out Of Service Order Operating Commercial
28-5242A		Failure To Register Vehicle - Interstate/Foreign Commerce
28-5242B		Operating Beyond Scope Of Registration Interstate/Foreign C
28-5242E	B27	Operating W/O Out-Of-Service Order - Interstate/Foreign Com
28-5243A		Motor Carrier Permitting Railroad Crossing Violations
28-5244A1		Foreign Motor Carrier No Certificate In Vehicle
28-5244A2		Foreign Motor Carrier Certificate Beyond Limitation Of Rest
28-5244A3		Foreign Motor Carrier Refusal To Show Certificate
28-5244A4		Foreign Motor Carrier Certificate Providing Point To Point
28-5244B1		Motor Carrier Registration With No Registration

Statute	ACD	Description
28-5244B2		Motor Carrier Registration Beyond Limitations Or Restriction
28-5244B3		Motor Carrier Registration Without Required Authority
28-5244E		Permanent Operating Authority With No 3-Year Inspection
28-5437		Operation With Excess Weight
28-5605		Violation Of Motor Fuel Procedure
28-5608,A		Exceeding The Capacity Of The Fuel Tank
28-5612,C		Violation Of Fuel Tax Refund Procedure
28-5617A		Violation Of Fuel Tax Collection By Vendor/No Receipt
28-5619		Failure To Maintain Req Distributor Or Buyer Records
28-5619A		Fuel Supplier Records Fail To Maintain 3yrs After Required
28-5619B		Fuel Supplier Records Fail To Maintain 3 Years After Filed
28-5620,C		Disclosure Of Confidential Information
28-5623		Failure To Maintain Required Reports
28-5623A		Purchase Of Fuel Not Exempt
28-5624		Failure To Maintain Required Reports
28-5624A		Failure To Maintain Required Reports/Motor Carriers
28-5624C		Failure To Maintain Required Manifest Forms
28-5625,A		Failure To Possess Waybills Or Manifest
28-5630		Display Of Distributors License
28-5630A1		Fuel Supplier License Not Assignable
28-5630A2		Fuel Supplier License Only Valid To Whom Issued
28-5630A3		Fuel Supplier License Displayed Conspicuously
28-5630B		Fuel Supplier Duplicate License Not Obtained
28-5635,A1A		Failure Of Distributor To Give Notice Of Transfer
28-5635A1		Failure Of Distrib To Give Notice Of Transf/No Date On Sale
28-5635A1B		Failure Of Give Name/Address Of Purchaser
28-5645A		Dyed Diesel Misuse In Fuel Tank
28-5647A		Sell Or Holding Of Diesel Fuel For Nontaxable Use
28-5647B		Use Or Holding Of Diesel Fuel For Non-Taxable Use
28-5647C		Willfully Intent To Evade Tax
28-5707		Violation Of Report Procedure For Use Fuel
28-5707A1		Violation Of Report Procedure/Refuses To Make Report
28-5707A2		Knowingly Makes False Statement In Report
28-5707A3		Knowingly Collects Refund W/O Being Entitled
28-5707A4		Violation Of Report Procedure For Refunds
28-5708		Improper Collection Of Use Fuel Tax
28-5718		Violation Of Fuel Tax Collection By Vendor
28-5731,A		Failure To Maintain Use Fuel Records
28-5733		Violation Of Use Fuel License Or Permit
28-5734A		Interstate Use License Requirement
28-5741		Failure To Display Use Fuel License
28-5742		Failure To Carry A Valid Cab Card
28-5742A		Evidence Of Valid License Who Is An Interstate User
28-5742B		Failure To Display Interstate User License
28-5744		Failure To Notify MVD Sale Of Use Fuel Vehicle
28-5857,C		Motor Carrier Transports Nonagric Product
28-5921A1A		Fuel Tax Corruptly Or By Force Impede An Employee Of The De
28-5921A1B		Fuel Tax Corruptly Or By Force Impede The Admin Of This Cha
28-5921A2		Fuel Tax Force/Threats To Prevent Communication Of Viol Of
28-5921A3		Fuel Tax Injures Person/Property Of Person Testifying
28-5921A4		Fuel Tax Intended To Evade Motor Fuel Taxes
28-5921B1		Fuel Tax Knowingly Fails To Pay Any Tax Administered
28-5921B2		Fuel Tax Fraudulent Documentation
28-5921B3		Fuel Tax Fraudulent Executes A License
28-5921B4		Fuel Tax Knowingly Fail To File Return Or Use Of False Doc
28-5921B5		Fuel Tax Knowingly Transport Motor Fuel W/Intent To Evade T
28-5921C1		Knowingly Fails To Make Statement/Motor Vehicle Fuel Tax
28-5921C2		Knowingly Makes False Statement/Motor Vehicle Fuel Tax
28-5921C3		Knowingly Collects Fuel Tax Refund
28-5921C4		Engages In Business As Distributor W/O License
28-5921C5		Selling Of Fuel/Unpaid Tax
28-5935,A		Disclosure Of Confidential Information
28-5938,B		Knowingly Disclosure Of Confidential Information
28-622,A	M08	Obedience To Police Officers
28-622.01	U01	Unlawful Flight From Pursuing Law Enforcement Vehicle
28-644,A,A1	M15	Failure To Obey Traffic Control Device

Statute	ACD	Description
28-644A2	M12	Driving Over/Across Gore Area
28-645	M16	Violation Of Traffic Sign Or Light Signal
28-645A1A,PE	M14	Green Light Violation
28-645A1B	M14	Green Arrow Violation
28-645A1B.PE	M16	Fail To Yield On Green Arrow
28-645A2B	M18	Pedestrian Yellow Light Violation
28-645A3A	M14	Failure To Stop For Red Light
28-645A3A.PE	M16	Fail To Stop For Red
28-645A3B,.PE	M14	Right Turn On Red Violation
28-645A3C	M14	Failure To Yield On Red Light
28-645A3C.PE	M16	Failure To Yield On Red
28-645A3D	M14	Pedestrian Red Light Violation
28-645B	M14	Violation Of Control Signal Other Than At Intersection
28-645C	M25	Failure To Stop & Yield To Driver On Right
28-646		Pedestrians Right Of Way In Cross Walks
28-646A1		Driver Failure To Yield Right Of Way To Pedestrian At Control
28-646A2		Pedestrian Violation/Walking Against Control Signal
28-646B		Pedestrian Violation/Loitering At Pedestrian Control Signal
28-647	M18	Violation Of Traffic Sign Or Light Signal
28-647.1	M18	Flashing Red Stop Signal Violation
28-647.2	M18	Flashing Yellow Caution Signal Violation
28-648		Display Of Unauthorized Signs
28-648A1		Display Of Unauth Signs/Resembles Official Traffic Control
28-648A2		Display Of Unauth Signs/Attempts To Direct Traffic
28-648A3		Display Of Unauth Signs Interferes With Traffic Control Dev
28-648B		Display Of Unauth Signs/Displaying Commercial Advertising
28-649A		Interference With Official Sign/Signal
28-649B		Possession Of Traffic Premption Emitter
28-650		Failure To Maintain Warning Devices At Construction Sites
28-651	M14	Use Of Private Property To Avoid Traffic Control Device
28-661,A	U31	Accident Involving Death Or Personal Injuries (H&R)
28-661A1	U31	Failure To Stop At Scene Of Injury Accident
28-661A2	U31	Failure To Remain At Scene Of Injury Accident
28-662	B04	Accident Involving Damage To Vehicle (H&R)
28-662A	B04	Accident Involving Damage To Vehicle/Failure To Stop Or Rem
28-662A1	B04	Accident Involving Damage To Vehicle/Failure To Stop
28-662A2	B04	Accident Involving Damage To Vehicle/Failure To Remain At S
28-662A3	B04	Failure To Stop At Scene W/O Obstructing Traffic
28-663	B01	Failure To Give Information And Render Aid In Accident
28-663A1	B01	Failure To Give Information In Accident/Name, Address, Registration
28-663A2	B01	Failure To Give Information In Accident/Exhibit Of Driver Lic
28-663A3	B01	Failure To Render Reasonable Assistance To Injured Person
28-664	B05	Failure To Stop After Striking Unattended Vehicle
28-664A	B05	Striking Unattended Vehicle
28-664A1	B05	Failure To Stop After Striking Unattended Vehicle
28-664A2	B05	Fail To Locate, Notify And Give Info Of Unattended Vehicle S
28-665,A1	B08	Duty Upon Striking Fixtures Upon A Highway
28-665A	B08	Striking Fixtures On A Highway
28-665A2	B08	Failure To Show Driver License/Striking Fixture On Hwy
28-666		Failure To Immediately Report Accident
28-672,A	M14	Accident Involving Serious Physical Injury Or Death
28-672C	U31	Accident Causing Death To Another Person
28-675A	U31	Causing Death By Use Of A Vehicle While Susp/Rev
28-676A	B20	Causing Serious Physical Injury By Vehicle When Susp/Rev
28-6807,D		Violation To Avoid Paying Toll
28-693,A	M84	Reckless Driving
28-695A	M42	Aggressive Driving
28-701	S94	Special Restrictions (Speed R&P)
28-701.02	S93	Excessive Speed
28-701.02A1	S93	Exceeding 35 Mph-School Crossing
28-701.02A2	S93	Exceed Limit By 20 Mph Or Over 45 Mph Business/Residential
28-701.02A3	S93	Exceeding 85 Mph
28-701A,.PE	S94	Reasonable And Prudent Speed Violation
28-701E	S94	Driving Vehicle At Speed Less Than Speed Reasonable And Prudent
28-702.01	S94	Maximum Speed Limit
28-702.01C,.PE	S94	Violation Of Maximum Speed Limit

Statute	ACD	Description
28-702.04	S93	Maximum Speed Limit On Interstate Highway
28-702.04B,.PE	S93	Violation Of Maximum Speed Limit Outside Urbanized Areas
28-704	S96	Minimum Speed Regulation
28-704A	S96	Speed Not To Impede Traffic
28-704C	S96	Requirement To Turn Off Road/Speed Less Than Normal Flow
28-705	S94	Special Speed Limit On Motor Driven Cycles
28-7053		Misuse Of Public Highways And Airports
28-7053A1		Misuse Of Public Highways And Airports/Places Obstruction O
28-7053A2		Places Obstruction On Hwy/Airport Unauth By Director/Politi
28-7053A3		Knowingly Molests/Destroys Any Part Of Public Highway
28-7053A4		Knowingly Destroys/Interferes With Crossing Of Creek/Stream
28-7053A5		Knowingly Places Vehicle Parked Within Highway
28-7053A6		Knowingly Works On Vehicle Other Than Temp Disabled On Hwy
28-7053A7		Knowingly Removes/Damages/Destroys Tree On Hwy Right Of Way
28-7053A8		Knowingly Obstructs/Injures A Public Hwy W/Water Seepage
28-7055,A		Leaving Gate Open When Road Crosses Fenced Land
28-7056,A		Dumping Refuse
28-706	S94	Special Speed Limitations
28-706A	S94	Special Speed Limitations/Solid Rubber Or Cushion Tires
28-706B	S94	Special Speed Limitations/Bridge Or Structure
28-708,A	S95	Racing On Highways
28-709A1	S93	Violation Of Maximum Speed Limit For Large Vehicles
28-709A2	S93	Viol. Of Maximum Speed Limit For Vehicle Drawing Pole Trail
28-710A,B	S93	Violation Of Maximum Speed - Highway Workzone
28-721,A	M40	Failure To Drive On Right Side Of Roadway
28-721B	M60	Failure To Drive On Right Side When Less Than Normal Speed
28-722	M75	Passing Vehicles Proceeding In Opposite Directions
28-723,.1	M73	Failure To Pass Vehicle On Left
28-723.2	M73	Failure To Give Way To Overtaking Vehicle
28-724,A	M73	Improper Overtaking On Right
28-724B	M73	Unsafe Conditions When Overtaking On Right
28-725	M77	Limitation Passing On Left Or In Face Of Oncoming Traffic
28-726	M71	Driving To The Left Of Center
28-726A1	M74	Driving Left Side When Approaching Crest/Or On Curve
28-726A2	M71	Driving Left Side/Intersection/Railroad Crossing/No Passing
28-726A3	M71	Driving Left Side When View Obstructed/Bridge Or Tunnel
28-727	M71	No Passing Zone - Overtaking Or Passing
28-728	N60	Passing On One Way Road Or Traffic Island
28-728B	N63	Failure To Drive Vehicle In Direction Designed/One-Way Road
28-728C	N61	Failure To Pass Rotary Traffic Island On Right Of Island
28-729	M42	Driving On Roadways Laned For Traffic
28-729.1	M42	Driving On Roadways Laned For Traffic/Single Lane
28-729.2	M42	Driving On Roadways Laned For Traffic/Center Lane Violation
28-729.3	M42	Failure To Obey Official Signs Directing Traffic
28-730,A	M34	Following Too Closely
28-730B	M34	Following Too Closely/Truck Or Vehicle Drawing Vehicle
28-730C	M34	Following Too Closely/Caravan
28-731	M51	Driving On Divided Highways
28-732	M46	Restricted Access
28-733,B	M50	Failure To Obey Access Restriction Signs
28-734	M12	Violation Of A Safety Zone
28-735A	M77	Overtaking Bicycles
28-736B1	M40	Designated Lane Viol/Veh Gross Weight Over 26,000 Lbs
28-736B2	M40	Designated Lane Viol/Veh Drawing Pole Trailer
28-737A	M49	Driving In HOV Lane With Fewer Than 2 Including Driver
28-751	N50	Improper Position And Method Of Turning
28-751.1	N54	Improper Position/Right Turn
28-751.2	N53	Improper Position/Left Turn
28-751.3	M03	Failure To Follow Markers Or Signs
28-751.4A	N53	Left Turn From Other Than Two-Way Left Turn Lane
28-751.4B	N56	Improper Driving In Two-Way Left Turn Lane
28-752	N50	Turning On Curve Or Crest Of Grade Prohibited
28-753	N83	Starting Parked Vehicle
28-754,A	N42	Turning Movements And Required Signals
28-754B	N43	Continuous Signal For 100 Feet Right Or Left Turn
28-754C	N43	Signal Given To Stop Or To Suddenly Reduce Speed

Statute	ACD	Description
28-755	N40	Signals By Hand Or Arm Or Signal Device/Improper Signal
28-771,A	N01	Failure To Yield The Right Of Way
28-771C	M46	Failure To Yield Right Of Way/Freeway Entrance
28-772	N31	Failure To Yield Right Of Way/Left Turn At Intersection
28-773,A,B	M46	Vehicle Entering Through Highways At Stop Signs
28-774	M25	Vehicle Entering Highway From Private Road Or Driveway
28-775	N04	Operation Of Vehicle On Approach Of Emergency Vehicle
28-775.C		Following Fire Apparatus/Closer Than 500 Ft
28-775A	N04	Yield Emergency Vehicle
28-775A1	N04	Failure To Yield Right Of Way/Emergency Vehicle
28-775A2	M33	Failure To Drive To Right/Emergency Vehicle Approaching
28-775A3	M33	Failure To Stop Until Emergency Vehicle Passes
28-775C	M32	Following Fire Apparatus/Closer Than 500 Ft
28-775D		Yield Emergency Vehicle Lights/Siren
28-775D1	N04	Approach Police Vehicle While In Emergency
28-775D2	M32	Following A Police/Closer Than 300 Ft
28-775E	N04	Yield Emergency Vehicle Stationary
28-775E1	N04	Approach Stationary Emergency Vehicle On Highway With 4 Lanes
28-775E2,E3	N04	Apprch Sttnry Emrgncy Vehicle Wthout Due Caution At Reduced Speed
28-776,A	N05	Failure To Yield To Funeral Procession Vehicles
28-776B		Improper Equipment/Marked Funeral Escort Vehicle
28-792,A	N20	Failure To Yield Right Of Way At Cross Walk
28-792B	N08	Overtaking Stopped Vehicle At Pedestrian Crosswalk
28-793,A,B,C		Failure Of Pedestrian To Cross A Roadway Properly
28-794,.1	N84	Failure To Exercise Due Care/Pedestrian
28-794.2	N84	Failure To Exercise Due Care/Sounding Horn
28-794.3	N84	Failure To Exercise Due Care/Child Or Incapacitated Person
28-7943,A		Failure To Obtain A Screen License For A Junk Yard
28-795		Failure To Use The Right Half Of A Pedestrian Crosswalk
28-796		Pedestrian Violation On Roadways
28-796A		Pedestrian Violation/Failure To Use Sidewalks
28-796B		Pedestrian Violation/Failure To Walk Facing Traffic
28-796C		Pedestrian Violation/Soliciting Ride
28-797	M13	School Zone Violation
28-797F	S15	Speed Greater Than 15 Mph In School Crossing
28-797G	N08	Failure To Stop At School Crossing/Crosswalk Occupied
28-797H	S15	Speed Greater Than 15 Mph In School Crossing Fines Doubled
28-797I	M12	Fail To Stop At School Crossing Fines Doubled
28-811		Violation Of Bicycle Regulation
28-811A		Parent/Guardian Responsibility/Operation Of Bicycles
28-813		Violation Of Bicycle Regulation
28-813A		Violation Of Bicycle Regulation/Seat Requirement
28-813B		Violation Of Bicycle Regulation/# Of Persons Carried
28-814		Violation Of Bicycle Regulation/Clinging To Vehicle
28-815		Violation Of Bicycle Regulation
28-815A		Violation Of Bicycle Regulation/Riding To The Right
28-815B		Riding More Than Two Abreast
28-815D	M47	Operating A Motor Vehicle In A Bicycle Path
28-816		Violation Of Bicycle Regulation/Carrying Package
28-817		Violation Of Bicycle Equipment Requirements
28-817A		Violation Of Bicycle Equipment/Lamp And Reflector
28-817B		Operating Bicycle Equipped With Siren Or Whistle
28-817C		Violation Of Bicycle Equipment/Brakes
28-8282,A1		Operating Aircraft While Under The Influence
28-8282A2		Operating Aircraft While Physically Or Mentally Disabled
28-8282C1		Operating Aircraft While .04 Alcohol In Blood
28-8282C2		Operating Aircraft W/In 8 Hours Of Consuming Liquor Or Drug
28-851,A	M22	Failure To Stop At Railroad Crossing
28-851B	M10	Driving Through, Around Or Under Crossing Gate
28-852	M22	Failure To Stop At Railroad Crossing/Stop Sign
28-853	M22	Failure To Stop At Railroad Crossing
28-853A	M22	Railroad Crossing/Stop Required Of Certain Vehicles
28-854	M22	Moving Heavy Equipment At Rail Road Grade
28-854A1	M22	Failure To Give Notice/Moving Heavy Equipment
28-854A2A	M22	Failure To Stop Heavy Equipment/Railroad Crossing
28-854A2B	M22	Failure To Look At Railroad Crossing

Statute	ACD	Description
28-854A3	M22	Moving Heavy Equipment At Rail Road Grade
28-854B	M22	Moving Heavy Equipment At Rail Road Grade/Against Signal
28-855	N26	Failure To Obey Stop Or Yield Sign
28-855B	M15	Failure To Stop At Stop Sign
28-855C	M19	Failure To Obey Yield Sign
28-856,.1	M25	Failure To Emerging From Alley/Driveway Properly
28-856.2	M25	Failure To Yield To Pedestrian At Alley/Driveway
28-856.3	M25	Failure To Yield Entering Road From Alley/Driveway
28-857	M75	Violation Of Overtaking And Passing School Bus
28-857A1,A2		Failure To Stop For School Bus Stop Signal
28-857B	M75	Unlawful School Bus Markings
28-857C		Failure To Conceal School Bus Markings
28-857D		Improper Stop Sign On School Bus
28-857D1		Improper Use School Bus Sign
28-857D2		Fail To Use School Bus Stop Sign
28-858	N84	Not Using Care When Approaching Horses Or Livestock
28-873	F34	Violation Of Stopping, Standing, Or Parking
28-874		Violation Of Parking Privileges
28-874A		Violation Of Parallel Parking
28-874C		Parking Violation/Interfering W/Movement Of Traffic On Hwy
28-884		Violation Of Handicapped Parking Privileges
28-884A		Parking In Disabled Persons Parking Space
28-891,A	N82	Limitations On Backing
28-891B	N82	Limitations On Backing/Access Road, Exit Or Entrance Ramp
28-892		Violation Of Operation Of Motorcycle
28-893,A	D70	Obstruction To Drivers View Or Driving Mechanism
28-893B		Obstruction To Drivers View/Driving Mechanism By Passenger
28-894		Driving On Mountain Highways
28-895,A	N80	Coasting Prohibited
28-895B	N80	Coasting Prohibited In Commercial Vehicle
28-896	N84	Driving At A Speed Which Causes Trailer To Sway
28-897	M56	Crossing Fire Hose
28-898,A		Placing Glass Or Other Objects On Roadway
28-898B		Failure To Remove Any Dropped Or Thrown Destructive Material
28-898C		Failure To Remove Wrecked Or Damaged Vehicle
28-899,.1		Allowing Barbed Wire To Lie Loose Along Highway
28-901		Violation Of School Bus Operation
28-901A1		Violation Of School Bus Operation/Carrying More Passengers
28-901A2		Violation Of School Bus Operation/While Person Standing
28-901B		Stopping School Bus On Side Of Hwy On Which School Is Located
28-902		Failure To Repaint School Bus After Sale By State
28-903	M41	Operating Motorcycle On Roadways Laned For Traffic
28-903A	M41	Driving In Manner To Deprive Motorcycle Full Use Of Lane
28-903B	M73	Operating Motorcycle/Passing In Same Lane Occupied By Vehicle
28-903C	M73	Operating Motorcycle/Between Lanes Or Adjacent Rows
28-903D	M41	Operating Motorcycle/More Than 2 Abreast In Single Lane
28-904,A	M58	Driving On Sidewalk
28-905		Opening And Closing Vehicle Doors
28-906		Mechanical Raising & Lowering Of Vehicles
28-907,A	F02	Child Passenger Restraint Requirements
28-911		Person Under 16 Yrs Operating Elec Personal Assistive Mobil
28-912A	E50	Compartment Violation - Transport Equine
28-912B1		Cargo Space Violation - Transport Equine
28-912B2		Failure To Segregate Aggressive Equine - Transport Equine
28-912B3		Insufficient Interior Height - Transport Equine
28-912B4	E50	Equipment Violation - Transport Equine
28-912C1		Improper Maintenance - Transport Equine
28-912C2A,B		Improper Loading - Transport Equine
28-912D1	N84	Failure To Properly Transport - Transport Equine
28-912D2		Failure To Observe/Check Condition - Transport Equine
28-912D3		Failure To Offload - Transport Equine
28-912D4		Improper Use Of Electric Prods - Transport Equine
28-921		Violation Of Equipment Requirements
28-921A1A		Equipment Violation/Vehicle In Unsafe Condition
28-921A1B		Equipment Violation/Veh W/Required Equipment Missing
28-921A1C		Equipment Violation/Illegally Equipped Vehicle

Statute	ACD	Description
28-921A2		Failure To Perform An Act In Violation Of Equipment Require
28-921D		Violation Of Equipment Requirements
28-922		Violation Of Lighted Lamps Requirement
28-924		Violation Of Head Lamps On Motor Vehicles
28-924A		Required Head Lamps, Other Than Motorcycle
28-924B		Required Head Lamps For Motorcycle
28-924C		Location Of Headlamps
28-925,A		Violation Of Tail Lamp Requirements
28-925B		Location Of Tail Lamp
28-925C		Lamp Required For License Plate
28-926,A1		New Motor Vehicles To Be Equipped With Reflectors
28-926A2		New Motorcycle To Be Equipped With Reflectors
28-926C		Improper Reflector Height/New Vehicles
28-927		Stop Lamps Required On Motor Vehicles
28-929		Violation Of Equipment Requirements
28-929.1		Number,Location Of Reflectors On A Bus Or Truck
28-929.2A		Number,Location Of Front Clearance Lamps/Additional Require
28-929.2B		Number,Location Of Rear Clearance Lamps/Additional Requirement
28-929.2C		Number,Location Of Marker Lamps/Additional Requirements
28-929.2D		Number,Location Of Reflectors/Additional Requirements
28-929.3A		Number,Location Front Clearance Lamps On Truck Tractor
28-929.3B		Number,Location Of Rear Clearance Lamps/Truck Tractor
28-929.4A		Number,Location Of Front Clearance Lamps/Trailer
28-929.4B		Number,Location Of Marker Lamps/Trailer
28-929.4C		Number,Location Of Reflectors/Trailer
28-929.4D		Number,Location Of Clearance Lamps/Trailer
28-929.5A		Number,Location Lamps/Pole Trailer
28-929.5B		Number,Location Rear Reflectors/Pole Trailer
28-929.6A		Number,Location Of Rear Reflectors
28-929.6B		Additional Stoplight, If Stoplight Obscured On Towing Vehicle
28-930		Special Lighting Equipment On School Buses
28-930B		Failure To Operate Warning Signal Properly On School Bus
28-931		Color Of Clearance And Side Lamps And Reflectors
28-931A		Color Of Reflectors And Lamps/Front Lamps
28-931B		Color Of Reflectors And Lamps/Rear Lamps
28-931C1		Improper Rear Lamp Color
28-931C2		Improper Color Backing Or License Plate Light
28-932		Violation Of Mounting Of Reflectors And Lamps
28-932A		Violation Of Relector Mounting Requirements
28-932D		Violation Of Clearance Lamp Mounting Requirements
28-933		Violation Of Visibility Of Reflectors And Lamps
28-933A		Violation Of Reflector Visibility Requirements
28-933B		Violation Of Clearance Lamp Visibility Requirements
28-933C		Violation Of Side Marker Lamp Visibility Requirements
28-934		Improper Vehicle Combo Lamps
28-935		Violation Of Lamp Or Flag On Projecting Load
28-935A		Lamp Or Flag On Projecting Load/Night
28-935B		Lamp Or Flag On Projecting Load/Day
28-936		Violation Of Lamps On Parked Vehicles
28-936B		Lamps On Parked Vehicles/Equipment Required
28-936C		Lamps On Parked Vehicles/Dimmed
28-937		Lamps On Other Vehicles And Equipment
28-938		Violation Of Spot Lamps And Auxiliary Lamps
28-938.1		Use Of Spot Lamp When Aimed, Used On Oncoming Vehicle
28-938.2		Number,Height Of Front Fog Lamps
28-938.3		Number,Height Of Front Auxiliary Lamps
28-938.4		Number And Height Of Front Auxiliary Lamps
28-939		Violation Of Signal Lamps And Signal Devices
28-939A1		Color Of Rear Stop Lamp Requirement
28-939A2		Visability Of Lamp Or Signal Device For Turning
28-939B		Improper Stop/Signal Lamp Visibility
28-939B1		Stop Lamp Not In Good Working Condition
28-939B2		Stop Lamp Projects Glaring Light
28-939C		Signal Device Self Illuminating When In Use
28-940		Violation Of Additional Lighting Equipment
28-940.1		Number,Color Of Side Cowl Or Fender Lamps

Statute	ACD	Description
28-940.2		Color,Location Of Running Board Courtesy Lamp
28-940.3		Number,Color,Location And Use Of Backup Lights
28-941		Violation Of Multiple Beam Road Lighting Equipment
28-941.1		Multiple Beam Road Lighting Equipment/Uppermost
28-941.2		Multiple Beam Road Lighting Equipment/Lowermost
28-941.3		No High Beam Indicator On New Vehicle
28-941.3A		No High Beam Indicator Lighted When In Use On New Vehicle
28-941.3B		High Beam Indictor Design And Location
28-941.4		Color Transparent Substance/Front Of Head Lamps
28-942		Violation In Use Of Lighting Equipment
28-942.1		Violation In Use Of Lighting Equipment/Lowermost
28-942.2		Proper Use Of Lighting Equipment While Passing
28-943		Violation Of Single Beam Road Lighting Equipment
28-943.1		Single Beam Road Lighting Equipment/Aimed Location
28-943.2		Single Beam Road Lighting Equipment/Intensity Sufficient
28-944		Violation Of Lighting Equipment On Motor Driven Cycles
28-944.1		Head Lamp Intensity Requirement On Motorcycle
28-944.2A		Multiple Beam Head Lamp/Upper Beam Requirement
28-944.2B		Multiple Beam Head Lamp/Lowermost Beam Requirement
28-944.3		Single Beam Lamp/Intensity And Aim Requirements
28-945		Alternate Road Lighting Equipment
28-946		Violation Of Number Of Driving Lamps Required Or Permitted
28-946A		Number Of Driving Lamps Required Or Permitted
28-946B		Number Of Auxiliary Lamps Permitted
28-947		Violation Of Special Restrictions On Lamps
28-947A		Improper Special Lamp Light Distance
28-947B		Improper Use Blue/Red Lights
28-947C		Improper Use Of Flashing Light On Vehicle
28-947D		Improper Warning Lights On Vehicle
28-947E		Improper Modulating Light On Motorcycle
28-948		Violation Of Standards For Lights On Snow Removal Equipment
28-948B		Standards For Lights On Snow Removal Equipment
28-949		Violation Of Selling Or Using Lamps Or Devices
28-949A		Selling Or Using Lamps Or Devices/Change Design
28-949B		Selling Or Using Lamps Or Devices/Without Trademark
28-949C		Selling Or Using Lamps Or Devices/Improper Mounting
28-952		Failure To Meet Brake Equipment Requirement
28-952.01		Unlawful Sale Of Brake Fluid
28-952A1		Failure To Meet Brake Equipment Requirement
28-952A2		Failure To Meet Brake Equipment Requirement/Motorcycle
28-952A3		Failure To Meet Brake Equipment Requirement/Trailers
28-952A4		Failure To Have Proper Brakes/New Vehicles
28-952A5		Improper Trailer Brake Operation
28-952A6A		Parking Brakes Inadequate On Grade
28-952A6B		Parking Brake Operation/Failure To Meet Requirements
28-952A6C		Parking Brake Design/Failure To Meet Requirements
28-952A7		Partial Brake Failure Leaves Vehicle W/O Brakes
28-952B		Brakes Fail To Slow/Stop As Required
28-952C		Failure To Maintain Brakes/Working Order
28-953,C		Failure To Meet Brake Standards/Motorcycle
28-954		Violation Of Horns And Warning Devices
28-954A		Failure To Have Horn In Good Working Order
28-954B		Failure To Use Horn Properly
28-954C		Unlawful Siren
28-954E		Unlawful Use Of Siren On Emergency Vehicle
28-955		Mufflers Prevention Of Noise And Air Pollution
28-955.01A		Improper Muffler On Motorcycle
28-955.01B		Unlawful Muffler Cutout/Motorcycle
28-955A		Failure To Have Muffler In Good Working Order
28-955B		Improper Muffler Cutout
28-955C		Excessive Exhaust Fumes
28-955D		Failure To Meet Emission Control Device Standards
28-956		Violation Of Mirror Requirements
28-957		Wipers On Windshields Required
28-957.01,A		Windshields Required
28-957A		Wipers On Windshields Required

Statute	ACD	Description
28-957B		Failure To Keep Wipers In Good Working Order
28-958		Violation Of Tire Equipment Restrictions
28-958.01,A		Violation Of Rear Fender Splash Guard Equipment
28-958.01B1		Improper Attachment Of Splash Guard
28-958.01B2		Splash Guard/No More Than 8 Inches From Ground
28-958.01B3		Splash Guard/Too Narrow To Cover Tread
28-958.01B4		Splash Guard/Not Control Side Throw
28-958.01B6		Splash Guard/Unlawful Attachment
28-958A		Failure To Meet Tire Requirements
28-958B		Unlawful Studs/Cleats On Tires
28-959		Violation Of Safety Glass Requirements
28-959.01		Improper Materials On Windows And Windshields
28-959.01B		Operating Vehicle W/Improper Materials On Windows/Windshield
28-959.01C		Placement Of Improper Materials On Windows/Windshields
28-959A		Violation Of Safety Glass Requirements
28-959E		Failure To Use Approved Safety Glass As Replacement
28-960		Violation Of Flare Requirements
28-960A1A		Failure To Use Flare/Lantern Requirements
28-960A1B		Failure To Use Flare/Torch Requirements
28-960A1C		Failure To Use Flares That Meet Requirements
28-960A1D		Failure To Carry Flares Properly In Vehicle
28-960A1E		Failure To Meet Requirements/Red Electric Lantern
28-960A2A		Failure To Meet Requirements/Red Fuses
28-960A2B		Failure To Meet Burning Requirements/Red Fuses
28-960A3		Failure To Meet Requirements/Red Flags
28-960B		Failure To Have Red Lanterns/Hazardous Materials
28-961		Display Of Warning Devices When Vehicle Is Disabled
28-961A1		Improper Warning Device Placement
28-961A2A,B		Improper Placement Of Fuse As Warning Device
28-961B1		Hazmat Vehicle/Improper Traffic Side Warning
28-961B2		Hazmat Vehicle/Improper Front/Rear Warning
28-961C		Improper Warning Device On Hazmat Vehicle
28-961D		Improper Display Of Flags As Warning Devices
28-961F		Failure To Meet Requirements/All Warning Devices
28-962		Violation Of Explosive Transport Regulations
28-962A1		Improper Placards On Vehicle With Explosives
28-962A2		Failure To Carry Fire Extinguisher/Vehicle With Explosives
28-963		Unlawful Placement Of Television In Vehicle
28-963.1		Unlawful Placement Of Television In Vehicle/Forward Driver
28-963.2		Unlawful To Have Tv Visible By Driver In Operation
28-964		Required Equipment On Motor Driven Cycles
28-964A		Improper Motorcycle Helmet/Eye Protection/Windshield
28-964B		Improper Motorcycle Seat/Footrests/Mirror
28-964C		Motorcycle Handlebars Above Shoulder
28-965		Violation Of Fuel Tank Cap Requirement
28-966	S94	Neighborhood Electric Vehicles;Speed;Restriction
28-966A	S93	Neighborhood Electric Vehicle/Over 25 Mph
28-966B	S93	Neighborhood Electric Vehicle/Unlawful On Highway
28-966C		Neighborhood Electric Vehicle/W/O Posted Restrictions
28-981,.1		Vehicle Unsafe For Operation On The Roadway
28-981.2	F66	Vehicle Unsafe Mechanical Condition
28-983		Failure To Comply With Inspection Laws
28-983A		Failure To Submit To Vehicle Inspection
28-983B		Failure To Comply With Repair Notice
28-983C		Operating Vehicle/With Repair Notice
28-983D2		Operating Vehicle W/O Certificate Of Adjustment
28-984,A2		Failure To Comply With School Bus Inspection Laws
28-995.04A		Commercial Vehicle Exhaust System
32-4		Notice To Police
32-5		Authority To Tow
32-6		Notice To Public Of Right To Tow
36-42,43,44		Speed Violation
36-45,46,48-51		Improper Turn
36-47		Improper U Turn
36-52,53		Wrong Way On One Way Street Or Alley
36-54		Temporary Markings-One Way Streets Or Alleys

Statute	ACD	Description
36-55,56		Failure To Stop
36-57		Impeding Other Traffic
36-58		Avoiding Stop Via Private Property
36-60		Limitations On Backing
36-61		Using An Alley As A Thoroughfare
36-63,63A		Driving On Sidewalk
36-64,64A,64B		Driving In A City Park
36-65		Following Or Parked Too Close To Emergency Vehicles
36-79		Impeding Other Traffic
36-80		Vehicles Not Part Of Authorized Procession
36-81		Location And Timing
4-241L	D06	Misrepresenting Age - Alcohol Related
4-241N		Misrepresentation Age - Fraud Id Alcohol Related
4-241P		Person With Intent To Sell/Give/Serve Sprtus Liqr To Prsns Underage
4-244.34	A60	Under Age Drinking While Driving
4-244.9	A31	Possession/Purchase Of Spirituous Liquor By Minor
4-251A1	A26	Consumption Of Liquor While Operating Or Riding In Vehicle
4-251A2	A35	Possession Of Open Container Of Liquor W/In Passenger Compa
5-395,A1-A4		Operation Of Motorized Watercraft While Intoxicated
5-396A		Aggravated Operation Of Motorized Watercraft While Intoxicated
5-396A1	W00	Agg OUI 3rd Or Sub Offense
5-396A2A	W00	Agg OUI Person Under Age 15
5-396A2B	W00	Agg OUI Person Under 15 2nd Offense
5-396A2C	W00	Agg OUI Person Under 15 With 5-397
5-397A1	W00	Extreme OUI BAC .15 To .19
5-397A2	W00	Extreme OUI BAC Over 020
8-232,B6		Defacing Or Damaging Property Of Another Person
8-323B6		Criminal Damage Under Town Or City Ordinance
R17-5-202	E01	Motor Carrier Regulations
R17-5-209	E53	Motor Carrier/Haz Mat Regulations

Point System Summary

The Arizona point system ranges from 2 to 8 points. 8 to 12 points attained in one year will result in either a suspension or assignment to Traffic Survival School. 13 points or more in a one-year period will result in suspension.

Aggressive Driving	Eight points.
Driving Over or Parking in a Gore Area (triangular area at on-ramps and off-ramps)	Three points.
DUI	Eight points.
Extreme DUI	Eight points.
Failure to Stop for Signal, Sign, or Yield, Causing Death	Six points.
Failure to Stop for Signal, Sign, or Yield, Causing Injury	Four points.
Leaving the Scene of Accident	Six points.
Racing on Highways	Eight points.
Reckless Driving	Eight points.
Speeding	Three points.
All Other Moving Violations	Two points.

Traffic Survival School

Attendance at a Traffic Survival School is mandated for convictions causing the accumulation of at least 8 points, but not more than 12 points, within a 12-month period, with no Traffic Survival School completed in the previous 24 months.

- Attendance can also be required for a conviction of one of the following violations:
- Aggressive Driving
- Moving Violation Resulting In An Accident Causing Serious Physical Injury
- Moving Violation Resulting In An Accident Causing Death
- For the first moving violation of a driver under 18 years of age
- For a conviction for Red Light Running

Arkansas

Administration

Tonie Shields, Administrator
Office of Driver Services
PO Box 1272, Room 2067
Little Rock 72203
501-682-7060
www.accessarkansas.org/dfa/motor_vehicle/mv_index.html

Note: The Office of Driver Services consists of five sections: Administrative, Driver's License Issuance, Safety Responsibility, Insurance Verification, Driver Control, and Traffic Violation Records.

Roger Duren, Administrator
Office of Motor Vehicles
PO Box 1272
Little Rock 72203
501-682-4661
www.dfa.arkansas.gov/offices/motorVehicle/Pages/default.aspx

Important Contacts

Driver License Issuance...........................501-682-7059
Driver Control 501-682-1631
Driving Records.......................................501-682-7207
Financial/Safety Responsibility...............501-682-7098
                                        or 501-682-7100
Insurance Verification 501-682-7930
Commercial Driver License.....................501-682-1400
Titles & Registration 501-682-3333
                                        or 501-371-5549
IRP...501-682-4651
State Dept of Insurance............................501-371-2600

State Statutes found at:

www.lexisnexis.com/hottopics/arcode/Default.asp

Driver's License Format, Issuance and Renewal

Classes, Restrictions and Endorsements Appear After the Driving Record Content Section

License Format

The current format is nine numbers. Until July 2003, the number consisted of either the Social Security Number (SSN) or nine numbers. Since 07/03, the SSN is no longer permitted to be used as the DL number. Prior to July 2003 and if the DL is not the Social Security Number, the first digit was "9," the next seven were sequential, and the last was a check digit.

Document Appearance

The current Driver's Licenses and ID Cards have been issued since June 2011. The previous version began issuance on December 11, 2006. Bothe are profiled below. Sample photos of newer format is shown at www.dfa.arkansas.gov/offices/driverServices/Pages/samples.aspx.

Current Documents

Security Characteristics: The new card has a number of redesigned security features to make stop tampering and counterfeiting. Most noticeable are the variable background colors and patterns. The biggest differences are in format and colors. Vertical cards are issued to drivers under 21. The License Class is indicated in a colorized outlined of the state appearing in the upper right corner. Class D is green; an Intermediate Class D is yellow; a Class D Lerner's Permit is white; a CDL is blue; and the ID Card is red.

Position of Photo: Lower left side, below license numbers. There is a smaller ghost image of card bearer located on the lower right edge.

Minor Age Driver Locator: Licenses and ID Cards are in a vertical format. *Under 21* is printed in red under the photo. *Under 18* is printed in yellow under the photo. See colors mentioned above.

CDL Indicator: The words *Commercial Driver License* appear to the left of the state name, and the state outline is in blue with "CDL" in white lettering inside the outline.

Older Documents

Security Characteristics: Core is card stock laminated with Advantage laminate.

Position of Photo: Shown on the middle left edge with a smaller portrait photo on the lower left edge card.

Minor Age Driver Locator: *Under 21* is printed in red under the photo. *Under 18* is printed in yellow under the photo. it.

CDL Indicator: COMMERCIAL DRIVERS LICENSE" is printed in heading above name, in red block.

Issuance

Location of Requirements for Proof of Identity:
www.dfa.arkansas.gov/offices/driverServices/Pages/FAQ's.aspx#e

Age Requirements

The Arkansas graduated licensing law, effective July 1st, 2002, provides for a progressive driver licensing program for young drivers. The three levels of licensing are Learner's, Intermediate and Regular licenses. The minimum for a Learner's License is fourteen; age sixteen to eighteen get an Intermediate License. All new licensees under eighteen must be accompanied by licensed adult for at least 6 months. A regular license is issued to a person at age 18 when the Intermediate License expires. Holders of an Intermediate Drivers License issued on or after July 31, 2009 are 1) Prohibited from operating a motor vehicle with more than one unrelated minor passenger unless accompanied by a licensed driver 21 years of age or older; 2) prohibited from operating a motor vehicle between the hours of 11:00 PM and 4:00 AM unless the licensee is: accompanied by a person 21 years of age or older; driving to or from a school activity, church-related activity, or job; or driving because of an emergency.

Applicants for a Regular License must have a record without any serious accidents or serious traffic convictions within the most recent 12 months. If the applicant has such accident or conviction within the most recent 12 months, he/she must retain the Intermediate License until such time that the record is free of these accidents/convictions for a period of 12 months. The age restrictions in this program do not apply to a person 16 years of age or older if such person is (A) married, (B) possesses a high school diploma, (C) has successfully completed a General Education Development test, or (D) is enlisted in the U. S. Military.

Residency

A person must obtain an AR Driver License within thirty days of establishing residency. If the out-of-state license is expired over 31 days but less than one year, the driver is be required to take the written and vision examination, but will not be required to take the road examination. If the out-of-state license is expired over one year, the driver is required to take the written, vision, and road examination.

Renewal

Renewal is on birth date of fourth year. Driver keeps same number when renewing. Renewal is not offered online. Military personnel may renew by mail, but they must pass a vision examination with the results and signature of the examiner shown on the state's application

Elderly-Related Restrictions
None.

Vehicle Insurance, Title and Registration Facts

Registration Renewal

One may renew by phone, mail or web if renewing previously issued car tags and if there is no need to change any information other than address. Annual renewal of registration is online at www.arstar.com/. Operators can also make addresses changes online.

New Residents

Non-residents must register vehicles within thirty calendar days of becoming a resident.

Inspections and Emissions Testing

At one time Arkansas had a required annual safety inspection, but this was no longer required as of 01/01/98. There is no statewide provision for emissions inspections.

Passenger Plate Facts

There is one plate with two decals (MO) (YR). The county of issuance is not coded or identified. When a passenger car and light truck is sold the plate remains with seller. For large trucks, the plate may either remain with seller or transfers to buyer.

Insurance and Financial Responsibility

Proof of insurance (compulsory) is required at registration, after a reportable accident, and upon demand from police. Minimum financial responsibility limits are $25,000/50,000/25,000. Proof of liability insurance is required for all personal watercraft and motorboats powered by engines of more than 50 horsepower. A $25.00 fine is charged to individuals who fail to present proof of insurance when requested by law enforcement.

Withdrawal Sanctions, and Alcohol and Drug Testing

Alcohol and Chemical Testing

The legal limit of alcohol level is .08 % for non-commercial drivers, .04 % for commercial drivers, and .02 % for drivers under 21. Arkansas will conduct urine, blood, and breathe tests. The Arkansas under-the-influence law contains a provision for implied consent.

Suspensions and Revocations

The state is in compliance with the mandatory CDL disqualifications per federal regulations as shown in the Appendix. Other mandatory suspension and revocations are shown below.

Accumulation of Points
Ten to Thirteen Points .... Warning Letter sent.
Fourteen to Seventeen Points............ Possible three- to six-month suspension.
Eighteen to Twenty-three Points....... Possible six- to twelve-month suspension.
Twenty-four or More Points .... Possible one-year suspension—may be subject to possible one-year revocation.
DWI Suspensions
First Offense).................................. Minimum 180 days.
Second Offense within 5 years .... Minimum 2 years.
Third Offense within 5 years .... Minimum 30 months.
Fourth Offense within 5 years .... Mandatory four-year revocation.
No Proof of Financial Responsibility .... Indefinite suspension.
Unsatisfied Judgment (accidents).......... Indefinite suspension.
Refused Chemical Test.......................... First offense - 180 day suspension.

Reinstatement Requirements

If convicted of DUI, driver must also complete a rehabilitation program before reinstatement. The reinstatement fees can be paid online. From www.dfa.arkansas.gov under *Drivers* click on *Driver's License Reinstatement*.
   Suspension   Determined by point accumulation and reason for suspension. $100.00 fee; $150.00 if DWI.
   Revocation   May reapply after one-year time-lapse, test required. $100.00 fee; $150.00 if DWI.
Note: If convicted of DUI, must also complete a rehabilitation program before reinstatement.

Record Access: Laws, Rules, and Forms

Note: Text below applies to both driver and vehicle records unless otherwise noted.

Governing Statutes and Rules

State Statutes found at   www.arkleg.state.ar.us/
Arkansas driving records are governed by Arkansas Code Section 27-50-901 et. Seq. These statutes are more restrictive regarding the release of personal information than DPPA. In accordance with Arkansas Code, authorization by the driver is required to obtain a driving record except for courts, law enforcement, governmental agencies showing cause, and the driver himself.
Arkansas Code Section 27-14-412 governs the release of vehicle information with or without personal information.

Policy Statement Regarding Permissible Uses

Permissible use requesters include a licensed attorney with copy of license, judgment or court order, and a private investigative agency or licensed security service with copy of license, and a written purpose for requesting records.
All requesters must have consent except for those requesters mentioned above. Authorization may be a signed release by the driver, a power of attorney, or (in the case of a minor) the parent or guardian. This release will remain in effect for 5 years. Employers and insurance companies must maintain the authorization on file. The authorization must be kept

on file by bulk users of records. This authorization prohibits any further resale of the driving record information by the end-user.

Request and Consent Forms

Driving Records One can use the *Driving Records Request* form or use a generic form. The signature of the subject is required, notarization is not required. The *Driving Records Release* form, *Driving Records Request* form, and *Driving Records Requestor* form all are available at www.dfa.arkansas.gov/offices/driverServices/Pages/DriverRecords.aspx
Vehicle Records There is not a recommended form to use, unless a subscriber - then at https://www.ark.org/subscribe/trl_agreement.html.

Vendor and Third Party Access Policy

Approved online vendors can access records for other vendors (who are not online, etc) who will then sell to an end user provided—

1. If contract between original vendor and reseller contains same language as contract between the state and the original vendor
2. If contract between reseller and end user contains same language as contract between the state and the original vendor.

Non-permissible Use Requests

With no consent, non-permissible requesters cannot obtain records, even records without personal information.

Access to Driver-Related Records

Driving Records

General Information and Fees

Department of Driver Services, Driving Records Division, PO Box 1272, Room 1130, Little Rock AR 72203, 501-682-7207.
www.dfa.arkansas.gov/offices/driverServices/Pages/DriverRecords.aspx
There are two types of records:

1. **Insurance Record** (Generally requested for insurance purposes, a 3-year record)
2. **Commercial Record** (Usually requested for commercial driver license holders for employment related purposes, may contain information longer than 3 years, see below).

The fees mail in-person records are $7.00 for the insurance record and $10.00 for the commercial (employment) record. Fees for online access are higher, see below. There is a full charge for "no record found" reports.
CDL Medical Certification is now displayed on driving records. See www.dfa.arkansas.gov/offices/driverServices/Pages/medCert.aspx.
In-Person – Records may be requested at the Office of Driver Services, 1900 West 7th, Ragland Bldg, Room 1130, Little Rock. This is the only location to request driving records on a commercial basis and will process up to five record requests while one you wait.
Mail – Requests mailed to the state are processed within twenty-four hours of receipt. State forms are not required when ordering but are available to customers who wish to use them. The driver's license number and date of birth are needed when ordering, and the fee must accompany each request.
Electronic – Arkansas.gov is the designated entity for online retrieval of driving records. Both a batch and interactive format is offered. The system is open 24 hours daily via the web. There is an annual $95.00 in addition to the record fee of $8.50 for insurance record or $11.50 for commercial record. Also, an online *Drivers Status Check* for a $2.00 fee is offered to car rental companies to validate that a license has not been restricted or revoked. For more info call Information Network of Arkansas (INA) at 800-392-6069 or visit http://portal.arkansas.gov/services/Pages/servicesINA.aspx.
Bulk – Commercial purchase of the driver license database not offered.
By Person of Record – Arkansas drivers may obtain their driving record by visiting the main office listed above or any Arkansas Revenue office. Same fees apply. Arkansas Drivers may also request, view and print their own record online at https://www.ark.org/personal_tvr/index.php. The name, DOB, DL, the DL issue date, and last five digits of the SSN are required along with a major credit card. The fee is $8.50 for an insurance record or $11.50 for a commercial record.

Mandatory Requirements for Employers

All employers of Arkansas commercial drivers are required to search the Arkansas Commercial Driver Alcohol and Drug Testing Database prior to hiring a commercial driver. Also per Arkansas law, employers are

required to report and submit to the database any positive alcohol and drug test results on commercial drivers as well as report drivers who refuse to submit to an alcohol or drug test. Registered service providers can act on behalf of employers. Online access is offered to this information; one must have a subscription account with INA. The fee is $2.50 per record. Employers that utilize a Service Provider are still required by the State to register.

Notification/Monitoring Program

A monitoring and notification system for approved requesters to track incidents of Commercial Drivers is available from Arkansas.gov (see above) at www.arkansas.gov/driverwatch/index.html. The Driver Watch Program permits employer subscribers to receive notification on the change in the driver license status for $1.00 per month. The fee for providing a record on a monthly basis is $11.50 per driver per month per registered employee.
Rental car companies can use this service for $1.00 per driver submitted, and will receive a **status check**.

Accident Reports

Reporting – A Safety Responsibility SR-1 accident report must be submitted within thirty days when damage to the property of any one person is in excess of $1,000 or results in the injury or death of any person regardless of who is at fault. The report is submitted to the police as well as the Safety Responsibility Section, Department of Revenue, PO Box 1272, Little Rock AR 72203 (501-682-7098). The report can be filed online at https://www.ark.org/dfa/sr1/index.html or downloaded at www.dfa.arkansas.gov/offices/driverServices/Documents/SR121.pdf or call Safety Responsibility at 501-682-7100 or 7098 for a copy. Otherwise visit www.asp.state.ar.us/divisions/rs/rs_crash.html or write to the State Police at #1 State Police Plaza, Little Rock AR 72209, 501-618-8130.

Record Access – Copies of accident reports are sold by the Arkansas State Police, Crash Records Section, #1 State Police Plaza, Little Rock AR 72209, 501-618-8130. It takes 3 to 5 days after a crash is investigated before new records are available for inquiry. Mail turnaround time is normally two to three weeks. Requests must include the name of the driver, the location, and the date of the accident. Enclose $10.00 for each request and include a SASE.
Access is also available online at https://www.ark.org/grs/app/asp. There is no fee to search, but a PDF copy of the report is $12.00. Use of a credit card is required unless requester has an account with Arkansas.gov. Records are available from 2000 to present. Note that not all crash reports are available for online purchase.

Access to Vehicle-Related Records

General Information

Office of Motor Vehicles, MV Title Records, PO Box 1272, Room 1100, Little Rock 72203, 800-662-8247, 501-682-4692, 501-682-3333, fax 501-682-4756. MVInformation@dfa.arkansas.gov

The Office of Motor Vehicles maintains title, registration, and lien records for vehicles and mobile homes. Also, this agency registers vessels; however, lien records on boats are found at the county level or at Secretary of State. Records are available from 1968 for plate information on microfiche. The agency films all records and does not hold paper copies. It takes 4 to 6 weeks before new records are available. Social Security Numbers are not released.

Mail or In-Person – The current fee for VIN, registration checks, vehicle lien records, or boat registration records is $1.00 per search and $1.00 per copy of a record. The state requires written, notarized consent as described above when ordering these searches. There is no form available at the web page.

Telephone or Fax – Established search accounts, law enforcement and government offices may request information by phone or fax. A $125.00 deposit is required.

Electronic – Arkansas.gov offers online access to title, registration or lien records to subscribers who have a permissible use. The cost is $1.50 per record plus an annual $95.00 subscription fee. The password entitles 10 users. Also, certified records may be ordered online. See: http://portal.arkansas.gov/services/Pages/servicesINA.aspx. This is the same system used to access driving records.

Bulk – The availability of commercial bulk or batch purchase of records, except for recall or statistical purposes, is prohibited by law.

Access to Vessel-Related Records

General Information, Access and Fees

All sail boats and all motorized boats must be registered with the Office of Motor Vehicles. Boat registrations may be applied for at any state revenue office. Vessels are not titled by the state. The state has determined access of boat registration records does not fall under the rule of DPPA. Title records are available from 1981, license plate records from 1971. Search by name or registration number or hull number. Lien information is not shown since it is recorded at the Secretary of State office or at the local county level. The search fee is $1.00 per search and $1.00 per copy of a record. Account holders may order by phone or fax. Bulk purchase is available via FTP. www.dfa.arkansas.gov/offices/motorVehicle/Pages/BoatRegistration.aspx.

Driving Record Content and Reciprocity

What's on or Not on the Record

- Convictions are shown on the **Insurance Record** is three years, suspensions indefinitely until requirements are met.
- Major convictions are shown on the **Commercial Record** for 55 years from conviction date. Serious violations, including railroad crossing are listed for 4 years; out of service order violations for 15 years; and all other convictions for 3 years from conviction date.
- The CDL Medical Certificate is displayed on commercial records.
- Violations on an interstate (not exceeding 75 mph) are not reported on an insurance record, but are listed if the record is requested for employment or law-enforcement purposes (commercial record).
- An accident will appear on the record only if the driver is at fault.
- Records contain the address and DOB. The SSN, race or gender are not listed on the insurance and commercial records.

Data Retention

CDL driver records are purged based on the timetable per federal regulations (see the appendix). Surrendered licenses are cancelled and are retained for one year from date of driver license expiration.

Court to Repository

Courts send conviction data to the state via paper. The state law requires courts to send ticket information within 5 days from the conviction. The information is entered online daily by state personnel, generally within thirty days of receipt from the courts.

State Reciprocity for Non-CDL Drivers

- Will suspend license of driver for unpaid out-of-state convictions.
- Record of new incoming driver is shown on MVR.
- Out-of-state convictions are shown on MVR.
- Out-of-state accidents are shown on MVR if sent electronically.
- Convictions of out-of-state drivers are sent to home state.
- Record is forwarded to new state upon surrender of license.

License Classes, Restrictions, Endorsements, and Status Codes

Commercial Classifications

Class A   Combination vehicle with a GVWR of 26,001 pounds or more, provided that the GVWR of the vehicle(s) being towed is in excess of 10,000 pounds. Minimum age is 18.

Class B   Any single vehicle with a GVWR of 26,001 pounds or more, and any such vehicle towing a vehicle less than 10,000 pounds. Minimum age is 18.

Class C   Any single vehicle with a GVWR of less than 26,001 pounds or any such vehicle towing a vehicle with a GVWR not in excess of 26,001 pounds or any such vehicle towing a vehicle with a GVWR less than 10,000 pounds, comprising:
- vehicles designed to transport sixteen (16) or more passengers, including the driver; and
- vehicles used in the transportation of hazardous materials which requires the vehicle to be placarded under 49 CFR, part 172, sub-part F. Minimum age is 18.

Restricted Commercial Classifications

Class B or C   Issued to seasonal drivers of farm retail outlets and suppliers, agri-chemical business, custom harvesters and livestock feeders. Restricts drivers to operating Class B or C vehicles only during a season not to exceed 180 days in a 12-month period.

Non-Commercial Classifications

Class D   Any vehicle which is not a commercial vehicle as defined above. Minimum age 14 with licensed adult; age 14 to 16 must hold adult restriction a minimum of 6 months.
Class ID   Identification Card.
Class M   Motorcycle only (over 250cc) - Minimum age 16.
Class MD   Motor Driver Cycle (50cc thru 250cc) - Minimum age 14, expires on 16th birthdate.
Class X   Dummy License.

Restrictions

A	With Licensed Adult	H	Passengers in Class B, C	S	School Bus and Class D Only
B	Corrective Lenses	I	Class C Only with Passengers	T	Seatbelts Required on all Passengers
C	Mechanical Aid	J	Other – (See Attachment)		
D	Prosthetic Aid	K	No Air-Brakes	U	Class D Only with Passengers
E	Automatic Transmission	L	Interlock Device	Y	Diesel Fuel, Fertilizer Only
F	Outside Mirror	Q	ID Card Issued (computer only/not shown on ID card)	Z	Seasonal Farm-Service Vehicle
G	Daylight Only				

Endorsements

H	Hazardous Materials	MD	Motor-Driven Cycle	V	Valid Without Photo (not on license)
N	Tank Vehicle	P	Passengers		
X	Combines H and N	S	School Bus		
M	Motorcycle	T	Double-/Triple-Trailers		

Note: There is no restriction or endorsement code shown on a driving record for a CDL Intrastate Only. This status is indicated on the header of the license document.

Status Codes

CAN	Cancelled	N/A	Not Applicable (CDL Only)	SUR	Surrender
DED	Deceased	PED	Pending	SUS	Suspended
DEN	Denied	PRO	Probation	UNJ	Unsatisfied Judgment
DIS	Disqualified	REV	Revoked	VAL	Valid
FIN	Financial Responsibility	RST	Restricted		

Conviction Table with Codes, ACD, and Points

The Withdrawal Table Follows

Reference Keys

- (F) in the Flag column means the violations could be flagged from view. For insurance records, speed violations S01, S06, S15, S16, S51, S92, and S93 are flagged, but it is not automatic. All D36 and B74 codes are automatically flagged from insurance only records. All F04, 67D and 33F codes are automatically flagged from commercial and insurance records.
- ## = Detail required (such as speed over limit)
- = Speed points for S50 and S92: 1-10 MPH over 3 points; 11-20 over 4 points; 21-30 over 5 points; 31+ over 8 points.
- Viewable on Tickets: 1 = Commercial   2 = Hazardous Materials

Note the conviction Table is presented in order of the 'Code' column, which is the state's native code. This Code appears on all driving records. Sometimes this code is identical to the ACD, but not always.

Description	Code	ACD	Flag	Pt	Full Text
DUI IN MTR BOAT	11B			0	Motor boat DUI
CELL PHONE VIO	11C			0	Cell Phone Warning
MTR BOAT REFUSE	12B				Motor boat refuse test
STAY OF SUSPENSION	1SS				Entered Stay of Suspension
SPILL R DRAG	23F			0	Spilling, dragging, unsecured or unsafe load
PARKN HANDIC	33F		(F)	0	Parking in a handicap zone
TR ALC ILLEG	51B			0	Transporting liquor illegally
LIQTR TO MINR	52B			0	Transporting liquor to a minor
LITTERING	67D		(F)	0	Littering from a motor vehicle
WARNING - FL SHOW INS	75B			0	Failure to show insurance
TEXT WHILE DRIVING	85M	M85		0	Texting while driving
TEXT MESSAGE WARN	85W			0	Texting while driving warning
HH PHONE WHILE DRI	86M	M86		0	Using a hand-held mobile device while driving
DUI@04BACPLI	A04	A04		14	Driving under the influence of alcohol with BAC at or over .04
DUI@)08BACPLI -#	A08	A08		14	Driving under the influence of alcohol with BAC at or over .08
DUI@10BACPLI	A10	A10		14	Driving under the influence of alcohol with BAC at over .10
DUI # @BAC ##	A11	A11		14	Driving under the influence of alcohol with BAC at or over (detail req)
REFUSE TEST	A12	A12		14	Refused to submit to test for alcohol - Implied Consent Law
DUI ALC/DRUG -#	A20	A20		14	Driving under the influence of alcohol or drugs

Description	Code	ACD	Flag	Pt	Full Text
DUI ALCOHOL* -#	A21	A21		14	Driving under the influence of alcohol
DUI OF DRUGS -#	A22	A22		14	Driving under the influence of drugs
DUI ACL&DRUG -#	A23	A23		14	Driving under the influence of alcohol or drugs
DUI MEDICATN -#	A24	A24		14	Driving under the influence of medication not intended to intoxicate
DRV IMPAIRED	A25	A25		14	Driving while impaired - ability definitely impaired
DRNK WH OPER	A26	A26		14	Drinking alcohol while operating a vehicle
POSS ALCOHOL	A31	A31		0	Illegal possession of alcohol
POSSESS DRUG	A33	A33		0	Illegal possession of drugs (controlled substances)
OPEN CONTAIN	A35	A35		0	Possession of open alcohol container
INTRLOCK VIOL	A41	A41		0	Driver violation of ignition interlock or immobilization device
VEH: CNTR SUB	A50	A50		0	Motor vehicle used in manufacturing, distribution or dispensing a controlled substance
UNAGE DUI -#	A60	A60		14	Underage convicted of drinking and driving at .02 or higher BAC
UNAGE D*DADM	A61	A61		0	Underage administrative Per Se - Drinking and Driving.02 or higher BAC
DUI@10ADMIN	A90	A90		14	Administrative Per Se for .10 BAC
DUI@ ADMIN	A91	A91		14	Administrative Per Se
DUI@04ADMIN	A94	A94		14	Administrative Per Se for .04 BAC
DUI@08ADMIN	A98	A98		14	Administrative Per Se for .08 BAC
ACCIDENT	AC			3	Accident
FATALITY ACCIDENT	AF			3	Fatality accident
AGE WAIVER ISSUED	AW1			0	Age waiver issued
REVOKE AGE WAIVER	AW2			0	Age waiver revoked
H&R AFTR ACC	B01	B01		3	Hit and run-failure to stop and render aid after accident fatal accident
H&R: FAT ACC	B02	B02		3	Hit and run-failure to stop and render aid after personal injury accident
H&R: IJN ACC	B03	B03		3	Hit and run-failure to stop and render aid after property damage accident
H&R: PDO ACC	B04	B04		0	Hit and run-failure to stop and render aid after accident
LVSC AFT ACC	B05	B05		8	Leaving accident scene before police arrive
LVSC: FAT ACC	B06	B06		8	Leaving accident scene before police arrive-Fatal accident
LVSC: INJ ACC	B07	B07		8	Leaving accident scene before police arrive-Personal injury accident
LVSC: PDO ACC	B08	B08		0	Leaving accident scene before police arrive-Property damage accident
FL RV ID ACC	B14	B14		0	Refusal to reveal identity after fatal or personal injury accident
D W LIC OOSL	B19	B19		3	Driving while out of service order is in effect and transporting 16 or more passengers including the driver and/or transporting hazardous materials
D W LIC WITH	B20	B20		3	Driving while license withdrawn
D W LIC BARR	B21	B21		3	Driving while license barred
D W LIC CANC	B22	B22		3	Driving while license canceled
D W LIC DENI	B23	B23		3	Driving while license denied
D W LIC DISQ	B24	B24		3	Driving while license disqualified
D W LIC REVK	B25	B25		3	Driving while license revoked
D W LIC SUSP	B26	B26		3	Driving while license suspended
D W LIC OOSO	B27	B27		3	Driving while our of service order is in effect
ALT/CFT DLID	B41	B41		0	Possess or provide counterfeit or altered driver license
EXP/NO DL/ID	B51	B51		0	Expired or no driver license (DL, CDL & instruction permit)
CMV NO CDL	B56	B56		0	Driving a commercial motor vehicle without obtaining a CDL
CMN NO CDL P	B57	B57		0	Driving a CMV without CDL DL in driver's possession
FL FILE ACCR	B61	B61		0	Failed to file accident report
FL FILE FUTP	B63	B63		0	Failed to file future proof of financial responsibility
FL FILE INSR	B64	B64		0	Failed to file insurance certification
FL FILE MEDC	B65	B65		0	Failed to file medical certification/disability information
FL SHOW INS	B74	B74	(F)	0	Failed to show insurance certification or proof of insurance
FL SHOW ID	B78	B78		0	Failed to show non-commercial driver license (includes Instruction Permit)
IMP CLS.NDOR	B91	B91		0	Improper classification or endorsement of driver license
MISREP ID DL	D02	D02		0	Misrepresentation of identity or other facts on applicator for DL, (DL, CDL & Instruction Permit
MISRP ID ALC	D06	D06		0	Misrepresentation of identity or other facts to obtain alcohol
MULTIPLE DLS	D07	D07		0	Possess multiple driver licenses (includes DL, CDL, and Instruction Permit)
MAKE FAKE DL	D10	D10		0	Manufacture or make false driver license (includes DL, CDL, and Instruction Permit)
USE IMP DLID	D16	D16		0	Show or use improperly-Drivers License (includes DL, CDL, and Instruction Permit)
VIO LTD LICN	D27	D27		0	Violate limited license conditions
VIO RESTRICT	D29	D29		0	Violate restrictions of driver license (includes DL, CDL, and Instruction Permit)
NO LIABL INS	D36	D36	(F)	0	Failure to maintain required liability insurance
FTP DAM/INST	D37	D37		0	Failure to pay for damages or make installment payment
NO SECURE/REL	D38	D38		0	Failure to post security or obtain release from liability

Description	Code	ACD	Flag	Pt	Full Text
UNSATIS JUDG	D39	D39		0	Unsatisfied judgment
FTA: TRIL/CT	D45	D45		0	Failure to appear for trial or court appearance
FTP: CH SUPT	D51	D51		0	Failure to make required payment of child support
FTP: FINE	D53	D53		0	Failure to make required payment of fine and costs
FTA: FOR ORG	D56	D56		0	Failure to answer a citation, pay fines, penalties and/or cost related to the original violation
VIEW OBSTRUC	D70	D70		0	Driver's view obstructed
NO CONTR VEH	D72	D72		3	Inability to control vehicle
OPER: DROWSY	D74	D74		0	Operating a motor vehicle improperly because of drowsiness
OPER W DISAB	D75	D75		0	Operating a motor vehicle improperly due to physical or mental disability
PERJURY VEHL	D78	D78		0	Perjury about the operation of a motor vehicle
DDC CLASS	DDC			0	Defensive driving course
OMIT EQUPMNT	E01	E01		0	Operating without equipment as required by law
OMIT BRAKES	E02	E02		0	Operation without brakes as required by law
OMIT HZM SAF	E03	E03		0	Operation without hazmat safety equipment as required by law
OMIT HZM MRK	E04	E04		0	Operation without hazmat placards/marking as required by law
OMIT LIGHTS	E05	E05		3	Operating without lights as required by law
OMIT S B EQP	E06	E06		0	Operating without school bus equipment as required by law
PROH RADAR/L	E23	E23		0	Use of radar of laser detector prohibited by law
DFCT BRAKES	E31	E31		0	Defective brakes
DFCT HZM SAF	E33	E33		0	Defective hazmat safety devices
DFCT LIGHTS	E34	E34		0	Defective lights
DFCT SB EQP	E36	E36		0	Defective school bus equipment
DFCT TIRES	E37	E37		0	Defective tires
NUSE EQUPMNT	E50	E50		0	Failure to use equipment as required
NUSE BRAKES	E51	E51		0	Failure to use brakes
NUSE HZM SAF	E53	E53		0	Failure to use hazmat safety devices as required
FT DIM LIGHT	E54	E54		3	Failure to use headlight dimmer as required
NUSE LIGHTS	E55	E55		3	Failure to use lights as required
NUSE S B EQP	E56	E56		0	Failure to use school bus safety equipment as required
NUSE SNO T/C	E57	E57		0	Failure to use snow tires or chains as required
MPRP EQUPMNT	E70	E70		0	Equipment used improperly or obstructed
MPRP BRAKES	E71	E71		0	Brakes used improperly
C/Y NOT USED	F02	F02		0	Child or youth restraint not used properly as required
M/C EQ N USD	F03	F03		0	Motorcycle safety equipment not used properly as required
S B NOT USED	F04	F04	(F)	0	Seat belt not used properly as required
PASS N OPN V	F05	F05		0	Carrying unsecured passengers in open area of vehicle
IMP OP/RD MC	F06	F06		0	Improper operation/ riding a motorcycle (no longer valid ACD Code)
OBSTR TRAFFC	F34	F34		0	Stopping, standing or parking: obstructing or impeding traffic
VEHIC UNSAFE	F66	F66		0	Unsafe condition of vehicle (no specified component)
FTO BARRIER	M02	M02		3	Failure to obey barrier - includes _Railroad Crossing_/barriers/saw horses
FTO CNST/MNT	M03	M03		3	Failure to obey construction or maintenance zone markers
FTO FLAGGER	M04	M04		3	Failure to obey flagger
FTO LANE MRK	M05	M05		3	Failure to obey lane markings or signal
FTO OFFICER	M08	M08		3	Failure to obey police or peace officer
FTO RR RESTR	M09	M09		3	Failure to obey railroad crossing restrictions
FTO RR GAT/S	M10	M10		3	Failure to obey railroad gates, signs or signals
FTO RST LANE	M11	M11		3	Failure to obey restricted lane
FTO SAF ZONE	M12	M12		3	Failure to obey safety zone - includes school zones
FTO SCH XING	M13	M13		3	Failure to obey school crossing guard
FTO SIGN/TCD	M14	M14		3	Failure to obey sign or traffic control device
FTO STP SIGN	M15	M15		3	Failure to obey stop sign
FTO TRF SGNL	M16	M16		3	Failure to obey traffic signal or light - includes red light or "stop" sign
FTO TRF SIGN	M17	M17		3	Failure to obey traffic sign; includes obscuring/tampering with road signs
FTO WARN LIT	M18	M18		3	Failure to obey warning light or flasher
FTO YLD SIGN	M19	M19		3	Failure to obey yield sign
FTO RR NSLOW	M20	M20		3	For drivers who are not required to always stop, failure to slow down at a railroad-highway grade crossing and check that tracks are clear of approaching train
FTO RR NSTOP	M21	M21		3	For drivers not required to always stop, failure to stop before reaching tracks at a railroad-highway grade crossing when track are not clear
FTO RR DRIVE	M22	M22		3	For drivers who are always required to stop, failure to stop as required before driving onto railroad-highway grade crossing
FTO RR SPACE	M23	M23		3	For all drivers, failing to have sufficient space to drive completely through the railroad-highway grade crossing without stopping
FTO RR CLRNC	M24	M24		3	For all drivers, failing to negotiate a railroad-highway grade crossing because

Description	Code	ACD	Flag	Pt	Full Text
					of insufficient undercarriage clearance
FAIL TO STOP	M25	M25		3	Fail to stop-basic rule at unsigned intersection/when entering road from private driveway, alley, etc.
FOL IMPROPER	M30	M30		3	Following improperly
NSF DIST PAS	M31	M31		3	Failure to leave sufficient distance for overtaking by other vehicle
FOL EMER VEH	M32	M32		3	Following emergency vehicle unlawfully
FOL FIRE EQU	M33	M33		3	Following fire equipment unlawfully
FOL TOO CLOS	M34	M34		3	Following too closely
IMPROPR LOCA	M40	M40		3	Improper lane or location
STRAY FRM LN	M41	M41		3	Failure to keep in proper lane
IMPR LANE CH	M42	M42		3	Improper or erratic (unsafe) lane changes
RAN OFF ROAD	M43	M43		3	Ran off road
IMP LOC XOVR	M44	M44		3	Improper lane or location-crossover
IMP LOC XWLK	M45	M45		3	Improper lane or location-crosswalk
IMP LOC RAMP	M46	M46		3	Improper land or location-entrance/exit ramp or way
IMP LOC BIKE	M47	M47		3	Improper lane or location-in bicycle lane
IMP LOC OCCL	M48	M48		3	Improper lane or location-in occupied lane
IMP LOC HOVL	M49	M49		3	Improper lane or location-in HOV or restricted lane
IMP LOC LTAC	M50	M50		3	Improper lane or location-limited access highway
IMP LOC MEDN	M51	M51		3	Improper lane or location-median
IMP LOC TRAK	M55	M55		3	Improper lane or location-on rail or streetcar tracks
IMP LOC FHOS	M56	M56		3	Improper lane or location-on fire hose
IMP LOC ONCM	M57	M57		3	Improper lane or location-oncoming traffic lane
IMP LOC SHLD	M58	M58		3	Improper lane or location-road shoulder, ditch or sidewalk
IMP LOC SLOV	M60	M60		3	Improper lane or location-slower vehicle lane
IMP LOC CNTR	M61	M61		3	Improper lane or location-straddling center line(s)
IMP LOC TURN	M62	M62		3	Improper lane or location-traveling in turn (or center) lane
IMPROPR PASS	M70	M70		3	Improper passing
PAS PST SIGN	M71	M71		3	Passing in violation of posted sign or pavement marking
PAS OP DIREC	M72	M72		3	Passing in violation of opposite directions restriction
PAS WRNG SID	M73	M73		3	Passing on wrong side
PASS HIL/CRV	M74	M74		3	Passing on hill or curve
PASS SCH BUS	M75	M75		8	Passing school bus displaying warning not to pass
PASS WH PROH	M76	M76		3	Passing where prohibited
PAS NSF DIST	M77	M77		3	Passing with insufficient distance or visibility
IN/CAREL/NEG	M80	M80		3	Inattentive or careless or negligent driving
CARELESS DRI	M81	M81		3	Careless driving
INATTENT DRI	M82	M82		3	Inattentive driving
NEGLIGENT DR	M83	M83		3	Negligent driving
RECKLESS DRI	M84	M84		8	Reckless driving
TEXT MSG VIO	M85	M85		0	Text message violation (was formerly State Code 12C)
TEXT WH DRIV	M85	M85		0	Texting while driving
HHMT WH DRIV	M86	M86		0	Using a hand held mobile telephone while driving
FT YLD R O W	N01	N01		3	Failure to yield right of way
FY 2 AN/RIDR	N02	N02		3	Fail to yield right of way to animal rider or animal-drawn vehicle
FY 2 CYCLIST	N03	N03		3	Fail to yield right of way to cyclist
FY 2 EMR VEH	N04	N04		3	Fail to yield right of way to emergency vehicle
FY 2 FUNERAL	N05	N05		3	Fail to yield right of way to funeral procession, procession or parade
FY 2 OTH VEH	N06	N06		3	Fail to yield right of way to other vehicle
FY 2 OVT VEH	N07	N07		3	Fail to yield right of way to overtaking vehicle
FY 2 PEDESTR	N08	N08		3	Fail to yield right of way to pedestrian
FY 2 SCH BUS	N09	N09		3	Fail to yield right of way to school bus
FTY ROW@XWALK	N20	N20		3	Fail to yield right of way at crosswalk
FTY ROW@ROTR	N21	N21		3	Fail to yield right of way at rotary
FTY ROW@STOP	N22	N22		3	Fail to yield right of way at stop sign
FTY ROW@T SN	N23	N23		3	Fail to yield right of way at traffic sign
FTY ROW@T SG	N24	N24		3	Fail to yield right of way at traffic signal
FTY ROW@UNSN	N25	N25		3	Fail to yield right of way at unsigned intersection
FTY ROW@YLDS	N26	N26		3	Fail to yield right of way at yield sign
FTY ROWWWWARN	N30	N30		3	Fail to yield right of way when warning displayed on other vehicle
FTY ROWWTURN	N31	N31		3	Fail to yield right of way when turning
IMPROPER SIG	N40	N40		3	Failure to use, or improper, equipment
FT CANC SGNL	N41	N41		3	Failure to cancel directional signals
FTS: PASSING	N42	N42		3	Failure to signal intention to pass
FTS CHNG/TRN	N43	N43		3	Failure to signal lane change or turn
WRONG SIGNAL	N44	N44		3	Giving wrong signal

Description	Code	ACD	Flag	Pt	Full Text
IMPROPR TURN	N50	N50		3	Improper turn
IMP TRN METH	N51	N51		3	Improper method of turning
IMP TRN PSTN	N52	N52		3	Improper position for turning
IMP LEFT TRN	N53	N53		3	Making improper left turn
IMP RGHT TRN	N54	N54		3	Making improper right turn
IM TRN ROUND	N55	N55		3	Making improper turn around (not U turn)
IMPROP U TRN	N56	N56		3	Making improper U turn
DR WRONG WAY	N60	N60		3	Driving wrong way
WW AT ROTARY	N61	N61		3	Driving wrong way at rotary intersection
WW ON DIV HW	N62	N62		3	Driving wrong way on divided highway
WW ON ONEWAY	N63	N63		3	Driving wrong way on one way street or road
DR WRONG SID	N70	N70		3	Driving on wrong side
WS ON DIV HW	N71	N71		3	Driving on wrong side of divided highway
WS ON UNDIVD	N72	N72		3	Driving on wrong side of undivided street or road
COASTING	N80	N80		3	Coasting (operating with gears disengaged)
IMPROP BACKN	N82	N82		3	Improper backing
IMPROP START	N83	N83		0	Improper starting
UNSAFE OPERA	N84	N84		3	Unsafe operation
NON-RESID ACTION	NR1			0	Non-Resident action
SP XS; 01-05	S01	S01	(F)	3	Speeding Excess in miles per hour - 01-05>Speed limit
SP XS; 06-10	S06	S06	(F)	3	Speeding Excess in miles per hour - 06-10>Speed limit
SP XS: 11-14	S14	S14		4	Speeding 11-14 mph over speed limit
SP XS; 15&GR	S15	S15	(F)	5	Speeding 15 mph or more above speed limit
SP XS; 16-20	S16	S16	(F)	4	16-20> Speed limit (detail optional)
SP XS; 21-25	S21	S21		5	21-25> Speed limit (detail optional)
SP XS; 26-30	S26	S26		5	26-30> Speed limit (detail optional)
SP XS; 31-35	S31	S31		8	31-35> Speed limit (detail optional)
SP XS; 36-40	S36	S36		8	36-40> Speed limit (detail optional)
SP XS; 41&GR	S41	S41		8	41+> Speed limit (detail optional)
SCHOOL ZONE	S50	S50	(F)	3	Speeding in school zone - 20
SP XS; 01-10	S51	S51	(F)	3	Speeding Excess in miles per hour - 01-10>Speed limit
SP XS; 21-30	S71	S71	(F)	5	Speeding Excess in miles per hour - 21-30>Speed limit
SP XS; 31-40	S81	S81	(F)	8	Speeding Excess in miles per hour - 31-40>Speed limit
SP XS; 41&GR	S91	S91		8	Speeding Excess in miles per hour - 41+>Speed limit
SPEED DTAIL	S92	S92	(F)	3	Speeding - Speed limit and actual speed (detail required)
SPEEDING	S93	S93	(F)	3	Speeding
PRIMA FACIE	S94	S94		3	Prima Facie-Speed violation or driving too fast for conditions
RACE CONTEST	S95	S95		8	Speed contest (racing) on road open to traffic
INSUFF SPEED	S96	S96		3	Speed less that minimum
ERRATC SPEED	S97	S97		3	Operating at erratic or suddenly changing speeds
WASTING FUEL	S98	S98		3	Speeding on freeway ("wasting fuel")
ADL INVALID MOVED	SE3			0	Licensee Moved
ADL CANCL DECEASE	SU1			0	Driver's license canceled deceased
VOL SURRENDER CDL	SU2			0	Voluntary surrender of CDL license
LICENSEE MOVED TO	SU3			0	Licensee moved to
VOLUNTARY SURR	SU4			0	Voluntary surrender of drivers license
RETURN TO ARKANSAS	SU5			0	Return to Arkansas
DEPARTMENT REASON	SU9			0	Canceled department reason
EVADING/FLEE	U01	U01		8	Fleeing or evading police or roadblock
RESIST ARRST	U02	U02		8	Resisting arrest
VEH IN FELNY	U03	U03		3	Motor vehicle in connection with a felony
VEH IN MSDEM	U04	U04		0	Using a motor vehicle in connection with a misdemeanor
AID/BET FEL	U05	U05		0	Using a motor vehicle to aid and abet a felon
VEH ASSAULT	U06	U06		3	Vehicular assault
VEH HOMICIDE	U07	U07		0	Vehicular homicide
V MANSLAUGTR	U08	U08		0	Vehicular manslaughter
CMV HOMICIDE	U09	U09		0	Negligent homicide while operation of a commercial motor vehicle
CMV FATALITY	U10	U10		0	Causing a fatality through the negligent operation of a commercial motor vehicle
IL OP EMRG V	U21	U21		0	Illegal operation of emergency vehicle
VEH FETIC 1	U27	U27		0	Vehicular Feticide (1st Degree)
VEH FETIC 2	U28	U28		0	Vehicular Feticide (2nd Degree)
VIO: FAT ACC	U31	U31		3	Violation resulting in fatal accident
FTS HME	W09	W09		0	Failure to surrender HAZMAT endorsement as required by the USA PATRIOT Act
PARNT CONSNT	W13	W13		0	Parental consent withdrawn

Description	Code	ACD	Flag	Pt	Full Text
PHY DISABLE	W14	W14		0	Physical or mental disability
PHYSICN REPT	W15	W15		0	Physicians' or specialists' report recommended
FAILED QUALIFICATIONS	W20			0	Failed qualifications
IMINT HAZAR	W70	W70		0	Physicians' or specialists' report recommended

Arkansas Withdrawal Table with Codes and ACD

Description	Code	ACD	Pt	Full Text
MUST PASS D/EXM TEST	18	W00		Must pass drivers license test
INSUFF FUNDS	22	W00		Insufficient funds
PTS WARNING	23			Points warning
VOL SURRENDER	24			Voluntary surrender
DEPT REASON	25	W00		Department reason
INTERLOCK DEVICE	34	W00		Interlock device
DUI/REF FEE	51	W00		DWI/REF fee
FEE DUI/REF	54	W00		DWI/REF fee
DISQ WARNING	56			Disqualified warning
HANDICAP PRKG	60	W00		Handicap parking
REHAB CERT	67	W00		Rehab certificate
F ATTEND SCH	70	W00		Fail to attend school
FUEL THEFT	72	W00		Fuel theft
REIN FEE CT	73	W00		Reinstatement fee
SUSP PENDING	76	W00		Suspension pending
DS REINSTATEMENT FEE	77	W00		DS reinstatement fee - DWI appealed
WEAPON/SCH	79	W00		Weapon at school
F ATTEND SCH	81	W00		Fail attend school
F ATTEND SCH	82	W00		Fail attend school
COURT FEIN F	88	W00		Court reinstatement fee
DUI FEE	92	W00		DUI fee
ACCIDENT	AC	U30		Accident
FINANCL RESP	D35	D35		Failure to comply with financial responsibility law
FTA NON-MOVE	NM		0	Fail to comply non-moving violation
NON-ACD	W00	W00		Non-ACD violation *****
ACCUM/HABVIO	W01	W01		Accumulation of Habitual Violations
FTS HME	W09	W09		Failure to surrender hazmat as required by Patriot Act
PARNT CONSNT	W13	W13		Parental consent withdrawn
PHYS DISABLE	W14	W14		Physical or mental disability
PHYSICN REPT	W15	W15		Physician's or specialists' report recommended
FAILED QUAL	W20	W20		Unable to pass DL test(s) or meet qualifications
ACCUM2VIOL	W30	W30		Two serious violation within three years (For a "60 day" penalty)
ACCUM3VIOL	W31	W31		Three serious violations within three years (For a "120 day" penalty)
ACCUM2MAJOR	W40	W40		The accumulation of two or more major offenses
ACCUM+ MAJOR	W41	W41		An additional major offense after reinstatement
PR DISQ CMV	W45	W45		Previous Disqualify Commercial Vehicle
ACCUM2 OOSO	W50	W50		The accumulation of tow out-of-service order general violation within ten years (violations not covered by W51)
ACCUM2 OOSOL	W51	W51		The accumulation of two out-of-service order general violation within ten years while transporting 16 or more passengers and or/hazardous materials
ACCUM3 OOSOL	W52	W52		The accumulation of three or more out-of-service order violations within three years
ACC2RR VIO1	W60	W60	3	The accumulation of two RRGC violations within three years
ACC3RR VIO1	W61	W61	3	The accumulation of three or more RRGC violations within three years
IMINT HAZAR	W70	W70		Imminent hazard

About the Point System

Points are assigned for various traffic violations ranging from 0 to 14 points depending on the severity of the violation. Accumulation of 10 through 13 points will result in a computer-generated warning letter. Accumulation of 14 or more points may result in a driving privilege suspension for up to one year.

California

Administration	Important Telephone and Web Contacts
George Valverde, Director Jim Woodward, Chief of Information Services Department of Motor Vehicles, M/S F101 2570 24th St, Sacramento 95818 Fax: 916-657-5907 www.dmv.ca.gov/ CA Code Book www.dmv.ca.gov/pubs/vctop/vc/vc.htm	Mandatory Actions......................................916-657 6525 Automated Service.......................................800-777-0133 Record Information ....916-657-8098 Commercial Requester Accounts ....916-657-5564 Financial Responsibility..............................916-657-6677 Commercial Driver License ....916-657-5771 State Department of Insurance ....213-897-8921 CA Only 800-927-4357 Highway Patrol Headquarters 916-843-3000

Driver's License Format, Issuance and Renewal

License Classes, Restrictions and Endorsements Appear After the Driving Record Content Section

License Format

The driver license or identification card (DL/ID card) number has one letter followed by seven numbers which is computer generated but not in any sequential order.

Document Appearance

Effective October, 2010 the CA DMV began issuance of the current,, more secure driver licenses and identification cards. It will take at least five years for the new documents to replace the older documents. Both are reviewed below.

New Documents

Security Characteristics   There are images that can be seen only with the use of ultraviolet lights. A 2D bar code on the back of the card that replicates and verifies only the information on the front of the card (similar to the current magnetic stripe); and a laser perforation outline of the California Brown Bear, which can be seen from the front of the card when a flashlight is pressed against the back of the card. The cardholder's signature is engraved with raised lettering.

Position of Photo Adult is middle left; minor top left

Minor Age Driver Locator The card is now in a vertical format. The DL number appears in red. "AGE 21 in (year)" is in red bar, or "AGE 18 in (year)" is in blue bar.

CDL Indicator   Commercial Driver License is printed in red letters.

Older Documents

This document began issuance on July 1, 200.

Security Characteristics   DL/ID number, expiration date, and birth date printed in red; a second, smaller picture of the holder; security features only seen under an ultraviolet light; fine line printing to deter scanning and photocopying; image of state flag across bottom; holograms of state seal and the DMV logo across the card; and a bar code and encoded magnetic stripe on back.   **Older versions** many contain the following: DL number printed in green; micro-printing of California DMV; variations of print size on face of card; holograms of state seal and the DMV logo across the card; reflective laminate security with bar code and encoded magnetic stripe on the back.

Position of Photo Adult is bottom left; minor bottom right.

Minor Age Driver Locator Photo location and "AGE 21 in (year)" is in a red bar, or "AGE 18 in (year)" is a in blue bar.

CDL Indicator   Commercial Driver License is printed in red letters.

Issuance

Location of Requirements for Proof of Identity:
www.dmv.ca.gov/dl/dlapp_lnks.htm

Age Requirements

A Minor's Provisional Permit is issued to drivers at least 15 1/2 but under 18. A Minor's Provisional License is issued to drivers at least 16 until age 18. There are a myriad of requirements and restrictions that apply to the provisional permit and license holders. See the California Driver Handbook or visit www.dmv.ca.gov.

Residency

Non-residents must obtain California license with 10 days of establishing residency. Visitors between the ages of 16 and 18 may only drive for 10 days with a home state license or instruction permit. After 10 days, these drivers must obtain a Nonresident Minor's Certificate or a CA license.

Renewal

The renewal license is valid for five birthdays from date of first application. The same DL/ID number is issued each time. Drivers may renew or make a change of address online at www.dmv.ca.gov/online/onlinesvcs.htm. See this site for eligibility information. Military personnel stationed outside of California may extend their licenses by mail (PO Box 942892, Sacramento 94290) or by telephone (916-657-7790). The license is considered valid beyond its normal expiration date while on active military duty in the U.S. Armed Forces.

Elderly-Related Restrictions

There are none, other than at age 70 a driver is not eligible for renewal by mail and the vision is checked once every renewal period or more often is required.

Vehicle Insurance, Title and Registration Facts

Registration & Renewal

Computer generated billing notices are mailed approximately 60 days prior to registration renewal date. The renewal of vehicles and vessels may be processed online at www.dmv.ca.gov/online/onlinesvcs.htm. The last five digits of the VIN or HIN (Hull Identification Number) are required, along with a credit card. If applicable, a change of address

must be first processed through the Change of Address System.
As of July 1, 2012, a used car dealer must first obtain the NMVTIS vehicle history report before offering or displaying the vehicle for sale. If the report indicates the vehicle has been declared a junk or salvage automobile, the law will require the dealer to post the disclosure and provide the purchaser a copy of the report.

Note about OHVs: Off-highway vehicles (OHV) must be operated exclusively off the highway on lands that are open and accessible to the public. The vehicle must display an identification plate issued by DMV. OHV vehicles include trail bikes, dune buggies, all-terrain vehicles, motorcycles, and snowmobiles.

For New Residents
Owners must register vehicles within twenty days of establishing residency or upon accepting employment.

Inspections and Emissions Testing
See www.smogcheck.ca.gov. Currently, smog inspections are required for automobiles and commercial vehicles, **except** diesel powered vehicles manufactured prior to 1998 or with a Gross Vehicle Weight (GVWR) of more than 14,000 lbs, electric, or natural gas-powered vehicles over 14,000 lbs, hybrids, motorcycles, trailers or gasoline-powered vehicles 1975 and older.

Vehicles registered in areas subject to the biennial smog certification program are required to submit evidence of a smog certification every other renewal period. Owners of vehicles six or less model years old will pay an annual abatement fee for the first six registration years instead of being required to provide a biennial smog certification.

Note: Upon initial registration, the *six or less years old* rule does not apply to diesel-powered vehicles manufactured in 1998 or after with a GVWR rating of no more than 14,000 lbs, and specially constructed vehicles 1976 and newer require smog certification. See www.smogcheck.ca.gov.

About Transfers: When a vehicle four years old or less is being transferred, a smog certificate is not required except if the vehicle is diesel powered, in which case a smog transfer fee is collected. When a vehicle is more than four model years old, the seller must provide evidence of a current smog certification except when one of the following occurs:

- The transfer occurs between a spouse, domestic partner, sibling, child, parent, grandparent or grandchild.
- A biennial smog certification was submitted to DMV within 90 days prior to the vehicle transfer date (a vehicle inspection may be required for proof of certification).

Smog certifications are valid for 90 days from the date of issuance.

Passenger Plate Facts
Passenger and pickups are issued and must display two plates with two stickers (mo) (yr) on the back plate. The county of issuance is not designated on the plate. Plates remain with the vehicle when sold except for special interest and personalized plates.

Insurance and Financial Responsibility
Minimum automobile liability insurance requirements are $15,000 for a single injury or death; $30,000 for injury to, or death of, more than one person; $5,000 for property damage caused by one accident. If a driver is under 18 years of age, the parents (or guardians) are responsible and liable for insurance and/or financial responsibility. A surety bond or cash deposit of $35,000 is an acceptable alternative (CVC §16434 and §16435). Proof of insurance or financial responsibility must be shown when requested by law enforcement, when renewing vehicle registration, and when the vehicle is involved in a traffic collision.

Withdrawal Sanctions, and Alcohol and Drug Testing

Alcohol and Chemical Testing
For anyone who drives a commercial or non-commercial vehicle or vessel, aquaplane, water skis or similar devices, the limits for alcoholic consumption are .08 percent for adults and .01 percent for persons under 21. For a commercial driver (CDL) or for those who operate any vessel other than a recreational one, the limit is .04 or more percent. Tests administered if arrested or detained for driving under the influence include blood or breath based, and urine under certain circumstances. One can also be cited for driving under the influence if using any drug that impairs. The law does not distinguish between prescription, over-the-counter, or illegal drugs.

Ignition Interlock Devices (IIDs) Per legislation (AB 91) the DMV implemented a pilot program effective July 1, 2010 through December 31, 2015, that requires individuals convicted for first and repeat driving under the influence (DUI) offenses in Alameda, Los Angeles, Sacramento, and Tulare counties to install a certified ignition interlock device (IID) on all vehicles they own or operate.

Suspensions and Revocations
See the Appendix for a list of the federally mandated disqualifications for offenses occurring in a CMV per MCSIA.

Failure to Appear

The Failure to Appear (FTA) in traffic court (ignoring a traffic ticket) or Failure to Pay (FTP) a fine will appear on the driving record, and may cause the Department to suspend a license. A holder of Provisional License will be suspended for a FTP and FTA.

For Conviction Points - Per Negligent Operator Treatment System

Class C or M
- Four or more points in twelve months
- Six or more points in twenty-four months
- Eight or more points in thirty-six months

Commercial Drivers and Fire-Fighters
- Six or more points in twelve months
- Eight or more points in twenty-four months
- Ten or more points in thirty-six months

Minor (Under 18) Drivers
- Two "At Fault" accidents of traffic convictions within 12 months - 30 day suspension
- Three "At Fault" accidents of traffic convictions within 12 months - 6 month suspension
- Four "At Fault" accidents of traffic convictions within 12 months - Classified as Unsafe Driver- suspension

In order for a commercial driver to be eligible for consideration under the higher point count, the commercial driver must request a hearing and appear. Additionally, the higher point count does not apply to certificate holders, drivers with hazardous materials endorsements or if the citations are attributable to the operation on a non-commercial vehicle.

Effective 2007, the state eliminated the issuance of a restricted commercial driver's license when privilege was suspended or because of serious family-related health problem. The CDL holder may still operate a non-commercial vehicle if issued a restricted Class C or M license.

The Department may suspend and place on probation or revoke the driving privilege of a negligent operator (as defined above). Although a Class A or B driver without a special certificate may be allowed two additional points, a violation received in a commercial vehicle carries one and one-half times the point-count normally assessed. A minor under eighteen may receive a thirty-day restriction for two points in twelve months or be suspended for three points in twelve months.

Conviction of Hit-and-Run or Reckless Driving Resulting in Injury ....License may be revoked.

Breaking Speed Laws (greater than 100 mph) or Reckless Driving

First Conviction ....Up to thirty-day suspension, and up to $1000 fine.

Subsequent Conviction Within Thirty-Six Months.....................Six-month suspension, and up to $1000 fine.

Subsequent Conviction Within Five Years.................................One-year suspension, and up to $1000 fine.

Refusal to Submit to Chemical Test (Blood, Breath, Urine or PAS) (All Ages)

First Offense ....One-year suspension.

Second Offense (within ten years):..Two-year revocation.

Third Offense (within ten years):...Three-year revocation.

Admin Per Se (APS) Actions

.08 BAC or Higher, Over 21, Non-CDL, First Offense ....Four-month suspension.

.01 BAC, Under 21, Non-CDL, First Offense ....One-year suspension.

CDL Driver in Non-CDL Vehicle, First Offense............................Four-month suspension.

CDL Driver in CDL Vehicle, First Offense....................................Four-month suspension.

Second Offense (within seven years), for All Above......................One-year suspension.

Note: An APS Zero Tolerance Law is in affect since 01/01/2009. If driver is on probation for a DUI offense and found operating a motor vehicle at any time with BAC of .0.01% or greater a one-year suspension is imposed. Refusal or failure to complete preliminary alcohol screening or chemical test while on probation will result in two-year revocation.

DUI Actions

Regarding Ignition Interlock Device (IID): If a driver with prior DUI conviction is convicted of driving with a suspended license, the DMV will require installation and use of Ignition Interlock Device. Current statutes authorize restricted driving privileges upon installation of an IID in lieu of a longer driver license suspension term.

Non-Commercial Drivers over 21 with BAC of .08 or higher

First Offense ....Six-month to one-year suspension.

Second Offense (within ten years)..18-month to two-year suspension.

Third Offense (within ten years)..Three-year revocation.

Fourth or Subsequent Offense (within ten years) ....Four-year revocation.

Non-Commercial Drivers over 21 with BAC of .20% or higher

Mandatory ten-month suspension and court ordered treatment program.

Note: As of 01/01/2012, courts can order a **10-year revocation** of any California motorist convicted of a third or subsequent DUI violation, with possible reinstatement after five years if specified conditions are met.

Commercial Driver in CDL Vehicle with BAC of .04% or higher

First Offense ....Three-year commercial disqualification.

Second Offense (within ten years)..Lifetime disqualification.

Third Offense (within ten years)..Three-year revocation.

Fourth or Subsequent Offense (within ten years) ....Four-year revocation.

Under 21 years of Age with BAC of .01 or higher

First Offense ....One-year suspension.

Commercial Drivers, but if offense did not occur in a commercial vehicle:

First Offense ....One-year disqualification.

Second and Subsequent Offense..Lifetime disqualification, but eligible for reinstatement in 10 years.

Habitual Truant-Minor

Persons aged 13 to 18 will lose license one year if convicted for being a habitual truant from school.

Possessing Firearms-Minor

Court will suspend or revoke driving privilege of any minor convicted of possessing a concealable weapon or live ammunition, or impose DL sanctions for minors convicted of misdemeanors involving firearms.

Road Rage

First Offense ....Six-month suspension.

Second or Subsequent Offense ....One-year suspension.

Other Convictions Which May Result in a Suspension or Revocation of Driving Privileges

- Errant in Family Support Payments
- Failure to Comply with Financial Responsibility Law
- Reckless Driving
- Recklessly Fleeing a Police Officer
- Unlawful Use of Driver License
- Vandalism
- Vehicle Theft

Lack of Insurance

Since October 1, 2006, vehicle registrations are subject to suspension when:

- DMV is notified that a policy has been cancelled and a replacement policy has not been submitted within 45 days.
- Insurance information is not submitted to DMV within 30 days of issuance of registration card upon initial registration or transfer of ownership.
- The registration is obtained by providing false evidence of insurance.

Reinstatement Requirements

Suspension...$55 fee; SR1P/SR-22 required in some cases.

Revocations ....$55 fee; SR-22 required in some cases.

If Admin Per Se Suspension or Revocation........ $125 fee ($100 if under 21); SR-22 required.

Excessive BAC... $100 fee; SR-22 in all cases; Drinking Driver Program completion.

Note: There is an additional $120 fee if a departmental review of an Admin Per Se hearing decision is requested.

Record Access: Laws, Rules, and Forms

Note: **This Section Applies to Both Driver and Vehicle Records.**

Governing Statutes and Rules

CA Code Book: www.dmv.ca.gov/pubs/vctop/vc/vc.htm

Below is the list of the laws that pertain to motor vehicle record access and confidentiality. In general, California law does not have/use the same language or wording of the federal statute. However, as one would surmise, the text associated with each of these laws is extensive. The text for these statues can be viewed from the CA Code Book at www.dmv.ca.gov/pubs/vctop/vc/tocd2c1a3.htm.

Following this list are selected portions of several of these laws which are most applicable to this book.

1807.5	Release of Conviction Information
1808	Records Open to Public Inspection
1808.1	Employer Notification
1808.2	Confidential Records: Address of Peace Officer
1808.4	Confidential Records: Address of Peace Officers and Employees
1808.5	Confidential Records: Physical, Mental Condition; Controlled Substance Offenses
1808.6	Confidential Records
1808.7	Confidential Records; Traffic Violator School Attendance
1808.8	Carrier Notification
1808.9	Confidential Records: Continued Eligibility
1808.21	Confidential and Suppressed Records
1808.22	Exemption: Financial Institution, Insurance Company, and Attorney
1808.23	Exemption: Vehicle Manufacturers, Dealers, and Electrical Corporations and Utilities
1808.24	Financial Responsibility: Disclosure
1808.25	Parking Restrictions: Residence Address
1808.45	Unauthorized Disclosure: Misdemeanor
1808.46	Unauthorized Access or Distribution: Civil Penalty
1808.47	Protection of Confidentiality
1808.51	Confidential Records: Department of Real Estate
1809	Traffic Accident Information
1810	Sale of Information: Identification of Requester; Notification of Subject
1810.2	Commercial Requester Accounts; Requester Codes
1810.3	Release of Accident Report Information
1810.5	Access to Records
1810.7	Direct Computer Access; Permit
1811	Sale of Records
1812	Free to Government Agencies
1813	Free Records

—

1808.22 Exemption: Financial Institution, Insurance Company, and Attorney (explained below)

1808.22. (a) Section 1808.21 does not apply to a financial institution licensed by the state or federal government to do business in the State of California, if the financial institution states under penalty of perjury that it has obtained a written waiver of Section 1808.21 signed by the individual whose address is requested, or to providing the address of a person who has entered into an agreement held by that institution prior to July 1, 1990, so long as that agreement remains in effect.

(b) (1) Section 1808.21 does not apply to an insurance company licensed to do business in California, or to an authorized contractor acting on behalf of that insurance company, pursuant to a contractual agreement, if the company or contractor, under penalty of perjury, requests the information for the purpose of obtaining the address of another motorist or vehicle owner involved in an accident with the company's insured.

(2) Section 1808.21 does not apply to an insurance company licensed to do business in California if the company, under penalty of perjury, requests the information on an individual who has signed a written waiver of Section 1808.21 or on the individuals insured under a policy if a named insured of that policy has signed a written waiver.

(c) (1) Notwithstanding any other provisions of the Vehicle Code and regulations adopted by the department, all information obtained from the department pursuant to the exemptions in subdivision (b) shall be subject to the existing use or disclosure limitations and data security requirements for the principal under applicable state and federal law.

(2) Use or disclosure limitations and data security requirements imposed on an authorized contractor by this subdivision shall be enforced by the department in compliance with its existing regulations governing the use or disclosure of information obtained from the department pursuant to subdivision (b).

(3) The use or disclosure of information obtained from the department by an authorized contractor of the insurance company pursuant to paragraph (1) of subdivision (b) shall be permitted only for the purpose of obtaining the address of another motorist or vehicle owner involved in an accident with the company's insured. The information shall not be used or disclosed for any other purpose, other than the reason for which the information was requested, or to any other person.

(4) An insurance company shall be responsible for any misuse of the information by the authorized contractor.

(5) An authorized contractor is subject to all of the following requirements:

(A) All information obtained by the contractor from the department pursuant to paragraph (1) of subdivision (b), and any copies made of that information, shall be destroyed by the contractor pursuant to Section 1798.81 of the Civil Code, once the contractor has used the information for the purpose of obtaining the address of a motorist or vehicle owner involved in an accident with individuals insured with the insurer.

(B) The contractor shall not sell the information obtained from the department or store, combine, or link that information with a database for resale or for any purpose other than obtaining the address of a motorist or vehicle owner involved in an accident with individuals insured with the insurer.

(C) The contractor shall maintain a log to track the receipt, use, and dissemination of the information. The log shall be immediately available to the department upon request and maintained for four years from the date of the request.

(D) The contractor shall maintain a surety bond in the amount of fifty thousand dollars ($50,000), consistent with subdivision (c) of Section 1810.2 and Section 350.24 of Title 13 of the California Code of Regulations.

—

1810.2 Commercial Requester Accounts; Requester Codes

1810.2. (a) The department may establish commercial requester accounts for individuals or organizations and issue requester codes for the purpose of obtaining information from the department's files, except as prohibited by Section 1808.21.

(b) Commercial requester account applications shall include the requester's name, address, type of business, a specific reason for requesting information, and the name of the person responsible for the business or firm.

(c) The department shall establish a commercial requester account when it determines that the applicant has a legitimate business need for the information requested and when the applicant files a bond in the amount of fifty thousand dollars ($50,000) and pays a two hundred fifty dollar ($250) filing fee. If the applicant does not request and is not issued a requester code permitting the applicant access to residence address information, only a filing fee of fifty dollars ($50) shall be required with the original application and each biennial renewal application.

(d) An individual requester code shall be issued for a period not to exceed five years and may be renewed upon application for additional periods not to exceed five years each.

(e) A requester code may be denied to any person unless the proposed use of the information from department records is related to legitimate business or commercial purposes of that person. A requester code may be canceled immediately if the requested information is used for a purpose other than the purpose for which the requester code was issued.

—

1810.7   Direct Computer Access; Permit
1810.7. (a) Except as provided in Sections 1806.5, 1808.2, 1808.4, 1808.5, 1808.6, 1808.7 , and 1808.21, the department may authorize, by special permit, any person to access the department's electronic database, as provided for in this section, for the purpose of obtaining information for commercial use.

(b) The department may limit the number of permits issued under this section, and may restrict, or establish priority for, access to its files as the department deems necessary to avoid disruption of its normal operations, or as the department deems is in the best interest of the public.

(c) The department may establish minimum volume levels, audit and security standards, and technological requirements, or any terms and conditions it deems necessary for the permits.

(d) As a condition of issuing a permit under this section, the department shall require each direct-access permittee to file a performance bond or other financial security acceptable to the department, in an amount the department deems appropriate.

(e) The department shall charge fees for direct-access service permits, and shall charge fees pursuant to Section 1810 for any information copied from the files.

(f) The department shall ensure that information provided under this section includes only the public portions of records.

(g) On and after January 1, 1992, the director shall report every three years to the Legislature on the implementation of this section. The report shall include the number and location of direct-access permittees, the volume and nature of direct-access inquiries, procedures the department has taken to ensure the security of its files, and the costs and revenues associated with the project.

(h) The department shall establish procedures to ensure confidentiality of any records of residence addresses and mailing addresses as required by Sections 1808.21, 1808.22, 1808.45, 1808.46, and 1810.2.

Summary of Policy Regarding Permissible Use
The Department provides records to two types of requesters: (1) "requester account holders" consisting of government entities, law enforcement agencies, and the private sector who have been pre-approved to receive record information fulfilling a specific business need, and (2) "casual requesters" who are not pre-approved and request department record information on a one-time or occasional basis.

Requester account holders are required to complete an agreement with the Department in order to become pre-approved to receive Department information.   The purpose and/or business use for which this information is being requested is required as part of this agreement.

If statutorily authorized to receive address information, a $50,000 surety bond is required. However, even with the bond process servers, self-insureds, dismantlers, and homeowner's associations cannot get addresses as there is no statute which currently authorizes them access. Also, the state may require a $50,000 surety bonds for Service Providers (Vendors or Agents) authorized to sell Department records to pre-approved requesters and "intermediate vendors" or indirect Service Providers (who submit requests received from pre-approved requesters to a pre-approved Service Provider). No notification process is provided in response to a request by a requester account holder as provided for in CVC §1810(b) unless the request is made by an attorney who is requesting the information to represent his client in a criminal or civil action which directly involves the use of the motor vehicle.   The information is immediately released to the attorney and post-notification is provided to the subject.

Request and Consent Forms
The *INF 70 Form* is used to request DL/ID or VR official record information on a one-time basis. *INF 1125* is used by individuals to request their own driving record or their vehicle/vessel information. The forms may be downloaded from the DMV's web page.

Vendor and Third Party Access Policy
Every vendor in the "chain" must be registered. See below for instructions on how to become a registered account.

Records Ordered For Non-permissible Uses
A casual requester must state the purpose and/or use of the information. In general, CVC Sections 1808 through 1810 states that DMV records are open to the public, except for portions of the records that are considered confidential and exempt from disclosure. Confidential information includes, but may not be limited to: certain DMV personnel matters; the physical and mental information in a driver's file; the residence address; Social Security Numbers; photographs; results of investigations in progress; and incomplete findings from research.

Access to Driver-Related Records

Driving Records
General Information and Fees
Department of Motor Vehicles, Information Services Branch, PO Box 944247, Mail Station G199, Sacramento 94244-2470.   Information: 916-657-8098.

Requester Accounts
A Requester Account will distinguish between an End-User and a Service Provider. To establish a Requester Account, applicants must complete an application, pay the appropriate enrollment fee, sign a Requester Account Agreement, and receive approval from the Department. The enrollment fee is based on the type of record information requested ($50 or $250). Applicants who are statutorily authorized and are requesting confidential residence address information as a Service Provider will be required to submit a $50,000 Surety Bond. For more information call 916-657-5564 or write to the following address: Department of Motor Vehicles, Account Processing Unit, Mail Station H221, PO Box 944231, Sacramento, California 94244-2310.

Non-Permissible Use Requesters
See detail description above. Non-permissible use requesters who want general information regarding forms, service fees, type of records available, record search criteria, etc., may telephone the Information Services Branch (ISB), Public Contact Unit, Monday through Friday, between the hours of 8:00am and 5:00pm at 916-657-8098, or write to: Department of Motor Vehicles, Public and Commercial Operations, Mail Station G199, PO Box 944247, Sacramento, California 94244-2470. General information is also available at www.dmv.ca.gov.

Use of Forms
Requests for forms (twenty-five or less) may be submitted in writing to the Department of Motor Vehicles, Public Contact Unit at the address listed above, or by telephone at 916-657-8098. Large requests for forms (over twenty-five) must be submitted in writing to: Department of Motor Vehicles, Forms and Accountable Items Unit, P.O. Box 932382, Sacramento, California 94232-3820 or fax your request on letterhead to 916-657-7243. Forms are provided at no fee to the requester. Visit the Department's website at www.dmv.ca.gov for information request

forms, publications, Vehicle Code and related information. California has an extensive coding system for violations. Driving records are coded with very brief citation descriptions provided. The table to follow provides these codes with extensive descriptions for convictions found on driving records.

Prices of Driver License Record Requests
Personal checks are accepted; credit cards are not accepted.
- Current Official Driver Record (by full name and DOB or name and DL number) is $5.00 for non-electronic means,
- Current Driver Record by electronic means (online access) is $2.00
- Copy of DL/ID application including guarantor's signature is $20.00 for each year
- DL/ID Photo is $20.00 for each year
- Status Response (restricted online) via an approved vendor is $1.00

In-Person – The public counter in Sacramento is closed to driving record requests. Individuals who submit their requests to a DMV Field Office will receive records only if they are subject of the records.

Mail – Requests mailed to the Department of Motor Vehicles are generally processed within ten days.

Electronic FTP Batch – The Department offers batch record requests through the Internet using file transfer protocol (FTP) through a Virtual Private Network (VPN). Contact the Automation Development Unit at 916-657-5582 for additional information.

Electronic Interactive – California offers online interactive service for DL record information. Authorized Requester End-Users can obtain access to DMV records through an authorized Service Provider/Reseller. Service Provider Resellers or End Users who access direct must: meet all DMV's programming, security, and technical requirement (see above section on *Requester Accounts*). The cost is $2.00 per record. For more information call the Electronic Access Administration Unit of the Information Services Branch at 916-657-5582.

Also, the DMV provides an **Occupational License Status Information** check at http://www.dmv.ca.gov/olinq2/welcome.do. This free search reports licensing information for these business categories: ATV School, Dismantler, Distributor, Driving School, Lessor-Retailer, Manufacturer, Mature Driver, Program, Registration Services, Remanufacturer, Traffic Violator School, Transporter, Vehicle Dealer (including Autobroker), and Vessel Agent..

Bulk – California offers bulk delivery of driver record/identification card information on electronic format or paper, written to special parameters (e.g., by county, make, etc.). The release of the information follows the statutory requirements and is not allowed for direct mail advertising purposes or solicitation. A written request explaining the purpose must be submitted to the Department of Motor Vehicles, Policy and Information Privacy Section, PO Box 942890, Mail Station H225, Sacramento 94290-0890. The cost is 10¢ per record plus programming and computer run time costs.

By Person of Record – CA drivers may obtain their driving record by mail or walk-in as described above. Use of Form INF 1125 is suggested (www.dmv.ca.gov/forms/inf/inf1125.pdf). Also, CA drivers may register, request, and print an unofficial driving record online. Visit www.dmv.ca.gov/online/dr/welcome.htm. Each record costs $2.00. The site has security blocks to prevent users from accessing any vehicle or driving record other than their own

Notification/Monitoring Program
The Department offers a Pull Notice Program to provide employers and regulatory agencies with an ongoing method to monitor driver records. The employer enrolls specified drivers in the program and is notified when the record has activity. For more information visit the website at www.dmv.ca.gov/vehindustry/epn/epnformlist.htm or write the DMV care of the Employer Pull Notice Unit - H265 or call 916-657-6346. The program does not allow insurance companies to register their insureds.

Accident Reports
Reporting – Reports must be filed immediately with the local police of the municipality for accidents involving injury, death or damage over $1,000. Accidents outside the municipality should be reported to the county sheriff or the nearest state police patrol. Accident reports completed by law enforcement must be filed in the same way. Commercial drivers must report convictions to employers within ten days of conviction and must report to their home state within thirty days of conviction. No special form is required; a letter with information is sufficient.

Record Access – Law enforcement accident reports may be obtained from the California Highway Patrol and local law enforcement agencies filing the report. Fees vary. If the accident was investigated by the California Highway Patrol, a copy may be obtained from the area office that conducted the investigation—there are 115 area offices. The SR-1 accident reports are provided (photo copy) to limited requesters by the Department of Motor Vehicles, PO Box 942884, Sacramento 94284-0001. The fee is $20.00.

Access to Vehicle and Vessel Related Records

General Information and Fees
Department of Motor Vehicles, Office of Information Services, PO Box 944247, Mail Station G199, Sacramento 94244-2470. Information: 916-657-8098. Requests for forms (twenty-five or less) may be submitted in writing to the Public Contact Unit at the address listed above or by telephone at 916-657-8098.

Liens are filed here. The Department began microfilming all vehicle and vessel documents in 1992, some records dating back to 1976 may be accessed. Records with no activity, such as tickets, renewals, transfers etc., are usually purged from the database after 4 years. Records and/or information specified by statute as confidential or non-reportable will not be provided by the Department.

Forms are provided at no fee to the requester. Requests for over twenty-five forms must be submitted in writing to: Department of Motor Vehicles, Forms and Accountable Items Unit, PO Box 932382, Sacramento, California 94232-3820 or fax your request on letterhead to 916-657-7243. Visit the Department's website at www.dmv.ca.gov for information request forms, publications, Vehicle Code and related helpful information.

Vehicle or Vessel Record Requests - Each Record Below is $5.00
- Current record by license, vehicle identification number, or vessel CF Number

- Current owner
- Current owner and generally the three previous owners
- All vehicles/vessels owned by am individual or business - usually no limited to groups of 8

A photocopy of hardcopy or microfilm documents is $20.00 per year, the last three years are available

Note electronic access for ongoing requesters is $2.00 (see below).

In-Person – Individuals may submit their requests to a DMV Field Offices for these purposes: (1) the subject of the record; (2) subject of record's spouse/minor child, provided address of subject and requester are same as on file at DMV; (3) lien sale; and (4) vehicle dealers. Requests for any other reason must be forwarded to the Casual Request Unit in Headquarters for processing

Mail – Requests mailed to the Department of Motor Vehicles are generally processed within ten days.

Electronic FTP Batch – The Department offers batch record requests through the Internet using file transfer protocol (FTP) through a Virtual Private Network (VPN). Contact the Automation Development Unit at 916-657-5582 for additional information.

Electronic Interactive – California offer online interactive service for DL record information. Authorized Requesters (End Users) can obtain access to DMV records through an authorized Service Provider/Reseller. Service Provider Resellers or End Users who access direct must. See the Requester Accounts in the Driving Records Section for the details on how account requirements and set-up fees. The cost is $2.00 per record. For more information call the Electronic Access Administration Unit of the Information Services Branch at 916-657-5582.

Bulk – California offers bulk delivery of registration information written, to special parameters (e.g., by county, make, etc.). The release of the information follows statutory requirements and is not allowed for direct mail advertising purposes or solicitation. A written request explaining the purpose must be submitted to the Department of Motor Vehicles, Policy & Information Privacy Section, PO Box 942890, Mail Station H225, Sacramento 94290-0809. The cost is 10¢ per record plus programming and computer run time fees.

More About Vessel Records

General Information, Access and Fees
Vessel records may also be obtained from the Department of Motor Vehicles as described above. Name searches are permitted, but you must use the state form.

This is a title and registration state. All motorized and sail, and watercraft over 8 ft (except rowboats) must be registered. This includes boats used or moored on private lakes. Vessels previously registered in other states must be registered in California within 120 days of being brought into the state, if it will be used upon California waterways the majority of the time. Liens are filed here. The state will not release bulk information for commercial purposes.

Commercial vessels of five net tons or more, or 30 feet or more in length must be registered (documented) by the U.S. Coast Guard. Visit www.dmv.ca.gov/boatsinfo/boat.htm for more information.

Driving Record Content and Reciprocity

What's On or Not On the Driving Record

- Records and/or information specified by statute as confidential or non-reportable will not be provided by the Department.
- Most non-moving violations are not reported.
- All accidents are reported, regardless if at fault

Data Retention and Reporting Periods
CDL driver records are purged per federal regulations, see the Appendix for this timetable.

Most convictions of traffic offenses, such as hit and run, and reckless driving will remain on the record for 7 years from the violation date. As of 01/01/07, a DUI remains on the record for 10 years and this rule is retroactive. Most other convictions of traffic offenses will remain on the record for 3 years from the violation date. Accidents are reported for 3 years from the accident date. Actions taken against driving privilege, such as a suspension or revocation due to a DUI or a failure to provide proof of financial responsibility, will be reported for 3 years from the proof termination date or the reinstatement date, whichever is earlier. A Failure To Appear for DUI offenses will be reported for 10 years from the violation date. All other Failure to Appear and Failure to Pay Fine citations will be reported for 5 years from the violation date.

Court to Repository
The California courts use tape, online, and paper to transfer conviction information to the Department of Motor Vehicles. CVC Section 1803 requires that courts report conviction information to the state within ten days of conviction. Usually convictions are entered within 5 days and convictions from out-of-state courts are entered on the record within 7 days.

State Reciprocity for Non-CDL Drivers
- Will not suspend license of driver for unpaid out-of-state convictions, but will not issue any licensing documents.
- Record of new incoming driver is shown on MVR.
- Out-of-state convictions are shown on MVR.
- Out-of-state accidents are shown on MVR.
- Convictions of out-of-state drivers are sent to home state.
- Record is forwarded to new state upon surrender of license.

Codes for License Classes, Restrictions, Endorsements, Certificates, Extensions, Statutes, and Courts

License Classes– Commercial and Non-Commercial *There are 10 classes of driver licenses.*

Class A	Allows any combination of vehicles, including Class B or a transit bus with a passenger transport endorsement and all vehicles listed under Class B and C. May tow any single vehicle with a GVWR of more than 10,000 lbs, more than one vehicle with endorsement, or a trailer bus with a passenger endorsement.
Class A Firefighter	Operate Class A and B defined combination fire fighting vehicles and all vehicles listed under Class C. May tow a single fire fighting vehicle with GVWR of more than 10,000 lbs.
Class A Noncommercial	Operate all vehicles listed under Class C. May tow a trailer coaches exceeding 10,000 pounds GVWR or any fifth-wheel travel trailer exceeding 15,000 pounds GVWR when not used in commerce or to transport passengers. With a vehicle weighing 4,000 lbs or more unladen, may tow a livestock trailer exceeding 10,000 lbs GVWR but not exceeding 15,000 GVWR if the vehicle is controlled and operated by a farmer, used to transport livestock to or from a farm, not used in commerce or contract carrier operations, and is used within 150 miles of the person's farm.
Class B	Operate any single vehicle in excess of 26,000 GVWR, a three-axle vehicle over 6,000 lbs gross, any bus (except a trailer bus) with endorsement, any farm labor vehicle with endorsement, and all vehicles listed under Class C. May tow a single vehicle with GVWR of 10,000 lbs or less.
Class B Firefighter	Operate only Class B defined single fire fighting vehicles and all vehicles listed under Class C. May tow a single vehicle with GVWR of 10,000 lbs or less or any vehicle under class.
Class B Noncommercial	Operate a house car that is over 40 feet, but not over 45 feet on specified highway with endorsement. May tow any vehicle listed under Class C.
Class C Commercial	Operate any Class C vehicle carrying hazardous materials or wastes which require placards. HAZMAT (hazardous materials) endorsement must be on license. Otherwise, may drive and tow the same vehicles listed in Class C.

Class C	Operate any two-axle vehicle with GVWR of 26,000 lbs or less; a motorized scooter, any three-axle vehicle weighing 6,000 lbs or less gross; any house car 40 feet or less; a vanpool vehicle designed to carry more than 10 but not more than 15 persons including the driver. (See website for more information.) May tow a single vehicle with a GVWR of 10,000 lbs or less including a tow dolly, if used; a boat trailer under 26,000 lbs for recreational purposes or repair. With a vehicle weighing at least 4,000 pounds GVWR may tow (when not for compensation) any trailer coach not exceeding 9,000 lbs fully loaded or a fifth-wheel trailer over 10,000 lbs GVWR, but under 15,000 lbs GVWR with endorsement. May operate Class M1, M2 or both with endorsement.
Class M1	May drive a two-wheel motorcycle or motor-driven cycle or motorized scooter.
Class M2	May drive any motorized bicycle, moped or any bicycle with an attached motor or motorized scooter.

Note: With Class A, B, or C license may drive an ambulance used commercially in emergency service with an Ambulance Driver Certificate.

About Commercial Vehicles

A **"commercial vehicle"** is defined as a motor vehicle or combination of vehicles used in commerce to transport passengers or property when any of the following conditions apply to the vehicle:

- A single vehicle with a GVWR of 26,001 pounds or more.
- A trailer with a GVWR of 10,001 pounds or more.
- Towing a set of double-trailers—regardless of weight.
- Towing a trailer-bus.
- Any vehicle which transports hazardous materials requiring placarding.
- A bus designed, used or maintained to transport more than ten passengers—including driver (except van-pools and vans designed to carry not more than fifteen persons while carrying only family members).

Note: The Commercial Vehicle Registration Act of 2001 (CVRA) requires most commercial vehicle registered owner(s)/lessee(s) to declare the operating weight of their commercial motor vehicle, or combination, and the heaviest load upon registration or renew whenever the operating weight changes.

About Implements of Husbandry

A driver license is not required when operating implements of husbandry incidentally operated or moved over a highway. A license of the appropriate class is required when operating other types of farm vehicles.

Restrictions

" * " = Signifies the Restriction is no longer used for Commercial Drivers, but can be valid for others.

01 Corrective Lenses Required
02 No Freeway Driving
03 Restricted to Driving to/from/during Course of Employment and Driving to and from DUI Treatment Program
04* Suspended Except During Course of Employment (Vehicles must be owned or leased in the name of the employer.)
06 Additional Right Rear View Mirror Required
07 Limited to Driving From Sunrise to Sunset Only
08 Restricted to Driving to/from/during Course of Employment and Driving to/from DUI Activities
09 Adequate Signaling Device Required
10 Class C - Automatic Transmission Required
11 Adjustable Seat or Support Required
13 Area Restriction
16 Hand Controlled Brakes
17 Steering Wheel Knob Required
18* Course of Employment Only
19 Must Wear Leg Prosthesis When Driving
22 Hand Controls Required
25 Restricted to Operating Buses per 15250(g) (Use for Firefighters Only)
27 Class B - May Operate Bus Subject to Restrictions on Special Certificate
29 May Not Transport Student Passengers Without a Valid School Bus Certificate
31* Restricted to Driving During Course of Primary Employment Per 16030.
32 Must Wear Hearing Aid While Driving CMV
34 Must Wear Corrective Lenses While Driving an Ambulance
35* Driving to And From Employment
36* Driving to, From, and During Employment
37* Driving to and From School
38 May not Drive on Saturday, Sunday or a Holiday
41 May Tow Fifth Wheel Recreational Trailer Between 10,001 and 15,000 GVWR
43 Restricted to Class M2 Motorcycle

44 Must Wear Bi-Optic Telescopic Lenses From Sunrise to Sunset
45 CL A or B-May Not Transport Passengers or Material Required Placards/Marking Per CVC 27903
46 Must Wear Corrective Lenses When Driving Commercially
47 First 6 months of License Issue May Not Transport Passengers Under Age 20 and First 12 Months May Not Drive Between 12 am and 5 am
48 Limited to Vehicles Without Air Brakes When Driving Commercially (Also used for house cars over 40' long)
50 Must Carry Special Restriction Card and Comply With Conditions
51* Restricted To Driving To/From Medical Treatment Per CVC 16077
52* Driving to And From and During Course of Primary Employment, Section 16072 CVC
53 Class A Operation Restricted to Tow Trucks Towing Disabled Vehicles
54* Court Restriction-Drive to and From Employment
55* Court Restriction-Drive During Course of Employment
56* Court Restriction-Drive to and From Treatment Program
57* Driver License Restricted By Court
58 Must Be Accompanied By Parent, Guardian or Spouse or Other Licensed Driver Over 25 Unless Class M Vehicle Without Passenger
59 Provisional License
62 May Tow Livestock Trailer Weighing 10,000 to 15,000 Pounds, Limited to Within 150 Miles of Farms
63 CL C Vehicles Only to And From And in the Course of Employment And to And From a Treatment Program
64 Automatic Transmission Drive-Class A or B
66 CL A/1 Towing Units Without Air Brakes
67 CDL-Driving Within California Only, May Not Be Used With HazMat
68 Disqualified From CDL Driving
69 Disqualified For Life-CDL
71 CL A Towing 1 Non-CDL Trailer-No CL B

72	CL A Towing 1 Non-CDL Trailer-CL B Ok	87	CL A-Firefighting Equipment or Towing 1 Non-CDL Trailer-CL Ok
73	CL A Towing 1 Non-CDL Trailer-CL C Ok - No CL B		
74	CL B- Limit Under 15 Passengers or up to Limit of Cert. in Possession	88	CL A-Restricted Combination Vehicles with GCWR of Less Than 26,001 lbs and GVWR of Vehicle(s) being Towed in Excess of 10,000 lbs Equipment Only. May Drive CDL Chassis
75	PV End.-15 Passengers or up to Limit of Cert. in Possession		
76	CL B & PV Endorsement-Buses Less Than 26,001 lbs. GVWR	90*	Vehicles Equipped With Ignition Interlock
77*	Restrict Driving to/From/During Course of Employment	91*	Immediate Family Member to/From Medical Treatment. 16077 CVC
78*	Restrict Driving to/From Treatment Program	92*	Minor Dependant to/From Primary or Secondary School. 16072 CVC
79	CL B-3-Axle Vehicles Less Than 26,001 lbs. GVWR		
80	CL B-Firefighting Equipment Only	93	Transit Bus Only
81	CL A/B-Firefighting Equipment Only	94*	Ignition Interlock Required CVC 23246B
82	CL B-Firefighting Equipment Only-CDL C Ok	96*	Court Ordered Ignition Interlock Device
83	CL A-Firefighting Equipment Only-CDL C Ok	97	Suspended From Driving a Vehicle With Hazardous Material
84	CL A-Firefighting Equipment Only-CDL B Ok	98	Suspended From Driving a Tank Vehicle CVC 22406.5
85	CL A-Firefighting Equipment or Towing 1 Non-CDL Trailer	99*	Restricted to Operating Vehicles Equipped With an Ignition Interlock Device
86	CL A-Firefighting Equipment or Towing 1 Non-CDL Trailer-CL B Ok		

Endorsements

T	Double Trailer Combination	N	Tank Vehicles
H	Hazardous Materials	P	Passenger Transport Vehicles
S	School Bus	X	Tank Vehicles Transporting Hazardous Materials

Certificates

Note: The *certificates* listed below are issued as a separate documents that a driver must have to operate a specified vehicle.

AMB	Ambulance Driver	TTD	Tow Truck Driver
F/L	Farm Labor	VDDP	Vehicle for Developmentally Disabled Persons Youth Bus Certificate
GPPV	General Public Para-transit Vehicle		
HAM	Hazardous Agricultural Materials	VTT	Verification of Transit Training Document
SCH	School Bus	YOB	Youth Bus
SPAB	School Pupils Activities Bus		

Extension Codes

RBM	Renewal By Mail Update	O/S	Out-of-State
RBMS	Renewal By Mail, Statement Mailed	MIL	Military
RBM1	1st Renewal By Mail	OSR	Out-of-State Renewal
RBM2	2nd Renewal By Mail	OSP	Out-of-State Renewal or Duplicate Application in Process

Editor's Note: There are certain "codes" that appear on driving record associated with accidents. However the CA DMV reports it is unlawful for the Agency to inform a record user the meaning of these codes or to release a master list of these codes with meanings. Therefore these codes are not included herein.

About California Court Codes

A driving record often will give the geographic court code number associated with the location of a violation. These five-digit numeric court codes are assigned in a systematic manner. They identify the county and the specific court location as follows:

- The first two digits denote the counties in alphabetical order. For example 01 is Alameda, 02 is Alpine, and 58 is Yuba.
- The third digit identifies the type of court. Usually 1, 4 or 6 denote a Superior Court, 2 denotes a Juvenile Court, and an 8 or 9 denote a US District Court.
- The last two digits specify a specific court. This is usually but not always divisible by 5. There can be cross-references as well.

Below is a sample list for Oakland County

01100	Superior in Oakland	01430	Superior Court in Fremont
01120	Juvenile Court in Hayward	01435	Superior Court in Pleasanton
01200	Juvenile Court in Oakland	01440	Superior Court in Oakland
01410	Superior Court in Alameda	01450	Superior Court in Hayward
01420	Superior Court in Berkeley	01800	U.S. District Court in Oakland

A complete list appears in *The California Courts Directory and Fee Schedule*, published annually by the California Court Association. See www.calcourt.org.

Statute Codes

Code	Abbrev.	Detail	Code	Abbrev.	Detail
A	VC	Vehicle Code	M	AGR	Agricultural Code
B	PC	Penal Code	N	F&G	Fish & Game
C	H&S	Health & Safety Code	O	M&V	Military & Veterans Code
D	W&I	Welfare & Safety Code	P	PR	Public Resources Code
E	M&I	Municipal & Traffic Code	Q	NA	Term of DUI treatment program
F	CO	County Ordinance	R	PU	Public Utilities Code
G	B&P	Business & Professional Code	S	OTH	Other
H	S&H	Streets & Highways	T	CAC	California Administrative Code
I	NA	Update Date (system generated)	U	NA	Term of Ignition Interlock Restriction
J	US	United States Code	V	NA	Court Verbal Service Data (5-88)
K	SFA	San Francisco Airport Code	X	NA	FTA/FTP Fine Amount
L	ED	Education Code	Y	H&N	Harbors & Navigation

California Violation Point Count Summary

To Summarize Most moving violation driving offenses, such as hit and run or reckless driving are designated as 2 points and will remain on the record for 7 years from the violation date. If DUI-related then 10 years. Most other offenses are designated as 1 point and remain on the record for 3 years from the violation date. An "at fault" accident is normally counted as 1 point.

The **California Motor Vehicle Code Section 12810** including parts **.2** thru **.5** determines the violation point count. Below is a reprint of these laws.

12810. In determining the violation point count, the following shall apply:

(a)   A conviction of failure to stop in the event of an accident in violation of Section 20001 or 20002 shall be given a value of two points.

(b)   A conviction of a violation of Section 23152 or 23153 shall be given a value of two points.

(c)   A conviction of reckless driving shall be given a value of two points.

(d)   (1) A conviction of a violation of subdivision (b) of Section 191.5 or (c) of Section 192 of the Penal Code, or of Section 2800.2 or 2800.3, subdivision (b) of Section 21651, subdivision (b) of Section 22348, subdivision (a) or (c) of Section 23109, Section 23109.1, or Section 31602 of this code, shall be given a value of two points.

(2) A conviction of a violation of subdivision (a) or (b) of Section 23140 shall be given a value of two points.

(e)   A conviction of a violation of Section 14601, 14601.1, 14601.2, 14601.3, or 14601.5 shall be given a value of two points.

(f)   Except as provided in subdivision (i), any other traffic conviction involving the safe operation of a motor vehicle upon the highway shall be given a value of one point.

(g)   A traffic accident in which the operator is deemed by the department to be responsible shall be given a value of one point.

(h)   A conviction of a violation of Section 27360 or 27360.5 shall be given a value of one point.

(i)   (1) A violation of paragraph (1), (2), (3), or (5) of subdivision (b) of Section 40001 shall not result in a violation point count being given to the driver if the driver is not the owner of the vehicle.

(2) A conviction of a violation of paragraph (1) or (2) of subdivision (b) of Section 12814.6, subdivision (a) of Section 21116, Section 21207.5, 21708, 21710, 21716, 23120, 24800, or 26707 shall not be given a violation point count.

(3) A violation of subdivision (d) of Section 21712 shall not result in a violation point count.

(4) A violation of Section 23136 shall not result in a violation point count.

(5) A violation of Section 38301, 38301.3, 38301.5, 38304.1, or 38504.1 shall not result in a violation point count.

(j)   A conviction for only one violation arising from one occasion of arrest or citation shall be counted in determining the violation point count for the purposes of this section.

12810.2.   Notwithstanding subdivision(e) of Section 12810, no violation point count shall be given for a conviction of a violation of Section 27315.

12810.3.   Notwithstanding subdivision (f) of Section 12810, a violation point shall not be given for a conviction of a violation of subdivision (a) of Section 23123, subdivision (a) of Section 23123.5, or subdivision (b) of Section 23124

12810.4.   Notwithstanding any other provision of law, no violation point shall be given for a conviction of a violation of Section 22526.

12810.5

(a)   Except as otherwise provided in subdivision (b), any person whose driving record shows a violation point count of four or more points in 12 months, six or more points in 24 months, or eight or more points in 36 months shall be prima facie presumed to be a negligent operator of a motor vehicle. In applying this subdivision to a driver, if the person requests and appears at a hearing conducted by the department, the department shall give due consideration to the amount of use or mileage traveled in the operation of a motor vehicle.

(b)   (1) Any class A or class B licensed driver, except persons holding certificates pursuant to Section 2512, 12517, 12519, 12523, 12523.5, or 12727, or an endorsement issued pursuant to paragraph (2) or (5) of subdivision (a) of Section 15278, who is presumed to be a negligent operator pursuant to subdivision (a), and who requests and appears at a hearing and is found to have a driving record violation point count of six or more points in 12 months, eight or more points in 24 months, or 10 or more points in 36 months is presumed to be a prima facie negligent operator. However, the higher point count does not apply if the department reasonably determines that four or more points in 12 months, six or more points in 24 months, or eight or more points in 36 months are attributable to the driver's operation of a vehicle requiring only a class C license, and not requiring a certificate or endorsement, or a class M license.

(2) For purposes of this subdivision, each point assigned pursuant to Section 12810 shall be valued at one and one-half times the value

(c)   The department may require a negligent operator whose driving privilege is suspended or revoked pursuant to this section to submit proof of financial responsibility, as defined in Section 16430, on or before the date of reinstatement following the suspension or revocation. The proof of financial responsibility shall be maintained with the department for three years following that date of reinstatement.

otherwise required by that section for each violation reasonably determined by the department to be attributable to the driver's operation of a vehicle requiring a class A or class B license, or requiring any certificate or endorsement described in this section.

Conviction Code Table with Statute, Points, and Explanation

The California Vehicle Code consists of a General Provisions section and 18 Divisions. We start with Division 2 since Division 1 is set aside for definitions of words and phrases found within the laws.

Administration, Division 2

Chapter 1 -Department of Motor Vehicles (1500-1825)
Chapter 2 -Department of CA Highway Patrol (2100-2478)
Chapter 2.5 - Licenses issued by Ca Highway patrol (2500-2574)
Chapter 3 - Reciprocity Commission (2600-2651)
Chapter 4 - Administration & Enforcement (2800-2818)
Chapter 5 - CA Traffic Safety Program (2900-2935)
Chapter 6 - New Motor Vehicle Board (3000-3079)

Code	Pts	Description
1808.1(a)		Employers of prospective drivers of hazardous material, ambulances, farm-labor vehicles, youth buses, specified limousines for hire, and para-transit required to obtain report of current driving record and maintain report until receipt of pull-notice system reports.
1808.1(b)		Employers of above-listed drivers to request participation in pull-notice system.
1808.1(c)		Employers of above-listed drivers to obtain pull-notice report at least every six months (over 500 drivers - at least every twelve months); review report and maintain in principal place of business.
1808.1(e)		If drivers are owners/operators/family/volunteers to be enrolled in pull-notice system.
1808.1(f)		Employment of driver after notice of conviction of driving offense.
1808.1(k)		Employers to obtain current driving record only for above-listed casual drivers (excluding those requiring passenger transportation endorsement).
1808.21		Any residence address in any record of the department is confidential and to be disclosed only to government, law enforcement, courts and those who have statutory authority.
1808.22(a)		Provides exemption to 1808.21 for financial institutions licensed by the state or federal government to do business in California.
1808.22(b)		Provides exemption to 1808.21 for insurance companies licensed to do business in California with restrictions for release.
1808.22(c)		Permits attorneys (under penalty of perjury) to obtain residence address information for a motor vehicle-related accident in order to represent a client in a civil or criminal action that is pending or filed or under investigation.
1808.22(b)		Also permits DMV to provide the record of a record subject, if that party has signed a waiver.
1808.22(c)		Requires the DMV to release addresses to an attorney who states under penalty of perjury that the information is necessary to represent a client. Except violations in furtherance of another crime, is subject to the same penalties as that other crime.
1808.23		Provides for release of residential addresses to licensed vehicle manufacturers, dealers, and persons who provide written assurance that information will be used for statistical research/reporting. Violators are also subject to any other penalties provided in the Vehicle Code.
1802.23(d)		Vehicle manufacturers not to release residential addresses for marketing or soliciting.
1808.45		Unauthorized disclosure of information from any DMV record or use of false representation to obtain information.
1808.46		Prescribes penalties for obtaining confidential information utilizing false representations or distribution of that information to unauthorized individuals.
1820(b)		Requires employers of a driver of a limousine for hire to comply with the requirements of current records and pull-notice.
1820(d)		Same as above.
2261		Unauthorized wearing of CHP or similar-type uniform.
2402.5		Sell or offer vehicle or equipment not in conformance with Federal standards.
2402.6(b)(c)		Violation of fuel system or container regulations.
2416(c)		Misuse of authorized emergency vehicle permit.
2417(a)		Suspension or revocation of permit issued for an authorized emergency vehicle
2418.5		Emergency ambulance must be equipped with resuscitator.
2420		Motorcycle dealer, selling after failure to furnish certificate.
2430.5(a)		Employer involved in freeway service patrol operations to obtain and maintain applicants tow truck driver certificate (effective 7/1/92).
2430.5(b)		Employer involved in freeway service patrol operations to obtain and maintain certificates for all tow-truck driver employees (effective 7/1/92).
2430.5(c)		Employer involved in freeway service patrol operations to maintain categorized list of tow-truck driver as specified.
2430.5(d)		Employer involved in freeway service patrol operations to remove tow-truck driver from freeway service patrol operations upon notice of arrest or conviction.
2432(a)		Tow-truck driver involved in freeway service patrol operations providing false information.

Code	Pts	Description
2432(b)		Failure of tow-truck driver involved in freeway service patrol operations to notify employer of arrest or conviction.
2436.3(a)		Employer involved in freeway service patrol operations to obtain carrier ID number for display on each tow truck operating freeway service patrol (effective 7/1/92).
2436.3(b)		Operating a tow truck involved in freeway service patrol operations with a suspended ID number.
2436.3(c)		Removal of ID number from tow truck involved in freeway service patrol operations upon sale/transfer or other disposition.
2462 thru 2478		All deal with records of or illegal transportation of kitchen grease.
2504		Violation of regulations governing ambulances, armored cars is an infraction.
2510(b)		Operating vehicle as ambulance without CHP inspection.
2525.2		Licensed fleet owners shall comply with regulations.
2525.6		Fleet owner, inspection-and-maintenance station placing sticker on vehicle not part of fleet.
2525.10		Stickers, unlawful to place on vehicle which does not comply with equipment requirements.
2545		Licenses issued by CHP license to be surrendered upon suspension or revocation.
2572(b)		Requires a valid license for the transportation of school pupils.
2800	1	Unlawful to willfully fail or refuse to comply with a lawful order, signal, or direction of a peace officer
2800(b)	1	unlawful to willfully fail or refuse to comply with a lawful order, signal, or direction of a peace officer (1)in regards to an out of service order or (2) no placard for HazMat or (3) when driver of a vehicle designed to transport 16 or more passengers, including the driver.
2800(c)	1	It is unlawful to fail or refuse to comply with a lawful out-of-service order issued by the United States Secretary of the Department of Transportation.
2800(d)	1	Failure to obey an out-of-service order including violations of Title 49 of the Code of Federal Regulations issued by any peace officer or commercial vehicle inspector.
2800.1(a)	1	Attempt to evade pursuing peace officer's motor vehicle.
2800.1(b)	1	Attempt to evade pursuing peace officer's bicycle.
2800.2(a)	2	Attempt to evade a pursuing peace officer in a reckless manner.
2800.3	2	Attempt to evade a pursuing peace officer causing injury.
2800.4	1	Evading a Peace Officer while willfully driving in the wrong lane (driving wrong way)
2801	1	Lawful order or direction, failure to obey fireman.
2803(a)	1	Refusal to adjust load or obtain special permit.
2803(b)		Weight certificate or bill of lading, shall submit to officer.
2803(c)	1	Refusal to obtain special permit prior to moving vehicle.
2807(b)		School bus, display CHP inspection certificate.
2807.1(b)		Other motor vehicles transporting pupils, display CHP inspection certificate.
2807.2		Failure to retain record of inspection on file for review by CHP upon request -display of appropriate certificate verifying inspection.
2807.3		Operation of youth bus without inspection
2810.1(b)		Rented commercial vehicle refusal to submit to inspection by traffic officer relative transportation of household goods.
2810.2		Peace officer inspection of vehicle transporting agricultural irrigation supplies that are in plain view to inspect the bills of lading, shipping, or delivery papers, or other evidence to determine whether the driver is in legal possession of the load, if the vehicle is on a rock road or unpaved road that is located in a county that has elected to implement this section and the road is located
2813		Commercial vehicle, stop and submit for sign-posted inspection.
2813.5(b)		Commercial vehicle, unauthorized inspection sticker.
2814		Vehicle must stop and submit to a roadside vehicle inspection checkpoint for smog
2814.1		Vehicle must stop and submit to a vehicle inspection checkpoint when signs and displays are posted
2814.2		Vehicle must stop and submit to a sobriety checkpoint when signs and displays are posted
2815	1	School crossing guard, failure to obey.
2816	1	Unlawful to load or unload children from a youth bus upon a highway where children must cross—unless traffic is controlled by a traffic officer or signal.
2817	1	Disregarding signal or direction of a peace officer escorting a funeral procession.
2818	1	Traversing a flare or cone pattern or electronic beacon established by public safety personnel.

Registration of Vehicles and Certificates of Title, Division 3

Chapter 1 - Original and Renewal Registration; Issuance of Certificates of Title (4000-5506)
Chapter 2 - Transfer of Title or Interest (5600-6105)
Chapter 2.5 - Misc. Title Provisions (6150-6172)
Chapter 3 - Liens or Encumbrances (6300-6303)
Chapter 4 - Permits to Nonresident Owners (6700-8204)
Chapter 5 - Offenses Against Registration Laws and Suspension, Revocation, and Cancellation of Registration (8800-8804)
Chapter 6 - Registration and Weight Fees (9101-9808)

Codes	Pts	Description
4000(a)		Vehicle on highway or off-street parking facility unregistered or with additional fees due.

Codes	Pts	Description
4000(b)		Vehicle on highway registered in violation of air pollution control regulations; exceptions.
4000.38		The department shall suspend, cancel, or revoke the registration of a vehicle when it determines that certain circumstances involving financial responsibility insufficiency have occurred.
4000.4(a)		Unregistered California-based vehicle.
4000.5		Pertaining to registration of Autoettes.
4000.6(d)		A person shall not operate a commercial motor vehicle, either singly or in combination, in excess of its registered declared gross or combined gross vehicle weight.
4001		Failure to register exempt vehicles and display license plate bearing distinguishing marks indicating exemption.
4004(a)		Foreign commercial vehicle - temporary operation permitted for temporary registration (90 days) or trip permit (4 days)
4152.5		Upon expiration of home-state license plates of a foreign vehicle, owner must make application for California registration within twenty days.
4159		Change of address, notify DMV within ten days.
4160		Change of address, owner to change on registration slip.
4161(a)		Motor change, notify DMV within ten days.
4301		Evidence of foreign registration, applicant to surrender.
4453		Contents on the registration card, including address, identification of rebuilt vehicle.
4453.6		Failure of leaser of vehicle to furnish name and address of lessee upon demand of peace officer.
4454(a)		Registration card, carry in vehicle.
4455		Foreign commercial vehicle, display of temporary permit.
4456		Use and display of report of sale forms
4457		Plates, tabs, certificates; obtain new when lost, mutilated, or illegible.
4458		Plates, both lost or stolen, notify police and apply for duplicates.
4459		Certificate of ownership, owner obtain duplicate when lost or mutilated.
4460		Peace officer may take possession of any certificate, card, placard, permit, license, or license plate issued under this code, upon expiration, revocation, cancellation, or suspension thereof or which is fictitious or which has been unlawfully or erroneously issued.
4461(a)		Evidences of registration, lending or allowing improper use.
4461(b)		Disabled person placard, lending or allowing improper use.
4461(c)		Disabled person placard, improper use or display of cancelled or revoked placard.
4461(d)		Vehicle displaying disabled plates shall not be parked in disabled stall unless transporting disabled person.
4462(a)		Evidences of registration, present to officer for examination.
4462(b)		Evidences of registration, presenting for wrong vehicle.
4462(c)		Unlawful possession of registration, ID, temporary receipt, certification of ownership, license plate or validation tab.
4462.5		Presenting or displaying false evidences of registration with the intent to avoid registration fees.
4463(a)		False evidences (forges, alters, counterfeits, falsifies) of registration (California or foreign) with intent to defraud.
4463(b)		Forges or counterfeits disabled person placard.
4463(c)		Displays a forged or counterfeit disabled person placard.
4463(d)		Disabled person, lending placard.
4463(e)		Displays a forged or counterfeit Clean Air Sticker.
4463.5(a)		Facsimile license plates, unlawful manufacture or sale.
4464		A person shall **not** display upon a vehicle a license plate **that is** altered from its original markings.
4601		Expiration and renewal of vehicle registration
4760		Refuse to register or renew vehicle for unpaid parking tickets.
4766		Refuse to register for failure to appear.
4770		Refuse to register or renew vehicle for unpaid toll fees - evasion.
5007.3(d)		Disabled person or veteran shall, upon request, present to a peace officer or authorized person a certification form that substantiates the eligibility of the disabled person or veteran to possess the plate or plates.
5011		Special construction, mobile, cemetery equipment, tow-dolly, and logging vehicle shall display I.D. plate.
5011.5		Charter Party Carrier-operated limousine, display special license plate required by Section 5385.6 PUC.
5015.5(d)		Use of display license plate on vehicle.
5017		Identification plate, attach to vehicle for which issued, surrender upon sale or destruction of vehicle.
5018		Transfer ownership of equipment, logging vehicle, or implement of husbandry.
5030		Motorized bicycle required to display special license plate.
5032		Operation of motorized bicycle without applying for a license plate within 5 days.
5035		Motorized bicycle using license plate on another motorized bicycle.
5037(a)		Motorized bicycle sold on or after July 1, 1981, on a highway without assigned plates.
5037(b)		Motorized bicycle sold prior to July 1, 1981, on a highway without assigned plates.
5109		Environmental license plates. Notify DMV upon transfer of plates.
5200		License plates, location, and number.
5201		License plates, securely attached and clearly visible, rear plate 12 to 90 inches high. Allows rear license plate on tow-truck mast. Includes installation of security plate cover.

Codes	Pts	Description
5201.1		License plates must be clearly visible and securely fashioned in correct locations.
5202		License plates or special permits in lieu of plates, operating vehicle without proper display of.
5204(a)		Current tabs, attached to rear license plate, except on truck tractor to front plate.
5205.5		Low emission vehicle identification for HOV lane use tolls
5206		Partial year registration, shall display certificate or insignia.
5302(d)		Display of name, trademark, or
5350.3		Sale of trailer coach without completion of certificate of origin.
5352		Trailer coach, current registration required, on or off highway.
5500(a)		Dismantling of a vehicle, person in possession surrender ownership and registration documents to DMV.
5602(c)		Failure of owner to notify DMV of sale or transfer.
5604		Insurance coverage, dealer to notify purchaser.
5753		Certificate of ownership and/or registration, sign and deliver to transferee.
5900(a)		Transfer of ownership, owner to notify DMV within five days.
5900(b)		Transfer of ownership, owner to notify DMV of mileage.
5900(c)		Transfer of ownership, person in possession of vehicle. Notify DMV of mileage.
5901(a)		Transfer of ownership, dealer notify DMV.
5901(b)		Transfer of ownership, dealer notify DMV of mileage.
5901(c)		Transfer of ownership, person in possession of vehicle notify DMV of mileage.
5902(a)		Transfer of ownership, transferee notify DMV within ten days.
5906.5(a)		Transfer of vehicles, no application required, transferee notify DMV of vehicle mileage.
5906.5(b)		Transfer of vehicle, no application required, person in possession notify DMV of vehicle mileage.
6700.3(a)		Filing with DMV for non-resident commuter indicia.
6700.4		Display of non-resident commuter indicia and identification card carried with vehicle.
6855		(Renumbered - see 34518) Foreign motor carrier.
8008		Reciprocity permit, owner's failure to obtain or carry with vehicle when required.
8057(a)		Apportioned registration, fleet records to be maintained for five years.
8100		Apportioned registration: application requirements.
8101		Grounds for refusal of application.
8102		Suspend the apportioned registration of a vehicle or a fleet.
8103		Suspension based on prohibited interstate operation.
8104		Suspended registration: vehicle or fleet operation by another person.
8800(a)		Suspend, cancel, or revoke registration or certificate of ownership, registration card, license plate, or permit under specific circumstances.
8802		Evidence of registration, surrender when canceled, suspended or revoked.
8803		Dealer, salesman, manufacturer, re-manufacturer, transporter or dismantler, surrender licenses when canceled, suspended, or revoked.
8804		Resident registering vehicle in a foreign jurisdiction.
9102.5(b)		Contract school bus, display of permit.
9400		Commercial vehicle weight fees due.
9400.1(f)		Proper display of gross vehicle weight decals.
9406		Alterations increasing weight fee, failure to report.
9553.5		Unpaid apportioned registration fees.
9564(b)		Scrap metal processor submit documents and certificate of title.
9564(c)		Reconstruction of vehicle delivered to scrap metal processor.

Registration and Transfer of Vessels, Division 3.5

3 Chapters – Chapter 2 Sections 9840 through 9928 relate to Vessels/Boats (Some omitted)

Code	Pts	Description
9850		Undocumented vessels shall be numbered prior to operation on waters.
9853.2		Undocumented vessels, display of required numbers.
9853.4(b)		Improper use of sticker, tab or device on vessel.
9853.8		Undocumented vessels: compliance with emissions standards.
9854		Out of state registration; make application within 30 days.
9865		Holder of a certificate of number, notify department within 15 days of change of address.
9866		Improper display of number on vessel.
9872		Defacing, destroying vessel number prohibited.
9901		Transfer of ownership, notify DMV within 10 days.
9910		Transfer of ownership, required delivery and endorsement.
9911		Transfer of ownership, notify DMV within 5 days.
9912		Dealer to notify DMV upon transfer of ownership.

Vehicle Sales, Division 3.6

4 Chapters (9950-9993)

Code	Pts	Description
9952		Unlawful to publish, offer for sale, sell, advertisement, brochure or manual in violation 9950, 9951. Dealer to repair safety defects
9953		If new motor vehicle cannot be operated with tire chains, manufacturer shall so indicate in owner's manual or other written material

Special Anti-Theft Laws, Division 4

7 Chapters (10500-10904)

Code	Pts	Description
10500(a)		Stolen vehicle or plates, police forward report to DOJ immediately.
10501(a)		False report of vehicle theft, with intent to deceive.
10502(b)		Report of embezzled vehicle, owner notify CHP upon recovery.
10551		Stolen undocumented vessel, police notify DMV of theft within 48 hours and immediately upon recovery.
10552		False report of theft of undocumented vessel.
10650(a)		Towing service, shall keep written record of stored vehicles.
10650(b)		Towing service, specific data on written records.
10650(c)		Towing service, records kept one year.
10650(d)		Towing service, statement of disposition upon termination of storage.
10653		Garage or repair shop notify sheriff or police of bullet marks within 24 hours.
10654		Renter of private building used as a private garage, notify sheriff or police of storage within 24 hours.
10655		Stored vehicles, keeper maintain records, make required reports.
10750(a)		Vehicle identifying numbers; altering, defacing or replacing.
10751(a)		Vehicle and component identifying numbers; knowingly buy, sell, or possess vehicle with such numbers removed, altered, defaced.
10752(a)(b)		Fraudulent acquisition or disposition of DMV- or CHP-issued vehicle identification number.
10801		No person shall own or operate a chop shop.
10802		Vehicle identification numbers: alteration, obliteration, defacement, or forgery - for the purpose of sale, transfer, import, or export.
10803(a)		Vehicles and components: buy to resell knowing vehicle identification numbers have been defaced, counterfeited, or obliterated.
10803(b)		Possession of vehicles or components with intent to sell or transfer knowing vehicle identification numbers have been defaced, counterfeited, or obliterated.
10851(a)		Auto theft, permanently or temporarily deprive owner of possession.
10851(b)(1)		Requires that two (2) previous misdemeanor/vehicle theft violations are punishable by imprisonment in the State Prison.
10851(b)(2)		Requires that one (1) or more previous felony/vehicle theft violations is punishable as set forth in Section 66.5 of the Penal Code.
10851(c)		Prescribes punishment for theft of ambulance, law enforcement, or fire vehicle on an emergency call or vehicle displaying disabled plate or placard modified for use by a disabled person.
10851.5		Binder chains, theft from load of metal products.
10852		Injuring or tampering, with vehicle or contents.
10853		Unattended vehicle, tampering with mechanism or setting in motion.
10854		Stored vehicle, unlawful use by keeper.

Occupational Licensing and Business Regulation, Division 5

11 Chapters that deal with: driver training school operators (licenses and registrations), auto dismantlers, salvage vehicles, lessors-retailers, dealers, advertisers (no "bait-and-switching"), manufacturers, distributors, re-manufacturers, salesmen, sale of house cars, sale of auto parts, private party vehicle markers, towing, sales of vehicles by private owners, and the Consumer Recovery Fund. (11100-12217)

Driver's Licenses, Division 6

Chapter 1 - Issuance of Licenses, Expiration, and Renewal (12500-13008)
Chapter 2 - Suspension or Revocation of Licenses (13100-13559)
Chapter 3 - Investigation and Hearing (13800-14401)
Chapter 4 - Violation of License Provisions (14600-14611)
Chapter 5 - License Fees (14900-14911)
Chapter 6 - Driver License Compact (15000-15028)
Chapter 7 - Commercial Motor Vehicle Safety Program (15200-15325)

Codes	Pts	Description
12500(a)		Driver, unlicensed.
12500(b)		Requires the driver of a motorcycle to be licensed.
12500(c)		Prohibits operation of vehicles if not properly licensed.

Codes	Pts	Description
12500(d)		A person may not drive a motor vehicle or combination of vehicles that is not of a type for which the person is licensed.
12500(e)		A motorized scooter operated on public streets shall at all times be equipped with an engine that complies with the applicable State Air Resources Board emission requirements.
12502(b)		Nonresident driver, medical certificate required when driving commercial vehicle.
12502(c)		Nonresident driver, shall comply with any restriction of the medical certificate issued to that nonresident.
12509		Issuance and use of instruction permits.
12509(c)		Instruction permit cannot he held for more than 24 months.
12509(d)		Person with instruction permit shall not drive motor vehicle unless a under the immediate supervision of a valid California licensed driver, who must occupy a position within the driver's compartment.
12509(e)		When taking driver training instruction administered by the California National Guard , a person with instruction permit may only operate a government-owned motor vehicle, other than a motorcycle, motorized scooter, or a motorized bicycle.
12509.5(a)		Person with instruction permit shall not drive a motorcycle unless successfully completing a motorcyclist safety program.
12509.5(c)		Person with instruction permit shall not drive a motorcycle during darkness, on a freeway, or with a passenger.
12511		Drivers license, possession of more than one.
12515(a)		Minor under 18, employed for purpose of driving.
12515(b)		Driver under 21, operating or employed to operate interstate commerce or hazardous substance vehicle.
12516		School bus driver, under 18.
12517(a)		School bus driver must possess both driver's license and certificate.
12517(b)		School pupil activity bus driver must possess both driver's license and certificate.
12517.45		Did not meet requirements for a charter bus transporting school pupils.
12517.5(a)		Operating a para-transit vehicle without valid, appropriate license.
12517.5(b)		Operating a para-transit vehicle without proper training.
12519(a)		Farm labor vehicle, endorsed drivers license required.
12519.5(a)		Tour bus operator, possession of valid license and CHP certificate.
12519.5(c)		Tour bus operator, use of safety belt; failure to report bus accident.
12520(a)		Operation of tow truck involved in freeway service patrol operations without valid CA driver's license and tow-truck driver certificate.
12521(a)		Requires tour bus operators to use safety belts.
12521(b)		Requires tour bus operators to report accidents.
12522(a)		School bus or youth-bus driver, first-aid qualification.
12523(a)		No person shall operate a youth bus without having in possession a valid driver's license of the appropriate class, endorsed for passenger transportation and a certificate issued by the department to permit the operation of a youth bus.
12523(d)		Youth bus operator-Use seat belt, refrain from smoking, report any accidents to CHP.
12523.5(a)		General public para-transit operator, driver's license, appropriate class and certificate.
12523.5(d)		General public para-transit operator; use seatbelts, refrain from smoking, report accident.
12523.6(a,d)		Driver of disabled, driver's license appropriate class and endorsement or employ without.
12524(a)		Radioactive materials drivers certificate - certificate required.
12804.6(a)		Transit bus operator; possess appropriate certificate.
12804.6(f)		Transit bus; employer permitting person to drive without a valid certificate on file in employee records.
12804.9		Examination and driving test classifications
12804.10		Class C drivers may operate house cars up to 40 ft in length; if over 40 ft, driver must possess Class B license with house car endorsement.
12804.11		Operating firefighting equipment without an endorsement issued by the Department and proper license.
12804.15		Driver of house car must possess appropriate class of driver's license, including endorsement if required
12813		Department imposes restrictions on the driver's license
12814		Provisions dealing with the renewal of the driver's license and examination by the Department
12814.5		Provisions related to license extension and renewal by mail
12814.6(a)		Provisions related to issuance of provisional driver's license to persons over 16 and under 18 years of age
12814.6(b)		For a Provisional License for a Minor, failure to obey restriction provisions
12815(a)		Driver's license lost or mutilated, obtain duplicate, destroy original if found.
12950		Signature of Licensee. Failure to sign usual signature
12951(a)		Driver's license, not in possession.
12951(b)		Driver's license, refusal to present to officer.
12952		Driver's license, display to court.
13003(a)		ID card; obtain duplicate if lost, stolen, mutilated, or name change.
13003(b)		ID card; surrender to DMV within 10 days after notification by DMV or law enforcement that document is mutilated.
13004(a)		ID card display or possession of, cancelled, altered, fictitious, fraudulently obtained.
13004(b)		ID card, lending or permitting another to use.
13004(c)		ID card, displaying another's.
13004(d)		ID card, permitting unlawful use.
13004(e)		To do any act forbidden by this article.

Codes	Pts	Description
13004(f)		ID card, reproducing or possession of facsimile.
13004(g)		ID card, unauthorized alteration.
13004.1(a)		Prohibits the manufacture or sale of an identification document which is substantially similar to a driver's license, or that purports to confer the same privileges, as the drivers' license issued by the Department.
13007		ID card holder must notify DMV change of address within ten days.
13007.5		Unlawful for applicant to knowingly declare to DMV that no birth certificate exists when, in fact, a birth certificate does exist.
13200		Suspension for speeding or reckless driving.
13200.5		Suspension for driving in excess of 100 MPH.
13201(a)		Suspension for failure to stop when involved with accident.
13201(b)		Suspension for reckless driving causing bodily harm.
13201(c)		Suspension for failure to stop at RR crossing.
13201(d)		Suspension for evading a peace officer.
13201(e)		Knowingly causing or participating in a vehicular collision, or any other vehicular accident, for the purpose of presenting or causing to be presented any false or fraudulent insurance claim.
13201.5		Suspension regarding prostitution.
13202		Controlled substance offense suspension or revocation.
13202.4		Minor's unlawful use of firearms: license suspension or delay.
13202.5		Suspension, underage controlled substances or alcohol-related offenses.
13202.6		Suspension, underage vandalism.
13202.7		Habitual truant - suspension or delay of driving privilege.
13202.8		Restricted driving privilege - ignition interlock device.
13203		Court cannot suspend license longer than code permits.
13206		Court requires surrender of license.
13207		Court suspends license and all related licenses held by subject.
13208		Recommendation of court to the Department.
13209		Court requests driving record from Department.
13210		Court-ordered suspension due to road rage.
13350		Department required revocation.
13350.5		Revocation for vehicular manslaughter.
13351(a1)		Department revocation for manslaughter.
13351(a2)		Department revocation for three violations (in 20001, 20002, 23103, or 23104) within twelve months.
13351(a3)		Department revocation associated with causing bodily harm (2800.3).
13351.5		Suspension for assault with deadly weapon: motor vehicles.
13351.8		Required suspension for road rage.
13351.85		Towing suspension, per 12110.
13352		Suspend or revoke for influence of alcohol or drugs; excess blood alcohol; addiction; or speed contest.
13352.1		Extended DUI suspension.
13352.3		Minor - revocation of driving privilege per 23152 or 23153.
13252.4(a,b)		First offense DUI Program.
13252.4(c,d)		Suspend for failure to supply proof of financial responsibility.
13352.4		Except as provided in subdivision (h), the department shall issue a restricted driver's license to a person whose driver's license was suspended under paragraph (1) of subdivision (a) of Section 13352, if the person specific requirements.
13352.5		Restricted driver's license issued – second offense.
13352.6		DUI Conviction of person under 21; required suspension.
13353		Suspension for refusal of chemical test.
13353.1		Suspension for refusal to take PAS preliminary alcohol screening test.
13353.2(a1)		Suspension for alcoholic content greater than .08 per cent.
13353.2(a2)		Suspension for alcoholic content greater than .01 per cent and under 21.
13353.2(a3)		Suspension of a commercial driver when driving CMV with alcohol content .04 percent or more.
13353.3		Order of suspension pursuant to conditions not met in 13353
13353.45		Treatment program: certification of completion.
13353.5		Restoration of driving privilege to a non-resident.
13353.6		Suspension and restriction of a CDL.
13353.7		Issuance of non-commercial driver's license.
13353.7(d)		CDL holder operating non-CDL that resulted in the suspension pursuant to Section 13353.2, the department shall restrict a class C or class M driver's license restricted in the same manner and subject to the same conditions
13353.8		Restricted license; person under 21.
13354		Consecutive suspensions, if so order by the court.
13355		Suspension for driving in excess of 100 MPH.
13357		Suspension or revocation for auto theft.

Codes	Pts	Description
13359		Department authorization to suspend or revoke upon grounds which authorize the refusal i=to issue a license,
13360		Suspension or revocation for violation of DL restriction.
13361(a)		Suspension for failure to stop at accident resulting in property damage only.
13361(b)		Suspension for second or subsequent conviction of reckless driving.
13361(c)		Suspension for manslaughter per paragraph 2 of subdivision (c) of Section 192 of the Penal Code.
13362		Surrender of license that was issued erroneously by the Department.
13363		Suspension or revocation for conviction in another state that would also be suspendable or revocated in this state.
13364		Suspension for bad or dis-honored check.
13365		Suspension for failure to appear.
13365.2		Suspension for failure to appear.
13365.5		Suspension for failure to comply with a court order.
13366		Effective date of suspension.
13367		Determining that minor's suspension cannot be lighter than that of an adult.
13368		Requirement to attend driving training, as part of re-issuance of DL.
13369		Refusal of Department to renew or issue certain CDL endorsements, and may suspend or revoke.
13370		Refusal of Department to renew or issue school bus endorsement, and may suspend or revoke.
13371		Denial, suspension, or revocation; request and scope of hearing.
13372		Denial, suspension, or revocation of ambulance driver certificate.
13373		Grounds for dismissal of ambulance driver or attendant.
13374		Refusal to issue or renew, suspend or revoke of ambulance driver certificate.
13376		Denial, revocation add or suspension of driver certificates involved with school bus or general public para-transit.
13377		Denial or revocation of tow truck driver certificate.
13378		Request for hearing, tow truck driver.
13380		Peace officer's report: service of order suspension
13382		Suspension or revocation of driving privilege; notice or confiscation of license or temporary license.
13384		Cannot issue license without written consent to chemical testing of blood, breath or urine.
13385		Preliminary alcohol screening or other chemical test: persons on probation for prior DUI.
13386		Ignition interlock verification (was 23235 until 07/01/99).
13388		Preliminary alcohol screening test or other chemical testing for person under 21.
13389		Preliminary alcohol screening or other chemical test: persons on probation for prior DUI.
13550		Surrender of license to the court.
13551		Surrender of license to the Department.
13552		Driving privileges of non resident may be suspend or revoked same as residents.
13553		When an unlicensed person is suspended or revoked of driving privileges.
13555		Pertaining to termination of probation and dismissal of charges.
13556		Pertaining to duration of suspension.
13557		Administrative review of order of suspension or revocation.
13558		Request or scope for hearing; suspension or revocation.
13559		Judicial review.
14600(a)		Change of address, notify DMV within ten days (DL).
14600(b)		Change address, mark-out on face, write-in on reverse (DL).
14601(a,b)	2	Driving when driver's license suspended or revoked for reckless driving, negligent or incompetent driving acts.
14601.1	2	No person shall drive a motor vehicle when his or her driving privilege is suspended or revoked for any reason other than those listed in Section 14601, 14601.2, or 14601.5.
14601.2(a)	2	Driving when driver's license suspended or revoked for driving under the influence of alcohol, drug, or combination.
14601.2(b)	2	Restricted license for alcohol and drug offenses, disobeying restrictions.
14601.2(d)	2	Certified ignition interlock device installed.
14601.2(h)	2	Court requires a person convicted of a violation of this section to install a certified ignition interlock device on a vehicle the person owns or operates.
14601.3(a)	2	Driver's license suspended or revoked - Habitual traffic offender.
14601.4(a)	2	Driving while license suspended or revoked pursuant to Section 14601.2 and causing an injury collision.
14601.5	2	DL suspended or revoked-chemical test refusal.
14602.6		Whenever a peace officer determines that a person was driving a vehicle while his or her driving privilege was suspended or revoked or without ever having been issued a driver's license, the peace officer may either immediately arrest that person and cause the removal and seizure of that vehicle or, if the vehicle is involved in a traffic collision, cause the removal and seizure of the vehicle, without the necessity of arresting the person
14602.7		Vehicle impoundment - fleeing a Peace Officer.
14602.8		Vehicle impoundment - DUI
14603	1	Restricted license, disobeying restrictions.
14604(a)		Motor vehicle owner, unlawful to loan to unlicensed driver. Must make reasonable effort to determine license status of person to whom car is loaned.

Codes	Pts	Description
14605(a)		Parking lot attendant, unlicensed.
14605(b)		Parking lot attendant, employing unlicensed.
14606(a)		Unlicensed person; employing, hiring, or knowingly permitting to drive.
14606(b)		Whenever a person fails to qualify, on reexamination, to operate a commercial motor vehicle, an employer shall report that failure to department within 10 days.
14607		Unlicensed person (under 21), permitting own child, ward, or employee to drive.
14608(a)		Renting motor vehicle, to unlicensed person.
14609(a)		Renting motor vehicle, maintain proper records.
14609(b)		Renting motor vehicle to unlicensed person, maintain proper records.
14610(1)(a)		Makes it unlawful to display or possess any cancelled, revoked, suspended, fictitious, fraudulently-altered, or fraudulently-obtained driver's license.
14610(2)(a)		Makes it unlawful to lend a driver's license to any person.
14610(3)(a)		Makes it unlawful for a person to represent their license is one not issued to them.
14610(4)(a)		Makes it unlawful to fail or refuse to surrender to DMV a driver's license which has been suspended, revoked. or cancelled.
14610(5)(a)		Makes it unlawful to permit any unlawful use of a driver's license.
14610(6)(a)		Makes it unlawful to do any act forbidden or fail to perform any act required by this division.
14610(7)(a)		Makes it unlawful to photograph, photostat, duplicate, or in any way reproduce any driver's license or facsimile so that it could be mistaken for a valid license.
14610(8)(a)		Makes it unlawful to alter any driver's license in any manner not authorized by the Vehicle Code.
14610.1(a)		Prohibits the manufacture or sale of an identification document which is substantially similar to a driver's license.
14610.5(a)		Sale or distribution of crib sheet on DMV drivers license examination; impersonation of a driver's license applicant.
14610.7		Knowingly assist an illegal alien in obtaining a driver's license.
14611		Knowingly directing hauling of radioactive materials by person not possessing certificate or valid license.
15220		Commercial motor vehicle driver shall report any out-of-state conviction involving the safe operation of a motor vehicle to DMV within thirty days.
15222		Commercial motor vehicle driver shall report any conviction involving the safe operation of motor vehicle to his or her employer within thirty days.
15224		Commercial motor vehicle driver shall notify employer of suspended or revoked drivers license before the end of business day following the action.
15226		Driver placed out-of-service for violation of Federal Motor Carrier Safety Regulations shall report to his or her employer within twenty-four hours.
15228		Driver placed out-of-service for violation of Federal Motor Vehicle Safety Regulations shall report to DMV within thirty days.
15230		Each person who applies for employment as a driver of a commercial motor vehicle shall provide employer with required information.
15240(a)		Employer knowingly allows a driver to drive a commercial motor vehicle with a suspended or revoked driving privilege.
15240(b)		Employer knowingly allows a driver with more than one driver's license to operate a commercial motor vehicle.
15250(a)1		A person may not operate a commercial motor vehicle unless that person has in his or her immediate possession a valid commercial driver's license of the appropriate class.
15250(a)2		A person may not operate a commercial motor vehicle while transporting hazardous materials unless that person has in his or her possession a valid commercial driver's license with a hazardous materials endorsement. An instruction permit does not authorize the operation of a vehicle transporting hazardous materials.
15250(b)1		Before an application for an original or renewal of a commercial driver's license with a hazardous materials endorsement is submitted to the United States Transportation Security Administration for the processing of a security threat assessment, as required under Part 1572 of Title 49 of the Code of Federal Regulations, the department shall complete a check of the applicant's driving record to ensure that the person is not subject to a disqualification under Part 383.51 of Title 49 of the Code of Federal Regulations.
15250(b)2		A person may not be issued a commercial driver's license until he or she has passed a written and driving test for the operation of a commercial motor vehicle which complies with the minimum federal standards.
15250.5(a)		Requires a person operating fire-fighting equipment to possess a valid driver's license for the appropriate class.
15250.6(a)		Operation of firefighting equipment. Driver shall have in immediate possession driver license of appropriate class.
15275(a)		A person may not operate a commercial motor vehicle described in this chapter unless that person has in his or her possession a valid commercial driver's license for the appropriate class, and an endorsement issued by the department to permit the operation of the vehicle unless exempt from the requirement to obtain an endorsement pursuant to subdivision (b) of Section 15278.
15275(b)1		An endorsement to drive vehicles specified in this ( )2 article shall be issued only to applicants qualified by examinations prescribed by the department and ( )3 who meet the minimum standards established in Part 383 of Title 49 of the Code of Federal Regulations.
15275(b)2		A hazardous materials endorsement shall be issued only to applicants who comply with paragraph (1) and the requirements set forth in Part 1572 of Title 49 of the Code of Federal Regulations.
15278(a)		Requires an endorsement to operate certain commercial vehicles.

Note: Chapter 7, Article 7 15300 - 15320 deal with sanctions as outlined below:

15300	Penalty: First Conviction
15301	Penalty if CDL driving transporting dangerous fireworks have gross weight of 10,000 pounds or more
15302	Penalty: Subsequent Conviction
15304	Penalty: Controlled Substance Offense
15306	Penalty: Second Offense Within Three Years
15308	Penalty: Third or Subsequent Offense Within Three Years
15309	Suspension for False Information on Application
15311	Suspension for Failure to Obey a Peace Officer
15311.1	Employer: Penalty for Allowing Employee to Violate Out-of-Service Order
15312	Commercial drivers prohibited from operating vehicle for specified time due to a violation of railroad grade crossing regulations.
15312.1	Employer: Penalty for Allowing Employee to Violate Railroad Crossing Laws
15315	Grounds for Refusal to Issue License, Surrender of Out-of-State License
15319	Departmental Administration
15320	Department Action Upon Receipt of Court Abstract
15325	Driver Disqualification: Imminent Hazard
15326	Upon receiving notification of an administrative action or conviction of a commercial licenseholder in a state, territory, or possession of the United States, the District of Columbia, the Commonwealth of Puerto Rico, or the Dominion of Canada, the department shall impose a suspension, revocation, or disqualification action on that person's commercial driving privilege based upon violations that would result in an administrative action or a conviction pursuant to Section 383.51 of Subpart D of Part 383 and Sections 384.206(b)(3), 384.213, and 384.231 of Subpart B of Part 384 of Title 49 of the Federal Code of Regulations.

Motor Vehicle Transactions With Minors, Division 6.5 (15500-15501)

Codes	Pts	Descriptions
15500		Driver's license, purchasing or obtaining motor vehicle without.
15501		Driver's license, presenting false license for leasing or purchasing of car.

Unattended Child in Motor Vehicle Safety Act, Division 6.7

3 Chapters (15600-15632)

Codes	Pts	Descriptions
15620		Children six (6) and under alone in vehicle when significant risk to health/safety exists.

Financial Responsibility Laws, Division 7

5 Chapters (16000-16560)

Codes	Pts	Descriptions
16000		SR-1 report, within ten days of reportable on-highway or off-highway accident.
16002		Employer's report, within ten days.
16003		Driver incapable, owner shall file report.
16004(a)		The department shall suspend the driving privilege of any person who fails, refuses, or neglects to make a report of an accident as required in this chapter.
16020(a)		Driver and owner must maintain a form of financial responsibility and shall carry evidence of financial responsibility in the vehicle at all times.
16020.3		Vanpool vehicle, employer must maintain proof of financial responsibility.
16025(a)		Exchange of information, including evidence of financial responsibility at the scene of the accident.
16028(a)		Display proof of financial responsibility when requested by a peace officer.
16028(c)		Display proof of financial responsibility when requested by a peace officer when involved in an accident.
16030(a)		Providing false evidence of financial responsibility.
16050.5		Owner shall furnish driver involved in reportable accident of his/her insurance information.
16054		Requires the owner of an insured vehicle to furnish insurance information to an individual involved in an accident while operating the vehicle with the owner's permission.
16070		Suspension for failure to provide evidence of financial responsibility when involved in accident.
16071		Suspension for failure of meeting the financial responsibility provisions, out of state violation.
16072		Period of suspension - restriction alternative
16073		Exemption from suspension - course of employment
16370		Suspension for judgment unsatisfied
16370.5		Suspension due to Small Claims Court judgment
16370.7		Dealing with suspension fees
16371		Period of suspension to remain in effect until debtor provides proof of financial responsibility
16373		Court report of judgment
16374		Suspension for judgments not covered by proof
16375		Affidavit of insurance

16376	Action against a non-resident
16377	When judgment deemed satisfied
16378	Disposition of money deposited
16379	Installment payments of judgments
16380	Conditions for installment payments
16381	Suspension for failure to pay court ordered installments towards a judgment
16457(a)	Driving a motor vehicle not covered by a certificate of insurance when proof of financial responsibility in damages is required.
16502	Commercial passenger vehicle, owner to maintain proof of ability to respond.
16503	Suspension for violation of 16502.
16560	Interstate highway carriers, failure to comply with PUC regulations.

Civil Liability, Division 9
2 Chapters (17000-17714)

Accidents and Accident Reports, Division 10 (20000-20018)

Codes	Pts	Descriptions
20001(a)	2	Hit-and-run, injury or death, immediate report of fatal.
20002(a)	2	Hit-and-run, property damage, including vehicles.
20002(b)	2	Hit-and-run, property damage, by runaway vehicle.
20003(a)(b)		Driver involved in accident resulting in injury or death shall provide information.
20004		Driver involved in accident resulting in death shall notify nearest Highway Patrol, if no peace officer present.
20006		Driver without license present other evidence of identification.
20008(a)		Accidents, injury or fatal, written report to law enforcement within twenty-four hours.
20008(b)		Common carrier file report by tenth of following month.
20010		Accident report, passenger comply when driver unable.
20011		Coroner's report, all MV fatales to CHP by tenth of following month.

Rules of the Road, Division 11
Chapter 1 - Obedience to and Effect of Traffic Laws (21000-21282)
Chapter 2 - Traffic Signs, Signals, and Markings (21350-21468)
Chapter 3 - Driving, Overtaking, and Passing (21650-21759)
Chapter 4 - Right of Way (21800-21809)
Chapter 5 - Pedestrians' Rights and Duties (21949-21971)
Chapter 6 - Turning and Stopping and Turning Signals (22100-22113)
Chapter 7 - Speed Laws (22348-22413)
Chapter 8 - Special Stops Required (22450-22456)
Chapter 9 - Stopping, Standing, and Parking (22500-22526)
Chapter 10 - Removal of Parked and Abandoned Vehicles (22650-22856)
Chapter 11 - Parking Lots (22950-22953)
Chapter 12 - Public Offenses (23100-23249.50)
Chapter 13 - Vehicular Crossings and Toll Highways (23250-23336)

Codes	Pts	Descriptions
21070		Unsafe operation of motor vehicle that causes bodily injury or great bodily injury.
21100.3	1	Failure to obey traffic direction of local authority.
21100.4		Violation of local licensing requirements.
21106(b)		Crosswalk, use of where prohibited by sign.
21113		School or public grounds, including grounds of public transportation agency, trespassing on with vehicle, animal, bicycle, skateboard, motorized bicycle, or roller skates.
21116(a)		Unlawful to drive upon roadway on a levee, canal bank, pipeline right-of-way, or natural waterline course.
21155		Driving golf cart on highway were prohibited.
21200.5		Riding a bicycle while under the influence of alcohol, drugs, or both.
21201(a)		Bicycle, single wheel brake required.
21201(b)		Bicycle, handlebars no higher than operator's shoulders.
21201(c)		Bicycle; rider unable to support in an upright position with at least one foot on the ground.
21201(d)		Bicycle, during darkness headlight, red reflector on rear, pedal reflectors and side reflectors required.
21201.3(b)		Steady or flashing blue light on bicycle.
21201.5(a)		Sale of unapproved, reflex reflector, or reflectorized tire.
21201.5(b)		Sale of bicycle without required reflectors on pedals and sides.
21202(a)		Bicyclist, failure to use right edge of roadway.
21203		Bicyclist, hitching ride on other vehicle.
21204(a)		Bicyclist, riding on other than permanent seat and/or passenger riding on other than permanent seat, unless bicycle was

Codes	Pts	Descriptions
		deigned by manufacturer to be ridden without a seat.
21204(b)		Bicyclist, permitting passenger on other than a permanent seat; minor passenger not retained in seat, unless bicycle was deigned by manufacturer to be ridden without a seat.
21205		Bicyclist, unable to keep at least one hand free to use on handlebars.
21207.5		Operation of motorized bicycle upon bikeway, equestrian, hiking or recreational trail without proper authority.
21208(a)		Failure to ride in a bicycle lane.
21208(b)		Bicyclist shall not leave bike lane until reasonably safe.
21209(a)	1	Driving in bicycle lane, except as provided.
21210		Bicycle lying on its side on a sidewalk.
21211(a)		Standing, stopping, sitting, or loitering on a Class I bikeway.
21211(b)		Placing or parking any bicycle, vehicle, or object upon a Class I bikeway which impedes the movement of a bicyclist.
21212(a)		Person under eighteen operating or riding as passenger on bicycle without wearing approved helmet.
21212(c)		Sale of bicycle helmet not meeting applicable safety standards.
21221.5		Operation of motorized scooter upon a highway while under the influence of an alcoholic beverage or any drug, or under the combined influence of an alcoholic beverage and any drug.
21223		Motorized scooter, during darkness-headlight, red reflector to the rear and side reflectors required.
21226(b)		Violation of motorized scooter muffler equipment requirements; maximum noise level.
21226(d)		Violation of motorized scooter exhaust/noise level requirements or operation with modified exhaust.
21228(a)a		Motorized scooter, failure to ride as close as practicable to the right hand curb or right edge of the roadway.
21229(a)		Motorized scooter, failure to ride within an established bicycle lane.
21229(b)		Prohibits the operator of a motorized scooter to exit a bicycle lane without signaling.
21230		Operating a motorized scooter on trail or pathway where prohibited.
21235(a-j)		Improper operation of motorized scooter on highway (A thru J).
21251		Low speed vehicles subject to motor vehicle provisions.
21260(a)		Exceeding speed limit of 35 MPH while operating a low-speed vehicle.
21266		Low-Speed Vehicles: Restrictions and Prohibitions By Local Authorities or Department of the California Highway Patrol
21281		Violations for equipment and devices on an electric personal assistive mobility device
21281.5		Unsafe operation of an electric personal assistive mobility device.
21281.5(a)		Unsafe operation of an electric personal assistive mobility device.
21281.5(b0		Unsafe operation of an electric personal assistive mobility device, speed that endangers the safety of persons or property.
21281.5(c)		Unsafe operation of an electric personal assistive mobility device, wanton disregard for the safety of persons or property.
21281.5(d)		Unsafe operation of an electric personal assistive mobility device, failure to yield to a pedestrian.
21367(a)	1	Disobedience to traffic signs/controller
21367(b)	1	Department of Transportation, disobeying traffic control at construction site.
21367(c)	1	Failure to obey warning devices at construction site.
21451(a)	1	Circular green signal; shall proceed, but shall yield to vehicles and pedestrians lawfully within intersection.
21451(b)	1	Green arrow; shall enter intersection only to make movement indicated.
21451(c)		Pedestrians facing circular green; may proceed, but must yield to vehicles lawfully within the intersection.
21451(d)		Pedestrian facing green arrow shall not enter roadway.
21452(a)	1	Illegal movement on yellow light or arrow.
21452(b)		Failure of pedestrian to properly respond to signal of yellow light or arrow.
21453(a)	1	Red or Stop; vehicles stop at limit line or X-walk.
21453(b)	1	After stopping, may turn right, or turn left from a one-way street to a one-way street (unless sign posted), but shall yield to pedestrians and traffic on cross street.
21453(c)	1	Red arrow, driver shall not enter intersection to make indicated movement.
21453(d)		Pedestrian facing circular red or red arrow, shall not enter roadway.
21454(a,b)	1	Traffic signals violation.
21454(c)	1	Lane use control signal, steady red, driver shall not enter or use.
21454(d)	1	Lane use control signal, flashing yellow, driver may use only for making left turn to or from the highway.
21455	1	Official traffic-control signal erected at other than an intersection, shall stop at sign, crosswalk, limit line, or if none, at the signal.
21456(a)		Walk pedestrian failure to yield right-of-way to vehicles already in crosswalk.
21456(b)		"Don't walk", or "wait", or "upraised hand"; pedestrian crossing against.
21457(a)	1	Flashing red; failing to stop for.
21457(b)	1	Flashing yellow, proceed only with caution.
21460(a)	1	Double solid lines; driving to left of—except driveway, intersection, or U-turn.
21460(b)	1	Solid-broken lines; driving to left when solid line placed on right.
21460.5(c)	1	Two-way, left-turn lane; driving in, or turning from through lane.
21461(a)	1	Traffic control sign; failure to obey regulatory provisions.
21461.5		Pedestrian; failure to obey any sign or signal.
21462	1	Traffic control signals; all traffic (sec. 620) to obey.

Codes	Pts	Descriptions
21463		Traffic signals; illegal operation.
21464(a)		Signs, signals, markers or motorist call boxes; damaging, removing, or attaching material to.
21464(b)		A person may not use, and a vehicle, other than an authorized emergency vehicle or a public transit passenger vehicle, may not be equipped with, any device, including, but not limited to, a mobile infrared transmitter, that is capable of sending a signal that interrupts or changes the sequence patterns of an official traffic control signal
21464(c)		A person may not buy, possess, manufacture, install, sell, offer for sale, or otherwise distribute a device described in subdivision (b),
21465		Traffic devices; display of unauthorized.
21466		Blinding lights; displayed toward highway.
21466.5		Display of light source impairing vision of drivers.
21650(a-f)	1	Right half of roadway; failure to drive on.
21650.1		Bicycle on roadway or shoulder required to be operated in same direction as motor vehicles.
21651(a)	1	Divided highways; driving over, upon, or across dividing section; left- or semi-circular U-turn—except through marked opening.
21651(b)	2	Driving the wrong way on a divided highway.
21651(c)	2	Driving the wrong way on a divided highway which causes injury or death.
21652	1	Service road; entering or leaving adjacent highway from other than lawful opening.
21654(a)	1	Slower vehicle, in left lane(s).
21655(b)	1	Certain vehicles (22406) using left lane(s), or passing in lane other than adjacent to right lane. Trailer buses allowed in HOV lane.
21655.5(b)	0	Failure to obey sign posted preferential traffic lanes; exceptions - motorcycles and mass transit vehicles.
21655.8(a)	1	Crossing over double yellow lines to enter or exit a preferential use traffic lane.
21655.8(b)	1	Failure to yield to emergency vehicle within exclusive or preferential lane
21655.9	1	HOV lanes: Use by ultra-low emission vehicles
21655.9(b)	1	No person shall drive a vehicle described in 5205.5 unless the proper decal, label, or other identifier is displayed.
21655.9(c)	1	No person shall operate or own a vehicle displaying a decal, label, or other identifier as described in 5205.5, if that decal, label, or other identifier is not assigned to that vehicle.
21656	1	Slow vehicle, failure to use sign-posted turnout or safe area.
21657	1	One-way street, highway; driving against traffic.
21658(a)	1	Laned roadways (two or more lanes in direction of travel); straddling or changing when unsafe.
21658(b)	1	Designated lanes; failure to obey signs.
21659	1	Three-lane highway; driving in far left lane, or using center lane when unsafe.
21660	1	Meeting vehicles; failure to pass to right, and/or yield half of roadway.
21661	1	Descending narrow grade; yield to ascending vehicle.
21662	1	Mountain driving; hold motor vehicle under control.
21662(a)	1	Mountain driving; drive as near the right edge as possible.
21662(b)	1	Mountain driving; roadway with insufficient width, driver to give audible warning where view obstructed within 200 feet.
21663	1	Driving on sidewalk—except when permitted.
21664	1	Exiting or entering a freeway at other than a designated on-ramp or off-ramp.
21700	1	Obstructing driver's view or control, by passengers or load.
21700.5		Operation of bus with school pupils standing in city of San Diego.
21701	1	Interfering with driver's control of vehicle.
21702(a)	1	Driving Hours - Persons, not to exceed ten hours.
21702(b)	1	Driving Hours - Property, not to exceed twelve hours.
21703	1	Following too closely; not reasonable and prudent.
21704(a)	1	Distance between trucks; 300 feet on two-lane highway.
21705	1	Caravans; maintain at least 100 feet distance between vehicles.
21706	1	Authorized emergency vehicles; following within 300 feet.
21706.5(b)	1	Operate a vehicle in an unsafe manner within an emergency incident zone.
21707	1	Fire area; operating vehicle within the block or 300 feet.
21708		Fire hoses; driving over unprotected.
21709	1	Safety zone; driving through.
21710		Coasting; in neutral on downgrade.
21711	1	Towed vehicle; whipping, swerving, or failing to track properly.
21712(a)	1	Permitting person to ride where unlawful.
21712(b)		Unlawful riding on portion not intended for passengers or load.
21712(c)		A person driving a motor vehicle shall not knowingly permit a person to ride in the trunk of a motor vehicle.
21712(d)		A person shall not ride in the trunk of a motor vehicle.
21712(e)		Unlawful towing of bicycle, skis, sled, etc.
21712(g)		Permitting riding in trailer coach or trailer carrying vessel unlawful.
21712(h)		Unlawful towing of bicycle, skis, sled, etc.

Codes	Pts	Descriptions
21713		Privately-owned armored car; operated without CHP license.
21714(a)		Operating fully enclosed 3-wheeled motor vehicle described in 27803(f) in any lane established in under 21655.5 as preferential lane.
21714(b)		Operating fully enclosed 3-wheeled motor vehicle described in 27803(f) adjacent to lane markings or between vehicles.
21715(a)	1	Passenger vehicle towing more than one other vehicle (see 36625 and 36626 for exceptions).
21715(b)	1	Motor vehicle under 4,000 pounds towing any vehicle over 6,000 pounds.
21716		Operating golf cart in speed zone above 25 mph.
21717	1	Motor vehicle turning across a bicycle lane.
21718(a)		Stopping or parking on freeway having full access and no crossing grades.
21720		Illegal to operate a pocket bike on a sidewalk, roadway, or any other part of a highway, or on a bikeway, bicycle path or trail, equestrian trail, hiking or recreational trail, or on public lands open to off-highway motor vehicle use.
21750	1	Overtaking vehicle; failure to pass safely to left.
21751	1	Overtaking vehicle; passing without sufficient clearance.
21752(a)	1	Driving left of center, when view limited by curve or hill crest.
21752(b)	1	Driving left of center, when view limited approaching bridge, viaduct or tunnel.
21752(c)	1	Driving left of center; traversing intersection or RR crossing.
21752(d)	1	Driving left of center, traversing any intersection.
21753	1	Overtaken vehicle; not moving to right on audible signal, or increasing speed.
21754	1	Passing on right, when unlawful.
21755	1	Passing on right, when unsafe, or on shoulder.
21756(a)	1	Passing streetcar when receiving or discharging passengers.
21756(b)	1	Passing streetcar at unsafe speed.
21756(c)	1	Passing trolley coach at unsafe speed.
21757	1	Passing streetcar on left.
21758	1	Passing too slowly on grade (ten mph faster, complete pass one-quarter mile).
21759	1	Passing animals; stop or reduce speed as necessary.
21800(a)	1	Uncontrolled intersection; yield to first vehicle within.
21800(b)	1	Uncontrolled intersection; yield to vehicle on right.
21800(c)	1	Intersection controlled from all sides (four-way stop); yield to vehicle on right.
21800(d)	1	Inoperative traffic signals; stop and proceed when safe.
21800(d)(1)	1	Driver shall stop at intersection with inoperative signals.
21800(d)(2)	1	Two vehicles at intersection with inoperative signals; driver on left yield right-of-way
21801(a)	1	Left turns or U-turns; yield until reasonably safe.
21801(b)	1	Failure to yield; turning vehicle having yielded (lane-by-lane).
21802(a)	1	Entering through highway; yield until reasonably safe.
21802(b)	1	Failure to yield; by vehicle not a hazard.
21803(a)	1	Yield signs; yield until reasonably safe.
21803(b)	1	Failure to yield; by vehicle not a hazard.
21804(a)	1	Public or private property; yield to approaching traffic so close as to constitute an immediate hazard.
21804(b)	1	Failure to yield, by vehicle not a hazard.
21805(b)	1	Equestrian crossings; failure to yield by driver.
21805(c)		Horseback rider proceeding into path of vehicle.
21806(a)	1	Emergency vehicles; other driver failing to yield.
21806(b)		Emergency vehicles; motorman failing to yield.
21806(c)		Emergency vehicles; pedestrian failing to yield.
21807	1	Unsafe operation of an emergency vehicle.
21809(a)	1	No displaying due caution when on freeway approaching stationary authorized emergency vehicle or tow truck is displaying emergency lights or flashing amber warning lights
21809(a1)	1	Improper lane change per when approaching stationary emergency vehicle or tow truck.
21809(a2)	1	Unsafe maneuver when approaching stationary emergency vehicle or tow truck.
21810(a)	1	Not yielding right of way to transit bus.
21950(a)	1	Crosswalks; failure to yield to pedestrians within.
21950(b)		Crosswalk; pedestrian running in front of vehicle.
21950(c)		Not exercising due care to safeguard safety of pedestrian.
21951	1	Crosswalk; overtaking and passing vehicle stopped for pedestrian within.
21952	1	Sidewalk; failure to yield to pedestrian on.
21953		Pedestrian yield, if protected crossing available.
21954(a)	1	Pedestrian yield, upon roadway outside crosswalk.
21954(b)	1	Due care for pedestrian safety outside crosswalk.
21955		Jaywalking; between signal controlled intersections.
21956		Walking on roadway, other than pedestrian's left edge.

Codes	Pts	Descriptions
21957		Hitchhiking; while standing in roadway.
21959		Skiing, tobogganing, on or across highway—interfering with traffic.
21960(a)	1	Prohibited or restricted use of freeway.
21963	1	Fail to yield right of way to blind pedestrian.
21964		Other than blind person carrying white cane.
21966		Pedestrian in a bicycle lane where pedestrian facility.
21967		Riding skateboard on highway, sidewalk, or roadway where prohibited.
21968		Motorized skateboard on highway, bikeway, or trail.
21970(a)		Stopping unnecessarily and blocking a crosswalk or sidewalk
22100(a)	1	Right turn at intersection; improper position.
22100(b)	1	Left turn at intersection; improper position.
22100.5	1	U-turn at traffic signal; only from left lane.
22101(d)	1	Required or prohibited turn; failure to obey official sign.
22102	1	U-turn in business district; other than from extreme left-hand lane at an intersection or opening in divided highway.
22103	1	U-turn in residence district; vehicle approaching within 200 feet.
22104	1	U-turn at fire station; in front of or using entrance.
22105	1	U-turn; vision obstructed within 200 feet.
22106	1	Starting or backing when unsafe.
22107	1	Unsafe turn; and/or without signaling.
22108	1	Turning without signaling last 100 feet.
22109	1	Stopping suddenly without signaling.
22110	1	Signal device; required body or load more than 24 feet to left of steering wheel center, or when arm signal not clearly visible—except implements of husbandry.
22111(a)	1	Left turn hand signal; improperly given.
22111(b)	1	Right turn hand signal; improperly given.
22111(c)	1	Stop hand signal; improperly given.
22112(a)	1	School bus driver must activate flashing red signal lights, amber warning lights, and stop signal arm system at School bus stop.
22112(b)		School bus driver, stop to load or unload pupils only at designated School bus stops.
22112(c)		School bus driver, check traffic, check lights, escort students with hand held stop sign at School bus stops.
22112(d)		School bus driver not escorting children on or off when traffic not controlled
22112(e)		School bus driver, may not activate the amber warning light system at specified locations, except where pupils must cross the highway.
22112(f)		Activation of either the amber warning light system or the flashing red light system at a location determined by the CHP as necessary.
22348(a)	1	Speed.
22348(b)	2	Driving in excess of 100 mph.
22348(c)	1	Vehicle subject to 22406 using left lane(s) or passing in lane other than lane immediately adjacent to right lane.
22349(a)	1	Exceeding 65 mph maximum speed limit.
22349(b)	1	Exceeding 55 mph speed limit on a two-laned undivided highway.
22350	1	Unsafe speed for prevailing conditions (use for all prima facie limits).
22351	1	Violation of basic speed law
22352(a,b)	1	Establishes a prima facie speed limit of 25 miles per hour when passing a senior center.
22354	1	Reduced prima facie speed limits.
22355	1	Variable speed limits.
22356(b)	1	Exceeding the maximum speed limit, as posted.
22357-58.4	1	Speed in excess of local limits.
22359	1	Speed limits
22360	1	Speed limits
22361	1	Speed limits
22362	1	Speed limit where persons at work, in construction zone.
22363	1	Restricted speed; weather conditions.
22364	1	Restricted speed; lanes.
22400(a)	1	Minimum speed; impeding normal flow of traffic.
22400(b)	1	Minimum speed; below sign-posted limit.
22405(a)	1	Unsafe speed (sign-posted) for condition of bridge, structure, tube, or tunnel.
22406(a)	1	55 mph limit; truck or truck tractor (3 axle or any combo).
22406(b)	1	55 mph limit; passenger car, or bus, towing any vehicle.
22406(c)	1	55 mph limit; school bus with pupils.
22406(d)	1	55 mph limit; farm labor vehicle.
22406(e)	1	55 mph limit; any vehicle transporting explosives.

Codes	Pts	Descriptions
22406(f)	1	55 mph limit; trailer bus.
22406.1(a)	1	A person who operates a commercial motor vehicle, as defined in subdivision (b) of Section 15210, upon a highway at a speed exceeding a posted speed limit established under this code by 15 miles per hour or more.
22406.1(b)	1	A person who holds a commercial driver's license, as defined in subdivision (a) of Section 15210, and operates a non-commercial motor vehicle upon a highway at a speed exceeding a posted speed limit established under this code by 15 miles per hour or more.
22406.5	1	Speeding or reckless driving; tank veh. transporting more than 500 gallons of flammable liquid.
22407	1	Truck speed on downgrade; exceeding posted limit 10,000 pounds or over.
22409	1	Solid tire vehicle; speed restricted by weight.
22410	1	Metal tire; vehicle exceeding 6 mph.
22411		No person shall operate a motorized scooter at a speed in excess of 15 miles per hour.
22413	1	Decreasing speed limit on grades.
22450(a)	1	Stop sign; failure to stop at limit line, crosswalk, or entrance to intersection.
22450(b)	1	Stop sign at railroad crossing, stop at a limit line, first track or entrance to railroad grade crossing.
22451(a)	1	Railroad crossing; failure to stop for signal device or closely approaching train.
22451(b)	1	Railroad crossing; driving through closed crossing gate.
22452(b)	1	Railroad crossing, certain vehicles, including farm labor vehicles and any school bus transporting pupils, must stop.
22452(c)	1	The driver of a CMV driving too fast or without caution upon approaching a railroad grade crossing.
22454(a)	1	Passing school bus; stop when red lights flashing.
22455(a)		Commercial vending vehicle failing to properly stop while vending
22456(d)		Ice cream truck shall be equipped while vending in residential areas with legible signs.
22456(e)		A person may not vend from an ice cream truck that is stopped, parked, or standing on any public street, alley or highway as specified.
22500(a)		Parking unlawfully; within intersection.
22500(b)		Parking unlawfully; on crosswalk.
22500(c)		Parking unlawfully; adjacent to safety zone.
22500(d)		Parking unlawfully; within 15 feet of fire station driveway.
22500(e)		Parking unlawfully; blocking any driveway.
22500(f)		Parking unlawfully; on a sidewalk.
22500(g)		Parking unlawfully; blocking excavation.
22500(h)		Parking unlawfully; double parking.
22500(i)		Parking unlawfully; in posted bus loading zone.
22500(j)		Parking unlawfully; in tube or tunnel.
22500(k)		Parking upon any bridge; unless posted to permit.
22500(l)		Parking unlawfully; blocking sidewalk wheelchair access.
22500.1		Parking unlawfully; in posted fire lane.
22502(a)		Park parallel on right, and/or within 18 inches if curbed; motorcycle, one wheel at curb.
22502(e)		Parking on one-way streets; parallel parking on left permitted within 18 inches of curb—except upon divided highways.
22504(a)		Stopping or parking; on roadway outside city limits.
22505(b)		Stop, park, or leave standing on state highway where sign posted.
22506		Local regulation of state highway: stopping, standing, or parking.
22507.1		Violation of local regulations for parking privileges in a car share or ridesharing program.
22507.8(a)		Parking in spaces; on public streets or public or privately owned off-street parking facilities designated for handicapped prohibited.
22507.8(b)		Obstruct or block designated handicapped parking space, except as provided.
22507.8(c)		Makes it unlawful to park on the lines marking the boundaries of a parking stall or space designated for disabled persons or an area designated for the loading and unloading of vehicles.
22510(a,c)		Parking in snow areas; when sign-posted by local jurisdictions or by Caltrans.
22511		Off-street parking for electrical vehicles - in a designated space.
22511.1(a)		Park or leaving standing a vehicle is space designated for electrical vehicles unless the vehicle is connected for electric charging purposes.
22511.1(b)		Block parking space designated for electrical vehicles.
22511.3		Veterans with special license plates: parking in metered spaces.
22511.56		Placards or plates: evidence of issuance misuse.
22511.57		Local restrictions for placards or disabled plates
22511.7		Parking for the disabled.
22511.85		Off street parking in area designated for disabled.
22513(b)		Tow truck, unauthorized stopping at accident or for disabled to solicit services.
22513(c)		Tow truck, unauthorized moving of vehicle.
22514		Fire hydrant; parking unattended vehicle within fifteen feet.
22515(a)		Unattended motor vehicle; motor running and/or brakes not set.
22515(b)		Unattended vehicle; wheels not blocked, and/or not set.

Codes	Pts	Descriptions
22516		Locked vehicle; with person who cannot escape.
22517		Vehicle doors; opening to traffic when unsafe, leaving open.
22518		Using or parking in a transportation corridor parking facility
22520		Stopping or parking, on freeway having full control of access and no crossings at grade.
22520.5(a)		Person who solicits, displays, sells, or vends within the freeway right of way.
22520.5(a)		Person who solicits, displays, sells, or vends within the freeway right of way. Second offense is misdemeanor.
22520.6(a)		Person who solicits, displays, sells, or vends within a highway rest area or vista point.
22520.6(a)		Person who solicits, displays, sells, or vends within a highway rest area or vista point. Second offense (misdemeanor).
22521		Unlawful to park within seven and one-half feet of railroad track.
22522		Parking within three feet of a sidewalk access ramp.
22523(a)		Abandoning vehicle on highway.
22523(b)		Abandoning vehicle on public or private property.
22526(a)		Entering intersection without sufficient space to clear intersection.
22526(b)		Driver making left turn; facing yellow traffic signal, entering an intersection without sufficient space to clear intersection.
22526(c)		Entering railroad without sufficient space to clear the railroad. Driver's prohibited from traversing railroad crossings unless vehicle's undercarriage has sufficient clearance to cross intersection.
22526(d)		Entering railroad or rail transit crossing without sufficient space to clear the crossing and to accommodate the vehicle driven and any railway vehicle.
25258		Vehicle shall not be equipped with a device that emits any illumination or radiation that is designed or used for the purpose of controlling official traffic control signals.
22650		Unauthorized removal of unattended vehicle from highway.
22651.1		Persons operating storage facility, where vehicles are stored pursuant to Section 22651, shall accept a valid credit card or cash for payment of towing and storage fees.
22651.3		Impoundment of vehicle in an off street parking facility for excessive parking tickets
22651.7(b)		Immobilization of vehicle by unauthorized person.
22658(1)		Tow company shall maintain the original written authorization.
22658(e)(2)		Property owner or agent's responsibility for vehicle removal
22658.1(a)		Tow company failure to notify property owner of damage sustained while removing vehicle.
22659.5		Impoundment of Vehicle Used in Commission of Act of Prostitution or Illegal Dumping of Commercial Quantities of Waste
22951		Parking lot operator; patrons vehicle on street or alley.
22952(a)		Parking lot operator; having vehicle removed within 24 hours.
22952(b)		Parking lot operator; having vehicle removed for nonpayment when no pay facilities available.
22953(a)		Towing of a vehicle parked in a no-cost, privately-owned, off-street parking facility within one hour of the vehicle being parked; prohibited.
23103(a)	2	Reckless driving; no injury.
23103(b)	2	Reckless driving; off-street parking facility
23104(a)	2	Reckless driving; causing injury.
23104(b)		Defines fines for reckless driving when causing great bodily injury with specified prior convictions.
23105	2	Reckless driving: specified injuries.
23109(a)	2	Speed contest; engage in.
23109(b)	1	Speed contest; aid or abet.
23109(c)	2	Exhibition of speed; engaged aid or abet.
23109(d)	1	Speed contest; blocking or obstructing highway.
23109(e)(2)		Gives details to fines and imprisonment for engaging in a speed contest, causing specific injury.
23109.1	2	Speed contest: specified injuries caused by violation of 23109 applies additional punishment
23110(a)		Throwing substances at vehicle or occupant thereof.
23110(b)		Throwing missile with intent to do serious bodily harm.
23111		Lighted substance; throwing from vehicle on rural highway.
23112(a)		Litterbug; depositing glass or trash on highway.
23112(b)		Litterbug; depositing rocks or dirt anywhere on right of way.
23112.5(a)		Hazardous material spill; notification to CHP.
23112.7		Illegal dumping: impoundment of vehicle.
23113(a)		Failure to remove spilled material immediately.
23114(a)		Spilling load; other than clear water and feathers from live birds.
23114(b)		Aggregate material; failure to comply with equipment requirements.
23114(e)		Aggregate material; failure to cover load (effective 9/1/90).
23114(f)		Failure to provide a location for operators to cover load.
23115(a)		Rubbish vehicle; cover required to prevent spilling load.
23116(a)	1	Unlawful to transport person in back of motor truck.
23116(b)		Unlawful to ride in back of motor truck.

Codes	Pts	Descriptions
23117(a)		Unrestrained animal in space intended for load.
23118		Unlicensed Repossession: Tow Vehicle Impoundment
23120		Obstructed side vision; by wide earpiece on glasses.
23123		Driving a motor vehicle while using a wireless telephone - unless that telephone is specifically designed and configured to allow hands-free listening and talking, and is used in that manner while driving.
23123(a)		Wireless telephone, person prohibited from operating motor vehicle while using wireless telephone without a hands free device, with exceptions.
23123.5		Text-messaging while driving - A person shall not drive a motor vehicle while using an electronic wireless communications device to write, send or read a text-based communication.
23124(b)		Wireless telephone, person under 18 prohibited from operating motor vehicle while using a wireless telephone or mobile service device. This is a secondary violation.
23125(a)		Driving school bus or transit vehicle while using wireless phone.
23127	1	Riding; bicycle path or hiking trail, unauthorized motor vehicle on.
23128(a)		Snowmobile; operating on highway except in crossing.
23128(b)		Snowmobile; careless or negligent operation.
23128(c)		Snowmobile; pursuing game animal with intent to harass.
23128(d)		Snowmobile; operating for purpose of violating 602 PC.
23129		Operation of vehicle with camper with obstructed or inoperable exits in which persons are riding.
23130(a)		Operating vehicle in excess of specified noise limits.
23130.5(a)		Operating vehicle in excess of specified noise limits—level roadways.
23135		Operating motorized bicycle modified to no longer conform to definition.
23136		Unlawful for a person under the age of 21 years who has a blood-alcohol concentration of 0.01 percent or greater to drive a vehicle.
23140(a,b)	2	Minor driving with BAC of .05 percent or more.
23152(a)	2	Under influence of alcohol, drug, or combination; drive a vehicle.
23152(b)	2	Driving with a BAC of .08 percent or more.
23152(c)	2	Addict; except on methadone program.
23152(d)	2	Commercial Driver; driving with a BAC of .04 percent or more (effective 1/1/92).
23152(e)		It is unlawful for a person who is under the influence of any drug to drive a vehicle (effective 1/1/2014).
23152(f)		It is unlawful for a person who is under the combined influence of any alcoholic beverage and drug to drive a vehicle (effective 1/1/2014).
23153(a,c)	2	Under influence of alcohol, drug, or combination, causing injury or death to another on highway or other than a highway.
23153(b)	2	Driving with a BAC of .08 percent or more, causing injury or death to another.
23153(d)	2	Commercial Driver; driving with a BAC of .04 percent or more, causing injury or death to another.
23153(e)		It is unlawful for a person, while under the influence of any drug, to drive a vehicle and concurrently do any act forbidden by law, or neglect any duty imposed by law in driving the vehicle, which act or neglect proximately causes bodily injury to any person other than the driver (effective 1/1/2014).
23153(f)		It is unlawful for a person, while under the combined influence of any alcoholic beverage and drug, to drive a vehicle and concurrently do any act forbidden by law, or neglect any duty imposed by law in driving the vehicle, which act or neglect proximately causes bodily injury to any person other than the driver (effective 1/1/2014).
23154		Prohibits a person who is on probation for DUI to operate a motor vehicle at any time with a BAC of .01 percent or greater.
23175(a)		Driving under the influence; fourth or subsequent offense within seven years.
23190(a)		Driving under the influence causing injury; third and subsequent offense within seven years.
23190(b)		Driving under the influence causing great bodily injury; fourth or subsequent offense within seven years.
23213		Unlawful for patient or person residing at a social rehabilitation facility to have a motor vehicle registered in their name on or near the rehabilitation facility.
23220(a)	1	Drinking alcoholic beverage while driving a motor vehicle on highway.
23221(a)		No driver shall drink any alcoholic beverage while in a motor vehicle upon a highway.
23221(b)		No passenger shall drink any alcoholic beverage while in a motor vehicle upon a highway.
23222(a)	1	Alcohol; personal possession of an opened container while driving a motor vehicle.
23222(b)	1	Marijuana, possession of less than one ounce while driving a motor vehicle.
23223(a,)		No driver shall have in possession an alcoholic beverage in a motor vehicle on a highway.
23223(b)		No passenger shall have in possession an alcoholic beverage in a motor vehicle on a highway.
23224(a)		Driver under 21; knowingly operating vehicle carrying alcohol.
23224(b)		Passenger under 21; personal possession of alcohol in motor vehicle.
23225(a)(1)		Owner or driver allowing opened container in passenger area.
23225(b)		Driver allowing opened container in passenger area, registered owner not present.
23226(a)		No driver shall allow alcoholic beverages in passenger compartment, living quarters of campers and housecars exempted.
23226(b)		No passenger shall allow alcoholic beverages in passenger compartment, living quarters of campers and housecars exempted.
23229.1		Possession of alcohol in limousine passengers under age 21

Codes	Pts	Descriptions
23247(a)		Ignition interlock device, knowingly renting, leasing, or lending motor vehicle.
23247(b)		Ignition interlock device, soliciting another person to start vehicle.
23247(c)		Ignition interlock device, activating vehicle for driver.
23247(d)		Ignition interlock device, tampering with or circumventing operation of.
23247(e)		Operation of a vehicle which has been prohibited by a court order.
23253	1	Vehicular crossing or toll highway; failure to obey officer's lawful order.
23270(a)	1	Vehicular crossing; unauthorized towing or pushing.
23270(b)		Charging excessive fee for towing on vehicular crossing.
23301		Failure to pay toll crossing.
23302		Failure to pay the Pay-by-Plate toll payment
23302(a)		Vehicular crossing or toll highway; refusing to pay toll charge.
23302(b)		Failure to display transponder on specified vehicle crossing or toll highway.
23302(c)		Pay by plate vehicular crossing or toll highway, failure to have valid vehicle license plates and/or full monetary or electronic payment.
23302(d)		Pay by plate, electronic (only) vehicular crossing or toll highway, failure to have valid license plates and/or transponder or other electronic device payment in full.
23302.5(a)		Vehicular crossing or toll highway; evading toll charge.
23330		Vehicular crossing; (a) unauthorized use by animals, (b) bicycles, (c) overwidth vehicles, (d) carrying items prohibited by the Department of Transportation.
23330(c)	1	Overwidth.
23331		Vehicular crossing; unauthorized use by pedestrians.
23332		Vehicular crossing; person in unauthorized area.
23333		Vehicular crossing; unauthorized standing or parking.
23336	1	Vehicular crossing; failure to obey any sign or regulation.

Sentencing for Driving While Under the Influence, Division 11.5

Chapter 1 - Court-Imposed Penalties: Persons Less than 21 Years of Age (23500-23521)
Chapter 2 - Court Penalties (23530-23598)
Chapter 3 - Probation (23600-23602)
Chapter 4 - Procedures (23610-23675)
Chapter 5 - Ignition Interlock Device (23700-23702)
Selected entries displayed below are infractions that may show on a driving record

Codes	Pts	Descriptions
23502		DUI penalties for persons under 21 years of age: driving-under-the-influence-program
23520		Minors: alcohol or drug education program required
23521		Minors: out-of-state offence
23536		Minors: alcohol or drug education program required
23538		Conditions of probation: first conviction
23540		Penalty: second offense within ten years
23542		Conditions of probation: second offense within ten years
23546		Penalty: third conviction within ten years
23548		Conditions of probation: third conviction within ten years
23550		Driving under the influence, fourth or subsequent conviction within ten years.
23550.5(a)		Driving under the influence, within ten years of prior felony DUI conviction.
23552		Conditions of probation
23554		Penalty: first conviction
23556		Conditions of probation: first conviction
23558		Multiple victims: enhanced penalty
23560		Penalty: second conviction within ten years
23562		Conditions of probation: second offense within ten years
23566		Penalty of third or subsequent conviction within to years.
23568		Conditions of probation: third or subsequent conviction within ten years
23700		Ignition interlock device: pilot program - person is required to have a certified ignition interlock device installed
23572		Minor passenger: enhanced penalty
23573		Ignition interlock device: installation requirement
23575		Authorized and mandatory installation of ignition interlock device
23576		Exception for operation of vehicle
23577		Chemical testing: refusal to take or failure to complete: enhanced penalties
23578		Excessive blood alcohol or refusal to take chemical testing: enhanced penalties
23580		Repeat offenders: mandatory imprisonment
23582		Speeding: additional penalty

Codes	Pts	Descriptions
23592		Vehicle is impounded because of conviction of a serious nature
23593		Driver has been officially advised by the court about the dangers of driving under the influence
23594		The owner of a vehicle is notified that the vehicle was involved in a violation of Section 23152 or 223153 and that vehicle will be subject to being impounded
23596		Vehicle is declared to be a nuisance and will be sold – notification to legal owner
23600		Sentencing of DUI – minimum probation conditions
23601		Sentencing of DUI – payment of money
23602		Sentencing of DUI – penalty for violation of probation
23612		Implied Consent of chemical testing – testing procedures
23700		Pilot Program – Ignition Interlock Device – per rules under Section 13386

Equipment of Vehicles, Division 12

Chapter 1 - General Provisions (24000-24018)
Chapter 2 - Lighting Equipment (24250-26106)
Chapter 3 - Brakes (26301-26522)
Chapter 4 - Windshields and Mirrors (26700-26712)
Chapter 5 - Other Equipment (27000-28150)

Codes	Pts	Descriptions
24002(a)	1	Unsafe condition of vehicle, load, or equipment presenting immediate safety hazard.
24002(b)	1	Vehicle not properly equipped.
24002.5		Operating a farm labor vehicle that is in unsafe condition.
24003		Unlawful lights; other than those required or permitted.
24004	1	Unlawful operation; after notice by peace officer.
24005		Unlawful equipment; selling, offering for sale, installing, or replacing with.
24005.5		Sale of synthetic rope or webbing not certified to CHP.
24006		Unapproved equipment; selling or offering for sale.
24007(a)		Dealer; selling vehicle not in compliance with code.
24007(b)		Any person selling vehicle not in compliance with smog requirements.
24007.5(a)		Auctioneer, or public agency; vehicle not in compliance with code.
24007.5(b)		Auctioneer, or public agency; notify bidder that certificate of compliance required.
24007.5(c)		Auctioneer, or public agency; surrender certificates of registration, ownership, and plates to DMV.
24007.5(d)		Auctioneer, or public agency; provide bill of sale and license plate number.
24008(a)		Passenger vehicle or commercial vehicle under 6,000 pounds; clearance modified to less than rim height.
24008.5		Maximum frame height of vehicle less than 10,000 pounds; operation prohibited.
24009		Dealer; sale of new truck, truck-tractor, or bus without ID plate and GVW rating.
24010(a)		Vehicle rental; necessary equipment, conform to safety standards mechanically safe and sound.
24010(b)		Vehicle rental; vehicle not in compliance.
24010(c)		Vehicle rental agreement to include specified information.
24011		Sale of vehicle or equipment not in compliance with federal standards or not properly marked.
24011.3(a)		Manufacturer sticker affixed to passenger vehicle - bumper strength notice.
24012		Lighting equipment or devices; failure to comply with mounting requirements.
24013		Seller to inform buyer of minimum fuel-octane rating.
24013.5(a)		Light duty trucks; dealers not affixing pricing information.
24014(a)		Dealer offering for sale motorcycle without specific items.
24014(b)		Dealer offering motorcycle for sale without specified information on label.
24015(a)		Motorized bicycle; comply with National Motor Vehicle Act.
24015(b)		Motorized bicycle; mirror and muffler.
24016(b)(1)		Motorized bicycle; operation without properly fitted and fastened bicycle helmet.
24016(b)(4)		Motorized bicycle; operation by person under 16 years of age.
24016(b)(5)		Motorized bicycle; manufacturer shall certify compliance with equipment and manufacturing requirements for bicycle.
24016(c)		Motorized bicycle; tampering with or modifying to increase speed capability.
24017		Transit bus required to be equipped with a speedometer in good working order
24018(a)		Transit bus required to carry two-way communications device.
24026(b)(4)		Motorized bicycle; operation by person under 16 years of age.
24250	1	Driving without lights during darkness.
24252(a)		Lighting equipment of required type; maintain in good working order.
24252(b)		Voltage of required lamps to be 85 percent of design voltage.
24252(c)		Combined lamps; reflectors shall meet department specifications: (1) Turn signal shall not be combined with stop lamp (certain exceptions), (2) Clearance lamps shall not be combined with tail or identification lamps.
24253(a)		Adequate battery required on motor vehicle first registered after 1/1/70.
24253(b)		Adequate battery required on motorcycles first registered after 1/1/70.

Codes	Pts	Descriptions
24255(a)		Infrared lighting equipment violation
24255(b)		Operation of infrared lighting system without use of headlights.
24400(a)		Headlamps; at least two during darkness, height 22 to 54 inches.
24400(b)		Operated during darkness, inclement weather, or both with at least two lighted headlamps that comply with 24400(a).
24401		Parked vehicle; with lights on high beam.
24402(a)		Auxiliary driving lamps; two maximum, height 16 to 42 inches. Cannot be lighted with lower beam.
24402(b)		Auxiliary passing lamps; two maximum, height 24 to 42 inches.
24403		Fog lamps; number two, height 12 to 30 inches, properly adjusted.
24404(a)		Spotlamps; number two, not substituted for headlamps, white only.
24404(b)		Spotlamps; exceeding 32 c.p. or glaring light ahead.
24404(c)		Spotlamps; improper use on highway.
24404(e)		Spotlamps; directed to illuminate moving vehicle.
24405(a)		Forward lamps; not to exceed four lighted.
24406		Dimmer switch; driver unable to select proper light distribution.
24407(a)		High beam; project at least 350 feet.
24407(b)		Low beam; project at least 100 feet without glare.
24408(a)		High beam indicator required.
24408(b)		Readily visible; red or amber on exterior.
24409(a)	1	Failure to dim; within 500 feet of approaching vehicle.
24409(b)	1	Failure to dim; within 300 feet of overtaken vehicle.
24410(a)		Single beam; proper adjustment.
24410(b)		Single beam; project at least 200 feet.
24411		Off-highway lamps; more than allowed, not mounted properly, not covered, and fuses removed when operated on the highway.
24600		Tail lamp; during darkness, single vehicles and vehicles at end of combination must be equipped as follows:
24600(a)		Tail lamp - one required all such vehicles.
24600(b)		Tail lamp - two, all vehicles manufactured after 1/1/58, except motorcycles, trailers, and semi-trailers less than 30 inches wide.
24600(c)		Tail lamp - two all vehicles subject to 22406a.
24600(d)		Tail lamp - when two required, must have one on left, one on right side at same level.
24600(e)		Tail lamp - red, visible at 500 feet, all vehicles manufactured after 1/1/69.
24600(f)		Tail lamp - must be mounted 15 to 72 inches on vehicles manufactured after 1/1/69—additional lamps allowed on tow-truck masts.
24601		License plate light - render clearly visible from 50 feet.
24602(a)		Not more than 2 red fog taillamps mounted on rear when visibility less than 500 feet.
24602(b)		Fog taillamps; mounted as close as practical to sides, between 15 and 60 inches, 4 inches from stop lamp, wired properly, with switch, with nonflashing amber pilot light.
24603		Stop lamps; single vehicles and vehicles at end of combination must be equipped with one or more mounted as follows:
24603(a)		Stop lamps - every vehicle must be equipped with one or more.
24603(b)		Stop lamps - two required, vehicles manufactured after 1/1/58 (except motorcycles, trailers and semi-trailers less than 30 inches wide).
24603(c)		Stop lamps - mounted 15 to 72 inches on vehicles manufactured after 1/1/69—additional lamps allowed on tow-truck masts.
24603(d)		Stop lamps - when two required, one must be on left, one on right at same level.
24603(e)		Stop lamps - red or amber, visible at 300 feet, vehicles of size requiring clearance lamps must be visible at 500 feet.
24603(f)		Must be activated by foot brakes and by hand valve for power brakes. May be activated by sudden release of accelerator. Manual transmission; mechanical device to activate stop lamps.
24603(g)		Supplemental stop lamps installed after 1/1/79 shall be red and mounted not lower than 15 inches above roadway.
24604	1	Projecting load, four feet to rear, two red lights at night, 16-inch red flag otherwise.
24605		A tow truck or an automobile dismantler's tow vehicle used to tow a vehicle shall be equipped with and carry a taillamp, a stoplamp, and turn signal lamps
24605(a)		Tow truck or dismantler's tow vehicle; carry stop and tail lamp with extension cord.
24605(b)		Tow truck or dismantler's tow vehicle; display tail and stop lamp on rear of disabled vehicle.
24606(a)		Backup lamp required on vehicles subject to registration manufactured after 1/1/69.
24606(b)		Backup lamp; white only, beam not over 75 feet to rear.
24606(c)		Backup lamp; used other than when backing.
24606(d)		Vehicle may be equipped with supplemental backup lamps, lighted only with backup lights.
24607		Reflectors; vehicles subject to registration must be equipped at all times, as follows:
24607(a)		Reflectors - every vehicle must have one, visible 350 to 100 feet with upper beams.
24607(b)		Reflectors - every vehicle manufactured and first registered after 1/1/65, except motorcycles, low speed vehicles, trailers,

Codes	Pts	Descriptions
		and semi-trailers less than 30 inches wide, must have two.
24607(c)		Reflectors - motortruck with unladen weight of 5,000 pounds, trailer coach, vehicle at end of combination, vehicles 80 inches or more wide manufactured after 1/1/69, must have two visible at 600 to 100 feet with upper beams.
24607(d)		Reflectors - when more than one required; one must be on right, one on left at same level—additional reflectors may be mounted at any height, additional reflectors allowed on tow cars.
24608(a)		Reflectors - motortrucks, semitrailers, buses 80 inches wide manufactured after 1/1/68 must have amber reflector on each side at front, red reflector on each side at rear.
24608(b)		Reflectors - such vehicle 30 feet or more in length, shall have amber reflector on each side at midpoint.
24608(c)		Reflectors - on sides, must be mounted 15 to 60 inches—additional reflectors may be mounted at any height.
24608(d)		Reflectors - required or permitted by (a) and (b) must be visible at 600 to 1,000 feet with upper beam.
24609(a)		Reflectors - white or amber on front to be mounted 15 to 60 inches.
24610		Reflectors - button type, to contain not less than seven units with total area of not less than three square inches.
24612		Trailers/semitrailers of specified height/weight to be equipped with conspicuity system per federal standards.
24615		Slow-moving vehicle emblem; vehicles designed and operated 25 mph or less.
24616		Vehicles allowed one/two rear-facing auxiliary lamps meeting specified mounting standards.
24617		Violation of yield right of way, transit bus.
24800		Parking lights; driving with, unless headlamps also lighted.
24950		Trailer coach; turn signal lamps required.
24951(b1)		Turn signals required; passenger vehicles, trucks, truck tractors, buses manufactured and first registered after 1/1/58.
24951(b2)		Turn signals required; trailers and semitrailers manufactured and first registered between 12/31/57 and 1/1/69.
24951(b3)		Turn signals required; trailers and semitrailers 80 inches or more in width manufactured after 1/1/69.
24951(b4)		Turn signals required; motorcycles manufactured and first registered after 1/1/73. Except motor-driven cycles whose speed attainable in one mile is 30 mph or less.
24951(c)		Turn signals; vehicles manufactured after 1/1/69, 15-inch minimum height.
24952		Turn signal lamps; clearly visible 300 feet front and rear (500 feet for vehicles with clearance lamps).
24953(a)		Turn signal lamps; white or amber to front, red or amber to rear.
24953(b)		Side-mounted turn signals; mounted to rear of center must be red.
24953(c)(d)		Improper signal lamps
25100(a)		Vehicle over 80 inches: (1) clearance lamps - one amber each side on front, one red each side on rear; (2) Side-marker lamps - one amber each side near front, one red each side near rear; (3) One amber each side near center, if trailer over 30 feet; (4) One amber side marker midpoint of multi-purpose passenger vehicles, motor trucks, buses 30 feet in length manufactured after 1/1/69.
25100(b)		Vehicle over 80 inches not equipped under (a): (1) Truck-tractor, one amber clearance lamp each side on front of cab or sleeper, amber side-marker lamps ok on sides; (2) Truck-tractor manufactured and first registered after 1/1/69 one amber side marker on each side near front; (3) Pole or logging dolly, one red combination clearance and side-marker lamp each side; (4) Vehicles (except tractors) over 80 inches for three feet or less - if one near front, one amber combination lamp each side, if near rear, one red combination lamp each side; (5) Drive-away/tow-away towing vehicle - one amber clearance lamp each side on front, one amber side-marker lamp each side near front; (6) Drive-away/tow-away towed vehicle - one amber side-marker each side of intermediate vehicles one red side-marker lamp each side, and one red clearance lamp near each side on rearmost vehicle.
25100(c)		Loads over 80 inches extending beyond side: one amber combination lamp on side at front and red combination lamp on side at rear. If projecting load not over three feet front to rear - one amber combination lamp on side, if load near front, one red combination lamp on side if near rear of vehicle.
25100(e)		Visibility requirements.
25100(f)		Mounting requirements; required positions.
25102		Side lamps; recessed, not to exceed 2 c.p. or use color red.
25103(a)	1	Projecting load to left; amber light to front and rear.
25103(b)	1	Projecting load to left; amber light to front, red light to rear if projection exceeds 120 inches.
25104		Overwidth vehicles; display 16-inch red flag, left front and rear.
25105(a)		Running board lamps; 6 c.p., white or green without glare.
25105(b)		Door-mounted lamps or reflectors; 6 c.p., red.
25105(c)		Entrance/exit exterior lamps lighted only when vehicle motionless, lamp not to exceed 32 c.p. or 30 watts.
25106(a)		Front cowl or fender lamps, white or amber; 1 amber side lamp near front, 1 red side lamp near rear, 4 c.p. maximum.
25106(b)		Lamps installed within 24 inches of rear shall be red; all other locations amber.
25107		Cornering lamps; not over two, to reveal object while turning.
25108(a)		Exterior signal indicator lamps; amber, properly mounted, not exceeding 5 c.p., at night or 15 c.p. day.
25108(b)		Pilot indicators; steady burning, lighted lens area of not more than 3/4 of an inch, no more than 5 c.p., and not red.
25108(d)		Tow vehicle equipped with exterior mounted pilot lamp for antilock braking system; readily visible, not more than 5 c.p., shall not show to sides or rear, not red.
25109		Running lamps; two on front, white or amber, not lighted at night.
25110(b)		Utility flood or loading lamps; improper use of such devices.
25250		Flashing lights prohibited; exceptions listed.

Codes	Pts	Descriptions
25251(b)		Disabled vehicle on roadway; failure to activate flashing signal lamps.
25252		Authorized emergency vehicle; red lamp required.
25252.5(a)		Authorized emergency vehicles; flashing headlamps prohibited during darkness.
25252.5(c)		Flashing headlamps; permitted only (1) during emergency call or when in pursuit, (2) when red warning light displayed and siren is sounded.
25253(a)		Tow trucks; flashing amber warning lamps required.
25253(c)		Tow truck; shall not display flashing amber warning lamps on a freeway except when an unusual traffic hazard or extreme hazard exists.
25254		Marshal's cars; misuse of flashing amber warning lamp.
25257(a)		School bus; flashing red signal system required.
25257(b1)		School bus manufactured on or after 9-1-92, stop signal arm required.
25257(b2)		School bus manufactured on or after 7-1-93, amber warning light system required.
25257.2		School bus; transporting developmentally disabled, unlawful use of flashing red light signal.
25258.1		Use of flashing light by Sergeant at Arms or Court employees in emergency situations only.
25259(c)		Authorized emergency vehicles; not more than two flashing white lights to the front mounted on roof-line if concurrently displaying three red, blue or amber warning lights to the front.
25259.1(c)		Disaster service worker, must cover or remove flashing amber lights when not in use.
25259.5		American National Red Cross; flashing amber warning lights on other than emergency or disaster service vehicles.
25260.4		Amber warning lights on hazardous substance spill response vehicle must be covered when not engaged in a cleanup
25262		Armored cars; misuse of red light.
25265		Warning lights on sanitation vehicles not to be lighted when vehicle in motion.
25266		State aqueduct vehicle; misuse of flashing amber warning lamp.
25268		Flashing amber warning lights; improper use.
25269		Red warning lights; improper use.
25270		Pilot cars and vehicles; improper use of or failure to cover amber warning lamps.
25270.5		Livestock herding vehicles; misuse of flashing amber warning lamps.
25275.5		Improper use of flashing crime lights by bus driver.
25276(a)		Improper use of warning lamps by vehicle used to transport handicapped or mentally retarded.
25279(b)		Private security vehicle; misuse of flashing amber lights; distinctively marked on rear and two sides.
25279(d)		Private security vehicle; flashing amber warning system installed without written authorization of CHP.
25281		Water tender vehicles; misuse of flashing amber lights.
25300(a)		Warning devices required on vehicles subject to 25100 and any truck tractor.
25300(b)		Display; when truck or any trailer disabled on roadway.
25300(c)		Display; when parked or disabled within ten feet of roadway during darkness.
25300(e)		Display continuously during darkness; if disabled on roadway or parked within 10 feet.
25301(a)		Utility vehicles; failure to display proper warning devices during daylight.
25301(b)		Utility vehicles; failure to display proper warning device during darkness.
25305(a)		Fusee; used on highway.
25305(b)		Unlawful to use other than red fuse.
25350		Noncompliance with Vehicle Code Standards for illuminated identification signs.
25351(a)		Commercial vehicles and vehicles 80 inches or more in width; ID lamps front or rear but front not below windshield.
25351(b)		Vehicles manufactured prior to 1/1/68; ID lamps amber, green or white to front; red to rear.
25351(c)		ID lamps, vehicles manufactured after 1/1/68, may exhibit only amber to front and red to rear.
25351(d)		ID lamps unlawful on passenger vehicles.
25352(a)		Devices affecting traffic control signals on buses visible light not to exceed an average of .0003 candela per flash.
25352(b)		Public transit bus using signal sequence changing device on other than authorized routes.
25352(c)		Failure to give emergency vehicles priority in changing traffic control signals. 23353(a)Public transit buses, light and sign regulations.
25400(a)		Exterior light or device not to emit light more than .05 candela per sq inch of surface.
25400(b)		Diffused light; no red to front or interference with required lamps.
25400(c)		Diffused light; 720 square inches maximum, rental use limited.
25400(d)		Internally illuminated sign, no white background.
25401		Diffused light on vehicle resembling official traffic control device.
25452		Acetylene headlamps; emitting glaring light.
25500(a)		Reflectorizing material resembling or conflicting with any warning device or signal.
26506(b)		Airbrake warning device readily visible or audible with continuous warning.
25650		Motorcycles headlamps; one required, two permitted.
25650.5		Motorcycle have lighted headlamp if manufactured after 1/1/78.
25651(a)		Motor driven cycle headlamps; reveal person at 100 feet at 25 mph, 200 feet up to 35 mph, 300 feet over 35 mph.
25651(c)		Motor driven cycle; single beam headlamp adjustment.
25803(a)		All other vehicles - display white light front, red to rear, visible 500 feet.

Codes	Pts	Descriptions
25803(b)		All other vehicles - also display reflectors, amber left front and red left rear, height 16 to 60 inches, visible at 500 feet.
25803(c)		All other vehicles over 100-inch width - display on left extremity amber light at night, a red flag otherwise.
25805		Forklift trucks; not equipped with required lights when towed upon highway.
25950(a)		Front lights and reflectors; white or amber unless specifically permitted.
25950(b)		Rear lights; red unless specifically permitted.
25951		Front lights; adjustment of beam for other than driving lights.
25952(a)		Lamps, reflectors on load; failure to comply with mounting regulations.
25952(b)		Lamps on vehicle carried as load unlawfully lighted.
26100		Lighting equipment or devices; selling or using unapproved type.
26101		Lights or devices; selling or using unapproved modifying devices.
26301	1	Power brakes required on new motor vehicles 14,000 pounds; two stage actuators less than 18,000 pounds.
26301.5	1	Passenger vehicles manufactured after 1/1/73, except motorcycles; required to have dual master cylinder.
26302(a)	1	Brakes required on semi-trailer over 6,000 gross.
26302(b)	1	Brakes required on semi or trailer over 3,000 gross manufactured after 1/1/66.
26302(c)	1	Brakes required on all wheels of trailer or semitrailer manufactured after 1/1/82 and equipped with air brakes.
26302(d)	1	Brakes on trailers or semitrailers must be adequate to supplement brakes on towing vehicle.
26303	1	Brakes required in trailer coaches over 1,500 gross.
26304(a)	1	Breakaway device; required on certain trailers or semitrailers.
26304(b)	1	Breakaway device; required for trucks or truck tractors in combination.
26307	1	Brakes required on forklift-truck manufactured after 1/1/70 when towed upon highway.
26311(a)	1	Brakes required on all wheels of motor vehicles; exceptions.
26311(b)	1	Reduced braking to front wheels by manual means permitted only under adverse weather conditions.
26450	1	Brake systems; both service and parking required on motor vehicles.
26451(a)	1	Parking brake; adequate for load and grade.
26451(b)	1	Parking brake; separate means of application.
26451(c)	1	Parking brake held solely by mechanical means.
26452	1	Brakes on motor vehicle; adequate to stop vehicle after motor failure.
26453	1	Brake system defective; not in good working order or proper adjustment.
26454(a)	1	Service brakes; adequate for load and grade.
26454(b)	1	Service brake stopping distance requirements:
		(1) Passenger vehicle, 25 feet @ 20 mph;
		(2) Single vehicle under 10,000 pounds, or any bus, 30 feet @ 20 mph;
		(3) Vehicle in (1) or (2) in combination, 40 feet @ 20 mph;
		(4) Single vehicle over 10,000 pounds or any bus, 40 feet @ 20 mph;
		(5) All other combinations, 50 feet @ 20 mph.
26456	1	Brake tests in excess of 25 mph prohibited.
26457	1	Certain vehicles, 32 feet @ 15 mph, or not exceed speed permitting stop within 32 feet.
26458(a)	1	Single control; if motor vehicle or combo required to be equipped with power brakes.
26458.5	1	Additional control to operate the brakes on a trailer shall not be used in lieu of the service brake.
26502(a)	1	Airbrakes capable of full service application; deliver 90 percent of reservoir pressure.
26503	1	Safety valve; properly installed, adjusted and maintained.
26504	1	Air governor; adjust within CHP regulations.
26505	1	Pressure gauge required; maintain good condition, legible at all times.
26506(a)	1	Airbrakes, required warning system.
26507	1	Check valve; properly installed and properly maintained.
26508		Vehicles using compressed air to apply service brakes shall meet the following requirements:
	1	1a. Motor or towed vehicle - must have emergency stopping system;
	1	1b,c. Motor vehicle combo - both manual and automatic means to actuate emergency system of towed vehicle;
	1	1e. Service brake and emergency system - failure of one system not to affect other;
	1	1f. Emergency system - manually applied, released, and reapplied from drivers seat;
	1	1g. Service brake air failure - vehicle not to be driven;
	1	1h. Emergency system - must not increase stopping distance, nor interfere with service brake operation;
	1	1i. Energy-storing device - operating requirements;
	1	1j. Axle-by-axle protection system - separate air tank each axle or each valve;
	1	1k. Stopping distance requirements;
	1	1o. Owner instruct driver - driver able to demonstrate operation.
26520	1	Vacuum gauge; accurate and visible.
26521	1	Warning device; audible or visible, operate eight inches mercury.
26522	1	Check valve; between vacuum source and reserve.
26700		Windshields; required on passenger vehicle, trucks and fire apparatus.
26701(a)		Safety glazing material; required wherever glass is used.

Codes	Pts	Descriptions
26701(b)		Safety glazing material in campers; manufactured 1/1/68. Also in internal partitions and openings in the roof.
26701(c)		Safety glazing material; MC windshields manufactured after 1/1/69.
26701(d)		Prohibits red, blue, or amber translucent aftermarket material in partitions, windows, windshields of motor vehicles.
26701(e)		Safety glazing material in windows, doors, interior partitions, openings in roof of towed trailer coach.
26703(a)		Safety glazing material; replacing with other than.
26703(b)		Safety glazing material; replacing with anything other than.
26705		Motorcycle windshield; after 1/1/69 unlawful to sell unless contains safety glazing material.
26706(a)		Windshield wipers; required on all motor vehicles (except motorcycles).
26706(b)		Windshield wipers; two required vehicle first registered 1/1/50.
26707		Windshield wipers; maintain good condition, use when necessary.
26708(a)1		A person shall not drive any motor vehicle with any object or material placed, displayed, installed, affixed, or applied upon the windshield or side or rear windows.
26708(a)2		A person shall not drive any motor vehicle with any object or material placed, displayed, installed, affixed, or applied in or upon the vehicle that obstructs or reduces the driver's clear view through the windshield or side windows.
26708(13)(B)		Failure to post notice in of video recording in visible location.
26708(13)(C)		Storing more that 30 seconds of video either before or after a triggering event.
26708(13)(F)		Failure to provide unedited copies to employees/representatives free of charge within 5 days of request
26708.2		Sunscreen devices shall be removable.
26708.5		Application of transparent material to windows.
26708(14)		Placement of video camera in CDL – where located
26709(a)		Rear view mirror; required on all motor vehicles subject to registration, two on motor vehicle subject to California registration, with one on left-hand side.
26709(b)		Two side-view mirrors; required on certain vehicles or combos.
26710		Defective windshield or rear window; impaired drivers view, correct within 48 hours.
26711		Sun visor required on bus or trolley coach, except pre-60 in urban service.
26712		Adequate defroster required; for-hire passenger vehicle.
27000(a)		Horn required in good working order, audible within 200 feet but shall not emit unreasonably harsh or loud sound.
27000(b)		Garbage truck purchased after 9/1/83 equipped with automatic back-up alarm audible within 100 feet.
27000 (c)		Garbage truck purchased after 01/01/2010 shall also be equipped with a functioning camera providing a video display for the driver to use for safely maneuvering truck
27000(d)		Construction vehicle with GVWR in excess of 14,000 pounds equipped with automatic back-up alarm audible within 200 feet.
27001(a)		Shall use horn when reasonably necessary.
27001(b)		Use of horn, only as reasonably necessary.
27002		Siren; vehicle illegally equipped with or used on, or unapproved type.
27003		Armored car; misuse of siren.
27007		Outside speakers; except to warn of hazard or request assistance.
27150(a)		Mufflers; vehicle subject to registration not equipped with, or emitting excessive. noise
27150(b)		Mufflers; off-highway passenger vehicle not equipped with, or emitting excessive noise. Exceptions
27150.1		Exhaust system; sale, offering for sale, or installing system not in compliance with CHP regulations.
27150.3		Motorcycle exhaust system - whistle tip; offering for sale when not in compliance with CHP regulations.
27151		Exhaust systems; modified to amplify or increase noise.
27152		Exhaust pipes; directed to side between 2 to 11 feet.
27152.5		Prohibits on or after 1/1/93, the operation of any 1993 or later model-year bus which operates on diesel fuel unless the exhaust system discharges upward or to the rear.
27153		Exhaust products, excessive smoke, flame or residue.
27153.5(a)		New vehicle registered after 1/1/71 cannot discharge from exhaust more than ten seconds: (1) excess of No. 1 on Ringelman chart; (2) Smoke equal to opacity of No. 1 Ringelman.
27153.5(b)		Vehicle sold prior to 1/1/71 limited to: (1) No. 2 on Ringelman chart; (2) Smoke equal to opacity of No. 2 Ringelman.
27154		Exhaust system; not maintained in gas tight condition.
27155		Fuel tank caps required; of noncombustible material.
27156(a)		Gross Polluter, operated or left standing on a highway.
27156(b)		Smog Device, vehicle not equipped with device when required, or device has been disconnected or modified.
27156(c)		Smog device; shall not install, sell, offer for sale, or advertise any device which modifies pollution control device or system.
27156(f)		Smog Device, continued operation in violation after notice by peace officer.
27158		Motor vehicle smog device; unlawful to operate after 30 days following notification by traffic officer (except 1955-1965 year models).
27158.5		Motor vehicle smog device; unlawful to operate after 30 days following notice by peace officer (1955-1965 year model vehicles only).
27200(d)(e)		No person shall sell or offer for sale a motor vehicle not in compliance with noise standards.

Codes	Pts	Descriptions
27202.1		A person shall not park, use, or operate a motorcycle registered in this state that does not bear the federal exhaust system label. Applicable to motorcycles manufactured on or after January 1, 2013.
27302		Safety belts; selling approved type.
27304		Driver training vehicle; seat belts not installed or not in use.
27305		Fire-fighting vehicles; publicly owned, seat belts for all personnel.
27314(a)		Dealer selling 1962 or later used car without safety belts.
27314(b)		Dealer selling 1968 vehicle without belt for each passenger position.
27314(c)		Seatbelts to comply with CHP regulations.
27314.5(a)		Dealer selling or offering for sale 1972 to 1990 vehicle without seatbelt warning affixed to vehicle.
27314.5(b)		Dealer to affix notice, if supplied as specified, to rear seat lap belt of used 1972 to 1990 model vehicles.
27315		Mandatory seat belt laws
27315(d)		Safety belts; drivers, or passengers four years or older in private passenger motor vehicle (exempts taxi drivers on city streets).
27315(e)		Passenger over sixteen years restrained by safety belt.
27315(f)		Private-passenger vehicle safety belts; maintained in good working order.
27315.3(b)		Requires law enforcement agencies to maintain safety belts in good working order.
27317		Cannot improperly install or modify air bag, or install if the air bag has already been deployed.
27360	1	Unlawful for a parent or legal guardian to permit a child under eight years of age to be transported by vehicle without a child passenger-seat restraint system in rear seat unless the parent or legal guardian is also present and not driving.
27360.5	1	Unlawful for a driver, parent or legal guardian to permit a child over eight but under sixteen years of age to be transported by vehicle without a child passenger-seat restraint system unless the parent or legal guardian is also present and not driving.
27360.6		Child passenger restraint system: penalties and fines
27362(a)		Selling an unimproved child passenger-seat restraint system.
27362.1(a)		No person shall sell or offer for sell a child passenger restraint system that was in use during a traffic collision.
27363(b)	1	Violation child seat belt .
27363.5(a)		Hospitals to provide information on child passenger-seat restraint system law.
26365(a)		Car rental agencies shall post child restraint system notice as specified, 15X20 inches or larger.
26365(b)		Car rental agencies to provide child passenger restraint system.
27400		Wearing headset which covers both ears.
27450(a)		Solid tire; three to six inches wide, thickness one inch.
27450(b)		Solid tire; six to nine inches wide, thickness one and one-quarter inch.
27450(c)		Solid tire; over nine inches wide, thickness one and one-half inches.
27452		Solid tire; even thickness without flat spots, securely attached.
27453		Dual solid tires; diameters not to exceed one-eighth-inch variance.
27454		Projection on tires; metal studs, cleats, or flanges prohibited (snot studs OK first day of November through first day of April).
27455(a)		Selling unauthorized inner tube for use in a radial tire.
27455(b)		Installing unauthorized inner tube for use in a radial tire.
27459		Tire chains or snow-tread tires required when sign-posted; exceptions
27459.5		Selling, leasing, installing, or replacing unauthorized tire chains.
27460		Four-wheel driver with snow tires in lieu of chains, operated under adverse roadway conditions or when posted to require chains.
27460.5		Regrooved tire; selling passenger-type tire or vehicle so equipped.
27461		Regrooved tire; operating or permitting use on highway, except on commercial vehicle.
27465(a)		Dealers selling, installing tires with less than 1/32-inch tread.
27465(b)		Use of tire in chain control area with less than 6/32 inch tread, use of tires on motor vehicles specified in 34500 with less than 4/32 or 2/32 inch of tread.
27501(a)		Dealers, retail sellers prohibited from selling, installing tire not conforming with CHP regulations.
27501(b)		No person shall use tire not in conformance with CHP regulations.
27502		Dealers, retail sellers prohibited from selling, installing tire not in compliance with CHP tire-noise regulation.
27600		Mudguards required on vehicles subject to registration over 1,500 pounds.
27601		Radiator ornaments; selling or operating vehicle with protruding.
27602(a)		Operation of motor vehicle containing unauthorized video screen or TV monitor within view of driver.
27603		Former school bus; not repainted a different color (except 90-day transfer).
27604		Resale of police vehicles; removal of marking required.
27605		Operation of a vehicle painted in the same manner as a police vehicle described in Section 40800 prohibited.
27606(a)		Light bar or facsimile; owning or operating vehicle to resemble law enforcement vehicle.
27700(a)		Tow trucks; carry broom, shovel, and fire extinguisher.
27800	1	Motorcycle or motorized bicycle passenger; not provided with seat and footrests. Passenger not using footrests.
27801(a)	1	Motorcycle seat; operator unable to reach ground with feet.
27801(b)	1	Motorcycle handlebars; higher than 15 inches above depressed seat.

Codes	Pts	Descriptions
27802(b)		Sale of motorcycle safety helmets not meeting federal requirements prohibited.
27803(a)		Driver and passenger, wear approved helmet when riding on a motorcycle, motor-driven cycle, or motorized bicycle.
27803(b)		Unlawful to operate a motorcycle, motor-driven cycle, or motorized bicycle if driver or passenger is not wearing a safety helmet.
27083(c)		Unlawful to ride as a passenger on a motorcycle, motor-driven cycle, or motorized bicycle if driver or any passenger is not wearing a safety helmet.
27900(a)		For hire vehicles, or three-axle- truck or tractor, or tractor-semi combination; not displaying identifying name on both sides.
27900(b)		Identifying names; change within sixty days of changing ownership.
27901		For-hire vehicles; name or trade mark not readily legible.
27903		Hazardous cargo; not displaying signs in accordance with Health and Safety Code.
27904		Pilot cars; must display company name on both sides of the car.
27904.5		Pilot cars; shall display signs containing the word "oversize" or acceptable substitute, as required by permit.
27905		Fire or Fire Department signs; on other than authorized vehicle.
27906(a)		School bus shall bear word "School bus" in letters 8 inches high or greater on front and rear.
27906(c)		School bus, shall bear on rear below window sign with words "Stop When Red Lights Flash" 6 inches high or greater.
27906.5		Youth bus, transporting school pupils, signed front and rear with "Youth Bus" eight inches in height.
27907		Tow trucks; not displaying identifying name on both sides.
27908(a)		Operating taxicab without proper display of interior sign.
27909		Vehicle using liquified petroleum gas shall display letters "CNG," "LNG," or "LPG," one inch high near tank. After 1/1/83, may not dispense LPG into tank not marked.
28000		Refrigerator van; emergency exit required.
28050		Odometer alteration device; sell, offer for sale, install or use.
28050.5		Odometer defective; operation with fraudulent intent.
28051		Odometer disconnected, advanced, or turned back.
28051.5		Odometer; advertising for sale device designed to reset odometer.
28053(b)		Odometer repair; failure to adjust or affix notice.
28053(c)		Odometer notice affixed; remove or alter with intent to defraud.
28060(a)		Sale of recreational vehicle with cooking equipment without fire extinguisher.
28060(b)		Operator to maintain fire extinguisher.
28071		Passenger vehicles required to be equipped with bumpers, exception
28080(a)		Camper required to have passenger-signaling device.
28080(b)		Operating a camper which does not have a visual or audible signaling device.
28085(c)		Vehicle-theft alarm activated other than when parked.
28085(d)		Vehicle-theft alarm; emit sound of siren.
28090		Cellular telephone; failure of motor-vehicle renter to provide written instructions.
28100		Pilot car, display at least one flag (as specified) on each side of the vehicle. Remove when not operating as pilot car.
28101(a)		Pilot car, less than 60 inches in width.
28103		Pilot cars, failure to comply with provisions or equipment requirements.
28111		Any 1993 or later model-year vehicle which is capable of operating on methanol or ethanol shall be equipped with an anti-siphoning device.
28150(a)		Vehicle equipped with radar jamming device.
28150(b)		Possession of radar jamming device.
28150(d)		Possession of four or more radar jamming devices.

Towing and Loading Equipment, Division 13
2 Chapters Numbered 1 and 5 (29000-31560)

Codes	Pts	Descriptions
29001	1	Fifth wheel halves; not securely attached to vehicle.
29002	1	Fifth wheel; locking device inoperable or defective.
29003(a)	1	Hitch or coupling structurally inadequate or improperly mounted.
29003(b)	1	Drawbar or other connection; improperly attached or structurally inadequate.
29003(c)	1	Tow dolly; raised end of towed vehicle improperly secured.
29004(a)	1	Every towed vehicle shall be couple to towing vehicle using a safety chain or equivalent device in addition to regular connection.
29004(b)	1	Safety connection must be of sufficient strength to control towed vehicle.
29004(c)	1	Safety chain or equivalent device, no more slack than necessary
29004.5		Recreational vehicle; sold, manufactured without safety chain.
29005		Length of drawbar or connection not to exceed 15 feet.
29006(a)	1	Towing on freeway prohibited unless coupled by rigid device.
29200(c)		(Repealed) Logs and poles; transporting in violation of CHP regulations.
29201	1	(Repealed) Logs and poles; exempt from CHP regulations required to be safely loaded.

Codes	Pts	Descriptions
29800(c)		(Repealed) Lumber and lumber products; transporting in violation of CHP regulations.
30800(b)		(Repealed) Baled hay and straw; transporting in violation of CHP regulations.
31301(a)	1	Caldecott tunnel restrictions.
31303(b)	1	Transportation of hazardous waste on most direct route.
31303(c)	1	Hazardous waste transporter to avoid congestion, crowds, and residential districts.
31303(d)		Hazardous waste transport vehicles not to be left unattended.
31303(e)	1	Hazardous waste transporter; comply with provisions of transportation safety plan.
31304		No person shall transport specified hazardous materials near a reservoir owned or operated by a public water system or near a reservoir that directly serves a water treatment plant.
31307(a)		Owner or agent direct or permit the driving of a vehicle in violation of 31303 or 31304.
31400(a)		Workmen on trucks used regularly, seats securely mounted.
31400(b)		Workmen on trucks, side and end railing at least 46 inches high.
31400(c)		Workmen on trucks, steps or stirrups required.
31401(b)		Operating farm labor vehicle without required certificate.
31401(d)(f)		Farm labor buses and trucks; violation of CHP regulations.
31402	1	Operation of farm labor vehicle after notification that it is in an unsafe condition or not equipped as required.
31403		Owner or operator transporting passengers in farm-labor bus which is in an unsafe condition or not equipped as required.
31405(d)		No person may operate a farm labor vehicle on highway unless the driver and passengers are restrained by seatbelts.
31406(b)		Installation of seat or seating system in farm labor vehicle that is not compliant with Vehicle Code.
31407		Farm labor vehicle in motion with sharp tool unsecured or blocking aisle or exit.
31408		No person may operate a farm labor vehicle on highway unless both headlamps required under existing laws are lighted, regardless of time of day.
31500		(Repealed 2007) Trailer as a load; securely bound.
31501		(Repealed 2007) Rails and chocks for logging dolly; securely attached.
31510(d)		(Repealed 2007) Loads of metal products; in violation of CHP regulations.
31520(b)		(Repealed 2007) Baled cotton, paper or jute; violation of CHP regulations.
31530(b)		(Repealed 2007)Empty wooden boxes; transporting in violation of CHP regulations.
31540(b)	1	Removable freight van or tank containers; violation of CHP regulations.
31560(a)		Person operating a vehicle or combination of vehicles while transporting waste tires, shall be registered with the California Integrated Waste Management Board, unless specifically exempted.
31602(a-c)	2	Routes to be used for explosives transportation.

Transportation of Explosives, Division 14 (31600-31620)

Codes	Pts	Descriptions
31602(a)	2	License required to engage in such transportation.
31602(b)	2	Operating (or owner permitting) explosive vehicles outside designated routes.
31602(c)	2	Stopping at other than designated safe-stopping place.
31607(a)		Inspection required prior to transporting and other places.
31609		Record of inspection; maintain and display on demand.
31610		Required equipment; maintained in good order.
31610(a)		Vehicles transporting explosives; brakes and brake system maintained in good working order.
31610(b)		Vehicles transporting explosives; ignition and lighting maintained in good working order.
31610(c)		Vehicles transporting explosives; tires in good condition and properly inflated.
31610(d)		Vehicles transporting explosives; carry fire extinguishers.
31610(e)		Vehicles transporting explosives; shall not carry flame producing signal device.
31611		Owner supply map of routes, safe stopping places, and summary.
31612		Shipping instructions; carry and display on demand.
31613		Prohibited cargo; flammable or corrosive fluid, combustible material, detonators, etc.
31614(a)	1	Prescribed route through city.
31614(b)	1	Avoid congested areas.
31614(c)		Motor off and brakes set when loading or unloading.
31614(d)	1	Load contained entirely within body.
31614(e)	1	Load enclosed or covered.
31614(f)	1	Care in passing fire.
31614(g)		Vehicle unattended.
31614(h)	1	Smoking or open flame around vehicle.
31614(i)	1	Explosives in passenger vehicle subject to regulations.
31618		Violation of provision relating to transportation of explosives where not otherwise specified is a misdemeanor.

Transportation of Hazardous Material Division 14.1 (32000-32053)

Codes	Pts	Descriptions
32000.5(a)		Hazardous material; licensed, displayed.
32000.5(d)		Fireworks transportation; carry copy of license and present to peace officer upon request.
32001(c)		Hazardous material; motor carrier directing transportation.
32002(a)		Hazardous material; violate provisions of Division 14.1, or regulations.
32002(b)		Hazardous-material transportation; valid license.
32052(a)		Transportation of certain hazardous chemicals (32050); carrier must provide advanced notification.

Transportation of Inhalation Hazards, Division 14.3 (32100-32109)

Codes	Pts	Descriptions
32103(a)		Inhalation-hazard transporter; must have latest map showing routes, safe stopping places, and inspection stops.
32104(a)	1	Inhalation-hazard transporter; driving on other than designated route.
32104(b)	1	Inhalation hazard transporter; stopping or parking except where permitted.
32105(a)	1	Inhalation-hazard transporter; avoid listed areas, when possible.
32105(b)		Inhalation-hazard transporter; vehicle left unattended on highway.
32105(c)	1	Inhalation-hazard transporter; perform required inspection preceding. Transportation.
32105(d)	1	Inhalation-hazard transporter; perform required inspections at designated locations.
32105(e)	1	Inhalation-hazard transporters; maintain record of every inspection.
32106(a)	1	Vehicles transporting inhalation hazard; brakes maintained in good condition.
32106(b)	1	Vehicles transporting inhalation hazard; steering and lighting system maintained in good condition.
32106(c)	1	Vehicles transporting inhalation hazard; tires in good condition, matched, and inflated.
32106(d)	1	Vehicles transporting inhalation hazard; carry fire extinguishers as required.
32107		Inhalation-hazard transporter; must have self-contained breathing apparatus and communication equipment.

Transportation of Radioactive Materials, Division 14.5 (33000-33002)

Codes	Pts	Descriptions
33002		Notification to the CHP required prior to the transportation of any hazardous radioactive materials.

Flammable Liquids, Division 14.7 (34000-34100)

Codes	Pts	Descriptions
34049		Change of address; registrant notify CHP within fifteen days.
34100		Tank vehicle on highway; unregistered with CHP (exceptions).
34101		Tank vehicle; operation without valid certificate of compliance.
34101.5(a)		Cargo tank certificate of compliance; unauthorized possession or display.
34101.5(b)		Cargo tank certificate of compliance; unauthorized manufacture, possession, issue or display of facsimile.
34101.5(c)		Cargo tank certificate of compliance; alter, counterfeit, or falsify.
34102	1	Tank vehicle; failure to obey commissioner's regulations.

Safety Regulations, Division 14.8 (34500-34520.5)
Motor Carriers of Property Permit Act, Division 14.85 (33600-34672)

Codes	Pts	Descriptions
34500.3		Violation of cargo securement standards.
34501(a)	1	Limitation on driving hours.
34501(e)		Bus terminal or maintenance facility, bus operation without CHP inspection.
34501.1		Manufacturers and distributors of wheelchair lifts shall submit proof of safety certification to the CHP.
34501.2(b)1	1	Driving hours and duty status.
34501.2(b)2		Motor carrier requiring driver to exceed maximum hours of service.
34501.2(c)	1	Driving hours and duty status, agricultural drivers.
34501.3		Motor carriers - permit unlawful schedule
34501.3(a)		Motor Carrier requiring driver to exceed maximum hours of service.
34501.8(b)		General public para-transit vehicle; operation without required inspection. certificate
34501.10		Required records; employer must notify CHP of address where records are available for inspection.
34501.12(e)		Motor carrier; failure to submit application and fees for original and subsequent inspection.
34501.12(f)		Motor carrier; operating without having submitted inspection application and fees.
34501.12(g)		Unlawful for motor carrier to operate any vehicle without inspection performed and safety compliance report issued within the prescribed period (effective 7/1/92).
34501.12(h)		Failure to apply for re-inspection.
34501.14(b)		Failure to apply on or before 7-1-93 for grape gondola inspection.
34501.14(c)		Operation of grape gondola on or after 7-1-93 not having applied for inspection.

Codes	Pts	Descriptions
34501.14(d)		Operation of grape gondola on and after 1-1-95 without being inspected and certified.
34501.15(a)		The regulations adopted pursuant to Section 34501 shall require that any driver of a commercial motor vehicle, as defined in Section 15210, be ordered out of service for 24 hours if the driver is found to have 0.01 percent or more, by weight, of alcohol in his or her blood.
34501.17(a)		Failure to inspect, maintain or lubricate para-transit vehicle.
34501.17(b)		Failure to document inspection and maintenance information; maintain records at place of business; present documentation to CHP; maintain odometer or para-transit vehicle.
34501.18		Motor carriers employing more than 20 full-time drivers required to report to CHP when more than half of their drivers are replaced in a 30 day period.
34505(a)		Tour bus required to be inspected every 45 days.
34505(b)		Tour bus not to be operated until defects corrected.
34505(c)		Tour bus records of inspection to be retained in garage where tour bus kept for 1 year and include specified information. Records must be maintained at motor carrier's terminal, include specified information, and retained for 2 years.
34505.5(a)		Motor carrier inspect vehicles every 90 days.
34505.5(b)		All defects noted must be repaired prior to operation.
34505.5(c)		Records must be maintained at motor carrier's terminal for 2 years.
34505.10		Motor carriers failure to retain required records of contracted transportation service.
34506(a)	1	Driving hours; failure to comply.
34506(b)	1	Hazardous materials; failure to comply.
34506(c)	1	School bus construction, design, color, equipment, maintenance, or operation; failure to comply.
34506(d)	1	Provides a penalty for failing to comply with regulations regarding youth bus equipment, maintenance or operation.
34506(e)	1	Provides a penalty for failing to comply with regulations regarding tour-bus equipment, maintenance or operation.
34506(f)	1	Commercial vehicles; failure to comply with any equipment, maintenance, or operation regulation.
34506(g)	1	School pupil activity bus; equipment, maintenance or operation.
34506.3	1	Inspection of vehicles; failure to comply.
34506.4(a)		Any motor truck with a gross vehicle weight rating of more than 10,000 pounds, which is in an unsafe condition can be placed in storage by Highway patrol.
24506.4(b)		Motorized farm equipment which is in an unsafe condition can be placed in storage by Highway patrol.
34507		Failure of motor carrier subject to PUC or ICC to have such identifying number or symbol displayed on vehicle.
34507.5(a)		Motor carrier; must make application for a carrier identification number unless exempted.
34507.5(b)		Motor carrier; failure to display carrier identification number.
34507.5(e)		Identification number shall be legible from a distance of 50 feet.
34507.7(f)		When no longer in business, identification markings shall be removed.
34507.6(a)		Bus carrier identification number, shall obtain from CHP.
34507.6(b)		Bus carrier identification number, properly displayed.
34509(a)		Vanpool vehicle, equipped with fire extinguisher.
34509(b)		Vanpool vehicle, equipped with first aid kit.
34509(c,d)	1	Vanpool vehicle, inspections must be documented and maintained with vehicle for one year, present to any authorized representative of CHP.
34509(e)		Proper display, identifying as a vanpool vehicle.
34510(a)		Vehicles transporting hazardous material subject to Division 14.8 shall carry shipping papers; must display to officer upon demand.
34510(b)		Intermodel transportation vehicles with cargo weight exceeding 10,000 pounds shall carry certificate of actual gross cargo weight and description of container contents; must display to officer upon demand.
34510.5		Failure of broker of construction truck services to secure a surety bond while providing services.
34516		Prohibits the use of certain vehicles to transport food products for human consumption, if the vehicles have been used to transport solid waste.
34517(a)		Prohibits operation outside boundaries of designated commercial zone of vehicle from another country without prior approval of US DOT.
34518		Violation of regulation for foreign motor carriers.
34518(a)		Foreign motor vehicle, operation without certificate.
34518(b)		Foreign motor vehicle, operating beyond limitations or restrictions of certificate.
34518(c)		Foreign motor carrier shall not operate a vehicle unless inspected by a Commercial Vehicle Safety Alliance inspector every three months.
34520(a)		Motor carriers and drivers comply with federal drug and alcohol use and testing requirements.
34520(b)		Motor carrier make available copies of results and records of drug and alcohol use and testing.
34520(c)		Testing consortium mail positive drug and alcohol test results summaries to the California Highway Patrol within 3 days of test.
34520(e)		Motor carriers and drivers must comply with federal drug and alcohol testing, including when hired.
34520.5(a)		Failure of employer of driver of para-transit vehicle to participate drug and alcohol testing program.
34520.5(c)		Failure of employer of driver of para-transit vehicle to participate in pull notice program.

Codes	Pts	Descriptions
34620(a)		Motor carrier of property, operating without registering is carrier ID with DMV.
34620(b)		Contracting or subcontracting with motor carrier of property without certification.
34623(c)		Motor carrier permits suspended for failure to comply with Section 34520.
34623(g)		Motor carrier of property operating when permit suspended.
34623(h)		Motor carrier of property who is suspended may not operate vehicles under suspension when suspended.
34623.1		The motor carrier permit of a licensee may be suspended if a licensee's name is included on a certified list of tax delinquencies provided by the State Board of Equalization or the Franchise Tax Board pursuant to Section 7063 or Section 19195, respectively of the Revenue and Taxation Code.
34660(a)		A motor carrier of property which continues to operate as a motor carrier after its permit has been suspended by the Department of Motor Vehicles.

Motor Vehicle Damage Control, Division 14.9 (34700-34725)

Codes	Pts	Descriptions
34715(a)		Sale of passenger vehicle manufactured after 9/1/73 without warranty of energy- absorption system.

Size, Weight, and Load, Division 15

Chapter 1 - General Provisions (35000-35003)
Chapter 2 - Width (25100-35111)
Chapter 3 - Height (35250-35252)
Chapter 4 - Length (35400-35414)
Chapter 5 - Weight (35550-35796)

Codes	Pts	Descriptions
35100(a)		Limitations on width.
35100.5		Cotton module mover; width 130 inches.
35101		Width; 108 inches to outside of tires.
35102		Loose agricultural products; 120 inches.
35103(a)		A vehicle used for recreational purposes may exceed the maximum width established under Section 35100 if the excess width is attributable to an appurtenance, excluding a safety device, that does not exceed six inches beyond either sidewall of the vehicle.
35104		Special mobile or construction equipment; not to exceed 120 inches.
35106(a)		Motor coaches and buses, maximum width 102 inches.
35106(b)		Specified motor coaches and buses, maximum width 104 inches.
35106(c)		Specified motor coaches and buses operating within a local ski area, maximum width 106 inches.
35109		Required devices; ten inches each side, not to exceed 120 inches total width.
35110		Projecting equipment; three inches each side.
35111		Passenger vehicles; projecting load to left, or over six inches to right.
35231		Boom or mast with hydraulic mechanism secured by chain while vehicle being transported.
35250		Height; vehicle 14 feet.
35251(a)		Boom or mast with hydraulic mechanism secured by chain while vehicle being transported.
35252(b)		Pilot car; vertical measuring device securely attached with no damage to overhead structures and no hazard to surrounding traffic.
35252(c)		Pilot car operator; shall not slow 20 mph below speed limit or exit vehicle to measure clearance.
35400(a)		Length; single vehicle 40 feet.
35400(b0(6)		An operator of a school bus shall not extend a crossing control arm while the School bus is in motion.
35400(e)		Properly mount bicycle on front of bus or trolley.
35401(a)		Length of combinations; 65 feet (exceptions).
35401(b)		Length of combinations; 75 feet (exceptions).
35401.3		Combination of Vehicles: Additional Exceptions
35401.5		Combination of Vehicles: Additional Exceptions
35401.7		Combination Vehicles: Access Limits: Exception
35401.8		Vehicle Length: Transportation of Agricultural Biomass
35402		Extension Devices
35403		Safety Devices
35404		Prohibiting Highway Use; Vehicle Size
35406(a)		Load to front; not over three feet (with exceptions).
35406(b)		Load of motor vehicles; not to extend over four feet to front.
35408		Front bumper; not to extend over two feet forward.
35410		Projections to rear; not to exceed two-thirds wheelbase.
35411(a)		Length of combination and load, 75 feet (except poles or pipes).
35411(b)		Load shall be contained within the exterior dimensions of the vehicle, when the combination of vehicle exceeds 75 feet.
35550(a)		Weight on axle, 20,000 pounds; one end of axle, 10,500 pounds; steering axle motor vehicle, 12,500 pounds.

Codes	Pts	Descriptions
35551(a)		Exceeding allowable weights for consecutive axles.
35551.5		Exceeding allowable weight limits for consecutive axles.
35554		Weight on any one axle of a bus not to exceed 20,500 pounds.
35600		Solid tires; weight not to exceed 600 pounds per inch of base width.
35601		Metal tires; not to exceed 500 pounds per inch of base width.
35655(a)		Load restriction on state highway; exceeding posted limit.
35655.6		Except as provided in subdivision (b), a person shall not drive a commercial vehicle with three or more axles, or a gross vehicle weight or a combined gross weight of 9,000 pounds or more, on the segment of State Route 2 (SR-2) that is located between Interstate Route 210 (I-210) in the City of La Canada Flintridge and County Route N4 (Big Pine Highway) in the County of Los Angeles
35700.5		Requires special permits designated for overweight vehicles in designated routes
35753(a)		Weight limit on bridges; exceeding posted limit.
35780.5		Permit ofr exceeding maximum width: unlawful to violate special regulations.
35783		Special permit; carry and display upon demand.
35783.5		Warning signs removed or covered.
35784(a,b)	1	Special permit (size, weight, etc.); violation of terms.
35784(c)		Extra legal load; not on prescribed route.
35784.5(a,b)	1	Extra legal load; transporting without permit.
35785(b)		Single saw log under permit; 15 mph on bridge, 25 mph on highway.
35786(b)		Truck booster power unit operating in violation of permit.
35789		House mover; notify R.R. 36 hours before crossing.
35790(g)		Overwidth manufactured home; permit to be carried in manufactured home or power unit.
35790(h)		Violating terms of permit.
35790.1 (b-n)		Overwidth Manufactured Homes: Additional Requirements for Movement on Highway

Implements of Husbandry, Division 16
8 Chapters (36000-36800)

Codes	Pts	Descriptions
36300		Driver of farm tractor required to possess license of proper class.
36305		Implement of husbandry; driver towing or operating combination of vehicles in excess of 25 mph, not possessing valid Class 3 driver's license.
36400	1	Lift-carrier; 35 mph speed limit.
36508		Slow-moving vehicle emblem; display of, on implements of husbandry only.
36509(b)		Implement of husbandry or farm vehicle towing loads exceeding 120 inches in width, not displaying flashing amber signals or red flags.
36510		Implement of husbandry stopping distance, 32 feet at 15 mph, or speed permitting stop within 32 feet.
36600(b)		Implements of husbandry on federal highway operating in excess of 25 miles of point of origin; operator not a farmer or farm employee, operator does not possess written origin and destination.
36600(c)		Implement of husbandry on highway operating in excess of 25 miles from point of origin; operator not a farmer or farm employee, operator does not possess written origin and destination.
36605		Trailers and lift-carriers used exclusively, width not to exceed 120 inches. Trailers transporting grain harvesters not to exceed 144 inches.
36705	1	Automatic bale wagon exceeding 96 inches wide or load exceeding 100 inches wide operated on highway during darkness.

Off-Highway Vehicles, Division 16.5
5 Chapters – (38000-38506)

Codes	Pts	Descriptions
38010(a)		Vehicles not registered and used exclusively off-highway required to display I.D. plate. Exceptions.
38020		Off-highway vehicles, not registered, required to be identified.
38026.5(b)		Prohibited operation of off-highway vehicles on designated combined-use highways.
38027		Off-highway vehicles moved by non-mechanical means.
38060(a)		Change of address, notify DMV within 10 days.
38060(b)		Change of address, owner to change on certificate.
38085(a)		Identification certificate, owner maintain with vehicle.
38090		I.D. certificate or plates, stolen, lost, mutilated, or illegible, owner immediately apply for duplicate.
38095		Certificate of ownership, stolen, lost, mutilated, or illegible, owner immediately apply for duplicate.
38170(a)		I.D. plate required to be displayed.
38170(b)		I.D. plate, securely attached and clearly visible. No covering.
38170(c)		ID plates, properly displayed.
38200(a)		Transfer of ownership, dealer notify DMV.
38200(b)		Unlicensed dealer of off-highway vehicles immediately notify DMV of change of ownership.
38205		Transfer of ownership, transferee notify DMV within 10 days.

Codes	Pts	Descriptions
38300		Failure to obey any sign, signal, or traffic control device.
38301		Prohibited operation of a vehicle in violation of special regulations which have been promulgated by the governmental agency having jurisdiction over public lands.
38301.3		Prohibited operation of a vehicle in a designated wilderness area.
38302		Unlawful to erect any sign, signal, or traffic control device unless authorized by law.
38304		Operator unable to reach or operate all vehicle controls.
38304.1		Ability to reach and operate controls: persons under 14.
38305		Off-highway prima facie speed limit.
38312		Unsafe start.
38314		Unsafe turning movement.
38316(a)		Reckless driving; willful and wanton disregard for safety of persons or property.
38317		Reckless driving causing injury.
38318(a)		Throwing a substance at an off-highway motor vehicle or occupant.
38318(b)		Throwing a substance with intent to do great bodily injury.
38318.5(a)		Maliciously removes or alters trail, danger, or directional markers.
38318.5(b)		Maliciously with intent to do great bodily harm, erects or places chain, cable, rope, etc.
38319		Illegal to operate or own vehicle which is operated in a manner which harms the environment.
38320(a)		Littering.
38320(b)		Illegal dumping.
38330		Unsafe vehicle; condition.
38335		One lighted headlamp required during darkness.
38345		One lighted red taillamp required during darkness.
38346		Shall not display a flashing or steady burning red or blue warning light on an off-highway motor vehicle except as permitted by Section 21055 or when an extreme hazard exists.
38355(a)		Service brake required on off-highway vehicles.
38365(a)		Adequate mufflers required on off-highway vehicles.
38370		Persons selling new off-highway vehicles subject to identification which produces maximum noise.
38390		Off-highway vehicle without emission control.
38391		Illegal to offer/sell off-highway vehicle without emission control.
38393		Operating off-highway vehicle after notification of no/illegal emission control.
38503		Person under 18 operating all-terrain vehicle on public lands without safety permit.
38504 (&.1)		Person under 14 operating all-terrain vehicle on public lands not supervised by adult.
38504.2		Court ordered safety training course.
38505		Must wear safety helmet when operating or riding all-terrain vehicle on public lands.
38506		No operator of an all-terrain vehicle shall carry a passenger when operating on public lands except under specific circumstances.
38601		A person shall not operate, or allow a passenger in, a recreational off-highway vehicle unless the person and the passenger are wearing safety helmets meeting the requirements established for motorcycles and motorized bicycles
38602		A person operating, and any passenger in, a recreational off-highway vehicle shall wear a seatbelt and shoulder belt or safety harness that is properly fastened when the vehicle is in motion.
38603		A person operating a recreational off–highway vehicle shall not allow a passenger to occupy a separate seat location not designed and provided by the manufacturer for a passenger.
38604		A person operating a recreational off–highway vehicle shall not ride with a passenger, unless the passenger, while seated upright with his or her back against the seatback, can grasp the occupant handhold with the seatbelt and shoulder belt or safety harness properly fastened.

Autonomous Vehicles, Division 16.6
(38750)

Registration and Licensing of Bicycles, Division 16.7
(39000-39011)

Codes	Pts	Descriptions
39002(a)		Operation of unlicensed bicycle where license required.
39002(b)		Tampering, mutilating or altering bicycle license indicia, registration forms, bicycle serial numbers or identifying mark on bicycle frame.
39006(a)		Bicycle retailer to provide bicycle ID information.
39007		Sale of bicycle after 12/31/76 without ID number stamped in frame.
39008(a)		Failure to notify licensing agency of sale of bicycle, within 10 days.
39008(b)		Failure of owner to apply for transfer of license, within 10 days.
39009(a)		Failure to notify within ten days of address change.
39009(b)		Bicycle license indicia or registration form lost, stolen, or mutilated; immediately notify licensing agency and apply for duplicate within 10 days.

Offenses and Prosecution, Division 17

Chapter 1 - Offenses (40000-40273)
Chapter 2 - Procedure on Arrests (40300-40618)
Chapter 3 - Illegal Evidence (40800-40834)
Chapter 3.5 - Evidence (40900-40903)
Chapter 4 - Presumptions (41100-41104)
Chapter 5 - Defenses (41400-41403)
Chapter 6 – Non-prosecution of Violations (41500-41501)
Chapter 7 - Arrest Quotas (41600-41603)
Chapter 8 - Consolidated Disposition (41610)

Codes	Pts	Description
40000.7		Salvage vehicle rebuilder, failing to provide buyer with CHP inspection report or DMV verification form.
40000.20		Classifies as a misdemeanor a third or subsequent violation of Section 23225, relating to the storage of an opened container of an alcoholic beverage, or Section 23223, relating to the possession of an open container of an alcoholic beverage, of a driver of any vehicle used to provide transportation services on a prearranged services
40001(a)		Owner, or person directing driver, causing unlawful operation on highway; including railroad-highway grade crossing.
40001(b)	1	Owner requesting or permitting operation of a vehicle which: **(no points if driver is not owner)**
	1	(1) Is unregistered or has fees due;
	1	(2) Is not equipped as required;
	1	(3) Does not comply with size, weight, or loading requirements;
	1	(4) Does not comply with administrative regulations;
	1	(5) Does not comply with smog device requirements.
40005		Owner or person directing driver; failure to dispose of driver's citation after agreement.
40008(a)		Violating VC Sections 21701, 21703, or 23103 with the intent to get a visual image, sound recording, or other physical impression of another person for a commercial purpose.
40008(b)		Violating VC Sections 21701, 21703, or 23103 with the intent to get a visual image, sound recording, or other physical impression of another person for a commercial purpose and endangering the person or health of a minor child or children.
40240		Parking violation on transit-only traffic lane, video imaging of
40254(b)		Notice of toll evasion violation; tampering with notice.
40500		Alter, conceal, modifies, nullifies, or destroys citation before it is filed with magistrate.
40504(b)		False signature; given on written notice to appear.
40505		Traffic Officer failing to include all court information on violator's copy of citation.
40508(a)		Failure to appear after signing citation or court continuance.
40508(b)		Failure to pay installment fine for violation of Division 11.
40508(c)		Failure to comply with condition of a court order.
40509		Notice to Department by court – failure to appear, pay fine, or obey court order
40509.1		Person has willfully failed to comply with a court order, except a failure to appear, to pay a fine, or to attend traffic violator school, which was issued for a violation of this code, the court may give notice of the fact to the department.
40509.5		Failure to appear – Notice given to Department by the court
40512		Forfeiture of bail
40518		Automated traffic enforcement systems notice to appear
40519(b)		Failure to appear; written plea.
40610		Notice to correct violation.
40614		Signing a notice to correct or a certificate of correction with a false or fictitious name.
40616		Willful violation of a written promise to correct or willfully failing to deliver proof of correction.

Penalties/Disposition of Fees, Fines, and Forfeitures, Division 18

Chapter 1 - Penalties (42000-42032)
Chapter 2 - Disposition of Fees, Fines, and Forfeitures (42200-42235)
Chapter 3 - Motor Vehicle Account (42270-42277)

Codes	Pts	Descriptions
42003(a)		Failure to pay fine; contempt.
42005(e)		Failure to attend traffic school or court ordered driving instruction.
42032		Authorizes assessment of a civil penalty against local public agencies operating garbage/refuse/rubbish collection vehicles that continuously violate weight limits.

California Penal Code Violations

Driving records may have indications about Penal Code violations, with a "PC" indicator. The general topics of the subjects are listed below.

Section	Penal Code Subject
16	Crimes- How Divided
19c	Punishment For Infractions
19d	Application Of Provisions Of Law To Infractions
118	Penalty Of Perjury
118.1	Penalty Of Perjury
146b	Simulating Official Inquiries
146e	Simulating Official Inquiries

Section	Penal Code Subject
148	Resisting, Delaying, Obstructing Officer
148.3	False "Emergency" Reports
148.5	False Report Of Criminal Offense
171 D	Bringing Loaded Firearm To Residences Or Adjoining Grounds Of State Officials
191.5	Gross Vehicular Manslaughter While Intoxicated
192	Manslaughter
192.C1	Vehicular Manslaughter
192.C2	Vehicular Manslaughter
192.C3	Vehicular Manslaughter
192.5	Vehicular Manslaughter
193	Manslaughter
193.5	Manslaughter Committed With Operation of a Vessel
193.7	Habitual Traffic Offender
193.8	Adult Allows Intoxicated Minor to Operate Motor Vehicle
219.1	Throwing Objects At Common Carrier Vehicles
219.2	Throwing Objects at Train, Bus, or Vessel
219.3	Throwing Objects From Toll Bridge
243A	Battery
243B	Battery-Officer
245A	Assault With A Deadly Weapon
246	Discharging A Weapon Where Prohibited
247	Shooting At Aircraft
369G	Trespassing On Railroad Right Of Way
370	Public Nuisance
374	McCarthy-Walsh Anti Litter Act
374c	Shooting Firearms From A Public Highway
415	Penal Code - Disturbing The Peace
417A	Weapon In Vehicle
459	Penal Code - Burglary
466.5	Master Keys
466.9	Master Keys
470	Forgery
470A	Forgery Of Drivers License Or Identification Card
470B	Possession or Permits Display Of Forged Drivers License Or Identification Card
484A	Penal Code - Theft By Fraudulent Means
484	Theft By Fraud
490.5	Petty Theft From A Library
496d	Obtain Motor vehicle, Vessel or Special Construction Equipment By Theft
499	Anti Theft Laws
529a	False Birth Identification Document
529.5C	Deceptive Identification Document
529.7	Assist With Deceptive Identification Document
530.5	Deceptive Identification Document
530.6	Deceptive Identification Document
530.7	Deceptive Identification Document
550A4	Penal Code- False/Fraudulent Insurance Claim
570	Unlawful Subleasing
571	Unlawful Subleasing of Motor Vehicle
572	Unlawful Transfer or Assignment of Interest in Motor vehicle
602(n)	Trespassing With Vehicle
602.8	Trespass
818	Issuance Of A Notice To Appear
830	Peace Officers
830.3	Peace Officers
1320A	Failure To Appear As Required
2813.5	Director Of Corrections: Sale Of Vehicles
11102	Penal Code - Fingerprinting
22900	Knowing Sells, Possess or Transports Tear Gs Weapons

Out-Of-State Violations

Report Code meanings:

01	Non reportable
03	Report for 36 months from violation date
07	Report for 7 years from violation date
CDL	Report for 55 years from violation date

NOTE: Violations which occur while driving a commercial or hazardous material vehicle are assessed a point count of 1.5 times greater than listed.

Codes	Pts	Report Code	Descriptions
01	1	03	Speed too fast or over speed limit
02	2	07	Speed contest and/or aiding or abetting
03	1	03	Speed; too slow, impeding, blocking, or failure to turn out
04	1	03	Passing; illegal, improper or unsafe
05	1	03	Following too close
06	1	03	Failure to yield right-of-way
07	1	03	Lane change: Illegal, unsafe use of change lanes
08	1	03	Turns: Illegal or unsafe turns
09	1	03	Failure to signal when turning or stopping or giving improper signal
10	1	03	Failure to stop or obey traffic signal, light, sign/device when
11	1	03	Crossing over double lines, markers or dividers
12	1	03	Driving wrong way on one-way street
13	1	03	Defective, unsafe or inadequate brakes
14	1	03	Defective, unlawful, inadequate lights or lamps or failure to use legally
15	2	07	Reckless driving, without injury
16	2	07	Reckless driving, with injury
17	2	07/CDL	Drunk driving
18	2	07/CDL	Drunk driving, with bodily injury
19	2	07/CDL	Hit-and-Run violation
20	2	07	Driving while suspended or revoked
21	1	03	Violation of a restricted license except insurance restrictions
22	0	03	Violation of insurance restrictions
23	0	03	Unlawful use of license
24	0	03	Unlicensed Driver; License expired, none in possession, driving out of class or failure to display on lawful demand
25	0	03	Permitting an unlicensed driver to operate a motor vehicle
26	1	03	Negligent, careless or inattentive driving
27	1	03	Illegal or improper starting or backing
28	1	03	Prohibited driving; driving in or across prohibited area
29	0	03/CDL	Illegal possession of alcohol or drugs in motor vehicle
30	1	03	Obedience to lawful order; Failure to obey order of police officer, fireman or school safety patrol
31	1	03	Improper, unsafe, or illegal towing
32	1	03	Obstructing driver's view or interfering with driver or mechanism
33	1	03	Unlawful riding on a motor vehicle
34	1	03	Illegal entry or exit from main thoroughfare
35	2	07	Habitual offender
36	0	03	Opening vehicle closure into moving traffic or while vehicle is in motion
37	2	07/CDL	Driving under the influence of narcotics
38	2	07/CDL	DUI; other than narcotics
39	0	03	Littering
40	1	03	Modified vehicle
42	0	03	Length or improper loading violation
43	0	03	Failure to appear
44	0	03	Failure to pay fine
45	1	03	Violation of regulations for carrying explosions
46	2	07	Manslaughter; without gross negligence
47	2	07	Manslaughter; with gross negligence
48	0	03	Grand theft of motor vehicle
49	0	03	Joy Riding
50	0	03	Failure to change address
51	1	03	Equipment; unsafe, illegal, improper or defective
52	0	03	Registration violation
53	1	03	Coasting
54	0	01	Use or possession of narcotics or dangerous drugs
55	0	03	Falsifying information to obtain license
56	0	03	Tampering with a motor vehicle/malicious mischief
57	0	03	Failure to fulfill legal obligations following an accident
58	1	03/CDL	Driving while impaired
59	0	03	Violation of safety belt requirement (driver)
60	0	03	Violation of safety belt requirement (passenger)
61	1	03	Child passenger-seat restraint

Codes	Pts	Report Code	Descriptions
62	0	03	No evidence of required financial responsibility
63	0	03	False evidence of financial responsibility
64	0	03/CDL	Refusal to submit to chemical test
65	0	03	Leaving unattended vehicle with engine running
66	0	03	Creating unlawful noise with vehicle or accessory
67	1	03	Defective headlights
68	0	03	Using a motor vehicle in connection with illegal activity, except felony
69	1	03	Following an emergency vehicle unlawfully
70	1	03/CDL	Using a motor vehicle in connection with/or aid and abet a felony
71	0	03	Sex offense in a motor vehicle
72	1	03	Operating at erratic or sudden-changing speeds
73	1	03	Evading arrest by extinguishing lights (when lights required)
74	1	03	Unsafe operation of vehicle
75	1	03	Ran-off road or driving on road shoulder, in ditch, or on sidewalk
76	1	03	Crossing fire hose with vehicle
77	1	03	Operating without required equipment or use of prohibited equipment
78	0	03	Required reports, appearance or documents
79	0	03/CDL	Administrative Per Se
80	1	03	Ignition interlock
81	2	07	Driving a commercial vehicle with BAC of .04 or greater
82	2	07/CDL	DUI in a commercial vehicle
83	0	03	Refusal chemical test, commercial vehicle
84	2	07/CDL	Driving commercial vehicle while under influence of controlled substance
85	2	07/CDL	Leaving scene of an accident involving commercial vehicle
86	1	03/CDL	Felony involving the use of a commercial motor vehicle
87	1	03/CDL	Use of commercial vehicle in commission of felony involving a controlled substance
88	1	03	Speeding in a commercial vehicle 15 MPH or more over posted limit
89	2	07	Driving commercial vehicle in willful or wanton disregard for safety
90	2	07	Reckless driving in a commercial vehicle
91	1	03	Improper or erratic lane changes in commercial vehicle
92	1	03	Following too closely in a commercial vehicle
93	1	03	Violation arising in connection with fatality, in commercial vehicle
94	0	03	Mutilated document
95	0	03	False report
96	0	03	Stopping, standing, and parking
98	0	01	Other
99	0	01	Minor traffic violations, unable to interpret
A1	2	07/CDL	Driving under the influence of alcohol or drugs
A2	2	07/CDL	Driving under the influence of alcohol and drugs
A3	0		Disobedience of lawful order OR Underage convicted of drinking and driving at .02 or higher BAC. 03
A4	0	03	Underage Administrative Per Se, drinking at .02 or higher BAC
AA	0	03	Illegal possession of weapon including firearm
AB	0	03	Transporting liquor to a minor
AC	2	07	Failure of duties upon damaging unattended vehicle or injuring animal
AD	2	07	Driving after withdrawal
AE	1	03	Driving while out of service order in effects
AF	0	03	Mutilated registration card or title
AG	0	03	Failed to show document as required
AH	0	03	Misrepresentation of identity or other facts
AI	0	03	Misrepresentation of identity or other facts to avoid arrest or prosecution
AJ	0	03	Misrepresentation of identity or other facts to obtain alcohol
AK	0	03	Manufacture or make false driver license (includes DL, CDL and Instruction Permit)
AL	0	03	Show or use improperly-document or item not specified
AM	1	03	Show or use improperly-operator's (driver's) log
AN	0	03	Failure to pay for damages or make installment payment
AP	0	03	Failure to post security or obtain release from liability
AQ	0	03	Unsatisfied judgment
AR	0	03	Failure to make required payment of child support
AS	0	03	Failure to pay
AT	0	03	Littering harmful substance
AU	1	03	Miscellaneous duty failure
AV	0	03	Failure to correct defects after inspection failure or notice
AW	0	03	Failure to weigh vehicle or stop at weight station
AX	0	03	Abandoned vehicle
AY	1	03	Failure to obey

Codes	Pts	Report Code	Descriptions
AZ	1	03	Improper lane or location
B1	2	07/CDL	Vehicular manslaughter
B2	0	03	Theft and damage
B3	1	03	Violation resulting in accident
B4	1	03	Violation resulting in fatal accident
B5	1	03	Violation resulting in personal injury accident
B6	1	03	Violation resulting in property damage
B7	1	03	Speeding in school zone
B8	1	03	Driving while license disqualified
B9	1	03	Vehicular manslaughter
BA	1	03	FTO railroad crossing restrictions
BB	1	03	Failure to obey railroad crossing restrictions
BC	1	03	RR crossing violation
BI	1	03	Driving a commercial motor vehicle without obtaining a CDL
BJ	0	03	Failure to appear or pay fines
BK	0	03	Perjury about the operation of a motor vehicle
BN	1	03	Speeding 11-15 mph over speed limit
BP	2	03	Speeding 15 MPH or more over the speed limit
BR	2	07	Leaving accident scene before police arrive
BT	2	07	Hit and run failure to stop and render aid after a Personal Injury accident
BU	2	07	Hit and run failure to stop and render aid after property damage accident
BV	2	07	Leave scene of accident-injury/fatal
BX	2	07	Leaving property damage accident scene before police arrive

Colorado

Administration	Important Telephone and Web Contacts
Office of the Director Division of Motor Vehicles Denver 80261-0016 303-205-5600 www.colorado.gov/revenue/dmv	General Driver Information .... 303-205-5613 Titles .... 303-205-5608 Registration .... 303-205-5607 Enforcement .... 303-205-5609 Division of Insurance .... 303-894-7499 State Police Headquarters................................... 303-239-4500

Link to Auto Industry Laws and Regulations: www.colorado.gov/revenue/AID
Link to Motor Vehicle Rules and Regulations: www.colorado.gov/cs/Satellite/Revenue-MV/RMV/1222771319447

Driver's License Format, Issuance and Renewal

License Classes, Restrictions and Endorsements Appear After the Driving Record Content Section

License Format

Since January 30, 1994, a permanent nine-digit numeric number has been issued to each driver. The format of the number is the Julian Date and a random four number sequence.

Document Appearance

The current document has been in force since October 2003. Both current and previous documents have a photographic backdrop of the mountains. All licenses and ID cards are laminated and tamper-proof. All previously issued documents are valid until expiration. The probationary driver's license is red in color.

Current Documents

Security Characteristics: A repeating, optically variable, UV-sensitive gold state seal is across the bottom of adult documents and down the left side of Under 21 documents. All documents contain guilloche security designs and micro printing. All documents have a magstrip and a 2D barcode on the back with the demographic information that appears on the front.

Position of Photo: Left side, above name and address of card bearer. There is a ghost image of card bearer located under the demographic data on the front of the card.

Minor Age Driver Locator: Under 21 documents are in a vertical format. *Under 21* is printed in red in the center.

CDL Indicator: The words *Commercial Driver License* appear underneath the header "Colorado," otherwise the CDL format is identical to basic license.

Older Documents

Security Characteristics: The repeating, optically variable gold state seal, UV-sensitive as of July 2002, is across the bottom of adult documents and is down the left side of Under 21 documents. All documents have a magstripe and 2D barcode on the back with the demographic information that appears on the front.

Position of Photo: Left side, above name and address of card bearer. There is a ghost image of card bearer located under the demographic data on the front of the card.

Minor Age Driver Locator: Under 21 documents are in a vertical format. *Under 21* is printed in red in the center.

CDL Indicator: The words *Commercial Driver License* appear underneath the header "Colorado," otherwise the CDL format is identical to basic license.

Issuance

Direct Location of Requirements for Proof of Identity:
Go to www.colorado.gov/revenue/dmv then Click on the Driver's License button

Age Requirements

The minimum age is 21 for a full Adult license. Minor licenses expire 20 days after the 21st birthday. For drivers under 18, there are specific permits available. The ages and available permits for these teen drivers are as follows:

- Driver Education Permit: 15 years to 15 years 6 months. Valid for 3 years.
- Driver Awareness Permit: 15 years 6 months to 16 years. Valid for 3 years.
- Minor Instruction Permit: 16 years to 21 years of age. Valid for 3 years.

All permits for anyone under 18 years must be held at least 12 months. Regardless when license issued, age under 18 cannot drive a vehicle carrying a passenger under 21 unless the driver license has been held for at least 6 months, and cannot drive a vehicle carrying more than one passenger under 21 unless license held for at least one year. See the web page for exceptions. Every applicant under 18 years of age must submit an 'Affidavit of Liability and Guardianship' DR2460 signed by a parent, stepparent, guardian or grandparent with Power of Attorney.

A 6-hour Behind the Wheel (BTW) certificate is required for any minor who is under the age of 16 years 6 months at the time they apply for their license. *Exception*: 12 hours of behind the wheel training may be administered by a parent, guardian or alternate permit supervisor if no approved school is offering at least 20 hours of driver education per week located within 30 miles of the permit holders residence.

Residency

Colorado defines a resident as any person who: 1) owns or operates a business in Colorado, or 2) obtains gainful employment in Colorado, or 3) has resided in Colorado continuously for a period of 90 consecutive days. After becoming a Colorado resident, the driver has 30 days to obtain a Colorado driver license and register their vehicle.

Renewal

Drivers can renew a DL and make a change of address at the same time online at https://www.colorado.gov/vroom/renewlicense/index.jsf. One can renew an expired driver's license or State ID online if it has not been expired for more than one year. If the license is expired one year, both the written and drive tests are required and additional identification may be required if the license is not presented. A credit card and an email address are required. This program is not available to drivers with a CDL. Renewal is organized as follows:

- Licenses issued May 26, 2005 forward: Birth month of fifth year.
- Licenses issued from July 2001 through May 26, 2005: Birth month of tenth year.
- Licenses issued August 1989 through June 200: Birth month of fifth year.

- CDL License: Four years.
- Under 21 licenses: Twenty days after the twenty-first birthday.

The driver keeps the same license number when renewing. Colorado drivers holding a regular license may request a *Driver License Renew By Mail Application* from the Colorado Department of Revenue's web page. Only Colorado drivers with clear driving records may renew their driver license by mail or online. When relocating, Colorado drivers have 30 days to change the address on their license.

An out-of-state extension is a sticker that is issued to extend the expiration date of a license if a person is out-of-state when the license expires. A civilian extension is for one year from the expiration date and can only be issued once, unless the person is out of the country then a second extension can be issued with a separate request done within 90 days of expiration of the first extension. Due to medical and testing requirements for CDL drivers, only a 30-day extension is available. A military extension is good for three years from the expiration date of the license and you may only be issued one military extension.

Elderly-Related Restrictions

None reported, however drivers 60 years of age and older may not renew online.

Vehicle Insurance, Title and Registration Facts

Registration Renewal

Registration is required on all passenger vehicles, commercial vehicles, motorcycles, mopeds, trailers and special mobile machinery used upon the highways. Boats, ATVs, OHVs, and snowmobiles are registered through the Colorado State Parks. Exemptions are manufactured homes, U.S. Government vehicles, firefighting vehicles, police, ambulances, patrol wagons and farm implements.

Renewal applications are mailed to the registered owners prior to expiration. Registration may be renewed in person, by mail, or online. Registration expiration for most vehicles is on a monthly staggered basis.

New Residents

Vehicles must be registered within 90 days after establishing residency. Residency is established when one of the following occurs: 1) own or operate a business in CO; 2) be gainfully employed in CO; 3) reside in CO for 90 consecutive days.

Inspections and Emissions Testing

Emission testing of gas powered vehicles is required when registering, re-registering or selling vehicles in the following Colorado counties known as the *Enhanced Area:* the full counties of Boulder, Broomfield, Denver, Douglas and Jefferson as well as parts of the counties of Adams and Arapahoe, Larimer and Weld. The diesel emissions program area consists of the full counties of Boulder, Jefferson, Broomfield, Denver, and Douglas, and the partial counties of Adams and Arapahoe, Larimer, Weld, and El Paso.

Testing of gas powered vehicles is also required in parts of two counties (Larimer, and Weld) known as the *Basic Area.* The gas vehicle emissions program has ended in El Paso County, but the diesel program is still in effect. Contact the respective county clerk's office for assistance to determine if an address is in or out of the program area in the partial counties of Adams (720-654-6010), Arapahoe (303-795-4500), and in El Paso (719-520-7302), Larimer (970-498-7878) or Weld (970-304-6520). For emissions information call 303-205-5603.

Tests for 1982 and newer vehicles in the Enhanced Area are done by Envirotest Inc. Tests for 1981 and older vehicles are performed by Air Care Colorado or independent testing facilities within the Enhanced Area. Vehicles registering in the three Basic Area counties may be tested at Basic Area stations or Air Care stations.

Colorado has no statutes requiring a safety inspection. Contact the respective county clerk's office for assistance to determine if an address is in or out of the program area in the partial counties as listed above.

Passenger Plate Facts

There are two plates with two decals (MO) (YR) on rear plate. Since January 1, 2000, re-issued license plates do not display county designations. Until that date, Colorado used extensive coding patterns, incorporating the county and the alpha characters on the plate, for all classes of vehicles. When a vehicle is sold the plates remain with seller.

Insurance and Financial Responsibility

The state's minimum financial responsibility limits are $25,000/50,000/15,000. Proof of liability insurance must be shown when reinstating driving privileges upon conviction of being an owner/operator of vehicle and not having liability insurance. SR-22 forms are used and must be shown for any financial responsibility suspension, or most revocations, for cancel & deny for physical or mental disabilities, or for cancellation of a CDL/PDL.

Withdrawal Sanctions, and Alcohol and Drug Testing

Alcohol and Chemical Testing Limits

Colorado has a "violation of driving under the influence," if alcohol content is .08 percent or greater, .02 or greater if the driver is under 21. If content is .05 percent to .079 percent, the violation is "driving while impaired." Colorado also has an "expressed consent" law, which allows the administration to revoke for failure to take a test for alcohol or drugs. Also allows for revocation if BAC is .08 or greater (.04 for commercial drivers and .02 for under 21). Only breath or blood tests are sanctioned for alcohol; urine and blood tests are sanctioned for drugs.

Suspensions and Revocations

The state is in compliance with the federally mandated disqualifications on CDLs. See the Appendix for these disqualifications.

If alcohol or drug-related offenses, leaving the scene of an accident, or felony involving use of a CMV:

First offense .... One-year revocation.

First offense while transporting hazardous materials requiring placarding.......................... Three-year revocation.

Second offense.. Lifetime revocation.

Conviction of the use of a CMV vehicle in the commission of a felony involving
the manufacturing, distribution, or dispensing of a controlled substance .... Lifetime revocation.

For Points

An up to one- year suspension is given for the following:

Driver 16-17 ....Six points in twelve months or seven points prior to turning 18.

Driver 18-20 ....Nine points in twelve months or twelve points in twenty-four months or fourteen points
for period of license.

Over 21 ....Twelve points in twelve months or eighteen points in twenty-four months.

Colorado does not have what is commonly referred to as a chauffeur license however, if a driver proves at a hearing that they are employed as a driver and received all of their tickets in the course of their employment, they are not subject to suspension until they receive 16 points in 12 months, 24 points in 24 months or 28 points in 4 years.

Ignition Interlock

Repeat alcohol offenders are required to have an ignition interlock device installed on their vehicle(s) before they can reinstate their driving privileges (Colorado Revised Statute 42-2-132.5). Reinstated licenses are restricted to the use of vehicles equipped with an approved ignition interlock device for a period of at least one year.

Other reasons the driving privilege may be suspended, revoked or canceled and denied:

- Accumulation of serious violations (speeding 15+ over, reckless,fatal, etc.)
- Alter or deface driver's license
- Conviction of manslaughter as a result of motor vehicle accident
- Failure to report an accident or leaving scene of accident
- Failure to pay fine
- Failure to appear
- Failure to pay child support
- Failure to provide evidence of insurance when requested by law enforcement officer
- Failure to register all vehicles owned within 30 days of becoming a CO resident
- Give false information on driver license application
- Lend license to another or misuse it in any way
- Outstanding Judgment Warrant (OJW). If an OJW is incurred a fee is still owed to the court on a ticket (citation). If an OJW is put on the record, it must be resolved or the license may be cancelled or denied.

Reinstatement Requirements

Suspension $95.00 fee; SR-22, or evidence of insurance.
FRA Suspension $95.00 fee; SR-22; also, release from liability or waiver of security.
Revocation $95.00 fee; SR-22. May also require Alcohol Education Program and therapy and interlock device.

Record Access: Laws, Rules, and Forms

Note: This Section Applies to Both Driver and Vehicle Records.

Governing Statutes and Rules

For **State Statutes:**
www.lexisnexis.com/hottopics/colorado/
For **Motor Vehicle Industry Laws and Regulations:**
 www.colorado.gov/revenue/AID
For **Motor Vehicle Rules:**
 www.colorado.gov/cs/Satellite/Revenue-MV/RMV/1185957917647
Per Statute CRS 42-1-206, and through administrative changes, the state adopted the provisions of DPPA. The release of driving and vehicle records and use of Form DR-2489 is governed by CRS 42-1-206 and 24-72-204. Colorado has all of the federal permissible uses and added the following: For use by the federally designated organ procurement agency for the purposes of creating and maintaining the organ and tissue registry. CRSA §24-72-204(7)(b)(XV). Below is a portion of CRS 42-1-206:

CRS 42-1-206 (3.7) (a) The department shall establish a system to allow bulk electronic transfer of information to primary users and vendors who are permitted to receive such information pursuant to section 24-72-204 (7), C.R.S. Bulk transfers to vendors shall be limited strictly to vendors who transfer or resell such information for purposes permitted by law. Such information shall consist of the information contained in a driver's license application under section 42-2-107, a driver's license renewal application under section 42-2-118, a duplicate driver's license application under section 42-2-117, a commercial driver's license application under section 42-2-403, an identification card application under section 42-2-302, a motor vehicle title application under section 42-6-116, a motor vehicle registration application under section 42-3-113, or other official record or document maintained by the department under section 42-2-121.

Request and Consent Forms

Driving Records: High volume, ongoing accounts must complete an agreement with the DMV. If the permissible user is not an ongoing account, *Form DR 2489 Requestor Release and Information Request/Notice of Intended Use* must be presented and signed by the requester. Also, the record can be released with permission of the subject (not notarized) and a copy of *DR 2559 Permission for Release of Individual Records* signed by the individual in question. Forms are accessible at www.colorado.gov/revenue/dmv. Records released contain address, height, weight, and DOB, but not the SSN.

Vehicle Records: The *DR 2539 Title Information Request and Receipt, DR 2489A Requestor Release and Affidavit of Intended Use* and *DR 2444 Statement of Fact* must be submitted for all record search and title history requests.

The *DR 2539 Title Information Request and Receipt* must include the vehicle identification number (VIN), year and make of the vehicle, the Colorado title number if available and the name and address of the requestor at the top of the form. The *DR 2489A* form must include the VIN, name and address of the requestor, Secure and Verifiable Identification, firm name (if applicable), date, signature and one box checked for 'approved permissible use'. The *DR 2444 Statement of Fact* must include how, when, and from whom the vehicle in question was obtained as well as how much was paid for the vehicle. It must also include why the person is requesting a title search or history. Copies of additional documents may be required to determine if information may be released to be in compliance with Driver Privacy Protection Act. All forms can be downloaded from the home page at www.colorado.gov/revenue..

Vendor and Third Party Access Policy

Permissible users can purchase records as a single request or in bulk or database format and then resell to another permissible user or another vendor selling to a permissible user, with the following restrictions—
a. Contract between original vendor and reseller must contain same language as contract between the state and the original vendor.
b. Contract between reseller and end user must contain same language as contract between the state and the original vendor.
Complete records of these transactions must be maintained for five years. Large users and information provider companies must sign an agreement that restricts the use, storage, and/or resale of driving records.

Non-permissible Use Requests

Records without personal information are not available.

Access to Driver-Related Records

Driving Records

General Information and Fees

Division of Motor Vehicles. The mailing address is: Motor Vehicle Division, Driver Control/Traffic Record Room 150, Denver 80261-0016. The express mail or delivery address is Motor Vehicle Division, Driver Control Section, 1881 Pierce Street, Room 150, Lakewood, CO 80214. Phone: 303-205-5613.

The record fee from Driver Control is $2.20, add $.50 for certification. The last fee increase was July of 1991 and no increases are planned for the near future. The DMV charges for "no record found" requests.

In-Person — Requests for up to fifty records can be processed over-the-counter while you wait at the address listed above. The same procedures and fee apply as listed above.

Mail — Record requests mailed to the state are generally processed within twenty-four hours of receipt. The driver's last name, first name, and date of birth are required when ordering. The license number and middle initial are optional, but suggested. The $2.20 fee must accompany each request.

Electronic — Colorado Interactive, 600 17th Street, Ste. 2150 South, Denver, CO 80202 800-970-3468, www.colorado.gov. Colorado Interactive is the entity designated by the state to provide online access to driving records to registered users. An interactive service allows user to input the DL and either the last name or DOB and then view and print the record. A point-to-point service allows batching of requests, with data returned in a database format. Requesters must be approved per state compliance requirements with DPPA. There is an annual $75.00 registration fee, records are $2.00 each. For more information, visit www.colorado.gov/registration. The Colorado Interactive person to contact for more information is Amy Sawyer at 303-534-3468 extension 102.

Bulk — Bulk sale for driver content is not offered to the public or to the insurance or trucking industries.

By Person of Record — Colorado drivers may obtain their driving record by mail or walk-in as described above. Drivers may also obtain a copy of their record at any Colorado License Office; however, certified record copies may only be purchased at Lakewood address. At present, there is no program for drivers to order or view their own record online.

Notification/Monitoring Program

Colorado Interactive manages the Driver Monitoring service; requesters must be approved as described above. Fees are based on number of individuals monitored, starting at $.06 per record for 1 to 400,000 records monitored. Requesters submit names and indicate if term is to be for 1 month, 6 months or 1 year. Monitoring is monthly, results are provided within 6 days. The service is open to insurers, trucking companies, employers, and third party providers.

Accident Reports

Reporting — Accidents involving damage or any injury or death must be reported immediately to the local law enforcement agency. If no police officer was called to the scene of the accident, driver can obtain the form to file an accident report or can file online at https://crash.state.co.us/. If a police officer was called to the scene to obtain all the needed information, the person does not need to provide any forms unless he/she receives a letter from this department.

Record Access — Motor Vehicle Division, Traffic Records, Driver Services, Room 150, Denver CO, 80261-0016, 303-205-5613 or 303-205-5793. https://crash.state.co.us

Copies of accident reports may be obtained by written requests. The request must include name, date of birth, date of the accident, license plate number, name and DOB of each driver involved, and your mailing address. The fee is $2.20 for the report or $2.70 to have it certified. Giving the location is helpful. If requester was not involved, permission must first be given by one of the involved drivers. Use *Form DR 2559*. These requests are subject to the same restrictions to access as driving records. *Form 2489 Requestor Release and Information Request/Notice of Intended Use* must also be submitted. Records are held for current year plus 6 years, records (except photographs and witness statements) are microfilmed for past 10 years. It can take 4 weeks before a new record is available.

Access to Vehicle-Related Records

General Information and Fees

Division of Motor Vehicles, Title & Registration Sections, Denver 80261-0016, Title and Registration Section 303-205-5608, fax 303-205-5765.

The search fee is $2.20 for vehicle, plate, lien and ownership records including mobile homes. Certification is an additional $.50 per record. Lien filing is handled at the County Motor Vehicle office in the county where the vehicle is located Lien extensions are processed at the local county clerk's office.

Note: The Department requires that the Statement of Fact be included with the Title Information Request and Receipt and Requestor Release and Affidavit of Intended Use for all record search and title history requests. The Statement of Fact is required to explain the reason the information is being requested. In order to process the request these forms need to be completed in full.

The *DR 2539 Title Information Request and Receipt* must include the vehicle identification number (VIN), year and make of the vehicle, the Colorado title number if available and the name and address of the requestor at the top of the form. The *DR 2489A Requestor Release and Affidavit of Intended Use* must include the VIN, name and address of the requestor, Secure and Verifiable Identification, firm name (if applicable), date, signature and one box checked for 'approved permissible use. The *DR 2444 Statement of Fact* must include how, when, and from whom the vehicle in question was obtained as well as how much was paid for the vehicle. It must also include why the person is requesting a title search or history. Copies of additional documents may be required to determine if information may be released to be in compliance with Driver Privacy Protection Act. All forms can be downloaded from the home page at www.colorado.gov/revenue.

Records are maintained for the current year plus 7 years past.

Mail — The same procedures and fees apply as listed above. A self-addressed, stamped envelope is suggested if the department determines the information should be released, the current title information will be mailed in approximately 3 weeks from receipt of the request. Written notification will be sent to the applicant for all requests that the department determines will not be provided. In those cases the applicant can pursue a subpoena or court order.

In-Person — The address is 1881 Pierce Street, Lakewood, CO 80214. Requests for up to three records can be processed over-the-counter while you wait.

Electronic — Colorado does not offer online retrieval.

Bulk — Division of Motor Vehicles, Title and Registration Sections Room 146, 1881 Pierce Street Lakewood, CO 80214. For information regarding bulk request of vehicle information write to the address listed.

Access to Vessel-Related Records

General Information, Access and Fees

Colorado State Parks, Registration, 13787 S Highway 85, Littleton 80160, 303-791-1920. www.parks.state.co.us

This agency maintains records for boats, snowmobiles, and off-highway vehicles. Lien information is not recorded here and must be searched at the Department of Revenue. All sail and motorized vessels must be registered. Vessels from other states may be operated in Colorado for up to 60 days with a current registration from the owner's state. A *Release of Registration Records Form* must be completed and signed by the requester. The form is not available online. Records can be searched by registration number, last name and DOB, or serial number going back 5 years. After 5 years, records are put on microfilm and can only be accessed by registration number. The fee is $2.00 per search and $1.25 per copy per page. Records can be accessed by mail, or fax 303-470-0782. The owner's DOB is not released.

Driving Record Content and Reciprocity

What's On or Not On the Driving Record

- The length of time violations and activities are listed on the public record is for seven years.
- Records released contain address, height, weight, and DOB, but not the SSN.
- Parking, pedestrian, and bicycle violations are not listed on the driving record. All other convictions and points will appear.
- An entry on the record shown as OJW stands for Outstanding Judgment Warrant.
- Convictions on the record indicate an accident occurred or not by a "Y/N." Thus, accidents are not reported on the record if the driver was not convicted of a violation.
- Colorado does not permit driver school attendance in lieu of conviction.

Data Retention

CDL driver records are purged based on the timetable per federal regulations, see the Appendix for this timetable. Records are kept on microfilm since 1983.

Court to Repository

The courts submit conviction information via electronic transmission, or on paper for data entry. The state mandates that conviction information be forwarded to the state within 10 days of disposition and five days for commercial drivers.

State Reciprocity for Non-CDL Drivers

- Will suspend license for unpaid out-of-state convictions.
- Record of new incoming driver is not shown on MVR.
- Only out-of-state convictions for DUI, felony or death/injury related incidents are shown on MVR.
- Out-of-state accidents not shown on MVR unless there is major conviction.
- Convictions of out-of-state drivers are sent to home state.
- Record is not automatically forwarded to new state upon surrender of license.

License Classes, Restrictions, and Endorsements Abbreviations

Colorado began issuing the CDL in January 1991. New classifications replaced old classified system on April 1, 1992.

License Classes– Commercial

Class A	Any vehicle combination 26,001 pounds or more GCWR which tows another vehicle 10,001 pounds or more GVWR; includes Class B and C.
Class B	Any single unit vehicle 26,001 pounds or more GVWR. May tow another vehicle (provided it weighs 10,000 pounds or less; includes Class C.
Class C	Any single unit vehicle (including buses) 26,000 pounds or less. May tow another vehicle provided it weighs 10,000 pounds or less.

License Classes– Non-Commercial

Class R	Regular operator
Class M**	Motorcycle (** = Since October 1, 1999, Class M licenses have not been issued. Now "M" is an endorsement on Class R or on CDL.

Restrictions

A	Automatic Transmission Only	H	Hand Controls		M	Left Side Rear View Mirror
D	Daylight Driving Only	L	No Air Brakes		E	Either V or M
K	CDL Intrastate	V	Vision (Corrective Lens Needed)		3	Three-Wheel Motorcycle

Endorsements

H	Hazardous Materials	P1	Class C Passenger	T	Double-/Triple-Trailers
M	*Motorcycle	P2	Class B Passenger	X	Hazardous/Tankers
N	Tank Vehicles	P3	Class A Passenger	S	School Bus

Conviction Table with Codes, ACD, and Points

This table is presented in order of the "Code" column. This code appears for each conviction on the driving record.
Note: "00" found in the points column can mean "department action" takes place.

Code	ACD	Description	Points
001	S95	Speed Contest	12
002	S95	Drag Racing *	12
003	S93	Speeding - Speed Not Specified*	03
004	S51	Speeding - 5-9 Over Limit	01
005	S93	Speeding - 10-19 Over Limit	01
006	S71	Speeding - 20 Or More Over	06
007	S94	Too Fast For Conditions*	03
008	S96	Impeding Traffic	03
009	-	Too Fast On Elevated Structure	03
010	S95	Speed Contest Aid & Abet	12
011	U01	Eluding Police	12
012	U01	Vehicular Eluding-Cl 5 Felony	00
013	U01	Vehicular Eluding-Inj (Felony)	00
014	U01	Vehicular Eluding Cause Death	00
015	S51	Speeding - 10-14 Mph Over CMV	04
016	S41	Speeding - 40 Or More Over	12
017	S95	Speed Exhibition	05
018	-	Aid/Facilitating Speed Exhibit	05
019	-	Under Min Speed Left Lane 1-70	00
020	S51	Speeding - 1-4 Mph Over Limit	00
028	B54	Fail Obtain Reg 2nd 5 Years	00
029	-	Failed To Register Vehicle(S)	00
030	-	No Registration	00
031	-	30 Day License Plate Requirement	00
032	-	No Registration In Vehicle	00
033	-	License Plate Violation*	00
034	-	Misused License Plates	00
035	-	No License Plate(S)	00
036	-	Plates Not Legible	00
037	-	Vehicle Had Only One Plate	00
038	-	Expired License Plates	00
039	-	Expired Temporary Permit	00
040	-	Improper Registration	00
041	-	Improper Registration	00
042	-	Improper Registration	00
043	-	Misused Metro Plate	00
044	-	30 Day License Plate Requirement	00
045	-	30 Day License Plate Requirement	00
046	-	Register In County Of Residence	00
048	-	All Terrain Vehicle	00
049	-	License Plate Obscured/Device	00
050	B60	Fl To Notify-Change Body Color	00
056	-	No Motorized Bike Registration	00
060	B51	Drove Without Valid Dr License	03
061	D29	Violate Dr License Restriction	00/03
062	D29	Violate Lic Permit Restriction	03
063	B51	No Driver Lic In Possession	00
064	B91	No Motorcycle Endorsement	03
065	D29	Violate Dr License Restriction	00/03
066	-	Fail Change Address On Dr Lic	00
067	B41	Unlawful Use Of License	00
068	D02	False Affidavit - Driver Lic	00
069	D16	Drive When Dr License Expired	00
069	B51	Drive When Dr License Expired	03
070	-	Permit Unauth Minor To Drive	00
071	-	Permit Unauthorized Driver	00
072	D16	Frgn Lic Invalid During Susp	00
073	-	Rent/Loan Veh To Unlicensed Dr	00
074	-	Permit Unlawful Driving	00
075	B26	Drive When Priv Suspended FRA	00
076	B26	Drive When Privilege Suspended	00

Code	ACD	Description	Points
077	B25	Drive When Privilege Revoked	00
078	B23	Drive When Privilege Denied	00
079	B22	Drive When Dr License Canceled	00
080	U03	Drive When Rev/Hto/Felony/Aggr	00
081	-	Dr Motorized Bike W/O License	00
082	B63	No Proof When Required *	00
083	-	No Driver Lic 30 Day Resident	03
084	B91	Driver License Class/Type	03
085	B25	Dr Under Alcohol Related Actn	00
089	-	Refused To Show Dr License	00
090	-	Drive When Priv Rev/Hto/Misdmn	00
091	-	Fl To Surr Dr Lic As Required	00
100	A21	Drive Under Influence Alcohol*	12
101	A25	Driving Impaired By Alcohol*	08
102	-	Rode Animal While DUI *	00
103	-	Pedestrian On Hwy While DUI *	00
104	A24	Unlawful Use Control Substance*	00
105	U08	Manslaughter	00
106	U07	Vehicular Homicide When DUI *	00
107	U06	Vehicular Assault When DUI*	00
108	U07	Criminally Negligent Homicide	00
109	U07	Vehicular Homicide	00
110	U06	Vehicular Assault*	00
111	A10	DUI/BAC 0.15 Or More	12
112	U03	Felony Motor Vehicle Used	00
113	A22	Drive Under Influence Of Drugs*	12
114	A25	Driving Impaired By Drugs*	08
115	A10	DUI/BAC 0.10 Or More *	12
116	A33	Felony/Drugs *	00
117	A31	Buy/Possess Alcohol	00
118	A12	Refused BAC Test	00
119	A98	Failed BAC Test	00
120	B06	Leave Scene Accident Death/Inj	00
121	B08	Leaving Scene Of An Accident	12
122	B14	Fail Give Info/Aid In Accident	12
123	B05	Strike Unattended Veh/Property	12
124	B08	Strike Hiwy Fixture	12
125	B05	Duty To Report Accident	12
126	B05	Fail To Stay/Return To Accident	12
130	B20	Driving W/License Withdrawn	00
131	B21	Driving With License Barred	00
132	B22	Driving W/License Canceled	00
133	B24	Driving W/ License Disqual.	00
138	M81	Careless Drive Cause Inj/Death	04
138	M81	Careless Driving Causing Death	04
139	M81	Careless Driving Cause Injury	08
140	M84	Reckless Driving	08
141	M81	Careless Driving	04
142	M34	Following Too Closely	04
143	M30	Follow Too Close In Motorcade	04
144	N83	Improper Start/Parked Position	03
145	M12	Driving Through Safety Zone	03
146	M40	Improper Driving On Mtn Hiway	03
147	N80	Coasting Prohibited	03
148	N80	Coasting Prohibited In CMV *	03
149	M33	Follow Too Close/Fire Vehicle	03
150	M56	Crossing Fire Hose	00
151	-	Obstruct Inters Crosswalk Or RRr *	00
152	M46	Imp Dr On Divided/Control Hiwy	03
153	N82	Unsafe Backing	02
154	N82	Unsafe Backing/Shoulder Of Road	02
156	-	Riding In Trailer	00
157	F06	Improper Riding On Motorcycle	03
158	-	Person Clinging On Motorcycle	03
159	-	Illegal Operation Veh Rec Area	00
160	-	Stop To Pick Up Ped On Road	00

Code	ACD	Description	Points
161	F03	Violate Motorcycle Safety Law	00
162	N05	Escorted Processions *	00
163	-	Funeral/Failed Maintain Lights *	00
164	M30	Unlawful Procession *	00
165	M34	Follow Too Close To Towing Veh	04
166	M58	Driving On Sidewalk	03
167	D29	Unlawful Oper Mid-5am / Age 17 *	02
168	D29	Unlawful Oper Mid-5am / Age 18	02
169	D29	Unlaw Minor Passenger-Under 18	02
170	E56	Mc/Moped No Helmet-Under 18	03
171	S15	Speeding 15 Or More Over Limit	00
172	S16	Speeding 16-20 Over Limit	00
173	S21	Speeding 21-25 Over Limit	00
174	S26	Speeding 26-30 Over Limit	00
175	S31	Speeding 31-35 Over Limit	00
176	S36	Speeding 36-40 Over Limit	00
177	S41	Speeding 41+ Over Limit	00
178	S71	Speeding 21-30 Over Limit	00
179	S81	Speeding 31-40 Over Limit	00
180	S91	Speeding 41+Over Limit	00
181	S92	Speeding	00
182	S14	Speeding 11-15 Over	00
190	M73	Fl Pass Right Of Oncoming Traffic	04
191	M70	Improper Passing *	04
192	M73	Imp Pass/Overtaking On Left	04
193	N07	Fail To Give Way/Overtaken	03
194	M73	Imp Pass/Overtaking On Right	04
195	M70	Passed On Left When Not Clear	04
196	M70	Imp Pass/100' Rr/Intersection	04
197	M74	Pass On Hill/Curve View Obstructed	04
198	M77	Passed When View Obstructed*	04
199	M70	Passed On Left When Prohibited	04
200	M70	Pass Within 100' Bridge/Tunnel	04
201	M70	Imp Pass/Insufficient Clearance	04
203	M76	Overtake Vehicle Stop For Ped	03
204	M71	Dr In Passing Lane Prohibited	03
208	A04	DUI Alcohol W/BACc<.04	00
209	A11	DUI With bACc .04 Or More	00
211	B01	Hit And Run Fail To Stop	00
212	B03	Hit/Run Fail To Stop P.I. Acc	00
213	B07	Leave Scene Of Accident	00
214	B02	Hit/Run Fatal Accident	00
215	B04	Hit/Run Property Damage Acc	00
220	M05	Vio Of Lane-Dir Control Signal	00/03
221	M42	Unsafe Lane Change	03
222	M73	Passed On Shoulder On Right	00/03
223	M41	Failed To Drive In Single Lane	03
224	M62	Unnecessarily Dr/Center Lane	03
225	M40	Fail To Dr In Designated Lane	03
226	-	Illegal Operation Of Motorcycle	03
227	M51	Unlawful Crossing Median	00/03
228	M46	Improper Entering Freeway *	00/03
229	M40	Roadways Laned For Traffic *	03
230	M49	Drove In Bus Only Lane *	00/03
231	M11	Unlawful Use Of Runaway Ramp	03
232	M49	HOV Lane Violation	00
233	-	Operate Nev Where Prohibited *	00
250	N70	Drove On Wrong Side Of Road	04
251	N70	Driving On Left Side Of Road	04
252	N70	Driving On Wrong Side Of Road	04
253	N71	Dr Wrong Side Of Divided Hiway	00/03
254	N63	Dr Wrong Way/One-Way Street	03
255	N63	Dr Wrong Way/One-Way Alley *	03
256	N61	Dr Wrong Way/Rotary Island	03
260	A90	Admin Per Se > .10 BAC	00
261	A23	DUI Alcohol And Drugs	00

Code	ACD	Description	Points
262	A11	DUI BAC Between .04-.79	00
270	N56	Made 'U' Turn Where Prohibited	03
271	N54	Right Turn Red Light/Prohibited	04
272	N53	Left Turn One Way Street *	04
273	N52	Left Turn From Wrong Lane	03
274	N52	Right Turn From Wrong Lane	03
275	N50	Prohibited Turn *	03
276	N50	Fail Turn From Turn Only Lane	03
277	N56	Made 'U' Turn On Hill Or Curve*	03
278	N31	Turn Left/Oncoming Traffic	03
279	N50	Improper Turn Across Median	03
280	N50	Improper Turn At Intersection	03
281	N50	Unlawful Turn Alley/Driveway*	03
282	N50	Unlawful Turn Alley/Driveway *	03
300	M16	Fail To Observe Traffic Device	00/03
301	M17	Disregard School Stop Or Sign*	00/03
302	M17	Disregard Warning/Slow/Const Sign*	00/03
303	M17	Disobeyed Direction Signs *	00/03
304	M16	Violation Of Red Signal Light	04
305	M16	Stop Wrong Place At Signal	04
306	M16	Red Signal W/Green Arrow *	04
307	M16	Green Light W/Green Turn Arrow*	04
308	M16	Green Turn Arrow Alone*	00/03
309	M16	Green Strght Thru Arrow Alone *	00/03
310	M18	Violation Flash Signal Light	04
311	-	Display Unauth Traf Cntrl Sign	00
312	D73	Interfere/Remove Traffic Sign	00/03
313	-	Alter/Deface Traffic Sign	00
314	-	Damage/Knock Down Traffic Sign	00
315	M10	Disregard RR Sign/Barricade	04
316	M09	Fail Stop At Marked RR Cross	04
317	M21	School Bus/Cmv Stop/RR Crossng	00/03
318	-	Unlaw Move Hvy Eqp/RR Crossing	00
319	M15	Disregard Stop Sign	04
320	M25	Caution At Malfuncting Cntrl Sig	00/03
321	-	Drove Across Wet Paint*	00
322	M14	Traffic Device/Markings *	03
323	M16	Interfere Traf Signal-Injury	03
324	-	Sell/Possess Device -Traf Sign	00
350	-	Parked/Paved Portion Of Hiway	00

Note: Codes 351 thru 363 are no point parking violations and are not shown on a driving record.

Code	ACD	Description	Points
370	N24	Row Right Turn On Red Light	03
371	N25	Right Of Way At Intersection	03
372	N26	Row At Yield Intersection	03
373	N22	Fail Yield Row At Stop Sign	03
374	N01	Failed Yield Row Entering Hwy	03
375	N04	Yield Row To Emergency Vehicle	04
376	N08	Right Of Way To Pedestrian	04
377	N08	Row To Pedestrian/Walk Signal	04
378	N08	Row To Pedestrian Alley/Drive	04
379	N01	Yield Row Emerging Alley/Drive*	03
380	N08	Row To Handicapped Person	06
381	N08	Fl Use Due Care For Pedestrian	04
382	N01	Right Of Way In Work Area	03

Note: Codes 400 thru 411 are no point pedestrian violations and are not shown on a driving record.

Code	ACD	Description	Points
417	-	Buy/Poss Alcohol Fail Comply *	
420	M75	Pass Stop School Bus W/Lights	04/05/06
421	M58	Illegal School Bus Stop	03
422	-	Duty Of School Bus Driver	02
430	N40	Fail To Signal For Turn - 200' *	02
431	N40	Fail To Signal Turn - 100' *	02
432	N40	Fail To Signal Turn 4 Lane Hwy *	02
433	N40	Fail To Give/Improper Signal	02
434	N43	Failure To Signal For Turn*	02

Code	ACD	Description	Points
435	N40	Fail To Signal For Stop	02
436	N40	Failed To Use Turn Signal *	02
437	N43	Failed To Signal Turn Or Stop	02
438	N40	Improper Hand Signals *	02
439	N40	Unlaw Use Flash Turn Signals *	02
450	D70	Too Many Front Seat-Obstruct	00
451	D70	Too Many Front Seat-Interfere	00
452	E70	Obstructed Windows	00
453	D70	Passenger Interfere W/Driver	00
454	D70	Driver Allow Passenger Interfere	00
455	D70	Passenger Obstructed Vision	00
456	-	Clinging To Outside Of Vehicle*	00
457	-	Allow Unlawful Riding *	00
458	D70	Obstructed Windows*	00
459	D70	Unclear Windows *	00
460	D70	Vision Obstructed *	00
461	D70	Windshield Obstructed *	00
462	D70	Load Obscured Vision	00
463	D70	Objects/Other Obstruct Vision *	00
464	D70	Passenger Obstruct Bus Dr View *	00
465	D70	TV Visible To Vehicle Operator	00
466	-	Tinted Windows	00
467	-	Unlawful Use Headset/Earphones	00
468	-	More Pass Than Seatbelt/Age 17	00
471	-	No Towing Flag	00
472	-	No Chain On Towed Vehicle	00
473	-	Unlawful Drawbar	00
488	D65	Throw/Deposit Human Waste-Hwy	00
489	D65	Misdemeanor -Throw Burning Mat	00
490	-	Threw/Left Foreign Matter Hwy	00
491	-	Left/Threw Burning Matter/Hwy	00
492	-	Excavate Highway W/O Authority	00
493	-	Construct On Highway W/O Auth	00
494	-	Spill Load On Highway	00
495	-	Damage To (Damaging) Highway	00
496	-	Littering Highway*	00
497	-	Obst Hwy W/Structure Debris	00
498	-	Pick-Up/Car Spilling Load-Hwy	03
499	F23	Spilled Load Causing Injury	03
510	-	Width Of Veh Exceeded 8'6"*	00
511	-	Bus Width Exceeded 8'6"*	00
512	-	Farm Tractor Exceeded 10'6" W *	00
513	-	Load Of Loose Hay/Exceed 12' W*	00
514	-	Unlawful Load On Passenger Veh	00
515	-	Load Project Past Left Fender *	00
516	-	Load Project More 6" On Right *	00
517	-	Load Project Beyond Headlamps *	00
518	-	Vehicle Height Exceeded 13' *	00
519	-	Vehicle Height Exceeded 14'6" *	00
520	-	Single Vehicle Exceeded 45' *	00
521	-	Vehicle Exceed 4 Or Length 70'*	00
522	-	Overweight Axles	00
523	-	Unlawful Gross Weight	00
524	-	Tailgate Down	00
525	-	Fail To Stop For Weighing Load*	00
526	-	Refused To Stop For Weighing *	00
527	-	Special Permit Violation *	00
528	-	Objects Protruding In Traffic	00
529	-	Unlawful Rear Proj Of Load	00
530	-	Exceeding Posted Maximum Load	00
531	-	No/Improper Mobile Home Permit	00
532	-	Fl Comply/Super Load Permit	00
533	-	Vio CDOT Os/Ow Permit Rules	00
534	-	Vio CDOT Divisible Load Permit	00
539	-	Unauth Use Green Marker Light	00
540	E05	No Turn Signal On Vehicle*	00

Code	ACD	Description	Points
541	-	Unauthorized Insignia	00
542	-	Defective Or Unsafe Vehicle	2
543	-	No Red Light/Flag Rear	00
544	-	Improper Spot/Auxiliary Lights *	00
545	-	Insuff Emergency Equipment	00
546	-	Defective Emergency Equipment	00
547	E50	Fail To Use Emergency Equipment	00
548	-	Defective Hand/Foot Brakes *	2
549	-	Defective Breakaway Brake*	00
550	-	Defective Or No Horn	00
551	-	Operate Vehicle W/Unauth Siren	00
552	-	Unlawful/Defective Muffler	00
553	-	No Rear View Mirror(S)	00
554	-	Mirror Not Permit Vision 200'	00
555	-	No/Defective Windshield Wipers	00
556	-	Unsafe Tires	00
557	-	Veh W/Glass Not Safety Glass	00
558	-	Imp Emergency Light Equipment	00
559	-	Explosives Carrier Not Marked	00
559	-	Improp Oper Low Speed Elec Veh	00
560	E03	Explsv W/O 2 Fire Extinguisher	00
561	-	Unlawful Chains Dragging	00
562	E57	No Tire Chains Or Snow Tires	00/03
563	-	Pollution Control Device	00
564	-	Altered Suspension System	00
565	-	Slow Moving Veh Disp Of Emblem	00
566	-	Veh Equip To Meet State Req	00
567	-	Installed Unlawful Muffler	00
568	-	Illegal Device-Ignite Exhaust	00
569	-	No/Unlawful Wheel Fenders	00
570	-	Unlawful Object Attached Veh	00
571	-	Improper Equipment-School Bus	00
572	-	Drove Vehicle W/O Safety Glass	00
573	-	Air Pollution Violation	00
574	F02	Child Restraint Systems	00
575	F04	Safety Belt Required	00
576	-	Unsafe Vehicle	00
577	F02	Child Restraint Under Age 16	00
578	-	No Snow Tires/Chains-Rd Closre	00
579	-	No Rear Flaps/Tarp Aggrgt Mat	00
580	-	Oper Under 17 No Seatblt/Passn	02
581	-	Engine Brake- Muffler Required	00
582	E20	Misuse Mobile Comm Device	01
583	E23	Oper Mv W/Radar Jamming Dev	03
584	-	Sell/Possess Radar Jam Device	00
585	M85	Misuse Mob Comm Device-Adult	01
586	M85	Misuse Mob Comm Dev-Adult 2nd	01
587	E20	Misuse Mob Comm Dev-Under 18	01
588	E20	Misuse Comm Dev- Under 18 2nd	01
609	-	Defective Headlamps	01
610	E55	Lights Required *	02
611	E55	Headlamps To Be Lit	02
612	-	Improper Headlights	02

Note: Most codes from 613 thru 674 are obsolete, zero points, deal with defective lights and most have been omitted from this table. Codes that are shown within this range are still in use.

Code	ACD	Description	Points
675	-	Mechanic Issue Invalid Sticker	00
676	-	Emissions Law Violation-Oper	00
677	-	Fail Comply Idling Standard	00
679	U26	Criminal Trespass / MV	00
680	-	Joy Riding	00
681	-	Stripping (Felony) Aid & Abet *	00
682	-	Stripping Less Than $20 Value	00
683	-	Stripping More Than $20 Value	00
684	-	Fail To Report Stored Vehicle	00
685	-	Theft Of A Motor Vehicle	00

Code	ACD	Description	Points
686	-	Trespass Motor Vehicle	00
687	-	Removed/Altered Vin Number	00
688	-	Possess Vehicle W/Altered Vin	00
689	-	Fl To Maintain Business Record	00
690	-	Fl Submit Records For Inspect	00
691	-	Fl To Register Full Name/Add	00
692	-	Failure To Examine Vin	00
693	-	Fl Notify Police - Altered Vin	00
694	-	Fl Notify Discrepancy Vin/Reg	00
695	-	Fail Deliver Title Upon Sale	00
696	U26	Aggravated Motor Vehicle Theft	00
696	-	Aggravated Motor Vehicle Theft	00
697	-	Theft By Receiving	00
698	-	Criminal Conspiracy	00
699	U26	Criminal Mischeif/Damage Mv *	00
700	-	No Tire Chains When Req-CMV	00
701	-	No Camp License	00
701	E57	No Tire Chains -CMV Lane Close	00
702	-	No Port Of Entry Clearance	00
703	-	Illegal Transport Of Xmas Tree *	00
704	-	Common Carrier - No PUC Permit	00
705	-	Fail To Comply With PUC Rules	00
708	-	Contract Carrier-No PUC Permit	00
709	-	Fail To Comply With PUC Rules	00
710	-	Unlawful Use Dyed Diesel Fuel	00
711	-	No Motor Fuel License *	00
712	-	PUC Rules Transport Haz Mat	00
713	-	Fl To Comply W/Dot Safety Rule	00
714	-	Fail Maintain True/Correct Rec *	00
715	-	No/Improper Gas Decal *	00
720	-	Haz Mat Permit Required	00
721	-	Haz Mat Permit/Possession	00
722	-	Haz Mat Regulations	00
723	-	Haz Mat Unauthorized Route	00
724	-	Haz Mat Permit Violation	00
725	-	Haz Mat Violation Aid & Abet	00
730	-	Nuc Mat Log Book	00
731	-	Nuc Mat Medical Cert	00
732	-	Nuc Mat License Violation	00
733	-	Nuc Mat Passenger	00
734	-	Nuc Mat Out Of Service Order	00
735	-	Nuc Mat Unsafe Vehicle	00
736	-	Nuc Mat Vehicle Defects	00
737	-	Nuc Mat Placard Violation	00
738	-	Nuc Mat Parking Violation	00
739	-	Nuc Mat Improper Papers	00
740	-	Nuc Mat Incident	00
741	-	Nuc Mat Unauthorized Route	00
742	-	Nuc Mat Radiation	00
743	-	Nuc Mat Max Index	00
748	U09	Negligent Homicide CMV	00
749	U09	Negligent Homicide Haz	00
750	A50	Felony Drugs Commercial Vehicle	00
752	B05	Leave Scene Accident CMV	12
753	A04	Dui/Alcohol CMV	12
754	A22	Controlled Substance CMV	00
755	A94	Per Se .04 CMV	00
756	U03	Felony Motor Veh Used CMV	00
757	A22	Controlled Substance Haz Mat	00
758	U03	Felony Motor Veh Used Haz Mat	00
759	A94	Per Se .04 Haz Mat	00
760	A04	Dui/Alcohol Haz Mat	12
761	B05	Leave Scene Accident Haz Mat	12
762	A12	Refused bac Test Haz Mat	00
763	B20	Drove CMV Under Cdl Restraint	00
764	B20	Drove CMV Under Cdl Rest. Haz	00

Code	ACD	Description	Points
765	U10	Cause Fatal/Neglig Oper CMV	00
766	U10	Cause Fatal/Neg Oper CMV Haz	00
767	M85	Texting While Driving CMV	01
768	M86	Use Handheld Dev/W Drive CMV	00
769	S71	Excessive Speed CMV 20 & Over	06
770	S15	Excessive Speed CMV 15-19 Over	04
771	M84	Reckless Driving CMV	08
772	U31	Accident - Fatal CMV	00
773	M42	Lane Change CMV	03
774	M34	Follow Too Close CMV	04
775	M10	Fail To Obey Rail Crossing-Cmv	04
776	M20	Fail Slow/Check Tracks-Cmv	00
777	M22	Fail To Stop Rr Gate	04
778	M23	Fail To Leave Space Rr Gate	00
779	M24	Fail Suff Clearance Rr Gate	00
780	A12	Refused bac Test CMV	00
781	M84	Disregard/Safety CMV	08
782	B56	Driving A CMV W/O Obtain Cdl	03
783	B51	Drove A CMV W/O CDL In Poss.	03
784	B91	Drove CMV W/O Prop Class/End	03
785	A60	DUI/BAC .02-.04 CMV Under 21	04
786	A04	DUI/BAC 0.04 Or More	00
787	A33	Possess Alcohol/Drug CMV	00
788	B27	Violate Out Of Service Order	00
789	B19	Vio Out Of Serv Order Haz/Pass	00
790	D02	Illegal Use Of CDL	00
800	A21	Drive Under Influence Alcohol	12
801	A25	Driving Impaired By Alcohol	08
802	-	Rode Animal While DUI	00
803	-	Pedestrian On Hwy While DUI	00
804	A24	Unlawful Use Control Substance	00
806	U07	Vehicular Homicide When DUI	00
807	U06	Vehicular Assault When DUI	00
808	A21	DUI Alcohol And/Or Drugs	12
809	A25	Dr Impaired Alcohol And/Or Drg	08
810	A60	DUI/BAC .02-.04 Under 21	04
811	A33	Non-Felony Drug*	00
812	A08	DUI/BAC .08 More	12
813	A22	Drive Under Influence Of Drugs	12
814	A25	Driving Impaired By Drugs	08
815	A10	DUI/BAC 0.10 Or More *	12
816	A41	Tamper With Ignition Device	00
817	A41	Operate Veh W/Tamprd Interlock	00
818	A41	Violate Lic Restrict Interlock	00
900	M08	Disregard Police Officer	03
901	-	Skis/Sleds On Roadway	00
902	D45	Fail To Appear In Court*	00
903	D45	Fail To Obey Summons	00
904	-	Permitted Livestock On Highway	00
905	-	Shoot From/Across Highway	00
906	-	False Report Of Explosives*	00
907	-	Hunt/Carry Weapons - Snowmoble	00
908	-	Release Held Veh W/O Authority	00
909	-	Coasters/Skates Restricted *	00
910	F34	Obstructing Traffic *	03
911	-	False Report To Authorities*	00
913	M02	Drove Thru/Around Barricades *	03
914	M04	Disregard Flagperson	00
915	-	Enter/Emerge From Parked Veh *	00
916	-	Door Open Into Lane Of Traffic	00
917	-	Hindering Transportation	00
918	-	Throw Missles At Vehicles	00
920	-	Unlaw Deviation Truck Routes	00
921	-	Unlaw Deviation Trk Rt Explosv *	00
922	-	Operate Truck At Unlawful Hour*	00
923	-	Trash Truck/Interstate Highway *	00

Code	ACD	Description	Points
924	-	Bike Obedience Control Devices	00
925	-	Persons Riding On Bicycles	00
926	-	Riding On Rdwys And Bike Paths	00
927	-	Speeding On Bicycle	00
928	-	Bike Emerge Alley/Driveway	00
929	-	Reckless Driving / Bicycle	00
930	-	Careless Driving / Bicycle	00
931	-	Bicycle Lights And Other Equip	00
932	-	Resisted Arrest *	00
933	-	Assault & Battery To Patrolman *	00
934	-	Carrying Concealed Weapon	00
935	A33	Possession Of Narcotics*	00
936	-	Snowmobile Registration	00
937	-	Issuance Of Registrtn Snowmble *	00
938	-	Transfer Of Ownership Snowmble	00
939	-	Training Courses Snowmobiles *	00
940	-	Rest On Young Operator Snowmbl*	00
941	-	Snowmble Prohibited On Streets	00
942	-	Snowmble Operate Right Of Way	00
943	-	Snowmobile Cross Rds/Hwys/Rr	00
944		Oper Snowmble On Private Prop	00
945	-	Required Equipment Snowmobiles *	00
946	-	Notice Of Accident/Snowmobile	00
947		Other Operating Rest Snowmbles *	00
948	-	Abandoned Motor Vehicle	00
949	-	Regulation By Political Subdvs*	00
950	-	Penalties - Enforcement *	00
951	-	Fail Surrender Title *	00
952	M48	Stop When Traffic Obstructed	00
953	D35	No Insurance In CMV	00
954	D35	No Liability Insurance	00/04
955	-	Fail To Sign Insurance Affirm	00
956	D36	Drove Vehicle W/O Insurance	04
957	D36	No Insurance In Possession	04
958	-	Toll Violation	00
959	-	Personal Mob Dev-Where Prohib	00
960	-	Safety Belt Passenger	00
961	-	Defaced Property / Cave *	00
962	A35	Open Container MVProhibited	00
963	A31	Provide Alcohol To Minor	00
964	DI5	Permit Use Of Id By Minor Alc	00
965	U04	Fuel Piracy	00
966	-	Fail To Pay Toll/Fee	00
990	-	Municipal Code Violation	00
997	-	CDL Miscellaneous	00
998	-	Parties To A Crime Aid & Abet	00
999	-	Unspecified Violation	00

Department Actions Table with Codes and Full Descriptions

Note: The Code-2 column is used by the DMV, but sometime the code is an ACD.

Code	Description	ACD
CAUR	Cancel Applied Under Restraint	W00
CBCD	Cancel Bad Check Driver License	W00
CDAM	Cancel/Deny Alter/Misuse License	B41
CDDR	Cancel/Deny Felony Drugs CD	A50
CDFC	Cancel/Deny False Statement CDL	D02
CDFN	Cancel/Deny False Statement NDR	D02
CDFR	Cancel/Deny Failed Reexam	W20
CDFS	Cancel/Deny False Statement	D02
CDF5	Cancel/Deny Failed Five Drives	W20
CDHS	Cancel/Deny Surrender Haz Mat	W09

Code	Description	ACD
CDJD	Cancel/Deny Oj-Ur Not Clear	D45
CDLD	C&D Lifetime CDL Disqual	W41
CDL2	Cancel/Deny Level 2 Incomplete	W00
CDMD	Cancel/Deny Cdl Multiple Disq	W40
CDME	Cancel/Deny Mental Disability	W14
CDMI	Cancel/Deny Mental Incompetnce	W14
CDNR	Cancel/Deny Not Colo Resident	D02
CDOF	Cancel/Deny Out Of State Ftp	D45
CDPD	Cancel/Deny Physical Disability	W14
CDPH	Cancel/Deny Physical	W14
CDUP	Cancel/Deny Unlawful Presence	D02
CEXM	Cancel Expired Medical	B65
CFPD	Cancel Fail Provide Accpt Doc	-
CFRD	Cancel Fail Register Veh-Dl	W00
CFRI	Cancel Fail Register Veh - Id	W00
CFSI	Cancel False Statement Id Card	W00
CLIE	Cancel License Issue Error	W00
COSW	Cancel Out Of State Withdrawal	W00
CSSN	Cancel Invalid SSN	D01
CSWD	Cancel Signiture Withdrawn	W00
CWMW	Cancel Withdrawn Med Waiver	W14
DAEX	Deny Extended-Accident	W01
DARN	Deny Renewed-Accident	W01
DCEX	Deny Extended-Citation	W01
DCRN	Deny Renewed-Citation	W01
DDAR	Deny 2 Dus/D/R 5 Yrs-4 Year	W01
DDUR	Deny 2 Dus/D/R/5 Yrs-3 Year	W01
DFIH	Disqualify Fed Imminent Hazard	W70
DOSH	Vio Out/Serv Ord. Haz/Pass	B19
DOSO	CDL Vio. Out Of Sevide Order	B27
DOS2	Vio Out/Ser Order 2nd/10 Years	W50
DOS3	Vio Out/Ser Order 3rd/10 Years	W52
DSH2	Vio Out/Serv Ord. Haz/Pass 2nd	W51
DSH3	Vio Out/Serv Ird, Haz/Pass 3rd	W52
RACD	Revoke DWAI CDL Holder	A25
RAEC	CDLRevoke Extended - Accident	W01
RAES	Revoke Extendacc-Sr22 Exempt	W01
RAEX	Revoke Extended-Accident	W01
RAOC	Revoke Dui/Alcohol CMV	A21
RAOH	Revoke Dui Alcohol Haz	A21
RAON	Revoke Dui/Alcohol Non-CMV	A21
RARC	CDL Renewed-Accident	W01
RARN	Revoke Renewed-Accident	W01
RARS	Revoke Renewed Acc-Sr22 Exempt	W01
RCEC	CDL Revoke Extended-Citation	W01
RCES	Revoke Extend Conv-Sr22 Exempt	W01
RCEX	Revoke Extended-Citation	W01
RCMT	Revoke Crimian Mischief Theft	W00
RCRC	CDL Revoke Renewed - Citation	W01
RCRN	Revoke Renewed-Citation	W01
RCRS	Revoke Renew Conv-Sr22 Exempt	W01
RCSU	Revoke Concurrent Southern Ute	A21
RDPP	Rev Deface Public/Private Prop	W00
RDRC	Revoke DUI/Drugs CMV	A22
RDRH	Revoke DUI/Drugs Haz	A22
RDRN	Revoke Dui Drugs Non-Cmv	A22
RDSI	Revoke Drove Under Ins Susp	W01
RDUI	Revoke DUI Conviction	A21
RECC	Revoke Refusal CMV	A12
RECH	Revoke Refusal Haz	A12
RECN	Revoke Refusal Non-CMV	A12
RECR	Revoke Refusal	A12
REC2	Revoke Two Refusals	W01
REC3	Revoke Three/More Refusals	W01
RFCM	Revoke Felony CMV	U03
RFCN	Revoke Felony Non-CMV	U03

Code	Description	ACD
RFEL	Revoke Felony MV/Used	U03
RFHZ	Revoke Felony Haz	U03
RFNH	Rev Neg Oper Causing Death Haz	U10
RFNO	Rev Neg Oper Causing Death CMV	U10
RFSR	Revoke Failed Stop/Render Aid	B01
RHTO	Revoke Habitual Traffic Offndr	W01
RLSC	Revoke Leave Scene Acc CMV	B05
RLSH	Revoke Leave Scene Acc Haz	B05
RLSN	Revoke Leave Scene Acc Non-CMV	B05
RMAO	Revoke Alcohol Offense-Minor	A21
RMFD	Revoke Felony Drug Multiple	W01
RMPS	Revoke Per Se 0/10 Multiple	W01
RM08	Revoke Per Se .08 Multiple	W01
RND1	Revoke Conviction .02	A60
RND2	Revoke 2nd Conviction .02	W01
RND3	Revoke 3/More Convictions .02	W01
RNRD	Revoke Controlled Substance	A24
ROCH	Rev Oper CMV Under CDL Rst Haz	B25
ROCR	Rev Oper CMV Under CDL Rest.	B25
RPAO	Rev Alcohol Offense-Provsion	A21
RPC1	Revoke Per Se .02 CMV	A61
RPC2	Revoke Per Se .02 CMV-2nd	W01
RPC3	Revoke Per Se .02 Cmv3/More	W01
RPER	Revoke Perjury/False Affidavit	W00
RPN1	Rev .02-.04 Under 21 Non-CMV	A61
RPPS	Revoke Per Se 0.15 Or More	A90
RPSC	Revoke Per Se 0.04 CMV	A94
RPSH	Revoke Per Se 0.04 Haz	A94
RPSN	Revoke Per Se .08 Non-CMV	A98
RPS1	Revoke Per Se .02	A61
RPS2	Revoke Per Se .02-2nd	W01
RPS3	Revoke Per Se .02-3/More	W01
RTCS	Revoke Possess/Distribute Drug	A50
RTID	Revoke Violate Lic Restriction	A41
RVAS	Revoke Vehicular Assault	U06
RVHM	Revoke Vehicular Homicide	U08
R1BP	Revoke Buy/Possess Alcohol	A31
R1FD	Revoke Felony Drug	U03
R1ND	Revoke Non-Felony Drug	A33
R1PS	Revoke Per Se 0.10	A90
R108	Revoke Per Se .08	A98
R2BP	Revoke 2 Buy/Possess Alcohol	W01
R2DC	Revoke 2 Alcohol - Conv Date	W01
R2DV	Revoke 2 Alcohol - Vio Date	W01
R2ND	Revoke 2nd Non-Felony Drug	W01
R2PS	Revoke 2nd Per Se	A98
R3AO	Revoke 3 Alcohol Convictions	W01
R3BP	Revoke 3/More Buy/Poss Alcohol	W01
R3ND	Revoke 3/More Non-Felony Drug	W01
R3PS	Revoke 3-More Per Se	W01
R3RK	Revoke 3 Reckless In 2 Years	M84
SAEC	CDL Susp Extended - Accident	W01
SAEX	Suspend Extended - Accident	W01
SAIN	Susp Administrative Insurance	D36
SAI2	Suspend Admin Ins-2nd Notice	W01
SAI3	Suspend Admin Ins-3rd Notice	W01
SARC	CDL Susp Renewed - Accident	W01
SARN	Suspend Renewed - Accident	W01
SCEC	CDL Susp Extended - Citation	W01
SCEX	Suspend Extended - Citation	W01
SCPT	Suspend Chauffeur Points	W01
SCRC	CDL Susp Renewed - Citation	W01
SCRN	Suspend Renewed - Citation	W01
SDIR	Suspend Direct Excess Points	W01
SDUI	Suspend Drove Under Influence	A21
SECR	Suspend Refusal - Interlock	A12

Code	Description	ACD
SEC2	Suspend Two Refusals - Interlock	W01
SEC3	Suspend 3/More Refusal- Interlock	W01
SFCE	Sus Lic Restriction Extended	A41
SFP1	Suspend Fuel Piracy First	W00
SFP2	Suspend Fuel Piracy Second	W00
SFRA	Suspend Financial Responsibility	D35
SFTC	Suspend Child Support Nonpayment	D51
SHTO	Susp Habitual Offndr-Interlock	W01
SINS	Suspend Insurance Terminated	B63
SJDG	Suspend Unsatisfied Judgment	D39
SMCS	Sus-Controlled Sub Vio-Multi	W01
SMPS	Suspend 0.10 Multiple Interlck	W01
SNCR	Suspend Co Resident SR22 Reqrd	B63
SND1	Suspend Conviction .02	A60
SND2	Sus 2nd Conviction .02-Intrlck	W01
SND3	Suspend 3/More Conv .02-Intrlk	W01
SNLI	Suspend No Liability Insurance	D35
SNRV	Suspend Non-Resident Violator	D56
SPAI	Sus Provide Alcohol/Id - Minor	A31
SPAO	Sus Alcohol Off-Provsnl-Intrlk	A21
SPC1	Suspend Per Se .02 Cmv	A61
SPRO	Suspend Excess Points	W01
SPSR	Suspend Per Se Revocation	A90
SPS1	Suspend Per Se .02	A61
SPS2	Suspend Per Se .02-2nd-Intrlck	W01
SPS3	Sus Per Se .02 - 3/More-Intrlk	W01
SPTS	Suspend Excessive Points	W01
SPT9	Suspend Excessive Points	W01
SRC1	Sus-Rail Crossing Vio 1st	M--
SRC2	Sus-Rail Crossing Vio 2-3 Yrs	W60
SRC3	Sus-Rail Crossing Vio 3-3 Yrs	W61
SSRO	Suspend Sr22 Required Owner	B63
STLA	Suspend No Interlock Lease	A41
S1CS	Sus-Controlled Sub Vio - 1st	A33
S1PS	Suspend Per Se 0.10 - Interlock	A90
S2DC	Susp 2 Alcohol-Conv Date- Interlock	A21
S2DV	Susp 2 Alcohol-Vio Date- Interlock	W01
S2SV	Suspend 2 Serious Vios/3 Years	W30
S3AO	Suspend 3 Alcohol Conv-I Interlock	W01
S3SV	Suspend 3 Serious Vios/3 Years	W31
TRAN	CDL Os Dept Action Received	0

Point System Summary

Colorado points range from 1 to 12 points. The following are point accumulations that result in suspension:

- Adult Driver (21 and older) - 12 points in any 12 consecutive months or 18 points in any 24 consecutive months.
- Minor Driver (18 thru 20 years of age) - 9 points in any 12 consecutive months or 12 points in any 24 consecutive months or 14 or more points between the ages of 18-21.
- Under the Age of 18 - 6 points in 12 consecutive months or 7 points prior to turning 18.

Connecticut

Administration	Important Telephone and Web Contacts
Driver Services Division Department of Motor Vehicles 60 State Street, Wethersfield 06161-1896 860-263-5720 www.ct.gov/dmv	Telephone Center ....860-263-5700 Suspension/Restoration ....860-263-5720 Driver Improvement..860-263-5720 Vehicle and Driver Record Information ....860-263-5154 State Department of Insurance ....860-297-3804 State Police (DPS)...860-685-8000 General Email Contacts at: www.ct.gov/dmv/cwp/view.asp?a=803&q=244560
Motor Vehicle Laws at: www.cga.ct.gov/current/pub/title14.htm Motor Vehicle Regulations at: www.ct.gov/dmv/cwp/view.asp?a=803&q=396292	

Driver's License Format, Issuance and Renewal

Classes, Restrictions and Endorsements Appear After the Driving Record Content Section

License Format

The DL document is nNine numbers. The first two digits indicate, by odd or even year, the driver's month of birth and the seven additional numbers are the next available sequential numbers.

Document Appearance

Current Documents

On October 4, 2011, the Connecticut Department of Motor Vehicles began a new program with verified identity protection for people obtaining new or renewing driver licenses and DMV-issued identification cards. The new license features a salmon-colored banner across the top and the non-driver identification cards have a green banner. The new cards will also feature more prominently the license or identification number, date of birth, and expiration date in bold letters. Through the SelectCT ID program, people verifying will get a gold star on the license or ID card. Those declining will have one stamped "Not for Federal Identification."

Security Characteristics: 1) An embedded graphic of the Charter Oak Tree within the center of the card that is only visible when held up to a bright light. 2) An image of a lighthouse that will appear as a hologram when the credential is held under ultra-violet light. 3) A special laminate with security features that will cover both sides of the card. 4) A second bar code and unique serial number located on the back of each card. The serial number, which is also contained within the bar code, will be connected to the customer's identity record.

Position of Photo: Lower right, also, a smaller ghost image on lower left. Applicants under 21 years old have image in upper center on left side of card, smaller ghost image on lower right of card.

Minor Age Driver Locator: The date when 16 and 17-year-old card holders will turn 18 appears in a yellow box running vertically and adjacent to the person's photo. The words "Under 21 Until xx-xx-xxxx" appear in a red box running vertically and adjacent to the person's photo or else next to the under 18 yellow box. Also, all cards for applicants under 21 years of age are printed in a vertical format.

CDL Indicator: A green box appears in the top banner with class and "Commercial Driver's License" is printed in green under the salmon bar. If the license holder has a commercial instruction permit, the indicators are the same except the color is yellow, not green.

Older Documents

There are three older versions of the driver license documents in circulation. The general descriptions below are for all three.

Security Characteristics Optical Variable Device (State of Connecticut seal and "DMVCT") embedded in overlay. Back laminate includes a State outline map image, visible under a black light, with the word Connecticut running through the image. Connecticut banner for all cards are color-coded. (CDL – Green; Permits – Yellow; Driver License – Blue; Identification Card – Red)

Position of Photo Lower right, also, a smaller ghost image on lower left. Applicants under 21 years old have image in center right of card, smaller ghost image on lower right of card.

Minor Age Driver Locator The words "Under 21 Until xx-xx-xxxx" appear on the lower front of card in red block. Also, all cards for applicants under 21 years of age are printed in a vertical format.

CDL Indicator   "Commercial Driver's License" is printed in green on upper right corner; also, "learner's" or "CD instruction permit" printed here in orange.

Issuance

Location of Requirements for Proof of Identity:

www.ct.gov/dmv/cwp/view.asp?a=805&q=244772&dmvPNavCtr=|41640|41679|#52709

Age Requirements

There is a mandatory Graduated Licensing Program for young drivers with specific restrictions in place for the first and the second three-month period of drivers aged 16 and 17. Those obtaining a Learner's Permit on or after 08/2008 have a "Photo Permit" and those who obtained the permit prior to 08/2008 have a "Paper Permit." Since 01/01/2009, all 16 and 17-year-olds seeking a driver's license need to pass a second written test called the DMV Final Exam. Passenger restrictions for 16-and-17-year-old motorcycle operators' license dictate they may not transport any passengers during the first six months they hold the endorsement. Motorcycle drivers 18 years-old or older may not transport passengers for the first three months. The web gives extensive details on all the requirements for the Graduated Licensing Program.

Residency

License must be obtained within thirty (30) days of establishing residency.

Renewal

Renewal is the birth date of sixth year, CDL is for four years, see below for over 65. Driver keeps same number when renewing. All renewals, including for military, require a photo. Out-of-state military personnel may began renewal process up to 4 months prior to expiration. An application, with signature of commissioned officer in charge, is required. Call 860-263-5148 for information on renewal while out of state. Renewal cannot be done online, but a driver or ID holder may request a change of address form. For more information see www.ct.gov/dmv/cwp/view.asp?a=4078&q=477742.

Elderly-Related Restrictions

A Limited License Program for older drivers (and for those drivers whose abilities have changed since their initial licensing) is offered. The license will contain limitations (such as daylight driving only) noted as restrictions on the physical document. Vision tests are not required at renewal or for new license after age 65. If requested, a 2-year license renewal is offered for those over 65.

Vehicle Insurance, Title and Registration Facts

Registration

Plates are issued on a biannual basis. CT eliminated vehicle registration stickers on August 1, 2010.

Renewal

Renewal information is mailed or online renewal is available at www.ct.gov/dmv (click on Online Services) for those who have no record changes, parking violations or property tax issues (and have received a PIN with the renewal notice). A verification site is provided for those who renew by mail, to confirm that payment has been received. Click on *Registration Lookup* under the Online Services tab. Renewal is blocked to those who have unpaid municipal property taxes or more than five unpaid parking violations.

New Residents

License plates must be purchased within sixty days of establishing residency. An emissions test and vehicle identification number (VIN) verification are both required and performed at the emissions station.

Inspections and Emissions Testing

Connecticut has required emissions tests for gasoline and diesel powered vehicles up to 10,000 pounds (motorcycles, composite vehicles, and farm vehicles are exempt). Testing every two years is required for vehicles 4 to 24 years old. Vehicles exempt from emissions testing will require a VIN verification inspection if previously registered out-of-state.

Safety inspections are required for certain vehicles including taxis, ambulances, school transportation vehicles, driver education vehicles if over 100,000 miles, homemade trailers, non-commercial trailers 10,000 GVWR and under, non-commercial trailers 10,000 over GVWR if less than 10 years old, and certain imported vehicle over 10 years old among others. The complete list is available on the web.

Passenger Plate Facts

Most vehicles were issued two plates, with the exception of trailers and motorcycles which are issued one plate. The county of issuance is not indicated on the plate. As of August 1, 2010, CT vehicle owners may legally drive without registration stickers on the front windshield or on the license plate. Prior to that date one decal (MO-YR), was shown on the windshield. When vehicle is sold, plate can be transferred to another vehicle by the same owner, otherwise it must be returned to the Department of Motor Vehicles.

Insurance and Financial Responsibility

Connecticut requires liability insurance. Minimum financial responsibility limits are $20,000/40,000/10,000. The state does not have a security type law in effect for verification of insurance. The state's enforcement program is based on mandatory cancellation reporting by insurance companies.

Withdrawal Sanctions, and Alcohol and Drug Testing

Alcohol and Chemical Testing

Connecticut's legal intoxication standard is .08 percent and .02 percent for those under 21. The state has an implied-consent law as well as an administrative license-suspension law. Blood, urine, and breath tests are permissible. CDL holders are subject to a standard of .04 percent when operating a commercial motor vehicle.

Suspensions and Revocations - Alcohol Related

See the Appendix for a list of the federally mandated disqualifications for offenses occurring in a CMV per MCSIA.

Department Sanctions - Admin Per Se

The license suspension periods outlined below have been recently revised and will be imposed in addition to criminal penalties (see 2nd chart below.) In most cases, the motor vehicle sanctions will be imposed much earlier.

Admin Per Se Sanctions - Drivers 21 Years and Older	First Offense	Second Offense	Third Offense
Refusal to submit to a blood, breath or urine test	6 months	1 year	3 years
Test results of .08 or higher up to .16	90 days	9 months	2 years
Test results of .16 or higher	120 days	10 months	2½ years

Admin Per Se Sanctions - Drivers 18-20	First Offense	Second Offense	Third Offense
Refusal to submit to a blood, breath or urine test	1 year	2 years	6 years
Test results of .02 or higher up to .16	6 months	18 months	4 years
Test results of .16 or higher	240 days	20 months	5 years

Admin Per Se Sanctions - Drivers 16 and 17	First Offense	Second Offense	Third Offense
Refusal to submit to a blood, breath or urine test	18 months	3 years	6 years
Test results of .02 or higher up to .16	1 year	2 years	4 years
Test results of .16 or higher	1 year	30 months	5 years

Criminal Law Penalties for Test Results of .08 or Higher

The Table below is for Operating Under the Influence of Alcohol or Drugs, C.G.S §14-227a, §14-227g or §14-111n conviction **on or after January 1, 2012**. Under Connecticut's criminal law, the driver arrested for DUI will receive both a summons and court date. If the court proceedings result in a conviction, the following penalties must be imposed:

First Conviction	Second Conviction	Third or Subsequent Conviction
45 days license suspension. All other terms of suspensions must be served except 14-227b. One year IID requirement from restoration date. If previously convicted of 53a-56b or 53a 60d, it's considered the 2nd offense.	45 days license suspension or until 21st birthday, whichever is longer. All other terms of suspensions must be served except 14-227b. Three years IID requirement from restoration date. Effective July 1, 2012, if driver serves less than a one year suspension, is restricted to drive to or from work or school, an alcohol or drug abuse treatment program or an ignition interlock device service center for the first year. (Must carry the appropriate schedule at all times.)	Permanent Revocation. May request a hearing after at least 6 years after date of revocation.

This Table is for **Operating Under the Influence of Alcohol or Drugs**, C.G.S §14-227a, §14-227g or §14-111n Conviction **prior to January 1, 2012**.

	First Conviction	Second Conviction	Third or Subsequent Conviction
Under 21 years old for OUI convictions prior to January 1, 2012	1-year license suspension.	3 years license suspension or until 21st birthday, whichever is longer. Two years IID requirement from restoration date. Effective July 1, 2012, if driver serves less than a one year suspension, is restricted to drive to or from work or school, an alcohol or drug abuse treatment program or an ignition interlock device service center for the first year. (Must carry the appropriate schedule at all times.)	Permanent Revocation. May request a hearing after at least 6 years after date of revocation.
21 and older for OUI convictions prior to January 1, 2012.	1 year license suspension.	1 year license suspension. Two years IID requirement from restoration date. Effective July 1, 2012, if driver serves less than a one year suspension, is restricted to drive to or from work or school, an alcohol or drug abuse treatment program or an ignition interlock device service center for the first year. (Must carry the appropriate schedule at all times.)	Permanent Revocation. May request a hearing after at least 6 years after date of revocation.

About Ignition Interlock Device Program

The Department's Ignition Interlock Device (IID) Program provides any operator, who has been convicted under (C.G.S) §14-227a, §14-227g or §14-111n, Operating Under the Influence of Alcohol or Drugs (OUI), §53a-56b, Vehicular Manslaughter or §53a-60b, Vehicular Assault, the ability to operate a motor vehicle. For more information on IID see www.ct.gov/dmv/cwp/view.asp?a=813&q=309844&dmvPNavCtr=|#44832.

Suspensions and Revocations - Non-Alcohol Related

The state is in compliance with the federally mandated disqualifications on CDLs. See the Appendix for details. The following are violations that will result in a suspension

- 4 or More Moving Violations in 2-Year Period
- 4 or More Speeding Violations in 2-Year Period
- Assault in the 2nd Degree With a Motor Vehicle
- Child Restraint
- Dishonored Check to DMV
- Disobeying Signal of Officer
- Evading Responsibility
- Failure to Complete Retraining Class
- False Statements or Reports
- High Points
- Improper Use of Marker, Registration or License
- Interfering or Tampering with a Motor vehicle
- Manslaughter With Motor Vehicle
- Medical Qualification
- Operating Under Suspension
- Operating Under the Influence
- Racing
- Reckless Driving
- Using Motor Vehicle or Vessel Without Owner's Permission

Young Drivers: 16 and 17 year old drivers receive a 48 hour suspension if cited for:
- Violating any of the driving restrictions that apply after licensure.
- Driving 20 miles per hour or more above a posted speed limit.
- Driving under the influence of alcohol or drugs.
- Driving recklessly.
- Racing a motor vehicle on a public highway.

Reinstatement Requirements

There is a $175.00 fee for reinstatement from either a suspension or revocation.

Substance Abuse Treatment Program - A substance abuse treatment program is required prior to restoration of a license or operating privilege when a second offense of either refusing or failing a chemical alcohol test on or after October 1, 1995 or a conviction of operating while under the influence of liquor or drug on or after October 1, 2003.

Record Access: Laws, Rules, and Forms

Note: This Section Applies to Both Driver and Vehicle Records.

Governing Statutes and Rules

Motor Vehicle Laws at:
    www.cga.ct.gov/current/pub/title14.htm
Motor Vehicle Regulations at:
    www.ct.gov/dmv/cwp/view.asp?a=803&q=396292
C.G.S. §14-10 defines and regulates the disclosure of personal information from records. Public Act 97-266, adopting provisions similar to DPPA, went into effect 7/1/97. §14-50a of the Connecticut General Statutes regulates the fees for copies, abstracts, duplicates, replacements and searches. Specific applicable request codes for permissible uses listed on the back of the Request Form J-23.

Connecticut does not have the following federal DPPA exceptions: 5, 10, and 14. Connecticut added the following exceptions to C.G.S. §14-10(f) (see www.cga.ct.gov/current/pub/chap246.htm#Sec14-10.htm):

(A) In connection with matters of motor vehicle or driver safety and theft, motor vehicle emissions, motor vehicle product alterations, recalls or advisories, performance monitoring of motor vehicles, and dealers by motor vehicle manufacturers, motor vehicle market research activities including survey research, motor vehicle product and service communications and removal of non-owner records from the original owner records of motor vehicle manufacturers to implement the provisions of the Federal Automobile Information Disclosure Act, 15 USC 1231 et seq., the Clean Air Act, 42 USC 7401 et seq., and 49 USC Chapters 301, 305 and 321 to 331 inclusive, as amended from time-to-time, and any provision of the general statutes enacted to attain compliance with said federal provisions;

(D) In connection with matters of motor vehicle or driver safety and theft, motor vehicle emissions, motor vehicle product alterations, recalls or advisories, performance monitoring of motor vehicles and motor vehicle parts and dealers, producing statistical reports and removal of non-owner records from the original owner records of motor vehicle manufacturers, provided the personal information is not published, disclosed or used to contact individuals except as permitted under subparagraph (A) of this subdivision;

(H) In connection with any lawful purpose of a labor organization, as defined in C.G.S. §31-77, provided (i) such organization has entered into a contract with the commissioner, on such terms and conditions as the commissioner may require, and (ii) the information will be

used only for the purposes specified in the contract other than campaign or political purposes;

(J) For the purpose of preventing fraud by verifying the accuracy of personal information contained in a motor vehicle record, including an individual's photograph or computerized image, as submitted by an individual to a legitimate business or an agent, employee or contractor of a legitimate business, provided the individual has provided express consent in accordance with subdivision (5) of subsection (a) of this section.

Request and Consent Forms

Driving Records: Requesters must complete *Copy Records Request Form J-23*. The form can be ordered by calling the Telephone Information Center at 860-263-5700 or download or fill it out at www.ct.gov/dmv/lib/dmv/20/29/j23.pdf. The form still must be mailed.
Vehicle & Vessel Records: The form to use for **registration** records is the *J-23* mentioned above. The form to use to obtain a copy of a **title** is *J-23T* found at www.ct.gov/dmv/lib/dmv/20/29/j-23t.pdf. For vessel records use *J-23B* found at www.ct.gov/dmv/lib/dmv/j-23b.pdf. The Telephone Information Center is accessible 24 hours a day, and provides voice mail ordering forms. Personal information is released to those requesters who sign under penalty of false statement on the permissible use on most records.

Vendor and Third Party Access Policy

Approved electronic vendors can access records for other vendors (who are not online, etc.) who will then sell to a permissible end user, subject to these restrictions—
a. If contract between original vendor and reseller contains same language as contract between the state and the original vendor
b. If contract between reseller and end-user contains same language as contract between the state and the original vendor.
Vendors may not transmit records via the Internet unless acceptable safeguards are imposed.

Records Ordered For Non-permissible Uses

Records with personal information are not released without consent or a permissible use. Public Act 08-150 Sec. 3 added a penalty for misuse of personal information contained in DMV records to CGS Sec. 14-10(g).

Access to Driver-Related Records

Driving Records

General Information and Fees
Department of Motor Vehicles, Copy Records Section, 60 State Street, Wethersfield CT 06161-0503, 860-263-5154.
The fee is $20.00 for a certified driving record, or $15.00 if obtained electronically to those who qualify for the volume contract.

In-Person — Counter service is no longer offered from this location. Individuals can walk in to any branch and obtain a copy of their own record. But those requesting record on others, even with a permissible use, must mail in the *J-23* request form.
Mail — The fee includes certification. A license status report is also available for the same price. Standard record requests mailed to the above address are processed within five to ten working days. The driver's license number and name are needed when ordering; the DOB may also be helpful. A photo ID of the person signing the *J-23 Form* is required. The fee must accompany each request. Connecticut charges for no record found requests. Turnaround time is typically 5 to 10 business days. Sending a SASE is encouraged for faster turnaround time.
Electronic — The online system is operational in interactive and batch

modes. The fee is $15.00 for each inquiry made to the online system, including no record found reports. The driver's license number, first name, last name, middle initial and DOB are required when ordering. A prepayment/deposit for the first 2,500 records is required upon approval of a contract for the online service. Thereafter, the state bills per inquiry. This prepayment is non-refundable and must be used within the term of the agreement. A first-time contract term is for one year; a renewal contract term is two years. For more information write to the Data Access unit at the same address listed above.
Editor's Note:
    The state's Judicial Branch offers a free look-up of motor vehicle convictions at www.jud2.ct.gov/crdockets/SearchByDefDisp.aspx. Search by name and court location.
Bulk — The DMV may provide the operator license file (names and addresses, class, restrictions and endorsements) on a contractual basis. This decision is based on a case-by-case basis and use of the records. For more information write to the Data Access Unit at the same address listed above.
By Person of Record — CT drivers may obtain their driving record by mail (at Wethersfield Office only) or walk-in at any full service DMV Branch Office, as described above. Use of the *J-23 Form* is

required. At present, there is no program for drivers to order or view their own record online.

Notification/Monitoring Program

At present, Connecticut does not offer a monitoring system or notification program to employers or insurance companies to track incidents of submitted drivers.

Accident Reports

Reporting - Accident reporting is not under the jurisdiction of the Department of Motor Vehicles but under the Department of Public Safety. Motorists are required to report motor vehicle accidents to police if there is an injury, death or property damage (no minimum limit designated) and if they are unable for any reason to share information with the injured party or property owner. Motorists are not, however, required to file written accident reports, which are the responsibility of the investigating police agency.

Record Access - Reports (officer copy) of accidents occurring on a state roadway or investigated by the state law enforcement officials can be obtained from the Dept. of Public Safety, Reports and Records Unit, 1111 Country Club Rd, Middletown CT 06457, 860-685-8250, fax-860-685-8675, www.ct.gov/despp/cwp/view.asp?a=4212&q=494530. Requests must be in writing and include name and address of requester, date and location of incident, names of operators, and the eight digit case number if known. Search fee is $16.00 search fee per uncertified report or $17.00 if certified. Use of their Form DPS-96C (www.ct.gov/despp/lib/despp/reports_and_records/dps-0096-c.pdf) is suggested. Forms may be downloaded from the web. Normally accident reports are available within ten business days following the date of the accident. Turnaround time can take as long as ten weeks. The agency will not release criminal cases still pending in the court system. Normally, records are destroyed after 10 years.

Online access of traffic crash reports is now available via a designated vendor – see www.docview.us.com. A $6.00 convenience fee is added. Please note, not all accidents will be available on Docview.

Access to Vehicle-Related Records

General Information and Fees

Department of Motor Vehicles, Copy Record Unit, 60 State Street, Wethersfield 06161-1896, 860-263-5154.

The release of vehicle title and registration information is restricted to permissible users or those who have authorization from the subject of the record inquiry. requesters can search by name and vehicle plate number, or vehicle plate number and description (VIN is helpful). The standard fee is $20.00 for a title search (includes lien data), a current owner file information, a copy of Application for Title, or an original registration certificate. Certification for any document is an additional $20.00. Use forms as indicated below. If the request does not fall under a permissible use, then written authorization from the subject must be presented. Paper records are kept a minimum of three years after expiration.

In-Person – Counter service is no longer offered from this location. Individuals can walk in to any branch and obtain a copy of their own record. But those requesting records on others, even with a permissible use, must mail in the *J-23* form to the Wethersfield office.

Mail – A photo ID of the person signing the *Copy Records Request Form (J23/J23T)* is required. Mail turnaround time is estimated at 5 to 10 working days. Use of SASE is suggested for faster service.

Electronic – There is no online access to records, but one may verify or check registration expiration dates by entering the plate number at www.dmvselfservice.ct.gov/RegistrationVerificationService.aspx.

Bulk – Connecticut does not make available any select or customized dumps of registration or vehicle information. However, the state may provide a complete set of all the records to approved businesses with a permissible use and an agreement with the Department. For more information write to the Data Access Unit at the address listed above.

Access to Vessel-Related Records

General Information, Access and Fees

The DMV maintains the registration file for boats. All motorized boats and all boats over 19 1/2 ft must be registered. Boats are not titled. For record requests, the *J-23/J23B Form* must be filled out and processed by the Marine Vessel Section at 60 State Street, Wethersfield, CT 06161-5031 860-263-5151. The fee is $20.00 for a current owner print-out or

for a copy of the registration. A complete boat history is $20.00 plus $20.00 per copy of the registration. Turnaround time is 7-14 days working days. The request form (J-23B) is available at www.ct.gov/dmv/lib/dmv/j-23b.pdf.

Also, batch and bulk records are available, subject to DPPA standards.

Driving Record Content and Reciprocity

What's On or Not On the Driving Record

- Driver history records do not contain address information.
- Connecticut does not report accidents on the driving record, but reports all convictions and administrative suspensions.
- The state does not permit driver school attendance in lieu of conviction.
- First time DUI offenders may be eligible for a court-sanctioned alcohol education program. Upon completion, the criminal case is dismissed. Program participation is listed on the driving record for seven years.
- The length of time that convictions are shown on the public driving record is three years for moving violations for non-CDL, if for CDL then four; ten years for DUI, Evading Responsibility, Driving Under Suspension for non-CDL, if CDL then 55 years. Suspensions are indefinite until restored.

Data Retention

CDL driver records are purged based on the timetable per federal regulations (see the Appendix). Surrendered licenses (to other states) can be retained as part of the public file for up to seven years before being purged from the system.

Court to Repository

The Judicial Department transfers conviction information to the Department daily. It can take 5 to 7 days to update new records on an operator's driving history record.

State Reciprocity for Non-CDL Drivers

- Will suspend driver for unpaid out-of-state convictions if a "fail to appear."
- Record of new incoming driver is not shown on MVR.
- Some out-of-state convictions are shown on MVR if other state is a Compact member.

- Out-of-state accidents are not shown on MVR.
- Convictions of out-of-state drivers are sent to home state

- Record forwarded to new state upon surrender of lic - if requested.

Abbreviations That May Appear on a Driving Record

CDL DISQ	CDL License Disqualified
CDLIS Inquiry Data	Last Date of Inquiry to Commercial Drive License Information System
IID REQ	Ignition Interlock Devise Required
NDR Inquiry Date	Last Date of Inquiry to National Driver Registry

License Classes, Restrictions, and Endorsements

Overview

Connecticut made major changes in 2006 to their License Classes, Restrictions, and Endorsements, as noted below. The state will support both old and new Classes, Restrictions, and Endorsements until a subject's record is modified. The renewal cycle is 4 to 6 years. Connecticut began issuing the CDL in April 1992.

License Classes– Commercial

Class A   Any combination of vehicles with a gross combined weight rating (GCWR) of 26,001 pounds or more, provided the GVWR of the vehicles being towed is in excess of 10,000 pounds.

Class B   Any single vehicle with a GVWR of 26,001 pounds or more, or any such vehicle towing a vehicle not in excess of 10,000 pounds.

Class C   Any single vehicle not in excess of 26,001 pounds, or any such vehicle towing a vehicle not in excess, including vehicles required to be placarded for hazardous materials; or any vehicle designed to transport 16 or more passengers, including the driver. Also, vehicles designed to transport more than ten passengers (including the driver), and used to transport students under the age of twenty-one years to and from school

License Classes– Non-Commercial

Class D   (Issued as of 01/01/2006) Any motor vehicle including a combination of motor vehicle and trailer or trailing unit used exclusively for camping or any other recreational purposes regardless of the gross weight of the trailer or trailing unit, except a commercial motor vehicle or an articulated vehicle or any other combination of motor vehicle and trailer where the gross weight of the trailing unit or trailer is more than 10,000 pounds.

Class 1   **(Has not been issued since 01/01/2006)** Any motor vehicle except a commercial motor vehicle.

Class 2   **(Has not been issued since 01/01/2006)** Any motor vehicle including a combination of motor vehicle and trailer or trailing unit used exclusively for camping or any other recreational purposes regardless of the gross weight of the trailer or trailing unit, except a commercial motor vehicle or an articulated vehicle or any other combination of motor vehicle and trailer where the gross weight of the trailing unit or trailer is more than 10,000 pounds.

Class M   **(Made an Endorsement 01/01/2006)** Alone or combined with any other class evidence the holder is licensed to operate a motorcycle.

Restrictions

* = No longer issued as of 01/01/2006. Will still show on license document until renewed.

B	Corrective Lenses	R	No Limited Access Roads
C	Mechanical Aid	*T	Taxicab, Service Bus, Motor Vehicle in Livery Service, Coach, Motorbus
D	Prosthetic Aid		
E	Automatic Transmission	U	Hearing Aid Required
F	Outside Mirror	*V	STVs and vehicles listed Under Restriction T; drivers with V restriction will not be allowed to drive students to home or school
G	Limited to Daylight Only		
K	CDL Intrastate Only		
L	Vehicle Without Air Brakes	W	Medical Waiver Required
*Q	Any Vehicle Exempt from the CDL Program with a GVWR of 26,001 or More Pounds Excluding Recreational Vehicles	*Z	School Bus - CDL only

Endorsements

A	Activity Vehicle	S	School Bus - includes Student Transportation Vehicle, Activity Vehicle, Taxi, Livery, Service Bus and Motor Coach
F	Taxi/Livery/Service Bus/Motor Coach		
H	Hazardous Materials	T	Tandem Double/Triple
M	Motorcycle	V	Student Transportation Vehicle - includes Activity Vehicle, Taxi, Livery, Service Bus and Motor Coach
N	Tank Vehicle		
P	Passenger	X	Endorsements N & H Combined
Q	Fire Apparatus		

Connecticut Conviction Tables

Connecticut has converted many of their *Reason Codes* to the ACD Code Set. Thus, when a violation has a corresponding ACD code, the driving record shows the ACD Code. However, there are many state violations (with no points) that are not applicable to an ACD Code. For those convictions, only the Reason Code is shown on the driving record. And, if there is an out of state conviction for a law not on the CT books, then only the ACD Code is shown and the conviction does not have a Reason Code.

Therefore two tables are presented as listed below. If only the ACD Code is shown without a reason code OR if the ACD Code and the Reason Code are identical, then refer to the AAMVA Code in the back of this book. The two tables are:

1. **Conviction Table 1 sorted by ACD Code.**
2. **Conviction Table 2 sorted by Reason Code.**

Conviction Table 1 with ACD Code and Statute

If a violation appears on a driving with an ACD Code not found on this list, the probability is that the violation occurred out of State. Please refer to the back of this book for the complete ACD Code set.

ACD	Statute	Description	Points
A04	14111n	Reports of comparable convictions	
A04	14227A	Operation while under the influence of liquor or drugs while having an elevated blood alcohol content	
A08	14111n	Reports of comparable convictions	
A08	14227A,ACZ,AZ	Operation while under the influence of liquor or drugs while having an elevated blood alcohol content	
A08	14386A3	Operation under influence-snowmobile	
A10	14111n	Reports of comparable convictions	
A11	14111n	Reports of comparable convictions	
A12	14227b	Refused to submit to test for alcohol-implied consent law under 18 years old	
A12	14227b	Refused to submit to test for alcohol-implied consent law 18 to 20 years of age	
A12	14227b	Refused to submit to test for alcohol-implied consent law	
A20	14111n	Reports of comparable convictions (Driving under the influence of alcohol or drugs)	
A21	14111n	Reports of comparable convictions (Driving under the influence of alcohol)	
A22	14111n	Reports of comparable convictions (Driving under the influence of drugs)	
A23	14111n	Reports of comparable convictions (Driving under the influence of alcohol and drugs)	
A25	14227AB	Driving while impaired (repealed)	
A31	3089B1	Possession of alcohol on any public street or highway, by a minor	
A31	3089B2	Possession of alcohol in any other public or private location, by a minor	
A33	21a279a1,a2	Possession of less than one half ounce of cannabis type substance	
A33	PA1171	Possession of less than one half ounce of cannabis type substance	
A41	14-111	Failure to comply (calibration of IID)	
A41	14227J	Court order prohibiting operation of motor vehicle not equipped with ignition interlock device	
A41	14227K	Avoidance of or tampering with ignition interlock device	
A41	14227KA1	Avoidance of ignition interlock device requirements	
A41	14227KA2	Operation of vehicle not equipped with a required ignition interlock device	
A41	14227KB	Tampering, Altering, or Bypassing a required ignition interlock device	
A50	21A277a,b	Motor vehicle used in commission of felony involving the manu, distrib, or dispensing of a controlled substance	
A50	21A278a,b	Motor vehicle used in commission of felony involving the manu, distrib, or dispensing of a controlled substance	
A60	14111n	Reports of comparable convictions (Underage convicted or Drinking and Driving at .02 or higher BAC)	
A60	14227G	Operation while under the influence of liquor or drugs while having an elevated blood alcohol content	
A61	14227b	Implied consent to test operator's blood, breath or urine	
A61	14227b	Implied consent to test operator's blood, breath or urine	
A61	14227b	Implied consent to test operator's blood, breath or urine	
A61	14227b	Implied consent to test operator's blood, breath or urine	
A94	14227b	Implied consent to test operator's blood, breath, or urine	
A94	1444kc	Administrative Per Se- CMV	
A98	14227b	Implied consent to test operator's blood, breath, or urine	
B01	14111n	Reports of comparable convictions	
B02	14224A,ACZ.AZ	Evading responsibility serious injury	
B03	14224B,BCZ,BZ	Evading responsibility	
B05	14111n	Reports of comparable convictions (Leaving scene before police arrive)	
B05	1444kb	Leaving scene before police arrive	
B06	14111n	Reports of comparable convictions (Leaving scene before police arrive- Fatal accident)	
B07	14111n	Reports of comparable convictions (Leaving scene before police arrive- Personal injury)	
B19	14163C8B2	Operating a CMV transporting Hazardous materials requiring a placards or operating a motor vehicle designed to transport 16 or more passengers including the driver in violation of out of service order as prescribed in 49CFR395.13(d)	
B19	14163C8B4	Operating a CMV transporting Hazardous materials requiring a placards or operating a motor vehicle designed to transport 16 or more passengers including the driver in violation of out of service order as prescribed in 49CFR396.9(c)(2)	
B20	1444kb		
B20	5476l(h) YO, 14215	Operation while registration or license is refused, suspended or revoked.	
B24	1444kb	Operation while registration or license is refused, suspended or revoked.	
B26	14215,C,CCZ,CZ, Z	Operation while registration or license is refused, suspended or revoked.	
B27	14163C8B1	Operating a CMV in violation of the out of service order as prescribed in 49CFR395.13(d)	
B27	14163C8B3	Operating a CMV that has been declared out of service in violation of the out of service order as prescribed in 49CFR396.9(c)(2)	
B41	14147A	Improper use of marker, registration or license	

ACD	Statute	Description	Points
B51	14215b1	Operating motor vehicle 60 days or less after expiration of suspension of license- Failure to renew operator's license under 14-41(c)	
B51	14215b2	Operating motor vehicle more than 60 days after expiration of suspension of license (1st offense) Operating without a license under 14-36	
B51	1436A	Motor vehicle operator's license required for operation of motor vehicle	
B51	1436B	Allowing person under sixteen years to operate a motor vehicle	
B51	1436B	Instruction of persons eighteen years of age or older	
B51	1436B	Operation of motor vehicle by a person 18 years of age or older in violation of learners permit requirements	
B51	1441D	Expiration and renewal of operator's licenses and permits	
B56	1439A1,A2	No nonresident shall operate a CMV without a CDL	
B56	1444A	Commercial driver's license required for operation of a commercial motor vehicle	
B65	14111(a)	Failure to comply with the Commissioner (Medical)	
B65	14275C	Violation of regulations re school buses and motor vehicles used to transport special education students	
B91	1444	License endorsement for operators of commercial motor vehicles used for passenger transportation	
B91	14276	School bus operators to hold valid passenger and school endorsement.	
B91	1436A	Classification of operators' license	
B91	1436AD	Operation of motor vehicle in violation of the classification of the license issued	
B91	1436AD	Operation of motor vehicle in violation of the classification of the license issued (subsequent offense)	
B91	1436AE	Illegal operation of motor vehicle - violation license class	
B91	1436AE	Illegal operation of motor vehicle - violation license class (2nd Offense)	
B91	1440AA	Operating motorcycle without motorcycle endorsement	
B91	1440AA,AB,AC,AD	Motor vehicle operator's license with a motorcycle endorsement; requirements.	
D02	1443	Misrepresentation renders license void	
D02	14110	Oaths and subpoenas. False statements or reports	
D02	1444F	False information	
D02	53A157	False statement in the second degree	
D02		Falsification of information or certification on application for CDL or CDIP	
D06	3088A	Operator's license as proof of age. Misrepresentation of age to procure liquor	
D06	3089A	Procuring liquor by person forbidden to purchase or by false statement, public possession of liquor by minors prohibited.	
D07	1444B	Prohibition re more than one driver's license	
D16	14147C	Improper use of marker, registration or license	
D16	53A130	Criminal impersonation: Class B misdemeanor	
D27	1436F	Motor vehicle operator's license (Limited License)	
D29	1436C	Motor vehicle operator's license. (Learner's permit)	
D29	1436F	Motor vehicle operator's license (Limited License)	
D36	1414	Registration of motor vehicles owned by minors. Proof of financial responsibility	
D36	14216	Operation by persons under eighteen without insurance	
D36	14213B,BCZ,BZ	Operation prohibited when insurance coverage fails to meet minimum requirements. Evidence of insurance coverage required to restore suspended license	
D36	14216CZ	Operation by persons under eighteen without insurance	
D36	14216Z	Operation by persons under eighteen without insurance	
D36	14289F	Liability insurance required for motorcycles	
D36	1429A	Owners of motor service buses, taxicabs, school buses and motor vehicles in livery service to furnish insurance or bond	
D45	14140	Failure to appear	
D51	46B221	Failure to make required payment of child support	
D53		Failure to appear	
D56	14140B	Failure to pay fines and fees (Motor Vehicle)	
D70	1499F	Defective windshield or wipers	
D70	1499FB	Obstruction View (windshield)	
D70	1499FC	Obstruction View (stickers on windshield)	
E01	14104A	Operating a motor vehicle without fenders	
E01	14104B	Operating commercial vehicle without wheel protectors	
E01	14105a	Improper Television Installation	
E01	14105b	Improper use of video monitor for backing	
E01	14296AAB	no person shall operate a motor vehicle upon a highway, while using a hand-held mobile telephone to engage in a call or while using a mobile electronic device while such vehicle is in motion. Includes texting	
E01	14296AAC	Use of hand held phone or hands free mobile telephone or other electronic devices while operating a moving school bus carrying passengers. Includes texting	
E01	14296AAD	Use of hand held or hands free mobile telephone or a mobile electronic device by individual with learner's permit or an individual under 18 while operating a moving motor vehicle. Includes texting	
E06	14278	Violation of school bus operation requirements	
E36	1497	No defroster on motor vehicle used to transport passengers for hire or school bus	

ACD	Statute	Description	Points
E36	14275c42	Failure to comply with Commissioner. Failure to have required repairs made to school bus per inspection results, causing plate suspension	
E37	1498A	Tires to be in safe operating condition	
E50	14228	Leaving motor vehicle without setting brake	
E50	14106a	Failure to have tamper proof odometer	
E50	1480BA	Ball joints, tie-end rods, concealing play or motion	
E50	1480H	Brake equipment of motor vehicles	
E50	1480HC	Ineffective parking brake system	
E50	1480IA	Motorcycle brakes, defective	
E50	1480IB	Motorcycle Handlebars, excessive height	
E50	1481A	Improper brakes on trailers	
E54	1496U	Improper use of high beam of lights	
E55	14220B,BCZ,BZ	Failure to use flashing lights by a slow moving CMV	
E55	14289BC	Motorcycle- failure to illuminate headlamp	
E55	1496A	Failure to have lights lit and devices illuminated	
E55	1496Q	Special restrictions on lamps. Flashing lights	
E55	1496Z	Improper use of additional lights	
E55	1497A	Improper emergency lights/failure to carry	
E56	14281AB,BCZ,BZ	School bus/STV failure to display lighted headlamps while transporting school children	
E70	14164C	Motor vehicle emissions systems	
E70	14164CN	Violation of exhaust emission standards/periodic inspection requirements	
E70	1496P	Use of unauthorized colored or white lights	
F02	14100AD	Transportation of child 6yrs or younger or less than 60 lbs w/o child restraint system	
F02	14100AD	Transportation of child 7yrs or older, 60 lbs or more w/o child restraint system or seat safety belt	
F02	14100AD	Failure to require child under 1yr or less that 20lbs to ride in child restraint system that is rear facing	
F02	14100AD	Transportation of child 4 yrs or older in student transportation veh w/o child restraint system or seat safety belt	
F02	14100AD	Transportation of child under 4 and less than 40 lbs in student transportation vehicle w/o child restraint system	
F02	14100AD	Securing child in booster seat w/o a safety belt which includes shoulder belt	
F02	14100AD	Child restraint systems	
F03	14289G	Protective headgear for motorcyclists and passengers under 18 years old	
F04	14100AC	Seat safety belts	
F05	14272A	Carrying of children in pickup trucks or open-bed vehicles	
F06	14289A,ACZ,AZ	Riding on motorcycle. Carrying of passenger	
F06	14289BA,BCZ,BZ	Motorcycle-operator prohibition of more than two abreast	
F17	14227b	Implied consent to test operators blood, breath, or urine	
M08	14223,CZ,Z	Failure to bring motor vehicle to full stop when signaled. Disregard of signal.	2
M10	14249A	Certain motor vehicles to stop at railroad crossing.	2
M12	14304	Safety zones	2
M13	14300F	Failure to obey school crossing guard	
M15	14301	Through ways. Stop sign	2
M16	14299	Traffic control signals. Right turn on red.	2
M17	14298	Failure to observe parkway or expressway restrictions	2
M17	14248A,ACZ,AZ	Cattle crossings (Failure to obey traffic sign)	
M20	14249C	Certain motor vehicles to stop at railroad crossing.	2
M21	14249B	For drivers who are not required to always stop, failure to stop before reaching tracks at a railroad-highway grade crossing when the tracks are not clear	2
M22	14250A	For drivers who are always required to stop, failure to stop as required before driving onto railroad-highway grade crossing	2
M23	14250C	For all drivers, failing to have sufficient space to drive completely through the railroad-highway grade crossing without stopping	2
M24	14250B	For all drivers, failing to negotiate a railroad-highway grade crossing because of insufficient undercarriage clearance	2
M32	14283F	Prohibits following an ambulance with sirens or lights more closely than 100 feet	3
M33	14296	Following fire apparatus, parking near fire apparatus, driving over hose prohibited	
M34	14240	Vehicles to be driven reasonable distance apart	3
M34	14240,A,CZ,Z	Failure to drive a reasonable distance apart by commercial vehicle combination	3
M34	14240A,ACZ,AZ	Vehicles to driven reasonable distance apart. Intent to harass or intimidate	4
M34	14240CZ,Z	Vehicles to be driven reasonable distance apart	3
M40	14230,ACZ,AZ	Use of restricted left lane by CMV	1
M40	14230A,ACZ,AZ	Failure to drive right- except wide load vehicle	1
M40	14230C,CCZ,CZ	Failure to drive right- wide load vehicle	
M41	14235,CZ,Z	Vehicle not to be driven on left side of highway on curve or upgrade	3
M42	14236,CZ,Z	Failure to drive in proper lane, multiple-lane highway	1
M42	14289B2	Failure to keep in lane; erratic lane changes (CDL Serious Traffic Violation)	1

ACD	Statute	Description	Points
M42	14289BB2	Motorcycle-operating between lanes of traffic	1
M46	14238	Controlled-access highways	2
M46	14238A,ACZ,AZ	Illegal entry on limited access highway	2
M46	14238CZ,Z	Controlled-access highways	2
M48	14289BA,BAZ	Operation of motorcycle two abreast in single lane	1
M48	14289BB1,B1Z,BCZ ,B27,BB1,BZ	Operation of motorcycles	1
M58	14250A	Vehicles prohibited on sidewalks	
M58	14250ACZ,AZ	Parking motor vehicle on sidewalk (excludes electric personal assistive mobility devices)	
M58	14250ACZ,AZ	Vehicles prohibited on sidewalks	
M60	14230B,BCZ,BZ	Improper lane or location - slower vehicle lane	
M70	14232A1,A1Z	Passing	3
M70	14232B	Unsafe Passing	3
M71	14234	Determination of no-passing zones.	3
M72	14231,CZ, Z	Vehicles in opposite directions to pass on right	3
M73	14233,CZ,Z	Passing on right	3
M75	14279,CZ,Z	Vehicles to stop for school buses	4
M76	14248B	Illegal passing of vehicle at marked crossing path	
M80	14163	Driving on ice (Reckless, careless or negligent driving)	
M80	14163	Driving on ice (Inattentive, careless or negligent driving)	
M82	14296aai	Distracted driving behavior while committing a moving violation	
M83	53A64	Reckless endangerment in the second degree: Class B misdemeanor	
M84	14111n	Reckless driving	
M84	14222CZ,Z	Reckless driving	
M85	14296AAE	Texting while operating a commercial motor vehicle	
M86	14296AAB	No person shall operate a motor vehicle upon a highway, while using a hand-held mobile telephone to engage in a call or while using a mobile electronic device while such vehicle is in motion. Includes texting	
M86	14296AAC	Use of hand held phone or hands free mobile telephone or other electronic devices while operating a moving school bus carrying passengers. Includes texting	
M86	14296AAD	Use of hand held or hands free mobile telephone or a mobile electronic device by individual with learner's permit or an individual under 18 while operating a moving motor vehicle. Includes texting	
N01	14247	Failure to grant ROW at private road or driveway	3
N01	14245,CZ,Z	Failure to give right of way at an intersection	3
N01	14245BRW	Failure to grant right of way at intersection to person riding bicycle	3
N01	14246A,ACZ,AZ	Failure to grant right of way at junction of highway	3
N01	14246BRW	Failure to grant right of way at junction of highway to person riding bicycle	3
N01	14247A,ACZ,AZ	Failure to grant ROW to pedestrian or traffic on emerging	3
N01	14247BRW,CZ,Z	Failure to grant ROW to person riding bicycle at private road or driveway	3
N01	53A63	Reckless endangerment in the first degree: Class A misdemeanor	
N03	14242EBR	Failure of driver making a left turn to grant right of way to person riding bicycle	1
N03	14242F	Failure of driver to grant ROW to person riding bike	
N04	14283B	Fail to reduce speed and/or move over upon approach of emergency vehicle.	
N04	14283E,ECZ,EZ,G,GZ	Rights of emergency vehicles	3
N04	14283GCZ	Rights of emergency vehicles	3
N04	14283H	Obstruct or retard ambulance or vehicle operated by emergency personnel while on emergency call	
N04	PA09121	Reduce speed upon approach of emergency vehicle	
N06	PA09171	Entering intersection which results in blocking passage of traffic	
N07	1499	Motor vehicles with commercial registration to allow others to pass	
N07	14-232A2,A2Z	Increasing speed while being passed	3
N08	14300	Failure to exercise due care to avoid colliding with pedestrian or person propelling a human-powered vehicle	3
N08	14300C	Overtaking and passing vehicle stopped at cross-walk to permit pedestrian to cross	3
N08	14300CA	Failure of operator of motor vehicle crossing sidewalk to yield right of way to pedestrian and all other traffic on the sidewalk	3
N08	14300D	Failure to yield right of way to pedestrian who is blind.	3
N26	14302	Yield sign	2
N31	14242E	Failure of driver making left turn to grant ROW	
N40	14101	Signal device, violations concerning	
N40	14242,CZ,Z	Restricted Turns- Failure to signal	1
N40	14244,CZ,Z	Improper signaling for turns or stopping	1
N50	14241,CZ,Z	Making an improper right turn	2
N60	14239,CZ,Z	Driving wrong way on one-way highway	1
N61	14239,CZ,Z	Rotaries improper direction	1
N63	14303	Designation of one-way streets	1

ACD	Statute	Description	Points
N71	14237,CZ,Z	Driving on divided highways	1
N82	14243,CZ,Z	Unsafe backing	1
N84	14242C	Unsafe/hazardous stopping	1
N84	14243A,ACZ,Z	Unsafe movement of stopped, standing, or parked vehicle	1
N84	14273,CZ,Z	Public Service overcrowding, exceeding capacity, person outside veh, improper seating	
S92	14218A	Travel unreasonably fast	1
S92	14219a2	Speeding >55 mph upon a highway other that specified in subsection (b) of 14-218a	1
S92	14219a4,b4	Speeding-over 20 mph on a highway or road with established speed limit under 65 mph	1
S92	14219b3	Speeding Violation. Travelling over 55mph but less than 60 mph on a highway not under section 14-218b	1
S93	14219	Speeding	
S93	14219	Driving to endanger; motor vehicles other that trucks	1
S93	14219	Violation of 14-219(a)(1)* in a school and construction or utility zone	1
S93	14219	Violation of 14-219(a)(1)* in a school zone	1
S93	14219	Violation of 14-219(a)(1)* in construction or utility zone	1
S93	14219	Driving to endanger; for all trucks defined by 14-260n	1
S93	14219,B	Speeding infraction; motor vehicles other than trucks	1
S93	14219,BCZ,BZ,C2,C CZ,CZ,Z	Speeding	
S93	14219,CZ,CCZ,	Speeding	
S93	14219a2	Speeding >55 mph upon a highway other that specified in subsection (b) of 14-218a	1
S93	14219a4	Speeding-over 20 mph on a highway or road with established speed limig under 65 mph	1
S93	14219B	Violation of 14-219(b)(1)* in a school and construction or utility zone	1
S93	14219B,CZ	Speeding	
S93	14219b2	Speeding violation; trucks; limited access highway under 14-218a; 66-70 mph	1
S93	14219b2S	Violation of 14-219b(2) in a school and construction or utility zone	1
S93	14219b2Z	Violation of 14-219b(2) in construction or utility zone	1
S93	14219BCZ,BZ	Speeding violation; trucks; limited access highway under 14-218a; 56-70 mph	1
S93	14219bSZ	Violation of 14-219b in a school and construction or utility zone	1
S93	14219C1	Speeding violation; motor vehicles other than trucks; greater than 70 mph	1
S93	14219C1	Violation of 14-219(c)(1)* in a school and construction or utility zone	1
S93	14219c1S	Violation of 14-219(c)(1) in a school zone	1
S93	14219c1Z	Violation of 14-219(c)(1) in construction or utility zone	1
S93	14219CZ	Violation of 14-219(a)(1) in a construction zone	1
S93	14219SZ	Violation of 14-219b in a school zone	1
S93	14219Z	Violation of 14-219b in construction or utility zone	1
S93	14219Z,CZ,Z	Violation of 14-219(a)(1) in a construction or utility zone	1
S94	14218A,ACZ,AZ	Travel unreasonably fast	1
S94	14281A,ACZ,AZ	Speeding school bus	5
S95	14224C,CCZ,CZ,C1	Racing	4
S95	14224C2A	Possession of a motor vehicle intended to be used in a race or event under 14-224(c)(1)	4
S95	14224C2B	Acting as starter, timekeeper, judge or spectator in a race or event under 14-224(c)(1)	4
S95	14224C2C	Wagering on the outcome of a race or event under 14-224(c) (1)	4
S96	14220A,ACZ,AZ	Slow speed	2
S96	14221,CZ,Z	Low-speed vehicles carrying passengers for hire	
U01	14223B,BCZ,BZ	Failure to bring motor vehicle to full stop when signaled. Disregard of signal.	
U03	1444kb	Disqualification from operation of commercial motor vehicles	
U06	53A60D	Assault in the second degree with a motor vehicle	
U07	14111n	Reports of comparable convictions	
U08	53A56B	Manslaughter in the second degree with a motor vehicle: Class C felony	
U08	53A57	Misconduct with a motor vehicle	
U09	14222AB,ABZ	Negligent homicide with a motor vehicle	5
U10	14111n	Reports of comparable convictions	
W00	14111gc	Operator suspended for conviction of moving violation after completing operator retraining class	
W00	14140B	Failure to pay fines and fees (Criminal)	
W00	14163D	Failure to update USDOT # and/or file commercial insurance. Reg priv and/or reg suspension	
W01	14111	4 moving violations	
W01	14137a8	High Points	
W13	1436C	Parental consent withdrawn	
W15	14111(a)	*must change to 145 for outside driving history (Physicians' or specialists' report recommended)	
W20	1436B	Unable to pass DL test(s) or meet qualifications	
W30		Disqualification from operation of commercial motor vehicles. Disqualification offenses. Lifetime disqualifications. Mitigation of lifetime disqualification	
W31		Disqualification from operation of commercial motor vehicles. Disqualification offenses. Lifetime disqualifications. Mitigation of lifetime disqualification	
W40		Disqualification from operation of commercial motor vehicles. Disqualification offenses. Lifetime	

ACD	Statute	Description	Points
		disqualifications. Mitigation of lifetime disqualification	
W41		Disqualification from operation of commercial motor vehicles. Disqualification offenses. Lifetime disqualifications. Mitigation of lifetime disqualification	
W45		This ACD withdrawal code will be used when we receive a B20-B26 from out of state, and the history shows prior violations were in a CMV	
W50		Motor carrier regulation fro intrastate or interstate commerce	
W51		Disqualification from operation of commercial motor vehicles. Disqualification offenses. Lifetime disqualifications. Mitigation of lifetime disqualification	
W52		Disqualification from operation of commercial motor vehicles. Disqualification offenses. Lifetime disqualifications. Mitigation of lifetime disqualification	
W60		The accumulation of two RRGC violations within three years	
W61		The accumulation of three or more RRGC violations within three years	
W70	1444KJ	Disqualification from operation of commercial motor vehicles. Disqualification offenses. Lifetime disqualifications. Mitigation of lifetime disqualification	
W72		Suspension pending final disposition (Administrative Suspension)	
W80		Failed employer-directed drug test	
W81		Refusal to submit to an employer-directed drug test	
	14227AI	Installation of ignition interlock device	
	14250B	Illegal obstruction at intersection	
	5456G	Alcohol Education Program Completed	

Conviction Table 2 with Reason Code and Statute

This table is sorted in order of the **R-Code** column, also known as the **Reason Code**. These violations are in-state code specific and usually have no points.

R-Code	Statute	Pts	Statute Description
001	1444C		License endorsement for operators of commercial motor vehicles used for passenger transportation
002	14257A,Z		Operating vehicle with crowded front seat
002	14257A,CZ,Z,CZ		Operating vehicle with rider outside
002	14257B,CZ,Z		Operating vehicle used to transport passenger for hire with seats in aisles
002	14262,D		Width and length of vehicles
002	14262A		Limitation on towing of disabled trucks and trailers by tow truck
002	14264		Special permits for vehicles of excessive height
002	14264		Height of vehicle, excessive, without permit
002	14266,CZ,Z		Operating vehicles of over four tons' capacity on restricted highways
002	14267A		Weight restrictions for vehicles, trailers or other objects. Penalties for overweight violations
002	14267		Failure to stop at the weighing area if indicated scale is in operation
002	14267		Failure to comply with weighing direction
002	14267		Parking on a limited access hwy newar weigh of safety inspection to avoid same
002	14269		Weight of vehicles and trailers engaged in construction work
002	14270		Permits required for nonconforming vehicles
002	14270G1		Operating a CMV that exceeds weight specified in permit
002	14270G2		Operating a CMV, without a permit, that exceeds statutory weight limit
002	14270G3		Operating a CMV that exceeds length specified in permit
002	14270G4,H		Operating a CMV that exceeds width specified in permit
002	14270G5		Operating a CMV that exceeds height specified in permit
002	14270G6		Operation on routes not specified in permit/exceeding length, width or height
002	14270GOW		Operating on routes not specified in permit/exceeding weight
002	14271		Securing of loads
002	14271A,CZ,Z		Operating vehicle improperly loaded or constructed to carry load
002	14271,CZ		Operating with unsecured load
002	14271CCZ,CZ		Securing of loads
006	14283G		Officers authorized to remove vehicles from obstruction of emergency personnel
006	14300A		Designation of crosswalk signs or signals
006	14300B		Pedestrians to cross hwy as indicated by signal.
007	14314		Penalties
008	14289C		Motorcycle-illegal passengers
008	14289D		Motorcycle-no face protection
009	14163A		Commissioner to furnish lists of motor vehicle and snowmobile owners to town assessors
009	14214,CZ,Z		Instruction of a person to operate a motor vehicle-limitations on
009	14260		Filling gas tank while motor is running
009	14261CZ,Z		Towing vehicles with excessive distance between, pushing vehicles restricted
009	14261AC		Illegal operation of uninspected commercial vehicle
009	14285		Failure of vehicle, other than motor vehicle, to be equipped with mirror
012	14222A,ACZ,AZ	5	Negligent homicide with a motor vehicle

013	1436c2	Operation of a motor vehicle by a person 16 or 17 years of age without having learner's permit in immediate possession
014	1436c2	Operation of a motor vehicle without proper instructor
016	14102	View in and exits from motor vehicles used to transport passengers for hire
016	1427B	Number plates for public service motor vehicles
016	1427B	Interstate motorbus-failure to display Connecticut number plates
016	1444C	Hearing held
019	14224D	Failure to remove motor vehicle from highway
020	14307	Parking restrictions
021	1436c3,c4	Violation of passenger restrictions imposed on learner's permit holders who are 16 or 17 yrs of age
022	3089A1	Permitting minor to possess alcoholic liquor -first offense
022	3089A2	Failure to halt possession of alcoholic liquor by a minor
025	14270H1	Operating in violation of conditions specified in permit
025	14270H2	Operating in violation of days of travel specified in permit
026	15133D	Operation of vessel while under the influence of liquor or drugs
026	15140LA1	Reckless operation of a vessel in the first degree while under the influence of alcohol or drug resulting in serious injury or death
026	15140LA2	Reckless operation of a vessel in the first degree while under the influence of alcohol or drug resulting in damage to property in excess of two thousand dollars
026	15140N	Reckless operation of a vessel in the second degree while under the influence of alcohol or drugs
026		Manslaughter in the second degree with a vessel Class C felony
029	14105	Television screen location restricted/failure to siable closed video monitor
029	1417	Failure to notify DMV of change of appearance or mechanical equipment of vehicle
029	1421B	Failure to display reflectorized safety number plates
029	14275	Equipment and color of school bus
029	14280	School marking concealed for use other than school bus
029	14282	Painting former school bus required
029	14292	Student driver, failure to mark vehicle
029	1480	Mechanical equipment
029	1480A,AA	Unnecessary or unusual noise, operating causing (AA =exceeding decibel level)
029	1480B	Improper muffler; defective muffler installation
029	1480C	Excessive fumes or exhaust smoke
029	1480D	Exhaust pipe requirements
029	1480E	Defective horn
029	1480F	Using a siren without a permit
029	1481A	Hydraulic brake fluid
029	1481B	Restrictions on used brake drums and brake discs
029	1498	Tire and wheel requirements (up to 4 tires + 1 violation)
029	1499	Operating a motor vehicle with a commercial registration below limit to allow passing
029	1499G	Tinted or reflectorized windows
029	14275a	Illegal operation of non-standard school bus
031	1445A1	Failure of holder of motor vehicle license to notify of change of address
031	1445A2	Failure of holder of identity card to notify of change of address
032	14270C	Failure to carry permit for nonconforming vehicles
033	14253AM	Use of a placard or special license plate issued to a person after the death of such person
034	53A119BA,B	Using motor vehicle or vessel without owner's permission. Interfering or tampering with a motor vehicle.
036	1435A	Motor Carrier prohibited from operating with suspended or revoked registration
037	14286b	Use of bicycle, motor driven cycles and high mileage vehicles
037	14286F	Improper operation of motor-driven cycle on public highway
038	21A267D1	Possession of drug paraphernalia related to less than one half ounce of cannabis type substance
038	21A267D2	Delivery of or Possession of drug paraphernalia related to less than one half ounce of cannabis type substance
039	1480HF	Operating vehicle with GVWR > 9999 lbs w/defective brakes
040	14289hb	Violation of personal assistive mobility device required equipment
040	14289hd	Violation of personal assistive mobility device on sidewalk or highway. Operators to yield ROW. Placard required. Must be 16 or older
040	14289he	Violation of personal assistive mobility device on limited access highway
040	14-289hf	Violation of personal assistive mobility device more than 15 mph
046	14148	Abandoned markers
046	14149	Mutilated or removed vehicle identification
046	1416A,D,F	Transfer of ownership
046	1417A	Failure of holder of motor vehicle registration to notify of change of address
046	1418,C	Violations concerning mutilated or illegible plates, report of lost plates, improper attachments on plates
046	1418A	Failure to display number plates and valid sticker; improper location of sticker
046	1418D	Failure to return plates on expiration of registration
046	1418E	Improper use or display of a sample number plate
046	14213,CZ,Z	Operation without carrying operator's license
046	1439B	Failure of nonresident to display on motor vehicle distinguishing number or mark

046	1413,A,B	Registration certificate and insurance identification card to be carried in vehicle
052	14112F	Failure to return license or registration after suspension of canceled insurance
052	1412D	Failure to return registrations on demand
052	1412g	Insurance Compliance
058	1496A	Lighted lamps and illuminating devices required
058	1496AA	Lamp requirements for snow removal and highway maintenance equipment
058	1496BB	Every motorcycle shall be equipped with at least one and not more than two head lamps
058	1496C	Failure to have tail lamps or to illuminate rear registration plates
058	1496D	Failure to have reflectors
058	1496E	Failure to have stop lamps or turn signals
058	1496F	Failure to equip buses, trucks, trailers, truck tractors as required
058	1496G	Failure to have reflectors or lighting devices of proper color
058	1496I	Visibility of reflectors and lamps, failure to comply
058	1496J	Failure to have proper front or rear lights on combination vehicles
058	1496K	Extended load of more that 4 feet with out red flag; projecting loads; improper carrying of animals
058	1496L	Failure to have proper head and rear lights, lights on parked vehicle
058	1496M	Failure to have proper lamps on farm vehicles
058	1496N	Failure to have proper lighting devices on other vehicles leading animals
058	1496O	Limitation on spot lamps, fog lamps, auxiliary lamps
058	1496R	Improper color of stop lamps and turn signals
058	1496S	Improper fender, back-up or identification lamps
058	1496T	Multiple-beam road light requirements
058	1496X	Motorcycles, improper headlamps
058	1496Y	Improper number of headlights
058	1496B	Failure to have headlamps
060	14147B	Improper use of marker, registration or license
067	1439,A2	Nonresident operators. Reciprocity concerning equipment, marking and inspection of vehicles
067	1441C	Failure to renew operators license
068	14276	Operating a school bus/student transportation vehicle without complying with certain operating requirements
069	1426A	No registration for motor bus, taxicab, school bus or motor vehicle in livery service; improper use of registration; failure to keep record of operator
070	14291	Violation of special occasion traffic regulations
071	1436C	
072	14250A	Parking motor vehicle on sidewalk (excludes electric personal assistive mobility devices)
072	14251	Improper parking
072	14252	Blocking driveway
072	14253AC	Parking in a parking space designated for blind persons or persons with disabilities
072	14253A	Unauthorized display or use of plate or placard of blind person or person with disability
072	14253A	Failure to return plate of blind person or person with disabilities
072	14253A	Improper parking facilities for blind person or person with disabilities
072	14305B	Bus stops and public service motor vehicle stands
072	14308	Loading and unloading
073	14217	Refusal to show or surrender license or registration
075	1436d	Improper issuance of operator's license to a person sixteen or seventeen years of age
076	14164IC	Failure to have required emissions repairs made to diesel powered commercial motor vehicles following inspection resulting in plate suspension
077	14111(a)	Subject to a federal out of service order
078	53A119C	Using motor vehicle or vessel without owner's permission. Interfering or tampering with a motor vehicle.
083	1412AF	Failure to register commercial motor vehicle
083	1434AE	Violation of registration requirements- commercial motor vehicles with gross weight of 60,000 lbs. or less
083	1448A	Registration of commercial truck/tractor
083	1412	Operating or towing an unregister vehicle
083	1412	Operating or towing unregistered motor vehicle
083	1412D	False statement- obtain motor vehicle registration
083	1412A	Registration of certain motor vehicles garaged or operated in Connecticut (Expired or no registration or title)
087	14217	Refusal to show or surrender insurance identification card
097	14150	Abandoned or unregistered motor vehicles and motor vehicles which are a menace to traffic
102	1435,D	Violation of motor vehicle transporter's registration regulation
102	1452	License required for selling or repairing motor vehicles
102	1460	Use of dealer's and repairers' plates
102	1466,B	Wreckers Towing and transporting Distinguishing number plates
102	1466A	Failure to maintain wrecker records
107	1412A	Failure to renew registration; registration of motor vehicle by non-owner
107	1412A2	Operator owns motor vehicle with out of state plates
107	14164IF	Operating a diesel-powered commercial motor vehicle in violation of emission requirements
107	1426B	Failure to carry registration for motor bus, service bus, taxicab, school bus or motor vehicle in livery service
107	1427D	Lack of, or improper use of, necessary credentials for an activity related to motor vehicles

107	1467		Qualifications of licensee; bond; fees. Solicitation of service contracts
107	1467I		Certificate of approval of location; license required
107	1467N		Use of general registration restricted Number plates for motor vehicles being towed
107	14161		Impersonation of inspector or agent
107	14164CJ		Equipment used improperly or obstructed
107	1427G		Lack of, or improper use of, necessary credentials for an activity related to motor vehicles
114	14111(a)		Failure to appear at a hearing
116	1412B		Presentation of insurance identification card or policy and statement that minimum security will be continuously maintained required for issuance of registration.
116	1412c		Verification of security coverages.
116	1415		Insurance for leasing or rental MV (Reg # Suspension)
116	1429		Motor or Service Bus Insurance (Reg # Suspension)
116	1435		Insurance on Transporter's (Reg # Suspension)
117	14215A,AA,AB		Operation while license is suspended pursuant to section 14-140
119	14198		
121	1444C		Criminal Record
122	14163D		Failure to update USDOT # and/or file commercial insurance. Reg priv and/or reg suspension
124	14111(a)		Parent or guardian permission withdrawn
125	14141		Court ordered juvenile withdrawal
127	53A125		Larceny in the fourth degree: Class A misdemeanor.
130	1444JC		Failure to notify Employer of suspended, revoked, cancelled, or disqualified operating privilege.
132	1449		Fees for miscellaneous registration and other fees (returned check)
132	1450		Fees for operator's license, passenger endorsement and examination (returned check)
136	14141		Court Order Suspension
137	14274		Hours of operators of motor vehicles with commercial registration or requiring a passenger endorsement or a passenger and school endorsement
140	1444JA		Failure of person who holds CDL to notify Commissioner of DMV of conviction
140	1444JB		Failure of person who holds CDL to notify employer of conviction
140	1444JD		Failure of person to provide prospective employer with required information re: employment as driver of commercial motor vehicle
142	1444JF		Employer permit or require a driver to drive a CMV
143	1444JE		Information on previous employment
145	14111		Failure to comply (Reg Priv Suspension)
145	1445		Notice of change of operator's address
145	14103c1,c2		Defective equipment (Reg # Suspension)
145	14111,(A)		Failure to Comply with the Commissioner
145	14111		Fingerprints required
145	14111g		Operator's retraining program
146	1446		Report of names of persons with chronic health or vision problems
146	1433		Delinquent Tax (Reg Priv Suspension)
150	14147A		Theft or illegal possession of number plate or sticker
151	1499GB		Operation of vehicle with obstructed view, placement on vehicle window of material altering color or reducing light transmittance
152	1499GG		Obstruction View (Tinted Windows after factor delivery)
153	1436B2		Operation of a motor vehicle with valid out of state license beyond 30 days
153	14111		Powers of the Commissioner
154	1499GD		Sale of motor vehicle with window(s) exceeding luminous reflective standards
155	14252AA		Operator of non commercial motor vehicle to remove accumulated snow from vehicle
155	14252AB		Injury or property damage caused by failure to remove snow from non commercial veh
155	14252AC		Operator of commercial motor vehicle to remove accumulated snow from vehicle
155	14252AD		Injury or property damage caused by failure to remove snow from commercial veh
155	1499GE		Failure to carry tinted glass sticker
165	14277	1	Operator's duties on stopping bus. Prohibition on idling of bus
166	14300		Failure to yield right of way to vehicle when crossing not within a crosswalk
166	14300		Crossing intersection diagonally
166	14300		Failure to cross within marked crosswalk between adjacent intersection at which traffic or pedestrian control signals operate
166	14300		Failure to travel upon right half of crosswalk
166	14300		Walking on roadway where sidewalk is provided and use thereof is practicable
166	14300		Failure to walk on shoulder properly when no sidewalk provided
166	14300		Failure to walk on left side of road when neither sidewalk nor shoulder is available
166	14300		Suddenly leaving place of safety adjacent to or upon a road and walking into path of vehicle as to constitute immediate hazard
166	14300		Walking or standing upon any part of a road while under influence of alcohol or any drug to a degree which renders such pedestrian a hazard
166	14300		Failure to yield right of way to authorized emergency vehicle
166	14300		Failure to yield right of way to each vehicle

171	14289JB	No person shall operate a mini-motorcycle or ride as a passenger on a mini-motorcycle on any highway, public sidewalk or public property of this state. No owner of a mini-motorcycle shall permit a person to operate the owner's mini-motorcycle or to ride
171	14289JC	Violation mini MC req OP/passenger private property
171	14289JD	Violation mini MC owner req private property
171	14289JF	Violation mini MC req sale/lease/rental
172	14298A	Failure to obey posted hieght requirement
173	14286	Failure to ride bicycle as near to right side of road as possible
173	14286	Riding bicycle with more that two abreast
173	14286	When riding two abreast-impeding movement to traffic-failure to ride within single lane on a laned roadway
173	14286	Riding upon bicycle, roller skates, sled, skateboard, coaster or toy vehicle attaching the same or himself to vehicle on public road
173	14286	Operator permitting rider of bike, roller skates, skateboard, coaster, sled or toy to attach to vehicle
173	14286	Carrying passenger on bicycle when bicycle is not equipped or designed to carry passengers except for children under 4 years of age
173	14286	Carrying package or other article which prevents using both hands in operation of bicycle
173	14286	Failure to keep at least one hand on handlebar of bicycle when bicycle is in motion
174	13B344A	Cross Railroad tracks after warning
175	14111a	Possession of alcoholic liquors in motor vehicle by minor
176	14380	Operating prohibited without valid registration
176	14381	Improper display of registration number or plate; failure to carry registration
176	14382	Failing to report change of address
176	14385	Renting or leasing without safety devices and equipment as required by law
176	14385	Renting or leasing of snowmobiles or ATV, records required
176	14386B	Failure to stop snowmobile or all terrain vehicles.
176	14386A1	Unreasonable speed-snowmobile or ATV
176	14386A2	Negligent operation- snowmobile
176	143871	Operating on a public highway; failure to stop or yield right of way before crossing public highway
176	143872	Excessive or unusual noise from exhaust system
176	143873	Operating with out functioning muffler or improper brakes or insufficient lighting and reflecting devices
176	143873	Operating a ATV with an engine size of 90 c.c. or less after dark
176	143874	Harassment of game or domestic animal
176	143875	Operating on fenced agricultural land or state-owned land or municipality-controlled land without written permission
176	143875	Failure to carry written permission to operate
176	143876	Operating on any used railroad right of way
178	14261A	Regulation of commercial vehicle combinations
178	14261AA	Illegal operation of overlength vehicle
178	14261AA	Exceeding length limit-combination vehicle
178	14261AB	Failure to have license to operate Commercial vehicle combination or semitrailer
179	5476l(h) YO	Reckless driving
179	5476l(h) YO	Failure to bring motor vehicle to full stop when signaled. Disregard of signal. (Fleeing or evading police or roadblock)
179	5476l(h) YO	Evading Responsibility (Hit and run-failure to stop and render aid after accident- personal injury accident)
179	5476l(h) YO	Racing (Speed contest on road open to traffic)
184	14163C1	Controlled Substances and Alcohol Use & Testing-49 CFR 382 (General Violation)
184	14163C1	Controlled Substances and Alcohol Use & Testing-49 CFR 382 (Out of Service)
184	14163C10	General Violation of 49CFR 392
184	14163C10	General Violation of 49CFR 392 (out of service)
184	14163C11	Driver Hours of Service- 49 CFR 396 (General Violation)
184	14163C11	Driver Hours of Service- 49 CFR 396 (Out of Service)
184	14163C12	Inspection, Repair and Maintenance- 49 CFR 396 (General Violation)
184	14163C12	Inspection, Repair and Maintenance- 49 CFR 396 (Out of Service)
184	14163C13	Hazardous Materials Transportation- 49 CFR 397 (General Violation)
184	14163C13	Hazardous Materials Transportation- 49 CFR 397 (Out of Service)
184	14163C2	Commercial Drivers License Stds- 49 CFR 383 (General Violation)
184	14163C2	Commercial Drivers License Stds- 49 CFR 383 (Out of Service)
184	14163C3	Safety Fitness Procedures - 49 CFR 385 (General Violation)
184	14163C3	Safety Fitness Procedures - 49 CFR 385 (Out of Service)
184	14163C4	Rules of Practice for Motor Carrier Safety and Hazardous Materials Proceedings
184	14163C5	Financial Responsibility Regs - 49 CFR 387 (General Violation)
184	14163C5	Financial Responsibility Regs - 49 CFR 387 (Out of Service)
184	14163C6	MC Safety Regulations- 49 CFR 390 (General Violation)
184	14163C6	MC Safety Regulations- 49 CFR 390 (Out of Service)
184	14163C7	Driver Qualifications - 49 CFR 391 (General Violation)
184	14163C7	Driver Qualifications - 49 CFR 391 (Out of Service)
184	14163C8	Motor Vehicle Driving - 49 CFR 392 (General Violation)

184	14163C8		Motor Vehicle Driving - 49 CFR 392 (Out of Service)
184	14163C9		Safety Parts and Accessories - 49 CFR 393 (General Violation)
184	14163C9		Safety Parts and Accessories - 49 CFR 393 (Out of Service)
184	14163C14		Inspection, Repair and maintenance- 49 CFR 396
184	14163C15		Hazardous material, driving and parking rules-46CFR397
188	1436ga1		Violation of motor vehicle passenger restrictions imposed on persons 16 or 17 years old during the period six months after issuance of license
188	1436ga2		Violation of motor vehicle passenger restrictions imposed on persons 16 or 17 years old during the period six months and ending one year after issuance of license
188	1436ga3		Operation of motor vehicle requiring a public transportation permit by a person 16 or 17 years old
188	1436ga4		Transporting more passengers than numbers of seat belts in motor vehicle by 16 or 17 year old
188	1436ga5		Violation of motorcycle passenger restriction imposed on persons 16 or 17 years old during period six months after issuance of license
188	1436ga6		Operation of a motor vehicle by a person 16 or 17 between 11:00 p.m. and 5:00 a.m.
189	14223A		Striking an officer with a motor vehicle
191	14111		Powers of the Commissioner (Improperly Issued License)
192	13B410A		Failure to comply with Unified Carrier Regulations
193	13B410B		Violation of regs, payment of fees by intrastate motor carriers for hire exempt from filing proof of insurance
194	13B410C		Violation of regs, payment of fees by intrastate motor common and carriers, fail to apply to transp commissioner, proof of insurance.
195	13B410		Failure to comply with DOT regulations
205	14277A	1	Operator's duties on stopping bus.
205	14277B	1	Prohibition on idling of bus

Point System Summary

Disobeying Orders of an Officer ....Two points.
Driving While Impaired ....Three points.
Entering or Leaving Controlled-Access Highway at Other Than Designated Entrance or Exit ....Two points.
Entry Upon a Limited Access Highway Other Than a Highway Intersection or Designated Point...............Two points.
Executing a Turn from the Wrong Lane or Contrary to Traffic-Control Device.....................................Two points.
Failure to Drive in Right-Hand Lane..One point.
Failure to Drive Reasonable Distance Apart ....Three points.
Failure to Drive Reasonable Distance Apart, Intent to Harass ....Four points.
Failure to Give Proper Signal..One point.
Failure to Grant Right-of-Way at an Intersection...Three points.
Failure to Grant Right-of-Way if Emerging from an Alley, Driveway, or Building.............................Three points.
Failure to Grant Right-of-Way at Intersection...Three points.
Failure to Grant Right-of-Way to Emergency Vehicles or Pedestrians ....Three points.
Failure to Keep Right or Keep Right on Curve, Grade, or Approaching an Intersection....................Three points.
Failure to Obey Railroad Crossing, a Stop or Yield Sign, or a Traffic-Control Signal........................Two points.
Failure to Observe Parkway or Expressway Restrictions ....Two points.
Failure to Stop at Railroad Crossing by School Bus, Commercial Motor Vehicle Carrying Flammable or Explosive .Two points.
Failure to Yield When Emerging from a Driveway or Private Road..Three points.
Illegal Use of Limited-Access Highway by Bus, Commercial Vehicle, or Vehicle With Trailer..................One point.
Improper Backing or Starting..One point.
Improper Operation on Divided Highway or Multiple-Lane Highway ....One point.
Improper Turn, Illegal Turn, Illegal Stopping, Failure to Signal Intention to Turn ....One point.
Negligent Homicide With a Motor Vehicle..Five points.
Operating a Vehicle Through Pedestrian Safety-Zone ....Two points.
Operating at Unreasonable Rate of Speed ....One point.
Operation of Motorcycles Abreast, Illegal Passing ....One point.
Operation of School Bus at Excessive Speed...Five points.
Operator's Duties on Stopping a School Bus...One point.
Passing a Stopped School Bus...Four points.
Passing in a No-Passing Zone or Passing on the Right...Three points.
Slow Speed, Impeding Traffic...Two points.
Speeding...One point.
Wagering, Speed Records ....Four points.
Wrong Way on One-Way Street...One point.

Note: There is a 30 day suspension for more than 10 points within a 2 year period. However, the Department is not permitted to assess points if the violation is paid by mail to the Centralized Infractions Bureau.

Operator Retraining Program

A driver must attend an Operator Retraining Program if:
- A driver who is 24 years of age or younger has two violations specified in Connecticut State Law - Section 14-111g(a) - involving either a moving violation or a suspension violation on his or her driving record.
- A driver who is 25 years of age or older has three violations specified in Connecticut State Law - Section 14-111g(a) - involving either a moving violation or a suspension violation on his or her driving record.

Delaware

Administration	Important Telephone and Web Contacts
Jennifer Cohan, Director Division of Motor Vehicles Safety and Homeland Security Building 303 Transportation Circle, Dover 19901 PO Box 698, Dover 19903 302-744-2510 - Fax: 302-739-3152 www.dmv.de.gov/default.shtml Note: All DMV offices have hours of operation from 8:00 am to 4:30 pm (EST), except Wednesday hours are noon to 8 pm.	Driver Licensing/Records ....302-744-2506 Vehicle Records...302-744-2531 License Suspensions..302-744-2509 License Revocations...302-744-2508 Financial Responsibility ....302-744-2513 Commercial Driver License ....302-744-2572 State Department of Insurance ....302-674-7300 State Police ....302-739-5901 Email........................ dot-public-relations@state.de.us Laws and Regulations: www.dmv.de.gov/information/laws_regs.shtml

Driver's License Format, Issuance and Renewal

License Classes, Restrictions and Endorsements Appear After the Driving Record Content Section

License Format

Format is one to seven numbers and is computer generated, there is no coding. Zeros are not placed in front if number is less than seven digits.

Document Appearance

Current Format

The current card, issued since 07/2010, is a digital license on a hard plastic card with a blue strip at the top.

  Security Characteristics: Caesar Rodney in laminate, bar code, UV image and DOB.

  Position of Photo: Top, left hand side, Ghost Image middle bottom.

  Under 21 Age Driver License; Vertical format, red rectangle with white letters stating, "21 on mm/dd/year and 18 on mm/dd/year."

  CDL Indicator: Written clear letters on green strip on top.

Older Format

This format may still be in use by military personnel. This older digital license is a hard plastic card with blue on top and was issued since 03/2003.

  Security Characteristics: Caesar Rodney in laminate, bar code..

  Position of Photo: Top, left hand side.

  Under 21 Age Driver License: Vertical format, red rectangle with white letters stating, "21 on mm/dd/year and 18 on mm/dd/year."

  CDL Indicator: Written in white letters on green strip on top.

Issuance

Location of Requirements for Proof of Identity:

www.dmv.de.gov/services/driver_services/drivers_license/pdfs/DL_ID_procedures_111111.pdf

Age Requirements

The minimum age is 16 years. A Graduated Driver License (GDL) took effect on July 1, 1999. A permit holder who is at least 17 years old, but less than 18 years old, may obtain a Class D operator's license when the driver has held a Level One Learner's Permit for at least 12 months, the sponsor has not withdrawn his/her endorsement, and the applicant's driving privileges are not suspended, revoked, canceled, denied, or surrendered. For the first six months after issuance of a Level One Learner's Permit, the permit holder may only drive when supervised.

Residency

A non-resident must obtain a Delaware license within sixty days of establishing residency.

Renewal

Since December 2011, the renewal cycle is on the birthdate randomized between five to eight years; prior was the birthdate of fifth year. Driver keeps same number when renewing. Online renewal is not offered. Military may renew by mail.

Elderly-Related Restrictions

None reported by state.

Vehicle Insurance, Title and Registration Facts

Registration Renewal

Applications for registration renewals are accepted at any of four branch offices. Applications are accepted by mail and there are no additional fees unless renewal is late. Renewals cannot be accomplished online.

New Residents

New residents must obtain title and registration within 60 days of establishing residency.

Inspections and Emissions Testing

Delaware requires a safety inspection, fuel tank pressure, fuel cap test, brake, emissions tests, and on-board diagnostics testing for 1996 and newer vehicles (1997 and newer if diesel powered). Inspections are performed at state operated inspection stations. Delaware exempts the first five model year vehicles (weighing less than 10,000 lbs.) from inspections. All vehicles older than five (5) years can renew registrations for one or two years. All vehicles must pass inspection prior to registration.

Emissions tests are required on automobiles and on trucks with a manufacturer's gross vehicle weight rating (MGVWR) of 8,500 pounds or less. Emission exceptions include vehicles manufactured before 1968, diesel-fueled vehicles manufactured before 1997, motorcycles, and kit cars.

Passenger Plate Facts

There is one plate and one decal with (MO) (YR) (Day). Delaware does not indicate the county or city of issuance on the plate. There is one plate and one decal with (MO) (YR) (Day). The plate remains with vehicle when sold unless the seller requests to retain the tag for a new vehicle.

Insurance and Financial Responsibility

Delaware has compulsory liability insurance requirements of $15,000/30,000/10,000. Delaware vehicle owners must carry a valid insurance identification card in the vehicle at all times. Proof of insurance must be presented to the Division at the time of registration or renewal or upon the request of a police officer or any other party involved in an accident with the insured. Vehicles are audited for proof of insurance as a result of notification of cancellation by insurance companies. Failure to comply with an audit, maintain continuous liability insurance or surrender tags prior to insurance cancellation may result in fines and registration and owner's drivers license suspensions.

Withdrawal Sanctions, and Alcohol and Drug Testing

Alcohol and Chemical Testing Limits

The legal limit is .08 percent (non-commercial) and to .02 percent for drivers under 21. The CDL legal limit is .04 percent; additionally, drivers will be placed out-of-service for twenty-four hours for any measurable alcohol content. The driving-under-the-influence laws include implied-consent as well as administrative revocations. The following tests are permissible: breath, blood, and urine.   Any person who has been convicted of a driving under the influence of alcohol charge may be required to have an Ignition Interlock Device installed on all vehicles owned by the offender.

The Ignition Interlock Program

An Ignition Interlock Program is available to DUI offenders on a voluntary basis and is mandatory for those with one or more DUI convictions. Various eligibility requirements must be met before installation of the device and issuance of a special IID license. The IID license is valid for Class "D" vehicles only.

Suspensions and Revocations

See the Appendix for a list of the federally mandated disqualifications for offenses occurring in a CMV per MCSIA.

Drag Racing, Speed Exhibition
  First Offense .... One-month suspension.
  Second Offense .... Twelve-month suspension.
Driving While License Suspended or Revoked:
  Suspension or revocation period is doubled up to one year.
Passing a Stopped School Bus .... One- to twelve-month susp.

Point Accumulation in One Year
  Calculated points are credited at full point value for the first 12 months from the date of violation. After the initial 12 months have expired, the calculated points will be credited at one-half point value for the next 12 months. All actions are based upon total calculated points within a 24-month period following the offense.
  Fourteen Points .... Four-month suspension.
  Sixteen Points .... Six-month suspension.
  Eighteen Points .... Eight-month suspension.
  Twenty Points .... Ten-month suspension.
  Twenty-two Points .... Twelve-month suspension.
  Note: At twelve points or more a driver must complete a behavior modification/attitudinal-driving course within 90 days after notification (unless extended by DMV). A mandatory 2-month suspension will be imposed for failure to comply.
Refusal to Pay Child Support ....Suspension until matter resolved.
Failure to adhere to Level 1 Learner's Permit or Driver's Education Permit (other than using cell phone)
  First Offense .... Two-month suspension.
  Second Offense .... Four-month suspension.
Level 1 Learner's Permit or Driver's Education Permit and using a cell phone while driving:
  First Offense .... One-month suspension.
  Second Offense .... Three-month suspension.
Alcohol-Related (Any person who drives under the influence is subject to both administrative and criminal penalties.)
Driving Under the Influence (non-commercial)
  First Offense (Probable Cause).......... Three-month revocation.
  Second Offense .... Twelve-month revocation.
  Third Offense................................... Eighteen-month revocation.
  Criminal Penalties include................ One- to Five-year revocation.
Driving Under the Influence (holder of CDL)
  First Offense .... One-year disqualified.
  First Offense with Hazardous Material.. Three-year disqualified.
  Second Offense................................. Lifetime disqualified.
Zero Tolerance - Under 21 Administrative & Criminal Penalties:
  First Offense .... Two-month revocation.
  Second Offense .... Six-month revocation.
  Third offense .... One-year revocation.

Refusal to Submit to Chemical Test (non-commercial)
  First Offense.....................................Twelve-month revocation.
  Second Offense ....Eighteen-month revocation.
  Third or Subsequent Suspension ....Two-year revocation.
Refusal to Submit to Chemical Test (holder of CDL)
  First Offense.....................................One-year disqualified.
  First Offense with HazMat.................Three-year disqualified.
  Second Offense ....Lifetime disqualified.
Serious Offenses in a Commercial Vehicle:
  Two in three years..............................Disqualified for sixty days.
  Three in three years...........................Disqualified for 120 days.

Speeding Related Suspensions
  • The driver will be suspended for one (1) month when convicted of driving 25 MPH over the posted speed limit. The suspension length will increase by one month for each additional 5 MPH over the initial 25-MPH threshold. The driver may elect to attend the behavior modification/attitudinal-driving course in lieu of license suspension when driving 25-29 MPH over the posted limit. When speeding 30 MPH or more over the suspension is mandatory.
  • One-year suspension when convicted of driving 50 MPH or more over the posted speed limit or driving 100 MPH on a highway.

Other Actions Which May Result in a Suspension Include:
  • Altering a driver's license or using a fraudulent license.
  • Driving an uninsured motor vehicle
  • Failing to answer a court summons in any state.
  • Giving a fictitious name or address or making a false statement in applying for a license.
  • Has by reckless or unlawful operation of a motor vehicle contributed to an accident resulting in injury or death to any person or caused serious property damage.
  • Has driven a motor vehicle without consent of its owner.
  • Has issued a non-collectible check to the Division.
  • Is incompetent to drive a motor vehicle for serious medical or mental conditions.
  • Loaning a driver's license to another person
  • Speed exhibition and spinning wheels.
  • Unlawful manufacture or possession of a false insurance document.
  • Use of fictitious, suspended, revoked or borrowed driver's license.

The Following Offenses Require Mandatory Revocation:
  • Any drug offense that results in a conviction
  • Attempting to flee from a police officer after having received a visual or audible signal to stop your vehicle
  • Contributing to the death of anyone by operating a vehicle

- Driving while under the influence of intoxicating liquor or narcotic drugs
- Leaving the scene of accident involving death or injury to another person or property damage
- Making a false statement or using fraudulent information
- The crime of assault in which a death occurs from operating a vehicle
- Three convictions for reckless driving in a period of twelve consecutive months
- Underage possession/consumption of alcohol by persons under 21 years of age
- Using a motor vehicle in committing any serious crime

Habitual Offender Revocation

After an accumulation of certain types of traffic violation convictions, the driver may be declared a habitual offender and his/her license may be revoked for up to five (5) years. No work or hardship licenses are issued to those convicted of being a habitual offender. Any combination of three of the following offenses in a five (5) year period may convict driver as a habitual offender:

- Driving during suspension or revocation
- Driving while under the influence of alcohol or drugs
- Driving without a license

- Failing to identify yourself at the scene of an accident
- Failing to stop at the scene of an accident
- Failing to stop on the command of a police officer
- Making a false statement to the Division of Motor Vehicles
- Manslaughter
- Reckless driving
- Use of a motor vehicle in the commission of a felony
- Violation of an occupational license
- Also, any combination of the above offenses and lesser offenses, such as speeding, that result in 10 convictions in 3 years may convict driver as a habitual offender.

Aggressive Driving

Violators committing a combination of 3 or more specific violations may, in addition to those violations or in lieu of those violations, may be charged with *aggressive driving*. Violations include: disregarding a traffic device; speeding; improper passing; improper lane change; following too close; fail to yield right of way; failing to signal; passing a stopped school bus; and, disregard a stop sign. Violators convicted of aggressive driving are required to complete a behavior modification/attitudinal driving course that is offered statewide. Failure to attend course will result in suspension.

Reinstatement Requirements

Suspension $25.00 fee; time lapse.
Revocation $143.75 fee; time lapse; re-examination in some cases.
Disqualification $25.00 fee; time lapse; re-examination in some cases.

- Alcohol-related violations also require satisfactory completion in a designated alcohol education/rehabilitation program and may be required to have character background review.
- Delaware *may* issue a conditional/restricted/occupational and/or temporary license for individuals revoked, suspended or in the Ignition Interlock Program.

Record Access: Laws, Rules, and Forms

Note: This Section Applies to Both Driver and Vehicle Records.

Governing Statutes and Rules

Laws and Regulations:

www.dmv.de.gov/information/laws_regs.shtml

The current statute—Title 21 Section 305, enacted 7/17/96 and amended July 26, 2000—placed the state in compliance with DPPA.

Policy Statement Regarding Permissible Uses

The state adopted 12 permissible uses from DPPA. Uses not adopted by statute are #12 and #13. All permissible users must be pre-approved to become authorized account holders.

Request and Consent Forms

Those routinely seeking information on an electronic basis must complete an *Application and a Contract for Direct Access*. Authorized access account holders may obtain information in accordance with their contracts. Otherwise, third-party requests must be accompanied by a valid court document or a completed *Personal Information Request*

Form MV703. The form must be notarized (requester's signature) if sent by mail is found at www.dmv.de.gov/forms/forms_manuals.shtml,

Vendor and Third Party Access Policy

Requesters of data must sign a contract stating that the information will only be used by the requester for the stated purpose and will not be sold by any of their client companies. Certain end users (employers) may obtain electronic records from an approved employment screening company via an authorized vendor. Otherwise, vendors cannot obtain records for other vendors.

Non-permissible Use Requests

Records may be released on a case-by-case determination, but personal information is blocked. No record with personal information shall be cleared without notarized written consent from the individual, use of the form mentioned above is recommended.

Access to Driver-Related Records

Driving Records

General Information and Fees

Driver's License Unit, Division of Motor Vehicles, PO Box 698, Dover DE 19903, Attn: Driver Services Dept., 302-744-2506.

The current fee is $15.00 per search, add $5.00 for certification. No fee increases are planned in the near term. Delaware charges for "no record found" requests. DMV hours of operation are 8:00 am to 4:30 pm (EST) except Wednesday hours are noon to 8 pm.

In-Person – The Division of Motor Vehicles will process up to three requests immediately, additional requests are processed overnight from

the address listed above. Over-the-counter requests require a valid ID and payment of $15.00 for each request. If requesting information on a third party, a notarized *MV703 Form* or valid court document is required. Records may also be requested over-the-counter from Division of Motor Vehicles locations in Wilmington, New Castle, Dover, and Georgetown.

Mail – Requests mailed to the Division of Motor Vehicles office processed in three-to-five working days. The driver's license number or name and date of birth are needed when ordering. Requesters must use *Form MV703* and the request must be notarized when sent by mail. Payment and a SASE must accompany all mail requests.

Electronic – The Direct Access Program is provided 24 hours via the web. The fee is $15.00 per name. Requests must include the driver's license number. Requesters must be pre-approved; a signed contract application is required. Online searching is by single inquiry only; no batch request mode is offered. For more information about establishing an account, call Ms. Stephani Jackson at 302-744-2726.

Bulk – Purchase of records in bulk or database format is not available.

By Person of Record – DE drivers may obtain their driving record by mail or walk-in as described above. The person of record may order a three-year, five-year, or a complete record. DE motorists can access their own personal driving record by using the expanded "MyDMV" account service located at www.dmv.de.gov. The same $15.00 fee applies and use of a credit card is required. Record is provided in PDF format and available for 90 days.

Notification/Monitoring Program

At present, Delaware does not offer an automated monitoring system or notification program for employers or insurance companies to track incidents of submitted drivers.

Accident Reports

Reporting – Accidents involving damage in excess of $500.00, injury, death, or if it appears an involved driver has been impaired as a result of drug or alcohol use, then the accident must be reported to local police, but not with the Motor Vehicle Division.

Record Access – Accident reports are held by the Delaware State Police, Traffic Records, PO Box 430, Dover 19903, 302-739-5931, fax: 302-739-5936.

Access to records is restricted to insurance companies, attorneys, and those involved with the incident. Otherwise a signed release is necessary. The fee is $25.00 for each report or $60.00 for a copy of a fatal accident report. It takes 2 weeks before new records are available for inquiry. Paper records maintained since 1984. Average turnaround time is 5 to 10 days; 30 to 90 days for a fatal report. Include the full name, location, date, and complaint number of the incident. One cannot search by phone, but one may call for verification if a report exists.

Access to Vehicle-Related Records

General Information and Fees

Correspondence Section, Division of Motor Vehicles, PO Box 698, Dover DE 19903, 302-744-2500.

The fee for VIN, lien and registration checks is $15.00 per record inquiry or $20.00 for a certified copy. Those routinely seeking information must complete an *Application* and a *Contract for Direct Access*. Authorized access account holders may obtain information in accordance with their contracts. Otherwise, third-party requests must be accompanied by a valid court document or a completed, notarized *Personal Information Request Form (MV703)*. DMV hours of operation are 8:00 am to 4:30 pm (EST), on Wednesday hours are noon to 8 pm. Find forms at www.dmv.de.gov/forms/forms_manuals.shtml.

In-Person or Mail – Over-the-counter requests for vehicle records must be made at the Dover location of the Division of Motor Vehicles. The physical address is 303 Transportation Circle, Dover, across Hwy

113 from the Blue Hen Corporate Center. Those requesting information in person must pay $15.00 for each record requested, and must provide a valid ID, complete the *MV703* and explain the purpose for seeking such information. A notarized release or valid court document is required for third-party information. Mail-in requests must also be accompanied by payment and a self-addressed stamped envelope, and mailed to the address above. Turnaround time for mail-in requests is 3 to 5 days.

Electronic – The Direct Access Program is provided 24 hours via the web. The fee is $15.00 per record. Requesters must be pre-approved; a signed contract application is required. Online searching is by single inquiry only; no batch request mode is offered. For more information about establishing an account, call Ms. Stephani Jackson at 302-744-2726.

Bulk – Per state law, the bulk database sale of records is not provided.

Access to Vessel-Related Records

General Information, Access and Fees

Department of Natural Resources and Environmental Control, 89 Kings Highway, Dover DE 19901, 302-739-9916
www.dnrec.delaware.gov/fw/Services/Pages/Licenses.aspx.

As a rule, every boat, vessel, jet ski, surf jet, ski craft or any other personal watercraft operated by Delaware residents on Delaware waterways must be registered. Non-resident boats/vessels using the waters of Delaware for principal use over 60 days and non-residents owning a boat docked and/or stowed in waters of Delaware for over 60 days must be registered in Delaware.

Records are available from 1979 to present. Records are for registration

only (not titles) and are indexed on microfiche from 1978 to 1989. Records are computer indexed from 1990 to the present. It takes 3 days for new records to become available. All motorized craft are registered. Registration information is considered confidential and this agency follows stricter guidelines than DPPA standards. However, the agency will often verify information over the phone with a "yes" or "no" response only.

Liens are filed at the Secretary of State and are not found at this location.

Note that boat trailers are titled and registered by the DMV.

Driving Record Content and Reciprocity

What's On or Not On the Driving Record

- All moving violation convictions are reported on the MVR.
- Accidents are reported only when a conviction is rendered.
- The record contains address, height, weight and DOB. The SSN is not released.
- The length of time that convictions, DUIs and suspension are listed on the public record is three years; however, if CDL then items may be reported back as far as 55 years.
- Only the driver has the choice of obtaining a three year or five year or a full lifetime record.
- The state does not permit Defensive Driver School attendance in lieu

of conviction, but one may earn a three-point credit once every three years for attendance.

Data Retention

Surrendered license information remains in the system for at least three years. CDL driver records are purged based on the timetable per the federal regulations (see the Appendix).

Court to Repository

Violations are entered via electronic processing and/or from paper abstracts sent from the courts to the DMV. Courts must submit convictions immediately. Tickets are entered upon conviction and sentencing, generally it takes two-to-three weeks to be entered.

State Reciprocity for Non-CDL Drivers

- Will suspend license of driver for unpaid out-of-state convictions.
- Record of new incoming driver is shown on MVR.
- Out-of-state convictions are shown on MVR.
- Out-of-state accidents are shown on MVR only if there is a conviction involved.
- Convictions of out-of-state drivers are sent to home state.
- Record forwarded to new state upon surrender of license upon request or if revoked/suspended.

License Classes, Restrictions, and Endorsements

License Classes

Code	Literal	Remarks
CA	CDL Class A	Over 26,000 pounds combination vehicle with trailer over 10,000 pounds.
CB	CDL Class B	Over 26,000 pounds single vehicle or combination vehicle with trailer 10,000 pounds or under.
CC	CDL Class C	26,000 pounds or under, if used to transport sixteen or more passengers (including the driver) or any vehicle requiring placarding for HazMat.
D	Class D	All non-CDL vehicles 26,000 pounds or under or if used to transport sixteen or more passengers (including the driver) or any vehicle requiring placarding for HazMat. Includes Level 1 Learners' Permit.
DA	Denied (Admin)	Denied license in Administration Office.
DG	Denied in Georgetown	Denied license in Georgetown Office.
DN	Denied in New Castle	Denied license in New Castle Office.
DW	Denies in Wilmington	Denied license in Wilmington Office.
GDL	Level 1 LP	Learner's Permit for Graduated Driver License.
LP	DE Learners' Permit	Permit for Driver Education students, adult students and *CDL permits*.
NA	Non-CDL A	Class A vehicle under Farmer or Fire-fighter waiver.
NB	Non-CDL B	Class B vehicle under Farmer or fire-fighter waiver.
NO	None	Violations/History on file or license issue denied.
OT	Out-Of-State	Violations/History on file.
PA	Perm Non-CDL A	Permanent non-CDL A, Class NA vehicle.
PB	Perm Non-CDL B	Permanent non-CDL B, Class NB vehicle.
PD	Perm D	Upgraded from old Class A or new Class D.
T	Temporary LIC	A Temporary License, giving short term driving authority for all license classes except learner permits.

Restrictions

B	Corrective Lenses	F	Outside Mirror	K	CDL Intrastate Only
C	Mechanical Aid	G	Limit to Daylight Only	L	Vehicles Without Air-Brakes
D	Prosthetic Aid	I	Limit - Other	W	Medical
E	Automatic Transmission	J	Other	Y	Convicted Sex Offender

Endorsements

H	Hazardous Materials	P	Passenger (all CMVs)	T	Double-/Triple-Trailer
M	Motorcycle	Q	Passenger B and C CMVs	X	Tank and HazMat Combined
N	Tank Vehicle	R	Passenger C CMVs	Z	Taxicab
O	Other	S	School Bus		

Conviction Table with ACD and Legal Reference

A blank in the **ACD** column usually indicates a conviction that is "retired" but may still show on a driving record. Sometimes all or part of the **Abbreviation** may appear on the conviction description line if it is an ACD out-of-state conviction.

The **Legal Reference** refers to generally refers to Title 21 with the middle numbers reference to section within. See http://delcode.delaware.gov/title21/index.shtml#. The last set of numbers reference the law codes and if researched on the web they will indicate the associated Revocation/Suspension/Disqualification lengths.

Description of Conviction	ACD	Abbreviation	Legal Reference
# Plate Sec'd To Veh<21"F/Gd		# PLT SEC	21-2126-000B
12yr Oper Ohv W/I Compliance		>12YR OPER OHV	21-6824-000B
12yr Oper Ohv W/I Compliance		EXP/NO DL/ID	21-6824-000B
1st Off Contrl Subst Dev Prrm	A33	1ST OFF CONTRL	16-4764-0000
3rd Dr Und Influ Alchl/Drugs	A20	DUI ALC/DRUG	21-4177 000A
3rd Dr Und Influ Of Alcohol	A20	DUI ALC/DRUG	21-4177 00A1
3rd Dr Und Influ Of Alcohol/Drugs	A23	DUI ALC/DRUG	21-4177 00A3
3rd Dr Und Influ Of Drugs	A22	DUI ALC/DRUG	21-4177 00A2
4th Dr Und Influ Alchl/Drugs	A20	DUI ALC/DRUG	21-4177 000A

Description of Conviction	ACD	Abbreviation	Legal Reference
4th DR Und Influ of /Drugs	A22	DUI ALC/DRUG	21-4177 00A2
4th DR Und Influ of Alcohol	A20	DUI ALC/DRUG	21-4177 00A1
4th DR Und Influ of Alcohol/Drugs	A23	DUI ALC/DRUG	21-4177 00A3
Aggressive Driving	M84	RECKLESS DRI	21-4175-A000
Allow Overtake Veh To Pass		ALLOW OVERTAKE	21-6519-000B
Alter/Forge Manu Cert Orgin		ALT/FORG CO	21-2316-0002
Alter/Forge Reg Card/Sticker		ALT/FORG REG	21-2316-0003
Altered Bumper Heights		DFCT EQUPMNT	21-4318-0000
Altering/Forging Cert Title		ALT/FORG TITLE	21-2316-0001
Ark In Handicapped Zone		PARKN HANDIC	21-4183-0000
Assault - 2nd Degree	U06	ASSAULT-2ND	11-0612-00A1
Auth/Permit Operate By Other		PERMIT UNLIC	21-2755-0000
Avoid Sp Weight Operation		NO WEIGHING*	21-4506-00C3
Axle Load Exceed 20000 Lbs		XS SIZ/WT/CR	21-4502-00C1
Back Veh On Shoulder/Rdway	N82	IMPROP BACKN	21-4126-00A6
Braking Distance Inadequate	E31	DFCT BRAKES*	21-4303-000B
Careless Driving	M81	CARELESS DRI	21-4176-000A
Carry No More Design Seat Mc	F06	IMP OP/RD MC	21-4185-000A
Carry Parcel Which Hinder Ster		PARCEL HINDER	21-4197-0000
Clinging To Vehicle		CLINGING TO*	21-4195-0000
Complete Stop/Red Signal	M15	FTO TRF SGNL	21-4108-0A3C
Criminal Neg Homicide	U07	CRIM NEG HOM	11-0630-0000
Deliver Narcotic Sch I Ccs	A33	POSS W/INTENT	16-4751-000A
Deliver Narcotic Sch I Cs	A33	POSS W/INTENT	16-4751-000A
Deliver Narcotic Sch Ii Ccs	A33	POSS W/INTENT	16-4751-000A
Deliver Narcotic Sch Ii Drugs	A33	POSS W/INTENT	16-4751-000A
Delv Sch Iii Contrld Substance	A33	DELV SCH III	16-4752-0000
Dest/Damage Wgt Equipment	E70	DEST/DAM WGT E	21-4506-00C4
Disclose Mile On Cert Tit/Orgn		FAIL TO FILE	21-6410-0000
Disobey Rest Traf Dev/Ent	M14	IMPROPR LOCA	21-4126-0A13
Disp Contrd Substn W/O Rx	A33	POSSESS DRUG	16-4755-00A1
Disp Fraudulently Alt Lic	B41	ALT/CFT DLID	21-2751-000G
Disp Lights Traction/Tractor		DISP LIGHTS	21-6509-0000
Disp Proof Of Registration		FL SHOW REGI	21-6801-000B
Disp Reg Plate Traction/Tractor		DISP REG PLATE	21-6507-0000
Disp Unauthorized Sign/Signal		TAMPER T C D	21-4111-0000
Disp/Rep Lic/ID Card Another	D16	USE OTH DLID	21-2751-000N
Display Of Cancelled License	B22	P W LIC CANC	21-2751-000C
Display Of Fictitious Lic	B41	ALT/CFT DLID	21-2751-000F
Display Of Revoked License	B25	DW LIC CANC	21-2751-000D
Display Of Suspended License	B26	DW LIC SUSP	21-2751-000E
Disregard Flashing Signal	M18	FTO WARN LIT	21-4110-00A1
Disregard Lane Change Device	M14	FTO SIGN/T CD	21-4122-0004
Disregard Marked Lane	M14	FTO LANE MARK	21-4122-0003
Disregard Minimum Speed	S96	INSUFF SPEED	21-4171-000A
Disregard No Passing Zones	M76	PAS PST SIGN	21-4120-000A
Disregard No Passing Zones	M76	PASS WH PROH	21-4120-000B
Disregard One Way Road	N63	WW ON ONEWAY	21-4121-000A
Disregard Pedestrian Signal		FTO TRF SIGN	21-4109-0002
Disregard Red Light		FTO TRF SGNL	21-4108-0A3D
Disregard Red Light	M14	FTO TRF SGNL	21-4108-0A3A
Disregard RR Barrier/Gate	M10	FTO RR GAT/S	21-4161-000B
Disregard Speed Limit Bridge	S92	R/B/T WEIGHT	21-4173-000A
Disregard Tow To Emergency Veh	N04	DIS ROW TO EMER	21-4106-0000
Disregard Traffic Control Device	M14	FAIL TRAF CONTL	21-4107-000A
Disregard Traffic Sign	M14	FTO TRF SIGN	21-4107-000B
Disregard Traffic Sign	M15	FTO TRF SIGN	21-4107-000C
Disregard Weight Limit Bridge		PRIMA FACIE*	21-4173-000B
Dissemin/Adv/Sell Master Key		DIS/ADV/SELL KEY	21-4601-000B
Dist/Poss Drugs W/I 1000 School	A33	DIST/POSS SCH	16-4767-00A1
Distribute Drugs To Minors	A33	DIST DRUGS	16-4761-0002
Dr On/Frm Rdway Except Et/Ex	M46	IMP LOC RAMP	21-4126-00A5
Dr Over/Upon Curb/Div Sec/L	M02	FTO BARRIER	21-4126-00A1

Description of Conviction	ACD	Abbreviation	Legal Reference
Dr Over/Upon Curb/Div Sec/L	M02	FTO BARRIER	21-4126 A1
Dr Slow Speed/Impede Traffic	S96	DR SLOW SPEED	21-4171-000B
Dr Und Influ Alcohol/Drugs	A23	DUI ALC/DRUG	21-4177 00A3
Dr Veh From Local Service Rd	M50	IMP LOC LTAC	21-4126-00A4
Dr W/Lic Susp/Rev-Fail Pay	B26	D W LIC SUSP	21-2756-000D
Dr W/o Learn permit	B78	POSSESS LRN PER	21-2710-00CI
Dr W/O Qualified Supervisor	D29	DR W/O QUAL DR	21-2710-00C2
Dr While CDL Lic Disq	B24	DR CDL DISQ	21-2607-000B
Dr Wrong Dir At Rotary Inter	N61	WW AT ROTARY	21-4121-000B
Drinking While Driving	A26	DRINK WH OPER	21-4177 000G
Drive After Judgment Prohibit	D35	FINANCL RESP	21-2810-000a
Drive Consume Alcohol <21	A60	UNAGE D*DCOV	21-4177-000I
Drive During Denial Period	B23	DR DRG DENIAL	21-2758-000B
Drive In Improper Lane	M62	IMP LOC TURN	21-4122-0002
Drive MV Over Fire Hose	M56	IMP LOC FHOS	21-4188-000B
Drive MV Sidewalk/Bike Path	M58	IMP LOC SHLD	21-4136-0000
Drive Thru Safety Zone	M12	FTO SAF ZONE	21-4199-0000
Drive Under Infl Alcohol	A20	DUI ALC/DRUGS	21-4177 00A1
Drive Under Infl Alcohol Drugs	A20	DUI ALC/DRUG	21-4177 000A
Drive Under Infl Drugs	A22	DUI ALC/DRUG	21-4177 00A2
Drive Veh W/O Consent Owner		NO OWNR CONS	21-6702-000A
Drive W/Imp Class Type Lic	B51	IMP CLS/NDOR	21-2701-000C
Drive W/O Lp In Possession	B78	VIO LP POSS	21-2710-00C1
Drive While Lic Susp/Rev	B26	D W LIC SUSP	21-2756-000A
Drive While License Expired	B51	EXP/NO DL/ID	21-2701-000D
Drive With >2 Passengers	D29	DR W/2 PASS	21-2710-00C5
Duty To Sign/Carry License		EXP/ NO DL/ID	21-2721-000A
Eave Motor Vehicle Unattended		VEH UNATTEND	21-4182-0000
Employer Violation CDL		EMP VIOL CDL	21-2606-00B1
Employment Of Unlicensed Person		PERMIT UNLIC	21-2754-0000
Enter/Cross Div Hwy Crossover	N06	IMP LOC XOVR	21-4135-0000
Evade Toll Bridge		FTP: TOLL***	21-4128-000A
Evade Turnpike Toll		FTP: TOLL***	21-4127-000A
Exceed Reasonable Speed	S94	PRIMA FACIE*	21-4168-000A
Exceed Weight/Length Reg Size		XS SIZ/WT/CR	21-4501-0000
Exp Reg Upon Transfer Of Title		EXP REG ON TRAN	21-2501-0000
Expired CDL License	B51	EXP/NO DL/ID	21-2609 E
Expired Registration		EXP/NO RG/TL	21-2109-000A
Extended Load/Wdt/Hgt/Len		XS SIZ/WT/CR	21-4502-00B2, 00B6
Fail Destroy Exp T-Tag		EXP/NO PLATE	21-2131-000A
Fail Destroy Exp T-Tag		EXP/NO PLATE	21-2131-000B
Fail Dim Headlgts Follow MV	E54	MPRP EQUPMNT	21-4350-0002
Fail Obey Traffic Cont Dev		FTO SIGN/TCD	21-4506-00C1
Fail T/Change Address On CDL		FAIL TO COA CDL	21-2609-000B
Fail T/Give Identity At Accident	B14	RFID AFT ACC	21-4201-000B
Fail T/Remove Deposit Material		LFT HARM SUB	21-4506-000B
Fail To Cover Animal Scraps		SPILL R DRAG	21-4372-0000
Fail To Cover School Bus Marks	E56	NUSE S B EQP	21-4362-000B
Fail To Dim Headlights	E54	MPRP EQUPMNT	21-4350-0000, 0001
Fail To Display Lic Plate		FAIL TO DISP PLT	21-2126-000A
Fail To Display Ins ID Card	B74	FAIL SHOW INS	21-2118-000P
Fail To Display Ins ID Card	D36	NO LIABL INS	21-2118-000O
Fail To Exercise Due Care	M82	INATTENT DRI	21-4144-0000
Fail To File Ins Certificate	B64	FAIL FILE INS	21-2118-000M
Fail To Issue Title 30 Days		FAIL TO ISSUE 30	21-2509-0002
Fail To Obtain Title		FAIL OBTAIN TITL	21-2503-000A
Fail To Pay Reinstatement Fee		FTP: FEE****	21-2737-0000
Fail To Perform/Operate		EXP/NO RG/TL	21-2115-0008
Fail To Renew Registration		EXP/NO RG/TL	21-2110-000A
Fail To Rep Acc Invol Alc/Drug	B61	FL FILE ACCR	21-4203-00A3
Fail To Report Accident	B61	FL FILE ACCR	21-4203-00A2, 000A, 000B, 21-4203-000D, 000E
Fail To Report Per Inj Accident	B61	FL FILE ACCR	21-4203-00A1
Fail To Stop At Command	U01	EVADING/FLEE	21-4103-000B

Description of Conviction	ACD	Abbreviation	Legal Reference
Fail To Stop At RR Crossing	M22	FTO RR DRIVE	21-4163-000A
Fail To Yield In Const Area	N01	FAIL TO YEILD	21-4105-000B
Fail To Yield Right Of Way	N01	FY 2 OTH VEH	21-4133-0000
Fail To Yield Rotary Inter	N21	FTY ROW@ROTR	21-4121-000C
Fail To Yielld Row To Overtaking Veh	N07	FY 2 OVT VEH	21-4116-0002
Fail Yield Row To Pedestrian	N20	FY 2 PEDESTR	21-4142-0000
Fail/Improper Signal	N40	IMPROPER SIG	21-4155-000B, 000C, 000D
Failed To Obtain Title		FAIL TO TITLE	21-2301-000B
Failed To Remain Stopped	M15	FTO STP SIGN	21-4164-000A, 000B
Failed To Use Due Care	S94	PRIMA FACIE*	21-4168-000B
Failed Yield At Yield Sign	M19	FTY ROW@YLDS	21-4164-000C
Failure Obey Lawful Order Pd	M08	FAIL OBEY LAW	21-4103-000A
Failure To Answer Summons	D45	FAIL TO APPEAR	21-0702-0000
Failure To Have License in Possession	B78	POSS OF LIC	21-2721-000B
Failure To Reinstate License	B20	EXP/NO DL/ID	21-2701-000B
Failure To Rpt Change of Address		FAIL RPT COA	21-0315-0000
False Info On Temp Tag		MISREP ID RT	21-2133-00A1
False Info T/Obtain Ha Tag		FALSE INFO TTAG	21-2134-0000
False Statement License	D02	MISREP ID DL	21-2751-000A
False Statement On Application		FALSE STATE APP	21-2315-0000
False Statement On ID Card		FALSE ID STATE	21-3107-0000
False Statement On License	D02	FALSE STATEM	21-2752-0000
False/Incomplete Info-CDL	D02	MISREPIDOL	21-2620-0000
Fed Motor Carrier Violation		FTO MT C REG	21-4702-000A
First Offense Election	A20	DUI ALC/DRUG	21-4177 000B
First Offense Election	A20	DUI ALCOHOL	21-4177 B000
Foe-IID Diversion	A20	DUI ALC/DRUGS	21-4177 B00G
Follow Fire Apparatus	M33	FOL FIRE EQU	21-4188-000A
Follow To Close/Motorcade	M34	FOL TO CLOSE M	21-4123-000C
Following Too Closely	M34	FOL TOO CLOS	21-4123-000A
Following Too Closely Towing	M30	IMPROP TOW/P	21-4123-000B
FTY ROW To Emergency Vehicle	N04	FY 2 EMR VEH	21-4134-000A
Habitual Offender		HABITUAL OFFEN	21-2802-0001
Helmet/Eye Protection	F03	M/C EQ N USD	21-4185-000B
Hold/Use Alter/Forge Title		HLD/USE TITLE	21-2316-0004
Ident Marker Affixed-View		MPRP EQUPMNT	21-5211-0000
Illegal Use Of Siren		PROH LT/SIRN	21-4307-0000
Imp Front Lights/Reflectors		DFCT LIGHTS*	21-4339-000A
Imp Issuance Of Temp Tag		IMP ISS TTAG	21-2133-00A2
Imp Mat/Top Edge Windshield		DFCT EQUPMNT	21-4313-000B
Imp Move Heavy Equip @ Rr Xx	M09	FTO RR DRIVE	21-4167-000A
Imp Parking Yellow/Line		STOP WH PROH	21-4179-0A17
Imp Projection From Tires	E37	DFCT TIRES**	21-4302-000A
Imp Rear Lights/Reflect/Signal Lgts		MPRP EQUPMNT	21-4339-000C
Imp Rear Lights/Reflectors		DFCT EQUPMNT	21-4339-000B
Imp Removal Veh Frm Accid Scene	B05	LVSC AFT ACC	21-4206-0000
Imp Towing/Pushing Vehicle		IMPROP TOW/P	21-4191-A00A
Imp Transfer Title W/O Cert		IMP TRANS TITLE	21-2510-0000
Imp Transfer Title W/O Cert		USE IMP RGTL	21-2510-000A
Imp/Fail To Use S/B Signals	E56	IMP/FAIL SB SIGN	21-4166-000B
Imp/Fail To Use S/B Signals	E56	NUSE S B EQP	21-4166-00B3
Imp/Use Of Handle Bars MC		M/C EQ N USD	21-4185-000C
Improper Bumper Height		DFCT EQUPMNT	21-4318-000A
Improper Clearance Equipment	E34	DFCT LIGHTS*	21-4338-0000
Improper Clearance Lights	E34	DFCT LIGHTS*	21-4335-0000
Improper Coasting	N80	COASTING ***	21-4187-0000
Improper Crossing Of Barrier	M02	FTO BARRIER*	21-4124-0000
Improper Flashing School Bus Lights	E06	MPRP EQUPMNT	21-4364-0000
Improper Front Light On MV	E05	DFCT LIGHTS*	21-4333-000B
Improper Front Light On MV	E34	DFCT LIGHTS*	21-4333-000A
Improper Front Lights	E55	DFCT LIGHTS*	21-4352-000A
Improper Front Lights On MV	E34	DFCT LIGHTS*	21-4333-0000
Improper Hand Arm Signal	N44	WRBONG SIGNAL	21-4157-0001

Description of Conviction	ACD	Abbreviation	Legal Reference
Improper Headlights	E34	DFCT LIGHTS*	21-4349-0000
Improper Lane Change	M42	IMP LANE CHG	21-4122-0001
Improper Left Turn	N06	IMP LEFT TRN	21-4132-0000
Improper License Plate Tint		IMP LIC PLT TINT	21-2126-000C
Improper Light Equipment	E34	DFCT EQUPMNT	21-4348-0000
Improper Light/Reflector	E34	DFCT LIGHTS*	21-4314-0000
Improper Mud Flap/Protectors		DFCT EQUPMNT	21-4317-000A
Improper Muffler		DFCT/NOIS EX	21-4311-000A
Improper Muffler		DFCT/NOIS EX	21-4311-000B
Improper Opening Of Vehicle Door		OPN DOOR: TR	21-4190-0000
Improper Operate Bicycle		IMP OPR BIKE	21-4196-000A
Improper Parking		STOP WH PROH	21-4179-0A10
Improper Parking From Curb		STOP WH PROH	21-4180-000A
Improper Pass On Curve/Grad	M74	PASS HIL/CRV	21-4119-00A1
Improper Passing	M70	IMPROPR PASS	21-4119-00A2
Improper Passing On Right	M70	PAS WRNG SID	21-4117-0000
Improper Passing On Right	M70	PAS WRNG SID	21-4117-000A
Improper Rear View Mirror		DFCT EQUPMNT	21-4308-0000
Improper Reg Plate Light	E34	DFCT LIGHTS*	21-4334-000A
Improper Safety Glass		DFCT EQUPMNT	21-4312-000A
Improper Safety Glass		DFCT EQUPMNT	21-4312-000B
Improper Signal Device	E55	DFCT LIGHTS*	21-4347-000A, 21-4347-000C
Improper Signal Device	E55	OMIT LIGHTS*	21-4347-0000
Improper Signal Device	N40	IMPROPER SIG	21-4156-000A
Improper Signal Lamps	E70	MPRP EQUPMNT	21-4156-000B
Improper Signal Lights	E34	DFCT LIGHTS*	21-4316-0000
Improper Slow Moving Vehicle	N06	FY 2 OTH VEH	21-4125-0000
Improper Stop Dev On School Bus	E06	NUSE S B EQP	21-4365-0000
Improper Studded Tires	E70	MPRP EQUPMNT	21-4302-000B
Improper Tail Lights On MV	E34	DFCT LIGHTS*	21-4334-000
Improper Tires	E37	DFCT TIRES**	21-4301-0000
Improper Turn	N50	IMPROPR TURN	21-4152-00A1, 21-4152-00A2 21-4152-00A3, 21-4152-000B
Improper Turn/Stop Signals	E34	DFCT LIGHTS*	21-4336-0000
Improper Use Of Color Lights		IL OP EMRG V	21-4356-0000
Improper Use Of Ct/Dealer Tag		IMP USE OF CT	21-2124-000A
Improper Use Of Flares		NO FLAG/FLAR	21-4357-0000
Improper Use Of Headlights	E55	MPRP EQUPMNT	21-4331-000A
Improper Use Of Horn		NO USE SAFEQ	21-4306-000B
Improper Use Of Light Device	E55	MPRP EQUPMNT	21-4353-0000, 21-4353-000B, 21-4353-000C
Improper Use Of Lights	E55	MPRP EQUPMNT	21-4346-000C
Improper Use Windshield Wipers	E70	MPRP EQUPMNT	21-4310-0000
Improper U-Turn	N50	IMPROP U TRN	21-4152-0000
Improper U-Turn	N56	IMPROP U TRN	21-4153-000A, 21-4153,000B
Improper Windshield/Front Window		DFCT EQUPMNT	21-4313-000A, 000A
Inadequate Brakes	E31	DFCT BRAKES*	21-4303-000A
Inadequate Hand Brakes	E31	DFCT BRAKES*	21-4304-000B
Inadequate Headlights On Mc	E05	DFCT LIGHTS*	21-4351-0000
Inadequate Horn		DFCT EQUPMNT	21-4306-00A
Inadequate Lights On Mc		INADQ LIGHT MC	21-2351-0000
Inadequate Service Brakes	E31	DFCT BRAKES*	21-4304-000C
Inadequate Stop Distance	E31	DFCT BRAKES*	21-4304-000A
Inadequate Tire/Chain On School Bus	E06	OMIT S B EQP	21-4361-0000
Inadequate Trailer Brakes	E31	DFCT BRAKES*	21-4305-0000
Inattentive Driving	M82	INATTENT DRI	21-4176-000B
Injury Veh/Obstructing Operation		INJURY VEH/OBS	21-6701-0000
Ins/Execution Search Warrant		INS/EXE SEARCH	21-6717-000B
Interfer W/Traf Control Dev Rr		TAMPER T C D	21-4112-0000
Intr/Sell/Dist MV Master Key		INTR/SELL KEY	21-4601-000 A
Invalid Temporary Reg Plate		INVAL TEMP REG	21-2133-00A3
Issue Permit Excess Weight		ISS PERMIT EXCE	21-6514-0000
Lane Signal Control	M10	FTO LANE MARK	21-4108-000B
Leave Scene Acc Invol CMV	B05	LVSC: AFT ACC	21-2612-00A3

Description of Conviction	ACD	Abbreviation	Legal Reference
Leave Scene Of Per Inj Accident	B06	LVSC AFT ACC	21-4202-000A
Leaving Scene Of Accident	B08	LVSC:PDO ACC	21-4201-000a
Left/U-Turn Where Allowable	N50	IMPROPR LOCA	21-4126-00A2
Lia Parent/Guardian Of Minor		LIA PARENT MINO	21-6105-0000
Lic Susp-Tag No Surr-No Ins	D36	NO LIABL INS	21-2118-00M1
Limit On Overtaking On Left	M72	PAS WRNG SID	21-4118-0000
Limitations On Backing	N82	IMPROP BACKN	21-4184-000A
Loaning License		LOAN LIC	21-2751-000M
Lost/Destroyed Reg Plate		LOST/DEST REG	21-2127-0000
Maint Mileage Statement 4 Yrs		MAIN MILEAGE	21-6408-000C
Maintain Records Rented Vehicles		MAIN RECD RENT	21-6104-0000
Malicious Mischief By MV	M84	UNSAFE OPERA	21-4172-A00A
Manslaughter	U08	MANSLAUGHTER	11-0632-0001
Mfg Narcotic Sch I Ccs Drugs	A33	POSS W/INTENT	16-4751-000A
Mfg Narcotic Sch I Controlled Sub	A33	POSS W/INTENT	16-4751-000A
Mfg Narcotic Sch II Ccs Drugs	A33	POSS W/INTENT	16-4751-000A
Mfg Narcotic Sch II Controlled Substance	A33	POSS W/INTENT	16-4751-000A
Mfg Sch I Contrld Substance	A33	MFG SCH SUBST	16-4752-0000
Mfg Sch II Controlled Substance	A33	MFG SCH II SUBST	16-4752-0000
Mfg Sch III Controlled Substance	A33	MFG SCH III SUB	16-4752-0000
Mfg/Deliver/Witd Controlled Sub	A33	MFG/DEL/PWITD	16-4751-000C
Mfg/Disp/Distb/Cont Substance	A33	MFG/DISP/CONT S	16-4755-00A2
Mfg/dlvr/Poss W Intent Drugs	A33	MFG/DLVR/POSS	16-4752-0000
Misrep/Buy/Sell Of Vehicle		STOLEN VEHIC	21-6705-000D
Moped/Triped Where Not Perm		VEH WHR PROH	21-4194-00AD
Mounted Height Of Lamps	E34	MNT HGT LMPS	21-4332-000B
Must Dr Right Side Of Road	N70	DR WRONG SID	21-4114-000C
Must Drive Right Side Of Road	N70	DR WRONG SID	21-4114-000A
Must Drive Right Side Road	N70	DR WRONG SID	21-4114-000B
No Child Passenger Restraint	F02	C/Y NOT USED	21-4803-000A
No Flag/Light On Extended Load		NO FLAG/FLAR	21-4343-0000
No Heavy Equip <10mph	M09	IMP LOC TRAK	21-4167-000B
No Lic Non-Resid Aft 30 Day	B51	EXP/NO DL/ID	21-2706-000B
No License W/I 60 Days Resid	D16	EXP/NO DL/ID	21-2704-000A
No Lights On Horse Drawn Vehs	E05	NO LGTS HRS VE	21-4345-0000
No Ohv Eye/Helmet Protection		M/C EQ N USD	21-6823-0000
No Parking In loading Zone		STOP WH PROH	21-4180-000E
No Possession Reg Card		FL SHOW REGI	21-2108
No Reg W/I 60 Days Residence		EXP/NO RG/TL	21-2102-000A
No Seat Belt/Restrnt <16 Yrs	F02	C/Y NOT USED	21-4803-000B
No Valid License	B51	EXP/NO DL/ID	21-2701-000A
No Valid Motorcycle License	B51	IMP CLS/NDOR	21-2701-000A
No Vehicle Shall Exeed 102"		XS SIZ/WT/CR	21-4502-00B1
Non-Res Ident Reg T For Cont		NON-RES ID REG	21-2112-0008
Notif Owner Intent To Rent		NOT OWNER RENT	21-6103-0000
Obstruction Of Traffic	F34	OBSTR TRAFFC	21-4130-0000
Obstruction Of View	D70	VIEW OBSTRUC	21-4309-0000
Offers False Instrument	D02	OFFERS FALSE	11-0877-0000
Ohv Dealer Safe Oper Rent/Ls		OHV DLR SAFE	21-6813-000A
Ohv Disobey Command To Stop		FAIL TO OBEY	21-6830-0000
Ohv Registration		OHV REG	21-6801-000A
Ohv-Leave Scene Accident		LVSC AFT ACC	21-6827-000D
Ohv-Prima Facie		PRIMA FACIE*	21-6829
Oper Moped/Triped W/O Lic		USE IMP DLID	21-4194-00AB
Oper Mv In Violation Restrict	D27	MV VIOL REST	21-2722-000D
Oper Mv Or Ohv On Private Prop		IMPROP TOW/P	21-4191-0000
Oper Ohv Acc Priv W/I 48 Hrs		FL FILE ACCR	21-6827-000B
Oper Ohv Malicious Exc Damage		RECKLESS DRI	21-6819-000A
Oper Ohv Uncontrol Excess Speed		OPER OHV SPEED	21-6815-0000
Oper Ohv Under Infl Alr/Drugs		DUI ALC/DRUG	21-6816-0000
Oper Ohv Viol Traf Control Dev		FTO TRF SIGN	21-6822-0000
Oper Ohv W/O Spark Arr Muffler		OMIT EQUPMNT	21-6820-000A
Oper Rented Veh W/O Liability Ins	D36	NO LIABL INS	21-6102-000A

Description of Conviction	ACD	Abbreviation	Legal Reference
Oper Unregistered Vehicle		EXP/NO RG/TL	21-2101-000A
Oper Veh Proh Traffic Dev	M14	FTO TRF SIGN	21-4126-0A12
Oper/Dr Bike-Cont Acc Hwy	N71	OPER BIKE HWY	21-4126-00A7
Operate CMV Felony	A50	VEH:CNTR SUB	21-2612-000D
Operate CMV W/O Proper CDL	B56	EXP/NO DL/ID	21-2607 A
Operate MV Causing Death	U31	CARELESS DRI	21-4176-A00a
Operate MV W/O Reg Insurance	D36	OPER W/O REG IN	21-2118-000B
Operate OHV W/O Brakes		DFCT BRAKES*	21-6818-0000
Operate OHV W/O Lights		DFCT LIGHTS*	21-6817-0000
Operate Taxi W/O Taxi License	B51	EXP/NO DL/ID	21-2761-0000
Operate Uninsured MV	D36	OPER UNREG MV	21-2118-000A
Operate Unregister Vehicle		EXP/NO RG/TL	21-2115-0001
Operate Unregistered Vehicle		EXP/NO RG/TL	21-2101
Operate Unsafe MV	F66	UNSAFE OPERA	21-4355-0000
Operate Unsafe MV	F66	UNSAFE OPERA	21-4355-000A
Operation Of Unreg Taxicab		EXP/NO RG/TL	21-2171
Opr CMV BAC .04 Or Above	A04	CMV BAC.04	21-4177-000M
Opr CMV BAC .04 Or Above	A04	DUI 04BACPLI	21-2613-000C
Overload Mc.Interfere W/Drvr		MC XS CRGO/P	21-4185-000E
Overload MV/Obstruct Dr View	D70	VIEW OBSTRUC	21-4186-000B
Overload/Mv Obstruct Driv View	D70	VIEW OBSTRUC	21-4186-000A
Overweight		VT XS WEIGHT	21-4503-0000
Overweight		VT XS WEIGHT	21-4503-00E2
Overweight Vehicle Limits		VT XS WEIGHT	21-4503-00C1
Park In No Parking Zone		STOP WH PROH	21-4180-000B
Park W/O High Lights	E34	MPRP EQUPMNT	21-4344-000C
Park W/O Lights On Road	E34	MPRP EQUPMNT	21-4344-000B
Pass Veh Proceed Opp Dir	M72	PAS OP DIREC	21-4115-0000
Pass/Overtake Stop Sch Bus	M75	PASS SCH BUS	21-4166-000D
Passing Weight Station		NO WEIGHING*	21-4506-00C2
Permit Drag Racing	M84	DRAG RACING	21-4172-000C
Permit Drag Racing	M84	RACE CONTEST	21-4172-A00B
Permit Unlawful Use Lic/ID	D16	LOAN DL LICN	21-2751-000P
Permit Unlicensed Minor Oper Mv	B51	PERMIT UNLIC	21-2753-0000
Poss Alter/Deface Vin On Ohv		FALSE VIN/PL	21-6811-000B
Poss Fraudulently Alter Lic	B41	ALT/CFT DLID	21-2751-000L
Poss Noncontrld Prscrptin Drugs	A33	POSS NONCONTR	16-4754-A000
Poss Of Blank Cert Of Title		ALT/CFT RGTL	21-6708-000A
Poss Of Cancelled License	D16	USE IMP DLID	21-2751-000H
Poss Of Fict License/ID Card	B41	ALT/CFT DLID	21-2751-000K
Poss Of Revoked License	B25	USE IMP DLID	21-2751-000I
Poss Suspended License	B25	USE IMP DLID	21-2751-000J
Poss W/I Mfg Nrctic Sch 1 Ccs	A33	POSS W/INTENT	16-4751-000A
Poss W/Int Dlvr Contrld Subst	A33	POSS W/INTENT	16-4752-0000
Poss W/Int Dlvr Sch I Cont Sub	A33	POSS W/INTENT	16-4752-0000
Poss W/Int Mfg Contrld Subst	A33	POSS W/INTENT	16-4752-0000
Poss W/Int To Dlvr Sch V Drugs	A33	POSS W/INTENT	16-4752-0000
Poss W/Intent Mfg Drugs	A33	POSS W/INTENT	16-4751-000A
Poss W/Intent Mfg Sch I Cs	A33	POSS W/INTENT	16-4751-000A
Poss W/Intent Mfg Sch II Ccs	A33	POSS W/INTENT	16-4751-000A
Poss/Consume Alcohol <21	A31	POSS/CONS ALC	04-0904-000F
Poss/Mfg Blank Ins Card		POSS/MFG BLK CD	21-2118-A00B
Possess Altered License	B41	POSS ALT LIC	21-2760-00A1, 21-2760-00A2
Possess Controlled Substance	A33	POSS CONTL SUB	16-4753-0000
Possess W/Intent To Deliver	A33	POSS W/INTENT	16-4751-000A
Possess/Use/Consume Drugs	A33	POSS/CONS DRGS	16-4754-000A, 16-4754-000B, 16-4754-0000
Probable Cause	A98	DUI@10ADMIN	21-2742-000C, 21-2742-00C1
Probable Cause <21	A61	UNAGE D*DADM	21-2742-00C2
Railroad Stop - 15 to 50	M09	FTO RR DRIVE	21-4161-000A
Reckless Driving	M84	RECKLESS DRI	21-4175-000A
Reckless Driving ALR	M84	RECKLESS DRI	21-4175-00AB
Refuse Breath/Blood Test CMV	A12	REFUSED TEST	21-2612 A5, 21-2614-000D
Refuse/Evade Turnpike Toll		FTP: TOLL***	21-4127-000B

Description of Conviction	ACD	Abbreviation	Legal Reference
Refused Chemical Test	A12	REFUSED TEST	21-2742-00B1
Refused Chemical Test <21	A61	UNAGE D*DADM	21-2742-00B2
Reg Reinstated-Insur Furn	D36	NO LIABL INS	21-2118 S3
Reg Susp - No Insurance	D36	NO LIABL INS	21-2118-00S2
Reg/Lic T/Oper Tracton/Tractor		REG/LIC T/OPER	21-6502-0000
Register Junk/Salvage Business		REG JUNK/SAL	21-6717-000A
Rem/Alter Veh Ident Plt/Strk		TAMPER W VEH	21-6709-000A
Remove/Affix Reg Plate Veh		FALSE VIN/PL	21-6705-000E
Rep Ohv/Acc Result Inj/Death		FL FILE ACCR	21-6827-000A
Report Poss/Master Keys T/Sec		RPT POSS/KEYS	21-4603-0000
Req 12 W/Shpu>18 Oper Ohv		REQ 12 W/SUPR	21-6824-00A1
Ride Mc Sitting Astride	F06	IMP OP/RD MC	21-4185-000D
Right Of Way At Intersection	N06	FT YLD R O W	21-4131-000A, 21-4131-0000, 21-4131-000B
Right-Of-Way From Driveway	N01	FAIL TO STOP	21-4165-0000
Safely Overtake Veh On Left	M31	PAS NSF DIST	21-4116-0000, 21-4116-0001
Sell Alter/Counterfeit Lic	B41	ALT/CFT DLID	21-2760-000B
Sell/Buy/Dispose Of Vehicle		STOLEN VEHIC	21-6705-000C
Sell/Deliver Blank Cert Titl		MISREP ID RT	21-6708-000B
Speed Exhibitions Aid	S95	RACE CONTEST	21-4172-000A
Speeding	S93	SPEEDING	21-4169
Spinning Wheels	S97	ERRATC SPEED	21-4172000B
Stamp/Affix Ohv To Vehicle		DFACE PLATES	21-6811-000A
Starting Parked Vehicle	N84	START PARKD VEH	21-4154-0000
Stop Command Of Property Owner		FAIL TO OBEY	21-6825-0000
Stop Stnd Prk Traf Dev Pro		STOP WH PROH	21-4179-0A15
Stop/Pass Horse Drawn Vehs		STOP/PASS HOR	21-6519-000A
Stop/Stand/Park On Highway	F34	STOP WH PROH	21-4178-000A
Stop/Stand/Park/Bridge Tun		STOP WH PROH	21-4179-0A14
Stop/Stank/Pk Div Hwy X/Ov		STOP WH PROH	21-4179-0A18
Stop-Obst Passg		OBSTR TRAFFC	21-4179-0A16
Surrender Ohv Reg Cert		FL SUR:DL/RG	21-6806-000B
Tamper W/Veh W/O Consent Owner		TAMPER W VEH	21-6703-0000
Throw Litter/Inj Matter Hwy		PUT HARM SUB	21-4189-000A
Throw Litter/Inj Matter On Hwy		PUT HARM SUB	21-4189-000C
Tract/Tractor Len Exc 75 Ft		TRACT/TRACTOR	21-6511-000B
Traction/Tractor Speed Limit		TRC/TRL SPEED	21-6518-0000
Traffic Cocaine >100 Gram	A33	TRAFFIC DRUGS	16-4753-AA2C
Traffic Cocaine 2.5gr-10grm	A33	TRAFFIC DRUGS	16-4753-AA3A
Traffic Cocaine 50-100grm	A33	TRAFFIC DRUGS	16-4753-AA2B
Traffic Phencyclidine 5-50 Grm	A33	TRAFFIC DRUGS	16-4753-AA6A
Transfer Title W/O Dsclos Lien		TRANS TITLE	21-2341-0000
Transferee Follow Regulation		TRASF FOL REG	21-2185-000B
Unauth Use Veh W/O Consent			11-0853-0001
Unauth Use Veh W/O Consent			11-0853-0002
Unauth Use Veh W/O Consent			11-0853-0003
Unauth Use/Addition To Plate		UNAUTH USE	21-2122-0000
Uninsur Veh Penalty Fee Due	D36	NO LIABL INS	21-2118-00M4
Unlawful Com Dr Sch W/O Lic		UNLAW COM SCH	21-8303-000A
Unlawful Delv Noncont Subst	A33	UNLAW DELV NON	16-4752-A0A1, 16-4752-A0A2
Unlawful Instr W/O Appl/Lic		UNLAW INSTR	21-8304-000A
Unlawful Master Key/Lock/Pck		UNLAWFUL MAST	21-4604-000A
Unlawful Oper Ohv Hwy/St/Sdw		IMPROP VEHIC	21-6814-000A
Unlawful Oper Veh School Bus	M75	OMIT S B EQP	21-4166-00D1
Unlawful Poss Tit/Reg/Ident		MISREP ID RT	21-6710-000A
Unlawful Sell/Install Odmt Dev		TAMPER ODOM	21-6403-0000
Unlawful Stop/Stnd/Prk Fire Ln		STOP WH PROH	21-7001-0000
Unlawful Use Ohv<12 Yrs		PERMIT UNLIC	21-6824-000C
Unlawful Use Tract/Tractor Hwy		USE TRACT/TRL	21-6517-0000
Unlawful Use Veh By Minor		PERMIT UNLIC	21-6106-0000
Unlawful Wgt Equipment		UNLAWFUL WGT	21-6512-0000
Unlawful Wgt Traction/Tractor		UNLAWFUL MGT	21-6510-0000
Unqualified T/Oper Sch Bus	B91	IMP CLS/NDOR	21-2708-000A
Unreg Moped/Triped		EXP/NO RG/TL	21-4194-00AA

Description of Conviction	ACD	Abbreviation	Legal Reference
Unsafe Movement Of Motor Veh	N84	IMPROP START	21-4154000A
Use CMV Committing Felony	U03	VEH IN FELNY	21-2612 A4
Use Of Cell By Sb Driver	M80	CELL SB DRVR	21-4176-B00a
Veh Assault-1st-Dui-Neglig Inj	U06	VEH ASSAULT	11-0629-0000
Veh Assault-2nd-Crim Neglig	U06	VEH ASSAULT	11-0628-0001
Veh Assault-2nd-Dui-Neglig Inj	U06	VEH ASSAULT	11-0628-0002
Vehicle Homicide 2nd Degree	U07	VEH HOM 2ND	11-0630-00A1
Vehicle Homicide/Dui 1st Degree	U07	VEH HOM/DUI 1S	11-0630-000A
Vehicle Homicide/Dui 2nd Degree	U07	VEH HOM/DUI 2D	11-0630-00A2
Vehs Yield Row To Ped On Sdwlk	N08	FTY ROW@XWLK	21-4151-0000
Viol Moving Permit/Size/Wght		VIOL PERMIT*	21-4504-000A
Viol Of Local Ord Speed Limit	S92	SPEEDING****	21-4170-0000
Viol Of Occupational License	D27	VIOL COND LIC	21-2733-000I
Viol Of Terms Or Conditions		VIOL PERMIT*	21-4504-000B
Viol Single Trip Permit		VIOL PERMIT*	21-4504-000D
Viol Temp Instruction Permit	D29	VIO TEMP INST	21-2710-000A
Violate Learners Permit	D29	VIO RESTRICT	21-2710-0000
Violate Learners Permit <16	D29	VIO RESTRICT	21-2710-00A1
Violate Learners Permit 18>	D29	VIO RESTRICT	21-2710-00A2
Violation Of Conditional Lic	B27	VIO LTD LICN	21-4177 E
Violation Of IRP		EXP/NO RG/TL	21-2115-0007
Violation of Out-of-Service-Order	B27	VIOL OOSO	21-2612-000H
Visibility Distance	E34	VIS DISTANCE	21-4332-000A
Visibility Reflector/Clearance		DFCT LIGHTS*	21-4341-0000
Willfully Abandon Veh On Hwy		ABANDN VEHIC	21-4414-0000
Window Tint W/O Manuf Certif		DFCT EQUPMNT	21-4313-000C

Point System Summary

Delaware points range from 2 to 6. An accumulation of 8 or more points in a 24-month period identifies problem drivers. An advisory letter is sent at point levels of 8 to 11.5. A driver is required to complete a behavior modification/attitudinal driving course at point levels of 12 to 13.5. A point level of 14 or greater results in a mandatory suspension of 4 months to 1 year, depending on point level. The behavior modification/attitudinal driving course is offered statewide. Drivers passing an approved **defensive driving** course may have 3 points deducted from their points total once every three years.

A speeding violation of 1 to 14 mph over the posted speed limit will not be assessed points, **IF** (a) it is the first violation within any three (3) year period and (b) the ticket is paid through the Voluntary Assessment Center or Alderman's Court and recorded as a "guilty mail-in."

Aggressive driving...6 points
Disregarding stop sign or red light...3 points
Passing a stopped school bus ....6 points
Reckless driving...6 points
Speeding 1-9 miles per hour (MPH) over posted limit ....2 points
Speeding 10-14 MPH over posted limit..4 points
Speeding 15-l9 MPH over posted limit...5 points
Speeding 20 MPH or more over posted limit...5 points
Other moving violations (contained in Chapters 27, 41, 42 of Title 21)..2 points

District of Columbia

Administration	Important Telephone and Web Contacts
Lucinda Babers, Director Joan B. Saleh, Driver Services Administrator Department of Motor Vehicles 95 M Street, SW Washington, DC 20024 202-737-4404 http://dmv.dc.gov/	Driver Licensing..202-737-4404 SR-22 & Financial Responsibility...............202-737-4404 Commercial Driver License.........................202-576-8278 Vehicle Information.....................................202-737-4404 State Department of Insurance ....202-727-8000 Metropolitan Police Department..................202-727-9099 Email Questions To:...................................dmv@dc.gov DC Municipal Regulations - Title 18 vehicle & Traffic: http://www.dcregs.org/

Driver's License Format, Issuance and Renewal

License Classes, Restrictions and Endorsements Appear After the Driving Record Content Section

License Format

A seven-digit number is issued. There is no numerical code sequence used to create license numbers, they are randomly generated. Previously, the SSN was used, but there are few left in circulation.

Document Appearance

The license is plastic and became digitized in July 2000.

Security Characteristics: Overlay with a repetitive pattern in gold "The American Experience in Washington DC."

Position of Photo: Lower left corner, also ghost image is in upper right corner.

Minor Age Driver Locator: Vertical card. The statement "Under 21 until XXX" is printed in red.

CDL Indicator: "CDL" printed on license.

Issuance

Location of Requirements for Proof of Identity:
http://dmv.dc.gov/service/proof-identity-name-and-date-birth

Age Requirements

The DMV introduced its GRAD (Gradual Rearing of Adult Drivers) program on September 1, 2000. GRAD involves three stages: a supervised learner's period; an intermediate licensing phase using a Provisional License that permits unsupervised driving only in less risky situations; and a full-privilege license with conditions that can apply at age 17. For age for a Learner's Permit or Provisional License is sixteen; under eighteen must have written permission of parent/guardian. The minimum age for a full license is eighteen. No one under age 21 may have a CDL.

Residency

License must be obtained within thirty days of establishing residency.

Renewal

Renewal is from the birthdate in the eighth year. The driver keeps the same number if the DL is the seven digit license number. If the DL was the SSN, the DL is converted to the seven-digit number. Military personnel holding a valid DC license may retain the license for 6 years while on active duty outside the District. However, application for extension must be made in each eight year period.

Renewal for regular drivers may be made by mail or online at http://dmv.dc.gov/node/344042. Online renewal available for every other renewal period providing the license is not suspended or revoked, or the driver has not yet reached age 70, or the license has not been expired over 90 days. One may make addresses changes online. CDL drivers cannot renew online.

If the DC driver's license has been expired over 90 days but not more than 180 days, the driver must pass a knowledge test. If the DC driver's license has been expired for more than 180 days months, driver must pass a knowledge test and a road test.

Elderly-Related Restrictions

Drivers 70 years or older must pass an eye test and have their physician complete the certification on the driver's license application.

Vehicle Insurance, Title and Registration Facts

Registration & Renewal

Plates are issued annually. Registrations can only be renewed by mail or online. As of July 13, 2009, in-person renewals were eliminated. One may renew online at http://dmv.dc.gov/node/156122 providing there is no address change, no administrative actions pending, or the license vehicle has not been expired for more than 90 days, or the emission inspection has not expired.

New Residents

DC law requires that all vehicles housed and operated in the District be registered in the District unless the owner displays a reciprocity sticker issued by the DMV. Vehicles must be registered at expiration of time allowed by reciprocity agreement (within 30 days). A DC title and current DC insurance are required before registration.

Inspections and Emissions Testing

Any motorized vehicle that is operated in the District of Columbia must be emission tested/inspected. This includes passenger cars, taxis, buses, snowmobiles, commercial, and government vehicles. Privately owned/not-for-hire vehicles must pass emissions inspections every two years. The only vehicles which are exempt from the emissions test process are new vehicles which have a Certificate of Origin (i.e., original title from the dealer), zero emission vehicles, passenger vehicles that are pre-1968, motorcycles and trail bikes.

The District's safety inspection program for most private cars was discontinued in October 2009. Commercial vehicles are inspected annually and vehicles for hire are inspected every six (6) months. During inspection, lights, brakes, suspension, emissions, and other safety components will be checked. Sticker is on front windshield.

Passenger Plate Facts

There are two plates and one validation sticker placed on front windshield. When a vehicle is sold the must be surrendered to the DC DMV by the seller or may be transferred to another vehicle.

Insurance and Financial Responsibility

The Compulsory/No-Fault Motor Vehicle Insurance Act requires that every person applying for registration or a reciprocity sticker in DC have valid DC vehicle insurance. The insurance must be maintained as long as the vehicle is registered. Lapses in coverage are subject to fines. Minimum coverage limits are: $25,000/50,000 for bodily injury and $10,000 for property liability. Uninsured Motorist property damage minimum is $5,000 subject to $200 deductible. Insurance for personal injury is optional. Liability insurance is mandatory. Evidence of insurance is required upon registration or if stopped for any reason by law enforcement officials. DC does use SR-22 forms.

Withdrawal Sanctions, and Alcohol and Drug Testing

Alcohol and Chemical Testing Limits

A level of .07 percent constitutes a driving-under-the-influence violation. A level of .08 percent or more constitutes an intoxication violation. Urine, blood, and breath tests are all legal. There is zero tolerance if driver is under 21. The District of Columbia may also suspend under Administrative Authority.

Suspensions and Revocations

Note: It is assumed DC is in compliance with the federally mandated disqualifications on CDLs. See the Appendix for a list of these disqualifications.

Point Accumulation of Points within Two Years

Ten or eleven points ....Suspension of ninety-days.
Twelve or More Points ....Revocation for minimum of six
                                  months.

Repeated Convictions

If convicted of certain criminal traffic violations in DC, including driving while intoxicated or driving under the influence, the license is revoked for 6 months for the first offense, 1 year for the second offense, and 2 years for the third or subsequent offense. The driving privileges are revoked until they have been officially reinstated and the reinstatement fee is paid.

Conviction of Any of the Following Twelve Point Convictions Will Result in Automatic Revocation—

- Committing a felony crime involving the use of a motor vehicle
- Committing any violation while operating a vehicle without the permission of the owner
- Conviction for an assault or homicide committed with an automobile
- Fleeing or attempting to elude a police officer
- Leaving the scene of a collision in which personal injury occurs (hit and run)
- Making a false affidavit or statement under any law relating to motor vehicles
- Operating a vehicle after your driver's license has been suspended or revoked
- Operating a vehicle under the influence of or impaired by intoxicating liquor and/or narcotics
- Operating a vehicle with any measurable amount of alcohol if the person is under 21 years old
- Reckless driving
- Using the driver's license of another person

In addition, the Director of the Department of Motor Vehicles has the authority to suspend or revoke a driver's license (at his discretion) for just cause, including non-payment for child support and outstanding traffic tickets (uncontested and unpaid after 30 days).

Reinstatement Requirements

Suspension $98.00 fee.
Revocation $98.00 fee and re-examination.

Record Access: Laws, Rules, and Forms

Note: This Section Applies to Both Driver and Vehicle Records as Indicated

Governing Statutes and Rules

To find the DC Municipal Regulations, from home page click on *About DMV*, then Click on *DC Code*. This takes you to Title (Chapter) 18 Vehicle and Traffic. The direct link is:
www.dcregs.org/Gateway/TitleHome.aspx?TitleNumber=18

Summary of Permissible Uses

At present, DPPA and the Federal Freedom of Information Act are cited in relation to information release. All other regulations are by administrative rule. Within its statutes, the District of Columbia does not have any of the exceptions that the federal statute does. However, the DC DMV protects the privacy of individuals by closely adhering to the DPPA. All requesters must bring the client's name, date of birth, and license or Social Security Number.

Driving Records: All requesters must provide the client's name, date of birth, and driver's license or Social Security Number. The following individuals may request driving records:

- Driver of record with identification listed above
- Driver of record's representative (for example, a spouse) with written authorization from the driver, a copy of the driver's proof of identification, bearing a discernable signature
- Law enforcement representatives with documentation showing a connection to an investigation
- Government entities as part of an established activity requiring records (for example, security clearances, investigations, and recruitment)
- Attorneys with written authorizations for releasing records from their clients
- Insurance company representatives with written authorizations from the driver as part of an established investigation

Vehicle Records: Records are classified as either "Authorized Records" or "General Records." Authorized Records are used for law enforcement and jurisdictional needs, and may be provided (upon request) to the person of record. General Records suppress the Social Security Number, date of birth, height, weight, and certain medical restrictions; these are the records issued to insurance companies, record-retrieval firms, lien-holders, etc. Also financial information is never released.

Request and Consent Forms

Driving Records: There is no required form. Written requests should state reason of the request and contain the requester's signature and the other proof of identification documents as required.

Vehicle Records: There is no required form. Written requests should state reason of the request and contain the requester's signature. Vehicle registration information is only released with the permission of the driver/owner.

Vendor and Third Party Access Policy

Approved vendors can access records for other vendors in order to service a permissible end-user. Third party requesters and their customers have the same responsibilities to adhere to DPPA guidelines.

Records Ordered For Non-permissible Uses

Except for the DL verification and vehicle status reports, records are not available without permissible use or consent, even records without personal information.

Access to Driver-Related Records

Driving Records

General Information and Fees

Department of Motor Vehicles, ATTN: Driving Records, PO Box 90120, Washington DC 20090, 202-737-4404.

The current fee is $7.00 for a three- or five-year record and $13.00 for a ten-year record. The last fee increase was in March of 2003 and there are no increases planned. The District of Columbia charges for *no record found* reports. Major credit cards (except American Express) are accepted. All requests must include the name, DOB and either the DL or SSN.

In-Person – Records may be requested over-the-counter at the Penn Branch Service Center at 3220 Penn Ave SE and the Southwest Service Center at 95 M Street SW. Records are processed immediately if staff available, unless lengthy lists submitted.

Mail – Requests mailed to the District of Columbia are processed within five to ten days of receipt. The above address is the only location to mail a request for a certified driving record. The driver's license number, name, and DOB are needed when ordering. The fee must accompany the request.

Electronic – The District offers an online inquiry system of the ten-year record to high volume, ongoing requesters. Each requester/vendor must be approved by the Department and sign a contract. There is an annual fee of $100. The system is interactive with immediate output available. The permit or Social Security Number is needed for inquiry in addition to the first name, last name, and date of birth (middle initial and sex is optional). The driver's address appears on the record. Call 202-737-4404 for further information.

DC also offers driver's the ability to order their own record online – see that section below.

License Verification

A Driver's License Verification and an ID Card Verification site is at:

https://public.dmv.washingtondc.gov/BusinessPages/DL/DriverLicense Verification.aspx

Bulk – All requests for the purchase of the driver license file are reviewed on an individual basis by the Department Chief. The same annual fee mentioned above applies to the access method as well.

By Person of Record – DC drivers may obtain their driving record in person or by mail as described above, and online. One may request a non-certified record is at http://dmv.dc.gov/service/online-services, click on *Driver Record Request*. Online choices include a 3-year record, 5-year record, 10-year record, or full history. Use of a credit card is required. The DL number or SSN, DOB and full name are required. There is no charge if the DL or SSN is not found. Certified copies can only be obtained in person. Proof of identity must be presented when in person.

Notification/Monitoring Program

At present, the District does not offer a monitoring system or notification program to employers or insurance companies to track incidents of drivers.

Accident Reports

Reporting – Accidents involving personal injury, death, or damage must be investigated by the Metropolitan Police. Since 12/12/03, individual reports need not be filed with the Department of Motor Vehicles.

Record Access – Copies of accident reports are available from the Metropolitan Police, 300 Indiana Ave NW, Rm 3075, Washington DC, 202-727-4357. An officer may write an Accident Report (PD-10) or an Incident/Offense Report (PD-251). This report is given a six-digit identifying number (often referred to as the CCN). The fee is $3.00 per record, use a SASE if requesting by mail. Personal checks are not accepted, but corporate checks are. Searches purely by name are not performed.

Access to Vehicle-Related Records

General Information

Southwest Service Center, 95 M Street SW, Washington 20024, 202-737-4404, fax is 202-673-9908. New records are available for inquiry in 24 hours. Paper records are held for thirteen years.

In-Person, Mail – The current fee for VIN, registration information, and vehicle lien records is $7.00. VISA, MasterCard, and Discover are accepted. DC requires use of their request form when ordering these searches. The typical turnaround time is 10 working days.

Electronic – DC provides a Vehicle Registration Verification at https://public.dmv.washingtondc.gov/BusinessPages/VR/VehicleRegistr ationVerification.aspx and an Out-of-State Title Status at https://public.dmv.washingtondc.gov/scripts/VS/OutOfStateTitleStatus.aspx.

Bulk – Bulk release of ownership or registration information is not available to the public, unless it is determined that the requested use "is for the public interest." This is determined by first submitting a written request to the Office of the Director, Department of Motor Vehicles. As a general rule, vehicle and ownership information is not released for commercial purposes. Once approved, the costs are based on a programming rate of $150.00 per hour and $ .05 per record. There is also a $1,200 annual fee. Monthly transmittals are available. Please contact the Office of the Director for further details.

Access to Vessel-Related Records

General Information, Access and Fees

All vessels, regardless of size and with or without mechanical propulsion, must registered by the Metropolitan Police Department, Harbor Patrol - Boat Registration, 550 Water St SW, Washington DC 20024, 202-727-4582, http://mpdc.dc.gov/node/207802. All watercraft are required to be registered: canoes, kayaks, sailboats, powerboats, Coast Guard documented, rentals, clubs and commercial. Liens are

shown on titles. Note Coast Guard documented vessels are not titled, but must be registered. Records are not open to the public, although some discretionary uses are approved if they are considered to be for the public good. Verifications are available on a case-by-case basis from the Public Information Section. Bulk purchase must be arranged via a FOIA.

Driving Record Content and Reciprocity

What's On or Not On the Driving Record

- All convictions with points are placed on the MVR.
- Accidents are listed if there is a conviction, but fault is not shown.
- The driver's address is provided as part of the record.
- The District of Columbia does not permit driver school attendance in lieu of conviction.

Data Retention

Convictions for CDL and non-CDL drivers are retained indefinitely. CDL driver records are purged based on the timetable per the federal regulations see the Appendix. The records of surrendered licenses are retained in the database indefinitely and can be accessed for seven years.

Court to Repository

Conviction information is transferred from the courts to the state via online. There are no laws mandating the time-period in which the information must be submitted or entered onto the record.

State Reciprocity for Non-CDL Drivers

- Will suspend license of driver for unpaid out-of-state convictions.
- Record of new incoming driver is shown on MVR.
- Out-of-state convictions are shown on MVR.
- Out-of-state accidents are shown on MVR.
- Convictions of out-of-state drivers are sent to home state.
- Record is forwarded to new state upon surrender of license if suspended or revoked.

License Classes, Types, Restrictions, and Endorsements

License Classes– Commercial

Class A	All vehicles except motorcycles.
Class B	Vehicles 26,001 pounds GVW or more, towing trailers under 10,000 pounds GVW, except motorcycles. Also mopeds.
Class C	Vehicles under 26,001 pounds, towing trailers under 10,000 pounds GVW, except motorcycle. Also mopeds.

License Classes– Non-Commercial

Note: The DC Department of Motor Vehicles introduced its graduated licensing program September 1, 2000. The program is designed for first-time drivers under the age of 21. The graduated licensing program involves three stages: a supervised learner's period; an intermediate licensing phase with a provisional license that permits unsupervised driving only in less risky situations; and a full-privilege license with conditions that apply age 18.

Class D	Vehicles under 26,001 pounds for non-commercial and personal use, except motorcycles. Also mopeds.
Class M	Motorcycles (endorsement).
Class N	Mopeds and motor-driven cycles.

License Types

CDL	Commercial Driver's License
LNR	Learner's Permit
RGL	Regular Driver's License
PDL	Provisional Driver License

Restrictions

0.	None	I.	Daylight driving only
1.	Must wear glasses or contact lenses	J.	Two outside mirrors properly placed
2.	May not operate a vehicle with air brakes	K.	Telescopic lens
3.	May not operate vehicles for compensation prior to age eighteen	L.	Steering requiring much less than 1 lb of pressure to operate
4.	Must be accompanied by driver who is authorized to operate class of vehicle being driven	M.	No driving during rush hours
		N.	Spinner knob for steering wheel
5.	May not operate Class A, B, or C vehicles in interstate commerce	O.	Turn signal switch lever-right hand extension
		P.	Other - see official documents
8.	May not operate tractor and semi-trailers	Q.	Automatic transmission left foot accelerator
A.	Work restriction (see official documents	R.	Automatic transmission all hand controls
B.	Automatic transmission	S.	Must use portable oxygen while driving
C.	Left outside mirror properly placed	T.	Automatic transmission poser brakes
D.	Hand controls (brake and throttle)	U.	IID program (interlock device)
E.	Diabetes	V.	Exempt from the use of seat belts
F.	Elevation of seat appropriately & use floor extension pedals	W.	Must wear hearing aid while driving
G.	Left foot accelerator	X.	Hand control for brakes only
H.	Hand dimmer switch with horn button attached		

Endorsements

0.	None	P.	Transport Passengers
H.	Hazardous Materials	S.	School Bus
I.	Professional Instructor	T.	Double-/Triple-Trailers
M.	Motorcycles	X.	N and H Endorsements
N.	Tankers		

Conviction Code Table with Statutes and ACD

About the Statutes

All statute referrals in the Conviction Table are per the DC Municipal Regulations - Title 18 Vehicle and Traffic. This document is found at http://www.dcregs.org/. To view the statutes associated with moving violations, enter "18-22" in the "By Chapter Number" box.

18-2200	Speed restrictions
18-2201	Driving on the right side of the roadway: proper use of the roadway
18-2202	Overtaking and passing
18-2203	Turning at intersections
18-2204	Turning requirements and restrictions
18-2205	Proper signals for turning and stopping
18-2206	Starting, stopping, and backing
18-2207	Right-of-way: between intersections
18-2208	Right-of-way: intersections
18-2209	Right-of-way: school buses
18-2210	Emergency vehicles and apparatus
18-2211	Streetcars, railroad trains, and safety zones
18-2212	Coasting
18-2213	Obstruction of driver's view or driving mechanism: improper riding
18-2214	Entering and leaving a vehicle: vehicle doors
18-2215	Riding on motorcycles
18-2216	Railroad crossings
18-2217	Closed streets, play streets, bus streets, bus restricted streets
18-2218	Funeral processions, parades, and other authorized processions
18-2219	Severe weather traffic controls: snow emergency route
18-2220	Restricted lanes
18-2221	Miscellaneous moving violations
18-2222	[Reserved]
18-2223	[Reserved]
18-2224	Alcoholic beverages in motor vehicles

About The Conviction Table

- The table below is presented in order of the four-digit code. If the code starts with the letter "P" it generally means the violation is associated with a parking ticket. All violations that have an entry in the Statute column indicate a Moving Violation that is enforced by the Metropolitan Police Department, and has a civil fine.
- The Hack column refers to a specific violation involving a taxicab.

Code	ACD	Description	Statute	Hack
-		Taxi, fail to notify about a change of information	822.8	Y
P122		Taxi, parked more than 5 feet from curb	822.8	Y
P123		Taxi, parked off stand	821.2	Y
P125		Taxi, soliciting for fares	819.1, 819.2	Y
P205		Taxi, signs, fail to exhibit license to	2829(e)(1)	Y
P206		Taxi, signs, fail to have proper colors, numbers, insignia, and phone number	503.8, 503.1-5, 504	
P208		Taxi, fake or fraudulent identification	822	Y
P210		Taxi, parked less than 100 feet off stand	821.2	Y
P212		Taxi, fail to have DCTC license	2829(e)(1)	Y
P330		Permitting driver to drive public vehicle, taxi, etc.	822.3	Y
R587		Loaning registration to another		
T001	A20	Driving under influence of alcohol/drug		
T002	M84	Reckless driving		
T003	B25	Operating after revocation		
T004	B26	Operating after suspension		
T005	B51	No DC permit		
T006	B07	Leaving scene of accident, personal injury		
T007	B08	Leaving scene of accident, property damage		
T008		Colliding with fixed object; no damage or injury	2200.4	
T009	D02	Obtaining permit by misrepresentation		
T010	D02	Aid to obtain permit by misrepresentation		
T012	M25	Fail to stop when emerging from alley	2207.1	
T013	M82	Failing to give full time and attention to operation of vehicle	2213.4	
T014		Failing to secure loads	2503.4	
T016	D02	False statements to secure permit		

Code	ACD	Description	Statute	Hack
T017	N82	Backing to turn		
T018	N82	Backing without caution	2206.3	
T019	M02	Driving through barricade	2217.3	
T024		Bad foot brakes	720.2	
T025		Bad hand (parking) brake	720.4	
T026	E31	Permitting bad brakes		
T027		Fail to set hand brakes		
T028		Bridge load limit violation	2510.2	
T034		Fail to turn wheels to curb		
T035	N83	Pull from curb and interfere with moving traffic	2206.1	
T036		Fail to back into parking space	2212.2	
T038	M33	Entering block with fire apparatus	2210.4	
T039	N04	Fail to pull to curb for fire apparatus or emergency vehicle	2210.1	
T040	M33	Following within 500 feet of fire apparatus	2210.4	
T042	M56	Driving over fire hose	2210.5	
T043	M34	Following vehicle too closely	2201.9	
T045	F03	No rear view mirror/motorcycles	731.6	
T046		Defective or no speedometer on motorized bicycles	735.1	
T047		Operating unregistered motorized bicycle	411.1	
T048	F66	Operating unsafe vehicle	700.2	
T049		Operating motorized bicycle without helmet, windshield or protective glasses	2215.3, 2215.4, 2215.5	
T050		Operate unregistered motor vehicle		
T051	M58	Driving on or over sidewalk	2221.3	
T052	F66	Permitting operation of unsafe vehicle	700.2	
T057	N25	Fail to slow down for intersection	2200	
T058	M41	Fail to keep in proper lane	2201.8	
T059	M42	Changing lane(s) without caution	2201.6(a)	
T064		Hitching on vehicle	1201.16	
T065	E55	No lights running when required	703.1	
T066		Bicycle, harass or interfere to signal	1201.14, 1201.15	
T067		Bicycle, impeding or obstructing traffic	1201.3, 1201.7	
T068		Bicycle, hazardous driving	1201	
T069		Bicycle, riding abreast	1201.7	
T070		Bicycle, excessive speed	1201	
T071		Bicycle, fail to yield right-of-way on roadway	1201.12	
T072		Bicycle, disobey traffic-control device	1201.14, 1201.15	
T080		Failure to display permit upon demand	40-301(c)	
T082	N63	Driving wrong way on one-way street	2201.2, 2201.4, 2201.7	
T083		Opening door on traffic side	2214.4	
T088	M73	Passing on right where prohibited	2202.5	
T095		Unauthorized use of a license by another	1100.7	
T096		Permitting unlicensed driver to operate a vehicle	1100.12	
T097		Loaning or permitting use of permit		
T098		Using another person's permit		
T100		Fail to surrender permit after suspension or revocation		
T101	D29	Driving in violation of restriction on permit	1100.9	
T105	E01	Driving on rim		
T106	M40	Fail to keep to right	2201.1	
T107	N01	Fail to yield right-of-way		
T108	M12	Driving through safety zone	2211.6	
T109	F66	Vehicle operation in unsafe mechanical condition	600.2	
T110	M12	Occupying Safety Zone	2101.1	
T112	M17	Disobeying official sign or signal device	2000.4	
T113	M16	Fail to come to complete stop before turning right; passing red light	2103.7	
T114	M18	Passing flashing red light	2104.2	
T115	N40	Failing to give hand or mechanic signal	2204.3, 2205	
T116	N54	Violation of "No Turn on Red" sign; Fail to come to complete stop before turning right on red	4013, 2103.7	
T117	M08	Disobeying officers signal		
T118	S51	Up to 10 mph in excess of speed limit	2200.1	
T119	S93	11 to 15 mph in excess of speed limit	2200.1	
T120	S16	16 to 20 mph in excess of speed limit	2200.1	
T121	S21	21 to 25 mph in excess of speed limit	2200.1	
T122	S26	25 to 30 mph in excess of speed limit	2201.1	

Code	ACD	Description	Statute	Hack
T123	S31	Speed in excess of 30 mph over limit		
T124	S96	Driving too slowly	2200.1	
T125	S93	Unreasonable speed	2200.3	
T126		Making a right turn around bus stopped at bus stop located at an intersection	50-2201.28a	
T127	N70	Driving on wrong side of street	2201.1	
T128	M15	Passing stop sign	2208.3	
T129		Drive truck through restricted street; Violation of truck route	2505.6	
T130		Drive Bus through restricted street	2217.8	
T133		Improper use of dealer tags	503.1	
T134	E55	Failure to use cruising/running lights at night	703.1, 605	Y
T135	E34	Broken cruising light	605.9	Y
T136		Displaying altered insurance sticker	902	Y
T137		Fail to properly attach insurance sticker	902.1	Y
T138		Fail to properly complete/maintain manifest	823	Y
T139		Fail to provide manifest to government agency	823	Y
T140		Altering manifest	823.5	Y
T141		No smoking in taxi per passenger's request	807	Y
T142	M08	Fail to obey orders of hack/enforcement personnel	822.9	Y
T143	B51	Unlicensed operator (Class - S)		
T144		Taxi, fail to post notification of seatbelt requirement	607	Y
T150		Covered Tag	422.8	
T151		Open container	2224.4	
T155	D16	Altering permit		
T165		Permitting unlicensed hacker/taxi driver to operate	822.3	Y
T166		Fail to pay bus fare or valid token		
T167		Weight limit violation; 5,000 pounds over weight limit	2505	
T168		Fail to pay bus fare or valid token		
T169		Permit unlicensed operator to drive public vehicle		
T170		Unlicensed public vehicle by DC resident	1000.2	
T171		Operating taxi/limo w/o ID card; non-resident or DC resident	822.2, 1209, 1218	Y
T178	F34	Obstructing traffic		
T181	N50	Improper turn at intersection	2203	
T183	N53	Left turn at no left turn	2204.6	
T184	N56	U-turn at no U-turn	2204.6	
T185	N51	Turn from wrong lane	2203.11, 2203.4	
T189	D70	Rear (front or side) vision obstructed	2213.1	
T190	D70	Objects hanging so as to obstruct vision	2213.7	
T192		Defective windshield	731.5	
T193	E70	Obstructed windshield	731.5	
T194	E01	Operating vehicle without windshield	731.3	
T196	B61	Failure to report accident		
T200	M18	Passing yellow light	2103.5	
T201	N04	Fail to yield or pull to curb for an emergency vehicle	2210.1	
T202	N54	Right turn at no right turn	2204.6	
T203	M18	Signal device, flashing yellow light		
T204	M16	Disobeying green arrow signal	2103.4, 2103.8	
T205	F34	Obstructing crosswalk or intersection		
T206	F34	Failing to clear intersection	2201.11	
T207		Television visible to operator	735.2	
T208	B91	Improper Class or Endorsement on driver license		
T210	N06 (M19)	Fail to yield to another vehicle	2207, 2208	
T211		Board/alighting from vehicle in motion		
T212	N80	Coasting with gears unmeshed or in neutral	2212.1	
T213		Dealer's certificate (fictitious content)		
T214	N25	Fail to yield emerging from driveway	2207.1	
T215		Highway permit violation		
T216	E55	Unauthorized lights	703	
T217	M51	Driving through median strip	2201.8	
T218	F03	Fail to wear helmet, goggles, safety glasses or windshield while driving MC	2215.3 and 2215.4	
T219	M70	Improper passing without caution	2202.2	
T220	M74	Passing on hill		
T222		Obtain registration by misrepresentation		

Code	ACD	Description	Statute	Hack
T223		Altered registration card		
T224	M43	Driving off roadway	2201.8	
T225	N09	Passing a stopped school bus with lights flashing	2209	
T227		Improper display of tags	422.4	
T229		Unapproved advertising on taxi	1217.1	Y
T230		Unkempt/improperly dressed operator (taxi)	822.1	Y
T232		Fail to have proper colors, numbers or insignia on taxi	503, 504	Y
T233		Fail to remove expired insurance sticker	902.9	Y
T234		Overloading passengers in taxi	822.14	
T235		Fail give receipt for fare to passenger on request	803	Y
T241		Taxi, defective speedometer	601.7	Y
T242		On taxicab stand/not for hire	821.1	Y
T243		Operating uninsured taxi		
T244		No zone map displayed	801.14	Y
T245		Altered certificate of title		
T246		Obtain title by misrepresentation		
T247		Using or permitting use of unregistered vehicle		
T248	E23	Radar device		
T278	S15	Speed violation 15 MPH in excess of limit - CMV		
T301	A20	Driving under influence, 1st offense		
T302	A20	Driving under influence, 2nd offense		
T303	A20	Driving under influence, 3rd offense		
T304	A20	Driving while intoxicated, 1st offense		
T305	A20	Driving while intoxicated, 2nd offense		
T306	A20	Driving while intoxicated, 3rd offense		
T310	A50	Motor vehicle – felony		
T311	A90	Administrative Per Se for .10 BAC		
T312	A94	Administrative Per Se for .04 BAC		
T313	A98	Administrative Per Se for .08 BAC		
T314	B01	Hit and Run – failure to stop and render aid after an accident		
T315	B02	Hit and Run – failure to stop and render aid after an accident – fatal accident		
T316	B03	Hit and Run – failure to stop and render aid after an accident – personal injury		
T317	B04	Hit and Run – failure to stop and render aid after an accident – property damage		
T318	B05	Leaving accident scene before police arrived		
T319	B06	Leaving accident scene before police arrived – fatal accident		
T320	B19	Driving while out of service – 16 or more passengers		
T321	B20	Driving while license withdrawn		
T322	B21	Driving while license barred		
T323	B22	Driving while license canceled		
T324	B23	Driving while license denied		
T325	B24	Driving while license disqualified		
T326	B27	General, driving while and out of service order is in effect		
T327	B56	Driving a CMV without obtaining a CMV permit		
T328		Out of State conviction		
T329	U08	Vehicular manslaughter		
T330	U09	Negligent homicide while operating a commercial motor vehicle		
T331	U10	Causing a fatality through negligent operation of commercial motor vehicle		
T332	U31	Violation resulting in fatal accident		
T333		Failure to provide proof of insurance	31-2413 (a) (7)	
T335	S94	Failure to control speed to avoid colliding	2200.4	
T336		Operating vehicle of greater width than permitted	2500, 2501, 2511	
T339		Operating vehicle of greater height than permitted	2501, 2511	
T340		Truck, violation of permit conditions	2508.6	
T340		Truck, violation of tunnel restrictions	2509	
T342		Unauthorized traffic control device	2102	
T343		Operating with an unsafe bumper	733.5, 733.6	
T396		Violation not detailed elsewhere		
T401	A25	Operating while impaired, 1st offense		
T402	A25	Operating while impaired, 2d offense		
T403	A25	Operating while impaired, 3rd offense		
T501	N05	Driving through funeral processions	2218.2	
T502	M40	Fail to keep right of funeral procession	2218.3	
T509	M43	Driving over lawn in federal park	4.10(a)	

Code	ACD	Description	Statute	Hack
T511	E55	Illegal headlight device	718	
T512		Dealing in vehicles w/o registration		
T513		Giving driving instruction w/o license		
T514	B51	Operating school bus without permit		
T515		Smoke screens		
T516		Tampering with locked or secured bike		
T517		Unauthorized use of emergency parking permit		
T518	F66	Permitting operation of unsafe vehicle		
T519	F66	Operating unsafe vehicle		
T523	M70	Passing at intersection	2202.3(b)	
T524	M74	Passing on curve	2202.3(a)	
T525	M77	Passing when view obstructed	2202.7	
T526	S95	Increasing speed to prevent passing	2202.4	
T527		Pedestrian, crossing against red light	2301.4	
T528		Pedestrian, walking suddenly into vehicle path	2303.2	
T529		Pedestrian, fail to yield right-of-way to emergency vehicle	2305.5	
T530		No motorcycle permit		
T531		Two on a seat of a motorcycle		
T533	N40	Fail to give signal	1201.1	
T535	M17	Disregarding slow sign	1201.15	
T539	D29	Violating restriction of learner's permit	102.9, 102.11, 1100.9	
T542		Improper use of dealer tags		
T547		Tamper with auto-move or cause to be moved		
T549	D02	False statement on application		
T550	D02	Obtain ID card by misrepresentation		
T555		Violation of towing regulations	2504	
T556		Violation of towing regulations, no safety chain		
T558	E01	No safety chain while towing		
T559	M17	Violation of no turn sign	2204, 4012-4015, 4018	
T560		Operating unapproved auto		
T561		Permitting operation of unapproved auto		
T562	F05	Improper riding on motorcycle	2215	
T563	F05	Permitting passenger to ride on vehicle; Unlawful riding on vehicle	2213.6	
T564		Operating with open doors	2214.3	
T567	N04	Passing or approaching within prohibited distance of fire apparatus	2210.4	
T568		False statement to obtain registration		
T569	N08	Fail to yield right-of-way to pedestrian		
T571	N50	Improper turn	2203, 2204	
T572	B25	Operating after revocation (non-resident)		
T573	B26	Operating after suspension (non-resident)		
T574	D36	Fail to have auto insurance		
T575		Pedestrian walking against "Don't Walk" or "Wait" signal	2302.3	
T576		Pedestrian crossing between intersection	2304.1	
T577		Pedestrian obstructing traffic in roadway	2305	
T579		Pedestrian crossing diagonally at intersection (no signal)	2303.3	
T580		Pedestrian walking in roadway (sidewalk provided)	2305.2	
T581		Pedestrian walking on wrong side of roadway (no sidewalk)	2305.3	
T582		Soliciting rides while standing in roadway	2305.4	
T583		Parading without permit	2218.1	
T585	U06	Collide with pedestrian	2300.2	
T586		Pedestrian fail to provide ID		
T590		Distracted driving-cell phone	50-1731.01	
T591		Cellular phone or other electronic device, use of without hands-free accessories while driving	50-1731.01	
T592		School bus; using cellular phone or other electronic device while driving	50-1731.01	
T600	M08	Fail to obey officer's orders		
T601		Fail to abide by parade regulation	2218.1	
T602		Displaying fictitious sticker		
T603		Removing inspection sticker		
T604		Fail to display ID card for passenger(s) view	814.5	
T605		Unlicensed hack/taxi vehicle, non-DC resident	1000.2	
T607	No1	Fail to yield right-of-way (can be on sidewalk)	1201.10 & 1201.11	
T609		Riding bicycle on sidewalk	1201	
T610		Excessive number or riders	1201.5	

Code	ACD	Description	Statute	Hack
T611		Fail to register bicycle	1202.1	
T612		Operating unregistered bicycle	1202.1	
T613		Furnishing false information; bike registration	1202.1	
T614		Improper equipment on bicycle	1204	
T615		Mounting rack violation-vehicle	1206	
T616		Improper securing of bicycle	1209	
T617		Not riding on seat of bicycle	1201.4	
T618		Carry object prevent keeping hands on bike	1201.6	
T619		Sounding of warning device (bicycle)	1204.14	
T620		Removing registration plate or number from bicycle	1202.9	
T621		Renting an unregistered bicycle	1207.7	
T622		Unauthorized device upon highway (bicycle)		
T623		Violation not enumerated (bicycle)	1210	
T624		Spilling load from commercial vehicle	2503.2	
T625		Operating commercial vehicle in national park	7.96 (f) (1)	
T626		Excessive idling; more than three (3) mins.	2418.3	
T627		Operating with torn fender or no fender	733.5, 733.4	
T629	E01	Inaudible or no horn	730.1	
T630	E70	Horn, Unnecessary	730.2	
T631		Fail to lock ignition		
T632		Operating on expired sticker or red sticker	602.4, 604.3	
T633		Fail to report for inspection	601.1	
T634		Fail to replace lost/mutilated inspection sticker	608/1	
T635		Operating vehicle greater that length that permitted by law	2502	
T636	E55	Improper lights	703-711	
T637	E05	No rear lights	705.1	
T638	E05	No stop lights	706.1	
T639	E05	One light running	704.1	
T640	E54	Operating with high beams	715.5	
T641		Failure to keep open load tightly covered	2503.2, 2503.4	
T642		Failure to secure shipping crates		
T643		Load extending over fenders	2503.1	
T644		Load more than 8 ft wide moving	2501.1	
T645		No red flag at end of load(s)		
T646		No rear view-mirror motorized bicycles	731.6	
T647	E01	No rear view-mirror	731.6	
T649		Motor running unattended		
T651		Defective muffler		
T652	E01	No muffler on vehicle		
T653		Unnecessary or disturbing noise	2221.1	
T654	N63	Violation of one-way street	2201.4	
T655		Fail to change address on permit	109.3, 109.4	
T656		Defaced permit	1100.2	
T657		Fail to change address on registration	414.1	
T658		Fail to exhibit registration	421.1	
T659		Unauthorized use of or possession of siren	712.4, 730.4	
T660		Excessive smoke	750.3	
T661	E57	No chains or snow tires		
T662		Defective speedometer	735.1	
T663	E01	Fail to have speedometer on vehicle	735.1	
T664		Steam shovel, etc., restricted hours		
T666	E34	Inadequate illumination of tags	705.4	
T667		Dead tags		
T668		No DC tags	429.1	
T669		Fail to turn in DC tags when required	415, 2706	
T670		Fail to secure DC tags	429.1	
T671		Permitting use of dead tags	1101.1	
T672		Fail to have or display current tags	422.1, 422.3	
T673		Loaning tags		
T674		Altering tags		
T675		Fail to have cruising light	605.1	Y
T676		Dirty taxi inside or outside	822.18	Y
T677		Fail to notify office of change in information	822.8	Y

Code	ACD	Description	Statute	Hack
T678		Fail to remove ID card from taxi	814.4	Y
T679		Loitering (taxi)	819.3	Y
T680		No approved manifest form in possession	823	Y
T681		Failure to report property left in taxi	822.19	Y
T682		Taxi, soliciting fares		Y
T683		Fail to display zone rate sticker	801.2	Y
T684		Fail to pull to curb to transfer passenger	822.16, 822.17	Y
T685		Fail to have insurance; fail to have insurance sticker	814.4, 902.1	Y
T686		Taxi, refuse to haul passenger	819.04	Y
T687		Unlicensed hack - DC resident		
T688		Failure to display off-duty sign	820	Y
T689		Improper use of off-duty sign; improper use while on call	820	Y
T690		Improper use of on-call sign; improper use while on call	820	Y
T691		Improper use of out-of-service sign	820	Y
T692		Unauthorized sign on taxi	1217.1	Y
T693		Failure to charge proper fare	801.6	Y
T694		Failure to display PSC license		
T695		Taxi, no zone rate sticker	801.2	
T696		Fail to exhibit taxi license to police	814	Y
T697		Fail to have proper colors, phone and vehicle number, insignia	503, 504	Y
T698		Failure to report accident to insurance carrier in specified time906.3		Y
T699		Impersonation of PSC license		
T700		Loading or unloading passenger in crosswalk	822.16	Y
T701		Refusing to pay fare	601, 802	Y
T702	E37	Driving on unsafe tire, or no rubber, or on rim without tire	732, 732.3	
T703		DC fail to transfer title	402	
T705	F02	Violation of child-restraint act	50-1703 & 1706	
T710		Violation of truck restriction on route	2505.6	
T711	D36	Operating uninsured vehicle - vehicle owner permitting or operating without proper insurance	31-2413 (a) (3)	
T712	B51	Driving with expired permit over 90 days		
T713	F04	Fail to wear or properly wear seat belt, driver	50-1802, 1806	
T714	E01	Fail to have hub cap / wheel cover	601.16	Y
T715	F04	Fail to wear or properly wear seat belt, passenger	50-1802, 1806	
T716		Obtained tags by misrepresentation		
T720	U07	Homicide involving a vehicle		
T721	U03	Felony involving a vehicle		
T722	S93	Speed in excess of limit		
T723	M70	Improper passing		
T724	D29	Fail to wear glasses		
T725		Fail to use caution at loading platform		
T726		Driving left of loading platform		
T727	E34	Defective lights		
T728		Defective mirror		
T729	F66	Unsafe mechanical condition		
T730		Unnecessary noise (tires)		
T731		Cruising taxi		
T732	E70	Improper use of sign		
T733		Leaving the scene, no personal injury		
T735		Altered title		
T736		Unapproved auto parked		
T737	E70	Unapproved sticker or sign		
T738		Permitting improper use of dealer tags		
T740	B61	Fail to file accident report		
T741		Inaccurate or incomplete accident report		
T742		Fail to display current inspection sticker	602.4	
T743		Operating while condemned sticker	606.3	
T744		Illegible tag	422.5	
T745		No front tag	422.1, 422.3	
T746		No rear tag	422.1, 422.3	
T747		Obstructed tag	422.6	
T748		Fail to affix validation sticker(s)	422.7	
T749	M51	Drive over raised strip, island or zone with curb	2201.8	
T750	M49	HOV violation		

Code	ACD	Description	Statute	Hack
T755		Fail to obey hack inspector		
T756		No passenger rights information displayed in taxi	701.2	Y
T757		Operate vehicle without effective snow tires or chains	2219.1	
T758		Tinted windows violation	50-2207.02(c)	
T759	N08	Fail to yield to a pedestrian (not in crosswalk)	2201.28, 2103.4, 2103.7, 2207.2, 2208.4, 2208.6, 2211.2, 2300.2	
T760	B51	No permit/ expired DC permit over	1401.01(d-1)	
T761		Improperly operating taxi air conditioning	601	Y
T762		Improperly operating taxi heating system	601	Y
T763		Other violation		
T764		Driving with expired permit, under 90 days		
T765		Over 21 MPH in excess of speed limit		
T766		Using another person's permit		
T767	U04	Any misdemeanor involving use of vehicle		
T768		Fail to pull to curb or yield to emergency vehicle		
T769		Violating while operating without owner's permission		
T770	D29	Driving in violation of permit restriction		
T771	S51	Speed up to 10 MPH in excess of speed limit		
T772	S93	Speed 11 to 15 in excess of speed limit		
T773	S21	Speed 21 to 25 MPH in excess of speed limit		
T774	S26	Speed 26 to 30 MPH in excess of speed limit		
T775	S93	Unreasonable speed		
T776	M75	Fail to stop for school vehicle w/flashing lights		
T777	N08	Fail to yield right of way to pedestrian		
T778	D29	Driving with improper class of license		
T779	D29	Oper veh learners permit / no permit		
T780	E55	Turning off lights to avoid identification		
T781	D16	Using another person`s permit		
T782	D51	Driving with expired permit under 90 days		
T783	U01	Fleeing or attempt to elude police officer		
T784		False statement or affidavit under oath		
T785	A60	Alcohol in blood, breath, urine -under 21		
T786	N04	Fail to pull to curb or yield emer vehicle		
T793	D02	Misrepresentation of identity or other facts on application for driver license		
T794	D45	Failure to appear for trial or court appearance		
T795	D53	Failure to make required payment of fine and costs		
T796	D56	Failure to answer a citation, pay fines, penalties and/or cost related to the original		
T901	A04	Driving under the influence of alcohol with BAC at or over .04		
T902	A08	Driving under the influence of alcohol with BAC at or over .08		
T903	A10	Driving under the influence of alcohol with BAC at or over .10		
T904	A11	Driving under the influence of alcohol with BAC at or over XX		
T905	A12	Refused to submit to test for alcohol – Implied Consent Law		
T906	A21	Driving under the influence of alcohol		
T907	A22	Driving under the influence of drugs		
T908	A23	Driving under the influence of alcohol and drugs		
T910	U05	Using motor vehicle to aid and abet a felon		
T911	A61	Underage Administrative per Se – driving and driving at .02 or higher BAC		
T913	F04	Fail to use seat belt – before law		
T916	M14	Right turn on red violation - before law		
T950	M49	HOV violation - before law		
T980	M09	Failure to obey RR highway grade crossing Highway Grade Crossing (HGC) restrictions		
T981	M10	Failure to obey RR HGC gates, signs or signals		
T982	M20	Failure to slow down at RR HGC		
T983	M21	Failure to stop at RR HGC		
T984	M22	Failure to stop as required before driving into RR HGC		
T985	M23	Failure to have sufficient space to drive completely through RR HGC		
T986	M24	Failure to negotiate RR HGC because of insufficient space under carriage clearance		
T987	W60	Second RR HGC violation during a three year period		
T988	W61	Accumulation of three or more RR HGC violations during a three year period		
T999		Unknown violation		
W00		Withdrawal		
W01		Habitual offender		

About the Point System

If 10 or 11 points are accumulated, the license will be suspended for up to 90 days. If 12 or more points, license will be revoked until DC DMV reinstates license, generally 6 months after revocation. A driver is eligible for one safe driving point for any calendar year in which a moving violation point was not assessed. A safe driving point may be used to offset a moving violation point and expires in 5 years.

Any moving violation that does not contribute to an accident and is not listed here	2-3 Points
Committing a misdemeanor crime involving the use of a motor vehicle	6 Points
Fail to comply with seatbelt law	3 Points
Failing to give right-of-way to a pedestrian	5 Points
Failing to report an accident	5 Points
Failing to stop for a school vehicle with alternately flashing lights	4 Points
Failing to yield to an emergency vehicle	6 Points
Following another vehicle too closely	2 Points
Leaving the scene of a collision in which no personal injury occurs	8 Points
Operating a motor vehicle in violation of a restriction on your license	4 Points
Operating a vehicle with a learner's permit unaccompanied by a licensed driver	5 Points
Operating a vehicle with an improper class of license	2 Points
Operating a vehicle with a license expired less than 90 days	2 Points
Speeding 11-15 miles per hour above posted speed limit	3 Points
Speeding 16-20 miles per hour above posted speed limit	4 Points
Speeding 21 miles per hour or more above posted speed limit	5 Points
Turning off headlights of a vehicle to avoid identification by a police officer	8 Points
Violations that contribute to an accident	3 Points

The license will be taken if convicted of the following:

Committing any violation while operating a vehicle without the permission of the owner	12 Points
Committing a felony crime involving the use of a motor vehicle	12 Points
Conviction for an assault or homicide committed with an automobile	12 Points
Fleeing or attempting to elude a police officer	12 Points
Leaving the scene of a collision in which personal injury occurs (hit and run)	12 Points
Making a false affidavit or statement under any law relating to motor vehicles	12 Points
Operating a vehicle after your driver's license has been suspended or revoked	12 Points
Operating a vehicle under the influence of or impaired by intoxicating liquor and/or narcotics	12 Points
Operating a vehicle with any measurable amount of alcohol if the person is under 21 years old	12 Points
Reckless driving	12 Points
Using the driver's license of another person	12 Points

Note: If 10 or 11 points are accumulated, the license will be suspended for up to 90 days. If 12 or more points, license will be revoked until DC DMV reinstates license, generally 6 months after revocation. A driver is eligible for one safe driving point for any calendar year in which a moving violation point was not assessed. A safe driving point may be used to offset a moving violation point and expires in 5 years.

Florida

Administration	Important Telephone and Web Contacts
Julie L. Jones, Executive Director Dept of Highway Safety and Motor Vehicles Clayton Boyd Walden, Director Division of Motorist Services B-443 Neil Kirkman Building Tallahassee 32399, 850-617-3100 www.flhsmv.gov	Driver/Vehicle/Vessel Records ....850-617-2000 SR-22 and Financial Responsibility ....850-617-2000 State Department of Insurance ....850-413-3100 Motor Carrier Services ....850-617-2909 Highway Patrol..850-617-2301 For other numbers see: www.flhsmv.gov/html/contact.html Statutes at: www.leg.state.fl.us

Driver's License Format, Issuance and Renewal

License Classes, Restrictions and Endorsements Appear After the Driving Record Content Section

License Format

One letter followed by twelve numbers. The letter corresponds to the first letter of the last name, and the numbers reflect a code representing the name, date of birth, and sex. The HSMV has indicated that this code is classified, and not released to the public.

Document Appearance

The current license and ID cards, issued since June 16, 2004, are laminated with a digital photo. Previously issued Florida driver licenses and identification cards remain valid until their expiration dates.

Current Format

Security Characteristics: The technology includes a 2-D barcode, magnetic stripe, digitized portrait image, signature, and various security features such as ghost image, UV image and text, and overlapping data. Florida's image is depicted with a beach scene and the state seal.

Position of Photo: Left side.

Minor Age Driver Locator: "UNDER 21 until xx-xx-xx" in red bar on left side of photo. License and ID cards are vertical with text at the top and a vertical photo. The cardholder's 21st birthday is indicated in the photo image area.

CDL Indicator: Blue bar at top of license - CDL designation under color bar at top.

Older Format (pre-2004)

Security Characteristics: The license is a digitized photo card. The state map appears under the photo on the right side.

Position of Photo: Left side.

Minor Age Driver Locator: "UNDER 21 until xx-xx-xx" across the face of license.

CDL Indicator: CDL class designation on left side of photo.

Issuance

Location of Requirements for Proof of Identity:
www.gathergoget.com/

Age Requirements

The minimum age is 16 and 15 for a Learner's License. To earn a regular Class E license, drivers under the age of 18 must have parent/guardian signature, hold Learner's Permit for 12 months, complete a Traffic Law & Substance Education Course or high school driver's education, not incur any moving traffic convictions, and be certified by a parent or guardian to have at least 50 hours of behind-the-wheel training, 10 of which must be at night. A Learner's License (Class E-Learner) is issued at age 15 with these requirements: may operate

vehicle only between 6 AM and 7 PM (after 3 months may drive until 10 PM); licensed driver 21 or older must accompany and sit in closest seat to the right of the driver; Class E-Learner does not permit operation of a motorcycle if under the age of 16. 16 year-olds cannot drive from 11 PM to 6 AM unless accompanied by a licensed driver 21 or older, or driving to or from work; 17 year olds cannot drive from 1 AM to 5 AM unless accompanied by licensed driver 21 or older, or driving to or from work.

Effective July 1, 2008, anyone under 16 who operates an off-highway vehicle on public land must complete an approved safety course and have the certificate in their possession while riding. Also, all motorcyclists must pass a basic rider course before receiving a motorcycle endorsement.

Residency

Drivers must surrender an out-of-state license and secure a Florida license within thirty days of establishing residency, enrolling children in school, registering to vote, filing for homestead exemption, or obtaining employment (including part-time employment)

Renewal

A clear license can be renewed for 8 years for persons 79 years of age and younger, and for 6 years for persons 80 years of age and older, except non-immigrants. The driver keeps the same number when renewing. Military personnel and their dependents serving outside the state are granted an automatic extension without renewal if their driver license status is valid. The extension is valid for 90 days after their return to Florida or separation from the military.

Renewal and address changes can be made online at www.GoRenew.com by all except immigrants. Individuals may renew a DL one time by a convenience method (Internet or mail). However, the next renewal must be made in a driver license office. Commercial driver licenses and licenses expired over one year cannot be renewed online or by mail.

Elderly-Related Restrictions

Since October 1, 2008, drivers who are 79 years of age and under are issued eight-year licenses while drivers 80 years of age and older continue to receive six-year licenses. Since January 1, 2004, all drivers 80 years of age or older must pass a vision test before renewing their driver license. The test may be administered at the driver license office or completed by a licensed health care practitioner, such as a medical doctor, osteopath or optometrist and submitted to the Department.

Vehicle Insurance, Title and Registration Facts

Registration Renewal

Renewal and address changes can be made online at www.GoRenew.com. Drivers have the option of renewing for one year or two years.

New Residents

New residents must register vehicles within ten days of obtaining employment or placing children in public school.

Inspections and Emissions Testing

Florida has no statewide regulation concerning safety inspections or emission testing. The emissions inspection program became obsolete July 1, 2000.

Passenger Plates Facts

The name of the county of issuance, the words *In God We Trust* or the words *Sunshine State* appear on bottom of license plate.
Passenger cars and light trucks display one plate, one decal (MO/YR). Commercial vehicles with GVW exceeding 26,000 pounds display two plates.
When vehicle is sold, the license plate remains with the original owner.
Note: Florida Off-Highway Vehicle (OHV) Titling Law requires OHV owners to apply for a Certificate of Title and obtain an OHV decal to be affixed on his/her OHV for use on OHV trails.

Insurance and Financial Responsibility

The Florida No-Fault law was re-enacted on January 1, 2008; the minimum mandatory requirements are $10,000 each of personal injury protection (PIP) and property damage liability (PDL) coverage. This is required throughout the registration period and whenever asked for by a law enforcement officer. Bodily Injury liability with limits of $10,000 per person, $20,000 per occurrence and $10,000 property damage coverage are required when: a crash is caused resulting in injury; or for some types of convictions; or when there is a judgment pursuant to a law suit. Commercial vehicles require personal injury protection and bodily injury liability coverage at all times with higher limits. Since October 1, 2007, the minimum mandatory requirements for a motorist convicted of a Driving Under the Influence (DUI) after that date must be able to provide coverage of the higher bodily injury liability limits of $100,000 per person, $300,000 per occurrence and $50,000 property damage on the date of the arrest for a DUI conviction.

Withdrawal Sanctions, and Alcohol and Drug Testing

Alcohol and Chemical Testing Limits

The unlawful blood-alcohol level or breath-alcohol level is.08 for an Administrative Suspension. CMV operators who have any alcohol in their system may not drive or be in actual physical control of a commercial motor vehicle and can be placed out of service for 24 hours. A blood-alcohol level or breath-alcohol level of .04 in a CMV is considered impairment, and the driver will be arrested for DUI. An administrative suspension is ordered if the operator's blood-alcohol level or breath-alcohol level is .08 or higher while operating a motor vehicle or a CMV, or is a CDL holder and operating a motor vehicle, or for Driving with an Unlawful Blood- or Breath-Alcohol Level (DUBAL), or refuses to submit to a breath, blood, or urine test (REFUSAL) test. Further, the CMV driver/CDL holder will also be disqualified from operating a CMV.
For a non-CDL driver or holder .05 BAC while operating a motor vehicle is considered impairment and the driver can be arrested for a DUI.
Persons under 21 years of age with a BAC of .02 will be administratively suspended. If the BAC level is higher than .02 they can be arrested and charged with DUI. If the BAC is above a .08 they can be administratively suspended as an adult. The determination is made by the police officer.
Alcohol testing includes urine, blood, and breath. Blood and urine tests are used for chemical and controlled substances. Operating any vehicle under the influence is also a violation that results in revocation of the driving privilege, if convicted. Effective July 1, 2005, drivers are required to install and use an ignition interlock if convicted of multiple DUIs, or if a first-time offender with a BAC of 0.15 or more (law changed from .20 to .15 effective October 1, 2008), or a minor was in the vehicle at the time of the offense.

Suspensions and Revocations

See the Appendix for a list of the federally mandated disqualifications for offenses occurring in a CMV per MCSIA.

Point Accumulation

Twelve Points in Twelve Months	Thirty-day suspension.
Eighteen Points in Eighteen Months	Three-month suspension.
Twenty-four Points in Thirty-six Months	One-year suspension.

Note: Three points will be deducted from the driving record of any person whose driving privileges have been suspended only once under the point system and reinstated, if such a person has complied with all other requirements.

Teen Drivers

Any Moving Violation if Learner's Permit	The one year period required for Learner's License is extended for one year from the date of the conviction or driver is 18.
Six Points in Twelve Months	Restricted driving privileges until 18 or for 12 months.
Truant in School Attendance	Suspension.
Possession of tobacco products	Suspension.

Note: Drivers under the age of 21 with a blood alcohol level of .02 or more will have their license immediately suspended for six months. This administrative action is for a first offense; a second offense will result in a one year suspension. Refusal to submit to testing (first offense) results in a suspension of twelve months; eighteen months on a second offense.

Giving False Information or Identification ...... Fraudulent license is cancelled and privilege suspended for one year.

Violations Which May Result in Suspension

- Admin Per Se .08 and above or .02 and above for CDL
- Allowing License to be Used for Illegal Purposes
- Child Support Delinquency
- Court-Ordered Suspension
- Dropping Out of School
- Failure of Road Test (5 attempts)
- Driving Without Insurance
- Failure to Pay Fine or Appear in Court
- Judged Mentally/Physically Incapacitated
- Loaning Vehicle to person who has Suspended License, and Crash Results with Injury or Death
- Making a Fraudulent License Application
- Point Accumulation
- Possession of Tobacco and Misrepresent Age to Obtain Tobacco, by a Minor

- Pending outcome of court conviction of incident which resulted in death and driver was charged

Violations Which May Result in Revocation

- An Immoral Act in Which a Motor Vehicle was Used
- Driving Under the Influence of Alcohol or Controlled Substance
- Failure to Stop and Render Aid in an Accident Resulting in Death or Personal Injury
- Felony Conviction of Drug Possession
- Felony Involving the Use of a Motor Vehicle
- Fleeing or Attempting to Elude a Police Officer
- Other Medical Problems
- Perjury or Misrepresentation of Truth in Ownership or

Other Violations Causing Revocations

DUI Convictions

First Conviction .... Revocation of 180 days to one year.
Second Conviction... Revocation minimum five years (if within five years of a prior conviction).
Second Conviction... Revocation minimum of 180 days (if outside of five years of a prior conviction).
Third Conviction.. Revocation minimum ten years (if within ten years of a prior conviction).
Four or More Convictions in Lifetime (chronic offenders) ... License permanently revoked.
DUI Resulting in Death .... Minimum three-year revocation involving serious bodily injury, a conviction of manslaughter resulting from the operation of a motor vehicle, or a conviction of vehicular homicide.
DUI Manslaughter .... License revoked permanently.
Street Racing -3rd Violation .... Minimum four-year revocation.

Note: If there is a term of incarceration and the driver is eligible for hardship consideration, the eligibility waiting period, if applicable, commences on the release date of the incarceration.

Violations Which May Result in a Disqualification

- Driving any vehicle, as a CDL holder, and arrested for DUI (post arrest they may have a BAC of .08 or above or refuse to submit to testing.)
- Driving a commercial vehicle without obtaining a CDL.
- Driving a commercial vehicle without the proper class of license or proper endorsement.
- Driving a commercial vehicle without having the driver license in possession.
- Driving a commercial vehicle while the operator's license is suspended, revoked, or canceled.
- Causing a fatality through the negligent operation of a commercial motor vehicle.
- Providing false information when applying for CDL results in a 60-day disqualification.
- A person who operates a commercial motor vehicle bearing a false or fraudulent identification commits a misdemeanor of the 1st degree

Note: Drivers are required to install and use an ignition interlock if convicted of multiple DUIs, as well as those first-time offenders with a BAC of 0.15 or more, or those who had a minor in the vehicle at the time of the offense.

Reinstatement Requirements

Suspension... $45 fee; time lapse and completion of Advanced Driver Improvement Course.
Revocation.. $75 fee.
DUI Revocation................................. $75 fee; plus administrative fee for DUI of $130; completion of DUI school if otherwise eligible.
DUI Administrative Suspension .... $45 fee; plus administrative fee for DUI of $130; DUI school enrollment if otherwise eligible.
For Insurance Suspensions .... $150 up to $500 for No-Fault and DUI cases and $15 for liability cases.
For Worthless Checks......................... $55 fee.

Note: Some reinstatements require DUI School and Advanced Driver Improvement School.

- Refusal to Submit to Breath, Blood or Urine Test
- Violation of Restriction

Operation of a Motor Vehicle
- Three Convictions of Reckless Driving in One Year
- Theft of Motor Vehicle Parts or Components
- Three Major Convictions, or Fifteen Pointable Convictions in Five Years (Habitual Offender Law)
- Vision Worse Than Standard Minimum Requirements
- Youthful Offender: Possession of Alcohol by a Minor, Gun Control, Criminal Mischief, Violation of Chapter 893 Controlled Substance

Record Access: Laws, Rules, and Forms

Note: This Section Applies to Both Driver and Vehicle Records.

Governing Statutes and Rules

Statutes at: www.leg.state.fl.us

Within the Florida Statutes, Title X, Chapter 119 places Florida in compliance with DPPA. Florida law changed in 2009 to adopt federal law by reference. Title X Section 119.0712(2) specifies when personal information in motor vehicle and driver license records can be released. The text is as outlined in 18 United States Code, section 2721 (DPPA). The back of the consent form (see below) provides a list of permissible uses - taken from DPPA.

Request and Consent Forms

Driving Records: Use of *Form HSMV 85054 – Driver License, Motor Vehicle/Vessel Records Request* is advised; fillable or downloadable at www.flhsmv.gov/dmv/forms/BTR/85054.pdf.

Vehicle Records: Use of *Form HSMV 85054 – Driver License, Motor Vehicle/Vessel Records Request* is advised: fillable or downloadable at www.flhsmv.gov/dmv/forms/BTR/85054.pdf.

Vendor and Third Party Access Policy

In order to receive records with personal information, **authorized accounts** must be pre-approved, or written requests must give the reason for the record request, with the signature of the requester.

All records containing personal information released to a third party must be maintained for a period of 5 years, including records identifying each person or entity that receives the personal information and the permitted purpose for which it will be used as per FS Title X; 119.071(2). The requesting party shall make these records available for inspection upon request by the providing agency.

Non-permissible Use Requests

Except for the driver license number and vehicle status checks described below, records with personal information are not released unless signed authorization is provided.

Access to Driver-Related Records

Driving Records

General Information and Fees

Division of Motorist Services, Bureau of Records, PO Box 5775, Tallahassee FL 32314-5775, 850-617-2000.

The fee for a three-year record is $8.00 and for either a seven-year record or a complete record the fee is $10.00. The fee for a no record found is $2.00. A request for a document, such as an application, citation, or address on file is $2.00 per record to search. An additional $0.50 for each document or a $1.00 for a certified document is required.

In-Person – Requests can no longer be made over-the-counter.

Mail – Requests mailed to the Division of Motorist Services are processed within 10 working days from receipt. The driver's license number, or name, date of birth and sex are needed when ordering. Payment must be submitted with each request.

FTP/Cartridge – The input cut-off time is 3:30 p.m. with output available after 7:30 a.m. the next working day. The driver's license number is required when ordering. No monthly minimum order is required, but accounts must be approved before orders can be placed. Payment is debited from the requester's bank account.

Online – The state differentiates between high and low volume users. Those businesses processing more than 5,000 transactions per month are considered Network Providers. Prospective Network Providers should contact the Data Processing Unit at DataProcessingUnit@flhsmv.gov.

Requesters needing less than 5,000 records per month are called Individual Users and are directed to a commercial vendor who is a Network Provider. Service fees will vary by vendor, state fees are as described above. A list of these companies is found at www.flhsmv.gov.

Bulk – The Florida public records law exempts personal information contained in motor vehicle or driver license records from disclosure except under specific exemption as outlined in 119.071(2) Florida Statutes. Fees are quoted per 322.20(11)(a).

By Person of Record – FL drivers may obtain their driving record by mail as described above. A record may also be requested from the Clerk of Court, local tax collector's office or other offices authorized by the DHSMV. No program is offered for drivers to order or view their own record online; however as described below, a site is offered for parents to view the record of the children under the age of 18.

Notification/Monitoring Program

Florida gives employers and insurers the ability to monitor drivers using a program that essentially permits approved entities to purchase in bulk based on new activity. Contact the Department's Data Processing Unit at DataProcessingUnit@flhsmv.gov.

DL Check

Visit https://services.flhsmv.gov/DLCheck/ for a free online check of any FL driver license number. Note this web address is case sensitive. Only the license number is used to access. No personal information is released.

Young Drivers – The DL Check site listed above also gives parents and guardians the ability to check the driving history of their children under 18 years of age. The last four digits of the SSN and the DOB are needed to view the record.

Crash Reports

Reporting – The requirements for law enforcement to utilize a long-form crash report include crashes 1) Resulting in death of, personal injury to, or any indication of complaints of pain or discomfort by any of the parties or passengers involved in the crash, 2) Leaving the scene involving damage to attended vehicles or property (F.S. 316.061 (1)), 3) Driving while under the influence (F.S. 316.193), 4) Rendered a vehicle inoperable to a degree that required a wrecker to remove it from the scene of the crash, and 5) Involved a commercial motor vehicle.

If the threshold for a long form is not met, the officer can write a short form. The short form is the same form as the long form but no narrative or diagram are required.

Crash reports must be submitted to the Department of Highway Safety and Motor Vehicles, Traffic Crash Records Section, Tallahassee FL 32399 within ten days of the completion of the investigation. A traffic crash or driver exchange reporting form is found at www.flhsmv.gov/ddl/ecrash/HSMV90011S.pdf

Record Access – Records are kept for a 10 year period from the date the crash report was filed. Traffic crash reports are exempt from public disclosure for 60 days after the date the report is filed, except for parties involved in the crash and other specific parties outlined in the statute (Section 316.066).

Mail request to Crash Records - MS-28, DHSMV, 2900 Apalachee Parkway, Room B231, Tallahassee, FL 32399-0538, 850-617-3416, fax is 850-617-5134. A downloadable crash report request form is available at www.flhsmv.gov/fhp/html/general/RequestForReport.pdf.

Homicide reports are kept in the local districts for 5 years from the date of crash. To order a traffic crash report older than 2 years, the cost is $10.00; a homicide report older than 5 years is $25.00. To order call 850-617-2306. To order traffic homicide photographs, call 850-617-3409.

Crash reports may be purchased online at www.buycrash.com. The fee is $16.00. Use of a credit card or PayPal is required. The orders can be placed over the telephone, call 866-495-4206. To obtain a report by mail, the driver's name, date of crash, and county are needed. It takes approximately 3 to 4 weeks to receive the report. The cost is $10.00 per report.

Access to Vehicle-Related Records

General Information and Fees

Division of Motorist Services, Record Information & Research Unit - MS91, Neil Kirkman Building, Room B-231, Tallahassee 32399. The mail address is 2900 Apalachee Parkway, Neil Kirkman Building, Mail Stop 91, Tallahassee, FL 32399-0620. 850-617-2000. www.flhsmv.gov/html/titlinf.html.

Names and current title histories are available for 10 years to present. To research by name for current vehicle information, the DOB and city are required. The fee for non-certified computer printouts for current registration information is $.50 per record. A specific title transaction is $1.00 per page. The fee for a complete title history record is $1.00 per page (the Agency recommends mail-in requesters send in a minimum of $15.00). A $3.00 certification fee is required if a document needs certification. **Liens** show on all records. The SSN is not released.

Mail and In-Person – Any fee required must accompany each request. Turnaround time is 10 days to 3 weeks. Also, one may do a plate search at a local Tax Collector's office.

Electronic – Motor Vehicle Data Listing Information Services, Neil Kirkman Building, MS-89, Tallahassee, FL 32399, 850-617-2634. For electronic access, Florida has contracted with several approved vendors to release information contained in the various Department of Highway Safety and Motor Vehicle's databases. For more information contact the Department's Data Processing Unit at DataProcessingUnit@flhsmv.gov. The link to the list of vendors on the Dept web site is at http://flhsmv.gov/data/internet2.html.

The SSN is not released. The access is transactional oriented. The cost will vary usually between $.52 and $1.25 per record fee plus a transactional fee based on the type of connection and software. Accounts work from a prepaid bank. However all new subscribers must first complete an application with this state agency.

Status Check – Enter title # or VIN to check vehicle status at https://services.flhsmv.gov/MVCheckWeb/. The vehicle status lets a customer know if the plate is renewable. A personalized license plate inquiry at https://services.flhsmv.gov/MVCheckPersonalPlate/ lets user know availability.

Bulk – The state will provide bulk data on CD only in conjunction with their DPPA compliant policy. Records are not released for marketing purposes. Customized search parameters are offered. Typical fees are $.01 per record, $1.00 for the CD and $4.50 for shipping. For further information, please contact Motorist Services, Data Listing Unit, MS-89; 2900 Apalachee Parkway; Tallahassee, FL 32399-0500 or phone 850-617-2805

Access to Vessel Records

General Information, Access and Fees

Motorist Services, Data Listing Unit; 2900 Apalachee Parkway, MS-91, Tallahassee, FL 32399-0500, 850-617-2908.

All motorized vessels must be titled and registered, regardless of size. Non-motor powered vessels less than 16 ft. in length and any non-motor powered canoe, kayak, racing shell, or rowing scull, regardless of length, are not required to be registered. However, non-powered vessels 16 ft. and over must be titled. A written request is required for all searches. Florida works with the local county tax collectors' offices in recording titles and registrations; this permits real-time connection. See www.flhsmv.gov/dmv/faqboat.html for additional information.

Name searches should include DOB and county. Fee is $.50 per page for computer print-out; microfilm copy of a title transaction is $1.00 per page, add $3.00 to certify. A complete title history is approx $15.00 or more.

Note: Florida recognizes valid registration certificates and numbers issued to visiting boaters for a period of 90 days. An owner who intends to use his/her vessel in Florida longer than 90 days must register it with a county tax collector. However, he/she may retain the out-of-state registration number if he/she plans to return to his/her home state within a reasonable period of time.

Driving Record Content and Reciprocity

What's On or Not On the Driving Record

- All convictions appear on the driving record.
- Collisions are only listed if convicted of a violation.
- Florida permits driver improvement school attendance in lieu of a court appearance for certain non-criminal traffic violations.
- Individuals who receive a Florida citation can keep points from being assessed by attending a driver improvement course in Florida. Individuals can attend driver improvement school once every twelve months and no more than five times in a lifetime. Florida law prohibits CDL holders from making this election.

Data Retention

Conviction information is not purged from the computer system until at least 3 to 5 years from conviction date for most offenses, or later for serious and DUI related offenses. Expired licenses are purged from the system 18 months after the expiration date if no convictions appear on

the record. Florida is working to establish a purge program for CDL holders based on the timetable per federal regulations (see Appendix).

Court to Repository

The courts must send conviction information within 10 days after adjudication of the case. Information is electronically transferred from all the county courts to the state.

State Reciprocity for Non-CDL Drivers

- Will suspend license of driver for unpaid out-of-state convictions.
- Record of new incoming driver is shown on MVR.
- Out-of-state convictions are shown on MVR.
- Out-of-state accidents are not shown on MVR.
- Convictions of out-of-state drivers are sent to home state.
- Record is forwarded to new state upon surrender of license.

Important Withdrawal and Licensing Codes

Revocation Codes

01	Perjury/False Affid/Oath - I.D. Applic	26	Metro Juvenile Traffic Violation
06	Viol Chapter 893 Controlled Substance	27	Theft of MTR VH/Parts/Components
07	Re-Imposed -- Reinstatement Rescinded	28	Viol - Ignition Interlock Device
08	Inadequate Vision-Out-State Residen	29	Inadequate Vision - Medical
09	Manslaughter/DUI/Dubal/Veh Hom	30	Inadequate Field of Vision
10	Manslaughter/DUI/Dubal/DUI Manslaughter	31	Fail Stop, Rend Aid Involving Inj/Death
11	Driving Under the Influence	32	Fleeing or Att Elude Police Officer
12	DUI Phy Ctl - Narc, Barb, Stim	37	Poss/Sell/Traf/Consprcy - Contrld Sub
13	Dui/Act Phy Ctl - Narc, Barn, Stim	38	Provide Alcohol to Minor
14	Habitual Traffic Offender	40	Murder Involving A Motor Vehicle
15	Driv W/An Unlaw Blood Alchl Lev	41	Manslaughter
16	Ordered By Circuit Ct, Juvenile Div	42	DUI Manslaughter
17	Conv Viol - Court Recommended Revoc	43	4 or more DUIs (Can apply for hardship consideration after five years from revocation. Manslaughter is NOT included
18	Ordered By Court As Term of Probation		
19	Reinstatement Rescinded - Revocation Reimposed	44	DUI/Manslaughter/DUI-no hardship license
20	Vehicular Homicide	46	Directed By CT. Contempt (Juvenile)
21	Using MV in Connection With Felony	47	Vio 790. 22(3) - Unlawful Poss Firearm
22	Felony - Poss of Controlled Substance	48	Vio 790. 22(9) - Com Off/Use/Pos F. Arm
23	DUI Serious Bodily Injury	51	Perjury/False Affid/Oath - DL Applic
24	DUI - Property Damage/Personal Injury	60	Rev. Extended - Contempt (Juvenile)
25	Juvenile Traffic Violation	61	Three Conv Rd Committed in 12 Mos

63	CT Dir Posses of Tobacco/Minor
64	CT Dir Misrepes/Age - Tobacco/Minor
68	Fraudulent Insurance Claims
69	Theft - Vio 812.0155
70	Rev Amend/Extended for Theft - Vio 812.0155
71	Immoral Act Involving MTR Vehicle
72	Immoral Act Involving MTR Vehicle Passenger
74	CT Directed Rev/Sus - Vio 569.11(5)
75	CT Directed Rev/Sus - Extend - Vio 569.11(5)
76	Court Directed Revocation
78	Incapable Operate Motor Vehicle Safely - Medical
79	Rev Extended For Viol of 806.13
80	Reinstatement Rescinded - Susp Imposed
81	Reinstatement Rescinded - Viol Restr
82	Incapable Op MV - Blackouts
83	Requested By Fla Parole Commission
84	Conv Viol - Court Directed Revoc

85	Rev Amend/Extend For Vio 562.11(2)
86	Rev Amend/Extend For Vio 562.111
87	Rev Amend/Extend For Vio Chapt 893
88	Rev Amend/Extend Vio Contrld Sub
89	Rev. Extended For Viol of 790.22(3)
90	Rev Extended For Viol of 790.22(9)
91	Reinstate Rescinded - Conv Mand Viol
92	Rev Extended 3 Mos - Conv Driv W/Rev
93	Failure to Surrender Driver Lic
94	Fail to Submit Vision Report As Req
95	Inadequate Vision
96	Incapable Operating MV Safely
97	Incapable OP MV - Subject to Seizures
98	Fail to Submit Med Report As Req
99	Racing on Public Traffic Way
100	Msrp/age obtain Alchl vio S.562.11(2)
101	Posses Alchl bev/minor S. 562.111

Suspension Codes

06	Incapable OP MV Safely - Failed Exam
07	Adj. Mental/Physical Incapacitated
09	DRV W/Unlaw Bal (.08% Or Above)
10	DRV W/Unlaw Bal (.10% Or Above)
14	Juvenile Traffic Violation
15	Metro Juvenile Traffic Violation
16	Ordered By Circuit CT. Juvenile Div
17	Failure to Pass - Driving Test Only
18	Failure to Report - Driving Test Only
19	Fail Pass DL Exam-Out-State Resid
20	Fail Report DL Exam-Out-State Resid
21	Violation of Restriction
22	Drive W/Unlaw Bal .02 (Under 21)
23	Refuse Sub Breath Test (Under 21)
24	Unlawful BAL (under 21) .05 or Higher
25	FTR for Re-Exam Investigation
26	Manslaughter
27	Using MV in Connection With Felony
28	Perjury/False Affid/Oath - DL Applic
29	MV Used - Immoral Act
30	Three Conv RD Committed in 12 Months
31	Comm Offense - Revoc Required If Conv
32	Viol Resulting Death/Pers Injury
33	Comm Out-State Viol - Ground Rev/Susp
34	Out-State Conv Grounds Rev - Susp
35	Driv/Act Phy Control While Intox
36	Conv/Viol - Court Recommended Susp
38	DWI/Act Phy Ctl - Narc, Barb, Stim
39	DWI/Act Phy Ctl - Narc, Barb, Stim
40	Driv W/An Unlaw Blood Alchl Lev
41	Permitting Unlawful Use of License
42	Conspiracy/Misrep Ident/Fact OBT DL
43	Display/Represent DL Not Ones Own
44	Display Alt/Fict/Rev/Susp/Canc DL
45	Obtaining A License By Fraud
46	Directed By CT.-Contempt (Juvenile)
47	Driving While License Suspended
48	Provide Alcohol to Minor- 562.11(1)(a)
49	Reinstatement Rescinded - Susp Imposed
50	Reinstatement Rescinded - Viol Restr
51	Adjudged Incompetent
52	Inadequate Vision
53	Incapable OP MV - Subject to Seizures
54	Incapable OP MV - Habitual Drunkard
55	Incapable OP MV - Addict/Hab Use Narc
56	Incapable OP MV - Blackouts
57	Failed D/L Exam 5 Times
58	Incapable Operating MV Safely

59	Vio 322.058 F.S. Child Support Delq
60	Susp. Extended - Contempt (Juvenile)
61	Failure to Report For Req D/L Exam
62	Failure to Pass Req D/L Exam
63	CT Dir Posses of Tobacco/Minor
64	CT Dir Misrepresents Age - Tobacco/Minor
65	Reinstate Rescinded - Conv Mand Viol
66	Refuse Sub Breath/Urine/Blood Test
67	Requested By Fla Parole Commission
68	Involved in Acc - Death Resulting
69	Involved in Acc - Per Inj Resulting
70	Fail to Submit Report of Vision Ex
71	Susp Extended 3 Mo - Conv Driv W/ Susp
72	Failure to Surrender Driver Lic
73	Conv Viol-Court Directed Susp
74	Court Directed Rev/Sus - Vio 569.11 (S)
75	Court Directed Rev/Susp Ext - Vio 569.11 (S)
76	Court Directed Suspension
77	Non-Compliance School Attendance
78	Education Non-Compliance S.322.091
79	Susp Extended For Viol of 806.13
80	Passing Stopped School Bus
81	Failure to Stop For School Bus
82	Unauthorized interlock removal
84	Vio resulting death/ser bodily inj
85	Sus Amend/Extend For Vio 562.11(2)
86	Sus Amend/Extend For Vio 562.111
87	Sus Amend/Extend For Vio Chapt 893
88	Sus Amend/Extend Vio Contrld Sub
89	Susp Extended For Viol of 790.22(3)
90	Susp Extended For Viol of 790.22(9)
91	Obtaining An I.D. Card By Fraud
92	Petit Theft for Gas
93	Refused to Submit to BAL Test (BUI)
94	Operating a Vessel BAL .02 (Under 21)
95	Failed to Appear - Worthless Check
96	Load Dropping/Shifting/Escaping
97	Theft Vio 812.0155
98	Susp Amend/Extended for Theft 812.0155
99	Failure secure load serious inj/death
100	Load drop/shft/esc & fail sec inj/death
101	Is incompetent to drive a motor veh
103	Vio. 322.36 Permit Unauth OP to Drive
107	Fail to Pay CT Financial Obligation
108	MSRP/Age Obtain Alchl Vio S. 562.11(2)
109	Posses of Alchl Bev/Minor S. 562.111
110	Viol Chapter 893 controlled substance
110	Non-Compliance Genetic Testing

D6 Suspension Codes

01	Failed to Appear on Traffic Summon	05	Failed to Pay Traffic Fine (Penalty)
02	Failed to Complete CT Ordered Sch	06	Criminal Fail to Pay
03	School Elected When Not Eligible	07	Criminal Fail to Appear
04	Fail to Comply Traf Summons	08	Sch Election Made Failed to Attend

Point Suspension Codes

11	12 Points Within 12 Months
12	18 Points Within 18 Months
13	24 Points Within 36 Months

License Classes, Restrictions, and Endorsements

License Classes– Commercial

Florida began issuing the CDL in April 1991.

Class A   Combination vehicles with a GVWR of 26,001 lbs. or more, provided towed vehicle is more than 10,000 lbs.

Class B   Any single motor vehicle that has GVWR of 26,001 lbs. or more, or any such vehicle towing a vehicle of 10,000 lbs. or less.

Class C   Vehicles less than 26,001 lbs. that are designed to transport 16 or more persons including the driver, OR transporting placardable amounts of hazardous materials.

CDL Exemptions

The following persons are exempt from the requirements to obtain a commercial driver license:

- Drivers of authorized emergency vehicles that are equipped with extraordinary audible warning devices that display red or blue lights and are on call to respond to emergencies. Military personnel driving military vehicles.
- Farmers transporting agricultural products, farm supplies, or farm machinery to or from their farms and within 150 miles of their farm, if the vehicle operated under this exemption is not used in the operations of a common or contract motor carrier.
- Drivers of recreational vehicles used for recreational purposes.
- Drivers who operate straight trucks (single units) that are exclusively transporting their own tangible personal property which is not for sale.
- An employee of a publicly owned transit system who is limited to moving vehicles for maintenance or parking purposes exclusively within the restricted-access confines of a transit system's property.

License Classes– Non-Commercial

Effective July 1, 2005, Class D licenses were converted to Class E. Drivers may continue to possess valid Class D licenses until their licenses are renewed or otherwise reissued. This includes farmers and emergency vehicle operators who are exempt from commercial driver license requirements.

Class D   (No Longer Issued) Any truck or truck tractor that has an actual weight, declared weight or GVWR of 8,000 lbs or more but less than 26,001 lbs. or is more than 80 inches wide. A resident who holds a valid Florida chauffeur license may continue to operate vehicles for which a Class D driver license is required, until the chauffeur license expires. This includes farmers and emergency vehicle operators who are exempt.

Class E   Regular operator's license. Any non-commercial motor vehicle with GVWR less than 26,001 lbs. A resident who holds a valid Florida operator license may continue to operate vehicles for which a Class E driver license is required, until the operator license expires.

Class E-L   Learner's permit. A resident who holds a valid Florida learner license may continue to operate vehicles for which a Class E Learner license is required, until the license expires.

MTCY ALSO   Authorized to **also** operate motorcycle.

MTCY ONLY   Authorized to **only** operate motorcycle.

Restrictions

A	Corrective Lenses	K	Hearing Aid	1	Vehicles Without Air-Brakes
B	Outside Rearview Mirror	L	Seat Cushion	2	CDL Intrastate Only
C	Business Purposes Only	M	Hand Controls or Pedal Extension	3	CDL Bus Only
D	Employment Purposes	N	Left-Foot Accelerator	4	CMV <26,001 GVWR
E	Daylight Driving Only	P	Probation-Interlock Device	5	No Tractor/Trailers
F	Automatic Transmission	S	Other Restrictions	6	No Class A Passenger Veh
G	Power Steering	T	No Passengers on Motorcycle	7	No Class B Passenger Veh
I	Directional Signals	X	Medical-Alert Bracelet		
J	Grip on Steering Wheel	Y	Educational Purposes		

Endorsements

H	Placarded HazMat		Passengers (including driver)		Trailers
N	Tank Vehicle	S	School Bus	X	Endorsements H and N
P	Designed to transport 16 or more	T	Combination with Double/Triple		

Traffic Violation Classifications Table with Points, ACD, Class, and Department Codes

Class/Charge Reference Keys

B	Bicyclist
C	Criminal violation
M	Moving infraction
N	Non-moving infraction
P	Pedestrian
R	Mandatory Revocation/Suspension
m	Fines/Fees mailable within 30 Calendar days (except as noted)
a	Mandatory appearance at Courthouse Traffic Violation Bureau (TVB), within 30 days or as noted
c	Mandatory Court appearance

"**" in the ACD Code column means there is no ACD code. The violation code is maintained for historical purposes only until retention period is met or the violation is a non-ACD conviction.

The Table is presented in order of the Description.

Code	ACD	Class	Pts	Description
410	N84	N/m	0	2 Rear Red Reflectors Tow Vehicles
212	**	N/m	0	Addition Runboard Lamp Improper
212	**	N/m	0	Additional ID Lamps Improper
833	A12			Admin Refuse Breath/Urine Test
832	A12			Admin Refuse Submit Breath Test <21
16	A20			Administrative Per Se
828	A94			Administrative Per Se For .04 BAC
829	A98			Administrative Per Se For .08 BAC
827	A90			Administrative Per Se For .10 BAC
830	A61			Administrative unlawful BAL(<21).05/HIGHER
384	**			All Other FHP
380	**	N/m	0	All Other Non-Traffic & Non-Criminal Infractions
383	**	C/c	0	All Others Not Specified Above (Criminal - will not go to record as conviction)
214	F03	N/m	0	All-Terrain Vehicles (ATV) Operators Under 16 Yrs of Age Must Wear Head-Helmet And Eye-Protection
541	**	C/c	0	Alter/Deface/Remove etc. A Traffic Control Device/Railroad Signs/Signals
133	**	N/m	0	Altered Exhaust System
380	**	N/m	0	Animals/Animal-Drawn Vehicles to Obey Traffic Laws
616	**	C/c	0	Any Person Permitting Unauthorized Person to Drive
471	**	C/c	0	Attaching Tag (License Plate) Not Assigned
458	**	N/m	0	ATV-Improper Operation on Certain Roadways
137	**	N/m	0	Auto Trailer Brake/Breakaway Improper
212	**	N/m	0	Auxiliary Driving Lamps Improper
212	**	N/m	0	Auxiliary Front Lights – Violation of Usage
137	**	N/m	0	Auxiliary Front Lights/Driving Lamps-Number Required
212	**	N/m	0	Auxiliary Passing Lamps Improper
392	N82	M/m	3	Backing – Improper/Backing, on Limited Access Facility
212	**	N/m	0	Back-Up Light on Going Forward
137	**	N/m	0	Beam Indicator None/Improper
482	**	M/m	0	Bicycle Offense Over 14 Yr of Age
382	**	B/m	0	Bicycle Offense with no or Improper light (1st offense dismissed upon proof of purchase and installation of proper lighting equipment)
396	F34	M/m	3	Blocking An Intersection Or Crosswalk
137	**	N/m	0	Brake Equipment Performance Requirements (Motorcycle/Motor Driven Cycle)
137	**	N/m	0	Brake Force Improper Type For Vehicle
137	**	N/m	0	Brake Stop Improper Distance
137	**	N/m	0	Brake Stop Improper For Gross Weight
137	**	N/m	0	Brakes – Electric Powered Vehicles
137	**	N/m	0	Brakes – Improper Adjustment
137	**	N/m	0	Brakes – Improper Type For Vehicle
137	**	N/m	0	Brakes-No/Improper
221	**	M/m	3	Bumper Law (Every Vehicle of Not More Than 5,00 Lbs Shipping Weight Shall Be Equipped As Indicated)(New Motor Vehicles S.319.001(4), Antique Automobiles S.320.08, Horseless Carriages S.320.086, Street Rods 3.320.0863 Are Excluded From Requirement)
211	E01	N/m	0	Bus Exhaust System Leak
211	E01	N/m	0	Bus Seats Unsecured
137	**	N/m	0	Bus/Truck 2 Frontside Clear Lamp
137	**	N/m	0	Bus/Truck 2 Rearside Clear Lamp
137	**	N/m	0	Bus/Truck 2 Rearside Reflectors And 1 Stop Light

Code	ACD	Class	Pts	Description
137	**	N/m	0	Bus/Truck 2 Side Marker Lamps
137	**	N/m	0	Bus/Truck Side Front/Back Reflectors
456	M81	M/m	3	Care When Approaching/Passing Person Riding/Leading An Animal on Shoulder/Roadway
455	M81	M/m	3	Careless Driving
432	M81			Careless Or Improper Driving
386	A34			Carry/Unlaw Conceal/Possess Firearm
404	F02	M/m	3	Child Restraint – Infant Thru 3 Yrs Must Be in Separate Carrier, 4-5 Years in Carrier/Seat Belt. Applies to Any Location in Vehicle (Driver to Be Cited)
404	F02	M/m	3	Child Restraint required
137	**	N/m	0	Clear/Id Lamp Visibility Improper
137	**	N/m	0	Clear/Side Marker Lamp Bad Mount
804	E01	N/c	0	CMV – Company ID Not in Compliance With Federal Regulations; Hazardous Materials
383	**	C/c	0	CMV – Criminal Action Not Specified
807	**	N/c	0	CMV – Disregard Required Hours of Rest
809	A04	M/m	0	CMV – Driving With Alcohol Concentration .04 Or Higher
816	A26	M/m	3	CMV – Driving With Alcohol Concentration Greater Than .00 to Less Than .04
802	E01	N/m	0	CMV – Fail to Display Required ID on Commercial Vehicle Readily Visible And Readable From 50 Ft
805	E70	N/c	0	CMV – Failure to Remove ID From Vehicle
806	**	N/c	0	CMV – Falsification of Time Records
483	**	C/c	0	CMV - ID Number Violation
380	**	N/m	0	CMV – Infraction Not Specified
801	B51	N/m	0	CMV – Operator Under 18, Vehicle Gross Weight 26,000 Lbs. Or More
625	**	N/m	0	CMV – Physical Examination Form in Possession
803	**	N/c	0	CMV – Removable Device Violation
822	E01			CMV - Violation of Identification Requirement
540	M09	M/m	3	CMV Fail to slow before RR tracks
540	M09	M/m	3	CMV Fail to slow before RR tracks
433	E53	C/c	0	CMV: Disregard Safety Regulations For Transporting Hazardous Materials
316	U02	C/c	0	CMV-Fail to Submit to Inspection of Vehicle (Resisting Officer With Violence)
317	U02	C/c	0	CMV-Fail to Submit to Inspection of Vehicle (Resisting Without Violence)
434	N80	M/m	3	Coasting Downgrade in Neutral (repealed 4/27/2011)
448	D02	C/c	0	Commercial Motor Vehicle – Possession of More Than One Driver License
139	D02	C/c	0	Committing Perjury to Obtain ID Card
400	F34	N/m	0	Crash – Disabled Vehicle Obstructing Traffic – Failure of Driver to Move/Solicit Help to Move Vehicle
312	**	N/m	6	Crash – Fail to Leave Information (Unattended Vehicle Property Damage)
400	F34	N/m	0	Crash – Fail to Remove Obstructing Attended Vehicle – Property Damage
400	F34	N/m	0	Crash – Fail to Remove Obstructing Unattended Vehicle
400	F34	N/m	0	Crash – Fail to Remove Obstructing Vehicle (Involving Death/Injury)
451	B61	N/m	0	Crash – Fail to Report to Police If Injured/Attending Person Unable to Receive Information
451	B61	N/m	0	Crash – Failure of Driver to Make Written Report of Accident When Required
451	B61	N/m	0	Crash – Failure of Driver to Report Accident Resulting in Injury/Death/Property Damage (>$500) to Law Enforcement Agency
282	B74	C/c	0	Crash – Failure of Each Party to The Accident to Provide Proof of Insurance to The Investigating Officer Within 24 Clock Hours
451	B61	N/m	0	Crash – Failure of Vehicle Occupant to Make Report If Driver Incapable
451	B61	N/m	0	Crash – Failure of Vehicle Owner to Make Report If Driver Incapable
450	**	C/c	0	Crash – Gave False Information At Crash
318	**	C/c	0	Crash – Leaving Scene of Accident Without Giving Information, $50 Or Less (Specify Amount)
313	B05	C/c	6	Crash – Leaving Scene Without Leaving Information More Than $50 Damage (Specify Amount)
311	B01	C/c	R	Crash – Leaving Scene Without Rendering Aid (Involving Death/Injury)
451	B61	N/m	30	Crash- Failure of Driver to submit SUPPLEMENTAL report of crash when required
1	**			Crash With Citation Issued
451	B61	N/m	0	Crash-Occupant/Owner Failure to Make Report If Driver Incapable
383	**	C/c	0	Criminal Mischief (Under 18 Years of Age)(If Court Does Not Direct to Suspend)
533	M02	M/m	3	Crossing/Driving on Median Strip Or Marked Divider of Divided Highway
617	U08	C/c	0	Culpable Negligence Using A Motor Vehicle
133	**	N/m	0	Cycle/Vehicle Exceed Noise Limit
212	**	N/m	0	Deceleration Lamps Improper
135	F66			Def Equip-Inability to Control MV
132	E31			Defective Equip-Brakes
378	E30	N/m	0	Defective Equipment – Owner Permitting Use With (All Vehicles) Driver Operating Vehicle With Unsafe/Defective Equipment.
2	F66			Defective Equipment Condition
137	**	N/m	0	Defective Equipment-1 Defect Per Citation-Defective Lights/Brakes/Tires/Steering/Defective Muffler/Other Defective Equipment
136	F66			Defective Steering

Code	ACD	Class	Pts	Description
399	**	N/m	0	Department of Transportation Obey Safety Regulation
536	**	N/m	0	Detour Signs/Barricade – Defacing/Tearing Down
533	M02	M/m	3	Detour Signs/Barricade – Driving Around
379	D02	C/c	0	DHSMV Issued Identification Card – Unlawful Use Of
3	W14			Disability Condition
383	**	C/c	0	Disabled Person's Parking Permit B Making False Statements on Applications
449	**	C/c	0	Disabled Persons Parking Permits – Fraudulently Obtained/Unlawful Use/Replica
332	M40	M/m	3	Disobey No Change of Lane Device
411	M76	M/m	3	Disobey No Passing Zone Sign
534	M17			Disobeyed Bus/Car Pool Lane Sign
379	D02	C/c	0	Display Another Persons Id
471	**	C/c	0	Display of Truck Tags – Fail to Display License Plates on Front & Rear of Trucks of 26,000 Lbs Or More Gross Vehicle Wt. Or on Front of Truck-Tractor
471	**	C/c	0	Display of Truck Tags: Fail to Display License Plates on Front & Rear of Trucks of 26,000 Lbs Or More
475	**	M/m	3	Display of Truck Tags: Fail to Display License Plates on Front & Rear of Trucks of 26,000 Lbs Or More - effective 10/1/2008
622	**	N/A	0	Dl Not Carried/Exhibit on Demand (If valid at time citation was issued, a dismissal fee up to $10 can be paid, when proof submitted to Clerk of Court).
397	F34	N/m	0	Double Parked
354	**	M/m	3	Dragging Part of Load
190	D70	N/m	0	Drapes/Blinds Restriction Behind Driver
158	A20			Driv W/An Unlaw Blood Alchl Lev
138	A20			Driv/Act Phy Control W/Intox
148	A20			Driv/Act Phy Control W/Intox-Bike
152	A22			Driv/Act Phy Ctl-Narc, Barb, Stim
816	A26			Driv/Phy Ctrl CMV with any Alcohol
168	A20			Driv/Wan Unlaw Blood Alch Lev-Bike
594	**	N/m	0	Driver License - Fail to change LEGAL address on DL
373	**	C/c	0	Driver License - False Display
613	B22	C/c	0	Driver License - Operating Vehicle While DL Suspended/Cancelled/Revoked (Specify Reason -Fail to Appear/Pay Fine/Complete Traffic School/Points/Habitual Traffic Offender)
377	**	C/c	0	Driver License - Permitting use of DL by Another Person
377	**	C/c	0	Driver License - Possession/Display/Permitting any Unlawful Use of DL
372	B41	C/c	0	Driver License - Possession/Display/Permitting Use of Suspended or Revoked or Cancelled or Fictitious or Altered DL
453	**	C/c	0	Driver License - Refusal to Surrender
613	B22	C/c	0	Driver License - Using DL From Another State While Under Suspension/Revocation
614	D27	C/c	0	Driver License - Violation of Restriction
604	D29	M/m	3	DRIVER LICENSE - Violation of RESTRICTION Operate against License Restrictions - special mechanical control devices required.(effective 10/1/2010)
383	**	C/c	0	Driver License Unlawful Use Of
253	D78	C/c	R	Driver License/ID Card - Unauthorized Use/Fraudulent DL/ID Card Application
374	D16	C/c	0	Driver License/ID Card - Unauthorized Use/Possession If Violation Is For DL
379	D02	C/c	0	Driver License/Id Card - Unauthorized Use/Possession If Violation Is For ID Card
137	**	N/m	0	Driver Operating Vehicle With Unsafe/Defective Equipment
190	D70	N/m	0	Driver's View/Driving Mechanism Obstructed By Load Or Passenger
190	D70	N/m	0	Driver's View/Driving Mechanism Obstructed By Load Or Passenger/Driver's View Impaired By Sign/Poster/Nontransparent Material
808	A50	C/c	0	Driving a CMV while in possession of a controlled substance
810	A33	C/c	D	Driving A CMV While in Possession of A Controlled Substance (Disqualified From Driving CMV)
631	N63	M/m	3	Driving in Wrong Direction on One-Way Roadway
632	N72	M/m	3	Driving Left of Center Line on Any Roadway Having Four Or More Lanes
411	M76	M/m	3	Driving on Left Side in No Passing Zone
454	**	M/m	3	Driving on Rim Damaging Road
632	N72	M/m	3	Driving on Wrong Lane Or Side or Failed to Drive Upon Right Half of Roadway
632	N72	M/m	3	Driving on Wrong Side of Divided Highway
129	F66	N/m	0	Driving Vehicle in Unsafe Condition
613	B22	C/c	0	Driving While License Permanently Revoked (Officer Should Specify Permanent)
611	B25			Driving While Revoked
612	B26			Driving While Suspended
190	D70	N/m	0	Driving While View Obstructed
190	D70	N/m	0	Driving While View Obstructed by Material
800	A25			Driving With Ability Impaired By Alcohol
352	**	N/m	0	Drop/Secure Load (Infraction)
647	A20	C/c	R	DUI - Driving Under The Influence
657	A20	C/c	R	DUI - Driving Under The Influence (Bicycle)

Code	ACD	Class	Pts	Description
172	U08	C/c	R	DUI - Manslaughter
171	U08	C/c	R	DUI - Manslaughter; Bicycle
648	A20	C/c	R	DUI - Property Damage/Personal Injury
658	A20	C/c	R	DUI - Property Damage/Personal Injury (Bicycle)
649	A20	C/c	R	DUI - Serious Bodily Injury
659	A20	C/c	R	DUI - Serious Bodily Injury (Bicycle)
379	D02	C/c	0	Duplicate/Possess Fake Id
528	F04	N/m	0	Effective Jan. 1, 2008, Farm Labor Vehicle - Proper Seat Belt assembly not installed for each passenger in vehicle with GVWR under 10,000 lbs. Or less
405	**	M/m	3	Electric Personal Assistive Mobility Device B Improper Operation on Certain Roadways
133	**	N/m	0	Emit Excess Exhaust Fumes
380	**	N/m	0	Employing Unlicensed Driver (For Type Vehicle Operated)
11	E70			Equipment Misuse
516	N01	M/m	3	Erected OTHER THAN at intersection, vehicle facing, failed to obey
212	**	N/m	0	Excessive Lights - (Back-Up/Clearance) - Improper Operation
817	B51	N/m	0	Expired CDL (30 Days Or Less)
817	B51	N/m	0	Expired CDL (30 Days Or Less)[If Expired More Than 30 Days See 322,54(4)(A)]
819	B51	C/c	0	Expired CDL (More Than 30 Days)/No Proper Endorsement
818	B51	C/c	0	Expired CDL (More Than 30 Days)/Out of Class CDL
606	B51	C/c	0	Expired DL (6 months or less) (effective 1/1/2013) (use 619 for Expired DL 4 months or less for offenses prior to 1/1/13)
618	B51			Expired DL Less Than 12 Months
216	**			Fail Comply Faulty Equip Notice
379	D02	C/c	0	Fail Comply ID Requirements
212	**	N/m	0	Fail Comply Light Requirements
210	E34	N/m	0	Fail Dim Headlights Parked Vehicle
195	E54	M/m	3	Fail Dim Headlights/Improper Adjustment
195	E54	M/m	3	Fail Dim Lights From Rear
211	E01	N/m	0	Fail Display 2 Warning Devices
211	E01	N/m	0	Fail Display 3 Emergency Devices
211	E01	N/m	0	Fail Display Slow Moving Emblem
614	D27	C/c	0	Fail Obey Driver License Restrictions
605	D27	M/m	3	Fail obey driver license restrictions - misuse of time and purpose (effective 10/1/2010)
211	E01	N/m	0	Fail Pass/Post Examine Certificate in Bus
211	E01	N/m	0	Fail Place Emergency Device Properly
211	E01	N/m	0	Fail Place Required Emergency Device
211	E01	N/m	0	Fail Place Warning Device Hill/Curve
211	E01	N/m	0	Fail Place Warning Device Properly
553	N41			Fail to Cancel Signal Directions
594	**	N/m	0	Fail to Change Address on DL
594	**	N/m	0	Fail to Change Name on DL
472	**	N/a	0	Fail to Display Registration - Possession Required
472	**	N/a	0	Fail to Display Registration/Temporary Internet Receipt; Possession Required
410	N84	N/m	0	Fail to Display Slow Emblem
211	E01	N/m	0	Fail to Display Warnings on Vehicle Used to Sell Ice Cream/Other Frozen Confections
332	M40	M/m	3	Fail to Drive in Single Lane
632	N72	M/m	3	Fail to Drive to Right When Driving Less Than Normal Speed of Traffic
314	U01	C/c	R	Fail to Obey Police Officer/Flee (Revoked By Court)
544		M/m	3	Fail to obey traffic control device(effective 10/1/2009)
543	M14		4	Fail to Obey Traffic Control Signal (Effective 10/1/05) Fail to obey traffic control device (Eff. 7/1/2010 new fee)
539	N30			Fail to Observe Warning on Vehicle
410	N84	N/m	0	Fail to Show Slow Move Farm Vehicle Emblem
551	N40	M/m	3	Fail to Signal Turn Properly
545	M16	M/m	4	Fail to stop at STEADY RED signal- (Eff. 10/1/2009- new code) (Eff. Fee change 7/1/2010)
545	M16	M/m	4	Fail to stop at STEADY RED signal before making right turn(Eff. Fee change 7/1/2010)
545	M16	M/m	4	Fail to stop at STEADY RED signal, one way street, before making left turn- (Eff. Fee change 7/1/2010)
332	M40	M/m	3	Fail to Use Designated Lane/Failed to Drive Within Single Lane
516	N01	M/m	3	FAIL to YIELD - to oncoming traffic/vehicle passing on left when MAKING LEFT TURN
193	**	M/m	3	Fail Tow Vehicle Properly
593	N50	M/m	3	Fail Turn As Directed
532	M17	M/m	3	Failed to Obey Flashing Red Stop Signal
532	M17	M/m	3	Failed to Obey Flashing Yellow Caution Signal
351	**	N/m	0	Failed to Remove Glass Or Other Injurious Substance From The Road (Wrecker Operator/Other Persons)
551	N40	M/m	3	Failed to Signal Change in Direction/Slowing
512	N23	M/m	3	Failed to Stop At A Stop/Yield Intersection
603	D07	M/m	3	Failed to surrender DL/CDL (effective 10/1/2010) Note: No longer classified as criminal (violation code 453

Code	ACD	Class	Pts	Description
				used until 10/1/2010)
453	**	C/c	0	Failed to Surrender Dl/CDL Note: as of 10/01/2010 no longer classified as criminal
603		M/m	3	Failed to Surrender Dl/CDL Note: effective as of 10/01/2010
332	M40	M/m	3	Failed to Use Designated Lane
514	N08	M/m	3	Failed to Use Due Care Toward Pedestrian
514	N08	M/m	3	FAILED TO USE DUE CARE TOWARD PEDESTRIAN
513	N25	M/m	3	Failed to Yield - Approaching/Entering Intersection (1. Vehicle in Intersection All Others Must Yield) (2. Vehicles Arriving At Same Time - Vehicle on Left Yields to Vehicle on Right) (3. State Roads Has Right-Of-Way Over Other Roads If Intersection Is Unmarked) (4. Paved Roads Have Right-Of-Way Over Unpaved Roads)
512	N23	M/m	3	Failed to Yield Or Stop At Sidewalk - From Alley/Bldg/Private Road Or Driveway
514	N08	M/m	3	Failed to Yield Right-Of-Way to Pedestrian
514	N08	M/n	3	FAILED TO YIELD right-of-way to PEDESTRIAN at crosswalk with signage. Effective July 1, 2008
511	N04	M/m	3	Failed to Yield to Emergency Vehicle
532	M17	M/m	3	Failed to Yield to Flagperson/Escort Vehicle-Oversized Vehicle
532	M17	M/m	3	Failed to yield to Highway Worker/Flagperson
512	N23	M/m	3	Failed to Yield/Stop At Sidewalk-From Alley/Bldg/Private Road Or Driveway to vehicles approaching
435	N04	M/m	3	Failure of An Emergency Vehicle to Use Warning Device
595	**	C/c	0	Failure of Registered Owner to Notify DHSMV of "Change of Address" Within 20 Days
444	M08	C/c	0	Failure to Allow Fingerprint
452	D45			Failure to Appear For Hearing Or Trial
451	B61	N/m	0	Failure to File Notice of ATV Accident
9	**			Failure to Have DL Or Registration
385	D72			Failure to Have Vehicle Under Control
333	M40	M/m	0	Failure to Obey High Occupancy Vehicle Lane Requirement
380	**	N/c	0	Failure to Obey Safety Rules For Non-Public Sector Bus
511	N04	M/m	3	Failure to Over For Emergency Vehicle/Wrecker
511	N04	M/m	3	Failure to Slow Down For Emergency Vehicle/Wrecker
428	N08	M/m	3	Failure to Stop For Mobility Impaired Pedestrian Carrying A White Stick/Cane Crossing An Intersection with assistance of guide dog, white stick/cane, walker or wheelchair
428	N08	M/m	3	Failure to Stop For Person Carrying A White Stick Or Cane/Guide Dog
516	N01	M/m	3	Failure to Yield right-of-way while in funeral procession
516	N01	M/m	3	Failure to yield to Public Transit Vehicles
530	B50	N/m	0	Farm Labor Vehicle - No/not clearly displayed seat belt notification instructions
529	B50	N/m	0	Farm Labor Vehicle - No/not clearly displayed sticker authorizing the transport of farm workers [sticker per s. 450.33(12)]
410	N84	N/m	0	Farm Tractor 2 Rear Red Reflectors
410	N84	N/m	0	Farm Tractor Light/Reflector Violation
410	N84	N/m	0	Farm Tractor Rear Red Lamp No/Improper
410	N84	N/m	0	Farm Tractor Warn Light No/Improper
4	U08			Fatality
613	B22	C/c	0	Financial Responsibility - Driving While DL Suspended
453	**	C/c	0	Financial Responsibility - Refusal to Surrender Driver License/Registration
17	D35			Financial Responsibility Condition
394	M56	M/m	3	Fire Hose - Crossing Unprotected
395	**	P/m	0	Fishing From Bridge
623	B51	C/c	0	Fl Resident Driving A CMV in Fl Must Have A CMV License Issued By Fl
532	M17	M/m	3	Flag person Or Worker-Failed to Yield To
211	E01	N/m	0	Flares - No/Improper
211	E01	N/m	0	Flares/Flags/Fuses-Failed to Display
532	M17	M/m	3	Flashing Control Signals - Fail to Obey
314	U01	C/c	0	Fleeing/Attempting to Elude A Police Officer (Not Revoked By Court)
314	U01	C/c	R	Fleeing/Attempting to Elude A Police Officer (Revoked By Court)
314	U01	C/c	R	Fleeing/Elude Officer After Crash (Revoked By Court)
314	U01	C/c	R	Fleeing/Elude Officer After Crash Involving Property Damage Injury (Revoked By Court)
315	U01	C/c	R	Fleeing/Elude Officer After Crash Involving Serious Bodily Injury Or Death (Revoked By Court)
314	U01	C/c	R	Fleeing/Elude Officer in Patrol Vehicle (Revoked By Court)
315	U01	C/c	R	Fleeing/Elude Officer Resulting in Serious Injury Or Death (Revoked Indefinite By Court)
314	U01	C/C	R	Fleeing/Elude Officer/Disregard Safety of Others (Revoked By Court)
408	F04	N/m	0	Florida Seat-Belt Law (Not A Primary Stop)
212	**	N/m	0	Fog Lamps Violation
271	M34	M/m	3	Follow Motorcade Too Close
271	M34	M/m	3	Follow Safe Distance Funeral Procession
273	M32			Following Emergency Vehicle Unlawfully
272	M33	M/m	3	Following Fire Apparatus Within 500 Feet
271	M34	M/m	3	Following Too Closely
271	M34	M/m	3	Following Too Closely With Tow/Truck

Code	ACD	Class	Pts	Description
410	N84	N/m	0	Front Amber Reflector Required
505	**	N/m	0	Golf Cart - Person Under Age 14 Operating on Public Road
405	**	M/m	3	Golf Carts - Improper Operation of on Certain Roadways - No/Improper Equipment (headlight, breaklight, turn signal and windshield)
137	**	N/m	0	Golf Carts-Improper/Defective Equipment (Brakes & Steering)
395	**	P/m	0	Green Circular Light, Pedestrian Failed to Cross Within Marked Or Unmarked Crosswalk
7	W01			Habitual Violator
552	N44	M/m	3	Hand Signals - Improper
397	F34	N/m	0	Handicap Parking - Obstructing Access to Parking Space
397	F34	N/m	0	Handicap Parking Area Illegally Parking in Space (Citation Must Be Hand Delivered to Driver)
397	F34	N/m	0	Handicap Parking in Governmental Parking Area - With No Sticker. Citation Must Be Hand Delivered to Driver)
397	F34	N/m	0	Handicap Parking in Private Parking Area - With No Sticker (Citation Must Be Hand Delivered to Driver)
448	D02	C/c	0	Having More Than One Valid Fl Driver License
137	**	N/m	0	Head Lamp Violation
410	N84	N/m	0	Headlight - (Single Beam) Farm Tractors
410	N84	N/m	0	Headlight - Farm Tractors
137	**	N/m	0	Headlight/Auxiliary/Driver/Passenger Lamp Select
137	**	N/m	0	Headlights - At Least 1 on Each Side of A Motor Vehicle, Showing A White Light Not More Than 54" Or Less Than 24"
436	E05	M/m	3	Headlights - Driving Without (Twilight to Sunrise, Smoke/Rain/Fog)
195	E54	M/m	3	Headlights - Fail to Dim
137	**	N/m	0	Headlights Required/Tinted
137	**	N/m	0	Headlights-Improper Distribution/Adjustment/Visibility
137	**	N/m	0	Headlights-Minimum Requirements For Motor Vehicles
219	M55	M/m	3	Heavy Equipment (No Stop R/R Before Crossing)
219	M55	M/m	3	Heavy Equipment Cross R/R After Warned
211	E01	N/m	0	Highway Service Vehicle Light Standard
211	E01	N/m	0	Highway Service With Improper Lamps
6	B01			Hit & Run
218	E70	N/m	0	Horn - Improper Use
212	**	N/m	0	Horn - Loud/Harsh Sound of Horn/Warning Device
137	**	N/m	0	Horn - No/Defective
399	**	N/m	0	Husbandry/Agriculture Trailer Safety Violation
137	**	N/m	0	Hydraulic Brake Force Improper Gross Weight
137	**	N/m	0	Hydraulic Brake Stop Improper Distance
137	**	N/m	0	Hydraulic Brake Stop Improper Ft Per Sec
196	U04			Illegal Activity With Motor Vehicle
825	A31			Illegal Possession Alcohol
154	A31			Illegal Possession Alcohol Or Drugs
824	A33			Illegal Possession Drugs
395	**	C/c	0	Illegally Carrying A White Or White Tipped in Red Cane/Walking Stick in A Raised/Extended Position Unless Totally/Partially Blind
402	**	C/c	0	Immoral Act Involving A Motor Vehicle
585	S96	M/m	3	Impeding Traffic
430	**	N/m	0	Improper Amount/Type/Mount Red Light
392	N82	M/m	3	Improper Backing
392	N82	M/m	3	Improper Backing on Limited Access Facility
137	**	N/m	0	Improper Brake Reservoir Safeguard
137	**	N/m	0	Improper Brake Reservoir/Air Brake
137	**	N/m	0	Improper Brake Reservoir/Vacuum Brake
332	M40	M/m	3	Improper Center Lane Use
331	M42	M/m	3	Improper Change of Lane, Pulling Out in Front of Vehicle Going in Same Direction
137	**	N/m	0	Improper Combo Brake Warning Device
430	**	N/m	0	Improper Display As A Regular Light
430	**	N/m	0	Improper Display/Use of Red Lights/Other Equipment Authorized For Use of Volunteer Firemen/Medical Staff
212	**	N/m	0	Improper Flashing Lights
137	**	N/m	0	Improper Front Lamp/Reflector Color-Improper
552	N44	M/m	3	Improper Hand Signal/Left
552	N44	M/m	3	Improper Hand Signal/Right
552	N44	M/m	3	Improper Hand Signal/Stop
430	**	N/m	0	Improper Inscription on Red Light
13	M40			Improper Lane Condition
482	**	M/m	0	Improper Left Turn By Bicycle
430	**	N/m	0	Improper Lens Dimensions
430	**	N/m	0	Improper Lens on Red Light
429	E34	N/m	0	Improper Mounting of Special Warning Lights

Code	ACD	Class	Pts	Description
219	M55	M/m	3	Improper Moving of Heavy Equipment At RR Crossing
526	M70	M/m	3	Improper overtaking and passing bicycle improper distance between(effective 10/01/06)
397	F34	N/m	0	Improper Park Safety Zone/Curb
397	F34	N/m	0	Improper Park Sale/Rent Without Permission
397	F34	N/m	0	Improper Parking (Two-Way Roadway/One-Way Roadway/Angle)
397	F34	N/m	0	Improper Parking Against Flow/Curb One-Way
397	F34	N/m	0	Improper Parking Two-Way Roadway
420	M70	M/m	3	Improper Passing (If Not Specified)
412	M73	M/m	3	Improper Passing of Vehicle Proceeding in Opposite Direction
412	M73	M/m	3	Improper Passing on Right
412	M73	M/m	3	Improper Passing on Right-Driving Off Pavement
137	**	N/m	0	Improper Reflector
391	N83	M/m	3	Improper Start of Vehicle From A Parked/Stopped/Standing Position. Do Not Use For Spinning Tires From A Start
397	F34	N/m	0	Improper Stop Bridge/Tunnel/Elevation
397	F34	N/m	0	Improper Stop Limited Access Facility
397	F34	N/m	0	Improper Stop Load Passenger Limited Access Facility
397	F34	N/m	0	Improper Stop on Bike Path
397	F34	N/m	0	Improper Stop on Crosswalk
397	F34	N/m	0	Improper Stop on R/R Track
397	F34	N/m	0	Improper Stop on Sidewalk
549	**	N/m	0	Improper stop School Bus (previously violation code 397) Effective October 1, 2009, fines for (1)(a) and (1)(b) increased by $65 and completion of traffic school is required even if adjudication is withheld for any offenses in 316.172
397	F34	N/m	0	Improper Stop Within Intersection
397	F34	N/m	0	Improper Stopping/Standing/Parking (Double) - Bridge, Tunnel. Crosswalk, Intersection, Railroad Tracks, Bicycle Bath - Where Sign Prohibits, Etc
397	F34	N/m	0	Improper Stopping/Standing/Parking (Double) Bridge, Tunnel, Crosswalk
190	D70	N/m	0	Improper Sunscreen At Top of Windshield
137	**	N/m	0	Improper Tow/No 2 Means of Emergency Brake
593	N50	M/m	3	Improper Turn - Left
593	N50	M/m	3	Improper Turn - Right
212	**	N/m	0	Improper Use Amber Lights
212	**	N/m	0	Improper Use Green and Amber Lights
430	**	N/m	0	Improper Use of Red Light By Fireman
212	**	N/m	0	Improper Use of Theft Alarm Signal Device
212	**	N/m	0	Improper Use White/Strobe Lights
211	E01	N/m	0	Improper Warning Device
137	**	N/m	0	Improper/No Air Brake Warning Device
137	**	N/m	0	Improper/No Rear Stop Lamps
137	**	N/m	0	Improper/No Single Control Brake Opening
137	**	N/m	0	Improper/No Turn Signals
137	**	N/m	0	Improper/No Vacuum Brake Warning Device
413	M77	M/m	3	Improper-Change-Of-Lane - Passing When Meeting Oncoming Vehicle
137	**	N/m	0	Inadequate Service Brakes
137	**	N/m	0	Incorrect Mount of Reflector
538	M17	M/m	3	Inoperative Traffic Light - Failed to Stop
445	A41	N*	R	Interlock Device Violation
438	**	C/c	0	Knowingly & Willfully Falsely Certifies That Air Pollution Control Equipment Has Not Been Tampered With And Is in Place And Appears Properly Connected & Undamaged
438	**	C/c	0	Knowingly & Willfully Offer/Display For Retail Sale/Lease/Transfer Title to A Motor Vehicle With Tampered Pollution Control Devices
445	A41	N*	R	Knowingly Lease/Lend A Motor Vehicle Without A Functioning, Certified Ignition Interlock Device
380	**	N/m	0	Knowingly Rent Bike to Person Under Age of 16
210	E34	N/m	0	Lamps Improper Aim/Adjustment
137	**	N/m	0	Lamps on Other Vehicles/Equipment
210	E34	N/m	0	Lamps Sell/Use Unapproved
410	N84	N/m	0	Lamps/Reflectors/Emblems on Farm/Agriculture Equipment - No/Improper
212	**	N/m	0	Lamps/Spot/Fog/Auxiliary - Violation of Intensity/Use/Number/ Color/ Installation
532	M17	M/m	3	Lane Direction Control Signals - Violation of
211	E01	N/m	0	Lantern/Reflectors None/Improper Flammable
599	D29	M/m	3	Learner Dl/Operate Invalid Hours
599	D29	M/m	3	Learner's DL Violation Restriction- Holds Valid License For Type Vehicle
599	D29	M/m	3	Learner's DL Violation Restriction- Person Accompanying Driver
599	D29	M/m	3	Learner's DL Violation Restriction- Person Less Than 21 Years of Age
599	D29	M/m	3	Learner's DL Violation Restriction- Person Not in Seat Closest to Right of Driver

Code	ACD	Class	Pts	Description
406	U04	N/m	0	Leaving Child Unattended in Vehicle
406	U04	N/C	0	Leaving Unattended Child in Vehicle - With Vehicle Running/Health of Child in Danger
427	U04	C/c	0	Leaving Unattended child in vehicle --in excess of 15 minutes
379	D02	C/c	0	Lend ID to Another
399	**	N/m	0	Length Load Extend Front
399	**	N/m	0	Length Violation
399	**	N/m	0	Length/Flag Violation
399	**	N/m	0	Length/Width Bus/Coach Violation
410	N84	N/m	0	Lights Obstructed By Load
137	**	N/m	0	Lights-Clearance/Side Marker (Bus/Truck/Truck Tractor/Trailer)
137	**	N/m	0	Lights-Clearance/Side Marker-No/Improper (Improper Color)
137	**	N/m	0	Lights-Clearance/Sidemarker (Defective/Improper Visibility)
137	**	N/m	0	Lights-Clearance/Sidemarker (Improper Mounting)
482	**	M/m	0	Limited Access Facilities, Interstate Highways; Use Restricted- Bike on Roadway/Shoulder of Interstate
380	**	M/m	0	Limited Access Facilities, Interstate Highways; Use Restricted: Animal-Drawn Vehicle - Operating Upon
335	M46	M/m	3	Limited Access Facilities, Interstate Highways; Use Restricted: Improper Entrance/Exit
337	S96	M/m	3	Limited Access Facilities, Interstate Highways; Use Restricted: Motor Driven Cycle - Operating Upon
380	**	N/m	0	Limited Access Facilities, Interstate Highways; Use Restricted: Riding Animal Upon
380	**	N/m	0	Litter Law (Only When Motor Vehicle Is Involved) Dumping on Any Public Highway/Street/Alley/Thoroughfare Including Right-Of-Ways Thereof/Public Lands. Amount Not Exceeding 15 Lbs/ 27 Cubic Ft.
353	**	N/c	0	Litter Law (UTC Required If Motor Vehicle Is Involved) Dumping on Any Public Highway/Street/Alley/Thoroughfare Including Right-Of-Ways Thereof/Public Lands. Amount Not Exceeding 15 Lbs/27 Cubic Ft. (Noncommercial)(Additional Penalties May Be Imposed)
356	**	C/c	**	Litter Law (UTC Required) - Amount Exceeding 15 Lbs/27 Cubic Ft., But Not Over 500 Lbs/100 Cubic Ft. (Noncommercial) ** 3 Points Awarded Upon A Finding of Guilty With A Motor Vehicle Involved
355	**	C/c	0	Litter Law (UTC Required) - Amount Exceeding 500 Lbs/100 Cubic Ft Or For Commercial Purposes (3rd Degree Felony)
383	**	C/c	0	Litter Law -Amount Exceeding 500 Lbs/100 CF Or For Commercial Purposes
383	**	C/c	0	Litter Law Litter on Private Land (Felony) With Motor Vehicle
383	**	C/c	0	Litter Law Litter Public Highway With Motor Vehicle (Felony)
380	**	N/m	0	Litter on Private Land (Infraction) With Motor Vehicle
356	**	C/c	3	Litter on Private Land (Misdemeanor) With Motor Vehicle
356	**	C/c	3	Litter Public Highway With Motor Vehicle (Misdemeanor)
350	**			Littering
349	**	C/c	S	Load Dropping/Shifting/Escaping Resulting in Serious Bodily Injury Or Death (Criminal)
352	**	N/m	0	Load Dropping/Shifting/Leaking/Blowing Off & Not Covered
440	E01	N/m	0	Load Not Secure By Chain/Stays/Stanchions/Etc
399	**	N/m	0	Load Oversized/Length Straight Truck
399	**	N/m	0	Load Oversized/Width
133	**	N/m	0	Loud Defective Muffler
190	D70	N/m	0	Louvered Restriction Behind Driver
405	**	M/m	3	Low Speed Vehicle - Improper Operation of on Certain Roadways - No/Improper Equipment
137	**	N/m	0	Low Speed Vehicle - No/Improper Equipment
436	E05	M/m	3	Low-Beam Headlights - Fail to Use During For/Smoke/Rain/Twilight Hours
436	E05	M/m	3	Low-Beam Headlights-Fail to Use During Fog/Smoke/Rain/ Twilight Hours
137	**	N/m	0	Lower Beam Improper Adjustment/Distribution
255	D02	C/c	0	Made False Affidavit Concerning License
253	D78	C/c	R	Making False Affidavit For A DL - Perjury
592	N53			Making Left Turn From Wrong Lane
591	N54			Making Right Turn From Wrong Lane
254	U08	C/c	R	Manslaughter-Involving The Use of A Motor Vehicle U.T.C. Must Be Written
221	**	M/m	3	Maximum Bumper Heights/None (Bumper Law)
399	**	N/m	0	Maximum Height/Length/Width For Operating Vehicle
380	**	N/m	0	Maximum Height/Length/Width Inspection - No Special Permit
399	**	N/m	0	Maximum Weights, Exceeding
211	E01	N/m	0	Migrant Farm Workers - Required Vehicle Equipment For Carrying
380	**	N/m	0	Migrant Farm Workers - Required Vehicle Equipment For Carrying
134	E37	N/m	0	Migrant Farm Workers - Vehicle With Improper Tires
211	E01	N/m	0	Migrant Farm Workers-Required Vehicle Equipment For Carrying
211	E01	N/m	0	Migrant Transport Equipment Violation
211	E01	N/m	0	Migrant Transport Improper Communication Devices
211	E01	N/m	0	Migrant Transport Improper Door/Gate
211	E01	N/m	0	Migrant Transport Improper Emergency Exit
211	E01	N/m	0	Migrant Transport Improper Exits
211	E01	N/m	0	Migrant Transport Improper Floor
211	E01	N/m	0	Migrant Transport Improper Handholds

Code	ACD	Class	Pts	Description
211	E01	N/m	0	Migrant Transport Improper Ladder/Step
211	E01	N/m	0	Migrant Transport Improper Seats
211	E01	N/m	0	Migrant Transport Improper Side/End
211	E01	N/m	0	Migrant Transport Improper Weather Cover
211	E01	N/m	0	Migrant Transport Nails Protrude
211	E01	N/m	0	Migrant Transport Use of Exhaust Heater
211	E01	N/m	0	Migrant Transport Use of Flame Heater
211	E01	N/m	0	Migrant Transport Use of Heater Not Securely Fastened
211	E01	N/m	0	Migrant Transport Use of Heater Permitting Air Contamination
211	E01	N/m	0	Migrant Transport Use of Heater With Leak
608	**	N/C	0	Misrepresent Age in Order to Obtain Tobacco Products
383	**	C/c	0	Misrepresent/Mistake One's Age/Age of Another in Order to Obtain Alcoholic Beverages (If Court Does Not Direct to Revoke/Suspend-When A UTC Is Written) (Does Not Go on Driver Record As A Conviction)
14	D02			Misrepresentation
281	D36	C/c	0	Misrepresentation of Insurance
214	F03	N/m	0	Moped - No/Improper Headgear (Helmet) on Rider/Operator (Under 16 Yrs Age)
514	N08	M/m	3	Mopeds - Fail to Yield Right of Way/Give Audible Signal Before Overtaking & Passing Pedestrian (Propelled By Human Power Only)
330	M40	M/m	3	Mopeds - Riding Too Far From Curb
137	**	N/m	0	Motor Driven Cycle-Headlamp/Multibeam Improper
137	**	N/m	0	Motor Driven Cycles Brakes
137	**	N/m	0	Motor Driven Cycles Operating Disapproved Brakes
137	**	N/m	0	Motor Driven Cycle-Types And Intensity of Headlamps
399	**	N/m	0	Motor Home Exceed 45 Feet
133	**	N/m	0	Motor Vehicle Noise (Operating With Improper Noise Limits)
137	**	N/m	0	Motorcycle - Multi-Beam Road Lighting Equipment
214	F03	N/m	0	Motorcycle - No Approved Eye Protection Device Over Operator's Eyes
214	F03	N/m	0	Motorcycle - No Headgear (Helmet)/No $10,000 Medical Benefit on Rider/Operator Over Age 21
214	F03	N/m	0	Motorcycle - No/Improper Headgear (Helmet) on Rider/Operator
332	M40	M/m	3	Motorcycle - Operating Between Lanes/Rows of Vehicles/Passing in Lane Occupied By Vehicle/Riding More Than Two Abreast in A Single Lane
189	B27	M/m	3	Motorcycle - Under 16 Years of Age Operating A Motorcycle That Has A Motor With More Than 150 Cubic Cm Displacement
137	**	N/m	0	Motorcycle Brake Force Improper to Gross Weight
137	**	N/m	0	Motorcycle Brake Stop Improper Distance
137	**	N/m	0	Motorcycle Brake Stop Improper Ft Per Sec
133	**	N/m	0	Motorcycle Exceed Noise Limit
137	**	N/m	0	Motorcycle Headlight Height Violation
436	E05	M/m	3	Motorcycle Headlights - Driving Without Being Lit
137	**	N/m	0	Motorcycle Headlights - No/Improper
590	F06	M/m	3	Motorcycle- Moped - tag improperly affixed, concealed or obscured
137	**	N/m	0	Motorcycle No/Improper Tag Light
332	M40	M/m	3	Motorcycle Operating Between Lane/Vehicle
332	M40	M/m	3	Motorcycle pass within occupied lane
137	**	N/m	0	Motorcycle Tail lamps-No/Improper
137	**	N/m	0	Motorcycle With Handlebars Higher than Shoulders
137	**	N/m	0	Motorcycle Without Footrest For Passenger
332	M40	M/m	3	Motorcycle, more than 2 abreast in a single lane
192	F06	M/m	3	Motorcycle/Moped - Carrying More Persons Than Designed/Improper Riding (Astride)/Carrying Bundle Preventing Both Hands on Handlebars
525	B43	N/m	0	Motorcycle/Moped-Person under 21, Failed to display Unique License Plate/Minor (effective 01/01/07)
218	E70	N/m	0	Motorcycle/Motor Driven Cycle - Improper Use of Horn
212	**	N/m	0	Motorcycle/Motor Driven Cycle - Improper Use of Theft Alarm Signal Device
212	**	N/m	0	Motorcycle/Motor Driven Cycle - Loud/Harsh Sound of Horn/Warning Devices
212	**	N/m	0	Motorcycle/Motor Driven Cycle - Unlawful Siren/Bell/Whistle
137	**	N/m	0	Motorcycle/Motor Driven Cycles-Brake Equipment Required.
137	**	N/m	0	Motorcycle-High Beam Light Improper/Defective
210	E34	N/m	0	Motorcycle-Lamps on Parked Cycles
137	**	N/m	0	Motorcycle-Low Beam Light Improper/Defective
192	F06	M/m	3	Motorcycle-Moped - Carrying More Persons than Designed
192	F06	M/m	3	Motorcycle-Moped-Carrying Bundle Preventing Both Hands on Handlebars
192	F06	M/m	3	Motorcycle-Moped-Improper Riding (Astride, both wheels on ground)
192	F06	M/m	3	Motorcycle-Moped-Riding Position Interference
137	**	N/m	0	Motorcycle-Multi-Beam Road Lighting Equipment
137	**	N/m	0	Motorcycle-No Footrest For Passenger/Handlebars Higher than Shoulders
137	**	N/m	0	Motorcycle-No/Improper Rear Reflector Device

Code	ACD	Class	Pts	Description
137	**	N/m	0	Motorcycle-No/Improper Stop Lamp on Cycle
330	M40	M/m	3	Motorcycles/Mopeds - Riding Too Far From Left-Hand Curb/Edge of Roadway When Making Left Turn
330	M40	M/m	3	Motorcycles/Mopeds - Riding Too Far From Right-Hand Curb/Edge of Roadway When Slower Than Normal Traffic Flow (No Turn Intended)
219	M55	M/m	3	Move Heavy Equipment Over R/R Violation
219	M55	M/m	3	Move Heavy Equipment Over R/R Without Notice
397	F34	N/m	0	Move Vehicle to Prohibited Area
129	F66	N/m	0	Mud Flaps-Required For Any Truck With Gross Weight of 26,000 Lbs Or More, Truck Tractor, Trailer, Semi-Trailer of 2,000 Lbs Or More. (Vehicles Used Exclusively For Agriculture/Horticulture/ Forestry Are Exempt)
133	**	N/m	0	Muffler/No/Improper/Unlawful Cutouts/Bypass/Device
133	**	N/m	0	Muffler-No/Improper (Cutouts, Bypass, Etc.)
249	U07	C/c	R	Murder Resulting From The Operation of A Motor Vehicle. U.T.C. Must By Written
436	E05	M/m	3	No Brake/Turn/Signal Lighted
623	B51	C/c	0	No CDL
623	B51	C/c	0	No Class D License With Proper Endorsement
817	B51	N/m	0	No Driver License - Expired CDL (30 Days Or Less)
623	B51	C/c	0	No Driver License - Never Had One Issued (If Valid At Time Citation Was Issued, A Dismissal Fee Up to $10.50 Can Be Paid, When Proof Submitted to Clerk of Court)
615	B51	C/c	0	No Driver License For The Operation of Motorcycle
399	**	N/m	0	No Escort Vehicle
211	E01	N/m	0	No Fire Extinguisher on Bus
211	E01	N/m	0	No First-Aid Kit on Bus
211	E01	N/m	0	No Flags/Emergency Reflectors
436	E05	M/m	3	No Head Lamps Rain/Fog/Smoke/Etc.
213	**			No Inspection Sticker
395	**	P/m	0	No Jump/Dive Off Public Bridge
217	**	N/m	0	No Lamp/Flag on Projecting Load
436	E05	M/m	3	No Lamps Or Illuminating Devices
471	**	C/c	0	No Motor Vehicle Registration
812	D36	N/m	0	No Proof of Insurance (CMV)
819	B51	C/c	0	No Proper Endorsement on CDL (Non-Resident)
624	B51	C/c	0	No Proper Endorsement on DL (Motorcycle, School Bus)
137	**	N/m	0	No Stop Lamp
540	M09	M/m	3	No Stop/Shift At R/R Crossing
137	**	N/m	0	No Tag Light
215	E05			No Turn Indicator
137	**	N/m	0	No Turn Signal Light
211	E01	N/m	0	No Warn Device When Disabled
211	E01	N/m	0	No Warn Lights Vehicle Disabled
399	**	N/m	0	No Warning Light
137	**	N/m	0	No/Defective Horn/Warning Devices (Motorcycle/Motor Driven Cycle)
193	**	M/m	3	No/Defective/Improper Chains While Towing
615	B51	C/c	0	No/Improper Driver License
615	B51	C/c	0	No/Improper Driver License (Driving Outside of Classification)
211	E01	N/m	0	No/Improper Rear View Mirror
551	N40	M/m	3	No/Improper Turn/Stop Signal Given
514	N08	M/m	3	No/Inoperative Traffic Light - Failed to Yield Right of Way
137	**	N/m	0	None/Improper Brakes
812	D36	N/m	0	Non-Public Sector Buses Additional Liability Insurance Coverage
471	**	C/c	0	Nonresident Tag Exemption Not Allowed. (Fl Tag Required Within 10 Days If Employed in Fl/Enters Children in Public Schools). Migrant Farm Workers/Some Students Exempt
633	N61	M/m	3	Not Driving to Right Around Rotary Traffic Island
426	**	C/c	0	Obscene Bumper Sticker/Decal/Emblem Or Other Device Attached to A Motor Vehicle (Must Relate to Obscene)
397	F34	N/m	0	Obstruct By Stopping/Standing/Parking Alongside Excavation
380	**	N/m	0	Obstruct/Digging Up Road
255	D02	C/c	S	Obtaining 2 Or More Photographic Dl's in Different Names
371	**			OOS CDL Conviction N/A Fl Statutes
370	**			OOS Conviction N/A to Fl Statues
130	E01			Op MV Improperly Equipped
178	D75			Op MV While Disabled
424	A35	M/m	3	Open Alcohol Container Law (Driver Cited)
425	A35	N/m	0	Open Alcohol Container Law (Passenger Cited)
424	A35	M/m	3	Open Container/Or Consumption of Alcohol In/On Vehicle (Driver Cited)
425	A35	M/m	3	Open Container/Or Consumption of Alcohol In/On Vehicle (Passenger Cited)
393	**	N/m	0	Opening Door Into Moving Traffic
614	D27	C/c	0	Operate Against License Restrictions

Code	ACD	Class	Pts	Description
197	**			Operate or Using MV W/O Consent Owner
812	D36	N/a	0	Operating A CMV Not Properly Insured (Disqualified From Operating A CMV)
812	D36	N/m	0	Operating A CMV Not Properly Insured (Specify CMV) *If Valid At Time Citation Was Issued, A Dismissal Fee Up to $7.50 Can Be Paid, When Proof Submitted to Clerk of Court) *Disqualified From Operating A CMV only if operator is owner or registrant of vehicle
137	**	N/m	0	Operating A Moped That Does Not Have Required Equipment
473	**	N/a	0	Operating A Motor Vehicle/Using A Mobile Home With An Expired Registration Expired 6 Months Or Less
473 or 381	**	N/a	0	Operating A Motor Vehicle/Using A Mobile Home With An Expired Registration Expired For 6 Months Or More - First Offense
474	**	C/c	0	Operating A Motor Vehicle/Using A Mobile Home With An Expired Registration Expired For 6 Months Or More - Subsequent Offense
280	B74	N/a	0	Operating A Non-CMV not properly -Proof of Insurance Required (Required By Owners/Lessee of Vehicle Only) Only Exclusions Are Taxicabs/Limousines/Motorcycles
812	D36	N/m	0	Operating CMV Not Properly Insured
613	B22	C/c	0	Operating Commercial Motor Vehicle (CMV) While DL Is Suspended/Cancelled/Revoked/Disqualified
442	**	N/m	0	Operating Diesel Powered Motor Vehicle Which Emits Visible Emissions More Than Five Continuous Seconds
133	**	N/m	0	Operating Exhaust System Noise/Abate Modify
436	E05	M/m	3	Operating Funeral Procession Vehicle Without Headlights Lit
442	**	N/m	0	Operating Gasoline Powered Motor Vehicle Which Emits Visible Emissions More Than Five Continuous Seconds
441	**	N/m	0	Operating Motor Vehicle That Has A Tampered With Air Pollution Control Device/System
129	F66	N/m	0	Operating Vehicle in Unsafe Condition/Improper Equipment (Not Corrected Within 30 Days)
613	B22	C/c	0	Operating While DL Revoked For Habitual Traffic Offender
600	B26	C/c		Operating while DL SUSPENDED/CANCELLED/REVOKED (specify reason) if no prior forcible felony (Previously 613)
613	B22	C/c	0	Operating While DL Suspended/Cancelled/Revoked 1st Conviction
613	B22	C/c	0	Operating While DL Suspended/Cancelled/Revoked 2nd Conviction
613	B22	C/c	0	Operating While DL Suspended/Cancelled/Revoked 3rd Or Subsequent Conviction
131	E34			Operating With Defective Lights
430	**	N/m	0	Operating Without Permit For Red Light
380	**	N/m	0	Operation Not Pertaining to Law - Special Permits
399	**	N/m	0	Operational/Safety Stipulation - Exceeding Vehicle Weight/Length/Width
621	**			Operator of Mot Veh Without DL Or Failed to Display A Dl
399	**	N/m	0	Over Height of Load
399	**	N/m	0	Over Height of Load
417	M77	M/m	3	Overtaking & Passing A Vehicle - Cutting In
416	N07	M/m	3	Overtaking & Passing A Vehicle - Failure to Give Right-Of-Way
412	M73	M/m	3	Overtaking on Right - Driving Off Pavement
527	E01	N/m	0	Owner/Operator Farm Labor Vehicle /Safety Standards
380	**	N/m	0	Parent/Guardian Allow Bike Violation
137	**	N/m	0	Park Brake Improper/Inadequate
397	F34	N/m	0	Park Handicapped Zone
210	E34	N/m	0	Park Lights None/Defective
210	E34	N/m	0	Park Lights Not Display Non municipality
397	F34	N/m	0	Park Prohibited R/R Crossing
397	F34	N/m	0	Park Where Prohibited By Traffic Device
397	F34	N/m	0	Parked in Signed No Park Zone
397	F34	N/m	0	Parking – Improper – Within 30' of Rural Mailbox Between 8 A.M. And 6 P.M.
210	E34	N/m	0	Parking Lamps – No/Improper on Parked Vehicles
397	F34	N/m	0	Parking Vehicle For Sale After Written Notice (Owner Must Be Present If Uniform Traffic Citation Issued)
397	F34	N/m	0	Parking Within One Block of Fire Apparatus
380	**	N/m	0	Passenger Exceed Seatbelts in Pickup
380	**	N/m	0	Passenger Obstructing Driver's View
380	**	N/m	0	Passenger Riding on Exterior of Vehicle
411	M76	M/m	3	Passing in No Passing Zone
418	M74	M/m	3	Passing on A Grade (Hill)
423	M74	M/m	3	Passing on A Grade (Hill) on A Curve
421	M70	M/m	3	Passing on A Grade (Hill) With Obstructed View Within 100' of Bridge/Viaduct/Tunnel (Specify)
422	M70	M/m	3	Passing on A Grade (Hill) Within 100' of Intersection Approach
419	M70	M/m	3	Passing on A Grade (Hill) Within 100' of R/R Crossing Approach
395	**	P/m	0	Pedestrian – Obstructing/Hindering Traffic/Highway
395	**	C/c	0	Pedestrian – Obstructing/Hindering Traffic/Highway Plus Soliciting Without Permit
514	N08	M/m	3	Pedestrian Control – Fail to Yield Right of Way to Pedestrian at intersection with traffic control device. Effective July 1, 2008
395	**	P/m	0	Pedestrian Control Signals – Pedestrian Fail to Obey
395	**	P/m	0	Pedestrian Crossed Intersection Diagonally
395	**	P/m	0	Pedestrian Enter/Remain Beyond Bridge/RR Gate

Code	ACD	Class	Pts	Description
395	**	P/m	0	Pedestrian Facing, Must Not Enter Roadway on Red Light
395	**	P/m	0	Pedestrian Fail to Obey Traffic Signal At Intersection
395	**	P/m	0	Pedestrian Fail to Walk Left Side When No Sidewalk
395	**	P/m	0	Pedestrian Failed to Cross At Right Angle/Shortest Route
395	**	P/m	0	Pedestrian Failed to Cross in Crosswalk
395	**	P/m	0	Pedestrian Failed to Move Right Half of Crosswalk
395	**	P/m	0	Pedestrian Failed to Use Sidewalk
395	**	P/m	0	Pedestrian Failed to Yield to Emergency Vehicle
395	**	P/m	0	Pedestrian Failed to Yield to Traffic
395	**	P/m	0	Pedestrian Leave Place of Safety And Enter Path of Vehicle
395	**	P/m	0	Pedestrian on Limited Access Facility
395	**	P/m	0	Pedestrian Proceed Safe Distance After R/R Signal
395	**	P/m	0	Pedestrian Proceed Safe Distance R/R Signal
395	**	P/m	0	Pedestrian Proceed Safe Distance R/R Train Visible
395	**	P/m	0	Pedestrian Stand in Road/Solicit Ride/Business
395	**	P/m	0	Pedestrian Standing On/In Proximity to Roadway to Guard/Watch Vehicle
395	**	P/m	0	Pedestrian Violation – Must Cross With Light/Walk on Provided Sidewalk/Walk on Shoulder of Road Facing Traffic If No Sidewalk. Standing in The Road to Hitch-Hike /Solicit/Jaywalking (Sidewalk Provided (Officer Must Specify Offense)
411	M76	M/m	3	Pedestrian Violation – Passing Vehicle Stopped For Pedestrian At Sidewalk
524	F02	N/m	0	Permit Passenger under 18 years to ride within open body of pickup or flatbed truck if not properly restrained
379	D02	C/c	0	Permit Unlawful Use of Id
198	F05	M/m	3	Permitting Passenger to Ride on Exterior of Vehicle
616	**	C/c	0	Permitting Unauthorized Minor (Under 18) to Drive (Must be Parent/Guardian to be cited under this statute)
247	**	C/c	S	Petit Theft ($100 to $299) [See 812.0155]
383	**	C/c	0	Petit Theft B Property Valued At $100 - $299 (If Court Does Not Direct to Suspend)
383	**	C/c	0	Petit Theft B Theft of Property Not Specified in Subsection [812.0155(2)] If Court Does Not Direct to Suspend
248	U04	C/c	S	Petit Theft of Gasoline From Retail Establishment [See 812.014(5)(B)]
383	**	C/c	0	Petit Theft With Previous Conviction (If Court Does Not Direct to Suspend)
247	**	C/c	S	Petit Theft With Previous Conviction [See 812.0155]
247	**	C/c	S	Petit Theft-Theft of Property Not Specified in Subsection (2) [See 812.0155]
211	E01	N/m	0	Place/Correct Number/Improper Flammable Device
351	**	N/c	0	Placing Injurious Substance on Road
137	**	N/m	0	Pole Trailer 1 Each Side Marker/Clear Lamp
137	**	N/m	0	Pole Trailer 2 Rear Reflectors
258	A33			Poss/Sell/Traf/Consprcy-Contrld Sub
379	D02	C/c	0	Possess False ID Card
153	**			Possess/Consume Alcohol/Drugs-Minor
383	**	C/c	0	Possession of A Controlled Substance B If Court Does Not Direct to Revoke/Suspend (When A UTC Is Written)(Does Not Go on Driver Record As A Conviction)
338	B46	C/c		Possession of a Counterfeit/Fictitious Motor Vehicle Registration
447	A31	C/c	R/S	Possession of Alcoholic Beverage By A Minor
383	**	C/c	0	Possession of Alcoholic Beverage By A Minor (Except Exempt Under F.S. 562.13)(If Court Does Not Direct to Revoke/Suspend- When A UTC Is Written)
147	A33	C/c	R	Possession of Controlled Substance – Violation of Chapter 893
372	B41	C/c	0	Possession of Driver License With Altered Date of Birth
372	B41	C/c	0	Possession of Driver License With Altered Date of Birth w/ none/altered sexual predator/offender markings
379	D02	C/c	0	Possession of Driver License/ID Card w/none/altered sexual predator/offender markings
379	D02	C/c	0	Possession of ID Card With Altered Date of Birth
424	A35	M/m	3	Possession of Open Container in Motor Vehicle (Driver Cited)
425	A35	M/m	3	Possession of Open Container in Motor Vehicle (Passenger Cited)
424	A35	M/m	3	Possession of Open Container Parked Vehicle (Driver Cited)
425	A35	M/m	3	Possession of Open Container Parked Vehicle (Passenger Cited)
607	**	N/C	0	Possession of tobacco product by a minor - Do Not write Uniform Traffic Citation for this charge. For use ONLY by courts to report suspensions through a Court Ordered Report of Disposition.
257	A33	C/c	R	Prohibited Acts/Penalties; Felony Possession of Controlled Substance While in Physical Control of A Motor Vehicle – UTC Is Mandatory As Per F.S. 316.650(10)
212	**	N/m	0	Prohibited Lights on Vehicle-Blue
212	**	N/m	0	Prohibited Lights on Vehicles – Red/Blue
212	**	N/m	0	Prohibited Lights on Vehicles – Red/Blue/Flashing
217	**	N/m	0	Projected Load Strobe Light
217	**	N/m	0	Projecting Load – Lamp/Flag Required If 4' Or More
357	**	N/m	0	Projecting Load on Passenger Type Vehicle (Any Load Beyond Line of Fender on Left Side & More Than 6" Beyond Line of Fender on Right Side
399	**	N/m	0	Projecting Load on Passenger Type Vehicle (Any Load Beyond Line of Fender on Left Side & More Than 6" Beyond Line of Fender on Right Side

Code	ACD	Class	Pts	Description
334	M58	M/m	3	Propelling A Moped Upon And Along A Sidewalk While Motor Is Operating
401	**	C/c	0	Prostitution/Lewdness – Involving Use of A Motor Vehicle
157	**	C/c		Public Drunkenness-Passenger
156	**	C/c		Public Drunkenness-Pedestrian
540	M09	M/m	3	R/R Crossing – Driving Around/Under/Through Barrier
540	M09	M/m	3	R/R Crossing – Fail to Obey Traffic Control Device At
395	**	P/m	0	R/R Crossing – Pedestrian to Obey Traffic Control Device
540	M09	M/m	3	R/R Crossing –Driving Safe Distance From R/R After Signal
540	M09	M/m	3	R/R Crossing Failed to Stop At (Only Applied to School Bus/Commercial Passenger Carriers/Flammable Or Explosive Carrying Vehicles; Except Taxi)
540	M09	M/m	3	R/R CROSSING- insufficient space to drive completely through
540	M09	M/m	3	R/R CROSSING- insufficient undercarriage clearance
540	M09	M/m	3	R/R Crossing –Vehicle Drive Safe Distance R/R Train Visible
571	S95	C/c	R	Racing on Highway – (Spinning Tires From A Start)
571	S95	C/c	R	Racing on highway - Coordinate, facilitate, and collect monies Effective 10/1/2010
571	S95	C/c	R	Racing on highway - Driving a motor vehicle
571	S95	C/c	R	Racing on highway - Knowingly ride as a passenger; Eff. 10/1/2010
571	S95	C/c	R	Racing on highway - Purposely stop or slow traffic; Eff. 10/1/2010
571	S95	C/c	R	Racing on Highway (Any Manner of Participation) (Effective October 1, 2002)
571	S95	C/c	R	Racing on Highway (Any Manner of Participation) [See 316.191(2)(A)]
588	S95	M/m	3	Racing on Highway Spectator
537	M17	M/m	3	Ran A Stop Sign
137	**	N/m	0	Rear Lamp/Reflector Color Improper
137	**	N/m	0	Rear Light/Reflector Color Improper
190	D70	N/m	0	Rear Window Nontransparent
137	**	N/m	0	Rearview Mirror – No/Improper
137	**	N/m	0	Rearview Mirror/No/Improper (Motorcycle/Motor Driven Cycle)
431	M84	C/c	4	Reckless Driving
457	M84	C/c	4	Reckless Driving - When Reduced From Dui
431	M84	C/c	4	Reckless Driving-Property Damage/Personal Injury
550	U03	C/c	R	Reckless Driving-Serious Bodily Injury [See 322.26(3)](previously violation 252)
211	E01	N/m	0	Red Fuse/Lantern/Reflectors Improper Amount
547	M16	M/m	0	Red Light Camera - Fail to stop at STEADY RED light for procedures see 316.0083 (Effective 7/1/2010)
547	M16	M/m	0	Red Light Camera Violations Only - Fail to obey traffic control device for procedures see 316.0083 (Effective 7/1/2010)
430	**	N/m	0	Red Light to Bright
137	**	N/m	0	Reflector Visibility Improper
410	N84	N/m	0	Reflector/Tape Fail Show Width
646	A12	C/c	R	Refusal to Submit to Bal Test
453	**	C/c	0	Refusal to Surrender License Plate/Dl/Registration Certificate
173	A12			Refuse Sub Breath/Urine/Blood Test
531	M08	C/c	0	Refused Obedience to Police/Fire Officers
811	A12			Refused Test to Determine Alcoholic Content – CMV
403	**	M/m	3	Refused to Obey Traffic Laws
10	**			Registration And Titling Condition
137	**	N/m	0	Registration Plate (Tag) Light-White Light Illumination From A Distance of 50'
383	**	C/c	0	Renting Motor Vehicle to Unlicensed Driver
15	W01			Repeated Violation Conditions
445	A41	N*	R	Requested/Solicited A Person to Blow Into An Ignition Interlock Device
211	E01	N/m	0	Required Equipment For School Buses & Physical Certificate For Driver
8	**			Required Reports Or Appearances
388	U04	N/m	0	Riding in House Trailer
211	E01	N/m	0	Safety Glass Required on Bus
535	M12	M/m	3	Safety Zone – Driving Through Or Within
380	**	N/m	0	Sale/Install Unlawful Sun Screen
414	M75	M/C	4	School Bus – Passing on Enter/Exit Side While Bus Is Stopped
415	M75	M/m	4	School Bus – Passing While Stopped (School Election to Have Adjudication Withheld)
540	M09	M/m	3	School Bus Fail Stop R/R Crossing
211	E01	N/m	0	School Bus Violation-Not Enough Seats
407	F04	N/m	0	Seat-Belt Law – Driver Not Belted – to Be Cited
409	F04	N/m	0	Seat-Belt Law – Front Seat Passenger Over 18 Yrs Not Belted B Passenger to Be Cited
408	F04	N/m	0	Seat-Belt Law – Front Seat Passengers Under 18 Yrs Not Belted Or in A Device- The Driver to Be Cited
380	**	N/m	0	Sell Bike Without ID Number
380	**	N/m	0	Sell Equipment Without Trade Mark
137	**	N/m	0	Semi/Trailer 2 Front Clearance Lamps (One on Each Side)
137	**	N/m	0	Semi/Trailer 2 Rear Clear/Reflectors And 1 Stop Lamp

Code	ACD	Class	Pts	Description
137	**	N/m	0	Semi/Trailer 2 Side Marker Lamps
137	**	N/m	0	Semi/Trailer 2 Side Reflectors
399	**	N/m	0	Semitrailer Length Specific Equipment
399	**	N/m	0	Semitrailer Length Violation
212	**	N/m	0	Side Fender Lamps Improper
137	**	N/m	0	Side Marker Visibility Improper
190	D70	N/m	0	Side Windows – Restriction on Sunscreen Material
334	M58	M/m	3	Sidewalk/Bicycle Path – Driving On
551	N40	M/m	3	Signal Improperly Used
137	**	N/m	0	Signal Lights Or Device (Stop/Turn Signal) No/Improper
211	E01	N/m	0	Signs on Slow Moving Vehicles – No/Improper
410	N84	N/m	0	Single Beam Improper Aim Tractor/Vehicle
410	N84	N/m	0	Single Beam Improper Intensity Tractor/Vehicle
212	**	N/m	0	Siren/Bell/Whistle – Unlawful Use/Equipment
212	**	N/m	0	Siren/Bell/Whistle – Unlawful Use/Equipment
410	N84	N/m	0	Slow Move Emblem Not State Approved
443	**	N/m	0	Sound Louder Than Necessary/Vehicle
443	**	N/m	0	Sound Making Device Violation
437	M82	M/m	3	Speed – Failed to Use Due Care
581	S93	M/m	3	Speed – Florida Turnpike As Posted
582	S93			Speed – Interstate – Radar/Time
581	S93	M/m	3	Speed – Interstate System in Area of 65 Mph Limit
573	S93	M/m	3	Speed – No Speeds Are Indicated on Citation
577	S93	M/m	3	Speed – Posted on County Roads
577	S93	M/m	3	Speed – Posted State Road Or Intersection
577	S93	M/m	3	Speed – Posted Within Any Municipality
578	S93			Speed – Posted Zone – Radar/Time
577	S93	M/m	3	Speed – School Zone
573	S93	M/m	3	Speed - School Zone(no speeds indicated)
580	S94	M/m	3	Speed - Special Hazard - Too Fast For Conditions
820	S15	C/c	R	Speed 16 Or More Mph Over Limit
573	S93	M/m	3	Speed B Unlawful Speed (If No Speeds Are Indicated on Citation)
575	S93	M/m	3	Speed B Unlawful Speed (Requires Speed)
584	S93			Speed on 4 Lane Hwy - 20 Med Radar/Time
575	S93	M/m	3	Speed Posted Municipality/County Road (Requires Speed)
572	S94	M/m	3	Speed Too Fast For Conditions Approaching Hill
572	S94	M/m	3	Speed Too Fast For Conditions Narrow/Winding Road
572	S94	M/m	3	Speed Too Fast For Conditions on Curve
572	S94	M/m	3	Speed Too Fast For Conditions R/R Intersection
572	S94	M/m	3	Speed Too Fast For Conditions Special Hazard
573	S93	M/m	3	Speed/65 Highway/Turnpike (If No Speeds Are Indicated on Citation)
575	S93	M/m	3	Speed/65 Highway/Turnpike (Requires Speed)
573	S93	M/m	3	Speed/70 Interstate (If No Speeds Are Indicated on Citation)
575	S93	M/m	3	Speed/70 Interstate (Requires Speed)
573	S93	M/m	3	Speed/Roadways (If No Speeds Are Indicated on Citation)
575	S93	M/m	3	Speed/Roadways (Requires Speed)
589	S41	M/c	4	Speeding > 50 MPH
815	S93			Speeding 15 Or More Mph Over Limit - CMV
573	S93	M/m	3	Speeding State Posted (If No Speeds Are Indicated on Citation)
575	S93	M/m	3	Speeding State Posted (Requires Speed)
573	S93	M/m	3	Speedposted County Road Non-Business/Residential (If No Speeds Are Indicated on Citation)
575	S93	M/m	3	Speedposted County Road Non-Business/Residential (Requires Speed)
573	S93	M/m	3	Speedposted County Road Residential/Business (If No Speeds Are Indicated on Citation)
575	S93	M/m	3	Speedposted County Road Residential/Business (Requires Speed)
573	S93	M/m	3	Speedposted Municipality/County Road (If No Speeds Are Indicated on Citation)
129	F66	N/m	0	Splash/Spray Suppressant Device (Mud Flaps)
212	**	N/m	0	Spot Lamp(S) Improperly Aimed
397	F34	N/m	0	Stand Where Traffic Device Prohibits
397	F34	N/m	0	Stand/Park Prohibited Bike Lane
397	F34	N/m	0	Stand/Park Prohibited Crosswalk At Intersection
397	F34	N/m	0	Stand/Park Prohibited Driveway
397	F34	N/m	0	Stand/Park Prohibited Fire Hydrant
397	F34	N/m	0	Stand/Park Prohibited Fire Station Driveway
397	F34	N/m	0	Stand/Park Prohibited Stop/Signal
211	E01	N/m	0	Standards For Lights on Maintenance Equipment
546	N24	M/m	3	Steady RED light, one way street, vehicle facing, fail to yield right-of-way to other traffic when making left turn

Code	ACD	Class	Pts	Description
				(previously violation code 516 - Effective 10/1/2009)
548	N08	M/m	3	Steady RED light, one way street, vehicle facing, fail to yield right-of-way to pedestrian when making left turn (previously violation code 514 - Effective 10/1/2009)
548	N08	M/m	3	Steady RED light, vehicle facing, fail to yield right of way to pedestrian while making right turn (previously violation code 514 - Effective 10/1/2009)
546	N24	M/m	3	Steady RED light, vehicle facing, failed to yield right-of-way while turning (previously violation code 516 - Eff.10/1/2009)
546	N24	M/m	3	Steady RED light, vehicle facing, failed to yield right-of-way to other traffic while making right turn (previously violation code 516 - Effective 10/1/2009)
395	**	P/m	0	Steady Yellow Traffic Light - pedestrian facing must not start to cross roadway
137	**	N/m	0	Stop Lights/Turn Signals-No Improper
551	N40	M/m	3	Stop Or Sudden Decrease in Speed Without Signal
398	F34	M/m	3	Stopping/Standing/Parking on Highway Outside of Municipalities
383	**	C/c	0	Submit False Affidavit Regarding Toll
190	D70	N/m	0	Sunscreen Violation
190	D70	N/m	0	Sunscreening - Illegal Operation With
405	**	M/m	0	Swamp Buggy - Improper Operation on Public Roadway
472	**	N/m	0	Tag - None/Obscured/Defaced/Improper Display
471	**	C/c	0	Tag - Unlawful Alteration
601	**		3	TAG - unlawful alteration - effective October 1, 2010 Note: Reclassified from Criminal to Non-Criminal (previously violation code 471 was applied)
601		M/m	3	Tag/Vehicle Registration - Unlawful Alteration-effective 10/01/2010 (Includes Temporary Tags)
137	**	N/m	0	Tail Lights None/Improper
137	**	N/m	0	Taillights - No/Improper - 2 Red Lights Required Except on Vehicles Made Prior to 01/72 With 1 Light
445	A41	N*	R	Tampered With/Circumvented Operation of Court Ordered Ignition Interlock Device
399	**	N/m	0	Tandem Trailer City/County Violation
399	**	N/m	0	Tandem Trailer Improper Length
399	**	N/m	0	Tandem Trailer Terminal Violation
212	**	N/m	0	Television in View of Driver
212	**	N/m	0	Television in View of Driver
471	**	C/c	0	Temporary Tag - Any Unlawful Use of -Knowingly
602	**	M/m	0	TEMPORARY TAG - must be displayed in the license plate bracket on the exterior of the vehicle. (effective 10/1/2010) Changed to Non-Criminal (violation code 471 was previously applied)
602	**	M/m	0	TEMPORARY TAG - Unlawful use of (effective 10/1/2010) Changed to Non-Criminal (violation code 471 was previously applied)
470	**	N/m	0	Temporary Tag –Expired 7 Days Or Less
251	**	C/c	R	Theft - Motor Vehicle Parts [See 322.274]
212	**	N/m	0	Theft Alarm Signal Device - Improper Use
247	**	C/c	S	Theft Any Violation Given As F.S. 812.015
251	**	C/c	R	Theft of A Motor Vehicle)[See 322.274]
380	**	N/m	0	Throwing Advertising Material in Vehicle
446	D06	C/c	R/S	To Misrepresent/Misstate One's Age/Age of Another in Order to Obtain Alcoholic Beverages
390	**	M/m	3	Toll - Failed to Pay
572	S94	M/m	3	Too Fast For Conditions
399	**	N/m	0	Tour Train Restriction Violation
399	**	N/m	0	Tow Non-Conforming Vehicle
399	**	N/m	0	Tow Tractor/Trailer Improper
399	**	N/m	0	Tow Without Special Weight Permit
193	**	M/m	3	Towing Requirements-No Improper Safety Chains, Cables Or Other Safety Devices
389	**			Towing Vehicle on Expressway
137	**	N/m	0	Tractor Brakes Improper
336	M40	M/m	3	Traffic Control Device - Cutting Across to Avoid
516	N01	M/m	3	Traffic Control Device - Erected Other Than At Intersection, Vehicle Facing, Fail to Obey in Entirety
532	M17	M/m	3	Traffic Control Device - Fail to Obey traffic control device (sign)
532	M17	M/m	3	Traffic Control Device - Green Arrow, Vehicle Facing, proceeded straight through, failed to yield right-of-way while turning
395	**	P/m	0	Traffic Control Device - Green Circular Light, Pedestrian Facing Failed to Obey in Entirety
532	M17	M/m	3	Traffic Control Device - Green Circular Light, Vehicle Facing, Failed to yield right-of-way while turning
395	**	P/m	0	Traffic Control Device - Pedestrian Facing, Must Not Enter Roadway on Red Light
516	N01	M/m	3	Traffic Control Device - Steady Red Light, Vehicle Facing, Failed to Obey in Entirety
395	**	P/m	0	Traffic Control Device - Steady Yellow Traffic Light. Pedestrian Facing, Must Not Start to Cross Roadway
536	**	N/m	0	Traffic Control Device/Railroad Signs/Signals - Alter/Deface/Remove/Etc
536	**	N/m	0	Traffic Device - Unlawful Display/Obscuring
137	**	N/m	0	Trailer 2 Rearside Reflectors And 1 Stop Light
137	**	N/m	0	Trailer Air Reservoirs Improper
137	**	N/m	0	Truck Tractor 1 Rear Stop Light

Code	ACD	Class	Pts	Description
137	**	N/m	0	Truck Tractor 2 Side Front Clearance Lamps (One on Each Side)
593	N50	M/m	3	Turn - Improper on Hill/Curve
137	**	N/m	0	Turn Signals-Vehicle Not Equipped With
551	N40	M/m	3	Turned Without/Improper Signal
399	**	N/m	0	Turnpike Width/Height/Length Violation
210	E34	N/m	0	Unapproved Lamps/Equipment - Selling/Using
191	**	N/m	0	Unattended Vehicle Left Running/Keys in Ignition/Wheels Not Turned to Curb
381	**			Unauthorized Fishing From Bridge
380	**	N/m	0	Under 16/Rent A Motorcycle Or Moped
380	**	N/m	0	Under Age of 16 Not Wearing Bicycle Helmet on Electric Personal Assistive Mobility Device
831	A61			Underage Admin Per Se/.02 or > BAC
439	**	N/m	0	Unknowingly & Unwillfully Falsely Certifies That Air Pollution Control Equipment Has Not Been Tampered With And Is in Place & Appears Properly Connected & Undamaged
439	**	N/m	0	Unknowingly & Unwillfully Offer/Display For Retail Sale/Lease/Transfer Title to A Motor Vehicle With Tampered Pollution Control Devices
609	B20	M/m	3	Unknowingly Operating Vehicle While DL Suspended-Canceled-Revoked {Used For Fail to Pay Or Financial Responsibility Per 322,34(2)}
821	U04			Unlawful Conveyance of Fuel in a CMV
252		C/c	R	Unlawful Conveyance of Fuel in a Non-CMV (using a motor vehicle in connection with a felony)
430	**	N/m	0	Unlawful Display Red Flash Light
536	**	N/m	0	Unlawful Display/Obscuring Traffic Device
443	**	N/m	0	Unlawful Operation of Radios/Sound-Making Devices Or Instruments (If Plainly Audible At A Distance of 25 Ft Or More, Or Plainly Audible to Persons Outside of The Vehicle When in Areas Adjoining Churches, School, Hospitals)
536	**	N/m	0	Unlawful Placement of Traffic Device Bearing Commercial Advertising
542	M01	M/m	4	Unlawful Possess/Use of traffic signal Pre-Emption device
383	**	C/c	0	Unlawful Possession of A Firearm By A Minor Under 18 Years of Age (If Court Does Not Direct to Revoke-When A UTC Is Written) (Does Not Go on Driver Record As A Conviction)
212	**	N/m	0	Unlawful Siren/Bell/Whistle
212	**	N/m	0	Unlawful Siren/Bell/Whistle
583	S93	M/m	3	Unlawful Speed - 4 Lane With 20' Median/Outside of Business/Residential District
586	S93	M/m	3	Unlawful Speed - Exceeding Posted Speed in A School Zone
586	S93	M/m	3	Unlawful Speed - Exceeding Posted Speed in A Work-Zone
587	M82	M/m	3	Unlawful Speed - Failed to Use Due Care
581	S93	M/m	3	Unlawful Speed - Interstate
574	S96	M/m	3	Unlawful Speed - Less That Posted Minimum
576	S93			Unlawful Speed - Radar/Time
572	S94	M/m	3	Unlawful Speed - Too Fast For Conditions (Intersection/Rr/Curve/Hill/Narrow Or Winding Road/Respect to Pedestrians, Weather Or Highway Conditions
572	S94	M/m	3	Unlawful Speed - Too Fast For Conditions (Streets/Roadways)
573	S93	M/m	3	Unlawful Speed (If No Speeds Are Indicated on Citation)
575	S93	M/m	3	Unlawful Speed (Requires Speed)
573	S93	M/m	3	Unlawful Speed/County Roads (If No Speeds Are Indicated on Citation)
575	S93	M/m	3	Unlawful Speed/County Roads (Requires Speed)
573	S93	M/m	3	Unlawful Speed; Interstate (If No Speeds Are Indicated on Citation)
575	S93	M/m	3	Unlawful Speed; Interstate (Requires Speed)
602		M/m	3	Unlawful Use of Temporary Tag(effective as of 10/01/2010)
471	**	C/c	0	Unlawful Use of Temporary Tag-Note prior to 10/01/2010
430	**	N/m	0	Unlawful Use Red Light By Medical
445	A41	N*	R	Unlawfully Blowing Into An Ignition Interlock Device Or Starting A Vehicle So Equipped
137	**	N/m	0	Upper Beam Improper Adjustment/Distribution
808	A50	C/c	D	Use of CMV in The Commission of Any Felony Involving The Manufacturing, Distributing, Or Dispensing of Controlled Substance (Disqualified From Driving CMV)
220	**	M/m	3	Using Airless Tires
212	**	N/m	0	Using Unapproved Warning Lights
380	**	N/m	0	Using Unapproved Warning Lights
405	**	M/m	3	Utility Vehicles-Homeowner's Association-Improper Operation on Certain Roadways
462	**	N/m	0	Utility Vehicles-Homeowner's Association-Improper Operation on Certain Roadways(under age 14)
461		M/m	3	Utility Vehicles-Homeowner's Association-No/Improper Equipment
593	N50	M/m	3	U-Turn - Improper/Unsafe/Prohibited
332	M40	M/m	3	Vehicle Deprive Motorcycle of Lane
540	M09	M/m	3	Vehicle Drive Safe/Proper Distance R/R Crossing
212	**	N/m	0	Vehicle Equipped With Open Toilet
133	**	N/m	0	Vehicle Exceed Noise Limit
436	E05	M/m	3	Vehicle Without Lights At Night
250	U07	C/c	R	Vehicular Homicide [See 322.28(4)]

Code	ACD	Class	Pts	Description
160	**	C/c	R	Vio 790.22(3) Unlawful Possession of A Firearm
161	**	C/c	R	Vio 790.22(9) Committing Offense/Use/Possession of A Firearm - under the age of 18 years old.
399	**	N/m	0	Violation Auto Tow Away/Driveway Restriction
573	S93	M/m	3	Violation Municipal Speed/Posted (If No Speeds Are Indicated on Citation)
575	S93	M/m	3	Violation Municipal Speed/Posted (Requires Speed)
610	D29	M/m	3	Violation of DL Restriction For Age 17 Operating Vehicle After Curfew (1 Am - 5 Am)
610	D29	M/m	3	Violation of DL Restriction For Minors Under 17 Operating Vehicle After Curfew (11 P.M. - 6 A.M.)
12	E50			Violation of Equipment Regulations
615	B51	C/c	0	Violation of Nonresident Requirements For A Dl
399	**	N/m	0	Violation of Operational/Safety Stipulation in Special Permit
823	B27			Violation of OSS Order
826	B19			Violation of OSS Order in Veh Req P/H
599	D29	M/m	3	Violation of Restriction For Learner's Driver License
516	N01	M/m	3	Violation of Right-Of-Way While Doing Improper Passing of Vehicle Proceeding in Opposite Direction
162	**	C/c	S	Violation of S 806.13 - Criminal Mischief
399	**	N/m	0	Violation Refuse Collection/Transportation Restriction
813	U31			Violation Resulting in A Fatality
5	U08			Violation Resulting in One's Own Death
814	**			Violation Resulting in Personal Injury
211	E01	N/m	0	Violation School Bus Safety Equipment
387	**	N/m	0	Wearing Headsets (Covering Both Ears)
193	**	M/m	3	Weight Violation Tow/Bridge/Culvert
212	**	N/m	0	Wheels - Rough Surfaced
383	**	C/c	0	Willful Refusal to Accept/Sign A Citation For A Traffic Violation
190	D70	N/m	0	Windows Behind The Driver-Restrictions on Sunscreen Material
190	D70	N/m	0	Windows Behind The Driver-Restrictions on Sunscreen Material
380	**	N/m	0	Windscreen Required on Grove Equipment
137	**	N/m	0	Windshield Wipers - Faulty
137	**	N/m	0	Windshield Wipers - None
137	**	N/m	0	Windshields - Not Equipped Or Upright
190	D70	N/m	0	Windshields-Sign/Covering/Sunscreen Material On
632	N72	M/m	3	Wrong Side of Roadway - Driving on
511	N04	M/m	3	Yield Right-Of-Way to Funeral - Driving Between Moving Funeral Vehicles
511	N04	M/m	3	Yield Right-Of-Way To Funeral - failure to

Point System Summary

Points range from three to six. Twelve or more points in a twelve-month period will result in a suspension. An FL licensed driver can elect to go to traffic school to avoid points on a ticket 5 times in a lifetime. A driver can elect to attend driver improvement only one time in a twelve (12) month period. A CDL holder is not eligible to attend traffic school to avoid points being placed on their record.

Speeding
    15 MPH or less over the limit .... 3 points
    Speed in excess of 15 MPH over the limit .... 4 points
    Unlawful speed resulting in an accident .... 6 points
Any moving violation resulting in a crash .... 4 points
Child restraint violation .... 3 points
Driving during restricted hours .... 3 points
Failing to stop at a traffic signal .... 4 points
Improper lane change .... 3 points
Leaving the scene of an accident resulting in property damage of more than $50 .... 6 points
Open container as an operator .... 3 points
Passing a stopped school bus .... 4 points
Reckless Driving .... 4 points
Violation of a traffic control signal/sign/device .... 4 points
Violation of curfew .... 3 points
All other moving violations .... 3 points

Georgia

Administration	Important Telephone and Web Contacts

Alan Watson, Director
Department of Driver Services
2206 East View Parkway, PO Box 80447
Conyers, GA 30013
678-413-8400
www.dds.ga.gov (driver)
 	
Vicki Lambert, Director
Department of Revenue, Motor Vehicle Division
PO Box 740381
Atlanta, GA 30374-0381
404-968-3690
http://motor.etax.dor.ga.gov/motor/MVDOnline.aspx (vehicle)
	All Driver License Related Questions are Directed to
	       678-413-8400/8500/8600
	License Status Check 404-657-9300
	Vehicle Information 404-968-3800
	Tag and Title 555-406-5221
	Commercial Vehicle Registration 404-968-3850
	State Commissioner of Insurance......................404-656-2056
	Georgia State Patrol, North Adjutant 404-624-7451
	       South Adjutant.................404-624-7718
	
	General Email Vehicle motorvehicleinquiry@dor.ga.gov
	
	Rules and Regulations www.dds.ga.gov/rules/index.aspx

Driver's License Format, Issuance and Renewal

License Classes, Restrictions and Endorsements Appear After the Driving Record Content Section

License Format

The current format is nine numbers or Social Security Number (SSN), but SSNs are being phased out. There is no code or sequential arrangement that determines the characters making the license number.

Document Appearance

Georgia began issuance of the current DL and ID card in November 2009. All previously issued Georgia licenses and IDs will remain valid until the expiration date when they will be exchanged for the newly-designed card. Both versions, which have digital imaging, a hologram, and a barcode on the back, are described below.

Current Documents

Security Characteristics: Security features include ghost photos, a laser-engraved signature over the primary photo to minimize alterations and a tamper resistant coating placed over the card. The cards feature machine-readable barcodes that can be used by banks, retailers and other businesses to verify the information printed on the front. The State Seal over the front of the card responds to ultra-violet light.

Position of Photo: Left edge, with a double ghost photo in lower right corner.

Minor Age Driver Locator: This vertical card has photo on middle left edge and a double ghost image photo on lower right corner. The words "Under 21" is printed in read to the right of the photo. The DL and ID cards do NOT specifically show the date when a teen under 21 reaches age 21.

CDL Indicator: The new Commercial DLs and permits are labeled with the word "Commercial" and are printed in a distinctive blue text.

Older Documents

Issued November 2006, these driver's licenses show "Issue Date" instead of "Exam Date" on the face of the license.

Security Characteristics: Barcode on back. Hologram in laminate "Georgia" on new cards. Small state seal on top to left of photo next to governor's signature. "Georgia" appears upper left corner.

Position of Photo: Right side, governor's signature is on top.

Minor Age Driver Locator: "UNDER 21" appears vertically on the left edge of photo, in brown.

CDL Indicator: CDLs have the word Georgia in yellow, while non-CDL is in green. "Commercial Driver's License" is stated on top of the license in yellow.

Issuance

Location of Requirements for Proof of Identity:
www.dds.ga.gov/secureid/index.aspx.

Age Requirements

The minimum age is eighteen for Class C; sixteen for Class D; fifteen for a Learner's License (Class CP). All teenagers wishing to obtain a Class D license when turning 16 must have a completed driver's education course from a DDS approved provider and have completed a cumulative total of at least forty (40) hours of other supervised driving experience, including at least six (6) hours at night. Otherwise the Class D license then cannot be obtained until age 17.

Residency

New residents must obtain license within thirty days

Renewal

Birth date of fifth or eighth year. An ID can be tenth year. Driver keeps the same number when renewing unless SSN, then driver must change to the computer-generated number. If there is no address change, non-CDL licenses may be renewed online at www.dds.ga.gov/ if a Customer Account is first established. Military personnel may renew by mail.

Elderly-Related Restrictions

The Dept. of Driver Services is required by Georgia law to administer a vision test to customers age 64 or older prior to renewing or issuing a Georgia driver's license. Because the vision test can only be taken in person at a Customer Service Center, customers age 64 or older are not eligible for auto-renewal services.

Vehicle Insurance, Title and Registration Facts

Registration & Renewal

There are three (3) different types of registration systems in Georgia: year-round registration (in the majority of counties); four-month staggered registration (Talbot county); and a four-month non-staggered registration system. The registration period depends upon what county the primary owner resides. Tag renewals are available at https://mvd.dor.ga.gov/tags/index.aspx. A "RIN" (registration ID) is needed and the address must be correct.

New Residents

Non-resident visitors may stay in Georgia on a reciprocal basis for ninety days. New residents must register their vehicle within thirty days.

Inspections and Emissions Testing

There are no statewide laws governing either safety inspections or emission testing. However, thirteen counties in the Metro Atlanta area do require an annual emissions test: Cherokee, Clayton, Cobb, Coweta, DeKalb, Douglas, Fayette, Forsyth, Fulton, Gwinnett, Henry, Paulding, and Rockdale. The three most recent model years are exempt each year.

Passenger Plate Facts

There is one plate, one decal for the year. County codes are not necessary as county of issue appears on the plate for typical plate patterns. However, certain license plates do not have county designation per legislative statute. When a vehicle is sold the plate remains with the owner.

Insurance and Financial Responsibility

Georgia has compulsory-insurance laws. Failure to comply with compulsory-insurance laws may result in vehicle registration (not driver license) suspension. Minimum financial responsibility limits are $35,000/50,000/25,000. Proof of insurance must be carried in the vehicle or proof must reside in the Dept. of Revenue database. SR-22 forms are used.

Withdrawal Sanctions, and Alcohol and Drug Testing

Alcohol and Chemical Testing

The prohibitive alcohol level is .08% or excess of .05%, .04% for CDL, and .02 % if under 21 years. Legal testing means include blood, urine, and breathe testing.

Suspensions and Revocations

Although suspensions and revocations are designated for specific time periods, many convictions require that the license physically be held for the specified period before the licensee is eligible to reinstate. Also, the state is in compliance with the federally mandated disqualifications on CDLs. See the Appendix for details.

Suspensions

Administrative License Suspension (40-5-67.1)... One to five years.

Failure to Appear .... Indefinite.

Implied Consent (CDL or regular DL) .... One year.

Safety Responsibility .... Until requirements of 40-9-33, 5, and 61 are complied with.

Also, a driver's license will be suspended if convicted of possession, distribution, manufacture, cultivation, sale or transfer of a controlled substance or marijuana.

Suspensions (First Conviction in Five Years)

DUI, Under 21 if Alcohol Level less than .08% ... Six months.

DUI, Under 21 if Alcohol Level .08% or More .... Twelve months.

Driving Without Insurance .... 60 to 90 day suspension.

Driving While Suspended or Revoked .... Six months, beginning at conviction date.

Driving Under Influence (1st Offense) .... Minimum 120 days from disposition date.

Eluding a Police Officer (1st Offense) .... Minimum 120 days from date of conviction.

Fraudulent or fictitious use of, or application for a license ... Varies.

Homicide by Vehicle (1st Offense) .... Three years from date of conviction.

Homicide by Vehicle (2nd degree) .... Minimum 120 days from date of conviction.

Leaving Scene of Accident; Hit-and-Run;
    Failure to Stop and Give Aid .... Minimum 120 days from date of conviction.

No Proof of Insurance.. Sixty days from date of conviction.

Racing (1st Offense)... Minimum 120 days from date of conviction.

Serious Injury by Vehicle .... Three years from date of conviction.

Suspensions (Second Conviction in Five Years)

Driving Under Influence .... Not eligible for permit for twelve months, reinstatement for eighteen months; Installation of ignition interlock device then required and completion of alcohol/drug risk clinical treatment; All license plates registered in driver's name must be surrendered to the court.

Homicide by Vehicle (second degree) .... Three years from conviction date.

No Proof of Insurance.. Ninety days.

Point Accumulation

First Fifteen Points in Twenty-four Months.......... One year with early return option.

Second Fifteen Points in Twenty-four Months ..... Three years with early return option.

Third Fifteen Points in Twenty-four Months .... Two years from SD; no permits or early reinstatement options.

Revocations

Habitual Violator .... Any third conviction of a mandatory offense within five years is a five-year revocation from surrender date.

Medical Revocation .... Indefinite from surrender date.

Under 21, If Four Point Offense .... Six months first offense; one year second or subsequent offense;

Under 21 DUI... .02-.07 alcohol level, six month suspension; .08 or higher, one year suspension.

Under 18, If Four Points Accumulated in
    Twelve Months .... Six months first offense; one-year second or subsequent; if .02-.07 alcohol level, six-month revocation; if .08 or higher one-year suspension.

Additional Mandatory Suspensions for Drivers Under 21
- Any offense for which four or more points are assessable
- Aggressive driving
- Exceeding the speed limit by 24 mph or more
- Hit and run
- Improper passing on a hill or a curve
- Leaving the scene of an accident
- Misrepresenting age for purpose of illegally obtaining any alcoholic beverage
- Misrepresenting identity or using false identification for purpose of purchasing or obtaining any alcoholic beverage
- Purchasing an alcoholic beverage
- Racing on highways or streets
- Reckless driving
- Unlawful passing of a school bus
- Using a motor vehicle in fleeing or attempting to elude an officer

Note: All "Under 21" revocations require that the license be held by the agency for the specified revocation period before the licensee will be eligible for reinstatement.

Other Mandatory Revocations Include:
- Any third conviction of a suspendable offense within 5 years.
- Refusal to submit a reexamination of driving skill or knowledge of driving rules after receiving notice giving reasonable grounds for such a request.
- Sufficient evidence of incompetence or unfitness to drive, due to incapability by reason of disease, mental or physical disability, or by alcohol or drug addiction.

About the Super Speeder Program
If DDS receives notification of a conviction of speeding 75 mph on a two-lane road or highway, or 85 mph on any road or highway, the customer will be notified by first class mail of the $200 Super Speeder fee, and will have 120 days from the date of the notice to pay the fee to DDS.   Failure to pay the Super Speeder fee to DDS within 120 days will result in the suspension of the customer's license, permit, or driving privilege in Georgia.

Reinstatement Requirements

Suspension   Any mandatory suspension is $200 fee by mail, $210 fee in-person; approved DUI or defensive driving course certificate. If for Insurance, then $50 fee by mail, $60 fee in person; proof of insurance required. If Super Speeder suspension, there is an additional $50 fee.

Revocation   HV is $200 fee by mail, $210 fee in-person; time lapse and possible DUI course certificate.

Record Access: Laws, Rules, and Forms

Note: This Section Covers Both Driver and Vehicle Records.

Governing Statutes and Rules

Rules & Regulation: www.dds.ga.gov/rules/index.aspx
Statutes: www.lexisnexis.com/hottopics/gacode/Default.asp

Driving Records

The Georgia law regulating the release of driver records, OCGA 40-5-2, severely restricts access and calls for a number of requirements for ongoing users and vendors. The operating records and personal information on each driver are excluded from the Georgia Open Records Law. The statute specifies which specific users are entitled to records including: CDL employers; insurance companies or insurance support organization; rental car companies; certain public employment such as law enforcement, bus drivers, and fire fighters; special businesses, pursuant to a contract, who can verify accuracy of personal information submitted to a business; governmental agencies; and organ procurement companies.

The law is summarized as follows: The department shall furnish a driver's operating record or personal information from a driver's record under the following circumstances:

(A)   With the written instructions and consent of the driver upon whom the operating record has been made and compiled;

(B)   (i) Pursuant to a written request or a request made in accordance with a contract with the Georgia Technology Authority for immediate on-line electronic furnishing of information, for use by any insurer or insurance support organization, or by a self-insured entity, or its agents, employees, or contractors, in connection with claims investigation activities, anti-fraud activities, rating, or underwriting involving the driver; provided, however, that notwithstanding the definition of personal information under Code Section 40-5-1, personal information furnished under this division shall be limited to name, address, driver identification number, and medical or disability

information. The person who makes a request for a driver's operating record shall identify himself or herself and shall have certified or affirmed that the information contained in the record will be used only for the purpose specified in the request. Further, the person making the request shall certify or affirm that he or she has on file an application for insurance or for the renewal or amendment thereof involving the driver or drivers; or

(ii) For the purpose of ascertaining necessary rating information by an insurance agent pursuant to an insurer's contract with the Georgia Technology Authority for the immediate on-line electronic furnishing of limited rating information to such insurer's agents. **Limited rating information** furnished under this division shall include only the number of violations of Code Section 40-6-391, relating to driving under the influence of alcohol, drugs, or other intoxicating substances, and the number and type of other moving traffic violations which were committed by the proposed insured driver or drivers within the immediately preceding three or five years, which period shall be specified by the person making the request. The provisions of division (i) of this subparagraph notwithstanding, no other information concerning a driver's operating record shall be released to such agents for purposes of rating;

(C)   In accordance with Article 7 of this chapter, the "Georgia Uniform Commercial Driver's License Act";

(D)   To a judge, prosecuting official, or law enforcement agency for use in investigations or prosecutions of alleged criminal or unlawful activity, or to the driver's licensing agency of another state;

(E)   Pursuant to a request from a public or private school system concerning any person currently employed or an applicant for employment as a school bus driver who agrees in writing to allow the department to release the information;

(F)   With the written release of the driver, to a rental car company for use in the normal course of its business; provided, however, that notwithstanding the definition of personal information under Code Section 40-5-1, personal information furnished under this subparagraph shall be limited to name, address, driver identification number, and medical or disability information. Such access shall be provided and funded through the GeorgiaNet Division of the Georgia Technology Authority, and the department shall bear no costs associated with such access.

(G)   For use in the normal course of business by a legitimate business or its agents, employees, or contractors, but only:

(i) To verify the accuracy of personal information submitted by the individual to the business or its agents, employees, or contractors; and

(ii) If such information as so submitted is not correct or is no longer correct, to obtain the correct information, but only for the purposes of preventing fraud by, pursuing legal remedies against, or recovering on a debt or security interest against, the individual; provided, however, that notwithstanding the definition of personal information under Code Section 40-5-1, personal information furnished under this subparagraph shall be limited to name, address, and driver identification number and shall not include photographs, fingerprints, computer images, or medical or disability information. The personal information obtained by a business under this subparagraph shall not be resold or redisclosed for any other purpose without the written consent of the individual. Furnishing of information to a business under this subparagraph shall be pursuant to a contract entered into by such business and the state which specifies, without limitation, the consideration to be paid by such business to the state for such information and the frequency of updates.

Vehicle Records

The Georgia Laws regulating the release of vehicle records, OCGA 40-2-130 and 40-3-23, severely restricts access and calls for a number of requirements for ongoing users and vendors. The operating records and personal information on each driver are excluded from the Georgia Open Records Law. Present law is stricter than DPPA.

The following parties are authorized to receive tag, title and/or lien information with acceptable proof of interest as shown below, when required, and the required research fees.

- **Licensed Motor Vehicle Dealer.** If you are a licensed Georgia motor vehicle dealer, your twelve-digit (12) permanent MVD-issued dealer identification number must be submitted with your request for information. If you are an out-of-state dealer, a copy of your valid state-issued license and proof of interest in vehicle must accompany your request.
- **Owner of Vehicle.** If you are not the owner of the vehicle, according to our current tag and title records, proof of ownership must be submitted with your request for tag, title and/or lien information that includes the purchase or transfer of the vehicle from the vehicle owner according to our current tag and title records.
- **Judgment Creditor** of the vehicle's owner. A certified copy of the fi.fa. must be submitted with the required research fees, and your request for tag, title and/or lien information.
- **Attorney-at-Law.** An attorney's letterhead request for the information, signed by the attorney must be submitted with the required research fees, Form MV20, a copy of the attorney's Bar Association card, proof of pending litigation involving a motor vehicle accident and a copy of the accident report or a certified copy of a fi.fa. Information will only be released with proof of pending litigation involving a motor vehicle accident and a copy of the accident report or a certified copy of a fi.fa. A paralegal or a member

of the attorney's staff may receive the information if they submit a copy of the attorney's Bar Association card, a letterhead request for the information signed by the attorney, the required research fees, a copy of pending litigation involving a motor vehicle accident and a copy of the accident report or a certified copy of the fi.fa. and the submitter's valid driver's license or government-issued identification card.

- **Bank or Lending Institution.** The bank's or lender's signed letterhead request must be submitted with the required research fees. If the bank's or the lender's lien or security interest is not perfected in our records, a copy of the contract between the record owner and the requesting bank or lender and Form MV 20A must also be submitted.
- **Insurance Company.** A signed letterhead request from the insurance company, the required research fees and a copy of the accident report or other proof of interest and Form MV 20A must be submitted.
- An individual involved in an accident as a passenger, vehicle operator or pedestrian. A copy of the accident report must be submitted along with the required research fees.

Request and Consent Forms

Driving Records: Written requests must indicate the purpose of the request and include the signature of the subject. Use of *Form DDS-18 Request for Motor Vehicle Report/MVR* is suggested; the form is at www.dds.ga.gov/FormsandManuals/index.aspx.

For high volume, ongoing requesters, a separate application must be filled out and approved by DDS for each purpose that the company has for requesting driver license reports. There are five purposes for requesting Motor Vehicle Reports: insurance, employment, credit, rental car agency and limited rating information. For each purpose and user applied for, user will be assigned a separate user ID and password in order to log onto the Motor Vehicle Reports web page.

Vehicle Records: For those who qualify, an order form (MV20) is found at http://motor.etax.dor.ga.gov/motor/dealers/researchfees.asp. The form also explains who can obtain the record information.

Attorneys can receive vehicle information by submitting a request on their letterhead along with proof of pending litigation involving a motor vehicle accident, an accident report, and a copy of the attorney's Bar Card. If a vehicle record is requested for any other reason, a subpoena to release information must be served and *Form MV-20A* must be used.

Vendor and Third Party Access Policy

Driving Records: Approved vendors cannot access records for other vendors, unless authorized. The forms described above state that records are used exclusively by the specified end-user. The agent for the end user must have a signed release from the driver. Georgia prohibits the further resale of records after a completed transaction.

Vehicle Records: Approved vendors cannot access records for other vendors. The agent for the end-user must have a signed release from the vehicle owner. Georgia prohibits the further resale of records after a completed transaction.

Records Ordered For Non-permissible Uses

Driving Records: If no consent, casual requesters cannot obtain records, with or without personal information.

Vehicle Records: An individual can request non-personal motor vehicle information. The printout will NOT reflect personal information such as name and address of owner, name and address of lien holder or security interest holder, title issuance date, title number, and registration information. It makes no difference if the casual requester has the consent of the vehicle owner or title-holder, only non-personal information is released.

Access to Driver-Related Records

Driving Records

General Information and Fees

Customer Services, Licensing and Records, PO Box 80447, Conyers, GA 30013, 678-413-8400.

The current fee is $6.00 for a three-year history or $8.00 for a seven-year history. Personal checks are not accepted. Georgia charges a full price for a "no record found" report.

In-Person – Up to three requests are processed over-the-counter while one waits, additional requests are processed overnight. Walk-in service is also available at many DDS Customer Service Centers throughout the state.

Mail – Mail-in requests are available only from the address above and are processed within two weeks. The driver's license number, last name, and date of birth must be submitted to receive a driving record, although a "hit" may be possible with two out of the three. The fee (money order or cashier's check) must accompany the request.

Fax – Approved requesters can order by fax (701-328-2435). Use of a credit card is required with expiration date and signature included.

Electronic – There are five purposes for requesting Motor Vehicle Reports: insurance, employment, credit, rental car agency and Limited Rating Information. For each purpose and use, a requester is assigned a separate user-ID and password.

Both the $6.00 three-year history and $8.00 seven-year history are available online.

The **Limited Rating Information** (LRI) is a specific type of record available only to the insurance industry. The fee is $1.70 for either a three-year or a five-year record. There is a full fee for a no record found. The LRI reports the license status and a summary of the number of violations relating to; driving under the influence of alcohol, drugs, or other intoxicating substances; and the number and type of other moving traffic violations committed by the subject. No withdrawal information is included on a LRI.

Requesters for any of these services must complete a series of application forms and user agreement forms. For further information, visit https://onlinemvr.dds.ga.gov/mvr/gettingcert.aspx or call 404-463-2300 and ask for Bulk Sales. There is an initial subscription account fee of $100.00. The agreement form is found at https://onlinemvr.dds.ga.gov/mvr/pdf/lri.pdf.

Database Sale – The state does not sell its license database, or portions there of. However, note that the DMV uses the term *Bulk Requester* when describing users who request a specific group or batch of records by name.

By Person of Record – GA drivers may obtain their driving record by mail or walk-in as described above. Also, drivers may view or download a non-certified copy of their driving record at https://online.dds.ga.gov/OnlineServices/MVRIntro.aspx. The same fees apply. Users can revisit and view their record for 30 days. Use of a credit card is necessary. A certified record is not viewable, but will be mailed within 7 days. Also, a driver may check the status of his/her license by call 404-657-9300.

Notification/Monitoring Program

At present Georgia does not offer a monitoring system or notification program to employers or insurance companies to track incidents of drivers.

DL Status Check

One may conduct an immediate driver's license status check at https://online.dds.ga.gov/DLStatus/default.aspx. Users of this free service are prompted to enter a nine digit Georgia driver's license number. An immediate answer of "license is valid" or "license is invalid" will be immediately displayed.

Crasht Reports

Reporting – Georgia requires crashes involving death, injury, or damage in excess of $250.00 to be investigated upon request by the Department of Transportation. The GDOT Crash Reporting Unit is at Shackleford Building #24, 935 East Confederate Ave, Atlanta GA 30316, 678-635-8109. Note that the DOT web page (www.dot.state.ga.us) has a crash reporting form that is downloadable. However, the form is for personal use only, since the law Enforcement Agencies send reports. The DOT states that it will throw away the personal use reports if mailed to them.

Record Access – Crash reports are maintained by the Department of Transportation, The GDOT Crash Reporting Unit, Shackleford Building #24, 935 East Confederate Ave, Atlanta GA 30316, 678-635-8109. Normally, new records are available for inquiry in 30 days. Records are available for 10 years to present. To access from this agency, the requester must have a letter from the subject or proof of legal representation to obtain a record. Include the following in the request; full name, date and location of accident. The fee is $5.00 per report. There is no charge for a no-record found. Turnaround time is 1 week to 10 days.

The agency has outsourced the online purchase of crash reports through a private vendor. See www.buycrash.com. Users can search for their crash reports utilizing a number of search options including their name, date of crash, road of occurrence and VIN. This agency also accepts mail requests; a form is at the web page. The fee for reports will vary between $6.00 and $12.00 depending on who is the investigating agency supplying the report to the DOT.

Access to Vehicle-Related Records

General Information and Fees

Attention: Research Unit, DOR/Motor Vehicle Division, PO Box 740381, Atlanta, GA 30374-0381, for Tag and Title - 855-406-5221; for CDL Registration 404-968-3850; fax is 404-362-2729.

Certified copies and microfilm histories can be obtained from this department. The fee for a printout of tag or title or lien information is $1.00 per vehicle or name. For a microfilm search (title history) of five years the fee is $5.00. Certification is an additional $10.00 and must be requested 7 days in advance. Major credit cards are accepted. The fee still applies if no record is found. It takes about 2 weeks before new records are available for inquiry on microfilm histories. For those public entities who qualify, records are available going back for 5 years. General questions can be directed to motorvehicleinquiry@dor.ga.gov.

About liens on non-title vehicles: Liens or security interest is recorded with Clerk of the Superior Court's office in the county where the vehicle owner resides under the provisions of the Uniform Commercial Code. See www.gsccca.org/filesandforms/uccforms.asp.

Mail – VIN, title, plate, and registration checks are subject to strict access and are only available under the criteria as provided above. Turnaround time is 2 weeks. A SASE is requested, but not required.

In-Person – In-person requests require a completed and signed *Request for Motor Vehicle Data Form MV-20*, bill or sale or contract between two parties, accompanied by the requester's valid driver's license or state-issued ID card. Turnaround time is while you wait, except if a certified document is needed it can take 7 days. The physical address is Motor Vehicle Division, 4125 Welcome All Road, Atlanta, GA 30349.

Electronic – Georgia does not offer a general online inquiry access program; however, there are several online systems for specific uses. The MVD provides a free public **Vehicle Insurance Status Check** at http://onlinemvd.dor.ga.gov/vinstatuscheck/vinstatus.aspx and also at https://mvd.dor.ga.gov/vincheck/VinCheck.aspx. Enter a VIN or title number.

At the same web page there is a more robust **Vehicle Insurance Status Report** available to **authorized users only**. Also, the DMV provides a web inquiry program for GA dealers. The Georgia Trucking Portal for commercial drivers and carriers is https://www.cvisn.dor.ga.gov/.

General email requests or questions may be sent to motorvehicleinquiry@rev.dor.ga.gov.

Bulk – Due to the strict public access laws, vehicle information is not available in bulk or batch mode for any type of commercial purpose.

Access to Vessel-Related Records

General Information, Access and Fees

Georgia Department of Natural Resources, License and Boat Registration Unit, 2065 U.S. Highway 278 SE, Social Circle, GA 30348-5310, 800-366-2661, http://www.georgiawildlife.com/boating.

All motorized boats and all sailboats over 12 ft must be registered. Exceptions include canoes, kayaks and rubber rafts with no mechanical propulsion, and boats operated exclusively on private ponds or lakes. Titles are not required for watercraft or for boat trailers. Records are available from 1986 and are computerized since 1990. Paper records are maintained for three years.

Request records by fax or mail. Requests should include name, registration # or hull number. There is no fee to do a name or registration search. Turnaround time is one week or longer. The agency will provide verification of data only by phone.

Download of stats of boat registration data by county or statewide at https://hfwa.centraltechnology.net/gdnr_vrs/downloads/boatData.do. ou must have MS Access or Excel.

Liens are filed at the county level and do not show on records found at this agency. See www.gsccca.org/filesandforms/uccforms.asp.

Driving Record Content and Reciprocity

What's On or Not On the Driving Record

- As mentioned, there is a three-year record, a seven year record, and a Limited record. See above for a complete description.
- The driver's address is included as part of the record.
- The state does not permit driver school attendance in lieu of conviction.
- The length of time convictions are listed on the record is 3 or 7 years depending on record requested, and 10 to 55 years for CDL drivers (depending on conviction).

Data Retention

The purging procedure used depends on the violation listed and the action taken. Non-CDL surrendered licenses are purged if they expire in less than two years from surrender date. When a CDL holder moves, the state forwards the CDL driver's record to the new state of residence; but the record is not purged.

Court to Repository

The court systems are mandated by law to forward their copies of citations within 10 days of the case being adjudicated. The convictions are then entered into the system.

State Reciprocity for Non-CDL Drivers

- Will suspend license of driver for unpaid out-of-state convictions.
- Record of new incoming driver is not shown on MVR.
- Out-of-state convictions are shown on MVR.
- Out-of-state accidents are shown on MVR only if a conviction is reported.
- Convictions of out-of-state drivers are sent to home state.
- Record is forwarded to new state upon surrender of license only if requested.

License Classes, Restriction and Endorsements

License Classes

Georgia began issuing the CDL in April 1990

Commercial Classifications

Class A   Any combination of vehicles with a GVWR of 26,001 pounds or more, provided the GVWR of the vehicle(s) being towed is in excess of 10,000 pounds. Includes vehicles in Classes B and C.

Class B   Any single vehicle with a GVWR of 26,001 pounds or more, or any such vehicle towing another vehicle not in excess of 10,000 pounds. Includes vehicles in Class C.

Class C   Can also be non-commercial. Any single vehicle with a gross vehicle weight rating not in excess of 26,000 pounds, or any such vehicle towing a vehicle with a gross vehicle weight rating not in excess of 10,000 pounds, any such vehicle towing a vehicle with a gross vehicle weight rating in excess of 10,000 pounds, provided that the combination of vehicles has a gross combined vehicle weight rating not in excess of 26,000 pounds, and any self-propelled or towed vehicle that is equipped to serve as temporary living quarters for recreational, camping, or travel purposes and is used solely as a family or personal conveyance. Class C commercial licenses are issued only if the vehicle is designed to carry sixteen or more passengers (including the driver), or utilized to transport hazardous materials in quantities that require placarding.

Non-Commercial Classifications

Note: **Effective March 25, 2011**, the Department of Driver Services (DDS) implemented a **License Class change** for drivers of non-commercial motor vehicles. Prior to that date, Class A and B licenses were either Commercial or Non-Commercial. Now anyone who previously would have been issued a non-commercial Class A driver's license is issued a non-commercial **Class E** license. Non-commercial Class B driver's licenses changed to a non-commercial **Class F** driver's license. The qualifications, testing procedures, and issuance process for each class of license remain the same. Vehicles which require a non-commercial Class E or F license are agricultural vehicles, military vehicles, and firefighter /emergency vehicles.

Class E   **[Was Class A]** Any combination of vehicles with a GCWR of 26,001 or more pounds provided the GVWR of the vehicle(s) being towed is in excess of 10,000 pounds.

Class F   **[Was Class B]** Any single vehicle with a GVWR of 26,001 or more pounds, or any such vehicle towing a vehicle not in excess of

10,000 pounds GVWR.

Class C   See above.

Class CP   Applicant must be at least 15 years old and be able to pass the vision and knowledge test. When driving, there must be a licensed driver at least 21 years old in the front seat with driver at all times. The permit is valid for 24 months. Parental consent is required for applicants under 18 years of age.

Class D   Provisional License for Class C vehicles, with restrictions and driving hours and passengers.

Class M   Motorcycles. [Regular Non-commercial Vehicle/Motorcycle combination license AM changes to EM. Regular Non-commercial Vehicle/Motorcycle combination license BM changes to FM.]

Class P   Instructional Permit. Note that CP, MP, AP, and BP are all instructional permits issued with the class designation followed by the letter P. [BP will become FP; AP will become EP]. Applicants under 18 years of age must hold a Class CP a minimum of 12 months before obtaining a Class D license.

Restrictions

Note: Effective January 30, 2012, extensive changes where made to the Restriction Code table. Since the older codes may show on the license documents, both the old and new lists are shown below **and changes are indicated in bold.**

Restrictions Prior to January 30, 2012	Restrictions Effective January 30, 2012
A – None	A – None
B – Corrective lenses required	B – Corrective lenses required
C – Vehicle mechanical aids required	C – Vehicle mechanical aids required
D – Business purpose only	**D – Prosthetic aids required**
E – Automatic Transmission only	**E – No manual transmission equipped CMV**
F – Right exterior mirror required	F – Right exterior mirror required
G – Daylight hours only	G – Daylight hours only
H – Employer vehicle only	H – Employer vehicle only
I – Left outside mirror required	I – Left outside mirror required
J – Prosthetic aids required	**J – Automatic transmission required**
K – Restricted to GA only	**K – Intrastate commerce only**
L – No Air Brakes Allowed	**L – No air brake equipped CMV**
M – No Highway/Interstate	**M – No class A passenger busses**
N – Power Brakes Required	**N – No class A or B passenger busses**
O – Power Steering Required	**O – No tractor trailer CMV**
P – Ignition Interlock Required	**P – Power steering required**
Q – No Passengers Allowed	Q – No passengers allowed
R – Not in use	**R – No highway/interstate**
S – To and From School only	**S – Power brakes required**
T – To and from medical only	**T – Disabled parent**
U – Not in use	**U – Accompanied by visually impaired parent**
V – No class A busses	**V – Medical variance**
W – No class A or B busses	**W – Valid farm waiver required**
X – Not in use	**X – No cargo in CMV tank vehicle**
Y – Valid farm waiver required	**Y – Hearing aid required**
Z – Accompanied by visually impaired parent	**Z – No full air brake**
0 – New	0 – Reserve for future use
1 – Bi-optic lenses required	1 – Bi-optic lenses required
2 – Personal vehicle only	2 – Personal vehicle only
3 - To and From employment/medical care/school/court ordered driver improvement/driver education/drug/alcohol program, scheduled meetings of organizations for persons who have alcohol/drug addiction/abuse problems or ignition interlock station. Interlock Device is required.	3 - To and From employment/medical care/school/court ordered driver improvement/driver education/drug/alcohol program, scheduled meetings of organizations for persons who have alcohol/drug addiction/abuse problems or ignition interlock station. Interlock Device is required.
4 – No Tractor Trailers	**4 – Blank**
5 – Disabled parent	**5 – Business purpose only**
6 – Not currently in use	**6 – To and from medical only**
7 – Not currently in use	**7 – To and From School only**
8 – Not currently in use	**8 – Ignition Interlock Required**
9 – Not currently in use	**9 – Valid in GA only**

Endorsements (Commercial Only)

P	Passenger Vehicles (sixteen or more, including driver)	H	Hazardous Material Haulers
T	Double-/Triple-Trailers	S	School Bus
N	Tank Vehicles	X	Combination of N and H Endorsements

Conviction Table with ACD, Legal Reference, and if Suspended

- An "X" in the CDL Column indicates that this conviction will ONLY show on the driving records of Commercial Drivers. If this violation is issued to a non-commercial driver, the conviction will not appear on the driving record.
- When two asterisks "**" are indicated next to the Statute it means this will result in a suspension if the driver is under 21 years of age.

Description	Legal Reference	CDL Only	Suspend	ACD
Acquiring License Plate To Conceal Vehicle Identity	40-2-5	X		
Administrative Action - Security Risk	40-5-150I2			W09
Administrative Per Se	40-5-67.1C		Susp	A98
Aggressive Driving	40-6-397**			
Agricultural Vehicle Light Violation	40-8-33	X		E05
All Parts Must Be Safely Maintained – *vehicle equipment violation*	40-8-2			E01
Altered Suspension	40-8-6	X		
Altered/Counterfeit Certificate Or Title	40-3-90	X		
Altering Ephedrine Products	16-13-30.3D		Susp	A33
Amber Light Violation	40-8-32	X		
Attempting To Purchase {alcohol}	3-3-23A2B**			A31
Auxiliary Light Violation	40-8-29	X		E55
Brake Light/Turn Signal Violation	40-8-26	X		E05
Brake Light/Turn Signal Violation	40-8-25	X		E34
Brake Violation	40-8-53	X		E02
Center Lane Violation	40-6-126			M62
Child Endangerment	40-6-391L		Susp	A20
Child Or Youth Restraint Not Used Properly	40-8-76			F02
Clinging to Another Vehicle	40-6-313			
Coasting Prohibited	40-6-246			N80
Commercial Driving Impaired	40-6-391I	X	Susp	A20
Commercial Driving W/Measurable BAC	40-5-152	X		A26
Commercial Misdemeanor	32-1-10	X		
Conspiracy To Possess Controlled Substance	16-13-33		Susp	A33
Construction Site Speed Violation *(not reported is speed less than 15 over unless in a CMV, then reported)*	40-6-188 ** *if over 24 MPH or more over the limit*			S92
Defective Brakes	40-8-51, 40-8-54	X		E31
Defective Or Insufficient Brakes	40-8-50	X		E31
Defective Or Missing Speedometer	40-8-8	X		E01
Defective Or No Headlights	40-8-22, 40-8-22B	X		E34
Defective Or No Lights	40-8-21	X		E34
Defective or No Reflectors	40-8-24	X		
Defective Or No Taillights	40-8-23	X		E34
Defective Tires	40-8-74	X		E37
Disregarding Signs Or Control Devices/RR	40-6-142A			M22
Driver's View Obstructed	40-6-242			D70
Driving CMV Without CDL	40-5-146A1	X		B51
Driving CMV Without CDL on Person	40-5-146A2	X		B51
Driving CMV Without Obtaining CDL	40-5-151F	X		B56
Driving in Circular of Zig-Zag Course "laying Drags"	40-6-251			N83
Driving In Left Lane Of 2 Lanes (Big Trucks)	40-6-52C			M49
Driving In Left Lane Of 3+ Lanes (Big Trucks)	40-6-52B			M49
Driving Over RR Crossing W/Out Sufficient Space	40-6-140E			M23
Driving Over RR Crossing When Train Approaching	40-6-140D			M21
Driving Over RR Xing W/Out Sufficient Clearance	40-6-140F			M24
Driving Under Influence - Inhalants	40-6-391A3		Susp	A23
Driving Under Influence Drugs/Alcohol	40-6-391 & A		Susp	A20
Driving Under The Influence – Alcohol – per se	40-6-391A5		Susp	A20
Driving Under The Influence/Alcohol	40-6-391A1		Susp	A21
Driving Under The Influence/Drugs	40-6-391A2		Susp	A22
Driving While License Withdrawn	40-5-121		Susp	B20
Driving While License Withdrawn – Felony (4th within 5 years if after 07/08)	40-5-121F		Susp	B20
Driving With No Or Without Lights	40-8-1	X		E05
Driving Without A License - Failure To Obtain In 30 Days	40-5-20A			B51
Driving Without a License – Felony (4th within 5 years)	40-5-20F			B20
Driving Without Proper CDL	40-5-146B1	X		B20
Driving Wrong Side Of Undivided Street	40-6-40A			N72
Drug-Free Commercial Zone	16-13-32.6		Susp	A33

Description	Legal Reference	CDL Only	Suspend	ACD
Drug-Free Recreation/Housing Project Zone	16-13-32.5		Susp	A33
Drug-Free School Zone	16-13-32.4		Susp	A33
DUI - Felony	40-6-391C4		Susp	B20
DUI – Minor Under Age 21	40-6-391K1		Susp	A60
DUI- Drugs And Alcohol Combined	40-6-391A4		Susp	A21
DUI- Marijuana	40-6-391A6		Susp	A22
Ecstasy Trafficking	16-13-31.1		Susp	A33
Emergency Vehicle Violation	40-6-6			
Emergency Vehicle Violation	40-8-96	X		
Emerging From Alley, Driveway, Or Building	40-6-144			N01
Emission Violation	40-8-130, 40-8-182 40-8-183	X		
Ephedrine Sales For Purposes Of Manufacturing	16-13-30.4G2		Susp	A33
Ephedrine Storage And Licensing Requirements	16-13-30.4		Susp	A33
Equipment Used Improperly-Excessive Noise	40-6-14	X		
Exceed/Violate Height Limit of Truck/Vehicle	32-6-22	X		
Exceed/Violate Size Limit of Truck/Vehicle	32-6-24	X		
Exceed/Violate Size, Weight, Pass/Cargo Limit	32-6-20	X		
Exceed/Violate Width Limit of Truck/Vehicle	32-6-23	X		
Exhaust System Used Improperly/Obstructed	40-8-181	X		
Exhaust System Violation	40-8-71	X		
Expired License	40-5-32	X		
Expired or No Drivers License	40-5-149, 40-5-20&20A, 40-5-32A	X		B51
Expired or No Drivers License	40-5-32A	X		B51
Expired or No license on Person	40-5-20	X		B51
Expired or No License Plate Or Decal	40-2-44, 44-2-8	X		
Expired or No License Plates Or Decal	40-2-20	X		
Expired or No Registration Or Title	40-2-38, 40-2-88, 40-2-90	X		
Expired or No Registration Or Title	48-2-31, 48-8-9, 48-9-38, 48-9-39	X		
Fail To Rpt Striking Fixed Object	40-6-272			B08
Failure of School Bus To Yield Right Of Way	40-6-165	X		N01
Failure of School Bus To Yield Right Of Way	40-6-164	X		N08
Failure To Appear For Trial Or Court Appeal	40-5-56		Susp	D45
Failure To Dim Lights	40-8-31	X		E54
Failure To Dim Lights When Parked	40-8-28, 40-8-28D	X		E54
Failure To Exercise Due Care	40-6-241			M81
Failure to Have License on Person	40-5-29, 40-5-29A	X		B51
Failure To Keep In Proper Lane	40-6-50 & B & D			M51
Failure to Keep in Proper lane (Bus or Motorcoach)	40-6-53			M49
Failure to Keep in Proper Lane (Truck Using Wrong Lane)	40-6-52			M49
Failure To Maintain Insurance	40-6-10 (also A & B)		Susp	D36
Failure To Obey Construction Markers	40-6-75			M03
Failure To Obey Motor Carrier Rules/Regs	46-7-3, 46-7-15, 46-7-16, 46-7-27, 46-7-38, 46-7-39	X		
Failure To Obey Police/Peace Officer	40-6-2			M08
Failure To Obey RR Crossing Restrictions	40-6-140			M10
Failure To Obey RR Crossing Restrictions –Driving Over or Around RR Barrier	40-6-140B			M10
Failure To Obey RR Gates/Signs/Signals	40-6-141			M10
Failure To Obey RR Grade Crossing Restrictions	40-6-140A			M10
Failure To Obey Safety Zone	40-6-98			M12
Failure To Obey Signs Or Control Devices	40-6-20			M14
Failure To Obey Stop Sign	40-6-72, 40-6-72B			M15
Failure To Obey Traffic Sign	40-6-23, 40-6-51			M17
Failure To Obey traffic Sign	40-6-51			M17
Failure To Obey Traffic Signal Or Light	40-6-21			M16
Failure To Obey Yield Sign	40-6-72C			M19
Failure To Remove Accident Vehicle	40-6-275	X		F34
Failure To Report Accident	40-6-273			B05
Failure To Report Name or Address Change	40-5-149B	X		
Failure To Secure Load	32-6-254			
Failure to Secure Load	40-6-254			
Failure To Secure Load --- *Resulting In Littering*	40-6-248.1	X		
Failure To Signal Lane Change Or Turn	40-6-123			N43
Failure To Signal/Improper Signal	40-6-124			N40
Failure To Slow For RR Grade Crossing	40-6-140C			M20
Failure To Stop At Railroad Grade Crossing	40-6-142			M22

Description	Legal Reference	CDL Only	Suspend	ACD
Failure To Use Visual Signals, By School Bus	40-6-162			E50
Failure to Weigh or Stop at Weigh Station	32-6-30	X	Susp	
Failure to Yield to Cyclist	40-6-56			N03
Failure To Yield Right Of Way	40-6-71			N31
Failure To Yield Right Of Way - Agricultural Pedestrian/Cyclist	40-6-77			N01
Failure To Yield Right Of Way At Crosswalk	40-6-91A			N20
Failure To Yield Right Of Way To Emergency Veh	40-6-74 & A			N04
Failure To Yield Right Of Way To Pedestrian - Blind	40-6-94			N08
Failure To Yield Right Of Way To Pedestrian – Exercise Due care with a Blind Pedestrian	40-6-93			
Failure To Yield Right Of Way To Pedestrian – Passing a vehicle Stopped for a Pedestrian	40-6-91D			N08
Failure To Yield Right Of Way To Vehicle	40-6-70, 40-6-73			N06
Failure To Yield To Funeral Procession	40-6-76			N05
False Report/Application For Driver License	40-5-125		Susp	D02
False Statements	16-10-20	X		D78
Falsification Of VIN Or Registration Plate	40-4-21	X		
Felony Driving Without a License (4th in 5 years)	40-5-20F			B20
Felony Fleeing Police Or Roadblock	40-6-395B5A		Susp	U01
Fleeing or Attempting to Elude Police	40-6-395 & A		Susp	U01
Following Emergency Vehicle	40-6-247			M32
Following Too Closely	40-6-49 (A & B)			M34
Following Too Closely In Convoy	40-6-49C			M34
Giving Wrong Signal	40-6-123B			N44
Habitual Violator	40-5-58		Susp	B25
Habitual Violator Misdemeanor	40-5-58C			B25
Hazardous Materials Violation	46-11-4	X		
Hit And Run-Failure To Stop And Render Aid	40-6-270		Susp	B01
Ignition Interlock Violation	40-8-117			
Illegal Possession of a Controlled Substance	16-13-30A,B		Susp	A33
Illegal Possession Of Controlled Substance, *(including felony marijuana possession; must use 16-13-2 or 16-13-2B for a nolo plea on misdemeanor poss. of marijuana)*	16-13-30		Susp	A33
Illegal Possession Of Dangerous Drugs	16-13-72		Susp	A33
Illegal Stop/Stand/Park Where Prohibited	40-6-203	X		
Imminent Hazard (Federal Determination)	40-5-151J1			W70
Improper Backing	40-6-240			N82
Improper Class/Endorsement	40-5-150D	X		B91
Improper Driving - Canyon/Mountain/Highway	40-6-245			M81
Improper Driving in Bicycle lane	40-6-55			M47
Improper Lane Usage	32-9-4, 40-6-54			M49
Improper Lane Useage	40-6-54			M49
Improper Lane/Loc On Fire Hose	40-6-248			M56
Improper Left Turn	40-6-120A2			N53
Improper Passing	40-6-46B			M71
Improper Passing	40-6-42			M73
Improper Passing In No Passing Zone	40-6-46 & A			M76
Improper Passing In No Passing Zone – in Intersection or RR Grade	40-6-45A2			M71
Improper Passing In No Passing Zone – Near Bridge or Tunnel	40-6-45A3			M76
Improper Passing Of Emergency/Towing/Hwy Vehicle	40-6-16			M18
Improper Passing On Hill/Curve	40-6-45A1**			M74
Improper Passing On Right	40-6-43 (A & B)			M70
Improper Right Turn	40-6-120A1			N54
Improper Signal	40-6-123D			N40
Improper Starting	40-6-122	X		N83
Improper Stopping	40-6-123C			N40
Improper Turn	40-6-120B			M50
Improper Turn	40-6-120			N50
Improper Use - Driver License	40-5-120		Susp	D16
Improper Use Of Hand Signal	40-6-125			N40
Improper/Erratic Lane Change	40-6-123A, 40-6-48			M42
Interlock Probation Violation	42-8-117			
Lane Direction Violation	40-6-24			M62
Lane Violation	40-6-40C			M62
License Plate Specifications	40-2-31	X		
Light Violation	40-8-30, 40-8-34	X		E05

Description	Legal Reference	CDL Only	Suspend	ACD
Littering From a Motor Vehicle	40-6-249	X		
Load Dragging on Highway	40-8-3	X		
Low Speed Vehicle Light Violation	40-8-35	X		E05
Making Improper U Turn	40-6-121			N56
Misrepresenting Age To Purchase Alcohol	3-3-23A3**			A31
Missing/Defaced/Obscured License Plate	40-2-6	X		
Motor Vehicle Used In Felony	40-5-54A2		Susp	U03
Motorcycle Equipment Not Used Properly - Headgear	40-6-315A			F03
Motorcycle Equipment Not Used Properly – Windshield/eye Protection	40-6-315B			F03
Motorized Cart Violation	40-6-331			M11
Moving Heavy Equipment At RR Grade Crossing	40-6-143			M24
Mud Flap Violation	40-8-75	X		
Name Requirements Not Properly Displayed	40-8-9	X		E01
No Proof Of Insurance - Motorcycle	40-6-11			D36
No Warning For Projecting Load	40-8-27	X		
Not Paying For Gasoline	40-6-255		Susp	
Obscured Or Missing License Plate	40-2-41	X		
Obstructing Flow Of Traffic	40-6-40B			S96
Obstructing Intersection	40-6-205			F34
Obstructing Traffic/FTY Row	40-6-40			N72
Obstructing/Impeding Traffic	40-6-40D			F34
Opening Door Into Traffic	40-6-243			
Operate Vehicle Where prohibited	40-6-26B			
Operating a Vehicle while Text messaging (18 or older)	40.6.241.2			N84 (M85)
Operating MV W/Other Lic While Susp/Rev	40-5-65		Susp	B20
Operating School Bus Without Using Headlights	40-6-161	X		E55
Operating Vehicle With Susp/Canc/Rev/Registration – Suspension imposed	40-6-15		Susp	
Operating W/Out Lights Required By Law	40-8-20	X		E05
Parking Brake Violation	40-8-52	X		E02
Parking Violation	40-6-201	X		
Parking Violation	40-6-252			N84
Passing School Bus -Loading/Unloading	40-6-163**			M75
Passing With Insufficient Clearance	40-6-44			M77
Possess Multiple Driver Licenses	40-5-143	X		D07
Possessing Substance To Manufacture Controlled Substance	16-13-30.5		Susp	A33
Possession Of Alcohol By Minor	3-3-23A2C**			A31
Possession Of Certain Amounts Of Ephedrine	16-13-30.3B1		Susp	A33
Possession Of Drug Related Object	16-13-32.2		Susp	A33
Possession Of Imitation Controlled Substance	16-13-30.2		Susp	A33
Possession Of Marijuana, Less Than One Ounce	16-13-2, 16-13-2B		Susp	A33
Possession Of Multiple Drivers Licenses	40-5-20C	X		D07
Possession Of Non-Controlled Substance	16-13-30.1		Susp	A33
Possession Of Open Alcohol Container (driver only)	40-6-253			A35
Possession Of Vehicle W/Altered VIN	40-4-22	X		
Purchasing Alcohol Under 21	3-3-23A2A**			D06
Racing	40-6-186		Susp	S95
Rear View Obstruction	40-8-72	X		E01
Reckless Driving	40-6-390 & A**			M84
Refused Test - Implied Consent	40-5-55		Susp	A12
Required Emblem Not Used	40-8-4	X		E01
Restrictions On Commercial Sales Of Ephedrine	16-13-30.3B1.1		Susp	A33
Safety Equipment Not Used Properly	40-6-352			
School Bus Equipment Violation	40-8-111	X		E06
School Bus Marking Violation	40-8-110, 40-8-115, 40-8-116	X		E06
School Bus Specification Violation	40-8-112	X		E06
School Bus Speeding	40-6-160	X		S92
Seat Belt Violation	40-8-76.1			F04
Serious Injury By Vehicle	40-6-394		Susp	U03
Show/Use Improperly-Insurance Cert	40-6-10C		Susp	
Speed Less Than Minimum	40-6-184			S96
Speeding (Actual amount shown) *(not reported is speed less than 15 over unless in a CMV, then reported)*	40-6-181 *** if over 24 MPH or more over the limit*			S92
Started Parked Vehicle Unsafely	40-6-122	X		N83

Description	Legal Reference	CDL Only	Suspend	ACD
Steering/Controlling Towed Vehicle Without License	40-5-20B	X		B51
Striking Unattended Vehicle	40-6-271			B08
Tampering With Odometer	40-8-6.1	X		
Tampering With Odometer	40-8-5	X		E01
Tampering With Traffic Signs or Signals	40-6-26A	X		
Theft By Bringing Stolen Property Into State	16-8-9			
Theft By Conversion	16-8-4			
Theft By Deception	16-8-3			
Theft By Receiving Property Stolen In Other State	16-8-8			
Theft By Receiving Stolen Property	16-8-7			
Theft By Taking	16-8-2			
Theft Of Lost Or Misplaced Property	16-8-6			
Theft Of Services	16-8-5			
Too fast for Conditions/Prima Facia Speed	40-6-180	X		S94
Too Fast For Conditions/Prima Facie Speed	40-5-7	X		S94
Traffic Control Device Preemption Emitter Violation	40-6-17			
Trafficking In Controlled Substance	16-13-31		Susp	A33
Transactions Of Drug Related Objects To Grow	16-13-32.1		Susp	A33
Transactions Of Drug Related Objects To Use	16-13-32		Susp	A33
Transportation Of Etiologic Agent	40-6-253.1			E04
Unlawful Operation Motor Truck	40-2-114	X		
Unlawful Use of Wireless Device (Under 18)	40.6.241.1			N84 (M86)
Unlawfully Dispensing Prescriptions	16-13-42		Susp	A33
Unlawfully Distributing Prescriptions	16-13-43		Susp	A33
Unsafe Operation Of Emergency Vehicle	40-6-74B			N84
Unsafe Operation Of Motorcycle	40-6-311			F06
Unsafe Operation Of Motorcycle – (various)	40-6-312(A thru E) - 40-6-314A&B			F06
Unsafe Operation Of Vehicle	40-6-244			N84
Unsafe Vehicle or Equipment	40-8-7	X		
Unsecured Passengers In Open Area/Vehicle	40-8-79	X		F05
Use Of Communication Facility To Commit Felony	16-13-32.3		Susp	A33
Use of Equipment Prohibited by Law	40-6-250			
Use Of Lights/Siren Prohibited	40-8-90	X		
Use Of Lights/Siren Prohibited	40-8-92	X		
Use Of Nitrous Oxide In Passenger Car	40-8-10	X		
Using False ID To Purchase Alcohol	3-3-23A5**			D06
Vehicle Used In Felony Controlled Substance	40-5-151.E		Susp	A50
Vehicular Feticide - 1st Degree	40-6-393.1B			U27
Vehicular Feticide - 2nd Degree	40-6-393.1C			U28
Vehicular Homicide - 1st Degree	40-6-393A,B, D		Susp	U07
Vehicular Homicide - 2nd Degree	40-6-393C		Susp	U08
Violate Excess Size/Weight Permit	32-6-28	X		
Violate Limited License Conditions – HV Probationary License	40-5-58E		Susp	D27
Violate Limited License Conditions – Limited Permit	40-5-64		Susp	D27
Violating Out Of Service Order	40-5-146.B2	X		B27
Violating Out Of Service Order - HAZMAT	40-5-151.G3	X		B19
Violating Restriction Of Driver License - *for medical or equipment requirements to operate*	40-5-30		Susp	D29
Violation Involving Fatal Accident	40-5-142.22E			U31
Violation of Handicap Parking	40-6-226	X		
Warning Device Violation	40-8-70	X		E01
Window Tint Violation	40-8-73.1	X		D70
Window, Windshield, Or Wiper Violation	40-8-73	X		E01
Wrong Side Of Road	40-6-41			N70
Wrong Way On One-Way Street	40-6-47			N63

About the Point System

The Georgia point system ranges from 2 to 6. A driver with 15 points in a 24 month period will be suspended. The state assesses no points for speeding convictions less than 15 miles-per-hour over the posted speed limit and for convictions of driving Too Fast For Conditions, as per O.C.G.A. Sec. 40-6-180. No points are assessed against non-residents of Georgia.

Aggressive Driving...Six points.
Child Safety Restraint
   1st Offense...One point.
   2nd Offense and Subsequent Offense...Two points.
Driving too Fast for Conditions ....Zero points.

Failure to Adequately Secure Load... Two points.
Failure to Adequately Secure Load (except fresh farm produce), Resulting in an Accident .... Three points.
Failure to Obey Police Officer .... Three points.
Failure to Obey Traffic-Control Device.. Three points.
HOV Lane Violation - 4th and Subsequent Offense ....One point.
Improper Passing on Hill or Curve .... Four points.
Possessing an Open Container of an Alcoholic Beverage While Driving .... Two points.
Operating a Vehicle while Text Messaging (Violation of usage of wireless telecommunications device requirements).........................One point.
Reckless Driving .... Four points.
Speeding:
    Fifteen to eighteen mph over limit.. Two points.
    Nineteen to twenty-three mph over limit... Three points.
    Twenty-four to thirty-three mph over limit .... Four points.
    Thirty-four or more mph over limit ....Six points.
Unlawful Passing School Bus ....Six points.
All Other Moving Violations .... Three points.

About the Super Speeder Conviction

- If DDS receives notification of a conviction of speeding 75 mph on a two-lane road or highway, or 85 mph on any road or highway, the customer will be notified by first class mail of the $200 Super Speeder fee, and will have 120 days from the date of the notice to pay the fee to DDS.
- Failure to pay the Super Speeder fee to DDS within 120 days will result in the suspension of the customer's license, permit, or driving privilege in Georgia. The customer must pay a $50 reinstatement fee in addition to the $200 Super Speeder fee in order to reinstate their license, permit, or driving privilege.
- Payment of Super Speeder fees and reinstatement fees can be made in person, by mail, and through the DDS website.
- Out of state drivers are subject to the same requirements as Georgia drivers.
- There are no points assessed. Just a fine.

Hawaii

Administration	Important Telephone and Web Contacts
Hawaii does not have a central agency that manages and regulates motor vehicle and driver functions.	**County of Hawaii**

Administration

Hawaii does not have a central agency that manages and regulates motor vehicle and driver functions.

The Hawaii Department of Transportation, Motor Vehicle Safety Office is responsible for the program co-ordination of five separate county-responsible agencies that oversee driver licensing matters and vehicle registration or titling matters.

The State Judiciary is responsible for Traffic Abstracts and Traffic Court Reports. In each county there is a **Traffic Violation Bureau,** which is part of the State Judiciary, which manages the county's driving record convictions. The Traffic Violations Bureau in Honolulu is the centralized agency that processes most of the manual record requests. Electronic access to driving records is provided by the Hawaii Information Consortium (HIC).

Motor Vehicle Safety Administrator
Motor Vehicle Safety Office
601 Kamokila Blvd #511, Kapolei 96707
808-692-7650
http://hawaii.gov/dot/highways/about/hwy-v/mvso.htm

Traffic Violations Bureau)
1111 Alakea St, 2nd Floor, Honolulu, HI 96813
808-538-5500, www.courts.state.hi.us

Administrative Rules governing Driver Licensing at:
http://hawaii.gov/dot/highways/admin-rules/ruleshwy.htm
Chapter 286, Hawaii Revised Statutes, sections 101-140, that govern Driver Licensing found at:
www.capitol.hawaii.gov/site1/docs/docs.asp?press1=docs

Important Telephone and Web Contacts

County of Hawaii
www.hawaiicounty.gov/finance-dl-general-info

    Driver Licensing....................................808-961-2222
    Vehicle..808-961-8351
    Traffic Violation Bureau 808-961-7470

City and County of Honolulu
www.co.honolulu.hi.us/csd/vehicle/dlinformation.htm

    Driver Licensing..................................808-532-7730
    Vehicle..808-532-7700
    Traffic Violation Bureau 808-538-5500

County of Kauai
www.kauai.gov

    Driver Licensing..................................808-241-4242
    Vehicle..808-241-4256
    Traffic Violation Bureau 808-482-2355

County of Maui
http://www.mauicounty.gov/index.aspx?NID=1328

    Driver Licensing..................................808-270-7363
    Vehicle..808-270-7840
    Traffic Violation Bureau 808-244-2800

    State Department of Insurance 808-586-2790
    Consumer Protection Office..................808-586-2636

The district traffic courts in each county manage that county's driving record convictions.
County police agencies handle all law enforcement duties. There is no Central Highway Patrol or DPS-type agency.

Driver's License Format, Issuance and Renewal

License Classes, Restrictions and Endorsements Appear After the Driving Record Content Section

License Format

Since 01/01/2001, a nine-character license is issued to all new and renewal drivers. This number consists of the letter "H" followed by eight numbers, selected on a random basis. Previous license numbers formatted using the Social Security Number are valid until expiration. There is no "code" used for the nine-character license.

Document Appearance

The current digital document has been in use since 03/2005. Additional security features were adopted after 2005 but prior to 2012.

Current Document

Security Characteristics: Pink stripe on top containing "USA" and the Hawaii state flag. 2D barcode on rear. Hologram includes the state seal and a rainbow.

Position of Photo: Top left with ghost image on the right.

Minor Age Driver Locator: "UNDER 21 UNTIL..." is indicated under the top bar. The document is vertical. The photo is along the left edge at top, a smaller ghost photo appears on lower left corner with license class in black overtop.

CDL Indicator: "CDL" appears on the lower right corner, as do the endorsement and restriction fields.

Old Document

Security Characteristics: Since 06/01 this document was issued with a 2-D barcode below address along bottom of license. The graphics show "Aloha State" with hibiscus.

Position of Photo: Top left (also, barcode below photo).

Minor Age Driver Locator: "UNDER 21 UNTIL..." appears in red and is under the license number.

CDL Indicator: A red "CDL" appears next to the endorsement/restriction fields.

Issuance

Requirements for Proof of Identity:

Effective March 5, 2012, anyone applying for an original or renewal of their Hawaii driver's license or permit must show proof of legal presence in the U.S. See http://hawaii.gov/dot/hawaiis-legal-presence-law for a complete analysis of necessary documents.

Age Requirements

A Class 3 Driver License may be issued at 17 years of age. A Graduated Driver License Program (GDL) was implemented in 09/2006. The minimum age to obtain an Instruction Permit is 15 1/2 years of age. A Provisional License may be issued at 16 years of age and must be held a minimum of 180 days. Other factors in the program include a driver education certification, and while operating a motor vehicle must be seated next to a person who is at least 21 years of age and licensed to operate the same type of motor vehicle. However, between the hours of 11:00 p.m. and 5:00 a.m., the supervising parent or guardian must be seated next to the minor driver.

Residency

Non-residents (eighteen and over) from any state, U.S. territory, or Canada are permitted to drive on Class 1, 2 or 3—as long as home-state license remains valid.

Renewal

Since November 3, 2008, HI driver's licenses issued to applicants age 24 thru 71 expire in eight years. Applicants under age 25 expire in 4 years except provisional licenses expire on the applicant's 19th birthday. Previously, if the driver was under 18 years of age, the license was issued for four years and for drivers between 18 and 71 the license was issued for 6 years. The driver keeps the same number when renewing. Each license holder is limited to two consecutive renewals by mail. Resident military personnel and their immediate family may request for renewal by mail as many times as necessary if they reside outside the state of Hawaii on official military duty. An expired Hawaii driver license while deployed (military) outside of the U.S. shall remain valid for 90 days after return to the U.S.

Elderly-Related Restrictions

If the driver is 72 or older the license is issued every two years, this includes CDL holders.

Vehicle Insurance, Title and Registration Facts

Registration & Renewal

The registration of all vehicles in Hawaii must be renewed every year in the county where the vehicle is registered and being driven.
Kauai, Oahu, Hawaii and Maui counties offer online renewal (except for trailers) at https://mvr.ehawaii.gov/renewals/index.html.

New Residents

Non-residents must register vehicles within ten days after arrival. However, an Out-of-State Permit is available. The permit has to be applied for within 30 days of arrival, proof of arrival (bill of lading), and the vehicle has to pass a safety check. This permit is good for 12 months or until the out-of-state plates expire, which ever comes first.

Inspections and Emissions Testing

Hawaii requires a yearly safety inspection, but not emission testing.

Passenger Plate Facts

There are two plates with decal (MO & YR) on rear plate.
The first alpha digit on a plate refers to the county of issue as follows:

H	Hawaii
K	Kauai
M	Maui
All other alpha	Honolulu

When a vehicle is sold, the plates remain with the car – not the owner.

Insurance and Financial Responsibility

Hawaii has mandatory no-fault insurance. Minimum financial responsibility limits are $35,000/10,000. Proof of insurance is required as part of the annual vehicle inspection program and after reportable accidents and after "certain" violations. Hawaii uses SR-22 forms.

Withdrawal Sanctions, and Alcohol and Drug Testing

Alcohol and Chemical Testing Limits

Hawaii's alcoholic content provision is .08 %, .04 % for CDL, and zero tolerance if driver under 21 years old. Testing is done by breath or blood. There is an implied-consent law and administrative revocation provisions.

Suspensions and Revocations

Hawaii is in compliance with the federally mandated disqualifications on CDLs per MCSIA. See the Appendix for details – or see a site maintained by Hawaii at http://hawaii.gov/dot/highways/hwy-v.

Under the Influence of Intoxicant .... One-year revocation.
Second DUI Offense within Five Years .... 18-month to two-year revocation.
Third DUI Offense within Five Years .... Two-year revocation.
Driving While License Suspended or Revoked for DUI .... See various penalties below.

Periods of Administrative Revocation of Driver License and Criteria:
1. No prior alcohol contacts during five-year period preceding the date of arrest ... One-year revocation.
2. If one prior alcohol enforcement contact within a five-year period .... 18-month revocation.
3. If two prior alcohol enforcement contacts within a five-year period .... Two years.
4. If three or more priors in the ten years preceding .... Five- to ten-year revocation.
5. Refusals under [(1), (2),] first and [(3)] subsequent are revoked for respective periods of [one, two,] 12 months and [four] two to five years.

Penalties for Driving While License is Suspended or Revoked for DUI:
1. For a first offense, or any offense not preceded within a five-year period by a conviction under this section:
   a. A term of imprisonment at least three consecutive days, but not more than thirty days;
   b. A fine not less than $250, but not more than $1,000; and
   c. License suspension or revocation for an additional year.
   d. Loss of ignition interlock driving privileges
2. For an offense which occurs within five years of a prior conviction under this section:
   a. Thirty-days imprisonment;
   b. A fine of $1,000; and
   c. License suspension or revocation for an additional two years.
   d. Loss of ignition interlock driving privileges
3. For an offense that occurs within five years of two or more prior convictions under this section:
   a. One-year imprisonment;
   b. A $2,000 fine; and
   c. Permanent revocation of the person's license
   d. Loss of ignition interlock driving privileges

Reinstatement Requirements

Suspension or Revocation $10.00 or higher fee; time lapse; SR-22. The fee is $20.00 if for a DUI or OVUII.
To be eligible for re-licensing after a period of administrative revocation has expired, the person shall:

1. Submit to the Director proof of compliance with all conditions imposed by the Director or by the court;
2. Obtain a certified statement from the director indicating eligibility for re-licensing;
3. Present the certified statement to the appropriate licensing official;
4. Pay all applicable fees; and
5. Successfully complete each requirement for obtaining licensure in the state.

Record Access: Laws, Rules, and Forms

Note: This Section Applies to Both Driver and Vehicle Records.

Governing Statutes and Rules

Administrative Rules governing Driver Licensing at:
    http://hawaii.gov/dot/highways/admin-rules/ruleshwy.htm
Chapter 286, Hawaii Revised Statutes, sections 101-140, that govern Driver Licensing may be found at:
    www.capitol.hawaii.gov/docs/HRS.htm
Driving Records: Per §286-172, furnishing of information is very specific as to whom may receive driving records. Hawaii has the following listed as exceptions:
(a) Subject to authorization granted by the chief justice with respect to the traffic records of the violations bureaus of the district courts and of the circuit courts, the director of transportation shall furnish information contained in the statewide traffic records system in response to:

(1) Any request from a state, a political subdivision of a state, or a federal department or agency, or any other authorized person pursuant to rules adopted by the Director of Transportation under chapter 91;
(2) Any request from a person having a legitimate reason, as determined by the director, as provided under the rules adopted by the director under paragraph (1), to obtain the information for verification of vehicle ownership, traffic safety programs, or for research or statistical reports; or
(3) Any request from a person required or authorized by law to give written notice by mail to owners of vehicles.

Vehicle Records: Chapter 286, Hawaii Revised Statutes, sections 41 to 69, relate to Vehicle Registration. Chapter 19-132.2, Hawaii Administrative Rules, relates to the Periodic Inspection of Vehicles. Per

§286-172, VIN and registration information is not available to the public except of certain requests that are in the interest of public health safety and welfare, when a party has a fiduciary interest, or if a subpoena is presented, and via the online system described below. The state laws are more restrictive than DPPA.

Forms & Consent

When a driver gives consent to release of information, personal information is still not released. Also, the subject can state the desired limitations of data release for both driver license and motor vehicle registration information. A special release form is needed when obtaining the driving record of a juvenile. A request form is found at http://hawaii.gov/dot/highways/hwy-v/dhrReqMay2010.PDF to use for a record on a CDL driver.

Vendor and Third Party Access Policy

Approved service vendors can access records for another vendor who represents an end user, as long as the end user has given written consent. It is the responsibility of the original vendor/service provider to ensure that the request is in compliance with the state statutes and the federal DPPA law. The information may not be used to compile a list of individuals for the purposes of any commercial solicitation by mail or otherwise.

Non-permissible Use Requests

With no consent, non-permissible requesters cannot obtain records, even records without personal information.

Editor's Note:
Hawaii does not have a central agency that manages and regulates motor vehicle and driver functions. The Hawaii Department of Transportation, Motor Vehicle Safety Office is responsible for the program co-ordination of five separate county-responsible agencies that oversee driver licensing matters and vehicle registration or titling matters. The State Judiciary is responsible for Traffic Abstracts and Traffic Court Reports.
In each county there is a Traffic Violation Bureau (TVB), which is part of the State Judiciary, which manages the county's driving record convictions. But the TVB in Honolulu is the centralized agency that processes most of the manual record requests. Electronic access to driving records is provided by the Hawaii Information Consortium (HIC).

Access to Driver-Related Records

Driving Records

General Information and Fees
Traffic Violations Bureau (TVB), 1111 Alakea Street, Honolulu HI 96813, 808-538-5500, www.courts.state.hi.us/. The TVB and the traffic courts in each county issue three types of certified documents that report a person's traffic history: traffic abstracts and traffic court reports. The driver's license number, full name, and date of birth are needed when ordering. The TVB also provides a CDL Driving History. Hawaii Information Consortium (HIC) provides online access to records on behalf of Traffic Violations Bureau. The fees are listed below with each record type.

1)**Traffic Abstract** (sometimes called a "public" or "abbreviated"

abstract), shows moving violations and alleged moving offenses, but does **not** show juvenile records unless a *Juvenile Information Release Form* is signed by the juvenile and a parent or legal guardian. If an adult has a juvenile traffic record and would like it displayed on the public record, a signed consent form must be provided.

If requested by mail or in-person the fee is $20.00 per record. The fee is $23.00 if accessed electronically (see below). Traffic Abstracts are normally used for insurance purposes. See www.courts.state.hi.us/self-help/traffic/traffic_abstracts.html.

2)**Traffic Court Report** (sometimes called a "complete" or "court" abstract) shows all cases including juvenile (with signed release form), parking, miscellaneous, dismissed and found not guilty cases.

A photo ID is required from the individual requesting this abstract. If an individual has juvenile record but release form is not provided, an abbreviated abstract without juvenile record will be issued.

The fee is $1.00 for the first page and $.50 for each additional page. Since this record can go back as far as 55 years, the record of drivers with extensive activity can be quite costly to obtain. This document can only be ordered in-person (by the person for whom the record is for) with a photo ID. Traffic Court Reports, which are essentially internal court records, are normally provided to government agencies and attorneys or to the subject person.

3) **Driver History, including commercial driver records,** may be requested by a holder of a CDL or by motor carrier provided that the request is made by the driver in person or the notarized form must be used – see http://hawaii.gov/dot/highways/hwy-v/request-a-copy-of-your-hawaii-driver-history.

The fee is $9.00 per record. If the record is ordered for the motor carrier, the results are mailed directly to the carrier. The results include all accidents, moving violations, FTPs for three years and withdrawal actions for five years. This record is actually maintained by the Department of Transportation but sold by the Traffic Violations Bureaus.

Also, copies of traffic citations issued from October 2005 and forward are available from the Traffic Violations Bureau. Copies of citation issued prior to October 2005 must be obtained from the court of record. The fee is $1.00 for the first page and $.50 for each additional page. There is an additional $5.00 fee if the document is certified.

In-Person – Driving records ordered at the TVB counter are processed in five-to-twenty minutes. Each county will process a limited number of walk-in requests for driving records at their office. The phone numbers of these agencies appear at the front of this chapter. Credit cards are accepted, checks are not. Walk-in requesters may purchase any of the records abstracts with a VISA or MasterCard.

Mail – The TVB—located at the above address—processes the mail-in requests for Traffic Abstracts only. Note that the Traffic Court Reports cannot be ordered by mail. Requests are done on a first-come-first-served basis and may take up to 5 working days to process, depending on volume. The fee must accompany each request. Cashier's checks or money orders should be made payable to "District Court." Include a self-addressed, stamped envelope (SASE).

Electronic – Online ordering of driving records by DPPA compliant requesters is available from the state's designated entity - Hawaii Information Consortium (HIC). Record requests are accepted via FTP. Results, if clear, are returned via FTP. The record fee is $23.00 per record. Record requesters must register with HIC and then be authorized and approved by the state judiciary. An annual $75.00 registration fee is required. HIC offers many additional subscriber services. Visit http://portal.ehawaii.gov/subscriber-services.html or call 808-695-4620 for more information.

There is another means to view moving violations online. Hawaii's Judiciary Information Management System (JIMS) eCourtKokua provides access to information from traffic cases in the district courts of the State of Hawaii. Drivers and the general public can view records by going to www.courts.state.hi.us, then click on "search court records" and choose the "eCourt Kokua" option. The information displayed is not the official record for a case and does not comprise all information from official court records available to the public. Case information provided by the Judiciary through this Web site is made available for public viewing "as is," with no warranties.

Bulk – The state does not offer the driver license database for sale.

By Person of Record – HI drivers may obtain their certified traffic abstract by mail or walk-in as described above at any of the District Courts at the county level. The Traffic Court Report can only be obtained in-person. Phone numbers are found at http://hawaii.gov/dot/news/highways/about/hwy-v/mvso.htm. To view tickets, drivers may visit the Judiciary online system described above.

License Status Check
Kauai County will verify a license status for $5.00.

Notification/Monitoring Program
The Hawaii Information Consortium (HIC), described above, offers a driver monitoring program to approved subscribers. The fee is $.15 per registered driver per month. Fees are billed. Call 808-695-4624 to learn more about this program.

Crash Reports
Reporting – Hawaii has a security-type law for accidents involving death, personal injury, or damage in excess of $3,000.

Accidents within Hawaii County must be reported immediately to the Police Department at 349 Kapiolani Street, Hilo HI 96720. Reports are filed by the police and need not be filed by those involved.

In the City and County of Honolulu, accident reports must be filed if no report is made at the scene. Reports should be filed with the Honolulu Police Department, 801 South King Street, Honolulu 96813.

For Kauai County, accidents must be reported immediately to the Kauai Police Department, 3060 Umi Street, Lihue 96766. Reports must be filed only if the earlier reports were insufficient in the opinion of the Police Dept.

Within Maui (Islands of Maui, Lanai, and Molokai) accidents must be reported immediately to the Police Department at 55 Mahalani Street, Wailuku 96793. No reports need to be filed by those involved in the crash, the police will collect all necessary information.

Record Access – There is no centralized agency to process statewide record keeping for accident reports. The police department in each county must be contacted (see above). For example, in Honolulu reports are available from the Records Division (808-529-3271) 7 days after the accident.

Access to Vehicle-Related Records

General Information and Fees
Vehicle Registration is managed by each county's government. Contact information is shown below.

County of Hawaii
East: Aupuni Center, 101 Pauahi Street, Suite 5, Hilo, HI 96720
West: 75-5751 Kuakini Hwy, Suite 107, Kailua-Kona, HI 96740
www.hawaii-county.com/
Phone: (East) 808-961-8351, Phone: (West) 808-327-3543

City & County of Honolulu
Division of Motor Vehicles and Licensing
PO Box 30320, Honolulu, Hawaii 96820-0320
www.co.honolulu.hi.us/csd/vehicle/dlinformation.htm
Phone: 808-532-7700

County of Kauai
Treasury Division (MVR)
4444 Rice St., Ste 466, Lihue, HI 96766-1340
www.kauai.gov (click on Government, then Treasury)
Phone: 808-241-4256

County of Maui
Department of Finance, Division of Motor Vehicles & Licensing
Maui Mall Shopping Center, 70 E. Kaahumanu Avenue, Suite A-17
Kahului, HI 96732-2176
http://www.co.maui.hi.us/index.aspx?NID=1328
E-mail: maui.dmvl@co.maui.hi.us
Phone: 808-270-7363 Fax: 808-270-7858

Record Request Methods
Each County provides limited counter service for records. With the

exception of the City and County of Honolulu, Hawaii counties do not offer any online record access programs to vehicle or ownership records at this time. Requesters needing bulk records for vehicle recall purposes are asked to contact the dealers.

Online – The City and County of Honolulu provides online title inquiry at www4.honolulu.gov/mvrtitleinq/. Requesters must provide last four digits of VIN and plate number.

Access to Vessel-Related Records

General Information, Access and Fees
Land and Natural Resources, Div. of Boating & Recreation, 333 Queen Street Room 300, Honolulu 96813, http://hawaii.gov/dlnr/dbor/dbor.html, 808-587-1966. Requests must be in writing and describe reason for the search. Liens are filed at the Bureau of Conveyances, but information is made available from this agency. There is no fee to do a registration or lien search. Copies are $.50 per page. Records are maintained since the 1950s (if still active); on microfiche from 1987-1994, and on computer and hard copy from 1994 forward (records are dropped from computer when not renewed). A boat or hull number is needed, but they can do a name search on the computer. Online renewal is available.

Driving Record Content and Reciprocity

What's on or Not on the Abstract Record
- The abstract shows all alleged moving violations, failures to appear, any judgments arising from the operation of a motor vehicle, and any administrative license revocation pursuant to law.
- Parking and equipment violations do not appear on the traffic abstract.
- Juvenile records are not subject to disclosure.
- The driver's address, DOB and other personal information are not part of the record.
- Accidents are only listed if a citation is issued for the accident per above.
- The state does not permit driver school attendance in lieu of conviction. Hawaii's CDL reporting-mandate laws now match the Federal Law.

Data Retention
Until 11/7/05, all violations were purged from record 10 years from final disposition of case. Since that date, CDL record keeping criteria is held to comply with the federal regulations (see Appendix). The courts hold the traffic records for 55 years.

Court to Repository
The courts input conviction data direct into the computer system.

State Reciprocity for Non-CDL Drivers
- Will suspend license of driver for unpaid out-of-state convictions.
- Record of new incoming driver is shown on MVR.
- Out-of-state convictions are shown on MVR.
- Out-of-state accidents are shown on MVR if sent electronically.
- Convictions of out-of-state drivers are sent to home state.
- Record is forwarded to new state upon surrender of license.

License Classes, Restrictions, and Commercial Endorsements

License Classes– Commercial
Class A	Any combination of vehicles with a GCWR of 26,001 pounds or more; GVWR of vehicles towed is in excess of 10,000 pounds.
Class B	Any single vehicle with a GVWR of 26,001 pounds or more; the GVWR of a towed vehicle is 10,000 pounds or less.
Class C	Any single vehicle or combination of vehicles that meets neither the definition of A or B and is designed to transport sixteen or more passengers, or used to haul hazardous materials requiring placards.

License Classes– Non-Commercial
Class 1	Motor scooters 5hp or less.
Class 2	Motorcycles over 5hp and motor scooters.
Class 3	Any single vehicle with a GVWR of 15,000 pounds or less and vehicles designed to transport fifteen or fewer passengers (including the driver).
Class 4	Any single vehicle with a GVWR of 15,001 to 26,000 pounds.

Restrictions
A	Corrective Lenses	I	Hearing Aid	Q	Mechanical Aid
B	Outside Mirror	J	Power Brakes	R	Prosthetic Aid
C	Automatic Transmission	K	Vehicle Without Air-Brakes	S	Limit to Employment
D	Daylight Hours Only	L	Steering Knob	T	Limited - Other
E	Full Hand-Equipment	M	Cushion	V	CDL Intrastate Only
F	Mechanical Signals	N	Medical Requirements	X	Except Class A Bus
G	Taxi	O	Others	Y	Except Class A & B Bus
H	Power Steering	P	Three-Wheel Motorcycles	Z	Except Tractor-Trailer

Endorsements
H	Placarded Hazardous Material	S	School Bus
T	Double-/Triple-Trailers	N	Tank Vehicles
P	Passengers (sixteen or more including driver)	X	Tank/HazMat Vehicles

Conviction Table with Statutes and ACD

Each moving violation is indicated with a statute number. Hawaii Revised Statutes Chapter 286 sections 101-140 that govern Driver Licensing may be found at: http://www.capitol.hawaii.gov/docs/HRS.htm

The table below has two description columns. The shorter version in all capital letters is used (we believe) on the abstract. The longer version may be helpful when trying to decipher meanings.

Note that Hawaii does NOT employ a points system.

Statute	ACD	Short Description	Long Description
264-64	M50	CONTROLLED ACCESS FACILITY	Controlled Access Facility
281-101.5	A31	ALCOHOL PROHIBITIONS RE MINORS	Alcohol Prohibitions Re Minors
286-102	B51	NO MOTOR VEH DRIVER'S LICENSE	Driving w/o Valid Motor Veh. Driver's Lic.
286-102.6		PROVISIONAL LICENSE, UNDER 18	No Motor Veh Driver's License
286-102.6(b)		PROVISIONAL LICENSE REQUIREMENT VIOLATION	Provisional License, Under 18
286-102.6(c)		PROVISIONAL LICENSE REQUIREMENT VIOLATION	Provisional License Requirement Violation
286-102(a)	B91	DRIV W/O VALID DRIVER LICENSE	Provisional License Requirement Violation
286-102(b)	B91	IMPROPER DL CLASS	Driving without Valid Driver License
286-102(e)	D51	FAIL TO PAY CHILD SUPPORT	Improper Dl Class
286-103	D29	SPECL RESTRICS ON DRIVERS LIC	Special Restrictions on Driver's Lic.
286-103(a)	D29	SPECL RESTRICT ON DR LIC-MOPED	Special Restrict On Dr License for-Moped
286-104(1)	W20	DL SUSPENSION	Driver License Suspension
286-104(2)	W20	EXAM REQUIRED	Exam Required
286-104(3)	W20	MUST SHOW PROOF FINANCIAL RESP	Must Show Proof Financial Responsibility
286-104(4)	W14	PHYS OR MENTAL DISABILITY	Phys Or Mental Disability
286-105	D29	OPR FARM EQP ON HWY UND AGE 13	Operate Farm Equipment on Hwy Under Age 13
286-106	B51	EXPIRED DRIVER'S LIC	Expired driver's license
286-108.5		DRIVER IMPROVEMNT PROGRAM-D	Driver Improvement Program-D
286-109		UNPAID FEE/FINE	Unpaid Fee/Fine
286-109(c)	D56	UNPAID FEE/FINE	Unpaid Fee/Fine
286-110	B51	INSTRUCTION PERMIT	Instruction permit
286-110(d)	D29	INSTR PERM (NO LIC DRVR PRES)	Instruction permit (no licensed driver present)
286-110(e)	D29	MC/MS NO PASNGR, NO NITE DRVNG	Motorcycle/motorscooter no passenger, no night driving
286-111		PERMIT & FL FEES	Permit & FL Fees
286-112	W13	PARENT/GUARDIAN LIABILITY	Parent/Guardian Liability
286-113	W13	RELEASE FROM LIABILITY	Parental consent withdrawn
286-114	W13	PARENT/GUARDIAN DEATH	Parental consent withdrawn
286-116		NO DRIVER'S LIC ON PERSON	No Driver's License on Person
286-116.5		DRV LIC HLDR-NOTIC CHG NAME	Drv Lic Holder-Notice of Change Name
286-116(a)	B78	FAIL TO SHOW NON-COMM DRV LIC/PERMIT	Fail To Show Non-Commercial Driver Lic/Permit
286-116(c)		REGIS OWNER CITED-NO INS CARD	Registration owner cited-no insurance card
286-116(d)		LIC-INS ID CARD-POSSESS/EXHIBT	License-insurance id card-possess/exhibit
286-116(e)		PERMIT UNINSD MV ON HWY	Permit Uninsured MV on Hwy
286-117		ILLEGIBLE DRIV PERMIT OR LICENSE	Illegible Driving Permit Or License
286-119	W20	DL EXAMNR DETERMINE DR INCOMPETENT	DL Examiner Determine Dr is Incompetent
286-120		DR EX CANCEL DRV LIC	Driving on expired Cancel Drive License
286-122		SUSPENSION OF LICENSE;SURRENDR	Suspension of license; surrender
286-123		DL SUSP/REV DUE TO CONVICTION	Dl Susp/Rev Due To Conviction
286-128	W01	ORDER TO SHOW CAUSE (POINT S	Order To Show Cause (Point S
286-128(b)		ORDER TO SHOW CAUSE-12 PTS	Order To Show Cause-12 Pts
286-128(M)	W01	ORDER TO SHOW CAUSE-6 PTS	Order To Show Cause-6 Pts
286-128(d)		FAILURE TO REPORT	Failure To Report
286-130	B26	NO OPS FRGN LIC DRNG REVOC/SUS	Operating w/foreign lic during rev/suspension
286-131	D16	FRAUDULENT USE OF LICENSE	Fraudulent Use of License
286-131 (1)	D16	FRAUDULENT USE OF LICENSE	Fraudulent Use of License
286-131 (5)	D02	FALSE INFO ON DL APPLICATION	False Info On Dl Application
286-131 (6)	B41	FRAUDULENT USE OF LICENSE	Fraudulent Use of License
286-132	B26	DRVNG WHILE LIC SUSP OR REVOKD	Driving With Revoked or Suspended Lic.
286-133		PERMIT UNLIC DRIVER TO DRIVE	Permitting an Unlicensed Driver. To Use Veh.
286-133 (a)		MOPED-PERMIT UNLIC DR TO DR	Moped-Permit Unlic Dr To Dr
286-134		EMPLOY UNLIC DRIVER TO DRIVE	Employing an Unlicensed Driver to Drive
286-151	A12	REFUSAL TO SUBMIT TO SOBRI TEST	Refusal To Submit To Sobriety Test
286-151.5	A12	REFUSAL TO SUBMIT TO SOBRI TEST UN 21	Refusal To Submit To Sobriety Test Un 21
286-155	A12	REFUSAL TO SUBMT TO SOBRI TEST	Refusal To Submit To Sobriety Test
286-155.5	A12	REFUSAL TO SUBMT TO SOBRI TEST	Refusal To Submit To Sobriety Test
286-157.3	A12	REFUSAL TESTING, DRUGS	Refusal Testing, Drugs
286-181		TRANSP OF STUDNTS & SAFETY REQ	Trans. Students & safety req

Statute	ACD	Short Description	Long Description
286-202.6		REQD COMMERCIAL MV MARKIN	Required Commercial MV Marking
286-21	F66	UNSAFE CONDITION OF VEH	Unsafe Condition of Vehicle
286-210		SAFETY STICKER DECAL	Safety Sticker Decal
286-223		TRNSPRTG HZDS MTRL	Transporting hazardous materials
286-223(c)		PACKAGG/MARKG/HANDLG HZDS MTRL	Package/marking/handling hazardous material
286-223(d)		SPILL/DUMP HAZARDOUS MATERIAL	Spill/dump hazardous material
286-224		INSPCTG MV TRNSPRTG HZDS MTRL	Inspecting MV transporting hazardous material
286-225		RPRTG INCIDENT W/HZDS MTRL	Reporting incident w/hazardous material
286-226		NOTC-INTRASTAT SHPMT OF XPLOSV	NOTC-Intrastate Shipment of Explosives
286-232	D07	LIMIT ON COMMERCL DRIVR LICENS	Limit on commercial driver license
286-233		NOTC OF VIOLATN-CDL DRIVER	Notice of Violation-CDL Driver
286-233(a)		NOTC OF VIOLATN-CDL DRIVER	Notice of Violation-CDL Driver
286-234		EMPLOYER RESP CMV APPLICANTS	Employer responsible CMV applicants
286-234(a)		EMPLOYER RESP CMV APPLICANTS	Employer responsible CMV applicants
286-234(b)		EMPLYR RSPNSBLTY-CDL DRIVER	Employer responsibility-CDL driver
286-234(b1)		EMPLOYING DIS/SUSP/REVOK DRIV	Employing Dis/Susp/Revok Driv
286-234(b2)		EMPLOYING DRIV W/>1 LICENSE	Employing Driv W/>1 License
286-234(b3)		EMPLOYING OUT OF SERVICE	Employing Out Of Service
286-234(b4)		EMPLOYING VIOL RAIROAD XING	Employing Viol Railroad Xing
286-235	B51	CDL REQRD	CDL required
286-235(a)	B56	DRVING CMV W/O CDL LIC/PERM	CDL required - Driving a CMV without a CDL license and /or permit
286-235(b)	B57	DRG CMV W/O CDL IN DRIVER'S POSSESSION	Driving a CMV without a CDL in the driver's possession
286-235(c)	B20	DRIVG W/SUSPD,RVOKD CDL LIC	Driving w/suspended, revoked CDL license
286-235(d)	B27	DRG WHILE OUT-OF-SERVICE ORDER IN EFFECT	Driving While Out-Of-Service Order In Effect
286-236(f)	D29	DRV W/PERMIT W/O LIC DRV ACCOMP	Driving W/Permit W/O Lic Driver Accompanied
286-240	W30	TWO SERIOUS VIOLATIONS WITHIN THREE YRS	Two Serious Violations Within Three Yrs
286-240(a4)	U03	USING CMV IN ANY FELONY	Using CMV In Any Felony
286-240(a5)	B01	LEAVE CDL ACC SCENE	Leave CDL Acc Scene
286-240(a6)	A33	UNLAWFUL CONTROLLED SUB /ON DUTY	Unlawful Controlled Sub /On Duty
286-240(a7)	W45	DRVG CMV WHILE PR DISQ CMV	Driving CMV While Previously Disq CMV
286-240(c)	W40	TWO OR MORE MAJOR OFFENSES	Two Or More Major Offenses
286-240(d)	A50	CDL USE/FELONY W/CONTROL SUB	CDL - Use/Felony W/Control Sub
286-240(e)	W31	THREE SERIOUS VIOLATIONS WITHIN THREE YRS	Three Serious Violations Within Three Yrs
286-240(f)	D02	FALSE INFO/FAIL TO REPORT	False Info/Fail To Report
286-240(g)	B27	VIOLATE OUT-OF-SERVICE ORDER	Violate Out-Of-Service Order
286-240(h)	B19	DRVG W/OOS ORDER ON EFF-16 PASS/HAZMAT	Driving W/Out of Service Order On Eff-16 Pass/Hazmat
286-240(i)	W61	THREE RRGC VIOLATIONS WITHIN THREE YRS	Three RR Grade Crossing Violations Within Three Yrs
286-240(i)	W60	TWO RRGC VIOLATIONS WITHIN THREE YRS	Two RR Grade Crossing Violations Within Three Yrs
286-240(i1)	M20	FAIL TO SLOW DOWN AT RRGC,TRACKS NOT CLEAR	Fail To Slow Down At RR Grade Crossing, Tracks Not Clear
286-240(i2)	M21	FAIL TO STOP AT RRGC, TRACKS NOT CLEAR	Fail To Stop At RR Grade Crossing, Tracks Not Clear
286-240(i3)	M22	FAILURE TO STOP AT RRGC	Failure To Stop At RR Grade Crossing
286-240(i4)	M23	FAIL TO HAVE SUFFICIENT SPACE AT RRGC	Fail To Have Sufficient Space At RR Grade Crossing c
286-240(i5)	M10	FAIL TO OBEY TRAFFIC CONTROL, DIRECTIONS	Fail To Obey Traffic Control, Directions
286-240(i6)	M24	FAIL AT RRGC DUE TO INSUFF UNDER CLEARANCE	Fail At RR Grade Crossing c Due To Insuff Under Clearance
286-240(j)	W70	DRIVER AN IMMINENT HAZARD	Driver An Imminent Hazard
286-240(g)	W50	TWO OOS ORDER GEN VIOLATIONS WITHIN TEN YRS	Two Out of Service Order Gen Violations Within Ten Yrs
286-240(g)	W52	THREE OR MORE OOS ORDER VIOL WITHIN 10 YRS	Three Or More Out of Service Order Viol Within 10 Yrs
286-240 (h)	W51	TWO OOS ORDR VIOL TEN YR 16+ PASS OR HAZMT	Two Out of Service Order Viol Ten Yr 16+ Pass Or Hazmat
286-241.4	W09	FAIL TO SURRENDER HME	Fail To Surrender Hazmat Endorsement
286-241.4(a)	W72	SUSPENDED PENDING FINAL DISPOSITION	Suspended Pending Final Disposition
286-242(a)	A26	COMM DRVR - ALCOHOL PROHIB	Commercial driver-alcohol prohibited
286-242(c)	A04	DRVG CMV UNDER INFLU LIQUOR WITH .04 BAC	Driving CMV Under Influ Liquor With .04 BAC

Statute	ACD	Short Description	Long Description
286-243	A12	CMV IMPLIED CONSENT	CMV implied consent
286-243(a)	A94	IMPLIED CONSENT-CMV DRVR	Implied consent-CMV driver
286-25		VEH W/O INSPECTION CERT	Veh Without Inspection Certification
286-30		MAK/ISS/USE FALS VEH INSP CERT	Make/Issus/Use False Veh Insp Cert
286-41(a)		FAIL REG MTR VEH BY CORP OWNR	Fail Reg Mtr Veh By Corp Ownr
286-44		UNL TO POSS CERT MTR VEH,PR	Unl To Poss Cert Mtr Veh,Pr
286-47.2		CERTIFICATE OF TRAILER REGISTR	Certificate Of Trailer Registr
286-47(3)		REGIST NOT IN VEH (ALSO MC)	Registration Not In Veh (Also Mc)
286-52.5		PROC WHEN TITLE TRANSFRD; NOTIC	Proc When Title Transfrd; Notice
286-54		REGIS OUT-OF-ST PLTS W/IN 10 D	Regis Out-Of-St Plates W/In 10 Days
286-81	F03	MTRCYCLE PROTECTIVE DEVIC	Motorcycle Protective Device
286-85		NO RECONSTRUCTION PERMIT	No Reconstruction Permit
286PARTXIV	A98	ADMIN HRNG FOR DUI	Administrative Hearing for DUI
287-16	D39	UNSATISFIED JUDGEMENT	Unsatisfied judgment
287-20	B63	LIC SUS FAIL TO POST FINAN RES	Lic Suspended-Failed to Post Financial Responsibility
287-4	B61	RPT REQ AFT ACCIDENT	Report required after accident
287-41		FAILURE TO SURRENDER LICENSE	Failure to surrender license
287-44	D35	LIC SUSP-FAIL POST FINANCIAL	Lic suspension--fail post financial
287-44(c)	D35	GIVING FALSE INFORMATION	Giving false information
287-44(d)	B26	DRIVNG W/SUSPENDED/REVOKED LIC	Driving while license susp/rev
287-5	B64	SECURITY REQD OR EVIDC OF INSU	Security required or evidence of insurance
287-6	D38	FAILURE TO POST SECURITY	Failure To Post Security
291-11		CARRY PASS UND 7 YRS ON MC/MS	Carry Pass Under 7 Years on motorcycle/motorscooter
291-11.5	F02	CHILD PASSENGER RESTRAINT	Child Passenger Restraint
291-11.5(1)	F02	CHILD PASSENGER UNDER 3 YRS	Child Passenger Under 3 Yrs
291-11.5(2)	F02	3 YRS < 4 YRS OLD-STBLT & HAR	3 Yrs < 4 Yrs Old-Stblt & Har
291-11.6	F04	MANDATORY USE OF SEAT BELTS	Mandatory Use Of Seat Belts
291-12	M82	INATTENTION TO DRIVING	Inattention To Driving
291-14	F05	PICKUP TRUCKS; PASS RESTR	Pickup Trucks; Pass Restr
291-14(a)	F05	PICKUP TRUCKS; PASSENGER RESTR	Pickup Trucks; Passenger Restr
291-14(c)	F05	UNDER 12 YRS OLD IN P/U TRUCKBED	Under 12 Yrs Old In P/U Truckbed
291-17(a)	M85	CDL DRIVER TEXTING WHILE DRVG CMV	CDL driver texting while driving a CMV
291-2	M84	RECKLESS DRIVING	Reckless Driving
291-21.5		TINT GLAZE-GLASS SUNSCREENING	Tint Glaze-Glass Sunscreening
291-24		MTRCY/MOPED NOISY MUFFLER	Motorcycle/Moped Noisy Muffler
291-25	E55	USE OF LIGHTS REQUIRED	Use Of Lights Required
291-25(a)	E34	DEFEC HEADLIGHT (MV,MC/MS)	Defective Headlight (MV or MCycle or MS)
291-28		RED FLG OR LT ON REAR LOAD OUT	Red Flag Or Lt On Rear Load Out
291-3.1	A26	CONSM OR POS INTOX LIQ OPER MV	Consuming or possessing liquor (operator)
291-3.1(a)	A26	CONS INTOX LIQ OPER MV PUB STR	Consuming intox liq operating motor vehicle on public street
291-3.2	A31	CONSUM/POS LIQ AS PSNGR IN MV	Consume or possess liquor as passenger in motor vehicle
291-3.2(a)	A31	CONSUM LIQ PSGR IN MV PUB STR	Consume liquor passenger in motor vehicle on public street
291-3.2(b)	A35	PSGR W/RECEP LIQ SEAL BROKEN	Passenger w/recep liq seal broken
291-3.3	A35	STORG OPEND CNTNR W/INTOX LIQ	Storing opened Container w/Intox Liq
291-3.3(a)	A35	REMV LIQ-SEAL BRKN-FR IN CAR	Remove liq-seal broken-front in car
291-3.3(b)		INTOX LIQUOR SCENIC LOOKOUT	Intox liquor scenic lookout
291-31	E55	USE OF TAIL LIGHTS REQRD	Use Of Tail Lights Required
291-33		DRVNG VEH W/WHEELS W/RIBS,ETC	Driving Veh W/Wheels W/Ribs,Etc
291-34		SIZE OF VEHICLE VIOLATIONS	Size Of Vehicle Violations
291-35		WEIGHT-LOAD OF VEH VIOLATIONS	Weight-Load Of Veh Violations
291-35.1		REGULATION OF BUMPER HEIGHT	Regulation Of Bumper Height
291-36		PRMT TO OP VEH EXCD HWL & WGHT	Permit To Operate Veh Excd Hwl & Wght
291-39(e)		REFUSING TO SUBMIT TO WEIGHING	Refusing To Submit To Weighing
291-4	A21	DRIVING UNDER INFL OF ALCOHOL	Driving Under Infl Of Alcohol
291-4.3	A60	UNDER 21 DRV; .02 BAC OR MORE	Under 21 Drv; .02 BAC Or More
291-4.4	A20	HABITUALLY DRIVING UNDER IN	Habitually Driving Under In
291-4.4(a1)	A20	HABITUALLY DRIVING UNDER INFLU	Habitually Driving Under Influ
291-4.4(a2)	A08	HABITUAL DUI WITH .08 ALCOHOL	Habitual Dui With .08 Alcohol
291-4.4(a3)	A22	HABITUAL DUI WITH DRUGS	Habitual Dui With Drugs
291-4.5	B26	DRIV AFTER LIC SUS/UNDER IN	Driv After Lic Sus/Under In
291-4.(a)(1)	A21	DRIV UND INFLU INTOX LIQUOR	Driv Und Influ Intox Liquor
291-4.(a)(2)	A08	DRIV WITH .08 BLOOD ALC LEV	Driv With .08 Blood Alc Lev
291-7	A22	DRIVING UNDER INFL OF DRUGS	Driving Under Influence Of Drugs

Statute	ACD	Short Description	Long Description
291-8		LOAD PROJ BYND WDTH VEH/TRK	Load Projecting Beyond Width Veh/Trk
291C-101	S94	SPEED RESTR UNDER CERT CONDS	Speed restriction under cert conditions
291C-102	S92	NONCOMPLIANCE-SPEED LIMIT	Noncompliance-Speed Limit
291C-102(a)	S93	NONCMPLN W/SPEED LIM - CTY ORD	Non-compliance with speed limit – county ordinance
291C-102(b)	S93	NONCMPLN W/SPEED LIM-DOT SIGN	Non-compliance with speed Limit – DOT Sign
291C-102-UND	S96	NONCOMPLIANCE-SPEED LIMIT	Non-compliance with speed limit
291C-103	S95	RACING ON HIGHWAYS	Racing on highways
291C-103(a)	S95	EXHIBIT SPEED OR ACCELERATION	Exhibit Speed Or Acceleration
291C-103(b)	S95	RACING ON HIGHWAY-SPEED CONTE	Racing on highways-speed contest
291C-103(d)	S95	EXHIBIT SPEED OR ACCELERATION	Exhibit speed or acceleration
291C-104	S93	SPEEDING SCHOOL/CONSTRUCTON ZN	Speeding in school/construction zone
291C-105	S92	EXCESSIVE SPEEDING	Excessive Speeding
291C-105A1(2c3)	S92	SPEED 30+/80+ MPH 5YRS 2 PRIOR	Speed 30+/80+ MPH 5yrs 2 Prior
291C-12	B02	ACC INVLVG DEATH/SERIOUS INJRY	Accident involving death/serious personal Injury
291C-12(a)	B06	ACC INVLVG DEATH/SERIOUS INJRY	Accident involving death/serious personal Injury
291C-12.5	B07	ACCDNTS INV SUBST BODILY INJRY	Accident involving substantial bodily injury
291C-12.6	B03	ACCDNTS INVOLVNG BODILY INJURY	Accident involving bodily injury
291C-121		UNATT VEH	Unattended Veh
291C-121(a)		KEYS IN CAR	Keys In Car
291C-121(b)		MOTOR RUNNING	Motor Running
291C-122	N82	UNSAFE BACKING	Unsafe backing
291C-123	M47	DRIVING UPON BIKEWAY	Driving on sidewalk, bike lane
291C-124	D70	OBSTRUCTION OF DRIVER'S VIEW	Obstruction to driver's view
291C-124(a)	D70	OBSTRUCTION OF VIEW BY OVERLD	Obstruction to driver's view by overload
291C-124(b)	D70	HOLDING PERSON/ANIMAL ON LAP	Holding person or animal on lap
291C-125		UNSAF OPENING & CLOSING VEH	Unsafe opening & closing Vehicle
291C-126		RIDE IN HOUSE TRAILER WHEN MOV	Ride in house trailer when moving
291C-127	N80	COASTING (DRIVER OF VEH)	Coasting (Driver of Vehicle)
291C-128	M32	FOLLOWING EMERGENCY VEH	Following emergency vehicle
291C-129	M56	VEH CROSSING OVER FIRE HOSE	Veh crossing over fire hose
291C-13	B08	ACCIDTS INV DAMAGE TO VEH/PROP	Accident involve damage to veh or property
291C-131		SPILL LOADS ON HIGHWAY	Spill Loads On Highway
291C-131(a)		VEH NOT CONSTRUCTED, COVERED, OR	Vehicle Not Constructed, Covered, Or
291C-131(b)		LOAD NOT ENTI W/IN BOD OF VEH	Load Not Entirely within Body Of Vehicle
291C-131(d)		LOAD NOT COV CARGO NT,TARP,CAN	Load Not Covered Cargo Nt,Tarp,Can
291C-131(e)		UNCOVERED GRANULAR LOAD	Uncovered Granular Load
291C-132		LITTER FRM VEH – DRIVER CIT	Litter Farm Veh – Driver Cit
291C-14	B05	ACC: DUTY TO GIV INF-REND AID	Accident: Duty to Give Info-Render Aid
291C-14(a)	B14	ACC: DUTY TO GIV INF-REND AID	Accident: Duty to Give Info-Render Aid
291C-147		LAMPS/EQMT ON BICYCLES	Lamps/Equipment On Bicycles
291C-148(a)	M58	DRIVING UPON SIDEWALK-VEHICLE	Driving Vehicle On The Sidewalk
291C-148(b)		DRVNG ON SIDEWALK—BICYCLE	Driving On Sidewalk—Bicycle
291C-15	B04	ACCID-STRKNG UNATT VEH/PROPTY	Accident: Duty if Striking Unatt Veh/Prop
291C-152		RIDING ON MOTORCYCLES	Riding on Motorcycles (not in seat)
291C-153(a)	M48	MOTORCYCLE ENTITLED TO LANE	Motorcycle Entitled to Full Use of Lane
291C-153(b)	M48	NO PASSING VEH IN SAME LANE	Motorcycle no passing veh in same lane
291C-153(c)	M48	NO RIDING BETWEEN LANES	Motorcycle no riding between lanes
291C-153(d)	M48	NO MORE THAN 2 ABREAST IN LANE	Motorcycle no more than 2 abreast in lane
291C-154		MOTORCYCLE ATTACH TO VEHICLE	Motorcycle Rider Clinging to Veh on Rd
291C-16	B61	ACCIDENT: IMMED NOTICE OF ACCI	Accident, must give Immediate Notice
291C-17		WRITTEN REPORTS OF ACCIDENTS	Written Reports Of Accidents
291C-172		REFUSE TO PROV IS—POLICE OR	Refuse To Prov Is—Police Or
291C-18		ACCIDENT: GIVING FALSE REPORT	Accident: giving false report
291C-194	B51	DRIVER LIC REQD FOR MOPED	Driver license required for moped
291C-195(a)		NO PERSON<15 TO DRIV MOPED	Operate moped under age 15
291C-195(c)		NO PASS PERM ON MOPED	No Pass Perm On Moped
291C-206		MODIFY MOPED MOTR-1 ½ HP MAX	Modify Moped Motr-1 ½ Hp Max
291C-222	M49	HIGH OCCUPANCY VEHICLE LANE	High occupancy vehicle lane
291C-23	M08	OBED TO POLICE DIR (DIR TRAF)	Failed to obey Police Order/Direction
291C-31	M14	OBED TO & REQD TRAF-CTL DEVCES	Failed to obey Required Traffic control Devices
291C-32	M16	DISREGD TRAF CTL SIGNAL LEGEND	Disregard traffic control legend
291C-32(a3a)	M16	DISREGARDING RED SIGNAL	Disregarding Red Signal
291C-32(a3b)	M14	NO RIGHT TURN ON RED (POSTED)	No Right Turn On Red (Posted)
291C-32(a3c)	N53	LEFT TURN RED PROH.L-WAY ST	Left Turn Red Prohibited lane or one way street
291C-32(3a)	M16	DISREGARING RED SIGNAL	Disregarding Red Signal
291C-34	M18	FLASHING SIGNALS	Flashing signals

Statute	ACD	Short Description	Long Description
291C-34(a)(1)	M18	FAIL TO STOP ON FLASHING RED	Fail to Stop on Flashing Red
291C-34(a)(2)	M18	SLOW & PRCD W/CAUT ON FLSH YEL	Slow & Proceed w/Caution on Flashing Yellow
291C-35	M40	LANE-DIRECTION-CONTROL SIGNALS	Lane-direction-control signals
291C-38	M05	DISREGARD TRAF LANE MARKINGS	Disregard traffic lane markings
291C-38(c)(1)	M05	BROKEN WHITE LINE;SAFE CROSSNG	Broken white line; safe crossing
291C-38(c)(12)	M11	VEH PROHIBITED ON BICYCLE LANE	Veh Prohibited on Bicycle Lane
291C-38(c)(2)	M05	CROSSING BROKEN YELLOW LINE	Crossing broken yellow line
291C-38(c)(3)	M05	DISREG SINGLE-SOLID WHITE LINE	Disregard single-solid white line
291C-38(c)(5)	M05	DISREGARDNG DBLE SOLID WHITE	Disregarding double solid white
291C-38(c)(6)	M05	DISREGARDING SOLID YELLOW LINE	Disregarding solid yellow line
291C-38(c)(8)	M05	DOUBLE SOLID YELLOW LINE	Double solid yellow line
291C-38(c)(9)	M05	CROSG SLD YEL LINE OF DBL LINE	Crossing solid yellow line of dbl line
291C-41	M57	DRIVG ON RIGHT SIDE OF ROAD	Driving on right side of road
291C-41(b)	M60	SLOW VEH TO DRIVE IN RT LANE	Slow vehicle to drive in right lane
291C-42	M72	PASSNG VEH PROCEEDG IN OPP DIR	Passing vehicle proceeding in opposite direction
291C-43	M72	OVERTAKING VEHICLE ON THE LEFT	Overtaking vehicle on the left
291C-43(1)	M72	OVRTAKG IN SAME DIR:SAFE CLRNC	Overtaking at safe distance left side
291C-43(2)	N07	VEH TO GIVE WAY WHEN OVERTAKEN	Vehicle to Give Way When Overtaken
291C-44	M76	OVRTKNG VEH ON RIGHT SHOULDER	Overtaking Vehicle on Right Shoulder
291C-44(b)	M43	OVRTAKG ON RT-SAFE MOVMNT	Overtaking on right-safe movement
291C-44(2)	M73	OVRTKNG VEH – EMERGENCY LANE	Overtaking VEH – EMERGENCY LANE
291C-45	M77	UNSAFE OVERTAKING ON LEFT SIDE	Unsafe overtaking on left side
291C-46	M57	DRIVING ON LEFT OF CTR OF RDWY	Driving left of center of roadway
291C-46(a)	M57	NO DRIVG ON LT SIDE OF ROADWAY	No driving on left side of roadway
291C-46(a)(1)	M74	DRIVG ON LT:APPRCHG GRAD,CURV	Driving on left-approaching grad, curve
291C-46(a)(2)	M57	DRIVG ON LT:APPRCHG INTERSECT	Driving on left-approaching intersect
291C-46(a)(3)	M57	DRIVG ON LT:APPRCHG BRIG,TUNL	Driving on left-approaching brig, tunnel
291C-47	M71	NO PASSING ZONES	No passing zones
291C-47(a)	M71	NO PASSING ZONES	No passing zones
291C-47(b)	M71	NO PASSING ZONES	No passing zones
291C-48	N63	DRV ON ONE-WAY RDWY & TRAF ISL	Driving on One-Way Rd & Traffic Island
291C-48(b)	N63	VEH DRIVEN IN DSGNATD DIR ONLY	Veh driven in designated dir only
291C-48(c)	N61	DRIV ON RT OF ROTARY ISLAND	Driving on right of rotary island
291C-49	M42	DRIVG ON RDWY LANED FOR TRAF	Unsafe Changing of Lanes
291C-49(1)	M42	UNSAFE LANE CHANGE (SINGLE LN)	Unsafe lane change (single lane)
291C-49(3)	M05	DISRG TRF CTL DEV INCL LN DESG	Driving on One-Way Rd & Traffic Island
291C-49(4)	M05	OBEY DIR OF TRAF CTROL DEV	Obey dir of traffic control dev
291C-50	M34	FOLLOWING TOO CLOSELY	Following too closely
291C-50(a)	M34	FOLLOWG VEH TOO CLOSE PROHIB	Following vehicle too closely
291C-50(b)	M31	TOW VEH TO LV SPAC FOR OVRTAKG	Failure to leave space for overtaking tossed vehicle
291C-50(c)	M31	CARVN TO LV SPAC FOR OTR VEH	Caravan to leave space for other vehicle
291C-51	M51	DRVNG OVER/ACR MED STRP, SPACE	Driving over/across med strip space
291C-52	M46	RSTR ENTR & EXIT TO CTLD AC HY	Restr enter & exit to controlled access hwy
291C-53	M40	RESTR USE OF CTRL RD/HWY	Restricted use of controlled rd/hwy
291C-53(c)	M40	RESTR USE OF CTRL RD/HWY	Restricted use of controlled rd/hwy
291C-61	N25	FAIL TO YIELD RT OF WAY AT INT	Fail to Yield Right of Way at Intersection
291C-62	N31	TURN'G VEH TO YIELD RT-OF-WAY	Turning veh to yield right-of-way
291C-63	N22	VEH ENTRG STOP,YIELD INTERSECT	Vehicle entering stop or yield at intersection
291C-63(b)	M15	DISREGARDING STOP SIGN	Disregarding stop sign
291C-63(c)	M19	DISREGARDING YIELD SIGN	Disregarding yield sign
291C-64	N01	UNSAFE EMRGNG FRM PRV ROAD/HWY	Unsafe emerging from private road/hwy
291C-65	N05	RIGHT OF WAY OF EMERGENCY VEHS	Right of Way Emergency Vehicles
291C-72	N20	VH YLD RT OF WY TO PED IN CROS	Vehicle yield Right of Way to Ped in Crosswalk
291C-72(a)	N20	VH YLD RT OF WY TO PED IN CROS	Vehicle yield Right of Way to Ped in Crosswalk
291C-74	M81	DRVRS EXER CARE CHLDN/DISABLED	Driver must exercise care children/disabled
291C-75	M40	PEDESTRN TO USE (R) HALF X-WLK	Pedestrian to use (r) half x-wlk
291C-77	M40	PEDESTRN SOLICIT RIDES/ATTENTION	Pedestrian solicit rides/attention
291C-78	M12	VEH DRIVE THROUGH SAFETY ZONE	Vehicle driven through safety zone
291C-79	N20	VEH YLD RT OF WY PEDS ON SIDWK	Failed to yield Right of Way Peds in Sidewalk
291C-81	N51	IMPROPER RT OR LFT TURN AT INT	Improper Left or Right Turn At Intersection
291C-81(1)	N54	MAKG RT TURN AT INTERSECT	Making right turn at intersect
291C-81(3)	M14	OBEY TRAF-CTL DEV AT INTERSECT	Obey traffic-control dev at intersect
291C-82	N55	TURN'G TO PROCEED IN OPP DIRCT	Turning to proceed in opposite direct
291C-82(a)	N56	UTURN AT CURV/NR GRAD,CREST	U-turn at curve/near grad crest
291C-82(c)	N56	NO U-TURN ON HIGHWAY-SIGN POST	U-Turn on Hwy (Sign Posted)
291C-83	N83	UNSAF MVEMT FRM STOP,STND,PARK	Starting Parked Vehicle (unsafe movement)

Statute	ACD	Short Description	Long Description
291C-84	N40	TURNG MOVEMENT/REQD SIGNAL	Turning movement required signal
291C-84(a)	N52	UNSAFE MOVEMENT WHEN TURNING	Unsafe movement when turning
291C-84(b)	N43	TURN SGNL W/IN 100' OF TURN	Turn Signal W/In 100 Feet of Turn
291C-84(c)	N40	NO STOP'G, SLOW'G W/OUT SIGNAL	No stopping/slowing w/out signal
291C-84(d)	N43	TURN SIGNL FOR LANE CHANGE	Turn signal for lane change
291C-85	N40	SIGS BY HND & ARM OR SIG LAMPS	Signals by Hand & Arm or Signal Lamps
291C-85(a)	N40	SIG BY HND & ARM/SIG LAMPS	Signals by Hand & Arm or Signal Lamps
291C-85(b)	N40	SIG BY HND & ARM/SIG LAMPS	Signals by Hand & Arm or Signal Lamps
291C-91	M09	OBEDNC TO SIG FOR APPCHG TRAIN	Obedience to signal for approaching train
291C-92	M09	NO DRIVG THRU CLOSD CROSG GATE	No driving thru closed crossing gate
291C-94	M25	STOP-EMERGNG ON SIDWK FR DRWY	Stop-emerging from alley, driveway bldg
291C-95	M75	OVRTKNG & PASSNG MKD SCH BUS	Overtaking & passing marked sch bus
291E-11	A12	REFUSAL TO SUBMIT TO SOBRI TEST	Refusal to submit to sobriety test
291E-15	A12	REFUSAL TO SUBMT TO SOBRI TEST	Refusal to submit to sobriety test
291E-61	A21	DRIVING UNDER INFL OF ALCOHOL	Driving under influence of alcohol
291E-61(a)	A21	DRVNG UNDR INFL OF INTOXICANT	Driving Under Influence of Alcohol
291E-61(a)(1)	A21	DRIVING UNDER INFL OF ALCOHOL	DUI by impairment of person
291E-61(a)(1),(a)(2)	A21	DRV UNDR INFL ALCOHOL/OR DRUGS	Driving under influence alcohol/or drugs
291E-61(a)(1),(a)(3)	A21	DUI W/.08 ALCOHOL BY BREATH	DUI w/.08 alcohol by breath
291E-61(a)(1),(a)(4)	A08	DUI W/.08 ALCOHOL BY BLOOD	DUI w/.08 alcohol by blood
291E-61(a)(1)(3)(4)	A08	DUI W/.08 ALCOHOL BREATH/BLOD	DUI W/.08 alcohol by breath or blood
291E-61(a)(2)	A22	DRIVNG UNDR INFL OF DRUGS	Driving Under Influence of Drugs
291E-61(a)(2)(b)(4)	A22	HABITUAL DUI WITH DRUGS	Habitual dui with drug
291E-61(a)(3)	A21	DUI W/.08 ALCOHOL BY BREATH	DUI w/.08 alcohol by breath
291E-61(a)(3)(b)(2)(b)(5)	A21	DUI<.08BRTH-1ST W/PSGR<15	DUI<.08 Bresth-1ST W/ passenger<15
291E-61(a)(4)	A21	DUI W/.08 ALCOHOL BY BLOOD	DUI w/.08 alcohol by blood
291E-61(b)(4)	A20	DUI W/PASSENGER<15	DUI w/passenger < 15
291E-61(a)(b)(1)(2)	A20	DUI ALCOH/DRUGS HI INTX 1ST	DUI Alcohol/Drugs Hi Intox 1st
291E-61.5	A20	HABTLY OPERG VEH UNDR INFLUENC	Habitual operating veh under influence
291E-62	B26	DRIV AFTER LIC SUSP/REVOKED	Driving after license suspended/revoked
291E-62(a)	B26	DRIV AFTER LIC SUS/UNDER INFL	Driving after license suspended/under influence
291E-62(a)(1)	B26	RESTRICTIONS PLACED ON LICENSE	Restrictions placed on license
291E-62(a)(1),(a)(2)		DRVNG WHILE LIC SUSPEND/REV	Driving while license suspended/revoked
291E-62(a)(1)(b)(3)	B26	DRV W/REST LIC; 5YRS; 2+ PRIOR	Drive with Rest Lic; 5yrs; 2+ Prior
291E-62(a)(2)	B26	DRIV AFTER LIC SUS/REVOKED	Driving after license suspended/revoked
291E-64	A60	DUI (ALCOHOL) UNDER 21	DUI (alcohol) under 21
291E-64(a)	A60	DUI (ALCOHOL) UNDER 21	DUI (alcohol) under 21
291E-64(a)(b)(2)(d)	A60	DUI (ALC) <21 -5YRS PRIOR; DEP	DUI (alcohol) <21 -5yrs prior; dep
291E-65	A12	REFUSAL TO SUBMIT TO SOBRI TEST UN 21	Refusal to submit to sobriety test under 21
291E-65 (a)	A61	UNDERAGE ADMIN PER SE W/.02 BAC	Underage admin per se w/.02 BAC
291EPART3	A98	ADMIN PER SE FOR .08 BAC	Admin per se for .08 BAC
291EPRTIII	A98	ADMIN PER SE FOR .08 BAC	Admin per se for .08 BAC
431:10C	D36	NO MOTOR VEH INSURANCE	No motor vehicle insurance
431:10C-104	D36	NO MOTOR VEH INSURANCE	No motor vehicle insurance
431:10C-107	B74	NO MOT VEH INS CARD IN VEHICLE	No Card in Vehicle
431:10C-108		FICTITIOUS OR ALTERED CARD	Fictitious or Altered Card
431:10C-110	D36	EXPIRED INSURANCE	Driving with expired insurance
431:10C-114		FAIL TO SURR CERT,PLTS-TERM IN	Fail to Surrender Cert, Plates-Term Indicated
431:10C-501	D36	MC/MC LIABILITY INSURANCE R	Failed to maintain liability insurance on motorcycle
431:10G	D36	MOTORCYCLE INSURANCE	Failed to maintain liability insurance on motorcycle
431:10G-102	D36	MC/MS LIABILITY INSUR REQD	Motorcycle/motorscooter liability insur required
431:10G-106		MC/MS INSURANCE CARD REQUIRED	Motorcycle/motorscooter insurance card required
710-1027	U01	OBDNCE TO POLICE OFFICER	Obedience to police officer
710-1077	D45	CRIMINAL CONTEMPT OF COURT	Criminal contempt of court
803-6(e)	D45	FAIL TO APPEAR	Fail to appear

Common Acronyms Found on the Hawaii Driver History Record

DLN   Driver's License Number
FTA   Failure to Appear
FTC   Failure to Comply
FTP   Failure to Pay
HME   Hazardous Material Endorsement
RRGC   Railroad Grade Crossing or Railroad-Highway Grade Crossing or Railroad-Rail Grade Crossing

Idaho

<table>
<tr><td>

Administration

Motor Vehicle Administrator
Idaho Transportation Department
P.O. Box 7129
Boise 83707-1129
208-334-4443

www.itd.idaho.gov/dmv/
http://trucking.idaho.gov/
General Email: DMV-info@itd.idaho.gov

</td><td>

Important Telephone and Web Contacts

Driver Services...208-334-8735
SR-22 and Financial Responsibility 208-334-8736
Motor Carrier...208-334-8611
Vehicle Titles 208-334-8663
Vehicle Registrations 208-334-8649
Highway Patrol...208-884-7200
State Department of Insurance 208-334-4250
Motor Vehicle Laws:
     www.legislature.idaho.gov/idstat/Title49/T49.htm
Administrative Rules: http://adminrules.idaho.gov/

</td></tr>
</table>

Driver's License Format, Issuance and Renewal

License Classes, Restrictions and Endorsements Appear After the Driving Record Content Section

License Format

The Current License Format has been in place since 05/1/93. Idaho law Code 49-306(2) prohibits disclosing the Social Security Number. Note that old formats may still be valid for certain license holders.

- Current License Format - 9 characters—2 alpha, 6 numeric, 1 alpha
- Format 1/1/93 - 5/1/93 - 9 numeric beginning with 910, 920, 930 or 940
- Format Prior to 1/1/93 - 9 numeric beginning with 910, 920, or SSN

Document Appearance

The current format has been in circulation since mid-2011. These documents are issued from a central location; Idaho no longer produces ID driver licenses and ID cards at County Driver Licensing Offices. The newer cards changed in appearance and have additional security characteristics. This new driver's license is not a "enhanced driver's license" (EDL) and cannot be used for border crossings.

Current Format
Security Characteristics: A plastic card with micro-printing and lamination difficult to duplicate. A laser-perforated pattern in the shape of the state of Idaho will give immediate validation. A bar code is on the rear.
Position of Photo: Left edge with ghost photo on lower right corner.
Minor Age Driver Locator: Licenses issued to individuals under 21 are in a vertical format. "UNDER 21 UNTIL XXXX" or "UNDER 18 UNTIL XXXX" is printed below the date of birth line in red (for under 21) or in green (for under 18).
CDL Indicator: A CDL is indicated by the class code and the designation "CDL" or the words "Commercial Drivers License" appear on the top of the card.

Older Format
Security Characteristics: A plastic card with laminate. A gold, repetitive design is embossed in the laminate.

Position of Photo: Bottom left.
Minor Age Driver Locator: Licenses issued to individuals under 21 are in a vertical format. "UNDER 21 UNTIL XXXX" or "UNDER 18 UNTIL XXXX" is printed below the date of birth line. Under 21 licenses have a red border around the photo. Under-18 licenses have a green border around the photo.
CDL Indicator: A CDL is indicated by the class code and the designation "CDL," or the words "Commercial Drivers License" appear on the top of the card.

Issuance
Location of Requirements for Proof of Identity:
www.itd.idaho.gov/dmv/DriverServices/driver_license_facts.htm#Bring
Age Requirements
The minimum age is fifteen with Driver Education; otherwise seventeen. For an Instruction Permit, driver must be accompanied by a licensed adult (eighteen or older).
Residency
Persons residing within the state for ninety continuous days are considered residents.

Renewal
For persons of age 21 or more renewal is the birthdate of fourth year. The driver keeps the same alpha-numeric license number when renewing. Military personnel can extend by mail for up to four year increments while on active duty outside of Idaho. The HAZMAT endorsement cannot be extended by mail. Upon discharge or return to Idaho, the license must be renewed within 60 days.
Elderly-Related Restrictions
None, unless the Department is notified in writing by a family member, physician, law enforcement officer or driver license examiner about an individual's inability to safely operate a motor vehicle.

Vehicle Insurance, Title and Registration Facts

Registration & Renewal
Online renewal is available for registrants in the following counties: Ada, Adams, Bannock, Bear Lake, Bingham, Blaine, Boise, Bonner, Bonneville, Boundary, Camas, Canyon, Caribou, Cassia, Clark, Clearwater, Custer, Elmore, Franklin, Fremont, Gem, Gooding, Idaho, Jefferson, Jerome, Kootenai, Latah, Lemhi, Madison, Minidoka, Oneida, Owyhee, Payette, Power, Shoshone, Teton, Twin Falls, Valley, and Washington County residents. Additional counties may participate

in this program in the future. However, this web service is not available for the renewal of the following plate types: Boats, Classic, Dealer, Exempt, Legislative, Loaner, Off-Road, Old Timer, Repossession, Snowmobiles and Transporter.
Go to https://www.accessidaho.org/secure/itd/vehicle/renewal.html.

New Residents
Persons whose primary home has been in the state for ninety days are considered residents for the purpose of driver's license, title, and

registration. Persons whose primary home is in Idaho may declare residency earlier than 90 days and may apply for the Idaho drivers license, title or registration.

Inspections and Emissions Testing

Idaho has no statewide, passenger vehicle-safety inspection program or emission-testing program. However in ADA and Canyon counties emission testing is required for vehicles owned by Ada or Canyon county residents.

Passenger Plate Facts

There are two plates with one decal (MO & YR) on each plate. The prefix to the passenger plates designates the county of issuance. The code is the numeric sequence of the first initial of the county with that initial (i.e. Butte is the 10th county starting with the letter "B," so the prefix is "10B"). Plates do not remain with vehicle when sold - they remain with seller.

Insurance and Financial Responsibility

Idaho has a compulsory insurance law. Minimum financial responsibility limits are $25,000/50,000/15,000. Proof of insurance must be carried at all times and is required to be shown when an officer asks for it under registration law. SR-22 forms are used.

Withdrawal Sanctions, and Alcohol and Drug Testing

Alcohol and Chemical Testing Limits

Idaho's alcoholic content level law is .08 percent, for CDL is .04 percent, if under 21 is .02 percent. It is possible a driver's CDL privileges can be disqualified while the operator's privileges are not. Urine, blood, and breath are legal. There is an implied-consent violation provision.

Suspensions and Revocations

The state is in compliance with the federally mandated disqualifications on CDLs. See the Appendix for details.
Point Accumulation
　Twelve or more points in twelve months..Thirty-day suspension.
　Eighteen or more points in twenty-four months...Ninety-day suspension.
　Twenty-four or more points in thirty-six months..Six-month suspension.
Conviction of Driving Under the Influence of Alcohol, Drugs or any Other Intoxicating Substance
　First Offense ....May include up to 180-day suspension.
　Second Offense Within Ten Years..May include one-year suspension.
　Third Offense Within Ten Years ....May include one- to five-year suspension.
Conviction of Aggravated Driving While Under Influence of Alcohol, Drugs
　or any Other Intoxicating Substance..May include one- to five-year suspension.
Leaving the Scene of an Accident Resulting in Death or Injury ....One-year revocation.

Other Reasons for Suspension

Judges and the Idaho Transportation Department are authorized under state statute to suspend, disqualify, deny, cancel, or revoke the license of drivers convicted of violating certain laws, no matter what the driver's point-system count. Those violations include:

- Alcohol-age violation (possession, use, or procurement).
- Administrative license suspension (for failing a breath, blood, or urine test when tested for DUI).
- Any court or the Department of Health and Welfare may order the Idaho Transportation Department to suspend the driver license and privileges of any person who fails to pay child support, fails to comply with visitation rights, or fails to comply with a subpoena for a paternity suit or child support proceeding.
- Conviction or action in another state for an offense that, if committed in Idaho, would be grounds for suspension.
- Driving while under the influence of alcohol or other drugs.
- Driving with a suspended license (driving without privileges).
- Failing to pay a fine for conviction on an "infraction" charge. (Infractions are a step below misdemeanors and include such minor violations as parking tickets.)
- Failing to pay a judgment for damages in an accident.
- Failure to carry motor vehicle insurance.
- Fleeing from or eluding a peace officer.
- Leaving the scene of an accident in which you were involved, when the accident caused property damage.
- Leaving the scene of an accident resulting in injury or death.
- Making false statements, oral or written, to the Transportation Department while under oath.
- Reckless driving.
- Refusal to Submit to an evidentiary test for DUI.
- Repeat violations under age 17.
- School districts may order the Idaho Transportation Department to suspend the driver's license and privileges of a minor who fails to attend school or does not comply with school requirements.
- Underage possession of marijuana or drug paraphernalia.
- Unlawful use of a driver's license or ID card.
- Using a motor vehicle to commit a felony.
- Violation of restriction.
- Violation of restrictions of supervised instruction permit.

Other Violations Causing Revocations
DUI Convictions
　First Conviction ....Revocation of 180 days to one year.
　Second Conviction within five years ....Revocation minimum five years.
　Second Conviction outside of five years................................Revocation minimum of 180 days.

Third Conviction..Revocation minimum ten years (if within ten years of a prior conviction).
Four or More Convictions in Lifetime (chronic offenders) .....License permanently revoked.
DUI Resulting in Death ....Minimum three-year revocation involving serious bodily injury, a conviction of manslaughter resulting from the operation of a motor vehicle, or a conviction of vehicular homicide.
DUI Manslaughter ....License revoked permanently.
Street Racing -3rd Violation...Minimum four-year revocation.

Note: If there is a term of incarceration and the driver is eligible for hardship consideration, the eligibility waiting period, if applicable, commences on the release date of the incarceration.

Violations Which May Result in a Disqualification

- Driving any vehicle, as a CDL holder, and arrested for DUI (post arrest they may have a BAC of .08 or above or refuse to submit to testing.)
- Driving a commercial vehicle without obtaining a CDL.
- Driving a commercial vehicle without the proper class of license or proper endorsement.
- Driving a commercial vehicle without having the driver license in possession.
- Driving a commercial vehicle while the operator's license is suspended, revoked, or canceled.
- Causing a fatality through the negligent operation of a commercial motor vehicle.
- Providing false information when applying for CDL results in a 60-day disqualification.
- A person who operates a commercial motor vehicle bearing a false or fraudulent identification commits a misdemeanor of the 1st degree

Note: Drivers are required to install and use an ignition interlock if convicted of multiple DUIs, as well as those first-time offenders with a BAC of 0.15 or more, or those who had a minor in the vehicle at the time of the offense.

Reinstatement Requirements

Suspension.......................$25.00 to $245.00 fee; SR-22 in most cases. Other requirements may apply.
Revocation.......................$85.00 fee in most cases; time lapse; SR-22 or other requirements in some cases.
In State DUI conviction.................$285.00 fee; time lapse; SR-22 in some cases.
Out of State DUI Conviction.........$245.00 fee; time lapse; SR-22 in some cases.

Record Access: Laws, Rules, and Forms

Note: **This Section Applies to Both Driver and Vehicle Records.**

Governing Statutes and Rules

Motor Vehicle Laws:
www.legislature.idaho.gov/idstat/Title49/T49.htm
Adminstrative Rules: http://adm.idaho.gov/adminrules/
Per Statutes 49-202, 49-203 and Administrative Rule 39.02.41, the state adopted the provisions of DPPA, although the text for #11 and #13 is not specifically in the statute. Idaho Code 49-306(2) prohibits the Transportation Department from disclosing an individual's Social Security Number on any information made available to the public.
Categories of requesters who may be authorized to receive personal information are listed in Idaho Code 49-203. Release of an individual's photograph, digitized image of a photograph, digitized signature, Social Security Number, and medical or disability information may not be disclosed without the written consent of the person to whom such information pertains, except for uses permitted under Idaho Code Section 49-203, subsections (4)(a) and (4)(d).

Consent Forms

Driving Records: The *Idaho Driver's License Record Request Form ITD 3120*, found at http://itd.idaho.gov/forms.htm, must be submitted if records are released to permissible users. If the request is attested to as having a permissible purpose, only the signature of the requester is needed. Using this same form, non-permissible use requesters can obtain records with personal information, provided that the subject of the record provides a signature of consent. Regardless, SSNs and medical information are not released. The form does not require the signature of the subject. For mass inquiries or high volume, ongoing accounts, contracts must be executed.
Vehicle Records: Use of the *Motor Record Request Form* is recommended. This form requires signature of the requester, but does not need notarization. The form is available at all Idaho county assessor offices or can be downloaded from the website at http://itd.idaho.gov/dmv/vehicleservices/documents/3374.pdf. For mass inquiries, contracts must be executed.

Vendor and Third Party Access Policy

The contract specifies that the information is to be used for the stated purpose, and cannot be "resold" again for direct marketing purposes. Approved online vendors can access records for other vendors (who are not online, etc.) who may then sell to an end-user as long as the use is for a permitted purpose and there is written prior approval from the Department.

Records Ordered For Non-permissible Uses

Other than the free status checks, driver and vehicle records are not released online to non-permissible requesters without consent. A public accessible record containing no personal information can be made directly to the Department by mail only

Access to Driver-Related Records

Editor's Note: Be aware that both Driver Services and Access Idaho refer to a driving record as a Driver License Record (DLR) and refer to a record related to vehicle title or registration as an MVR.

Driving Records

General Information and Fees
Drivers Services, PO Box 34, Boise 83731-0034, 208-334-8736, fax 208-334-8739.
The fee for a driving record is $7.00 if processed manually, records access online have a slightly higher fee as described below. Certification of a single record is an additional $14.00. A photocopy of a document (i.e., Citations, Suspension Orders, etc.) is $7.00 per document. Drivers Services accepts checks, money orders, VISA and MasterCard. There is a full fee charged for "no record found" reports for mail and fax requests. Records are reported for the last 3 years, unless an "all year"

record is requested.

In-Person – Counter service from the Headquarters is not offered. Service is available at the Public Service Counters at any of the county driver licensing locations. A list of addresses is found on the webpage.

Mail & Fax – Requests mailed or faxed to the state are processed within three business days of receipt. The driver's address is provided as part of the public record to authorized permissible users or with driver's consent. The driver's license number and date of birth are needed when ordering. If no record is found, a secondary search is performed using the name and date of birth, or name and license number. The fee must accompany the request, credit cards are accepted for fax requests.

Electronic – Access Idaho is the state designated portal for online retrieval of driving records. Records can be retrieved in a batch mode (FTP) or via interactive. The Division must first approve all accounts. There is an annual subscription fee of $95 (for Premium Service which includes 100 user IDs) and $9.00 per driving record. Records can be accessed via their web site at www.accessidaho.org. For more information, see www.accessidaho.org/ai/subscription.html.

Note: Access Idaho is master portal site for many of Idaho's government agencies. Their Premium Service offers access to other commercial records including corporation and UCC records from the Secretary of State. Also, more records will be added periodically. The subscription fee allows users to access one or more of the premium services plus all of the standard services offered by Idaho.gov. No prepayment is required, and the fee will appear on the first monthly invoice. Download the agreement at https://www.accessidaho.org/ai/universal_agreement.pdf.

Bulk – This service is not offered.

By Person of Record – ID drivers may obtain their driving record by mail or walk-in as described above and online. The online application is designed to allow private citizens to audit their driver's license record as maintained by the Idaho Dept. of Transportation. A printable copy is $9.56. In order to verify the holder of the identity of the driver, the application requires the driver's license number, name, DOB, and receipt number exactly as they appear on the license. Go to https://www.accessidaho.org/secure/itd/dlr/interactive/search.html. Access Idaho accepts MC/Visa/Discover/Am Ex credit cards for payment of records.

DL Status Check

Through Access Idaho, ID provides a free DL status check at https://www.accessidaho.org/secure/itd/reinstatement/index.html. Look up the status by entering the name as it appears on the license document, the DOB and either the SSN or the DL#.

HAZMAT Endorsement Status Look-up

Using the Carrier' Account Number, a free HAZMAT status check is at https://www.accessidaho.org/secure/itd/motorcarrier/unitsearch/hazmat/tportal/search.html. Enter the 7-digit Motor Carrier account number.

Notification/Monitoring Program

Access Idaho (https://www.accessidaho.org/online_services/) provides a driver monitoring program for a subscribers that wish to monitor driving records for violations and suspensions. The program works on a monthly basis. The user supplies a driver list for a fee of $.14 per driver for each month checked (the check can go back in time). If there is activity, the system automatically generates a driving record for the $9.00 fee. Activity includes moving violations and withdrawal actions. The program is available for DPPA permissible user clients including employers and insurance companies.

Access Idaho also offers a **Youthful Driver Check** that operates on a similar basis. For $.03 per month per driver, this program will alert insurance companies of recently issued driving privileges for operators between the ages of 16 and 21 within in the household of existing insureds. For more information on either program, call 208-332-0102.

Accident Reports

Reporting – Accidents resulting in death, personal injury, or damage in excess of $1,500 must be reported immediately to the local police; however, written reports do not have to be filed by the driver. Idaho reports no variations in this method for commercial drivers.

Record Access – Copies of accident reports can be obtained from the sheriff, or from city or state police. They can also be obtained by calling or writing to: Idaho Transportation Department, Office of Traffic and Highway Safety, Records, PO Box 7129, Boise ID 83707-1129, 208-334-8111, fax is 208-334-4430.

The cost is $7.00 per report. Please send a self-addressed stamped envelope as well to avoid handling fees. Pre-payment is required. Turnaround time is 2 weeks. Requests phoned or faxed in are still returned by mail. Items required for search include full name, driver license number, date and location of incident.

An online system is also available. View and download reports at https://www.accessidaho.org/secure/itd/ohs/crashreports/search.html. The total fee is $9.00. It can take several weeks or more before new records are available on this system.

Access to Vehicle-Related Records and Vessel Title Records

General Information and Fees

Vehicle Record Services, Titles MVR Desk, Idaho Transportation Department, PO Box 34, Boise 83731-0034, 208-334-8649 or 8663.

Idaho maintains title, registration, and lien records for vehicles, and for manufactured homes and mobile homes not declared real property. This agency also maintains title records since 01/2000 on watercraft for model year 2000 or if there is a permanently attached mode of propulsion or if longer than 12 feet unless exempt. If a lien is placed on a vessel that is older than model year 2000, that vessel must be titled. Note that vessels are registered with the Parks and Recreation Department (see below).

The fee for obtaining a hard copy of a title record, lien record, or registration record is $7.00. A complete title history is $14.00. The certification of a record is an additional $14.00 per vehicle per record. Fees for online access differ (see below). Medical information and SSNs are not released. The same fees for vehicle ownership searches apply to vessel ownership searches.

Lien record information on vessels must be searched at the UCC Division of the state for liens recorded prior to 01/01/00, or recorded against vessels exempt from titling after 01/01/00 (call 208-334-3191)

or at vehicle services for liens recorded against title-able vessels since 01/01/00. Note there is a $6.00 fee for UCC data.

In-Person – The counter on State Street is closed except for motor carrier and commercial trucking needs. However, records may be requested from any county assessor auto licensing location statewide. The completion of the record request form mentioned above is required. The form is available at county offices.

Mail or Fax – Vehicle records may be requested directly from the Idaho Transportation Department (ITD) by mail or by fax using the MVR request form referred to above. All replies are mailed to the requestor. Records (except complete history records) can be returned by fax to a local or toll free number for no extra fee. Turnaround time is generally 3 business days. Title histories can only be requested through the ITD and turnaround time is normally 5 to 10 days. Idaho will accept MasterCard and Visa for fax requests of the $7.00 record searches at 208-334-8542. Title histories cannot be faxed.

Telephone – Access to records is not available by telephone.

Electronic – Access Idaho at Idaho.gov is the state designated portal for online retrieval of motor vehicle records. The fee for a vehicle record (known as an MVR) is $8.50 per record. Records can be accessed from www.accessidaho.org in batch or interactive mode Idaho.gov is a master portal site for many of Idaho's government agencies. Their Premium Service offers access to other commercial records including driving record and corporation and UCC records from the Secretary of State. An annual $95 subscription fee allows up to 100 users on an account to access one or more of the premium services plus all of the standard services offered by Idaho.gov. No prepayment is required; the fee will appear on the first monthly invoice. To download the agreement at, see this web page: https://www.accessidaho.org/ai/universal_agreement.pdf.

Vehicle Registration Status Check – A free status check is on the web: https://www.accessidaho.org/secure/itd/vehicle/status.html. Search by plate number. An Idaho DL number for the registrant is required.

Bulk – Idaho offers bulk retrieval of registration, ownership, and vehicle information for authorized purposes. A user (with a signed contract) is charged a minimum $75.00 set-up fee and must also pay for computer time which varies based on the request. Idaho offers a variety of sorts or parameters. The output media is cartridge, paper, disk, zip disk or CD. For more information, contact Economics and Research, Transportation Department, PO Box 7129, Boise ID 83707-1129, 208-334-8601.

By Person of Record –Counter service from the Headquarters was discontinued 01/01/2009. But counter service is available at the Public Service Counters at any county driver licensing location. A list of addresses is found on the web at www.itd.idaho.gov/dmv/.

Access to Vessel Registration Records

General Information, Access and Fees
Idaho Parks & Recreation, Public Affairs Officer, PO Box 83730, Boise 83720-0065 208-334-4199, ext 306, fax is 334-2639
http://parksandrecreation.idaho.gov/activities/boating
All boats with either a motor or permanently attached sail must be registered. Registration records are open to the public but phone numbers and addresses are not released unless written consent given.

Record information can be verified or provided; however state statutes forbid the release of commercial lists. A written request is required. Access is by mail and in-person only. Turnaround time by mail is within 10 working days. Simple ownership and registration verification are provided for no fee, but fees are charged for custom data searches. Requesters must provide name or hull number or registration number.

Driving Record Content and Reciprocity

What's On or Not On the Driving Record
- The length of time convictions are listed is three years, regardless of violation or if CDL, unless an "all year" record is requested.
- Accidents are not reported on the driving record.
- Bond forfeitures and withheld judgments do not appear on the driving record, unless committed by a CDL driver or in a CMV.
- When requesting driver records, if you do not provide the individual's SSN/DLN or if it differs from the information you provide, the driver's license number will not be disclosed; SSN/DLN matches will be returned as usual, but the SSN is not returned as a part of the record, even if submitted with the request.
- The state does not permit traffic school attendance in lieu of conviction.

Data Retention
CDL driver records are purged based on the timetable per federal regulations (see the Appendix). Non-CDL convictions are purged from the active file no sooner than seven years.

State Reciprocity for Non-CDL Drivers
- Will suspend license of driver for unpaid out-of-state convictions.
- Record of new incoming driver is not shown on MVR.
- Out-of-state convictions are shown on MVR.
- Out-of-state accidents are not shown on MVR.
- Convictions of out-of-state drivers are sent to home state.
- Record is forwarded to new state upon surrender of license.

Important Abbreviations Used on Driving Records

A series of Abbreviations and the codes used for Action and Withdrawals are shown below. This is followed by license classes, restriction, and endorsements.

License Issue Type

DL	Driver's License
DT	Driver Training
CT	Same as DT except the trainer is a private or commercial business and not a driver training program through public schools
IP	Instruction permit, allows the driver to operate a vehicle when an individual properly licensed to operate the vehicle is in the passenger seat
ID	Identification card only

Operator Status

CANCEL	Driving privileges have been canceled	DISQ	Disqualified (Class A, B, C license only)
CDEYES	County denial of license; failed eye exam	EXPIRE	Expired
CDMEDC	County denial of license; medical certificate needed	INVALD	Invalid
CDMEDR	County denial of license; for medical reasons	NOTLIC	Not licensed
CDOTHR	County denial of license; other/special reasons	OTHER	Other
CDSOUT	County denial of license: suspended out of state	PENDNG	Pending Issue
CLCSOR	CDL; changed state of residence, no longer licensed in Idaho	RDP	Restricted Driving Permit (Issued by Department)
CRLP	Court suspension; restricted driving permit has been issued by the court	REVOKE	Revoked (which is treated the same as suspended)
		SUSPND	Suspended
DECEAS	Deceased	VALID	Valid license

Type (type of event on driving record)

CANC   Cancellation for the following reasons: committing fraud while making application, failure to provide correct information while making application, failure to provide correct information while making application, not entitled to driver's license, withdrawal of signature.
CITN   Citation; only shown on DLR (MVR) if found guilt of offense. Date shown is date the citation was issued.
CONV   Conviction. Date shown is when driver was found guilty of offense.
CRLP   Court (issued) Restricted License Permit
CSUS   Court ordered suspension; all suspensions that do not show CSUS are Department suspensions
DDC   Defensive Driving Course
DENY   Denial
DISQ   Disqualification, type of withdrawal, applies to the commercial license status only.
ORD   Ordinance degree:
       INF -   Infraction
       MISD -   Misdemeanor
       FEL -   Felony
PEND   Action is pending
RDP   Restricted Driving Permit (issued by Department)
RVOK   Revocation
SUSP   Suspension

Data/Format of Suspension Notation (Disqualifications Follow Same Format)

CLS   License class of privileges affected.
CSUS   Court-ordered suspension. Department-ordered suspensions are blank where "CSUS" is normally shown.
DATE   Date when driving privileges were suspended.
DESC   Reason for privileges being suspended. If driver is found guilty of offense, the offense will be shown. However, if driver received a withheld judgment, "COURT ORDERED" will be shown. Reason for suspension will not be released.
GLTP   Guilty, plea.
NRVC   Non-Resident Violator Compact
TO DATE   The date suspension time is completed. However, driver does not receive driving privileges until reinstatement requirements are met. Note that suspension time may be different for OPR and CDL privileges.
REIN DATE Date when privileges are reinstated. Suspension records are immediately removed from the record when privileges are reinstated for the following:
- Certified proof of liability insurance to be carried in motor vehicle
- Failure to attend school
- Failure to pay penalty for infraction of judgment
- Failure to maintain proof of liability insurance
- Family responsibility law
- Financial responsibility
- Out-of-state family responsibility law
- Required motor vehicle insurance
- Unsatisfied judgment

Other Abbreviations of Importance

CRT   Location of court where fine was paid or a decision was made regarding citation
DOC   #Case or file number
GLTP   Guilty, plead guilty or found guilty due to a failure to appear
LOC   Location where citation issued (can be city, county, or state)
PTS   Points
INFR   Infraction
MISD   Misdemeanor

License Classes, Restrictions, and Endorsements

License Classes

CDL Class A   Enables a driver to operate combination vehicles with a GCWR over 26,000 pounds—provided the GVWR of the vehicle(s) being towed is greater than 10,000 pounds. A driver with a Class A license is properly licensed to operate Class A, B, C, and D vehicles.
CDL Class B   Enables a driver to operate single vehicles with a GVWR of over 26,000 pounds, or any such vehicle towing a vehicle not in excess of 10,000 pounds GVWR. A driver with a Class B license is properly licensed to operate Class B, C, and D vehicles.
CDL Class C   Enables a driver to operate vehicles that do not fall into Class A or B, but are designed to carry sixteen or more passengers (including the driver) or carry hazardous materials in quantities which require placards. A driver with a Class C license is properly licensed to operate Class C and D vehicles.
Seasonal CDL   Special, restricted Class B or C license to operate certain commercial vehicles in farm-related industries under restrictions imposed by the Depart. Must be accompanied with a valid Class D license. Not valid for driving vehicles containing quantities of HAZMAT requiring placarding except for diesel fuel in quantities of 1,000 gallons or less, liquid fertilizers (3,000 gallons or less), and solid fertilizers not mixed with any organic substance.

Class D	Enables a driver to operate a vehicle that is not a commercial vehicle.
Class NA	Non-resident Class A CDL.
Class NB	Non-resident Class B CDL.
Class NC	Non-resident Class C CDL.
Class XA	This person has a class A CDL in another state.
Class XB	This person has a class B CDL in another state.
Class XC	This person has a class C CDL in another state.
Class XD	This person has a class D or CDL in another state, or a base record was created to add a withdrawal.

Endorsements

H	Hazardous Materials	S	School Bus
M	Motorcycles	T	Double-/Triple-Trailers
N	Tank Vehicles	X	N & H Combined
P	Passengers, 16 or more		

Restrictions

Abbreviation	Code	Description
DAY/16	A	Can Only Drive During Daylight Until Sixteenth Birthday, Non-CDL Only
LENSES	B	Corrective Glasses or Lenses Required While Driving
MECAID	C	Mechanical Aid Required (such as a special brake or hand controls
PROAID	D	Prosthetic Aid is Required
AUTO T	E	Restricted to Vehicles With Automatic Transmissions
MIRROR	F	Outside Mirrors Required
DYLGHT	G	Daylight Driving Only
EMPLOY	H	Can Drive for Employment Only
OLIMIT	I	Limited - Other
ATTACH	J	Other Special Restrictions (such as fifteen-mile radius from home)
INTRA	K	CDL, Intrastate Only. Can Only Operate a Commercial Vehicle Within Idaho.
W/OAIR	L	Can Only Operate Vehicles Not Equipped With Air-Brakes
A BUS	M	Except Class A Bus
A/BBUS	N	Except Class A and B Buses
TRCTOR	O	Except Tractor Trailer
WLADLT	P	Must be Accompanied by a Driver Properly Licensed to Operate that Class of Vehicle, in Front Seat Next to Driver
1UND17	Q	In First 6 Months of Licensure, Only One Person Under 17 In Vehicle Who is Non-relative
3WHEEL	R	3-Wheel Motorcycle Only
SEACDL	S	Seasonal CDL
CBIRTH	T	Identity Not Verified - Certified birth certificate/legal presence documentation must be reviewed before driver's license can be issued
NOPSGR	U	Motorcycle, No Passenger Permitted
DL/POS	V	Idaho DL in possession
INTRLK	W	Ignition Interlock Device Required
N/FRWY	X	Restricted to Non-Freeway Driving
CWC	Y	Community Work Center
A/B SB	Z	Except Class A and B School Bus
A BUS	M	Except Class A Bus
DL/POS	V	Idaho DL in possession

Conviction Table With Record Display, ACD, Points, and Descriptions

* Any violations marked with an asterisk * are not for insurance purposes.

Display	Pts	ACD	Description
2 VIOL/3-YEARS	0	W30	Driver convicted of 2 serious violations in a 3 year period
3 VIOL/3-YEARS	0	W31	Driver convicted of 3 serious violations in a 3 year period
2/MOREMAJVIO	0	W40	Two or more major violations
2ND OFFENSE	0	W01	2nd offense any combination of serious violations
2 VIO OOSGEN	0	W50	Accumulation of two out of service orders violations within 10 years
3+VIO OOSO	0	W52	Accumulation of three or more out of service orders- violations within 10 years
AC MISC	0	U30	Accident - miscellaneous
ADDLMAJOFREN	0	W41	Additional major offenses after reinstatement
AGGRAVTD DUI	0	A20	Aggravated driving under the influence of alcohol/drugs/intoxicating substance
AID/ABET FEL	0	U05	Using a motor vehicle to aid and abet a felon
ALCO/TOB AGE	0	A52	Beer/wine/other alcohol, tobacco age violations
ALS 08+/DRUG	0	A98	Administrative license suspension BAC .08+/drugs/intoxicating substances
ALS.04/.07	0	A94	Administrative license suspension BAC .04 to .07
ALS02+UNDER21	0	A61	Administrative license suspension BAC .02 to .07 under 21
ALT LICENSE	0	B41	Unlawful use of license - possess or provide counterfeit or altered drivers license or ID card
FTY PDSTRN	3	N08	Drivers to exercise due care - Failed to yield right of way to pedestrian

Display	Pts	ACD	Description
BACKING	1	N82	Limitations on backing
BASIC RULE	3	S92	Basic rule/Speeding
BASIC RULE	3	S93	Basic rule/Speeding
BLIND BENFITS	0	W20	Blind benefits - Unable to pass DL tests or meet qualifications
C AGRVTD DUI	0	A20	Aggravated DUI involving a commercial motor vehicle
C/FATAL ACC	0	U31	Serious violation - viol/connection with fatal accident
C/FOLLOW CLS	3	M34	Serious violation - following too close
C/LANE USAGE	1	M42	Serious violation - lane usage
C/LT CNTR HY	3	M74	Limitations driving left of center of highway: passing on hill or curve
CDLALS08+DRG	0	A98	CDL Administrative license suspension with BAC .08 or more drugs and/or intoxicating substances
CDLDMGACCNCV	0	B05	Leaving the scene of an accident involving CDL holder in a non-commercial vehicle
CDLFELACCNCV	0	B05	Felony leaving the scene of an accident involving CDL holder in a non-commercial vehicle
CHZ ALS 04/07	0	A94	Commercial motor vehicle, administrative license suspension for BAC .04 to .08 with hazardous material
CHZ ALS 08+ DRG	0	A98	Commercial motor vehicle, administrative license suspension for BAC .08 or greater with hazardous material
CM04/08DUI21	0	A04	Under age 21 - alcohol concentration is .04 - .08%
CMANSLAUGHTR	0	U08	Manslaughter involving commercial motor vehicle
CMV ALS04/07	0	A94	CMV Administrative license suspension with BAC .04 to .07
CMV ALS02+<21	0	A61	CMV Administrative license suspension with BAC .02 or more and under 21 years of age
CMV DMG ACC	0	B08	Leaving the scene of an accident involving a CMV
CMV DUI .04%	0	A04	Driving CMV while alcohol concentration is 0.04 percent or more
CMV-DQ-DRVR	0	B20	Motor Carrier - disqualified driver (DWP)
CMV DUI CS	0	A22	Driving CMV under influence of a controlled substance
CMV DUI/LAW	0	A20	Driving CMV under influence of alcohol or drugs
CMV FEL ACC	0	B05	Felony leaving the scene of accident involving a commercial vehicle
CMV FEL/CSUB	0	A50	Felony use CMV involving manufacturing, distribution or dispersion of control substance
CMV FEL/OTHR	0	U03	A felony involving use of a CMV other than described
CMVHMNEGHOM	0	U09	Negligent homicide while operating a commercial motor vehicle involving hazardous materials
CMVHMVEHHOM	0	U07	Commercial motor vehicle - vehicular homicide involving hazardous material
CMV NEG HOM	0	U09	Negligent homicide while operating a commercial motor vehicle
CMV PASS RGT	2	M73	Improper passing right
CMV RCKLS DR	0	M84	Serious violation - reckless driving in CMV
CMV RTS TST	0	A12	Refusal to test to determine alcohol concentration while operating CMV
CMV SAFETY	0	W10	Serious violation - driving CMV in disregard for safety
CMV STRK FIX	4	B08	Leaving the scene of an accident involving a CMV – failure to notify owner or person in charge
CMVRRBUS/TRK	4	M09	CMV-comply with stopping requirements at all RR crossings
CMV-RRSIGNL	4	M10	CMV-obedience to signal indicating approach of train
CMV VEH HOM	0	U07	Commercial motor vehicle - vehicular homicide
CO DENY EYE	0	W20	County denial for failed eye examination
CO DENY MED	0	W15	County denial for medical certificate
COASTING	0	N80	Coasting or operating with gears disengaged
CONST SPEED	3	S93	Construction danger zone speed limits
CONTR ACCESS	1	F41	Entering controlled access roadway/restricted access
CPASS NO CLR	3	M77	Limitations on overtaking on the left/insufficient clearance or visibility
CRLSS DRVNG	3	M81	Careless driving
CRT BURGLARY	0	W10	Burglary (for court suspension purposes only)
CT DRV/INVLD	0	B20	Driving while invalid (for court suspension purposes only)
CT MISC/SUSP	0	W10	Miscellaneous offenses (for court suspension purposes only)
CT VIOL/PROB	0	W10	Violated probation (for court suspension purposes only)
CV-DWP-CDLWD	0	B20	CMV - driving without privileges due to prior CM offenses
OS REFUSAL	0	A12	Out of state refusal to submit test by a CDL holder in a non-commercial vehicle
CVHZDWPCDLWD	0	B20	CMV - driving without privileges due to prior CM offenses involving hazardous materials
CV STRK UNAT	4	B08	Leaving the scene of an accident involving a CMV
DE MISC	0	E30	Defective equipment - miscellaneous
DEFECT BRAKE	0	E31	Operating with defective brakes
DEFECT EQUIP	0	F66	Defect equipment resulting/inability/control vehicle movement properly
DEFECT EX SYS	0	E35	Operating with defective muffler or exhaust system
DEFECT HDLGT	0	E34	Operating with defective headlights
DEFECT TIRES	0	E37	Operating with defective tires
DI MISC	0	A99	DUI - miscellaneous
DIVIDED HWY	1	M51	Divided highway
DRAG RACING	0	S95	Contest racing on public traffic way
DRVCMVW/OCDL	0	B56	Driving a CMV without obtaining a CDL
DRVCMVW/OCDL	0	B57	Driving a CMV without a CDL in the driver's possession

Display	Pts	ACD	Description
DRV RT SIDE	3	N70	Driving right side of roadway - exceptions
DUI	0	A20	Driving under influence alcohol/drugs/intoxicating substance
DUI .20 OR	0	A20	Excessive alcohol concentration
DUI CDL NCV	0	A20	DUI by CDL holder in a non-commercial vehicle
DUI FELONY	0	A20	DUI felony
DUI UNDER 21	0	A60	Under age 21 - DUI alcohol/drugs/intoxicating substance
DW/O FIN RES	0	D35	Driving without financial responsibility
DWP FELONY	0	B26	DWP felony
DWP REVOKED	0	B25	Driving without privileges - revoked
DWP SUSPEND	0	B26	Driving without privileges - suspension
ELDE PCE OFC	0	U01	Fleeing or attempting to elude a peace officer
EM MISC	0	E50	Equipment misuse - miscellaneous
ER MISC	0	E01	Equipment regulations - miscellaneous
ERREATIC SPD	0	S97	Operating at erratic or suddenly changing speed
EXC SPD CMV	0	S93	** Excessive speeding in a commercial vehicle
EXHIB ACCL	4	S95	Exhibition of acceleration
EXHIB SPEED	4	S95	Exhibition of speed
EXP/NOCDL/IP	0	B51	Expired or no driver's license - includes CDL and instruction permits
EXP/NO DL/IP	0	B51	Expired or no driver's license - includes instruction permits
F/DISC OP MV	0	W14	Fail/discontinue operation of vehicle after onset physical/mental disability
FAIL AID/INJ	0	B01	Fail/stop/render aid after involvement in accident result/bodily injury
FAIL ATD SCH	0	W24	Failure to attend school
FAIL DIM LGT	0	E54	Failure to dim lights as required
FAIL MNT INS	0	D36	Proof required upon certain convict/financial responsibility
FAIL SIGNAL	3	N40	Turning movements and required signals
FAIL WRT TST	0	W20	Failure to pass written test
FAILED INFO	0	D02	Failed to give required information on application
MISREPRESENTATION	0	D02	False information on application
FAM RESP LAW	0	D51	Family responsibility law
FATNEGCVOPHM	0	U10	Causing a fatality through negligent operation of a commercial motor vehicle involving hazardous materials
FAT/NETCMVOP	0	U08	Causing a fatality through negligent operation of a commercial motor vehicle - Could be U10
FE MISC	0	W10	Felony - miscellaneous
FEL/CSUB NCF	0	A50	Non CMV used in commission of felony involving manufacturing, distribution, dispensing of controlled substance
FEL ELDE OFC	0	U01	Felony fleeing or attempting to elude a peace officer
FEL LV ACC	0	B07	Felony leaving scene of accident - injury/death
FELDUI .20 OR >	0	A20	Felony - excessive alcohol concentration .20 or greater
FLASHING SGL	3	M18	Flashing signals
FLDSCHCOMPLY	0	W24	Not entitled - fail to show school comply
FOLLOW CLOSE	3	M34	Following too closely
FOLLOW EM MV	0	M32	Following emergency vehicle unlawfully
FR MISC	0	W10	Financial responsibility - miscellaneous
FRD ID CRD	0	D06	Fraudulent misrepresentation of identification card to obtain alcohol
FTA TRIAL	0	D45	Failure to appear for hearing or trial
FTF ACC RPT	0	B61	Failure to file report of accident as required
FTM COMP INS	0	D36	Failure to maintain required compulsory liability insurance
FTO RR BUS	4	M22	CMV-failure to stop as required before driving onto RR crossing
FTO RR CLRNC	0	M24	CMV-insufficient undercarriage clearance for RR crossing
FTO RR NSLOW	0	M20	CMV-failure to slow down at RR crossings
FTO RR NSTOP	4	M21	CMV-fail to stop when RR crossing not clear
FTO RR SPACE	0	M23	CMV-fail to have sufficient space for RR crossing
FTO TRF INST	0	M14	Fail/obey traffic instructions, sign, or control device
FTO WARNINGS	0	M03	Failure to obey construction/maint. zone markers
FTY EMER VEH	3	N04	Operation of vehicle on approach of authorized emergency or police vehicle
FTY LEFT TRN	3	N31	Vehicle turning left
FTY PDSTRN	3	N20	Pedestrian's right of way in crosswalks
FTY PED/ANML	0	N02	FTY right of way to pedestrian, animal rider or animal-drawn vehicle
FTY PRV ROAD	3	M25	Vehicle entering highway
FTY RGT/WAY	0	N26	FTY right of way yield sign, after stop sign, emerging from private traffic way
FTY SCHL BUS	0	N09	Failure to yield to school bus as required
FTY SIGN	3	M19	Yield sign
FTY UNS INTR	3	N25	Vehicles approach/enter unmarked/uncontrolled intersection
HAB DRNKARD	0	W10	Habitual drunkard
HABITUAL	0	W01	Habitual violator (as verified per D20)
H-H WHL DRVG	0	M86	Using a hand-held mobile telephone while driving

Display	Pts	ACD	Description
HAZ W/O SAFE	0	E53	Transport haz sub without required safety devices or precautions
HC02/07DUI21	0	A04	Under age 21 - alcohol concentration is .02 - .07% with haz mat
HM C DMG ACC	0	B05	Leaving the scene of an accident involving a CMV - haz/met
HM C DUI .04%	0	A04	Driving CMV while alcohol is 0.04% or more hazardous material
HM C DUI CS	0	A22	Driving CMV under influence of a controlled substance/haz mat
HM C DUI/LAW	0	A20	CV DUI of alcohol, as prescribed by law with haz mat
HM C RTS TST	0	A12	Refuse to test for alcohol concentration while operating CMV/haz mat
HMC AGVT DUI	0	A20	Aggravated DUI involving a commercial motor vehicle with haz mat
HMC C FEL ACC	0	B05	Felony leaving the scene of accident involving CMV - haz/mat
HMC FEL/OTHR	0	U03	A felony involving use of a CMV other than described - haz mat
HMC STRK FIX	0	B08	Leaving the scene of an accident involving a CMV - haz/mat
HMC STRKUAT	0	B08	Leaving the scene of an accident involving a CMV - haz/mat
HMCMNSLAGHTR	0	U08	Manslaughter involving commercial motor vehicle with haz mat
HMFTRIDF/ACC	0	B14	Fail to reveal ID after fatal/personal injury accident in a commercial moto vehicle with hazardous material
HV MISC	0	W01	Habitual violator - miscellaneous
IL MISC	0	M40	Improper lane operations where prohibited - miscellaneous
IL USE N/FEL	0	U04	Using motor vehicle connection with illegal activity other than felony
ILLEG S BUS	0	M75	Illegally passing school bus
IMM HAZ	0	W70	Imminent hazard
IMPCLSCDL/EN	0	B91	Improper classification or endorsement of driver license - includes CDL and instruction permits
IMP ENT/EXIT	0	M46	Making improper entrance to or exit from traffic way
IMP PASS LFT	3	M73	Overtaking vehicle on the left: Passing on wrong side
IMP PASS RT	3	M73	Passing on wrong side
IMPAIRED	0	A25	Driving while impaired
IMPROPER TRN	0	N50	Making improper turn
INATT DRVNG	3	M82	Inattentive driving
INFO DMGE MV	4	B13	Duty to give information in ACC involving damage to vehicle
INFRACTIONS	0	D53	Infractions – failure to make required payment of fines and costs
LANE USAGE	1	M42	Driving on highways laned for traffic
LFT CNTR HWY	3	M74	Further limitations on driving on left of center of highway – Passing on hill or curve
LOAN DL	0	B92	Loaning a driver license
LT/RT LANE	0	N53	Making left turn from right turn lane
LV DMGE MV	0	B08	Accidents involving damage to vehicle
LV SC ACC	0	B05	Leaving scene of accident
LV SC BFR PL	0	B05	Leaving scene of accident provide aid or ID but before arrival police
MANSLAUGHTER	0	U08	Manslaughter by a motor vehicle
MEDICAL EXAM	0	W15	Medical examination
MEDICAL STND	0	W14	Medical standards
MINIMUM SPD	3	S96	Minimum speed
MISC OS CONV	0	-	Miscellaneous out of state conviction
MJ/DRG PARA	0	A30	Possession marijuana/drug paraphernalia by a minor
MNTL/PHY DIS	0	D75	Operate motor vehicle improperly because of physical/mental disability
MS MISC	0	W10	Miscellaneous – Miscellaneous
MV CON W/FEL	0	U03	Using a motor vehicle in connection with a felony
MV FELONY	0	U03	Using a motor vehicle as the device for committing a felony
N/PF LIA INS	0	B74	Certification of proof of liability insurance to be carried in motor vehicle
NCOMP	0	D51	Failure to make required payment of child support
NGLGNT DRVNG	3	M83	Negligent driving
NO LIAB INS	0	D36	Required motor vehicle insurance
NO PASS TEST	0	W20	Inability to pass one or more tests required for drivers license
NO PASSING	4	M76	Duties of the department – no passing zones
NON SUFF FUN	0	W26	Non-sufficient funds
NOT ENTITLED	0	W20	Not entitled to driver's license
NRVC	0	D53	Non resident violator compact
O/S ALC/AGE	0	A52	Out of State Beer/Wine/other alcohol violations
O/S ALS04/07	0	A94	Out of state administrative license suspension with BAC .04 to .07
O/S ALS.08+	0	A98	Out of state administrative license suspension with BAC .08 or more
O/S CMV MNSL	0	U08	O/S manslaughter involving a commercial motor vehicle
O/S CMV RTS	0	A12	Out of state refusal to under go test as by law
O/S DMGE ACC	0	B08	Out of state – accidents involving damage to vehicle
O/S DUI	0	A20	Out of state – DUI alcohol/drugs/intoxicating substance
O/SDUICDLNCV	0	A20	Out of state DUI by a CDL holder in a non commercial vehicle
O/S DUI FEL	0	A20	Felony out of state DUI
O/S DWP SUSP	0	B26	Out of state – driving without privileges
O/S ELDE OFC	0	U01	Out of state – eluding peace officer

Display	Pts	ACD	Description
O/S FEL ACC	0	B07	Out of state felony leaving the scene of accident – injury/death
O/S MJ/DRUG	0	A33	Possession marijuana/drug paraphernalia
O/SNCOMP VIS	0	D51	Out of state non compliance with order of visitation – Failure to make payment of child support
O/S RCKLS DR	0	M84	Out of state – reckless driving
O/SRTSCDLNCV	0	A12	Out of state refusal to submit test by a CDL holder in a non commercial vehicle
O/S RTS TEST	0	A12	Out of state refusal to submit BAC tests
O/S VIO RSTR	0	D29	Out of state – violation of restricted license
O/SMNSLAGHTR	0	U08	Out of state manslaughter by a motor vehicle
ONE-WAY	1	N60	One-way highways
OSALS02+21	0	A61	Out of state administrative license suspension with BAC .02 or more and under 21 years of age
OSCALS02+>21	0	A61	Out of state CDL administrative license suspension with BAC .02 or more and under 21 years of age
OS C DUI .04%	0	A04	Out of state driving CMV alcohol concentration is 0.04% or more
OS C DUI/LAW	0	A20	Out of state driving CMV under influence of alcohol, as prescribed by law
OSCDLALS.08+	0	A98	Out of state CDL administrative license suspension with BAC .08 or more
OSCVALS04/07	o	A94	Out of state CDL administrative license suspension with BAC .04 to .07
OSCVDWPCDLWD	0	B20	Out of state CMV – driving without privileges due to prior CM offenses
OSDMGACCNCV	0	B08	Out of state leaving the scene of an accident involving CDL holder in a non-commercial vehicle
OSDUI 20OR	0	A20	Out of state – excessive alcohol concentration
OSDUIUNDER21	0	A60	Out of state – DUI under 21 years of age
OSFELACCNCV	0	B05	Out of state felony leaving the scene of an accident involving CDL holder in a non-commercial vehicle
OSFELCSUBNCV	0	A50	Out of state non CMV used in commission of felony involving manufacturing, distribution, dispensing of controlled substance
OSFELDUI20	0	A20	Out of state felony – excessive alcohol concentration
OSFELELDEOFC	0	U01	Out of state felony eluding a peace officer
OSHMCDUI .04%	0	A04	OS Driving CMV alcohol concentration is 0.04% or more with haz mat
OSHMCDUI/LAW	0	A20	Out of state driving CMV DUI, as prescribed by law with haz mat
OSHMCVRTSTST	0	A12	Out of state refusal to submit to test for alcohol concentration in CMV with hazardous material
OSHMDWPCDLWD	0	B20	Out of state CMV with hazmat Driving without privileges due to prior CMV offenses
OVERLOAD P/C	0	F11	Overloading vehicle with passengers or cargo
PA MISC	0	M70	Passing – miscellaneous
PASS INS CLR	3	M77	Limitations on overtaking on the left
PASSING	2	M72	Passing vehicles proceeding in opposite directions
PERJURED	0	D05	Perjured, made false affidavit/statement (court conviction)
POINTS/DISCR	0	W01	Accumulation of violations resulting in discretionary action
POINTS/MAND	0	W01	Points
POS DRG CSUB	0	A33	Illegal possession of drugs (controlled substance)
PROP DMG ACC	0	-B08	Failure stop/reveal identity after accident result in property damage only
PROPER LANE	0	M41	Failure to keep in proper lane
RACE ON HWY	4	S95	Drag racing, race on highway
RAN OFF ROAD	0	M43	Ran off road
RCKLSS DRVNG	0	M84	Reckless driving
RECURR VIOL	0	W01	Recurrence of violations requiring mandatory action
REFUSED TEST	0	A12	Test/driver for alcohol concentration, presence of drugs/other intoxicating substances
REG LIC TYPE	0	B51	Driving w/o being licensed or w/o lic required for type of vehicle operated
RESTR ACCESS	1	F41	Restricted access
RK DR 3/1 YR	0	M84	Reckless driving (3 in a 12 month period)
RK MISC	0	M80	Inattentive, reckless, careless or negligent driving – miscellaneous
ROAD TEST	0	W21	Road test
RR MISC	0	B70	Required reports, appearances or documents – miscellaneous
RR SIGNAL	4	M10	Obedience to signal indicating approach of train
RR-CROSSING	4	M09	Compliance w/stopping requirement at all RR crossings
RRGC2 A VIOL	0	W60	Two RR grade crossing violations within three years
RRGC3 A VIOL	0	W61	Three RR grade crossing violations within three years
RR-STOP SIGN	4	M10	RR Crossing – all vehicle stop
RT/LT LANE	0	N54	Making right turn from left turn lane
RTMISC	0	D21	Registration and titling – miscellaneous
RTSTSTCDLNCV	0	A12	Refusal to submit test by a CDL holder in a non-commercial vehicle
RV MISC	0	W01	Repeated violations – miscellaneous
RW MISC	0	W10	Right of way – miscellaneous
SAFETY ZONE	2	M12	Driving through safety zone prohibited
SHO/DTC/SDWK	0	M58	Driving on road shoulder, in ditch, or on sidewalk
SI MISC	0	N43	Signaling intentions – miscellaneous
SP 70/I ONLY	0	S93	Serious violation – excessive speeding/interstate 70 mph only
SP MISC	0	S93	Speeding – miscellaneous

Display	Pts	ACD	Description
SPD 15+OVR	3	S92	Serious violation – excessive speeding/15 mph over
SPEC LICNESE	0	D27	Unlawfully used special license for unspecified purpose
SPEED SPCL	3	S94	Special speed limit
STOP ALLEY	3	M25	Emerging from alley, driveway or building
STOP SIGN	3	M15	Stop signs
STP SCHL BUS	4	N09	Overtaking and passing school bus
STRK FIX HWY	4	B13	Duty upon striking fixture upon or adjacent to highway
STRK UNAT MV	4	B13	Duty upon striking unattended vehicle
STRT PKD VEH	2	N83	Starting parked vehicle
SURREND DOCS	0	B80	Fail/surrender driver license, registration, title documents
SUS ANTHR ST	0	W10	Suspended in another state
TRF CTRL DVC	3	M14	Obedience to and required traffic – control devices
TRF CTRL SGL	3	M16	Traffic – control signal legend
TRFC BARRIER	0	M02	Pass thru/around barrier position to prohibit/channel traffic
TRK INS CLR	0	M31	Fail/truck to leave sufficient distance overtaking by other vehicle
TU MISC	0	N50	Turns – miscellaneous
TURN-NO VIS	3	N55	Limitations on turning around
TURN-WR LANE	3	N50	Required position and method of turning
TXT WHL DRVG	0	M85	Texting while driving
TWOOOSPAS/HM	0	W51	Two out of service orders with passengers and/or hazardous materials
UNLAW USE DL	0	D16	Unlawful use of license
UNSAFE OP	0	N84	Unsafe operation of vehicle
UNSAT JUDGE	0	D39	Suspension for non-payment of judgments
VIO LIA INS	0	B74	Financial responsibility (violation of liability insurance)
VIOL OOS ORD	0	B27	Violation of out of service order
VIOL OOSW/HM	0	B19	Violation of out of service order with haz mat
VIOL RESTR	0	D29	Violation of restricted license
VIOL SIP	0	W20	Unable to pass DL tests or meet qualifications
VIOL<17	0	W01	Repeat violations under 17
VISUAL EXAM	0	D43	Visual examination
VISUAL REV	0	W20	Visual review
VISUAL STAND	0	W20	Visual standards
VEH HOMICIDE	0	U07	Vehicle homicide
VOL SURREND	0	W10	Voluntary surrender of driver's license
VR MISC	0	B20	Violations of driving while license is withdrawn
WDRAW SIGN	0	W13	Withdrawal of parent or guardians signature
WJ DISMISSED	0	W10	Withheld judgment/probation dismissed-miscellaneous charges
WJ DSMSS ALS	0	W10	Withheld judgment/probation dismissed-ALS charges
WJ DSMSS DUI	0	W10	Withheld judgment/probation dismissed-DUI charges
WO REQ EQUIP	0	E01	Operating without equipment required by law
WRNG WAY/INT	0	N61	Driving in wrong direction at rotary intersection
WRONG SIGNAL	0	N44	Giving wrong signal
WW MISC	0	N60	Wrong way, side or direction miscellaneous

Summary of Points and Point Assessment

The following moving violations chart shows the section of Idaho Code that applies to each violation, and lists the assessment of points for each type of moving violation.

    *   = CMV Serious Moving Violations
   ** = CMV Railroad Crossing Violations

Code	Violation Description	Points	CMV
49-603	Starting parked vehicle	2	
49-604	Limitation on backing	1	
49-615	Drivers to exercise due care	3	
49-616	Driving through safety zone prohibited	2	
49-624	Duty upon approaching stationary police vehicle or emergency vehicle displaying flashing lights	3	
49-625	Operation of vehicles on approach of authorized emergency police vehicle	3	
49-630	Drive on right side of roadway – exceptions	3	
49-631	Passing vehicles proceeding in opposite direction	2	
49-632	Overtaking a vehicle on left	3	
49-633	When passing on right is permitted	2	*
49-634	Limitations on overtaking on the left	3	*
49-635	Further limitation on driving on left of center of highway	3	*
49-636	One-way highways	1	

49-637	Driving on highways laned for traffic	1	
49-638	Following too closely	3	
49-640	Vehicle approaching or entering unmarked or uncontrolled intersection	3	
49-641	Vehicle turning left	3	
49-642	Vehicle entering highway	3	
49-644	Required position and method of turning	3	
49-645	Limitation on turning around	3	
49-648	Obedience to signal indicating approach of train	4	**
49-649	Compliance with stopping requirements at all railroad grade crossings	4	**
49-650	Failure to allow for sufficient undercarriage clearance at railroad grade crossing	3	**
49-651	Emerging from alley, driveway, or building	3	
49-654	Basic rule and maximum speed limits/ CMV failure to slow down at railroad grade crossing ***	3-4	*/**
49-655	Minimum speed regulations	3	
49-656	Special speed limitations (1 to 15 miles per hour over the speed limit = 3 points. 16 or more miles per hour over the speed limit = 4 points)	3-4	*
49-657	Work zone speed limit	3	
49-658	School zone speed limit	3	
49-702	Pedestrian's right-of-way in crosswalk	3	
49-801	Obedience to and required traffic control devices	3	
49-802	Traffic control signal legend	3	
49-804	Flashing signals	3	
49-807(2)	Stop signs	3	
49-807(3)	Failure to yield – signed intersections	3	
49-808	Turning movement and required signals	3	
49-1302	Duty to give information in accident involving damage to a vehicle	4	
49-1303	Duty upon striking unattended vehicle	4	
49-1304	Duty upon striking fixtures upon or adjacent to a highway	4	
49-1401(3)	Inattentive driving	3	
46-1419	Obedience to traffic direction	2	
49-1421(1)	Driving on divided highways	1	
49-1421(2)	Restricted access	1	
49-1422	Overtaking and passing school bus	4	
49-1424	Racing on public highways	4	

About Point Assessment

Point accumulation is shown for the last 12 month, 24 month, and 36 month period. Each minor moving violation is given a value of one to four points. The conviction and the points assessed are entered on the driver's records and maintained for three years following the conviction date. Driving privileges will be suspended for:

-30 days if a driver accumulates 12-17 points in any one year period.

-90 days for an accumulation of 18-23 points in any two year period.

-6 months for an accumulation of 24 or more points in any three year period.

Once every three years, a driver may reduce his/her point total by three points by completing an approved defensive driving course. Point reduction cannot be saved up or credited toward future convictions. Completing a course does not remove the conviction from the record.

Illinois

Administration	Important Telephone and Web Contacts
Michael J. Mayer, Director Drivers Services Department 2701 S Dirksen Parkway Springfield, IL 62723 Ernie Dannenberger, Director Vehicle Services Department 501 S 2nd Street Room 312 Springfield, IL 62756 www.cyberdriveillinois.com	Driver Licensing .... 217-782-6212 SR-22 & Financial Responsibility.............. 217-782-3720 Mandatory Insurance .... 217 524-4946 Driver Services .... 217-782-2720 PDPS Help Desk.. 217-785-3108 Commercial Driver License .... 217-524-1350 Vehicle Information.................................... 217-782-6992 State Police (Springfield District) .... 217-786-7107 State Department of Insurance .... 217-782-4515 **Vehicle Code:** www.ilga.gov//legislation/ilcs/ilcs2.asp?ChapterID=49

Driver's License Format, Issuance and Renewal

License Classes, Restrictions and Endorsements Appear After the Driving Record Content Section

License Format

The format is one letter and eleven numbers. The format is coded,, however the coding "translation" is not available to the public

Document Appearance

Two changes (01/01/2005 and 01/01/2008) were made to the DL and ID documents. Older licenses are being phased out as new licenses are issued. All three documents are listed below.

Current Documents Issued Since 10/2007

Security Characteristics: Security features include kinetic movement and color shifting designs, a UV feature, microtext, a ghost image of the photo and incorporation of the date of birth in two locations on the cards.

Overall Description: The photo with blue background is on the upper left, a ghost image is found in the lower right corner. Colors across the card tops indicate card types. Red is used for standard DLs and CDLs. ID cards are in green and Temporary Visitor DLs are in purple.

Minor Age Driver: All Illinois Under 21 driver's licenses, identification cards, and commercial drivers licenses (DLs, IDs, and CDLs) are a vertical design. The "Under 21 until MO/DAY/YR" and "Under 18 until MO/DAY/YR" text appears in red and yellow bars next to the photo. The header bar above the photo is blue and identifies card type (DL, ID or CDL).

Temp Visitor: Known as the TVDL (Temporary Visitor Driver's License), the standard card and under 21 card look like the associated DL or ID card, except the color header across the top is purple. Front has text "Not Valid for Identification" in red under purple header bar and TVDL in a blue bar.

CDL Indicator: "CDL" appears in a blue bar on right side under the header.

Documents Issued 2005 Through Fall 2007

Security Characteristics: The appearance of the digital license is similar to a credit card. There is a hologram across the bottom of license and a "Safer State with .08" 1-D bar code on back contains driver's license number. A 2-D bar code on the back contains data from the front. Blue header is above photo for drivers over 21.

Position of Photo: Photo with blue background is on right.

Minor Age Driver: These Illinois Under 21 driver's licenses, identification cards, and commercial drivers licenses (DLs, IDs, and CDLs) are a vertical design with a blue pattern across much of the card. The actual text that appears on the card remains the same. The

card back is unchanged from the pre-2005 document. The "Under 21 until MO/DAY/YR" and "Under 18 until MO/DAY/YR" text appears in red and yellow bars next to the photo. The header bar above the photo is blue and identifies the card type (DL, ID or CDL). The DL/ID number, issue date and expiration date appear in a blue block beneath the signature. The date of birth appears beneath an image of the State Seal. The retro-reflective "Safer State with .08" optical variable device runs through the side of the card lengthwise, over part of the photo and signature and DL/ID number.

Temp Visitor Under 21: The Under 21 Temporary Visitor Driver's License looks like other Under 21 cards, but the background color is green. The header bar above the photo is green instead of blue and includes the text "Temporary Visitor Drivers License". The bar containing the text "Under 21 until MO/DAY/YEAR is green instead of red. The block containing DL number, issue date and expiration date is green instead of blue. The text "Not Valid for Identification" is in red above the name. The expiration date will indicate either 3 years from date of issuance or less if the authorized length of stay in the U.S. is less.

CDL Indicator: CDL" appears at top of the photo.

Pre-2005 Documents

Security Characteristics: State's outline in data area; hologram in laminate which covers portions of both the data and photo areas; a three digit security plate number appears vertically in top left of photo area.

Position of Photo: Lower right

Minor Age Driver: Red header above photo, red printing and borders on license laminate and red background. Minor's license is indicated by "under 21 until xx/xx/xx" (or under 18 if applicable), across top. Photo position is in lower right.

CDL Indicator: "CDL" in blue background appears in data area of license, and directly above photo area.

Issuance

Location of Requirements for Proof of Identity:
www.cyberdriveillinois.com/publications/pdf_publications/dsd_x173.pdf

Age Requirements

The minimum age for a full license is eighteen; sixteen with completion of approved driver education course (minimum of 50 hours including 10 hours of night-time practice) holding Learner's Permit nine months. Unless emancipated, all applicants under 18 must have parent/guardian consent. A Learner's Permit, which is required first, is valid for two years and is issued at age 15. These drivers must be accompanied by parent, legal guardian or licensed adult age 21 or older with one year of driving experience and face night time driving restrictions.

Drivers under age 21 are not allowed to drive for-hire a second division vehicle transporting more than 10 passengers, or drive a commuter van, religious organization bus, school bus, vehicle transporting senior citizens, or a child-care vehicle.

Residency

Non-resident's home-state license honored on a reciprocal basis; one must secure Illinois license within 90 days of establishing residency. CDL holders must obtain an Illinois CDL within 30 days of becoming an Illinois resident.

Renewal

Normal renewal is birthday of fourth year, except for drivers over 81 years of age (see below), or drivers under 21 (license expires three months after 21st birthday). Driver keeps same number when renewing unless change of name, DOB, and/or gender.

In 2011, the agency eliminated the use of the Safe Driver Renewal stickers which allowed qualified drivers to place a sticker on the back of the expiring license and use the document for an additional four years. Instead, qualified drivers may renew by mail and will then receive a new document in the mail.

Active military personnel serving outside IL may obtain a Military Deferral Card to be carried with the expired license. The card is also available for spouses and dependents. The card, which can be secured from the Driver Services Department (217-782-2720), is valid for 90 days after discharge or reassignment to a military base in IL.

Online renewal at www.ilsos.gov/SafeDriverWeb is available to drivers who have a clean record for the 4 preceding years.

Elderly-Related Restrictions

All persons aged 75 or older must take a driving test at each renewal. Drivers aged 81-86 must have their licenses renewed every two years, while persons aged 87 and older must renew annually.

Vehicle Insurance, Title and Registration Facts

Insurance and Financial Responsibility

Liability insurance is required for all motor vehicles that must display license plates and are being driven, including cars, vans, motorcycles, recreational vehicles, trucks and buses. Trailers are not required to have liability insurance.

Minimum financial responsibility limits are $20,000/40,000/15,000. If stopped for a traffic violation or involved in an accident, a law enforcement officer may issue a traffic citation if driver is unable to provide evidence of insurance. If convicted, the license plates will be suspended. Proof of financial responsibility is required after an uninsured at fault accident, revocations and mandatory insurance offenses. Proof of financial responsibility (SR-22 Certificate) is required for three years on: unsatisfied judgment suspensions related to an accident; and safety responsibility suspensions and revocations. Also since 01/01/2008, proof of financial responsibility is required for three years as a condition of supervision for violations of the mandatory insurance law and those receiving three convictions for mandatory insurance violations.

A Circuit Court or the Department of Healthcare and Family Services may request the Secretary of State suspend the driving privileges of a parent who is 90 days behind on child support payments. The court ordered suspension will appear as a FR (Family Financial Responsibility) on the driving record.

Registration Renewal

License plate registrations are renewed annually. Online renewals (see home page) are available for motorists using a Renewal Code and Personal Identification Number (PIN) printed on the renewal notice. Also, renewals can be processed via a touch-tone phone system by

calling 866-545-9609 using a major credit card. Renewals of snowmobiles, jet-skis, boats less than 16 feet, and boats over 16 feet are handled by the Illinois Department of Natural Resources. They can be contacted at 217-782-2138. Off-road motorcycles and ATVs are titled but are not registered.

New Residents

Non-residents must register vehicles within thirty days of establishing residency.

Inspections and Emissions Testing

Although Illinois has no mandatory statewide emission testing program, certain counties and parts of counties require emissions testing including all of Cook, DuPage and Lake counties, and parts of Kane, Kendall, Madison, McHenry, Monroe, St. Clair, and Will counties. All cars and trucks are tested every two years beginning when four years old, except vehicle model year 1995 or older and diesel-powered vehicles, must be tested. There is no cost to the vehicle owner.

The Secretary of State does not require a safety inspection except before a rebuilt title may be issued for all salvage vehicles that are eight model years old or newer. Also a safety inspection on certain commercial vehicles is required by the IL Dept. of Transportation. See 625 ILCS 5/13-100.1 for the standards.

Passenger Plate Facts

For passenger cars two plates are issued with one decal on rear with MO-YR. Every truck tractor is issued one plate, which is displayed on the front of the vehicle. There is no county coding on the plates that indicate county of issuance. When a vehicle is sold the plates remain with seller.

Withdrawal Sanctions, and Alcohol and Drug Testing

Alcohol and Chemical Testing Limits

Illinois' alcoholic provision limit is .08% with .04% for CDL and .00% (zero tolerance) if under 21 years of age. Legal testing means include urine, blood, and breathe. Illinois has provisions within its laws for an implied-consent violation and an administrative suspension. Effective 2009, certain individuals convicted of a DUI are required to have an ignition Interlock device installed in their vehicles. See Public Act 095-0400.

Suspensions and Revocations

Point Accumulation: If three or more point assessed violations are committed within a 12-month period, or two or more point assessed violations are committed by a driver under the age of 21 within a 24-month period, the driver's record is reviewed for possible suspension or revocation. If the driver's record shows no prior suspensions or revocations in the previous seven-year period, the following tables are used to determine the length of the suspension or whether revocation is to be entered:

Point Accumulation - Under Age 21

    10 thru 34 points ....One-month suspension.

35 thru 49 points ....Three-month suspension.
50 thru 64 points ....Six-month suspension.
65 thru 79 points ....Twelve-month suspension.
80 or more points ....Revocation.

If the driver is under the age of 21 and has previously been suspended for being convicted of 2 or more point assigned violations within a 24 month period and is convicted of another point assigned violation... OR... If a person under the age of 21 is convicted of the violations illegal possession or consumption of alcoholic beverages, the driving privileges shall be suspended or revoked as follows—

First offense ....Six-month suspension.
Second offense ....Twelve-month suspension.
Third of subsequent offense ....Revocation.

If the driver was previously revoked and is convicted of another point assigned violation, driving privileges will be revoked.

If the driver is under age 21 and is placed on Court Supervision for a violation of illegal possession or consumption of alcoholic beverages the driving privileges shall be suspended for three months.

Point Accumulation - Over Age 21
15 thru 44 points ....Two-month suspension.
45 thru 74 points ....Three-month suspension.
75 thru 89 points ....Six-month suspension.
90 thru 99 points ....Nine-month suspension.
100 thru 109 points ....Twelve-month suspension.
110 or more points ....Revocation.

DUI Convictions - Under Age 21
First Offense ....Minimum two-year revocation.
Second Conviction..Minimum five year revocation.
Third Conviction...Minimum ten-year revocation.
Fourth Conviction...Lifetime revocation.

DUI Convictions - Age 21 or Older
Same as above except if 2nd conviction in twenty years   Minimum five-year revocation.

Statutory Summary Suspension for Refusal to Submit to Chemical Test Indicating .08 BAC or higher
First Offense (prior to 01/01/2009)...Three-month suspension.
First Offense (01/01/2009 or thereafter) ....Twelve-month suspension.
Subsequent Offenses within five years ....Twelve-month suspension.

Statutory Summary Suspension for Refusal to Submit to Chemical Test
First Offense (prior to 01/01/2009)...Six-month suspension.
First Offense (01/01/2009 or thereafter) ....Twelve-month suspension.
Subsequent Offenses within five years ....Thirty-six-month suspension.

Refuses to submit to a chemical or other test per implied consent provision
Revocation when that person has been driving or in actual control of a motor vehicle which has been involved in a personal injury or fatal motor vehicle accident; person shall not be eligible for restricted driving permit.

Illegal Transportation of Open Alcoholic Beverages-Drivers Under Age of 21
First Offense ....Twelve-month suspension.
Subsequent Offenses..Revocation.

Illegal Transportation of Open Alcoholic Beverages-Drivers Over Age of 21
First Offense ....No action.
Second Offense within one year ....Twelve-month suspension.
Third or Subsequent Offense ....Revocation.

Zero Tolerance Law Under 21 with BAC of more than .00%
First Offense ....Three-month suspension.
Subsequent Offenses..Twelve-month suspension.

Zero Tolerance Law Under 21--Refusal to Submit to Chemical Test
First Offense ....Six-month suspension.
Subsequent Offenses..Twenty four-month suspension.

Zero Tolerance Law School Bus Drivers BAC of more than .00 - Any Offense .... Cancellation of Permit.

Notes: Effective January 1, 2012, the agency will suspend for three years the **school bus permit** of a driver who **refuses to submit to a test** or fails to obtain a **zero tolerance** for the presence of alcohol, drugs or intoxicating compounds.

Drivers convicted of **speeding 40 mph above the posted speed limit** are not eligible for court supervision.

Driving While License Suspended or Revoked

Extension of revocation or suspension or loss of full driving privileges, if privileges have been reinstated.
Felony DUI...Minimum one-year revocation.
Reckless Homicide Class 2 Felony..Minimum two-year revocation.
Leaving the Scene of a Fatal or Personal Injury Accident ....Minimum three-year revocation.
Graduated Drivers License Denials: ....One serious violation (majors plus speeding 30+ over) means a denial for six months or until the 18th birthday, which ever is shorter. A moving violation conviction results in nine months waiting period before applying for a driver's license. Driving with no valid license or committing an offense that would result in a mandatory revocation of a license or permit will deny the applicant until 18 years of age.

These additional violations may trigger a revocation or suspension. Termination dates vary according to offense.
Revocations:
• Aggravated DUI (minimum revocation lengths vary according to type of offense and previous history)

- Aggravated Fleeing the Police
- Auto Theft
- Drag Racing or Street Racing
- Felony Offense (vehicle used when serious crime committed)
- Fraudulent ID
- Perjury (gave false information to the Secretary of State)
- Reckless Conduct (involving a vehicle resulted in injury or danger to another person)
- Reckless Driving (convicted of three reckless driving offenses in 12 months)
- Second or Subsequent Conviction of Driving While Revoked When Already Revoked for Reckless Homicide
- Violation of any offense regulating the movement of traffic that was the proximate cause of death of any person

Suspensions:

- Drug or Sex Offense (committed a drug or sex crime while operating or in direct physical control of an automobile)
- Failure to Appear (failed to appear for any traffic citation)
- Failure to Pay Child Support
- Failure to Pay Five or More Automated Traffic Law Violations
- Failure to Pay Five or More Tollway Violations
- Failure to Yield and Proceed with Due Caution Upon Entering a Construction Zone or When Workers are Present
- Failure to Yield Right of Way to Emergency Vehicles
- Failure to Obey a Railroad-Crossing Signal (second violation)
- Fraudulent License/ID Application
- Illegal Transportation of Alcohol (convicted of illegally transporting alcohol twice in 12 months)
- Obstructing Railroad Crossing For Use by Trains or Railroad Equipment
- Parking Violations (failure to pay fines or penalties for 10 or more unpaid parking violations)
- School Bus Violations (failed to stop as required by law for a school bus that was picking up or dropping off children)
- Speeding in a Construction Zone (second or subsequent violation within two years)
- Theft of Motor Fuel
- Traffic Crashes (convicted for refusal or neglect to report a traffic accident)
- Uninsured Crashes

Illinois is in compliance with the mandatory CDL disqualifications. See the Appendix for these disqualifications.

Reinstatement Requirements

Suspension	$70 fee; time lapse. If under 21, may be required to attend remedial education and be re-examined. $100 for Mandatory Insurance Conviction Suspension
DUI or Admin "Per Se"	$250 fee, first offense; $500 subsequent offenses.
Revocation	$500 fee; $30 license fee; time lapse (at least one year); proof of financial responsibility (SR-22) insurance for three years; application for renewal of license; re-examination; formal/informal hearing required.

Record Access: Laws, Rules, and Forms

Note: This Section Applies to Both Driver and Vehicle Records.

Governing Statutes and Rules

Rules of the Road Laws:
www.cyberdriveillinois.com/publications/motoristpub.html#trafficsafety

Vehicle Code:
www.ilga.gov//legislation/ilcs/ilcs2.asp?ChapterID=49

Illinois Complied Statutes:
www.ilga.gov/legislation/ilcs/ilcs.asp

Driving records are deemed public information. Vehicle Code Law 2-123 fully explains who may request information and at what price. The driver's address and personally identifiable information are only provided to requesters who are exempt as defined under Section 2-123(3) of the Illinois Compiled Statutes.

Illinois does not provide the same text as stated in DPPA for exceptions 11 and 13.   Illinois added the following exceptions: "For use by members of the news media, as defined in Section 1-148.5, for the purpose of news gathering when the request relates to the operation of a motor vehicle or public safety." The state carefully screens for requesters who are exempt and who must provide the purpose of the request.

Exempt requesters can receive full information in a timely manner. Exempt requesters include those affiliated with law enforcement, court officials, legal representatives (including IL licensed private investigators), parent or guardian, prospective employer, the insurance industry, vehicle dealers, tow truck firms, and representatives of financial institutions with a legitimate business need. If the subject submits a court order of protection no one other than law enforcement, courts and the individual will receive all information.

Request and Consent Forms

Driving Records: There is a state form, but the state form is not required as long as a written request stipulates the purpose of the request and contains the requester's signature. Family members requesting a driving record and parents or legal guardians of a minor under 18 years of age must submit the notarized, written permission of the person listed on the request form. *Form DC164* is found at:
www.cyberdriveillinois.com/publications/pdf_publications/dsd_dc164.pdf

Vehicle Records: The state form is recommended; visit the web at www.cyberdriveillinois.com/publications/pdf_publications/vsd375.pdf for *Form VSD 375*. Signature of the requester is required, but does not need to be notarized.

Vendor and Third Party Access Policy

The liability of DPPA compliance is the responsibility of the vendor. Certain end users (employers) may obtain electronic records from an approved employment screening company via an authorized vendor. Otherwise, vendors cannot obtain records for other vendors.

Non-permissible Use Requests

A non-exempt requester must provide the purpose of the request and receives data without addresses and personal information. However, before information is released there is a ten-day waiting period while the Abstract Information Unit will notify the subject person of the name of the individual who is requesting a copy of the record. A court order of protection will completely stop everyone except law enforcement, courts, insurance companies, and the subject from obtaining an individual's driving record.

Access to Driver-Related Records

Driving Records

General Information and Fees

Abstract Information Unit, Driver Analysis Section, Driver Services Department, 2701 S. Dirksen Parkway, Springfield IL 62723, 217-782-2720.

The current fee is $12.00, certification included if a paper record is purchased. The state charges for "no record found" reports.

In-Person – Individuals may obtain certified driving records at any full-time Driver Services Facility. No personal identifiable information will be provided to the requester unless they are exempt from this provision by law. Up to five records may be requested over-the-counter; more than five are considered to be "mail-in" requests. Credit or debit cards are not accepted at Driver Services facilities.

Mail – Requests are processed within approximately ten working days. The driver's name, date of birth, and sex or DL number are needed when ordering a manual record search. The fee must accompany the request. No personal identifiable information will be provided to the requester unless they are exempt from this provision by law.

FTP – Contract Sales, Driver Services Department at 217-785-3094. This is a batch program. Only non-certified records are sold in this manner and the fee is $12.00 per record. The state receives input file before 6:00 p.m. and makes output available after 10:00 p.m. The driver's license number is the only identifier needed when ordering; however, a secondary search can be made using the driver's name, sex, and date of birth. The driver's address is provided as part of the public record. The minimum order is 200 requests per day. Payment is made daily via direct-payment from a specified bank account.

Electronic – This interactive program for online access to records is limited to a number of current requesters who obtain records. Call the number above for further information. There is also a free, Parental Access Program (see below).

Bulk – The driver license database is not sold to commercial vendors.

By Person of Record – IL drivers may obtain their driving record by mail or walk-in as described above. At present, there is no program for drivers to order or view their own record online.

Parental Access Program

The parents or guardians of persons under 18 years of age may view the teen's record for free online at https://www.ilsos.gov/parentalaccess/.

Some of the data appearing on the record is not included on the public driving record.

Notification/Monitoring Program

Illinois does not offer program to enable employers or insurance companies to monitor drivers about incidents of selected drivers.

Obtaining Crash Reports

Reporting – Crashes resulting in property damage in excess of $1,500 ($500 if any of the vehicles involved in the accident is not covered by liability insurance), injury, or death must be re ported in-person or by phone to the nearest law enforcement agency. Within ten days, form "SR-1" must be filed with the Department of Transportation, Accident Report Office, 1340 North 9th Street, Springfield 62766. The "SR-1" form is for both personal and commercial vehicles. A box on the form is checked for "driving in the course of employment." Drivers at fault in the crash must also meet the requirements of Safety Responsibility Law. This law requires a security (a guarantee of payment) if there is no insurance coverage or another acceptable form of payment.

Record Access – Copies of crash reports are available to drivers, their attorneys and the courts, from the Illinois State Police, Patrol Records Section, 801 South 7th Street, Ste 400-M, Springfield 62794, 217-785-0612.

The fee is $5.00 per crash report or $20.00 for a reconstruction report, a self-addressed stamped envelope is required. Limited information is given over the phone at no charge. A written request and the fee are required to receive a report. Turnaround time is 10 days. Also, it can take 10 days before new reports are ready for inquiry. Items needed by the requester include date, names of drivers, and crash report number.

One may request and pay for a copy of a crash report online using a credit card. Go to www.isp.state.il.us/traffic/crashreports.cfm. There is an additional $1.00 fee plus the $5.00 per record fee for this service. Credit cards are accepted for payment online. Using E-PAY, one may also request, pay for and receive the traffic crash report by email.

Copies of accident reports that occurred on the IL Tollway System may be obtained for $5.00 per report from: IL Toll Highway Authority, Attn: IL State Police Dist. 15, One Authority Dr, Downers Grove, IL 60515.

Access to Vehicle-Related Records

General Information and Fees

Vehicle Record Inquiry, Vehicle Services Department, 501 S. 2nd Street Room 408, Springfield, IL 62756, 217-782-6992 or 217-785-3000.

The database also contains registration information on unattached mobile homes, but not on watercraft. Off-road motorcycles and ATVs are titled but are not registered. In general, records are available for last 10 years. It takes one to two weeks before new records are available for inquiry.

There is a $5.00 fee per vehicle record for either a title search or a registration search. A combined Title & Registration record is $10.00. Add $5.00 per document for certification. The request form is at www.cyberdriveillinois.com/publications/pdf_publications/vsd375.pdf

Mail and In-Person –The state requires that a written request be submitted to the address listed above or a "sale of information" form be used. The fee must accompany each request. Personal information is not released for non-business purposes. Only exempt requesters receive subject's name and address. The state processes walk-in requests, **but non-exempt requesters must wait 10 days for results.**

Electronic Status Check – Illinois provides a free Title and Registration Status Inquiry at www.ilsos.gov/regstatus/. Enter the VIN to check the status of a vehicle.

Bulk – Records are available for statistical purposes only. Please contact Becky Tipps, Secretary of State's Office, Data Processing Division, Room 400, Howlett Building, Springfield 62756.

Access to Vessel-Related Records

General Information, Access and Fees

Department of Natural Resources, Records and Legal Services, One Natural Resources Way, Springfield 62702-1270, 217-557-0180 or 217-782-2138. www.dnr.illinois.gov/boating Snowmobiles, jet-skis, boats less than 16 feet, and boats over 16 feet are handled by the Illinois Department of Natural Resources._All watercraft must be registered and titled unless non-motorized craft is only used on one's own property. Liens are recorded with this agency. The watercraft and snowmobile records are maintained on computer from 1982 to present. A title history

record costs $5.00 and can take up to 6 weeks. The record will include any lien. Snowmobile records are also available. It can take as long as 6 to 8 weeks for new records received by this office on paper format to be input into the system. Bulk information may be purchased only on a FOIA basis.

Driving Record Content and Reciprocity

What's On or Not On the Driving Record

- SSNs and most non-moving violations do not appear on the driving record.
- The state does permit driver school attendance in lieu of conviction. Illinois has child restraint and seat-belt laws in effect. Illinois has a system of "court supervision" that gives courts the discretion to substitute a requirement (e.g. additional fine, Traffic Safety School, time frame not to receive additional tickets, etc.) in a traffic case.

The length of time convictions are listed on the driving record is:

- **Moving Violations:** Four to four and one-half years from date of conviction *(unless used for driver control action)*.
- *Accidents:* Four to four and one-half years, unless fatality involved then five years.
- **DUI:** Lifetime.
- **Suspensions:** Seven years from the termination date.
- **Other Serious Convictions (any vehicle):** Ten years past reinstatement date.

For Commercial Motor Vehicle Serious Violations

- **DUI, Leaving the Scene of Accident, Felony Convictions:** Fifty-five years past conviction date.
- **Minor Convictions:** Three years past conviction date.
- **Accidents:** Ten years past accident date.
- **Withdrawal Actions:** Fifty-five years past withdrawal date or three years past reinstatement date.

Data Retention

CDL driver records are purged annually based on the timetable per federal regulations (see the Appendix). Otherwise, convictions are purged from the state system twice a year using the above timetable. Surrendered licenses are purged from the system using a method based on the expiration date and the status of the driving record.

Court to Repository

Conviction information must be submitted to the state within five days of the conviction date by input file (FTP) or paper. Mandatory paper violation transcripts are usually input into the system within two to three days of receipt from the courts; minor moving violations are input into the system within thirty days of receipt.

State Reciprocity for Non-CDL Drivers

- Will suspend license of driver for unpaid out-of-state convictions from NRVC states.
- Record of new incoming driver is not shown on MVR.
- Out-of-state convictions is shown on MVR.
- Out-of-state accidents are not shown on MVR.
- Convictions of out-of-state drivers are sent to home state.
- Record is not forwarded to new state upon surrender of license, unless suspended, revoked or canceled.

Important Abbreviations and Codes on Driving Records

Codes and Descriptions

AV	Abandon vehicle		16	Collision involving fatal injury
CC	Certificate of Completion-Drivers Education		17	Statutory summary suspension
DN	Denial of license or permit		18	Vehicle emissions suspension (obsolete as of 01/01/08)
DQ	Disqualification		19	Collision involving personal injury
ES	Extension of Statutory Summary Suspension		27	License surrendered to another state
EZ	Extension of zero tolerance suspension		28	Reported deceased
FE	Safety & Responsibility fee status item		32	Denial of restricted driving permit
IV	Invalidation of a license or permit		33	Denial of license
FP	Failure to pay court-imposed fine/penalty		34	Extension of revocation
FR	Family financial responsibility suspension		35	Extension of suspension
MC	Mandatory insurance conviction		37	Extension of statutory summary suspension
MP	Monitoring Device Driving Permit		39	Medical Certificate
NP	License issued valid without photo and/or signature		40	Formal hearing
SC	Supervision/conviction (offense committed in CMV)		41	CDL Disqualification hearing
OS	Out of service		43	DCFS child-care driver
SD	Start/End date of 3-yr period (CDL holders)		45	School bus history item
SR	Sworn report		46	Religious organization bus or senior-citizen transportation driver
ZT	Zero Tolerance Suspension		47	FR Future proof required
01	Mandatory revocation		48	School bus driver permit
02	Discretionary revocation		49	Certification Safety Officer or Commercial Driver Training Instructor
03	Discretionary suspension		50	Informal conference held
04	Safety responsibility suspension		51	Family financial responsibility history item
05	Financial responsibility suspension		52	Show cause hearing; recommended action
06	Unsatisfied judgment suspension		53	Show cause hearing; recommended no action
07	Parking/Tollway suspension		55	Driver remedial program and/or court supervision
08	Cancellation of license		60	Warning letter issued
09	Failure to appear suspension		68	Out-of-state conviction (record-history item only)
10	Amended order issued		70	Family financial responsibility permit
12	Cited for examination			
14	Collision involving property damage			

71	Probatory or temporary instruction permit, or temporary driver's license issued, or seasonally restricted CDL
78	Restricted occupational driving permit
79	Judicial driving permit issued (Obsolete as of 01/01/09)
80	Out-of-state accident
82	Out-of-state conviction (DL and/or CDL sanctions imposed)
83	Out-of-state conviction (immediate action)
84	FR future proof filings completed
85	Out-of-state conviction (no points assigned)

87	Out-of-state conviction (points assigned)
89	Out-of-state withdrawal
91	Convictions of drivers under age 15 at time of arrest
93	Immediate action bond forfeiture (no points assigned)
94	Immediate action conviction (no points assigned)
95	Bond forfeiture (no points assigned)
96	Conviction (no points assigned)
97	Bond forfeiture (points assigned)
99	Conviction (points assigned)

License Classes, Restrictions, Endorsements, and Permit Codes

License Classes

A		Any combination of vehicles with a GCWR of 26,001 pounds or more, provided the GVWR of the vehicle(s) being towed is in excess of 10,000 pounds.
B		Any single vehicle with a GVWR of 26,001 or more pounds, or any such vehicle towing a vehicle not in excess of 10,000 pounds GVWR.
C	1.	Any single vehicle with a GVWR of 16,001 or more pounds, but less than 26,001 pounds GVWR, or any such vehicle towing a vehicle not in excess of 10,000 pounds GVWR;
or	2.	Any vehicle less than 26,001 pounds GVWR designed to transport sixteen or more people (including the driver) or used in the transportation of Hazardous Materials (HazMat) which requires the vehicle to be placarded;
or	3.	Any vehicle less than 26,001 pounds GVWR designed to transport sixteen or more people (including the driver) or used in the transportation of HazMat which requires the vehicle to be placarded, towing a vehicle with a GVWR of 10,000 pounds or less or with a GCWR of less than 26,000 pounds.
D	1.	Any single vehicle with a GVWR of 16,000 pounds or less that is not designed to transport sixteen or more people, or not used in the transportation of HazMat which requires such vehicle to be placarded.
or	2.	Any single vehicle with a GVWR of 16,000 pounds or less that is not designed to transport sixteen or more people, or not used in the transportation of HazMat which would require such vehicle to be placarded, towing any vehicle providing the GCWR is less than 26,001 pounds.
L		Any motor-driven cycle with less than 150 cc displacement.
M		Any motorcycle.
R-CDL		A Restricted CDL is available to drivers employed by farm retail outlets and suppliers, agri-chemical business, custom harvesters and livestock feeders. The R-CDL can be issued for no less than 90 days and no more than 180 days within a 12-month period and is valid only within 150 miles of the employer's place of business. The R-CDL must be accompanied by an Illinois Class B driver's license and letter of employment verification

Endorsements — (For Commercial Driver's License Only.)

T	Double/Triple Trailers			(HazMat)
P	Passenger Carrying Vehicles (16 or more persons including driver)		X	Combination of Tank and Hazardous Materials Endorsement
N	Tank Vehicles		C	Charter Bus (used for the transportation of students to and from school functions)
H	Vehicles Carrying Hazardous Materials requiring placard		S	School Bus (Effective 2006)

Restrictions

A	None
B	Corrective Lenses
C	Mechanical Aid
D	Prosthetic Aids
E	Automatic Transmission
F	Outside Mirrors
G	Limited to Daylight Only
K	Intrastate Only
L	Restricted to a vehicle without air brakes (CDL only)
V	Medical Variance/Waiver/Exception
JO1	Driver has been issued an Illinois medical restriction card that must be carried in addition to a valid Illinois license.
JO2	Driver authorized to operate a religious organization bus within classification as provided in section 6-106(2) of IVC.
JO3	Driver authorized to operate a religious organization bus or van within Class D only (the driver took the religious organization bus test in a Class D vehicle, but may hold a Class A, B, or C license).
JO4	Driver authorized to operate a religious organization bus or van within Class C only (the driver took the religious organization bus test in a Class C vehicle, but may hold a Class A or B license).
JO5	Driver authorized to operate a senior-citizen organization

vehicle within classification (the driver operates a vehicle which is used solely for the purpose of providing transportation for senior citizens, as provided in section 6-106.3 of the IVC).

JO6	Driver authorized to operate a senior-citizen organization vehicle within Class D only (the driver took the senior-citizen organization vehicle test in a Class D vehicle, but may hold a Class A, B, or C license).
JO7	Driver authorized to operate a senior-citizen organization vehicle within Class C only (the driver took the senior-citizen organization vehicle test in a Class D vehicle, but may hold a Class A or B license.)
JO8	Driver authorized to operate a commuter van in a for-profit, ride-sharing arrangement within Classification as provided in section 6-106.4 of IVC.
JO9	Driver who is sixteen or seventeen years of age is authorized to operate Class M motorcycles as provided in section 6-103(2) of IVC.
J10	Restricts the driver to vehicles with a GVWR of 16,000 pounds or less (the driver would, with proper endorsement, be authorized to transport certain hazardous materials in a Class D vehicle, but must hold a Class C Commercial Driver's License).

J11	Authorizes an applicant holding a Class L or M license to operate a three-wheel motorcycle or motor-driven cycle only in these classes.
J12	The driver has a "P" endorsement valid in Class B (or lesser classification) vehicle only.
J13	The driver has a "P" endorsement valid in Class C (or lesser classification) vehicle only.
J14	The driver is restricted to the use of a non-standard lens arrangement when operating a motor vehicle (lens arrangement may be designed for monocular or binocular vision).
J15	This is an "either/or" restriction, applying only to variations of C, D, or E restrictions.
J16	Authorizes an applicant holding a Class L license to operate a pedal-cycle only.
J33	Non-standard lens - unrestricted hours
J48	Limited CDL - school bus only
J50	Farm waived Non-CDL(Class A only) - Allows farmer or member of family who is 21 or older and completed all applicable exams to operate truck/tractor semi-trailer to transport farm products, equipment, or supplies to or from a farm, if used within 150 miles of the farm, and not used in the operations of common or contract carrier.
J71	A driver's license valid without photo or signature for an Illinois resident temporarily out-of-state.
J72	A driver's license valid without photo or signature for an Illinois resident temporarily out-of-country.
J73	A driver's license valid without photo or signature for an individual in the military or military dependent who is stationed out-of-state or out-of-country.
J74	A card issued to defer the expiration date of an expired license for a military person, spouse, or dependent who is out-of-state or out-of-country.
J75	A driver's license valid without photo or signature for a person having established religious conviction or facial disfigurement that would prevent having a photo license.
J88	This restriction indicates that the driver is deaf/hard of hearing: requires alternative forms of communication.
J89	This restriction indicates that the driver is Aphasic which is defined as a partial or total loss of the ability to articulate ideas or comprehend spoken or written language. This type of restriction requires alternative forms of communication.

Special Permits

Restricted CDL........... Issued for seasonal employees of farm services companies.

Probationary .... A conditional license, issued after the completion of a Defensive Driving Course conducted through the National Safety Council (NSC), which grants full driving privileges during a period of suspension. Commercial licensed drivers are restricted to an automobile only.

Restricted Local .... This special license may be issued to drivers who live in communities with less than 3,500 residents and who drive only within certain areas of the community.

Restricted Permits

Restricted Driving (RDP) .... Allow driving only during certain times and along specified routes for work-related or educational purposes or to receive medical care or drug treatment. A restricted driving permit cannot be issued to a motorist under the age of 16.

Judicial Driving (JDP)........... Issued, following a circuit judge's order, to a first offender serving a statutory summary suspension following an arrest for driving under the influence of alcohol, other drugs and/or intoxicating compounds (DUI). Judicial driving permits have the same restrictions and provisions as restricted driving permits. A judicial driving permit will not be issued to a motorist under age 18. (Note - this is obsolete 12 of 12/31/2008)

Monitoring Device Driving Permit (MDDP).... Issued, following a Circuit Judge's order, to a first offender serving a Statutory Summary Suspension following an arrest for driving under the influence of alcohol, other drugs, and/or intoxicating compounds (DUI). The driver's vehicle must be equipped with an ignition interlock device (BAIID).

Family Financial Responsibility Driving (FRP) This permit is issued, following a circuit judge's order, to a driver who has been suspended under the Family Financial Responsibility Law for nonpayment of court-ordered child support. No permit will be issued to a person under the age of 16 years who possesses an instruction permit.

Conviction Table with Statute and ACD Code

This Table is presented in order of the "first digit" under the IVC/Code column.

Note: Some violation records may be coded with a "UART" prefix which pertain to violations that occurred prior to 1970. The DHR code of the "UART" violation will correspond to the DHR code on the regular violation description. Some violations may indicate "Adverse Conditions" and are basically obsolete since 1974, however the phrase must stay on the listing because some records with old revocations indicate these older codes.

A law effective January 1, 2013 bans the use of hand-held cell phones by Commercial Drivers License (CDL) holders operating commercial motor vehicles and upgrades the offense to a serious violation for truck drivers ticketed for texting while driving.

IVC/Code	EDPM	Pts	ACD	Description
1104	001104	00	F02	Unrestrained Child Under Age Four
1104(A)	101104	00	F02	Unrestrained Child Age Four But Under Age Six
1105	001105	00	-	See Correct EDPM #101104
11-1002(A)	100201	20	N08	Failure to Yield to Pedestrians
11-1002(B)	100202	20	M70	Passing Vehicle Stopped for Pedestrians
11-1002(D)	100204	20	M70	Passing Vehicle Stopped for Pedestrians
11-1002(E)	100205	20	N08	Yield Right-of-Way to Pedestrian/Intersect
11-1003 1	100301	10	N01	Failure to Exercise Care for Pedestrian/Bicyclist

IVC/Code	EDPM	Pts	ACD	Description
11-1004	100400	20	N08	Failure to Yield to Impaired Pedestrian
11-1008	100800	20	N08	Failure to Yield to Pedestrian on Sidewalk
11-1101	110100	10	M70	Improper Passing of Street-Car on Left
11-1102	110200	20	M70	Improper Passing or Fail to Stop for Street-Car
11-1103	110300	05	F34	Obstructing Street-Car Traffic
11-1104	110400	20	M12	Driving Through Safety-Zone
11-1201	120100	20	M10	Failure to Stop for Railroad Train or Signal
11-1201(a)	120110	20	M21	Fail to Stop at Railroad Crossing if Track Not Clear
11-1201(a-2)	120112	20	M10	Fail to Obey Traffic Control at Railroad Crossing
11-1201(a-5)	120115	20	M20	Failure to Slow Down to Check if Railroad Tracks Clear
11-1201(d-1)	120141	20	M24	Fail to Manage Crossing, Insufficient Clearance
11-1202	120200	20	M09	Failure to Stop at Railroad Grade Crossing
11-1203	120300	05	M09	Improper Movement/Heavy Equipment/RR Crossing
11-1204	120400	20	M15	Disregarding Stop/Yield Sign at Intersection
11-1205	120500	20	M25	Failure to Yield from Alley or Driveway
11-1301 3A-2	301312	-	-	Unauthorized Use of Handicap Placard/Device
11-1301 5 B1	301521	00		Unlawful use of disabled license plate or decal
11-1301 5 B7	301527	-	-	Falsify a Certification That a Person is Disabled
11-1301 6 B1	301621	00		Fraudulent use of disabled license plate or decal
11-1401	140100	00		Failure to Observe Regulations; Unattended Vehicle
11-1402	140200	05	N82	Limitations on Backing
11-1402(A)	140201	10	N82	Limitations on Backing
11-1402(B)	140202	20	N82	Limitations on Backing; Controlled-Access Highway
11-1403 1	140301	05	N84	Motorized Pedal-cycle Operating Violation
11-1403 2	140302	55	M84	Operation of Motorcycle/Motor-Driven Cycle on One Wheel
11-1403	140300	05	F03	Motorcycle Operating or Passenger Equipment Violation
11-1404	140400	05	F03	Motorcycle Glasses, Shield, or Goggles Violation
11-1404(B)	140402	05	F03	Motorcycle Violation; Glasses, Goggles, Shield
11-1405	140500	05	F03	Motorcycle Equipment Violation
11-1406	140600	00	D70	Obstruction to Driver's View of Control
11-1407	140700	00		Improper Opening of Door into Traffic
11-1410	141000	00	N80	Coasting on Downgrade
11-1411	141100	00	M33	Following Fire Apparatus
11-1412 1	141201	20	M58	Driving upon Sidewalk
11-1412	141200	00	M56	Crossing Fire-Hose
11-1414(A)	141401	25	M75	Passing Stopped School Bus
11-1414(A)	141400	00	M75	Passing Stopped School Bus
11-1414(A)	141410	00	M75	Failure to Stop for School Bus
11-1414(F)	141460	00	M75	Failure to Stop for School Bus
11-1416	141600	00	F34	Obstructing Traffic
11-1418	141800	10	M50	Illegal Operation of Farm-tractor upon Highway
11-1420	142000	00	N05	Funeral Procession Violation
11-1425(B)	142520	00	M23	Fail to have Space to Drive Through RR Crossing
11-1425(D)	142540	00	M23	Obstructing Railroad Crossing for Use of Trains or Railroad Equipment
11-14262(G)	142627	15		Operating a Low Speed Vehicles Without a Valid License
11-1505 1	150501	10	N84	Riding Motorized-Pedal-cycle More Than Two Abreast
11-1505	150500	10	N84	Improper Position Motorized Pedal-cycles on Roadway
11-1507 1	150701	10	N84	Violation of Lamps on Motorized Pedal-cycles
11-1510(B)	151020	10	N84	Improper Left-Turn on Pedal-cycle
11-15 1	011151	00	U03	Soliciting for a Juvenile Prostitute
11-19 1	011191	00	U03	Juvenile Pimping
11-203	020300	10	M08	Failure to Obey Officer
11-204 1	020401	00	U01	Aggravated Fleeing or Eluding a Peace Officer
11-204	020400	00	U01	Fleeing or Attempting to Elude a Peace Officer
11-204(B)	020420	00	U01	Eluding or Fleeing from a Police Officer
11-204(B)	204002	00	U01	Eluding or Fleeing from a Police Officer
11-305	030500	20	M16	Disregarding Official Traffic-Control Device
11-306	030600	20	M16	Disregarding Traffic-Control Light
11-308	030800	20	M05	Disregarding Lane-Control Signal
11-309	030900	20	M18	Disregarding Flashing Traffic Signal
11-401	040100	00	B07	Leaving Scene of Accident; Death or Personal Injury
11-402	040200	25	B04	Leaving Scene of Accident; Vehicle Damage Only
11-402(A)	040201	25	B04	Failed to Stop/Exchange Information/Report; Property Damage Accident
11-402(B)	040202	00	B08	Leaving Scene of Accident; Damage in Excess of $1,000
11-403	040380	50	B14	Failure to Stop/Exchange Information; Fatality Accident
11-403	040370	50	B14	Failure to Stop/Exchange Information; Personal Injury Accident

IVC/Code	EDPM	Pts	ACD	Description
11-403	040300	25		Failed to Stop/Exchange Information; Property Damage Accident
11-403(A)	040310	50	B14	Failure to Stop/Exchange Information; Personal Injury Accident
11-404	040400	15	B08	Failed to Notify Owner; Property Damage Accident
11-405	040500	00		Failure to Notify Owner; Property Damage Accident
11-406	040600	00	B61	Fail to Report Collision; Property Damage/Personal Injury
11-406(A)	040610	00	B61	Failure to Make Report of Vehicle Accident
11-406(B)	040620	00	B61	Failure to Make Report of School Bus Accident
11-406(E)	040650	00	B61	Failure to Report Accident
11-407	040700	00	B61	Fail to Report Accident; Property Damage/Personal Injury
11-407(A)	040710	00	B61	Failure of Driver to Give Notice of Accident
11-407(B)	040720	00	B61	Failure of Passenger to Give Notice of Accident
11-501	050100	00	A21	Driving Under Influence Liquor or Drugs
11-501 1	050101	00	A12	Statutory Summary Suspension
11-501 8	050108	00	A61	Zero tolerance suspension
11-501(A)	050110	00	A21	Driving under the influence of intoxicating liquor
11-501(A)1	050111	00	A10	DUI; Alcohol Concentration .08 or More
11-501(A)2	050112	00	A21	DUI; Alcohol
11-501(A)3	050113	00	A22	DUI; Any Other Drug or Combination of Drugs
11-501(A)4	050114	00	A23	DUI; Alcohol and Other Drug(s)
11-501(A)5	050115	00	A22	DUI; Any Amount of a Drug Substance or Compound
11-501(B)	050120	00	A22	Driving Under Influence of any narcotic drug
11-501(C-1)1-3	501311-3	00	A20	DUI While Rev/Susp for DUI/Reck Hom/leave Scene
11-501(C-4)1-4	501341-4	00	A20	DUI BAC 16 or More Transport Children Under 16
11-501(D)	050140	00	A20	Driving a School Bus While Under the Influence
11-501(D)1	050141	00	A20	Conviction of 3 or more viol 11-502(A) DUI
11-501(D)1a	501411	00	A20	Conviction of Three of More Violations of 11-501(A) DUI
11-501(D)1b	501412	00	A20	Conviction of Violation of 11-501(A) While Driving a School Bus
11-501(D)1c	501413	00	A20	Conviction of Violations of 11-501(A) Accident w/Bodily Harm
11-501(D)1d	501414	00	A20	Conviction of 11-501(A) and Previous Conviction of Reckless Homicide
11-501(D)1e	501415	00	A20	DUI in School Zone with Accident with Bodily Harm
11-501(D)1f	501416	00	A20	DUI Violation Resulting in Death to Another Person
11-501(D)2	050142	00	A20	Conviction of Violation of 11-501(A) While Driving School Bus
11-501(D)3	050143	00	A20	Conviction of Violation of 11-501(A) Accident Involving Bodily Harm
11-501(D)4	050144	00	A20	Conviction of 11-501A and Previous Conviction of Reckless Homicide
11-501(E)	050150	00	A20	DUI; Accident Resulting in Bodily Harm or Disability
11-501(F)	050160	00	A20	DUI; Accident Resulting in Bodily Harm or Disability
11-502A	050201	25	A31	Illegal Transportation of any Alcoholic Liquor
11-503	050300	55	M84	Reckless Driving
11-503(B-1)	503201	00	U03	Reckless Driving
11-503(c)	050303	00	U03	Aggravated Reckless Driving
11-503(d)	050304	00	U03	Aggravated Reckless Driving
11-504	050400	00	S95	Drag Racing
11-505	050500	10	N84	Squealing or Screeching Tires
11-506(a)	050601	00	S95	Street Racing
11-506(b)	050602	00	-	Vehicle Owner Permitting Street Racing
11-507	050700	20		Supervising Minor driver while under the influence
11-601(A)	060100	10	S94	Speeding Too Fast for Conditions
11-601(B)	060101	05	S51	Speeding 1-10 mph Above Limit
11-601(B)	060103	15	S93	Speeding 11-14 mph Above Limit
11-601(B)	060105	20	S15	Speeding 15-25 mph Above Limit
11-601(B)	060107	50	S15	Speeding Over 25 mph Above Limit
11-601(B)	060108	50	S15	Speeding Over 25 mph Above Limit
11-601(B)	060109	50	S15	Speeding Over 29 mph Above Limit
11-605	060500	20	S94	Exceeding Max Speed Limit in School/Construction Zone
11-605(A)	060501	20	S94	Exceeding Max Speed Limit in School Zone
11-605(B)	060502	20	S94	Exceeding Max Speed Limit in Construction Zone
11-605.10	060510	20	S94	Exceeding Max Speed Limit in Construction Zone
11-606	060600	05	S96	Driving Below Minimum Speed Limit
11-606(A)	060601	05	S96	Driving Below Minimum Speed Limit
11-606(B)	060602	20	S96	Driving Below Minimum Speed Limit on Illinois Tollway
11-607	060700	10	E01	Driving Tractor Less Than 20 mph Without Red Flag
11-608	060800	10	S93	Speeding on Bridge or Elevated Structure
11-609	060900	12	E50	Failure to Use Warning Equipment; Emergency Vehicle
11-701	070100	20	N72	Failure to Drive on Right Side of Roadway
11-702	070200	20	M70	Improper Passing Meeting Approaching Vehicle
11-703(A)	070301	20	M70	Improper Passing on Left

IVC/Code	EDPM	Pts	ACD	Description
11-703(B)	070302	20	N07	Failed to Yield Right-of-Way to Vehicle Passing on Left
11-703(C)	070303	20	M70	Improper Passing with a Two-Wheeled Vehicle
11-703(D)	070304	20	M70	Improper Passing of Bicycle or Individual
11-703(E)	070305	20		Driving close to pedestrian or person operating a non-motor vehicle
11-704	070400	20	M70	Improper Passing on the Right
11-705	070500	20	M70	Improper Passing on the Left
11-706	070600	20	N70	Driving on Left Side of Roadway/Prohibited
11-707	070700	20	M71	Driving on Left Side of Roadway/No-Passing Zone
11-707(B)	070702	20	M71	Driving on Left Side of Roadway/No-Passing Zone
11-707(D)	070704	10	M76	No Passing/Unincorporated Areas/School Speed Zone
11-708	070800	05	N63	Driving Wrong Way on One-Way Street/Highway/Around Island
11-709 1(A)	070911	20	M58	Pass on Shoulder While Merging into Traffic
11-709(A)	070901	20	M41	Improper Traffic Lane Usage
11-709(B)	070902	20	M62	Improper Center Lane Usage
11-709(C)	070903	20	M40	Improper Traffic Lane Usage
11-709(D)	070904	20	M40	Improper Traffic Lane Usage
11-710	071000	25	M34	Following Too Closely
11-711(A)	071101	10	M46	Improper Entry or Exit; Controlled-Access Roadway
11-711(B)	071102	10	M50	Improper Vehicle on a Controlled-Access Roadway
11-801	080100	10	N50	Improper Turn at Intersection
11-802	080200	20	N56	Improper U-Turn
11-803	080300	15	N83	Unsafe Movement of Vehicle From Parked Position
11-804	080400	15	N40	Failure to Give Stop or Turn Signal
11-805	080500	15	N44	Improper Stop or Turn Signal
11-806	080600	15	N44	Improper Arm Signal
11-90101	090101	15	N25	Failure to Yield Right-of-Way at "T" Intersection
11-901	090100	15	N25	Failure to Yield Right-of-Way at Intersection
11-902	090200	25	N53	Improper Left-Turn with On-Coming Traffic
11-903	090300	20	N08	Failure to Stop or Yield to Pedestrians
11-904	090400	20	M14	Failure to Observe Stop/Yield/Right-of-Way Sign
11-905	090500	20	M48	Improper Merging into Traffic
11-906	090600	20	N01	Failure to Yield from Private Road/Driveway
11-907	090700	15	N04	Failure to Yield Right-of-Way to Emergency Vehicle
11-907(C)	090703	00	N04	Failure to Yield to Stopped Emergency Vehicle
11-908(A)	090801	15	N01	Failure to Yield to Vehicle or Pedestrian
11-908(A)1	090811	00	M03	Failure to Yield Entering Construction Zone
11-908(B)	090802	15	N30	Failure to Yield to Authorized Vehicle
11-908(C)	090803	15	M03	Failure to Stop at Highway Construction Sign
12-13	012013	00	U03	Criminal Sexual Assault
12-14	012014	00	U03	Aggravated Criminal Sexual Assault
12-15	012015	00	U03	Criminal Sexual Abuse
12-16	012016	00	U03	Aggravated Criminal Sexual Abuse
12-101	210100	00	F66	Driving Unsafe/Improperly Equipped Vehicle
12-102	210200	10	E05	Head, Tail or Side Light Violation
12-103(A)	210301	00	E01	Clearance, Ident or Side Market Violations; Second Division
12-103(B)	210302	00		No Reflectors on Rear of Trailer
12-104	210400	00	E05	Front or Rear Light Violation on Parked Vehicle
12-105	210500	00		Projecting Load on Vehicle
12-106	210600	00	E05	Failure to Display the Safety Lights Required
12-108	210800	00		Spot Light Violation
12-109	210900	05	E05	No Stop or Turn Signal Lights
12-111	211100	00	E54	Failure to Dim Headlights
12-112(A)	211201	00		Headlight Violation
12-112(B)	211202	00		Front Light Violation
12-113	211300	00		Front Red, Flashing Light Violation
12-114	211400	05	E56	School Bus Warning Light Violation
12-115	211500	05	E50	Rural Mail Delivery Vehicle Warning Light Violation
12-118	211800	09	E31	Defective Brakes
12-121	212100	00		Muffler Violation
12-122	212200	00	E01	No Rear-View Mirror
12-123(A)	212301	00	D70	Driver's View Obstructed
12-123(B)	212302	00	D70	Driver's View Obstructed
12-123(C)	212303	00	E01	No Windshield Wipers
12-123(D)	212304	00	D70	Obstruction to Driver's View
12-128(B)	212802	10		Failure to Display Flares Warning Flags; Vehicle Parked
12-131	213100	10	E04	Improperly Market Vehicle/Explosives/Flammable Liquid

IVC/Code	EDPM	Pts	ACD	Description
12-201	220100	10	E05	Head, Tail, or Side Light Violation
12-201(B)	220102	10	E05	Head, Tail, or Side Light Violation
12-201(C)	220103	00	E34	Registration Light Violation
12-202(A)	220201	00	E05	Clearance, Ident or Side Marker Light Violation; Second Division
12-202(B)	220202	00	E52	No Reflectors on Rear of Trailer
12-203	220300	00	E55	Lamps on Parked Vehicle
12-204	220400	00	F22	Projecting Load on Vehicle
12-205	220500	00	E55	Failure to Display the Safety Lights Required
12-207	220700	00	E20	Spot Light or Auxiliary Light Violation
12-208	220800	05	E01	No Stop or Turn Signal Lights
12-208(A)	220801	05	E05	No Stop Lights
12-208(B)	220802	05	E05	No Turn Signal Lights
12-208(C)	220803	05	E05	No Turn Signal Lights on Trailers or Semi-Trailers
12-209	220900	00	E20	Other Light Violation
12-211(A)	221101	00	E24	Headlight Violation
12-211(B)	221102	00	E24	Front Light Violation
12-212	221200	00	E21	Front Red or Flashing Light Violation
12-213	221300	05	E56	School Bus Warning Light Violation
12-214	221400	00	E34	Special Lighting Equipment on Rural Mail Delivery Vehicle
12-215(F)	221560	00	U03	Conviction of 12-215 Without Lawful Authority to Stop
12-215(G)	221507	00	U03	Conviction of 12-215 Without Lawful Authority to Stop
12-301	230100	20	E31	Defective Brakes
12-502	250200	00	E01	No Rear-View Mirror
12-503(A)	250301	00	D70	Driver's View Obstructed
12-503(B)	250302	00	D70	Driver's View Obstructed
12-503(C)	250303	00	E01	No Windshield Wipers
12-503(D)	250304	00	D70	Obstruction to Driver's View
12-601	260100	00	E73	Failure to Use/Improper Use of Horn
12-602	260200	00	E35	Muffler Violation
12-603 1	260301	00	F04	Violation of the Seat-Belt Act
12-610.10	261010	10	N84	Driver Under Age 19 Using a Wireless Phone
12-610(B)	261012	10	N84	Driver Underage 18 using a Wireless Phone
12-610.1e	261015	15	M86	Using a Wireless Phone in a School or Construction Zone
12-610.2b	261022	20	M85	Using an Electronic Communications Device to Compose, Send, or Read a Message
12-610.5b	261052	05		Unlawful Use of Registration Plate covers
12-702(B)	270202	10		Failure to Display Flares Warning Flags; Vehicle Parked
12-704	270400	10	E04	Improperly Marked Vehicle/Explosives/Flammable Liquid
12-712(A)	271201	00	E23	Possession of Radar Detector in CMV
12-713(A)	271301	00	E23	Possession of Radar Jamming Device in CMV
12-714(A)	271401	00	E23	Possession of Radar Detector in CMV
12-715(A)	271501	00	E23	Possession of Radar Jamming Device in CMV
12-804	280400	05		School Bus Identification and Warning Light Violation
12-805	280500	05	E56	School Bus Warning Light Violation

> **Note:** Illinois carries a series of "124" codes in their table. The associated violations deal with ID Cards, including false, fraudulent, allowing others to use, not entitled, etc. While codes are obsolete, a 124 may appear on a record. Most of the 124 series codes were replaced by codes in the "335" series.

IVC/Code	EDPM	Pts	ACD	Description
13-112(B)	311122	00	W00	Vehicle Emissions Inspection Law
13B 55B	132552	00	W00	Vehicle Emissions Inspection Law
1401 1(A)	140111	00	U03	Controlled Substance Trafficking
1401(A)	140101	00	U03	Violation Chapter 56 1/2, Section 1401; Controlled Substances Act
1401(B)	140102	00	U03	Violation Chapter 56 1/2, Section 1401; Controlled Substances Act
1401(C)	140103	00	U03	Violation Chapter 56 1/2, Section 1401; Controlled Substances Act
1401(D)	140104	00	U03	Violation Chapter 56 1/2, Section 1401; Controlled Substances Act
1401(E)	140105	00	U03	Violation Chapter 56 1/2, Section 1401; Controlled Substances Act
1401(F)	140106	00	U03	Violation Chapter 56 1/2, Section 1401; Controlled Substances Act
1401(G)	140107	00	U03	Violation Chapter 56 1/2, Section 1401; Controlled Substances Act
1402(A)10	014210	00	U03	Violation Chapter 56 1/2, Section 1402A; Controlled Substances Act
1402(A)11	014211	00	U03	Violation Chapter 56 1/2, Section 1402A; Controlled Substances Act
1402(A)1	014201	00	U03	Violation Chapter 56 1/2, Section 1402A; Controlled Substances Act
1402(A)2	014202	00	U03	Violation Chapter 56 1/2, Section 1402A; Controlled Substances Act
1402(A)3	014203	00	U03	Violation Chapter 56 1/2, Section 1402A; Controlled Substances Act
1402(A)4	014204	00	U03	Violation Chapter 56 1/2, Section 1402A; Controlled Substances Act
1402(A)5	014205	00	U03	Violation Chapter 56 1/2, Section 1402A; Controlled Substances Act
1402(A)6	014206	00	U03	Violation Chapter 56 1/2, Section 1402A; Controlled Substances Act
1402(A)7	014207	00	U03	Violation Chapter 56 1/2, Section 1402A; Controlled Substances Act

IVC/Code	EDPM	Pts	ACD	Description
1402(A)8	014208	00	U03	Violation Chapter 56 1/2, Section 1402A; Controlled Substances Act
1402(A)9	014209	00	U03	Violation Chapter 56 1/2, Section 1402A; Controlled Substances Act
1402(B)	014220	00	U03	Violation Chapter 56 1/2, Section 1402B; Controlled Substances Act
1402(C)	014230	00	U03	Possession of Controlled/Counterfeit Substance
1407 1	014071	00	U03	Violation Chapter 56 1/2, Section 1407 1; Controlled Substances Act
1407	014070	00	U03	Violation Chapter 56 1/2, Section 1407; Controlled Substances Act
140-43	140043	00		Illegal Transportation of Liquor
146 OA	146001	00	U07	Manslaughter or Reckless Homicide
15-101	510100	00		Illegal Size, Weight, or Load
15-102	510200	00		Illegal Width or Height
15-105	510500	00		Illegal Projecting Load on Passenger Vehicle
15-106	510600	15	F66	Failure to Fasten/Secure Protruding Component
15-107	510700	00		Illegal Length
15-107(D)	510704	10		Improper Pushing of Another Vehicle
15-109	510900	15	F66	Spilling or Unsafe Load
15-110	511000	10	N84	Improper Towing of a Vehicle
15-114	511400	10	N84	Improper Pushing of Another Vehicle
16J-15	161015	00		Theft of Motor Fuel
16K-15	161115	00		Theft of Motor Fuel
183-43	183043	00	A31	Illegal Possession of Liquor by a Minor
193-38	193038	00	-	Intoxication, Other than Driving
204 01	204001	00	E01	Light Violation on Horse-Drawn Vehicles
2103	021003	00	U03	Violation Chapter 56 1/2, Section 2103, Illinois Revised Statutes
22-51	022051	00	U03	Violation Chapter 38, Section 22-51, Illinois Revised Statutes
24-1 5(B)0	241520	00	U03	Reckless Discharge of a Firearm
25/4	250400	00	F02	Violation of Child Passenger Protection Act child under age 8
25/4A	250401	00	F02	Unrestrained Child age 8 but under age 16
25/4B	250402	00	F02	Unrestrained Child age 8 but under age 18
3-413(G)	413007	10	-	Operating a Motor Vehicle Equipped With Registration Plate Covers
3-413(J)	413010	-	-	Violation of Modification of Rear Registration Plate
3-707(c-1)	707301	00	D36	Convicted of Driving Without Liability
335-13(B)1	013201	00		Not Entitled to Identification Card
335-13(B)2	013202	00		False Statement/Concealed Material Fact
335-13(B)3	013203	00		Display/Represent Identification Card Not Issued to Him
335-13(B)4	013204	00		Permitted Display/Use of Identification Card by Other Person
335-13(B)5	013205	00		Signature of Applicant or Signature on Card Forgery
335-13(B)6	013206	00		Identification Card Used for Unlawful Fraudulent Purpose
335-13(B)7	013207	00		Identification Card has been Altered or Defaced
335-13(B)8	013208	00		Identification Card Duplicated for Any Purpose
335-13(B)9	013209	00		Identification Card Utilized to Counterfeit Such Cards
335-13(B)10	013210	00		You are Not a Disabled Person
335-13(B)11	013211	00		Holder Failed to Appear for Re-issuance of an ID Card
335-14B(B)1	014221	00	B41	Possess Fraudulent Identification Card
335-14B(B)2	014222	00	B41	Possess/Display Fraudulent Identification Card
335-14B(B)3	014223	00	B41	Possess Fraudulent Identification Card
335-14B(B)4	014224	00	B41	Possess Fraudulent Identification Card
335-14B(B)5	014225	00	B41	Possess Fraudulent Identification Card
335-14B(B)6	014226	00	B41	Possess Fraudulent Identification Card
335-14B(B)7	014227	00	D10	Possess License-Making Implement
335-14B(B)8	014228	00	D10	Possess Stolen Illinois Identification Card-Making Implement
335-14B(B)9	014229	00	D10	Duplicate/Sell Fraudulent Identification Card
335-14B(B)10	014210	00	U03	Advertise or Distribute Fraudulent Card
335-14A(B)11	014211	00	U03	Obtain Services of person for Fictitious Card
335-14C(A)1	014311	00	D02	Present False Information in Application for Identification Card
335-14C(A)2	014312	00	D02	Accept False Information in Application for Identification Card
335-14C(A)3	014313	00	D02	Make False Affidavit/Swear or Affirm Falsely
335-14C(A)4	014104	00		Lend Identification Card for Use by Another
335-14C(A)5	014105	00		Fail/Refuse to Surrender Revoked/Canceled Identification Card
335-14(A)1	014101	00		Display/Possess Canceled/Revoked Identification Card
335-14(A)2	014102	00		Display/Represent as Own Identification Issued to Another
335-14(A)3	014103	00		Allow Unlawful Use of Your Identification Card
335-14(A)4	014104	00		Lend ID Card for Use by Another
335-14(A)5	014105	00		Fail or Refuse to Surrender Revoked or Canceled ID Card
335-14(A)6	014106	00		Possess/Use and ID Card-Making Implement
4-102	102000	00		Motor Vehicle Anti-Theft Law; Misdemeanor
4-102(A)	102001	00		Theft of a Motor Vehicle

IVC/Code	EDPM	Pts	ACD	Description
4-102(B)	102002	00		Unauthorized Possession of a Motor Vehicle
4-102(C)	102003	00		Damage/Removal of Parts from Motor Vehicle
4-102(D)	102004	00		Tampering with Motor Vehicle
4-103	103000	00	U03	Motor Vehicle Anti-Theft Law; Felony
4-103 1	103100	00	U03	Motor Vehicle Anti/Theft Law; Felony
43-131(A)	431311	00	D06	Violation of 6-16 of the Liquor Control Act
6-20 (a,c,d or e)	006020	00	D06	Conviction of Section 6-20 of the Liquor Control Act
6-101	101000	00	B51	Driving Without Valid License or Permit
6-104(A)	104001	00	B91	Violation of License Classification
6-104(B)	104002	00	B91	Classification Violation Transporting for Hire
6-104(C)	104003	00	B91	Classification Violation Transporting for Hire
6-104(D)	104004	00	B91	Violation of School Bus Driver Permits
6-104(E)	104005	00	B91	Violation of Religious Bus Driver Endorsement
6-104(F)	104006	00	B91	Violation of Class for Transportation of Elderly
6-105	105000	00	D29	Violation of Instruction Permit
6-105(B)	105200	00	W00	No Longer in Driver Education
6-106 1	106001	00		School Bus Permits Transaction
6-107(E)	107005	10		Exceeding Passenger Restrictions
6-107(F)	107006	10		Restrictions on Passenger Seat Belt/Child Restraints
6-107(G)	107007	10		Restrictions on Number of Passengers
6-107.1(a)	107110	00	D29	Violation of Instruction Permit
6-107.1(b)	107102	00	B51	Violation of Nighttime Driving Restrictions
6-108(1)	108001	00	W13	Withdrawal of Consent
6-108(2)	108002	00	W00	Death of Person Giving Consent
6-108(3)	108003	00	W00	Person Giving Consent no Longer has Legal Custody
6-108(B)	180200	00	A33	Violation of Cannabis Control/IL Controlled Substances
6-110(A)	110000	00	B51	Violation of Curfew Law; Under Age Seventeen
6-110(A-1)	110101	00	B51	Violation of Night-time Driving Restrictions
6-113(C)	113001	00	D29	Violation of Driver's License Restriction
6-113(C)	113300	00	W00	Violation of Restriction on a License or Permit
6-113(D)	113400	00	D29	Violation of Restriction of License or Permit
6-113(D)	113002	00	D27	Violation of Restriction on Special Restricted License
6-113(E)	113501	00	D29	Violation of Driver's License Restriction
6-113(E)	113502	00		Violation of Restriction on Special Restricted License
6-113(E)	113500	00	D29	Violation of Restriction on License or RDP
6-119(C)	119300	00	D29	Violation of Restriction on a License or Permit
6-119-01	119001	00	D29	Violation of License Restriction
6-119-02	119002	00	D27	Violation of License Restriction
6-201(A)0	201100	00	W20	Fraud in Application or Ineligible Under Section 6-103
6-201(A)1	201101	00	W00	Not Entitled to License or Permit
6-201(A)2	201102	00	W00	Failed to Give the Required or Correct Information
6-201(A)3	201103	00	W00	Failed to Pay Fees/Taxes
6-201(A)4	201104	00	W00	Committed Any Fraud in Making of Application
6-201(A)5	201105	00	W00	Ineligible Under the Provisions of Section 6-103
6-201(A)6	201106	00	WOO	Refused to Submit to Exam/Re-exam as required
6-201(A)7	201107	00	A33	Violation of Cannabis Control/IL Controlled Substances
6-201(A)8	201108	00	W00	Failed to Notify Sec of State of Medical Condition
6-201(A)9	201109	00	W00	Conviction of a Sex Offense as Defined in the Sex Offender Registration Act
6-201(A)11	201111	00	W00	Refusal to Appear for New License - Driver Failed to Appear to obtain a Re-Issuance of a Driver's License
6-205(A)0	205100	00	W00	Revocation of a RDP
6-205(A)10	205110	00	M80	Reckless Conduct; Section 12-5 Criminal Code
6-205(A)11	205111	00	U01	Aggravated Fleeing or Eluding Peace Officer
6-205(A)12	205112	00	B20	Unlawful Operation of a Commercial Motor Vehicle
6-205(A)13	205113	00	A31	Second or Subsequent Conviction of 11-502(A) Under Age 21
6-205(A)14	205114	00	S95	Street Racing
6-205(A)15	205115	00	B25	Second or more conviction for driving while revoked after revoked for reckless
6-205(A)16	205116	00	U31	Traffic Violation resulting in death of any person
6-205(A)17	205117	-		Conviction/Illegal Possession controlled Substance/Cannabis
6-205(A)18	205118	-		Unauthorized use of Handicap Placard Device
6-205(A)1	205101	00	U07	Reckless Homicide; Motor Vehicle
6-205(A)2	205102	00	A20	DUI Alcohol, Other Drug, or Combination Thereof
6-205(A)3	205103	00	U03	Any Felony in Commission of Which Motor Vehicle Used
6-205(A)4	205104	00	B07	Leaving Scene of Accident; Death or Personal Injury
6-205(A)5	205105	00	D78	Convicted of Perjury of False Affidavit
6-205(A)6	205106	00	W01	Three Convictions of Reckless Driving Committed in a Twelve-Month Period

IVC/Code	EDPM	Pts	ACD	Description
6-205(A)7	205107	00	W00	Drag Racing Under Section 11-504 IVC
6-205(A)9	205109	00	D35	Violation of FR in Operation of Vehicle for Hire, Chapter 8/Rent, Chapter 9
6-205(B)1	205201	00	U03	Violated Section 4-103; Anti-Theft Laws
6-205(B)2	205202	00	W00	Violated Law Requiring Suspension or Revocation
6-205(B)3	205203	00	WOO	Committed Gang Related Offense Involving Motor Vehicle or DL
6-205(B)4	205204	00		Violated Law Requiring Suspension or Revocation
6-205(B)	205200	00	A50	Manufacture/Sell/Deliver/Controlled Substance
6-205(C)	205300	00	W00	Revocation/Suspension/Cancellation of a RDP
6-205(D)	205400	00	A20	Person Under Age Twenty-One Convicted Under 11-501
6-205(E)0	205500	00	W00	Subsequent Sex Offense
6-205(F)	205600	00		Revocation Under 6-205(B)2 or 3 Converted to a Suspension
6-205-03	205003	00	U03	Any Felony in Commission of Which Motor Vehicle Used
6-205-05	205005	00	D78	Perjury/False Statement
6-206(A)1	206101	00	W0	Committed Off Requiring Revocation on Conviction
6-206(A)2	206102	00	W01	Three or More Convictions of Moving Traffic Violation in Twelve Months
6-206(A)3	206103	00	W01	Habitually in Violation of Vehicle Laws
6-206(A)4	206104	00	W00	Accident Resulting in Death or Injury
6-206(A)5	206105	00	W00	Permitted Unlawful Use of License/Identification Card/Permit
6-206(A)6	206106	00	W00	Out-of-State Conviction of Off Requiring Suspension/Revocation
6-206(A)7	206107	00	W00	Refused or Failed to Submit to an Examination
6-206(A)8	206108	00	W00	Ineligible for License or Permit under Section 6-103
6-206(A)9	206109	00	D02	False Statement/Used False Information/Identification
6-206(A)10	206110	00	W00	Displayed/Fraudulently Used License/Identification Card
6-206(A)11	206111	00	B25	Driving While License or Permit Revoked/Suspended
6-206(A)12	206112	00	D02	Submitted to/Obtained Services of Another
6-206(A)13	206113	00	B51	Violation of Night-time Driving Restrictions
6-206(A)14	206114	00	D16	Unlawful Use of License/Permit/ID Card Under Section 6-301/124
6-206(A)15	206115	00	W00	Criminal Trespass to Vehicle; Section 21-2/Criminal Code
6-206(A)16	206116	00	U01	Violation of Section 11-204; Fleeing from Peace Officer
6-206(A)17	206117	00	A12	Refused to Submit to Test Under Section 11-5-1 1
6-206(A)18	206118	00	W14	Mental Disability/Disease
6-206(A)19	206119	00	B51	Has Violated Section 6-101; Driving Without Valid License
6-206(A)20	206120	00	B91	Has Violated Section 6-104; Classification on Driver's License
6-206(A)21	206121	00	B08	Leaving Scene of Accident; Vehicle Damage in Excess of $1,000
6-206(A)22	206122	00	W00	Unlawful Use of Weapons Violation of Chapter 38, Section 24-1
6-206(A)23	206123	00	W01	Two or More Convictions of Section 11-502(A)
6-206(A)24	206124	00	W00	Convicted of/Committed Offense on Military Base
6-206(A)25	206125	00	W00	Permitted Identification to be used by Another in Application Process
6-206(A)26	206126	00	B41	Altered or Possessed Altered License/Identification Card
6-206(A)27	206127	00	W00	Violated Section 6-16 of the Liquor Control Act
6-206(A)28	206128	00	A33	Conviction of Illegal Possession of Controlled Substance/Cannabis
6-206(A)29	206129	00	W00	Conviction of Certain Sex or Drug Offenses
6-206(A)30	206130	00	W00	Conviction of Second or Subsequent Sex or Drug Offenses
6-206(A)31	206131	00	A12	Refused to Submit/Failed Test Required by Section 11-501 6
6-206(A)32	206132	00	U03	Conviction of Aggravated Discharge of a Firearm
6-206(A)33	206133	00	A31	Conviction of Section 11-502(A) Under Age 21
6-206(A)34	206134	00	W000	Unlawful use of Disabled License Plate/Decal/Device - effective 08/11/98, prior was 6-206(A)36
6-206(A)35	206135	0	W00	Unlawful Use of Disabled License Plate/Decal/Device - effective 08/11/98), prior was 6-206(A)36
6-206(A)36	206136	00	W01	Two or more convictions of moving violations in 24 months - effective 08/11/98
6-206(A)37	206137	00	N04	Convicted of Fail to Yield to Stopped Emergency Vehicle
6-206(A)38	206138	00	W00	Violated 6-20 of the Liquor Control Act
6-206(A)39	206139	00	M09	Second or Subsequent Conviction of 11-1201
6-206(A)40	206140	00	M03	Failure to Yield Entering Construction Zone
6-206(A)41	206141	00	W00	Two or More Convictions for Speeding in a Construction Zone
6-206(A)42	206142	00	W00	Unauthorized Use of Handicap Placard/Device
6-206(A)43	206143	00	W00	Supervision for Violation of Section 6-20 of the Liquor Control Act
6-206(A)44	206144	00	W01	Convicted of Moving Violation After Being Suspended or Revoked Pursuant to 6-206(A)36
6-206(A)45	206145	00		Perjury or Submitted False Documents at a Hearing
6-206(a)46	206146	-	-	Has committed a violation of subsection J of section 3-413 - Violation of modification of rear registration plate
6-206(B)2	206202	00		Convicted of Offense While Holding a RDP
6-206 2(C)	206203	00	A41	Tampering With or Circumventing Interlock Device
6-206(C)0	206300	00	D27	Violation of RDP

IVC/Code	EDPM	Pts	ACD	Description
6-206(C)2	206302	00	W01	Suspended/Two of Five Convictions While Operating Commercial Vehicle
6-206(C)3	206303	00	W00	Revocation/Suspension/Cancellation of RDP
6-210(1)	210001	00	B26	Driving During the Period of Suspension/Revocation
6-210(2)	210002	00	B25	Driving During the Period of Revocation/Suspension
6-301 1	301100	00	D10	Conviction of False Driver's License
6-301 1(B)1	301121	00		Possess Fictitious/Altered Driver's License/Permit
6-301 1(B)2	301122	00	D02	Possess/Display/Alter Fictitious Driver's License or Permit
6-301 1(B)3	301123	00	D02	Possess Fictitious/Altered Driver's License/Permit
6-301 1(B)4	301124	00	D02	Possess Fictitious/Altered Driver's License/Permit
6-301 1(B)5	301125	00	D02	Possess Fictitious/Altered Driver's License/Permit
6-301 1(B)6	301126	00	D02	Possess Fictitious/Altered Driver's License/Permit
6-301 1(B)7	301127	00	D02	Issue Fictitious Driver's License/Permit
6-301 1(B)8	301128	00	B41	Altered/Attempt to Alter Driver's License/Permit
6-301 1(B)9	301129	00	D02	Provide Identification for Obtaining Fictitious Driver's License/Permit
6-301 1(B)10	301120	00		Use Fictitious/Altered License or Permit
6-301 1(B)11	011211	00		Possess Fictitious/Altered License or Permit
6-301 2(B)1	301221	00	B41	Possess Fraudulent Driver's License/Permit
6-301 2(B)2	301222	00	B41	Possess/Display Fraudulent Driver's License/Permit
6-301 2(B)3	301223	00	D10	Possess Fraudulent Driver's License/Permit
6-301 2(B)4	301224	00	D10	Possess Fraudulent Driver's License/Permit
6-301 2(B)5	301225	00	D10	Possess Fraudulent Driver's License/Permit
6-301 2(B)6	301226	00	D10	Possess Fraudulent Driver's License/Permit
6-301 2(B)7	301227	00	D10	Possess Driver's License Making-Implement
6-301 2(B)8	301228	00	D10	Possess Stolen Driver's License-Making Implement
6-301 2(B)9	301229	00	D10	Duplicate/Sell Fraudulent Driver's License/Permit
6-301 2(B)10	301220	00	D10	Advertise or Distribute Fraudulent Driver's License/Permit
6-301 2(B)11	012211	00		Use Fraudulent License or Permit
6-301 2(B)12	012212	00		Possess Fraudulent License or Permit
6-301(1)	301001	00	D16	Conviction of Unlawful Use of License/Permit
6-301(2)	301002	00	D16	Conviction of Unlawful Use of License/Permit
6-301(3)	301003	00	D16	Conviction of Unlawful Use of License/Permit
6-301(4)	301004	00		Conviction of Unlawful Use of License/Permit
6-301(5)	301005	00	D16	Conviction of Unlawful Use of License/Permit
6-301(6)	301006	00	D02	Conviction of Unlawful Use of License/Permit
6-301(7)	301007	00	D16	Conviction of Unlawful Use of License/Permit
6-301(8)	301008	00	B41	Possess or Sell Blank License/Permit
6-301(9)	301009	00	D16	Conviction of Unlawful Use of License/Permit
6-302	302000	00	D78	Perjury
6-302(A)1	302101	00	D78	Present False Information on Application for Driver's License/Permit
6-302(A)2	302102	00	D02	Accept False Information/Identification on Application for Driver's License/Permit
6-302(A)3	302103	00	D78	Make False Affidavit Swear or Affirm Falsely
6-303(A)1	303101	00	B26	Driving During a Suspension/Revocation
6-303(A)2	303102	00	B25	Driving During a Revocation/Suspension
6-303(B)	303200	00	B26	Driving While License or Permit Revoked/Suspended
6-303(D)	303400	00	B25	Driving While License or Permit Revoked/Suspended
6-306 1	306001	00	W00	Outstanding Warrant(s); Parking or Traffic Violations
6-306 2	306002	00	D45	Failure to Appear
6-306 3	306003	00	D45	Failure to Appear After Depositing License
6-306 5	306005	00	W00	Ten or More Violations of Standing/Parking Regulations
6-306 6	306006	00	D56	Failure to Pay Traffic Fines and Court Costs
6-306	306000	00	D45	Lieu of Bail
6-306(D)	306400	00	D45	Lieu of Bail
6-501	501000	50	D07	Violation of More Than One Driver's License
6-507(A)	507100	50	B56	Driving Commercial Motor Vehicle Without Valid License
6-507(B)	507200	00	B20	Driving Commercial Motor Vehicle While License/Permit Revoked/Suspended/Disqualified
6-507(B)1	507201	00	B20	Driving CMV While License/Permit Revoked/Suspended/Canceled/Disqualified
6-507(B)2	507202	00	B27	Driving Commercial Motor vehicle While License/Permit Subject to Out-of-Service Order
6-507(B)3	507203	00	B19	Driving Commercial Motor vehicle While License/Permit Subject to Out-of-Service Order While Transporting Passengers or Hazardous materials
6-514(A)1	514101	00	A12	Refusal to Submit/Failure to Complete Chemical Test
6-514(A)2	514102	00	A04	Operating Commercial Motor Vehicle; Alcohol Concentration .04 or More
6-514(A)3I	514131	00	A20	Driving Under Influence of Alcohol/Other Drug(s)
6-514(A)3II	514132	00	B05	Leaving Scene of Accident While Operating Commercial Motor Vehicle
6-514(A)3III	514133	00	U03	Driving Commercial Motor Vehicle While Committing Any Felony

IVC/Code	EDPM	Pts	ACD	Description
6-514(B)	514200	00	W01	Second Conviction of Violating Section 60514(A)
6-514(C)	514300	00	A50	Conviction of Felony Drug Offense(s) Using Commercial Motor Vehicle
6-514(E)	514500	00	W30	Conviction of Two or More Serious Traffic Violations in Three Years
6-514(i)1	514901	00	B27	Driving CMV While in Violation of Out-of-Service Order
6-514(i)2	514902	00	W50	Driving CMV While in Violation of Out-of-Service Order
6-514(i)3	514903	00	W50	Driving CMV While in Violation of Out-of-Service Order
6-514(i)4	514904	00	B19	Driving CMV While in Violation of Out-of-Service Order
6-514(i)5	514905	00	W51	Driving CMV While in Violation of Out-of-Service Order
6-514(i)6	514906	00	W51	Driving CMV While in Violation of Out-of-Service Order
6-514(J)2I	514021	00		Convicted for First Violation of Railroad Crossing
6-514(J)2II	514022	00	W60	Convicted for Second Violation of Railroad Crossing
6-514(J)2III	514023	00	W61	Convicted for Third or More Violation of Railroad Crossing
6-515	515000	00		Twenty-Four-Hour Out-of-Service Order
704(a)	070401	00	A33	Violation Chapter 56 1/2, Section 704, Cannabis Control Act
704(b)	070402	00	A33	Violation Chapter 56 1/2, Section 704, Cannabis Control Act
704(c)	070403	00	U03	Violation Chapter 56 1/2, Section 704, Cannabis Control Act
704(d)	070404	00	U03	Violation Chapter 56 1/2, Section 704, Cannabis Control Act
704(e)	070405	00	U03	Violation Chapter 56 1/2, Section 704, Cannabis Control Act
705	000705	00	U03	Violation Chapter 56 1/2, Section 705, Controlled Substances Act
707	000707	00	U03	Violation Chapter 56 1/2, Section 207, Controlled Substances Act
708	000708	00	U04	Violation Chapter 56 1/2, Section 708, Controlled Substances Act
7-201	201000	20	M16	Disregarding Official Traffic-Control Device
7-202	202000	20	M16	Disregarding Traffic-Control Light
7-203	203000	20	M18	Disregarding Flashing Traffic Signal
7-204	204000	20	M05	Disregarding Lane-Control Light
7-205	205000	20	M16	Avoiding Official Traffic-Control Device
7-210	210000	10	M46	Driving Motor-Driven Cycle on Access Roadway
7-211	211000	20	M41	Improper Traffic Lane Usage
7-212 01	212001	05	S51	Speeding 1-10 mph Above Limit
7-212 03	212003	15	S93	Speeding 11-15 mph Above Limit
7-212 05	212005	20	S15	Speeding 16-25 mph Above Limit
7-212 07	212007	50	S15	Speeding Over 25 mph Over Limit
7-212	212000	10	S94	Speeding Too Fast For Conditions
7-213	213000	05	S96	Driving Below Minimum Speed Limit
7-214	214000	10	N50	Improper Turn at Intersection
7-215	215000	20	N50	Improper or Illegal Turn on Red Signal Light
7-216	216000	10	N56	Improper U-Turn
7-217	217000	10	N56	Improper U-Turn in Loop District
7-218	218000	10	M17	Disobeying No-Turn Sign
7-219	219000	05	N63	Driving Wrong Way on One-Way Street
7-220	220000	05	N63	Driving Wrong Way on One-Way Street; Restricted Period
7-221	221000	20	M15	Disregarding Stop Sign At Intersection
7-222	222000	20	N22	Failure to Yield Right-Of-Way at Stop Intersection
7-223	223000	20	N25	Failure to Yield From Alley or Driveway
7-224	224000	20	N01	Entering Intersection When Traffic Obstructed
7-225	225000	20	N01	Failure to Observe Yield Right-Of-Way
7-226	226000	20	M10	Failure to Stop for Railroad Train or Signal
7-227	227000	20	M16	Failure to Observe Bridge Signal
7-228	228000	15	N04	Failure to Yield Right-of-Way to Emergency Vehicle
7-229	229000	20	N08	Failure to Yield Right-of-Way to Pedestrian
7-230	230000	15	N25	Failure to Yield Right-of-Way at Intersection
7-231	231000	20	N08	Failure to Yield Right-of-Way to Pedestrian
7-232	232000	20	N02	Failure to Yield Right-of-Way to Equestrian
7-233	233000	20	N08	Failure to Yield Right-of-Way to Blind Person
7-235	235000	00	N05	Driving Through a Funeral Procession
7-236(A)	236001	20	M70	Improper Passing on the Left
7-236(B)	236002	20	N07	Failure to Yield to Vehicle Passing on Left
7-237	237000	20	M70	Improper Passing on the Right
7-238	238000	20	M70	Improper Passing on the Left
7-239	239000	05	N72	Failure to Drive on Right Side of Roadway
7-240	240000	00	M75	Passing Stopped School Bus
7-241	241000	20	N08	Passing Vehicle Stopped for Pedestrian
7-244	244000	10	M08	Failure to Obey Lawful Order or Officer
7-245	245000	00	M33	Following Fire Apparatus
7-246	246000	00	M56	Crossing Fire-Hose
7-247	247000	20		Driving in Area Designated as Play Street

IVC/Code	EDPM	Pts	ACD	Description
7-248	248000	20	M58	Driving on Sidewalk or Parkway
7-249	249000	20	M12	Driving Through Safety-Zone
7-250	250000	20	M49	Driving in Bus Lane
7-251	251000	20	N72	Driving on Left Side of Roadway Where Prohibited
7-252	252000	10	N82	Improper Backing
7-253	253000	10	M46	Improper Entry or Exit; Controlled-Access Roadway
7-254	254000	00	F34	Obstructing Traffic
7-255	255000	10	M83	Negligent Driving
7-256	256000	25	M34	Following Too Closely
7-257	257000	10	N08	Failure to Exercise Due Care for Pedestrian
7-258	258000	00	F66	Driving Vehicle Which is in an Unsafe Condition
7-259	259000	00	N80	Coasting on Downgrade
7-260	260000	15	N83	Unsafe Movement of Vehicle From Parked Position
7-261	261000	15	N40	Failure to Give Stop or Turn Signal
7-262	262000	15	N40	Improper Stop or Turn Signal
7-264	264000	00		Failure to Use/Improper Use of Horn
7-265	265000	00	D70	Driving with View Obstructed
7-266	266000	10		Improper Towing or Pushing of Vehicle
7-267	267000	00	E54	Failure to Dim Headlights
7-268	268000	00		Fail to Observe Unattended Vehicle Regulations
7-270	270000	20	M41	Failure to Drive Within Bus Lane; Bus Drivers
7-271	271000	20		Failure to Observe Mass-Transit Vehicle Regulations
7-274	274000	00	N05	Driving in a Funeral Procession
7-275	275000	00		Driving Freight-Hauling Vehicles on Boulevard
7-276	276000	00	F34	Obstructing Traffic Buses and Cab Drivers
7-277	277000	00	F34	Taxi-Cab Cruising; Obstructing Traffic
7-278	278000	10		Illegal Operation of Motorcycle or Motor-Driven Cycle
7-342 1	342001	00	F04	Violation of the Seat-Belt Law
7-342	342000	20	E31	Defective Brakes
7-343	343000	00	D70	Driver's Vision Obstructed
7-344	344000	00	E01	Defective Windshield Wipers
7-346	346000	10	E05	Head, Tail, or Side Light Violation
7-347	347000	00		Spot Light Violation
7-348	348000	00		Other Light Violation
7-349	349000	00		Front Red/Flashing Light
7-351	351000	00	E01	No Rear-View Mirror
7-352	352000	00		No Reflectors on Rear of Trailer
7-358	358000	00		Projecting Load On Vehicle
7-359	359000	10		Towing Vehicles Without Bar/Other Safety Device
7-369	369000	25		Failure to Notify Owner; Collision, Unattended Vehicle
70402(C)	402003	10	M17	Restricted Turn Signs; Prohibited Right or Left
8-101	008000	00	D35	Failure to Show Proof of Financial Responsibility
C/C 12-5	012005	00	M80	Conviction of Reckless Conduct
C/C 18-3	018003	00	U03	Vehicular Hijacking
C/C 18-4	018004	00	U03	Aggravated Vehicular Hijacking
C/C 21-2	021002	00		Criminal Trespass Inv Motor Vehicle
C/C 24-1(A)3	241103	00		Conviction of Unlawful Use of Weapons
C/C 24-1(A)4	241104	00		Conviction of Unlawful Use of Weapons
C/C 24-1(A)7	241107	00	U03	Conviction of Unlawful Use of Weapons
C/C 24-1(A)9	241109	00	U03	Conviction of Unlawful Use of Weapons
C/C 24-1 2	241200	00	U03	Conviction of Aggravated Discharge of Firearm
C/C 9-3	009003	00	U07	Reckless Homicide

Point System

Points vary from two to fifty. If three or more point assessed violations are committed within a 12-month period, or two or more point assessed violations are committed by a driver under the age of 21 within a 24-month period, the driver's record is reviewed for possible suspension or revocation.

Indiana

Administration	Important Telephone and Web Contacts
R. Scott Waddell, Commissioner Bureau of Motor Vehicles (BMV) 100 North Senate Avenue Indianapolis, IN 46204 888-692-6841 www.myBMV.com	Driver Licensing.......................................888-692-6841 SR-22 & Financial Responsibility..........................888-692-6841 Commercial Driver License medical Div................317-615-7335 Title Tracing for Government and Law Enforcement Agencies Only.....................317-234-3712 State Dept of Insurance ....317-232-2385 State Police, General Operations............................317-232-8248 State Police, Motor Carrier Enforcement ....317-615-7373 State Statutes www.in.gov/legislative/ic/code/

Driver's License Format, Issuance and Renewal

License Classes, Restrictions and Endorsements Appear After the Driving Record Content Section

License Format

The license has ten numbers. Since July 1988, the first 3 digits denote the License Branch where the credential was first issued. Otherwise, Indiana reports that no codes or sequential arrangements are used to determine license number.

Document Appearance

Effective June 2007, the state began issuing new driver's licenses and ID cards. The previous digital format had been issued since July 1, 1999. It will be at least 2014 before the new license is completely phased in.

Current License

Effective 01/01/2010, IN began issuing new *SecureID* driver's licenses and ID cards designated by a gold star, or a hollow star if issued after December 9th, 2012, in the upper right-hand corner. Persons making application for a new driver's license or ID card must provide specified documents for identity, lawful status, Social Security Number (SSN) and Indiana residency/legal address. Persons renewing or replacing their current Indiana driver's license, permit, or identification card can choose to apply for a "Legacy" license by verifying their name, date of birth, SSN and legal address as it appears on the BMV record or the customer can provide original versions or certified copies of documents so they can obtain a SecureID credential. Persons amending their credentials must provide documentary evidence supporting the change.

Note: As of 11-19-2009, Indiana no longer issues a Driver Education Learner's Permit. If the driver is attending a driver education program, the DE Permit restriction is added to the Learner's Permit.

Current Documents

The color strip across the top is a pinkish dusty rose, unless it is an ID card; then the strip is green. Different credential types are indicated by different header colors of map icon in upper left corner. Brown is an Operator's Driver License, Public Passenger Chauffeur's License, and Chauffeur's License. Red designates a CDL and Green an ID. Purple is a Learner's Permit or Learner's Permit with a DE permit restriction.

Security Characteristics: Security features include printed variable data only detectable with a black light, IDMarc, a security feature only detectable by a validation device offered by Indiana's vendor, UV ghost portrait, 2D Barcode and ID card EIN Barcode on back.

Position of Photo: The picture is placed in the mid to upper left hand corner.

Minor Age Driver: In vertical format. "Under 21 until..." or "Under 18 until ..." appears vertically to the right of the photo.

CDL Indicator: CDL is indicated with a red state icon in upper left corner.

Older Documents

Different licenses are indicated by different header colors: green for IDs, purple for all learner and driver education permits, red for CDLs, and gold for operators.

Security Characteristics: Indiana torch and stars are embedded as an OVD, 2 dimensional bar code on rear.

Position of Photo: The picture is placed in the lower left hand corner.

Minor Age Driver Locator: "Under 21 until..." or "Under 18 until ..." appears in red, and the DOB is also in red. If under 18, "Probationary" is printed under the license type on front.

CDL Indicator: CDL is indicated with a red band across the top, as well as by classification.

Issuance

Location of Requirements for Proof of Identity: www.in.gov/bmv/2767.htm

Age Requirements

License issuance minimum age is 16 years and 180 days with completion of driver education course; otherwise, 16 years and 270 days. A Learner Permit with the DE Permit restriction can be issued at age 15 and 180 days, if enrolled in approved driver education course; upon completion, learner must be accompanied by parent, guardian or relative 21 or older with a valid license. A Learner's Permit can be issued at 16; must be accompanied by parent, guardian or relative 21 or older with a valid license.

Drivers under the age of 18 are issued a Probationary Operator's License that restricts the driver's cell phone use, nighttime driving, and passengers for the first 180 days, and probationary drivers do not qualify for court diversion programs.

Residency

Non-residents must obtain an Indiana license within sixty days of establishing residency; exceptions are persons attending an institution of higher learning or active-duty military personnel.

Renewal

The validity period of an operator's license may be between 4 and 6 years; for a CDL the period is 4 years. Older drivers have different periods (see below). Drivers keep the same driver's license number when renewing. US Citizens may renew their license or ID card up to one year in advance of their expiration. Permanent and temporary lawful residents may renew 30 days in advance of their expiration. When the operator's license of an Indiana operator who is in the military and stationed outside of Indiana has expired, the license remains valid for 90 days following the person's discharge. Persons may renew online every other issuance if they meet the following requirements:

- Are under 75 years old.
- Are within 12 months of the renewal date.
- Current license is not expired more than 180 days.
- Customer record does not have certain restrictions.
- Do not require any testing or medical certifications.
- Hold an operator's license, chauffeur's license or ID card. Commercial driver's licenses or public passenger chauffeur's licenses cannot be renewed online.
- Is a citizen of the United States.
- No change in name, address, or other information.
- Previous photo is on file.

- Are not suspended or invalidated.
- Do not have six or more active points on driver record.
- Are not switching from a non-SecureID to a SecureID.
- No points on current license, if customer is under 21 years old.

Elderly-Related Restrictions
Licenses issued after December 31, 2005 for drivers 75 to 84 years old expire at midnight on the birthday of the holder three years following the date of issuance. Licenses issued after June 30, 2005 for drivers at least 85 years old expire at midnight on the birthday of the holder two years following the date of issuance. The same timelines are applied to motorcycle endorsements.

Vehicle Insurance, Title and Registration Facts

Registration Renewal
Vehicle registration is staggered by month corresponding to owner's last name initial. Company owned vehicles are registered in January. Registrants may renew vehicle registrations online, at www.myBMV.com. An Indiana Driver License, Social Security Number and zip code are needed. Renewal is not available with this system if additional documentation is required, such as with many special group recognition plates. Since 2011 all customers receive their registration cards, stickers and license plates through the mail under a centralized distribution system.

Note: Since 01/01/06, Indiana Code specifies all "off road" vehicles purchased or sold as new or used and are less than five (5) model years old must obtain a certificate of title.

New Residents
New residents must title and register vehicles within sixty days of establishing residency.

Inspections and Emissions Testing
Indiana has no provision for statewide vehicle safety inspections or emissions testing. However vehicles registered in Lake and Porter counties are required to undergo emissions tests and tampering inspections every two years for passenger vehicles, vans and trucks with a gross vehicle weight rating (GVWR) of 9,000 pounds or less. 1976 and older model year vehicles and the four newest model year vehicles are exempt.

Passenger Plate Facts
There is one plate, 2 stickers that have different coloring indicating date of expiration (7th, 14th, 21st or 28th) and year of expiration. For

standard passenger plates, the name of the county of issuance appears on the top of the plate along with a corresponding number from 1 to 98 per an alphabetical list of the 92 counties. Thus 1 is Adams, 2 is Allen, etc. Two counties have additional assigned numbers—Marion County has 93, 95, 97, 98, and 99 while Lake County has 94 and 96 assigned. When a vehicle is sold, the plate remains with the seller.

Insurance and Financial Responsibility
Insurance is mandatory; minimum limits for financial responsibility are $25,000/50,000/10,000. Proof of financial responsibility must be shown on these occasions:

- If involved in a traffic accident;
- If a traffic ticket is received within one year of receiving two other traffic tickets;
- If convicted of a misdemeanor or felony involving a motor vehicle; or
- Any traffic violation by a driver who was previously suspended for failing to provide proof of financial responsibility.

If any of the preceding situations occur, a Certificate of Compliance must be submitted to the BMV electronically by the insurance provider verifying proof of insurance for the date of the incident. The penalty for non-compliance is a 90-day license suspension and a graduated reinstatement fee. The 1st offense is $150.00, 2nd offense $225.00, and 3rd offense $300.00; each additional offense is $300.00. In addition, if there is a second occurrence within three years, there is an additional one-year license suspension. After the suspension period ends, the driver's insurance provider must submit current proof of insurance (SR-50) electronically to the BMV and the driver must pay the appropriate reinstatement fee.

Withdrawal Sanctions, and Alcohol and Drug Testing

Alcohol and Chemical Testing Limits
Indiana's illegal intoxication level is .08 %, .02 % for drivers under 21, and .04% for drivers of CMVs. Urine, blood, and breath testing are used. Indiana has an implied-consent violation, as well as a provision for an administrative suspension. Operating a horse or bicycle under the influence is also considered illegal.

Suspensions
Note: Indiana does not have a "Revocation" status. The state is in compliance with the **federally mandated disqualifications on CDLs**. See the Appendix for details.

- Altering a Driver's License   90-day suspension.
- Allowing Another Person to Use Your License   90-day suspension.
- Criminal Recklessness   60-day to two-year suspension.
- Driving While Intoxicated   180-day probationary license or 90-day to five-year suspension.
- Driving While Suspended   90-day to two-year suspension.
- Failure to Pass Chemical Test (DUI)   180-day suspension *(minimum thirty days)*.
- Failure to pay Child Support   Indefinite Suspension until Payments Made Satisfactorily to Court or Administration.

- Financial Responsibility-Failure to Show Proof (Accidents or conviction of a violation of motor vehicle law.)
    First Offense   90-day suspension; $150.00 fee.

Second Offense	90-day suspension; $225.00 fee.
Third or Subsequent Offense	90-day suspension; $300.00 fee.
If Twice Within Three-Year Period	Additional one-year suspension.
• Graffiti	Up to one-year suspension.
• Habitual Traffic Violator (scenarios below are within a ten-year period)	
1 Major and 9 Minor Traffic Offenses	Five-year suspension.
3 Major Traffic Offenses	Ten-year suspension.
2 Alcohol Traffic Offenses Resulting in Injury or Death	Ten-year suspension.
• Leaving the Scene of an Accident	Six-month suspension.
• Perjury or Making a False Affidavit	Up to one-year suspension.
• Possession, Use or Sale of Controlled Substances Involving Use of Motor Vehicle	Six-month to five-year suspension.
• Reckless Homicide or Manslaughter Resulting from Operation of a Motor Vehicle	Two to five-year suspension.
• Refusal to Take Chemical Test	One- to two-year suspension.
• Suspension or Expulsion from School (Under 18)	Minimum 120-day suspension.
• Three Convictions of Criminal Recklessness in Twelve Months	Six-month to two-year suspension
• Using a Motor Vehicle to Commit a Felony	Six-month suspension.
• Writing a Bad Check to the License Bureau	Indefinite suspension.

Note: Any person who, within a 12-month period, commits two or more traffic offenses that result in convictions will be required by the BMV to attend a BMV-approved driver safety program. Failure to complete the course or pay the fee within the specified time period will result in the suspension of the individual's driving privileges.

For Points: Motorists who accumulate 18 or more active points during a 2-year period will be notified and placed on administrative probation and/or suspended. Periods of probation and/or suspension are outlined in the Indiana Administrative Code, and vary from 30 days to 1 year, depending on the number of points accumulated.

CDL & MCSIA Compliance

The Indiana BMV is in compliance with the provisions of the Motor Carrier Safety Improvement Act (MCSIA). See the Appendix for more information about all of the mandatory CDL disqualification sanctions.

Reinstatement Requirements

Depending on the type of suspension, the driver may be required to complete one or more of the following requirements.
• Proof of current financial responsibility (SR50)
• Proof of future financial responsibility (SR22) ; an SR22 will suffice for SR50 filing requirement (but not vice-versa)
• Reinstatement fee(s) - $10 (only prior to 7/1/05); $150/225/300 for insurance suspensions

Record Access: Laws, Rules, and Forms

Note: This Section Applies to Both Driver and Vehicle Records.

Governing Statutes and Rules

State Statutes: www.in.gov/legislative/ic/code/
Indiana Code (IC) chapters 9-14-3 and 9-14-3.5 set forth the requirements for disclosing personal information contained in motor vehicle records.
Pursuant to IC 9-14-3, the BMV must deliver motor vehicle records upon written request or upon request received through the computer gateway administered by the Indiana Office of Technology. However, the BMV may not disclose personal information without consent from the individual whose personal information is being requested, unless a statutory exception is met (IC 9-14-3.5). Personal information is defined in IC 9-14-3.5-5 as including an individual's digital photograph, Social Security Number, driver's license or ID number, name, address (not including the 5-digit zip code), telephone number, or medical or disability information.
All related records will contain only the personal information that the requesting party submitted with their request unless laws permit the party to obtain records containing additional personal information.

Policy Statement Regarding Permissible Uses

The statutory exceptions include, for example: use by a government agency, such as a court or law enforcement agency, in carrying out its functions; use in connection with a civil, criminal, administrative, or arbitration proceeding; for use in providing notice to the owners of towed or impounded vehicles; and other limited uses permitted by law.

Request and Consent Forms

Driver Records: Use of the *Request for Driver Records - State Form 53789* is recommended. The form, found at https://forms.in.gov/Download.aspx?id=6912, requires the signature of the requester, but does not need to be notarized. If the permission of the subject is needed, attach to this form a notarized authorization granting the requester access to personal information and include a copy of the subject's DL or other form of ID.
Vehicle Records: Use of the *Request for Motor Vehicle or Watercraft Records - State Form 46449* is suggested. If the permission of the subject is needed or if the requester is a legal guardian or has power of attorney, attach to this form a notarized authorization granting the requester access to personal information and include a copy of the subject's DL or other form of ID. The form is available at https://forms.in.gov/Download.aspx?id=8281.

Vendor and Third Party Access Policy

Indiana expects all vendors and service companies acting as an agent for a permissible end-user to be in compliance with DPPA. Indiana restricts further use, storage or resale of records after a completed transaction. Driver licensing and vehicle records are not available in bulk for commercial purposes.

Records Ordered For Non-permissible Uses

Without consent, non-permissible requesters can obtain records, but records display no personal information.

Access to Driver-Related Records

Driver Records

General Information and Fees

Bureau of Motor Vehicles, Driver Records, 100 N Senate Ave, Room N412, Indiana Government Center North, Indianapolis 46204, 888-692-6841.

There are four general types of driver-related records available:

1. Certified Official Driver Record (ODR/MVR)
2. Proof of Insurance at the time of an accident or ticket
3. Certified Driver History
4. DL Status

The Certified Driver History includes an Official Driver Record plus photocopies of specified underlying documents. The current fee for a Certified Official Driver Record or Proof of Insurance is $4.00, or $8.00 for a Certified Driver History. The state does not charge for a "no record found" report. Use of *State Form 53789 (Request for Driver Records)* mentioned above is suggested. Electronic request accounts, including requests for the Status, must obtain records through IN.gov (see below). Proof of Insurance reports cannot be produced until 120 days after the accident.

In-Person – Counter service is no longer offered.

Mail – The $4.00 records are processed within 10 working days; a complete driver history record can take from 2 to 4 weeks to obtain. The license number or name and date of birth are required when requesting a record search; the driver's address is sometimes helpful. The correct fee must accompany the request.

Electronic – IN.gov, Market Tower Building, 10 W. Market Street #600, Indianapolis, IN 46204, 317-233-2010, fax 317-233-2011. IN.gov is the state-designated interactive information and communication system operating under the Authority of the Indiana Intelenet Commission and is the designated agency to provide online batch and interactive access to Indiana driver records (as well as vehicle title, registration, and lien records). Subscribers must be approved and sign an agreement and pay an annual $95.00 fee. The SSN, driver's license number, or name and DOB are required to retrieve a record. Records are $7.50 each. The system is available 24/7. For information on how to subscribe, visit www.in.gov/accounts. Driver records are only one segment in a full range of information available from IN.gov. Click on Premium Services to find other Indiana record data available.

Bulk – Indiana does not offer a program to sell the driver license file to exempt entities or commercial vendors.

By Person of Record – Indiana drivers may obtain their driver record by mail or online at www.myBMV.com by creating an account and sufficiently establishing identity. The record can be viewed (but not printed) free of charge. The customer may purchase their Certified Official Driver Record for $4.00.

Electronic Status Report

Existing driver record subscribers to the IN.Gov system may also verify Indiana driver's licenses for just $1.00 per transaction. The program, called ValIDate, allows one to confirm a person's identity using the Indiana driver's license.

Notification/Monitoring Program

At present, Indiana does not offer an automated monitoring system or notification program to allow employers or insurance companies to track incidents of drivers.

Accident Reports

Reporting – Any accident involving injury, death, or entrapment must be reported to the local police. Failure to do so may result in the suspension of driving privileges.

Record Access – Records have been privatized. Copies of accident reports may only be obtained from Open Portal Solutions at 374 Meridian Parke Lane, Ste B, Greenwood, IN 46142, 317-215-8300, fax 317-234-2041, www.buycrash.com.

Records are available for 20 years. It takes from 2 hours to 2 weeks before new records are available for inquiry. The fee is $12.00 per report. If more research must be performed, add $25.00 per hour. Major credit cards are accepted. Items required include full name, specific date and location of the incident. Normal turnaround time is 10 days. If only a name is given, then turnaround time can be 4-6 weeks. The agency will not disclose SSNs or driver's license numbers. The agency will sell a downloadable PDF file of records.

Access to Vehicle-Related Records

General Information and Fees

Bureau of Motor Vehicles, Vehicle Records, Government Center North, 100 N Senate Ave., Room N412, Indianapolis IN 46204, 888-692-6841.

There are four general types of vehicle records available: title inquiry, title history, registration inquiry, and registration history. Use of the *Request for Motor Vehicle or Watercraft Records - State Form 46449* is suggested (https://forms.in.gov/Download.aspx?id=8281).

1. **A certified title inquiry** ($4.00) contains information pertaining to the current owner and includes information regarding liens; vehicle make, model, year, and VIN; odometer reading; and vehicle purchase date.
2. **A certified title history** ($8.00) includes information pertaining to all previous Indiana owners for the prior ten (10 years, or the prior five (5) years if no changes were made to the title during the prior five (5) years.
3. **A certified registration inquiry** ($4.00) contains: information pertaining to the current registrant and includes county and township of registration; registration fees and county tax paid; vehicle purchase date; vehicle make, model, year, VIN, type and color; and plate number with expiration date.
4. **A certified registration history** ($8.00) includes the registration inquiry information for the previous four years.

One of the following is required when requesting a record: make of vehicle and VIN; SSN or Federal ID#; plate number, plate type and plate year; or title # (accesses title file only).

Records will contain only the personal information submitted with request unless otherwise authorized by law.

If the permission of the subject is needed or if the requester is a legal guardian or has power of attorney, attach to this form a notarized authorization granting the requester access to personal information and include a copy of the subject's DL or other form of ID. The last 4 digits of the requester's SSN are required.

In-Person – Counter service is no longer offered.

Mail – The normal turnaround time for a mail-in request is ten to fourteen business days; however, lists of requests may take longer. Address the envelope to either Vehicle Registration Requests or Vehicle Title Requests.

Electronic – IN.gov, Market Tower Building, 10 W. Market Street #600, Indianapolis 46204, 317-233-2010, Fax 317-233-2011. IN.gov is the state-designated interactive information and communication agency which provides online batch and interactive access to vehicle title, registration, and lien records (and driving records).

There are two distinct vehicle searches available. Search the Indiana Bureau of Motor Vehicles database for **title and lien information** by VIN number, title number, or Social Security Number. Search includes salvage titles as well. The fee is $5.00. Also, search the Indiana Bureau of Motor Vehicles database for **vehicle registration information** by plate number, social security number, or VIN number. The system is available 24/7. Batches are generally available 6 hours after transmission. Information on how to become a subscriber is found at www.in.gov/accounts/. There is an annual $95.00 fee.

Either record type is $15.00 per record for subscribers. **Non-subscribers** may purchase either of the two records for $16.32 per record; use of a credit card is required. All records returned through this service will contain only the personal information that the requesting party submitted with their request.

Bulk – Any entity, including any governmental entity, requesting bulk information (50 or more records in a single request) in Motor Vehicle Records shall enter into a contract for such data or establish an IN.gov account.

Access to Vessel-Related Records

General Information, Access and Fees

Records are maintained by the Bureau of Motor Vehicles. Requests for watercraft title and registration records must be submitted by mail. Fees and required form are described above.

Indiana is a title and registration state. All motorboats (and jet skis) and sailboats valued $3,000 and over when new must be titled. A vessel does not need to be titled if: the watercraft was purchased before January 1, 1986; or the watercraft was valued under $3,000 when new; or the watercraft was home built and not intended for resale. An Indiana certificate of registration is required to legally operate a vessel on public waters unless the vessel is non-motorized (excluding sailboats).

Driving Record Content and Reciprocity

What's On or Not On the Driver Record

- All convictions and suspensions are present on the driver history, regardless of the age of the conviction or suspension.
- Indiana does not report non-motor vehicle violations on the public record unless the court has authority to suspend driving privileges for specific non-motor vehicle violations.
- Indiana displays accidents as received by the Indiana State Police on the Official Driver Record if the driver fails to provide proof of financial responsibility for the accident.
- Although the state does not permit driver school attendance in lieu of conviction, it does require a Driver Safety Program in certain instances.
- The points are active on the record for a 2-year period; however, they then become inactive and the conviction stays on the public record indefinitely.

Data Retention

In general, records and files that are no longer shown on the MVR are not necessarily purged for many years. CDL driver records are purged annually based on the timetable per federal regulations (see the Appendix for this list).

Court to Repository

Conviction data is transmitted by courts to the state via paper, electronic files (FTP), and online. Indiana courts are required to report convictions within ten (10) days of final determination.

State Reciprocity for Non-CDL Drivers

- Will suspend license of driver for unpaid out-of-state convictions.
- Record of new incoming driver is not shown on MVR.
- Out-of-state convictions are shown on MVR.
- Out-of-state accidents are not shown on MVR.
- Convictions of out-of-state drivers are sent to home state.
- Record is forwarded to new state upon surrender of license only upon request.

License Classes, Restrictions, and Endorsements

License Classes– Commercial

Indiana began issuing the CDL in September of 1990.

Class A	Any combination of vehicles with a GCWR of 26,001 or more pounds provided GVWR of the vehicle(s) being towed is in excess of 10,000 pounds.
Class B	Any single vehicle with a GVWR of 26,001 or more pounds or any such vehicle towing a vehicle not in excess of 10,000 pounds GVWR.
Class C	Any single vehicle, or combination of vehicles, that does not meet the definition of group A or group B as contained herein, but that either is designed to transport 16 or more passengers including the driver, or is placarded for hazardous materials.

License Classes– Non-Commercial

OPR	Operator
CH	Chauffeur (GVWR between 16,000 and 26,000 when used to transport property for hire; 15 passengers or less only if operating a bus for certain benevolent organizations)
PPC	Public Passenger Chauffeur (15 passengers including the driver or less) (also, can be PPCH)

Restrictions and Endorsements

To comply with a final rule issued last year by the Federal Motor Carrier Safety Association (FMCSA), the BMV is transitioning to new standardized codes for all restrictions and endorsements on driver's licenses. Effective December 10, 2012, the Indiana BMV began issuing credentials with the new codes. Refer to the Restriction and Endorsement Code Conversion Charts below for more information.

Restriction Code Conversion Chart

New Code	Old Code	Printed Description	AAMVA Meaning / Description
B	A	Corrective Lenses	Corrective lenses must be worn
C	4	Mechanical Aid	Mechanical Aid (Special Brakes, hand controls, or other adaptive devices)
D	New	Prosthetic Aid	Prosthetic Aid
No Change	E	Auto Transmission CMV	No Manual transmission equipped CMV
F	B	Outside Mirror	Outside Mirror
G	C	Limit Day Only	Limited to Daylight Only
H	4	Limit to Employment	Limited to Employment
I	4	Limit Other	Limited - other
J	4	Other	Other
No Change	K	CDL Intrastate Only	CDL Intrastate Only
No Change	L	No Airbrake CMV	No Air brake equipped CMV
M	O	No Class A Pass Vehicle	No Class A passenger vehicle
N	P	No A/B Pass Vehicle	No Class A and B passenger vehicle
O	S	No Tractor-Trailer CMV	No Tractor-Trailer CMV
No Change	V	Med Variance Doc Req	Med Variance Doc Required
W	New	Farm Waiver	Farm Waiver
No Change	Q	Bus Only	Bus Only
No Change	T	Hazmat Prohibited	Haz Mat Prohibited
Z	New	No Full Airbrake CMV	No Full air brake equipped CMV
R	New	Valid for Restricted Agricultural CDL Privileges Only When Presented with Seasonal Authorization Document	
*No longer a Restriction	Z	Blind	Blind
2	2	HTV Conditional	HTV Conditional
3	3	Photo Exempt	Photo Exempt
4	4	BMV Rest	Miscellaneous
5	5	Conditional	Conditional
6	6	Interlock Device	Interlock
7	7	Seatbelt Exempt	Seat Belt Exempt
8	8	Medical Condition	Medical Condition Exempt
9	9	Temporary	Temporary

*Blind designation will now be placed as a "Medical Condition" on the back of the card.

Endorsement Code Conversion Chart

New Code	Old Code	Printed Description	AAMVA Description
No Change	T	Doubles/Triples	Doubles/Triples
No Change	P	Passenger Transpt	Passenger
No Change	N	Tank Vehicle	Tank
No Change	H	Haz Material	Hazard Materials
No Change	X	Haz Materials & Tank	Combined Haz Mat/Tank
No Change	S	School Bus	School Bus
L	M	Motorcycle	Motorcycle

License Status Table - Non-CDL

Driver's License Status (Non CDL)	Description
BMV PROBATION	This may appear in combination with any other DL status; Driver has been placed on an administrative probation by the BMV.
CANCELLED	Driving record has been cancelled by the BMV
CONDITIONAL	Driver has restricted driving privileges (e.g., privileges are restricted to the parameters of hardship license or probationary license)
FRAUDULENT	Driving privileges are invalid; license was obtained fraudulently
HABITUAL TRAFFIC VIOLATOR	Driving privileges are suspended as a habitual traffic violator
HABITUAL TRAFFIC VIOLATOR – LIFE	Driving privileges are forfeited for life as a habitual traffic violator
INVALID – REVOKED	Driver has no driving privileges (e.g., this status may represent: a driver who is less than eighteen (18) years of age and is a habitual truant, is under a suspension or an expulsion or has withdrawn from school; a minor who has had an individual sign the minor's license or permit application and then later requests to be relieved from liability; or a previously licensed driver whose Social Security number is not verified with the Social Security Administration)

Driver's License Status (Non CDL)	Description
SUSPENDED – INFRACTION	Driving privileges are suspended as a result of an infraction
SUSPENDED – MISDEMEANOR	Driving privileges are suspended as a result of a misdemeanor
SUSPENDED – PRIOR	Driving privileges are suspended, and driver has been convicted of Driving While Suspended within the previous ten (10) years
UNLICENSED	Driver has a record with the BMV, but has not been licensed in Indiana
VALID	Driver has full driving privileges

License Status Table -CDL

CDL Status	Description
CANCELLED	CDL is cancelled because facts reveal that driver did not qualify for CDL
DISQUALIFIED	Commercial driving privileges are disqualified
NONE	Driver has no privileges to operate a commercial motor vehicle
PENDING TRANSFER	Driver has commercial driving privileges, which are being transferred to a new state of record
RETEST	Commercial driving privileges are suspended pending a required retest
TRANSFERRED	Commercial driving privileges have been transferred to a new state of record
VALID	Driver has privileges to operate a commercial motor vehicle within the specified class
VOLUNTARY SURRENDER	Driver has no privileges to operate a commercial motor vehicle because driver has voluntarily surrendered commercial driving privileges

Other Driving Record Abbreviations of Note

ACC	Accident	HTV	Habitual traffic violator
AH	Automatic hearing	IC	Indiana Code
AUTH	Authorize	IMPROPR	Improper
BAC	Blood alcohol content	INCL	Includes
BMV	Indiana Bureau of Motor Vehicles	MB	Motorboat
CMV	Commercial Motor Vehicle	MC	Motorcycle
CONTR	Control	OWI	Operating While Intoxicated
DEV	Device	ROW	Right of Way
DIRECT	Direction	RR	Railroad
DISR	Driver improvement/safety responsibility	SIG	Signal
DISRS	Driver improvement/safety resp. system	SR-22	Proof of financial responsibility required
DL	Driver's License	SUSP	Suspension
DOB	Date of birth	SUSP ID	Suspension identification number system
DR	Driver	TEMP	Temporary
DSP	Driver Safety Program	TITLE 16&12	Deferred prosecution
ED	Education	TRAF	Traffic
EMER	Emergency	UNLIC	Unlicensed
EST	Eastern Standard Time	VEH	Vehicle
EXC/EXCESS	Excess (damages exceed $1000.00)	VIOL	Violation
FIN	Financial	W/ -	With
FLASH	Flashing	WARN	Warning
FTA	Failure to appear	WHL	While
FTP	Failure to pay	X-ING	Crossing
HTO	Habitual traffic offender		

Suspensions, Disqualifications, and Administrative Actions Section

There is also a Suspension Section on the driver record. The suspension information includes a unique suspension identifier ("Susp ID"), type of action ("Type"), description of the suspension ("Suspension Reason") including the case number, court and court phone number associated with the suspension, the date the suspension starts or started ("Suspension Effective Date"), the date the suspension ends or ended ("Suspension Expiration Date"), the date the suspension notice was mailed to the individual ("Mail Date"), the unique address to which the suspension notice was mailed ("Address ID"), and any fees associated with that suspension which are due to the BMV ("Fee Due"). An asterisk (*) next to the suspension description denotes the suspension is active. Suspensions with an expiration date of "Indefinite" denote suspensions which require reinstatement notification from the associated court or are life-long suspensions. A **pending suspension** may appear on a record. Below are examples of common suspensions:

- Failure to provide proof of insurance to the BMV following a conviction for a traffic offense
- Failure to provide proof of insurance to BMV following an accident
- Failure to appear for driver safety program (DSP)
- Failure to Pay (the driver has failed to pay court costs/fines following a conviction)
- Failure to Appear

The Disqualification Information will also appear on the record. Disqualifications and Pending Disqualifications are associated with the loss of commercial driving (CDL) privileges.

Conviction Table with Code, Descriptions, ACD, and Points

- Each conviction in the driver record shows the following information: Conviction date, points, offense description, offense date, and court case number.
- On the driver record, when an "*" appears next to a reason this means the points for that reason are currently being applied towards the total number of points on that driver's license.
- This table contains some ACD codes which may be no longer in use. Please refer to the ACD Code Dictionary at the back of this book for ACD removals and changes.

Code	Description	Pts	ACD	If Mand. Suspension
001	No valid license for type of vehicle that was operated	0	B51	
002	Never received a valid license	6	B51	Yes, if convicted after 6/30/2010
003	Learner permit violation	4	D27	
004	Driver's Education Permit Violation	4	D16	
005	Temporary motorcycle learner permit violation	4	D27	
006	Motorcycle learner permit violation	4	D27	
007	Improper Motorcycle license endorsement	6	B91	
008	Violation of driver's license restriction	4	D27	
009	Unlawful use of license	8	D16	
010	Allow unlicensed individual to operate vehicle	4		
011	Allow unlawful use of vehicle	4		
012	Drive while suspended	8	B26	Yes
014	Unlawful license use to obtain alcohol	8	D06	Yes
015	Operating while registration is suspended	8		
016	Disregard traffic officer	6	M08	
017	Disregard traffic control device	6	M14	
018	Disregard traffic signal	4	M16	
021	Accident-leaving the scene-injury/death/entrapment	8	B07	Yes
021	Accident-leaving the scene-injury/death/entrapment – {fatality}	8	B06	Yes
022	Accident-leaving the scene-vehicle damage	8	B05	
023	Accident-failure to report-excess damage	0		Yes
025	Accident Leaving the scene-parked vehicle	8	B04	
026	Accident-leaving the scene/failure to report-property damage	8	B08	
027	Criminal recklessness with vehicle-misdemeanor	8	U04	Yes
028	Criminal mischief with vehicle-misdemeanor	8	U04	
029	Reckless driving	6	M84	
030	Reckless driving-property damage	8	M84	Yes
031	Failure to dim lights	4	E54	
032	Speeding, speed not indicated	2	S93	
	Speeding, 1 - 15 mph	2	S92	
	Speeding, 16 - 25 mph	4	S92	
	Speeding 26+ mph	6	S92	
033	Slow vehicle blocking traffic	2	S96	
034	Unsafe speed on bridge	4	S94	
035	Driving left side of road	4	N70	
036	Truck in restricted lane	4	M11	
037	Slow vehicle improper lane	2	M60	
038	Improper passing/refuse to give way	4	M70	
039	Improper passing to left	6	M77	
040	Improper passing to right	4	M70	
042	Failure to obey signs or markings	4	M71	
043	Wrong way on one-way road	4	N63	
044	Unsafe lane movement	4	M42	
045	Improper use - center lane	4	M62	
046	Following too closely	6	M34	
047	Truck follow too closely	6	M34	
048	Road entrance/exit violation	4	M46	
049	Improper turn at intersection	4	N50	
050	Improper u-turn	4	N56	
051	Unsafe start from park	4	N83	
052	Failure to use/improper signal	2	N40	
054	Failure to yield right of way	6	N01	
055	Yield sign violation	6	N26	

Code	Description	Pts	ACD	If Mand. Suspension
056	Fail to Yield to moving emergency vehicle	6	N04	
057	Fail to yield to pedestrian	6	N08	
058	Fail to stop-rail road crossing	6	M21	
060	Failure of CMV/special vehicles to stop-rail road crossing	8	M22	Yes
061	Disregarding stop sign	6	M15	
062	Improper parking	2		
063	Improper passing of school bus	8	M75	
064	Speed contest on road	8	S95	
067	Failure to use headlights	2	E55	
068	Improper headlights	2	E34	
069	Improper tail lights	2	E34	
070	No brake or turn signal lights	2	E05	
071	Improper use lights/reflectors	2	E34	
072	No required lights/reflectors	2	E05	
073	Projecting load violation	2		
074	Light device violation	2		
075	No or improper brakes	4	E31	
078	No or improper muffler	2	F66	
079	Improper bumper height	2	E01	
080	Improper emergency devices	2	E03	
081	Depriving motorcycle of full lane	4	M48	
082	Motorcycle headlights not illuminated	2	E55	
083	More than 2 motorcycles abreast	4	M48	
084	Motorcycle passenger violation	4	F06	
085	Improper parcel on motorcycle	4	F06	
086	Improper motorcycle headgear	4	F03	
087	Motorcycle equipment violation	2	E01	
088	No/improper flashing lights slow moving vehicle	2	E50	
089	Child restraint violation	0	F02	
090	Operating per se .08 alcohol concentration	8	A08	Yes
091	Operating while intoxicated (OWI)	8	A20	Yes
093	Prior OWI within 5 years	8	A20	Yes
094	OWI resulting in injury	8	A20	Yes
095	OWI resulting in death	8	A20	Yes
096	Violation of probationary license	8	D27	
097	Operating while habitual traffic violator/misdemeanor	8	B26	
098	Operating while habitual traffic violator/felony	8	B26	Yes
099	Operating during life suspension	8	B26	Yes
100	Speeding school bus		S93	
101	Failure of operator of school bus to stop at railroad crossing	8	M22	Yes
102	School bus-improper loading/unloading	4	M40	
103	School bus-no stop arm signal	4	E56	
104	School bus-no directional signal	4	N43	
105	School bus-no flashing lights	4	E56	
113	Seat belt violation	0	F04	
117	Probable cause - refusal	0	A12	Yes
118	Probable cause – failure {non-CMV}	0	A98	Yes
118	Probable cause – failure {CMV}	0	A94	Yes
120	Non-pointable violation	0		
121	Local ordinance violation	0		
122	Equipment violation	0	E01	
126	Dealing or possessing controlled substance-juvenile	0		Yes
127	Operating vehicle without financial responsibility	2	D35	Yes
128	Driving while suspended for criminal offense	8	B26	Yes
129	Violation of ignition interlock device court order	8	A41	
130	Ignition interlock device-soliciting another to start vehicle	8	A41	
132	Reckless driving in commercial motor vehicle	8	M84	
134	Violation of probationary license	8	D27	Yes
135	Operating per se-.04 alcohol concentration in commercial motor vehicle	8	A04	
136	Driving commercial motor vehicle while disqualified	8	B24	
137	Driving left of rotary island	4	N61	
138	Follow too close to motorcade/caravan	6	M31	
139	Involuntary manslaughter with vehicle	8	U08	Yes

Code	Description	Pts	ACD	If Mand. Suspension
140	Reckless homicide with vehicle	8	U07	Yes
142	Criminal recklessness with vehicle-felony	8	U03	Yes
143	Obstruction of traffic with vehicle-felony	8	U03	Yes
144	Felony in a motor vehicle	0	U03	Yes
146	Failure to provide proof of financial responsibility to Bureau	2	D35	Yes
149	Operator consuming alcoholic beverage	6	A35	
151	Failure to provide financial responsibility for accident	2	D35	Yes
152	Non-motor vehicle violation	0		
153	No commercial driver license when required	8	B56	
154	Probable cause refusal-accident with injury/death	0	A12	Yes
155	Drug violation with vehicle misdemeanor	0	A33	Yes
156	Drug violation with vehicle felony	0	A50	Yes
157	Alcohol minor-less than 18 years old with vehicle	6	A31	Yes
158	Alcohol minor-at least 18 years old with vehicle	6	A31	Yes
159	Probable cause-Refusal/motorboat	0		Yes
160	Probable cause-Failure/motorboat	0		Yes
161	Operating while intoxicated/motorboat	8		Yes
162	Operating while intoxicated with a prior within 5 years/motorboat	8		Yes
163	Operating while intoxicated with a prior within more than 5 years but less than 10 years/motorboat	8		Yes
164	Operate motorboat under influence of controlled substance	8		Yes
165	Operating motorboat while suspended			Yes
166	Unsafe operation of a motorboat	8		
167	No valid license/motorboat	0		
168	Resisting arrest with vehicle-felony	8	U02	Yes
170	Minor operating per se with alcohol concentration .02-.08	6	A60	
171	Resist arrest with vehicle - misdemeanor	8	U02	
172	Driving while suspended-resulting in bodily injury/death	8	B26	Yes
173	Driving while suspended - prior within 10 years	8	B26	Yes
174	Failure to yield to stationary emergency/maintenance/recovery vehicle	8	N01	
175	Violation of minor's probationary license	4	D27	
176	Operating per se-.08 alcohol concentration-motorboat	8		Yes
177	Court order/juvenile	0	A60	Yes
178	Failure to yield to stationary emergency vehicle resulting in property damage	8	N04	Yes
179	Failure to yield to stationary emergency vehicle resulting in injury	8	N04	Yes
180	Failure to yield to stationary emergency vehicle resulting in death	8	N04	Yes
181	Failure to yield to stationary maintenance/recovery vehicle resulting in property damage	8	N01	Yes
182	Failure to yield to stationary maintenance/recovery vehicle resulting in injury	8	N01	Yes
183	Failure to yield to stationary maintenance/recovery vehicle resulting in death	8	N01	Yes
185	Operating out of service - no Hazmat checked	0	B27	
185	Operating out of service - Hazmat checked	0	B19	
186	Fuel theft misdemeanor	0	U04	Yes
187	Fuel theft felony	0	U03	Yes
189	Throwing burning material from moving vehicle	0		
190	Watercraft accident--leaving the scene -felony	0		
191	Watercraft accident--leaving the scene-misdemeanor	0		
192	Operating motorboat while suspended	0		Yes
193	Speeding in motorboat	0		
194	Operating under influence of control subs	8	A22	Yes
198	Heavy equipment railroad crossing violation	8	M09	
200	Violation of driver license restriction	4	D29	
201	Violation of driver license restriction- causing bodily injury or death	0	D29	Yes
205	Funeral procession violation	0	N05	
208	Operating motorboat while intoxicated causing death	8		Yes
209	Operating under influence of controlled substance causing injury	8	A22	Yes
210	Operating under influence of controlled substance causing death	8	A22	Yes
211	Tampering with ignition interlock misdemeanor	8	A41	
212	Interlock device in lieu of chemical test failure	0		
213	Interlock device in lieu of chemical test refusal	0		
217	Speeding in work zone	6	S93	
218	No license or permit in possession (CMV not checked)	0	B78	
218	No license or permit in possession (CMV checked)	0	B51	

Code	Description	Pts	ACD	If Mand. Suspension
220	Aggressive driving	0	N84	
221	Operating while intoxicated endangering a person	8	A20	Yes
222	Operating while intoxicated felony with passenger < 18 years of age	8	A20	Yes
223	Obstruction of Traffic- misdemeanor	0	F34	
225	Reckless operating in work zone	0	U03	Yes
226	Falsify Driver License application	8	D02	Yes
227	Improper class/endorsement	0	B91	
228	ACD Violation	0		
229	Out of service order violation- bus/hazmat	0	B19	
230	Vehicular homicide- CMV	0	U07	
231	Negligent operation/fatality- CMV	0	U10	
233	Out of state administrative per se .04	0	A94	
234	Out of state administrative per se .08	0	A98	
235	Out of state administrative per se .10	0	A90	
236	Accident-failure to notify-injury/death/entrapment	8		
237	Criminal mischief-graffiti	0		
238	No insurance-previously uninsured motorist registry	2		Yes
240	Criminal mischief with vehicle-felony	8	U03	
241	Reckless operation in workzone-misdemeanor	0		
242	Improper passing – opposite direction	4	M57	
243	Improper passing at worksite	8	M70	
244	Violation by a minor	0		Yes
245	False statements of age	0		Yes
246	Voluntary manslaughter with vehicle	0	U08	Yes
247	Manufacturing, distributing, dispensing controlled substance with vehicle-felony	0	A50	Yes
248	Texting while driving	0	M85	
249	Restricted license violation	0	D27	Yes
252	Operating motorboat while intoxicated causing bodily injury	0		Yes
253	Transportation of food; violations of rules and regulations	0		
254	Recklessly, knowingly or intentionally transporting food ordered to be disposed	0		
255	Dangerous operation of a motorboat	0		
257	Operation of non-complying vehicle	0		
258	Operating while intoxicated with prior causing death	8	A20	Yes
259	Operating vehicle while suspended for delinquent child support	0	B26	Yes

Point System Overview

Points range from 2 to 8. State law requires a driver who commits two or more traffic offenses resulting in convictions within a 12-month period to complete a BMV-approved DSP. Drivers who are under 18 years of age are required to complete a DSP if, within a 12-month period, they are convicted of two or more traffic offenses, involved in two or more accidents, or a combination of the two. Failure to complete the course and/or pay all applicable fees will result in suspension until completion or payment.

As an added incentive to those who have completed the course in order to improve their driving habits, a four-point credit will appear on the driver record for a period of 3 years.

Iowa

Administration	Important Telephone and Web Contacts
Kim Snook, Office Director Kathy McLear, Records Manager Office of Driver Services, PO Box 9204 Des Moines 50306-9204, 515-237-3253 Tina Hargis, Office Director Office of Vehicle & Motor Carrier Services PO Box 9278 Des Moines 50306-9278, 515-237-3110 www.iowadot.gov/mvd/index.htm	General Number for Driver Licensing, Accidents, Financial Responsibility, Commercial Driver Licensing is: 515-244-8725 or 800-532-1121 Vehicle Services..515-237-3110 Iowa State Patrol ....515-725-6250 State Department of Insurance ....515-281-5705 General Email ods@dot.iowa.gov For Iowa Codes and Administrative Rule see https://www.legis.iowa.gov/index.aspx

Driver's License Format, Issuance and Renewal

License Classes, Restrictions and Endorsements Appear After the Driving Record Content Section

License Format

Since July 1, 2001, a randomly assigned nine-digit number is issued. Prior to this date, the nine-digit driver's license number was primarily the Social Security Number or nine characters alpha-numeric combination (fourth and fifth were alpha characters).

Document Appearance

The state changed the license document in 2005 and in 2010. Both versions are profiles below. All license documents are issued from a central location; the DL Stations around the state issue temporary documents used until the real document arrives by mail.

Current Version

Appearance: Tamper resistant laminated coating. The standard license has a blue bar on header. ID cards have a brown bar.

Security Characteristics   2-D barcode on back contains all the data on the front of the license. The photo has an issuing office number and Director's signature overlapping the edge. A ghost image of photo is on front. The front has an optical variable pattern that changes color when the document is tilted.

Position of Photo: Left edge in middle. Ghost image on lower right.

Minor Age Indicator: Vertical format. The Instruction Permit has a Orange bar at top, the Intermediate License has a purple bar at top. "Under 21 until dd/mm/yyyy" is in yellow wording and appears to the right of the photo.

CDL Locator: The license class and associated restrictions or endorsements are indicated in the "class" section of the license. There is a green bar at top.

Prior Version

Appearance: Tamper resistant laminated coating. The document as a pinkish colored header, ID cards have a green header.

Security Characteristics: 2-D barcode and magnetic stripe on back contains all the data on the front of the license. The photo has an issuing office number and Director's signature overlapping the edge. A ghost image of photo is on front. The front has an optical variable pattern that changes color when the document is tilted.

Position of Photo: Left edge in middle. Ghost image on lower right.

Minor Age Indicator: Vertical format. A red bar with "Under 21 until dd/mm/yyyy" is in yellow wording and appears to the right of the photo.

CDL Locator: The license class and associated restrictions or endorsements are indicated in the "class" section of the license. There is no special heading or color.

Issuance

Location of Requirements for Proof of Identity:
www.iowadot.gov/mvd/ods/identity.htm

Age Requirements

Iowa initiated a Graduated Driver's License (GDL) program on January 1, 1999, for drivers age 14 to 18.

Instruction Permit: Eligible at age 14, must be held at least 6 months to be eligible for Intermediate License. The driver is required to: limit the number of passengers to the number of seatbelts; log 20 hours of supervised driving of which 2 must be between sunset and sunrise; driving accident-free (at fault) and conviction-free for 6 months prior to obtaining the Intermediate License; and complete Driver Education.

Intermediate License: Eligible at age 16 after meeting all conditions of the Instruction Permit. This license must be held at least 12 months with the limitations of: same number of riders as seatbelts; log 10 hours of supervised driving of which 2 must be between sunset and sunrise; driving accident-free (at fault) and conviction-free for 12 months; and able to drive between 5am and 12:30am without supervision. The Intermediate driver must be accompanied between the hours of 12:30am and 5am unless carrying a waiver.

Full Privilege License: Eligible at age 17 after all previous conditions met. Beginning drivers over 18 are exempt from GDL requirements.

Residency

A person is considered an Iowa resident for the purposes of driver licensing and vehicle registration when at least one of the following happens: registered to vote; enrolled children in public school; accepted a permanent job; or resided in Iowa for 30 continuous days

Renewal

Since July 1, 2002, the license is renewed on a five year basis except if age 18 or under then two years. Previously the renewal was the licensee's option of the birth month of second or fourth year. At present, renewal is not available online. There are two six (6) month extensions available if temporarily absent from Iowa. The driver keeps the same number when renewing. A vision screening test each time license is renewed. If license has been expired for more than one year, the driving test and written knowledge are both required. Military extensions are available by mail and are valid until six months following initial separation from active service.

Elderly-Related Restrictions

If the driver is age 70 or older, the license is renewed every two years. IDs for those non-drivers over 70 do not need to be renewed.

Vehicle Insurance, Title and Registration Facts

Registration & Renewal

Renewal is annual and is administered by the County Treasurer. At present, online renewal is available in all counties, but not from the Department of Transportation.

New Residents

One is considered a resident for the purposes of driver licensing /vehicle registration when one of the following takes place: register to vote; enroll children in public school; accept a permanent job; or reside in IA for 30 continuous days.

Inspections and Emissions Testing

The state of Iowa has no mandatory safety inspections or emission testing programs; however, commercial vehicles are subject to the Federal Motor Carrier Safety Laws.

Passenger Plate Facts

There are two plates with one decal (MO & YR) on rear plate only. County name (where issued) will appear on plate. When a vehicle is sold, the plates remain with the seller.

Insurance and Financial Responsibility

Iowa does not have a compulsory insurance law, but has a Financial & Safety Responsibility Act with the following criteria:
- Suspends the operating and registration privileges of a driver or owner who hasn't been able to show immediate financial responsibility following an accident; and,
- Requires anyone whose driver's license has been suspended or revoked because of a conviction, unsatisfied judgment or violation of the OWI law to prove financial responsibility for any future damages or injuries that driver may cause.

Thus, any suspension as a result of moving convictions or revocation for OWI and implied consent (Chapter 321J) requires compliance with Iowa's financial responsibility law. This requirement is normally met by filing proof of at least $55,000 insurance coverage. Otherwise, the driver must post security of $55,000 by certified check, cashier's check, money order, or surety bond. This filing must be maintained for two years.

Withdrawal Sanctions, and Alcohol and Drug Testing

Alcohol and Chemical Testing Limits

Iowa uses blood, breath or urine tests to determine alcohol content. Iowa statutes contain an implied-consent law and also allow for administrative revocations for .08 or more or test refusal. Implied consent affects CMV operators if .04 or higher and persons under 21 who test .02 or more but less than .08. Operating a motorized bicycle under the influence is also illegal. Iowa uses urine and blood tests to determine drug content. The same penalties apply for drugged driving as drunk driving.

Suspensions and Revocations

See the Appendix for a list of the federally mandated disqualifications for offenses occurring in a CMV per MCSIA.

The Following Can Cause a Suspension

About Countable Moving Violations: Conviction of six moving violations committed within a two-year period may cause driver to be barred for one year from the date of judgment. Includes all moving violations except the first two speed convictions within a 12-month period which occur in speed zones between 34 and 56 mph and if convicted of speed 10 mph or less over the posted speed limit.

Driving While Suspended...Suspension may be doubled.
Drug or Drug Related Conviction...180 days.
Failure to Attend School...Until Age 18.
Failure to Pay College Fees...Indefinite until satisfied.
Habitual Recklessness or Negligence...Three or more tickets or accidents in twelve months   Sixty days to one year.
Habitual Violator Bars..Ninety days to six years.

Three or more of any combination of the following convictions in a six-year period may cause a two-year to six-year bar:
Manslaughter with a motor vehicle
Conviction of operating while under the influence of alcohol or drugs (Iowa Code Chapter 321J)
Conviction for driving while license is suspended, revoked or barred; eluding or attempting to elude pursuing law enforcement vehicles
Serious injury by vehicle
Failure to stop and leave information or render aid at the scene of an accident as required by Iowa Code 321.263.

Juvenile Actions:
Purchase or Attempt to Purchase Alcohol ....One year.
Possession of a Controlled Substance...One year.
Public Intoxication or Public Consumption..One year.
Juvenile Possession of Alcohol - Second or Subsequent Violation ....One year.
Non-Resident Violator Compact...Indefinite until satisfied.
Non-Payment of Fines...Indefinite until satisfied.
Operating While Under the Influence; Administrative Test Result ....180 days to one year.
Operating While Under the Influence; Administrative Test Refusal ....One year to two years.
Operating with Alcohol Content of .02 or more person under age 21 ....Sixty days to ninety days.
Serious Violation (twenty-five miles or more over limit).................................Sixty days to one year.
Unlawful Use of License or Falsifying Information ....Thirty days to one year.
Violation of License Restriction ....Thirty days to one year.
Violation of Minor's Restricted License ....Thirty days.
Violation of School License ....Thirty days.
Violation of School License (second conviction)..One year.

OWI (Operating While Intoxicated) Revocations (Criminal penalties for OWI offenses are determined by the court.)

First Offense (12 year period)...180 days revocation
Second Offense (12 year period) ....One-year revocation
If Under 18 ....Revocation until 18 years of age
Third Offense (Court ordered)..Six-year revocation
Any Offense – If Personal Injury involved ....Additional one-year revocation
Any Offense – If Death Involved ....Six-year revocation

The driver's license of a person under age 21 who submits to a chemical test that indicates an alcohol level of .02 or more, but less than .08, will be revoked for 60 days on a first violation and 90 days on subsequent violations. If a person is suspected of operating a motor vehicle with an alcohol level of .02 or more, and refuses chemical testing, the driver's license revocation will be one year for a first violation and two years on a second or subsequent violation. These revocations (.02/"zero tolerance") are administrative and are not dependent upon criminal charges being filed. If a driver's license is revoked for a .02/"zero tolerance" violation, the driver is not eligible for a temporary restricted license at any time during the revocation period.

The Following Can Cause a Revocation with License Revoked for Thirty Days to Six Years
- Drag Racing
- Eluding or Trying to Elude a Marked Law Enforcement Vehicle
- Failure to Stop and Give Aid at the Scene of an Accident Involving Death or Injury in Which You Were Involved
- Homicide by Vehicle if Operated while Intoxicated
- Manslaughter Resulting From Driving a Motor Vehicle
- Perjury or Making False Affidavit About the Ownership or Operation of a Motor Vehicle
- Refusing a Chemical Test Requested by Peace Officer
- Second Conviction for Reckless Driving
- Using a Motor Vehicle When Committing a Felony.

Reinstatement Requirements

When the Department suspends, revokes, or bars a person's motor vehicle license or non-resident operating privilege under chapter 321A and 321J; or suspends, revokes, or bars a person's motor vehicle license or non-resident operating privilege for a conviction under Chapter 321, the department shall assess the person a civil penalty of $200.00. However, for persons under age twenty, the civil penalty assessed is $50.00 for sanctions under 321A & 321 only.

Suspension $20.00 fee; knowledge and vision test; $1.00 duplicate license; and—in most cases—proof of financial responsibility. A driving test is required if license was not valid for more than 12 months.

Revocations $20.00 fee plus fee for new license; knowledge and vision test; and—in most cases—proof of financial responsibility. OWI requires payment of $200.00 civil penalty. A driving test is required if the license was not valid for more than one year.

Record Access: Laws, Rules, and Forms

Note: This Section Applies to Both Driver and Vehicle Records.

Governing Statutes and Rules

State Statutes: https://www.legis.iowa.gov/index.aspx
Per Section 321.11, Code of Iowa, the state adopted the provisions of DPPA. Iowa does not enumerate the exceptions but simply states, "personal information shall not be disclosed to a requestor, except as provided in 18 U.S.C. § 2721, unless the person whose personal information is requested has provided express written consent allowing disclosure of the person's personal information." Thus, the state adopted all permissible uses from DPPA, except for Section 14(d), the waiver procedure.

Also, per 321.11, *personal information* is defined as: "...information that identifies a person, including a person's photograph, social security number, driver's license number, name, address, telephone number, and medical or disability information, but does not include information on vehicular accidents, driving violations, and driver's status or a person's zip code."

Request and Consent Forms

Use of the state's form is required for either a vehicle or driving record, unless requested by an approved ongoing requester. *Form 431069, Privacy Act Agreement for Request of Motor Vehicle Records(s)* is found at www.iowadot.gov/mvd/forms.html. Signature of the requester is required, but does not need to be notarized. With the signature, the requester certifies the permissible reason for the request. If ordered by a private investigator, the form mandates that a copy of the PI license be attached to the form.

All ongoing requesters must sign an agreement to establish an account. If a requester is asking for a record, based on a permissible use, the requester must furnish proof of eligibility and must sign the agreement.

Vendor and Third Party Access Policy

Approved vendors or service providers can access records for other vendors (who are not online, etc.) who will then sell to an end user (who is permissible or has a signed release) as long as the original vendor accepts responsibility for compliance with DPPA. Records may not then be resold by either a vendor or end-user.

Records Ordered For Non-permissible Uses

Driver and vehicle records are released to non-permissible requesters without consent, but no personal information is released. This includes vehicle information requested by plate number, VIN, name or title number; but personal information will not be included on the record.

Access to Driver-Related Records

Driving Records

General Information and Fees

Driver Services Records Section, Department of Transportation, PO Box 9204, IA Des Moines (6310 SE Convenience Blvd, Ankeny IA 50021)

50306-9204, 515-244-9124 or (800) 532-1121 (IA).
The current fee for a certified paper record is $5.50 and for an electronic record the fee is $8.50. Credit and debit cards are not accepted. A copy of a ticket can be obtained for $.50 per copy.

In-Person – Records requested over-the-counter are processed while you wait, time permitting and if lists not lengthy. There is no charge for "no record found" reports.

Mail – Requests mailed to the above address are processed within 14 days of receipt. The driver's license number or full name and date of birth are required to make a record match. The fee must accompany the request.

Electronic – All ongoing, higher volume, requesters must establish an Internet access account with Iowa Interactive. The fee is $8.50 per record. Both batch and interactive access is provided. A set-up fee is not required. Other search services are available. For more information, call 515-323-3468 or 866-492-3468. Information about signing up or using this service is not available on the web.

By Person of Record – Iowa drivers may obtain their driving record by mail or walk-in and Iowa drivers may view their own record online for free at https://mymvd.iowadot.gov/Account/Login. The fee to order a certified record is $7.00, use of a credit card or debit card is required. One must submit the last 5 digits of the SSN to order the record.

Notification/Monitoring Program

At present, Iowa does not offer a monitoring system or notification program to employers or insurance companies to track incidents of drivers. However, reportedly there are vendors who offer this service. The DOT feels these vendors are using the Iowa court system to collect conviction information.

Accident Reports

Reporting – An accident occurring anywhere within the State of Iowa causing death, personal injury, or total property damage of $1,500 or more must be reported within 72 hours on Iowa Accident Report Form #433002 and sent to the Department of Transportation, Driver Services, PO Box 9235 Des Moines IA 50306-9204. The form is found at https://forms.iowadot.gov/FormsMgt/External/433002.pdf. Failure to return an accident report form within 72 hours may result in suspension of driving privileges. If the accident is investigated by law enforcement and the investigating officer files a report, the driver then is not required to file a report. There are no special reporting requirements for commercial drivers.

Record Access – Department of Transportation, Office of Driver Services, PO Box 9204, Des Moines 50306-9204, 515-244-9124. Courier address is 6310 SE Convenience Blvd, Ankeny 50021. Also, direct questions to ods@dot.iowa.gov.

Accident reports filed by law enforcement are only available to persons involved in the accident, the person's insurance company, or the person's attorney. However, the agency will provided limited information such as date, time, location, circumstances. Records are usually available within 3 days receipt by this office. To obtain a copy of the report, send $4.00 with a written request with the date of the accident, time, location, and names and driver license numbers of the drivers involved. Turnaround time is 2 to 3 weeks. Records are maintained for 5 years.

The state's accident report form provides an excellent job explaining all the codes and abbreviations found on an accident report, go to https://forms.iowadot.gov/FormsMgt/External/433002.pdf. County sheriffs in Iowa are authorized to furnish copies of accident reports, but not all do.

Accident reports filed by drivers are confidential.

Access to Vehicle-Related Records

General Information and Fees

Office of Vehicle & Motor Carrier Services, Department of Transportation, PO Box 9278, Des Moines IA 50306-9278, (6310 SE Convenience Blvd, Ankeny IA 50021), 515-237-3110.

Although Iowa titles are recorded at the county level, the title, registration, and liens are updated immediately on the DOT system and are thus provided from this office.

Record services available include: vehicle histories, liens, title research, registration research, and owner name research, and are all available on vehicles, mobile homes, motorcycles, and trailers. A search fee of $5.00 per quarter-hour or a fraction thereof is applied. Computer printouts are $1.00 each; photocopies are $.10 each, and certified copies are $.50 each. No fees applied if no record found. Ongoing, approved requesters may establish an escrow account. Requests on plate information are subject to Statute 321.11 and personal information is blocked. Registration and titles records are indexed on computer and are retained for seven years.

In-Person, Mail, Fax – The state suggests using Form 431069 described earlier (www.iowadot.gov/mvd/forms.html). Turnaround time for a record request can take up to 30 days. Note that fax inquiry is available, the fax number is 515-237-3056. Prepayment is required prior to release of records.

Electronic – A web service is limited to specific users that are privacy act qualified including vehicle dealers, Iowa licensed private investigators, and security companies. To set up an account, one must first write to the Office of Vehicle Services and explain the need for the records. Upon approval, access is free of charge.

Bulk – Iowa provides a service by which vehicle registration and titling data is available subject to DPPA and Iowa Code Chapter 321.11. A copy of the entire database file is available on DVD. Weekly transactions and some generic data selects (i.e. batch plate extracts) are also available upon request. The weekly transactions and unique selects are provided to customers electronically by FTP. The cost of the data is $0.0003 per record. Requests for the entire database file, weekly transactions or selected data should be sent to: Iowa Department of Transportation, Motor Vehicle Division, Office of Vehicle & Motor Carrier Services, 6310 SE Convenience Blvd, Ankeny IA 50021. 50306-9278. Requests may also be emailed to vehser@dot.state.ia.us.

Access to Vessel-Related Records

General Information, Access and Fees

Iowa Department of Natural Resources, License Records Section, Wallace State Office Building, 509 East 9th Street, Des Moines, IA 50319-0034, 515-242-5818 or 515-281-5918.
www.iowadnr.gov/Recreation/Boating/BoatingRegistration.aspx

All titles, registrations, and liens are handled by the county recorder's office. However, this office does have a database of titles and registration information and does permit record searching, except for liens.

All boats 17ft long or longer and any boat that carries a lien need to be titled. The exceptions are canoes, kayaks, and inflatable vessels regardless of length. Boats, snowmobiles, and all-terrain vehicles are registered and titled at the county recorders' offices.

Note that Boater Education is mandatory for any person 12 - 17 years old who will operate a motorboat over ten horsepower or personal watercraft (PWC).

Driving Record Content and Reciprocity

What's On or Not On the Driving Record

- All convictions are listed on the record.
- "Countable Moving Violations" shown include all moving violations. A moving violation is defined to include all violations not specifically excluded by Iowa Code 321.210. (Examples of excluded violations include parking violations, failure to appear, and disturbing the peace with a motor vehicle.)
- All reportable accidents are also listed; however, fault is not shown.
- Child-restraint and seat-belt law convictions are shown.
- The state does not permit driver school attendance in lieu of conviction.

The length of time that convictions are listed is:

Non-Moving Violations.......Three years.
Moving Violations...............Five to seven years (unless CMV).
OWI....................................Twelve years (unless CMV).
Suspensions ....If reinstated, six months to twelve years; if open, indefinite.

Data Retention

CDL driver records are purged based on the timetable per the federal regulations (see the Appendix). The state did not indicate when non-CDL records are purged.

Court to Repository

Convictions are submitted by the courts via paper or electrical transmission. Courts must certify convictions to the Department of Transportation within ten days. There is no statutory time period for input, but convictions are usually entered within two to three days.

State Reciprocity for Non-CDL Drivers

- Will suspend license of driver for unpaid out-of-state convictions.
- Record of new incoming driver is shown on MVR.
- Out-of-state convictions are shown on MVR.
- Out-of-state accidents are shown on MVR.
- Convictions of out-of-state drivers are sent to home state.
- Record is forwarded to new state upon surrender of license.

License Classes, Restrictions, and Endorsements Codes

License Classes– Commercial

Iowa began issuing the CDL in November 1990. The designation "Commercial Driver License" will appear on the Drivers License; "Commercial" on the Driver Record Abstract.

Class A	Vehicle with 26,001 pounds GCWR or more. Towed unit(s) is 10,001 pounds GCWR or more.
Class B	Vehicle with 26,001 pounds GVWR or more. Towed unit(s) is less than 10,001 pounds GVWR.
Class C	Vehicle with 26,000 pounds GVWR or less, and either sixteen passenger design or placarded for Hazardous Materials.

License Classes– Non-Commercial

Class C	Non-commercial vehicle
Class D	Chauffeur
Class L	Motorcycle Only (only issued for operating motorcycle. If operator has existing license, then an L Endorsement is added to current license.
Class O	Non-Driver - Identification Only

Restrictions

Note: Certain codes for License Restrictions were recently changed. Older codes are indicated in parentheses below.

B	Corrective Lenses	R	Maximum Speed of 35 mph
C	Mechanical Aid	S	SR required
D	Prosthetic Aid	U	Not Valid For Two-Wheel Vehicle
E	Automatic Transmission	V	Left and Right Outside Mirrors
F	Outside Mirror	T	(W) Medical Report Required Upon Renewal
G	No Driving When Headlights Required	W	(H) Restricted CDL
H	(J) Temporary Restricted License	Y	Intermediate License
I	Limited Other - Ignition Interlock required	1	Motorcycle Instruction Permit
J	(X) Restrictions Shown on Back of Card	2	Non-Commercial Instruction Permit (vehicle less than 16,001 pounds GVWR)
K	CDL Intrastate Only		
L	Vehicle Without Air-Brakes	3	Commercial Instruction Permit
M	(8) Except Class A Bus	4	Chauffeur Instruction Permit
N	(9) Except Class A Bus and B Bus	5	Moped License
O	Except Tractor-Trailer (not in use at this time)	6	Minor Restricted License
P	Special Permit	7	Minor School License
Q	No Interstate or Freeway Driving		

CDL Endorsements

H	Hazardous Materials	T	Double-/Triple-Trailer
P	Passenger	S	School Bus
N	Tank	X	Hazardous Materials and Tank

Non-CDL Endorsements

1	Truck-Tractor-Semi-Trailer Combination	L	Motorcycle (can be an endorsement with any type of license)
2	Vehicle With 16,001 Pounds GVWR or more. Not Valid for Truck-Tractor-Semi-Trailer Combination		
3	Passenger Vehicle Less Than Sixteen-Passenger Design		

Conviction Table with Iowa Code, ACD, and Actions

Notes:

- If the violation occurred in a commercial motor vehicle, "CMV" will precede the explanation in the uncoded version of the record.
- An "accident trailer" is placed on the record when the DOT receives a report that a person was involved (not at fault) in an accident with a minimum of $1,500 damage or personal injury.
- The state's accident report form provides an excellent job explaining all the codes and abbreviations found on an accident report. Go to https://forms.iowadot.gov/FormsMgt/External/433002.pdf.

Iowa Code	ACD Code	If Moving Violation	Offense Description	Action
1	W00	n/a	Not entitled to issuance/unpaid fees	Cancel
2	none	Yes	Allow unauthorized person to drive	Conviction
3	F02	No	No child restraint	Conviction
4	M81	Yes	Careless driving	Conviction
5	F04	No	Seat belt violation	Conviction
6	M56	Yes	Crossing fire hose	Conviction
7	E50	No	Defective equipment	Conviction
8	D37	n/a	Default in payment	Suspend
9	S95	Yes	Drag racing	Conviction
9	S95	n/a	Drag racing	Revoke
10	M40	Yes	Driving where prohibited	Conviction
11	D29	n/a	Minor restricted license	Revoke
11	D29	n/a	Minor restricted license	Suspend
12	B20	Yes	Driving while suspended, denied, cancelled, revoked	Conviction
12	B25	n/a	Driving while revoked (in CMV)	Disqualify
12	B25	n/a	Driving while revoked	Revoke
12	B26	n/a	Driving while suspended	Suspend
13	N63	Yes	Driving wrong way on one way street	Conviction
14	S96	Yes	Driving too slow	Conviction
15	E55	Yes	Driving without headlamps or with park lamps	Conviction
17	U01	Yes	Eluding	Conviction
17	U01	n/a	Eluding	Revoke
18	M57	Yes	Fail to yield one-half of roadway	Conviction
19	D38	n/a	Fail to post security	Suspend
20	B63	n/a	Fail to re-file SR-22	Suspend
21	U03	Yes	Felony in use of motor vehicle	Conviction
21	U03	n/a	Felony in use of motor vehicle	Disqualify
21	U03	n/a	Felony in use of motor vehicle	Revoke
22	D45	No	Fail to appear	Conviction
23	M08	Yes	Fail to obey officer	Conviction
24	B61	Yes	Violation of accident requirements	Conviction
25	E54	Yes	Fail to dim headlights	Conviction
26	none	No	Giving false report (720.2)	Conviction
27	N01	Yes	Fail to yield right of way	Conviction
28	N04	Yes	Fail to yield to emergency vehicle	Conviction
29	M14	Yes	Fail to obey traffic sign/signal	Conviction
30	M34	Yes	Following too close	Conviction
31	D72	Yes	Fail to have vehicle under control	Conviction
32	W01	n/a	Habitual offender	Bar
33	W01	n/a	Habitual violator	Suspend
34	N82	Yes	Improper backing	Conviction
35	M42	Yes	Improper lane (changing lanes)	Conviction
36	none	No	Improper muffler	Conviction
37	none	No	Improper parking on highway [321.354 (2)]	Conviction
38	None	No	Improper registration	Conviction
39	none	No	Improper use of registration	Conviction
40	M70	Yes	Improper passing	Conviction
41	N40	Yes	Improper signal or failed to signal	Conviction
42	N83	Yes	Improper start	Conviction
43	N50	Yes	Improper turn	Conviction
44	A12	n/a	OWI test refusal (in CMV)	Disqualify
44	A12	n/a	OWI test refusal	Revoke
45	W20	n/a	Incapable of operating a motor vehicle safely	Deny
45	W20	n/a	Incapable of operating motor vehicle safely	Suspend
46	W20	n/a	Voluntary surrender	Deny
46	W20	n/a	Voluntary surrender	Suspend

Iowa Code	ACD Code	If Moving Violation	Offense Description	Action
47	-	Yes	Injurious material on highway	Conviction
49	-	Yes	Interfere with signs or signals (321.260)	Conviction
50	D39	n/a	Judgment	Suspend
51	E55	Yes	Lamps on parked vehicle (321.395)	Conviction
52	-	Yes	Larceny of motor vehicle	Conviction
53	-	No	Miscellaneous	Conviction
54	B07	Yes	Leaving scene of personal injury accident	Conviction
54	B07	n/a	Leaving scene of PI accident	Disqualify
54	B07	n/a	Leaving scene of personal injury accident	Revoke
56	U08	Yes	Manslaughter	Conviction
56	U08	n/a	Manslaughter	Disqualify
56	U08	n/a	Manslaughter	Revoke
57	U07	Yes	Vehicular homicide	Conviction
57	U07	n/a	Vehicular homicide	Disqualify
57	U07	n/a	Vehicular homicide	Revoke
58	W01	n/a	Habitually reckless/negligent	Suspend
59	B51	No	Expired driver's license	Conviction
60	B51	Yes	No driver's license	Conviction
61	D70	Yes	Obstructed vision	Conviction
62	A20	Yes	Operating while intoxicated	Conviction
62	A20	n/a	Operating while intoxicated	Disqualify
62	A20	n/a	Operating while intoxicated	Revoke
63	A41	Yes	Ignition interlock device	Conviction
63	A41	n/a	Ignition interlock device	Revoke
63	A41	n/a	Ignition interlock device	Suspend
64	F34	No	Obstructing traffic	Conviction
65	D78	No	False statement under oath (321.217)	Conviction
65	D78	n/a	False statement under oath	Revoke
67	M84	Yes	Reckless driving	Conviction
68	M75	Yes	Passing school bus	Conviction
70	A20	Yes	Deferred judgment OWI	Conviction
70	A20	n/a	Deferred judgment OWI	Disqualify
70	A20	n/a	Deferred judgment OWI	Revoke
71	F06	Yes	Violation of motorcycle or moped	Conviction
72	S92	Yes	Speed	Conviction
75	F03	No	Violation of MC law (helmet-goggles)	Conviction
76	Code of conviction	n/a	Serious violation	Suspend
77	D53	n/a	Non-payment of Iowa fine	Suspend
78	D53	n/a	Fail to satisfy a non-Iowa citation	Suspend
79	W01	n/a	Two reckless driving convictions	Revoke
80	D16	Yes	Unlawful use of license	Conviction
80	D16	n/a	Unlawful use of license	Suspend
81	D29	Yes	Violation of restricted license	Conviction
81	D29	n/a	Violation of restricted license	Suspend
82	D36	Yes	Violation of SR restriction	Conviction
83	D29	Yes	Violation of school license	Conviction
83	D29	n/a	Violation of school license	Revoke
83	D29	n/a	Violation of school license	Suspend
84	A98	n/a	OWI test result	Disqualify
84	A98	n/a	OWI test result	Revoke
85	none	Yes	Operating without owner's consent	Conviction
86	none	No	Failure to display flags and flares	Conviction
87	E50	No	Slow moving vehicle emblem	Conviction
88	none	No	Non traffic convictions	Conviction
89	W00	n/a	Violation of moped law	Cancel
90	none	n/a	Accident owners failed to post security	Suspend
91	none	Yes	Offense by owner (conviction)	Conviction
93	M32	Yes	Following emergency vehicle	Conviction
94	W13	n/a	Withdrawal of parent's consent	Cancel
96	S92	No Only 321.210 sanctions	Speed (10 mph & under 35-55 mph zone)	Conviction
96	S92	Yes	Speed (10 mph & under 35-55 mph zone) (3rd conviction in 12 months)	Conviction

Iowa Code	ACD Code	If Moving Violation	Offense Description	Action
97	W00	n/a	Not entitled to issuance	Cancel
100	A94	n/a	.04 BAC or more (in CMV)	Disqualify
102	A50	Yes	Felony or aggravated misdemeanor involving disp/dist/mfg of drugs	Conviction
102	A50	n/a	Felony involving disp/dist/mfg drugs	Disqualify
103	B51	Yes	No commercial driver's license (321.174(3))	Conviction
104	B24	Yes	Driving a CMV while disqualified	Conviction
104	B24	n/a	Driving while disqualified (in CMV)	Disqualify
105	W30	n/a	Multiple serious violations (CDL) 2 serious violations	Disqualify
105	W31	n/a	Multiple serious violations (CDL) 3 serious violations	Disqualify
106	D02	n/a	Not entitled to issuance (CDL)	Cancel
107	none	n/a	Not entitled to issuance (ID)	Cancel
107	none	No	Not entitled to issuance (ID)	Conviction
108	B21	Yes	Driving while barred	Conviction
108	B21	n/a	Driving while barred (in CMV)	Disqualify
109	B27	Yes	Violation of out-of-service order (CMV)	Conviction
109	B19	Yes	Violation of out-of-service order (CMV-HAZ or passengers)	Conviction
109	B27	n/a	Violating out-of-service order (CMV)	Disqualify
109	B19	n/a	Violating out-of-service order (CMV-HAZ or passengers)	Disqualify
109	W50	n/a	Violating out-of-service order (CMV) 2 violations	Disqualify
109	W51	n/a	Violating out-of-service order (CMV-HAZ or passengers) 2 violations	Disqualify
109	W52	n/a	Violating out-of-service order (CMV) 3 violations	Disqualify
110	U07	Yes	Vehicular homicide-OWI	Conviction
110	U07	n/a	Vehicular homicide-OWI	Disqualify
110	U07	n/a	Vehicular homicide-OWI	Revoke
111	D06	Yes	Unlawful use of license-alcohol related	Conviction
111	D06	n/a	Unlawful use of license-alcohol involved	Suspend
112	A33	No	Drug/drug related conviction (not vehicle)	Conviction
112	A33	n/a	Drug/Drug related conviction	Revoke
113	W00	n/a	Fail to attend school	Suspend
114	D06	n/a	Purchase or attempt to purchase alcohol	Suspend
115	A33	n/a	Possession of a controlled substance	Suspend
116	W00	n/a	Public intox or public consumption	Suspend
118	A31	No	Possession alcohol under legal age	Conviction
118	A31	n/a	Possession alcohol under legal age	Suspend
119	D38	n/a	Fail to post security: Driver only	Suspend
120	A35	Yes	Open container	Conviction
121	A61	n/a	Under 21, Al Con.02 but less than .08	Revoke
122	A41	Yes	Violation of impoundment or immobilization (321J.4B)	Conviction
123	D51	n/a	Non-payment of child support	Suspend
124	W00	n/a	Delinquent account owed to state	Suspend
125	none	No	Vehicle overweight	Conviction
126	B65	No	Medical card violation	Conviction
127	none	No	Logbook/hours of service	Conviction
128	E53	No	Hazardous materials	Conviction
129	none	No	Vehicle over length	Conviction
130	none	No	Vehicle over width	Conviction
131	none	No	Vehicle over height	Conviction
132	none	No	Violation of commercial vehicle permit	Conviction
135	B08	Yes	Leaving the scene of PD ACC (321.263)	Conviction
135	B08	n/a	Leaving the scene of PD ACC	Disqualify
136	M40	Yes	Improper lane use	Conviction
137	B64	No	No insurance card	Conviction
138	D29	Yes	GDL violation	Conviction
138	D29	n/a	GDL violation	Suspend
139	W00	n/a	Unpaid college loans	Suspend
140	D27	n/a	Probation violation	Suspend
141	W00	n/a	Juvenile weapons school	Suspend
142	W00	n/a	Juvenile assault school	Suspend
143	D16	Yes	Unlawful use of license-Tobacco	Conviction
143	D16	n/a	Unlawful use of license-Tobacco	Suspend
144	M22	Yes	Fail to stop before crossing railroad	Conviction
144	M22	n/a	Fail to stop before crossing railroad	Disqualify
145	M20	Yes	Fail to slow/check RR crossing	Conviction
145	M20	n/a	Fail to slow/check RR crossing	Disqualify

Iowa Code	ACD Code	If Moving Violation	Offense Description	Action
146	M21	Yes	Fail to stop/RR track not clear	Conviction
146	M21	n/a	Fail to stop/RR track not clear	Disqualify
147	M23	Yes	Blocks RR crossing	Conviction
147	M23	n/a	Blocks RR crossing	Disqualify
148	M10	Yes	Disobeys traffic control at RR	Conviction
148	M10	n/a	Disobeys traffic control at RR	Disqualify
149	M24	Yes	Not enough clearance/RR	Conviction
149	M24	n/a	Not enough clearance/RR	Disqualify
150	M09	Yes	Violation of RR crossing	Conviction
151	M40	Yes	Unsafe approach to certain vehicles	Conviction
152	F34	Yes	Stopping on traveled way	Conviction
153	W60	n/a	Violation of RR crossing - 2 violations	Disqualify
153	W61	n/a	Violation of RR crossing - 3 violations	Disqualify
154	W09	n/a	Hazmat threat assessment	Cancel
154	W09	n/a	Hazmat threat assessment	Deny
154	W09	n/a	Hazmat threat assessment	Revoke
155	W40	n/a	Two or more major offenses	Disqualify
156	W41	n/a	A major offense after reinstatement	Disqualify
157	B91	Yes	Improper class or endorsement on CDL (321.174(2))	Conviction
158	B56	Yes	Driving a CMV without obtaining CDL (321.174(1))	Conviction
159	W70	n/a	Imminent hazard	Disqualify
160	E01	Yes	Operating without equipment	Conviction
161	E23	No	Prohibited use of radar detector	Conviction
162	E31	No	Defective brakes	Conviction
163	E34	No	Defective lights	Conviction
164	E36	No	Defective school bus equipment	Conviction
165	E37	No	Defective tires	Conviction
166	U04	No	Theft of motor fuel	Conviction
166	U04	n/a	Theft of motor fuel	Suspend
167	U31	Yes	Violation contributing to fatal accident (out of state)	Conviction
168	none	Yes	Serious injury	Conviction
169	M85	No	Texting while driving	Suspend
170	W00	n/a	Court-ordered sanction	Suspend

Point System Summary

The Iowa Point System is used to determine if a driver is to be declared a *habitual offender*, and to determine the length of time the person is barred from operating a motor vehicle, as shown below.

Driving while barred .... 4 Points
Driving while under Iowa Code Chapter 321J revocation or denial .... 3 Points
Driving while under suspension, revocation or denial (except 321J) .... 2 Points
Eluding or attempting to elude a pursuing law enforcement vehicle (Code 321.279) .... 5 Points
Failure to stop and leave information or render aid .... 5 Points
Felony in the commission of a motor vehicle or felony as defined by vehicle laws .... 5 Points
Manslaughter resulting from the operation of a motor vehicle .... 6 Points
Operating a motor vehicle in violation of 321J.2 - (OWI) .... 4 Points
Perjury or making false affidavit or statement under oath to the DPS .... 2 Points
Serious injury by a vehicle - 707.6A(3) .... 5 Points

Points and Length of Bar, for Habitual Offenders

6-7 points .... Two years
8-9 points .... Three years
10-12 points .... Four years
13-15 points .... Five years
16+ points .... Six years

Kansas

Administration	Important Telephone and Web Contacts
Donna Shelite, Director of Vehicles Department of Revenue Division of Vehicles Topeka 66626-0001 785-296-3601 http://ksrevenue.org/vehicle.html Policy Information Library: http://rvpolicy.kdor.ks.gov/	Suspension/Reinstatement...........................785-296-3671 Financial Responsibility..............................785-296-3671 Title and Registration Information..............785-296-3621 Commercial Driver License........................785-296-3963 Motor Carrier Services-Apportioned Veh...785-296-6541 State Department of Insurance...................785-296-3071 Highway Patrol...785-296-6800 Email contacts www.ksrevenue.org/contactus.html

Driver's License Format, Issuance and Renewal

License Classes, Restrictions and Endorsements Appear After the Driving Record Content Section

License Format

Since July 1, 2004, all KS licenses are issued a randomly assigned number consisting of the letter "K" plus eight numbers.

Document Appearance

Effective 10/8/2012 Kansas began issuing driver's licenses and ID cards with a new look and added security features to guard against counterfeiting and fraud. Each card is laminated with a tamper resistant coating. There are 1D and 2D barcodes on the back of each card that contains text data from the front of the card. The magnetic stripe was removed from the back of card. There are two ghost images of the cardholder's portrait in addition to the conventional photograph on the card. The Capital building on the card is made up of a dynamic screen patterns that are not commercially available. The Under 21 cards remain in vertical format.

Other Security Characteristics (after 10/7/12): Guilloche printing, microprint, ghost image, UVR security features.

Security Characteristics (prior to 07/04): Wheat pattern and Advantage™ transparent coating security feature.

Position of Photo: Left side.

Minor Age Driver Locator: Vertical format; under 21 has red strip under photo that states "Not 21 until MM-DD-YYYY". Under 18 has green strip under photo that states "Not 18 until MM-DD-YYYY".

CDL Indicator: "Commercial Driver's License" indicated in red letters at top of license.

Issuance

Location of Requirements for Proof of Identity:
http://ksrevenue.org/dmvproof.html

Age Requirements

A GDL law that took effect 01/01/2010 placed additional driving restrictions on young drivers, added a Lesser Restricted License, and changed the minimum age for having an unrestricted license from sixteen to seventeen. An excellent overview is found at www.ksrevenue.org/pdf/GDL_public.pdf. An Instruction Permit can be secured by a fourteen year old, and a Restricted License can be secured by a fifteen year old. The Restricted License allows driving to and from work/school; must be accompanied by a licensed driver at all other times; cannot operate vehicle with a minor passenger(s) who is not a member of the immediate family. An Instruction Permit or Farm Permit can be obtained at age fourteen.

Residency

Non-residents (sixteen or older) may use home-state license; however, a Kansas license must be obtained if driving Kansas-registered/plated vehicle in excess of ninety days.

Renewal

Non-commercial drivers 21 years of age or over but less than 65 years of age are issued a valid license for 6 years from the DOB nearest application date. Drivers under 21 or over 65 and all commercial license holders are issued a license valid for 4 years from DOB nearest application date. At present, renewal is not available online but change of address is at https://www.kdor.org/dl/default.aspx. The driver keeps same number when renewing (unless SSN used, then a new number is issued). Military personnel may renew by mail; current copy of a military ID is required. If driver is out of state, but not in military, a 6-month extension is available with form DEMI-1.

Elderly-Related Restrictions

If over 65, then license renewed every 4 years.

Vehicle Insurance, Title and Registration Facts

Registration Renewal

Renewal is annual and handled locally by the county treasurer's motor vehicle offices. If the address on the renewal notice is current, renewal is available by touchtone phone at 866-457-8247 and also online at www.kswebtags.org.

New Residents

New residents must secure KS plates within thirty days. Non-residents may drive vehicles without Kansas registration on a home-state reciprocal basis for ninety days (exceptions are military and students).

Inspections and Emissions Testing

Kansas does not have a provision for mandatory statewide emission testing or annual safety inspection of vehicles. Kansas does require VIN inspections of vehicles that request to be titled in Kansas from another state. Additionally, inspections are required for specially constructed vehicles such as street rods and assembled vehicles.

Passenger Plate Facts

There is one plate, three decals (MO) (YR) (County). The county designation is applied to the plate by decal only. It is not part of the plate. The license plate stays with the registrant when the county of residence changes. When a vehicle is sold the plate remains with the vehicle unless personalized plates at owner's option.

Insurance and Financial Responsibility

Kansas has compulsory no-fault insurance. Evidence of insurance is required at registration, renewal, upon suspension and after an accident, or certain violations. Minimum financial responsibility limits are $25,000/50,000/10,000. A driver (including a driver licensed in another state) may be required to provide proof of insurance to any law enforcement officer. SR-22 forms are used.

Withdrawal Sanctions, and Alcohol and Drug Testing

Alcohol and Chemical Testing Limits

The Kansas illegal intoxication level is .08 percent and above for non-commercial drivers and .04 percent for commercial drivers and .02 for under 21 years of age. Urine, blood, and breath testing are used. Kansas has an implied-consent violation, as well as the provision for an administrative suspension.

Suspensions and Revocations

The state is in compliance with the federally mandated disqualifications on CDLs. See the Appendix for these disqualifications.

Conviction of Any of the Following May Result in Suspension or Revocation

- Aggravated Vehicular Homicide
- Attempting to Elude a Police Officer
- Committing a Felony While Using a Car
- Driving Under the Influence of Alcohol or Drugs
- Failure to Appear in Court
- Failure to Maintain Liability Insurance
- Failure to Stop and Give Aid When Involved in an Accident
- Minor Testing .02 to .0799 Percent Blood Alcohol
- Reckless Driving
- Refusal to Submit to a Chemical Test
- Testing .08 Percent or Above for Blood Alcohol
- Three or More Moving Violations in Twelve Months
- Transporting an Open Container of Liquor

Note: Kansas law does not provide for the issuance of a hardship license that would allow a person to drive during the length of their suspension, revocation, cancellation or disqualification period

Reinstatement Requirements

Suspensions and Revocations

Failure to Comply	$59.00 fee; comply with citation.
Insurance	$100.00 to $300.00 fee; file evidence of insurance for one year; obtain release of liability.
DUI	Reinstatement fee varies, depending on number of alcohol occurrences; $25.00 reexamination fee.

Record Access: Laws, Rules, and Forms

Note: This Section Applies to Both Driver and Vehicle Records.

Governing Statutes and Rules

Policy Information Library: http://rvpolicy.kdor.ks.gov
Legislation: www.kslegislature.org/li/statute/
Per Statutes K.S.A. 74-2012, 74-2022 (both found in Article 20), and 45-219, Kansas became compliant with the provisions in the DPPA. The state adopted the permissible uses outlined in the DPPA with the exception of #12 (bulk distribution of surveys, marketing or solicitations). A list of all permitted exemptions is found on the *TR/DL 302 Form* (see below).

Request and Consent Forms

There are two primary forms which are used for both driver and vehicle records. The *TR/DL 301-Third Party Consent* form (http://ksrevenue.org/pdf/trdl301.pdf) is used for temporary consent for someone else to obtain a motor vehicle record other than their own. *TR/DL 302-Request for Copies or Access* is a general request form for access to records. This may be downloaded from (http://ksrevenue.org/pdf/trdl302.pdf). For all forms, the requestor's signature is required, but notarization is not necessary.

Vendor and Third Party Access Policy

Permissible users qualifying under K.S.A. 74-2012 can purchase in batch format. Contracts vary in purpose and therefore, the resell ability is unique to each contract. Any authorized re-seller must be in compliance with the state's contract and must maintain records identifying each person or entity that received information and the permitted purpose for 5 years. Statutes prohibit acquiring records for the purpose of obtaining addresses and lists for the sale or offering for sale any property or services.

Non-permissible Use Requests

Generally, motor vehicle records cannot be released without consent. Statistical information (record information without personal information) can be released as long as it does not identify an individual or group of individuals.

Access to Driver-Related Records

Driving Records

General Information and Fees
Division of Vehicles, Driver Control Bureau, PO Box 12021, Topeka KS 66612-2021, 785-296-3671. The physical location is at the Docking State Office Building, 915 SW Harrison Room 100.

The current fee is $10.00 per record and $20.00 for a driver's license folder for mail or in person searches, $6.00 for online batch, and $6.60 for online interactive. Kansas does charge for "no record found" reports. The last fee increase was effective 07/01/09. A search by name only is not available.

Mail and In-Person
Requesters should use the general request for records (TR/DL 302 form - http://ksrevenue.org/pdf/trdl302.pdf) and use the above referenced addresses. Remittances should be made payable to the Kansas Department of Revenue and must accompany the TR/DL 302 form. The turnaround time for a mail in request is approximately 5 days, while walk-in requests are processed while you wait.

Electronic
Kansas contracts with the Kansas.gov to service all electronic media requests of driver license histories, title, registration and lien searches. Both single inquiry and batch modes are available for driving records. For batch requests, the record fee is $6.00. Requests received before 10:00 p.m. are returned before 7:30 a.m. the following morning. The driver's license number is required for an interactive online search. The full name and DOB are required when ordering an online batch record search. Single record requests processed for $6.60 per record. Records are available 24/7 (excluding brief periods for computer maintenance).

There is a $95 annual fee to become a subscriber and a $15.00 per month minimum if paid by check. Billing is monthly, but there is a 3% surcharge if EFT (electronic funds transfer) is not in place. Credit cards are not accepted for payment. Other subscriber services include: vehicle record data, court data, legislation, UCC filings, District Court access, library data, business and commerce information, some local government data, and many state agency services. The website is www.kansas.gov/subscribers/, click on Subscriber Center or call 800-452-6727.

Bulk
Kansas Motor Vehicle Records are available at a contract/bulk rate only to parties who qualify for a contract/bulk rate pursuant to K.S.A. 74-2012. An example of a qualifying party would be the Selective Service or Automobile Manufacturers when used to notify owners of safety related defects. For additional information contact Sandra Bach at 785-296-3013.

By Person of Record
KS drivers may obtain their driving record by mail or walk-in as described above. Also, Kansas drivers may purchase a copy of their "limited" driving record online for $6.60 at https://www.accesskansas.org/ssrv-mvr-ltd/. A fee is charged for a "Record Not Found" message.

DL Status Check
Kansas offers a free driver's license status check at https://www.kdor.org/DLStatus/login.aspx?ReturnUrl=%2fdlstatus%2fsecure%2fdefault.aspx. (Or you can go to home page and click on a link.) The information must be entered as it appears on the driver's license, with no dashes or spaces. The DL #, full name and DOB are required.

Notification/Monitoring Program
Kansas offers a notification program for insurance companies to monitor any changes that occur during the month for records with a traffic conviction and/or administrative action added to the record. Entity sends a file to Kansas.gov of DL #s they want to monitor, the cost is $.06 per record.

Kansas also offers a monitoring system for employers to monitor commercial drivers. The fee is $6.00 per driver. The file is generated monthly and the fee is applied to each monitored driving record.

Accident Reports
Reporting
Any accident resulting in death, injury, or total damage in excess of $1,000.00 must be reported immediately to the nearest law enforcement agency. It is not necessary to file a separate accident report with the state. The Motor Vehicle Division may request that the vehicle owner submit insurance information, if the data is incomplete on the police report. Motor Carriers licensed by the State Corporation Commission must file a report with the Commission at 1500 SW Arrowhead Road, Topeka, KS 66604. There are no special state reporting requirements for commercial drivers.

Record Access
If the accident was investigated by the Kansas Highway Patrol, the record may be accessed for a $2.00 minimum fee. All requests must in writing. Write to KS Highway Patrol, GHQ – Records Section, 720 SW Jackson, Topeka KS 66603, phone is 785-296-6800. Records are maintained for 10 years. It generally takes 10 days for new records to become available, longer if a fatality. The fee is $2.00.

A 30-day Crash Log is online at https://www.accesskansas.org/ssrv-khp-crashlogs/index.do. Search the crash logs by date, county, and type of crash. Crash reports cannot be sent electronically. The Crash Log does not release reports of accidents that occur on the Kansas Turnpike.

Access to Vehicle-Related Records

General Information and Fees
Division of Vehicles, Title and Registration Bureau, Verification Section, Docking State Office Bldg, 915 SW Harrison Rm 155, Topeka 66626-0001, 785-296-3621, fax is 785-296-3852.

The current fee per vehicle registration or motor carrier registration record is $10.00 (except online, see below). A vehicle title history is $25.00; a certified title history is $30.00. Requesters should use the general request for records (TR/DL 302 form - http://ksrevenue.org/pdf/trdl302.pdf) and use the above referenced addresses. A search using the name only is not available.

Records are computerized since 1988. Records from 1970-1987 are stored on microfiche and microfilm. The state maintains registration and lien information on vehicles and mobile homes (if unattached). It generally takes eight weeks from the date of application before new records are available for inquiry. Kansas charges for "no record found" reports. For apportioned vehicle records, call the Motor Carrier Services at 785-296-6541.

Mail and In-Person
Request turnaround time is 5 to 10 days for mail requests, immediate for walk in requests. Use one of the above mentioned forms. Remittances should be made payable to the Kansas Department of Revenue.

Electronic
Kansas contracts with the Kansas.gov to service all electronic media requests for title, registration and lien searches. Kansas.gov is located at 524 S Kansas Ave #1210, Topeka KS, 66603. The website is www.kansas.gov/subscribers/, click on Subscriber Center or call 800-452-6727.

The fee is $6.50 to search by title number or by plate number or by VIN. No name searching is permitted. Records are available 24/7 (excluding brief periods for computer maintenance). Input requirements are available upon request.

There is a $95 annual fee to become a subscriber and there is a $15.00 per month minimum. Billing is monthly, but there is a 3% surcharge if EFT (electronic funds transfer) is not in place. Credit cards are not accepted for payment. Other subscriber services include: driving records, legislation, UCC filings, District Court access, library data, business and commerce information, some local government data, and many state agency services.

Access to Vessel-Related Records

General Information, Access and Fees

Kansas Department of Wildlife, Parks & Tourism, Boat Registration, 512 SE 25th Ave, Pratt 67124-8174 620-672-5911 http://www.kdwpt.state.ks.us/news/Boating.

All vessels powered by gasoline, diesel, electric or sail must be registered, including sailboards and personal watercraft. Boats are not titled in this state. Record requests need to me submitted via email, mail, or fax. A specific form is not needed. All requests should include a brief statement indicating the registration number or manufacturer's hull identification number of the vessel in question, the purpose of the request, and a contact name and number that could be reached. It is also helpful to include the fax number, or mailing address the print out needs sent to. The request does not have to come from the owner of the vessel as Department does not include personal or contact information for the owner of record on what is sent.

Liens are recorded at the Secretary of State's UCC Department – 785-296-4564 – and must be searched there.

Driving Record Content and Reciprocity

What's On or Not On the Driving Record

- The driver's address is included as part of the record.
- The state does not report violations of the following on a driving record: ten mph or less over in a fifty-five to a seventy-five zone, six mph or less in a thirty to fifty-four zone, and diversion agreements or expungements.
- All accidents are reported-fault is not shown.
- Local jurisdictions may permit driver school attendance in lieu of conviction; however, the Division does not permit this on administrative actions

The length of time that convictions are listed is:

Minor Moving Violations .... Three years.
Major Moving Violations .... Five years.
DWI, Chemical Test Failure, Refusal........... Lifetime.
Suspensions .... Three to five years.

Data Retention

Violations are purged based on conviction date based on the timetable per the federal regulations (see Appendix). In most cases, non-CDL surrendered or expired licenses are purged from the system after one year.

Court to Repository

Effective July 1, 2007, courts are required to electronically submit to the DMV all convictions and also all suspension/reinstatements due to failure to comply with a traffic citation.

State Reciprocity for Non-CDL Drivers

- Will suspend license of driver for unpaid out-of-state convictions for moving violations with NRVC members.
- Record of new incoming driver shown on MVR, but for only moving violations.
- Out-of-state convictions are shown on MVR.
- Out-of-state accidents are not shown on MVR.
- Convictions of out-of-state drivers are sent to home state.
- Record is forwarded to new state upon surrender of license.

Important Abbreviations Found on Driving Records

Miscellaneous Codes

ADM	Administrative	EXP	Expired	SUS	Suspended
CAN	Cancelled	OTH	Other not valid	VAL	Valid
CON	Conviction	RES	Restricted driving privileges	WTH	Withdrawal
DEN	Denied	REV	Revoked		
DIS	Disqualified	SUR	Surrendered		

Additional SVRTY Codes for ACC Listings

1	Fatal	4	Possible Injury
2	Incapacitating Injury	5	Property Damage Only
3	Non-Incapacitating Evident Injury	9	Unknown

Additional Abbreviations Found on a Driving Record

ACTION:	Type of entry, usually as follows: CON-conviction; WTH-withdrawal of license; ADM-administrative action; RES-restricted license; AC4-accident.
ACTION DATE:	Date action was taken. Conviction date for a conviction, order date for a withdrawal, reinstatement date.
OCCUR DATE:	Date of arrest, also could be order date for a withdrawal or reinstatement.
VIOL TYPE:	Code or abbreviation for conviction or action.
STT JUR:	State of offense.
LCL JUR:	Local Jurisdiction.
CRT TYP:	Type of court which convicted (DIS=District, MUN=Municipal).
CMV:	If event occurred in a commercial motor vehicle.
HAZMAT:	If hazardous material was involved with a commercial motor vehicle event.
REAS:	The reason the action was taken. This entry does NOT represent a separate conviction.
EFF DATE:	Effective date. Date action is effective.
LGTH:	Length of suspension or revocation if applicable.

ELIG DATE: Date person is eligible for reinstatement; does not mean person will be reinstated on that date.
REINS DATE: Date of actual reinstatement.
EXT SEV: Accident severity.

License Classes, Restrictions, and Endorsements

License Classes

Class A   Motor vehicles which include any combination of vehicles with a GCWR of 26,001 pounds or more, provided the GCWR of the vehicle or vehicles being towed is in excess of 10,000 pounds, and all other lawful combinations of vehicles with a GCWR of 26,001 pounds, or more; except that Class A does not include a combination of vehicles that has a truck registered as a farm-truck under subsection (2) of K.S.A. 8-143, and amendments thereto.

Class B   Motor vehicles which include any single vehicle with a GVWR of 26,001 pounds or more, or any such vehicle towing a vehicle not in excess of 10,000 pounds GVWR. Class B motor vehicles do not include a single vehicle registered as a farm-truck under subsection (2) of K.S.A 8-143, and amendments thereto, when such farm-truck has a GVWR of 26,001 pounds or more, or any fire truck operated by a volunteer fire department.

Class C   Motor vehicles which include any single vehicle with a GVWR less than 26,001 pounds, or any such vehicle towing a vehicle not in excess of 10,000 pounds GVWR, or any vehicle with less than a 26,001 pound GVWR towing a vehicle in excess of 10,000 pounds GVWR, provided the GCWR of the combination is less than 26,001 pounds, or any single vehicle registered as a farm-truck under subsection (2) of K.S.A. 8-143, and amendments thereto, when such farm-truck has a GVWR of 26,001 pounds or more.

Class M   Motor vehicles which include motorcycles.

Restrictions and Non-Commercial Endorsements

B	Corrective Lenses	M	No CDL - A Bus	J08	Seasonal CDL
C	Mechanical Aid	N	No CDL - A/B Bus	J09	Farm Permit
D	Prosthetic Aid	O	No Tractor-Trailer	J10	Non-Resident CDL
E	Automatic Transmission	J01	Outside Business Area	J11	Rest. - 5 Miles of Home
F	Outside Mirror	J02	Under Age Sixteen	J12	Rest. - 10 Miles of Home
G	Daylight Only	J03	No Freeway Driving	J13	Rest. - 15 Miles of Home
H	Employment Only	J04	Rest. - 25 Miles From Home	J14	Rest. - 20 Miles of Home
I	Limited - Other	J05	Within City Limits	J15	Rest. - 30 Miles of Home
K	Intrastate Only	J06	Licensed Driver - Front Seat	J20	Temporary Resident
L	Without Air-Brakes	J07	Moped		

Commercial Endorsements

T	Double-/Triple-Trailers	H	Placarded Hazardous Material
P	Passenger Vehicle	X	Combination Tank/Hazardous Material
N	Tank Vehicle	S	School Bus

Kansas Conviction Code Table

Editor's Notes:

- **Kansas does not have a Point System.**
- At this time the Department of Revenue does not have the ability to produce a conviction table with ACD Code Translations. However, the Department is planning to implement a new motor vehicle system, this will result in a new code set. The new code set is tentatively scheduled to be published in mid to late 2013.
- The Department of Revenue indicates there may be codes that appear on a commercial driving record that are not listed here. These instances will be rare; however, if you have questions you may phone the Driver Control Bureau at 785-296-3671 for help.

Code	Description	Code	Description
AC4	Involvement in an accident	B57	Drive a CMV without a CDL in driver's possession
A10	Driving under the influence with BAC .15 or greater – court conviction	B91	Improper classification/endorsement on driver's license
A12	Chemical test refusal - court conviction	CA2	DUI Conviction expunged
A30	Minor possess/consume alcohol	CA4	Juvenile offender
A33	Unlawful Possession of Controlled Substance or Controlled Substance Analog	CA5	School safety violation - administrative suspension
A61	Under 21 with BAC of .02 but less than .08	C11	Operating CMV with .04 blood alcohol content or higher
A90	Chemical test failure for alcohol BAC .15 or greater, administrative suspension	C12	Operating CMV under the influence of alcohol (DUI)
		C13	Refusal to submit to a test for alcohol or drugs after operating a CMV
B19	Driving while out of service order in effect and transporting 16+ passengers and/or transporting HazMat that requires a placard	C14	Operating CMV under the influence of a controlled substance
		C15	Operating CMV and leaving the scene of an accident
B27	CMV-Violation of out-of-service order	C16	Operating CMV involving a felony
B51	Driving with expired license or no driver's license	C17	Operating CMV in commission of a felony involving manufacturing, distributing, or dispensing of a controlled substance
B56	Driving a CMV without obtaining a CDL	C18	Operating a CMV in excess of 15 mph or more

C19	Operating a CMV in willful/wanton disregard for the safety of persons or property
C20	Reckless driving in a CMV
C21	Improper or erratic lane change in a CMV
C22	Following too closely in a CMV
C23	Violation of a traffic control law in a CMV, arising in connection with a fatal accident
C51	One-year disqualification for driving a CMV with BAC at .04 or higher
C52	One-year disqualification for driving a CMV under the influence of alcohol (DUI)
C53	One-year disqualification for refusal to submit to a test for alcohol or drugs after operating a CMV
C54	One-year disqualification for driving a CMV under the influence of a controlled substance
C55	One-year disqualification for leaving the scene of an accident involving a CMV
C56	One-year disqualification for a felony involving use of a CMV
C61	Three-year disqualification for driving a CMV with a BAC of .04 or higher while transporting hazardous material
C62	Three-year disqualification for driving a CMV under the influence of alcohol, while transporting placarded hazardous material
C63	Three-year disqualification for refusal to submit to a test for alcohol or drugs after operating a CMV while transporting hazardous material
C64	Three-year disqualification for driving a CMV under the influence of a controlled substance, while transporting placarded hazardous material
C65	Three-year disqualification for leaving the scene of an accident involving a CMV, while transporting placarded hazardous material
C66	Three-year disqualification for a felony involving use of a CMV, while transporting placarded HazMat
C70	Lifetime disqualification for using a CMV in the commission of a felony involving manufacturing, distributing or dispensing of a controlled substance
C71	Lifetime disqualification for a second offense for any combination of C11, C12, C13, C14, C15 and C16
C80	60-day disqualification for a second offense in a three-year period for any combination of C18, C19, C20, C21, C22, and C23 in separate incidents
C81	120-day disqualification for a third offense in a three-year period for any combination of C18, C19, C20, C21, C22, and C23 in separate incidents
C99	24-hour out-of-service order in a CMV
DI0	Limited driving privileges with ignition interlock - KSA 8-292
DI1	Driving under the influence of alcohol, narcotics or pathogenic drugs or excessive blood alcohol - court conviction
DI2	6 months ignition interlock
DI3	Refusal to submit to a test for alcohol or drugs - administrative suspension
DI4	Illegal transportation of alcohol or drugs in a motor vehicle
DI5	Chemical test failure for alcohol - administrative suspension
DI6	Limited driving privileges with ignition interlock
D17	Voluntary ignition interlock
DI8	Entered diversion agreement after DWI arrest
DI9	Ignition interlock required
D37	Default on Payment Agreement
D51	Failure to pay child support
D37	Default on payment agreement
D51	Failure to pay child support
D70	Driving with view obstructed to front or sides
EM1	Leaving vehicle unattended with engine running
EM2	Exceeding weight limits
EM3	Towing or pushing vehicle improperly
EM5	Failure to dim lights as required or driving without lights

E01	Operating without proper equipment as required by law
E70	Equipment used improperly or obstructed
FA1	Violation of a motor vehicle law resulting in the death of a person (includes vehicular homicide)
FE2	Using a motor vehicle in connection with a felony (includes aggravated vehicular homicide and manslaughter)
FL5	Failure to pass required examination
FL6	Failure to submit required medical/vision report
FL7	Medical problem indicated on driver's license application
FL8	Failure to complete required alcohol program
FO1	Following too close
F02	Child or youth restraint not used properly as required
F04	Seat belt not used properly as required
FR2	Failure to meet requirements for financial security following an accident - administrative suspension
FR4	Failure to maintain continuous liability insurance or file evidence of insurance - administrative suspension
FR5	Failure to maintain required compulsory liability insurance - court conviction
F02	Child or youth restraint not used properly as required
F04	Seat belt not used properly as required
FR2	Failure to meet requirements for liability insurance following an accident - administrative suspension
FR4	Failure to maintain continuous liability insurance or file evidence of insurance – administrative suspension
FR5	Failure to maintain required liability insurance - court conviction
F66	Unsafe condition of vehicle (no specified component)
HR1	Failure to stop and render aid after involvement in an accident resulting in bodily injury
HR2	Failure to stop and reveal identity after involvement in accident resulting in property damage only
HR4	Evading arrest
M09	Failure to obey railroad-highway grade crossing not specifically noted in related codes while operating a CMV
M10	Failure to obey traffic control device or directions of an enforcement official at a railroad-highway grade crossing while operating a CMV
M20	Failure to slow down at railroad-highway grade crossing while operating a CMV
M21	Failure to stop before railroad-highway grade crossing while operating a CMV
M22	Failure to stop as required before driving onto railroad-highway grade crossing while operating a CMV
M23	Failure to have sufficient space to drive completely through the railroad-highway while operating a CMV
M24	Failure to negotiate a railroad-highway grade crossing due to insufficient undercarriage clearance while operating a CMV
M25	Failure to stop before sidewalk when emerging from an alley, building private road, or driveway
M45	Entering an intersection, marked crosswalk or railroad crossing when there is insufficient space to cross over
MR1	Misrepresentation of identity or other facts to obtain a driver's license - administrative action
MS1	Starting improperly from a parked position
MS2	Improper backing
MS8	Suspended/revoked out-of-state
MS9	Insufficient check
M81	Careless driving
M82	Inattentive driving
N08	Failure to take action to avoid colliding with a pedestrian
N80	Coasting with the gears or transmission in neutral
N84	Allowing an under 14 aged passenger to ride on the vehicle while in motion
PA1	Passing improperly or where prohibited
RE8	Diversion Agreement for a chemical test refusal
RK1	Heedless, willful, wanton, or reckless disregard of the rights or

safety of others in operating a motor vehicle, endangering persons or property

RK2   Vehicle battery; with DUI

RK7   Vehicle battery; with eluding or reckless driving

RR2   Failure to comply with a traffic citation

RR3   Accumulation of violations resulting in the administrative suspension of driving privileges

RV3   Accumulation of violations resulting in the suspension of driving privileges

RV4   Habitual violator - three-year loss of driving privileges - administrative suspension

RW3   Failure to yield right-of-way in manner required

SC1   Failure to obey traffic instructions of police officer or fireman, or traffic sign or control device

SI1   Failure to give proper signal

SP1   Contest racing on public roads or highways

SP2   Driving too fast for conditions

SP3   Driving in excess of posted maximum speed limit

SP4   Driving less than posted minimum speed limit

TF1   Theft of motor fuel dispensed in a vehicle at a gas station

TU3   Making improper turn

VR1   Driving while revoked

VR2   Driving while suspended

VR3   Violation of probation

VR4   Operating contrary to conditions specified on driver license or without being licensed

VR7   Driving while revoked as habitual offender

VR9   Circumventing or tampering with ignition interlock

WW1   Driving wrong way, in wrong direction, or in wrong lane or improper lane changing

W60   Accumulation of two or more railroad-highway grade crossing violations within three years

W61   Accumulation of three or more railroad-highway grade crossing violations within three years

Kentucky

Administration	Important Telephone and Web Contacts
Bill Heise, Director Doug Sutton, Assistant Director Division of Driver Licensing 502-564-6800 http://transportation.ky.gov/Driver-Licensing/Pages/default.aspx Godwin Onodu, Assistant Director Division of Motor Vehicle Licensing 502-564-5301 http://transportation.ky.gov/motor-vehicle-licensing/Pages/default.aspx Transportation Office Building, 2nd Fl 200 Mero Street 40622	Driver Licensing..................................502-564-1257 Reinstatement......................................502-564-0278 Commercial Driver License ....502-564-0279 Vehicle Title Information...................502-564-2737 Vehicle Registration Information ......502-564-5301 Motor Carriers....................................502-564-4540 State Police...502-695-6300 Motor Vehicle Enforcement..............502-227-8780 General Email Drivers: kytc.ddlwebservices@ky.gov General Email Vehicle: KYTCMVLHelpDesk@ky.gov Statutes: www.lrc.state.ky.us/krs/titles.htm Title 601 Regs: www.lrc.state.ky.us/kar/TITLE601.HTM

Driver's License Format, Issuance and Renewal

License Classes, Restrictions and Endorsements Appear After the Driving Record Content Section

License Format

The DL or ID consists of a combination of a single alpha and eight numerals. The alpha corresponds to the first initial of last name, but if name changes license number does not.

Document Appearance

Kentucky began issuing the current license and permit documents in December 2001. The older license is a photo paper card that is laminated after picture is developed. Some may still be in use.

Current Documents

Security Characteristics: KY Transportation Cabinet logo is optical variable device across front.

Position of Photo: Horizontal on left edge, bluish background for regular documents, red if an ID document, and purple if a permit.

Minor Age Driver Locator: Vertical format, date when age 18 and age 21 in upper right.

CDL Indicator: New Green background color, indicated under license type and class.

Older Documents - Pre 2001

Security Characteristics: A 1/4 inch clear laminate border, "KENTUCKY DRIVER LICENSE" is across top in blue.

Position of Photo: Lower right, bluish background.

Minor Age Driver Locator: Special laminate "UNDER 21" printed vertically on sides.

CDL Indicator: Indicated under license type and class.

Issuance

Location of Requirements for Proof of Identity:

http://transportation.ky.gov/Driver-Licensing/Pages/Driver-License-ID-Card-General-Information.aspx

Age Requirements

The minimum age for obtaining a permit or license is sixteen. Kentucky has a Graduated Driver's License program for drivers under 18 years of age. This program defines driving privileges and responsibilities using three phases: Permit, Intermediate License, Full Unrestricted License. All student 16 and 17 years old must present a School Compliance Verification Form in order to obtain the permit or license. An Instruction Permit is required of operator, motorcycle, and CDL applicants; must be accompanied by licensed driver 21 years or older

(except motorcycle). Extensive changes were made to the GDL in 2007 regarding the Intermediate Stage. Intermediate License holders are not permitted to drive between the hours of 12 midnight and 6 a.m. unless the driver can demonstrate a good cause for driving such as emergencies, school or work related activities.

A commercial driver's license may be issued to an individual 18 years of age who holds a valid automobile Class D driver's license who has passed the vision and knowledge test required for a commercial driver's license of the class vehicle to be driven, if the individual only drives a commercial motor vehicle in intrastate commerce and does not drive a school bus or a vehicle hauling hazardous material. The license shall be class specific and shall contain an "I" restriction noting that the commercial driver is limited to Kentucky intrastate commerce. For school bus or hazardous materials endorsements, the minimum age is 21.

Note a CDL permit/license cannot be issued until the applicant has provided a copy of the CDL application to the Division of Driver Licensing and DDL has posted the application to the driver's record. This process could take up to 48 hours. It is the applicant's responsibility to provide the Division of Driver Licensing a copy of the 10 Year History Application prior to the issuance of the CDL permit/license.

Residency

Non-resident's home-state license honored on a reciprocal basis; Kentucky license must be secured upon establishing residence.

Renewal

Birth date of 4th year expiring 30 days after birthday, if a under 21 license then expires 90 days after 21st birthday. Driver keeps same number when renewing even if last name changes. If the license is expired for more than one year, a vision and written test is required. All Class D drivers (except military personnel) must appear in the clerk's office for license issuance. Military personnel stationed out-of-state may renew by mail to the county where the license was issued. The county will issue an ID w/o photo. This must be done every 4 years.

Elderly-Related Restrictions

None are reported.

Vehicle Insurance, Title and Registration Facts

Renewal

Renewal is annual. Vehicles registered with standard issue passenger car plates can renew online from web page at https://mvl.ky.gov/MVLWeb/requirementpage.jsp providing the address on the renewal notice is correct.

New Residents

Non-residents must register vehicles within 15 days upon establishing residency.

Inspections and Emissions Testing

Kentucky has neither a mandatory safety inspection nor emission testing required with a vehicle registration; however, some local jurisdictions do have emissions testing. However, all cars entering Kentucky must have the vehicle identification number inspected by the sheriff in the county in which they are to be registered. The only exception belongs to new cars handled by Kentucky dealers which do not have to be inspected.

Passenger Plate Facts

There is one plate with one decal (MO & YR). Passenger plates have county of issue printed on bottom; commercial plates do not. When a vehicle is sold, the plate remains with the vehicle.

Insurance and Financial Responsibility

Kentucky has compulsory liability and no-fault insurance laws. Insurance cards must be kept in the vehicle. Compulsory insurance limits are $25,000/50,000/10,000. Proof of insurance is required at registration and renewal of the vehicle. SR-22 forms are not used.

Withdrawal Sanctions, and Alcohol and Drug Testing

Alcohol and Chemical Testing Limits

Kentucky's illegal intoxication level is .08 BAC and .04 BAC for drivers of commercial vehicles. All drivers under the age of 21 are subject to Zero Alcohol Tolerance (defined as .02 Blood Alcohol Concentration). Urine, blood, and breath testing are used. Operating a horse, bicycle or any non-motor vehicle under the influence is also considered illegal.

Suspensions and Revocations

The state is in compliance with the mandated disqualifications on CDLs per MCSIA. See the Appendix for details.

Attempt to Elude a Peace Officer, First Offense .... 3-month suspension discretionary.
Failure to Answer Court Summons .... Indefinite.
Failure to Enroll in or Complete State Traffic School .... Indefinite.
Failure to Maintain Liability Insurance, Second Offense .... 1-year suspension.
Driving While License Suspended or Revoked .... Fine and/or jail and 6-month suspension.
    (If under the influence: fine and/or jail and suspension is doubled.)
Third/Subsequent Offense .... 2-year suspension.
False Application .... 6-month suspension.
Leaving Scene of an Accident, First Offense .... 6-month suspension.
Racing on a Public Highway, First Offense .... 3-month suspension discretionary.
Speeding Twenty-six mph or More Over Limit, First Offense .... 3-month suspension discretionary.

Alcohol-Related Withdrawals

Driving Under the Influence of Alcohol or Other Substance Which May Impair Driver Ability, if Within 5 Year period
Over Age Eighteen
    First Offense .... 30 to 120 days suspension, 2 to 30 days jail time, education program.
    Second Offense .... 12 to 18 months suspension, 7 days to 6 months jail time, education program.
    Third Offense .... 24 to 36 months suspension, 30 days to 12 months jail time, education program.
    Fourth Offense .... 60 months suspension, Class D felony, education program.
Under Age Eighteen
    Suspensions for first, second, and third offenses are identical to the periods of time listed above *or* until the eighteenth birthday, whichever is longer.
Under Twenty-One with BAC .02 to .08 ... Thirty days to six months.
Regarding CDL Drivers: If a driver tests from .01% BAC to .039% BAC, that driver shall be put out of service for 24 hours. Drivers testing at .04% BAC or higher will be disqualified for one year. A second conviction carries a penalty of disqualifying a commercial driver for life. Penalties apply to the commercial driving privileges only.
Refusal to Submit to Breathalyzer Test -- The court of jurisdiction imposes a pre-trial suspension for refusal to submit to breathalyzer test. Suspension periods for pre-trial suspensions and/or refusal convictions are:
    First Offense .... Up to 6-month suspension.
    Second Offense .... Up to 18-month suspension.
    Third Offense .... Up to 3-year suspension.
    Fourth or Subsequent Offense .... 5-year suspension.
DUI with Aggravating Circumstances - mandatory jail time if convicted of DUI while:
- .18 BAC or higher
- Causing accident resulting in death or serious physical injury
- Going wrong way on limited access highway
- In excess of 30 mph above posted speed limit
- Refusal to take blood, breathe or urine test
- Transporting a passenger under 12 years of age

Other Facts Regarding Second or Subsequent DUI
- Drivers convicted of a second or subsequent DUI will forfeit their license plates to the courts during the period in which the driver license is suspended. The court may order an ignition interlock device to be installed on the violator's vehicle after the driver serves a

statutory suspension period.

Other Facts Regarding Young Drivers

- A "No Pass/No Drive Law" states that all students ages 16 or 17 can be denied a driver's license or have a license revoked for academic deficiency.
- A driver under the age of 18 who accumulates more than 6 points, or a driver age 18 and over who accumulates 12 points may have their driving privilege suspended.

Reinstatement Requirements

Suspension $40.00 fee; re-examination if suspended for one year or more.
Revocation $50.00 fee; re-examination if suspended for one year or more.

Record Access: Laws, Rules, and Forms

Note: **This Section Applies to Both Driver and Vehicle Records.**

Governing Statutes and Rules

Title 601 Regs (For Vehicle Regulation):
www.lrc.state.ky.us/kar/TITLE601.HTM
KY Statutes: www.lrc.state.ky.us/krs/titles.htm
(Chapters for Driver Licensing are 159, 186, 187, 189, 189A and 281A)
Per Statute KRS 61.874, and per 601 KAR 2:020. Drivers' privacy protection form Title 601, the state adopted the provisions of DPPA. This statute included provisions for release of boat records as well as vehicle records. However, Kentucky did not specifically adopt federal exemption 14.
In 601 KAR 2:020, Kentucky combined the 11, 12, and 13 of the federal exceptions into the following section:

"Section 6. Disclosure with Consent. Personal information referred to in Sections 1 and 2 of this administrative regulation may be disclosed to any requestor, if the requestor provides a written statement of consent that has been notarized, from the person who is the subject of the information being requested. (601 KY ADC 2:020)"

Request and Consent Forms

Driving Records: The state does not mandate use of a specific form. A permissible use requester should provide, in writing, reason for request and the requester's signature.

Vehicle Records: The needed request form *Request for Motor Vehicle Record Which Includes Personal Information TC96-16A* is found at https://mvl.ky.gov/MVLWeb/pdf/TC96-16A.pdf. Request must be in writing stating purpose of request. The form requires a notarized signature of the requester attesting that use of the record is permissible.

Vendor and Third Party Access Policy

Per KRS 61.874, there are no restrictions as long as vendors comply with statute and do not create a commercial mailing list. Approved online vendors can access records for other vendors (who are not online) who will then sell to an end-user, providing the end user is permissible per DPPA.

Non-permissible Use Requests

Non-permissible use requesters without consent receive records with personal information cloaked. A three-year driving record is a public record in accordance with KRS 186.018. This record does not contain accident information or any of the driver's personal information such as address, sex, date of birth, or SSN. The Public online access for driving records described below is open to non-permissible use requesters.

Access to Driver-Related Records

Driving Records

General Information and Fees
Attention: MVRs, Division of Driver Licensing, Transportation Office Building, 200 Mero Street, Frankfort KY, 40622, 502-564-6800, ext. 2250. https://dhr.ky.gov/DHRWeb/index.jsp
The current fee for the public three-year record, commercial or non-commercial driver records is $3.00; the fee for electronic access is $5.00. Credit cards are accepted. The last fee increase was December 2006 when the electronic record fee increased from $4.50 to $5.00.
In-Person – Walk-in requests can be made at the State Office Building or at one of twelve field offices in the state. Individual requests are processed while you wait; lists are processed overnight. The field offices are located in Bowling Green, Catlettsburg, Elizabethtown, Florence, Frankfort, Hazard, Lexington, Louisville, Madisonville, Paducah, Prestonsburg, and Somerset.
Mail – Mail-in requests are processed in three-to-five days. The driver's license number or SSN, or name and DOB must be submitted with request. The fee must accompany each request.
Electronic Batch – Electronic access in batch mode is available to approved, ongoing requesters with a permissible use. The system, run by Kentucky.gov, is open 24/7 and provides immediate results after requests are sent. The driver's license number or Social Security Number is needed when ordering. The fee is $5.00 per record and monthly billing is offered. Requesters must be approved by the Commissioner's office and have an account with Kentucky.gov. The records provided contain personal information. There is a $75.00 annual subscription fee. Information about this service is not available on the web. For more information, call Kentucky.gov at 502-875-3733 or email support@kentucky.gov.
Electronic Public Online – The general public may obtain a three-year driving record at https://dhr.ky.gov/DHRWeb/. This record provided the driver status, license expiration, driving restrictions, and traffic violations. The record does not contain accident information or any of the driver's personal information such as address, sex, date of birth, and SSN. Up to 50 records may be ordered at one time and then can be viewed and printed within minutes. Records are available for further viewing for 2 weeks. A $5.00 fee applies, records must be ordered with a credit or debit card. The service is closed from 11:30 pm until 5:00 am. If questions, call 502-564-1257.
Bulk – The Commonwealth of Kentucky does not sell driving records in bulk.
By Person of Record – KY drivers may obtain their driving record by mail, walk-in or online interactive as described above. A five-year record with personal information is available to the driver, but this record cannot be obtained electronically, nor is it available to the public.

Notification/Monitoring Program

At present, Kentucky does not offer a monitoring system or notification program to employers or insurance companies to track incidents of drivers.

Accident Reports

Reporting – Any accident resulting in property damage in excess of $200.00—which is not investigated by a law enforcement agency—must be reported in writing within ten days to the KY State Police, Records

Branch, 1250 Louisville Road, Frankfort KY 40601 502-227-8700. The form is available at www.kentuckystatepolice.org in the Forms/Download tab.

Record Access – To obtain a copy of a traffic collision report a person needs to contact the Investigating Agency. Each agency has a different dissemination procedure. The Kentucky State Police procedure for requesting a copy of a collision report is shown below.

Accident reports can be obtained from the Kentucky State Police, Criminal Identification and Records Branch, 1250 Louisville Road, Frankfort 40601 502-226-2175, fax 502-226-7418. Records are maintained from 1998. Requests must be in writing and include the exact date, county, roadway, and the driver's name.

Per KRS 189.635 - To obtain a copy of a vehicle accident report, one must be a party to the accident, the parent or guardian of a minor who is party to the accident, insurers of any party who is the subject of the report, or an attorney of the parties. Requests must be in writing and include the exact date, county, roadway, and the driver's name.

The cost is $5.00 per report. The report may also be accessed using the microfilm number appearing on the driving record entry. In-person and fax searching are available. Turnaround time is normally 1 to 2 weeks. Statistical reports are available to the general public

Online access to records is provided by a designated vendor. Go to https://www.buycrash.com/Public/Home.aspx. Fee is $10.00 per report.

Access to Vehicle-Related Records

General Information and Fees

Division of Motor Vehicle Licensing, Transportation Office Building, 200 Mero Street 2nd Fl, Frankfort 40622, 502-564-2737 for Title History, 502-564-5301 for Registration, 502-564-3298 for other requests. Email questions to KYTCMVLHelpDesk@ky.gov.

The current fee for VIN, registration, ownership, vehicle information, and lien checks is $3.00. Records include those of boats and mobile homes. Records are computerized or microfilm since 1992 for title histories, 1999 to present for current titles only. Please note this agency will not do a search using only the name and DOB. Also, this agency will not search using a SSN.

Mail and In-Person – Normal turnaround time is 5 to 10 days. Generally, records are available for 10 years to present. Expedited service is available for ongoing requesters. Use PO Box 2014, Frankfort KY 40622-2014 as the mail address.

Electronic – Electronic access is available to the Online Vehicle Information System (OVIS) to approved, ongoing requesters with a permissible use. Available records include title, lien, registration, and dealer assignment category. Search by VIN or title number. OVIS, operated by Kentucky.gov, is open 24/7 and provides immediate results after requests are sent. Requesters must be approved by the Commissioner's office and have an account with Kentucky.gov. There is a $75.00 annual subscription fee, and a $.44 charge for each record accessed. Information about this service is not available on the web. For more information, call Kentucky.gov at 502-875-3733 or visit http://kentucky.gov/register/Pages/subscribe.aspx.

Bulk – Kentucky will supply large bulk- or batch-orders of registration information to specific users; customization is available as well. Address information is released if the use is permissible per DPPA. The user must send a written request specifying the purpose, what information they wish, and how they want the data returned (record layout). Programming development cost and record fees are determined upon the extent of the request. For further information contact: Division of Motor Licensing, Transportation Office Building, 200 Mero Street, Frankfort, KY 40622, 502-564-5301.

Access to Vessel-Related Records

General Information, Access and Fees

Records can be obtained from the Division profiled above. Only motorized boats must be titled and registered. Title and registration information is available from 1992 to present. Prior records are kept by county clerks. Direct questions to 502-564-2737.

Driving Record Content and Reciprocity

What's On or Not On the Driving Record

- Kentucky reports all moving violation convictions, and all out-of-state convictions except non-CDL speeding violations.
- The public three-year driving record does not contain accident information or any of the driver's personal information such as address, sex, date of birth, and Social Security Number.
- KY drivers may purchase their own five-year record, but the public may not.
- Any entry over three years is "masked" for insurance and employers. Most moving violation convictions remain part of the record for a period of five (5) years from the conviction date.
- The court of adjudication is permitted to allow driver school attendance in lieu of conviction.

Data Retention

Records of surrendered licenses are available for 3 years. CDL driver records are purged based on the MCSIA timetable (see the Appendix).

Court to Repository

All courts submit information electronically. Law mandates that courts submit conviction information to the state as follows: five days for DUI and fifteen days for other moving violations. Conviction information is input into the state system within five-to-seven days of receipt from the court.

State Reciprocity for Non-CDL Drivers

- Will suspend license of driver for unpaid out-of-state convictions.
- Record of new incoming driver is not shown on MVR
- Out-of-state convictions is shown on MVR, except speeding (all if CDL).
- Out-of-state accidents are not shown on MVR.
- Convictions of out-of-state drivers are sent to home state.
- Record is forwarded to new state upon surrender of license.

Abbreviations of License Classes, Restrictions, and Endorsements

License Classes– Commercial

Kentucky began issuing the CDL in October of 1991.

Class A   Any combination of vehicles with a GVWR of 26,001 or more pounds, provided the GVWR of the vehicle(s) being towed is in excess of 10,000 pounds.

Class B   Any single vehicle with a GVWR of 26,001 or more pounds, or any such vehicle towing a vehicle not in excess of 10,000 pounds GVWR.

Class C   Any single vehicle less than 26,001 pounds GVWR, or any such vehicle towing a vehicle not in excess of 10,000 pounds GVWR. This group applies to vehicles which are placarded for hazardous materials or designed to transport sixteen or more people (including the driver).

License Classes– Non-Commercial

Class D   Operator
Class E   Moped
Class M   Motorcycle

Restrictions

0	Valid KY Only	6	Hand Accelerator
1	Corrective Lenses	7	Hand Brake
2	Power Brakes	8	Other: miscellaneous restriction assigned by the license examiner
3	Automatic Transmission		
4	Daylight Driving	9	Ignition Interlock
5	Power Steering		

CDL Restrictions Only

F	Farm-Related Services (see accompanying document)	L	Except Class A Bus
I	Intrastate Driving Only	O	Except Tractor/Trailer
J	Except Class A and B Bus	Z	Except Intra-city
K	No Air Brakes		

Endorsements

H	Hazardous Materials	T	Triple-/Double-Trailers
N	Tank	X	Combination HazMat-Tanker
P	Passenger	S	School Bus

Conviction & Action Table with Points and ACD

Code	Num	ACD	Pts	Description
A1	411			Operator's Test Authorized - A1 Letter
A3	691			CDL Test Authorized - A3 Letter Sent
A30	041	A30		Possession
A31	042	A31		Illegal Possession of Alcohol
A33	043	A33		Illegal Possession of Drugs (Controlled Substance)
A4	692			Operator/CDL Test Authorized - A4 Letter Sent
A61	267	A61		Non KY Under 21 Admin Per Se BAC .02 or higher
A90	268	A90		Non KY Admin Per Se .10 BAC
A91	272	A91		Administrative Per Se BAC ( )
A94	269	A94		Non KY Admin per Se .04 BAC
A98	270	A98		Non KY Admin Per Se .08 BAC
AD1	514			Referred to Alcohol School/DUI
AD4	592			Referred to Alcohol School/Fraud
AD7	547	A20		Out-of-State DUI/Request Hearing
AIE	484			Authorized in Error
ALT	341	B41		Altered or Fictitious Driver's License
ANT	449			Administrative Notice of Transfer
APL	448			Conviction Appealed
AS	266	D02		Administrative Suspension
ATC	508			Alcohol Treatment Program Completion
B19	733	B19		Driving While Out of Service With Endorsement for 16 passengers or More, or With Hazmat
B27	722	B27		Driving While License Out of Service
BIL	823			Begin Intermediate License Phase
BK	452			Bankruptcy on Unsatisfied Judgment
C11	701	A04		Driving Under Influence - .04 to .07

Code	Num	ACD	Pts	Description
C13	715	A12		Refused Chem Test In Commercial Motor Vehicle - Out of State
C17	712	A50		Use of Commercial Motor Vehicle - Cont Substance Felony
C18	600	S15		Speed 15 mph or More - CMV - Out-of-State
C23	683	U31		Violation Result In Fatal Accident - Commercial Motor Vehicle
C51	718			Commercial Driver License Disqualified - DUI .04 to .07
C52	704			Commercial Driver License Disqualified - DUI .08 or More
C53	702			Commercial Driver License Disqualified For Refused Chemical Test
C55	706			Commercial Driver License Disqualified - Leaving Scene of Accident
C56	708			Commercial Driver License Disqualified for Felony
C59	716			Commercial Driver License Disqualified - Murder/Manslaughter
C61	719			Commercial Driver License Disqualified - DUI .04 to .07 - Haz/Mat
C62	705			Commercial Driver License Disqualified - DUI .08 or More - Haz/Mat
C63	703			Commercial Driver License Disqualified for Refused Chemical Test - Hazardous Material
C65	707			CDL Disqualified - Leaving Scene - Hazardous Material
C66	709			CDL Disqualified for Felony - Hazardous Material
C69	717			Commercial Driver License Disqualified - Murder/Manslaughter Hazardous Material
C70	720			Disqualified - Use Commercial Motor Vehicle in Commission of Felony
C71	713	W40		Disqualified – Two or More Major Violations
C80	710	W30		Two Serious Violations in Three-Year Period
C81	711	W31		Three Serious Violations in Three-Year Period
C86	672			Request To Keep Out-of-State License
C99	695			Twenty-four-Hour Out-of-Service Order - Commercial Motor Vehicle
CA	505			Court Approval On Habitual Violator
CAN	590			License Cancellation Letter Sent
CAP	657			Commercial License Application Received
CAS	539			Completed Alcohol School
CCS	731	B20		Driving CMV While CDL Suspended or Cancelled
CD	006	M81	3	Careless Driving
CDM	023	M82	4	Changing Driver in Moving Vehicle
CDR	422			Commercial Driver License - Life Disqualified. Reduced to Ten Years
CDU	796			Commercial Driver License Disqualified - U-Civil Judgment
CDW	714	W45		Commercial Driver License Disqualified - Driving While Suspended
CEA	815			Commercial Driver License Endorsement Added
CED	816			Commercial Driver License Endorsement Dropped
CFA	625			Cancelled Federal Amputee Waiver
CFC	732	U10		Causing Fatality - Negligent CMV Operator
CGL	545			Graduated License Course Completed
CHD	673			Completed STS Home/Diversion
CHR	538			Completed Hearing
CJS	435			Civil Judgment Satisfied
CLR	436			Clearance Letter Received
CLS	504			Clearance Letter Sent
CMR	721	D02		Commercial Driver License Disqualified for Misrepresentation - 186.610
CNT	427			Commercial Driver License Test Not Taken
CO	457			Court Order To Return License
COR	688			Student Driver License Court Order
COS	271			Court Ordered Suspension
CPG	433			Citation Pending Conviction
CR	453			Agreed Order on Civil Judgment
CRD	568			Combined Records
CS	679			Change State of Record
CSC	477			Complied With Child Support Arrears
CSD	481			Change State-of-Record/DLR
CSF	821			CDL Skills Test Fee
CT1	537			Completed Traffic School - Court Referred
CT2	544			Completed Traffic School - Probation
CT5	575			Completed Traffic School - Out-of-state Driver
CT6	659			EXT To Complete STS Out-Of-State
CT8	559			Completed STS/Probation/Home Study
CT9	564			Completed STS/O.O.S/Home Study
CTD	678			Completed STS/Diversion Program
CTF	451			Commercial Driver License Test Failed
CTH	676			Completed Traffic School - Home School Study
CTR	465			Commercial Driver License Test Reinstated
CVS	418			Commercial Driver License Voluntarily Surrendered
CWC	046	B56		Driving CMV Without Obtaining a CDL

Code	Num	ACD	Pts	Description
CWE	048	B91		Driving CMV Without Proper CMV Class or Endorsement
CWP	047	B57		Driving CMV Without CDL Document in Possession
D02	321	A60		Driving Under the Influence .02 to .07
D51	264	D51		Failure to Pay Child Support
DAO	313	D37		Default On Agreed Order/Judgment
DIP	824			Duplicate Permit/Intermediate
DLA	401			Driver License Application
DLI	618			Duplicate License Issued
DLR	423			Driver License Received
DMI	682			Duplicate Moped License Issued
DML	602			Duplicate Motorcycle License Issued
DMP	403			Duplicate Motorcycle Permit Issued
DNV	476			Duplicate License Issued - Not Valid
DPA	478			Duplicate Class A Permit Issued
DPB	425			Duplicate Class B Permit Issued
DPC	415			Duplicate Class C Permit Issued
DPI	620			Duplicate Permit Issued
DPV	644			Duplicate Permit Issued - Not Valid
DS	454			License Denial Statement
DS1	316	B26		Driving While Suspended – DUI
DS2	345	B26		Driving While Suspended on DUI - 2nd
DS3	346	B26		Driving While Suspended on DUI - 3rd
DS4	347	B26		Driving While Suspended - Aggravate - 1st
DS5	348	B26		Driving While Suspended - Aggravate - 2nd
DS6	349	B26		Driving While Suspended - Aggravate - 3rd
DU1	320	A20		Driving Under Influence - Non-Motor Vehicle
DU6	322	A20		Driving Under Influence - Under Eighteen Years
DVS	445			Operator License - Voluntary Surrender
DW1	324	A20		Driving Under Influence - First Offense
DW2	325	A20		Driving Under Influence - Second Offense
DW3	326	A20		Driving Under Influence - Third Offense
DW4	327	A20		Driving Under Influence - Fourth Or Subsequent Offense
DWI	301	A20		Driving Under Influence - CV
DWS	302	B26		Driving While Suspended
EAR	404			Court Order for Early ADE Release
ECR	576			Employer Certification Received
EGL	543			Graduated License Course - Enrolled
ELU	105	U01		Eluding Police Officer - CV
ENR	486			Employer/Employee NDR Request
ER1	801			Reinstated by MRB/Fee Required
ERL	434			Driver Eligibility Letter Sent
EVS	446			Moped License - Voluntary Surrendered
FA	407			False Affidavit Letter Sent
FA2	216			Failure To Enroll STS; Court Referral
FA3	217			Failure To Complete STS; Court Referral
FA4	214			Fail to Attend Graduated License Course
FAC	408			False Application Letter Sent - Commercial Driver License
FAH	535			Failure To Appear For Hearing
FAP	202	D02		Suspended For False Application
FAS	225	D56		Failure To Answer Court/Summons
FAW	619			Federal Amputee Waiver
FCA	227			Failure to Complete Alcohol Education School
FCT	536			Failure to Complete Traffic School
FDC	611			Federal Diabetic Waiver Cancelled
FDH	025	E54	3	Failure to Dim Headlights
FDR	612			Federal Diabetic Waiver Reinstated
FDW	615			Federal Diabetic Waiver
FFI	810			Firefighter ID Issued
FHL	265	D02		False Application - Hardship License
FIH	026	E55	3	Failure To Illuminate Headlights
FLN	306	U03		Felony - Motor Vehicle Involved
FMR	209			Failure to Obey Motorcycle Rules
FPA	741			Failure to Provide CDL Application
FPR	211			Failure to Pay Restitution
FRA	319	D06		Fraud Attempt To Purchase Alcohol
FSC	495			Farm Services - Restricted Commercial Driver License

Code	Num	ACD	Pts	Description
FSH	751	W09		Fail to Surrender HAZMAT – US Patriots Act
FSS	213	B70		Failure To Supply Social Security Number
FTC	012	M34	4	Following Too Closely; Car; Truck Vehicles
FTE	420			Failure To Enroll in Traffic School
FVC	609			Federal Vision Waiver Cancelled
FVR	610			Federal Vision Waiver Reinstated
FVW	604			Federal Vision Waiver
GLN	556			Graduated License Course Non Attend
GLR	540			Graduated License Course Required
GLT	541			Tran Driver Graduated Lic Info Letter
GRS	546			Graduated License Course - Rescheduled
GT	318	U04		Gasoline Theft
GWR	218	W13		Parent/Guardian Withdraw Responsibility
HAP	640			Hazmat Application
HCO	521			Hardship License - Court Order
HDL	507			Hardship License Issued
HDR	530			Hardship License Received
HER	686			Hazmat Endorsement Removed
HLC	524			Hardship License Cancelled
HLR	512			Hardship License Re-issued
HLS	804			Hazmat 60 Day Letter Sent
HR1	525			Hearing Requested - False Application - CDL
HR3	527			Hearing Requested - NE
HR4	528			Hearing Requested - Suspension
HR6	570			Hearing Requested - OOS Record
HR7	409			Hearing Requested - Out-of-State DUI
HRC	599			Hardship Court Order Restitution
HRI	517			Hardship License Issued - Restitution
HRM	573			Hearing Scheduled - Medical Review Board
HRR	597			Hardship License Issued - Restitution
HRS	542			Hearing Rescheduled
HS	661			Discretionary Hearing Scheduled
HTA	616			Hazmat TSA Approved
HTD	617			Hazmat TSA Denied
HTR	613			Hazmat TSA Revoked
HVC	314	W01		Habitual Violator Conviction
HVD	414			Habitual Violator - Dismissed
HWR	472			Hearing Waiver Received
IAR	419			Intrastate Waiver Appeal Received
ICN	494			Insurance Cancellation Notice
ID	007	N84	3	Improper Driving
IDD	632			Duplicate ID Issued
IDI	631			ID Card Issued
IDO	577			Medical Waiver - Denial Overturned
IDR	633			Reprint ID Card
IDU	601			Medical Waiver - Denial Upheld
IH	750	W70		Imminent Hazard
IHR	623			Imminent Hazard Rescinded
IID	594			Ignition Interlock Device Required
IIR	596			Ignition Interlock Device Removed
ILC	045	M42	3	CDL Conviction - Improper or Erratic Lane Change
ILL	034	M50	3	Improper Use - Left Lane/Limited Access Highway
ILU	013	M40	3	Improper Lane Usage
ILV	052		3	Intermediate License Violation
IMD	605			Intrastate Medical Waiver Denied
IMG	630			Intrastate Medical Waiver Granted
IMP	595			Vehicle Plates Impounded
IMR	674			Intrastate Medical Request Received
INS	526			Enter INS Information
INT	431			Internal Office Use Only
IP	010	M70	5	Improper Passing
IPB	033	M75	6	Failure To Stop For School/Church Bus
IPR	667			Instruction Permit Received
IPS	443			Permit Surrendered to Another State
IPV	051		3	Instruction Permit Violation
IS	003	N83	3	Improper Start

Code	Num	ACD	Pts	Description
ISI	825			Ineligible Skills Test - Intermediate Phase
IST	614			Intrastate Skills Test Required
IT	014	N50	3	Improper Turn
ITR	658			Intrastate Skills Test Results
IUR	607			Intrastate Medical Update - Received
IUS	649			Intrastate Medical Update - Sent
IWC	799	W14		Intrastate Medical Waiver - Cancelled
LC2	624			License Type Changed from OPR/Motorcycle
LC6	456			License Class Changed from OPR/Commercial Driver License
LCA	817			License Class Added
LCD	818			License Class Dropped
LCS	444			License Surrendered To Another State
LOA	342	B92		Lend License to Other
LOS	740			CDL Disqualification/License Out of Service
LRF	455			License Surrendered From Another State
LRS	459			License Reported Stolen or lost
LSA	308	B05		Leaving Accident Scene - Hit-and-Run
LTR	417			Personal Letter Sent
LVS	473			License - Voluntary Surrender
M09	724	M09		Fail to Obey RR Crossing-Restrictions
M10	725	M10		Fail to Obey Railroad Track Control Device or Directions of Officer
M20	726	M20		Fail to Slow Down and Check Railroad Crossing
M21	727	M21		Fail to Stop When Railroad Track not Clear
M22	728	M22		Fail to Stop as Required at Railroad Crossing
M23	729	M23		Fail to Obey Railroad Crossing - Space
M24	730	M24		Fail to Obey Railroad Crossing - Clearance
M85	734	M85		Texting While Driving
MCA	654			Motorcycle License Added
MCR	828			Medical Certification Received
MC1	826			Medical Certification - 1st Notice
MC2	827			Medical Certification - 2nd Notice
MDE	548			Medical Driver Evaluation Required
MDF	549			Medical Driver Evaluation Failed
MDP	550			Medical Driver Evaluation Passed
MFS	586			Medical Form Sent
MIL	053			Military Exemption - Graduated License
MIN	315			Court Suspension of Minor
MLI	651			Moped License Issued
MLR	685			Moped License Renewed
MMV	323	U08		Murder Or Manslaughter - Motor Vehicle
MNT	432			Motorcycle Test Not Taken
MNV	487			Moped License Issued - Not Valid
MOF	099		6	Multiple Offenses/Convictions
MON	650			Modified License Issued - Not Valid
MOP	562			Medical Review Board - Ophthalmology Exam Required
MPR	684			Motorcycle Permit Renewed
MQ3	522			Meets Qualifications of FMCSA 391
MR	797	D02		Misrepresentation of CDL / 186.610
MR1	798	D02		False Affidavit Suspension - Commercial Driver License
MRB	442			Medical Review Board Case Created
MRD	591			Medical Report Received
MRF	566			Medical Road Test Failed
MRI	621			Modified/Replacement Issued
MRP	532			Medical Road Test Passed
MRR	579			Medical Review Released
MRS	208	W14		Medical Review Board Suspension
MRT	563			Medical Review Board Road Test Required
MTF	410			Motorcycle Test Failed
MVA	024		6	Traffic Violation Resulting in Accident
MVS	447			Motorcycle License - Voluntary Surrender
N84	040	N84		Unsafe Operation of Vehicle
NAI	441			DI Interview - No Action
NCA	511			Name Change Affidavit
NCD	696			Prior Conviction - Not Commercial Driver License - Disqualified
NCI	803			NCIC/LINC Check

Code	Num	ACD	Pts	Description
NCT	822			NCIC/LINC Check – Transfer Driver
NDR	299			NDR Hit - Must Furnish Clearance Letter
NIR	571			No Impoundment Reported
NLI	317	D36		No Liability Insurance in Force
NOL	303	B51		Operating With No License or Permit
NPL	593			Non-Payment License Fee - Cancel
NS1	554			STS Court Referral - Not Eligible
NS2	652			STS Referral Returned To Court
NS3	523			Not Subject to FMCSA 391
NVO	583			Not a Vehicle Owner
OCI	603			Commercial Driver License Added
OL1	416			Data Purge - KRS 186.018; Five Years Old
OLA	660			Operator License Added
OLI	636			Original License Issued
OLM	438			Original Motorcycle License Issued
OMV	032	N84		Any Other Moving Hazard Violations
ONT	450			Operator Test Not Taken
ONV	680			Original License Issued - Not Valid
OPA	589			Original Class A Permit Issued
OPB	479			Original Class B Permit Issued
OPC	424			Original Class C Permit Issued
OPI	606			Original Permit Issued
OPM	437			Original Motorcycle Permit Issued
OS1	670			Driver License Received - Returned to Issue State
OS2	671			Conviction Forwarded/Out-of-State License Not Received
OSC	405			Out-of-State Clearance Required - REN
OSR	111			Out-of-State Record - Must Clear
OSS	634			Override SSN Verification
OTF	413			Operator Test Failed
OWS	009	N63	3	Wrong Way On One-Way Street
P	402			Placed On Probation
PA	488			Previous Address
PAM	648			Permit To Add Motorcycle
PAO	647			Permit To Add Operator
P-C	463			Plate and/or Certificate Received
PCA	819			Permit Class Added
PCD	820			Permit Class Dropped
PCS	503			Police Demand Order - Cancellation Letter Sent
PDO	471			Police Demand Order
PDR	485			Police Demand Order - Returned
PDW	723			Privilege Disqualified - Operating CMV With No License
PGR	643			Parent/Guardian Restored Responsibility
PGS	426			Parent/Guardian Signature
PJR	305	D78		Perjury - License Application
PM1	580			Periodic Medical Required - Quarterly
PM2	581			Periodic Medical Required - Semi-Annual
PM3	582			Periodic Medical Required - Annual
PNV	483			Instruction Permit Issued - Not Valid
POI	496			Proof of Insurance
PR	428			Restitution Paid
PSA	493			Proof Of Citation Satisfied
PSD	257	W72		Pretrial Suspension on a DUI
PSR	261	W72		Pretrial Suspension on a Refusal Chemical Test
PSS	201	W01		Accumulation Twelve or More Points in Two Years
PTD	531			Pre-trial Suspension Termination - DUI
PTR	533			Pre-trial Suspension Termination - Refusal Chemical Test
PTS	252			Pre-trial Suspension
PTT	598			Pre-trial Suspension Terminated
PV2	584			Periodic Visual Required - Semi-Annual
PV3	585			Periodic Visual Required - Annual
PVS	466			Permit Voluntary Surrendered
PVW	662			Points Violation Warning
R1	412			Operator Reinstated - Notified
R2	665			Traffic School Suspension Rescinded
R3	693			Commercial Driver License Reinstated - Notified
R4	694			Operator/Commercial Driver License Reinstated - Notified

Code	Num	ACD	Pts	Description
R5	558			Suspension Order Rescinded
R6	689			Court-Ordered School Reinstatement
R7	462			Driving Privilege Restored
R8	499			Reinstate Motorcycle License Permit
RAC	108	S95		Racing
RCM	474			Resolved CDLIS Matches
RCT	311	A12		Refusal of Chemical Test
RD	005	M84	4	Reckless Driving
RDR	307	W01		Third Reckless Driving Conviction
REP	344	D02		License Misrepresentation
RH1	516			Notice To Request Hearing - Notification Sent/FA
RH3	518			Notice To Request Hearing - Notification Sent/NE
RH4	519			Notice To Request Hearing - Notification Sent/Suspension
RH6	569			Notice To Request Hearing - Notification Sent/Clearance
RHM	572			Notice To Request Hearing - Notification Sent/Medical Review Board
RIE	467			Reinstated in Error
RKM	400			Resolved KY Match Only
RLI	635			Renewal License Issued
RMI	656			Renewal Motorcycle License Issued
RNM	469			Resolved NDR Matches
RNS	490			Reinstatement Letter Not Sent - National Driver Register Hit
RNV	464			Renewal License Issued/Not Valid
ROP	653			Refunded Overpayment
ROW	008	N01	3	Failure To Yield Right-of-Way
RPA	561			Renewal Class A Permit Issued
RPB	406			Renewal Class B Permit Issued
RPC	482			Renewal Class C Permit Issued
RPI	639			Renewal Permit Issued
RPN	681			Renewal Permit Issued - Not Valid
RR	501			Reinstatement Fee
RR2	440			Commercial Driver License Reinstatement - Re-licensing Fee
RRF	567			Refunded Reinstatement Fee
RSA	813			Restriction Added
RSC	831			Self Certification Received
RSD	814			Restriction Dropped
RSF	565			Refunded Traffic School Fee
RSS	629			Resolved SSN Verification
RST	608			Restrictions Appeal Received
RTM	439			Undelivered Mail Returned
S14	044	S14		Speeding 11-14 MPH Over Limit
S15	049	S15		Out 0f State Speeding/ 15+ Over Limit
S93	050	S93		Out of State Speeding – No Detail
SAS	690			School Academic Sufficiency
SBF	806			School Bus Exemption Check: Failed
SBP	805			School Bus Exemption Check: Passed
SC1	829			Self Certification - 1st Notice
SC2	830			Self Certification - 2nd Notice
SC4	492			Court Summons Notice
SC5	645			Social Security Letter Sent
SCM	502			Status Changed
SCR	807			School Bus Certification Received
SD2	220	S26		Speed Over 25 MPH
SD3	221	U01		Elude Police Officer Suspension
SD4	222	S95		Racing Suspension
SD6	224			Suspended Out-of-State
SHL	802			Hazmat 60 Day letter Sent
SHS	668			Special Hearing Scheduled
SP1	001	S93	3	Speeding Under 16 mph Over Limit
SP2	002	S16	6	Speeding 16-25 mph Over Limit
SP3	029	S93		LTD Access - Speeding Under 16 mph
SP4	035	S93	3	Speeding 11-15 mph Over Limit; Limited Access
SP5	036	S51		Speeding 1-10 mph Over Limit; Limited Access
SP6	037	S15	3	Speeding 15 mph Over Limit in a Commercial Motor Vehicle
SPS	102	S15		Speeding 26 mph or More Over Limit
SSD	698			Selective Service Declined
SSF	628			SSN Verification Failed

Code	Num	ACD	Pts	Description
SSR	697			Selective Service Registration
SSS	646			Social Security Number Supplied
SSV	626			Social Security Verified
SSX	669			Social Security Batch Letter
ST1	510			Referral To Traffic School By Court
ST5	513	D45		Referred to STS - Out-of-State Driver
STD	509			Referred to STS - Diversion Program
SV	004	M15	3	Disregard of Stop Sign
SVN	253	W24		School Verification Notice (KRS 159.051)
TCD	030	M14	3	Failed To Obey Traffic-Control Device
TFC	018	S94	3	Driving Too Fast for Conditions
TMV	309			Theft of Motor Vehicle/Parts
TNV	458			Test Issued - Not Valid
T-R	460			Passed Test - License Reinstated
TRS	529			Traffic School - Rescheduled
TS1	520			Traffic School - Enrollment; Court Referred
TS2	552			Traffic School - Enrollment; Probation
TS5	574			STS Enrollment - Out-of-State Driver
TSC	017	S96	3	Driving Too Slowly For Conditions
TSD	677			Enrolled STS/Diversion Program
TYC	812			Ten Year History Completed
TYS	811			Ten Year History Started
UCI	506			Upgrade Commercial Driver License Issued
UCJ	310	D39		Unsatisfied Civil Judgment - Accident
UOV	228	N84		Unlawful Operation Of Motor Vehicle
VFS	587			Vision Form Sent
VHC	578			Vehicle Hardship Condition
VNC	015	D72	4	Vehicle Not Under Control
VPA	204	W01		Probation Violation - Abstract
VPC	203	W01		Probation Violation - Traffic School
VPH	340	D27		Violation Provisions of Hardship License
VVV	996			Withdrawal Transmitted From Out of State
VWL	663			First Serious Violation Warning/CDL
W41	735	W41		Additional Major Offense After Reinstatement
W50	736	W50		Accumulate Two Out-of-Service Orders in 10 years
W51	737	W51		Accumulate Two Out-of-Service Orders in 10 years, Having 16 Passenger or Hazmat Endorsement
W52	738	W52		Accumulate Three Out-of-Service Orders in 10 years
W60	794	W60		2 Railroad Grade Crossing Violations in a 3 Year Period
W61	795	W61		3 Railroad Grade Crossing Violations in a 3 Year Period
WRR	793			CDL Disqualified - FTO Railroad Crossing
WSR	011	N70	4	Driving On Wrong Side of Road
WT2	664			Suspension Order Issued - Traffic School
WT6	687			Suspension Order Issued - School Academic Violation
WTH	421			Suspension Order Issued
X-W	016	N08	3	Failure to Yield to Pedestrian
XXX	997			Conviction Transmitted from Out-of-State
Y	627			"Y" Flagged Record
YEM	019	N04	4	Failure to Yield to Emergency Vehicle
YTS	110	B01		Failed to Stop - Accident
YYY	998			Conviction Loaded - Change SOR
ZZZ	999			Withdrawal Loaded - Change SOR

Summary of Point System

Points assessed under the Kentucky Point System expire two (2) years from the date of conviction. However, the conviction entry remains part of the driver's record for a period of five (5) years from the conviction date.

Upon the accumulation of twelve (12) or more points against a driver age eighteen (18) or older, or 7 points against a driver under age 18, the Transportation Cabinet conducts a hearing concerning the driver's privileges to operate a motor vehicle. Failure to appear for the hearing results in a driving suspension for a period of six (6) months for the first such accumulation of twelve (12) points, one (1) year for the second such accumulation of twelve (12) points, and two (2) years for any subsequent accumulation of twelve (12) points within the two (2) year period.

After a hearing, the department may require the driver to be placed on "probation" in lieu of suspension and attend a driver improvement clinic (State Traffic School) approved by the Transportation Cabinet.

Once a driver has been placed on "probation" by the department, he/she shall not be considered for probation again until a lapse of two (2) years from the ending date of any previous probation period granted, whether served or not.

Points	Description
0	10 MPH or Less Over Speed Limit on Limited Access Highway
0	15 MPH or More in CMV (out-of-state conviction listed as serious offense only, no points)
3	Careless Driving
3	CDL Conviction - Improper or Erratic Lane Change
3	Disregard of Stop Sign
3	Driving Too Fast for Conditions
3	Driving Too Slowly For Conditions
3	Failed To Obey Traffic-Control Device
3	Failure to Dim Headlights
3	Failure To Illuminate Headlights
3	Failure To Yield Right-of-Way
3	Failure to Yield to Pedestrian
3	Improper Driving
3	Improper Lane Usage
3	Improper Start
3	Improper Turn
3	Improper Use - Left Lane/Limited Access Highway
3	Speeding 11-15 mph Over Limit; Limited Access
3	Speeding 15 mph Over Limit in a Commercial Motor Vehicle
3	Speeding Under 16 mph Over Limit
3	Wrong Way On One-Way Street
3	Any Other Moving Hazardous Violations
4	Changing Driver in Moving Vehicle
4	Driving On Wrong Side of Road
4	Failure to Yield to Emergency Vehicle
4	Following Too Closely; Car; Truck Vehicles
4	Reckless Driving
4	Vehicle Not Under Control
5	Improper Passing
6	Commission of Moving Hazardous Violation Involving an Accident
6	Failure To Stop For School/Church Bus
6	Combination of any Two or More Moving Hazardous Violations in Any One Continuous Occurrence
6	Speeding 16-25 mph Over Limit
6	Traffic Violation Resulting in Accident

Louisiana

Administration	Important Telephone and Web Contacts

Stephen F Campbell, Commissioner
Office of Motor Vehicles
PO Box 64886, Baton Rouge 70896
Phone: 225-925-6161
 	
Main Web Page: www.expresslane.org
 	
Laws and Statutes:
   www.legis.state.la.us/searchlegis.htm
 	
Policies and Procedures:
   http://dpsweb.dps.louisiana.gov/omv1.nsf//
	General Information 225-925-6146
	Driver Licensing..225-922-1175
	Driving Records/Record Discrepancies...............225-925-6388
	Financial Responsibility 225-925-6388
	Suspensions & Revocations 225-925-6388
	Commercial Driver License 225-925-6277
	Vehicle Registration...225-925-6146
	State Dept of Insurance 225-342-5900
	State Patrol 225-925-6006
	Email Contacts: https://dpsweb.dps.louisiana.gov/OMVContactUs.nsf

Driver's License Format, Issuance and Renewal

License Classes, Restrictions and Endorsements Appear After the Driving Record Content Section

License Format

The format is eight digits preceded by one zero (e.g., 012345678). Louisiana reports there is no code or sequential arrangement which determines the characters making the license number other than the zero at the beginning.

Document Appearance

Horizontal licenses are issued to license holders age 21 and over. Class I (ID cards) and H (Handicap) cards will specify "THIS IS NOT A DRIVER'S LICENSE." The state capitol drawing coordinates with the header bar with blue for Class E (personal), green for Class D (chauffeur), blue of all ID cards and Handicap Placards, gold for CDL, and red as indicated below for under 21. A duplicate license is shown by "DUP" in the license header.

Security Characteristics: The license has a reflective security strip in the shape of the state, across the text.

Position of Photo: The photo is on the right side, a signature is above the photo.

Minor Age Driver: Vertical licenses are issued to those under 21. Text will indicate "Under 21/18 until xxxx". There is a red border around photo.

CDL Indicator: "COMMERCIAL LICENSE" is printed across top. The header bar is gold, unless driver is under 21 then header is red.

Veteran: "VETERAN" is printed in black below the photo.

Sex Offender: "SEX OFFENDER" is printed in orange below the photo.

Issuance

Location of Requirements for Proof of Identity:
http://dpsweb.dps.louisiana.gov/omvfaqs.nsf?OpenDatabase&Start=1&Count=1200&Expand=2

Age Requirements

The age requirement for a full Class E license is seventeen years of age as is the age requirement for a Class D license.

A graduated licensing system exists for those under seventeen years of age. The minimum ages are fifteen for Learner's Permit, sixteen for Intermediate License, and seventeen for a regular Class E License. After completing the learner's permit stage and upon reaching at least sixteen years of age, a minor may apply for a Class "E" Intermediate License. This license must be maintained for a minimum of one year from the date of issuance or until the driver has reached the age of seventeen. This license allows the minor to drive alone or with other passengers in the vehicle, but restricts him from driving between the hours of 11:00 p.m. to 5:00 AM unless he is accompanied by a licensed parent, guardian, or adult at least twenty-one or older. After the one-year period or once the driver reaches age seventeen, the minor may qualify for a regular Class E license.

Residency

Non-resident's home-state license honored for ninety days; however, Louisiana license must be secured within thirty days of establishing residency.

Renewal

Birth month of fourth year, except sex offenders are issued driver's license/ID cards valid for one year. Driver keeps same number when renewing. Renewal for the driver's license or ID card is available online. But making changes in personal information, including address, is not permitted when renewing on the web, by telephone, or by mail. In accordance with R.S 32:412F, any Louisiana out-of-state military personnel is not subject to renewal until 60 days after returning or discharge. Note that nothing is permanent except a Mobility Impaired Handtag or Senior ID.

Elderly-Related Restrictions

None are reported.

Vehicle Insurance, Title and Registration Facts

Registration Renewal

Online renewal is available at the home web page. Motorcycles expire after four years, motor homes two years, boat and light utility trailers four years, trucks up to 6000 GVW four years, trucks 6001-10000 GVWR one or four years, trucks 10001+ GVWR one year, commercial vehicles one year, and passenger cars two years (one year if commercial plate). Trailers 1500 pounds or greater can be one year, four years or permanent.

New Residents

Non-residents must register vehicles immediately upon obtaining employment or establishing residence. When applying for a license plate for any motor vehicle, the applicant must have proof of the required liability insurance or other allowable substitute.

Inspections and Emissions Testing

Every automobile, truck, trailer, boat trailer and motorcycle operated on the highways of this state must have a current motor vehicle safety inspection sticker. Testing a vehicle for its emissions is part of the annual safety inspection of the vehicles in Louisiana. The City of New Orleans, the City of Kenner and the City of Westwego have their own inspection programs. Also there is now an Inspection and Maintenance (I/M) Program for the five parishes of Ascension, East Baton Rouge, Iberville, Livingston, and West Baton Rouge.

Passenger Plate Facts

There is one plate with one decal (YR). The state indicates there is no coding designation on the plates to indicate the parish of issuance.. When a vehicle is sold the plate does not remain with the car, it is destroyed by the dealer or returned to the state, except for very special circumstances. If one is going to cancel the liability insurance on the vehicle the license plate must be surrendered within 10 days from the date of the cancellation notice to avoid a fee.

Insurance and Financial Responsibility

Louisiana has a compulsory insurance law but not a no-fault insurance

provision. Minimum financial responsibility limits are $15,000/$30,000/$25,000 for vehicles with a gross vehicle weight of 20,000 pounds or under. Vehicles with a GVW of 20,001 to 50,000 pounds must have insurance coverage of at least $25,000/$50,000 bodily injury and $25,000 property damage or a single combined limit of no less than $75,000. The limits for vehicles with GVW over 50,000 pounds is at least $100,000/$300,000 bodily injury and $25,000 property damage or a combined single limit of $300,000. Proof of financial responsibility is required following an accident wherein a judgment is rendered, or for DWI convictions and refusals. SR-22 forms are used by the state.

When applying for a license plate for any motor vehicle, the applicant must have proof of the required liability insurance or other allowable substitute. Proof of insurance must be maintained in the vehicle when the vehicle is operational and must be presented any time a law enforcement officer requests that such proof be provided. If unable to provide the proof upon request, the vehicle's license plate will be seized and the vehicle may be impounded.

Withdrawal Sanctions, and Alcohol and Drug Testing

Alcohol and Chemical Testing Limits

Louisiana's illegal intoxication level for the purpose of convicting individuals of driving while intoxicated is .08 percent and above for non-commercial vehicles and .04 for commercial vehicles. In addition, individuals under the age of 21 can be convicted for underage driving while intoxicated with a .02 to . 079 percent intoxication level, but will be charged with driving while intoxicated if they test at or over the .08 level. Blood, urine, and breath tests are all permissible for measurement purposes. Louisiana has an administrative per se suspension as well as conviction-based suspensions for driving while intoxicated or underage driving while intoxicated. The crime of operating a vehicle while intoxicated is the operating of any motor vehicle, aircraft, water craft, vessel, or other means of conveyance.

Suspensions and Revocations

The state is in compliance with the federally mandated disqualifications on CDLs per MCSIA. See the Appendix for details.

Driving While License Suspended ....Suspension extended for one year.
Driving Under the Influence (at any age)
    First Conviction............................. .... One-year suspension; SR-22 or bond required.
    Second Conviction................................ ....Two-year suspension; SR-22 or bond required.
    Third or Subsequent Conviction... ....Three-year suspension; SR-22 or bond required.
Refusal to Submit to a Chemical Test
    First Conviction .... Six-month suspension.
    Second or Subsequent Conviction .... One and one-half-year suspension.
Vehicular Negligent Injury 1st ....One-year suspension.
Vehicular Negligent Injury 2nd .... Two-year suspension.
Vehicular Negligent Injury 3rd.......... .... Three-year suspension.

Driving Privileges Will be Suspended or Revoked for Any of the Following Violations
- Committing an Offense in Another State, if Committed in LA Would be Punishable by Suspension or Revocation
- Failure to Answer Traffic Violation Charge
- Failure to Comply with Financial Responsibility Law
- Failure to Maintain Liability Insurance
- Felony Conviction While Operating Motor Vehicle (Two years)
- Habitual Offender
- Hit & Run (Two years)
- Homicide Committed While Operating a Motor Vehicle, Manslaughter, Negligent Homicide, Felony with MV Used (All are two year suspensions)
- Three Convictions for Reckless Driving in Twelve Months (Two years)
- Violation of License Restrictions

Ignition Interlock and Interlock Hardship

Any restricted driver's license issued on or after August 15, 2007 for a Refusal/Submit, DWI or Vehicular Negligent Injury, including underlying Driving Under Suspension convictions, requires an ignition interlock device to be installed in the vehicle being driven prior to the issuance of an interlock hardship.

Reinstatement Requirements

Suspension   Expiration of mandatory suspension period; SR-22 for DWI convictions/refusals; payment of reinstatement fee.
Revocation   Expiration of mandatory revocation period; payment of reinstatement fee.
Note: Any reinstatement processed on or after August 15, 2007, regardless of the offense/conviction date, which requires an ignition interlock to be installed as a condition of reinstatement will be required for no less than 6 months or for the length of original suspension period, whichever is longer. If an interlock hardship was issued during the course of the suspension period, credit will be given for time the interlock was installed.

Record Access: Laws, Rules, and Forms

Note: This Section Applies to Both Driver and Vehicle Records.

Governing Statutes and Rules

Laws and Statutes: www.legis.state.la.us/lss/tsrssearch.htm
Policies and Procedures: http://dpsweb.dps.louisiana.gov/omv1.nsf/
Louisiana does not specifically enumerate the exceptions of the federal statute, but Louisiana states "the purpose of its statute is to implement the federal Driver's Privacy Protection Act and to substantially comply with the DPPA." Thus, the state refers to US Code, Title 18 §2721 through 2725 and 350 of Public Law 106-69 as the reason for compliance with DPPA. For example this statement appears on the web page where one can obtain their own driving record online. There is no specific law or statute with this text.

Policy Statement Regarding Permissible Uses

The state adopted the 14 permissible uses as outlined in DPPA.

Request and Consent Forms

Driving Records: A two-sided form *Request for Louisiana Driver's License Information* must be completed. At present, the form is not available at the web page. If the requester states the purpose of the request abides by the law, signature of the subject is not required.
Vehicle Records: There is no required form. Businesses should submit written requests on letterhead, indicating the reason for the request. A signature is required, but it does not need to be notarized.

Vendor and Third Party Access Policy

The purchaser can not disseminate or publish the information obtained from the department on the Internet or permit another to do so. Approved online vendors who access records for other vendors (who are not online, etc.) may sell to a permissible end user; however, records of such transactions must be maintained for 5 years and these records must be made available to the Office of Motor Vehicles upon request.

Non-permissible Use Requests

No records, even record without personal information, are released to casual requesters if consent is not given by the subject.

Access to Driver-Related Records

Driving Records

General Information and Fees

Office of Motor Vehicles, Attn: ODR, PO Box 64886, Baton Rouge LA 70896, 225-925-6388.
Note that this agency often refers to a driving record as an ODR - which means Official Driving Record. Use of *Request for Louisiana Driver's License Information Form* is required. Note this form cannot be downloaded from the web. This requires signed release of subject. The current fee for a driving record is $15.00, $6.00 electronically for approved requesters and businesses, and $17.00 via the web for license holders. The fee for a copy of a driver license application or basic driver license information is $5.00 per record.

In-Person – Office of Motor Vehicles, 7979 Independence Blvd, Baton Rouge 70806. The state charges for "no record found" reports. Records may also be requested from the Motor Vehicle Offices in Alexandria, Lake Charles, Monroe, Baton Rouge, or Shreveport.

Mail – Requests mailed to the state are processed in approximately ten working days. The driver's license number, name, date of birth, and race/sex are needed when ordering. The fee must accompany each request and use of a special form is requested.

Electronic – The online subscription system is offered only to approved high volume, ongoing requesters. The minimum order requirement is 2,000 requests per month. Users must post a bond or submit a deposit; thereafter, the state bills monthly. Users also must pass background checks and vetting. The fee is $6.00 per record. The DPS charges for no record found reports. Inquiries can be made between 7:00 am and 9:30 pm daily. Requests are processed interactively; batch retrieval is not available. Network protocols will be disclosed when contract is approved. The driver's address is included as part of the record. Only the driver's license number is required when ordering.
For more information, contact Ms. Tammy LeBlanc, Executive Staff Officer, DPS USEC's Office MFN, PO Box 66614, Baton Rouge, LA 70896-6614, 225-925-6032.
There is a second online system designed for the license holder. See *By Person of Record* below.

Bulk – Requests for bulk purchase are handled in accordance with the DPPA. All requesters must address written inquires to both the Director of Information Services for the Department of Public Safety as well as to the Undersecretary's Office within the Office of Management and Finance. For detailed information on the requirements, it is suggested to contact Ms. Tammy LeBlanc, Executive Staff Officer, DPS USEC's Office MFN, PO Box 66614, Baton Rouge, LA 70896-6614, 225-925-6032.

By Person of Record – LA drivers may obtain their driving record by mail as described above. A walk-in requester may view his/her own record for free.
An individual may view and print his/her driving record at https://omv.dps.state.la.us/pp_odr/odr.asp. The cost is $17.00; use of a credit card or debit card is required. This is an interactive system; the record can be printed immediately. Order requirements include name, address, DL number, DOB and license class. The most current version of the official driving record may be re-viewed and/or re-printed for 30 days after the record is purchased. Personal information is released since a disclaimer is used.

Notification/Monitoring Program

At present, Louisiana does not offer a monitoring system or notification program to employers or insurance companies to track incidents of drivers.

Crash Reports

Reporting – Any crash resulting in death or injury must be reported immediately to the nearest police department. SR claim forms maybe filed, but it is not required.
Record Access – Louisiana State Police, Traffic Records Unit - A27, PO Box 66614, Baton Rouge 70896, 225-925-6156.
Copies of crash reports can be purchased in person at any Louisiana State Police Troop or online at www.lsp.org/technical.html#traffic.
Online: The request requires first and last name, date of crash, and parish location of crash. The initial search is free and a limited preview is shown. To view and download a PDF version of the report, the fee is $8.50, use of credit card required. Records go back 5 years.
In Person or Mail: If purchasing a crash report at a Louisiana State Police Troop, a certified check, company check, or money order of $7.50 must accompany the request for all non-fatal crashes and $15.00 for all crashes resulting in a fatality. Crashes resulting in a fatality are only available at a local Louisiana State Police Troop. Personal checks, cash and credit cards will not be accepted at Troop locations.

Access to Vehicle-Related Records

General Information and Fees

Department of Public Safety and Corrections, Office of Motor Vehicles, Attn: Research, PO Box 64886, Baton Rouge LA 70896, 225-925-6146. Requesters must have a license plate number or VIN to do a search. The current fee for VIN, registration, lien or plate checks is $10.00 per record ($8.00 to search and $2.00 per page to certify). It can take 4 to 6 weeks before new records are ready for inquiry. If a personal or business check is sent, the requester's DL # must be included, or the request will be returned.

Note the state closed the walk-in counter; in person search requests are not accepted.

Mail, Fax – A written letter must be submitted with each mailed request. Requests can also be faxed to this office by pre-approved requesters. Turnaround time is 2 to 4 weeks. Personal checks are accepted, but either a DL # or federal tax ID # must be on the check.

Electronic – This service is not offered except to the contracted towing/recovery/storage related-industries.

Bulk – Purchase of statistical information, without personal identifiers, is permitted. VIN numbers disclose nothing about a vehicle buyer and are not considered private information as long the VIN is not coupled with owner information. The Department does not provided database dumps unless there is a valid reason, purpose, exemption, and the use is covered by DPPA. The request must be cleared by Legal. Minimum fees start at $500.00 plus cost of records.

By Person of Record – Counter service is available at the Public Service Counters at any county driver licensing location. A list of addresses is found on the web. Since 01/01/2009, counter service from the Headquarters was discontinued.

Access to Vessel-Related Records

General Information, Access and Fees

Department of Wildlife & Fisheries, PO 14796, Baton Rouge, LA 70898, 225-765-2898 www.wlf.louisiana.gov/boating. All motorized boats and all sail boats over 12 ft must be registered. On August 25, 2009, Louisiana became a titling state for certain boats and this agency is the authorizing entity for securing liens on titles. Until that date no titles were issued and lien information was found at the parish level. Now both locations (this agency and parishes) should be checked. The

release of records is subject stricter criteria than vehicle records. Consent must be given, including for insurance purposes. Records can be searched by name, hull number or registration number and from whom the boat was acquired. Records are indexed on computer since 1970. There is no fee; turnaround time is 7-10 days.

Copies of boat accidents are available for a $10.00 fee. See www.wlf.louisiana.gov/boating/boating-incident-reporting

Driving Record Content and Reciprocity

What's On or Not On the Driving Record

- All convictions (except non-moving violations) and the address are reported.
- Accidents that occurred on 08/15/2001or thereafter are displayed only if the individual's driving privileges are suspended because of non-compliance, such as failure to show proof of insurance. The accident is shown on the official record until compliance is met, then no longer displayed. If an accident is shown, it does not mean the driver was at fault or was given a citation.
- DUI (DWI), Vehicle Negligent Injury and Out-of-Service convictions remain on the record for 10 years from the date of conviction.
- An Underage DUI is kept 2-4 years or until all requirements have been met.
- Other major traffic convictions (suspendable/disqualifying) remain on the record for 5 years from the date of conviction.
- Minor traffic convictions remain on the record for 3 years from the date of conviction.
- Suspensions are kept on the record 5-10 years or as long as the suspension is active.
- State law permits driver school attendance in lieu of conviction.

Data Retention

Records of commercial drivers are purged based on the timetable per the MCSIA (see Appendix). In general, records for non-commercial drivers and for surrendered licenses are purged ten years for DWI related convictions, five years for "mandatory" convictions, and three years for accidents.

Court to Repository

Most courts report conviction information electronically to the state through a program administered by the Louisiana Supreme Court; however, some courts still send paper abstracts for key-in by OMV personnel or to the DPS Information Technology Center for upload from CD or by FTP. There is no effective law mandating the time period in which conviction information must be submitted to the state or added to the record.

State Reciprocity for Non-CDL Drivers

- Will suspend driver for unpaid out-of-state convictions.
- Record of new incoming driver is not shown on MVR.
- Out-of-state convictions are shown on MVR.
- Out-of-state accidents are not shown on MVR
- Convictions of out-of-state drivers are sent to the home state.
- Upon request, record is forwarded to new state upon surrender of license

License Classes, Restrictions, and Endorsements

License Classes– Commercial

Louisiana began issuing the CDL in December 1990.

Class A	Any single vehicle, or any combination of vehicles, with a GVWR of 26,001 pounds, or more, or towing a vehicle in excess of 10,000 pounds GVWR. This license also permits the operation of all other classes of vehicles.
Class B	Any single vehicle with a GVWR of 26,001 pounds or more, or towing a vehicle not exceeding 10,000 pounds GVWR without a movable joint in its frame. This license also permits the operation of Class C, D, and E vehicles.

| Class C | Any single vehicle with a GVWR of 26,001 pounds or less, or towing a vehicle not exceeding 10,000 pounds GVWR, or designed to transport sixteen or more passengers (including the driver), which are not within Class A or B, or is utilized for the transportation of hazardous materials. This license also permits the operation of Class D and E vehicles. |

License Classes– Non-Commercial

Class D	(Louisiana Commercial) Any single vehicle less than 26,001 pounds GVWR or any such vehicle designed or utilized for the transportation of passengers for hire or fee or which are not within the definition of vehicles within groups A, B, or C, including all vehicles with three or more axles or having GVW in excess of 10,000 pounds, and not utilized in the transportation of materials found to be hazardous. This license also permits the operation of Class E vehicles.
Class E	(Operators) Any single motor vehicle under 10,000 pounds GVWR, excluding motorcycles or motor scooters, not utilized to transport passengers for hire. This class includes all personal use vehicles, recreational vehicles, and farm vehicles operated within 150 miles of the owner's farm.
Class H	Mobility impaired picture identification card.
Class I	Personal Identification Card (no driving privileges).

Restrictions

00	No Restrictions	36	Extension Bar for Gas Pedal
1	Corrective Lens (Glasses/Contacts)	37	Dimmer Switch on Steering Column
2	Operating A Vehicle With Licensed Driver Only	38	Specific Driving Route Must Accompany License
3	Using Left Outside Rearview Mirror	39	Light Traffic in The Parish Of Residence Only
4	Eyes Cannot Be Improved	40	Wearing Of Artificial Limb
5	Automatic Transmission	41	Inside and Outside Rearview Mirror
6	Power Steering	42	Left and Right Rearview Mirrors
7	Cycle Endorsement	43	Specific Visual for CDL
8	Daytime Driving Only	44	Eyeglasses/Contacts, Left Outside Rearview Mirror Eyes Cannot Be Improved
9	Special Restrictions or 4+ Restrictions Used (**Note:** No longer used, converted to code 60)	45	Eyeglasses/Contacts, Left Outside Rearview Mirror, Eyes Cannot Be Improved, Daytime Driving Only
10	Hearing Cannot Be Improved	46	Restricted To Driving A Vehicle Equipped With Automatic Transmission, Power Steering, Mechanical Turn Signals, Hand Controls, Extension Bar For Gas Pedal
11	Must Wear Hearing Aid		
12	Restricted To No More Than a 5 Mile Radius Of Home	47	CDL Waiver for Farm Related Service Industries
13	Restricted To No More Than a 10 Mile Radius Of Home	48	Light Traffic Only
14	Restricted To No More Than a 15 Miles Radius Of Home	49	Air Over-Hydraulic Brake System
15	Restricted To No More Than a 20 Mile Radius Of Home	50	Hardship Restricted License
16	Restricted To No More Than a 25 Mile Radius Of Home	51	Interlock Device
17	Restricted To Rural Area Only	52	Intra-State Only (Under the Age Of 21)
18	No Interstate Highway Driving	53	Intra-State Only (Medical Condition)
19	Driving Only Within Parish of Principal Residence	54	Air-Brakes Restriction
20	Restricted To Driving A Maximum of 50 MPH	55	No 18 Wheelers
21	Restricted To Driving A Maximum of 45 MPH	57	Interlock/Condition of Reinstatement
22	Restricted To Driving A Maximum of 40 MPH	58	FMCSA Medical Variance Document Required (CDL)
23	Restricted To Driving A Maximum of 35 MPH	60	Restriction Card
24	Vision Medical Exam Required Every 6 Months	61	Intermediate License
25	Vision Medical Exam Required Every Year	62	Front/Side Fender Mirrors
26	Vision Medical Exam Required Every 2 Years	63	Class B Passenger Endorsement (CDL)
27	Complete Medical Exam Required Every 6 Months	64	Class C Passenger Endorsement (CDL)
28	Complete Medical Exam Required Every Year	65	School Bus Only
29	Complete Medical Exam Required Every 2 Years	66	Bioptic Lens Required
30	Driving Only Between the Hours Of 9:00 am To 3:00 pm	70	Loss of Vision in Left Eye
31	Seat Cushion Required	71	Loss of Vision in Right Eye
32	Accelerator Pedal on Left Side	72	Vision Medical Every 4 Years
33	Mechanical Turn Signals		
34	Hand Controls Required		
35	Brake and Accelerator Controls Required		

Endorsements

T	Double/Triple Trailers	P	Passenger	L	Restricted To No Airbrakes
H	Hazardous Materials	S	School Bus	M	Motorcycles
N	Tank	K	Restricted To Driving Intrastate Only	E	Emergency Endorsement
X	Combination Tank and Hazmat				

Notes

- If a driver with an "H" endorsement receives a second conviction of any combination of reckless and/or negligent violations, the hazmat "H" endorsement will be permanently revoked. Once the hazmat endorsement is removed, it cannot be added back in Louisiana.
- If a driver with an "X" endorsement receives a second conviction of any combination of reckless and/or negligent violations, the "X" endorsement will be permanently revoked. The driver may, however, keep his tank "N" endorsement. Once the hazmat endorsement is removed, it cannot be added back in Louisiana.
- If a driver with an "S" endorsement receives a DWI or Refusal while operating any vehicle, the "S" endorsement will be revoked for ten (10) years.

Important Abbreviations and Codes
Common Abbreviations and Interpretations

BINDER	Licensee provided proof of insurance, insurance binder valid for 90 days only
CAN/CANC	License canceled due to new state of residency/license issuance or parents/guardian of minor requested license be canceled
COMP SEC	Compulsory insurance required by law
CRIM/REFUS	Crime of refusal
DAYS DISQ	Indicates number of days disqualified
DISC 3	Disclosure of personal information prohibited per PDDA
DISQ/PERM	Indicates the individual's driving privileges to operate a commercial vehicle has been withdrawn (disqualified)
DRIVER	Accident involvement when individual was driving someone else's vehicle
DUP	Duplicate license
ENDR	Endorsement
EX/EXP	Indicates license has expired
FATAL	Fatality in accident
FATALITY	Someone was killed in an accident
FEE	Reinstatement fee required following suspension or revocation
FEE ONLY	Only a fee is required to reinstate driving privileges
FILED	SR-22 insurance certificate on file
GP STATUS	The following appear after GP STATUS and deal with the Gun Permit Status for an Individual

	DENIED	Permit denied
	EXPIRED	Permit expired
	INVALID	Permit no valid
	ON-HOLD	Permit applied for, pending further investigation
	PENDING	Permit applied for
	REVOKED	Permit revoked
	SUSPEND	Permit suspended
	VALID	Individual has valid permit

HARDSHIP	Hardship license issued
HD or HS	Hardship license issued
IMPOUNDED	Vehicle impounded for operating without proper evidence of liability insurance in vehicle
INDEF	Indefinite suspension
INJURY	Someone was injured in accident
INS	Insurance (individual's vehicle insured)
INSURANCE SUSPENDED	SR-22 required
INSTALLMENT	Installment agreement entered into in reference to an accident
INST AGR	Installment agreement entered into in reference to an accident
INV	Invalid
MIN	Minor
MIR	Mail-in drivers license renewal program
NO ENTRIES	No moving violations appear on the official driving record
N/R	No moving violations appear on the official driving record
NI	Indicates the individual's license is blocked against renewal or re-issuance. Does not mean a suspension is imposed. Used for record keeping purposes, showing when money is owed.
NSF	Driving privileges suspended as a result of dishonored check (insufficient funds)
OTHER	Individual involved in accident and complied in some other manner than having insurance
OWNER	Someone else is driving individual's vehicle
PARISH	Parish in which individual stopped for chemical test
PEN/PEND/PND	Pending (suspension is pending)
PENDING	Pending (suspension is pending)
PER STATUS	Status of individual's personal driving privileges
PETITION	Petition filed
PRIV	Operating private vehicle
PROPERTY	Property damage only (accident involvement)
PUL or PICKUP DRIVERS LICENSE	
	Indicates the individual's driving privileges are withdrawn for an accident or a moving violation such as a DUI, Refusal, Submit, etc. However, the Dept. is not in possession of the individual's license or a non-possession affidavit nor has his license expired. When the individual complies with this requirement the "PUL" will be updated to indicate "SUS" indicates that the driving privileges have been or will be withdrawn.
REI	Driving and/or registering privileges reinstated
RELEASE	Individual released of all claims by other party(s) involved in accident
SEC	Individual posted security due to involvement in accident
SUS/AF	Indicates a suspension based on a failure to appear in court for a traffic offense. This offense does not show on the driving record as state statutes prohibit it from being shown, the suspension shows in the master only.
SUS/DI	Indicates a suspension for a moving violation such as DWI, Refusal, Submit, habitual Offender, School Bus violations and Revocation violations.
SUS/FR	Indicates a suspension following an accident in which the individual provided no evidence of insurance or other compliance. It

may also indicate a suspension for failure to file the required SR-22 as a result of a DWI or judgment filed against him.

TEMP	Temporary permit issued in lieu of picture license
TESS	Motor Carrier Safety Violation - individual must contact State Police Motor Carrier Safety at (225) 295-8550. License is blocked against renewal or re-issuance - does not mean suspension
VAL/MLTRY	Licensee is in military service and driver's license is valid even though it displays an expired expiration date

Court Codes

1	City Court	4	Parish Court	7	Juvenile
2	Judicial District Court	5	U.S. District Court	8	Non-conviction-administrative action
3	Mayor Court	6	Out-of-state	9	Hardship

Conviction Table with Abbreviations and ACD

Louisiana provides a shortened or abbreviated description of each conviction. Below, you will find these abbreviated versions listed in alphabetical order and cross referenced to the full description and matching ACD Code. **The state does not have a point system.**

About the Note Column

All violations are displayed on the driver history record internally; however, they may or may not be displayed on the official driving record history, depending on state statutes. A suspension flag displayed in the status field is indication the person's driving privileges are suspended in the State of Louisiana. The **Note Column** indicates the following:

- (1) If violation is not displayed on the official driving record history.
- (2) If violation is not displayed on the official driving record history. However, suspension flag is displayed in personal status field on the official driving record history.
- (3) If violation is not displayed on the official driving record if conviction is pending.

Abbreviation	Description	ACD	Note
	Withdrawals, Non-ACD	W00	
3 Reckless	Three Reckless Driving Offenses	W00	
Accident Violation - Fatal	Violation resulting in fatal accident	U31	
Brakes Used Improperly	Brakes used improperly	E71	(1)
Careless Driving	Careless driving	M81	
Carrying Unsecured Passengers-open Area	Carrying unsecured passengers in open area of vehicle	F05	(1)
Child Restraint Used Improperly	Child or youth restraint not used properly as required	F02	(1)
Child Support	Failure to make required payment of child support	D51	(2)
Coasting	Coasting (operating with gears disengaged)	N80	
Controlled Substance	Motor Vehicle used in the commission of a felony involving manufacturing, distributing, or dispensing a control substance	A50	(1)
Crime of Refusal	Crime of Refusal	W00	
Defective Brakes	Defective brakes	E31	(1)
Defective HAZMAT Devices	Defective HAZMAT safety devices	E33	(1)
Defective lights	Defective lights	E34	(1)
Defective School Bus Equipment	Defective school bus equipment	E36	(1)
Defective Tires	Defective tires	E37	(1)
Denial of Driving Privileges for Adult	Denial of Driving Privileges (For Adult)	W00	(2)
Denial of Driving Privileges For Youth under 19	Denial of Driving Privileges (For Youth under 19	W00	(2)
Departmental Driving Under Suspension	Department Action	W00	(2)
DOE Disciplinary	DOE Disciplinary Suspensions	W00	(2)
Drag Racing	Speed contest (racing) on road open to traffic	S95	
Drinking Alcohol	Drinking alcohol while operating a vehicle	A26	
Driver-Interlock Violation	Driver violation of ignition interlock or immobilization device	A41	(1)
Driver's View Obstructed	Driver's view obstructed	D70	(1)
Driving CMV No CDL	Driving a CMV without obtaining a CDL	B56	
Driving on Wrong Side	Driving on wrong side	N70	
Driving While Barred	Driving while license barred	B21	
Driving While Canceled	Driving while license canceled	B22	
Driving While Denied	Driving while license denied	B23	
Driving While Disqualified	Driving while license disqualified	B24	
Driving While Impaired	Driving while impaired - ability definitely impaired	A25	
Driving While Revoked	Driving while license revoked	B25	
Driving While Suspended	Driving while license suspended	B26	
Driving While Withdrawn	Driving while license withdrawn	B20	
Driving Wrong Side - Divided Highway	Driving on wrong side of divided highway	N71	
Driving Wrong Side - Undivided Road	Driving on wrong side of undivided street or road	N72	
Driving Wrong Way	Driving wrong way	N60	
Driving Wrong Way - Divided Highway	Driving wrong way on divided highway	N62	
Driving Wrong Way - One Way	Driving wrong way on one way street or road	N63	

Abbreviation	Description	ACD	Note
Driving Wrong Way - Rotary	Driving wrong way at rotary intersection	N61	
DUI - Alcohol	Driving under the influence of alcohol	A21	
DUI - Alcohol or Drugs	Driving under the influence of alcohol or drugs	A20	
DUI - Alcohol/Drugs	Driving under the influence of alcohol and drugs	A23	(1)
DUI - Drugs	Driving under the influence of drugs	A22	
DUI - Medication	Driving under the influence of medication not intended to intoxicate	A24	
DUI (detail	Driving under the influence of alcohol with BAC at (detail field required)	A11	
DUI .04	Driving under the influence of alcohol with BAC at least .04 but not greater than .079	A04	
DUI .08	Driving under the influence of alcohol with BAC at or over .08	A08	
DUI .10	Driving under the influence of alcohol with BAC at or over .10	A10	
Equipment Used Improperly	Equipment used improperly or obstructed	E70	(1)
Evading Police	Fleeing or evading police or roadblock	U01	
Expired or no License	Expired or no driver license (includes DL, CDL, and Instruction Permit)	B51	
Failed DL Exam	Unable to pass DL test(s) or meet qualifications	W20	(2)
Failed to File Insurance	Failed to file insurance certification	B64	(1)
Failed to File Medical	Failed to file medical certification/disability information	B65	(1)
Failed to File SR-22	Failed to file future proof of Financial Responsibility	B63	(1)
Failed to Report	Failed to file accident report	B61	(1)
Failure to Attend RR Course	Failure to Attend Safe DR course RR	W00	(2)
Failure to Cancel Signals	Failure to cancel directional signals	N41	(1)
Failure to Complete DL Requirement	Failure to Complete DL Requirement	W00	(2)
Failure to Dim Headlights	Failure to use headlight dimmer as required	E54	
Failure to Obey Barrier	Failure to obey barrier	M02	
Failure to Obey Construction Zone	Failure to obey construction or maintenance zone markers	M03	
Failure to Obey flagger	Failure to obey flagger	M04	
Failure to obey Lane Markings or Signal	Failure to obey lane markings or signal	M05	
Failure to Obey Police	Failure to obey police or peace officer	M08	
Failure to Obey Railroad Restrictions	For all drivers, failure to obey railroad-highway crossing restrictions no specifically noted in other railroad-highway grade crossing related codes	M09	
Failure to Obey Railroad Traffic Device/Officer	For all drivers, failure to obey traffic control device or the directions of an enforcement official at railroad-highway grade crossing	M10	
Failure to Obey Restricted Lane	Failure to obey restricted lane	M11	
Failure to Obey Safety Zone	Failure to obey safety zone	M12	
Failure to Obey School Guard	Failure to obey school crossing guard	M13	
Failure to Obey Signal/Lights	Failure to obey traffic signal or lights	M16	
Failure to obey Stop Sign	Failure to obey Stop Sign	M15	
Failure to Obey Traffic Sign	Failure to obey traffic sign	M17	
Failure to Obey Warning Light	Failure to obey warning light or flasher	M18	
Failure to Obey Yield Sign	Failure to obey yield sign	M19	
Failure to Pay Criminal Fines	Failure to Pay Criminal Fines	W00	
Failure to Pay Fine	Failure to make required payment of fine and costs	D53	(1)
Failure to Pay Tax	Failure to pay required tax	W00	(2)
Failure to Pay/Make Installments	Failure to pay for damages or make installment payment	D37	(1)
Failure to Post Security/Release	Failure to post security or obtain release from liability	D38	(1)
Failure to Signal – Lane Change/Turn	Failure to signal lane change or turn	N43	
Failure to Signal - Passing	Failure to signal intention	N42	
Failure to Slow Down-Railroad	For drivers who are not required to always stop, failure to slow down at a railroad-highway grade crossing and check that tracks are clear of approaching train	M20	
Failure to Stop - Before Railroad Track	For drivers who are always required to stop, failure to stop as required before driving onto railroad-highway grade crossing	M22	
Failure to Stop – Railroad Track Not Clear	For drivers who are not required to always stop, failure to stop before reaching tracks at a railroad-highway grade crossing when the tracks are not clear	M21	
Failure to Stop – Unsigned Intersection	Failure to stop - basic rule at unsigned intersection or when entering roadway from private driveway, alley, etc.	M25	
Failure to surrender HAZMAT	Failure to surrender HAZMAT endorsement as required by the USA Patriot Act	W09	
Failure to Use Brakes	Failure to use brakes	E51	(1)
Failure to Use Equipment	Failure to use equipment as required	E50	(1)
Failure to use HAZMAT Devices	Failure to use HAZMAT safety devices as required	E53	(1)
Failure to Use Lights	Failure to use lights as required	E55	(1)
Failure to Use School Bus	Failure to use school bus safety equipment as required	E56	(1)
Failure to Use Snow Tires/Chains	Failure to use snow tires or chains as required	E57	(1)
Failure to Yield	Failure to yield right of way (FTY ROW)	N01	
Failure to Yield – Animal Rider/Vehicle	FTY ROW to animal rider of animal-drawn vehicle	N02	
Failure to Yield - Crosswalk	FTY ROW at crosswalk	N20	

Abbreviation	Description	ACD	Note
Failure to Yield - Cyclist	FTY ROW to cyclist	N03	
Failure to Yield - Emergency Vehicle	FTY Row to emergency vehicle (i.e. ambulance, fire equipment, police, etc.	N04	
Failure to Yield - Funeral/ Parade	FTY ROW to funeral procession, procession or parade	N05	
Failure to Yield – Overtaking Vehicle	FTY ROW to overtaking vehicle	N07	
Failure to Yield - Pedestrian	FTY ROW to pedestrian (includes handicapped or blind)	N08	
Failure to Yield - Rotary	FTY ROW at Rotary	N21	
Failure to Yield – School Bus	FTY ROW to school bus	N09	
Failure to Yield - Stop Sign	FTY ROW at stop sign	N22	
Failure to Yield – Traffic Sign	FTY ROW at traffic sign	N23	
Failure to Yield – Traffic Signal	FTY ROW at traffic signal	N24	
Failure to Yield - Turning	FTY ROW when turning	N31	
Failure to Yield – Unsigned Intersection	FTY ROW at unsigned intersection	N25	
Failure to Yield - Vehicle	FTY ROW to other vehicle	N06	
Failure to Yield – Vehicle Warning	FTY ROW when warning displayed on other vehicle	N30	
Failure to Yield - Yield Sign	FTY ROW at yield sign	N26	
Fake license	Manufacture or make false driver license (includes DL, CDL and Instruction Permit)	D10	(1)
Felony	Using a motor vehicle in connection with a felony (not traffic offense)	U03	
Felony	Using a motor vehicle to aid and abet a felon	U05	(1)
Financial Responsibility	Failure to comply with financial responsibility law	D35	(1)
Following Improperly	Following improperly	M30	
Following Improperly-Overtaking	Failure to leave sufficient distance for overtaking by other vehicles	M31	
Following to Closely	Following to closely	M34	
Following Unlawfully- Emergency Vehicle	Following emergency vehicle unlawfully	M32	
Following Unlawfully- Fire Equipment	Following Fire equipment unlawfully	M33	
FTA - Written Promise, In-lieu or OOS	Failure to appear for trial or court appearance	D45	(2)
FTA-DOTD, TESS/MC	Failure to answer a citation, pay fines, penalties and/or costs related to the original violation	D56	(2)
Habitual Offender	Accumulation of convictions (including point systems and/or being judged a habitual offender or violator	W01	(2)
Hit and Run	Hit and run - failure to stop and render aid after accident	B01	
Hit and Run - Fatal accident	Hit and run - failure to stop and render aid after accident - Fatal after accident	B02	
Hit and Run - Injury	Hit and run - failure to stop and render aid after accident - Personal injury accident	B03	
Hit and Run - Property	Hit and run-failure to stop and render aid after accident - Property damage accident	B04	
Illegal Operation	Illegal operation of emergency vehicle	U21	
Illegal Possession-Alcohol	Illegal possession of alcohol	A31	(1)
Illegal Possession-Drugs	Illegal possession of drugs (controlled substances)	A33	(1)
Imminent Hazard	Imminent Hazard	W70	
Impeding Traffic - Stop Stand/Park /	Stopping, standing, or parking: obstructing or impeding traffic	F34	(1)
Improper Backing	Improper backing	N82	
Improper Class/Endorsement	Improper classification or endorsement on driver license (includes DL, CDL, and Instruction Permit)	B91	
Improper Lane	Failure to keep in proper lane	M41	
Improper Lane/Location	Improper lane or location	M40	
Improper Lane/Location -	Improper lane or location - road shoulder, ditch or sidewalk	M58	
Improper Lane/Location - bike Lane	Improper lane or location - in bicycle lane	M47	
Improper Lane/Location - Center Line	Improper lane or location - straddling center line(s)	M61	
Improper Lane/Location - Entrance/Exit	Improper lane or location -entrance/exit ramp or way	M46	
Improper Lane/Location - Fire Hose	Improper lane or location - on fire hose	M56	
Improper Lane/Location - Limited Access	Improper lane or location - limited access highway	M50	
Improper Lane/Location - Occupied Lane	Improper lane or location - in occupied lane	M48	
Improper Lane/Location - Oncoming Traffic	Improper lane or location - oncoming traffic lane	M57	
Improper Lane/Location - Rail/Streetcar Track	Improper lane or location - on rail or streetcar tracks	M55	
Improper Lane/Location - Restricted	Improper lane or location - in HOV or restricted lane	M49	
Improper Lane/Location - Slower Lane	Improper lane or location - slower vehicle lane	M60	
Improper Lane/Location - Turn Lane	Improper lane or location - traveling in turn (or center) lane	M62	
Improper Lane/Location -Crosser	Improper lane or location - crossover	M44	
Improper Lane/Location -Crosswalk	Improper lane or location - crosswalk	M45	
Improper Lane/Location -Median	Improper lane or location - median	M51	
Improper Left Turn	Making Improper left turn	N53	
Improper Operation MC	Improper operation of or riding on a motorcycle	F06	

Abbreviation	Description	ACD	Note
Improper Passing	Improper passing	M70	
Improper Passing - Direction Restriction	Passing in violation of opposite direction restriction	M72	
Improper Passing - Distance/Visibility	Passing with insufficient distance or visibility	M77	
Improper Passing - Hill/curve	Passing on hill or curve	M74	
Improper Passing - Prohibited	Passing where prohibited	M76	
Improper Passing - School Bus	Passing school bus displaying warning not to pass	M75	
Improper Passing - Sign/ Pavement Restriction	Passing in violation of posted sign or pavement restriction	M71	
Improper Passing - Wrong side	Passing on wrong side	M73	
Improper Position -Turning	Improper position for turning	N52	
Improper Right Turn	Making Improper right turn	N54	
Improper Signal	Failure to use or improper signal	N40	
Improper Starting	Improper starting	N83	
Improper Turn	Improper turn	N50	
Improper Turn Around	Making Improper turn around (not U turn)	N55	
Improper Turning	Improper method of turning	N51	
Improper U Turn	Making Improper U turn	N56	
Improper/Erratic Lane Changes	Improper or erratic (unsafe) lane changes	M42	
Inability to control vehicle	Inability to control vehicle	D72	
Inattentive Driving	Inattentive driving	M82	
Insufficient Undercarriage Clearance - Railroad	For all drivers, failing to negotiate a railroad-highway grade crossing because of insufficient undercarriage clearance	M24	
Insurance Violation	Failure to maintain required liability insurance	D36	(1)
Interlock Required	Ignition interlock violation	W00	
Leaving the Scene	Leaving accident scene before police arrive	B05	
Leaving the Scene - Fatal	Leaving accident scene before police arrive - Fatal accident	B06	
Leaving the Scene - Injury	Leaving accident scene before police arrive - Personal injury accident	B07	
Leaving the scene - Property	Leaving accident scene before police arrive - Property damage accident	B08	
Limited DL Condition Violation	Violate limited license conditions	D27	
Major CMV Offense - 2nd	The accumulation of 2 or more major offenses	W40	
Major CMV Offense after Reinstatement	An additional major offense after reinstatement	W41	
MC Safety Equipment Used Improperly	Motorcycle safety equipment not used properly as required	F03	(1)
Medical Statement	Physician's or specialists' report recommended	W15	(2)
Misdemeanor	Using a motor vehicle in connection with a misdemeanor (not traffic offense)	U04	(1)
Misrepresentation-DL Application	Misrepresentation of identity or other facts on application for driver license (includes DL, CDL, and Instruction Permit)	D02	(1)
Misrepresentation-Obtain alcohol	Misrepresentation of identity or other facts to obtain alcohol	D06	(1)
Multiple License	Possess multiple driver licenses (includes DL, CDL, and Instruction Permit)	D07	(1)
NDR Withdrawal	NDR Withdrawal OOS/DL Compact	W00	(2)
Negligent CMV Fatal	Causing a fatality through the negligent operation of a CMV	U10	
Negligent Driving	Negligent driving	M83	
Negligent Homicide CMV	Negligent homicide while operating a CMV	U09	
Negligent Injury	Negligent Injury	W00	
NSF	NSF	W00	
OOS Refusal	Refused Alcohol Analysis/OOS DL	W00	(2)
OOS Submit	Submit Test/OOS DL	W00	(2)
OOS Submit Underage	Submit Underage/OOS DL	W00	(2)
Open Container	Possession of open alcohol container	A35	(1)
Operate CMV Required	Operate CMV w/o CDL	W00	
Operating improperly-Drowsy	Operating a motor vehicle improperly because of drowsiness	D74	
Operating without Equipment	Operating without equipment as required by law	E01	(1)
Operating without HAZMAT Placards/Markings	Operating without HAZMAT placards/markings as required by law	E04	(1)
Operating without HAZMAT Safety Equipment	Operating without HAZMAT Safety equipment as required by law	E03	
Operating without lights	Operating without lights as required by law	E05	
Operating without School Bus Equipment	Operating without school bus equipment as required by law	E06	(1)
Operation without Brakes	Operating without brakes as required by law	E02	(1)
Operator Disabled	Operating a motor vehicle improperly due to physical or mental disability	D75	
Out of Service Order	Driving while out of service order is in effect and transporting 16 or more passengers, including the driver and/or transporting hazardous materials that require a placard	B19	
Out of Service Order	General, driving while out of service order is in effect	B27	
Out of Service Order - 2nd	The accumulation of 2 out of service order general violations within 10 years	W50	
Out of Service Order - 3rd +	The accumulation of 3 or more out of service order general violations within 10 years	W52	

Abbreviation	Description	ACD	Note
Out of Service Order HZ -2nd	The accumulation of 2 out of service order general violations within 10 years while transporting 15 or more passengers, including the driver and or transporting hazardous materials that require a placard	W51	
Perjury	Perjury about the operation of a motor vehicle	D78	(1)
Physical or Mental Disability	Physical or mental disability	W14	(2)
Purchase/Poss Alcohol < 21	Purchase/Possession alcohol < 21	W00	(2)
Purchase/Poss Alcohol < 21	Purchase alcohol for < 21	W00	(2)
Radar Detector Prohibited	Use of radar or laser detector prohibited by law	E23	(1)
Railroad Violation - 2nd	Two accumulated RRGC (railroad grade crossing) violations within three years	W60	
Railroad Violation - 3rd	Three or more accumulated subsequent RRGC violations within three years	W61	
Ran Off Road	Ran off road	M43	
Reckless Driving	Reckless driving	M84	
Reckless/Careless/ Negligent Driving	Reckless, careless, or negligent driving	M80	
Recommended by Court	Recommended by Court	W00	
Refusal	Refused to submit to test for alcohol - Implied Consent Law	A12	
Refusal to Reveal Identity – fatal or injury	Failure to reveal identity after fatal or person injury accident	B14	(1)
Resisting Arrest	Resisting arrest	U02	(1)
Restriction Violation	Violate restrictions of driver license (includes DL, CDL, and Instruction Permit)	D29	
Seatbelts used Improperly	Seatbelts not used properly as required	F04	(1)
Serious CMV Violation - 2nd	Two serious violations within three years	W30	
Serious CMV Violation - 3rd	Three serious violations within three years	W31	
Speed Erratic	Operating at erratic or suddenly changing speeds	S97	
Speed Less than Minimum	Speed less than minimum	S96	
Speeding	Speeding	S93	
Speeding - Conditions	Prima Facie speed violation or driving too fast for conditions	S94	
Speeding - Wasting Fuel	Speeding on freeway ("Wasting Fuel)	S98	
Speeding (01-05 MPH)	01-05> Speed limit (detail optional)	S01	
Speeding (01-10 MPH)	01-10> Speed limit (detail optional)	S51	
Speeding (06-10 MPH)	06-10> Speed limit (detail optional)	S06	
Speeding (15+ MPH)	Speeding 15 mph or more above speed limit (detail optional)	S15	
Speeding (16-20 MPH)	16-20> Speed limit (detail optional)	S16	
Speeding (21-25 MPH)	21-25> Speed limit (detail optional)	S21	
Speeding (21-30 MPH)	21-30> Speed limit (detail optional)	S71	
Speeding (26-30 MPH)	26-30> Speed limit (detail optional)	S26	
Speeding (31-35 MPH)	31-35> Speed limit (detail optional)	S31	
Speeding (31-40 MPH)	31-40> Speed limit (detail optional)	S81	
Speeding (36-40 MPH)	36-40> Speed limit (detail optional)	S36	
Speeding (41+ MPH)	41+ > Speed limit (detail optional)	S41	
Speeding (41+ MPH)	41+ > Speed limit (detail optional)	S91	
Speeding - details "Posted/Actual"	Speeding - Speed Limit and actual speed (detail required	S92	
SR22 Insurance	SR22 Insurance	W00	(2)
Stopping on Railroad Track	For all drivers, failing to have sufficient space to drive completely through the railroad-highway grade crossing without stopping	M23	
Submit .04+	Administrative Per Se for BAC of at least .04 but not greater than .079	A94	(3)
Submit .08+	Administrative Per Se for BAC at or over .08	A98	(3)
Submit .10+	Administrative Per Se for BAC at or over .10	A90	(3)
Submit	Administrative Per Se for BAC at ____	A91	(3)
Theft of Fuel	Theft of Fuel	W00	(2)
Underage DUI .02+	Underage convicted of drinking and driving at .02 percent or higher BAC	A60	
Underage Submit .02+	Underage administrative per se drinking and driving at .02 % or higher BAC	A61	(1)
Unlawful Use of DL or Fraudulent DL	Possess or provide counterfeit or altered driver license (includes DL, CDL, Instruction Permit) or ID	B41	(1)
Unsafe Operation	Unsafe operation	N84	
Unsafe Vehicle	Unsafe condition of vehicle (no specified component)	F66	(1)
Unsatisfied Judgment	Unsatisfied judgment	D39	(1)
Use license Improperly	Show or use improperly - Driver license (includes DL, CDL, and Instruction Permit	D16	(1)
Vehicle Negligent Injury	Vehicle Negligent Injury	W00	
Vehicular Assault	Vehicular assault	U06	
Vehicular Feticide (xth Degree)	Vehicular Feticide	U28	
Vehicular Homicide	Vehicular homicide	U07	
Vehicular Manslaughter	Vehicular manslaughter	U08	
Wrong Signal	Giving wrong signal	N44	

Maine

Administration	Important Telephone and Web Contacts
Patty Morneault, Director of Driver License Svcs Garry Hinkley, Director of Vehicle Services Bureau of Motor Vehicles 29 State House Station Augusta 04333-0029 207-624-9000 www.maine.gov/sos/bmv/ **Motor Vehicle Laws and Rules** may be accessed from the home page. **State Statutes** are found at http://janus.state.me.us/legis/	Driver Licensing............................ 207-624-9000 x52114 Driver Records .... 207-624-9000 x52116 Financial Responsibility (SR-22) .. 207-624-9000 x52108 Commercial Driver License........... 207-624-9000 x52122 OUI.. 207-624-9000 x52104 Titles.. 207-624-9000 x52138 Registrations.................................. 207-624-9000 x52149 Commercial Registrations .... 207-624-9000 x52151 State Police.....................................207-624-7200 State Department of Insurance ....207-624-8475 Email questions to: sos.office@maine.gov

Driver's License Format, Issuance and Renewal

License Classes, Restrictions and Endorsements Appear After the Driving Record Content Section

License Format

The format is seven numbers. Maine reports there is no code or sequential arrangement which determines the characters of the license number.

Document Appearance

Maine integrated the current digital license design effective March 2011. The previous document was introduced in October 1999. It will take approximately 9 years to completely replace all drivers' licenses.

Current Documents

Security Characteristics: New technology and security features were added. The backside includes a 1-D barcode with a unique identification number and a 2-D bar code with all the information contained on the front of the card captured. Blue print on top middle indicates a cardholder over 21 years of age.

Position of Photo: Large photo on left edge, ghost portrait on right edge.

Minor Age Driver Locator: Drivers license and identification cards issued to individuals under 21 are issued in a vertical format. Red text will indicate "Under 18 until xx/xx/xx and "Under 21 Until xx/xx/xx". Vertically formatted credentials bear the title of the credential in red.

CDL Indicator: The words "CDL Operator" appears in blue lettering at the top right of license.

Previous Documents

Security Characteristics: Information on the front of the card is stored on a bar code on the rear. Heading is orange-ish with word "Maine" written in middle.

Position of Photo: Right edge; if an ID Card, then on left edge. A small ghost photo image is on the opposite side of photo, with an embedded hologram.

Minor Age Driver Locator: There is a red notation in the bottom center with "Under 21 Until xx/xx/xx".

CDL Indicator: The words "CDL Operator" appears in blue lettering under the Maine Banner.

Non-Photo License: Since 01/03, non-photo licenses are issued with the same format as the digital driver's license with the words "valid without photo" placed where the image would appear.

Issuance

Proof of Authorized Presence

Any resident seeking to **acquire or renew** a Maine driver license or non-driver ID card must provide documentary evidence of legal presence and residency. For a list of the acceptable documents to prove identity visit www.maine.gov/sos/bmv/licenses/legalpresence.htm.

Age Requirements

Maine's 3-step graduated drivers licensing system for new drivers who are under 18 years of age was introduced in September, 2003. The minimum age for an Intermediate License is 16 with approved driver education course. There are many driving restrictions with this license. A Learner's Permit is required for all new drivers. That person must hold the permit for 6 months before applying for a road test and is prohibited from using a cellular phone while operating with a permit. While driving, the permit holder must be accompanied by a licensed driver at least 20 years of age and has held a valid license for two years.

Proof of Authorized Presence

Individuals applying for a Maine driver license or non-driver ID card must establish that they are legally present in the U.S. and a resident of the State of Maine.

Residency

A non-resident's home-state license honored is on a reciprocal basis. A Maine license is required within thirty days of declaring or establishing residency.

Renewal

If age less than 65, then birth month of 6th year, photo license required; if age 65 or older, then birth month of 4th year, photo license required. In an effort to improve customer service and reduce wait times in regional branch offices, some license holders have been renewed for 8 years instead of 6. Renewals are available online for persons having already proven legal residency and legal presence. This service is available for any Maine licensed driver with an active license, motorcycle license or motor driven cycle restricted license and any holder of a Maine ID card. This service is not available for commercial driver license holders, driver's who require a vision test or drivers over 62. Driver keeps same number when renewing.

Active military personnel stationed out-of-state need not renew. Upon discharge, they must renew within 30 days.

Elderly-Related Restrictions

None, other than the shorter renewal period as mentioned above.

Vehicle Insurance, Title and Registration Facts

Registration Renewal

Vehicle registration renewal is available online for passenger vehicles, commercial vehicles, and non-excisable trailers if the town where the vehicle is garaged participates. Rapid Renewal may be accessed through https://www1.maine.gov/online/bmv/rapid-renewal/. Registrations not eligible to renew online include island use, emergency/coach, vehicles over 12,000 pounds GVW, apportioned, special mobile equipment, tractors, municipal and state vehicles which all must be renewed in person.

New Residents

Non-residents must register vehicles within thirty days of declaring or establishing residency.

Inspections and Emissions Testing

Maine requires an annual safety inspection on all vehicles. All vehicles in Cumberland County are subject to an Enhanced Auto Inspection.

Passenger Plate Facts

There are two plates in force with two decals (MO) (YR) on both plates. There is no coding on the plate designating the county of issuance. When a vehicle is sold the plates remain with seller.

About Motorcycle Registrations

Per a recent Maine law, all motorcycle registrations, issued on or after March 1, 2012, will expire on March 31st of 2013. Under this law, Maine Inspection Stations are required to issue a certificate of inspection and an official inspection sticker for each motorcycle. Motorcycle registration stickers will include the month and year of expiration and must be placed in the upper right corner of the plate.

Insurance and Financial Responsibility

Maine has a compulsory insurance law, but does not require no-fault insurance. Minimum financial responsibility limits are $50,000/100,000/25,000. Proof is required at registration, renewal, after an accident and after certain violations. Maine uses SR-22 forms.

Withdrawal Sanctions, and Alcohol and Drug Testing

Alcohol and Chemical Testing Limits

Maine's illegal intoxication level is .08 percent and above; .04 percent if operating a CMV; and if driver is under twenty-one years or has a conditional license, the level is any amount. Blood and breath testing are authorized. Maine has both an implied-consent violation and a provision for an administrative suspension.

A driver's license may be reinstated prior to the expiration of the total suspension period with installation of an approved ignition interlock device in the motor vehicle of the driver.

Suspensions and Revocations

See the Appendix for a list of the federally mandated disqualifications for offenses occurring in a CMV per MCSIA. See www.maine.gov/sos/cec/rules/29/250/250c006.doc to view the rules for suspension for CDL drivers.

Aggravated Assault with a Motor Vehicle (Class B)	3-year revocation.
Altering License/registration	30-day suspension.
Assault with a Motor Vehicle (Class C)	3-year revocation.
Assault with a Motor Vehicle (Class D)	2-year revocation.
Criminal Threatening with a Motor Vehicle (Class D)	2-year revocation.
Displaying Suspended License	30-day suspension.
Drag Racing	90-day suspension.
Elevated Aggravated Assault with a Motor Vehicle (Class A)	3-year revocation.
Eluding a Police Officer	90-day suspension.
Failure to Stop for Police Officer	30-day suspension.
False Application for License/registration	30-day suspension.
False Information to Police	30-day suspension.
Illegal transportation of liquor or drugs by minor	30-day suspension.
Leaving Scene of Injury Accident	30-day suspension.
Loaning License	30-day suspension.
Operating After Suspension	60-day suspension.
Operating Alone on Permit	30-day suspension.

Operating Under the Influence (OUI)

First Offense	Minimum 90-day suspension; for refusal to take test—275 days.
Second Offense - Violation Date Prior to 09/01/2008	18-month suspension.
Second Offense - Violation Date On or After 09/01/2008	3-year suspension. (Could be reduced to 9 months with an ignition interlock device)
Third Offense - Violation Date Prior to 09/01/2008	4-year suspension.
Third Offense - Violation Date On or After 09/01/2008	6-year suspension.
Fourth or Subsequent Offense - Violation Date Prior to 09/01/2008	6-year suspension. (Could be reduced to 3 years with an ignition interlock device)
Fourth or Subsequent Offense - Violation Date On or After 09/01/2008	6-year suspension with Restoration Requirement that Ignition Interlock Device is installed for four years.

Administrative Imposed Suspensions for OUI

1st Provisional (teen)	1 year
1st Provisional (refusal)	18 months
2nd & Subsequent provisional (teen)	2 years
2nd Provisional (refusal)	30 months

1st	90 days
1st (refusal)	275 days
2nd	3 years (could be reduced to 9 months with an ignition interlock device)
2nd (refusal)	18 months
3rd	6 years (could be reduced to 3 years with an ignition interlock device)
3rd (refusal)	4 years
4th & Subsequent	6 years
4th & Subsequent (refusal)	6 years

Operating Under the Influence - CDL Holders

First Offense	1-year suspension.
First Offense w/HAZMAT	3-year suspension.
Second Offense	Permanent suspension.
Operating Without License	30-day suspension.
Passing a Roadblock	90-day suspension.
Passing Stopped School Bus	30-day suspension.
Reckless Conduct with a Motor Vehicle (Class D)	2-year revocation.
Speed Thirty Miles or More Over Limit	30-day suspension.
Three License Suspensions in Three Years Plus Subsequent Conviction	120-day suspension.
Twelve Demerit Points within One Year Period	15-day suspension.
Unlawful Use of License	30-day suspension.

Underage Suspensions: A juvenile provisional license holder within the first two years of the license, a conviction for any moving violation will result in the following suspension:

First violation	30-day suspension
Second violation	180-day suspension
Third and subsequent violation	1-year suspension

Reinstatement Requirements

Suspension $50.00 fee; time lapse; state conditions.
Revocation $50.00 fee; time lapse; financial responsibility; re-examination, if applicable, payment of license fees.
Higher reinstatement fees may apply, depending on the violation.

Record Access: Laws, Rules, and Forms

Note: This Section Applies to Both Driver and Vehicle Records.

Governing Statutes and Rules

Motor Vehicle Laws and Rules can be accessed from the home page. **State Statutes** are found at http://janus.state.me.us/legis/.

29-A MRSA Section 256 & 153 establishes the procedure for the disclosure of personal information contained in motor vehicle records and implements compliance with the requirements of DPPA. This was amended June 1, 2000. An excellent summary can be found at www.maine.gov/sos/cec/rules/29/chaps29.htm.

Personal information will not be released to the following unless an affirmation statement has been filed with the BMV asserting the entity is entitled to personal information under DPPA:

- Agencies conducting vehicle recalls
- Insurance companies
- Businesses, in order to verify information already given by a person or to prevent fraud or to recover on a debt or lien
- Parties involved with a federal or state court case or arbitration, including attorneys
- Towing companies that tow abandoned or impounded vehicles
- An employer verifying information related to a CDL
- Private investigators acting for any purpose stated above

Request and Consent Forms

Driving Records: A written request that includes the signature of the requester and reason for the request will be accepted. There is a state form, but it is not available from the web. Once the subject gives written permission, this permission stays in effect for 12 months for that specific requester. See www.maine.gov/sos/bmv/privacy.htm.

Vehicle Records: A written request that includes the signature of the authorized requester and reason for the request will be accepted. DPPA information and an affirmation statement form can be obtained at www.maine.gov/informe/subscriber/dppa.htm. The form can be used for both driver and vehicle records.

Vendor and Third Party Access Policy

Maine does not provide any restrictions upon the use, storage, or resale of records after a completed transaction, providing the authorized requester complies with permissible use regulations. Approved vendors can access records for other vendors who will then sell to an end-user, as long as the original vendor assumes the responsibility of the sales chain. Also, per statute the statute mentioned above:

"A recipient of personal information under Sections 4 and 7, other than a recipient under Section 7(3)(B), who resells or rediscloses personal information must keep for a period of five years records identifying each person who receives that information and the permitted purpose for which the information will be used and must make such records available to the Bureau or another person or state agency designated by the Bureau upon request."

Non-permissible Use Requests

Driver Records: Non-permissible requesters without consent can obtain records, but personal information is shielded except for the personal information submitted with the request. For example, if a record is requested with the name and DOB, but not the license number, the record will be returned without the license number and address, etc.

Vehicle Records: Without consent, the records are released but contain no personal information.

Access to Driver-Related Records

Driving Records

General Information and Fees

Driver License Services, 29 State House Station, 101 Hospital Street, Augusta 04333-0029, 207-624-9000 x52116, the fax is 207-624-9090. The current fee for a three-year record is $5.00; a ten-year record is $10.00. Add $2.00 if requested online or faxed back. Add $1.00 for certification. The state charges for "no record found" reports only if request is mailed. A document copy of a conviction, suspension or revocation notice is $10.00.

In-Person – Counter requests are processed while you wait with a maximum of five requests per person per day. A certified record can be purchased for $6.00. There is no charge for a "no record found" request.

Mail – Mail-in requests are processed in about three days. The above address is the only location to secure a driving record in-person or through the mail. The full name and DOB are required when ordering; the license number is optional. Payment must be made in advance of receiving the report.

Auto Fax Back – This program enables the requester to order a driving record over an automated telephone system. After entering the account number (pin), DL number, and a fax number, the state will respond within 10-30 minutes, by fax, with a driving record. There is an additional $2.00 for this service. Pre-approved, established accounts can also request records by fax for an additional $2.00; turnaround time is 2 days or less.

Electronic – There are two programs.

1) Maine offers online interactive access to all users 24 hours daily through Driver Record Check at www.informe.org/bmv/drc/. The electronic, uncertified record displays driving history information only- no personal information is provided. A credit card is needed. The requester must supply either the name and DOB or the license number. Three-year records are $7.00 each; ten-year records $12.00 each.

2) There is also a subscription service which gives an approved requester full information. Three-year records are $7.00 each; ten-year records $12.00 each. There is an annual $95.00 fee for the subscription service. For more information, call 207-621-2600 or visit www.maine.gov/informe/subscriber/services.htm. (The subscription service offers access to a variety of government records from this web page.)

Bulk – Bulk sales are not offered, except for vehicle recall purposes.

By Person of Record – Maine drivers may obtain their driving record by mail, walk-in, and via online as described above.

Notification/Monitoring Program

Driver CrossCheck is an innovative service that allows employers to automatically receive notification about changes to the driving records of registered employees. This program is offered by InforME (see above). Requesters submit a driver list for $15.00 for the 10 first drivers and $1.00 for each additional driver. Subscribers can determine how often to run a check (monthly, quarterly, etc.). The fee is $7.00 per check to see changes, but there is no fee if no changes are indicated. Results are sent via email.

Crash Reports

Reporting – Crashes involving death, injury or property damage in excess of $1000.00 must be reported immediately to the nearest law enforcement agency. There are no special CDL reporting requirements.

Record Access – Copies of crash reports may be obtained in person, by mail or online from the Maine State Police, Traffic Division, Crash Records, State House Station #20, Augusta 04333-0020, 207-624-8944. The URL is https://www1.maine.gov/online/mcrs/. Records are available from 1975 to 2002 on microfilm and 2003 forward on computer. New records are available anywhere from 5 to 30 days after the incident. Requests must include the drivers' names and DOBs, date of crash and location. The fee is $10.00 per report (either manual or online), $15.00 per 25 pages for a fatality report. Photos and mapping reports range from $10.00 to $35.00. Turnaround time is 1 day if on computer, 5 days if on microfilm.

Records from 01/2003 forward may be ordered from the web page by using a credit card or by subscription via an InforME account. Resulting reports are returned by email in a PDF format. There is no charge if no record is found. One may search by name, date of birth, crash location, crash date, or investigating agency (police department). Records occurring prior to 2003 must be ordered manually.

Also, subscribers may purchase records in bulk ($.50 per record) on a monthly or annual basis, as well participate in the "Crash Tracker" notification program (free).

Access to Vehicle-Related Records

General Information and Fees

Registration Section, 29 State House Station, Augusta ME 04333-0029, 207-624-9000 x52138-Titles, x52149-Registration.

Records are held from 1982. Besides record on passenger and commercial vehicles, the Bureau of Motor Vehicles maintains records for certain RV vehicles—motor homes and camper trailers. All other RV (ATV and snowmobile) records as well as boat records are maintained by the Department of Inland Fisheries and Wildlife. Mobile homes are only required to be registered if they are being moved, hence the Bureau of Motor Vehicles only maintains records of those mobile homes that are registered.

All mobile homes records (including lien records) are maintained by the municipality in which the mobile home is located.

Mail or In-Person – All requests must be submitted in writing. Registration search records are $5.00 each for uncertified and $6.00 for certified. A certified title record is $33.00. Submit the subject's DOB when requesting a name search. Title information, which includes **lien records** if applicable, can be requested by submitting VIN, plate number or name and date of birth There is no special form required when submitting a request for information, but an Affirmation Statement must be completed agreeing to abide by the provisions of the Maine law

mentioned previously and DPPA, and the fee must accompany the request. Records may be faxed back for an additional $2.00. Turnaround time is usually 7 to 10 days.

Telephone or Fax – If the requesting party establishes an account, they can receive information via telephone and are billed. Records may be faxed back for an additional $2.00.

Electronic – Maine offers online interactive access to title and registration records 24 hours daily through InforME's Interactive Services. This is a subscription service and is open only to those who qualify as permissible users. The fee is $5.50 per title and $5.00 per registration record plus there is an additional $2.00 portal fee. Search by name and DOB or plate number for registration records, by VIN or by title application number for title records. With the annual $95.00 subscription fee, subscribers have access to a variety of Maine information, including corporation, UCC filings and criminal history records. Subscribers may also go online to release vehicle liens.

For more information email customerservice@informe.org. or visit www.maine.gov/informe/subscriber/services.htm,

Bulk – Registration and ownership information is not available for commercial use through the BMV office. Contact InforMe [see above].

Access to Vessel Records

General Information, Access and Fees

Department of Inland Fisheries and Wildlife, 41 State House Station, Augusta ME 04333-0041, 207-287-5232 (certified docs), 207-287-2043 (look-ups), http://www.maine.gov/ifw/

All motorized boats must be registered, boats are not required to be titled. Registration records can be searched by name or registration number. Records go back on the computer to 1989 for those who have renewed. There is a $5.00 if searching is done by staff. Turnaround time for mail requests is up to two weeks. The fee is $25.00 if the search requires accessing older records on microfiche in another building (some have been destroyed by weather.). Credit cards are accepted for payment.

Liens are not shown and must be searched with the Secretary of State at 207-624-7752.

Driving Record Content and Reciprocity

What's On or Not On the Driving Record

- Maine reports all convictions on a driver's record for the last 3 years or 10 years, per the type of record ordered.
- Maine provides a record without personal information to the general public and a record with personal information to those permitted by law.
- Crash reports are shown if reported to State Police (effective 10/01/03) if damage is more than $1000 or if there is an injury; however, fault is not shown.
- Medical information is not released on non-CDL records.
- The state does not permit driver school attendance in lieu of conviction, but a 3 point credit is given (once every 12 months).

Data Retention

Driver information is not purged from the state database, but is restricted from access after 3 years. This includes records of drivers who have surrendered their licenses to another state. See the Appendix for the federally mandated data retention policies on CDL drivers.

Court to Repository

Violation and conviction information is transferred from the courts to the state via paper and electronically. There is no law mandating when the information must be submitted to the DMV, generally this information is input within thirty days.

State Reciprocity for Non-CDL Drivers

- Will suspend license for unpaid out-of-state convictions.
- Record of new incoming driver is shown on MVR
- Out-of-state convictions are shown on MVR if NRVC state.
- Out-of-state accidents are not shown on MVR
- Convictions of out-of-state drivers are sent to home state.
- Record is forwarded to new state on license surrender.

License Classes, Restrictions, Endorsements, and Status

License Classes– Commercial

Maine began testing and implementation of the CDL in October 1991

Class A	A combination of vehicles with a GVWR or registered weight of 26,001 or more pounds, providing the GVWR or GW of the vehicle or vehicles being towed is in excess of 10,000 pounds. A Class A license is a commercial driver's license. Holders of a Class A license may—with any appropriate endorsements—operate all vehicles in Class B and Class C.
Class B	A single vehicle with a GVWR or registered weight of 26,001 or more pounds, or any such vehicle towing a vehicle not in excess of 10,000 pounds GVWR or GW. A Class B license is a commercial driver's license. Holders of a Class B may—with any appropriate endorsements—operate all vehicles in Class C.
Class C	A Class C License (see below) is a commercial driver's license if it carries a bus or hazardous materials endorsement.

License Classes– Non-Commercial

Class C	A single vehicle or combination of vehicles that does not meet the definition of Class A or Class B license. Holders of a Class C license may—with any appropriate endorsements—operate all vehicles in that class.

Restrictions

A	Corrective Lenses	G	Geographical	V	CDL Medical Variance
B	Daylight Operation	Q	Conditional License	W	Operation of Vehicles Equipped with Air-Brakes Not Allowed
C	Driver Improvement	R	Moped		
D	Motorcycle	S	Special Equipment	Z	Ignition Interlock

Endorsements

H	Hazardous Materials	P	Passenger (bus) Vehicle	Y	(No longer used) School Bus Over Fifteen Passengers
I	Motorcycle	T	Double-/Triple-Trailer		
K	Valid Until Thirty Days after Discharge from Armed Forces	X	Combination Tank/ Hazardous Materials	Z	School Bus Fifteen Passengers or Less (including driver
N	Tank Vehicle	S	School Bus Over Fifteen Passengers		

Status Codes

A	Active	I	Deceased	V	Voluntary Surrender
C	Cancelled	R	Revoked	X	Pending Suspension
D	Deleted - Name Change	S	Suspended		

Conviction Table with Abbreviated Text, Points, and ACD

Conviction	ACD	Pts	Explanation
ABAND VEH			Abandoning Vehicle On Public Way
ACTIVATE IID FOR OP MV			Activating Ignition Interlock Device For Purpose Of Providing An Operable MV
AGG ASSAULT-MV	U06		Aggravated Assault - Motor Vehicle
AGG GROSS WGHT			Aggravated Gross Weight Violation
AL OP UNQUAL DR			Rule Violation Allowing Op By Unqualified Driver
AL UNRG M/V HWY			Allowing Unregistered Motor Vehicle On Highway
ALL ILLEG OP MV			Allowing Illegal Operation Of A Motor Veh
ALTER DL	B41		Alteration Of Driver License
ASSAULT BY M/V	U06		Assault By Motor Vehicle
ASSAULT-MV-C	U06		Assault - Motor Vehicle - C
ASSAULT-MV-D	U06		Assault - Motor Vehicle - D
ATT OUI DRUGS	A20		Attempting To OUI (Drugs)
ATT OUI LIQUOR	A20		Attempting To OUI (Liquor)
AUTOCYCLE VIOL		2	Operating Autocycle In Violation Of Highway Restrictions
BAC .08 OR MORE	A08		Blood Alcohol Content .08 Plus
BAC .10 OR MORE	A10		Blood Alcohol Content .10 Plus
CARELESS DRIVIN	M81		Careless Driving
CHG CRS UNSAFE	M70	2	Changing Course Of Travel When Unsafe
CRIM THREAT-MV	M84		Criminal Threatening - Motor Vehicle
CRIMINAL SPEED	S15		Speeding - Criminal Violation
CROSSOVER VIOL	M44	2	Crossover Violation
CS OP OVR 70/60			Rule Violation Cause Op Over 70/60 Rule
DEAL TRANSFER			Dealer Ft Possess Transfer Form
DEF BRAKE ADJ	E31		Defective Brake Adjustment
DEF BRAKE HOSE	E31		Defective Brake Hose
DEF COUPLING			Rule Violation Defective Coupling
DEF FRAME			Defective Frame
DEF INTERN VALVE			Defective Internal Valve
DEF STEERING			Rule Violation Defective Steering
DEF SUSPENSION			Defective Suspension
DISP BLUE LIGHT		2	Displaying Blue Light On Motor Vehicle
DISP MUTILAT L			Displaying Mutilated License
DISP RED LIGHT		2	Displaying Red Light
DISP SUSP LIC	D16		Displaying A Suspended License
DLR FAIL FILE TITLE APP			Failure to Deliver Title to Secretary of State
DR ACROSS ROTARY	N61	2	Driving On/Across Center Part Of Rotary/Tr Circles
DR TO ENDANGER	M84		Driving To Endanger
DR WH IMPAIRED	A25		Driving While Impaired
DR WH INTOX	A20		Driving While Intoxicated
DR WRONG SIDE	N70	6	Driving Wrong Side
DR WRONG WAY	N63	6	Driving Wrong Way
DRAG RACING	S95		Drag Racing
DRV TAMP W/OP OF IID	A41		Driver Tampering W/Or Circumvent The Operation Of An Ignition Interlock
DUI DRUGS	A20		Driving Under Influence Drugs
DUI LIQUOR	A20		Driving Under Influence Liquor
E/A ASSAULT-MV	U06		Elevated Agg. Assault - Motor Vehicle
ELUDING POL OFF	U01		Eluding A Police Officer
ENTER LIMIT ACCESS	M50	2	Entering/Leaving Limited-Access Way Improperly
EV REG FEES/TAX			Evasion Reg Fees And Taxes
EX OV HEIGHT			Exceeding Overhead Clearance Height Of Way
EX REG WEIGHT			Op Veh In Excess Of Registration Wght
EX SD SYS NOISE			Excessive Sound System Noise
EX VEH WEIGHT			Excess Vehicle Weight
EXCESS ACCEL	S98	4	Excessive Acceleration
EXCESS NOISE			Excessive Noise
EXP INSPEC STKR			Expired Inspection Sticker
FAIL DIM H/L	E54	2	Failure To Dim Headlights
FAIL FURN SEC	D38		Failure To Furnish Security
FAIL KEEP RITE	N70	4	Failure To Keep Right
FAIL PRO EV INS	D36		Failure To Produce Evidence Of Insurance
FAIL RPT ACCD	B61		Failure To Report Accident
FAIL RPT ACCD BI CMV	B14		Failure To Report Accident CMV
FAIL RTRN RIGHT	N70	4	Failure To Return To The Right
FAIL SIGNAL	N43	2	Failure To Signal

Conviction	ACD	Pts	Explanation
FAIL SUB EXAM			Failure To Submit To Examination
FAIL TO PAY UCR FEES			Failure to pay UCR Fees
FAIL TO SURR HAZMAT END	W09		Failure To Surrender Hazmat Endorsement As Required By USA Patriot Act
FAIL YLD EM VEH	N04	4	Failure To Yield For Emergency Vehicle
FAIL YLD NO SGN	N25	4	Failure To Yield/ No Sign
FAIL YLD PEDSTR	N08	4	Failure To Yield For Pedestrian
FAIL YLD SIGN	N26	4	Failure To Yield/Sign
FALS APP OF REG			Falsifying Application Of License/Registration
FALS INFO TO PO	D78		Giving False Information To A Police Officer
FALS INFO TO PO CMV	D78		Giving False Information To A Police Officer CMV
FALSE ID LIQ	D06	6	Misrepresentation Of Identity Or Other Facts To Obtain Alcohol
FL AP RES LI 30			FL Apply Resident Lic Within 30 Days
FL CARRY R/C			Failure To Carry Registration Certificate
FL CMPLY W/FINAN RESP	D35		Failure To Comply With Financial Responsibility
FL CMPLY W/IRP			Failure To Comply With IRP Registration
FL CROSS CLRNC	M24		Failure To Cross Railroad Grade Crossing Clearance
FL DIS FLGS/FLR			Failure To Provide Or Display Flags/Flares
FL DIS NM/TKTR	E01		Failure To Display Name On Truck/Tractor
FL DIS VLD I/S			Failure To Display Valid Inspection Sticker
FL DIS VLD R/P			Failure To Display Valid Registration Plate
FL DSP F/U DCAL			Failure To Obtain Or Display F/U Decal
FL FLG/LT EX LD			Failure To Flag/Light Extended Load
FL GV WAY OT VH	N06	4	Failure To Give Way To Overtaking Vehicle
FL INS BOND	D38		Failure To Have Insurance Bond
FL KEEP RT CUR	N70	2	Failure To Keep Right On Curve
FL OB RR GT/SGN	M10		Failure To Obey Railroad Gate/Sign
FL OB TR ISLAN	M02	2	Failure To Obey Traffic Island
FL OBEY RR XING	M09	2	Failure To Obey Railroad Grade Crossing
FL OBEY STP SGN	M15	4	Failure To Obey Stop Sign
FL PR V/R DMAN			Failure To Produce Valid Reg On Demand
FL PRD RT PLN RDACT MAT			Failure To Produce Routing Plan Radioactive Material
FL PROD DOC A+B EXP			Failure To Produce Document A&B Explosive
FL PROD INST FLAM CYR LIQ			Failure To Produce Instruction For Flammable Cryogenic Liquid
FL PROD OPR LI			Failure To Produce Operators License
FL PROD RT PLAN A+B EXP			Failure To Produce Routing Plan A&B Explosives
FL PRODU L-BOOK			Failure To Produce Log Book
FL PROR R/C			Failure To Produce Registration Certificate
FL RDU SP GR CR	M20	2	Failure To Reduce Speed At Grade Crossing
FL RDU SP ON GR/CRV	S94	2	Failure To Reduce Speed On Grade / Curve
FL REMOVE I/S STICK			Fail To Remove Prior Inspection Sticker
FL STOP POL OFF	M08		Failure To Stop For Police Officer
FL STOP RED LIT	M16	4	Failure To Stop For Red Light
FL STP SUFF SP	M23		Failure To l Stop Sufficient Space – Railroad Crossing
FL STP TRK BFR CROSSING	M22		Always Required To Stop But Fails To Before Driving Onto Crossing
FL STP TRK OBS	M21		Failure To Stop at Railroad Tracks When Not Clear
FL STP WGH STA			Failure To Stop At Weighing Station
FL SUR SUSP FUD			Fail To Sur Susp F/U Dcal
FL SUR SUSP L/R			Fail To Sur Susp Lic/Reg
FL TITLE W/IN REG			Fail To File Title W/In Required Time
FL YL RT OF WAY-CRIMINAL	N01	4	Failure To Yield Right Of Way - Criminal
FL YL RT OF WAY-TRAFF INFRAC	N01	4	Failure To Yield Right Of Way - Traffic Infraction
FLR PROVIDE SSN			Failure To Provide Social Security Number
FOLL TOO CLOSE	M34	2	Following Too Close
FT CHG NAME/ADD			FT Notify Of Name/Address Change On Reg/Lic
FT DIS DOT/MC			Failure To Display DOT Or MC Number
FT MAINTAIN CNTL MV		2	Failure To Maintain Control Of Motor Vehicle
FT NTF ADDR CHG			Fail To Notify Address Change On Reg/Lic
FT NTF NAME CHG			Fail To Notify Name Change On Reg/Lic
FT OBEY TC DVC	M14	2	Fail To Obey Traffic Control Device
FT PROD COM/ISP			Failure To Produce Proof Of Comm Inspect
FT TINT REP CRT	E01		Ft Issue Tinted Window Replacement Cert
HITCHHIKING			Hitchhiking
HLINTE WO ME RG			Hauling Interstate Commerce W/O Maine Reg
IL DISPLAY PLTS			Illegal Display Of Plates
ILL ATH I-STK			Illegal Attachment Inspection Sticker
ILL ATH PLATES			Illegal Attachment Of Plates/Improper Plates

Conviction	ACD	Pts	Explanation
ILL LEFT TURN	N53	2	Illegal Left Turn
ILL POSS DRUGS	A33		Illegal Possession Of Drugs
ILL POSS LIQUOR	A31		Illegal Possession Of Liquor
ILL RIGHT TURN	N54	2	Illegal Right Turn
ILL TRAN DRUGS	A33		Illegal Transportation Drugs
ILL TRAN LIQUOR	A31	6	Illegal Transportation Liquor
ILLEGAL DUMPING			Illegal Dumping
ILLEGAL PARKING			Illegal Parking
ILLEGAL U-TURN	N56	2	Illegal U-Turn
IMP BLOCK BRACING	E50		Improper Blocking And Bracing
IMP COLORED HL	E01		Improperly Colored Headlamp
IMP DIS REG PLATE			Improper Display Of Registration Plate
IMP DIS REG PLT			Improper Display Of Reg Plate
IMP SHIP PAPERS			Improper Shipping Papers
IMPED FLOW TRAF	F34	2	Impeding Normal Flow Of Traffic
IMPROP FOG AUX			Improper Mounting/Use/Color Of Fog/Auxiliary Lights
IMPROP RED AUX		2	Improper Display/Use Of Red Auxiliary/Emergency Light
IMPROPER COURSE	M40	2	Improper Course
IMPROPER LANE CHANGE	M42	6	Improper Or Erratic Lane Change
IMPROPER PASS	M70	6	Improper Passing
IMPROPER TURN	N50	2	Improper Turn
IMPRUDENT DR	M82	4	Imprudent Driving
IMPRUDENT SPEED	S94	4	Imprudent Speed
INAD BINDING			Inadequate Bindings
INAD EXH SYS	E01		Inadequate Exhaust System
INAD HAZ WASTE	E04		Inadequate Hazardous Waste Manifest
INAD LOAD SECURE			Inadequate Load Securement
INAD MUFFLER	E01		Inadequate Muffler
INAD OR DEF EQ	E01		Inadequate Or Defective Equipment
INAD PACKAGE MARK			Inadequate Bulk/Non-Bulk Package Marking
INAD PACKING			Inadequate Packaging
INAD PLACARD	E04		Inadequate Placarding
INAD SFTY DEV	E01		Rule Violation Inadequate Safety Device
INAD SHIP PAPERS			Inadequate Shipping Papers
INAD TAIL LIT	E05		Inadequate Tail Light
INAD TANK MARK	E01		Inadequate Cargo Tank Marking
INAD/FIRE EXT	E01		Inadequate Or No Fire Extinguisher
INADE BRAKES	E31		Inadequate Brakes
INADE EXH SYS	E01		Op With An Incomplete/Leaking Exhaust System
INADE FLARE KIT	E01		Inadequate Flag/Flare Kit
INADE MIRROR	F66		Op With Inadequate Mirror
INADE PLATE LIT	E01		Inadequate Plate Light
INADE SAFETY CHAIN	E57		Op With Inadequate Safety Chain/Cable
INADE SUSP	F66		Inadequate Suspension
INADE TIRES	E37		Inadequate Tires
INOP LIGHTS	E55		Inoperative Lights
INTER WITH TRAF	F34		Interfering With Traffic
JUVENILE OFF			Juvenile Offense
LACK REQ EQUIP	E01		Lack Of Required Equipment
LAMP COLOR	E01		Signal Lamps Not Proper Color
LANE CONV	M41	2	Lane Violation
LITTERING		2	Littering From Motor Vehicle
LOADED OVER STA			Loaded Over Stakes
LOANING DL			Loaning Driver License
LOG NOT CURRENT			Log Book Not Current
LV SCENE ACC BI	B07		Leaving Scene Accident/Bodily Injury
LV SCENE ACC PD	B08	6	Leaving Scene Accident/Property Damage
LV STA MV ON HW			Leaving Stationary Vehicle On Highway
MANSLAUGHTER	U08		Manslaughter
MANSLAUGHTER CMV	U09		Manslaughter CMV
MC WHEEL OFF RD	N84	2	Raising Motorcycle Front Wheel Off Road
MIS DISABLE PLACARD			Misuse Of Disability Reg Plates/Placard
MIS FACT	D02		Misstatement Of Fact
MISUSE DEAL PLATES			Misuse Of Dealer Plate
MISUSE TEMP PLATE			Misuse Of Temporary Plate
MISUSE WRECK PLATE			Misuse Of Dealer Wrecker Plate

Conviction	ACD	Pts	Explanation
MV COMMISSION DRUG OFFENSE			Use of Motor Vehicle in Commission of Drug Offense
MV INVLV FEL W/CON SUB	A50		MV Used In Felony Act Involving Controlled Substance
MV USED COMMIT FELONY	U03		Using Motor Vehicle To Commit Felony
NO BRK PRESSR	E31		Rule Violation No Brake Action Pressure
NO EMG RES INFO	E03		No Emergency Response Information
NO INSP STICKER			No Inspection Sticker
NO PLACARD WRONG CLASS	E04		No Placarding Or Wrong Class
NO REG CERT			No Registration Certificate
NO SHIPPING PAPER			No Shipping Paper
NO TEST DATES			No Test Dates
NON-DRV TAMP W/OP OF IID			Non-Driver Tampering W/Or Circumvent The Operation Of An Ignition Interlock
NON-SPEC CARGO TANK			Non-Spec Cargo Tank
NPP ADV REPORT	D75		Not A Proper Person - Adverse Report
NPP PHY OR MENT	D75		Not A Proper Person - Physical Or Mental
OAR	B25		Operating After Habitual Offender Revocation
OAS - TRAF INFRAC	B26	8	Operating After Suspension - Traffic Infraction
OAS CHILD SUP	B26		Operating After Suspension/Child Support
OAS CR	B26		Operating After Suspension/Court Record
OAS FR (no longer used)	B26		Operating While Suspended FR
OAS FTA CMV	D56		Operating After Suspension/Failure To Appear CMV
OAS FTA/FPF	B26		Operating After Suspension/Failure To Appear
OAS FTP CMV	D56		Operating After Suspension/Failure To Pay Fine CMV
OAS OUI	B26		Operating After Suspension/OUI Liquor
OBST FLOW OF TR	F34	2	Obstructing Flow Of Traffic
OBST TRAFFIC	F34	2	Obstructing Traffic
OFF FOG LIGHTS	E55		Ft To Turn Off Fog Lights
OP AFT REVK	B25		Operating After Revocation
OP AFT WITHDRWL	B20	2	Operating After Withdrawal
OP ALONE PERMIT	B51		Operating Alone/Permit
OP BEY RD RES			Operating Beyond Road Restriction
OP BEYOND RES	D29	6	Operating Beyond Restriction
OP BRKDN LANE	E01		Opr Breakdown Lane
OP COM VEH OOS	B27		Operating Com Veh Out Of Service
OP COM VEH OOS HM OR P16	B19		Operating Com Veh Out Of Service Hazmat Or Passengers > 16
OP DEF EXHAUST	E01		Operating With Defective Exhaust
OP DEF F/S	E01		Operation W/Defective Fuel System
OP DEF M/V	E01		Operating Defective Motor Veh
OP EXP INS STKR			Operating Expired Inspection Sticker
OP EXP LICENSE	B51	4	Operating With Expired License Within 90 Days
OP FLSG DTY STA			Cause Operation With Falsifying Log Book
OP INOP BKWY DV	E01		Rule Violation Operating W/Inoperative Breakaway D
OP LEFT RR XING	M71	2	Operating Left At Intersection/Railroad Crossing
OP LOW AIR WARN	E01		Operation W/Defective Low Air Warn
OP M/C BEY RES	D29	6	Operating Motorcycle Beyond Restriction
OP M/C W/O LIT	E05	2	Operating Motorcycle W/O Lighted Headlamp
OP M/C W/O REG			Operating Motorcycle Without Registration
OP M/C W/O V/L	B51	4	Operating Motorcycle Without Valid License
OP M/V OB VIEW	D70	4	Operating Motor Vehicle With Obstructed View
OP M/V WITHOUT IID	A41		Operate A Motor Vehicle Without Ignition Interlock Device
OP MV CONS LIQ	A26	2	Operating MV While Consuming Intox Liquor
OP MV OVR 10 HR			Rule Violation Cause Operation Over 10 Hrs
OP MV USING MO PHONE/ELEC DEV	M86		Operating MV While Using Mobile Phone Or Electronic Device
OP MV VISIBLE EM		2	Operating Motor Vehicle With Visible Emissions
OP MV WO 7 PREV			Causing Op Of MV Without 7 Days Prev Log
OP MV WO T/LIT	E05	2	Operating Motor Vehicle Without Tail Light
OP OFF-RD VEH PUB WAY PK LOT			Op Unauth Off-Road Veh On Public Way Or Parking Lot
OP OV HGT RES			Operating Over Height Restriction
OP OV LGHT RES			Operating Over Length Restriction
OP OV LMT P/R			Op Beyond Over Limit Permit Restrictions
OP OV WIDTH			Operating Over Width Restriction
OP OVER 15 HR			Operation Over 15 Hour Rule
OP OVERWIDTH W/O PERMIT			Op Overwidth Vehicle Without Permit
OP OVR PSTD WT			Operating Over Posted Weight
OP UNQ DRVR	B91		Rule Violation Op By Unqualified Driver
OP UNSAFE M/V	N84		Operating Unsafe Motor Vehicle

Conviction	ACD	Pts	Explanation
OP VEH 1916 REQ	E01		Op/Causing Op Of Veh Not Meeting #1916 Req
OP VEH BRKDN LN	M40	2	Operating Vehicle In Breakdown Lane
OP W/IMPRO LIC	D27	6	Operating With An Improper License
OP W/O AUTH LIC	B51		Operating Without Authority License
OP W/O AUTH LIC CMV	B56		Operating Without Authority License CMV
OP W/O BRAKES AXLES	E31		Op Without Adequate Brakes On All Axles
OP W/O COR-LENS	D29	6	Operating Without Corrective Lenses
OP W/O CR PERS			Operating Without Registration On Person
OP W/O DUTY STA			Rule Violation Cause Operation W/Out Log
OP W/O ID DEVIC	E01		Operating Without Identification Device
OP W/O LIGHTS	E05	2	Operating Without Lights
OP W/O MED CERT	B65		Cause Operation Without Valid Medical Certificate
OP W/O PROP P/B	E02		Operating Without Proper Parking Brake
OP W/O REG			Operating Without Registration
OP W/O VLD STK			Operating Without Valid Inspection Sticker
OP W/SUSP REG			Operating With A Suspended Registration
OPAQUE WINDOW	D70	2	Operating MV W/Opaque Material In Window
OPR ALCOH P-W	A26	2	Opr Consuming Alcohol In A M/Veh On A Public Way
OPR LEFT CURVE	N70	6	Operating Left On Curve
OPR M/C W/O MIR	E01		Operating Motorcycle Without Mirror
OPR POSS ALCOH	A35	2	Opr Possessing Open Alcoholic Container On A P-W
OPR UNREG MV			Operating Unregistered Motor Vehicle
OTH IMPROP PASS	M70	6	Other Improper Passing
OTH MOV VIOL		2	Moving Violation
OTH VIOL			Other Violation
OUI CLASS B	A21		OUI Class B
OUI CLASS C	A21		OUI Class C
OUI DRUGS	A22		Operating Under The Influence Of Drugs
OUI LIQUOR	A21		Operating Under The Influence Of Liquor
OVER LNGTH COMB VEH			Over Length Trailer/Semi-Trailer/Combination Veh
OVERTIME PARKIN			Overtime Parking
OWL	B51		Operating Without License
OWL MC	B51		Operating Motorcycle Without License
OWN PASS ST BUS	M75		Reg Owner Of Veh Passing Stopped Sch Bus
P W/O H ON M/C	F03		Passenger Without Helmet On Motorcycle
PARK DISABILITY ACCESS AISLE			Park Disability Access Aisle
PARK DISABILITY RESTRICTED SP			Park Disability Restricted Space
PARK ON HWY			Parking On Highway
PARK REST AREA			Parking In A Restricted Area
PASS 100FT INTE	M77	6	Passing Within 100 Feet Of An Intersection
PASS CURVE HILL	M74	6	Passing On Curve/Hill
PASS M/C W/O SE	F03	6	Carrying Passenger On M/C, Seat Not Provided
PASS ON RIGHT	M70	6	Passing On The Right
PASS ROAD BLOCK	U01		Passing Police Road Block
PASS RR SCH BUS	M18		Passing Stop Signal - Railroad
PASS STP SCH BS	M75		Passing Stopped School Bus
PASS VEH STP XING	M76	2	Passing Vehicle Stopped At Crosswalk
PASS WRONG SIDE	M73	6	Passing On Wrong Side
PED OBEY SIGNAL			Pedestrian Disobeying Control Signal
PED ON ACCESS			Pedestrian On Access Way
PED ON TPK			Pedestrian On Turnpike
PED ON WAY			Pedestrian On Limited-Access Way
PENDING INS	D36		Pending Insurance Filing
PK 6000 REG AUT			Pickup Over 6000 Lbs Registered As Auto
PK ON DRIVE LAN			Parking On Paved Driving Lane
PK UNREG M/V HW			Parking Unregistered Motor Vehicle On Public Way
PK W/O LIGHTS	N40		Parking Without Lights
POSS ALC IN CMV	A31		Possessing Of Alcoholic Beverages In A CMV
POSS VALID LIC	D07		Possessing More Than One Valid License
PR OP UNISP M/V			Permitting Operation Of Uninspected Motor Vehicle
PR UNA PRS DRI			Permitting Unauthorized Person To Drive
PROHIB VEH TRNPK			Op Or Allowing Prohibited Vehicle On Turnpike
PROVIDE MV W/OUT IID			Renting/Leasing/Lending MV Without Ignition Interlock
PSG CONS ALCOH	A35		Op W/Psgr Consuming Alcohol In MV On A Public Way
PSG POSS ALCOH	A35		Op W/Psgr Possessing Open Alcoholic Cont't On P/W
PSGR FIRST 90	D29	2	Carrying Passenger Within 90 Days Of Lic

Conviction	ACD	Pts	Explanation
RECK DRIVING	M80		Reckless Driving
RECK HOMICIDE	U08		Reckless Homicide
RECKLESS CON-MV	M84		Reckless Conduct - Motor Vehicle
RED LITE VIOL	M16	4	Red Light Violation
RED SP W/O SIGNAL	S97	2	Stopping/Suddenly Reducing Speed W/O Signal
REF FIL FUEL TX			Refuse To File Fuel Tax Reports
REF SIGN UTT			Refusing To Sign Uniform Traffic Ticket
REG OWN FL YLD EM VEH	N04		Reg. Owner/Veh Fail to Yield Right-Of-Way To Emergency Veh
REQ ACTIVATE/IID	A41		Requesting/Soliciting Another Person To Activate Ignition Interlock
SALE VEH NOT MEET I/S			Permitting Sale Of Vehicle Not Meeting Inspection Standards
SEAT BELT VIOL	F04		Violation Seat Belt Law
SEMI MARKED LIGHTS	E05		Semitrailer Not Properly Marked W/Lights/Warnings
SEMITLR EX 48 FT			Over Length Semitrailer Exceeding 48 Ft
SNOW/SLUSH P-W			Placing Snow/Slush On Public Way
SPD UND PST MIN	S96	2	Speed Under Posted Minimum
SPEED UNDER 15	S93	4	Speeding 1-14 Mph Over Speed Limit
SPEEDING 15-29	S15	6	Speeding 15-29 Mph Over Speed Limit
SPEEDING 30+	S15		Speeding 30 Mph Or More Over Speed Limit
SQUEALING TIRES		2	Squealing Tires
STOP ON H/W			Stopping On Highway
STOP ON TRNPK			Unnecessary Stopping On Turnpike
TAMP WITH M/V			Tampering With A Motor Vehicle
TEST DATES NOT CURRENT			Test Dates Not Current
TEXTING WHILE OP AN MV	M85	2	Texting While Driving
TK M/V W/O CONS			Taking Motor Vehicle Without Consent
TLR W/O LIGHTS	E70	2	No Display Of Lights On Trailer
TOW 53 W/O PERMIT			Towing A 53 Ft Semitrailer W/Out A Permit
TOW UNREG TLR			Towing Unregistered Trailer
TOW UR MV W/O P			Towing Unregistered Motor Vehicle Without Permit
TOW W/O S-CHAN	E01		Towing Without Safety Chain
TOWBAR W/O SAFETY	E01		Towing Without Towbar/Safety Chain
TRANS FORB ITEMS			Transporting Forbidden Items
TRK -150 APAR	M31	2	Trucks Traveling Less Than 150 Feet Apart
TW 2TLR WO CHAI	E01		Towing 2 Trailers Without Safety Chain
TW OW TL WO PRM			Towing Overwidth Trailer Without Permit
TW UTLR INS FAS			Towing Utility Trailer With Insecure Fastening
UN			Unknown
UNINSP MOTOR V			Uninspected Motor Vehicle
UNLAWF DR TRAF INFRAC	D16		Permitting Unlawful Use-Driver Commits Traffic Infraction
UNLAWF USE D/L	D16		Unlawful Use Of Driver License
UNLAWF USE D/L – TRAF INFRA	D16	4	Unlawful Use Of Driver License – Driver Commits Traffic Infraction
UNLIC LOCATION			Operating At Unlicensed Location
UNLIC OP TO DR			Allowing Unlicensed Operator To Drive
UNSECURE LOAD			Unsecured Load On Vehicle
UNSFE SEMI TRLR			Rule Violation Unsafe Semi Trailer
UNSP SEMI TLR	B55		Uninspected Semi Trailer
VEH EQUIP	E01		Violation Of Vehicle Equipment Rule
VEH EQUIP BLUE LIGHT		2	Vehicle Equipped With/Displaying Blue Light
VEH NO PSG ZONE	M76	2	Passenger Veh Traveling Same Direction In No Passing Zone
VEHICLE HOMICIDE CMV	U10		Vehicle Homicide In A CMV
VIO DO NOT PAS	M71	6	Violation Of Do Not Pass Sign
VIO HAZMAT RULE	E03		Causing Op Of MV In Violation Of Hazmat Rules
VIO INST PERMIT	B51	6	Violation Instruction Permit
VIOL INSP STND			Violation Of Inspection Standards
VIOL INTERM	D29		Violate Restrictions Of Driver License
VL LAW RES DTH	U31		Violation Of Law Resulting In Death
WRECKER FLASH AMBER	E55		Wrecker Not Equipped W/Using Flashing Amber Light
YELLOW LINE-VI	M71	2	Yellow Line Violation

Point System Summary

The Maine point system ranges from two to eight points. There is a 15-day suspension due to accumulation of 12 or more points within a one-year period. With 12 months of a clear record, a driver can "earn" a free violation credit point, with a maximum of 4 points. Also, one 3 point credit can be given to a person for successful completion of an authorized Defensive Driving Course or a Motorcycle Defensive Driver Course. The credit will be given only once in a twelve month period and the credit of points will be erased one year from the completion date.

Maryland

Administration	Important Telephone and Web Contacts
John T. Kuo, Administrator Motor Vehicle Administration 6601 Ritchie Highway Glen Burnie 21062 410-768-7274 www.mva.maryland.gov Motor Vehicle Laws: http://mlis.state.md.us	Driver Licensing..................301-729-4550 or 410-768-7000 Driver Records... 410-787-7758 Financial Responsibility .... 410-768-7431 Vehicle Information... 410-768-7508 State Police... 410-486-3101 Maryland Insurance Division........................... 410-468-2000 Email List: www.mva.maryland.gov/General-Information/contact.htm

Driver's License Format, Issuance and Renewal
License Classes, Restrictions and Endorsements Appear After the Driving Record Content Section

License Format

The format is 1 letter and 12 numbers. The letter represents the first letter of the driver's last name. The twelve numbers are coded in groups of three, creating a unique total number: the first three digits are coded to the last name; the second three to the first name; third group to the middle name; and the last group is coded to the month and day of birth.

Document Appearance

Security Characteristics: Advantage transparent coating security feature, bar code of license. Magnetic strip on back contains license number and identifying information.
Position of Photo: Top left with ghost imaging technique.
Minor Age Driver: Card is vertical, "Under 21 alcohol restricted" printed in red.
CDL Indicator: Document I.D. line (under state name) states "CDL".

Issuance

As of June 1, 2009, new applicants for a learner's permit, license, moped operator's permit or ID card must present (1) document to prove age and identity, (1) document to prove they possess a valid, verifiable Social Security Number (SSN) or proof of ineligibility for an SSN, (1) document to prove lawful status and (2) residency documents. The applicant must bring original documents or copies certified by the issuing agency. Photocopies, notarized copies, and documents with alterations or erasures are not accepted. Under the provisions of the law, individuals holding a valid Maryland driver's license or ID card prior to April 19, 2009 but cannot provide proof that they are in the United States legally will be allowed to renew their license or identification card until June 30, 2015, but their product may not be acceptable for federal purposes. After June 30, 2015, any renewal will require all individuals to provide proof of legal presence utilizing acceptable documents outlined above. For more information visit: www.mva.maryland.gov/Driver-Services/Apply/proof.htm

Age Requirements

One cannot obtain a full license until reaching the age of 18.
A Graduated Licensing System with three levels of licensing - Learner's Permit; Provisional License, Full driver's license - is in effect. In 2005 and 2009, modifications were made to the program. Those who hold a Learner's Permit must wait a full nine months before being eligible for a Provisional License. The nine-month period is restarted should the person be convicted or granted *probation before judgment* (PBJ) for a moving violation. The holder must be at least age 16 years and 6 months before being eligible for a provisional license after holding the learner's permit for the mandatory 9 months. Provisional License Holders must hold the Provisional License for a minimum of 18 consecutive months without violation before conversion to a full license. The 18-month period will be restarted for any convictions or PBJ's for moving violations or violations of license restrictions.

Residency

New resident's home state license is honored on reciprocal basis. New residents if currently licensed must pass a vision test and obtain an MD license within sixty days of establishing residency for a non-commercial license and within thirty days for a commercial license. Applicants who have not previously held a driver's license for eighteen months or more, conviction free, will be issued a Provisional driver's license.

Since October 1, 2003, Maryland non-commercial drivers operating a commercial motor vehicle in intrastate commerce (within the state of Maryland) and if the vehicle weight is between 10,001 and 26,000 pounds are required to hold a valid Federal Motor Carrier (DOT) physical card in their possession. If driver is licensed prior to October 1, 2003 and has a pre-existing medical condition, and the onset was prior to that date, the driver is exempt from this requirement for a 20-year period, provided the pre-existing condition does not worsen. All CDL holders must meet FMCSA medical requirements in accordance with 49 CFR 391.41-49.

Renewal

The validity period for drivers 21 or older changed effective Oct 1, 2012. Until that date license expiration occurs on birth day and month of 5th year. Since then the document expires on birth day and month of 8th year. If the driver is under 21, the period expires 60 days after the 21st birthday. Products for individuals, with temporary lawful status, will reflect an expiration date that coincides with the individual's lawful status in the U.S. Driver keeps same license number when renewing, unless name or date of birth change. Drivers have up to one year after expiration to renew without having to take additional tests.

There is no online renewal available. In addition to issuing renewal licenses by mail for eligible applicants (if a current photo image is on file), MD issues a photo license for applicants who are MD residents but temporarily outside the state.

Maryland active duty military personnel stationed out-of-state are not required to renew, but may do so to obtain a valid "absentee photo license." They must renew within 30 days of discharge or return to state. Renewal can be done in-person or by mail for certain drivers.

Also, Maryland's law requires individuals who are 40 and older to obtain vision certification or submit to an MVA vision screening each time a license is renewed. Individuals under the age of 40 are required to obtain a vision certification every 10 years.

Elderly-Related Restrictions

There are no restrictions in place for renewing drivers. Individuals 70 years or older who are applying for an original (first time issued anywhere) Maryland license must provide proof of satisfactory operation of a motor vehicle or a written certification from a licensed physician attesting to the general physical and mental qualifications of the applicant.

Vehicle Insurance, Title and Registration Facts

Registration Renewal

Online registration renewal via the web is available through a program called "FastTrack." The link is easily found at www.mva.maryland.gov. A change of address can also be performed online. Owners can also go to a private tag and title service or renew by mail when they receive their notices. Or they can renew by telephone by calling 888-834-7344.

New Residents

New residents must register their vehicles within sixty days of establishing residence.

Inspections and Emissions Testing

Maryland requires a safety inspection for all used vehicles at the time of transfer.

Emission testing is required every two years in 14 counties and in the City of Baltimore. An On-Board Diagnostics (OBD) test is required for; 1) model year 1996 and newer passenger vehicles and light duty trucks, 2) model year 2008 and newer heavy duty vehicles up to 14,000 pounds. The Idle Tailpipe test is required for; 1) model year 1977 - 1995 passenger vehicles and light duty trucks, 2) model year 1977 - 2007 heavy duty vehicles up to 14,000 pounds, 3) model year 1977 and newer heavy duty vehicles 14,000 - 26,000 pounds. New vehicles are exempt from testing for the first two years with testing scheduled between 30 and 36 months. Senior citizens 70 years of age or older that drive less than 5,000 miles per year may apply for an exemption.

Passenger Plate Facts

There are two plates with two decals (MO) (YR) on rear. The state does not designate the county of issuance on the plate. When a vehicle is sold the plates remain with seller.

Withdrawal Sanctions, and Alcohol and Drug Testing

Alcohol and Chemical Testing Limits

Maryland's illegal alcoholic levels are: .08 % or higher is "under the influence;" .10 % and above is "intoxicated." The legal limit for drivers under 21 is .02, if driving a CMV .04. Blood and breath testing are authorized. Maryland has both an implied-consent violation and a provision for an administrative suspension. Operating a horse or bicycle under the influence is also considered illegal.

Suspensions and Revocations

Maryland completed structure testing and received CDLIS certification in 2006. See the Appendix for more information about the mandatory CDL disqualification sanctions.

Driving While Intoxicated
    First Conviction   Minimum six-month revocation.
    Second Conviction   Twelve-month revocation.
    Third and Subsequent Convictions   Eighteen-month revocation.
Driving While Under the Influence
    First Conviction   Up to sixty-day suspension.
    Second and Subsequent Convictions   Up to 120-day suspension.
Refusal to Submit to Chemical Test
    First Offense   120-day suspension.
    Second and Subsequent Offenses   One-year suspension.
Administrative Per Se (for test results .08 percent alcohol concentration or more)
    First Offense   Forty-five-day suspension.
    Second Offense   Ninety-day suspension.

The Administration May Cancel, Revoke, Refuse, or Suspend a License for any of the Following Reasons:

- Accumulation of 8 to 11 points in a two-year period (suspension)
- Accumulation of 12 or more points in a two-year period (revocation)
- Commission of an offense in another state, which would require revocation or suspension in Maryland.
- Disregard of traffic laws and the safety of others
- Making a false certification of insurance on any application for a title or vehicle registration
- Outstanding arrest warrants—law enforcement agencies notify the MV Administration which places a flags/suspends the license
- Permitting unlawful or fraudulent use of a driver license
- Provisional Driver under age 18 operating a motor vehicle while using a wireless communication device and or cell phone
- Suspension or revocation in another state
- Unfit, unsafe, habitually negligent or reckless driver
- Violation of license restrictions

Repeat Offender - A Repeat Offender is anyone who has received more than one "driving under the influence" (DUI) violation within a 5-year period. A Repeat Offender will be suspended for a one-year period. After the one-year suspension period has ended, the person then must maintain an ignition interlock device on his or her vehicle(s) for one year.

Reinstatement Requirements

Suspension   Time lapse (reinstatement procedure not required for suspension.
Revocation   Time lapse and reinstatement process.
Fees $15.00 filing fee; $30.00 approval fee; $60.00 approval fee if revocation due to alcohol/drug-related motor vehicle violation).

The reinstatement process includes: a reinstatement application; $15.00 filing fee; and current close-up photograph (applicant's) signed "Authorization for Release of Information Form." Could also include Driver Improvement Program; interview with Medical Advisory Board; or Alcohol Treatment or Education Program. If applicant has been involved in two alcohol incidents in preceding five years or three or more alcohol incidents during any time period, must submit evidence of current on-going satisfactory treatment, along with reinstatement application. There is a $30.00 restoration fee for those licenses flagged and suspended for outstanding arrest warrants.

Insurance and Financial Responsibility

Maryland law requires that all motor vehicles registered in Maryland be insured by a company licensed in Maryland and carry coverage of $30,000 for bodily injury per person, $60,000 for bodily injury for two or more people, and $15,000 for property damage. The state has optional add-on no-fault insurance (PIP coverage of $2,500) and compulsory insurance. The state does not use insurance cards; vehicle owners must self-certify when registering or upon renewal. Proof is required when the state is notified by the insurance company of a cancellation (FR-19 needed), through random selection, and when a warning letter is issued for accumulation of bad driving points.

Penalties Assessed Against Uninsured Drivers—If insurance certification Form FR-19 is not submitted to verify continuous insurance of a vehicle, penalties are assessed at the rate of $150 for the first 30 days the vehicle is uninsured and $7.00 for each additional day. Non-compliance also results in suspension of the uninsured vehicle registration and future registration privileges.

Record Access: Laws, Rules, and Forms

Note: **This Section Applies to Both Driver and Vehicle Records.**

Governing Statutes and Rules

Motor Vehicle Laws–Transportation Article   http://mlis.state.md.us
Per Transportation Article §12-111, §12-112, §12-113, §16-117, the state adopted the provisions of DPPA. State Government Article 10-610, 10-611, 10-616 and 10-626 deal with permitted release of personal information.

Maryland does not have the following Federal exceptions: 11, 12, and 13. Maryland added the following exceptions:

(xi) for use by an applicant who provides written consent from the individual to whom the information pertains if the consent is obtained within the 6-month period before the date of the request for personal information;

(xii) for use in any matter relating to:
the operation of a Class B (for hire), Class C (funeral and ambulance), or Class Q (limousine) vehicle; and
public safety or the treatment by the operator of a member of the public;

(xiv) for use by a hospital to obtain, for hospital security purposes, information relating to ownership of vehicles parked on hospital property.

As part of the agreement, direct access/online subscribers are required to state the purpose for which records will be accessed, which must be in accord with DPPA. No other screening is done at this time

Request and Consent Forms

Request for MVA Records for Businesses (Form # DL-015) is used for a business to request multiple records. The form must be filled and submitted with the required fee. Non-permissible use requesters must provide the consent of the subject using *Form DL# 57*. This form requires proof of the requester's identity - a notary is not required. Both forms may be downloaded from the Forms tab at www.mva.maryland.gov.

Vendor and Third Party Access Policy

Approved vendors may access records for other approved vendors. Maryland will not approve vendor access, resale, or use for purposes other than authorized by DPPA. To become an approved vendor, it is suggested to call the MVA Driver Records Unit or email to mvrsdatarequests@mdot.state.md.us.

Records Ordered For Non-permissible Uses

Without consent or permissible use, driving records are not released.

Access to Driver-Related Records

Note: In Maryland a driving record is referred to as a "Driver History Record" or "DLR." A title or registration record is referred to as a" Motor Vehicle Record" or "MVR."

Driving Records

General Information and Fees

MVA, Driver Records Unit, 6601 Ritchie Highway NE, Rm 145, Glen Burnie 21062, 410-787-7758.

The fee for a driving record is $9.00. There is an additional $3.00 fee to certify a non-electronic record. The state does charge for "no record found" reports, except for walk-in requests. The fee must accompany requests except for online service which is billed monthly and tape which is pre-paid. The last fee increase was in July 2004.

In-Person – Records may be requested from MVA office and Express locations in 19 cities. Up to 6 requests will be processed while you wait. If more than 6 requests are presented, the results are available in 1-3 business days. Credit cards are accepted. There is no charge for "no record found" reports.

Mail – Records are processed in two-to-three days. The driver's license number, or name and date of birth are needed when ordering.

Electronic – Effective May 1, 2012, the Maryland Motor Vehicle Administration began partnering with NICUSA regarding the access of driver and vehicle records previously accessed through MVA's subscription services (DARS, LMS, etc.). The fee is $12.00 per record for either interactive or batch access.

There is a $95.00 subscription fee (which was waived for existing subscribers to DARS). For more information call 888-963-3468 or visit https://www.egov.maryland.gov/register/. A business can request an information package for MVA's Direct Access Record System by email to mvrsdatarequest@mdot.state.md.us.

Bulk – The MVA provides bulk release of record data (partial records or elements of MVA's vehicle record) to authorized entities (e.g. law enforcement, courts, businesses, etc.) via a secure electronic method (FTP) or encrypted CD. Examples of authorized entities include courts that request a file of names & addresses of vehicle owners who fail to pay parking citations, or a vendor providing vehicle recall data.

By Person of Record – An individual may order an electronic copy of their driving record to be mailed within 10 business days to the individual's address currently on record with the MVA. Go to https://secure.marylandmva.com/emvaservices/VRR/DrRecord_Entry.asp?sku=drrecord. Either a certified or non-certified copy can be requested. If the individual has an MVA PIN, the record may be viewed online and the record also will be mailed. If an individual who moved out-of-state needs a copy of the MD driving record, the transaction must be done by mail or in person. The same $9.00 or $12.00 fee applies. Checks (with bank routing number) and credit cards are accepted.

Notification/Monitoring Program

As mentioned above, the MVA has contracted NICUSA regarding the **License Monitor System (LMS)** for employers and insurance companies that need to monitor their employees' or insured drivers' driving records for violations and suspension.

Approved requesters use batch file transfer (FTP) to register drivers for monitoring. Each night, the system inspects the records of monitored drivers and generates a result file containing either the changes to each driver record or the entire driver record. Only those updates that have been deemed as moving violations, suspensions, cancellations, revocations, and restrictions are provided to the subscribers of LMS. By this means, subscribers only receive new activity that is meaningful. A three-year driving record is produced and sent to the customer whenever a new Driver's License number is submitted. Upon the anniversary date of the subscriber's participation in the program, a new three-year driving record for each Driver's License is produced and the client is billed accordingly at the current rate. The fee for the batch access for monitoring (LMS) is $0.08 per record. The fee is $12.00 when a driving record is produced.

There is a $95.00 subscription fee, which was waived for existing subscribers to DARS. For more information go to https://www.egov.maryland.gov/register/ or call 888-963-3468.

Accident Reports

Reporting – Every operator involved in an accident resulting in injury or death—regardless of fault—must report the accident to the Motor Vehicle Administration (6601 Ritchie Highway, Glen Burnie MD 21062) within fifteen days. No report is required from the operator if the accident is investigated by a law enforcement officer and involves property damage only.

Record Access – Copies of accident reports investigated by the State Police (except for occurrence in the city of Baltimore) can be requested from: Maryland State Police, Central Records Division, 1711 Belmont, Woodlawn MD 21244, 410-298-3390. http://www.mdsp.org/. Requests should include report number, date of incident, driver(s) names, self-addressed stamped envelope, and $4.00 check or money order for each record. If there was a fatality involved, please state so since these records are handled by a different unit. In can take 20 days before new records are available for inquiry. Turnaround time can take 3 to 4 weeks. Records are kept for 5 years plus present year. There is a downloadable request form from the web page.

For reports in Baltimore, call 410-396-2663 or 2222; the record center closes at 3PM.

Access to Vehicle-Related Records

General Information and Fees

Vehicle Registration Division; 6601 Ritchie Highway NE, Room 204; Glen Burnie 21062; 410-768-7508, fax 410-768-7529. The fee for VIN, plate, ownership, title histories and lien searches (including unattached mobile homes/house trailers) is $9.00 per non-certified record and $12.00 per certified record or electronic record. Medical information is not released. Title service agents (private businesses) may also supply certified copies of title and registration documents.

In-Person, Mail, Fax – No special forms are needed, but the fee must accompany the request. Major credit cards are accepted at the counter. Mail requests will take up to one week to process. Requests on letterhead are preferred.

Title service agents offer services related to MVA certificates of title, registrations, drivers' licenses, certified copies of records, and other related documents. Fees may vary. The MVA does not maintain information of the services each agent provides, but provides a list of agents at www.mva.maryland.gov/VehicleServ/REG/titleagents.htm.

Electronic – Requesters can access the vehicle records in the same manner as described under the Driving Records section. The same access and subscription fees apply. A business can request an information package for MVA's Direct Access Record System by email to mvrsdatarequest@mdot.state.md.us. The link to sign up for online access is at https://egov.maryland.gov/register

Also a monitoring program is offered for vehicle records. The electronic batch service allows customers to securely upload specifically formatted request files containing identifying information for vehicles for which they need records. Each night the system processes the request files, looks up the requested vehicle records, and returns a results file which is securely downloaded by the customer.

Bulk – The MVA VORS program provides larger volumes of record data (partial records or elements of MVA's vehicle record) to authorized entities (e.g. law enforcement, courts, businesses, etc.) via a secure electronic method (FTP). An example of a typical reason for a Data Client to obtain a high volume of partial records is a court that requests a file of names & addresses of vehicle owners who fail to pay parking citations; a research company for vehicle recalls, etc. For questions or to request application forms, visit https://egov.maryland.gov/register or email MVRSDataRequests@mdot.state.md.us.

Access to Vessel-Related Records

General Information, Access and Fees

Department of Natural Resources, Licensing & Watercraft Division, 1804 West St #300, Annapolis 21401 410-260-3220, fax 410-260-4339, http://dnr.maryland.gov/service/.

All motorized boats must be titled and registered. Vessels 16 feet in length or less and/or propelled by a motor of 7.5 hp or less must display a 2-year registration decal but are exempt from the registration fee. The 2-year registration decal is valid for the calendar year in which it is issued and the subsequent year, expiring on December 31. Boat trailers are registered with the Maryland Motor Vehicle Administration. Records are maintained since 1962; paper records kept 5 years before conversion to digital imaging.

Three types of records are released: certified true copy for $10.00; microfiche history file for $5.00; and a current computer file copy for $5.00. Lien records are blocked and are not released. However, when asked the Department will indicate with a yes or no if a lien exists. A Maryland boat number, tidal fish license number, or name and address of boat owner or tidal fish license holder are needed for look-up. At most, it takes about 2 weeks to process a request. The home address, phone and DOB of a subject will not be released. There are 6 additional Regional Service Centers in the state that will process in-person record requests.

Driving Record Content and Reciprocity

What's On or Not On the Driving Record

- The driver's address is part of the record in compliance with DPPA or if consent given.
- All convictions are listed on the public record. Accident indicators are shown on the MVR only if citation is issued.
- For CDL holders, until programming is completed, a "full" or complete history may be provided particularly if a written request is sent by mail. Otherwise, and if another state submits the request electronically, a 10-year CDL record is returned electronically.
- For non-CDL holders, the length of time that convictions are listed on the drivers record is governed by statute 16-117.1 is as follows, all from date of last moving violation: Moving Violations - Three

years; DWI or 2 or more Suspensions - Ten years; Single Suspension - Five years from date of last moving violation.
- The state does not permit driver school attendance in lieu of conviction.

Data Retention

Violations shall be automatically purged from the driving records of non-flagrant violators. The law requires a request from drivers to have other violations purged from the driving record. This purge is made using the above timetable. The length of time a record is accessible for a surrendered license is determined by the purge criteria. CDL driver records are purged based on the timetable per the federal disqualification rules (see the Appendix)

Court to Repository

The MD court system reports convictions within five to ten days, via electronic media or paper to the MVA or the driver's home state.

State Reciprocity for Non-CDL Drivers

- Will suspend license of driver for unpaid out-of-state convictions.
- Record of new incoming driver is shown on MVR.

- Out-of-state convictions are shown on MVR.
- Out-of-state accidents are not shown on MVR.
- Convictions of out-of-state drivers are sent to home state.
- Record is forwarded to new state upon surrender of license upon request.

License Classes, Restrictions, and Endorsements Codes

License Classes– Commercial

Class	One May Drive	And May Tow	Exceptions
Class A	Any single combination of vehicles	Any trailer	Motorcycles
Class B	Motor vehicles 26,001 or more pounds (GVW)	Trailers 10,000 pounds or less	Combination of Class F (tractor) and Class G (trailer), Motorcycles
Class C	Motor vehicles under 26,001 pounds (GVW)	Trailers to 10,000 pounds or less	Motorcycles

License Classes– Non-Commercial

Class	One May Drive	And May Tow	Exceptions
Class A	Any single or combination of non-commercial motor vehicles	Any non-commercial trailer	Commercial Motor Vehicles, Motorcycles
Class B	Any non-commercial vehicle 26,001 or more pounds (GVW)	Any non-commercial trailer	Commercial Motor Vehicles, Combination of Class F (tractor) and Class G (trailer), Motorcycles
Class C	Any non-commercial combination of motor vehicles with a GCW less than 26,001 pounds	Any non-commercial trailer	Commercial Motor Vehicles, Motorcycles
Class M	Motorcycles	Motorcycle trailer	Commercial & Non-Commercial Motor Vehicles - Classes A, B & C

Restrictions

B	Corrective Lenses	H	Limited (see restriction card)	L	Vehicles Without Air-Brakes
C	Special Brakes, Hand-Controls/Other	I	Limited (see restriction card)	M	Except Class A Bus
D	Prosthetic Aid	J	Other Customized Text Including Alcohol, Interlock Device, Employment, and Education.	N	Except Class A and B Bus
E	Automatic Transmission			O	Except Tractor-Trailer
F	Outside Rearview Mirror			Z	Organ Donor, Hearing/Speech Impaired
G	Limited to Daylight Only	K	CDL Intrastate Only		

Endorsements

T	Double-/Triple-Trailers	H	Hazardous Materials	TPXS	All CDL Endorsements
P	Passenger Transport	S	School Bus Authorized		
N	Tank Vehicle	X	N and H Combined		

Unique Abbreviations Found on Maryland Driving Records

*	Points Expired	CG	Corrected gratis license	EC	Express consent
A	License class	CIR	Circuit	EFF	Effective
A/A	Administrative adjudication	CLF	Central license file	ELEC	Electric
ABEY	Abeyance	CLR	Clearance	EMP	Employee, Employment
A/C	Air conditioning	CONTR	Control	ENT	Entry
ACC	Accident	COR	Corrected	EX	Expired, expiration
ACCUM	Accumulate-accumulated	CR	Corrected renewal license; or credit	EXC	Exceeding
ACT	Action-acted			EXD	Excluded driver case
ADM	Administration/administrative	CSE	Child Support Enforcement	EXP	Explosives
AEP	Alcohol education program	CT	Court	FA	Fatal accident
AFF	Affirmed	D	Days (30D)	FC	Full credit
AOM	Age of majority	D	License class	FI	Fictitious
APP	Application	D-1	Duplicate license	FPF	Fail to pay fine
APPR	Approved or approval	D/R	Driver Records	F/R	Financial responsibility
A/R	Alcohol related	DEC	Decision	FR#()	Financial responsibility case (date)
ATT	Attend	DEV	Device		
AUM	Accident - uninsured	DIP	Driver improvement program	FT	Feet, Failed test
B	License class	DIS	Displaying	FTA	Fail to appear
BAC	Blood Alcohol Level	DIST	District	H	Hearing (Hearing officers initials)
B/S	Blackout/seizure	DR	Drive, driving, driver	HFA	Hearing - failed to appear
C	Corrected license	D/R	Driver records	HGT	Height
C	License class	DRC	Driver rehabilitation clinic	HW	Hearing waived
C/FS	Complaint of false statement	DT	Date	IC	Implied Consent
CDS	Controlled dangerous substance	DTO	Dealer tags only	IMP	Improper, improvement
CESA	Child Enforcement Safety Admin	E	License class	INC	Increase

IND	Indefinite	PI	Personal injury	SCH	Scheduled
INF	Influence	POS	Possession	SER	Serial
INJ	Injury	PROB	Probated or probation	SIGN	Signed
INS	Insurance	PROH	Prohibited	SNL	Signed statement no license in possession
INTER	Interest	PROP	Property		
INVEST	Investigation	PSYS	Point system	SPA	Suspended pending appearance
ISS	Issued	PT	Passed test	SPEC	Special
IVP	Insurance verification program case	PUR	Purpose	SS	Sentence suspended
		PWV	Probation without (or before) verdict	ST	Student
J	MVA Judgment case			STAT	Statement
LEA	Law enforcement agency	R	Refused	SUB	Substitute
LO	Violation of local ordinance	R	Renewal license	SUBST	Substance
M	Months; or license class (motorcycle)	RA	Application for reinstatement	SUR	Surrender
		RE	Reissued	SUS	Suspended or suspension
(MV)	Moving Violation	RECD	Received	SW	Suspension withdrawn
MAB	Medical Advisory Board case	RECIP	Reciprocity	SYS	System
MAG	Magistrate	REF	Refused or refusal	TP	Test place
MAIF	Maryland Automobile Insurance Fund	REHEAR	Rehearing	TRANS	Transportation or transporting
		REL	Relative, related	TRK	Truck
MISREP	Misrepresentation	REM	Remand, remanded	TUN	Tunnel
MO	Motorcycle or Motorscooter	REQ	Requirement, require	TV	Television
MODI	Modified	RES	Resident	TY	Regular or photo license
MUT	Mutilated	RESC	Rescinded	UL	Investigation - unable to locate
MV	Moving Violation	RESCH	Rescheduled	UMC	Uninsured motorist complaint case
MVA	Motor Vehicle Administration	RET	Return		
NC	Nolo contendere	RETRO	Retroactive	UN	Under
NEGL	Negligent	RI	Reinstated	VER	Verdict
NRS	Non-Resident student	RP	Reprimand	WARR	Warrant
OBT	Obtain	RPA	Refused or revoked pending appearance	WDN	Withdrawn
O/C	Out-of-country			WL	Warning letter
OP	Operating	RR	Railroad, restriction removed	W/O	Without
O/S	Out of state	R/R	Review and reinstatement	X	Involved in an accident
PAR	Parent	RS	Random selection	YDIP	Youth driver improvement program
PBJ	Probation before judgment	RTT	Brake reaction time test		
PED	Pedestrian	S	Substitute license	YLCP	Youth license control program
PD	Property damage	SAT	Satisfied		

Conviction Table with ACD, State Code, and Points

- The State Code column is an internal code used by the MVA. While this code does NOT appear on the driving record, it is a code reference point for discussion with the MVA about a specific conviction.
- Some driving records may show a four digit number that indicates the court of conviction. For example 6325 is the code for the District Court in Baltimore County and 6005 is the code of the District Court in Baltimore City. These codes are not violation codes and should not be confused with the State Code column.
- Any conviction shown as a one or two point violation becomes a three point violation if the violation contributes to an accident.

Description	Points	State Code	ACD
1st Order Of Suspension Issued Alcohol Content .08 Or More		5846	A98
2nd Order Of Suspension Issued Alcohol Content .08 Or More		5847	A98
Note: Will continue to 8th Order, the State Code increasing by one count each time			
1st Order Of Suspension Issued Alcohol Content .10 Or More		5710	A12
2nd Order Of Suspension Issued Alcohol Content .08 Or More		5711	A12
Note: Will continue to 8th Order, the State Code increasing by one count each time			
1st Order Of Suspension Issued Alcohol Content .15 Or More		6021	A98
2nd Order Of Suspension Issued Alcohol Content .15 Or More		6022	A98
Note: Will continue to 8th Order, the State Code increasing by one count each time			
A/R Cancel Lic-Ref Pend Clr In		1521	A20
A/R Hear-Fail To Appear-Ref		1509	A20
A/R Hear-Fail To Appear-Rev		1511	A20
A/R Hear-Fail To Appear-Sus		1510	A20
A/R Hear-Fail To Appear-Sus Refused 1st Chemical Test		5613	A12
A/R Hear-Fail To Appear-Sus Refused 2nd Chemical Test		5614	A12
A/R Hear-Fail To Appear-Sus Refused 3rd Chemical Test		5615	A12
A/R Hear-Fail To Appear-Sus Refused Chemical Test		5612	A12
A/R Hearing Waived-Refused		1506	A20
A/R Hearing Waived-Refused		5634	A21
A/R Hearing Waived-Revoked		1508	A20
A/R Hearing Waived-Revoked		5636	A21
A/R Hearing Waived-Suspended		1507	A20

Description	Points	State Code	ACD
A/R Hearing Waived-Suspended		5635	A21
A/R Hearing-.10 Or More Failed To Appear-Suspended		5772	A90
A/R Hearing-1st .10 Or More Failed To Appear-Suspended		5773	A90
A/R Hearing-2nd .10 Or More Failed To Appear-Suspended		5774	A90
Note: Will continue to 8th hearing, the State Code increasing by one count each time			
A/R Hearing-Failed To Appear Refused		5637	A21
A/R Hearing-Failed To Appear Revoked		5639	A21
A/R Hearing-Failed To Appear Suspended		5638	A21
A/R Hearing-License Cancelled		1523	A20
A/R Hearing-License Cancelled		5647, 5649	A21
A/R Hearing-License Cancelled Refused Pending Clearance In		5647	A21
A/R Hearing-License Suspended For		5646	A21
A/R Hearing-Mab Refusal Withdrawn		5655	
A/R Hearing-Mab Suspension Withdrawn		5654	
A/R Hearing-Privilege To Drive In MD-Suspended		5633	A21
A/R Hearing-Refused		1501	A20
A/R Hearing-Refused		5601	A21
A/R Hearing-Refused Pending Clearance By Mab		5653	A21
A/R Hearing-Revocation Continued		5676	A21
A/R Hearing-Revocation Retro-Active To		5675	
A/R Hearing-Revocation To Stand		5600	
A/R Hearing-Revoked		1503	A20
A/R Hearing-Revoked		5611	A21
A/R Hearing-Sus Concurrent		1513	A20
A/R Hearing-Sus Consecutive		1514	A20
A/R Hearing-Suspended		5621	A12
A/R Hearing-Suspended		1505	A20
A/R Hearing Suspended Alcohol Content .15 or More		6056	A98
A/R Hearing Suspended 1st Offense Alcohol Content .15 or More		6057	A98
A/R Hearing Suspended 2nd Offense Alcohol Content .15 or More		6058	A98
Note: Will continue to 8th Suspension, State Code increasing by one count each time			
A/R Hearing-Suspended For 1 Year		5632	A21
A/R Hearing-Suspended For 10 Days		5622	A21
A/R Hearing-Suspended For 120 Days		5629	A21
A/R Hearing-Suspended For 180 Days		5631	A21
A/R Hearing-Suspended Pending Clearance By Mab		5652	A21
A/R Hearing-Suspended Refused 1st Chemical Test		5603	A12
A/R Hearing-Suspended Refused 2nd Chemical Test		5604	A12
A/R Hearing-Suspended Refused 3rd Chemical Test		5605	A12
A/R Hearing-Suspended Refused Chemical Test		5602	A12
A/R Hearing-Suspended Retro-Active To		5674	
A/R Hearing-Suspension Concurrent		5640	A21
A/R Hearing-Suspension Consecutive		5641	A21
A/R Hear-Ref 1st Chemical Test Failed To Appear-Rev Continued		5666	A12
A/R Hear-Ref 2nd Chemical Test Failed To Appear-Rev Continued		5667	A12
A/R Hear-Ref 3rd Chemical Test Failed To Appear-Rev Continued		5668	A12
A/R Hear-Revocation Continued Refused 1st Chemical Test		5658	A12
A/R Hear-Revocation Continued Refused 2nd Chemical Test		5659	A12
A/R Hear-Revocation Continued Refused 3rd Chemical Test		5660	A12
A/R Hear-Revocation To Stand		1500	
A/R Hear-Sus-R-Chemical Test		1502	A12
A/R H-Lic Canc-Ref Pend Clr In		1520	A20
A/R License Cancelled- Refused Pending Clearance In		5648	A21
A/R License Suspended For		5645	A21
A/R License Suspended For X		1519	A29
A/R Mab Refused		5651	A21
A/R Mab Suspended		5650	A21
A/R Mab-Refused		1525	W14
A/R Mab-Suspended		1524	W14
A/R Point System-Revoked		5642	A21
A/R Pt Sys Sus-Lic Not Surr		1522	A20
A/R Pt System-Revoked		1516	A20
A/R Pt System-Suspended		1515	A20
A/R Rev Failed To Attend Aep		1527	A20
A/R Revocation Continued		1518	
A/R Revocation Continued		5644	A21
A/R Revoked		1517	A20
A/R Revoked		5643	A21
A/R Revoked-Failed To Attend Alcohol Education Program		5657	

Description	Points	State Code	ACD
A/R Sus Failed To Attend Aep		1526	A20
A/R Sus-Hfa-R-Chemical Test		1504	A12
A/R Suspended Alcohol Content .10 Or More		5727	A90
A/R Suspended For Misrepresentation Of Age		6000	
A/R Suspended Refused 1st Chemical Test		5719	A12
A/R Suspended Refused 2nd Chemical Test		5720	A12
A/R Suspended Refused Chemical Test		5718	A12
A/R Suspended-Failed To Attend Alcohol Education Program		5656	
A/R Suspension Imposed		5680	A21
A/R Suspension Imposed Violation Of Lic Restriction		5688	
A/R-Suspended-1st Offense Alcohol Content .10 Or More		5728	A90
A/R-Suspended-2nd Offense Alcohol Content .10 Or More		5729	A90
A/R-Suspended-3rd Offense Alcohol Content .10 Or More		5730	A90
A/R-Suspended-Alcohol Content .15 Or More		6029	A98
A/R-Suspended-1st Offense Alcohol Content .15 Or More		6030	A98
A/R-Suspended-2nd Offense Alcohol Content .15 Or More		6031	A98
Note: Will continue to 8th Suspension, State Code increasing by one count each time			
Act as Dr Instructor w/o License		2148	
Aggressive Driving	5	2983	
Alcohol Concentration .04 Or More While Driving CMV		5677	
Allow Minor Under Age 15 To Dr	5	0409	
Alter Forge Documents/Plates	12	0107	
Alter/Change Veh Equipment After Inspectio/Repair Cert Iss		3952	
Alter/Reduce Effectiveness of Vehicle Bumpers		3460	E01
Altered Or Forged Documents	12	0108	
Altered Or Forged Plates	1	0610	
Approved For Operator License Only By Medical Advisory Board		4506	
Attempting Op Under Inf Drugs		0841	A22
Attempting Op Under Inf Liquor		0840	A21
Authorize/Permit Violation By A Minor Or Ward		3242	
Automatic Signal	1	0703	M16
Bench Warrant Dist Court Sus		1385	
Cause/Knowingly Permit Unauth Minor To Drive Motor Veh	5	2310	
CDL Dr Fail To Notify MVA Within 30 D Name/Add Change		2314	
CDL License Downgraded To Non-Commercial License		4263	
Clearance Received		5678	
Coasting Down Grade	1	0730	N80
Coasting Downgrade In Neutral With Clutch Disengaged	1	3130	N80
Commercial Driver License Disqualification Withdrawn		4962	
Commit fraud in appl for cert of title/reg of veh (MV)	12	1880	
Commit Life Threatening Injury By Means Of A Vehicle	12	4192	
Completed Dr Improve Program Revocation Withdrawn		5324	
Conducting driving school without license		2147	
Consent Filed-Sus Withdrawn		1041	
Consent Withdrawn-Suspended		1040	W13
Consuming Alc Bev In Pass Area Of Mtr Vehicle On Hwy	1	3042	
Cross Property/Leave Roadway To Avoid Traf Control Dev	1	2461	
Crossing Center Line	1	0706	M41
Crossing Over Fire Hose	1	0741	M56
Damaging/tampering/entering vehicle without owners consent		2000	
Dealer fail collect tax/fees/keep required dealer records		1900	
Defaulted In Judgment Payments License And Veh Tags Suspended		4807	D37
Dis 120days CMV Three Separate Serious Conv Within 3yr Period		4956	W31
Dis 1yr For A Crime Punishable By Death/One Year Imprisonment		4937	U04
Dis 3yr Dr CMV With Hazmat And .04 Or More Alcohol Conc		4942	A94
Dis 3yr Dr CMV With Hazmat And Leaving Scene Of Accident		4946	B01
Dis 3yr Dr CMV With Hazmat And Refused Test For Alcohol Conc		4944	A12
Dis 3yr Dr CMV With Hazmat And Under Inf Of Controlled Subst		4945	A22
Dis 3yr Dr CMV With Hazmat And Under Influence Of Alcohol		4943	A21
Dis 3yr For A Crime Punishable By Death/One Year Imprisonment		4948	U04
Dis 3yr For A Felony Involving The Use Of CMV With Hazmat		4947	U03
Dis 60 Days CMV Two Separate Serious Conv Within 3yr Period		4955	W30
Dis Canc Rev Sus Fi License		0848	B20
Dis Canc Rev Sus Fi-Alter Lic	12	0203	B41
Dis Lifetime CMV Used Comm A Felony Mfg/Dist/Dispensing Cs		4953	A50
Dis Lifetime Viol Part 49 Code		4938	W40
Dis Lifetime Viol Part 49 Code Fed Regs 383.51b3iv In CMV		4954	
Dis/permit dis of reg plate issued to other veh/person		1687	
Dis/sell/deliver unapproved equip or w/o appr trademark		3451	

Description	Points	State Code	ACD
Discharge Refuse From Vehicle	1	0771	
Discriminate against employee use of company van pool		1744	
Dispensing of mtr fuel to dirt bike from retail pump in balt		3249	
Display/Possess Altered License	12	2283	D16
Display/Possess Canceled License	12	2276	D16
Display/Possess Fictitious License	12	2279	D16
Display/Possess Revoked License	12	2277	D16
Display/Possess Suspended License	12	2278	D16
Display/Represent License Not Own	12	2285	D16
Displaying expired plates issued by any state		1686	
Displaying License Of Another	12	0207	
Displaying License Of Another	1	0737	
Disqualification Of Commercial Driver License		4957	
Disqualified-120 Days Railroad Crossing Violation In CMV		4965	W60
Disqualified-1yr Dr CMV Under Inf Of Controlled Substance		4934	A22
Disqualified-1yr For A Felony Involving The Use Of CMV		4936	U03
Disqualified-1yr For Dr A CMV When Alch Conc .04 Or More		4931	A94
Disqualified-1yr For Dr A CMV When Under Inf Of Alcohol		4932	A21
Disqualified-1yr Leaving Scene Of Accident Involving A CMV		4935	B01
Disqualified-1yr Refused Test For Alcohol Concentration		4933	A12
Disqualified-1yr-Railroad Crossing Violation In CMV		4966	W61
Disqualified-60days-Railroad Crossing Violation In CMV		4964	
District Court Fail To Appear Suspension Withdrawn		4221	
District Court-Fail To Appear Suspended		4217	D45
District Of Columbia Recip Suspension Withdrawn		4251	
Dr Ability Impaired By Alcohol	6	0350	A25
Dr Ability Impaired By Drugs	6	0351	A22
Dr Across Center Line/Fail To Dr Right Side Of Rdwy	1	2520	N70
Dr After Ref Canc Sus Or Rev	12	0001	B20
Dr After Suspended For Ins Vio	3	0551	B26
Dr Alone On Instruction Lic	5	0405	D29
Dr CMV subj to OOS trans 16 or more pass including dr (MV)	12	2337	
Dr CMV While Lic/Priv Canceled By Any Other State	12	2321	B22
Dr CMV while lic/priv disqual by U.S. Dept of Trans (MV)	12	2334	
Dr CMV While Lic/Privilege Canceled In This State	12	2319	B22
Dr CMV While Lic/Privilege Disq In This/Any State	12	2326	B24
Dr CMV While Lic/Privilege Ref In This/Any Other State	12	2318	B23
Dr CMV While Lic/Privilege Revoked By Any Other State	12	2325	B25
Dr CMV While Lic/Privilege Revoked In This State	12	2324	B25
Dr CMV While Lic/Privilege Susp By Any Other State	12	2323	B26
Dr CMV While Lic/Privilege Suspended In This State	12	2322	B26
Dr CMV While Subject To Out-Of		2331	
Dr CMV Without A Valid CMV License In Possession		2332	B51
Dr CMV Without Authorization/ without obtaining a CDL		2333	
Dr CMV Without Required Lic For Class Of Vehicle	2	2313	B91
Dr fail to notify police after strike/injure domestic animal		2420	
Dr Fail To Use School Bus Zone	1	0798	M40
Dr Foreign Lic-Sus/Rev In Md	12	0224	B26
Dr In Improper Manner To Cause Skid/Spin Wheels/Noise	1	3210	N83
Dr Inf Drugs Or Drugs/Alcohol	6	0352	A20
Dr low spd veh across hwy pst spd exc 45 mph no trf dev (MV)	1	3248	
Dr low spd veh on hwy posted spd exceeds 30 mph (MV)	1	3245	
Dr low spd veh on prohibited county, municipal hwy (MV)	1	3247	
Dr M/V On Learner Permit With Unauth Person In Front Seat		2181	
Dr M/V While Consuming Alcohol	1	0578	A26
Dr Of CMV Fail To Apply Within 30 D For Cdl License		2315	B51
Dr Over Unprotected Fire Hose W/O Consent Of Fire Dept	1	3150	M56
Dr pass emer veh in proc of park or back w/in 100' of sta		3142	
Dr Privilege Suspension Wdn By Medical Advisory Board		4503	
Dr School Veh W/O Proper Class Lic/Endorsements/Cert	8	2329	B91
Dr School Veh With Passengers In Excess Of 45 Mph	1	2960, 2959	S93
Dr Veh In Race/Spd Contest On Hwy/Pri Prop Used By Publ	5	3201	S95
Dr Veh On Vehicular Crossing Exceeding Hgt/Wgt/Width	1	3410	
Dr veh unauth flasning lights/ color lamps/signals		3680	
Dr Veh While Wear Headset/Ear Phones/Earplugs Both Ears	1	3240	
Dr Veh Without Equip Meeting Minimum Equipment Standards		3940	E01
Dr Veh/Trailer Without First Line Tires/Approved Recaps		3810	E37
Dr w/o medical examiner cert showing physically qualified		4139	
Dr While Lic/Privilege Sus	3	0549	B26

Description	Points	State Code	ACD
Dr While Under Inf Of Cds	12	0220	A24
Dr Without Lic for Veh Class	2	0577	
Dr Without Lic For Veh Class	5	0408	B91
Dr Without Lic For Veh Class	2	0611	B91
Dr/Att Dr Snow Emergency Route W/O Snow Tires/Chains	1	3230	
Dr/Att Dr Under Inf Of Drugs/ Comb Drugs And Alcohol	8	3030	
Dr/attempt dr while under inf of alc per se trans minor (MV)	12	3002	
Dr/attempt to dr impaired by CDS transporting minor (MV)	12	3022	
Dr/Attempt To Dr Mv/Motorbike On Highway Without License	5	2150	B51
Dr/attempt to dr while imp by alc transporting minor (MV)	8	3012	
Dr/Attempt To Drive CMV W/O Appropr Lic/Endorsements	8	2328	B91
Dr/Cause/Permit Veh Be Driven Without Rear Wheel Flaps		3880	E01
Dr/Op/Physical Control Of CMV While Alcohol In Blood/Breath		2327	A04
Dr/op/physical control of CMV while possess/consume alcohol		4138	
Dr/Participate As Time Keeper In Race/Speed Contest	5	3200	S95
Dr/Permit Driving Of Unsafe/ Improperly Equipped Vehicle		3450	F66
Dr/permit driving of vehicle exceeding max width limit		3960	
Driv Fail To Make Required Stop At (Sig,Sign,Pave Mark	2	2467	
Driv Fail To Stop At Red Traff Sig Before Any Other Turn	2	2465	
Driv Fail To Stop At Red Traff Signal Before Left Turn	2	2464	
Driv Fail To Stop At Red Traff Signal Before Right Turn	2	2463	
Driv Thru/In A Safety Zone	1	2730	M12
Drive At A Speed Not Reasonable And Prudent	1	2900	
Drive Below Minimum Posted Speed Limit	1	2940	
Drive CMV In Willful/Wanton Disregard Safety Of Pers/Prop		2982	M84
Drive CMV On Instructional Permit Unaccompanied in MV	5	2317	B91
Drive In Intoxicated Condition	12	0217	A20
Drive low spd vehicle on expressway/cont access highway	1	3246	
Drive Motor Veh On Hwy While Consuming Alcoholic Bev in MV	1	3040	
Drive Motor Vehicle In A Careless Manner		2974	M81
Drive Motor Vehicle In A Negligent Manner	1	2980	M83
Drive Motor Vehicle In A Reckless Manner	4	2970	M84
Drive Motor Vehicle In An Inattentive Manner		2975	M82
Drive On Median Strip	1	0777	M51
Drive oversize/overweight veh across/through toll facility		4102	
Drive Passenger Vehicle With Improper Projecting load		3970	
Drive passenger vehicle with improper projecting load		3970	
Drive School Veh With Improper Class License/Certificate	2	2160	B91
Drive Thru Or In Safety Zone	1	0769	M12
Drive Under Inf Of Alcohol	8	0306	A21
Drive Under Inf Of Alcohol	6	0353	A21
Drive Under Inf-Drugs/Alcohol	8	0308	A21
Drive Under Influence Of Drugs	12	0219	A22
Drive Under Influence Of Drugs	8	0307	A22
Drive veh exceeding gross max weight on other than state hwy		4050	
Drive Veh Not In Compliance With Hazardous Materials		3850	E53
Drive Veh On Hwy With Tires		3791	
Drive veh on hwy with tires not complying with standards		3791	E37
Drive veh w/dis park placard hanging in rearview mirror		1837	
Drive Veh W/O Required Warning Device for Disabled Vehicle		3830	E01
Drive Veh With Illegal Tires/ Suds/Cleats/Spikes		3800	E37
Drive Veh With Load Improperly Covered/Loaded/Fastended		4010	
Drive Vehicle In Violation Of License Restriction		2220	D29
Drive vehicle with television receiver visible to driver		3890	
Drive While Lic/Priv Suspended For Unsatisfied O/S Ticket	3	2301	B26
Drive While License/Driving Privilege Suspended	3	2300	B26
Drive With View Obstructed/		3770	D70
Drive Without/Unauthorized Use Of Slow Moving Veh Emblem	1	2950	E01
Drive/Attempt Dr Under Inf Of Controlled Dangerous Subst	12	3020	A22
Drive/Attempt Dr While Under The Inf Of Alcohol Per Se	12	3001	A20
Drive/Attempt To Dr Impaired By Drugs/Comb Drugs & Alc	8	3031	A23
Drive/Attempt To Dr Motor Veh On Hwy With Expired License		2240	B51
Drive/Attempt To Dr Motor Veh With Improper Class Lic	2	2170	B91
Drive/Attempt To Drive Impaired By Cds	12	3021	A22
Drive/Attempt To Drive M/V On Learner Permit W/O Supervision	5	2180	D29
Drive/Attempt To Drive Motor Veh On Highway Without Lic	5	2145	B51
Drive/Attempt To Drive While Impaired By Alcohol	8	3011	
Drive/Attempt To Drive While Under Inf Of Alcohol	12	2991	A20
Drive/cause driving of veh in violation of road restriction		4100	

Description	Points	State Code	ACD
Drive/Knowingly Permit Veh Be Driven W/O Req Security	5	2370	D36
Drive/Move Heavy Equipment Veh On/Across RR Crossing	1	2840	M09
Drive/move veh/object on hwy/road to cause unusual damage		4090	
Drive/permit driving of veh w/o current reg card/plates		1850	
Drive/permit driving of veh with canc/sus/rev registration		1860	
Drive/permit operation veh w/o current tags/tags of other		1680	
Drive/Permit Vehicle Be Driven		3920	E70
Drive/Sell/Equip Vehicle Without Safety Glass		3820	E01
Driver Fail Stop/Remain At Acc Scene Of Bodily Inj/Death	12	2380	B03
Driver fail to give required veh insurance information		2411	
Driver Fail To Stop At Steady Circular Red Signal	2	2468	M16
Driver Fail To Stop At Steady Red Arrow Signal	2	2469	
Driver Fail To Stop/Give Info Pd Accident/Unattended Veh	8	2410	
Driver Fail To Stop/Remain At Property Damage Accident	8	2390	B04
Driver Passing Veh Stopped For Pedestrian At Crosswalk	1	2711	N08
Driver Privilege Refusal Wdn By Medical Advisory Board		4505	
Driver Privilege Refused By Medical Advisory Board		4504	W14
Driver Privilege Suspended By Medical Advisory Board		4502	W14
Drivers View Obstructed	1	0734	D70
Driving A Motor Vehicle On A Sidewalk	1	3090	M58
Driving A Vehicle With View Obstructed/Not In Control	1	3100	D70
Driving After License Refused/ Canceled/Suspended/Revoked	12	2290	B20
Driving Commercial Motor Veh With More Than One Dr Lic	12	2316	D07
Driving Improperly On Divided Highway	1	2610	N71
Driving limited speed veh on hwy w/o affixed emblem	1	2951	
Driving limited speed veh on prohibited highway	1	2947	
Driving On Controlled Access Highway When Prohibited	1	2630	
Driving On Sidewalk	1	0767	M58
Driving To The Left In A No Passing Zone	1	2570	N70
Driving To The Left Of Center Of Road Where Prohibited	1	2560	N70
Driving Too Slow	1	0713	S96
Driving unregistered veh/allow unregistered veh to be driven		1640	
Driving While Lic Sus/Rev/Ref In Another Jurisdiction	12	2270	B26
Driving Without A License	5	0404	B51
Driving/Attempting To Dr While Under Influence Of Alcohol	8	3010	A21
Driving/Attempting To Drive While Intoxicated	12	2990, 3000	A20
Driving/attempting to drive while intoxicated (MV)	12	2990, 3000	
Driving/Damaging Highway/		3190	M02
Driving/taking vehicle without owners consent	12	1980	
Driving/using special reg plate on unauthorized vehicle		1840	
Drop/Throw/Place Trash/ Injurious Substance On Hwy	2	3160	
Dump Truck Speed Violation	1	0600	S93
Enter Highway From Crossover W/O Yielding Right Of Way	1	2690	N23
Enter/Emerge From Alley/Drvwy/ Bldg Without Stopping	1	2850	M25
Equip Vio Transport Explosives	1	0765	E53
Exc 40 Mph-Transport Explosive	1	0305	S93
Exceed Highway Work Zone Speed	1	2934	S51
Exceed max gross wgt allowed vehicle/combination vehicle		4060	
Exceed Maximum Speed Limit On Bridge/Elevated Structure	1	2961	S93
Exceed Posted School Zone Speed By 10-19 Mph	2	2942	
Exceed Posted School Zone Speed By 20-29 Mph	2	2943	
Exceed Posted School Zone Speed Limit By 1-9 Mph	1	2941	
Exceed Posted Speed Limit Of 65 Mph By 20 Mph Or More	5	2938	S92
Exceed Speed Limit By 10 Mph	2	0502	
Exceed Speed Limit By 30 Mph	5	0402	S81
Exceed Speed Limit By 40 Mph	5	0412	S91
Exceed Speed Limit By Ten Mile	3	0602	S06
Exceed Speed Limit By Ten Mph	2	0575	S06
Exceeding Maximum Speed Limit By 10 Mph	2	2930	
Exceeding Maximum Speed Limit By 15 Mph	2	2933	S15
Exceeding Maximum Speed Limit By 1-9 Mph	1	2932	S51
Exceeding Maximum Speed Limit By 30 Mph	5	2920	S71
Exceeding Speed Limit 65 Mph By 20 To 39 Mph	5	2944	
Exceeding Speed Limit 65 Mph By 30 To 39 Mph	5	2945	
Exceeding Speed Limit 65 Mph By 40 Mph Or Over	5	2946	
Exceeding Speed Limit/Failure To Reduce Speed When Req	1	2890	S94
Fail apply duplicate license/surrender original lic to MVA		2230	
Fail by licensee to surrender cancelled license to MVA		2260	
Fail by new owner to apply for/obtain new reg prior dr veh		1770	

Description	Points	State Code	ACD
Fail by owner to apply to MVA for registration of vehicle		1660	
Fail by transferee to obtain reg prior to driving vehicle		1760	
Fail Comply With Requirement of Child Safety Seat/Belts		3870	F02
Fail destroy temp reg plates upon expiration of temp reg		1796	
Fail dis disabled placard as required		1822	
Fail display tab on plates of veh as required by admin		1671	
Fail display temp number plate upon loss/theft/destruction		1720, 1740	
Fail Display Warning Device		0811	E05
Fail Drive Extreme Right Side	1	0755	
Fail Equip Veh Multiple Beam		3630	E05
Fail Equip Veh With Marker/ID/Clearance Lamps/Reflectors		3520	
Fail Equip Veh With Required		3700	E02
Fail Equip Veh With Seat Belts Transporting Retarded Children		3860	F04
Fail Give Right Of Way To Ped		2471, 2742	N08
Fail Give Right Of Way To Ped Blind/Deaf/Mobility Impaired		2741	N08
Fail Give Right Of Way To Ped Blind/Deaf/Mobility Impaired	2	2742	N08
Fail Grant Ped-Right Of Way	1	0605	N08
Fail keep records four years/available for inspection		4104	
Fail keep rental records		2374	
Fail Leave Car Tracks	1	0729	M55
Fail Maintain Posted Min Speed On A Vehicular Crossing	1	3400	S96
Fail Make Required Stop	1	0728	M15
Fail notify adm of instructor termination		2149	
Fail Obey Flashing Signal	1	0727	M18
Fail Obey Officer Signal/Order	1	0724	M08
Fail obey OOS drive com m/v on hwy w/trans non hazmat (MV)	12	2335	
Fail obey OOS order dr com m/v on hwy trans haz w/o placq (MV)	12	2336	
Fail Obey Police-Weighing Sign	1	0790	
Fail Obey Police-Weighing Sign		1402	M17
Fail Obey Traffic Device	1	0726	M16
Fail Obtain Chauffeur License	1	0748	B91
Fail Obtain Spec Chauf Lic	1	0720	B91
Fail possess/display license		2190, 2200	
Fail Reduce Speed To Avoid Acc	3	0550, 0607	S94
Fail register/display reg for school vehicle		1741	
Fail report recovered vehicle to MVA after notice of theft		2010	
Fail return disabled parking permit within 5 days of exp		1811	
Fail return reg card/plates to MVA after vehicle scrapped		1775	
Fail Stop After Acc-Veh Or Pd	8	0301	
Fail Stop At Through Highway	1	0738	N25
Fail Stop For Stopped Vehicle Operating Flashing Red Lts	3	2862	
Fail Stop Overtaking/Passing School Veh Flashng Red Lt	3	2863	
Fail Stop Overtaking/Passing School Veh Flashng Red Lt	2	2860	M75
Fail Stop Railroad Crossing	1	0733	M09
Fail submit title certificate within 10 days of total loss		1776	
Fail to affix permit in conspicuous place		3059	
Fail to apply duplicate reg if lost/stolen/mutilated		1730	
Fail to carry reg card in veh/display it upon demand		1670	
Fail To Change Name Or Address		0803	
Fail to comply with law when not use as school vehicle (MV)		3692	
Fail To Control/Reduce Speed When Required To Avoid Acc	3	2910	S94
Fail To Dim Headlights	1	0711	E54
Fail To Display Identification		3780	E01
Fail To Display Lamps/Flags/Reflectors on Projected Load		3560	E55
Fail To Display Lights/Lamps When Using Windshield Wipers		3471	E50
Fail To Display Tow Truck Reg		1922	B51
Fail To Drive On Extreme Right Side Of Roadway	1	2530	N70
Fail To Equip School Vehicle With Seatback Crash Pads		3910	E56
Fail To Equip Trailer/Semi Trailer with Metal Frame		3856	E01
Fail to equip vehicle with required lights		3694	
Fail To Equip/Display Lamps/ Reflectors on Farm equipment		3567	E05
Fail To Equip/Display Parking/Dimming Lights on Veh		3564	E54
Fail to flash amber lights at required distance (MV)		3693	
Fail To Give Hand Signal	1	0717	N40
Fail To Give Information-Aid	8	0302	
Fail To Give Information-Aid		0800	
Fail To Give Required Signal	1	0768	N40
Fail To Grant Right Of Way	1	0604	N01
Fail To Have Required Front/Rear Seat Belts		3857	

Description	Points	State Code	ACD
Fail To Keep Right Of Center	1	0705	M41
Fail to make lane change/slow down while passing emerg veh	1	2703	
Fail to notify MVA in 30 days of change of name/address		2250	
Fail to notify police of repossession		2005	
Fail To Obey A Lane Direction Control Signal	1	2490	M16
Fail To Obey Court Order		0872	D45
Fail To Obey Instructions Of Traffic Control Device	2	2462	
Fail To Obey Instructions Of Traffic Control Device	1	2460	M14
Fail To Obey Officers Order		4135	M08
Fail To Obey Stop/Yield Sign	1	0791	M14
Fail To Obey Traffic Signal/ Sign	1	2470	M16
Fail To Obey Written Citation		0817	D45
Fail To Obtain License Within 30 Days		2151	B51
Fail to obtain permit before moving ovweight/ovsize load		4081	
Fail To Pay Fine In District Court Sus Withdrawn-Fine Paid		4224	
Fail To Perform Required Act Pertaining To Drivers Lic	12	2288	
Fail to provide unobstructed entrance for handicapped		3068	
Fail To Reduce Speed	1	0772	S94
Fail to reg veh when public service permit required		1745	
Fail to reg vehicle used in inerstate pass transport		1746	
Fail to register van pool veh		1742	
Fail To Remain Stopped For School Veh Flashng Red Lt	2	2861	
Fail To Remain Stopped For School Veh Flashng Red Lt	3	2864	
Fail To Remove/Unload Excess		4080	M08
Fail to report address change within 30 days		2061	
Fail to return license upon suspension/revocation		2062	
Fail to return veh title/reg after cancel/sus/rev		1890	
Fail to secure public service/appropriate agency permit		1747	
Fail to sign in presence of officer		2209	
Fail To Sign License		0828	D16
Fail To Stop After Acc Death	12	0014	B02
Fail To Stop After Acc Pi	12	0015	B03
Fail To Stop And Grant Blind/ Deaf Ped Right Of Way	1	2740	N08
Fail To Stop At Rr Crssng When Carrying Passenger/Cargo	1	2830	M09
Fail To Stop For Emergency Veh	1	0718	N04
Fail To Stop For School Bus	2	0576, 0609	M75
Fail To Stop Right Turn On Red	1	0780	M17
Fail to stop/obey sign/signal to weigh/measure vehicle		4070	
Fail To Stop/Yield At Inter- Section/Thru Highway	1	2670	M25
Fail to Surrender ID When License Issued	12	1611	
Fail To Surrender License	12	0209	
Fail To Use Hand/Arm Signal/ Signal Lamp When Required	1	2790	N40
Fail To Wear Motorcycle Helmet	1	0751	F03
Fail To Yield Right Of Way At Intersection	1	2650	N25
Fail To Yield Right Of Way To A Funeral Procession	1	2510	N05
Fail Use Reasonable Care	1	0770, 0773	M81
Fail verify/inspect license of leasee		2372	
Fail/Comply Child Safety Seats		1403	F03
Fail/Improper Mount Reflector/		3540	E05
Fail/refusal to pay toll		3440	
Failed Comply Medical Advisory Board Refusal Withdrawn		4511	
Failed Comply Medical Advisory Board-Dr Privilege Suspended		4508	W14
Failed Comply Medical Advisory Board-Driver Privilege Refused		4510	W14
Failed Comply Medical Advisory Board-Suspension Withdrawn		4509	
Failed Re-Examination Suspended		5510	
Failed Re-Examination-Driving Suspended		5511	
Failed Re-Examination-Law Suspended		5512	
Failed Re-Examination-Vision Suspended		5513	
Failed To Appear Circuit Court Bench Warrant Sus Withdrawn		4209	
Fail-Obey Spec Restr On Lamps	1	0608	
Failure by Owner to Maintain Ins On File		2330	B64
Failure Equip/Properly Locate Headlamps on Vehicle		3480	E05
Failure Obey Sign/Signal/Order Direction At Veh Crossing	1	3380	M17
Failure Of Driver In Pi/Death Acc To File Rep In 15 Days	5	2430	B61
Failure to attach plate to rear of vehicle		1682	
Failure to attach plates to front and rear of vehicle		1681	
Failure To Comply With School Vehicle Regulations	1	3220	
Failure to comply with school vehicle regulations (MV)	1	3220	
Failure To Display Amber/Red		3530	E05

Description	Points	State Code	ACD
Failure to display disabled persons parking permit		1824	
Failure To Display Lighted lamps When Required		3470	E55
Failure To Display/Carry Rear Vehicle Reflectors		3500	E55
Failure To Drive In Designated Direction On One Way Rdwy	1	2580	N63
Failure To Drive On Roadway In Designated Lane	1	2590	
Failure To Equip Veh With Rear Stop Lights		3610	E05
Failure To Equip Veh With Stop Lamps/Turn Signals		3510	E05
Failure To Equip Vehicle With Proper Equipment		3760	E01
Failure to equip vehicle with proper fog/spot/driving lamps		3580	E05
Failure To Equip Vehicle With Proper Lights		3570, 3580	E05
Failure to equip vehicle with required lamps/reflectors		3570	E05
Failure To Exercise Due Care For Pedestrian	1	2720	
Failure to flash red lights upon stop		3696	
Failure To Maintain And Adjust		3710	E31
Failure To Obey A Flashing Traffic Signal	1	2480	M18
Failure To Obey Bridge/Culvert		4110	M17
Failure To Obey Stop Sign At Railroad Grade Crossing	1	2820	M10
Failure to properly maintain/fasten/position visible plate		1683	
Failure To Render Aid And Give Required Information		2400	B04
Failure To Report An Accident	5	0401	B61
Failure To Stop And Proceed Safely At RR Grade Crossing	1	2810	M21
Failure To Stop At Stop Sign/ Yield At Yield Sign	1	2870	M19
Failure To Stop For Livestock At Livestock Crossing	1	2880	N01
Failure To Stop For Pedestrian In Crosswalk	1	2710	N20
Failure To Stop/Yield Right Of Way When Entering Highway	1	2680	M25
Failure To Yield Right Of Way At Intersection	1	2640	N25
Failure To Yield Right Of Way To Emergency Vehicle	1	2700	N04
Failure To Yield Right Of Way When Making Left Or U Turn	1	2660	N31
False Affidavit Or Statement	12	0005	
False Certification For Lic	12	0105, 0106	
False claim/fraudulently obtain motor fuel tax refund		4106	
False evidence of required security		2365	
False Evidence Of Title-Regis	12	0805	
False-Fi Name On App For Lic	12	0104	D02
Falsify App For Lic-Reg-Title	12	0221	
Falsify/attempt to falsify official document/plate	12	2050	
Felony Involving Use of Motor Vehicle	12	4195	
Fin Resp-Lic + Tags Sus Wdn		0953	
Fin Resp-Lic + Tags Suspended		0952	D36
Fin Resp-Pay Agree Sat-Sus Wdn		0955	
Fin Resp-Suspended		0948	D36
Fin Resp-Tags Suspended		0950	
Fin Resp-Vio Pay Agree-Sus		0954	D37
Flee-Attempt To Elude Officer	12	0012	U01
Fleeing/Attempting To Elude Police Officer	12	3050	U01
Follow Fire Apparatus To Close	1	0735	M33
Follow W/In 500 Ft/Park W/In 300 Ft Fire Apparatus	1	3140	M33
Following Another Vehicle Too Closely	2	2600	M34
Following Too Closely	1	0708	M34
Fraud App Reg Or Title	12	0010	
Fraud give/sell/attempt sell title/ownership document/reg	12	2041	
Fraud In Application For Lic/ Misuse Of License To Drive	12	2280	D02
Fraud In Application For License	12	2275	D02
Fraud in applying for disabled parking permit (MV)	12	1825	
Fraud in using disabled persons parking permit		1826	
Fraud Use Of Document Or Plate	12	0013	
Fraud/Misrep Applying For/ Using Reservd Parkng Perm	12	3060	
Fraud/misrep applying for/prep emissions control program		3954	
Fraud/misrep in app for use reg/disabled park permit (MV)	12	1830	
Fraud/Misrep In Use Of Reserved Parking Space Permit		3061	
Fraud/Misrepresentation	12	1610	D02
Fraudulent application for special registration plate (MV)	12	1831	
Fraudulent use of disabled persons parking plate		1832	
Fraudulently Obtain/Attempt To Obtain A License	12	2274	D02
Front Seat Passenger In Mv		3874	F04
Fta Sus-Bench Warr Circuit Ct		1027	
Fta Sus-Wdn Bench Warr Cir Ct		1029	
Give false identity to officer		2210	
Giving Information In Oral Or Written Report Knowingly False		2440	

Description	Points	State Code	ACD
Hear-Fail To Appear-Suspended		0992	
Hear-Fta-Mab Suspended		1347	W14
Hearing - Interlock Removed - Revoked		5336	
Hearing - Interlock Removed Suspended		5335	
Hearing Cancelled		1001	
Hearing Suspended Alcohol Content .10 Or More		5754	A90
Hearing Suspension To Stand		4927	
Hearing Waived-Refused		0976	
Hearing Waived-Revoked		0980, 1002	
Hearing Waived-Suspended		0978	
Hearing-Fail To Appear-Refused		0990	
Hearing-Fail To Appear-Revoked		0994, 1000	
Hearing-Failed To Appear Ign. Interlock-All Vehicles Owned		5984	
Hearing-Failed To Appear Mab Suspended		5405	
Hearing-Failed To Appear Mab Suspension Upheld		5404	
Hearing-Failed To Appear- Suspended		4920	
Hearing-Ign.Interlock Hardship Vehicle Waived		5985	
Hearing-Ignition Interlock All Vehicles Owned		5986	
Hearing-Interlock Restriction Employer Vehicle Excluded		5332	
Hearing-Interlock Restriction On All Vehicles Operated		5326	
Hearing-License Restricted To Interlock		5331	
Hearing-License Suspended For		4924	
Hearing-Licenses Cancelled		0996	
Hearing-Mab Refusal Withdrawn		5403	
Hearing-Mab Suspension Not Upheld		5408	
Hearing-Mab Suspension Upheld		5407	
Hearing-Mab Suspension Withdrawn		5401	W14
Hearing-Privilege To Drive In Maryland-Suspended		4921	
Hearing Rescheduled Alcohol Content .15 Or More		6047	
Hearing-Rescheduled 1st Offense Alcohol Content .15 Or More		6048	
Hearing-Rescheduled 2nd Offense Alcohol Content .15 Or More		6049	
Note: Will continue to 8th Suspension, State Code increasing by one count each time			
Hearing-Refused		0964	
Hearing-Refused Pending		5402	W14
Hearing-Revocation Withdrawn		0997	
Hearing-Revoked		0970	
Hearing Scheduled Alcohol Content .15 Or More		6038	
Hearing-Scheduled 1st Offense Alcohol Content .15 Or More		6039	
Hearing-Scheduled 2nd Offense Alcohol Content .15 Or More		6040	
Note: Will continue to 8th Suspension, State Code increasing by one count each time			
Hearing-Suspended		0972	
Hearing-Suspended 1st Offense Alcohol Content .10 Or More		5755	A10
Hearing-Suspended 2nd Offense Alcohol Content .10 Or More		5756	A90
Note: Will continue to 8th Suspension, State Code increasing by one count each time			
Hearing-Suspended 1st Offense Alcohol Content .15 Or More		6057	
Hearing-Suspended 2nd Offense Alcohol Content .15 Or More		6058	
Note: Will continue to 8th Suspension, State Code increasing by one count each time			
Hearing-Suspended Alcohol Content .15 Or More		6056	
Hearing-Suspended 8th Offense Alcohol Content .10 Or More		5762	A90
Hearing-Suspended Pending		5400	W14
Hearing-Suspended Pending Completion Of Dip		4925	
Hearing-Suspended Retro-Active To		4929	
Hearing-Suspension Concurrent		1007	
Hearing-Suspension Consecutive		1008	
Hearing-Suspension Modified		4930	
Hearing-Tags Revoked		0984	
Hearing-Tags Suspended		0982	
Hearing-Tags Suspended		4928	
Hear-Sus Pend Completion Dip		1343	
Hear-Suspended-R-Chemical Test		0963	A12
Hear-Suspended-R-Chemical Test		0963	A12
High risk driving		3049	
Holder Learner's Permit Mtrcycle Drive W/Unauth Rider		2182	
Homicide By Motor Vehicle	12	4182	
Homicide By Motor Vehicle While Intoxicated	12	4190	U07
Homicide By Motor Vehicle While Under The Influence	12	4191	U07
Homicide By Mtr Veh/Vessel While Imp By Alcohol	12	4174	U07
Homicide By Mtr Veh/Vessel While Imp By Cds	12	4176	U07
Homicide By Mtr Veh/Vessel While Imp By Drugs	12	4175	U07

Description	Points	State Code	ACD
Homicide By Mtr Veh/Vessel While Under Inf Of Alcohol	12	4173	U07
Homicide By Mtr Veh/Vessel While Under Inf Of Cds	12	4193	U07
Homicide By Mtr Veh/Vessel While Under Inf Of Drugs	12	4194	U07
Homicide Or Assault By Vehicle	12	0215	U07
Homicide-Mtr Veh While Intox	12	0216	U07
Ign Interlock Noncompliance- Revoked		5988	
Ign Interlock Notice Mailed Repeat Offender		5980	
Ign Interlock-Noncompliance- Suspended		5989	
Illegal Duplication/ Reproduction Of Id/License	12	2281	B41
Illegal Facsimile Production Of Identification Or Lic	12	2282	B41
Illegal Light or Signal Device	1	0304, 0756	
Illegal Light or Signal Device	1	0774	
Imp Motorcycle Rider Equip	1	0793	F03
Imp Op Motorcycle On Laned Hwy	1	0785	M40
Imp stop/park/leave/stand veh		3051	
Imp Use Of Lamps-Parked Veh		0888	E55
Imp Use Spec Equip School Bus	1	0797	N56
Imp/unauth park/stand/stop or move vehicle		3052	
Improper dis of current and vintage registration plates		1688	
Improper Display/Use Of Rural Letter Carrier Warning Device		3600	
Improper Equipment	1	0745	
Improper Hand/Arm Signal To Stop/Turn/Decrease Speed	1	2800	N44
Improper Lane Changing	1	0750	M42
Improper License	1	0712	B91
Improper Lights	1	0743	E55
Improper Loading	1	0747	
Improper Operation Motorcycle On Laned Highway	1	3340	M40
Improper Passing	1	0702	M70
Improper Passing/Fail Permit Vehicle To Pass	1	2540	M70
Improper Registration		0806	
Improper Riding/Trans Person/ Articles On Motorcycle	1	3330	
Improper riding/trans person/articles on motorcycle (MV)	1	3330	
Improper temp registration		1792	
Improper Towing	1	0789	
Improper towing equipment/fail display white towing flag		4040	
Improper Truck Loading	1	0742	
Improper Turn	1	0716	N50
Improper Use Of Alternate Road Lighting Equipment		3660	
Improper Use Of Audible/Visual Sign Device		3590	E70
Improper use of common carrier special reg plates		1849	
Improper use of farm tractor		1932, 1942	
Improper use of finance reg		1973	
Improper Use Of Multiple Beam Lights		3640	E54
Improper use of recycler reg		1972	
Improper use of special mobile equipment registration		1974	
Improper use of special registration plate		1835	
Improper Use Of Vehicle Horn/		3730	E70
Improper use transporter reg		1975	
Improper Veh Tail Lamps/Fail Illuminate Rear Reg Plate		3490	E05
Improper visibility marker is/clearance lamps/reflectors		3550	
Improper window tinting		3821	
In fuel business/receive motor oil without license		4105	
Inadequate Brakes	1	0723	E31
Inadequate Muffler		0804	
Injurious Subst/Refuse On Hwy	1	0784	
Ins Can Sus-Fail To Sur Tags		1380	D36
Ins Certified-Sus Withdrawn		1361	
Ins Hear Fail To Appear-Sus		1378	
Ins Hear License Suspended For		1379	D36
Insurance Hearing-Failed To Appear-Suspended		5316	
Insurance Hearing-License Suspended For		5317	D36
Insurance Suspension Withdrawn		4814	
Inten op mtr veh door strike interfere w/bike/mtr sctr rider		3322	
Interfere With Bicycle Rider		3315	M84
Interfere With Traffic Control Device/Railroad Sign/Signal		2505	
Interlock Removed - Revoked		5338	
Interlock Removed - Suspended		5337	
Involved In Fatal Accident		6400	U08
Jr11 Cancelled-Suspended		1030	

Description	Points	State Code	ACD
Jr11 File-Sus Withdrawn		1031	
Jr11 Relieved-Sus Withdrawn		1033	
Judg Def-Lic + Tags Suspended		1054	D39
Judg-Lic + Tags Suspended		1050	D39
Judgment-Driver License And Vehicle Tags Suspended		4805	D39
Judgment-Installment Agreement Dr Lic And Vehicle Tag Sus Wdn		4806	
Know permit minor/ward to vio bicycle,play veh, mtr sctr law		3244	
Know rent M/V to person under infl/impaired by alco/drug/cds		2376	
Knowingly holding falsified document/registration		2053	
Knowingly make false report of stolen veh to MVA/police		2020	
Knowingly Permit Unauthorized Person To Drive Vehicle	5	2320	
Knowingly Permit/Require operator of Vehicel to Violate Law		4150	U04
Knowingly rent veh to person under inf of alcohol/drugs		2375	
Knowingly using falsified document/registration		2054	
Leave unattended animal in parked/standing vehicle		3053	
Legally Adjudicated Insane		0009	
Lic Sus Fail To Comply-Ins Req		1366	D36
Lic Sus Fail To Report Acc		1367	B61
Lic Suspended For Non-Payment		1032	
Lic/Id Reprinted		4309	
License Cancelled		1060	
License Issued In Another State-Md Lic Not Surrendered		4248	
License Restriction	1	0721	D29
License Sus For Failure Comply With Insurance Requirements		4813	D36
License Suspended-Failed To Report Accident		4815	B61
License Suspended-Lea Flag		5963	W00
Life Threatr Inj By Mot Veh/VESS While Under Influence of Alcohol	12	4181	
Lighted Lamps Required	1	0788	E05
Loaded vehicle exceeding maximum height limits		3980	
Loan Borrow Alter A Permit	12	0205	
Loaning Or Altering A Permit	12	0201	
Loaning Or Borrowing A License	12	0223	
Mab Refused/Failed To Comply		1086	B65
Mab Sus Wdn/Failed To Comply		1085	
Mab Suspended/Failed To Comply		1084	B65
Mab-Refused		1080	W14
Mab-Suspended		1078	W14
Mab-Suspension Withdrawn		1079	
Make A Prohibited Turn On Vehicular Crossing/Crossover	1	3390	N50
Make A U Turn On Curve/Crest Of Grade Where Prohibited	1	2760	N52
Manslaughter By Automobile	12	4180	U08
Manslaughter Or Negl Homicide	12	0007	U08
Manslaughter While Intoxicated		4179	
Manslaughter While Under The Influence Of Alcohol/Drugs	12	4178	
Medical Advisory Board Suspension Held In Abeyance		4514	
Misleading/false information temporary registration plate		1810	
Misrep Age for Alcohol		4196	
Misrep Age For Beer/Light Wine		4199	D06
Misrep Age To Induce		4198	D06
Misrep Age To Obtain Alcoholic		4197	D06
Misrepresentation in apply for disabled parking permit (MV)	12	1827	
Misrepresentation in apply for special registration plate (MV)	12	1833	
Misrepresentation in use of disables parking permit		1828	
Misrepresentation in using special registration plate		1834	
Mo w/blue dot illum (improperly placed, exc allowed size (MV)		3622	
Mo w/impr lighting (attach to whls emit red/blue light (MV)		3621	
Mobile seafood vendor sell/offer sale w/o permission		4122	
Mobile seafood vendor sell/offer sale without permit		4121	
Motor carrier fail display valid ID marker on CMV		4103	
Motor carrier Operator fail to comply with rules/regulations		4136	
Mva Notified-Licensee Deceased		4200	
Negligent Driving	1	0766	M83
No Headlights	1	0740	E55
No Id-Commercial Vehicle		0852	E01
No Insurance-License And Vehicle Tags Suspended		4812	D36
No Insurance-Suspended		1360	D36
No License In Possession		0801	
No Rear Flaps		0833	E01
No Reg Card In Possession		0802	

Description	Points	State Code	ACD
Non Comm Cl A Driver Dr/Att To Dr Mv Not Auth By Lic Type	2	2171	B91
Non Comm Cl B Driver Dr/Att To Dr Mv Not Auth By Lic Type	2	2172	B91
Non Comm Cl C Driver Dr/Att To Dr Mv Not Auth By Lic Type	2	2173	B91
Non Comm Cl M Driver Dr/Att To Dr Mv Not Auth By Lic Type	2	2174	B91
Notified Md Drivers License Surrendered To Out-Of-State Mv		4214	
Obscure/Modify Veh Plate With Intent To Avoid Ident	1	3175	
Obstruct Drivers View/Control		3101	D70
Obtain farm truck registration by fraud/misrepresentation (MV)	12	1930	
Obtain Lic-Misrepresentation	12	0011	D02
Op After Ref Canc Sus Or Rev	12	0202	B20
Op Alone On Instruction Lic	1	0722	D29
Op Driving Ability Impaired	6	0407	A25
Op Dump Semitrailer Vehicle In		1940	S93
Op Dump Truck veh Excess of WT Limit for 4 or More Axles		1921	
Op Emergency Veh Unsafely	1	0725	N84
Op Motor Assisted Bicycle Without Req Lic/Permit	5	2146	B51
Op Motorcycle Unlawfully	1	0731	N84
Op Motorcycle With Improper x		3360	E01
Op MV dis disabled parking permit without or not disables		1829	
Op Mv Headset Earphone/Plugs		1404	M82
Op MV while op unauthorized TV/video equip visible to driver	1	3233	
Op Mv While Operator/Occupant Not Retsrained by Seatbelt		3873	F04
Op MV with removable placard hanging rearview mirror (MV)	1	1823	
Op of handheld telephone while operating a motor vehicle		3232	
Op of handheld telephone while operating a motor vehicle	1	3234	
Op On Suspended-Revoked Tags	1	0759	
Op Un Inf Intox Liq Or Drugs	12	0002	A20
Op Unregistered Motor Vehicle	1	0719	
Op Veh Ins Lapsed/Terminated	3	0558	D36
Op Veh Not Equipped-Seat Belts	1	0757	F04
Op veh w/out shuttle permit/required security		1847	
Op veh with out gross weight veh trailer		1915	
Op/Sus Circuit Court Fta	3	0557	D45
Op/Sus District Court/Fpf	3	0553	D53
Op/Sus District Court/Fta	3	0552	D45
Op/Sus Reciprocity Fta	3	0554	D45
Op/Sus U S District Court Fpf	3	0556	D45
Op/Sus U S District Court Fta	3	0555	D45
Op-Driving Ability Impaired	1	0758	A25
Open Door Intent Inj Bicyclist		0882	N84
Open Veh Door When Unsafe	1	0762	
Open/Fail Close Vehicle Door When Unsafe	1	3110	
Oper Veh With Power Booster Without Required Decal	5	3812	
Operate A (Moped,Mtr Scooter) On Hwy W/O Req Lic Or Perm	5	2152	
Operate motor scooter in excess of 30 mph		3285	
Operate Motor Vehicle/Trailer Dfct Tires		3790	E37
Operate Motorcycle With Dfct Brakes		3720	E31
Operate motorcycle with improper lighting equipment		3650	
Operate Mv With Propane Fuel W/O Hazmat		3781	E04
Operate On Unauth Roadway With Improper Horse Power M/C	1	3341	
Operate School Veh Flashing Red Signal When Moving		3690	E70
Operate school vehicle flash red light when moving		3691	
Operate Truck With Passenger Under 16 In Unenclosed Bed	1	3241	
Operate veh exceeding maximum load extension limit		4000	
Operate vehicle exceeding maximum length limit		3990	
Operate vehicle w/o fastening/enclosing material transported		4030	
Operate vehicle without proper registration plates/stickers		1684	
Operate Without Mirrors	1	0764	E01
Operate/carry/load vehicle with loose material		4020	
Operate/Ride Motorcycle		3370	F03
Operating Dump Truck Vehicle		1920	S93
Operating On Expired License	1	0710	B51
Operating Unfit Vehicle	1	0736	E01
Operating Uninsured Vehicle		0829	D36
Operating Vehicle With Power Booster	5	3811	
Operating Without A License	1	0709	B51
Operation of a text messaging device While op a MV	1	3238	M85
Operation Of A Wireless Comm Device While Op A MV	1	3237	M86
Order Of Suspension Issued		6020	A90

Description	Points	State Code	ACD
Order Of Suspension Issued		5845	A98
Order Of Suspension Issued Alcohol Content .10 Or More		5709	A12
Order Of Suspension Issued Alcohol Content Of .08 Or More		5845	A98
Order Of Suspension Issued Refused 1st Chemical Test		5701	A12
Order Of Suspension Issued Refused 2nd Chemical Test		5702	A12
Order Of Suspension Issued Refused 3rd Chemical Test		5703	A12
Order Of Suspension Issued Refused Chemical Test		5700	A12
Owner fail to return spec ret within 30 days of termination		1836	
Owner Permit Op Veh/Uninsured	5	0413	
Owner permit vehicle operation without proper plates/stickers		1685	
Owner/Insurer Fail Notify Mva		2350	D36
P Sys-Refused		1108	W01
P Sys-Revoked		1106	W01
P Sys-Suspended		1100	W01
Par/guar auth minor/ward vio bicycle, play veh,mtr sctr law		3243	
Parental/Guardian Consent Withdrawn-Suspended		6200	W13
Park in space designated for individuals with disabilities		3065	
Park veh in reserved space without displaying permit		3062	
Parked-Roadway Without Lights		0837	E05
Particip As Timekeeper/Flagman In Race/Speed Contest	5	3202	S95
Participate In Speed Contest	5	0406	S95
Passed Re-Examination Suspension Withdrawn		5506	
Passing An Emergency Veh	2	2701	M70
Passing Emergency Vehicle	1	0606	N04
Passing On The Right When Not Permitted	1	2550	M73
Pedestrian Entering Roadway Against Red Traffic Signal		2466	
Permit unauth use/display reg card/plate/cert of title		1870	
Permit Unauthorized Pers To Dr	5	0410	
Permit Unlawful Use Of Lic	12	2287	
Permit Unlic Opr To Drive	5	0403	
Permit Unlic Opr To Drive	4	0501	
Permit Unlic Person To Drive	12	0213	
Permit Use Of License By Another	12	2284	
Permit/Occupy Area Of Vehicle Intended To Carry Cargo	1	3125	
Permit/Occupy Mobile Home While Being Towed On Hwy	1	3120	
Permitting unauthorized person to drive rented vehicle		2377	
Person Occupy Area Of Vehicle Intended To Carry Cargo	1	3126	
Place cnty sticker on special/commerative reg plate		1673	
Place/maintain/display in view of hwy unauth sig/signal/mark		2500	
Placing Traffic Hazard On A Highway		3180	
Point System Hearing Cancel Failed To Appear-Suspended		4923	
Point System Revoked		5808	W01
Point System Suspended		5806	
Point System Suspended- License Not Surrendered		5800	
Point System Suspension Withdrawn		5807	
Possess fraud intent ownership document/card/plate/vin		2040	
Possess More Than One Drivers		2185	D07
Possess paraphernalia used for falsification of documents		2051	
Possess/give/sell falsified document/plate		2052	
Prov driver under 18 may not use wire com while driving (MV)		3239	
Prov Driver Under Age 18 With Passengers Under Age Of 18	1	3236	
Pt Sys Sus-Lic Not Surrendered		0989	W01
Racing Or Speed Contest	1	0714	S95
Reciprocity Suspension Withdrawn		4220	
Reckless Driving	4	0510	M84
Reckless Driving	3	0601	M84
Reckless/ Exceed Speed 20 Mph Or More Above Speed Limit		2915	
Refuse To Surrender Lic	12	2286	
Refused		5809	
Refused 30 Days After Age 16		5810	
Refused By Medical Advisory Board-Alcohol Related		4516	W14
Remove Or Alter Safety Device		0887	E70
Remove/alter position of light at guard closing part of hwy		3195	
Remove/Alter Required Veh Safety Device or Equipment		3457	E01
Remove/falsify/unauthorized ID/registration card/plate		2030	
Rent M/V know indiv under infl impaired by alco/drugs/cds		2378	
Rent veh inaccurate odometer/deceived distance traveled		2373	
Rent veh to unlic opr		2371	
Repeat Offender-Ignition Int. Restriction		5987	

Description	Points	State Code	ACD
Require employee participate in company van pool		1743	
Restricted Use Of Television	1	0744	
Revocation Imposed For Viol Of License Restriction		5844	
Revocation Imposed For Violation Of Alcohol Rest		5841	
Revoked		1160, 5811	
Revoked - Subsequent Alcohol Violation		5791	
Revoked For Using Lic/Id In An Unlawful Or Fraud Manner		5794	
Revoked-Driv Ability Impaired		1161	A25
Revoked-Fail To Complete Driver Improvement Program		5323	
Ride Animal/Dr Animal Drawn Veh On Prohibited Highway		2453	
Riding Motorcycle While Attached To Another Veh	1	3350	
School Bus	1	0707	M75
School Bus Speed Violation	1	0794	S93
Sell/Offer Veh W/O Required Front/Rear Seatbelts		3858	
Sell/Offer Veh With Seat Belt Fail to Meet Standards		3859	
Sell/offer/use unapproved/improper lamp/reflector		3695	
Speeding	1	0701	S93
Speeding	1	2905	S93
Spinning Wheels	1	0749	N83
Start/Move Veh Unsafely W/O Giving Adequate Signal	1	2770	N84
Stop Sign	1	0704	M15
Stop/Prk/Lv Veh Unattended W/O Removing Key/Setting Brake	1	3070	
Stop/stand/park vehicle on vehicular crossing		3287	
Sus Abey Pend Add Moving Viol		1344	
Sus Wdn-Court-Fail To Appear		1388	
Sus-Fail Comply Dr Control Req		1154	
Suspended- 90 Days Minor Passenger Conviction		6006	
Suspended By Medical Advisory Board-Alcohol Related		4515	W14
Suspended For Child Support Non-Compliance		5697	
Suspended For Using Lic/Id In An Unlawful Or Fraud Manner		5695	
Suspended-90 Days Wireless Communication Device Violation		6008	
Suspended-Court-Fail To Appear		1376	D45
Suspended-Fail To Appear-Bench Warrant Issued-Circuit Court		4207	D45
Suspended-Fail To Attend Alcohol Education Program		5322	
Suspended-Fail To Pay Fine		1390	D53
Suspended-Failure To Pay Fine In District Court		4223	D53
Suspended-HFA-R-Chemical Test		0971	A12
Suspended-Theft Of Motor Fuel		6003	W00
Suspended-Violated District Of Columbia Recip Agreement		4250	D45
Suspended-Violated Reciprocity Agreement		4219	
Sus-Pending Payment Of Lic Fee		1194	
Suspension Imposed For Violation Of Lic Restr		5691	
Suspension Notice Mailed-Minor Passenger		6005	
Suspension Notice Mailed-Wire- Less Communication Device Conv		6007	
Suspension Withdrawn For Child Support Non-Compliance		5698	
Suspension Withdrawn-Fine Paid		1391	
Suspension/Revocation Action Taken By The State Of Xx		7060	
Tamper/alter/damage vehicle odometer		3900	
Throw obj at/in dir of person ride bike/mtr sctr		3321	
Towing Occupied House Trailer	1	0753	
Traffic Court-Suspended		1192	
Transp Danger Article Across/ Thru Veh Crossing/Hwy	3	3420	
Transport Dangerous Substances	1	0786	
Transport Dangerous Substances	3	0559	E53
Turn Off Light To Avoid Ident	1	0006	U01
Turn Off Lights To Avoid Id	8	0303	U01
Turning Off Vehicle Lights To Avoid Identification	8	3170	U01
U S District Court-Ftp Suspended		4261	D45
Unauthorized Entering/Leaving Controlled Access Highway	1	2620	M46
Unauthorized Number Of Vehicle Auxiliary/Spot/Head Lamps		3670	
Unauthorized Turning/Slowing/ Stopping W/O Req Signal	1	2780	N40
Unauthorized use of class 1A- dealer registration plate		1950	
Unauthorized use of class 1B- motorcycle dealer reg plate		1960	
Unauthorized use of class 1C- trailer dealer reg plate		1970	
Unauthorized use of state hwy for truck testing purposes		4120	
Unlawful issuance by dealer of more than one temp reg plate		1780	
Unlawful possession of motor vehicle master key		1990	
Unlawful Taking Of Mtr Veh	1	0739	
Unlawful taking or unauth use of a motor vehicle (MV)	12	1982	

Description	Points	State Code	ACD
Unlawful Use Of License	12	0211, 0810	
Unlawful/Improper Use Of Vehicle Lamps/Lighting Equip		3620	E55
Unlicensed activity		2064	
Unnecessary Noise	1	0760	E70
Unnecessary Use Of Horn		0813	E70
Unsafe Backing	1	0761	N82
Unsafe Backing Of A Motor Vehicle	1	3080	N82
Unsafe Driving By Emergency Vehicle Driver	1	2702	
Unsafe Operation Of Emergency Vehicle	1	2455	U21
Use force to remove animal used by police/animal control		3054	
Use hwy bridge when prohibited by state highway adm		4101	
Use Improper Position/Method Making A Turn	1	2750	N52
Use Of CMV In Comm Of Felony Involve Mfg/Dist/Disp A Cs		2981	A50
Use of finance co registration plate in unauthorized manner		1843	
Use of recycler registration plate in unauthorized manor		1842	
Use of sound amplification sys noise limitations		3235	
Use of special dealer reg upon expiration of temp reg		1841	
Use of transferred reg plates after expiration of permit		1764	
Use reg plates w/o written consent/beyond allowed time		1750	
Use transporter ret plates in unauthorized manner		1846	
Use Unauthorized Crossover	1	0776	M44
Veh driv fail exer care avoid col w/bike/mtr sctr op by per		3319	
Veh Driver Follow/Park W/In Prohib Dist Of Fire App	1	3141	
Veh Operated While Uninsured	5	0411	D36
Veh owner fail change name/address within 30 days		1710	
Veh owner fail sur evidence of reg in 48 hrs notice os susp		2360	
Veh subject to registration		1645	
Vehicle Used In A Felony	12	0008	U03
Vehicles Abreast In Same Lane	1	0754	M48
Vio Contributing To An Acc	3	0603	
Vio Controlled Access Highway	1	0781	M50
Vio of dealer location/fail to keep req books/records		2060	
Vio Of School Bus Operator	1	0795, 0796	N84
Vio Reciprocity-Refused		1118	D56
Vio Reciprocity-Suspended		1116	D56
Vio Slow Moving Vehicle Emblem	1	0783	N01
Vio Special Provision/Tunnels	1	0787	
Vio Transporting Haz Material	1	0732	
Vio While Trans Exp	1	0102	E53
Vio-Funeral Procession	1	0778	N05
Vio-Hgt Wgt Width Length	1	0746	
Viol rules/reg of inspection procedures/inspect requirement		3955	
Violate Out-Of-Service Order While operating a CMV		4140	B27
Violate Special Provisions Driving Thru Tunnel	1	3430	M41
Violate state highway adm rule/regulation for highway use		4091	
Violate/rail comply with adm rule/order		2144	
Violating school buss operating regulations		4130	
Violation Alcohol Restriction Under 21 Years Of Age		2221	A61
Violation Of Court Ordered Alcohol Restriction		2223	
Violation Of Ignition		4161	A41
Violation of motor fuel business regulation		4107	
Violation Of Provisional License Restriction		2222	
Violation Open Container Law		3041	
Violation Sign Restriction	1	0782	M17
Violation Snow Emergency	1	0763	E57
Violation Truck Testing Permit	1	0799	
Vio-Mo Goggles Or Face Shield	1	0752	F03
Vio-Skidding-Spinning Wheels	1	0792	S97
Willfully disobey order of school crossing guard		2456	
Willfully Disobey Order/ Dir/Summons Of Officer	1	2450	M08
Wrong Way-1 Way Street	1	0715	N63
Wrong Way-Divided Highway	1	0775	N62
Yield Sign	1	0779	M19

About the Point System

The Maryland point system ranges from one to twelve points. Any conviction shown as a one or two point violation becomes a three point violation if the violation contributes to an accident. A driver will be assigned to attend a Point System Conference (PSC) if there are 5, 6, or 7 points accumulated on the driving record within any two-year period. The PSC is a 2-hour program that is intended to acquaint drivers with Maryland law regarding the Point System and the possible suspension or revocation of their driving privilege due to accumulated points.

Massachusetts

Administration	Important Telephone and Web Contacts
Rachel Kaprielian Registrar of Motor Vehicles PO Box 55889, Boston, MA 02205-5889 857-368-9460 www.massdot.state.ma.us/rmv/ Mary Ann Mulhall Director of the Merit Rating Board PO Box 55889, Boston, MA 02205-5889 617-267-3636 www.massdot.state.ma.us/rmv/MeritRatingBoard.aspx For Motor Vehicle Laws: www.malegislature.gov/	Driver Licensing..............................857-368-8000 Suspensions/Revocations ....857-368-8200 Current Insurance Carrier.........................857-368-8000 Commercial Driver License.........................857-368-8110 Merit Rating Board Consumer Service Section ....857-368-8100 Vehicle Information..............................857-368-8000 State Police....................................508-820-2300 State Division of Insurance.......................617-521-7794 General Email: www.mass.gov/rmv/feedback/index.htm

Driver's License Format, Issuance and Renewal

License Classes, Restrictions and Endorsements Appear After the Driving Record Content Section

License Format

A computer generated number with one letter (usually an "S") and eight numbers is automatically issued.

Document Appearance

The current driver license and ID format has been in use since April 2010, replacing the previous documents which have been in circulation since 2004. It will take over 5 years to phase in the newer 2010 documents.

Current Version

Security Characteristics: New features include a perforated outline of Massachusetts that can be seen when held up to any light. Ghost imaging on all licenses and cards, 2D barcode. The license is lighter in appearance, the greenish look was removed. The barcode on the back is in the upper right corner.

Position of Photo: Flush left with a ghost image to the right.

Minor Age Driver Locator: The Under 21 license is printed vertically. "UNDER 21" or "JUNIOR OPERATOR" is in bold red lettering with date printed under message indicating when driver turns 18 or 21.

ID Card Indicator: A vertical card, with the initials "ID" are in bold red just to the left of the picture. The words "Identification Card" are in red under the state name, across the top. There is no color bar across the top.

CDL Indicator: "CDL Driver's License" is printed on upper portion; class description and any endorsements or restrictions are printed on the reverse side. If under 21, is vertical format.

Veteran's Indicator: The word "Veteran" can be printed in the lower right-hand corner of a license or ID card for customers who are veterans of the U.S. Armed Forces and were honorably discharged.

Older Version (pre-2010)

Security Characteristics: Multiple ghost images of the bearer's image, a kinegram or metalized optical device and ultraviolet sensitive inks. The background color is greenish. The barcode on the back is in the middle of the card.

Position of Photo: Flush right with ghost image to the left for both License and ID card. Previous ID card if only adult ID was bottom left.

Minor Age Driver Locator: The Under 21 license is printed vertically. "UNDER 21" is in bold red lettering with date printed under message indicating when driver turns 18 or 21.

ID Card Indicator: A vertical card, with the initials "ID" are in bold red just to the left of the picture. The words "Identification Card" are in red under the state name, across the top. There is no color bar across the top.

CDL Indicator: "CDL Driver's License" is printed on upper portion; class description and any endorsements or restrictions are printed on the reverse side. If under 21, is vertical format.

Issuance

Location of Requirements for Proof of Identity:

https://secure.rmv.state.ma.us/policybrowserpublic/splash.aspx

Age Requirements

The state has a Graduated Licensing Law. The minimum age is to obtain a learner's permit is 16. A driver must first have had a Learner's Permit for a period of at least 6 months, have a clean driving record, and complete a driver's education course to receive the Junior Operator License (JOL). Further restrictions are placed on JOLs holders including carrying passengers under the age of 18 for the first 6 months after receiving the JOL, unless it is an immediate family member or are accompanied by a licensed driver 21 years of age or older and is occupying the seat beside them; and driving is prohibited between 12:30 am and 5:00 am, unless accompanied by parent/guardian. Conviction of certain offenses will require the Junior Operator to complete retraining courses including a Driver Attitudinal Retraining Course and State Courts Against Road Rage (SCARR) program and retesting may also be required.

The minimum age for obtaining an ID Card is 14 years old.

Residency

Home-state license honored on a reciprocal basis; Massachusetts license must be secured immediately upon establishing legal residence. If the out-of-state license is expired for more than one year, an exam is required; if more than 4 years an exam and a road test are required.

Renewal

Renewal is birth date of fifth year. Driver keeps same number when renewing. Drivers may renew their license and make address changes from the web page under a program called RMV Express Lane. One cannot renew DL online if license photo was taken before age 21 or is more than nine years old, or if holding a CDL. Military personnel are not required to renew while on active duty, but can do so by mail. A non-photo license is issued until their discharge or return to Mass.

Elderly-Related Restrictions

None is reported by RMV, however online renewal is not available to those at age 75 or older.

Vehicle Insurance, Title and Registration Facts

Registration Renewal

Vehicles registration may be renewed by phone at 866-627-7768 or from the web at www.massdot.state.ma.us/rmv - provided there are no outstanding parking tickets, unpaid excise taxes or if the registration is suspended or revoked. An owner of a vehicle or trailer who purchases a new vehicle or trailer from a dealer or purchases a used vehicle or trailer from a private party may transfer the registration to the newly acquired vehicle within a 7-day grace period.

New Residents

Non-residents must register vehicles within 30 days of residency. Non-residents (except exempted students) who own motor vehicles or trailers that are registered in other states or countries must register those vehicles and trailers in Massachusetts if Massachusetts residents have or control those vehicles or trailers for more than 30 total days in one calendar year. Note that boats, snowmobiles, and ATVs are titled and registered by the Massachusetts Division of Law Enforcement, Massachusetts Environmental Police.

Inspections and Emissions Testing

The Massachusetts Vehicle Check program can consist of an annual safety inspection and an emissions test. All vehicles registered in MA must receive a safety inspection annually. The emissions On-Board Diagnostic Test (ODB Test) is given to: a) model year 1998 and newer passenger cars, trucks, SUVS, and light-duty diesel weighing 8,500 pounds or less; b) model year 2007 and new diesel vehicles weighing 8,501 to 14,000; c) and model year 2008 and news for non-diesel vehicles weighing 8,501 to 14,000. All incoming vehicles, motorcycles and mopeds, and vehicle in above categories but are 15 or more model years old are exempted. The web page for the Massachusetts Vehicle Check program is at http://massvehiclecheck.state.ma.us/. An in-depth description of commercial vehicle inspection process is found at www.mass.gov/rmv/inspect/commercial_regs.pdf.

Passenger Plate Facts

Currently two plates (red and white) are issued with one sticker (YR) only applied to rear plate. The single plate in green and white is no longer issued. The plate has no county or coding to indicate the county of issuance. When a vehicle is sold, the plates remain with the seller.

Insurance and Financial Responsibility

The state has compulsory financial responsibility laws which require a motor vehicle insurance policy or bond, or security deposit in lieu of a motor vehicle insurance policy or bond pursuant to M.G.L. c. 90, § 34D, must be in force for any vehicle. See M.G.L. c. 90, § 34A, et seq. Massachusetts also has a no-fault insurance provision. Minimum financial responsibility limits for motor vehicle policies and bonds are $20,000/40,000 per person/per accident for bodily injury liability coverage. Proof of compliance with the financial responsibility provisions of M.G.L. c. 90 must be electronically present on the Registry's file or must be provided at the time a vehicle is registered or renewed.

Withdrawal Sanctions, and Alcohol and Drug Testing

Alcohol and Chemical Testing

Massachusetts' illegal intoxication level is .08 percent and above, .02 for under age 21 drivers, and .04 for CDL drivers. Blood (by registered physician, nurse, or certified medical technician only), and breath (breathalyzer or infra-red) testing are used. Massachusetts has an implied-consent violation as well as the provision for an administrative suspension. Operating a horse, boat or bicycle under the influence is also considered illegal.

Suspensions and Revocations

The state is in compliance with the federally mandated disqualifications on CDL related infractions. See the Appendix for a list of these disqualifications. The RMV provides an excellent overview of suspensions and revocations at www.mass.gov/rmv/dmanual/chapter2.pdf. Below is a partial, but representative list.

Failure to Make Court Ordered Child Support Payments .... Indefinite suspension.
Habitual Traffic Offender .... Four-year suspension.
> (Note: This suspension is triggered by an accumulation of a total of three major moving violations or any combination of 12 major or minor moving violations within a five-year period. This period is calculated back from the most recent finding/conviction date. If another state reports an event, it will be included in the calculation. Surchargeable accidents are not part of HTO calculations.)

Junior Operator One Speeding Offense in Twelve Month Period .... Six-month suspension.
Leaving Scene of Accident with Property Damage Only, First Offense .... Sixty-day suspension.
Leaving Scene of Accident with Property Damage Only, Second Offense .... One-year suspension.
Leaving Scene of Injury Accident, First Offense .... One-year suspension.
Leaving Scene of Injury Accident, Second Offense .... Two-year suspension.
Motor Vehicle Homicide   Fifteen-year to permanent suspension.
Operating MV Without Owner's Authority, First Offense .... One-year suspension.
Operating MV Without Owner's Authority, Second Offense .... Three-year suspension.
Three Speeding Offenses in Twelve Month Period .... Thirty-day suspension.

Surchargeable Events
Three Surchargeable Events in 24 Months (effective 9/30/2010)...................................... Take Course or Indefinite suspension.
Five Surchargeable Events in 36 Months (for violations prior to 9/30/2010).................... Take Course or Indefinite suspension.
Seven Surchargeable Events in 36 Months.. Sixty-day suspension.

OUI
First Offense within 10 Years.. One-year suspension.
     Alternative First Offense within 10 Years .... 45 to 90-day suspension, plus Alcohol Program.
First Offense (under twenty-one) .... 210-day suspension, plus Alcohol Program.
Second Offense in Life of Operator... Two-year revocation.
Third Offense in Life of Operator .... Eight-year revocation.
Fourth Offense in Life of Operator.. Ten-year revocation.
Fifth Offense in Life of Operator .... Lifetime revocation.

OUI Homicide by Motor Vehicle OUI or Neg. Operation Fatality ....Ten-year revocation.
   (Note: If previous OUI or Fatality, then lifetime revocation.)
Under 21 years of Age and Buy or Try to Buy Alcohol .... 180-day suspension.

Chemical Tests
Failures (.08 BAC or more) .... 30-day suspension.
Failures - Under Age 21 (.02 BAC)... 30-day suspension.
Refusals with:
No Prior OUI offenses   ....180-day suspension; three-year if under 21.
One OUI Prior in Life of Operator ....Three-year suspension.
Two OUI Prior in Life of Operator...Five-year suspension.
Three or more OUI Prior in Life of Operator ....Lifetime suspension.

Other Reasons a Driver May Be Suspended
- Failed to pay required child support
- Have an outstanding arrest or default warrant
- Have been convicted of a drug offense
- Have failed to pay Massachusetts income tax
- Have failed to register as a sex offender
- Have made a bad payment to the RMV

About Ignition Interlock Devices

Since January 1, 2006, any driver with a second or subsequent OUI offense who is eligible for a hardship license or is eligible for a license reinstatement is required to have an Ignition Interlock Device (IID) on all associated vehicles. A driver with a hardship license must use the IID for the entire period of the hardship license and fro an additional two years after the license has been reinstated. If a driver with two or more OUI offenses is eligible for license renewal, the IID will be required for a mandatory two years.

Reinstatement Requirements

Reinstatement fees range from $50.00 - $1,200, depending upon the offense. In addition, some offenses may have additional requirements, such as a learner's permit exam and road test. Typical fees are:
Minor Suspension........$100.00 fee.
Major Suspensions.......$500.00 fee.
OUI..............................$500.00 first offense, $700.00 2nd offense, $1,200.00 third+.

Record Access: Laws, Rules, and Forms

Note: This Section Applies to Both Driver and Vehicle Records.

Governing Statutes and Rules

Massachusetts General Laws:
   www.mass.gov/legis/laws/mgl/index.htm
A specific law or statute was not passed to place the state in compliance with DPPA. Many changes were done administratively, and specific statutes cover certain requesters. For example; MGL Chapter 90, §§ 1A, 34A, 34B, and 34H deal with record usage by insurance companies, or authorized agent or service carrier; MGL Chapter 90F deals with holders of a CDL; MGL Chapter 147, § 25 deal with use by private investigator. MGL Chapter 6C § 57A is the enabling legislation for the Merit Rating Board and regulates records released to the auto insurance industry.
Uses #11 and #12 from DPPA are not allowed. Bulk purchase for marketing or solicitation purposes is prohibited.

Request and Consent Forms

There are two important forms and both can be downloaded from the web. A *Request for Personal Information in RMV Records* is a four-page form, the last page is the consent portion and requires the notarized signature from the subject. The *Request for a Driving Record* form also

is available. Both forms are found at www.massdot.state.ma.us/rmv within the *Forms & Manuals* section.

Vendor and Third Party Access Policy

Driving Records: Approved vendors cannot access records for other vendors who sell to an end-user, even if the end user has a permissible purpose with the exception of consumer reporting agencies. Otherwise, a vendor chain is not permitted.
Vehicle Records: Bulk retrieval media is available for permitted commercial vendors. Exclusive of bulk marketing and solicitation purposes, the state does not restrict further resale of purchased records to other permitted users only.

Records Ordered For Non-permissible Uses

Driving Records: Any requester without consent can obtain a record, but the driver's license number must be submitted with the request and the resulting record will not show personal information.
Vehicle Records: Without consent, requesters with a non-permissible use can obtain records that contain no personal information

Access to Driver-Related Records

Driving Records

General Information and Fees
Driving Records, Registry of Motor Vehicles, Court Records Department, P.O. Box 55889, Boston, MA 02205-5896. 857-368-8000 www.massdot.state.ma.us/rmv/
Two different types of driving records are provided by the Registry and are used for employment or personal use.
   1) The **Registry's Driving Record.** The Driving Record will go back ten years, plus the current year, and contain Civil Motor Vehicle

Infractions (CMVI's) and criminal violations where the individual has been found guilty or responsible, and motor vehicle accidents where the individual has been found to be more than 50 percent at fault. All serious offenses where the individual has been found guilty, such as operating under the influence, vehicular homicides and drug related offenses, etc., will display regardless of how far back they occurred.
   2) The **Registry's Driving History.** A Driving History goes back for as long as the RMV has the data and contains everything a Driving Record does, plus administrative actions, any Civil Motor Vehicle Infraction or criminal violation where the individual has been found

not responsible or not guilty, any amendments and corrections made to the record, and file notes requests made for the record.

Each of the above records also has two "types" or available versions:

- A **True and Attested Driving Record (or History)** is on MassDOT RMV Division letterhead and is certified with the Registrar's signature. Cost $20.00
- An **Unattested Driving Record (or History)** can only be obtained online and is downloaded rather than mailed. This version contains the same information as a True and Attested but is not certified and does not contain the Registrar's signature. Cost $6.00

In-Person & Mail – Walk-in public service for the RMV is at 25 Newport Avenue Extension, Quincy, MA 02171; however, a driver can request a driving record at any full service RMV branch.

Up to ten records may be requested immediately. Requests of more than ten are processed overnight (larger lists may take longer). It takes an average of 8 working days to process mail-in requests. The driver's license number, name, and date of birth are needed when ordering. Payment must be made with the request. There is a full charge for a "no record found" report.

Electronic – Electronic driving records and **status checks** are available for high volume requester or users. The record most often accessed by vendors for permissible use clients is the Unattested Record which is available electronically for $8.00 per record. The driver license number is needed for input. Contact the Registrar's office for details.

Bulk – Not offered.

By Person of Record – MA drivers may obtain their driving record online [see below}, by mail or walk-in as described above. Any full service branch can supply walk-in records. In addition, drivers may order their own record from the Registry by telephone at 857-368-8000 using a credit card. The record is mailed to the address on file.

Online ordering system. One may purchase the Unattested Driving Record or "True and Attested Driving Record" online. The Unattested Record is viewable online in PDF format. The True and Attested Record is not viewable online but is mailed within ten days to the address on file for the Record Holder; an alternate mailing address cannot be used. The name of the requestor will appear on the printed record. Use of a credit card is required for either record. To purchase, click on "Other: Request Driving Records" from the home page.

Status Check

Drivers may verify the status of their MA License or ID. The screen indicates the class/type and status, expiration date, method of next renewal (online or in person), and if the licensee has outstanding obligations associated with the MA License/Permit or ID number provided. No personal information is displayed at this site. See https://secure.rmv.state.ma.us/LicInquiry/intro.aspx.

Notification/Monitoring Program

The RMV offers a Driver Verification System (DVS). DVS is a web based application that allows companies, cities, towns, state agencies and authorities to track the license statuses of their employees. When an employee's license status changes, the employer will receive an e-mail notification from the RMV. The users can then log into the DVS Web application to view the status change. DVS WEB will only provide license status e.g. active, expired, suspended, revoked, and cancelled. DVS WEB will <u>not</u> provide a driving record or the reason why a license has been suspended, revoked, etc. To request more information, email dvs@state.ma.us or call 617-351-9521.

Crash Reports

Reporting – All accidents resulting in death, personal injury, or over $1,000.00 in property damage must be reported within five days to the local police, to the insurance company, and to the RMV Crash Records at the address above. A driver does not need to file a report if the crash occurred on a private road, driveway, private parking lot or other private way. Forms are available from the police, the Registry, and at www.massdot.state.ma.us/rmv/. There are no special reporting requirements for commercial drivers.

Record Access – Copies of accident reports may be obtained from the Registry of Motor Vehicles, Crash Records, PO Box 55889, Boston 02205, 857-368-8190 for a fee of $20.00 per report. The request must include full name, date of incident, location and license or registration number. Allow 4 weeks after the incident before new records are available. Normal turnaround time is 7 to 10 days; however, it can take as long as 4 weeks. Records are available from 2 years to present. Criminal offender record information will not be released. In-person searches are available while you wait. View a crash report online at https://secure.rmv.state.ma.us/CrRequest/Public/Intro.aspx. Use of a credit card is required. Quarterly or yearly electronic updates are available for purchase.

About The Merit Rating Board (MRB)

The Important Role of the Merit Rating Board

The Merit Rating Board (MRB), part of the Massachusetts Department of Transportation (MassDOT), is a section within the Registry of Motor Vehicles. The address is PO Box 55889, Boston MA 02205-5889, phone: 857-368-8100, fax: 857-368-0810. The home page is www.massdot.state.ma.us/rmv/MeritRatingBoard.aspx.

The Merit Rating Board maintains operator driving records consisting of traffic law violations, at-fault and comprehensive insurance claim records, and out-of-state driving records. The primary responsibilities of the MRB are:

- The maintenance and update of operator driving history record information for Massachusetts auto insurers and other government agencies involved in transportation and public safety.
- The administration of the state's Safe Driver Insurance Plan (SDIP). In Massachusetts, auto insurers may offer different prices for different insurance packages. Insurers may use the point-based system of the SDIP or develop their own merit rating plan to determine discounts for safe drivers and surcharges for drivers with at-fault accidents and traffic violations.

MRB's Driving Record Service for the Insurance Industry

The MRB's operator driving history records contain surchargeable incidents, such as at-fault accidents and traffic violations as defined in 211 CMR 134.00 Safe Driver Insurance Plan.

An online service is available to authorized insurance companies and agents to view driving records maintained by the MRB. This service is available through the RMV Uninsured Motorist System (www.mass.gov/rmv/ums/). There are no MRB fees and no per-transaction fees. The MA private passenger insurance industry is assessed for expenditures of the Merit Rating Board including fringe benefits and indirect costs. An FTP site is used for file transfers between the MRB and insurers. The MRB receives claim and Out-of-State driving record information from insurers. The MRB transfers driving history record information containing surchargeable incidents to insurers.

The MRB also has a notification program (Notice to Re-inquire) that notifies an insurer when the driving record information on a policy inquiry record previously reported to an insurer changes. This Notice to Re-inquire feature is available to insurers that use the MRB Policy Inquiry application. The information may be used to adjust automobile insurance premiums.

Per statute, access to the MRB data as described above is not available to the general public.

Access to Vehicle-Related Records

General Information and Fees

Registry of Motor Vehicles, Document Control, PO Box 55889, Boston MA 02205-5889 857-368-8000.

The Title Department can be reached at PO Box 55885. The current fee for a computer printout of a VIN or registration record, or a history search is $5.00. An "Attested Copy" of information is $10.00. A photocopy of an original RMV-1 Applications is $10.00. Credit cards are accepted for payment. Lien information is automatically provided as part of registration and title information. Records are available from 30 years to present. Use of the forms described earlier is needed to obtain personal information. Personal information is not released when requested by non-permitted users. Fax requests are only accepted from government agencies.

Mail or In-Person – Turnaround time for walk-in requests is immediate, except microfilm lookups may take up to 3 days. Turnaround time for mail-in requests is 7 to 10 days.

Electronic –There are two online inquiry systems open to the public.

1) The Title/Lien Inquiry Transaction is for vehicle owners and lienholders to track a title, to verify lienholder accuracy, or to ensure a title has been sent to the appropriate party. Requester must supply the VIN or the actual Title number, found on the vehicle registration document. The on-screen message displays the date the title was issued, to whom the title was (or will be) mailed, and the name of the lienholder if applicable. No personal information is ever displayed. Visit https://secure.rmv.state.ma.us/TitleLookup/intro.aspx.

2) The Registration Inquiry Transaction works in a similar manner. Requesters must have the vehicle's registration plate type and registration number as printed on the vehicle registration card. Once the information is validated, the displayed results will include registration status, registration expiration date, a link to associated registration fees, last vehicle inspection date with result and insurance information. Additional information may be obtained by providing subsequent user validation details. Transactions for the following registration types are not available: dealer/manufacturer, repair, farm, owner contractor, transport and apportioned. No personal information is ever displayed.

Visit https://secure.rmv.state.ma.us/RegInquiry/intro.aspx

Certain permissible use requesters such as Massachusetts-based insurance companies and some Massachusetts insurance agents are online to the Registry's computer, for whom there is no cost beyond the line charge. However, this availability is restricted solely to such users and is not open to the general public.

Bulk – Massachusetts provides a "mechanism" whereby outside govt. agencies can obtain bulk records in electronic format or paper format (for smaller runs). The charge for such records is $2,500.00. An automated inquiry request form must be submitted to begin any processing. For further information, please contact the Production Control Office at the address above.

Access to Vessel-Related Records

General Information

Massachusetts Environmental Police, 251 Causeway St, #101, Boston 02114 617-626-1610 http://www.sport.state.ma.us/

Note that boats, snowmobiles, and ATVs are titled and registered by this agency. State law requires all boats 14 ft or over to be titled and requires the registration of any boat powered by a motor and operated on public waterways in Massachusetts. Registration is required even if the motor is not the primary means of propulsion for that boat.

Examples of boats requiring registration include fishing boats with motors, recreational motorboats, canoes or sailboats that use motors (includes electric motors), and personal watercraft such as jet skis or wet bikes. Boats exempt from registration requirements include those that do not use motors, and documented vessels (large boats that are issued a marine document and registration through the U.S. Coast Guard). Vessels used solely by a city, county, state, or federal agency will be issued a certificate of registration and number at no charge.

Access and Fees

There is no charge for a record search. Name searches may be conducted by fax at 617-626-1630. Records maintained from 1998 to present. Records from 2000 forward are available by telephone. SSNs, DOBs, and subject phone numbers are not released. This agency maintains lien record information and will release lien holder names and addresses.

Driving Record Content and Reciprocity

What's On or Not On the Driving Record

- Registry MVRs show suspensions and revocations.
- Only surchargeable at fault accidents ($500 damage or more) on the driving record, meaning if a person is involved, but not at fault, the accident will not appear.

Data Retention

CDL driver records are purged based on the timetable per federal regulations (see the Appendix). The Registry did not indicate when non-CDL records are purged.

Court to Repository

Court to Central Repository - The state requires a court to notify the Registry forthwith of a disposition on a criminal motor vehicle violation. This conviction information is passed to the Registry via paper abstract. All convictions are keyed into the system within one week of receipt. **Police Department to Central Repository** - The state requires that a police department mail a copy of a citation containing one or more civil motor vehicle violations to the Registry no later than the end of the sixth business day after the date of violation. Payments and court hearing requests for minor civil (non-criminal) motor vehicle violations are processed at the Registry.

State Reciprocity for Non-CDL Drivers

- Will suspend driver for unpaid out-of-state convictions if NRVC state.
- Record of new incoming driver is shown on MVR.
- Out-of-state convictions are shown on MVR.
- Out-of-state accidents are shown on MVR.
- Convictions of out-of-state drivers are sent to home state upon request.
- Record is forwarded to new state when driver moves upon request.

Codes for License Classes, Restrictions, and Endorsements

License Classes– Commercial

Class A   Any combination of vehicles with a GCWR of 26,001 or more pounds—provided the GVWR of the vehicle(s) being towed is in excess of 10,000 pounds, except a school bus, (includes Class B and C with appropriate endorsements).

Class B   Any single vehicle with a GVWR of 26,001 or more pounds, or any such vehicle towing a vehicle not in excess of 10,000 pounds GVWR, except a school bus, (includes Class B and C with appropriate endorsements).

Class C   Any single vehicle that is less than 26,001 pounds GVWR, or any such vehicle towing a vehicle not in excess of 10,000 pounds GVWR that is placarded for hazardous materials or designed to transport sixteen or more persons (including the operator), except a school bus.

License Classes– Non-Commercial

Class D   Any motor vehicle or combination, except a semi-trailer unit, truck trailer combination, tractor, or truck having a registered gross weight in excess of 26,000 lbs., a bus or a school bus.

Class M   A motorcycle or any other motor vehicle having a seat or saddle for the rider and designed to travel with no more than three wheels in contact with the ground.

Note: "**JOL**" if indicated refers to Junior Operator License.

Restrictions

B	Corrective Lenses	M	Except Class A Bus
C	Mechanical Aid	N	Except Class A and B Bus
D	Prosthetic Aid	O	Except Tractor Trailer
E	Automatic Transmission	P	Use with certified Driving Instructors Only (Permit Only)
F	Outside Mirror	R	Bioptic Telescopic lens
G	Limit to Daylight Only	S	Proof of Current Blood Sugar Level
H	Limit to Restricted Hours	V	CDL – CMV Interstate Federal Medical Variance
I	Limit - Junior Operator Only	W	CMV – Intrastate only with Medical Waiver
J	Other - Restriction Defined on Card (Must be Carried)	Q	CMV Medical Waivers Must Be Carried
K	CDL Intrastate Only (for drivers under age 21)	Y	Restrict to 14 passengers or Less
L	Only CDL Vehicles without Air Brakes	Z	Ignition Interlock Device Required

Endorsements

H	Hazardous Materials	S	School Bus
N	Tank Vehicles	T	Doubles/Triples
P	Passenger Transport	X	Hazardous Material and Tank Vehicles

More About CDL Endorsements:

- A Class A license can have all endorsements.
- A Class B license can have all endorsements except for Combination and Doubles/Triples.
- A Class C license can only have HAZMAT, Tank, School Bus, and Passenger endorsements.
- If driver passes a CDL road test in a vehicle equipped with air brakes, driver will be permitted to operate a vehicle with air brakes.
- Transporting school-aged children and/or operation of a 'school bus' requires state-issued special authority.

Conviction Table with Statute, ACD, and Points

The state of Massachusetts does not have a point system for license suspensions or revocations. Suspensions and revocations are in accordance with specific statutes. Thus the Points Column in this table is indicative of either a Minor or Major Surchargeable Traffic Violation – for purposes of the MRB Safe Driver Insurance Plan. Two points are assigned to a Minor and five points to a Major violation.

Following this Conviction Table are these components of the MRB Safe Driver Insurance Plan (SDIP):

- Major Surchargeable Traffic Violation Table
- Minor Surchargeable Traffic Violation Table
- MRB - Accident At-Fault Surcharge Codes

In this table in the **Points Column**, an asterisk "*" next to the point count indicates this particular violation is classified as a **criminal traffic violation**.

Description	State Code/Law	ACD Code	Pts
2 Railroad Viols	W60	W60	
24 Hour Out Of Service Order	C99	B27	
2nd/Sub Conv Cl A Sub W/Intent To Dist	94C32B	A33	
2nd/Sub Conv Cl C Sub	94C32BB	A33	
2nd/Sub Conv Cl C Sub W/Intent To Dist	94C32-AB, AD, CB, DB	A33	
3 Railroad Viols	W61	W61	
3 Speeding Citations	TSP	W01	
5 Surcharge Events	FSU	W01	
7 Surcharge Events	RV1, SSE, SSU	W01	
Abandonment Of Veh	90 22A,B	F66	

Description	State Code/Law	ACD Code	Pts
Accid And Bi	AC1	B03	
Accid And Pd	AC2	W00	
Accid Fault Unk	AC4	W00	
Accid With Viol	AC3	W00	
Accident	AC	W00	
Accum Of 2 Out-Of-Serv W/10 Years While	W51	W51	
Accum Of 3 Or More Out-Of-Serv W/Ten Years	W52	W52	
Accum Of Two Out-Of-Serv Order W/Ten Years	W50	W50	
Accumulation Of Two Or More Major Offens	W40	W40	
Additional Major Offense After Reinstate	W41	W41	
Admin Per Se	DI5	A04, A08, A10, A11, A61, A90, A94, A98	
Administrative Per Se	ADM	A08	
Adult Drag Racing	90 17B AD	S95	2*
Aftermarket Lighting	5402207		2
Allow Op W/O Ign Lck	90 12E		2*
Allow Unlic Operate	90 12	D16	2
Allow Unlic/Susp Opr	90 12C	W00	2*
Alter Vin	266139	W00	
Altering/Transferring License Or Id	13834B	B41	
Attach Imporoper Plate	90 2	E01	
Attach Impropr Plate	RT1, 90 2	E01	
Attaching Plates	90 23 AP	E01	
Bad Check	BCK	W00	
Bad Check Payment	BCN	W00	
Bad Credit Card Pymt	BCC	W00	
Being Present Where Heroin Is Kept	94C35	A33	
BK TPK Negl Loading	730708		2
Boat Refuse to Obey	90B38	M08	
Boating Fatal OUI	90B8B FO	U31	
Brake Linings	90 7H	E31	
Brakes Violation	97 7 BV	E31	2
BV TPK Brakes Viol	730705		2
BV TPK Breakdwn LN Viol	730708		2
Careless Driving	M81		2*
Cargo Transport Violation	730708 CT	E50	
CDL Adm Haz Mat	C61	A04	
CDL Adm Per Se	C51	A04	
CDL Admin Per Se	C11	A04	
CDL Chem Test Refuse	C13, C53	A12	
CDL Csor Surrender	CS	D16	
CDL Ctr Haz Mat	C63	A12	
CDL Drive To Endanger	C19	M84	
CDL Driving While OOS Effective	C30	W50	
CDL DWI Drugs	C14 , C54	A22	
CDL DWI Drugs Haz Mat	C64	A22	
CDL DWI Haz Mat	C62	A21	
CDL DWI Liquor	C12, C52	A21	
CDL Following Too Close	C22	M34	
CDL Homicide/Negligent Operation	C28, C58	U09	
CDL Homicide/Negligent Operation Haz Mat	C68	U09	
CDL Illegal Status Response	INQREV	B91	
CDL Improper Class	C26	B91	
CDL Leaving The Scene Of Pd/Pi	C15, C55	B05	
CDL Lifetime Disqualification	C71	W40	
CDL Lve Scene Pd/Pi Haz Mat	C65	B05	
CDL No License In Possession	C25	B51	
CDL Operating Recklessly	C20	M84	
CDL Operating Unlicensed	C24	B56	
CDL Operating While Revoked	C27, C57	B25	
CDL Operating While Revoked Haz Mat	C67	B25	
CDL Out Of Serv Order Effective	C94, C95, C96	B27	
CDL Out Of Serv Transport 16 Pass Or Haz	C91, C92, C93	B19	
CDL Out Of Service	90F9E.51 &.53	B27	
CDL Out Of Service Hazmat	90F9E.52	B19	
CDL Out Of Service Order Employer	90F4C	B27	
CDL Pending Withdrawal	INQPEND	B91	

Description	State Code/Law	ACD Code	Pts
CDL Railroad Crossing Violation	C32	M10	unk
CDL Speed	C18	S15	
CDL Stv Disqual	C80	W30	
CDL Stv Disqual	C81	W31	
CDL Veh Felony Drugs	C17	A50	
CDL Veh To Commit Felony	C16, C56	U03	
CDL Veh To Commit Felony Drugs	C70	A50	
CDL Veh To Commit Felony Drugs Haz Mat	C60	A50	
CDL Veh To Commit Felony Haz Mat	C66	U03	
CDL Vehicular Homicide	C23	U07	
CDL Voluntary Surrender	VS	D16	
CDL Weaving Between Lanes	C21	M42	
Chem Test Refusal	CTR, D13	A12	
Compl Improp Oper	CLI	W70	
Complaint Fraudulent License/Id	CFL	B41	
Complaint General	CLG	W70	
Complaint Medical	CLM	D75	
Complaint Regulatory	CLR	W70	
Conceal Identity	90 23 CI	B41	
Conspiracy To Viol Controlled Sublaw	94C40	A33	
Conv Cl A Traff/ Manuf/Distrib/Dispen	94C32E CA	A33	
Conv Cl B Traff/ Manuf/ Distrib/ Dispen	94C32E CB	A33	
Conv Cl D Traff/ Manuf/ Distrib/ Dispen	94C32E CD	A33	
Court Default	DEF, RR2	D45	
Court Ordered Drug Revocation	CTORE	A22	
Court Ordered Drug Suspension	CTOSU	A22	
Court Ordered Liquor Revocation	CTLRE	A21	
Court Ordered Liquor Suspension	CTLSU	A21	
Court Ordered Suspension	COS	W00	
Court Ordered Suspension, MV Fatality	COF	U31	
CR TPK Cross Over Viol	730708		2
Cross Fire Hose	MS4	M56	2
CV Ovrsze Const VH N/PT	730706		2
CV TPK Coasting Viol	730708		2
CZ TPK Speed Const Zne	730708		2
Dangerous Animals	85 19	N84	
Defacing Property	266126A	W00	
Defect Brakes	DE2	E31	2
Defect Equip	DE5	E70	
Defect Equipment	DE	E33, E36, E70	2
Defect Exhaust	DE3	E70	2
Defect Tires	DE4	E37	2
Defective Lights	DE1	E34	2
Disability	DS	B65, W14	
Disable Con Oper	DS3	D74	
Dispensing Controlled Substances	94C5	A33	
Display Number Plate	RR5, 90 6	E01	
Display Red Lights	90 7E	E34	
Display Single Plate	90 6B	E01	
Disposal Of Garbage	27016	W00	
Disposal Of Vehicle	90 24 H	F66	
Disposal Of Vehicle	EM3	F66	2*
Disturb Funeral	27242		2*
DPW Sign/Devices	85 2	M14	
DPW Sign/Devices	SC2	M05, M09, M10, M14, M15, M16, M17, M19, M20, M21, M22, M23, M24, R24, W60, W61	2
DPW State Hway Regs	85 2		2
Dpw/Fed Regs Haz Mat	720803	E03	
Dpw/St Pol Restrict	7201000RS	M40	
Drag Racing	90 17B	S95	
Drag Racing by JR License/Permit Holder	90 17B DR	S95	ink
Drink Open Container	90 24 I	A35	
Driv Intoxicated	DI	A20	
Driv Medi/Sub	DI2	A24	5*
Driv On Shoulder	IL4	M58	2

Description	State Code/Law	ACD Code	Pts
Driving CMV Without CDL	B56	B56	2
Driving Denied	VR3	B23	2
Driving School Viol	90 32G	D16	
Driving To Endanger	90 24 DE	M84	5*
Driving To Endanger	RK1	M84, U06	2*
Driving To Endanger	RK2,	M84	2*
Driving To Endanger	RK4	N80	2*
Driving While Out-Of-Service Is In Effect	B19	B19	
DV TPK Disabled Veh Vio	730708		2
DWI Alcoh/Drug	DI1	A20, A21, A22, A23, A60	5*
DWI Alcohol Program	90 24 D	A21	5*
DWI Drug Program	90 24 DP	A21	5*
DWI Drugs	90 24 DD	A22	5*
DWI Liquor	90 24 DI	A21	5*
DWI Serious Injury	90 24 L	A21	5*
EA TPK Restricted Area	730708		2
EC TPK Restricted CZ	730708		2
EE TPK Enter/Exit Impr	730708		2
Electronic Message – Operator Send Receive	90 13B	M82	unk
EM TPK Median/Excl Area	730708		2
Equipment Violation	90 7 EV		2
Equipment Violation	ER	D70	2
Equipment Violation	ER	F05, F66	
Equipment Violation	ER, ER1, ER2	E01	
Equipment Violation	ER1	E02, E03, E04 E05, E06	
Equipment Violation	ER2	E23	2
Erratic Speeds	SP5		2
ET Explsv Veh Too Close	730706		2
EV Explsv Veh Stop Impr	730706		2
Evading Arrest	HR5	U01	
Excess Running Motor	90 16A	F66	
Excess Running Motor	EM1	F66	2
Excise Tax Lic	EXL	W00	
Excise Tax Reg	EXR	W00	
Exhibit Anothers Lic	90 23 EL	D16	2*
Expired Reg Sticker	540205	E01	
Expired Registration Sticker	540224 CR	E01	
Fail Canc Direct	SI3	N41	2
Fail Dim Lights	540212	E54	2
Fail Dim Lights	540225	E54	2/0
Fail Finan Resp	FR3	B63, B64	
Fail Observ Warn	SC4	M18	2
Fail Sec Require	FR2	D38	
Fail Show Insurance	B74		2
Fail Stop At Toll	730703		2
Fail Stop For School Bus	90 14 SB	N09	2
Fail To Dim Lights	EM5	E54	2
Fail To Give Signal	SI1, 90 14B	N43	2
Fail To Keep Right	89 1	M41	2
Fail To Keep Right	IL2	M11, M41	2
Fail To Return Plate	90 6C	D16	
Fail To Rpt Accd	90 26 , RR1	B61	
Fail To Rpt Name/Add	RR	W15	
Fail To Rpt Name/Add	RR, 90 26A	B61	
Fail To Signal	PA5	N40, N42	2
Fail To Use Safety	90 14	E50	2
Failure To Answer Citation, Pay Fines, Penalties	D56	D56	
Failure To Obey	SC1	M08, W00	2*
Failure To Register	90 3	E01	
Failure To Reveal ID After Fatal Or Personal Injury	B14	B14	
Failure To Stop	89 9	M15	2
Failure To Yield	PA6	N01, N07	2
False Citation	90C10	D02	
False Lic, Reg, Etc	MR2	B41	2*
False Lic, Reg, Etc.	90 24 B	B41	
False Statement Weight Sticker	90 19D FS	D02	

Description	State Code/Law	ACD Code	Pts
False Statements	MR	D02, D06, D07, W13	
False Statements	MR5, 90 24 FS, MR1	D02	
False Title	90D32	B41	
False Weight Sticker	90 19D	D02	
Fatal Accd Prelim	FA, FAP	U08	
Fatal Accid Final	FAF	U08	
Felony	FE	U03	
Financial Respon	FR4	B64	
FL Follow Too Closely	730400, 730706, 730707, 730708		2
Fl Obs Safe Zone	SC5	M03, M12	2
Fl Rmv/Prod Stck Cert	90 19D FL	E01	
Flare Violation	85 14B	F34	
Follow Too Close	FO	M30	2
Follow Too Close	FO, FO1, FO2	M34	2
Follow Too Close	FO2	M31	2
Fraud Register Mv	90 2 FR	D02	
Fraudulent Claim	RT3, 26 8B	D02	
FS Sum/Cal Tunl Other	730300		2
FS TPK Fl Signl STP TRN	730708		2
FTO RR Clrnc	M24	M24	2
FTO RR Drive	M22	M22	2
FTO RR Gat/S	M10	M10	2
FTO RR Nslow	M20	M20	2
FTO RR Nstop	M21	M21	2
FTO RR Restr	M09	M09	2
FTO RR Space	M23	M23	2
Gubernatorial By Law	85 23	N84	2
Habitual Traf Offndr	HTO, HV	W01	
Hazardous Material	730710	E53	
Hazardous Sub	RK3	E03, E04, E53	
Headlights – Alternating Flashing	540225 AF	E70	2
Heavy Veh County	85 30 CT	F66	
Heavy Veh Mun	85 30 MU	F66	
Heavy Veh State	85 30	F66	
Hit And Run	HR	B01, B02	2*
Hitch Mechanism Violation	90 19K	E70	
Horn Violation	90 7 HV		2
HP Plate/Placard Misuse	90 2 B	W00	
HV TPK-High Beam Viol	730708		2
Hvy Veh Ns County	85 30A CT	F66	
Hvy Veh Ns Mun	85 30A MU	F66	
Hvy Veh Ns State	85 30A	F66	
IF Sum/Cal TNL Insp Stk	730300		2
Ilegal Veh State Hwy	85 2E	M40	
Illegal Operation	90 16	M40	2
Illegal Operation	MS6	F06, N84	2
Illegal Possession Of Class A Substance	94C34 CA	A33	
Illegal Possession Of Class B Substance	94C34 CB	A33	
Illegal Possession Of Class C Substance	94C34 CC	A33	
Illegal Possession Of Class D Substance	94C34 CD	A33	
Illegal Possession Of Class E Substance	94C34 CE	A33	
IM Failed Inspection	IMF	E70	
IM Non-Compliance	IMR	E70	
Immediate Threat	CIT	W70	
Immediate Threat-Medical	CIM	D75	
Imminent Hazard	W70	W70	
Impaired	DI6	A25	
Impede Fire Aparatus	89 7A	N04	unk
Impede Fire Aparatus	RW1	N04, N05, N30	2
Impeding Operation	90 13	F34	2
Improp Backing	MS2	N82	2
Improp Entrance	IL5	M25, M46	2
Improper Equipment	90 7	E70	2
Improper Lane	IL	F34, M40, M44, M45, M47, M48, M49, M50, M51, M55, M60, M61, M62	2
Improper Lane	IL1	M42	2

Description	State Code/Law	ACD Code	Pts
Improper Passing	PA1	M71, M74	2
Improper Passing	PA1, 89 2	M70	2
Improper Saddlemount	90 19C	F03	
Improper Turn	90 14 TU	N50	2
Improper Turn	TU3	N50	2
Impropr Equipment Ns	90 7 NS	E01	
Inatt, Careless, Negl	M80		2*
Inducing Minor To Sell Controlled Subst	94C32K	A33	
Ins Cancellation	FR5	B64, D36	2
Ins Cancellation	INS	D36	
IS Inspection Stk Viol	730708	E01	2
JOL CDL Vehicle	90 8 JL	D27	2
JOL Lic Time Restriction	90 8 TR		2
JOL Mult Speed Or Racing Violations	JSP	W01	
JOL Operator-Use Mobil Phone Device	90 *M	M82	
JOL Pass Restriction	90 8 JO	D29	2
JOL Perm Time Rest	90 8B TR		2
JOL Permit No Lic Dr	90 8BUS		2
JOL Permit Not Accomp by Lic Driver	90 8B UA	D29	unk
JOL Time Restriction	90 10 JO		2*
Jun Oper Lic Time Rest	90 10 JO	D29	
Keep In Right Lane	89 4B	M41	2
Keep Right No View	89 4	M41	2
Lane Violation	89 4A	M41	2
Larceny Of A Controlled Substance	94C37	A33	
Large Tandem Unit Violation	730707	F66	
Learner Permit	90 8B	D29	2
Lease Veh Park	LVP	F34	
Lease Veh Viol/Intoxicated/Unauthorized	90 32C	A21	
Lease Vehicle Violation	90 32E	D16	
Leav The Scene	HR3	B05, B06	2*
Leav the scene Accident Before Police Arrive	B05	B05	2*
Leave Fatal Acc Before Police Arrive	B06	B06	*
Leave Scene Fatal Accident	90 24 FA	B06	5*
Leaving Scene Pers Inj	90 24 PI	B07	5*
Leaving Scene Pers Inj	HR1	B03, B07	2*
Leaving Scene Prop Dam	90 24 PD	B08	5*
Leaving Scene Prop Dam	HR2	B04	2*
Left Lane Exclusion	89 4C	M49	2
Lessee Fraud	26664	D02	
Lic Test Failure	DS1	W14, W20	
License Class Viol	540206		2
License Restriction	90 8	D27	2
License Restriction	VR4	B91, D27, D29	2
License Restriction Violation	VR	B20, B21, B22, B24	
License Revoked	90 23 RE	B25	5*
License Suspended	90 23 SU		5*
Lights Violation	85 15	E55	2
Limit/Prohibited Use	730705	M40	2
Liq Poss/Carry By Minor	13834C NS	A31	
Liq Trans By Minor	13834C	A31	2
Liq Trans By Minor	13834C LQ	A31	2*
Litter From Vehicle	LI, LI1, LI2, LI3	W00	
Littering A False Prescription	94C33	A33	
LL TPK left land Rest	730708		2
Load No Cover/Escape	85 36	F66	
Loan Lic/Permit	MR4, 90 24 LP	D16	2*
Logan Traffic Viol	7402100TV	M17	2
Lt Turn From Rt	TU2	N53	2
Lv Fatal Acc Bfr Pol	B06		2
Manslaughter By Motor vehicle	26513	U08	5*
Manslaughter Whl OUI	2651312		5*
Manuf/Distrib/Dispen To Minors Cl A, B, C	94C32F	A33	
Mass Pike Equip Viol	730500 EQ	E01	
Mass Pike Ex Wght	730500 EW	F66	
Mass Pike Excess Vio	730500 EV	F66	

Description	State Code/Law	ACD Code	Pts
Mass Pike Park Zone	730500 P1	F34	
Mass Pike Parking	730500 P3	F34	
Mass Pike Parking Hp	730500 P4	F34	
Mass Pike Parkwalk	730500 P2	F34	
Mass Pike Tandem Trl	730400	F66	
Mass Pike Viol Ii	730500 V2	N84	
MC TPK Muffler Cutout	730708		2
MDC Excluded Vehicle	350401 CV	M40	2
MDC Fail Stop/Yield	350401 SY	M17	2
MDC Rec/Snow Viol	350200	E01	
MDC Sign/Signal	350401	M17	2
MDC Violation	350401 OT	N84	2
MDC Watershed Reserve	350801	M40	
MDC Way Speeding Over Posted Limit	350401 PL	S93	2
Military Plate Misuse	90 5A	E01	
Minor Att Purch Liquor	13834P	A31	
Minor Purchase/Att Liquor	13834A	A31	
Minor Traffic	MRBSDIP, ORDTOWN, 7401100NS, 7401100OT, 7402100OT	N84	2
Minor traffic- Tobin Bridge	7001000 OT	M14	2
Misc Condition	MS	W00	
Miscellaneous Condition	MS	A41, D10	
Misrep Avoid ARR	MR6	D02	2
ML TPK- marked Lane Viol	730708		2
Mobile Phone – Public Transport Non-MV Oper	90 12A NM	M82	unk
Mobile Phone Use – Public Transport Oper	90 12A PT	M82	unk
Modify Veh Height	90 7P		2
Moped Violation	90 1B	M40	
Motorcycle Handlebar	90 7J	F03	
Motorcycle Noise	90 7U	E70	
Motorcycle Pasenger Violation	90 7 PV	F06	unk
MS TPK Min Speed Viol	830708		2
MTR-Cucle Equip Viol	90 7 ME		2
MV Hmcide/Drug&Negl	90 24 GD	U07	5*
MV Hmcide/Drugs&Rkls	90 24 GE	U07	5*
MV Homicide/Liq&Negl	90 24 GG	U07	5*
MV Homicide/Liq&Rkls	90 24 GH	U07	5*
MV Homicide/Negl Op	90 24 GA	U07	5*
MV Homicide/OUI Drug	90 2 4GC	U07	5*
MV Homicide/OUI Liq	90 24 GF	U07	5*
MV Homicide/Rkls Op	90 24 GB	U07	5*
MV Malicious Damage	26628D	W00	unk
MV Where Excluded	90 18 EX	M40	2
Natl Network Viol	7201000OT	M40	
NC TPK-Ngl Op/Constrct Zone	730708		2
NE TPK-Negl Operation	730708		2
Neg Op Inj Mobile Dev	90 24 MP		5*
Neg Open MV Door	90 14 MV	M84	2
Negligent Operation/Boat	90B8B NG	W00	
New Hampshire Reciprocity	NHR	W00	
No Child Restraint	90 7AA	F02	
No Inspection Sticker	90 20 IS	E01	2
No Inspection Sticker	90 7A	E01	2
No Liability Policy	90 34J	D36	2*
No Liability Policy	90 34J CV		2
No Liability Policy	FR	D35, D36, D37, D51, D53	
No Polution Control	90 7O	E70	
No Reg/Lic In Possess	RR4	D16, W00	
No Transparnet Window	90 9D	E70	
Non-ACD Code Withdrawal	W00	W00	
Non-Pay Child Support	NPC	W00	
Number Plate Missing	90 9 NP	E01	
NV TPK Noise violation	730708		2
Obs Traff Device	SC6	M14	
Obstruct Emergency Vehicle	89 7C	N04	unk

Description	State Code/Law	ACD Code	Pts
Obstruct RR/Mbta	16194	M55	
One Way Street	WW1, 89 10	N63	2
One Way Street (wrong way)	89 10	N63	
OOS At-Fault Minor	AF3		3
Op W/Sus Or Rev Lic	90 23 CV	B25	2
Oper Improperly	DS2	D75	
Oper On Bet Or Wager	SP1, 90 24 BW	S95	2*
Oper Unlicense	VR5	B51, B56, U21	2*
Oper Unlicensed	90 10	B51	
Oper W/O Ign Intlock	90 24 S		5*
Oper W/O Safety Glas	90 9A	E01	2
Oper W/Susp Lic/OUI	90 23 J		5*
Operate Expired Reg	RT2		2
Operating After Revocation	VR1, 90 23 RE	B25	
Operating After Suspension	VR2, 90 23 SU	B26	
Operating Expired Registration	RT2	E01	
Operating Recklessly	90 24 OR	M84	2*
Operating Recklessly	RK	D72, M80, M81, M82, M83, M84	2*
Operator Unlicensed	90 10	B51	2*
Opr After Revocation	VR1		2*
Opr After Suspension	VR2		2*
OT Minor Traffic	740300 NS, OT	N84	2
Oth Bypas Ign Intlck	90 24UA		5*
OUI Boating	90B8	A21	
OUI W/Child Endanger	90 24VA		5*
Out Of State Administrative Revocation	ODARE	W00	
Out Of State Administrative Suspension	ODASU	W00	
Out Of State Court Default	ODF	W00	
Out Of State Drugs	ODD	A22	
Out Of State Fatal	OFA	U08	
Out Of State Liquor	ODI	A21	
Out Of State Ser Inj	OAC	B03	
Oversize Vehicle	90 19	F66	2
Oversize Vehicle Ns	90 19 NS	F66	
Overweight Irriducible	90 19A IL	F66	
Overweight Veh Fed Law	90 19E	F66	
Overweight Vehicle	EM2, 85 34, 90 19A	F66	
Overwght Veh Bridge	85 35	F66	
Parking Prohibitions	730708 PK	F34	
Pass Condition	PA	M70, M72, M76	2
Pass Suff Dist	PA3	M77	2
Pass Wrong Side	PA2	M73	2
Passing Barrier	SC3	M02	2
Passing School Bus	90 14	E50	
Patriot Act	W09	W09	
Payment Default	RDF	D53	
Perjury About The Operation Of A Motor V	D78	D78	
Person Under 21 – Attempt Procure Liquor	13834A AP	W00	unk
Person Under 21 – Procure Liquor	13834A PR	W00	unk
PF TPK-Fail Obey Police	730708		2
PL TPK Speed/over Limit	730708		2
Poss Alcoh/Drugs	DI4	A26, A27, A31, A33, A35, A50	
Poss Class A Sub W/Intent To Distribute	94C32A	A33	
Poss Class B Sub W/Intent To Distribute	94C32AA	A33	
Poss Class C Sub W/Intent To Distribute	94C32BA	A33	
Poss Class D Sub Intent To Distribute	94C32C	A33	
Poss Class E Sub Intent To	94C32D	A33	
Poss Cocaine W/Intent To Distribute	94C32AC	A33	
Poss Of Hypo Needle/Syringe	94C27	A33	
Poss Within A 1000 Ft Of A School	94C32J	A33	
Possession Of A Hypodermic Syringe	94C38 HS	A33	
Practitioners Violations	94C24 A, 94C25, 94C26, 94C38 PV, 94C39, 94C21, 94C22	A33	
Property Damage Claim	FR1	D39	
Propty Damage Clm	PDC	D39	
Protective Headgear	540228	E50	2

Description	State Code/Law	ACD Code	Pts
PV TPK Passing Viol	730708		2
RA TPK Equipment Viol	730708		2
Ran Off Road	IL3	M43	2
Rec/Snow Violation	323300	E01	
Reckless Driving	M84		2
Refusal Submit To Po	90 25	M08	
Refuse Give Name/Adr	85 16	B01	
Refuse Obey Police	90 25		5*
Refuse Obey Police	HR4	U01	2*
Refuse To Be Weighed	90 19A RF	F66	
Reg Elsewhere + 30	90 3 RG	E01	
Reg Suspend/Revoked	90 23 RG		2*
Reg Suspend/Revoked	RT4	W00	2*
Reg/Title Cita	RT	E01	
Registrar Rule/Reg	90 31		2
Registrar Rule/Reg	RV3	W00	
Repair/Dealer Plate Misuse	90 5 G	D16	
Repair/Remove Vehicle	730711	F66	
Repeated Viol	RV	W01	
Research Projects	94C8	A33	
Restriction Viol	VR	D29	2
Right Of Way	RW	N01, N03, N06, N20, N21, N24, N31	2
RL Fail Opr in Right Lane	89 4B	M41	2
RL TPK Fail Keep Right	730708		2
RMV ID Card Viol	90 8G, 90 8H, 90 8J	B41	
RMV/Fed Regs Haz Mat	5401403	E03	
RMV/Fed Safety Regs	5401403OT	E01	
Rp/Dlr Plate Misuse	90 5	D16	
Rt Of Way Emerg Vehc	89 7	N04	2*
Rt Of Way Emerg Vehc	FO3	M32, M33, N04	2*
Rt Of Way Intersection	RW3	N25	2
Rt Of Way Intersectn	89 8	N25	2
Rt Turn From Lt	TU1	N54	2
Rules/Reg Violation	90 31 NS	D02	
RV (Revoke) Dangerous Oper	90B26	M80	
RV Drugs/Firearm	90B26 RE	A33	
RV Fail To Rpt Accid	90B27	B61	
RV Improper Equipt	90B24	E01	
RV Operating Without headgear	90B26 HG	E01	
RV Public Ways	90B25	M40	
RV Reciprocal Priv	90B30	M40	
RV Refusal To Submit	90B32	A12	
RV Unregistered	90B21	E01	
Safety Standards	90 20 SS	E70	
Safety Standards	EM	E50, E51, E55, E56, E57, E70, E71	2
Sale Of Counterfeit Substances	94C32G	A33	
Sale Of Drug Paraphenalia	94C32IA	A33	
Sale Of Drug Paraphenalia To Minors	94C32IB	A33	
Sb Instrt Nolicense	90 8A SB	D27	
SB TPK Stp/Bck/Trn Viol	730708		2
Sch Bus Cross RR W/E	90 15 EF	M22	2
Sch Bus-Op Too Close	90 14 WT	M34	2
Schl Bus Oper/Equipt	90 7B	E06	2
Schl Bus Overloaded	90 7B EP	F66	
School Bus Inspect – Fail Perform Post trip	90 7B IS	E56	unk
School Bus – Use Mobile Phone While driving	90 7B MP	M86/F66	unk
Schl Bus Regulations	90 7C	E06	
Schl Bus Vocational	90 7D12	E06	
Schl Bus/Sta Wgn Reg	90 7D	E06	
Schl Bus/Sta Wgn Reg	90 7D PT	F66	
School Bus License	90 8A	W00	2*
School Bus Seating	90 7L	F66	
SD TPK Speed/Endanger	730708		2
Seat Belt Violation	90 13A	F04	
Seatbelt	90 7BB	F04	
Sell Retread Tires	90 7M	E01	

Description	State Code/Law	ACD Code	Pts
Sex Offense	MS5	W00	
SF Spec Fuel Stop Impr	703706		2
Signaling	SI	N40	2
Signs	SC	M04, M13, W00	2
Snowmobile Op Refuse	90B33	M40	
SP Mass Pike Speed	730400, 730500, 730707		2
SP Speeding	730708, 740300		2
SP Sum/cal Tunl Speed	730300		2
Spd Less Pst Min	SP4	S96	2
Spd Metal Tires Cnty	85 31 CT	E01	
Spd Metal Tires Mun	85 31 MU	E01	
Spd Metal Tires St	85 31 ST	E01	
Special Permit Viol	730706		2
Speed County Bridge	85 20		2
Speed Drag Racing	90 17B	S95	2
Speed Metallic Tires	85 31	E01	
Speed-Constr Zone	90 17 CZ	S93	2
Speeding	350401 SP	S93	2
Speeding	703708 SP		
Speeding	7401100 SP, 7402100 SP		2
Speeding	90 18 FS	S93	2
Speeding	90 17 & 90 18	S93	2
Speeding	SP, SP2, 90 17, 90 18	S93	2
Speeding	SP2, SP3	S01, S06, S15, S16, S21, S26, S31, S41, S51, S71, S81, S91, S92,S93	2
Speeding Massport	7401100SP, 7402100SP, 740300 SP	S93	
Speeding On Bridges	85 20	S93	
Speeding Overweight	90 17 OW	S93	2
Speeding-Tobin Bridge	7001100 SP	S93	2
St Hway Parking	720900 PK	F34	
St Hway Violation	720900 OT	N84	2
Starting Improp	MS1	N83	2
State Highway – Left Lane Restriction Violation	720900 LL	M50	2
State Highway Ramp – Back On/Off	720900 RP	N82	2
State Highway South Boston Haul Road Viol	720900 HR	M40	2
State Highway Traffic Violation	720900 TR	M08	2
State Highway Traffic Violation	720900 TV	N01	2
State Highway Wrong Way Viol	720900 WW	N62	2
Stop At RR Crossing	90 15	M09	2
Stop St Railway Car	89 6A	M55	
SU Sum/Cal Negligent Op	730300	M83	2
Suicide By M/V	FA3	U31	
Sum/Cal Inl Insp Stk	730300 IF	E01	
Sum/Cal Negligent OP	730300SU	M83	unk
Sum/Cal Serious Viol	730300 TL	N84	
Sum/Cal Tunl Viol	730300 OT	N84	
Sum/Cal Tunnel Speed	730300 SP	S93	unk
Tagging/Defacing	266126B	W00	
Tamper Odometer	266141A	E50	
Tax And Title Viol	5401803	D02	
Theft/Concealment Of Mv Or Trl	26628	W00	
Tire Tread	540404, 90 7Q	E37	2
Tires Minimum Safety	90 7K	E37	
Tires On Trucks	90 9C	E37	
TL TPK Fail Obey Light	730708		2
Tmpr Wth Ign Intlock	90 24 T		5*
Tobin Bridge Equipment Viol	7001105 EQ	M50	2
Tpk Left Lane Restri	703708 LL		
Tpk-Left Lane Restri	730700 LL		2
Traffic Violation	90 18 OT	S93	2
Traffic/Safety Viol	730708	N84	2
Tran Unsafe Material	85 2B	M17	
Tran Unsafe Material	85 2B UM	E53	
Trans Pupil W/O Lic	90 8A12	W00	
Transport Regulation	90 31A	E50	
Transporting Unprotected Animals	90 22H	E50	

Description	State Code/Law	ACD Code	Pts
Trespass With MV	266121A	M40	
Trns Spec Nds Children	90 7CC	F02	
TU TPK Tunl Wrong Way	730705		2
Tunnel Haz Mat	720900 HM	M40	
Tunnel Violation	720900 TN	N84	
Turn Condition	TU	N50, N51, N52, N55, N56	2
UE TPK Enter/Exit Viol	730705		2
Under Age 18 C90 S24 Violation	90 24 P 2	A61	
Unlic Person To Oper	VR6		2
Unlic Person To Oper	VR6, 90 12	D16	
Unreasonable Noise	EM4	E70	2
Unreg/Improper Equip	90 9	E01	2
Unsafe Lane Changes	M42		2
Unsafe Operation Boat	90B8B UN	W00	
Use Boat Without Authority	90B8B WA	W00	
Use M/V Non Fel	EM6	U04	
Use/Avoid Electronic System	730704	E50	
Used Brake Drums	90 7G	E31	
Using False Registration Number	94C33 A	B41	
Using W/O Authority	90 24 WA	D16	2*
Using W/O Authority	EM7	D16	2*
Uttering A False Prescription	94C33 B	A33	
V1 Mass Pike Viol	730500		2
Veh Commit Felony - Controlled Substance	A50	A50	
Veh Feticide 1st Deg	U27	U27	5*
Veh Feticide 2nd Deg	U28	U28	5*
Veh To Commit Felony	FE1, FE2, FE3, 90 24A	U03	
Veh To Commit Felony	FE3	U05	
Vehc Into Traffic	MS3	W00	2
Vehicular Homicide	90 24 G	U07	5*
Vehicular Homicide	FA1	U07, U08, U09, U10, U31	5*
Viol Mandat Actn	RV2	W01	
Viol Own Death	FA2	U31	
Violation Fatal Acci	FA4		5*
Warn Device Misused	90 7I	E01	
Warrant	WRT	W00	
Weaving Between Lanes	89 4A	M41	
Wrong Dir In Rotary	WW3	N61	2
Wrong Side Of Road	WW2	N70, N71, N72	2
Wrong Signal	SI2	N44	2
Wrong Way	WW	M57, N60, N62	2
WT TPK WM Tunnel Viol	730705		2
WW TPK Wrong Way	730707		2
Yield Blind Person	90 14A	N08	2
Yield School Bus	RW5	N09	2
Yield Sign	RW2	N22, N23, N26	2
Yield To Pedestrian	89 11	N08	2
Yield To Pedestrian	RW4	N02, N08	2
Youth Alcohol Pgm	YAP	A61	

The MRB Safe Driver Insurance Plan (SDIP)

The Safe Driver Insurance Plan (SDIP) is a state designated rating system that outlines specific surcharges for certain traffic violations and accidents, and applies specific credits for clean driving records. Each operator is assigned an Operator SDIP Rating based on the operator's driving history record within the 6-year policy experience period. The Merit Rating Board is the only authorized source of Safe Driver Insurance Plan (SDIP) driving records for all insurance companies. As of April, 2008, Massachusetts auto insurers may elect to either use the SDIP as their Merit Rating Plan or they may elect to develop their own rating system. Automobile policies that are assigned through the Massachusetts Auto Insurance Plan (MAIP) are subject to the SDIP. Detailed information about the Safe Driver Insurance Plan (SDIP) is available on the Merit Rating Board's website at www.massdot.state.ma.us/rmv/MeritRatingBoard.aspx.

Below is an explanation of the rating portion of the SDIP. A "surchargeable incident" as defined in 211 CMR 134.00 (SDIP) may result in an increase in auto insurance premium as a:

Minor At-Fault Accident

An "at-fault" accident is one in which the insurance company determines that the operator is more than 50% at fault. A Minor at-Fault claim is for damage to someone's property, bodily injury liability, collision or limited collision, of more than $500 and under $2,001.

Major At-Fault Accident

An "at-fault" accident is one in which the insurance company determines that the operator is more than 50% at fault. A Major at-Fault claim is for damage to someone's property, bodily injury liability, collision or limited collision, of more than $2,000.

Major Traffic Law Violation

Includes violations such as: vehicular homicide, driving under the influence (including assignment to a driver alcohol or drug education program), driving to endanger or reckless driving, leaving the scene of an accident, refusing to obey a police officer, driving after license suspension or revocation.

Minor Traffic Law Violation

Includes violations such as: speeding, operating a vehicle without a valid inspection sticker, failure to obey traffic lights.

Note: **Out-of-State Incidents** can be classified in any of the above categories. For additional information, Massachusetts advises contacting the Merit Rating Board at 857-368-8100 or by visiting the website at www.massdot.state.ma.us/rmv/MeritRatingBoard.aspx.

About the Date used for a Surchargeable Incident

The surcharge date is NOT the incident date. It is:

- the disposition date and/or judgment date entered by a court on a citation for a traffic law violation
- the date the Registry of Motor Vehicles applies the payment of the fine assessed for a civil traffic law violation
- the date of assignment to a driver alcohol education (or substance abuse) program
- the fine payment default date, or the court hearing default date
- the conviction date of an out-of-state traffic law violation from an out-of-state driving record
- the date of notice entered by an insurer on the at-fault accident Surcharge Notice

SDIP Appendix A: Traffic Law Violations

Table of Major Surchargeable Traffic Violations

Notes: In the Statute Column, M.G.L. refers to the Massachusetts General Laws. CMR refers to the Code of Massachusetts Regulations.

"*" = For incidents that occur on or after October 28, 2005.

"**" = For incidents that occur on or after January 1, 2006.

Major Traffic Violation Description	Statute
Bypass ignition interlock for another**	M.G.L. c. 90, § 24U (a)(1)
Child endangerment while OUI*	M.G.L. c. 90, § 24V
Driving to endanger or reckless driving	M.G.L. c. 90, § 24
Leaving Scene of Accident after Injuring a Person	M.G.L. c. 90, § 24
Leaving Scene of Accident after Injuring a Property	M.G.L. c. 90, § 24
Leaving Scene of Personal Injury and Death	M.G.L. c. 90, § 24
Liquor and narcotics, operating under the influence of (including assignment to a driver alcohol education program or controlled substance treatment or rehabilitation program under M.G.L. c. 90 § 24D)	M.G.L. c. 90, § 24
Liquor and Narcotics, operating under the influence of and reckless operation causing serious injury	M.G.L. c. 90, § 24L
Manslaughter (only if by Motor Vehicle)	M.G.L. c. 265, § 13
Manslaughter while OUI*	M.G.L. c. 265, § 13 1/2
Operate without ignition interlock**	M.G.L. c. 90, § 24S(a)
Operating after revocation of license	M.G.L. c. 90, § 23
Operating after Suspension of Drivers License	M.G.L. c. 90, § 23
OUI while license suspended for OUI*	M.G.L. c. 90, § 23
Permit operation without ignition interlock**	M.G.L. c. 90, § 12(c)
Permit unlicensed suspended operation of MV**	M.G.L. c. 90, § 12(b)
Refusing to Stop for Officer	M.G.L. c. 90, § 25
Tamper with ignition interlock**	M.G.L. c. 90, § 24T(a)
Vehicular homicide	M.G.L. c. 90, § 24G

Out-of-State incidents to be counted as Major Violations

- Operating under the influence of liquor and/or narcotics (including assignment to a driver alcohol education program)
- Vehicular homicide

Table of Minor Surchargeable Traffic Violations

Note: In the Statute Column, M.G.L. refers to the Massachusetts General Laws. CMR refers to the Code of Massachusetts Regulations.

Minor Traffic Violation Description	Statute
Accident, hit and run	M.G.L. c. 90, § 24
Alleys and driveways, emerging from, must stop	720 CMR 9.06(20)
Allowing vehicle to stand unattended, motor running	M.G.L. c. 90, § 13
Anything on or in vehicle or on person interferes with operation	M.G.L. c. 90, § 13
Attempting a speed record	M.G.L. c. 90, § 13
Backing and U-turns prohibited	730 CMR 7.08(17)(b)
Backing up for missed ramp	720 CMR 9.08(3) 730 CMR 7.08(17)(b)
Blind pedestrians, must stop for	M.G.L. c. 90, § 14A

Minor Traffic Violation Description	Statute
Blow horn when necessary	720 CMR 9.06(15)
Brakes, inadequate	730 CMR 7.05(5)(g)
Brakes, operating without	M.G.L. c. 90, § 7
Bridges, speed law	M.G.L. c. 85, § 20
Careless operation - construction zone	730 CMR 7.08(12)(c)
Careless or negligent operation	730 CMR 7.08(5)(a)
Channelizing island, no driving on	720 CMR 9.06(22)
Coasting	730 CMR 7.08(16)
Crossing solid pavement markings	730 CMR 7.08(8)
Crosswalk, motor vehicle not to enter if car will block	M.G.L. c. 89, § 11
Crosswalk, operator yield to pedestrian	M.G.L. c. 89, § 11
Cutting in after passing	720 CMR 9.06(3)
Deploying unauthorized sign	730 CMR 7.08(1)(a)
Directional signals, devices required	M.G.L. c. 90, § 7
Directional signals, hand or mechanical required for lane change	M.G.L. c. 90, § 14B
Drag racing, speeding	M.G.L. c. 90, § 17B
Driving in "breakdown lane"	M.G.L. c. 89, § 4B
Driving within eight feet of street car stopped for passengers	M.G.L. c. 90, § 14
Emergency vehicles, right of way	M.G.L. c. 89, § 7
Employ unlicensed operator (Only for incidents that occur on or after January 1, 2006)	M.G.L. c. 89, § 12(a)
Entry into excluded area - construction zone	730 CMR 7.08(12)(b)
Entry into restricted area - general	730 CMR 7.08(11)(a)
Entry into restricted area - left lane restrictions	730 CMR 7.08(11)(b)
Exhibit another license	M.G.L. c. 90, § 23
Failure to ascertain if it is safe to change lanes	M.G.L. c. 89, § 4A
Failure to comply with orders	730 CMR 7.08(1)(b)
Failure to keep to the right when turning right	M.G.L. c. 90, § 14
	350 CMR 4.01(4)
	720 CMR 9.06(16)
	730 CMR 7.08(17)(c)
Failure to keep to the far left when turning on a one/two way street	M.G.L. c. 90, § 14
Failure to fasten a trailer to a tow vehicle with proper safety chains	M.G.L. c. 90, § 7
Failure to give proper stopping or turning signals	M.G.L. c. 90, § 14
	350 CMR 4.01(4)
	730 CMR 7.08(17)(c)
Failure to keep in right lane	M.G.L. c. 89, § 4B
	350 CMR 4.01(4)
	720 CMR 9.06(16)
	730 CMR 7.08(13)(a) & (b)
Failure to keep to right when view is obstructed up to 400 feet	M.G.L. c. 89, § 4
	720 CMR 9.06(16)
Failure to obey sign	730 CMR 7.08(1)(a)
Failure to obey traffic control signal	730 CMR 7.08(2)
Failure to see that movement can be made in safety before starting, stopping, turning or backing up	720 CMR 9.06(9)
Failure to stop at sign or signal at intersection	M.G.L. c. 89, § 9
Failure to stop at toll booth	730 CMR 7.03(2)
Failure to use care in stopping or turning - hand signals	730 CMR 7.08(17)(c)
Failure to use child restraint	M.G.L. c. 90, § 7AA
Fire apparatus, driving within 300 feet if going to a fire	M.G.L. c. 89, § 7A
Fire apparatus, failing to pull to right and stop	M.G.L. c. 89, § 7A
Fire Department, interfering with	M.G.L. c. 89, § 7A
Flashing red traffic signal, failure to stop	M.G.L. c. 89, § 9
	730 CMR 7.08(2)
Following too closely	720 CMR 9.06(7)
	730 CMR 7.08(15)
Hand signals, failure to give	M.G.L. c. 90, § 14B
	350 CMR 4.01(4)
Headlights, dimming from high beam	M.G.L. c. 90, § 31
	540 CMR 22.00
	730 CMR 7.08(22)(b)
Headlights, one half hour after sunset	M.G.L. c. 90, § 7
Headlights, improper use of	730 CMR 7.08(22)(a) & (b)
Headphones, wearing while operating	M.G.L. c. 90, § 13
Height, operating vehicle when elevated or lowered	M.G.L. c. 90, § 7P
Hit and run, person injured	M.G.L. c. 90, § 24
Hit and run, property damage	M.G.L. c. 90, § 24

Minor Traffic Violation Description	Statute
Horn, improper use of	730 CMR 7.08(21)
Horn, operating without	M.G.L. c. 90, § 7
Horn, sound when necessary	720 CMR 9.06(15)
Ignition key, remove from unattended vehicle	M.G.L. c. 90, § 13
Improper entry to a way	730 CMR 7.08(7)
Improper passing	M.G.L. c. 89, § 1
Improper use of cutouts	730 CMR 7.08(20)
Inadequate equipment (brakes, directional signals, lights or safety devices)	730 CMR 7.08(27)
Inspection sticker, failure to display	M.G.L. c. 90, § 20
	730 CMR 7.08(26)
Inspection sticker, operating without	M.G.L. c. 90, § 7A
	M.G.L. c. 90, § 20
	730 CMR 7.08(26)
Interfering with sign	730 CMR 7.08(1)(a)
Intersecting way, slow down when approaching	M.G.L. c. 90, § 14
Junior operator's license, operating in violation of	M.G.L. c. 90, § 8
Keeping to the right when overtaking another vehicle	730 CMR 7.08(13)(a) & (b)
Lane, marked, no straddling	720 CMR 9.06(1)
Learner's permit, motorcycle, violation of	M.G.L. c. 90, § 8B
Learner's permit, operating in violation of	M.G.L. c. 90, § 8B
License, Class 1-2-3	M.G.L. c. 90, § 8A,
	540 CMR 2.06
License, operating when not properly licensed	M.G.L. c. 90, § 10
License, violation of restriction	M.G.L. c. 90, § 8
Lights, operating motor vehicle with improper lights	M.G.L. c. 90, §§ 7 & 16
Liquor, operation of motor vehicle containing alcoholic beverage, minor (under age 21)	M.G.L. c. 138, § 34C
Making a turn from the wrong lane of traffic	M.G.L.c.90,§14
Making a right turn on a red light where prohibited	M.G.L. c. 89, § 8
Meeting other vehicles, exercise due care when	M.G.L. c. 89, § 1
Minimum separation	730 CMR 7.06(5)(f)4.
	730 CMR 7.06(6)(e)4.
Mirrors and reflectors, operating without proper	M.G.L. c. 90, § 7
Motorcycle, operating without proper equipment, lights and headgear	M.G.L. c. 90, § 7
Motorcycle, no more than two abreast	M.G.L. c. 89, § 4A
Motorcycle, no passenger unless machine so designed	M.G.L. c. 90, § 13
Motorcycle, single file when passing	M.G.L. c. 89, § 4A
Negligent loading	730 CMR 7.08(5)(b)
Negligently operating	M.G.L. c. 90, § 24
	730 CMR 7.08(5)(a)
No stopping	730 CMR 7.06(5)(f)5.
	730 CMR 7.06(6)(e)5.
Not reasonably to right for vehicle approaching from the opposite direction	M.G.L. c. 89, § 1
Noise, offensive, unreasonable (squealing tires)	M.G.L. c. 90, § 16
Not slowing down and keeping right of center on approaching intersection or corner where view is obstructed	M.G.L. c. 90, § 14
Not yielding to oncoming vehicles when making a left turn	M.G.L. c. 90, § 14
Obstructing emergency vehicle	M.G.L. c. 89, § 7
One way street	M.G.L. c. 89, § 10,
	720 CMR 9.05(1)& (2)
	730 CMR 7.05(1)
One way street, left turn from	M.G.L. c. 90, § 14
Operating after suspension or revocation of registration	M.G.L. c. 90, § 23
Operating, at crosswalk yield to pedestrian	720 CMR 9.06(27)
Operating, being overtaken, must not increase speed	720 CMR 9.06(5),
	730 CMR 7.08(14)
Operating on a bet or wager	M.G.L. c. 90, § 24
Operating car not properly registered	M.G.L. c. 90, § 9
Operating, disobeying sign, signal or marker	350 CMR 4.01(1), (7)
	720 CMR 9.06(10) (11), (12),(17)
	720 CMR 9.07(4)
	730 CMR 7.08(1)(a)
Operating, don't enter intersection or crosswalk unless crossing can be completed	720 CMR 9.06(6)(b)
Operating, don't obstruct movement of traffic	720 CMR 9.06(6)(a),
Operating, don't pass unless safe	720 CMR 9.06(3)& (4)
	730 CMR 7.08(14)
	720 CMR 9.06(24)
Operating, funerals and processions	M.G.L. c. 272, § 42

Minor Traffic Violation Description

Minor Traffic Violation Description	Statute
Operating in violation of license restrictions	M.G.L. c. 90, § 8
Operating, men & equipment in highway	720 CMR 9.06(25)
Operating at speed greater than reasonable or proper	M.G.L. c. 90, § 17
Operating, marked lanes staying within	720 CMR 9.06(1)
Operating, motorcycle without permanent seat	M.G.L. c. 90, § 13
Operating motor vehicle without liability policy	M.G.L. c. 90, § 34J
Operating, no driving on sidewalks	720 CMR 9.06(19)
	M.G.L. c. 89, § 1
Operating, obey traffic signs, signals, markings	M.G.L. c. 90, § 18
	350 CMR 4.01(1)& (7)
	720 CMR 9.06(10), (11), 12),(17),
	720 CMR 9.07(4)
	730 CMR 7.08(1)(a)
	730 CMR 7.08(2)
Operating on road surface closed to travel due to construction or repair	720 CMR 9.06(18)
Operating, obey yield signs	720 CMR 9.06(14)
Operating on ways divided into lanes	M.G.L. c. 89, § 4A
Operating through peekhole in snow on windshield	M.G.L. c. 90, § 13
Operating truck or bus, using passing lane where signs prohibit	720 CMR 9.08(5)
Operating, turning where signs prohibit	720 CMR 9.06(21)
Operating, U-turn contrary to sign	720 CMR 9.06(22)
Operating unregistered car	M.G.L. c. 90, § 9
Operating, use right lane	720 CMR 9.06(2)
Operating without proper mirrors and reflectors	M.G.L. c. 90, § 7
Operator not to obstruct passing vehicle	M.G.L. c. 89, § 2,
	730 CMR 7.08(14)
Parking lights	M.G.L. c. 90, § 7
Passing a vehicle stopped for a pedestrian in a crosswalk	M.G.L. c. 89, § 1
	350 CMR 4.01(8)
Passing bicycles, slow down	M.G.L. c. 90, § 14
Passing, care in passing another vehicle	730 CMR 7.08(14)
Passing, commercial vehicles, excess 2 ½ tons (except busses) use right lane pass in adjacent lane	M.G.L. c. 89, § 4C
Passing, don't obstruct passer	M.G.L. c. 89, § 2
Passing horses, use care	M.G.L. c. 90, § 14
Passing on right, unless vehicle being passed is (a) making a left turn, (b) on one way street (c) on a divided highway	M.G.L. c. 89, § 2
Passing school bus when flashers are on	M.G.L. c. 90, § 14
Passing vehicle forbidden if view is obstructed for less than 400 feet	M.G.L. c. 89, § 4
Pedestrian, failing to exercise due care to avoid colliding with	720 CMR 9.06(28)
	350 CMR 4.01(8)
Pedestrian, must slow down for	M.G.L. c. 90, § 14
	350 CMR 4.01(8)
Permitting Operation by a person who has no legal right	M.G.L. c. 90, § 12
Procession, following vehicle ahead as closely as is practical and safe	720 CMR 9.06(24)
Racing	M.G.L. c. 90, § 24
Railroad crossing, failure to slow down	M.G.L. c. 90, § 15
Railroad crossing, failure to stop while lights are flashing or gate lowered	M.G.L. c. 90, § 15
Rear lights, must have	M.G.L. c. 85, § 15
Rear lights, operating without	M.G.L. c. 90, § 7
Red flag or light, rear of load	M.G.L. c. 90, § 7
Red flashing signal, stop	M.G.L. c. 89, § 9
	730 CMR 7.08(2)
Right of way, fire engines, patrol wagons, ambulances	M.G.L. c. 89, § 7
Right of way, failure to yield to an approaching vehicle	720 CMR 9.06(14)
Right of way, pedestrian in a crosswalk	M.G.L. c. 89, § 11
Safety glass, operating or permitting operation without	M.G.L. c. 90, § 9A
School bus, driver's responsibilities	M.G.L. c. 90, § 7B
School bus, railroad crossing, must stop and open door	M.G.L. c. 90, § 15
School bus, speed limited	M.G.L. c. 90, § 17
School zone, speed limit	M.G.L. c. 90, § 17
Siren law	M.G.L. c. 90, § 16
Slow down to pass pedestrian	M.G.L. c. 90, § 14
Slow moving vehicles, keep right on upgrade	M.G.L. c. 89, § 4
Slow moving vehicles, keep 200 feet apart	720 CMR 9.06(8)
Space between vehicles	730 CMR 7.08(15)

Minor Traffic Violation Description	Statute
Speed at railroad crossings	M.G.L. c. 90, § 15
Speed, bridges	M.G.L. c. 85, § 20
Speed, certain vehicles to operate five m.p.h. below speed posted	M.G.L. c. 90, § 17
Speed, decrease for special hazards (pedestrians, traffic, weather)	M.G.L. c. 90, § 17
Speed, excess speed - construction zone	730 CMR 7.08(12)(a)
Speed, failure to regulate when men and equipment are on road	M.G.L. c. 90,§ 17
Speed, faster than posted	M.G.L. c. 90, § 17
	M.G.L. c. 90, § 18
	350 CMR 4.01(2)
	730 CMR 7.08(6)(c)
Speed, greater than reasonable and proper	M.G.L. c. 90, § 17
	730 CMR 7.08(6)(a)
Speed limit 15 m.p.h. near vehicle peddling merchandise, when flashing lights	M.G.L. c. 90, § 17
Speed limits, thickly settled district, school zone	M.G.L. c. 90, § 17
Speed, maximum speed	730 CMR 7.08(6)(c)
Speed, minimum speed	730 CMR 7.08(6)(c)
Speed, operating at dangerous speed	730 CMR 7.08(6)(b)
Speed, reasonable and proper	730 CMR 7.08(6)(a)
Speed, special regulations	M.G.L. c. 90, § 18
Speed, school bus	M.G.L. c. 90, § 17
Stolen car, operating	M.G.L. c. 90, § 24
Stop before passing school bus	M.G.L. c. 90, § 14
Stop sign, failure to completely stop	720 CMR 9.06(13)
Stop signs	M.G.L. c. 89, § 9
Stopping, standing, or parking	730 CMR 7.08(17)(a)
Street car, care in passing	M.G.L. c. 90, § 14
Street car, eight foot stopping law	M.G.L. c. 90, § 14
Tailgating	720 CMR 9.06(7)
Television in operator's view	M.G.L. c. 90, § 13
Throughways, right of way	M.G.L. c. 89, § 9
Tires too wide	M.G.L. c. 90, § 19
Traffic, refusing to comply with lawful order of police officer when directing	720 CMR 9.07(3)
	350 CMR 4.01(6)
	730 CMR 7.08(1)(b)
Traffic control lights, failure to obey	720 CMR 9.06(10)
	730 CMR 7.08(2)
Traffic signals, flashing red is same as stop sign	M.G.L. c. 89, § 9
Tread depth, tires	M.G.L. c. 90, § 7Q
	540 CMR 4.04
Turning where signs prohibit	720 CMR 9.06(23)
Turning improperly	M.G.L. c. 90, § 14
Unauthorized entry or exit from a way	730 CMR 7.05(3)
Unauthorized or dangerous crossing of median or other area	730 CMR 7.08(10)(a)
Unauthorized use of breakdown lane	730 CMR 7.08(9)
Unauthorized use of cross-over	730 CMR 7.08(10)(b)
Unlawful speed on County Bridge	M.G.L. c. 85, § 20
Unattended vehicle, stop engine, set brakes, remove key from switch and from vehicle	M.G.L. c. 90, § 13
U-turn where signs prohibit	720 CMR 9.06(26)
Vehicles excluded area, operating or permitting one's vehicle to be operated where posted	M.G.L. c. 90, § 16
	350 CMR 4.01(10)
Violation of Department of Highways rule or regulation or by-laws relative to signs, lights, signal systems, traffic devices markings	M.G.L. c. 85, § 2
Violation of left lane exclusion of heavy vehicles	M.G.L. c. 89, § 4C
Violation of right of way at intersecting ways	M.G.L. c. 89, § 8
Violation of gubernatorial by-laws on ways of the Commonwealth	M.G.L. c. 85, § 23
Wrong direction in Sumner, Callahan, or Ted Williams Tunnel	730 CMR 7.05(2)
Wrong way travel	730 CMR 7.05(1)
"Yield sign," failure to surrender to oncoming traffic, stop if necessary	720 CMR 9.06(14)

Out-of-State Incidents to be Counted as Minor Violations

All out-of-state Minor Traffic Violations which can be classified in any one of the above categories shall be counted as Minor Traffic Violations for the purposes of 211 CMR 134.00, Safe Driver Insurance Plan.

MRB - Accident At-Fault Surcharge Codes

Note: At-Fault Accident "Standards of Fault" surcharge codes used by the insurance company to determine fault in excess of 50%. The following are situations in which fault is presumed to be more than 50%.

(01) Collision with a Lawfully or Unlawfully Parked Vehicle. The operator of a vehicle subject to the Safe Driver Insurance Plan shall be presumed to be more than 50% at fault when operating a vehicle which is in collision with a lawfully or unlawfully parked vehicle.

(03) Rear End Collision. The operator of a vehicle subject to the Safe Driver Insurance Plan shall be presumed to be more than 50% at fault when operating a vehicle which is in collision with the rear section of another vehicle.

(05) Out of Lane Collision. The operator of a vehicle subject to the Safe Driver Insurance Plan shall be presumed to be more than 50% at fault when operating a vehicle which is partially or completely out of its proper lane and is in collision with another vehicle:

a. while being passed by the other vehicle, the passing vehicle being in its proper lane;

b. while passing the other vehicle, the other vehicle being in its proper lane; or

c. while changing or turning into or across the other vehicle's lane.

(07) Failure to Signal. The operator of a vehicle subject to the Safe Driver Insurance Plan shall be presumed to be more than 50% at fault when operating a vehicle which is in collision while failing to signal as required by law before turning or changing lanes.

(08) Failure to Proceed with Due Caution from a Traffic Control Signal or Sign The operator of a vehicle subject to the Safe Driver Insurance Plan shall be presumed to be more than 50% at fault when the operator fails to obey a traffic control signal or sign, or fails to proceed with due caution therefrom, and whose vehicle is thereafter in a collision with another vehicle.

(09) Collision on Wrong Side of Road. The operator of a vehicle subject to the Safe Driver Insurance Plan shall be presumed to be more than 50% at fault when operating a vehicle which is in collision with another vehicle which is moving in the opposite direction on the proper side of the roadway or center line.

(10) Operating in the Wrong Direction. The operator of a vehicle subject to the Safe Driver Insurance Plan shall be presumed to be more than 50% at fault when operating a vehicle in the wrong direction on a travel lane, one-way street, or highway, and whose vehicle is thereafter in a collision with another vehicle.

(11) Collision at an Uncontrolled Intersection. The operator of a vehicle subject to the Safe Driver Insurance Plan shall be presumed to be more than 50% at fault when operating a vehicle which is in collision with another vehicle at an uncontrolled intersection:

a. if the operator's vehicle enters a main road from a secondary road,

b. b .if both vehicles enter the intersection at the same time, and such operator's vehicle entered the intersection from the left of the other vehicle, failing to allow the vehicle on the right to proceed, or

c. if the operator's vehicle enters the intersection at a point in time later than the other vehicle.

(14) Collision While in the Process of Backing Up. The operator of a vehicle subject to the Safe Driver Insurance Plan shall be presumed to be more than 50% at fault when operating a vehicle which is in the process of backing up and whose vehicle is thereafter in a collision with another vehicle.

(15) Collision While Making a Left Turn or U-Turn Across the

Travel Path of a Vehicle Traveling in the Same or Opposite Direction. The operator of a vehicle subject to the Safe Driver Insurance Plan shall be presumed to be more than 50% at fault when operating a vehicle making a left turn or U-turn across the path of travel of another vehicle moving:

a. in the same direction, or

b. in the opposite direction, and whose vehicle is in a collision with such vehicle.

(17) Leaving or Exiting from a Parked Position, Parking Lot, Alley or Driveway. The operator of a vehicle subject to the Safe Driver Insurance Plan shall be presumed to be more than 50% at fault when operating a vehicle which is leaving or exiting from a parked position, parking lot, alley or driveway, and whose vehicle is in a collision with another vehicle.

(18) Opened or Opening Vehicle Door(s). The operator of a vehicle subject to the Safe Driver Insurance Plan shall be presumed to be more than 50% at fault when the vehicle's door or doors are opened or opening resulting in a collision with another vehicle.

(19) Single Vehicle Collision. The operator of a vehicle subject to the Safe Driver Insurance Plan shall be presumed to be more than 50% at fault when operating the only vehicle involved in a collision.

(20) Failure to Obey the Rules and Regulations for Driving. The operator of a vehicle subject to the Safe Driver Insurance Plan shall be presumed to be more than 50% at fault when the operator violates any provision of M.G.L. Chapter 85, 89 or 90, or fails to obey the following regulations: the Metropolitan District Commission (350 CMR), Registry of Motor Vehicles (540 CMR), MA Department of Highways (720 CMR), MA Turnpike Authority (730 CMR), or MA Port Authority (740 CMR), and whose vehicle is in a collision with another vehicle.

(21) Unattended Vehicle Collision. The operator of a vehicle subject to the Safe Driver Insurance Plan shall be presumed to be more than 50% at fault when the vehicle is left unattended and rolls resulting in a collision.

(26) Collision While Merging onto a Highway, or into a Rotary. The operator of a vehicle subject to the Safe Driver Insurance Plan shall be presumed to be more than 50% at fault when operating a vehicle merging onto a highway, or into a rotary when the other vehicle is already on the highway, or in the rotary, resulting in a collision.

(27) Non-Contact Operator Causing Collision. The operator of a vehicle subject to the Safe Driver Insurance Plan shall be presumed to be more than 50% at fault when operating a vehicle which is not in a collision, but whose actions cause the collision of one or more other vehicles.

(29) Failure to Yield the Right of Way to Emergency Vehicles when Required by Law. The operator of a vehicle subject to the Safe Driver Insurance Plan shall be presumed to be more than 50% at fault when the operator fails to yield the right of way to emergency vehicles (as required by M.G.L. c. 89, § 7) resulting in a collision.

(31) Collision at a "T" Intersection. The operator of a vehicle subject to the Safe Driver Insurance Plan shall be presumed to be more than 50% at fault when operating a vehicle coming from a roadway that terminates onto a throughway and whose vehicle is in a collision with another vehicle traveling on that intersecting throughway.

Michigan

Administration	Important Telephone and Web Contacts
Director Driver and Vehicle Records Division Department of State 7064 Crowner Drive, Lansing 48918 888-767-6424 www.michigan.gov/sos	Driver Licensing..888-767-6424 Driving Records ....517-322-1624 Financial Responsibility & SR-22...............517-322-6406 Commercial Driver License ....888-767-6424 Vehicle Information ....888-767-6424 State Police..517-332-2521 State Department of Insurance ....877-999-6442 Send questions to: soswebmaster@michigan.gov

Driver's License Format, Issuance and Renewal

License Classes, Restrictions and Endorsements Appear After the Driving Record Content Section

License Format

The format is one letter followed by twelve numbers. The numbers are coded as follows: three numbers for the last name, three numbers for the first name, three numbers for the middle name, and three numbers for the birth month and day. Because a small number of drivers' names and birth dates have the same number, MI began using the first initial of the last name with the code 726 or 727 to assign drivers a unique driver license number.

Note: Michigan will eventually change the numbering system with the implementation of its Business Application Modernization (BAM) project. No firm BAM implementation date is set at this time.

Document Appearance

The SOS Office provides an Enhanced driver's license and ID as an alternative to the standard license and ID. The Enhanced driver's license or ID card contains a Radio Frequency Identification chip to facilitate border crossings and homeland security efforts. The unique reference number assigned to the RFID chip allows the Customs and Border Protection agent to quickly and accurately verify identity and citizenship. Both the regular license and Enhanced license have the same characteristics shown below.

Appearance: A digital image document with signature.

Security Characteristics: Magnetic strip and bar code with a PolaPrime UV security feature only visible under black light.

Position of Photo: Bottom left, since 07/01/03 a ghost image appears in upper right.

Minor Age Driver Locator: "Under 21 Until dd/mm/yy" appears above photo. Since 07/01/03 those under the age of 21 are issued a vertical (portrait) style driver license.

CDL Indicator: "COMMERCIAL DRIVER LICENSE" printed in green above license number.

Issuance

Age Requirements

One must be at least 16 years old to take a driving skills test. One must pass a driving skills test if never been licensed before and is applying for an original driver's license, or if the driver's license has been expired for more than four years. A graduated licensing for drivers up to 18 years old includes three levels. A full description of this program is found in the Section about License Classes.

Individuals with a valid out-of-state operator's license applying for a Michigan chauffeur's license, Commercial Driver License or a motorcycle endorsement, or whose license has been expired for at least four years, must pass the required written or driving skills tests before a license can be issued.

Location of Requirements for Proof of Identity:
www.michigan.gov/documents/sos/SOS-428_275188_7.pdf

Residency

A Michigan license must be secured immediately upon establishing residency. Proof of residency is required at driver's license application.

Renewal

Renewal is based on the birth month of fourth year. A driver keeps same number when renewing, unless there is a change in name or date of birth which would require issuing a new license number. (When the DL format changes with the implementation of the Business Application Modernization project, drivers will no longer be assigned a new license number if there is name change.) A driver's license can be renewal by mail or in-person at a branch, and online but only for an operator, chauffer or moped license and not for CDL. See https://onlineservices.michigan.gov/ExpressSOS.

Elderly-Related Restrictions
None reported by the state.

Vehicle Insurance, Title and Registration Facts

Registration Renewal

All motor vehicles and trailers used on Michigan roads must be registered and display valid license plates. Renewal for passenger vehicles is set at one year. Trailers and trailer coaches are registered with a permanent, non-expiring trailer plate based on the unit's weight. These trailer plates are non-transferable. Renewal is available online 24/7 at www.michigan.gov/sos. Owners can use this service if the renewal notice contains a PIN (proof of mandatory insurance) and if the owner's name, address, and vehicle information are all correct. If not, renewal must be done at a branch office or by mail or telephone.

New Residents

New residents must title and register their vehicles immediately. Non-residents must register vehicles after ninety days. Motor vehicles, trailer coaches, trailers weighing 2,500 pounds or more empty, off-road vehicles, pickup campers, and watercraft 20 feet and over or with a permanently affixed engine must be titled.

Inspections and Emissions Testing

Michigan has no statewide provisions for either emission testing or vehicle safety inspections.

Passenger Plate Facts

There is one plate, one decal with the plate number and both expiration month and year. Current renewals are issued one decal with expiration month and plate number. The county of issuance is not shown or coded on the plate. An owner may purchase a plate in any county. When a vehicle is sold, plates remain with the vehicle.

Insurance and Financial Responsibility

The state has a compulsory no-fault insurance law. Proof of insurance must be presented when purchasing a registration and must be shown at the request of a law enforcement officer. About 80% of proofs of insurance are obtained through an Electronic Insurance Verification (EIV) program. Customers whose insurers participate in this program receive a Personal Identification Number (PIN) as proof of insurance. Minimum financial responsibility limits are $20,000/40,000/10,000. A driver's license may be suspended if the driver fails to satisfy a Financial Responsibility (FR) court judgment within thirty days for damages arising out of the ownership, maintenance, or use of a motor vehicle. A suspension becomes effective thirty days after preparation of suspension order, and remains in effect until the driver satisfies the judgment. A restricted license may be issued to the driver if the court approves a partial-payment agreement and proof of financial responsibility insurance is provided.

Withdrawal Sanctions, and Alcohol and Drug Testing

Alcohol and Chemical Testing Limits

Under Michigan law, it is illegal to drive:

- While intoxicated or impaired by, alcohol, illegal drugs, and certain prescribed medications.
- With a bodily alcohol content of 0.08 or more (driving while intoxicated).
- With any presence of a Schedule 1 drug or cocaine.

If under age 21 it is against the law:

- To drive with a bodily alcohol content of 0.02 or greater, or have any presence of alcohol other than that consumed at a generally recognized religious ceremony.
- To buy, possess, or consume alcoholic beverages. One may transport alcohol in a vehicle only when accompanied by an adult age 21 or older. If caught with alcohol in a vehicle and if no adult accompanying, the young driver you can be charged with a misdemeanor, whether on the road or in a parking lot.

Suspensions and Revocations

See the Appendix for a list of the federally mandated disqualifications for offenses occurring in a CMV per MCSIA.

Extensive information about suspensions and revocations including corresponding statutes is found at: www.michigan.gov/documents/offensecode_73877_7.pdf

As of October 31, 2010, a person convicted of **Operating with Blood Alcohol Content of .17 or More (HBAC)** receives an automatic one-year suspension. This can be amended to a restricted license after the 1st 45 days of suspension has been served and the installation of an Interlock Device is installed. The restrictions are valid for the remainder of the one-year HBAC suspension period. This also affects a driver's CDL privileges; the privilege to operate a commercial vehicle is suspended/revoked even if the driver was operating a non-commercial vehicle.

Habitual-Offender Revocation

Persons who repeatedly operate a motor vehicle during periods of suspension, revocation, and/or denial or who repeatedly violate the state's drinking/driving laws are subject to repeat offender penalties. These penalties may include plate confiscation, vehicle immobilization, registration denial, ignition interlock, and vehicle forfeiture.

- First revocation is for a minimum of one year; second is for a minimum of five years.
- *Two convictions in seven years for DUI alcohol or drugs, unlawful blood alcohol level, or impaired driving.
- Two convictions in seven years for reckless driving.
- Two convictions in seven years for felonies involving a motor vehicle.
- *Three convictions within ten years for any alcohol violation.
- One conviction of DUI or impaired driving causing injury or death.

* = One conviction of child endangerment will count same as alcohol conviction.

Child Support Suspension

The driver and occupational licenses of parents in arrears in their child support are suspended. This suspension is identified as an FCJ and requires an $85.00 reinstatement fee.

Reinstatement Requirements

Suspension or Revocation $125.00 fee ($85.00 if Child Support); re-examination.

Record Access: Laws, Rules, and Forms

Note: This Section Applies to Both Driver and Vehicle Records.

Governing Statutes and Rules

Michigan Complied Laws: www.legislature.mi.gov/
Michigan Vehicle Code: www.michigan.gov/sos/0,4670,7-127-1627_46351_46353---,00.html

Per Public Acts 99, 100, 101, and 102 of 1997, Public Act 192 of 2000, and Public Act 362 of 2004, the state adopted provisions to comply with DPPA. MVC 257.40b defines personal information and highly restricted personal information as follows:

(1) "Personal information" means information that identifies an individual, including the individual's photograph or image, name, address (but not the zip code), driver license number, social security number, telephone number, digitized signature, and medical and disability information. Personal information does not include information on driving and equipment-related violations or civil infractions, driver or vehicle registration status, vehicular accidents, or other behaviorally-related information.

(2) "Highly restricted personal information" means an individual's photograph or image, social security number, digitized signature, medical and disability information, and source documents presented by an applicant to obtain an operator's or chauffeur's license under section 307(1).

Michigan added the following exceptions at Michigan Vehicle Code 257.208c(3):

(j) For use by a car rental business, or its employees, agents, contractors, or service firms, for the purpose of making rental decisions.

(l) For use by a news medium in the preparation and dissemination of a report related in part or in whole to the operation of a motor vehicle or public safety. "News medium" includes a newspaper, a magazine or periodical published at regular intervals, a news service, a broadcast network, a television station, a radio station, a cablecaster, or an entity employed by any of the foregoing.

(m) For any use by an individual requesting information pertaining to himself or herself or requesting in writing that the Secretary of State provide information pertaining to himself or herself to the individual's designee. Only the individual, however, may submit a request for disclosure to a designee.

Medical and disability information is a record maintained under this act may be used and disclosed for purposes of subsection 3(a), (d) or (m).

Request and Consent Forms

To request a copy of another person's driving or vehicle record, the *BDVR-154 Commercial Record Request Form* must be submitted. The record requester must select at least one of the permissible reasons found on Section 4 of the form that pertains to the request and give an explanation in Section 6 stating the reason of the record request.

High volume requesters (15 or more record requests per month) may establish an account for monthly billing. Form *BDVR-153* is used for record holders requesting their own records. Both forms are easily found at the home page - www.michigan.gov/sos. For assistance in completing the form or to establish an account, call 517-322-1624.

Vendor and Third Party Access Policy

Approved vendors can provide or share records to other vendors (who are not online, etc.) who will then sell to an end-user provided that the contract between reseller and end-user contains same privacy provisions as the contract between the state and the original vendor.

Michigan requires the purchaser to establish and maintain records in a secure environment and keep for five years a list of recipients of record information and the permissible purpose under which the record was released. Purchasers may not use or resell record information for survey, marketing or solicitation purposes and must abide by DPPA provisions by selling records only for a reason permitted under DPPA. Audits of compliance may be required at the expense of the vendor.

Records Ordered For Non-permissible Uses

Driving Records: Records cannot be obtained by a non-permissible use requester who does not have consent, this includes records with no personal information.

Vehicle Records: Casual requesters can obtain records if required fees are paid; however, personal information is redacted.

Access to Driver-Related Records

Driving Records

General Information and Fees

Department of State, Record Lookup Unit, 7064 Crowner Drive, Lansing MI 48918, 517-322-1624, fax 517-322-1181.

The current fee is $7.00 per record by mail or $8.00 at certain walk-in locations. The $8.00 record is considered to be certified. The full fee is charged for a no record found request. The last fee increase was effective October 1, 2003; fee increases are determined by the legislature. If the requester anticipates a high volume of requests (15 or more records per month), then call 517-322-6714 or 877-570-6714 to establish an account with the Department of State.

In-Person – Processing is available at the address listed above or at any branch office. Note the fee is $8.00 per record when purchased at the "Secretary of State Plus" or at a "Super! Center Branch store." Discover and MasterCard are accepted. Same day service is only available for walk-in customers who are requesting their own driving records (See **By Person of Record** below). If requesting another person's record, requests will be available for pick-up 24 hours after submitting a request. Records stored on microfilm or unusual circumstances take longer to process.

Mail – The processing time for manual requests is 10 working days, microfilmed documents may take longer. The driver's license number or full name and date of birth are needed when ordering. The Department will not perform searches with partial driver license numbers or partial names. The fee must accompany the request, unless the requestor has a Michigan Department of State account.

Telephone – Call the Record Look-up Unit at 517-322-1624. Phone service is available for pre-approved, established accounts or for those obtaining their own records. Results are returned by mail. Major credit cards are accepted.

Fax – The Record Look-up Unit fax is 517-322-1181. Anyone can order by fax if using a credit card, otherwise fax service is available only to account holders. Results are returned by mail. Major credit cards are accepted. Requests are typically processed within 3 weeks.

Electronic Batch – Commercial Services Section, 517-322-6281. Transmissions made by 7:00 pm are available after 8:00 am the next morning. The driver's license number or full name and date of birth are needed when ordering. The minimum order requirement is 100 records. Billing is monthly by account.

Electronic Online Interactive – Commercial Services Section, 7064 Crowner Drive, Lansing MI 48918, 517-322-6281. The Direct Access Program provides single inquiry access over the web, 24/7. The driver's license number or full name and DOB are needed for an inquiry.

A contractual agreement and $25,000 surety bond is required, billing is monthly.

Bulk – List Sales Technician, 517-322-1042. Michigan offers information extracted from the driver's license database for sale. This information is sold in strict compliance with Michigan law, as well as the Michigan and federal Driver Privacy Protection Acts. A written request-letter, stating the purpose of request, must be approved. A usage contract is required and a $25,000 surety bond must be placed with the state. The information is dispensed via CD-ROM or DVD-ROM. The Department's current standard charges are $16.00 per thousand entries for information not subject to particular selection parameters. The charge is $64.00 per thousand entries for information subject to one or more specific criteria. There is a minimum purchase of $500.00.

By Person of Record – MI drivers may obtain their driving record by mail, walk-in (at any Branch Office or at the Crowner Drive address as described above), fax or telephone. One cannot order a request by phone to be mailed to a different address not on file. Branch office records are certified and cost $8.00 each; no form is required. Drivers wishing to order their own record via the mail or fax are advised to use Form BDVR-153, downloadable. At present, there is no program for drivers to order or view their own record online. However, drivers may enter information on an online form, then print, mail or fax the record request to the Record Lookup Unit previously mentioned. Go to www.michigan.gov/sos and click on Forms & Resources.

Notification/Monitoring Program

The Commercial Services Section (517-322-5281) provides a program that sends driving records to employers and insurance companies annually or whenever there is activity on the driving record. There is no set-up cost for this subscription service, but a fee of $7.00 per record generated is charged. Government agencies are not charged a fee.

Crash Reports

Reporting – The driver in a crash involving death, injury or damage in excess of $1,000 must immediately report that crash to the nearest or most convenient police agency. Crashes in excess of $1,000 require completion of a written report by the police officer receiving a report. There are no state special requirements for commercial drivers.

Record Access – Copies of crash reports are available from the Department of State, Record Lookup Unit for drivers convicted of a violation in conjunction with the accident, call 517-322-5509, fax 517-322-5350. It will take 6 to 8 weeks for a new incident to be available for a search. Requests will be accepted in-person, but responses will be mailed. Turnaround time is up to 10 days. Procedures for obtaining the accident report are the same as described above. Records are available from 1983 to present or 10 years using the TCPS (see below). Fax requests are also accepted.

The Traffic Crash Purchasing System (TCPS) offers traffic crash reports, provided by all Michigan law enforcement agencies online at http://mdotjboss.state.mi.us/TCPS/login/welcome.jsp. The fee is $10.00; a credit card may be used unless billing arrangements are made. Online requests are viewable/printable when ordered – records are not mailed. For specific questions email CrashPurchaseTCPS@michigan.gov or call 517-241-1699.

Access to Vehicle-Related Records

General Information and Fees

Department of State, Record Lookup Unit, 7064 Crowner Drive, Lansing MI 48918, 517-322-1624, Fax 517-322-1181.

Alpha-searches can be made with complete name and street address. Title records are available for 10 years to present and 4 years to present for registration. The current fee for VIN, registration, and lien holder searches is $7.00 per transaction. For a complete title history, there is a $7.00 fee incurred for each title change or correction. There is an additional $1.00 fee if the record must be certified. If both a registration and current title record are ordered, the requester is charged for 2 records ($14.00). There is a full charge for a no record found. Records are available on vehicles, mobile homes, and watercraft.

In-Person – Walk-in customers may request their own vehicle records at the address above and receive same-day service. If requesting another person's record, must go through the Crowner Drive address and requests will be available for pick-up 24 hours after submitting a request. Lengthy lists or unusual circumstances may take longer. The Department does not perform searches with partial names. Pay by check, Discover or MasterCard. Note: Visa is also accepted at the SOS, Secondary Complex at 7064 Crowner Drive, Lansing 48918.

Mail – The processing occurs at the address above. On average, mail requests are returned in 10 working days. The fee must accompany the request, unless the requestor has an established billing account.

Fax – Fax is 517-322-1181. Fax requesting is available for pre-approved, established accounts or for customers paying with a valid credit card. Results are returned by mail.

Telephone – Record Look-up Unit, 517-322-1624. Phone requests are available for pre-approved, established accounts.

Electronic – Commercial Services Section, 517-322-6281. Plate, VIN, and registration information is available via a program called Direct Access. This is a single inquiry method using the Internet or computer-to-computer socket layer connectivity. A usage agreement is required and a $25,000 surety bond must be placed with the state. The plate or VIN number (as opposed to name) is required to access this service.

A unique service offered is the Repeat Offender Inquiry. This web search function allows dealers and others to learn if a vehicle purchaser is ineligible for license plates and subject to registration denial under Michigan's "Repeat Offender Law" (MCL 257.219). This law prohibits the Department of State from registering any vehicle owned, co-owned, leased, or co-leased by certain repeat offenders. The search verifies if the name, DOB, and driver license number or state identification card number appearing on a Michigan DL or ID card match department records. Search results state if the purchaser is eligible, not eligible, or if not on file. The web site is https://services.sos.state.mi.us/RepeatOffender/Inquiry.aspx.

Bulk – List Sales Technician, 517-322-1042. Michigan offers information extracted from the vehicle database for sale. This information is sold in strict compliance with Michigan law, as well as the Michigan and federal Driver Privacy Protection Acts. A written request-letter, stating the purpose of request, must be approved. A usage contract is required and a surety bond must be placed with the state. The information is dispensed via CD-ROM or DVD. The Department's current standard charges are $16.00 per thousand entries for information not subject to particular selection parameters. The charge is $64.00 per thousand entries for information subject to one or more specific criteria. A usage contract and $25,000 surety bond must be placed with the state. There is a minimum purchase of $500.00. Fees for records are waived for governmental agencies; however, some fees for set-up and distribution may apply.

Access to Vessel Records

General Information, Access and Fees

Department of State, Record Lookup Unit, 7064 Crowner Drive, Lansing MI 48918, 517-322-1624, Fax 517-322-1181

Vessel records are administered by the same agency that handles vehicle records, hence record access procedures and fees are the same. All motorized boats must be registered; if 20 ft or over they must also be titled. Vessel records can be searched by either name or MC number or registration number with same restrictions as vehicle record requests.

Driving Record Content and Reciprocity

What's On or Not On the Driving Record

- The public record contains all convictions as required by law.
- Accidents are displayed on the public record if the driver is convicted of a traffic violation in relation to the accident.
- The state does not permit driver school attendance in lieu of conviction.

The standard length of time convictions appear on the driving record for moving violations is seven years from conviction date for moving violations(ten to fifty-five if CDL); Ten years from conviction date for OWI, and seven years from suspension date (ten to fifty-five if CDL). Repeat Offenders and other situations may cause a violation to remain on the record for a longer period of time.

Data Retention

CDL driver records are purged quarterly based on the timetable per the MCSIA (see Appendix). Surrendered licenses are purged seven years after the date of surrender. Surrendered out-of-state licenses with violations are purged three years after expiration; those without violations are purged one year after expiration.

Court to Repository

Conviction information is transferred to the state by the courts via direct connection, FTP, or by paper abstracts. The court is to forward all conviction information within five days of conviction date. Local courts notify the Michigan Department of State to suspend the driver license of persons who fail to respond to a Michigan traffic citation (FAC) or fail to comply with a court judgment (FCJ). Sometimes these abbreviations will appear on driving records.

State Reciprocity for Non-CDL Drivers
- Will suspend license of driver for unpaid out-of-state convictions.
- Record of new incoming driver is shown on MVR.
- Out-of-state convictions are shown on MVR.

- Out-of-state accidents are not shown on MVR.
- Convictions of out-of-state drivers are sent to home state.
- Record is forwarded to new state upon surrender of license.

License Classes, Restrictions, and Endorsements

Michigan began issuing the CDL in January 1990. On 4/1/97, the state began a graduated licensing which includes 3 levels.

License Classes– Commercial

Class A Operation of vehicle towing a vehicle or trailer with a GVWR over 10,000 pounds.
Class B Operation of a single vehicle with a GVWR of 26,001 pounds or more, **or** a combination of vehicles having a GCWR of 26,001 pounds or more, with the vehicle being towed having a GVWR of 10,000 pounds or less.
Class C Operation of a small vehicle or combination of vehicles (with a GVWR of 26,000 pounds or less) designed to carry sixteen or more people (including the driver), **or** a small vehicle carrying hazardous materials in amounts requiring the display of a placard.

License Classes– Non-Commercial

Class O1 Operator, Level 1
Class C1 Chauffeur Level 1
Class O2 Operator, Level 2
Class C2 Chauffeur Level 2
Class O   Operator (Level 3)
Class C   Chauffeur (Level 3)
Class M   Moped

Note: A Chauffeur License is required if someone is not required to obtain a commercial classification but:
- Is employed for the principal purpose of operating a motor vehicle with a gross vehicle weight rating (GVWR) of 10,000 pounds or more.
- Operates a motor vehicle as a carrier of passengers or as a common or contract carrier of property.
- Operates a pupil transportation vehicle used for the regularly scheduled transportation of pupils between school and home, a bus or a school bus.
- Operates a taxi or limousine.

Graduated Driver License Program

On April 1, 1997, Michigan began a graduated licensing for drivers up 18 years old which includes three levels:

Level 1 A driver must be at least 14 years 9 months, completed segment one of a driver education course, pass a vision test and meet health standards, and obtain written approval from a parent or legal guardian.

Level 2 Driver must be at least 16 years of age, successfully completed 6 months of practice driving at level 1, completed segment two of a driver education course, have no convictions/civil infractions, suspensions, or crashes during the 90-day period immediately prior to applying for a Level 2. Driver must also complete a minimum of 50 hours behind-the-wheel practice driving, including 10 hours of nighttime driving that is certified by parent or legal guardian, and pass a road test conducted by an independent testing agency.

Level 3 Full operator's license. Driver must be at least 17 years of age, held a Level 2 license for 6 months, and completed 12 consecutive months of driving without a moving violation, and at-fault crash, a suspension or violation of graduated license restrictions.

Transaction Types (Found Next to License Type)

R = Renewal
O = Original

D = Duplicate
C = Correction

Restrictions

Most restrictions are spelled-out on both the driver's license and the driving record. The term "Verify restrictions on record" may appear.
Accelerator on Left-Side
All Hand Controls
Artificial Arm
Artificial Arms
Artificial Legs
Artificial Leg
Automatic Transmission
CDL Not Valid for Vehicles with Air Brakes
CDL-P Endorsement Valid in Group B or C Vehicle Only
CDL-P Endorsement Valid in Group C Vehicle Only
Corrective Lens
Cushions
Daylight Driving Only
Designated Radius
Electric Turn-Signals
Emancipated Minor
Foot Pedestal Extension

Full Moped Privileges
Hand-Operated Headlight Beam Switch
Hand-Operated Accelerator
Hand-Operated Clutch
Hand-Operated Brake
No Alcohol usage Before Driving
No Expressway Driving
No GCWR Over 26,000, if Towed Vehicle Over 10,000
No Single Vehicle/Power Unit Over 26,000 GVWR
Not Valid for Two-Wheel Cycle
Power Brakes
Power Steering
Right Outside Mirror
Special Steering Knob
Specified Hours
Steering Knob or Power Steering
Telescopic Lens
Tinted Windows
Turn Signal Extension

Other CDL Restrictions:

Code 28 Restriction	CDL not valid for operating vehicles equipped with air brakes.
Code 29 Restriction	CDL-P endorsement valid in Group B or C vehicles only.
Code 30 Restriction	CDL-P endorsement valid in Group C vehicles only.
Seasonal Restricted CDL	A special seasonal restricted CDL available for agri-business employees operating Group B and C vehicles on routes within 150 miles from the place of business. Buses and school buses cannot be operated with this restricted license

Endorsements

T	Double-Trailers		P	Passenger Vehicles
N	Tankers		S	School Bus
H	Hazardous Materials		X	Combination H and N

Endorsements - Other

CY	Operation of Motorcycle
F	Farm Endorsement
R	Recreational Double (A "recreational double" is a pickup

truck pulling a fifth wheel trailer designed for recreational living purposes, with a second trailer attached to the rear of the fifth wheel trailer.)

Other Important Abbreviations and Codes on Driving Record

Codes of Vehicle Types

The following vehicle codes may appear in a conviction/crash record as the type of vehicle at time of incident

AA	Group A Vehicle		CX	C & Tank & Hazardous
AH	A & Hazardous		CY	Cycle
AL	A & Tank & Double/Triple, Hazardous		GC	Go Cart
AN	A & Tank		H1	Hazardous Cargo Truck - Single Vehicle
AP	A & Passenger		H2	Hazardous Cargo Truck-Cab (Tractor) Plus Trailer H3-Hazardous
AS	A & School Bus			
AT	A & Double/Triple		H3	Cargo Truck-Cab (Tractor) Plus Double Bottom Trailer
AX	A & Tank & Hazardous		HV	CDLIS Hazardous Veh. From CSOR
AY	A & Tank & Double/Triple		MD	Medium Duty Trucks
AZ	A & Double/Triple & Hazardous		MO	Moped
BB	B Vehicle		NC	CDLIS Non-Comm. Veh. From CSOR
BH	B & Hazardous		OR	Off Road Vehicle
BN	B & Tank		PA	Passenger (2 Dr, 4 Dr, Sta. Wagon)
BP	B & Passenger		PU	Pick Up Truck
BS	B & School Bus		SB	School Bus
BX	B & Tank & Hazardous		SM	Snowmobile
BU	Bus		ST	Small Truck (Under 10,000 Pounds) [Obsolete]
CG	Go Cart		T1	Truck – Single Vehicle [Obsolete]
CH	C & Hazardous		T2	Truck – Cab (Tractor) Plus 1 Trailer [Obsolete]
CP	C & Passenger		T3	Truck – Cab (Tractor) Plus Double Bottom Trailer [Obsolete]
CS	C & School Bus		VA	Van
CV	CDLIS Veh From CSOR		WC	Watercraft

Common Abbreviations Found on Driving Records

ACC	Crash		EMERG	Emergency
ADDL	Additional		EQUIP	Equipment
ADMIN	Administrative		FAC	Failure To Appear In Court
AHSP	Alcohol Highway Safety		FCA	Failure To Change Address
APP	Application		FCJ	Failure To Comply With Judgment
APPR	Approved		FCPV	Failure To Clear Parking Violations
APT	Apartment		FED	Federal
AUTH	Authority, Authorized		FR	Financial Responsibility
CDL	Commercial Driver License		FTA	Failed To Appear
CDSS	County Driver Safety School		GRP	Group
CF#	Court File Number		GVW	Gross Vehicle Weight
CIRC	Circuit (Court)		HOSP	Hospital
CIR CT	Circuit Court		HWY	Highway
CONTD	Continued		INC	Incorporate
DEPT	Department		INDEF	Indefinitely
DI	Driver Improvement		INFO	Information
DIAG	Diagnostic		INFL	Influence T
DLAD	Driver License Appeal Division		INJ	Injured
DR STMT	Doctor's Statement		INSTR	Instruction
EFF	Effective		INTOX	Intoxicated
ELIG	Eligible		LATERECD	Late Received Abstract

LIC	License		REST	Restrictions Or Restricted
LIQ	Liquor		RETD	Returned
MAG	Magistrate (Court)		REV	Revocation
MAND	Mandatory		SO	Sheriffs Office
MCL	Michigan Complied Laws		SOS	Secretary Of State
MED	Medical		SPEC	Special
MS	Mandatory Suspensions		ST	Street
MSP	Michigan State Police		STMT	Statement
MTR	Motor		SUBJ	Subject
MUN	Municipal (Court)		SUPT	Superintendent
NEG	Negligent		SUSPENSION	Suspensions
NUM	Number		TEMP	Temporary
ORIG	Original		TERM	Terminate
OUCS	Operating Under Influence Controlled Substance		TIP	Temporary Instruction Permit
OUIL	Operating Under Influence Of Liquor		TRAF	Traffic (Court)
OWI	Operating While Impaired		UA	Under Age (Under 21)
P.D.	Property Damage		UBAC	Unlawful Body Alcohol Content
PD	Police Department		UDAA	Unlawfully Driving Away Auto (Joyriding)
PET	Petitioner		UDR	Unsatisfactory Driving Record
P.I.	Personal Injury		UJ	Unsatisfied Judgment
PROB	Probation		UUA	Unlawful Use Of Motor Vehicle
RD	Road		VEH	Vehicle
RECOM	Recommend (Ed)		VIOL	Violation
REFD	Referred		W/O	Without
REQ	Requirements		X-WAY	Expressway Or Freeway
RESP	Responsible Or Responsibility		YR	Year

Conviction Table with Statute, ACD, and Points

- Violations and other descriptive data on records are spelled-out.
- "DI" signifies a warning letter sent to individuals who have four or more points on their record and advising them of the consequences if they receive too many points.
- If the violation occurred in an off road vehicle, snowmobile, or vessel the description line will begin with ORV or Snowmobile or Marine.
- See the end of this table for the Speed Violation with points. Also, see Violation of Basic Speed Law.
- Multiple ACD codes map show for a violation. This is because the violation description is somewhat generic and must be mapped to the exact ACD Code. See the back of this book for the ACD mapping suggestions.

About the Convert Column (CVT)

The Convert Column (CVT) indicates how incoming ACD codes convert to a Michigan conviction or how outgoing convictions are converted. The **R**, **S**, and **B** stand for **Received**, **Sent** or **Both Received and Sent**. An incoming ACD code will always convert back to the same ACD code whenever the Michigan record is passed to another state. Also, a single ACD Code could convert to one of several Michigan convictions depending on the circumstances, such as the driver's age at time of violation or if driving a commercial motor vehicle.

Statute	ACD	Description	Pts	CVT
750.321,324, 316,317		A Fatality Through Negligent Or Criminal Operation Of A CMV	6	
257.257		Alter/ Forge/ Falsify Vehicle Document Or License Plate	0	
257.324	B41	Altered Driver License	0	B
257.626B	M80, M83	Careless Driving	3	R
257.626B	M81	Careless Driving	3	B
257.319B	U10	Causing A Fatality Through Negligent Or Criminal Operation Of A CMV	0	B
333.7341,7401	A50	CDL Manu/Distrib Controlled Substance (CMV)	6	B
257.648	M42	Changing Lanes To Interfere	2	B
257.625(7)		Child Endangerment	6	
257.669(A)(4)	M23	CMV Failed To Drive Completely Through Railroad Crossing Without Stopping	2	B
257.669(A)(3)	M24	CMV Failed To Negotiate Railroad Crossing-Insufficient Undercarriage Clearance	2	B
257.667,257.668,257.669(a)(1)	M20	CMV Failed To Slow Down At Railroad Crossing	2	B
257.667,257.668	M22	CMV Failed To Stop At Railroad Crossing	2	B
257.667,257.668	M21	CMV Failed To Stop At Railroad Crossing When Tracks Are Not Clear	2	B
257.625	A21	Combined Operated Under Infl Liq/Unlawful Bodily Al Content (Eff. With Arrest Date< 09/302003)	6	S
257.625(1)		Combined Operated Under Influence Liquor And Controlled Substance	6	
257.625(3)	A25	Combined Operated While Impaired By Liquor And Controlled Substance	4	S
257.613D	M13	Disobey School Crossing Guard	3	B
257.668	M10	Disobey Stop Sign At Railroad Crossing (Effective Before 10/1/2002)	3	B

Statute	ACD	Description	Pts	CVT
257.611	M02, M03, M04, M05, M11, M12, M17	Disobeyed Traffic Control Device	2	R
257.602	M08	Disobeyed Police Officer Directing Traffic Flow	2	B
257.613d	M13	Disobey School Crossing Guard	3	B
257.649,671	M15	Disobeyed Stop Sign	2	B
257.611	M02, M12, M17	Disobeyed Traffic Control Device	2	R
257.612	M16	Disobeyed Traffic Signal	3	B
257.626A	S95	Drag Racing	4	B
257.312e		Driving A CMV Without Obtaining A CMV License or Without CMV in Driver's Possession	2	
257.319(B)	B91	Driving A CMV Without Proper Endorsement Or Designator (CMV)	0	B
257.312e		Driving A CMV Without Proper Endorsement Or Designator (Various Descriptions)	2	
257.319B	B21, B22, B23, B24, B26	Driving CMV While Commercial Driver License Is Suspended, Revoked Denied Or Cancelled	0	R
257.319B	B20	Driving CMV While Commercial Driver License Is Suspended, Revoked Denied Or Cancelled	0	B
257.319(B)	B56	Driving CMV Without Obtaining A CDL	0	B
257.625(1)	A20	Driving Under Infl Alc And Drugs (Effective With Arrest Date < 9/30/2003)	6	S
257.625(1)	A23	Driving Under Infl Alc And Drugs (Effective With Arrest Date < 9/30/2003)	6	R
257.319(d)	B27	Drove CMV During Out Of State Service Order	2	B
257.319(d)	B19	Drove CMV During Out Of State Service Order - Hazardous/Bus	2	B
257.904	B24	Drove CMV While Disqualified (Effective Before 10/1/2005)	2	B
257.319(B)	B57	Drove CMV With No License In Possession (CMV)	0	B
257.634	M57, M62	Drove Left Of Center	2	R
257.640	N72	Drove Left Of Center	2	R
257.634, 639	N70	Drove Left Of Center	2	B
257.634, 639, 640	M40, M41, M60, M61	Drove Left Of Center	2	R
257.679A	M50	Drove Moped On Sidewalk or Limited Access Hwy	2	R
257.312	D29	Drove W/O Corrective Lens	2	S
257.301,312A, 312E	B91	Drove W/O Proper License/Endorsement/Veh Group Designator (Non-CMV)	2	B
257.301	B51	Drove While License Expired (CMV) (Effective With Arrest Date >/= 08/01/2011)	2	S
257.301	B51	Drove While License Expired (Non-CMV) (Effective With Arrest Date < 02/01/2006)	2	
257.301,312A, 904A	B51	Drove While License Not Valid Or Improper License	2	S
257.904		Drove While License Susp/Rev/Denied	2	
257.904		Drove While License Suspended By FAC/FCJ	2	
257.904(4)	U31	Drove While License Suspended, Revoked, Denied Causing Death	6	S
257.904(5)	M80	Drove While License Suspended, Revoked, Denied Causing Serious Injury	6	S
257.904	B20	Drove While License Suspended/Revoked/Denied (Non-CMV)	2	B
257.904	B21, B22, B23, B25, B26	Drove While License Suspended/Revoked/Denied (Non-CMV)	2	R
257.904a, 312a, (2)	B51	Drove While Unlicensed Or Without Cycle Endorsement	2	B
257.627(1)	M82	Drove Without Due Care And/Or Caution	2	B
257.627(1)	D74	Drove Without Due Care And/Or Caution	2	R
257.641	N71	Drove Wrong Side Of Divided Hwy	2	R
257.641	N61	Drove Wrong Way	2	R
257.641	N60, N62	Drove Wrong Way On One-Way Street	2	R
257.641	N63	Drove Wrong Way On One-Way Street	2	B
333.7401-7455, 1766A	A33	Drug Crime		B
333.7401-7455		Drug Crime	0	
257.653b	M18	Due Care and Caution for Waste-Utility-Road Maintenance Vehicles	2	S
	S93	Energy Speed (<03/31/1997)		S
257.611	M14	Failed To Comply With Traffic Control Device	2	B
257.700	E54	Failed To Dim Lights	2	R
257.311	B78	Failed To Display A Valid License	0	
257.310e(14)		Failed To Display Valid Graduated License Status	0	

Statute	ACD	Description	Pts	CVT
257.268(5)	S96	Failed To Drive Minimum Speed	2	B
257.627(1)	D72	Failed To Have Car Under Control	2	R
257.648	N40	Failed To Signal And/Or Observe	2	B
257.648	N42, N43, N44	Failed To Signal And/Or Observe	2	R
257.648		Failed To Signal And/Or Observe (Various Descriptions)	2	
257.667	M09	Failed To Stop At Railroad Crossing (Effective Before 10/1/2002)	3	R
257.667-669		Failed To Stop At Railroad Crossing (Various Descriptions)	3	
257.682	M75	Failed To Stop For School Bus	3	B
257.652	M25	Failed To Stop Leaving Alley Or Private Drive	2	B
257.618	B04, B05, B08	Failed To Stop Or Identify After P.D. Acc	6	R
257.618, 620		Failed To Stop Or Identify After P.D. Accident (Also Hit & Run, Leaving Scene Etc.)	6	
257.617A	B03	Failed To Stop Or Identify After P.I. Acc - Misdemeanor	6	B
257.617A	B07	Failed To Stop Or Identify After P.I. Acc - Misdemeanor	6	R
257.617A	B06	Failed To Stop Or Identify After P.I. Accident Causing Death or Serious Bodily Impairment - Felony	6	R
257.617(3)	B02	Failed To Stop Or Identify After P.I. Accident Causing Death - Felony	6	B
257.617(2)	B03	Failed To Stop Or Identify After P.I. Accident Causing Serious Injury	6	S
257.617(2)	B14	Failed To Stop Or Identify After P.I. Accident Causing Serious Injury	6	R
257.627(1)	S94	Failed To Stop Within Assured Clear Distance Ahead	2	S
257.724		Failed To Submit To Truck Weighing When Required	2	
257.649	N09, N21, N23, N24, N25, N26, N30	Failed To Yield	2	R
257.649	N01	Failed To Yield Right Of Way	2	B
257.649	N02, N03	Failed To Yield Right Of Way	2	R
257.649	N22	Failed To Yield Right Of Way At A Stop Sign	2	R
257.653a(1)(a)	N04	Failed To Yield To Emergency Responder	4	S
257.653	N04	Failed To Yield To Emergency Vehicle	2	B
257.654	N05	Failed To Yield To Funeral Procession	2	R
257.612	N08	Failed To Yield To Handicapped/Blind Individual	2	S
257.649	N06	Failed To Yield To Oncoming Traffic	2	R
257.612	N08	Failed To Yield To Pedestrian	2	B
257.612	N20	Failed To Yield To Pedestrian	2	R
257.65	N31	Failed To Yield When Turning Left	2	R
257.321A(13)	D45	Failure To Appear In Court	0	B
257.321A(13)	D53	Failure To Comply With Judgment	0	B
257.321A(13)	D56	Failure To Comply With Judgment	0	R
257.667	M09	Failure To Obey Railroad Crossing Restrictions	3	B
257.668-257.669	M10	Failure To Obey Traffic Control Device Or Enforcement Official At Railroad Crossing	3	B
257.601c(2)	U31	Failure To Use Due Care And Caution Causing Death Of A Person Operating An Implement Of Husbandry	6	S
257.601b(3)	U31	Failure To Use Due Care And Caution Causing Death To A Construction Worker	6	S
257.601c(1)	M80	Failure To Use Due Care And Caution Causing Injury Of A Person Operating An Implement Of Husbandry		S
257.601b(2)	M80	Failure To Use Due Care And Caution Causing Injury To Construction Worker	6	S
257.653b	M82	Failure To Use Due Care Caution For Waste-Utility-Road Maintenance Vehicles	?	S
257.653a(1)(b)	M81	Failure To Use Due Caution For Emergency Responder - Misdemeanor	4	S
257.653	M81	Failure To Use Due Caution for Stationary Authorized Emergency Responder	4	S
257.653a(4)	U31	Failure To Yield For An Emergency Responder Causing Death	6	S
257.653a(3)	M80	Failure To Yield For An Emergency Responder Causing Injury - Felony	6	S
257.903,217(1),226(10),233A	D78	False Certification Under Vehicle Code (Perjury)		B
750.411a(2),327-8		False Report Or Threat Of Bomb/Harmful Device (School)	0	
257.626C	U06	Felonious Driving	6	B
	U04	Felony With Auto Used / Attempt Is Misdemeanor	6	B
Various	U03	Felony With Auto Used / Attempt Is Felony	6	B
257.732(5),73	U03	Felony/Auto Used	6	B
257.602A	U01	Fleeing/Eluding Officer 1st Degree	6	R
257.602A(4)	U01	Fleeing/Eluding Officer 2nd Degree	6	S

Statute	ACD	Description	Pts	CVT
257.602A(3)	U01	Fleeing/Eluding Officer 3rd Degree	6	S
257.602A(2)	U01	Fleeing/Eluding Officer 4th Degree	6	B
257.643,643A	M30, M31	Followed Too Closely	2	R
257.643,643A	M34	Followed Too Closely	2	B
258.602A	M33	Following Fire Truck too Closely	?	B
257.324	D02	Fraud In Obtaining License	0	B
257.315(4)		Fraudulent Change Of Address	2	
257.617A	B14	Gave False Info - Personal Injury Accident	6	S
257.618	D78	Gave False Info - Property Damage Acc	6	S
257.324	D78	Gave False Information To Police Officer	0	S
257.625(2)	A41	Ignition Interlock Device Violations	0	B
257.647(1)	N56	Illegal (Prohibited) Turn	2	R
257.644(1)	M44	Illegal Crossover On Limited Access Highway	2	B
257.645(1)	M46	Illegal Entrance/Exit - X-Way	2	B
257.656b	F34	Impeded Traffic	?	S
257.644	M51	Improper Crossing - Divided Hwy	2	R
257.642(1)	M62	Improper Lane Use	2	R
257.642,634(3)	M41	Improper Lane Use	2	R
257.718, 720-21		Improper Load Or Towing (Various Descriptions)	2	
257.698(5)	N84	Improper Operation - Emergency Equipment (Misdemeanor)	2	S
257.603	N84	Improper Operation - Emergency Vehicle	2	S
257.1855, 1855(1), 1855(5)	E56	Improper Operation Of School Bus	2	B
257.636,637	M71, M73, N07	Improper Passing	3	R
257.636,637	M70	Improper Passing	3	B
257.636,637,639	M77	Improper Passing	3	R
257.636,637,640	M72, M76	Improper Passing	3	R
257.639	M74	Improper Passing On Hill	3	R
257.647, 612	N50	Improper Turn	2	B
257.647	N52, N54, N55	Improper Turn	2	R
257.650	N31	Improper Turn	2	R
257.647,650	N53	Improper Turn	2	R
257.649	N01	Interfere With Traffic	2	S
257.679,680	M56	Interfered With Fire Apparatus	2	R
257.620	B01	Leaving The Scene Of An Accident	6	B
257.628,629B	S92	Limited Access Speed	2	S
750.382(2)		Malicious Destruction (Turfing) <$200.00	0	
750.382(1)(b		Malicious Destruction (Turfing) >$200.00	0	
324.80147		Marine Safety - Reckless Operation	0	?
257.660(2)	M40	Motorcycle/Moped Over Two Abreast	2	S
257.601d(1)	U31	Moving Violation Causing Death (Effective With Arrest Date > 10/30/2010)	?	B
750.91	U03	Murder/Auto Used	6	S
257.626B	M83	Negligent Driving	3	R
750.324	U07	Negligent Homicide (Effective With Arrest Date < 10/31/2010)	6	B
750.324	U09	Negligent Homicide (CMV) (Effective With Arrest Date < 10/31/2010)	6	B
257.328(1)	B74	No Proof of Insurance or No Insurance	0	B
500.3101-03	B74	No Insurance Under the Insurance Code - Misdemeanor	0	B
257.709	D70	Obscured Vision	2	B
257.682B	F05	Occupant Under The Age Of 18 In Open Bed Of Pickup Truck	2	S
257.624A	A26	Open Intoxicants In Vehicle/Driver	2	R
257.624A	A35	Open Intoxicants In Vehicle/Driver	2	B
257.624A	A35	Open Intoxicants In Vehicle-Passenger	2	S
257.625M	A04	Operated Commercial Motor Vehicle With BAC .04-.07	0	B
257.625M	A94	Operated Commercial Motor Vehicle With BAC .04-.07 [If Veh Type CMV]	0	R
257.625M	A11	Operated Commercial Motor Vehicle With BAC .04-.07 [If Detail >=,04 And <.08 And Veh Type CMV]	0	R
257.625(4)	A21	Operated Under Influence Or While Impaired By Liquor Causing Death	6	S
257.625(1)	A22	Operated Under Influence Controlled Substance (Effective With Arrest Date < 09/30/2003)	6	B
257.625(1)	A24	Operated Under Influence Controlled Substance (Effective With Arrest Date <	6	R

Statute	ACD	Description	Pts	CVT
		09/30/2003)		
257.625(1)		Operated Under Influence Liquor	6	
257.625	A21	Operated Under Influence Liquor (Effective With Arrest Date < 09/30/2003)	6	B
257.625(1)	A90	Operated Under Influence Liquor (Effective With Arrest Date < 09/30/2003)	6	R
257.625	A20	Operated Under Influence Liquor (Effective With Arrest Date < 09/30/2003)	6	R
257.625(1)	A21	Operated Under Influence Liquor (Effective With Arrest Date < 09/30/2003)	6	B
257.625(4)	A22	Operated Under Influence Of Controlled Substance Causing Death	6	S
257.625(5)	A22	Operated Under Influence Of Controlled Substance Causing Serious Injury	6	S
257.625(4)(b)	A21	Operated Under Influence Or While Impaired By Liquor Causing Death Of An Emergency Responder	6	S
257.625(5)	A21	Operated Under Influence Or While Impaired By Liquor Causing Incap Injury	6	S
257.625(3)	A25	Operated While Impaired By Controlled Substance	4	S
257.625(3)	A25	Operated While Impaired By Liquor	4	B
257.625(3)	A08	Operated While Impaired By Liquor (Effective With Arrest Date< 09/30/2003)	4	R
257.625(3)	A11, A98	Operated While Impaired By Liquor [If Detail>.07 And <.10] (Effective With Arrest Date < 09/30/2003)	4	R
257.625(7)	A25	Operated While Impaired By Liquor Occupant Less Than 16	6	S
257.625(1)	A08, A10, A11, A21, A22, A23, A24, A90, A98	Operating While Intoxicated (Effective With Arrest Date > 09/30/2003)	6	R
257.625(1)	A20	Operating While Intoxicated (Effective With Arrest Date > 09/30/2003)	6	B
257.625(8)	A33	Operating With Presence Of Drugs (Effective With Arrest Date >09/30/2003	6	S
257.319B(1)	A12	Out-Of-State Implied Consent	0	B
257.677	F05	Permit Passenger(S) To Ride On Outside Of Car	2	R
436.1703(1)	A31	Person Under 21 Purchase/Consume/Possess Liquor	0	S
257.625a(2)		Person Under 21 Refused Preliminary Breath Test	2	
257.624B	A31	Person Under 21 Transport/Possess In Vehicle -Driver	2	B
257.624B	A31	Person Under 21 Transport/Possess In Vehicle -Passenger	2	S
436.1703(2)	D06	Person Under 21 Used Fraudulent Id To Purchase Liquor	0	B
257.625(6)	A60	Person Under 21 With BAC .02 < .08	4	B
257.625(6)	A61	Person Under 21 With BAC	4	R
257.625(6)	A94	Person Under 21 With BAC [If Veh Type Not CMV, & Age < 21 At Violation]	4	R
257.625(6)	A11	Person Under 21 With BAC [If Detail <.08, Veh Type Not CMV, & Age < 21 At Violation]	4	R
257.625a		Preliminary Breath Test Refusal In CMV	0	
257.625a(2)		Preliminary Breath Test Refusal In Non-CMV		
257.647(1)	M18	Prohibited Turn	2	S
257.626	M84	Reckless Driving	6	B
257.647	N51	Right (Left) Turn - Wrong Lane	2	R
257.642	M60	Slow Vehicle Failed To Keep Right	2	R
257.627,628	S93	Speed (Details Unknown)	2	R
257.627(9)	S92	Speeding In A Construction Zone	3-5	S
257.642	M48	Straddling Lanes	2	R
	M85	Texting While Driving CMV - [CMV only] Effective With Arrest Date >/= 10/28/2013		
750.367c		Theft Of Motor Vehicle Fuel	0	
257.642	M40	Through Left (And Right) Turn Only Lane	2	R
750.414		UDAA W/O Intent To Steal (Joyriding)	2	
257.698	E55	Unauthorized Or Improper Use Of Lights (various descriptions)	2	B
257.700	E50	Unauthorized Or Improper Use Of Lights (various Descriptions)	2	R
257.625(1)		Unlawful Bodily Alcohol Content (.10)	6	
257.625(1)	A11	Unlawful Bodily Alcohol Content (.10) [If Detail>=.10] (Effective With Arrest Date < 09/30/2003)	6	R
257.625(1)	A10	Unlawful Bodily Alcohol Content (.10) (Effective With Arrest Date < 09/30/2003)	6	B
750.413		Unlawful Driving Away Auto	6	
257.658(2), (3)		Unlawful Rider On Motorcycle/Moped	0	
257.324	D16	Unlawful Use Or Display Of License (Various Descriptions)	0	B
257.627(1)	N84	Unsafe Manner	2	R
750.321	U08	Vehicular Manslaughter	6	B
257.312	D29	Viol Of License Restrictions	2	B
257.312	D27	Viol Of Restricted License	2	B

Statute	ACD	Description	Pts	CVT
257.627(1)	S94	Violation Of Basic Speed Law	2	B
257.627(1)	S97	Violation Of Basic Speed Law	2	R
	F02	Violation Of Child Restraint Law (FCJ Only)		S
257.905	D35	Violation Of Financial Responsibility Law	2	S
257.310E(11)	D29	Violation Of GDL Permit	2	S
257.642(2)	M49	Violation Of High-Occupancy Vehicle/Land (HOV)	2	B
257.306	D29	Violation Of Instruction Permit	2	S
	F04	Violation Of Safety Belt Law (FCJ Only)		S

Note About Off-Road Vehicles:

When a person is convicted on a violation performed while in an Off Road Vehicle, this conviction will be indicated with the letters ORV in front of the explanation field as shown above. The section of Michigan law that deals with the operation of ORV is 324.81134.

About Speeding

Michigan statues involved are 257.627-629 and 257.722. On the driving record, the "actual speed" is followed by the posted speed limit (48/35, etc.)

Speed	Points	Limited Access Speed	Points	In Construction Zone	Points
No amount given	2	1 - 5 mph over	0	1 - 10 mph over	3
1 - 10 mph over	2	6 - 10 mph over	1	11 - 15 mph over	4
11 - 15 mph over	3	11 - 15 mph over	2	16 and over	5
16 and over	4	16 - 25 mph over	3		
		26 and over	4		

Withdrawal Table with ACD Translations

ACD	Description	Convert
W01	Accum/Hab Vio Conv of Multiple Serious Offenses Resulting In Long Term Removal of License	B
W50	Accumulation Of Two Out Of Service Order General Violations Within 10 Years	B
W52	Accumulation of Three Or More Out of Service Order Violations Within 10 Years	B
W61	Accumulation of Three or More RRGC Violations Within 3 Years	B
W40	Accumulation of Two Or More Major Offense	B
W50	Accumulation of Two Out of Service Order General Violations Within 10 Years	B
W51	Accumulation of Two Out of Service Order Violations With 10 Yrs Transporting 16 Or More Pass Or Hazmat	B
W60	Accumulation of Two RRGC Violations Within 3 Years	B
W01	Accumulation of Viol Resulting In Discretionary Action By Lic Authority	B
W01	Accumulation of Viol Resulting In Mandatory Action of The Lic Auth Because of A Statutory Pt System	B
W41	Additional Major Offense After Reinstatement	B
W30	CDL Privilege Withdrawal For 2 Serious CMV Violations Within 3 Years	B
W31	CDL Privilege Withdrawal For 3 Serious CMV Violations Within 3 Years	B
W09	Failure To Surrender Hazmat Endorsement As Required By The USA Patriot Act	B
D51	Friend of the Court Suspension (Effective as Withdrawal Only)	S
W70	Imminent Hazard	B
W00	Non-ACD Withdrawals	B
A90, A91 A94, A98	Out-Of-State Admin Per Se Alcohol Violations (Effective With Arrest Date >/= 01/01/2004)	R
W13	Parent Consent Withdrawn - Cancellation [With Reason Code 10]	S
W14	Physical Or Mental Disability -Suspensions [With Reason Codes AB, AC, or AV]	S
W15	Physician's Or Specialist' Report Recommended [Doctor Statement Required]	S
W01	Recurrence of Viols Requiring Mandatory Action of The Lic Auth Because of Statutory Pt System	B
W20	Unable To Pass Dl Test(S) Or Meet Qualifications - Cancellation	B
W14	Unfavorable doctors Statement	S
W45	Withdrawal For Driving A CMV While Disqualified For Previous Violations In A CMV	B

Point System Summary

Points range from 2 to 6 and remain on driving record for two years. Michigan operates on a 12 point system. Four points in any two year period triggers an initial letter and the need to be careful. At eight points, drivers receive a warning letter which advises that they will be scheduled for a re-examination if driving habits do not improve. At twelve points, a driver re-examination is scheduled at which time driving privileges could be suspended.

Also, points **assessments** are assessed once annually for drivers who accumulate and maintain seven or more points on their driving record. Drivers are assessed each year in which seven or more points remain. The fees begin at $100 for seven points and increase by $50 for each additional point on the record. In addition, Category 2 Fees are imposed for specific offenses as defined by law. This fee is assessed for two years in a row. Fees range from $150 to $1,000.

Note that snowmobile and off-road vehicle (ORV) alcohol-conviction points are placed on a driver record and may result in licensing action against driving privileges even though the violation happened while operating a snowmobile or ORV.

Point System - Selected Violations	Points
10 mph or less over the legal speed limit.	2
11 through 15 mph over the legal speed limit.	3
16 mph or more over the legal speed limit.	4
All other moving violations of traffic laws.	2
Careless driving.	3
Disobeying a traffic signal or stop sign or improper passing.	3
Drag racing.	4
Failing to stop and give identification at the scene of a crash.	6
Failure to stop at railroad crossing.	3
Failure to stop for a school bus or for disobeying a school crossing guard.	3
Failure to yield/show due caution for emergency vehicles.	4
Fleeing or eluding a police officer.	6
Manslaughter, negligent homicide, or other felony involving use of a motor vehicle.	6
Open alcohol container in vehicle.	2
Operating under the influence of liquor or drugs.	6
Operating while visibly impaired.	4
Reckless driving.	6
Refusal of Preliminary Breath Test (PBT) by anyone under age 21.	2
Refusal to take a chemical test.	6
Under age 21 with any bodily alcohol content.	4
Unlawful bodily alcohol content of 0.08 or more.	6

Minnesota

Administration	Important Telephone and Web Contacts
Jennifer Cohan, Director Division of Motor Vehicles Safety and Homeland Security Building 303 Transportation Circle, Dover 19901 PO Box 698, Dover 19903 302-744-2510 - Fax: 302-739-3152 www.dmv.de.gov/default.shtml Note: All DMV offices have hours of operation from 8:00 am to 4:30 pm (EST), except Wednesday hours are noon to 8 pm.	Driver Licensing/Records ....302-744-2506 Vehicle Records...302-744-2531 License Suspensions...302-744-2509 License Revocations..302-744-2508 Financial Responsibility....................................302-744-2513 Commercial Driver License ....302-744-2572 State Department of Insurance ....302-674-7300 State Police ....302-739-5901 Email........................ dot-public-relations@state.de.us Laws and Regulations: www.dmv.de.gov/information/laws_regs.shtml

Driver's License Format, Issuance and Renewal

License Classes, Restrictions and Endorsements Appear After the Driving Record Content Section

License Format

The DL format is one letter followed by twelve numbers. The number is randomly generated with no significance to the card holder's name or date of birth and is assigned to the card holder for a lifetime.

Document Appearance

The current license document has been issued to new drivers and renewals since 12/12/2004.

Current Document

Security Characteristics Front: A holographic state seal that appears only under ultraviolet light. A virtual image of a loon appears to float above or sink below the surface as the viewing angle changes. A digital image of the cardholder is fused with heat into the card plastic with fine print over the image and a rainbow print pattern.

Security Characteristics Back: A 1-D bar code, 2-D bar code, and a magnetically encoded strip.

Position of Photo: Always on left.

Minor Age Driver Locator: A red border around photo image indicates "Under 21." Age 18 birth date (if applicable) is printed in red to the right of the date of birth.

CDL Indicator: The word "Commercial" is printed under the driver's license in the header area.

Older Document (prior to 12/12/2004)

The license card, issued in 1999 through late 2004, has a polymer core with a front and back laminate.

Security Characteristics Front: An encrypted 2-D bar code, holograms depicting snowflakes and the word Minnesota, loons printed with ultraviolet sensitive ink and micro-printing in the shape of a star. Digital image and ghosted image of the card holder. No embossing.

Security Characteristics Back: A 1-D bar code and magnetically encoded strip.

Position of Photo: 21 and over - right side; under 21 - left side.

Minor Age Driver Locator: Photo on left. "Under 21" is printed in the header and 21st birth date is printed directly underneath 2-D bar code. Beginning 02/01/00, 18th birth date is printed directly underneath 21st birth date.

CDL Indicator: "CDL" printed directly under colored header.

Issuance

Age Requirements

The state's Graduated Driver's License law provides for three phases of licensing for persons under 18 years of age: Phase I-Instruction Permit; Phase II-Provisional License; and Phase III-Full License. Limitations on teens in the first 6 months of licensure include a nighttime driving prohibition between midnight and 5am, and only one passenger under the age of 20 permitted, unless driver accompanied by a parent or guardian. During the second 6 months of licensure, 3 passengers under 20 are permitted (family members exempted).

Instruction Permit: Must be at least 15 years of age, pass vision and written test. If under 18, be enrolled in behind-the-wheel instruction, must complete 30 hours of classroom instruction, and only operate the vehicle when accompanied by a licensed driver age 21 years or older.

Provisional License: Must be at least 16 years of age, have completed driver education, held an instruction permit for 6 months with no convictions for moving violations or convictions for alcohol/controlled substance violations, and pass road test.

Under 21 Full License: Must be at least 18 years of age or must have held a provisional license for at least 12 consecutive months with no convictions for alcohol/controlled substance violations or crash-related moving violations, and with not more than one conviction for a moving violation that is not crash-related. If under 18, the person who approves the application also certifies that the applicant has driven under the supervision of a licensed driver at least 21 years of age for not less than 10 hours on the provisional license. If age 18, must have held an instruction permit for 6 months. If age 19 or older, must have held an instruction permit for three months. License expires at age 21 and may be renewed without additional written or road tests.

Location of Requirements for Proof of Identity:
  https://dps.mn.gov/divisions/dvs/forms-documents/Documents/IdentificationRequirements_English.pdf

Residency

Non-resident's home-state license honored if age 15 or older, but must secure Minnesota license within sixty days (within thirty days if CDL) of establishing permanent residency.

Renewal

Birthday of fourth year. Driver keeps same driver's license number for life, regardless if name is changed. At present, renewal is not available online. MN law states that military personnel need not renew their license, but after discharge, the license renewal transaction is required to be completed within 90 days. Those MN drivers who are temporarily out-of-state may renew by mail, but must appear for a new photo within 30 days of their return to the state.

Elderly-Related Restrictions

None indicated.

Vehicle Insurance, Title and Registration Facts

Registration Renewal

Online registration is available for passenger vehicles, recreational vehicles, motorcycles, mopeds, trailers, and some trucks provided the gross weight of the truck does not need to be changed and it is not required to have a U.S. DOT number. One can also change an address online. Renew vehicles online at https://www.mvrenewal.state.mn.us/ with a credit card or ACH. Registration stickers will be mailed within 10 days of the Internet transaction.

New Residents

New residents have a 60-day grace period to register a passenger vehicle, motorcycle, utility trailer or house trailer. If the registration displayed on the vehicle expires before the 60-day grace period ends, the owner must apply for Minnesota registration immediately.

Inspections and Emissions Testing

There are no provisions for statewide safety inspections or emission testing.

Passenger Plate Facts

2 plates are issued with 2 decals (MO) (YR) on both plates for normal passenger plates, but the number of plates and stickers vary based on the class of registration. Counties are coded on the plate in alphabetical order respectively from 01 to 87. The coding is as follows: 01 is Aitkin, 02 is Anoka..... and 87 is Yellow Medicine. Code 88 is used for Foreign; for the life of the vehicle Plates remain with vehicle when sold except certain specialty and unique symbol plates, restricted use plates, and prorate class plates are retained by owner. Note that passenger plates are replaced at seven-year intervals

Insurance and Financial Responsibility

Proof of insurance must be provided upon request of a law enforcement officer. Minimum liability requirements are $30,000/60,000/10,000. MN state law also requires all licensed vehicle to have Personal Injury Protection (PIP), Uninsured, and Underinsured coverage.

Suspensions and Revocations, Alcohol and Chemical Testing

Alcohol and Chemical Testing Limits

Minnesota's illegal intoxication level is an alcohol concentration of .08 percent and .04 percent for CMV drivers. There is zero tolerance for drivers under 21. Urine, blood, and breath testing are authorized, and there is a one-year revocation for refusal to submit to a test. Minnesota has provisions for administrative revocation.

Suspensions and Revocations

See the Appendix for a list of the federally mandated disqualifications for offenses occurring in a CMV per MCSIA.

Any Misdemeanor Offense Resulting in Fatality ....180-day suspension.
Any Misdemeanor Offense Resulting in Class A Injury to Another ....90-day suspension.
Criminal Vehicular Operation .... One- to 10-year revocation.
Driving While License Revoked, Suspended, or Cancelled ....30-day to one-year suspension.
DUI -
    First Offense .... 90 days or if under 21 6-month revocation if BAC <. .16; One-year revocation if BAC >.16.
    Second Offense in 10 years .... 1 year <.10; Two year revocation if BAC > .10.
Failure to Maintain or Provide Proof of Insurance
    No other violations .... 30-day revocation.
    One other violation .... 90-day revocation.
    Two other violations .... 180-day revocation.
    Three or more other violations...One-year revocation.
Felony Involving Motor Vehicle ....One-year revocation.
Fleeing a Police Officer.. 1 or 3-year revocation.
Habitual Offender
    Four violations in 12 months ....30-day suspension.
    Five offenses in 12 months ....90-day suspension.
    Six offenses in 12 months ....180 day suspension.
    Seven offenses in 12 months ....365 day suspension.
    Five offenses in 24 months ....30-day suspension.
    Six offenses in 24 months ....90-day suspension.
    Seven offenses in 24 months ....180-day suspension.
    Eight or more offenses in 24 months ....One-year suspension.
Leaving the Scene of an Accident ....6-month(if personal injury) to one-year revocation (if fatal).
Multiple Misdemeanors Revocations
    Two misdemeanors in 12 months .... 30-day suspension warning letter sent.
    Three misdemeanors in 12 months .... 30-day revocation.
    Four misdemeanors in 12 months.. 90-day revocation.
    Five or more misdemeanors in 12 months..One-year revocation.
Perjury or False Statement (relating to operation/ownership of motor vehicle) .... 180-day revocation.
Refusal to Submit to a Drug or Alcohol Test ....One-year revocation.
School Bus Stop Arm Violation
    One gross misdemeanor or more .... 90-day to one-year revocation.
    Two petty misdemeanors (or 1 petty misdemeanor + 1 misdemeanor) in 5 years ....30-day suspension.
    Three petty misdemeanors in 5 years..90-day suspension.
    Four or more petty misdemeanors in 5 years ....1-year suspension.
    Two misdemeanors in 5 years .... 30-day revocation.

Three misdemeanors in 5 years.. 90-day revocation.
Four misdemeanors in 5 years .... 180-day revocation.
Five or more misdemeanors in 5 years .... 1-year revocation.

Editor's Note: The Minnesota legislature structured the stop arm violation law in response to a public outcry that sanctions were too harsh or not harsh enough. As a result, a stop arm violator's conviction (from the courts) is based on the nature of his/her violation. For example, passing a bus on the right with a child present gets a higher sanction than passing on the left with no child present. It is rare for someone to get more than three petty misdemeanors of this violation in 5 years.

Speed in Excess of 100 mph..6-month revocation.
Theft of Gas..30-day suspension.
Unlawful/Fraudulent Use of Driver's License ....90-day to 180-day suspension.

Reinstatement Requirements

Suspension $20.00 fee.
Revocation   30.00 or $680.00 (for alcohol-related offenses) fee; time lapse; reapply for license, written test required

Record Access: Laws, Rules, and Forms

Note: This Section Applies to Both Driver and Vehicle Records.

Governing Statutes and Rules

Minnesota Statutes: https://www.revisor.mn.gov/
DVS Rules: https://dps.mn.gov/divisions/dvs/news/Pages/Public-Notices.aspx.
Access to personal data is governed by M.S. 168.346, subd. 7 and M.S. 171.12, subd 7a, and United States Code, Title 18, Chapter123 section 2721.
Information collected by Driver and Vehicle Services falls into three classifications:
1. Public – Anyone may see this data. (M.S.13.03, subd. 1). The following are classified as public information; driver's license status, Zip Code, convictions, unpaid fines information, and physical description.
2. Private – Only the subject of the data and those specifically authorized by the statutes cited are entitled to see data unless subject has given written authorization to release. The following are classified as private data:
* personal name and date of birth, address; driver's license number (18 U.S.C. § 2725);
* crash report information (M.S. 169.09, Subd. 13); medical data (13.69, Subd. 1 (a)(1));
* designated caregiver data (must be given to law enforcement M.S. 13.69 (4));
* disability parking certificate data (non-medical data only) may be released to law enforcement agencies pursuant to M.S. 13.69 subd. 1(a) (2);
* motor vehicle lessee data is only available to the subject of the data and those specifically authorized pursuant to M.S.168.345, subd.2);
* Social Security Number (SSNs) must be provided to the Department of Revenue for tax administration and the Department of Labor and Industry for workers' compensation administration and enforcement), and Department of Natural Resources for purposes of license application, M.S. 13.69, Subd 1 (3).

3. Confidential – No one may see this information, including the subject, except authorized department personnel. Driving ability information received by a family member is classified as confidential.

Request and Consent Forms

Individual requesters are required to submit a *Record Request Form (PS2502)*. The requestor must specify on the form how the requester is authorized under the DPPA to obtain the identified records and personal information or provide written consent of the subject. The Department of Public Safety approves access to the *Grant Access to Record Form (PS2503)*. The notarized the signature of the subject is required. These same forms can be used for requesting either driver or vehicle records. These record request forms and multiple record supplements are available online at https://dps.mn.gov/divisions/dvs/Pages/records-request-procedure.aspx. Forms are also available at the division's central office, and may be requested by phone at 651-296-2940.

Vendor and Third Party Access Policy

Approved online vendors can access records for other service providers, such as a consumer reporting company who is not online, etc., providing the end-user is in compliance with the provisions of DPPA. The original vendor is responsible. Records cannot be re-disclosed in a bulk fashion.

Non-permissible Use Requests

Records with public data (see above) can be obtained. Per M.S.13.03, subd. 1, a driver license status is considered public information.

Access to Driver-Related Records

Driving Records

General Information and Fees
Driver and Vehicle Services Division; Driver License Record Requests, 445 Minnesota St, #161 St Paul MN 55101, 651-215-1335, fax: 651-282-5512.
Fees vary by who is ordering and by access method. A non-electronic request is $9.50 per record display or $9.00 if the requester is subject. Add $1.00 for certification. In addition add a $1.00 "correspondence fee" for each page printed. High volume requesters obtain records electronically for $5.00 per record.
Mail or In-Person – Driver and Vehicle Services central office is located at 445 Minnesota Street, St Paul. Turnaround time for mail is generally within one week or less.
Telephone - Status Only – One may verify the status of a submitted driver license number for free by calling 651-284-2000. This service is available 24/7.

Electronic – Online access to records is offered to entities with an approved Business Partner Records Access Agreement. The use of the data must comply with statutes and DVS business practices. DVS establishes a unique account for each customer. The customer must maintain funds in the account sufficient to cover customer use. The fee for each inquiry is $5.00. The account balance is displayed at time of log on. For more information call 651-297-5352.
Electronic - Status Only – DL status information is available at https://dutchelm.dps.state.mn.us/dvsinfo/info/DLTitleStatus/DLTitle_main.asp. The requester must submit the DL#, there is no fee. No personal information is displayed - only public information is disclosed.
Bulk – If the use of the data is within DPPA provisions, record retrieval is available based on customized requests. Fees depend on media and type of data requested. The data cannot be used for marketing purposes. Call Data Services at 651-297-5352.

By Person of Record – MN drivers may obtain their own driving record by mail or walk-in as described above. The fee is $9.00 or $10.00, if certified. Online service is not available.

Notification/Monitoring Program

At present, Minnesota does not offer a distinctive monitoring system or notification program to employers or insurance companies to track incidents of drivers. However the bulk purchase program can be configured to operate in this manner.

Crash Reports

Reporting – Accidents involving death, injury or damage to an apparent extent of $1,000 or more must be reported immediately to the local or state police. Drivers must file a written report of the accident with the Department within ten days of the accident. Report forms can be found online at https://dps.mn.gov/divisions/dvs/forms-documents/Documents/MinnesotaMotorVehicleAccidentReport.pdf then send to Department of Public Safety (DPS), Driver and Vehicle Services, 445 Minnesota St, Ste 181, St. Paul 55101, 651-296-3279. If a commercial driver is issued a citation in another state, they must report it to DPS per the Commercial Motor Vehicle Safety Act of 1986 - Federal Statute 383.31.

Record Access – Crash information may only be disclosed to authorized requestors, their legal representatives, or insurance representatives (M.S. 169.09, subd. 13). The current fee is $5.00 per record. Records are indexed from 1998 forward, electronically imaged. Requests should be submitted to Driver & Vehicle Services; Crash Records, 445 Minnesota St. #161, St Paul 55101.

Download a request form (PS2503-06) at https://dps.mn.gov/divisions/dvs/forms-documents/Documents/CrashRecordRequestForm.pdf.

Escrow account holders may fax requests to: (651) 282-5512 or e-mail to: dvs.records@state.mn.us. Processing time is usually one week. Records are usually available 3 weeks after the incident. A driver can obtain, upon written request, a free copy of his own citizen report. For questions, email to dvs.records@state.mn.us or call 651-215-1335.

Access to Vehicle-Related Records

General Information and Fees

Driver and Vehicle Services Division, Record Requests, 445 Minnesota St., Ste 161, St Paul 55101-5161, 651-296-2940, fax: 651-282-5512. Records released include ownership and vehicle information and are available for the past 7 years. Fees vary by who is ordering and by access method. A non-electronic request is $9.50 per record display or $9.00 if the requester is subject. Add $1.00 for certification. In addition add a $1.00 "correspondence fee" for each page printed. High volume requesters obtain records electronically for $5.00 per record.

In-Person – Driver and Vehicle Services central office is located at 445 Minnesota Street, St Paul. Up to three requests are processed per visit. Turnaround time varies depending on each day's customer demand.

Mail – Send completed request forms and fees to the address above. Turnaround time is generally one week or less plus mail time.

Electronic – Approved accounts have the ability to request and receive title and registration records. DVS establishes a unique account for each customer. The customer must maintain funds in the account sufficient to cover customer use. The fee for each inquiry is $5.00. The account balance is displayed at time of log on. For more information call 651-297-5352.

Electronic Status Check – Enter a MN plate or registered VIN at https://dutchelm.dps.state.mn.us/dvsinfo/info/DLTitleStatus/DLTitle_main.asp to get a status report. Only public information is released. There is no fee.

Bulk – Records & Information Management, 651-297-1714. Record can be purchased only for permissible use purposes. Commercial use is not permitted. Records can be retrieved in bulk based on individual requests and sorted according to customer needs. Call for fees and media methods.

Access to Vessel-Related Records

General Information, Access and Fees

Department of Natural Resources, License Center, 500 Lafayette Rd, St. Paul 55155-4026, 651-296-2316
www.dnr.state.mn.us/boating/index.html
Records are maintained 15 years for watercraft, snowmobiles, and off-highway vehicles (all terrain) and off-highway motorcycles. A watercraft must be titled if over 16 feet and 1980 model or newer. All motorized and sailboats must be registered. Non-motorized boats and duck hunting boats are exempt.

Recent amendments to the law have defined access regulations to personal information to be very similar to the state's regulations for driver and vehicle records. To view the statute and related material visit https://www.revisor.mn.gov/statutes/?id=84.0874.

Driving Record Content and Reciprocity

What's On or Not On the Driving Record

- The following are classified as private data and are shown only to Permissible Users: date of birth, address, DL number, and crash record information.
- The data that is public and shown on all records includes driver's license status, Zip Code, convictions, unpaid fines information, physical description.
- The numeric county code shown indicates the location of the infraction. Counties are coded in alphabetical order respectively from 01 to 87; 01 is Aitkin and 87 is Yellow Medicine.
- Convictions not reported include speeding 10 mph or less in a 55 mph zone and certain non-moving violations as determined by statute and department rules and regulations.
- Accidents are not shown on the driving record.
- On may not take driver school in lieu of conviction.

The length of time that convictions are displayed is:

Moving Violations	Five year minimum (ten if CDL)
DWI	Displayed indefinitely
Suspensions	Five years minimum
Open Revocation	Ten years minimum

Data Retention

Surrendered licenses with clean records are purged from the system one year after expiration; records with violations are purged after five years. DWIs are retained indefinitely. CDL driver records are purged annually using an automated program based on the timetable per the federal regulations (see the Appendix).

Court to Repository

Courts are required to forward convictions within ten days. Input is done either by data entry operators at the state or online by the courts (passed daily to Central Office via a data link). Records are input as they are received, usually within five days of receipt.

State Reciprocity for Non-CDL Drivers

- Will suspend license of driver for unpaid out-of-state convictions.
- Record of new incoming driver is shown on DL records.
- Out-of-state convictions are shown on DL records.
- Out-of-state accidents are not shown on DL records.
- Convictions of out-of-state drivers are sent to home state.
- Record is forwarded to new state upon surrender of license.

License Classes, Restrictions, Endorsements and Codes

License Classes– Commercial

Minnesota began issuing the CDL in March 1990.

Class A   Valid for any vehicle or combination.

Class B   Valid for any Class D/C single unit motor vehicle, including with passengers endorsement buses. May tow only vehicles with GVW of 10,000 pounds or less.

Class C   Valid for Class D vehicles with hazardous materials or school bus endorsement. May tow vehicles with GVW of 10,000 pounds or less. Towed vehicles may exceed 10,000 pounds only if combined weight 26,000 pounds or less GVW.

License Classes– Non-Commercial

Class D   Valid any single unit 26,000 pounds GVWR or less; emergency equipment operated by firefighters on-duty; all farm-trucks and recreational vehicles, except buses or vehicles requiring hazardous material endorsement. May tow vehicle with GVW of 10,000 pounds or less. Towed vehicles may exceed 10,000 pounds only if combined weight 26,000 pounds or less GVW.

Restrictions

A	Any Use of Alcohol or Drugs Invalidates License	K	Intrastate Only (CDL – under 21 years old)
B	Hand Operated Brakes	L	Driving Only Vehicles Without Air-Brakes (CDL)
C	Complete Hand Control	O	Valid for Vehicles With Less Than 26,001 GVWR
D	Prosthetic Aid	Q	Hand-Operated Light Beam Controls
E	Automatic Transmission	R	Elevated Driver Seat
F	Left Outside Mirror	U	No Freeway Driving
G	Daylight Driving Only	W	Valid for vehicles Less Than 26,001 GVWR and Buses With Passenger Capacity Under 24
I	Also Valid for 3-Wheel Motorcycle	Y	Over 26,000 GVWR Towed
J	Till Age 16—Farm Work & Driver Educ Instr Permit		

Endorsements

H	Hazardous Materials	S	School Bus
M	Motorcycle	T	Double-/Triple-Trailers
N	Tanker	X	Tanker and HazMat
P	Passenger		

Common Abbreviations Found On Driving Records

Abbreviation	Description
AAI	Alcohol assessment interviews
BATCH STORES CODE	The number that is entered behind a conviction indicates where the ticket is stored
C	This letter entered behind a conviction indicates if an offense was in a commercial vehicle
CANC	Driving privileges cancelled
CANC-IPS	Driving privileges cancelled inimical to public safety
COUNTY CODE	Number behind an alcohol related offense where the incident occurred
COURT RECOMMENDATION	Recommendation from the court to take action on a driver license
DEV	Driver evaluation
H	The letter entered behind the conviction indicates the offense was while driving hazardous materials
IC-1	Implied Consent, refusal
IC-3	Implied Consent, test failure
IC-6	Implied Consent refusal (old history)
IPS	Inimical (hostile or unfriendly) to Public Safety
L-W	Living will; the current year entered behind this indicates the driver does have a living will
LIMITED MOBILITY	"L" entered on record indicates eligibility for a reduced public transit pass
M	This letter before a conviction indicates that it is a misdemeanor. A misdemeanor is an offense which is hazardous or endangers a person's life or property. Convictions may be misdemeanors if designated by the court or if it is the third petty misdemeanor in a one-year period on a driving record.
N	This letter entered behind the conviction indicates if the offense was in a non-commercial vehicle
PSD-DT	Passed driver test
PSD-WT	Passed written test
RECD	Received
REIN	Driving privileges reinstated

REV ....Driving privileges revoked
SPECIAL REVIEW ....An interview that is held with an evaluator when a driver has had two alcohol incidents in ten years or three on the record
STATE CODE...............................The state is listed if the conviction occurred in another state
STMT RE (DL, ID) ....A statement was made regarding a driver's license or identification card
SUSP ....Driving privileges Suspended
UNCODED ....A conviction that is entered on the computer that does not have an assigned code for entry into the computer

Special Status Code: Conax

On very rare occasions, the term "**Conax**" may show as a license status. This term refers to the type of record created when a driver has no current driver's license number in Minnesota. The reason could be the driver is licensed in another state, is no longer a MN resident, or has received a violation in Minnesota.

Conviction Table with Statute, ACD, and State Code
(A Withdrawal Table Follows)

Notes on this Conviction Table

- The Minnesota Conviction Table is presented in the order of the Description field, which appears on the driving record. The MN Code is a native, internal use code, does not appear on the driving record, and is only presented below as a courtesy.
- Certain Descriptions indicate a retired statute. These convictions are shown on this table because they could possibly appear on older driving records.
- **Minnesota does not have a point system**

Conviction Description	Statute	ACD	MN Code
Agg Drive While Undr Influence of Cont. Substance - Pled	Retired	A22	DI7
Agg Driving Under Influence Cont. Substance IC-1	Retired	A22	DJ8
Agg Driving Under Influence Cont. Substance IC-3	Retired	A22	DJ9
Agg Driving While Under Influence IC-1	Retired	A21	DJ5
Agg Driving While Under Influence IC-6	Retired	A21	DJ4
Agg Driving While Under the Influence - Pled	Retired	A21	DI3
Agg Driving While Under the Influence IC-3	Retired	A21	DJ3
Aggravated Drive Undr Influenc of Cont. Substance	Retired	A22	DI8
Aggravated Driving Under the Influence	Retired	A21	DI4
Alcohol Related Driving .04 or More Conviction	169A.20.1(6)	A04	DI9
Allow Alcohol or Cntrl Sub	169A.78		DI0
Allow Another to Use Driver License/MN ID Card	171.22.1(2)	D16	MR7
Allow Careless or Reckless Driving	None		RK0
Allow Change Of Course Violation	None		CC0
Allow Criminal Negligence	None		CN0
Allow Driving After Withdrawal	None		DA0
Allow Equipment Violation	None		EQ0
Allow Expired, Improper or No Driv Lic Possession	None		DL0
Allow Fail In Duties Of Driver At Accident	None		AC0
Allow Fail to Appear	None		FA0
Allow Fail to Obey Peace Officer	None		PO0
Allow Fail to Obey Traffic Control Devices	None		SC0
Allow Fail to Stop for School Bus	169.444.6(a)		SB0
Allow Flee From Peace Office	None		FP0
Allow Headlight Violation	None		HL0
Allow Illegal Operation	169.90.2		IO0
Allow Illegal Or Improper Backing	None		BA0
Allow Illegal or Improper Follow	None		FO0
Allow Illegal Use of Driver License/MN ID Card	171.22.1(2)	D16	MR0
Allow Interference With Control, Vision or Hearing	None		IN0
Allow Juvenile Use DL/MN ID Card Purc Tobacco	171.22.1(1)	D16	JV0
Allow Lane Usage Violation	None		IL0
Allow Leave Scene of Accident	None		HR0
Allow No Driver License, Class or Endors Violation			LC0
Allow No Fault	None		NF0
Allow Open Bottle	169A.35.4		OB0
Allow Passing Violation	None		PA0
Allow Restriction Violation	None		RV0
Allow Right of Way Violation	None		RW0
Allow Speed or Fail to Exercise Due Care	None		SP0
Allow Theft of Motor Vehicle			WP0

Conviction Description	Statute	ACD	MN Code
Allow Traffic Hazard	None		TH0
Allow Unsafe Start	None		ST0
Allow Use DL/MN ID Card - Attempt Purchase Alcohol	340A.503.2(3)	D06	AL0
Allow Use Motor Vehicle in Commission of a Felony	None		FE0
Careless Driving	169.13.2	M81	RK1
Careless Driving (Amended for DWI)	Retired	M81	RK3
Child Restraint Violation	169.685.5	F02	CR1
Criminal Negligence	169.11	U31	CN1
Criminal Vehicular Operation - Bodily Harm	609.21.1a(d)	U06	CV5
Criminal Vehicular Operation - Fatal	609.21.1a(a)	U07	CV2
Criminal Vehicular Operation - Great Bodily Harm	609.21.1a(b)	U06	CV3
Criminal Vehicular Operation - Injury to Unborn Child	Retired	U06	CV6
Criminal Vehicular Operation - Substantial Bodily Harm	609.21.1a(c)	U06	CV4
Crossing Median or Center Lane	169.18.9	M44, M51	SC7
Crowded Driver Seat	169.37		IN1
Defaced or Mutilated DL, IP, or ID			MR2
Drive Motorcycle Without Headlight	169.974.5(i)	F03, E05	HL3
Drive While Undr Influence of Cont. Substance - Pled	169A.20.1	A22	DI5
Drive While Undr the Influence of Cont. Substance	169A.20.1(2)	A22	DI6
Drive With Equipmnt Interfering Vision or Hearing	169.471.1, 169.471.2		IN2
Driver Without Headlights	169.48.1	E55, E05	HL2
Driving After Inimical Cancellation	171.24.5	B20	DA5
Driving After Withdrawal	171.20.2	B20	DA1
Driving After Withdrawal - No Action	171.17.1(b)		DA7
Driving After Withdrawal - Petty	171.20.2(a)	B20	DA6
Driving in Prohibited Area	160.2715(14)	M02	SC6
	169.25, 169.40.2	M12	
	169.41	M56	
Driving on Shoulder	169.18.4(4)	M58	IL5
Driving Under Influence of Cont. Substance IC-1	Retired	A22	DJ6
Driving Under Influence of Cont. Substance ICD	Retired	A22	DJ7
Driving Under the Influence - Pled	169A.20.1	A21	DI1
Driving While Under the Influence	Retired	A21	DI2
Driving While Under the Influence IC-1	Retired	A21	DJ0
Driving While Under the Influence IC-3	Retired	A21	DJ1
Driving While Under the Influence IC-6	Retired	A21	DJ2
DUI - .20 or More IC-9	Retired	A21	DK1
DUI - Child Endangerment	169A.31.2.1		ED1
DUI - Child Endangerment - .20 or More	None	A21	ED2
DUI - Child Endangerment - .20 or More Rec Vehicle	None		ED4
DUI - Child Endangerment - Off Road Vehicle	None		ED3
DUI - Pled .20 or More	169A.54.5	A08, A21	DH1
DUI - Railroad Crossing	Retired	A21	DH3
DUI - Railroad Crossing .20 or More	Retired	A21	DH4
DUI - Railroad Crossing .20 or More Rec Vehicle	Retired		DH6
DUI - Railroad Crossing Off Road Rec Vehicle	Retired		DH5
DUI .20 or More in Off Road Rec Vehicle			XY4
DUI In Off Road Recreational Vehicle			XY3
Equipment Violation		E01	EQ1
Erratic Driving		S97	SP4
Exhibition Driving		S97	SP3
Expired Driver License or Instruction Permit	Retired	B51	DL2
Expired Motorcycle Instruction Permit	169.974.2(b)	B51	LC6
Fail to Allow Passing	169.18.3(2)	N07	PA2
Fail to Appear	169.92	D45	FA1
Fail to Dim Headlights	169.61(c)	E54	HL1
Fail to Display Driver License	171.08	B51	DL5
Fail to Exercise Due Care or Control	169.14.1, 169.21.3(d)	S94, D72	SP6
Fail To Give Insurance Information After Accident	169.09.3(b)	B74	AC5
Fail To Give Required Information At Accident	169.09.3(a)	B74	AC1
Fail To Leave Information At Accident	169.09.4		AC2
Fail to Obey Peace Officer	169.02.2	M08	PO1
Fail to Obey Semaphore	169.06.5(a)(3)(i), 169.06.5(a)(3)(iii)	M16	SC2
	169.06.7	M18	
	169.06.8	M16	
Fail to Obey Sign	169.06.4(a)	M14, M15	SC1

Conviction Description	Statute	ACD	MN Code
	169.06.4(e)	M04	
	169.20.3	N22	
	169.30(b)	M15	
	169.305.1(d)	M17	
Fail to Provide Insurance Info - Conviction	169.791.2, 169.791.3, 169.791.4		NF9
Fail To Report Accident	169.09.6	B61	AC3
Fail To Signal	169.19.5	N40	CC5
Fail to Stop at Pedestrian Crosswalk	169.21.2(a)	N08, N20	RW4
Fail to Stop at Railroad Crossing	169.26	M10, M22	SC3
	169.26.1(c)	M10	
Fail to Stop at School Crossing or Patrol	169.21.2(c)	M13	RW5
Fail to Stop at Sidewalk or Leaving Alley	169.31	M25	RW3
Fail to Stop for School Bus	169.444.1	N09	SB1
Fail to Stop for School Bus - Gross Misdemeanor	169.444.2(b)(1), 169.444.2(b)(2)	M75	SB2
Fail to Stop for School Bus - Petty	169.444.1, 169.444.1a	M75	SB4
Fail to Surrender Withdrawn DL/MN ID Card	None		DA4
Fail to Yield to a Pedestrian	169.202.2	N08	RW2
	169.21.2(b)	N06	
Fail to Yield to Motor Vehicle	169.06.5(a)(1)(i)	N01	RW1
	169.20.1	N25	
	169.20.2	N31	
	169.20.4	N06	
	169.20.5, 169.20.5(a)	N04	
	169.20.5(b), 169.20.5(c)	N04	
	169.20.6	N05	
	169.20.7	N01	
	169.201	N26	
Five False Information On Accident Report	169.09.7	B61	AC4
Flee an Officer - Great Bodily Harm	609.487.4(b)	U01	FP3
Flee Peace Officer	609.487.3	U01	FP1
Flee Peace Officer - Fatal	609.487.4(a)	U01	FP2
Flee Peace Officer - Substantial Bodily Harm	609.487.4(c)	U01	FP4
Follow Emergency Vehicle	169.18.8(c), 169.40.1	M32	FO2
Follow Too Close	169.18.8(a), 169.18.8(b)	M34	FO1
Give False Information to Police Officer	169.791.7, 171.22.1(8)		MR8
IC Test .20 or More in Off Road Vehicle			XY7
IC Test .20 or More in Off Road Vehicle			XY7
IC Test In Off Road Recreational Vehicle			XY6
IC Test Refusal Conviction Off Road Veh			XY5
IC Test Refusal In Off Road Rec Vehicle			XY2
Illegal Change Of Course	169.19.4	N52, N55	CC1
Illegal Operation	169.90.1, 169.90.2	N84	IO1
Illegal Or Improper Backing	169.305.2	N82	BA1
Illegal or Improper Passing	169.18.3(1), 169.18.3(3)	M70	PA1
	169.18.4(1),(2), (3)	M73	
	169.18.5(b)(2), 169.18.11	M70	
Illegal Or Improper Turn	169.19.1(a)	N50	CC2
Illegal or Improper Use of Lane	169.18.1, 169.18.2	M40	IL1
	169.18.7(a)	M41	
	169.18.7(b)	M62	
	169.18.7(c)	M60	
	169.18.7(d)	M47	
	169.18.10	M60	
Illegal Or Improper U-Turn	169.19.2	N56	CC3
Illegal Parking	169.32, 169.34	F34	TH4
	169.36	E51	
Impede Traffic	169.15	S96, F34	TH5
Implied Consent - Refusal	169A.52	A12	IC1, IC7
Implied Consent - Refusal	Appears in history	A12	IC6
Implied Consent - Test		A90	IC3, IC4
Implied Consent - Test .20 or More		A11	IC9
Implied Consent - Test Drugs		A22	ICD
Implied Consent - Test Drugs Off Road Rec Veh			ICE
Implied Consent - Test Refusal Conviction	169A.20.2	A12	ICR
Improper Address on Driver License	171.11	D16	DL4
Improper Lane Change	169.18.7	M42	CC4

Conviction Description	Statute	ACD	MN Code
Improper Signal	169.19.7	N40, N44	CC6
Inattentive Driving	None	M82	IN6
Instruction Permit / Provisional License Violation	171.05	D29	LC4
Invalid Driver License	Retired	B51	LC4
Juvenile Use DL/MN ID Card Attempt Purch Alcohol	340A.503.2(2)	D06	DL3
Juvenile Use DL/MN ID Card Attempt Purch Tobacco	609.685.2(b)	D16	JV1
Leave Scene of Accident - Fatal	169.09.1	B02, B06	JV2
Leave Scene of Accident - No Personal Injury	169.09.2, 169.09.5	B05	HR1
Leave Scene of Accident - Personal Injury	169.09.1	B03, B07	HR3
Littering	169.42		HR2
Make Fraudulent Driver License	171.22.1(7)	D10	EQ3
Minimum Speed	169.14.8	S96	MR4
Motorcycle Equipment Violation	169.974	F03	SP2
Motorcycle Instruction Permit Violation	169.974.2(c)	D29	EQ2
Motorcycle Lane Violation	169.974.5(e)	M48, M40	LC5
	169.974.5(f)		IL4
No Driver License		B51	LC8
No Driver License in Possession	171.08	B78, B51	DL1
No Fault			NF1
No Insurance Conviction	169.797.2, 169.797.3, 169.797.3a	D36	NF6
No Minnesota Driver License	171.03(g)	B51	LC9
No Moped Permit	171.02.3	B91	LC3
No Motorcycle Endorsement	169.974.2(a)	B91	LC1
No Proof of Insurance			NF2
No Proof of Insurance - Court Admin		D36	NF8
No Proof of Insurance Conviction			NF4
No Proof of Insurance Report			NF3
No Proof Report - Police Issue		D36	NF7
No School Bus Endorsement	171.321.1	B91	LC2
Open Bottle	169A.35.2	A26	OB1
	169A.35.3, 169A.35.4	A35, A35	
Open Door Into Traffic	169.315		TH3
Over Center Line		M61	IL2
Pass on Shoulder	169.18.4(4)	M76, M73	PA3
Passenger on Moped	169.223.3		IN5
Perjury, False Affidavit	171.17.1(a)(5)	D78	PR1
Possess Another Driver License/MN ID Card	171.22		MR6
Possess or Display Fictitious/Altered DL, IP, or ID	171.22.1(1), 171.22.1(5)	B41	MR1
Possession or Display of Withdrawn DL/MN ID Card	171.22.1(9)	D16	DA3
Racing	169.13.1(b)	S95	SP8
Railroad Grade Crossing Violation	MS 169.28	M10	SC8
Railroad Xing Viol Fail To Slow Down	383.51	M20	RR0
Railroad Xing Viol Fail to Stop As Required	169.28.1(a), 383.51	M22, M10	RR2
Railroad Xing Viol Fail to Stop B4 Reaching Tracks	383.51	M21	RR1
Railroad Xing Viol Insuff Undercarriage Clearance	383.51	M24	RR4
Railroad Xing Viol Stop on Tracks	383.51	M23	RR3
Reckless Driving	169.13.1	M84	RK2
Restriction Violation	171.09	D29	RV1
Sale, Manufacture, Distribution or Pss of Drugs	152.0262	A33, A50	FE2
School Bus - Headstart Driver Not a Drop	169A.31.1		ED5
School Bus Driver Violation	169.443	E56	SB3
Serious Speed	169.14.2(d)?	S15	SP7
Service Lane Infraction			SC5
Sold / Possessed Controlled Substance	152.021, 152.022, 152.023, 152.024, 152.025, 152.0261, 152.0262, 152.027	A33	FE3
Speed	169.14.2	S01	SP1
	169.14.2(a)	S06	
	169.14.2(a)(1)	S14	
	169.14.2(a)(2)	S15	
	169.14.2(a)(4)	S16	
	169.14.2(a)(5)	S21	
	169.14.2(a)(6)	S26	
	169.14.2(a)(7)	S31	
	169.14.5	S36	
	169.14.5a(b)	S41	
	169.14.5b	S51	

Conviction Description	Statute	ACD	MN Code
	169.14.5c	S71	
	169.14.5d	S81	
	169.14.5d(b)	S91	
	169.14.5d(e)	S92	
	169.14.5e, 169.16(a)	S93	
Speed - Over 100 MPH	169.14.1a	S15	SP9
Stop on Highway or Freeway	169.32	F34	TH2
Take Any Part of Driver License Exam For Another	171.22.1(6)	D02, D16	MR9
Texting While Operating a Motor Vehicle	169.475.2		DL6
Theft of Gas	171.175.1		TG1
Theft of Gas	609.52.2(17)		WP1
Too Many Passengers on Motorcycle	169.974.5(a)	F06	IN4
Traffic Hazard		F34	TH1
Uncoded, Not Counted Toward Any Department Action	169.7995.2		UC3
Uncoded, Petty Misdemeanor, Moving Violation			UC1, UC2
Uncoded, Review by DEV Required	609.20, 609.205		UC4
Under 21 Drinking and Driving	169A.33.2	A60	JA1
Unreasonable Acceleration		S97	SP5
Unsafe Start	169.19.3	N83	ST1
Use DL In Attempt to Purchase Alcohol	171.171(1)	D06	MI1
Use DL/MN ID Card - Attempt Purchase Alcohol	171.171.1	D06	AL1
Use Fictitious Name to Police/Application	171.22.1(4)	D02	MR3
Use Motor Vehicle to Patronize Prostitution	609.324.5	U04	XY1
Use of Motor Vehicle in Commission of a Felony	609.19.1(2)	U03	FE1
Use or Display Anothers Driver License/MN ID Card	171.22.1(3)	D16	MR5
Violation of Controlled Access	169.305.1(a), 169.305.1(b)	M50	SC4
Violation of Limited License	171.30.4	D27	DA2
Violation of Out-of-Service Order	221.605.1	B27, B19	VO1
Vision Obstructed	169.37	D70	IN3
Wrong Class License	171.02.1(a)	B91	LC7
Wrong Way	169.18.6(a)	N63	IL3
	169.18.6(b)	N61	

Minnesota Conviction Table with Statute and ACD

Withdrawal Description	Withdrawal Length	ACD	Internal Code
Amended Limited Commercial License			598
Amended Limited Issued Until		W00	401
Canc		W00	399
Canc - Dishonored Check		W00	321
Canc - Fail To Appear Dev Interview		W00	308
Canc - Fail To Appear For Apa		W00	306
Canc - Fail To Comp Apa		W00	305
Canc - Fail To Comp Driver Clinic		W00	301
Canc - Fail To Comp Driver Exam		W20	314
Canc - Fail To Comp Driver Training		W00	322
Canc - Fail To Comp Dwi Clinic		W00	302
Canc - Fail To Comp Req Of Apa		W00	307
Canc - Fail To Comp Req Of Spec Rev		W00	304
Canc - Fail To Comp Spec Rev		W00	303
Canc - Fail To Compl Department Req		W20	325
Canc - Fail To Pay Rein Fee		W00	316, 331, 335
Canc - Fail To Pay Rein Fee ($30)		W00	315
Canc - Fail To Provide Resident Doc		W00	333
Canc - Fail To Submit Birth Cert		W00	327
Canc - Fail To Submit Immigrat Card		W00	328
Canc - Fail To Submit Med Statement		B65	326
Canc - Fail To Submit Physical Exam		B65	311
Canc - Fail To Submit Reinstatement		W00	329
Canc - Fail To Submit Vision Exam		B65	309
Canc - Fail To Surr Dl-Dept Request		W00	332
Canc - Fail To Surrender Os Dl		W00	330
Canc - Inimical To Pub Sfty		W00	323
Canc - Insufficient Vision		W14	310
Canc - Insurance Denied		D36	300
Canc - Not Entitled To Issuance		W20	313

Withdrawal Description	Withdrawal Length	ACD	Internal Code
Canc - Not Physically Qualified		W14	312
Canc - Ordered By Court		W00	320
Canc - Ordered By Juvenile Court		W00	319
Canc - Parental Consent Withdrawn		W13	317
Canc - Voluntary Surrender Of Dl		W00	318
Canc & Deny - Inimical To Pub Sfty		W01	324
Canc & Deny - Inimical To Pub Sfty		W00	334
Canc- Fail To Surr Hazmat Endrsmt		W09	336
Class A Limited Until			403
Class B Limited Until			404
Comm Status/Fail To Pay Income Tax			141
Disq - 2 Alcohol Related Driving .04 Or +	Lifetime CDL disqual	W40	512
Disq - 2 Rr Xing Violations In 3 Yrs		W60	539
Disq - 2nd Alcohol Content .04 Or +		W40	515
Disq - 2nd Conv Leave Scene Of Accident		W40	503
Disq - 2nd Driving Under Influence	Lifetime CDL disqual	W40	509
Disq - 2nd Refuse To Test		A12	518
Disq - 2nd Sb/Headstart Driver Not A Drop		W00	525
Disq - 2nd Serious Violation In 3 Years		W30	500
Disq - 2nd Use Motor Vehicle In Felony		W40	506
Disq - 2nd Violate Out-Of-Service Order	2 year CDL disqual	W50	562
Disq - 3 Or More Rr Xing Viol In 3yrs		W61	540
Disq - 3rd Serious Violation In 3 Years		W31	501
Disq - 3rd Violate Out-Of-Service Order	3 year CDL disqual	W52	564
Disq - 3rd Violate Out-Of-Service Order W/Pass And/Or Hazmat			565
Disq - Additional Major Offense After Reinstatement		W41	549
Disq - Alcohol Content .04 Or +		A04	514
Disq - Alcohol Content .04 Or + (Hazmat)		A04	516
Disq - Alcohol Related .04 Or + (Hazmat)	3 year CDL disqual	A04	513
Disq - Alcohol Related Driving .04 Or +	1 year CDL disqual	A04	511
Disq - Canc - Fail To Complete CDL Rd Test		W00	560
Disq - Child Endangerment .04 Thru .20		A21	526
Disq - Child Endangerment .20 Or More		A21	527
Disq - Combination Of Major Offenses	Lifetime CDL disqual	W40	520
Disq - Crim Veh Op - Bodily Harm		U06	531
Disq - Crim Veh Op -Bodily Harm Haz Mat		U06	536
Disq - Crim Veh Op-Great Harm		U06	529
Disq - Crim Veh Op-Great Harm Haz Mat		U06	534
Disq - CVO - Fatal		U07	528
Disq - CVO - Fatal (Haz Mat)		U07	533
Disq - CVO Injury To Unborn Child		U06	532
Disq - CVO Injury To Unborn Child Haz Mat		U06	537
Disq - CVO-Substantial Bodily Harm		U06	530
Disq - CVO-Substantial Bodily Harm Haz Mat		U06	535
Disq - Drive Under The Influence (Hazmat)	3 year CDL disqual	A21	510
Disq - Driving After Withdrawal		B20	546
Disq - Driving After Withdrawal (Haz Mat)		B20	547
Disq - Driving Under Influence	1 year CDL disqual	A21	508
Disq - Fail To Obey Traffic Cntrl Or Enforcement At Rr Xing	60 day CDL disqual	M10	543
Disq - Fail To Slow At Rr Xing	60 day CDL disqual	M20	541
Disq - Fail To Stop As Required At Rr Xing		M22	538
Disq - Fail To Stop When Trks Not Clear At Rr Xing	60 day CDL disqual	M21	542
Disq - Imminent Hazard	From 30 days to 1 year CDL disqual	W70	548
Disq - Implied Consent Test-Drugs		W00	523
Disq - Insufficient Undercarriage Clearance At Rr Xing	60 day CDL disqual	M24	545
Disq - Leave Scene Of Accident		B05	502
Disq - Leave Scene Of Accident (Hazmat)		B05	504
Disq - Refuse To Test		A12	517
Disq - Refuse To Test (Hazmat)		A12	519
Disq - Sale, Manuf, Distrib, Poss - Drugs	Lifetime CDL disqual	A50	521
Disq - Sb/Headstart Driver Not A Drop		W00	524
Disq - Use Motor Vehicle In Felony		U03	505
Disq - Use Of Mv In Felony (Hazmat)		U03	507
Disq - Violate Out-Of-Service Order		B27	522
Disq - Xing Without Enough Space At Rr Xing	60 day CDL disqual	M23	544
Disq- 2nd Violate Out-Of-Service Order W/Pass And/Or Hazmat	3 year CDL disqual	W51	563

Withdrawal Description	Withdrawal Length	ACD	Internal Code
Disq- Violate Out-Of-Service Order W/Pass And/Or Hazmat	2 year CDL disqual	B19	561
Limited Commercial License			599
Limited Issued By Juvenile Court		W00	402
Limited Until		W00	400
Rev		W00	199
Rev - 2 Under Influence In 10 Yr		W01	156
Rev - 2 Under The Influence In 5 Yr		W01	113
Rev - 3 Misd / 5 Vios. In 12 Mos.		W01	131
Rev - 3 Misd/6 Or More Vios. 24 Mos		W01	132
Rev - 3 Or More Misdemeanors 12 Mos	1st (3 tickets): 30 days 2nd (4 tickets): 90 days 3rd (5 tickers): 365 days	W01	100
Rev - 3 Under Influence In 10 Yr		W01	157
Rev - 3 Under The Influence In 5 Yr		W01	114
Rev - 3 Under The Influence On Recd		W01	115
Rev - 4 Misd/6 Or More Vios. 24 Mos		W01	133
Rev - 4 Under Influence In 10 Yr		W01	158
Rev - 4 Under The Influence In 5 Yr		W01	116
Rev - 4 Under The Influence On Recd		W01	117
Rev - 5 Under The Influence On Recd		W01	118
Rev - 6 Under The Influence On Recd		W01	119
Rev - Alcohol Content .10 Or More		A90	110, 122, 153, 160
Rev - Alcohol Content .20 Or More		A11	147, 163
Rev - Allow Control Substance		W00	120, 159
Rev - Attempt To Purchase Alcohol		D06	125
Rev - Crim Veh Op - Bodily Harm		U06	145
Rev - Criminal Veh Op - Fatal		U07	106
Rev - Criminal Veh Op In CMV - Fatal	1st: 1 year CDL disqual 1st with hazmat: 3 year disqual 2nd: lifetime disqual	U10	129
Rev - CVO Crim-Veh-Op-Bodily-Harm		U06	172
Rev - CVO Injury To Unborn Child		U06	173, 146
Rev - CVO-Crim-Veh-Op - Fatal		U07	169
Rev - CVO-Great-Bodily Harm		U06	170
Rev - CVO-Substantial Bodily Harm		U06	144, 171
Rev - Driving Under Influence		A21	112, 124, 155, 162
Rev - DUI- .20 Or More		A21	148, 164
Rev - DUI- Child Endang .20 Or More		A21	150, 166
Rev - DUI- Child Endangerment		A21	149, 165
Rev - Fail To Provide Ins Info Conv	1st in 5 yrs: 30 days 2nd in 5 yrs: 90 days 3rd in 5 yrs: 180 days 4th in 5 yrs: 365 days	B63	139
Rev - Fail To Stop For Sch Bus G.M.		M75	136
Rev - Fail To Stop For School Bus		M75	135
Rev - Flee Officer - Great Harm		U01	142
Rev - Flee Officer-Substantial Harm		U01	143
Rev - Flee Peace Officer		U01	126
Rev - Flee Peace Officer - Fatal		U01	130
Rev - Flee Peace Officer-Felony	OK	U01	109
Rev - Implied Consent		W00	198
Rev - Implied Consent Test - Drugs		A22	151, 167
Rev - Implied Consent Test Drugs Orrv		A22	168
Rev - Juvenile Attempt Purch Alcohl	365 days or until age 18, whichever is greater	D06	127
Rev - Leave Acc - Personal Injury	180 days	B07	102
Rev - Leave Scene Accident - Fatal	1 year	B06	103
Rev - No Fault Conviction	1st in 5 yrs: 30 days 2nd in 5 yrs: 90 days 3rd in 5 yrs: 180 days 4th in 5 yrs: 365 days	D36	101
Rev - No Fault Conviction		D36	105
Rev - No Proof Ins - Court Admin		D35	138
Rev - No Proof Of Insurance	1st in 5 yrs: 30 days 2nd in 5 yrs: 90 days 3rd in 5 yrs: 180 days	D36	128

Withdrawal Description	Withdrawal Length 4th in 5 yrs: 365 days	ACD	Internal Code
Rev - No Proof Rpt Police Iss Deny		D35	137
Rev - Perjury, False Affidavit	180 days	W00	107
Rev - Refuse To Test		A12	111, 123, 154, 161
Rev - Rev-Crim Veh Op-Great Harm		U06	121
Rev - School Bus Driver Violation		W00	134
Rev - Sold/Possessed Controlled Sub		A33	140
Rev - Speed Over 100 Mph	365 days	S15	174
Rev - Theft Of Motor Vehicle		W00	104
Rev - Use Motor Vehicle In Felony	1 year	U03	108
Rev Implied Consent Test Drugs Orrv		A22	152
Susp		W00	299
Susp - 2 Misdemeanors In 12 Months	30 days (if DEV WL sent)	W01	204
Susp - 2nd Conv - Ip Conditions		D29	222
Susp - 2nd Conv - Mc Equipment Vio		E01	217
Susp - 2nd Conv - No Moped Permit		B51	219
Susp - 2nd Conv - No Motorcycle End		B91	221
Susp - 2nd Conv - No School Bus End		B91	218
Susp - 2nd Conv - Wrong Class Dl		B91	220
Susp - 2nd Conviction - No Dl		B51	216
Susp - 2nd Driving After Withdrawal	90 days	B20	201
Susp - 3rd Driving After Withdrawal	180 days	B20	202
Susp - 4 Violations In 12 Months	30 days (if DEV WL sent)	W01	245
Susp - 4th Driving After Withdrawal	365 days	B20	256
Susp - 5 Violations In 12 Months	90 days	W01	255
Susp - 5 Violations In 24 Months	30 days	W01	205
Susp - 6 Violations In 24 Months	90 days	W01	206
Susp - After Preliminary Hearing		W01	241
Susp - Alcohol Content .08 Or More		A98	243
Susp - Allow Another To Use Dl		W00	224
Susp - Allow Attempt Purch Alcohol		W00	252
Susp - Allowed Another To Take Exam		D02	239
Susp - Alw Juvenile Purch Tobacco		W00	266
Susp - Attempt Purch Alcohol Juv Ct	90 days	D06	253
Susp - Attempt To Purchase Alcohol		D06	228
Susp - Conviction - Fatal Accident	180 days	U31	236
Susp - Conviction Personal Inj Acc	90 days	W00	257
Susp - Criminal Complaint 171.18(1)		W00	254
Susp - Criminal Neg Indictment		W00	229
Susp - Days Or Dic Comp		W00	248
Susp - Days Or Dic-A Comp		W00	249
Susp - Default In Agreement On Judg		D37	235
Susp - Denial Of Ins Coverage Acc		D35	270
Susp - Denial Of Ins Coverage Rs			272
Susp - Dishonored Check		W00	273
Susp - Driving After Withdrawal	30 days	B20	200
Susp - Fail Dhs Subpoena/Child Sup		D51	264
Susp - Fail Rpt Loss Of Consciousns		W14	262
Susp - Fail To Appear Or Pay Fines		D56	226
Susp - Fail To Attend Hearing		W01	232
Susp - Fail To Complete Apa		W00	230
Susp - Fail To Complete Apa Req		W00	231
Susp - Fail To Provide Ins Info Rs			271
Susp - Fail To Provide Ins On Acc		D35	269
Susp - Fail To Stop For School Bus		M75	259, 261
Susp - Fail To Surr Withdrawn Dl		W00	242
Susp - Fail-DHS Agrmt/Child Sup		D51	265
Susp - Failure To Pay Child Support		D51	263
Susp - Flee Peace Office-Gross Misd		U01	250
Susp - Fraudulent Dl Application		D02	240
Susp - Insurance Denied		D36	233
Susp - Juvenile Purchased Tobacco		W00	267
Susp - Lawsuit		D37	247
Susp - Misuse Of Driver License	DEV interview	B41/ D02	258
Susp - More Than 6 Vios In 24 Mos	1st: 180 days	W01	207

Withdrawal Description	Withdrawal Length	ACD	Internal Code
	2nd: 365 days		
Susp - No Fault - Accident		D35	209
Susp - No Fault Conviction		D36	237
Susp - No Proof Of Insurance		D36	251
Susp - Ordered By Court		W00	213, 214, 215
Susp - Ordered By Juvenile Court		W00	210, 211, 212
Susp - Out Of State Accident		W00	246
Susp - Refuse To Test		A12	244
Susp - Theft Of Gas	30 days	W00	274
Susp - Took Exam For Another		D02	238
Susp - Under 21 Drinking & Driving		A60	260
Susp - Under 21 Drinking & Driving	1st: 30 days	A60	268
	2nd: 180 days		
Susp - Unpaid Fine(S)		D53	227
Susp - Unsatisfied Judgment		D39	234
Susp - Use Fictitious Dl		B41	223
Susp - Violation During Withdrawal		B20	203
Susp - Violation Of Agreement		W00	208
Susp - Violation Of Limited License	1st in 5 yrs: 30 days	D27	225
	2nd in 5 yrs: 90 days		
	3rd in 5 yrs: 180 days		
	4th in 5 yrs: 365 days		

Minnesota Index of Statutes for Traffic Regulations

Note: This table shows the MN statute regulating the indicated topic. Statutes may be found at https://www.revisor.mn.gov/. Another resource in Minnesota is the Administrative Rules. This index presents category breakdowns by topic. For example, Chapter 7503 is Driver's License Revocation, Incidents. The rules may be found at https://www.revisor.mn.gov/rules/?view=list.

Mississippi

Administration	Important Telephone and Web Contacts
<u>Major Chris Gillard</u> Director of Driver Services Driver Services Bureau PO Box 958, Jackson 39205 Barbara Ford, Director Motor Vehicle Licensing Division PO Box 1140, Jackson 39215 601-923-7131 www.dps.state.ms.us (driver) www.dor.ms.gov/mvl/main.html (vehicle)	Driver Licensing ....601-987-1281/1283 Financial Responsibility/SR-22 ....601-987-1230 Reinstatements...601-987-1224 MVR ....601-987-1275 Commercial Driver License ....601-987-1334 Vehicle Registration..601-923-7100 Vehicle Title ....601-923-7200 Highway Patrol ....601-987-1212 State Department of Insurance ....601-359-3569 Use the web page for Driver License questions. For Vehicle questions, use the email submission form at www.dor.ms.gov/perl/ContactUs_new.pl

Motor Vehicle and Traffic Regulations - Title 63: www.mscode.com/free/statutes/63/index.htm

Motor Vehicles and Titles Regulations - Title 35: www.dor.ms.gov/info/rules/main.html

Driver's License Format, Issuance and Renewal

License Classes, Restrictions and Endorsements Appear After the Driving Record Content Section

License Format

The license number is a randomly generated nine-digit number in the same format as a Social Security Number with the first three digits assigned as 800 (i.e. 800-11-1111). Until several years ago the Social Security Number was used as the DL unless the license holder specifically requested an assigned number. Now DPS issues an assigned number to all new license holders and renewals.

Document Appearance

The current format for driver's license and ID cards has been issued since in November 2002. Since some older cards may remain in force if used by military personnel both old and new are described below.

Current Format

Security Characteristics: These digital documents are highly durable plastic with a laminate security coating. The coating contains a hologram of the state seal and the letters DPS. There is a "ghost" photo image in the lower right corner. A 2D bar code is on the back of the card containing the bearer's demographic data and medical codes if pertinent. State outline in green indicates regular operator; blue indicates an ID card; if red then CDL.

Position of Photo: Left edge, smaller ghost image in lower right corner.

Minor Age Driver: The DL and ID documents are in a vertical format. "Under 21 Until---" appears in red under photo, "Under 18 Until---" appears in yellow under photo.

CDL Indicator: Red indicates CDL. "COMMERCIAL LICENSE" in red box appears above personal information.

Old Format

Security Characteristics: The **old** documents are laminated with digital image photo. The Commissioner's signature is shown.

Position of Photo: Left.

Minor Age Driver: A vertical document with "Under 21 Until---".

CDL Indicator: "COMMERCIAL DRIVER LICENSE" is at top of document in state heading.

Issuance

Location of Requirements for Proof of Identity:
www.dps.state.ms.us/driver-services/new-drivers-license/

Age Requirements

The minimum age for a Class R is sixteen years of age and applicant must have held a Learner's Permit for a minimum of one year. Twenty-one is the minimum age for Class A, B, and C Commercial, except for persons aged eighteen authorized to operate a vehicle transporting sixteen or more passengers within the state. For an Intermediate License, the age is sixteen years and has 6AM-10PM restrictions. For a Learner's Permit the age is fifteen years; age fourteen can drive but only when in driver education car.

Residency

A non-resident must secure Mississippi license after sixty days, unless a tourist, out-of-state student, or a military person.

Renewal

On birthday every eight years. Sixteen and seventeen year-olds are good for one year or until their birth date. The driver is assigned the 9-digit license number at renewal, if the previous license was using the driver's SSN. Driver keeps same number when renewing.

Online renewal is available but only to holders of a Class R license and up to one year after the expiration date. One can renew the license online every other time when the card is up for renewal. To renew online, driver must live at the address that is printed on current license that is expiring. Renewal is available at self-service kiosks in at least 30 counties as well. Out-of-state military personnel can renew by mail as long as a letter with a copy of current military ID is submitted.

Elderly-Related Restrictions

None, unless state personnel at the renewal station detect a reason the person is unfit to drive.

Vehicle Insurance, Title and Registration Facts

Registration & Renewal

Motor vehicle with a Gross Vehicle Weight (GVW) of 10,000 lbs or less must be registered receive tags from the local county tax collector's office where the vehicle is garaged or domiciled. For motor vehicles with a GVW of over 10,000 lbs and which travels in Mississippi only, register in the local county tax collector's office and receive their tags from the State Office. For motor vehicles with a GVW of over 10,000 lbs and which travels across state boundaries, vehicle must register at the State Office in Clinton, Mississippi.

Online renewal is offered for the following counties through www.ms1stop.com: Alcorn, Attala, Desoto, Hancock, Harrison, Jackson, Lafayette, Lee, Madison, Pearl River, Rankin, and Warren. Also, renewal for Hinds County is found at www.co.hinds.ms.us/pgs/apps/tags/tag_renewal_query.asp, for Lauderdale County at www.lauderdalecounty.org.

New Residents

New residents must register vehicles within thirty days.

Inspections and Emissions Testing

Mississippi has a required annual safety inspection for vehicles. There is no statewide provision for emission testing.

Passenger Plate Facts

There is one plate with two decals (MO) (YR). The county name of issuance is indicated at the bottom of the plate.

The tag is issued to both the vehicle and the owner. If one or the other changes, the tag must be removed and surrendered to the issuing authority.

Insurance and Financial Responsibility

Mississippi has compulsory insurance laws, but not no-fault insurance laws. Financial security minimum limits are $10,000/20,000/5,000. SR-22 may be required. Proof is required after a reportable accident and certain violations. Proof is not required when vehicle registrations are renewed.

Withdrawal Sanctions, and Alcohol and Drug Testing

Alcohol and Chemical Testing

Mississippi's illegal intoxication level is .08 percent and above, for drivers of CMVs the level is .04 percent and above, for drivers under 21 years old the level is .02 percent. Urine, blood, and breath testing are authorized. Mississippi has an implied-consent violation, as well as the provision for an administrative suspension.

Suspensions and Revocations

The state is in compliance with the federally mandated disqualifications on CDLs per MCSIA. See the Appendix for details. Below are listed suspensions associated with driving under the influence.

Driving Under the Influence

First Conviction .... One-year suspension.
(Ninety-days, if driver completes MASEP; not less than thirty days with hardship order.)
Second Conviction in Five Years .... Two-year suspension.
(This can be reduced to one year with completion of alcohol and/or drug abuse treatment.)
Third or Subsequent Conviction in Five Years.. Five-year suspension.
(This can be reduced to three years with completion of alcohol and/or drug abuse treatment.)

DUI Conviction with Refusal to Submit to a Chemical Test

First Refusal .... Ninety-day administrative suspension.
(In addition to any other suspensions upon conviction of DUI.)
Second or Subsequent Refusal .... One-year suspension.
(In addition to any other suspensions upon conviction of DUI.)

Driving While License Suspended for DUI...Six months added to original suspension.

Reinstatement Requirements

Suspension $25.00 fee; time lapse of thirty days to five years; SR-22 filing required for three years from date of DUI and three years from date of accident, if driver was uninsured on accident date and could be held liable for property damages or injuries.

Revocation $100.00 reinstatement fee on DUIs or Drug-Related Convictions

Record Access: Laws, Rules, and Forms

Note: This Section Applies to Both Driver and Vehicle Records.

Governing Statutes and Rules

Motor Vehicle and Traffic Regulations - Title 63:
www.mscode.com/free/statutes/63/index.htm
Title 35, Part VII Motor Vehicles and Title Regulations:
www.dor.ms.gov/info/rules/main.html
Per Statute §25-61-5, the state adopted the provisions of DPPA, except for exceptions 11 and 12. In accordance with DPPA, the Mississippi State Tax Commission promulgated Revenue Rule #3 to protect information contained on motor vehicle records. All employees, agents or contractors of the State Tax Commission must adhere to this policy and not knowingly disclose or make available any information based on a motor vehicle record, except where otherwise permitted in the rule.

35.VII.01.01 Mississippi Administrative Code Part VII, Subpart 1, Chapter 1 provides Motor Vehicle Records Disclosure. This document and the Amended Public Record Resolution govern the price and many of the access and storage procedures of the records in the custody of the Mississippi State Tax Commission.

Request and Consent Forms

Driving Records: If the requester is not pre-approved, a signed, notarized state form signed by the subject is required. Two request forms are available from the web at the Driver's License Info menu: *Consent to Release Records DPPA-2* is used by individuals to request a certified copy of his/her own record. The *Driver Record Request DDPA-3* is used by employers, courts, etc. to request a certified copy of a person's driving record. (Must have DDPA-2 attached.).

Both forms are found at www.dps.state.ms.us/driver-services/new-drivers-license/applications-forms/.

Vehicle Records: Use of the *MVLB* form found on the web at www.dor.ms.gov/title/forms/77969ALLN1.pdf is recommended. Note this Web form has not been revised since July 2006, and therefore it does not reflect the current prices for vehicle related records. Signature (not notarized) of the requester is required. Ongoing, high volume users sign agreements instead. The form still shows the MLVB as being part of the Tax Commission, but it is the form to use.

Vendor and Third Party Access Policy

Vendors obtaining driving records online are prohibited from creating a

database. Otherwise, Mississippi does not provide any restrictions upon the use, storage, or resale of vehicle-related records after a completed transaction, provided the user complies with usage guidelines. There are no restrictions upon resale of records after a completed transaction, providing the end-user is within the boundaries of the listed permissible uses.

Non-permissible Use Requests

Without consent, records are not available, including records without personal information. Casual requesters must provide notarized consent of subject before any data is released.

Access to Driver-Related Records

Driving Records

General Information and Fees

Driver Records Branch, PO Box 958, Jackson MS 39205, 601-987-1275.

The driver record fee is $11.00 per record, electronic access for high volume requesters is $14.00 per record. There is a $6.00 fee for a copy of a driver license application; a copy of a suspension/reinstatement letter is $5.00. The last fee increase went into effect October 13, 2004. Email questions to acline@mdps.state.ms.us.

In-Person – The only location that processes record requests on other drivers is the Department of Public Safety Headquarters at 1900 East Woodrow Wilson, Jackson 39216. Requests are processed in five-to-ten minutes and up to ten may be requested at one time.

Mail – Per compliance with DPPA as described above, mail-in requests are processed in approximately two days. The driver's full name, license number, and/or DOB are needed. The fee must accompany each request. Cash, certified check, or money order is accepted, but enclose a pre-addressed, stamped envelope. The agency charges a full fee for "no record found" reports on walk-in and mail-in requests.

Electronic – In 2012, the processing of electronic driving record requests was taken over by Mississippi Interactive (MSI), an affiliate of NIC. This was in concert with the new state portal for Mississippi. The fee is $14.00 per record. All requesters are required to be initially approved by the DPS and must sign a subscription agreement with MS.gov. There is an annual $95 subscription fee for new accounts. Billing is monthly.

At present there are no details about this service on the web page, but details will be added. Interested new subscribers should contact the MSI at 877-290-9487.

Bulk – Mississippi no longer offers bulk purchase of records.

By Person of Record – Drivers may view their own record at https://www.ms.gov/hp/drivers/license/motorVehicleReportBegin.do. The MVR shows the current status of the license and the moving

violations on record. A non-certified copy of the record can be printed from the screen. The fee is $11.00 and a $2.14 convenience fee is added for using a credit or debit card. Private individuals wishing to obtain a certified copy of their own driving record must bring a notarized copy of the completed *Consent to Release Records Form (DPPA-2)* to the nearest driver license location.

Notification/Monitoring Program

Mississippi does not offer a monitoring system or notification program to employers or insurance companies to track incidents of drivers.

Accident Reports

Reporting – Accident reports should be filed with the nearest law enforcement agency when damage is in excess of $500.00. For accidents involving death, personal injury, or damage in excess of $1,000.00, an individual accident report must be filed with the Highway Patrol, Safety Responsibility Branch, PO Box 958, Jackson 39205, 601-987-1256. There are no special state reporting requirements for commercial driver.

Record Access – Accident reports require authorization for release. Records may only be obtained through written request by a person involved in the accident or the legal counsel, or a representative of the insurer. Requests should be sent to Highway Patrol: Safety Responsibility, Accident Records, PO Box 958, Jackson 39205 601-987-1255 or 967-1254. Records are available for three year to present, but some older records are kept. The fee is $15.00 per copy. No personal checks accepted. Turnaround time is 5 working days. Only the name is needed to search recent records. All requests must be in writing, in-person requests are mailed back if more than two records sought. Mail requests must include a SASE with $.65 postage.

Persons legally eligible to obtain a copy of the report can do so online by visiting www.reportbeam.com. Select "Purchase a Report" under the "Public Access" tab. The fee is $20.00.

Access to Vehicle-Related Records

Editor's Note:

The Department of Revenue has two separate bureaus — the Title Bureau and the Motor Vehicle Licensing Bureau (MVLB) — which are respectively responsible for the titling and the registration of motor vehicles. Both Bureaus are physically located at 1577 Springridge Rd, Raymond MS 39154, but use different mailing addresses. Be sure to address mail requests accordingly.

General Information

Motor Vehicle Licensing Bureau, PO Box 1140, Jackson, MS 39215, 601-923-7100. www.dor.ms.gov/mvl/main.html

Title Bureau, PO Box 1033, Jackson MS 39215, 601-923-7200. www.dor.ms.gov/title/main.html.

Records are available from July 1, 1969. Record information can also be obtained at the county level. Boat trailers may be voluntarily titled if less

than 5000 pounds Gross Vehicle Weight (GVW.) If the trailer is over 5000 pounds GVW, then it is required to be titled.

Mail and In-Person –

Licensing and Registration: The MVLB provides a print of the registration information screen for $3.00, if certified then $8.00. Recent records have a turnaround time of 2 days. Note that records over 4 or 5 years old must be searched in a different history file and will take up to 14 working days to process.

Title Bureau: Data (i.e., title history, lien data) is available by written request only. The fees are follows: $5.00 for a screen print showing title and lien holder information; $8.00 for a title verification letter; $8.00 for a certified letter of no title; and $8.00 for a title history for each time the vehicle has been issued a title. A title history will include the front and back of each title, title application, replacement title application if applicable, and any other included documentation such as power of attorney. Records are available on microfiche from July 1, 1969 to present; images are available from June 2005 forward.

Fax – Fax requests are accepted from approved, ongoing accounts, see above for fees. Fax for Registration is 601-923-7134. Fax for Titles is 601-923-7224.

Electronic – Online access to vehicle title information is available for approved, DPPA-compliant users. Subscribers must pay an annual $100 registration fee; record fees are the same as described above. The log-in

is at www.dor.ms.gov/inquiry.html?dept=MVL. Contact the Title Bureau for details. An online search of registration is not offered.

Bulk – To obtain bulk orders of VIN and registration information, a written request must be submitted to: Barbara J. Ford, MVLB, PO Box 1140, Jackson 39215. There are some standardized media files available, but Mississippi also has the capacity to customize a request (geographical area, type of vehicle, etc.) with an additional programming fee. The state will research the request and will respond with costs and availability of the data requested.

Access to Vessel-Related Records

General Information, Access and Fees

Wildlife, Fisheries and Parks Department, PO Box 451, Jackson MS 39205, 601-432-2186

www.mdwfp.com/license/boating-registration.aspx.

All motorized boats and all sailboats must be registered. Since 07/98, boats are titled at the option of the owner. The department will do a

record search with a boat number or name at no fee; however, they will screen calls to insure that the purpose of the request complies with DPPA. Liens are shown on this database. One may do a search at the registration renewal site at https://www.ms.gov/gf/boating/index.jsp. There is no name searching, use the "MI" number or Hull number.

Driving Record Content and Reciprocity

What's On or Not On the Driving Record

- Accidents and non-moving violations do not appear on driving records.
- The driver's address is provided for permissible uses or if consent is provided by the subject.
- The state permits driver school attendance in lieu of conviction at the option of the court only for a person under twenty-one years of age.

The length of time non-CDL convictions are listed on public record is three years, but indefinite for unpaid traffic conviction and reinstatement fees.

Data Retention

CDL driver records are purged based on the timetable per the MCSIA (see the Appendix). Surrendered licenses are not purged; however, the surrendered status is shown on the record. Such a record can be

obtained by manual search only—up to five years from the license expiration date.

Court to Repository

An "e-citations" program is in affect that enables to be entered online by the courts. All or nearly all courts now report online. Courts not online must report within forty-five days of the conviction via paper abstracts

State Reciprocity for Non-CDL Drivers

- Will suspend license of driver for unpaid out-of-state convictions.
- Record of new incoming driver is not shown on MVR.
- Out-of-state convictions are shown on MVR.
- Out-of-state accidents are shown on MVR.
- Convictions of out-of-state drivers are sent to home state.
- Record is forwarded to new state upon surrender of license only upon Request.

Codes for License Classes, Restrictions, and Endorsements

License Classes– Commercial

Class A	Any Combination of vehicles with a gross vehicle weight rating of 26,001 pounds or more, or towing a vehicle with a GVWR of 10,001 pounds or more.
Class B	Single vehicle 26,001 pounds or more GVWR.
Class C	Vehicle less than 26,001 pounds GVWR with placard for hazardous materials or designed to transport sixteen or more people including driver.
Class D	All other vehicles or combination of vehicles which are not included in Class A, Class B or Class C and for which a Commercial License is required to be issued as provided by Section 63-1-43.

License Classes– Non-Commercial

Class R	Regular operator license.
Class LP	Learner's permit
Class Y	Intermediate license

Restrictions

1	Corrective Lenses		A	Daylight Driving
2	Restricted for Use Between Hours of 6 am and 10 pm.		B	Custom Equipment
3	Outside Rear-View Mirror		C	Forty-five mph
4	Except Class A Bus		D	Re-examination Before Renewal
5	Automatic Transmission		F	CDL Intrastate Only
6	Except Class A & B Bus		G	Prosthetic Aid
7	Bioptic Lens		K	CDL Vehicle Without Air-Brakes
8	Motorcycle Only		M	Insulin Dependent - Shots
9	Company-Owned Vehicle		N	Insulin Dependent - Pills

S	School Bus Related Functions Only	
T	Interlock Device	

U	Must be Accompanied by Farm Service Waiver Card

Endorsements

E	Motorcycle	P	Passenger Vehicle
H	Hazardous Materials	S	School Bus
K	Air Brakes	T	Double-/Triple-Trailers
N	Tank Vehicle	X	Tank Vehicle With Hazardous Endorsement

Table 1: Convictions with Description, ACD, and Severity

(A Traffic Regulations and Rules Table Follows)

The Conviction Table displays both convictions and withdrawals. Mississippi uses the ACD Codes and ACD abbreviations for their conviction table. Mississippi does not add codes on a regular basis unless directed by AAMVA. The master table has not been updated since 2006 and thus is not in concert with recently revised ACD Codes.

Please note the following about this table—

- The **column labeled "SEV"** is a subcode and relates to the severity of the violation. The subcode will distinguish the amount of fine and length of suspension or revocation (if any). The SEV does not indicate points: **Mississippi does not have a point system.**
- The **column labeled "COM"** relates to commercial licensed drivers as follows—
    C indicates a **CDL offense**
    H indicates a **CDL offense with a hazardous materials endorsement**

Violation Description	ACD	SEV	COM
.04% Or Greater BAC - CMV	A94		C
.04% Or Greater BAC - Haz	A94		H
.08% Or Greater BAC	A98		
.10% Or Greater BAC	A90		
2 Out Of Serv Viol – CMV	W50		
2 Out Of Serv Viol – Haz	W51		
3 or More Out Of Serv Viol	W52		
3 Or More Serious CMV Viol	W31		
Breath Test Refusal	A12		
Breath Test Refusal - CMV	A12		C
Breath Test Refusal - Haz	A12		H
Careless Driving	M81		
Careless Driving - Haz	M81		H
Careless Driving _ CMV	M81		C
Child Restraint Vio	F02		
Coasting - Gear Disengage	N80		
Controlled Sub -CMV	A22		C
Controlled Sub -Haz	A22		H
Counterfeit Or Altered DL	B41		
Counterfeit Or Altered DL	B41		C
Counterfeit Or Altered DL	B41		H
Crossing Firehose	M56		
Disq DUI CMV	A20		C
Disq DUI Haz/Mat	A20		H
Disregard for Traffic Control Device	M14		
Disregard for Traffic Control Device - CMV	M14		C
Driving CMV Without CDL Lic	B56		
Driving on Wrong Side of Road	N70		
Driving Too Slow	S96		
Driving While Disq - CMV	B24		C
Driving While Disq - Haz	B24		H
Driving While Revoked	B25		
Driving While Susp (Impl Consent)	B26	02	
Driving While Suspended - DUI	B26		
Driving With Suspend Lic	B26	01	
Driving Wrong Way	N60		
Drug Felony - CMV	A50		C
Drug Felony - Haz	A50		H
DUI 1st Offense	A20	01	

Violation Description	ACD	SEV	COM
DUI 2nd Offense	A20	02	
DUI 3rd Offense	A20	03	
DUI 4th/Sub Offense	A20	04	
DUI CMV 1st Offense	A20	01	C
DUI CMV 2nd Offense	A20	02	C
DUI CMV 3rd Offense	A20	03	C
DUI CMV 4th Offense	A20	04	C
DUI CMV OOS Offense	A20	09	C
DUI Haz 1st Offense	A20	01	H
DUI Haz 2nd Offense	A20	02	H
DUI Haz 3rd Offense	A20	03	H
DUI Haz 4th Offense	A20	04	H
DUI Haz OOS Offense	A20	09	H
DUI Out-Of-St Offense	A20	09	
Expired Or No DL	B51		
Expired Or No DL - CMV	B51		C
Expired Or No DL - Haz	B51		H
Fail To Appear Or Pay	D56		
Fail To File Ins Cert	B64		
Fail To File Med / Disab	B65		
Fail To Obey Barrier	M02		
Fail To Obey Officer	M08		
Fail To Obey RR (Non CDL)	M09		
Fail To Obey RR Clearance	M24		C
Fail To Obey RR Drive	M22		C
Fail To Obey RR Gates	M10		C
Fail To Obey RR Nslow	M20		C
Fail To Obey RR Space	M23		C
Fail To Obey RR stop	M21		C
Fail To Observe Safety Zone	M12		
Fail To Pay Child Support	D51		
Fail To Post Security	D38		
Fail To Surr Hazmat End	W09		
Failure To File Acc Rept	B61		
Failure To Signal	N40		
Failure To Yield	N01		
False Application	B41		
Fatality	U08		
Fatality By Neg Oper CMV	U10		C
Fatality By Neg Oper Haz	U10		H
Financial Responsibility	D35		
Follow Too Close CMV	M34		C
Follow Too Close Haz	M34		H
Following Too Close	M34		
FTO Sign / Traf Cntl Dev	M14		C
FTO Sign / Trfc Cntl Dev	M14		
Gas Drive Off - 1st Offense		01	
Gas Drive Off - 2nd Offense		02	
Gas Drive Off - 3rd Offense		03	
Imminent Hazard	W70		
Improper / No Inspec Stkr			
Improper / No Tag			
Improper Class Or End	B91		
Improper Class Or End-CMV	B91		C
Improper Class Or End-Haz	B91		H
Improper Lane Chg	M42		
Improper Lane Chg - CMV	M42		C
Improper Lane Chg - Haz	M42		H
Improper Lane Usage	M40		
Improper Or Defective Equ	E01		
Improper Passing	M70		
Improper Passing - CMV	M70		C

Violation Description	ACD	SEV	COM
Improper Passing _ Haz	M70		H
Improper Turn	N50		
Imprpr Or Def Equip-CMV	E01		C
Inability To Pass Test	W20		
Leaving Scene/Inj Acc	B07		
Leaving Scene/Inj Acc - CMV	B07		C
Leaving Scene/Inj Acc - Haz	B07		H
Leaving Scene/Prop Dmg	B08		
Leaving Scene/Prop Dmg - CMV	B08		C
Leaving Scene/Prop Dmg - Haz	B08		H
Life Disq – 10yr Rein	W40		
Life Disq – No Rein	W41		
Misrepresentation	D02		
Negligent Homicide - Vehicle	U08	01	
Negligent Homicide CMV	U09		C
Negligent Homicide Haz	U09		H
No Proof Of Liab Ins	D36		
Non-Compliant Sex Offndr			
Obstructing / Impeding Traffic	F34		
Out Of Serv Order Vio CMV	B27		
Out Of Serv Order Vio Haz	B19		
Outside Auth Lane	M41		
Outside Auth Lane- CMV	M41		C
Outside Auth Lane- Haz	M41		H
Passing School Bus	M75		
Physical Or Mental Disability	W14		
Railroad grade Crossing Disq 1 Year	W61		
Railroad grade Crossing Disq 120 Days	W60		
Reckless Driving	M84		
Reckless Driving CMV	M84		C
Reckless Driving Haz	M84		H
Repeated Violations	W01		
Requ Proof Of Ins (Sr22)	B63		
Seatbelt Violation	F04		
Show / Use Improperly - Dl	D16		
Signature Withdrawn	W13		
Speed 15 Over	S15	01	
Speed 15 Over CMV	S15	01	C
Speed 15 Over Haz	S15	01	H
Speed 20 Over CMV	S15	02	C
Speed 20 Over Haz	S15	02	H
Speed Too Fast / Cond	S94		
Speed Too Fast / Cond CMV	S94		C
Speeding	S93		
Speeding - CMV	S93		C
Speeding 10-19 Mph	S92	02	
Speeding 10-19 Mph CMV	S92	02	C
Speeding 1-9 Mph	S92	01	
Speeding 1-9 Mph CMV	S92	01	C
Speeding 20 & Over Mph	S92	03	
Speeding 20 & Over Mph CMV	S92	03	C
Sudden/Erratic Speed	S97		
Susp W / Intrlck Dev	A41	01	
Suspended – Bad Chk	W00		
Trans Haz W/O Safety Dev	E03		
Two Serious CMV Viol	W30		
Underage .02% Or Greater	A61		
Underage DUI 1st Offense	A60	01	
Underage DUI 2nd Offense	A60	02	
Underage DUI 3rd Offense	A60	03	
Underage DUI Out-Of-State	A60	09	
Unsafe Operation	N84		

Violation Description	ACD	SEV	COM
Unsatisfied Judgment	D39		
Using Veh Felony - Haz	U03		H
Using Veh In Felony	U03		
Using Veh In Felony - CMV	U03		C
Using Veh In Misdeamor	U04		
Valid W / Intrlck Dev	A41	02	
Vehicular Homicide	U07		
Vehicular Homicide - CMV	U07		C
Vehicular Homicide - Haz	U07		H
Vehicular Manslaughter	U08		
Vehicular Manslaughter CMV	U08		C
Vehicular Manslaughter Haz	U08		H
Viol Cntrl Subs Act	A33		
Withdrawal Non ACD Viol	W00		

Table 2: Traffic Regulations and Rules Table

The table below is taken from Chapter 003 - Traffic Regulations and Rules of the Road. This chapter appears in Title 63 of the Motor Vehicles and Traffic Regulations. The complete Motor Vehicle Laws for the State of Mississippi is found at www.mscode.com/free/statutes/63/index.htm.

Statute	Title
63-3-101.	Applicability of definitions.
63-3-103.	Vehicles.
63-3-105.	Tractors.
63-3-107.	Trailers.
63-3-109.	Railroads.
63-3-111.	Tires.
63-3-113.	Explosives and flammable liquids.
63-3-115.	Department of public safety.
63-3-117.	Local authorities.
63-3-119.	Police officers.
63-3-121.	Individuals.
63-3-123.	Traffic.
63-3-125.	Streets, roads, and highways.
63-3-127.	Crosswalks.
63-3-129.	Intersections.
63-3-131.	Safety zones.
63-3-133.	Traffic signals or devices.
63-3-135.	Right-of-way.
63-3-137.	Stopping, standing, and parking.
63-3-139.	Districts.
63-3-201.	Offenses and penalties generally.
63-3-203.	Failure or refusal to comply with order or direction of police officer.
63-3-205.	Applicability of chapter to various public officers and employees.
63-3-207.	Applicability of chapter to persons riding bicycles or animals or driving animal-drawn vehicles.
63-3-208.	Use of electric personal assistive mobility devices allowed on highways and sidewalks; restrictions.
63-3-209.	Uniformity of application of chapter throughout state; local traffic regulation generally.
63-3-211.	Enactment of traffic regulations by local authorities.
63-3-212.	Localities prohibited from enacting ordinances restricting cell phone use in motor vehicles.
63-3-213.	Effect of chapter upon rights of owners of certain real property.
63-3-301.	Adoption of uniform system of traffic-control devices.
63-3-303.	Placing and maintaining of traffic-control devices upon state and county highways; placement of devices upon such highways by local authorities.
63-3-305.	Placing and maintaining of traffic-control devices upon highways under local jurisdiction.
63-3-307.	Reflectors on bridges in state highway system.
63-3-309.	Traffic-control signal colors and rules.
63-3-311.	Flashing signal colors and rules.
63-3-313.	Disobedience of official traffic-control devices.
63-3-315.	Obedience of official traffic-control devices by emergency vehicles.
63-3-317.	Unauthorized signs, signals, markings and devices.
63-3-319.	Interference with official traffic-control devices or railroad signs or signals.
63-3-321.	Destruction, removal, etc., of detour sign, warning sign, barricade, or fence; offenses.
63-3-323.	Destruction, removal, etc., of detour sign, warning sign, barricade, or fence; definitions.
63-3-325.	Destruction, removal, etc., of detour sign, warning sign, barricade, or fence; penalties.

Statute	Title
63-3-1013.	Moving heavy equipment at railroad grade crossing.
63-3-1101.	Pedestrians subject to traffic-control signals at intersections; privileges and restrictions at other locations.
63-3-1103.	Pedestrians' right-of-way at crosswalks lacking traffic control signals; duty of vehicle approaching vehicle stopped for pedestrian.
63-3-1105.	Pedestrians crossing roadways at locations other than crosswalks.
63-3-1107.	Pedestrians to use right half of crosswalks.
63-3-1109.	Solicitation of rides by pedestrians.
63-3-1111.	Rights of blind and otherwise incapacitated pedestrians crossing at or near intersections or crosswalks; effect of failure to employ cane or guide dog; regulation of use of canes.
63-3-1112.	Duty of driver to avoid collision with pedestrian or person propelling human-powered vehicle; warning signal.
63-3-1113.	Driving through safety zone.
63-3-1201.	Reckless driving.
63-3-1203.	Operation of vehicle under circumstances which interfere with driver's view or control over driving mechanism; interference with driver's view or control by passenger.
63-3-1205.	Driving through defiles or canyons or on mountain highways.
63-3-1207.	Coasting upon down grade.
63-3-1209.	Crossing unprotected fire hose.
63-3-1211.	Throwing, etc., of glass or other injurious material on highway; removal of glass or other injurious material by person removing wrecked or damaged vehicle from highway.
63-3-1213.	Careless driving

Missouri

Administration	Important Telephone and Web Contacts
Jackie Bemboom, Director Motor Vehicle and Driver Licensing Division P.O. Box 629, Jefferson City 65105 573-526-1827 Phil Reed, Client Services Manager Office of Administration, Information Technology Services Division - Revenue PO Box 41, Jefferson City 65105 573-751-3100 http://dor.mo.gov/drivers/ (Drivers) http://dor.mo.gov/motorv/ (Vehicles)	Interactive Voice Response System.................573-526-2407 Points, Tickets, Revocations, Suspensions ......573-751-4475 Driver Licensing...573-751-1887 Financial Responsibility, Accidents ....573-751-1887 Administrative Alcohol ....573-751-1887 Vehicle Information ....573-526-3669 Commercial Driver License..............................573-751-1887 Highway Patrol..573-751-3313 State Department of Insurance ....573-751-4126 General E-mail ....dlbmail@dor.mo.gov Motor Vehicle Laws.....................www.moga.mo.gov Driver License Bureau Rules: www.sos.mo.gov/adrules/csr/current/12csr/12c10-24.pdf

Driver's License Format, Issuance and Renewal

License Classes, Restrictions and Endorsements Appear After the Driving Record Content Section

License Format

The format is a randomly assigned number consisting of one alpha and five to nine numbers or of nine numbers only. There is no coding based on last name or county of issuance. In 2005, Missouri implemented the requirements of the Federal Intelligence Overhaul Legislation (S2845) which prohibited states from displaying the Social Security Number (SSN) on any driver license or personal identification card. Prior to 12/17/05, the SSN could have been assigned as a DL number.

Document Appearance

The Missouri Department of Revenue began issuing newly designed driver licenses, non-driver identification cards, and instruction permits on December 10, 2012. The rollout to all license offices statewide should be completed in April 2013. All previously issued documents will remain valid until the expiration date.

Format Used from December 2012 to Present

Security Characteristics: The most evident new feature is a laser perforation of "MO" that can be seen when held up to a light source. Other security features include a laminate that contains the state seal which will change color when the card is tilted for review and certain graphics that will appear green under UV light.

Position of Photo: Left side for minor and adult.

Minor Age Driver Locator: Vertical vs. horizontal format and the license indicates "Under 21 until MM-DD-YY" in red on the right side above the ghost portrait of the applicant.

CDL Indicator: "Commercial Driver License" appears in green in the heading.

Anatomical Gift: Red donor heart with green ribbon in lower right corner

Temporary Document: Applicants will receive a temporary paper license valid for 30 days until their permanent license arrives in the mail. The temporary license has the same identifying information and photo that will be on the permanent license. The paper license also has the state seal and the word "TEMPORARY" printed in blue, with temperature-sensitive security ink that fades with exposure to warmth.

Format Used From April 2003 to December 2012

Security Characteristics: The most evident new feature is a "ghost" portrait of the applicant at the bottom of the license. Other security features include an outline of the state of Missouri and the words "Show Me" across the front of the license visible under ultraviolet light, printed data overlapping the ghost portrait, and a two dimensional barcode on the back of the license.

Position of Photo: Lower right.

Minor Age Driver Locator: The photo appears on the left side of the card and the license indicates "Under 21 until MM-DD-YY" in red on upper right.

CDL Indicator: "Missouri Commercial Driver License" appears in green on the heading.

Anatomical Gift: Red donor heart with green ribbon in lower left corner (right corner for minor licenses).

Oldest Format (Prior to April 2003)

The only valid document still in circulation with this format is the non-driver, non-expiring document.

Security Characteristics: A pattern of red-colored state seals, easily visible under normal light, appears across the identifying data on the bottom of the card. These seals shift in color as the card is tilted. The front contains an outline of the state and the word "Missouri" slanted through the outline that is visible only under ultraviolet light.

Position of Photo: Lower right.

Issuance

Location of Requirements for Proof of Identity:
http://dor.mo.gov/drivers/idrequirements.php

Age Requirements

The minimum age for Class F or M is 16. For Classes A, B, C, or E it is 18. A Graduated Drivers License Law went into effect 01/01/01 as follows:

Instruction Permit An individual who is at least 15 years of age can obtain a Temporary Instruction Permit. The holder of a temporary instruction permit who is less than 16 years of age may only operate a motor vehicle with a licensed parent, grandparent, legal guardian, or certified driving instructor. The holder of a temporary instruction permit who is 16 years of age or older may operate a motor vehicle with any licensed driver who is 21 years of age or older. Under any condition, the licensed driver riding with the permittee must occupy the seat next to the driver.

Intermediate License For ages 16 to 18, must have driven with an instruction permit for a minimum of 6 months. The parent, grandparent, legal guardian or certified instructor with a federal residential job training program must certify the driver has received 40 hours of behind-the-wheel instruction with a minimum of 10 hours of nighttime driving. The applicant must have no alcohol-related offenses in the last 12 months, and no traffic convictions in last 6 months. Seat belts required for all passengers and no driving alone between 1 a.m. and 5 a.m. During the first 6 months, an Intermediate driver is limited to only one passenger who is under 19 and who is not a member of their immediate family. After the first 6 months, an Intermediate driver is limited to less than 3 passengers who are under 19 and who are not members of the driver's immediate family.

Residency

As soon as one establishes residency a Missouri license must be secured. If a new resident surrender a valid current driver license or one that is expired 184 days or less from another U.S. Missouri waives the skills and written tests. All applicants are required to pass the Missouri road sign recognition and vision tests. Non-resident's home-state license is honored on a reciprocal basis.

Renewal

Intermediate license expires in two years or less based on proof of identity verification. Drivers 18-20 years or drivers age 70 and over receive a license expiring in three years or less based on proof of identity verification. Drivers 21-69 years of age receive a license expiring in six years or less based on proof of identity verification. Applicants for CDL with a hazmat endorsement are limited to a license term of five years or less based on federal regulations. Driver keeps same assigned license number when renewing.

Active-duty armed forces members (temporarily mobilized and deployed outside of Missouri) may obtain a new, renewal, or duplicate permit/driver/non-driver license via a mail-in process or through a power of attorney when required documentation is submitted.

Elderly-Related Restrictions

Ages 70 and over renew on DOB of third year.

Vehicle Insurance, Title and Registration Facts

Registration Renewal

Drivers are eligible to renew vehicle registration online with the Missouri Online Registration Exchange (MORE), if a PIN (Personal Identification Number) is recorded on the renewal application. The web page is http://plates.mo.gov. A vehicle can be operated for 30 days beyond the vehicle's registration date if it is being driven to reset the vehicle's readiness monitors in order to pass the on-board diagnostic (OBD) emission inspection.

One has 60 days from the date of purchase to title a newly purchased boat/vessel/outboard motor.

New Residents

Non-residents must register (and title) vehicles within thirty days of establishing residency. If a boat, then the requirement is sixty days if the boat is kept in Missouri for sixty days, regardless if owner is out-of-state.

Inspections and Emissions Testing

A vehicle safety inspection is required statewide. Since January 1, 2010, vehicles are exempt for the first five years following the model year of manufacture, as well as vehicles registered in excess of 24,000 pounds or above for a period of less than 12 months.

Certain areas require an emissions inspection. Vehicles 1995 and older are exempt from emissions testing requirements. All inspections are good for two years, unless the vehicle is sold in that two-year period. Even model year vehicles must be inspected when the registration expires in even years and odd model year vehicles when the registration expires in odd years. Emissions inspections only apply to residents of St. Louis, St. Charles, Franklin and Jefferson counties, and the City of St. Louis. The program, known as the Gateway Vehicle Inspection

Program (GVIP) combines safety inspections and emission testing into one program.

Note: Franklin County vehicle owners are not required to have emissions inspections every year. Instead, emissions inspections are good for two years and due in conjunction with safety inspections. Registration renewal will require an emissions test for odd model years only in odd years and even model year vehicles only in even years. A number of different vehicles are exempt from an emissions inspection for a variety of reasons. See the web page for details.

Passenger Plate Facts

One plate is issued, the year shows in the upper left corner. The plates do not indicate the county or city where the plates were issued. When a vehicle is sold, the plates remain with owner.

Insurance and Financial Responsibility

Missouri has compulsory insurance and requires all vehicle owners and drivers to be financially responsible and show proof of financial responsibility to the Department of Revenue or to any law enforcement officer when requested. Minimum liability limit amounts are $25,000/50,000/10,000. MO law also requires owners to have uninsured motorist coverage of $25,000 for bodily injury per person and $50,000 for bodily injury per accident.

Proof must be carried in the vehicle at all times. The state does not have a no-fault insurance provision. Anyone renewing license registration for their vehicle must present their insurance card or other acceptable proof of insurance. Proof is required normally for reinstatement after suspension or revocation and for "certain" violations. SR-22 forms are normally used, but in some instances insurance companies send this information electronically.

Withdrawal Sanctions, and Alcohol and Drug Testing

Alcohol and Chemical Testing

Missouri's illegal intoxication level is .08 percent and above, .04 percent if operating a CMV. If blood alcohol content is .08 percent or higher (.02 if under 21), a provision for "license withdrawal" is instituted. Saliva, urine, blood, and breath testing are authorized. Missouri has both an implied-consent violation and a provision for an administrative suspension. Minors arrested or stopped with .02 or more blood alcohol content are also subject to administrative sanctions.

Point System and Suspensions

The Missouri point system ranges from 1 to 12 points. Drivers could be suspended with an accumulation of 8 or more points in 18 months or revoked for an accumulation of 12 or more points in 12 months, 18 or more points in 24 months and 24 or more points in 36 months.

Suspensions and Revocations

See the Appendix for a list of the federally mandated disqualifications for offenses occurring in a CMV per MCSIA.

Point Accumulation

Eight or More Points in Eighteen Months:

    First Suspension... Thirty days.

    Second Suspension .... Sixty days.

    Third or Subsequent Suspension... Ninety days.

Twelve or More Points in Twelve Months .... One-year revocation.

Eighteen or More Points in Twenty-Four Months .... One-year revocation.

Twenty-four or More Points in Thirty-Six Months.................................... One-year revocation.

Three years with No New Points Added... Points reduce to zero.

    In certain cases, a Driver Improvement Program (DIP) is offered in order to reduce the points on a driver record for a ticket.

Failure to Have Financial Responsibility:

    First Offense .... Zero days.

    Second Offense... Ninety-days.

    Third Offense... One year.

Other Reasons for Suspensions or Revocations:

Abuse and Lose	In-State or Out-of-State Failure to Appear Suspension
Administrative Fraud Suspension	Mandatory Insurance
Child Support Arrearage Suspension	Minor in Possession
Citation Revocation	Misrepresentation
Court Ordered (i.e. fail to stop for school bus, FTY)	Motor Fuel Theft
Failure to File an Accident Report	Motor Vehicle Accident Judgment
Failure to Appear in Court or Pay Fine for CDL holders in one of these States- AK, CA, MI, MT, OR, WI	Out-of-state Accident
	Refusal for Not Taking Alcohol or Drug Test
Failure to Maintain Insurance or Having False Insurance	Security Accident
Failure to Maintain Ignition Interlock Device (IID)	Zero Tolerance or Administrative Alcohol

About Alcohol-Related Offenses

- Any person convicted of two intoxication-related traffic offenses within a five-year period is denied all driving privileges for five years. After five years the privilege to drive can only be restored by court order.
- Any person convicted more than twice of an intoxication-related traffic offense is denied all driving privileges for ten years. After ten years the privilege to drive can only be restored by court order.
- Individuals with more than one alcohol offense on their driving record must have an **ignition interlock device (IID)** installed prior to reinstatement of their driving privileges OR issuance of a Limited Driving Privilege (LDP) or Restricted Driving Privilege (RDP). The IID must be maintained for the duration of the LDP/RDP and for six months following the reinstatement date, and the driver is required to report to a certified IID vendor each month for maintenance to ensure the device is working properly. Failure to maintain or removal of the device during the six-month period will result in a re-suspension of driving privileges.

Notes:

1. The Department issues Restricted Driving Privileges only for certain alcohol-related suspensions. The driver must serve the first 30 days of the suspension and file proof of liability insurance (i.e., SR-22 form) and proof of installation of an IID (if required) with the Driver License Bureau. A person cannot obtain an RDP to drive a commercial motor vehicle.
2. The Department or Circuit Court provides a Limited Driving Privilege (LDP) to those who have lost their driving privilege, but need to drive for employment or other important matters. Eligible drivers may obtain an LDP unless they have certain convictions or losses of license on the driver record. Some convictions or loss of license are so serious that an LDP may not be granted. Details are found at http://dor.mo.gov/drivers/ldp.php. A person cannot obtain an LDP to drive a commercial motor vehicle.

Reinstatement Requirements

Reinstatement information is available by telephone at 573-526-2407. Reinstatement fees may also be paid by telephone with use of a debit or credit card.

Suspension	$20 fee; proof of financial responsibility.
Revocation	$20 fee; proof of financial responsibility; re-examination (except for chemical refusal revocation).

If For Financial Responsibility Suspension

First Offense	$20 fee; proof of financial responsibility.
Second Offense	$200 fee; proof of financial responsibility.
Third or Subsequent Offense	$400 fee; proof of financial responsibility.

Note: An additional $25 fee is assessed when the suspension/revocation is alcohol related (unless it was based on an out-of-state alcohol conviction). Successful completion of a Substance Abuse Traffic Offender Program or comparable program is also required. If more than one alcohol offense is showing on the record, an IID will be required.

Record Access: Laws, Rules, and Forms

Note: This Section Applies to Both Driver and Vehicle Records.

Governing Statutes and Rules

Motor Vehicle Laws: ....www.moga.mo.gov

Driver License Bureau Rules:
www.sos.mo.gov/adrules/csr/current/12csr/12c10-24.pdf

Title 12 CSR 10-42.050 (Disclosure of public records and confidentiality of closed records) states that all records retained by government agencies are public records unless there is specific authority to close those records. Section 17 (A) states "...title history, dealer sales reports, license registration information and driving records are not confidential..." The Department of Revenue has issued administrative rules which specifically identify public and confidential records. Missouri has the same exceptions as the federal statute. Missouri statute 32.091(2) states that the "department of revenue may disclose individual motor vehicle records pursuant to Sections 2721(b)(11) . . . and 2721(b)(12) of Title 18 of the United States Code." Missouri statute 32.091(4) states that the "department of revenue shall disclose any motor vehicle record or personal information permitted to be disclosed pursuant to Sections 2721(b)(1) to 2721(b)(10) and 2721(b)(13) to 2721(b)(14)."

An opt-in policy is in place. Departmental policy for electronic requesters requires written approval from the Division.

Request and Consent Forms

Driver and Vehicle Records: A Security Access Code assignment is required for business and entities entitled to receive records with personal information, per federal law. Request a security access code using *Form 4678, Request For Security Access Code.* Note this form requires the notarized signature of the requester.

If requester is the search subject, then submit notarized *Form 4681, Request From Record Holder.* This form is used to obtain either driving record information or vehicle history. Also, *Form 4803* may be used to request vehicle related information.

All forms are found at http://dor.mo.gov/forms/. One may also obtain copies of forms from any license office or the Department of Revenue.

Vendor and Third Party Access Policy

Vendors must ensure that those receiving requested records are authorized under the DPPA to receive such information. However, the vendor must ensure the person/entity they are reselling to is also exempt under the DPPA. Vendors that resell or re-disclose personal information must keep for a period of five years, records identifying each person or entity that receives such information and the permitted purpose for which the information will be used.

Records Ordered For Non-permissible Uses

Without consent, records are still released, but personal information is withheld. Personal information includes the person's name, address, date of birth, sex, height, weight, eye color, driver license number, SSN, photograph, telephone number, medical or disability information including restrictions, and all information contained on a tax return or application.

Casual requesters can obtain records with personal information if consent is given. Use *Form 4681* as mentioned above. Notary of subject's signature is required.

Access to Driver-Related Records

Driving Records
General Information and Fees
Motor Vehicle and Driver Licensing Division, Record Sales, PO Box 2167, Jefferson City, MO 65105 [301 West High Street Rm 360] 573-526-3669.

Fee is $5.88 for manual processed records and those accessed through the Dialing for Records process. Electronic access fees vary. There is a surcharge to use a credit card or debit card, this fee will vary from 3% to 2.6% with a minimum of $1.00. Frequent requesters of driving records should establish an account with the Record Sales area and obtain records through the Dialing for Records process.

As mentioned above, a Security Access Code assignment is required. The electronic access of driving records in Missouri is very unique, see below. For questions about driving records, e-mail dlrecords@dor.mo.gov.

Note: One may request driver records by mail or walk-in that do not contain the personal information of an individual. Non-personal information includes the driving history showing speeding tickets and other violations.

In-Person – Counter service available at the central office in Jefferson City. Most license offices in the state process requests for the record subject, but an additional $2.00 processing fee is charged.

Mail – Requests should include the driver's full name, date of birth, and/or license number. Requests are processed within two days of receipt of the request. The fee must accompany all requests. No record found requests are charged the full fee.

Telephone and Fax – This is only available for approved account holders. Requesters can dial the Bureau's Interactive Telephone Driver Record System via a touch-tone telephone. Fax requests should be faxed to 573-526-7367. Requester must include a major credit card. Driving records will be mailed or faxed within 24 hours. There is an additional $.50 fee per page to fax back. Both certified and non-certified records can be ordered. Driver records will be mailed the following day by first class mail, or faxed to a fax machine within 24 hours of the request. To establish an account, contact Records Sales at 573-526-3669.

E-mail – Requests for driver records may be e-mailed to dlrecords@dor.mo.gov. Customers request must include all credit card information (type, number, expiration date, etc.) in order for the request to be processed.

Editor's Note on Electronic Access:
The electronic access of driving records in Missouri is very unique. The fee schedule is not based the traditional method used in other states of using a per-record cost per the specific names submitted in a request. Approved users and vendors may purchase electronic records in either a batch or database mode. See the next section for details.

♦

FTP – The order and delivery of Missouri driving records is provided by File Transfer Protocol (FTP) to approved requesters with a security access code. Records are processed Monday through Saturday. Batches sent by 2AM will be available for pick-up at 6AM the same day. The fee is $52.00 per batch submitted, regardless of the number of requests within the batch. For further information, call 573-526-3669 or e-mail dlrecords@dor.mo.gov.

Bulk – The Office of Administration Information Technology Bureau provides a driver license database purchase program that enables approved users to purchase the entire driver file with or without driver history information. In addition, the user can purchase monthly or daily updates. At press time the fee for the initial purchase of the entire database is $2035 with driver history data or $1035 without the driver history data. Monthly or daily updates are then priced on a per record basis ($.0043 per record for the first 50,000 records and $.0003 per record for every record over 50,000). Users must also initially pay for programming set-up time. For more information, call 573-526-3669.

By Person of Record – Missouri drivers may obtain their driving record by mail or walk-in as described above. Use of Form 4681 is suggested. (http://dor.mo.gov/forms/4681.pdf). At present, there is no program for drivers to order or view their own record online.

Notification/Monitoring Program
Missouri does not offer a specific monitoring system or notification program to employers or insurance companies to track incidents of drivers. However, the Bulk Purchase Program enables entities to construct their own monitoring programs for themselves or clients.

Crash Reports
Reporting – All crashes resulting in damage, injury, or death must be reported to the Missouri State Highway Patrol within 20 days by the local police or investigating jurisdiction. Reports are made to Missouri State Highway Patrol, P.O. Box 568, Jefferson City, MO 65102. In

addition, all accidents occurring in Missouri that result in property damage in excess of $500, death or personal injury and which involve an uninsured motorist must be reported to the Department of Revenue. Reports are accepted for up to one year after the accident occurs. Copies of statements from the attending physician or an appraiser's estimate of damage must accompany reports involving personal injury or property damage. The *1140 Form* is found at http://dor.mo.gov/forms/.

Record Access – Missouri State Highway Patrol, Traffic Records Division, PO Box 568, Jefferson City 65102, 573-522-2590. www.mshp.dps.missouri.gov/MSHPWeb/PatrolDivisions/TFD/index.html Requests for report copies of crashes that occurred in 1997 or later can either be forwarded to the Highway Patrol headquarters of the troop where the motor vehicle crash occurred, or to the Traffic Records Division. Requests for report copies of crashes that occurred in 1996 or earlier, certified crash reports, crash report photographs or crash reconstruction reports must be forwarded to the Traffic Records Division.

The fee is $3.75 for the standard 4-page report. Add $2.00 for certification. Personal checks are accepted. In general, the records are open to the public from 1941 to present. Requests must be in writing or in person and should include the driver's name and date and location of the accident. A form is available at the web page. A self-addressed stamped envelope is recommended. Note that while crash reports are always available, crash reconstruction reports may be closed due to an ongoing investigation. The reconstruction reports may be ordered on CD. Records cannot be e-mailed.

Also, preliminary information within the last 29 days on crash reports only investigated by the Highway Patrol is found at www.mshp.dps.mo.gov/HP68/search.jsp.

Access to Vehicle-Related Records

General Information and Fees

Department of Revenue, Motor Vehicle and Driver Licensing Division, PO Box 2167, Jefferson City MO, 65105, 573-526-3669; fax is 573-526-7367.

The Department of Revenue maintains record information on all terrains, boats, motors, mobile homes, trailers, and motorcycles as well as passenger and commercial vehicles. Lien information shows on title records. Registration/title records are computerized. Records are available from 1968 to present. All requesters of personal information must qualify to receive such information under the DPPA. The SSN, sales and use tax information is not shown on records. The Department of Revenue will not take vehicle record requests by phone, nor does it offer billable accounts for customers. The fee is $5.88 per record. There is a surcharge to use a credit card or debit card, this fee will vary from 3% to 2.6% with a minimum of $1.00.

Use of Form 4803 is suggested (http://dor.mo.gov/forms/4803.pdf).

In-Person or Mail – See fees above. The physical address is Motor Vehicle and Driver Licensing Division, Room 370, Harry S. Truman Office Building, 301 West High Street, Jefferson City, MO 65101. Credit cards are accepted. One may also visit a licensing office, an additional $2.00 processing fee is charged. For mail requests, an SASE is requested.

Fax – Records may be returned by fax for an additional $.50 per page.

Electronic – Vehicle lienholder data, registration and ownership information is available to registered requesters. There is an approval process since records are only released per permissible use. Two forms are required. The applicant must qualify to have a security access code (DPPA number) issued by the Department. Application is made using *Form 4678*, Request for Security Access Code. Customer must also complete an Application for Online Account (Form 5017), accessible at the web page. The service allows qualified businesses (lienholders, motor vehicle and boat dealers, etc.) to file notices of lien (NOLs) online. The $.0382 record fee is automatically debited from the requester's ACH (Automated Clearing House) account or credit card account. For more information, call 573-526-3669.

Bulk – The Office of Administration Information Technology Bureau has a number of databases and files available for extraction. Most of the file purchases are affected by the DPPA. Therefore, the requester will be required to obtain a Security Access Code, as described above and submit a Bulk/Customized Record Request Form, Form 5153. Fees vary. For more information, call 573-526-3669.

Access to Vessel-Related Records

General Information, Access and Fees

Records are available from the Motor Vehicle and Driver Licensing Division, see http://dor.mo.gov/motorv/watercraft/. Missouri law requires that all motorized boats/vessels and any boat/vessel more than twelve feet in length powered by sail alone be titled and registered, unless exempt by law. This includes jet skis and motorized water bikes. Any vessel regardless of length which is solely propelled by oars or paddles is not required to be titled or registered. Also, trolling motors are exempt from title and registration requirements.

Driving Record Content and Reciprocity

What's On or Not On the Driving Record

- Records without personal information are released to casual requesters.
- Records with personal information are provided to authorized requesters.
- Accident involvement is stored in the Department's computer, but does not appear on the driving record unless a related suspension or revocation action is taken.
- The state does not permit completion of a driver improvement program in lieu of conviction, but will permit such attendance in lieu of assessment of points. The conviction will display on the record with zero points assessed.
- SSNs, medical information, and eye exam data is not shown.

Data Retention

Non-major convictions are retained on a CDL driving record for a minimum of four years and major convictions are permanently retained. Non-CDL convictions are retained on the driving record for a minimum of three years. DWI-related Convictions, Suspensions and Revocations and Mandatory Insurance Suspensions are permanent. All other Suspensions and Revocations are retained for a minimum of five years after reinstatement.

Non-CDL records are purged from the system using the timetable listed above. CDL driver records are purged per Federal guidelines (see the Appendix). Surrendered licenses are held until reinstated or expired.

Court to Repository

Conviction information is sent from the courts to the state via either paper abstracts or electronic reporting. The courts must forward convictions to the DMV within 7 days, who, in turn, must forward to the Missouri State Highway Patrol within 15 days.

State Reciprocity for Non-CDL Drivers

- May suspend driving privilege of Missouri driver for out-of-state convictions and for failure to appear or pay for moving violations occurring out-of-state;
- Prior state's driving history of new incoming driver is not shown on MVR;
- Out-of-state convictions are shown on MVR; and
- Out-of-state accident suspensions are shown on MVR.
- Record is forwarded upon request to new state upon surrender of license.

License Classes, Restrictions, and Endorsements

How License Class is Displayed on License Document

The CDL driver's license will have either the words "Commercial Driver License" or the letters "CDL" on the face of the license. All CDL driver records will show Class A, B, or C. No other field in the record will indicate CDL. Any driver with Class E, F, or M will be a non-CDL driver

License Classes— Commercial

Class A Combination vehicle 26,001 pounds GVWR or more with trailer over 10,000 pounds GVWR.
Class B Single vehicle 26,001 pounds or more GVWR.
Class C Vehicle under 26,001 pounds GVWR or placarded for hazardous materials or designed to transport sixteen or more people, including the driver.

License Classes— Non-Commercial

Class E Operator for hire not required to have Class A, B, or C - single vehicle under 26,001 GVWR.
Class F Operator.
Class M Motorcycle.
Class ND Non-Drivers (ID Card).

Also, a Limited Driving Privilege (LDP) hardship license is issued for those in work or alcohol programs, medical treatments, school, etc.

Restrictions

A	Corrective Lenses	M	Extension Foot Operated Device
B	Outside Rearview Mirror	N	Leg Brace or Braces
C	Daylight Driving Only	O	Foot-Operated Emergency Brake
D	Automatic Trans/Power Steering	P	Accelerator on Steering Column
E	Seat Cushion	R	Back Cushion
F	Restricted to 45 MPH	T	Right Outside Mirror
G	Restricted to 25 Mile Radius	U	Uncoded (Restrictions) Special
H	Special Hand Devices	W	Three-Wheel Motorcycle
I	Intermediate License	Y	Left Outside Mirror
J	Electrical Turn Signals	Z	More Than 5 Restrictions
K	Intrastate Driving Only	#	Information Restricted
L	CDL Vehicle Without Air-Brakes		

Endorsements

B	Passenger Endorsement Restricted to Class B	N	Tank Vehicle
C	Passenger Endorsement Restricted to Class C	P	Passenger Vehicle
CCW	Concealed Carry*	S	School Bus
H	Hazardous Material Vehicle	T	Double-/Triple-Trailer
M	Motorcycle	X	Tank/Hazardous Material Vehicle

Note: *Missouri has a Concealed Carry endorsement that is noted on the face of the license for concealed carry permit holder. This will show license or non-driver document as *CCW Until mm-dd-yyyy*, which reflects the expiration date of the concealed carry permit issued by the local sheriff or designee.

Important Abbreviations on Driving Records

ERS Action Status Description Codes

A	Active	IAP	Awaiting Processing	R	Reinstated
AC	Active	IAR	Arrest Rejected	RES	Restored
ADN	Active-Denovo	IAT	Awaiting Test	S	Stayed
ALP	Active-Litigation Pending	IPR	Information Petition Review	SAP	Stayed Appealed
APR	Active-Petition Review	IVF	Citation Forfeiture	SBA	Stayed Bankruptcy
C	Cancelled	M	Complied	SHP	Stayed Hearing Pending
CCC	Cancelled-Case Closed	P	Pending Description	SMA	Stayed Military Appeal
CN	Cancelled	PDN	Pending De Novo	SPR	Stayed Petition Review
CNC	Cancelled-No Current Address	PE	Pending	T	Terminated
D	Deleted	PLP	Pending Litigation Pending	TM	Terminated
EX	Expired	PPR	Pending Petition Review	TNP	Terminated No Point Reduction
I	Informational	QU	Quashed		

ERS Pending Activity Codes

A	Appeal	G	GRS Suspension	R	Revocation
C	CDL Disqualification	K	Appeal-License Required	S	Suspension
D	Denial	O	CDL Disqualification - DWOS	V	CDL Disqualification-No Test

ERS Operator Status Codes

C	Cancelled	O	Other Not Valid	VR	Valid-Registration Suspension Only
CS	Cancelled-OS Surrender	R	Revoked	VX	Valid Expired
D	Denied	RR	Revoked - No Test Required	W	Walk-in Eligible
E	Reinstated-Must Test	S	Suspended	WE	Walk-in Reinstated Must Test
LT	Limited	V	Valid	WV	Walk-in Reinstated Valid

Commercial Status Codes

C	Cancelled	E	Restored Test	S	Suspended
CC	Cancelled CDL	LT	Limited	V	Valid
CS	Surrendered License Out Of State	NO	Not Eligible	VX	Valid Expired
D	Denied	O	Other Not Valid	WE	Walk-In Restored - Must Test
DO	Disqualified - DWOs	R	Revoked	WV	Walk-In Restored Valid
DQ	Disqualified	RC	Revoked CDL		
DS	Restored - Must Test	RR	Revoked - No Test		

Accident Severity Codes

1	Fatal	3	Non-Incapacitating Evident Injury	5	Non-Injury (Property Damage)
2	Incapacitating Injury	4	Possible Injury	9	Unknown Severity

Conviction Court Type

ADM	Administrative Adjudication	HUS	Hustings	SUM	Summary Court Martial
CHA	Chancery	JPC	Justice Of Peace	SUP	Superior Court
CIR	Circuit	JUS	Justice Court	TJC	Trial Justice
CIT	City Court	JUV	Juvenile	TRA	Traffic
CIV	Civil	LEC	Law & Equiry	TRI	Tribal
COC	County	MAG	Magistrate	TWN	Town
COR	Corporation	MAY	Mayor's	UNK	Unknown
CRI	Criminal	MUN	Municipal	USC	U.S. Commissioner
DIS	District	POL	Police	USM	U.S. Magistrate
DOT	Secretary USDOT	SJC	Special Justice	USS	U.S. Supreme
FED	U.S. District	SPL	Special Court Martial		
GEN	General Court Martial	SSP	State Supreme Court		

ERS School Bus Status

I	Invalid
S	Suspended
V	Valid

ERS Must Test Codes

A	All Privileges
C	Commercial Privileges Only
O	Operator Privileges Only

ERS Eye Color Codes

1	Brown
2	Gray
3	Green
4	Black
5	Hazel
6	Blue
7	Pink
8	Dichromatic
9	Unknown

ERS Sex Codes

B	Business
F	Female
M	Male
U	Unknown

Withdrawal Types

1	Revoked
2	Barred
3	Suspended
4	Cancelled
5	Denied
6	Disqualified
7	Other Withdrawal

Conviction Table with Codes, Points and ACD

(An **Administrative Action Codes Table** follows this table)
There are four columns: **Desc. ACD Conviction Text Points**
The numbers under the Desc column below denote where the type of conviction.

- The 1000 series denotes **Municipal** convictions
- The 2000 series denotes **County** convictions
- The 3000 series denotes **State** convictions

- The 4000 series denotes **Miscellaneous** convictions
- The 5000 series denotes **SIS (Suspended Imposition of Sentence)** commercial convictions
- The 6000 series denotes **Federal** convictions.

In actuality, each of the first three series have nearly identical conviction explanations and point total, for example 1001, 2001 and 3001 all are stop sign convictions of 2 points, and so forth. In the interest of not duplicating three like columns, the multiple corresponding codes if they are identical for the 2000 and 3000 series are printed using only the "1000 series." But any conviction in the 2000 or 3000 series that do not appear in the 1000 series or have a different point total are shown in the tables to follow.

DESC	ACD	Conviction Text	Points	DESC	ACD	Conviction Text	Points
1001	M15	Stop Sign	01	1058	B41	Altered Driver's License	02
1002	M08	Disobeyed Traffic Officer	02	1059	M82	Inattentive/Careless Driving	02
1003	N70	Driving on Wrong Side of Road	02	1060	-	Operation of ATV With Passenger	02
1004	S96	Driving Under Min. Speed Limit	02	1061	-	Open Car Door into Traffic	02
1005	D70	Driver's View Obstructed	02	1062	-	Excessive Vehicle Noise	02
1006	M41	Failure to Keep Right	02	1063	S15	Excessive Speeding	02
1007	E54	Failure to Dim Lights	02	1064	A04	Driving Under the Influence BAC .04	02
1008	N43	Failure/Improper Signal	02	1065	B56	Drive CMV Without Obtaining a CDL	02
1009	N42	Failure to Sound Horn	02	1066	B91	Operation w/o Passenger Endorsement	02
1010	N08	Failure to Yield to Pedestrian	02	1067	B91	Operation w/o HazMat Endorsement	02
1011	N26	Failure to Yield Right-of-Way	02	1068	B91	Operation w/o Tank Vehicle Endorse	02
1012	M34	Following Too Close	02	1069	B91	Operation w/o Double/Triple Endorse.	02
1013	N82	Improper Backing	02	1070	B91	Operation w/o School Bus Permit	02
1014	M42	Improper Lane	02	1071	-	Warning of Radar	02
1015	M71	Improper Passing	02	1072	B74	Failure to Produce Proof of Insurance	04
1016	F34	Impeding Traffic Movement	02	1073	-	Activated Red Light w/Non-Emergency	02
1017	N83	Improper Start From Parked Position	02	1074	A50	Felony-Drug Trans/Manufacturing	00
1018	N50	Improper Turn	02	1075	N09	Failure to Stop For School Bus	02
1019	S97	Increased Speed When Passed	02	1076	S15	Excessive Speed-Non Assessable	00
1020	-	No Motorcycle Qualification	02	1077	U31	CMV/CDL Holder Fatality	00
1021	M58	Operating Where Prohibited	02	1078	B24	Driving While Disqualified	00
1022	B51	No Driver's License	02	1079	B27	Driving While Out of Service	02
1023	N56	Prohibited U-Turn	02	1080	B91	Improper CDL Class/Endorsement	02
1024	E01	Failure to Wear Protective Headgear	02	1081	-	Interfere w/Officer or Traffic System	02
1025	D29	Violation of Restricted License	02	1082	M40	Cruising	02
1026	M16	Traffic Turn Signal Violation	02	1083	-	Overtake/Strike Rear of Vehicle	02
1027	N63	Wrong Direction-One Way Street	02	1084	N06	Improper Emerging From Drive	02
1028	N62	Wrong Direction-Divided Street	02	1085	N06	Obstructing Traffic	02
1029	S93	Speeding	02	1086	A25	Driving While Impaired	02
1030	B05	Leaving Scene of Accident	06	1087	N80	Coasting With Gears Disengaged	02
1031	M84	Careless & Imprudent Driving	02	1088	S94	Driving Too Fast For Condition	02
1032	B26	Driving While Susp/Revoked/Denied	12	1089	S97	Erratic Speed	02
1033	D02	Obtained License By Misrepresentation	12	1090	A20	Driving While Intoxicated	08
1034	A20	Driving While Intoxicated	08	1091	A10	Excess Blood Alcohol Content	06
1035	A22	Driving Under the Influence of Drugs	08	1093	-	Operating ATV on Highway	02
1036	A10	Excess Blood Alcohol Content	06	1094	E55	Operating Mot. Veh. W/O headlights	02
1037	U03	Felony Involving Motor Vehicle	12	1095	S93	Failed to Reduce Speed	02
1038/1039		Not in Use		1096	M10	Disobey Traffic Device - Railroad	02
1040	-	Permitting Unlicensed Driver to Drive	04	1097	N05	Disobey Funeral Procession Ordinance	02
1041	N84	Driving Motorcycle Between Vehicles	02	1098	B19	Drove out of Service - 15 Pass/Hazmat	02
1042	B61	Failure to Report Accident	02	1099	-	Strike a legally Stopped Car	02
1043	N84	Weaving	02	1100	-	Loan Driver License to Another	00
1044	M56	Driving Across Fire Hose	02	1101	A41	Viol of Ignition Interlock	02
1045	-	Violation of Instruction Permit	02	1102	A41	Viol Ignition Interlock - SIS	00
1046	M58	Driving Over Sidewalk	02	1103	D78	Gave false Information to Officer	02
1047	D16	Using Another's Driver's License Own	02	1104	M05	Unauthorized Lane Use	02
1048	M58	Driving Over Curb	02	1105	A08	Excess Blood Alcohol Content	08
1049	N84	Driving With Child On Lap.MC Tank	02	1106	A08	Excess Blood Alcohol Content	08
1050	-	Excessive Passengers	02	1107	M58	Driving on Shoulder	02
1051	-	Collision With Other Vehicle	02	1108	M02	Driving through Barricade	02
1052	-	Failure to Remain in Moving Vehicle	02	1109	U06	Assault_3rd Degree involving Motor Veh	02
1053	S95	Engage in Speed Competition	02	1110	-	Operated an ATV - Under age of 16	02
1054	M80	Fishtailing	02	1111	M14	Disobey Traffic Control Device	02
1055	A35	Violation of Open Container Law	02	1112	M43	Leave Main Portion of Highway	02
1056	-	Operate Motorcycle with 3 Passengers	02	1113	N04	Disobey Emergency Vehicle Ordinance	02
1057	U01	Eluding Police Officer	02	1114	-	15 1/2 Years Old - Operate at Night Ord	02

Code	Abbr	Description	Pts
1115	-	Driving a Motor Veh w/o Owner's Consent	02
1116	-	Failure to Stop and Render Aid	02
1117	B78	No License - Possess or on Demand	02
1118	D16	Fictitious/Canceled/Susp/Revd/Alt Lic	02
1119	-	Altered Counterfeit Insurance Card	02
1120	F06	Riding Sidesaddle on Motorcycle	02
1121	-	Attempted Leave Scene - Accident	02
1122	S94	Hot Roding	02
1123	M83	Aggressive Driving	02
1124	-	Tampering with Motor Vehicle	02
1126	A41	Tampering with Ignition Interlock	02
1129	M58	Failure to Stay on Pavement	02
1130	A25	Operate ATV Under Alcohol or Drugs	02
1132	B01	Out-of-State Hit & Run	02
1133	B02	Out-of-State Fatality	02
1134	B14	Fail to Reveal ID - Accident	00
1135	U07	Vehicular Homicide	12
1136	U08	Vehicular Manslaughter	12
1137	U09	Negligent Homicide - CMV	12
1138	U10	Negligent Operate CMV - Fatality	12
1139	M31	Follow with Insufficient Space	02
1140	M09	Failure to Obey Railroad Restriction	02
1141	M10	Failure to Obey Railroad Device	02
1142	M20	Failure to Slow at Railroad Crossing	02
1143	M21	Failure to Stop at Railroad Crossing	02
1144	M22	Failure to stop before railroad crossing	02
1145	M23	Insufficient space to drive thru RR	02
1146	M24	Insufficient clearance for railroad crossing	02
1151	-	Unlawful Tow Truck Stop	04
1153	-	Texting While Driving	02
1998	A20	DWI - Prior to S.B. 513	12
1999	N84	Misc-Convert from Prior System	02
2001	M15	Stop Sign	02
3001	M15	Stop Sign	02
3029	S93	Speeding	03
3038	U08	Involuntary Manslaughter - DWI Felony	12
3039	U06	Assault Vehicular Injury - Felony	12
3040	D16	Permit Unlicensed Driver to Drive	02
3125	N07	School Bus Driver Not Allowed to Pass	02
3127	-	Attempted DWI	02
3128	-	Motor Fuel Theft	02
3131	-	Use TSPS to Control Traffic	02
3147	-	Endanger Welfare of Child	02
3148	A31	Minor in Possession	02
3149	M84	Endanger Highway Worker	04
3150	M84	Aggravated Endanger Highway Worker	12
3152	U03	Murder 2nd Vehicle/Intoxicated	12
3153	M85	Texting While Driving	02
3205	A08	Excessive Blood Alcohol - Felony	08
3222	B51	No Drivers License - Felony	12
3230	B05	Leave Scene of an Accident - Felony	12
3232	B26	Driving While Susp/Rev/Denied - Felony	12
3234	A21	Driving While Intoxicated - Felony	08
3235	A22	Driving Under Influence Drugs - Felony	08
3999	N84	Misc Convert From Prior System	02
4001	M15	Stop Sign (Accident)	02
4022	B51	No Driver's License	02
4029	S93	Speeding	02
4030	B05	Leaving Scene of Accident	02
4031	M84	Careless & Imprudent 304.016	04
4034	A21	Driving While Intoxicated	08
4035	A22	Driving Under the Influence Drugs	08
4036	A10	Excessive Blood Alcohol Content	06
4038	U08	Involuntary Manslaughter - DWI - Felony	12
4039	U06	Assault Vehicle Injury - Felony	12
4063	S15	Excessive Speeding	02
4064	A04	Driving Under the Influence - BAC .04	02
4072	B74	Fail to Produce Proof of Insurance	02
4091	A10	Excessive Blood Alcohol	06
4105	A08	Excessive Blood Alcohol	08
4128	-	Motor Fuel Theft - Felony	12
4131	M84	Careless and Imprudent	02
4140	M09	Failure to Obey Railroad Restriction	02
4141	M10	Failure to Obey Railroad Device	02
4142	M20	Failure to Slow at Railroad Crossing	02
4143	M21	Failure to Stop at Railroad Crossing	02
4144	M22	Failure to Stop Before Railroad Crossing	02
4145	M23	Insufficient Space to Drive Through RR Crossing	02
4146	M24	Insufficient Clearance for RR Crossing	02
5000	-	Chem Refusal When Driving CMV	00
5012	M34	Following Too Close "SIS"	00
5014	M42	Improper Lane "SIS"	00
5030	B05	Leaving Scene of Accident "SIS"	00
5031	M84	Careless & Imprudent "SIS"	00
5032	B26	Driving While Sus/Rev/Dis "SIS"	00
5033	D02	Obtaining Lic by Misrepres. of "SIS"	00
5034	A20	Driving While Intoxicated "SIS"	00
5035	A22	DUI of Drugs "SIS"	00
5036	A10	Excessive Blood Alcohol "SIS"	00
5037	U03	Felony Involving Motor Veh "SIS"	00
5038	U08	Involuntary Manslaughter DWI "SIS"	00
5039	U06	Assault Vehicular Injury "SIS"	00
5063	S15	Excessive Speed in CMV "SIS"	00
5064	A04	DUI BAC .04 "SIS"	00
5065	B56	No Commercial Driver's Lic "SIS"	00
5074	A50	Felony-Drug Transp/Manufact. "SIS"	00
5076	-	Excessive Speed-Non Assessable "SIS"	00
5077	U31	Commercial Vehicle Fatality "SIS"	00
5078	B24	Driving While Disqualified "SIS"	00
5079	B27	Driving While Out of Service "SIS"	00
5098	B19	Driving Out-of-Serv-15 Passenger "SIS"	00
5140	M09	Failure to Obey Railroad Restriction "SIS"	02
5141	M10	Failure to Obey Railroad Device "SIS"	02
5142	M20	Failure to Slow at Railroad Crossing "SIS"	02
5143	M21	Failure to Stop at Railroad Crossing "SIS"	02
5144	M22	Failure to Stop Before Railroad Crossing "SIS"	02
5145	M23	Insufficient Space to Drive Thru RR Cross"SIS"	02
5146	M24	Insufficient Clearance for RR Crossing "SIS"	02
6034	A20	Federal Drove While Intoxicated	00
6035	A22	Federal Drove Under Influence Drug	00
6036	A10	Federal Excess Blood Alcohol Content	00
7000	D56	Fail to Appear/Pay	00
7001	D45	Fail to Appear/Pay	00

Point System Summary

The Missouri point system ranges from 1 to 12 points. Drivers could be suspended with an accumulation of 8 or more points in 18 months or revoked for an accumulation of 12 or more points in 12 months, 18 or more points in 24 months and 24 or more points in 36 months.

Missouri ERS Administration Action Codes with ACD

Code	ACD	Description	Code	ACD	Description
AC00	-	Accident Security/Mandatory Insurance	CM52	A21	1st DWI Disqualification
AC01	B61	Failure to File Suspension	CM53	A12	1st Chemical Disqualification
AC02	D38	Security Suspension (Driver Only)	CM54	A22	1st DUI Disqualification
AC03	-	Security Suspension (Registration Only)	CM55	B05	1st Leaving/Scene Disqualification
AC04	D38	Security Suspension (Driver/Registration)	CM56	U03	1st Felony Disqualification
AC05	D38	Security Suspension (Converted)	CM57	W45	Disqual - Drive While Withdrawn - 1st
AC10	D36	1st Mandatory Insurance Suspension (Driver/Regist.)	CM61	A04	1st DUI Disqualification (Hazmat Involved)
AC11	D36	2nd Mandatory Insurance Suspension (Driver/Regist.)	CM62	A21	1st DWI Disqualification (Hazmat Involved)
AC12	D36	3rd or Higher Mandatory Ins. Suspension (Driver/Regist.)	CM63	A12	1st Chemical Disqual (Hazmat Involved)
AC13	-	1st Mandatory Insurance Susp (Regist. Only)	CM64	A22	1st DUI Disqualification (Hazmat Involved)
AC14	-	2nd Mandatory Insurance Susp (Regist. Only)	CM65	B05	1st Leave/Scene Disqual (Hazmat Involved)
AC15	-	3rd or Higher Mandatory Ins. Susp (Regist. Only)	CM66	U03	1st Felony Disqualification (Hazmat Involved)
AC16	D36	1st Mandatory Insurance Susp (Driver Only)	CM67	W45	Disqual - Drive While Withdrawn - Hazmat Invl
AC17	D36	2nd Mandatory Insurance Susp (Driver Only)	CM70	A50	Disqualification-Felony-Transport-Manufact. Drugs
AC18	D36	3rd or Higher Mandatory Ins. Susp (Driver Only)	CM71	W40	2nd or Higher DUI Disqualification
AC19	D36	1st Mandatory Suspension (Converted)	CM72	W40	2nd or Higher DWI Disqualification
AC20	D36	2nd Mandatory Suspension (Converted)	CM73	W40	2nd or Higher Chemical Disqualification
AC21	D36	3rd or Higher Mandatory Suspension (Converted)	CM74	W40	2nd or Higher DUID Disqualification
AC30	D36	Mandatory (Driver/Registration)	CM75	W40	2nd or Higher Leaving/Scene Disqualification
AC31	D36	Mandatory -2nd (Driver/Registration)	CM76	W40	2nd or Higher Felony Disqualification
AC32	D36	Mandatory -3rd (Driver/Registration)	CM77	W40	Disqual - Drive While Withdrawn - Substance Invl
AC33	-	Mandatory (Registration Only)	CM80	W30	Disqual for 2nd Serious Traffic Violation
AC34	-	Mandatory -2nd (Registration Only)	CM81	W31	Disqual for 3rd Serious Traffic Violation
AC35	-	Mandatory -3rd (Registration Only)	CM89	-	Out of State CDL Denial
AC36	D36	Mandatory (Driver Only)	CM90	W70	Imminent Hazard
AC37	D36	Mandatory -2nd (Driver Only)	CM91	W70	Imminent Hazard - 1 Year
AC38	D36	Mandatory -3rd (Driver Only)	CM93	B19	1st Out-of-Service Disqual, 15 Passenger
AC90	D37	Security Default Suspension	CM94	W51	2nd or Higher Out-of-Service Disqual, 15 Passenger
AD00	-	Administrative DUI Action	CM95	B27	1st Out-of-Service Disqual, No Haz Mat
AD01	A98	Administrative Alcohol Suspension	CM96	W50	2nd Out-of-Service Disqual, No Haz Mat
AD02	A94	Administrative Zero Tolerance Suspension	CM97	W52	3rd/Higher Out-of-Service Disqual, No Haz Mat
AD03	A94	Administrative Zero Tolerance Suspension	CM98	B19	1st Out-of-Service Disqual, Haz Mat
AD50	A98	Administrative Alcohol Revocation	CM99	W51	2nd/Higher Out-of-Service Disqual, Haz Mat
AD51	A94	Administrative Zero Tolerance Revocation	CO16	D36	Mandatory (Driver Only)
AD52	A94	Administrative Zero Tolerance Revocation	CO17	D36	Mandatory -2nd (Driver \Only)
AD99	-	Zero Tolerance Action	CO18	D36	Mandatory -Subsequent (Driver \Only)
AL00	-	Abuse and Lose Action	CS01	D51	Child Support Enforcement Suspension
AL01	A31	Abuse And Lose Suspension	CT50	W20	Citation Revocation
AL50	A31	Abuse And Lose Revocation	CT51	W20	Citation Revocation
AL51	A33	Abuse And Lose Revocation (Driver Over 21 Years)	CT52	W20	Citation Revocation
CH01	A12	Chemical Refusal Revocation	CT53	W20	Citation Revocation
CH02	-	Out of State Chemical Revocation	CT54	W20	Citation Revocation
CM01	D02	CDL Canceled For Misrepresentation of Fact	CT55	W20	Citation Revocation
CM02	D45	Failure to Appear/Pay Disqualification	CT56	W20	Citation Denial
CM05	B56	CDL Revocation For Driving Without CDL License	CT57	W20	Citation Denial
CM18	M09	1st RR Disqualification	CT58	W20	Citation Denial
CM19	M10	1st RR Disqualification	CT59	W20	Citation Denial
CM20	M20	1st RR Disqualification	CT60	W20	Converted Citation Revocation
CM21	M21	1st RR Disqualification	CT61	W20	Converted Citation Revocation
CM22	M22	1st RR Disqualification	CT62	W20	Citation Revocation
CM23	M23	1st RR Disqualification	DS16	D36	Mandatory (Driver Only)
CM24	M24	1st RR Disqualification	DS17	D36	Mandatory -2nd (Driver Only)
CM25	W60	2nd RR Disqualification	DS18	D36	Mandatory -Subsequent (Driver Only)
CM26	W61	3rd RR Disqualification	DS26	D36	Sample Mandatory (Driver Only)
CM41	W41	Disqualification - DUI - Perm	DS27	D36	Sample Mandatory -2nd (Driver Only)
CM42	W41	Disqualification - DWI - Perm	DS28	D36	Sample Mandatory -Sub (Driver Only)
CM43	W41	Disqualification - Chem - Perm	DS36	D36	Mandatory (Driver Only)
CM44	W41	Disqualification - DUID - Perm	DS37	D36	Mandatory -2nd (Driver Only)
CM45	W41	Disqualification - Leaving Scene - Perm	DS38	D36	Mandatory -Subsequent (Driver Only)
CM46	W41	Disqualification - Felony - Perm	DS98	-	ESP Mandatory Sampling
CM47	W41	Disqualification - Drive While Withdrawn - Perm	FA01	D56	Failure to Appear Suspension
CM51	A04	1st DUI Disqualification	FA02	D56	Instate Failure to Appear Suspension

FI02	D35	Fraud Insurance (Driver Only)
FI03	-	Fraud Insurance (Regist Only)
FI04	D35	Fraud Insurance (Driver/Regist)
FJ01	D39	Judgment Suspension
FJ02	D39	Out-of-state Judgment
FJ90	D39	Judgment Default
FJ91	D39	Judgment Revived
FJ93	D39	Judgment Re-suspension
GT00	W00	Fuel Theft Suspension
GT01	W00	Fuel Theft Suspension (60 day)
GT02	W00	Fuel Theft Suspension (90 day)
GT03	W00	Fuel Theft Suspension (180 day)
ID01	W00	Issuance Denial
ID51	-	Issuance 5 Year Denial
ID52	-	Issuance 10 Year Denial
IG01	W00	Failure to Maintain IGIN Device
IN01	D36	Failure to Maintain Proof of Insurance Suspension
JV01	-	Juvenile Denial
LB01	-	Hold License in Lieu of Bail
ME01	W14	Court Ordered Denial
MP01	A31	Minor in Possession Suspension-1st
MP02	A31	Minor in Possession Suspension-2nd
MP50	A31	Minor in Possession Revocation
MR01	-	Special Investigation
MR30	D02	Fraud Denial
MR50	D02	Revocation for Misrepresentation of Fact
ON00	-	Mandatory Insurance Officer Note
ON10	D36	1st Mandatory Insurance Susp (Driver/Regist.)
ON11	D36	2nd Mandatory Insurance Susp (Driver/Regist.)
ON12	D36	3rd of Higher Mandatory Insurance Suspension (Driver/Regist.)
ON13	-	1st Mandatory Insurance Susp (Regist. Only)
ON14	-	2nd Mandatory Insurance Susp (Regist. Only)
ON15	-	3rd or Higher Mandatory Insurance Suspension (Regist. Only)
ON16	D36	1st Mandatory Insurance Susp (Driver Only)
ON17	D36	2nd Mandatory Insurance Susp (Driver Only)
ON18	D36	3rd or Higher Mandatory Insurance Suspension (Driver Only)
OS01	D38	Out of State Accident Suspension (Driver Only)
OS02	D38	Out of State Accident Susp (Driver/Regist.)
OS03	-	Out of State Accident Suspension (Regist. Only)
PT01	W01	30 Day Point Suspension
PT02	W01	60 Day Point Suspension
PT03	W01	90 Day Point Suspension
PT04	W01	Point Suspension - 1st Alcohol
PT40	A41	Ignition Interlock, 1 yr
PT41	A41	2nd or higher Ignition Interlock, 5 yrs
PT45	D02	Fraud Revocation
PT50	W01	Point Revocation
PT51	W01	5 Year Denial (Alcohol Involved)
PT52	W01	10 Year Minimum Denial
PT53	W01	Permanent Denial
PT54	U08	5 Year Denial (Vehicular Manslaughter Involved)
RW01	N26	Right of Way Suspension
RW02	N26	Right of Way Suspension
RW03	N26	Right of Way Suspension
SB01	-	School Bus Permit Suspension
SB02	N09	Court Order School Bus Suspension - 1st
SB03	N09	Court Order School Bus Suspension – Subsequent
ST03	-	Skills Test Denial
ST04	-	Skills Test Denial
ST05	-	Skills Test Denial
ST06	-	Skills Test Denial

Montana

Administration	Important Telephone and Web Contacts
Bob Pesta, Bureau Chief Motor Vehicle Division, Department of Justice Operations and Customer Support 302 N Roberts, Helena 59620-1430 406-444-3933 Greg Noose, Bureau Chief Motor Vehicle Division, Department of Justice Records and Driver Control Bureau 302 N Roberts, Helena 59620-1430 406-444-3288 Kristine Thatcher, Bureau Chief Motor Vehicle Division, Department of Justice Field Operations Bureau 302 N Roberts, Helena, MT 59620-1430 406-444-3933 Joann Loehr, Bureau Chief, Title and Registration Bureau 1003 Buckskin Drive, Deer Lodge, MT 59722 406-444-3661	Driver Licensing Customer Srv ....406-444-3933 Financial Responsibility/SR-22 ....406-444-3288 Commercial Driver License 406-444-3244 or 444-3667 Vehicle Information......................................406-444-3661 State Department of Insurance ....406-444-2040 Highway Patrol..406-444-3780 https://doj.mt.gov/driving/ General Email for vehicle questions mvdtitleinfo@mt.gov General Email for driver licensing mvd@mt.gov The Montana Code is found at http://data.opi.mt.gov/bills/mca_toc/61.htm

Driver's License Format, Issuance and Renewal
License Classes, Restrictions and Endorsements Appear After the Driving Record Content Section

License Format

Since October 2005, all Montana driver licenses and IDs are issued with a system-generated 13 numeric number. For individuals licensed prior to 2005 who requested to use their SSN as a driver license number, the electronic system would pre-fill four zeros (0000) at the end of the SSN. Prior to this, the SSN or a nine digit (*made-up number*) was used.

All previously issued licenses and ID cards remain valid until the card expiration date or another transaction that would provide for the opportunity to change the customer's driver license number. Since October 2005, driver licenses and ID cards are not issued using the SSN as the license number or ID card number. Below is a description of the prior card numbering systems.

Issued From October 2000 to Present. Below example is of a system generated 13 numeric license number 0100019544114.

First 2 digits:	Month of birth (01)
Next 3 digits:	Sequence numbers assigned by Driver License Application System (000)
Next 4 digits:	Year of birth (1954)
Next 2 digits:	Montana statehood (41)
Last 2 digits:	Day of birth (14)

Issued July 1994 to October 2000. Now only applicable for military personnel.

(Made-Up Number) When a made-up number comes up on-terminal as belonging to someone else, the same number is used, but at the end of the number (male/female) a "2" is placed instead of the "0" or "1"; if the "2" is also a duplicate, succeeding numbers are used (i.e., "3" or "4", etc.)   The following describes the construction of made-up numbers for Angela Rae Olson, DOB 07-02-68, whose license number is F8702ANG1.

Position 1:..............An alpha character (A-L) corresponding to the decade in which the year of birth falls: i.e., 1910=A, 1920=B, 1930=C, 1940=D, 1950=E, 1960=F, 1970=G, 1980=H, 1990=I, 1900=J, 1890=K, 1880=L

Position 2:	A number corresponding to the year of birth within the decade. (8)
Position 3:	A number or alphabetic character (1-9, A-C) corresponding to the month of birth: January=1, February=2, etc. to September=9, then October=A, November=B, December=C. In the example above "7" is used.
Positions 4 & 5:.....	Numbers (01-31) corresponding to the day of birth. (02)
Positions 6, 7 & 8:.	Alpha characters representing the first three letters of the individual's first name (use a dash where there is no letter). (ANG)
Position 9:	A number designating sex; 0=male, 1=female.

Document Appearance

Since 1994, Montana has issued digital licenses and ID cards. In 2008, Montana introduced the "Current Style" driver licenses and ID cards. The card formats and security features on the New-Style cards comply with AAMVA standards. These include: color-coded banners; custom lettering; quick reference codes; repeated, overlapping data and photos; a retro reflective surface with a "Grizzly Bear" design that sinks and floats within the card overlay; and special ultraviolet and shadow features that appear within the card stock. A pamphlet that fully describes New-Style card security features is available and may be obtained by emailing mvd@mt.gov. Driver licenses and ID cards with the previous design are valid until their expiration date.

Security Characteristics: Licenses issued between Jan 1994 and July 1995 - a state seal hologram covers name, DOB, and a portion of the photo. Licenses issued after July 1995 - the security feature changed to a series of grizzly bears. driver licenses produced between October 2000 and July 2008 contain a ghost image as well as previous security features.

Position of Photo: Current–Style: Regular license, CDL and over 21 ID card- left side; under 21 ID card and under 21 driver license card printed vertically- photo upper left; all cards have ghost photo image-lower right. **Old–Style:** Regular license, CDL and over 21 ID card-lower left; under 21 ID card and under 21 driver license-lower right.

Minor Age Driver Locator New-Style: Minor age cards have yellow or red banners next to portrait with *Under 18 OR Under 21 until...* **Old-Style:** Photo position as described above and the date the driver turns 21 is printed under the license number.

CDL Indicator: Current-Style: Gold-colored upper banner - Quick Reference Code "CDL" and adjacent Class A, B or C. **Old-Style:** Text is printed in red, "COMMERCIAL DRIVER'S LICENSE" appears under number..

Motorcycle Only: Effective October 2000, Montana began issuing a new license valid only for the operation of a motorcycle. It follows the same expiration pattern as any other license. **Current-Style:** Quick Reference Code "ML" with adjacent Class M. **Old-Style:** header is black and contains the words "MOTORCYCLE ONLY".

Issuance

Age Requirements
In 2006 Montana adopted a Graduated Licensing Program with three stages. The minimum age for the first stage - an Instruction Permit -is 14 1/2. The next step is the Restricted License; then a Full Privilege License is issued on or before the age of 18. A driver under the age of 16 must participate in an approved driver education course.

Proof of Authorized Presence
Since December 2005, individuals who apply for a Montana driver license must provide proof that their presence in the United States is authorized under federal law. Applicants must prove that they are either a U.S. citizen or that they are legally authorized to be in the U.S. In the case of authorized non-citizens, the card expiration date is concurrent with the documented end date for lawful presence. More detailed information regarding this along with identification and Montana residency requirements is available at: https://doj.mt.gov/driving/required-docs/#proofidentity.

Residency
Non-resident's home-state license honored as long as it is valid and in good standing. Montana license must be applied for within 60 days; commercial license within 30 days.

Renewal
Renewal is the birth month of eighth year for all applicants aged 21-67 years old receive an 8 yr license. New applicants 15-21 receive license pro-rated to 21st birthday. Qualified military personnel are exempted from DL expiration (as long as it is not suspended or revoked) and need not renew their license. For exempted military personnel, a driver license is valid for 30 days following honorable separation from military service. Driver license renewal is not available online. Those who live in a county that does not provide driver license services - Carter, Garfield, Golden Valley, Jefferson, Judith Basin, Madison, Petroleum, Prairie, Treasure and Wibaux – or those who are temporarily out-of-state may apply for a renewal of a regular Class D Montana driver license through the mail. Driver license mail-in renewal forms are available online at www.doj.mt.gov/driving/forms.asp.

Other Age Related Restrictions
Applicants aged 67-75 receive license pro-rated to 75th birthday. All applicants 75 and over receive four-year license.

Vehicle Insurance, Title and Registration Facts

Registration Renewal
Under state law, all motor vehicles including motor homes; motorcycles and quadricycles; travel trailers; utility trailers; all-terrain vehicles; sailboats over 12 feet in length; motorboats, jet skis and other motorized vessels; and snowmobiles must be registered with the state.
Registration must be renewed annually for passenger cars and trucks unless eleven years old or older and registered permanently. Permanent registration is used for motor cycles, trailers, boats, and quads. Vehicle registration renewal is available online at www.doj.mt.gov/driving.

New Residents
New residents must apply for a Montana vehicle title and register their vehicles within 60 days of establishing residency. Non-resident military personnel stationed in Montana may register their vehicles in their home jurisdictions or in Montana, unless they are gainfully employed in Montana outside of their military duties. If they are gainfully employed outside those duties, they must title and register their vehicles in Montana.

Inspections and Emissions Testing
Montana has neither an emissions test provision nor an annual safety inspection provision. Drivers may only use studded tires on Montana roads from October 1 until May 31.

Passenger Plate Facts
There two plates and one decal (MO & YR) on rear plate. The first two digits of the plate represent the county of issuance. These numbers range from 1 to 56. The counties are not assigned in alphabetical order and are assigned a random number. Please contact the Title and Registration office if an exact listing of these codes is needed. The plates remain with the seller when a vehicle is sold.

Insurance and Financial Responsibility
Motor vehicle liability insurance is mandatory; it is unlawful to operate a vehicle without a valid motor vehicle liability insurance policy. Minimum financial responsibility limits are $25,000/50,000/10,000. Under Montana law, motorists stopped for a traffic violation or involvement in a motor vehicle collision are required to show proof of insurance to law enforcement, in addition to displaying their driver license and vehicle registration. And when the Motor Vehicle Division revokes the driver license of any person, proof of financial responsibility (SR22) is required to be provided prior to reinstatement. The Division will suspend license plates for up to 180 days following multiple convictions of either failure to have or failure to provide proof of required motor vehicle liability insurance.

Withdrawal Sanctions, and Alcohol and Drug Testing

Alcohol and Chemical Testing Limits
Montana's illegal intoxication level is .08 percent and above, .02 percent if under 21 years old, and .04 percent if operating a commercial vehicle. Blood and breath testing are authorized. Montana has an implied-consent violation. Since 2003, drivers convicted of a second or subsequent offense of driving under the influence of alcohol or drugs shall, in addition to other punishments imposed in accordance with law, have their motor vehicle seized and subjected to forfeiture or equipped with an ignition interlock device for a twelve-month period following reinstatement.

Suspensions and Revocations

The state is in compliance with the federally mandated disqualifications on CDLs. See the Appendix for details.

Note: Montana has an excellent resource – the **MT Bond Book** – which provides a wealth of information regarding maximum penalties and mandatory minimums for felonies and misdemeanors, including all vehicle related incidents. The latest version is as of June 2011. To view the book, visit http://courts.mt.gov/content/lcourt/training_guides/2010_bondbook.pdf.

Suspensions

Under Montana law, the following are examples of suspensions:

Driving Under the Influence or Operating a Motor Vehicle with a Blood Alcohol Content of 0.08% or Greater:

First Offense .... Six-month suspension

Second, Third or Subsequent Offense............. One-year suspension with provisions for Ignition Interlock, DUI Court Participation or 24/7 Alcohol Testing

Refusal to Submit to Alcohol Testing (Implied Consent or Preliminary Alcohol Screening Test):

First Refusal... Six-month suspension

Second or Subsequent Refusal........................ One-year suspension

Operation of a Vehicle by a Person Under 21 Years of Age with an Alcohol Concentration of 0.02% or More:

First Conviction .... 90-day suspension

Second Conviction.. Six-month suspension

Third Conviction... One-year suspension

A Commercial Driver Operating a Commercial Motor Vehicle with an Alcohol Concentration of 0.04% or More:

First Violation - 1 Year Suspension (3 Year Suspension if Transporting Placardable Hazardous Materials)

Second or Subsequent Violation Suspension for Life (Reinstatement May be Reconsidered after Ten Years)

Minor in Possession of Alcohol (MIP):

MIP convictions are not recorded on an individual's Montana Driving Record. However, as part of the penalty for an MIP, judges have the authority to order the suspension of an offender's driver license. If a judge sends notice of a license suspension resulting from an MIP conviction, the MVD will suspend the offender's driver license for the number of days ordered by the court and permanently record the withdrawal action on the offender's driving record.

Note: As provided by law, all alcohol-related suspensions may also include jail time and fines.

Other Suspensions that may mandate a driver's license will be suspended for varied periods lasting from 30 days to 1 year (or in some cases, even indefinitely) include, but are not limited to

- 3 reckless driving offenses committed within a period of 12 months
- Altering a driver's license or ID card to obtain alcohol
- Any unlawful use of a driver's license
- Authorizing another to use ones license or ID card to obtain alcohol
- Default on a student loan
- Driver medically unable to safely operate a motor vehicle
- Failure to pay child support
- Failure to obtain required medical evaluation or submit to testing
- Falsifying a date of birth on a driver's license application
- Fraudulent application for a license to drive
- Non-Payment of fines or non-appearance on a notice to appear
- Unsatisfied judgment
- Use a motor vehicle in the theft of motor vehicle fuel

Revocations

Upon receiving notice of a conviction from a court for any of the following violations, a driver's license will be revoked for one year:

- Conviction for negligent homicide resulting from the operation of a motor vehicle
- Conviction for any felony in the commission of which a motor vehicle is used (including 4th offense DUI / BAC violations)
- Failure to stop and render aid as required from motor vehicle accident resulting in the death or personal injury of another
- Negligent vehicular assault involving a motor vehicle
- Perjury or the making of false affidavit or statement under oath relating to the ownership or operation of motor vehicles

For Habitual Traffic Offenders:

- Any person who accumulates 30 or more conviction points within a three-year period - license revoked for three years

Cancellations - Examples Include:

- Death of a person signing a minor's application
- Fraud and/or falsifying information on an application for a license to drive
- License is suspended or revoked in another state
- Paying for a driver's license service with a non-sufficient funds check
- Removal of parental consent
- Voluntary surrender of a license.

Reinstatement Requirements

Driver's license reinstatement is based upon time lapse for periodic suspension requirements and payment of reinstatement fees ranging from $100 (non-alcohol) to $200 (alcohol). Other requirements may include substance abuse treatment, proof of financial responsibility, application fees, and taking tests for new licenses.

Record Access: Laws, Rules, and Forms

Note: This Section Applies to Both Driver and Vehicle Records.

Governing Statutes and Rules

Montana Code: http://data.opi.mt.gov/bills/mca_toc/61.htm
Montana Code Annotated § 61-11-501 through 516 is the Montana Driver Privacy Protection Act (MDPPA) which regulates the release of individual driving records. The provisions for permitted disclosure are found in MCA § 61-11-509. MCA § 33-18-210(9) and MCA § 61-5-208 of the Montana Code Annotated restrict how aspects of a driving record may be used.

MCA. 61-11-105(2) and 61-11-501 through 516 are the statutes governing the release of motor vehicle records. All vehicle registration information is available for access for those with a permissible purpose: https://app.mt.gov/dojvs/public.

Policy Statement Regarding Permissible Uses

Montana does not have the following federal DPPA exceptions (18 USC Sec. 2721): 10, 11, and 12. Any person who qualifies under MCA § Title 61 Chapter 11 Part 5 (MDPPA) may obtain a driver history record upon paying the appropriate fees and presenting identification. Highly restricted personal information including address, SSN, photo and medical information is not released. Mailing list purchases are prohibited. The authorized usage list to obtain driving records is found on the back of request form and also at https://app.mt.gov/dojdrs/authuse.html.

Request and Consent Forms

Driving Records: The *Release of Driving Records Form (34-0100)* can be downloaded at https://doj.mt.gov/driving/forms/. The intended use of the request must be divulged. Page two of the Form is the *Personal Information Express Consent* form. Unless a copy of the requester's driver's license or state issued ID card is included with the request, the signature of the requester must be notarized. Most personal information, including address, is not released to requesters.

Vehicle Records: Use of *MV210 Form - Release of Motor Vehicle Records* - is required. The form can be can be downloaded at https://doj.mt.gov/driving/forms/. The signature of the requester is required and must be notarized unless a copy of the requester's DL or ID is attached.

Vendor and Third Party Access Policy

Driving Records: Approved electronic vendors cannot access records for other vendors who would then sell to a permissible end-user, unless the secondary vendor has been authorized.

Vehicle Records: Permissible users purchase in bulk or database format for authorized purposes, but records cannot be resold to another permissible user or another vendor selling to a permissible user.

Records Ordered For Non-permissible Uses

Driving Records: Anyone may request a driving record; however, personal information (address, SSN, photo, and medical information) is not released.

Vehicle Records: Casual requesters without consent can obtain records that have no personal information.

Access to Driver-Related Records

Driving Records

General Information and Fees

Motor Vehicle Division, PO Box 201430, Helena MT 59620-1430, 406-444-3292, fax 406-444-7623.

The current fee is $4.00 per record or $10.00 for a Certified Driver Record, and $7.25 if record is secured electronically. There may be additional fees to fax or mail back a driving record, see below. The MVD charges for "no record found" reports.

In-Person – Motor Vehicle Division Office, Scott Hart Building, Second Floor, 302 N. Roberts, Helena. Requesters must present picture ID. Each record requests must include 2 of the 3 following pieces of information; full name, date of birth, driver's license number. Any amount of records may be ordered at the Division office in Helena, although the records may not be available the same day.

Mail & Fax – Mail-in requests, available only at the Helena location, are processed in about three days. The driver's license number or full name and date of birth are needed when ordering. Requesters are required to submit funds with the request. Use of the state's form, which can be downloaded from the web site, is required. The fee is $4.00 per record. A SASE is required or a $3.00 fee is incurred. Alternately, one may request the record sent via fax for an additional $3.00 for each record, and the SASE is not needed.

Electronic – Both a **Public User** and **Registered User** interface are offered.

The **Registered User** system is for ongoing, pre-approved accounts. There is an annual $100.00 Registration Fee for 10 users. Subscribers must sign a Restricted Use Agreement for Driving Record Information stating agreement to use the information only for allowable purposes. The fee is $7.25 per record. The web portal offers many other services including vehicle history searches and business entity searches. Address information is not released. To find out more about this driving records program, see https://app.mt.gov/registered or call 406-449-3468.

The **Public User** system is available to anyone who is licensed to drive in Montana. Licensed drivers who establish a permissible use may obtain their own driver record or the record of another Montana driver. Personal information, including SSN or address is not released. There is a $7.25 fee. A credit card must be used or the requester must have an ePass Montana account. The requester must identify the permissible use. Before searching for a driver record online, a requestor must identify themselves by providing: 1. their own first and last name, 2. their Montana driver license number and 3.the last four digits of their own SSN. Once the requestor's identity is verified electronically, a search for a driver record may be conducted online by providing the name, date of birth and the Montana driver license number of the driver who is the subject of the record. See https://app.mt.gov/dojdrs.

Bulk – Montana does not offer database sales of the license header or history.

By Person of Record – MT drivers may obtain their driving record by mail, walk-in, or via online as a Public User as described above.   A request form is downloadable at www.doj.mt.gov/driving/forms/34-0100.pdf.

Notification/Monitoring Program

Montana has a License Status Conviction Activity (LSCA) process that enables requesters to track lists of drivers on a monthly basis. The requester submits an electronic file each month; the fee is $.15 per driver submitted. The MVD, through the Montana Interactive portal, checks the database and responds with a Y/N indicator. The Y/N is based upon a conviction of an ACD Code-related violation. For each "Y", the requester is sent a driver record and charged $7.25.

Note the the MVD is not monitoring an ongoing list; **a new list must be re-submitted each month.**

Crash Reports

Reporting – Accidents resulting in death, injury, or property damage in excess of $500 to any one person must be reported immediately to law enforcement. If the investigating officer or agency does not produce a written report and the damage is in excess of $1,000 then the operator must report the crash within ten days in writing to the Montana Highway Patrol, 2550 Prospect Ave, Helena 59620. The reporting form is at https://files.doj.mt.gov/wp-content/uploads/HQ1598.pdf..

Record Access – In accordance with the provisions of MCA § 61-7-114, the Montana Highway Patrol regulates who may receive a copy of a Crash Report in Montana. (https://doj.mt.gov/highwaypatrol). Reports by individuals (the requestor filled out the crash report themselves) may be released only to the person who submitted the original report or by someone designated in writing by that person. Reports completed by an officer may be released to the following individuals:

a. Any person named on the report (including companies, businesses, etc.);

b. Any driver, passenger or pedestrian involved in the crash, or any person whose property was damaged in the crash;

c. A party to a civil action arising from the crash;

d. If the person is deceased, his executor or administrator or the attorney representing his executive or administrator designated in writing;

e. Anyone designated in writing by persons in categories a. and b;

f. Any insurance carrier for categories a. and b. Insurance carrier includes life, health, auto and workers compensation carriers.

To request a copy of a crash report, requestors must read and complete the required form and submit to 2550 Prospect Ave., Helena, MT 59620. Information about obtaining crash photos can also be found at this website. Requests are generally processed in 10 to 14 days from the date of crash. A $2.00 non-refundable search fee is required. All forms may be downloaded at https://doj.mt.gov/highwaypatrol/forms.

Access to Vehicle-Related Records

General Information and Fees

Title and Registration Bureau, Dealer and Specialized Services Section, 1003 Buckskin Dr, Deer Lodge MT 59722, 406-444-3661; fax: 406-846-6039.

The Title and Registration Bureau regulates the titling and registration of motor vehicles. Under state law, all motor vehicles including motor homes; motorcycles and quad-cycles; travel trailers; utility trailers; all-terrain vehicles; sailboats over 12 feet in length; motorboats, jet skis and other motorized vessels; and snowmobiles must be registered with the state.

The fee for a VIN, registration or lien check is $6.00 per request, this includes records on mobile homes and vessels. The Bureau cannot look up information by plate alone and must have second identifier. (There is no cost for the registration history or current information for obtaining data on requester's own vehicle.) Requesters must use Form MV210. The requester must provide the reason for the request, a SSN or federal tax ID number, and agree to indemnify and hold harmless the state of Montana.

For the purposes of *Form MV210*, the term "motor vehicle" includes all passenger cars, trucks, trailers, campers, off-highway vehicles, snowmobiles and boats/vessels/personal watercraft.

In-Person, Mail, Fax – These methods are only available to permissible users or with the consent of the subject. Usually, walk-in requesters have results returned by mail. Normal turnaround time is 5-7 working days. Proper request forms must be presented. Records can be returned by fax if arrangements are made, the fee is $3.00 for the first 5 pages and $1.00 each additional page.

Electronic – Both **Public User** and a **Registered User** interface are offered. The service allows users to instantly search for and view **vehicle and vessel** record information including owner information, title history and registration information.

The **Registered User system** is for ongoing registered accounts approved by the Motor Vehicle Division. Depending on the level of authority granted, the following is available: Vehicle Information, License Plate Information, Vehicle Owner Information, Lien History, Title History and Registration Information. Also, registered users can obtain ownership and lien history by submitting either a title number, VIN or license plate number. The fee is $2.25 per search. There is an annual $100.00 Registration fee for 10 users. The web portal offers many other services including driving record searches and business entity searches. For more information call 406-449-3468 or visit https://app.mt.gov/registered/.

The **Public User system** is designed for Montana citizens or users with an occasional need to know the ownership history of a pre-owned car. Sensitive information, such as the SSN or home address is not released. The requester must identify the purpose for the request and provide the first and last name, DL#, and last four digits of the SSN in order to access the inquiry screen. The fee is $5.00 per record search and use of a credit card is required. There are seven portions of data on each record received: Vehicle Data, License Information, Owner, Title, Lien, Title History, and Registration

See https://app.mt.gov/dojvs/public.

The **Temporary Registration Permit** site at https://app.mt.gov/trp/client allows registered users to create, reissue and void Temporary Registration Permits for recently purchased vehicles. Searching for a vehicle by VIN is also available.

Bulk – Bulk or batch ordering of registration information is available on CD, FTP, tape, disk, or paper. The user must fill out a specific form, which gives the user the capability of customizing by results. For further information, contact the Bureau at the address above.

Access to Vessel-Related Records

General Information, Access and Fees

All boats must be titled and registered. All sailboats over 12 feet in length; motorboats, jet skis and other motorized vessels must be registered. Vessel records, including liens, are maintained at the Title and Registration Bureau as mentioned above. Online access is available (see above), otherwise the $6.00 search fee must be included with requests. All requests in writing must be on the state form. Turnaround time is normally 10 to 12 days. Lien information shows on the title.

Driving Record Content and Reciprocity

What's On or Not On the Driving Record

An individual Montana driving record contains a comprehensive record of convictions and driver improvement actions. With limited exceptions, current practice is to retain this history, especially the record of serious traffic convictions, in conjunction with a permanent driving record. Montana statutes restrict how aspects of driver history may be used.

A DUI or BAC conviction qualifies as a subsequent offense if less than 5 years have passed between commission of present offense and a previous conviction. After three convictions, all prior offenses count toward subsequent prosecutions.

Traffic conviction points (Habitual Traffic Offender) expire after three years from conviction date, and insurance companies are prohibited from using conviction history older than three years for purposes of rate setting or determining eligibility.

The length of a driver license suspension varies in accordance with the underlying violation from thirty days to indefinite.

- Seatbelt convictions are not listed on the driving record.
- Driver address and SSN not provided as part of the public record.
- Accidents are not reported unless the damage is over $1000 and a conviction is rendered.
- The state does not permit driver school attendance in lieu of conviction removal or removal/reduction of conviction points.

Data Retention

Traffic violations remain in the state database indefinitely. Surrendered licenses are purged from the computer system five years after the expiration date. To view the mandatory retention requirements for CDL holders, see the Appendix.

Court to Repository

The courts must submit information to the Motor Vehicle Division within five days after a conviction is final. (Violators have a ten day window to appeal a traffic conviction – most convictions are final upon expiration of time of appeal.) Most convictions are reported electronically from court to Motor Vehicle Division. Paper conviction reports are recorded on a driver record within five to ten days.

State Reciprocity for Non-CDL Drivers

- Will not suspend license of driver for unpaid out-of-state convictions.
- Record of new incoming driver is shown on MVR.
- Out-of-state convictions are shown on MVR.
- Out-of-state accidents are shown on MVR.
- Convictions of out-of-state drivers are sent to home state.
- Record is forwarded to new state upon surrender of license upon request

Abbreviations for Classes, Restrictions, Endorsements, Status

License Classes– Commercial

Montana began issuing the CDL in October of 1990 with red text and containing the words "COMMERCIAL DRIVERS LICENSE." Existing Chauffeurs' Licenses remain valid as a Class D until they expire. CDL is not noted on Driving Record abstract, except through classification

Class A	Any combination of two or more vehicles, including trailer(s) in excess of 10,000 pounds, articulated buses with a GVWR exceeding 26,000 pounds, and all vehicles authorized to be driven under Class B, C, or D.
Class B	Any single vehicle in excess of 26,000 pounds GVWR, or any such vehicle towing a vehicle not in excess of 10,000 pounds GVWR, or any school bus and any vehicle designed to carry and capable of carrying more than sixteen passengers (including the driver), and all vehicles under Class C or D.
Class C	A single vehicle under 26,000 pounds GVWR which may tow a trailer under 10,000 pounds GVWR which hauls hazardous materials in an amount sufficient to require placarding under "CFR391," and any such vehicle which transports sixteen or more passengers (including the driver), and all school buses.
Type 1	Allows a driver to operate a commercial motor vehicle (CMV) in interstate commerce.
Type 2	Montana Only - Allows a driver to operate a CMV intrastate (only within the state of Montana) commerce.

License Classes– Non-Commercial

Class D	Regular non-commercial license.

Notes:

- A Learner Licensee allows an individual who has paid the license fees and passed the vision and written tests to operate a vehicle when accompanied by a driver who has a valid license of the same class and type as that of the vehicle being driven. A learner's license is valid for up to one-year from the date of successfully passing the knowledge test.
- "Motorcycle; motor-driven cycles" is shown as an endorsement (Standard Motorcycle), not as a class. One can get a motorcycle license only, but there is no separate license class indicated.
- Seasonal CDL is valid 03/15 to 09/10—180 day period of the current year.

Restrictions

AT	Automatic Transmission Only		LM	Left Outside Mirror
BB	B or C Bus		MA	Mechanical Aid
BU	To and From Bus Only		MO	Montana Only
CB	C Bus		MV	Med Variance
CL	Corrective Lenses		NB	No Airbrake Equipped Vehicles
DO	Daylight Hours Only		NI	No Interstate
EO	Essential Driving Only		NR	No Recreational
FA	FARSI CV Waiver		NT	No Tractor Trailer
FI	FARSI Waiver Inactive		NW	No Inclement Weather Driving
IL	Interlock Device		PA	Prosthetic Aid
LL	Learner License		PR	Probation Restriction

| RA | Restricted Area | | RS | 45-55 Miles Per Hour Speed Limitation |
| RL | 1st Year Restricted Graduated DL | | SC | To and From School Only |

Endorsements

			N	Tanker
H	Hazardous Materials		P	Passenger; sixteen or more
T	Double/Trailer		M	Motorcycle
S	School Bus			
O	Other			

Motorcycle Endorsements

			8	Fail Skills Test
1	Standard Motorcycle Endorsement		9	Learner Motorcycle Endorsement
3	3 / 4 Wheeler Only			
7	Fail Written			

License Type Codes

			07	RECORD ONLY	Record Only
00	NO LICENSE	No License	08	DECEASED	Deceased
01	DRIVER	Driver	10	MC ONLY	Motorcycle Only
02	COMMERCIAL	Commercial	16	SURRENDERED	Surrendered
03	PROB DRIVER	Probationary Driver			
05	ID CARD	Identification Card			

License Status Codes

			NL	NO LCE	No License
CA	CNCLD	Canceled	NR	NEWSOR	Driver Changed to New SOR
CL	CDLTEMP	Commercial Temp learner License	PT	PEND TRAN	Pending Transaction (RIP)
CR	SORINP	Change SOR in Progress	RV	REVOKE	Revoke
DN	DENIED	Denied	SU	SUSPEND	Suspended
DR	FAILDR	Drive test Failure	TL	TELL	Traffic Ed Learners License
EX	EXP	Expired	VA	VALID	Valid
IA	IA	Inactive	WF	WF	Written Test Failure
IC	INCMPL	Incomplete			
LL	LLIC	Learners License			

Montana Conviction Table with ACD, Statute, and Points

In Montana, a Uniform Violation Code (UVC) is used to record a conviction on a driver record. If a UVC has an assigned ACD Code, then conviction information is transmitted and shared with other states. If a UVC has no assigned ACD Code, then the corresponding conviction is only recorded on the Montana motor vehicle record only and is not shared with other states.

Note: Montana has an excellent resource – the **MT Bond Book** – which provides a wealth of information regarding maximum penalties and mandatory minimums for felonies and misdemeanors, including all vehicle related incidents. Visit http://courts.mt.gov/content/lcourt/training_guides/2010_bondbook.pdf.

Following this table are:
- **Table of Federal Regulations Code with MVR Descriptors**
- **Table of Driver Improvement (DI) Actions**
- **Summary of Points**

MVR Descriptor	MCA	UVC	ACD	Points
.02 blood alcohol content under 21	61-8-410(1)	V0017	A60	2
3-axle truck with insufficient reserve or vacuum reservoir	61-9-310(2)	V7272	E31	2
Aggravated DUI	61-8-465	V5107	A20	10
Aiding or abetting in speed contest on highway	61-8-308 [2]	V5132	S95	5
Allowing vehicle to coast downgrade	61-8-362	V5730	N80	2
Alter or forge certificate of reg or ownership	61-3-603	V8170	U03	12
Alter/deface/remove traffic control device-RR sign	61-8-713(2)	V5100		0
Assist person restricted to interlock	61-8-440(2)	V1132		2
Back-up lamps illuminated when veh in forward motion	61-9-219(3) [2]	V7185	E34	2
Basic rule - reasonable and prudent	61-8-303(3)	V5140	S94	2
Binders fail to meet minimum specifications	61-9-414(2)(a)	V7065	E50	2
Brakes required on all wheels	61-9-304	V7259	E02	2
Careless driving	61-8-302(1)	V5134	M81	2
Careless driving w/ death/serious bodily injury	61-8-302(1) [2]	V5135	M81	2
Carry package, etc, wh/interfere w/operation of mc/quad	61-8-359(3)	V5703	F66	2
Carry passenger on mc/quad which interferes w/driver	61-8-359(2)	V5702	F66	2
Change lanes when unsafe to do so	61-8-328(1)	V5280	M42	2
Circumvent the operation of an interlock device	61-8-440(3)	V1131	A41	2
CMV w/engine comp brake not equipped with working muffler	61-9-321(1)	V7281	E01	2
Committing perjury concerning D/L matters	61-5-303(2)	V1161	D78	0

MVR Descriptor	MCA	UVC	ACD	Points
Concealing a material fact in DL/ID application	61-5-302(5) [4]	V1157	D02	2
Crossing fire hose	61-8-364	V5750	M56	2
Deface/damage/interfere with traffic device	61-8-713	V5041		2
Deface/damage/remove highway sign/signal/marker	61-8-713(1)	V5040		0
Defective brakes--motor-driven cycle	61-9-315(1)	V7280	E31	2
Defective horn--warning device	61-9-401(1) [1]	V7290	E01	2
Defective lights--motor-driven cycle	61-9-223(1)	V7210	E34	2
Defective or improper mud flaps	61-9-407(2)	V7341	E01	2
Defective or removed seat belts	61-9-409(3) [2]	V7370	E01	2
Defective or shattered windshield	61-9-405(2)(b)	V7317	E70	2
Defective rear-view mirror	61-9-404 [2]	V7311	E01	2
Defective signal lamps	61-9-218(2)	V7172	E34	2
Defective signal lamps on school bus	61-9-402(3) [2]	V7162	E36	2
Defective taillamps--insufficient visibility	61-9-204(1) [2]	V7031	E34	2
Defective windshield wipers	61-9-405(3) [1]	V7321	E01	2
Deprive mc/quad of full use of traffic lane	61-8-359(7)	V5713	M40	2
Disobedience to direction of safety/peace officer	61-8-105	V5000	M08	2
Disobey local turn signs and markers	61-8-333(3)	V5337	M05	2
Disobey signals indicating approach of rr train	61-8-347(1)	V5570	M10	2
Display invalid D/L (cancel, rev., susp. fict or altered)	61-5-302(1) [1]	V1150	B41	2
Display or represent as one's own the DL/ID of another	61-5-302(3)	V1153	D16	2
Display unauthorized blue light	61-9-402(7)	V7167	E70	2
Display unauthorized flashing headlamps/backup lamps	61-9-402(9)	V7169	E70	2
Display unauthorized green light	61-9-402(8)	V7168	E70	2
Display warning signs that do not meet specs	61-9-416(1)(b)	V7601	E70	2
Displaying fictitious, altered, etc., license plates	61-3-301(3) [1]	V8122		0
Displaying license plates assigned to another vehicle	61-3-301(3) [2]	V8124		0
Displaying prior design license plates after 18 months	61-3-301(3) [3]	V8127		0
Displaying unauthorized red light	61-9-226(2)	V7231	E70	2
Drawing more than three motor vehicles by saddlemount	61-10-104(3) [2]	S2080		2
Drive across central divide of controlled access hwy	61-8-331(2)	V5311	M51	2
Drive on other than right-hand roadway of div highway	61-8-330 [1]	V5300	N71	2
Drive over/etc divided space or barrier of div highway	61-8-330 [2]	V5301	M02	2
Driver fails to exercise due care/observing pedestrian	61-8-504	V5470	N08	2
Driver of slow-moving veh fail/pull off rdway as reqd	61-9-415(3)	V7143	M60	2
Driving a CMV while disqualified/federal law	61-5-212(1)(ii)	V1171	B24	6
Driving commercial vehicle with BAC .04 or greater	61-8-406(1)(b)	V5115	A04	10
Driving in special left turn lane when prohibited	61-8-333(4)(b)	V5339	M62	2
Driving into/parking within 1 block of fire apparatus	61-8-363 [2]	V5741	F34	2
Driving MV in signed/delineated bicycle lane	61-8-328(6)	V5287	M47	2
Driving through barrier or gate at rr crossing	61-8-347(2)	V5571	M10	2
Driving under the influence of alcohol	61-8-401(1)(a)	V5110	A21	10
Driving under the influence of alcohol and drugs	61-8-401(1)(d)	V5114	A23	10
Driving under the influence of any drug (narcotic etc.)	61-8-401(1)(b)	V5111	A22	10
Driving under the influence of non-narcotic drugs	61-8-401(1)(c)	V5113	A24	10
Driving w/o a valid D/L	61-5-102(1) [2]	V1100	B51	2
Driving while privilege to do so is suspended/revoked	61-5-212(1)(i)	V1170	B26	6
Driving without a valid D/L	61-5-102(1) [1]	V1000	B51	0
Employing unlicensed cvo	61-5-305	V1190		0
Exceed 35 MPH maximum speed limit for haystack movers	61-10-123(4)	S2121	S92	3
Exceed 55 mph limit for triples 12 miles over or more	61-10-124(4)(g)[3]	S2090	S92	3
Exceed 55mph limit for triples 6-12 miles over	61-10-124(4)(g)[2]	S2128	S92	3
Exceed 95' max length w/o permit	61-10-124(2) [2]	S2068		0
Exceed overall length - tks / tk tractors	61-10-104(5)[2]	S2086		0
Exceeding 11,000 lb single axle wt (exclude steering axle)	61-10-107(2)(a) [1]	S2097		0
Exceeding 14'0" height limit	61-10-103	S2075		0
Exceeding 20,000 pounds single axle weight limit	61-10-107(1) [1]	S2093		0
Exceeding 34,000 pounds tandem axle weight limit	61-10-107(1) [2]	S2094		0
Exceeding 500 lb psi width on single axle	61-10-107(2)(a) [2]	S2098	E37	2
Exceeding 53' maximum semi trailer length	61-10-104(2)[a]	S2088		0
Exceeding 55' maximum bus length	61-10-104(1)[2}	S2077		0
Exceeding 55' maximum truck length	61-10-104(1)[1]	S2076		0
Exceeding 75' maximum combo vehicle length	61-10-104(2)[c]	S2089		0
Exceeding 75 mile limit (haystack movers)	61-10-123(2)	S2120		2
Exceeding Maximum GVW	61-10-107(1) [3]	S2095		0
Exceeding maximum size (haystack movers)	61-10-123(1)	S2119		0

MVR Descriptor	MCA	UVC	ACD	Points
Exceeding number of driving lamps permitted	61-9-225(2)	V7220	E70	2
Exceeding permit GVW	61-10-146(2)(a)	S2109		0
Exceeding the 102" width limit	61-10-102(1)	S2070		0
Expired transit plates	61-4-301(2) [2]	S3210		0
Fail other vehicles/equipment with proper lighting-dark	61-9-216	V7140	E55	2
Fail to affix decal to collectors motor vehicle	61-3-412(4)	V8012		0
Fail to affix validating sticker to rear license plate	61-3-332(2)	V8001		0
Fail to carry 2 fire extinguishers--veh carrying expl	61-9-413(3)	V7401	E01	2
Fail to carry extension cord for towed vehicle-tow truck	61-9-416(1)(g) [1]	V7607	E01	2
Fail to carry fire extinguisher-tow truck	61-9-416(1)(c)	V7605	E01	2
Fail to carry flares/lanterns/warning lights	61-9-416(1)(a)	V7600	E01	2
Fail to carry receipt for special mobile equipment	61-3-434 [1]	V3176		0
Fail to carry shovel and/or spread dirt on oil/grease-tow	61-9-416(1)(f)	V7606	E01	2
Fail to comply with duties applicable to mc operator	61-8-359(8)	V5707	F06	2
Fail to comply with written notice of mech defects	61-9-503(2)	V7501		2
Fail to dim within 1000 feet of oncoming traffic	61-9-221(1)	V7200	E54	2
Fail to disp dlr/equip plate on spec mobile vehicle	61-3-431(1)(a)	V3175		0
Fail to disp MT plates - veh used for hire	61-3-701(2)	V8151		0
Fail to display D/L when demanded	61-5-116 [2]	V1061	B78	2
Fail to display foreign base plates with r.p.o. plate	61-3-702	V8160		0
Fail to display lamp on projecting load at night	61-9-213(2)	V7111	E70	2
Fail to display lamp or flag on projecting load	61-9-213(1)	V7110	E70	2
Fail to display special receipt for inspection	61-3-434 [2]	V3177		0
Fail to display stop/turn/tail lights on towed vehicle	61-9-416(1)(g) [2]	V7671	E05	2
Fail to display warning devices--disabled vehicle	61-9-412	V7390	E50	2
Fail to drive to right of roadway except when passing	61-8-321(1)	V5200	M41	2
Fail to drive to the right/slow traffic	61-8-321(3)	V5206	M60	2
Fail to exhibit proof of insurance upon demand	61-6-302(2)	V9019	B74	5
Fail to follow directions/requirements of spec permit	61-10-146(1) [2]	S2111		0
Fail to give approaching vehicle half of roadway	61-8-322	V5210	N06	2
Fail to give complete accurate information on CV app	61-5-107(2) [2]	V1041	D02	2
Fail to give complete accurate information on D/L app	61-5-107(2) [1]	V1040	D02	2
Fail to give notice of accident by quickest means	61-7-108	V4050	B61	4
Fail to give right of way to a funeral procession	61-8-380(1)	V5822	N05	2
Fail to have 2 headlamps properly operating on mtr veh	61-9-203(1)	V7020	E05	2
Fail to have 2 lighted headlamps during hours of dark	61-9-225(1)	V7219	E05	2
Fail to have 40 day temp reg permit - fert app veh	61-3-431(1)(b)	S3174		0
Fail to have at least two binders on loaded log truck	61-9-414(2)(c)	V7064	E01	2
Fail to have beam indicator, when required	61-9-220(3)	V7190	E05	2
Fail to have binder secured by fastner	61-9-414(2)(b)	V7066	E50	2
Fail to have both ends of short logs secured by binder	61-9-414(2)(d)	V7067	E01	2
Fail to have both red/amber signal lts on school bus	61-9-402(3) [1]	V7161	E06	2
Fail to have clearance lamps on trailer or semitrailer	61-9-208(4)(a)	V7058	E05	2
Fail to have clearance lamps on truck tractor	61-9-208(3)	V7056	E05	2
Fail to have clearance lamps/reflectors on trailer	61-9-208(4)(d)	V7083	E05	2
Fail to have D/L in immediate possession	61-5-116 [1]	V1060	B78	2
Fail to have emergency warning devices in vehicle	61-9-411(1)	V7380	E01	2
Fail to have lamps lighted on parked or disabled veh	61-9-214(2)	V7120	E70	2
Fail to have lamps lighted when required	61-9-201	V7010	E05	2
Fail to have mc/quad or mtr driven cycle equip w/refl	61-9-205(1) [2]	V7043	E05	2
Fail to have motor vehicle equipped with windshield	61-9-405(1) [1]	V7312	E01	2
Fail to have pilot cars properly equipped	61-10-123(3) [2]	S2118	E01	2
Fail to have police vehicle equipped with siren	61-9-402(1)	V7160	E01	2
Fail to have proof of separation military D/L	61-5-104(5) [2]	V1013		2
Fail to have proper emblem/slow moving veh when reqd	61-9-415(1)	V7141	E01	2
Fail to have proper headlamps on motorcycle	61-9-203(2) [1]	V7021	E05	2
Fail to have rear reflectors trailer less than 3000 gvw	61-9-208(6)(b) [1]	V7075	E05	2
Fail to have rear-view mirror	61-9-404 [1]	V7310	E01	2
Fail to have reflectors on pole trailer over 3000 gvw	61-9-208(5)(b)	V7074	E05	2
Fail to have reflectors on trailer or semi-trailer	61-9-208(4)(c)	V7069	E05	2
Fail to have safety chain when required on trailer	61-9-208(6)(a)	V7068	E01	2
Fail to have sidemarker lamp & clearance lamp pole tr	61-9-208(5)(a)	V7073	E05	2
Fail to have stoplamp trailer less than 3000 gvw	61-9-208(6)(b) [2]	V7076	E05	2
Fail to have temporary driving permit in possession	61-5-106(3)(b)	V1032		2
Fail to have two pilot cars (haystack movers)	61-10-123(3) [1]	S2117		2
Fail to have veh equipped with 1or 2 taillamps as req	61-9-204(1) [1]	V7030	E05	2

MVR Descriptor	MCA	UVC	ACD	Points
Fail to have veh equipped with mud flaps as required	61-9-407(1)	V7340	E01	2
Fail to have veh equipped with signal lamps when req	61-8-337(2)	V5370	E05	2
Fail to have vehicle equipped with license plate lamp	61-9-204(3) [1]	V7033	E05	2
Fail to have vehicle/trlr equipped with brakes	61-9-301	V7260	E02	2
Fail to have windshield wipers	61-9-405(3) [2]	V7322	E01	2
Fail to id self and vehicle when involved in accident	61-7-105 [1]	V4020	B14	4
Fail to identify disabled veh w/proper equip while tow	61-9-416(1)(d)	V7603	E01	2
Fail to keep seat belts in working order	61-9-409(3) [1]	V7367	F04	2
Fail to keep vehicle under control on mountain highway	61-8-361 [1]	V5720	N84	2
Fail to leave identity in struck vehicle	61-7-106 [2]	V4031	B08	4
Fail to maintain brakes in good working order	61-9-313(1) [1]	V7270	E02	2
Fail to maintain lamps in proper working order	61-9-109(5)	V7006	E34	2
Fail to meet height requirements for taillamps	61-9-204(2)	V7032	E70	2
Fail to notify department of change of address	61-5-115 [1]	V1090		0
Fail to notify department of change of name	61-5-115 [2]	V1091		0
Fail to notify owner/damage to prop/fixtures along hwy	61-7-107	V4040	B08	4
Fail to obey direction to be weighed	61-10-141(1) [1]	S2100	M14	2
Fail to obey instructions of traffic control devices	61-8-201	V5050	M14	2
Fail to obey peace officer/highway patrol/public safety wrk	61-9-105	V7003	E55	2
Fail to obey red (stop) traffic signal	61-8-207(3) [1]	V5063	M16	2
Fail to obtain trip permit by non-resident	61-10-211(1)	S3130		0
Fail to pay addl GVW fees to cover overload	61-10-233(2)	S3164		0
Fail to permit officer to inspect special permit	61-10-142 [2]	S2114		
Fail to place red flare/lantern/warning light/reflector	61-9-431(5)	V7610	E55	2
Fail to place warning signs as required	61-9-431(1)	V7602	E50	2
Fail to proceed w/caution past red or blue light	61-9-402(5)	V7163	N04	2
Fail to properly display trip permit in vehicle	61-10-212(1)	S3140		0
Fail to properly secure license plates	61-3-301(1) [3]	V8123		0
Fail to provide supplemental info of accident	61-7-109(2)	V4061	B61	4
Fail to purchase trip permit immed upon arrive in st	61-10-213 [1]	S3150		0
Fail to reduce spd - lane next to stationary ER/police veh	61-8-346(4)	V5433	N84	3
Fail to reg o/s mv - for hire/gainfully employed	61-3-701(1)	V8150		0
Fail to remain at acci scene where person injured	61-7-103(1) [2]	V4001	B07	8
Fail to remain at acci scene where person killed	61-7-103(1) [4]	V4003	B06	8
Fail to remain at property accident scene	61-7-104(1) [2]	V4011	B08	4
Fail to render reasonable assistance to injured	61-7-105 [3]	V4022	B07	8
Fail to renew D/L within 30 days from milit separation	61-5-104(5) [1]	V1012	B51	2
Fail to renew pioneer/vintage plates when veh change owners	61-3-411(4)	V8011		0
Fail to replace lost/mutilated cert of registration	61-3-341	V8214		0
Fail to secure leverage handle	61-9-414(2)(b)(iii)	V7054	E50	2
Fail to secure load	61-8-370	S5810		2
Fail to show DL to other parties involved in accident	61-7-105 [2]	V4021		2
Fail to signal intention to turn within 300 feet/turn	61-8-336(3)	V5364	N43	2
Fail to slow for sch bus prep to stop for school child	61-8-351(2)	V5631	M75	2
Fail to slow/use caution for stationary emergency veh	61-8-346(3)	V5432	N84	2
Fail to sound horn to insure safe operation	61-9-401(1) [2]	V7291	E50	2
Fail to stop and id self after striking unattended veh	61-7-106 [1]	V4030	B08	4
Fail to stop at intersection w/ inoperative electronic TCD	61-8-212	V5091	M16	2
Fail to stop at rr crossing when carrying explosives	61-8-349(1) [3]	V5592	M22	2
Fail to stop at rr crossing when carrying flamm liquid	61-8-349(1) [4]	V5593	M22	2
Fail to stop at rr crossing when driving school bus	61-8-349(1) [2]	V5591	M22	2
Fail to stop at rr crossing when stop sign erected	61-8-348	V5580	M10	2
Fail to stop for red or blue light	61-9-402(4)	V7164	N04	2
Fail to stop immed at acci scene where person injured	61-7-103(1) [1]	V4000	B03	8
Fail to stop immed at acci scene where person killed	61-7-103(1) [3]	V4002	B02	8
Fail to stop immed at prop damage acci scene	61-7-104(1) [1]	V4010	B04	4
Fail to submit vehicle to inspection	61-9-503(1)	V7500		2
Fail to submit written report of acc w/n 10 days	61-7-109(1)	V4060	B61	4
Fail to surrender all D/L in poss before rec prob D/L	61-5-206(2) [2]	V1111		0
Fail to surrender amateur radio plates when required	61-3-425 [2]	V8030		0
Fail to surrender o/s D/L	61-5-102(1) [3]	V1001		0
Fail to surrender suspended, revoked or canceled DL/ID	61-5-302(4)	V1154	D16	0
Fail to surrender viol spec permit to officer when ordered	61-10-143	S2115		2
Fail to use sign/flare/reflector as required - flag persons	61-9-431	V7374	E01	2
Fail to wear protective eyeware with no windshield	61-9-405(1) [2]	V7313	E01	2
Fail to Yield - Blind Pedestrian	61-8-516	V5503	N08	2

MVR Descriptor	MCA	UVC	ACD	Points
Fail to yield row to ped when obeying green traffic signal	61-8-207(1) [2]	V5061	N24	2
Fail to yield row to veh when obeying grn traf signal	61-8-207(1) [1]	V5060	N24	2
Fail to yield to overtaking vehicle	61-8-323(2) [1]	V5221	N07	2
Fail/adjust brakes w/respect to wheel on opposite side	61-9-313(1) [2]	V7271	E31	2
Fail/carry special permit in vehicle to which it refer	61-10-142 [1]	S2113		0
Fail/dim within 300 feet when approach veh from rear	61-9-221(2)	V7201	E54	2
Fail/dr to rt side of rd in canyons, defiles, mountain road	61-8-361 [2]	V5721	N70	2
Fail/equip auth emerg veh with red sig lamps alternate	61-9-402(2)(b)	V7166	E05	2
Fail/equip auth emerg veh with siren and flash red lit	61-9-402(2)(a)	V7165	E05	2
Fail/exhibit certificate of reg when requested	61-3-322(3)	V8053		0
Fail/have auto breakway brakes/trlr over 3000 lbs gvw	61-9-305	V7263	E02	2
Fail/have bus or truck properly equip w/clearance lamp	61-9-208(2)(a)	V7061	E05	2
Fail/have bus or truck properly equip w/side mark lamp	61-9-208(2)(c)	V7062	E05	2
Fail/have bus/truck properly equipped with reflectors	61-9-208(1)	V7060	E05	2
Fail/have child under 6 years old properly restrained	61-9-420	V7361	F02	2
Fail/have side marker lamps on trailer or semitrailer	61-9-208(4)(b)	V7059	E05	2
Fail/have supply air reservoir safeguard agnst backflo	61-9-307	V7264	E31	2
Fail/have taillamps wired to illuminate with headlamps	61-9-204(3) [2]	V7034	E34	2
Fail/have veh equipped w/two reflectors when required	61-9-205(1) [1]	V7040	E05	2
Fail/mark trailer w/ident number assigned by registrar	61-3-107	V8054		0
Fail/prevent escape of excessive fumes/smoke from mv	61-9-403(2)	V7301	E01	2
Fail/remove unloaded excess commodities from hwy r.o.w	61-10-141(2)	S2108		2
Fail/stop at rr cross when carrying passenger for hire	61-8-349(1) [1]	V5590	M22	2
Fail/stop school bus stopped (load or unload sch child)	61-8-351(1)	V5630	M75	2
Fail/Unload excess weight/load when directed to do so	61-10-141(1) [2]	S2101	M14	2
Fail/yield row to ped or traf when obey grn arrow sig	61-8-207(1)(b)	V5064	N24	2
Failure of passenger to give immed notice/driver unable	61-7-110(2)	V4070	B61	4
Failure of veh owner to submit written report/dr unable	61-7-110(3)	V4071	B61	4
Failure to surrender license	61-6-112	V1205	D27	0
Falsifying affidavit to obtain DL/ID	61-5-302(5) [1]	V1080	D02	2
Fl to carry broom and/or clean debris from road-tow truck	61-9-416(1)(e)	V7604	E01	2
Fl to have bus/truck >80" wide equipped with reflectors	61-9-208(2)(d)	V7082	E05	2
Fl to have bus/truck >80" wide with clearance lamps (rear)	61-9-208(2)(b)	V7077	E05	2
Fl to obey trfc cntrl dev designating specific lane	61-8-328(3)	V5282	M42	2
Fl to stop rr w/o stop sign view impaired-train approach	61-8-348(2)	V5581	M20	2
Flashing signal violation (red or yellow)	61-8-209(1)	V5080	M18	2
Fleeing/eluding a peace officer	61-8-316(2)(a)	V5198	U01	5
Fleeing/eluding a peace officer w/mv inj-death	61-8-316(2)(b)	V5199	U01	5
Fog lamps used as headlamps	61-9-217(2) [2]	V7155	E70	2
Following fire apparatus closer than 500 ft	61-8-363 [1]	V5740	M33	2
Following to closely--reasonable and prudent	61-8-329(1)	V5290	M34	2
Following too close-insuff space between veh or combo	61-8-329(2)	V5291	M34	2
Front side window tinting-allows less than 24% light	61-9-405(4)(b)	V7323	E70	2
FTO conditions of triples permit	61-10-124(4)(g)[1]	S2067		2
FTO traffic control device prohibiting lane change	61-8-328(5)	V5286	M14	2
FTY row for hwy maintenance veh flashing lights	61-8-317	V5201	N06	2
FTY row to bicycle within designated bicycle lane	61-8-320(2)	V5284	N03	2
Giving false info in written accident report	61-7-110(4)	V4072	B61	4
Habitual offender operating motor vehicle	61-11-213	V1203	B25	6
Hauling hay over 16 1/2ft w/o flag escort	61-10-102(2)(b)	S2085	E50	2
Having in possession or control more than one MT D/L	61-5-102(1) [5]	V1050	D07	2
Holding a race or speed contest w/o written permit	61-8-308 [1]	V5130	S95	5
Holding a speed contest, which is not patrolled	61-8-308 [3]	V5133	S95	5
Husbandry/comb - no lamps indicating projections	61-9-215(4)(c)	V7134	E55	2
Illegal entrance or exit to restricted access highway	61-8-331(1)	V5310	M50	2
Illegal use of spotlights, etc.	61-9-217(1)	V7150	E70	2
Improper aiming of single beam lamp – motorcycle	61-9-223(3)	V7212	E55	2
Improper approach when making left turn	61-8-333(1)(b) [2]	V5333	N53	2
Improper approach when making right turn	61-8-333(1)(a) [2]	V5331	N54	2
Improper color backup light	61-9-209(3)(c)	V7079	E70	2
Improper color license plate light	61-9-209(3)(b)	V7078	E70	2
Improper color of signal device on rear of vehicle	61-9-209(3)(a)	V7084	E70	2
Improper color of stop lamps	61-9-206(2) [2]	V7170	E70	2
Improper color signal lamp	61-9-218(1) [3]	V7176	E70	2
Improper color undercarriage lights	61-9-226(4) [2]	V7238	E70	2
Improper color, reflectors	61-9-209(3)	V7072	E70	2

MVR Descriptor	MCA	UVC	ACD	Points
Improper color,clearance lamp	61-9-209(1)	V7070	E70	2
Improper color,side marker lamp	61-9-209(2)	V7071	E70	2
Improper color--cowl or fender lamps	61-9-219(1) [2]	V7181	E70	2
Improper color--running board lamps	61-9-219(2) [2]	V7183	E70	2
Improper display of transit plates	61-4-307	S3220		0
Improper distribution of light - high beam	61-9-220(1)	V7188	E34	2
Improper distribution of light - low beam	61-9-220(2)	V7189	E34	2
Improper left turn onto one-way roadway	61-8-333(1)(c)	V5335	N53	2
Improper markings--vehicle carrying explosives	61-9-413(2)	V7400	E70	2
Improper method of hand/arm signals	61-8-338	V5371	N44	2
Improper mount of clearance lamps bus/trk/trlr	61-9-210(4)	V7081	E70	2
Improper mount of reflectors (24"--60") bus/trk/trlr	61-9-210(1)	V7080	E70	2
Improper mounted signal lamps	61-9-218(1) [2]	V7173	E70	2
Improper mounting of emblem denoting slow-moving veh	61-9-415(2)	V7142	E70	2
Improper mounting of headlamps	61-9-203(3)	V7022	E70	2
Improper mounting of reflectors	61-9-205(2) [1]	V7041	E70	2
Improper mounting or adjustment - fog lamps	61-9-217(2) [1]	V7151	E70	2
Improper mounting--auxiliary driving lamps	61-9-217(3) [2]	V7153	E70	2
Improper operation of a vehicle in procession	61-8-382	V5824	N84	2
Improper or illegal use of lic plates before transfer	61-3-335(1)	V8212		0
Improper parking at injury/fatality crash scene	61-7-103(1) [5]	V4004	F34	2
Improper parking at property damage accident scene	61-7-104(1) [3]	V4012	F34	2
Improper pass-appro w/n 100 ft bridge etc whn view obstr	61-8-325(2)(c)	V5252	M77	2
Improper pass-approach crest of grade (hill) or curve	61-8-325(2)(a)	V5250	M74	2
Improper passing--approaching intersection	61-8-325(2)(b)	V5251	M70	2
Improper passing--crowding overtaken vehicle	61-8-323(1)	V5220	M70	2
Improper passing--highway ahead obstructed	61-8-325(1)	V5240	M70	2
Improper passing--in no-passing zone	61-8-326(1)	V5260	M71	2
Improper starting--fail to start vehicle in safety	61-8-335	V5350	N83	2
Improper turn – grade, curve, traffic approach w/n 500 ft	61-8-334(2)	V5341	N56	2
Improper turn--crest of grade or on curve	61-8-334(1)	V5340	N56	2
Improper turn--not in required position	61-8-336(1) [1]	V5360	N52	2
Improper use of a funeral vehicle	61-8-381(1)	V5823		2
Improper use of amber light-use only for funeral	61-8-381(2)	V5826	E70	2
Improper use of center lane of three-lane roadway	61-8-328(2)	V5281	M62	2
Improper use of four-way emergency signal lamps	61-9-219(4)	V7186	E70	2
Improper use of off road lamps	61-9-217(4)	V7156	E70	2
Improper use of siren, whistle, or bell	61-9-401(4)	V7294	E70	2
Improper use of theft alarm when vehicle is in motion	61-9-401(3)	V7295	E70	2
Improper use of transit plates	61-4-301(2) [1]	V8128		0
Improperly adjusted supplementary light	61-9-226(1)	V7230	E70	2
Improperly retain/fail to sur spl mil/vet license plate	61-3-458	V8049		0
Inadequate lights	61-9-221	V7004	E55	2
Inadequate or defective parking brake	61-9-303	V7262	E31	2
Inadequate or defective service brakes	61-9-302	V7261	E31	2
Increasing speed when being overtaken	61-8-323(2) [2]	V5222	S97	2
Insufficient lamps on combination of vehicles	61-9-212	V7100	E05	2
Insufficient or inadequate reservoir for brakes	61-9-310(1)	V7268	E31	2
Insufficient visibility of reflectors	61-9-205(2) [2]	V7042	E70	2
Insufficient visibility of stop lamps	61-9-206(2) [1]	V7052	E70	2
Insufficient visibility—clearance lamps bus/trk/trl	61-9-211(2)	V7091	E70	2
Insufficient visibility—side marker lamps bus/trk/trl	61-9-211(3)	V7092	E70	2
Insufficient visibility—signal lamps	61-9-218(1) [1]	V7174	E70	2
Insufficient visiblility—reflectors bus/trk/trlr	61-9-211(1)	V7090	E70	2
Interference with a funeral procession	61-8-383	V5825	N05	2
Interfering with driver's view or control over vehicle	61-8-360(2)	V5711	D70	2
Interfering with traffic by opening vehicle door	61-8-368	V5790	N84	2
Interfering with traffic while backing	61-8-358	V5690	N82	2
Left turn from other than special left turn lane	61-8-333(4)(a)	V5338	N52	2
Lighter trailer in front of heavier trailer	61-10-124(4)(g)	S2091		2
Logs over 15 ft w/o permit	61-10-104(5)[1]	S2082		0
Making a false statement in DL/ID application	61-5-302(5) [3]	V1156	D02	2
Making false affidavit concerning D/L matters	61-5-303 [1]	V1160	D02	0
Making left turn from improper lane	61-8-333(1)(b) [1]	V5332	N52	2
Making right turn from improper lane	61-8-333(1)(a) [1]	V5330	N52	2
Mc/Quad passenger not seated on firmly attached seat	61-8-359(1) [2]	V5701	F66	2

MVR Descriptor	MCA	UVC	ACD	Points
Misrepresent size/weight/load when obtaining permit	61-10-146(1) [1]	S2110		0
More than one on one-seated mc/quad	61-8-359(1) [1]	V5700	F66	2
Motor Fuel Theft	45-6-301	V0611	U04	0
Motor-driven cycle over 35mph without headlights	61-8-312(3) [2]	V5185	E55	2
Moving defective vehicle beyond specified limits	61-9-503(3)	V7502		2
MT res operate w/foreign D/L over 60 days	61-5-103(1)	V1006	B51	2
Mufflers defective or improper	61-9-403(1)	V7300	E01	2
Multi beam headlamps fail to meet requirement	61-9-223(2)	V7211	E05	2
No commercial driver license when required	61-5-102(2)(b) [1]	V1052	B56	2
No motorcycle endorsement	61-5-102(2)(a)	V1051	B91	2
No seat belt front left/right side	61-9-409(1)	V7360	F04	2
No seatbelts in vehicle manufactured after 1964	61-9-409	V7359	E01	2
No seatbelts in vehicle manufactured 1968 or newer	61-9-409(2)	V7365	F04	2
Not equipped with chains, cables, straps, webbing	61-9-414(1)	V7055	E01	2
Not having required id card on private veh with red light	61-9-227(2)	V7241	E70	2
Obstruct traff (slow veh fail to pull over)	61-8-311(2)	V5171	F34	2
Obstruct traffic, under minimum speed	61-8-311(1)	V5170	S96	2
Obstructing driver view/control over driving mechanism	61-8-360(1) [2]	V5710	D70	2
Op electric veh w/o proper lights/equip	61-9-432	V7611	E01	2
Op mv w/ exhaust noise in xs 95 decibels	61-9-435(1)	V7615	E01	2
Op non-divisible w/o permit	61-10-124(2)(f)(I)	S2084		0
Op veh w/ more than 3 people-front seat	61-8-360(1) [1]	V5714	D72	2
Oper a mtr veh in unsafe cond w/o proper lights/equip.	61-9-109(1) [1]	V7000	E05	2
Oper coll mc w/o taillamp during darkness	61-9-204(4)	V7035	E05	2
Oper emerg veh- fl drive w/due regard to sfty of others	61-8-346(2)	V5431	U21	2
Oper veh btw 5/31 and 10/1 w/stud tires excpt sch bus	61-9-406(3) [2]	V7333	E70	2
Oper veh whole laden GW exceeds GVW on own cert of reg	61-10-233(1)	S3161		0
Oper veh without traction devices when required	61-9-406(5)	V7334	E01	2
Operat mc/quad on public highway or st without lights	61-8-359(5)	V5705	E05	2
Operate a CMV without proper endorsement	61-5-102(2)(b) [2]	V1053	B91	2
Operate a veh which has not been properly registered	61-3-301(1) [2]	V8121		0
Operate assistive mobility device where prohibited	61-8-376	V5792		0
Operate CMV (HAZ) while subject to OOS order	61-8-812(1)[2]	V5102	B27	6
Operate CMV (PA) while subject to OOS order	61-8-812(1)[3]	V5103	B27	6
Operate CMV while subject to out-of-service order	61-8-812(1)[1]	V5101	B27	6
Operate dealer exempt veh in viol of exempt authorized	61-10-214(3)	V3172		0
Operate impl of husb over 12'6" w/o flag escort	61-10-102(2) [5]	S2074	E50	2
Operate implement of husbandry w/o lights	61-10-102(2)(a)	S2083	E50	2
Operate in excess of gvw license	61-10-233	V3168		0
Operate in state in excess time limit of trip permit	61-10-212(2)	S3141		0
Operate motor vehicle with obstructed windshield	61-9-405(2)(a)	V7314	E70	2
Operate overwidth impl of husbandry hours of darkness	61-10-102(2) [3]	S2072		2
Operate overwidth impl of husbandry over 100 mi w/o flag	61-10-102(2) [4]	S2073		2
Operate triple combo outside 2 mile limit	61-10-124(4)(a)	S2078		2
Operate veh (new or used) w/o permit display rear vehicle	61-3-317 [1]	V8078		0
Operate veh carry explosives/flammables w/o elect sgnl	61-9-411(2) [1]	V7381	E01	2
Operate veh in excess of gvw w/o obtaining spec permit	61-10-146(1) [3]	S2112		0
Operate veh in excess of season weight/speed restr (st/loc)	61-10-128(2)	S2116	S92	3
Operate veh w/o app for reg transfer-40 day grace period	61-3-317 [2]	V8213		0
Operate veh w/tires having illegal studs, etc.	61-9-406(3) [1]	V7332	E70	2
Operate vehicle w/expired staggered tlr Regis	61-3-721	S8163		0
Operating "exempt" city vehicle beyond 15 mile limit	61-10-214(1)	V3170		0
Operating a CMV with foreign CVOL/ENDR over 30 days	61-5-103(2)	V1007	B51	2
Operating a veh upon public highways w/o lic plates	61-3-301(1) [1]	V8120		0
Operating dual-wheel tractor +15 w/o flag veh	61-10-102(2) [1]	S2069	E01	2
Operating haystack mover during hours of darkness	61-10-123(5)	S2122		2
Operating haystack mover on interstate	61-10-123(6)	S2123		2
Operating in violation of restrictions imposed on D/L	61-5-113(4)	V1070	D29	2
Operating MC with modulating headlight after sunset	61-9-203(2) [2]	V7023	E70	2
Operating more than two mc abreast in traffic lane	61-8-359(6)	V5706	F06	2
Operating motor veh with BAC 0.08 or greater	61-8-406(1)(a)	V5112	A08	10
Operating motor veh without liab insurance in effect	61-6-301(4)	V9017	D36	5
Operating motorcycle/quad without helmet-under 18	61-9-417(1)	V5708	F03	2
Operating mv reg -10,000lbs w/o front or rear bumper	61-9-430(1)	V7375	E01	2
Operating overweight vehicle on highway	61-10-109	S2096		0
Operating veh with license plates obstructed to view	61-3-301(1) [4]	V8125		0

MVR Descriptor	MCA	UVC	ACD	Points
Operating vehicle not equipped with stop lamp	61-9-206(1) [2]	V7051	E05	2
Operating vehicle on highway with metal tires	61-9-406(2)	V7331	E70	2
Operating vehicle over 10,000 gvw w/o proper markings	61-3-709(1)	V8162		0
Operating vehicle with obscured/tinted headlights	61-9-203(4)	V7026	E70	2
Operating vehicle with obscured/tinted rear lights	61-9-204(5)	V7037	E70	2
Operating vehicle without interlock	61-8-440(1)	V1130	A41	2
Operating w/foreign D/L when privilege sus/rev by mont	61-5-210	V1140	B26	2
Operating with defective solid rubber tires	61-9-406(1)	V7330	E37	2
Operating with expired registration (reregister)	61-3-312	V8129		0
Operating with prohibited flashing lights	61-9-226(3)	V7232	E70	2
Operating without noise suppression device on mc/quad	61-9-418	V5709	E01	2
Operating without ssrs regulations	61-3-708	V8161		0
Operator allow passenger under 18 without headgear	61-9-417(2)	V5712	F06	2
Operator of mv interfering w/person riding bicycle	61-8-320(1)	V5283	N03	2
Overtaking vehicle stopped at crosswalk	61-8-502(2)	V5452	N20	2
Overweight/fail/use retract axle when required	61-10-145(2)	S2200		2
Overwidth impl of husbandry over 100 miles w/o permit	61-10-102(2) [2]	S2071		2
Owner allow unsafe vehicle to be driven on highway	61-9-109(1) [2]	V7001	F66	2
Owner permits operation of motor veh w/o insurance	61-6-301(1)	V9009	D36	5
Parking on road when practical to park off road	61-8-353(1) [1]	V5650		0
Pass to left of rotary traffic island	61-8-327(3)	V5270	N61	2
Passing on right when prohibited	61-8-324(2)	V5230	M73	2
Performance ability of brakes	61-9-312	V7274	E31	2
Permitting the use of your D/L by another	61-5-302(2)	V1152	D16	2
Permitting unauthorized minor to drive	61-5-304	V1180		0
Permitting unlawful use of DL/ID	61-5-302(6)	V1159	D16	0
Possess flame device in veh carrying expl/flm liquid	61-9-411(2) [2]	V7382	E70	2
Possessing an invalid DL/ID	61-5-302(1) [2]	V1151	B41	2
Possessing more than one MT D/L	61-5-102(1) [4]	V1002	D07	2
Rear/rear side window tinting-allows less than 14% light	61-9-405(4)(c)	V7324	E70	2
Reckless driving	61-8-301(1)(a)	V5120	M84	5
Reckless driving passing stopped school bus	61-8-301(1)(b)	V5122	M84	5
Reckless driving w/ death/serious bodily injury	61-8-301	V5125	M84	5
Reckless endangerment of a highway worker	61-8-301(4)(a)	V5123	M84	5
Reckless or unsafe operation of auth emergency vehicle	61-8-107	V5010	U21	2
Resident operating with foreign lic and registration	61-3-302	V8140		0
Riding motorcycle/quad (side-saddle)	61-8-359(4)	V5704	F06	2
Riding or allowing person to ride on fender	61-8-366	V5770	N84	2
Riding/allow person to ride in trailer house in tow	61-8-367	V5780	N84	2
Row violation - fail to yield to pedestrian	61-8-502(1) [1]	V5450	N08	2
Row violation--fail to obey requirements of yield sign	61-8-342	V5420	N26	2
Row violation--fail to yield to authorized emergcy veh	61-8-346(1)	V5430	N04	2
Row violation--fail to yield to veh on through highway	61-8-341 [1]	V5400	N25	2
Row viol-fail to yield to veh entering or crossing hwy	61-8-341 [2]	V5401	N06	2
Row viol-fail to yld to sch children/sch safety patr	61-8-502(3)	V5453	M13	2
Row viol-fail/yield to haz traf when making left turn	61-8-340 [1]	V5390	N31	2
Row viol-fail/yield to veh on right	61-8-339(1)	V5380	N25	2
Row viol-fail/yield when enter hwy frm prvt rd or drve	61-8-343 [1]	V5410	N01	2
Row viol-fl/approach driv to yld to veh making lft trn	61-8-340 [2]	V5391	N31	2
Row viol-no yield when enter hwy frm public approach	61-8-343 [2]	V5411	N01	2
School bus fail to activate amber lights bef stopping	61-8-351(3)	V5633	E56	2
School bus signs not covered in non-school function	61-8-351(5)	V5634	E56	2
Single beam road-lighting requirements	61-9-222	V7202	E55	2
Slow moving veh f/drive right lane	61-9-415(4)	V7770	M60	2
Snow removal equipment improperly equipped	61-9-228	V7250	E70	2
Speed: exceed restricted spd limit est by locally	61-8-310(1)	V5160	S92	3
Speed: exceed restricted spd limit established by dept	61-8-309(1)	V5150	S92	3
Speeding interstate urban-exceed 65mph	61-8-303(1)(a) [4]	V5147D	S92	3
Speeding interstate urban-exeed 65mph	61-8-303(1)(a) [1]	V5147N	S92	3
Speeding on hwy 93-exceed 65mph day	61-8-303(2) [2]	V5143D	S92	3
Speeding on hwy 93-exceed 65mph night	61-8-303(2) [1]	V5143N	S92	3
Speeding on interstate-exceed 75 mph	61-8-303(1)(a) [3]	V5145N	S92	3
Speeding on interstate-exceed 75 mph	61-8-303(1)(a) [2]	V5145D	S92	3
Speeding on non interstate-exceed day limit-70mph	61-8-303(1)(b) [1]	V5144D	S92	3
Speeding on non interstate-exceed night limit-65mph	61-8-303(1)(b) [2]	V5144N	S92	3
Speeding truck non interstate - day 60mph	61-8-312(1)(b) [1]	V5180D	S92	3

MVR Descriptor	MCA	UVC	ACD	Points
Speeding truck non interstate - night 55mph	61-8-312(1)(b) [2]	V5180N	S92	3
Speeding: 25 mph urban district	61-8-303(1)(c)	V5142	S92	3
Speeding: Exceeding 55 mph triple unit trk speed	61-8-312(2)	V5184	S92	3
Speeding: exceeding 65 mph truck speed on interstate	61-8-312(1)(a)	V5183	S92	3
Speeding: Exceeding posted spd over elevated structure	61-8-313(2)	V5190	S92	3
Speeding: Motor-driven cycle night speed	61-8-312(3) [1]	V5181	S92	3
Speeding – Violate 61-8-309	61-8-303(4)[1]	V5138	S92	3
Speeding – Violate 61-8-310	61-8-303(4)[2]	V5139	S92	3
Stop light projecting glaring light	61-9-206(3)	V7053	E34	2
Stop or signal lamp projecting glaring light	61-9-218(4)	V7175	E34	2
Stop violation-emerging from alley, rd, bldg or driveway	61-8-345	V5620	M25	2
Stop/stand/park veh less than 500 ft visibility to drivers	61-8-353(1) [2]	V5651		0
Stopping or slowing without giving appropriate signal	61-8-336(4)	V5363	N40	2
Stop-sign violation	61-8-344(4)	V5610	M15	2
Throw match/cigarette/flame on roadway or RR	61-8-372	V0051		0
Tinted windshield exceeds limits	61-9-405(4)(a)	V7320	E70	2
Tow more than 1 trailer w/veh less than 2,000 lbs GVW	61-10-104(4)	S2081		0
Tow more than 1 vehicle in combination	61-10-104(3) [1]	S2079		2
Tow veh w/air brks nt equpd w/2 means apply emerg brks	61-9-308(1)	V7265	E01	2
Tow veh w/vac brake-not equip with 2nd control devic	61-9-308(2)	V7266	E01	2
Towed husbandry - no red lamps indicating projections	61-9-215(4)(b)	V7132	E55	2
Tractor brakes protected	61-9-306	V7275	E31	2
Traffic control signal at a place other than intersection	61-8-207(4)	V5065	M14	2
Trailer-air or vacuum reservoir with no check valve	61-9-310(3)	V7273	E31	2
Transfer/sell/encumber veh that is to be seized-felony	61-8-422 [1]	V5117	U03	0
Transferor fails to remove lic plates from transfrd veh	61-3-334	V8211		0
Travel wrong direction--one-way street or highway	61-8-327(2)	V5271	N63	2
Triple operating without permit	61-10-124(1)	S2124		0
Turn or move R/L w/o signal given	61-8-336(1) [3]	V5365	N43	2
Turning when unsafe to do so	61-8-336(1) [2]	V5361	N50	2
Turning without giving proper signal 100 feet	61-8-336(2)	V5362	N43	2
Unauthorized license plate light	61-9-226(4) [1]	V7235	E70	2
Unauthorized veh using/equipped with siren, bell, etc	61-9-401(2)	V7293	E70	2
Unlawful issue of Montana DL/ID card	61-5-309	V1204	D10	0
Unlawful operation of nonstandard motorized vehicle	61-8-375	V5791	F66	2
Unlawful use flashing lights on school bus(amber/red)	61-8-352	V5640	E56	2
Unnecessary use of horn or warning device	61-9-401(1) [3]	V7292	E70	2
Unsafe left turn across lane marked with two yellow lines	61-8-328(4)	V5285	N53	2
Use "pioneer" or "vintage" plates/veh for general use	61-3-411(1)	V8010		0
Using driving lamps as headlamps	61-9-217(3) [1]	V7154	E70	2
Using false or fictitious name on DL/ID application	61-5-302(5) [2]	V1155	D02	2
Veh equip w/more than 1 running board lamp each side	61-9-219(2) [1]	V7182	E70	2
Veh left of center fails to yield	61-8-321(2)	V5205	N07	2
Vehicle equip with more than two side or fender lamps	61-9-219(1) [1]	V7180	E70	2
Vehicle equipped with more than two back-up lamps	61-9-219(3) [1]	V7184	E70	2
Vehicle filming movies or tv w/o reg ov 180 days	61-3-520(1)	V8044		0
Vehicle not equip w/single control to operate all brak	61-9-309	V7267	E31	2
Vehicle not equipped with air brake warning device	61-9-311	V7269	E01	2
Viol in display/use of amateur radio license plates	61-3-425 [1]	V8020		2
Viol in use of red blinker light for private vehicle	61-9-227(1)	V7240	E70	2
Viol of D/N travel restrict - comm hay hauler	61-10-102(2)(c)	S2087		2
Violate 1st year restriction on D/L issued to minor	61-5-133	V1063	D29	2
Violate D/L privilege of govt veh drivers	61-5-104(1)	V1010		2
Violate gvw licensing requirement	61-10-232	V3167		0
Violate limitations put on restricted access highway	61-8-332(1)	V5320	M14	2
Violate of D/L privilege granted road machinery, etc.	61-5-104(1)(d)	V1011		2
Violate restriction of 1st year driver license	61-5-134	V1064	D29	2
Violate use of vehicle exempted 15-6-201	61-10-213 [2]	S3151		0
Violating mileage payment of trip permit	61-10-211(2)	S3131		0
Violation in a construction zone	61-8-314(2) [1]	V5195	M03	3
Violation in a work zone	61-8-314(2) [2]	V5196	M03	3
Violation in moving heavy equipment across rr crossing	61-8-350(1)	V5600	M24	2
Violation in use of single movement permit	61-4-310	V8130		0
Violation in use of traffic ed learners license	61-5-106(2)	V1031	D29	2
Violation of medical assessment and rehab driving permit	61-5-120	V1062	D27	2
Violation of restrictions imposed on probationary D/L	61-2-302	V1108	D29	2

MVR Descriptor	MCA	UVC	ACD	Points
Violation of restrictions on instruction permit	61-5-106(1)	V1030	D29	2
Violation/use of exempt vehicle of agricultural worker	61-10-214(2)	V3171		0
Violations of triples permit	61-10-124(2) [1]	S2125		2

Table of Federal Regulations Code with MVR Descriptors

Per Montana Code 44-1-1005, citations can be issued for violations of the Code of Federal Regulations (CFR). The table below indicates the CFR Statute with the associated Montana codes and descriptions.

MVR Descriptor	CFR Per MCA 61-10-154	UVC Code	ACD
General brake violations	393.41 to 393.51, 396.3A1B - 396.3A1BL	V4431	E31
Defective coupling devices	393.7 to 393.71	V4432	E01
Defective exhaust system	393.83A to 393.83H	V4433	E01
Defective fuel system	393.65 to 393.67C8	V4434	E70
Defective lighting devices	393.11 [1] to 393.2, 393.25F, 393.28, 393.33, 393.9H, 393.9T	V4435	E34
Defective steering mechanism	393.209A to 393.209D	V4437	E01
Defective tires	393.75A to 393.75F	V4440	E37
Defective vehicle frame	393.201 to 393.201D	V4439	E01
Defective vehicle suspension	393.207A to 393.207F	V4438	E01
Defective wheels and rims	393.205A to 393.205C	V4441	E01
Driver disqualified under 391.11 or 391.15DD	391.15A	V4406	B24
Driver hazardous material laws (general)	177.804 to 177.87, 397.11A to 397.1B, 397.5 to 397.7	V4452	F66
Driver under 21 years of age	391.11B1	V4401	B51
Driver violations (general)	391.11B2, 392.16, 392.6, 392.7, 395.8, 397.3	V4450	
14 hour driving rule	395.3A2	V4414	
11 hour driving rule	395.3A1	V4413	
Duty status inaccurately reflects actual status	395.8E	V4418	
Fail have duty status current on day of inspection	395.8F1	V4417	
No or improper medical certificate	391.41A, 391.45B	V4402	B65
Fail to have proper haz. mat shipping papers	107.62, 171.2A to 171.4, 172.2, 172.201 to 172.205, 172.6 to 172.7	V4463	
Impaired driver - to sick or tired to continue	392.3	V4405	D74
Improper hazmat packaging	173.24B1	V4442	
Not licensed to drive type of veh being operated	391.11B5	V4403	B51
No emergency warning device	392.22, 393.95F	V4462	E01
No/bad/inadequate load securement	393.1	V4410	
No record of duty status in possession w/required	395.8A, 395.8K2	V4416	
No MCS82/MCS90 form	387.31F - 387.7F	V4409	D35
No HM shipping paper in possession	172.200A	V4412	
No waiver of physical disqualification in poss.	391.43E, 391.49J	V4404	B65
No/improper flag on projected load	393.87	V4411	E01
General placarding requirements	172.504A	V4443	E04
Onboard recording info not available	395.15G	V4457	E01
Operating MV while driver out of service	395.13D1	V4453	B27
Operating out-of-service vehicle	396.9C	V4454	B27
Possess or use drugs or other substances	392.4	V4407	A33
Possess or use intox bev or other substances	392.5	V4408	A31
Rear vision mirrors inadequate/broken	393.8	V4461	E01
Trans haz. mat w/o placards properly displayed	172.5 to 172.502A2, 172.516 to 172.516C6	V4460	E04
Unsafe loading	392.9	V4436	
Use of electronic device for texting by CMV operator	390.17	V4471	N84
Using/equipping CMV with radar detector	392.71	V4448	E23
Vehicle maintenance (general)	390.21, 393.106, 393.203, 393.63, 393.3, 393.6, 393.63, 393.76, 393.77, 393.79, 393.81, 393.82, 393.84, 393.86, 393.88, 393.9, 393.91, 393.92, 393.93, 393.95A, 396.17, 396.3A, 396.5B	V4451	F66
Working more than 60/70 hrs in 7/8 day period	395.3B	V4415	

Table of Driver Improvement (DI) Actions

* = ACD Assigned to Original UVC

DI	MVR Description	Long Description	DI Action Implemented	ACD
080	PERIODIC REQMT	Periodic Requirement – Required to File Certificate of Proof of Financial Responsibility (SR-22)	3 Year Sr-22 Filing	B64
081	ADMIN REVIEW	Driver License Under Administrative Review	Valid Pending Full Compliance – May Be Converted To DI Action: 630, 680 Or 681	W15
096	STAY ORDER	Stay Order, Prior Withdrawal Removed Pending Other Action	Indefinite Stay	W10
097	STAY ORDER A12	Stay Order, Breath Test Refusal-Court Hearing Pending	Indefinite Stay	A12
098	STAY ORDER A04	Stay Order-CDL Alcohol Concentration Certification-Court Hearing Pending	Indefinite Stay	A04
099	DC REQUIREMENT	Driver Control Requirement	Misc Court Ordered Req	*
100	STUDENT LOAN	Driver License Suspension After Failure to Repay Student Loans	Indefinite Suspension	W00
110	REV HO DECLARED	Revoked After Habitual Offender Declared	3 Year Revocation	W01
112	REREV –VIO REST PROB	Re-Revoke After Conviction for Violating Restrictions on Probationary Driver License	Revocation Of Probationary Driver License	D29
113	REREV ADDL SUMM	Re-Revoke New Conviction During Revocation	Re-Revoke Until End Of Original Revocation	D29
114	RESUS/REV F/TMT	Re-Suspend / Re-Revoke – Fail to Attend Required Substance Abuse Treatment	Indefinite Suspension/Revocation	*
115	REREV F/MAIN PRF	Re-Revoke – Fail to Maintain Proof of Financial Responsibility	Re-Revoke Until End Of Original Revocation	D35
118	REREV F/COMP REQ	Re-Revoke – Fail to Complete Requirements (Removed Ignition Interlock before Eligible)	Re-Revoke	*
120	ADDL 1 YEAR DWHO	Additional 1 Year Revocation – Driving While Declared Habitual Offender	Revoke Additional 1 Year	W01
208	SUSP 1ST BAC .08	Suspend 1st Violation Breath Alcohol Concentration 0.08% or Greater	Suspension 6 Months	A08
209	RESUS AFT STA OR	Re-Suspend After Stay Order	Indefinite Suspension	A12
212	RESUSP VIO RESTR	Re-Suspend After Violation of Restrictions on Probationary Driver License	Re-Suspend Until End Of Original Suspension	D29
213	RESUSP ADDL SUMM	Re-Suspend After Additional Conviction (Summons)	Re-Suspend Until End Of Original Suspension	D29
214	RESUSP NO CT SCH	Re-Suspend – 1ST Offense – Fail to Attend Court Ordered Chemical Dependency Assessment – Course – Treatment (ACT)	Re-Suspend For Time Period Calculated By Driver Control Analyst In Accordance With Dl Restrictions	-
218	SUSP 1ST DUI .08	Suspend 1st Violation Driving Under the Influence – 0.08% BAC or Greater	Suspension 6 Months	A20
223	SUSP 3rd + DUI	Suspend 3rd Violation Driving Under the Influence	Suspension 1 Year	A20
225	SUSP 2nd DUI	Suspend 2nd Violation Driving Under the Influence	Suspension 1 Year	A20
227	SUSP 2ND DUI .08	Suspend 2nd Violation Driving Under the Influence – 0.08% BAC or Greater	Suspension 1 Year	A20
230	1ST .02 BAC < 21	1st Offense – Breath Alcohol Concentration 0.02% or Greater by Person Under 21 Years of Age	Suspension 90 Days	A61
240	2ND .02 BAC < 21	2nd Offense – Breath Alcohol Concentration 0.02% or Greater by Person Under 21 Years of Age	Suspension 6 Months	A61
250	3RD+ .02 BAC <21	3rd or Subsequent Offense – Breath Alcohol Concentration 0.02% or Greater by Person Under 21 Years of Age	Suspension 1 Year	A61
280	1ST BAC.08INTRLK	1st Violation Breath Alcohol Concentration 0.08% or Greater – Ignition Interlock Required	Suspension 6 Months	A08
281	1ST DUI.08INTRLK	1st Violation Driving Under the Influence - Breath Alcohol Concentration 0.08% or Greater – Ignition Interlock Required	Suspension 6 Months	A20
287	1 YR INTRLK RQMT	1 Year Requirement Breath Alcohol Ignition Interlock Device (Link to DUI DI Action 227)	Additional 1 Year Suspension Commencing On Conclusion Of Original Suspension	A41
323	SUSP 3rd + BAC	Suspend 3rd Violation Breath Alcohol Concentration	Suspension 1 Year	A08
325	SUSP 2ND BAC	Suspend 2nd Violation Breath Alcohol Concentration	Suspension 1 Year w/Prob DL - – 45 Days with Interlock	A08
327	SUSP 2ND BAC .08	Suspend 2nd Violation Breath Alcohol Concentration 0.08% or Greater	Suspension 1 Year	A08

DI	MVR Description	Long Description	DI Action Implemented	ACD
330	SUSP IMP CONSENT	Suspend After Implied Consent Breath Test Refusal (1st Violation)	Suspension 6 Months	A12
342	SUSP 2ND/SUB IC	Suspend After Implied Consent Breath Test Refusal (2nd or Subsequent Violation)	Suspension 1 Year	A12
345	SUSP P.A.S.T.	Suspend After Preliminary Alcohol Screening Test Refusal (1st Violation)	Suspension 6 Months	A12
352	SUSP P.A.S.T.	Suspend After Preliminary Alcohol Screening Test Refusal (2nd or Subsequent Violation)	Suspension 1 Year	A12
387	1 YR INTRLK RQMT	1 Year Requirement Breath Alcohol Ignition Interlock Device (Link to BAC DI Action 327)	Suspension 1 Year	A41
418	RESUSP F/CMP REQ	Re-Suspend – Fail to Complete Requirements (Ignition Interlock)	Indefinite Suspension	A41
450	SUSP UNSAT JUDGMT	Suspend Subsequent to Unsatisfied Judgment	Suspension 6 Years	D39
451	FL GV PRF/JUGMNT	Suspend – Fail to Maintain Proof of Financial Responsibility Subsequent to Unsatisfied Judgment	Indefinite Suspension	B63
452	RESUSP NON PAY AGR	Re-Suspend Following Non Payment of Judgment in Accordance with Agreement	Suspension 6 Years	D39
510	ADDL SUSP DWLS	Additional Suspension Following Conviction for Driving While License Suspended	Suspension 1 Year	B26
520	ADDL REV DWLR	Additional Period of Revocation Following Conviction for Driving While License Revoked	Revoke For Additional 1 Year	B25
601	SUSP NON PAY/FIN	Non-Payment of a Fine	Indefinite Suspension	D53
602	SUSP NO APPR/CRT	Non-Appearance in Court	Indefinite Suspension	D45
603	SUSP FTP BND/APP	Failed To Post Set Bond Amount Or Appear Upon Issued Summons, Complaint Or Court Order	Indefinite Suspension	D45
604	SUSP DL I/L BND	Failed to Appear After Posting a Driver's License in Lieu of Bond	Indefinite Suspension	D56
605	SUSP FTP FN/RES	Failed to Pay Assessed Fine, Costs or Restitution of $100 or More	Indefinite Suspension	W00
606	SUSP FL TO CMPLY	Failed to Comply with a Penalty, Restriction or Condition of Sentence	Indefinite Suspension	W00
612	FAIL TO APPEAR	Fail to Appear for Trial or Court	Indefinite Suspension	D45
613	FTC-TRAFFIC	Fail to Comply with Condition of Sentence – Traffic Violation	Indefinite Suspension	D56
614	FTC-NON TRAFFIC	Fail to Comply with Condition of Sentence – Non-Traffic Violation	Indefinite Suspension	W00
630	SUSP INELIGIBLE	Suspension After Driver Becomes Ineligible	Medical Indefinite Suspension	W14
632	CDL INELIGIBLE	Medical Indefinite Suspension – Commercial Driver License Only	Medical Indefinite Suspension	W20
640	SUSP UNLAWFL USE	Suspension Unlawful Use	Suspension 6 Months	D06
650	SUSP FRAUD APP	Suspension Subsequent to Application Fraud	Suspension 6 Months	D02
661	SUSP DRUG/FELONY	Felony Drug Conviction	Suspension 6 Months	U03
665	INS VIOLATION	Suspension – Failure to Maintain Required Motor Vehicle Liability Insurance (4th Offense)	Indefinite Suspension	D36
670	SUSP CAR/NEG DRV	Suspension – Conviction for Careless or Negligent Driving	Suspension 6 Months	D29
680	SUSP F/RE-EXAM	Medical Suspension – Fail to Complete Required Re-Examination (Attempted)	Medical Indefinite Suspension	W15
681	SUSP F/COMP REEX	Medical Suspension – Fail to Comply with Required Re-Examination (Not Attempted)	Medical Indefinite Suspension	W15
685	F/EYE TEST	Failed Eye Test	Medical Indefinite Suspension	W15
690	CRT ORDERED SUSP	Court Ordered Suspension	Suspension Set By The Court	*
698	FUEL THEFT	Fuel Theft	Suspension Set By The Court	W00
708	REV DRUG FELONY	Revoked – Drug Felony	Revocation 1 Year	U03
710	REV NEG HOMICIDE	Revoked – Negligent Homicide	Revocation 1 Year	U07
720	REV FELONY W/MV	Revoked – Felony with a Motor Vehicle	Revocation 1 Year	U03
730	REV F/ST REN AID	Revoked – Failure to Stop and Render Aid at an Injury / Fatal Accident	Revocation 1 Year	B03
740	REV PERJRY F/AFF	Revoked – Perjury or False Affidavit	Revocation 1 Year	D02
752	FLEE/ELUDE PO	Revoked – Fleeing or Attempting to Elude a Peace Officer	Revocation 1 Year	U01
757	SUSP 3RCKLS 12 MO	Suspended Subsequent to 3 Convictions for Reckless Driving Within 12 Months	Suspension 1 Year	W01
760	REV/CRT ORDER	Revoked – Court Order	Revocation – Time Period Set By The Court	*
770	REV NEG VEH ASLT	Revoked – Negligent Vehicular Assault	Revocation 1 Year	U06
810	CANC PAR CONSENT	Cancelled – Withdrawn Parental Consent	Cancelled Until 18th Birthday	W13
820	CANC DEATH OF PT	Cancelled Due to Death of Parent Signing Original Application	Cancelled	W13
830	CANC NSF CHECK	Cancelled – Non-Sufficient Funds Check	Renewal Or New	W00

DI	MVR Description	Long Description	DI Action Implemented	ACD
			Application Cancelled	
840	CANC INELIGIBLE	Cancelled Subsequent to Becoming Ineligible	Cancelled	W20
850	CANC FRAUD APPL	Cancelled Subsequent to Application Fraud	Cancelled	W20
860	CANC F/MAIN PRF	Cancelled - Fail to Maintain Proof of Financial Responsibility	Cancelled	D35
870	CANC VOL SURR	Cancelled – Driver License Voluntarily Surrendered	Dl Initially Inactive - May Be Cancelled	W00
880	CANC F/REQ RE-EX	Cancelled – Failed Required Re-Examination	Cancelled	W20
890	CANC DENIED	Cancelled – Denied	Cancelled	W00
900	RV RENST FEE DUE	Revoked – Reinstatement Fee Due	Indefinite Revocation	*
901	REREV RENST NSF	Re-Revoked – Reinstatement Fee Paid by Non-Sufficient Funds Check	Indefinite Revocation	W00
910	SUSP RENST FEE DUE	Suspended – Reinstatement Fee Due	Indefinite Suspension	*
911	RESSUS RENST NSF	Re-Suspended – Reinstatement Fee Paid by Non-Sufficient Funds Check	Indefinite Suspension	W00
920	60 DAYCVSUSP MLTV	60 Day CDL/CV Suspension – Multiple Qualifying Offenses (Serious Traffic Violations)	Suspension 60 Days	W30
921	120 DAYCVSUSP MLTV	120 Day CDL/CV Suspension – Multiple Qualifying Offenses (Serious Traffic Violations)	Suspension 120 Days	W31
922	LIFESUSPCVDRGFEL	Lifetime Suspension – Drug Felony Involving Commercial Motor Vehicle	Lifetime CDL Suspension	A50
923	1YRSUSCDLMAJ-A94	1Year CDL Suspension – Major Offense – 0.04% Breath Alcohol Concentration	Suspension 1 Year	A94
924	3YRSUSCDLMAJ-A94	3Year CDL Suspension – Major Offense – 0.04% Breath Alcohol Concentration	Suspension 3 Years	A94
925	1YRSUSCDLMAJ-A08	1Year CDL Suspension – Major Offense – 0.08% Breath Alcohol Concentration	Suspension 1 Year	A08
926	1YRSUSCDLMAJ-B05	1Year CDL Suspension – Major Offense – Leaving Scene of Accident	Suspension 1 Year	B05
927	3YRSUSCDLMAJ-B05	3Year CDL Suspension – Major Offense – Leaving Scene of Accident	Suspension 3 Years	B05
928	3YRSUSCDLMAJ-A08	1Year CDL Suspension – Major Offense – 0.08% Breath Alcohol Concentration	Suspension 3 Years	A08
929	1YRSUSCDLMAJ-U03	1Year CDL Suspension – Major Offense – Felony in a Motor Vehicle	Suspension 1 Year	U03
930	3YRSUSCDLMAJ-U03	3Year CDL Suspension – Major Offense – Felony in a Motor Vehicle	Suspension 3 Years	U03
937	1YRSUSCDLMAJ-A12	1Year CDL Suspension – Major Offense – Alcohol Breath Test Refusal	Suspension 1 Year	A12
938	3YRSUSCDLMAJ-A12	3Year CDL Suspension – Major Offense – Alcohol Breath Test Refusal	Suspension 3 Years	A12
940	1YRSUSCDLMAJ-B26	1Year CDL Suspension – Major Offense – Driving While CDL Suspended	Suspension 1 Year	B26
941	1YRSUSCDLMAJ-U10	1Year CDL Suspension – Major Offense – Causing Fatality Through Use of CMV	Suspension 1 Year	U10
942	3YRSUSCDLMAJ-B26	3Year CDL Suspension – Major Offense – Driving While CDL Suspended	Suspension 3 Years	B26
943	1YRSUSCDLMAJ-A20	1Year CDL Suspension – Major Offense – Driving Under the Influence	Suspension 1 Year	A20
944	3YRSUSCDLMAJ-A20	3Year CDL Suspension – Major Offense – Driving Under the Influence	Suspension 3 Years	A20
945	LIFECVSUSPMAJOFF	Lifetime CDL Suspension – 2nd Major Offense	Lifetime CDL Suspension	W40
946	SUSP FEDERL DISQ	CDL Suspension – Federal Disqualification	Indefinite Suspension	W70
947	CV FRAUD APPL	CDL Cancelled Subsequent to Application Fraud	Indefinite Cancellation	D02
949	SUSPVIOLOOSORDER	CDL Suspended – 1st Violation Out-of-Service Order	Suspension 6 Months	B27
950	SUSP 2ND VIOLOOS	CDL Suspended – 2nd Violation Out-of-Service Order	Suspension 1 Year	W50
951	3YRSUSCDLMAJ-U10	3Year CDL Suspension – Major Offense – Causing Fatality Through Use of CMV	Suspension 3 Years	U10
952	CHILD SUPPORT	Suspension for Failure to Pay Child Support	Indefinite Suspension	D51
953	2ndVIOLOOSHAZ/PA	CDL Suspended – 2nd Violation Out-of-Service Order While Hauling Hazardous Materials or Passengers	Suspension 3 Years	W51
954	VIOL OOS 3+	CDL Suspended – 3rd or Subsequent Violation Out-of-Service Order	Suspension 3 Years	W52
955	RRGC 2 AVIOL	Railroad Grade Crossing Violation – 2ND Offense Within 3 Years	Suspension 120 Days	W60
956	RRGC 3 AVIOL	Railroad Grade Crossing Violation – 3RD or Subsequent Offense Within 3 Years	Suspension 1 Year	W61
958	FTO RR GAT/S	Failure to Obey Railroad Grade Crossing Signal -	Suspension 60 Days – 1st Offense	M10
959	FTO RR NSLOW	Failure to Obey Railroad Grade Crossing Signal - Vehicle Not Required to Slow	Suspension 60 Days – 1st Offense	M20
960	FTO RR NSTOP	Failure to Obey Railroad Grade Crossing Signal - Vehicle Not Required to Stop	Suspension 60 Days – 1st Offense	M21
961	FTO RR DRIVE	Failure to Obey Railroad Grade Crossing Signal - Space	Suspension 60 Days – 1st Offense	M22
962	FTO RR SPACE	Failure to Obey Railroad Grade Crossing Signal - Clearance	Suspension 60 Days – 1st Offense	M23

DI	MVR Description	Long Description	DI Action Implemented	ACD
963	FTO RR CLRNC	Failure to Obey Railroad Grade Crossing Signal -	Suspension 60 Days – 1st Offense	M24
964	CMV HOMICIDE	Homicide Involving Use of a Commercial Motor Vehicle	CDL Major Offense Suspension	U09
965	ADDCDLMAJ/REINST	Additional CDL Major Offense After Reinstatement	Lifetime CDL Suspension	W41
966	1stVIOLOOSHAZ/PA	CDL Suspended – 1st Violation Out-of-Service Order While Hauling Hazardous Materials or Passengers	Suspension 3 Years	B19
967	60 DAY SUS - VIOFTL	Violation resulting in a fatal accident	60 Day Suspension	U31
968	120DAYSUS - VIOFTL	Violation resulting in a fatal accident	120 Day Suspension	U31
972	RESUS CHILD SUP	Failure to Pay Child Support – Re-suspend After Stay Order	Indefinite Suspension	D51
973	1YRSUSCDLMAJ-A04	CDL Suspension – Major Offense	Suspension 1 Year	A04
974	3YRHAZCDLMAJ-A04	CDL Suspension – Major Offense - HazMat	Suspension 3 Years	A04
976	SUSP CDL SOW-W00	CDL Suspension – Help Desk Withdrawal	CDL Help Desk Withdrawal	W00

Point System Summary

- Traffic conviction points range from 2 – 12 per offense (MCA 61-11-203) and are tallied based upon 36 months between the most recent conviction and a prior conviction.
- For multiple convictions that occur during a single incident, only the violation with the highest number of points is counted.
- Traffic offenses with zero points may or may not appear on a driver record (and may not be available to the public).
- A driver accruing 30 or more traffic conviction points during a 36 month period is subject to driver license revocation as a habitual traffic offender.

Nebraska

Administration	Important Telephone and Web Contacts

Beverly Neth
   Director of Motor Vehicles
Betty Johnson
   Driver & Vehicle Records Administrator
Sara O'Rourke
   Driver Licensing Services Administrator
Kathy Hraban
   Financial Responsibility Manager
 	
301 Centennial Mall South
Lincoln, NE 68509
www.dmv.ne.gov
	Driver Licensing..402-471-3861
	Financial Responsibility/SR-22.................402-471-3985
	Commercial Driver License........................402-471-3861
	Driver Records 402-471-3918
	Vehicle Information.....................................402-471-3918
	State Department of Insurance 402-471-2201
	Highway Patrol..402-471-4545
	Rules and Regulations are found at:
	   www.dmv.ne.gov/rulesandregs.html
	General Email Address dmv.dvrweb@nebraska.gov

Driver's License Format, Issuance and Renewal

License Classes, Restrictions and Endorsements Appear After the Driving Record Content Section

License Format

One letter (A, B, C, E, G, H, or V) and 3 to 8 digits make up the license number.

Document Appearance

The current driver licensing document has been in production since July 2009. Until July 20, 2009, the DMV used an over-the-counter process to produce the driver licenses and state ID cards. Since that date, the cards are issued from a central issue location and mailed within 30 days.

Current Document

The background of the driver license contains an image of the Nebraska State Capitol on both the adult and minor license designs. The current identification card design contains a background image of the Sower and the State Seal.

Security Characteristics: Security features include a ghost photo image imprinted over vital information to minimize alterations, a tamper resistant coating placed over the card and machine readable technology via a barcode printed on the back of the card. The tamper resistant coating contains an optically variable image of the state that changes color as the license is tilted and an ultraviolet image of the state seal visible under a UV light source. The back of the card also includes an ultraviolet ghost photo image on the right-hand side. The advantages of the document include increased fraud protection, added security features, machine-readable technology and increased readability.

Position of Photo: Middle, left-hand side.

Minor Age Driver Locator Printed vertically and will include cardholder specific items such as, "Under 21 until xx/xx/xx" and Under 18 until xx/xx/xx".

CDL Indicator: Commercial or non-commercial designation is printed in a solid colored header bar directly under "Nebraska." All possibilities include: "Commercial Driver's License," "Commercial Learner's Permit," or "Operator's License," "School Permit," etc.

Old Document

The background of the driver license contains an image of the Nebraska State Capitol on both the adult and minor license designs. The current identification card design contains a background image of the Sower and the State Seal.

Security Characteristics: Security features include a ghost photo image imprinted over vital information to minimize alterations, a tamper resistant coating placed over the card and machine readable technology via a barcode printed on the back of the card. The tamper resistant coating contains an optically variable image of the state seal that changes color as the license is tilted. The advantages of this document include increased fraud protection, added security features, machine-readable technology and increased readability.

Position of Photo: Upper right-hand corner

Minor Age Driver Locator: Printed vertically and will include cardholder specific items such as, "Under 21 until xx/xx/xx" and Under 18 until xx/xx/xx".

CDL Indicator: Commercial or non-commercial designation is printed in a solid colored header bar directly under "Nebraska." All possibilities include: "Commercial Driver's License," "Commercial Learner's Permit," or "Operator's License," "School Permit," etc.

Issuance

Requirements for Proof of Identity and Address Verification:
See www.dmv.ne.gov/examining/pdf/verificationdocs.pdf

Residency

Non-resident's home-state license honored for up to thirty days of continuous residence.

Age Requirements

A graduated driver's licensing program regulates the age and licensing requirements of the following documents:

School Learner's Permit (LPE) ....Fourteen; required for two months to obtain an SCP.

School Permit (SCP) ....Fourteen and two months.

Learner's Permit (LPD) ....Fifteen; required for six months to obtain a POP.

Provisional Operator's Permit (POP).......................Sixteen but less than eighteen.

Regular License (Class O)...Eighteen or after POP held one year.

Renewal

Renewal is on birthday of fifth year after issuance. The driver keeps the same number when renewing. Individuals who hold a Class O or Class M license may renew online at www.clickdmv.ne.gov.

Military personnel and their spouses or dependents who are stationed out-of-state may renew by mail. Proof of active duty is required. "Military" will be indicated on driving records.

Elderly-Related Restrictions

None reported by the state.

Vehicle Insurance, Title and Registration Facts

Registration Renewal

Renewal is annual. Registrations may be renewed online at www.clickdmv.ne.gov.

New Residents

Non-residents must register vehicles within 30 days of their arrival. The exceptions to this are individuals coming into Nebraska from the states – currently Wyoming and North Carolina – with whom Nebraska has a reciprocity agreement.

Inspections and Emissions Testing

Nebraska has no provisions for a mandatory annual vehicle-safety inspection or for statewide emission testing.

Passenger Plate Facts

There are two plates, one decal (MO & YR) on both plates. Note there is a single plate for trailers, motorcycles, mini-trucks, semi-tractors, buses, dealers, special interest vehicles, and pull types of mobile homes. The first number(s) of the plate designate county of issuance, except in Douglas, Lancaster and Sarpy counties. The list of the 93 numbers and counties can be obtained from the DMV. Plates do not remain with vehicle when sold.

Insurance and Financial Responsibility

Minimum limits of financial responsibility are $25,000/50,000/25,000. Liability insurance is compulsory, no-fault is not. Nebraska's financial responsibility laws provide that proof of insurance can be required by the Motor Vehicle Department for liability reasons. Proof may be required at registration, renewal, upon an accident or certain violations. SR-22 forms are used.

Withdrawal Sanctions, and Alcohol and Drug Testing

Alcohol and Chemical Testing Limits

Nebraska's illegal intoxication level is .08 percent and above; .02 for drivers under 21 years of age, and .04 for drivers of CMVs. Urine, blood, and breath testing are authorized. Nebraska does have an implied-consent violation. DUI offenders arrested on or after Jan. 1, 2012, may be eligible to apply for an ignition interlock permit.

Suspensions and Revocations

See the Appendix for a list of the federally mandated disqualifications for offenses occurring in a CMV per MCSIA.

Point Suspensions

For the accumulation 12 or more points within a two (2) year time period is a revocation for six (6) months. Subsequent revocations within a five (5) year time period are for a three (3) year time period. The subject can apply for an Employment Drive Permit if there are no other open suspensions/revocations/impounds on the record.

Underage Points: If driver is under the age of 21, and accumulates six (6) or more points within a 12-month time period, the driver will be required to complete a Defensive Driving Course to prevent suspension. This course must be completed within 3-months of the date the Department of Motor Vehicles sends notification.

Other Violations That Could Result in Suspension or Revocation:

- Administrative License Revocation (ALR)—Immediate seizure of license for refusal or failure of alcoholic content testing.

- Alcoholism or Drug Addiction
- Allowing Another Person to use Your License
- Failure by Individuals Under 21 to Complete a Driver Improvement Course After Accumulating 6 Points in One Year
- Failure to Comply with a Child or Alimony Support Order
- Failure to Pay Out-of-State Ticket
- Failure to Provide Proof of Financial Responsibility Following Involvement in an Accident.
- Failure to Settle Citations or Court Judgments
- Failure to Submit to a Chemical Test
- Falsifying/Withholding Information on License Application
- Fleeing to Avoid Arrest
- Leaving the Scene of an Accident
- No Proof of Insurance (owner only)
- Reckless Driving

Reinstatement Requirements

Court /Revocations	$125.00 fee; re-examination; SR-22 for three years.
Point Revocations	$125.00 fee; re-examination; SR-22 for three years; completion of approved driver improvement course.
Administrative License Revocation	$125.00 fee: re-examination.
Support Child/Alimony	$50.00 fee: proof of support settlement
Failure to Settle Citation	$50.00 fee; proof of court settlement.
Accident Related Suspensions	$50.00 fee; proof of damage/injury settlement.

Record Access: Laws, Rules, and Forms

Note: This Section Applies to Both Driver and Vehicle Records.

Governing Statutes and Rules

Rules and Regulations: www.dmv.ne.gov/rulesandregs.html

By passage of the Nebraska Uniform Vehicles Records Disclosure Act (Neb.Rev.Stat. 60-2901 through 60-2913) the state adopted the provisions of DPPA, including Public Law 106-69. Neb.Rev.Stat. 71-3201 to 71-3213 governs use by a private detective, plain clothes investigator, or private investigative agency licensed under for purposes permitted under this act. Neb.Rev.Stat. 20-145 governs use, including redisclosure through news publication, for a member of a medium of communication in connection with news involving motor vehicle or driver safety or vehicle theft.

Nebraska does not have the federal exception #11 from DPPA. Nebraska added the following exceptions:

(13)   For use, including redisclosure through news publication, of a member of a medium of communication as defined in section 20-145 who requests such information in connection with preparing, researching, gathering, or confirming news information involving motor vehicle or driver safety or motor vehicle theft.

And as amended and effective July 1, 2004:

(14) For use by the federally designated organ procurement organization in Nebraska to establish and maintain the Donor Registry of Nebraska as provided in section 7 of this act.

As such, it was determined the news media had an exemption including redisclosure in connection with preparing, researching, gathering or confirming news information involving motor vehicle or driver safety, or motor vehicle theft.

Request and Consent Forms

Driving Records: The two state forms are downloadable from the web site. An *Application for Copy of Driving Record* is required for a single inquiry (www.dmv.ne.gov/dvr/pdf/drvrecapp.pdf). An *Application for Copies of Multiple Records* should be submitted (www.dmv.ne.gov/dvr/pdf/multidrvrec.pdf) when records are requested on more than one driver. Notarized signature of the requester is required if either form is mailed to the DMV and if the use of the record is for an exempted use.

Vehicle Records: Use of *Application for Copy of Vehicle Record* (www.dmv.ne.gov/dvr/pdf/vehrecapp.pdf) is required for one record or *Application for More Than One Vehicle Record* (www.dmv.ne.gov/dvr/pdf/multivehrec.pdf) for multiple records is

required. Notarized signature of the requester is required, if purpose of request is not an exempted use.

For **both driver and vehicle record** requests, if the purpose of request is not associated with a listed exempted, then the subject must give notarized consent before records with personal data are released.

Vendor and Third Party Access Policy

Approved vendors can access records for other vendors (who are not online, etc.) who will then sell to an end user if—

a. Contract between original vendor and reseller contains same language as contract between the state and the original vendor.

b. Contract between reseller and end user contains same language as contract between the state and the original vendor.

The reseller shall make and keep for five years record identifying each person to whom the record was disclosed.

Records Ordered For Non-permissible Uses

Without consent or an exempted use, driving records without personal information are released via the public One-Time Driver Record Search described below.

Access to Driver-Related Records

Driving Records

General Information and Fees

Driver & Vehicle Records Division, 301 Centennial Mall South, PO Box 94789, Lincoln NE, 68508, 402-471-3918. dmv.dvrweb@nebraska.gov.

The fee is $3.00 for manual or online requests. The last fee increase was 1997 and no increases are planned for the near future. The state charges for "no record found" reports.

In-Person – Requests may be made over-the-counter at the above location, and up to six requests will be processed while you wait. When requesting seven or more records, record results are available the next business day for pick-up. This is the only location for processing manual orders. The driver's full name and date of birth or license number is needed when ordering. The fee, an application for copy of driving record, and proof of identification must accompany each request.

Mail – Requests mailed-in are processed within twenty-four hours of receipt. The driver's full name and date of birth or license number is needed when ordering. The fee and the *Application for Copy of Driving Record* form must accompany each request.

Electronic – Electronic access of driving records in Nebraska is through a designated third party—Nebraska.gov. The online system is interactive and open 24 hours a day, 7 days a week. There is an annual fee of $50.00 plus a $.12 per minute connect fee IF the Internet is not used for access, in addition to the record fee. Nebraska.gov offers other interactive services for the legal and banking communities. For more information, call Nebraska.gov at 800-747-8177 or visit www.nebraska.gov and click on Subscribe on the lower left.

One Time Driver Record Search – This online search is offered to any individual or business who requests a copy of a driving record. Records returned from this process contain no privacy protected data. The service is available at www.clickdmv.ne.gov. Select Driver Record Search (One-time). The fee is $3.00.

Bulk – The driver record header information is available to approved entities. The fee is $18.00 per thousand records. Monthly updates are also available.

By Person of Record – Nebraska drivers may obtain their driving record by mail or walk-in as described above or online at www.clickdmv.ne.gov. In person, drivers can view their own records for no fee.

Online License Status

Another online service offered is the License Status Check. Enter the full name, DOB and either the DL or SSN. Results include DL reinstatement requirements if any, license status including points, and ending date for SR-22 Insurance Form. There is no fee. Visit www.clickdmv.ne.gov and click on *Check Your Points Total*.

NDR Access

Form DMV 07-71 must be completed by either the current or prospective employer, or the current or prospective employee. A fee of $2.00 per record request is required. Any mailed NDR record check request must be notarized. Requests made in person will require U.S. based proof of identification to be provided for the person signing the request. Completed form DMV 07-71 should be returned to the address listed above. Requests can only be processed for the employer if the employee holds a Nebraska Driver's License or if the employee is domiciled in Nebraska and does not hold a driver's license. If the employee holds an out-of-state license, requests must be processed through the employee's state of licensure.

Notification/Monitoring Program

Nebraska offers a monitoring system to employers or insurance companies to track incidents of drivers. Subscribers submit an electronic list of drivers to be monitored. The charges for program include a monthly fee of $.06 per driver involved plus a $3.00 fee for each record provided when a change or incident occurs. Call Nebraska.gov at 800-747-8177 for more information or sign-up.

Accident Reports

Reporting – A driver who has been involved in a collision, regardless of fault, is required to show proof of motor vehicle liability insurance if the collision resulted in personal injury or death, or damage to property exceeding $501. Accidents involving property damage in excess of $501, injury, or death must be reported to the local police or state troopers. An Accident (Crash) Report form is required when there is a crash resulting in either an injury or total property damage of $2,000 or more. This report is not required if the crash was investigated by a peace officer. This report must be filed within ten days with the Department of Administration, Division of Motor Vehicles, PO Box 110221, Juneau, AK 99811-0221. The report can be made directly via the Web; go to http://www.dot.state.ak.us/stwdplng/accreptapp/index.shtml. There are no special reporting requirements for commercial drivers.

Record Access – Accident reports are required for incidents with property damage in excess of $1,000 or if death or injury. Reports are maintained by the Department of Roads, Accident Records Bureau, Box 94669, Lincoln 68509, 402-479-4645 www.dor.state.ne.us/highway-safety/. Records may be purchased either in-person or by mail. The fee is $15.00.Records are available from 1978 to the present and the index is

computerized since 1988. Hard copies are kept for 1 year then placed on a document imaging system (1998 to present). Microfilm records are from 1978 to 1994, on CD 1995 to 1997. New records become available in 6 weeks or less. The name, date and county of location are needed when ordering.

Access to Vehicle-Related Records

General Information
Driver & Vehicle Records, 301 Centennial Mall South, Lincoln NE, 68509, 402-471-3918. www.dmv.ne.gov
The state maintains current title, registration and lien record database for vehicles and mobile homes. Title information is available from 1939 to present. To complete a search on vehicle license plate number, vehicle identification number, title number or name of person(s) on the title/registration, an *Application for Copy of Vehicle Record* (or use the form for multiple records, see below) must be submitted. The applicant must sign the application and indicate the applicable exempted use. If reason is an exempted use, consent of the record holder is not required. The applicant's signature must be notarized. If not for an exempted purpose, consent is needed with the notarized signature of record holder required.

In-Person or Mail – The current fee for VIN, registration, title history, and lien searches is $1.00 per record. Normal turnaround time is 5 to 7 days. The state requires the use of a special form when requesting record searches. If request is by mail the signature of an exempted user or record holder must be notarized.

Electronic – Electronic access of title, lien and registration records in Nebraska are processed by a designated third party—Nebraska.gov. There is a start-up fee and line charges are incurred. The online system is interactive and open 24/7. There is an annual fee of $50.00 and a $1.00 fee per record. Nebraska.gov offers other interactive services for the legal and banking communities. For more information, call Nebraska.gov at 800-747-8177 or visit www.nebraska.gov.

Bulk – Large-bulk orders of registration/ownership information can be selected by make, county, statewide, etc. A written statement, explaining the purpose of the request, must be submitted. The initial setup fee for bulk retrieval is $55 - $500. Record fees are $75 per run up to 2,000 records and over 2,000 records there will be an additional $18 per thousand. For more information, contact either the DMV at 402-471-3885 or Nebraska.gov.

Title Inquiry Site
Title Status, lien notation confirmation and brand information may be obtained at no fee using the Vehicle Identification Number (VIN), go to www.clickdmv.ne.gov or www.nebraska.gov/dmv/els/index.cgi.

Access to Vessel-Related Records

General Information, Access and Fees
All motorized boats manufactured after 11/01/72 must be titled and registered. All motorboats are required to have a 12-digit Hull Identification Number. All vessels powered by any mechanical device capable of propelling the vessel over any public or private waters in NE must be registered, except the following:
a. Vessels not powered by machinery at any time
b. Motorboats registered in another state and housed in Nebraska less than 60 consecutive days
c. Vessels owned by any government or political subdivision
d. Racing-type motorboats when competing in state-approved races and during trial runs 48 hours prior to or 48 hours after competition
e. Vessels documented by U.S. Coast Guard

Registration Records
Nebraska motorboat **registrations** are issued only from the county treasurer of the boater's county of residence, but watercraft registration

records are held by the Nebraska Game and Parks Commission, 2200 North 33rd Street, Lincoln, NE 68503, 402-471-5579, http://outdoornebraska.ne.gov/boating/

Title Records
Watercraft titles are held by the DMV. Lien records, including liens on vessels, are retained on the title, lien and registration records held by the DMV, but are recorded by the County Treasurer in the county where the owner resides. See (www.dmv.ne.gov/dvr/mbtitles/title.html).
Requesters are asked for reason of request. If purpose is termed legitimate, then record is released. There is no fee for searching or copies, unless extensive lists provided. Verifications and simple requests are handled by phone, if the reason for request is valid. The SSN is not entered into the database. The DOB has not been entered into the database since late 2006. See *Vehicles Records* for information on **vessel titles**.

Driving Record Content and Reciprocity

What's On or Not On the Driving Record
- The driver's address is provided as part of the record, unless the record is purchased through the One-Time Driver Record Search process.
- Non-moving violations and SSNs are not reported on the driving record.
- Any accident involving damage in excess of $1,000.00 is reported. The inclusion of an accident on a driving record does not in any way indicate a driver's fault. All records note at the bottom—"Any entry for an accident which may appear on the MVR is for statistical purposes and does not indicate a determination of fault."
- The state does not permit driver school attendance in lieu of conviction; however, some county courts provide dismissal of violations upon completion of a driver improvement class.

- Convictions show on the public record for CDL drivers for a minimum of ten years.
- Medical certification information for CDL drivers (limited to in-person/mail requests or electronic single record searches for employers of CDL holders only).
The length of time non-CDL convictions are retained on the public driving record is five years, except DWIs which are reported for fifty-five years.

Data Retention
CDL driver records are purged based on the timetable per the federal regulations (see the Appendix). Surrendered licenses are purged from the system one year after the actual date of expiration. All information is purged to microfiche.

Court to Repository

County courts are mandated to transfer conviction information to the state within thirty days of adjudication. All Nebraska counties transfer violation data electronically.

State Reciprocity for Non-CDL Drivers

- Will suspend license of driver for unpaid out-of-state convictions.

- Record of new incoming driver is not shown on MVR.
- Out-of-state convictions are shown on MVR.
- Out-of-state accidents are not shown on MVR.
- Convictions of out-of-state drivers are sent to home state
- Record is forwarded to new state upon surrender of license if requested

Classes, Endorsements, Restrictions, and Status Abbreviations

License Classes

Nebraska began issuing the new CDL license in September of 1990. Commercial or non-commercial designation is printed in the header bar. Possibilities include: "Commercial Driver's License," "Commercial Learner's Permit," or "Operator's License," "School Permit," etc. Driving record abstracts have a "CDL Status" area with classes and CDL restrictions listed.

Class A	Vehicle with 26,001 pounds GVWR or more; towed unit is 10,001 pounds GVWR or more.
Class B	Vehicle with 26,001 pounds GVWR or more; towed unit is less than 10,001 pounds GVWR.
Class C	Vehicle with 26,000 pounds GVWR or less, and either sixteen-passenger or more design or for vehicles transporting placarded amounts of hazardous material.
Class O	Represents a regular license for automobiles and small trucks.
Class M	Motorcycle qualified only.

Restrictions

B	Corrective Lenses		V	Restricted Geographical Area
C	Mechanical Aids on Vehicle		W	No One-Way Streets or Roadways
E	Automatic Transmission		X	Maximum Speed Restriction
F	Outside Mirror		Y	Two Lanes, Two-Way Traffic Only
G	Limited to Daylight Only		Z	Special, as Specified by DMV
Q	No Interstate Driving			(Restrictions V, X & Z are described on individual's driving record)
U	Automatic Turn Signals Required			

CDL Restrictions

I	Intrastate Only (Impaired)		O	Except Tractor Trailer
K	Intrastate Only		M	Except Class A Bus
N	Except Class A & B Bus		W	Restricted CDL (farming purposes only, requires SEP)
L	Vehicle w/out Air Brakes		V	Medical Variance Required

Endorsements

M	Motorcycle		T	Double/Triple Trailers
N	Tank Vehicle		P	Passenger Vehicle
H	Hazardous Material		S	School Bus (Eff. 09/30/05)
X	Combination Tank Vehicle and Hazardous Material			

Other Abbreviations Used

Permits

BUS	School Bus Driver Permit		MHP	Medical Hardship Permit
FHP	Farm Husbandry		POP	Provisional Operator's Permit
ID	Identification Card		SCP	School Permit
IIP	Ignition Interlock Permit		SEP	Seasonal Permit
LPC	Commercial Learner		TPL	Temporary Permit
LPD	Class O/M Learner		WRK	Work Permit
LPE	School Learner's Permit			

Race

I	American Indian or Alaskan Native		H	Hispanic
A	Asian or Pacific Islander		O	Other
B	Black		U	Unknown
W	White			

License Status

The following is a list of the possible statuses. When there is more than one possible status, the most severe appears.

Blank	No regular license, privilege is valid.
Deceased	Department has been notified of death.
Revoked	Privileges have been revoked. Further information under "Conviction/Administrative Adjudications" or "Administrative Withdrawals."

Suspended	Privileges have been suspended. Further information under "Conviction/Administrative Adjudications" or "Administrative Withdrawals."	
Impounded	License has been impounded by order of a county or district court, in conjunction with a conviction.	
Cancelled	Driver's license has been cancelled. Further information under "Conviction/Administrative Adjudications" or "Administrative Withdrawals."	
Confiscated	Privileges are valid. License has been confiscated by the Department pending Administrative License Revocation procedures.	
Expired	Privileges are valid, license has expired.	
Valid	Privileges and license are valid.	
Surrendered	Privileges are valid. License has been surrendered. Type of surrender is listed under Administrative Withdrawals."	
Dis/Rein	CDL disqualified then reinstated; has not obtained a valid CDL.	
Rev/Rein	Privileges revoked then reinstated; has not obtained a valid license.	

Note: When the Department has been notified of the military status, it is indicated on the record by the word "Military" directly below the status area.

Conviction Table with ACD, NE Code, Points and Statutes

The Administrative Withdrawal Table follows.

Note: This table is sorted in the order of the NE Code Column. Please note the following:
- If "Abey" or "Held in Abeyance" appears as part of an entry, the restrictive action is temporarily dormant pending a court finding.
- All driving records obtained are five-year records unless the word "Complete" appears in the top left-hand corner.
- If "***" appears, the retention period is 55 years if the violation is flagged "commercial" and the conviction date is greater than 04/01/1992.

All driving records obtained are five-year records unless the word "Complete" appears in the top left-hand corner.

ACD	NE Code	Points	Description	Statute
	AC		Accident	CDLIS
A20	AC1	6	Ser Inj-Drv U/Infl	60-6,198
A20	AC2B	12	MV Homicide-DUI	28-306
A20	AC2C	12	MV Hmcd-DUI 2nd	28-306
	C1	0	FHWA Serious Offense	CDLIS
U10	C09	1	Fatality Neg CMV	60-6,186(1)(f)
B20	C10	1	Drv CMV Lic W/D	60-4,141.01
A94	C11	0	.04% Alcohol	60-4,164
A20	C12	6	Drv U/Infl-1st	60-6,196
A10	C12A	6	.10% Alcohol	60-6,196
A20	C12B	6	Drv U/Infl-2nd	60-6,196
A20	C12C	12	Drv U/Infl-3rd	60-6,196
A20	C12D	12	Drv U/Infl-4th	60-6,196
A20	C12E	12	Drv U/Infl-5th	60-6,196
A20	C12F	6	Drv U/Infl-.15 1st	60-6,196
A20	C12G	6	Drv U/Infl-.15 2nd	60-6,196
A20	C12H	12	Drv U/Infl-.15 3rd	60-6,196
A20	C12I	12	Drv U/Infl-.15 4th	60-6,196
A20	C12J	12	Drv U/Infl-.15 5th	60-6,196
A12	C13	1	Refuse Alcohol Test	60-4,164
A20	C14	6	Driving U/Infl Cntl Sub	60-4,168 (a)
A20	C14A	6	Ser Inj-Drv U/Infl (OBSOLETE)	60-6,198
A20	C14B	12	MV Homicide-DUI	28-306
A20	C14C	12	MV Hmcd-DUI 2nd	28-306
A20	C14D	12	MV Hmcd-Unbrn C-DUI	28-394
A20	C14E	12	MV Hmcd-Unbrn -DUI -S	28-394
B01	C15	4	Lv Scn Ac W/I 12 Hr	60-696
B01	C15A	8	Lv Scn Ac R/O 12 Hr	60-696
B03	C15B	6	Lv Sen Acc-Inj/Dth	60-698
B01	C15C	6	Lv Scn Acc/Damge	60-696
U03	C16	0	Commit Felony MV	60-4,168 (a)
A50	C17	0	Commit Felony MV CSub	60-4,168 (a)
S15	C18	3	Spd 15/Ovr MPH Muni OR Spd 15-35 MPH Muni	60-6,186
S15	C18A	3	Spd Ovr 15 MPH C/S OR Spd 16-35 MPH C/S	60-6,186
S15	C18B	3	Spd Ovr 15 MPH NIS OR	60-6,186

ACD	NE Code	Points	Description	Statute
			Spd 16-35 MPH NIS	
S15	C18C	2	Spd 15 MPH C/S	60-6,186
S15	C18D	2	Spd 15 MPH NIS	60-6,186
S36	C18K	4	Spd Ovr 35 MPH Muni (OBSOLETE)	60-6,186
S36	C18L	4	Spd Ovr 35 MPH C/S	60-6,186
S36	C18M	4	Spd Ovr 35 MPH NIS	60-6,186
M84	C19	6	Wil Reck Drv-1st	60-6,216
M84	C19A	6	Wil Reck Drv-2nd	60-6,217
M84	C19B	6	Wil Reck Drv-3rd	60-6,218
	C2	0	FHWA Serious Offense	CDLIS
M84	C20	5	Reckless Dr-1st	60-6,215
M84	C20A	5	Reckless Dr-2nd	60-6,217
M84	C20B	5	Reckless Dr-3rd	60-6,217
M42	C21	1	Impr Lane Chnge	60-6,139
M34	C22	1	Folw/Close	60-6,140
U31	C23		Violation Fatal/Acc	60-4,168 (5)
B57	C24	1	Drv CMV no CDL on P	60-489
B56	C25	1	Drv CMV no CDL	60-4,141 (1)
B91	C26	1	Drv CMV no Clas/End	60-4,141 (1)
B27	C30	1	Vio Out-of-Ser CMV	60-4,141.01
B19	C31	1	Vio Out-of-Ser Pas/Hz	60-4,141.01
M09	C40	1	Fail Obey RR Rest	60-6, 170 – 60-6, 174
M10	C41	1	Fail Obey RR Gts/S	60-6, 170 – 60-6, 174
M20	C42	1	Fail Slow Down RR	60-6, 170 – 60-6, 174
M21	C43	1	Fail Stop RR no/clr	60-6, 170 – 60-6, 174
M22	C44	1	Fail Stop RR	60-6, 170 – 60-6, 174
M23	C45	1	Fail Provide RR Spc	60-6, 170 – 60-6, 174
M24	C46	1	Fail Prvde RR u/cl	60-6, 170 – 60-6, 174
	DE		Defect Equipment	CDLIS
E34	DE1	1	No Headlight	60-6,219
E31	DE2	1	Defective Brakes	60-6,244
	DE2A	1	Fail Set Hndbrake	60-6,244
	DE3	1	Excess Noise/Smoke	60-6,286
	DE5	1	Defect Equipment	
D70	DE5A	1	Obstruct Wndshield	60-6,256
	DI		Driving Under Influ	CDLIS
A20	DI1	6	Drv U/Infl-1st	60-6,196
A10	DI1A	6	.10% Alcohol	60-6,196
A20	DI1B	6	Drv U/Infl-2nd	60-6,196
A20	DI1C	12	Drv U/Infl-3rd	60-6,196
A20	DI1D	12	Drv U/Infl-4th	60-6,196
A20	DI1E	12	Drv U/Infl-5th	60-6,196
A20	DI1F	6	Drv U/Infl-.15 1st	60-6,196
A20	DI1G	6	Drv U/Infl-.15 2nd	60-6,196
A20	DI1H	12	Drv U/Infl-.15 3rd	60-6,196
A20	DI1I	12	Drv U/Infl-.15 4th	60-6,196
A20	DI1J	12	Drv U/Infl-.15 5th	60-6,196
A25	DI1M	1	Drv While Impaired	60-6,196
A25	DI2	1	.02 Pr Fel DUI Conv	60-6,196.01
A12	DI3	1	Refuse Alcohol Test	60-6,197
	DI3B	1	Refuse Pre Test	60-6,211.02 (2)
	DJ		Underage .02 BAC	CDLIS
A60	DJ1T	0	.02 Underage D/D	60-6,211.02 (3)
A12	DJ3R	0	Underage Refuse	60-6,211.02 (3)
	DR		Refuse Alcohol Test	CDLIS
	DS		Disability	CDLIS
	EM		Equipment Misuse	CDLIS

ACD	NE Code	Points	Description	Statute
	EM2	1	Spilling Load	6-6,179, 60-6,304, 60-6,301
S95	EM4	1	Exhibition Driving	60-6,195
E54	EM5	1	Fail to Dim Lights	60-6,224, 60-6,221
U04	EM6A	1	Hunt From Roadway	39-313
	ER		Equip Regulation	CDLIS
E01	ER1A	1	No Slow Veh Emblem	60-6,241
E01	ER1B	1	No Splash Aprons	60-6,283
E05	ER1C	1	No Taillight	60-6,162
E05	ER1D	1	Driving W/O Lights	60-6,219
F02	ER1E	1	Child Restraint	60-6,268
F03	ER1F	0	No M/C Helmet	60-4,182, 60-6,282
E05	ER1G	1	No Clearance Lights	60-6,235
	ER1H	1	No Flags or Flares	60-6,243
F04	ER1I	0	Occupant Protection	60-6,270
F02	ER1J	1	Intox Trans Child	28-1,254
	ER2A	1	Vio Use Stud Tires	60-6,250
	ER2B	0	Over Dimension	60-6,288
E55	ER2C	1	Improper Lights	60-6,225, 60-6,229
	ER2D	1	TV Screen Visible	60-6,287
	FA		Fatality	CDLIS
U07	FA1	12	MV Homicide	28-306
U07	FA1A	0	Attempt MV Homicide	
U31	FA2		Violation Fatal/Acc	60-4,168(5)
A20	FA3	12	MV Hmcd Unbrn C-DUI	28-394
A230	FA3A	12	MV Hmcd Unbrn -DUI -S	28-394
	FE		Commit Felony MV	CDLIS
U03	FE1		Commit Felony MV	60-4,168(1) (d)
	FO		Follow Improperly	CDLIS
M34	FO1	1	Follow to Close	60-6,140
	FO2	1	F Cls Ped/Bic/Mbl D	60-6,133
M32	FO3	ˑ1	Follow Emergency V	60-6,183
	FR		Financial Resp	CDLIS
D36	FR5	0	No Proof of Ins	60-528, 60-570
B01	HR		Leave Scn/Evade Arr	CDLIS
B03	HR1	6	Lv Scn Acc-Inj/Dth	60-698
B01	HR2		Hit and Run	CDLIS
B01	HR2A	4	Lv Scn Acc W/I 12 Hr	60-696
B01	HR2B	8	Lv Scn Acc R/O 12 Hr	60-696
B01	HR2C	6	Lv Scn Acc/Damge	60-696
U01	HR4	1	Flee Avoid Arrest	28-905
	HV		Habitual Violator	CDLIS
	IL		Improper Lane Use	CDLIS
M42	IL1	1	Impr Lane Change	60-6,139
M41	I11A	1	Move Over Law	60-6,378
M41	IL2	1	Fail Keep Proper Ln	60-6,131, 60-6,136
F34	IL2A	1	Impeding Traffic	60-6,139, 60-6,193, 60-6,180
F34	IL2B	1	Obstruct Traffic	60-6,193, 60-6,166
M58	IL4	1	Dr Crb/Sdwlk/Shldr	60-6,178
M46	IL5	1	Impr Access Ramp	60-6,143
IM	IM		Imminent Hazard	60-4,168.02
	LI		Littering	CDLIS
	LI1	1	Deface Rd Surface	
MI	MI		Misrepresentation	
F06	MR	1	Acts Declare Unlaw Motorcycle/Moped Related	60-6,307 (2)(3), 60-6,308 (6), 60-6,312 (2)(3)(5)
A41	MR1	1	Tamper Ignition Interlock	60-6,211.05 (3)
A41	MR1A	1	Vio Interlock Pard	60-6,211.05 (3)
A41	MR1B	1	Vio Interlock Rein	83-1,127.02 (3)
A41	MR1C	1	Vio Interlock Rest	60-6,211.05 (3)
M22	MR2	1	Bus/Vio RR Stop	60-6,172
M09	MR2A	1	Fail Obey RR Rest	60-6, 170 – 60-6, 174
	MR2B		Graffiti Offense	28-524

ACD	NE Code	Points	Description	Statute
	MS		Miscellaneous	CDLIS
N82	MS2	1	Improper Backing	60-6,169
M56	MS4	1	Fire Hose/Barrier	60-6,184
D72	MS6A	1	Fail to Maintain Control	60-6,166 (2)
W00	NT		Non-Traffic Vio	CDLIS
W00	NT1A		Juvenile Drug Violation – 1st	28-416 (18) (a) (i)
W00	NT1B		Juvenile Drug Violation – 2nd	28-416 (18) (a) (ii)
W00	NT1C		Juvenile Drug Violation – Subsequent	28-416 (18) (a) (iii)
W00	NT2A		Minor in Poss 1st	53-181 (1) (a)
W00	NT2B		Minor in Poss 2nd	53-181 (1) (b)
W00	NT2C		Minor in Poss - Subsequent	53-181 (1) (c)
W00	NT9		Juvenile Violation	43-287
	PA		Passing Vio	CDLIS
M71	PA1	1	Improper Passing	60-6,132, 60-6,137
M75	PA3	3	Pass Stopped Schl Bus	60-6,175
M75	PA4	3	Pass Stopped Schl Bus	60-6,175
	PO		Possession	CDLIS
	RK		Reckless/Carless/Neg	CDLIS
M84	RK1	6	Wil Reck Drv-1st	60-6,216
M84	RK1A	6	Wil Reck Drv-2nd	60-6,217
M84	RK1B	6	Wil Reck Drv-3rd	60-6,218
M81	RK2	4	Careless Driving	60-6,212
M84	RK2A	5	Reckless Dr-1st	60-6,215
M83	RK2B	3	Negligent Driving	60-4,182
M84	RK2C	5	Reckless Dr-2nd	60-6,217
M84	RK2D	5	Reckless Dr-3rd	60-6,217
F05	RK2E	1	Prmt Rider O/S V (permit rider outside of vehicle)	36-140
M86	RK2F	3	V HH WRLS COM DV 1st (operating vehicle using a handheld wireless communications device – i.e. texting while driving)	60,6,179.01 (4) (a)
M86	RK2G	3	V HH WRLS COM DV 2nd	60,6,179.01 (4) (b)
M86	RK2H	3	V HH WRLS COM DV 3rd	60,6,179.01 (4) (c)
N80	RK4	1	Coast Downgrade in Neutral	60-6,182
	RR		Required Reports	CDLIS
B61	RR1	1	Fail Report Acc	60-696
	RR4	0	No Lic on Person	60-489
	RT		Registration and Titling	
	RT1		Invalid Registration	
	RT4		Improper Plates	
	RV		Repeated Violations	CDLIS
	RW		Right of Way	CDLIS
N23	RW2	1	Fail Yield R-O-W	60-6,147, 60-6,151
N08	RW4	2	Fail Yield R-O-W Ped	60-6,153
N08	RW4A	4	Fail Yield R-O-W/Inj	60-4,182 (12)
	SA		Controlled Substances Act	CDLIS
A50	SA1		Commit Felony Contl Sub	60-4,168 (3) (b)
	SC		Control Devices	CDLIS
M08	SC1	1	Fail Obey Officer	60-6,110
M17	SC2	1	Violate Stop/Trfc	60-6,213, 60-6,119
M14	SC2A	1	Disobey Traf Device	60-6,119, 60-6,143, 60-6,144
M02	SC3	1	Trespass Closed Rd	60-6,115
M10	SC5A	1	Violate RR Sngl/Gts	60-6,171, 60-6,170, 60-6,173
	SC6	1	Destroy Traf Device	60-6,130
	SD		School Dropout Minor	CDLIS
	SI		Signaling Devices	CDLIS
N43	SI1	1	Fail to Signal	60-6,161, 60-6,162
N40	SI2	1	Impr Signal	60-6,161, 60-6,162, 60-6,163
	SP		Speeding	CDLIS
S95	SP1	1	Engage Spd Contest	60-6,195
S94	SP2	1	Too Fast Conditions	60-6,186 (Basic Rule)

ACD	NE Code	Points	Description	Statute
	SP3		Speeding	CDLIS
S01	SP3A	1	Spd 1-5 MPH Muni	60-6,186
S06	SP3B	2	Spd 6-10 MPH Muni	60-6,186
S06/S92***	SP3C	3	Spd Ovr 10 MPH Muni OR Spd 11-15 MPH Muni	60-6,186
S51	SP3D	1	Spd 1-10 MPH C/S	60-6,186
S06/S92***	SP3E	2	Spd 11-15 MPH C/S	60-6,186
S15	SP3F	3	Spd Ovr 15 MPH C/S OR Spd 16-35 MPH C/S	60-6,186
S51	SP3G	1	Spd 1-10 MPH NIS	60-6,186
S06/S92***	SP3H	2	Spd 11-15 MPH NIS	60-6,186
S15	SP3I	3	Spd Ovr 15 MPH NIS OR Spd 16-35 MPH NIS	60-6,186
S16	SP3J	3	Spd Ovr 15 MPH Muni OR Spd 16-35 MPH Muni	60-6,186
S36	SP3K	4	Spd Ovr 35 MPH Muni	60-6,186
S36	SP3L	4	Spd Ovr 35 MPH C/S	60-6,186
S36	SP3M	4	Spd Ovr 35 MPH NIS	60-6,186
S96	SP4	1	Driving Too Slow	60-6,193
	SR		Court Requested	
	TU		Improper Turn	CDLIS
N50	TU3	1	Improper Turn	60-6,159, 60-6,160
	VR		Vio of Lic Rest	CDLIS
B20	VR1A	1	Dr During Revo/Imp	60-4,108
B20	VR1B	1	Dr During Revo-Subs	60-4,108
B20	VR1C	1	Dr During Revo Enh	60-6,197.06
B20	VR2	1	Dr During Susp	60-557, 60-4,107, 60-4,108
B20	VR2A	1	Dr During Susp-Subs	60-4,108
D29	VR4	1	Violate Lic Restr	60-4,118, 60-4,141
D27	VR4A	1	Violate WP	60-4,129
D29	VR4B	1	Violate LP/SP/POP	60-4,123 (LPD), 60-4,124 (LPE, SCP), 60-4,141 (LPC), 60-4,120.02 (POP)
D27	VR4C	1	Violate POP Pass Lt	60-4,120.01(3)(b)
D27	VR4D	1	Violate Inter Wire D	60-4,120.01(3)(c)
B51	VR5A	1	No Drivers License	60-484, 60-490 (Expired), 60-488 (Non-Resident)
B91	VR5B	1	Impr Lic Class	60-4,127, 60-4,141
	WW		Wrong Way/Side	CDLIS
N63	WW1	1	Wrong Way/One Way	60-6,138

Administrative Withdrawal Table with NE Code, ACD Code, and Retention Period

ACD	NE Code	Description	Retention Period
	C5	FHWA Dis – 1 Yr	*
M10	C41	Dis/R One RR V-60D	*
M20	C42	Dis/R One RR V-60D	*
M21	C43	Dis/R One RR V-60D	*
M22	C44	Dis/R One RR V-60D	*
M23	C45	Dis/R One RR V-60D	*
M24	C46	Dis/R One RR V-60D	*
D02	C47	Dis/R App Fraud-60D	60-487 *
A94	C51	Dis/R .04-1Y	+
A20	C52	Dis/R DUI-1 Yr	+
A12	C53	Dis/R Ref Test-1 Yr	+
A20	C54	Dis/R Cntrl Sub-1 Yr	+
B01	C55	Dis/R LvScn Ac-1 Yr	+
U03	C56	Dis/R CMV Felny-1 Yr	+
U10	C57	Dis/R CMV Neg Fa-1Y	+
B20	C58	Dis/R Dr CMV W/D 1Y	+
	C6	FHWA Dis – 3 Yr	+
A94	C61	Dis/R .04 Haz-3 Yr	+
A20	C62	Dis/R DUI Haz-3 Yr	+

ACD	NE Code	Description	Retention Period
A12	C63	Dis/R Ref T Haz-3 Yr	+
A22	C64	Dis/R Ctrl S Hz-3 Yr	+
B01	C65	Dis/R Lv Scn Hz-3 Yr	+
U03	C66	Dis/R Cmt Fe Hz-3 Yr	+
U10	C67	Dis/R CMV Neg Fa H3	+
B20	C68	Dis/R Dr CMV W/DH3	+
	C7	FHWA Dis – Life	++
A50	C70	Dis/R Cmt Fe Sub-L	++
W40	C71	Dis/R 2nd CMV-Life	++
	C8	FHWA Dis – 60/120 D	*
W30	C80	Dis/R Two CMV-60	*
W31	C81	Dis/R Three CMV-120	*
W60	C82	Dis/R Two RR V – 120 D	*
W61	C83	Dis/R Three RR V – 1 Y	*
	C9	FHWA 24 Hour OOS	***
B27	C90	Dis/R OS-90D	***
B27	C90A	Dis/R OS-180 DY	***
W50	C91	Dis/R OS-2nd 2 YR	***
W52	C92	Dis/R OS-3rd 3 YR	***
B19	C93	Dis/R OS-Haz/P 180D	***
W51	C94	Dis/R OS-H/P Sub 3 Y	***
W70	C97	Imminent Hazard - 60-4,168.02 49C.F.R. 383.52	***
	CS	Change SOR Surrender	**
A12	DI3B	Revo-Implied Cons	*
A12	DI3C	Admin Lic Revo-1 Yr (Refusal)	***
A98	DI5	Admin Lic Revo-90 D	***
A41	DI51	Violate Int Rest (Violate Interlock Restriction)	
A98	DI5A	Admin Lic Revo-1 Yr	***
W01	DI5P	Vio Pard Brd Rein (Violating Pardons Reinstatement Board)	*
W20	DS1	Recall/Cancel	*
D39	FR1A	Susp-Unsat Judg	*
D39	FR1B	Susp-DIP-Uns Jud	*
D38	FR2A	Susp-Acc	*
D38	FR2B	Susp-DIP-Acc	*
D35	FR3	Susp-Ins Can	*
D35	FR5A	Susp-No Proof FR	*
D02	MR1A	Lic Cancel-DMV	*
D02	MR1B	Lic Can-Compact	*
W14	MR1D	Lic Cancel-M/V	*
D56	RR2	Failure to Comply	*
D51	RR3	Violate Support Order	*
W01	RV2A	Revo-Points 6 Mo	*
W01	RV2B	Revo-Points 3 Yr	*
W01	RV2C	Susp-Fail Comp DRI	*
W00	NT	None Traffic W/drwl	*
W09	MR1H	Fail to Sur Haz End	U.S. Patriot Act *
	VS	Voluntary Surrender	**

*	= Ten years from reinstatement date, or if not reinstated, retained permanently.
**	= One year from reinstatement date. (Complete record is purged if all other retention periods are met).
***	= Fifteen years from reinstatement date, or if not reinstated, retained permanently.
+	= Fifty-five years from reinstatement date, or if not reinstated, retained permanently.
++	= Lifetime.

Point System Summary

The points range from 1 to 12, accumulation of 12 or more points in a two year period can result in a suspension. If an individual who has less than 12 points assessed against his/her driving record completes a Driver Improvement Course for a two-point credit, it will appear on the record as "Driver Improvement Credit" with the date of completion.

Nevada

Administration	Important Phone and Web Contacts
Troy L. Dillard, Administrator Rhonda Bavaro, Administrator Lori Warren, Record Manager 555 Wright Way Carson City 89711 775-684-4549 www.dmvnv.com General Email info@dmv.nv.gov Motor Vehicle Laws www.dmvnv.com/codebook.htm Traffic Laws: www.leg.state.nv.us/NRS/NRS-484.html	Driver Licensing & Records Las Vegas 702-486-4368 Driver Records - Reno/Carson City.......775-684-4590 Driver Licensing - Reno/Carson City....775-684-4368 SR-22 and Financial Responsibility ......775-684-4368 Help Line (Toll free) ....877-368-7828 CDL Carson City.................................775-684-4368 CDL Las Vegas ....702-486-5655 Vehicle Information ....775-684-4368 State Insurance Division......................775-687-0700 Highway Patrol...................................775-687-4808

Driver's License Format, Issuance and Renewal

License Classes, Restrictions and Endorsements Appear After the Driving Record Content Section

License Format

Since 1/1/98, Nevada has issued a ten-digit number and reports the number is made randomly: there is no specific code.

Document Appearance

The current driver license and ID documents were introduced in October 2008. The previous document was initially issued in April 2002. Both cards are described below.

Current Documents

Security Characteristics: Micro-printing, ghost images, Guilloche security design, laser perforation, overlapping data, and a laser-engraved outline of the state. A 1D bar code and 2D bar code appear on the backside of the card. The documents are issued using facial recognition software, allowing the Department to compare new photos with other photos in the database as a further guard against identity theft.

Position of Photo: For adult licenses, the photo is positioned on the left with a ghost image on the right side.

Minor Age Driver Indicators: The minor cards are vertical. The photo is on the upper left side and the ghost image on the upper right. Underneath the ghost photo appears "Under 18 or 21 until xx/xx/xxxx" in red ink. The location of the laser perforation is in a different location than the adult card.

CDL Indicator: License header shows "Nevada Commercial Driver License."

Older Documents (pre-Oct 2008)

Security Characteristics: State seal on laminate; see above.

Position of Photo: Old - bottom right: Current - top right.

Minor Age Driver Locator (since 04/02): "Nevada Minor Driver (Under 21)" is laminated on license; photo is side profile. If under 21 is a vertical license with no side view photo, yellow bar indicates "Under 21 until xx."

Minor Age Driver Locator (prior 04/02)   "Nevada Minor Driver (Under 21)" is laminated on license; photo is side profile. If under 18 the license header is light blue, "Under 21" written in yellow. If under 21 but over 18 the license header is yellow, "Under 21" written in red.

CDL Indicator (since 04/02): Gold bar header shows "Commercial Driver License."

CDL Indicator   (prior 04/02): License header shows "Nevada Commercial Driver License."

Issuance

Location of Requirements for Proof of Identity:
www.dmvnv.com/dlresident.htm

Age Requirements

The minimum age for a learner's or instruction permit is fifteen and one-half. Nearly all Nevada beginning drivers under 18 must complete a driver education course. The course is not a requirement to obtain an instruction permit; it is a requirement for a driver license. Young drivers can enroll at age 15.   Exceptions are not made for home-schooled students. Young drivers are required to complete 50 hours of behind-the-wheel experience (10 hours of which completed in darkness) and must have a licensed driver, who is 21 or older and has been licensed for at least one year, seated next to them at all times. An excellent description with complete details of the program is found at www.dmvnv.com/nvdlteens.htm.

Residency

New residents must secure Nevada license within thirty (30) days of establishing residency. New residents under 21 must take a written test.

Renewal

A Nevada driver's license is valid for 4 years and expires on the birthday of the 4th year unless immigration documents are presented as evidence of the name and date of birth. If immigration documents are used, the expiration of the license will coincide with the departure date on the immigration documents, or in 4 years, whichever is sooner. NV allows active military personnel, federal government employees, and dependents of either, to renew by mail unless the document has been expired 2 years.

Drivers may renew online once every 8 years. To qualify for web kiosk or mail renewals, a driver must have obtained or renewed in person within the last 4 years, be at least 20 years old on the next birthday, and must not have had more than two moving violations or any license suspension, revocation, cancellation or denial within the last 4 years. Also, if a license holder has moved and the address shown on the card is incorrect, the license holder must renew by mail or in person.

Elderly-Related Restrictions

Drivers age 71 and older who wish to renew by mail must provide a medical evaluation signed by a physician. Drivers age 71 and older are not eligible to renew online or at kiosks.

Vehicle Insurance, Title and Registration Facts

Registration Renewal

Vehicle renewal for NV vehicles is available online at https://dmvapp.nv.gov/dmv/vr/vrrenewal/vr_ren_input.aspx. If a smog (emissions) check is required the vehicle registration may be renewed online if the Department received an electronic record stating the vehicle passed. Also, online registration renewal for motor carriers is available through the Nevada Commercial Online Registration System (NCORS), call 775-684-4711 for more information.

New Residents

New residents must register (and have inspected) vehicles within thirty (30) days of establishing residency. This includes a non-resident who furnishes a vehicle to a Nevada resident for continuous use here.

Inspections and Emissions Testing

Nevada has no annual vehicle-safety inspection, but does have provisions for annual emission testing in Clark and Washoe counties. The following vehicles are exempt from emission testing: new motor vehicles on their first and second registration; new hybrid-electric vehicles for the first five model years; 1967 or older; motorcycle or moped; vehicles based in remote areas of Clark and Washoe counties and all other Nevada counties; alternative fuel vehicles; Diesel vehicles with a gross vehicle weight up to 14,000 pounds; vehicles registered with Classic Vehicle or Classic Rod license plates and driven 5,000 miles or less per year. A vehicle identification number inspection is required for all vehicles not previously registered or titled in Nevada.

Passenger Plate Facts

There are two plates with one sticker (MO & YR) on rear plate. If a vehicle is not equipped by the manufacturer for a front display, then one plate is okay. Pre-1982 plates, some of which are in use, are coded with the alpha(s) designating the county. Since 1982, there are no county codes.

Plates remain with seller when vehicle is sold. One must surrender the license plates if the liability insurance on the vehicle is dropped for any reason.

OHV Note: Any motorized vehicle which does not have the normal safety equipment such as lights and mirrors or is not built to federal vehicle standards is an off-road vehicle and is restricted to off-road use only. There is no driver license minimum age requirement for off-road vehicles. Nevada stopped issuing titles on OHVs on August 15, 2005. On July 1, 2012, the state began requiring registration of OHVs and snowmobiles 1976 and newer and registration and titling of any OHV sold on or after that date.

Insurance and Financial Responsibility

A Nevada Evidence of Insurance card must be carried in the vehicle at all times and presented to any law enforcement officer upon request. Minimum automobile liability insurance coverage is $15,000 for bodily injury or death of one person in any one accident; $30,000 for bodily injury or death or two or more persons on any one accident; and $10,000 for injury to or destruction of property of others in any one accident. Coverage must be reported by an insurance company authorized to do business in the State of Nevada. Motorists with driver license suspensions or revocations may be required to file a SR-22 with the DMV to regain driving privileges. The state does not have a provision for no-fault insurance.

Withdrawal Sanctions, and Alcohol and Drug Testing

Alcohol and Chemical Testing

Nevada's illegal intoxication level is .08 percent blood alcohol level or any detectable amount of a controlled substance; .02 if under 21; and .04 for anyone driving a commercial motor vehicle. Urine, blood, and breath testing are authorized. Nevada has an administrative license revocation provision. This provision also applies to juveniles with .02 - .08 percent intoxication level.

Suspensions and Revocations

The state has implemented the federally mandated disqualifications for offenses occurring in a CMV. See the Appendix for a list of these disqualifications. Below are examples of driver license suspensions and revocations. Juveniles may have additional offense that can suspend or delay their licenses.

Possible Suspensions

- Accumulation of Twelve or More Points in Twelve Months
- Aggressive Driving First Offense- Court Order
- Various CDL Disqualifications
- Child Support Arrearage
- Collision with Bicyclist or Pedestrian
- Court Recommendations due to Traffic Violation Conviction
- Driving Uninsured (3rd Offense)
- Failure to Appear in Court or Pay Fines
- Failure to Maintain Insurance
- Failure to Pay Delinquent Fine
- Failure to Properly Secure a Child
- Firearm - Juvenile
- Graffiti
- Illegal Per Se - Juvenile .02-.08%
- Out-of-State Offense Which in this State Would Require Suspension
- Street Racing
- Passing a School Bus
- Truancy

Possible Revocations

- Aggressive Driving Second Offense- Court Order
- Conviction of Three Charges of Reckless Driving Within Twelve Month
- Failure to Stop When Involved in an Accident Resulting in Death or Personal Injury
- Felony Involving the Use of a Vehicle or Car Theft
- Manslaughter

DUI Revocations

- First Violation in Seven Years   Ninety days.
- Second Violation in Seven Years   One year.
- Third or Subsequent Violations   Three years.

Cancellations

- Failure to Give Correct or Required Information When Applying for a Driver's License or to Meet Department Requirements
- Fraud Committed When Applying for a Driver's License
- If the Driver is Under Eighteen, a Parent or Guardian May Request Cancellation of the License
- If the Driver Voluntarily Surrenders his/her Driver's License for Medical Reasons

Reinstatement Requirements

Suspension....................................$40.00 to $120.00 fee; re-examination.
Revocation...............................$75.00 to $125.00 fee; re-examination; SR-22.
If for driving while uninsured, fees will range from $250 to $1,750 for serious repeat offenders.

Record Access: Laws, Rules, and Forms

Note: **This Section Applies to Both Driver and Vehicle Records.**

Governing Statutes and Rules

Traffic Laws: http://www.leg.state.nv.us/NRS/NRS-484.html
Motor Vehicle Laws: www.dmvnv.com/codebook.htm

Statute NRS 481.063 brought the state into compliance with the Driver's Privacy Protection Act (DPPA). The release of DMV records is governed by NRS 481.063, NRS 485.316, and Nevada Administrative Code 481.500-481.600 and DPPA.

Nevada does not have the following federal exceptions: 1, 6, 10, 11, 13, and 14. Nevada added the following exceptions:

(h) By a reporter or editorial employee who is employed by or affiliated with any newspaper, press association or commercially operated, federally licensed radio or television station for a journalistic purpose. The Department may not make any inquiries regarding the use of or reason for the information requested other than whether the information will be used for a journalistic purpose.

(i) In connection with an investigation conducted pursuant to NRS 253.0415 or 253.220.

However, Nevada modified the exception in connection with motor vehicles as follows

(c) In connection with matters relating to:
 (1) The safety of drivers of motor vehicles;
 (2) Safety and thefts of motor vehicles;
 (3) Emissions from motor vehicles;
 (4) Alterations of products related to motor vehicles;
 (5) An advisory notice relating to a motor vehicle or the recall of a motor vehicle;
 (6) Monitoring the performance of motor vehicles;
 (7) Parts or accessories of motor vehicles;
 (8) Dealers of motor vehicles; or
 (9) Removal of non-owner records from the original records of motor vehicle manufacturers.

Nevada modified the exception regarding *bulk distribution of surveys* as follows:

(k) In the bulk distribution of surveys, marketing material or solicitations, if the Director has adopted policies and procedures to ensure that:

(1) The information will be used or sold only for use in the bulk distribution of surveys, marketing material or solicitations;
(2) Each person about whom the information is requested has clearly been provided with an opportunity to authorize such a use; and
(3) If the person about whom the information is requested does not authorize such a use, the bulk distribution will not be directed toward that person.

In summary, what the above means is that personal information, defined as information which reveals the identity of a person including SSN, photo, driver's license number, address, medical conditions, cannot be released to requesters of driver and vehicle records, except to specifically defined users. This group includes insurers (and their vendors), employers (and their vendors), process servers, court and litigation matters, towing, among others. The notable exception to the permissible uses defined in the DPPA is the NV statute authorizes access by reporters and editorial employees of newspapers, press associations, and federally licensed radio or television stations.

Request and Consent Forms

All third party requesters and insurance companies must complete an *Application for Records Service* which includes an Affidavit requiring a notarized signature. The package may be downloaded at www.dmvnv.com/pdfforms/ir001.pdf. Any third party who requests driver license or registration records must complete the *Application for Individual Record Information (IR-002)*. To download, go to www.dmvnv.com/pdfforms/ir002.pdf.

Vendor and Third Party Access Policy

Approved online vendors can access records for other vendors (who are not online, etc.) who will then sell to an end user if contract between reseller and end user contains same language as contract between the state and the original vendor.

Non-permissible Use Requests

Records are released, but all personal information is blocked.

Access to Driver-Related Records

Driving Records

General Information and Fees

Department of Motor Vehicles, Records Section, 555 Wright Way, Carson City NV 89711-0250. For Reno/Sparks/Carson City use 775-684-4590; for Las Vegas use 702-486-4368; For rest of state or out-of-state use 877-368-7828. The fax number is 775-684-4899. Email questions to info@dmv.nv.gov.

Three records are available: 3-year, 10-year, and School Bus records. Only the 3-year record is available online. The current fee for a driving record is $7.00; for driver's license information the fee is $5.00; certification is $4.00; and a photo copy of a document is $3.00. The last fee increase was in July 2003 and no increases are planned for the near future. The state charges for "no record found" reports.

In-Person – Walk-in requests are processed while you wait at the location listed above. Drivers may obtain their own record at any DMV Office, but the address above is the only location to obtain a certified record. Credit cards are accepted for payment. Also, one may receive a

3-year, School Bus or 10-year history from self-service kiosks at larger DMV offices and a number of private locations. If for person of record, see Kiosk Services at the web page.

Mail – Requests mailed to the state are processed within 10 days. Specific forms are required when requesting information. Please call to request forms or visit the web site to download forms.

Telephone, Fax – Nevada offers a retrieval phone-in system at 775-684-4590. Callers must have an assigned five-digit account number for access. Pre-approved callers can request up to 5 MVRs at a time over the phone. The driver's license number or name and date of birth are needed when ordering. NV will also mail-back phone-in requests, if requested. Billing is monthly, and must be paid within 30 days. Pre-approved accounts may fax requests.

Electronic – Nevada accepts input files for its External Agency Driver History Inquiry interface on an FTP file server. Each ordering entity with an account has an assigned directory on the file server. All input and output files are exchanged within these directories. Only three-year histories are available. Nevada processes all batch input files received by 5:30 PM daily, except Sunday. The output files are written to their corresponding vendor directories by 6:30 PM for download. For further information, call 775-684-4702. Interactive service was recently made available, also.

Bulk – Records can be sold to business entities upon meeting the same criteria as an individual request for information. An application must be submitted to the Record Section of the DMV. Costs vary from $500 to $2,500.

By Person of Record – Individuals may obtain their own 3-year driving record by mail, fax, kiosk, in person from any DMV Office or online at https://dmvapp.nv.gov/dmv/dl/OL_DH/Drvr_Usr_Info.aspx, note the record must be printed at the time ordered. The fee is $7.00. A 10-year record can only be requested in person or by mail. If request is mailed, requester must mail a signed letter which contains the full name, address, daytime telephone number, date of birth, Social Security Number, driver license number if available and a reason for the request. Please enclose a check or money order payable to DMV. If a certified copy or if original issue date is needed please enclose an additional $4.00.

Driver Notification/Monitoring Program

At present, Nevada does not offer a monitoring system or notification program to employers or insurance companies to track incidents of drivers. However, reportedly there are vendors offering this service. The DMV feels the vendors are obtaining the records via the court system.

Accident Reports

Reporting – A written report is required when: an accident was not investigated at the scene by law enforcement; damage occurred in excess of $750 to any one person; the accident resulted in an injury or death. Reports must be filed within ten days with the Department of Motor Vehicles, Central Services & Records Division, Driver License Review, 555 Wright Way, Carson City NV 89711-0400. There are no additional state reporting requirements for commercial drivers at this time.

Record Access – There is no centralized database of Highway Patrol investigated accident reports; the reports must be ordered from one of the three regional offices. Note that the Nevada Highway Patrol headquarters will accept orders, but still sends all requests to the appropriate office. The fee to obtain an accident report is $10.00 for a non-fatality and $20.00 if fatality involved. The only access method is by mail, which takes one week.

The addresses and phone numbers of the regional office and of headquarters are listed below;

- Headquarters, 555 Wright Way, Carson City, NV 89711, 775-684-7381
- Las Vegas Div., 4615 Sunset, Las Vegas, NV 89118, 702-486-4100
- Reno Div., 357 Hammell Lane, Reno, NV 89511, 775-688-2500
- Elko Div., 3920 E Idaho St, Elko, NV 89801, 775-753-1111

Access to Vehicle-Related Records

General Information and Fees

Department of Motor Vehicles, Motor Vehicle Record Section, 555 Wright Way, Carson City, NV 89711-0250, 775-684-4590.

Owners of off-road vehicles (ORVs or OHV) must now register their vehicles with the DMV. The current fee for vehicle title or registration information is $5.00; for a vehicle history the fee is $7.00; and a title verification letter or vehicle history is $7.00. Certification of any document is an additional $4.00. A photocopy of each page of a document is an additional $3.00 per page. Records requested for insurance purposes from an insurance company or agent must provide the NAIC number of the insurance company.

In-Person & Mail – Current records only are available on computer and on microfilm back to 1980. Plate numbers are not released when doing a name search. Turnaround time for mail-in requests is 10 days. Specific forms are required (see earlier section) when requesting information. Please call to request forms, or obtain from the web site.

Telephone – The same phone-in request system offered for driving record searches (see Driving Records section) is available for vehicle and ownership information at 775-684-4590. Callers must have an assigned five-digit account number for access. Pre-approved callers can request up to five records at a time over the phone.

Electronic Status – Although full title and registration records cannot be accessed online, the DMV offers an online registration status inquiry. The requester must submit the license plate number and last four digits of the VIN to display the record information. Go to https://dmvapp.nv.gov/dmv/vr/vr_dev/VR_reg/VR_Reg_Default.aspx. There is no fee.

Bulk – Records can be sold to business entities upon meeting the same criteria as an individual request for information. An application must be submitted to the Record Section of the DMV. Costs can vary from $500 to $2,500.

Access to Vessel-Related Records

General Information, Access and Fees

Department of Wildlife, Attn: Boat Registration, 4600 Kietzke Lane, D-135, Reno NV 89502 775-688-1511, Fax is 775-688-1509. www.ndow.org/boat/index.shtm.

All motorized boats must be registered and titled. Records are open to the public, but the SSN is blocked. The boat registration or hull number, or name of owner or SSN is needed to do a search. The SSN is blocked. Records are available from 1972 to present on microfilm and computer.

There is a $10.00 fee per boat or person which includes computer printout. Photocopies are $.50 per page. The information will include current lien-holder name and address. Turnaround time is within 1 week. Bulk lists, labels and tapes are available for purchase. Fees depend on the media type and can be $1,000 or more.

Note that there are three Regional Offices and four Field Offices in the state, and all offices provide counter and mail service. A list of offices is found at the web page.

Driving Record Content and Reciprocity

What's on or Not on the Record

- Information about traffic accidents and convictions are a part of the driving record, including incidents that occur out-of-state.
- Social Security Numbers are not released.
- Withdrawal actions and accidents are **not** released on a three-year record, but show on a ten-year record.
- Non-moving violations (except for commercial drivers) are not listed

on the driving record.

- Using a three-digit numeric code, the conviction line indicates the Justice or District Court presiding over the citation. This code list can be found at www.dmvnv.com/pdfforms/courtcodes.pdf.
- The length of time that convictions appear on the public driving record is three years; a suspension or revocation will be reported indefinitely if the license is not reinstated.

- The state does not permit driver school attendance in lieu of conviction. However, demerit points may be reduced by attending a state authorized driver training course.

Data Retention

Information on most serious violations is kept and available to all 50 state DMVs for a period of 10 years after the conviction or license reinstatement. License suspensions and revocations which are not reinstated will remain on the record indefinitely. Convictions remain on file indefinitely with the court which handled the case and in state and local criminal history files. The state purges CDL records based on the timetable per federal regulations, see the Appendix for this table.

Court to Repository

All convictions are sent via paper from the courts to the state within twenty days for input on the driving record; however, DUIs can be reported by law enforcement or the courts. DUIs are usually entered on the driving record within twenty-four hours of being received by the state; moving violations are added within thirty days.

State Reciprocity for Non-CDL Drivers

- Will suspend license of driver for unpaid out-of-state convictions.
- Record of new incoming driver is not shown on MVR.
- Out-of-state moving violation convictions are shown on MVR.
- Out-of-state accidents are not shown on MV.
- Convictions of out-of-state drivers are sent to home state.
- Record is forwarded to new state upon surrender of license if requested.

License Classes, Restrictions, and Commercial Endorsements

License Classes

Nevada license classes and common endorsements are listed below. Nevada does not issue any type of Chauffeur or other special license.

Class A   Required to drive combination vehicles, such as tractor-trailers, with a gross combination weight rating (GCWR) of 26,001 pounds or more, provided the vehicle being towed has a gross vehicle weight rating (GVWR) of 10,001 pounds or more.

Class B   Required to drive any single vehicle with a GVWR of 26,001 or more pounds, or any such vehicle towing a vehicle weighing 10,000 pounds GVWR or less.

Class C   Required to drive cars, vans, pickups, mopeds, and other vehicles with a GVWR of 26,000 pounds or less; allows towing of a vehicle with a GVWR of 10,000 pounds or less.

Class M   Required is for motorcycles. Motorcycle classification and a Class A, B, or C will show up as both classes on the driver's license, provided all other requirements were met. Additionally, Nevada has a Class M license with a U Restriction that limits riders to mopeds, tri-mobiles, and motorcycles that are less than 90 cc and do not exceed 6 1/2 horsepower.

Common Commercial Endorsements

J   Allows Class C license to tow a vehicle over 10,000 pounds GVWR. Additional written and skills tests are required.

R   **(No longer issued as of 1/28/2013)** Allows Class C license to tow a combination of vehicles not to exceed 70 feet in length. Additional written and skills tests are required.

F   For firefighters, farmers and military members who drive non-commercial heavy equipment. This endorsement is a limited exemption from commercial licensing requirements.

T   Double/Triple-Trailers-CDL

P   Passengers-CDL

N   Tankers-CDL

S   School Bus

X   Hazardous Materials & Tankers

H   Hazardous Materials-CDL

Restrictions

Nevada is scheduled to implement extensive revisions to its list of restrictions on January 28, 2013 (after the publication date of the book). The following table shows both the old and the new lists. Designations listed on existing licenses will be changed automatically when a new card is issued for any reason.

Prior to 1/28/13	On/ after 1/28/13	Restriction Description	Prior to 1/28/13	On/ after 1/28/13	Restriction Description
F	A	Auto Trans only	XI	J	Drive NCMV B Rec Veh
A	B	Corrective Lenses	L	J	Left Foot Accelerator
K	C	Mechanical/Adaptive devices	XL	J	Trimobile
Q	D	Prosthetic Aid	9	J	Class A tow car only
XP	E	Auto Trans CMV wgt only	XN	J	Instruction Permit
C	F	Outside Mirrors	XO	J	Driver Educ Only
D	G	Daylight driving only	5	J	Tow veh >10000 lb CMV C
none	H	Limited to Employ	6	J	Tow NCMV <10000 lb <70'
none	I	Limited Other	none	J	3 wheel MC w/1 rear pwr wheel
X	J	Other	XM	J	Low-Speed Vehicles Only
XA	J	Must Carry Detail Form			
XB	J	Drive Test Every 6 months	XM	J	Low-Speed Vehicles Only
XC	J	Eye Test Every 6 Months	E	J	Speed less than 45 MPH
XD	J	Drive Fire Equip NCMV A	P	J	Phys Exam Reqd
XG	J	Drive Fire Equip NCMV B	7	J	NV Med Waiver
XF	J	Must Have Wink Mirrors	W	J	Dir visual sup 21+ yrs
XE	J	Motorcycle w-Sidecar	2	K	CMV intrastate only
XH	J	Trnsprt Handicapped Only	1	L	No air brakes CMV wgt only
XJ	J	Drive NCMV A Rec Veh	3	M	No Class A Psngr veh

4	N	No Class A/B Psngr veh	Y	Y	Ignition interlock
none	O	No tractor trailer CMV wgt only	none	Z	No Full Air brake Equip CMV
none	P	No Psngr in CMV bus	B	1	Telescopic Device
Z	Q	Moped	I	2	Hearing Aids
R	R	No Plac HazMat or Psngrs	XQ	3	No fwy driving
V	S	No Passengers	H	4	Grip/Power Steering Wheel
T	T	To-from school only	G	5	Directional Signals
U	U	MC not to exceed 90 cc	M	6	Yearly vision exam
7	V	Med Variance Docs Reqd	N	7	Yearly medical Letter
none	W	Farm Waiver	O	8	Yearly drive test
none	X	No cargo in CMV tank veh	J	9	Seat Cushion/Auto Seat

Conviction Table with Codes, ACD, Statute, and Description

The Withdrawal Table Appears Next, Followed by Demerit Point System

On the table below, the numeric codes that appear under the Code column will appear on driving records and signify the violation for which the motorist was convicted.

- An asterisk "*" in the Code column signifies an obsolete code that could still show on a driving record. Note these codes are not shown on the actual Nevada traffic citation.
- The ACD is the code reported to each motor vehicle agency in the U.S.
- The "WD" column signifies if there is a **withdrawal action** associated with the conviction. A separate Withdrawal Table follows this table.
- In the Statute column, items starting with 483 or 484 or 485 refer to the Nevada Revised Statutes (NRS). 49 CFR refers to the Code of Federal Regulations.
- **The first number of the Code** indicates the number of demerit **points** assigned for that offense. Codes beginning with zero indicate serious offenses in which the motorist's driving privilege may be revoked, suspended or cancelled
- On the driving record, the conviction line uses a three-digit numeric code to indicate the **Justice or District Court** presiding over the citation. This code list is found at www.dmvnv.com/pdfforms/courtcodes.pdf.

Code	ACD	WD	Description	Statute (State or Federal)
*001	B05	Y	Leaving accident scene before police arrive	484.221-225:49 CFR 383.51
002	B06	Y	Leaving accident scene before police arrive-fatal accident	484.221-225:49 CFR 383.51
003	B07	Y	Leaving accident scene before police arrive-personal injury	484.221-225:49 CFR 383.51
*004	B08	Y	Leaving accident scene before police arrive-property damage accident	484.221-225:49 CFR 383.51
005	D45	N	Failure to appear for trial or court appearance	483.465
006	D56	N	Failure to answer a citation, pay fines, penal ties and/or cost related to the original violation	484.807
007	D53	N	Failure to make required payment of fine and costs	483.465
008	D51	N	Failure to make required payment of child support	483.443
*009	U04	N	Using a motor vehicle in connection with a misdemeanor (not traffic offense)	484.37937
010	A41	N	Driver violation of ignition interlock or immobilization devices	483.46
011	B25	Y	Driving while license revoked	483.560.5B
012	U08	Y	Vehicular manslaughter/involuntary manslaughter	483.460.B1
013	B02	Y	Hit and run-failure to stop and render aid after accident-fatal accident	484.219:49 CFR 383.51
014	B26	Y	Driving while licensed suspended	483.560(5)(a)
015	U01	Y	Fleeing or evading police or roadblock-failing or refusing to stop a vehicle on a signal of a peace officer, attempting to elude or fleeing a peace officer, evade a police officer	484.348
*016	U31	Y	Violation resulting in fatal accident	49 CFR 383.51
017	W00	Y	Violation resulting in personal injury accident/driver in accident causing substantial bodily harm	483.470B
018	U03	Y	Using a motor vehicle in connection with a felony (not traffic offense)	483:460
020	D36	N	Failure to maintain required liability insurance - no insurance -owner operator are different	485.187
021	D29	Y	Violate restrictions of driver license (includes DL, CDL, and instruction permit)	483:360
023	A50	Y	Driving a CMV while in the commission of a felony involving the manufacturing, distributing, or dispensing a controlled substance	49 CFR 383.51
024	B22	Y	Driving while license cancelled	483.560(5)(D)
025	D27	Y	Violate limited license conditions/hardship license	483.49
026	B27	Y	General, driving while an out of service order is in effect (for violations not covered by B19)	49 CFR 383.51
027	D36	Y	Failure to maintain required liability insurance-no insurance-owner/operator-suspend driver's license only	485.187
028	W00	N	Failed to show insurance certification to officer	484.792
029	W00	Y	Aggressive driving	484.3765
030	B19	Y	Driving while out of service order is in effect and transporting 16 or more passengers,	49 CFR 383.51

Code	ACD	WD	Description	Statute (State or Federal)
			including the driver and/or transporting hazardous materials that require a placard	
*031	B01	Y	Hit and run-failure to stop and render aid after accident	484.219:49 CFR 383.51
032	B03	Y	Hit and run-failure to stop and render aid after accident-personal injury accident	494.219:49 CFR 383.51
033	U31	Y	Violation resulting in fatal accident	483.46
035	B91	N	Improper classification or endorsement on driver license (includes DL, CDL, and instruction permit) - 1st Offense	48 CFR 383.51
037	M86	N	Using a hand-held mobile telephone/device while driving	-
040	U07	Y	Vehicular homicide/manslaughter causing fatality through negligent operation of a CMV	49 CFR 383.51
041	A08	Y	Driving under the influence of alcohol with BAC at or over .08	484.379 CFR 383.51
042	A10	Y	Driving under the influence of alcohol with BAC at or over .10	484.379 49 CFR 383.51
043	A11	Y	Driving under the influence of alcohol with BAC at or over (detailed field required)	484.379 49 CFR 383.51
*044	A24	--	Driving under the influence of medication not intended to intoxicate	----
045	W09	Y	Failure to surrender hazmat endorsement as required by USA Patriot Act	----
*046	A61	N	Underage administrative per se-drinking and driving at .02 or higher BAC	----
*047	A31	N	Illegal possession of alcohol	----
*048	A33	N	Illegal possession of drugs (controlled substances)	----
*049	A35	N	Possession of open alcohol container	----
051	M10	Y	For all drivers in a CMV, failure to obey a traffic control device or the directions of an enforcement official at a railroad-highway grade crossing	49 CFR 383.51
052	M20	Y	Failure to slowdown at R/R crossing and check that tracks are clear	49 CFR 383.51
053	M21	Y	Failure to stop before reaching R/R crossing when tracks are not clear	49 CFR 383.51
054	M22	Y	Failure to stop as required before driving on R/R crossing	49 CFR 383.51
055	M23	Y	Failure to have sufficient space to drive completely through R/R crossing without stopping	49 CFR 383.51
056	M24	Y	Failure to negotiate R/R crossing because of insufficient undercarriage clearance	49 CFR 383.51
057	U10	Y	Causing a fatality through the negligent operation of a CMV	49 CFR 383.51
058	U09	Y	Negligent homicide while operating a CMV	49 CFR 383.51
065	B56	Y	Driving a CMV without obtaining a CDL	49 CFR 383.51
069	B51	N	Expired or no driver license (includes DL, CDL, and instruction permit)	483.380: 483.350:49 CFR 383.51
*070	B50	--	Expired or no document which is required	----
*071	E01	N	Operating without equipment as required by law	49 CFR 383.51
*072	E20	--	Use of equipment prohibited by law	----
*073	E50	N	Failure to use equipment as required	49 CFR 383.51
*074	F20	--	Failure to weight vehicle or stop at weigh station	----
*075	F23	--	Spilling, dragging, unsecured or unsafe load	----
*076	D71	--	Exceeding hours on duty limitations	----
*077	B30	--	Permit unlicensed person to drive	----
080	A60	Y	Underage convicted of drinking and driving at .02 or higher BAC/juvenile DUI-court finding	484.461
081	A21	Y	Driving under the influence of alcohol	484.379 49 CFR 383.51
082	A22	Y	Driving under the influence of drugs	484.379 49 CFR 383.51
083	A04	Y	Driving under the influence of alcohol with BAC at or over .04	49 CFR 383.51
084	A12	Y	Refused to submit to test for alcohol-implied consent law	484.379 49 CFR 383.51
085	A90	Y	Administrative per se for .10 BAC	49 CFR 383.51
086	A23	Y	Driving under the influence of alcohol and drugs	484.379
087	A20	Y	Driving under the influence of alcohol or drugs	484.379 49 CFR 383.51
088	A94	Y	Administrative per se for .04 BAC	49 CFR 383.51
089	A98	Y	Administrative per se for .08 BAC	484.385: 49 CFR 383.51
*090	D16	N	Show or use improperly-driver license (includes DL, CDL, and instruction permit)	484.53
*091	E30	--	Defective equipment	----
*092	E31	N	Defective brakes	484.595
*093	F10	--	Exceeding or violating size, weight, or passenger/cargo limits	----
*094	B54	--	Expired or no registration or title	----
*095	B54		Operating with w\expired registration	----
*096	E37	N	Defective tires	484.541
*097	E70	N	Equipment used improperly or obstructed	484.541
*098	D20	--	Show or use improperly-registration, plates or decal/sticker	----
*99	N84		Unsafe operation of vehicle (operating out of service)	
100	S51	N	Speeding 1 to 10 miles over the posted speed limit	484.361
101	M58	N	Improper lane or location-road shoulder, ditch or sidewalk	484.451
103	M32	N	Following emergency vehicle unlawfully/following within 500 feet of a fire truck	484.461
104	N05	N	FTY ROW to funeral procession, procession or parade	484.467
105	N40	N	Failure to use or improper signal/failure to sound horn when required	484.607
108	N44	N	Giving wrong signal	484.283

Code	ACD	WD	Description	Statute (State or Federal)
109	F05	N	Carrying too many or unsecured passengers in open area of vehicle or motorcycle	486.181
110	M33	N	Following fire equipment unlawfully	484.461
201	N83	N	Improper starting	484.341
202	N82	N	Improper or unsafe backing	484.449
*204	F41	--	Driving on highway closed to traffic	----
205	M50	N	Improper lane or location-limited access highway	484.311
206	M56	N	Improper lane or location-driving over fire hose	484.463
210	F06	N	Improper operation of or riding on a motorcycle-failure to keep one hand on motorcycle handle bars	486.211
212	F03	N	Motorcycle safety equipment not used properly as required/failure to wear protective headgear, glasses or have windshield (motorcycle, etc.)	486.231
213	M48	N	Improper lane or location-in occupied lane/riding a motorcycle between vehicles occupying adjacent lanes	486.351
220	S94	N	Prima facie speed violation or driving too fast for conditions	484.361
223	S92	-	Speeding 11-20 MPH over the posted limit - speed limit and actual speed detailed required	----
227	S96	N	Speed less than minimum-impede or block traffic-too slow, move to right	484.373
228	F34	N	Stopping standing or parking; obstructing or impeding traffic	484.3732
230	M60	N	Improper lane or location-slower vehicle lane	484.373
233	E54	N	Failure to use headlight dimmer as required	484.589
234	N84	N	Unsafe operation/failure to use headlights/obstructing drivers view	----
235	E55	N	Failure to use lights as required	484.545
240	S93	-	Speeding	----
300	S71	N	Speeding 21-30 MPH over the posted speed	484.361(3)
*304	M15	N	Failure to obey stop sign	484.283-285
*308	M14	N	Failure to obey sign or traffic control device	484.283-285
319	N56	N	Making improper or prohibited U turn/U-turn on a curve or hill	484.337-339
*325	N54	N	Making improper right turn	484.333
326	N53	N	Making improper left turn	484.333
*340	S93	N	Speeding	484.361
400	S81	N	Speeding 15 MPH or more above speed limit	483.900-940
401	M02	N	Failure to obey barrier/disregard road block sign or control	484.3595
402	N80	N	Coasting (operating with gears disengaged)/coasting prohibited	484.459
403	M12	N	Failure to obey safety zone	484.495
*404	S16	N	Speeding 16 to 20 miles over the posted speed limit	484.361(3)
405	M15	N	Failure to obey stop sign	484.283-285
406	M71	N	Passing in violation of posted sign or pavement marking	484.301
407	M82	N	Inattentive driving/driving without due care/failure to decrease speed	484.363
408	N03	N	FTY row to cyclist or exercise due care to avoid a collision with a person riding a bicycle	484.363
409	M14	N	Failure to obey sign or traffic control device	484.283-285
410	M34	N	Following too closely/failure to leave sufficient distance between vehicles	484.307
411	M83	N	Negligent driving/full attention/imprudent	Local code
412	M77	N	Passing with insufficient distance or visibility/cutting in before it is safe in overtaking a vehicle	484.295
413	M76	N	Passing where prohibited	484.299
414	M73	N	Passing on wring side/unsafe passing vehicle on right side	484.297
417	N25	N	FTY ROW at unsigned intersection	484.315
419	N26	N	FTY ROW at yield sign	484.319
420	N22	N	FTY ROW at stop sign	484.319
421	N01	N	Failure to yield right of way-includes private driveway	484.322
422	N04	N	FTY ROW to emergency vehicle (i.e. ambulance, fire equipment, police, etc)	484.323
423	N31	N	FTY ROW when turning	484.333
425	N08	N	FTY ROW to pedestrian or exercise due care to avoid a collision with a pedestrian (includes handicapped or blind)	484.325-328
428	M75	N	Passing school bus displaying warning not to pass	484.357
*429	S99	--	Speeding in a school zone at least 1 but not more than 15 MPH over the posted speed limit	----
*431	S71	N	Speeding 21 to 30 MPH over the posted speed limit	484.361(3)
432	N50	N	Improper turn/unsafe turn using improper position and method	484.333
433	M42	N	Improper or erratic (unsafe) lane changes	484.305(1)
437	M86	N	Using a hand-held mobile telephone while driving - 2nd offense	-
438	N63	N	Driving wrong way on one way street or road	484.303
439	N61	N	Driving wrong way at rotary intersection	484.303
440	M62	N	Improper lane or location-traveling in turn (or center) lane	484.305(2); 484.305(3)
442	N70	N	Driving on wrong side	484.291.293

Code	ACD	WD	Description	Statute (State or Federal)
445	N71	N	Driving on wrong side of divided highway/gore	484.309
446	M41	N	Failure to keep in proper lane/failure to keep to the right on a mountain highway	484.305
449	M08	N	Failure to obey police or peace officer	484.253
450	M04	N	Failure to obey flagger	484.254
452	M17	N	Failure to obey or disregard traffic control device/control signal or school crossing guard	484.278-335
453	M16	N	Failure to obey traffic signal or light	484.283-285
454	N24	N	FTY row at traffic signal	484.278
456	M09	N	For all drivers in a NCMV, failure to obey railroad-highway grade crossing restrictions	484.353
*460	B13	--	Duty to stop upon damaging unattended vehicle or property -	----
461	M18	N	Failure to obey warning light or flashers	484.349; 484.364
462	M19	N	Failure to obey yield sign	484.319
463	M05	N	Failure to obey lane markings or signal	484.278; 484.283; 484.305
464	M86	N	Using a hand-held mobile telephone/device while driving - Second Offense	-
500	S91	N	Speeding 31 to 40 MPH over the posted speed limit	484.361
501	A26	N	Drink alcohol while operating a vehicle/open container	484.448(1)
*600	S91	N	Speeding at least 41 MPH or more over the posted speed limit	484.361
*601	S99	--	Speeding in a school zone	----
604	B08	-	Leaving accident scene before police arrive - Property damage accident	----
610	B05	-	Leaving accident scene before police arrive	----
612	M81	N	Careless driving/unlawful manner of driving	Local code
614	B04	N	Hit and run-failure to stop and render aid after accident-property damage accident	484.221:49 CFR 383.51
615	B14	N	Failure to reveal identity after fatal or personal injury accident	484.223
631	B01	Y	Hit and run - failure to stop and render aid after accident - CMV Violations ONLY	484.223:49 CFR 383.51
701	A25	N	Driving while ability impaired	Local code
*810	A21	Y	Driving under the influence of intoxicating liquor/drugs	
831	M84	N	Reckless driving	484.377 and local code
833	S95	N	Speed contest (racing) on road open to traffic	484.377

Nevada Withdrawal Table

A *withdrawal* is any adverse action taken against a driver's privilege. Withdrawals are NOT listed on the three-year driving record, but ARE listed on the ten-year record and on the school bus record. Violation codes are used only by the Nevada DMV. Nevada refers to ACD codes as "Off Ty" or Offense Type codes. The "Status" shown on a driving record indicates the specific type of withdrawal and helps determine reinstatement requirements.

- An asterisk "*" in the Code column signifies an obsolete code that could still show on a driving record. Note these codes are not shown on the actual Nevada traffic citation.

Table Keys

WD Column: S = Suspension, R = Revocation, C = Cancellation, D = Denial, PRS = Permanent Suspension
Extent Column: Indicates the extent of the withdrawal, i.e. CDL, Non-CDL or Both.

Code	WD	Extent	ACD	Description
*A1A	S	CDL	W00	Illegal Per Se-CDL/NCDL In CMV With/Without/Haz Mat (BAC 0.04/more) By Law
A1B	S	CDL	W00	Illegal Per Se (1st Off)-CDL In CMV/NCMV Without/Haz Mat (BAC 0.04-0.079)
A1C	S	CDL	W00	Illegal Per Se - CDL In CMV/NCMV Without/Haz Mat (BAC 0.04-0.079) After Hear
*A1D	S	CDL	W00	Illegal Per Se-(1st Off) CDL In CMV With/Haz Mat (BAC 0.04/more) issued by Law
*A1E	S	CDL	W00	Illegal Per Se-(1st Off) CDL In CMV With/Haz Mat (BAC 0.04/more) issued by Law
*A1F	S	CDL	W00	Illegal Per Se-(1st Off) CDL In CMV With/Haz Mat (BAC 0.04/more) issued by Law or DL - After Hearing
*A2A	S	CDL	A98	ILLEGAL PER SE (1ST) - CDL/NCDL IN CMV/NCMV WITHOUT/HAZ MAT (BAC 0.08/MORE-DRUGS - BY LAW)
*A2B	S	CDL	A98	ILLEGAL PER SE (1ST) - CDL/NCDL IN CMV/NCMV WITHOUT/HAZ MAT (BAC 0.08/MORE-DRUGS - BY DL)
*A2C	S	CDL	W00	Illegal Per Se (1st) - CDL In CMV/NCMV Without/Haz Mat (BAC 0.08/Drugs) Iss By Dl After Hearing
*A2D	S	CDL	A98	Illegal Per Se (1st) - CDL In CMV/NCMV Witht/Haz Mat (BAC 0.08/Drugs) By Law
*A2E	S	CDL	W00	Illegal Per Se (1st) - CDL In CMV/NCMV Witht/Haz Mat (BAC 0.08/Drugs) By Dl
*A2F	S	CDL	W00	Illegal Per Se - CDL/NCDL In CMV/NCMV (BAC 0.08/More/Drugs)Iss By Dl After Hear
*A2M				ILLEGAL PER SE (1ST) - CDL IN CMV WITHOUT/HAZ MAT (BAC 0.08/MORE DRUGS - BY DL)
*A4A				ILLEGAL PER SE - (1ST OFFENSE) - CDL IN NCMV -(BAC 0.08/MORE - LAW)
*A5A				ILLEGAL PER SE - (1ST OFFENSE) - CDL IN NCMV-(BAC 0.08/MORE-DL)
ADA	S	NCDL	W00	Accident Resulting In Death/Injury/Serious Damage
ADB	S	NCDL	W00	Accident Resulting In Death/Injury/Serious Damage - After Hearing
AGA	S	NCDL	M80	Aggressive Driving First Offense - Time Determined By Court Order - 30 days max
AGB	R	NCDL	M80	Aggressive Driving Second Offense - 1 Year Suspension

Code	WD	Extent	ACD	Description
*AIA				ILLEGAL PER SE (1ST OFFENSE) - CDL IN CMV WITHOUT/HAZ MAT (BAC 0.04/MORE
*APA				ILLEGAL PERSE-(1ST) CDL-NCMV/CMV -NCDL WD-90 DAY REVOKE (BAC OBSOLETE 0.08/MORE BY LAW)
*B1A				FAILING TO OBEY RAILROAD-HIGHWAY GRADE CROSSING RESTRICTION OBSOLETE
B2A	S	CDL	M10	Failing To Obey A Traffic Control Device Or Directions Of An Enforcement Official At A Railroad-High Grade Crossing
B2B	S	CDL	M10	Convicted Of Railroad Highway Grade Crossing- After Hearing
B3A	S	CDL	M20	Failing To Slow Down At A Railroad Highway Grade Crossing And Checking That Tracks Are Clear
B4A	S	CDL	M21	Failing To Stop Before Reaching Tracks At A Railroad-Highway Grade Crossing When The Tracks Are Not Clear
B5A	S	CDL	M22	Failing To Stop As Required Before Driving Onto Railroad-Highway Grade Crossing
B6A	S	CDL	M23	Failing To Have Sufficient Space To Drive Completely Through The Railroad-Highway Grade Crossing Without Stopping
B7A	S	CDL	M24	Failing To Negotiate A Railroad-Highway Grade Crossing Because Of Insufficient Undercarriage Clearance
B8A	S	CDL	W60	Convicted Of Two Railroad-Highway Grade Crossings Violations Within Three Years
B8A	S	CDL	W61	Convicted Of Two Railroad-Highway Grade Crossings Violations Within Three Years - After Hearing
B9A	S	CDL	W61	Convicted Of Three Separate Railroad-Highway Grade Crossings Violations Within Three Years
B9B	S	CDL	W61	Convicted Of Three Railroad-Highway Grade Crossings Violations Within Three Years - After Hearing
C2A	S	CDL	W00	Failure To Surrender Hazmat Endorsement As Required By Us Patriot Act
C2B	S	CDL	W00	Failure To Surrender Hazmat Endorsement As Required By Us Patriot Act - After Hearing
*CAA				PROOF OF AGE/DOB
CAB	C	ID CARD Suspend	D02	No Proper Proof Of Age Or Identity - ID Card Cancellation
CAC	C	ID CARD Suspend	D02	No Proper Proof Of Age Or Identity - ID Card Cancellation - After Hearing
CCA	C	NCDL	W00	Unpaid Check
CCB	C	NCDL	W00	Unpaid Check After Hearing
CDA	C	NCDL	W00	Incorrect/Missing Endorsement
CDB	C	NCDL	W00	Incorrect/Missing Endorsement - After Hearing
CFA	C	NCDL	B41	Committed Fraud On Application
CFB	C	NCDL	B41	Committed Fraud On Application After Hearing
CFC	C	ID CARD Suspend	B41	Committed Fraud On ID Card Application
CFD	C	ID CARD Suspend	B41	Committed Fraud On ID Card Application After Hearing
CFE	S	CDL	D02	Committed Fraud While Obtaining a CDL
CFF	S	CDL	D02	Committed Fraud While Obtaining a CDL
CIA	C	NCDL	D02	Ineligible To Be Licensed (Withdrawn In Another State)
CIB	C	NCDL	D02	Ineligible To Be Licensed (Withdrawn In Another State) - After Hearing
CLA	C	NCDL	W13	Release From Liability
CLB	C	NCDL	W13	Release From Liability Due To Death Of Liable Person
CLC	C	NCDL	W13	Release From Liability- After Hearing
COA	S	NCDL	W00	Court Ordered Suspension
*COB				COA AFTER HEARING
COC	S	NCDL	W00	Minor Use/Possession/Sale/Violation of a Minor Traffic Offense
COD	D	NCDL	W00	Minor Use/Possession/Sale/Violation of a Minor Traffic Offense
*COE				COC AFTER HEARING
*COF				COURT ORDER DENIAL MINOR
COH	S	NCDL	W00	Court Ordered Suspension for Collison with Pedestrain or Bicylist (6 mths to 2 years)
*CPA				INCORRECT INFO ON APPL
*CPB				CPA AFTER HEARING
CSA	S	NCDL	D51	Child Support Court/DA Ordered
CSC	S	NCDL	D51	Child Support Court/DA Ordered
CUA	S	NCDL	W14	Failure To Voluntarily Surrender License
CUB	S	NCDL	W14	Failure To Voluntarily Surrender License - After Hearing
*CY				FAIL TO MEET DEPARTMENT REQUIREMENTS
CYA	C	NCDL	W00	DOB Wrong
*CYB				INCORRECT NAME ON LICENSE
CYC	C	NCDL	W00	SSN Incorrect
CYD	C	NCDL	W20	Drive Required
CYE	C	NCDL	W20	Written Test Required
CYF	C	NCDL	W20	Vision Test Required

Code	WD	Extent	ACD	Description
CYG	C	NCDL	W00	Failure Of Responsible Party To Sign License Application - Need Parent Signature
CYH	C	NCDL	W00	Omitted Or Incorrect Restriction On License
CYI	C	NCDL	W00	Incorrect Expiration Date On License
CYJ	C	NCDL	W00	Incorrect Class On License
CYK	C	NCDL	B63	Failure To Provide Sr-22 Prior To Issuance Of License
CYL	C	NCDL	W00	Uncharged Fees At Time Of Transaction
CYM	C	NCDL	W15	Medical Letter Required Or Confidential Physicians Report
CYN	C	NCDL	W15	Vision Report Required
CYO	C	NCDL	W00	Failure To Surrender License And Obtain Permit
CYP	C	NCDL	B80	Failure To Surrender License And Obtain Permit After Hearing
CYQ	C	NCDL	W00	License Currently Under Withdrawal (Reinstated Prior To Withdrawal Action)
CYT	C	NCDL	W00	Failure To Meet Department Requirements - After Hearing
CYU	C	NCDL	W00	Failure To Meet Department Requirements
*CYV				VOLUNTARY SURRENDER
CYW	C	NCDL	D07	Multiple State Licenses
CYY	C	NCDL	D50	Failure To Pay Victim's Fee
*CZA				ISSUED LICENSE IN ERROR
D1A	S	CDL	A20	DUI - Alcohol Or Drugs (1st Offense) - CDL/NCDL In CMV/NCMV Without Haz Mat No Illegal Per Se
D1B	S	CDL	A20	DUI - Alcohol Or Drugs (1st Offense) - CDL/NCDL In CMV/NCMV Without Haz Mat W/ Illegal Per Se
D1C	S	CDL	A20	DUI - Alcohol Or Drugs (1st Offense) - CDL/NCDL In CMV/NCMV Without Haz Mat-After Hearing
D1E	S	CDL	A20	Out Of State DUI Conviction For Alcohol Or Drugs While Driving CMV/NCMV 1st Offense
D1F	S	CDL	A20	Out Of State DUI Conviction For Alcohol Or Drugs While Driving CMV/NCMV 1st Offense - After Hearing
D3A	S	CDL	A20	DUI - Alcohol Or Drugs (1st Offense) - CDL/NCDL In CMV With Haz Mat No Illegal Per Se
D3B	S	CDL	A20	DUI - Alcohol Or Drugs (1st Offense) - CDL/NCDL In CMV With Haz Mat W/ Illegal Per Se
D3C	S	CDL	A20	DUI - Alcohol Or Drugs (1st Offense) - CDL/NCDL In CMV With Haz Mat-After Hearing
D3D	S	CDL	A20	Out Of State DUI Conviction For Alcohol Or Drugs While Driving CMV With Hazmat 1st Offense
D3E	S	CDL	A20	Out Of State DUI Conviction For Alcohol Or Drugs While Driving CMV With Hazmat 1st Offense - After Hearing
*D9A				DUI -ALCOHOL OR DRUGS (2ND OR SUBSEQUENT OFFENSE)-NCDL/CDL IN CMV/NCMV WITH/WITHOUT HAZ MAT
*D9C				DUI-ALCOHOL/DRUGS (2ND/SUBSEQUENT OFFENSE)-NCDL/CDL IN CMV/NCMV WITH/WITHOUT HAZ MAT-AFTER HEARING
*D9E				OUT-OF-STATE DUI CONVICTION FOR ALCOHOL OR DRUGS IN CMV/NCMV 2ND OFFENSE
*D9K				DUI - ALCOHOL OR DRUGS (1ST OFFENSE) - CDL IN NCMV
DAA	S	NCDL	D37	Default On Agreement
DAB	S	NCDL	D37	Default On Agreement After Hearing
*DCA				DRIVING UNDER CANCELLATION
DCS	Pending	NCDL	N/A	District Court Stay
DDA	R	NCDL	A20	Out Of State DUI After Hearing
*DDB				ILLEGAL PER SE
*DDC				ILLEGAL PER SE
DDD	R	NCDL	A21	2nd DUI In 7 Years - No Illegal Per Se
DDE	R	NCDL	A21	3rd DUI In 7 Years - No Illegal Per Se
DDF	R	NCDL	A21	DUI Already Rev With Illegal Per Se
DDG	R	NCDL	A21	2nd DUI In 7 Years/Rev For Illegal Per Se
*DDH				REVOKED AFTER HEARING ILLEGAL PER SE
DDI	R	NCDL	A21	DDD or DDG After Hearing
DDJ	R	NCDL	A21	DDE or DDF After Hearing
DDK	R	NCDL	A21	DUI/Allowed Treatment
DDL	R	NCDL	D44	DUI/Treatment Refused
DDM	R	NCDL	D44	DUI/Treatment Incomplete
DDN	R	NCDL	A21	DUI (1st Offense) Already Revoked For Illegal Per Se
DDQ	R	NCDL	A20	DUI/Death Or Bodily Harm (3 Years)
DDT	R	NCDL	A21	Out Of State DUI
DDU	R	NCDL	A21	DUI (1st Offense) - 90 Day Revocation Without IP
DDW	R	NCDL	D44	DUI/Incomplete Education Course
DDX	R	NCDL	A20	DUI/Death Or Bodily Harm (3 Years)
DDY	R	NCDL	A20	DUI (1st Offense) Reinstated On Illegal Per Se (90-Day Revocation)
DDZ	R	NCDL	A21	DUI or DDU - After Hearing (89- Day)
DEA	D	NCDL	W00	Withdrawn In Another State
DEB	D	NCDL	W00	Withdrawn In Another State After Hearing
*DEC				WITHDRAWN IN ANOTHER STATE
*DED				DEC AFTER HEARING
DFA	D	NCDL	D53	Delinquent Fine - Delay Of Issuance Of Drivers License
DFB	S	NCDL	D53	Delinquent Fine - Suspension
DFC	D	NCDL	D53	Delinquent Fine - Delay Of Issuance Of Drivers License - After Hearing

Code	WD	Extent	ACD	Description
DFD	S	NCDL	D53	Delinquent Fine - Suspension - After Hearing
DJA	S	NCDL	D37	Default On Installment To Satisfy Judgment Resulting From Vehicle Accident
DJB	S	NCDL	D37	Default On Installment To Satisfy Judgment Resulting From Vehicle Accident-After Hearing
DPA	S	NCDL	W00	Reg Only Suspension For 2nd Or Subsequent DUI
DRA	R	NCDL	B25	Driving Under Revocation
DRB	R	NCDL	B25	Driving Under Revocation After Hearing
DSA	S	NCDL	B26	Driving Under Suspension
DSB	S	NCDL	B26	Driving Under Suspension After Hearing
DSC	S	NCDL	B22	Driving Under Cancellation
DSD	S	NCDL	B22	Driving Under Cancellation After Hearing
DWA	R	NCDL	D27	Driving On Restricted License
DWB	R	NCDL	D27	Driving On Restricted License After Hearing
ELA	R	NCDL	U01	Eluding Police Officer
ELB	R	NCDL	U01	Eluding Police Officer After Hearing
F1A	R	CDL	U03	Felony Use Of CMV (1-year)
F1B	R	CDL	U03	Felony Use Of CMV- After Hearing (1-year)
F2A	S	NCDL	D45	Out-Of-State Failure To Appear/Pay/Comply
F2B	S	NCDL	D45	Out-Of-State Failure To Appear/Pay/Comply - After Hearing
F3A	S	CDL	U03	Felony Use Of CMV W/ Hazmat
F3B	S	CDL	U03	Felony Use Of CMV W/ Hazmat - After Hearing
F9C	Perm S	CDL	A50	CMV In Commission Of Felony Involving A Controlled Substance
F9D	Perm S	CDL	A50	CMV In Commission Of Felony Involving A Controlled Substance - After Hearing
FDA	S	NCDL	W00	Permitted Unlawful Or Fraudulent Use Of Drivers License
FDB	S	NCDL	W00	Permitted Unlawful Or Fraudulent Use Of Drivers License - After Hearing
FDC	R	NCDL	A21	Felony DUI
FDD	R	NCDL	A21	Felony DUI - After Hearing
FMA	S	NCDL	B63	Fail To Maintain Proof Of FR - Drivers License And Registration Suspension
FMB	S	NCDL	B63	Fail To Maintain Proof Of FR - Drivers License And Registration Suspension -After Hearing
FMC	S	NCDL	B63	Fail To Maintain Proof Of FR - Drivers License Suspension Only
FMD	S	NCDL	B63	Fail To Maintain Proof Of FR - Drivers License Suspension Only- After Hearing
FRA	S	NCDL	B61	Fail To Report Accident
FRB	S	NCDL	B61	Fail To Report Accident- After Hearing
FSA	S	NCDL	W00	Fail To Submit To Examination
FSB	R	NCDL	W00	Fail To Submit To Examination - After Hearing
FTA	S	NCDL	D45	Failure To Appear
FTB	S	NCDL	D45	Failure To Appear - After Hearing
FTC	S	NCDL	D56	Failure To Comply
FTD	S	NCDL	D56	Failure To Comply - After Hearing
FVA	R	NCDL	U03	Use Of Motor Vehicle In Felony
FVB	R	NCDL	U03	Use Of Motor Vehicle In Felony - After Hearing
*G1A				FOLLOWS THE VEHICLE TOO CLOSELY CDL IN CMV/NCMV (2ND OFFENSE)
*G3A				MAKES IMPROPER OR ERRATIC TRAFFIC LANE CHANGES CDL IN CMV/NCMV
GRA	S	NCDL	W00	Juvenile Graffiti/Court Order - Suspension Of License
GRC	D	NCDL	W00	Juvenile Graffiti/Court Order - Delay Of Issuance Of License
GRE	S	NCDL	W00	Adult Graffiti - Suspension Of License
GRG	D	NCDL	W00	Adult Graffiti - Delay Of Issuance Of License
GUA	S	NCDL	W00	Juvenile Firearms (1st) Court Ordered
GUC	D	NCDL	W00	Juvenile Firearms (1st) Court Ordered
GUE	S	NCDL	W00	Juvenile Firearms (2nd) Court Ordered
GUG	D	NCDL	W00	Juvenile Firearms (2nd) Court Ordered
*HNA				HABITUAL NEGLIGENCE
*HNB				HNA AFTER HEARING
HRA	R	NCDL	B05	Leaving Scene Of Accident Before Police Arrive In CDL/NCDL In NCMV
HRB	R	NCDL	B05	HRA (Leaving Scene Of Accident) After Hearing
HSA	C	NCDL	W00	Dept of Homeland Security Unable to verify Documents/DL Cancellation
HSB	C	NCDL	W00	Dept of Homeland Security Unable to verify Documents/DL Cancellation - After hearing
HSC	C	NCDL	W00	Dept of Homeland Security Unable to verify Documents/ID Card Cancellation
HSD	C	NCDL	W00	Dept of Homeland Security Unable to verify Documents/ID Card Cancellation - After hearing
*HVA				HABITUAL VIOLATOR
*HVB				HVA AFTER HEARING
I1A	S	CDL	U07	Causing A Fatality Through The Negligent Operation Of A CMV (Vehicular Manslaughter, Homicide
I1B	S	CDL	U07	Causing A Fatality Through The Negligent Operation Of A CMV (Vehicular Manslaughter/Homicide-After Hearing
I3A	S	CDL	U07	Causing A Fatality Through The Negligent Operation Of A CMV While Transporting Haz Mat
I3B	S	CDL	U07	Causing A Fatality Through The Negligent Operation Of A CMV While Transporting Hazmat (V-Aft Hear)
*ICA				IMPLIED CONSENT CDL/NCDL IN CMV-NCDL WD-90-DAY REVOCATION (1ST OFFENSE)

Code	WD	Extent	ACD	Description
*ICB				IMPLIED CONSENT CDL/NCDL IN CMV-NCDL WD-90-DAY REVOCATION (2ND OFFENSE)
*ICC				ICA HEARING OVER 60 DAY LIMIT
*ICD				IMPLIED CONSENT (PREV REV FOR SAME REASON)
*ICE				IMPLIED CONSENT (BEFORE 7/83)
*ICF				ICE HEARING REQUET BEYOND LIMIT
*ICG				ICE AFTER HEARING (90 DAY IMP CONS BY LAW ENF)
*ICH				90 DAY IMP CONS BY LAW ENF
*ICI				1 YEAR IMP CONS BY LAW ENF
*ICJ				3 YEAR IMP CONS BY LAW ENF
*ICK				ICH AFTER HEARING
*ICL				ICI AFTER HEARING
*ICM				ICJ AFTER HEARING
*ICN				1 YEAR IMP CONS BY DRIV LIC
*ICO				90 DAY IC BY DRIVER LICENSE
*ICP				1 YEAR IC HEARING CANCELLED
*ICV				3 YEAR IC HEARING CANCELLED
IDA	R	NCDL	W00	Illegal Per Se - Drugs - NCDL Withdrawal-90 Day Revocation
IDB	R	NCDL	W00	Illegal Per Se-Drugs-NCDL Withdrawal- (90 Day Revoke/After Hear)
IDF	R	NCDL	W00	CDL Illegal Per Se-Drugs-NCDL Withdrawal- (90 Day Revoke/After Hear)
IIA	R	NCDL	A41	1st Violation Of Ignition Interlock Device
IIB	R	NCDL	A41	1st Violation Of Ignition Interlock Device - After Hearing
IIC	R	NCDL	A41	2nd Violation Of Ignition Interlock Device
IID	R	NCDL	A41	2nd Violation Of Ignition Interlock Device - After Hearing
IIO	Pending	NCDL		Court Ordered Interlock Device
IMA	R	NCDL	U08	Involuntary Manslaughter
IMB	R	NCDL	U08	Involuntary Manslaughter - After Hearing
IPA	R	NCDL	W00	Ill Per Se (BAC 08 Or More By Law Enforcement 90 Day)
IPB	R	NCDL	W00	Ill Per Se (BAC 08 Or More By Drivers License 90 Day)
IPC	R	NCDL	W00	Ill Per Se (BAC 08 Or More-90 Day) After Hearing
IPF	R	NCDL	W00	CDL Illegal Per Se (BAC .08 or More) NCDL Internal Withdrawal (90-Day Rev)
IPG	R	NCDL	W00	CDL Illegal Per Se (BAC .08 or More) NCDL Internal Withdrawal (90-Day Rev) - After Hearing
JDA	R	NCDL	W00	Juvenile DUI/Court Ordered
JDB	R	NCDL	W00	Juvenile DUI/Court Ordered- After Hearing
*JIA				RECKLESS DRIVING - CDL IN CMV/NCMV (2ND OFFENSE)
JPA	S	NCDL	W00	Juvenile Illegal Per Se (.02) 90 Day Suspension By Law Enforcement
JPB	S	NCDL	W00	Juvenile Illegal Per Se (.02) 90 Day Suspension By Drivers License
JPC	S	NCDL	W00	Juvenile Illegal Per Se (.02) 90 Day Suspension - After Hearing
*KKA				DUI - CDL/NCDL IN CMV - NCDL WITHDRAWAL-90 DAY REVOCATION (1ST CONVICTION - IP REINSTATE
*KMA				DUI - CDL IN NCMV - NCDL WITHDRAWAL-90 DAY REVOCATION (1ST CONVICTION - IP NOT REINSTAT
*KNA				DUI - CDL IN NCMV - NCDL WITHDRAWAL-1 YEAR REVOCATION (2ND OR SUBSEQUENT CONVICTION - IP
L1A	R	CDL	B01	Hit And Run/Leaving Scene Of Accident Before Police Arrive (1st Offense)
L1B	R	CDL	B01	Hit And Run/Leaving Scene Of Accident Before Police Arrive (1st Offense) - After Hearing
L3A	S	CDL	B01	Hit And Run/Leaving Scene Of Accident Before Police Arrive In CMV W/ Hazmat (1st Offense)
L3B	S	CDL	B01	Hit And Run/Leaving Scene Of Accident Before Police Arrive In CMV W/ Hazmat(1st Off)- After Hearing
M1A	S	CDL	W45	Driving A CMV While Withdrawn As A Result Of Prior CDL In CMV Offenses (1st Offense)
M1B	S	CDL	W45	Driving A CMV While Withdrawn As A Result Of Prior CDL In CMV Offenses (1st Off) - After Hearing
M3A	S	CDL	W45	Driving A CMV With Hazardous Materials While Withdrawn As A Result Of Prior CDL In CMV
M3B	S	CDL	W45	Driving A CMV With Hazardous Materials While Withdrawn As A Result Of Prior CDL In CMV - After Hearing
MDA	S	NCDL	W14	Deteriorating Medical Condition
MDB	S	NCDL	W14	Deteriorating Medical Condition - After Hearing
*MLA				MULTIPLE STATE LICENSES
*MLB				MULTIPLE STATE LICENSES - AFTER HEARING
MOA	S	NCDL	W01	Habitual Offender - 6 Convictions of 4 Demerits or More in 5-Year Period
MOB	S	NCDL	W01	Habitual Offender - 6 Convictions of 4 Demerits or More in 5-Year Period - After Hearing
MRA	R	NCDL	W00	Rev By Military Installation
MRB	S	NCDL	W00	Military Suspension
MRC	R	NCDL	W00	MRA After Hearing
MRD	S	NCDL	W00	MRB After Hearing
*NIA				DRIVER/REG OWNER NO INSURANCE
*NIB				NIA AFTER HEARING
*NIC				REG OWNER NO INSURANCE
*NID				NIC AFTER HEARING

Code	WD	Extent	ACD	Description
NIE	S	NCDL	D36	Driver & Registered Owner Convicted Of Driving With No Insurance - DL Suspension Only
NIF	S	NCDL	D36	Driver & Registered Owner Convicted Of Driving With No Insurance - DL Suspension Only after Hearing
NLA	Pending	NCDL		NV Live Indicator/SR22 Required to Reinstate NV Live Sanction - Not DL Withdrawal
NLB	S	NCDL	D36	3rd or Subsequent Offense of Fialing to Maintain Liability Insurance - Reported from NVLive
NLC	S	NCDL		3rd or Subsequent Offense of Fialing to Maintain Liability Insurance - Reported from NVLive After Hearing
P1A	S	CDL	A04	DUI (1st Offense) - CDL In CMV Without Haz Mat (BAC 0.04 Or Over)
P1B	S	CDL	A04	DUI (1st Offense) - CDL In CMV Without Haz Mat (BAC 0.04 Or Over) - After Hearing
P3A	S	CDL	A04	DUI (1st Offense) - CDL In CMV With Haz Mat (BAC 0.04 Or Over)
P3B	S	CDL	A04	DUI (1st Offense) - CDL In CMV With Haz Mat (BAC 0.04 Or Over) After Hearing
*P9A				DUI (2ND OR SUBSEQUENT OFFENSE) - CDL IN CMV WITH/WITHOUT HAZ MAT (BAC 0.04 OR OVER)
*PS				POINT SYSTEM
*PSA				POINT SYSTEM
*PSB				PSA AFTER HEARING
PVA	S	NCDL	W01	Point Violator 12 Demerits In A One Year Period (6 Months)
PVB	S	NCDL	W01	Point Violator Second Accum 12 Demerits In a 3-Year Period
PVC	S	NCDL	W01	Point Violator Third Accum 12 Demerits In a 5-Year Period
PVD	S	NCDL	W01	Point Violator 12 Demerits In A One Year Period After Hearing
PVE	S	NCDL	W01	PVB or PVC - After Hearing
*PYA				FAIL TO UPDATE CDL PHYSICAL
*R1A				IMPLIED CONSENT WHILE DRIVING CMV (OUT OF STATE - 1ST OFFENSE)
R1B	S	CDL	A12	Implied Consent While Driving CMV (Out Of State - 1st Offense) -
R1C	S	CDL	A12	Implied Consent While Driving CMV (Out Of State - 1st Offense) - After A Hearing 1-year
R3B	S	CDL	A12	Implied Consent While Driving CMV W/Hazmat (Out Of State - 1st Offense) - 3 Years
R3C	S	CDL	A12	Implied Consent While Driving CMV W/Hazmat (Out Of State - 1st Offense) - After Hearing (3 Years)
R6A	S	CDL	A98	Illegal Per Se - OOS CDL In CMV/NCMV Without/Haz Mat (Alcohol/Drugs)
R6B	S	CDL	A98	Illegal Per Se-OOS-CDL-CMV/NCMV Without/Haz Mat (Alcohol/Drugs) After Hear
R7A	S	CDL	A98	Illegal Per Se - OOS CDL/NCDL In CMV/NCMV With/Haz Mat (Alcohol/Drugs)
R7B	S	CDL	A98	Illegal Per Se - OOS CDL/NCDL-CMV/NCMV With/Haz Mat (Alcohol/Drugs) After Hear
*R9B				Implied Consent While Driving CMV (Out of sstate, subsequent offense)
RDA	R	NCDL	M84	3 Reckless Driving Convictions In A 1 Year Period
RDB	R	NCDL	M84	3 Reckless Driving Convictions In A 1 Year Period - After Hearing
REA	S	NCDL	D29	Fail To Comply With Restriction - 2nd Or Subsequent conviction Received
REB	S	NCDL	D29	Fail To Comply With Restriction - 2nd Or Subsequent Conviction Received - After Hearing
RHA	R	NCDL	M84	Reckless Driving - Substantial Bodily Harm or Death
RHB	R	NCDL	M84	Reckless Driving - Substantial Bodily Harm or Death - After Hearing
*RPA				OUT OF STATE DL/ONLY WD OR CONV
*RPB				OUT OF STATE DL WD OR CONV
*RPC				OUT OF STATE DL WD OR CONV AFTER HEARING
*RPD				OUT OF STATE DL WD OR CONV AFTER HEARING
*RPE				OUT OF STATE DL/REG WD OR CONV
*RPF				OUT OF STATE DL/REG WD OR CONV
*RPG				OUT OF STATE DL/REG WD OR CONV
*RPH				RPG AFTER HEARING
*RPI				LICENSE WITHDRAWAN IN ANOTHER JURISDICTION
*RPJ				OUT OF STATE DL WITHDRAWAL
*RPK				OUT OF STATE DL ONLY
RPL	S	NCDL	W00	License Withdrawn In Another Jurisdiction - After Hearing
*RPM				OUT OF STATE REG ONLY
*RPN				OUT OF STATE REG ONLY
*RPO				RPM AFTER HEARING
*RPP				RPN AFTER HEARING
*S1A				SPEEDING EXCESSIVELY IN A CMV INVOLVING ANY SPEED OF 15 MPH OR MORE (2ND OFFENSE)
*S2A				SPEEDING EXCESSIVELY IN A CMV INVOLVING ANY SPEED OF 15 MPH OR MORE (3RD OR SUBSEQUENT
SBA	S	NCDL	M75	Passing A School Bus Displaying Warning Not To Pass (2nd Offense)
SBB	S	NCDL	M75	Passing A School Bus Displaying Warning Not To Pass (2nd Offense) - After Hearing
SBC	S	NCDL	M75	Passing A School Bus Displaying Warning Not To Pass (3rd Offense)
SBD	S	NCDL	M75	Passing A School Bus Displaying Warning Not To Pass (3rd Offense) - After Hearing
SDA	S	NCDL	D38	Security Deposit Resulting From Vehicle Accident- Drivers License & Registration Suspension
SDB	S	NCDL	D38	Security Deposit Resulting From Vehicle Accident- Drivers License Suspension
SDC	S	NCDL	D38	Security Deposit Resulting From Vehicle Accident- Registration Suspension
SDD	S	NCDL	D38	Security Deposit Resulting From Vehicle Accident- Drivers License & Registration Suspension - After hearing
SDE	S	NCDL	D38	Security Deposit Resulting From Vehicle Accident- Drivers License Suspension - After Hearing

Code	WD	Extent	ACD	Description
SDF	S	NCDL	D38	Security Deposit Resulting From Vehicle Accident- Registration Suspension - After Hearing
SPA	S	NCDL	W00	Court Order Suspension (Disregard Safety - Driving/Organize Speed Contest)
SSA	S	NCDL	W00	Court Order Suspension (3rd Offense failure to Secure Child in Child Restraint System in Vehicle
T2A	S	CDL	W30	2 Serious Violations In CMV Within A 3 Year Period
T2B	S	CDL	W30	2 Serious Violations In CMV Within A 3 Year Period - After Hearing
T4A	S	CDL	W31	3 Serious Violations In CMV Within A 3 Year Period
T4B	S	CDL	W31	3 Serious Violations In CMV Within A 3 Year Period - After Hearing
TLC	C	NCDL	W00	Cancellation Of A Temporary License
TLS	Pending	NCDL	W00	Temporary License Issued Pending Hearing
TSA	D	NCDL	W00	Truancy-Juvenile (1st Offense) - 30-Day Delay Of Drivers License
TSC	D	NCDL	W00	Truancy-Juvenile (2nd Offense) - 60-Day Delay Of Drivers License
TSE	S	NCDL	W00	Truancy-Juvenile (1st Offense) - 30-Days - 6 Months, Determined By The Court
TSG	S	NCDL	W00	Truancy-Juvenile (2nd Offense) - 30-Days - 1 Year, Determined By The Court
*TSH				FIRST/SECOND TRUANCY AFTER HEARING
TXA	S	NCDL	W00	Administrative Fine/CODs Owed to NV Transportation Authority
TXB	S	NCDL	W00	Administrative Fine/CODs Owed to NV Transportation Authority - After hearing
TXC	S	NCDL	W00	Default on Agreement of Repayment of Fine/Cost to NV Transportation Authority
TXD	S	NCDL	W00	Default on Agreement of Repayment of Fine/Cost to NV Transportation Authority - After Hearing
USA	S	NCDL	D39	Unsatisfied Judgment Resulting From A Vehicle Accident
USB	S	NCDL	D39	Unsatisfied Judgment Resulting From A Vehicle Accident - After Hearing
V1A	S	CDL	B27	Driving While Out Of Service Order Is In Effect - CDL In CMV - (1st Offense)
V1B	S	CDL	B27	Driving While Out Of Service Order Is In Effect - CDL In CMV - (1st Offense) - After Hearing
V2A	S	CDL	B27	Driving While Out Of Service Order Is In Effect - CDL In CMV - (2nd Offense in 10 Years)
V2B	S	CDL	B27	Driving While Out Of Service Order Is In Effect - CDL In CMV - (2nd Offense in 10 Years)- After Hearing
V3A	S	CDL	B27	Driving While Out Of Service Order Is In Effect - CDL In CMV - (3rd Offense in 10 Years)
V3B	S	CDL	B27	Driving While Out Of Service Order Is In Effect - CDL In CMV - (3rd Offense in 10 Years) - After Hearing
V4A	S	CDL	B19	Driving While Out Of Service Order Is In Effect While Transporting Hazardous Materials
V5A	S	CDL	B19	Driving While Out Of Service Order Is In Effect While Transporting Hazardous Materials (2nd Offense in 10 Years)
V6A	S	CDL	W52	Driving While Out Of Service Order Is In Effect While Transporting Hazardous Materials(>=3 Off in 10 Years)
VCA	S	NCDL	D45	Failure To Appear In An Out Of State Court
VCB	S	NCDL	D45	Failure To Appear In An Out Of State Court- After Hearing
VSA	C	NCDL	W15	Voluntary Surrender Drivers License
VSB	C	NCDL	W15	Voluntary Surrender Drivers License - After Hearing
W00		NCDL	W00	Withdrawal For a Non-ACD Violation by State of Record
W01		NCDL	W01	Accumulation of Convictions (Including Point Systems and/or being Judged a Habitual Offender or Violator
W1A	C	CDL	W00	Failure To Submit Required Medical Waiver Document
W1B	C	CDL	W00	Failure To Submit Required Medical Waiver Document - After Hearing
W2A	C	CDL	W00	Failure To Meet Physical Requirements For CDL Medical Waiver
W2B	C	CDL	W00	Failure To Meet Physical Requirements For CDL Medical Waiver - After Hearing
W30		CDL	W30	Two Serious Violations Within Three years
W31		CDL	W31	Three Serious Violations Within Three years
W3A	C	CDL	B65	Failure To File Medical Certification As Required For CDL
W3B	C	CDL	B65	Failure To File Medical Certification As Required For CDL - After Hearing
W40		CDL	W40	The Accumulation of Two or More Offenses
W41		CDL	W41	An Additional Major Offense After Reinstatement
W4A	C	CDL	W00	Voluntary Surrender Of Commercial Driver License
W4B	C	CDL	W00	Voluntary Surrender Of Commercial Driver License After Hearing
W50		CDL	W50	Accumulation of Two Out-of-Service Order Violations (not covered by W51) Within 10 Years
W51		CDL	W51	Accumulation of Two Out-of-Service Order Violations Within 10 years Where the Second is while Transporting 16 or More passengers, Including the Driver and./or Transporting HAZ MAT That Required a Placard
W5A	S	CDL	W00	Failed To Voluntary Surrender CDL
W5B	S	CDL	W00	Failed To Voluntary Surrender CDL After Hearing
W60		CDL	W60	The Accumulation of Two RRGC Violations Within Three Years
W61		CDL	W61	The Accumulation of Three or More RRGC Violations Within Three Years
W72		NCDL	W72	Suspended pending Final Disposition
W80		CDL	W80	Failed Employer-Directed Drug Test
W81		CDL	W81	Illegal Per Se - CDL in NCMV/CMV W/O Haz Mat (BAC 0.10 or More)
*Y1A				Illegal Per Se - CDL In NCMV/CMV Without/Haz Mat (BAC 0.10 Or More) - Issued By Dl
*Y3A				Illegal Per Se - CDL In CMV Witht/Haz Mat (BAC 0.10 Or More)
*Y3B				Illegal Per Se - CDL In CMV Witht/Haz Mat (BAC 0.10 Or More) After Hearing
Z2A	S	CDL	W70	Imminent Hazard
Z2B	S	CDL	W70	Imminent Hazard - After Hearing
*Z3A				Accumulation Of Two Or More Major Offenses - CDL

Code	WD	Extent	ACD	Description
*Z3B				Accumulation Of Two Or More Major Offenses - CDL - After Hearing
Z5A	Perm S	CDL	W41	An Additional Major Offense After Reinstatement Of A Z3A
Z5B	Perm S	CDL	W41	An Additional Major Offense After Reinstatement Of A Z3A - After Hearing
Z6A	S	CDL	W00	Illegal Per Se (Possible 2nd Major) - CDL in CMV/NCMV W/O Haz Mat (BAC .04 or More Issued DL)
Z6B	S	CDL	W00	Illegal Per Se (Possible 2nd Major) - CDL in CMV/NCMV W/O Haz Mat (BAC .08 or More Issued DL)
Z6C	S	CDL	W00	Illegal Per Se CDL/NCDL In CMV (BAC 0.04-0.07999) After Hearing
Z6D	R	NCDL	W00	Illegal Per Se - CDL-CMV/NCMV (BAC 0.08/More-Alcohol/Drugs) After Hear

Summary of the Demerit Point System

The State of Nevada has an extensive demerit point system with the following provisions:

- Drivers receiving twelve or more points in any twelve-month period will have their licenses suspended.
- Drivers accumulating three to eleven points may have three points removed by completing a traffic safety course approved by the DMV.
- The record of convictions remains as part of the driver history record after point reductions.
- Conviction of a major traffic offense, such as DUI, by itself results in license withdrawal. No demerit points are assigned to DUI offenses.

Careless driving..6 Points
Carrying too many passengers on motorcycle ....1 Point
Changing lanes improperly..4 Points
Coasting prohibited ....4 Points
Commercial motor vehicle (CMV) speeding at least 15 MPH over the posted speed limit..........4 Points
Commercial motor vehicle speeding 11-14 MPH over the posted speed limit ....2 Points
Cutting in before it is safe in overtaking a vehicle ....4 Points
Disobeyed authorized flag person ....4 Points
Disobeyed police officer..4 Points
Disregard official traffic control device exhibiting colored lights ....4 Points
Disregard railroad signal or crossing gate ....4 Points
Disregard road block or sign ....4 Points
Disregard traffic control device, including signs and markings...4 Points
Drinking an alcoholic beverage while driving...5 Points
Driving a school bus at any speed in excess of the posted speed limit ....4 Points
Driving in center lane when unnecessary ....4 Points
Driving on a highway closed to traffic ....2 Points
Driving on sidewalk ....1 Points
Driving onto or from controlled access highway where prohibited ....2 Points
Driving over fire hose..2 Points
Driving the wrong side of a divided highway...4 Points
Driving the wrong way on a one-way street ....4 Points
Driving through funeral or other procession..1 Points
Driving through safety zone ....4 Points
Driving too fast for conditions..2 Points
Driving while ability impaired ....7 Points
Driving without due care/failure to decrease speed ....4 Points
Duty (failure) to give information and render aid at the scene of an accident ....6 Points
Duty to stop at scene of an accident, damage to vehicle or property ....6 Points
Duty to stop upon damaging unattended vehicle or property ....4 Points
Excessive speed for conditions, with no actual speed indicated ....2 Points
Fail to dim headlights ....2 Points
Failing to stop at railroad crossing...4 Points
Failure to give appropriate signal when required ....1 Points
Failure to give information or render at scene of accident..6 Points
Failure to keep one hand on motorcycle handlebars..2 Points
Failure to keep to the right on a mountain highway ....4 Points
Failure to sound horn when required ....1 Points
Failure to wear protective headgear, glasses or have windshield (MC, etc.).............................2 Points
Failure to yield at open intersection right of way ....4 Points
Failure to yield entering highway...4 Points
Failure to yield from stop or yield at controlled intersection ....4 Points
Failure to yield to a pedestrian ....4 Points
Failure to yield to emergency vehicle...4 Points
Failure to yield to person riding bicycle ....4 Points
Following too closely or failure to leave sufficient distance between vehicles ....4 Points
Following within 500 feet of fire truck..1 Points
Impede or block traffic/too slow, move to right ....2 Points

Improper or prohibited U-turn, or U-turn on a curve or hill ....3 Points
Imprudent/full attention ....4 Points
Miscellaneous/minor violations ....2 Points
Not driving on right side when required ....4 Points
Passing in a no-passing zone or over double yellow line ....4 Points
Passing school bus when signal flashing ....4 Points
Passing Where prohibited or w/o sufficient clearance (except no passing zone) ....4 Points
Prima facie speed - 25 MPH if not posted ....2 Points
Reckless driving ....8 Points
Riding a motorcycle between vehicles occupying adjacent lanes or operating more than two abreast in a single lane ....2 Points
Speeding 1-10 MPH over the posted speed limit (excluding energy violation) all vehicles ....1 Points
Speeding 16-20 MPH over the posted speed limit (non-commercial) ....3 Points
Speeding 21-30 MPH over posted limit ....3 Points
Speeding 31-40 MPH over posted limit ....4 Points
Speeding 41 MPH or more over posted limit ....5 Points
Speeding in a school zone 1-15 MPH over the posted speed limit ....4 Points
Speeding in a school zone at least 16 MPH over the posted speed limit ....6 Points
Starting improperly from parked position ....2 Points
Unsafe backing ....2 Points
Unsafe passing vehicle on right side ....4 Points
Unsafe turn using improper position and method..4 Points
Using a hand-held mobile telephone while driving - 2nd offense ....4 Points

New Hampshire

Administration	Important Telephone and Web Contacts
Richard C. Bailey Jr., Director William Joseph, Deputy Director Arthur Garlow, Assistant Director Division of Motor Vehicles 23 Hazen Drive, Concord 03305-0002 603-227-4050 www.nh.gov/safety/divisions/dmv Administrative Rules and a link to Title XXI - Motor Vehicle Laws are found under *Rules and Laws* at the home page.	Driver Licensing, CDL................................603-227-4020 Driving Records ....603-227-4040 SR-22 & Financial Responsibility ....603-227-4010 Registration Information ....603-227-4030 Title Information ....603-227-4150 State Police..603-271-3636 State Department of Insurance ....603-271-2261 Contacts: www.nh.gov/safety/divisions/dmv/contactus.html

Driver's License Format, Issuance and Renewal

License Classes, Restrictions and Endorsements Appear After the Driving Record Content Section

License Format

The format is two numbers, three letters, and five numbers. The license number is coded as follows:

- birth month (two digits);
- the first letter of the last name;
- the last letter of the last name;
- the first letter of the first name;
- the year of birth (two digits);
- day of month (two digits);
- and a computer "twin" number (usually one, never a zero).

Document Appearance

The current license and ID card documents have been in circulation since May 30, 2008 and are issued to all first-time drivers and renewal licensees. Presently, all DMV card customers are issued a temporary license or temporary non-driver ID card while their permanent license or ID card is being processed and then mailed. It will take at least five years to replace the older documents. Both document types are listed below.

Current Document

Security Characteristics: Features holographs, small windows and a bar code with the driver's description and license restrictions.

Position of Photo: Left side, ghost image on right.

Minor Age Driver Locator: Vertical, photo on top, ghost photo on bottom, statement shows date when driver is 21.

CDL Indicator: The fact that the driver is CDL qualified is indicated.

Older Document

Security Characteristics: Hologram of New Hampshire, license is laminated.

Position of Photo: Top left.

Minor Age Driver Locator: Red border around photo, also statement on card showing date when driver is 21.

CDL Indicator: "CDL" appears next to the class designation.

Issuance

Location of Requirements for Proof of Identity:

www.nh.gov/safety/divisions/dmv/forms/documents/identification-residency.pdf

Age Requirements

One must be at least 16 years of age to get a New Hampshire driver license. Persons 16 and 17 years of age may get a New Hampshire driver license only with successful completion of an approved driver education program. Persons under 18 years of age cannot get a commercial driver license. Any person 16 years of age or older and under 21 years of age is issued a Youth Operator license. Non-licensed learners must be accompanied by a licensed parent, guardian, certified driving instructor, or responsible adult aged twenty-five or older.

Residency

Non-resident's home-state license honored on a reciprocal basis; New Hampshire license must be secured within sixty days of establishing residency. Note NH law requires the DMV be notified within ten days of a change of address.

Renewal

All licenses shall expire on the fifth anniversary of the license holder's date of birth following issuance. All youth operator licenses expire on the holder's 21st birthday. The driver keeps same number when renewing. Renewal by mail is available for New Hampshire residents temporarily living out-of-state. The online renewal system permits non-commercial drivers to renew a five-year license once every ten years. From the home page, click on "online driver license renewal."

Elderly-Related Restrictions

A driving test is required when drivers renew at age 75 or older.

Vehicle Insurance, Title and Registration Facts

Registration Renewal

Registration renewal is on an annual basis. Note that registering a vehicle in New Hampshire is a actually two-part process. All motor vehicles (except mopeds) must begin their registration process at the town or city clerk in the town or city in which they reside. The second part of the process is the state transaction. However, a Town/City Clerk who is a Municipal Agent of the State may be able to complete the state transaction for an additional fee. Some towns or cities may offer online registration.

New Residents

New residents must register vehicles upon the expiration of time period granted by home-state reciprocity agreement or within sixty days of establishing residency—whichever is first.

Inspections and Emissions Testing

New Hampshire's program of vehicle safety inspections is as follows: all non-commercial vehicles, annually; all commercial vehicles (over 10,000 pounds GVW) and all buses, semi-annually. Visual inspection of several emissions components is included in the annual statewide safety inspection for light-duty vehicles.

All 1996 and newer model year vehicles are subject to emissions testing and must pass the On-Board Diagnostics (OBD) inspection. New Hampshire incorporated OBD inspections into the safety inspection program beginning in May 2005 as a requirement of the Federal Clean Air Act. The program enables licensed inspection stations to perform OBD inspections and allows the state to comply with Environmental Protection Agency regulations.

Passenger Plate Facts

There are two plates with two decals (MO) (YR) on both plates Counties of issuance are not designated on the plate. When a vehicle is sold the plates remain with seller.

Insurance and Financial Responsibility

Although the state does not have a mandatory insurance law, the state requires financial responsibility proof (SR-22) in case of the following convictions:

1. Driving under the influence of alcohol or drugs.
2. Failing to stop and report when involved in a crash.
3. Homicide arising out of the operation of a motor vehicle.
4. The second time for reckless driving.
5. After review of a person's driver record for any traffic violation (just cause after hearing).

The DMV strongly recommends and urges all owners of motor vehicle to carry standard liability and property damage insurance with minimum requirements of $25,000/50,000/25,000. SR-22 forms are used by the state.

Withdrawal Sanctions, and Alcohol and Drug Testing

Alcohol and Chemical Testing

Evidence that there was an alcohol concentration of more than .03% but less than .08% is relevant evidence (not prima facie) and may be considered with other competent evidence to determine guilt or innocence. Drivers under 21 years of age have a limit of .02 percent, if driving a CMV then .04%. Urine, blood, and breath testing are authorized.

New Hampshire has provisions for implied-consent and administrative license suspensions. Operating a horse, boat, ORHV, or bicycle under the influence is also considered illegal.

Suspensions and Revocations

The state is in compliance with the federally mandated disqualifications on CDLs. See the Appendix for details.

Point Accumulation

Drivers Under Twenty Years of Age

Any violation ....20-day suspension; 45-day for second offense.

Third violation ....90-day suspension.

Drivers Under Eighteen Years of Age

Six points in one calendar year or third violation ....Up to three-month suspension.

Twelve points in two consecutive calendar years ....Up to six-month suspension.

Eighteen points in three consecutive calendar years ....Up to one-year suspension.

Drivers Aged Eighteen to Under Twenty-One

Nine points in one calendar year....................................Up to three-month suspension.

Fifteen points in two consecutive calendar years..............Up to six-month suspension.

Twenty-one points in two consecutive calendar years......Up to one-year suspension.

Drivers Twenty-One Years or Older

Twelve points in one calendar year.................................Up to three-month suspension.

Eighteen points in two consecutive calendar years...........Up to six-month suspension.

Twenty-four points in three consecutive calendar years ...Up to one-year suspension.

Transporting Alcoholic Beverages ....Up to sixty-day suspension.

Intoxication or Under the Influence of Drugs

1st Offense...Revocation from ninety days to two years.

2nd offense Within a Ten-Year Period ....Revocation of driving privileges for at least three years.

Refusal to Submit to a Chemical Test or Prior NH Refusals:

First conviction with no prior DWI convictions ....180-day revocation.

Prior refusal to submit or DWI conviction.......................Two-year revocation.

Note: Since 01/01/2009, drivers with outstanding E-Z Pass violations are no longer be subject to suspension; however, outstanding violations will block the driver from renewing registrations.

Reinstatement Requirements

Suspension or Revocations $100.00 fee; SR-22 (in some cases).

DUI Suspension $100.00 fee; SR-22; successful completion of approved alcohol program; installation of Ignition Interlock Device (in some cases). SR-22

Record Access: Laws, Rules, and Forms

Note: This Section Applies to Both Driver and Vehicle Records.

Governing Statutes and Rules

Administrative Rules and a link to **Title XXI - Motor Vehicle Laws** are found under *Laws & Rules* at the home page.

Title XXI, RSA 260:14 Records and Certification, amended per Laws of 2002 (House Bill 1456) effective January 1, 2003, provides the governing rules for the release of motor vehicle records. The New Hampshire Administrative Rules pertaining to Confidentiality of Motor Vehicle Records are found in Chapter Saf-C 5600. (Driver Privacy).

Policy Statement Regarding Permissible Uses

Per the above laws, the Dept. of Safety is required to keep personal information on drivers' records confidential. The information is only available to certain persons who need the information to conduct their businesses, such as law enforcement, insurance companies or government agencies. Persons requesting records are screened to see if they fall within one of the permissible user groups.

New Hampshire does not have the following federal exceptions: 10 and 14. New Hampshire added the following exceptions:

(9) For use with respect to a request for a named person's motor vehicle records by a public utility, as defined in RSA 362:2 and over which the public utilities commission exercised jurisdiction on July 1, 1996, to perform its public service obligations, provided that the named person's express consent has been obtained. Such consent may be withdrawn at any time.

(10) For use by life insurance companies authorized to write life insurance policies, or their authorized agents, on a case-by-case basis, in connection with claims investigation, rating, and underwriting, provided that the insurance company has provided written notice to the named person that the person's motor vehicle records will be accessed.

A person's photograph, computerized image and SSN are not released to any user.

Request and Consent Forms

A *Certificate of Authority* must be filed with the state when an agent or employees of an agent is permitted to obtain records (Saf-C 5603.2). Frequent requesters may establish an account with the state if the requester expects to make more than 20 requests in a one year period (Saf-C 5604).

Authorized requesters of driver, vehicle, or accident records must complete form *DSMV 505 - Release of Motor Vehicle Records*. The form can be downloaded from the web at www.nh.gov/safety/divisions/dmv/forms/dsmv505.pdf. If the reason is a permissible use, all written requests must indicate the reason for the request and be signed by the requester. If not for a permissible use, consent must be given; the subject's signature must be notarized on *DSMV Form 505*. All requests for pre-employment screening must be submitted on this form.

Vendor and Third Party Access Policy

One vendor may not resell to another record vendor, even if there is a signed release or the reason is for a permissible use, unless a telecommunication link has been established and both vendors have been approved. In this situation, the original vendor must maintain a record of all such transactions for a minimum of five years.

Records Ordered For Non-permissible Uses

Without consent or a permissible use all motor vehicle records cannot be obtained, even a record without personal information.

Access to Driver-Related Records

Driving Records

General Information and Fees

Driving Records, 23 Hazen Drive, Concord NH, 03305, 603-227-4040. As indicated above, if a requester does not fall into one the permitted use groups, the requester is required to present a document notarized by the licensee in order to obtain information.

There are three records available - **The Insurance Report**, the **Certified Report**, and the **Non-Certified Report**. The fee for each report (unless obtained online) is $15.00. An Insurance Report has only violations and accidents. A Certified or Non-Certified Report has detailed information regarding past history including present and/or prior suspensions, restorations, convictions, and crash involvement. Credit cards are accepted for payment. New Hampshire charges for a no record found report.

In-Person – Five walk-in requests can be processed while you wait. The Concord Office listed above is the only location that processes manual search requests. The driver's full name and date of birth are needed when ordering (the license number and last known address are helpful). Certified records are also sold across-the-counter.

Mail – Mail-in requests are processed in seven to ten working-days. The Concord office listed above is the only location that processes mail requests. The driver's full name and date of birth are needed when ordering (the license number and last known address are helpful). If ordering

Fax – Per Administrative Rule (Saf-C 5602.07), established accounts may fax requests to 603-271-1555.

Electronic FTP – DMV data is available via File Transfer Protocol (FTP). FTP transmissions to be processed in batch mode are scheduled at the Data Processing Center. The record fee is $12.00. The input cut-off time is 3 pm with output available at 8 am the next day. There are three ways to search the record: license number; license number and last name; or full name and date of birth. Billing is available on a monthly basis. The minimum daily order requirement is fifty requests. If more information is required, call 603-227-4050.

Electronic Online – New Hampshire offers interactive online inquiry for commercial accounts, the system is open approx. 22 hours

per day. The record fee is $12.00. Searches are by license number or by name and DOB. For more information, call 603-227-4050.

Bulk – Information from the NH driver license file can be provided upon request, with output on printed lists or mailing labels, or on tape. Costs will vary. Call 603-227-4050 for further information.

By Person of Record – NH drivers may obtain their driving record by mail or walk-in as described above. At present, there is no program for drivers to order or view their own record online.

Notification/Monitoring Program

New Hampshire does not offer a monitoring or notification program to employers or insurance companies to track incidents of drivers.

Accident Reports

Reporting – An accident report must be filed within fifteen days for accidents involving death, injury, or combined property damage in excess of $1,000.00. Reports are written and filed by the police if they investigate. If the police did not respond and the accident involving death, injury, or combined property damage in excess of $1,000.00, then an Individual Operator's Report must be filed with the Department of Safety, Department of Motor Vehicles, 23 Hazen Drive, Concord, 03305. There are no special requirements for commercial drivers.

Record Access – Copies of accident reports may be obtained by written request from the Department of Safety, Attention: Crash Section, 23 Hazen Drive, Concord NH, 03305, 603-227-4040. If crash involved fatality, please indicate so in request. The department follows the privacy regulations in effect per RSA 260:14. The notarized *DSMV 505 Form* www.nh.gov/safety/divisions/dmv/forms/documents/dsmv505.pdf (the same form used to request a driving record) must be completed by the subject involved or an insurance representative licensed to write automobile policies in the state of NH. In-person requesters are required to have notarized paperwork if not involved in the incident. The fee is $1.00 per page, with a minimum of $5.00. Both drivers' names and dates of birth, and the date and location of the accident are needed when ordering. Records are maintained for five years. New incidents are ready for inquiry in four to six weeks.

Access to Vehicle-Related Records

Note: There are two different Bureaus with two counter locations that process record requests. Each is separately profiled below

Bureau of Titles

General Information and Fees

Bureau of Titles, Department of Safety, DMV, 23 Hazen Drive, Concord 03305, 603-227-4150.

The Bureau of Title oversees requests for title and lien information. The current fee for a title search (includes lien data) is $20.00 per request. VIN and fee must be submitted with each written request. Photos and SSNs are not released to record requesters.

In-Person, Mail – Vehicle records are available for up to 15 years. Turnaround time is normally up to 5 days.

Electronic – This method is not available.

Bulk – This method is not available.

Bureau of Registration

General Information and Fees

Bureau of Registration, Department of Safety, 23 Hazen Drive, Concord, NH 03305, 603-227-4030, the fax is 603-271-1061.

The Registration Bureau is responsible for the registration of vehicles, boats, mopeds, motorcycles, construction equipment, agricultural and farm equipment, tractors, and trailers. The fee for a current registration listing is $5.00 per record; a certified copy is $15.00. Credit cards are accepted. Photos and SSNs are not released to record requesters.

In-Person, Mail – The owner's name, DOB, the plate number or VIN and fee must be submitted with each written request. Records are available for current registrations only. Turnaround time is normally up to 5 days.

Electronic – This method is not available.

Bulk – New Hampshire offers several means of obtaining registration information, for those are qualified. Output can be given electronically or via paper, including specific (custom) requests. Costs vary. For more information, please contact Information Services at 603-271-2314.

Access to Vessel-Related Records

General Information, Access and Fees

The Department of Safety, Division of Motor Vehicles, Bureau of Registrations also maintains the database of boat registrations. The same privacy provisions apply as those to vehicle records. All motorized boats and all sailboats over 12 ft must be registered. Mail requests should be sent to the attention of the Boat Registration Section. A name or registration search is $5.00 per name (or per registration) for current year only. The direct line is 603-227-4030. Liens on boats are recorded with the Secretary of State, Office of Commercial Code. For more information call 603-271-3276.

Driving Record Content and Reciprocity

What's On or Not On the Driving Record

- All convictions are reported on a New Hampshire driving record. SSNs are not released.
- Accidents are reported, but fault is not shown.
- See above for the differences between the Insurance Report and the Certified Report.
- The state does not permit driver school attendance in lieu of conviction.
- With the exception of the ten-year certified record, the period of time convictions are listed on the public record is seven years for moving violations (non-CDL, major & minor), and ten years for DWIs.
- A driving record will indicate whether or not an individual is required to file proof of insurance. This information is displayed either as:
  o "No proof of financial responsibility is required."
  or
  o "Proof of financial responsibility is required."

Data Retention

Records are purged, using an automated procedure, based on the timetable per federal regulations (see the Appendix). Surrendered licenses remain on the system for at least five years after the expiration date.

Court to Repository

Courts must report conviction information to the Director within seven days (RSA263:60). The Department enters convictions manually from paper.

State Reciprocity for Non-CDL Drivers

- Will suspend license of driver for unpaid out-of-state convictions if state is member of NRVC.
- Record of new incoming driver is shown on MVR.
- Out-of-state convictions are shown on MVR.
- Out-of-state accidents are not shown on MVR.
- Convictions of out-of-state drivers are sent to home state.
- Record is forwarded to new state upon surrender of license only upon request.

License Classes, Restrictions, and Endorsements

License Classes– Commercial

New Hampshire began issuance of the CDL in April of 1990.

Class A	Any combination of vehicles with a GVWR of 26,001 or more pounds provided the GVWR of the vehicle(s) being towed is in excess of 10,000 pounds. Holders of Group A licenses may—with any appropriate endorsements—operate all vehicles within groups B and C.
Class B	Any single vehicle with a GVWR of 26,001 or more pounds, or any such vehicle towing a vehicle not in excess of 10,000 pounds GVWR.
Class C	Any single vehicle that is less than 26,001 pounds GVWR, or any such vehicle towing a vehicle not in excess of 10,000 pounds GVWR, that is placarded for hazardous materials or designed to transport sixteen or more persons (including the operator).

License Classes– Non-Commercial or Older Licenses Still In Circulation

Codes	Description	Explanation
A	CDL-A	Class A - CDL
A M1	CDL-A MC	Class A - CDL with motorcycle
A M2	CDL-A MDC	Class A - CDL with motor-driven cycle
B	CDL-B	Class B - CDL
B M1	CDL-B MC	Class B - CDL with motorcycle
B M2	CDL-B MDC	Class B - CDL with motor-driven cycle
C	CDL-C	Class C – CDL **(Must have HAZMAT or Passenger Endorsement)**
C M1	CDL-C MC	Class C - CDL with motorcycle **(Must have HAZMAT or Passenger Endorsement)**
C M2	CDL-C MDC	Class C - CDL with motor-driven cycle **(Must have HAZMAT or Passenger Endorsement)**
D	OPERATOR	Operator
D M1	OPR-MC	Operator with motorcycle
D M2	OPER-MDC	Operator with motor-driven cycle
M1	MOTORCYCLE	Motorcycle
M2	MTR-DRVN-CYC	Motor-driven cycle
M3	MOPED	Moped
M4	3 WHL MC ONLY	Trike
NO	NON-DRIVER ID	Non-driver ID
YO	YOUTH OPERATOR	Youth Operator

Restrictions

B	Corrective Lenses	M	Class A CDL Restricted to Class B Bus
C	Mechanical Aid	N	Class B CDL Restricted to Class C Bus
D	Prosthetic Aid	O	Except Tractor-Trailer. As of September 3, 1991, a combination of vehicles over 26,000 pounds either not hooked by a fifth-wheel or straight-truck towing a trailer with electric brakes.
E	Automatic Transmission		
F	Outside Mirror		
G	Limited to Daylight Only		
K	CDL Intrastate Only	Z	Ignition Interlock Device Required
L	Vehicles Without Air-Brakes		

Endorsements

H	Hazardous Materials	T	Double-/Triple-Trailers
N	Liquid Bulk/Cargo Tank	S	School Bus
P	Passenger/Transportation		

Conviction Table with ACD, NH Code, and Statute

The table is ordered by the **Description** column since violations, types of accidents, etc., are spelled-out on all abstracts whether acquired manually or electronically. The **ACD** column reflects how convictions are translated when they are transmitted to other states. Some of the listed **NH Codes** are only for internal/computer use.

Description	RSA Number	ACD	NH Code
2 or more major offenses	263:94	W40	0090
2 out of serv viol 10 yrs 16+ pass or haz	263:93	W51	0072
2 out of serv viol w/in 10 years	263:93	W50	0071
2 serious violations – comm. veh	263:94	W30	CS80
3 convictions in calendar year	263:55	W01	0039
3 out of serv viol 10 yrs 16+ pass or haz	263:93-a	W52	0074
3 serious violations – comm. veh	263:94	W31	CS81
3+ out of serv w/in 10 years	263:93-a	W52	0073
Administrative per se for .10 bac	265-A:4	A90	AC16
Allow improper person	263:1A		VR60
Alteration of title	262:1		RR30
Altered license	268:12	B41	0046
Binder chains	266:66	E01	ZZ28
Cancellation of insurance	264:21	D36	0002
Cause fatal neg hom oper CMV	263:94 (i)(g)	U10	RK51
Coasting	265:99	N80	IL50
Comm veh admin per se	265-A:25(iv)	A94	D163
Comm veh admin per se 2nd	265-A:25(iv)	A94	D164
Conduct after accident	264:25	B05	HR60
Conv refusal of implied consent	265-A:25	A12	D165
Corrective lens	263:13	D29	DS40
Court ordered	263:57	W00	0037
Court recommended	263:57	W00	0036

Description	RSA Number	ACD	NH Code
Crossing median	265:26	M51	IL60
CV refusal implied consent 2nd	265-A:25	A12	D166
Default agreement	264:3	D37	0044
Default child support	161:B:11	D51	0060
Default court admin fee	263:56A	D53	0054
Default court summons	263:56A	D45	0031
Default motor vehicle hearing	263:56A	D45	0030
Default payment	263:56A	D53	0041
Direct course	265:11-A	M41	IL30
Disobey license restrictions	263:13	D29	DS30
Disobey police officer	265:4	M08	HR40
Disobeying terms of probation		W00	0023
Drive out of serv 16+ pass or haz	263:93A	B19	0070
Drive while OODO in effect	263:93A	B27	0075
Driving comm. veh w/out CDL	263:92	B56	RT51
Driving CV w/out CDL – 2nd	263:92	B56	RT52
Driving CV w/out CDL – 3rd or subsequent	263:92	B56	RT53
Driving on sidewalk	265:26A	M58	IL40
Driving to left of center	265:21	M57	IL25
Driving while intoxicated	265-A:2	A20	D110
Driving while license barred	263:64	B21	AC25
Driving while license canceled	263:64	B22	AC22
Driving while license denied	263:64	B23	AC23
Driving while license disqualified	263:64	B24	AC24
Driving while license withdrawn	263:64	B20	AC20
DWI – 3rd offense	265-A:2	A20	D125
DWI – 4th or subsequent	265-A:2	A20	D124
DWI - aggravated	265-A:3	A20	D130
DWI – boat	265-A:2	W00	DB10
DWI – default	263:56A	D45	D131
DWI – OHRV	265-A:2	A20	OH10
DWI – second offense	265-A:2	A20	D120
DWI .04-.09 comm veh	265-A:23	A04	D160
DWI .04-.09 comm veh subsequent	265-A:23	A04	D162
DWI aggravated – boat	265-A:3	W00	DB30
DWI aggravated – OHRV	265-A:2	A20	OH30
DWI alcohol	265-A:2	A21	AC13
DWI alcohol and drugs	265-A:2	A23	AC14
DWI alcohol w/BAC at/over w/dtl	265-A:2	A11	AC12
DWI alcohol w/BAC gt eq .08	265-A:2	A08	AC08
DWI alcohol w/BAC gt eq .10	265-A:2	A10	AC10
DWI drugs	265-A:2	A22	D115
DWI drugs – boat	265-A:2	W00	DB15
DWI drugs – OHRV	265-A:2	A22	OH15
DWI second offense – boat	265-A:2	W00	DB20
DWI second offense – OHRV	265-A:2	A20	OH20
DWI subsequent – boat	265-A:2	W00	DB25
DWI subsequent offense – OHRV	265-A:2	A20	OH25
Emergency veh	265:8	U21	ZZ53
Excessive noise	266:59		EM40
Excessive smoke	266:59		ZZ44
Excessive speed in comm. veh	259:98-A	S93	SP60
EZPass violation 1st offense	263:31	W00	EZ01
EZPass violation 2nd offense	263:31	W00	EZ02
EZPass violation 3rd offense	263:31	W00	EZ03
EZPass violation 4TH Offense	263:31	W00	EZ04
Fail dim lights	265:114	E54	ZZ11
Fail reveal ident – fatal inj acc	265:4	B14	HR41
Fail surrender hazmat endorse	1808	W09	0079
Fail to answer summons	263:56A	D45	RR20
Fail to keep right	265:16	M41	IL20
Fail to obey officer	265:3	MO8	ZZ47
Fail to obey RR – second offense	265:52	W60	RW67
Fail to obey RR – third offense	265:52	W61	RW68

Description	RSA Number	ACD	NH Code
Fail to obey RR gates and signs	265:48	M10	RW61
Fail to obey RR slow down	265:48	M20	RW62
Fail to obey RR stop as required	265:48	M22	RW64
Fail to obey RR stop before tracks	265:48	M21	RW63
Fail to obey RR sufficient space	265:48	M23	RW65
Fail to obey RR under car clearance	265:51	M24	RW66
Fail to yield from private way	265:32	N25	ST25
Fail to yield right of way	265:28	N01	RW30
Fail to yield to emergency vehicle	265:33	N04	RW35
Fail to yield turning left	265:29	N31	ST15
Failure to file – fatal accident	264:25	B61	RR15
Failure to file accident report	264:25	B61	0001
Failure to pay court fine	263:56A	D56	0043
Failure to report accident	264:25	B61	RR10
Failure to stop	265:31	M15	ST10
Failure to use due care	265:37	M82	RW50
Failure to yield	265:30	N01	ST20
Failure to yield	265:9	N01	ZZ04
Failure yield pedestrian	265:35	N08	RW40
False statement on license	263:12V	D02	0032
False statement on license	263:12V	D02	MR10
Fatal accident/immed susp	263:59	W70	0057
Felony administrative per se	265-A:30	A98	FE50
Felony administrative per se – subsequent	265-A:30	A98	FE52
Felony comm. veh – 1st	263:94	A20	FE10
Felony comm. veh – 1st	263:94	U03	FE10
Felony comm. veh – 2nd	263:94	A20	FE20
Felony comm. veh – 2nd	263:94	U03	FE20
Felony comm. veh - drugs	263:94	A50	FE30
Flaps/guards	266:57	E01	ZZ51
Following fire apparatus	265:100	M33	F020
Following too close	265:25	M34	F010
Habitual offender	262:19	W01	0035
Hardship registration abuse	261:180		HE75
Hit & run – fail to stop render aid	264:25	B01	AC61
Hit & run – fail to stop render aid – fatal	264:25	B02	AS62
Hit & run – fail to stop render aid PDO	264:25	B04	AC64
Hit & run – fail to stop render aid pers	264:25	B03	AC63
Illegal backing	265:94	N82	ZZ10
Illegal possession alcohol	179:10	A31	VR80
Illegal towing	265:108		ZZ06
Illegal transportation – drugs	265-A:43	U04	0018
Imminent hazard	263:59	W70	0068
Impeding traffic	265:64	S96	RK60
Implied consent – subsequent	265-A:14	A12	0016
Improper class/ndors on driver license	263:92	B91	RT50
Improper lane change	265:44	M42	IL05
Improper loading	263:61		EM21
Improper operation of vehicle	265:37	M82	0038
Improper passing	265:18	M70	ZZ05
Improper turn	265:42	N50	0009
Improper turn	265:42	N50	TU30
Incompetency /improper driving	263:59	W14	0014
Indefinite suspension original license	263:14	W00	0064
Lack of insurance	263:63	D36	0049
Lane control	265:24	M41	ZZ09
Leave acc scene – fatal acc	264:25	B06	AC71
Leave acc scene – pers inj acc	264:25	B07	AC72
Leave acc scene – prop damage acc	264:25	B08	AC73
Leaving scene	264:25	B05	HR10
Major offense after reinstate	263:94	W41	0091
Manslaughter	630:2	U08	RK30
Medical reasons	263:59	W14	0007
Misuse of license	263:57A	D16	0045

Description	RSA Number	ACD	NH Code
Misuse of plates	261:176		RT40
Misuse of registration	261:61		RT30
Modified exhaust	266:59		ZZ24
Modified height	266:9		ZZ49
Modify sticker or decal	262:16		ZZ40
More than 1 license	263:4	D07	VR40
Motor Carrier regulation	375:B		ZZ29
Motorcycle requirement	265:122	F03	MC10
Negligent driving	265:79B	M83	RK12
Negligent homicide	630:3	U07	RK40
Negligent homicide operating CMV	263:94 IG	U09	RK41
No child restraint	265:107A	F02	ZZ56
No child restraint – 2nd offense	265:107A	F02	ZZ57
No financial proof	263:63	D36	FR40
No flares	266:72A		ER40
No hand signal	265:45	N40	S110
No signal	265:45	N40	ZZ25
Non-emergency stop	265:69		ZZ34
Obstructed vision	265:95	D70	ZZ23
Odometer tampering	262:17		MR30
Open container	265-A:44		OC10
Open container – subsequent	265-A:44	A35	OC15
Operating after alcohol revocation	263:64 IV	B25	0011
Operating after revocation	263:64	B25	VR10
Operating after rights	263:64	B25	VR30
Operating after suspension	263:64	B26	VR20
Operating to endanger	265:79	M84	RK20
Operating w/o comm. lic	263:92	B91	ZZ02
Operating w/o license	263:1	B51	VR50
Operating w/o lights	265:109	E55	ZZ12
Operating w/o mc lic	263:30	B91	ZZ03
Operating while habitual offender	262:23	B25	RV20
Original and youth license	263:14	D29	0065
Original and youth license – subsequent	263:14	D29	0066
Over road limit	266:25		ZZ43
Overheight	266:10		OV10
Overlength	266:11		OV30
Overload	266:25		OV40
Overwidth	266:12		OV20
Parental consent withdraw	263:17	W13	0042
Parking on highway	265:68		MS70
Pass on right	265:19	M70	IL70
Passengers in improper truck	265:106		MS80
Perjury about operation of veh	265:4	D78	HR42
Point system suspension	263:56	W01	0053
Possession master keys	262:13	W00	EM80
Prob lic – admin per se	265-A:35	A94	D153
Prob lic – admin per se subsequent	265-A:35	A94	D154
Prob lic – refusal implied cons	263-A:35	A12	0056
Prohibition	263:12	B41	ZZ46
Prohibition license	263:12	B41	ZZ16
Protested check – bus off	6:11-a	D35	0052
Protested check – RT	6:11-a	D35	0051
Protested check – TC	544-B	D35	0050
Protested or invalid ck – court	263:56A	W00	0024
Railroad crossing	265:48	M09	RW60
Reckless death	630:2	U31	RK50
Reckless operation	265:79	M84	RK10
Red light	265:10 III	M16	ZZ21
Refusal of implied consent law	265-A:14	A12	0005
Road racing	265:75	S95	SP10
Rubbish on highway	265:102		L110
Safety chains	266:63	E01	ZZ27
School bus violation	265:54	N09	PA44

Description	RSA Number	ACD	NH Code
Speed too fast for road condition	265:60	S94	SP30
Speeding 01-05 over limit	265:60	S01	SP01
Speeding 06-10 over limit	265:60	S06	SP06
Speeding 15 over limit	265:60	S15	SP15
Speeding 16-20 over limit	265:60	S16	SP16
Speeding 21-24 over limit	265:60	S21	SP21
Speeding 21-30 over limit DTL OPT	265:60	S71	
Speeding 25 over limit	265:60	S21	SP24
Speeding 26-30 over limit	265:60	S26	SP26
Speeding 31-35 over limit DTL OPT	265:67	S31	SP31
Speeding 31-40 over limit DTL OPT	265:60	S81	
Speeding 36-40 over limit DTL OPT	265:67	S36	SP36
Speeding 41+ over limit DTL OPT	265:67	S41	SP41
Speeding 41+ over limit DTL OPT	265:67	S91	
Speeding -Construction Zone	265:6-A	S93	0020
Speeding over +25	265:60	S93	SP25
Speeding spd lim octl spd DTL req	265:60	S92	
Speeding under +25	265:60	S93	SP20
Spillage	266:72		ZZ19
Squealing tires			ZZ13
Subsequent operation of vehicle	263:64	B26	HE76
Take without consent	262:12	W00	EM70
Tinted windows	266:58-A		EM30
Traffic signal	265:9	M16	ZZ22
Trailer brakes	266:30	E31	ZZ45
Trailer lights	266:44	E34	ZZ48
Transporting alcohol beverage	265-A:44		0010
Transporting drugs	265-A:43	U04	D140
Transporting drugs	265-A:43	U04	0006
Unattended vehicle	265:72		EM10
Uncovered load	266:72	E50	ZZ32
Under 20 prog 3 or more offense	263:14	W00	0063
Under 20 prog first offense	263:14	W00	0061
Under 20 prog second offense	263:14	W00	0062
Underage admin per se – subsequent	265-A:30	A61	D155
Underage administrative per se	265-A:30	A61	D151
Underage DWI	265-A:2	A60	D111
Underage DWI – aggravated	265-A:3	A60	D132
Underage DWI – second offense	265-A:2	A60	D121
Underage DWI – subsequent off	265-A:2	A60	D126
Underage DWI Drugs	265-A:2	A22	D116
Uninsured accident	264:3	D35	0003
Unsafe start		N83	ZZ33
Unsafe tires	266:52		DE40
Unsafe vehicle	261:178	F66	0026
Unsafe vehicle	261:178	F66	ZZ54
Unsatisfied judgment	264:3	D39	0040
Use MV felony – not traffic offense	630:3	U03	RK45
Using a motor vehicle in connection with a felony (not traffic offense)	630:3	U03	RK45
Vehicular assault	265:79A	U06	RK11
W/O NH license	263:35	B51	ZZ42
Withdrawal, non-ACD violations	263:59	W00	1000
Wrong way	265:23	N60	ZZ18
Yellow line	265:22	M70	IL10

Point System Summary

The point system ranges from 1 to 6 points. 12 or more points in a calendar year may result in a suspension. The point assessment total will be reduced by 3 points if the driver shows that he/she has completed a driver improvement course. This reduction is only available once every three years, for suspension purposes only.

1 Point:
- Failing to obey inspection requirements.
- Failing to obtain a N.H. driver's license.
- Operating without vehicle registration available in the vehicle.

2 Points:
- Allowing an improper person to operate a commercial motor vehicle.
- Allowing an improper person to operate a motor vehicle.
- Driving an unregistered vehicle.
- Failing to abide by license restrictions.
- Failing to comply with directions from a police officer.
- Failing to produce a license when requested by a police officer.
- Operating a vehicle with improper class of license.
- Operating without a motorcycle license.

3 Points:
- Abandoning a vehicle.
- Carrying passengers in a truck not so designed.
- Coasting.
- Disobeying any traffic control device.
- Driving on a sidewalk.
- Failing to obey stop and yield signs.
- Failing to obey yield sign.
- Failing to signal a turn.
- Failing to use due care when blind person crosses the street.
- Failing to yield right of way.
- Following fire trucks too closely.
- Following too closely.
- Illegal backing.
- Improper conduct at a railroad crossing.
- Misuse of plates.
- Misuse or failure to display plates.
- Obstructing the driver's view (by persons, objects, etc.).
- Opening and closing vehicle doors improperly.
- Speeding at less than 25 MPH above the posted limit.

4 Points:
- Driving without a license.
- Driving without required insurance.
- Failing to drive on the right side of the road.
- Improper passing.
- Speeding at 25 MPH or more above the posted limit.
- Yellow line violation.

6 Points:
- Aggravated DWI.
- Conduct after an accident
- Disobeying a police officer.
- Driving a motor vehicle while in possession of controlled drug(s).
- Driving after license revocation or suspension.
- Driving while under the influence of drugs or alcohol.
- Failure to stop immediately after a crash.
- False report of a theft.
- Improper use of a registration certificate.
- Improper use of license.
- Lending a driver's license to an underage person to buy alcoholic beverages.
- Modifying or forging inspection sticker or registration decal.
- Odometer tampering.
- Racing and/or reckless driving.
- Removal or changes to vehicle identification number.
- School bus violation.
- Taking motor vehicle without the owner's consent.
- Title alteration.

New Jersey

Administration	Important Telephone and Web Contacts
Raymond P. Martinez, Chief Administrator Motor Vehicle Commission Donna Pennabere, Director Compliance and Safety Motor Vehicle Commission 225 East State Street, PO 174 Trenton , NJ 08666 www.state.nj.us/mvc/	Driver Licensing and CDL ....609-292-6500 Driver Licensing (In-State Only)....................888-486-3339 Suspensions ....609-292-7500 Vehicle Information ....609-292-6500 State Department of Insurance ....609-292-5360 State Police...609-882-2000 Email: www.state.nj.us/mvc/About/ContactEmail.htm Statutes and Laws Look-up: www.njleg.state.nj.us

Driver's License Format, Issuance and Renewal

License Classes, Restrictions and Endorsements Appear After the Driving Record Content Section

License Format

The format is the first letter of last name and fourteen numbers. For example, DL Number "S5778-40771-01024" is interpreted as follows:

S — first initial of last name of the driver (i.e., Smith)
5778 — coded next four letters of last name (i.e., mith)
407 — coded first name (John)
71 — coded middle initial (J.)
01 — coded birth month for males (January)
02 — year of birth (1902)
4 — coded eye color (blue)

In another example, if the driver was a female, Christine J. Smith, with the same date and year of birth and eye color, the driver license number would be "S5778-12471-51024" and would be interpreted as follows:

S — first initial of last name of the driver (i.e., Smith)
5778 — coded next four letters of last name (i.e., mith)
124 — coded first name (Chris)
71 — coded middle initial (J.)
51 — coded birth month for females (January)
02 — year of birth (1902)
4 — coded eye color (blue).

Document Appearance

Currently Issued Documents

The current Enhanced Digital Driver License began issuance May 2011.

Security Characteristics: Features similar to previous license, but location of redundant data and 2D barcode shifted to right, the EIN/1Dbarcode is now positioned vertically at the far left. The photo position of under 21 drives changed (see below). Back has gray MVC logo and black silhouette of the state of the state. The new document is more secure and made with tamper-evident material. The background security has pre-print design and is continuous edge-to-edge. The cardholder name is formatted on two lines, the last name on the top and first name below.

Position of Photo: Left edge, ghost image on lower right side. Regular license has red bar above photo with "AUTO DRIVER LICENSE" in white letters.

Minor Age Driver Locator: Vertical format. Type of license is in yellow bar across top, under state name. The larger photo is on the left side half way up the document. The ghost photo is to the right. Along right edge of large photo is "UNDER 21 UNTIL xx-xx-xxxx".

CDL Indicator: Indicated by class below the header bar.

Older Issued Documents

This generation license (DDL) began issuance in mid-January 2004.

Security Characteristics: Virtually counterfeit-proof digital license contains nearly two dozen security features.

Position of Photo: Lower side, ghost image on lower right side. Regular license has red bar above photo with "AUTO DRIVER LICENSE" in white letters.

Minor Age Driver Locator: Vertical format. Type of license is in yellow bar across top, under state name. Photo is on bottom left, along right edge of photo is "UNDER 21 UNTIL xx-xx-xxxx".

CDL Indicator: Indicated by class.

Issuance

Location of Requirements for Proof of Identity:
www.state.nj.us/mvc/Licenses/6PointID.htm

Age Requirements

The minimum age for "Agricultural Pursuit" is 16, for a CDL is 18 for interstate driving and 21 to drive with a passenger and/or HAZMAT. The minimum age for a motorboat or jet ski license is 16, but if under 17 a letter with parental or guardian consent must be provided.

New Jersey's Graduated Driver License Program has three steps. Step One starts with a Special Learner's Permit or Student Permit issued at age 16. Driver must be accompanied by adult at all times and can only drive from 5AM to 11PM. Next, at 17 and after 6 months of supervised driving and passage of a road test, a Provisional Photo License is issued for one year. Step Three is the basic license at 18.

NJ law requires new drivers aged 21 years old and younger to display identifying decals on the front and rear licenses plates of their vehicles.

Residency

Non-resident's home-state license honored on reciprocal basis; drivers must secure a New Jersey license within sixty days of establishing residency. A license cannot be transferred to a New Jersey license if the driver is under 18 years old. Instead, the driver must complete the Graduated Driver License (GDL) program requirements.

Renewal

Four years from initial or renewal issue date. Drivers born on or before December 1, 1964, may skip the trip to an agency and renew by mail for the present renewal cycle. All other drivers must renew in person. Drivers keep the same number when renewing unless there is a change or correction to name, sex, date of birth, or eye color.

Active military duty members, including New Jersey National Guard and Reserve, are entitled to automatic extensions for driver license, registration and inspection requirements. The license, registration and inspection documents will remain valid for long as the subject is actively serving. Once the driver is demobilized, the document must be renewed within two weeks of the demobilization date.

Elderly-Related Restrictions

None are reported.

Vehicle Insurance, Title and Registration Facts

Registration Note

As of 2010, NJ law requires new drivers aged 21 years old and younger to display identifying decals on the front and rear licenses plates of their vehicles.

Renewal

Renewal is annual. Online renewal is available at www.state.nj.us/mvc/About/mymvc_page.htm. Vehicles eligible for renewal by Web or by phone include passenger vehicles, pleasure boats, trailers under 55,000 lbs and motorcycles. All others must renew at an MVC agency. Effective 2012, renewal is available by mail.

New Residents

Non-residents must register vehicles within sixty days of establishing residency. The "touring privileges" law is no longer valid.

Inspections and Emissions Testing

Effective August 1, 2010, NJ passenger vehicle inspections entail only an emissions check and the four-year exemption for new and used vehicles was extended to five years. Previously a bi-annual car and truck safety inspection was required for all gasoline-powered cars, motorcycles and trucks. All NJ registered diesel-powered motor vehicles over 18,000 GVWR (heavy duty diesel vehicles) are required to be tested annually for smoke emissions.

Passenger Plate Facts

There are two plates. One decal (MO & YR) is found on the windshield. The county of issuance is not designated on the plate. When a vehicle is sold the plates remain with the seller.

Insurance and Financial Responsibility

New Jersey has compulsory insurance for liability, personal injury protection (PIP), and uninsured motorist coverage. Minimum liability financial responsibility limits are $15,000/30,000/5,000. Proof is required after certain violations and for accidents resulting in death, injury, or damage in excess of $500.00. There is no provision in force for SR-22 forms. Special automobile insurance policies are available for eligible low income individuals.

Withdrawal Sanctions, and Alcohol and Drug Testing

Alcohol and Chemical Testing Limits

New Jersey's intoxication level is .08 % and above; .01% for drivers under 21, and .04% if driving a CMV. Urine, blood, and breath testing are authorized. NJ has an implied-consent violation, and a provision for an administrative suspension for out-of-state convictions. Operating a horse or bicycle under the influence is also considered illegal.

Suspensions and Revocations

See the Appendix for a list of the federally mandated disqualifications for offenses occurring in a CMV per MCSIA. Also, an excellent overview is provided at www.state.nj.us/mvc/pdf/Violations/cdl_chart.pdf.

Alcohol- or Drug-Related Convictions
- First Offense if BAC.08% but less than .10%...............................Three-month suspension.
- First Offense if BAC.10% or higher...Seven-month to one-year suspension.
- Second Offense...Two-year suspension.
- Third Offense..Ten-year suspension.

DUI or Refusing Chemical Test in School Zone or Crossing
- First Offense ....One- to two-year suspension.
- Second Offense...Four-year suspension.
- Third Offense..Twenty-year suspension.

Under Age 21 Alcohol and Convicted for Driving or Boating with a BAC or .01 or higher:
- First Offense ....Thirty-day to ninety-day suspension or DUI sentence above.
- Second Offense...Two-year suspension.
- Third Offense..Ten-year suspension.

If suspended because of a DUI offense, the court may require an ignition interlock device to fully restore driving privileges.
- First DUI Offense ....Installation of interlock device for six months to one year if B.A.C. is less than .15%.

First DUI offense with B.A.C. of .15% or above and for second or subsequent DUI offenses:
.... The court shall order the installation of an ignition interlock during the suspension term and as a condition of restoration. First offense – six months to one year; second and subsequent DUI offenses – one to three years.

Driving While Suspended for DWI   Additional one- to two-year suspension.

No Insurance
- First Offense ....One-year suspension.
- Second Offense...Two-year suspension.

Driving With Drugs in Possession ....Two-year suspension.

Refusal to Take Chemical or Breath Test
- First Offense ....Seven-month to one-year suspension.
- Second Offense...Two-year suspension.
- Third or Subsequent Offense ....Ten-year suspension.

Habitual Offender..Up to three-year suspension.

Point Accumulation Suspensions
Note: All point suspension terms listed below are proposed; discretion allowed by the Motor Vehicle Commission.
- Twelve to Fifteen Points in up to Two Years ....Thirty days.
- Twelve to Fourteen Points in a Period Greater than Two Years.......Thirty days.

Sixteen to Eighteen Points in up to Two Years.................................Sixty days.
Nineteen to Twenty-one Points in up to Two Years ....Ninety days.
Twenty-two to Twenty-four Points in up to Two Years ....120 days.
Twenty-five to Twenty-seven Points in up to Two Years.................150 days.
More than Twenty-eight Points in up to Two Years..........................180 days.
Fifteen to Eighteen Points in More than Two Years........................Thirty days.
Nineteen to Twenty-two Points in More than Two Years.................Sixty days.
Twenty-three to Twenty-six Points in More than Two Years...........Ninety days.
Twenty-seven to Thirty Points in More than Two Years..................120 days.
Thirty-one to Thirty-five Points in More than Two Years................150 days.
Thirty-six Points in More than Two Years ....180 days.

Other possible reasons for suspensions:
- Driving with a suspended license
- Failure to appear in court or to pay fines
- Failure to pay surcharges
- Fault in a fatal accident
- Physical or mental disqualification
- Reckless driving
- Vehicle abandonment on a public highway

Note: The MVC does not provide a conditional or special work license. If a license is suspended, the driver cannot drive for any reason until the license is restored.

The **Probationary Driver Program (PDP)** program is mandated for new (probationary) drivers who are convicted of two or more moving violations totaling four or more points in their first two years of driving. A driver who does not successfully complete the 4-hour program (that provides up to a three-point reduction on the driver's record) or does not pay the class fee will be suspended indefinitely. A driver who commits a violation within a year after finishing the class will receive a scheduled suspension; the amount of days depends on when the violation was committed: within 0-6 months will receive a 90- day scheduled suspension, 6-9 months will receive a 60-day scheduled suspension, and 9-12 months will receive a 45-day scheduled suspension.

Reinstatement Requirements

Driving License Suspension ....$100.00 fee, suspension term served, all compliance obligations satisfied.
Registration Suspension ....$100.00 fee and compliance obligations satisfied.

Record Access: Laws, Rules, and Forms

Note: This Section Applies to Both Driver and Vehicle Records.

Governing Statutes and Rules

Statutes and Laws Look-up: www.njleg.state.nj.us
Per Statute N.J.S.A. 39:2-3.3 et seq., the state adopted the provisions of DPPA. The Open Public Records Act (OPRA) (N.J.S.A. 47:1A-1 et seq.) was enacted to give the public greater access to government records maintained by public agencies in New Jersey. Specifically, Statute N.J.S.A. 39:2-3.4(c) Disclosure of personal information connected with motor vehicle record. sets the permissible uses.

Policy Statement Regarding Permissible Uses
The public has the right under OPRA to examine or obtain copies of those public records that are not subject to exceptions from disclosure. OPRA expands the intent of the *Right to Know* law by re-defining what records are available to the public, by setting standards for accessing those records, and penalties for failing to disclose them. New Jersey does not sell or otherwise provide its vehicle database for commercial or political solicitation, marketing or campaigning.
The uses set forth in N.J.S.A. 39:2-3.4(c) are:

1. For use by any government agency, including any court or law enforcement agency in carrying out its functions, or any private person or entity acting on behalf of a federal, State or local agency in carrying out its functions

2. For use in connection with matters of motor vehicle or driver safety and theft; motor vehicle emissions; motor vehicle product alterations, recalls, or advisories; performance monitoring of motor vehicles, motor vehicle parts and dealers; motor vehicle market research activities, including survey research; and the removal of non-owner records from the original owner records of motor vehicle manufacturers.

3. For use in the normal course of business by a legitimate business or its agents, employees or contractors, but only:

a. to verify the accuracy of personal information submitted by the individual to the business or its agents, employees, or contractors; and
b. if such information as so submitted is not correct or is no longer correct, to obtain the correct information, but only for the purposes of preventing fraud by, pursuing legal remedies against, or recovering on a debt or security interest against the individual.

4. For use in connection with any civil, criminal, administrative or arbitral proceeding in any federal, State or local court or agency or before any self-regulatory body, including service of process, investigation in anticipation of litigation, and the execution or enforcement of judgments and orders, or pursuant to an order of a federal, State or local court.

5. For use in educational initiatives, research activities, and for use in producing statistical reports, so long as the personal information is not published, redisclosed, or used to contact individuals and, in the case of educational initiatives, only to organ procurement organizations as aggregated, non-identifying information.

6. For use by any insurer or insurance support organization, or by a self-insured entity, or its agents, employees, or contractors, in connection with claims investigation activities, antifraud activities, rating or underwriting.

7. For use in providing notice to the owners of towed or impounded vehicles

8. For use by an employer or its agent or insurer to obtain or verify information relating to a holder of a commercial driver's license that is required under the "Commercial Motor Vehicle Safety Act," 49 U.S.C.App.s.2710 et seq.

9. For use in connection with the operation of private toll transportation facilities.

10. For use by any requestor, if the requestor demonstrates it has obtained the notarized written consent of the individual to whom the information pertains.

11. For product and service mail communications from automotive-related manufacturers, dealers and businesses, if the commission has implemented methods and procedures to ensure that:

    a. individuals are provided an opportunity, in a clear and conspicuous manner, to prohibit such uses; and

    b. product and service mail communications from automotive-related manufacturers, dealers and businesses will not be directed at individuals who exercise their option under subparagraph (a) of this paragraph.

12. For use by an organ procurement organization designated pursuant to 42 U.S.C.s.1320b-8 to serve in the State of New Jersey, or any donor registry established by any such organization, exclusively for the purposes of determining, verifying, and recording organ and tissue donor designation and identity. For these purposes, an organ procurement organization shall have electronic access at all times, without exception, to real-time organ donor designation and identification information. An organ procurement organization may also have information for research activities, pursuant to paragraph (5) of subsection c. of this section.

Request and Consent Forms

Driving Records: Requesters submitting on *Form DO-21 (Driver History Abstract Request)* will be provided records with personal information. Signature of the requester is required. Also, if a copy of an application is needed, use *Form DO-11 (Driver License Application Request)*. Both forms call for notarized consent of individual if request does not comply with uses permitted by N.J.S.A. 39-2-3.4(c). Use *Notarized Authorization Form DO-21A*. Forms are found at www.state.nj.us/mvc/About/Forms.htm.

Vehicle Records: There are state forms required if the requester is not an ongoing account. Requests must be submitted on *Form DO-11A* for registration requests, *Form DO-22A* for title requests, and *Form DO-22* for lien searches. Requests must be submitted on the appropriate form which calls for notarized consent of the subject if request does not comply with uses permitted by N.J.S.A. 39-2-3.4(c). If notarization is needed, use *Notarized Authorization Form DO-21A*. Forms are found at www.state.nj.us/mvc/About/Forms.htm.

Vendor and Third Party Access Policy

Approved online vendors may access records for other vendors who represent an end-user authorized under DPPA, unless the secondary vendor has been authorized. See below additional restriction placed on online requesters who are also vendors. New Jersey does not permit the use, storage or resale of records for commercial solicitation for profit or political canvassing or campaigning or any similar purpose.

Records Ordered For Non-permissible Uses

Records are not released to requesters not specifically mentioned in N.J.S.A. 39:2-3.4(c) and who do not present consent. Records without personal information are not released.

Access to Driver-Related Records

Driving Records

General Information and Fees

Motor Vehicle Commission, Abstract Unit, PO 142, Trenton NJ 08666, 609-984-7771 or 609-292-0698.

The fee for a driver history record is $15.00 per look-up for either a certified complete record or certified five-year record. Submit requests using *Form DO-21*. Established accounts pay $12.00 when record is obtained electronically. For the driver's license application information, the fee is also $15.00 per record and use of *Form DO-11* is required. Completed *DO-11* forms and applicable fees are to be mailed to the Certified Information Unit, PO Box 146, Trenton, NJ 08666-0146.

In-Person – Only the five-year driver history abstract of the driver's own record can be processed in-person.

Mail – The state charges for "no record found" reports. Requests mailed to the state are processed within ten-to-fifteen working days. The driver's license number, full name, date of birth, sex, and eye color may all be submitted when requesting a manual record. If the driver's license number is not provided, then the address must be provided along with the full name and date of birth. The driver's address is provided as part of the record. Fee must accompany each request.

Electronic – The MVC offers the Customer Abstract Information Retrieval (CAIR) program for online access of driving records to approved users. Visit www.state.nj.us/mvcbiz/Records/CAIR.htm. The system is only available to those with a permissible use such as insurance companies, bus and truck companies, and highway/parking authorities. Both batch (SFT) and individual (interactive) modes are offered. Records can only be requested by using a driver license number, which will provide a five-year driver history abstract no *name only* searching is offered). Records are $12.00 each and batch requests are processed overnight. Two important items must be noted:

1. Vendor's representing end-user clients with a permissible use, must first submit a client list complete with name, address, phone number, and client's intended use.

2. Vendors or end users may not store the data or create a database for use beyond the initial use.

For more information, call 609-292-4572.

Bulk – The state does not sell its license database, or portions there of.

By Person of Record – New Jersey drivers may order their own record at www.state.nj.us/mvc/Licenses/driver_history_page.htm. The driver must first have a MyMVC Account Number to obtain a User ID number. It will take 7 to 10 days to receive this number, sent by mail. Then to access one must submit their DL number and last 4 digits of the SSN. The fee is $15.00 plus a credit card service fee of $.75 which is required for the online orders. NJ drivers may also order their record in person or by mail. Walk-in requests are processed while the customer waits. Proof of identity is required. Walk-in requests can be made at any of the 43 motor vehicle agencies. Use of the *DO-21 Form* is required and a copy of the DL must be submitted.

Status Check Program

CAIR also provides driver status information to entities such as school transportation providers, vehicle rental companies, and other approved businesses for a fee of $2.00 per inquiry. Account holder may obtain a driver's license expiration date, endorsements, restrictions and class of license, as well as verify whether or not a driver's current license privilege is suspended or is in good standing.

Notification/Monitoring Program

At present, New Jersey does not offer a monitoring system or notification program to track incidents of drivers.

Accident Reports

Reporting – If an accident involves damage in excess of $500.00, injury, death, or if it appears that a driver has been impaired as a result of drug or alcohol use, then the accident must be reported to local police, but not with the Motor Vehicle Division.

Record Access – There are a variety of sources for accident reports, depending on who investigated the accident.

- If the accident was investigated by the New Jersey State Police, contact their Criminal Justice Records Bureau at PO Box 7068, West Trenton NJ 08628-0068, 609-882-2000, ext. 2382. Typical turnaround time is up to 3 weeks. No counter service is offered. New records are ready for inquiry in 2 to 3 weeks. Records are maintained for past 6 years. The drivers' names, date, and location of the incident is required. A report is availableat a cost of $10.00 if 1-5 pages, $16.00 if 6 or more pages. Photographs are $5.00 each for 1-10 photos, additional photos are $3.00 each. Typical turnaround time is three weeks.

- If investigated by local police, contact either the local department (costs will vary) or to obtain a copy of an accident report from the NJ MVC submit a completed DO-21 form, along with a $5.00 fee to the MVC Abstract Unit, PO Box 142, Trenton, NJ 08666-0142.

- If the accident occurred on a toll-road, contact the following: New Jersey Turnpike Authority at 732-442-8600 ext 2908; Garden State Parkway at 732-442-8600 ext.2419; Atlantic City Expressway at 609-965-7200, ext. 108.

Both the Turnpike Authority and Garden State Parkway have contracted with www.buycrash.com for the online purchase of accident reports. The fee is $5.00. Use of a credit card or PayPal is required.

Access to Vehicle-Related Records

General Information and Fees

NJ Motor Vehicle Commission, Certified Information Unit, PO Box 0146, Trenton, NJ 08666, 609-292-4102 or in-state at 888-486-3339.

The NJ Motor Vehicle Commission maintains registration, title, and lien information on all vehicles including mobile homes, and boats. Also, the MVC issues motorboat and Jet Ski licenses for use on fresh, non-tidal waters or lakes, creeks or rivers not affected by tidal conditions. SSNs and medical information are not released. The fee for a record request is $15.00 unless processed online then fee is $12.00.

In-Person – Counter service is not offered.

Mail – The state requires using the appropriate request form when reqesting any of the information described above (DO-11 for registration information, DO-22 for lien information and DO-22A for title information). Turnaround time can take as long as 6 weeks.

All requests for registration records, title histories and lien searches must be submitted through the mail and payment must be in the form of a check or money order (no cash or credit cards are accepted). All records provided will be certified.

Electronic – Online access is available for insurance companies, bus and truck companies, highway/parking authorities, and approved vendors via the same Customer Abstract Information Retrieval (CAIR) program described in the Driving Records section. For details visit www.state.nj.us/mvcbiz/Records/CAIR.htm. The contact information is: New Jersey Motor Vehicle Commission, Business & Government Services, PO Box 122, Trenton, NJ 08666-0122. All records are $12 -

including ownership history.

A user can make any inquiry by simply entering a license plate number, or a vehicle identification number (VIN). Name searching is not offered. The license plate number will provide immediate access to the owner's name, address, vehicle information, expiration date and, leased vehicle status.

The VIN number will produce the mileage, mileage status, owner/lien holder names and addresses and lessee information if the vehicle is leased.

If using the Ownership History option (only available to insurance companies), the New Jersey VIN data will also be provided.

Social Security numbers will never appear through any search option. A completed application must be submitted for service. Two important items must be noted:

1. Vendor's representing end user clients with a permissible use, must first submit a client list complete with name, address, phone number, and client's intended use.
2. Vendors or end users may not store the data or create a database for use beyond the initial use.

Bulk – New Jersey does not sell or otherwise provide its vehicle database for commercial or political solicitation, marketing or campaigning. The state will consider all other requests on an individual basis. The purpose of the request must be put in writing and sent to the office of the Director of Motor Vehicles. New Jersey will "out-source" the programming costs.

Access to Vessel-Related Records

General Information, Access and Fees

The same forms and fees for access to vehicle records apply to vessels. Turnaround time for registration or title information is the same as stated above for vehicle records.

Boats greater than 12 feet in length regardless of propulsion means must

be titled and registered at a MVC Agency. Exception include ship's lifeboat, canoe, kayak, inflatable, surfboard, rowing scull, racing shell, tender/dinghy used for direct transportation between a vessel and shore for no other purposes. Also, registration is waived if used exclusively on small lakes and ponds on private property.).

Driving Record Content and Reciprocity

What's On or Not On the Driving Record

- Non-moving violations (i.e., seat-belt and inspection), SSNs, and medical information are not reported on the driving record.
- Records are available for 5 years for the public, 10 years if a CDL driver; complete history for attorneys.
- New Jersey does have child-restraint and seat-belt laws in effect. Accidents involving death, injury, or property damage in excess of $500.00 are reported on the record; however, fault is not shown.
- The state does not permit driver school attendance in lieu of conviction, but they will deduct up to two points after completion of an MVC approved defensive driving class.
- All records contain the personal information allowable by law. The state does not provide a record w/o personal information.

Data Retention

The length of time convictions are maintained for moving violations is permanently if point-carrying and with subsequent penalties. DWIs and suspension are kept permanently with subsequent penalties. Surrendered

records or no point records with no additional penalties are usually kept for five years. CDL driver records are purged based on the timetable per the MCSIA (see the Appendix).

Court to Repository

Convictions must be submitted to the Department within three days of adjudication in court. New Jersey has converted court violation transfer of data from paper to electronic file transfer. There is no time requirement for entry into database

State Reciprocity for Non-CDL Drivers

- Will suspend license of driver for unpaid out-of-state convictions.
- Record of new incoming driver is not shown on MVR.
- Out-of-state convictions are shown on MVR, but only if moving violation.
- Out-of-state accidents are not shown on MVR.
- Convictions of out-of-state drivers are sent to home state.
- Record is forwarded to new state upon surrender of license upon request.

License Classes, Restrictions, and Endorsements

License Classes– Commercial

New Jersey began issuing the CDL in September of 1991.

Class A   Any combination of vehicles with a GCWR of 26,001 or more pounds, provided the GVWR of the vehicle(s) being towed is in excess of 10,000 pounds.

Class B   Any single vehicle with a GVWR of 26,001 or more pounds; or any such vehicle towing a vehicle not in excess of 10,000 GVWR; or any vehicle with a GVWR of 26,001 pounds and designed to transport sixteen or more passengers (including the driver) whether used for hire or not.

Class C   Any single vehicle with a GVWR of less than 26,001 pounds, or any such vehicle towing a vehicle not in excess of 10,000 pounds GVWR provided that the vehicle is placarded to transport hazardous materials; or the vehicle is designed to transport sixteen or more passengers (including the driver) whether for hire or not; or the vehicle is designed to transport eight to fifteen passengers including the driver and is used for hire; or the vehicle is designed to transport eight to fifteen persons including the driver for hire on a daily basis to and from places of employment; or the vehicle is used for the transportation of more than 6 passengers to or from summer day camps or summer residence camps; or the vehicle is required to be registered as a school bus except that a person licensed as a bus driver on or before 12/31/90 may operate a bus required to be registered as a school bus but without a CDL provided the vehicle is designed to carry not more than passengers including the driver.

License Classes– Non-Commercial

Class D   **Auto** - This class is for all types of motor vehicles, except motorcycles used for non-commercial transportation.

Class E   **Motorcycle** - This class is for vehicles with less than four wheels; motor bikes and scooters included.

Class F   **Moped** - This class is for unlicensed drivers fifteen years and older operating a motorized bicycle.

Class G   **Agricultural** - This class is for farming purposes only and may be granted to persons between sixteen and seventeen years of age. Note that this class is subject to the Graduated Driver License Program.

Class I   **Identification** - This class is for any individual seventeen years of age or older who cannot/do not want to qualify for a driver's license. This identification is valid for four years.

Restrictions

1	Corrective Lenses Required	O	Except Tractor-Trailers (tow trucks only)
2	Prosthetic Device	P	Passenger End: School Bus Capacity 15 Only **
3	Mechanical Device	Q	Except Passenger Vehicles Capacity 16+
4	Hearing Impaired	R	Bus Mechanic (no passengers)
5	Attached Restrictions	S	Except School Age Passengers
K	Intrastate Only *	U	Class I Owner Only (was ID3)
L	To Drive Vehicles with Air-Brakes	V	Class I Violator Only (was ID5)
M	Except Class A Passenger Vehicles	W	Class I Misc (was ID2, ID4, IDx)
N	Except Class A and B Passenger Vehicles		

*   This is a CDLIS restriction code. It will only be used by the New Jersey Classified Licensing System when communicating via CDLIS.

**   This restriction applies to drivers holding a Bus 2 endorsement on or before December 31, 1990. CDL testing was not required for these drivers prior to April 1, 1992. These drivers were issued a Class D (auto) with a "P" endorsement and a "P" restriction.

Endorsements

T	Double- and Triple-Trailer - Class A licenses for vehicles pulling two or three trailers.	L	Needed to drive vehicle with airbrakes
P	Passenger - Buses and/or vans used to transport passengers.	M	Motorcycle
N	Tank vehicle	S	School Bus
H	Hazardous materials	F	Moped

Other Important Codes and Abbreviations on Records

Court Codes (Event Responsibility)

A	Atlantic	R	Passiac
B	Bergen	S	Salem
C	Burlington	T	Somerset
D	Camden	V	Sussex
E	Cape May	W	Union
G	Essex	Y	Warren
H	Gloucester	Z	Foreign State
J	Hudson	X	U.S. Comm Court
K	Hunterdon	01-94	Municipal Court
L	Mercer	95	County Dist Court
M	Middlesex	96	County Court
N	Monmouth	97	Juvenile Court
P	Morris	M-99	Misc Court Rptd Action
Q	Ocean	CRT	Misc Court Rptd Action

Event Responsibility Codes

ACP	Alcohol countermeasures (Health Dept)
CIS	Compulsory insurance/accident reporting
COO	Business license compliance
CON	Conference unit
DIP	Driver improvement program
DMV	Division Director
DRT	Driver testing
DVR	Driver
FAR	Fatal accident review
FRJ	Financial responsibility/judgment
ISS	Insurance surcharge
MFR	Medical fitness review
OAL	Office of Administrative Law Liaison
PDP	Probationary driver program
RES	Restoration authorization
RSU	Reexamination scheduling
SEC	Security responsibility
SUS	Suspension authorization
UCJ	Unsatisfied claims and judgments
UMS	Uninsured Motorist System

Event Type Code

A	Accident Reported by Police (Note: POLC indicates Investigated by Police)
B	Billing
C	Conference
D	Fee Due
E	Reexamination Activity
F	Fee Payment
I	Initial Medical Request
J	Referral
K	Referral with Interval Reporting
L	Limitation
M	Memo Entry
N	Advisory Notice
O	Suspension Order
P	Program Activity
R	Restoration
S	Scheduled Suspension
V	Violation
W	Warning Notice
Z	Point Credit (can also be PC)

Other Abbreviations of Note

CMV "X"	Violation committed in a commercial vehicle
HZM "X"	Violation committed while carrying hazardous materials
FTL "X"	Violation resulted in a fatality
1.	

Violation Event Table with ACD, Codes and Statutes

Note that two tables are presented, followed by the Points System.

2.   The first table is the **Violation Event Table**. Notice "V" at the beginning of each Code.
3.   The second table is the **Order Table**, notice the "O" at the beginning of each Code.

Multiple possibilities of corresponding ACD codes are indicated. The exact ACD Code assigned could depend if the violation occurred in a CMV and/or if Hazardous Materials were involved and /or the level of the BAC.

Code	Event Description	Statute	ACD Code Possibilities
V 0804	Failure To Make Repairs	390080004	E50
V C804	Failure To Make Repairs	390080004	E36, E50
V H804	Failure To Make Repairs	390080004	E50
V 010A	Possession Controlled Dangrs Subst	2C035010A	A33
V 010B	Under Inflnc Controlled Dangrs Subst	2C035010B	A22
V 018F	Stop Pick Up/Discharge On Parkway	1900800018F	F34
V 0310	Unlicensed Driver	390030010	B51, W20
V 0311	Oper MV In Viol Of DL Condi/Restri	390030011	D27, D29
V 0312	Illegal Securing Of Driver License	390030012	D02, D06, D07
V 0320	Constructor Vehicle Exceeding 30 Mp	39003020B	S93
V 0334	Applying For Dr Lic/Reg During Susp	390030034	D02
V 0336	Fail To Notify DMV-Address Change	390030036	D02
V 0337	Falsify Appl Or Sell/Loan ID Doc	390030037	D02
V 0340	Operate While Suspended Or Revoked	390030040	B20, B21, B22, B23, B24, B25, B26
V 0343	Equipment Violation:MVS Regulations	390030043	E01
V 0344	Unsafe Vehicle	390030044	E02, E56, F66
V 0347	Operate Vehicle Without Lights	390030047	E05, E34, E35
V 0348	Improper Visibility/Lights	390030048	E54
V 0349	Vehic Not Equipd W/Approved Headlamps	390030049	E01
V 0353	Spot Lamps Prhibited	390030053	E70
V 0354	Spec Restrictions-Lamps/Warn Lights	390030054	E55
V 0360	Improper Use Of Multi Light Beams	390030060	E54
V 0361	Lamps And Reflectors Required	390030061	E01
V 0366	Maintenance Of Lamps	390030066	E34
V 0367	Defective Brakes Equipment	390030067	E31
V 0367	Defective Brakes Equipment	390030067	E51
V 0370	Improper Muffler	390030070	F66
V 0372	Drive/Move Mtr Veh W/Unsafe Tires	390030072	E37, E57
V 0374	Windshield/Windows Obstructed	390030074	D70
V 0375	Safety Glass/Broken Or Distorted	390030075	F66

Code	Event Description	Statute	ACD Code Possibilities
V 0376	Dangerous Exhaust Gases	390030076	F66
V 0377	Selling/Using-Unapproved Equipment	390030077	E70
V 0380	Improper Or Not Equip Approved Tire	390030080	E37
V 039B	App/Renewal DL Street Address	390030009B	D02
V 0435	Fail Allow Pedestrian Complete Cross	390040035	N08
V 0436	Failure Yield Rt Way To Pedestrian	390040036	N08
V 0440	Improper Passing Of Street Car	390040040	M70
V 0441	Driving Through Safety Zone Prohibi	390040041	M12
V 0446	No Name/Place Owner-Commercial Vehi	390040046	E01
V 0448	Use Motor Veh Without Owner Consent	390040048	D78, U21
V 0449	Tampering With Vehicle	390040049	E70
V 0450	Operate Under Influence Liq/Drugs	39004050A	A08, A10, A20, A21, A23
V 0452	Racing On Highway	390040052	S95
V 0455	Improper Act Steep Grades Or Curves	390040055	N80
V 0456	Delaying Traffic	390040056	F34
V 0457	Failure To Comply Police Instruction	390040057	M08, M13, U02
V 0458	Dri Veh W View Side/Rear Obstructed	390040058	D70
V 0467	Obstructing Passage Of Other Vehicle	390040067	F34
V 0471	Improper Driving On Sidewalk	390040071	M58
V 0480	Disregard Officer Directing Traffic	390040080	M04
V 0481	Fail To Observe Traff Cntrl Device	390040081	M14, M16
V 0481	Disregard Stop Sign Regulations	390040081	M17
V 0482	Failure To Keep Right	390040082	M41
V 0483	Failure To Keep Right-Intersection	390040083	N25
V 0484	Fail To Pass Right Proc In Oppos Di	390040084	M70
V 0485	Improper Passing	390040085	M70, M71, M72, M73, M74, M76, M77
V 0486	Improper Pass/Cross No Pass Line	390040086	M70
V 0487	Fail To Give Way To Overtaking Vehicle	390040087	N07
V 0488	Improper Oper-Hwys W/Marked Lanes	39004008800	M42
V 0489	Following Too Closely	390040089	M34
V 0490	Failure To Yield Right Of Way	390040090	M19, N01, N02, N03, N06, N20, N21, N22, N23, N24, N26, N30, N31
V 0491	Failure Yield To Emergency Vehicle	390040091	N04
V 0492	Fail Stop/Yield To Emergency Vehicle	390040092	N04
V 0493	Failure To Yield To Procession	390040093	N05
V 0496	Reckless Driving	390040096	M84
V 0497	Careless Driving	390040097	D72, D74, M25, M80, M81, M82, M83, S94, S97
V 049C	Failure Yield To Emergency Vehicle	390040091	N04
V 049H	Failure Yield To Emergency Vehicle	390040091	N04
V 0530	Susp/Revoke Dl-Reciprocity	390050030	B26
V 0535	Failure Surrender Susp License Cert		W09
V 0540	Trailer-Improper Equip,Towing,Etc.	390040054	E01
V 0541	Poss/Cons Alc Bev By Minor In Mv	2a1700054001	A31
V 05C1	Racing On Highway	3905c0001	S95
V 06B2	No Liability Insurance On Mtr Veh	3906b0002	D36
V 0804	Failure To Make Repairs	390080004	E36
V 0804	Failure To Make Repairs	390080004	E50
V 0806	Fail To Display-Approval Certificate	390080006	B65
V 1011	Violation With A Fatality In CMV	390030010110	U31
V 1013	Commercial Oper Under Infl Liq/Drug	390030010130	A04, A11, A20
V 1018	Operate CMV While Com Priv Suspend	39003001018b	B20, B21, B22, B23, B24, B25, B26
V 1019	Fail To Pay Toll On Turnpike	190090001019	D35
V 101D	Felony In Non-Cmv/Ctrld Dangr Subst	39003001011d	A50
V 1020	Felony In A Commercial Motor Vehicle	390030010200	U03
V 1024	Commercial Refusal Of Alcohol Test	390030010240	A12
V 1026	Oper Com Veh Restricted To One Lic	39003001026	D02
V 102E	Felony In CMV/Controlled Dang Substa	39003001020e	A50
V 10A1	Possess Cds Sched I,II,III or Iv	2c03510a1	A33
V 10A4	Possession 50grs Or Less Marijuana	2c03510a4	A33
V 10A6	Violation With Fatality In Non-CMV	390031020a6	U31
V 10J4	Felony In A Non-Commercial Vehicle	390031020j4	U03
V 1151	Leave Scene Accident - Death	2c0110005001	B02, B06
V 118A	Operate CMV Without A CDL	39003001018a	B56, W20
V 120A	Possession Of Narcotic Drugs	24021002000a	A33
V 120B	Under Influence Of Narcotic Drug	24021002000b	A22

Code	Event Description	Statute	ACD Code Possibilities
V 121B	Aggravated Assault	2c012001b001	U06
V 1271	Improper Crossing Railroad Grade	390040127001	M10
V 1272	Failure Comply With Signal On Bridge	390040127002	M18
V 1281	Passing Stopped School Bus	390040128001	M75, N09
V 1284	No Stop/Improper Passg Dessert Trk	390040128004	M70
V 1292	Fail To Reveal Identity After Accident	390040129c2	B14
V 129A	Leave Scene Accident-Personal Injury	39004012900a	B03, B07
V 129B	Leave Scene Accident-Property Damage	39004012900b	B04, B08
V 129C	Fail To Give Info/AID After Accident	39004012900c	B01, B05,
V 129D	Leave Scene Accident-Unattended Prop	39004012900d	B08
V 12A2	Speeding	19009000102a	S92
V 12A4	Speeding	19009000102a	S92
V 12A5	Speeding	19009000102a	S92
V 12B2	Speeding	19009000102b	S92
V 12B4	Speeding	19009000102b	S92
V 12B5	Speeding	19009000102b	S92
V 12C2	Speeding	19009000102c	S92
V 143E	No Insurance-Moped	39004001403e	D36
V 143G	Driving Under Influence On A Moped	39004001403g	A20
V 143Q	Operate Moped-No Helmet	39004001403q	F03
V 19A1	Possess CDS W/Intent To Distribute	2402119a1	A33
V 20A1	Possess Controlled Dangerous Subst	2402120a1	A33
V 2118	Possess CD$ Not In Orig Container	240210018	A35
V 2121	Counterfeit/Fraudulent DL/ID	2C00210002001	B41
V 2121	Counterfeit/Fraudulent DL/ID	2C0210002001	D10, D16
V 212C	Counterfeit/Fraudulent DL/ID	2C00210002001	B41
V 212C	Counterfeit/Fraudulent DL/ID	2C0210002001	D10, D16
V 212H	Counterfeit/Fraudulent DL/ID	2C00210002001	B41
V 212H	Counterfeit/Fraudulent DL/ID	2C0210002001	D10, D16
V 2147	Possess Drug Paraphernalia	240210047	A33
V 2151	Possess Hypodermic Syringe/Needle	24021051c	A33
V 2910	Moving Against Traffic Tpk/Pkwy/Exw	270230029000	N60
V 2920	Illegal Use Of Medial Strip	270230029001	M11
V 2930	Vehicle In Hazardous Condition	270230029002	F66
V 2940	Use Of Improper Lane	270230029003	M42
V 2950	U Turn Prohibited	270230029004	N56
V 2962	Speeding	270230029	S92
V 2964	Speeding	270230029	S92
V 2965	Speeding	270230029	S92
V 3101	Special Bus Driver License Noncompl	390030010001	B51
V 3104	Physicians/Specialists Report Reco		W15
V 3105	Fail To Notify DMV/Seizure Disorder	390030010005	D75
V 3105	Fail To Notify DMV/Seizure Disorder	390030010005	W14
V 3111	Improper Use Agricultural License	390030011001	D29
V 3130	Regular Learner Permit Noncomplianc	390030013	B51
V 3191	Trans Pass For Hire W/O Omnibus Reg	390030019001	B51
V 3261	Operate Under Influence Liq/Drugs	270230026	A20
V 3262	Careless Driving	270230026001	M81
V 3298	Misuse Of Identification Cards	390030029008	D02
V 3315	Possess/Consume Alc Bev-Underage	2c0330015	A31
V 333K	Vehicle In Hazardous Condition	0a003000303k	E71
V 339A	Loaning Driver License	39003039a	D02
V 340C	Allowing Susp Driver To Operate Veh	3900300401c	B26
V 340H	Allowing Susp Driver To Operate Veh	39003040h	B26
V 340I	Driving While Revoked Prk Tickets	39003040i	B26
V 3602	Use Or Possess Drug Paraphernalia	2c0360002	A33
V 3606	Possess Hypodermic Syringe/Needle	2c0360006	A33
V 3702	Emission Of Smoke Or Contaminants	390030070002	F66
V 371A	Loaning Driver License	3900300371a	D02
V 371B	Allow Unlicensed Driver To Operate	3900300371b	D02
V 3762	No Child Restraint System	390030076 2a	F02
V 3767	Operate/Ride Motorcycle-No Helmet	390030076007	F03
V 3B25	Cell Phone While Oper A School Bus	3903b0025	M86
V 3B54	Operation School W/O Proper Equiptm	3903b0005004	E06
V 3C20	No Liability Insur-Snowmobile/Atv	3903c0020	D36
V 4100	Speeding Across Sidewalk	390040100	S93

Code	Event Description	Statute	ACD Code Possibilities
V 4102	Speeding By A Physician	390040102	S93
V 4105	Impr Oper At Intersect Traf Signal	390040105000	M16
V 4115	Improper Turn Traffic Control Signal	390040115	M16
V 4116	Improper Turn Green Arrow Traf Cntr	390040116	M16
V 4117	Failure Observe Pedestrian Interval	390040117	N08
V 4119	Failure Stop Flashing Red Signal	390040119	M18
V 4122	Failure To Stop For Police Whistle	390040122	M08
V 4123	Improper Right And Left Turns	390040123	N53, N54
V 4124	Improper Turn Marked Course	390040124	N50, N51, N52, N55
V 4125	U Turn Prohibited	390040125	N56
V 4126	Failure To Give Proper Signal	390040126	N40, N41, N42, N43, N44
V 4127	Illegal Backing/Turning In Street	390040127	N82
V 4128	Failure To Stop At Railroad Crossing	390040128	M09
V 4129	Fail To Obey Traffic Control Dev	390040120009	M14
V 4130	Failure To Report Accident	390040130	B61
V 4144	Disregard Of Stop Sign Regulations	390040144	M15
V 4145	Fail Yield Line Vehicle Through St	390040145	M19
V 4215	Failure To Obey Directional Signals	390040215	M16
V 436A	Failure Yield Right Way To Driver	39004036a	N01
V 4371	Failure To Yield To Blind Person	390040037001	N08
V 4491	Operate MV While In Poss Of Narcotics	390040049001	A33
V 4501	Chemical Analysis-Presumtion	390040050001	A20
V 4504	Refusal To Submit To Chemical Test	39004005004a	A12
V 450B	Operating While Impaired	39004050b	A25
V 450G	Oper Under Influence School Zone	390040050g	A20
V 4515	DWI With Minor Passenger	39004005015b	A20
V 4519	Failure To Install Interlock Device	390040050019	A41
V 451A	Consuming Alco Bev Oper/Pass In Mv	39004051a	A26
V 451B	Open Container In A Motor Vehicle	39004051b	A35
V 45G1	DWI:1000 Ft On Or Near School Grounds	390040050g1	A20
V 45G2	DWI:Driving Though School Crossing	390040050g2	A20
V 45G3	DWI:Driving With Juveniles Near Cro	390040050g3	A20
V 4661	Improper Entering Or Leaving Highway	390040066001	M25
V 4662	Avoiding A Traffic Control Signal	390040066002	M14
V 4771	Snow/Ice Dislodged From Moving Veh	3900400771	F66
V 4821	Improper Use Of Divided Highway	390040082001	N62, N71
V 4851	Wrong Way On One Way Street	390040085001	N63
V 488A	Improper Oper Highway W/Mark Lanes	39004008800a	M05, M11, M40, M41, M43, M44, M45, M46, M47, M48, M49, M50, M51, M55, M56, M57, M60, M61, M62
V 489A	Following Unlawfully Or Improperly	39004008900a	M30. M31, M32, M33
V 4901	Failure To Use Proper Entrance/Exit	390040090001	M25
V 4942	Disregard Of Posted Notice/Barricade	390040094 2b	M02, M03
V 4942	Disregard Of Posted Notice/Barricade	390040094 2b	M03
V 4971	Operate At Slow Speed/Block Traffic	390040097001	S96
V 4972	Careless Driving	3900400972	F06,N83
V 4973	Using Hand Held Cell While Driving	39004009703	M85,M86
V 4982	Speeding	390040098	S01, S06, S51, S92
V 4984	Speeding	390040098	S15, S16, S21, S26, S71, S92
V 4985	Speeding	390040098	S15, S26, S31, S36, S41, S71, S81, S91, S92
V 4992	Exceeding Speed Limitations	390040099	S92
V 4994	Exceeding Speed Limitations	390040099	S92
V 5014	Driving After Underage Drinking	39004005014	A60, A61
V 5B29	Failure To Use Hazmat Safety Device	3905b0029	E53
V 5B32	Oper Interstate W/O Hazmat Placard	3905b0032	E03, E04
V 5D41	DWI Administrative Per Se .10 BAC	39005d4.10	A90, A91
V 5D44	DWI Administrative Per Se .04 BAC	39003005d4.04	A91, A94
V 5D48	DWI Administrative Per Se .08 BAC	39005d4.08	A91, A98
V 6A15	Insurance Fraud	3906a0015	D36
V 6B01	Liability Insurance Of Coverage	39006b001	B64
V 762F	Failure To Wear Seat Belt	3900300762f	F04
V 762F	Failure To Wear Seat Belt	3900300762f	F05
V 8113	Fail To Observe Traffic Control Device	190080001013	M16
V 8122	Speeding	190080001002	S92
V 8124	Speeding	190080001002	S92
V 8125	Speeding	190080001002	S92

Code	Event Description	Statute	ACD Code Possibilities
V 815A	Failure To Keep Right	19008000105a	M41
V 815B	Improper Passing	19008000105b	M70
V 819A	Illegal Entry Onto The Parkway	190080001 9a	M25
V 9116	Consume Intox Beverage On Turnpike	190090001016	A26
V 9122	Speeding	190090001002	S92
V 9124	Speeding	190090001002	S92
V 9125	Speeding	190090001002	S92
V 913C	Fail To Obey Traffic Cntrl Device	19009000103c	M16
V 9140	Tpk-Uniform Direction Traffic	190090001 04	N60
V 914A	Moving Against Traffic	19009000104a	N60, N61, N70, N72
V 914B	Use of Proper Lane	19009000104b	M42
V 972G	Unsafe Operation - Cell Phone	3900400972.G	N84
V 9813	Retarding Traffic	190080001003	F34
V 9814	Moving Against Traffic Tpk/Pkwy/Exw	190080001004	N60
V 9815	Improper Passing	190080001005	M70
V 9816	U Turn Prohibited	190080001006	N56
V 9817	Illegal Use Of Medial Strip	190080001007	M11
V 9819	Vehicle In Hazardous Condition	1908800019b6	E33
V 9824	Gsp-Parade,Demonstration Prohibited	190080002004	F34
V 9829	Gsp-Obstruction/Interference	190080002009	F34
V 9831	Refuse To Pay/Evade Toll Payment	190080003001	D35
V 9915	U Turn Prohibited	190090001005	N56
V A011	Operate At Slow Speed/Block Traffic	0a0010001002	S96
V A112	Speeding	0a0010001001	S92
V A114	Speeding	0a0010001001	S92
V A115	Speeding	0a0010001001	S92
V A222	Illegal Backing Or Turning In Street	0a0020002002	N82
V A223	Improper Passing	0a0020002003	M70
V A224	Improper Use Of Divided Highway	0a0020002004	M11
V A225	Illegal Use Of Medial Strip	0a0020002005	M41
V A227	Failure To Use Proper Entrance/Exit	0a0020002007	M25
V AB33	Purchase Alcoholic Beverage-Underage	330010081	A31
V C014	Driving After Underage Drinking	39004005014	A60
V C046	Obstruct Passage Vehicle	390040067	F34
V C053	Leaving Vehicle With Engine Running	390040053	N84
V C104	Physicians/Specialists Report Reco		W15
V C105	Fail To Notify DMV/Seizure Disorder	390030010005	D75, W14
V C114	Aggravated Assault By Auto	2c0110004	U31
V C115	Vehicular Homicide	2c0110005	U07, U08, U09, U10
V C119	Failure Stop Flashing Red Signal	390040119	M18
V C121	Assault By Auto	2c012001c	U06
V C124	Speeding In A Commercial Vehicle	190080001002	S92
V C125	Speeding In A Commercial Vehicle	190080001002	S92
V C126	Failure To Give Proper Signal	390040126	N40, N41, N42, N53, N44
V C127	Illegal Backing/Turning In Street	390040127	N82
V C129	Fail To Reveal Identity After Accident	39004012902c	B14
V C12C	Assault By Auto	2c012001c	U06
V C12H	Assault By Auto	2c012001c	U06
V C130	Failure To Report Accident	390040130	B61
V C144	Disregard Of Stop Sign Regulations	390040144	M15
V C14A	Moving Against Traffic	19009000104a	N60, N61, N70, N72
V C14B	Use Of Improp Lane In Commerc Vehicle	19009000104b	M42
V C15B	Improper Passing	19008000105b	M70
V C19A	Oper Snowmbl/Atv Without Helmet	3903c019a	F03
V C1A3	Vehicular Homicide In A CMV	390031020a3	U07, U08, U09, U10
V C202	Automobile Theft	2c0200002	D78
V C20B	Under Influence Of Narcotic Drug	24021002000b	A24
V C215	Failure To Obey Directional Signals	390040215	M16
V C222	Illegal Backing Or Turning In Street	0a0020002002	N82
V C223	Improper Passing	0a0020002003	M70
V C24C	Improper Turn Marked Course	380040124	N50, N51, N52, N55
V C281	Passing Stopped School Bus	390040128001	M75, N09
V C291	Interfering With An Officer	2c0290001	M08
V C292	Fleeing/Eluding An Officer	2c0290002	U01
V C29A	Leave Scene Accident-Pers Inj-Com Veh	39004012900a	B03, B07
V C29B	Leave Scene Accd-Prop Dam-Comm Vehi	39004012900b	B04, B08

Code	Event Description	Statute	ACD Code Possibilities
V C29C	Fail To Give Info/AID After Accident	39004012900c	B01, B05,
V C29D	Leave Scene AccID Unatten Prop/CMV	39004012900d	B08
V C2A4	Speeding In A Commercial Vehicle	19009000102a	S92
V C2A5	Speeding In A Commercial Vehicle	19009000102a	S92
V C2B4	Speeding In A Commercial Vehicle	19009000102b	S92
V C2B5	Speeding In A Commercial Vehicle	19009000102b	S92
V C311	Oper MV In Viol Of DL Condi/Restrict	390030011	D27, D29
V C312	Illegal Securing Of Driver License	390030012	D02, D06, D07
V C33K	Vehicle In Hazardous Condition	0a003000303k	E71
V C343	Equipment Violation:MVS Regulations	390030043	E01
V C344	Unsafe Vehicle	390030044	E02, E56, F66
V C347	Operate Vehicle Without Lights	390030047	E05, E34, E55
V C367	Defective Brakes Equipment	390030067	E31, E51
V C372	Drive/Move Mtr Veh W/Unsafe Tires	390030072	E37, E57
V C374	Windshield/Windows Obstructed	390030074	D70
V C376	Dangerous Exhaust Gases	390030076	F66
V C411	Improper Turn Traffic Control Signa	390040115	M16
V C43Q	Operate Moped-No Helmet	39004001403q	F03
V C448	Use Motor Veh Without Owner Consent	390040048	D78, U21
V C450	Oper Under Influence/Commer Vehicle	39004050a	A08, A10, A11, A20, A21, A23
V C451	Consuming Alco Bev Oper/Pass In MV	39004051a	A26
V C454	Refusal To Submit To Chem Test/CMV	39004005004a	A12
V C455	Improper Act Steep Grades Or Curves	390040055	N80
V C457	Failure To Comply Police Instruction	390040051	M08, M13, U02
V C467	Obstructing Passage Of Other Vehicle	390040067	F34
V C481	Fail To Observe Traff Cntrl Device	390040081	M14, M16
V C481	Disregard of Stop Sign Regulations	390040081	M17
V C484	Fail To Pass Right Proc In Oppos Di	390040084	M70
V C485	Improper Passing	390040085	M70, M71, M72, M73, M74, M76, M77
V C486	Improper Pass/Cross No Pass Line	390040086	M70
V C488	Improp Oper-Hwys W/Marked Lane-CMV	39004008800	M42
V C489	Following Too Close In Commerc Vehicle	390040089	M34
V C48A	Improper Oper Highway W/Mark Lanes	39004008800a	M05, M11, M40, M41, M43, M44, M45, M46, M47, M48, M49, M50, M51, M55, M56, M57, M60, M61, M62
V C490	Fail To Yield Right Of Way	390040090	M19, N01, N02, N03, N06, N20, N21, N22, N23, N24, N26, N30, N31
V C491	Operate MV While In Poss Of Narcoti	390040049001	A33
V C494	Speeding In A Commercial Vehicle	390040099	S92
V C495	Improper Passing	390040085	M70
V C496	Reckless Driving In A Commercial Vehicle	390040096	M84
V C497	Careless Driving In A Commercial Vehicle	390040097	D72, D74, M25, M80, M81, M82, M83, S94, S97
V C501	Driving After Underage Drinking	39004005014	A60, A61
V C50B	Operating While Impaired	39004050b	A25
V C519	Failure To Install Interlock Device	390040050019	A41
V C51B	Open Container In A Motor Vehicle	39004051b	A35
V C535	Failure Surrender Susp License Cert		W09
V C541	Poss/Cons Alc Bev By Minor In MV	2a1700054001	A31
V C5C1	Racing On Highway	3905c0001	S95
V C62F	Failure To Waer Seat Belt	3900300762f	F04, F05
V C661	Improper Entering Or Leaving Highway	390040066001	M25
V C762	No Child Restraint System	3900300762a	F02
V C767	Operate/Ride Motorcycle-No Helmet	390030076007	F03
V C806	Fail To Display-Approval Certificate	390080006	B65
V C813	Retarding Traffic	190080001003	F34
V C815	Improper Passing	190080001005	M70
V C819	Vehicle In Hazardous Condition	1900800019b6	F66. N62
V C821	Improper Use Of Divided Highway	390040082001	N71
V C831	Refuse To Pay/Evade Toll Payment	190080003001	D35
V C851	Wrong Way On One Way Street	390040085001	N63
V C89A	Following Unlawfully Or Improperly	39004008900a	M30, M31, M32, M33
V C924	Speeding In A Commercial Vehicle	190090001002	S92
V C925	Speeding In A Commercial Vehicle	190090001002	S92
V C930	Vehicle In Hazardous Condition	270230029002	F66
V C940	Use Of Improper Lane In Commerc Vehicle	270230029003	M42

Code	Event Description	Statute	ACD Code Possibilities
V C942	Disregard Of Posted Notice/Barricade	3900400942b	M02
V C942	Disregard Of Posted Notice/Barricade	3900400942b	M03
V C964	Speeding In A Commercial Vehicle	270230029	S92
V C965	Speeding In A Commercial Vehicle	270230029	S92
V C971	Operate At Slow Speed/Block Traffic	390040097001	S96
V C972	Unsafe Operation Of A Motor Vehicle	3900400972	N84
V C972	Careless Driving in a Commercial Vehicle	3900400972	F06, N83
V C981	Failure To Wear Seat Belt	1900800019b6	F04
V C982	Speeding	390040098	S01, S06, S51, S92
V C982	Speeding In A Commercial Vehicle	390040098	S92
V C984	Speeding In A Commercial Vehicle	390040098	S15, S16, S21, S26, S71, S92
V C985	Speeding In A Commercial Vehicle	390040098	S15, S26, S31, S36, S41, S71, S81, S91, S92
V CA14	Speeding In A Commercial Vehicle	0a0010001001	S92
V CA15	Speeding In A Commercial Vehicle	0a0010001001	S92
V CA21	Operate CMV - CDL Not In Possession	390031018.A21	B57
V CA22	Operate CMV- Wrong CDL Class/Endors	390031018a22	B91
V CB01	Liability Insurance Of Coverage	39006b001	B64, D36
V CB54	Operation School W/O Proper Equipment	3903b0005004	E06
V CCDS	Under Influ Control Dang Subs/CMV	39003001013a	A22
V CD41	DWI Administrative Per Se .10 BAC	39005d4.10	A90, A91
V CD48	DWI Administrative Per Se .08 BAC	39005d4.08	A91, A98
V CLRN	Fail To Obey Rr Under Clearance	390040128024	M24
V COOS	Driving Com Veh While Out Of Service	390031018b1	B27
V D143	Unlicensed Moped Operator	3900400143.D	B51
V FRRS	Failure To Stop At Railroad Cross	493830051	M21
V H011	Violation With A Fatality In Cmv	390030010110	U31
V H020	Felony With Hazardous Material	390030010200	U03
V H02E	Felony In Hazmat/Contrld Dangr Subs	39003001020e	A50
V H104	Physicians/Specialists Report Reco		W15
V H105	Fail To Notify DMV/Seizure Disorder	390030010005	D75
V H105	Fail To Notify DMV/Seizure Disorder	390030010005	W14
V H113	Oper Under Infl Liq/Drugs-Haz/Mat	390030010130	A04, A11, A20
V H126	Failure To Give Proper Signal	390040126	N40, N41, N42, N43, N44
V H127	Illegal Backing/Turning In Street	390040127	N82
V H129	Fail To Reveal Identity After Accident	3900401290c2	B14
V H130	Failure To Report Accident	390040130	B61
V H1A3	Vehicular Homicide In A Hazmat	390031020a3	U07, U08, U09, U10
V H20B	Operate Hazmat While Com Priv Suspd	39003001020b	B20, B21, B22, B23, B24, B25, B26
V H24C	Improper Turn Marked Course	390040124	N50, N51, N52, N55
V H281	Passing Stopped School Bus	390040128001	M75, N09
V H29A	Leave Scene Accd-Persnl Injur/Hazmat	39004012900a	B03, B07
V H29B	Leave Scene Accd-Prop Damage/Hazmat	39004012900b	B04, B08
V H29C	Fail To Give Info/AID After Accident	39004012900c	B01, B05,
V H29D	Leave Scene AccID Unat Prop/Hazmat	39004012900d	B08
V H311	Oper MV In Viol Of DL Condi/Restri	390030011	D27, D29
V H312	Illegal Securing Of Driver License	390030012	D02, D06, D07
V H344	Unsafe Vehicle	390030044	E02, E56, F66
V H347	Operate Vehicle Without Lights	390030047	E05, E34, E55
V H367	Defective Brakes Equipments	390030067	E31, E51
V H372	Drive/Move Mtr Veh W/Unsafe Tires	390030072	E37, E57
V H374	Windshield/Windows Obstructed	390030074	D70
V H448	Use Motor Veh Without Owner Consent	390040048	D78, U21
V H450	Oper Under Influence/Hazard Material	39004050a	A08, A10, A11, A20, A21, A23
V H454	Refusal To Submit Chem Test/Hazmat	39004005004a	A12
V H455	Improper Act Steep Grades Or Curves	390040055	N80
V H457	Failure To Comply Police Instruction	390040057	M08, M13, U02
V H485	Improper Passing	390040085	M70, M71, M72, M73, M74, M76, M77
V H486	Improper Pass/Cross No Pass Line	390040086	M70
V H489	Following Too Close In Commerc Vehicle	390040089	M34
V H48A	Improper Oper Highway W/Mark Lanes	39004008800a	M05, M11, M40, M41, M43, M44, M45, M46, M47, M48, M49, M50, M51, M55, M56, M57, M60, M61, M62
V H490	Failure To Yield Right Of Way	390040090	M19, N01, N02, N03, N06, N20, N21, N22, N23, N24, N26, N30, N31
V H494	Speeding In A Commercial Vehicle	390040099	S92
V H496	Reckless Driving In A Commercial Vehicle	390040096	M84

Code	Event Description	Statute	ACD Code Possibilities
V H497	Careless Driving In A Commercial Vehicle	390040097	D72, D74, F06, M25, M80, M81, M82, M83, S94, S97
V H519	Failure To Install Interlock Device	390040050019	A41
V H535	Failure Surrender Susp License Cert		W09
V H5C1	Racing On Highway	3905c0001	S95
V H661	Improper Entering Or Leaving Highway	390040066001	M25
V H804	Failure To Make Repairs	390080004	E36, E50
V H806	Fail To Display-Approval Certificate	390080006	B65
V H821	Improper Use Of Divided Highway	390040082001	N62, N71
V H831	Refuse To Pay/Evade Toll Payment	190080003001	D35
V H851	Wrong Way On One Way Street	390040085001	N63
V H89A	Following Unlawfully Or Improperly	39004008900a	M30, M31, M32, M33
V H942	Disregard Of Posted Notice/Barricade	3900400942b	M02, M03
V H971	Operate At Slow Speed/Block Traffic	390040097001	S96
V H972	Unsafe Operation Of A Motor Vehicle	3900400972	N84
V H972	Careless Driving in a Commercial Vehicle	3900400972	F06, N83
V H984	Speeding In A Commercial Vehicle	390040098	S15, S16, S21, S26, S71, S92
V H985	Speeding In A Commercial Vehicle	390040098	S15, S26, S31, S36, S41, S71, S81, S91, S92
V HA21	Operate CMV - CDL Not In Possession	390031018.A21	B57
V HA22	Operate Cmv- Wrong CDL Class/Endors	390031018a22	B91
V HB01	Liability Insurance Of Coverage	39006b001	B64
V HB54	Operation School W/O Proper Equipment	3903b0005004	E06
V HCDS	Under Influ Contrl Dang Sub/Hazmat	39003001013b	A22
V IBTG	Illegal Backing/Turning In Street	111111111111	N82
V IUEE	Failure To Use Proper Entrance/Exit	111111111111	M25
V IUMS	Illegal Use Of Medial Strips	111111111111	M11
V NSTP	Failure To Obey Railroad Stop	390040128021	M21
V OSHM	Commercial Out Of Service Hazmat	390031018b2	B19
V RRCL	Fail Under Clr For RR Crossing	493830051	M24
V RRCR	Fail To Make Required RR Stop	493830051	M22
V RRDR	Fail To Make Required RR Stop	493830051	M22
V RRDR	Fail to Obey Stop RR Cross-Required	390040128022	M22
V RRRC	Failure To Obey RR Crossing Restri	390040128	M09
V RRRG	Failure To Obey Railroad Gates/Sig	390040128010	M10
V RRSL	Failure To Slow Down At RR Crossing	390040128020	M20
V RRXV	Failure To Obey RR Crossing Restric	390040128009	M09
V RSPA	Fail To Make Space RR Stop	493830051	M23
V SLRR	Fail Rr Cross To Slow	493830051	M20
V SPED	Speeding	111111111110	S93, S98
V SPRR	Fail To Obey RR Space Stopping	390040128023	M23
V SSBT	Operate At Slow Speed/Block Traffic	111111111111	S96
V T113	Transferred Comerc Oper Und Influe		A20
V TC45	Transferred Oper Und Influence/CMV		A20
V TC54	Transferred Refusal Chem Test/CMV		A12
V TH13	Transferred Oper Under Influ/Hazmat		A20
V TH45	Transferred Oper Under Infl/Hazmat		A20
V TH54	Transferred Refusal Chem Test/Hazmat		A12
V UNRR	Fail Rr Clearance Undercarriage	493830051	M24
V UTRN	U Turn Prohibited	111111111111	N56
V VIHC	Vehicle Hazardous Condition	111111111111	F66

New Jersey Order Table with ACD

Note: "Cds" refers to Controlled Dangerous Substance.

Event Code	Event Description	ACD Code
O 0059	Begging Rides	W00
O 010A	Possession Controlled Dangrs Subst	A33
O 010B	Under Inflnc Controlled Dangrs Subst	A22
O 018F	Stop Pick Up/Discharge On Parkway	F34
O 0304	Unregistered Motor Vehicle	W00
O 0311	Oper MV In Viol Of DL Condi/Restri	D27, D29
O 0312	Illegal Securing Of Driver License	D02, D06, D07
O 0313	Parental Consent Withdrawn	W13
O 0320	Constructor Vehicle Exceeding 30 Mp	S93
O 0329	No Lic,Reg Or Ins ID In Possession	W00
O 0330	Improper Transfer/Destruction Of MV	W00
O 0332	Defaced Plates	W00
O 0333	Improper Display/Fictitious Plates	W00
O 0334	Applying For Dr Lic/Reg During Susp	D02
O 0336	Fail To Notify DMV-Address Change	D02
O 0337	Falsify Appl Or Sell/Loan ID Doc	D02
O 0338	Use Of Counterfeit Plate Or Marker	W00
O 0340	Operate While Suspended Or Revoked	B26
O 0343	Equipment Violation: MVS Regulations	E01
O 0344	Unsafe Vehicle	E02, E56, F66
O 0347	Operate Vehicle Without Lights	E05, E55
O 0348	Improper Visibility/Lights	E54
O 0349	Vehicle Not Equipped W/Approved Headlamps	E01
O 0353	Spot Lamps Prohibited	E70
O 0354	Spec Restrictions-Lamps/Warn Lights	E55
O 035C	Vehicle With Improper Light Color	W00
O 0360	Improper Use Of Multi Light Beams	E54
O 0361	Lamps And Reflectors Required	E01
O 0366	Maintenance Of Lamps	E34
O 0367	Defective Brakes Equipment	E31, E51
O 0370	Improper Muffler	F66
O 0372	Drive/Move Mtr Veh W/Unsafe Tires	E37, E57
O 0374	Windshield/Windows Obstructed	D70
O 0375	Safety Glass/Broken Or Distorted	F66
O 0376	Dangerous Exhaust Gases	F66
O 0377	Selling/Using-Unapproved Equipment	E70
O 0380	Improper Or Not Equip Approved Tire	E37
O 039B	App/Renewal DL Street Address	D02
O 0435	Fail Allow Pedestrian Complete Cros	N08
O 0436	Failure Yield Rt Way To Pedestrian	N08
O 0440	Improper Passing Of Street Car	M70
O 0441	Driving Through Safety Zone Prohibi	M12
O 0446	No Name/Place Owner-Commercial Vehicle	E01
O 0448	Use Motor Veh Without Owner Consent	D78, U21
O 0449	Tampering With Vehicle	E70
O 0450	Operate Under Influence Liq/Drugs	A08, A10, A11, A20, A21, A23
O 0452	Racing On Highway	S95
O 0455	Improper Act Steep Grades Or Curves	N80
O 0456	Delaying Traffic	F34
O 0457	Failure To Comply Police Instruction	M08, M13, U02
O 0458	Dri Veh W/View Side/Rear Obstructed	D70
O 0467	Obstructing Passage Of Other Vehicle	F34
O 0471	Improper Driving On Sidewalk	M58
O 0480	Disregard Officer Directing Traffic	M04
O 0481	Fail To Observe Traffic Control Dev	M14, M16
O 0481	Disregard of Stop Sign Regulations	M17
O 0482	Failure To Keep Right	M41
O 0483	Failure To Keep Right - Intersection	N25
O 0484	Fail To Pass Right Proc In Oppos Di	M70
O 0485	Improper Passing	M70, M71, M72, M73, M74, M76, M77
O 0486	Imp Passing/Crossing No Passing Lin	M70
O 0487	Fail To Give Way To Overtaking Vehicle	N07
O 0488	Improper Oper-Hwys W/Marked Lanes	M42

Event Code	Event Description	ACD Code
O 0489	Following Too Closely	M34
O 0490	Failure To Yield Right Of Way	M19, N01, N02, N03, N06, N20, N21, N22, N23, N24, N26, N30, N31
O 0491	Failure Yield To Emergency Vehicles	N04
O 0492	Fail Stop/Yield To Emergency Vehicle	N04
O 0493	Failure To Yield To Procession	N05
O 0496	Careless Driving	M80, M84
O 0496	Reckless Driving	M84
O 0497	Careless Driving	D72, D74, M25, M81, M82, M83, N83, S94, S97
O 049C	Failure Yield To Emergency Vehicles	N04
O 049H	Failure Yield To Emergency Vehicles	N04
O 0530	Susp/Revoke Dl-Reciprocity	B26
O 0535	Failure Surrender Susp License Cert	W09
O 0540	Trailer-Improper Equip,Towing, Etc.	E01
O 0541	Poss/Cons Alc Bev By Minor In MV	A31
O 05C1	Racing On Highway	S95
O 0682	No Liability Insurance On MV	D36
O 06B2	No Liability Insurance On Mtr Veh	D36
O 0804	Failure To Make Repairs	E36, E50
O 0806	Fail To Display-Approval Certificat	B65
O 0818	Affix Sticker Without Reinspection	W00
O 1011	Violation With A Fatality In CMV	U31
O 1013	Commercial Oper Under Infl Liq/Drug	A04, A20
O 1018	Operate CMV While Com Priv Suspend	B20, B21, B22, B23, B24, B25, B26
O 1019	Fail To Pay Toll On Turnpike	D35
O 101D	Felony In Non-CMV/Ctrld Dangr Subst	A50
O 1020	Felony In A Commercial Motor Vehicle	U03
O 1024	Commercial Refusal Of Alcohol Test	A12
O 1026	Oper Com Veh Restricted To One Lic0	D02
O 102E	Felony In CMV/Controlld Dang Substance	A50
O 10A1	Possess CDS Sched I,III, III Or IV	A33
O 10A4	Possession 50grs Or Less Marijuana	A33
O 10A6	Violation With Fatality In Non-CMV	U31
O 10J4	Felony In A Non-Commercial Vehicle	U03
O 1151	Leave Scene Acdt - Death	B02, B06
O 118A	Operate CMV Without A CDL	B56
O 120A	Possession Of Narcotic Drugs	A33
O 120B	User Of Narcotics	A22
O 120C	Withdrawal, Non ACD Violation	W00
O 120E	Withdrawal, Non ACD Violation	W00
O 120H	Withdrawal, Non ACD Violation	W00
O 121B	Order Of Susp.- Aggrevated Assault	U06
O 1231	Failure To Pay Citation Or Fines	D56
O 1271	Improper Crossing Railroad Grade	M10
O 1272	Failure Comply With Signal On Bridge	M18
O 1281	Passing Stopped School Bus	M75, N09
O 1284	No Stop/Improper Passg Dessert Trk	M70
O 1292	Fail To Reveal Identity After Acc Identity	B14
O 129A	Leave Scene MV-Personal Injury	B03, B07
O 129B	Leave Scene Acc Identity-Property Damage	B04, B08
O 129C	Fail To Give Info/Aid After Acc Identity	B01, B05
O 129D	Leave Scene Acc Identity-Unattended Prop	B08
O 12A2	Speeding	S92
O 12A4	Speeding	S92
O 12A5	Speeding	S92
O 12B2	Speeding	S92
O 12B4	Speeding	S92
O 12B5	Speeding	S92
O 12C2	Speeding	S92
O 143E	No Insurance - Moped	D36
O 143G	Operate Under Influence Liq/Drugs	A20
O 143K	No License Plate On Moped	W00
O 143Q	Operate Moped-No Helmet	F03
O 19A1	Possess Cds W/Intent To Distribute	A33
O 20A1	Possess Controlled Dangerous Subst	A33
O 2118	Possess Cds Not In Orig Container	A35

Event Code	Event Description	ACD Code
O 2121	Show Or Use Improperly DLN	D16
O 2121	Counterfeit/Fraudelent DL/ID	D16, D10
O 2147	Possess Drug Paraphernalia	A33
O 2151	Possess Hypodermic Syringe/Needle	A33
O 2910	Moving Against Traffic Tpk/Pkwy/Exw	N60
O 2920	Illegal Use Of Medial Strip	M11
O 2930	Vehicle In Hazardous Condition	F66
O 2940	Use Of Improper Lane	M42
O 2950	U Turn Prohibited	N56
O 2962	Speeding	S92
O 2964	Speeding	S92
O 2965	Speeding	S92
O 3101	Special Bus Driver License Noncmpl	B51
O 3104	Physicians/Specialists Report Reco	W15
O 3105	Fail To Notify DMV/Seizure Disorder	D75
O 310D	Failure To Change Name	W00
O 3111	Improper Use Agricultural License	D29
O 3115	Improper Use Of Drvr Lic By Militar	D16
O 3130	Regular Learner Permit Noncompliance	B51
O 3171	Cont Of Nonres Right After Res Identity	B41
O 3191	Trans Pass For Hire Wo Omnibus Regi	B51
O 3261	Operate Under Influence Liq/Drugs	A20
O 3262	Careless Driving	M81
O 3298	Misuse Of Identityification Cards	D02
O 3315	Possess/Consume Alc Bev-Underage	A31
O 3317	Purchasing Alcohol For Minors	A31
O 333K	Vehicle In Hazardous Condition	E71
O 3381	Counterfeit DL/Reg/Insurance ID Card	B41
O 339A	Loaning Driver License	D02
O 339C	Exhibit DL Of Another-Operating MV	D16
O 339D	Exhibit DL Of Another-Not Oper MV	D16
O 340C	Allowing Susp Driver To Operate Veh	B26
O 340H	Allowing Susp Driver To Operate Veh	B26
O 340I	Driving While Revoked Prk Tickets	B26
O 3602	Use Or Possess Drug Paraphernalia	A33
O 3606	Possess Hypodermic Syringe/Needle	A33
O 3702	Emission Of Smoke Or Contaminants	F66
O 371A	Loaning Driver License	D02
O 371B	Allow Unlicensed Driver To Operate	D02
O 3762	No Child Restraint System	F02
O 3767	Operate/Ride Motorcycle-No Helmet	F03
O 3B54	Operation School W/O Proper Equipment	E06
O 3C03	Unregistered ATV-Snowmobile	W00
O 3C20	No Liability Insur-Snowmobile/ATV	D36
O 4100	Speed Across Sidewalk	S93
O 4102	Speeding By A Physician	S93
O 4105	Improper Oper At Intersect Traffic Signal	M16
O 4115	Improper Turn Traffic Control Signal	M16
O 4116	Improper Turn-Green Arrow Traf Control	M16
O 4117	Failure Observe Pedestrian Interval	N08
O 4119	Failure Stop At Flashing Red Signal	M18
O 4122	Failure To Stop For Police Whistle	M08
O 4123	Improper Right And Left Turns	N53, N54
O 4124	Improper Turn Marked Course	N50, N51, N52, N55
O 4125	U Turn Prohibited	N56
O 4126	Failure To Give Proper Signal	N40, N41, N42, N43, N44
O 4127	Illegal Backing/Turning In Street	N82
O 4128	Failure To Stop At Railroad Crossing	M09
O 4129	Fail To Obey Traffic Control Dev	M14
O 4130	Failure To Report Acc Identity	B61
O 4141	Under The Influence On A Moped	A20
O 4144	Disregard Of Stop Sign Regulations	M15
O 4145	Fail Yield Line Vehicles Through St	M19
O 4215	Failure To Obey Directional Signals	M16
O 436A	Failure Yield Right Way To Driver	N01
O 4371	Failure To Yield To Blind Person	N08

Event Code	Event Description	ACD Code
O 4491	Operate MV While In Poss Of Narcoti	A33
O 4501	Chemical Analysis-Presumption	A20
O 4504	Refusal To Submit To Chemical Test	A12
O 450B	Operating While Impaired	A25
O 450G	Oper Under Influence School Zone	A20
O 4515	DWI With Minor Passenger	A20
O 4519	Failure To Install Interlock Device	A41
O 451A	Consuming Alcohol Beverage In A MV	A26
O 451B	Open Container In A Motor Vehicle	A35
O 45G1	Dwi:1000 Ft On Or Near Sch Grounds	A20
O 45G2	DWI:Driving Though School Crossing	A20
O 45G3	DWI: Driving With Juveniles Near	A20
O 4661	Improper Entering Or Leaving Highwa	M25
O 4662	Avoiding A Traffic Control Signal	M14
O 4771	Snow/Ice Dislodged From Moving Veh	F66
O 4821	Improper Use Of Divided Highway	N62, N71
O 4851	Wrong Way On One Way Street	N63
O 488A	Improper Oper Highway W/Mark Lanes	M05, M11, M40, M41, M43, M44, M45, M46, M47, M48, M49, M50, M51, M55, M56, M57, M60, M61, M62
O 489A	Following Unlawfully Or Improperly	M30, M31, M32, M33
O 4901	Failure To Use Proper Entrance/Exit	M25
O 4942	Disregard Of Posted Notice/Barricade	M02, M03
O 4971	Operate At Slow Speed/Block Traffic	S96
O 4972	Unsafe Operation Of A Motor Vehicle	N84
O 4972	Carless Driving	F06, N83
O 4973	Using Hand Held Cell While Driving	M85,M86
O 4982	Speeding	S01, S06, S51, S92
O 4984	Speeding	S15, S16, S21, S26, S71, S92
O 4985	Speeding	S15, S26, S31, S36, S41, S71, S81, S91, S92
O 4992	Exceeding Speed Limitations	S92
O 4994	Exceeding Speed Limitations	S92
O 5014	Driving After Underage Drinking	A60, A61
O 5B29	Failure To Use Hazmat Safety Device	E53
O 5B32	Oper Interstate W/O Hazmat Placard	E03
O 5B32	Oper Interstate W/O Hazmat Placard	E04
O 5D41	DWI Administrative Per Se .10 BAC	A90, A91
O 5D44	DWI Administrative Per Se .04 BAC	A91,A94
O 5D48	DWI Administrative Per Se .08 BAC	A91,A98
O 655A	Altering/Forging Of Insurance Card	B64
O 655B	Failure To Return License Or Regist	W00
O 6A15	Insurance Fraud	D36
O 6B01	Liability Insur Amount Of Coverage	B64
O 762F	Failure To Wear Seat Belt	F04
O 762F	Failure To Wear Seat Belt	F05
O 8113	Fail To Observe Traffic Control Device	M16
O 8122	Speeding	S92
O 8124	Speeding	S92
O 8125	Speeding	S92
O 815A	Failure To Keep Right	M41
O 815B	Improper Passing	M70
O 819A	Illegal Entry Onto The Parkway	M25
O 9116	Consume Intox Beverage On Turnpike	A26
O 9122	Speeding	S92
O 9124	Speeding	S92
O 9125	Speeding	S92
O 913C	Fail To Obey Traffic Control Device	M16
O 9140	Turnpike Uniform Direction Of Traffic	N60
O 914A	Moving Against Traffic	N60, N61, N70, N72
O 914B	Use Of Improper Lane	M42
O 972G	Unsafe Operation - Cell Phone	N84
O 9813	Retarding Traffic	F34
O 9814	Moving Against Traffic Turnpike/Pkwy/Expw	N60
O 9815	Improper Passing	M70
O 9816	U Turn Prohibited	N56
O 9819	Vehicle In Hazardous Condition	E33

Event Code	Event Description	ACD Code
O 9824	GSP-Parade, Demonstration Prohibited	F34
O 9829	GSP-Obstruction/Interference	F34
O 9831	Refuse To Pay/Evade Toll Payment	D35
O 9915	U Turn Prohibited	N56
O A011	Operate At Slow Speed/Block Traffic	S96
O A112	Speeding	S92
O A114	Speeding	S92
O A115	Speeding	S92
O A222	Illegal Backing Or Turning In Street	N82
O A223	Improper Passing	M70
O A224	Improper Use Of Divided Highway	M11
O A225	Illegal Use Of Medial Strip	M41
O A227	Failure To Use Proper Entrance/Exit	M25
O AB33	Purchase Alcoholic Beverage-Underage	A31
O BFNJ	Bond Forfeiture DWI	D45
O BFOS	Bond Forfeiture O/S DWI	D45
O BSED	Disqualified School Bus Driver Doe	W01
O C014	Driving After Underage Drinking	A60
O C104	Physicians/Specialists Report Reco	W15
O C105	Fail To Notify DMV/Seizure Disorder	D75
O C114	Aggravated Assault By Auto	U31
O C115	Vehicular Homicide	U07
O C119	Failure Stop Flashing Red Signal	M18
O C121	Assault By Auto	U06
O C124	Speeding In A Commercial Vehicle	S92
O C125	Speeding In A Commercial Vehicle	S92
O C126	Failure To Give Proper Signal	N40
O C127	Illegal Backing/Turning In Street	N82
O C129	Fail To Reveal Identity After Acc Identity	B14
O C12C	Assault By Auto	U06
O C12H	Assault By Auto	U06
O C130	Failure To Report Acc Identity	B61
O C144	Disregard Of Stop Sign Regulations	M15
O C14A	Moving Against Traffic	N60
O C14B	Use Of Improper Lane In Commercial Vehicle	M42
O C15B	Improper Passing	M70
O C19A	Oper Snowmbl/ATV Without Helmet	F03
O C1A3	Vehicular Homicide In A CMV	U07, U08, U09, U10
O C202	Automobile Theft	D78
O C20B	Under Influence Narcotic Drug	A24
O C215	Failure To Obey Directional Signals	M16
O C222	Illegal Backing Or Turning In Street	N82
O C223	Improper Passing	M70
O C231	Failure To Pay Citation Or Fines	D56
O C24C	Improper Turn Marked Course	N50
O C281	Passing Stopped School Bus	M75
O C291	Interfering With An Officer	M08
O C292	Fleeing/Eluding An Officer	U01
O C29A	Leave Scene Acc Identity-Pers Inj-Com Veh	B07
O C29B	Leave Scene Accd-Prop Dam-Comm Vehi	B08
O C29C	Fail To Give Info/Aid After MV	B01
O C29D	Leave Scene Accid Unatten Prop/CMV	B08
O C2A4	Speeding In A Commercial Vehicle	S92
O C2A5	Speeding In A Commercial Vehicle	S92
O C2B4	Speeding In A Commercial Vehicle	S92
O C2B5	Speeding In A Commercial Vehicle	S92
O C311	Oper MV In Viol Of DL Condi/Restri	D29
O C312	Illegal Securing Of Driver License	D02
O C313	Parental Consent Withdrawn	W13
O C33K	Vehicle In Hazardous Condition	E71
O C343	Equipment Violation: MVS Regulations	E01
O C344	Unsafe Vehicle	F66
O C347	Operate Vehicle Without Lights	E55
O C353	Spot Lamps Prohibited	E70
O C367	Defective Brakes Equipment	E31
O C372	Drive/Move Mtr Veh W/Unsafe Tires	E37

Event Code	Event Description	ACD Code
O C374	Windshield/Windows Obstructed	D70
O C376	Dangerous Exhaust Gases	F66
O C381	Counterfeit Dl/Reg/Insurance ID Card	B41
O C39C	Exhibit DL Of Another-Operating MV	B41
O C411	Improper Turn Traffic Control Signal	M16
O C43Q	Operate Moped-No Helmet	F03
O C448	Use Motor Veh Without Owner Consent	D78
O C450	Oper Under Influence/Commer Vehicle	A20
O C451	Consuming Alco Bev Oper/Pass In MV	A26
O C454	Refusal To Submit To Chem Test/CMV	A12
O C455	Improper Act Steep Grades Or Curves	N80
O C457	Failure To Comply Police Instruction	M08
O C467	Obstructing Passage Of Other Vehicle	F34
O C481	Fail To Observe Traff Control Device	M14
O C484	Fail To Pass Right Proc In Oppos Di	M70
O C485	Improper Passing	M70
O C486	Improper Pass/Cross No Pass Line	M70
O C488	Improp Oper-Hwys W/Marked Lane-CMV	M42
O C489	Following Too Close In Commerc Vehicle	M34
O C48A	Improper Oper Highway W/Mark Lanes	M05
O C490	Fail To Yield Right Of Way	N01
O C491	Poss/Cons Alc Bev By Minor In MV	A33
O C494	Speeding In A Commercial Vehicle	S92
O C495	Improper Passing	M70
O C496	Reckless Driving In A Commerc Vehicle	M84
O C497	Careless Driving In A Commerc Vehicle	M81
O C501	Driving After Underage Drinking	A60
O C50B	Operating While Impaired	A25
O C519	Failure To Install Interlock Device	A41
O C51B	Open Container In A Motor Vehicle	A35
O C535	Failure Surrender Susp License Cert	W00, W09
O C541	Poss/Cons Alc Bev By Minor In MV	A31
O C55A	Altering/Forging Of Insurance Card	B64
O C5C1	Racing On Highway	S95
O C62F	Failure To Wear Seat Belt	F04
O C661	Improper Entering Or Leaving Highway	M25
O C762	No Child Restraint System	F02
O C767	Operate/Ride Motorcycle-No Helmet	F03
O C804	Failure To Make Repairs	E50
O C806	Fail To Display-Approval Certificate	B65
O C813	Retarding Traffic	F34
O C815	Improper Passing	M70
O C819	Vehicle In Hazardous Condition	F66
O C821	Improper Use Of Divided Highway	N62
O C831	Refuse To Pay/Evade Toll Payment	D35
O C851	Wrong Way On One Way Street	N63
O C89A	Following Unlawfully Or Improperly	M30
O C924	Speeding In A Commercial Vehicle	S92
O C925	Speeding In A Commercial Vehicle	S92
O C930	Vehicle In Hazardous Condition	F66
O C940	Use Of Improper Lane In Commercial Vehicle	M42
O C942	Disregard Of Posted Notice/Barricade	M02
O C964	Speeding In A Commercial Vehicle	S92
O C965	Speeding In A Commercial Vehicle	S92
O C971	Operate At Slow Speed/Block Traffic	S96
O C972	Unsafe Operation Of A Motor Vehicle	N84
O C984	Speeding In A Commercial Vehicle	S92
O C985	Speeding In A Commercial Vehicle	S92
O CA14	Speeding In A Commercial Vehicle	S92
O CA15	Speeding In A Commercial Vehicle	S92
O CA21	Operate CMV - CDL Not In Possession	B57
O CA22	Operate CMV- Wrong CDL Class/Endorsement	B91
O CB01	Liability Insurance Of Coverage	D36
O CB54	Operation School W/O Proper Equipment	E06
O CBIP	Medical Info Not Returned-License	W14
O CBMU	Med Unqualified To Drive-License	W14

Event Code	Event Description	ACD Code
O CCDS	Under Influ Control Dang Subs/CMV	A22
O CDB1	Commercial Driver Disqualified Type B-1	W30
O CDB2	Commercial Driv Disqualified Type B-2	W31
O CDLM	Medical Commercial Order Of Suspen	W14
O CFPR	Commercial Failed To Pass Reexam	W20
O CFTA	Commercial Failed To Appear Reexam	W20
O CHIP	Medical Info Not Returned-Hazmat	W14
O CHMU	Med Unqualified To Drive-Hazmat	W14
O CLRN	Fail To Obey RR Under Clearance	M24
O COFA	Court Ordered Susp: Fail To Appear	D45
O COOS	Driving Comm Veh Out Of Service	B27
O COPF	Court Ordered Sus:Fail To Pay Fine	D56
O CPCR	Disqualifying Record-Pass	W01
O CPDE	Dept Of Ed Disqualification-Pass	W01
O CPDF	Fail To Submit Declaration Flyer	W20
O CPIA	Fail To Sub Comp Initial Pass App	W20
O CPID	Need Proof Of 3yrs Drv Exper - Pas	W20
O CPIP	Medical Info Not Returned-Pass	W14
O CPIS	Fail Sub Initial Schl Bus App-Pass	W20
O CPLF	Fail To Submit Fingerprint Card	W20
O CPMU	Med Unqualified To Drive-Pass	W14
O CPO1	Fail To Supply Date Of Phys Ex-Pas	W15
O CPO2	Failed To Supply Health Hist Pass	W15
O CPO3	Fail Comp Visual Requirements-Pass	W15
O CPO4	Fail To Complete Audio Requir-Pass	W15
O CPO5	Fail To Provide Blood Pressure-Pas	W15
O CPO6	Doctor Fail To Comp Phys Form-Pass	W15
O CPO7	Medical Exam Cert Miss/Incomp-Pass	W15
O CPO8	Fail To Sub Required Screening-Pas	W15
O CPPE	Fail To Submit Physical Exam-Pass	W15
O CPPT	Disq Accum 12 Or More Pts - Pass	W01
O CPRI	Fail To Submit Required Info-Pass	W15
O CPRS	Fail To Sub School Bus Renewal-Pas	W20
O CPSA	Disq-Cdra/Alcohol Conv-Pass	W01
O CSBT	Chemical Test Refusal-Compact State	A12
O CSDD	Drive Under Influence-Compact State	A20
O D143	Unlicensed Moped Operator	B51
O DBIP	Medical Info Not Returned-License	W14
O DBMU	Med Unqualified To Drive-License	W14
O DHIP	Medical Info Not Returned-Hazmat	W14
O DHMU	Med Unqualified To Drive-Hazmat	W14
O DPIP	Medical Info Not Returned-Pass	W14
O DPMU	Med Unqualified To Drive-Pass	W14
O EFTL	Fatal Acc Identity-Emergent	U10
O FARX	Fail To Appear Driver Reexam	W20
O FCAC	Fail To Comply Countermeasure Program	W00
O FCCS	Fail To Comply-Community Service	D45
O FCIO	Fail To Comply Court Install Order	D53
O FCSC	Fatal Ord:Fail To Comply Settl/Con	W20
O FFTL	Fatal Acc Identity-Foreign State	U31
O FPCS	Court-Ordered Sus: Child Support	D51
O FPIX	Driv Lic Suspd By DMV-Reexam Reqd	W20
O FPRX	Failure To Pass NJ Driver Re-Exam	W20
O FRRS	Failure To Stop At Railroad Cross	M21
O FSFA	Failure To Appear	D45
O FSSC	Failure To Appear-Scofflaw	D53
O GBIP	Medical Info Not Returned-License	W14
O GBMU	Med Unqualified To Drive-License	W14
O GHIP	Medical Info Not Returned-Hazmat	W14
O GHMU	Med Unqualified To Drive-Hazmat	W14
O GPIP	Medical Info Not Returned-Pass	W14
O GPMU	Med Unqualified To Drive-Pass	W14
O H011	Violation With A Fatality In CMV	U31
O H020	Felony With Hazardous Material	U03
O H02E	Felony In Hazmat/Contrld Dangr Subs	A50
O H104	Physicians/Specialists Report Reco	W15

Event Code	Event Description	ACD Code
O H105	Fail To Notify DMV/Seizure Disorder	D75
O H113	Oper Under Infl Liq/Drugs-Haz/Jat	A20
O H113	Oper Under Infl Liq/Drugs-Haz/Mat	A20
O H126	Failure To Give Proper Signal	N40
O H127	Illegal Backing/Turning In Street	N82
O H129	Fail To Reveal Identity After Acc Identity	B14
O H130	Failure To Report Acc Identity	B61
O H1A3	Vehicular Homicide In A Hazmat	U07
O H20B	Operate Hazmat While Com Priv Suspd	B26
O H231	Failure To Pay Citation Or Fine	D56
O H24C	Improper Turn Marked Course	N50
O H281	Passing Stopped School Bus	M75
O H29A	Leave Scene Accd-Persnl Injur/Hazmat	B07
O H29B	Leave Scene Accd-Prop Damage/Hazmat	B08
O H29C	Fail To Give Info/Aid After Acciden	B01
O H29D	Leave Scene Accid Unat Prop/Hazmat	B08
O H311	Oper MV In Viol Of DL Condi/Restri	D29
O H312	Illegal Securing Of Driver License	D02
O H313	Parental Consent Withdrawn	W13
O H344	Unsafe Vehicle	F66
O H347	Operate Vehicle Without Lights	E55
O H353	Spot Lamps Prohibited	E70
O H367	Defective Brakes Equipments	E31
O H372	Drive/Move Mtr Veh W/Unsafe Tires	E37
O H374	Windshield/Windows Obstructed	D70
O H381	Counterfeit Dl/Reg/Insurance ID Card	B41
O H448	Use Motor Veh Without Owner Consent	D78
O H450	Oper Under Influence/Hazard Material	A20
O H454	Refusal To Submit Chem Test/Hazmat	A12
O H455	Improper Act Steep Grades Or Curves	N80
O H457	Failure To Comply Police Instruction	M08
O H485	Improper Passing	M70
O H486	Improper Pass/Cross No Pass Line	M70
O H489	Following Too Close In Commercial Vehicle	M34
O H48A	Improper Oper Highway W/Mark Lanes	M05
O H490	Failure To Yield Right Of Way	N01
O H494	Speeding In A Commercial Vehicle	S92
O H496	Reckless Driving In A Commercial Vehicle	M84
O H497	Careless Driving In A Commercial Vehicle	M81
O H519	Failure To Install Interlock Device	A41
O H535	Failure Surrender Susp License Cert	W09
O H55A	Altering/Forging Of Insurance Card	B64
O H5C1	Racing On Highway	S95
O H661	Improper Entering Or Leaving Highwa	M25
O H806	Fail To Display-Approval Certificat	B65
O H821	Improper Use Of Divided Highway	N62
O H831	Refuse To Pay/Evade Toll Payment	D35
O H851	Wrong Way One One Way Street	N63
O H89A	Following Unlawfully Or Improperly	M30
O H942	Disregard Of Posted Notice/Barricade	M02
O H971	Operate At Slow Speed/Block Traffic	S96
O H972	Unsafe Operation Of A Motor Vehicle	N84
O H984	Speeding In A Commercial Vehicle	S92
O H985	Speeding In A Commercial Vehicle	S92
O HA21	Operate CMV - CDL Not In Possession	B51
O HA22	Operate CMV- Wrong CDL Class/Endors	B91
O HB01	Liability Insurance Of Coverage	D36
O HB54	Operation School W/O Proper Equipment	E06
O HBIP	Medical Info Not Returned-License	W14
O HBMU	Med Unqualified To Drive-License	W14
O HCDS	Under Influ Contrl Dang Sub/Hazmat	A22
O HHIP	Medical Info Not Returned-Hazmat	W14
O HHMU	Med Unqualified To Drive-Hazmat	W14
O HPIP	Medical Info Not Returned-Pass	W14
O HPMU	Med Unqualified To Drive-Pass	W14
O IBTG	Illegal Backing/Turning In Street	N82

Event Code	Event Description	ACD Code
O ICLC	Uninsured Motor-Insur Cancel-Licens	D36
O IDRC	Fail To Comply- Intox Driv Rsc Ctr	W00
O IHAZ	Imminent Hazard Commercail Disqual	W70
O ILEX	Comml DL Suspd By DMV-Reexam Reqd	W20
O IODC	Fail To Comply Court Install Order	D53
O IUEE	Failure To Use Proper Entrance/Exit	M25
O IUMS	Illegal Use Of Medial Strip	M11
O J1LR	Unsatisfied Judgment-Driver/Owner	D39
O J2LR	Unsatisfied Judgment-Driver/Owner	D39
O J3LR	Unsatisfied Judgment-Driver/Owner	D39
O J4LR	Unsatis Ucj Installmt Jdgmt-Dri/Own	D39
O J5LR	Unsatis Ucj Installmt Jdgmt-Dri/Own	D39
O MBIP	Medical Info Not Returned-License	W14
O MBMU	Med Unqualified To Drive-License	W14
O MEOD	Phys Unqual-Med Exam Other Defects	W14
O MHIP	Medical Info Not Returned-Hazmat	W14
O MHMU	Med Unqualified To Drive-Hazmat	W14
O MLCD	MCSIA Lifetime CDL Disqualification	W41
O MLDF	MCSIA Life CDL Disqual-Felony-Cds	A50
O MNTL	Phy Unqual Mental/Nervous Disabilit	D75
O MPIP	Medical Info Not Returned-Pass	W14
O MPMU	Med Unqualified To Drive-Pass	W14
O MSMC	MCSIA Second/Subseq Major Convict	W40
O NBIP	Medical Info Not Returned-License	W14
O NBMU	Med Unqualified To Drive-License	W14
O NFTL	Fatal Acc Identity-Non Emergent	U31
O NHIP	Medical Info Not Returned-Hazmat	W14
O NHMU	Med Unqualified To Drive-Hazmat	W14
O NPIP	Medical Info Not Returned-Pass	W14
O NPMU	Med Unqualified To Drive-Pass	W14
O NSTP	Failure To Obey Railroad Stop	M21
O OSDD	Driv Under Influence-Noncomp State	A20
O OSHA	Out Of Service Commercial Hazmat	W50
O OSHB	Out Of Service Commercial Hazmat B	W51
O OSHC	Out Of Service Commercial Hazmat C	W52
O OSHM	Commercial Out Of Service Hazmat`	B19
O PFDC	Dishonored Check Court Fine Pmt	D53
O POAA	Parking Offenses	D53
O PVPS	Persistent Violator	W01
O RRCA	Comm Railroad 'A' Level Suspension	W60
O RRCB	Comm Railroad 'B' Level Order	W60
O RRCC	Comm Railroad 'C' Level Order	W61
O RRDR	Fail to Obey RR Cross-Required	M22
O RRRC	Failure To Obey RR Crossing Restri	M09
O RRRG	Failure To Obey Railroad Gates/Sig	M10
O RRRS	Failure To Stop At Required RR Cros	M22
O RRSL	Failure To Slow Down At RR Crossing	M20
O RRST	Failure To Stop At Rr Crossing	M21
O RRXV	Failure To Obey Rr Vrossing Restric	M09
O SANQ	Haz Security Assessment Not Qualif	W09
O SBIP	Medical Info Not Returned-License	W14
O SBMU	Med Unqualified To Drive-License	W14
O SDLC	Suspend Dl-Security Responsibility	D38
O SHIP	Medical Info Not Returned-Hazmat	W14
O SHMU	Med Unqualified To Drive-Hazmat	W14
O SODL	Fail To Dep Security O/S Dvr Lic	D37
O SPED	Court-Ordered Suspension-Speeding	S93
O SPED	Court-Ordered Suspension-Speeding	S98
O SPIP	Medical Info Not Returned-Pass	W14
O SPMU	Med Unqualified To Drive-Pass	W14
O SPRR	Fail To Obey Rr Space Req To Stop	M23
O SSBT	Operate At Slow Speed/Block Traffic	S96
O T113	Transferred Comerc Oper Und Influe	A20
O TC44	Transferred Under Influence/CMV	A20
O TC45	Transferred Oper Und Influence/CMV	A20
O TC54	Transferred Refusal Chem Test/CMV	A12

Event Code	Event Description	ACD Code
O TH13	Transferred Oper Under Influ/Hazmat	A20
O TH45	Transferred Oper Und Influ/Hazmat	A20
O TH54	Transferred Refusal Chem Test/Hazmat	A12
O UNLC	Uninsured Motor-Insur Cancel-License	D36
O USDS	Unanswered Summons: Drive While Sus	D45
O UTRN	U Turn Prohibited	N56
O VCCB	No Payment-VCCB Penalty Assessment	D56
O VIHC	Vehicle In Hazardous Condition	F66
O ZBIP	Medical Info Not Returned-License	W14
O ZBMU	Med Unqualified To Drive-License	W14
O ZHIP	Medical Info Not Returned-Hazmat	W14
O ZHMU	Med Unqualified To Drive-Hazmat	W14
O ZPIP	Medical Info Not Returned-Pass	W14
O ZPMU	Med Unqualified To Drive-Pass	W14

Point System

Points range from 2 to 8 points per violation. A driver accumulating of 6 or more points within three years will be assessed a surcharge. A driver accumulating 12 or more points accumulated in any period will receive a notice of suspension. Also, drivers may earn 3 point deductions by remaining violation and suspension-free for one year or 2 point deduction by taking qualified driving courses approved by MVC.

NJSA Section	Points	Offense
27:23-29	2	Moving against traffic: NJ Turnpike, Garden State Parkway and Atlantic City Expressway
27:23-29	4	Improper passing: New Jersey Turnpike, Garden State Parkway and Atlantic City Expressway
27:23-29	2	Unlawful use of median strip: NJ Turnpike, Garden State Parkway and Atlantic City Expressway
39:3-20	3	Operating constructor vehicle in excess of 45 mph
39:4-14.3	2	Operating motorized bicycle on a restricted highway
39:4-14.3d	2	More than one person on a motorized bicycle
39:4-35	2	Failure to yield to pedestrian in crosswalk
38:4-36	2	Failure to yield to pedestrian in crosswalk; passing a vehicle yielding to pedestrian in crosswalk
39:4-41	2	Driving through safety zone
39:4-52	5	Racing on highway
39:4-55	2	Improper action or omission on grades and curves
39:4-57	2	Failure to observe direction of officer
39:4-66	2	Failure to stop vehicle before crossing sidewalk
39:4-66.1	2	Failure to yield to pedestrians or vehicles while entering or leaving highway
39:4-66.2	2	Driving on public or private property to avoid a traffic sign or signal
39:4-71	2	Operating a motor vehicle on a sidewalk
39:4-80	2	Failure to obey direction of officer
39:4-81	2	Failure to observe traffic signals
39:4-82	2	Failure to keep to right
39:4-82.1	2	Improper operating of vehicle on divided highway or divider
39:4-83	2	Failure to keep right at intersection
39:4-84	5	Failure to pass to right of vehicle proceeding in opposite direction
39:4-85	4	Improper passing on right or off roadway
39:4-85.1	2	Wrong way on a one-way street
39:4-86	4	Improper passing in a no passing zone
39:4-87	2	Failure to yield to overtaking vehicle
39:4-88	2	Failure to observe traffic lanes
39:4-89	5	Tailgating
39:4-90	2	Failure to yield at intersection
39:4-90.1	2	Failure to use proper entrances to limited access highways
39:4-91	2	Failure to yield to emergency vehicles
39:4-92	2	Failure to yield to emergency vehicles
39:4-96	5	Reckless Driving
39:4-97	2	Careless Driving
39:4-97a	2	Destruction of agricultural or recreational property
39:4-97.1	2	Slow speed blocking traffic
39:4-97.2	4	Driving in an unsafe manner. (Points only assessed for 3rd and subsequent violation within five- year period of the most recent violation.)
39:4-98	2	Exceeding maximum speed 1-14 mph over limit
39:4-99	4	Exceeding maximum speed 15-29 mph over limit
39:4-99	5	Exceeding maximum speed 30 mph or more over limit
39:4-105	2	Failure to stop for traffic light

39:4-115	3	Improper turn at traffic light
39:4-119	2	Failure to stop at flashing red signal
39:4-122	2	Failure to stop for police whistle
39:4-123	3	Improper right or left turn
39:4-124	3	Improper turn from approved turning course
39:4-125	3	Improper "U" turn
39:4-126	2	Failure to give proper signal
39:4-127	2	Improper backing or turning in street
39:4-127.1	2	Improper crossing of railroad grade crossing
39:4-127.2	2	Improper crossing of bridge
39:4-128	2	Improper crossing of railroad grade crossing by certain vehicles
39:4-128.1	5	Improper passing of school bus
39:4-128.4	4	Improper passing of a frozen dessert truck
39:4-129	2	Leaving the scene of an accident – no personal injury
39:4-129	8	Leaving the scene of an accident – personal injury
39:4-144	2	Failure to observe "stop" or "yield" signs
39:5C-1	5	Racing on highway
39:5D-4	2	Moving violation out-of-state

New Mexico

Administration	Important Telephone and Web Contacts
Alicia Ortiz, Deputy Director Motor Vehicle Division PO Box 1028 Santa Fe NM 87504-1028 505-827-2296 www.mvd.newmexico.gov	Integrated Voice Response System ....888-683-4636 This system connects caller to specific departments. Commercial Driver License ....505-827-1036 Heavy Vehicle Registration IRP Unit..........505-827-0392 State Department of Insurance ....505-827-4601 State Police..505-827-9300 Email general questions to MVDHelp@state.nm.us

The **NM Motor Vehicle Code (Chapter 66)** and other NM statutes can be found online at: www.nmonesource.com/nmnxtadmin/NMPublic.aspx

Regulations can be found in **Title 18** in the **NM Administrative Code** at: www.nmcpr.state.nm.us/nmac/

Driver's License Format, Issuance and Renewal

License Classes, Restrictions and Endorsements Appear After the Driving Record Content Section

License Format

The license consists of nine numbers. New Mexico reports there is no code or sequential arrangement determining the numbers in the license.

Document Appearance

The current document has been issued since the Spring of 2008.

Current Document

Security Characteristics: A Guilloche security design is present in several locations on the face of the card. There is micro-print across the bottom of the card. The card has a Zia design laser perforation, which can be seen with the naked eye by holding the card up to the light or shining a light through the card from behind. The photo is on left side with a ghost photo on the bottom right. The driver's signature is under the photo. There are 1-D and 2-D bar codes and a magnetic strip. The card also has UV features on the front pattern.

Minor Age Driver Locator: In a vertical format. The photo is positioned in the bottom left. Across the top or under the top bar (older license) is text explaining the type of license issued.

CDL Indicator: "Commercial Driver License" is printed in red lettering on top of license.

Older Document (pre 2008)

Security Characteristics: There is a slight trim around the edge in a dark color and is a combination of three technologies; a digital image that is stored as part of the driving record; a digital signature that is also captured and stored; and a magnetic stripe that encodes the printed information on the license. The Photo is found at the bottom left, the driver's signature to the right of the photo. There is a yellow bar across the top with the words "New Mexico" inside.

Minor Age Driver Locator: In a vertical format. The photo is positioned in the bottom left. Across the top or under the top bar (older license) is text explaining the type of license issued.

CDL Indicator: "Commercial Driver License" is printed in red lettering on top of license.

Issuance

First-time driver's license applicants, out-of-state driver's license applicants, renewals, replacements and ID card applicants are issued a temporary extension while their regular license is being processed and mailed. Also, all first-time NM licensees age 18 to 24 are required to take the "None for the Road" self-study DWI awareness class. Written tests are required for all applicants who are applying for a first time driver's license or for those whose licenses that have been expired for

one year or more. Road tests are required for first time applicants or those with licenses expired over 5 years.

Location of Requirements for Proof of Identity/Residency: www.mvd.newmexico.gov/Drivers/Licensing/Pages/Proof-of-New-Mexico-Residency.aspx

Age Requirements

A Graduated Driver License System affects all drivers under 18 until they meet the requirements for an unrestricted license. Requirements vary by age and stage, as stated below:

Stage 1   Instructional Permit, also known as a Learners Permit - 15; must be accompanied by licensed driver (while enrolled in approved driver education course), must hold 6 months and have 50 hours of supervised driving, 10 of which at night.

Stage 2   Provisional License - Fifteen and six months; successful completion Stage 1; prohibited driving from midnight to 5 a.m.; no more than 1 passenger younger than 21 except family members.

Stage 3   Unrestricted Drivers License - 16 and 6 months; successful completion Stage 2; under 18 must have completed driver education.

Note: All first-time licensees in New Mexico who are 18 to 24 years of age are required to take the *None for the Road* awareness class.

Residency

Once a motor vehicle driver establishes residency in New Mexico the person is required to obtain a New Mexico Driver's License. A driver's license held by a person who is on active duty in the armed forces of the U.S. and is absent in this state, or is in this state only on leave status, remains valid beyond the expiration date of the license. This provision also applies to spouses of such military personnel.

Renewal

Renewal is for either four years or eight years with expiration one month after the individual's birthday (choice is based on driver's preference). Shortened renewal periods apply with prorated fees, for individuals who will turn 21 or 75 in less than four years. Expiration for those individuals is one month after the 21st or 75th birthday. Renewal is not available online. CDL drivers who have a HAZMAT Endorsement may only receive a four-year renewal. The driver keeps same number when renewing.

Elderly-Related Restrictions

At age seventy-five, the license must be renewed annually (with no fee).

Vehicle Insurance, Title and Registration Facts

Registration Renewal

Vehicles can be renewed for either one year or two years. The Motor Vehicle Division's Integrated Voice Response (IVR) and Internet systems allow customers to renew vehicle registration on the Internet or by telephone with a major credit card (MasterCard or VISA only). To access the MVD Integrated Voice Response system, call 888-683-4636. Online renewal is found at https://efile.state.nm.us/renewal/home1.aspx.

New Residents

New residents must register vehicles within thirty days of establishing residency. In addition, a Vehicle Identification Number (VIN) Inspection is required for every vehicle coming to New Mexico from another state.

Inspections and Emissions Testing

New Mexico has no statewide provisions for either an annual vehicle safety inspection or emissions test. However, residents of the Bernalillo County and others who commute into Bernalillo County 60 or more days per year are required to have their vehicles tested and to provide proof that the vehicles have passed an emissions inspection test. More information is available from the Vehicle Pollution Management Division at 505-764-2273.

Passenger Plate Facts

The two basic plate options have for the last several years been the yellow and the balloon plates. Effective 2010 the turquoise centennial plate has replaced the balloon plate in production. There is one plate with one decal (MO & YR). There are no codes or number sequence which indicates the county of issuance. When a vehicle is sold the plate remains with the seller.

Withdrawal Sanctions, and Alcohol and Drug Testing

Alcohol and Chemical Testing

New Mexico's illegal intoxication level is .08 % and above for persons 21 and older, .02 % for persons less than 21 years of age, and .04% for drivers of CMVs. Use of breath and blood test(s) is authorized. New Mexico has both an implied consent administrative revocation and a DWI criminal action provision.

Suspensions and Revocations

The New Mexico DMV is in compliance with the provisions of the Motor Carrier Safety Improvement Act (MCSIA). See the Appendix for more information about these mandatory CDL disqualification sanctions.

Alcohol or Drug Related:

It is illegal to drive with a breath or blood alcohol concentration of .08 or more if you're 21 or over, or .02 if under 21, or .04 if driving a commercial vehicle.

Driving Under the Influence of Liquor/Drugs
First Conviction	One-year revocation.
Second Conviction	Two-year revocation.
Third Conviction	Three-year revocation.
Fourth Conviction	Lifetime revocation.

Illegal Blood Alcohol Content – **Implied Consent** (21 and Over)
First Administrative Revocation	Six-month revocation.
First Offense for Refusing a Test	One-year revocation.
Second or Subsequent	One-year revocation.

Illegal Blood Alcohol Content – Implied Consent (under 21)
First and Subsequent	One-year revocation.
Refusal to Submit to Chemical Test	Administrative revocation.

DWI - CDL License Holder – Regardless if driving a CMV
First Conviction	One-year disqualification.
Second Conviction	Lifetime disqualification.

Note: If a driver's license is revoked for DWI, the driver may be eligible for an ignition interlock license but is not eligible for a limited license under any circumstances, including personal or family hardship.

Other Suspensions and Revocations of Note—
Accumulation of Seven to Ten Points in a Twelve-Month Period	Ninety-day Suspension.
Accumulation of Twelve Points in a Twelve-Month Period	One-year Suspension.

(A judge may also recommend a longer suspension for accumulation of 7 to 10 points in a twelve month period.)

Any Offense Committed in Another State, Which, If Committed in New Mexico,	
Would Result in Suspension or Revocation	Period specified by New Mexico Statute.
Delinquent with Regard to Child Support Obligations	
	Suspension until judgment satisfied and reinstatement fee paid.
Driving While License is Revoked	Revocation extended one additional year.
Failure to Appear in Court	Indefinite suspension.
Failure to Pay Penalty Assessed for Traffic Citation	Suspension until terms of citation complied with.
Failure to Pay Judgment Resulting From an Accident	
Suspension until judgment satisfied, proof of insurance, and reinstatement fee paid. (14 year time limit.)	
Manslaughter/Negligent Homicide	One-year revocation.
Perjury or Making a False Statement to Motor Vehicle Division	One-year to Indefinite Suspension.
Permitting Fraudulent or Unlawful Use of a Driver's License	One-year suspension.

Reinstatement Requirements

Suspension.........$25.00 fee; proof of financial responsibility if for unpaid liability in accident. If suspended for points, must complete Driver Improvement Course.

Revocation.........$100.00 fee.

Insurance and Financial Responsibility

Everyone who operates a motor vehicle in New Mexico must have a motor vehicle liability insurance policy. The Mandatory Financial Responsibility Act requires that proof of such insurance be carried in the vehicle at all times. Registered vehicles must have a motor vehicle liability insurance policy with minimum limits of $25,000/50,000/10,000 or evidence of financial responsibility in the amount of $60,000 cash deposit or surety bond deposited with the New Mexico State Treasurer's Office. The state does not have a no-fault insurance provision. Insurance information from insured vehicles is matched electronically between insurance companies and the Motor Vehicle Division to ensure insurance is current. Violation will result in suspension of vehicle registration. Only vehicles currently insured are eligible for registration and/or registration renewal.

Record Access: Laws, Rules, and Forms

Note: This Section Applies to Both Driver and Vehicle Records.

Governing Statutes and Rules

The **NM Motor Vehicle Code (Chapter 66)** and other NM statutes can be found online at:
http://www.nmonesource.com/nmnxtadmin/NMPublic.aspx
Regulations can be found in **Title 18** in the **NM Administrative Code** at: www.nmcpr.state.nm.us/nmac/.
Per NMSA 66-1-4.14 through 66-2-14, NM adopted the provisions of DPPA. Sec. 66-2-7.1 is the Records Confidentiality Statute.

Policy Statement Regarding Permissible Uses

The above mentioned statute lists 9 permissible user groups including insurance, government agencies, research and statistical purposes, notice regarding towed or impounded vehicles, and employers. It also states that records are released with written consent. New Mexico does not have the following federal exceptions: 3A, 3B, 4, 8, 10, 11, 12, and 14. New Mexico added the following exceptions:

(1)   to the individual or the individual's authorized representative;

(9)   for use by an insured state-chartered or federally chartered credit union; an insured state or national bank; an insured state or federal savings and loan association; or an insured savings bank, but only:

(a)   to verify the accuracy of personal information submitted by an individual to the credit union, bank, savings and loan association or savings bank; and

(b)   if the information as submitted is not correct or is no longer correct, to obtain the correct information, but only for the purpose of preventing fraud by pursuing legal remedies against or recovering on a debt or security interest from the individual;

(10) for providing organ donor information as provided in the Uniform Anatomical Gift Act or Section 66-5-10 NMSA 1978; or

(11) for providing the names and addresses of all lienholders and owners of record of abandoned vehicles to storage facilities or wrecker yards for the purpose of providing notice as required in Section 66-3-121 NMSA 1978.

Request and Consent Forms

Driving Records: To obtain the MVD-11260 *Confidential Records Release* go to the All MVD Forms link at the home page at www.mvd.newmexico.gov. Person of record must sign a notarized waiver before information is released. This must be on letterhead.
There is a specific contract for all organizations or people requesting ten or more records. The contract must state the purpose of request, be approved by state administrators, and renewed annually.
Businesses that have a permissible use can order records online. Certain document must be signed including: *Agreement For Access to Drivers License and Motor Vehicle Records* and the *New Mexico Driver Privacy Protection Agreement Online.*
Vehicle Records: A contract is required or waiver of consent provided on letterhead. Notarized signature of the subject required. Use *Form MVD-10705 Request For Vehicle Or Hull Identification Number Verification* at www.mvd.newmexico.gov:
Use of the *MVD11260 Confidential Records Release* mentioned above is also advised.

Vendor and Third Party Access Policy

Online vendors must sign an *Agreement for Access to Drivers License and Motor Vehicle Records.* Since online access from NM is provided by a designated vendor – New Mexico Interactive – the Agreement refers to MVR vendors as "sub-vendors." The Agreement specifies the following:
1. The sub-vendor or end user may not use the information in direct mail usage or sell, resell, assign or transfer any information for such usage.
2. Once a sub-vendor has made a resale for an approved use, the record may not be sold again.

Records Ordered For Non-permissible Uses

Driving Records: Records are not released to other individuals if there is no consent. Records without personal information are released to businesses.
Vehicle Records: Without consent no records are released, even records without personal information.

Access to Driver-Related Records

Driving Records

General Information and Fees

Driver Services Bureau, PO Box 1028, Santa Fe NM 87504-1028, 888-683-4636, fax 505-827-2792.
There is no fee for mail-in or over-the-counter requests, there is a fee for online services, see below. Personal information is not released except to specified groups or if subject gives notarized approval.
In-Person – Requests for up to 2 records are processed as soon as possible. The DMV headquarters in Santa Fe is the only location for manual requests that involve multiple records. All state field offices can service single record requests. The driver's Social Security Number or license number, and name and date of birth are needed when ordering.
Mail – Requests mailed to the state are processed in 10-15 days. The driver's SSN and DL with name and DOB are needed when ordering.
Electronic – The New Mexico DMV contracts with New Mexico Interactive to provide all electronic media requests of driver license histories, title, registration and lien searches. Two online access programs are available or driving records.

1) **Non-Subscriber** Individual History Records are available to those who attest they have a permissible use. The DOB and last 4 digits of the SSN are required. The fee is $6.63 per record, use of a credit card is required. This is for a non-certified, three-year history record. Go to https://secure.mvd.newmexico.gov/RenewalServices/DHR/Individual/default.aspx. This service is also accessible from the home page.

2) **Subscribers** who meet federal and state standards have access to both single inquiry and batch (called Point-to-Point) modes are available for driving records. The annual subscription fee is $75.00 for up to 10 users. The fee for a driving record is $6.50. A non-hit result incurs a fee. Monthly billing is provided. Subscribers also have access to Driver Monitoring, and vehicle lien and registration records searches. For more information call New Mexico Interactive at 877-660-3468 or visit the Online Services section at www.mvd.newmexico.gov/Online-Services/subscriber-services.html#motor.

DUI Search – Also, visit www.nmcourts.gov/dwi.html for a free DUI Offender History search. This is not and MVD service and not an official record, it may not contain all court records.

Bulk – All inquiries must be made through New Mexico Interactive at 877-660-3468.

By Person of Record – NM drivers may obtain their driving record by phone, mail or walk-in as described above. Drivers may also order a three-year copy of their record online from the Non-Subscriber system described above. At the home page, click on *Drive History Records Search*. The fee is $6.63; use of a credit card is required.

Driver Monitoring Programs

New Mexico Interactive provides both a **Driver Monitoring** and a **Youthful Driver Monitoring** program for subscribers who wish to monitor driving records for violations and suspensions. The subscriber supplies a driver list for a fee of $.12 per driver for each to month

checked (the check can go back in time 1, 6 or 12 months). If there is activity, the system automatically generates a driving record for the $6.50 fee. Activity includes moving violations and withdrawal actions. The program is available for DDPA permissible use clients including employers and insurance companies. For more information on either program, call New Mexico Interactive at 877-660-3468.

Obtaining Accident Reports

Reporting – The nearest law enforcement agency should be notified of accidents resulting in injury, death, or damage in excess of $500.00. Within five days, an accident report must be filed with the Department of Highways and Transportation, P.O. Box 1149, Santa Fe NM 87504. The form will be provided by the investigating officer.

Record Access – Department of Public Safety, Attention: Records, PO Box 1628, Santa Fe NM 87504, 505-827-9182. www.dps.nm.org/ Local accidents that occur within cities, such as Albuquerque, are handled by individual city police departments and record copies must be secured from those entities.

At the DPS location, there is no charge for person directly involved. For others, the fee is $1.00 first page and $.25 for each additional copy, and $10.00 if placed on a CD or disk. When ordering by mail, the name, date, and city or county location are needed when ordering. Please call first to determine number of pages before sending check. One may also order by phone. Prepayment is required. Turnaround time is about 2 weeks. It takes up to 15 days before new accident information is available. Records are available 5 years to present on computer and 25 to present if fatality involved. Older records are archived. Arrest information is not released. One may also make a request online, but results are not shown online. See www.dps.nm.org/index.php/criminal-history-records/records-request/.

Access to Vehicle-Related Records

General Information and Fees

Vehicle Services Bureau, PO Box 1028, Santa Fe NM 87504-1028, 505-827-4636 or (888) 683-4636.

There is no fee for manually processed record requests for VIN, plates, registration or lien information, certified copies or histories from microfilm. However, fulfillment can take 2-3 weeks and regular customers should contact New Mexico Interactive-See **Electronic**.

In-Person, Mail – Information is available 6 years to the present except vehicle history searches which are only 4 years. Turnaround time is 3 to 6 weeks. A SASE required.

Electronic – The New Mexico DMV contracts with New Mexico Interactive to provide all electronic media requests of title, registration and lien searches, as well as driving records. Records are available to subscribers that meet federal and state standards. The annual

subscription fee is $75.00 for up to 10 users. The fee for a record check is $4.95 per record. One record showing registration, lien, and title information is generated. The VIN or plate number must be submitted – a name search is not available. Monthly billing is provided. For more information call New Mexico Interactive at 877-660-3468 or visit the Online Services section at www.mvd.newmexico.gov/Online-Services/subscriber-services.html#motor.

Bulk – Bulk requests for release of vehicle or ownership information must be approved by the Director's office on an individual basis. The purpose is reviewed and a specific contract is required. As stated above, once a sale is made, further resale of the records by the requester is prohibited.

Access to Vessel-Related Records

General Information, Access and Fees

Records are available from the agency above. All motor or sail boats and jet skis over 10 ft must be titled and registered. Motor and sail boats under 10 ft must be registered. UCCs on boats are filed here and will

show on title searches.

However, lien information on boats under 10 feet in length and on jet skis is filed with UCCs at the Secretary of State's office (www.sos.state.nm.us/sos-ucc.html).

Driving Record Content and Reciprocity

What's On or Not On the Driving Record

- Speeding violations of fifty-six to seventy-five mph in a fifty-five mph zone and sixty-six to seventy-five mph in a sixty-five mph zone appear on the "life" record, but may not be used for revocation/suspension or for insurance rating purposes.
- Accidents are not reported on the driving record.
- Records will show suspensions for failure to pay or failure to

appear.

- The length of time convictions appear for public driving records is three years for moving violations (ten years if in CMV); for DUI convictions fifty-five years, and for suspensions three years, unless still in force.
- The state does not permit driver school attendance in lieu of conviction; however, the local courts may do so.

Data Retention

CDL driver records are purged based on the timetable per the federal regulations (see the Appendix). Surrendered licenses are purged from the system after three years.

Court to Repository

Convictions are transferred from the courts to the state via tape, paper, and online. The courts are mandated to report within ten days after disposition. Convictions are input within thirty days of receipt from the courts.

State Reciprocity for Non-CDL Drivers

- Will suspend license of driver for unpaid out-of-state convictions.
- Record of new incoming driver is not shown on MVR.
- Out-of-state convictions are shown on MVR.
- Out-of-state accidents are not shown on MVR.
- Convictions of out-of-state drivers are sent to home state.
- Record is forwarded to new state upon surrender of license upon request.

Abbreviations for Classes, Restrictions, Endorsements, and Medical

License Classes– Commercial

Class A   Any combination of vehicles with a GCWR of 26,001 pounds or more—provided the GVWR of the vehicle(s) being towed is in excess of 10,000 pounds GVWR.

Class B   Any single vehicle with a GVWR of 26,001 or more pounds, or any such vehicle towing a vehicle not in excess of 10,000 pounds GVWR.

Class C   Any single vehicle less than 26,001 pounds GVWR, or any such vehicles towing a vehicle not in excess of 10,000 pounds GVWR. Applies only to vehicles placarded for hazardous materials or designed to transport sixteen or more passengers (including driver).

License Classes– Non-Commercial

Class D   Single vehicles weighing less than 26,001 pounds, and to tow another vehicle provided that: (1) the towing vehicle is of equal or greater weight than the vehicle being towed; or (2) if the towing vehicle weighs less than the towed vehicle, the weight in the towed vehicle does not exceed the manufacturer's rated capacity and:

    a.   the towing vehicle has either a class 4 or higher equalizing hitch or a fifth wheel;

    b.   the vehicle being towed is a trailer; or

    c.   the vehicle combination properly displays slow-moving insignia and moves at speeds of 25 mph or less.

Class M   Authorizes licensee to drive a two- or three-wheeled motorcycle. This class of license is issued to drivers who drive only a motorcycle, and must have an endorsement of Z, Y or W to be valid.

Class E   (CDL-Exempt) Issued only to individuals who are exempt from the requirements of the New Mexico Commercial Driver's License Act, including: drivers of non-commercial recreational vehicles, farm and ranch vehicles, firefighting equipment; and military vehicles.

Restrictions

Code		Applies to:
B	Corrective Lenses	Commercial and Non-Commercial
C	Mechanical Aids	Commercial and Non-Commercial
D	Prosthetic Aids	Commercial and Non-Commercial
E	Automatic Transmission	Commercial Vehicles Only
F	Outside Mirrors	Non-Commercial Vehicles Only
G	Limited to Daylight Only	Non-Commercial Vehicles Only
H	Limited to Employment	Non-Commercial Vehicles Only
I	Limited/Other - Local	Non-Commercial Vehicles Only
J	Other; Auto Transmission	Non-Commercial Vehicles Only
K	CDL - Intrastate Only	Commercial Vehicles Only
L	Vehicles w/o Air-Brakes	Commercial Vehicles Only
V	Medical Variance	Commercial Vehicles Only
X	Medical (6-month permit)	Non-Commercial Vehicles Only
Y	Yearly Renewal	Non-Commercial Vehicles Only

Endorsements

H	Any Vehicle Used to Transport Hazardous Materials
N	Any Vehicle Intended for Hauling Liquids in Bulk
P	Any Vehicle Designed to Transport Sixteen or More Passengers (including driver)
S	Authorizes Driving a School Bus
T	Combination Vehicles with Double- or Triple-Trailers
V	Victim of Identity Theft
W	Any Two- or Three-Wheeled Motorcycle With an Engine Piston Displacement of More Than 100 Cubic Centimeters
X	Combination of N and H
Y	Any Two- or Three-Wheeled Motorcycle With an Engine of Fifty, But Not More Than 100 Cubic Centimeter Piston Displacement
Z	Any Two- or Three-Wheeled Motorcycle With an Automatic Transmission and Engine of Less Than Fifty Cubic Centimeter Piston Displacement

Medical Transactions

AL1	Alcoholism	GE1	Medical General
CA1	Cardiovascular	LC1	Lapses of Consciousness
DA1	Diabetic	NE1	Neurological
DR1	Addiction	OR1	Orthopedic
DV2	Diabetic and Vision	PS1	Psychological
EN2	Epilepsy and Neurological	VI1	Vision
EP1	Epilepsy	VI2	Federal vision waiver granted - 1 year

New Mexico Citation and Code Index with ACD and Statute

- Please note the New Mexico **Withdrawals and Administrative Actions Index** follows this table.
- All tables are ordered by the state's Code column. The table includes some Administrative Transactions.
- The MVD indicated that out-of-state violations are often posted using the true ACD Codes as a code, especially when that code does not match into their own code. The table below will show the State Code and ACD Code as being identical only if a NM statute is specifically in place for that conviction. The complete AAMVA ACD Code list is found at the back of this book.

Code	ACD	Statute	Citation Description
AC1		66-8-101B	Violation of a motor vehicle law resulting in bodily injury
AC2		66-7-205	Violation of a motor vehicle law resulting in property damage
AC3			Violation of a motor vehicle law not resulting in damage to persons or property but considered an accident
AC4			Involvement in an accident, no indication of fault
AC5	B61	66-7-207	Failure to file accident report
BA1	A61	66-8-111C2	Revocation based on a blood alcohol content in excess of statutory limit-under age 21-1st offense
BA2	A61	66-8-111C3	Revocation based on a blood alcohol content in excess of statutory limit-under age 21-subsequent offense.
BA3	A98	66-8-111	Revocation based on a blood alcohol content in excess of statutory limit-age 18 and over-1st offense
BA4	A61	66-8-111C2	Revocation based on a blood alcohol content in excess of the statutory limit-under age 21-1st offense, lab tested
BA5	A61	66-8-111C3	Revocation based on a blood alcohol content in excess of the statutory limit-under age 21-subsequent offense, lab tested
BA6	A98	66-8-111	Revocation based on a blood alcohol content in excess of statutory limit-age 21 and over-1st offense, lab tested
BA7	A98	66-8-111	Revocation based on blood alcohol content in excess of statutory limit-age 21 and over-subsequent offense
BA8	A98	66-8-111	Revocation based on blood alcohol content in excess of statutory limit-age 21 and over-subsequent offense, lab tested
B19	B19	66-5-59B	Driving while OOSO in effect while transporting 16 or more passengers including driver and/or transporting hazmat requiring placard
B62	B62	66-5-22	Failure to give notice for address change
B72		65-5-16	Failure to show driver license or related document
CC1		65-2-83	Failure to comply with SCC rules or regulations
CC2		65-2-84	Failure to obtain intrastate authority
CC3		65-2-105	Failure to register lease
CC4		65-2-115	Failure to obtain interstate authority
CR1	F02	66-7-369	Child-passenger restraint
C11	A04	66-5-68.1	Driving a commercial vehicle while person's alcohol concentration is .04% or more; commercial motor vehicle only
C12	A21	66-8-102	Driving under the influence of alcohol as prescribed by state law while operating a commercial motor vehicle
C13	A12	66-8-111	Refusal to undergo testing required by state or jurisdiction in the enforcement of the laws relating to driving while under the influence of alcohol when operating a commercial motor vehicle
C14	A22	66-8-102B	Driving a commercial motor vehicle while under the influence of a controlled substance; commercial motor vehicle only
C15	B01	66-7-206	Failure to give immediate notice of an accident involving injury, death, or property damage in excess of $100.00 Leaving the scene of an accident involving a commercial motor vehicle in a commercial motor vehicle
C16	U03		A felony involving the use of a commercial motor vehicle; commercial motor vehicle only
C17	A50		Use of a commercial motor vehicle in the commission of a felony involving manufacturing, distribution, or dispensing of a controlled substance; commercial motor vehicle only
C18	S15		Excessive speeding, involving any single offense for any speed of 15 or more mph above the posted speed limit; commercial motor vehicle only
C19	M81	66-8-114	Driving a commercial motor vehicle in willful or wanton disregard for the safety of persons or property (careless driving)
C20	M84	66-8-113	Reckless driving as defined by state or local law or regulation including driving in willful or wanton

Code	ACD	Statute	Citation Description
			disregard for safety of persons or property while operating a commercial motor vehicle
C21	M42	66-7-317	Failure to keep in proper lane _improper or erratic traffic lane changes_ while operating a commercial motor vehicle
C22	M34	66-7-318A	Following the vehicle ahead too closely while operating a commercial motor vehicle
C23	U31	66-8-101	Violation of state or local law (arising in connection with fatal accident) relating to motor vehicle traffic control while operating a commercial motor vehicle
DE1	E34	66-3-804	Operating with defective headlights
DE2	E31	66-3-840	Operating with defective brakes
DE3		66-3-844	Operating with defective muffler or exhaust system
DE4	E37	66-3-847	Operating with defective tires
DE5	F66	66-3-801,66-3-807,66-3-901	Operating with any defective equipment resulting in inability to control vehicle movement properly (three points prior to 7/1/92)
DF1		66-5-135G	Court deferment (excluding DWI citations)
DI0	A20	66-8-102	Driving while intoxicated; first offense, DWI school (code valid for DWI violation occurring prior to 7/1/90)
DI1	A21	66-5-5	Revocation based on at least 3 convictions of driving under the intoxicating influence of alcohol, narcotics, or pathogenic drugs (Editor's Note: rarely seen - most DI1 convictions are for 66-8-102)
DI1	A21	66-8-102	Driving under the intoxicating influence of alcohol, narcotics, or pathogenic drugs
DI2	A24		Driving while under the intoxicating influence of medication or other substances not intended to produce intoxication as a result of normal use
DI3	A12	66-8-111	Revocation based on refusal to submit to tests for alcohol after arrest for DWI or suspicion of intoxication
DI4			Illegal possession of alcohol or drugs in motor vehicle
DS2	D75		Operating a motor vehicle improperly because of physical or mental disability
DS3	D74		Failure to discontinue operating vehicle after onset of physical or mental disability (including uncontrolled drowsiness)
EB1	F66	65-3-9B	Absence of braking action
EB2	F66	65-3-9B1	Damaged brake lining or pads
EB3	F66	65-3-12A	Loose or missing brake components
EB4	F66	65-3-12A1	Inoperable breakaway braking system
EB5	F66	65-3-12A2	Defective or damaged brake tubing
EB6	F66	65-3-9B2	Inoperable low pressure warning device
EB7	F66	65-3-12A4	Reservoir pressure not maintained
EB8	F66	65-3-9B3	Inoperative tractor protection valve
EB9	F66	65-3-12B4	Damaged or loose air compressor
EC1	F66	65-3-12A5	Audible air leak at brake chamber
EC2	F66	65-3-9E	Defective safety devices-chains or hooks
EC3	F66	65-3-9E1	Defective towing or coupling devices
EC4	F66	65-3-9H	Defective exhaust systems
ED2	F66	65-3-8A	Unsafe loading
ED3	F66	65-3-9N	Defective or missing windshield wipers
ED4	F66	65-3-9M	Defective or inoperative emergency exit - bus
EF1	F66	65-3-12B4	Frame defects - trailers
EF2	F66	65-3-9I	Frame defects - other
EF3	F66	65-3-9D	Defective fuel systems
EH1	F66	65-3-13A1	Cargo tank not meeting specifications
EH2	F66	65-3-13A2	Internal valve operation violations
EL1	E34	65-3-9A	Missing or inoperative lamps
EL2	E34	65-3-9A1	Missing lamps on projecting loads
EL3	E34	65-3-9A2	Missing or inoperative turn signal
EM1		66-7-353	Leaving vehicle unattended with engine running
EM2		66-7-357	Overloading vehicle unattended with passengers or cargo (three points prior to 7/1/92)
EM3		66-7-408	Towing or pushing vehicle improperly
EM4		66-3-843	Creating unlawful noise with vehicle or accessory
EM5	E54	66-3-831	Failure to dim lights as required by law (three points prior to 7/1/92)
EM6	U04		Using a motor vehicle in connection with illegal activity other than felony
EM7	U25	66-3-504,A	Operating or using a vehicle without consent of owner
EM8	E55		Failure to turn on lights
EM9	D70		Driving with obstructed vision
ER1	E01	66-7-356	Operating without equipment required by law
ER2		66-7-358	Use of equipment prohibited by law
ES1	F66	65-3-9K	Excessive steering wheel play
ES2	F66	65-3-9K1	Steering column defects
ES3	F66	65-3-9K2	Steering box, steering system defects
ES4	F66	65-3-9K3	Suspension system defects
ES5	F66	65-3-9J	Defective springs or spring assembly

Code	ACD	Statute	Citation Description
ET1	E37	65-3-9F	Defective tires - steering axle
ET2	E37	65-3-9F1	Defective tires - other axles
ET3	E37	65-3-9F2	Defective wheels and rims
FA1	U31	66-8-101	Violation of a motor vehicle law resulting in the death of another person
FA2	--		Violation of a motor vehicle law resulting in one's own death
FA3	--		Suicide by motor vehicle
FA4	U31	66-8-101	Violation of a motor vehicle law resulting in the death of another person
FE1	U03		Using a motor vehicle as the device for committing a felony
FE3	U05		Using a motor vehicle to aid and abet a felon
FO1	M34	66-7-318,A	Following too closely
FO2	M31	66-7-318B	Failure of truck to leave sufficient distance for overtaking by other vehicles
FO3	M32	-	Following emergency vehicle unlawfully
FR4	B63	66-5-205	Failure to file future proof of financial responsibility as required under any other provisions of the FR law
FR5	D36	66-5-205B, 66-5-229,C	Failure to maintain required compulsory liability insurance
HM1	-	65-3-13A	Placarding violations
HM2	-	65-3-13A3	Hazardous materials packaging violations
HM3	-	65-3-13A4	Insecure load - hazardous materials
HM4	-	65-3-13A5	Shipping papers violations
HM5	-	65-3-13A6	Shipment of forbidden combination of hazardous materials
HM6	-	65-3-13A7	No hazardous waste manifest
HM7	-	65-3-13A8	Bulk packaging marking violations
HM8	-	65-3-13A9	Cargo tank marking violations
HR1	B03	66-7-201	Failure to stop and render aid after involvement in an accident resulting in bodily injury
HR2		66-7-204, 66-7-205	Failure to stop and reveal identity after involvement in an accident resulting in property damage only
HR3	B05	66-7-205	Leaving the scene of an accident after providing aid or identity before arrival of police
HR4	U01		Evading arrest by fleeing the scene of citation or road block
HR5	U01		Evading arrest by extinguishing lights (when required)
IL1	M42	66-7-317	Improper lane changing
IL2	M41	66-7-317	Failure to keep in proper lane
IL3	M43	-	Ran off road
IL4	M58	-	Driving on road shoulder, in ditch or on sidewalk
IL5	M46	-	Making improper entrance to or exit from trafficway
LI1		30-8-10, 66-7-364	Depositing injurious or harmful substance on trafficway
LI2			Throwing from vehicle any burning or smoldering substance
LI3			Littering from a motor vehicle
M10	M10	66-7-341A1	Failing to obey traffic control devices, gates or barriers or directions of officer at RR grade crossing
M20	M20	66-7-341A2B	Failing to stop at proper distance, RR crossing, approaching train
M21	M21	66-7-341A2A	Failing to stop at proper distance, RR crossing, while train moving through crossing
M23	M23	66-7-341A3	Failing to proceed properly thru RR grade crossing, only if safe
M24	M24	66-7-341B3	Failing to have proper undercarriage clearance at RR crossing
MC1		65-1-12	Failure to register motor carrier vehicle
MC2		65-1-26	Failure to produce registration or tax card
MC3		65-5-1	Failure to produce manifest or stop at designated POE
MC4		65-5-2	Failure to produce tax receipt or tax card
MC5		65-5-3	Failure to obtain clearance certificate
MC6		65-5-4	Failure to obtain short term registration
MR1	D02	66-5-37E	Misrepresentation of identity or other facts to obtain a driver's license
MR2	B41	66-5-37F	Displaying a driver's license which is invalid because of alteration, counterfeiting, or withdrawal (revocation, suspension, etc.)
MR3	D16	66-5-37C	Displaying the driver license of another person
MR4		66-5-37B	Loaning a driver license
MR5	D02		Obtaining or applying for a duplicate driver license during withdrawal
MR6			Misrepresentation of identity or other facts to avoid arrest or prosecution
MS1	N83	66-7-324	Starting improperly from a parked position
MS2	N82	66-7-354	Improper backing
MS3		66-7-367	Opening vehicle closure into traffic, or while vehicle in motion
MS4	M56	66-7-362	Crossing fire hose with vehicle
MS5	D77		Sex offense in a motor vehicle
MS6	N84	66-7-359	Unsafe operation of vehicle
OH1	M40	66-3-1010	Not meeting safety requirement while operating an off-highway vehicle
OL1		66-7-401	Violation of state size and weight law
OL2		66-7-407	Failure to secure load
OL3		66-7-408	Inadequate trailer connection or unbalanced loading
OL4		66-7-409	Overweight on axles
OL5		66-7-410	Gross weight or bridge weight exceeds limits

Code	ACD	Statute	Citation Description
OL6		66-7-411	Shipper loading violation; or refusal to submit to weighing; or gross/comb weight exceeds max
OL7		66-7-413	Oversize/overweight permit violation
OL8		66-7-416	Damage to highway structure or surface
OL9		66-7-413	Transport of reducible load with special permit more than 6 miles from border crossing
OS1		66-7-402	Violation of state width law
OS2		66-7-403	Violation of lateral projection law
OS3		66-7-404,E	Violation of maximum height or length law
OS4		66-7-406	Violation of front or rear overhang law
PA1	M76	66-7-315	Passing where prohibited by posted signs, pavement marking, or hill or curve
PA2	M73		Passing on the wrong side
PA3	M77	66-7-312	Passing with insufficient distance allowed for other vehicles or with inadequate visibility
PA4	M75	66-7-347	Passing school bus taking-on or discharging passengers or displaying warning not to pass
PA5	N42		Failure to signal intention to pass
PA6	N07	66-7-332.1	Failure to yield to overtaking vehicle
PR1		40-5A-12	Parental responsibility surcharge fee
RF1		66-5-33.1	Reinstatement fee
RF2		66-5-33.1	Reinstatement fee
RK1	M84	66-8-113	Heedless, willful, wanton, or reckless disregard of rights and safety of others in operating a motor vehicle, endangering persons or property (reckless driving)
RK2	M81	66-8-114,B	Operating a motor vehicle without the exercise of care and caution required to avoid danger to persons or property (careless driving)
RK3	E53	66-3-858	Transporting hazardous substance without required safety devices or precautions
RK4	N80	66-7-360	Coasting or operating with gears disengaged
RR1	B61	66-7-210	Failure to file report of accident as required
RR2	D45	66-8-126	Failure to appear for hearing or for trial
RR3		66-5-37D	Failure to surrender driver license, registration, or title documents as required
RR4		66-3-13, 66-4-16	Failure to keep driver license or registration certificates in possession while driving or in vehicle as required
RR5		66-3-17,C, 66-3-18, A	Operating motor vehicle with registration plates missing, defaced, or obscured
RT1		65-3-4, 66-3-19,E	Operating a vehicle without registering it as required
RT2		66-3-19C	Operating with expired registration
RT3		66-8-3	Misrepresentation of identity or other facts to obtain title or registration
RT4		66-8-2, 66-8-3	Displaying a registration or title which is invalid because of alteration, counterfeiting, or withdrawal (revocation, suspension, etc.)
RT5			Displaying a registration or plates which are invalid - other
RT8		66-3-18B	Improper use of evidences of registration
RW1	N04	66-7-332	Operation of vehicle on approach of emergency vehicle
RW2	N01	66-7-345/346	Failure to yield right-of-way at YIELD sign, after STOP sign, or when emerging from private trafficway
RW2	N26	66-7-345C	Failure to yield right-of-way at YIELD sign, after STOP sign, or when emerging from private trafficway
RW3	N25	66-7-328	Failure to yield right-of-way in manner required at unsigned intersection
RW4	N08	66-7-334	Failure to yield right-of-way to pedestrian, animal rider, or animal-drawn vehicle as required (66-7-337 was three points prior to 7/1/92)
RW5	N09		Failure to yield to school bus as required
RW6	N01	-	Failure to yield right of way
SA1	-	65-1-9	Federal hazardous materials violation
SA2	-	65-3-3	General state safety regulation violation
SA3	-	65-3-7	Driver qualification - state
SA4	-	65-3-8	Driving of motor vehicles - state
SA5	E01	65-3-9	Parts and accessories - state
SA6	-	65-3-11	Driver hours of service - state
SA7	-	65-3-12	Inspection, repair & maintenance violation - state
SA8	E53	65-3-13	State hazardous materials violation
SB1	F04	66-7-372 & 373	Safety belt use required
SB1	F04	66-7-373	Child restraint use required
SC1	M08	66-7-4	Failure to follow instructions of police officer
SC2	M17	66-7-105 & 342	Failure to obey traffic instructions stated on traffic sign or shown by traffic-control device
SC3	M02	66-7-319	Passing through or around barrier positioned to prohibit or channel traffic
SC4	M30		Failure to observe warnings or instruction on vehicle properly displaying them
SC5	M12	66-7-303.1,C,D	Failure to observe safety zone
SC6		66-7-108, 6-7-109	Obscuring, tampering with, or illegally displaying traffic-control devices, warning, or instructions
SI1	N40	66-7-325	Failure to signal intention to change vehicle direction or to reduce speed suddenly (three points prior to 7/1/92)
SI2	N44	66-7-326	Giving wrong signal (three points prior to 7/1/92)
SI3	N41		Failure to cancel directional signals after executing maneuver

Code	ACD	Statute	Citation Description
SN1	E70	66-3-846.1	Violation of sun screening material on windshield and windows, requirements, violations and penalties
SP1	S95	66-8-115	Contest racing on public trafficway
SP2	S94		Prima facie speed violation or driving too fast for conditions
SP3	S93	66-7-306	Speed in excess of posted maximum
SP4	S96	66-7-305	Speed less than posted minimum (three points prior to 7/1/92)
SP5	S97		Operating a erratic or suddenly changing speeds
SP6	S93		Excessive speed in commercial vehicle
SP9			Speeding in a school zone
TK2	-	-	Case dismissed (DWI - criminal)
TK3	-	-	Failure to appear in court (DWI - criminal)
TK4		-	Reduction in offense (DWI - criminal)
TL1	--	66-8-111.1	Temporary permit, implied consent violations
TM2	N51		Turning on curve or crest of grade prohibited
TU1	N54		Making right turn from left turn lane
TU2	N53		Making left turn from right turn lane
TU3	N50	66-7-322/3	Making improper turn
VA1	D29	65-3-7B	Driver's age
VA2	B91	65-3-7B5	Driver not licensed for the type of vehicle being operated
VA3	B56	66-5-59A	Failure to have valid commercial driver's license in possession
VA4	-	65-3-7B3	No waiver of physical disqualification in possession
VA5	D74	65-3-8B2	Sickness or fatigue
VA6	B24	65-3-7B4	Driver disqualification
VB1	-	65-3-11	Exceeding the 10 hour driving rule
VB2	-	65-3-11A	Exceeding the 15 hour on duty rule
VB3	-	65-3-11A1	Exceed the 60 hours in 7 days on duty rule
VB4	-	65-3-11A2	Exceed the 70 hours in 8 days on duty rule
VB5	-	65-3-11A3	False log book
VR1	B25	66-5-39	Driving while revoked
VR2	B26	66-5-39	Driving while suspended
VR3	B23		Driving after license denied
VR4	D29	66-5-19,E	Operating contrary to conditions specified on driver license
VR5	B51	66-5-2/59	Operating without being licensed or without license required for type of vehicle operated
VR5	B51	66-5-21	Invalid driver license
VR5	B51	66-5-37	Unlawful use of license
VR6		66-5-41	Allowing an unlicensed operator to drive
VR7	B27	66-5-59D	Driving CMV when out-of-service order is in effect
WA1		MVC5-30:4	MVD warning notice for point accumulation
WW1	N63	66-7-316,B	Driving wrong way on one-way street
WW2	N72	66-7-317	Driving on wrong side of road
WW3	N61	66-7-316,C	Driving in wrong direction at rotary intersection
WW4	M40		Driving in wrong lane
XA1	A31	66-8-138	Illegal consumption or possession of alcoholic beverages in open containers in a motor vehicle
XA2	A33	32-1-34E5	Illegal possession, use, or abuse of controlled substance or certain chemical substances by a minor (adjudicated as a delinquent)
XA3	A04	66-8-111C	Operating a commercial motor vehicle with a blood alcohol content in excess of the statutory limit; age 21 and over, first offense
XA4	A04	66-8-111C1	Operating a commercial motor vehicle with a blood alcohol content in excess of the statutory limit; age 21 and over, first offense, lab tested
XA5	A04	66-8-111C3	Operating a commercial motor vehicle with a blood alcohol content in excess of the statutory limit; age 21 and over, subsequent offense
XA6	A04	66-8-111C3	Operating a commercial motor vehicle with a blood alcohol content in excess of the statutory limit; age 21 and over, subsequent offense, lab tested
XB1		66-3-505	Receiving or transferring stolen vehicle or motor vehicle
XB2		66-5-38	Perjury conviction
XB3	U03	30-3-8	Shooting at or from a motor vehicle
XB4	U03	30-3-8	Conspiracy or Attempt to shoot at or from a motor vehicle
XF1	B04	66-7-202	Failure to stop, reveal identity and/or render aid
XF2	B01	66-7-206	Failure to give immediate notice of an accident involving injury, death, or property damage in excess of $100
XG1	M40	66-7-308	Drive on right side of roadway
XG2	M72	66-7-309	Passing vehicle proceeding in opposite direction
XG3	M70	66-7-310/311/312	Improper overtaking or passing of a vehicle
XG4	M40	66-7-313	Driving to the left of center of roadway when prohibited
XG5	M40	66-3-1011 & 1012 & 1013, 66-7-320 & 321	Operation of a vehicle where prohibited
XG6	N51	66-7-329	Vehicle turning left at intersection

Code	ACD	Statute	Citation Description
XG7	M22	66-7-343	Certain vehicle must stop at railroad grade crossings
XG8	M09	66-7-344	Moving heavy equipment at railroad grade crossing
XG9	--	66-7-366	Riding in or towing occupied house-trailer
XH1	S01	66-7-301	Speed 1 to 5 mph over if the posted limit is 15, 30 or 75
XH2	S92	66-7-301	Speed 6 to 15 mph over if the posted limit is 15, 30 or 75
XH3	S92	66-7-301	Speed 6 to 15 mph over if the posted limit is other than 15, 30 or 75 and the speed is at least 76
XH4	S15	66-7-301	Speeding 16 to 25 over if the posted limit is 15, 30 or 75
XH5	S15	66-7-301	Speeding 16 to 25 over if the posted limit is other 15, 30 or 75 and the speed is at least 76
XH6	S92	66-7-301	Speeding 26 or more over the posted limit if limit is 15, 30 or 75
XH7	S15	66-7-301	Speeding 26 or more over if the posted limit is other 15, 30 or 75 and the speed is at least 76
XH8	S92	66-7-301	Speeding 1 or more over posted limit if limit is other than 15 or 30 and speed was less than 76 mph
XJ1	E55	66-3-802	Failure to turn on headlights
XJ2	E55	66-3-853 thru 857	Improper emergency signal
XJ3	E50	66-3-887	No slow-moving vehicle emblem or flashing amber light
XJ4	F66	66-3-846	Operating with any defective equipment resulting in inability to control vehicle movement properly
XJ5	E34	66-3-805	Defective tail lamps
XK1		30-8-4	Littering
XK2		66-3-851/852, 66-7-349-352	Improper or dangerous parking
XK3		66-5-40	Permitting unauthorized minor to drive
XK4	--	66-5-37G	Do any forbidden act or fail to perform any act required by the New Mexico Motor Vehicle Code
XM1	B41	66-5-18A	Possession of altered, forged, or fictitious license
XM2	D10	66-5-18B	Forging or making a fictitious driver's license or permit
XM3	D16	66-5-37A	Display, permit to be displayed, or possess any canceled, revoked, or suspended driver's license or permit
XM4		66-5-37D	Fail or refuse to surrender a driver's license or permit
XM5	--	66-5-37F	Permit any unlawful use of driver's license or permit
XN1	S92	66-7-301	Speeding in CMV 6 to 14 over limit when posted limit is 15 or 30
XN2	S15	66-7-301	Speeding in CMV 15 or more over limit when posted limit is 15 or 30
XN3	S92	66-7-301	Speeding in CMV 6 to 14 over limit when posted limit is other than 15 or 30 and speed is at least 76 mph
XN4	S15	66-7-301	Speeding in CMV 15 or more over limit when posted limit is other than 15 or 30 and speed is at least 76 mph
XN5	S92	66-7-301	Speeding in CMV 6 to 14 over limit when posted limit is other than 15 or 30 and speed is less than 76 mph
XN6	S15	66-7-301	Speeding in CMV 15 or more over limit when posted limit is other than 15 or 30 and speed is less than 76 mph
XP1	S92	66-7-301	Speeding in any vehicle 1 to 14 mph over the posted speed limit on a public highway in a zone where the posted speed limit is less that 55 mph
XP2	S15	66-7-301	Speeding in a commercial vehicle 15 to 30 mph over the posted speed limit on any trafficway where the posted speed limit is less than 55 mph
XX1	M01	66-7-333	Pedestrians subject to traffic regulations
XX2	-	66-7-340	Pedestrians soliciting rides of business

New Mexico Withdrawals and Administrative Actions Index

The Withdrawals and Administrative Actions are indicated in the Type column as follows:

SUSP	=	**Suspension**
REV	=	**Revocation**
DISQ	=	**Disqualification**
CAN	=	**Cancellation**
DEN	=	**Denial**
OTH	=	**Other Administration Actions**

The table is presented in order of the **Code** column, which shows on the driving record. The MVD indicated that out-of-state violations are often posted using the true ACD Codes as a code, especially when that code does not match into their own code. The table below will show the State Code and ACD Code as being identical only when a NM statute is specifically in place for that conviction. The complete AAMVA ACD Code list is found at the back of this book.

Type	Code	ACD	Statute	Description
DISQ	A04	A04	66-5-68	Disqualification for first A04 violation
DISQ	A08	A08	66-5-68	Disqualification for first A08 violation
DISQ	A10	A10	66-5-69	Disqualification for first A10 violation
DISQ	A11	A11	66-5-68	Disqualification for first A11 violation
DISQ	A12	A12	66-5-68	Disqualification for refusal to submit to test for alcohol - implied consent law
DISQ	A20	A20	66-5-68	Disqualification for first A20 violation

Type	Code	ACD	Statute	Description
DISQ	A21	A21	66-5-68	Disqualification for a major violation for driving a motor vehicle or commercial vehicle while under the influence of alcohol
DISQ	A22	A22	66-5-68	Disqualification for first A22 violation
DISQ	A23	A23	66-5-68	Disqualification for first A23 violation
DISQ	A50	A50	66-5-68	Lifetime disqualification for using a CMV in the commission of a felony involving manufacturing, distributing or dispensing a controlled substance
DISQ	A61	A61	66-5-68	Underage administrative per se - drinking and driving at .02 or higher BAC
DISQ	A90	A90	66-5-68	1-Year disqualification for administrative per se - blood alcohol content in excess of statutory limit
DISQ	A91	A91	66-5-68	Disqualification for first A91 violation
DISQ	A94	A94	66-5-68	Disqualification for first A94 violation
DISQ	A98	A98	66-5-68	Disqualification for first A98 violation
REV	AC1		66-5-29	Revocation based on conviction of violation of a motor vehicle law resulting in bodily injury
DISQ	B01	B01	66-5-68	Disqualification for first B01 violation
DISQ	B02	B02	66-5-68	Disqualification for first B02 violation
DISQ	B03	B03	66-5-68	Disqualification for first B03 violation
DISQ	B04	B04	66-5-68	Disqualification for first B04 violation
DISQ	B05	B05	66-5-68	Disqualification for first B05 violation
DISQ	B06	B06	66-5-68	Disqualification for first B06 violation
DISQ	B07	B07	66-5-68	Disqualification for first B07 violation
DISQ	B08	B08	66-5-68	Disqualification for first B08 violation
DISQ	B20	B20	66-5-68	Disqualification for first B20 violation
DISQ	B21	B21	66-5-68	Disqualification for first B21 violation
DISQ	B22	B22	66-5-68	Disqualification for first B22 violation
DISQ	B23	B23	66-5-68	Disqualification for first B23 violation
DISQ	B24	B24	66-5-68	Disqualification for driving while disqualified
DISQ	B25	B25	66-5-68	1-year disq for CDL holder convicted of driving while license is revoked, disq or susp
DISQ	B26	B26	66-5-68	1-year disq for CDL holder convicted of driving CMV after CDL is revoked, disq or susp
DISQ	B27	B27	66-5-71	1-year disq for driving CMV when out-of-service order in effect
DISQ	B27	B27	66-5-68	Disqualification for first B27 violation
DISQ	B51	B51	66-5-68	1-year disq for CDL holder convicted of driving while CDL license is cancelled for a violation committed while oper a CMV
REV	BA1	A61	66-8-111C2	Revocation based on a BAC in excess of statutory limit - under age 21 1st offense
REV	BA2	A61	66-8-111C3	Revocation based on a BAC in excess of statutory limit - under age 21 subsequent offense
REV	BA3	A98	66-8-111C1	Revocation based on a BAC in excess of statutory limit - age 21 and over, 1st offense
REV	BA4	A61	66-8-111C2	Revocation based on a BAC in excess of the statutory limit - under 21, 1st offense, lab tested
REV	BA5	A61	66-8-111C3	Revocation based on a BAC in excess of the statutory limit - under 21, subsequent offense, lab tested
REV	BA6	A98	66-8-111C1	Revocation based on a BAC in excess of statutory limit - age 21 and over, 1st offense, lab tested
REV	BA7	A98	66-8-111C3	Revocation based on a BAC in excess of statutory limit - age 21 and over, subsequent offense
REV	BA8	A98	66-8-111C3	Revocation based on a BAC in excess of statutory limit - age 21 and over, subsequent offense, lab tested
OTH	BC1			Dishonored check for ID, driver license, permit, registration, plate, title, or other doucment
OTH	BC2			Dishonored check for penalty assessment
REV	C13	A12	66-8-111	Rev based on refusal to undergo testing required by state or jurisdiction in the enforcement of the laws relating to driving while under the influence of alcohol when operating a CMV
DISQ	C51	A04	66-5-68A2A	Disqualification for driving a commercial motor vehicle while person's alcohol concentration is .04 percent or more while transporting placarded quantities of HAZMAT
DISQ	C52	A21	66-5-68	Disqualification for violation of Section 66-8-102; driving under the intoxicating influence of alcohol in a commercial motor vehicle
DISQ	C53	A12	66-5-68	Disqualification for violation of 66-8-111; refusal to submit to test for alcohol after arrest for DWI or suspension of intoxication in a commercial motor vehicle
DISQ	C54	A22	66-5-68A1	Disqualification for driving a commercial motor vehicle while under the influence of a controlled substance
DISQ	C55	B05	66-5-68A2	Disqualification for leaving the scene of an accident involving a commercial motor vehicle
DISQ	C56	U03	66-5-68C	Disqualification for felony involving a commercial vehicle; other than a felony involving manufacturing, distribution, or dispensing of a controlled substance
DISQ	C61	A04	66-5-68C	Disqualification for driving a commercial motor vehicle while person's alcohol concentration is .04 percent or more while transporting placarded quantities of HAZMAT
DISQ	C62	A21	66-5-68C	Disqualification for first conviction of section 66-8-102; driving under the intoxicating influence of alcohol in a commercial vehicle transporting placarded quantities of hazardous materials
DISQ	C63	A12	66-5-68A1	Disqualification for violation 66-8-111; refusal to submit to test for alcohol after arrest for DWI or suspension of intoxication in a commercial vehicle transporting placarded quantities of hazardous materials
DISQ	C64	A22	66-5-68A1	Disqualification for driving a commercial motor vehicle transporting placarded quantities of hazardous materials while under the influence of a controlled substance
DISQ	C65	B05	66-5-68A2B	Disqualification for leaving the scene of an accident involving a commercial motor vehicle transporting placarded quantities of hazardous materials

Type	Code	ACD	Statute	Description
DISQ	C66	U03	66-5-68A2C	Disqualification for a felony involving a commercial motor vehicle transporting placarded quantities of hazardous material; other than a felony involving manufacturing, distribution or dispensing of a controlled substance
DISQ	C70	A50	66-5-68C	Disqualification for felony involving manufacturing, distribution or dispensing of a controlled substance, or possession with intent to manufacture, distribute or dispense a controlled substance act in a commercial motor vehicle
DISQ	C71	W01	66-5-68B	Lifetime disqualification for two or more convictions of DUI alcohol or controlled substance, leaving the scene of an accident involving death or serious injury, or commission of a felony not involving manufacturing, distribution or dispensing a controlled substance in a commercial motor vehicle
DISQ	C72	D02	66-5-60E	One Year Disqualification committing an offense when taking CDL test specified per 66-5-60. Driver required to reapply for CDL.
DISQ	C80	W30	66-5-68E	Disqualification for conviction of two serious traffic violations in separate incidents during any three-year period
DISQ	C81	W31	66-5-68E	Disqualification for conviction of three serious traffic violations in separate incidents during any three-year period
DISQ	C82	D02	18.19..5.15	60 day DQ for providing false information to obtain CDL
DISQ	C83	B27	66-5-71 (1)	Disqualification for 1st conviction for driving CMV when driver or vehicle out of service order in effect-Disq 1-year
DISQ	C84	B27	66-5-71	Disqualification for 2nd conviction for driving CMV when driver or vehicle out of service order in effect-Disq 1 year
DISQ	C85	B27	66-5-71	Disqualification for 3rd or subs conviction for driving CMV when driver or vehicle out of service order in effect-Disq 3 years
DISQ	C86	B19	66-5-68F	Disqualification for violating a driver or vehicle out of service order while transporting HAZMAT - 1st offense-Disq 180 days
DISQ	C87	B19	66-5-68F	Disqualification for violating a driver or vehicle out of service order in CMV while transporting 16 or more passengers - 1st offense-Disq 180 days
DISQ	C88	B19	66-5-68F	Disqualification for violating a driver or vehicle out of service order while transporting HAZMAT - subsequent offense-3 years
DISQ	C89	B19	66-5-68F	Disqualification for 2 or more violations of either driver or vehicle out-of service orders within 10 years-while driving a vehicle designed for 16 or more passengers-Disq 3 years
DISQ	C90	B26	66-5-68D	1-year disqualification for driving CMV after CDL is revoked, suspended, disq or cancelled for violations while operating a CMV
DISQ	C91	B02	66-5-68E	1-year disqualification for being convicted of causing a fatality in unlawful operation of a CMV pursuant to Sec 66-8-101
REV	CA1	A94	66-8-111C	Revocation based on BAC of .04% or more in CMV - 1st offense
REV	CA2	A94	66-8-111C	Revocation based on BAC of .04% or more in CMV - subsequent offense
REV	CA3	A94	66-8-111C	Revocation based on BAC of .04% or more in CMV - 1st offense - Lab tested
REV	CA4	A94	66-8-111C	Revocation based on BAC of .04% or more in CMV - subsequent offense - Lab tested
SUR	CS		66-5-55	Voluntary surrender of NM commercial driver license
DISQ	D51	D51	40-5A-6	Disqualification for failure to make required child support payment
SUSP	D51	D51	40-5A-6	Suspension for failure to make required child support payments
CANC	DED			Deceased
OTH	DF1		66-5-135G	Court Deferment (excluding DWI citations)
DEN	DI1	A21	66-5-5D	Ineligible to apply for license for a period of 10 years - 3 DWIs within ten year period
REV	DI1	A21	66-5-5	Revocation based on at least three convictions of driving under the intoxicating influence of alcohol, narcotics, or pathogenic drugs
REV	DI1	A21	66-5-29	Revocation based on first or second conviction of driving under the intoxicating influence of alcohol, narcotics, or pathogenic drugs in 10 year period
REV	DI3	A12	66-8-111	Revocation based on refusal to submit to tests for alcohol after arrest for DWI or suspicion of intoxication
REV	DI5	A21		Administrative per se
DEN	DS1	W20	66-5-5F	Inability to pass one or more tests required for driver license or meet qualifications
DEN	DS4		66-5-5H	Inimical to public safety
REV	EM7		66-5-29	Revocation based on conviction of operating or using a vehicle without consent of owner
REV	FA1	U31	66-5-29	Revocation based on conviction of violation of a motor vehicle law resulting in the death of another person
SUSP	FA1		66-5-30	Violation of a motor vehicle law resulting in the death of another person
REV	FA4	U31	66-5-29	Violation of a motor vehicle law resulting in the death of another person (alcohol related)
OTH	FDL		66-5-24	Cancellation for failure to give the required or correct information in application or committed any fraud in making the application
REV	FE2	U03	66-5-29A4	Revocation based on conviction for using a motor vehicle in connection with a felony
OTH	FID		66-2-9	Seizure of any documents including but not limited to permit, license, which is fictitious or which has been unlawfully or erroneously issued
SUSP	FR1	D39	66-5-236A1	Suspension for unsatisfied judgment rendered as a result of an automobile accident
SUSP	FR2	D38	66-5-210B	Suspension for failure to meet requirements of the security following accident provisions of the FR

Type	Code	ACD	Statute	Description
				law, (default in payment under settlement agreement)
SUSP	FR3	B63	66-5-205D	Suspension for failure to file future proof of financial responsibility following conviction for violation of motor vehicle law
SUSP	FR4	B63	66-5-205	Suspension for failure to file future proof of financial responsibility as required under any other proof of financial responsibility law
SUSP	FR4	B63	66-5-205	Suspension for failure to file future proof of financial responsibility as required under any other provision of financial responsibility law
OTH	HG1		66-5-30B	Hearing requested/granted (suspension)
OTH	HG2		66-5-30B	Hearing requested/granted (revocation)
OTH	HG5		66-8-112B	Hearing requested/granted (implied consent act)
REV	HR1	B03	66-5-29	Revocation based on conviction of failure to render aid after involvement in an accident resulting in bodily injury
DISQ	M10	M10	66-5-68H(1)	Disqualification for 1st offense of violation driver or vehicle with out of service order in a CMV or the directions of an enforcing official at a railroad-highway grade crossing-60 days
DISQ	M10	M10	66-5-68	Disqualification for first M10 violation
DISQ	M20	M20	66-5-68H(1)	Disq-1st offense-failing to stop not more than 50 feet, and not less than 15 feet from the nearest rail of a crossing if a train is plainly visible and approaching within HAZ prox-60 days
DISQ	M21	M21	66-5-68K(1)	Disq-1st offense failing to stop more than 50 feet, not less than 15 feet from the nearest rail of a crossing when a train is moving through or blocking the crossing-60 days
DISQ	M22	M22	66-5-68K1	Disq- certain vehicles must stop at railroad highway grade crossing 1st offense-60 days
DISQ	M23	M23	66-5-68K1	60 day disq - going through RRGC when unable to go through without stopping completely pass through the entire RRHGC without stopping
DISQ	M24	M24	66-5-68K1	Disq - passing thru RRGC with insufficient undercarriage clearance - 1st offense 60 days
SUSP	MR1	D02	66-5-30	Misrepresentation to obtain license or has permitted an unlawful or fraudulent use of license
SUSP	MR2	B41	66-5-30	Suspension for displaying a driver's license which is invalid because of alteration, counterfeiting, or withdrawal
SUSP	MR3	D25	66-5-30	Suspension for displaying the driver license of another person
SUSP	MR4		66-5-30	Suspension for loaning a driver license
CANC	MR7	D02	66-5-24	Cancelled for misrepresentation of identity or facts to obtain a NM driver's license
OTH	PR1		40-5A-12	Parental responsibility surcharge fee
SUSP	RR3		66-5-30	Suspension for failure to surrender driver license, registration, or title documents as required
SUSP	RT3		66-8-4	Suspension for misrepresentation of identity or other facts to obtain title or registration
SUSP	RT4		66-8-4	Suspension for displaying a registration or title which is invalid because of alteration, counterfeiting, or withdrawal (revocation, suspension, etc.)
REV	RV1	W01	66-5-29A7, 66-8-139B	Revocation based on recurring violations requiring mandatory action of licensing authority as specified by law
SUSP	RV2	W01	MVCS-30:5	Suspension based on accumulation of violations resulting in mandatory action of the licensing authorities because of state point system
SUSP	RV3	W01	66-5-30A3	Suspension based on accumulation of violations resulting in discretionary action by the licensing authority
OTH	SH2		MVC5-32:1	Driver improvement school completed (point suspension)
OTH	SH4		MVC5-32:1	Failure to complete driver improvement school as required
DISQ	U03	U03	66-5-68	Disqualification using a motor vehicle in connection with a felony (not traffic offense)
DISQ	U07	U07	66-5-68	Disqualification for first U07 violation
DISQ	U08	U08	66-5-68	Disqualification for first U08 violation
DISQ	U10	U10	66-5-68	Disqualification for first U10 violation
DISQ	U31	U31	66-5-68	1-year disq for any CDL holder who causes a fatality in the unlawful operation of a CMV pursuant to section 66-8-101
REV	VR1	B25	66-5-39	Revocation based on conviction of driving while revoked
SUSP	VR2	B26	66-5-39	Suspension based on conviction of driving while suspended
SUSP	VR4	D29	66-5-19D	Suspension based on conviction of operations contrary to conditions specified on driver license
SUR	VS		66-5-49	Voluntary surrender of NM driver license
DISQ	W30	W30	66-5-68	Disq for two serious traffic convictions
DISQ	W31	W31	66-5-68	Disq for more that two serious traffic convictions
DISQ	W40	W40	66-5-68	Lifetime disqualification for 2 or more major offenses accumulated
DISQ	W41	W41	66-5-68	An additional major offense after reinstatement
DISQ	W50	W50	66-5-68	Accumulation of 2 out of service orders general violations within 10 years
DISQ	W51	W51	66-5-68	Second out of service order violation within ten years while transporting 16 or more passengers incl driver and/or transporting HAZMAT that requires placard
DISQ	W52	W52	66-5-68	Accumulation of 3 or more out of service orders general violations within 10 years
DISQ	W60	W60	66-5-68	Accumulation of 2 RR grade crossing violations within three years
DISQ	W60	W60	66-5-68	Disqualification for 2nd RRGC violation within 3 years
DISQ	W61	W61	66-5-68H	Accumulation of three or more RRGC violations within three years-Disq for 1 year
DISQ	W61	W61	66-5-68	Disqualification for 3rd RRGC violation within 3 years
DISQ	W70	W70	66-5-68	Imminent Hazard - CMV only

Type	Code	ACD	Statute	Description
OTH	W80		65-3-14	Drug and alcohol testing program-report of positive test
OTH	W81		65-3-14	Drug and alcohol testing program-report of positive test
OTH	WA1		MVC5-30:4	MVD warning notice (point accumulation based on traffic violation convictions)
REV	XA1	A31	66-8-139B	Revocation based on conviction of illegal consumption or possession of alcoholic beverages in containers in a motor vehicle
DEN	XA2	A33	32-1-34J	Denial based on illegal possession, use or abuse of controlled substance or certain chemical substances by a minor (adjudicated as a delinquent)
REV	XA2	A33	32-1-34J	Revocation based on illegal possession, use, or abuse of controlled substance or certain chemical substances by a minor (adjudicated as a delinquent)
REV	XA3	A08	66-8-111C1	Revocation based on a BAC in excess of the statutory limit - age 18 and over while operating a commercial motor vehicle
REV	XA4	A08	66-8-111C1	Revocation based on a BAC in excess of the statutory limit - age 18 and over, 1st offense, lab tested
REV	XA5	A08	66-8-111C3	Revocation based on a BAC in excess of statutory limit - age 18 and over, subsequent offense, while operating a commercial motor vehicle
REV	XA6	A08	66-8-111C3	Revocation based on a BAC in excess of the statutory limit - age 18 and over, subsequent offense, while operating a commercial motor vehicle, lab tested
REV	XB1		66-5-29	Revocation based on conviction of receiving or transferring stolen vehicle or motor vehicle
REV	XB2		66-5-29	Revocation based on perjury conviction
REV	XB3	U03	66-5-29	Revocation based on conviction for the offense of shooting at or from a motor vehicle
REV	XB4	U03	66-5-29	Revocation based on conviction for conspiracy or attempt to commit the offense of shooting at or from a motor vehicle
SUSP	XC1		66-5-31	Suspension for refusal to take examination as required
SUSP	XC2	W10	66-5-25a	Suspension or revocation of driving privileges of non-residents
SUSP	XC3	D53	66-5-30	Suspension for failure to remit penalty assessment
SUSP	XC4	D45	66-5-30	Suspension for failure to appear in court
SUSP	XC5	D53	66-8-137.1	Suspension for failure to comply with terms of traffic citation issued in another jurisdiction (NRVC)
DEN	XC6	W20	66-5-5E	Denied, medically disqualified
SUSP	XC6	W20	66-5-31	Suspended; medically disqualified
SUR	XD1		66-5-49	Surrendered a CDL license for a Class D or an ID card
CANC	XD2	W13	66-5-12	Canceled, parental consent withdrawn; minor under age eighteen
CANC	XD3	D02	66-5-24	Canceled for misrepresentation of identify or facts to obtain a New Mexico driver license
CANC	XD4		66-6-141	Cancellation due to dishonored check
CANC	XD5		66-5-401A	Cancelled for misrepresentation of identity or facts to obtain a NM Identification card
SUSP	XK4		66-5-30	Suspension for doing any forbidden act or failure to perform any act required by the New Mexico motor vehicle code
SUSP	XM1	B41	66-5-30	Suspension for possession of altered, forged, or fictitious license
SUSP	XM2	D10	66-5-30	Suspension for forging or making a fictitious driver's license or permit
SUSP	XM3	D16	66-5-30	Suspension for display, permitting to be displayed or possess, any cancelled, revoked, or suspended driver's license or permit
SUSP	XM4		66-5-30	Suspension for failing or refusing to surrender a driver's license or permit
SUSP	XM5		66-5-30	Suspension for permitting any unlawful use of driver's license of permit

Point System Summary

The points range from 2 to 6 points. The accumulation of 7 to 10 points in a 12-month period *may* result in a suspension of period of 3 months. The accumulation of 12 points in a 12 month period will result in a 12-month suspension.

New York

Administration	Important Telephone and Web Contacts

Barbara Fiala, Commissioner
Department of Motor Vehicles
6 ESP, Swan Street, Albany 12228
www.dmv.ny.gov
 	
Administrative Codes, Rules and Regulations:
     www.dos.ny.gov/info/nycrr.html
State Laws and Regulations:
     http://public.leginfo.state.ny.us/menugetf.cgi
	Call Center (Upstate)..................................518-486-9786
	Call Center (Downstate) 718-477-4820
	Driver Improvement....................................518-474-0774
	Financial Responsibility............................518-474-0700
	Request Driving Record 518-486-9786
	Commercial Driver License Policy Unit 518-473-9938
	State Department of Financial Services - Consumer Hotline
	          ... 518-474-6600, NY only 800-342-3736
	State Police...518-457-6811

Driver's License Format, Issuance and Renewal

License Classes, Restrictions and Endorsements Appear After the Driving Record Content Section

License Format

New York assigns randomly selected nine-digit numeric Client Identification Numbers to all driver licenses and non-driver ID cards.

Document Appearance

The current license format has been issued since 2005. Also in 2008 the DMV began issuing the WHTI-Compliant Enhanced Driver Licenses and non-driver photo IDs all using the newer format. It will take at least eight years for the new format to replace the old.

Current Format

Security Characteristics: A two-dimensional barcode is on the back of the document that verifies information contained on the front of the document. Prismatic or "rainbow" printing and duplex patterns within the design and fine line structures enhance the security features. An "optical variable device" (OVID) is imbedded within the laminate to prevent forgery. The wavy line, a feature unique to New York State, appears to float above the surface of the license.

On September 16, 2008, NYS began issuing WHTI-Compliant Enhanced driver licenses (EDL) (includes Enhanced learner permits) and Enhanced non-driver photo ID cards (ENDID) to applicants who can prove U.S. citizenship and NYS residency. An EDL or ENDID can be used instead of a passport for travel by land and sea between the United States and Canada, Mexico and some countries in the Caribbean. Features of an EDL/ENDID include "Enhanced" in white text within a red-orange bar, the U.S. flag at the lower right and a 2D barcode and machine readable zone on the back. License is made from "Teslin," a thick, durable material.

Position of Photo: Left.

Minor Age Driver Locator: All documents issued to individuals under the age of 21 have "under 21" printed vertically in red to the right of the photo. Client ID, DOB and expiration date are also printed in red.

CDL Indicator: "Commercial Driver License" printed in brown above client ID. Expiration date printed in red. All other pertinent information is in black.

Color Indicators: Color coding of the title line located underneath "NEW YORK STATE" distinguishes the document type: driver license - blue; restricted use - purple; conditional - purple; learner permit - green; commercial - brown; identification card - gold.

Old Format (prior to 2005)

Security Characteristics: Digital Imaging is used. Signature and image are digitally stored. Light blue and green security image of the NYS Coat of Arms in the background. The security CONFIRM laminate features the State Coat of Arms in a repetitive

arrangement. Current license is made from "Teslin," a thick, durable material.

Position of Photo: Bottom left.

Minor Age Driver Locator: "Under 21" printed in red right of photo. Client ID, DOB, and expiration date printed in red.

CDL Indicator: "Commercial Driver License" in brown above driver name. Expiration date printed in red. All other pertinent information in black.

Issuance

Location of Requirements for Proof of Identity:

See www.dmv.ny.gov/idlicense.htm

Age Requirements

The minimum age for a Class A commercial driver license is 21. The minimum age for a Class B or C license is 18; however, drivers are limited to driving in NYS only and may not transport hazardous materials or operate a school bus until they reach age 21. The minimum age is 18 for an unrestricted (non-commercial) driver license, or 17 with a driver education certificate.

Since September 1, 2003 a graduated licensing program is offered with three levels of permits for youthful drivers. Major changes were made to the program in February 2010. For example, an intermediate step between the Learner Permit and a "full" Junior License was eliminated. A Junior Permit must be held for at least 6 months before a Junior or Senior license may be issued. There are a myriad of restrictions to these levels, including regional restrictions in the New York City Boroughs and also Long Island. For details of these restrictions, visit www.dmv.ny.gov/youngerdriver/gradLicense.htm.

Residency

While a non-resident's home-state license honored, one must secure New York License within thirty days of establishing residency. Those under sixteen with an out-of-state licensees are not permitted to drive regardless of license type. Proof of New York State residency is required for issuance of a commercial driver license or an Enhanced driver license/learner permit or for an Enhanced non-driver ID card.

Renewal

A renewal is on the birth date every 8 years for all license classes. Online renewal is available at www.dmv.ny.gov/licrenew/default.html except for: learner permits; conditional or restricted licenses; licenses with an ignition interlock restriction; a commercial driver license that requires a medical certification for renewal; if a regular driver license/non-driver ID card is converted to an Enhanced Driver License (EDL) upon renewal; and licenses that are valid without photo. An Eye Test Report (*form MV-619*) is required. The driver keeps the same license number when renewing.

NYS Law automatically extends a valid driver license, for drivers on active military duty, throughout their military service for up to 6 months after the extended expiration. No more than 30 months may have passed since discharge (6-month extension plus 24-month grace period).

Once notified of military status, the DMV sets an indicator on the license record.

Elderly-Related Restrictions

None are reported.

Vehicle Insurance, Title and Registration Facts

Registration Renewal

Renewal is available by mail, in person or online at www.dmv.ny.gov. To renew online, the mailing address must be correct.

New Residents

New residents must register vehicles within thirty days of establishing residency.

Inspections and Emissions Testing

New York requires annual safety and emissions inspections or when the ownership of a vehicle is transferred. The DMV has the authority to require an additional inspection after involvement in an accident.

The **emissions inspection** requirement is based on the model year, fuel, weight, and the county where the vehicle is registered.

- Statewide, 1996 and newer light duty vehicles weighing 8500 lbs or less (except as noted below) receive an OBD II test, which is a test of the vehicles on-board diagnostic computer system. This includes gasoline, CNG and propane powered vehicles.
- Statewide, 1995 and older light duty non-OBD II equipped vehicles (except as noted below) weighing 8500 lbs or less receive a Low Enhanced inspection which is a visual check of the emissions control devices, including a visual check of the gas cap. This visual check is also required on OBD II inspections.
- Diesel powered vehicles registered in the New York Metropolitan Area (NYMA), which includes the 5 boroughs of NYC, Nassau, Suffolk, Rockland and Westchester counties, that are registered at more than 8500 lbs. receive a Diesel Emissions Inspection. All vehicles, regardless of year, registered at more than 8500 lbs. GVWR in the NYMA require the opacity test.

Vehicles less than 2 model years old, or more than 25 model years old, electric-powered, motorcycles, vehicles registered as Historical, and diesel powered vehicles (except those diesel vehicles listed above) are exempt from emissions testing.

Vehicles registered in New York State must also receive a **safety inspection**. Certain vehicles, such as Special Purpose Commercial, Farm vehicles, and some Limited Use vehicles are exempt from any inspection requirement.

Passenger Plate Facts

There are two plates with one decal (MO & YR) on front windshield for regular passenger vehicles and for most commercial vehicles. But many other vehicles have only one plate and a plate sticker that is valid for one year. The plates do not show where vehicle was registered. When a vehicle is sold, the plates remain with registrant to be transferred to another vehicle or must be surrendered to the DMV.

Insurance and Financial Responsibility

New York has a provision for compulsory insurance; proof of insurance must be in the vehicle at all times. Insurance companies must file electronic notices of new insurance, cancellation and reinstatement. Minimum financial responsibility limits are 25,000/50,000 for bodily injury, $50,000/100,000 for death, and $10,000 for property damage. The state has no-fault insurance provision.

Proof is required at registration, renewal of most-for-hire registrations and late renewal, when an accident occurs, and upon certain violations. All paper proof of insurance submitted must be electronically verified by the insurer.

Withdrawal Sanctions, and Alcohol and Drug Testing

Alcohol and Chemical Testing Limits

NY has varying provisions for illegal intoxication levels. A level of .08 percent and above (Driving While Intoxicated) is a misdemeanor; while a level .05 to .07 (Driving While Ability Impaired), is a traffic infraction. For commercial drivers, blood alcohol content levels .04 or above will result in revocation of commercial driving privileges. For drivers under 21, BAC levels of .02 or above will result in suspension or revocation of driving privileges. If you drive a motor vehicle in NY, you are considered to have already given your consent to submit to a chemical test. Urine, blood, saliva and breath testing are authorized.

Suspensions and Revocations - Non-CDL

Penalties for Alcohol-related and Drug-Related Violations

Violation (1)	Mandatory Driver License Action (3)
Aggravated Driving While Intoxicated (A-DWI)	Revoked for at least one year
Second A-DWI in 10 years (E felony)(1)	Revoked for at least 18-months (5)
Third A-DWI in 10 years (D felony)(1)	Revoked for at least 18-months (4,5)
Driving While Intoxicated (DWI)	Revoked for at least six months
Driving While Impaired by Drugs	Suspended for at least six months
Second Drug violation in 10 years (1)	Revoked for at least one year
Third -Drug violation in 10 years (1)	Revoked for at least one year (4)
Driving While Ability Impaired by a Combination of Alcohol/Drugs (DWAI-Combination)	Revoked for at least six months
Second DWAI/Combination in 10 years (E felony)(1)	Revoked for at least one year/18 months (5)
Third DWAI/Combination in 10 years (D felony)(1)	Revoked for at least one year/18 months (4,5)
Driving While Ability Impaired by Alcohol (DWAI)(3)	Suspended for 90 days
Second DWAI violation in 5 years(3)	Revoked for at least six months
Zero Tolerance Law	Suspended for six months
Second Zero Tolerance Law	Revoked for one year or until age 21

Violation (1)	Mandatory Driver License Action (3)
Chemical Test Refusal	Revoked for at least one year; 18 months if commercial driver.
Chemical Test Refusal within five years of a previous DWI-related charge/Chemical Test Refusal	Revoked for at least 18 months; one-year or until age 21 for drivers under age 21; permanent CDL revocation for commercial drivers.
Chemical Test Refusal - Zero Tolerance Law	Revoked for at least one year.
Chemical Test Refusal -Second or subsequent Zero Tolerance Law	Revoked for at least one year.
Driving Under the Influence - (Out-of-State)	90-day revocation. If less than 21 years of age, revoked at least one year.
Driving Under the Influence - (Out-of-State) with any previous alcohol-drug violation	90-day revocation. If less than 21 years of age, revoked at least one year or until age 21 (longest term).
Driving while Impaired by Drugs-(Out-of-State)	Suspended for 6 months
Drug Possession	Suspended for 6 months
Drug Possession-(Out-of-State)	Suspended for 6 months

Notes:
1. Surcharges are added to misdemeanors ($160) and felonies ($270).
2. The driver license penalties for drivers under the age of 21, and for drivers of commercial motor vehicles and other professional drivers, are different.
3. Since November 1, 2006 three or more alcohol or drug-related convictions or refusals can result in **permanent revocation**, with a waiver request permitted after at least 5 years. Three convictions within four years or four convictions within eight years.
4. A driver with an Aggravated DWI violation conviction within the prior 10 years will receive a minimum 18-month revocation if convicted of DWI, DWAI/Drugs or DWAI/Combination. Also a driver with a prior DWI, Aggravated DWI, DWAI/Drugs or DWAI/Combination with the prior 10 years will receive a minimum 18-month revocation.
5. An Aggravated DWI/Child in Car is when a DWI occurs with a child of 15 or younger in the car, is a Class E Felony.
6. Effective August 15, 2010, a driver sentenced for a DWI must have an Ignition Interlock Device installed on any vehicle they operate, plus an Ignition Interlock Restriction is placed on the license.

Other Suspensions/Revocations of Note

Leaving the Scene of a Personal Injury Accident ....Six-month revocation.
Operating an Uninsured Vehicle/Uninsured Accident....................................One-year revocation.
Operating an Uninsured Vehicle(Insurance Lapse) ....Registration/driver's license suspension period equals length of
 insurance lapse.
Three Speeding and/or Traffic Misdemeanors Within Eighteen Months..........Six-month revocation.

Suspensions and Revocations of CDLs and Drivers of Commercial Vehicles

See the Appendix for a list of the federally mandated disqualifications for offenses occurring in a CMV per MCSIA. Please review this list for Major Offenses, Serious Offenses, Railroad Grade Crossing Offenses and Out-Of-Service Violations.

Reinstatement Requirements

Suspension.....................................$25 to $100 suspension termination fee. The fee is a minimum of $50 if the suspension date was after July 6, 2009.
Revocation.....................................Re-application fee is $50 (if license was revoked before July 6, 2009) or $100 (if license was revoked on or after July 6, 2009); sanction time served; and payment of civil penalty fees of between $100 and $750 may apply. If out-of-state resident, $25 reinstatement fee; sanction time served, and payment of civil penalties between $100 and $750 may apply. The fee to reinstate a Refusal is between $100 and $750, depending on age and license type.
Suspension For Insurance Lapse....Registration must be surrendered for the length of lapse. If the lapse is 90 days or less, a civil penalty may be paid in lieu of surrender. Driver's license is suspended if the lapse is over 90 days. Suspension period is equal to the lapse and a $25 or $50 suspension termination fee must be paid.

Note: For a **Revocation for Uninsured Operation/Accident**, there is a required application for new license plus license application fees, FS-15 Affirmation form, $750 civil penalty.

Note: There are a number of proposed 2012-13 regulatory changes that are pending official adoption. These regulations will impose extended waiting periods for re-licensing for persons convicted of multiple alcohol/drugged driving-related offenses.

Record Access: Laws, Rules, and Forms

Note: This Section Reviews Both Driver and Vehicle Records.

Governing Statutes and Rules

Administrative Codes, Rules and Regulations (NYCRR) Motor Vehicles is Title15: - www.dos.ny.gov/info/nycrr.html
State Laws and Regulations: - http://public.leginfo.state.ny.us
Access to records is regulated by the following: the federal DPPA (18 U.S.C. § 2721, et seq.); the NY State Information Security Breach and Notification Act (ISBNA) (G.B.L. §899-aa; State Technology Laws §208); NYS Vehicle and Traffic Law (VTL) §§ 201, 202 & 354; and the NY Freedom of Information law (FOIL) (Public Officers Law, Article 6).
New York does not specifically enumerate the federal exceptions, but did make changes administratively to comply with DPPA. NY VEH &

TRAF §313(4)(h) states. Notwithstanding "any other provision of law, information obtained by the department pursuant to this section shall not be disclosed, used, sold, accessed, utilized in any manner or released by the department to any person, corporation, or state and local agency, except in response to a specific, individual request for such information authorized pursuant to the federal Driver's Privacy Protection Act (18 U.S.C. 2721 et. seq.). The department shall institute measures to ensure that only authorized persons are permitted to access such information for the purposes specified by this section..."
The DMV redacts account numbers, SSNs, home telephone numbers, photographs, and medical information from all released records. The history of a vehicle's ownership contains private/personal information

which is protected by law from disclosure and requests for such information can only be honored in certain circumstances as provided by law (e.g., DPPA-permissible use). *Request Form MV-15* lists the permissible uses.

Request and Consent Forms

Form MV-15 is required to obtain certified records by mail order. Frequent requesters and government entities should establish accounts for direct access to electronic records and to directly order certified records. If the requester does not have a permissible use, consent is required to receive records with personal information.

DMV *MV-15GC* (general consent form) on which a requester may document the motorist's consent before obtaining a record.

Form MV-15F is used to request DMV records under the state's Freedom of Information law and only for records not available per MV-15.

Form MV-15D is used by for government, commercial, and not-for-profit organizations, volunteer fire companies, and volunteer ambulance services.

To download a form, go to www.dmv.ny.gov/forms.htm.

Vendor and Third Party Access Policy

Both DPPA and ISBNA regulate the use, storage, and dissemination of DMV records. Qualifying persons or entities may purchase records for resale to resellers or end-users. All such transactions are subject to audit by DMV. See pages 3 and 4 on *DMV Form MV-15D* for Terms of Service.

Records Ordered For Non-permissible Uses

Driving Records: The record without personal information (masked) the DMV provides is the printed "Abstract of Operating Record" (driver license abstract). Note this shortened version of the abstract will show license status and type, traffic convictions, suspensions, revocations and accidents, but not the motorist's address. This "masked" abstract is available only by mail order or at the counter at the Department address in Albany.

Vehicle Records: Requesters without permissible use or consent may not obtain vehicle records. There are no records without personal information provided to the public other than the online title status report listed below.

Access to Driver-Related Records

Driving Records

General Information and Fees

The fees are $10.00 per driving record search for mail-in, over-the-counter, and website requests; $15.00 for telephone requests by record-holder, and $7.00 for searches performed using the Dial-In Display (Dial-In service) or License Event Notification Service (LENS). The driver license (client identification) number or name and date of birth are required for all searches. Search fees apply whether or not a record is found. See below for more detailed information about search methods. Note that the masked abstract does not show the personal information of the driver. A masked abstract is available by mail or at the DMV Customer Service Counter of the Central Office in Albany.

In-Person – Driver records may be requested over the counter at any Motor Vehicles office; the office produces the record immediately. Office addresses are available at www.dmv.ny.gov. Records are also available at the Customer Service Center in Room 136 of the Swan Street Building in Albany. The requester's photo ID, form *MV-15C* and the $10.00 fee are required at the time of the request. The *MV-15C* is available at each office or online at www.dmv.ny.gov. Government organizations are exempt from the fee.

Mail – Requesters must complete form *MV-15*, attach a copy of the requestor's photo ID and include the $10.00 fee. The *MV-15* is available at www.dmv.ny.gov. Mail requests to MV-15 Processing, NYS Department of Motor Vehicles, 6 Empire State Plaza, Albany NY 12228.

Electronic – The "Dial-In Search Account" service permits online access to Motor Vehicle records 24/7. Certified records may be ordered through the service. Record retrieval is subject to DPPA. The driver license (client identification) number or driver's name and date of birth are necessary to retrieve driving records. A $7.00 fee per search is collected through an escrow account. Any public organization, its officers, a volunteer fire company, or volunteer ambulance service that makes a search for a public purpose is exempt from the search fee. For more information, visit www.dmv.ny.gov/dialin.htm or call 518-473-3959.

Bulk – The state does not sell its license database, or portions thereof.

By Person of Record – Drivers may obtain a copy of their own record by mail, walk-in, phone, or at the DMV web site. To order online, go to https://my.dmv.ny.gov/crm/. The driver must provide information from the driver license to prove identity and must use a credit card to pay the $7.00 fee.

To order by telephone, the driver must provide information from the

driver license to prove identity and must use a credit card to pay the fees. The total fee if ordered by telephone is $15.00 (search fee of $10.00 and processing fee of $5.00). It takes two weeks for the driver's abstract to arrive by mail. To order, call 518-473-5595.

Notification/Monitoring Programs

The **License Event Notification Service (LENS)** enables an organization to file with the DMV a roster of employees or volunteers who drive on the organization's behalf. The LENS program will notify the organization if a new event posts to a registered driver's record. Organizations may choose to receive notifications for any combination of the following events: suspension or revocation orders, expiration, convictions, reportable accidents, restoration of driving privilege or Point Insurance Reduction course completion. Accounts are charged a $7.00 fee to register each driver in the program and a $1.00 fee for each notification LENS provides thereafter. When adding a driver the fee includes a driving record. The fees are collected through an escrow account. Government organizations are exempt from fees. For more information, visit www.dmv.ny.gov/LENS/, call the Help Line at 518-486-4480, or email LENS@dmv.ny.gov.

The **TEENS (Teen Electronic Event Notification Service)** program is a voluntary free notification service provided by NYS DMV that notifies a parent or guardian of teenage drivers under age 18, when a ticket, conviction, suspension, revocation, or accident has appeared on the younger driver's license record. Parents or guardians can enroll in this program by creating a MyDMV on-line account (my.dmv.ny.gov), downloading an enrollment form (MV-TEENS) from the DMV website (www.dmv.ny.gov) or when accompanying their teen to a DMV office to get their Junior Permit. For more information please visit: www.dmv.ny.gov/youngerdriver/teensprogram.htm.

Accident Reports

Reporting – Motorists must report within 10 days any accident occurring in NY State that involves a fatality, personal injury, or damage of $1,001 or more to property of any one person. Motorist reports on *Accident Report Form MV-104* should be sent to: Accident Records Bureau, P.O. Box 2925, 6 Empire State Plaza Albany NY 12220-0925. Police agencies are required to file reports, forthwith for any accident involving fatalities, property damage is $1,001 or more, or personal injuries. If a fatality occurred, in addition to the Police Accident Report (MV-104A), an *Early Notification of a Fatal Accident (MV-104EN)* must be filed within the first 24 hours and a *Police Report for Fatal Motor Vehicle Accidents (MV-104D)* must be filed afterwards. A *Truck and Bus Supplement Police Accident Report (MV-104S)* is required to be submitted for each qualified commercial vehicle involved in the accident. Currently, a police officer may indicate whether they feel there was property damage to any one vehicle that met the reporting criteria. Form MV-104 may be downloaded from www.dmv.ny.gov/forms.htm.

Record Access – Only accidents that are reported are those that meet the reporting threshold to appear on a driver's file. The DMV reporting threshold for accidents is one that involves a death, personal injury or property damage to any one person in excess of $1,000. Available records go back 4 years.

Manual: Copies of accident reports may be requested by submitting *Form MV-198C* found at www.dmv.ny.gov/forms/mv198c.pdf. Record retrieval is subject to DPPA. For mail requests, there is a $10.00 search fee plus an additional $15.00 fee for each report produced per accident.

In-person searching is not permitted. In general, requests take 2-3 weeks to process. Fax requests are accepted at 518-474-0718 from escrow account holders.

Electronic: There is no charge to view a list of accident case files for a particular date and county. There is a $7.00 fee to choose one of the accidents or a $7.00 fee to search by case number or by plate number or by the DL number of a person involved. An additional $15.00 fee is charged if a copy of the report is ordered. Visit www.dmv.ny.gov/AIS.

Copies of Tickets

Copies of tickets, suspension orders, and license and registration/title applications may be requested using Form MV-15. The fee is $11.00 per photocopy. Copies of parking tickets are not available from DMV.

Access to Vehicle-Related Records

General Information and Fees

The DMV maintains title and registration records on all registered vehicles and lien records on all titled vehicles including boats and manufactured homes. There are two abstracts available; the **Vehicle Title Record** and the **Registration Plate Record**. The Vehicle Title Record reports lienholders and odometer readings. The Registration Plate record reports all vehicles registered using that plate number and any events that affect the status (such as lapse in insurance coverage). The fee for either record is $10.00 per search for mail-in and over-the-counter requests, $15.00 for telephone requests, and $7.00 for searches performed using the Dial-In Display (see Electronic). The plate number or the registrant's name and date of birth are required for all registration searches, and the Vehicle Identification Number (VIN) is required for all title searches. Search fees apply whether or not a record is found. See below for more detailed information about search methods.

In-Person – Vehicle records may be requested over the counter only at the DMV Customer Service Center, 6 Empire State Plaza Rm 136, Albany NY, 12228. Please note that documents will not be available until the next business day, at which time they may be picked up or mailed back to the requestor. The requester's photo ID, *Form MV-15*, and the $10.00 fee are required at the time of the request. Government organizations are exempt from the fee.

Mail – Requesters must complete *Form MV-15*, attach a copy of their photo ID and include the applicable fee. The plate number, and VIN, or registrant's name are needed when ordering. Mail requests to: MV-15 Processing, NYS Department of Motor Vehicles, 6 Empire State Plaza Albany NY 12228. Frequent commercial requesters and government organizations should establish accounts with the Department. Read Dial-In Display in the Electronic section below for further information.

Telephone – Vehicle owners and drivers may order their own registration abstract or title abstract by telephone. The person must provide the information from the driver license to prove identity and must use a credit card to pay the fees. The total fee is $15.00 (a search fee of $10.00 and a processing fee of $5.00). It will take one week for the abstract to arrive by mail. To order, call 518-473-5595.

Electronic – The "Dial-In Search Account" program permits interactive access to Motor Vehicle records. The program is available 24/7, certified records may be ordered through the program. Record retrieval is subject to DPPA. The plate number or registrant's name and date of birth are required to retrieve registration records. The VIN is required to retrieve ownership records. The plate number or the registrant's name and date of birth, along with the VIN or year, make, and model of the vehicle are required to retrieve insurance coverage information for the vehicle. Fees are collected through an escrow account. Non-escrow accounts are available to government entities. For more information, visit dmv.ny.gov/dialin.htm.

Electronic Batch –This method of obtaining registration and plate data is only offered to government entities. For more information concerning electronic batch requests contact the DMV by email at preedmail@dmv.ny.gov

Lien/Title Status – Use this online application to check the status of a NYS-issued vehicle title. Status Check displays the date the title was issued by the DMV, number of liens (if any), and the lien holder. No personal information is displayed. You must enter the VIN, vehicle model year, and vehicle make. For more information, go to dmv.ny.gov/titlestat. The status of a title or lien on watercraft is not available online.

Insurance Status – A unique service that NY offers to NY drivers is the ability to check vehicle insurance status online. The driver must have a letter or notice from the NYS DMV related to automobile liability insurance. The letter or notice will include a 10-digit Document Number and the vehicle plate number. Go to www.dmv.ny.gov/InsStatus/. Enter the document number to view current information about the status of the insurance case related to the vehicle plate number. This data may include status of the vehicle registration and/or DL.

Database Purchase – DMV awards contracts for the sale of access to bulk registration and ownership files to third party vendors, via a competitive bidding process. For additional information, contact the DMV by email at DataServices@dmv.ny.gov.

Access to Vessel-Related Records

General Information, Access and Fees

The law requires any boat that is powered by a motor and operated on public waterways in New York to be registered and titled. The DMV issues titles for boats that are model year 1987 or newer, which are at least 14 feet long and registered in NYS. This includes homemade boats

manufactured on or after August 1, 1986 if a model year was not designated. All 1973 model year and newer boats must have a 12-digit Hull Identification Number before being registered.

Lien information is included on some registrations. Same fees and turnaround times as for vehicle record requests apply.

Driving Record Content and Reciprocity

What's On or Not On the Driving Record

- Driving records contain license class and status as well as a record of convictions, suspensions, and revocations.
- Most equipment violations (except inadequate brakes) and most non-moving violations are not reported on the driving record.
- Accidents are shown on the record for any driver involved, but fault is not shown.
- For those record requesters that do not qualify or have consent to receive an unredacted license abstract, a masked abstract is issued that contains no address information. This abstract will contain either the DL Number or the name and DOB as an identifier.
- All driving records show the same length of activity, based on data retention requirements. This means there is only one type of driving record available to the public. Generally, the length of time license events are listed on the driving record is as follows:
  - Moving Violations...Remainder of calendar year of the date of conviction plus three years.
  - Accidents... Remainder of calendar year of the date of the accident plus three years.
  - DWI or DWAI...Ten years from the conviction date.
  - Serious accidents and convictions...Can be more than ten years and may be displayed permanently.
  - Suspensions-Closed...four years from closure date.
  - Suspension for Refusal to Submit to a Chemical Test - Closed...five years from closure date
  - Suspensions-Open...indefinitely until closed, then four years from closure date.
- The state does not permit driver school attendance in lieu of conviction.
- Each NY driving record has a Record Summary Line that reports the license or document type, status, and when the license or document expires. If the individual is unlicensed or licensed by another jurisdiction, that information appears as NO NY LICENSE. There will be more than one Record Summary Line if the motorist has a valid license in one class and a valid permit in another. It is possible to have a valid non-commercial license when a CDL held by the driver is revoked or suspended
- "Scofflaw" found on a New York record means the driver Failed to Appear.

Data Retention

A driver record is normally accessible for five years after the driver license expires and is not renewed, unless there is a suspension, conviction, accident or other activity with a longer retention period on the record. CDL driver records are purged based on the timetable per the MCSIA (see the Appendix).

Court to Repository

Convictions are entered either manually from paper source (hard copy) or electronically, depending on the court. Convictions are entered as soon as possible after adjudication.

State Reciprocity for Non-CDL Drivers

- Will suspend license of driver for unpaid out-of-state convictions except in Alaska, California, Michigan, Montana, Oregon or Wisconsin.
- Record of new incoming driver is not shown on MVR.
- Out-of-state convictions shown on MVR only include DUIs, Veh. manslaughter and homicide; moving violations from the provinces of Quebec and Ontario are also shown on the driving record.
- Out-of-state accidents are shown on MVR.
- Convictions of out-of-state drivers are sent to home state.
- Record is forwarded to new state upon surrender of license upon request.

License Classes, Restrictions, and Endorsements

License Classes– Commercial

Note: Effective July 26, 2005, the DMV eliminated the Non-CDL Class C license. In addition, the gross vehicle weight rating (GVWR) and gross vehicle combination weight rating (GCWR) of vehicles that a driver can operate with a Class D license increased.

Class A Any vehicle or combination (such as tractor-trailer or truck trailer) with a GCWR of more than 26,000 pounds-provided the GVWR or GCWR of vehicle(s) being towed is more than 10,000 pounds. Minimum age is 21.

Class B A single unit vehicle (such as a heavy single unit truck or bus) with a GVWR of more than 26,000 pounds. (Class B may tow vehicles with a GVWR of 10,000 pounds or less or may tow a vehicle of more than 10,000 pounds providing the GCWR is not more than 26,000 pounds). Minimum age is 18. Drivers under age 21 are restricted to operation in NYS only and may not transport hazardous materials or operate a school bus.

Class C A single unit vehicle (such as a truck or bus) with a GVWR of 26,000 pounds or less that transports fifteen or more passengers or transports passengers under Article 19-A of the "V and T" Law, or carries hazardous materials (Class C may tow vehicles with a GVWR of 10,000 pounds or less or may tow a vehicle of more than 10,000 pounds providing the GCWR is not more than 26,000 pounds). Minimum age is 18. Drivers under age 21 are restricted to operation in NYS only and may not transport hazardous materials or operate a school bus.

License Classes– Non-Commercial

Class C **This class is in the process of being eliminated** and is only issued when a Farm (F)(G) and/or Tow Truck (W) endorsement is applied for. Valid for operation of a single-unit vehicle (such as medium trucks, farm vehicles and some heavy recreational vehicles) with a GVWR of 26,000 pounds or less that does not require a CDL endorsement. Also valid for the operation of a passenger vehicle, Class B or Class C Limited Use Motorcycle, or Limited Use Automobile.

Class D A single unit vehicle (such as passenger cars and light trucks with a GVWR of 26,000 pounds or less. May tow a vehicle with a GVWR 10,000 pounds or less or may tow a vehicle of more than 10,000 pounds providing the GCWR is not more than 26,000 pounds. Limited-use automobiles; Class B and/or C limited use motorcycles; Recreational vehicles with a GVWR of 26,000 pounds or less. Minimum age 18 or 17 with Driver Education.

Class DJ Junior Driver (minimum age is 16). Valid for operation of a single-unit vehicle with a GVWR of 10,000 pounds or less, a passenger vehicle, Class B or Class C Limited Use Motorcycle, or Limited Use Automobile. Issued only to drivers younger than 18 years of age; automatically becomes a Class D license on the individual's 18th birthday. Subject to Junior License Restrictions.

Class E   GVWR of 26,000 pounds or less used to transport fourteen or less passengers for hire, and does not fall under Article 19-A of the "V and T" Law. May tow a vehicle with a GVWR 10,000 pounds or less or may tow a vehicle of more than 10,000 pounds providing the GCWR is not more than 26,000 pounds. Recreational vehicles with a GVWR of 26,000 pounds or less. Minimum age is 18.

Class M   Motorcycle. Minimum age 18 or 17 with Driver Education. Allows operation of motorcycles and limited use motorcycles (mopeds).

Class MJ   Junior motorcycle (minimum age is 16). Allows operation of motorcycles and limited use motorcycles (mopeds). Subject to Junior License Restrictions.

Note: On the Record Summary Line, if the driver does not have a NY License or learner permit, the lien will read NO NY LICENSE. If the driver only has a non-driver ID Card, the Record Summary Line will read ID ONLY.

Restrictions

A	Accelerator Left of Brake	L2	Not valid for Class B Air Brakes
A1	Temporary Visitor	M	Pass Restricted to Class B Veh
A2	Limited Use Ending Date - for Graduated JR Lic	N	Pass Restricted to Class C Veh
A3	Limited CDL for only School Vehicle or Municipal Vehicle	N1	No Vehicle Designed for 15 or More Adults
		N2	No Vehicle Designed for 8 or More Adults
A4	Interlock Device	O	Truck/Trailer Combo Only
B	Corrective Lenses	O1	Truck/Trailer Combo Not Over 26,000 lbs
C	Mechanical Aid	P	Power Brakes
D	Prosthetic Device	Q	Power Steering
E	Automatic Transmission	R	Built Up Seat/Pedal/Shoe
F	Hearing Aid or Full View Mirror	S	School Vehicle (**no longer issued**)
G	Daylight Driving Only	T	CMV Tractor Only (**no longer issued**)
H	Limited to Employment	U	Hand Operated Brake
I	Limited Use Auto Max 40 MPH	V	Foot Oper Parking Brake
I1	Limited Use MCY MAX 40 MPH	W	No Veh Over 18,000 lbs GVWR (**no longer issued**)
I2	Limited Use MCY MAX 30 MPH	X	Full Hand Control
I3	Limited Use MCY MAX 20 MPH	Y	Shoulder Harness Use
I4	Three Wheel MCY	Z	Wheel Spinner
K	CDL Intrastate Only	4	Telescopic Lens 4
L	Not Valid for Air Brakes	5	No Limited Access Rds
L1	Not valid for Class A Air Brakes		

Endorsements

F	Farm Class A Vehicles (Valid on Non-CDL Only)	S	School Bus -Starting 10/1/05
G	Farm Class B Vehicles (Valid on Non-CDL Only)	S	Tow Truck -Valid Until 09/30/05, then converted to W
H	Hazardous Materials	T	Doubles/Triples
M	Metal Coil	W	Tow Truck -Valid as of 05/01/03
N	Tank Vehicles	X	HazMat and Tank
P	Passenger Transport	Z	Farm HazMat (Valid on Non-CDL Only)
R	RV over 26,000 lbs GVWR		

Special or Limited License Privileges

The type of special driving privilege follows the license class on the Record Summary Line.

CONDITIONAL: A limited driving privilege granted to NYS licensed drivers who are suspended/revoked for alcohol or drug-related convictions.

CONDITIONAL PRIVILEGE: A limited driving privilege granted to drivers licensed in other states who are suspended/revoked in NYS for alcohol or drug-related convictions.

PRE-CONVICTION CONDITIONAL LICENSE: A limited driving privilege granted to NYS licensed drivers who have been suspended in NYS for alcohol or drug-related violations (not yet convicted).

PRE-CONVICTION CONDITIONAL PRIVILEGE: A limited driving privilege granted to drivers licensed in other states who are suspended in NYS for alcohol or drug-related violations (not yet convicted).

RESTRICTED USE: A limited driving privilege granted to NYS licensed drivers who are suspended/revoked for reasons other than alcohol/drug-related convictions.

RESTRICTED USE PRIVILEGE: A limited driving privilege granted to drivers licensed in other states who are suspended/revoked in NYS for reasons other than alcohol/drug-related convictions.

POST REVOCATION CONDITIONAL LICENSE: A limited driving privilege granted to NYS licensed drivers who have ignition interlock devices as a probation condition and who have completed the minimum revocation period required after an alcohol or drug-related conviction. (Formerly known as INTERLOCK CONDITIONAL.)

LIMITED USE ENDING DATE MM/DD/YYYY: A limited driving privilege granted to junior drivers who pass their road test within 6 months of receiving a Learner's Permit. After the ending date, full driving privileges are granted

Conviction Table with ACD Code and Full Explanation

- "Scofflaw" found on a New York record means the driver Failed to Appear.
- There may be a series of numbers after a non-conviction incident (e.g. 510-4-A) which refers to a specific "Traffic Law" and not to a conviction of a violation. These numbers should not be confused with the Conviction Code Table listed below.

Short Description	ACD	Long Description
19-a no affiv compl	n/a	No article 19-a affidavit of compliance
2 os vio 10yr pas/hz	W51	Two out-of-service order violations in 10 years/transporting passengers or hazmat
2 serious vio/3y	W30	Two serious traffic violations committed while operating a commercial motor vehicle within 3 years
2 spd wk zn/rst hwy	S93	Two speeds in a work zone or a restricted highway
3 or mor os vio 10yr	W52	Three or more out-of-service order violations in 10 years
3 serious vio/3y	W31	Three serious traffic violations committed while operating a commercial motor vehicle within 3 years
3 speed/misd	n/a	3 speeding or misdemeanor violations
3 speed/misdem 18 mo	W01	Three speeding violations or misdemeanors in 18 months
abandon vehicle	n/a	Abandoned vehicle
admin per se - oos	A94	Admin per se - out-of-state
administrative review	W14	Administrative action by department
advctg overthrow gv	n/a	Advocating the overthrow of the government
agg DWI .18+ bac	A21	Aggravated DWI - blood alcohol content .18 or higher
agg DWI child in veh	A21	Aggravated DWI-child in vehicle
agg DWI chld cmv/hzm	A21	Aggravated DWI-child in vehicle-in a commercial vehicle or carrying hazardous materials
agg DWI chld/sp veh	A21	Aggravated DWI-child in vehicle – special vehicle
agg DWI CMV/hzmt	A21	Aggravated DWI - blood alcohol content .18 or higher in a commercial vehicle or carrying haz. materials
agg DWI spec veh	A21	Aggravated DWI - blood alcohol content .18 or higher - special vehicle
agg homicide/mot veh	U07	Aggravated vehicular murder
agg unl op 3rd misd	B20	Aggravated unlicensed operation 3rd degree misdemeanor
agg unl op alc-misd	B20	Aggravated unlicensed operation, second degree misdemeanor - alcohol
agg unl op fel	U03	Aggravated unlicensed operation, first degree, felony
agg unl op inf	B20	Aggravated unlicensed operation, third degree infraction
agg unl op misd	B20	Aggravated unlicensed operation, second degree misdemeanor
agg veh manslaughter	U08	Aggravated vehicular manslaughter first degree
aggr veh assault	U03	aggravated vehicular assault
aggr veh homicide	U07	aggravated vehicular homicide
al/drg incd cdl hldr	A21	Alcohol/drug incident - CDL holder
alj find purs 509-j	n/a	Alj findings pursuant to section 509-j of the Vehicle and Traffic law
allow op unin fh veh	D35	Permitting operation of an uninsured for hire vehicle
alt bridge notice	n/a	Altering bridge closed notice
alter conv stub	n/a	Altered conviction stub
alter document/plate	n/a	Altered document/plate
altered license	B41	Altered license
art 19a violation	n/a	VIN block per section 509j(g) of article 19a of the vehicle and traffic law
article 48c atv viol	n/a	Article 48c all terrain vehicle operating violation
assault - traf enf	n/a	Assault of a traffic enforcement agent
assault-mot veh-fel	U03	Assault due to the operation of a motor vehicle - felony
assault-mot veh-misd	U06	Assault due to the operation of a motor vehicle - misdemeanor
avoid int/traf dev	M16	Avoiding traffic device or intersection
backing unsafely	N82	Backing unsafely
ban use of radar	n/a	Banned use of radar
bckg ctr acces high	N82	Backing on controlled access highway
bicycle red lgt viol	n/a	Disobeying a red light on a bicycle
bicycle violation	n/a	Bicycle violation other than red light
bus on park/parkway	n/a	Operating a bus in a park on a parkway without a permit
boating while imprd	n/a	Boating while ability impaired
boating imprd drugs	n/a	Boating while ability impaired-drugs
boating while intox	n/a	Boating while intoxicated
boating intox .08	n/a	Boating while intoxicated/.08
boat intx pub vsl .04	n/a	Boating while intoxicated-public vessel/.04
cau fat neg oper CMV	U10	Causing a fatality through the negligent operation of a CMV
cert isud w/o inspec	n/a	Inspection certificate issued without an inspection
chem test ref - oos	A12	Chemical test refusal out-of-state
chem test ref 1194a	n/a	Chemical test refusal 1194a
chem test ref 19/21	A12	Refused to submit to a chemical test, under age 21
chem test ref boat <21	n/a	Chemical test refusal-operating vessel after consuming alcohol under 21-navigation law 49b
chem test refsl-cdl	A12	Chemical test refusal - CDL holder
chgd lanes unsafely	M42	Changed lanes unsafely
cl/rl other	D27	Other occurrence and/or failure to comply with conditional/restricted license

Short Description	ACD	Long Description
cl/rl - drop out	D27	Failure to attend or satisfactorily participate in NYS drinking driver program
cl/rl - fail attend	D27	Failure to attend or satisfactorily participate in NYS drinking driver program
cl/rl - term af hear	n/a	Conditional/restricted license - order terminated after hearing
cl/rl - withdrawal	D27	Conditional/restricted license - failed to register in program
cl/rl conv traffic	D27	Traffic offense occurring during conditional/restricted license program
cling to moving veh	n/a	Clinging to a moving motor vehicle
CMV conv w/fatal	U31	Commercial motor vehicle conviction with fatal
CMV-2 rrgc vio-3 yrs	W60	CMV-two railroad-highway grade crossing violations in three years
CMV-3 rrgc vio-3 yrs	W61	CMV-three railroad-highway grade crossing violations in three years
CMV-fld lv room/rrgc	M23	Failure of CMV to leave enough room to drive through railroad-highway grade crossing without stopping
CMV-fld slow at rrgc	M20	Failure of CMV to slow down at railroad-highway grade crossing and to check tracks
CMV-fld stop at rrgc	M21	Failure of CMV to stop before railroad-highway grade crossing when tracks are not clear
CMV-insuf clear/rrgc	M24	Failure of CMV to negotiate railroad-highway grade crossing-insufficient clearance
CMV-no stop/rrgc req	M22	Failure of CMV to stop at railroad highway grade crossing when required
consume alc under 21	A61	Operating after consuming alcohol, under 21 years of age
contact bdcu	n/a	Contact BDCU
Contact CDL Policy	N/A	Contact CDL Policy Unit
contact dfi	n/a	Contact DFI
contact title bureau	n/a	Contact title bureau
court probation	n/a	Court probation
court revocation	n/a	Court revocation
crim neg-fatality	U07	Criminal negligence in a fatality
crm neg/hom cdl hldr	U07	Criminal negligence and/or homicide with a motor vehicle- CDL holder
crm neg/hom CMV/hzmt	U07	Criminal negligence and/or homicide with a motor vehicle operating a CMV and/or carrying hazmat
crossed fire hose	M56	Crossed fire hose
cstng gears neutral	N80	Coasting with gears in neutral
dangerous driving	M80	Dangerous driving
dec speed w/o signal	N40	Decreased speed without signaling
dec sp-sto wo signal	N43	Decrease speed/stopping without signaling
def court ord ins fs	D37	Default in court order - insurance - fs
def court ord ins sr	D37	Default in court order - insurance - safety responsibility
default agree to pay	D37	Default in agreement to pay
dfi – junk invs	N/A	DFI – junk vehicle investigation **(DFI= Division of Field Investigation)**
dfi – title stop	N/A	DFI – title stop
dfi exam required	N/A	DFI exam required
dfi no show	N/A	Field investigation no-show
dfi review	N/A	Division of Field Investigation review
dis steady red arrow	M16	Disobeyed steady red arrow
Dishonored check	n/a	Dishonored check
disobeyed grn arrow	M16	Disobeyed green arrow
disobeyed traf dev	M14	Disobeyed traffic device
document obtd unlaw	n/a	Using a document or plate which was unlawfully obtained
dot out of service	B27	Violation of a DOT out of service order while operating a commercial motor vehicle
dot out srv pas/haz	B19	Violation of a DOT out of service order while operating a commercial motor vehicle used to transport passengers or hazardous material
dr .08%+DWI-sp-ve-2n	A21	Driving while intoxicated and with .08% or more alcohol in the blood, special vehicle, second offense
dr CMV w/o obtan cdl	B56	Driving a CMV without obtaining a CDL
dr intox & .08% alch	A21	Driving while intoxicated and with .08% or more alcohol in the blood
dr intox &.08% al-pi	A21	Driving while intoxicated and with .08% or more alcohol in the blood, personal injury accident involvement
dr intox os CMV/hzmt	A21	Driving while intoxicated out-of-state in a CMV or while carrying hazmat
dr over dividing spc	M51	Driving over dividing space
dr under influence	A21	Driving under the influence - out-of-state
dr.08%+DWI-pi-sp-veh	A21	Dr.08%+DWI-personal injury-special vehicle
dr.08%+DWI-pi-sv-2nd	A21	Dr.08%+DWI-personal injury-special vehicle-second offense
dr.08%+DWI-spec veh	A21	Driving while intoxicated and with .08% or more alcohol in the blood, special vehicle
dr.08%-spec veh-2nd	A21	Dr.08%-special vehicle-second offense
dr.08%-spec vehicle	A21	Driving a special vehicle with .08% blood alcohol content
drivers view obstrd	D70	Driver's view obstructed
driving on shoulder	M58	Driving on shoulder
driving on sidewalk	M58	Driving on sidewalk
driving too slow	S96	Driving too slowly
driving while intox	A21	Driving while intoxicated
drove left on curve	M41	Drove left on curve
drove wrong dir	N63	Drove wrong direction on a one way street
drug felony w/CMV	A50	Motor vehicle used in the commission of a felony involving the manufacturing, distributing, or dispensing of a

Short Description	ACD	Long Description
		controlled substance
drv .08%+ CMV-hzmt	A21	Driving with a blood alcohol content of .08% in a commercial motor vehicle carrying hazardous materials
drv .08%+ in CMV	A21	Driving with a blood alcohol content of .08% in a commercial motor vehicle
drv across hzrd mark	M71	Drove across no-passing markings
drv CMV .04-.06%	A04	Driving with a blood alcohol content of .04% to .06% in a commercial motor vehicle
drv CMV .06-.08%	A04	Driving with a blood alcohol content of more than .06% but less than .08% in a commercial motor vehicle
drv drugs CMV-hz	A22	Driving a commercial motor vehicle carrying hazardous materials while impaired by drugs
drv drugs in CMV	A22	Driving a commercial motor vehicle while impaired by drugs
drv hzmt .04-.06%	A04	Driving with a blood alcohol content of .04% to .06% in a commercial motor vehicle carrying haz. materials
drv hzmt .06-.08%	A04	Driving with a blood alcohol content of more than .06% but less than .08% in a commercial motor vehicle carrying hazardous materials
drv imp drg cdl hldr	A22	Driving while impaired by drugs- CDL holder
drv left at bridge	M41	Driving left at bridge or tunnel
drv left pav mark	M41	Driving left of pavement markings
drv left rr cross	M41	Driving left at railroad crossing
drv lft crst grd/crv	M41	Driving left at the crest of a grade or curve
drv thru safety zone	M12	Driving through safety zone
drv too slow in zone	S96	Driving too slow in zone
drv while use drugs	A22	Driving while ability impaired, using drugs
drvg drugs pi acc	A22	Driving while ability impaired, using drugs, personal injury accident
drvg in center lane	M62	Driving in center lane
drvg intox pi acc	A21	Driving while intoxicated, personal injury accident involvement
drvg left ctr line	M41	Driving to left of center line
drvg left no pas zon	M42	Driving to left in a no passing zone
drvg on bicycle lane	M47	Driving a motor vehicle on bicycle lane
drvg on restr street	n/a	Driving on street restricted for playing
drvg w/ impaired os	A25	Driving while impaired out-of-state
drvg w/.08% alch pi	n/a	Driving with .08% or more alcohol in blood, personal injury accident involvement
drvg w/.12% alch pi	n/a	Driving with .12% or more alcohol in blood, personal injury accident
drvg w/.15% alch pi	n/a	Driving with .15% or more alcohol in blood, personal injury accident
drvg w/intox os	A21	Driving while intoxicated out-of-state
drvg while impaired	A25	Driving while ability impaired by alcohol
drvg with .08% alch	A21	Driving with .08% or more alcohol in blood
drvg with .12% alch	n/a	Driving with .12% or more alcohol in blood
drvg with .15% alch	n/a	Driving with .15% or more alcohol in blood
drvg/wanton disr	M80	Driving with a wanton disregard for human life
dui .04+	A04	Driving under the influence .04+
dui drugs	A22	Driving under the influence drugs
dui in CMV	A21	Driving under the influence - out-of-state in a commercial motor vehicle
dui in CMV/hzmt	A21	Driving under the influence - out-of-state in a commercial motor vehicle carrying hazardous materials
dup title verif inv	n/a	Invalid verification for a duplicate title
DWAI dr/al CMV/hz pi	A23	DWAI - operator impaired by combining multiple drugs or drugs/alcohol, physical injury accident in a commercial vehicle or carrying hazardous materials
DWAI dr/al sp veh pi	A23	DWAI- operator impaired by combining multiple drugs or drugs/alcohol, physical inj. accident, special veh.
DWAI drg/alc CMV/hzm	A23	DWAI - operator impaired by combining multiple drugs or drugs and alcohol in a commercial vehicle or carrying hazardous materials
DWAI drg/alc sp veh	A23	DWAI - operator impaired by combining multiple drugs or drugs and alcohol - special vehicle
DWAI drgs/alc w/pi	A23	DWAI - operator impaired by combining multiple drugs or drugs and alcohol, physical injury accident
DWAI drugs/alcohol	A23	DWAI - operator impaired by combining multiple drugs or drugs and alcohol
DWAI drugs-pi-sp veh	A22	Driving while ability impaired, using drugs, personal injury accident, special vehicle
DWAI drugs-pi-sv-2nd	A22	Driving while ability impaired, using drugs, personal injury accident, special vehicle, 2nd offense
DWAI drugs-spec veh	A22	Driving while ability impaired, using drugs, special vehicle
DWAI in CMV	A25	Driving a commercial motor vehicle while ability was impaired
DWAI in CMV/hzmt	A25	Driving a commercial motor vehicle carrying hazardous materials while ability was impaired
DWAI mult cdl hldr	A23	DWAI- operator impaired by combining multiple drugs or drugs and alcohol- CDL holder
DWAI os CMV/hzmt	A25	Driving while impaired out-of-state in a CMV or while carrying hazmat
DWAI-drugs-sp ve-2nd	A22	Driving while ability impaired, using drugs, special vehicle, second offense
DWAI-spec veh-2nd	A21	DWAI-special vehicle-second offense
DWAI-special vehicle	A25	Driving while ability impaired, special vehicle
DWI in CMV	A21	Driving a commercial motor vehicle while intoxicated
DWI in CMV-hzmt	A21	Driving a commercial motor vehicle carrying hazardous materials while intoxicated
DWI/.08% CMV-hazmat	A21	DWI with .08% or more alcohol in blood while operating a commercial motor vehicle while carrying hazardous materials
DWI/.08% in CMV	A21	DWI with .08% or more alcohol in blood while operating a commercial motor vehicle
DWI-pi-spe veh-2nd	A21	DWI-personal injury-special vehicle-second offense
DWI-pi-spec veh	A21	DWI-personal injury-special vehicle

Short Description	ACD	Long Description
DWI-spec veh-2nd	A21	DWI-special vehicle-second offense
DWI-special vehicle	A21	Driving while intoxicated, special vehicle
earphone violation	M82	Earphone violation
ent ext ctr ac hwy	M46	Entering exit ramp of controlled access highway
equipment	n/a	Equipment
esc w/cancld cert	n/a	Escorting with cancelled certification
esc w/o cert	n/a	Escorting without certification
evading prosecution	U01	Evading prosecution
exam reqd/call title	n/a	Salvage examination required - call title
excess passngr on mc	n/a	Carrying excess passenger on a motorcycle
excess speed 4/76	S15	Speeding 25 mph or more above legal limit
fac agg unl op fel	n/a	Facilitating aggravated unlicensed operation felony
fac agg unl op inf	n/a	Facilitating aggravated unlicensed operation
fac agg unl op misd	n/a	Facilitating aggravated unlicensed operation misdemeanor
fail appr 19a reexam	n/a	Failed to appear for 19-a re-examination
fail comp sec req ny	D38	Failure to comply with financial security requirements, new york state
fail comp sec req os	D38	Failure to comply with financial security requirements, out of state
fail notify chg addr	n/a	Failure to notify of change of address
fail to appr re-exam	n/a	Failed to appear for a re-examination
fail to del reg/lic	n/a	Failure to deliver registration/license after suspension or revocation
fail to pay fine-os	D56	Failure to pay out of state fine
fail to pay surcharg	D56	Failure to pay surcharge
fail to surr fin sec	n/a	Misdemeanor failure to surrender after financial security revocation
failed special exam	W20	Failed special examination
failed to attend dss	n/a	Failure to attend driver safety school
failed to delv lic	n/a	Failure to deliver license after suspension or revocation
failed to keep right	M41	Failed to keep right
failed to report acc	B61	Failure to report an accident
failed to signal	N43	Failed to signal as required
failed to verify vin	n/a	Failure to verify vehicle identification number
failed to yield row	N24	Failure to yield right of way - green light
failure to pay fine	D56	Failure to pay fine
failure to post bond	n/a	Failure to post bond
fals temp ind regis	n/a	Falsification of temporary indicia of registration
false statement-reg	n/a	Making a false statement on registration application
false stmt -document	D02	Making a false statement on a document or plate application
faulty lights	E34	Faulty lights
faulty muffler	n/a	Faulty muffler
fel dis drg cdl hldr	A50	Felony distributing drugs - CDL holder
felony conv cdl hldr	U03	Felony conviction - CDL holder
felony conviction	n/a	Felony conviction
felony in CMV hz	U03	Commission of a felony using a commercial motor vehicle carrying hazardous materials
felony using CMV	U03	Commission of a felony using a commercial motor vehicle
fh ins cancelled	B64	For-Hire insurance CANCELLED
fictitious insp cert	n/a	Misdemeanor fictitious inspection certificate
fictitious insp lic	n/a	Fictitious inspection station license
fld 19a road reexam	n/a	Failed 19-a road test re-examination
fld adbl warn mt hw	n/a	Failure to give audible warning on a mountain highway
fld allow suff space	M31	Failed to allow sufficient space (caravan or motorcade)
fld ans/pay cdl os	D56	Failure to answer a citation, pay fines, penalties and/or costs related to the out-of-state violation. CDL holder and/or CMV violation
fld ans or pay-pvb	n/a	Failure to answer or pay - parking violations bureau
fld answer summons	D56	Failure to answer a summons
fld attnd hearg-acc	n/a	Failure to attend accident hearing
fld attnd hearg-pv	n/a	Failure to attend persistent violator hearing
fld comply with ord	M08	Failure to comply with a lawful order
fld due care w/pi	M81	Failure to exercise due care with physical injury
fld due care w/spi	M81	Failure to exercise due care with serious physical injury
fld due care-emr/haz	M70	Failed to exercise due care when passing a stopped, standing or parked emergency vehicle
fld give one half rd	M41	Failed to give one half of roadway
fld give way	N07	Failure to give way
fld keep rt-slow veh	M60	Slow moving vehicle failed to keep right
fld kep scl b hlt/lt	E56	Failure to keep school bus halted or lighted while discharging pupils
fld leave suff space	M31	Failed to leave sufficient space (combination of vehicles)
fld obey tr sig ahed	M16	Failure to obey a traffic signal ahead
fld pay child supp	D51	Failed to pay child support

Short Description	ACD	Long Description
fld pay driv assess	n/a	Failure to pay driver responsibility assessment
fld pay fine cdl os	D53	failed to pay fine for a violation out-of-state cdl holder and/or cmv violation
fld pay supp crt ord	D51	Failed to pay child support court ordered
fld prelim t reexam	W20	Failed preliminary test - re-examination
fld prelm 19A reexam	W20	Failed preliminary 19-A re-examination
fld road test reexam	W20	Failed road test re-examination
fld stop mlfunc lght	n/a	Failed to stop as required at malfunctioning traffic light
fld stop-yield sign	M19	Failure to stop at yield sign when required
fld surr after rev	n/a	Failed to surrender after revocation
fld surr hzmt endors	W09	Failed to surrender hazmat endorsement
fld tape in-line ska	n/a	Failed to use reflective tape on in-line skates
fld to answer cdl os	D45	Failed to answer citation for a violation out-of-state CDL holder and/or CMV violation
fld to dim hdlights	E54	Failed to dim headlights
fld to gv corr inf	D02	Failed to give correct information
fld to gve way-right	N01	Failed to give way - right
fld to pay fine/sur	D56	Failed to pay fine/surcharge
fld to stop	M25	Failure to stop emerging from alley, driveway, private road or building
fld to stop as rqd	N01	Failure to stop as required
fld to stop at sign	M15	Failure to stop at stop sign
fld to stop-schl bus	M75	Failed to stop for a school bus
fld to turn as reqd	M14	Failure to turn as required
fld to use desg lane	M40	Failure to use designated lane
fld to use due care	N01	Failure to use due care or sound horn for bicyclist, pedestrian or domestic animal
fld to yield row-ped	N08	Failed to yield right of way to a pedestrian
fld to yield row-ped	N08	Failed to yield right of way - pedestrian
Fld use care app hrs	N01	Failed to use due care approaching a horse
fld yield row-blind	N08	Failed to yield right of way to a blind person
fld yield row-right	N01	Failed to yield right of way to the right
fld yield-grn arrow	N24	Failure to yield - green arrow
fld yld - caused dth	N01	Failed to yield right of way that causes death
fld yld row tunl-ped	n/a	Failure to yield right of way to a pedestrian in a tunnel
fld yld row-emer veh	N01	Failure to yield right of way to an emergency vehicle
fld yld row-ent rdwy	N01	Failure to yield right of way entering a roadway
fld yld row-intersec	N01	Failure to yield right of way at an intersection
fld yld row-lf tr rd	N24	Failure to yield right of way - left turn on red
fld yld row-lft turn	N01	Failure to yield right of way on a left turn
fld yld row-loc ord	N01	Failure to yield right of way, according to local ordinance
fld yld row-rt tr rd	N24	Failure to yield right of way, right turn on red
fld yld row-stp sign	N01	Failure to yield right of way at a stop sign
fld yld row-trf circ	N01	Failure to yield right of way at a traffic circle or island
fld yld row-yld sign	N01	Failure to yield right of way at a yield sign
fld yld-caused spi	N01	Failed to yield right of way that causes serious physical injury
fld/imp use flashers	n/a	Failure to use, or improper use of four way flasher
fls bomb rep/plac	n/a	False report or placement of false bomb on school grounds
fls stmt reg/ttl fel	n/a	False statement on registration/title - felony
fmcsa out of service	n/a	FMCSA - ordered out of service
fol fire app too cls	M33	Following fire apparatus too closely
followed too closely	M34	Followed too closely
followed too closely	M34	Following too closely
fraud id-contact dfi	B41	Fraudulent photo ID - contact DFI
fraudulent activity	D02	Made false statement or provided fraudulent documents in application for a NY state identification document
fs-55 suspension	D35	SUSPENSION - registration irregularly obtained
fs7 rv30 day-no ins	D35	FS-7 revocation - 30 days
fto rr gat/s	M10	Failure to obey a traffic control device or the directions of an enforcement official at a RR highway grade crossing
fto rr restr	M09	Failure to obey railroad-highway grade crossing restrictions
glass distrg vsblty	D70	Glass disturbing visibility
gross neg oper of mv	N84	Gross negligence in the operation of a motor vehicle
hansom cab violation	n/a	Hansom cab violation
hld nylic/other juri	D07	Holding a NY license and one from another location
hldg more 1 lic-inf	D07	Holding more than one license - infraction
homicide/mot veh	U07	Homicide with a motor vehicle
horn - no danger	n/a	Horn - no danger
hov lane violation	n/a	Unlawful use of high occupancy vehicle lane
hvy veh exc emission	n/a	Heavy duty vehicle exceeds environmental conservation laws emissions levels
ill dumping fail pay	n/a	Illegal dumping failure to pay fine

Short Description	ACD	Long Description
illegal brake fluid	n/a	Sale of illegal brake fluid
illg label brake fld	n/a	Illegally labeled brake fluid
imminent hazard	W70	Imminent hazard
imp left turn-1 way	N53	Improper left turn onto one way street
imp left turn-2 way	N53	Improper left turn onto two way street
imp use bus lane nyc	M40	Improper use of bus lane NYC
impop use tank veh	n/a	Improper use of a tank vehicle
impr use farm plate	n/a	Improper use of farm plate
improp cls/end dl	B91	Improper classification or endorsement on driver license
improp rt turn inter	N52	Improper right turn at intersection
improp wiper/sticker	F66	Improper wipers/unauthorized sticker
improper hand signal	N44	Improper hand signal
improper passing	M70	Improper passing
improper passing-mcy	M70	Improper passing, motorcycle
improper plates	n/a	Improper plates
improper reg	n/a	Improper registration
improper reg/snow	n/a	Failure to properly register a snowmobile as required by Section 2222 of the V&T
improper registration	n/a	Improper registration- incomplete response to multiple political subdivision eligibility requests
improper right turn	N54	Improper right turn
improper signal	N44	Improper signal
improper turn	N50	Improper turn
improper u turn	N56	Improper u turn
imprud spd app horse	N01	Imprudent speed while approaching a horse
imprud speed/snomobl	n/a	Imprudent speed - snowmobile
imprudent driving	M81	Imprudent driving
inadeq brake-non own	E31	Inadequate service brakes, non owner
inadequate brakes	E31	Inadequate brakes, misdemeanor
inadequate brakes-mc	E31	Inadequate brakes, motorcycle
ins. Not in effect	D35	Insurance not in effect
insuff turn signal	N43	Insufficient turn signal - less than 100 feet
insufficient acc rpt	B61	Insufficient accident report
insurance lapse	D35	Insurance lapse
interfd drivers view	D70	Passenger interfering with driver's view or control
interfd w safe oper	M77	Interfered with safe operation
interlock cond disch	n/a	Ignition interlock conditional discharge
interlock crt prob	n/a	Ignition interlock device - court probation
intrf fir ap mov vil	M33	Following emergency vehicle too closely
invalid f.h. cert.	n/a	Invalid for hire certificate
invalid f.h. trans	n/a	Invalid for hire transaction
invld proof of insur	n/a	Invalid proof of insurance
irp non-payment	n/a	International registration plan non-payment
JR driver violation	D29	Junior driver violation
know operate w/o ins	D35	Knowingly operating without insurance
leav scene inc - ani	n/a	Leaving the scene of an incident involving an animal without reporting
leav scene inc - pd	B05	Leaving the scene of a property damage incident without reporting
leaving scene inc in	B05	Leaving the scene of a personal injury accident
leaving scene of acc	B05	Leaving the scene of an accident
left around traf ild	N61	Drove left around a traffic island
lic irreg issued	n/a	License irregularly issued
lic irreg obtained	D02	License irregularly obtained
lien omitted mv999	n/a	Lien omitted MV999
limited use veh vio	n/a	Driving a limited use vehicle in an unauthorized area
local for-hire viol	n/a	Operating or permitting operation of a vehicle for-hire without a license from the local licensing authority or without for-hire insurance
logs insecure fasten	n/a	Logs insecurely fastened
lpb review	n/a	License production bureau review
lv scn acc cdl hldr	B05	Leaving the scene of an accident - CDL holder
lv scn acc w/o exhbt	B14	Leaving the scene of an accident without exhibiting identification and vehicle insurance card or exchanging information as required
lv scne acc cmv hzmat	B05	Leaving the scene of an accident while operating a CMV carrying hazardous materials
lv scne acc op CMV	B05	Leaving the scene of an accident while operating a commercial motor vehicle
lv scne acc cmv hzmat	B05	Leaving the scene of an accident while operating a CMV carrying hazardous materials
maj rnst imp cdl/cmv	W01	Major offense after reinstatement, with at least one driving while ability impaired offense, committed by CDL holder or in a CMV or HazMat vehicle
Menacing - traf enf	n/a	Menacing a traffic enforcement agent
misc atv violation	n/a	Miscellaneous all terrain vehicle violation

Short Description	ACD	Long Description
misc violation	E01	Miscellaneous or equipment violation
miscellaneous	n/a	Miscellaneous
mjr off rnst cdl/cmv	W41	Major offense after reinstatement - CDL holder and/or CMV violation
more than 3 in front	D70	More than 3 in front
mtc - between lanes	M40	Riding motorcycle between lanes or depriving of a full lane
mtc-more 2 abreast	M40	Operated motorcycle more than two abreast
mult maj imp cdl/cmv	W01	Multiple major offenses, with at least one driving while impaired offense, committed by CDL holder or in a CMV or HazMat vehicle
mult mjr off cdl hld	W40	Multiple major offenses - CDL holder
multi/no sticker/veh	n/a	No sticker or more than one sticker on vehicle
multiple open stops	n/a	Multiple open stops
mv82 outcharge dfi	n/a	Form MV-82 outcharged to DFI
mvd fm lane unsafely	M42	Moved from lane unsafely or weaving
ndr inquiry	n/a	National driving record inquiry
neg hom oper CMV	U09	Negligent homicide while operating a CMV
nj vin - dfi invst	n/a	NJ VIN - division of field investigation
no child rest backs	F02	No child restraint device - back seat
no child rest front	F02	No child restraint device - front seat
no child restr dev	F02	No child restraint device
no cntrl strg mechan	n/a	Not in control of steering mechanism
no conspec marking	n/a	No conspec marking
No convex mirror cmv	E01	Operation of a CMV without a convex mirror
no fire extinguisher	E01	No fire extinguisher
no headlamps/weather	E55	No headlamps/inclement weather
no headlights	E05	No headlights
no insp over 60 days	n/a	No inspection - over 60 days
no instructors cert	n/a	No Instructor's certificate
no marking	E04	No markings
no nassau local lic	n/a	Operating without a local license from the Nassau county taxi and limousine commission
no nyc local lic	n/a	Operating without local license from the New York city taxi and limousine commission
no s belt 4-15 backs	F02	No seat belt, back seat, passenger aged 4 to 15
no s belt 4-15 front	F02	No seat belt, front seat, passenger aged 4 to 15
no s belt 4-9 backs	F02	No seat belt, back seat, passenger aged 4 to 9
no s belt adult pass	F04	No seat belt, adult passenger
no safety chain	E01	No safety chain
no safety glass	E01	No safety glass
no seat belt adult	F04	No seat belt adult
no seat belt driver	F04	No seat belt driver
no seat belt learner	F04	Learner operating without a seat belt
no seat belt sch-bus	E01	No seat belt - school bus
no splash guard	E01	No splash guard
no taxi s belt sign	n/a	Taxi/livery failed to post a conspicuously visible and legible notice to passengers that seat belts are available and should be used.
no/inad mark-msd/fel	E04	No or inadequate marking on vehicle carrying hazardous material, misdemeanor or felony
not seated prop - mc	F06	Not seated properly on motorcycle
obstr view fnrl plac	n/a	Obstructed view-oversized funeral placard
obstrction rr xing	M09	Obstructing a railroad crossing
obstruct intersect	F34	Obstructing intersection
obstructing traffic	F34	Obstructing traffic
op CMV with CMV sanc	W45	Operating a CMV while license is withdrawn-CMV sanctions
op CMV wo cdl dr pos	B57	Operating a commercial motor vehicle without a CDL in the driver's possession
op esc veh - dot	n/a	Operating escort vehicle in violation of commissioner of transportation rules and regulations
op lic rev/susp-al	B20	Operating while license revoked or suspended for an alcohol related offense
op lic rev/susp-ins	B20	Operating while license revoked or suspended - insurance
op lic/reg susp/rev	B20	Operating while license or registration revoked or suspended under article 7 - misdemeanor
op mv - mobile phone	M86	Operation of a motor vehicle while using a hand held mobile phone
op mv port elec dev	M85	Operating a motor vehicle while using a portable electronic device
op out cls < 60 days	B91	Operating out of class, less than 60 days
op out/cls < 60 days	B91	Operating out of class less than 60 days, junior operator
op out intrlck restr	A41	Operating out of ignition interlock restriction-misdemeanor
op sch bus stand pas	n/a	Operating school bus with standing passengers
op unreg minibik-inf	n/a	Operating unregistered minibike - infraction
op veh on cl bridge	n/a	Operating a vehicle on a closed bridge
op ves cons alc<21	n/a	Operating vessel after consuming alcohol under 21 navigation law 49b
op vio rest (lp-inf)	D29	Operating in violation of restriction, learner permit - infraction

Short Description	ACD	Long Description
op w/out lic < 60 dy	B51	Operating without a license, less than 60 days
Open	n/a	open
drvg impair cdl	A25	Driving while impaired- CDL holder
oper boat while susp	n/a	Operation while boating privileges suspended
oper heavy exceed em	n/a	Operating a heavy duty diesel vehicle while exceeding the emissions levels
oper heavy w/o insp	n/a	Operating a heavy duty diesel vehicle without an inspection sticker
oper out of cl jr op	B91	Operating out of class junior operator
oper out of rest-cl	D29	Operating out of restriction - conditional license
oper out of rest-inf	D29	Operating out of restriction - infraction
oper snow while susp	n/a	Operating while snowmobiling privileges suspended
oper w/o ins - inf	D35	Operating without insurance - infraction
oper w/o ins-os	D35	Operating without insurance, out-of-state
operat lic rev/susp	B20	Operating while license revoked or suspended
operat out of class	B91	Operating out of class
operat reg susp/rev	n/a	Operating while registration revoked or suspended
operat w/o a license	B51	Operating without a license
operating reg revoke	n/a	Operating with registration revoked
operating w/o ins	D35	Operating without insurance
operating w/o proof	D35	Operating without proof of insurance
operating w/susp	B20	Operating while suspended
osid/save prohibit	n/a	Social Security Number or immigration and naturalization service verification pending-requires osid action
out of state	n/a	Out of state
ovrwght/ovrsze veh	n/a	Overweight or oversize vehicle
ovrwght/size veh nyc	n/a	Overweight/oversize vehicle NYC
ovrwt/ovrsize esc	n/a	Overweight/oversize vehicle violations escalating fines- NYC regs 301 & 415 -other than (8)(9)(10)- v&t 385- other than (8)(9)(10)
parkway violation	n/a	Parkway violation
pass flash red light	M16	Passed flashing red light
pass stp veh intrsec	M76	Passed stopped vehicle at intersection
passed on right	M70	Passed on right
passed red light	M16	Passed red light
penalty fee due	n/a	Penalty fee due
pend auto theft invs	n/a	Pending auto theft investigation
pend investgn - ia	n/a	Pending investigation - IA
pend dfi inst-sl283	n/a	Pending DFI investigation - sl283
pend dfi invest	n/a	Pending DFI investigation
pend pros-ct bac	w72	Pending prosecution by court, blood alcohol count
pend pros - ct jr	w72	Pending prosecution by court-junior operator
Pend prosecution OOS	W72	Pending prosecution – out of state
pend prosecution-ct	W72	Pending prosecution by court
pend prosecution-dmv	W72	Pending prosecution by department
pend review (title)	n/a	Pending review (title)
pendg pass spec exam	D02	Pending passing special examination
pending hearing	W72	Pending hearing
pending tvb hearing	D56	Indefinite suspension, pending appearance or determination pursuant to VTL sect. 226 2(b) or 227
per oper w/o ins-inf	D35	Permitting operation without insurance - infraction
per othr use lic-inf	n/a	Permitting another to use license - infraction
per unlic op - inf	n/a	Permitting unlicensed operation - infraction
per unlic op mc -inf	n/a	Permitting unlicensed operation of a motorcycle - infraction
per use veh in crime	U04	Permitting use of vehicle in a crime
permit oper w/o ins	D35	Permitting operation without insurance
permt clinging to mv	N84	Permitting another to cling to a moving motor vehicle
persistent violator	W01	Persistent violator
persistnt violator-g	W01	Persistent violator - g
pndg submissn to crt	W72	Pending submission to the court
png submsn to crt-al	W72	Pending submission to court - alcohol
png submsn to crt-os	D56	Pending submission to court, out-of-state
pos and/or sale drgs	A33	Possession and/or sale of drugs
poss dup record	n/a	Possible duplicate record
poss fict lic-inf	B41	Possessing fictitious license or altering date of birth - infraction
poss stolen veh-fel	n/a	Possession of stolen vehicle - felony
prd inv ins id cd-ms	n/a	Produced an invalid insurance identification card
pri ord reinstatd-cl	n/a	Prior order reinstated by court - conditional license
prior order reinst	n/a	Prior order reinstated
prl-wrttn test cheat	n/a	Written test substitution or cheating
Psd susp pend rev	n/a	Registration suspended pending administrative review-failure to respond to multiple political subdivision

Short Description	ACD	Long Description
		eligibility requests
purch alc bev ill	D06	Purchasing alcoholic beverages illegally
pved susp. (5 in 12)	n/a	Parking violations suspension - 5 tickets/notices of suspension within 12 months
pved susp. (default)	n/a	Parking violations suspension - default
rcvd cdl wo ny res	n/a	Obtained NYS CDL without a NYS residence address
reck dr jr op misd	M84	Reckless driving junior operator misdemeanor
reck dsrgd life/prob	M80	Reckless disregard of life or property
reckless driving	M84	Reckless driving
reckless operation	n/a	Reckless operation
reckless opr-2 in 18	n/a	Reckless operation-2 within 18 months
reckless opr-3 in 18	n/a	Reckless operation 3 times within 18 months
reckless opr-speed	n/a	Reckless operation - speed
ref chem tst CMV	A12	Refused a chemical test while driving a commercial motor vehicle
ref chem tst hzm	A12	Refused a chemical test while driving a commercial motor vehicle carrying hazardous materials
ref find purs 510-3a	n/a	Referee finds pursuant to 510-3(a)
refsd sub chem test	n/a	Refused to submit to a chemical test-oprhp 25.24(6)
refsd sub chem boat	n/a	Refused to submit to chemical test - boat
reg ovrwt < 18000 esc	n/a	Registration overweights less than 18000 lbs escalating fines V&T 401
reg ovrwt > 18000 esc	n/a	Registration overweight more than 18000 lbs escalating fines (V&T 401) (NYC regs 415)
reg susp nav law 49a	n/a	Registration suspended under navigation law 49a
reg susp oprhp 25.24	n/a	Registration suspension under office of parks and historic preservation law 25.24
reinstated by ct ord	n/a	Reinstated by court order
reinstd by ct ord-cl	n/a	Conditional license reinstated by court order
request dot (fs)	n/a	Request to department of transportation - FS
request of court	n/a	Suspension requested by the court
request of oprhp	n/a	Suspension requested by NYS dept parks and recreation
resch hearing-vessel	n/a	Rescheduled hearing - vessel
rev-fed veh inspect	n/a	Revoked - failed vehicle inspection
revoked by court	n/a	Revoked by court
revoked prob lic	D29	Revoked probationary license
revoked prob lic-cl	D29	Revoked probationary conditional license
rfsd breath test-inf	A12	Refused breath test - infraction
rfsd sub chem test	A12	Refused to submit to a chemical test
rules road vio bicyc	n/a	Rules of the road violation-bicycle
s370 bnd-fh acc-msd	D35	Section 370 indemnity bond; notice of for hire accident, misdemeanor
sal alt vin busn fel	n/a	Sale of altered vehicle identification number by a business - felony
sal alt vin felony	n/a	Sale of altered vehicle identification number - felony
sale false doc/plate	n/a	Sale of false or fraudulent document or number plate
seat belt violation	F04	Seat belt violation
see case folder	n/a	See case folder
see overflow record	n/a	See overflow record
smoking during oper	N84	Misdemeanor smoking during operation
smoking vehicle	n/a	Smoking vehicle
snd horn app horse	N01	Sounded horn while approaching a horse
spc cond contact diu	n/a	Special conditional contact driver improvement unit
sp CMV/radar 10+	S92	Speeding 10+ mph in a commercial motor vehicle equipped with a radar detector and with a vehicle defect present or while carrying hazardous materials
sp CMV/radar 20+	S92	Speeding 20+ mph in a commercial motor vehicle equipped with a radar detector
spd not reas/prudent	S94	Speed not reasonable and prudent
spd past schl jr op	S93	Speeding past school junior operator
spd past school	S93	Speeding past school
spd wk zone/rst hwy	S93	Speeding in a work zone or on a restricted highway
speed +15	S15	Speeding +15
speed contest	S95	Speed contest
speed contest	S95	Speed contest
speed contest jr op	S95	Speed contest junior operator class
speed in zone	S93	Speed in zone
speed in zone jr op	S93	Speed in zone junior operator
speed junior operatr	S93	Speeding junior operator
speed plus radar	S92	Speed with radar in a CMV (over 10,000 lbs)
speed/radar/other	S92	Speed with radar in a vehicle over 18,000 lbs
speeding	S93	Speeding
speeding - vessel	n/a	Speeding - vessel
speeding/snowmobile	n/a	Operating a snowmobile on public trails or lands over 55 mph
substitution in exam	D02	Substitution In examination
Sus/rev sr w/jr vio	D29	Suspend or revoke senior license for violation committed with junior license

Short Description	ACD	Long Description
susp by court 510	n/a	Suspended by court under V&T law section 510
susp pend hg nav 49b	n/a	Suspended pending hearing under navigation law 49b
susp pend pros/swi	n/a	Suspension pending prosecution/snowmobiling while intoxicated
susp term fee reqd	n/a	Suspension termination fee required
susp/rev jr lic	D29	Suspension or revocation of junior license
suspended by court	n/a	Suspended by court
suspended prob lic	D29	Suspended probationary license
suspnded prob lic-cl	D29	Suspended probationary conditional license
susp-pend veh inspec	n/a	Suspended pending vehicle inspection
swai	n/a	Snowmobiling while ability impaired
Snow impaired drugs	n/a	Snowmobiling while ability impaired-drugs
swi	n/a	Snowmobiling while intoxicated
Snow intox .08	n/a	Snowmobiling while intoxicated/.08
switched plate	n/a	Switched plate
t&I-road test sub	n/a	Road test substitution
tax and tran law	n/a	Violation of tax or transportation law
taxi belt not usable	n/a	Taxi/livery failed to ensure all seat belts were clearly visible, accessible, or in good working order; or seat belts were removed.
temp - pdg c/t hrg	w72	Suspension pending chemical test refusal hearing
temp susp pdg c/t hr	n/a	Temporary suspension pending court hearing
temp-pdg cthrg	n/a	Temporary pending court hearing
title returned check	n/a	Title returned check
transp hazard matl	n/a	Transporting hazardous material
truck mil tax	n/a	Truck mileage tax violation
truck rte viol-nyc	n/a	Truck route violation, New York City
trv ln ctr red sig	M16	Traveling in lane controlled by red signal
turn w/o signalling	N43	Turning without signaling
two o/s viol 10 yrs	W50	Two out-of-service order violations in 10 years
unauth for hire veh	n/a	Unauthorized for-hire vehicle
unauth remov tag-msd	n/a	Misdemeanor unauthorized removal of tag or sticker
unauthorized towing	n/a	Unauthorized towing
uncovered load	n/a	Uncovered load
unins acc-o/s reg	D35	Accident with uninsured out of state vehicle
unins f.h. veh-msd	D35	Uninsured for hire vehicle
unins for hire veh	D35	Uninsured for hire vehicle
uninsp heavy vehicle	n/a	Operating a heavy duty vehicle without valid inspection sticker
uninspected vehicle	n/a	Uninspected vehicle
uninsured accident	D35	Uninsured accident
uninsured operation	D35	Uninsured operation
uninsured vehicle	D35	Uninsured vehicle
unlaw dispos summons	n/a	Misdemeanor unlawful disposition of a summons
unlaw sale hlight dv	n/a	Unlawful sale of a headlight device
unlaw sol grd trans	n/a	Unlawful solicitation of ground transportation at an airport
unlaw trans hazd mat	n/a	Misdemeanor or felony unlawful transportation of hazardous waste
unlaw trans hzrd wst	n/a	Misdemeanor unlawful transportation of hazardous waste
unlaw validation dev	n/a	Unlawful use of a validation device
unlic instructor-inf	n/a	Unlicensed instructor - infraction
unlic op glasses	D29	Unlicensed operation - glasses
unlic op inf	B51	Unlicensed operation - infraction
unlic op learner per	n/a	Unlicensed operation - learner permit
unlic op,glasses-inf	D29	Unlicensed operation, glasses - infraction
unlic op,lp-inf	B51	Unlicensed operation, learner permit - infraction
unlic op,mcycle-in	B51	Unlicensed operator, motorcycle - infraction
Unlic oper for hire	B91	Unlicensed oepration of a for hire vehicle
unlic op-misd	B51	Unlicensed operation - misdemeanor
unlic opmyc-inf <60d	D29	Unlicensed operation of a motorcycle, less than 60 days
unlicensed chauffeur	B51	Unlicensed chauffeur
unreg atv	n/a	Unregistered all terrain vehicle
unreg boat	n/a	Unregistered boat
unreg lu vehicle	n/a	Unregistered limited use vehicle
unreg mcy < 61 days	n/a	Unregistered motorcycle, less than 61 days
unreg mcy/mini-bike	n/a	Unregistered motorcycle or mini-bike
unreg mot veh	n/a	Unregistered motor vehicle
unreg mot veh - inf	n/a	Unregistered motor vehicle - infraction
unreg mtcycle/snmble	n/a	Unregistered motorcycle or snowmobile
unreg tow truck	n/a	Unregistered tow truck

Short Description	ACD	Long Description
unreg veh < 61 days	n/a	Unregistered vehicle, less than 61 days
unsafe starting	N83	Unsafe starting
unsafe pass bicycle	M70	Failed to safely pass a bicycle
unsatisfied judgment	D39	Unsatisfied judgment
unsupervised learner	D29	Unsupervised learner
unver ssn contct dfi	D02	Pending investigation. Failure to comply with requested information for identity verification
unverified ssn	D02	Failure to provide information to verify your social security number
used another lic	n/a	Using another's license
used fict license	B41	Used a fictitious license
use/plce unath post	n/a	Use or placing of unauthorized posters or stickers on windshield or rear window
veh aslt 2nd/veh man	n/a	Vehicular assault 2nd degree/vehicular manslaughter
veh mansltr cdl hldr	U08	Vehicular manslaughter- CDL holder
veh mansltr CMV/hzmt	U08	Vehicular manslaughter operating a CMV and/or carrying hazmat
veh not under cntrl	N84	Vehicle not under control
vehic aslt - 1st deg	U03	Vehicular assault in the first degree
vehic aslt - 2nd deg	U03	Vehicular assault in the second degree
vehic manslaughter	U08	Vehicular manslaughter/manslaughter
vio grad lic rest	D29	Operating out of graduated license restriction
vio intlck-loan	A41	Violating ignition interlock restriction-knowingly leasing/renting/loaning a vehicle without interlock device to a person with interlock restriction
vio intlck-solicit	A41	Violating the ignition interlock restriction by soliciting or allowing another person to blow into the device-misd.
vio intlck-strt othr	A41	Violating the ignition interlock restriction by blowing into device to start a MV for another person-Misdemeanor
vio intlck-tampr dev	A41	Violating the ignition interlock restriction by tampering with a device-misdemeanor
voided summons	n/a	Voided summons
voluntary surrender	n/a	License cancelled at the request of the licensee
weaving	M42	Weaving
wthdrwl cnst jr op	W13	Withdrawal of parental consent, junior operator

Point System Summary

Points range from 2 to 11 points. The accumulation of 11 points in an 18-month time period may result in a suspension. The accumulation of 6 or more points in an 18-month time period, where the violations occurred on or after November 18, 2004, will result in an assessment payable to the DMV. Points are not added to a NY driver record for an out-of-state traffic violation, except for traffic violations occurring in Ontario or Quebec. Drivers who take a DMV-approved course may reduce their driver violation point total by 4 points. The web page has a list of courses.

Failing to obey traffic signal or stop sign .... 3 Points
Failing to stop for school bus .... 5 Points
Failing to yield right of way .... 3 Points
Following too closely .... 4 Points
Improper passing, unsafe lane change, drove left of center, drove wrong direction .... 3 Points
Inadequate brakes... 4 Points (2, if while driving employer's car)
Leaving scene of incident involving property damage or injury to animal... 3 Points
Passenger safety violations, including seat belts, child safety seats, and passengers under age 16 .... 3 Points
Railroad crossing violation... 3 Points
Reckless Driving .... 5 Points
Safety restraint violation involving person under 16 .... 3 Points

Speeding

1 to 10	3 Points	31 to 40	8 Points
11 to 20	4 Points	41+	11 Points
21 to 30	6 Points		
Speeding MPH not specified	3 Points		

Stop sign, traffic signal, yield sign .... 3 Points
Using handheld electronic device while driving.. 3 Points
Any other moving violation.. 2 Points

North Carolina

Administration	Important Telephone and Web Contacts
J. Eric Boyette, Commissioner Division of Motor Vehicles 3101 Mail Service Center, Raleigh 27699-3101 www.ncdot.gov/DMV Statutes: www.ncleg.net/gascripts/statutes/Statutes.asp	Driver Licensing...919-715-7000 SR-22 & Financial Security.........................919-715-7000 Traffic Records Section...............................919-861-3062 Safety Responsibility...................................919-715-7000 Commercial Driver License.........................919-715-7000 Vehicle Information......................................919-715-7000 IRP Unit ....919-861-3720 State Department of Insurance ....919-807-6750 Highway Patrol..919-733-7952 General Email List www.ncdot.gov/dmv/contact/

Driver's License Format, Issuance and Renewal

License Classes, Restrictions and Endorsements Appear After the Driving Record Content Section

License Format

The format is one to twelve numbers. Although DMV indicates there is no code or sequential arrangement which determines the digits on the license number, the DMV indicates most new numbers start with leading zeros, such as "00008..."

Document Appearance

The DMV has used the same documents for a number of years. The creation of the license document uses a computerized process called digital imaging.

Security Characteristics: Holographic overlay on the front and bar code on the rear. On December 2006, a holographic security patch was added to newly issued North Carolina driver licenses, but this patch was removed effective October 21, 2008.

Position of Photo: Bottom left corner and ghost image on bottom right corner, for drivers over 21.

Minor Age Driver Locator: Since October, 2008, the DMV issues a vertical license for drivers under the age of 21. The license includes color-coded bars that highlight the driver's 18th and 21st birthdays. Drivers between the ages of 15 and 18 receive licenses with two color bars, red and yellow, next to their photos listing the dates they turn 18 and 21. Drivers between the ages of 18 and 21 receive licenses with one red color bar listing the date they turn 21. Previously, if under 18, the picture is framed in red as is border; if age 18, 19 & 20, picture framed in yellow as is the border; if age is 21 & over, picture is framed in green as is the border.

CDL Indicator: DMV logo is printed in amber and license indicates the commercial driver license number in amber.

Issuance

Location of Requirements for Proof of Identity:
www.ncdot.gov/dmv/driver/

Age Requirements

The minimum age for Class A and B is 18, but driver would not be eligible for the Hazardous Material Endorsement and will be restricted to drive inside North Carolina only (Intrastate Restriction 4) until age 21. Minimum age for Class C is 16. A full description of the Graduated License Process is presented in the License Classes section.

One must be age 16 or older to operate a moped on North Carolina highways or public vehicular areas. A driving license is not required, and the moped does not have to be registered, inspected or covered by liability insurance.

Residency

New residents must secure a North Carolina license within 60 days of establishing residency or within 30 days if transferring a commercial license. If age sixteen or older, a non-resident's home state or home country license honored.

Renewal

Renewal is the birth date of eighth year for those 18 through 65 years old; birthdate of the fifth year for those 66 years old and older. The driver keeps same number when renewing. On July 1, 2008, the Division implemented a central issuance of driver licenses instead of an over-the-counter issuance program. At renewal or after a new driver completes a test, the driver receives a Temporary Driving Certificate valid for 20 days. One may keep the older license to use for photo identification until the new one arrives by mail. Renewal is not available online. Military personnel may renew by mail (write to the DMV,C/O Temporary DL Unit) every other renewal period.

Elderly-Related Restrictions

None reported other than the five-year renewal period described above for drivers 66 years old and older.

Vehicle Insurance, Title and Registration Facts

Registration Renewal

Renewal of registration is annual. Renewal is available online at www.ncdot.gov/dmv/. Since 2006, a staggered registration system is used for Apportioned Motor Carrier, Commercial Vehicles, Special Mobile, For-Hire, Transporters, Drive Away vehicles and Taxis. In the past, these vehicles were registered on an annual basis with all registrations expiring on December 31st of each year.

New Residents

Non-residents must register vehicles within 60 days (or longer, depending on reciprocity agreement with prior state of residence) or when gainful employment is accepted, which ever comes first. New residents must obtain a North Carolina Driver License prior to registering a vehicle in North Carolina.

Inspections and Emissions Testing

An NC Vehicle Safety Inspection is required annually before the vehicle's registration can be renewed. The Safety Inspection is waived for vehicles 35 years or older.

An Emissions Inspection (OBD) is also required in 48 counties (see www.ncdot.gov/dmv/vehicle/registration/inspection/). The emissions inspection is waived for vehicles 35 years or older, Model 1995 vehicles or older, diesel-operated vehicles, and famer-rate licensed vehicles. New residents can register a vehicle without getting an inspection, but the vehicle cannot be renewed until the inspection is passed.

Passenger Plate Facts

There is one plate and two decals (MO) (YR). The state does not designate the county of registration on the plate. When a vehicle is sold the plate remains with seller. However, an owner's license plate may be transferred to a different vehicle if the insurance was secured on the new vehicle at the same time the insurance was deleted on the old vehicle.

Insurance and Financial Responsibility

Insurance is compulsory. North Carolina law requires the registered owner of a motor vehicle to maintain continuous liability insurance coverage as long as there is a valid license plate for that vehicle. Minimum financial responsibility limits are $30,000/60,000/25,000. Per federal law, for CDL drivers the minimum liability limit is $750,000. Proof is required upon registration or renewal, when obtaining a driver's license, and when involved in an accident or "certain" violations. The state does not use SR-22 forms.

Withdrawal Sanctions, and Alcohol and Drug Testing

Alcohol and Chemical Testing Limits

North Carolina's legal intoxication level is .08 percent and above, for CDL drivers or drivers of CMVs .04 percent, and if under 21 years old there is zero (.00) tolerance. Commercial drivers are also subject to sanctions if blood alcohol content level of .00 percent. Blood and breath testing are authorized. North Carolina has both an implied consent violation and a provision for an administrative suspension.

Suspensions and Revocations

The North Carolina DMV is in compliance with the provisions of the Motor Carrier Safety Improvement Act (MCSIA). See the Appendix for these CDL mandatory disqualifications.

Accumulation of 12 points within three years (Note: The accumulation of eight points within three years following the reinstatement of the license can result in a second suspension.)

First Offense	Sixty days.
Second Offense	Six months.
Third Offense	Twelve months.
Assault With a Motor Vehicle	One year.
Betting, Watching, or Allowing the Use of Your Vehicle for Racing	Three years.
Death by Vehicle	One year.

Driving Under the Influence of an Impairing Substance

First Offense	One year.
Second Offense	Four years.
Third Offense	Permanent.

Other Suspensions

Failure to Stop When Involved in an Accident	One year.
Getting a License or Learner Permit under False Pretense	One year.
Making False Application for License	One year.
Manslaughter	One year.
Manslaughter While Under the Influence	Permanent.
Pre-arranged Racing	Three years.
Refusal to Submit to Chemical/Breath Test	One year.
Second Conviction Speeding Violation Within Twelve Months	Sixty days.
Speeding in Excess of 55 MPH and at Least 15 MPH Over Legal Limit	Thirty days.
Speeding in Excess of 55 MPH and at Least 15 MPH Over the Legal Limit While Attempting to Avoid Arrest	One year.
Two Reckless Driving Convictions in Twelve Months	One year.

Provisional Licensed Drivers

Two Moving Violations in Twelve Months	Thirty days.
Three Moving Violations in Twelve Months	Ninety days.
Four Moving Violations in Twelve Months	Sixth months.

Other Student Suspensions—

- A loss of license will occur if a student receives a suspension for more than 10 consecutive days or receives an assignment to an alternative educational setting due to disciplinary action for more than 10 consecutive days.
- Failure to appear or to pay fine

The DMV can also suspend a license for the following—

- Two convictions of speeding over 55 mph during the same year
- One conviction of speeding over 55 mph and one conviction of reckless driving within a year
- A conviction of willful racing with another motor vehicle, whether it is pre-arranged or unplanned
- A court ordered sentence or part of a sentence mandating that driver must not operate a motor vehicle for a specified time period
- A conviction for speeding over 75 mph
- Speeding conviction plus reckless driving conviction on the same occasion

CDL and Alcohol

Driver will lose CDL for one year for first offense, will lose for life for second offense. If the blood alcohol concentration is less than 0.04% but with any detectable amount, the driver will be put out-of-service for 24 hours.

Reinstatement Requirements

Suspension or Revocation...$50.00 fee; $100.00, if DWI-related.

Record Access: Laws, Rules, and Forms

Note: This Section Applies to Both Driver and Vehicle Records.

Governing Statutes and Rules

Statutes: www.ncleg.net/gascripts/statutes/Statutes.asp
North Carolina does not specifically enumerate the federal exceptions. Per NCGS 20-43.1, North Carolina law states that:

(a) The Division shall disclose personal information contained in motor vehicle records in accordance with the federal Driver's Privacy Protection Act of 1994, as amended, 18 U.S.C. §§ 2721, et seq.

(b) As authorized in 18 U.S.C. § 2721, the Division shall not disclose personal information for the purposes specified in 18 U.S.C. § 2721(b)(11).

(c) The Division shall not disclose personal information for the purposes specified in 18 U.S.C. § 2721(b)(12) unless the Division receives prior written permission from the person about whom the information is requested.

Policy Statement Regarding Permissible Uses

Personal information MAY be disclosed as follows:

1. For the applicant's own personal record.
2. For use by any government agency in carrying out its function, or for use by any private person or entity acting **on behalf of** a government agency.
3. For use in matters of motor vehicle or driver safety and theft, motor vehicle emissions, motor vehicle product alterations, recalls or advisories, performance monitoring of motor vehicles, motor vehicle parts and dealers, motor vehicle market research activities, including survey research, and removal of non-owner records from the original owner records of motor vehicle manufacturers.
4. For use in the normal course of business by a legitimate business, but only:
   a.   To verify accuracy of personal information.
   b.   To obtain correct information, but only for the purpose of:
      i.   Preventing fraud by the individual.
      ii. Pursuing legal remedies against the individual.
      iii. Recovering a debt or security interest against the individual.
5. For use in connection with any civil, criminal, administrative or arbitral proceeding in any federal, state or local court or agency (includes the execution or enforcement of judgments and orders or court orders).
6. For use in research activities and statistical reports, provided that personal information must not be:
   a.   Published.
   b.   Re-disposed.
   c.   Used to contact individuals.
7. For use by insurance companies in connection with claims investigation, anti-fraud activities, rating or underwriting.
8. For use in providing notice to owners of towed or impounded vehicles.
9. For use by private investigators or licensed security service for any purpose listed herein.
10. For use by employers to verify information regarding CDL.
11. For use by any requester who has obtained written consent of the individual to whom the information pertains.
12. For use in connection with the operation of private toll transportation facilities.

No individual authorization or certification need be submitted with the request for a driving record. However, companies requesting large numbers of records must be pre-approved and have a certificate on file with the DMV.

Request and Consent Forms

Driving Records: Complete the *Driver Privacy Protection Act Form 1 (DL-DPPA-1)*, or use *Driver Privacy Protection Act Form 2 (DL-DPPA-2)* if driver wants to give someone else permission to receive record copy. The *DL-DPPA-1A* form is used as a continuation sheet in conjunction with the *DL-DPPA-1* if a requester needs more than five MVRs. One may request up to 22 additional MVRs, be sure to provide all needed for each MVR request. See http://www.ncdot.gov/dmv/forms/ for either form. The form requires the signature of the requester. If the requester does not have a permissible purpose, signature of the subject is also required. Neither signature needs to be notarized. Licensed private investigators must report their state PI license number on the form.

Vehicle Records: *Request Form MVR-605A* is required for new requesters. The form can be downloaded from either www.ncdot.gov/dmv/records or www.ncdot.gov/dmv/forms. Licensed private investigators must report their state PI license number on the form. No authorization or certification need be submitted with the request from ongoing requesters. Companies requesting large numbers of records must be pre-approved and have a certificate on file with the DMV.

Vendor and Third Party Access Policy

Approved vendors can access records for other vendors who supply the records to an end-user as long as the contract between original vendor and reseller contains same language as the contract between the state and the original vendor. Both vendors and the end-user must be in compliance with DPPA. Resale of data for bulk distribution for survey, marketing or solicitations is prohibited by NC General Statutes.

Records Ordered For Non-permissible Uses

The statute provides that personal information in DMV records be closed to the general public. The statute refers to name, address, DL or ID number, phone number, SSN, medical and disability information, and photos. Thus, if no consent, requesters without a permissible use cannot obtain records, even records without personal information.

Access to Driver-Related Record

Driving Records

General Information and Fees

Division of Motor Vehicles, Motor Vehicle Records Center, 3113 Mail Service Center, Raleigh, NC 27699-3113 919-715-7000, fax 919-861-3919. (www.ncdot.gov/dmv/records)
The current fee is $8.00 for either the **Limited** three-year (insurance) record or the **Complete** seven-year (employer) record. Add $3.00 for certification. The last fee increase was October 2005. The Division does not charge for "no record found" reports, except for requests mailed in for processing.

In-Person – Driver License Section is located at 1100 New Bern Avenue, Raleigh NC 27697, 919-715-7000. Requests will be processed over-the-counter while you wait; there is no limit based on staffing and number requested. This is the only location that processes record requests. The driver's license number, name, DOB, and a completed Request Form are required when ordering.

Mail – The address shown above is the only location that processes mail requests. The turnaround time for processing is generally 10 days, not including mail time. The driver's license number, name, DOB, SSN, and a completed *DL-DPPA-1 or DPPA-2 Form* (see above) are required when ordering. Payment must accompany the request.

Electronic, Commercial – Traffic Records Section, 3105 Mail Service Ct, Raleigh NC 27699-3105, 919-861-3062. To qualify for online availability, submit a written request to noted address stating how the information will be used. The agency will send applications forms or a denial letter. A security deposit is required (minimum $500.00; estimated at 150 percent of typical monthly bill), billing is monthly.

Electronic, Public Web – The Internet Driving Record Request service allows North Carolina citizens to purchase a NC driving record online. Requesters must first apply for a PIN which is sent by email. See https://edmv-dr.dot.state.nc.us/DrivingRecords/DrivingRecords.
Both certified and non-certified records are available, fees are the same as above: $8.00 fee for non-certified or $11.00 if certified. The non-certified driving record may be viewed, printed or stored during the online transaction. Certified driving records are mailed within 10 business days to the address provided. Each request requires the first and last name, driver's license or ID card number, the SSN, and the DOB. Any entity may request the driving record of an individual if that entity has a valid reason under the DPPA. As a part of the transaction, the requester must indicate the valid reason for the request. Payment must be made using either VISA or MasterCard.

Bulk – The Division does not offer bulk sale of records.

By Person of Record – NC drivers may obtain their driving record by mail, walk-in, or online as described above. Mail or walk-in requesters should use a specific form (DPPA-1) found at www.ncdot.gov/dmv/forms/.

Notification/Monitoring Program

At present, North Carolina does not offer the sale of information that can be used as a monitoring system or notification program to employers or insurance companies to track incidents of drivers.

Crash Reports

Reporting – Crashes resulting in death, injury, or property damage of $1,000.00 or more must be reported immediately to the nearest law enforcement agency. If additional information is needed, it will be requested by the Division of Motor Vehicles. Written reports of crashes must be filed with the *DMV, Traffic Records Section, 1100 New Bern Avenue, Raleigh 27697.*

Record Access – Records are maintained for 10 years electronically, hard copies are not kept once computerized. Traffic Records Section, Crash Reports Unit, 3105 Mail Service Center, Raleigh NC 27699-3105, 919-861-3098. Copies can be purchased for $5.00 per certified copy. Information on minor drivers is not released. The requester should submit a request form (*TR-67A*) indicating at least one of the names of the drivers, the county of occurrence, approximate date, and the exception under which he/she qualifies to receive personal information in accordance with DPPA. Normal turnaround time is 5 days. It will take 1 to 3 days before new records are available for research, once data is received by this office.
For a copy of the request form, call 919-861-3098 or visit www.ncdot.gov/dmv/records/ to fill out *Form TR-67A* online.

Access to Vehicle-Related Records

General Information and Fees
Registration/Correspondence Unit, 3157 Mail Service Center, Room 100, Raleigh, NC 27699-3157, 919-715-7000.
The DMV maintains records for vehicles, mobile homes and boat trailers. The current fee for VIN, ownership, lien and registration records is $1.00, or $10.00 for a certified copy. There are over 8 million vehicles registered in North Carolina.

In-Person or Mail – The state requires use of the request form mentioned above. Records and history is available for all years. There is a full charge for a no record found. Mail-in requests have a normal turnaround time of 3 days. For **uncertified records**, mail form & fee to NC Division of Motor Vehicles RTP Unit, 3148 Mail Service Center, Raleigh, NC 27699-3148. For **certified copies**, mail form &

fee to NC Division of Motor Vehicles, Room 100, 3157 Mail Service Center, Raleigh, NC 27699-3157.
Telephone – Subscribers who have been assigned a user code may request information by telephone.
Electronic – Online retrieval is not offered at this time.
Bulk – North Carolina offers a bulk method to qualified entities for retrieval of ownership and registration information. A request form is required detailing the specific information desired and the exception under which one must qualify to receive personal information in accordance with DPPA. There are a variety of generalized parameters from which to pull data. The cost includes CPU time, programming and postage. For more information call 919-861-3062.

Access to Vessel-Related Records

General Information, Access and Fees
NC Wildlife & Resource Commission, Transaction Management, 1709 Mail Service Center, Raleigh 27699 (800) 628-3773, fax is 919-707-0293 http://ncwildlife.org.
All motorized boats and all sail boats over 14 ft must be registered. Vessels under 14ft and if not a personal watercraft must be registered but do not need to be titled unless there is a lien - then title is optional. Note that since 01/07 titles are mandatory; previously this was

optional. Paper records maintained from 2003, computerized index from 1970. Record search fee is $20.00 but can be higher if extensive research is required. All requests must be in writing. Search by name, hull ID or registration #. Turnaround time is 1-2 days. Lien information will show on a Title Certificate if the vessel is titled here. Although liens could previously be filed at the state with the UCC filings, most lenders now file liens here.

Driving Record Content and Reciprocity

What's on or Not on the Record

- The state reports only moving violation convictions on the driving record as well as driver control actions.
- Medical information is not released.

- All accidents are reported—regardless of fault—if there is personal injury or damage of $1,000 or more.
- A "Prayer for Judgment" citation means that the court reserves the right to pass judgment later. The driver is charged the cost of court, no decision is rendered, and no points are assigned (except for a

third Prayer for Judgment citation within five years). The judge can finalize the citation later.

- The state does not permit driver school attendance in lieu of conviction.

Data Retention

Moving Violations are maintained at least 10 years; DUIs and suspension/revocations for over 10 years. CDL records follow federal regulation guidelines (see Appendix). Records for surrendered licenses are maintained for one year after the expiration dates.

State Reciprocity for Non-CDL Drivers
- Will suspend license of driver for unpaid out-of-state convictions.
- Record of new incoming driver is not shown on MVR
- Out-of-state convictions and fail to pay or appear are shown on MVR.
- Out-of-state accidents are note shown on MVR.
- Convictions of out-of-state drivers are sent to home state.
- Record is forwarded to new state upon surrender of license upon request.

License Classes, Restrictions, and Commercial Endorsements

License Classes

A Commercial Driver License (CDL) is required for most Class A & B vehicles. Class C vehicles that transport hazardous materials requiring placarding or that are designed to carry sixteen or more persons also require a CDL. A Non-Commercial license is known as a "Regular License" in this state. Each category uses the same Class A, B or C and each regular license has the same requirements in force as long as the vehicle is exempt from CDL requirements (such as an RV trailer or farm equipment). North Carolina began issuing the CDL in September 1990

Class A   Any combination of vehicles with a GVWR of 26,001 pounds or more, provided the GVWR of the vehicle(s) being towed is (are) in excess of 10,000 pounds. if the vehicle is exempt from CDL requirements—also required for combination vehicles less than 26,001 pounds if the vehicle being towed exceeds 10,000 pounds.

Class B   Any single vehicle with a GVWR of 26,001 pounds or more, and any such vehicle towing a vehicle not in excess of 10,000 pounds if the vehicle is exempt from CDL requirements.*

Class C   Vehicles under 26,001 pounds that are exempt from CDL requirements, and a combination of non-commercial vehicles that have a GVWR of more than 10,000 pounds but less than 26,2001 pounds. This sub-subdivision does not apply to a Class C license holder less than 18 years of age. Most drivers need only a Regular C License to operate their personal automobiles and small trucks.

Note: One must be age 16 or older to operate a moped on North Carolina highways or public vehicular areas. A driving license is not required, and the moped does not have to be registered, inspected or covered by liability insurance.

Graduate Licenses

(All levels require a driving eligibility certificate or a high school diploma or its equivalent.)

Level I   **Limited Learner's Permit:** This level requires a driving eligibility certificate or a high school diploma or its equivalent. Must be at least 15 and completed driver education; always accompanied by supervising driver; first 6 months can only drive between 5am and 9pm; after 6 months can drive anytime with supervising driver; everyone in car must wear seatbelt or be in child restraint system; mobile telephone restriction. Requires completion of a 60-hour driving log to advance to Level II.

Level II   **Limited Provisional License:** This level does not require a driving eligibility certificate or a high school diploma or its equivalent unless the driver has been suspended for grades or conduct. Must have had Level I at least 12 months with no convictions in last 6 months; pass road test; drive unsupervised from 5am to 9pm; drive anytime to and from work or with supervising driver; drive to or from an activity of a volunteer fire department, volunteer rescue squad or volunteer emergency medical service, if the driver is a member of the organization; passenger limitation restriction; everyone in car must wear seatbelt or be in child restraint system; mobile telephone restriction. Requires completion of a 12-hour driving log to advance to Level III

Level III   **Full Provisional License:** Must have had Level II at least 6 months with no convictions in last 6 months; mobile telephone restriction if under 18.

Restrictions

	Regular	Commercial		Regular	Commercial
L - No Air-Brakes		■	12 - 6:00 a.m. to 8:00 p.m.	■	■
S - School Bus Only (no longer used)		■	13 - Automatic Transmission	■	■
O - None	■	■	14 - Passenger Class B and C Only		■
1 - Corrective Lenses	■	■	15 - Passenger Class C Only		■
2 - Forty-five mph Speed Limit - No Interstate Driving	■	■	16 - Limited Learners Permit	■	
3 - Daylight Driving Only	■	■	17 - Limited Professional License	■	
4 - Intrastate Only		■	18 - No Passengers	■	■
5 - Wrecker Only		■	19 - BAC .04	■	■
6 - Mobile Home Transport Only		■	20 - BAC .04 / Ignition Interlock	■	
7 - Outside Mirror	■	■	21 - BAC .00	■	■
8 - No Tractor-Trailers		■	22 - BAC .00 / Ignition Interlock	■	
9 - Other-Shown on License Face	■	■	23 - Ignition Interlock Only	■	
10 - Accompanied by Driver Licensed for Class Shown	■	■			

Endorsements

H	Hazardous Material		N	Tank Vehicles
M	Motorcycle		S	School Bus
P	Passenger Carrying		T	Double-Trailers
X	Combination H and N			

Conviction Table with DMV Code and ACD

DMV Code	ACD	Description
027	-	Failure to Complete Community Service Requirements
028	A98	Civil Revocation
029	A41	Violation of Ignition Interlock Restriction
193	M86	Cell Phone Use by School Bus Driver
195	M85	Mobile Phone Violation While Less Than 18 Years Old
196	D29	Fail to Comply With Passenger Seating Less Than 18 Years Old (GDL)
197	F04	Seatbelt Violation - Less Than 18 years Old
198	D51	Fail To Make Child Support/Admin Office of Courts
199	D51	Fail to Make Child Support/DHR
201	D29	Allowing Unlicensed person to Drive (Obsolete - map to 205)
202	E70	Improper Equipment - Speedometer
203	S96	Driving Below Minimum Speed Limit
205	D29	Allowing Unlicensed To Drive
206	B51	Expired Operator's License (Expired Less Than 1 Year)
209	B91	Driving CMV Without Proper Endorsement
210	S94	Driving Too Fast For Conditions
211	N40	Fail To Give Signal
212	E50	Horn And Warning Device Violation
213	-	Littering - Using MV
214	S94	Failure to Reduce Speed
215	E55	Using Red or Blue Lights Prohibited By Law
216	M40	Fail To Use Truck Route
217	M33	Following a Fire Truck
218	S94	Fail to Reduce Speed (Overtaken Vehicle Increased Speed)
219	M40	Improper Use of Traffic Lane
220	M40	Interstate Highway Violation
221	F66	Improper Towing
222	N50	Improper Turn
223	M42	Improper or Erratic (Unsafe) Lane Change (Court Desc. is Marked Lane Violation)
224	M56	Drive Over Fire Hose or Equipment
225	N63	Driving Wrong Way - One Way Street
226	M33	Obstructing Fire Operations
227	N50	UnSafe Movement Violation
230	M40	Unlawfully Pass Emergency Vehicle
231	B51	License Not In Possession
231	B51	Fail To Display or Exhibit License
232	F34	Impeding Traffic - Sitting/Standing/Lying to Obstruct Traffic
234	M49	HOV Lane Or Restricted Lane Violation
237	B26	Driving After License Suspended (Obsolete - Use 606)
238	B25	Driving After License Revoked (Obsolete - Use 606)
239	S94	Exceed Safe Speed
240	-	Forfeiture Of Licensing Privileges
241	-	Non-Traffic Conviction (Used for Court Order)
242	S96	Speed Less Than Posted Minimum - Impeding Traffic
244	E55	Fail to Burn Headlamp
245	E55	Motorcycle - Fail to Burn Headlamp
246	E55	Motorcycle - Fail to Burn Taillight
247	M05	Fail To Stop/Weigh Vehicle At Station
248	D29	Overload/Crowd Vehicle
249	M51	Crossing Median
250	M09	Fail to Obey Railroad Signal - Stop At RR
251	F06	Motorcycle Overload / Crowd
252	S92	Speeding in Work Zone
253	F02	Child Not in Rear Seat Or Youth Restraint Not Used Properly
254	F02	Fail to Secure Passenger Under 16
255	F05	Carrying Unsecured Passengers in Open Area of Vehicle
301	B51	Driving No Operator License More Than One Year (Obsolete)

DMV Code	ACD	Description
302	B51	Driving No Operator License
303	D29	Fail To Comply With License Restrictions
304	B61	Fail To Report An Accident
305	M08	Fail To Stop or Heed For Siren Or Red Light
306	N01	Fail To Yield Right Of Way
307	D36	No Liability Insurance
308	M16	Running Red Light
309	M15	Running Stop Sign (Obsolete - map to 311)
311	M15	Stop Sign Violation
312	M12	Safety Zone Violation
313	S92	Speeding
314	S92	Speeding In A School Zone
317	B91	No Motorcycle Endorsement
318	A35	Transporting Open Container After Consuming
320	D29	Driving Outside Time Limit (Graduated License)
321	D29	Driving Without Supervising Driver (Graduated License)
322	D29	License/Permit Violation of Other Restriction, Under 18 Years of Age
401	N72	Driving Left of Center (Wrong Side Of Road)
402	M34	Following Too Close
403	B04	Hit And Run (Property Damage)
404	N08	Fail to Yield to Pedestrian
407	B08	Leaving Scene Of Accident (Property Damage)
408	M84	Reckless Driving
409	M70	Illegal Passing
410	B01	Hit And Run
411	M84	Reckless Driving (Offenses Prior to 10/1/83)
412	A31	Possession of Alcohol in Commercial Vehicle
501	M75	Fail to Stop for a Stopped School Bus
502	M20	For drivers who are not required to always stop, failure to slow down at a railroad-highway grade crossing and check that tracks are not clear
503	M21	For drivers who are not required to always stop, failure to stop before reaching tracks at a railroad-highway grade crossing when the tracks are not clear
504	M22	For drivers who are always required to stop, failure to stop as required before driving onto railroad-highway grade crossing
505	M10	Fail To Obey Railroad Gates/Signs/Signals (Fail to Stop Where Traffic Obstructed)
506	M84	Reckless Driving With CMV Load Permit
507	S15	Speeding 15 or More Over Limit With CMV Load Permit
508	M23	For all drivers, failing to have sufficient space to drive completely through the railroad-highway grade crossing without stopping
509	M24	For all drivers, failing to negotiate a railroad-highway grade crossing because of insufficient undercarriage clearance
510	M84	Aggressive Driving
601	B26	Driving While License Suspended (Obsolete)
602	U04	Larceny of Motor Vehicle - Felony - Car Value Exceeds $1,000
603	D16	Allow Use of License or Permit
604	S95	Willful Racing Or Speed Competition
605	A31	Transporting Intoxicants
606	B25	Driving While License Suspended or Revoked
607	A20	Driving While Intoxicated (Obsolete)
608	B03	Hit And Run (Personal Injury)
609	U08	Involuntary Manslaughter
610	B07	Leaving Scene Of Accident (Personal Injury)
611	U08	Manslaughter
612	S95	Prearranged Racing Or Speed Competition
613	B41	Fictitious License - Improper Use of License
614	D16	Unlawful Use Of License
615	B25	Use Foreign License While Driving While License Revoked
616	D02	Fraudulent License Permit - Obtain Driver's License by Fraud
617	D02	Allowing False Application
618	D27	Violation Of Limited Privilege
619	D56	Fail To Appear - Fail to Comply With Out-Of-State Citation
620	A20	BAC .10 Or More (Obsolete)
621	U08	Misdemeanor Death by Vehicle
622	U01	Speeding To Elude Arrest (Obsolete After 12/1/97)
624	U06	Assault With A Motor Vehicle
625	A20	Driving While Impaired
626	A20	Driving Under The Influence On Moped Or Bicycle (Obsolete)

DMV Code	ACD	Description
627	A20	Instructing While Under The Influence
628	U07	Death By Vehicle Involving DWI
629	U08	Manslaughter Involving DWI (Obsolete)
630	A60	Consuming Alcohol/Drugs While Less Than 21 - Provisional License
631	D06	Violation Of ABC Laws - Obtain/Attain Alcohol Using False ID
632	A20	Driving While Impaired (Moped Or Bicycle)
633	D27	Driving While License Revoked - Violation of Limited License Condition
634	D45	Failure To Appear in Court
635	D53	Fail To Pay Court
636	U03	Felony - Using A Motor Vehicle
637	U07	2nd Degree Murder - DWI
638	B24	Driving CMV While Disqualified
639	A04	BAC of .04 or More In A CMV
640	A20	Habitual Impaired Driving
641	U01	Misdemeanor Eluding Arrest
642	U01	Felony Eluding Arrest- 2 Aggravating Factors
643	U01	Felony Eluding Arrest- 3 Aggravating Factors
644	A50	Felony Involving a Controlled Substance in an CMV
645	A26	Driving CMV After Consuming Alcohol
646	A26	Driving School Bus/Activity Bus/Childcare Vehicle After Consuming Alcohol
647	B03	Hit and Run - Fail to Stop W/ Personal Injury (2-Year Revocation)
648	-	Property Damage by Explosion
650	-	False Bomb Report - Public Building
651	-	Hoax - False Bomb - Public Building
652	-	Possessing Explosive on Education Property
653	-	Aid Minor Possess Explosive on Education Property
654	B27	Driving While Service Order In Effect
655	B19	Violation of Out of Service Order
656	-	Aid Underage Purchase of Liquor
657	-	Purchase MTBV/U-WN - Under 21 years of Age
658	N01	Fail to Yield - Serious Injury
659	B41	False Lic/Permit in Committing Felony
661	B25	DWLR After DWI Revocation Notice Sent
662	D45	Failure to appear for 2 years on implied consent offense
664	-	Larceny of Motor Fuel
665	N04	Fail to Move Over – Serious Injury/Death
667	U03	Felony – Serious Injury by Vehicle
668	U03	Aggravated Felony Serious Injury by Vehicle
669	U07	Aggravated Felony Death by Vehicle
670	-	Give Alcohol to Underage Person
786	A12	Refused Chemical Test
787	D29	Violation of Alcohol Concentration Restriction
788	A41	Violation of Ignition Interlock Violation
789	W20	CDL Disqualification – Positive Drug Test (GS20-17.4(L))
790	W81	CDL Disqualification – Refused
S15	S15	Speeding 15 MPH or More Above Limit
S16	S16	Speeding 16-20 Over Limit
S21	S21	Speeding 21-25 Over Limit
S26	S26	Speeding 26-30 Over Limit
S31	S31	Speeding 31-35 Over Limit
S36	S36	Speeding 36-40 Over Limit
S41	S41	Speeding 41+ Over Limit
S51	S51	Speeding 01-10 Over Limit
S71	S71	Speeding 21-30 Over Limit
S81	S81	Speeding 31-40 Over limit
S91	S91	Speeding 41+ Over Limit
W09	W09	Failure to Surrender HAZMAT Endorsement as Required by US Patriot Act
W70	W70	Imminent Hazard

Point System Summary

Drivers accumulating seven points may be assigned to a Driver Improvement Clinic. Upon satisfactory completion of the clinic, three points are deducted from the driving record. Accumulation of as many as twelve points within a three-year period may cause license to be suspended. The accumulation of eight points within three years following the reinstatement of the license can result in a second suspension. When driving privilege is reinstated, all previous driver license points are canceled. Insurance companies use a different point system to determine insurance rates.

Point Schedule if Operating a Non-Commercial Motor Vehicle

Passing a stopped school bus loading or unloading children...5 Points
Aggressive driving ....5 Points
Reckless driving...4 Points
Hit and run, property damage only...4 Points
Following too closely...4 Points
Driving on wrong side of road ....4 Points
Illegal passing ....4 Points
Failure to yield right-of-way to pedestrian pursuant to GS 20-158(b)(2)b..4 Points
Failure to yield right-of-way to bicycle motor scooter, or motorcycle..4 Points
Running through stop sign ....3 Points
Speeding more than 55 mph..3 Points
Speeding through a school zone...3 Points
Failure to yield right of way ....3 Points
No driver's license or license expired more than one year ....3 Points
Running through red light ....3 Points
Failure to stop for siren ....3 Points
Driving through safety zone...3 Points
Failure to report accident where such report is required ....3 Points
No liability insurance...3 Points
Failure to properly restrain a child in a restraint or seat belt ....2 Points
Littering involving a motor vehicle..1 Point
All other moving violations..2 Points

Point Schedule if Operating a Commercial Motor Vehicle

Passing a stopped school bus loading or unloading children..8 Points
Rail-highway crossing violation..6 Points
Careless and Reckless driving in violation of G.S. 20-140(f) ....6 Points
Speeding in violation of G. S. 20-141(j3) ....6 Points
Aggressive driving ....6 Points
Reckless driving...5 Points
Hit and run, property damage only...5 Points
Following too closely...5 Points
Driving on wrong side of road ....5 Points
Illegal passing ....5 Points
Failure to yield right-of-way to pedestrian pursuant to G. S. 20-158(b)(2)b..5 Points
Failure to yield right-of-way to bicycle motor scooter, or motorcycle..5 Points
Running through stop sign ....4 Points
No liability insurance...4 Points
Speeding more than 55 mph..4 Points
Speeding through a school zone...4 Points
Failure to yield right of way ....4 Points
No driver's license or license expired more than one year ....4 Points
Running through red light ....4 Points
Failure to stop for siren ....4 Points
Driving through safety zone...4 Points
Failure to report accident where such report is required ....4 Points
Possessing alcoholic beverage in the passenger area of a commercial motor vehicle ....4 Points
All other moving violations..3 Points
Littering involving a motor vehicle..1 Point

No points shall be assessed for convictions of the following offenses:
   Carrying concealed weapon
   Failure to display current inspection certificate
   Illegal parking
   Improper display of license plates or dealer's tags
   Improper muffler
   Improper plates
   Improper registration
   Over height
   Over length
   Over loads
   Over width
   Unlawful display of emblems and insignia

North Dakota

Administration	Important Telephone and Web Contacts
Glenn Jackson, Director Driver's License Division 701-328-2600 Linda Sitz, Director Motor Vehicle Division 701-328-1986 608 East Boulevard Avenue Bismarck 58505-0750 www.dot.nd.gov/public/licensing.htm	Driver Licensing..701-328-4353 Suspensions & Driving Records..................701-328-2604 Financial Responsibility & SR-22..............701-328-2604 Commercial Driver License.........................701-328-2600 Vehicle Information.....................................701-328-2725 State Department of Insurance ....701-328-2440 Highway Patrol..701-328-2455 Rules of the Road handbook is found at www.dot.nd.gov/divisions/driverslicense/docs/rulesroad.pdf

Driver's License Format, Issuance and Renewal

License Classes, Restrictions and Endorsements Appear After the Driving Record Content Section

License Format

The alpha numeric combination used is comprised of nine characters beginning with the first three letters of the last name (if last name is only two letters, an "X" is added). Until April 1, 2003, at the option of the driver either the Social Security Number or an assigned nine digit number starting with a "9" was used. Since that date drivers with the SSN or a nine-digit number on their license are given a new alpha-numeric number when the license is renewed.

Document Appearance

Current Document

The current document, introduced in 2006, is plastic non-laminated with a security overlay on front.
  Security Characteristics: Ghost image of the holder on the bottom of the card; state seal overlapping the portrait; transparent hologram with alternating images of a meadowlark bird and prairie rose flower. "blue map" with pink sky indicates a regular driver license, motorcycle permit, regular instruction permit, temporary permit, and a motorized bicycle permit. The non-driver ID Card has a orange map with green sky.
  Position of Photo: Larger image on left edge middle, smaller ghost image lower right corner.
  Minor Age Driver Locator: Vertical design on cards issued to persons under 21. The card has a red bar with the date that the person will turn 21 or a yellow bar for person under 18 that states their 18th birthday.
  CDL Indicator: State map in green map with pink sky. The words *Commercial Driver License* appears in green in the middle of the card.

Older Document

The document is plastic non-laminated with a security overlay on front.
  Security Characteristics: Contains security patch over DOB.

Position of Photo: Lower right, for 21 and older.

Minor Age Driver Locator: Drivers 18 to 20 years of age have image on left side with a red border, DOB printed in red. Drivers under 18 have image on left side with a yellow border and DOB printed in red.

CDL Indicator: CDL has a green header and "COMMERCIAL DRIVER LICENSE" is printed along top.

Issuance

Location of Requirements for Proof of Identity:
http://www.dot.nd.gov/divisions/driverslicense/dlinfo.htm#id

Age Requirements

The minimum age is sixteen; fourteen (restricted) with completion of approved driver education course. A Learner's Permit is required.

Residency

Any person other than a nonresident student, a tourist, or a non-resident member of the Armed Forces who has lived in this state 90 consecutive days shall be deemed a resident of North Dakota for the purpose of driver licensing. A Non-resident's home-state license is honored for 60 days (30 days if CDL) after establishing residency.

Renewal

Driver license renewal is the birth month and day of fourth year. North Dakota photo identification cards issued after August 1, 2007 expire eight years from the date of issuance. At present, renewal is not available online, but change of address is.

Military licenses of personnel stationed out-of-state need not be renewed, but will only remain valid 30 days after discharge or return if expired.

Elderly-Related Restrictions

None indicated.

Vehicle Insurance, Title and Registration Facts

Registration Renewal

Online vehicle renewal is available from the home page for registration renewals vehicles except new vehicles, fleet vehicles, apportioned vehicles or trucks 55,000 pounds and greater may not be renewed online.

If a ND registered vehicle owner wishes to change a permanent address, it cannot be done at the online renewal. But there is a separate link to do this at https://apps.nd.gov/dot/mv/mvrenewal/addresschange.htm.

New Residents

New residents must register vehicles upon accepting employment or establishing residency; students displaying current home-state plates are exempt.

Inspections and Emissions Testing

North Dakota has no statewide provisions for emissions testing or mandatory vehicle safety inspections.

Passenger Plate Facts

There are two plates for each passenger car, house car (motor home), or pickup and one license plate for each motorcycle, trailer, travel trailer, off-highway vehicle, or unconventional vehicle, with one decal (MO & YR) on both plates. There is no coding depicting the county of issuance. When a vehicle is sold, the plates remain with the previous owner.

Insurance and Financial Responsibility

Mandatory insurance requires financial responsibility minimum limits of $25,000/50,000/25,000. North Dakota also has no-fault insurance. Proof is required after judgments, DUIs, reportable accidents, and when an authorized law enforcement officer stops a motor vehicle for any statutory violation. Proof of insurance is also required at registration and renewal.

Withdrawal Sanctions, and Alcohol and Drug Testing

Alcohol and Chemical Testing

North Dakota's illegal intoxication level is .08 percent and above; for drivers under 21 the limit is .02 percent, for drivers of CMVs the limit is .04 percent. Urine, blood, saliva, and breath testing are authorized. North Dakota has both an implied consent violation and a provision for an administrative suspension. Operating a horse or bicycle under the influence is also considered illegal.

Suspensions and Revocations

CDL Disqualifications: The state is in compliance with the federally mandated CDL disqualifications. See the Appendix for details.

Below are specific time periods on suspensions and revocations.

Point Accumulation:

Twelve Points ....Seven-day suspension.

Thirteen or More Points...Seven-day suspension for each point over eleven.

Drivers under eighteen accumulating six points ....Cancellation.

DWI and Refusals:

DWI Conviction - First Offense in Five Years..............................91-day suspension.

    If BAC .18 or Greater ....180-day suspension.

DWI Conviction - Second Offense in Five Years ....365-day suspension.

    If BAC .18 or Greater ....Two-year suspension.

DWI Conviction - Third or Subsequent Offense Within 5 Years

    OR Fourth or Subsequent Offense Within 7 Years ....Two-year suspension.

    BAC .18 or Greater...Three-year suspension.

ND has a zero tolerance for anyone under the age of 21 operating a motor vehicle when blood alcohol measures .02 and above.

Refusal to Submit to Chemical Test

    First Offense in Five Years...One-year revocation.

    Second Offense in Five Years..Three-year revocation.

    Third Offense in Five Years ....Four-year revocation.

Railroad Crossing Violation by a Commercial Driver

    First Offense in Three Years..60-day suspension, CDL only.

    Second Offense in Three Years ....120-day suspension, CDL only.

    Third Offense in Three Years ....One-year suspension, CDL only.

Failure to Provide Proof of Financial Responsibility

Drivers will be suspended until Proof of Financial Responsibility is provided to the director and maintained for the allotted time as required by law.

Conviction for No Liability Insurance

Drivers must provide A Certificate of Motor Vehicle Liability Insurance to the director and keep a valid certificate on file for three years.

Reinstatement Requirements

Suspension $50.00 fee, $100.00 if alcohol-related; proof of financial responsibility; time lapse; alcohol evaluation and treatment after conviction.

Revocation $50.00 fee, $100.00 if alcohol-related; proof of financial responsibility; time lapse; re-examination; alcohol evaluation and treatment after conviction; retesting of written and road.

Record Access: Laws, Rules, and Forms

Note: This Section Applies to Both Driver and Vehicle Records.

Governing Statutes and Rules

State Statutes: www.legis.nd.gov/information/statutes/
The 2001 state legislature enacted HB 1774 which placed the state in compliance with DPPA and Public Law 106-69.
Statute NDCC 39-33 governs driver and motor vehicle record privacy. Section 05 lists permitted disclosures. Also, 39-16-03 governs driving records release and fees; 39-16-03.1 governs when entries on driver's record abstract are considered confidential; 39-06-32(6) governs release of certain suspension records to the public. In general, the state has a strict policy regarding the release of records.

Policy Statement Regarding Permissible Uses

Although the statute did not include exemption #13 (For use by any requester, if the requester demonstrates it has obtained the written consent of the individual to whom the information pertains.), this policy is in place. In addition, the commissioner will send an additional copy of the abstract to the driver whose record was requested, accompanied by a statement identifying the requester, identifying the person or company for whom the request was made, identifying the intended recipient of the record, and providing the reason for the request. No copy is sent to the driver when the request for the record is made by the court, FBI, CIA, or by any law enforcement agency of the state.

Request and Consent Forms

Driving Records: A suggested form – *Request for Driver Abstract* – is available at www.dot.nd.gov/forms/sfn51386.pdf. No signatures need to be notarized, however if the record is for a prospective employer of a commercial driver then the requester must attach a signed release. Personal information is released to permissible users.

Vehicle Records: The suggested form – *Request for Vehicle Information* – is available at www.dot.nd.gov/forms/sfn51269.pdf. No signatures need to be notarized. Personal information is released to permissible users.

Vendor and Third Party Access Policy

Certain end-users (employers) may obtain electronic records from an approved employment screening company via an authorized vendor. Otherwise, vendors cannot obtain records for other vendors. The state requires any authorized recipient who resells or rediscloses personal information to maintain for a period of not less than five years records as to the person receiving the information and the permitted use for which it was obtained and to make these records available for inspection by the Department upon request.

Records Ordered For Non-permissible Uses

Both driver and vehicles records may be released without consent to non-permissible use requests, but these records do not contain personal information.

Access to Driver-Related Records

Driving Records

General Information and Fees

Driver License Division, 608 East Boulevard Avenue, Bismarck ND 58505-0750, 701-328-2603.

The current fee is $3.00. The last fee increase was in July of 1989 and no increases are planned for the near future. Credit cards are accepted for payment for both in-person and mail requesters.

Two types of records are available - a *limited, public record* and a *complete record*.

The **limited record** is available to the public A limited record does not include total points, violations or convictions that are more than three years old, violations that have been assigned less than three points, suspensions/revocations/cancellations that have been satisfied and are more than three years old, or any crash information.

The **complete record** has personal information and includes total points, all violations or convictions, including two points or less, and crash information. The Complete record is distributed only to the driver and or to requesters who have a provided a signed release - except the Complete Record is never, never given to an insurance company regardless if there is a signed release.

In-Person – Walk-in requests are processed only at the Bismarck address, usually limited to five requests which will be processed immediately. There is a charge for a "no record found" reports, but the staff usually asks the requester to return with more information to complete the search.

Mail – Requests mailed to the state are usually processed within seventy-two hours of receipt, but can take as long as ten days. The state charges for "no record found" reports. Bismarck is the only location in the state where a record can be ordered. The driver's license number, name, and date of birth are needed when requesting a manual search, but "two out of three" may produce a "hit." The fee must accompany the request. A copy of the record and the name of the requester is automatically sent to the driver when his/her record is requested.

Fax – All requesters can order by fax (701-328-2435). Use of a credit card is required with expiration date and signature included. Use of the *Request for Driver Abstract* form is recommended.

Commercial Electronic – This system is available to ongoing, higher volume requesters with a permissible use and a signed agreement in place. Approved requesters can receive records with personal information. The **Complete Record** described above is available, but not to the insurance industry. The insurance industry received the Limited Record electronically.

Note that a copy of the abstract with the name of the requester is automatically sent to the driver when his/her record is requested.

The $3.00 per record fee applies with monthly billing available. The minimum number of abstract requests per month is 100. There is no charge for a "no record found." Call 701-328-4790 for more information.

Public Online – Also, the **Limited Public Record** can be obtained online at https://secure.apps.state.nd.us/dot/dlts/dlos/welcome.htm. One may both view and print the record, but the record can not be downloaded and neither will a document be sent via mail. The fee is $3.00 per record and use of a credit card is required. No personal information is released unless the data is input when the request is made. The Complete Record is not available at this URL.

Bulk – The state does not sell its license database, or portions there of.

By Person of Record – ND drivers may obtain their complete driving record by mail, fax, walk-in or via online and may view and print the limited online record as described above. If a complete record is requested, it can only be sent to the driver's address on file with the Drivers License and Traffic Safety Division.

To request by fax, the current credit card number, expiration date and CVV number to 701-328-2435, the record will be mailed.

Status Check

Status Check – A free status check of a North Dakota driver's license is at https://apps.nd.gov/dot/dlts/dlos/requeststatus.htm. Access this information by DL number.

Notification/Monitoring Program

North Dakota provides approved entities the ability to determine if there has been a serious conviction on a driver. This is on a batch method, and not on an ongoing notification basis. Typical fees involved include $1.09 per name submitted and a $12.00 fee per batch or computer run, plus programming fees for the initial set-up. Call the Driver License Division for details.

Accident Reports

Reporting – Any accident resulting in death, injury, or damage in excess of $1,000.00 must be reported to the nearest law enforcement agency. If insurance information is not available at the time of the accident, it should be sent to Driver License Division, 608 East Boulevard Avenue, Bismarck, ND 58505. There are no special reporting requirements for commercial drivers.

Record Access – Copies of accident reports can be ordered from Driver License Division, 608 East Boulevard Avenue, Bismarck 58505-0750, 701-328-2601 or 2604. Download the request form at www.dot.nd.gov/forms/sfn04901.pdf. Records are stored since 2005. There are two parts of the report: 1) The front page (Officer's Report) includes the drivers, witnesses, and insurance information, the cost is $2.00 and can be ordered by anyone with a written request; 2) The investigating officer's detailed Opinion, available only to parties of a crash, their legal representatives or their insurer, sells for $5.00. Together the Officer's Report and the Opinion cost $7.00.

All requests must be in writing and state why this information is desired. Mail request turnaround time is typically 5 days. It can take 1 to 2 months before new records are ready for inquiry.

Access to Vehicle-Related Records

General Information and Fees
Motor Vehicle Division, Business Operations, 608 East Boulevard Avenue, Bismarck ND 58505-0780, 701-328-2725, Fax: 701-328-1487. The fee is $3.00 per vehicle record (including mobile homes) or $3.00 per search if no record found. Liens are automatically shown with an ownership search. Records with personal information are only available to requesters with a permissible use.

All trailers, semi-trailers, and farm trailers are required to be titled and licensed except:
- Trailers with a gross weight of 1,500 pounds or less and not for hire or commercial use.
- Trailers used to haul recreational vehicles such as a motorcycle not qualified for registration, ATVs, snowmobiles, boats, and personal watercraft.

Trailers used to haul recreational vehicles used in competitive events are required to be titled and licensed in spite of the weight.

In-Person, Mail, Fax – A written request using "Form SFN-51269" (www.dot.nd.gov/forms/sfn51269.pdf) is required. Turnaround time is usually within 3 to 5 days. Fax accounts are available to qualified requesters, call to make arrangements.

Electronic – North Dakota does not offer online inquiry at this time.

Bulk – North Dakota offers bulk or batch retrieval of VIN or ownership information of vehicles. The requester must explain the purpose and intent; there are no restrictions placed upon requests of a legal nature (DPPA). Customized or special runs (i.e., by county, sex, age, etc.) are available. The base cost is $40.00 per thousand records with a minimum cost of $50.00. For further information, contact Linda Sitz at the address listed above.

Access to Vessel-Related Records

General Information, Access and Fees
North Dakota Game & Fish Department, 100 N. Bismarck Expressway, Bismarck 58501 701-328-6336, fax 701-328-6374.
http://gf.nd.gov All motorized boats and all sailboats must be registered. No titles are issued here. This agency does not follow DPPA; records are considered open to the public. Boat registrations may be searched by mail, in-person, fax, or email (ndgf@nd.gov). Searches require the VIN, hull #, or name. All search requests must be in writing. Records are maintained for 5 years on computer, it takes 2 weeks for new records to appear on the system. There is no fee unless electronic lists are requested (call). Turnaround time is normally within 24 hours.

There is a free public inquiry system at the web page. Click on "Watercraft Registration and Renewals" to find registration number, or click on "Find Watercraft Safety Number" for that search.

Liens are filed with UCC filing locations at either the county or state.

Driving Record Content and Reciprocity

What's On or Not On the Driving Record
- As mentioned, there is a **limited** and a **complete record**. A limited record does not include total points, violations or convictions that are more than three years old, violations that have been assigned less than three points, suspensions/revocations/cancellations that have been satisfied and are more than three years old, or any crash information.
- Other information not shown on the limited record includes the SSN, medical information, the photo image on the driver license, and information from family members about an individual's driving ability.
- The driver's address is provided as part of the record to permissible use requesters
- The complete record can only be obtained by a written request. As stated above, a copy of the record is sent to the driver when ordered by another person or business.
- The state does not permit driver school attendance in lieu of conviction; however, a defensive driving course may be used in lieu of point assessment or to reduce a point count by three points.

The length of time convictions are listed on the public record for CDL drivers is 10 years, for non-CDL is three years, unless suspension/revocation is still active.

Data Retention
Non-CDL license holder records are kept for five years after the last activity on record. If the driver is suspended, revoked or canceled, the record is kept indefinitely. CDL driver records are purged based on the timetable per the MCSIA (see the Appendix).

Court to Repository
Paper copies of the tickets are submitted to the state by the courts and are keyed-in to the system online. This conviction information must be forwarded to the state within ten days and is usually entered within ten-to-fourteen days of receipt. Electronic copies of traffic convictions are submitted to the state by the court and are entered on the driver record within 24 hours.

State Reciprocity for Non-CDL Drivers
- Will suspend license of driver for unpaid out-of-state convictions if state is NRVC member.
- Record of new incoming driver's major or criminal convictions is shown on MVR.
- Out-of-state convictions are shown on MVR.
- Out-of-state accidents are not shown on MVR.
- Convictions of out-of-state drivers are sent to home state.
- Record is forwarded to new state upon surrender of license.

License Classes, Restrictions, and Endorsements

License Classes– Commercial
North Dakota began issuing the CDL in October of 1990.

Class A   Any vehicle or combination of vehicles, except Class M.
Class B   Single vehicle, trailers 10,000 pounds or less, and Class C or D. Not valid for Class A or M.
Class C   Single vehicle less than 26,001 pounds, trailers 10,000 pounds or less, must have endorsement "H" and/or "P": all Class D vehicles. Not valid for Class A, B, or M.

License Classes– Non-Commercial

Class D   Single vehicle less than 26,001 pounds, trailers not over 10,000 pounds. Trucks towing trailers, semi-trailers, or farm-trailers not over 16,000 pounds. Not valid for Class A, B, C, or M.

Class M   Any two or three-wheeled motorcycle.

The following may also be operated on a Class D License:

1. Age 14 or 15 may drive a farm vehicle within 150 miles of driver's farm, having a gross weight of not more than 50,000 pounds, when transporting agricultural products or farm supplies.
2. Any two-axle, tandem axle, triple axle, or truck-tractor farm vehicle controlled and operated by a farmer transporting agricultural products, farm machines, or farm supplies to or from a farm within 150 miles of the person's farm. Farm vehicle may tow a trailer, semi-trailer, or farm trailer **except** double or triple trailers or, if under 18 years of age, a truck-tractor.
3. Any farm vehicle operated by a farmer may transport hazardous material within 150 miles of the farm without a hazardous material endorsement on the operator's license.
4. Emergency vehicles, RV, camper, certain construction equipment, and vehicles driven by active duty members for military purposes.

Note: To operate a motorized bicycle or scooter, one must be at least 14 years of age and must have one of the following: operators license (minimum Class D, no motorcycle endorsement required); temporary permit; instruction permit; or motorized bicycle operators permit. NDCC 39-06-14(7)

Restrictions

0	Class A, B, or C Intrastate Only	5	Daylight Driving Only
1	Adequate Eye Lenses	6	Financial Responsibility
2	Outside Rear-View Mirror	7	Not Valid to Operate Truck-Tractor
3	Automatic Transmission	8	Non-Air-Brake Equipped Vehicle
4	Hand-Control Equipment	9	Other

Endorsements

H	Hazardous Material	S	School Bus
N	Tanker Vehicle	T	Double-/Triple-Trailer
P	Passenger Bus	X	Combination of H and N

Additional Abbreviations

Driver Status Table

Note: A letter "T" preceding the status indicates non-immigrant duration of stay per expiration date.

Status	Description	Status	Description
DOSX	Permit, License or ID Card expired (duration of stay)	PISP	Instructional permit suspended
ID	Identification record only (ND citizen with no permit or license)	PIX	Expired permit
		PO	Current temporary permit
LI	Current license	POSP	Temporary permit suspended
LI*	Renewal mailed - awaiting return	POSPO	Temporary permit suspended - occupational permit
LISP	License suspended	RO	Record only (Out-of-state drivers with record or ND citizen with no license or permit who have record)
LISPO	License suspended - occupational permit		
LISPR	License suspended - restricted permit for 24/7 Sobriety Program only	ROC	Record only cancelled
		ROCDL	Record cancelled - graduated driver license
LIX	Expired license	ROCO	Record only cancelled - occupational permit
MB	Current motorized bicycle permit	RORV	Record only revoked
NOMB	No motorized bicycle permit (Cancelled, revoked, suspended, or expired record only)	RORVO	Record only revoked - occupational permit
		RORVR	Record only revoked - restricted permit for 24/7 Sobriety Program only
OS	ND driver now licensed out-of-state		
OSSP	ND driver now licensed out-of-state suspended	ROSP	Record only suspended
OSSPO	ND driver now licensed out-of-state suspended - occupational permit	ROSPO	Record only suspended - occupational permit
		ROSPR	Record only suspended - restricted permit for 24/7 Sobriety Program only
PI	Current instructional permit		
Status	Description	RPD	Reported deceased

Other Abbreviations of Note

ADMIN	Administrative	SUSP	Suspension
CONV	Conviction	HEAR	Hearing
VIOL	Violation	REVO	Revocation
ACC	Accident	CANC	Cancelled

Conviction Table with ACD, Statute, and Points

- North Dakota does not provide statute codes or ACD type codes on any driving records. All violations are spelled out in English.
- The following table reflects the violations in North Dakota that have points, the ACD Code and statute associated with each conviction.
- An internally-used state offense code is also listed as a reference point, but this code does not show on the record.

ACD	Violation	Statute	Points	State Code
S92	1-10 MPH Over Speed Limit (effective 7-1-01)	39-06.1-10(3.a 30)	0	390
S92	11-15 MPH over 70/75 Speed Limit	39-06.1-10(3.a 33)	3	353
S92	11-15 MPH Over Speed Limit (effective 7-1-01)	39-06.1-10(3.a 30)	1	391
S92	1-5 MPH over 70/75 Speed Limit	39-06.1-10(3.a 33)	0	351
S92	16-20 MPH over 70/75 Speed Limit	39-06.1-10(3.a 33)	5	354
S92	16-20 MPH Over Speed Limit (effective 7-1-01)	39-06.1-10(3.a 30)	3	392
S92	21-25 MPH over 70/75 Speed Limit	39-06.1-10(3.a 33)	7	355
S92	21-25 MPH Over Speed Limit (effective 7-1-01)	39-06.1-10(3.a 30)	5	393
S92	26-30 MPH over 70/75 Speed Limit	39-06.1-10(3.a 33)	10	356
S92	26-35 MPH Over Speed Limit (effective 7-1-01)	39-06.1-10(3.a 30)	9	394
S92	31-35 MPH over 70/75 Speed Limit	39-06.1-10(3.a 33)	12	357
S92	36+ MPH over 70/75 Speed Limit	39-06.1-10(3.a 33)	15	358
S92	36-45 MPH Over Speed Limit (effective 7-1-01)	39-06.1-10(3.a 30)	12	395
S92	46 + MPH Over Speed Limit (effective 7-1-01)	39-06.1-10(3.a 30)	15	396
S92	6-10 MPH over 70/75 Speed Limit	39-06.1-10(3.a 33)	1	352
A20	Actual Physical Control	39-08-01	0	153
A98	Administrative Action /Implied Consent	39-20	0	151
A98	Administrative Action Out of State/Implied Consent	39-20	0	150
M84	Aggravated Reckless Driving	39-08-03	12	109
M82	Care Required	39-09-01.1	2	377
M81	Careless Driving, Basic Rule	39-09-01	6	310
F03	Carry Passenger Without Footrest	39-10.2-05	2	373
N04	Causing Crash with Emergency Vehicle or DOT Maintenance Vehicle	39-06.1-10(3.b 15) & 39-10-26	2	309
U03	Causing Serious Bodily Injury	39-06-31.2	0	441
F02	Child Not in Restraining Device	39-06.1-06(2.c) & 39-21-41.2	1	308
N80	Coasting Downgrade	39-10-56	0	457
M56	Crossing Fire Hose	39-10-58	0	424
M18	Disregard Flashing Light	39-10-07	0	445
M08	Disregarding the Commands of a Police Officer	39-06.1-10(3.a 15)	2	336
M14	Disregarding Traffic Control Device	39-10-04	2	329
S95	Drag Racing or Racing	39-08-03.1	10	323
B57	Driving a CMV without a CDL in the driver's possession	39-06.2-02(27)(e)	0	406
N70	Driving on Wrong Side of Highway	39-10-14 & 39-10-16	2	331
B25	Driving Under Revocation	39-06-42	0	207
B26	Driving Under Suspension	39-06-42	0	203
A20	Driving Under the Influence	39-08-01	0	152
B27	Driving While Placed Out-of-Service (CDL)	Admin. Rule 37-10-01-01	0	204
B19	Driving While Placed Out-of-Service with Hazmat or Passengers	Admin. Rule 37-10-01-01	0	205
W45	Driving While Previously Disqualified in a CMV	Admin. Rule 37-10-01-05	0	206
D36	Driving Without Liability Insurance (2nd Offense Within 18 Months)	39-08-20	12	162
D36	Driving Without Liability Insurance (No Crash Involved)	39-08-20	6	160
D36	Driving Without Liability Insurance (With Crash Driver is the Owner)	39-08-20	14	161
S97	Exhibition Driving	39-08-03.1	3	327
B53	Fail to Display Plates/Tabs	39-04-37	1	326
B61	Fail to Give Immediate Notice	39-08-09	6	364
M82	Fail to Have Motor Vehicle Under Control	39-10-30	0	417
M09	Fail to Stop at RR Crossing	39-10-41	3	343
N04	Fail to Stop for Emergency Vehicle	39-10-26	0	412
N08	Fail to Yield to Pedestrian	39-10-28	0	413
E54	Failure to Dim Headlights	39-21-21	1	332
E04	Failure to Display Placard While Transporting Hazardous Material	39-21-44	2	130
M24	Failure to Obey RR Crossing Clearance	39-06.2-10	3	317
M23	Failure to Obey RR Crossing Space	39-06.2-10	3	316
M10	Failure to Obey TCD at RR Crossing	39-06.1-10 & 39-06.2-10	3	312
M20	Failure to Slow Down at RR Crossing	39-06.2-10	3	313
M22	Failure to Stop at RR Crossing	39-06.2-10	3	315
M21	Failure to Stop Before Tracks When Tracks Not Clear	39-06.2-10	3	314
N05	Failure to Yield to Funeral Procession	39-10-72	2	325
N23	Failure to Yield/Stop Sign	39-10-44	2	311
U03	Felony Involving a Motor Vehicle	39-06.2-10.1(13)	0	216

ACD	Violation	Statute	Points	State Code
A50	Felony Involving a Motor Vehicle for Manufacturing, Distributing, Dispensing a Controlled Substance.	39-06.2-10.1(11)	0	217
U01	Fleeing Law Enforcement Officer in Motor Vehicle	39-10-71	24	119
M33	Following Emergency Vehicle	39-10-26	0	423
M34	Following to Close	39-10-18	0	449
M75	Illegal Passing of School bus (Driver)	39-10-46	6	339
M75	Illegal Passing of School bus (Owner Responsible)	39-10-46.1	0	440
F34	Impeding Traffic	39-09-09	0	466
N82	Improper Backing	39-10-52	0	455
E31	Improper Brakes	39-21-32 & 39-21-33	2	335
E70	Improper Equipment	39-21-46	2	349
M42	Improper Lane Usage	39-10-17	0	446
M48	Improper Motorcycle Laned Traffic	39-10.2-03	2	371
F66	Improper or Modified Motor Vehicle	39-21-45.1	2	320
E05	Improper Signals or Signal Not Working	39-10-38	0	453
N83	Improper Start from Parked Position	39-10-37	0	452
E37	Improper Tires	39-21-40	0	434
N50	Improper Turn/U-Turn	39-10-35	0	451
E70	Improper Wipers	39-21-39	0	463
F63	Leaving a Motor Vehicle Unattended	39-10-51	1	342
B06	Leaving the Scene of an Crash Involving Death	39-08-04	18	126
B07	Leaving the Scene of an Crash Involving Injury	39-08-04	18	125
B08	Leaving the Scene of an Crash Involving Property Damage	39-08-05, 39-08-07, 39-08-08	14	121
E55	Light Equipment Not Lighted	39-21-01	0	431
U08	Manslaughter with a Motor Vehicle	39-06-31	0	215
U07	Negligent Homicide with a Motor Vehicle	39-06-31	0	211
E01	No Slow Moving Emblem	39-21-50	0	439
D70	Obstructed View	39-10-54	0	422
D70	Obstructed Windows	39-21-39	0	462
A35	Open Container	39-08-18	2	363
B56	Operate a CMV Without a License	39-06-01 & 39-06.2-06	4	376
B51	Operate Motor Vehicle Without a License	39-06-01	4	375
F03	Operate Motorcycle Without Head Gear	39-10.2-06	2	374
F66	Operating an Unsafe Motor Vehicle	39-21-46(2)	2	131
E01	Operating Without Required Equipment	39-10-46	2	350
M70	Overtaking Where Prohibited or in an Unsafe Manner	39-10-11, 39-10-12, & 30-10-13	2	337
F34	Overtime/Double/Standing Abreast Parking	39-10-50	0	465
B30	Permitting Unauthorized Minor/Person to Drive	39-06-45	2	330
M84	Reckless Driving	39-03-08	8	105
D10	Reproducing Driver License	39-06-40.1	0	419
S92	Speeding 55-70 in a 55 Zone	39-09-02	0	401
M85	Texting While Driving	39-06.2-02(27)(g)	0	208
F34	Unlawful Parking in a Prohibited Place Obstructing Traffic or Handicap Parking	39-10-49	1	338
D16	Unlawful Use of Driver License	39-06-40	0	407
S93	Unsafe Speed (No Zone or MPH Listed)	39-09-02	0	402
F04	Use of Safety Belts Required	39-21-41.4	0	408
M86	Using a Hand-held Mobile Telephone While Driving	39-08.23	0	411
D29	Violated Eye Restriction	39-06-17 & 39-06.1-11	3	106
D29	Violated Restrictions other than 106	39-06-17	4	107
U10	Violation Resulting in a Fatal Crash - CDL Holder	39-06.2-02(25c)	0	210
N63	Wrong Way on a One Way	39-10-16	0	448

Point System Summary

Points range from 1 to 24 points. If the number of points assigned to a violation is two or less, the violation and points may not be entered on the driving record (and may not be available to the public). These points would be assessed as part of the record only for the purpose of point reduction or license suspension. A 7-day suspension can result from the accumulation of 12 or more points. Each additional point can add another 7 days. Drivers under age 18 accumulating 6 points can be cancelled.

Ohio

Administration	Important Telephone and Web Contacts
Mike Rankin, Registrar Ohio Bureau of Motor Vehicles PO Box 16520 Columbus 43216-6520 614-752-7600 www.bmv.ohio.gov/ Revised Code and the Administrative Code are found at: http://codes.ohio.gov/	Driver Licensing.................................614-752-7600 Accident and Insurance ....614-752-7700 Commercial DL.................................614-752-7600 Titles.................................614-752-7752 or 7671 Registration ....614-752-7800 The State Department of Insurance ....614-644-2658 Highway Patrol.................................614-466-2660 Contact List: www.bmv.ohio.gov/contact.stm Email the Registrar: www.bmv.ohio.gov/registrar_email.stm

Driver's License Format, Issuance and Renewal

License Classes, Restrictions and Endorsements Appear After the Driving Record Content Section

License Format

The format is two letters followed by six numbers. The state reports no special sequence to the letters or numbers issued.

Document Appearance

Ohio will offer the new driver license and state identification card design beginning with the release of the federally compliant "Ohio's Safe ID" in 2013. The new Safe ID includes additional security features, markings, a new card material and other federal requirements.

The license issued since November 3, 2008 is printed on standard plastic credit card stock with the color and design was changed significantly compared to previous documents. The oldest format is valid until expiration. Both formats are described below.

Current Documents (Prior to Safe ID)

Security Characteristics: The color Hologram overlay, 2-D bar code, magnetic strip and digital signature. A state of Ohio outline logo along the top edge indicates the type of card (DL, CDL, ID, etc.)

Position of Photo: The primary photo is on left side, with a secondary "ghost" picture on right side.

Minor Age Driver Locator: For those 21 and under, the card is vertical with an "under 21" message along the photo image. Header is red, if for an ID card, then header is green.

CDL Indicator: "Commercial Driver's License" shows on the top banner, header is blue.

Oldest DLs and IDs

Security Characteristics: Hologram overlay, secondary "ghost" signature, bar code, magnetic strip and digital signature. The Class, expiration and any endorsements appear in the bottom right corner.

Position of Photo: Right side.

Minor Age Driver Locator: The document is vertical (short sides on top and bottom). Photo is located on top left side.

CDL Indicator: "Commercial Driver's License" shows on the top banner.

Issuance

Location of Requirements for Proof of Identity:
http://bmv.ohio.gov/acceptable_id_documents.stm

Age Requirements

Under the BMV's Graduated Licensing Program a Temporary Instruction Permit may be granted at fifteen and one-half with completion of approved driver education course. A Probatory License can be issued at age 16, provided the permit is held for a period of 6 months and driver successfully completes written, vision, road and maneuverability examinations, and provides parental verification of 50 hours of driving experience. This license is good until age 21. A Probationary CDL is granted at 18 to 21 with completion of testing requirements. A Motorized Bicycle License is granted to 14 or older with completion of written, road, and vision testing. A Hardship License is granted at 14 to 15 with proof of hardship and approval of the Registrar of Motor Vehicles. A Temporary Instruction Permit is granted if driver is accompanied by licensee of same license class; valid for one year.

Residency

Non-resident's license honored on a reciprocal basis; Ohio license must be secured within thirty days of establishing residency.

Renewal

Licenses renew on the birthday of fourth year. Drivers keep the same DL number when renewing, thus making it a permanent license number. Military personnel stationed out of Ohio can renew by mail every 4 years

Elderly-Related Restrictions

Ohio's motor vehicle laws currently do not provide for mandatory retesting of elderly drivers. All drivers, regardless of age, are required to pass a vision screening prior to being issued a renewal driver license.

Vehicle Insurance, Title and Registration Facts

Registration Renewal

License plates expire on the owner's birthday. Or if the vehicle is leased the registration expires on the 20th of the month designated for the leasing company. There is a 7-day grace period for most registrations. If a registrant renews on the 8th day, then a $20.00 late fee is charged.

Registrations can be renewed by going to a Deputy Registrar license agency, mail-in registration, by logging onto www.OPLATES.com or by calling 1-866-OPLATES (1-866-675-2837). Online, one can also select specialty plates, change address, and check on renewal status.

New Residents

Ohio requires all out-of-state vehicles to be registered with Ohio plates within 30 days of becoming an Ohio resident or becoming employed in Ohio.

Inspections and Emissions Testing

Ohio does not have a statewide vehicle safety inspection program or an emissions testing program. However, there is an Automobile Inspection and Maintenance pollution control inspection program in Cuyahoga, Geauga, Lake, Lorain, Medina, Portage, and Summit counties.

Passenger Plate Facts

There are two plates, two decals (MO & YR) and a County Number on rear. The owner's county of residence on bottom center for older style plates or a numerical value in the lower left hand corner for the new style plates. Plates do not remain with vehicle when sold, they remain with seller.

Insurance and Financial Responsibility

The minimum financial responsibility limits are $12,500/25,000/7,500.

Ohio does not have a no-fault insurance provision. Licensed drivers and vehicle owners must maintain proof of financial responsibility by one of the following: liability insurance; $32,500 surety bond; $30,000 BMV Certificate for money or government bonds in the amount of $30,000 on deposit with the Ohio Treasurer; or a certificate of self-insurance that is issued by the Ohio Bureau of Motor Vehicles. A signed affidavit is a part of the license application.

Future proof is required after a reportable accident and court appearances for moving violations. SR-22 forms are used. An arresting officer must verify proof of insurance and mark the citation with a "yes" or "no."

Individuals unable to provide proof are permitted 30 days to submit proof to the BMV, or driving privileges are suspended. Limited driving privileges can be given to first and second offenders only. Other penalties include loss of license plates, vehicle registration, reinstatement fees and the requirement to have proof of financial responsibility on file with the BMV for three or five years. Financial responsibility proof must also be shown at all vehicle inspection stops and upon random checks by the Registrar of the BMV.

Withdrawal Sanctions, and Alcohol and Drug Testing

Alcohol and Chemical Testing

Ohio's illegal intoxication level is .08 percent and above, .02 and above for drivers under 21, .04 and above for CDL. Urine, blood, and breath testing are authorized. Ohio has both an implied consent violation and a provision for an administrative suspension. Operating a horse or bicycle under the influence is also considered illegal

Suspensions and Revocations

The Ohio BMV is in compliance with the provisions of the Motor Carrier Safety Improvement Act (MCSIA). See the Appendix for more information about these mandatory CDL disqualification sanctions.

Administrative License Suspension (ALS) Positive (alcohol tests results .08% or above)	Ninety days to five years.
Administrative License Suspension (ALS) Refusal (refusal to submit to chemical test)	One to five years.
Application for Ohio Driver License While under Suspension Elsewhere	Indefinite.
Child Support	Indefinite.
Civil Action Resulting from Accidents	Indefinite.
Court Actions From Violation Convictions	Variable.
Driver License Restriction Violation	Six months.
Driving Under Suspension	One year.
Driving Under the Influence	
First Offense	Determined by court, but usually 180 days to three years.
Second Offense	One year to five years.
Third Offense	Two years to ten years.
Driving Without Insurance	Ninety days first offense; one year second offense; two years subsequent offense.
Failure to File Reports for Accidents Involving Damage in access of $400.00 or personal injury	Indefinite.
Failure to Pay Fine or Appear in Court	Indefinite.
Failure to Provide Proof of Financial Responsibility	Ninety days first offense; one year second offense; Two years subsequent offense.
Falsifying a Driver's License	One year.
Habitual use of Alcohol/Drugs (three convictions in three years)	Indefinite suspension.
License Forfeiture	Indefinite.
Outstanding Ticket in One of the Forty-one Compact States	Indefinite.
Three Violation Convictions Before the Age of Eighteen	One year.
Two Violation Convictions Before the Age of Eighteen	Ninety days.
Twelve or More Points Accumulated Within Two Years	Six months.
Tobacco Violation When Under 18 years of Age	Thirty days.
Unauthorized Withdrawal from School (drop-out)	To age eighteen.
Unruly Delinquent	Until age eighteen or twenty-one.
Using License to Obtain Alcohol When Under Age	One year.
Various Medical Reasons	Indefinite.
Weapon on School Property	One to five years.

Reinstatement Requirements

Reinstatement fees vary based on the type of action, date and frequency of occurrence.
For an instructive, detailed overview visit http://www.bmv.ohio.gov/suspension_reinstatement.stm.

Suspension $!5.00 up to $650.00 fee; proof of financial responsibility.
Revocation   No fee; re-examination; proof of insurance for three years.

Record Access: Laws, Rules, and Forms

Note: This Section Applies to Both Driver and Vehicle Records.

Governing Statutes and Rules

Revised Code and Administrative Code: http://codes.ohio.gov/
Ohio Statutory Authority: Ohio Public Records Act, Revised Code (OCR) 149.4; Ohio Driver Privacy Protection Act (DPPA) ORC 4501.27 - 4501.272; additional ORC sections involving confidential personal information include 4501.15 and 4507.53. Ohio Administrative Code sections 4501:1-12-02 and 4501:12-03. Together these governing statutes and rules place the state in compliance with the provisions of DPPA. Personal information to be protected includes a person's name, SSN, DOB and address.

Policy Statement Regarding Permissible Uses

Ohio adopted all of the federal exceptions and added the following exception: ORC 4501.27 states

"...The registrar or an employee of contractor of the BMV may disclose personal information ... (e) pursuant to an order of a court of this state, another state, the United States, or a political subdivision of this state or another state."

The Ohio Bureau of Motor Vehicles (BMV) does not release personal information from an individual's driving record to bulk mail distributors for surveys, marketing or solicitations.

With Ohio's "opt-in" policy, the driver's personal information will only be released if the individual whose information is requested completes a form giving express written consent for disclosure. A driver's photograph, SSN, telephone number, and medical or disability information is never released. Personal information to be protected includes a person's name, SSN, DOB and address. (The SSN and sometimes the photo are released to authorized governmental entities for criminal justice purposes.)

Request and Consent Forms

All forms may be found at http://bmv.ohio.gov/bmv_forms.stm.
The form to use when consent is needed is *Form 5008* found at http://publicsafety.ohio.gov/links/bmv5008.pdf. The signature of the subject must be notarized.
The form to use if the requester has a permissible use, or for a person to request his/her own record, is *Record Request Form 1173*. It may be downloaded at http://publicsafety.ohio.gov/links/bmv1173.pdf.
Bulk requesters must sign an *Agreement for the Release of Information* in which the purchaser agrees not to provide information obtained pursuant to this agreement to any other person without entering into an agreement including these prohibitions.

Vendor and Third Party Access Policy

Approved online vendors can access records for other vendors (who are not online, etc.) who will then sell to an end-user as long as the approved vendor complies with DPPA and has a method of ensuring that their customers comply with DPPA. The approved vendors must keep copies of requests and proof that their customers comply and this information may be audited by the state of Ohio to ensure compliance. The burden of proof is on the purchaser (who purchases direct from Ohio). The following items are applicable—

1. The approved vendor must enter into an agreement for the release of information with the state of Ohio.
2. The approved vendor must hold end-users to requirements set forth in DPPA and enter into a contract with end users so stating.
3. Contract wording can and should be the same to ensure that all customers are in compliance with Ohio laws.
4. Any contracts used must follow the DPPA guidelines and Ohio laws.

Regarding Vehicle Records: The agreement states, in part; "Purchaser will not: 1) copy, give, or resell this information in its total form to any other person or organization, and 2) sell any or all parts of this information at a cost less than the acquisition cost..." Furthermore, the "Purchaser agrees that it will not provide information obtained pursuant to this agreement to any other person without entering into an agreement including these prohibitions."

Non-permissible Use Requests

Driving Records: If the requester does not have a permissible use or consent, driving records are not released. Records without personal information are not sold, however drivers may view their own driving record online for no charge.

Vehicle Records: If the requester does not have a permissible use or consent, vehicle records are not released. Records without personal information are not sold, however certain title information without personal information to vehicle and watercraft may be viewed online for no charge.

Access to Driver-Related Records

Driving Records

General Information and Fees

Bureau of Motor Vehicles, Records Request, 1970 W Broad St, Columbus 43223, or PO Box 16520, Columbus 43216-6520, 614-752-7600. This location is known as the Shipley Customer Service Center. The fee for a driving record is $5.00 or $8.50, depending where purchased.

In-Person — Over-the-counter requests are processed at the central office listed above and at regional offices. Up to eight records may be requested per day. The fee is $8.50 if purchased at the Shipley Customer Service Center in Columbus but is only $5.00 if purchased at one of the Regional Driver License Reinstatement Centers.

The driver's license number, Social Security Number, and DOB are needed when ordering.

Mail —The BMV requires specific identification before processing the request, therefore, it is unlikely to receive a "no record found" on a manual request. Requests mailed to the state are processed within 14 to 21 days of receipt. The driver's license number, DOB, and SSN should be submitted with each request, and the fee must accompany each request. Sending a SASE is not required. The fee is $5.00.

Telephone and Fax — Ohio offers a "Pre-Paid Driver Search Account" for searches by phone or fax. There is a $200.00 minimum deposit. Call to make arrangements.

Electronic – There are several online programs offered for accessing driving records.

1. A **free view** of an unofficial record, 2-year record is accessible from www.ohiobmv.com/driver_license.stm. The DL, DOB and last 4 digits of the SSN are needed.

2. A certified, three-year driver record abstract is available for purchase online at https://www.oplates.com/. Records are mailed. Either the DL and last 4 digits of the SSN, or the full name, DOB and last 4 digits of the SSN are needed to place the order. The fee is $5.00.

3. The BMV provides access for approved large commercial customers and users for both batch and interactive access. The fee is $5.00. A single shared connection to the AAMVA network is supported. Access to an FTP batch server is suggested for requesters who order 100 or more motor vehicle reports per day. The driver's license number and name, or SSN and name, plus appropriate form are needed when ordering. For more information, call the Bureau of Motor Vehicles at 614-752-7691.

The BMV offers a free status check of an auto dealer. Go to https://ext.dps.state.oh.us/BMVOnlineServices.Public/DealerSearch.aspx.

Bulk – All or selected portions of the license file only may be provided, based upon a written request with specifications and a signed Memorandum of Understanding Agreement. Fees will be charged in accordance with the Ohio public record law. Call 614-752-7691 for more information.

By Person of Record – Ohio drivers may obtain their driving record in-person or online as described above. Also, Ohio drivers may request an abstract of their driving record by calling 866-675-2837. The record is mailed to the address on file.

Notification/Monitoring Program

At present, Ohio does not offer a program or any means that would enable employers or insurance companies to notify or monitor incidents of drivers.

Crash Reports

Reporting – The driver of a vehicle involved in a motor vehicle accident may file a report to: Ohio Bureau of Motor Vehicles, Compliance Unit, PO Box 16520, Columbus, OH 43216-6520 within six months after the accident if both of the following apply: (1) there was any personal injury or there was property damage in excess of $400.00, and (2) the driver or owner of the other vehicle did not have insurance or other financial responsibility coverage at the time of the accident. The proper forms can be obtained from any law enforcement agency or at the address above. The form is found at http://publicsafety.ohio.gov/links/bmv3303.pdf.

Carriers (operating under the authority of PUCO) must report accidents resulting in death, injury, or property damage in excess of $500.00 within fifteen days to: Public Utilities Commission of Ohio, 111 North High Street, Columbus OH 43215. The *State Form EN-11* or the form provided by the U.S. Department of Transportation must be submitted. Ohio carriers must also submit their tax decal number and a copy of the driver's log for the day on which the accident occurred with report to the PUCO.

Record Access – Copies of crash reports and crash photos from crashes investigated by the Ohio State Highway Patrol may be obtained from the Ohio State Highway Patrol, DPS, Central Records Unit, PO Box 182074, Columbus 43218-2074, 614-466-3536. http://statepatrol.ohio.gov/crash.stm; oshpcrashreports@dps.state.oh.us

Records are available for 5 years to present. New crashes are available after 7 business days. The fee is $4.00 per report; normal turnaround time may vary from 2-3 days to 4 weeks. Personal checks are accepted. Reports of crashes may be ordered online at http://statepatrol.ohio.gov/crash.stm, a record is returned via email within 24 hours. Crash photographs purchased online will be sent on CD by mail. Use of credit card is required. SSNs are not released.

Access to Vehicle-Related Records

General Information and Fees

Bureau of Motor Vehicles, 1970 West Broad St, Columbus OH 43223, {mail to Attn: Record Requests, PO Box 16520 Columbus 43216-6520, 614-752-7752, (Titles at 614-752-7671) fax 614-752-7001.

The fee for a registration record or copy of title record is $5.00. Certification is an additional $3.00. Registration records are available for past seven years. The state requires use of *Record Request Form 1173* when making these requests. Vehicle title records include the lien information. A request for a title history requires the VIN, make and year of the vehicle. All previous owners and mileage figures are reported. Since September 23, 2008, Ohio titles and registers three-wheel motor vehicles as motorcycles if the Manufacturer's Certificate of Origin indicates the vehicle meets the federal specifications of a motorcycle. For questions on titles, email asktitles@dps.state.oh.us. Note that title issuance is performed by the county title clerks, not by the Ohio BMV.

Mail and In-Person – Look-ups can be done using the license plate number, owner's Social Security Number, or vehicle identification number (VIN). Walk-in requesters do not receive results immediately; results must be picked up the next day. Automated Title Processing System (ATPS) records are made available by written request and purchase contract.

Telephone – Ohio offers a Pre-paid Search Account for information on title or registration records. Requirements include a $200.00 minimum deposit and completion of BMV Form 1173. Call the Fiscal Section at 614-752-2091 to establish an account.

Fax – Faxes accepted from pre-approved accounts with funds on file.

Electronic – There is both a subscription service and a limited free service offer.

1. A subscription service is accessible through the AAMVA network to those who qualify under DPPA. A written request must be submitted and a purchase contract completed prior to the state's release of technical information. Vehicle registration and driver license information are supplied. For more information, contact Jeff Payne, Supervisor, BMV Records; 1970 West Broad Street, Columbus, Ohio 43223; 614-752-7548; fax 614-995-7946. Not that fees will vary depending on volume.

2. Also, the BMV offers a limited, free search at https://ext.dps.state.oh.us/BMVOnlineServices.Public/TitleSearch.aspx. Search by either title number or identification number. Results do not include personal information. The site also includes information on watercraft. The title information available from this web page is obtained from Ohio county title offices. Title information may not exist in the system and on this web page for titles issued prior to March 1993, because all Ohio county offices were not automated until March 1993. For more information call 614-752-7598.

Bulk – All drivers are opted out. Bulk requests must be accompanied by a written request explaining the purpose of the order. Bulk orders are not available for marketing or solicitation purposes. For more information contact Data Services Operations at 614-752-7691.

Access to Vessel-Related Records

General Information, Access and Fees
Natural Resources Department, Division of Watercraft, 2045 Morse Rd, Columbus Oh 43229, 614-265-6480, fax 614-784-5987. www.dnr.state.oh.us.
Ohio is a title state; all boats 14+ foot or have a 10 or greater HP motor even if less than 14 foot must be titled. All boats operated on public waters must be registered, unless issued commercial documentation and used exclusively for commercial purposes. Only Watercraft Agents issue registrations (at the county level). Only Country Clerks of Court write titles. But this agency has access to all records. Lien information will be provided, but you must first request in writing or use their form. There is

no fee for a registration check, but a $2.00 fee for a title search. There is limited phone searching (no more than 5 at a time). Mail requests normally are processed in one week. A serial or hull number and/or name are needed to search. SSNs are withheld.
A free search of a watercraft title is available at https://ext.dps.state.oh.us/BMVOnlineServices.Public/TitleSearch.aspx. Search by title number or Identification Number. Personal information is not displayed. A summary of Ohio boating laws is found at www.ohiodnr.com/watercraft/opsguide/tabid/2740/default.aspx.

Driving Record Content and Reciprocity

What's On or Not On the Driving Record
- All violations reported to the Bureau of Motor Vehicles by the courts are listed on the report.
- Anytime an individual is involved in a motor vehicle accident and a police report is made, all parties listed on the police report have an entry of that accident placed on their driving record. When this entry is placed on the record, there are no points assessed and it does not specify who was at fault.
- The driver's address is provided as part of the record to permissible users.
- The state does not permit driver school attendance in lieu of conviction. Judges may assess points at their discretion; they are not "locked into" the point codes.

The length of time convictions are listed on a record for CDL and non-CDL is: three years from **conviction date** for moving violations and accidents and three years from **closed date** for OVI and withdrawals.

Data Retention
CDL driver records are purged based on the timetable per the federal regulations (see the Appendix). Violations are purged from public view

after three years—insurance laws require thirty-six months of activity-history. Surrendered licenses are available for the same length of time.

Court to Repository
At least 50% of the Ohio courts submit conviction data to the state via diskette or FTP. The remaining courts submit paper copies, which are coded, key-entered, and verified. The courts have ten days to report convictions and the state normally will take two-to-five days to process.

State Reciprocity for Non-CDL Drivers
- Will suspend license of driver for unpaid out-of-state convictions.
- Record of new incoming driver is not shown on MVR.
- Only out-of-state convictions shown on MVR are out-of-state OVI and drug offenses, or if unpaid.
- Out-of-state accidents are not shown on MVR.
- Convictions of out-of-state drivers are sent to home state.
- Record is not forwarded to new state upon surrender of license, but will send to NDR.

Codes for License Classes, Restrictions, and Endorsements

License Classes– Commercial
Ohio began issuing the CDL in July of 1990.

Class A Any combination of vehicles with a GVWR of 26,001 pounds or more—provided the GVWR of the vehicle(s) being towed is in excess of 10,000 pounds.
Class B Any single vehicle with a GVWR of 26,001 pounds or more, or any such vehicle towing a vehicle not in excess of 10,000 pounds GVWR.
Class C Any single vehicle, or combination of vehicles that does not meet the definition of Class A or B (as above), but that is designed to transport sixteen or more passengers (including the driver), or is transporting hazardous materials in an amount requiring placarding; and any school bus with a GVWR less than 26,001 pounds and designed to transport less than sixteen passengers (including the driver).

License Classes– Non-Commercial
Class D Operator.
Class I Identification Card
Class T Temporary ID Card

Class M1 Motorcycle Only
Class M2 Motorized Bicycle Only
Class M3 Three-Wheel Motorcycle Only

Restrictions
All licenses issued on or after 11/03/2008 no longer have a "table of contents" on the backside; only the restrictions, if any, pertaining to the driver are listed.

A   None
B   Corrective Lenses
C1 No Special Attachments
C2 All Hand Controls
C3 Modified Dimmer Switch
C4 Spin Knob/Power Steering
C5 Modified Turn Signal
C6 Modified Accelerator

C7 Modified Brake
C8 Built-up Seat
C9 Modified Emergency Brake
D1 Artificial Limb Required
D2 Auto Drive/Artificial Limb
D3 Power Steering
D5 Medical on Renewal
D6 Medical Yearly

D7	Medical 6 Months	J5	Bioptic Daytime Only
E	Automatic Transmission	J6	Bioptic No Freeway
E1	Hardship	K	Intrastate Only (AAMVA Valid Code)
E2	Area/Time Restriction	K1	Intrastate Only - Under 21
F1	Left Outside and Inside Mirrors	K2	Intrastate - Vision. Fed Waiver Required to Operate Interstate
F2	Right Outside and Inside Mirrors	K3	Intrastate - Medical. Fed Waiver Required to Operate Interstate
F3	Inside and Dual Outside Mirrors		
G	Daytime Driving Only	L	Vehicles Without Air-Brakes
J1	Biotic Telescopic Lens Required	P1	No Passenger - Class A
J2	Ineligible for Hazmat Endorsement	P2	No Passenger - Class A, B
J3	Valid with Bioptic Trainer Only	P4	School Buses; Less than Fifteen passengers (plus Driver)
J4	Bioptic Night Driving Only	W	Farm Waiver

Endorsements

H	Hazardous Materials - CDL	P	Vehicles designed to transport sixteen or more passengers, including the driver
M	Motorcycle		
M2	2 Wheel Motorcycle	R	Three-Wheel Motorcycle
M3	3 Wheel Motorcycle	S	School Bus
N	Tank Vehicle - CDL	T	Double-/Triple-Trailers - CDL
O	Other	X	N and H Combined - CDL
P	Passenger - CDL		

Two-Part License

U	Two-Part License Required
V	Medical Two-Part License Required

Conviction Table with ACD, Statute, Code, and Points

Note: Three Tables are Presented
1. Conviction Table with ACD Codes, Statutes, Suspension Class, and Points
2. Withdrawal Actions Code Table
3. Suspension Explanation Table

Conviction Code Table Reference Keys Codes

* = Code is no longer in use, but retained for old records on file.
*** = Repealed

➤ for Code 24   Speed 4511.21DThe section of the Ohio Revised Code (ORC) that specifically refers to speeding violations on freeways and provides for accelerated point assessment by the court.

➤ for Code 27   Moving Violations 4507.021G-15The section of the ORC that specifies a two-point assessment for any moving violation that is not spelled-out as an item in the code.

➤ for Code 44   Failure to Control 4507.021GSimilar to Code 27, provides the arresting officer or the court with a "blanket-type" type of violation.

➤ for Code 64   Failure to Control 4511.202A section of the ORC relating to Reckless Operation of a vehicle, but a less severe penalty than a reckless operation charge.

Offense Code	ACD	Suspension Class	Pts	Violation	OH Revised Code Section
01	D78		0	Perjury/False Information	2921.11
02	A08	5	6	OVI - Alcohol &/or Drug(s) of Abuse	4511.19A
03	XXX		6	Driving w/out Owner Consent	2913.03
04	U03		6	Motor Vehicle Felony	2913.02
05***	U07		6	Vehicular Homicide	2903.07
06	B01	5	6	Hit Skip/Leaving Scene	4549.02/021
07	B26	7	2	Driving Under Susp/Revoke	4510.11(C)(1)
08	S95	7	6	Drag Racing/Street Racing	4511.251
09	U01	2	6	Flee/Elude Officer	2921.331
10	M15		2	Stop Sign	4511.43
11	M16		2	Traffic Control Lights	4511.13-15
12*	A22		6	DUI - Drugs/Opiates	4511.19
13	M10		2	Violation RR Crossings	4511.61-64
14	M14		2	Traffic Control Dev/Signs	4511.12
15*	M16		2	Violation to Avoid Light	
16	B05	5	2	Hit - Skip Private Property	4549.03
17*	A10		6	DUI/Alcohol Municipal	Muni Code
18	F02		0	No Child Restraint	4511.81
19	U06	4	6	Vehicular Assault	2903.08(A)(2)
20	S93		4/2/0	Speed	4511.21
21	S96		2	Slow Speed	4511.22

Offense Code	ACD	Suspension Class	Pts	Violation	OH Revised Code Section
22	B26	7	2	Driving under FRA Suspension.	4510.16(A)
23	M34		2	Following too Close	4311.34
24➤	S93		4/2/0	Speed 4511.21D	4511.21
25	S15		4/2/0	Speed Commercial Vehicles	4511.21
26	A04		Varies	DUI .04 Commercial	4506.15
27*➤	S93		2	Moving Violations 4507.021G-15	4507.021
28	M84		4	Disregard of Safety	4511.20
29	M84		2	Disregard Safety Private/Property	4511.201
30	N63		2	Violation One Way Traffic	4511.32
31	M57		2	Driving Left of Center	4511.29-30
32	N08		2	Failure to Yield Ped/Blnd	4511.46-47
33	M71		2	Crossing Yellow Line	4511.30
34*	N04		2	Fail Yield Emergency Vehicle/Funeral	4511.451
35	N70		2	Right Side of Roadway	4511.25
36	M44		2	Crossing Divided Highway	4511.35
37	M42		2	Violation Traffic Lanes/Lines/Safety Zone	4511.33 & 4511.60
38	N01		2	Failure to Yield Right of Way	4511.41-42
39	M72		2	Opposite Dir Veh Traffic Violation	4511.26
40	M70		2	Improper Passing	4511.28
41	N07		2	Violation When being Pass	4511.27
42	N09		2	Stopped School Bus Violation	4511.75
43*	A25		4	Specified Alcohol Content	4511.19
44*➤	D72		2	Fail Control 4507.40G13	4507.4
45	M84		2	W/O Due Regard Private Property	4511.201
46	N84		2	Unsafe Operator Private/Property	Muni Code
47	M84		2	Reckless Operation Private/Property	Muni Code
48	M84		4	Without Due Regard	4511.201
49	N84		4	Unsafe Operation	Muni Code
50	M84		4	Reckless Operation	4510.15
51	M08	2	2	Disobey/Interfere with Police Order	4513.36
52	M30		2	Assured Clear Distance	4511.21(A)
53	N82		2	Violation Starting/Backing	4511.38
54	M02		2	Driving on Closed Highway	4511.71
55	XXX		2	Dropping/Placing Material on Roadway	4511.74
56	D29		2	Violation of Restriction	4510.11
57*	S93		2	Moving Violation 4507.40G-13	4507.40G
58	B51	7	0	No Driver License	4510.12(A)
59	D72		2	Loss Physical Control	Muni Code
60	N56		2	Prohibited U Turn	4511.37
61	N50		2	Improper/Prohibited Turn	4511.36
62	N40		2	Violation Turn Signal	4511.39
63	N50		2	Failure To Turn	4511.36
64➤	D72		2	Fail Control 45011.202	4511.202
65	U07	1	6	Aggravated Vehicular Homicide	2903.06A(2)
66	F66		0	Operating Unsafe Vehicle	4513.02
67	E01		0	Violation Equip Regulations	4513.03-10 12-19, 201-262, 27,29
68	E01		0	Violation Slow Moving Vehicle Sign	4513.11
69	E70		0	Equipment Misuse	4513.02
70	E50		0	Disabled Vehicle Warning	4513.28
71	B27		Varies	Violation Out of Service Order	4506.16
72*	A60		2	Juvenile BAC	4511.19B
73	B26	7	6	Driving Under OVI Suspension	4510.14, 4511.19 4511.191
74*	XXX		0	Overweight Violation	4513.33
75	U03	3	6	Aggravated Vehicular Assault w/Alcohol	2903.08
76	U03	3	6	Aggravated Vehicular Assault	2903.08(A)(1)
77	U07	1	6	Vehicular Homicide w/Alcohol	2903.06(A)(1)
78	U08	1	6	Involuntary Manslaughter w/Alcohol	2903.04D
79	XXX		0	Failure to Show Driver License	4507.35
80	D02		0	Driver License Misrepresentation	4507.30/163
81*	D72		2	Physical Control	4511.79
82	B61		0	Failure to File Required Report	4509.74/99
83*	XXX		0	Registration/Title Violation	4505.18
84	F04		0	Violation of Seat Belt Law	4513.263

Offense Code	ACD	Suspension Class	Pts	Violation	OH Revised Code Section
85	E02		0	Violation of Brake Requirement	4513.20
86	D74		2	Impaired Alertness	4511.79A
87	A60		4	OMVUAC	4511.19B
88	XXX		Varies	Juvenile Miscellaneous	
89	XXX	7	0	Wrongful Entrustment	4511.203
90	N84		0	Vehicular Child Endangerment	2919.22(C1)
91	M41		2	Failure to Control/Weaving	Muni Code
92*	S95		6	Street Racing	4511.251
93	A21		6	OVI - 4th Degree Felony	4511.19/99
94	A35		0	Consume Alcohol - Motor Vehicle	4301.64
95*	A31		0	Illegal Purchase Alcohol	4301.632
96				No Corresponding Code: Use ACD	
97	D56		0	Ohio Turnpike	
98	D56		0	Highway Use Tax	5728.02
99	XXX		0	Miscellaneous	
AA	XXX		2	No Temp Permit/No Adult	4507.05 F1
AB	D29		2	Curfew Violation Temp Dr License	4507.05 F2
AC	D29		2	Curfew Violation Driver License	4507.071B
AD	F04		0	All Occupants Secure	4507.071D
AE	N05		2	Failure to Yield Funeral	4511.451
AF	N04		2	Unsafe Operation Around Emergency Vehicle	4511.213
AG	U07	1	6	Aggravated Vehicular Homicide w/Alcohol	2903.06(A)(1)
AH	U08	6	6	Vehicular Manslaughter	2903.06(A)(4)
AI	U07	4	6	Vehicular Homicide	2903.06(A)(3)
AJ	XXX	7	0	Physical Control	4511.194
AK	B20	7	2	Failure to Reinstate	4510.21(B)
AL	XXX		0	Soliciting	2907.24
AM	XXX		0	Soliciting with Positive HIV	2907.24(B)
AN	U03		6	Involuntary Manslaughter	2903.04
AO	B26	6	6	Driving under a 12 Point Suspension	4510.037(J) - 4510.11
AP	XXX		0	Gasoline Theft	2913.02(B)(9)
AQ	XXX		2	Weigh Station Violation	4511.121
AR	A50		6	Motor Vehicle Used in Manufacturing, Distributing, or Dispensing a Controlled Substance	4506.16(B)(4)
AS	A12	5	6	OVI/Refusal	4511.10(A)(2)
AT	B91		2	Driving Without Required Endorsement	4506.03(A)(1)
AU	S94		2	Unreasonable for Conditions	4511.21(A)
AV	B24		2	Driving a CMV While Disqualified	4506.15(A)
AW	U10		2	Fatality Through Operation of Commercial Motor Vehicle (CMV)	4506.15(A)(9)
AX	B56		2	Driving CMV Without Obtaining a CDL	4506.03; 4506.16(D)1
AY	B51		2	Driving a CMV Without CDL in Driver's Possession	4506.03(A)(1)
AZ	B19		0	Violation Out of Service Order Hazmat	4606.16(B)(1)
BA	A11		6	OVI BAC.17 or Above	4511.19(A)(1)f,g,h,i
BB	-		0	Registration Violation	4503.12
BC	-		0	Title Violation	4505.18
BD	-		0	Tag/Sticker Violation	4503.21
BE	-		0	Immobilization Device Operation	4510.44
BG	-		2	Unsafe Operation/Passengers	4511(D)(E)(F)
BH	-		2	Obstructed View	4511.70
BI	-		2	Headphones	4511.84
BJ	-		2	Towing Violation	4513.32
BK	B26		6	Driving Under Specified Lifetime Suspension	4510.18(A)
BL	U07		6	Aggravated Murder	2903.01
BM	U07		6	Murder	2903.02
BN	U03		6	Felonious Assault	2903.11
BO	F34-		2	Obstructing an Intersection	4511.712
BP	F05		2	Excess Passengers with Juvenile	4507.071(B)(4)
BQ	-		2	Driving Without a Parent (Restriction)	4507.071(D)(1)(a)
BR	M20		2	Failure to Slow Down at RR Crossing	4511.62(A)(1)(a)
BT	M21		2	Failure to Stop at RR Crossing	4511.63(A)
BU	M23		2	Insufficient Space at RR Crossing	4511.62(A)(1)(d)
BV	M24		2	Insufficient Undercarriage to Negotiate RR Crossing	4511.62(A)(1)(f)
BW	M22		2	Failure to Obey RR Stop Sign	4511.61(A)
BX	B26			Immobilization Waiver	4503.235
BY	-			OMWI Under Age of 21	1547.11(B)

Offense Code	ACD	Suspension Class	Pts	Violation	OH Revised Code Section
BZ	-			OMWI - Court Must Refer to the Ohio Dept of Natural Resources (ODNR)	1547.11(A)
CA	B26		2	Out of State Child Support – Failure to Pay or Appear	4510.11(C)(1)(B)
CB	B51		2	Driving Without Motorcycle Endorsement	4510.12 (B)(1)
CC	A11		varies	OVI Less Than .04 BAC	4506.15 (A)1
CD	E01		0	Motorcycle Temp Permit w/o Helmet	4511.53(C)(1)
CE	E01		0	Motorcycle Temp Permit Violation	4511.53(C)(2)
CL	B20		2	Driving Under Non Payment Judgment Suspension.	4510.16
CM	B51		0	Permitting Operation w/o Valid License	4507.02(A)
CN	-		0	Wrongful Entrustment	4511.203(A)(4),(5)
CP	M85		0	Texting While Operating a Commercial Vehicle	4506.01
CQ	B01		0	Failure to Stop After Accident	4506.15
CR	M85		0	Driving While Texting	4511.204
CS	M86	7	0	Driving Using Electronic Wireless Communication Device - Under 18	4511.205

Note: OMWI Refers to a watercraft OVI. These convictions are used when calculating subsequent OVI suspensions, and OMWI refusals are used to calculate subsequent ALS refused suspensions

Withdrawal Actions Table

(Found in the CODE column of the record)

AR	Administrative suspension	MF	Court suspension/major offense with FRA
AT	License cancellation - altered	MN	Court suspension/minor offense
A1	Accident report	MR	Moped revocation
BF	Bond forfeiture	NC	Non-compliance suspension
CC	License cancellation - cosigner	ND	National Driver Registry cancellation
CS	Co-signer	NR	General narrative
CT	License cancellation - court ordered	N6	6 point warning
CV	Court suspension-major offense w/o FRA	OS	Cancellation of a specific license number
C1	Conviction record	OW	Out-of-state withdrawal
C2	Commercial driver conviction record	PD	Probationary suspension/OVI
C3	Out-of-state conviction reported by driver license compact member state	PR	Permanent revocation
C4	In-state drug conviction	PT	Pre-trial suspension
C5	OVI/drug conviction for an Ohio resident/driver that occurred in another state	P1	Probationary suspension/OVUAC
		P2	Probationary suspension - two violations
DD	Out-of-state CDL disqualification	P3	Probationary suspension - three violations
DL	Commercial driver license disqualification record	RM	Remedial driving course
DX	License cancellation - ID card issuance	RS	Random selection/non-compliance
D1	Court suspension/first CVI	RV	Restriction violation suspension
FI	License cancellation - fraudulent license issuance	SD	School drop-out suspension
FPFP	Fee Payment Plan	SI	Administrative license suspension/refusal
FR	License cancellation - fraudulent issuance	SJ	Judgment suspension
FX	License cancellation - 4th failure of DL Exam	SP	Probationary revocation
HB	Habitual alcohol suspension	VS	License cancellation - voluntary surrender
JS	Juvenile suspension	SR	Failure to file crash report suspension in results of motor vehicle accident
KS	Child support suspension	SS	Security suspension
LF	License forfeiture	SW	School weapon suspension
LS	Suspension - violation of liquor law	S1	Twelve-point suspension
L1	Work related accident/line of duty	UA	Underage alcohol suspension
MD	Administrative suspension	VC	Violator compact
PH	Physical control while Under the Influence	WB	Warrant Block

Suspension Explanations Table

Suspension	Cause	Length
12-POINTS	Accumulation of 12 points within a two-year period	Six months.
ADMINISTRATIVE LICENSE SUSP. (ALS)/POSITIVE	Testing .08 or above to a blood alcohol content test	Ninety days.
ADMINISTRATIVE LICENSE SUSP. (ALS)/REFUSAL	Refusing to submit to a blood, breath or urine test when requested to do so by law enforcement	One year.
CHILD SUPPORT	A suspension imposed for failure to pay court ordered child support	Indefinite.
COURT SUSPENSIONS	A suspension limiting driving privileges, and invoked by a court within the state of Ohio	Variable.
FIRST OFFENSE - OVI	Driving under the influence of alcohol or drugs	Variable.

Suspension	Cause	Length
HABITUAL USE OF ALCOHOL/DRUGS	Conviction of three or more alcohol/drug related offenses within a three year period	Indefinite.
HIGH SCHOOL SUSPENSION	Unauthorized withdrawal from school, habitual absence without legitimate excuse, or suspension/expulsion for drugs or alcohol	Until age eighteen, or if terminated.
IN-STATE DRUG RELATED	Individual found guilty by an Ohio court of drug related offenses under Chapter 2925 of ORC	Six months to Five years.
JUDGMENTS	Unsatisfied civil judgment resulting from the use, care, or maintenance of a motor vehicle	Indefinite.
JUVENILE SUSPENSION	Under 18 and has been adjudicated unruly, delinquent, or juvenile traffic offender	Until age eighteen.
LICENSE FORFEITURE	Failure to pay a fine or appear in court in connection to a traffic offense within Ohio	Indefinite.
LIQUOR LAW VIOLATIONS	Person of insufficient age uses another person's driver license or alters one's own to purchase alcohol	One year.
MEDICAL (RESTRICTED OR SUSPENDED)	Suffering from a physical or mental disability or disease that prevents him/her from exercising reasonable/ordinary control of a motor vehicle	Six months/one year/ renewal.
MODIFYING ORDER	A court or administrative order modifying a suspension	Variable.
NATIONAL DRIVER REGISTRY (NDR) – INDEFINITE	Upon a check with other states, an individual is found to be under suspension	Indefinite.
NON-COMPLIANCE (CRASH REPORT/ACCIDENT/UTT TICKET)	An individual receives a ticket or is involved in a crash, randomly selected, and fails to show proof of being insured	Ninety days first/up to 2 years for mult offenses.
NON-RESIDENT VIOLATOR COMPACT	Ohio driver has an unpaid ticket from a court in another state	Indefinite.
OVUAC	Underage drinking with a BAC of .02 or more but less than .08	Ninety days – Five years.
OUT-OF-STATE ALCOHOL OR DRUG RELATED OFFENSES	An individual pleads guilty or is convicted of a OVI or Drug related offense in another state	Six months.
PROBATIONARY LICENSE SUSPENSION/OVI	The PD will be triggered by a conviction record with an offense date greater than 12/31/98, the driver is under the age of 18 at the time of the offense, with a BAC of .08% or above	Six months.
PROBATIONARY LICENSE SUSPENSION/OVUAC	The P1 will be triggered by a conviction record with an offense date greater than 12/31/98, the driver is under the age of 18 at the time of the offense, with at BAC of .02% or more but less than .08%	Six months.
PROBATIONARY REVOCATIONS (2 VIOLATIONS)	A person is convicted of two separate moving violations within any two year period prior to 18 years of age	Ninety days.
PROBATIONARY REVOCATIONS (3 VIOLATIONS)	A person is convicted of three separate moving violations within any two year period prior to 18 years of age	One year.
SECOND OFFENSE OVI	OVI coded by presiding court as a second or more offense within a six-year period	Determined by the court.
SECURITY	Damages from an accident where a "case" has been established by the BMV	Two years.
VIOLATION OF RESTRICTION	Driver has violated a driver license restriction (corrective lenses, etc.)	Six Months
WARRANT BLOCK	A block on either driver license and/or vehicle registration due to outstanding arrest warrant	Indefinite.
WEAPON ON SCHOOL PROPERTY	Under 19 yrs. old and conveying or possessing a deadly weapon or dangerous ordinance to, or on school property	One to Five years.

About Point System

Points range from 2 to 12. Accumulation of 12 points in a 24-month period can result in a suspension

Oklahoma

Administration	Important Telephone and Web Contacts

Michael C. Thompson, Commissioner
Department of Public Safety
3600 North Martin Luther King Blvd
Oklahoma City, OK 73111
405-425-2001
www.dps.state.ok.us/
 	
Russ Nordstrom, Director
Motor Vehicle Division
Oklahoma Tax Commission
2501 Lincoln Blvd, Oklahoma City 73194
405-521-2519
www.tax.ok.gov/motveh.html
	Driver Licensing......................405-425-2026
	MVR Desk................................405-425-2262
	Financial Responsibility 405-425-2098
	Vehicle Information 405-521-3221
	Vehicle Liens............................405-521-3344
	CDL Program Administration 405-702-0810
	Highway Patrol........................405-425-2424
	State Dept of Insurance............405-521-2828
	General Email (driver) comment@dps.state.ok.us
	Title 47. Motor Vehicles:
	   www.oscn.net/applications/oscn/index.asp?ftdb=STO
	   KST47&level=1
	Laws for Motor Carriers:
	   www.dps.state.ok.us/ohp/chapter56.pdf

Driver's License Format, Issuance and Renewal

License Classes, Restrictions and Endorsements Appear After the Driving Record Content Section

License Format

Since 2002 DPS assigns a ten-digit identifier which is randomly generated format. An example is A123456789. Previously the Social Security Number (SSN) or an assigned nine-digit number was used.

Document Appearance

The current license cards and ID cards, in circulation since 09/2003, are in a digitized format. Oklahoma is also currently in the process of implementing a new digital driver license version.

One fact not mentioned below is that "Interlock Required" will appear on the front of the DL document when required as a condition of reinstatement or modification.

Current Document

Security Characteristics: The document has optical variable ink images and is multicolored with ultra violet images. There is a ghosted image of the photo, overlapping seal on photo, gradient color pattern and barcode with unique numerical information. Licenses issued to sex offenders are indicated in three places. The regular license has blue background, DL in large type in lower right. The ID Card is in red.

Position of Photo: Currently, the regular license has picture on the right side, underage drivers and the ID Card has picture on left side. Small version of photo is also in middle.

New Format: Using the new format, the photo will be on the left side of a regular license and the right side for underage drivers and ID cards. The photo will also be slightly smaller.

Minor Age Driver Locator: Card is vertical, picture on left side. *Note for the Forthcoming New Format:* The picture will be on the right side.

CDL Indicator: Yellow background, large type CDL in lower right corner.

Sex Offender: The driver license or ID card is clearly labeled with the words "sex offender" in the color red, in three distinct places.

Non-US Citizen: The DL or ID is clearly labeled "Temporary."

Veteran Logo: With the **new format**, a veteran logo (American flag with the word "Veteran") can be requested. This will appear in the top left corner of card and would replace the current default Osage Indian shield logo.

Older Document - pre-2003

Security Characteristics: License is laminated. State symbol overlaps licensing information. Camera number and location number runs along side of photo.

Position of Photo: Top right.

Minor Age Driver Locator: "Under 21 Until (date)" appears above name, left side, with date of 21st birthday in light red block.

CDL Indicator: Gold area across top with notation "CDL" to the left of photo.

Issuance

Issuance and ID Requirements

Anyone applying for an original driver license or identification card or anyone with a driver license or ID card expired more than 30 days must show proof of legally being in the U.S. Acceptable documents include a U.S. state-issued birth certificate, certificate of born abroad, U.S. issued passport, certificate of naturalization or a valid immigration document issued by the U.S. Customs and Immigration Service (USCIS). A list of acceptable documents is at www.dps.state.ok.us/dls/pub/DOCS.pdf.

Age Requirements

A Graduated Driver Licensing is in place for drivers under the age of 18. The minimum age for a regular license is 16. A learner permit is issued at 15 1/2 to students participating in an approved driver education school or parental certification of required training. More privileges are granted as the driver becomes more experienced. To hold an intermediate license, one must have had the learner permit for a minimum of 6 months and have no traffic violations. For a regular license, one must have had the intermediate license for 6 months and have no traffic violations. If convicted of am offense, the current GDL level is in force until 6 months from the date the convection has elapsed. The GDL law was strengthened in 2009 to restrict teens' driving time to the hours of 5am to 10pm, with exceptions for driving to work, school, church or related activities, or if a licensed driver is seated next to the teenager.

Residency

Non-resident's home-state license honored; must secure Oklahoma license upon establishing residency. Change of address must be provided to DPS within 10 days of the change. Non-CDL licensees may do so online at www.dps.state.ok.us/addresschange/. Oklahoma law requires applicants for new license to provide proof of legal presence in the United States.

Renewal

Four years from date of issue on originals, renewals expire four years from previous expiration. Sex offenders are required to renew the license or ID card annually. Driver keeps same number when renewing or changes number, as long as the SSN is not used as the number. Renewal is not available online, but licensees may sign-up for an email renewal notice at https://www.dps.state.ok.us/renewal/. Class D licenses can be renewed by mail, reusing the photo and signature on file with DPS. Renewal can be made up to one year before expiration. Also, see Issuance Requirements above.

Elderly-Related Restrictions

None indicated.

Vehicle Insurance, Title and Registration Facts

Registration and Renewal

All vehicles, boats and outboard motors in excess of ten horsepower are registered annually. There is no exclusion made for vehicles, boats, or outboard motors not in use. Renewal is available online at www.tax.ok.gov/mvonlinereg.html for standard non-commercial vehicles, commercial trucks with laden weight not exceeding 15,000 lbs, and farm trucks if truck and load are under 55,001 lbs.

New Residents

New residents must register within thirty days of establishing residency.

Inspections and Emissions Testing

Oklahoma no longer requires an annual safety inspection for vehicles. There is no statewide emission testing program.

Passenger Plate Facts

There is one plate with two decals (MO) (YR). Oklahoma does not use an issuing system that indicates on the plate pattern the county of plate issuance. However, month decals do have a county identifier indicating the county in which the decal was purchased. The vast majority of plates remain with a sold vehicle. However, for an additional fee the vehicle owner may retain the plate if the vehicle is sold.

Insurance and Financial Responsibility

Oklahoma has compulsory liability insurance. Financial responsibility limit minimums are $25,000/50,000/25,000. The state does not have a no-fault insurance provision. Proof is required upon registration or renewal, after a reportable accident or certain violations. A *Liability Insurance Security Verification* form is used. Insurance is verified electronically at registration, at traffic stops, and during collision investigations.

The Oklahoma Compulsory Insurance Verification system, provides an electronic real-time means to law enforcement and the courts to verify compliance with the Compulsory Insurance Law of Oklahoma (47 O.S. §7-600 et seq.) as it pertains to privately-owner vehicles. Verification may be performed online at www.dps.state.ok.us/insver/ or at https://ocivs.dps.state.ok.us/.

Withdrawal Sanctions, and Alcohol and Drug Testing

Alcohol and Chemical Testing

It is a violation of Oklahoma Law for any person to drive/operate or be in actual physical control of a motor vehicle while under the influence of alcohol or other intoxicating substance or a combination thereof. For an individual 21 years of age or older, a blood or breath alcohol concentration of .08 or above is the statutory limit. For an individual under 21 years of age, any measurable amount, determined to be .02 or more by the Oklahoma Board of Tests for Alcohol and Drug Influence, is the statutory limit. If an individual is operating a CMV, the statutory limit is .04.

Suspensions and Revocations

Note the following:

- At the court's discretion, anyone under 18 can have their licensed suspended from 6 months to 2 years for any crime involving alcohol or a controlled dangerous substance.
- Ignition Interlock can be required for additional periods of time for certain repeat offenders upon reinstatement.
- MCSIA by state statute and federal law requires a CDL disqualification of 12 months for driving a CMV and convicted for DUS.
- A non-commercial driver will have an additional four (4) months added to the original revocation for every conviction added.
- A DUI conviction for any driver will result in a minimum six (6) month revocation, second revocation within the last 10 years shall be for a period of 12 months, third revocation within the last 10 years, shall be for a period of three(3) years.

Driving While License Suspended or Revoked Unexpired suspension is extended for three or four months.

Dropping Out of School While Under 18...... Indefinite suspension but minimum 2 months.

Point Accumulation of Ten Points Within 5 year Period:

    First Suspension.. One month.

    Second Suspension .... Three months.

    Third Suspension .... Six months.

    Fourth or Subsequent Suspensions .... Twelve months.

Attempting to Elude a Police Officer - incurs a one-month suspension on the first conviction, a six-month suspension on the second conviction, and a twelve-month suspension on the third or subsequent conviction

The following incur a two-month suspension on the first conviction and a six-month suspension on the second conviction:

- Display or Possession of a Driver's License Bearing Altered Information
- Giving False Information When Applying for a License
- Lending a Operator's or Chauffeur's License to any Other Person
- Presenting a License that is not Your Own for the Purpose of Committing Fraud
- To Make, Print, or Otherwise Produce False Oklahoma Driver's Licenses
- To Display or Knowingly Possess a Counterfeit License
- To Display or Possess a License Having a Forged Signature or Picture of a Person Other Than Licensee

The Following Offenses Result in a Six-Month to Three-Year Revocation:

- Any drug conviction in which a motor vehicle is used
- Any felony in which a motor vehicle is used
- Failure to pay for gasoline
- Failure to register vehicle
- Failure to stop and render aid if involved in a collision resulting in serious injury or death
- Manslaughter or negligent homicide resulting from operating a motor vehicle
- Perjury or making a false statement under oath to obtain a license or for any other legal matter related to the ownership or operation of a motor vehicle

Reinstatement Requirements

FR Suspension $100.00 fee; comply with requirements. Add-on a fee of $50.00 if failure to surrender driver license and registration tag within 30 days of suspension date. An additional $200.00 trauma care fee is assessed for certain violations.

DI Revocation   A DL revocation reinstatement fee for an arrest before November 1, 2011 is $340.00, if the arrest occurred after November 1, 2011, the reinstatement fee will be $390.00

Record Access: Laws, Rules, and Forms

Note: This Section Applies to Both Driver and Vehicle Records.

Governing Statutes and Rules

Title 47, Motor Vehicles:
www.oscn.net/applications/oscn/index.asp?ftdb=STOKST47&level=1
Laws for Motor Carriers: www.dps.state.ok.us/ohp/chapter56.pdf
Oklahoma Open Records Act Title 51 §24A.3 governs openness of records. Title 47 provides for laws for drivers and vehicles.

Record information is confidential under both federal and state law. The statute regarding privacy (effective December 9, 1992) requires the release of collision, conviction, and department action information; however, personal information such as address, height, weight, and eye color will not be released. Thus, the release of records with personal data is regulated administratively.

Policy Statement Regarding Permissible Uses

Information is available for insurance and law enforcement purposes and, in general, is available to the public. The only requesters who can receive the address of the driver are government agencies and users authorized by the Commissioner. Affirmation of permissible use by the person making the request is covered by 12 O.S. §426. Also, medical information is not public record information. The current statutes are more restrictive than the provisions in DPPA. Oklahoma does not have the following federal exceptions: (5), (9), (11), (12), and (13). Oklahoma added the following exception:

"For use by any person compiling and publishing motor vehicle statistics, provided that such statistics do not disclose the names and addresses of individuals. Such information shall be provided upon payment of a fee as determined by the DPS."

Request and Consent Forms

Driving Records: Personal information will be released if the requester attests to the reason as being permissible per the *Oklahoma State Records Request Form* or if the subject gives written consent. The signature does not need to be notarized. Download the records request form at www.dps.state.ok.us/recm/rrctl.pdf. This form is also used to obtain a copy of an accident report.

Subscribers to the commercial online system must be registered and complete a *Certificate of Acceptable Use Form*. The form is found at https://www.ok.gov/idlr/doc/DPPA_form_0305.doc.

Vehicle Records: *The Vehicle Information Request Form* is required, accompanied by the applicable fee. The form can be downloaded from the Internet at www.tax.ok.gov/mvforms/769.pdf. The requester's signature must be notarized (effective 01/01/2011).

Vendor and Third Party Access Policy

Approved electronic vendors access records for other vendors (who do not access electronically, etc.) who can then sell to an end user. However, the responsibility of compliance to current statutes rests with the original vendor. Oklahoma does not provide any bulk or database record sales.

Records Ordered For Non-permissible Uses

Records are not released without consent or with a permissible use, even records without personal information.

Access to Driver-Related Records

Driving Records

General Information and Fees
Records Management Division, Attn: MVR DESK, PO Box 11415, Oklahoma City OK 73136-0415, 405-425-2262.

The current fee is $25.00 for a paper record, $28.00 if certified, and $27.50 for an electronic non-certified record. The state does not charge for "no record found" reports when the record is requested over-the-counter, unless the requester asks for a printed report. There is a charge for a "no hit" report when the request is mailed to the state. The driver's license number, name, and date of birth are needed when ordering. Note that *requests* for records cannot be made by telephone or email AND *records* cannot be faxed or emailed.

In-Person — Records Management, 3600 North Martin Luther King Boulevard, Oklahoma City OK 73111, 405-425-2262. Driving records are also available from motor license agents - known as "Tag Agents" -

throughout the state. However, certified copies are available only from this location.

Mail — The fee must accompany each request; however, Oklahoma does have a billing system for large users. Including a self-addressed, stamped envelope is helpful. Turnaround time is usually one to two days.

Electronic — Electronic access is available for qualified, approved users through www.ok.gov. This is a batch mode process with plans for interactive service in the future. The $27.50 record fee includes a $2.50 service fee. There is an annual $75.00 subscription fee upon approval. Search by either the DL# or by the name, and DOB and gender. The full record fee applies for a no record found report.

For   more   information,   call   800-955-3468,   email helpdesk@www.ok.gov, or visit https://www.ok.gov/idlr/index.php.

Bulk — Oklahoma does not offer its driver license database file for sale to commercial users or vendors.

By Person of Record – OK drivers may obtain their driving record by mail or walk-in as described above. At present, there is no program for drivers to order or view their own record online. For those over 65, the Department provides individuals their own driving record at no charge.

Notification/Monitoring Program

In early to mid 2013 the Division will activate DSNS. This is an online subscription service for employers of people who have a commercial driver license and who operates a commercial motor vehicle in the course of employment.

The system will allow an employer to be automatically notified by email should the driving record of an employee reflect a traffic conviction in any court or an administrative action by the Department which alters the status of the commercial driving privileges of the person. The system will also provide electronic delivery of a driving record at least annually for any employee who is a CDL licensee or who operates a commercial motor vehicle, as required by 49 C.F.R. Section 391.25. For more information, contact Records Management.

Collision Reports

Reporting – Collisions involving death, personal injury, or damage in excess of $300.00 must be reported if a settlement is not reached within six months. If requested by the Department of Public Safety, a report must be filed within ten days. The report must be completed on required forms with accompanying doctor's statement of personal injury, and repair estimate dated and signed by an authorized representative of a garage or body shop, and/or itemized estimate by property owner for property damage. A reporting form can be downloaded at www.dps.state.ok.us/recm/omvcr.pdf. The report should be sent to: Financial Responsibility Division, Department of Public Safety, PO Box 11415, Oklahoma City OK 73136-0415

Record Access – Records Management Division, P.O. Box 11415, Oklahoma City OK 73136-0415, 405-425-2192

After the report is filed with the DPS, collision reports remain confidential for a period of 60 days before those not involved may have access. Those qualified to obtain reports include permissible users per DPPA plus the media (newspapers, radio, and television broadcasters). Copies of collision reports are available for a fee of $15.00 uncertified or $18.00 if certified. Records are generally available for at least 5 years to present. Turnaround time is generally 24 hours. The agency will check to see if a record is available, but will not release record information over the phone. Please indicate if a fatality is involved. Download the records request form at www.dps.state.ok.us/recm/rrctl.pdf.

Access to Vehicle-Related Records

General Information and Fees

Oklahoma Tax Commission, Motor Vehicle Division, 2501 Lincoln Boulevard, Attention: Research, Oklahoma City 73194, General number: 405-521-3770; Titles 405-521-3221; Registration 405-521-3101; Liens 405-521-3344.

The Motor Vehicle Division is the office of record for all vehicle/boat/outboard motor lien entries and releases.

Although telephone numbers are given above please be aware that under NO circumstances will vehicle information be given over the telephone. To obtain vehicle information, the requester MUST complete the *Vehicle Information Request Form 769* as explained above, and include the appropriate fees. Information is only released to statutorily qualified requestors. The fees are as follows:

- Computer screen printout of current ownership/lienholder information is $1.00.
- Computer generated title history (only 1992 or newer models) is $5.00.
- Microfilm Title history is $7.50.
- Certified copy of title history is $10.00.
- Copy of a lien release is $7.50, if certified then $10.00.

Vehicle records cannot be researched by the owner's name. All requests must include either the OK title number, license plate or registration decal number or VIN. If a boat, the hull ID or outboard serial number is also acceptable. Driver's license numbers and insurance information are not released.

The *Vehicle Information Request Form* can be downloaded from the Web at www.tax.ok.gov/mvforms/769.pdf. As of January 1, 2011, notarization of the requestor's signature is **required** on **all** *Vehicle Information Request Forms (Form 769)*.

Lien records go back to July 1, 1979 for vehicles, and July 1, 1990 for boats. Inactive vehicle, boat and outboard motor records without active liens are removed from the computer record periodically. However, most information is still available via microfilm and microfiche.

In-Person – Current ownership may be obtained by qualified requesters at any of the over 300 motor license agencies throughout Oklahoma. All information may be obtained by qualified requesters at the Oklahoma Tax Commission at the address listed above.

Mail – Mail the properly filled out Form 769 to the address listed above. If the requester needs lien information, it must be specified in the request. Mail turnaround time is usually 7 to 14 days.

About Title History Requests – If a **Standard Request** is made, all copies of available title transaction documentation will be provided for the prior 10 years. If an **Extended Request** is made, all copies of all available title transaction documentation will be provided; however, this may require an additional 2 weeks to process.

Electronic – Oklahoma does not offer online record access of registration and title records to the public or to permissible use requesters. However, Oklahoma does offer Insurance Verification online. The site allows one to verify compulsory liability insurance coverage on privately-owned vehicle insured by a personal policy of vehicle insurance. It does not verify coverage for a vehicle covered by a commercial policy. The request must include the VIN and Policy Number. Visit www.ok.gov/redirect.php?link_id=716.

Bulk – Bulk sales are only available to qualifying requesters meeting the Oklahoma statutory information release criteria.

Access to Vessel-Related Records

General Information, Access and Fees

Oklahoma is a title state for boats; every boat used for transportation on the water of the state and every outboard motor in excess of ten (10) horsepower must be titled and registered. Records are maintained by and accessible from the agency described above. Record access is limited to law enforcement, government agencies, and requests related to boating safety. Record access fees are the same as reported above for vehicles.

Driving Record Content and Reciprocity

What's On or Not On the Driving Record

- All moving violations appear on the driving record.
- Violations for speeding one to ten mph over the limit will not be included on the driving record unless the violation was committed while operating a commercial motor vehicle (CMV) or the operator was the holder of a CDL at the time of the violation.
- The length of time convictions are listed on the report is three years from date of conviction.
- Collisions are reported only if the licensee was issued a citation and convicted of the offense.
- Although the state does not permit driver school attendance in lieu of conviction, the courts have this option. Records can be ordered without personal information shown.

Data Retention

There is no statement regarding the purging of non-CMV related records. All CMV records are permanent records and will be on file with the Department..

Court to Repository

Conviction information is transferred from the courts to the state via paper and electronic transfer. The courts have five days after conviction to report violation information to the state. By policy and procedure, Driver Compliance provides that the Department will suspend or revoke on a conviction if the conviction was received within one (1) year from the conviction date if there are no prior revocations, two (2) years from the conviction date if there are prior license revocations.

State Reciprocity for Non-CDL Drivers

- Will suspend license of driver for unpaid out-of-state convictions.
- Record of new incoming driver is shown on MVR.
- Out-of-state convictions are shown on MVR.
- Out-of-state collisions are only shown on MVR with total record transfer.
- Only moving violations convictions of out-of-state drivers are sent to home state.
- Record is forwarded to new state upon surrender of license.

License Classes, Restrictions and Endorsement Codes

License Classes– Commercial

Oklahoma began issuing the CDL in January 1991

Class A — Any combination of motor vehicles with a GCWR of 26,001 pounds or more, providing the vehicle being towed has a GVWR of 10,000 pounds or more, with applicable endorsements.

Class B — Trucks or buses with GVWR of 26,001 pounds or more, or any such vehicle towing a vehicle weighing less than 10,000 pounds GVWR.

Class C — Trucks or buses weighing less than 26,001 pounds GVWR, or any such vehicle towing a vehicle less than 10,000 pounds GVWR. This class applies to vehicles which are placarded to transport hazardous materials or designed to carry sixteen or more passengers (including the driver).

License Classes– Non-Commercial

Class D — All other vehicles will be Class D and will include cars, pickups, all recreational vehicles, fire trucks, and certain farm vehicles.

ID — Identification License

Restrictions

1	Corrective Lenses	9	Accompanied by Licensed Driver Over Eighteen in Front Seat
2	Left Outside Rear-View Mirror		
3	Restriction #1 or #2	0	Motorcycle or Motor-Bike Restrictions
4	Automatic Transmission	A	Licensed Driver Twenty-one or Older in Visual Contact
5	Turn Indicators and Power-Steering, or Steering Knob	E	Passenger Bus Restricted to Class B or C
6	Food, Fruit, or Candy Within the Reach of Driver	G	Graduated Driver License
7	Adequate Artificial Limbs	KCDL	Intrastate Only
8	Detailed Restrictions on License - Inquire Oklahoma Driver License File	V	Vehicle Without Air-Brakes

Endorsements

T	Doubles/Triples (for Class A)	M	Motorcycle (ABCD)
N	Tank Vehicle (ABC)	X	Combination of H and N (ABC)
P	Passenger (ABC)	S	School Bus (new)
H	Hazardous Materials (ABC)		

Conviction Table with Codes, Statutes, Points and Withdrawals

Oklahoma Conviction Table with ACD Code, Statute, and Points Oklahoma driving records show each conviction or action with a full description. The VC (violation code) column below does not appear on a driving record, but this information can be helpful if talking to administration people about a specific violation. This table is presented in order of the Description column, which does appear on the driving record.

Note that **CDS** refers to **Controlled Dangerous Substance.**

About the "WA" - Withdrawal Action for Violation (first column below)

C	Cancellation
D	Denial
DQ	Disqualification
*DQ	Disqualification only if Operating a CMV
R	Revocation
S	Suspension
ST	Serious Traffic Offense/CMV

WA	Pts	VC	Description	Citation
R		HM1	2nd degree murder with a motor vehicle	21:701.8(2)
R		LI7	Abandon goods on highway	21:1465
		ST6	Abandoning a vehicle on highway or public property (over 48 hours)	901
		LP4	Affixing improper license plate to motor vehicle	4-107(d)
R		AG1	Aggravated DUI	11-902 D
		DL6	Allowing an unlicensed person to drive	6-305
		LP2	Altering or changing a license plate or decal	1151A.2
R		D17	APC of Motor Vehicle while under the influence of alcohol and other intoxicants	11-902 A.4
R		ES6	Attempting to elude an officer	21:540A
R		FE1	Attempting to elude an officer (causes an accident)	21:540A,C
R		FE1	Attempting to elude an officer (endanger any other person)	21:540A,B
	2	CD1	Careless driving	Municipal or OOS only
R		FE2	Cause great bodily injury collision while violation of 11-901A	11-904B.1
	1	IL1	Changing lanes unsafely	11-309.2
DQ		U31	CMV traffic offense which results in fatality	6-205.2 F.3
	1	RK4	Coasting in neutral operating with clutch disengaged	11-1107(a), (b)
R		MR1	Commit fraud in license application (fictitious name, etc.)	6-301.2.f
R		AD5	Consume, possess, purchase low point beer under 21	37:246 A
	2	S95	Contest racing (municipal only)	Municipal only
		EM4	Creating unlawful (excessive/unusual) noise with muffler	12-402
		TP4	Crossing center median (turnpike violation)	11-1401 I
		MS4	Crossing fire hose with vehicle	11-1109
	1	DE0	Defective or improper equipment	12-101, 12-405
		LI1	Depositing injurious or harmful substances on highway	11-1110(a)
R		LP5	Display another state's license plate when possessing an Oklahoma driver license	1151A.3
R		MR3	Display as one's own using other person's photo	6-301 2d
R		MR9	Display DL not own	6-301.2.e
R		MR2	Display/possess driver license with altered information (misdemeanor)	6-301.1.c
	1	SC5	Drive through/within safety zone	11-1301
R		AD1	Drive, operate or be in APC/alcohol/under 21	11-906.4.A.1
R		AD2	Drive, operate or be in APC/combined influence/under 21	11-906.4.A.2
R		AD3	Drive, operate or be in APC/combines influence/under 21	11-906.4.A.3
R		D10	Drive, operate, or APC of Motor Vehicle with BAC of .08 or more	11-902.A.1
		DL3	Driving after driver license is denied or canceled	6-111D, 6-303B
	2	WW3	Driving in wrong direction around rotary traffic island	434215
	1	IL3	Driving off of roadway when overtaking on right	11-304(b)
	2	WW2	Driving on wrong side of divided roadway	11-311
DQ		A08	Driving under influence alcohol .08 or more (CMV only)	6-205.2
R		D18	Driving while ability is impaired by alcohol or other intoxicating substance	761 A
		DL8	Driving while disqualified (CDL)	6-303B
		DL1	Driving while revoked	6-303B
		DL2	Driving while suspended	6-303B
R		D11	Driving while under the influence of alcohol	11-902.A.2
R		D13	Driving while under the influence of medication or other substance not intended to produce - intoxication as a result of normal use	11-902.A.3
R		D12	Driving while under the influence of narcotics or pathogenic drugs	11-902.A.3
		DL9	Driving without privileges, cause collision with injury or death	11-905 A,B,C
	2	WW1	Driving wrong way on one-way road	11-308(b)
R		D16	DUI/APC/after previous conviction in last 10 years (felony: 11-901C)	11-902, A.1, A.2, A.3,

WA	Pts	VC	Description	Citation
				A.4
		LI2	Dump trash or substance which may cause fire	21:1761.1 C D
		EW1	Endangerment of highway worker within maintenance/construction zone	11-1303
		TP2	Enter closed area (turnpike violation)	11-1401 G
*DQ	2	R04	Enter railroad crossing-insufficient space to clear	11-1115.1
R		AD5	Enter, attempt to enter area for those over 21 years of age	37:246 B
	2	S93	Excessive speed (no speed given) (only appears if CMV or CDL tickets)	Various Statutes
	1	SI2	Fail to give proper signal	11-605(b)
R		GO1	Fail to pay for gasoline	21:1740
		LI4	Fail to prevent sifting or dropping loads	14-105(a)
		LI6	Fail to secure or cover load	14-105(b)
	1	SI1	Fail to signal intention to stop or reduce speed suddenly/to change direction	11-604A, C
		SW4	Failure to carry or exhibit certificate or bill of sale	14-111 (b)
*DQ	2	R01	Failure to check for train traffic at railroad crossing	11-701c
S		FR6	Failure to comply with required compulsory insurance law (deferred sentence, court use only)	7-606A.1
S		FR5	Failure to comply with required compulsory liability insurance law or fail to carry security verification form	7-606A.1
	1	EM5	Failure to dim lights when meeting/following another vehicle	12-230.2 1,2
	1	EM6	Failure to display lighted lamps	12-201
	1	SC1	Failure to follow instructions of police officer	11-103
		RR4	Failure to have DL in possession while driving	6-112
	1	IL2	Failure to keep in proper lane	11-301B; 11-309.1, 3, 4
	2	LC1	Failure to keep left of center on roadway with 4 or more lanes	11-301(c)
		SW5	Failure to keep registration certificate in vehicle (If CMV, then indicted)	14-110; 1113D
	2	LC4	Failure to keep right on road of sufficient width	11-301(a)
	1	SC2	Failure to obey instructions of traffic control device (signal, sign)	11-201(a);11-1302D1
*DQ	2	R05	Failure to obey officer or signal at railroad crossing	11-701.B
R		SC9	Failure to obey traffic light/stop sign causing great bodily injury	11-201(a)
		TP1	Failure to pay toll	11-1401 B
		EX1	Failure to properly mark explosives or flammable load	12-409
	1	RK3	Failure to reduce speed when lawfully required	11-801E
	1	PA5	Failure to signal intention to pass	11-604A, 11-303.3
*DQ	2	R03	Failure to stop at railroad crossing-drive onto crossing	11-702
*DQ	2	R02	Failure to stop at railroad crossing-tracks not clear	11-701A.5
R		FE3	Failure to stop at roadblock	21:540B
	2	ST2	Failure to stop for red light	11-202.3.a
	4	ST4	Failure to stop for school bus loading or unloading	11-705A; 11-705.1A
R		ST9	Failure to stop for school bus loading or unloading	11-705A; 11-705.1A
	2	ST1	Failure to stop for stop sign	11-403 B
	2	RW0	Failure to yield right of way from alley/driveway/building	11-704
	2	RW5	Failure to yield right of way from private road or drive	11-401A ; 11-404
	2	RW8	Failure to yield right of way from sign/signal at intersection	11-403(d); 11-202.1.b
	2	RW3	Failure to yield right of way from stop sign	11-403(b)
	2	RW4	Failure to yield right of way from yield sign to pedestrian	11-403(c)
	2	RW2	Failure to yield right of way from yield sign to vehicle	11-403(c)
	2	RW7	Failure to yield right of way in intersection to vehicle while turning	11-402
	2	RW1	Failure to yield right of way to emergency vehicle	11-405
	2	RW6	Failure to yield right of way to vehicle on right	11-401B
	1	PA6	Failure to yield to overtaking vehicles	11-303.2
R		MR8	Fictitious or forged name or signature (felony)	6-301.2.c
	2	FO2	Following emergency vehicle	11-1108 a,b; 21:1211
	2	FO1	Following too closely	11-310(a,b,c,d)
R		HR1	Hit and run collision resulting (bodily injury) (death)	10-102A, B
		HR2	Hit and run collision resulting in property damage only	10-103
		TP2	Hitchhiking or illegal pedestrian on turnpike	11-1401 D
		TP2	Illegal vehicle on turnpike	11-1401 F
	1	S96	Impeding traffic	11-804(a); 11-301B; 11-309 3
	1	MS2	Improper backing	11-1102
		TP1	Improper entering or leaving turnpike	11-1401 A
	1	TU2	Improper left turn at an intersection	11-601.2, 3
	1	PA0	Improper passing	11-303.1, 3; 11-1302D2
	1	PA8	Improper passing of stationary emergency vehicle	11-314
	1	TU1	Improper right turn at an intersection	11-601.1, 3
	1	ST5	Improper stopping on roadway	11-1001

WA	Pts	VC	Description	Citation
	1	TU0	Improper turn (turn about, U-turn, etc)	11-601
	1	TU4	Improper turn from wrong lane	11-601.1, 2, 3
	1	IL0	Improper use of lane	11-309.1, 3, 4
	1	PA2	Improperly passing on the right	11-304(b)
		LP3	Improperly removing a license plate from vehicle/defacing license plate	4-107(d)
	2	IN3	Inattentive driving	11-901b
	2	IN1	Inattentive driving resulting in a collision	11-901b
	2	IN4	Inattentive driving while using cell phone or electronic communications device	11-901b
*DQ		E23	Install, possess, operate or use Radar Detector (CDL holder or CMV)	11-808.1
*DQ	2	R06	Insufficient undercarriage clearance at railroad crossing	11-1115.2
R		FE2	Involved in personal injury accident while in violation of 11-902A (2nd Offense)	11-904A.2
		DR6	Involved in personal injury collision while in violation of 11-902A (1st offense-misd)	11-904.A.1
R		FE2	Involved in personal injury collision while in violation of 11-902A (2nd offense-felony)	11-904 A.2
		EW2	Leave child or vulnerable adult unattended (forget-me-not)	11-1119B
	1	EM1	Leaving vehicle unattended with engine running	11-1101
	2	LC2	Left of center in marked zone	11-307(b)
	2	LC3	Left of center on curve or hill	11-306(a) 1
	2	LC3	Left of center when approaching bridge, viaduct or tunnel	11-306(a) 3
	2	LC3	Left of center when approaching intersection or railroad crossing	11-306(a) 2
R		MR4	Loaning a driver license (misdemeanor)	6-301.1.b
	1	IL4	Making improper entrance to or exit from controlled-access highway	11-312
R		HM2	Manslaughter with a motor vehicle (see 6-205A1)	21.711
DQ		D02	Misrepresentation of CDL application	6-301
R		MR6	Misrepresentation of identity (false presentation)	6-301 2e
		SW2	Move manufacture item without Special Permit / escort	14-103 D
R/DQ		U09	Negligent homicide while operating a CMV	6-205.2 B7
R		HM4	Negligent homicide with a motor vehicle (misdemeanor)	11-903(a)
		MS3	Opening vehicle door into traffic	11-1105
	1	RK2	Operate a motor vehicle at a speed greater or less that reasonable and proper	11-801A
	1	LI5	Operate a motor vehicle loaded so driver's view is obstructed	11-1104(a)
		LP1	Operate a motor vehicle without proper license plate/fail to pay all taxes due state	1134; 1151A.5; 1125; 68:607
		SW2	Operate special combination vehicle without special permit	14-121
		SW7	Operating a motor carrier vehicle without authority	166
		SW8	Operating a motor carrier vehicle without proper identification device	180
		RR5	Operating a motor vehicle with registration plates missing or obscured	1151A.9; 1113A.2
		RT1	Operating a vehicle w/o registering it as required or improper registration	1151 A, B
		DL4	Operating contrary to condition(s)/restriction(s) specified on driver license	6-113D, 6-111D
		SW3	Operating improper combination of vehicles	14-103 C.4; 14-118 D
	1	DE2	Operating with defective/improper brakes	12-301
	1	DE1	Operating with defective/improper headlights	12-203(a),(b),(c)
	1	DE6	Operating with defective/improper light (other than headlight)	12-101
	1	DE3	Operating with defective/improper muffler or exhaust system	12-402
	1	DE4	Operating with defective/improper tires	12-101, 12-405
	1	DL5	Operating without being licensed	6-303A
		DL7	Operating without license required for type of vehicle operated	6-101A
		TP1	Other turnpike violations	11-1401
		SW2	Over-length trailer	14-121
		SW2	Oversize violation	14-101 A C
		SW2	Oversize violation (with or without permits) violation of special permit	14-103A,B,C
		SW2	Oversize violation as auto transporter	14-103 B
		SW2	Oversize violation of manufactured home / industrialized housing	14-130 A
		SW1	Overweight violation	14101 A,C; 14-118G
		SW6	Overweight violation (owner Only – per 14-109 1)	14-109A
	1	PA7	Pass on left of vehicle attempting to turn left	11-604D
	1	PA4	Passing in a No-passing zone	11-307(b)
	1	PA7	Passing on left without sufficient clearance	11-305
	1	SC3	Passing through/around barrier/dividing section / median on divided highway	11-311, 11-1302B
	1	PA1	Passing when view obscured at intersection or railroad crossing	11-306(a) 2
	1	PA1	Passing when view obscured on hill or curve or at bridge	11-306(a) 1
	1	PA3	Passing with insufficient distance allowed for other vehicles or inadequate visibility	11-305
R		LA4	Person not entitled to possession of vehicle	4-103

WA	Pts	VC	Description	Citation
R		AD5	Possession of low point beer - under 21	21:1215
	2	IN2	Public transit driver operating MV while using cell phone or electronic communications device	11-901c
S		FR8	Purchase, display, possess security verification form which is counterfeit, bears altered or fictitious information.	7-612 C.1, C.2
	2	R07	Railroad crossing violation - not specifically covered	11-701
	4	RK1	Reckless driving	11-901A
R		RK9	Reckless driving without regard to safety of person	11-901A
R/DQ		A12	Refusal to submit to test for alcohol	6-205.2
	2	S11	Speeding (11-14 mph over limit)	11-801B,C,E; 11-806.1,2
			(**Note:** 11-806 1 & 2 refer to speeding in construction, school or tollbooth zone)	
	2	S16	Speeding (16-20 mph over limit)	11-801B,C,E; 11-806.1,2
	2	S21	Speeding (21-25 mph over limit)	11-801B,C,E; 11-806.1,2
	3	S26	Speeding (26-30 mph over limit)	11-801B,C,E; 11-806.1,2
	3	S31	Speeding (31-35 mph over limit)	11-801B,C,E; 11-806.1,2
	3	S36	Speeding (36-40 mph over limit)	11-801B,C,E; 11-806.1,2
	3	S41	Speeding (41 + mph over limit)	11-801B,C,E; 11-806.1,2
	2	S51	Speeding 1-10 mph over the limit (only appears if CMV or CDL tickets)	11-801B,C,E; 11-806.1,2
	2	S15	Speeding 15 mph over limit	11-801B,C,E; 11-806.1,2
	2	S99	Speeding in School Zone (Municipal only)	Municipal only
	1	MS9	Spinning wheels (excessive acceleration)	Municipal Ord.
	1	MS1	Starting unsafely from a parked position	11-603
*DQ		M85	Texting While Driving (CDL holder or CMV)	11-901C
R		LA5	Theft of a motor vehicle (felony)	21:1720
		LI3	Throw (deposit) litter from a vehicle upon Highway	21:1753.3 A
		LI2	Throwing from a motor vehicle any burning or smoldering substance	21:1753.3C
R		MR7	To display or possess counterfeit or fictitious driver license	6-301.2.b
	1	EM3	Towing trailer / another vehicle improperly	12-405F;14-106;1133 I
		RT1	Transport cotton modules without License (1st or 2nd offense indicated)	1134.4C
	1	EX3	Transporting hazardous substances w/o safety devices or precautions	12-409
		WE2	Transporting loaded pistol in MV without possessing hand gun permit	21-1289 13A
R		MR0	Unauthorized manufacture of driver license (felony)	6-301.2.a
R		LA3	Unauthorized use of a motor vehicle (felony)	4-102
		AT1	Unauthorized vehicle (all-terrain vehicle - ATV) on highway	11-1116 D
DQ		A04	Under influence .04 or more CMV	6-205.2
	1	TU3	Unsafely turn at an intersection	11-604A
	1	TU6	Unsafely turn to enter private drive	11-604A
*DQ		M86	Using a Hand-held Mobile Device (CDL holder or CMV)	11-901C
R		FE1	Using a motor vehicle in the commission of a felony (authority: 6-205A.3) Including:	Various Statutes
			Allow child in vehicle when driver is impaired or under influence	21:852.1 A.3
			DUI with child in vehicle	21:852.1 A.4
R		A50	Using MV in commission of felony involving CDS	63: chapter 2-various
R		DU4	Using MV in commission of misdemeanor involving CDS	63:2-10 et seq.
R		DU2	Using MV in commission of other felony involving CDS	63:2-101, et seq
R/DQ		U08	Vehicular manslaughter - CMV	6-205.2 B7
		B19	Violate out-of-service order (passenger or haz mat in CMV)	6-205.2
		SW2	Violation of Special Permit	13-103; 14-118 C

Point System Summary

Points range from 1 to 4. Accumulation of 10 points can result in a suspension. 2 points are deducted for each twelve-month period in which there are no convictions of any pointable traffic violations.

Careless driving... 2 Points
Driving wrong way on one way... 2 Points
Failure to obey stop sign or traffic light .... 2 Points
Failure to stop or remain stopped for a school bus loading or unloading .... 4 Points
Failure to yield right of way.. 2 Points
Following too close or improperly .... 2 Points
Left of center... 2 Points
Operating a defective vehicle .... 1 Point
Reckless driving .... 4 Points
Speed.. 2 Points
Speed in excess of 25 mph above posted limit .... 3 Points
Violation of license restriction .... 2 Points
All other violations (excluding the violations requiring suspension or revocation action)....... 1 Point

Oregon

Administration	Important Telephone and Web Contacts
Tom McClellan Administrator Driver and Motor Vehicle Services 1905 Lana Avenue NE Salem 97314 503-945-5000 www.oregon.gov/ODOT/DMV/	Driver Licensing...503-945-5000 Financial Responsibility/SR............................503-945-5400 Commercial Driver License............................503-945-5400 IRV (Interactive)..503-945-5300 Vehicle Information..503-945-5000 State Department of Insurance........................503-947-7980 State Police..503-378-3720 Contacts and Emails www.oregon.gov/ODOT/DMV/contact_us.shtml

Oregon Motor Carrier Laws and Rules:	www.oregon.gov/ODOT/MCT/LAWS.shtml
Oregon Revised Statutes:	www.leg.state.or.us/ors/
Oregon Administrative Rules:	http://arcweb.sos.state.or.us/banners/rules.htm

Driver's License Format, Issuance and Renewal

License Classes, Restrictions and Endorsements Appear After the Driving Record Content Section

License Format

The current format uses seven digits. An older format no longer used was one to seven numbers. License numbers are computer-generated in numeric order. Numbers are eventually recycled after they meet certain specific criteria.

Document Appearance

Oregon DMV has provided digital driver licenses and ID cards since November of 2003

Current Document

Security Features: Tamper-resistant laminate repeats "Oregon" across top; it varies in color depending on the viewing angle and glows under ultraviolet light. Has small "ghost image" of card holder's photo. There is overlapping type and graphics, including an image of the Capitol. The State of Oregon seal overlaps the card holder's photo. Bar-coded information is on the back of the card, and the card contains a digitized signature. Since July 1, 2008, the DMV has been using "facial recognition" software to prevent fraud and identity theft. The procedure is designed to prevent someone from obtaining a driver license or ID card under a false name or under multiple names

Minor Age Drivers: Cards held by minors will bear age notices for alcohol and tobacco vendors. The notices, printed in a red border around the bearer's photo, state "Under 18 until ..." and "Under 21 until ...." Under 18 also has "Provisional License" printed in white inside blue header bar. Also, minors' photos are on the right side of the card instead of on the left.

CDL Indicator: Looks the same as the regular license, except "Commercial Driver License" is in red header bar.

Class C: Standard Class C says "Driver License" in white print within blue header bar.

ID Card: Green header bar with "Identification Card" in white. Card says "Not A License to Drive."

Previous Documents

Appearance: Photographic, credit card style with overlay on the front only.

Security Features: Overlay with repetitive pattern of "OREGON" and gold state seals.

Position of Photo: Upper left.

Minor Age Drivers: All drivers under 18 years of age receive a license stating "PROVISIONAL DRIVER LIC" OR "PROVISIONAL LICENSE." Also "MINOR UNTIL (DATE)" appears on the right side of the license and is printed in red.

CDL Indicator: Classification code and heading across top with "COMMERCIAL DRIVER LICENSE" printed in red.

Issuance

Issuance Facts

The DMV has a centralized issuance of the documents. An interim paper driver license, driver permit, or identification card is provided to the applicant in the field office. After processing and verification has been completed, a secure plastic permanent card is mailed from a separate, centralized location.

As of Jan. 1, 2012, new motorcyclists aged 41 and under must complete an ODOT-approved motorcycle safety course before they can be issued a motorcycle endorsement by DMV. The exception is if the applicant has a valid motorcycle endorsement from another state, then the applicant is required to successfully complete the written knowledge test through the DMV.

Location of Requirements for Proof of Identity:

www.dps.state.ok.us/dls/pub/DOCS.pdf

Age Requirements

The minimum age is 16. Under the Graduated Driver License system, a Student Permit is issued at age 14 under special conditions. An Instruction Permit is issued at 15 and is required prior to issuance of a license, unless applicant is 18 years of age or older. Graduated licensing laws restrict the age and number of passengers that a driver under the age of 18 may have in a vehicle as well as the night time hours when the teenager may drive. Oregonians under 18 years of age who apply for their first driving privileges need to show proof of school attendance, completion of school, or exemption from attendance before DMV will issue a permit or a driver license. Proof of attendance or completion would include a *Statement of Enrollment Form* (available through the local school district or ESD), a diploma, or a GED certificate. If a person is home schooled or exempt from school attendance, he or she needs to obtain the form through the school district or ESD.

Residency

Non-resident's home-state license honored; Oregon license must be secured upon establishing residency. Oregon Revised Statute does not identify a time limit in days that an individual must secure a license or ID Card, however statute does state the circumstances that qualify a person as a resident of Oregon. It is typically a decision made and enforced by law enforcement as to the allowable timeframe for someone to get the license or ID before penalties are given. See ORS 807.062.

Renewal

Licenses are issued for eight years and expire on the person's birthdate. Renewal is not available online, but change of address is. Before the DMV will renew a driver license, an applicant must provide proof of legal presence, full legal name, identity, date of birth, and SSN, if not previously verified. The applicant must also submit proof of current residence address if the address has changed since the previous issuance date. An applicant who needs time to obtain the required proof of legal presence or proof of SSN or to take care of an issue with the Social Security Administration may be issued an Oregon Temporary Driver License/ID Permit up to two times for 90 days each.

Elderly-Related Restrictions

None, other than a vision test required for renewals over age 50.

Vehicle Insurance, Title and Registration Facts

Registration Renewal

Registration is renewed on a bi-annual basis. Renewal may be done online as long as vehicle does not require a DEQ test or registration has been expired more than 75 days. Go to https://www.oregondmv.com/online/index.htm. Renewal information for CMVs is at www.oregon.gov/ODOT/MCT/TOL.shtml.

New Residents

Non-residents must register vehicles upon establishing residency (within 30 days).

Inspections and Emissions Testing

There are no statewide provisions for safety inspections or emission testing of vehicles. However, two geographic areas require bi-annual emission testing: Portland Metro (if vehicle is 1975 or newer) and Medford (if vehicle less than 21 years old).

Passenger Plate Facts

There are two plates with two decals (MO) (YR) on both plates. The state does not employ a county coding system on the plates. Plates remain with vehicle when sold.

Insurance and Financial Responsibility

Oregon has mandatory liability insurance. Financial responsibility minimum limits are $25,000/50,000/20,000. There is a mandatory one-year license suspension for an uninsured driver involved in an accident. The state does not have no-fault insurance. With some exceptions, all motor vehicles registered in the state are required to meet the financial responsibility laws. Proof must be shown at time of drive test, renewal, when an accident occurs or upon a random sampling. SR-22 forms are used.

Withdrawal Sanctions, and Alcohol and Drug Testing

Alcohol and Chemical Testing

Oregon's illegal intoxication level is .08 percent. Breath, blood, and urine testing are authorized. Under Oregon's implied-consent law, drivers' licenses are suspended for failure or refusal of a test. Blood alcohol content levels for administrative suspensions are: Under twenty-one years of age - any amount; commercial vehicle offenses - .04 percent and above; all other operators - .08 percent and above.

Suspensions and Revocations

The state is in compliance with the federally mandated disqualifications on CDLs, see the Appendix for details.

Any of the Following Offenses May Result in a Suspension—
- Attempting to Elude a Police Officer
- Altering Any License or Permit
- Criminal Action of Financial Responsibility
- Exceeding the Speed Limit While Driving 100 MPH or More (In any vehicle, but holding a CML)
- Exceeding the Speed Limit by 30 MPH or More When the Court imposes a Suspension (in any vehicle, but holding a CDL)
- Failure to Appear in Court
- Failure to File an Accident Report as Required by the Law
- Failure to File Financial Responsibility When Required
- Failure to Give Required or Correct Information in the Application
- Failure to Obtain Required Medical Clearance
- Failure to Pay a Fine or Obey a Court Order
- Failure to Pay Child Support
- Failure to Perform Duties When Involved in an Accident Resulting in Property Damage
- Failure to Settle Judgment
- Failure to Take Or Pass Exam Upon Request of the Division
- Knowingly Allowing the Use or Display of (or Permitting Display of) a Fictitious or Altered License or Permit
- Making a Fraudulent Application
- Manufacturing, Possession or Delivery of Controlled Substance
- Permitting Misuse of a License or Permit
- Reckless Driving
- Reckless Endangerment, Criminal Mischief Resulting from the Operation of a Motor Vehicle

- Refusing or Failing a Breath, Blood or Urine Test
- School Enrollment/Expulsion
- Tobacco Offense by Minor
- Too Many Traffic Violations

Any of the Following May Result in License Cancellation—
- Failure to Give Required or Correct Information in the Application
- Person Not Entitled to License or Permit
- Error or Defect Found on the License
- At Request of Parent/Guardian/Employer Who Signed Driver's Application
- Operation of a Motor Vehicle for any Purpose other than one approved under an Emergency Student Driver Permit

Any of the Following May Result in License Revocation—
- Murder, Manslaughter, Criminally-Negligent Homicide, or Assault Resulting from the Operation of Motor Vehicle
- Perjury or Making a False Affidavit to the Division
- Third or Subsequent conviction of DUI
- Felony Convictions Involving the Use of a Motor Vehicle
- Failure to Perform Duties to an Injured Person When Involved in an Accident
- Habitual Offender (see below)

Any of the Following May Result in Court-Ordered Registration Suspension—
- Conviction of Driving While License Suspended or Revoked
- Second or Subsequent Conviction of Driving While Under the Influence of Intoxicants

The Habitual Offender Program

DMV will revoke driving privileges for five years for habitual offender if convicted of 20 or more traffic violations within five years, or if convicted of three or more of the following offenses within a five year period:

- Any degree of murder, manslaughter, criminally negligent homicide, assault, recklessly endangering another person, menacing or criminal mischief resulting from the operation of a motor vehicle.
- Driving while under the influence of intoxicants.
- Driving while your driving privileges are suspended or revoked.
- Reckless driving.
- Failure to perform the duties of a driver after a collision.
- Fleeing or attempting to elude a police officer.

More About Teen Drivers

For drivers under 18 who get: a) two convictions, b) two preventable accidents, or c) one of each, DMV will restrict driving privileges for 90 days to drive only for work purposes with no passengers except a parent, stepparent or guardian. For a third conviction or accident, DMV will suspend the teen's driving privileges for 6 months even if he or she turns 18 years of age during the suspension period. Each subsequent driver improvement violation or preventable accident will suspend driving privileges or right to apply for driving privileges for 6 months, regardless of a previous or current Driver Improvement Program suspension(s).

Reinstatement Requirements

Suspension $75.00 fee; time lapse, determined by reason; proof of financial responsibility (in many cases).

Revocation $75.00 fee; proof of future financial responsibility (in most cases); time lapse, determined by reason; complete licensing test and original fee.

Record Access: Laws, Rules, and Forms

Note: This Section Applies to Both Driver and Vehicle Records.

Governing Statutes and Rules

Oregon Revised Statutes: www.leg.state.or.us/ors/

Oregon Administrative Rules:
http://arcweb.sos.state.or.us/banners/rules.htm

Oregon Motor Carrier Laws and Rules:
www.oregon.gov/ODOT/MCT/LAWS.shtml

Per ORS 802.175-802.191, the state adopted modified provisions of DPPA. Oregon Administrative Rule 735-010-020 through 0200 states which entities may qualify for personal information and the uses of the information. In 2006, significant modifications were made by the legislature to 13(B) below, and changes were also made to the administrative rule set.

As defined in Oregon's Record Privacy Law, personal information means the following information that identifies an individual: Driver License, Driver Permit or Identification Card Number, Name, Address (excluding five-digit ZIP Code), Telephone Number.

Policy Statement Regarding Permissible Uses

Oregon's policy follows ORS 802.179. See selected text below:

(4) The department shall disclose personal information to:

(a) An attorney, a financial institution as defined in ORS chapter 706 or a collection agency registered under ORS 697.031 for use in connection with a civil, criminal, administrative or arbitration proceeding in any court, government agency or self-regulatory body. Permissible uses of personal information under this paragraph include but are not limited to service of process, investigation in anticipation of litigation and the execution and enforcement of judgments and orders.

(b) A process server acting as an agent for an individual for use in serving documents in connection with an existing civil, criminal, administrative or arbitration proceeding, or a judgment, in any court, government agency or self- regulatory body. Nothing in this paragraph limits the activities of a process server when acting as an agent for an attorney, collection agency or like person or for a government agency.

(5) The department shall disclose personal information other than names to a researcher for use in researching health and educational questions and providing statistical reports, as long as the personal information is not published, redisclosed or used to contact individuals. The department may disclose information under this subsection only for research sponsored by an educational institution

or a health research institution.

(6) The department shall disclose personal information to an insurer, an insurance support organization or a self-insured entity in connection with claims investigation activities, antifraud activities, underwriting or rating.

(7) The Department shall disclose personal information regarding ownership or other financial interests in a vehicle to a person who is required by the state or federal Constitution, a statute or an ordinance to give notice to another person concerning the vehicle. Personal information disclosed under this subsection may be used only for giving the required notice. Persons authorized to receive personal information under this subsection include, but are not limited to: (a) Tow companies; (b) Persons who have or are entitled to have liens on the vehicle; and (c) Persons taking an action that could affect ownership rights to the vehicle.

(8) The Department shall disclose personal information to any private security professional certified under ORS 181.878, to be used for the purpose of determining ownership of vehicles parked in a place over which the private security professional, acting within the scope of the officer's employment, exercises control.

(9) The department shall disclose personal information to the employer of an individual who holds a commercial driver license, or the insurer of the employer, to obtain or verify information about the holder of the commercial driver license.

(10) The department shall disclose personal information to the operator of a private toll facility for use in collecting tolls.

(11) The department may not disclose personal information for bulk distributors of surveys, marketing materials or solicitations except as provided in this subsection. The department shall implement methods and procedures to ensure:

 (a) That individuals are offered an opportunity to request that personal information about themselves be disclosed to bulk distributors; and (b) That the personal information provided by the department will be used, rented or sold solely for bulk distribution of surveys, marketing materials and solicitations.

(12) The department shall disclose personal information to a person who requests the information if the requester provides the department with written permission from the individual whose personal information is requested. The written permission from the individual must be notarized.

(13) The Department shall disclose personal information to a person

who is in the business of disseminating such information under the following conditions: (a) In addition to any other requirements under the contract executed pursuant to paragraph (b) of this subsection, the person requesting the information must file a performance bond with the department in the amount of $25,000. The bond must be executed in favor of the State of Oregon and its form is subject to approval by the Attorney General. (b) The disseminator shall enter into a contract with the department. A contract under this paragraph shall contain at least the following provisions: (A) That the disseminator will not reproduce or distribute the personal information in bulk but only in response to an individual record inquiry. (B) That the disseminator will provide the personal information only to a person or government agency authorized to receive the information under this section and only if the person or government agency has been authorized by the Department to receive the information. (C) That the disseminator will have a method of ensuring that the disseminator can delay for a period of up to two days the giving of personal information to a requester who is not a subscriber.

(14) The Department shall disclose personal information to representatives of the news media for the gathering or dissemination of information related to the operation of a motor vehicle or to public safety.

(15) The Department shall disclose personal information as provided in ORS 802.220 (5).

(16) The Department shall adopt rules providing for the release of personal information from motor vehicle records to a person who has a financial interest in the vehicle. Rules adopted under this subsection may include, but need not be limited to, rules establishing procedures for the department to verify the financial interest of the person making the request for personal information.

(17) The Department shall adopt rules providing for the release of personal information from motor vehicle records to a person who is injured by the unsafe operation of a vehicle or who owns property that is damaged because of the unsafe operation of a vehicle.

(18) The department shall disclose personal information to a private investigator licensed by any licensing authority within the State of Oregon, to be used for any purpose permitted any person under this section. A licensed private investigator requesting information must prove to the department that the person has a corporate surety bond, an irrevocable letter of credit issued by an insured institution as defined in ORS 706.008 or such other security as the Department of Public Safety Standards and Training may prescribe by rule in the minimum amount of $5,000 or errors and omissions insurance in the minimum amount of $5,000.

(19) The Department shall disclose personal information to a procurement organization defined in ORS 97.950 for the purpose of facilitating the making of anatomical gifts under the provisions of 97.952.

Request and Consent Forms

Entities and requesters who are eligible to receive personal information must submit a *Request for Information Form* which is found at www.odot.state.or.us/forms/dmv/7122.pdf. Proof of business identity and signature of the requester is required.

Ongoing requesters are encouraged to establish a **Record Inquiry Account** (see the next section). If established, then use of the form is not needed with each inquiry). Personal information is not released unless the requestor qualifies as a permissible user using a *Request for Information Form* and has a Record Inquiry Account or requester presents notarized written consent of the subject.

Vendor and Third Party Access Policy

Approved vendors can resell to other vendors, as long as the 2nd vendor is approved by the DMV and the end user has a permissible user. The authorized recipients of personal information are subject to the redisclosure requirements set forth in ORS 802.181. A person who receives personal information under ORS 802.179 (11) may not resell or redisclose the information except as provided in ORS 802.179. Oregon will sell portions of the driver license (not history) file to commercial vendors. The data can be resold from a database created by a vendor, within limitations set by state statute.

Non-permissible Use Requests

Without consent, there is a sanitized record (no personal information) available.

Access to Driver-Related Records

Driving Records

General Information and Fees

DMV Records Services, 1905 Lana Avenue NE, Salem OR 97314, 503-945-5254, fax 503-945-5425.

http://cms.oregon.gov/ODOT/DMV/Pages/records/index.aspx

The types of records available and fees are listed below.

Non-employment record $1.50: A three-year record including in-state accidents, diversion agreements and convictions, other than those in the employment driving record. $1.50

Open ended non-employment record $1.50: Contains same information as shown on a non-employment record, but is not limited to three years. Available only to insurer or to subject.

Employment driving record $2.00: Certified three-year record of Oregon employment-related convictions and accidents and commercial driver license entries. May contain some out-of-state commercial entries, multiple status entries and miscellaneous administrative entries

Certified Court Print $3.00: A certified court print includes major convictions for 10 years, minor convictions and accidents for 5 years for all driving.

Certified court print with CDL medical certification $3.00: Contains the same information as a certified court print record but includes CDL medical qualifications.

Driver license information $1.50: Includes name, address, license number, date of birth, license type, license issue and expiration dates, original business date, restrictions, endorsements, multiple status entries and ID card expiration date, if applicable. Information may be provided by computer-produced certified print or orally (to account users).

Suspension package $11.50: Certified copies of suspension documents relating to a particular court proceeding. Package includes certified court print. A $3.00 fee is charged for the court print even when there is not a suspension on the individual record.

Add $1.00 to certify any document not already certified. The state's charge for a "no record found" for most reports is $1.50.

A Fee List is shown at www.odot.state.or.us/forms/dmv/6691.pdf.

Note: Oregon law requires the Department (ODOT) to post positive drug test results to the employment driving record of commercial drivers who participate in federally mandated drug testing programs for Motor Carriers. A request for an employment driving record with positive drug test result information must be submitted on the Affidavit to Authorize Release of Employment Driving Record with Positive Drug test Result Information or the employer's waiver form. This form must be completed in full with a signature of the person whose driving record is being requested. A fee of $2.00 must be included with the request. Send the completed form and fee to the address above.

In-Person – This method is only available from field offices. However, field offices must submit all requests to DMV Headquarters for processing. DMV headquarters will mail the record. The service is only available for the following circumstances:

1. Person of record.
2. Parent or guardian of minor (not emancipated) for child's record.
3. A person (but not a business) with notarized power of attorney or permission.
4. Anyone or business can order a record as long as the record is mailed to the person of record (not to the requestor).

Mail – Requests mailed to the state are processed in three-to-five days. The complete name and date of birth must be provided. The fee must accompany the request. **Sanitized records** can only be ordered by mail, from DMV Headquarters in Salem. These records contain no personal information of the subject of the record.

About Record Inquiry Accounts

Entities qualified to receive personal information (as described in the previous section) may be eligible for a DMV Record Inquiry Account. Established account holders may request records via:

- Interactive Voice Response (IVR) system (telephone)
- Online ordering, mail back

Records can be returned by fax or mail.

To obtain an account, one must complete a Record Inquiry Account Application (at www.oregon.gov/ODOT/DMV/forms/records.shtml), submit the documents necessary to prove one qualifies for personal information, and submit a $70.00, non-refundable, application fee. Approved entities are pre-qualified to receive record information. Account holders are billed monthly for records requested, and have access to DMV's Interactive Voice Response System (IVR), see below. Call 503-945-7950 for more information or see http://cms.oregon.gov/ODOT/DMV/pages/records/recinquiry_daveaccts.aspx.

Telephone – IVR (Interactive Voice Response System

Established Record Inquiry Account Holders are approved to receive record information. IVR reads information from computer files in a human-sounding voice. Advantages for IVR users include 24-hour access to certain driver and vehicle record information, and overnight turnaround time for prints ordered through the system. Through IVR, requesters have the following six menu choices:

1. Listen to driver license name and address, description and status.
2. Listen to vehicle description and ownership.
3. Order a three-year non-employment driving record.
4. Order a complete or certified court print driving record.
5. Order a three-year employment driving record.
6. Order a vehicle record print.

Any prints ordered by 7:00 p.m. will be processed overnight and mailed the next business day. There is a 20 percent discount for all drivers license (no history) or vehicle information requests processed through IVR, including "no record found" reports. However, the normal fees apply to all records printed through IVR. IVR is not available to sanitized account holders. For questions about IVR call 503-945-5312.

Online (Record Ordering Only)

DMV Record Inquiry Account holders may submit online requests for driver, tow desk and vehicle records. Records are returned either via fax or first class mail. In general, records requested before 3 PM Monday through Friday are sent by the next business day. See http://cms.oregon.gov/ODOT/DMV/pages/records/request_records.aspx

Electronic Ordering and Receiving Records

The Oregon Department of Administrative Services (DAS) signed an agreement with NIC, Inc. for NIC to provide E-Government services on behalf of Oregon State Agencies.

Effective June 4th 2012, the NIC Oregon affiliate became the designated DMV source for providing electronic driving records to approved entities. The fee for an electronic driving record is $9.68; the no record

found fee is $9.18. At this time no other DMV records are available from this service. For more information about obtaining an account contact the Records Policy Unit at 503-945-7950.

Bulk – Driver and Motor Vehicle Services Branch, Records Policy Unit, 1905 Lana Avenue NE, Salem 97314, 503-945-8906. Oregon will sell all or portions of the driver license (not history) file via FTPS to qualified requesters for limited uses. The data can be resold from a database created by a vendor. The vendor must qualify under OR records privacy laws and enter into a contract with DMV. For more information, write or call.

By Person of Record – OR drivers may obtain their driving record by mail or walk-in as described above. If ordered by mail, the record will be returned to the address on the state computer for that license, unless a myriad of personal information is included with request, including mother's maiden name. At present, there is no program for drivers to order or view their own record online.

Notification/Monitoring Program

The Automated Reporting Service (ARS) Program allows users who have a Record Inquiry Account to submit a name list and DMV will automatically produce a printed driving record whenever a conviction, accident or suspension is posted to the record. There is always a $3.00 fee whenever a record is produced. The maintenance of adding or deleting drivers can be done free of charge via Oregon's online DMV service. But if adding or deleting names is done by the DMV, there is a $2.00 fee per name. For more information about ARS, call 503-945-5427 or email ARS@odot.state.or.us.

Crash Reports

Reporting – An Oregon Traffic Accident and Insurance Report must be filed with DMV within 72 hours when:

- Damage to the vehicle you were driving is over $1,500
- Damage to any vehicle is over $1,500 and any vehicle is towed from the scene as a result of damages from this accident
- Injury or death resulted from this accident
- Damages to any one person's property other than a vehicle involved in this accident are over $1,500
- The owner of the vehicle involved in a reportable accident and the driver fails to report the accident.

This written report must be filed with the DMV, Reporting & Insurance Verification, 1905 Lana Avenue NE, Salem 97314, or local law enforcement. Download an accident report form at www.odot.state.or.us/forms/dmv/32.pdf. The Motor Carrier Crash Report is a part of this form and is required to be completed if there is a loss of life, bodily injury treated away from the accident scene, or if any vehicle was towed from the scene. The full report is sent to DMV, Reporting & Insurance Verification, 1905 Lana Ave NE, Salem, OR 97314, or to local law enforcement

Record Access – Copies of police crash reports filed with DMV can be obtained from the DMV Accidents Reporting Unit, 1905 Lana Avenue NE, Salem 97314, 503-945-5098.

Copies of reports can be requested by Record Inquiry Account Holders or by non-account holders by using the Request for Information Form 7122. The report will be provided without personal information unless the requestor qualifies under Oregon's Privacy Law ORS 802.175-802.191. The fee is $8.50, $9.50 if certified, and turnaround time is usually 5 days plus mail time. It can take up to 3 months for reports to be filed with the DMV. Arrangements may be made only at the time of the request to pick up reports at DMV Headquarters office in Salem.

Copies of an individual's traffic accident report are not available, but information is provided in letter form to the individual family or personal representative. Certification for such a letter is $13.50.

Access to Vehicle-Related Records

General Information and Fees

Record Services Unit, 1905 Lana Avenue NE, Salem OR 97314, 503-945-5254. Personal information is not released unless the requester qualifies as a permissible user by completing a *Request for Information Form* or establishing a Record Inquiry Account. Account holders must first complete a Record Inquiry Account Application and pay the $70 fee. The current fee for vehicle record checks by mail or over-the-counter is $4.00, record information by phone only (IVR) is $2.50.

Other available reports include: vehicle title history, $22.50; previous owner, $14.00; insurance information, $10.00; and odometer history, $25.00 ($2.00 for current, $3.50 for previous).

Add $1.00 to certify any document not already certified. A fee of $2.50 is charged for most no record found items. For ongoing requesters, if a Record Inquiry Account is opened, there is a $70.00 application fee. Call 503-945-7950.

In-Person

This agency does not provide counter service to the public for the purpose of obtaining records.

Mail

Requests are processed in 3 to 5 days. The fee must accompany the request. **Sanitized records** can only be ordered by mail, from DMV Headquarters in Salem. These records contain only the personal information of the person receiving the record. For example, if DMV sends a sanitized vehicle history to John Doe, only John Doe's customer number, name, address, and telephone number will appear on the record. Any other person's personal information will be blocked out. Other information that is not personal, such as odometer readings, will still appear on the record.

About Record Inquiry Accounts

Vehicle records may be requested by an entity approved as a Record Inquiry Account, as described in the Driver-Related Records Section above. The two methods of inquiry are:

1. Telephone (IVR System)
2. Online (ordering only)

For more information, including the web page, refer to the section above or call 503-945-7950.

Electronic Ordering and Receiving

Oregon does not offer online access and retrieval for vehicle records at this time.

Bulk

Driver and Motor Vehicle Services, Records Policy Unit, 1905 Lana Avenue NE, Salem OR 97314, 503-945-8906. Oregon allows qualified entities to obtain name and vehicle information lists via FTPS. Customized selections are available that include vehicle year, make, class, body style, county, zip code, and combinations thereof, for registered vehicles. Output results produce all of the listed data, plus addresses and VINs. Lists based on driver criteria are also available. Call or write for further information.

Access to Vessel-Related Records

General Information, Access and Fees

Oregon State Marine Board, 435 Commercial St NE #400, Salem, OR 97301, 503-378-8587 fax 503-378-4597. www.boatoregon.com.

Titles and registrations are issued on all motorized boats and on sailboats over 12 ft. Title records are available from 1997. Registration records on are microfiche from 1978 to 1998, and on computer from 1999 forward. Lien information is shown on the title record. There is no fee for a registration or lien record search unless lists are presented, copies are $.25 per page if more than 5 pages. The certification fee is $5.00. Single records can be requested by mail, phone, fax, in person, and email. The telephone number and the signature of the requester are required. Mail turnaround time is 7 to 10 days.

Bulk mail lists may be purchased on paper or electronic format. There is an opt-out provision in effect regarding mail list purchases.

Extremely large boats that move along the OR-WA-CA border for 60 days or more are registered with the US Coast Guard. Call 800-799-8362 for more information

Driving Record Content and Reciprocity

What's On or Not On the Driving Record

- As described above there are four different record types, with two versions to each type - one with personal information and one without personal information.
- Parking and passenger offenses, SSNs, maiden names, and places of birth are not reported on the driving record.
- Accidents are reported if damage is more than $1,500 or if there is personal injury. Fault is not determined and only the police report is available to the public, unless authorized by the person who reported the accident. Police reports will not contain personal information.
- The length of time convictions appear on the driving record depends on whether a three or five-year record is ordered. Moving violations and DUIs are shown three or five years; major conviction for ten years.
- Suspensions are shown three or five years after reinstatement; closed suspensions do not show on three-year records.
- The state does not permit driver school attendance in lieu of conviction. There is a diversion program available for first time DUI offenders.

Data Retention

Inactive records are maintained for about ten years. A system purge is run annually (but not at a pre-set time) for inactive records and violations that have met the above time limits. CDL driver records are purged based on the timetable per the MCSIA (see the Appendix).

Court to Repository

Convictions are batch-processed from "Uniform Traffic Citation" for input into the computer system. The mandated time for convictions to be sent to DMV is twenty-four hours from the time of conviction but there is no time limit for the DMV data entry.

State Reciprocity for Non-CDL Drivers

- Will suspend license of driver for unpaid out-of-state convictions only with Washington.
- Record of new incoming driver's major or criminal convictions is shown on MVR.
- Out-of-state convictions are shown on MVR.
- Out-of-state accidents are NOT shown on MVR.
- Only major convictions of out-of-state drivers are sent to home state.
- Record is forwarded to new state upon surrender of license only upon request.

Codes for License Classes, Restrictions, Endorsements, and Status

License Classes– Commercial -

Oregon began issuing the CDL in April of 1990.

CDL-A   Any vehicle or combination of vehicles with the proper endorsement.

CDL-B   Any single vehicle with the proper endorsements. May tow a trailer up to 10,000 pounds GVWR. If the trailer has a GVWR of more than 10,000 pounds, the gross weight of the combination (towing vehicle and trailer) must be less than 26,001 pounds.

CDL-C   Any single vehicle with proper endorsements which does not weigh more than 26,001 pounds and is designed to transport sixteen or more passengers or hazardous materials.

PCDL   CDL instruction permit.

License Classes– Non-Commercial

C   Any single vehicle with proper endorsements weighing less than 26,001 pounds. Includes mopeds, vehicles designed to carry fewer than 16 passengers including driver, a motor home for personal use and any fire or emergency vehicle. May tow another vehicle with a loaded weight of 10,000 pounds or less. May also tow another vehicle over 10,000 pounds if the combined weight of the towing vehicle and trailer is not more than 26,001 pounds.

C   (Restricted) may only operate mopeds or person has student permit, emergency permit, or disabled golf cart permit.

PC   Class C non-commercial instruction permit.

PM   Motorcycle instruction permit.

LVIP   Limited Vision instruction permit.

Restrictions

2	Emergency Driver Permit; Issued to Persons at Least Fourteen Years of Age or Older	F	Outside Mirrors
3	Student Driver Permit; Issued to Persons at Least Fourteen Years of Age or Older	G	Daylight Driving only
		J	Other (Restriction letter maybe carried by license holder)
4	Disability Golf Cart Permit; Issued to Allow a Disabled-Person to Drive a Golf Cart on Restricted Routes	K	CDL Intrastate only
		L	Vehicle Without Air-Brakes (on CDLs only)
5	Limits an Individual to the Driving of Mopeds Only	M	No Class A Passenger Vehicles
8	Emancipated Minor	N	No Class A or B Passenger Vehicles
B	Wear Corrective Lenses	R	Hand-Operated Controls
D	Anatomical Donor	S	Turn Signals
E	Automatic Transmission	U	With Prosthetic Aid
		V	Federal CDL Medical Variance

Endorsements

H	(CDL) Hazardous Materials/Placards	S	(CDL)	School Bus
M	Motorcycle Endorsement for any Motorcycle Regardless of Displacement	T	(CDL)	Double-/Triple-Trailers
		X	(CDL)	Combination H and N
N	(CDL) Tank Vehicles	Y		Farm Endorsement for Class A Type License
P	(CDL) Sixteen or More Passengers	Z		Farm Endorsement for Class B Type License

Other Important Abbreviations Found on Driving Records

Additional Abbreviations Used in Status Field

APRD   Driver appeared in court on fail to appear suspension. No longer used.

BUS   Driving privileges partially reinstated. Hardship/Probationary permit issued.

RCV   DMV received the accident report form the driver

RC/H   Action is rescinded pending a hearing

CPLY   DMV was notified that driver complied with the requirements of the court

RND   Judgment was rendered by court against a driver

SAT   DMV received court documents satisfying the judgment.

REL   Indicates the date the driver was released from prison or was placed on parole or post-prison supervision for purposes of calculating reinstatement requirements.

VCTED   Action is vacated and has no effect on the person's driving record

Abbreviations Used in Accident Entry Fields

Type of Accident: 1 = One other vehicle. 2 = Three or more other vehicles. 3 =Pedestrian. 4 = Train. 5 = Motorized scooter. 6 = Bicycle. 8 = Animal. 9 = Light rail "MAX". X = Fixed object/property damage. R = Non-collision. P = Police report filed. * = Police report filed, fatal accident.

CMV   Commercial Motor Vehicle indicator

HAZ   CMV was carrying hazardous materials

Abbreviations Used in Driver Improvement Fields

PROV DI REST   **Provisional DI Restriction:** Driver is under 18 years old and received two convictions, two accidents or a combination of one conviction and one accident. Driving privileges restricted for 90 days to and from, or for, employment with no passengers except parent, stepparent or guardian.

ADULT DI REST   **Adult DI Restriction:** Driver is 18 years old or older and received three convictions, three accidents or a combination that totals three, in an 18-month period. Driving privileges restricted for 30 days to prohibit driving between midnight and 5 a.m. except to and from, or for, employment.

Abbreviations Used in CDL Medical Qualification Fields

UNKNOWN	A medical certificate has not yet been requested by DMV and medical certificate information is not available.
NOT QUALIFIED	The person is not qualified for issuance or retention of a CDL. Medical qualification has expired, person is no longer medically qualified after changing driving type or the person did not respond to a request to submit proof of medical qualification.
INTERSTATE	The person meets the medical qualification for all driving types.
INTERSTATE W/COR LENSES	The person meets the medical qualification for all driving types provided corrective lenses are worn.
INTERSTATE W/HEAR AID	The person meets the medical qualification for all driving types provided a hearing aid is worn.
INTERSTATE W/COR LENSE &HEAR AID	The person meets the medical qualification for all driving type provided corrective lenses and a hearing aid are worn.
INTERSTATE W/49 CFR 391.64EXEMPTION	The person meets the medical qualifications for all driving types provided the exemption letter is carried.
INTERSTATE W/COR LENS &49 CFR 391.64 EXEMPTION	The person meets the medical qualifications for all driving types provided corrective lenses are worn and the exemption letter is carried.
INTERSTATE W/HEAR AID &49 CFR 391.64 EXEMPTION	The person meets the medical qualifications for all driving types provided a hearing aid is worn and the exemption letter is carried.
INTERSTATE W/COR LENSHEAR AID & 49 CFR 391.64 EXEMPTION	The person meets the medical qualifications for all driving types provided corrective lenses and hearing aid are worn and the exemption letter is carried.
INTRASTATE	The person meets the medical qualifications for intrastate or excepted interstate, CMV operation only. A CDL with a 'K' restriction may be issued.

Conviction Abbreviations with Statute and ACD Translation

(A Suspensions, Revocations, and Cancellations Table Follows)

Literal	ORS Cite	Description	ACD
A DNG OP A/S	821250	Permitting Dangerous Operation Of A Snowmobile Or An ATV	
A MISUSE DL	807590	Permitting Misuse Of License	
A MISUSE ID	807430	Permitting The Misuse Of An Identification Card	
A OP NREG VH	803320	Permitting Unlawful Operation Of An Unregistered Vehicle	
A UNL OP VH	811255	Permitting Unlawful Operation Of A Vehicle	
ABAND VH	819100	Abandoning A Vehicle	
AGG DWS/DWR	C783	Aggravated Driving While Suspended Or Revoked	
ALT POL EQ	815305	Unlawful Disconnection Or Alteration Of Pollution Control Equipment	
ALT/I DS PLT	803550	Alteration Of, Or Illegal Display Of Plates	
ASSAULT MV 1	163185	Assault In The First Degree	U06
ASSAULT MV 2	163175	Assault In The Second Degree	U06
ASSAULT MV 3	163165	Assault In The Third Degree	U06
ASSAULT MV 4	163160	Assault In The Fourth Degree	U06
ASSLT B/P MV	811060	Assault On A Bicyclist Or Pedestrian	
ATT ASSAULT	163185	Attempted Assault (136.460)	
ATT DWS/DWR	811182	Attempted Criminal Driving While Suspended	
BLK DISBL PK	811617	Blocking A Parking Space Reserved For Disabled Persons	
C DOG EXT VH	811200	Carrying A Dog On External Part Of Vehicle	F05
C MNR EXT VH	8112051	Carrying Minor In Open Bed Or On External Part Of Vehicle	F05
C PAS MS	814530	Carrying A Passenger On A Motor Assisted Scooter	
CAR TFT 1	164055	Theft Of A Vehicle In The First Degree	U03
CAR TFT 2	164045	Theft Of A Vehicle In The Second Degree	U04
CARELESS DR	811135	Careless Driving	M81
CMV ALCOHOL	F3925	Possession/Consumption Of Intoxicating Beverage	A31
CMV DEF EQ	F3931-F39394	Defective Equipment	
CMV DR HRS	F3953	Driving And On-Duty Time	
CMV EM EQ	F39395	Emergency Equipment	E01
CMV HAZ	F3971	Admin. Rule Adopts North American Uniform Hazardous Material Out-Of-Service Criteria	E03
CMV HAZ ATND	F3975	Attendance And Surveillance Of Motor Vehicles	
CMV LOG BK	F3958	Driver's Record Of Duty Status	
CMV MED CERT	F39145	Medical Certification	B65
CMV UNSF LD	F393105-F393136	Unsafe Load. "Cite Also Includes f393.100, f393.101 and f393.103	
CMVP O/SVC	825.990(2)	Violation Of Out-Of-Service Notice; Passenger Vehicle Designed For 16 Or More People Including The Driver	B19
COASTING	811495	Unlawful Coasting On A Downgrade	N80
CRIM MIS MV1	164365	Criminal Mischief In The 1st Degree	U03
CRIM MIS MV2	164354	Criminal Mischief In The 2nd Degree	M80

Literal	ORS Cite	Description	ACD
CRIM MIS MV3	164345	Criminal Mischief In The 3rd Degree	M80
CRIM TRES MV	164245	Criminal Trespass In The Second Degree	M80
CRS CTR LINE	811310	Crossing The Center Line On A Two-Way, Four-Lane Road	M57
CRS PP INTR	L O	Local Ordinance; Crossing Private Property To Avoid An Intersection	
CS UNR NS VH	815025	Causing Unreasonable Noise With A Vehicle	
CTRL SUB	809413	CDL Holder Using A Non-CMV While Committing A Felony Offense Involving The Manufacturing, Distributing Or Dispensing Of A Controlled Substance (475.840-475.894)r	A50
CTRL SUB CMV	809413	Using a CMV While Committing a Felony Offense Involving The manufacturing, Distributing Or Dispensing Of A Controlled Substance (475.840-475.894)	A50
D PST WARN	811530	Failure To Post Warnings For A Disabled Vehicle	
DNG LFT TRN	811350	Dangerous Left Turn	N53
DNG MVMT VH	811565	Dangerous Movement Of A Stopped, Standing Or Parked Vehicle	N84
DNG OP A/S	821290	Dangerous Operation Of A Snowmobile Or An All-Terrain Vehicle	
DNG OP LVSTK	811510	Dangerous Operation Around Livestock	N02
DR F RPT AC	811725	Driver failed To File An Accident Report With Dmv Or Law Enforcement	B61
DR HWY DIV	811430	Driving On A Highway Divider	M51
DR O/SVC	825990	Violation Of Out Of Service Notice; Driver.	B27
DR ON BEACH	L O	Local Ordinance: Driving On Beach	
DR ON LFT	811305	Driving On The Left On A Curve Or Grade Or At An Intersection Or Rail Crossing	M76
DR ON SW	L O	Local Ordinance: Driving On Sidewalk	M58
DR SFT ZONE	811030	Driving Through A Safety Zone	M12
DR UNINS	806010	Driving Uninsured	D36
DR V SFT CDE	820070	Driver Violation Of Worker Transport Vehicle Safety Code	N84
DR WW TF ISL	811330	Driving The Wrong Way Around A Traffic Island	N60
DSRPT FUPRO	811810	Disrupting A Funeral Procession	N05
DUII	813010	Driving While Under The Influence Of Intoxicants	A20
DUII BYC	813010	Driving While Under The Influence Of Intoxicants	
DWR	811182	Criminal Driving While Revoked	B25
DWR-VC	811175	DWR (811.182r) Criminal Driving While Revoked - Violation	B25
DWR-VI	811175	Infraction Driving While Revoked	B25
DWS	811182	Criminal Driving While Suspended	B26
DWS-VC	811175	DWR (811.182r) Criminal Driving While Revoked – Violation	B26
DWS-VI	811175	Infraction Driving While Suspended	B26
END ATV OP	821292	Endangering A Class I or Class III ATV Operator	
END ATV OP/P	821203 811210 2011 Leg	Endangering a Class I, II, III, or IV ATV Operator Or Passenger -Or-Failure To Properly Secure Child Passenger On Class I or Class II ATV	
END CHD PAS	811210	Endangering Child Passenger; Failure To Use Safety Belts	F02
END MC PAS	814280	Endangering A Motorcycle Passenger	F03
END MS OP	814536	Endangering A Motor Assisted Scooter Operator	N84
END OP ATV	821291 (2011 Leg)	Endangering An Operator Of A Class I or Class IV ATV	
ENG BRK	811492	Unmuffled Engine Braking	E70
EXC SP FUPRO	811806	Exceeding The Maximum Speed For A Funeral Procession	S92
EXC TIRE NS	L O	Local Ordinance: Excessive Tire Noise	
F C OS ATV P	821142	Failure To Carry Out-Of-State ATV Permit	
F C OS SNO P	821140	Failure To Carry Out-Of-State Snowmobile Permit	
F C PRF INS	806012	Fail To Carry Proof Of Compliance With Financial Responsibility Requirements	B74
F C REG	803505	Failing To Carry Registration Card	
F C WARN DVC	815285	Failure To Carry Roadside Vehicle Warning Devices	E01
F CD CDL PLC	807570	Failure To Carry/Present (Display) Commercial License To Police Officer	B57
F CD DL PLC	807570	Failure To Carry/Present (Display) License To A Police Officer	B51
F CH N/AD DL	807560	Failure To Notify The Division Upon Change Of Driver Name/Address	
F CH N/AD ID	807420	Failure To Notify Division On Change Of Identification Card Holder Name/Address	
F CH N/AD VH	803220	Failure To Notify DMV Of Name/Address Change	
F D MH PLT	820550	Failure To Display Mobile Home Registration Plate	
F D OS PLT	803545	Failure To Display, Or Improper Display Of Out Of State Registration Plates	
F D PLT	803540	Failure To Display Registration Plates	
F DES ASM VH	803225	Failure To Designate An Assembled, Specially Constructed Vehicle	
F DLV VH DOC	803105	Failure To Deliver Vehicle Documents On Transfer	
F DR IN LN	811370	Failure To Drive Within A Lane	M42
F DR RT	811295	Failure To Drive On The Right	M41
F DR RT A/VH	811300	Failure To Drive On The Right Of An Approaching Vehicle	M41
F DR RT HWY	811320	Failure To Drive To The Right On A Divided Highway	M41
F DR RT LN	811325	Failure To Keep Camper, Trailer Or Truck In The Right Lane	M41
F DR Y RD	811280	Failure Of Driver Entering Roadway To Yield Right Of Way	N06
F EQ POL EQ	815295	Failure To Be Equipped With Required Pollution Control Equipment	E01

Literal	ORS Cite	Description	ACD
F FL ACC	806200	Failure To File After Accident	B63
F FL F VER	806220	Failure To File After Failing Verification	B64
F FLW RR PRC	811460	Failure To Follow Rail Crossing Procedures For High-Risk Vehicles	M22
F IN/USE IID	813602	Failure To Install/Use An IID.	A41
F INSP XV MR	815237	Failure To Inspect 'Forward Crossview Mirror'	E01
F MAINT S/BL	811225	Failure To Maintain Seat Belts In Working Order	
F MK END LD	815275	Failure To Mark End Of Load With Light Or Flag When Required	
F MNT SD EVA	811147	Failure To Maintain A Safe Distance From An Emergency Vehicle Or Ambulance	M32
F MRG DR Y	811285	Failure Of Merging Driver To Yield Right Of Way	N06
F NOT CND VH	819018	Failure To Notify A Subsequent Purchaser Of The Condition Of A Vehicle	
F OB NEW VIN	819420	Failure To Obtain A Vehicle Id Number For A Vehicle With An Altered Number	
F OB VIN	819410	Failure To Obtain A Vehicle Identification Number For An Unnumbered Vehicle	
F OBEY 1WAY	811270	Failure To Obey A One-Way Designation	N63
F OBEY HOVL	810140	Fail To Obey Traffic Control Device; Exclusive Use; High Occupancy Vehicle Lane	M49
F OBEY PLC	811535	Failing To Obey A Police Officer	M08
F OBEY TCD	811265	Failure To Obey Traffic Control Device	M14
F OBEY TF PT	811015	Failure To Obey A Traffic Patrol Member	N08
F PAY FEE	803315	Failure To Pay Appropriate Registration Fee	
F PFM DR	811700	Failure To Perform The Duties Of A Driver When Property Is Damaged	B04
F PFM DR INJ	811705	Failure To Perform The Duties Of A Driver To Injured Persons	B03
F PFM INJ AN	811710	Failure To Perform The Duties Of A Driver When An Animal Is Injured	
F PFM WIT	811715	Failure To Perform The Duties Of A Witness To An Accident	
F PR USE S/B	811210	Failure To Properly Use Safety Belt	F04
F PRC TLD VH	819012	A Person, Other Than An Insurer Failing, Failed To Follow Procedures For A Totaled Vehicle	
F REG MH	820540	Failure To Register Mobile Home	
F REG VH	803300	Failure To Register A Vehicle	
F RM INJ SUB	822225	Tow Vehicle Operator Failure To Remove Injurious Substance	
F RMV MV HWY	811717	Failure To Remove A Motor Vehicle From The Highway After An Accident	F34
F RNW SNO	821110	Failure To Renew Snowmobile Registration	
F RNW VH REG	803455	Failure To Renew Vehicle Registration	
F RTRN DL	809500	Failure To Return A Suspended, Revoked Or Cancelled License	
F RTRN ID	807430	Failure To Return A Cancelled Identification Card (809.500)	
F RTRN S/REG	809080	Failure To Return Suspended Registration	
F S/RS B PED	811035	F Stop/Remain Stopped For Blind Ped	N08
F S/RS PED	811028	Failure To Stop And Remain Stopped For A Pedestrian	N08
F S/RS TF/PT	811015	Failure To Stop/ And Remain Stopped For A Traffic Patrol Member	M13
F SEC VH	811585	Failure To Secure A Motor Vehicle	
F SIG LT RQ	811405	Failure To Signal With Lights When Required	N40
F SIG MS	814522	Failure To Signal For A Motor Assisted Scooter Maneuver	
F SLW DR RT	811315	Failure Of Slow Driver To Drive On Right	M60
F SLW DR Y	811425	Failure Of A Slow Driver To Yield To Overtaking Vehicle	N07
F STP BUS	811155	Failure To Stop For Bus Safety Lights	M75
F STP DRVWY	811505	Failure To Stop When Emerging From An Alley, Driveway Or Building	M25
F STP PAS LD	811165	Failure To Stop For Passenger Loading Of Public Transit Vehicle	N06
F STP RR	811455	Failure To Stop For A Railroad Signal	M10
F SUBM CERT	803440	Failure To Submit Certificate Of Weight	
F SUBM ODM	815425	Failure To Submit An Odometer Disclosure	
F SUR DL	807540	Failure To Surrender A Prior License	
F SUR FM PLT	805360	Failure To Surrender Farm Registration Plates	
F SUR OS REG	803380	Failure To Surrender Out Of State Registration	
F TTL SNO	821070	Failure To Title A Snowmobile	
F USE BYC LN	814514	Failure Of A Motor Assisted Scooter To Use A Bicycle Lane Or Path	
F USE SIG	811400	Failure To Use Appropriate Signal For Turn, Lane Change, Or Stop	N43
F USE TRACT	815140	Failure To Use Vehicle Traction Tires Or Traction Devices	E57
F USE TRN LN	811345	Failure To Use Special Left Turn Lane	N52
F VIOL FR FL	806230	Failure Of A Previous Violator To Make Future Responsibility Filing	D35
F Y A/EV	811145	Failure To Yield To An Emergency Vehicle Or Ambulance	N04
F Y BYC LN	811050	Failure To Yield To A Rider On A Bicycle Lane	N03
F Y BYC SW	811055	Failure To Yield Right Of Way To Bicyclist On A Sidewalk	N03
F Y FUPRO	811802	Failure To Yield The Right Or Way To A Funeral Procession	N05
F Y PED SW	811025	Failure To Yield To A Pedestrian On A Sidewalk	N08
F Y RNDABOUT	811292	Failure To Yield Right Of Way Within A Roundabout	N21
F Y TF PT	811017	Failure To Obey A Traffic Patrol Member	N08
F Y UNC INTR	811275	Failure To Yield Right Of Way At An Uncontrolled Intersection	N25
F Y UNC TINT	811277	Failure To Yield At Uncontrolled T Intersection	
F YLD RW HWK	811233	Failure To Yield The Right Of Way To A Highway Worker Who Is A Pedestrian	N08

Literal	ORS Cite	Description	ACD
F/C RQ DEST	819010	Failure To Comply With Requirement For Destruction Of Vehicle	
F/D LT MP/MC	814320	Failure To Display Lighted Headlights On A Moped Or Motorcycle At All Times	E55
F/D SNO REG	821120	Failure To Properly Display Snowmobile Registration Numbers	
F/P DUT A*	811705	Failure To Perform Duties Of A Driver Involved In A Fatal Accident	B02
F/S CC FR	806300	Failure To Surrender license And Registration On Cancellation Of Future Responsibility	
F/S CC R/TTL	809110	Failure To Surrender Cancelled Registration Or Title	
F/SLOW CK RR	811462	Failure Of Commercial Motor Vehicle Operator To Slow And Check Tracks For Train	M20
FL/AT ELUDE	811540	Fleeing Or Attempting To Elude A Police Officer (Changed From Elude)	U01
FLS APP DL	807530	False Application For A Driver License	D02
FLS APP ID	807430	False Application For An Identification Card	
FLS APP REG	803375	False Application For Vehicle Registration	
FLS APP TTL	803070	False Statement On Application For Title/Transfer	
FLS CERT FR	806050	Knowingly Certifying Falsely To Existence Of Liability Insurance or Other Means	
FLS EXMPT FR	806030	False Certification Of Exemption From Financial Responsibility	
FLS FR	806050	Falsification Of Financial Responsibility	
FLS INFO INS	806055	Giving False Information About Liability Insurance To A Police Officer	D78
FLS INFO PLC	807620	Giving False Information To A Police Officer	D78
FLS SWR DL	807520	False Swearing To Receive A Driver License	D02
FLS SWR FM	805370	False Swearing On Farm Registration Or Renewal	
FLS SWR REG	803385	False Swearing Relating To Registration Of Vehicle	
FLS SWR TTL	803075	False Swearing Relating To Titling Of Vehicle	
FLW TOO CLS	811485	Following Too Closely	M34
FORG TTL REG	803230	Forging, Altering, Or Unlawfully Producing/Using Vehicle Title Or Registration	
FRN VH N IID	813608	Furnishing a vehicle without an IID to someone who is not authorized to drive	
FTY RW TBUS	811167	Failure To Yield The Right Of Way To A Transit Bus	N06
FU VH IMP LT	811800	Operation Of A Funeral Escort Vehicle With Improper Lights	E55
FY UNC INTR	811275	Failure To Yield Right Of Way At An Uncontrolled T Intersection	
HAZ O/SVC	825990(2)	Violation Of Out Of Service Notice; Hazardous Waste	B19
HOLD MULT DL	807550	Holding Multiple Licenses	D07
HT/HR AN A/S	821260	Hunting Or Harassing Animals From A Snowmobile Or An All-Terrain Vehicle	
I A/EV SIREN	820380	Illegal Ambulance Or Emergency Vehicles Sirens	
I ALT MP	814310	Illegal Alteration Of A Moped	
I AMB LT EQ	820360	Illegal Ambulance Lighting Equipment	E05
I BCKG	811480	Illegal Backing	N82
I D BUS MK	820160	Illegal Display Of School Bus Markings	
I ODM TAMP	815410	Illegal Odometer Tampering	
I OP EV/AMB	820320	Illegal Operation Of An Emergency Vehicle Or An Ambulance	N84
I SLV PRC	819040	Illegal Salvage Procedures	
I U-TRN	811365	Illegal U-Turn	N56
I WDW TNT	815222	Illegal Window Tinting	
IL OP A/S	821190	Illegal Operation Of ATV/Snowmobile	
IMP CERT POL	815315	Use Of Improper Certificate For Pollution Control System	
IMP CTR LN	811380	Improper Use Of Center Lane On A Three Lane Road	M40
IMP D DE PLT	822045	Improper Display Of Dealer Plates	
IMP D P	803655	Improper Display Of Permit	
IMP D STKR	803560	Improper Display Of Validating Stickers	
IMP DE PLT	822045	Improper Use Of Dealer Plates	
IMP DIS HWAS	811172	Improperly Disposing Of Human Waste	
IMP EQ ATV	821220	Operating An Improperly Equipped All-Terrain Vehicle	
IMP EQ SNOW	821210	Improperly Equipped Snowmobile	
IMP FNDR/MG	815185	Operation Without Proper Fenders Or Mudguards	E01
IMP LFT TRN	811340	Improperly Executing A Left Turn	N53
IMP LT ATV	821230	Operating An All-Terrain Vehicle Without Proper Lighting Equipment	
IMP MVMT RR	811470	Improper Movement Of Heavy Equipment Across A Rail Crossing	
IMP OP MS HW	814518	Improper Operation Of A Motor Assisted Scooter On A Highway	
IMP OP MS LN	814520	Improper Operation Of A Motor Assisted Scooter In A Lane	
IMP OPN DOOR	811490	Improper Opening Or Leaving Open A Vehicle Door	
IMP RT TRN	811355	Improperly Executed Right Turn	N54
IMP TRN S/LT	811360	Improper Turn At A Stop Light	N50
IMP TRNS PLT	822315	Improper Use Of Vehicle Transporter Plates	
IMP USE TEMP	803635	Improper Use Of Temporary Registration Permit	
IMPED TF	811130	Impeding Traffic	S96
INTFR A/EV	811150	Interference With An Emergency Vehicle Or Ambulance	N04
INTFR STRCAR	811160	Interference With Streetcar Operation	N84
INTFR TCD/RR	810240	Unlawful Interference With A Traffic Control Device Or Railroad Sign	
INV DISBL PK	811627	Use Of An Invalid Disabled Person Parking Permit	

Literal	ORS Cite	Description	ACD
M SP LTRN LN	811346	Misuse Of A Special Left Turn Lane	M62
MANSL 1	163118	Manslaughter, First Degree	U08
MANSL 2	163125	Manslaughter, Second Degree	U08
MC CLING	814220	Motorcyclist Clinging To Another Vehicle	
MENACING MV	163190	By Word Or Conduct, Places Another In Fear Of Imminent Serious Injury	M80
MIN OP BUS	820190	Minor Operating A School Vehicle	B51
MIN OP PPVH	820200	Minor Operating A Public Passenger Vehicle	B51
MISUSE ID	807430	Misuse Of Identification Card	
MISUSE PLAC	811630	Misuse Of Program Placard	
MP/MC OP 2+	814250	Moped Or Motorcycle Operating More Than Two Abreast	N84
MP/MC UNL PS	814240	Motorcycle Or Moped Unlawfully Passing In A Lane With A Vehicle	M48
MURDER MV	163005	Criminal Negligence Causing Death	U07
MV FELONY	809409	Felony Conviction With A Material Element Involving The Operation Of A Motor Vehicle	U03
N HELMET ATV	821202	Failure Of A Class I Or Class III ATV Rider To Wear Protective Headgear	
N HELMET MC	814269	Failure Of A Motorcycle Operator To Wear Protective Headgear	F03
N HELMET MP	814260	Failure Of A Moped Rider To Wear Protective Headgear	F03
N HELMET MS	814534	Failure Of A Motor Assisted Scooter Operator To Wear Protective Headgear	F03
N LN MP/MC	811385	Depriving A Motorcycle Or Moped Of A Full Lane	M48
N PUC	825100	Operating Without Certificate Or Permit From Dept Of Transportation	
N RVW MIR	815235	No Rearview Mirror, Defective Rearview Mirror	E01
N TRIP P MH	820570	Moves A Manufactured Structure On A Highway Without A Trip Permit	
N/IMP BRK	815130	Driving Or Allowing Operation Of A Vehicle Without Brakes That Meet Requirement	E02
N/IMP WPR	815215	Failure To Have Windshield Wipers; Failure To Meet Windshield Wiper Requirement	E01
NEG HOM	163145	With Criminal Negligence, Causes Death	U07
OBS CRS TF	811290	Obstructing Cross Traffic	F34
OBS RR/LW VH	811475	Obstructing A Rail Crossing Due To Insufficient Undercarriage Clearance (Low Commercial Motor Vehicle)	M24
OBS RR/N SPC	811475	Obstructing A Rail Crossing Due To Insufficient Space On The Other Side To Accommodate The CMV	M23
OBS VH WDW	815220	Obstruction Of Vehicle Windows	D70
OC F RPT AC	811735	Occupant Of A Vehicle Failed To File An Accident Report With DMV Or Law Enforcement	B61
OP A/S C WPN	821240	Operating A Snowmobile Or All-Terrain Vehicle While Carrying A Firearm Or Bow	
OP ATV N P/D	821195	Operating An ATV Without A Permit And A Decal	
OP ATV PR AR	821295	Operating A Class Ii Or Class III All-Terrain Vehicle In A Prohibited Snow Area	
OP ATV RS AR	821192	Illegal Operation Of An ATV In A Restricted Area.	
OP CMV N CDL	807010	Operating A Commercial Motor Vehicle Without Commercial Driving Privilege	B56
OP I WDW TNT	815222	Operating A Vehicle With Illegal Window Tinting	
OP MP SW/TR	814210	Operation Of A Moped On A Sidewalk Or Bicycle Trail	
OP MS CRSW	814528	Operation Of A Motor Assisted Scooter In A Crosswalk	
OP MS UNL LD	814532	Operating A Motor Assisted Scooter With An Unlawful Load	
OP MV BYC TR	811435	Operation Of A Motor Vehicle On A Bicycle Trail	
OP N ATV PRV	821170	Operation Of A Class I Or Class III ATV Without Driving Privileges	
OP N EXH SYS	815250	Operation Without Proper Exhaust System	E01
OP N LT EQ	816330	Operation Without Required Lighting Equipment	E05
OP N MC ENDS	807010	Operating A Motorcycle Without The Proper Endorsement	B91
OP N REG SNO	821100	Operation Of An Unregistered Snowmobile	
OP N SN PRIV	821150	Operation Of A Snowmobile Without Driving Privileges	
OP NST LT EQ	816300	Operation With Nonstandard Lighting Equipment	
OP ORVH N EQ	821040	Operation Of Off-Road Vehicle Without Required Equipment	E01
OP RV U/DISP	815260	Operation Of A Recreational Vehicle With Unsealed Disposal System	
OP SMVH PR A	820220	Operation Of Low Speed Vehicle In Prohibited Area	
OP UNSF VH	815020	Operation Of An Unsafe Vehicle	F66
OP V EQ OAR	815100	Operation Of A Vehicle That Violates State Equipment Administrative Rules	
OP V GC REST	807210	Operating A Golf Cart In Violation Of Permit Restrictions (Driving In An Area With A Speed Designation Greater Than 25 MPH)	D29
OP V MBL DEV	811507	Offense For Using Mobile Communication Devise While Operating Motor Vehicle	M86
OP V REST	807010	Operating A Vehicle In Violation Of License Restrictions	D29
OP VH N DL	807010	Operating A Vehicle Without Driving Privileges	B51
OP VH N WDW	815210	Operation Of A Vehicle Without Approved Materials In Windows	E70
OP VHH N SPM	815255	Operation Of Vehicle For Hire Without Speedometer	E01
ORG SP RACE	811127	Organizing A Speed Racing Event	S95
OW F RPT AC	811730	Owner Failure To Report An Accident	B61
OW V SFT CDE	820060	Owner Violation Of Worker Transport Vehicle Safety Code	N84
P/USE OS VH	803325	Purchase And Use Of Out Of State Registered Vehicle	
PAS IN TRLR	811195	Passenger In Trailer	E70
PAS OBS DR	811190	Driver Operation With Obstructing Passenger	D70

Literal	ORS Cite	Description	ACD
PF/P USE S/B	811210	Passenger Failure To Properly Use Seat Belt	
POSS STLN VH	819300	Possession Of A Stolen Vehicle	
PROV CURFEW	807010	Provisional Violation Of Curfew Restrictions	D29
PROV PASS 1	807010	Provisional Violation Of Passenger Restrictions In First Six Months	D29
PROV PASS 2	807010	Provisional Violation Of Passenger Restrictions In Second Six Months	D29
PROV SBLT	811210	Provisional Failure To Use Seat Belt	F04
PS N/PS ZONE	811420	Passing In A No Passing Zone	M71
PS VH CRSWK	811020	Passing A Stopped Vehicle At A Crosswalk	M71
R END H/WKR	811231	Reckless Endangerment Of A Highway Worker	M84
R/OBEY FLGR	811232	Refusing To Obey Flagger In A Highway Work Zone	M04
RECK DR	811140	Reckless Driving	M84
RECK END MV	163195	Recklessly Endangering Another Person	M84
REFUSE TEST	813095	Refuse A Breath Or Urine Test	
RM ODM RPR	815420	Unlawfully Removing An Odometer Repair Notice	
SL N TTL VH	803085	Selling An Untitled Vehicle	
SOL IID OP	813610	Soliciting Another To Blow Into An IID, Or Starting The Motor	A41
SP RACE	811125	Speed Racing On A Highway Or Any Premises Open To The Public	S95
SUBM FLS ODM	815420	Submitting A False Odometer Disclosure	
SWTCH PLT	803540	Display Of Plates That Do Not Entitle Holder To Operate Vehicle	
TAMP IID	813614	Tampering With An Ignition Interlock Device	A41
TAMP VI BOOT	809702	Tampering With A Vehicle Immobilization Boot	A41
TFK ALT VIN	819430	Trafficking In Vehicles With Destroyed Or Altered Identification Numbers	
TFK STLN VH	819310	Trafficking In Stolen Vehicles	
TRNS N CERT	822300	Acting As A Vehicle Transporter Without A Certificate	
TRSFR MSREP	807510	Transfer Of Documents For The Purposes Of Misrepresentation	
UNAUTH TCD	815440	Unauthorized Possession, Use Or Distribution Of Traffic Control Device	E70
UNAUTH USE	164135	Unauthorized Use Of A Vehicle, Boat Or Aircraft	U03
UNL BLOW IID	813612	Unlawfully Blowing Into An IID Or Starting A Vehicle Equipped With An IID	
UNL C PAS MC	814325	Unlawfully Carrying A Passenger On A Motorcycle	
UNL CERT POL	815320	Unlawful Certification Of Compliance With Pollution Control Requirements	
UNL DISBL PK	811625	Unlawful Use Of Disabled Person Parking Permit By A Nondisabled Person	
UNL DMG A/S	821280	Unlawful Damage With A Snowmobile, class I Or class Ii All-Terrain Vehicle	
UNL DMG ATV	821285	Unlawful Damage With Class III All-Terrain Vehicle	
IDLE CMV	2011 Leg	Unlawful Idling The Primary Engine Of A Commercial Motor Vehicle	
UNL LT PAS	811390	Unlawful Use Of Lights To Signal For Passing	
UNL MP/MC OP	814200	Unlawful Moped Or Motorcycle Operation	N84
UNL OP F-ATV	821191 (2011 Leg)	Unlawful Use Of A Class I, II, Or IV ATV Used For Agricultural Purposes	
UNL OP LSP V	811512 811513	Unlawful Operation Of A Low Or Medium Speed Vehicle	
UNL OP MS	814512	Unlawful Operation Of A Motor Assisted Scooter	
UNL OP RAV	815514	Unlawful Operation Of A Racing Activity Vehicle	
UNL PAS MP	814330	Unlawfully Carrying A Passenger On A Moped	
UNL PK DISBL	811615	Unlawful Parking In A Space Reserved For Disabled Persons	
UNL PROD DL	807500	Unlawful Production Of License Or Camera Cards	D10
UNL PROD ID	807500	Unlawful Production Of License Or Camera Cards	
UNL PUB TTL	803080	Unlawful Publishing Of Title Forms	
UNL RPR ODM	815415	Unlawful Repair Of An Odometer	
UNL STP/DEC	811500	Unlawful Stop Or Deceleration	N40
UNL TRN	811335	Making An Unlawful Or Unsignaled Turn	N50
UNL/F USE LT	811520	Unlawful Use Of Or Failure To Use Lights	E55
UNL/U IMGD	815240	Unlawful Use Of Vehicle Image Display Device	
UNR SND 3X	815233	Three Or More Violations Of ORS 815.232, Unreasonable Sound Amplification From Veh	
UNR SND AMP	815232	Causing Unreasonable Sound Amplification From A Vehicle	
UNSF BUS OP	820180	Unsafe School Vehicle Operation	N84
UNSF LN CH	811375	Unsafe Movement From Lane	M41
UNSF MS B LN	814526	Unsafe Operation Of A Motor Assisted Scooter On A Bicycle Lane Or Path	
UNSF MS SW	814524	Unsafe Operation Of A Motor Scooter On A Sidewalk	
UNSF PS BYC	811065	Unsafe Passing Of A Person Operating A Bicycle	M70
UNSF PS LFT	811410	Unsafe Passing On The Left	M42
UNSF PS RT	811415	Unsafe Passing On The Right	M42
UNSIG LN CH	811375	Unsignaled Change Of Lane	N43
UNSIG TRN	811335	Making An Unlawful Or Unsignaled Turn	N43
USE INV DL	807580	Display/Possess Or Permit To Be Displayed, Any Driver License Known To Be Fictitious	B41
USE INV ID	807430	Display/Possess Or Permit To Be Displayed, Any ID Card Known To Be Fictitious	B41
USE OTHER DL	807600	Using Another's License	D16
USE OTHER ID	807430	Using Another's Identification Card (807.600)	

Literal	ORS Cite	Description	ACD
USE PR LT EQ	816360	Use Of Prohibited Lighting Equipment	
USE TWAY PR	811445	Use Of A Throughway When Prohibited	
V CL PAS VH	815245	Violation Of Minimum Clearance Requirements For Passenger Vehicles	
V DSG SPD	811111	Violating Designated Speed Class Code Depends On Speed	S92
V FM REG	805350	Violation Of Farm Registration Limits	
V MH TTL RQ	820530	Violating manufactured Structure Title Requirements	
V MS EQ RQ	815283	Violation Of Motor Assisted Scooter Equipment Requirements	E01
V OPEN CTNR	811170	Violation Of Open Container Law	A35
V PK HWY	811575	Violation Of Posted Parking Restrictions On State Highways	
V REG LMT	805030	Violation Of Registration Limits On Antique/Special Interest Vehicles	
V SMVH EMB	815115	Violation Of Slow-Moving Vehicle Emblem Requirements	E01
V SP SCH ZN	811111	Violating the Speed limit In a School Zone	S92
V TEMP PRC	803630	Agent Violation Of Temporary Registration Permit Procedures	
V TRK RTE	811450	Violation Of Posted Truck Routes	
V USE HORN	815225	Violation Of Use Limits On Horns And Sound Equipment	E70
V VARI PMT	818340	Violation Of A Variance Permit	N84
V VH SND EQ	815230	Violation Of Vehicle Sound Equipment Requirements	
V VH TTL RQ	803025	Violating Vehicle Title Requirement	
V VIS EMIS	815200	Violation Of Visible Emission Limits	
VBR	811100	Violating The Basic Speed Rule	S92
VEH HOM	163149	Aggravated Vehicular Homicide	U07
VH EQ OBS DR	815270	Vehicle Loaded Or Equipped To Obstruct Driver	D70
VH O/SVC	8259902(2)	Violation Of Out Of Service Notice; Vehicle	B27
VH UNQ DR	807610	Employing Or Providing A Vehicle To An Unqualified Driver	
VREGLMTRAC	805037	Violation Of Registration Limits On A Racing Activity Vehicle	

Suspensions, Revocations, and Cancellations Table

- Suspensions, revocations, cancellations, and violations are shown on driving record abstracts with abbreviations.
- In Oregon documentation, many of the abbreviations are accompanied by a paragraph of specific definitions—too lengthy to reproduce here. We are listing the pertinent abbreviations, along with a brief translation. Omitted are such sections as "Off-Road Vehicle" Convictions. A listing of abbreviations and definitions, as well as other valuable information, can be found in *Guide to Oregon Driving Records and Standard Conviction Abbreviation Manual* available at www.odot.state.or.us/forms/dmv/6665.pdf.
- Court-ordered suspensions and revocations will have "C" or "CO" in the abbreviation. Example: CO/CAR TFT (auto theft) or CO/MSRPAGE (misrepresent age).
- **An asterisk (*)** signifies that the action length will increase due to a prior offense.
- If **Obsolete** Indicated in Description, this means this is no longer used/entered, but may still appear on some driving records.

Literal	Type	Description
1 CO/DUII	S	First offense for DUII. Court ordered suspension for one year.
*CO/DUII	S	Second or subsequent DUII conviction. Court ordered suspension for three years.
1 CT DENY	S	First offense of a youth aged 13-17 for an offense involving the delivery, manufacture or possession of a controlled substance or for bringing/possession of guns or weapons in schools or other public buildings. Suspended for one year or until age 17, whichever is longer. May or may not involve a motor vehicle.
1ST DUII	S	Driver convicted of DUII. No other DUII convictions appear on driver's record within five years of the current conviction. Suspended for one year. (Used for out-of-state DUII.)
2 CT DENY	S	Second or subsequent offense of a youth aged 13-17 for offense involving the delivery, manufacture or possession of a controlled substance or from bringing/ possession of guns or weapons in schools or other public buildings. Suspended for one year or until age 18, whichever is longer. May or may not involve a motor vehicle.
2ND DUII	S	Driver convicted of second DUII. Offense committed within 5 years of conviction for a separate DUII offense. Suspended for three years. (Used for out-of-state DUII.)
3RD DUII	S	Driver convicted of third or subsequent DUII. Offense committed within 5 years of conviction for a separate DUII offense. Suspended for three years. (Used for out-of-state DUII.)
A DWS/R IN	R	Driver convicted of aggravated driving while suspended or revoked. Sentencing included incarceration. The revocation is imposed upon notice of conviction, but has no end date until DMV receives notice of the person's release from incarceration for this and any other crime arising from the same criminal episode. Driver is eligible to reinstate ten years from the date of release from incarceration.
A MIS DL/C	S	Allowing misuse of an Oregon driver license. Suspended for one year. The "C" in the literal means the suspension was based on a conviction.
A MIS DL/D	S	Allowing misuse of an Oregon driver license. Suspended for one year. The "D" in the literal means it was determined by DMV.
A MIS DL/H	S	After hearing suspension to A MIS DL/D suspension.
A MIS ID/C	S	Allowing an identification card issued by DMV to be misused. Suspended for one year. The "C" in the literal means the suspension was based on a conviction.
A MIS ID/D	S	Allowing an identification card issued by DMV to be misused. Suspended for one year. The "D" in the literal means it

Literal	Type	Description
		was determined by DMV.
A MIS ID/H	S	After hearing suspension to A MIS ID/D suspension.
AC N/RPT/H	S	After hearing suspension to ACCD N/RPT suspension.
AC UNINS/H	S	After hearing suspension to ACCD UNINS suspension.
ACCD N/RPT	S	Driver was involved in an accident and did not file accident report. Suspended until driver files accident report or five years from the suspension effective date.
ACCD UNINS	S	Driver was involved in an uninsured accident. Driving privileges are suspended for one year. Driver must comply with financial responsibility filing requirements.
ADLTACC/H	S	After hearing suspension to ADLTACCAPA suspension.
ADLTACCAPA	S	Driver suspended for 30 days based on having four or more preventable accidents, or a combination of accidents and driver improvement violations that totals four or more, within the 24-month period preceding the date of record review under the driver improvement program.
ADLTCONVAR	S	Driver suspended to 30 days based on receiving four or more driver improvement violations within the 24-month period preceding the date of record review under the driver improvement program.
AGG DWS/R	R	Driver convicted of aggravated driving while suspended or revoked. Revoked for ten years.
ASLT1/INC	R	Driver convicted of 1st degree assault resulting from the operation of a motor vehicle. Sentencing included incarceration. Revocation is imposed upon notice of conviction, but has no end date until DMV receives notice of the person's release from incarceration for this and any other crime arising from the same criminal episode. Driver is eligible to reinstate ten years from the date of release.
ASLT 2/INC	S	Driver convicted for 2nd degree assault resulting from the operation of a motor vehicle. Sentencing included incarceration. Suspension is imposed upon notice of conviction, but has no end date until DMV receives notice of the person's release from incarceration for the related conviction. The suspension period ends eight years from the date of release.
ASLT 3/INC	S	Driver convicted of 3rd degree assault resulting from the operation of a motor vehicle. Sentencing included incarceration. Suspension is imposed upon notice of conviction, but has no end date until DMV receives notice of the person's release from incarceration for the related conviction. The suspension period ends five years from the date of release.
ASLT 4/INC	S	Driver convicted of 4th degree assault resulting from the operation of a motor vehicle. Sentencing included incarceration. Suspension is imposed upon notice of conviction, but has no end date until DMV receives notice of the person's release from incarceration for the related conviction. The suspension period ends one year from the date of release.
ASSAULT	R	Driver revoked for ten years for a conviction of Assault in the 1st degree resulting from the operation of a motor vehicle. Older revocation entries will show a five or eight year revocation period. *At one time, this literal was used to suspend drivers convicted of Assault in the 2nd, 3rd, or 4th degree. The suspension type was used on a temporary basis in order to implement 1999 legislation. Suspension lengths varied, based on the offense, and whether or not there was a previous revocation for the same conviction.*
ASSAULT1/P	R	Driver convicted of assault in the 1st degree resulting from the operation of a motor vehicle. Revoked permanently by court order. Person may petition the court to restore driving privileges no sooner than ten years from the date the person is released from incarceration.
ASSAULT 2	S	Driver suspended for eight years based on conviction of assault in the 2nd degree, resulting from the operation of a motor vehicle.
ASSAULT 3	S	Driver suspended for five years based on conviction of assault in the 3rd degree resulting from the operation of a motor vehicle.
ASSAULT 4	S	Driver suspended for one year based on conviction of assault in the 4th degree resulting from the operation of a motor vehicle.
BAC FAIL	S	Breath test shows a blood alcohol content of .08% or more (any amount if under 21). Suspended for 90 days.
BAC FAIL*	S	Breath test shows a blood alcohol content of .08% or more (any amount if under 21). Increased suspension length because at the time of arrest, driver participated in an alcohol diversion program or, within five years preceding the arrest, driver began participation in an alcohol diversion program, began serving an Implied Consent suspension, or was convicted of DUII. Suspended for one year.
BFAIL CMV	S	Driver of a CMV failed breath test with a blood alcohol content of .04% or greater. Suspended for one year. (This suspension is of the person's CDL only.)
BFAIL CMV*	S	Driver of a DMV failed breath test with a blood alcohol content of .04% or greater. Suspension length is increased due to prior major CDL/CMV offense in Oregon or an equivalent prior offense in another state. Lifetime suspension of CDL only. Conditional reinstatement after 10 years.
BFAIL HAZ	S	Driver of a DMV transporting hazardous materials failed breath test with a blood alcohol content of .04% or greater. Suspended for three years. (This suspension is of the person's CDL only.)
BFAIL HAZ*	S	Driver of a DMV transporting hazardous materials failed breath test with a blood alcohol content of .04% or greater. Suspension length increased due to prior major CDL/CMV offense in Oregon or an equivalent prior offense in another state. Lifetime suspension of CDL only. Conditional reinstatement after 10 years. (see OAR 735-070-0200).
C/DUI CDL*	S	Driver of a CMV or a driver with a valid CDL at the time of offense was convicted of a DUII. Suspension length is increased due to prior major CDL/CMV offense in Oregon or an equivalent prior offense in another state. Lifetime suspension of CDL only. Conditional reinstatement after 10 years (seer OAR 735-070-0200).
C/DRGS CDL	S	Driver of a CMV or driver with a valid CDL at the time of offense committed a felony crime involving the manufacture, distribution or dispensing of a controlled substance. Lifetime suspension. (This suspension is of the person's CDL only.)
C/DUII CDL	S	Driver of a CMV was convicted of Driving Under the Influence of Intoxicants (DUII). Suspended for one year. (This suspension is of the person's CDL only.)
C/DUII HAZ	S	Driver of a DMV transporting hazardous materials was convicted of DUII. Suspended for three years. (This suspension

Literal	Type	Description
		is of the person's CDL only.)
C/FL/A/ELD	S	Driver convicted of fleeing or attempting to elude. See CO/CR MIS for suspension length.
C/FPD CDL*	S	Driver of a CMV or a driver with a valid CDL at the time of offense failed to perform the duties of a driver involved in an accident. Suspension length is increased due to prior major CDL/CMV offense in Oregon or an equivalent prior offense in another state. Lifetime suspension of CDL only. Conditional reinstatement after ten years (see OAR 735-070-0200).
C/FPDD CDL	S	Driver of a CMV or a driver with a valid CDL at the time of offense failed to perform the duties of a driver involved in an accident. The suspension period is for one year. (This suspension is of the person's CDL only.)
C/FPDD HAZ	S	Driver of a CMV transporting hazardous materials failed to perform the duties of a driver involved in an accident. Suspended for three years. (This suspension is of the person's CDL only.)
C/HR CDL	S	Driver of a CMV was convicted of Hit and Run. Suspended for one year. (This suspension is of the person's CDL only.)
C/HR CDL*	S	Driver of a CMV or a driver with a valid CDL at the time of offense was convicted of Hit and Run. Suspension length is increased due to prior major CDL/CMV offense in Oregon or an equivalent prior offense in another state. Lifetime suspension of CDL only. Conditional reinstatement after ten years (see OAR 735-070-0200).
C/HR HAZ	S	Driver of a CMV transporting hazardous materials was convicted of Hit and Run. Suspended for three years. (This suspension is of the person's CDL only.)
C/MFEL CDL	S	Driver of a CMV or a driver with a valid CDL at the time of offense was convicted of a crime punishable as a felony. Suspended for one year. (This suspension is of the person's CDL only.)
C/MFEL HAZ	S	Driver of a CMV transporting hazardous materials was convicted of a crime punishable as a felony. Suspended for three years. (This suspension is of a person's CDL only.)
C/MVF CDL*	S	Driver of a CMV or a CDL holder at time of offense was convicted of a crime punishable as a felony. Suspension length is increased due to prior major CDL/CMV offense in Oregon or an equivalent prior offense in another state. Lifetime suspension of CDL only. Conditional reinstatement after ten years (see OAR 735-070-0200).
C/O SPDG	S	Convicted of speeding while driving at least 31 MPH over the speed limit or designated speed and has one prior speeding conviction within 12 months of the current offense date. Suspended for a period determined by the court, up to 30 days.
C/O SPD 100	S	Convicted of speeding while driving over 100 MPH. Suspended for period determined by the court, between 30-90 days.
CO/VEH HOM	R	Driver convicted of aggravated vehicular homicide. Revoked for ten years. Older revocation entries will show eight year revocation period.
CARELSS DR	S	Driver convicted of careless driving and the offense contributed to serious physical injury or death of a vulnerable user of a public way. Suspended for one year.
CDL DISQ	S	Driver of a CMV or a driver with a valid CDL at the time of offense was convicted of a third CDL disqualifying offense (traffic crime) after imposition or reinstatement of a CDL lifetime (10 year) suspension. Lifetime suspension of CDL only – NOT eligible for conditional reinstatement after 10 years.
CDL FRAUD	S	Commercial Dl or permit holder submitted fraudulent information to obtain or maintain qualification for commercial driving privileges. This suspension is of the person's CDL only.
CDL FRAUD/H	S	After hearing suspension to suspension code 402.
CDL RAIL 1	S	Suspended for 60 days for having one CDL rail conviction within a three-year period. This suspension is of the person's CDL only.
CDL RAIL 2	S	Suspended for 120 days for having two CDL rail convictions within a three-year period. This suspension is of the person's CDL only.
CDL RAIL 3	S	Suspended 1 year for having three CDL rail convictions within a three-year period. This suspension is of the person's CDL only.
CDL/MED	S	Inability to meet CDL requirements under Oregon Administrative Rule. This suspension is of the person's CDL only.
CDLMEDQUAL	C	Commercial DL or permit holder has not submitted medical certificate as required. This cancellation is of the person's CDL only.
CDLMEDWAIV	C	Commercial DL or permit holder has not obtained a waiver or federal variance as required to prove medical qualification. This cancellation is of the person's CDL only.
CO A DWS/R	R	Driver convicted of aggravated driving while suspended or revoked. Court imposed revocation upon conviction. Revoked for ten years.
CO/A MIS DL	S	Allowing misuse of an Oregon driver license. Suspended for one year.
CO/A MIS ID	S	Court ordered a one year suspension for an offense under ORS 809.310.
CO/ASAULT1	R	Driver convicted of assault in the 1st degree resulting from the operation of a motor vehicle. Revoked for ten years. Older revocation entries will show a five or eight year revocation period.
CO/ASAULT2	S	Driver convicted of assault in the 2nd degree. Suspended for eight years.
CO/ASAULT3	S	Driver convicted of assault in the 3rd degree. Suspended for five years.
CO/ASAULT4	S	Driver convicted of assault in the 4th degree. Suspended for one year.
CO/CAR TFT	R	Auto theft. Revoked for one year.
CO/CR MIS	S	Driver was convicted of criminal mischief with a motor vehicle. The period of suspension is determined by the number of CRIMNL MIS, FL/AT/ELUD, RECKLSS DR, RECK ENDGR, F PER/DUTY and MENACING convictions within a five year period. Driving privileges are suspended for: 90 days for the first offense, one year for a second offense and three years for a third offense.
CO/CR TRES	S	Driver convicted of criminal trespass with a motor vehicle. Suspended for six months.
CO/DRIC	S	Court ordered driver to complete a defensive driving or other driver improvement course. Suspended until course has been completed.
CO/DUII	S	Driver convicted of DUII. Court imposed suspension; one year for first offense or three years if second offense committed within five years of another DUII offense.
CO/F AP DL	S	Suspended for making a false application for a driver license. Suspended for one year.

Literal	Type	Description
CO/F AP ID	S	Court ordered a one year suspension for an offense under ORS 809.310.
CO/F PLC DL	S	Making false statements to a police officer about a driver license. Suspended for one year.
CO/F PLC ID	S	Court ordered a one year suspension for an offense under ORS 809.310.
CO/FPDD	S	Failure to perform the duties of a driver involved in an accident. See CO/CR MIS for suspension length.
CO/FPDUTA*	R	Driver convicted of failure to perform the duties of a driver to injured persons, and there is indication on the conviction that a person was killed as a result of the accident. Revoked for five years.
CO/HIT RUN	R	Hit and run after an accident, which resulted in person injury or death to another person. Revoked for one year.
CO/INV DL	S	Using an invalid Oregon driver license. Suspended for one year.
CO/INV ID	S	Court ordered a one year suspension for an offense under ORS 809.310.
CO/LITTER	S	Suspended based on order of court – maximum 90 day suspension based on convictions for littering in violation of ORS 164.775.
CO/MANSL	R	Convicted of manslaughter with a motor vehicle. Revoked for ten years. Older entries will show a five year revocation period.
CO/MENCING	S	Menacing with a motor vehicle. See CO/CR MIS for suspension length.
CO/MSREPDL	S	Making an unlawful misrepresentation with a driver license. Suspended for one year.
CO/MSREPID	S	Court ordered a one year suspension for an offense under ORS 809.310.
CO/MSRPAGE	S	Court ordered a one year suspension for misrepresentation of age by a minor.
CO/MURDER	R	Driver convicted of murder resulting from the operation of a motor vehicle. Revoked for ten years. Older revocation entries will show a five or eight year revocation period.
CO/MV FLNY	R	Using a motor vehicle in the commission of a felony. Revoked for one year.
CO/NEGHOM	R	Convicted of negligent homicide with a motor vehicle. Revoked for ten years. Older entries will show a five or eight year revocation period.
CO/OTHER DL	S	Using another person's driver license. Suspended for one year.
CO/OTHER ID	S	Court ordered a one year suspension for an offense under ORS 809.310.
CO/PERJURY	R	Perjury or false affidavit to DMV under any law of this state requiring the registration of vehicles or regulating their operation on highways. Revoked for one year.
CO/PROD DL	S	Unlawfully producing a driver license. Suspended for one year.
CO/PROD ID	S	Court ordered a one year suspension for an offense under ORS 809.310.
CO/R EN HW	S	Driver recklessly endangered the life a highway worker in a highway work zone. See CO/CR MIS for suspension length.
CO/RECK DR	S	Reckless driving. See CO/CR MIS for suspension length.
CO/RECK EN	S	Reckless endangering with a motor vehicle. See FL/AT ELUD for suspension length.
CO/SWR DL	S	False swearing on application for driver license. Suspended for one year.
CO/UN USE	R	Unauthorized use of a motor vehicle. Revoked for one year.
CRIM TRES	S	Driver convicted of criminal trespass with a motor vehicle. Suspended for six months.
CRIMNL MIS	S	Driver convicted of criminal mischief involving the operation of a motor vehicle. See FL/AT ELUD for suspension lengths.
CT DENY A	S	Second or subsequent offense of a youth aged 13-20 for offense involving possession, use/abuse of alcohol. Suspended for one year or until age 18, whichever is longer. If age 18 or over, suspended for one year. May or may not involve a motor vehicle.
CT DENY A*	S	Second or subsequent offense of a youth aged 13-20 for offense involving possession, use/abuse of alcohol. Suspended for one years or until age 18, whichever is longer. If age 18 or over, suspended for one year. May or may not involve a motor vehicle.
CT DRUGS	S	Driver suspended for six months based on court notice – manufacturing, possession, or delivery of a controlled substance, or DUII of an inhalant or controlled substance.
DMVDNYTST1	C	DMV has denied further testing under OAR 735-062-0073.
DMVDNYTST2	C	DMV has denied further testing under OAR 735-062-0073 (immediate cancellation).
DMVDNYTSTH	C	After hearing cancellation to DMVDNYTST cancellation.
DR UNINSUR	S	Driver was convicted of driving uninsured. Suspended until the driver complies with Financial Responsibility Laws.
DRUGS CDL	S	Driver of a CMV or a driver with a valid CDL at the time of offense committed a felony crime involving the manufacture, distribution or dispensing of a controlled substance. Lifetime suspension of CDL only – NOT eligible for conditional reinstatement after 10 years.
DUII 1	S	First offense for driving under the influence of intoxicants (DUII). Suspended for one year. Used for Oregon DUII convictions.
DUII 2	S	Second DUII offense committed within five years of a prior DUII conviction. Suspended for three years. Used for Oregon DUII convictions.
DUII 3	S	Third or subsequent offense for DUII committed within 5 years of another DUII offense. Suspended for three years. Used for Oregon DUII convictions.
DUII CDL	S	Driver of a CMV or CDL holder at time of offense was convicted of Driver Under the Influence of Intoxicants (DUII). Suspended for one year. (This suspension is of the person's CDL only.)
DUII CDL*	S	Driver of a CMV or a driver with a valid CDL at the time of offense was convicted of a DUII. Suspension length is increased due to prior major CDL/CMV offense in Oregon or an equivalent prior offense in another state. Lifetime suspension of CDL only. Conditional reinstatement after ten years (see OAR 735-070-0200).
DUII FLNY	R	Driver Revoked for felony DUII. Permanent revocation ordered by court. Person may petition the circuit court in their county of residence to restore driving privileges. Petition can be filed no sooner than ten years after the date of release, on parole or post-prison supervision.
DUII HAZ	S	Driver of a CMV transporting hazardous materials was convicted of DUII. Suspended for three years. (This suspension

Literal	Type	Description
		is of the person's CDL only.)
DUII MISD	R	Driver revoked for 3rd or subsequent misdemeanor DUII. Permanent revocation ordered by court. Person may petition the circuit court in their county of residence to restore driving privileges. Petition can be filed no sooner than ten years after the date of release, on parole or post-prison supervision.
DWS/R CMV	S	Driver of a CMV received first conviction of driving while suspended or revoked for violations committed while operating a CMV. Suspended for one year. (This suspension is of the person's CDL only.)
DWS/R CMV*	S	Driver of a CMV received a 2nd conviction of DWS or DWR for violation committed while operating a CMV. Suspension length is increased due to prior major CDL/CMV offense in Oregon or an equivalent in another state. Lifetime suspension of CDL only. Conditional reinstatement after 10 years (see OAR 735-070-0200).
DWS/R HAZ	S	Driver of a CMV transporting hazardous materials received a first conviction of driving while suspended or revoked for violations committed while operating a CMV. Suspended for three years. (This suspension is of the person's CDL only and, for suspensions effective 11/10/08 or later, is used for out-of-state drivers only.)
F AP DL/C	S	Suspended for making a false application for a driver license. Suspended for one year. The "C" in the literal means the suspension was based on a conviction.
F AP DL/D	S	Suspended for making a false application for a driver license. Suspended for one year. The "D" in the literal means it was determined by DMV.
F AP DL/H	S	After hearing suspension to F AP DL/D suspension.
F AP ID/C	S	Driver suspended for submitting a false application for an ID card to DMV. The "C" in the literal means the suspension was based on a conviction.
F AP ID/D	S	Driver suspended for submitting a false application for an ID card to DMV. Suspended for one year. The "D" in the literal means it was determined by DMV.
F AP ID/H	S	After hearing suspension to F AP ID/D suspension.
F INST IID	S	Driver has not installed Ignition Interlock Device (IID) when required after DUII suspension. Suspended until driver installs (IID) or until ending date of IID requirement (one year from end of DUII suspension for a first conviction or two years for a 2nd or subsequent DUII conviction).
F PAY TAX	S	Driver suspended in accordance with request from the Oregon Department of Revenue, for failure to file a tax return or pay a tax. Suspended until a notice is received from the Oregon Department of Revenue allowing driver to reinstate. (This suspension is of the person's CDL only.)
F PAY TX/H	S	After hearing suspension to F PAY TAX suspension.
F PER/DUTY	S	Failure to perform the duties of a driver involved in an accident. See FL/AT ELUD for suspension lengths.
F PLC DL/C	S	Making false statements to a police officer about a driver license. Suspended for one year. The "C" in the literal means the suspension was based on a conviction.
F PLC DL/D	S	Making false statements to a police officer about a driver license. Suspended for one year. The "D" in the literal means it was determined by DMV.
F PLC DL/H	S	After hearing suspension to F PLC DL/D suspension.
F PLC ID/C	S	Giving false information to a police officer. Suspended for one year. The "C" in the literal means the suspension was based on a conviction.
F PLC ID/D	S	Giving false information to a police officer. Suspended for one year. The "D" in the literal means it was determined by DMV.
F PLC ID/H	S	After hearing suspension to F PLC ID/D suspension.
F SWR DL/C	S	Suspended for one year based on a conviction for false swearing on application for a driver license.
F/A BAIL/	S	Driver surrendered driver license to a court for security until court appearance date and then failed to appear in court. Suspended until the court submits a clearance or for ten years, whichever comes first.
F/A HEAR/	S	Failure to appear for a court hearing. Suspended until the court submits a clearance or for ten years, whichever comes first.
F/A MIP	S	Failure to appear in court on a minor in possession citation. Suspended until the court submits a clearance or for ten years, whichever comes first.
F/A RCTST	S	Driver failed to appear for recertification testing.
F/A RCTSTH	S	After hearing suspension to F/A RCTST suspension.
F/A TR CRM/	S	Failure to appear on a traffic crime. Suspended until the court submits a clearance or for ten years, whichever comes first.
F/BLD CMV	S	Driver of a CMV failed a blood test. Suspended for one year. (This suspension is of the person's CDL only.)
F/BLD CMV*	S	Driver of a CMV failed a blood test. Suspension length is increased due to prior major CDL/CMV offense in Oregon or an equivalent prior offense in another state. Lifetime suspension of CDL only. Conditional reinstatement after 10 years.
F/BLD HAZ	S	Driver of a CMV transporting hazardous materials failed a blood test. Suspended for three years. (This suspension is of the person's CDL only.)
F/BLD HAZ*	S	Driver of a CMV transporting hazardous materials failed a blood test. Suspension length is increased due to prior major CDL/CMV offense in Oregon or an equivalent prior offense in another state. Lifetime suspension of CDL only. Conditional reinstatement after 10 years.
F/BLD TST	S	Driver failed a blood test. Suspension is for 90 days.
F/BLD TST*	S	Driver failed a blood test. Suspension length is increased because at the time of arrest driver was participating in an alcohol diversion program or, within five years preceding the arrest, driver began participation in an alcohol diversion program, began serving an Implied Consent suspension, or was convicted of DUII. Suspended for one year.
F/C MEDRQ1	S	Driver failed to comply with medical recertification requirement
F/C MEDRQ2	S	Driver failed to comply with medical recertification requirement
F/C REQ/H	S	After hearing suspension to F/C/MED REQ suspension.

Literal	Type	Description
F/C TEST/H	S	After hearing suspension to DI F/C TST suspension.
F/C/MED REQ	S	Failure to provide medical information as required by DMV. Suspended until the person establishes eligibility under ORS 807.090 or ORS 807.070.
F/CHLD SUP	S	Failure to pay child support. Suspended until a notice is received from District Attorney or Support Enforcement Division (SED) allowing driver to reinstate.
F/COMPLY/	S	Failure to pay a fine or comply with a condition imposed by a court. Suspended until the court submits a clearance or for ten years, whichever comes first.
F/EST DL	C	Not entitled to a driver license or permit due to failure to establish identity through the 1:N check. Applicant must establish identity using an alternative method. Cancelled until applicant meets requirements.
F/EST ID	C	Not entitled to an identification card due to failure to establish identity through the 1:N check. Applicant must establish identity using an alternative method. Cancelled until applicant meets requirements.
F/F ACFR	S	Driver was required to file proof of FR with DMV because of uninsured accident. Proof has not been received. Suspended until driver complies with FR law. Follows an uninsured accident suspension.
F/F ACFR/H	S	After hearing suspension to F/F ACFR suspension.
F/F MAND	S	Driver was required to file proof of future responsibility with DMV because of a major suspension or revocation and proof has not been received. Suspended until driver complies with FR requirements. This suspension follows a major suspension or revocation.
F/F PRF	S	Driver required to file proof of future financial responsibility with DMV and the proof is not on file. Suspended until driver complies with future responsibility filing requirements.
F/F RS	S	Owner of a vehicle chosen by random sample to provide proof of liability insurance coverage did not provide DMV with the insurance information or the insurance company denied coverage. Suspended until owner complies with future responsibility filing requirements.
F/F RS/H	S	After hearing suspension to F/F RS suspension.
F/FILE	S	Driver was required to file proof of FR with DMV and the proof has not been received. Suspended until driver complies with future responsibility filing requirements.
F/FILE/H	S	After hearing suspension to F/FILE suspension.
F/P DUT A*	R	Driver was convicted of failure to perform the duties of a driver to injured persons, and the court indicated on the conviction that a person was killed as a result of the accident. Revoked for five years.
F/P RCTST	S	Driver failed to pass recertification testing.
F/P RCTSTH	S	After hearing suspension to F/P RCTST suspension.
F/P REEXAM	S	Suspended for failure to pass licensing tests as required by DMV. Suspended until all required tests are successfully completed.
F/P REXM H	S	After hearing suspension to F/P REEXAM suspension.
F/RP ACC/H	S	After hearing suspension to F/RPT ACC suspension.
F/RPT AC/H	S	After hearing suspension to F/RPT ACCD suspension.
F/RPT ACC	S	Failure to file an accident report. Suspended for five years or until the report is filed. Exempt from insurance requirements.
F/RPT ACCD	S	Failure to report an accident. Suspended until driver files an accident report or five years from the suspension effective date.
FC MEDRQ1H	S	After hearing suspension to F/C MEDRQ1 suspension.
FC MEDRQ2H	S	After hearing suspension to F/C MEDRQ2 suspension.
FINAL HAZ	C	DMV received a Final Determination of Threat Assessment for the driver from TSA. CDL is cancelled until driver brings in CDL to remove the hazmat endorsement.
FL/AT/ELUD	S	Driver convicted of fleeing or attempting to elude a police officer. Suspension length depends on prior convictions for CRIMNL MIS, FL/AT ELUD, RECKLSS DR, RECK ENDGR, F PER/DUTY, R END H/WKR and MENACING within a five year period. Driving privileges are suspended for: 90 days for the first offense, one year for a second offense and three years for a third offense.
FMCSA DISQ	S	MV has been notified that the FMCSA Asst Administrator has determined that operation of a CMV by the driver constitutes an imminent hazard. Suspended up to one year as specified by FMCSA. (This suspension is of the person's CDL only.)
FPDD*/INC	R	Driver convicted of failure to perform the duties of a driver to injured persons, and a person was killed as a result of the accident. Sentencing included incarceration. The suspension is imposed upon notice of conviction, but has no end date until DMV receives notice of the person's release from incarceration for the related conviction. The suspension period ends five years from the date of release from incarceration.
FPDUTY CDL	S	Driver of a CMV or a driver with a valid CDL at the time of offense failed to perform the duties of a driver involved in an accident. Suspended for one year. (This suspension is of the person's CDL only.)
FPDUTY CDL*	S	Driver of a CMV or a driver with a valid CDL at the time of offense failed to perform the duties of a drive involved in an accident. Suspension length is increased due to prior major CDL/CMV offense in Oregon or an equivalent prior offense in another state. Lifetime suspension of CDL only. Conditional reinstatement after 10 years (see OAR 735-070-0200).
FPDUTY HAZ	S	Driver of a CMV transporting hazardous materials failed to perform the duties of a driver involved in an accident. Suspended for three years. (This suspension is of the person's CDL only.)
FRS DL	S	Suspended for making a false application for a driver license or permit. Discovered during the 1:N biometric check process.
FRS DL/H	S	After hearing suspension to FRS DL suspension.
FRS ID	S	Suspended for making a false application for an identification card. Discovered during the 1:N biometric check process.
FRS ID/H	S	After hearing suspension to FRS ID suspension.

Literal	Type	Description
HAB OFF/AR	R	Driver has been revoked as a habitual offender (convicted of 20 minor or 3 major traffic crimes within 5 years). Eligible for reinstatement after five years.
HIT/RUN	R	Hit and run after an accident which resulted in personal injury or death of another person. Revoked for one year.
HR CDL	S	Driver of a CMV or a driver with a valid CDL at the time of offense was convicted of Hit and Run. Suspended for 1 year. (This suspension is of the person's CDL only.)
HR CDL*	S	Driver of a CMV or a driver with a valid CDL at the time of offense was convicted of Hit and Run. Suspension length is increased due to prior major CDL/CMV offense in Oregon or an equivalent prior offense in another state. Lifetime suspension of CDL only. Conditional reinstatement after 10 years (see OAR 735-070-0200).
HR HAZ	S	Driver of a CMV transporting hazardous materials was convicted of Hit and Run. Suspended for 3 years. (This suspension is of the person's CDL only.)
IMMED HAZ	C	DMV received an Initial Determination of Threat Assessment and Immediate Revocation for the driver from TSA. CDL is cancelled until driver brings in CDL to remove the hazmat endorsement.
INTER HAZ	C	Driver has not initiated required interim TSA security background check. CDL is cancelled until driver brings in CDL to remove the hazmat endorsement.
INV DL/C	S	Using an invalid Oregon driver license. Suspended for one year. The "C" in the literal means the suspension was based on a conviction.
INV DL/D	S	Using an invalid Oregon driver license. Suspended for one year. The "D" in the literal means it was determined by DMV.
INV DL/H	S	After hearing suspension to INV DL/D suspension.
INV ID/C	S	Using an invalid Oregon identification card. Suspended for one year. The "C" in the literal means the suspension was based on a conviction.
INV ID/D	S	Using an invalid Oregon identification card. Suspended for one year. The "D" in the literal means it was determined by DMV.
INV ID/H	S	After hearing suspension to INV ID/D suspension.
JUDG UNSAT	S	Judgment rendered against a person for damages in an automobile accident have not been paid. Suspended until the judgment is satisfied; or 7 years from judgment rendered date.
M/FEL CDL*	S	Driver of a CMV or CDL holder at the time of offense was convicted of crime punishable as a felony. Suspension length is increased due to prior major CDL/CMV offense in Oregon or an equivalent prior offense in another state. Lifetime suspension of CDL only. Conditional reinstatement after 10 years (see OAR 735-070-0200).
M10CDLRAIL	S	Driver of a CMV was convicted of failure to obey a traffic control device or the directions of an enforcement official at a railroad-highway grade crossing. Suspended for 60 days. This suspension is of the person's CDL only.
M20CDLRAIL	S	Driver of a CMV who is not required to always stop at a railroad-highway grade crossing was convicted of failure to slow down and check that tracks are clear of approaching train. Suspended for 60 days. This suspension is of the person's CDL only.
M21CDLRAIL	S	Driver of a CMV who is not required to always stop at a railroad-highway grade crossing was convicted of failure to stop before reaching track when the tracks are not clear. Suspended for 60 days. This suspension is of the person's CDL only.
M22CDLRAIL	S	Driver of a CMV who is not required to always stop at a railroad-highway grade crossing was convicted of failure to stop as required before driving onto the crossing. Suspended for 60 days. This suspension is of the person's CDL only.
M23CDLRAIL	S	Driver of a CMV was convicted of failing to have sufficient space to drive completely through a railroad-highway grade crossing without stopping. Suspended for 60 days. This suspension is of the person's CDL only.
M24CDLRAIL	S	Driver of a CMV was convicted of failing to negotiate a railroad-highway grade crossing because of insufficient undercarriage clearance. Suspended for 60 days. This suspension is of the person's CDL only.
MANSL/INC	R	Driver convicted of manslaughter resulting from the operation of a motor vehicle. Sentencing included incarceration. The revocation is imposed upon notice of conviction, but has no end date until DMV receives notice of the person's release from incarceration for this and any other crime arising from the same criminal episode. The revocation period ends ten years from the date of release from incarceration.
MANSLAUTR	R	Driver revoked for 10 years for a conviction of manslaughter resulting from the operation of a motor vehicle. If the person was incarcerated as a result of the conviction, the revocation period will not begin until DMV receives notice that they have been released from incarceration. Older revocation entries will show a five year revocation period.
MANSLTR/P	R	Driver convicted of manslaughter resulting from the operation of a motor vehicle. Revoked permanently by court order. Person may petition the court to restore driving privileges no sooner than ten years from the date the person is released from incarceration.
MDODNYTST1	C	Medical Determination Officer has denied further testing.
MDODNYTST2	C	Medical Determination Officer has denied further testing (immediate cancellation).
MDODNYTSTH	C	After hearing cancellation to MDODNYTST cancellation.
MED C	S	A court finds a person charged with a traffic offense guilty except for insanity and the person is committed to jurisdiction of the Psychiatric Security Review Board. A copy of the final judgment is sent to DMV to suspend the person's driving privilege. Suspended until the person establishes eligibility under ORS 807.090.
MED P	S	Present physical or mental condition renders it unsafe for the person to operate a motor vehicle. Suspended until the person establishes eligibility under ORS 807.090.
MED RECERT	S	Immediate suspension under the At-Risk Driver mandatory medical program recertification process.
MED S	S	State Hospital Superintendent informed DMV that driver is not competent to drive. Suspended until DMV receives recommendation of the State Hospital Superintendent, a judicial decree of competency, or a favorable determination from the Medical Determination Officer.
MED V	S	Driver's vision does not meet state vision standards. Suspended until driver's vision meets state vision standards.

Literal	Type	Description
MED1	S	Immediate suspension under the At-Risk Driver mandatory medical reporting program.
MED2	S	Immediate suspension under the At-Risk Driver mandatory medical reporting program.
MED3	S	Immediate suspension under the At-Risk Driver mandatory medical reporting program.
MED4	S	Immediate suspension under the At-Risk Driver mandatory medical reporting program.
MED5	S	Immediate suspension under the At-Risk Driver mandatory medical reporting program.
MENACING	S	Menacing with a Motor Vehicle. See FL/AT ELUD for suspension lengths.
MISREP AGE	S	Minor convicted of misrepresentation of age in order to purchase or consume alcohol. Suspended for one year.
MSREP DL/C	S	Making an unlawful misrepresentation with a driver license. Suspended for one year. The "C" in the literal means the suspension was based on a conviction.
MSREP DL/D	S	Making an unlawful misrepresentation with a driver license. Suspended for one year. The "D" in the literal means it was determined by DMV.
MSREP DL/H	S	After hearing suspension to MSREP DL/D suspension.
MSREP ID/C	S	Making an unlawful misrepresentation with an identification card. Suspended for one year. The "C" in the literal means the suspension was based on a conviction.
MSREP ID/D	S	Making an unlawful misrepresentation with an identification card. Suspended for one year. The "D" in the literal means it was determined by DMV.
MSREP ID/H	S	After hearing suspension to MSREP ID/D suspension.
MURDER	R	Driver revoked for ten years for a conviction of murder resulting from the operation of a motor vehicle. Older revocation entries will show an eight year revocation period.
MURDER/INC	R	Driver convicted of murder resulting from the operation of a motor vehicle. Sentencing included incarceration. The revocation is imposed upon notice of conviction, but has no end date until DMV receives notice of the person's release from incarceration for this and any other crime arising from the same criminal episode. The revocation period ends ten years from the date of release from incarceration. Older revocation entries will display an eight year revocation period.
MURDER/P	R	Driver convicted of murder resulting from the operation of a motor vehicle. Revoked permanently by court order. Person may petition the court to restore driving privileges no sooner than ten years from the date the person is released from incarceration.
MV FEL CDL	S	Driver of a CMV or a driver with a valid CDL at the time of offense was convicted of crime punishable as a felony. Suspended for one year. (This suspension is of the person's CDL only.)
MV FELONY	R	Using a motor vehicle in the commission of a felony. Revoked for one year.
MVFEL HAZ	S	Driver of a CMV transporting hazardous materials was convicted of crime punishable as a felony. Suspended for three years. (This suspension is of the person's CDL only.)
N/ENT CDL	C	Not entitled to a CDL for various reasons, such as a discrepancy with an SSN or CDL tests were improperly administered. Cancelled until driver meets requirements.
N/ENT DL	C	Not entitled to a driver license or permit for various reasons. Driving privileges may have been suspended/revoked in Oregon or another state when license or permit was issued; an error was made when the license was issued; a business address was used, rather than a residence address; or no further testing to obtain a license will be granted. Cancelled until driver meets requirements.
N/ENT ID	C	Not entitled to an identification card. An error may have been made when card was issued; a business address may have been used rather than a residence address; the person may not be an Oregon resident, etc. Canceled until the driver meets requirements.
N/ENT DL/H	C	After hearing suspension to N/ENT DL suspension.
N/ENT FARM	C	Driver is not qualified for a farm endorsement due to a lifetime CDL suspension. License is cancelled until farm endorsement is surrendered or CDL suspension is cleared.
NEG HOMC/P	R	Driver convicted of criminally negligent homicide resulting from the operation of a motor vehicle. Revoked permanently by court order. Person may petition the court to restore driving privileges no sooner than ten years from the date the person is released from incarceration.
NEGHOM/INC	R	Driver convicted of criminally negligent homicide resulting from the operation of a motor vehicle. Sentencing included incarceration. The revocation is imposed upon notice of conviction, but has no end date until DMV receives notice of the person's release from incarceration for this and any other crime arising from the same criminal episode. The revocation period ends ten years from the date of release from incarceration.
NSF CHECK	S	A check returned to DMV for non-sufficient funds and the person has not reimbursed DMV. Suspended indefinitely or until payment is made, including an NSF check fee.
NEG HOMICD	R	Driver was convicted of negligent homicide resulting from the operation of a motor vehicle. Revoked for ten years. If the person was incarcerated as a result of the conviction, the revocation period will not begin until DMV receives notice that they have been released from incarceration. Some older entries will appear on records showing a five or eight year revocation period.
O/SBFLCDL*	S	Driver of a CMV or a driver with a valid CDL at the time of offense failed a blood test in another state. Suspension length is increased due to prior major CDL/CMV offense in Oregon or an equivalent prior offense in another state. Lifetime suspension of CDL only. Conditional reinstatement after 10 years.
O/S BFLCMV	S	Driver of a CMV failed breath test in another state with a blood alcohol content of .04% or greater. Suspended for one year. (This suspension is of the person's CDL only.)
O/S BFLHAZ*	S	Driver of a CMV or driver with a valid CDL at the time of offense transporting hazardous materials failed a blood test in another state. Suspension length is increased due to prior major CDL/CMV offense in Oregon or an equivalent prior offense in another state. Lifetime suspension of CDL only. Conditional reinstatement after 10 years (see OAR 735-070-0200).
O/S REFUSE	S	Driver of a non-CMV refused a chemical breath test in another state. Suspended until the driver is cleared in the other

Literal	Type	Description
		state.
O/S RF CMV	S	Driver of a CMV or a driver holding a CDL at the time of the offense refused to submit to blood alcohol content test in another state. Suspended for three years. (This suspension is of the person's CDL only.)
O/S RF HAZ	S	Driver of a CMV transporting hazardous materials refused to submit to a blood alcohol content test in another state. Suspended for five years. (This suspension is of the person's CDL only.)
O/S RFCDL*	S	Driver of a CMV or a driver with a valid CDL at the time of offense refused to submit to blood alcohol content test in another state. Suspension length is increased due to prior major CDL/CMV offense in Oregon or an equivalent prior offense in another state. Lifetime suspension of CDL only. Conditional reinstatement after 10 years (see OAR 735-070-0200).
O/S RFHAZ*	S	Driver of a CMV transporting hazardous materials refused to submit to a blood alcohol content test in another state. Suspension length is increased due to prior major CDL/CMV offense in Oregon or an equivalent in another state. If driver has other open implied consent suspensions on their record (includes any pending suspension arising out of same arrest), this suspension begins on the ending date of that suspension. Lifetime suspension of CDL only. Conditional reinstatement after 10 years (see OAR 735-070-0200).
O/SBACFAIL	S	Driver of a non-CMV failed a breath test in another state with a blood alcohol content of .08% of more (any amount if under 21). Suspended until the driver is cleared in the other state.
O/SBFLCMV*	S	Driver of a CMV failed a blood test in another state. Suspension length is increased due to prior major CDL/CMV offense in Oregon or an equivalent prior offense in another state. Lifetime suspension of CDL only. Conditional reinstatement after 10 years (see OAR 735-070-0200).
O/SBFLHAZ	S	Driver of a CMV transporting hazardous materials failed breath test in another state with a blood alcohol content of .04% or greater. Suspended for three years. (This suspension is of the person's CDL only.)
O/SVC CDL3	S	Driver of a CMV violated an out-of-service order. Third or subsequent offense. Suspended for five years. (This suspension is of the person's CDL only.)
O/SVC HAZ	S	Driver of a commercial motor vehicle carrying hazardous materials, or a vehicle designed to carry 16 or more passengers (including the driver), violated an out-of-service order. Suspended for one year. (This suspension is of the person's CDL only.)
O/SVC HAZ*	S	Driver of a commercial motor vehicle carrying hazardous materials, or a vehicle designed to carry 16 or more passengers (including the driver), violated an out-of-service order. Second offense. Suspended for five years. (This suspension is of the person's CDL only.)
OS FAC CDL/	S	Driver of a CMV or driver with a valid CDL at the time of offense failed to appear or railed to comply as ordered by another state. Suspended for ten years or until a clearance is received from the other state, whichever occurs first. (This suspension is of the person's CDL only.)
OTHER DL/C	S	Using another person's driver license. Suspended for one year. The "C" in the literal means the suspension was based on a conviction.
OTHER DL/D	S	Using another person's driver license. Suspended for one year. The "D" in the literal means it was determined by DMV.
OTHER DL/H	S	After hearing suspension to OTHER DL/D suspension.
OTHER ID/C	S	Using an identification card belonging to another person. This applies only to cards issued by DMV. Suspended for one year. The "C" in the literal means the suspension was based on a conviction.
OTHER ID/D	S	Using an identification card belonging to another person. This applies only to cards issued by DMV. Suspended for one year. The "D" in the literal means it was determined by DMV.
OTHER ID/H	S	After hearing suspension to OTHER ID/D suspension.
OWNER AC/H	S	After hearing suspension to OWNER ACC suspension.
OWNER ACC	S	A vehicle registered to one person and driven by someone else was involved in an uninsured accident. Owner is suspended until they comply with future responsibility filing requirements. Note: It is possible to see this suspension even if there is no accident posted to the record.
PAR SIG	C	Withdrawal of parental signature on a license or permit for a driver under 18 years of age. May reapply with a new parental signature, if declared an emancipated minor by a court, reaches 18 years of age, or gets married.
PERJURY	R	Perjury or false affidavit to DMV under any law of this state requiring the registration of vehicles or regulating their operation on highways. Revoked for one year.
PROD DL/C	S	Unlawfully producing a driver license. Suspended for one year. The "C" in the literal means the suspension was based on a conviction.
PROD DL/D	S	Unlawfully producing a driver license. Suspended for one year. The "D" in the literal means it was determined by DMV.
PROD DL/H	S	After hearing suspension to PROD DL/D suspension.
PROD ID/C	S	Unlawfully producing an Oregon identification card. Suspended for one year. The "C" in the literal means the suspension was based on a conviction.
PROD ID/D	S	Unlawfully producing an Oregon identification card. Suspended for one year. The "D" in the literal means it was determined by DMV.
PROD ID/H	S	After hearing suspension to PROD ID/D suspension.
PROLIC ACT	S	Driver suspended in accordance with Professional License Act of 1993 for failure to pay child support. Suspended until a notice is received from a District Attorney or Support Enforcement Division (SED) allowing a driver to reinstate. (This suspension is of the person's CDL only.)
PRV/DRIC	S	Driver attended provisional driver improvement interview and was required by counselor to take a driver improvement course. Suspended for five years, or until course has been completed.
PRV/MJR	S	Driver is convicted of major traffic offense prior to their 18th birthday. Suspended for one year.
PRV/REF	S	Driver attended provisional driver improvement interview and was given a referral to another agency. Referral form,

Literal	Type	Description
		signed by representative of agency and returned to DMV has not been received by DMV within 30 days. Suspended for five years, or until referral form is signed and returned to DMV.
PRV/TEST	S	Driver attended a provisional driver improvement interview and was required by counselor to complete all tests for a driver license. Suspended for five years, or until tests have been completed.
PRV_ACC/H	S	After hearing suspension to PRV ACCAPA suspension.
PRV_ACCAPA	S	Provisional driver suspended for six months based on having three or more preventable accidents, or a combination of accidents and driver improvement violations that totals three or more, prior to reaching their 18th birthday.
PRV_CONVAR	S	Provisional driver suspended for six months based on receiving three or more driver improvement violations prior to their 18th birthday.
R/END H/WK	S	Driver recklessly endangered life of a highway worker in a highway work zone. See FL/AT ELUD for suspension lengths.
R/BLD CDL	S	Driver of a CMV refused to submit to blood test taken for blood alcohol content while receiving medical care in a health facility after a motor vehicle accident. Suspended for three years. (This suspension is of the person's CDL only.)
R/BLD CDL*	S	Driver of a CMV or a driver with a valid CDL at the time of offense refused to have a blood test taken for blood alcohol content while receiving medical care in a health facility after a motor vehicle accident. Suspension length is increased due to prior major CDL/CMV offense in Oregon or an equivalent prior offense in another state. Lifetime suspension of CDL only. Conditional reinstatement after 10 years (see OAR 735-070-0200).
R/BLD HAZ	S	Driver of a CMV transporting hazardous materials refused to submit to blood test taken for blood alcohol content while receiving medical care in a health facility after a motor vehicle accident. Suspended for five years. (This suspension is of the person's CDL only.)
R/BLD HAZ*	S	Driver of a CMV transporting hazardous materials refused to have a blood test taken for blood alcohol content while receiving medical care in a health facility after a motor vehicle accident. Suspension length is increased due to prior major CDL/CMV offense in Oregon or an equivalent prior offense in another state. Lifetime suspension of CDL only. Conditional reinstatement after 10 years (see OAR 735-070-0200).
R/BLD TST	S	Refused to submit to a blood test under Implied Consent Law, while receiving medical care in a health care facility immediately after a motor vehicle accident. Suspended for 1 year.
R/BLD TST*	S	Same as R/BLD TST (328). Suspension length is increased because at the time of arrest driver was participating in an alcohol diversion program or, within five years preceding the arrest, driver began participation in an alcohol diversion program, began serving an Implied Consent suspension, or was convicted of DUII. Suspended for three years.
R/UA CDL	S	Driver of a CMV or driver with a valid CDL at the time of offense refused to submit to a urine test. Suspended for three years. (This suspension is of the person's CDL only.)
R/UA CDL*	S	Driver of a CMV or a driver with a valid CDL at the time of offense refused to submit to a urine test. Suspension length is increased due to prior major CDL/CMV offense in Oregon or an equivalent prior offense in another state. Lifetime suspension of CDL only. Conditional reinstatement after 10 years (see OAR 735-070-0200).
R/UA HAZ	S	Driver of a CMV transporting hazardous materials refused to submit to a urine test. Suspended for five years. (This suspension is of the person's CDL only.)
R/UA HAZ*	S	Driver of a CMV transporting hazardous materials refused to submit to a urine test. Suspension length is increased due to prior major CDL/CMV offense in Oregon or an equivalent prior offense in another state. Lifetime suspension of CDL only. Conditional reinstatement after 10 years (see OAR 735-070-0200).
RECK ENDGR	S	Recklessly endangering another person with a motor vehicle. See FL/AT ELUD for suspension lengths.
RECKLSS DR	S	Reckless Driving. See FL/AT ELUD for suspension lengths.
REFUS BT	S	Driver refused a breath test. Suspended for one year.
REFUS BT*	S	Driver refused a breath test. Increased suspension length because at the time of arrest, driver participated in an alcohol diversion program, or within five years preceding the arrest, driver began participation in an alcohol diversion program, began serving an Implied Consent suspension, or was convicted of DUII. Suspended for three years.
REFUS CDL	S	Driver of a CMV or a driver with a valid CDL at the time of arrest refused a breath test. Suspended for three years. (This suspension is of the person's CDL only.)
REFUS CDL*	S	Driver of a CMV or a driver with a valid CDL at the time of arrest refused a breath test. Suspension length is increased due to prior major CDL/CMV offense in Oregon or an equivalent prior offense in another state. Lifetime suspension of CDL only. Conditional reinstatement after 10 years (see OAR 735-070-0200).
REFUS HAZ	S	Driver of a CMV transporting hazardous materials refused a breath test. Suspended for five years. (This suspension is of the person's CDL only.)
REFUS HAZ*	S	Driver of a CMV transporting hazardous materials refused a breath test. Suspension length is increased due to prior major CDL/CMV offense in Oregon or an equivalent prior offense in another state. Lifetime suspension of CDL only. Conditional reinstatement after 10 years.
REFUSE DISQ	S	Driver of a CMV or a driver with a valid CDL at the time of offense refused to submit to breath, blood or urine test after imposition of reinstatement of a CDL lifetime (10 year) suspension. Lifetime suspension of CDL only – NOT eligible for conditional reinstatement after 10 years.
REFUSE UA	S	Driver refused to submit to a urine test. If the driver has another current implied consent suspension on their record (includes any pending suspension arising out of same arrest), this suspension begins on the ending date of that suspension. Suspended for one year.
REFUSE UA*	S	Driver refused to submit to a urine test. Suspension length is increased because at the time of arrest driver was participating in an alcohol diversion program; or, within five years preceding the arrest driver began participation in an alcohol diversion program, began serving an Implied Consent suspension, or was convicted of DUII. If the driver has another open implied consent suspension on their record (includes any pending suspension arising out of same arrest),

Literal	Type	Description
		this suspension begins on the ending date of that suspension. Suspended for three years.
SCH ATTEND	S	Suspended based on notification by School Board/District that a student between the ages of 15 and 18 has withdrawn from school as defined in ORS 339.257(2).
SCHOOL 1	S	School Board or Superintendent requested suspension of driving privileges for student who was suspended or expelled from school for bringing weapon to school, assault, menacing or willful damage to school property. Suspension is for a maximum of one year.
SCHOOL 2	S	Second or subsequent request from School Board or Superintendent. Suspended until age 21.
SER ACC	S	A serious accident suspension may be ordered by DMV after a fatal accident if DMV has reason to believe the driver contributed to the accident by being incompetent, negligent, or recklessly or unlawfully operating a motor vehicle. Suspended for one year.
SER ACC/H	S	After hearing suspension to SER ACC suspension
SER VIOL1	S	Driver of a CMV was convicted of two serious traffic offenses within a three year period. Suspended for 60 days. (This suspension is of the person's CDL only.)
SER VIOL2	S	Driver of a CMV was convicted of three serious traffic offenses within a three year period. Suspended for 120 days. (This suspension is of the person's CDL only.)
SERIOUS AC	S	DMV imposed a serious accident suspension after a fatal accident and DMV had reason to believe the driver caused and contributed to the accident by being incompetent, negligent, or recklessly or unlawfully operating a motor vehicle. Suspended for one year.
SPL VIOL/H	C	After hearing cancellation to SPL VIOL cancellation.
SPL VIOL	C	Operating a vehicle outside restrictions designated on an Emergency Operator=s Permit or Student Permit. Permit is canceled until the person is 16 years old.
TAMP IID	S	Tampering with an Ignition Interlock Device (IID). Suspended until ending date of IID requirement (one year a first conviction or two years for a second or subsequent DUII conviction).
THEFT GAS	S	Convicted of theft when the theft was of gasoline. Suspended for six months.
TOBACCO	S	Suspended based on court notification – possession of tobacco through misrepresentation of age. Suspended for period of time determined by court, up to a maximum of one year.
UNAUTH USE	R	Unauthorized use of a motor vehicle. Revoked for one year.
UNSAT MED	S	Medical certification is denied by the Medical Determination Officer. Suspended indefinitely or until certification is approved.
UNSAT REQ	C	Canceled under At-Risk Driver mandatory medical reporting program for inability to meet medical requirement.
UNSAT REQ1	C	Cancellation - Inability to meet licensing requirement under mandatory medical reporting program (immediate cancellation).
UNSAT REQH	C	After hearing cancellation to UNSAT REQ cancellation.
V HOM/INC	R	Driver convicted of aggravated vehicle homicide. Sentencing included incarceration. The revocation is imposed upon notice of conviction, but has no end date until DMV receives notice of the person's release from incarceration for this and any other crime arising from the same criminal episode. The revocation period ends ten years from the date of release from incarceration.
V OUT/SVC	S	Driver of a commercial motor vehicle violated an out-of-service order. Suspended for 180 days. (This suspension is of the person's CDL only.) Older suspension entries will indicate a 90 day suspension period.
V/OUT SVC*	S	Driver of a commercial motor vehicle violated an out-of-service order. Second offense. Suspended for three years. (This suspension is of the person's CDL only.)
VEH HOM	R	Driver convicted of aggravated vehicular homicide. Revoked for ten years. Older revocation entries will show eight year revocation period.
VEH HOM/P	R	Driver convicted of aggravated vehicular homicide. Revoked permanently by court order. Person may petition the court to restore driving privileges no sooner than ten years from the date the person is released from incarceration.
VIOL CON/H	R	After hearing suspension to VIOL COND revocation.
VIOL COND	R	Driver violated the conditions of a hardship permit issued during a DUII suspension. The permit is revoked for one year or until the ending date of the DUII suspension, whichever comes first.
VIOL PRO/H	R	After hearing suspension to VIOL PROB revocation.
VIOL PROB	R	Driver violated the conditions of a probationary permit (issued during a habitual offender revocation). Permit is revoked for one year, during which driver is not eligible for any license or permit.
VIOL REQ	R	Driver violated the requirements of a hardship permit issued during any suspension other than a DUII. The permit is revoked for one year or until the ending date of the underlying suspension, whichever comes first.
VIOL REQ/H	R	After hearing suspension to VIOL REQ suspension.
VIOL RST	S	Usually second offense for violating a license restriction, such as not wearing corrective lenses. Suspended for 30 days. If restriction is removed prior to end date of suspension, driving privileges can be reinstated. If convicted or violating a Driver Improvement restriction, then 1st conviction results in suspension.
WDRAW MH/H	R	After hearing suspension or revocation to WITHDRW MH suspension.
WITHDRW MH	R	Withdrawal of mental health recommendation for a hardship permit issued during a suspension for a second or subsequent DUII. First withdrawal is a suspension until ending date of the DUII suspension or until a new recommendation is received by DMV. Second withdrawal is a one year revocation or until the ending date of the suspension, whichever comes first.

Pennsylvania

Administration	Important Telephone and Web Contacts

Janet Dolan, Director
Bureau of Driver Licensing
Department of Transportation
Riverfront Office Center, 4th Floor
1101 South Front Street
Harrisburg 17104
 	
www.dmv.state.pa.us
	Driver and Vehicle Services
	.... 717-391-6190, In-state only 800-932-4600
	Commercial Driver License.........................717-783-3653
	General Number 717-412-5300
	State Department of Insurance 717-787-2317
	State Police...717-783-5599
	Email contact list at:
	   www.dot4.state.pa.us/contact_us/index.shtml
	Vehicle Code - Title 75:
	   https://www.dot4.state.pa.us/vehicle_code/index.shtml

Driver's License Format, Issuance and Renewal

License Classes, Restrictions and Endorsements Appear After the Driving Record Content Section

License Format

The format is eight numbers. There is no code in the sequential arrangement determining the digits making the license number.

Document Appearance

The current version of the driver license has been in circulation since 07/31/2001, the current Temporary License/ID Card since 10/2007. The "PA" in the Keystone appears in all licenses and ID Cards effective 02/2008.

Security Characteristics: Features include a holographic overlay that displays the "Keystone" in the foreground and county names in the background. The cards have a thick security coating or hologram, an area to denote organ donors, and different colored bands to indicate product type. Regular licenses have a blue colored band appearing on left side, ID cards have a yellow band, under 18 drivers have a green band. There is a red banner on all restricted license documents. In the lower right corner of the license document is a visible box that indicates the type of license.

Position of Photo: On the left side, inside the colored band.

Minor Age Driver Locator: For driver under 21, cards are produced in a vertical format. Above the picture, the date the individual turns 18 is highlighted in yellow and the date they turn 21 is highlighted in red. Drivers under 21 have a blue band, drivers under 18 have a green band.

Occupational: The wording inside the red banner on the left side indicates Limited License. The Keystone in lower right corner indicates Occupational License.

Probationary: The wording inside the red banner on the left side indicates Limited License. The Keystone in lower right corner indicates Probationary License.

Ignition Interlock: The wording inside the red banner on the left side indicates Limited License. The Keystone in lower right corner indicates Ignition Interlock License.

CDL Indicator: "COMMERCIAL DRIVERS LICENSE" appears within blue band on left.

Note: Since October 2007, a *Temporary License/ID Card* is used to new applicants. This card looks like the other products except the banner is gray, the word "Temporary" is printed in red across the license and the expiration date is outlined in red. In addition, the overlay on the front is changed to include "PA" in the Keystone. The temporary product is valid for 15 days and provides PennDOT time to ensure the individual's photograph does not match another photograph in the database under a different driver name(s).

Issuance

Location of Requirements for Proof of Identity:
www.dmv.state.pa.us/licensing_master/identity.shtml

Age Requirements

The minimum age is sixteen; eighteen for CDL. Below is information on various permits.

Learner's Permit: Required; sixteen; mandatory six months on learner permit before eligible to take skills test; certification of 65 hours behind-the-wheel skill building prior to skills test; must have parent/guardian consent and be accompanied by a licensed driver, twenty-one or older, licensed in the same class; driving permitted only between 5AM to 11PM.

Junior License: Sixteen and six months; must have passed all skills requirements of leaner's permit. For the first six months, a driver is not permitted to have more than one passenger under age 18 who is not an immediate family member in the vehicle unless accompanied by a parent or legal guardian. If they have not been convicted of a driving violation or been partially or fully responsible for a reportable crash after six months, they may have up to three passengers under age 18 who are not immediate family members without a parent or legal guardian present. If they have any convictions or are partially or fully responsible for a reportable crash while a junior driver, they are once again restricted to one passenger.

Unrestricted License: Possible at seventeen and six months if crash and conviction free record for twelve months; completion of approved driver's education course.

Note: Occupational Limited Licenses can be issued under certain circumstances, except to drivers convicted of homicide by vehicle and other serious traffic offenses in Chapter 37 Subchapter B, as well as all Subchapter C, convictions relating to accidents and accident reports.

Residency

A non-resident's home-state license is honored on a reciprocal basis. One must secure a PA license within sixty days of establishing residency. A knowledge test is not required for new residents with out-of-state driver's licenses which are valid or expired six months or less.

Renewal

Licenses expire one day after the licensee's birthdate on fourth year; drivers over age sixty-five have the option of two-year renewals. Driver keeps same number when renewing. Renewal and address changes are available online, except for CDL drivers. Go to www.dot4.state.pa.us/centers/OnlineServicesCenter.shtml. Military personnel who have an expired license do not have to renew as long as they are active duty. In addition, if an out-of-state driver's license has been expired for more than six months, it cannot be transferred for a PA driver's license. The driver must apply for a PA Learner's Permit and complete all applicable knowledge and skills tests in order to obtain the driver's license.

Elderly-Related Restrictions
Individuals age 65 or older have the option of renewing their license every two years, instead of standard four years.

Vehicle Insurance, Title and Registration Facts

Registration Renewal
Renewal is annual. Renewal may be performed online for passenger cars, truck weighing less than 54,999 pounds (there are exceptions), and trailers; current insurance information is required. Renewal is available from the home page at www.dmv.state.pa.us, and from there view the exceptions list.

Also private businesses (Online Messengers - OLM) are contracted to provide vehicle registration services for customers. In many cases, the product can be handed immediately over the counter to the customer since the OLM has an online connection with PennDOT. The OLM charges the normal state fee plus a service fee for its service.

New Residents
All new residents are required to make application for Pennsylvania title and registration of their vehicle(s) within 20 days of establishing residency in Pennsylvania. A vehicle newly registered in Pennsylvania must be safety inspected within ten (10) days of the registration date.

Inspections and Emissions Testing
Pennsylvania has an annual vehicle safety inspection provision. There is no statewide emission testing program, but four regional areas require annual emission testing: Pittsburgh area (Allegheny, Beaver, Washington, and Westmoreland counties); South Central (Berks, Cumberland, Dauphin, Lancaster, Lebanon, Lehigh, Northampton, and York counties); Philadelphia area (Bucks, Chester, Delaware, Philadelphia, and Montgomery counties); and the Northern region

(Blair, Cambria, Centre, Erie, Lackawanna, Luzerne, Lycoming, and Mercer counties).

Thus, vehicles registered in 42 counties are not required to pass the emissions inspection. However, as part of the safety inspection most passenger vehicles and light trucks weighing 11,000 pounds and less are required to pass a visual anti-tampering check. The visual anti-tampering check is a visual inspection for the presence of emission control components that were installed on a vehicle by the manufacturer. Vehicles registered as classic or collectible are exempt from the anti-tampering portion of the safety inspection.

Passenger Plate Facts
There is one plate and one decal (MO & YR). There is no coding sequence which depicts county of issuance. When a vehicle is sold, the plate remains with the seller.

Insurance and Financial Responsibility
Pennsylvania has a compulsory liability insurance law in effect with minimum limits for responsibility at $15,000/30,000/5,000. The state has no-fault insurance provisions. The state requires proof of insurance or financial responsibility at registration or renewal and after an accident or certain violations. What constitutes acceptable proof of insurance is found at www.dmv.state.pa.us/insurance/proof.shtml. The SR-22 form is not used. A person or company desiring to qualify as a self-insurer must file a proposal of self-insurance with PennDOT for approval.

Withdrawal Sanctions, and Alcohol and Drug Testing

Alcohol and Chemical Testing Limits
The illegal intoxication level is 0.08 percent and above, .04 for CDL drivers except school bus drivers which is .02, and .02 for drivers under 21. There is a three-tier measurement system that dictates the penalties (.08 to .099%, .10 to .159%, and .16% and higher). Breath, blood, or urine testing are authorized. There is an implied-consent law, but not a provision for an administrative suspension per se. Operating a horse or bicycle under the influence is also considered illegal.

Suspensions and Revocations
See the Appendix for a list of the federally mandated disqualifications for offenses occurring in a CMV per MCSIA. Also, a Fact Sheet on CDL Sanctions is found at www.dmv.state.pa.us/pdotforms/fact_sheets/fs-pub7216.pdf.

DUI Convictions (Fines and jail sentences also imposed, which increase based on level and number of previous offenses.)
.08 to .099% BAC - 2nd offense or 3rd offense..Twelve-month suspension
.10 to .159% BAC
   1st or 2nd offense..Twelve-month suspension.
   3rd or 4th offense...Eighteen-month suspension.
.16% or higher BAC
   1st offense..Twelve-month suspension.
   2nd or greater offense ....Eighteen-month suspension.
DUI Commercial Driver, 2nd conviction..Lifetime disqualification.
DUI ARD (Accelerated Rehabilitation Program) ....Maximum ninety days suspension.
Careless Driving Causing Serious Bodily Injury...Three-month suspension.
Careless Driving Causing Unintentional Death...Six-month suspension.
Child Support or Domestic Relations Issues ....Indefinite.
Conviction of Thirty-one mph Over Limit ....Fifteen-day suspension.
Drivers under age of eighteen
   Accumulation of Six or More Points ....Ninety-day suspension.
   High Speed Conviction (26 or more over posted limit) ....Ninety-day suspension.
   Second occurrence of either above ....One hundred twenty-day suspension.
Driving Without Insurance ....Three-month suspension.

Failure to Attend Departmental Hearings	Sixty-day suspension.
Failure to Comply With Crossing Gate or barrier	Thirty-day suspension.
Failure to Stop for School Bus With Flashing Red Lights	Sixty-day suspension.
Habitual Offender	Five-year revocation.
Operating a Vehicle Without Insurance or Financial Responsibility	Three-month suspension.

Point Accumulation of Six Points

Second Time at Six Points (Departmental Hearing)	Fifteen-day suspension.
Failure to Attend Departmental Hearing	Sixty-day suspension.
Third Time at Six Points (Departmental Hearing)	Thirty-day suspension.
Failure to Attend Departmental Hearing	Indefinite suspension.

Point Accumulation of Eleven or More Points

First Suspension	Five days per point.
Second Suspension	Ten days per point.
Third Suspension	Fifteen days per point.
Subsequent Suspensions	One-year suspension.

Possession, sale, or delivery of controlled substance regardless if motor vehicle involved:

First Offense	Six-month suspension.
Second Offense	One-year suspension.
Third or Subsequent Offense	Two-year suspension.
Work Zone (active) Speeding if involved in accident or if 11 MPH or more over	Fifteen-day suspension.

Note About Points: Three points are removed from a driving record for every 12 consecutive months a person drives (from the date of the last violation) without a violation which results in points, license suspension or revocation.

Reinstatement Requirements

Suspension $25.00 to $100.00 fee; proof of financial responsibility.

Revocation $25.00 to $100.00 fee; proof of financial responsibility; must reapply for driving privilege by applying for learner's permit under some circumstances.

Record Access: Laws, Rules, and Forms

Note: This Section Applies to Both Driver and Vehicle Records.

Governing Statutes and Rules

Statutes: www.legis.state.pa.us/cfdocs/legis/LI/Public/cons_index.cfm
Vehicle Code: https://www.dot4.state.pa.us/vehicle_code/index.shtml
Title 75 § 6114 of the PA Consolidated Statutes and Section 6114 of the state Vehicle Code specifically denotes who can obtain driving records and accident report information, and under what circumstances.

Policy Statement Regarding Permissible Uses

Pennsylvania adopted the DPPA exceptions (uses) and added the following exceptions:

(1) Required or authorized under this title to be sold, published or disclosed.

(2) Authorized in writing by the person who is the subject of the record or report to be sold, published or disclosed. A police officer, or officer, employee or agent of a Commonwealth agency or local authority may rely on a certification from a person requesting a record or report under this paragraph that its sale, publication or disclosure has been authorized by the person who is the subject of the record or report. In the event such sale, publication or disclosure shall not have been authorized, the person who made the false certification, rather than the police officer or officer, employee or agent of the Commonwealth agency or local authority, shall be guilty of the offense defined by this section.

(3) Required to be released by order of court.

(4) Authorized by departmental regulation to be sold, published or disclosed to any Federal, State or local governmental agency for the sole purpose of exercising a legitimate governmental function or duty. Such records or reports shall not be resold, published or disclosed by the receiving agency for any commercial purpose or without prior departmental approval.

(4.1) Of a constituent released to a member of Congress or of the General Assembly or to an employee of a member of Congress or of the General Assembly. Under this paragraph, records or reports may not be sold, published or disclosed by the member or the employee for any commercial purpose without prior approval by the department.

(5) Purchased by a person who, in compliance with the Fair Credit Reporting Act (84 Stat. 1127-1136, 15 U.S.C. § 1601 et seq.), has filed with the department an affidavit, in form acceptable to the department, certifying the intended use of said records or reports.

(6) Obtained in any form, including computer access, by a messenger service which has filed an affidavit of intended use with the department and which maintains on file at its office of record an authorization in writing by the person who is the subject of the obtained record or report. The authorizations are subject to inspection by the department and shall be retained for a period of two years. The records or reports may not be accessed, sold, published or disclosed by the messenger service for any commercial purpose except the filed intended use without prior approval by the department.

Request and Consent Forms

Driving Record: Internet User Affidavit: A signed, notarized copy of *DL-9001 Internet User Application/Licensing Agreement* must be submitted by authorized users who wish to obtain records via the DOT Internet site. (Depending on type of requester, *DL9002, DL9004, or DL9005* may be required instead.) This form lists a series of restrictions including but not limited to:

- Requester understands that the driver record is confidential and restricted information and will establish procedures to protect the confidentiality of these records.
- Requester agrees not to sell, assign or otherwise transfer to any other party the information obtained from PennDOT.
- Requester understands that PennDOT retains exclusive ownership of all driver record information provided and Requester agrees not to combine and/or link in with any other data on any database except as may be required by law.
- Requester will not disseminate or publish on the Internet personal information obtained from PennDOT or allow any other person to disseminate or publish the personal information on the Internet without the express written permission of PennDOT.

- Requester understands that he/she is responsible for all actions taken with their assigned commercial account number and password and will establish procedures to protect this information. Requester understands that he/she must contact PennDOT immediately if they feel their account number and/or password has been used by any unauthorized person or for any fraudulent or non-legitimate purpose.
- Requester agrees that PennDOT, or an independent auditor selected by PennDOT, may audit their records as to their performance under this Licensing Agreement. The degree and conduct of any such audit, and the frequency of such audits, will be at the sole discretion of PennDOT and will focus on compliance with the terms of this Licensing Agreement. Requester agrees to fully cooperate with PennDOT's auditors and agrees to be responsible for ensuring cooperation by any and all employees.
- Requester understands that he/she must utilize Internet Explorer browser version 5.0 or higher with 128-bit encryption to perform online transactions. Requester agrees to limit the number of business transactions to 25 per session. Requester further understands that he/she must close their browser after each session.

Pre-employment screening companies can utilize the DOT Internet site to obtain driver records on behalf of their customers. An *Affidavit of Intended Use* must be submitted by all customers of approved wholesale accounts and pre-employment screening companies. This form requires the signature of the requester be notarized.

Driving Record: Non-Internet Requests: For the permissible use requesters that submit directly to the Department for records, *Form DL-503* must be used, which requires the notarized signature of the requester unless the requester is the subject of the request. The form (found at www.dmv.state.pa.us/forms/driversLicenseForms.shtm) remains valid for three months. All government requesters must submit the Government Agency Internet Application/License Agreement form.

Vehicle Records: Either a release signed by the owner or a statement of intended use must be submitted when requesting a vehicle record. *State Form DL-135* must be completed which requires the notarized signature of the requester and non-notarized signature of the subject. The form is at www.dot4.state.pa.us/pdotforms/dl_forms/dl-135.pdf.

Vendor and Third Party Access Policy

Wholesale vendors can only sell to end-users who are pre-approved by the state, otherwise record sold vendor-to-vendor is strictly forbidden. The state restricts the use, storage, or resale of records after a completed transaction.

See the **Internet User Affidavit above.**

Non-permissible Use Requests

No record information is released without consent, even records without personal information.

Access to Driver-Related Records

Driving Records

General Information and Fees

Driver Record Services, Department of Transportation, PO Box 68695, Harrisburg PA 17106-8695, 717-391-6190.

The in-state toll-free number for questions is 800-932-4600. A $5.00 fee is charged for each of four different record types:
1. basic information
2. three-year driving record
3. ten-year record on a commercial driver for employment purposes only
4. full history record on a commercial driver for employment purposes only.

A copy of a document may be obtained from microfilm. Pennsylvania charges for a no record found search. Add $5.00 for certification for any of the record types. The DL-503 Form is found at www.dmv.state.pa.us/pdotforms/dl_forms/dl-503.pdf.

Also, a Letter of Clearance may be requested for $5.00. Use DL-130 found at www.dmv.state.pa.us/forms/driversLicenseForms.shtml.

In-Person – This agency will process one driving record request over-the-counter at the 1st Floor Customer Service Area at 1101 S Front St in Harrisburg while you wait. More than one request can not be processed while waiting, but will be forwarded to the processing area and mailed upon completion. Records may also be obtained from PennDot's Driver License Centers. Note the Centers take only checks or money orders; no cash or credit cards are accepted at these locations.

Mail – The Harrisburg address is the only location to provide certified driving records, Clearance Letters and microfilm access. The driver's license number, name, and date of birth are needed when ordering. Casual requesters must submit *Form DL-503* (downloadable from web). The fee must accompany each request. Turnaround time is 7-10 days.

Electronic – Online access is available to approved requesters - usually businesses who obtain driver histories for the purpose of employment or insurance. The three-year driving record is released, unless the subject is a CDL holder, then the ten-year record is released. For more information on opening an account, visit the Department's web site (www.dmv.state.pa.us) and click on the *Business Partners* tab, then the *Online Business Driver History Request Service* link. If applying for service, *Form DL-9001* (mentioned above) must be submitted for

approval. Use of a credit card is required. Also, high volume vendors who directly represent permissible users may access on an interactive basis.

The driver's license number and first two letters of the last name are required when ordering. Payment in full is required before information is released. However, note that all signed agreements forbid the requester from using the Internet as a means to transmit data to end-user clients without express written permission from PennDOT. There is a $200 non-refundable application fee.

Also, the DOT offers another, unique, online service to driving records via *online messengers*. Located throughout the state, these messengers provide online access and processing for a variety of customer DOT needs. Additional fees apply. Visit the web page to find locations for over 200 approved messengers

Bulk – The state does not offer its driver license file for sale to commercial vendors or users.

By Person of Record – PA drivers may obtain their driving record by mail or walk-in as described above or may purchase online at www.dmv.state.pa.us/centers/OnlineServicesCenter.shtml. The driver must provide the DL or Photo ID number, the DOB and last four digits of the SSN. The fee is $5.00 for either the three-year record or ten-year CDL record. This record will not indicate the number of points associated with each conviction.

Notification/Monitoring Program

Although the DOT does not offer a monitoring system or notification program to employers or insurance companies, account holders who employ **commercial drivers or school bus drivers** can apply for unlimited electronic access to driver records. The $200.00 account fee mentioned must be paid and there is a $5.00 charge per driver. A form must be completed on an annual basis in order to maintain this service.

Accident Reports

Reporting – The police should be contacted immediately when there is an accident involving death, personal injury, or when a vehicle must be towed from the scene of the accident—regardless of the dollar amount of damage. If the police cannot be contacted, an "Operator's Report" must be filed within five days. Reports should be filed with Bureau of Highway Safety and Traffic Engineering, PO Box 2047, Harrisburg 17105-2047. Commercial carriers with operating authority of the Public Utilities Commission must file a report (with that agency) on any accident resulting in death, injury, or property damage in excess of $100.00. Fatal accidents must be reported within twenty-four hours; accidents involving injury should also be reported within twenty-four hours; and written reports should be filed for all accidents within thirty days.

Drivers of motor carrier vehicles, buses, school buses or vehicles transporting hazardous materials if involved in a reportable accident must submit to testing for alcohol and controlled substances. The cost is borne by the driver's employer.

Record Access – State Police Headquarters, Crash Reports Unit, 1800 Elmerton Avenue, Harrisburg 17110, 717-783-5516, fax is 717-705-6368. www.psp.state.pa.us. Copies of accident reports within last five years can be obtained. However per Section 3751(b) of the Vehicle Code, only those involved or attorney or insurer may request a copy. Reports are $8.00; prepayment is required. Requesters must include drivers" names, the date, and the incident number. It takes an average of 15 days before new records are ready for inquiry. Turnaround time on mail requests is usually 3 weeks. Reports can be returned by email, if so requested.

Access to Vehicle-Related Records

General Information and Fees

Vehicle Record Services, Department of Transportation, 1101 South Front St, PO Box 68691, Harrisburg 17106-8691, 717-391-6190, in-state 800-932-4600. Records are kept on all vehicles and unattached mobile homes. The following information is available for a fee of $5.00 per report:

Title History: A copy of the title transaction documents is provided.

Odometer: A copy of the title/renewal transaction is provided.

Basic: Includes name, address, title number, tag, VIN, make and expiration date of tag.

Encumbrance: Includes basic information listed above plus the lienholder's name and address and expiration date.

Insurance: A copy of the title/renewal transaction is provided.

Add $5.00 for certification. Note that encumbrance or lien information is not considered public information and is only available per DPPA guidelines.

In-Person or Mail – Requests must be submitted using *Form DL-135* (downloadable from web site). Walk-in requesters may order records, but the results will be mailed.

Electronic – Online inquiry is not available at this time.

Bulk – The state will sell some vehicle information depending on intended use. A written request to the address above is required for consideration. Certain statistical type user requests (i.e. vehicle recall) will be honored.

Access to Vessel-Related Records

General Information, Access and Fees

Fish and Boat Commission, Division of Licensing & Registration, PO Box 68900, Harrisburg, 17106-8900, 717-705-7940, fax is 717-705-7931, www.fishandboat.com.

Any boat powered by a gasoline, diesel or electric motor, including sailboats with auxiliary power, must be registered. Boats must be titled if with inboard motor or outboard motor and 14 ft or longer and has a manufacture year of 1997 or newer. The agency follows the FCRA regarding the release of boat registration and ownership information. Liens are filed here for $5.00 per lien. As of 1998, this agency issues

certificates of title. Search requests must be in writing and require signature of requester, reason for request, as much information about the boat or owner as possible. It can take as along as one month before new records are ready for inquiry.

The *Request Boat Title or Security Interest Information* form is found at www.fish.state.pa.us/images/pages/forms/pfbc_t9.pdf. There is a $5.00 fee for either current ownership information or lien information. The charge for a title history report is $5.00 for each owner shown on the record chain. Credit cards are accepted

Driving Record Content and Reciprocity

What's On or Not On the Driving Record

- The driver's address is part of the record, the SSN is not released.
- Any violation resulting in points being assessed against the record or a suspension/revocation of driving privileges is processed against the driver's record.
- Accidents are reported on the driving record as involvement only.
- The length of time convictions are shown on a driving record is dependent on the type of record ordered, as explained above.
- A record ordered online by the driver will not show points.

Data Retention

CDL driver records are purged based on the timetable per federal regulations (see the Appendix) and all drivers according to Departmental regulations or statutes; including surrendered licenses.

Court to Repository

Convictions and failure to respond to citations are transferred electronically or via paper. Major violations (i.e. misdemeanors and

felonies) are required by law to be mailed within 10 days of final judgment of conviction. The law further mandates that the Department shall promptly enter information on the records of the persons involved. Typically, a conviction will be placed on a record within 15 days of receipt via paper and the next day electronically.

State Reciprocity for Non-CDL Drivers

- Will suspend license of driver for unpaid out-of-state convictions, if NRVC member.
- Record of new incoming driver is not shown on MVR.
- Out-of-state convictions are shown on MVR only if major with suspension action.
- Out-of-state accidents are not shown on MVR.
- Convictions of out-of-state drivers are sent to home state.
- Record is forwarded to new state upon surrender of license when requested.

License Classes, Restrictions, and Endorsements

License Classes– Commercial

Pennsylvania began issuing the CDL in November 1990.

Class A   Minimum age 18, required to operate any combination of vehicles with a GVW rating of 26,001 pounds or more, provided the vehicle being towed is in excess of 10,000 pounds; also includes Classes B and C.

Class B   Minimum age 18, required to operate any single vehicle with GVW rating of 26,001 pounds or more; also includes Class C.

Class C   Minimum age 18, required to operate any single vehicle with a GVW rating of not more than 26,000 pounds that is designed to transport 16 or more passengers, including the driver; or is a school bus designed to carry 11 passengers or more, including driver; or is used to transport hazardous materials.

License Classes– Non-Commercial

Class A   Minimum age 18, required to operate any combination of vehicles with a gross weight rating of 26,001 pounds or more, where the vehicle(s) being towed is/are in excess of 10,000 pounds. Example: Recreational Vehicle, when the towing vehicle is rated at 11,000 pounds and the vehicle towed is rated at 15,500 pounds (total combination weight of 26,500 pounds).

Class B   Minimum age 18, required to operate any single vehicle rated in excess of 26,000 pounds. Example: Motor homes rated at 26,001 pounds or more.

Class C   Issued to persons 16 years of age or older to operate any vehicles, except those requiring a Class M qualification, and who do not meet the definitions of Class A or Class B. Any firefighter or member of a rescue or emergency squad who is the holder of a Class C driver's license and who has a certificate of authorization from a fire chief or head of the rescue or emergency squad will be authorized to operate any fire or emergency vehicle registered to that fire department, rescue or emergency squad or municipality. The holder of a Class C driver's license is also authorized to drive a motorized pedalcycle (a motor-driven cycle) or a three-wheeled motorcycle equipped with an enclosed cab, but not a motorcycle.

Class M   Issued to those persons 16 years of age or older to operate a motorcycle or motor-driven cycle. If a person is qualified to operate only a motorcycle or motor-driven cycle, he/she will be issued a Class M driver's license. If motorcycle is less than 50 CCs, an "8" restriction will appear on the driver's license and the license holder is prohibited from operating a motorcycle 50 CCs or larger.

Other License Types

- Occupational Limited License (OLL) for non-commercial classes. An OLL authorizes one to drive a designated motor vehicle, under certain conditions, when it is necessary for the driver's occupation, work, trade, medical treatment or study.
- Probationary Licenses for Class C only. Both limited licenses need an authorization letter that contains specific information pertaining to the operator, such as; vehicle information, operating hours, and destination. Both products must be carried together at all times.
- An Ignition Interlock License is issued to those individuals restricted to only driving vehicles with an ignition interlock device.

Restrictions

Medical Restrictions

B	Equip with Hand Emergency Brake	L	Must Wear Corrective Lenses
C	Classified Driver (see record)	N	Gear Shift on Steering Column
D	Hand Dimmer-Switch and/or Throttle	O	Special Hand-Control Equipment
E	Equip With Outside Mirror	P	Special Left- or Right-Side Gas Pedal
G	Extension on Gas and/or Brake Pedal	S	Equip With Automatic-Type Shift
H	All Hand Controls	V	Restricted Motorcycle
I	Equip With Power Brake and/or Power Steering	X	See Endorsement Card
J	Special Foot-Control Equipment	Z	Daylight Driving Only
K	Knob on Steering Wheel		

Commercial Licensing Restrictions

L	May Not Drive Air-Brake Equipped Vehicles	C	Restricts the Driver to C Bus
B	Restricts the Driver to B and C Buses		

Note: If an "8" restriction appears on the driver's license, the licensee is prohibited from operating a motorcycle 50 CCs or larger.
If an "9" restriction appears on the driver's license, the licensee may only operated a 3-wheeled motor cycle.

Endorsements

H	Hazardous Materials	S	School Bus
N	Tank Vehicles	T	Double-/Triple-Trailers
P	Passengers	X	Tank and Hazardous Materials

Pennsylvania Record Types and Status Codes

Record Types

A2	2 YR LIC/LP/ID	FI	FICT OPERATOR	JA	JR LIC/LP/ID
A4	4 YR LIC/LP/SB	ID	PHOTO ID	JB	JR LIC/LP
BP	SCHBUS/PERMIT	II	INTERLOCK LICENSE	JL	JR LICENSE
B2	2YR LIC/LP	IL	INTERLOCK DEVICE	JP	JR PERMIT
B4	4YR LIC/LP	IO	INTERLOCK PA MOVED OOS	LB	LICENSE/SB
CS	CHGSOR INPROG	IP	REG LP/ID	LI	JR LIC/ID
DC	DECEASED	IR	PHOTO ID REES	LL	OCC UM LIC

LM	OPER/MECHANIC	OM	OUT/STATE MEC	RA	REG LIC/LP/ID
LR	LIC RE-EST	OS	OUT OF STATE	RL	REG LICENSE
L2	REG 2YR LIC	PD	LP PD 2YR/ID	RP	REG LP
MI	MILITARY	PI	JR LP/ID	SB	SCHOOL BUS
ND	NON-DRIVER	PL	PROBATIONARY LIC	SI	2 YR LIC/ID
NI	INTERLOCK ND OOS	PP	JR LP PD	SL	SR LICENSE
OB	OUT OF ST SB	PR	LP RE-EST	SR	SCH BUS RE-ES
OI	REG LIC/ID	P2	LP PD 2 YRS	XX	INTERLOCK OLL
OL	OCCUPATIONAL LIC	P4	LP PD 4 YRS		

Driver Privilege Status Codes

AC	Appeal CDL Disq	NE	No point credit; school and exam	RC	Recall
AD	Administrative stop	NM	Non renewal medical	RE	Revocation
AN	Appeal non; points	NS	No point credit; school	RI	Recall Ignition Interlock
AP	Appeal points	OF	Old "F" stop	RO	Recall OLL
AQ	Acknowledge disq product recvd	OG	Old "G" stop	RP	Rest pend med/dual cont learner's permit
AS	Acknowledge suspension-product received	OH	Old "H" stop		
		OI	Old "I" stop	RR	Restr removal (vision and equip)
CA	Cancellation	OL	Occupational limited license	RX	Re-exam
CD	Cancellation - CDL retest	PA	Pending OLL appeal	SU	Suspension
CP	Cancel probatory license	PB	Pending PL appeal	UL	Pending underage lifetime disqualification
CS	Point credit; school	PC	Pending cancellation		
CV	Cancellation voluntary surrender	PD	Pending disqualification	UD	Pending underage drinking suspension
DD	Lifetime disqualification	PE	Pending PE exam		
DM	Deny the right to apply	PH	Pending PL hearing	UN	Unclaimed
DQ	Disqualification	PM	Pending medical	UQ	Pending underage disqualification
EC	Exam credit point exam	PO	Pending OLL recall	US	Pending underage suspension
EN	Exam non-point	PP	Pending PL recall	UT	Pending underage trespass suspension
EX	Exam points	PR	Pending recall		
FD	Federal Imminent Hazard	PS	Pending suspension	UV	Pending underage revocation
HE	Hearings	PV	Pending revocation	VB	Victim Bad Check
HS	Speed hearings	P3	Pending PL cancel	XE	Hold point exam credit
ME	Pending medical exam	RB	Rebuild	XH	Hold hearing credit
MW	Military waiver	RD	PL Recall		

Conviction Tables with ACD, Statute, and Points

The data for Pennsylvania is presented in **two tables**. The first table indicates convictions that incur points and the ACD translation. The second table shows non-point convictions that may result in a suspension. Pennsylvania MVRs indicate the state statue code for each conviction shown. Butt there may not be a PA code associated with the newer ACD codes that recently went into effect. PA will report the ACD code on Commercial Records only as defined by the Federal definition.

Note: As of 2012, motorists who drive around or through signs or traffic control devices closing a road or highway due to hazardous conditions will have two points added to their driving records and be fined up to $250.

Conviction Table with Points

PA Code	ACD	Description	Points
1512	D29	Violation of restrictions on drivers license - wearing glasses, etc.	2
1571	B41	Violation concerning license	3
3102	M08	Failure to obey policeman or authorized person	2
3112a3i/ii	M16	Failure to stop for a red light	3
3111.1	M14	Traffic control – Hazardous condition	2
3114(a)(1)	M18	Failure to stop for a flashing red light	3
3302	N01	Failure to yield half of roadway to oncoming vehicle	3
3303	M40	Improper passing - overtaken driver to maintain speed; passing in at safe distance	3
3304	M42	Improper passing on the right	3
3305	M42	Improper passing on the left - clear distance ahead	3
3306(a)(1)	M42	Improper passing on a hill	4
3306(a)(2)	M42	Improper passing, at a railroad crossing or intersection	3
3306(a)(3)	M42	Improper passing, at a bridge or tunnel	3
3307	M42	Improper passing, in a no-passing zone	3
3310	M34	Following too closely	3
3321	N06	Failure to yield to driver on the right at intersection	3
3322	N31	Failure to yield to oncoming driver when making left turn	3

PA Code	ACD	Description	Points
3323(b)	M15	Failure to stop for stop sign	3
3323(c)	M19	Failure to yield at yield sign	3
3324	N25	Failure to yield when entering or crossing roadway between intersections	3
3332	N55	Improper turning around - illegal U-turns	3
3341(a)	M10	Failure to obey signal indicating approach of train	2
3341(b)	M10	Failure to comply with crossing gate or barrier	4 *and 30-day suspension*
3342(b),(e)	M22	Failure to stop at railroad crossings	4
3344	M25	Failure to stop when entering from alley, driveway or building	3
3345(a)	M75	Failure to stop for school bus with flashing red lights	5 *and 60-day suspension*
3361	S94	Driving too fast for conditions	2
3362	S Series	Exceeding maximum speed -- Miles over speed limit:	
		6 to 10	2
		11 to 15	3
		16 to 25	4
		26 to 30	5
		31 and over - Note: Also, Departmental hearing and sanctions provided under Section 1538(d (If violation occurs in active work zone, then 15 day suspension triggered.)	5
3365(b)	S15/92/93	Exceeding special speed limit in school zone	3
3365(c)	S15/92/93	Exceeding special speed limit for trucks on downgrades	3
3542(a)	N08	Failure to yield to pedestrian in cross-walk	2
3547	N08	Failure to yield to pedestrian on sidewalk, (when entering from a driveway or alley)	3
3549(a)	N08	Failure to yield to blind pedestrians	3
3702	N82	Improper backing	3
3714(a)	M81	Careless driving	3
3745	B04	Leaving scene of accident involving property damage only	4

Table of Codes Appearing on Driving Records

That Carry No Point Value, But May Result in Suspensions

PA Code	ACD	Description
13a10	A50	Using a vehicle in the commission of a felony involving manufacturing, distributing or dispensing a controlled substance (federal description - is major offense if CMV or if CDL holder)
13a12	A33	Acquisition or obtaining of controlled substance
13a14	A33	Using a vehicle in the commission of a felony involving manufacturing, distributing or dispensing a controlled substance (federal description - is major offense if CMV or if CDL holder)(federal description - is major offense if CMV or if CDL holder)
13a16	A33	Possession of a controlled substance
13a30	A33	Delivery of a controlled substance
13a31	A33	Possession of marijuana
13a36	A33	Manufacture, distribution, possession of a designer drug
1333		Truancy
1371		Driving while vehicle registration is suspended
1501(a)	B51	Driver required to be licensed
1533(a)	D45	Failure to respond (in-state)
1533(b)	D45	Failure to respond (out-of-state)
1533(d)	D45	Default in failure to respond
1535(e)		Conviction of 3361 (too fast for conditions) while in an active work zone. 15-day suspension.
1535(e)		Conviction of 3362 (speeding), minimum 11+ over while in an active work zone. 15-day suspension.
1538		School, examination or hearing on accumulation of points or excessive speed
1539		Suspension of operating privilege on accumulation of points
1540		Surrender of license
1541		Period of revocation or suspension of operating privilege
1542		Revocation of habitual offender's license
1543	B20	Driving while operating privilege is suspended or revoked
1543(a)	B20	Driving when license is withdrawn, barred, or canceled
1543(b)	B20	Driving while operating privilege is suspended or revoked for a DUI violation
1543(b)(1.1)	B20	Driving while operating privilege is suspended or revoked for a DUI violation while under the influence of drugs or alcohol
1547	A12	Refusal to submit to alcohol test, Non-CMV

PA Code	ACD	Description
1547(b)(1)	A12	Refusal - driving under suspension without ignition interlock device
1554(h)1	D27	Violation of limited licensee condition
1606(a)	B51	Driving a CMV without obtaining a CDL or driving without a valid CDL in possession or without proper card or endorsement (federal description - is Serious Traffic Offense for drivers operating a commercial vehicle). Repealed as of 12/24/12- but remains on record.
1601(a)(1)	B56	Driving a CMV without obtaining a CDL (federal description is Serious Traffic Offense for drivers operating a commercial vehicle.)
1601(a)(2)	B57	Driving a CMV without a CDL in possession (federal description is Serious Traffic Offense for drivers operating a commercial vehicle.)
1601(a)(3)	B91	Improper classification or endorsement of drivers license (federal description is Serious Traffic Offense for drivers operating a commercial vehicle.)
1606(c)(1)	B20	Driving a CMV while the driver's CDL is revoked, suspended, cancelled or disqualified (federal description - is major offense if CMV or if CDL holder)
1613	A12	Refusal to submit to alcohol test, CMV
1786(f)	D36	Driving without financial responsibility
2503	U08	Causing a fatality through the negligent operation of a CMV (Federal description - is major offense if CMV or if CDL holder)
2504	U08	Causing a fatality through the negligent operation of a CMV (Federal description - is major offense if CMV or if CDL holder)
2702(a)1	U03	Vehicular assault
2706		Terroristic threats
3111	M14	Traffic control
3309	M42	Improper lane usage - CMV only
3326	M03	Duty of driver in construction and maintenance areas or on highway safety corridors (federal description - is major offense if CMV or if CDL holder, is violation of STO under PA law)
3342(a)	M22	Vehicles required to stop at railroad crossings (federal description is a railroad crossing offense for drivers operating a commercial vehicle.)
3342(g)(1)	M20	For drivers who are not required to alsway stop, failure to slow down at a railroad –highway grade crossing and check that tracks are clear of approaching train (federal description is a railroad crossing offense for drivers operating a commercial vehicle.)
3342(g)(2)	M21	For drivers who are not required to always stop failure to stop before reaching tracks at a railroad-highway grade crossing when the tracks are not clear. (federal description is a railroad crossing offense for drivers operating a commercial vehicle.)
3342(h)(1)	M23	For drivers failing to have sufficient space to drive completely through the railroad-highway grade crossing without stopping. (federal description is a railroad crossing offense for drivers operating a commercial vehicle.)
3342(h)(2)	M24	For drivers failing to negotiate a railroad-highway grade crossing because of insufficient undercarriage clearance. (federal description is a railroad crossing offense for drivers operating a commercial vehicle.)
3342(i)	M10	For drivers failure to obey a traffic control device or the directions of an enforcement official at a railroad-highway grade crossing.(federal description is a railroad crossing offense for drivers operating a commercial vehicle.)
3367	S95	Racing on highways
3714(b)	U31	Careless driving causing unintentional death - 6-month suspension
3714(c)		Careless driving causing bodily injury - 90-day suspension
3731	A20	Driving under the influence of alcohol or controlled substance
3732	U07	Homicide by vehicle
3733	U01	Fleeing or attempting to elude a police officer
3734	U01	Driving without lights to avoid identification or arrest
3735	U07	Homicide by vehicle while driving under the influence
3735.1	U06	Aggravated assault by vehicle while driving under the influence
3736	M84	Reckless driving
3742	B03	Accidents involving death or personal injury
3742.1	B03	Accidents involving death or personal injury while not properly licensed
3743	B01	Accidents involving damage to attended vehicle or property
3745	B04	Leaving the scene of an accident (federal description - is major offense if CMV or if CDL holder)
3802(a)(1)	A21	Driving under the influence of alcohol (general impairment)
3802(a)(2)	A08	Driving under the influence of alcohol (general impairment) w/BAC
3802(b)	A10	Driving under the influence of alcohol (.10% < .16%)
3802(c)	A11	Driving under the influence of alcohol (.16% or >)
3802(d)	A22	Driving under the influence of a controlled substance
3802(e)	A60	Driving under the influence of alcohol (minor with a BAC of .02% or >)
3802(f)(i)	A21	Driving dender the influence of alcohol (commercial driver with a BAC of .04% or >)
3802(f)(ii)	A04	Driving under the influence of alcohol (school bus or school vehicle with a BAC of .02% or >)

PA Code	ACD	Description
3808(a)	A41	Driving without ignition interlock
3808(b)	A41	Tampering with ignition interlock
3921	U26	Vehicle theft
3925	U03	Receiving or disposing of stolen vehicle or its parts
3928	U04	Illegal operation of an emergency vehicle
4355	D51	Child Enforcement
6307	D06	Misrepresentation of age to secure liquor or malt or brewed beverages
6308	A31	Purchase, consumption, possession or transportation of liquor or malt or brewed beverages
6310.3	D16	Carrying a false identification card
7102(b)		**(Repealed, driver can remove from record)** Removal or falsification of identification number
7103(b)		**(Repealed, driver can remove from record)** Dealing in vehicles with removed or falsified numbers
7111		Dealing in titles and plates for stolen vehicles
7121		False application for certificate of title or registration
7122		Altered, forged or counterfeit documents and plates
7514(a)	**A41**	**(Repealed, but stays on record)** Violation of Ignition Interlock

ARD Program

Some PA driving records with a DUI violation may include this description: "ARD-DUI GEN IMPAIRMENT." ARD, which stands for Accelerated Rehabilitation Program, is a pre-adjudication program that eliminates a criminal violation in the court system. The offender must meet certain criteria such as providing community service or taking a class. The DUI will show on the driving record for non-commercial drivers for 10 years, for commercial drivers it is not eliminated.

Enforcement Agreements

The Secretary may enter into agreements relating to enforcement of this title, including, but not limited to:

1. the Driver License Compact and any other agreements to notify any state of violations incurred by residents of that state;
2. agreements to suspend or revoke the operating privilege of Pennsylvania licensed drivers who are convicted of any offense essentially similar to 1532(a) and (b) (relating to revocation or suspension of operating privilege);
3. agreements to disqualify the commercial driving privilege of Pennsylvania drivers convicted in Federal court or in another state of offenses essentially similar to those resulting in disqualification under section 1611 (relating to disqualification);
4. agreements to establish procedures for the seizure of suspended, revoked or disqualified drivers' licenses of residents of other states; and
5. agreements to take measures to assure taking of chemical tests of breath, blood or urine and payment of fines or attendance at hearings by persons charged with these or other violations (May 30, 1990, P.L. 173, No. 42, effective November 1, 1990).

Point System Summary

Points range from two to five. When an accumulation of six points occurs for the first time, the driver will receive written notice to take a special point examination. If the record reduces below six points and then reaches six or more points a second or subsequent time, suspensions, and more testing will occur. Accumulation of 11 or more points in one year will result in a suspension. Points recorded against any person shall be removed at the rate of three points for each 12 consecutive months (using the violation date) in which such person has not committed any violation which results in the assignment of points or in suspension or revocation.

The driving privilege of a person under the age of 18 will be suspended if that person accumulates six or more points or is convicted of driving 26 miles per hour or more over the posted speed limit. The first suspension will be for a period of 90 days. Any additional occurrences will result in a suspension of 120 days. This suspension is in addition to the requirements of the point system.

Rhode Island

Administration	Important Telephone and Web Contacts
Administrator, Division Motor Vehicles Operator Control 600 New London Ave Cranston, RI 02920 www.dmv.ri.gov/ RI Statutes: http://webserver.rilin.state.ri.us/Statutes/	Operator Control..401-462-0800 Main Number...401-462-4368 Financial Responsibility ....401-462-5747 Titles/Research ....401-462-5720 Plates ....401-462-5801 State Department of Insurance......................401-462-9520 State Police..401-444-1000 To email questions, use the "Feedback" button on the left edge of the home page.

Driver's License Format, Issuance and Renewal

License Classes, Restrictions and Endorsements Appear After the Driving Record Content Section

License Format

The format is seven numbers. The first two numbers represent the year of issuance, the third digit represents the location where license was issued, and the last four digits are sequential numbers. A "V" and six numbers indicate a disabled veteran.

Document Appearance

The document is a plastic laminate over a photocard.

Security Characteristics: A picture of the state appears in solid blue; security features are embossed in laminate.

Position of Photo: Top right for regular license; smaller ghost image is next to picture.

Provisional License: Yellow map of state on top. License is vertical, picture on bottom left with ghost image to the right. Above the photo states the day the driver will be 21.

Under 21 License: Blue map of state on top. License is vertical, picture on bottom left with ghost image to the right. Above the photo states the date the driver will be 21.

CDL Indicator: "CDL" appears on the license; also, the classification indicates a CDL.

Issuance

Age Requirements

The minimum age is 16 years and 6 months for a provisional. A Limited Instruction Permit is available for those between the ages of 16 - 18 who have completed a 33-hour driver education course certified by the Rhode Island Department of Education. An Instruction Permit is available for those 18 or older who have never held a driver's license in Rhode Island. If the license has expired over five (5) years, driver must apply for an Instruction Permit. This does not entail taking any driver education course, but driver must pass written exam and road test given by the DMV.

Location of Requirements for Proof of Identity:

www.dmv.ri.gov/documents/forms/license/LI-1.pdf

Residency

Non-resident's license honored on a reciprocal basis; Rhode Island license must be secured within thirty days of establishing residency.

Renewal

Renewal is on the birth month of fifth year except for drivers over 70 (see below). Driver keeps same number when renewing. License renewal can be done in person or online but not by mail. A license held by a member of the U.S. Armed Forces is valid until 30 days after termination of service with Special Operator's License Form.

Elderly-Related Restrictions

Drivers who reach the age of 71 during a renewal cycle must renew their license in four years, drivers who reach the age of 72 must renew in three years, drivers 73 or older must renew every two years.

Vehicle Insurance, Title and Registration Facts

Registration & Renewal

Renewal is available online at https://www.ri.gov/DMV/vrr/, by mail, or in person at AAA (if a member) or by drop box at a DMV office. Renewal is NOT available in person at a DMV office. Renewal is annual for commercial trucks and semi-annual for passenger plates. The DMV cannot process a renewal that has outstanding property taxes owed, if there is a block for unpaid income tax, or if there is a registration suspension. If a person owes tax to a city or town, the person must first pay the tax and then have stamped. Minors under the age of 18 who want to process a registration in their name are required to have a GU-1338 certificate of insurance on record at the Cranston DMV.

New Residents

Non-residents must register vehicles within thirty days of establishing residency; non-resident must also register vehicle, if owner uses it in connection with an established place of business in Rhode Island, otherwise non-resident's registration honored on reciprocal basis.

Inspections and Emissions Testing

Every car and light truck weighing 8,500 pounds or less must be safety and emission inspected every two years. All new motor vehicles have two years or 24,000 miles, whichever comes first, to obtain an inspection sticker. Trailers, semi-trailers, livestock trailers, motorcycles, and all other vehicles over 8,500 lbs must be inspected once a year. Vehicles registered as antiques (over 25 years old) or as being electric are exempt from the emissions inspection, but not the safety inspection. All trailers, semi-trailers with a GVW over 1,000 lbs., livestock trailers, and all motorcycles must be inspected before June 30 of each year. See www.riinspection.org/.

Passenger Plate Facts

There are two plates with one decal (MO & YR) on each plate. There are no codes or indications to the county of issuance. When a vehicle is sold, the plates remain with seller.

Insurance and Financial Responsibility

Minimum liability limits are $25,000/50,000/25,000. The state has a compulsory insurance provision, but does not have no-fault insurance provision. Proof is required after insurance violations. SR-22 filing may be required.

Withdrawal Sanctions, and Alcohol and Drug Testing

Alcohol and Chemical Testing Limits

The illegal intoxication level is .08 percent and above, .04 for CDL. The fines and suspensions will vary (see Section 31-27-2) as the BAC percentage increases to .10 and .15 percent. The same levels apply to under 21 aged drivers, but penalties are increased. Urine, blood, and breath testing are authorized. The state has an implied-consent law, but not a provision for an administrative per se suspension. Operating a bicycle under the influence is also considered illegal.

Suspensions and Revocations

With regard to suspensions, there are many diverse reasons for which an individual may lose his/her license and registration. Some reasons are mandatory and many are at the discretion of the judge. The *Conviction Table* at the end of this chapter lists the mandatory suspensions and revocations with corresponding codes.

CDL Sanctions and MCSIA Compliance

Rhode Island is in compliance with the provisions of the Motor Carrier Safety Improvement Act (MCSIA). See the Appendix for a list of these mandatory CDL disqualification sanctions.

Reinstatement Requirements

To have a license reinstated, the driver must go to a DMV branch with the reinstatement clearance, one identity document such as a birth certificate or passport, Social Security card, and proof of current address.

Suspension: $151.50 reinstatement fee.
Revocation: $151.50 reinstatement fee; proof of insurance.
Reinstatement if DUI or Refusal Related: $351.50.
Reinstatement for Suspended Registration (license plates): $251.50.

Record Access: Laws, Rules, and Forms

Note: This Section Applies to Both Driver and Vehicle Records.

Governing Statutes and Rules

State Statutes: http://webserver.rilin.state.ri.us/Statutes
Section I. Chapter 27-49 of the general laws entitled Motor Vehicle Theft and Insurance Fraud Reporting - Immunity Act was amended to provide adoption of the provisions of DPPA. There are no provisions similar to those in DPPA for permissible uses (13 and (14).
State Code Sections 31-2-10 & 11 govern the release of the driver abstract.
Requesters must submit a sample and description of proposed use in advance for Department approval.

Request and Consent Forms

Driving Records: The state does not provide a specific form to use for obtaining a driving record. However, if consent of the driver is given in writing, casual requesters can obtain records with personal information.
Vehicle Records: Rhode Island has strict rules regarding access to vehicle and ownership records. Records are only released to casual requesters if written consent of the subject is given. A form is at www.dmv.ri.gov/documents/forms/registration/Reg_DL_App.pdf

Vendor and Third Party Access Policy

Driving Records: The official policy is that only insurance companies and employers with a signed release may request records from a vendor or via a "vendor chain." Information collected by the Division of Motor Vehicles may not be made available to any person for use in commercial solicitation or for the purpose of trade. Commercial solicitations and trade for this rule shall not include motor vehicle recall uses, statistical analysis, market research, the activities of insurance companies investigating claims or applications for insurance, and other uses allowed by statute.

Vehicle Records: Permissible users can purchase in bulk or database format, but cannot resell to another vendor. Information collected by the Division of Motor Vehicles may not be made available to any person for use in commercial solicitation or for the purpose of trade. Commercial solicitations and trade for this rule shall not include motor vehicle recall uses, statistical analysis, market research, the activities of insurance companies investigating claims or applications for insurance, and other uses allowed by statute.

Records Ordered For Non-permissible Uses

Driving Records: If there is no consent then no record is released to mail or walk-in requesters. A driving record without personal information is available online and can be ordered by a casual use requester; the consent of the subject not needed.
Vehicle Records: Non-permissible use requesters without consent cannot obtain vehicle records.

Access to Driver-Related Records

Driving Records

General Information and Fees

Operator Control, 600 New London Ave, Cranston, RI 02920-3024, 401-462-0800.
The fee for a driving record is $17.50 by mail or in person, $20.00 if online. There is a full charge for a no record found search.
In-Person − Most on-site requests can be processed within minutes. Otherwise, lists or record with extensive research must be picked up 3 to 4 days later or can be returned by mail in 7 to 10 days. The address shown above is the only location in the state that will process these on-site record requests. Hours are 8:30AM to 3:15PM.
Mail − Mail requests are processed by the state in 7-10 days. The driver's license number, name, and date of birth are needed when ordering. Payment must accompany each request.

Electronic − Driving records are available in two manners from the DMV web portal, plus a validity check..
1. Higher volume, ongoing requesters who qualify to receive records with personal information may obtain a subscription account for interactive service. A $20.00 per record fee applies. The subscription is $75.00 annually. For more information about becoming a subscriber visit www.ri.gov/subscriber or call 401-832-8099, ext 260, or email rihelp@nicusa.com.
2. Anyone may request a record online for the $19.50 fee. A credit card is required with and the record will be mailed. This three-year record does not contain the driver's address or SSN. The driver's name, DOB and license number must be submitted. Visit https://www.ri.gov/DMV/mvr/citizen/.
3. Rhode Island offers the ability to verify the validity of a record by

entering the driver record validation code (generated when ordering the record) at https://www.ri.gov/DMV/mvr/citizen/validate.php.

Bulk – Driver license data is not sold in database or bulk format for marketing purposes.

By Person of Record – RI drivers may obtain their driving record by mail, walk-in, or online as described above.

Notification/Monitoring Program

At present, Rhode Island does not offer a mechanism to permit employers or insurance companies, or their vendors, to monitor or track incidents of submitted drivers - or by data regular data updates. However a number of vendors are known to offer this service in Rhode Island. It is thought the vendors are likely using court records as a resource for this type of service.

Accident Reports

Reporting – The operator of any motor vehicle involved in an accident in RI resulting in injuries and/or property damage in excess of $1,000.00, is required to report this accident in writing, within 21 days, to the Division of Motor Vehicles, Accident Section, 600 New London Ave, Cranston RI 02920. If the operator is physically incapable of making out the report, it should be made by the owner within 21 days of

having learned of the accident. For more information, call 401-462-5710 or 401-462-4368. There is an accident report form available at www.dmv.ri.gov/forms/various/index.php.

Record Access – Rhode Island State Police, Record Division, 311 Danielson Pike, North Scituate 02857, 401-444-1143, www.risp.ri.gov/. The Police prefer that requesters use the online system. Requests must include drivers' names and date and location of the incident. The fee is $15.00 per record for mail in requests and $20.00 if online. Normal turnaround time is 1 week. There is no searching permitted by phone, but one may call to see if a report is available. Note the office is closed on Thursdays. Records are available since 2000; it will take 72 hours after occurrence for an incident to become available.

The agency has outsourced online record requests to a vendor at http://www.getcrashreports.com/. Search by name or by any number of factors. Fee is $20.00. Records include reports from at least 32 cities/towns in Rhode Island. The site works well, provides detailed information, but lacks upfront details on costs and record throughput. One must basically to go through the order process to find these details. There is a subscription program for ongoing requesters, but no details are given until the third step in the order process.

Access to Vehicle-Related Records

General Information and Fees

Registry of Motor Vehicles, 600 New London Ave, Cranston RI 02920, 401-462-4368 or 401-462-5774.

Requests are carefully screened for purpose. Records are not made available for commercial use, nor released over the phone. See www.dmv.ri.gov/documents/forms/registration/Reg_DL_App.pdf for a record request form.

In-Person or Mail – The fee for VIN, ownership registration, name searches, and plate information is $11.50 per search. The fee for a lien search and/or title information is $51.50. This fee includes the $1.50 surcharge imposed per record on all record requests. Title information can be obtained in person, registration information must be returned by mail. Write to above address and state your purpose for request. Requests may be made in-person and results are available the same day. Title information is available for 3 years after titled vehicle is 10 years old. Other information is available for 10 years. There is a full charge for a no record found.

Electronic – This application allows RI.gov subscribers (see Driving Records) to access title records currently on file with the Rhode Island Division of Motor Vehicles. Search by registration number or VIN number. The record presented is the most recent record on file with the Division of Motor Vehicles. Historical records must be obtained in person or by mail. The total fee for this service is $53.30. For more information on becoming a subscriber call 401-831-8099 x230 or visit www.ri.gov/subscriber.

Bulk – The strict access of records statutes and administrative rules in Rhode Island provide that vehicle ownership information is not available in bulk media for commercial or solicitation purposes. A sample and description of proposed use must be submitted in writing and in advance for Department approval.

Access to Vessel-Related Records

General Information, Access and Fees

Department of Environmental Management, Office of Boat Registration, 235 Promenade Rm 360, Providence 02908, 401-222-6647, fax (titles) 401-462-5783.

All boats over 14 ft must be titled and registered. Lien information will show on a title record. All requests must be in writing on the agency's request form, see www.dem.ri.gov/pubs/forms/recrdreq.pdf. The agency

will accept fax requests on their request form. The agency follows the same privacy mandates per the DPPA. Copies are $.15 per page. There is no fee to do a simple name, file or registration search; otherwise the search is at least $15.00 per hour. Generally the turnaround time is within 1 to 2 weeks. For casual requesters, this agency will not release the name and address of a lien holder, but will indicate whether a lien does exist.

Driving Record Content and Reciprocity

What's On or Not On the Driving Record

- All convictions are reported on the public driving record.
- Personal information is not shown on the public online record, but is shown on the record released to requesters with a verified permissible use.
- SSNs are not shown on either record.
- Accidents are reported, but fault is not shown, on either record.
- The state does not permit driver school attendance in lieu of conviction.

The length of time non-CDL convictions are listed on the public record is:

Moving Violations and Accidents: ....Three years.
Suspensions................................. Three years after reinstatement.
Alcohol-Related Violation or Suspension:....................Five years.

Data Retention

Surrendered licenses are purged from the system three years after expiration Any District or Superior Court conviction will remain on the record until the violator petitions the court for expungement. CDL records are purged based on the timetable per MCSIA (see Appendix).

Court to Repository

Conviction information must be forwarded from the courts to the state within ten days. There is no mandated time-period in which information must be entered on the record; however, it is usually input within twenty days.

State Reciprocity for Non-CDL Drivers

- Will suspend license of driver for unpaid out-of-state convictions.
- Record of new incoming driver is shown on MVR.
- Only major convictions out-of-state convictions shown on MVR
- Out-of-state accidents are not shown on MVR.
- Convictions of out-of-state drivers are sent to home state.
- Record is forwarded to new state upon surrender of license.

License Classes, Restrictions, and Endorsements

License Classes

Class 1	Jitney, taxi, bus
Class A	Any combination of vehicles with a GVWR of more than 26,000 pounds—provided the GVWR of the vehicle(s) being towed is in excess of 10,000 pounds.
Class B	Any single vehicle with a GVWR of more than 26,000 pounds, or any such vehicle towing a vehicle not in excess of 10,000 pounds GVWR.
Class C	Any single vehicle with a GVWR of 26,000 pounds or less. This group applies to vehicles which are placarded for hazardous materials or designed to transport fifteen or more people (excluding the operator); school buses must have a special permit.
Class O	Regular operator (Note: Can have "R" Restriction for Chauffeur)

Restrictions

A	Corrective Lenses		G	Special Equipment		M	Insulin Dependent
C	Brake, Clutch Extension		H	Valid for Motorcycle		U	Ignition Interlock Required
D	Inside and Outside Mirrors		K	Vision Waiver			
E	Hand Controls		L	No Air Brakes			

Endorsements

H							
Hazardous Material			T	Double-/Triple-Trailers		X	Combination N and H
N	Tank Vehicles		P	Passenger		S	School Bus (New)

Conviction Table with ACD Codes and Statute

A Suspension Reasons Code Table follows this table.
Statutes are found at http://webserver.rilin.state.ri.us/Statutes
Rhode Island does not use a point system.

Violation Description	Suspension	ACD	Statute
2 Out-Of-Service - 10 Year	1B	W50	-
3+ Out Service/10yr	3B	W52	-
3+ Out Service/10yr/16+Passen	2B	W51	-
Abandon Animal From MV/Dea		W00	4126
Abandoned Vehicles		W00	31-2213
Abandonment Animals From MV		U04	040126
Accident & Reports-General		W00	31-260115
Accident Chasing Tow Truck		W00	31-0330
Adminst.Paymnt Of Offenses		D53	31-4100
Advertis.Sale/Ste Highw		N84	24-10-19
Aggressive Driving		M84	31-27.1-4
Alteration Identification.No.		W00	31-0905
Altering Weight		W00	31-23131
Approaching Horses		N84	31-22-25
Apprv Types Seat Belts-Req		F04	31-2340
Apprvl Of Light.Equip Req.		E05	31-2449
Auth.Wgt Of Reg.Overweight		W00	31-25-16
Authr.Max.Wgt/Reg.Exceed		W00	31-2516
Authr.Max.Wgt/Reg.Exceed		W00	31-2516
Axle Load Lmt-22,400 Pds +		W00	31-25-13
Backing Up Prohibited		N82	24--1018
Back-Up Lamps		E05	312420
Bicycle Violations-General		W00	31-100121
Blnd/Deaf Ped W/O Dog-Cane		N08	31-1815

Violation Description	Suspension	ACD	Statute
Brakes Used Improperly		E71	-
Break Equipment Required		E02	31-2304
C- Lanes Of Operation		M40	31-2706
Card ID Misuse		B41	386
Care In Starting From Stop		N83	311601
Carry Load Firearm Rec Veh		W00	31329
Carry-Inspct Exces Ld Perm		W00	31-25-24
Chem Test Refusal - U18		A12	31-2725
Chemical Test Refusal	19	A12	31-27021
Child Passenger Restraint		F02	31-2222
Clearance For Overtaking		N07	31-1506
Clinging To Vehicles		W00	31-1905
Clrce/Mrkr Lamps,Refel Req		W00	31-2437
CMV-Comm.Lic.Viol/Penalty		D29	31-9331
CMV-DWI--Alcohol >=.04	AC	A04	31-9331B1B
CMV-DWI--Alcohol>.00 &<.04		A25	31-9331B
CMV-Employee Notification		D29	31-9328
CMV-Employer Responsibilty		D29	31-9329
CMV-Unauthor.Manuf. Cdl	UC	D10	31-9336
Coasting Prohibited		N80	31-2206
Color-Clearance/Marker Lamps		E55	31-2438
Commercial License Require		B91	31-9313
Commis Of Felony Cntr Subs	52	A50	31-2724
Conditns Req.Reduce Speed		S94	31-1403
Conection Bet.Coupled Vehs		W00	31-2511
Consuming.Alcohol While Driving	43	A26	31-2221
Contempt Of Court		W00	31-436
Contents Of Reg. Plate		W00	31-311
Cross Hway - Youth Opertr		W00	31-329
Cross.Center Divided Hiway		N71	31-1513
Crossing Fire Hose		M56	31-2208
Cycle Handlebar Violation		F03	31-10001-5
Dealer License Required		W00	3155
Defective Brakes		E31	-
Defective Tires		E37	31-2345
Dem Rules Park, Stnd, Stop		F34	3224
Dim Head Lamps-Parked Vehs		E54	31-2434
Dismantle Vehicles		W00	3148
Display Of Plates-Penlty		W00	31-0318
Dot,Dem,Other Agency/Depts		F34	31-43-1.2
Drive Inv License/Certain	76	B51	31-11181
Drive Without/Expired Lic	77	B51	31-11181
Driving After Susp,Deny,Rev	24	B26	31-11181
Driving School License Req		W00	31-1035
Driving Unsafe Vehicle		F66	31-2301
Driving W/Expired License		B24	31-1030
Driving W/Expired Registration		W00	31-0332
Driving While Impaired	53	A25	31-2727
Driving Wrong Way		N62	31-1509B
Drivng To Endnger,Pers.Inju	12	W00	31-27011
Drv Aft License Suspension	24	B26	31-1118
Drv CMV without CDL	SC	B56	-
Drv Endanger-Death Result	11	U08	31-2701
Drv Out Of Service 16+ Pas	8C	B19	-
Drv Thru Railroad Gate/Barrier	6C	M10	31-2002
Drv While Out Of Service	8C	B27	-
Drving W/O Owner Consent	08	U03	31-0901
Drvng W/Expired Comm.License		B51	31-9323
Dty Stop-Acc-Dead/Inj Anim		W00	31-26031
Due Care By Drivers		M80	31-1808
Due Care By Drivers		W00	31-188
Due Care By Emergency Vehs		U21	31-1209
DUI Commercial Vehicle	BC	A20	31-10331

Violation Description	Suspension	ACD	Statute
DUI Transp Child < 13 Yrs	74	A08	31-272
DUI/First Offense/.08	60	A08	31-272
DUI/First Offense/.10-.15	65	A10	31-272
DUI/First Offense/.15	66	A11	31-272
DUI/First Offense/Bal Unk	67	A20	31-272
DUI/Second Offense/.08	68	A08	31-272
DUI/Second Offense/.10-.15	69	A10	31-272
DUI/Second Offense/.15	70	A11	31-272
DUI/Second Offense/Bal Unk	71	A20	31-272
DUI/Sub Offense/<.15/Bal U	73	A10	31-272
DUI/Subsequent Offense/.15	72	A11	31-272
Dummy Code	88	W00	-
DWI - Bodily Injury		A20	31-2726
DWI - Liquor Or Drugs	10	A20	31-2702
DWI-Liq/Drugs-Death Result	27	U08	31-27022
DWI-Liquor/Drug>=.08<.1		A20	31-27-2
Earphones/Headsts Prohibit		F66	31-2351
Elude Police	14	U01	31-2741
Elude Police/Sub Offense	14	U01	31-2741
Eluding Police-High Speed		M84	31-274.1
Eluding Traffic Light		M16	31-1306
Entering From Private Road		M25	31-1705
Entr/Lvng-Ltd Access Rdway		M41	31-1514
Entrng Inters-Blkng Inters		N61	31-15121
Equip Improper/Obstructed		E70	-
Equip/Accessories-General		E01	31-230156
Evading Toll (Mt.Hope)		W00	24-1330
Expired Reg. By Transfer		W00	31-4-1
Fail Comply-Grad Lic Restriction		D16	31-106.4
Fail Info/Render Aid - Acc		W00	31-2603
Fail Notify-Chg Of Address		W00	31-0334
Fail Notify-Chg Of Name		D16	31-0335
Fail Stop Acc-Hiway Damage	16	B04	31-2605
Fail Stop Acc-Injury	15	B03	31-2601
Fail Stop Acc-Unattend.Veh	16	B08	31-2604
Fail Stop Acc-Veh.Damage	16	B08	31-2602
Fail Surrender Hazmat Endorsement	TC	W09	-
Fail to Obey (FTO) - RR Clrnc	5C	M24	-
Fail To Use Hazmat Safety		E53	-
Fail Yield Row-Intersectin		N25	31-1703
Fail.Maint.Proper Cntrl Mv	12	N84	31-1401
Fail.Obey Yield Sign		N26	31-1704
Fail.Stop - RR Crossing	5C	M09	31-2001
Fail.Yield Row-Emergy Veh		N04	31-1706
Fail.Yield Row-Fire Co.		N04	31-1707
Fail.Yield Row-Turn Left		N31	31-1702
Failre-Fendrs/Whls W/Flaps		E01	31-2328
Failure Equip Schbus Safty		E56	-
Failure File Accident Rpt	40	B61	31-3302
Failure To Stop		M25	-
Failure To Surrender Lic/R		W00	31-335
Failure To Use Brakes		E51	31-14-1
False Inspection Certifica		W00	31-3809
False Swearing/License		W00	31-1117
Falsify Accident Report		W00	31-333
Fastening Of Load/Covering		W00	31-2510
Fatal Negligent Op Of CMV	VC	U10	-
Fenders,Wheel Flaps Requrd		E01	31-2326
Flags Req-Tow Chains 12"		W00	3-12512
Flares/Warng Dev.- Trk/Bus		W00	31-2329
Flashing Signals		M18	31-1309
Flshng Lght-Auth.Veh-Types		E05	31-2431
Following Fire Apparatus		M33	31-2207

Violation Description	Suspension	ACD	Statute
Following Too Closely		M34	31-1512
Front Red Lights-Prohibitd		W00	31-2430
Front/Rear Extns.Load Exce		W00	31-2507
Ft ID Aft Fatal/Inj Accid	6A	B14	-
FTO - RR Drive	5C	M22	-
FTO - RR Not Slowing	5C	M20	-
FTO - RR Not Stopping	5C	M21	-
FTO - RR Space	5C	M23	-
FTO School Crossing Guard		M13	-
Ful Stp-Ped W/Guid Dog-Cne		N08	311814
H&R Fail Stop/Aid Fatalacc	3A	B02	-
H&R Failure Stop/Aid Accid	2A	B04	-
Habitual Offender	18	W01	31-4006
Handicap Parking Violation		W00	31-28073A
Hazard Switch/Flash Lights		W00	31-2452
Head Lamps-Motr Drvn Cycle		F03	31-2425
Head Lamps-Slow Moving Veh		E01	31-2426
Headlamps- Non-Cycle -Req		E05	31-2404
Headlamps-Cycle,Et Al Req		F03	31-2405
Height Of Head Lamps		E34	31-2406
Height Of Tail Lamps		E34	31-2408
Hitch-Hiking In Road		M03	31-1812
Horn Required		E01	31-2308
Hvy Duty Veh Emiss.Inspect		W00	31-47.2-6
ID-Trks/Trcts-No Wgt Print		W00	31-2517
Ignition Interlock System		A41	31-272D2
Illegal Evid Of Financial	44	D35	31-4791
Illegal Oper Emerg Vehicle	9A	U21	-
Illegal Operation Of Rv		W00	31-327
Illegal Possession Drugs	7A	A33	-
Illumination Of Rear Plate		W00	31-2409
Immediate Notice Of Accide		B61	31-2632
Imminent Hazard	4B	W70	-
Imp Class/Endorsment Cdl	9C	B91	-
Imp Location Not Nat Netwk		M50	-
Improper Backing		N82	31-2202
Improper Loc Hov/Restrictd		M49	-
Improper Riding On Motorcy		F06	31-2203
Improper School Bus Use		N84	31-22-11.5
Improper Use Evidence Regist		W00	31-0803
Injurng/Tampering W/Vehcls	08	W00	31-0903
Injury To Signs/Devices		W00	31-1311
Inspect/Purchased Out		W00	31-385
Inspection - General		W00	31-380120
Inspection Of School Bus		E06	31-2211
Inspection Sticker Requird	A2	W00	31-3804
Instr.Permit-Sch.Train.Prg		D29	31-1006
Instructors License Reqd		W00	31-1039
Intr Lgts-Oper.Police Stop		M08	31-2224
Inv License/Cert Viol/Sub	75	B51	31-11181
Issunce Of License-Probatn		D16	31-1026
Lamps On Animal Drawn Veh		E55	31-2435
Laned Roadway Violations		M41	31-1511
Leave Scene Aft Acc Before Police	4A	B05	-
Leave Scene Fat Acc Before Police	5A	B06	-
Leave Scene Pdo Acc Before Police	16	B08	-
License For Dealer Plates		W00	31-510
License Susp/Revok-General		D29	31-110121
License Violations-General		W00	31-10014
Light Equip/Reflect-Generl		E05	31-240153
Lighted Lamp Display-Req.		E05	31-2427
Lighting On Farm Tractors		E55	31-2421
Lighting-Snow Removal Equip		E05	31-2446

Violation Description	Suspension	ACD	Statute
Limitation On # Of License		D07	31-9327
Littering - Forestry Laws		W00	2157
Littering Prohibited		W00	37-1507
Littering-Creating Hazards		W00	31-2209
Loaded Weapons In Vehicle		W00	20138
Local Motor Vehicle		W00	31-1212
Make/Use False Inspection		W00	31-389
Making False Affidavit	31	D02	31-1117
Manip Control Malicious		W00	31-94
Manuf.Cntrfit Hcap Plac		W00	31-28-7
Marking Of Turn Path		N50	31-1630
Max Weight And Tandem Axel		W00	31-25-14
Max Width-102" Exceeded		W00	31-2503
Maxi #/Lgth - Coupled Vehs		W00	31-25-6
Maxi.Driving Hours-Comm.Vehs		W00	31-2705
Maxi.Hgt - 162" Exceeded		W00	31-2504
Maxi.Intensity Of Lights		E54	31-2429
Maxi.Number Lamps Lighted		E05	31-2428
Maxi.Wgt & Tandem Axles		W00	31-2514
Maxi.Wgt & Tandem Axles		W00	31-2514
Measure Of Height Of Lamp		E34	31-243
Measuring Dist Visability		M77	31-242
Mech Signl Dev - Self Illu		W00	31-2415
Mechanical Signal Dev. Req		E01	31-1609
Metal Tires Prohibited		E37	31-2319
Method Of Giving Signals		N44	31-1608
Minor Tran/Sell Sch Iii/Iv	7A	A33	21-284152B
Minor Trans/Sell Sch I/Ii	7A	A33	21--284152A
Minor Trans/Sell Sch V Drg	7A	A33	21284152C
Miscellnus Rules - General		M03	31-220126
Misuse Grp Handicap Plate		W00	31-2871E
Misuse Of Handicap Plates		W00	31-2871D
Motor Vehicle Offense-Gen		U03	3-1270119
Motor.Bike-Drvng Hiwy-Proh		W00	31-19001-2
Motor.Tric-Drvng Hiwy-Proh		W00	31-19002-2
Motorcycle Inspection Requ		W00	31-10001-7
Motorcycle Learnr Permt-Vio		F06	31-1012
Mount/Adjust Of Lamps		E34	31-2451
Mounting Of Reflectors		W00	31-2439
Mountng-Clearnce/Side Mrkr		W00	31-2440
Muffler Snow/Rec Vehicles		W00	31-328
Muffler Violation		W00	31-2313
Multiple Beam Lamps Req.		E05	31-2422
Negligent Homicide CMV	VC	U09	-
No Child Restraint/Belt		E06	31-2222B
No Cycle Helmet-Passenger		F03	31-10001-6
No Fuel Tax Stmp/Non-Ri Trk		W00	31-36001-17
No Helmet - U21 Or 1st Lic		F03	31-1014
No License On Pers-Demand	23	W00	31-1027
No Seat Belt-Operator		E06	31-2222G
No Seat Belt-Passenger		E06	31-2222GN
Noise In Vicinity Of Horse		N84	31-22-26
Noise Limits Exceeded		W00	31-4501
Non-Pay Toll-Newp Br		W00	24-12-37
Not Crossing At Crosswalk		W00	31-1805
Notice Of Change Of Addres		W00	31-1032
O/State Purch Reg Violatio		W00	31-0409
Obedience To Laws Required		M03	31-12-3
Obedience To Police Oficer		M08	31-1203
Obedience To Stop Sign		M15	31-2009
Obedience To Traffic Device		M14	31-1304
Obstructed Light Not Reqd		F66	31-2444
Obstructed View-Windshield/Sticker		D70	31-2316

Violation Description	Suspension	ACD	Statute
Offense Persons Dirct.Drvr		W00	31-2710
Opening Doors Of Vehicle		W00	31-2114
Oper Beach Veh W/O Permit		W00	31-81.1
Oper By Other Than Lessee		W00	31-3430
Oper Cycle W/O Eye Protect		F03	31-10001-4
Oper Cycle W/O Req License		F06	31-10001-1
Oper Foreign Licns-Suspend	24	B26	31-1112
Oper On Bike Trail/Path		M47	31-2719
Oper Snow/Rec W/I Marshes		E01	31-3271
Oper Snow/Rec W/O Land Per		W00	31-3241A
Oper Snow/Rec W/O Ownr Per		U03	31-3241B
Oper Unreg Snow/Rec Vehicl		W00	31-322
Oper Veh After Reg Canceld		W00	31-0802
Oper Veh W/O Evidnc Regist		W00	31-0801
Oper W/O Insurnce 3rd Offe		D35	31-4709
Oper When Reg Revoked		W00	31-82
Oper When Reg. Suspend		W00	31-82
Oper. On Foreign Regist		W00	31-0101
Oper. Unlicensed Tow Truck		W00	31-0329
Oper.Comm.Veh W/O Comm.Lic	SC	B91	31-9330
Operating - Habitual Offender		W01	31-4008
Operating - Restricted License		D29	31-1028
Operating Belw Mini. Speed		S96	31-1409
Operating Left Of Center		M72	31-1503
Operating Veh W/O Req License	23	B51	31-1001
Operating W/O Insurance	54	D35	31-4709
Operating With Disability	22	D75	-
Operation Of Unreg.Vehicle		W00	31-0301
Out-Of-Service Order		B27	31-103.31
Overloading Vehicles		W00	31-2204
Overtaking On Left		M70	31-1504
Overtaking On Right		M73	31-1505
Overtaking Prohibited		M76	31-1507
Overtaking Veh Stopped For Ped		N08	31-1804
Ovrwght Permit - No Sticker		W00	31-2522
Own/Op W/Unlaw Sunscr Matl		F66	31-2335
Owner Liab - Parking Ticke		W00	31-289
Owner/Owner Oper W/O Insur	44	D35	31-4709
Park/Ride Lot-Unauth.Veh		W00	24-10-20
Parking/Stopping Prohibited		F34	31-2104
Parties To Offenses		U04	31-2709
Passenger Prohib - Motorcycle		F06	31-22331
Passing/Lanes/Rules-General		M70	31-150116
Pedestrians - General		N08	31-180120
Pedestrians On Freeway		N84	31-18-17
Penalties For Civil Viols		N84	31-27-13
Penlty Emp Unlic/Unauth Op		W00	31-11211
Perjury: Operation Of Mv		D78	-
Permitting Minor To Drive	26	W00	31-1119
Permitting Unauth.Pers Drv	26	W00	31-1120
Permtng Juv.Oper.Unreg.Cyc		F06	31-2717
Posses.Veh W/Alter Id.No.		U03	31-0906
Possess.Bevg-Underage Pers	38	A31	030810
Possessin Stolen Veh/Parts	20	W00	31-0902
Posting No Pass Zone-Viol		M71	31-1508
Prelim.Chemcal Test Refusl		D45	31-27002-3
Pres.Alchl/Oper/Ride MV	62	A35	31-22-21.1
Present Comm.Lic.On Demand	RC	W00	31-9326
Prevention Of Load Leakage		W00	31-2509
Prevntin Excess.Fumes/Smok		W00	31-2314
Proh Oper Snow/Rec Vehicle		W00	31-327
Prohib Comm Veh Local Auth		W00	31-2526
Projecting Loads-Red Flag Req		W00	31-2445

Violation Description	Suspension	ACD	Statute
Proof Of Insurance/Rent	44	D35	31-342
Protuberances On Tires		E37	31-2320
PUC Violation		M03	39-1226
Radios,Stereo,Audio Sys		F66	31-4505
Rear Reflectors Required		W00	31-2410
Rear View Mirror Required		E01	31-2315
Rear Whl Flaps-Bus,Trk,Trl		E01	31-2327
Reasonable & Prudent Speed		S93	31-1401
Reckless Driving	12	M84	31-2704
Reckless Driving	12	M84	31-274
Reckless Driving/Sub Offense	12	M84	31-274
Reflect.In Lieu Warn.Devce		F34	31-2331
Refusal To Show Reg. Cert		W00	31-0309
Refusal-Wgt/Remve Exces Ld		W00	31-2520
Reg/Cert Lighting Equip.		E05	31-2447
Reg/Title Offenses-General		W00	31-08017
Remvl Exces From Ovwgt Veh		W00	31-2519
Repair Shop Plates-Temp Reg		W00	31-320.1
Restr. Use Coasters/Skates		W10	31-1919
Revoke Cert. Light Equip		W00	31-2448
Right Half Of Road		M41	31-1501
Road/Fog Lamps-Numb&Direct		E50	31-2417
Rotary Traffic Island		N21	31-1510
ROW - General		N01	31-17018
ROW At Rotary		N21	31-1708
ROW In Crosswalk		N20	31-1803
ROW On Sidewalks		N20	31-1818
Row-Absence Of Signs, Signl		N25	31-1701
Rules - Armed Forces License		D27	31-1010
Run Board - Courtesy Lamps		W00	31-2419
Safety Belt/Public Serv Veh		E06	31-23-41
Safety Lghts Req.Food Vendng		E05	31-2453
Sale Of New Bicycle		W00	31-1920
Sale Of Used Bicycle		W00	31-1921
Scattering Debis On Highwy		W00	112210
School Bus Stops - Routes		N09	31-20103
Sell/Poss Manip Device Auto		W00	31-911
Side Cowl And Fender Lamps		W00	31-2418
Signaling Of Stop		N40	31-1607
Single Beam Lamps		E05	31-2424
Single Veh/Ld-Max Lgt 40 Ft		W00	31-2505
Sirns,Bels,Whistls Prohibt		E55	31-2310
Size/Wgt/Local Limit-Genrl		W00	31-250129
Slow Movng Veh Emblems Req		E01	31-2347
Slow Traffic To Right		M60	31-1502
Soliciting Rides In Mv		M03	24-1017
Spec Restr/Drivers Compens		D29	31-105
Spec Speed Limts-Hgwy-Cnst		S94	31-1415.1
Special Mirrors On Sch Bus		E06	31-23421
Special Stops Req.-General		W00	31-200117
Specs For Reflectors		W00	31-2411
Specs Stop/Signl Lamps		W00	31-2414
Speed Limit-Bridges/Struct		S94	31-1412
Speed Restrictions-General		S93	31-140113
Speeding (11+ Mph Over)		S06	31-4104B
Speeding (11+ Mph Over)		S11	31-4104C
Speeding (11+ Mph Over)		S16	31-4104D
Speeding (11+ Mph Over)		S21	31-4104E
Speeding (11+ Mph Over)		S26	31-4104F
Speeding (1-10 Mph Over)		S94	31-4104A
Speeding>10mph Over Limit		S93	462295
Start/Stop/Turns-General		N53	31-160110
Stop And Turn Lamps Author		E01	31-2413

Violation Description	Suspension	ACD	Statute
Stop For School Bus Req		M75	31-2012
Stop Lamps Required		E05	31-2412
Stop Lamps-Numb & Directn		E34	31-2416
Stop Trvl Portion Of Hiway		F34	31-2101
Stop/Stand/Park - General		F34	31-210116
Stopping/X-Ing Guard Req.		N08	31-2017
Stops At Bridle Path Cross		N84	31-20-16
Tail Lamps Required		E05	312407
Television Recevers Prohib		F66	31-2338
Temp Reg-Invoic Vouchr Dlr		W00	31-0403
Temp Trans Of Reg Violatio		W00	31-0410
Temp. Plates-Dealer Issued		W00	31-0340
Temp.Drivers Permit >18yrs		B51	31-10-7
Theft/Related Offense-Gen	20	W00	31-090111
Throwing Articles At Moving Veh		W00	114422
Time Of Signaling Turn		N41	31-1606
Times When Lights Required		E55	31-2401
Tow Trucks-Ident. Required		W00	31-2223
Towing-Cost Paid By Owner		W00	31-2214
Trademark Shown On Equip		W00	31-2450
Trafc Cntrl/Constr.Oper		M14	31-13-12
Traff.Regulations-General		E50	31-120115
Traffic Law Applic-Bicycle		M47	31-1903
Trafic Cntrl Devic-General		W00	31-130113
Trans Explosives In Vehicl		E53	23282824
Trans.Alcoholic Bevg-Minor	38	A31	030809
Transp. Of Gasoline Vehicl		W00	31-2349
Transpt.Haz.Mat.-Incl.Gas		E03	31-2337
Trnsprt Anmals Unrestraine		M03	31-2228
Turn Signal Required		N40	31-1605
Turning Manner At Intrsect		N51	31-1602
U Turn Prohibited		N56	31-1604
Unattended Vehicles		W00	31-2201
Unauthr.School Bus Entr		W10	31-22-11.7
Unlaw Instl Sunscreen Matl		F66	31-2335
Unlawful Use Of Comm. Lic.		D29	31-9335
Unlawful Use Of Id	64	D02	3862
Unlawful Use Of License	25	B41	31-11-16
Unsafe Vehicle/Sticker Rqd	A1	F66	31-381
Uri,Ric,Ccri Parking Viol		F34	16-59-1
Use Of Multiple Beam Lamps		W00	31-2423
Use Of Transporter Plates		W00	31-0321
Using Aid & Abet Felon	20	U05	-
Using Brkdown Lane For Trvl		M58	31-1516
Using In A Misdemeanor		U04	-
Veh Regist-General Aad Use		W00	31-030151
Veh To Be Towed In Rght Ln		W00	31-25121
Veh. Emergng-Alleys/Drvway		M25	31-2010
Veh.Parked On Lighted Hiwy		F34	31-2432
Veh.Req.Special Lghts/Refl		E05	31-2436
Veh.Stoped On Lighted Hiwy		F34	31-2433
Vehicle Homicide	11	U07	-
Vehicular Assault	8A	U06	-
Vehicular Manslaughter	11	U08	-
Viol Restric Of License	1A	D29	-
Violate Limited License	1A	D27	31-10-6
Violation Of Inspectin Law		W00	31-3803
Violation Of Safety Zone		M12	31-2205
Visibility Of Plates		W00	31-0312
Visibility Of Reflectors		E55	31-2441
Visibility Side Markr Lamp		E55	31-2443
Visibility-Frt/Rear Clr Lamps		E55	31-2442
Wheel Safety Checks-Requrd		W00	31-2343

Violation Description	Suspension	ACD	Statute
Willful Glass Breaking-Hiway		W00	114429
Willful Interjct.Funeral Pr		N05	31-2716
Windshield Wipers		W00	31-2317
Withdrawal, Non-ACD Viol		W00	-
Wrong Way Rotary/Intersect		N61	-

Rhode Island Suspension Reasons Code Table

01	DWI-drugs	56	Chem test refusal/juvenile	A1	Fail to comply w/ notice
02	Negligent operation	57	Drive to endanger-personal inj	A2	Fail obtain inspection cert
03	Frequent offender	58	DWI-serious bodily injury	A3	Vehicle deemed unsafe
04	Fail to appear or pay fine/sanction	59	Court ordered restitution	A4	Fail submit state inspection
05	Fail complete drive school	60	DWI-liqur/drug	A5	Suspend transport passenger
06	Drive record-court order	61	Dvng no lic-refs/revkd	AC	CDL/CMV DWI .04%+
07	Fail appear acc hrg-summ	62	Pres.alcohol oper/ride	ACL	Test only
08	Oper w/o owners consent	63	Aggressive driving	B1	Improperly obtained regist
09	Fail pay AAC fine-summon	64	Unlawful/fraud.use id card	B2	Civil judgment
10	DWI-liquor	65	DUI/first offense/.10-.15	B3	Financial responsibility
11	Drive to endanger-death	66	DUI/first offense/.15	B4	Returned check
12	Reckless operation	67	DUI/first offense/bal unk	B5	Miscellaneous
13	Drag racing	68	DUI/second offense/.08	B7	AAC
14	Eluding police-(attempt)	69	DUI/second offense/.10-.15	B9	Other
15	Lvng scene-pers inj/death	70	DUI/second offense/.15	BC	CDL/CMV - DWI state law
16	Lvng scene-property damage	71	DUI/second offense/bal unk	C1	Fail to establish fin resp
17	Fatal accd involv neglig	72	DUI/subsequent offense/.15	C2	Failure to renew leasing
18	Habitual offender	73	DUI/sub offense/<.15/bal u	C3	Fail deposit secur/accident
19	Chemical test refusal	74	DUI transp child < 13 yrs	C5	No proof of ins filed
20	Use of M Vehicle in felony	75	Inv license/cert viol/sub	CC	CDL/CMV - chem test refusal
21	Per family court order	76	Drive inv license/certain	D1	Improper use of plates
22	Phys fitness or disability	77	Drive without/expired lic	D2	Unfit motor vehicle
23	Operate w/o license	88	Dummy code	D3	Request of tax assessor
24	Oper after lic/priv susp	92	Fail to pay income tax	D4	Isolated instances
25	Unlawful/fraud use of lic	93	Child support non-compilance	D6	Title block
26	Lic use by unauthrzd person	94	Refuse/deny CDL license	E1	emission block
27	DWI-resulting in death	95	Refuse/deny operator lic	EC	CDL/CMV-leave scene of acc
28	Alteration of license	96	Lic surr from out-of-state	FC	CDL/CMV-felony involvement
29	Lic in anothers possession	97	Voluntary surrender of lic	GC	CDL/CMV-dwi-0.04%+ w/haz
30	Allow illegal use of license	98	Out-of-state withdrawal	HC	CDL/CMV-dwi state law w/hz
31	Not entitled to lic issue	99	Reinstatement of lic/priv	IC	CDL/CMV-chem.test ref.w/hz
32	Providing incorrect info	1A	Viol restr/limited license	JC	CDL/CMV-dwi contrl sub/haz
33	Fail to pay required fee	1B	2 out-of-service - 10 year	KC	CDL/CMV-lve acc scene/hazm
34	Fail to appear-DMV hearing	1C	CDL/CMV-lv.scene-injury	LC	CDL/CMV-felony involve/haz
35	Request of parent/guardian	2A	H&r fail stop/aid accident	MC	CDL/CMV-comissn felon/drug
36	Fail to complete drive exam	2B	3+ out serv/10yr/16+passen	NC	CDL/CMV-2+CDL serious viol
37	Surrendered RI license	2C	CDL/CMV-pres.alchol in mv	OC	CDL/CMV-2 CDL viol in 3yrs
38	Transport alcohol by minor	3A	H&r fail stop/aid fatal acc	PC	CDL/CMV-3 CDL viol in 3yrs
39	Fail pay/appr out-of-state	3B	3+ out service/10yr	Q1	Parking priv plate viola
40	Fail file accident report	3C	CDL/CMV-pres.alchol mv/haz	Q2	Parking ticket
41	Fail deposit secur/accident	4A	Lvsc aft acc befor pol arv	QC	CDL/CMV 24 hr out of serv
42	Default of agreement	4B	Imminent hazard	RC	CDL/CMV - present comm license
43	Consumtion alcohol in veh	4C	CDL/CMV-aggressive driving	S1	Stolen plate
44	Fail maintain fin respon	5A	Lvsc fatl acc befor police	S2	Child support non-comply
45	Failure satisfy judgment	5C	CDL/CMV-1st rr gate crossing	SC	CDL/CMV oper w/o CDL
46	Fail appear breathalyzer	6A	Fail to ID accid fatal/inj	T1	Tax delinquency/title prob
47	Default/no show w/police	6C	CDL/CMV-2nd railroad gate cross in 3 yrs	TC	CDL/CMV-oper.w/o CDL/haz
48	Fail comply w/AAC appeal			UC	CDL/CMV-unauth.manuf.CDL
49	Fail perform public serv	7A	Illegal possession drugs	VC	CDL/CMV-drv endangr/death
50	Fail appear for evaluation	7C	CDL/CMV-3+ railroad gate cross in 3 yrs	WC	CDL/CMV-drv endgr/death-hz
51	Insufficient funds/check			XC	CDL/CMV-physical fitness
52	Commis of felony w/ controlled substance	8A	Vehicular assault	YC	CDL/CMV-drv endgr/per.inj
		8C	Drv out of service	ZC	CMV-drv engr/per.inj/hazmat
53	Drive while impaired age 18-21	9A	Illegal oper emerg vehicle		
55	Oper aftre susp-ser bodi	9C	Imp class/endorsment CDL		

South Carolina

Administration	Important Telephone and Web Contacts
Kevin Shwedo Executive Director Department of Motor Vehicles PO Box 1498 Blythewood 29016 803-896-5599 www.scdmvonline.com	Driver Licensing...803-896-5000 SR-22 & Financial Responsibility...................803-896-5000 Commercial Driver License............................803-896-2673 Registration & Title Information....................803-896-5000 Highway Patrol...803-896-7920 State Department of Insurance ....803-737-6160 Email Help help@scdmvonline.com SC Code of Laws www.scstatehouse.gov

Driver's License Format, Issuance and Renewal

License Classes, Restrictions and Endorsements Appear After the Driving Record Content Section

License Format
The South Carolina driver's license number consists of eleven numbers computer-generated on a sequential basis.

Document Appearance
The current license and ID credentials began issuance in November 2010. The previous format will stay in circulation until at least 2021.

Current Format
The document is a digitized license document with photo. The background of the credential now has colored lines, a blue palmetto tree with a crescent moon and images of leaves and small palmetto trees at the top and bottom of the credential.

Security Characteristics: There are three levels of security; the third level can only be identified by a SCDMV forensic specialist. There is a holographic laminate with the state seal and the SCDMV logo. The magnetic strip has been removed and a 2D barcode is on the back.

Position of Photo: Each document displays two photos; the larger photo is on the left, the smaller on lower right.

Minor Age Driver Locator: Under 21 drivers are issued a vertical document. There are two pictures - the larger photo is on top. The right side of the document indicates the drive is underage. The date the driver turns 21 is indicated in green at the bottom.

CDL Indicator: CDL is designated in upper right corner and C "COMMERCIAL DRIVER'S LICENSE" is across the top.

Previous Format
This document is a digitized license document with photo.

Security Characteristics: Stiff lamination with a magnetic strip is on the top of the back. The state seal is in center of license. The document includes a hologram with state seal and state emblem.

Position of Photo: Lower Right.

Minor Age Driver Locator: This is indicated across the top of the license.

CDL Indicator: A CDL driver is designated by "CDL" on the license by a dark aqua green stripe with "COMMERCIAL DRIVER'S LICENSE" on the document and shows license class.

Veteran Designation
SCDMV offers a "VETERAN" designation on driver licenses, identification cards and beginner permits for individuals who served honorably in the United States Armed Forces. To apply, veterans must present an acceptable document based on the SC Code of Laws 56-1-140 and the standards set by the South Carolina State Office of Veterans' Affairs.

Issuance and Renewal
Location of Requirements for Proof of Identity:
www.scdmvonline.com/DMVNew/default.aspx?n=accepted_forms_of_identification

Age Requirements
Beginner's Permits are issued in four classes according to the type of vehicle. One must be 14 years of age or older to drive a moped, Class G; 15 years of age or older to drive a passenger vehicle, Class D; motorcycle, Class M; and 18 years of age or older to drive a non-commercial, Class E or F vehicle. Beginner's Permit holders may drive from 6am to midnight. They must be accompanied by a licensed driver in the front seat who is 21 years of age or older, with at least one year of driving experience. A Conditional License is available to fifteen year and ½ olds, and a Special Restricted license is available to sixteen year olds.

 To drive a commercial vehicle Class A, B or C, you must be 18 years old to drive within the state of South Carolina and 21 years old to drive interstate.

Residency
Non-resident's home-state license honored for ninety days; South Carolina license must be obtained upon establishing residency (except students and military personnel and their dependents). CDL holders must apply to a CDL license within 30 days.

Renewal
Both five and ten-year licenses are processed. Ten-year licenses are issued in branch offices to U.S. citizens who are under the age of 65. Five-year licenses are issued by mail to eligible applicants under the age of 65. Licenses expire on the applicant's birthday in the expiring year. Vision examinations are required by law every five years for all age applicants. Because of this vision requirement, licenses may no longer be renewed online.

Elderly-Related Restrictions
Persons who are 65 years of age or older are issued a five-year license.

Vehicle Insurance, Title and Registration Facts

Registration Renewal
Renewal is annual. In South Carolina, payment of personal property taxes is required before a license plate can be renewed. Citizens can pay both the property taxes and renewal fees at the county treasurer's office. These counties provide the ability to pay both taxes and registration fees online; Beaufort, Berkeley, Charleston, Chester, Darlington, Dorchester, Greenville, Lexington, Pickens, Richland, Spartanburg, and York.

New Residents

Registration must be obtained within 45 days of establishing residency. Effective January 1, 2012, acceptable identification must be provided when applying for a title and/or vehicle registration. See http://www.scdmvonline.com/DMVNew/default.aspx?n=providing_id_for_title_and_registration.

Inspections and Emissions Testing

There are no provisions for statewide emission testing or annual safety inspections.

Plate Descriptions

There is one plate with two decals (MO) (YR). The county of issuance is not indicated on the plate. When the vehicle is sold the plate remains with seller.

Insurance and Financial Responsibility

Minimum financial responsibility limits are $25,000/50,000/25,000.

Current South Carolina law requires when a driver's license is issued or renewed or if involved in an accident, drivers must certify on the driver's license application (*DL 447*) that they are insured by an automobile liability policy. Owners are required to provide proof that the vehicle being operated is insured. If a driver is stopped by a law enforcement officer and unable to provide proof that the vehicle being operating is insured, the driver may be issued a citation and be subject to a fine or imprisonment. Also, South Carolina requires drivers to carry no-fault insurance.

The state uses SR-22 forms. South Carolina law requires that insurance companies notify the department when a liability insurance policy is cancelled.

Note that vehicle owners can pay a $550.00 Uninsured Motorist Fee for the privilege to drive and operate an uninsured motor vehicle. This is not an insurance payment: owners are still liable for damages for an at fault accident.

Withdrawal Sanctions, and Alcohol and Drug Testing

Alcohol and Chemical Testing Limits

South Carolina's level at which a person may be inferred to be intoxicated is .08 BAC percent and above; .02 BAC or greater if under 21, and .04 BAC or greater in a CMV. There is an implied consent violation if under 21. There is also a separate violation if BAC is .15 or greater. Levels of BAC between .04 and.10 can be used with other evidence for a conviction.

Suspensions and Revocations

South Carolina is in compliance with the provisions of the Motor Carrier Safety Improvement Act (MCSIA). See the Appendix for more information about these mandatory CDL disqualification sanctions.

The Following Violations Will Result in Driving Privileges Being Revoked—

- Conviction of Careless or Reckless Driving Resulting in Death
- Conviction of a Felony in Which a Vehicle Was Used
- Failure to Stop and Give Aid When Involved in an Accident Resulting in Death or Personal Injury
- Giving False Information Pertaining to Financial Responsibility or Vehicle Registration
- Mental or Physical Incompetence to Drive

The Following Violations Will Result in Driving Privileges Being Suspended—

Driving Under the Influence
    First Conviction .... Six-month suspension.
    Second Conviction .... One-year suspension.
    Third Conviction... Two-year suspension.
    Fourth and Subsequent .... License revoked.
Felony DUI Conviction .... License revoked 3 years if bodily injury, 5 years if death, plus time served.
BAC of .02 or greater while under the age of 21 .... Three-month suspension.
Refusal to Submit to a Chemical Test, 21 and older........ Six-month suspension.
Refusal to Submit to a Chemical Test, under the age of 21 .... Six-month suspension.
Previous offenses of;
    Implied Consent, DUI, Felony DUI, BAC of .15 or greater within past 10 years One hundred eighty days suspension.
    Implied Consent under 21 with BAC of .02 or greater .... One year suspension.
    Implied Consent, DUI, Felony DUI, BAC of .15 or greater within the past 5 years .... One year suspension.
    BAC of .15 or greater .... Thirty-day suspension.
Previous offenses of Implied Consent under 21 with BAC of .15 or greater;
    Implied Consent, DUI, Felony DUI, BAC of .02 or greater within the past 10 years.. Sixty-day suspension.
    Implied Consent, DUI, Felony DUI, BAC of .02 or greater within the past 5 years.... Six-month suspension.
    Second Conviction of Reckless Driving in Five Years................................. Three-month suspension.
    Each Subsequent Conviction in the Five-Year Period .... additional 3-month suspension.
Conviction for Hauling Illegal Whiskey... Suspension.
Failure to Pay Traffic Ticket .... Suspension.
Failure to Satisfy Judgment Rendered When Involved in an Accident............. Suspension.
Habitual Offender... Five-year suspension.
Point Accumulation of Twelve Points.. Suspension.
    Note: Under SC law, a driver gets half of accumulated points removed each year. Also, a driver can take a class and have 4 points removed, but only once every three years.
Taking Part in a Race on Any Public Road, Street, or Highway...................... One-year suspension of license and registration.
Assisting in a Race .... Three-month suspension of license and registration.

Any of the Following Will Result in Driving Privileges Being Canceled—
- If Driver is a Minor and Parent, Guardian, or Whomever Signed for Driver Withdraws his or her Signature from the License Application.
- Giving False Information on the Application.
- Driving While License Suspended, Revoked, or Canceled.

About Ignition Interlock

Since January 1, 2009, an **Ignition Interlock restriction** is required for persons who are convicted of a second or subsequent offense for the following violations:
1) driving under the influence of alcohol or drugs,
2) driving with an unlawful alcohol concentration, or
3) causing great bodily injury or death while driving under the influence of alcohol or drugs.

Reinstatement Requirements

Suspension....................$100.00 fee for each suspension; proof of insurance (SR-22); re-examination—varies depending on reason for suspension.

Revocation....................Proof of financial responsibility; re-examination—varies depending on reason for revocation and failure to provide financial responsibility liability statement (first time issuance of driver license).

Vehicle Reinstatement...When notified by department (liability insurance cancellation), the vehicle owner must reinstate insurance on the vehicle(s) or surrender license plates and registration to the department as soon as possible. Owner will be charged $5.00 per day, not to exceed $200.00, for a vehicle not insured, beginning on the date of the cancellation. If suspended, owner will be required to pay a $200.00 reinstatement fee.

Note: SCDMV offers a driver's license reinstatement fee payment program for SC residents that have a suspended driver's license. Qualified customers that enter into a payment plan agreement will be issued a valid driver's license during the six-month payment plan period

Record Access: Laws, Rules, and Forms

Note: This Section Applies to Both Driver and Vehicle Records.

Governing Statutes and Rules

SC Code of Laws: www.scstatehouse.gov

See Title 56 for Motor Vehicle Laws.

South Carolina indicates the federal Driver Privacy Protection Act (US Code, Title 18, §2721, et seq.), the South Carolina Family Privacy Protection Act (SC Code §30-2-10, et seq.), and the South Carolina Freedom of Information Act (SC Code §30-4-10, et seq.), control the release and use of personal information from DMV records.

Also, §56-3-510 provides that vehicle registration may be disclosed provided the request is submitted on a form prescribed by the Department.

Policy Statement Regarding Permissible Uses

South Carolina does not have any DPPA federal exceptions specifically enumerated by statute; however, South Carolina indicates the following exceptions on the *Form MV-70* request form for driver information:
- To carry out a governmental function.
- For a business to verify the accuracy of personal information previously provided to the business.
- To use in any court proceeding, or investigation in anticipation of litigation.
- For research and statistical purposes so long as the personal information is not published, redisclosed, or used to contact individuals. (Such requests are processed only in Blythewood DMV Headquarters. See special instructions on back of this form.)
- For use by an insurer for claims investigations, rating and underwriting.

- For use by an employer or their insurer to verify commercial driver license information.
- For any other use by the driver or by written consent of the driver.

Request and Consent Forms

Driving Records: Form *MV-70 Request for Driver Information* (www.scdmvonline.com/DMVNew/forms/mv-70.pdf)   must   be submitted. This does not require the driver's consent if request is for a permissible purpose, but does require the signature of the requester. Non-permissible use requesters can only obtain records with personal information with a signed release from the subject using the form mentioned above.

Vehicle Records: Use of *Form 5027-A Request for Vehicle Information* is suggested. Use *MV-82 Expedited Documents/Records Request* to expedite the request. Notarization is not required. Forms are at www.scdmvonline.com/DMVNew/forms.aspx.

Vendor and Third Party Access Policy

Third party entities can sell to a permissible user as long as all vendors and end users in the chain are in compliance with DPPA. Bulk requests for data are not honored for commercial solicitation purposes.

Records Ordered For Non-permissible Uses

Driving Records: Without consent or a permissible use, requesters cannot obtain a driving record but may obtain an online summary without personal data (see below).

Vehicle Records: Casual requesters can obtain records only with consent of the subject. The *Form 5027-A* can be used. No records are released if there is no consent.

Access to Driver-Related Records

Driving Records

General Information and Fees

Driver Records Mail-In Unit, Department of Motor Vehicles, PO Box 1498, Blythewood 29016-0028, 803-896-5000.

The fee is $6.00 for manual processing and $7.25 for electronic access. A $6.00 fee is also charged for a copy of a ticket or of a suspension notice.

In-Person – Requests may be made over-the-counter from DMV Branch office or Express Office. Generally, up to ten requests will be

processed while one waits; more than ten requests will take two days to process. Use *Form MV-70*.

Mail – A three or ten-year driving record may be ordered for the same fee. Requests mailed to the address above are processed within five working days. The driver's license number or full name and date of birth are needed when ordering. The fee must accompany each request. Address mail requests to Alternative Media

Electronic Commercial – Commercial records are available from the   portal   https://www.scdmvonline.com/dmvmember/.   Authorized businesses must establish an account through a formal approval and acceptance process. The fee is $7.25 per record and a $75.00 annual fee is required. Members have access to additional online services. For more information about opening an account, call 803-771-0131 or email help@scdmvonline.com.

Bulk – The state does not sell its license database, or portions there of.

By Person of Record – SC drivers more purchase a copy of their own driving record in person, by mail as described above. Also, one may purchase a three or ten-year record for $6.00 at https://www.scdmvonline.com/dmvpublic/trans/DrvRecWarn.aspx. No personal information is released. The unofficial record is viewed in a PDF format, and an "official" record is also mailed to the address of record. To order, the DL #, SSN, DOB, issue date of the DL, and exact address that appears on the license or ID Card.

Electronic Status Record

One may obtain a free summary of a driving record that includes the points and status. Submitting the DL#, SSN and DOB is required. Visit https://www.scdmvonline.com/dmvpublic/trans/DRecPoints.aspx.

Notification/Monitoring Program

At present, South Carolina does not offer a monitoring system or notification program to employers or insurance companies to track incidents of drivers. However, there is discussion about providing this service in the future.

Accident Reports

Reporting – Accidents resulting in death, injury, or property damage in excess of $1,000.00 must be reported immediately to the nearest law enforcement agency. At the time of an accident, South Carolina Law requires that the investigating officer issue a Notice of Requirement (Form FR-10) to verify that liability insurance was in effect. When the investigating officer issues the form, the owner is responsible for providing proof (via insurance company) that the vehicle involved in the accident was insured. Failure to provide insurance verification to the department within fifteen (15) days from the date of the accident may result in suspension of the owner's driver's license and/or registration privileges. The verification of liability insurance should be forwarded to the Department of Motor Vehicles, Financial Responsibility Office, PO Box 1498, Blythewood SC 29016-0050.

Record Access – Accident Reports, Financial Responsibility Office, PO Box 1498, Blythewood SC 29016-0050, 803-896-5000, fax is 803-896-8099.

Copies of accident reports may be obtained by sending the full name of all drivers, date of accident, drivers' license numbers, and the name of the county in which the accident occurred all to the address above. To request an accident report, it is suggested to complete *Form FR-50*, found at www.scdmvonline.com/DMVNew/forms/FR-50.pdf. The tag number of a vehicle involved is also helpful. The fee is $6.00 per accident research report or insurance report. Records are available from 10 years to present. Mail turnaround time is generally 7-10 days.

An account can be established with a deposit, the amount depends on volume of records requested. Call 803-896-9092 to establish an account. Accounts may request by phone, but no more than 5 requests per day.

Access to Vehicle-Related Records

General Information and Fees

Registration (or Titles) Section, Department of Motor Vehicles, PO Box 1498, Blythewood SC 29016-0024, 803-896-5000, fax: 803-896-6682, www.scdmvonline.com.

The DMV maintains the registration, title, and lien records for vehicles and mobile homes. The DMV will not release name and address information, but will confirm validity of name and address if provided by requester. The current fee for all VIN, registration, and lien checks is $6.00, add $20.00 for expedited counter service (see below). The title history contains odometer reading information, as known. Both title and registration records are held for 3 years on computer. Title records are held on microfiche since 1984.

In-Person, Mail – Mobile homes are researched by VIN and by name. Normal turnaround time for mail-in requests is 3 days. South Carolina permits pre-approved, established accounts to order records by phone. A deposit is required.

Expedited Service – There is an additional $20.00 fee for each document or record request completed within one day. All requests received after 2:00 PM will be counted as received on the following business day. DMV branch offices will process up to three expedited documents on the same business day. Use of *Form MV-82 Expedited Documents/Records Request* is suggested.

Fax – Fax searching is available but only to pre-approved, ongoing requesters. A deposit is required.

Electronic – South Carolina does not offer online inquiry at this time.

Bulk – South Carolina offers a batch-method of obtaining title and registration information, only for permitted requests described above (and not for commercial purposes). The cost is $.10 per record with a minimum charge of $1,000.00. For more information, call Customer Service Administration for automated searching at the number listed above.

Access to Vessel-Related Records

General Information, Access and Fees

Department of Natural Resources, Registration & Titles, PO Box 167, Columbia 29202, 803-734-3857, www.dnr.sc.gov/boating/index.html. All motorized boats must be titled and registered. All boat motors must be titled. There is a distinction between a boat title and a motor title. All outboard motors with five HP or greater are required to be titled. All sailboats must be titled. All sailboats over 14 foot must be titled and registered. Records are stored in a document imaging system.

A title search request will show any liens. The title search fee is $10.00 per record or if over 4 pages then $25.00 per hour. Thus, a search of boats with no motor is $10.00 and a search of a boat and an outboard motor is $20.00, if each is under 4 pages. Credit cards are accepted, but only in person. A *Title Search Form* is provided at www.dnr.sc.gov/boating/forms/pdf/TitleSearchForm.pdf.

The DNR suggests submitting VIN, hull # with description or with outboard motor serial #, but can run a name search if requested. SSNs are not released. Turnaround time is generally 7 to 10 days, but can take up to 3 weeks. State law prohibits the release for records for commercial purposes, but the DNR will sell the database in bulk to qualified entities.

Driving Record Content and Reciprocity

What's On or Not On the Driving Record

- South Carolina will not show most non-moving violations (e.g., seatbelt, open container) on the record, but will show the suspension if a non-moving violation fine ia not paid.
- Accidents resulting in at least $1,000.00 in damage or in personal injury will appear on the driving record, along with the date.
- South Carolina gives a second summary on CDL driver records. This summary separates all driver moving violations occurring while under a commercial status, including out-of-state violations. These second summaries show on all the access modes listed above.
- The driver's address is provided as part of the public record only to permissible users; the SSN and other personal information are not released.
- Both a three-year and a ten-year record can be provided. Three-year driving records will list convictions for the previous three years from the date of receipt.
- The state permits driver school attendance in lieu of conviction.

Data Retention

The length of time moving violations and DUI convictions are retained is at least ten years, longer if withdrawals are involved or if CMVs involved. A logical purge is done every three years on the birth date of posting. Surrendered licenses are not purged from the system, but are only available for public access for ten years. A physical purge is done periodically based on the timetable per the MCSIA (see the Appendix).

Court to Repository

The courts transfer data to the state via paper and must submit this data within five days of conviction. The violations are key-entered at headquarters within five days to three weeks of receipt.

State Reciprocity for Non-CDL Drivers

- Will suspend license of driver for unpaid out-of-state convictions.
- Record of new incoming driver is shown on MVR.
- Out-of-state convictions are shown on MVR.
- Out-of-state accidents are not shown on MVR.
- Convictions of out-of-state drivers are sent to home state.
- Record is forwarded to new state upon surrender of license.

License Classes, Restrictions, and Endorsements

License Classes– Commercial

South Carolina began issuing the CDL in July of 1990, and required commercial drivers to convert to the CDL by April 1992.
A CDL driver is designated by "CDL" on the license by a dark aqua green stripe with "COMMERCIAL DRIVER'S LICENSE" on the license itself, and shows class of license. The Driving Record abstract indicates: "CMV (Y/N)."

Class A	Any combination of vehicles with a GVWR of 26,001 or more pounds, provided the unit being towed is in excess of 10,000 pounds GVWR, (includes Class G, trike; but does not include motorcycle or motorcycle with sidecar.).
Class B	Any single vehicle with GVWR of 26,001 or more pounds, or any such vehicle towing a vehicle not in excess of 10,000 pounds (except motorcycles).
Class C	Any single vehicle less than 26,001 pounds. GVWR placarded for hazardous materials or designed to transport sixteen or more persons, including the driver (except motorcycles).

License Classes– Non-Commercial

Class D	All vehicles not exceeding 26,000 pounds GVW (except motorcycles) that do no meet the definitions of Classes A, B and C.
Class E	Single unit vehicles, including class D, exceeding 26,000 pounds GVW that do not meet the definitions of Classes A, B, & C (except motorcycles).
Class F	All vehicle combinations (including Class D and E) exceeding 26,000 pounds GVW that do not meet the definitions of Classes A, B, & C (except motorcycles).
Class M	Motorcycles (includes Class G, tike, and motorcycle with sidecar..
Class G	Moped.

Restrictions

A	Corrective Lenses		M	Outside Mirrors
B	Special Restricted		N	Turn Signals
C	No Interstate Driving		O	Day Driving Only
D	Not to Exceed 50 mph		P	(CDL) Government Vehicles
E	Neighborhood Only (ten-mile radius)		Q	Power Steering/Brakes
F	Previous DUI		R	Passenger Vehicle Only
G	Hand Control		S	Route Restricted
H	Steering Knob		U	Conditional/Provisional
I	(CDL) Interstate Only		V	(CDL) Class B Passenger Veh Also
II	Ignition Interlock Device		W	(CDL) Class C Passenger Veh Also
J	Automatic Transmission		X	Special Restricted Waiver
K	(CDL) Vehicle Without Air-Brakes		Z	(CDL) Except Tractor-Trailer
L	Other			

Endorsements

N	Tanker Vehicle		P	Passenger Vehicles
T	Double/Triple Trailer		S	School Bus
H	Hazardous Material		X	Hazmat & Tank Vehicle Combination

Pointable Conviction Table with ACD and Statute,

A Suspension Table and an Accident Table follow.

State Code	ACD	Pts	Statute	Violation
421	S51	2	56-5-1510	Speeding; ten mph or less
422	M42	2	56-5-1900	Shifting lanes improperly
423	F35	2	56-5-2510, 2530, 2540	Improper dangerous parking
424	S94	2	56-5-1510	Too fast for conditions; ten mph or less
425	E54	2	56-5-4780	Failure to dim lights
426	E05	2	56-5-4490, 4510, 4500, 4520, 4530	Operating with improper lights
427	N82	2	56-5-3810	Improper backing
428	F66	2	56-5-4410, 5310	Driving a vehicle in unsafe condition
429	M40	2	56-5-1810, 1820	Driving in improper lane
430	E34	2	56-5-4510	Defective tail-light
431	B91	0	56-1-2070	Violation of CDL Class/Restrictions or Endorsements
441	S61	4	56-5-1510	Speeding; more than 10, but less than 25 mph
442	M14	4	56-5-2740, 950, 970	Disobedience of any official traffic device
443	M08	4	56-5-740	Disobedience to officer directing traffic
444	N01	4	56-5-2310, 2320, 2330, 1840, 2350, 2340	Failure to yield right-of-way
445	N70	4	56-5-1810, 1820	Driving on wrong side of road
446	M70	4	56-5-1850, 1860, 1890, 1880	Passing unlawfully
447	N50	4	56-5-2120, 2140, 2130, 2150, 2160	Turning unlawfully
448	M12	4	56-5-3240	Driving through or within safety zone
449	S94	4	56-5-1510	Too fast for conditions; over ten mph
450	N40	4	56-5-2150	Failing to give or giving improper signal
451	M34	4	56-5-1930, 1940, 1950, 1960	Following too closely
452	E31	4	56-5-4850, 4860, 4870	Operating with improper brakes
461	M84	6	56-5-2920	Reckless driving
462	M75	6	56-5-2770	Passing stopped school bus
463	B04	6	56-5-1220	Hit-and-run (property damage only)
464	S92	6	56-5-1510	Speeding; 25 mph or more
465	N82	0	56-5-3810	Improper backing (Before 1-1-89)
466	U25	0	16-21-60	Operating vehicle without owner's consent
467	B92	0	56-1-510(2)	Lending or borrowing driver license
469	B51	0	56-1-40	No driver license
470	B30	0	56-1-480	Allowing unlicensed person to drive
472	U26	0	56-1-490	Theft/unlawful taking of motor vehicle
473	B82	0	56-3-1350, 56-10-240	Fail to surrender suspended plates/registration
475	M81	0	56-1-2030	Careless/negligent driving
476	B27	0	56-1-2060	Out-of-service; 24 hours or more
664	B56	0	-	Driving CMV without obtaining CDL
665	B51	0	-	Driving a CDV without CDL in possession
666	U01	0	-	Negligent or criminal operation of CMV - fatality
771	M10	4	56-5-2710	Disregard railroad sign or signal
772	M20	4	56-5-2710	Disobedience to signal of approaching train
773	M21	0	56-5-2720	Fail to stop for approaching train-no signal or barrier present
774	M22	0	56-5-2725	Failure to stop at railroad crossing
776	M09	0	56-5-2710	Failure to obey railroad crossing restriction
777	M23	0	56-5-2735	Failure to obey railroad crossing clearance for undercarriage
778	M24	0	-	Failure to obey railroad-highway crossing violation

Suspension Table - Includes Commercial Motor Vehicle (CMV) Suspensions

State Code	ACD	Statute	Description
001	A20	56-5-2990	Driving Under the Influence
002	B63	56-9-610	Failure to Maintain Proof of Financial Responsibility
003	W01	56-1-740	Point Suspension
004	M84	56-5-2920	Reckless Driving
005	B07	56-5-1210	Leaving Scene of Accident - Bodily Injury
006	W20	56-1-270	Failure to Pass Re-Exam
007	D02	56-1-240	False Information on Application
008	W14	56-1-270	Physically Disqualified
009	W20	56-1-270	Failure to Appear For Re-Examination
010	W13	56-1-120	Minor Signature Withdrawal
011	U08	56-1-280	Manslaughter / Involuntary Manslaughter
012	U07	56-5-2910	Reckless Homicide

State Code	ACD	Statute	Description
013	B26	56-1-460	Driving Under Suspension
014	W00	61-6-4290	Transporting Liquor Illegally
015	W00	56-2-2740	Failure to Pay Property Tax
016	S95	56-5-1620	Racing
017	D36	56-10-270	Operating or Allowing Operation of Uninsured Vehicle
018	U01	56-5-750	Failure to Stop for Blue Light
019	B64	56-10-260	Presenting False Insurance Certificate
020	U04	56-5-1620	Acquiescing In Racing
022	W01	56-1-1030	Habitual Offender
024	U04	16-13-185	Failure To Make Payment For Gasoline
025	B26	56-1-460	Driving Under Suspension - FTPTT
026	B26	56-1-460	Driving Under Suspension - DUI
027	B26	56-1-460	Driving Under Suspension - No Susp to attach
028	W01	56-1-185	Excessive Points
029	B26	56-1-460	Driving Under Suspension - FTPPT
030	-	56-1-125	Failure to Register Selective Service
033	W30	56-1-2110(F)	Serious Traffic Violations
034	W00	20-7-1333	Court Ordered Suspension
035	A31	56-1-746	Alcohol Violation
036	A33	56-1-745	Controlled Substance Violation
037	U01	56-5-750	Failure Stop for Blue Light with BI/Death
038	D51	20-7-945	Delinquent Child Support
039	U31	56-5-2780	Passing Stopped School Bus BI/Death
040	U04	56-1-290	Operating Unlicensed Vehicle or Taxi
041	D36	56-10-510	Insurance Verification Request
042	D36	56-10-240	Cancellation of Insurance
043	D36	56-10-520	Owner Operating an Uninsured Motor Vehicle
044	D36	56-10-520	False Insurance Certificate by Non-Owner
045	D36	56-10-520	False Insurance Certificate by Owner
046	D36	56-10-520	Non-Owners Operating Uninsured Motor Vehicle
047	D36	56-10-530	Accident - Uninsured
048	W40	56-1-2110	CMV Permanent
049	W70	Federal 383.52	Imminent Hazard
050	W00	56-1-240	Failure to Meet Licensing Requirements
051	W00	56-4-2110 (G)	CDL DRUG/ALCOHOL
052	W00	56-5-2951 (L)	Fail To Successfully Complete ADSAP
053	D02	56-1-2090 (D)	False Information on CDL Application
054	W00	56-5-1030	Altering or Defacing Signs or Signals
055	W00	56-5-2947	Child Endangerment
056	A12	56-1-286	Implied Consent Under 21
057	A90	56-5-2950	BAC of .15 or Greater
058	A61	56-1-286	BAC of .02 or Greater Under 21
059	D36	56-10-225	Failure to Show proof of Insurance at Time of Stop
060	D36	56-10-225	Failure to Show proof of Insurance
062	D36	56-10-240	No Insurance at time of Registration
063	B04	56-1-2110(A-3)	Hit and Run - Property and Damage only
064	B56	56-1-2110	Driving a CMV without obtaining a CDL (V664 - not in use)
065	B51	56-1-2110	Driving a CMV without a CDL in Possession (V665-not in use)
066	U10	56-1-2110 (7)	Negligent or Criminal Operation of CMV-Fatality
067	B24	56-1-460	Driving CMV Under Suspension
068	B41	56-1-746	Misrepresentation of Identity
071	U03	56-1-280	Felony in a Motor Vehicle
072	B19	56-1-2070 E (4)	Operating CMV-OS over 16 psgrs/Haz Mat
073	W00	FMCSA	CDLIS Disqualification from OOS
074	A50	56-1-2110 (E)	Felony - CMV - Controlled Substance
075	D37	56-9-490	Accident Judgment Default
076	W00	56-1-2120	CMV Out of Service Order Issued
077	D37	56-9-490 (J)	Accident Installment Default
078	D38	56-9-351	FR Accident
079	D39	56-9-430	Accident Judgment
080	W00	56-1-240	Dishonored Check
081	D35	56-10-225	Failure to Verify Insurance
084	A08	56-5-2933	Unlawful Alcohol Concentration
086	W00	Unsure	Tobacco Restriction - Minor
087	A41	56-5-2941/2990	IID Assessment Infringement
088	A41	56-5-2941/2990	IID Point Infringement

State Code	ACD	Statute	Description
089	A41	56-5-2941/2990	IID Unauthorized Vehicle
090	W00	56-2-240	Failure to Remit Fees
091	A12	56-5-2950	Implied Consent
092	A04	56-1-2110(A-2)	BAC of .04 or Greater
094	B27	56-1-2070	Operating CMV While Out of Service
095	A20	56-5-2945	Felony Driving Under the Influence
096	W00	56-1-146	Court Administration Cancellation
097	D56	56-25-10	Failure to Pay Traffic Ticket
098	W00	56-1-130	Departmental Action - ADSAP
099	W00	56-1-130	Departmental Suspension
100	W40	56-1-2060	CDL Disqualified for Life
775	M10	56-5-2710	Railroad-Highway Grade Crossing Disq
999	-		Temp Susp for Defining Rule No and Warning Letters

Accident Table

Code	ACD	Description
00	U30	Did not contribute
11	U32	Personal injury - property damage less than $1,000
21	U33	Property damage only - $1,000 or more
31	U31	Fatality with less than $1,000
41	U32	Personal injury & property damage $1,000 or higher
51	U33	Personal injury & fatality - property damage less than $1,000
61	U31	Personal damage & fatality - with or without personal injury of $1,000 or more
71	U33	Property damage & fatality ($400-$750). No injury or fatality (only used for accidents occurring before June 5, 1996)
81	U30	Less than $1000. No injury, no fatality (type 8 accident)

About the Point System

Points range from 2 to 6. Accumulation of 12 or more points in a 12-month period can result in a suspension. Half of the accumulated points can be removed each year. A driver may take a driving class to have 4 points removed, but the driver is limited to taking the class once every 3 years.

South Dakota

Administration	Important Telephone and Web Contacts
Cynthia Gerber, Director Driver Licensing Program Department of Public Safety 118 W Capitol, Pierre 57501 605-773-6883 http://dps.sd.gov/licensing/default.aspx Debra Hillmer, Director Motor Vehicle Division, Revenue Department 445 E Capitol, Pierre 57501-3185 605-773-3541 www.state.sd.us/drr2/motorvehicle/index.htm SD Codified Laws: http://legis.state.sd.us/statutes/index.aspx	Driver Licensing.....................................605-773-6883 Financial Responsibility/SR-22..............605-773-6883 Commercial Driver License....................605-773-6883 Accident Reports.....................................605-773-3868 Motor Carrier Services...........................605-773-4578 Title and Registration Information.........605-773-3541 State Department of Insurance.................605-773-3563 Highway Patrol.......................................605-773-3105 General Email for Driver Licensing: dps.sdlicensinginfo@state.sd.us General Email for Vehicles: motorv@state.sd.us Motor Vehicle Statutes - Title 32: www.state.sd.us/drr2/laws/motor_v/motorv_statutes.htm

Driver's License Format, Issuance and Renewal

License Classes, Restrictions and Endorsements Appear After the Driving Record Content Section

License Format

The current DL is an eight digit computer-generated sequential number. Until July 2006, Social Security Numbers were used at the DL number. Prior to December 4, 1989, license numbers had six digits. Military and old suspended/revoked drivers may still have older licenses.

Document Appearance

The state began issuing the current driver license and ID card documents in December 2009. The previous driver license document was originally issued in May 2000. Both documents are reviewed below.

Current Document

Security Characteristics: A ghost image of the driver's photo is in the lower right; 1 and 2-dimensional barcodes on rear; Mt Rushmore shows in the background. The laminate has various designs and includes the words "The Mount Rushmore State."

Position of Photo: Left.

Minor Age Drivers: The card is in a vertical format. A red colored header is used for driver license and ID Cards for ages 16 to 21. A green header is used for drivers under 18 driving on a restricted license. (Regular drivers have blue headers.) Date indicates when driver turns 21.

CDL Indicator: "COMMERCIAL DRIVER LICENSE" is printed in gold.

Older Document

Security Characteristics: Ghost image of the driver's photo is in the lower left corner; a 2-dimensional barcode on rear; the words "South Dakota" written all over the face of the document.

Position of Photo: Upper right.

Minor Age Driver Locator: red colored header is used for drivers 16 to 21. A green header is used for drivers under 18 driving on a restricted license. (Regular drivers have blue headers.) A gray header is used for ID cards. Date indicates when driver turns 21.

CDL Indicator: COMMERCIAL DRIVER LICENSE" is printed in gold header.

Issuance

Location of Requirements for Proof of Identity:
http://dps.sd.gov/licensing/driver_licensing/obtain_a_license.aspx

Age Requirements

Effective 01/01/99, South Dakota implemented a Graduated Licensing System.

Minimum Age: Sixteen for an operator license; fourteen for Instruction Permit.

Instruction Permit: Fourteen; valid from 6AM to 10PM when accompanied by licensed driver who is at least 18 years of age and who has at least one year of driving experience. From 10PM to 6AM, permit holder must be accompanied by a parent or legal guardian.

Restricted Minor's Permit: Must be at least 14 years of age and pass the vision, knowledge, and driving test, complete the requirements of the Instruction Permit, and have not been convicted of a traffic violation during the prior six months. An individual up to age 18 years of age may hold a Restricted Minor's Permit. This permit is valid from 6AM to 10PM; if accompanied by parent/guardian, valid from 10PM to 6AM.

Residency

Non-residents must secure a license within ninety days of establishing residency. CDL holders must secure a license within thirty days of establishing residency.

Renewal

Renewal occurs on the birth month of fifth year. Driver keeps the same number when renewing, unless number is SSN. As mentioned all SSNs are being converted to the computer-generated eight digit number. Active military licenses do not expire (as long as the person is active duty, out of state, and has the license in possession). Persons who have accumulated child support arrearages of $1,000 or more will be issued one 6-month temporary license.

Elderly-Related Restrictions

None reported.

Vehicle Insurance, Title and Registration Facts

Registration & Renewal

All motor vehicles, motorcycles, and trailers owned by South Dakota residents and operated on public highways must be registered with the County Treasurer of the applicant's residence. All snowmobiles used on public and private lands and any frozen public waters within territorial limits of South Dakota must be licensed.

Registration renewals are determined on a staggered registration renewal system based on the first letter of the last name. The chart is available at www.state.sd.us/drr2/motorvehicle/fee_schedule/fees.htm. Renewal is available online at www.sdcars.org unless an address change is necessary. This includes boats and snowmobiles that have been issued a multi-year license.

New Residents

New residents must register vehicles within ninety days, on reciprocal basis. However, per state law South Dakota residency is not required for titling and registration.

Inspections and Emissions Testing

South Dakota requires neither a vehicle safety inspection nor an emissions test.

Passenger Plate Facts

Two plates are issued with one decal (MO & YR) on both plates. The first 1 or 2 numeric characters designate the county of issuance. There are 66 (1-65 + 67) codes, but not in a matching alpha order. To obtain the code list, we suggest calling the DMV.

When a vehicle is sold, typical passenger and commercial plates no longer transfer with the vehicle and stay with the original owner. Organizational plates remain with the owner. Seller must provide purchaser with a seller's permit that is used by the new purchaser until plates can be obtained. A seller's permit can be obtained online at www.sdcars.org. A sale can be reported at the same web page, one must have a SD driver's license, with several exceptions. Seller must also report the sale on a private transaction within 15 days of the sale. A report of sale form is used if the form is not on the title. The form is available on the web at www.state.sd.us/drr2/motorvehicle/forms.htm.

Insurance and Financial Responsibility

Minimum limits are $25,000/50,000/25,000. South Dakota does not have no-fault insurance. Proof of financial responsibility is required for all residents and must be carried in the vehicle and presented at the request of law enforcement. Any operator who has had their driver license revoked or suspended following a judgment, a conviction for no insurance, vehicular homicide, DWI, or two convictions of reckless driving (within a one year period) must establish proof of financial responsibility for the future before he may drive or re-register any vehicle in this state. Most motorists provide this proof of financial responsibility by obtaining an SR22 insurance filing from their auto insurance company.

Withdrawal Sanctions, and Alcohol and Drug Testing

Alcohol and Chemical Testing Limits

South Dakota's illegal intoxication level is BAC .08 percent and above; .04 BAC if driving a CMV; and .02 BAC if under age 21. Urine, blood, and breath testing are authorized.

Suspensions and Revocations

The South Dakota DPS is in compliance with the provisions of the Motor Carrier Safety Improvement Act (MCSIA). See the Appendix for more information about these mandatory CDL disqualification sanctions.

Point Accumulation *(Fifteen points in twelve months or twenty-two points in twenty-four months)*

First Offense	Sixty-day suspension.
Second Offense	Six-month suspension.
Third or Subsequent Offense	One-year suspension.

Minor's Conviction of Class 1 Misdemeanor or Felony
Suspended until 16th birthday or as directed by the courts.

Restricted Minor License *Traffic Violation Conviction or License Restriction Conviction*

First Offense	Thirty-day suspension.
Second Offense	Suspension until sixteenth birthday or ninety days, whichever is longer.

Driving While Intoxicated

First Conviction	Thirty-day revocation.
Second Conviction Within Ten Year Period	One-year revocation.
Third Conviction Within Ten Year Period	One-year revocation from sentence date or release from incarceration, whichever is longer.
*Refusal to Submit to Chemical Test	One-year revocation.

The Following Violations Will Also Result in Revocation or Suspension of Driving Privileges

- Alcohol Possession (not in a Motor Vehicle) by a Minor Under 21
- Conviction for False Information on Application
- Conviction for Possession of Suspended, Revoked or Altered Driver License
- Court Ordered Suspension or Revocation
- Under 18 years of age, Violation of License Restriction
- Driving While Under the Influence
- Driving While License is Revoked or Suspended
- Eluding Law Enforcement
- Failure to Maintain Proof of Insurance
- Failure to Pay Child Support
- Failure to Pay a Fine
- Failure to Satisfy a Judgment as a Result of an Accident

- Point Accumulation
- Possession/Consumption of Alcohol in a Motor Vehicle (Driver only)
- Possession/Consumption of Drugs in a Motor Vehicle
- Providing Alcoholic Beverages to Person Under 21
- *Refusal to Submit to a Chemical Test (.02 BAC only)
- Two Convictions for Reckless Driving Within Twelve Months
- Under 16 Years of Age, Conviction of Any Traffic Offense
- Vehicular Homicide
-

Notes   1)   * = Implied Consent repealed except for .02 BAC, under age 21 arrests.
             2)   Restricted licenses for work purposes are available on some suspensions and revocations.

Reinstatement Requirements

Suspension $50.00 fee; eye exam and written test required if license is expired more than 30 days.
Revocation $50.00 to $200.00 fee; eye exam; knowledge test; financial responsibility required after DWI, no insurance, vehicular homicide,
                judgment, or 2nd offense of reckless driving in one-year period.
Note: There are specific and varying reinstatement fees for certain, specific revocations

Record Access: Laws, Rules, and Forms

Note: This Section Applies to Both Driver and Vehicle Records.

Governing Statutes and Rules

SD Codified Laws: http://legis.state.sd.us/statutes/index.aspx
Motor Vehicle Statutes - Title 32:
www.legis.state.sd.us/statutes/DisplayStatute.aspx?Statute=32&Type=Statute
SDCL 32-5-144 through 32-5-150 places the state into compliance with the provisions of DPPA.

Policy Statement Regarding Permissible Uses

Requesters shall not sell, retain, distribute, provide, or transfer any record information or portion of the record information acquired under any agreement except as authorized by the Department and DPPA.

Request and Consent Forms

Driving Records; The form to use for a request by third party (Insurance or Employer) is found online at http://dps.sd.gov/licensing/driver_licensing/driving_record.aspx. As long as the purpose of the request is a permissible use, the form does not need to be signed by the subject; however the notarized signature of the requester is required. These requesters must maintain a current list of names and individuals authorized to access Department records. This list must be available to the Department upon demand. Requesters with no permissible use can only obtain records with the notarized permission of the subject. The same web page mentioned above also is the source for those requesting their own record for personal use. One can use this form to authorize another person to have record, but request must have notarized signature of license holder.
Vehicle Records: South Dakota requires that all requests for vehicle-related records be on the state's vehicle record request form (*MV-*

DPPA). Download at www.state.sd.us/drr2/motorvehicle/forms.htm. As long as the purpose of the request is a permissible use, the form does not need to be signed by the subject, but does require the notarized signature of the requester. Private Investigators must submit their PI license number and state sales tax license number on the request form.

Vendor and Third Party Access Policy

Requesters must maintain a current list of names and individuals authorized to access Department records and make this list available to the Department upon demand.
Each Department-approved requester that resells or discloses personal information per statute must keep, for a period of five years, records identifying each person, or entity that receives such information and the permitted purpose for which the information will be used. These records shall be available to the Department upon request.
Approved online vendors may access records for other vendors (who are not online, etc.) who will then sell to an end user with the following restrictions—
a)   If contract between original vendor and reseller contains same language as contract between the state and the original vendor
b)   If contract between reseller and end-user contains same language as contract between the state and the original vendor

Non-permissible Use Requests

Without consent or permissible use, records are not released; even records with no personal information. A non-permissible use requester can only obtain records with the signed, notarized consent of the subject.

Access to Driver-Related Records

Driving Records

General Information and Fees
Driver License Program, 118 West Capital, Pierre SD 57501, 605-773-6883.
The current fee is $5.00; the last fee increase was in 2009. The agency does charge for "no record found" requests.
South Dakota has two different records available - the **Regular three-year record** and the **Complete three-year record.** The difference is the **Complete record** is only available to CDL holders, their employers, or prospective employers and displays all driver license suspensions, revocations, and disqualifications. The **Regular record** only includes convictions and accidents and is what the insurance industry uses.

In-Person – Records may be requested over-the-counter at Driver Licensing office listed above and at the Aberdeen, Brookings, Mitchell, Rapid City, Sioux Falls, Watertown, and Yankton Driver Exam Stations. Records are processed immediately. Up to and including five records may be ordered at once by businesses.
Mail – The driver's full name, date of birth, and driver's license number are needed when ordering. Requests mailed to the state are processed within forty-eight hours of receipt. The fee must accompany request.
Telephone – Pre-approved accounts may order records by phone.
Electronic – The system is open for pre-approved requesters 24 hours a day. Only the **Regular record** is available. There is a minimum of 250 requests daily. This is a batch system with an approximate 10 minutes

wait time to retrieve a batch after ordering. The fee is $5.00 per record. There are some start-up costs involved. The license number and date of birth are required to access a record. Billing is weekly.

Bulk – Bulk sales are not permitted.

By Person of Record – South Dakota drivers may obtain their driving record by mail or walk-in as described above. This is the only location in the state to obtain the **Complete record**. At present, there is no program for drivers to order or view their own record online.

Notification/Monitoring Program

At present, South Dakota does not offer a means for employers or insurance companies to monitor or track incidents of drivers.

Accident Reports

Reporting – A state reportable accident is an accident resulting in bodily injuries or death to any person or, if there was no personal injury, property damage to an apparent extent of $1,000 or more to any one person's property or $2,000 per accident. Accidents which occur in parking lots or on private property are not reportable to the Office of Accident Records. There are no special state reporting requirements for CDL.

Record Access – Copies of officer-completed reports are available from the Department of Public Safety, Office of Accident Records, 118 W Capitol Avenue, Pierre 57501, 605-773-3868.

A state reportable accident is an accident resulting in bodily injuries or death to any person or, if there was no personal injury, property damage to an apparent extent of $1,000 or more to any one person's property or $2,000 per accident. The fee is $4.00 per report. Records are available for ten years to present, five years on paper. The SSN is not released. New records are available for inquiry after one week, but can take twenty days. Full name, the date and location of the accident is required. Turnaround time is five to fifteen days.

To obtain an accident report request form go to www.dps.sd.gov/enforcement/accident_records/images/accrequest.pdf.

Access to Vehicle-Related Records

General Information and Fees

Division of Motor Vehicles, Information Section, 445 E. Capitol, Pierre SD 57501-3185, 605-773-3541.

Information is available on the following types of vehicles: cars, trucks, boats, snowmobiles, motorcycles, trailers, and motor-homes. The DMV took over the registration process for boats in 1992. Original paper documents are maintained for 18 months, but all records are maintained permanently on film.

The current fee for a computer printout of VIN, registration, ownership or a lien check is $2.00 per record. The fee is $5.00 for a complete title history from microfilm. Original paper documents are maintained for 18 months, but all records are maintained permanently on film. The DMV's vehicle record request form (*MV-DPPA*) is downloadable at www.state.sd.us/drr2/motorvehicle/forms.htm. The requester's signature must be notarized. If not for a permissible use, the form includes a release to be signed by the record holder. The registering of motor vehicles is performed at the local county treasurers' offices and the paperwork is sent to the DMV for issuance of title. All snowmobiles used on public and private lands and any frozen public waters within territorial limits of South Dakota must be licensed.

In-Person or Mail – Records are available for 20 years to present. Normal turnaround time for mail-in requests is up to 10 days. In-person requests are processed immediately when personnel are available.

Electronic – This method is not available to the public.

Bulk – Requests for a bulk registration lists are not available.

Access to Vessel-Related Records

General Information, Access and Fees

Vessel records are accessible the same as vehicle records described above. All boats over 12 feet in length and all motor boats regardless of length must be titled and registered; however, canoes, inflatable vessels, kayaks, sailboards and seaplanes are exempt from titling. Liens and registration records are available for boats 12 foot or longer and motorized boats. Liens on smaller boats are filed at the office of the Secretary of State. The fee is $2.00 for a title or registration check and $5.00 for a complete title history. Requesters must use the state's *DPPA Form* described above. The SSN is not released. Previous owner's address information is extremely limited.

Driving Record Content and Reciprocity

What's On or Not On the Driving Record

- Suspensions, revocations, speeding convictions ten miles per hour or less over the speed limit and out-of-state speeding violations are not listed on the regular driving record. They are listed in the Complete driving record if committed in a commercial vehicle.
- Accident involvement is listed but fault is not shown on either the Regular or Complete driving record. .
- The driver license status section on the driving record indicates suspended or revoked, however a further suspension or revocation statement does not print on the history portion of the Regular record. The suspension or revocation statement does appear on the Complete record.
- The driver's address is provided to permissible use requesters; the SSN is not.
- The state does not permit driver school attendance in lieu of conviction.
- The length of time convictions are listed on either type of driving record is three years.

Data Retention

South Dakota does not currently purge records nor has plans in place to do so.

Court to Repository

The courts are required to forward conviction information to the state within ten days. Most courts transmit conviction information electronically.

State Reciprocity for Non-CDL Drivers

- Will suspend license of driver for unpaid out-of-state convictions (fines) to NRVC members.
- Record of new incoming driver is not shown on MVR.
- Out-of-state convictions are shown on MVR except non-CDL speeding convictions.
- Out-of-state accidents are shown on MVR.
- Convictions of out-of-state drivers are sent to home state.
- Record is forwarded to new state upon surrender of license.

Codes for License Classes, Restrictions, and Endorsements

License Classes– Commercial

South Dakota began issuing the CDL in April of 1991.

Class A   Any combination of vehicles with a GCWR of 26,001 or more pounds—provided the GVWR of the vehicle(s) being towed is in excess of 10,000 pounds.

Class B   Any single vehicle with a GVWR of 26,001 or more pounds, or any such vehicle towing a vehicle not in excess of 10,000 pounds GVWR.

Class C   Any single vehicle less than 26,001 pounds GVWR, or any such vehicle towing a vehicle not in excess of 10,000 pounds GVWR. Applies only to vehicles placarded for hazardous materials or designed to transport sixteen or more passengers (including driver).

Note: Classes A3, B3, C3 are commercial driver license classes with motorcycle permit.

License Classes– Non-Commercial

1   Car/Light Truck/Moped
2   Class 1 and Motorcycle
3   Motorcycle Only

Restrictions

Non-CDL Restrictions

E   Automatic Transmission
F   Outside Rearview Mirror (Left)
G   No Night Driving
M   Medical Restriction
O   Corrective Lenses
R   Restricted Permit (6am - 10pm)
Q   No Driving Outside of Town
X   Fifty-mile Radius of Residence
Z   Special Equipped Vehicles

CDL Restrictions

B   Operation of CMV Not Equipped with Air-Brakes
K   No Class A or B Passenger Vehicle Privileges
J   No Class A Passenger Vehicle Privileges
V   Medical Variance
W   Restricted CDL (Validation Dates Required)

Endorsements

T   Double-Triple-Trailers
P   Passengers
S   School Bus
N   Tank Vehicles
H   Hazardous Materials
X   Combination Tank and Hazardous Materials

Conviction Table with Type, ACD, Points, and Statutes

The **column** marked **Type** indicates the following:

First Letter:
   A = Accident
   C = Conviction
   R = Revocation/Suspension/Disqualification
   O = Other
   S = comment

Second Letter (Vehicle Type):
   C = Commercial
   N = Non-commercial
   U = Unknown
   A = Administrative

Code	Type	ACD	Points	Description and Statute
ACC	AU			Accident (32-34; 32-35-101)
ACE	AU			Accident in emergency vehicle (32-35-101)
ADL	CU	B41		Possess an alt sus rev cancel lic or ID (32-12-17.3, 67)
BRK	CC			Failure to stop at brake checkpoint (32-29-11)
CA1	OA	W13		Cancelled - parental consent withdrawn
CA2	OA	W14		Cancelled - physical or mental disability
CA3	OA	W20		Cancelled - unable to pass test or meet qualifications
CA4	OA	W15		Cancelled - physicians or specialists report recommended
CAN	OA	W00		Cancelled by driver licensing (32-12-20,30)
CC1	OC	W09		Failure to surrender HAZ MAT endorsement
CDN	CU	N80	2	Coasting downhill in neutral (32-24-2)
CDR	CU	M81	2	Careless driving (32-24-8)
CIM	OA	W70		Imminent hazard (as determined by FMCSA)
CMD	CU	M51	2	Crossing median (32-26-9,10)
COV	SU		2	Clinging to other vehicle (MC only 32-20-65)
CPI	CC	B24	2	Drive CMV while privilege is invalid (32-12a-8)
D10	CC	W70		Disq - CDL driver determined imminent hazard by FMSCA (383.52)
DDC	OU		-3	Defensive Driving Course (obsolete, no longer used)
DFH	CU	M56	2	Drive over fire hose (32-31-8)

Code	Type	ACD	Points	Description and Statute
DIA	OU		-3	Alcohol Course (obsolete, no longer used)
DIM	CU	E54		Failure to use headlight dimmer (32-17-7)
DIS				Disqualification - out of state withdrawal
DO1	RC	B27		Disq violation out-of-service order 1st (90 days, 32-12A-52)
DO2	RC	B19		Disq violation out-of-service order w/hazmat/pass 1st (90 days, 32-12A-52)
DO3	RC	W52		Disq violation out-of-service order 3rd in 10 years (3 years, 32-12A-54)
DO4	RC	W52		Disq violation out-of-service order 3rd in 10 years w/hazmat/pass (3 years, 32-12A-54)
DO5	RC	W50		Disq violation out-of-service order 2nd in 5 years (32-12A-53)
DO6	RC	W51		Disq violation out-of-service order 2nd w/hazmat/pass (32-12A-53)
DOS	CU	M58	2	Drive on sidewalk (32-26-21.1)
DOT	CU	M14	3	Disobey traffic control device (32-28-6,10,14)
DOV	CU	N07	2	Duty of driver of overtaken vehicle (32-26-31)
DQ1	RC	A08		Disq - one year for DWI, DWL, HAR, FEL, RCT (32-12A-36 (1-5))
DQ2	RC	W40		Disq - lifetime (21-12A-36,37)
DQ3	RC	B01		Disq - 3 years - DQ1 violation with haz mat (32-12A-36)
DQ4	RC	W30		Disq - 60 days - two serious viol in 3 yr period (32-12A-40)
DQ5	RC	W31		Disq - 120 days - three serious viol in 3 yr period (32-12A-41)
DQ6	RC	B20		Disq - 1 yr - driving CMV with invalid privileges (32-12-66)
DQ7	RC	D02		Disq - 60 days - falsify CDL application (21-12A-18)
DQ8	RC	W41		Disq - additional major offense after reinstatement
DQ9	RC	A50		Disq - controlled substance felony - permanent lifetime
DR1	RC	M20		Disq - 60 days - Disqualification for first RR crossing violation (FSC) conviction (32-12A-59)
DR2	RC	W60		Disq - 120 days - Disqualification for second RR crossing violation (FSC) conviction (32-12A-60)
DR3	RC	W61		Disq - 1 yr - Disqualification for third RR crossing violation (FSC) conviction (32-12A-61)
DS1	RC	W45		Disq - 1 year - driving CMV while disqualified
DUC	CU	B22	2	Driving under cancellation (32-12-65)
DUR	CU	B25	2	Driving under revocation (32-12-98,66; 32-23-5)
DUS	CU	B26	2	Driving under suspension (32-12-98,66; 32-35-110)
DWI	CU	A08	10	Driving under the influence (32-23-1,2,3,4,4.6)
DWL	CC	A04	2	Driving CMV w/BAC >.04 but <.08 (32-12a-36,44)
DWS	CU	B20	2	Driving while suspended (32-35-110)
EPA	CU	U01	6	Aggravated Eluding (32-33-18.2)
EPO	CU	U01	6	Eluding a police office (32-33-18,19)
EPS	CU		2	Excessive number of passengers (32-26-43)
EXH	CU	S97	2	Exhibition driving (32-24-9; 41-2-18)
FCP	CC	D56		Failure to comply (CDL & CMV only)
FEL	CC	U03		Felony committed while driving a CMV (32-12a-36)
FEX	CC	A50	2	Using vehicle in commission of a drug felony
FFA	CU	M33	2	Following fire apparatus (32-31-7)
FGI	CU	D35		Gave forged or unauthorized proof of insurance
FGS	CU	N40	2	Fail to give signal (32-26-22,22.1,24)
FHD	CU	E55		Failure to use lights (32-17-4)
FIN	CU	D02		False info to obtain DL. or ID (32-12-75.1)
FOR	CU	M09		Failure to obey railroad crossing device
FOS	CU	M05	2	Fail to obey turn signal (32-26-20)
FR1	RU	D39		Suspension - failure to pay a judgment (32-35-52)
FR2	RU	n/a		Suspension - re-suspension due to judgment
FR3	RU	B63		Suspension - financial responsibility requirement (SR22) (32-35-43,44,45...)
FR4	RU	D36		Suspension - no insurance conviction (32-35-121)
FR5	RU	B63		Suspension - failure to maintain financial responsibility (32-34-43, 44, 45)
FR6	RU	B63		Suspension - FR Intent for out of state DWI/INS (32-35-43)
FRA	CU	B61	2	Fail to report accident (32-34-3.1,7)
FRR	CU	M22	2	Failure to stop – railroad (32-29-5)
FSA	CU	B08		Fail to stop at accident scene (32-34-4,6)
FSB	CU	M75	2	Fail to stop for school bus (32-32-6)
FSC	CU	M10	2	Fail to stop at railroad crossing (32-29-4,5,7,8,9)
FSL	CU	M08	6	Failure to stop at the signal of law enforcement (32-33-18)
FSR	CU	M02	2	Travel through roadblock (31-4-14.3; 32-33-13)
FSS	CU	M15	3	Fail to stop at sign or signal (32-28-7; 32-29-2.1,2.2)
FSW	CC	N/A		Fail to stop at weigh station (32-33-17)
FTA	CC	D45		Failure to appear (CDL or CMV only)
FTC	CU	M34	2	Following to close (32-26-40,42)
FTP	CC	D53		Failure to pay (CDL or CMV only)
FUE	CU	E50		Failure to use equipment as required (32-17-28, 32-17-46)
FYE	CU	N04	4	Fail to yield to emergency vehicle (32-31-6,6.1; 32-26-15)
FYP	CU	N08	2	Failure to yield to blind pedestrian (32-27-7)

Code	Type	ACD	Points	Description and Statute
FYR	CU	N01	4	Fail to yield right of way (32-26-13,14; 32-27-1; 32-29-3)
HAR	CU	B01		Hit and run (32-34-5)
HAZ	CC	E03		Violate HAZ MAT safety regulations
IBK	CU	N82	2	Improper backing (32-30-20,21)
ICL	CU	B91	2	Improper Classification or Endorsement on DL (32-12A-6)
ILC	CU	M42	2	Improper or erratic lane change (32-20-9.1; 32-26-6)
ILU	CU	M41	2	Illegal lane usage (32-26-8)
IMC	CU	F06	2	Improper operation of a motorcycle (32-20-6.1, 6.2, 6.3)
INS	CU	D35		No insurance conviction (32-35-113,120,121)
IPU	CU	M70	4	Improper passing (32-20-9.2; 32-26-26,27,28,30,34,35,37)
IRS	CU	M23	2	Insufficient railroad space
ITU	CU	N50	2	Improper turn (32-26-18.1,19)
IUL	CU	D16		Improper use of DL or ID card (32-12-17.4,17.5,17.6; 32-12-69,70,71)
IUT	CU	N56	2	Illegal u-turn (32-26-25)
JS1	RN	W00		Judicial suspension - DL held by the Clerk
LIT	CU	N/A		Littering (34a-7-7)
LSA	CU	B05	2	Leaving the scene of an accident (32-34-3)
MCH	CU	F03	2	Motorcycle helmet required (minor only 32-20-4)
MFD	CU	D10		Manufacture false driver license
MSL	CU	U08	2	Manslaughter/vehicle (22-16-15,20)
NCD	CU	B56	2	Driving a CMV without obtaining a CDL (21-12A-6)
NDL	CU	B51	2	No drivers license (32-12-22; 32-12a-6; 32-20-2)
OBR	CU	E02		Violate brake regulations (32-18-1, 32-18-17 thru 20)
ODV	CU	D70	2	Obstructed view - windshield/rearview (32-15-2.4, 2.5; 32-20-4)
ORC	CU	S94	2	Overdriving road conditions (32-25-3)
ORV	CU	n/a	2	Illegal operation of off road vehicle (32-20-12)
OSH	CC	B19		Violating out of service order-trans 16 or more pass or w/hazmat
OSR	CC	B27		CMV-24 hour out of service order (32-12a-8)
PRB	OU	n/a		Probation (no longer used)
PUD	CU	n/a	2	Permit unauthorized person to drive (32-12-72, 32-12-73)
R10	RU	W00		Revocation - provide alcohol to minor 1st (Under 18 yrs old)
R11	RU	W00		Revocation - provide alcohol to minor 2nd (Under 18 yrs old)
R12	RU	n/a		Revocation - booz (other than driver) - 1st (No Longer Used)
R13	RU	n/a		Revocation - booz (other than driver) - 2nd (No Longer Used)
R14	RU	W00		Revocation - suspended imposition of sentence
R15	RU	n/a		Rev - sell/provide alc to 18-20 yr old - 1st (No Longer Used)
R16	RU	n/a		Rev - sell/provide alc to 18-20 yr old - 2nd (No Longer Used)
R17	RU	U01		Revocation - eluding - 1st offense (32-33-18)
R18	RU	U01		Revocation - eluding - 2nd or subsequent offense (32-33-18)
R19	RU	U07		Revocation - vehicular homicide (22-16-41)
R20	RU	A12		Revocation - refusal of the chemical test (32-23-11,15)
R21	RU	U01		Revocation - aggravated eluding (32-33-18.2)
R22	RU	U06		Revocation - vehicular battery (22-16-42)
R23	RU	U07		Revocation - vehicular homicide (22-16-41)
R24	RU	M84		Revocation - 2nd reckless driving in 1 yr (32-24-3)
RAC	CU	S95	2	Racing (32-25-23,25)
RC1	RU	D51		Revocation for Child Support (32-12-116)
RCL	CU	M24	2	Insufficient railroad clearance (32-29-8)
RCT	CU	A12		Refusal of chemical test (32-23-11,15)
RRC	CU	M20	2	Railroad crossing violation (32-29-9)
RRV	CU	M21	2	Railroad violation (32-29-4)
RUD	CU	M84	8	Reckless driving (32-24-1,3)
RV1	RU	A10		Revocation - DWI 1st offense (32-23-1,2)
RV2	RU	A33		Revocation for drug offense (32-12-52.3)
RV3	RU	A21		Rev for multiple DWI (also RCT prior to 2-11-04) (32-23-3,4,4.6)
RV4	RU	W00		Revocation - court ordered
RV5	RU	W00		Rev - 2nd traffic conviction (under 16 yrs) (No Longer Used)
RV6	RU	B25		Revocation - driving under revocation conviction (32-12-65,66)
RV7	RU	n/a		Revocation - failed re-exam (No Longer User)
RV8	RU	n/a		Revocation - 1st alcohol offense (minor) (No Longer Used)
RV9	RU	n/a		Revocation - 2nd alcohol offense (minor) (No Longer Used)
S10	RU	W00		Suspension - felony or misdemeanor (under 16 yrs old) (32-12-15)
S11	RU	D29		Suspension - vrl for 16 or 17 yr olds (32-12-15.1; 32-12-38.1)
S12	RU	W00		Suspension - vandalism in MV (damage $200 or less) (22-34-29)
S13	RU	W00		Suspension - vandalism in MV (damage $201 to $999) (22-34-29)
S14	RU	W00		Suspension - vandalism in MV (damage $1000 or more) (22-34-29)

Code	Type	ACD	Points	Description and Statute
S15	RU	W00		Suspension - sell/provide alc to 18 to 20 yr olds - 1st offense (35-9-7)
S16	RU	W00		Suspension - sell/provide alc to 18 to 20 yr olds - 2nd offense (35-9-7)
S17	RU	W00		Suspension - minor in possession of alcohol (not driving a vehicle)1st offense (35-9-7)
S18	RU	W00		Suspension - minor in possession of alcohol (not driving a vehicle)2nd or sub offense (35-9-7)
S19	RU	D29		Suspension for driving in violation of the driver license restrictions (VRL) for individuals over 18 yrs of age (32-12-38,74)
S20	RU	W00		Suspension - 2nd traffic conviction (under 16 yrs old) (32-12-15)
SBE		E56		Failure to use school bus safety equipment
SPD	CU	S92		Speeding (32-25-1.1,3,4,6,6.1,7,11.2,12,14,15,19)
SPM	CU	S96	2	Driving below minimum speed
SPX	CU	S15		Speeding 15 mph or more over limit (32-25-1.1,3,4,6,6.1, 7,11.2,12, 14,15,19)
SU1	RU	W01		Suspension - excessive points (32-12-48, 49.2)
SU2	RU	W00		Suspension - court ordered
SU3	RU	B41		Suspension - altered/imp use of DL or ID (32-12-17.3,6; 32-12-67,69,70,71)
SU4	RU	D53		Suspension - non-payment of fine (32-12-49(6))
SU5	RU	W00		Suspension - 1st traffic conviction (under 16 yrs old) (32-12-15)
SU6	RU	B26		Suspension - driving under suspension conviction (32-12-65,66)
SU7	RU	D02		Suspension - false info to obtain DL or ID (32-12-75.1)
SU8	RU	A26		Suspension - alcohol offense by minor (driver) - 1st (32-12-52.4)
SU9	RU	A26		Suspension - alcohol off by minor (driver) - 2nd or subs (32-12-52.4)
SUS		n/a		Suspension - out-of-state driving history
SZ1	RU	A60		Suspension - zero tolerance - 1st offense (32-23-21)
SZ2	RU	A60		Suspension - zero tolerance - 2nd or subsequent offense (32-23-21)
TIR	CU	E37		Defective tires (32-19-12 & 13)
UPL	CU	n/a	2	Unlawful operation of vehicle on public land
VBT	CU	U06	2	Vehicular battery (22-16-42)
VHM	CU	U07	2	Vehicular homicide (22-16-41)
VLO	CU			Miscellaneous violation
VRL	CU	D29		Violate restricted license. (32-12-12,38,74)
VSZ	CU	M03	2	Violate safety zone (32-12-12,38,74; 32-25-19.1; 32-26-21)
WLT	CU	n/a		Warning letter for points (no longer used)
WMF	CU	S98		Wasting motor fuel
WOE	CU	E01		Operate vehicle without proper equipment (32-19-7, 32-19-9)
WOS	CU	N63	2	Wrong way on one way
WSR	CU	N70	4	Drive on wrong side of road (32-26-1,2,35,36)
WTH		n/a		Withdrawal out of state history
ZTL	CU	A60	2	Zero tolerance (minors w/ .02+ BAC) (32-23-21)

Point System Summary

Points range from two to ten points. When multiple pointable violations occur points are assessed on in-state and out-of-state convictions to determine if license should be suspended. Any operator who accumulates fifteen points in any twelve consecutive months, or twenty-two points in twenty-four consecutive months is subject to possible suspension.

Tennessee

Administration	Important Telephone and Web Contacts
Mike Hill, Director, Financial Responsibility Division Michael Hogan, Director, Driver Services Division Department of Safety, Nashville 37249-2000 615-251-5221 www.tn.gov/safety/dlmain.shtml Linda Kelly Vehicles Services Division 44 Vantage Way, Ste 160 Nashville 37243-8050 615-741-3101 www.tn.gov/revenue/vehicle/	Driver Licensing & CDL .... 615-253-5221 SR-22 & Financial Responsibility .... 615-741-3954 Suspension/Revocation/Records............ 866-903-7357 Vehicle Information .... 615-741-3101 or 888-971-3171 State Department of Insurance................ 615-741-2241 Highway Patrol .... 615-251-5175 General Email - Driver email.safety@state.tn.us General Email - Vehicle T&R@tn.gov Laws and Policies: www.tn.gov/safety/laws.shtml Statutes: www.lexisnexis.com/hottopics/tncode/

Driver's License Format, Issuance and Renewal

License Classes, Restrictions and Endorsements Appear After the Driving Record Content Section

License Format

The format is nine numbers (as of 2000), seven or eight numbers (pre-2000). Tennessee indicates the last digit is a check-digit based upon a confidential algorithmic formula. The older format was phased out as renewal licenses are issued, although military personnel may still have the old format. Those who still hold a valid license with only eight digits will have a leading zero (0) at the beginning of their current eight-digit number.

Document Appearance

The current document has been issued since 2003. The text below describes both old and new. Any Tennessee driver license issued to a minor has the word "INTERMEDIATE" as part of the license title.

Current Document

Appearance: Digitized photo and signature, laminated PVC card stock.

Security Characteristics: Ghost image of photo in lower right corner for over 18, lower left corner for under 18. Gold reflective "Tennessee - The Volunteer State" and state seal in top laminate.

Position of Photo: Top left corner for over 18, top right corner for under 18. For the ID only, the photo is in lower right corner and the document is in a vertical format.

Under 18 Age Driver: Photo on right with yellow header bar indicating "Intermediate" Restricted or Unrestricted Driver License.

Under 21 Age Driver: Photo on left with red bar running down left side of photo indicating "Under 21 Until xx-xx-xxxx."

CDL Indicator: "Commercial Driver License" on green header bar above the driver license number. Also, Tennessee state outline over lapping the ghost image with the letters "CDL" inside.

Old Document

Appearance: Digitized photo and signature, PVC card type, laminated.

Security Characteristics: A small ghost image of the photo was over data area. Reflective gold "Tennessee" and the state seal form a security pattern on front laminate; microdot signature line.

Position of Photo: Top left corner.

Minor Age Driver: Red portrait border, red header, "UNDER 21" to the left of the license number; twenty-first birthday in red in the data area.

CDL Indicator: "Commercial Driver License" on header above DL. May be abbreviated as "CDL" for temporary or seasonal CDLs, CDLs with CDL permit, or non-CDLs with CDL permit.

Issuance

Location of Requirements for Proof of Identity:
www.tn.gov/safety/driverlicense/dlnew.shtml

Age Requirements

The minimum age for a D Class license is eighteen. The Graduated Drive License Program provides that a Learner's Permit is granted at fifteen; which must be held sixteenth birthday; must be accompanied by a twenty-one or older who holds valid license.

A driver under eighteen is assigned an Intermediate Class D. Those with an Intermediate Restricted License must have held a permit for 180 days and can only have one other passenger in the vehicle unless: 1) one or more of the passengers is age 21 or older and has a valid, unrestricted license; 2) the passengers are brothers and sisters, step-brothers or step-sisters, adopted or fostered children residing in the same house as the driver and going to and from school AND the intermediate license holder has in their possession written permission from their parent or guardian to transport their siblings. Also those with an Intermediate License are prohibited from driving between the hours of 11pm and 6am unless they are: 1) accompanied by a parent or guardian; 2) accompanied by a licensed driver 21 or older who has been designated by the parent or guardian and this designation is in writing and be in the possession of the teen driver; 3) driving to or from a specifically identified school sponsored activity or event and have in their possession written permission from a parent or guardian to do this; 4) driving to or from work and have in their possession written permission from a parent or guardian identifying the place of employment and authorizing the driver to go to and from work; 5) driving to or from hunting or fishing between 4am and 6am and have in their possession a valid hunting or fishing license.

A Hardship License is granted at age fourteen or fifteen for those who have a legitimate need.

Residency

A non-resident must secure Tennessee license within thirty days of establishing residency and must provide examiner with two documents confirming Tennessee residence address. If a new resident brings a valid out-of-state driver license (or a certified driving record from that state showing the license has not expired), only the vision test is required, unless otherwise deemed necessary by the Examiner. However, if the license has expired over six months, all tests are required. New residents from other countries are required to take full tests: vision, knowledge and road tests.

Renewal

Licenses are renewed on a five-year cycle (birth date), but may be first issued for 3-7 years. Driver keeps same number when renewing. Drivers may renew their non-commercial license by mail or online every-other cycle at https://apps.tn.gov/tndlr/. Drivers will receive a new license produced with the current digitized image on file and new expiration date.

The Temporary Driver License (XD) or Identification (XID) will have the same expiration date as the holders authorized stay in the U.S. This could range from 2 days up to a maximum of 5 years.

Military personnel stationed outside Tennessee are granted a "Code30" which does not expire until they are discharged or re-assigned to TN. Renewal by mail then is only necessary for those who did not establish their military status beforehand. Once the person has been honorably discharged or separated from such services or has been reassigned to a duty station within the state, he or she must renew his/her license within sixty (60) days following the date of separation on the DD-214 Form.

Elderly-Related Restrictions

None indicated.

Vehicle Insurance, Title and Registration Facts

Registration Renewal

Registration is annual and is a process handled by the County Clerk in each county. The Department of Revenue does not offer online renewal, but many counties do. Visit a links list at www.tn.gov/revenue/vehicle/onlinetagrenewals.shtml.

New Residents

Non-residents employed in Tennessee must register vehicles after thirty days; new residents must register immediately.

Inspections and Emissions Testing

Tennessee has no statewide provisions for vehicle annual safety inspections.

Gasoline and diesel vehicles with a model year of 1975 and newer with a GVWR up to 10,500 lbs must pass an emissions test prior to registration renewal if registering in Hamilton, Davidson, Rutherford, Sumner, Williamson or Wilson Counties. Motorcycles are exempt.

Note in Memphis reportedly there an inspection is required for vehicles of all model years.

Passenger Plate Facts

There is usually 1 plate with 2 or 3 decals (MO) (YR) (County). There can be up to 5 decals if a wheel tax is applicable. The county of issuance appears on one of the stickers on the plate but there is no coding sequence with the plate number that indicates the county of issuance. When a vehicle is sold the plate remains with the seller.

Insurance and Financial Responsibility

Tennessee does not have compulsory liability insurance, but does require financial responsibility. The minimum limits are set at $25,000/50,000/15,000. At the time a driver is charged with any moving violation or involved in a motor vehicle accident, the officer will request evidence of financial responsibility. Such evidence may include proof of liability insurance, self-insured certificate, certificate that bond has been posted with the Commissioner in the amount of $60,000, or if vehicle is regulated by ICC. If such evidence is not provided, the driver will be issued a citation. If convicted, driver is subject to a fine of not more than $100 and the driver's privileges are suspended.

SR-22 forms are used when proof of financial responsibility for the future is required. The state has mandatory no-fault insurance if coverage is offered by the insurance company; otherwise, it is not mandatory. Questions may be emailed to FinResp.Safety@tn.gov.

Withdrawal Sanctions, and Alcohol and Drug Testing

Alcohol and Chemical Testing

Tennessee does not have a per se law, but rather a "presumptive" law. At .08 percent and above BAC, drivers are presumed to be driving while intoxicated; .04% if the driver has a CDL. If a person has one or more convictions of DUI, the presumptive BAC content level is .08%. For persons age 16 to 21, a BAC level of .02% creates a presumption the person is impaired. For persons age 21 or older. a BAC level of .08% creates a presumption the person is impaired. Urine, blood, and breath testing are authorized. If the court determines that test was refused, driving privileges are suspended for twelve months. Operating a horse or bicycle under the influence is also considered illegal.

Suspensions and Revocations

The Tennessee Department of Safety is in compliance with the provisions of the Motor Carrier Safety Improvement Act (MCSIA). See The Appendix for more information about these **mandatory CDL disqualification** sanctions.

Letter of Proposed Suspension

Drivers that accumulate twelve or more points on their driving record within any 12-month period are sent a notice of proposed suspension and given an opportunity to attend an administrative hearing. If they fail to request a hearing, their driving privileges are suspended for a period of six to 12 months. In most cases, when a driver requests a hearing, they are given the opportunity to attend a defensive driving class in lieu of suspension or a reduction of suspension time.

If a driver has accumulated twelve or more points within a twelve month period and attended a defensive driving course in lieu of suspension within the previous five years, then driver will have driver license suspended for six months.

Drivers less than eighteen years of age that accumulate six or more points on their driving record within any twelve-month period are sent a notice of proposed suspension from the Department of Safety and are placed in the Driver Improvement Program. The driver will be required to attend an administrative hearing, with their parent or guardian present, to discuss the points assigned to their driving record. Certain actions could be imposed based on the outcome of the hearing and the number of points accumulated on the driver's record.

Alcohol-Related Withdrawals:

Implied Consent.. Twelve months.
Implied Consent Involving Accident with Injury ..... Twenty-four months.
Implied Consent Involving Accident with Death...... Five years.
Driving While Impaired 2nd offense .... Two years, restricted license not available (repealed 07/03).

Driving Under the Influence with .08 BAC

    1st time .... One year.
    2nd time... Two years, restricted license available (Ignition Interlock required after one year).
    3rd time.. Three to ten years, restricted license not available.
    4th and subsequent time....................................... Five years, restricted license not available.

Other Violations Which May Result in Revocation or Suspension

- Aggravated Vehicular Homicide (while driving intoxicated)
- Allowing Unlawful Use of License
- Altering Driver's License
- Conviction of Failure to Provide Evidence of Financial Responsibility
- Drag Racing
- Driving Under the Influence
- Failure to Pay Fine and/or Appear in Court for Moving Violation
- Failure to Resolve, Discharge, or Satisfy a Court Judgment Involving an Accident
- Failure to Stop and Give Aid
- Felony Involving Use of a Motor Vehicle
- Frequent Convictions of Traffic Law Violations
- Habitual Offender
- Leaving the Scene of a Personal Injury Accident
- Mental or Physical Difficulties
- Most Aggravated Drunk Driver (.20 or more BAC)
- Perjury, or Giving False Information Pertaining to Use or Ownership of a Vehicle
- Two Convictions of Reckless Driving in Twelve Months
- Violation of Restriction Codes

Reinstatement Requirements

Requirements vary with the specific violations. The agency provides an overview at http://www.tn.gov/safety/financialresponsibility.shtml but specific list of with fees and requirements is not provided. Upon request, the individual is advised by letter of requirement for reinstatement.

Record Access: Laws, Rules, and Forms

Note: **This Section Applies to Both Driver and Vehicle Records.**

Governing Statutes and Rules

Laws and Policies:
  www.tn.gov/safety/laws.shtml
Rules for the Department of Safety:
  www.tn.gov/sos/rules/1340/1340.htm
Tennessee Statutes - Annotated Code:
  www.lexisnexis.com/hottopics/tncode/

TCA 55-50-204 regulates records to be kept by the Department and fees charged; however, it does not specifically regulate the release or restrictions of release of records.

TCA 55-25-101 et seq authorizes the conditions for release of personal information.

TCA 55-25-107 (Disclosure for Certain Purposes) lists the accepted reasons (permissible uses).

Request and Consent Forms

Driving Records: A state form can be used, found at www.tennessee.gov/safety/forms/recorddppa.pdf, but other written requests are accepted. If the request is for a permissible use, the requester must provide information about him/herself, the specific reason for the request, and sign the request. A notary is not needed. Requesters with a non-permissible use can obtain records with personal information only with the notarized consent of the subject. Online requesters must complete a Network Registration Agreement with TennesseeAnytime Subscriber Services.

Vehicle Records: Requesters with a permissible use should make their request on letterhead or complete the *Vehicle Information Request Form*. Requesters without a permissible use can obtain records with personal information only with the notarized written consent from the subject. Use the release form as well as the request form listed above. Forms are found at www.tn.gov/revenue/forms/index.shtml

Vendor and Third Party Access Policy

Approved online vendors can access records for other vendors (who do not access direct, etc.) who will then sell to an end user providing that all parties qualify under the provisions of DPPA. Tennessee does not provide any restrictions upon the use, storage or resale of records after a completed transaction; however, purchasers of the driver license database file must sign a written application stating the purpose of the information request subject to DPPA.

Records Ordered For Non-permissible Uses

Driving Records: Without consent or proper form, no records are released, even records without personal information.

Vehicle Records: Records requested without consent and not for a permissible purpose are strictly limited and requests are reviewed on a case-by-case basis. If released, personal information is blocked. If consent is provided, records with personal information are released.

Access to Driver-Related Records

Driving Records

General Information and Fees

Driver Dept of Public Safety, Financial Responsibility Section, MVR Request, PO Box 945, Nashville TN 37202, 615-741-3954 or 866-903-7357.

The fee for a three-year record is $5.00, $7.00 if obtained online.

Tennessee charges for "no record found" reports.

In-Person — Up to ten records at a time may be requested over-the-counter at any of full service or express service Driver Service Centers – a list is found at www.tn.gov/safety/driverlicense/dllocationmain.shtml.

Mail — Mail-in requests are processed within ten days to two weeks. The driver's license number and last name or and date of birth are needed. Payment must accompany the request

Electronic – Commercial online record service via the e-government services website at https://apps.tn.gov/imvr/ is available for a driving record and for a license status check. The driving record program is called the **Interactive Moving Violation Record** application (IMVR). Users must be authorized per DPPA and complete a Network Registration Agreement and be authorized per DPPA. The fee is $7.00 per three-year driving record or $1.25 for a DL number status report which gives name, DOB, address and DL expire date. An annual $75.00 registration fee is charged.   The IMVR Subscriber Service allows subscribers retrieving more than 500 records per month to use a batch process in which multiple license numbers are submitted and the results are returned in one file. For more information, call 1-866-886-3468. TennesseeAnytime also offers access to other TN records, such as corporation and UCC filings.

By Person of Record – TN drivers may obtain their driving record by mail or walk-in as described above. For a list of all the stations go to www.tn.gov/safety/driverlicense/dllocationmain.shtml. At present, there is no program for drivers to order or view their own record online.

Bulk – The Tennessee Department of Safety offers approved, DPPA permissible users the ability to purchase the entire database of driver information with monthly updates.   For the preparing and furnishing bulk portions of individual MVRs, we will charge the costs we incur to produce the MVRs.   In this case, bulk means one time requests for portions of individual MVRs, and the request should be made in electronic format.

For the recurrent preparing and furnishing portions of multiple or all individual MVRs, the Department will charge 4 cents per year for each licensed driver in TN.   The fee will be paid in 12 equal monthly payments.   The requests will be accepted in electronic format only. Call the Director's office for more information.

Status Check

Subscribers to the IMVR system may verify status information on a Tennessee driver license for $1.25 per search. The service is called **Driver License Inquiries**.

Notification/Monitoring Program

The Tennessee Department of Safety no longer offers a specific program to purchase activity updates on a submitted group of drivers. However, approved permissible user requesters may purchase the driver license file in **bulk** for this purpose – please refer to that section's description.

Accident Reports

Reporting – Accidents resulting in death, personal injury, or damage in excess of $400.00 to any one person's property must be reported immediately to any law enforcement agency. This is regardless which driver is at fault. A report must be filed within twenty days with the Financial Responsibility Section, TN Department of Safety and Homeland Security, PO Box 945, Nashville TN 37202, 615-741-3954. Report forms are available from the Department or use www.tn.gov/safety/forms/owneroperator.pdf. There are no special reporting requirements for commercial drivers.

Record Access – Copies of accident reports are available from the investigating agency or by mail from the Records Unit, Financial Responsibility Section, Department of Safety, PO Box 945, Nashville 37202. If the accident was investigated by the Tennessee Highway Patrol and 7 days have passed from the date of accident, the report can be purchased in person or via mail from the Tennessee Highway Patrol District Office for the county in which the accident occurred.

The driver's name, date of accident, and location (county) must be included with the request. The fee is $4.00 per Officer's Accident Report, $5.00 for Compliance of Accident report, and $5.00 for a Financial Responsibility Affidavit. For the latter reports, the requester must furnish the date and county of accident. For a request form see www.tennessee.gov/safety/forms/recorddppa.pdf.

Records are available at the above location for 3 years to present. It takes 30 days for a new incident to be available if investigated by the Highway Patrol and filed via paper; 10 days if filed electronically, and 60 days from other local law enforcement. Turnaround time for mail-in requests is 10 days to 2 weeks.

Access to Vehicle-Related Records

General Information and Fees
Vehicle Services Division, 44 Vantage Way Suite #160, Nashville TN 37243-8050, 615-741-3101 or 888-871-3171.
www.tn.gov/revenue/vehicle
The current fee for general inquiries, such as name and plate searches, is $1.00; a photocopy of the current title record the fee is $5.00; a certified computer printout of a vehicle record is $1.50 per record, and for an advanced search (including complete title history) the fee is $15.00. Records are maintained for at least twelve years.
Trailers used for the transportation of boats are exempt from both title and registration.
Liens on vehicles are secured at the local county clerk offices; they are not available from this agency. Temporary vehicle liens are serviced by the Secretary of State.
In-Person – **Counter service is no longer offered.**
Mail – Use the address mentioned above. Record requests must be either mailed or accessed online.

Electronic – Tennessee offers commercial online inquires on the Interactive Vehicle, Title, and Registration (IVTR) system. Search by plate license number or VIN. Users must complete a Network Registration Agreement and be authorized per DPPA and state law. The fee per is $2.00 per inquiry, regardless of search results. There is also a $75.00 annual registration fee. Records are available on an interactive basis only. For more information see https://apps.tn.gov/ivtr/ or call 866-886-3468.
Subscribers have access to other state records including corporation and UCC records as will as driving records (upon approval).
There is a free search for temporary vehicle liens (270 days or less) on the web site for the Secretary of State. Search by debtor last name or VIN at http://tn.gov/sos/bus_svc/MotorVehicleSearch.htm.
Bulk – Tennessee does not offer a bulk access of vehicle records to the public beyond assistance with vehicle recall address information.

Access to Vessel-Related Records

General Information, Access and Fees
Wildlife Resources Agency, Boating Division, PO Box 40747, Nashville TN 37204, 615-781-6585
www.state.tn.us/twra.
All motorized boats and all sailboats must be registered; there are no titles. It takes 30 days before new records are ready for inquiry. A TN

ID#, hull#, name, or SSN is needed to perform a search. Requests may be processed by phone or mail. There is no fee to do 1 or 2 searches. Turnaround time is normally 2-3 days. One may request records via email to darren.rider@state.tn.us.
Lien information is not available here and must be secured from the office of the Secretary of State.

Driving Record Content and Reciprocity

What's On or Not On the Driving Record

- Tennessee reports all convictions on the driver's record.
- All accidents are reported, but records do not indicate fault.
- All convictions are listed on the driver's record for three years if license is valid; for seven years, if not valid.
- If the driver status is revoked, suspended, restricted or cancelled, the report then shows seven years of activity.
- The state does permit the courts to allow driver school attendance in lieu of conviction, except commercial drivers

Data Retention

CDL driver records are not purged and the state follows the retention policy per MCSIA (see Appendix).

Court to Repository

Conviction information is transferred from the courts to the state via various electronic methods and paper. Statutes require submitted to the state and input to the record within thirty days.

State Reciprocity for Non-CDL Drivers

- Will suspend license of driver for unpaid out-of-state convictions.
- Record of new incoming driver is not shown on MVR.
- Out-of-state convictions are shown on MVR.
- Out-of-state accidents are not shown on MVR.
- Convictions of out-of-state drivers are sent to home state.
- Record is forwarded to new state upon surrender of license only upon request.

Codes for License Classes, Restrictions, and Endorsements

License Classes– Commercial

Tennessee began issuing the CDL in July of 1989.

Class A   Combination vehicles over 26,001 pounds GCWR, with trailers over 10,000 pounds.
Class B   Trucks/buses over 26,001 pounds GVWR and trailers equal to or less than 10,000 pounds.
Class C   Trucks/buses equal to or less than 26,000 pounds, requiring special endorsements H, X, P, or S.

License Classes– Non-Commercial

Class D   Vehicles equal to or less than 26,000 pounds. No special endorsements required.
Class ID   Identification only.
Class M   Motorcycles and motor-driven cycles.
Class H   Hardship limited and restricted use Class D or M (ages fourteen or fifteen only). Valid only for daylight hours and for travel to authorized locations as specified in the approval letter.
Class P   Learner permit for class indicated. Must be accompanied by licensed driver of same class.
Class TD   No longer issued. Previously, a Certificate for Driving (CFD) was available to persons who do not qualify for a Tennessee driver license, but this document was replaced by the TDL Class. As of October 1, 2007 the CFD is no longer issued to new applicants. Those holding an expired or expiring certificate will not be able to have it renewed and must apply for the new Temporary Driver License (Class XD) if they qualify.
Class XD   Effective October, 1 2007, the Tennessee Department of Safety began issuing a Temporary Driver License (TDL) to foreign nationals residing in Tennessee whose legal, temporary presence has been authorized by the federal government for an authorized stay at time of application. The new TDL documents are available only for non-CDL class licenses. The TDL Class is indicated by an "X" preceding the letter of the class (i.e. XD, XM, XPD, etc.) Only the "For Hire (F)" endorsement may be obtained on a TDL.
Class XID   A Temporary Identification License. This is for applicants who can provide federal proof of legal, temporary presence but do not drive. Requires proof of authorized stay at time of application.

Notes:
- On driving records, the License Class can show as a combination of the classification letters above. For example "Class BM" is a Class B License with a Class M and "Class DMB" is a Class D License with Motorcycle and Class B Permit.
- Motorcycle permit is the only "P Class" where holder is not required to be accompanied by licensed driver.

License Classes– Other

These do not exist after expiration of issue of July 1993, except for non-expiring military licenses.

Class OP   Operator
Class CH   Chauffeur
Class SC   Special Chauffeur
Class HS   Hardship

Restrictions

01	Corrective Lenses	28	Hearing Impairment
02	Auto Transmission	30	Active Military - Does Not Expire While in Military
03	Knob/Power Steering	50	See "L" for Details
04	Outside Mirror	51	CMV - Intrastate only
10	Daylight Only	52	Gov/Church vehicles only
11	Custom Controls	53	IntraCity Zone Only - CMV
12	Seat Cushion	54	Intrastate Only, Medical Limitation - CMV
14	Medical Alert	55	Any Vehicle Except Class A Bus
15	Special Restriction Order	56	Except Class A and B Bus
16	Ignition Interlock Device	57	Class A - Excluding Tractor-Trailers
20	Medical Problems (Driver Improvement)	L	Vehicles Without Air-Brakes (On some older records shows as "50" but printed on license as "L" per Federal Code)
26	Passed Special Exam		

Endorsements

CDL only

B	School Bus, Private	P	Passenger
C	Cargo Tank	S	School Bus, Public
H	Hazardous Material	T	Multiple Trailer
N	Cargo Tanker	X	Tanker and Hazardous Material

Non CDL only

F   For Hire - Non Commercial Class D

Conviction Table with Code, ACD, and Points

This table is sorted by the Code column, which is the state's native code.

Code	ACD	Points	Description
001	SP3	1	Speeding 1 to 5 over
		3	Speeding 6 to 15 over
		4	Speeding 16 to 25 over
		5	Speeding 26 to 35 over
		6	Speeding 36 to 45 over
		8	Speeding 46+ over
		3	Speed not indicated
002	M84	6	Reckless driving
003	M14	4	Failure to obey traffic instructions
004	M70	4	Improper passing
005	N60	4	Wrong way, side or direction
006	M34	3	Following improperly
007	N01	4	Failure to yield the right-of-way
008	N50	4	Making improper turn
009	N43	2	Fail to signal direction or reduce speed suddenly
010	M75	6	Passing stopped school bus
011	M32	2	Following emergency vehicle unlawfully
012	S96	3	Speed less than posted minimum
013	B51	3-8	No driver license; wrong license for type vehicle
014	M86	4	Careless or negligent driving
015	D29	6	Violation of driver license restrictions (first offense - glasses)
016	M84	8	Reckless endangerment by vehicle - misdemeanor
017	B05	5	Leaving scene of accident - no revocation action
018	E01	4	Conviction of violation of bumper law
019	N84	3	Miscellaneous - failure to maintain proper control
020	A20		Driving while intoxicated - revocation
021	U08		Violation resulting in death of another person (manslaughter) - revocation
022	B25		Driving while revoked - revocation
023	S95		Contest racing on public trafficway - revocation
024	D29		Violating conditions specified on license - revocation
025	B01		Hit-and-run; leaving scene; evading arrest - revocation
026	B41		Unlawful use of driver license - revocation
027	W01		Mandatory revocation due to reckless driving conviction - revocation
028	U03		Felony by a motor vehicle - revocation
029	A20		Allowing an intoxicated person to drive - revocation
030	D39		Accident (unsatisfied judgment) - revocation
031	U01		Vehicular homicide - revocation
032	W01		Motor vehicle habitual offender - revocation
033	U07		Vehicle homicide - Intoxication prob cause - revocation
034			Aiding or abetting prostitution - revocation
035	W00		Theft of a vehicle or part thereof - revocation
036	W00		Suspension due to two serious violations within 36 months
037	W01		Suspension due to three serious violations within 36 months
038			Motor vehicle habitual offender reinstatement
039			Reinstatement on 30 and 32 with no money
040	A20		Driving while intoxicated - suspension
041	U08		Violation resulting in death of another person (manslaughter) - suspension
042	B26		Driving on suspended license - suspension
043	S95		Contest racing on public traffic way - suspension
044	D29		Operating contrary to conditions specified on license - suspension
045	B03		Hit-and-run; leaving scene; evading arrest (personal injury accident) - suspension
046	D16		Unlawful use of driver license/fraudulent application - suspension

Code	ACD	Points	Description
047	U31		Contributing to the occurrence of a fatal accident - suspension
048	U03		Felony by a motor vehicle (vehicular homicide, etc.) - suspension
049	W01		Frequent traffic violator (12 or more points in a 12 month period) - suspension
050	W00		Failure to satisfy non-moving citation - suspension
051	D45		Failure to appear in court; out-of-state citation - suspension
052	D45		Failure to pay fine after conviction of traffic violation - suspension
053	A12		Failure to submit to blood alcohol test (IC) - suspension
054	M09		Fail to stop at railroad crossing - CMV
055	W00		Suspension action taken per court order
056	A12		Conviction under implied consent law - suspension
057	W00		Non-driving suspension - juvenile court; first denial
058	W00		Non-driving suspension - juvenile court; second denial
059			Reinstatement on 51 - 53, 55 with no money; test required
060	D02		Misrepresentation of identity or other facts to obtain a driver's license - cancellation
061	W13		Teen-age affidavit cancelled - cancellation
062	W00		Bad check or non-payment of fees - cancellation
063			Has license in another jurisdiction - TN DR Lic returned
064	W00		Out of state cancel (non-resident, cancellation due to revocation/suspension in other state)
065	W00		License voluntarily surrendered - cancellation
066	W00		Cancellation of special restricted driver's license
067	D45		Failure to answer traffic citation -license surrendered - cancellation
068			Deceased - cancellation
069			Reinstatement on 60-62, 64-68, 51 81, 267 - no test required
070			*no longer used* Accident; property damage
071			*no longer used* Accident; personal injury
072			*no longer used* Accident; involving fatality
073			*no longer used* Accident; property damage - private property
074			*no longer used* Accident; damage - private property, personal injury
075			*no longer used* Accident; damage - private property, fatality involved
076			*no longer used* Accident; property damage - fixed object
077			*no longer used* Accident; personal injury - fixed object
078			*no longer used* Accident; involving fatality - fixed object
080	B61		Failure to report accident as required under FR law - suspension
081	D35		Failure to meet requirements of security following accident - revocation
082	B64		Failure to file insurance following conviction of motor vehicle law - suspension
083	B63		Failure to maintain proof of insurance - suspension
084			Reinstatement on 80 (filed report and paid fee) - no test required
085			Reinstatement on 81 (sec, fee, proof) 83 (proof, fee) - test required
086			Reinstatement on 80 and 82 (three-year close) - test required
087			Reinstatement on 82 (filed, proof and fee) - test required
088			Reinstatement on 81 - revocation cleared by bankruptcy
089			Release with special restriction - (restricted license)
090			Reinstatement - special restrictions removed
091			Reinstatement on 20-29, 31, 34-35 (proof, fee) 30 (sec, fee, proof) - test required
092			Reinstatement on 40-49, 54, 56 (filed proof, fee) - test required
093			Eligible for license in other state
094			Reinstatement _ 110 (proof,fee) - test required
095			Reinstate –eligible for Non- CDL only, not eligible for CDL
096			Reduction of time of suspension
098			Reinstatement (filed proof) no fee on 80, 82-83; late insurance on 81 - no test required
100	S15	4	Excessive speed in commercial vehicle, speed not indicated
		2	Excessive speed in commercial vehicle, 1-5 mph over
		4	Excessive speed in commercial vehicle, 6-14 mph over
		5	Excessive speed in commercial vehicle, 15-25 mph over
		6	Excessive speed in commercial vehicle, 26-35 mph over
		8	Excessive speed in commercial vehicle, 36 or more mph over
101	D21		Driving a vehicle with revoked registration
103			Registration law (driving an unregistered vehicle)
105	M09		Failure to stop school bus at railroad crossing
110	W00		Conviction for failure to provide evidence of financial responsibility-suspensions
111	S93	2	Speeding in construction zone, 1-5 mph over
		4	Speeding in construction zone, 6-15 mph over
		5	Speeding in construction zone, 16-25 mph over
		6	Speeding in construction zone, 26-35 mph over

Code	ACD	Points	Description
		8	Speeding in construction zone, 36+ mph over
		4	Speeding in construction zone, speed not indicated
113	M49		Violation of HOV lane
114			Violation of truck lane restriction
115	F02		Child restraint violation-ages 4 thru 13
116	U03		Reckless endangerment by vehicle - felony
117	F04		Violation of seat belt law as driver
118	F04		Violation of seat belt law as passenger - age 18 or over
119	F04		Permitting minor to ride w/o proper restraint - age 16 or 17
120	B61	4	Conviction for failure to report accident
121	U01	6	Fleeing law enforcement officer (misdemeanor)
122	A25		Driving while impaired-2nd offense
123	A25		Driving while impaired-3rd offense - revocation
124	A25		Driving while impaired-4th offense - revocation
125	F02		Child restraint violation-ages 4 thru 15 - 2nd offense
126	W00	2	Driving without driver license in possession
127	N84	6	Fail to change lanes or slow down for auth veh on roadside
128	B25		Driving after convicted as Habitual offender-revocation - felony
129	F04		Violation of seat belt law driver/passenger age 16-17 - 1st offense
130	U07		Violation of seat belt law driver/passenger age 16-17 - 2nd offense
131			Aggravated vehicular homicide - revocation
132	U01		Fleeing law enforcement officer - felony
133	U06		Vehicular assault - felony
134	A20		Child Endangerment - DWI
135	A20		Child Endangerment; injury -DWI
136			Child endangerment; fatality
137	W00		Revocation for fatal accident - GDL program
138	W00		Suspension for acc/seat belt violation - GDL program
139	W00		Revocation for fraudulent documentation - GDL program
142	W00		Susp for driving off not paying for fuel - not stated
143	W00		Susp for driving off not paying for fuel - 1st offense
144	W00		Susp for driving off not paying for fuel - 2nd offense
145	W00		Susp for driving off not paying for fuel - 3rd offense
146			Presenting Fake ID to Purchase Alcohol – Suspension
147			Equipment law - commercial motor vehicle
148	A33		Driving While Possessing 5 or More Grams of Meth
149	D53		Default on a payment plan - notice sent
150			Illegal possession of a controlled substance - CMV
151			Illegal possession of a controlled substance - CMV
152			Furnish Alcohol/Entice to Purchase for Under 21
155	W00		Violation of Truancy Law; first offense
156	W00		Violation of Truancy Law; second offense
157	W00		Driving suspension - juvenile court; first denial
158	WOO		Driving suspension - juvenile court; second denial
159	WOO		Conviction - alcoholic beverage violation; first denial; non-driving-juvenile
160	W00		Conviction - alcoholic beverage violation; second denial; non-driving-juvenile
161	W00		Conviction - alcoholic beverage violation; first denial; driving - juvenile
162	W00		Conviction - alcoholic beverage violation; second denial; driving - juvenile
163	W00		Possession of weapon - juvenile court - first denial
164	W00		Possession of weapon - juvenile court - second denial
165	D51		Failure to pay child support - suspension
166	B27		1st Violation out of service order/CMV/susp
167	B27		2nd Violation out of service order/CMV/susp
168	B27		3rd Violation out of service order/CMV/susp
169	B19		1st Violation out of service order/CMV/Hazmat or bus/susp
170	B19		2nd Violation out of service order/CMV/Hazmat or bus/susp
171	D51		Failure to pay child support - court direct - suspend
172	W00		Rev/Susp/Canc/due to returned check
173			Railroad grade crossing - CMV
174	M21	8	*no longer used* CMV - Failure to stop before reaching tracks at a railroad-highway grade crossing when the tracks are not clear
175	M22		*no longer used* CMV - Failure to stop as required before driving onto railroad-highway grade crossing.
176	M23		*no longer used* CMV - Failure to have sufficient space to drive completely through the

Code	ACD	Points	Description
			railroad-highway grade crossing without stopping
177	M24		*no longer used* CMV - Failing to negotiate a railroad-highway grade crossing because of insufficient undercarriage clearance.
178	A35		Possession of open container of alcoholic beverage
179	N84		Child endangerment
180	N04	6	Failure to yield right of way to emergency vehicle
181			Violation of Motorcycle Helmet Law
182			Operating vehicle while using cell phone - under 18 years old
183			Operating improperly due to drowsiness - CMV
184			Operating improperly due to drowsiness - personal vehicle
185			Operating improperly - physical or mental disability - CMV
186	M85		Texting while driving
187	F34		Illegal parking - CMV
194			Fail to Satisfy Fine/Costs/Taxes on Criminal Off-Rev
195	D53		Suspension for failure to comply with fee installment agreement
196			Fail to Comply With Court Pay Plan or Stay Lifted – Rev
200			Administrative Per Se for .04 or Greater BAC - CDL
220	A20		Driving while intoxicated
221	A20		Driving while intoxicated; first offense
222	A20		Driving while intoxicated; second offense
223	A20		Driving while intoxicated; third offense
267	D45		Failure to answer traffic citation; license not surrendered - cancellation
400	A20		Driving while intoxicated - 4th offense
401	S93	5	Speeding in commercial vehicle hauling hazmat, speed not indicated
		3	Speeding in commercial vehicle hauling hazmat, 1-5 mph over
		5	Speeding in commercial vehicle hauling hazmat, 6-14 mph over
		6	Speeding in commercial vehicle hauling hazmat, 15-25 mph over
		7	Speeding in commercial vehicle hauling hazmat, 26-35 mph over
		8	Speeding in commercial vehicle hauling hazmat, 36-45 mph over
		9	Speeding in commercial vehicle hauling hazmat, 46 or more mph over
		7	Excessive speeding in commercial vehicle, at least 15 mph over, speed not indicated on court document (but on citation)
402	M84	8	Reckless driving; hazardous material
403	M14	5	
404	M70	5	Improper passing; hazardous materials
405	N60	5	Wrong way, side or direction; hazardous materials
406	M34	5	Following improperly; hazardous materials
407	N01	5	Failure to yield right-of-way; hazardous materials
408	N50	5	Making improper turn; hazardous materials
409	N43	4	Failure to signal direction or reduce speed suddenly; hazardous materials
410	M10	8	Passing stopped school bus; hazardous materials
411	M32	3	Following emergency vehicle unlawfully; hazardous materials
412	S96	5	Speed less than posted minimum; hazardous materials
413	B51		No driver license/wrong license for type vehicle; hazardous materials 3pts if valid, 8pts if rev/susp
414	M81	6	Careless or negligent driving; hazardous materials
418	E01	4	Violation of bumper law; hazardous materials
419	N84		Miscellaneous traffic violation; hazardous materials
420	A20		Driving while intoxicated; hazardous materials
421			Administrative per se - dui - hazardous materials
422	B25		Driving while revoked; hazardous materials
423	S95		Contest racing on public trafficway; hazardous materials
424	W00		Unattended vehicle containing med/hazmat - suspension
425	B01		Leaving scene of accident; hazardous materials
426	B41		Unlawful use of driver license; hazardous materials
428	U03		Felony by a motor vehicle; hazardous materials
429	A20		Allowing intoxicated person to drive; hazardous materials
430	A42	6	Improper or erratic lane change - CMV - hazmat
431	U07		Vehicular homicide; hazardous materials - revocation
432	U07		Aggravated vehicular homicide - CMV/hazmat - revocation
433	U07		Vehicular homicide; intoxication proximate cause; hazardous materials
437	B24	8	Conviction of driving while cancelled
439	B22	8	Conviction of driving while cancelled
447	U31		Contributing to the occurrence of a fatal accident; hazardous materials

Code	ACD	Points	Description
448	U03		Using a motor vehicle in connection with a felony
450	W00	6	Driving while intoxicated - juvenile court - no revocation
451	WOO	6	Leaving scene of accident - juvenile court - no revocation
452	W00	6	Vehicular homicide - juvenile court - no revocation
453			Driving while revoked - juvenile court - no revocation
454			Contest racing - juvenile court - no revocation
455			Unlawful use of driver license - juvenile court - no rev
456			Manslaughter - juvenile court - no revocation
472	B26		Driving on suspended license; hazardous materials
486	A12		Conviction under I.C law; hazardous materials
501	S93	4	Speeding in commercial vehicle, speed not indicated
		2	Speeding in commercial vehicle, 1-5 mph over
		4	Speeding in commercial vehicle, 6-14 mph over
		5	Speeding in commercial vehicle, 15-25 mph over
		6	Speeding in commercial vehicle, 26-35 mph over
		8	Speeding in commercial vehicle, 36 or more mph over
502	M84	7	Reckless driving; commercial motor vehicle
503	M14	4	Failure to obey traffic instructions; commercial motor vehicle
504	M70	4	Improper passing; commercial motor vehicle
505	N60	4	Wrong way, side, or direction; commercial motor vehicle
506	M34	4	Following improperly; commercial motor vehicle
507	N01	4	Failure to yield right of way; commercial motor vehicle
508	N50	4	Making improper turn; commercial motor vehicle
509	N43	3	Failure to signal direction or reduce speed suddenly; commercial motor vehicle
510	M75	6	Passing stopped school bus; commercial motor vehicle
511	M32	3	Following emergency vehicle unlawfully; commercial motor vehicle
512	S96	4	Speed less than posted minimum; commercial motor vehicle
513	B56		No driver license; wrong license for type of vehicle; commercial motor vehicle
514	M81	5	Careless or negligent driving; commercial motor vehicle
515	S93	2	Speeding in construction zone, 1-5 mph over
		4	Speeding in construction zone, 6-15 mph over
		5	Speeding in construction zone, 16-25 mph over
		6	Speeding in construction zone, 26-35 mph over
		8	Speeding in construction zone, 36+ mph over
		7	Speeding in construction zone, speed not indicated
516	B57		Driving commercial motor vehicle without CDL in possession
517	B91		Driving commercial motor vehicle without proper class or endorsement
518	F01	4	Violation of bumper law; commercial motor vehicle
519	N84	3	Miscellaneous traffic violation; commercial motor vehicle
520	A04		Driving while intoxicated; commercial motor vehicle
521			Administrative per se - DUI - commercial motor vehicle
522	B25		Driving while revoked; commercial motor vehicle
523			Drag Racing - CMV
525	B01		Leaving scene of accident; commercial motor vehicle
526	B41		Unlawful use of driver license; commercial motor vehicle
528	U03		Felony by a commercial motor vehicle
529	A20		Allowing intoxicated person to drive; commercial motor vehicle
530	M42	5	Improper or erratic lane change - CMV
531	U07		Vehicular homicide; commercial motor vehicle
532	U07		Aggravated vehicular homicide - CMV - revocation
533	U07		Vehicular homicide; intoxication proximate cause; commercial motor vehicle
534	W00		Aiding or abetting prostitution; commercial motor vehicle
535	M21		Railroad crossing suspension - CMV - 1st offense
536	W60		Railroad crossing suspension - CMV - 2 viol in 3 year period CMV
537	W61		Railroad crossing suspension - CMV - 3 or more in 3 year period - suspension
538			Lifetime Disqualification - 2 Major Offenses - CDL
539			Out of Service Disqualification - CDL
540	A25	8	Driving while ability impaired - no suspension
541			Imminent Hazard - CDL
542	B26		Driving on suspended license; commercial motor vehicle
547	U31		Contributing to occurrence of fatal accident; commercial motor vehicle
555	W00		Driver license reported stolen - case number will be new DL #
556	A12		Conviction under I.C. law; commercial motor vehicle
557			Implied Consent - Out of State - CMV

Code	ACD	Points	Description
560	D02		Misrep of identify to obtain CDL
561			Operating CMV with radar detector
575	A35		Possession of open container of alcoholic bev - CDL
630	W00		Duplicate number - case number will be new driver license
690			Reinstatement; test required
700			Crash - Government Vehicle - Emergency Run
701			Accident - property damage
702			Property damage accident - Gov't vehicle
703			Property damage accident - private
711			Personal injury accident
712			Personal injury accident - Gov't vehicle
713			Personal injury accident - Private
717			Leaving Scene of Crash - CDL - Property Damage
719	B02		Leaving scene of accident involving death-felony - revocation
720	A20		Driving while intoxicated; commercial motor vehicle; second offense
721	U31		Accident involving fatality
722	U31		Fatal accident - Gov't vehicle
723	U31		Fatal accident - private property
725	B01		Leaving scene of accident; commercial motor vehicle; second offense
728	U03		Felony by commercial vehicle- second offense
729	A50		Felony by commercial vehicle, involving a controlled substance
731			Contributing to Crash Resulting in Own Death
732	U31		Fatal accident - own death - Gov't vehicle
733			Accident resulting in own death - private property
741		3	Driver View Obstructed
742		3	Inability to Control Vehicle
743		3	Improper Operation/Riding a Motorcycle
744		3	Improper Lane or Location
745		3	Inattentive Driving
746		3	Coasting/Operating with Gear Disengaged
747		3	Improper Backing
748		3	Improper Starting
749		3	Prima Facia Speed Violation or Driving Too Fast for Conditions
750		3	Operating at Erratic or Suddenly Changing Speeds
751	S93	2-8	Speeding resulting in accident; CMV, 1 to 5 over 2 pts, 6-14 over or if not indicted 4 pts, etc
752	M84	6	Reckless driving resulting in accident; commercial motor vehicle
753	M17	4	Failure to obey traffic instructions resulting in accident; commercial motor vehicle
754	M70	4	Improper passing resulting in accident; commercial motor vehicle
755	N60	4	Wrong way, side, or direction resulting in accident; commercial motor vehicle
756	M34	3	Following improperly resulting in accident; commercial motor vehicle
757	N01	4	Failure to yield right of way resulting in accident; commercial motor vehicle
758	N50	4	Making improper turn resulting in accident; commercial motor vehicle
759	N43	2	Failure to signal or reduce speed suddenly resulting in accident; commercial motor vehicle
760	M75	6	Passing stopped school bus resulting in accident; commercial motor vehicle
761	M32	2	Following emergency vehicle unlawfully resulting in accident; commercial motor vehicle
762	S96	3	Speed less than posted minimum resulting in accident; commercial motor vehicle
764	M81	4	Careless or negligent driving resulting in accident; commercial motor vehicle
768	E01	4	Violation of bumper law resulting in accident; commercial motor vehicle
770			Property damage accident - Gov't vehicle
771			Personal injury accident - Gov't vehicle
772	U31		Fatal accident - Gov't vehicle
773			Property damage accident - private
774			Accident - property damage
775			Personal injury accident
776	U31		Accident involving a fatality
901			Re-examination - (passed)
902	W20		Re-examination (failed); not eligible for renewal - suspension
903			Re-examination (passed after failing prior exam)
921			Administrative probation
922	W01		Interviewed - suspend; not eligible for renewal
923	W00		Suspend - violation of probation; not eligible for renewal
924	W01		Suspend - frequent traffic violator; not eligible for renewal
928			Reinstatement (922, 923, and 924); test required
929			Reinstatement (922, 923, and 924); no test required

Code	ACD	Points	Description
930			*no longer used* Hearing disposition; failure to appear (6 months)
931	D40		Hearing disposition - FTA (12 months)
932			Hearing disp - Def Driving Course - no suspension
933			Hearing disp - Def Driving Course - 90 day suspension
934			Hearing disp - Def Driving Course - 6 month suspension
935			Hearing disp - 6 month suspension
936			Hearing disp - 12 month suspension
937			Hearing disp - medical upheld
938	W10		Hearing disp - withdrawal action
949			Frequent traffic viol-juvenile/suspension/notice sent
950	W14		Suspend - disability; not eligible for renewal
951	W00		Suspend - failure to appear for exam; not eligible for renewal
952	W01		Suspend - fail to appear for interview - suspended use 7/1/81
953	W00		Suspend - in-house suspension; no fee required
954	W14		Cancelled - mental or physical disability
957			Reinstatement (950, 951, and 952); test required
958			Reinstatement (950); no test required.
959			Reinstatement (951 and 952); no test required
960			Reduce time of suspension
972			*no longer used* Completed defensive driving course to reduce suspension time
975			*no longer used* Completed defensive driving course
985			*no longer used* Reinstatement - no test required

About Accidents

Accidents are shown as:

Accident - Government Vehicle - Do Not Use For Insurance Rating
Accident - Personal Injury
Accident - Personal Injury - Private Property
Accident - Property Damage
Accident - Property Damage - Private Property
Accident Involving Fatality
Accident Involving Fatality - Private Property

About the Point System

Points range from 1 to 9. Accumulation of 12 points in a 12-month period can result in a suspension.

Texas

Administration	Important Telephone and Web Contact
Rebecca Davio, Assistant Director Driver License Division Texas Department of Public Safety PO Box 4087 Austin 78773-0001 512-424-2600 www.dps.texas.gov Whitney Brewster, Executive Director Texas Department of Motor Vehicles Central Administration 4000 Jackson Ave Austin, TX 78731 888-368-4689 www.TxDMV.gov	Driver Licensing and Records .... 512-424-2600 Conviction Reporting .... 512-424-2031 SR-22 and Financial Responsibility .... 512-424-2600 Commercial Driver License .... 512-424-2600 Failure to Appear Programs............................... 800-686-0570 Enforcement and & Compliance Services............ 512-424-2600 (Fax 512-424-2501) Driver Responsibility Program........................... 800-688-6882 Title and Registration Information .... 888-368-4689 Texas Department of Insurance........................... 512-463-6169 Dept. of Public Safety (Highway Patrol).............. 512-424-2000 Email for Driver License: customerservicedl@dps.texas.gov Email Contacts for Vehicles: www.TxDMV.gov

Texas Statutes & Transportation Code:	www.legis.state.tx.us
Motor Carrier Rules and Notices:	www.dmv.tx.gov/motor_carrier/notices_rules.htm
Administrative Code Title 43 Transportation:	http://info.sos.state.tx.us/pls/pub/readtac$ext.ViewTAC?tac_view=2&ti=43

Driver's License Format, Issuance and Renewal

License Classes, Restrictions and Endorsements Appear After the Driving Record Content Section

License Format

The format is eight numbers, beginning with 0, 1, 2, or 3. License numbers are sequential and computer-generated.

Document Appearance

The current driver licenses and identification cards, redesigned with new and enhanced security features, were put into production April 15, 2009. The prior driver licenses and ID cards are still valid and will be phased out as they expire. An abbreviated description of the new documents is shown below.

Current Documents

License has digital photo with state capitol in light blue on right side on a beige background, with TEXAS at the top left side in blues

Security Characteristics: At this time, the agency has deferred from describing the security features.

Position of Photo: Photo is located on the left side.

Minor Age Driver Locator: This driver license is presented vertically and reads "Under 21 DL" on the top in red and "under 21 until MM/DD/YYYY" next to the photo

CDL Indicator: License reads "Commercial Driver License" in brown on top.

Limited Term Indicator: License reads "Limited Term" underneath the term "Driver License" or "Identification Card" on the header bar.

Identification Card Indicator: Identification card reads "Identification Card" in green on top.

Occupation License Indicator: Occupational reads "Occupational License" in black on top.

Donor Designation: Red heart appears at the bottom right hand corner of license.

DPS Audit number: Listed on the bottom of the driver license and identification card in blue.

Older Documents

License has digital photo with state capitol featured on a beige background, with TEXAS at the top in *red* and DEPARTMENT OF PUBLIC SAFETY in *blue* below. A color bar is displayed in the header behind TEXAS.

Security Characteristics: Security laminate has TEXAS printed in metallic ink across the entire face of the card, TEXAS will glow green under ultraviolet light. There is a bar code, magnetic strip and endorsement/restriction codes printed on back.

Position of Photo: Photo is located on the right side; the DPS audit number appears along the side of the photo and the director's signature falls halfway on the beige background on the top of the photo.

Minor Age Driver Locator: Vertical format license with forward facing photo at bottom right. For ages 18-21, "under 21 driver license" is printed in *red* across the top; if CDL, "under 21 commercial DL" is brown. Also, "under 21 until (MMDDYY)" appears in red on first detail line of license. For ages 16-18, "provisional driver license" is printed in *purple* across the top.

CDL Indicator: COMMERCIAL DRIVER LICENSE appears in brown in the header line. "CDL" appears in text next to the eight-digit license number.

Issuance

Age Requirements

The minimum age for a Regular License is 18; 16 with completion of approved driver education course. Texas adopted a graduated license program. A Learner License can be issued at 15 upon the completion of at least 6 hours of classroom instruction of driver education; and must be accompanied by licensed driver age 21 or over. The restriction "B" (for an accompanying licensed driver) will not be removed until an individual reaches the age of 16, has held a Learner License at least 6 months and completes the behind the wheel instruction of driver education and has passed a driving test, or has applied for a MRDL (Minor's Restricted Driver License), or has turned 18 years of age and has passed a driving test. If over the age of 18, driver may remove the "B" restriction once the road test is passed. If between ages 18 and 24, driver must complete an adult driver education course.

A Provisional License may be issued at 16: must have held a Learner License at least 6 months and complete Phase II of Driver's Ed. During Phase II, the minor is restricted for one year to:

1) No more than one non-family member passenger under 21.
2) No driving after midnight before 5am unless driving is necessary for employment, school or school related activity or medical

emergency. If an individual is accompanied by a licensed operator age 21 or over in the front seat, he/she is not limited to hours of operation or of passengers.

3) No operating vehicle when using a wireless communication device, including cell phones.

A Learner License is issued to a person, under the age of 18 and valid until the person's 18th birthday. A Hardship License can be issued at 15 until 18, under necessary conditions.

Residency

To be eligible for a Texas driver license or identification card, the applicant must be a resident of or domiciled in Texas. New residents must a secure Texas license 90 days after entry into the state and surrender any driver license from the prior state of residence.

Location of Residency Requirements:

Texas now requires proof of residency for non CDL holders and domicile for CDL holders. For non-CDL residency see www.dps.texas.gov/DriverLicense/residencyReqNonCDL.htm.   For CDL domicile see www.dps.texas.gov/DriverLicense/domicileReq.htm.

Renewal

Since 01/01/02, all renewals, with the exception of commercial driver licenses and limited term licenses, are issued for 6 years. Commercial licenses are issued for 5 years, and limited term licenses are issued for the length of lawful presence up to 6 years. Driver keeps same number when renewing. Non-CDL renewal and address changes are available online at www.texas.gov. Non-CDL renewal is available by phone at 866-357-3639. Address changes are not available by phone. Military personnel may renew their expired TX licenses by mail. Upon renewal, military personnel may be assigned a new driver license number. Although licenses carried by military personnel are legally valid, they may be purged if not renewed within two years of expiration. All drivers who renew in person, regardless of age, must take and pass a vision exam.

Elderly-Related Restrictions

Since September 1, 2007, state law requires drivers age 79 or older to visit a driver license office in person and prohibits renewing a driver license by alternative means such as by mail or through online services. Additionally, drivers age 85 or older receive a two-year renewal instead of the standard 6-year renewal.

Vehicle Insurance, Title and Registration Facts

Registration Renewal

Renewal is set on a 12, 24 or 36 month basis and can be done in person, by mail, or online (in participating counties). Counties and cities have the ability to enforce a program to block registration to those who have not paid traffic court fines. Currently, 19 counties have instituted this program.

New Residents

New residents must title and register their vehicle(s) within thirty days of establishing residency or accepting employment.

Inspections and Emissions Testing

All Texas registered vehicles are required to receive an annual inspection. This program is administered by the Texas Department of Public Safety (DPS). Visit www.txdps.state.tx.us/vi/ for details on criteria and locations.

Some vehicles are required to have an emissions test in addition to the safety inspection if registered in these designated counties and less than 24 years old: Brazoria, Collin, Dallas, Denton, El Paso, Ellis, Fort Bend, Galveston, Harris, Montgomery, Johnson, Kaufman, Parker, Rockwall, Tarrant, Travis, and Williamson counties. Diesel powered vehicles and motorcycles are exempt from the emissions standards, but are still required to have the annual safety inspection.

Passenger Plate Descriptions

There are two plates with one windshield decal. Vehicles with no windshield (trailers, motorcycles, etc.) have one plate with one decal showing MO/YR of expiration. Note as of July 2012, Texas began issuing a new license plate - called The Texas Classic - with a seven digit format. Older general issue plates with six and seven digit patterns are still in use, but will be replaced when the plate's age reaches seven years. Texas has no coding on license plates signifying the county of issuance.

When a vehicle is sold, the license plates should be removed and/or transferred upon sale of a vehicle. If the vehicle is sold by a dealer, the license plate must be returned to the seller or transferred to another vehicle owned by the seller. Owners of vehicles sold in private sale are encouraged, but not required, to remove or transfer the license plates. Specialty license plates remain with the owner.

Insurance and Financial Responsibility

The state has compulsory liability insurance, but does not have a no-fault insurance provision. Minimum financial responsibility limits effective 01/01/2011are $30,000/$60/000/$25,000. Proof of insurance is required upon request by a law enforcement officer at the time of vehicle registration or original driver license issuance, upon vehicle inspection, and upon a reportable crash. A second conviction for operating a vehicle without liability insurance results in automatic suspension.

Withdrawal Sanctions, and Alcohol and Drug Testing

Alcohol and Chemical Testing

Texas' illegal intoxication level is .08 percent for 21 years and older for Class C licensees. The level is .04 for CDL drivers and any detectable amount for persons under 21 years of age. Blood and breath testing are authorized; urine testing is authorized only for CDLs. Texas has an implied-consent law provision.

Suspensions and Revocations

See the Appendix for more information about the mandatory MCSIA CDL disqualification sanctions.

The Following can Trigger an Automatic Suspension or Revocation as Indicated—

Subsequent conviction of no liability insurance ....Two years.

   A $100 Reinstatement fee and SR-22 must be filed and maintained with the Department for two years from conviction date.

Child Support (No Reinstatement Fee)..Indefinite until in compliance (determined by court).

Drug Conviction ....180-day suspension.

Fraudulent Use of License ....90 days to one year (determined by the court).

Liability Judgment Rendered as Result of Automobile Crash ......10 years and can be renewed every 10 years.

Using Motor Vehicle to Transport, Conceal or Harbor an Alien ..Lifetime Disqualification.

DWI First Offense (includes watercraft for first/subsequent)   90-day to one-year suspension, determined by the court.

DWI Second Offense........................ 180-day to two-year suspension, determined by the court.

DWI Third or Subsequent Offense ... 180-day to two-year suspension, determined by the court.

Notes: 1)   DWI offenses have tougher punishments if a minor is found in the car. First-time offenders are automatically suspended and repeat offenders are subject to an extended suspension period.

2)   If the DWI is probated, the subject may be required to complete a DWI Education Program within 181 days of the conviction. Failure to do so may result in a revocation of driving privileges. Upon a subsequent conviction, the Department will impose a twelve-month suspension.

Motor Fuel Theft - Subsequent Conviction ....180-day suspension.

Note: ALR refers to the **Administrative License Revocation** law that provides for suspension due to .08 or higher BAC or refusal of driver to comply with officer's request for such a test. An administrative hearing may be requested within 15 days from the date the notice of suspension is received. A reinstatement fee of $125 is required for all suspensions.

ALR - Failure First Offense (includes when operating a watercraft) ....90-day suspension.

    Subsequent Offense ....One-year suspension.

    With prior alcohol-related conviction ....One-year suspension.

ALR - Refusal First Offense (includes when operating a watercraft) ....180-day suspension.

    Subsequent Offense ....Two-year suspension.

    With prior alcohol-related conviction ....Two-year suspension.

Drivers under 21 years of age ....

    DWI 1st Offense (includes when operating a watercraft) ....One-year suspension.

    DWI 2nd Offense..18-month suspension.

    ALR Failure 1st Offense...60-day suspension.

    ALR Failure 2nd Offense..120-day suspension.

    ALR Failure w/ Prior Alcohol Related Conviction...........................180-day suspension.

    ALR Refusal First Offense ....180-day suspension.

    ALR Refusal Subsequent Offense...Two-year suspension.

    ALR Refusal With prior alcohol-related conviction ....Two-year suspension.

    ALR 1st Offense/Any Detectable Amount ....60-day suspension.

    ALR 2nd Offense/Any Detectable Amount ....120-day suspension.

    ALR Subsequent Offense/Any Detectable Amount.........................180-day suspension.

Public intoxication, Alcohol Beverage Code Offenses (minor in possession, attempt to purchase, purchase of alcohol, consumption of alcohol, misrepresentation of age) - No reinstatement fee

    1st Offense...30-day suspension.

    2nd Offense..60-day suspension.

    3rd Offense ....180-day suspension.

Fail to Complete Minor Education Program..One month to 12 months (determined by the court).

Juvenile under 17 years of age:

    Drug and DWI ....365 days or until 19th birthday.

    Truancy..Not to exceed 12 months.

A driver issued a speeding ticket and found guilty of driving at a speed of 95 miles per hour or higher is prohibited from taking a driving safety class to dismiss the ticket. CDL holders are prohibited from taking a driver safety course to dismiss any ticket.

Suspension or revocation of driving privileges is automatic unless an administrative hearing (when authorized by law) is requested. The suspension period is 90 days or, in certain circumstances, an indefinite revocation is imposed.

An Administrative Hearing may be requested within 20 days from the date notice is received. The outcome can be suspension of the license for up to one year, probation up to two years, revocation of the license for an indefinite period, or dismissal of the hearing. A hearing may be held for any of the following reasons.

• Commission of Offense in Another State, which would be grounds for Suspension/Revocation in TX

• Driving While License Invalid

• Determined Medically Incapable by the Medical Advisory Board (results in revocation)

• Failure to Take or to Pass an Examination Required by the Department (results in revocation)

• Failure to Provide Medical Records Required by the Medical Advisory Board (results in revocation)

• Responsible as a Driver for Serious Personal Injury or Property Damage

• Habitually Reckless or Negligent

• Habitual Violator (defined as 4 moving violations in 12 months or 7 moving violations in 24 months)

• Incapability of Safe Driving (results in revocation)

• Minor, Failure to Appear for a Traffic or Non-Traffic related offense (results in revocation)

• Minor Restricted Driver License Holder, convicted on one moving violation within a 12-month period.

• Non-Compliance With the Terms of the Non-Resident Violator Compact (results in revocation)

• Provisional or Hardship License Holder, Convicted on Two or More Moving Violations Within a 12-Month Period

• Restriction Violations

Driver Responsibility Program (DRP) and Point System

The Driver Responsibility Program authorizes the DPS to assess surcharges to an individual based on certain traffic offenses that have occurred on or after September 1, 2003. Individuals are notified by mail each time a surcharge is added to their driver record. Surcharges are in addition to other fees and do not replace a suspension, revocation, denial, disqualification or cancellation resulting from the same conviction.

Point Assessment

Points are issued as part of DRP. Traffic offenses resulting in points are designated by Title 37 Texas Administrative Code Rule 15.89. Points are assessed to moving violations classified as Class C misdemeanors and remain on the driver history for a period of fifteen years from conviction date. Points are assigned as follows:

- Two points for a moving violation conviction in Texas or that of another state.
- Three points for a moving violation conviction in Texas or another state that resulted in a crash.

DPS assesses a surcharge when the driver accumulates a total of six (6) points or more on their driver history during a three-year period. Points are assigned for speeding less than 10% over the speed limit convictions. The driver must pay a $100 surcharge for the first six points and $25 for each additional point.

Annual Assessment

The surcharge assessment will be reviewed annually. If the driver history continues to reflect six or more points during the prior three-year period, the surcharge will be assessed. Therefore, drivers may be required to pay for **one or more years if six or more points continue to accumulate on the driver record**. Point surcharges are cumulative and may vary with each annual assessment if convictions are added or removed from the driver history. Failure to pay surcharges results in an indefinite suspension.

Conviction Based Surcharges

Drivers who receive a conviction for an offense listed below pay an annual surcharge for a period of three (3) years from date of conviction. No points are assessed for these offenses. Once the conviction is reported to DPS, the following surcharges are assessed:

Driving While Intoxicated, Boating While Intoxicated, Flying While Intoxicated, Assembling Amusement Park Ride While Intoxicated, Intoxication Assault, and Intoxication Manslaughter

First time offense	$1,000
Second or subsequent offense	$1,500
DWI 0.16 Blood Alcohol Content or greater	$2,000
Failure to Maintain Financial Responsibility	$250
Driving While License Invalid	$250
No Driver License	$100

The surcharges are cumulative; example, an initial conviction for DWI will be assessed $1000 annually, and a subsequent DWI conviction within the same three-year period will be assessed an additional $1500 annually.

Deferred Adjudication - Defensive Driving Course

No points will be assessed or surcharges applied if the conviction is deferred, or a DDC course is taken. Only non-CDL drivers may be granted deferred adjudication, and/or take a defensive driving course (DDC) for any points-based citation and No-DL citations. No-Insurance and DWLI offense are eligible for deferred adjudication. Intoxication offenses are NOT eligible for deferral.

Reinstatement Requirements

The renewal/issuance of a Texas license will be denied until the reinstatement fee is paid.

Suspension	$100 fee; SR-22, if mandatory or no insurance suspension.
Revocation	$100 fee.
ALR (blood/breath test refusal)	$125 fee.
Education Program	$100 ($50 if prior to 9-1-2010)

Record Access: Laws, Rules, and Forms

Note: This Section Applies to Both Driver and Vehicle Records.

Governing Statutes and Rules

Texas Statutes (Transportation Code) Look-up:
 www.legis.state.tx.us/
Motor Carrier Rules and Notices:
www.dmv.tx.gov/motor_carrier/notices_rules.htm
Per Texas Transportation Code Ch. 730 the state adopted the provisions of DPPA. Also governing the release of records are Transportation Code §502.008, §501.023, §502.151 and §552.130.
The Texas Transportation Code Ch. 730.007 states as follows:
"Sec. 730.007. PERMITTED DISCLOSURES. (a) Personal information obtained by an agency in connection with a motor vehicle record may be disclosed to any requestor by an agency if the requestor:
(1) provides the requestor's name and address and any proof of that information required by the agency; and
(2) represents that the use of the personal information will be strictly limited to:
 (A) use by:
  (i) a government agency, including any court or law enforcement agency, in carrying out its functions; or
  (ii) a private person or entity acting on behalf of a government agency in carrying out the functions of the agency;
 (B) use in connection with a matter of:
  (i) motor vehicle or motor vehicle operator safety;
  (ii) motor vehicle theft;
  (iii) motor vehicle product alterations, recalls, or advisories;
  (iv) performance monitoring of motor vehicles, motor vehicle parts, or motor vehicle dealers;
  (v) motor vehicle market research activities, including survey research; or
  (vi) removal of nonowner records from the original owner records of motor vehicle manufacturers;
 (C) use in the normal course of business by a legitimate business or an authorized agent of the business, but only:
  (i) to verify the accuracy of personal information submitted by the individual to the business or the agent of the business; and
  (ii) if the information is not correct, to obtain the correct information, for the sole purpose of preventing fraud by, pursuing a legal remedy against, or recovering on a debt or security interest against the individual;
 (D) use in conjunction with a civil, criminal, administrative, or arbitral proceeding in any court or government agency or before any self-regulatory body, including service of process, investigation in anticipation of litigation, execution or enforcement of a judgment or order, or under an order of any court;
 (E) use in research or in producing statistical reports, but only if the personal information is not published, redisclosed, or used to contact any individual;
 (F) use by an insurer or insurance support organization, or by a self-insured entity, or an authorized agent of the entity, in connection with claims investigation activities, antifraud activities, rating, or underwriting;
 (G) use in providing notice to an owner of a towed or impounded vehicle;
 (H) use by a licensed private investigator agency or licensed security service for a purpose permitted under this section;
 (I) use by an employer or an agent or insurer of the employer to obtain or verify information relating to a holder of a commercial driver's license that is required under 49 U.S.C. Chapter 313;

(J) use in connection with the operation of a private toll transportation facility;

(K) use by a consumer reporting agency, as defined by the Fair Credit Reporting Act (15 U.S.C. Section 1681 et seq.), for a purpose permitted under that Act; or

(L) use for any other purpose specifically authorized by law that relates to the operation of a motor vehicle or to public safety."

Consent Forms

Driver Records: Use of *Form DR-1* is required for a copy of a driving record, or *DR-36* for a copy of a certified abstract driver record. See www.dps.texas.gov/internetforms for the forms. The signature of requester is required but does not need to be notarized. Type 1, 2 and 2A driver records are available to anyone with *DR-1 Form* (or *DR-36* for certified abstract) who qualifies under one of the exceptions allowed in TRC Chapter 730. Casual requesters can obtain records with personal information with a *DR-1 Form* (or *DR-36* for a certified abstract) that contains a written authorization signed by the subject, as found on the form. A notary is not required. With this is a one-time release, Type 3 and 3A driver records are provided with the customer's consent.

Vehicle Records: *Form VTR-275 Request for Texas Motor Vehicle Information* is required. The form must be signed by the requester to certify that the information will be used in compliance with state and federal laws and that the information is for a "lawful and legitimate purpose." Requester must furnish a copy of government issued photo ID (driver license, passport, etc.) Casual requesters can obtain records with personal information only with permission of the subject. The requester must submit *Form VTR-275* and a current copy of gov-issued photo ID,

and attach to the form written authorization from the subject *Authorization for Release of Personal Information Form VTR-386.* Download both forms at www.TxDMV.gov.

Vendor and Third Party Access Policy

Driver Records: Approved vendors can access records for another vendor who will then sell to an end-user, as long as all vendors meet the privacy exceptions. The state suggests that all vendor chain implement an agreement specifying that each vendor meets a qualified exception (DPPA permissible use).

Vehicle Records: Permissible users can purchase in bulk or database format. They can then resell to another permissible user or another vendor selling to a permissible user. However, the motor vehicle record information obtained for a permitted use may not be resold or redisclosed unless the information is used only for the permitted use. Records must be maintained for a period of not less than 5 years by the original vendor and by the person or entity that received the information. The purchaser must also provide a copy of those vehicle records to the department upon request.

Records Ordered For Non-permissible Uses

Certain limited types of records, such as a driver license status or motor carrier compliant history, are released to the public. Otherwise specific driver or vehicle records are not released, even records without personal information, unless there is consent or the requested use is per one of the listed permissible uses and the stated procedures are followed.

Access to Driver-Related Records

Driver Records

Department of Public Safety, License and Record Service, PO Box 149008, Austin TX 78714-9008 512-424-2600.

See summary of fees below. **Note:** DPS sells a license status (see fees below). A certified copy of an original license or ID card application can be provided for $1.00. Also, a certified abstract with a summarization of crashes, convictions, and suspensions is available for $20.00 using *Form DR-36.* DPS charges for a no record found search.

Driver Record Types and Fees

The following types of records can be requested online at www.dps.texas.gov or by mail:

- **Status Record** (Type 1): name, date of birth (DOB), license status, and latest address. ($4.00, $4.50 if online)
- **3-year History Record** (Type 2): name, DOB, license status, list of crashes where a citation has been issued and violations within the immediate past 3-year period. ($6.00, $6.50 if online)
- **Certified 3-year History Record** (Type 2A): certified version of Type 2. This record is not acceptable for Defensive Driving Course (DDC). ($10.00, $12.00 if online)
- **List of all Crashes and Violations in Record** (Type 3): name, DOB, license status, list of all crashes and violations in record. ($7.00, $7.50 if online). **Only furnished to the license holder.**
- **Certified List of All Crashes and Violations in Record** (Type 3A): certified version of Type 3. This record is acceptable for Defensive Driving Course (DDC). ($10.00, $12.00 if online) **Only furnished to the license holder.**
- **Certified Abstract of Driver Record** ("AR"): Certified text abstract of complete driving record of a license holder. ($20.00, $22.00 if online)

The complete Type 3 records follow the purging criteria shown later in this section. There is no record offered that shows just CDL or CMV violations.

In-Person – The Driver License Division no longer offers counter service for driving record requesters.

Mail – Mail to DPS, Attn: L.R.S. PO Box 149008, Austin TX78714-9008. Requests mailed to the state are processed within fourteen to twenty-one days. The driver license number and name, or name and date of birth are needed when ordering, and use of Form DR-1 or DR-36 is required. The form can be downloaded from the Internet site. The fee must accompany each request.

Electronic – A commercial service is available to ongoing requesters and companies who have permissible use and have signed contracts with DPS. Access is by both interactive and batch methods. Call 512-424-2600 to receive a copy of the license agreement. Various record types are available as described above. An online service is also offered to eligible license holders; see *By Person of Record* below.

Bulk – The entire driver license file is available to permissible users. Output on a DVD, including names, addresses, and DOBs of all licenses, is sold for a fee of $2,000. Weekly updates may be purchased for $75.00. Driver history is not included.

By Person of Record – Eligible TX Driver License holders may purchase their own driver record online. The record must be printed when viewed; a copy will not be mailed. Online eligibility is determined by the system at log-in – see the frequently asked questions for information on the requirements. Upon verification of this data, the licensee may select from the six different types of records. Drivers must submit DL or ID number, DOB, last 4 digits of SSN and most currently issued DPS Audit number (appears on the DL card).

Notification/Monitoring Program

At present, Texas does not offer a monitoring system or notification program to employers or insurance companies to track incidents of drivers. However, Texas offers a free annual driving check of school bus drivers. The requester must complete a contract to be approved as a requester.

Crash Reports

Reporting – Crashes involving death, injury, or property damage in excess of $1,000 or more to one person's property must be reported immediately to the local authorities. If the crash is not investigated by the police, a written report (*Form CRB-2, Driver's Crash Report*) must be filed by the involved drivers within ten days with the Texas DOT, Crash Records, PO Box 149349, Austin TX 78714. Download crash report forms at www.txdot.gov.htm.

Record Access – Texas DOT, Crash Records, PO Box 149349, Austin TX 78714; 512-486-5780, fax 512-486-5794; www.txdot.gov/driver/laws/crash-reports.html

The Traffic Operations Division of the Texas Department of Transportation has the responsibility of maintaining crash records.

The fees are $6.00 per record, $8.00 if certified. Either the *CR-3* (copy of the peace officer's crash report) or *CR-2* (copy of driver's crash report) can be ordered. The request forms are available at the web page. Records are available for 5 years to present, first available 10 days after the event. Information needed must include two of the following: the date, specific location including city and county, and full name of one party involved. Normal turnaround time is 15 to 20 days, but can take as long as 4 weeks. Written requests should be mailed to the address above.

Access to Vehicle-Related Records

General Information

Vehicle Titles and Registration Division, Texas Dept of Motor Vehicles, Austin TX 78731, 888-368-4689 or 512-465-3000. www.TxDMV.gov

Records remain in the active files until the record has no activity for 18 months. After 48 months of inactivity records are archived. Title history information is available either on microfilm or digital imaging for 10 years.

The fee for VIN and plate checks is $2.30, $3.30 if certified. A title history is $5.75, if certified then $6.75. Searches by name and/or address are performed with certification of a permitted use.

In-Person & Mail – Research by license plate number or VIN is available at 16 Regional Service Centers. Title histories and registration information are only provided to requesters who certify the information is requested under a permitted use. Use of the request form *VTR-275 Request for Texas Motor Vehicle Information* mentioned earlier is required. Also a current photo identification containing a unique identification number is required. Permissible identification includes:

- Driver's license or state identification certificate issued by a state or territory of the United States
- United States or foreign passport
- United States military identification card
- United States Department of Homeland Security or United States Citizenship and Immigration Services identification document.

Electronic – There are several electronic access systems available.

1) The Technology Support Branch offers a **web inquiry system** for immediate VIN and plate look-ups. This requires a written service agreement, a $200.00 deposit, $23.00 fee per month, and a $ .12 fee per look-up. Searches based on a per name or owner lookup are not available. There are approximately 2,500 companies with nearly 16,000 users on the system, including car dealers, insurance companies, record-retrieval firms, and investigative companies. The use of personal information by approved requesters is strictly limited to only those entities as listed previously above in the *Governing Statutes and Rules* Section.

2) TxDMV provides access to various databases for use by the public to search for **Motor Carrier** records, such as registration, complaints, safety, and DPS records. The following database topics are searchable

at www.TxDMV.gov:

- Motor Carrier Registration (MCR) Database
- Motor Carrier Complaint History

3) TexasSure is a vehicle insurance verification system. This program uses a database to match vehicle registration information (such as the VIN, owner name and address, and make, model and year) and insurance policy information (such as address, insured drivers, insurance company name and policy effective dates). Access is only available to authorized users per DPPA, which include law enforcement, county tax assessor-collectors, the TxDMV, the TX Department of Insurance, the Department of Information Resources and the Office of the Attorney General.

Subscriptions – The TxDMV provides subscriptions to the e-Tag (Buyer's Tag) data and the Dealer Supplemental files. The e-Tag Files contain one record for each e-Tag created on a given day. Each record includes the Create Date (Date Time Stamp the tag is created), Tag Effective Date (For Buyers' Tags this is the Sale Date reported by the Dealer), Tag Type (Buyers Tag indicates a vehicle has been sold), VIN Number (for Buyers' Tags this represents the Vehicle being reported as sold. This field can be blank/null for some tags) and the Dealer License Number (License number issued by Motor Vehicle Division. This field this field can be blank/null for some tags). The resale of this information is not permitted without the State's prior written consent. The fee is $9.00 per day with an annual or yearly subscription minimum of 365 days or $3,285.

The Dealer/Supplemental Files contains dealer weekly sales transactions including dealer "P" number; document number; and VIN. The dealer name and address by dealer "P" number is provided in a second file. The fee is $95.00 per week with a minimum 12 week subscription.

Bulk – The TxDMV Technology Support Branch offers CD and FTP retrieval of VIN and plate numbers (but not by name) to eligible organizations under signed contract. Fees are based on the cost of a "computer run" and on a small fee per record. The entire vehicle database can also be purchased and weekly updates are available. Strict control is in place to assure that requesters must abide by DPPA provisions.

Access to Vessel-Related Records

General Information, Access and Fees

Parks and Wildlife Department (TPWD), 4200 Smith School Rd, Austin 78744, 512-389-4828, in-state at 800-268-2755, www.tpwd.state.tx.us/fishboat/boat/owner.

Boats, boat motors and personal watercraft are titled and registered with the Texas Parks and Wildlife Department: all motorized boats must be registered and titled; all sail boats 14 ft and over must be registered and titled. There are two type of records commonly requested: for **current data** including lien holders there is no fee, a **complete ownership history** is $11.00. Use of *Form PWD 763* is strongly advised. The form, downloadable from web, requires the signature of the requester and attests that the use of the data is for legal purposes. The signature of the

subject is not required. Record checks can be processed by any TPWD Law Enforcement Field Office or at a participating County Tax Assessor-Collector office, as well as the office listed above. If the form is not used, the name and/or registration number is required and request must contain the following phrase in the request: "*The information obtained will be used for a lawful purpose.*" Turnaround time is 2 days, can be longer in the summer months.

Online access to current owner/lienholder names, addresses, and vessel or outboard motor description is provided as long the user provides a valid TX number or serial number. Visit https://apps.tpwd.state.tx.us/tora/jump.jsf.

Driving Record Content and Reciprocity

What's On or Not On the Driving Record

Refer to the 6 types of driving records, described earlier.

- Moving violations appear on a Type 2 driver record for the past 3 years only.
- All moving and non-moving violations appear on a Type 3 driver record for a period of 15 years with the exception of serious offenses.
- All crashes that are investigated by a police officer are recorded on the individual's driver record. The driver record does not indicate fault on the part of the individual but shows the date and location of crash.

In general, the length of time convictions MAY be retained on the driving record is:

Moving Violations	Fifteen years.
DWI, No Insurance, and Drug-Related Violations	Indefinite.
Suspensions	Fifteen years.
SR Judgment	Eleven years.

Data Retention

Records of licenses are purged from the system after 125 years.

Court to Repository

As of January 1, 2013, courts must submit convictions using a secure web-based process to protect Personal Private Information (PPI). Convictions must be reported within seven days and are placed on the record in a timely manner.

Any necessary information omitted from the convictions will have to be obtained from the issuing court. The court information can be found on the ticket/citation/report and www.courts.state.tx.us/oca/. For questions regarding convictions please contact the Conviction Reporting Section at 512-424-2031.

State Reciprocity for Non-CDL Drivers

- Will suspend license of driver for unpaid out-of-state convictions.
- Record of new incoming driver is not shown on MVR.
- Out-of-state convictions are shown on MVR.
- Out-of-state crashes are shown on MVR.
- Convictions of out-of-state drivers are sent to home state.
- Record is forwarded to new state upon surrender of license if requested.

Codes for License Classes, Restrictions, and Endorsements

License Classes– Commercial

Texas began issuing the CDL in September of 1990.

The holder of a valid commercial driver license may drive all vehicles in the class in which he/she is licensed and all lesser classes of vehicles (except for motorcycles and mopeds).

Class A   Any combination of vehicles with a GCWR of 26,001 pounds or more—providing the GVWR of the vehicle or vehicles being towed exceeds 10,000 pounds.

Class B   Any single vehicle with a GVWR of 26,000 pounds or more, any one of those vehicles towing a vehicle that does not exceed 10,000 pounds GVWR, and any vehicle designed to transport twenty-four passengers or more (including the driver).

Class C   Any single vehicle or combination that is not a Class A or B if either vehicle is:

    a   Designed to transport sixteen to twenty-three passengers, (including the driver); or

    b   Used in the transportation of hazardous materials that require the vehicle to be placarded under 49 C.F.R. Part 172, Subpart F.

Note: Persons operating motorcycles which carry hazardous materials requiring a placard must hold a Class M license in conjunction with a Class A, B, or C - CDL license.

License Classes– Non-Commercial

The holder of a valid non-CDL may drive all vehicles in the class in which he/she is licensed and all lesser classes of vehicles except for motorcycles and mopeds. A driver may not operate a CMV with a non-CDL license unless they are specifically exempt from the CDL Act.

Class A   Any vehicle or combination of vehicles with a GCWR of 26,001 pounds or more—provided that the GVWR of the vehicle(s) being towed is in excess of 10,000 pounds.

Class B   A single vehicle with a GVWR of 26,001 pounds or more, and any such vehicle towing either a vehicle with a GVWR that does not exceed 10,000 pounds or a farm trailer with a GVWR that does not exceed 20,000 pounds; and a bus with a seating capacity of twenty-four passengers or more (including the driver).

Class C   A single vehicle or combination of vehicles that is not a Class A or B and a single vehicle with a GVWR of less than 26,001 pounds towing a trailer that does not exceed 10,000 pounds GVWR, or towing a farm trailer with a GVWR that does not exceed 20,000 pounds.

Class M   Motorcycle or moped.

Restrictions

A	With Corrective Lenses		M	CDL Intrastate Commerce Only
B	LOFS Age 21 or Over		N	Ignition Interlock
C	Daytime Only		O	Occupational/essential need DL-no CMV-see court order
D	Not to Exceed 45 mph		Q	LOFS 21 or Over Vehicle above Class B
E	No Expressway Driving		R	LOFS 21 or Over Vehicle above Class C
F	Must Hold Learner License to MM/DD/YY		S	Outside Mirror or Hearing Aid
G	TRC 545.424 applies until MM/DD/YY		T	Automatic Transmission
H	Vehicle Not To Exceed 26,000 lbs GVWR		U	Applicable Prosthetic Devices
I	Motorcycle Not To Exceed 250CC		V	Medical Variance Documentation Required
J	Licensed Motorcycle Operator; Age 21 or Over in Sight		W	Power Steering
K	Moped		X	Vehicle not to exceed Class C
L	Vehicle Without Air-Brakes-CDL only		Y	Valid TX vision or limb waiver required

Z	Applicable Vehicle Devices	P15	Operation Class A Exempt Vehicle Authorized
P1	For Class M TRC454.424 Until MM/DD/YY	P16	If CMV, School Buses (Interstate)
P2	To/From Work/School	P17	If CMV, Government Vehicles (Interstate)
P3	To/From Work	P18	If CMV, Only Transporting Personal Property (Interstate)
P4	To/From School	P19	If CMV, Transporting Corpse/Sick/Injure (Interstate)
P5	To/From Work/School Or A Licensed Driver 21 Years Of Age Or Older (LOFS) Must Be In The Front Seat	P20	If CMV, Privately Transporting Passengers (Interstate)
		P21	If CMV, Fire/Rescue (Interstate)
P6	To/From Work Or A Licensed Driver 21 Years Of Age Or Older (LOFS) Must Be In The Front Seat	P22	If CMV, Intra-City Zone Drivers (Interstate)
		P23	If CMV, Custom Harvesting (Interstate)
P7	To/From School Or A Licensed Driver 21 Years Of Age Or Older (LOFS) Must Be In The Front Seat	P24	If CMV, Transporting Bees/Hives (Interstate)
		P25	If CMV, Use In Oil/Water Well Service/Drill
P8	With Telescopic Lens	P26	If CMV, For Operation Of Mobile Crane
P9	LOFS 21 Or Over, Bus Only	P27	HME Expiration Date MM/DD/YY
P10	LOFS 21 Or Over, School Bus Only	P28	FRSI CDL Valid MM/DD/YY To MM/DD/YY
P11	Bus Not To Exceed 26,000 GVWR	P29	FRSI CDL MM/DD/YY – MM/DD/YY Or Exempt B Vehicles
P12	Passenger Cmvs Restricted To Class C Only	P30	FRSI CDL MM/DD/YY – MM/DD/YY Or Exempt A Vehicles
P13	LOFS 21 Or Over In Vehicle Equipped With Airbrake	P31	Class C Only; No Taxi/Bus/Emergency Vehicle
P14	Operation Class B Exempt Vehicle Authorized	P32	Other

Endorsements

T	Double-/Triple-Trailer	N	Tank Vehicle	S	School Bus
P	Passenger	H	Hazardous Materials	X	Combination N and H

Driver License Status Indicator

The status of a license is indicated without abbreviation on the driving record as one of the following:

- Eligible
- Not Eligible
- Eligible non-CDL-Not Eligible CDL

Conviction Table with ACD and Native Code

"**ALR**" found on a driving record means that there was a blood/breath test refusal or failure.

Native Code	Description	ACD Code
3040	Aggravated Assault With Motor Vehicle	U06
3716	Aid And Abet-Over Gross Wt. 15% Or Over	--
3717	Aid And Abet-Over Gross Wt. Under 15%	--
3241	Alcohol Beverage Code Offense	A31
3814	ALR CDL Disq Refusal ADM	A12
3815	ALR CDL Disq Refusal ADM >.08	A98
3815	ALR CDL Disq Refusal ADM >.08	A98
3816	ALR CMV and/or CDL Disq Failure ADM 0.08 or >-HAZMAT	A98
3820	ALR CMV and/or CDL Disq Failure ADM 0.10 or >	A90
3821	ALR CMV and/or CDL Disq Failure ADM 0.10 or >-MAZMAT	A90
3454	ALR CMV Hzmt .04>-Adm	A94
3453	ALR CMV-.04/> Adm	A94
3819	ALR Disq Boating Failure	A98
3818	ALR Disq Boating Refusal	A12
3452	ALR-CMV Hzmt Ref-Adm	A12
3451	ALR-CMV Refusal-Adm	A12
3652	Alter Or Forge Certificate Of Title	--
3651	Alter Vehicle Identification Number	--
3650	Alter/Change/Mutilate Transfer Papers	--
3329	Amusement Ride Intoxicated-Probated	--
3029	Amusement Ride Intoxication	--
3653	Apply For Registration W/O Motor Number	--
3501	Articles Interfered With Handling Bike	--
3801	Attempt To Purchase Alcohol - Minor	--
3901	Attempt To Purchase Alcohol-Minor-Deferred	--
3337	Bail Jumping - Failure To Appear	--
3507	Bike Rider-Fail To Use Due Care-Passing	--
3506	Bike Rider-Hazardous Traffic Violation	--
3023	Boating While Intoxicated	--
3324	Boating While Intoxicated-Probated	--
3215	Brakes Not On All Wheels When Required	E01
3132	Bus Failed To Stop At RR Crossing	M22
3133	Bus Shifting Gears While Cross RR Tracks	M09
3654	Buyer Accepts Papers Wholly/Part Blank	--
3313	Careless Driving (TX)	M81

Native Code	Description	ACD Code
3120	Carry Passenger Without Helmet (on motorcycle)	F03
3009	Changed Lane When Unsafe	M42
3034	Child Not Secured By Seat Belt	F02
3179	Clearance Lamps Improperly Mounted	E70
3189	Clearance Lights Not Visible Suff Dist	E70
3502	Clung To Vehicle	--
3194	Coasting (TX)	N80
3405	Completed Teen Court Program	--
3035	Consume Alcohol While Driving	A26
3803	Consumption Of Alcohol - Minor	--
3903	Consumption Of Alcohol - Minor-Deferred	--
3245	Controlled Substance Act Offense	A33
3353	Coroner Fail To Report To DPS	--
3041	Criminal Negligent Homicide	U07
3137	Cross Rail Road With Heavy Equip W/O Stop/Safety	M22
3136	Cross Rail Road With Heavy Equip Without Notice	M09
3589	Crossing Fire Hose Without Permission	M56
3028	Crossing Physical Barrier	M02
3081	Cut Across Driveway To Make Turn	N50
3013	Cut Corner Left Turn	N53
3092	Cut In After Passing	M70
3243	Dangerous Drug Act Offense	A33
3655	Dealers License Violation	D27
3213	Defective Brakes (TX)	E31
3229	Defective Exhaust Emission System	--
3162	Defective Head Lamps	E34
3174	Defective Parking Lamps	E34
3234	Defective Safety Glazing Material	--
3170	Defective Stop Lamps	E34
3167	Defective Tail Lamps	E34
3172	Defective Turn Signal Lamps	E34
3233	Defective Windshield Wiper	--
3376	Deposited Glass/Other Debris On Highway	--
3126	Did Not Use Designated Lane Or Direction	M40
3110	Display Altered Drivers License	B41
3142	Display DL/ID Issue To Another	D16
3656	Display Expired License Plates	--
3265	Display Fictitious Driver License	B41
3657	Display Fictitious License Plate	--
3267	Display Suspended Operator License	D16
3354	Display Traffic Sign/Signal W/Advertising	--
3658	Display Unclean License Plates	--
3121	Disregard Police Officer	M08
3581	Disregard Sole Green Turn Signal Arrow	M16
3342	Disregard Warning Signs Or Barricades	M14
3067	Disregarded Flashing Red Signal	M16
3008	Disregarded Flashing Yellow Signal	M18
3069	Disregarded Lane Control Signal	M05
3071	Disregarded No Lane Change Sign	M05
3019	Disregarded No Passing Zone	M76
3582	Disregarded Pedestrian Control Signal	--
3073	Disregarded RR Crossing Gate Or Flagman	M10
3072	Disregarded Signal At Rail Road Crossing	M10
3059	Disregarded Traffic Control Device	M14
3078	Disregarded Turn Marks At Intersection	M05
3065	Disregarded Warning Sign At Construction	M03
3146	Distribute/Sell Deceptive Driver License Or Identification	D10
3196	Drawbar Over 15 Feet	--
3590	Drive Into Block Where Fire Eng Stopped	M40
3321	Driver Opened Door In Moving Traffic	--
3341	Driving Around Barricades	M02
3401	Driving Safety Course	--
3336	Driving Under Influence	A20
3806	Driving Under Influence - Minor	--
3043	Driving Under Influence Of Drugs (TX)	A22
3906	Driving Under Influence-Minor-Deferred	--

Native Code	Description	ACD Code
3335	Driving While Impaired (TX)	A25
3042	Driving While Intoxicated	A21
3047	Driving While Intoxicated - Probated	A21
3246	Driving While Intoxicated 0.16 Or More	A21
3811	Driving While intoxicated W/Child >.016 Probated	A21
3812	Driving While intoxicated W/Child under 15 YOA Probated	A21
3242	Driving While Intoxicated-Under 21	A21
3347	Driving While License Disqualified-CMV	B24
3101	Driving While License Invalid	B20
3089	Drove Center Lane-Not Pass Or Left Turn	M62
3315	Drove On Sidewalk	M58
3129	Drove On Streetcar Tracks Where Prohibited	M55
3088	Drove On Wrong Side--Divided Highway	N71
3585	Drove On Wrong Side-RR Crossing	M09
3127	Drove Onto Controlled Access Hwy Where Prohibited	M46
3066	Drove Through Safety Zone	M12
3087	Drove To Left Of Rotary Traffic Island	N61
3198	Drove Without Lights When Required	E55
3090	Drove Wrong Way In Designated Lane	N60
3016	Drove Wrong Way On One-Way Roadway	N63
3240	Drug Offense	A33
3248	Drug Offense-Bond Forfeiture	A33
3745	Duty Status Not Current	--
3743	Duty Status Not Retained-Previous 7 Days	--
3048	DWI Bond Forfeiture	A21
3403	DWI Education Program Completed	--
3813	DWI Education Program Extended	--
3402	DWI Education Program Required	--
3404	DWI Education Program Waived	--
3247	DWI W/Child Under 15	A21
3148	DWLI - Bond Forfeiture	B20
3355	Employ Unlicensed Commercial Driver	--
3305	Endorsement Violation - CMV	B91
3392	Evade Arrest/Detention	U01
3311	Excessive Acceleration	S97
3260	Expired Commercial Driver License	B51
3259	Expired Driver License	B51
3272	Fail Comply Req Striking Unattended Veh	--
3273	Fail Comply Striking Fixtures On Highway	--
3659	Fail Del Cert Of Title At Time Of Sale	--
3661	Fail Present New Motor Num Rec/Tax Coll	--
3068	Fail Stop Proper Place-Flash Red Signal	M05
3662	Fail Surrender Cert Of Title-Veh Junked	--
3050	Fail To Control Speed	S97
3263	Fail To Display DL	--
3660	Fail To Display License Receipts-CMV	--
3503	Fail To Keep Bike On Right Side Of Road	--
3025	Fail To Maintain Fin. Responsibility-2nd Offense	D36
3331	Fail To Make Written Report Acc To DPS	B61
3371	Fail To Pay Toll	--
3720	Fail To Reduce/Shift Load	--
3356	Fail To Remove Injurious Material-Hwy	--
3286	Fail To Report Accident S/R Law	B61
3264	Fail To Report Change Of Address Or Name	--
3330	Fail To Report Injury Accident At Once	B61
3045	Fail To Stop And Render Aid	B01
3138	Fail To Stop From Alley Driveway Or Bldg	M25
3064	Fail To Stop Proper Place-Not Intersect	M40
3063	Fail To Stop Proper Place-Traffic Light	M05
3060	Fail To Stop-Designated Point-Stop Sign	M15
3061	Fail To Stop-Designated Point-Yield Sign	M19
3332	Fail To Surrender License Plates And/Or DL	--
3082	Fail Yield Right of Way On Left At Obstruction	N01
3114	Fail Yield Right of Way To Pedestrian At Signal Intersect	N08
3116	Fail Yield Right of Way To Pedestrian In Crosswalk--No Signals	N08
3115	Fail Yield Right of Way To Pedestrian On Sidewalk	N08

Native Code	Description	ACD Code
3118	Fail Yield ROW (FYROW) For Blind Or Incapacitated Person	N08
3611	Failed To Conceal Signs On School Bus	E50
3156	Failed To Dim Headlights--Following	E54
3155	Failed To Dim Headlights--Meeting	E54
3070	Failed To Drive In Single Lane	M40
3085	Failed To Give One-Half Of Roadway	M40
3124	Failed To Give Way When Overtaken	N07
3139	Failed To Keep To Right Of Mountain Road	M40
3086	Failed To Pass Met Vehicle To Right	M70
3302	Failed To Report Change Addr Or Name - CDL	--
3097	Failed To Signal Distance Before Turn	N40
3098	Failed To Signal --For Stop	N40
3084	Failed To Signal Lane Change	N43
3096	Failed To Signal Turn	N43
3113	Failed To Sound Horn--Mountain Road	E50
3074	Failed To Stop At Marked Rail Road Crossing	M22
3131	Failed To Stop For Approaching Train	M21
3021	Failed To Stop For School Bus	M75
3095	Failed To Stop For Streetcar or Stop Wrong Direction	N01
3117	Failed To Use Due Care For Pedestrian	M82
3154	Failed To Use Proper Headlight Beam	E55
3052	Failed To Yield At Stop Intersection	N01
3053	Failed To Yield At Yield Intersection	N26
3005	Failed To Yield Right Of Way	N01
3054	Failed To Yield Row At Open Intersection	N25
3287	Failed To Yield Turn Right On Red Signal	N24
3288	Failed To Yield When Changing Lanes	M42
3056	Failed Yield Right of Way Leaving Private Drive, Alley, Etc	N01
3058	Failed Yield Right of Way --On Green Signal	N24
3057	Failed Yield Right of Way To Emergency Vehicle	N04
3055	Failed Yield Right of Way--Turn Left	N31
3338	Failure To Identify	--
3271	False Affidavit--Felony	D02
3744	False Log - Making False Report	--
3145	False Statement DL/ID Application	D02
3304	False Statement On CDL Appl Or Cert	D02
3109	False Statement On Driver License Application	D02
3036	False Swearing DL Application	D02
3663	Farm License Violation	--
3344	Felony-Use Of CMV	U03
3346	Felony-Use Of CMV-Controlled Substance	A50
3266	Fictitious Driver License In Possession	B41
3149	Fictitious License Plate/Registration/Safety Inspection	--
3377	Flash Light/Sign Within 1000 Ft Intersection	--
3122	Fleeing From Police Officer	U01
3027	Flying While Intoxicated	--
3327	Flying While Intoxicated-Probated	--
3591	Following Fire Apparatus	M32
3017	Following Too Closely (TX)	M34
3105	Fraudulent Government Record	--
3381	Graffiti Offense	--
3237	Hazard Material Placard Violation	E04
3163	Head Lamps Glaring, Not Adjusted	E70
3075	Heavy Equipment Disregarded Signal Of Train	M10
3225	Horn Violation	E70
3190	ID Lamps Not Visible Suff Distance	E70
3316	Illegal Backing	N82
3316	Illegal Backing	N82
3612	Illegal Cleats	E70
3283	Illegal Load Extension	--
3020	Illegal Pass On Right	M70
3613	Illegal Use Of Metal Tires	E70
3094	Illegally Passed Streetcar	M70
3003	Impeding Traffic	S96
3277	Improper Flashing Lights	E70
3621	Improper Loading	E70

Native Code	Description	ACD Code
3741	Improper Log (Form Of Log)	--
3317	Improper Lookout	D70
3022	Improper Passing (TX)	M70
3614	Improper Signs On School Bus	E70
3746	Improper Time Base - 24 Hour Period	--
3014	Improper Turn	N51
3099	Improper Turn Or Stop Signal	N40
3152	Improper Use Of Auxiliary Driving Lamps	E70
3150	Improper Use Of Auxiliary Passing Lamps	E70
3175	Improper Use Of Back-Up Lamp	E70
3211	Improper Use Of Fog Lamps	E70
3209	Improper Use Of Spot Lamps	E70
3165	Improperly Directed Lamps	E70
3622	Improperly Secured Tailgate	E70
3624	Inadequate Bed-Sideboard Front/Rear	E70
3220	Inadequate Brake Reservoir	E70
3623	Inadequate Or Defective Bed	E70
3221	Inadequate Reservoir Safeguard	E70
3125	Increased Speed While Being Overtaken	N07
3314	Interfere With Funeral Procession	N05
3130	Interfere With Streetcar	M55
3391	Intoxication Assault	A21
3388	Intoxication Assault Motor Vehicle	A21
3390	Intoxication Manslaughter	U08
3389	Intoxication Manslaughter Motor Vehicle	A21
3046	Involuntary Manslaughter	U08
3519	Jaywalking-Cross Intersection Diagonally	--
3357	Judge/Clerk Fail To Report Convictions	--
3062	Lack Of Caution On Green Arrow Signal	M16
3358	Leave Refuse On Highway	--
3319	Leaving Scene Of Accident	B05
3141	Lend/Permit Use DL/ID	--
3748	Log Not Sent/More Than One Carrier	--
3625	Loose Material Not Removed-Loaded Veh	--
3626	Loose Material Not Remove-Unloaded Veh	--
3079	Made U-Turn On Curve--Or Hill	N56
3800	Minor In Possession	--
3900	Minor In Possession - Deferred	--
3230	Mirror Violation	E01
3804	Misrepresentation Of Age - Minor	--
3904	Misrepresentation Of Age-Minor-Deferred	--
3592	Modified Or Weighted Motor Vehicle	--
3157	More Than 4 Driving Lamps Lighted	E70
3300	More Than One DL In Possession - CMV	D07
3270	More Than One Valid DL In Possession	D07
3206	Motor Vehicle Fuel Theft	--
3409	Motorcycle Safety Course	--
3227	Muffler Violation	--
3044	Murder With Motor Vehicle	U07
3205	MVI Inspection Violation (Motor Vehicle Inspection)	--
3312	Negligent Collision	M80
3216	No Auto Brake Appl On Breakaway Trailers	E01
3275	No Beam Indicator	E01
3177	No Clearance Lamps	E01
3301	No Commercial Driver License	B56
3258	No Commercial Operator License	B51
3103	No Drivers License	B51
3278	No Fire Extinguisher	E01
3224	No Flags On Projecting Load Daytime	E01
3615	No Front And Rear Signs On School Bus	E56
3251	No Front Seat Belts When Required	E01
3161	No Head Lamps - When Not Equipped	E01
3664	No In-Transit License	--
3223	No Lamps Or Reflectors On Load At Night	E05
3274	No License Plate Light	E01
3603	No Light On Animal-Drawn Vehicle	E05

Native Code	Description	ACD Code
3049	No Motor Vehicle Liability Insurance	D36
3749	No Motor Vehicle Liability Insurance	--
3112	No Motorcycle License	B91
3238	No Mudflaps Or Improper Mudflaps	E01
3164	No Multiple-Beam Road Lighting Equipment	E01
3173	No Parking Lamps	E01
3740	No Record Of Duty Status	--
3176	No Reflectors When Required	E01
3032	No Seat Belt - Driver	F04
3033	No Seat Belt - Passenger	F04
3219	No Single Control To Operate All Brakes	E01
3169	No Stop Lamps	E01
3166	No Tail Lamps	E05
3303	No Texas CDL - Domiciled Over 30 Days	B51
3171	No Turn Signal Lamps--When Required	E01
3218	No Two Means Emergency Brake Operation	E01
3604	No Veh Haz Warning Light On Farm Equip	E05
3222	No Warning Signal For Brakes	E01
3197	No White Flag On Tow Chain Or Cable	E01
3232	No Windshield Wiper	E01
3602	No/Def Lamp Or Reflectors-Farm Equip	E34
3504	No/Defective Brake On Bike Or Motor-Bike	--
3505	No/Defective Light-Front Bike/Motor-Bike	--
3214	None Or Defective Parking Brakes	E02
3520	Non-Motorized Veh On Prohibited Roadway	--
3378	Obscure/Interfere Traffic Control Device	--
3231	Obstructed View Through Windshield	D70
3320	Obstructing Traffic	F34
3665	Obtain Unauthorized License Plate	--
3309	Open Container - Driver	--
3323	Open Container - Passenger	A35
3366	Open Door In Lane Of Traffic/Non-Driver	--
3666	Operate Motor Veh With Fictitious Plate	--
3667	Operate Motor Vehicle Without Plates	--
3207	Operate Motorcycle W/O Approved Headgear	F03
3668	Operate Unregistered Motor Vehicle	--
3201	Operate Vehicle More Than One Pass-Minor	D29
3038	Operate Vehicle With Child In Open Bed	F05
3669	Operate W/License For Other Class Veh	B91
3322	Operating Vehicle Where Prohibited	M40
3747	Orig. Log Not Sent To Carrier In 13 Days	--
3723	Over 20,000 Lbs Single Axle-Permit Viol	--
3703	Over 20,000 Single Axle	--
3724	Over 34,000 Lbs Tandem Axle-Permit Viol	--
3706	Over 34,000 Lbs. Tandem Axle	--
3711	Over 44,000lbs. Tandem - Cement	--
3713	Over 44,000lbs. Tandem - Solid Waste	--
3712	Over 64,000lbs. Gross Wt. - Cement	--
3714	Over 64,000lbs. Gross Wt. - Solid Waste	--
3722	Over Allowable Gross Weight-Permit Viol	--
3708	Over Axle Load (Zoned)	--
3707	Over Gross (Zoned)	--
3702	Over Gross Weight	--
3705	Over Permissible Wheel Weight	--
3709	Over Tandem Load (Zoned)	--
3704	Over Tire Size Limitation	--
3715	Over Weight Group Of Axles	--
3710	Over Wheel Load (Zoned)	--
3593	Overcrowded School Bus	--
3280	Overheight	--
3281	Overlength Vehicle	--
3701	Overweight Group Of Axles (B-Bridge Law)	--
3725	Overweight Grp Of Axles-Permit Violation	--
3279	Overwidth	--
3721	Ovrwght Grp Of Axles Bridge Lw Permit Bp	--
3360	Owner Permit Non-Hazard Violation	--

Native Code	Description	ACD Code
3359	Owner/Guardian Permit Hazard Violation	--
3550	Park Along/Opposite Street Excavation	F34
3566	Park Without Locking Ignition/Remove Key	M40
3552	Park/Stand In Front Of Public/Private Drive	M40
3570	Park/Stand W/In 20 Ft Crosswalk At Inters	M40
3571	Park/Stand W/In 20 Ft Fire Sta Driveway	M40
3572	Park/Stand W/In 30 Ft Traffic Cont Device	M40
3569	Park/Stand Within 15 Ft Of Fire Hydrant	M40
3551	Park/Stand/Stop Between Safety Zone-Curb	M40
3557	Park/Stop/Stand On A Railroad	M23
3556	Park/Stop/Stand On A Sidewalk	M40
3558	Park/Stop/Stand Prohibited Area-Hwy Sign	M40
3559	Parked All Night Where Prohibited	--
3256	Parked And Failed To Set Brakes	E51
3560	Parked At Angle-Not Permitted	M40
3284	Parked Double	F34
3561	Parked Facing Traffic	M40
3257	Parked Fail To Stop Engine	E70
3594	Parked In Block Where Fire Eng Stopped	M40
3562	Parked In Prohibited Military Zone	M40
3253	Parked On Crosswalk	M45
3255	Parked On Grade--Failed To Turn Wheels	F66
3563	Parked Overtime	--
3254	Parked Upon A Bridge Or In Tunnel	F34
3208	Parked With Head Lamps Not Dimmed	E54
3565	Parked Within 50 Ft Of Railroad Crossing	M09
3252	Parked Within An Intersection	F34
3199	Parked Without Lights	E70
3553	Parking In Prohibited Area	M40
3567	Parking Meter Violation	--
3026	Parking On Roadway	F34
3568	Parking Unlawfully-Unauthorized	M40
3564	Park-Wheel Over 18 In From Curb/Road Edge	M40
3093	Passed Vehicle Stopped For Pedestrian	M70
3018	Passed--Insufficient Clearance	M77
3361	Passenger Interfer W/Driver View/Control	D70
3160	Passenger/Load Obstruct View Of Driver	D70
3204	Passing Authorized Emergency Vehicle	N04
3517	Ped Cross Between Intersec Where Prohibited	--
3523	Ped Fail Yield Row When Not In Crosswalk	--
3522	Ped Fail Yield Row-Tunnel/Cross Provide	--
3525	Ped On/Adjacent To Hwy-Pub Intoxication	--
3518	Pedestrian Disobeyed Police Officer	--
3583	Pedestrian Disregard Red Signal-Regular Light	M16
3584	Pedestrian Disregarded Yellow Sig-Reg Light	M16
3521	Pedestrian Entering Path Of Vehicle	--
3524	Pedestrian On Prohibited Roadway	--
3516	Pedestrian-Use Left Half Of Crosswalk	--
3363	Permit Livestock To Roam	--
3107	Permit Unlawful Use Of Driver License	--
3364	Permit Unlicensed Minor To Drive-Guardian	--
3365	Permit Unlicensed Oper To Drive/Non-Guardian	--
3379	Place/Maintain Unauthorized Sign/Device	--
3144	Poss More Than 1 Valid DL/ID (TX)	D07
3147	Possess Deceptive DL/Id	B41
3671	Possess/Sell Veh W/Vin Removed/Altered	--
3111	Present Driver License Issued To Another Person	D16
3128	Prohibited Mtr Veh On Control Access Hwy	M40
3805	Public Intoxication - Minor	--
3905	Public Intoxication - Minor - Deferred	--
3282	Pull More Than One Trailer Or Vehicle	--
3802	Purchase Of Alcohol - Minor	--
3902	Purchase Of Alcohol - Minor - Deferred	--
3807	Purchase/Furnish alcohol to Minor	--
3004	Racing	S95
3007	Ran Red Light	M16

Native Code	Description	ACD Code
3006	Ran Stop Sign	M15
3123	Reckless Driving (TX)	M84
3276	Red Light On Front	--
3178	Reflectors Improperly Mounted	E70
3188	Reflectors Not Visible Sufficient Distance	E70
3143	Refuse To Surrender DL/ID	--
3108	Refuse To Surrender Driver License - Suspended	--
3228	Removed Orig Equip Exhaust Emission Syst	E01
3367	Rent Motor Vehicle To Unlicensed Person	--
3407	Repeat Offender Education Program Completed	--
3406	Repeat Offender Education Program Required	--
3408	Repeat Offender Education Program Waiver	--
3742	Required Information Not Shown On Log	--
3306	Restriction Violation - CMV	D29
3340	Ride in Semi Trailer	--
3368	Riding In House Trailer	--
3508	Rode Improperly On Bicycle	--
3509	Rode Improperly On Bicycle-Too Many	--
3510	Rode More Than Two Bicycles Abreast	--
3410	Safety Seat Course	--
3673	Sell Imitation License Plate	--
3674	Sell Unregistered Secondhand Vehicle	--
3146	Sell/Dist Deceptive DL/ID	B41
3672	Shop Fail Keep Repar Rec-Veh Bought/Sold	--
3191	Side Marker Lamps Not Visible Sufficient Dist	E70
3083	Slower Vehicle Failed To Keep To Right	M60
3039	Speed 15 Mph Or More Over Posted Limit (TX)	S15
3051	Speed Under Minimum (TX)	S96
3010	Speeding - Fuel Conservation Roadway	S93
3596	Speeding - School Zone	S93
3001	Speeding (TX)	S93
3586	Speeding 10% Above Posted Limit	S93
3554	Standing In Prohibited Area	M40
3527	Stood On/Near St/Hwy-Solicit Guard Veh	--
3526	Stood Rdwy To Solicit Ride/Contr/Employ	--
3555	Stopping In Prohibited Area	M40
3168	Tail Lamp Improperly Located	E70
3380	Tampering With Barricade	--
3675	Tax Collector Register Veh W/O Number	--
3250	Television Improper Located In Vehicle	E70
3153	Too Many Auxiliary Driving Lamps	--
3151	Too Many Auxiliary Passing Lamps	--
3212	Too Many Fog Lamps	--
3119	Too Many Riders On Motorcycle	F06
3210	Too Many Spot Lamps	--
3217	Tractor Brakes Not Pro Case Breakaway	E01
3369	Train Obstructing Crossing	--
3676	Transfer Vehicle-Papers Blank/Part Blank	--
3629	Transport Loose Materials	--
3076	Turned Across Dividing Section	N50
3011	Turned Left From Wrong Lane	N53
3012	Turned Right From Wrong Lane	N54
3077	Turned Right Too Wide	N54
3080	Turned When Unsafe	N50
3334	Unauthorized Glass Coating Material	--
3670	Unauthorized Motor Number On Motor Veh	--
3226	Unauthorized Siren Or Bell Or Whistle	--
3362	Unauthorized Traffic Device-Local Auth	--
3158	Unauthorized Use Of Siren, Bell, Whistle	--
3140	Unlawful Display/Poss DL/ID	D16
3031	Unrestrained Child-Safety Seat Violation	F02
3239	Unsafe Air Condition Equipment	E70
3002	Unsafe Speed	S94
3024	Unsafe Start from Parked, Stopped, Standing	N83
3628	Use Equipment Not Approved	--
3037	Use Of Illegally Obtained DL/ID	D16

Native Code	Description	ACD Code
3595	Use School Bus Signal-Wrong Purpose	E70
3308	Use Wireless Device While Driving - Bus	--
3307	Use Wireless Device While Driving - Minor	D29
3627	Veh W/O Req Equipment/Unsafe Condition	F66
3627	Veh W/O Req Equipment/Unsafe Condition	F66
3236	Vehicle Emblem Violation	E70
3134	Vehicle Haul Explosive Fail Reduce Speed Rail Road Crossing	M20
3135	Vehicle Haul Explosive Fail Stop At Rail Road Crossing	M22
3106	Violate DL Restriction	D29
3285	Violate DL Restriction On Occ License	D27
3202	Violate Operating Hours-Minor	D29
3349	Violate Out Of Service Order HAZMAT and/or Pass	B19
3333	Violate Promise To Appear	--
3348	Violated Out Of Service s	B27
3244	Volatile Chemical Act Offense	A33
3529	Walk On Roadway Where Sidewalk Provided	--
3528	Walked On Hwy With Traffic-No Sidewalk	--
3159	Warning Devices Not Displayed	--
3235	Warning Devices Not Installed Or Defect	E01
3718	Weight Violation - 2nd Offense	--
3719	Weight Violation - 3rd Offense	--
3370	Wrecker Driver Fail To Remove Glass-Hwy	--
3186	Wrong Color Backup Light	--
3180	Wrong Color Clearance Lights	--
3182	Wrong Color ID Lamp	--
3185	Wrong Color License Plate Light	--
3183	Wrong Color Reflectors	--
3181	Wrong Color Side Marker	--
3187	Wrong Color Signal Device	--
3184	Wrong Color Stoplight	--
3015	Wrong Side Of Road	N70
3091	Wrong Side Road-Not Passing	N70

Point System - Driver Responsibility Program

Effective September 30, 2004, the DPS instituted the Driver Responsibility Program (DRP). Points are issued as part of the program. Below is a description of the major components of the DRP.

Conviction Based Surcharges

Drivers who receive a conviction for an offense listed below pay an annual surcharge for a period of three (3) years from date of conviction. No points are assessed for these offenses. Once the conviction is reported to DPS the following surcharges are assessed:

Driving While Intoxicated, Intoxication Assault, and Intoxication Manslaughter:

If first time offense	$1,000
If second or subsequent offense	$1,500
DWI 0.16 or greater	$2,000
Failure to Maintain Financial Responsibility	$250
Driving While License Invalid	$250
No Driver License	$100

The surcharges are cumulative; example, an initial conviction for DWI will be assessed $1000 annually, and a subsequent DWI conviction within the same three-year period will be assessed an additional $1500 annually.

Point Assessment

Points are issued as part of DRP. Traffic offenses resulting in points are designated by Title 37 Texas Administrative Code Rule. Points are assessed to moving violations classified as Class C misdemeanors and remain on the driver record for a period of three years from conviction date. Points are assigned as follows:

- Two points for a moving violation conviction in Texas or that of another state.
- Three points for a moving violation conviction in Texas or another state that resulted in a crash.

Points will not be assigned for speeding less than 10% over the speed limit or seat belt convictions. DPS assesses a surcharge when the driver accumulates a total of six (6) points or more on their driver record during a three-year period. The driver must pay a $100 surcharge for the first six points and $25 for each additional point.

Annual Assessment

The surcharge assessment will be reviewed annually. If driver record continues to reflect six or more points during the prior three-year period, the surcharge will be assessed. Therefore, drivers may be required to pay for **one or more years if six or more points continue to accumulate on the driver record**. Point surcharges are cumulative and may vary with each annual assessment if convictions are added or removed from the driver record.

An offense committed prior to September 1, 2003 will not apply to the assessment of surcharges.

Failure to pay surcharges results in an indefinite suspension.

Utah

Administration	Important Telephone and Web Contacts

Nannette Rolfe, Director
Driver License Division
PO Box 144501
Salt Lake City 84114-4501
801-965-4437; 888-353-4224
http://publicsafety.utah.gov/dld/
 	
Brad Simpson, Director
Motor Vehicle Division
Tax Commission
801-297-7500
www.dmv.utah.gov/   (Vehicle)
	All Driver Licensing Contacts....................801-965-4437
	Vehicle Information....................................801-297-7780
	State Department of Insurance 801-538-3805
	Highway Patrol...801-965-4518
	
	Email Contacts:
	    http://publicsafety.utah.gov/dld/contact.html
	Utah Statutes:
	    www.le.state.ut.us/documents/code_const.htm

Driver's License Format, Issuance and Renewal

License Classes, Restrictions and Endorsements Appear After the Driving Record Content Section

License Format

Format can be four to ten numbers, but currently only nine digit numbers are being issued. Sometime in the future ten digit numbers will be utilized. Utah reports there is no code or sequential arrangement that determines the characters making the license number.

Document Appearance

The state has four versions of driver license and ID cards. The cards issued prior to August 2001 may still be held by military personnel. All versions are described below. Note the Division also issues a Driving Privilege Card (DPC) to individuals who do not meet the requirements to obtain a DL or ID. The card typically has a one-year expiration. The DPC changed its format and color as of September 1, 2009.

Document Issued Since 01/2010

Security Characteristics: All cards have laser perforation spelling the letters "DLD." Overlapping data can be seen over the image and a smaller "ghost" as well. An optical variable device appears on the card surface, forming an outline of the state with the letters "DPS" inset. A tamper-proof barcode is on the back. With this version the Division also changed the look of the Temporary Permit (paper document) for all driving certificates and ID cards.

Position of Photo: Left side, middle. There is also a smaller "ghost image" photo appearing in the lower right corner.

Minor Age Driver Locator: Card is vertical. The Under 21 designator is over the "ghost" in red; under 19 is in blue. The DOB is shown in red.

CDL Indicator: Commercial Driver printed on card.

Document Issued from 11/2006 to 01/2010

Security Characteristics: All cards have laser perforation spelling the letters "DLD." Overlapping data can be seen over the image and a smaller "ghost" as well. An optical variable device appears on the card surface, forming an outline of the state with the letters "PS" inset. A tamper-proof barcode is on the back.

Position of Photo: Left side, middle. There is also a smaller "ghost image" photo appearing to the right.

Minor Age Driver Locator Card is vertical. The Under 21 designator is over the "ghost" in red; under 19 is in blue. The DOB is shown in red.

CDL Indicator: Commercial Driver printed on card.

Older Document Issued from 08/2001 to 11/2006

Security Characteristics: A two dimensional barcode on the back is tamper proof and contains the bearer's demographic information found on the front. There is a one-dimensional barcode on the back with bearer's address only. Utah county names will be seen when viewed at an angle, transparent when viewed direct.

Position of Photo: Right side, there is also a smaller "ghost image" photo appearing on the left side.

Minor Age Driver Locator "Under 21 Until MM-DD-YY" appears in red. "Under 19 Until MM-DD-YY" appears in blue. After 07/01/03, the card is vertical with the picture in the bottom left corner. Prior to that date the card is horizontal.

CDL Indicator: License class appears in the upper right corner.

Oldest Document Issued Prior to 08/2001 (There may be military personnel who still hold this license.)

Security Characteristics: Laminated card with Utah Seal, color code over DOB, Utah embossing through laminate, color bar shows type of license.

Position of Photo: Right side.

Minor Age Driver Locator: Top left, Minor (under 21) or Adult (over 21).

CDL Indicator: CDL purple color bar at top and classification in code data area.

Issuance

Location of Requirements for Proof of Identity:
http://publicsafety.utah.gov/dld/acceptable_id.html

Age and Document Requirements

Effective January 1, 2010, the requirements to obtain a Utah driving certificate and/or ID card changed. The Utah Driver License Division issues a regular driver license, CDL, or ID card to applicants who are U.S. citizens; legal permanent residents, or U.S. nationals; a Limited-Term driver license, CDL, or ID card to applicants who provide proof of legal/lawful presence; and a Driving Privilege card to applicants who do not qualify for a regular or limited-term certificate.

A first time regular license holder one must be at least 16 years old, have held a Utah Learner Permit for 6 months if under 18 years old, furnish proof of a prior driver license or proof of driver education training, proof of resident address, proof of legal presence, and present one form of positive identification and acceptable evidence of SSN. An applicant who is at least 15 years of age may apply for a Learner Permit. If an applicant is 19 years old or older and has not completed an approved driver education course, a Learner's Permit must be held three months before applying for a regular Class D license.

About the Limited-Term Documents

The Limited-Term card is issued to an individual who is not a U.S Citizen, U.S. National, or Permanent Resident Alien but has documentation showing they are in the country legally. This certificate will be valid for their approved length of stay in the country or five years, whichever is shorter or one year if no ending date exists. The Division also changed the look of the Temporary Permit (paper document) for all driving certificates and ID cards.

Effective July 1, 2011 an applicant whose legal/lawful status is **Conditional Permanent Resident Alien** is only eligible for a Limited-Term certificate.

Residency

Utah law does not have a grace period in which to change an out-of-state driver license to a Utah license. It simply requires a resident to have a valid Utah driver license when driving in Utah. A person is considered a Utah resident if the person establishes a domicile, remains longer than six months, engages in other than seasonal employment, or obtains Utah privileges not ordinarily afforded nonresidents, such as obtaining a driver license, vehicle registration, or placing children in a Utah school etc.

Renewal

Birth day of fifth year and can be renewed within 6 months of expiration date. Driver keeps same number when renewing. With the new issuance laws in effect, renewal must be in-person. Online renewal will be available for eligible applicants in 2013. If a CDL driver moves or changes names at a time other than renewal, the driver is required to apply for a duplicate license within 30 days of the change. A military personnel or dependant license for individuals stationed outside of the state does not expire until 90 days after discharge or termination of orders.

Since July 1, 2011, all Driving Privilege Card (DPC) holders must submit a completed applicant fingerprint card and photograph upon renewal, duplicate or original application to the Driver License Division. Upon the renewal, duplicate or original application of the Driving Privilege Card, the Driver License Division will collect and verify the fingerprint card, photograph, and identity documents, social security card (SSN) or Individual Tax Identification Number (ITIN), proof of Utah residency, appropriate licensing fees and a $25.00 fingerprint process and storage fee. Once approved, submission of the fingerprint card and photograph will only be required one time.

Elderly-Related Restrictions

None are reported.

Vehicle Insurance, Title and Registration Facts

Registration Renewal

Renewal, which is annual, may be done online at https://secure.utah.gov/rex/index.html. The program, called Renewal Express, is available to people who received a mailed renewal notice which contains a designated PIN. To renew, the address and name submitted must match the current registration data on file. Vehicles currently registered can renew online within one month of the registration expiration, and no more than six months after the registration has expired. Campers may be renewed online.

New Residents

For vehicle registration purposes, a resident is anyone who engages in a trade, profession, occupation or gainful employment in Utah for more than sixty days.

Inspections and Emissions Testing

Vehicles with model years four, eight, and ten years old require a safety inspection. Vehicles with model years ten years old and older must pass safety inspections every year.

All vehicles registered in Davis, Salt Lake, Utah and Weber counties with model years less than six years old are required to have an emission test once every two years.. Vehicles with model years six years old and older (to 1967) must have an emission test every year. Vehicles less than two years old, based upon the model year, or model years 1967 and older are exempt from the requirement to obtain an emissions inspection.

See http://dmv.utah.gov/registerinspections.html.

Passenger Plate Facts

There are two plates with two decals (MO) (YR) on rear plate. Plates are no longer issued with codes indicating the county where issued. But older plates (issued until 05/02) had two alpha characters designating county of registration displayed on left of validation block. When a vehicle is sold the plates remain with the seller.

Insurance and Financial Responsibility

Utah has compulsory liability and no-fault insurance laws. Minimum liability limits are $25,000/65,000/15,000. Proof must be shown at the request of a police officer, after a reportable accident, and after certain violations. SR-22 forms are used.

Withdrawal Sanctions, and Alcohol and Drug Testing

Alcohol and Chemical Testing Limits

Utah's illegal intoxication level is .08 % and above for adults, .04 for drivers of CMVs, and a zero tolerance level if the driver is under 21. Breath, blood, oral fluids, and urine testing are authorized; the type of testing used is determined by the arresting officer. Utah has both an implied-consent violation and a provision for an administrative suspension.

Suspensions and Revocations

See the Appendix for a list of the federally mandated disqualifications for offenses occurring in a CMV per MCSIA.

DUI Sanctions if Under 21

Drivers under the age of 21 for Per Se arrests under UCA 53-3-223 or for Not-a-Drop arrests under UCA 53-3-231 face administrative actions not based on a criminal conviction of DUI, but on the arrest report itself. The individual may petition the court for a shortening of the suspension period for a first offense for a violation of 41-6a-502 (DUI) or 41-6a-517 (metabolite) if certain conditions have been met.

If driver is under the age of 19 at the time of arrest, the following are first offense suspension periods:

Not-a-Drop arrest...One-year suspension effective 30 days from arrest date.

Per Se arrest ....One-year suspension effective 30 days from arrest date.

If a driver is age 19 or 20 at the time of arrest, the following suspension periods will be imposed for a first offense:

Not-a-Drop arrest...Six-month suspension effective 30 days from arrest date.

Per-Se arrest..Six-month suspension effective 30 days from arrest date.

Note: Changes were made to suspension periods that have already been imposed for an arrest that occurred on or after July 1, 2009 to apply the suspension periods listed above retroactively. For arrests that occur on or after July 1, 2011, if a driver is under age 21 at the time of arrest and refuses to submit to a chemical test, the license will be revoked for a period of 2 years for a first offense. Previously the time period was 18 months.

Other Suspension and Revocation Periods:

Controlled Substance/Metabolite

First Offense .... 120-day Suspension or until age 21.

Second or Subsequent Offense .... Two-year Suspension or until age 21.

Controlled Substance or Paraphernalia .... Six-month Suspension.

Discharging (or Allowing) Firearm or Explosive Device or Chemical from Vehicle .... One to five-year Revocation.

DUI

First Offense .... 120-day Suspension.

Second or Subsequent Offenses .... Two-year Revocation.

Eluding a Police Officer .... One-year Revocation.

False Application .... Three-month to one-year Suspension.

Habitually-Negligent Driver .... One-year Suspension.

Leaving Scene of Accident Involving Personal Injury or Death .... One-year Revocation.

Manslaughter or Negligent Homicide .... One-year Revocation.

Per Se (DUI Arrest)

First Offense .... 120-day Suspension.

Second Offense .... Two-year Suspension.

Operating (or allowing) motor vehicle Without Insurance or FR .... Indefinite Suspension.

Point Accumulation .... One-month to one-year Denial or Suspension.

Reckless Driving, Second Offense in One Year .... One-year Revocation.

Refusal to Submit to Chemical Test

First Offense .... Eighteen-month Revocation.

Second or Subsequent Offense .... Thirty six-month Revocation.

Speed Contest or Exhibition on Highway

First Offense .... Sixty-day Suspension.

Second or Subsequent Offense .... Ninety-day Suspension.

Unlawful Use of a Driver's License .... Three-month to One-year Suspension.

Use of a Motor Vehicle to Commit a Felony .... One-year Revocation.

Other Sanctions of Note

Drivers may be designated "Alcohol Restricted." This means they must not drive with any alcohol in their system. Under this designation, the electronic driver history is updated to show the Alcohol Restricted Driver status, and the driver is notified by mail of the restriction. Law enforcement has access to the Alcohol Restricted Driver status and will issue a citation when they make contact with a driver who has alcohol in their system and is Alcohol Restricted. If a driver is convicted for a violation of the Alcohol Restricted Driver law, their driving privilege will be revoked for a period of one year from the conviction date. See www.publicsafety.utah.gov/dld/alcohol_restricted_driver.html.

- When individuals age 21 or older have been convicted of a first DUI, they are restricted to driving a vehicle that has an Ignition Interlock Device installed for a period of 18 months from the conviction date. If the individual is under age 21, they are restricted for a period of 3 years from the conviction date.
- When individuals have been convicted of a second or subsequent DUI or Alcohol Related Reckless Driving, or have been revoked for refusal to submit to a chemical test after being arrested for DUI, they are restricted to driving a vehicle that has an Ignition Interlock Device installed for a period of three years from the date of conviction or effective date of the revocation.
- A Felony DUI carries a 6-year Ignition Interlock Device restriction, and Automobile Homicide carries a ten-year Ignition Interlock Device restriction.

- If a restricted individual operates a vehicle without an Ignition Interlock Device installed, the vehicle may be impounded. In addition, the driver may be cited for violating the "IRD" law. A conviction for violating the IRD law will result in an additional 3-year Ignition Interlock Device restriction from the date of conviction and a one-year driver license revocation.
- A vehicle shall be impounded if the driver of the vehicle is suspended, revoked, or denied for refusal to submit to a chemical test, DUI, automobile homicide, driving with a metabolite of a drug in the body, impaired driving, or an alcohol restricted driver violation.
- Although effective July 2005, Utah no longer issues a "no alcohol conditional license," some of these licenses are still in effect and this license is described herein. A "no alcohol conditional license" dictates one must not drive with any alcohol in their system. The constraint period is in effect for two years from the issue date of the conditional licenses for a first "qualifying conviction," and ten years from the issue date of the conditional license for a second or subsequent "qualifying conviction." The "no alcohol" conditional license information is encoded on the new driver license certificate. Insurance companies and employers will not have access to this information, but it will be available to law enforcement, courts and other legitimate requesters.

Reinstatement Requirements

Suspension .... $30.00 fee ($65.00 if alcohol or drug-related); SR-22 for three years for financial responsibility actions; $170.00 administrative fee for alcohol/drug actions. Motor vehicle registration reinstatement fee for failure to have insurance or financial responsibility is $100.00.

Revocation .... $30.00 fee ($65.00 if alcohol or drug-related); must apply for new license; $170.00 administrative fee for alcohol/drug actions.

Denial .... $30.00 fee ($65.00 if alcohol or drug-related)

CDL Disqualification .... $30.00 fee ($65.00 if alcohol or drug-related); $170.00 administrative fee for alcohol/drug actions.

Record Access: Laws, Rules, and Forms

Note:　This Section Reviews Both Driver and Vehicle Records.

Governing Statutes and Rules

State Statutes:
　www.le.state.ut.us/documents/code_const.htm

State Administrative Codes:
　www.rules.utah.gov/publicat/code.htm#toc

Driving Records: Utah does not specifically enumerate the federal exceptions. However, the Administrative Code states, "MVRs shall only be released to qualified requesters in accordance with the DPPA" UT ADC R708-36. See www.rules.utah.gov/publicat/code/r708/r708-036.htm.

Disclosure of Division records other than driving records is controlled by the Utah Government Records Access and Management Act (GRAMA) Title 63G, Chapter 2, Administrative Rules. Release of driving records is governed by DPPA, and by state statutes UCA 53-3-104 and 53-3-109.

Vehicle Records: Access information in the motor vehicle database is controlled by the Utah Government Records and Management Act (GRAMA) and UCA 41-1a-116(4), 63G-2-201. Some information, such as Social Security Numbers or medical data, is considered private or controlled.

As of June 1, 2000, all motor vehicle records are classified as "protected." Under this designation, a motor vehicle record may only be released to the subject of the record, the subject's legal representative, law enforcement and others designated in the law.

Request and Consent Forms

Driving Records: All requests must be in writing; signature of the requester and the reason for the request must be submitted using one of the following forms:

- *Form DLD60* for a request made by the driver of a record;
- *Form DLD60* **and** *DLD266* for a Certified Driving Record, provided the request is made by the driver of a record;
- *Form DLD60A* for agencies with a permissible use under DPPA;
- *Form DLD60B* for requests made by someone other than the driver of record or to obtain a CDL MVR.

All of the forms may be downloaded at http://publicsafety.utah.gov/dld/drivingrecord12.html, If for a non-permissible use, the subject's notarized signature must be provided.

Vehicle Records: *Form TC-895 Application to Request a Motor Vehicle Account* is required to establish an ongoing account to obtain vehicle records. This form is used by qualified requestors to subscribe to the online service described below. For single or occasional use requesters wishing to purchase protected motor vehicle information, a completed *Release of Protected Motor Vehicle Information Form TC-890* must be presented to the DMV. This form requires the requester's signature and the reason for the request. If requested by a private investigator, a copy of the investigators license must also be submitted with the form. A notary is not required. Both forms are found at http://tax.utah.gov/forms.

Vendor and Third Party Access Policy

Driving Records: Permissible users may process record requests for another vendor who is selling the data to a permissible end-user. However, all parties must be in compliance with DPPA and state law. The responsibility for this compliance rests with the original vendor accessing the records from the Division.

Permissible users may purchase in bulk or database format, but are restricted to only provide data to an end-user with a permissible purpose. Vendors are restricted from selling to any other vendor who is selling the data to a permissible end user, meaning no vendor chains are permitted.

Vehicle Records: Permissible use requesters may purchase in bulk or database format, but are restricted to only provide data to an end-user with a permissible purpose. Vendors are restricted from selling to any other vendor who is selling the data to a permissible end-user, meaning no vendor chains are permitted.

Records Ordered For Non-permissible Uses

Without consent, no records are released (even without personal information) to requesters without a permissible use.

Access to Driver-Related Records

Driving Records

General Information and Fees

Driver License Division, 4501 South 2700 West, Salt Lake City UT 84129 (PO Box 144501, Zip 84114-4501), 801-965-4437, or toll free at 888-353-4224.

The Division hours are Monday through Friday from 8 a.m. to 5 p.m. Two field offices and the call center are open 7 a.m. to 6 p.m. Monday through Friday. The Division has several rural traveling locations with varied work days and hours.

The current fee is $6.00, $9.00 if online. A certified record is $10.75 for the first 15 pages. The state charges for "no record found" reports. Address questions regarding MVRS to nmitchell@utah.gov.

In-Person – Obtain records Monday through Friday 8 a.m. to 5 p.m. Generally up to ten requests will be processed while you wait. See http://publicsafety.utah.gov/dld/offices/admin_offices.html for a list of field offices where one can obtain driving records. The driver's full name, DOB and/or license number are needed when ordering.

Mail – Requests mailed to the state are processed within 1 week, and 2 weeks or more if for a certified record. The driver's full name, DOB and/or license number are needed when ordering. The fee must accompany each request. Use the request forms mentioned in the Request and Consent Forms section.

Electronic – There are three online records available.

1. Driving records are available online from Utah.gov at www.utah.gov/registration/. The service is available 24 hours a day, 7 days a week. This is an interactive system; results can be returned immediately. An annual subscription fee of $75 per year is required, plus $9.00 per record accessed. Eligible organizations may subscribe by visiting www.utah.gov/registration or call 801-983-0275.

2. Address Verification Service is for insurance organizations to check for uninsured drivers residing at the same address as current policyholders. Approval by the Department of Public Safety/Driver License Division is required. The fee is $5.00 per search.

3. DL Validate Check – Subscribers may also take advantage of a driver validation service. Users may validate the information found on driver license, ID cards and driving privilege cards. The fee is $1.50 per verification. Access is by the DL number.

Bulk – Utah will not sell its driver license file database, in part or whole, to commercial vendors.

By Person of Record – Utah drivers may obtain their driving record by mail or walk-in as described above, and online at https://secure.utah.gov/mvr-personal/public/index.html. The online fee is $9.00. Use of a credit card is required AND the billing address of the credit card must match the address the Division has on file for the driver. Only the driver may order his or her own record.

Notification/Monitoring Program

Through the online service provider Utah.gov, a notification program is offered that enables insurance companies and insurance support firms to track activity of submitted drivers. **By statute, the program is not**

available to employers. The subscriber submits a monthly list of drivers. If there has been activity in the preceding calendar month, a driving record is automatically issued. If there was no activity, the subscriber is also notified. The cost for the service is $.12 per driver and the driving record fee if issued. Eligible organizations may subscribe by visiting www.utah.gov/registration.

Accident Reports

Reporting – Accidents involving death, injury, or damage $1,500 or more must be reported to the local authorities. Reports are filed by the investigative agency.

Record Access – Copies of accident reports are protected and may only be obtained by a person involved in the accident, a person suffering loss or injury in the accident, an agent, parent or legal guardian of a person involved in the accident or suffering loss, government agencies using the report for official business, and private investigators. Members of the press or broadcast media are limited to the information they receive from reports.

The basic reports may be obtained from the Driver License Division, PO Box 144501, Salt Lake City 84114-4501, 801-965-4428. Note that this office is open Monday thru through Friday 8:00 a.m. to 5 p.m. Records are available for 10 years to present. Records from 2002 to present are available on an optical imaging system. The fee is $5.00 per report. Requests must be in writing; use of *Form DI-8* is recommended. Also, include the date of the incident. Turnaround time depends on staffing. It can take 2 weeks or more before new incidents are available.

Eligible requesters may order the report electronically and receive it instantly at https://secure.utah.gov/accidentreport/index.html. The fee is $7.50.

Also, the Utah Highway Patrol will sell the complete accident file to qualified parties. The fee is $5.00 for 1 to 10 pages and $25.00 for 11 to 50 pages. Photos can be purchased on a CD for $25.00. Visit http://publicsafety.utah.gov/highwaypatrol/index.html.

Access to Vehicle-Related Records

General Information and Fees

State Tax Commission, 210 North 1950 West, Salt Lake City, UT 84134, 801-297-3507. All state DMV offices are open Monday through Friday, from 8 am to 5 pm.

Records are available for past 15 years. The current fee for non-online VIN and registration information is $3.00, $4.00 if faxed, and $6.50 if the record must be searched on microfilm. A written request, stating the purpose, must be submitted with bulk requests.

The procedures described herein also are for obtaining ownership and lien records for watercraft, snowmobiles, and off-highway vehicles. Snowmobiles and off-highway vehicles must be titled if 1988 or newer. The state will not release medical records, SSNs, or insurance information. The required request forms described in an earlier section are found at http://tax.utah.gov/forms.

In-Person, Mail – See note above about days and hours. There is a limit to the number of across-the-counter records processed per requester per day. Credit cards are accepted for in person search requests. Utah also has a program for dealerships and financial institutions requesting lien-holder information. *Form TC-890* is needed for occasional requesters and requests must be accompanied by check. Walk-in requesters must shown proper identification.

Phone, Fax – Pre-approved requesters may order in this manner. The same request fees apply if ordered by phone or fax, but there is an additional $1.00 fee to fax back a record.

Electronic – Motor vehicle information is available by subscription to qualified requestors via the online "Title, Lien and Registration Information Service" (TLRIS) 24/7. A subscription to TLRIS is $75.00 per year, plus $2.00 per record accessed. In addition, one must be an overall subscriber to utah.gov, which also has a $75.00 annual fee. A user can search by a license plate number, VIN, or name to retrieve a record online using TLRIS. Eligible organizations will find subscription details at http://utah.gov/registration/.

Bulk – Tax Technology Mgmt 4th, Data Processing, 210 North 1950 West, Salt Lake City 84134, 801-297-2700. Only users with permissible purposes are permitted to purchase in bulk format. Each request is looked at on an individual basis. For more information, contact the agency listed above.

Access to Vessel-Related Records

General Information, Access and Fees

Record request procedures are as outlined above. All watercraft (including canoes and personal watercrafts) powered by a motor or a sail operated in Utah waters must be registered, but they are only titled if they are 1985 and newer. All outboard motors over 25 HP and built in 1985 or newer must be titled. An excellent description on registering and titling watercraft is found at www.dmv.utah.gov/vehicles-by-type/boats-and-watercraft. SSNs, insurance information and medical information are not released.

Driving Record Content and Reciprocity

What's On or Not On the Driving Record

- Drivers' addresses, SSNs, and medical records are not provided to the general public.
- The length of time convictions appear on the public record is three years for moving violations and withdrawals if not alcohol or drug related. All alcohol or drug related convictions and suspension, and mandatory conviction if for a CMV, are shown for ten years.
- The length of time convictions appear on a commercial (CDL) record is not limited. The record contains all convictions as well as pleas held in abeyance, suspensions, revocations, disqualifications, and out of state incidents.
- However, unless CDL license holder or in a CMV, interstate speeding violations less than 11 mph over the posted speed limit are only available with the written consent of the driver.
- Accidents are reported on the driving record only if convicted for a moving violation.
- Courts can require driver school attendance in lieu of conviction.

Data Retention

Convictions are purged from the system by using batch processing and following the above timetable. Purging of CDL driving records follow the federal standards as shown in the Appendix.

Court to Repository

Courts submit conviction information in a variety of methods; via file transfers, and paper that must be entered manually. It takes from two weeks to six months for violations to be added to the state database. Information for CDLIS must be entered within 10 days, otherwise there is no timeline mandate when data must be entered on the driving record.

State Reciprocity for Non-CDL Drivers

- Will suspend license of driver for unpaid out-of-state convictions if NRVC member.
- Record of new incoming driver is shown on MVR.
- Out-of-state convictions are shown on MVR.

- Out-of-state accidents are shown on MVR if in accordance with a conviction.
- Convictions of out-of-state drivers are sent to home state.
- Record is forwarded to new state upon surrender of license, if requested.

License Classes, Restrictions, and Endorsements

License Classes

Utah began issuing the CDL in February of 1990

Class	Age	Description
Class A	21	Over 26,000 pounds combination vehicle and over 10,000 pounds towed unit
	18-21	Intrastate Only Restriction
Class B	21	Over 26,000 pounds single or combination vehicle, under 10,001 towed unit.
	18-21	Intrastate Only Restriction
Class C		Under 26,001 pounds, if used to transport:
	21	1. Sixteen or more occupants;
	21	2. Placarded amounts of hazardous material
	21	Under 10,001 pounds towed unit "S" endorsement available
	Note:	A CDL Class C is required if any one of the above vehicles is used to haul hazardous materials or when carrying sixteen or more occupants. Classes A, B, and C can be issued to drivers that do not meet federal medical standards, but meet Utah medical standards. Such drivers are approved for intrastate only.
Class D	16	Regular Operator
Class M*	16	Motorcycle Only (No longer issued - see below)

*Note: On July 1, 2008, all class M licenses were repealed and replaced with endorsements. A regular operator license (Class D) or CDL (Class A, B, or C) must be obtained before a motorcycle endorsement (M) may be added to the license. All new motorcycle riders are restricted to riding a motorcycle based on the cc size of the motorcycle upon which the rider is tested with 3 restrictions used. If an operator is tested on a motorcycle 650 cc or greater, no restriction is placed on the license and the operator is permitted to ride any size motorcycle.

Restrictions

A	No Restrictions	J	Restricted Other	1	Interlock Device
B	Corrective Lenses	K	CDL Intrastate Only	2	249 cc or less Motorcycle
C	Mechanical Aid	L	Vehicle Without Air-Brakes	3	649 cc or less Motorcycle
D	Prosthetic Aid	M	Except Class A Bus	4	Street-legal ATV
E	Automatic Transmission	N	Except Class A and Class B Bus	5	90 cc or less Motorcycle
F	Outside Mirror	U	Three-Wheel Motorcycle	6	Speed posted mph or less
G	Limited to Daytime Only	V	Medical Variance		

Endorsements

H	21	Hazardous Materials	P	21	Passengers	X	21	Tank and Hazardous Material
M	16	Motorcycle	S	21	School Bus	Z	21	Taxicab
N	18	Tank Vehicles - Intrastate Only if Under 21	T	18	Double-/Triple-Trailers Intrastate Only if Under 21	-		

Conviction Table with ACD Code, Statute, and Points

(A second table showing Withdrawals Actions follows.)

Abbreviations

DQNP	= Disqualified; No Points	NP	= No Points This Violation	RNP	= Revoked; No Points
DISQ	= Disqualified	SNP	= Suspended; No Points	DNP	= Denied; No Points

About Points: Except for speeding tickets, points may vary plus or minus 10% depending upon the recommendation of the court.
About Codes: This Code column generally indicates the ACD Code translation of the violation. However, know that the ACD Code is not supplied on the driving record.

This table is ordered by the Violation Description column.

Statute	Code	Violation Description	Pts/Action
53-3-221(13)(b)	DMV	Admin action based on notification from DMV for revoked registration	SNP
53-3-221(6)	ORS	Admin action based on recovery services recommendation, suspension for nonpayment of child support – (on record 10 years or until cleared)	SNP
53-3-223	MEA	Admin action for driving with a metabolite of a drug in the system	SNP
53-3-418(1)(a)	A94	Administrative per se for .04 BAC (CDL only)	DQNP
53-3-223	A98	Administrative per se for .08 BAC	S/R
DLD Admin Action	A90	Administrative per se for .10 BAC (out of state only)	S/R/SDISQ
53-3-232	ACL	Alcohol conditional license – (on record 10 years)	RNP
41-6a-512	M8A	Alcohol related reckless driving	80

Statute	Code	Violation Description	Pts/Action
41-6a-530	ARD	Alcohol Restricted Driver	R/NP
76-5-207.5	TXH	Auto homicide while texting	R/NP
382.201	A04	BAC at or over .04	DQNP
41-6a-1715	M81	Careless driving (suspend if court ordered)	50 or SNP
383.51(b)(8)	U10	Causing a fatality through the negligent operation of a CMV	DISQ
41-6a-1805(1)(a)	F02	Child/youth restraint not used properly/required	NP
58-37-8(2)(g)	ADI	Controlled substance/caused bodily injury or death	SNP
76-5-303(4)	CIA	Custodial Interference Class A	SNP
76-5-303(3)	CIB	Custodial Interference Class B	SNP
76-5-303(5)	CIF	Custodial Interference Felony	SNP
41-6a-1636	E37	Defective tires	NP
32B-4-410	AAM	Driver under 21 in a bar or tavern – court ordered suspension on record until cleared unless extended	S/NP
41-6a-1705(2)	D70	Drivers view obstructed	NP
53-3-404	B57	Driving a CMV without a CDL in the driver's possession	DQNP
53-3-404(3)(b)	B24	Driving CMV while disqualified/CMV	DQNP
53-3-227(1)	B25	Driving on revocation	RNP
41-6a-712	N71	Driving on the wrong side of divided highway	60
41-6a-701	M40	Driving on wrong side	60
41-61-713	VOG	Driving over gore area	50
41-6a-1302	E55	Driving school bus without lights turned on	40
41-6a-502	A08	Driving under the influence alcohol and drugs	S/R/DQ NP
Out of State	A23	Driving under the influence of alcohol and drugs (out of state only)	S/R NP
41-6a-517	MEC	Driving under the influence of drugs metabolite (MEC)	S/R NP
City/county	A24	Driving under the influence of medication not intended to intoxicate	S/R NP
Out of State	A10	Driving under the influence w/BAC at/over.10 (out of state only)	S/R NP
41-6a-502(1)(b)	A08	Driving under the influence w/impaired	S/R NP
53-3-227(1)	B23	Driving while denied	DNP
City/county	D74	Driving while fatigued	40
Out of State	B22	Driving while license canceled/CMV	DQNP
53-3-404	B27	Driving while out of service order is in effect - No HAZMAT - No 16 passenger	DQNP
53-3-404	B19	Driving while out of service order is in effect, Hazmat or 16+ passengers	DQNP
53-3-227(1)	B26	Driving while suspended	SNP
41-6a-517	MEC	Driving with a metabolite of a drug in	S/R NP
41-6a-1639(2)(a)	E04	Driving without hazmat placards (hazmat flag req)	NP
41-6a-1639(2)(b)	E03	Driving without hazmat safety equipment (Hazmat flag req)	NP
41-6a-1603	E05	Driving without lights turned on	40
41-6a-709(2)	N60	Driving wrong way	60
41-6a-709(3)	N61	Driving wrong way at rotary intersection	60
41-6a-709	N63	Driving wrong way on one way street or road	60
41-6a-1601	E01	Equipment violation	NP
41-6a-1205(1)(d)(i)	M23	Fail to obey R/R space vehicle too large - CMV	50/DISQ
41-6a-1205(1)	M20	Fail to slow at R/RX - CMV not always req to stop	50/DISQ
41-6a-1205(2)(a)	M22	Fail to stop at R/RX - CMV always required to stop	50/DISQ
41-6a-1205(1)(b)	M21	Fail to stop at R/RX- CMV not always req to stop	50/DISQ
41-6a-1203	M10	Fail to stop R/R traffic control device or officer	50
41-6a-1302(5)	E55	Fail to use headlights as required	NP
41-6a-1613	E55	Fail to use lights as required	40
41-12a-411	B63	Failed to file future proof of financial response.	SNP
53-3-304	B65	Failed to file medical certification/send withdrawal only	NP
53-3-202	B51	Failed to show non-commercial driver license	NP
53-3-221(3)(a)	D56	Failure to answer a citation, pay fine, penalties	SNP
53-3-221-(2)(a)	D45	Failure to appear for trial/court appear.	SNP
53-3-231(11)	D44	Failure to appear or complete required rehab	D/NP
41-6a-702	M41	Failure to keep in proper lane	40
41-6a-711(b)	M34	Failure to leave sufficient distance for overtaking by other vehicles	60
78B-6-315	D51	Failure to make payment of child support/court ordered suspension	SNP
53-3-221(2)	FPJ	Failure to make required payment of fine & costs/JUV	D/SNP
72-6-114(2)	M02	Failure to obey barrier	50
41-6a-209(1)(c)	M04	Failure to obey flagger	50
41-6a-308	M05	Failure to obey lane markings or signal	50
41-6a-209(1)(a)	M08	Failure to obey police or peace officer	50
41-6a-1205	M22	Failure to obey R/R crossing restrictions	50
41-6a-209(1)(d)	M13	Failure to obey school crossing guard	60
41-6a-305	M14	Failure to obey sign or traffic control device	50
41-6a-304	M14	Failure to obey sign or traffic control device	50

Statute	Code	Violation Description	Pts/Action
41-6a-307	M18	Failure to obey warning light or flasher	50
41-6a-1202	M12	Failure to observe safety zone	50
41-12a-501	D38	Failure to post security or obtain release	SNP
53-3-202	B51	Failure to show driver license	NP
41-6a-804	N40	Failure to signal	50
41-6a-907	M25	Failure to stop when entering roadway from a private driveway/alley	6 50
41-6a-906	M25	Failure to stop/unsigned intersection/entering roadway from driveway/alley	50
41-6a-1613(1)(a)	E54	Failure to use headlight dimmer as required	40
41-6a-804	N40	Failure to use or improper signal	50
41-6a-804(1)	N40	Failure to use or improper signal	50
41-6a-804(1)(a)(ii)	N40	Failure to use or improper signal	50
41-6a-305(6)(b)	N01	Failure to yield right of way	60
41-6a-902	N23	Failure to yield right of way at traffic sign	60
41-6a-904(1)(a)	N04	Failure to yield to emergency vehicle	60 or SNP
41-1a-1314	U03	Felony with a vehicle (joy riding)	REV/DIS
41-6a-210	U01	Fleeing or evading police or roadblock	RNP
41-6a-711(1)	M34	Following too closely	60/DISQ
41-6a-711(1)(b)	M34	Following too closely	60/DISQ
41-6a-304(1)	M14	FTO instruction of official traffic control device	50
41-6a-1008	N20	FTY at crosswalk	60
41-6a-902(2)(b)	N01	FTY right of way	60
41-6a-901	N01	FTY right of way	60
41-6a-902(2)(a)	N22	FTY right of way at stop sign	60
41-6a-902(3)	N26	FTY right of way at yield sign	60
41-6a-1007	N08	FTY right of way to blind pedestrian	60
41-6a-904(1)(a)	N04	FTY right of way to emergency vehicle	60 or SNP
41-6a-903	N06	FTY right of way to other vehicle	60
41-6a-904(3)(a)	N04	FTY to emergency vehicle	60 or SNP
41-6a-904(2)(a)	N04	FTY to emergency vehicle/ambul/fire/police	60 or SNP
41-6a-1006	N08	FTY to pedestrian	60
41-6a-1002	N08	FTY to pedestrian/includes handicapped or blind	60
41-6a-905	N01	FTY to work vehicle or pedestrian	60
41-6a-903(2)	N01	FTY when enter/crossing highway	60
41-6a-903(3)	N01	FTY when merging	60
41-6a-401.3	B03	Hit and run - injury	R/DISQ
41-6a-401(1)	B04	Hit and run - property damage/regular operator	60
41-6a-401.5	B02	Hit and run/fatal	REV/DQ
41-6a-518.2	IID	Ignition interlock device violation - (result in 1 yr revocation)	Rev
41-6a-502.5	A25	Impaired driving	
41-6a-502.5(7)	IMP	Impaired driving - Utah Specific	
41-6a-1701	N82	Improper backing	50
41-6a-713	VOG	Improper entry/exit gore	40
41-6a-701	M40	Improper lane	40
41-6a-710	M40	Improper lane	40/DISQ
41-6a-710	M40	Improper lane or location	60
41-6a-701	M40	Improper lane or location	60
41-6a-706.5	M47	Improper lane or location - bicycle lane	40
41-6a-702(1)(a)	M49	Improper lane or location - in HOV or restricted lane	40
41-6a-714	M50	Improper lane or location - limited access hwy	40
41-6a-712(2)	M51	Improper lane or location - median	40
41-6a-710(1)(b)	M48	Improper lane or location - occupied lane	40
41-6a-1201	M55	Improper lane or location - on rail or streetcar tracks	40
41-6a-1702	M58	Improper lane or location - road shoulder, ditch or sidewalk (specific to sidewalk)	40
41-6a-701(3)	M60	Improper lane or location - slower vehicle lane	40
41-6a-710	M62	Improper lane or location - traveling in turn (or center) lane	40
41-6a-704	M70	Improper passing	50
41-6a-704	M70	Improper passing	50
41-6a-705	M70	Improper passing (generic)	50
41-6a-803	N83	Improper starting	50
41-6a-801	N50	Improper turn	50
41-6a-1708	D72	Improper/inability to control vehicle	50
41-6a-801 (3)(b)	N50	Making improper left turn	50
41-6a-801 (4)(b)	N50	Making improper right turn	50
41-6a-801	N50	Making improper turn	50
41-6a-802	N56	Making improper U turn	50

Statute	Code	Violation Description	Pts/Action
53-3-229(3)(a)	D10	Manufacture or make false DL/CDL/Instruction Per.	NP
32B-4-409	A31	Minor possession or consumption of alcohol	S/D/NP
53-3-229(1)(d)	D02	Misrepresentation of identity or other facts on application for driver license/CDL/Inst. Permit	RSD/DIS
53-3-414(5)	A50	Motor vehicle used in the commission of a felony involving the manufacturing, distributing or dispensing a controlled substance	S/DISQ
76-5-206(3)	U09	Negligent homicide while operating a CMV	DISQ
76-5-206(3)	NHM	Negligent homicide while operating a motor vehicle	REV
53-3-404	B57	No commercial driver license	DQNP
41-12a-302	D36	No insurance	SNP
41-12a-303.2	B74	No proof of insurance	S/NP
53-3-404(1)	B57	Operating a CMV without a CDL	
53-3-221(1)(c)	D75	Operating a motor vehicle improperly due to physical or mental disability	40
41-6a-1623	E02	Operating without brakes as required by law	NP
41-6a-1601	E01	Operating without equipment as required	NP
41-6a-703	M72	Passing in violation of opposite directions restrictions	50
41-6a-708	M71	Passing in violation of posted sign/pavement marking	50
41-6a-707	M74	Passing on hill/curve	50
41-6a-1302	M75	Passing school bus displaying warning not to pass	50
41-6a-706	M77	Passing with insufficient distance or visibility	50
58-37c-20.5	PSU	Pharmacist violation-Plea in Abeyance considered conviction	SNP
53-3-229(1)(g)	B41	Possess/provide counterfeit/altered DL/CDL/INST Permit/ID	NP/SNP
41-6a-526	A35	Possession of open alcohol container -	NP
41-6a-1205(1)(d)(ii)	M24	R/R clearance too low to clear tracks - CMV	50/DISQ
41-6a-512	M84	Reckless driving	80
41-6A-520	A12	Refusal to submit to testing implied Consent DLD Admin Action	REV/DQ
41-6a-1803	F04	Seat belt not used properly as required	NP
76-10-508.1	USV	Shooting gun from a vehicle/Criminal class required (felony only)	RNP
53-3-229	D16	Show or use improperly DL,CDL, Instr. Permit	SNP/DIS
41-6a-601	S51	Speed 1-10 mph over posted speed limit	35
41-6a-601	S61	Speed 11-20 mph over posted speed limit	55
41-6a-601	S16	Speed 15+ mph over speed limit	55
41-6a-601	S15	Speed 15+ mph over speed limit (Serious Violation CDL)	55
41-6a-601	S21	Speed 21-25 mph over posted speed limit (detail optional)	75
41-6a-601	S71	Speed 21-30 mph over posted speed limit	75
41-6a-601	S26	Speed 26-30 mph over posted speed limit (detail optional)	75
41-6a-601	S31	Speed 31-36 mph over posted speed limit (detail optional)	75
41-6a-601	S81	Speed 31-40 mph over posted speed limit	75
41-6a-601	S36	Speed 36-40 mph over posted speed limit (detail optional)	75
41-6a-601	S91	Speed 41+ mph over posted speed limit	75
41-6a-601	S41	Speed 41+ mph over posted speed limit (detail optional)	75
41-6a-606	S95	Speed contest (racing)(1st 60 days-2ndw/I 3 yrs 90 days)	S/NP
41-6a-606	S95	Speed contest(racing) on road open to traffic prior to 5/1/2006	60
41-6a-605	S96	Speed less than minimum OK	50
41-6a-209	S94	Speeding in a construction zone	50
41-6a-604	S99	Speeding in a school zone (Utah specific)	35/55
53-3-221(11)(a)	S98	Speeding on freeway (wasting fuel)//on MVR if CDL/CDL Holder	35
76-6-412(1)(a)(ii)	U26	Taking vehicle without consent/send withdrawal as W00	DISQ/NP
41-6a-1716	M85	Texting while driving – Either 50 points or court ordered suspension	50 or SNP
76-6-404	GAS	Theft of gas – suspend if court ordered	SNP
76-10-306(4)	UIV	Throwing incendiary device from vehicle	RNP
41-6a-701	M40	Travel in improper lane	40
53-3-231	A61	Underage administrative per se/drink/drive @ .02 higher(arrest)	
32B-4-411	POA	Unlawful proof of age	SUS
41-6a-1601	E01	Unsafe condition of vehicle	NP
41-6a-803	N84	Unsafe operation (416a1601)	50
41-12a-511	D39	Unsatisfied judgment	SNP
76-8-306(1)(f)	U05	Using a motor vehicle to aid and abet a felon	RNP
76-5-207	U07	Vehicular homicide	REV/DQ
76-5-205(3)	U08	Vehicular manslaughter/CMV	DISQ
53-3-208	D29	Violate restrictions of DL,CDL, Instr. Permit	SRNP
53-3-232	ACL	Violation alcohol conditional license	R/NP
41-6a-403	D35	Violation of FR law	SNP
41-6a-518	A41	Violation of ignition interlock device under 41-6a-518	NP
Title 58 Chapters 37, 37a, 37b, 37c, & 37d	A33	Violation of the Controlled Substance Act	SNP

Withdrawal Actions Table

Statute	Code	Withdrawal Description	Action
383.51	W50	Accumulation of 2 or more out-of-service order general violations within 10 years	DISQ1/5
383.51	W51	Accumulation of 2 or more out-of-service orders within 10 years while transporting 16 or more passengers including driver and/or transporting HAZMAT	DISQ3/5
383.51	W60	Accumulation of 2 railroad grade crossing violations within three years	DISQ
383.51	W52	Accumulation of 3 or more out-of-service order general violations within 10 years	DISQ3/5
383.51	W61	Accumulation of 3 railroad grade crossing violations within three years	DISQ
53-3-221	W01	Accumulation of convictions (points/habitual offender)	D/S/NP
383.51	W40	Accumulation of two or more major offenses	DQ/LIFE
383.51	W41	Additional major offense after reinstatement	DQ/LIFE
383.51(c)(2)(ii)	W31	Disqualified for 120 days– serious violations	DQNP
383.51(c)(2)(i)	W30	Disqualified for 60 days – serious violations	DQNP
383.51	W45	Driving a CMV while disqualified for previous violation in a CMV	DISQ
53-3-413(6)(b)	W09	Failure to surrender HAZMAT endorsement	DISQ
383.51	W70	Imminent Hazard	DISQ
	W26	Insufficient funds, bad check - withdrawal sent as W00	S/NP
	W10	Non-traffic DLD - withdrawal sent as W00	DNP
53-3-211(5)	W13	Signature withdrawn by parent or guardian	DS/NP
53-3-221	W20	Unable to pass DL test(s) or meet qualifications	NP
	W00	Withdrawal non-ACD violation - A withdrawal issued by another state (SOR) for a single conviction which is neither traffic safety related, driver control related, or federally mandated.	

Point System Summary

Points range from 35 to 88. Under the state point system, if a driver does not have any moving violation convictions for one full year, one-half of the points on the record will be removed. If the driver has two successive years with no convictions, all points on the record will be removed. Individual conviction points are automatically removed from the record three years after the date of violation. 50 points may be removed from the driving record after completion of a Department recommended Driver Improvement Course. This deduction is only allowed once every three years.

Vermont

Administration	Important Telephone and Web Contacts

Robert Ide, Commissioner
Department of Motor Vehicles
120 State Street, Montpelier 05603-0001
802-828-2011
http://dmv.vermont.gov
 	
See an assembled list Vermont DMV Laws at
    http://dmv.vermont.gov/safety/laws/statutes
 	
See Vermont State Statutes at
    www.leg.state.vt.us/statutesMain.cfm
	Driver Licensing...802-828-2000
	SR-22, Financial Responsibility..................802-828-2050
	Vehicle Information 802-828-2000
	Commercial Driver License 802-828-0597
	State Department of Banking/Insurance......802-828-3301
	State Police..802-244-7345
	
	Submit general question via email to
	    CommissionersOffice@state.vt.us

Driver's License Format, Issuance and Renewal

License Classes, Restrictions and Endorsements Appear After the Driving Record Content Section

License Format

Eight digits; the last digit is a check-digit which may be numeric or alpha "A." Vermont reports there is no code or sequential arrangement which determines the characters making the license number, other than numeric order from the computer.

Document Appearance

A photo license is mandatory for all licenses issued after 07/01/2005. In 2009, Vermont began issuing Enhanced Driver Licenses and ID Cards which allows holders to cross the United States-Canada border without a passport or other supporting documents. The cards denote both identity and citizenship, per the Western Hemisphere Travel Initiative. Anyone applying will have to present extensive documentation to prove their identity and be interviewed by a motor vehicle employee. The license is mailed once the information has been verified. The enhanced drivers' licenses contain an electronic transponder, like those used in E-Z Pass toll-paying systems.

Current Document

The card is laminated and has a "credit card" appearance. There is a bar code with information such as the name, DOB, height and weight encoded. Normal Operator Licenses have a green header.

Security Characteristics: Ghost image of photo appears on right side, state seal in middle towards right.

Position of Photo: Upper left for regular operator, lower left for Under 21 operator.

Underage: PURPLE header bar, The dates are shown when the driver is both 21 and 18.

CDL Indicator: "COMMERCIAL DRIVER LICENSE" appears in a BLUE header bar.

Old Document

Photo card is laminated. There is a magnetic strip with the name, DOB, height and weight encoded.

Security Characteristics: Ghost image of photo appears on right side, state seal in middle towards right.

Position of Photo: Upper left for regular operator, lower left for Under 21 operator.

Minor Age Driver Locator: "JUNIOR OPERATOR" appears in a Yellow header bar.

Age 18-19-20: PURPLE header bar, "UNDER 21 UNTIL XX-XX-XXXX" appears in red letters.

CDL Indicator: "COMMERCIAL DRIVER LICENSE" appears in a BLUE header bar.

Issuance

Location of Requirements for Proof of Identity:
http://dmv.vermont.gov/licenses/enhanced/general_info

Age Requirements

Individuals under eighteen are subject to the provisions of a Graduated Driver License Program. The first level is a Learner's Permit, the next level is the Junior Operator. The Senior Operator minimum age is eighteen; sixteen for a Junior Operator; fifteen for a two-year Learner's Permit and must be accompanied by licensed driver age twenty-five or over, or certified driver training instructor.

Residency

Vermont requires proof of residency to obtain licenses and ID cards. This must be done no later than 60 days after moving to Vermont. Non-resident's home-state license is honored on a reciprocal basis not to exceed thirty days. Vermont requires proof of residency to obtain licenses and ID cards.

Renewal

Renewal is birth month and day of second or fourth year. Driver keeps same number when renewing. Renewal is available by mail and in person. Online renewal is not available, but drivers may change their addresses at https://secure.vermont.gov/dmv/express. Military personnel (stationed out-of-state) licenses are valid for 4 years after expiration and until 30 days after discharge.

Elderly-Related Restrictions

None indicated.

Vehicle Insurance, Title and Registration Facts

Registration Renewal

Renewal is annual and is available at any DMV location online or by telephone. The site also allows one to change an address. Go to https://secure.vermont.gov/dmv/express or call 866-259-5368. This service is available 24/7. The registration and sticker are mailed.

New Residents

Non-residents must register vehicles at expiration of time period granted by home-state reciprocity agreement, not to exceed six months; or within six months of accepting employment.

Inspections and Emissions Testing

All motor vehicles registered must be inspected once each year at state approved inspection stations. Any newly registered vehicle not currently inspected in this state must be inspected within 15 days from the date of registration. Light trailers (less than 1,500 pounds) are exempt.

All 1996 and newer gasoline powered vehicles, and 1997 and newer diesel powered vehicles having a gross vehicle rating of 8,500 pounds or less, must have an On-Board Diagnostics (OBDII) examination as part of their annual safety equipment inspection. The OBDII examination tests the emission control system of the vehicle.

Passenger Plate Facts

There are two plates. Until July 1, 2009 two decals each with the MO & YR were issued, one decal per plate. Effective July 1, 2009 the state began to issue one decal only, which needs to be placed on the rear plate. Counties are not designated by code nor are they spelled out on the plate. When a vehicle is sold the plates remain with the seller.

Insurance and Financial Responsibility

Vermont has compulsory insurance. Minimum liability limits are $25,000/50,000/10,000. The state does not have a no-fault insurance provision law. Evidence of insurance is required after certain violations or an uninsured reportable accident and when the vehicle is inspected. SR-22 forms are used.

Withdrawal Sanctions, and Alcohol and Drug Testing

Alcohol and Chemical Testing

Vermont's illegal intoxication level is .08 percent and above; however, content of .05 to .08 percent can be used with other evidence for a conviction. Drivers under 21 have a legal limit of .02 percent, drivers of CMVs have a limit of .04 percent. Blood and breath testing are authorized. Vermont has both an implied-consent violation and a provision for an administrative suspension.

Suspensions and Revocations

The Vermont DMV is in compliance with the provisions of the Motor Carrier Safety Improvement Act (MCSIA). See the Appendix for more information about these mandatory CDL disqualification sanctions. Below is an overview of significant withdrawals.

Impersonating Another on an Application or Aiding an Applicant by False Representation
....Sixty-day suspension.
Refusal to Submit to Breath or Blood Alcohol Test -- Civil Violation......Six-month to life suspension.
Under the Influence of Alcohol or Drugs
   All Offenses, Blood Alcohol Content .08 Percent or More ....Ninety-day to life suspension.
Points Accumulation ....Ten or more points in two years will initiate suspension proceedings.
Habitual Offender (8 or more convictions with 6 or more points or major violations within 5 years)
....Two-year revocation.

- Vermont law requires that anyone suspended for an alcohol-related offense must complete an alcohol treatment program.
- The DMV now issues Ignition Interlock Device Restricted Drivers Licenses (RDL's) to applicants who are suspended for DUI offenses.
- Vermont law does not provide for a "hardship license" or a "work license."

Reinstatement Requirements

Suspension $71.00 fee; plus requirements specific to the suspension.
Revocation $71.00 fee; investigation (for DWI); plus requirements specific to the revocation.

Record Access: Laws, Rules, and Forms

Note: This Section Applies to Both Driver and Vehicle Records.

Governing Statutes and Rules

See assembled list **Vermont DMV Laws** at
   http://dmv.vermont.gov/safety/laws/statutes
See **Vermont State Statutes** at
   www.leg.state.vt.us/statutesMain.cfm
Vermont implemented a Driver Privacy Protection Policy in accordance with Title 23-VSA Chapter 3. The state did not specifically mention the following DPPA exemptions in the state policy: (11), (12), and (13). Vermont added the following exception: Unrestricted or specified use with written consent of the person who is the subject of the information. Release of personal information is restricted and only given to those demonstrating permissible use or signed release. Personal information includes photo or computerized image, SSN, address other than 5 digit ZIP Code, telephone number, and medical or disability information.

Request and Consent Forms

Ongoing requesters for driver and vehicle records must process a certain form depending on access mode. Ongoing requesters must also complete and submit a *VG118 - Agreement as to the Driver Privacy Protection Policy, State of Vermont, Department of Motor Vehicles* and a subscriber agreement with the Vermont Information Consortium, through whom records are disseminated. Occasional users with a permissible purpose must use form *VG116*. This form requires the signature of the subject, regardless if the request is a permissible use per statute. Both forms are found at http://dmv.vermont.gov/forms.

Vendor and Third Party Access Policy

The restrictions upon the use, storage or resale of records after a completed transaction coincide with the current disclosure and permissible user policies. Approved online vendors can access records for other vendors (who are not online, etc) who will then sell to an end use, providing the following—

1. If other vendor (reseller) is registered with the state
2. If contract between original vendor and reseller contains same language as contract between the state and the original vendor
3. If contract between reseller and end-user contains same language as contract between the state and the original vendor.
4. Records of all sales and purposes of the sales must be kept by the original vendor for five years

Records Ordered For Non-permissible Uses

Non-permissible use requesters must provide written authorization (by subject) using *Form VG116*. A notary is not needed. If no consent and/or for a non-permissible use, records without personal information are released.

Access to Driver-Related Records

Driving Records

General Information and Fees

Driver Improvement Information, 120 State Street, Montpelier VT 05603, 802-828-2050, fax is 802-828-2098.

The fee for a certified three-year driving record accessed by mail or walk-in is $13.00. The fee for complete (all years) record is $16.00. The fee for an electronic three-year record is $15.00. Fee increases are mandated by the legislature. The agency charges a full fee for processing a "no record found" report.

In-Person – The only location for walk-in or (mail-in) record requests is the address listed above. Requests made over-the-counter are processed while you wait.

Mail – Requests mailed to the state are processed within approximately six days of receipt. The driver's full name and date of birth are needed when ordering; the license number may be helpful, but is not required. The fee must accompany each request.

Electronic – Access is available to approved subscribers, but not the general public. Users must complete and submit *VG118* discussed above and have a subscriber agreement with Vermont Information Consortium, through whom records are disseminated. A $75.00 annual subscription fee is also required.

The fee is $15.00 per record, there is a full charge for a no hit. The system offers both immediate response single inquiry and a batch mode delivery for higher volume users. Records are available 24/7 except for periods of file maintenance. Only the driver's license number is needed when ordering; the system does not accept the driver name or date of birth.

All information concerning the forms and how to become a subscriber is found at https://secure.vermont.gov/DMV/mvr/help. Contact Vermont Information Consortium directly at 802-229-4171.

Bulk – The state will sell data from the license file, but cannot program or customize requests. Social Security Numbers are not released. Form VG-118a must be submitted (found at web site). Fees are indicated at http://dmv.vermont.gov/fees/misc. Call Information Management.

By Person of Record – VT drivers may obtain their driving record by mail or walk-in as described above. At present, there is no online method for drivers to view or order their own record. It is suggested to use the *Record Request Form VG116* found at http://dmv.vermont.gov/forms.

Notification/Monitoring Program

At present, Vermont does not offer a mechanism for employers or insurance companies to monitor or track drivers and be notified if there is active on a driver's record or license.

Crash Reports

Reporting – Crashes involving death, injury, or property damage in excess of $3,000.00 must be reported within seventy-two hours to the DMV, Agency of Transportation, 120 State Street, Montpelier VT 05603. Use *Form VA004* to file a report of a crash. The form is found at http://dmv.vermont.gov/forms. There are no other special state reporting criteria for commercial drivers.

Record Access – Copies of crash reports may only be obtained from at the 120 State Street location. Fax requests can be sent to 802-828-3577. The fee for a police report is $15.00, for an individual's crash report is $10.00, for insurance information of an accident is $6.00. The SSNs and individual's addresses are protected and are not released. Records are available for 4 years to present. Normal turnaround time is up to 15 days. If there is criminal action involved (DWI, fatality) it may take as long as three months after the crash to get a copy of the t report.

Access to Vehicle-Related Records

General Information and Fees

Department of Motor Vehicles, Registration-License Information, 120 State Street, Montpelier VT 05603-0001, 802-828-2000.

The DMV maintains records on vehicles, motor homes, trailers, and boats. Lien record information is provided for all of these conveyances. The fee for listings of up to four current or expired registrations is $6.00. A certified copy of an original registration application is $6.00. A certified copy of a title is $6.00. A certified copy of a vehicle title search, and title info, and lien info is $20.00. A certified copy of a vessel, snowmobile or ATV title search is $13.00. Vehicle and vessel records are available for fifteen years to present.

Potential lien-holders are provided a "yes or no" answer when asking about liens on a vehicle. If specific details (such as current lien-holder, etc.) are requested, a *VG116 Form* is required along with a title search fee. Statistical research is provided at $35.00 per hour.

At a minimum, a VIN or registration plate number must be provided by the requester.

In-Person or Mail – Across-the-counter printed records are available in 30-60 minutes. Also, there is a public access terminal available in Montpelier. Turnaround time for mail requests is 7-10 days.

Electronic – Vermont does not offer online inquiry access at this time.

Bulk – Vermont offers bulk retrieval of vehicle or ownership records by contract. Apply to the Office of the Director of Operations of Motor Vehicles, Linda Snyder at 802-828-2066. Fees are indicated at http://dmv.vermont.gov/fees/misc. Records are not released for marketing purposes.

Access to Vessel-Related Records

General Information, Access and Fees

Since July 1, 2007, Vermont titles all vessels that are 15 years old or newer, based on calendar year, with a length of 16 feet or longer (including shuttlecraft). Exceptions include any vessel which is a canoe, kayak, or similar watercraft designed to be manually propelled or such a vessel equipped with a motor of 10 horsepower or less. Previously, all boats that operate with an attached motor had to be registered. One may operate in Vermont for a period of 90 consecutive days if the home state grants like privileges to Vermont boats or if the boat has a federally issued number. However, if the vessel is used in Vermont waters for 30 days or more one must obtain a vessel validation sticker.

The agency above is the resource for records. A title search with lien information is $13.00; a registration check is $6.00. Use of the above mentioned *VG116 Form* is required.

Driving Record Content and Reciprocity

What's On or Not On the Driving Record

- For computer-printed driving records or records obtained online, the address of the driver does not appear.
- SSNs do not appear on the record.
- All convictions are reported on the driving record.
- Crashes which result in injury, death, or total damage of $3,000 or more are reportable, but fault is not shown on the record.
- The state does not permit driver school attendance in lieu of conviction.
- CDL drivers have convictions listed for life. The length of time convictions stay listed for non-CDL driver depends whether a three-year record or complete record is purchased.

Data Retention

CDL driver records are purged based on the timetable per the MCSIA (see the Appendix). Surrendered licenses (non-CDL) fall into the same purging criteria as listed above.

Court to Repository

Conviction information is keyed in from paper abstracts manually transmitted from the courts to the state. There is no law mandating when convictions must be submitted. State files are updated daily, and most convictions are entered within one week. Adjudications are transmitted electronically from the "VT Judicial Bureau" to the DMV.

State Reciprocity for Non-CDL Drivers

- Will suspend license of driver for unpaid out-of-state convictions.
- Record of new incoming driver is shown on MVR but only for majors.
- Out-of-state convictions are shown on MVR, but only for majors.
- Out-of-state accidents are not shown on MVR.
- Convictions of out-of-state drivers are sent to home state only if criminal conviction with a notice of suspension.
- Record is forwarded to new state upon surrender of license.

License Classes, Restrictions, Endorsements, and Status

License Classes– Commercial

Class A	Combination vehicles with GCWR of 26,001 pounds or more—provided towed vehicle is 10,001 pounds or more.
Class B	Single vehicles with GVWR of 26,001 pounds or more—provided towed vehicle is 10,000 pounds or less.
Class C	Single vehicles with GVWR of 26,000 pounds or less which transport placarded hazardous materials or sixteen or more passengers (including the driver).

License Classes– Non-Commercial

Class D	All motor vehicles except motorcycles and school buses, includes minors' licenses.
Class RDL	Ignition Interlock Device Restricted Drivers Licenses (RDL's) are issued to applicants who are suspended for DUI offenses.

License Status

S	Active Suspension	R	Revoke
P	Suspension Pending	N	Not Suspended

Restrictions

A	Accompanied by Licensed Operator 25 or older	N	Except Class A and B Bus
B	Corrective Lenses	P	Built-Up Pedals
C	Mechanical Aid (Special Brakes, Hand Controls or Other Controls	Q	Device to Operate Brake and Clutch Simultaneously
		R	Automatic Transmission and Hand Operated Dimmer
D	Prosthetic Aid	S	All Hand Operation
E	Automatic Transmission	T	Built-Up Seat
F	See Separate Card	U	Left Foot Accelerator
G	Daylight Only	V	Foot or Right Hand Operated Parking Brake
I	Three Wheel MTC Only	W	Hand Operated Dimmer Switch
J	Other	X	Hand Operated Parking Brake
K	Intrastate Only	Y	Power Steering or Wheel Knob
L	Vehicle Without Air-Brakes	Z	No Measurable Amount of Alcohol or Drug
M	Except Class A Bus		
s			

Endorsements

A	Motorcycle and Sch Bus I	P	Passenger
B	Motorcycle and Sch Bus II	S	Type I School Bus
H	Hazardous Material	T	Double-/Triple-Trailers
M	Motorcycle	V	Type II School Bus
N	Tanks; 1,000 Gal or More	X	Tank and Hazardous Materials

Conviction Table with Statute, ACD, and Points

This table is presented in order of the Code column. The first portion shows Codes that begin with a letter (alpha), followed by codes that begin with a number.

- In general, all **codes starting** with an **"8"** signify a **snowmobile** violation and **codes starting** with a **"9"** signify a **motorboat** violation.
- The DMV indicated out-of-state convictions may appear as an ACD Code. Please refer to the back of this book for the AAMVA ACD Code Table.
- If a driver has outstanding ticket in another state and is subject to the **Non-Resident Violator Compact**, this possible suspension is indicated with a **"N"** before the state's two-letter abbreviation (such as **NAL** for Alabama). The complete listing of every state is omitted.
- The Title and Section columns refer to the applicable law in the Vermont Statutes (www.leg.state.vt.us/statutes/statutes2.htm).
- The entries without data in the Title and Section Columns usually have a referring code to the U.S. Department of Transportation regulations, such as 49 C.F.R. Sec. 396.4

Here are the meanings for the **Type Column**:

B = Can be a conviction or suspension
C = Conviction
DQ = CDL Disqualification
O = Obsolete, no longer used but may appear on operating records
S = suspension

Code	ACD	Type	Title	Section	Pts	Description
ACC	D35	S	23	801	0	Financial responsibility required as a result of an uninsured accident
AEI	N25	C	23	1046	2	Vehicle approaching or entering intersection
AFC		C	23	2082	0	Altering, forging, or counterfeiting certificates
AID	W00	S	23	671	0	Overseer of the poor
ALT		C	23	1704a	0	Alteration of odometer/hubometer/clock meter
AND		C	23	3502(a)	0	(ATV VIOLATION) Operating ATV on a VASA trail with no trail access decal
APK		C	23	1105	0	Additional parking regulations
ASL	E05	C	23	1252(b)	0	Amber signal lamps
AT		C	23	3505(f)	0	(ATV VIOLATION) Spark arrester required
ATA		C	23	3502(a)	0	(ATV VIOLATION) Registration required
ATB		C	23	3504(b)	0	(ATV VIOLATION) Dealer registration
ATC		C	23	3505(a)	0	(ATV VIOLATION) Equipment required
ATD		C	23	3505(b)	0	(ATV VIOLATION) Muffler required
ATE		C	23	3505(c)	0	(ATV VIOLATION) Sales, no muffler
ATF		C	23	3506(b)	0	(ATV VIOLATION) Operation along public highway
ATG		C	23	3506(02)	0	(ATV VIOLATION) Operation across public highway
ATH		C	23	3506(03)	0	(ATV VIOLATION) Operation on private land/water
ATI		C	23	3506(04)	0	(ATV VIOLATION) Operation on public lands
ATJ		C	23	3506(05)	0	(ATV VIOLATION) Operation by person less than 12 years of age
ATK		C	23	3506(06)	0	(ATV VIOLATION) Operation to harass wildlife
ATL		C	23	3506(07)	0	(ATV VIOLATION) Display of plate
ATM		C	23	3506(08)	0	(ATV VIOLATION) Operating under the influence
ATN		C	23	3506(09)	0	(ATV VIOLATION) Careless or negligent operation
ATO		C	23	3506(10)	0	(ATV VIOLATION) Operation within a cemetery
ATP		C	23	3506(11)	0	(ATV VIOLATION) Operation on limited access highway
ATQ		C	23	3506(12)	0	(ATV VIOLATION) Operation on sidewalk
ATR		C	23	3509(a)	0	(ATV VIOLATION) Altered serial number
ATS		C	23	3509(b)	0	(ATV VIOLATION) Altered trail sign
ATT		C	23	3511(a)	0	(ATV VIOLATION) Failure to stop and render aid at scene of accident
ATU		C	23	3511(b)	0	(ATV VIOLATION) Failure to report an accident
ATV		C	23	3512	0	(ATV VIOLATION) Attempting to elude a police officer
ATW		C	23	3506(d)(1)	0	(ATV VIOLATION) Operate ATV w/exhaust system with cut out/bypass/similar device
ATX		C	23	3506(e)	0	(ATV VIOLATION) Illegal operation of ATV by person under the age of 18
ATY		C	23	3506(d)(2)	0	(ATV VIOLATION) Operate ATV w/spark arrester removed or modified
ATZ		C	23	3506(f)	0	(ATV VIOLATION) Failure to hold/exhibit safety education certificate
AU2	W00	B	23	201	0	Registration & other applications to be under oath
AUO	D02	B	23	201	0	License & driving permit applications to be under oath
AWD	A26	C	23	1134	2	Consuming alcoholic beverages while driving
BBP		C	23	1139	0	BICYCLE - Riding on roadways and/or bicycle path improperly
BC1	A21	S	23	1205	0	School bus driver - administrative per se suspension for operating a motor vehicle with an alcohol concentration of .02% or more, civil, 1st offense
BC2	A21	S	23	1205	0	School bus driver - administrative per se suspension for operating a motor vehicle with an alcohol concentration of .02% or more, civil, 2nd offense
BC3	A21	S	23	1205	0	School bus driver - administrative per se suspension for operating a motor vehicle with an alcohol concentration of .02% or more, civil, 3rd/subsequent offense
BCA		C	23	1140	0	BICYCLE - Carrying articles

Code	ACD	Type	Title	Section	Pts	Description
BD		C	23	1136	0	BICYCLE - Application of bicycle regulations to parents and children
BDE		C	23	1141	0	BICYCLE - Equipment on bicycles
BDL	W00	S	23	204(a)	0	Outstanding balance due for a DMV license transaction
BDR	W00	S	23	204(a)	0	Outstanding balance due for a DMV registration transaction
BE	E02	C	23	1307	0	Brake equipment required
BIC		C	23	1096(b)	0	Parent/guardian permitting child to violate T. 23, Sections 1136 thru 1141
BP		C	23	1453	0	Baled products
BR	S94	C	23	1081(b)	2	Basic rule (speeding)
BR2	A12	S	23	1205	0	School bus driver - administrative per se suspension for refusal to submit to test of alcohol concentration, civil, 2nd offense
BR3	A12	S	23	1205	0	School bus driver - administrative per se suspension for refusal to submit to test of alcohol concentration, civil, 3rd/subsequent offense
BRF	A12	S	23	1205	0	School bus driver - administrative per se suspension for refusal to submit to test of alcohol concentration, civil, 1st offense
BRN	W00	S	24	02201	0	Title 24, burning or causing to be burned solid waste
BRR		C	23	1138	0	BICYCLE - clinging to motor vehicles, riding on roadways and bicycle path wrong
BTR		C	23	1203b	0	Duty to report blood test results
BTW		C	23	1124	2	Position of operator (behind the wheel)
BU2	A21	B	23	1201(a)(1)	0	School bus driver - .02 or more BAC while operating a school bus, criminal offense, 2nd offense
BU3	A21	B	23	1201(a)(1)	0	School bus driver - .02 or more BAC while operating a school bus, criminal offense, 3rd/subsequent offense
BUS	A21	B	23	1201(a)(1)	0	School bus driver - Operating a school bus with a BAC of .02 or more
B74	B74	B	23	4115(c)	0	Failure to show insurance Certification
B78	B78	B	23	4115(c)	0	Failure to show license - Non-CDL
C04	A04	DQ	23	4116	0	Operating CMV with .04 or more BAC, CDL disqualification
C0H	A04	DQ	23	4116	0	Operating with 0.04or more BAC alcohol concentration w/haz-mat, CV disqualification
C41		S	23	1205		.04 or more BAC operating a commercial vehicle, first, civil suspension
C42		S	23	1205		.04 or more BAC operating a commercial vehicle, second, civil suspension
C43		S	23	1205		.04 or more BAC operating a commercial vehicle, third, civil suspension
CA1	A98	S	23	1205	0	Suspension for operating a motor vehicle with an alcohol concentration of .08% or more (First Offense)
CA2	A98	S	23	1205	0	Suspension for alcohol concentration of .08% , or more (Second Offense)
CA3	A98	O	23	1205	0	Suspension for alcohol concentration of .08%, or more (Third Offense)
CA4	A98	O	23	1205	0	Suspension for alcohol concentration of .08%, or more (Fourth, or subsequent, offense)
CAH	M50	C	23	1009	2	Restrictions of controlled access highways
CB1	A94	DQ	23	4116	0	Administrative per se disqualification for operating a commercial motor vehicle with alcohol concentration of .04%, or more (First offense)
CB2	A94	DQ	23	4116	0	Administrative per se disqualification for operating a commercial motor vehicle with alcohol concentration of .04%, or more, (subsequent disqualification offense)
CBR	S15	C	23	1081(b)	2	Commercial motor vehicle being operated at a speed of 15 MPH (or more) over the speed limit - basic rule
CC1		C	5	2101	0	Commercial Motor Carrier violation, Group #1 (Title 5)
CC2		C	5	2101	0	Commercial Motor Carrier violation, Group #2 (Title 5)
CC3		C	5	2101	0	Commercial Motor Carrier violation, Group #3 (Title 5)
CC4		C	5	2101	0	Commercial Motor Carrier violation, Group #4 (Title 5)
CCC	W00	S	23	671	0	Failure to obtain corrected CDL license
CCM		C	5	2101	0	Commercial Motor Carrier violation, Group #5 (Title 5)
CCN	W00	S				5 VSA - Commercial vehicle carrier non-compliance
CCS	D51	DQ	15	798	0	Suspension of Commercial Driver's License for non-payment of child support
CD1		C	5	2101	0	Commercial vehicle driver violation, Group #1
CD2		C	5	2101	0	Commercial vehicle driver violation, Group #2
CD3		C	5	2101	0	Commercial vehicle driver violation, Group #3
CD8	A08	DQ	23	4116	0	Commercial driver operating .08 or more BAC, criminal violation
CDC	A98	DQ	23	4116	0	Commercial driver .08 or more BAC, civil
CDF	D02	B	23	4110(d)	0	Falsify CDL application information or certifications, revocation
CDH	A21	B	23	4116	0	Disqualification for operating a commercial motor vehicle (transporting hazardous materials) while under the influence of liquor
CDI	A08	O	23	1214	5	(Civil) traffic ticket for operating with an alcohol concentration of .08% or more
CDM		C	5	2101	0	Commercial vehicle driver violation (Miscellaneous)
CDO	B26	DQ	23	4116	0	Commercial driver operating while suspended for prior CMV violations
CDR		C	23	462	0	Failure to return dealer registration certificate/plates
CDS	B24	DQ	23	4116	0	Driving a CMV while suspended or disqualified for a prior CMV violation
CDW	A21	DQ	23	4116	0	Operating a commercial motor vehicle while under the influence of liquor (disqualification)
CEC	M02	C	23	1006a	2	CMV operated on a highway - emergency closing 02

Code	ACD	Type	Title	Section	Pts	Description
CES	S15	O	23	4103	2	C/D, Operating commercial vehicle 15 MPH or more above posted speed limit
CFE	U03	DQ	23	4116	0	Commission of a felony while operating a commercial motor vehicle
CFH	U03	DQ	23	4116	0	Commission of a felony while operating a commercial motor vehicle (transporting hazardous materials)
CFN	U10	DQ	23	4116	0	Causing a fatality through the negligent operation of a commercial vehicle
CHU	W00	S	7	1007	0	Title 7, failure to pay penalty for furnishing tobacco product(s) to a minor
CI2	W00	S	7	1005	0	Title 7, failure to pay penalty for (minor's) possession of tobacco product(s) - unlicensed individual, Second/Subsequent Offense
CIG	W00	S	7	1005	0	Title 7, failure to pay penalty for minor's possession of tobacco product(s) - unlicensed individual, First Offense
CIV	A98	S	23	1205	0	Administrative per se for alcohol concentration of .08% or more (3rd or subsequent offense)
CJ1	A04	DQ	23	4116a(a)	0	Operate commercial motor vehicle with .04 BAC (operator from non-reciprocating jurisdiction), 1st offense
CJ2	A04	DQ	23	4116a(b)	0	Operate commercial motor vehicle (carrying hazardous materials) with .04 BAC (operator from non-reciprocating jurisdiction), 1st offense
CJ3	A04	DQ	23	4116a(c)	0	Operate commercial motor vehicle with .04 BAC (operator from non-reciprocating jurisdiction), 2nd/subsequent offense
CJ4	W30	DQ	23	4116a(d)	0	Two serious traffic violations while operating commercial motor vehicle (operator from non-reciprocating jurisdiction)
CJ5	W31	DQ	23	4116a(d)	0	Three serious traffic violations while operating commercial motor vehicle (operator from non-reciprocating jurisdiction)
CJ6	A50	DQ	23	4116a(e)	0	CMV used in manufacturing/distributing/dispensing a controlled substance (operator from non-reciprocating jurisdiction)
CL	E05	C	23	1250	0	Clearance lights
CLF	B02	DQ	23	4116	0	Commercial driver leaving the scene of a fatal crash
CLH	B01	DQ	23	4116	0	Leaving the scene of an accident while operating a commercial motor vehicle (transporting hazardous materials)
CLR	S15	C	23	1081(b)	2	(Local) Commercial motor vehicle being operated at a speed of 15 MPH (or more) over the speed limit - basic rule
CLS	B01	DQ	23	4116	0	Commercial driver leaving the scene of an accident
CM1		B	23	2031	0	Counterfeit plates and/or sticker
CM2	B41	B	23	2032	0	Display fictitious or altered license and/or registration
CM3		B	23	2033	0	Loaning license
CM4	D16	B	23	2034	0	Display as own license one not issued
CM5		B	23	2035	0	Permit unlawful use of license
CM6	D02	B	23	2036	0	Fraud in obtaining or attempting to obtain documents
CM7	D02	B	23	2038	0	Loaning identity documents to aid in applicant's attempted fraud
CM8	W00	B	23	2037	0	Attempt to obtain or obtain any license/permit or special privilege from DMV by false information
CME		C	23	1399	0	Construction and maintenance equipment
CMU			23	4116	0	Convicted of two (or more) major violations while operating a commercial motor vehicle
CN	M80	O	23	1091	*10	Careless and negligent driving
CNC		C	5	2101	0	Commercial vehicle carrier non-compliance
CNF	U31	O	23	1091(d)	*10	Careless and negligent driving, fatality resulting
CNL	B56	C	23	4107	2	Commercial driver license required
CO	W00	S	23	671	0	Court order
CON		C	23	1283(b)	0	School bus converted for use
COV		C	23	1116	2	Clinging to other vehicles (while on motorcycle/moped)
CP	N80	C	23	1121	2	Coasting prohibited
CPH	D27	B	23	614(a)	2	Carrying passengers for hire, Junior Operator violation
CPL	N02	C	23	1127	2	Control in presence of livestock
CPU	A50	DQ	23	4116(e)	0	Commercial driver use of vehicle in commission of a felony involving the manufacture, distribution, or dispensing of a regulated drug, or possession with intent to manufacture, distribute, or dispense a regulated drug
CR2	A12	DQ	23	4116	0	Administrative per se disqualification for subsequent refusal to submit to BAC test
CRH	A12	DQ	23	4116	0	Refusal to submit to test of alcohol concentration while operating a commercial motor vehicle that is transporting hazardous materials
CRI	A08	O	23	1208	0	(Criminal) Operation with alcohol concentration of .08% or more (3rd or subsequent offense)
CRS	F02	C	23	1258	0	Child restraint system
CRT	A12	DQ	23	4116	0	Administrative per se disqualification for refusal to submit to test of alcohol concentration
CS2	W30	DQ	23	4116	0	Commercial driver convicted of 2 serious violations in 3 years
CS3	W31	DQ	23	4116	0	Conviction of 3 serious traffic violations (while operating a commercial motor vehicle) in preceding 3 years

Code	ACD	Type	Title	Section	Pts	Description
CSI	B03	DQ	23	4116	0	Commercial driver leaving the scene of a crash - injury resulting
CSP	A33	C				Possession of controlled substances (ticket) 49 CFR 391.15(C)(2)(iii)
CT1	A12	S	23	1205	0	Administrative per se, suspension for refusal to submit to test of alcohol concentration (first offense)
CT2	A12	S	23	1205	0	Administrative per se suspension for refusal to submit to test of alcohol concentration (Second offense)
CT3	A12	O	23	1205	0	Administrative per se suspension for refusal to submit to test of alcohol concentration (Third offense)
CT4	A12	O	23	1205	0	Administrative per se suspension for refusal to submit to test of alcohol concentration (Fourth offense)
CT5	A12	O	23	1205	0	Administrative per se suspension for refusal to submit to test of alcohol concentration (Fifth or subsequent offense)
CV1		C	5	2101	0	Commercial vehicle equipment violation, Group #1
CV2		C	5	2101	0	Commercial vehicle equipment violation, Group #2
CV3		C	5	2101	0	Commercial vehicle equipment violation, Group #3
CVA	B24	C	23	0677(a)	2	Operating commercial motor vehicle while disqualified (civil violation)
CVB	B24	C	23	0677(b)	2	Operating commercial motor vehicle while disqualified (criminal violation)
CVC	B24	C	23	0677(c)	2	Three (or more) civil violations of Title 23, Section 7 (criminal offense)
CVF	W00	DQ	23	4116	0	Commercial driver violation resulting in fatal crash
CVM		C	5	2101	0	Commercial vehicle equipment violation, miscellaneous
CWD	A22	DQ	23	4116	0	Commercial driver operating under the influence of controlled substances
CWH	A22	DQ	23	4116	0	Commercial driver under the influence of controlled substances while transporting hazardous materials
CX1	A90	O	23	1205	0	Administrative per se suspension for operating with an alcohol level of .10%, or more (First offense)
CX2	A90	O	23	1205	0	Administrative per se suspension for operating with an alcohol level of .10%, or more (Second offense)
CX3	A90	O	23	1205	0	Administrative per se suspension for operating with an alcohol level of .10%, or more (Third offense)
CX4	A90	O	23	1205	0	Administrative per se suspension for operating with an alcohol level of .10%, or more (Fourth offense)
CX5	A90	O	23	1205	0	Administrative per se suspension for operating with an alcohol level of .10% , or more (Fifth or subsequent offense)
DA1	A08	B	23	1206	0	(Criminal) violation of operating with an alcohol concentration of .08%, or more (First offense)
DA2	A08	B	23	1208	0	(Criminal) violation of operating with an alcohol concentration of .08%, or more (Second offense)
DA3	A08	B	23	1208	0	(Criminal) violation of operating with an alcohol concentration of .08%, or more (Third offense)
DA4	A08	B	23	1208	0	(Criminal) violation of operating with an alcohol concentration of .08%, or more (Fourth, or subsequent, offense)
DC2	A04	B	23	1208	0	Operating a CMV with .04% or more BAC, second offense
DC3	A04	B	23	1208	0	Operating a CMV with .04% or more BAC, third or subsequent offense
DCS	B26	C	23	679	2	Operating commercial motor vehicle while privilege to operate a commercial motor vehicle has been suspended
DCV	A04	B	23	1206	0	Operating a CMV with .04% or more BAC, First offense
DD1	A22	B	23	1206	0	Driving while under the influence of drugs (First offense)
DD2	A22	B	23	1208	0	Driving while under the influence of drugs (Second offense)
DD3	A22	B	23	1208	0	Driving while under the influence of drugs (Third offense)
DD4	A22	B	23	1208	0	Driving while under the influence of drugs (Fourth offense)
DD5	A22	B	23	1208	0	Driving while under the influence of drugs (Fifth, or subsequent, offense)
DDH	N71	C	23	1040	3	Driving on divided highways
DEF		C	23	1221	0	Defective equipment
DEL		S	23	0462(a)	0	(DEALER) Cancellation of dealer's registration
DFE	D27	B	23	614(a)	2	Driving for employer/employment, Junior Operator violation
DFH	M56	C	23	1123	2	Driving over fire hose prohibited
DFV		C	23	3027	0	Diesel fuel violation
DHM	B24	DQ	23	4116	0	Driving a CMV while disqualified or suspended for previous CMV violations - with hazardous materials
DIS		C	23	1223	0	Affix inspection sticker not assigned
DKR		C	23	466	0	(DEALER) Failure of dealer to keep records
DLD	B26	C	23	0674(b)	*10	"DLS" while suspended or revoked for a violation of Title 23, §1201
DLR	B26	C	23	674	0	After 07/01/2012 "DLS" while suspended or revoked for a violation of Title 23, §1201
DLS	B26	C	23	674	*10	Driving after license/privilege suspended or revoked
DLT	M42	C	23	1038	0	Driving on roadways laned for traffic.
DLW			23	674	0	After 07/01/2012 "DLS" while suspended or revoked

Code	ACD	Type	Title	Section	Pts	Description
DNH	U09	DQ	23	4116	0	Negligent homicide while operating a CMV
DOP		C	23	1058	0	PEDESTRIAN - Duties of pedestrians
DOR		C	23	1119	0	Opening and closing vehicle doors when unsafe
DP		C	23	511	0	Failing to display registration plates
DP2		C	23	511	0	No display of plates (front and rear)
DPS		C	23	467	0	(DEALER) Failure of dealer to report purchase and sale of vehicle
DPT		C	23	512	0	Failing to display registration plates on a trailer or semi-trailer
DQD	B24	C/DQ				Operating while disqualified 49 CFR 391.14(A)
DR	N70	C	23	1031	2	Driving to the right
DRB	W00	S	23	607a	0	Diversion/Reparative Board recall
DRS		C	23	1092	0	Damaging the road surface
DSL	E01	C	23	1249	0	Directional signal lamps
DSW	M58	C	23	1132	0	Driving on sidewalk
DSZ	M12	C	23	1059	0	Driving through safety zone
DTE	M84	C	23	1091	*10	Driving to endanger
DTP		C	23	3024(b)	0	Failure to obtain/display diesel permit
DTR		C	23	3024(b)	0	Diesel Tax Regulations
DUM		C	23	454	0	Dealer's use of motor vehicle(s)
DUP	D02	C	23	1205(s)	0	Applied for duplicate operator's license while (civil) DUI action is pending
DUT		C	23	460	0	Dealers use of temporary number plates restricted
DW1	A21	B	23	1206	0	Driving under influence of liquor, 1st offense, criminal
DW2	A21	B	23	1208	0	Driving under influence of liquor, 2nd offense, criminal
DW3	A21	B	23	1208	0	Driving under influence of liquor, 3rd offense, criminal
DW4	A21	B	23	1208	0	Driving under influence of liquor, 4th offense, criminal
DW5	A21	B	23	1208	0	Driving under influence of liquor, 5th or subsequent offense, criminal
DWD	A22	B	23	1206	0	Driving under the influence of drugs
DWI	A21	B	23	1206	0	Driving while under the influence of intoxicating liquor, criminal
DX1	A10	O	23	1206	0	Alcohol content of .10% or more, 1st offense, criminal
DX2	A10	O	23	1208	0	Alcohol content of .10% or more, 2nd offense, criminal
DX3	A10	O	23	1208	0	Alcohol content of .10% or more, 3rd offense, criminal
DX4	A10	O	23	1208	0	Alcohol content of .10% or more, 4th offense, criminal
DX5	A10	O	23	1208	0	Alcohol content of .10% or more, 5th or subsequent offense, criminal
ED1	W00	B	13	1753	0	False public alarm(s), licensed, 1st offense
ED2	W00	B	13	1753	0	False public alarm(s), licensed, subsequent offense
ED3	W00	B	13	1753	0	False public alarm(s), underage, 1st offense
ED4	W00	B	13	1753	0	False public alarm(s), underage, subsequent offense
ED5	W00	C	13	1753	0	False public alarm(s), unlicensed and 15 years of age or older
EDP		C	23	456	0	Employee's use of dealer's plates restricted
EE	E01	C	23	1301	0	Emergency exits
EFD	M25	C	23	1074	0	Vehicle emerging from driveway
EPR	N01	C	23	1049	4	Vehicle entering from private road
ER		C	23	4106	0	Employer responsibilities (CDL)
ERR		C	23	4123	0	Employer requiring/permitting violation of 23 VSA 1076 (CDL)
ES	S92	O	23	1003	6	Excessive speed (20 mph or more over the speed limit)
ES2	S92	O	23	1003	0	Exceeding the speed limit (subsequent offense).
ESA	S94	C	23	1081	2	Excessive speed, accident involvement
ESD	S94	O	23	1081(d)	2	Excessive speed
ESE		C				Failure to meet or refusal to test the exhaust-smoke emission standards
ESL	S92	O	23	1003	3	Exceeding the speed limit
FA8	D45	S	23	671	0	Failure to appear/pay fine to court for the offense of operating with .08 or more BAC
FAA	D45	S	23	671	0	Failure to appear/pay fine to court for the offense of leaving the scene of an accident
FAB	D45	S	23	671	0	Failure to appear/pay fine to court for the offense of operating with .02 or more BAC while operating a school bus
FAC	D45	S	23	671	0	Failure to appear/pay fine to court for the offense of driving a CMV with .04 or more BAC
FAD	D45	S	23	671	0	Failure to appear/pay fine to court for the offense of driving while suspended
FAE	W00	S	23	671	0	Failure to appear for a special written examination
FAF	D53	S	23	2307	0	Failure to pay fine
FAH	D45	S	23	671	0	Failure to appear/pay fine to court for the offense of leaving the scene of an accident resulting in a fatality
FAI	D45	S	23	671	0	Failure to appear/pay fine to court for the offense of operating under the influence
FAL	D45	S	23	671	0	Failure to appear/pay fine to court for the offense of leaving the scene of an accident resulting in injuries
FAM	W00	S	23	671	0	Failure to appear in court for a major violation
FAN	D45	S	23	671	0	Failure to appear/pay fine to court for the offense of negligent operation
FAO	W00	S	23	671	0	Failure to appear/pay fine to court for the offense of operating without owner's consent

Code	ACD	Type	Title	Section	Pts	Description
FAP	W00	S	23	2205(d)	0	Failure to appear in court (non-major violation)
FAR	D45	S	23	671	0	Failure to appear/pay fine to court for the offense of refusal to obey a law enforcement officer
FAS	D45	S	23	671	0	Failure to appear/pay fine to court for the offense of refusal to take the evidentiary test
FAT	W00	S	23	636	0	Failure to appear for the special exam road test
FAU	D45	S	23	671	0	Failure to appear/pay fine to court for the offense of negligent operation resulting in a fatality
FAW	W00	S	23	671	0	Failure to appear/pay fine to court for the offense of operating without the owner's consent, aggravated
FAX	D45	S	23	671	0	Failure to appear/pay fine to the court for excessive speed
FCC		C	23	307	0	Failure to carry registration certificate
FCD			23	0671	0	Failure to comply with diversion contract
FCJ			23	0671	0	Failure to comply with the agreement with the Vermont Judicial Bureau
FCP		C	23	1392	2	Failure to carry overweight permit in vehicle
FDC		C	23	451	0	(DEALER) Dealer's display violation
FDT		C	23	2083b	0	Failure to deliver title within 10 days of sale of vehicle
FFA	M33	C	23	1122	2	Following fire apparatus prohibited (within 500 feet)
FIE	W00	S	23	636	0	Failure to appear for initial special exam
FLR	E01	C	23	1303	0	Violation of the flare law
FNL	B51	C	23	602	0	Operating farm tractors or highway equipment without license
FOO	M08	C	23	1012(b)	4	Failure to obey officer
FPE	W20	S	23	636	0	Failure to pass special written examination
FPI		C	23	1012(a)	4	Failure to provide identity to an enforcement officer
FPR	W00	S	23	636	0	Failure to pass the special examination road test
FR1	B63	S				Failure to maintain mandatory proof of financial responsibility
FRA	B61	C	23	1129(a)	0	Failure to file an accident report
FRC		C	23	322	0	Failure to return certificate on sale of vehicle
FRI		C	23	1129(c)	0	Notification of liability insurance information
FRL		C	23	204	0	Failure to return license
FRR		B	23	1213F	0	Continuing to drive after failing rolling test
FRT		S	23	636		Motor carrier fails to pass special road test - third failure
FS	M16	C	23	1024	0	Flashing signals
FSB	F04	C	23	1259	0	Failure to use seat belts
FSE	W15	S	23	636	0	Failure to submit eye report
FSH	W09	DQ	23	671	0	Failure to surrender CDL with Hazmat per Patriot Act
FSL	M16	O	23	1022(c)	2	Failure to stop for a light
FSO	M08	C	23	1013	4	Authority of enforcement officer
FSP	W15	S	23	636	0	Failure to submit psychiatric report
FSR	W15	S	23	636	0	Failure to submit medical report
FSS	M23	C/DQ	23	1076	0	For all CMV drivers failing to have sufficient space to completely cross without stopping
FST	W00	S	23	636	0	Failure to schedule the special road test within thirty days
FTC	M34	C	23	1039	3	Following too closely
FTN		S	23	1213(e)	0	Failure to notify Commissioner of removal of IID or sale of vehicle
FTS	M22	C/DQ	23	1072	0	For CMV drivers required to stop, failing to stop before driving onto the crossing
FTT		C	23	370	0	Registration of farm tractors & trailers
FVU	M30	C	23	1039(a)	3	Carelessly following and passing a vulnerable user
FYB	N08	C	23	1057	4	Failure to yield to blind person
FYE	N04	C	23	1050	5	Failure to yield to emergency vehicle
FYL	N53	C	23	1047	2	Vehicle turning left
FYP	N08	C	23	1051	4	Failure to yield to pedestrian
FYY	N01	C	23	1048(c)	0	Failure to yield right of way
GL		O	23	1094	10	Grand larceny of motor vehicle
GN	M84	C	23	1091(b)	10	Grossly negligent operation (First offense)
GN2	M84	C	23	1091(b)	10	Grossly negligent operation (subsequent offense)
GNF	U10	C	23	1091(b)	10	Grossly negligent operation (fatality resulting)
GNI	M84	C	23	1091(b)	10	Grossly negligent operation w/serious bodily injury
HEC	M50	C	23	1006a	2	Highways; emergency closure
HFC	U10	DQ	23	4116	0	Causing a fatality by negligent operation of a CMV - with hazardous materials
HH		C	23	1056	0	PEDESTRIAN - Hitch-hiking
HM1		C	5	2001	0	Commercial vehicle haz-mat violation, group #1
HM2		C	5	2001	0	Commercial vehicle haz-mat violation, group #2
HM3		C	5	2001	0	Commercial vehicle haz-mat violation, group #3
HMA		C	5	2001	0	Hazardous Material, Air
HMH	E53	C	5	2001	0	Hazardous Material, Highway, Title 5 .
HMM		C	5	2001	0	Commercial vehicle haz-mat violation, miscellaneous

Code	ACD	Type	Title	Section	Pts	Description
HMR		C	5	2001	0	Hazardous material, railway
HMW		C	5	2001	0	Hazardous material, water
HO	W01	C	23	0673a	0	Habitual offender
HP		C	23	0304a(e)	0	Handicap parking
HRR		C	23	0421(a) (03)	0	Failure to file reports
HS	N40	C	23	1065	2	Hand signals
HUB		C	23	0421(a) (05)	0	Highway use by an out-of-state bus
HUF		C	23	0421(a) (4)	0	Failure to keep records
HUP		C	23	0421(a) (01)	0	No highway use permit
HUR		C	23	0421(a) (2)	0	Violation of regulations
IA		O	23	671	0	Involved in an accident
IAF		O	23	671	0	Involved in an accident, fatality resulting
IB1		C	23	473	0	Illegally engaged in business of buying/selling/offering for sale motor vehicles (First offense)
IB2		C	23	473	0	Illegally engaged in business of buying/selling/offering for sale motor vehicles (subsequent offense)
IDS		C	23	1028	0	Interference with devices or signals
IEL	B91	C	23	4103	2	Improper classification/endorsement on license or permit
IES	S92	O	23	1004	0	Excessive speed (20 over)
IFR	D02	B	23	202	0	Impersonating another in an application, or aiding an applicant by false representation
IH	W00	O	23	671	0	Improper handling of a motor vehicle
IHA	W00	O	23	671	0	Improper handling of a motor vehicle, accident resulting
IHH		C	23	1004	0	PEDESTRIAN - Hitch-hiking on interstate highway
IIE		C	23	1705	0	Impersonating a DMV Inspector or Examiner
IIR		S	23	1213(g)	0	RDL holder convicted of a Title 23 criminal offense
IMH	W70	DQ	23	4116	0	Imminent hazard
INS	D36	C	23	800	2	No insurance
IOP		C	23	1253	0	Inspection of permits (issued by commissioner of DMV)
IP	W00	S	23	671	0	Improper person
IP5	W00	S	23	0671(b)	0	Improper person - the safety of the public will be imperiled by your operation
IPI	W00	S	23	0671(b)	0	Improper person - the safety of the public will be imperiled by your operation
IR	E34	C	23	1244	0	Illumination required
IRM	F03	C	23	1245	0	Illumination required on motorcycles
IRV	N84	C	23	1004	2	Violation of interstate regulations (except speeding)
IS	S92	C	23	1004	2	Excessive speed on interstate highway (20 mph or more over speed limit)
ISC	S15	C	23	1004	2	Commercial motor vehicle being operated at a speed of 15 MPH (or more) over the speed limit on an interstate/limited access/controlled access highway
ISL	S92	C	23	1004	2	Speeding on interstate highway (1-19 mph over speed limit)
IUC	M24	C/DQ	23	1076(b)(3)	0	CMV drivers failing to cross because of insufficient undercarriage clearance
IWT		C	10	6607a(d)	0	Title 10 VSA, illegal waste transport
JNL	D29	C	23	614	2	Rights under junior license
JR1	A60	O	23	1216(a) (01)	0	Persons under 18/alcohol concentration of .02% or more, 1st offense, civil violation
JR2	A60	O	23	1216(a) (02)	0	Persons under 18/alcohol concentration of .02% or more, subsequent offense, civil violation
JR6	W01	S	23	607a	0	Junior Operator points accumulation recall
JRP	W00	S	23	607a	0	Junior Operator recall, 3-point speeding
JRR	A12	O	23	1216(c)	0	Persons under 18/refusal to submit to BAC test, civil violation
JRS	A12	O	23	1216(a) (02)	0	Persons under 18/refusal to submit to BAC test, subsequent, civil violation
JRT	W00	S				Junior operator or learner permit recall-texting
JW		C	23	1052	0	PEDESTRIAN - crossing except at crosswalks
LAL		C	23	1391	0	(LOCAL) Over the axle limit (T. 23, §1391a(d))
LAS	S92	C	23	1081(a)	2	(LOCAL) Excessive speed, accident involvement
LBK	N82	C	23	1113	2	Limitations on backing
LBR	S92	C	23	1081(b)	2	(LOCAL) Basic rule
LCM		C	23	1399	0	(LOCAL) Construction and maintenance equipment (T. 23, §1391a(d))
LCS	M16	C	23	1026	2	Lane control signals
LD		C	23	1241	0	Locking device
LDP		C	23	465	0	Loaning dealer's number plates prohibited
LES	S92	C	23	1081(d)	2	(LOCAL) Excessive speed
LEW		C	23	1400	0	(LOCAL) Permit to operate in excess of weight limits (T. 23, §1391a(d))
LFH	B02	DQ	23	4116	0	Commercial driver leaving the scene of a fatal crash - with hazardous materials
LIF	A12	S	23	1205(a)	0	Admin per se suspension - Refusal to submit to evidentiary test of BAC, third or subsequent offense (life revocation)
LIH	B03	DQ	23	4116	0	Commercial driver leaving the scene of a crash with injury - with hazardous materials
LIT	W00	S	24	2201	0	(Title 24) Throwing, depositing and dumping refuse (littering from a motor vehicle)
LK	E05	C	23	1243	2	Lights (what kind shall be installed)

Code	ACD	Type	Title	Section	Pts	Description
LLL		C	23	1400a	0	(LOCAL) Special local highway/bridge limits (T. 23, §1391a(d))
LN1		C	23	1434	0	Operation of over-size vehicle with no permit - local, First offense (CDL)
LN2		C	23	1434	0	Operation of over-size vehicle with no permit - local, subsequent offense in 24 months (CDL)
LN3		C	23	1434	0	Operation of over-size vehicle with no permit - local, third or subsequent offense in 24 months (CDL)
LNL	D07	C	23	4104	0	Limitation on number of driver licenses (CDL)
LNO	E55	C	23	1362	0	Night operation (of other vehicles)
LNV	E34	C				Lamps-other than head lamps-must be visible - 49 CFR 393.25(B)
LOG		C	23	3025	0	Log book
LOH		C	23	1431	0	(LOCAL) Over legal height
LOL		C	23	1432	0	(LOCAL) Over legal length
LOP	M70	C	23	1035	3	Limitations on passing
LOT		C	23	1408	0	(LOCAL) Overloaded truck (T. 23, §1391a(d))
LOV		C	23	1407	0	(LOCAL) Operation of over-weight vehicles (T. 23, §1391a(d))
LOW		O	23	1431	0	(LOCAL) Over legal width
LP		C	23	310	0	Loaning number plates
LP1		C	23	1434	0	Operation of over-size vehicle in violation of permit - local, First offense (CDL)
LP2		C	23	1434	0	Operation of over-size vehicle in violation of permit - local, subsequent offense in 24 months (CDL)
LP3		C	23	1434	0	Operation of over-size vehicle in violation of permit - local, third or subsequent offense in 24 months (CDL)
LPC		C	23	1451	0	Loads on passenger cars
LRL		C	23	1392	0	(LOCAL) Gross limits on highways (T. 23, §1391a(d))
LSA	B01	C	23	1128	*10	Leaving the scene of an accident
LSB	S92	C	23	1083(b) & (c)	2	(LOCAL) Special speed restrictions (bridge)
LSF	B02	C	23	1128(c)	*10	Leaving the scene of an accident with death resulting
LSI	B03	C	23	1128(b)	*10	Leaving the scene of an accident with serious bodily injury resulting
LSL	S92	C	23	1083(a) & (d)	2	(LOCAL) Special speed limitations
LSR	U21	C	23	1255(2)	0	Improper use of a vehicle with emergency lights and/or siren
LSV	S96	C	23	1082	2	(LOCAL) Slow-moving vehicle
LTP		C	23	493	0	Loaned transporter plates prohibited
LTS	E55	C	23	1243	0	Head or rear light violation
LVO	E55	C	23	1361	0	Lights on vehicles other than motor vehicles
M80	M80	B	23	4115(c)	0	Inattentive -careless-or negligent driver
MAR	W41	DQ	23	4116	0	Additional major offense after reinstatement
MCA		C	7	657(a)(3)	0	Minor (under-age) person consumed alcoholic beverage, 1st offense
MDP		C	23	455	0	Use of dealer's number plates by others than a dealer
MEP	F03	C	23	1257	2	No goggles or windshield (motorcycle)
MEQ	F03	C	23	1117	2	Footrest and handlebars (MOTORCYCLE)
MES	S81	C	23	1097	2	Exceeding speed limit traveling 60 mph or more and at least 30 mph in excess of limit
MFC	W00	O	7	656(f)	0	Minor (under-age) person failure to complete alcohol screening/counseling/therapy
MFT	W00	O	7	656(f)	0	Minor (under-age) person failure of timely completion of other diversion conditions
MIC		C	23	2302(c)	2	Any moving violation not covered by a specific code
MIS	W00	S	23	671	0	Any suspension not covered by a specific code
MLT	M40	C	23	1115	2	Operating motorcycles on roadways laned for traffic (properly)
MP		C	23	468	0	Misuse of plates
MPA	A31	C	7	657(a)(2)	0	Minor (under-age) person in possession of alcoholic beverage, 1st offense
MPF		C	23	368	0	Misuse of farm registration
MRA	D06	C	7	657(a)(1)	0	Minor (under-age) person misrepresenting age to procure alcoholic beverage, 1st offense
MSV		CB	23	1212(h)	0	RDL holder missed a service visit
MT1		C	23	0367a	0	Special purpose truck misuse (First offense)
MT2		C	23	0367a	0	Special purpose truck misuse (subsequent offense in 12 months)
MTM	E01	C	23	1305	0	Motor truck, mirror required
MV2	A31	S	7	657(d)(2)	0	Minor (under-age) person subsequent violation of Title 7, Section 656 or Title 7, Section 657
NAC		C	23	205	0	Notification of change of name or address
NCB			23	1452	0	Insufficient cross-binders, or insecure load
NE2		C	23	1091(a)	10	Negligent operation (subsequent offense)
NEF	U31	C	23	1091(b)	10	Negligent operation (fatality resulting)
NEG	M84	C	23	1091(a)	*10	Negligent Driving
NH	F03	C	23	1256	0	No helmets (MOTORCYCLE)
NL	B51	C	23	601	2	No operator's license
NLP	B51	C	23	615	2	No learner's permit

Code	ACD	Type	Title	Section	Pts	Description
NP1		C	23	1434(a)	0	Operation of over-size vehicle with no permit (First offense)
NP2		C	23	1434(a)	0	Operation of over-size vehicle with no permit (subsequent offense in 24 months)
NP3		C	23	1434(a)	0	Operation of oversize vehicle with no permit - third or subsequent offense in 24 months
NPZ	M71	C	23	1036	3	No passing zones
NR		C	23	301	0	Operating an unregistered vehicle
NRD		O	23	4105	0	Notification required by driver (CDL)
NRT		C	23	413	0	Registration of motor trucks (VT reg)
N83	N83	B	23	4115(c)	0	Improper start from parked position
OAL		C	23	1391	0	Over the axle limit
OBL		C	23	1396	0	Special limits for bridges and highways
OCA		C	23	1094(b)	10	Aggravated operation without consent of owner
OCD	A35	C	23	1134	2	Person operating a motor vehicle with an open alcoholic beverage container on a highway
OCF	U31	O	23	3905	0	Out-of-state careless & negligent driving, fatality resulting
OCP	A35	C	23	1134A	0	Passenger in a motor vehicle on a highway with an open alcoholic beverage container
ODI	A21	O	23	3905	0	Out-of-state DWI
OEI	E06	C	23	1282	0	Operator: Equipment and Inspection (FOR SCHOOL BUSES)
OGC	M09	C	23	1073	2	Heavy equipment operation at railroad grade crossings
OIL		C	23	711	0	Operates a driver training school or acts as an instructor without a license
OLF	D02	O	23	671	0	Obtained license fraudulently (revocation)
OLH		C	23	1431	0	Over the legal height of vehicle
OLL		C	23	1432	0	Over-length vehicle
OLS	B01	O	23	3905	0	Out-of-state leaving the scene of an accident
OLT		C	23	1408	0	Overloaded truck
OLW		C	23	1431	0	Overwidth vehicle
OOC		C	23	1094	*10	Operating without the owner's consent
OOS	B27	C	23	4120	0	5 VSA §2101, Commercial vehicle out-of-service violation
OOV		C	23	1407	0	Operation of over-weight vehicles
OPB		B	23	1213(h)	0	RDL Holder solicits another person to activate the IID
OPT		B	23	1213(k)	0	Other person tampering with an IID or otherwise assist the circumvention of an IID
ORL		C	23	1392	0	Gross limits on highways
ORR	N61	C	23	1037	2	One-way roadways and rotaries
OS1	B27	C/DQ	23	4120	0	Violation of out-of-service order
OS2	B27	C/DQ	23	4119	0	Violation of out-of-service order, second offense
OS3	B27	C/DQ	23	4119	0	Violation of out-of-service order, third or subsequent offense
OS4	B19	C/DQ	23	4119	0	Violation of out-of-service order while transporting hazardous materials and/or 15 (or more) passengers, including the driver, First offense
OS5	B19	C/DQ	23	4119	0	Violation of out-of-service order while transporting hazardous materials and/or 15 (or more) passengers, including the driver, second or subsequent offense
OSC	B26	C	23	0676(a)(b)	5	Operating after suspension/revocation/refusal, civil violation
OSI	D36	O	23	0801(a) (05)	0	Out-of-state insurance
OSX		C	23	4120	0	Employer's violation of an out-of-service order, or employer who knowingly requires or permits a driver to violate or fail to comply with an out-of-service order
OUS			23	0676	5	Operating under suspension/revocation/refusal, civil violation - post diversion
OWI		B	23	1213(f)	0	RDL holder operating vehicle without ignition interlock device installed in the vehicle
OWP		C	23	311	0	Operating unregistered motor vehicles without permit
OWS	E70	C	23	1125	0	Obstructing windshields
PAB	E31	C	23	1308	0	Performance ability of brakes
PAC	W00	O	23	671	0	Pending accident investigation
PAL	D02	B	23	201	0	Perjury in applying for a license
PAR	W00	B	23	201	0	Perjury in applying for a registration
PAV	D27	B	23	615(a)	2	Passenger age violation
PB	M02	C	23	1112	0	Passing barrier (Closed highways - restricted travel)
PC	W00	S	23	110	0	Protested check (written to DMV)
PCC		C	23	1054	0	PEDESTRIAN - crossing except at crosswalks, pedestrians to use right half of crosswalks
PCR		C	23	1055	0	PEDESTRIAN - Pedestrians on roadways
PCS		C	23	1023	0	PEDESTRIAN - Pedestrian control signals
PD	W14	S	23	671	0	Unresolved physical disability preventing safe operation of a motor vehicle
PDI		C	23	1130	0	Permitting Driving while intoxicated
PDM	W14	S	23	671	0	Physical disability - medical report
PDP	W14	S	23	671	0	Physical disability - psychiatric report
PDR		C	23	1130	0	Permitting driving while license revoked
PDS		C	23	1130	0	Permitting driving while license under suspension
PDV	W14	S	23	671	0	Physical disability - visual acuity
PED		C	23	1095(a)	2	Person under 18 yrs of age (Jr operator) using a portable electronic device while

Code	ACD	Type	Title	Section	Pts	Description
						operating a moving vehicle
PER		C	23	1130	0	Permitting illegal operation of a motor vehicle
PEW		C	23	1400	0	Permit to operate in excess of weight limits
PFA	W00	O	23	671	0	Pending investigation of a fatal accident
PGH		C	23	1126	0	Putting glass, etc. on highways prohibited
PKR		C	23	1101	0	Stopping, standing, or parking in restricted areas
PL		C	23	611	2	Possession of license
PM1		C	23	1401(d)	0	Category I violation of 1401 regarding contents of permit
PM2		C	23	1401(d)	0	Category II violation of 1401 regarding contents of permit
PNA		C	23	513	0	Plates not assigned
PNL		C	23	1130	0	Permitting operation without a license
POD	M72	C	23	1032	2	Passing vehicles in opposite direction
POL	M70	C	23	1033	3	Passing on the left
POR	M73	C	23	1034	3	Passing on right
PPC	W00	S	23	110	0	Protested check - CVO - PTO
PR	D27	C	23	614(a)	0	Passenger restrictions, Junior Operator violation
PRA		C	23	1014	0	Persons riding animals
PRK		C	23	1005	0	Parking regulations
PRW	N20	C	23	1053	2	Pedestrian right of way in crosswalks (drivers to exercise due care)
PSB	M75	C	23	1075	5	Passing a stopped school bus
PT	W00	O	23	604	0	Delinquent poll tax
PT1	W00	S	23	3009(b)	0	Privilege to operate (other than diesel tax reports)
PTC	W01	S	23	2506	0	Points suspension (changed)
PTO	W00	S	23	3009(b)	0	Privilege to operate
PTS	W01	S	23	2506	0	Points Suspension
PU	W00	S	32	8909	0	Non-payment of purchase and use tax
PV1		C	23	1434(b)	0	Operation of over-size vehicle in violation of permit limitations (First offense)
PV2		C	23	1434(b)	0	Operation of over-size vehicle in violation of permit limitations (subsequent offense in 24 months)
PV3		C	23	1434(b)	0	Operation of oversize vehicle in violation of permit limitations - 3rd or subsequent offense within 24 months
PVU	M70	C	23	1033(b)	3	Improperly passing a vulnerable user
RAR	M46	C	23	1041	2	Restricted access roadways
RBI		C	23	1137	0	BICYCLE - Riding on bicycle improperly
RCC	M10	C/DQ	23	1076	0	CMV drivers failing to obey traffic control device or enforcement official at railroad crossing
RCT	A12	O	23	1205	0	Refused chemical test
RD	M84	C	23	1091	*10	Reckless driving
RDP		C	23	464	0	Return of number plates by dealer
RE2	A12	B	23	1208	0	(CRIMINAL) Refusal to submit to evidentiary test (one previous conviction of Title 23, §1201)
RE3	A12	B	23	1208	0	(CRIMINAL) Refusal to submit to evidentiary test (previous convictions of Title 23, §1201)
RED	E01	C	23	0371a(b)	0	Red reflector on wood splitters and pole dinkeys
REF	A12	B	23	1206	0	(CRIMINAL) Refusal to submit to evidentiary test of BAC (accident involvement)
RL1			23	2592	0	Failure to return rented/leased motor vehicle within 72 hrs. (first offense)
RL2			23	2592	0	Failure to return rented/leased motor vehicle within 72 hrs. (subsequent offense)
RMC	F06	C	23	1114	2	Riding on motorcycles (properly)
RNL	D29	C	23	612	2	Restricted license
ROF	B08	C	23	1133	10	Refusal to obey an officer - Fatal
ROI	B08	C	23	1133	10	Refusal to obey an officer - Injury
ROL		C	23	1213c(m)	0	Renting/owning/leasing a vehicle after issuance of immobilization/forfeiture order
ROO	M08	C	23	1133	*10	Refusal to obey an officer
RPL		C	23	1246	0	Restrictions (Prohibited lights)
RRC	M09	C	23	1071	2	Railroad grade crossings
RRL		C	23	1411	0	Refusal to weigh vehicles or remove load
RRT		C	5	3408(c)	0	Trail use rule for railroad rights-of-way
RSS		C	23	1013	2	Refusal to stop on signal
RSV		C	23	2084	0	Report of theft, recovery of unclaimed vehicle
RTA	D29	S	23	1209a	0	Violation of conditions of total abstinence reinstatement
RTP	F05	C	23	1344	0	Riding in trailer coaches (Prohibited)
RTT	E37	C	23	1302(a)	0	Rubber tires on trucks (Required)
S00	S92	C	23	1003	2	Speeding (1-10 mph over speed limit) violation of 1.3
S02	S92	C	23	1003	3	Speeding (11-20 mph over speed limit) violation of 1.3
S03	S71	C	23	1003	5	Speeding (21-30 mph over speed limit) violation of 1.3
S04	S92	C	23	1003	8	Speeding (31 or more mph over speed limit) violation of 1.3

Code	ACD	Type	Title	Section	Pts	Description
S05	S15	C	23	1003	3	Operate a commercial motor vehicle 15-20 MPH above the posted speed limit
S14	S14	B	23	4115(c)	0	Speeding 11-14 over the limit
SAF		C	23	1285	0	Failure to provide instruction in safe riding practices (school bus)
SB1	A12	B	23	1206	0	(School bus driver) criminal refusal to submit to evidentiary test, 1st offense
SB2	A12	B	23	1208	0	(School bus driver) criminal refusal to submit to evidentiary test, 2nd offense
SB3	A12	B	23	1208	0	(School bus driver) criminal refusal to submit to evidentiary test, 3rd/subsequent offense
SBD	M09	C	23	1072(c)	2	School bus door not opened
SBE		C	23	1284	0	Failure to identify, equip and maintain (school bus)
SBL	E56	C	23	1072	0	School bus driver failure to use flashing signal lamps
SCL		C	23	1251	0	Sirens and colored lamps
SC1		S	23	4116	0	.02 BAC or more operating a school bus - civil
SC2		S	23	4116	0	.02 BAC or more operating a school bus - second or subsequent - civil suspension
SCL			23	1251	0	Sirens and colored lamps
SDC	M20	C/DQ	23	1076	0	CMV drivers not required to stop failing to slow and check tracks are clear of trains
SDE	E06	C	23	1281	0	Additional equipment (for school buses)
SEL		S	23	801	0	Sealed record
SEV		C	23	1213c(n)	0	Selling/encumbering vehicle prohibited
SG	E01	C	23	1242	0	Safety glass (cars shall have)
SGC	M22	C	23	1072(a)	2	Certain vehicles must stop at railroad grade crossings
SHM	B26	DQ	23	4116	0	Commercial driver operating while suspended for prior CMV violations - with hazardous materials
SIG	N40	C	23	1064	2	Signals required
SL		C	23	1454	0	Securing loads
SL1	S92	C	23	1007	2	(LOCAL) Speeding (1-10 mph over speed limit) violation of 1.7
SL2	S92	C	23	1007	3	(LOCAL) Speeding (11-20 mph over speed limit) violation of 1.7
SL3	S71	C	23	1007	5	(LOCAL) Speeding (21-30 mph over speed limit) violation of 1.7
SL4	S92	C	23	1007	8	(LOCAL) Speeding (31 or more mph over speed limit) violation of 1.7
SL5	S15	C	23	1007	3	(LOCAL) Operate a commercial motor vehicle 15-20 MPH above the posted speed limit
SLL		C	23	1400a	0	Special local highway/bridge limits
SMV		C	23	1082	2	Slow-moving vehicle
SNO		C	23	1126a	0	Depositing snow onto or across certain highways
SO		C	23	1010	2	Special occasions (town ordinance)
SOC	S15	O	23	1010	2	Commercial motor vehicle being operated at a speed of 15 MPH (or more) over the speed limit - special occasions (town ordinance)
SOE	E06	C	23	1281(a)	0	Optional equipment (for school buses)
SP6	S15	O	23	4103	0	(Commercial driver) Operating commercial vehicle 15 mph (or more) above posted speed limit
SPL		C	29	170	0	Title 29, violation in State of Vermont parking lot
SPV	N83	C	23	1063	2	Starting parked vehicles
SRR		O	23	1283(a) (04)	2	School bus signal lamps lighted at railroad grade crossings
SS	M15	O	23	1048(b)	2	Failing to stop at a stop sign
SSA	W00	S	23	671(e)	0	Failure to correct social security number discrepancy with the Social Security Administration
SSB		C	23	1083(b)& (c)	2	Special speed limitations (bridge)
SSD		C	23	1093	2	Smokescreen device (prohibited)
SSL	S93	C	23	1083(a)& (d)	2	Special speed limitations
SSM		C	23	1027	0	Unauthorized signs, signals or markings
STR		C	23	495	0	Failure of transporter to return registration certificate/plates
SUP	D51	S	15	798	0	Suspension for non-payment of child support, Title 15.
T13		C	13		0	Unknown violation of Title 13 amended to a DMV violation
TAN		C	10	1454	0	Title 10 - Transport aquatic plants and aquatic nuisance species
TCD	M16	C	23	1021	2	Traffic control devices (failure to obey)
TCI		B	23	1213(f)	0	RDL Holder tampering with an IID or otherwise Circumventing the IID
TCS	M16	C	23	1022	2	Traffic control signals (failure to obey)
TFE	E01	C	23	1342	0	Trailer coaches (fire extinguisher required)
TI	N50	C	23	1061	0	Turning at intersections
TID	A41	C	23	1213a(h)	0	Tampered with immobilization device or mobilized vehicle subject to an immobilization order
TKR		C	23	496	0	Transporter required to keep written records
TL	E05	C	23	1248	0	Tail lights (required)
TMD		C	23	1135	2	Trespass by motor vehicle (with damage caused)
TMT		C	23	1302(b)	0	Number of trailers
TMV		C	23	1135	2	Trespass by motor vehicle (no damage caused)
TNC	M21	C/DQ			0	CMV drivers not required to stop failing to stop if the tracks are not clear
TNP		C	23	458	0	Limitation of use of temporary number plates
TO2	W00	S	7	1005(a)	0	Title 7, failure to pay penalty for selling/furnishing tobacco product(s) to a minor -

Code	ACD	Type	Title	Section	Pts	Description
						licensed individual, Second/SUBSEQUENT OFFENSE
TOB	W00	S	7	1005(a)	0	Title 7, failure to pay penalty for selling/furnishing tobacco product(s) to a minor - licensed individual, First OFFENSE
TP	N56	C	23	1062	2	Turning prohibited
TPD		C	23	461	0	Failure to destroy temporary plates
TR	A12	O	23	1205	0	Refusal to chemical test, 1st offense (civil)
TR2	A12	O	23	1205	0	Refusal of chemical test, 2nd offense (civil)
TR3	A12	O	23	1205	0	Refusal of chemical test, 3rd offense (civil)
TR4	A12	O	23	1205	0	Refusal of chemical test, 4th offense (civil)
TR5	A12	O	23	1205	0	Refusal of chemical test, 5th or subsequent offense (civil)
TSC		C	23	1341	0	Trailer coaches - safety chain required
TV		C	23	1095	2	Television installed
TVU		C	23	1039(a)	3	Throwing an object at a vulnerable user
TX2	M85	C	23	1099	2	Texting while operating a moving motor vehicle on a highway - second or subsequent offense
TXD	M85	C	23	1099	5	Texting while operating a moving motor vehicle on a highway
UD	A22	O	23	0671(a)	0	Use of drugs
UFL		C	23	1304	0	Use of flares
UJ	D39	S	23	605	0	Unsatisfied judgment
UL	A21	O	23	0671(a)	0	Use of liquor
UMV		C	23	1111	0	Unattended motor vehicle
UTP		C	23	491	0	Use of transporter plates restricted
VES	S92	O	23	1007(b)	6	Excessive speed - local ordinance (20 mph or more over speed limit)
VIN		C	23	1701	0	Possession of motor vehicle w/serial or motor numbers defaced
VLP		C	23	1104	0	Stopping prohibited (in restricted areas)
VLR	N84	O	23	2302(c)	0	Violation of the law of the road
VNI		C	23	1222	0	Vehicle not inspected
VO	N84	O	23	1008	0	Violation of a local ordinance
VSL	S92	O	23	1007(a)	3	Local (ordinance) speed limits
VTF	U03	C	23	4116	0	Any offense state/federal law punishable by more than one year imprisonment
WDA		B	23	1208	0	Conviction of 1201 D - BAC of .16 or more
WDC		S	23	1205	0	Civil suspension - .02 BAC with second or previous 1201 BAC of .16 or more
WDD		B	23	1208	0	Third or subsequent 1201 .02 BAC with second or previous 1201 BAC of .16 or more
WF	E01	C	23	1306	0	Rear wheel flaps (required)
WPC	W13	S	23	0607a(d)	0	Withdrawal of parental consent
WS		C	23	1131	0	Warning signal (horn)
W60	W60		23	4116	0	Second CMV railroad violation in three-year period
W61	W60		23	4116	0	Third CMV railroad violation in three-year period
W81	W81	B	23	4115(c)	0	Refused to submit to employer directed drug test
ZAK	W00	S	23	671	0	Under suspension in the State of Alaska

Note: See violation listed above (ZAK). If a driver is under suspension in another state, this is indicated with a "Z" before the two-letter abbreviation. The complete listing of every state is omitted.

Code	ACD	Type	Title	Section	Pts	Description
16A	D06	B	7	656(a)(1)	0	Minor (over 16 years of age) misrepresenting age to procure alcoholic beverage
16B	A31	B	7	656(a)(2)	0	Minor (over 16 years of age) in possession of alcoholic beverage(s)
16C	A31	B	7	656(a)(3)	0	Minor (over 16 years of age) consumed alcoholic beverage(s)
21A	A60	B	23	1216(a)(1)	0	Persons under 21 years of age with alcohol concentration of .02 (or more), First offense
21B	A60	B	23	1216(a)(2)	0	Persons under 21 years of age with alcohol concentration of .02 (or more), subsequent offense
21C	A12	B	23	1216(d)	0	Persons under 21 years of age refusal to submit to evidentiary test, First offense
21D	A12	B	23	1216(d)	0	Persons under 21 years of age refusal to submit to evidentiary test, subsequent offense
2RR	W60	DQ				Second CMV RR violation in three year period
3RR	W61	DQ	23	4116		Third CMV railroad violation in three-year period
4P		C	23	1118	2	Four (or more) persons in front seat
5PT	B63	S	23	801(a)(1)(G)	0	Financial Responsibility Insurance required for not providing proof of liability insurance coverage at the time of a moving violation when 5 points are already on record

Note: In general, all codes starting with "8" signify a snowmobile violation.

Code	Type	Title	Section	Pts	Description
81N	O	23	3206(b))	0	Operating a snowmobile without liability insurance
8AE	C	23	3212	0	Failure to stop, attempting to elude an officer

Code	Type	Title	Section	Pts	Description
8AH	C	23	3206(b)(02)	0	Operation along public highway
8AL	C	23	3206(b)(20)	0	Trail access limited to after 11 PM and before 6 AM when less than 500 feet from a residence
8CD	C	23	3206(b)(19)(D)	0	Failure to display commercial identification
8CE	C	23	3206(b)(14)	0	Operation within a cemetery
8CI	C	23	3206(b)(19)(C)	0	Display of improper TMA by a snowmobile used in a commercial operation
8CL	C	23	3206(b)(19)(B)	0	Commercial operation on public land/body of water without written consent
8CN	C	23	3206(b)(13)	0	Operating in a careless and negligent manner
8CP	C	23	3206(b)(19)(A)	0	Commercial operation on private land/body of water without written consent
8CS	C	23	3206(b)(22)	0	Operating a snowmobile on the trail system during the closed season
8DE	C	23	3205(a)	0	Defective or inadequate equipment
8DI	B	23	3207a	0	Operation while under the influence of drugs or intoxicating beverages
8DN	C	23	3209(a)	0	Defacing a motor or serial number
8DP	C	23	3206(b)(03)	0	Distance from plowed portion of highway
8FR	C	23	3211(b)	0	Failure to report an accident within 72 hours
8FS	C	23	3211(a)	0	Failure to stop after accident, failure to give identity
8HW	C	23	3206(b)(10)	0	Harassing wildlife
8ID	C	23	3206(b)(11)	0	No registration or consent form with vehicle, registration number improperly displayed
8IN	C	23	3206(b)(19)	0	Operating a snowmobile without liability insurance
8J1	B	23	3207f(a)(01)	0	Persons under 21 years of age operating a snowmobile with .02 (or more) BAC, First offense
8J2	B	23	3207f(a)(02)	0	Persons under 21 years of age operating a snowmobile with .02 (or more) BAC, subsequent offense
8J3	B	23	3207f(d)	0	Persons under 21 years of age refusal to submit to evidentiary test, First offense
8J4	B	23	3207f(d)	0	Persons under 21 years of age refusal to submit to evidentiary test, subsequent offense
8LA	C	23	3206(b)(15)	0	Operation on a limited access/interstate highway
8MD	C	23	3205(b)	0	Improper muffling device
8MR	C	23	3204(b)	0	Misuse of manufacturer's/seller's registration or number plate
8MS	C	23	2302 (c)	0	Any snowmobile violation without a specific offense code
8MU	C	23	3206(b)(04)	0	On/across a municipal highway
8NC	C	23	3206(b)(08)	0	Snowmobile operated by a person born after July 3, 1983 without Snowmobile Education Certificate
8NH	C	23	3206	0	Operate, ride on, or be pulled by a snowmobile without proper protective headgear
8OH	C	23	3206(b)(01)	0	Operation on or across a public highway
8OR	C	23	3203	0	Failure to return transferred registration
8OS	C	23	3206(b)(16)	0	Operation on a sidewalk
8PO	C	23	3206(a)	0	Permitting operation of an unregistered snowmobile
8PR	C	23	3206(b)(06)	0	Operation on private land or private body of water
8PS	C	23	3206(b)(17)	0	Operating snowmobile after privileges suspended
8PU	C	23	3206(b)(07)	0	Operation on public land/in a natural area
8RP	C	23	3206(b)(18)	0	Operation of a snowmobile in an unreasonable manner
8SE	C	23	3205(c)	0	Sale without required equipment
8SS	C	23	3206(b)(23)	0	Operating a snowmobile in the open season when trail system not officially opened by *VAST*
8TS	C	23	3209(b)	0	Damaging or removing trail signs
8U8	C	23	3206(b)(07)	0	Snowmobile operated by a child under 8 years of age
8UN	C	23	3206(b)(09)	0	Operation by a person under 16 years of age
8UO	C	23	3206(b)(08)	0	Operation by a person under 12 years of age
8US	C	23	3202	0	Operation of an unregistered snowmobile
8WP	C	23	3206B	0	Operating snowmobile after 11PM and before 6AM when prohibited

Note: In general, all codes starting with "9" signify a motorboat violation.

Code	Type	Title	Section	Pts	Description
910	C	10	1424	0	Violation of Title 10
9AE	C	23	3311(f)	0	Attempting to elude a law enforcement officer
9AO	C	23	3311		Authority of law enforcement officer to stop and board vessel
9BC	C	23	3305(b)	0	Operating without a boating certificate
9BR	C	23	3316	0	Boat races
9CA	C	23	3305(h)	0	Failure to notify DMV of change of address
9CN	C	23	3311(a)	0	Careless and negligent operation
9DD	C	23	3381	0	Diver down flag
9DI	B	23	3323	0	Operation of vessel with .08% (or more) BAC
9DR	C	23	3311(c)	0	Distance requirements
9FA	O	12	5704	0	Failure to appear or answer uniform snowmobile/boating complaint
9FC	C	23	3829	0	Altering, forging, or counterfeiting vessel certifications
9FI	C	23	3327(a)	0	Person operating vessel shall give information to law enforcement officer
9FR	C	23	3313(b)	0	Failing to file an accident report
9FS	C	23	3327(b)	0	Operator of vessel shall stop when signaled by law enforcement officer

Code	Type	Title	Section	Pts	Description
9HP	C	23	3311(d)	0	Underwater historic preserve area
9ID	C	23	3305(e)	0	Compliance with federal motorboat identification
9IN	C	23	3305(i)	0	Incorrect number displayed on boat
9J1	B	23	3323a(a)(1)	0	Persons under 21 years of age operating a vessel with .02 (or more) BAC, First offense
9J2	B	23	3323a(a)(2)	0	Persons under 21 years of age operating a vessel with .02 (or more) BAC, subsequent offense
9J3	B	23	3323a(d)	0	Persons under 21 years of age refusal to submit to evidentiary test, First offense
9J4	B	23	3323a(d)	0	Persons under 21 years of age refusal to submit to evidentiary test, subsequent offense
9LE	C	23	3306	0	Lights and equipment
9LS	C	23	3313(a)	0	Leaving the scene of an accident
9MD	C	23	3309	0	Muffling device
9MT	C	23	3306(e)	0	Marine toilet (improper/illegal emptying)
9NB	C	23	3303	0	Unnumbered boat
9OR	C	23	3305(d)	0	Old registration certificate to be returned
9OV	C	23	3311(e)	0	Overloaded vessel
9PI	C	23	3311(b)	0	Permitting use by an intoxicated person
9PS	C	23	3305(a)	0	Operating privileges suspended
9PW	C	23	3312(a)	0	Operation of personal watercraft
9QP	C	23	3305(a)	0	Qualified person may operate
9RP	C	23	3311(g)	0	Residential vessel prohibited
9RR	C	23	3308	0	Boat rental records
9RT	B	23	3326	0	Refusal to submit to a chemical test to determine alcohol content
9RV	C	23	3312	0	Rules between vessels
9SO	C	23	3315(a)	0	Water ski observer
9ST	C	23	3315(c)	0	Improper ski towing
9TR	C	23	3305(j)	0	Temporary registration
9UB	C	23	3305(a)	0	Unregistered boat
9UI	B	23	3323	0	Operating a vessel while under the influence
9UO	C	23	3305(a)	0	Under age operation
9VS	C	23	3307(a)	0	Documented boat validation sticker
9WR	C	10	1424	0	Surface water rules
9ZM	C	10	1266	0	Transportation of zebra mussels

Point System Summary

Points range from 2 to 10. There is an automatic suspension for accumulation of 10 points within 2 years

Virginia

Administration	Important Telephone and Web Contacts
Richard D. Holcomb, Commissioner Millicent N. Ford, Director, Driver Services Department of Motor Vehicles PO Box 27412, Richmond 23269 804-367-6602 www.dmvnow.com Virginia Statutes: http://leg1.state.va.us/000/src.htm	Driver Licensing .... 804-497-7100 SR-22, Financial Responsibility .... 804-497-7100 Commercial Driver License .... 804-497-7100 Vehicle Information .... 804-497-7100 Bureau of Insurance .... 804-371-9741 State Police .... 804-674-2000 General Email Contacts: www.dmvnow.com/webdoc/utilities/contact.asp

Driver's License Format, Issuance and Renewal

License Classes, Restrictions and Endorsements Appear After the Driving Record Content Section

License Format

All licenses issued since July 1, 2003 display a computer generated random number consisting of an alpha character followed by eight numbers. Social Security Numbers were once used as the driver license number, but they are nearly all phased out.

Document Appearance

Virginia rolled out a newly designed license and ID documents in July 2009. The new cards are made of laser engraved polycarbonate. It will take at least 8 years to phase-in these new cards. The existing style of digitized driver's licenses has been in production since April 1999. Both styles are reviewed below.

Current Format

Security Characteristics: Driver's licenses banners have blue lettering; ID card banners have green lettering; and children's ID card banners have gold lettering. Cards for individuals age 21 and over bear an image of the Virginia state capitol building; cards for individuals under 21 show images of the state flower - the dogwood. Polycarbonate card construction features include security printing on internal layers and a clear window secondary photo. Laser engraved personalization features include black printing burned into card body, grayscale photos burned into card body, and tactile raised engraving.

Position of Photo: All primary photographs are grayscale, full faced and are displayed on the left side of the cards. Secondary photographs are grayscale, full faced and displayed in a clear window, visible from the front and back of the cards.

Minor Age Driver Locator: Minors aged 15 to 21 have a vertical card; minors under 15 have a horizontal card. Licenses and ID cards for minors show the date that the individual turns 18 and 21.

CDL Indicator: Indicated by class. License reads "Commercial Drivers License" across the top.

Previous Format (Issued prior to July 2009)

Security Characteristics: A blue band runs across the top portion of the license. The security laminate contains small outlines of the state and the word Virginia that changes color depending on the angle viewed. The word Virginia appears across the top of the license. Bar codes on the back of the license replicate information on the front, providing added security.

Position of Photo: All photographs are taken full faced and are displayed in the lower left corner (lower right corner on ID cards).

Minor Age Driver Locator: Minors aged 15 to 21 have a vertical card; minors under 15 have a horizontal card Licenses and ID cards for minors show the date that the individual turns 18 and 21 (printed in red next to photo.)

CDL Indicator: Indicated by class. License reads "Commercial Drivers License" across the top.

Issuance

Location of Requirements for Proof of Identity:

https://www.dmv.virginia.gov/webdoc/pdf/dmv141.pdf

Age Requirements

The minimum age is 18 for full license privileges. A Learner's Permit is issued at 15 years, 6 months—there are passenger and curfew restrictions. At age 16, 3 months and after holding the Learner's Permit for 9 months, a limited driver's license is issued. There are restrictions on passenger limits and curfew until the driver reaches the age of 18. Also, any teen under the age of 19 must complete a state-approved driver education program.

Residency

Individuals moving to VA have 60 days to obtain a VA driver's license, or 30 days if for a CDL. Non-resident's home-state driver's license honored for up to one year after expiration for the purpose of exchange for a VA license without testing requirement. Applicants must be a resident of Virginia in order to obtain any type of license or ID card.

Renewal

Since July 1, 2008, driver's licenses issued are valid for 8 years instead of 5. However, the validity period for ID cards remained at 5 years. Other exceptions to the 8-year validity law include teens, registered sex offenders and those with limited duration driver's licenses issued to customers who are in the United States for a limited amount of time. Previously, all renewals expire on a year when the driver's age is divisible by 5 (i.e., 25, 30, 35, 40, etc.). Driver keeps same number when renewing. Renewals and address changes can be done online.

When renewing a driver's license at age 20, the driver is required to take the knowledge test if driving record reflects at least one demerit point conviction. If a demerit point conviction (including safety belt or child restraint violations) while driver is under age 20, driver is required to attend a driver-improvement clinic (web-based clinics may not be taken).

A Military Extension is granted and valid for 3 years, including for spouses and dependents; additional extensions may be granted.

Note the DMV does not issue driver's licenses and ID cards in DMV customer service centers. Customers receive new secure licenses and ID cards by mail.

Elderly-Related Restrictions

None indicated.

Vehicle Insurance, Title and Registration Facts

Insurance and Financial Responsibility

Minimum liability limits for insurance and financial responsibility are $25,000/50,000/20,000. Proof of financial responsibility, when requested, shall be made by filing with the Commissioner the written certificate of any insurance carrier authorized to do business in the Commonwealth certifying there is in effect a motor vehicle liability policy for the benefit of the person required to furnish proof of financial responsibility. *Form SR 22* can be used for this filing. However, persons required to provide proof of financial responsibility due to a driving under the influence related conviction must have an insurance policy with double the minimum limits ($50,000/$100,000/$40,000). *Form FR-44* is used for this filing.

Virginia law requires a vehicle to have liability insurance or pay a $500 Uninsured Motor Vehicle (UMV) fee at the time of registration. The UMV fee does not provide any insurance but allows one to drive an uninsured vehicle at one's own risk for a one-year period.

Virginia has an electronic Insurance Verification program that requires insurance companies to report automobile liability insurance for new business and cancellations. In addition, there are other verification activities including, suspected uninsured accidents, police accident reports, citizen information and law enforcement notification. It is unlawful to register or operate or permit the operation of an uninsured motor vehicle, subject to Virginia registration, without vehicle owners having liability insurance on their vehicle or paying the UMV fee upon registration. Virginia is not a mandatory insurance state.

Registration Renewal

One may renew for one, two, or three years. Renewal may be performed online, by mail, or by phone by using DMV's automated phone service at 804-497-7100. The DMV charges extra fees if renewal is done at a Customer Service Center or a Satellite Office.

New Residents

Every person residing in the state who owns a motor vehicle must register their vehicle within 30 days of purchase. Non-resident owners of passenger vehicles with current out-of-state (or country) registration may operate the vehicle for 6 months, then the vehicle must be registered in Virginia. There is an exception for a non-Virginia resident active duty military service member, activated reserve or national guard member, or mobilized reserve or national guard member living in Virginia and the sole owner of a vehicle that is titled and registered in another state - these people are not required to title or register their vehicle in Virginia.

Inspections and Emissions Testing

An annual safety inspection on all vehicles is required. The inspection is governed by the Virginia State Police.   There is no statewide emission test law, but an emissions inspection is required for vehicle more than 2 years old that are garaged in the counties of Arlington, Fairfax, Loudoun, Prince William, or Stafford, or the cities of Alexandria, Fairfax, Falls Church, Manassas or Manassas Park, must meet the emissions inspection requirement before registering the vehicle with the DMV.   The emissions inspections are valid for two years. Motor vehicles exempted from emissions inspections include any gasoline powered passenger or property carrying vehicle with a model year that is more than 25 model years old before January 1 of the current calendar year, passenger or property carrying vehicle with a manufacturer's designated gross vehicle weight rating of more than 10,000, diesel powered vehicles, qualified hybrid vehicles, vehicles exclusively powered by clean fuel (natural gas, solar, electric) l, and motorcycles.

Passenger Plate Facts

There are two plates with two decals (MO) (YR) on both plates. County of issuance is not designated on the license plate. When a vehicle is sold the plates remain with seller.

Withdrawal Sanctions, and Alcohol and Drug Testing

Alcohol and Chemical Testing

The illegal intoxication level is .08 % and above, .02% and above for drivers under 21, and .04% for CDL. Breath testing is authorized. Virginia has an implied-consent violation. A refusal to submit to a breath test or having a BAC of .08% or greater will result in an immediate 7-day administrative license suspension. Second offense of refusal and/or BAC of .08% or greater is 60 days or until trial; third offense is until trial. Anyone driving during a DUI suspension or DUI restricted license with a BAC of .02% or greater is subject to an additional one-year revocation. Also, driving on a DUI-related suspended or revoked license results in a 30-day impoundment of the vehicle being operated.

Suspensions and Revocations

The Virginia DMV is in compliance with the provisions of the Motor Carrier Safety Improvement Act (MCSIA). See the Appendix for more information about these mandatory CDL disqualification sanctions.

Child Support.. Suspension initiated by Department of Social Services.
Driving While Intoxicated
    First Offense ....One-year revocation or restricted driving privileges.
    Second Offense (within 5 years).............................. Three-year revocation or one-year revocation and two years restricted driving privileges. Ignition interlock required.
    Second Offense (within 10 years)........................... Three-year revocation or four-month revocation and two years and eight months restricted driving privileges. Ignition interlock required.
    Third Offense... Indefinite revocation. Eligible to petition the court for restricted privileges after three years and for full restoration after five years. Ignition interlock required as of 2009 if not court ordered DMV takes administrative action regardless.
    Driving While Under the Influence .... Felony—six points.
Note: Drivers under 21 with BAC of .02 or more will be suspended for one year.
Failure to Have Liability Insurance .... Suspension (driver must also pay the uninsured motor vehicle fee of $500 and file proof of financial responsibility for three years from the date of suspension).
Failure to Pay Fines-Motor Vehicle/Criminal Offenses.... Court suspension.
Making a Bomb Threat
    First Offense .... One-year revocation or until age 17 (whichever is longer).
    Second Offense... One-year revocation or until age 18 (whichever is longer).
    If Over 18 Years Old .... One-year revocation, Class 5 Felony.

Manslaughter (Voluntary or Involuntary).........................Indefinite revocation, eligible for restricted privileges in three years, six points. Full restoration after 5 years.

Providing Alcohol to Minor or Intoxicated Person...........One-year suspension.

Point Accumulation
   Eight Points in Twelve months or
     Twelve Points in Twenty-four Months ....Advisory letter.
   Twelve Points in Twelve Months or
     Eighteen Points in Twenty-four Months ....Driver improvement clinic; 6-month probation; 18-month control period.
   Eighteen Points in Twelve Months or
     Twenty-four Points in Twenty-four Months ....90-day suspension (rapid violator) and Driver Improvement clinic; 6-month probation; 18-month control period.

Point Violation While Driving When on Driver Improvement Probation
   Three-Point Violation ....45-day Suspension.
   Four-Point Violation..60-day Suspension.
   Six-Point Violations...90-day Suspension.

Taking a Driver's License Test for Another Person or Appearing as Another.
     Person to Renew Their License ....One-year revocation.

Under 18 Safety Belt/Child Restraint or Demerit Point Violation
   1st Conviction...Driver Improvement Clinic and passenger restriction until 18.
   2nd Conviction ....*Ninety-day suspension.
   3rd Conviction ....One-year revocation or until 18, whichever last.

   * = May petition the Juvenile and Domestic Relations Court for restricted privileges from home to place of employment and/or an institution of higher learning only.

Restricted Driving Privileges

In certain instances, when a driving privilege is suspended or revoked, the driver may be eligible for restricted driving privileges. Restricted driving privileges are granted either by a court or by DMV, depending on the nature of the suspension or revocation. If the driver is a CDL holder and the privilege to drive commercial motor vehicles has been disqualified, the driver is not eligible for restricted privileges to drive commercial motor vehicles. For more information, visit www.dmvnow.com/webdoc/citizen/drivers/restrict_privs.asp.

Reinstatement Requirements

Reinstatement fees for suspensions and revocations range from $145.00 to $220.00. If the driver has two or more outstanding suspension/revocation orders in effect, the driver must pay an additional $5.00 for each second/subsequent suspension/revocation order to reinstate driving privileges. Depending upon the suspension or revocation order, other applicable compliance item(s) may apply. Persons with DWI revocations must provide proof of insurance for three years from the revocation end date, complete an alcohol treatment/education program, and have ignition interlock equipment installed on all vehicles owned/co-owned.

Record Access: Laws, Rules, and Forms

Note: This Section Applies to Both Driver and Vehicle Records.

Governing Statutes and Rules

State Statutes: http://leg1.state.va.us/000/src.htm
Sections 46.2-208, 46.2-209, 46.2-210, 46.2-211, 46.2-212, and 2.2-3800 through 2.2-3809 of the Code of Virginia outline the circumstances under which entities may be authorized to access vehicle and driver records and the limitations on use of such records. Virginia statutes stipulate that all DMV records are privileged and are not available to the general public. DMV may only release driver, vehicle and personal information from their records under the conditions specified in the statutes mentioned above. The purpose must be stated and access is restricted to insurance, employment, school boards, law enforcement, and courts. Records must be used strictly for the purpose stated in the request, and cannot be reused. A signed contract is required to obtain records online. The Virginia rules are stricter than DPPA, but broader in scope by outlining specific groups entitled to records. 46.2.208 B Virginia lists 28 specific entities or rules of or about who are entitled to records. See this list at http://leg1.state.va.us/cgi-bin/legp504.exe?000+cod+46.2-208.
It is worth noting in the description text for numbers 8, 9, 11, 12, 13, 15, 18, 22, 24, 25, and 26 the following phrase appears..."the Commissioner shall (i) compare personal information supplied by the company or agent with that contained in the Department's records and, when the information supplied by the {company or agent} is different from that contained in the Department's records, provide the {company or agent} with correct information as contained in the Department's record."

Specific About Vehicle Records: The state permits private investigation and security agents, who are licensed in Virginia and are listed as a "compliance agent" by the Department of Justice Services, to receive address information when submitting a license plate number. Users must also be pre-approved by the Department.

Request and Consent Forms

Written requests for driving records, accident reports, and vehicle records may be submitted on the same *Form CRD-93* found at www.dmvnow.com/webdoc/pdf/crd93.pdf. The form requires the signature of the requester, and if for a driving record from the subject as well.

Non-governmental entities who request records on an ongoing basis may apply for access to DMV records by downloading an *Information Use Agreement Application US531A* document found at www.dmvnow.com/webdoc/pdf/us531a.pdf. Mail the completed application and a $25.00 non-refundable application fee to the address printed on the front of the application. (The fee is $12.50 for non-profits and charities.) The $25.00 fee may be paid by check, cashier's check or money order made payable to DMV. Also, one can order the application by calling 804-497-7155.

The application requests specific information about the requester's DMV records access needs, including the purpose(s), security measures to ensure protection of records, and the names of authorized users. DMV must approve the application before the requester can gain access to DMV records. Otherwise consent from the driver is required for release unless the record is being provided to law enforcement, a government entity, the DMV or if an employer is requesting on a CDL driver.

Vendor and Third Party Access Policy

Approved online vendors may access records for other vendors (who are not online, etc.) who will then sell to an end user, provided the following occurs—

- Contract between original vendor and reseller contains same language as contract between the state and the original vendor.
- Contract between reseller and end-user contains same language as

contract between the state and the original vendor.

Information cannot be sold for marketing purposes. Non-individual specific information can be provided for statistical purposes.

Records Ordered For Non-permissible Uses

Not available. Without consent or a permissible use, records, even without personal information, are not provided.

Access to Driver-Related Records

Driving Records

General Information and Fees

Department of Motor Vehicles, Customer Records Work Center, PO Box 27412, Richmond VA 23269, 804-497-7100, fax is 804-367-0390. The release of records is restrictive, as mentioned above. The current fee is $7.00 for online record requests and $8.00 for manually ordered records. Add $5.00 for certification. The last fee increase was May 2002 and no increases are planned in the near future. The DMV charges for "no record found" reports.

In-Person – There are 76 locations within the state to order manual searches, requests are processed while waiting. The Customer Records Work Center above is open 8AM to noon on Sat.

Mail – Requests mailed to the state are processed in five working days. The driver's name, date of birth, and sex must "match" to get a record. The fee must accompany the request. Businesses can get "name and address only" records if they are pursuing a remedy which requires locating the individual and can first furnish a name and address for comparison purposes. A written request on a DMV form or letterhead must be accompanied by the $8.00 fee.

Fax – This service is only offered to pre-approved, ongoing account holders. Call to make arrangements.

Electronic – The DMV must approve all customers. Visit www.dmvnow.com to request an *Information Use Application*. There is a $25.00 application fee valid for two years for new accounts and the search fee is $7.00 per record. Either a five year insurance record or seven year employment record can be ordered. The system is open 24/7 and is Internet-based. The driver's address is provided as part of the record. The driver license number or name, date of birth and sex are needed to search. Billing is monthly.

Bulk – The state does not sell its license database, or portions there of.

By Person of Record – Walk-in customers receive their records immediately at the location. Mail-in requests are returned within 7-10 days When a subject orders own record for insurance companies a 5-year history is produced. If for employment purposes, the subject will receive a 7-year history. If a reason not specified, subject will receive an 11-year history. The same $8.00 fee, $13.00 if certified, applies. The online form is available at www.dmvnow.com.

One may use an online site to order a driving record or use **Record at a Glance** to take a free look at limited driver, vehicle and address information the DMV has on file. The web page to visit for either of these services is: https://www.dmv.virginia.gov/dmvnet/online.asp. For either record, the subject must obtain a PIN. After obtaining the PIN, VA drivers may request a copy of their own driving record (or vehicle record) or request the record be sent to a third party, such as a prospective employee. Once the fee is paid, one may view the record again anytime within five days for no additional charge.

Notification/Monitoring Program

Two programs exist.

1) The DMV provides a **Voluntary Monitoring Program** called **Driver Alert** to monitor the driving records of individuals employed by participating public and private transportation companies and other organizations employing large numbers of drivers. The fee for the program is $25 for two years. Participants may select one or any combination of electronic notification criteria such as, immediate pre-employment driving record access, immediate alert of moving violation convictions, immediate alert if drivers accumulate seven adverse points within a calendar year, immediate alert of suspensions, revocations, disqualifications, reckless driving or driving while intoxicated convictions, month and day to receive annual risk management driver records. Participants are billed $9 for each driving record generated. The $25 program fee is waived for public organizations and $12.50 for non-profits and charitable entities.

To apply, use *Form US531A* found online at www.dmvnow.com/webdoc/pdf/us531a.pdf. For questions about the application process, call Use Agreement Services at 804-497-7155, or fax a request to 804-367-2536, or send an email to useagreement@dmv.state.va.us.

2) A **Mandatory Driving Record Monitoring Program** is available to actively monitor the driving records of public school bus drivers, public and private school driver education instructors and commercial driving school instructors. If their driver licenses are suspended, revoked or disqualified if convicted of driving while intoxicated or reckless driving, the DMV will provide a copy of driving record to the local school division, private school or licensing authority that employs the subject. Additionally, if the driver is a driving instructor and accumulates more than 6 demerit points, DMV will notify the employer. Virginia law requires the DMV to monitor these drivers.

Crash Reports

Reporting – Accidents involving death, injury or total damage to an apparent extent of $1,500.00 or more must be reported by the investigating police/law enforcement officer to the DMV. The police must submit all necessary accident reports within 24 hours of completing an investigation.

Record Access – Copies of crash reports are available from the Department of Motor Vehicles, Attention: Customer Records, Rm 514, PO Box 27412, Richmond VA 23269-0001, 804-497-72100, 866-368-5463. Records are not considered open and are only released to persons involved in the crash or their representatives. A written request (including the driver, date and location of accident) must be submitted. Use of *Form CRD93* at www.dmvnow.com/webdoc/pdf/crd93.pdf is suggested. The fee is $8.00 per report. Credit cards are accepted. Turnaround time is 5 days. It takes 25 to 30 days before new records are available for inquiry. Records are maintained for 40 months.

Access to Vehicle-Related Records

General Information

Department of Motor Vehicles, Customer Records Work Center, PO Box 27412, Richmond 23269 804-497-7100, fax is 804-367-9705. Online and bulk access of records is provided by the Department. The state permits private investigation and security agents, who are

licensed in Virginia and are listed as a "compliance agent" by the Department of Justice Services, to receive address information when submitting a license plate number. Users must also be pre-approved by the Department.

In-Person, Mail – The fee for vehicle ownership and registration information is $8.00 per record, add $5.00 for certification. Approved, on-going requesters must sign an agreement and are issued a "User ID." Normal turnaround time for mail-in requests is 7 to 10 working days. Lien information is available upon written request from lending institutions, collection agencies, and businesses. The counter is also open on Sat. from 8AM to noon

Fax – Fax requests are accepted for pre-approved, ongoing accounts.

Electronic –.   The DMV must approve all customers. Visit: www.dmvnow.com to request an *Information Use Application*. There is a $25.00 application fee valid for two years for new accounts and the search fee is $7.00 per record. The system is open 24 hours daily and is Internet-based. The service provides lienholder information including title history, but does not include personal information. The license plate number, VIN or title number is required for vehicle information. Billing is monthly.

By Vehicle Owners: The same online service described under Driving Records is available for vehicle owners. One may order a complete vehicle record or use **Record at a Glance** which is a free look at limited like of the driver, vehicle and address information the DMV has on file. For either record, the subject must obtain a PIN. With the PIN, VA

drivers may request a copy of their own or vehicle record or request the record be sent to a third party. Once the fee is paid, one may view the record again anytime within five days for no additional charge.

The web page to visit for either of these services is: www.dmvnow.com.

Prospective Purchase Inquiry: Prospective Purchaser Inquiry (PPI) allows individual or business customers to obtain information on a vehicle that they are considering purchasing. Use this application to find information such as odometer reading at time of titling, special notes about water damage or demolition status, vehicle history. The fee for the service is $12.00 per vehicle.   This service is available online at https://www.dmv.virginia.gov/dmvnet/ppi/intro.asp or by visiting a Customer Service Center.

Bulk – Bulk information may be obtained through the Department for statistical and vehicle recall purposes. No bulk records are available for sale for marketing purposes. Records are sold for $30.00 per 1,000 records. Additional fees may apply for required programming changes.

Access to Vessel-Related Records

General Information

Game & Inland Fisheries Department, 4010 W. Broad Street, Richmond VA 23230-1104, 800-898-2628, 804-367-6135 www.dgif.virginia.gov. All motorized boats must be registered and titled. Non-motorized boats sailboats over 18 ft are titled. Liens are included on the record. The records are open to the public to the extent that information is released with either a title or hull #. Submit either the title or hull #. Name searches are not performed by this agency. Records are available from 1989 to present.

In-Person, Mail – If history or extensive research is required, there is a fee of $50.00 per boat. There is no fee for a simple name search or registration search. Mail turnaround time is 3-4 days.

Phone, Fax – The Dept. will report the owner's name if a boat number is given or if a lien exists. This is done on a single request basis.

Simple questions may be submitted by fax (804-367-1064).

Electronic – Virginia Interactive, 1111 E. Main Street #901, Richmond 23219, 804-786-4718, http://portal.virginia.gov/online/premium_services/dgif/boat_registrations/ The VA boat registration database may be searched on the web. A subscription is required; there is a $95.00 annual fee. There are two options, one for commercial use, and for non-commercial use. Fees for watercraft records: Individual - $1.00 per record for 1-50 record requests with a $25.00 minimum purchase; Packet Request - $50.00 for a batch record query of 50-2500 record requests; Entire Database: $3,000 for initial access to the entire database; $500 for each request thereafter. Additional services are provided to subscribers. A subscription agreement is required.

Driving Record Content and Reciprocity

What's On or Not On the Driving Record

- All convictions are reported on the driving record.
- Accidents are maintained on the driving record for 40 months
- Accidents are only reported if damage is $1,000 or more, or if there is personal injury or death.
- **Insurance** records display the last **five** years of the record; **Employment** records display the last **seven** years of the record; and **Unrestricted records (available only to subject)** display the last **eleven** years, unless a conviction resulting in suspension or revocation is still in force.

Data Retention

Surrendered non-CDL licenses are purged five years after the license expiration date. CDL convictions are retained by the state for 55 years, per federal regulations (see the Appendix).

Court to Repository

Convictions are received electronically from the courts or input manually from paper abstracts sent by the courts.   Abstracts of conviction must be forwarded to the Department within eighteen days of the conviction date.

State Reciprocity for Non-CDL Drivers

- Will suspend license of driver for unpaid out-of-state convictions, if NRVC member.
- Record of new incoming driver is shown on MVR.
- Out-of-state convictions are shown on MVR.
- Out-of-state accidents are not shown on MVR.
- Convictions of out-of-state drivers are sent to home state.
- Record is forwarded to new state upon surrender of license upon request.

Classes, Restrictions, Endorsements and Important Abbreviations

License Classes– All

Virginia began issuing the CDL in January of 1990.

Note: There is no class code for a non-commercial license. The state refers to this document as the "Diver License."

Class A   Any combination of vehicles with a GVWR or a gross combination weight rating of 26,001 pounds or more, providing the vehicle(s) being towed is in excess of 10,000 pounds. Holders of a Class A license may, with appropriate endorsements, also

Class B   operate vehicles listed under Classes B and C.

Class B   Any vehicle with a GVWR of 26,001 pounds or more, or any such vehicle towing a vehicle not in excess of 10,000 pounds. Holders of a Class B license may, with appropriate endorsements, also operate vehicles listed under Class C.

Class C   Any vehicle that does not fit the definition of a Class A or Class B vehicle and is either designed to transport sixteen or more passengers (including the driver) or is used to transport hazardous materials.

Class M   Motorcycles - This class may be added to a driver's license or CDL or holder may be licensed to operate motorcycles only.

Restrictions

Note: The first column is the Internal State Code, the second column is what will appear on the document itself. A code "9" restriction indicates a medical disability.

Code		Description		Code		Description
1A	1	Automatic transmission		2O	Y	Corrective lenses when operating a CMV
1B	2	Mechanical signal device		2P	9	Artificial limb when operating standard shift vehicle
1C	3	Side view mirror - hearing impaired		2Q	9	Hearing Impaired
1D	5	All hand controls		2R	9	Speech Impaired
1E	9	Quad grip with pin		2S	9	Turn Signal In Floor
1F	9	Yoke spinner		3A	6	Driving privilege restricted to motorcycle only
1G	9	Tri-post spinner		3B	7	"S" endorsement - less than 16 pass veh
1H	9	Amputee ring spinner		3C	8	Valid 1/2 hr after sunrise and 1/2 hr before sunset
1I	9	Steering knob		3D	9	Insurance restriction
1J	9	Turn lever extension		3E	9	Class "S" Restriction
1K	9	Gear shift extension		3E	9	Restricted to School Bus-Less than 32 passengers
1L	9	Power steering		3F	9	Restricted from interstate highway driving
1M	9	Power brakes		3G	9	Restricted to 5 mile radius of home
1N	9	Accelerator on left side		3H	9	Restricted to 10 mile radius of home
1O	9	Built up clutch pedal		3I	9	Restricted to 25 mile radius of home
1P	9	Built up brake pedal		3J	9	Corrective lenses for night only
1Q	9	Built up accelerator		3K	9	Restricted from hwy w/posted speed in excess of 45 MPH
1R	9	Built up dimmer		3L	9	Must be accompanied by licensed driver
1S	9	Hand control clutch		3M	9	Valid operating Dept of Corrections vehicles only
1T	9	Hand control brake		3N	9	See court order for restriction
1U	9	Hand control accelerator		3O	G	CDL restricted to town, city, county, state owned veh only
1V	9	Hand control dimmer		3P	-	City, county, state employee endorsement fee waiver
1W	9	Auto dimmer switch		3Q	J	CDL restricted to school and/or school activity bus only
1X	9	All foot controls		3R	K	CMV without air brakes
1Y	9	Auto steering rod & power steering gloves		3S	L	CDL valid only in Virginia
1Z	9	Panoramic mirror		3T	9	MC Class valid only when in employ city, county state
2A	9	Back brace		3U	9	Waiver/variance required
2B	9	Left leg brace		3V	9	HO restored CT-order, see restrictions
2C	9	Right leg brace		3W	9	Drive only under supervision of rehab services
2D	9	left arm brace		3X	-	Diplomatic learners permit
2E	9	Right arm brace		3Y	W	CDL seasonal restricted license
2F	9	Pressure suit		3Z	9	Not elig for DL w/o J&D Court Judge authorization
2G	9	Chest harness		4A	M	Not allowed to transport more than three passengers
2H	9	Seat cushion		4B	M	Operation of Pass Bus - restricted to Class B passenger vehicles
2I	9	Specially built seats		4C	N	Operation of Pass Bus - restricted to Class B passenger vehicles
2J	X	Corrective lenses				
2K	4	Artificial limb		5A	9	Limited duration (see expiration date on front)
2L	9	Carrier lenses w/btl		7A	O	Valid only in VA
2M	9	Hearing aids		6A	9	Hurricane Katrina Evacuee
2N	9	Insulin dependent diabetic				

CDL Restrictions

J   May only operate school/activity bus, and no other commercial vehicles. This only applies if CDL fees are not paid.
K   Cannot operate a vehicle with airbrakes
L   Cannot operate a vehicle outside of Virginia
N   Operation of a passenger bus restricted to a Class C passenger vehicle
Y   Must wear corrective lenses

CDL Endorsements

H	Vehicles Transporting Hazardous Materials		S	School Bus
M	Motorcycle Operation		T	Double- and Triple-Trailers
N	Tank Vehicles			
P	Vehicles Carrying Passengers			

Court Restrictions

A	To and from work
B	To and from ASAP Meetings
C	During work hours for employment
D	To and from school
E	Medically Necessary Travel
F	Ignition Interlock System
G	Transporting Child
H	Child Visitation

I	To and from court appearances when subpoenaed as witness or a party/appointments with probation officer, and to and from any programs required by court or as condition of probation
J	To and from worship place
K	To and from child support program appointments
M	To and from jail/work release
O	Based on Court Order
P	To and from higher learning institution

Accident Information

DRIVER	Driver of the vehicle
OWNER	Owner of the vehicle
IC	Incapacitation
PD	Property Damage

PI	Personal Injury With Visible Signs of Injury
FA	Fatality
NI	Property Damage
VN	Personal Injury With No Visible Signs of Injury

Court Types

ADM	Administrative Adjud
CHA	Chancery Court
CIR	Circuit Court
CIT	City Court
CIV	Civil Court
COR	Corporation Court
CRI	Criminal Court
DIS	General District Court
DOT	Secretary USDOT
FED	US District Court
GEN	General Court Martial
HUS	Hustings Court

JPC	Justice of Peace Court
JUS	Justice Court
JUV	Juvenile and Domestic Relations Court
LEC	Law & Equity Court
MAG	Magistrate Court
MAY	Mayor's Court
MUN	Municipal Court
POL	Police Court
SJC	Special Justice Court
SPL	Special Court Martial
SPR	Superior Court

SSP	State Supreme Court
SUM	Summary Court Martial
SUP	Supreme Court
TJC	Trial Justice Court
TRA	Traffic Court
TRI	Tribal Court
TWN	Town Court
UNK	Unknown
USC	United States Commissioner's Court
USD	United States District Court
VCA	Virginia Court of Appeals

Miscellaneous

ACC	Accident
ALIAS	Other/Previous Names
ANS	Answer
ASAP	Alcohol Safety Action Program
CI	City
COM VEH	Commercial Motor Vehicle
CMV	Commercial Motor Vehicle
COMBVEH	Combination Motor Vehicle
CONTL	Control
CONV	Conviction
CROSSREF	Cross reference-other/previous names
CT	Court
DELD	Delivered
DISQUAL	Commercial Driver Disqualified
DI	Driver Improvement
DR	Driver or Driving
DWI	Driving While Intoxicated
EFF	Effective Date
ENDR	Endorsement
EXP	Expire
FR	Financial Responsibility
GCWR	Gross Combination Weight Rating
GVWR	Gross Vehicle Weight Rating
HAZMAT	Hazardous Materials
HGT	Height
INS	Insurance
INTOX	Intoxicated
INTRVW	Interview
JURSD	Jurisdiction
JUV	Juvenile

LIC	License
MV	Motor Vehicle
MOTVEH	Motor Vehicle
OALS	Operate after license suspended
OFF	Offense
OFFEND	Offender
OPR	Operate/Operation
PER	Personal
PROB/NOTC	Probation Notice
PRGM	Program
PTS	Points
RC	Record Control (DMV use)
RD	Reckless Driving
REHAB	Rehabilitation
RECD	Received
RESTR	Restriction
RETD	Returned
REP	Representative
SAT	Satisfied
SECT	Section
SUR	Surrendered
SUSP	Suspended
TREAT	Treatment
UNINS	Uninsured
UNDEL	Undelivered
UNLIC	Unlicensed
UR	Unrestricted
VASAP	Virginia Alcohol Safety Action Program
VEH	Vehicle
WGT	Weight

Conviction Table with ACD, Statute, and Points

View statutes at http://leg1.state.va.us/000/src.htm

Description	Points	Statute	ACD
Abandoned Motor Vehicle Violation		46.2-1200.1	
Access Highway Viol (Operator) 4th/Subsq		B46.2-819.5(4)	
Access Highway Viol (Own/Oper) 4th/Subsq		A46.2-819.5(4)	
Access Highway Viol (Owner/Operator) 1st		A46.2-819.5	
Access Highway Viol (Owner/Operator) 2nd		A46.2-819.5(2)	
Access Highway Viol (Owner/Operator) 3rd		A46.2-819.5(3)	
Access Highway Violation (Operator) 1st		B46.2-819.5	
Access Highway Violation (Operator) 2nd		B46.2-819.5(2)	
Access Highway Violation (Operator) 3rd		B46.2-819.5(3)	
Administrative Suspension		46.2-391.2	
Aggressive Driving	4	46.2-868.1	
Aids And Abets Racing	6	46.2-866	
Air Brake Reservoir Required		49CFR393.50	E31
Air Pressr Warn Signl,Vacm Hose-Inop/Mis		49CFR393.51	E31
Allow Load To Leak, Escape		46.2-1156	
Allow Use Disabled Park Plates/Placard		46.2-1253	
Alter Disabled Parking Plates/Placard		46.2-1249	
Alter/Forge Cert Of Title/Registration		46.2-605	
Altered Or Forged License Plates		46.2-722	
Altered Temporary Tags		46.2-1561	
Antique Motor Veh-License Plate Violation		46.2-730	
Apply Tint,Sign,Decal On Wndshld-2nd/Sub		B46.2-1052	E70
Apply Tint,Signs,Decal On Windsheild-1st		A46.2-1052	E70
Attempt, Aid Or Abet		4.1-323	
Auth Persn DUI Or H.O./DUI Susp To Dr	6	46.2-301.1E	
Blocking Access To Service Facility	6	46.2-818(2)	
Brake Away/Emerg Brake-Inoper Or Missing		49CFR393.43	E31
Brake Performance-Inoperative Or Missing		49CFR393.52	E31
Brake Tubes/Hoses-Inoperative Or Missing		49CFR393.45	E31
Brakes On All Wheels Inoper Or Missing		49CFR393.42	E31
Brakes-Inoperative		49CFR393.48	E31
Brk Slack Adjr,Pads,Lining,Drum-Inop/Mis		49CFR393.47	E31
Bus Violation-Aisle Seat Prohibited		49CFR393.91	E01
Bus Violation-Drive Shaft		49CFR393.89	E01
Bus Violation-Standee Line Bar		49CFR393.90	E01
Bus/Truck Unloading On Highway		46.2-893	
Causing Fatality/Negligent Oper CMV		49CFR383.51B8	U10
CDL Driver: Fail To Change Address		46.2-341.11	
CDL Instruction Permit Violation		46.2-341.10	D29
Change Course After Signal	3	46.2-850	N44
Child Restraint Viol(Age 7 & Und)2nd/Sub		C46.2-1095	F02
Child Restraint Violation		46.2-1095	F02
Child Restraint Violation(Age 7 & Under)		A46.2-1095	F02
CMV-Fail To Place Red Flags/Flares-Emerg		46.2-111	
Cntrl Vale For Brakes-Inoper Or Missing		49CFR393.49	E31
Coasting Gears In Neutral	3	46.2-811	N80
Contract Passenger Carrier Violation		46.2-2099.1	
Counterfeit Disabled Park Plates/Placard		46.2-1247	
Coupling/Towing Devic/Multiple Veh		49CFR393.70	
Coupling/Towing Devices		49CFR393.71	
Damaging Highway Signs		46.2-832	
Damaging Vehicle/Vehicular Assault	6	46.2-818(3)	U06
Defective Cab/Body Components		49CFR393.203	
Defective Speedometer		46.2-1080	E01
Defective Suspension System		49CFR393.207	
Defective Wheels And Rims		49CFR393.205	
Dimensions/Hood Scoop		46.2-1088.1	
Disable Parking Violation		46.2-731	
Display Of Non-Permissable Lights		46.2-1020	E55
Disregard Crossing Guard/Officer Signal	4	46.2-834	M13
Disregard Officers Signal	4	46.2-1309	M08
Dr CMV Influ Drugs And Alcohol, 1st	6	D46.2-341.24	A23

Description	Points	Statute	ACD
Dr CMV Influ Drugs And Alcohol, 2nd	6	I46.2-341.24	A23
Dr CMV Influ Drugs, 1st	6	C46.2-341.24	A22
Dr CMV-BAC .08 Or More, 2nd W/In 5 Yrs	6	E46.2-341.24	A08
Dr CMV-BAC .08 Or More, 3rd	6	F46.2-341.24	A08
Dr Commercial Veh Left Lane Interstate	3	46.2-803.1	M41
Dr During DUI/Invol Mansltr Misdemeanor	6	A18.2-36.1F	B25
Dr Elec Device/Toy Veh/Bike On Highway	3	46.2-908.1	
Dr Under Infl Drugs & Alcohol,3rd Or Sub	6	I18.2-266	A23
Dr Under Influence Drugs & Alcohol, 1st	6	G18.2-266	A23
Dr Under Influence Drugs & Alcohol, 2nd	6	H18.2-266	A23
Dr Under Influence Drugs, 3rd Subsequent	6	F18.2-266	A22
Drinking While Operating A Vehicle	3	18.2-323.1	A26
Drive Away-Non-Payment Of Fuel		46.2-819.2	
Drive CMV In Violation Of Restriction	3	46.2-341.7C	D29
Drive CMV Influ Drugs And Alcohol, 3rd	6	J46.2-341.24	A23
Drive CMV Influence Drugs, 2nd	6	G46.2-341.24	A22
Drive CMV Influence Drugs, 3rd	6	H46.2-341.24	A22
Drive CMV W/Out Cdl-Proper Class/Endors	3	46.2-341.7A	B91
Drive CMV Without Cdl In Possession	3	46.2-341.7B	B51
Drive CMV-BAC .04 Or More, 1st	6	B46.2-341.24	A04
Drive CMV-BAC .08 Or More 1st	6	A46.2-341.24	A08
Drive CMV-More Than One License	3	46.2-341.6	D07
Drive On Suspended License/Fine &Cost	6	A46.2-301	B26
Drive Susp/Rev No Endangement-Misdemeanr		46.2-391D1	B25
Drive Susp/Revoked Endangement-Felony		46.2-391D2	B25
Drive Susp/Revoked-2nd/Subseq-Felony		46.2-391D3	B25
Drive Suspended Before Giving Proof Fr	6	46.2-302	B26
Drive Through Safety Zone	3	46.2-814	M12
Drive Vehicle Without Windshield		46.2-1057	E01
Drive W/O Lights/Excessive Lights	3	46.2-1030	E55
Drive While License Withdrawn		49CFR383.51B7	B20
Drive Without License Endorsements	3	46.2-328	B91
Drivers License Violation		46.2-346	B41
Driving CMV While Disqualified	6	46.2-341.21	B24
Driving In Excess 13 Hrs In 24 Hrs	3	46.2-812	
Driving Influence Drugs,1st	6	D18.2-266	A22
Driving Influence Drugs,2nd	6	E18.2-266	A22
Driving Over Fire Hose	3	46.2-922	M56
Driving Requirement Violation		49CFR391	
Driving Under Influ/Drug	6	X18.2-266	A22
Driving Under Influ/Drug/Alcohol	6	Y18.2-266	A20
Driving Under Revocation Or Suspension	6	B46.2-301	B25
Driving Veh When Removed From Service		46.2-1001	
Driving While Disqualified	6	49CFR391.15	B24
Driving While Intox 3rd, Or Subsequent	6	C18.2-266	A08
Driving While Intox, 1st	6	A18.2-266	A08
Driving While Intox, Maiming		18.2-51.4	A08
Driving While Intoxicated		36CFR4.23	A21
Driving While Intoxicated With Bac.08		36CFR4.23A2	A21
Driving While Intoxicated,2nd	6	B18.2-266	A08
Driving Wrong Way On One-Way Highway	4	46.2-806	N63
Driving/Riding On Sidewalk	3	46.2-903	M58
Drv In Violation Of Curfew/Learner Pmt		46.2-335D	D29
Drv In Violation Pass Rest/Learner Pmt		46.2-335C	D29
Drv Sch Bus W/Child/Posses/Consume Alcoh	6	4.1-309.1	A35
Drv W/Out Or Defect Defroster/Defogger		46.2-1055.1	E01
Drv Wrong Way @ Rotary,Roundabout,Circle	4	46.2-807	N61
Elude/Disregard Police Death-Felony		46.2-817C	U08
Eluding/Disregard Police-Felony		46.2-817B	U03
Eluding/Disregard Police-Misdemeanor		46.2-817A	U01
Emergency Equipment-Inspection Use		49CFR392.8	
Enter/Set In Motion Vehicle		18.2-147	
Equipment-Inspection/Use		49CFR392.7	
Evasion Of A Traffic Control Device	3	46.2-833.1	
Excess Wgt/Hgt/Size/Spd On Rest Hgw		46.2-1104	
Excessive Veh Length/Two Lane Hiway		B46.2-1112	

Description	Points	Statute	ACD
Excessive Vehicle Length		A46.2-1112	
Excessive Vehicle Length		46.2-1114	
Excessive Vehicle Width		46.2-1105	
Expired Registration		46.2-646	
Expired Temporary Registration		46.2-1565	
Fail Carry/Exhibit Regis Card/License		46.2-104	
Fail Dim Headlights	3	46.2-1034	E54
Fail Drive Right/Stop - Emergency Veh	4	A46.2-829	N04
Fail Give Way In Favor Of Overtaking Veh	3	46.2-842	N07
Fail Give Way When Abreast Another Veh	3	46.2-842.1	N06
Fail Keep Right When Xing Intersection	4	A46.2-803	M40
Fail Keep Right When Xing Railroad	4	B46.2-803	M09
Fail Leave Acc Under Dirctn Of Officer	3	46.2-902	M08
Fail Pay Toll-Photo (Operator) 3rd		B46.2-819.1(3)	
Fail Pay Toll-Photo (Operator) 4th/Sub		B46.2-819.1(4)	
Fail Pay Toll-Photo (Operator)1st		B46.2-819.1	
Fail Pay Toll-Photo (Operator)2nd		B46.2-819.1(2)	
Fail Pay Toll-Photo (Own/Opr) 1st		A46.2-819.1	
Fail Pay Toll-Photo (Own/Opr) 2nd		A46.2-819.1(2)	
Fail Pay Toll-Photo (Owner/Oper)3rd		A46.2-819.1(3)	
Fail Pay Toll-Photo (Owner/Oper)4th/Sub		A46.2-819.1(4)	
Fail Pay Toll-Video (Operator) 1st		B46.2-819.3:1	
Fail Pay Toll-Video (Operator) 2nd		B46.2-819.3:1-2	
Fail Pay Toll-Video (Operator) 3rd		B46.2-819.3:1-3	
Fail Pay Toll-Video (Operator) 4th/Subsq		B46.2-819.3:1-4	
Fail Pay Toll-Video (Own/Oper) 4th/Subsq		A46.2-819.3:1-4	
Fail Pay Toll-Video (Owner/Operator) 1st		A46.2-819.3:1	
Fail Pay Toll-Video (Owner/Operator) 2nd		A46.2-819.3:1-2	
Fail Pay Toll-Video (Owner/Operator) 3rd		A46.2-819.3:1-3	
Fail Report Structure Damage	3	D46.2-1110	
Fail Rtrn Susp'd Or Rvk'd Dr Lic Or Plt		46.2-370	
Fail Sound Horn Overtaking Another Veh		46.2-840	N42
Fail Stop And Yield Right-Of-Way Priv Rd	4	46.2-826	N01
Fail Stop For Pedestrian With White Cane	4	46.2-933	N08
Fail Stop Scene Accident/Death-Felony		E46.2-894	B02
Fail Stop Scene Accident/Injury-Felony		D46.2-894	B03
Fail Stop/Yield Entering Hwy	4	46.2-821	N22
Fail Stp @ Acc-Prop Damg $1000/More-Felo	6	C46.2-894	B04
Fail Stp @ Acc-Prop Damg =/<$1000-Misd	4	B46.2-894	B04
Fail To Answer Summons		46.2-936	D45
Fail To Attend/View-Explosive Carry Veh		49CFR397.5A	
Fail To Attend/View-Hazmat Carrying Veh		49CFR397.5B	
Fail To Carry/Exhibit License		A46.2-104	B78
Fail To Carry/Exhibit Registration Card		B46.2-104	
Fail To Change Address		46.2-324	
Fail To Comply With The URCA		46.2-703D	
Fail To Consent Blood/Breath Test-Boat		29.1-738.2	
Fail To Deliver Title		46.2-628	
Fail To Destroy Temporary Plate		46.2-1564	
Fail To Discontinue Operating CMV		46.2-1134	
Fail To Display Both License Plates		46.2-715	
Fail To Display Inspection Sticker		46.2-1163	
Fail To Drive On Right Half Of Highway	4	46.2-802	N70
Fail To Fix Defects After Inspection		B46.2-1158	
Fail To Give Full Time Attention	4	NOSTAT-E	M82
Fail To Have License Revalidated		46.2-330	B51
Fail To Negotiate Insuf Undercarriage		49CFR383.51D6	M24
Fail To Obey Highway Lane Markings	4	A46.2-804	M05
Fail To Obey Highway Sign	3	46.2-830	M17
Fail To Obey Highway Sign Sleep/Rest	0	46.2-830.1	
Fail To Obey Lane Directional Signal	4	46.2-805	M05
Fail To Obey RR Crossing Signal	4	46.2-884	M10
Fail To Obey Traffic Signal	4	46.2-833	M16
Fail To Obtain Driver's License	3	46.2-308	
Fail To Obtain Registration Title		46.2-600	
Fail To Pay Toll		46.2-819	

Description	Points	Statute	ACD
Fail To Register Farm Vehicle		46.2-666	
Fail To Report Accident To DMV		46.2-372	
Fail To Rept Accident/Unattend Property	3	A46.2-896	B61
Fail To Return License		46.2-709	
Fail To Rpt Acc/Unattn Prop-$249 Or Less	3	B46.2-896	B61
Fail To Rpt Acc/Unattn Prop-$250 Or More	4	C46.2-896	B61
Fail To Secure Roll On/Off Hook Lift		49CFR393.134	
Fail To Show Ins Card/Umv Fee-Law Enforc		46.2-902.1	B74
Fail To Signal When Moving From Curb	4	46.2-851	N40
Fail To Stop Pass Carry Veh At Rr Cross	4	46.2-886	M22
Fail To Stop Rr Grade Crossing	4	46.2-885	M22
Fail To Surr Cert Title Or Lic Plates		46.2-612	
Fail To Update Registration Address		46.2-606	
Fail To Use Truck Route		46.2-1304	
Fail Use Chains, Snow Tires		46.2-1302	E57
Fail Use Headlights W/Windshield Wipe		A46.2-1030	E55
Fail Yield At Uncontrolled "T" Intersec	4	46.2-824	N25
Fail Yield Right Of Way To Pedestrians	4	46.2-924	N08
Fail Yield Right-Of-Way At Traffic Circl	4	46.2-822	N21
Fail Yield Right-Of-Way To Us Forces/Ng	4	46.2-827	N01
Fail Yield To Funeral Procession	4	46.2-828	N05
Fail Yield Turning Left	4	46.2-825	N31
Fail/Refuse Surr Plate/Reg/Title		46.2-613(4)	
Failure To Yield Right Of Way	4	46.2-820	N01
False Statement/Identy-Reg/Title		46.2-613(5)	
Felony-Motor Vehicle Used		18.2-8	
Follow, Park Within 500 Ft Of Fire Appar	3	46.2-921	M33
Following Too Closely	4	46.2-816	M34
Frame-Cracked/Loose/Sagging/Broken		49CFR393.201	
Fraud Obtain Disabled Parking Plts/Plcrd		46.2-1251	
Fraud Use Of Drivr Lic Or Idcard-Alcohol		46.2-347	D06
Fraudulent Application For Lic - Felony		A46.2-348	D02
Fraudulent Application For License-Misd		B46.2-348	D02
Front Brake Lines-Inoperative Or Missing		49CFR393.44	E31
Front End Structure		49CFR393.106	
Fuel Leak/Cap		49CFR393.67	
Fuel Tank Securement		49CFR393.65	
Golf Cart & Util Veh On Public Hiway		46.2-916.1	
Grand Larceny Vehicle/Parts		18.2-95	
Haul Prohibited Cargo Through Tunnel		46.2-815	
Have Poss Cert Title Issued To Another		46.2-618	
Hazmat/Fail To Have Route Plan		49CFR397.67	
Hazmat/Instructions And Document Violate		49CFR397.19	
Hazmat/Smoking Violation		49CFR397.13	
Hazmat-Improper Operation Near Fire		49CFR397.11A	
Hazmat-Improper Parking Near Fire		49CFR397.11B	
Hearing Aid Violation		49CFR391.41B11	
Height Violation	3	A46.2-1110	
High Mount Brake Light Violation		46.2-1014.1	E55
HOV Viol 2nd Offense Planning Dist 8	3	B33.1-46.2	M49
HOV Viol 4th/Subseq Planning Dist 8	3	D33.1-46.2	M49
HOV Violation		33.1-46.2	M49
HOV Violation 3rd Off Planning Dist 8	3	C33.1-46.2	M49
HOV Violation-Planning District 8	0	A33.1-46.2	M49
IFTA Violation		46.2-2130	
Ill/Fatigued Driver		49CFR392.3	D74
Illegal Handlebar On Motorcycle		46.2-1085	
Illegal Park Space Reserved For Disabled		46.2-1242	
Impede Traffic-Slow Speed	3	46.2-877	S96
Impede/Disrupt Funeral Procession	4	46.2-828.1	N05
Improp Lights On Bicycles Or Mopeds		46.2-1015	E70
Improper Brake Lights		46.2-1014	E55
Improper Brakes		46.2-1066	E02
Improper Display Of Plates		46.2-711	
Improper Display Of Registration Number		46.2-712	
Improper Driving	3	46.2-869	

Description	Points	Statute	ACD
Improper Equipment		46.2-1003	E70
Improper Exhaust System		46.2-1049	
Improper Horn		46.2-1059	E01
Improper Lights		46.2-1010	E05
Improper Load Fastening		46.2-1155	
Improper Loading		46.2-1111	
Improper Medical Examiner's Certificate		A49CFR391.43	
Improper Mirror		46.2-1082	E01
Improper Oper Crawl-Tract Over RR Cross	4	46.2-887	M22
Improper Operation/Riding Motorcycle	3	46.2-909	F06
Improper Or Erratic Lane Change	4	B46.2-804	M42
Improper Or No Pollution Control		46.2-1048	
Improper Parking-Commuter Lot		46.2-1219.2	
Improper Parking-Explosive Carrying Veh		49CFR397.7A	
Improper Parking-Hazmat Carrying Vehicle		49CFR397.7B	
Improper Passing	3	46.2-838	M70
Improper Passing On Right	3	46.2-841	M73
Improper Signal	4	46.2-849	N40
Improper Signal Back, Stop Or Turn	4	46.2-848	N40
Improper Steering Gear		46.2-1065	F66
Improper Stop On Highway	3	46.2-888	F34
Improper Stud,Cleat,Chain On Tires		46.2-1044	E70
Improper Tail Lights		46.2-1013	E55
Improper Towing		46.2-1118	
Improper Turn	3	46.2-846	N50
Improper U Turn	3	46.2-845	N56
Improper Use Farm Vehicle On Highway		46.2-665	
Improper Use Of Auxillary Lights		46.2-1028	E55
Improper Use Of Dealer Plates		46.2-1550	
Improper Use Of Drive Away Tags		46.2-733	
Improper Use Of Plates/Registration		46.2-1543	
Improper Use Of State Tags		46.2-720	
Improper Windshield Wiper		46.2-1055	E01
Improper/Fictitious Reg/Title/Plate		46.2-613(2)	
Improper/No Emergency/Parking Brakes		46.2-1068	E02
Improperly Mounted License Plates		46.2-716	
Improperly Parked		46.2-889	
Inadequate Hazard Lights	3	46.2-1040	E55
Inj Or Death-Fail Notify Police Of Accid		46.2-371	B61
Inoperative Brakes On Trailer		46.2-1070	E31
Inspection-Fail/Refuse Correct Defect		B46.2-1157	
Insufficient Tread On Tires		46.2-1043	E37
Intrastate Oper Authrty Viol-Pass Carrie		46.2-2011.21	
Invalid Medical Examiner's Certificate		B49CFR391.43	
Invol Manslaughter/Alcohol-Boating		18.2-36.2	
Involuntary Manslaughter In Vehicle	6	18.2-36	U08
Involuntary Manslaughter/Aggravated	6	B18.2-36.1	U08
Juv Drive In Violation Of Curfew	0	46.2-334.01C	D29
Juv Passenger Restriction Violation	0	46.2-334.01B	D29
Learner's Permit Viol-Drv W/Out Lic Drvr		46.2-335H	D29
Leaving Veh Running Unattended		46.2-1209	
Lights On Other Vehicles/Reflectors		46.2-1016	E55
Local Ordinance Violation		46.2-LOCAL	
Log Book Violation/No Log Book		49CFR395.8	
Manslaughter In Vehicle	6	18.2-35	U08
Markings On Commercial Motor Veh Viol		49CFR390.21	
Motor Carrier Fail To Display Id		46.2-2129	
Motorcycle Helmet/Equipment Violation		46.2-910	F03
Move Hazmat Vehicle-Emergency		49CFR177.823	E04
No Commercial Lic Endorsement		49CFR383.23	B91
No County Or City Tag		NOSTAT-G	
No County Or City Tag		46.2-752	
No Driver Vehicle Inspection Report		49CFR396.11	
No Drivers License-Vehicle/Motorcycle	3	46.2-300	B51
No Fire Extinquisher		49CFR393.95A	E01
No Headlights		46.2-1011	E05

Description	Points	Statute	ACD
No Marker Lights		46.2-1017	E55
No Medical Card		49CFR391.41A	
No Medical Waiver		49CFR391.49	
No Name/Address For Hire Vehicle		46.2-1076	
No Periodic Inspection		49CFR396.17	
No Placards (CMV/Hazmat)		49CFR172.504	E04
No Seatbelt While Operating CMV		49CFR392.16	F04
No Shipping Papers (CMV/Hazmat)		49CFR177.817	
No Slow-Moving Vehicle Emblem		46.2-1081	E01
Noncompliance Of OOS Citation		46.2-946	D45
Non-Motor Vehicle Related		18.2-000	
Obscene Video Image Visible Outside Veh		46.2-1077.01	
Obstructing Traffic	3	NOSTAT-D	F34
Obtaining Documents Not Entitled To		46.2-105.2	
Offens Desc In VA Code Sec 46.2-341.18:2		18.2-251.4	
Offense Desc In VA Code Sec 46.2-390.1		18.2-247	A33
Offense Desc In VA Code Sec 46.2-390.1		18.2-248	A33
Offense Desc In VA Code Sec 46.2-390.1		18.2-248.01	A33
Offense Desc In VA Code Sec 46.2-390.1		18.2-248.1	A33
Offense Desc In VA Code Sec 46.2-390.1		18.2-248.1:1	A33
Offense Desc In VA Code Sec 46.2-390.1		18.2-248.4	A33
Offense Desc In VA Code Sec 46.2-390.1		18.2-248.5	A33
Offense Desc In VA Code Sec 46.2-390.1		18.2-249	A33
Offense Desc In VA Code Sec 46.2-390.1		18.2-250	A33
Offense Desc In VA Code Sec 46.2-390.1		18.2-250.1	A33
Offense Desc In VA Code Sec 46.2-390.1		18.2-251	A33
Offense Desc In VA Code Sec 46.2-390.1	0	18.2-251.2	A33
Offense Desc In VA Code Sec 46.2-390.1		18.2-251.3	A33
Offense Desc In VA Code Sec 46.2-390.1		18.2-252	A33
Offense Desc In VA Code Sec 46.2-390.1		18.2-253	A33
Offense Desc In VA Code Sec 46.2-390.1		18.2-254	A33
Offense Desc In VA Code Sec 46.2-390.1		18.2-255	A33
Offense Desc In VA Code Sec 46.2-390.1		18.2-255.1	A33
Offense Desc In VA Code Sec 46.2-390.1		18.2-255.2	A33
Offense Desc In VA Code Sec 46.2-390.1		18.2-256	A33
Offense Desc In VA Code Sec 46.2-390.1		18.2-257	A33
Offense Desc In VA Code Sec 46.2-390.1		18.2-258	A33
Offense Desc In VA Code Sec 46.2-390.1		18.2-258.01	A33
Offense Desc In VA Code Sec 46.2-390.1		18.2-258.02	A33
Offense Desc In VA Code Sec 46.2-390.1		18.2-258.1	A33
Offense Desc In VA Code Sec 46.2-390.1	0	18.2-258.2	A33
Offense Desc In VA Code Sec 46.2-390.1		18.2-259	A33
Offense Desc In VA Code Sec 46.2-390.1		18.2-259.1	A33
Offense Desc In VA Code Sec 46.2-390.1		18.2-260	A33
Offense Desc In VA Code Sec 46.2-390.1		18.2-260.1	A33
Offense Desc In VA Code Sec 46.2-390.1		18.2-261	A33
Offense Desc In VA Code Sec 46.2-390.1		18.2-262	A33
Offense Desc In VA Code Sec 46.2-390.1		18.2-263	A33
Offense Desc In VA Code Sec 46.2-390.1		18.2-264	A33
Op Susp/Rev/Rest W/Bac-.02 Or More	4	18.2-272B	B25
Oper Motrcycle W/O Hdlights/Horn/Mir		46.2-912	E01
Oper Bus Transp Sch Chldrn W/O Safty Blt	3	46.2-1091	F04
Oper Motorcycle W/Out Muffler		46.2-1050	E01
Oper Public Pass Carrying Veh Under Age	3	46.2-810	
Oper Susp/Rev W/Out Interlock-Dmv Requir	6	18.2-272C	A41
Oper Susp/Revoked 3rd In 10 Yrs-Felony	6	18.2-272A	B25
Oper With Obstructed Windshield Or Glass		46.2-1054	D70
Oper/Permit Oper Of Unlicensed Mv		46.2-613(1)	
Oper/Permit Oper Unins Mv (Non Owner)		C46.2-707	
Operate All-Terrain Vehicle On Hgw		46.2-915.1	
Operate Boat While Intoxicated Under 21		29.1-738.02	
Operate CMV W/Alcohol In Blood	3	46.2-341.31	
Operate For Hire W/O Required Lic Pl		46.2-724	
Operate In Violation Restricted License	3	46.2-329	D29
Operate Moped On Hwy Above 35mph		46.2-914A	
Operate Moped On Interstate Highway	3	46.2-914C	

Description	Points	Statute	ACD
Operate Mtr Veh Under Foreign Dealer Lic		46.2-1556	
Operate MV W/Below Standard Tires		46.2-1042	E37
Operate MV W/Working N2o Device		46.2-1088.4	
Operate Or Prmit Oper Of Veh W/Out IRP		46.2-703	
Operate Out Of Service Vehicle		49CFR396.9	B27
Operate Overweight Or Before Pymt Of Fee		A46.2-704	
Operate Passr Veh W/Out Paymt Of Reg Fee		46.2-687	
Operate School Bus Under Age	3	46.2-919	
Operate School Bus W/Out Warning Device		46.2-1090	E36
Operate School Bus Without License	3	46.2-339	B91
Operate Suspended Or Revoked	6	18.2-272	B25
Operate Uninspected Vehicle		A46.2-1157	
Operate Uninspected Vehicle		A46.2-1158	
Operate Unsafe Vehicle	0	49CFR396.7	F66
Operate Veh W/Device To Detect Mcrowaves		46.2-1079	E23
Operate Veh W/Expired Rejection Sticker		46.2-1158	
Operate Vehicle Overweight		46.2-1123	
Operate Vehicle W/O Vin Or Serial Nmbr		46.2-1072	
Operate While Using Earphones	3	46.2-1078	
Operate With Altered Suspension System		46.2-1063	
Operate With Smoke Screen/Felony		46.2-1086	
Operate With Solid Rubber Tires		46.2-1041	E37
Operate With Tint,Sign,Decals On Wndshld		46.2-1052	E70
Operate With TV Screen Visable To Driver	3	46.2-1077	
Operate Without Flag/Light		46.2-1121	
Operate Without Mud Flaps		46.2-1083	E01
Operate Without Safety Glass		46.2-1056	E01
Operate Without Signal Device		46.2-1038	E55
Operating After Declared H.O.- Felony	6	B46.2-357	B25
Operating After Declared H.O.-Misdemr	6	A46.2-357	B25
Operating Boat-Reckless Or Intoxicated		29.1-738	
Overweight Bed - Coal Haulers		46.2-1143	
Owner Oper/Prmit Operation Unins Mtr Veh		A46.2-707	D36
Park Without Proper Lights Displayed	3	46.2-1037	E55
Park Without Setting Hand Brake		46.2-1071	E51
Park/Interfer With Emergency Vehicle		46.2-890	
Parking Brake System Inoperative		49CFR393.41	E31
Passenger Fail To Report Accident		46.2-895	
Passenger-Failed To Report Accident		46.2-897	B61
Passing Left Of Approaching Vehicle	4	46.2-837	M73
Passing Stopped School Bus(Non Reckless)	4	46.2-844	M75
Passing When Unsafe	4	46.2-843	M70
Pedestrian Impeding Traffic		46.2-923	
Perjury		46.2-105	D78
Permit Unlicensed Person To Drive	3	46.2-349	
Petit Larceny Vehicle/Parts		18.2-96	
Poss/Lend Reg/Lic-Not Entitled		46.2-613(3)	
Possess Motor Veh Without Vin Number		46.2-1075	
Possess/Oper Unapp/Altered Safety Equip		46.2-1002	
Possession Of Alcohol		49CFR392.5	A31
Possession Of Drugs		49CFR392.4	A33
Prk Frnt Private Drive/Hydrant/Fire Sta		46.2-1239	F34
Prohibit Use Wireless Dev-Oper Schl Bus		46.2-919.1	
Prohibiting Placarding		49CFR172.502	
Purchase Alcohol For Unauthrzd Person		4.1-306	
Purchase/Possess Alcohol		4.1-305	A31
Purchase/Possess Alcohol		4-62	A31
Railroad Crossing, Stopping	4	49CFR392.10	M22
Railroad Crossing/Fail To Slow Down		49CFR383.51D1	M20
Rd/Racing - Misdemeanor	6	A46.2-865	M84
Rear End Protection Required		49CFR393.86	
Reck Drv-Improper Control/Brakes-Felony	6	C46.2-853	U08
Reckdrv-Pass/Overtake Emergency Veh-Misd	6	B46.2-829	M84
Reckdrv-Speed 20/More Above Spd Lmt-Misd	6	C46.2-862	M84
Reckdrv-Speed 20/More Abv Spd Lmt-Felony	6	D46.2-862	U08
Reckdrv-Speeding Excess Of 80 Mph-Felony	6	B46.2-862	U08

Description	Points	Statute	ACD
Reckless Driv-Death While Racing-Felony		A46.2-865.1	
Reckless Driv-Dr Too Fast For Cond-Misd	6	A46.2-861	M84
Reckless Driving/Racing-Death-Felony	6	B46.2-865	U08
Reckless Driving-Generally-Felony	6	B46.2-852	M84
Reckless Driving-Generally-Misdemeanor	6	A46.2-852	M84
Reckless Driving-Pass School Bus-Misd	6	A46.2-859	M84
Reckless Driving-View Obstructed-Misd	6	A46.2-855	M84
Reckless Driv-Injury While Racing-Felony	6	46.2-865.1	
Reckless Drivng-Drvtwo Veh Abreast-Misd	6	A46.2-857	M84
Reckless Driv-On Parking Lots, Etc-Misd	6	A46.2-864	M84
Reckless Driv-Pass Two Veh Abreast-Misd	6	A46.2-856	M84
Reckless Drv-Dr Too Fast For Cond-Felony	6	B46.2-861	U08
Reckless Drv-Drv Two Veh Abreast-Felony	6	B46.2-857	U08
Reckless Drv-Fail Stop Entering Hwy-Misd	6	A46.2-863	M84
Reckless Drving-Pass At Rr Crossing-Misd	6	A46.2-858	M84
Reckless Drving-Pass School Bus-Felony	6	B46.2-859	U08
Reckless Drving-View Obstructed-Felony	6	B46.2-855	U08
Reckless Drv-On Parking Lots,Etc-Felony	6	B46.2-864	U08
Reckless Drv-Pass At Rr Crossing-Felony	6	B46.2-858	U08
Reckless Drv-Pass On Crest Of Hill-Misd	6	A46.2-854	M84
Reckless Drv-Pass Two Veh Abreast-Felony	6	B46.2-856	U08
Reckls Drv-Improper Control/Brakes-Misd	6	A46.2-853	M84
Reckls Drv-Speeding Excess Of 80mph-Misd	6	A46.2-862	M84
Recklsdrv-Fail Give Proper Signal-Felony	6	B46.2-860	U08
Recklsdrv-Pass/Overtake Emerg Veh-Felony		C46.2-829	M84
Recklss Drv-Fail Give Proper Signal-Misd	6	A46.2-860	M84
Recklss Drv-Pass On Crest Of Hill-Felony	6	B46.2-854	U08
Recklssdrv-Fail Stop Entering Hwy-Felony	4	B46.2-863	U08
Refuse Blood/Breath Test While Oper CMV	6	46.2-341.26:3	A12
Refuse To Have Vehicle Weighed		B46.2-704	
Refused Blood/Breath 2nd Offense	6	A18.2-268.3	A12
Refused Blood/Breath 3rd Offense	6	B18.2-268.3	A12
Refused Blood/Breath Test	6	18.2-268.3	A12
Refusing To Drive To Weigh Station		46.2-1137	
Registration Violation - Non-Resident		46.2-656	
Represents No Statutory Definition		46.2-0000	
Rmve, Chg, Altr Or Conceal Vehicle Vin #		46.2-1074	
RR Xing/Fail Obey Traffic Ctrl Device		49CFR383.51D5	M10
RR Xing/Fail To Have Sufficient Space		49CFR383.51D4	M23
RR Xing/Fail To Stop Before Crossing		49CFR383.51D3	M22
RR Xing/Fail To Stop Track Not Clear		49CFR383.51D2	M21
Run Red Light	4	NOSTAT-A	M16
Safe Loading (Secured)		B49CFR392.9	
Safety Belt Viol (8-17 Yrs) 2nd/Subsequ		D46.2-1095	F02
Safety Belt Viol/Minor(Ages 8 To 17 Yrs)		B46.2-1095	F02
Safety Belt Violation		46.2-1094	F04
Safety Lap Belt/Shoulder Harness Viol		46.2-1092	F04
Sale Of Mtr Veh W/O Securing Title Cert		46.2-617	
Securely Affix Seat For Veh Driver		46.2-1084	
Securement System Devices Required		49CFR393.102	
Sell,Give Or Distrib Fraudulent License		46.2-105.1D	
Sell/Drive Vehicle With Muffler Cutout		46.2-1047	
Sell/Exchange Disabled Park Plts/Placard		46.2-1252	
Service Hours Violation		49CFR395.1	
Spd Rural Rust Rd 20mph Or More Abv Lmt	4	C46.2-873.2	S15
Speed 15 Mph Above Speed Limit In A CMV	4	H46.2-878	S15
Speed In Highway Work Zone	4	46.2-878.1	S93
Speed Rur Rust Rd 10-14mph Above Spd Lmt		F46.2-873.2	S92
Speed Rur Rust Rd 15-19mph Above Spd Lmt		G46.2-873.2	S15
Speed Rural Rust Rd 1-9mph Above Spd Lmt	3	A46.2-873.2	S92
Speeding 10-14 Mph Above Speed Limit	4	F46.2-878	S92
Speeding 10-14 Mph Abv Spd Lmt - Ex55	4	F46.2-870	S92
Speeding 15-19 Mph Above Speed Limit	4	G46.2-878	S15
Speeding 15-19 Mph Abv Spd Lmt - Ex55	4	G46.2-870	S15
Speeding 1-9 Mph Above Speed Limit	3	A46.2-870	S92
Speeding 1-9 Mph Above Speed Limit	3	A46.2-878	S92

Description	Points	Statute	ACD
Speeding 20 Mph Or Above	6	C46.2-870	S15
Speeding 20 Or More Above Speed Limit	6	C46.2-878	S15
Speeding At School Crossing 10-14 Mph	4	F46.2-873	S92
Speeding At School Crossing 15-19 Mph	4	G46.2-873	S15
Speeding Bus/Res Dist 10-14 Mph	4	F46.2-874	S92
Speeding Bus/Res Dist 15-19 Mph	4	G46.2-874	S15
Speeding City Or Town 10-14 Mph Av Lt	4	F46.2-875	S92
Speeding City Or Town 15-19 Mph Abv Lt	4	G46.2-875	S15
Speeding Generally	4	D46.2-870	S93
Speeding In Sch Bus 1-9 Mph Abv Sp Lmt	3	A46.2-871	S92
Speeding In Sch Bus 20 Mph Or Abv Sp Lmt	6	C46.2-871	S15
Speeding In School Bus 10-14 Ab Sp Lt	4	F46.2-871	S92
Speeding In School Bus 15-19 Ab Sp Lt	4	G46.2-871	S15
Speeding On Bridge 10-14 Mph Ab Sp Lt	4	F46.2-881	S92
Speeding On Bridge 15-19 Mph Ab Sp Lt	4	G46.2-881	S15
Speeding On Bridge 1-9 Mph Abv Sp Lmt	3	A46.2-881	S92
Speeding On Bridge 20 Mph Or Abv Sp Lmt	6	C46.2-881	S15
Speeding Residential District/Excessi	4	46.2-878.2	S93
Speeding W/Sp Permit 1-9 Mph Abv Sp Lmt	3	A46.2-872	S92
Speeding W/Special Permit 10-14 Mph	4	F46.2-872	S92
Speeding W/Special Permit 15-19 Mph	4	G46.2-872	S15
Speeding While Towing 10-14 Mph Ab Sp	4	F46.2-876	S92
Speeding While Towing 15-19 Mph Abv Sp	4	G46.2-876	S15
Speedng At A Sch Xing 1-9 Mph Abv Sp Lmt	3	A46.2-873	S92
Speedng At Sch Xing 20 Mph Or Abv Sp Lmt	6	C46.2-873	S15
Speedng Bus/Res Dist 1-9 Mph Abv Sp Lmt	3	A46.2-874	S92
Speedng Bus/Res Dist 20 Mph Or Abv Sp Lt	6	C46.2-874	S15
Speedng City/Town 20 Mph Or Abv Sp Lmt	6	C46.2-875	S15
Speedng In City/Town 1-9 Mph Abv Sp Lmt	3	A46.2-875	S92
Speedng W/Sp Permit 20 Mph Or Abv Sp Lmt	6	C46.2-872	S15
Speedng While Towing 1-9 Mph Abv Sp Lmt	3	A46.2-876	S92
Speedng While Towing 20 Mph Or Abv Sp Lt	6	C46.2-876	S15
Steering System-Defective		49CFR393.209	
Stop Vehicle To Impede Travel	6	46.2-818(1)	
Subseqnt Offense Oper Boat Recklss/Intox		29.1-738.4	
Sunshielded Windows		46.2-1053	
Suspension Modification-Lift Blocks		46.2-1064	
Tampering With Vehicle		18.2-146	
Temporary Exemption Violation		46.2-662	
Texting/Emailing While Driving-1st	3	A46.2-1078.1	
Texting/Emailing While Driving-2nd/Subq	3	B46.2-1078.1	
Theft Of Motor Vehicle/Parts		46.2-390	
Tire Exceeds Weight Limit		49CFR393.75	
Toll Violation 1st		A46.2-819.3	
Toll Violation 2nd		B46.2-819.3	
Toll Violation 3rd		C46.2-819.3	
Toll Violation 4th/Subsequent		D46.2-819.3	
Trailer Restriction Violation		46.2-1116	
Trans Flam Liq Non-App Container		10.1-1450	E03
Trans Hazmat W/O Shipping Papers		49CFR172.201	
Transport Juvenile In Bed Of Pickup		46.2-1156.1	F05
Tunnel Height Viol(Subsequnt Offense)	3	C46.2-1110	
Tunnel Height Violation	3	B46.2-1110	
Unapproved Glass		46.2-1058	E01
Unauth Use Cross-Over Control Access Hwy	3	46.2-808.1	M44
Unauthorized Use Disable Park Plts/Plcrd		46.2-1250	
Unauthorized Use Of Dmv Materials		46.2-105.1	
Unauthorized Use Of Inspection Sticker		46.2-1172	
Unauthorized Use Of Motor Veh - Felony		A18.2-102	
Unauthorized Use Of Motor Veh - Misd		B18.2-102	U04
Unauthorized Use On Controlled Highway		46.2-808	
Under Age Operating Moped/No Id	3	46.2-914	
Underage-Driving After Consuming Alcohol	6	18.2-266.1	A60
Unlawful Sale Of Motor Vehicles		46.2-1508	
Unlawful Use Reg/Identification Marker		46.2-2011.20	
Unlawful Use Regist/Fail To Pay Taxes		46.2-609	

Description	Points	Statute	ACD
Unlawful/Improper Use Warning Device		46.2-1060	
Unnecessary Noise		NOSTAT-H	
Use CMV To Dist Control Substance		46.2-341.19	A50
Use Counterfeit Disable Park Plts/Placrd		46.2-1248	
Use Of Counterfeit Inspection Sticker		46.2-1173	
Use Radar Detector Device		49CFR392.7A	E70
Use Radar Detector Device		49CFR392.71	E23
Using A Hand-Held Mobile Telephone		49CFR392.82	M86
Vehcle Viol/Flashing Lights-Inj/Prop Dam	4	A46.2-921.1	N04
Vehcle Violation/Flashing Lights-2nd/Sub	3	C46.2-921.1	N04
Vehicle Equipment Violation		49CFR393.1	E70
Vehicle Improperly Parked On Highway		46.2-1224	F34
Vehicle Maintenance (General)		49CFR396.3	
Vehicle Violation/Flashing Lights	3	46.2-921.1	N04
Vehicle Violation/Flashing Lights-Death	6	B46.2-921.1	U31
Viol Of Cell Phone/Wireless Device	0	46.2-334.01C1	
Viol Out Service Veh W/16+ Pass/Hazmat		46.2-341.18:01	B19
Viol Resulting In Fatal Accident		46.2-341.20A3	U31
Violate 10-Hour Rule, 15-Hour Rule		A49CFR395.3	
Violate 60/70-Hour Rule Logbook		B49CFR395.3	
Violate Highway Haul Permit		46.2-1139	
Violating Out Of Service Order	6	A46.2-341.21	B27
Violation Of 3-Day One-Trip Permit		46.2-651	
Violation Of A Cruising Ordinance		46.2-1219.1	
Violation Of Left Turn On Red	3	46.2-836	N53
Violation Of Right Turn On Red	3	46.2-835	N54
Violation Resulting In Fatal Accident		D20-U31	U31

Point System Summary

Points range from 3 to 6. For drivers age 18 or older, accumulation of 18 points in a 12 month period can result in a suspension. Different requirements apply to drivers under age 18. Points are dropped after 2 years from the offense date. A Points Assessment brochure is viewable at www.dmvnow.com/webdoc/pdf/dmv115.pdf

Virginia gives *safe driving* points. For every full calendar year a driver has no violations or suspensions, the driver earns one safe driving point. A driver may earn up to five safe points to offset demerit points. Also, attending a Driver Improvement program can delete points or allow one to earn safe driving points.

Washington

<table>
<tr><th>Administration</th><th>Important Telephone and Web Contacts</th></tr>
<tr>
<td>

Julie Knittle, Assistant Director
Programs and Services Division
Department of Licensing
PO Box 9030, Olympia 98507-9030
360-902-3850

Mykel Gable, Assistant Director
Customer Relations Services Division
Department of Licensing
PO Box 9020, Olympia 98507-9020
360-902-3820

www.dol.wa.gov/
</td>
<td>

Driver License Information 360-902-3900
Commercial Driver License....................360-902-3900
Vehicle Information................................360-359-3600
Registration 360-359-4002
Office of the Insurance Commissioner 800-562-6900
State Police..360-753-6540

Driver License Laws may be accessed from:
www.dol.wa.gov/about/publicdisclosurelawsandrules.html

General Email Help:
    Drivers: drivers@dol.wa.gov
    Vehicles: titles@dol.wa.gov
</td>
</tr>
</table>

Driver's License Format, Issuance and Renewal

License Classes, Restrictions and Endorsements Appear After the Driving Record Content Section

License Format

First five letters of last name, first initial, middle initial, three numbers, and two letters or numbers (i.e., WASHI G E 222 O3). Asterisks (*) are used to fill in the digits if the person's last name has fewer than five letters and/or the person has no middle initial (no middle name). Coding of the last five characters is not released due to security reasons; however, this code is widely known among commercial record vendors, insurance industry personnel, and motor carrier firms.

Document Appearance

Enhanced Document (Issued Since December 2007)

The *Enhanced* Driver Licenses (EDLs), CDLs, and ID card documents are similar overall to the documents issued since 2001, but with several important upgrades. There is an updated format with a ghost photo on the right side of the card, the U.S. flag overlapping the photo, and on the back is a machine-readable zone. The licenses have a salmon color header bar with fish and evergreen trees; for ID cards the header bar is light green in color.

Prior to enhancement, the current digitized license began statewide distribution on July 1, 2001. It will take a number of years before all the older license documents are phased out. The information below describes the old and new license cards as some older cards may still be in use by military personnel.

Document 2001 to December 2007

Security Characteristics   These licenses are created using a digital imaging process. An optically variable ink coats the inside of the front laminate. The ink changes color with changes in the angle of viewing under normal light. Ultraviolet sensitive inks used in printing the card are visible under normal light but fluoresce under any "black light." If the laminate is tampered with, the word VOID displays across the document. The front of every card features a view of Mt. Rainier, larger and bolder printing, and a digital portrait of the individual. Printed on the back are the individual's endorsements and restrictions along with barcodes containing machine-readable information matching the printed information on the card's face.

Position of Photo   Right 1/3 of document.

Minor Age Driver Locator   The Intermediate License features a vertical orientation and includes the words "Intermediate License." Minors are indicated by "Age 21 on mm/dd/yy" or "Age 18 on mm/dd/yy" in a vertical orientation.

CDL Indicator   Shown in endorsement field below license number and expiration, and above yellow highlight bar.

Issuance

Location of Requirements for Proof of Identity:

www.dol.wa.gov/driverslicense/edlproof.html

Age Requirements

An Instruction Permit may be issued to those reaching age 15. The minimum age for a regular license is 18; or 16 with completion of approved driver education course. The DOL issues an Intermediate Driver License to all drivers under age 18. The Intermediate License has the following restrictions: For the first 6 months after issuance, the holder of the license may not have any passengers in the car under the age of 20, except for members of the holder's immediate family. After the first 6 months, the holder may not have more than 3 passengers in the car under the age of 20, except for members of the holder's immediate family. The holder of an Intermediate Driver's License may not operate a vehicle between the hours of 1 a.m. and 5 a.m. except when the holder is accompanied by a parent, guardian, or a licensed driver who is at least 25 years of age. The Intermediate License holder may not operate a wireless device (talking and texting) while driving unless it is to summons medical or emergency help.

Residency

Non-resident's home-state license honored; must secure Washington license within thirty days of establishing residency.

Renewal

The license expires after 6 years. Driver keeps same number when renewing, unless a name change or date of birth correction. Online renewal is available at https://fortress.wa.gov/dol/olr/. Licenses can be renewed or extended by mail for individuals who are out of the state when the license expires. Military personnel and their dependents can have a military designated expiration date on the license, which expires 90 days after discharge. A military driver license issued to a reservist who has been called to active duty, or the spouse or dependent child of the reservist, remains in effect only while the person remains on active duty.

Elderly-Related Restrictions

None indicated.

Vehicle Insurance, Title and Registration Facts

Insurance and Financial Responsibility

Insurance is compulsory; motorists are required to carry proof of insurance or financial responsibility in the form of one of the following:

- Auto Insurance - Minimum limits are $25,000/50,000/10,000.
- Self-Insurance - Must have 26 or more vehicles to qualify
- Certificate of Deposit -with $60,000 value or greater.
- Liability Bond - with $60,000 value or greater.

Washington does not have a no-fault insurance provision. Proof is required upon reinstatement of a suspension or revocation, accident involvement, and before a drive test is administered. SR-22 forms are used. Operators of vehicles registered as antique vehicles, collector vehicles older than 30 years, state or publicly owned vehicles, motorcycles, motor-driven cycles, mopeds, or vehicles registered with the Washington Utilities and Transportation Commission as common or contract carriers are exempt from mandatory insurance requirements.

Registration Renewal

Registration renewals are required annually. Renewal options for vehicles and vessels are available by mail, or online at www.dol.wa.gov, or in person at any County Auditor or vehicle licensing subagent office statewide. RCW 46.16 defines what vehicles are required to be registered in Washington.

New Residents

Non-residents must register vehicles within thirty days of establishing residency. Annual renewal is required for all vehicles operated on highways, unless exempted.

Inspections and Emissions Testing

Washington does not require an annual vehicle safety inspection, but does require a VIN inspection if a discrepancy is noted for an incoming out-of-state vehicle or a destroyed vehicle that was rebuilt.

There is no provision for a statewide emission test program; however, residents in Spokane, King, Pierce, Snohomish, and Clark Counties may be required to obtain an emission test every two years. Certain hybrid vehicles with a 50 MPG rating, certain diesel vehicles, and most 2009 and new vehicles certified to California emissions standards are exempt.

Passenger Plate Facts

The state issues replacement license plates every seven years. There are two plates with one decal with (MO) (YR) on rear plate only. Plates are not coded to indicate the county of issuance, nor is the county spelled out on plate. Plates remain with a vehicle when sold unless they are special/personalized. However, standard issue plates may be transferred to a replacement vehicle for a fee.

Withdrawal Sanctions, and Alcohol and Drug Testing

Alcohol and Chemical Testing

Washington's illegal intoxication level for adults is .08 %, .04% for CDL drivers, and .02 % for drivers under 21. Blood and breath testing is authorized. Washington has an implied-consent violation and an administrative per se law. Based on breathalyzer reading level and number of arrests, subject may be suspended, revoked or disqualified. A probationary license is required when a person enters into a deferred prosecution or is convicted of a DUI or Physical Control. Operating a vessel or bicycle under the influence is also considered illegal.

Suspensions and Revocations

The Washington Department of Licensing is in compliance with the provisions for mandatory Federal CDL disqualification sanctions per the Motor Carrier Safety Improvement Act (MCSIA) – see the Appendix.

To view additional information about DL Penalties and Administrative Actions visit www.dol.wa.gov/forms/500014.pdf.

Administrative Per Ser
    First Incident - Adult ....Ninety-day suspension.
    Second/Subsequent Incident - Adult...............................Two-year revocation.
    First Incident - Minor..Ninety-day suspension.
    Second/Subsequent Incident - Minor..............................Revocation for 1 year or until age 21, whichever is longer.
Aiding or Abetting an Applicant in Falsifying an Application. Thirty to 364-day suspension.
Alcohol & Possession of Firearms Offenses - Minors, Thirteen to Seventeen
    First Offense ....One-year, or until age seventeen, whichever is longer.
    Second or Subsequent Offense ....Two-years, or until age eighteen, whichever is longer.
Cancellation of Fraudulent Driver License..............................Five-year cancellation.
Child Support Enforcement (fail to meet obligations)..............Suspension until obligation met.
Display Another's License..Thirty to 364-day suspension.
Display or Possess a Counterfeit or Altered License................Thirty to 364-day suspension.
Driver Awareness Program
    Continuing Offenses...Thirty to 364-day suspension.
    Habitual Traffic Offender ....Revoked until reinstated (see below)
Driving Under the Influence (penalty depends on BAC)
    First Breath/Blood Conviction in Seven Years.................Ninety-day suspension or one-year revocation.
    Second Breath/Blood Conviction in Seven Years............Two-year or 900 days revocation.
    Third Breath/Blood Conviction in Seven Years ....Three-year or four-year revocation.
    First Refusal Conviction in Seven Years ....Two-year revocation
    Second Refusal Conviction in Seven Years......................Three-year revocation.
    Third Refusal Conviction in Seven Years.........................Four-year revocation.
Driving While Suspended/Revoked...Additional one-year suspension/revocation.
Driving While Revoked - HTO ....Additional one-year revocation.
Drug Offenses - Minors, Thirteen through Twenty
    First Offense ....One-year, or until age seventeen, whichever is longer.
    Second or Subsequent Offenses......................................Two-years, or until age eighteen, whichever is longer.
Eluding a Police Officer ....One-year revocation.
Failure to Appear or Respond to Traffic Citation or Infraction Suspended until adjudicated.

Failure to Pay Judgment Resulting From Collision .... Suspension until judgment satisfied.
Failure to Submit Alcohol Report or Report
    Indicates Non-Satisfactory/Incomplete Treatment............... Variable length suspension
Felony in Which a Vehicle is Used... One-year revocation.
Fraudulent Application .... Thirty to 364-day suspension.
Hit-and-Run (attended vehicle, injury, or fatality)................... One-year revocation.
Intermediate (Minor) License Holder convicted of:
    2nd traffic violation or violation of license restriction...... Six months suspension or until age 18, whichever first.
    3rd traffic violation or violation of license restriction ...... Suspension until age 18.
Leaving Children Unattended in Vehicle
    First Conviction.. No action.
    Second Conviction .... One-year revocation.
Leaving Scene of Fatality Accident .... One-year revocation.
Loaning a Driver's License .... Thirty to 364-day suspension.
Manufacturing Counterfeit License .... Thirty to 364-day suspension.
Motor Fuel Theft .... Up to six months (court determination).
Perjury or Making a False Affidavit Under Any Law
    Relating to the Operation of a Motor Vehicle..................... One-year revocation.
Physical Control .... Same as DUI.
Racing... Same as Reckless Driving.
Reckless Driving
    First Conviction in Two Years... Thirty-day suspension.
    Second Conviction in Two Years .... Thirty-day suspension.
    Third Conviction in Two Years .... One-year revocation.
Reckless Endangerment - Construction Zone......................... Sixty-day suspension.
Refuse Breath/Blood Test - Based on Court Conviction
    First Incident... Two-year revocation.
    Second Incident .... Three-year revocation.
    Third/Subsequent Incident.. Four-year revocation.
Refuse Breath/Blood Test - Based on DUI Arrest
    First Incident - Adult .... One-year revocation.
    Second/Subsequent Incident - Adult................................ Two-year revocation.
    First Incident - Minor... One-year revocation.
    Second/Subsequent Incident - Minor............................... Revocation for 2 years or until age 21, whichever longer.
Unattended Child in Running Vehicle (2 or more offenses) .... One-year revocation.
Unauthorized Person Signing for a Minor .... Thirty to 364-day suspension.
Unlawful Application for Driver License .... Thirty to 364-day suspension.
Vehicular Assault .... One-year revocation after release from total confinement.
Vehicular Homicide.. Two-year revocation after release from total confinement.
Vehicular Manslaughter.. One-year revocation after release from total confinement
Violation of Court Probation .... Thirty- or Extended Thirty-day Suspension.
Violation of License Restrictions .... 120-day suspension.

Vehicle Collision with Lack of Financial Responsibility

If driver/owner insurance information not provided and there is a reasonable possibility of judgment being entered against the driver owner, the license is suspended up to three years or until one of the following is met:
- Enter into payment agreement with adverse party for damages
- Provide proof of insurance in force at time of collision
- Pay claim and provide signed release by adverse party
- Deposit security, amount based on damages/injuries
- Provide civil court decision showing no liability for damages
- Submit an affidavit of non-suit (3 years from date of collision)

Ignition Interlock

Those convicted of an alcohol-related DUI or Physical Control of a motor vehicle, or granted a deferred prosecution, must have an IID: 1 year for the first offense, 5 years for the second offense, and 10 years for subsequent offenses.

Habitual Traffic Offender

A habitual traffic offender (HTO) is a driver who, within a 5-year period, has been convicted of 3 or more offenses listed in RCW 46.65.020(1) OR been found to have committed or convicted of 20 or more of the moving violations listed in WAC 308-104-160. The violation dates of all the offenses must have occurred within the 5-year period. However, if more than one of these offenses are committed within a 6-hour period, they are only counted as 1 offense on the first occasion. If a driver is found to be a habitual traffic offender, the driver license will be revoked until it is eligible to be reinstated

Reinstatement Requirements

Suspension	$75.00 to $150.00 fee; SR-22 may be required.
Revocation	$75.00 to $150.00 fee; SR-22 may be required; reexamination (written and driving); apply for new license.
If DUI Related	The reissue fee is $150. In addition, evaluation from a state-approved facility for alcohol/drugs and satisfactory progress in any required treatment must be completed. Actions on DUI related convictions and Deferred Prosecution include issuance of probationary license.

If DUI Conviction	Proof of installation of an ignition interlock device (IID) is required
If CDL Positive Test	Evaluation from a substance abuse professional (SAP) is required
If Medical	A current Medical/Visual Certification and/or re-exam may be required
If Child Support	Compliance with DSHS rules and agreements

Record Access: Laws, Rules, and Forms

Note: This Section Pertains to Both Driver and Vehicle Records.

Governing Statutes and Rules

To view **Washington Statutes and motor vehicle regulations,** go to www.dol.wa.gov/about/publicdisclosurelawsandrules.html
Washington has strict public disclosure laws (RCW 46.12.380 and 46.52.130) which restrict driver and vehicle information from being released (per request) to the public. Washington adopted an amendment to an administrative rule - WAC 308-10-050 - to acknowledge DPPA, but the state did not specifically enumerate the federal exceptions. Release of **vehicle records** is specifically governed by RCW RCW 42.56, RCW 46.12.370, RCW 46.12.380, WAC 308-10, and WAC 308-93-087.

Policy Statement Regarding Permissible Uses

The department will not release personal information, as defined in 18 USC 2725(3), from records pertaining to motor vehicle operator's licenses and permits, motor vehicle titles, motor vehicle registrations, and identification cards, unless the release both is considered a permissible use under 18 USC 2721 and is otherwise permitted by state law. In construing 18 USC 2721 (b)(2), the release of personal information for use in connection with matters of motor vehicle safety or driver safety shall be deemed to include the physical safety of persons as drivers, passengers or pedestrians and their motor vehicles or property.
Driving Records: The regulations encompass the permissible uses. In general, the following groups may obtain a copy of another person's driving record: attorneys; law, justice, or other government agencies; employers, prospective employers, or their agents; insurance companies or their agents; transit authorities or their agents; volunteer organizations; school districts, state colleges and state universities; and local government. Upon approval, vendors with legitimate purposes, such as driver-record service companies or insurance companies, can access the driving record data. Third party agents that merely act as a conduit, and do not make any hiring decisions, are permitted to act on behalf of employers. Collision reports are redacted of personal information if ordered by a party not authorized.
Vehicle Records: Individuals and businesses should use request forms to request copies of vehicle records - see next section.

Request and Consent Forms

Driving Records: All service providers must have a contract with the DOL. Once approved, accounts do not have to provide the DOL with signatures of drivers with each request. If the account has not been pre-approved, use of *Driving Request Form TR-500-09* is required. The form requires the signature of the requester and the subject, and a statement as to the purpose of the request. The form can be downloaded at www.dol.wa.gov/forms/formspd.html.
Vehicle Records: The *Vehicle/Vessel Information Disclosure Request Form* is used to make a one-time request for information about a vehicle or vessel. Neither form requires notarization. Forms are available online at www.dol.wa.gov/forms/formspd.html. Businesses must include a copy of their business license with their request, and attorneys must provide a copy of their BAR card. Individuals and businesses should use the *Vehicle/Vessel Disclosure Agreement Application* to apply for a contract for ongoing access about vehicles or vessels.

Vendor and Third Party Access Policy

Driving Records: The WA statutes prohibit disclosure to any third party, but an agent or service provider is acting on behalf of an insurer or employer. Vendors may not access records for other vendors. Electronic service providers must have subscriber certificates with the employers or insurance companies. Paper requesters must have a contract if requests exceed 100 requests per month. If not, requests must include properly signed release.
Vehicle Records: An authorized vendor or user may not resell to any third party, including another permissible user or another vendor selling to a permissible user. In general, bulk delivery of vehicle information is available for statistical purposes, but is not available for commercial resale purposes.

Records Ordered For Non-permissible Uses

Without a permissible use, requesters cannot obtain records. The requester will be notified in writing of the denial and provided the statutory exemption which applies and an explanation of how the exemption applies. A driver license status report with no personal information is provided online (see below)

Access to Driver-Related Records

Driving Records

General Information and Fees

Department of Licensing, Revenue Accounting - Driver Record Section, PO Box 3907, Seattle WA 98124-3907, 360-902-3900.
Detailed information on access to records, required forms and when releases are necessary can be found at the website www.dol.wa.gov.
Note that the DOL refers to a driving record as an **Abstract of Driving Record** and uses the abbreviation **ADR**. The driving record fee is $13.00. There are eight different types of driving records that can be ordered. Listed below are record types with typical requesters.

1. **Complete record:** the driver, justice agencies, attorneys
2. **3-year noncommercial insurance abstract:** the driver, insurance industry
3. **3-year commercial insurance abstract:** the driver, insurance industry
4. **3-year life insurance abstract:** the driver, insurance industry
5. **Employment record:** the driver, current employer, prospective

employer (to determine if driver can be hired as a CDL driver)
6. **Volunteer vanpool record:** the driver, employees of agents of a transit authority
7. **Volunteer for organization record:**   the driver, volunteer organizations
8. **School bus driver record:** the driver, school districts

Address Only Request – One may request an address of an individual who has a WA driver license, identification card, or permit number. Use *Form DR-500-002* (www.dol.wa.gov/forms/500002.pdf). The fee is $2.00 for each address up to ten and $.15 for each additional.

In-Person – Walk-in requests of five or less records are processed over-the-counter while you wait. Requests in excess of five are processed with a one-day turn-around time.

Mail – Mail requests are processed within ten to fifteen days. The driver's address is provided as part of the record for permissible users or with signed release. The driver's license number or full name (including middle initial) and date of birth are needed when ordering.

The fee must accompany the request. A refund is not processed if the Department owes less than $10.00 fee if for overpayment or if no record is found.

Electronic (FTP Batch) – Department of Licensing, Data Sales Management, PO Box 9030, Olympia WA 98507, 360-902-3851.

The type of record requested and either the driver's license number or full name (including middle initial) and date of birth are needed when ordering. If a request is submitted using the license number, name and date of birth, the state will still only search using only the license number.

Note: Most high volume requesters prefer to not submit the license number and instead use the name and date of birth. This is because the license number can be confusing as it may contain "Os," "0s," and asterisks (*).

The minimum order requirement is 2,000 records per month. Accounts must be pre-paid and funds must be on-deposit with the state or files will be held until payment is made. Washington charges a full fee for a no record found search.

Bulk – The state will sell data from the driver license file, but only in compliance with DPPA.

By Person of Record – A driver can request his/her own record by mail or walk-in. as described above. Online access is also available at https://fortress.wa.gov/dol/dsdiadr/. Requesters can view and print a PDF copy of the record. Use of a credit card is required. The driver's SSN must be on file.

Status Check

Washington offers a free online inquiry called Driver Status Display. The user may verify if a person has a valid state DL, CDL, ID card, motorcycle endorsement or permit. All responses are in a yes or no format, no personal information is provided. Visit https://fortress.wa.gov/dol/dolprod/dsdDriverStatusDisplay/.

Notification/Monitoring Program

The Department operates a monitoring system for insurance companies to review the driving records of existing policyholders for changes to the driving record. The program is only available to entities with an account (as described above) that access 2,000 or more records per month. Service bureaus (MVR vendors) can provide the service for the insurance companies. The program requires the subscriber to pay a monthly $.06 fee per driver on the list. When there is activity on a driver's record, the $13.00 record fee is incurred to obtain the MVR. Note that employers, such as firms employing CDL drivers, are not able to participate per the legislation that enabled this monitoring program.

Collision Reports

Reporting – Collisions involving death, injury, or property damage in excess of $700.00 (that are not investigated by law enforcement) must be reported immediately to the nearest law enforcement agency having jurisdiction over the collision. Within four days the original report must be filed with the Washington State Patrol, Records Section, PO Box 42628, Olympia WA 98504; call 360-570-2355. There are no special state reporting requirements for commercial drivers.

Record Access – Records are stored for 6 years plus the present year at the Washington State Patrol, Collision Records Section, PO Box 47382, Olympia, WA 98504-2628, 360-570-2355. These reports are written for each vehicle collision resulting in injury or death of any person, or damage to the property of any one person to an apparent extent of $700 or more. The fee is $9.50 per report. It may take 2 to 4 weeks before new reports are ready for access. Entitled parties have access to the complete reports. If the requesting party is not involved or is not an authorized representative, then a redacted report is provided. Include the name, date of accident, location of accident. Use of the agency's request form - *Form 300-345-008* - is required. The agency will fax a copy of the form, upon request. The request form is found at http://www.wsp.wa.gov/publications/collision.htm.

Also, one may purchase a collision report online at https://fortress.wa.gov/wsp/wrecr/WSPCRS/Search.aspx

Access to Vehicle-Related Records

General Information and Fees

Department of Licensing, Public Disclosure Unit, PO Box 2957, Olympia WA 98507-2957, 360-359-4002 *fax* is 360-570-7088. Email questions to vsdisclose@dol.wa.gov.

This department maintains the database for registrations, titles, and liens for vehicles, mobile homes, and vessels. Records are available for six years, plus the current year. Generally new records are placed in the system within one day. Copies of imaged documents, such as title history documents, may take 2-3 weeks to be available.

Washington can search for vehicle information by name of registered owner, as long as the requester is entitled to the information and has a permissible use.

Note: The DOL works with the Department of Social and Health Services Division of Child Support (DCS) to enforce child support and collect delinquent payments. If someone owes child support, the DCS will place a lien on the person's vehicle or vessel through the DOL.

In-Person, Mail – The fee for a photo copy or printout is $.15 each. A special request form is required (see above). Requests sent by mail are responded to within 5 business days from the date received and are either: provided the records, provided an explanation of why access to the records was denied, or provided an estimated date of when the records will be provided. There is no charge to "view" records in person.

Phone, Fax, Email – Requests may be sent by fax or email to the address on the request form. Requests are processed within 5 business days from the date received. Requests for vehicle records must be in writing and may not be requested by phone. IVIPS account holders (see below) may request records by email without using the request form. See below for more information.

Electronic – An online search is available for pre-approved users to access a system known as **IVIPS** (Internet Vehicle/Vessel Information Processing System). With an IVIPS account, you can obtain lien holder name(s). There is a one-time deposit of $25 and a charge of $.04 per inquiry. Approved users may access IVIPS online 24/7. Contact the Public Disclosure Section at 360-359-4001 during normal business hours for more information about applying for IVIPS access.

Bulk – Large bulk requests of vehicle and ownership information cannot be released for any commercial purpose. For more information, please contact: The Department of Licensing, Public Disclosure Section, PO Box 2957, Olympia, WA 98507, 360-359-4002 or email: vsdisclose@dol.wa.gov.

Access to Vessel-Related Records

General Information, Access and Fees

All vessels with propulsion machinery are required to be titled or registered. This requirement also includes sailboats 16 feet and over without any propulsion machinery. The Department keeps records for 7 years. Access, forms, and fee requirements are the same as mentioned for vehicles. You must title and register a boat in Washington State within 60 days of moving to Washington with your boat, or within 1(?) days of buying the boat if living in Washington and bought the boat i(?) another state.

Driving Record Content and Reciprocity

What's On or Not On the Driving Record

- Registration or non-traffic violations and SSNs are not reported on the driving record. Neither is the original date when the license was first issued - only the renewal issuance date is shown.
- While Washington has laws banning the use of a cell phone or texting while driving, the law also states these convictions may not be available to insurance companies or employers.
- The 3-year insurance company record includes employment OR non-employment violations as described. This record also includes convictions, collisions, and overall status of the record only for the past three years, except for seat belt and open container citations
- The 3-year abstract related to insurance requests will not show suspensions, revocations, or disqualifications.
- The full employment record includes employment AND non-employment violations, convictions, collisions, suspensions, revocations, disqualifications, and overall status of the record
- Accidents are placed on the record regardless of who is at fault and shows number of vehicles involved, if legally parked or moving, whether the vehicles were occupied at the time of the collision, and whether the collision resulted in any injury or fatality.
- Drivers' addresses are shown.
- The state does not permit driver school attendance in lieu of conviction.

Data Retention

Moving violations and departmental action (suspensions, revocations, disqualifications) are maintained for a minimum of five years from conviction or final release date and purged from the computer system weekly when appropriate. Non-commercial vehicle collisions are reported for 5 years from collision date; commercial vehicle collisions are reported 10 years from the collision date. Fail to Appear (FTA) convictions are kept ten years from notification date or until resolved - whichever is earlier. Since 07/26/2009, a DUI or any alcohol related conviction is kept a lifetime. Vehicular Assault, Vehicular Homicide, and Deferred Prosecution are also kept a lifetime. Driver records and files that have been inactive for 5 years are purged yearly. CDL data is kept for the mandatory periods per MCSIA (see the Appendix).

Court to Repository

Most violations are entered by data-entry staff from paper abstracts submitted by the courts. RCW 46.20.270 requires convictions to be forwarded immediately upon conviction date.

State Reciprocity for Non-CDL Drivers

- Will suspend driving privilege of driver for unpaid out-of-state citations/convictions.
- Record of new incoming driver is only shown on MVR for certain mandatory convictions.
- Out-of-state convictions are shown on MVR.
- Out-of-state accidents are not shown on MVR.
- Convictions of out-of-state drivers are sent to home state.
- Record is forwarded to new state upon surrender of license.

Classes, Restrictions, Endorsements and Important Abbreviations

License Classes– Commercial

Class A   Any vehicle or combination of vehicles (except motorcycles). Class A required for combination vehicles only when both the GCVWR exceeds 26,000 pounds, and the GVWR of towed vehicle(s) exceeds 10,000 pounds.

Class B   Any vehicle except Class A, combination vehicles and motorcycles. All single vehicles with a weight rating (GVWR) of more than 26,000 pounds.

Class C   Vehicles rated less than 26,000 pounds, provided they are designed to carry 16 or more passengers and/or hazard materials requiring placards.

Note: Additional vehicles included in the CDL program:
- Vehicles designed to transport 16 or more persons (including driver);
- Public school buses, regardless of size. Private and parochial school buses are covered if and when they carry 16 or more persons (including driver);
- Any size vehicles carrying hazardous materials which require vehicle to be placarded

License Classes– Non-Commercial

The "Basic License," while not considered a class, is valid for any vehicle with GVWR or GCVWR of 26,000 pounds or less (except motorcycles).
The "Instruction Permit" requires supervision from the passenger seat by a licensed driver with at least five years of driving experience.
The "Intermediate License" has special restrictions for drivers 16 and 17 years of age, regarding passengers, night time driving, and cell phones.
The "IIL – Ignition Interlock License" allows a person to drive vehicles equipped with an IID while their license is suspended for an alcohol-related DUI.
The "ORL - Occupational/Restricted Driver License" is used for the following reasons:
- Employment
- Undergoing continuing healthcare or providing continuing care for yourself or to another person who is dependent on you
- Enrolled in an educational institution and pursuing a course of study leading to a diploma, degree or other certification
- Court-ordered community service
- Work First, apprenticeship, or on-the-job training
- Attending substance abuse treatment, or 12-step meetings (unless transit service is available)
- The Ignition Interlock License (IIL), used for DUI/alcohol related suspensions. Requires installation of device, no driving restrictions.

Endorsements

I	Commercial Instruction Permit	X	Both Tank Vehicles and HazMat (CDL)	7	Two-Wheeled and Three-Wheeled Motorcycle
H	Placarded Hazardous Materials (CDL)	Y	Motorcycle Instruction Permit	9	Commercial and MC Instruction Permits
N	Tank Vehicles (Liquids/Gasses) (CDL)	3	Two-Wheeled Motorcycle Only		
T	Double or Triple Trailers (CDL)	5	Motorcycle with Sidecar/Trike Only		
U	CDL Medical Waiver				

Restrictions

*	Indicates Probationary Driver	L	Medical on File	S1	School Buses (CDL - Effective 09/06)
C	Corrective Lenses	P1	Class B Passenger Vehicles (Except School Buses) (CDL)	S2	School Buses (CDL)
E	Emancipated Minor			V	Agriculture Permit
F	Financial Responsibility	P2	Class C Passenger Vehicles Under 26,000 lbs (Except School Buses) (CDL)	Z	Special Restrictions on File
G	Ignition Interlock Device				
K	No Air-Brakes (CDL Only)				

Common Abbreviations Found on Driving Records

AKA	Also known as	ENDR	Endorsement	ORL	Occupational restricted license
AL	Alcohol requirement	EXP	Expiration	ODL	Occupational driver's license
CANC	Cancelled license	F	Failure to appear	PDL	Personal driver's license
CDL	Commercial Driver License	FED	Federal	PEND	Pending
CLR	Clear	FR	Financial responsibility	PROB	Probation
CM	Commercial license	FTA	Failure to appear	REIN	Reinstatement
CO	County	I/D	Identification	REL	Release
COMP	Compliance	IID	Ignition Interlock Device	RESTR	Restriction
COND	Conditional	IIL	Ignition Interlock License	REV	Revocation
CONV	Conviction	ILL	Illegal	SR	Safety responsibility
CRT	Court	I/P	Instruction permit	STAY	Stay action pending court
D	Deferred	INV	Invalid	SUP	Superior
DEF PROS	Deferred prosecution	ISS	Issue	SURR	Surrendered
DI	Driver improvement	J	Jail	SURV	Surveillance
DIS	District	JUV	Juvenile	SUSP	Suspension
DISQ	Disqualification	LIC	License	TRI	Tribal Court
DR	Driver responsibility	M/C	Motorcycle	TVB	Traffic Violations Bureau
DS	Driver services	MPH	Miles per hour	VIOL	Violation
DSP	Disposition	MUN	Municipal	Y	Deferred prosecution
ELIG	Eligible	N/A	No action		

Conviction Table with ACD Code, State Code, and Statute

This table is presented in order of the Description column. The ACD Code is to be C23 if any fatal accident is indicated on the citation. The State Code column is for internal use by the DOL, but this code will appear on letters and other communications to the driver. See the short table to follow regarding when criminal or felony action is required.

- For help with statutes, go to www.dol.wa.gov/about/publicdisclosurelawsandrules.html.
- For help with DL Penalties and Administrative Actions go to www.dol.wa.gov/forms/500014.pdf
- For help with DL penalties following convictions go to www.dol.wa.gov/forms/500015.pdf

Description	ACD	RCW	State Code
1st Out-Of-Serv/Hazmat	B19		Z4
1st Per Se >0.02 Bac	A61		TJ
1st Refus Breath/Blood Tst	A12		RJ
1st Vio Out-Of-Service	B27		Z1
2nd Adm Per Se Incident	A90		RB
2nd Adm Per Se/Bl	A90		RY
2nd Or Subse >0.02 Bac	A61		TM
2nd Vio Out-Of-Service	B27		Z2
2nd/CDL Major Offense	W40		LT
2nd/Subse Ref Breath/Blood	A12		RM
2nd/Subse-Ref Bac Test	A12		RC
3rd/Sub Out-Of-Service	B27		Z3
A & Ab Unlawful Application	D02		AB
A/B Commission Of Crime	U05	46.64.048	1B
Adm Per Se Time Served	A90		Y1
Adm Per Se/1st	A90		YB
Adm Per Se/Bl-1st	A90		YA

Description	ACD	RCW	State Code
Adm Per Se/Bl-2nd/Sub	A90		YC
Adm Per Se-2nd/Sub	A90		YD
Admin Per Se	A98		TA
Affidavit/FR Law	D35		AF
Alco Cond/Chem Dependency	W14		BD
Altered License	B41		AL
Assist In Start Interlock	A41	46.20.750.2	13
Breath Test .04 & Above	A94		T4
Cancelled Insurance	B63		CI
Causing Fatal/Neg-CMV	U10	46.25.090.1g	BH
CDL Endorsement Viol	B91	46.25.080, 46.20.400, 46.20.440	3D
Child Restraint Law Viol	F02	46.61.687	43
Child Sup Enforcement	D51		ZA
Coasting On Downgrade	N80	46.61.630	4K
Continuing Offenses	W01		CO
Crossing Fire Hose	M56	46.61.640	76
Default On Agree To Pay	D37		DE
Defective Equipment	E50	46.32.060, 46.37.500, 46.37.005, 46.37.513, 46.37.518, , 46.37.050, 46.37.200	68
Defective/Imp. Muffler	E50	46.37.390	69
Deposit-On File	D35		DP
Dept Occupational Viol	D27	46.20.391, 46.20.394, 46.20.400, 46.20.410	E2
Disobey Road Sign/Signal	M17	46.61.050, 46.61.070, 46.61.075, 46.61.140.3, 46.61.140.4, 46.61.450,	12
Disobey School Patrol	M13	46.61.385	34
Disobey Signalman/Officer	M08	46.61.015, 46.61.020, 46.61.021, 46.61.022	32
Display Another Lic Or ID	D16		DL
Dr Wrong Side Rd/Cros Div	N70	46.61.150	26
Driving On Shoulder	M58	46.61.670	58
Driving On Sidewalk	M58	46.61.606	57
Driving Under Influence	A20	46.61.502	A0
Driving Under Influence – No Suspension	A20	46.61.515	A1
Driving W/O Future Proof	D36	46.29.440	71
Driving W/O Liability Ins	D36	46.30.020, 46.72.100	7S
Driving While Canc	B22	46.25.090.1F, 46.20.342, 46.25.050.2	C5
Driving While Disq	B24	46.25.090.1F, 46.20.342, 46.25.050.2	B5
Driving While Susp	B26		DS
Driving Without CDL Lic	B51	46.25.030, 46.25.050.1, 46.25.060, 46.25.070, 46.25.160	95
Driving Without Lights	E05	46.37.020, 46.37.160, 46.37.184, 46.37.185, 46.37.215, 46.37.220, 46.37.260, 46.37.270	36
DUI - < 0.15 Bac -2nd Ofns	A21	46.61.5055	GU
DUI <0.15 Bac	A21	46.61.5055	GQ
DUI <0.15 Bac	A21	46.61.5055	JF
DUI - <0.15 Bac	A21	46.61.5051	GC
DUI - >0.15 Bac	A21	46.61.5051	GD
DUI - No Susp Recom	A21	46.61.5051	GN
DUI - Prior Conviction	A21	46.61.5053	GK
DUI - Refused Test	A12	46.61.5051	GE
DUI - While Susp/Rev	A21	46.61.5053	GL
DUI .04 BAC	A04	46.25.090(1)(b)	DW
DUI .08 BAC	A08	46.61.502	DX
DUI .10 BAC	A10	46.61.502	DY
DUI <0.15 Bac-2nd Ofns	A21	46.61.5055	JJ
DUI <0.15bac -3rd/Sub	A21	46.61.5055	GX
DUI <0.15bac-3rd/Sub	A21	46.61.5055	JM
DUI =>0.15 3rd/Sub	A21	46.61.5055	GY
DUI =>0.15-2nd Ofns	A21	46.61.5055	JK
DUI =>0.15-3rd/Sub	A21	46.61.5055	JN
DUI =>0.15bac	A21	46.61.5055	GR
DUI =>0.15bac	A21	46.61.5055	JI
DUI =>0.15bac-2nd	A21	46.61.5055	GV
DUI Alcohol And Drugs	A23	46.61.502	DA
DUI Bac Detail Required	A11	46.61.502	DZ
DUI Pl - <0.15 Bac	A21	46.61.5052	GF
DUI Pl - >0.15 Bac	A21	46.61.5052	GH
DUI Time Served	A21	46.61.5055	G1

Description	ACD	RCW	State Code
DUI W/Rt	A12	46.61.5055	JP
DUI W/Rt -2nd Ofns	A12	46.61.5055	GM
DUI W/Rt -2nd Ofns	A12	46.61.5055	GW
DUI W/Rt-2nd Ofns	A12	46.61.5055	JS
DUI W/Rt-3rd/Sub	A12	46.61.5055	GP
DUI W/Rt-3rd/Sub	A12	46.61.5055	GZ
DUI W/Rt-3rd/Sub	A12	46.61.5055	JT
DUI/Drugs	A22	46.61.5055	UA
DUI/Drugs Time Served	A22	46.61.5055	U1
DUI/Drugs/Rt	A12	46.61.5055	UE
DUI/Drugs/Rt-2nd Ofns	A12	46.61.5055	UL
DUI/Drugs/Rt-3rd/Sub	A12	46.61.5055	UY
DUI/Drugs-2nd Ofns	A22	46.61.5055	UD
DUI/Drugs-2nd Ofns	A22	46.61.5055	UJ
DUI/Drugs-3rd/Sub	A22	46.61.5055	UH
DUI/Drugs-3rd/Sub	A22	46.61.5055	UQ
DUI/Drugs-W/Rt	A12	46.61.5055	UB
DUI/Drugs-W/Rt	A12	46.61.5055	UX
DUI/Drugs-W/Rt-2nd Ofns	A12	46.61.5055	UG
DUI/Drugs-W/Rt-2nd Ofns	A12	46.61.5055	UW
DUI/Drugs-W/Rt-3rd/Sub	A12	46.61.5055	UI
DUI/Drugs-W/Rt-3rd/Sub	A12	46.61.5055	UV
DUI-Drugs	A22	46.61.5055	UF
DUI-W/Rt	A12	46.61.5055	GJ
DUI-W/Rt	A12	46.61.5055	GT
DWLS 3rd	B20	46.20.342, 46.25.050.2	B8
DWLS 3rd	B21	46.20.342, 46.25.050.2	C9
DWLS 3rd	B23	46.20.342, 46.25.050.2	C8
DWLS/R 1st Dg	B25	46.20.342.1A..C	D1
DWLS/R 1st Dg/Non Ext	B25	46.20.342	D4
DWLS/R 2nd Dg	B26	46.20.342.1B.C, 46.20.342.1B	D2
DWLS/R 2nd Dg/Non Ext	B26	46.20.342, 46.25.050.2	D5
DWLS/R 3rd Dg	B26	46.20.342.1C, 46.20.342.1C.C	D3
Eluding Police Vehicle	U01	46.61.024	A9
Fail To Dim Headlight	E54	46.37.230	38
Fail To Keep Right	M41	46.61.100, 46.61.135.3	05
Fail To Report Acc/Injury	B61	46.52.030, 46.52.035, 46.52.040	01
Fail To Submit Med	B65		MC
Fail to Yield - Rotary	N21	46.61.190.3	3Q
Fail To Yield Rt Of Way	N01	46.61.180, 46.61.185, 46.61.190, 46.61.205, 46.61.235, 46.61.245, 46.61.427, 46.61.212 (1), 46.61.212.(3), 46.61.261	30
Fail To Yield-Bus	N09	46.61.220	3N
Fail To Yield-Constr	M03	46.61.215	3M
Fail To Yield-Emgy Veh	N04	46.61.210	3J
Fail To Yield-Safety Zone	M12	46.61.260	3L
Fail/Improper Signal	N40	46.61.305	50
Fail/Keep Right-Hvy Veh	M41	46.61.100.3	3E
Failed CDL Re-Exam	W20		CE
Failed Exam	W20		FX
Failure To Comply Trm Pgm	W14		UC
Failure To Maintain Cntl	W14		FM
Failure To Stop	M25	46.61.065, 46.61.200, 46.61.340, 46.61.345, 46.61.365, 46.61.370, , 46.61.190.2, 46.61.195	10
Felony Involving Drugs	A50	46.61.285	FD
Felony Involving Vehicle	U03	46.20.285	B4
Fictious/Altered Lic	B41	46.20.0921, 46.20.336	96
Fictitious Driver Lic / ID	B41		FL
Follow Emergency Equip.	M32	46.61.635	84
Following Too Close	M34	46.61.145	40
Fraudulent Application	D02		FA
FTA/Unpaid Ticket	D53		FT
FTA-14 Day Lic-App/Ojt	D27		FZ
FTA-Apprentice/Ojt	D27		FV
FTA-Limited Lic-A/D	D27		FU
FTA-Workfirst Program	D27		FY

Description	ACD	RCW	State Code
Fail to Appear	D45		F1
Fail to Comply	F56		F2
Failure to Appear	D45		8R
Failure to Pay	D53		8P
Failure to Respond/Comply	D56		98
Habitual Offender	W01		HO
Handle Bars Over Height	F03	46.61.611	47
Haz Mat Violation	E03	46.48.170	7Z
Hearing A & Ab	B41		HB
Hearing Altered Lic	B41		HA
Hearing Display Lic	D16		DH
Hearing Fictitious Lic	D01		HF
Hearing- Fraud App	D02		FE
Hit & Run (Fatality)	B02	46.52.020	H1
Hit & Run (Occupied)	B03	46.52.020	A8
Hit & Run (Body)	B03		HJ
Hit And Run	B01	46.25.090.1C	LQ
Hit And Run -Fatality	B02	46.25.090.1C	LF
Hit And Run-Personal Inj	B03	46.25.090.1C	LO
Hit And Run-Prop Damage	B04	46.25.090.1C	LG
Hit/Run (Unattended)	B04	46.52.010	52
Il Canceled-Alco Vio	D02		XR
Il Canceled-Traf Vio	D02		XQ
Illegal use/Disp Lic/ID Card	D16	46.20.0921	75
Imminent Hazard	W70		HZ
Impeding Traffic	F34	46.61.202, 46.61.425, 46.61.427	56
Improper Backing	N82	46.61.605	80
Improper Lane Change	M42	46.61.140	14
Improper Lane Travel	M62	46.61.140	16
Improper Mirrors	E70	46.37.400	37
Improper Overtake/Pass	M70	46.61.110, 46.61.115, 46.61.120, 46.61.125, 46.61.130	44
Improper Starting	N83	46.61.300	3S
Improper Turn	N50	46.61.290	42
Inattention	M82		88
Individual Interview	W01		II
Inter Lic-Restr Vio-2nd	D29		XL
Inter Lic-Restr Vio-3rd	D29		XN
Inter Lic-Traf Conv-2nd	D29		XM
Inter Lic-Traf Conv-3rd	D29		XO
Interest Of Safety	W01		IS
Interview A &Ab	B41		IB
Interview Altered Lic	B41		IA
Interview Display Lic	D16		IL
Interview Ficitious Lic	B41		IF
Interview-Fraudapp	D02		FF
Judgment	D39		JD
Leaving Scene Bf Pol Arr	B05	46.25.090.1C	LA
Leaving Scene Prop Dmg	B08	46.25.090.1C	LP
Leaving Scene-Fatal	B06	46.25.090.1C	LE
Leaving Scene-Per Injury	B07	46.25.090.1C	LN
License Cancelled	D01		LC
License Manufacturing	D10		LM
License Restriction Viol	D29	46.20.041	60
Limited Access Roadway	M50	46.61.155	4F
Medical	W14		MS
Medical Hearing Against	W14		MH
Medical Interview Against	W14		MA
Minor => .02-2nd/Sub	A61		MT
Minor =>.02-1st Ofns	A61		MJ
Minor 1st Incid/Bl	A61		MK
Minor In Possession	A31		MP
Minor In Possession/Alchol	A31		MB
Minor In Possession/Alchol	A31		MX
Minor In Possession/Drugs	A33		MD
Minor In Possession/Drugs	A33		MY
Minor In Possession	A31		MV

Description	ACD	RCW	State Code
Minor Operates Veh/Alco	A60	46.61.503,	1A
Minor Time Served	A61		M1
Minor-2nd/Sub-Blood	A61		ML
Minor-Physical Control	A60	46.61.503	1D
Mip-Alcohol-Diversion	A31		MM
Mip-Alcohol-Diversion	A31		MQ
Mip-Drugs-Diversion	A33		MN
Mip-Drugs-Diversion	A33		MR
Misrepresentation of Identity	D02	46.20.0921	8X
More Than One License	D07	46.20.021.2	31
Motorcycle Helmet Req	F03	46.37.530	79
Mult Vio-14 Day Lic-App/Ojt	D27		OT
Mult Viol-Apprentice/Ojt	D27		OJ
Mult Viol-Limited Lic-A/D	D27		OA
Mult Viol-Workfirst Program	D27		OW
Multiple Cycle Violation	F03	46.37.530.1C	99
Neg Driving-1st Deg/Al	M83	46.61.5249	2A
Negligent Driving	M83	46.61.525	22
Negligent Driving - 2nd Deg	M83	46.61.525	2C
Negligent Driving - 1st Deg	M83	46.61.5249	2B
Negligent Driving ****	M83	46.61.525	23
Negligent Homicide - CMV	U09	46.61.520	B0
No CDL Re-Exam	W20		CF
No Func Iid	A41		IT
No License On Person	B51	46.20.017, 46.20.190	92
No Motorcycle License	B51	46.20.500, 46.20.510	93
No Proof of Liability Ins	B74	46.30.020	6S
No Shield Or Mirrors M/C	F03	46.37.530.1A	83
No Valid License****	B51	46.20.021	53
No Valid License/C	B51	46.20.005	21
No Valid License/I	B78	46.20.015, 46.20.190	29
No/Illegal Helmet (Dr)	F03	46.37.530.1C, 46.37.535	7V
No/Illegal Helmet (Pass)	F03	46.37.530.1C, 46.37.535	7W
Obstructed Vision/Ctl	D70	46.61.615, 46.37.410	82
Occ / Restr Driver License	D27		OL
Open Container Law (1)	A35	46.61.519	45
Open Container Law (3)	A35	46.61.519.3	65
Open Container Law (4)	A35	46.61.519	49
Open Container Law (5)	A35	46.61.519.5	51
Open Container-Passenger	A35	46.61.519.3	55
Oper Mc W/O Lights	F03	46.37.522	35
Oper Mc W/O Prop Equip	F03	46.37.250, 46.37.522, 46.37.530, 46.37.530.1A, 46.37.530.1C, 46.37.535, 46.37.536, 46.61.611	8V
Out-Of-State	D35		OS
Over/Stradl Center Line	M61	46.61.140	25
Pass Stopped School Bus	M75	46.61.375, 46.61.370	54
Pc Time Served	A21	46.61.5055	K1
Pc/Drugs Time Served	A22	46.61.5055	W1
Pc/Prob Lic-Refused Test	A12	46.61.5052	KI
Person/Animal O/Side Veh	F05	46.61.660	78
Phy Ctl - <0.15 Bac	A21	46.61.5051	KD
Phy Ctl <0.15bac -3rd/Sub	A21	46.61.5055	KX
Phy Ctl <0.15bac -3rd/Sub	A21	46.61.5055	TU
Phy Ctl =>0.15-3rd/Sub	A21	46.61.5055	KY
Phy Ctl =>0.15-3rd/Sub	A21	46.61.5055	TY
Phy Ctl - >0.15 Bac	A21	46.61.5051	KE
Phy Ctl - No Susp Recom	A21	46.61.5051	KN
Phy Ctl - Pl - <0.15 Bac	A21	46.61.5052	KG
Phy Ctl - Pl - >0.15 Bac	A21	46.61.5052	KH
Phy Ctl - Prior Conviction	A21	46.61.5053	KJ
Phy Ctl - Refused Test	A12	46.61.5051	KF
Phy Ctl - While Susp/Rev	A21	46.61.5053	KL
Phy Ctl <0.15 Bac	A21	46.61.5055	KR
Phy Ctl <0.15 Bac	A21	46.61.5055	TH
Phy Ctl <0.15bac-2nd Ofn	A21	46.61.5055	TK
Phy Ctl <0.15bac-2nd Ofns	A21	46.61.5055	KU

Description	ACD	RCW	State Code
Phy Ctl =>0.15bac	A21	46.61.5055	KS
Phy Ctl =>0.15bac	A21	46.61.5055	TI
Phy Ctl =>0.15bac 2nd Of	A21	46.61.5055	TO
Phy Ctl =>0.15bac 2nd Ofn	A21	46.61.5055	KV
Phy Ctl W/Rt	A12	46.61.5055	KA
Phy Ctl W/Rt	A12	46.61.5055	KT
Phy Ctl -W/Rt	A12	46.61.5055	TN
Phy Ctl W/Rt -3rd Sub	A12	46.61.5055	KZ
Phy Ctl W/Rt -3rd Sub	A12	46.61.5055	TR
Phy Ctl W/Rt -3rd Sub	A21	46.61.5055	KC
Phy Ctl W/Rt-2nd Ofns	A12	46.61.5055	KB
Phy Ctl W/Rt-2nd Ofns	A12	46.61.5055	KW
Phy Ctl/Drugs	A22	46.61.5055	WA
Phy Ctl/Drugs	A22	46.61.5055	WH
Phy Ctl/Drugs/Rt	A12	46.61.5055	WJ
Phy Ctl/Drugs/Rt-2nd Ofn	A12	46.61.5055	WP
Phy Ctl/Drugs/Rt-3rd/Sub	A12	46.61.5055	WY
Phy Ctl/Drugs-2nd Ofns	A22	46.61.5055	WC
Phy Ctl/Drugs-2nd Ofns	A22	46.61.5055	WK
Phy Ctl/Drugs-3rd/Sub	A22	46.61.5055	WE
Phy Ctl/Drugs-3rd/Sub	A22	46.61.5055	WU
Phy Ctl/Drugs-W/Rt	A12	46.61.5055	WB
Phy Ctl/Drugs-W/Rt	A12	46.61.5055	WX
Phy Ctl/Drugs-W/Rt-2nd Of	A12	46.61.5055	WD
Phy Ctl/Drugs-W/Rt-2nd Of	A12	46.61.5055	WW
Phy Ctl/Drugs-W/Rt-3rd/Sb	A12	46.61.5055	WF
Phy Ctl/Drugs-W/Rt-3rd/Sb	A12	46.61.5055	WV
Phy Tl W/Rt-2nd Ofns	A12	46.61.5055	TQ
Physical Control	A20	46.61.504	A5
Physical Control – No Suspension	A20	46.61.515	A7
Pos More Than One Lic	D07	46.20.020, 46.20.021.2	7X
Poss Fictious License	B41	46.20.0921, 46.20.336.1	7T
Prob Lic - Refused Test	A12	46.61.5052	GI
Prohibited Turn	N50	46.61.295	18
Racing	S95	46.61.530	A4
Railroad Crossing Viol-2nd	W60		XY
Railroad Crossing Viol-3rd	W61		XZ
Reckless Driving	M84	46.61.500	A2
Reckless Driving ****	M84	46.61.500	A3
Refus Breath/Blood Test	A12		RA
Refusal Time Served	A12		R1
Refuse Empl Test	W81		PP
Refuse Test	A12		RT
Refuse Test	A12		TB
Refuse To Take Exam	W20		FQ
RR Crossing Viol-1st (M09)	M09		XX
RR Crossing Viol-1st (M10)	M10		X1
RR Crossing Viol-1st (M20)	M20		X2
RR Crossing Viol-1st (M21)	M21		X3
RR Crossing Viol-1st (M22)	M22		X4
RR Crossing Viol-1st (M23)	M23		X5
RR Crossing Viol-1st (M24)	M24		X6
RR-Fail Oby Signal/Off	M10	46.61.340	6E
RR-Fail Stop Not Clear	M21	46.61.340	6B
RR-Fail Stp Before Xing	M22	46.61.350	6C
RR-Fail To Slow/Check	M20	46.61.400 (3)	6A
RR-Insuf Clearance	M24	46.61.355	6F
RR-Insuf Space To Cross	M23	46.61.202	6D
RR-Other Violation	M09	46.61.340	6G
Seat Belt Law Violation	F04	46.61.688	41
Seat Belt Viol - Passenger	F04	46.61.688	39
Serious Traffic Offenses	W30		SO
Serious Traffic Offns >3	W31		S3
Six Violations/1 Year	W01		VY
Spec Exam Hearing Against	W20		SH
Spec Exam Interview Agnst	W20		SA

Description	ACD	RCW	State Code
Special Exam	W20		SX
Speed	S93	46.61.400	04
Speeding	S92	46.61.400	06
Speeding 15 MPH Over	S15	46.61.400	08
Speeding 1-10 MPH Over	S51	46.61.400	0G
Speeding 11-14 MPH Over	S14	46.61.400	0M
Speeding 16-20 MPH Over	S16	46.61.400	0A
Speeding 21-25 MPH Over	S21	46.61.400	0B
Speeding 21-30 MPH Over	S71	46.61.400	0H
Speeding 26-30 MPH Over	S26	46.61.400	0C
Speeding 31-35 MPH Over	S31	46.61.400	0D
Speeding 31-40 MPH Over	S81	46.61.400	0I
Speeding 36-40 MPH Over	S36	46.61.400	0E
Speeding 41+ MPH Over	S91	46.61.400	0J
Speeding 41-45 MPH Over	S41	46.61.400	0F
Sub Out-Of-Serv/Hazmat	W51		Z5
Tamper Interlock	A41	46.20.750.1, 46.20.750	1T
Test Positive Alco/Drug	W80		PT
Too Fast For Conditions	S94	46.61.400.1,	02
Unable To Qual On Spec Ex	W20		SR
Uninsured Accident/Fr Law	D35		CV
Unlawful Oper MC Roadway	F06	46.61.608, 46.61.612, 46.61.614	4H
Unsafe Condition Of Veh	F66	46.12.075, 46.12.080, 46.32.010 (7), 46.32.060, 46.61.620	8U
Unsafe/Improper Tires	E37	46.37.420, 46.37.423, 46.37.425, 47.36.250	6J
Unsat Progress During Trm	W14		UP
Using Another's License	D16	46.20.0921	73
Vehicle Accident/Fr Law	D35		FC
Vehicular Assault	U06	46.61.522(1)(B)	V1
Vehicular Assault	U06	46.61.522	VA
Vehicular Homicide	U07	46.61.520(1)(A)	V2
Vehicular Homicide	U07	46.61.520	VH
Vehicular Homicide	U27	46.61.520	VE
Vehicular Homicide	U28	46.61.520	VF
Vehicular Manslaughter	U08	46.61.520	B2
Viol Of Interlock Rest	A41	46.20.740, 46.20.720	5C
Viol Of Rest Hearing Agnst	D29		RH
Viol Of Restr Against	D29		VI
Viol Of Restriction(S)	D29		VR
Viol Out-Of-Serv Order	B27	46.32.100	1Z
Viol Out-Of-Serv Order/Haz	B19	46.25.090, 46.32.100	4Z
Viol Out-Of-Serv Order/Pass	B19	46.25.090, 46.32.100	6Z
Viol Resulting Fatal Acc	U31	FMCSA	2E
Viol Trans/Carpool Lane	M49	46.61.165	4G
Vision Below Standards	W14		VS
Wrong Way On One-Way St	N63	46.61.135	24
Wrong Way on Rotary	N61	46.61.135.3	3R

When Criminal/Felony Action Required

(Can involve suspension or revocation)

- Driving revoked/HTO
- Driving while intoxicated
- Driving while license revoked
- Driving while license suspended
- Eluding police
- Felony involving vehicle
- Hit-and-run (occupied vehicle)
- Manslaughter
- Minor in possession/alcohol (minors age thirteen through seventeen)
- Minor in possession/drugs (minors of age thirteen through twenty)
- Negligent homicide
- Physical control
- Racing
- Reckless driving
- Unattended children in running vehicle (second charge)
- Vehicular assault
- Vehicular homicide
- Violation of occupational driver's license

No Point System

Washington does not have a point system. However, 4 moving violations within 12 months or 5 within 24 months will bring about a suspension.

West Virginia

Administration	Important Telephone and Web Contacts

Joe E. Miller, Commissioner
Division of Motor Vehicles
5707 MacCorkle Ave SE
PO Box 17300
Charleston 25317-7300
304-926-3871
www.transportation.wv.gov/dmv/Pages/default.aspx
 	
State Statutes:
   www.legis.state.wv.us/WVCODE/Code.cfm
	Driver Licenses, CDL.....................................304-926-3801
	Driving Records 304-926-3802
	Citations Unit - Point System.........................304-926-2505
	Revocation or Suspension Due to DUI............304-926-2506
	Compulsory Motor Vehicle Insurance.............304-926-3802
	Ignition Interlock..304-926-2507
	Titles, Registration, or Plates........................304-926-3840
	State Department of Insurance 304-558-3386
	West Virginia State Police..............................304-746-2100
	Code of State Rules - Title Series 91
	   http://apps.sos.wv.gov/adlaw/csr/index.aspx

Driver's License Format, Issuance and Renewal

License Classes, Restrictions and Endorsements Appear After the Driving Record Content Section

License Format

A seven digit alpha/numeric series, with no correlation to type of license issued, is used as follows—

0000001 - 0999999	E000001 - E999999
1X00001 - 1X99999	F000001 - F999999
A000001 - A999999	G000001 - G999999
B000001 - B999999	S000001 - S999999
C000001 - C999999	XX00001 XX99999
D000001 - D999999	

Document Appearance

As of January 1, 2012, card holders may also choose between two types of driver's licenses and ID cards: those FOR federal identification purposes and those NOT FOR federal identification purposes. Per the requirements of the REAL ID Act, WV is encouraging all drivers to include the full middle name when applying for a new or renewal license. The current Driver License Cards and Identification Cards are issued by all Regional Offices since July 28, 2011.

Current Document Issued

Cards FOR federal identification license have a gold star in the corner and will take approximately 10 business days to ship directly to the customer via UPS. The other type will have "Not For Federal Identification" has printed across the regular license and ID cards and is give at the time of issuance.

Security Characteristics: Built in micro-printing, there is a holographic overlay featuring the state with the new River Gorge bridge. A colored coded map appear on top, right side. The map is blue for Class E & D licenses; gold for A, B, and C; Green for Identification cards; and the state has a red outline for Instruction Permits.

Position of Photo: Left edge. For drivers 21 and older, a smaller ghost image appears in lower right corner. A signature appears partially over the ghost photo.

Underage: Vertical format, picture in left corner. All licenses for driver 15-17 are Red, if 18-21 are Blue. A signature appears partially over the ghost photo on lower right corner.

CDL Indicator: "COMMERCIAL DRIVER LICENSE" appears in a header bar.

Previous Document

Security Characteristics: License is a digital/PVC card, overlay with WV outline in bold (hologram).

Position of Photo: Top left.

Minor Age Driver Locator: Vertical format, picture in left corner. All licenses for drivers 15-17 are Red, if driver is 18-20 then Blue.

CDL Indicator: "COMMERCIAL DRIVER LICENSE" is printed across the top of the license.

Issuance

Location of Requirements for Proof of Identity:

Visit www.transportation.wv.gov/dmv/Drivers-Licenses/Pages/default.aspx

Age Requirements

A Graduated Driver's License Program was instituted 01/2001 with three levels or licensing steps, as related below. An Instruction Permit minimum age is 15, valid until 18th birthday with a 30-day extension. An Intermediate License minimum age is 16; minimum 6 months infraction-free driving at Instruction Permit level. A Full License is the level three and is valid until age 21. One must have a minimum of 12 months infraction-free driving at Intermediate Level. A Class E minimum age is eighteen; which is the adult license.

Residency

Non-resident's home-state license is honored on a reciprocal basis for up to 30 days.

Renewal

WVDMV issues driver licenses with expiration of up to 5 years. Renewal is not available online at this time. Vision screening is required. Driver keeps the same number when renewing. Licenses of military personnel out-of-state do not expire, but must be renewed within 6 months after discharge. Any driver whose license has been expired for more than 6 months will be required to retest.

Elderly-Related Restrictions

None are reported.

Vehicle Insurance, Title and Registration Facts

Insurance and Financial Responsibility

Liability insurance is compulsory; minimum liability limits are 20,000/40,000/10,000. West Virginia does not have no-fault insurance. Proof is required at registration or renewal, vehicle inspection and after an accident or certain violations. Vehicle registrations are randomly sampled for validity. SR-22 forms are not used by the state. A violation of the compulsory insurance law may result in the suspension of the driver license and revocation of the license plate. Failure to satisfy a civil judgment resulting from an accident requires an indefinite suspension until restitution is made. Motorists are required to carry a proof of insurance form *Certificate of Insurance* in their vehicle at all times. Law enforcement officers will request this information during any traffic stop or crash

Registration Renewal

Renewal is annual. At this time renewal is not available online. However, the new West Virginia Vehicle Registration System (VRS) online filing system allows one to enter vehicle purchase information and generate a temporary tag or transfer registration and necessary DMV forms - through an authorized dealer.

New Residents

Non-residents must register vehicles if stay exceeds 30 days. New residents must title the vehicle in West Virginia within 30 days of establishing residency.

Inspections and Emissions Testing

West Virginia requires a routine safety inspection every twelve (12) months for all vehicles. Inspections are performed at any official inspection station licensed by the State Police. A sticker is placed on the inside of the windshield. New residents have 10 days from the date they title a vehicle to have a West Virginia inspection. West Virginia has reciprocity with Louisiana, Mississippi, Missouri, New Hampshire, New York, Oklahoma, Texas, Utah, and Wyoming. Therefore, out of state inspection stickers from these states are valid in West Virginia until expiration. Any vehicle purchased or otherwise acquired within West Virginia not having a valid inspection sticker must be inspected within ten days.

There is no provision for vehicle emission testing.

Passenger Plate Facts

There is one plate and one decal (yr). County of issuance is not designated by codes or printed on the plate. When a vehicle is sold the plate remains with the seller.

Withdrawal Sanctions, and Alcohol and Drug Testing

Alcohol and Chemical Testing

West Virginia's illegal intoxication level is .08 percent and above,15 percent and above for aggravated DUI, .05 percent and above for administrative driver's license suspension, .04 percent for drivers of CMVs, and .02 percent for drivers under 21. Blood tests can be requested or obtained with a search warrant. Breath tests are the designated secondary chemical tests. West Virginia has an implied-consent violation provision, an administrative suspension provision, and any measurable alcohol provision for drivers under the age of 21 with BAC of .02 and less than .08.

Suspensions and Revocations

Mandatory Suspension will occur with accumulation of 12 or more points within a 2-year period as follows:

12-13 Points	Thirty Days.
14-15 Points	Forty-five Days.
16-17 Points	Sixty Days.
18-19 Points	Ninety Days.
20+ Points	License is Suspended until Accumulated Points are Reduced to 11 or Less.

Note: License suspensions run consecutively; points accumulated by drivers already under suspension will result in an additional license suspension, to begin after the original suspension period ends. However, suspensions received upon reaching 20+ points shall run concurrently.

Mandatory Revocation (three months to one year) For Conviction of any of the Following:

* Manslaughter or Negligent Homicide
* Felony Involving a Motor Vehicle
* Leaving the Scene of an Accident Resulting in Death or Personal Injury
* Court Ordered Judgments.
* Three Reckless Driving Convictions in Twenty-four Months
* Drag Racing
* Driving While License Suspended/Revoked

DUI Revocations

First Offense	Varies, 15 day minimum suspension.
Second Offense	Will include one-year suspension.
Third Offense	Will include one-year suspension of driving privileges.

No Proof of Insurance

For failure to show proof of insurance during a notice for verification of coverage, ticket, crash report or insurance company cancellation; the driver's license may be subject to suspension for 30 days. There is no provision in the Motor Vehicle code for a driving permit during a suspended period.

CDL Suspensions, Revocations, and Disqualifications

West Virginia is in compliance with the provisions of the Motor Carrier Safety Improvement Act (MCSIA), see the Appendix. Below is an overview of many CDL sanctions.

Any one of the following will disqualify a WV Commercial Driver's License holder:

* Causing fatality thru negligent operation of a CMV
* Controlled substance DUI
* Driving a CMV while suspended, revoked, or disqualified
* Driving Under the Influence (DUI), blood alcohol content (BAC) .04 or above
* Drug felony while operating a commercial motor vehicle
* FMSCA Notice that driver poses an imminent hazard
* Leaving the scene of an accident
* Violation of an out-of-service order
* Railroad crossing violation committed in a CMV
* Refusal to submit to a BAC test

A 60-day suspension will be assessed against any person who operates a commercial vehicle:

* Without a valid CDL
* Without proper license endorsements
* While serving a disqualification

DMV disqualifies CDL holders who are convicted of two or more of these offenses in a CMV within a 3-year period:

* Reckless driving
* Improper lane changes
* Following too closely
* Speeding 15 MPH or more above limit
* Any violation of traffic law in connection with a fatal accident
* Driving a CMV without obtaining a CDL
* Driving a CMV without a CDL in possession
* Driving a CMV without proper license class or endorsements

Reinstatement Requirements

If alcohol or drug related, completion of Safety & Treatment Program is required. Aggravated DUI offenders and Repeat offenders must participate in the WV Alcohol Test & Lock program. All suspension and revocation fees are $50.00 with the exception to Compulsory Insurance files which are: revocation of license plate is a $100.00 reinstatement fee; secure order to State Police for license plate is a $50.00 penalty fee.   Should an administrative hearing be held additional costs may apply.

Record Access: Laws, Rules, and Forms

Note: This Section Applies to Both Driver and Vehicle Records.

Governing Statutes and Rules

Code of State Rules - Title Series 91:
   http://apps.sos.wv.gov/adlaw/csr/index.aspx
State Statutes: www.legis.state.wv.us/WVCODE/Code.cfm
Per the State's Uniform Motor vehicle Records Disclosure Act (Statute 17A-2A-1 et seq), the state adopted the provisions of DPPA.
Section 17A-2A-6 discusses "disclosure with consent." Section 17A-2A-7 outlines "permitted disclosures." Although the state enforces the permissible uses per DPPA, the statute did not adopt the following DPPA exemptions (uses): (11), (12), and (13). Ongoing requesters should establish an account.

Request and Consent Forms

Driving Records: The *Request for Driving Records Form DMV-101-PS-1* must be used unless an account has been established. If mailed, the form requires a copy of a valid state-issued driver's license or identification card of the requester. The form is found at www.transportation.wv.gov/dmv/Forms/DMVForms/DMV-101-PS1_PS2-wf.pdf. The form includes a *Release Authorization* page, if the request is for a non-permissible use. Also, if mailed a copy of a valid state-issued drivers license or identification card of the requester is required.
Vehicle Records: *Request for Vehicle Information Form* is known as *Form DMV 100*. The form is not easily found on the Web; we suggest using the search feature to find the form. The form requires signature of the requester and a copy of a state-issued picture ID

Vendor and Third Party Access Policy

Any authorized recipient who resells or rediscloses personal information shall:
  1. Maintain for a period of not less than five years, records as to the person or entity receiving information, and the permitted use for which it was obtained;
  2. Upon request make the records available for inspection by the division;
  3. Only be disseminated in accordance with express consent obtained pursuant to section four of this article.
Approved, high volume vendors can access records for other vendors (who will then sell to an end-ser with the following restrictions—
  1. Contract between original vendor and reseller contains same language as contract between the state and the original vendor
  2. Contract between reseller and end user contains same language as contract between the state and the original vendor
Records on subjects who have opted-in are available for commercial purposes; however, further resale is prohibited.

Records Ordered For Non-permissible Uses

If no consent or permissible use is presented, records are not released. However, the state permits the requester of a driving record to use the Message Forwarding Service that enables the state to forward a request to the license holder to approve the record request.

Access to Driver-Related Records

Driving Records

General Information and Fees

Division of Motor Vehicles, Driving Records/Insurance Section, PO Box 17020 Charleston WV 25317, 304-926-3802.
For mail or walk-in requests, if the driver's license number is provided the fee is $5.00 for a non-certified record and $6.00 for a certified record. However, if the driver's license number is NOT provided, the fee is $6.00 for a non-certified record and $7.00 for a certified record. The fee is $9.00 for a record obtained electronically.
The **Message Forwarding Service** (see above) fee is $5.00. All fees are non-refundable. The state charges for "no record found" reports. All requests for a driving record on an employee or client must have a completed DMV-101-PS-2 form.
The agency will provide a copy of a suspension revocation, or disqualification file for $.25 per page.
In-Person – Up to five requests may be obtained over-the-counter with immediate service; otherwise the records are available the next day. Physical address is 5707 MacCorkle Ave SE, Ste 200 Charleston 25317.
Mail – Requests may be mailed to the above address. The driver's license number and last name are needed for a search. The fee must accompany the request.
Electronic – The designated service manager for online access to WV driving records is at WV.gov (handled by WV Interactive, an NIC affiliate). All requesters must complete three agreement documents necessary for account approval. The system processes requests on an interactive basis. The fee is $9.00 per record; there is a $100.00 subscription fee that permits 10 users. Subscribers have access to other information services. For more info call WV.gov at 304-414-0265.
Bulk – The state will sell all or part of its driver license database (no histories) to approved authorized accounts, per provisions of DPPA. Call Information Services at the phone number listed above for more information. A signed contract is required and records may not be sold or released to individuals or other vendors.

By Person of Record – West Virginia drivers may obtain a copy of their driving record by either mail or walk-in at the address above. At present, drivers may not order their own record online, but can use the Status Check mentioned above.

Notification/Monitoring Program

A monitoring system for employers and other approved entities to track incidents of drivers is in the works. The DMV indicates the program is in a testing stage and may be available sometime in the near future. For more information, call WV.gov (WV Interactive, an NIC affiliate) at 304-414-0265.

Status Check

West Virginia offers a free Driver's License Status Check at www.transportation.wv.gov/dmv/Pages/dlverify.aspx.

Crash Reports

Reporting – Crashes involving death, injury, or damage in excess of $250.00 must be reported immediately to the nearest police department. There are no special reporting criteria for commercial drivers.
Record Access – West Virginia State Police, 725 Jefferson Road, South Charleston WV, 25309-1698, 304-746-2128; fax is 304-746-2206. www.statepolice.wv.gov/Pages/default.aspx
The WV State Police Records Section sells copies of the crash reports they have investigated. To obtain a copy, send $20.00 per request and a written letter explaining the purpose and requester's involvement (family member, lawyer, participant, etc.) to the address above. Approved requesters can order by phone. Add $5.00 for certification or $5.00 to have copied fax back. Records are available for 10 years to present. Normal turnaround time is 1 to 6 weeks. Expedited fax service is available for an extra $5.00. Approved requesters can order by phone. Juvenile names will not be released. Obtain request form at: www.statepolice.wv.gov/forms/Documents/crashReportRequestForm.pdf.
If the incident was not investigated by the State Police, the report must be obtained from the local investigating jurisdiction.

Access to Vehicle-Related Records

General Information and Fees

Division of Motor Vehicles, Vehicle Records - Box 17150, 5707 MacCorkle Ave SE, Ste 200, Charleston 25317, 304-926-3909.

The DMV maintains records for vehicles, boats, and unattached mobile homes. The fee for a VIN, plate and registration checks is $1.00; $5.00 per vehicle for lien information with registration; $5.00 per title copy; $10.00 for certified title copy; $25.00 per vehicle for a complete title history (which includes lien data), and $5.00 Message Forwarding fee (as described in the Driving Records section above). Title copies are available from the early 1960's. Lien Perfection information (which must include Dealer's fax date) is $20.00.

Form DMV 100, The Request for Vehicle Information Form, is found at www.transportation.wv.gov/dmv/Forms/Pages/default.aspx.

In-Person, Mail – Requests are available by mail or over-the-counter. All requests must include a copy of a state-issued photo ID. The fee and proper documentation as listed on the request form must accompany the request. Mail requests are returned within three to five days. Turnaround time is immediate for in-person requests if data is on the computer, otherwise results are returned by mail. Note that a copy of the request **may** be forwarded to the record holder.

Electronic – West Virginia does not offer online inquiry at this time.

Bulk – Requests for bulk orders must be submitted in writing to Joyce Abbott, Legal Services, stating the purpose of the request. Costs for custom runs are based on programming run-time and clerical help. A dump of the entire vehicle file is available. For cost and further information, call 304-926-0730.

Access to Vessel-Related Records

General Information, Access and Fees

The same vehicle records access methods, requirements, and fees apply as described above.

All boats propelled by machinery, including gasoline, diesel and electric motors, and principally operated on West Virginia waters must be registered and issued a West Virginia Certificate of Number

(Registration) by the West Virginia Department of Motor Vehicles. Motorboat registrations are on a three year cycle with each cycle year ending every March 31st, and starting over every April 1st.

All boats with a motor or a sail must be titled and registered. Registration records are available from 1975.

Driving Record Content and Reciprocity

What's On or Not On the Driving Record

- West Virginia does not report accidents or speeding on interstate if less than eleven MPH over the limit for non-CDL only. These events will show on a CDL-holder's record.
- All remaining convictions and actions are listed on the driving record for five years. This includes suspensions and DUIs.
- The state does not permit driver school attendance in lieu of conviction.

Data Retention

Convictions are not purged from the computer system—only from public record. CDL driver records are maintained per the timetable per federal regulations as shown in the Appendix.

Court to Repository

All convictions are entered manually from paperwork received from the courts. DUIs are entered within one to two weeks; suspensions within thirty-five days, unless appealed; and all other moving violation convictions are entered within four weeks.

State Reciprocity for Non-CDL Drivers

- Will suspend license of driver for unpaid out-of-state convictions.
- Record of new incoming driver is shown on MVR
- Out-of-state convictions are shown on MVR
- Out-of-state accidents are not shown on MVR.
- Convictions of out-of-state drivers are sent to home state.
- Record is forwarded to new state upon surrender of license.

Abbreviations for Classes, Types, Restrictions, and Endorsements

License Classes– All

Class A	Any combination of vehicles with a GCWR of 26,001 or more pounds, providing the GVWR of the vehicle(s) being towed is in excess of 10,000 pounds.
Class B	Any single vehicle with a GVWR of 26,001 pounds or more, or any such vehicle towing a vehicle not in excess of 10,000 pounds GVWR.
Class C	Any single vehicle or combination of vehicles less than 26,001 pounds GVWR, or any such vehicle towing a vehicle not in excess of 10,000 GVWR. This group applies to vehicles which are placarded for hazardous materials or designed to carry sixteen passengers or more (including the driver).
Class D	Commercial vehicles; non-CDL for hire classes (e.g., taxi cabs, delivery vans, etc.).
Class E	Operator's license; operation of a vehicle for personal use.
Class F	Motorcycle license only. The holder of this license class may not possess any other type of license. West Virginia began issuing "Motorcycle Only" licenses as of July 1, 1992.
Class X	Identification Cards Only (Non-Driver)
Class G	Bioptic licensed drivers.

License Types

Note: West Virginia has a Graduated Driver's License Program with three levels: Instruction Permit, Intermediate License, and Full License (good until 21).

1. Level 1 Instruction Permit
2. Level 2 Intermediate License
3. Level 3 Full E License
5. Operator Instruction Permit

6.	Operator	10.	Motorcycle Instruction Permit
7.	Operator/Motorcycle Endorsement	11.	Motorcycle Only License
8.	Operator/Motorcycle Endorsement/CDL	12.	CDL Instruction Permit
9.	Operator/CDL	13.	Level 2 License/Motorcycle Endorsement

Historical Note: Motor Vehicle Truck registration classes 'K' and 'E' are eliminated. These vehicles were issued Class 'B' registration plates. Trailer registration class 'L' are eliminated and replaced with Class 'C' registration plates, however class 'L' registrations will be renewed as usual.

Restrictions

1.	Artificial Limbs	D.	Daylight Driving Only
2.	Corrective Lenses	K.	CDL Intrastate Only
3.	Automatic Transmission	L.	CDL Vehicle Without Air-Brakes
4.	Mechanical Signals	M.	CDL Class B or C Bus Only
5.	Hand Controls	N.	CDL Class C Bus Only
6.	Outside Mirror	Q.	Power Steering and Brakes
7.	Corrective Lenses and Outside Mirror	S.	Spinner Knob
9.	Other		

Endorsements

H	Hazardous Materials	F	Motorcycle
N	Tanker Vehicle	X	Tank/Hazardous Materials
S	School Bus	T	Double-/Triple-Trailers
P	Passenger Vehicle	I	Interlock

Conviction Table with ACD, Statute, and Points

About CMV Convictions:

Note that the CMV convictions are Conviction Code 109 through 161. Conviction codes 128, 130-135 were removed form the CMV-only violations to that the convictions could be properly recorded on operators of CMV's weighing less than 26,001 pounds and are not regulated through MCSIA. These violations were moved to 221-227.

Convictions of serious violations 101, 118-124, 160, 161; 2ND conviction in 3 years causes 60-day disqualification; 3RD conviction in 3 years causes 120 days disqualification. Out-of-service violations 127 & 136 -2nd and -3rd must occur within 10 years of each other.
In the Points/Action Column:
    (S) denotes a serious violation under MCSIA
    (R) denotes a revocation or suspension
    (D) denotes a disqualification

WV Code	PTs/Action	Conviction Description	ACD
001	0	Driving Under The Influence	A20
002	0	Knowingly Permitting Intox Driving	
003	R/D	Hit And Run – Bodily Injury Or Death	B03
004	R/D	Leaving Accident – Bod Injury Or Death	B07
005	R/D	Negligent Homicide	U07
006	R/D	Vehicular Manslaughter	U08
007	R	Contest Racing – Public Traffic way	S95
008	R	Aid Or Abet In Drag Racing	
009	R	Driving With Suspended License*(Do Not Use After 1/4/04)*	B26
010	R	Driving With Revoked License*(Do Not Use After 1/4/04)*	B25
011	R/D	Using Veh As Device For A Felony	U03
012	R/D	Using Veh – Connection W/ Felony	U03
013	R	Using Veh To Aid And Abet Felon	U05
014	6	Reckless Driving	M84
015	6/S	Speeding In A School Zone (Considered Serious if in CMV)	S92
016	2	Speeding 5 – 9 Mph Over The Limit	S92
017	5	Speeding 15 Mph Or More Above Limit	S15
018	3	Speeding 10 – 14 Mph Over The Limit	S92
019	R/D	Using Veh-Felony Drug	A50
020	6/D	H & R/Leaving Accident	B08
021	R	Passing Stopped School Bus	M75
022	3	Improper Passing	M70
023	3	Pass In Face Of Oncoming Traffic	M72
024	3	Pass Where Prohibited – Signs/Unsafe	M71
025	3	Passing On The Wrong Side	M73
026	3	Pass – Inadequate Distance/Visibility	M77

WV Code	PTs/Action	Conviction Description	ACD
027	2	Failure To Signal Intent To Pass	N42
028	3	Failure To Yield To Overtaking Veh *(Do Not Use After 1/4/04)*	N07
029	3	Fail To Obey Traffic Sign/Control	M17
030	3	Failure To Obey Stop Sign	M15
031	3	Failure To Obey Traffic Light	M16
032	3	Driving Left Of Center	N70
033	3	Driving Too Fast For Conditions	S94
034	3	Fail To Maintain Control/Use Due Care	N84
035	3	Hazardous Driving	S94
036	3	Careless Driving	M81
037	3	Failed To Yield	N01
038	2	Following Too Closely	M34
039	2	Oper/More Than 3 People In Front	
040	3	Driving Wrong Way On One-Way Str	N63
041	3	Driving On Wrong Side Of Road	N70
042	2	Making Improper Turn	N50
043	2	Improper Backing	N82
044	2	Improper Signal Or No Signal	N40
045	3	Improper Lane Changing	M42
046	3	Failure To Keep In Proper Lane	M41
047	3	Fail To Follow Instr Of Police Officer	M08
048	3	Failed To Yield To Emergency Veh	N04
049	0	Failure To Appear/Answer Citation	D56
050	0	Failure To Pay Citation	D56
051		*Not Used*	
052	2	Oper Without Lights When Required	E05
053	2	Driving W/ Improper, Defective Lights	E34
054		*Not Used*	
055	2	Driving With No Lights	E55
056	0	Defective/Improper/Unsafe Equipment	F66
057		*Not Used*	
058	0	Causing Illegal Noise W/ Veh/Acc	
059	0	Expired/Improper Registration	
060	0	Expired/No MVI Sticker	
061		*Not Used*	
062	0	Violating Size, Wgt Or Pass/Cargo Limit	
063		*Not Used*	
064	0	Accident Involvement Not At Fault	
065		*Not Used*	
066	0	Illegal Possession Of Drugs	A33
067	0	Illegal Possession Alcohol	A31
068	0	Towing Or Pushing Veh Improperly	
069	0	Failure To Dim Lights As Required	E54
070		*Not Used*	
071	0	Using Equipment Prohibited By Law	
072		*Not Used*	
073	2	Improper Entering/Exiting Traffic-way	M46
074	3	Littering	
075	0	Apply For Dup Lic During Withdrawal	D02
076		*Not Used*	
077	3	Speed Less Than 81 In 65 Mph *(Do Not Use After 1/4/04)*	S93
078		*Not Used*	
079	3	Failure To Observe Safety Zone	M12
080	0	Illegal Use Of Traffic Control Dev	
081	0	Violation Of Restrictions	D29
082	0	Allowing Unlicensed Person To Drive	
083	0	DUI-Controlled Substance	A22
084	0	Violation Of Child Restraint Law	F02
085	0	Operate Vehicle Without Insurance	D36
086	R	Driving While Suspended/Revoked	B26
087	R	Weapon Possess/Sec School (<18)	
088	R	Weapon Possession Over 18 Yrs	
089	0	Under 21 – Measurable Alcohol	A60
090	0	< 21 – Meas Alcohol – W/ Injury	A60
091	0	< 21 – Meas Alcohol – Death Misd	A60
092	0	< 21 – Meas Alcohol – Death Fel	A60

WV Code	PTs/Action	Conviction Description	ACD
093	0	Knowingly Permitting/Control Sub	
094	0	DUI W/ Unemancipated Minor In Veh	A20
095	2	Interlock Restriction Violation	A41
096	2	Driving Susp/Revoked – Mun Court	B26
097	2	Driving Susp/Revoked – Non-Dui	B26
098	0	DUI With Bodily Injury	A20
099	0	DUI With Death – Misdemeanor	A20
100	0	DUI With Death – Felony	A20
101	R/D (S)	Driving Without CDL License	B56Y
102	0	Failure To Pay For Gasoline	U04
103	8	Fleeing/Evading Officer	U01
104	0	Driving W/O Supervising Adult L1	D29
105	0	Driving During Restricted Hours	D29
106	0	Violating Passenger Limit Level1	D29
107	0	Driving W/0 Supervising Adult L2	D29
108	0	Violating Passenger Limit Level2	D29

Begin CMV Convictions

WV Code	PTs/Action	Conviction Description	ACD
109	0	Admin Per Se .08 /CDL	A98
110	0	Admin Refusal /CDL	A12
111	D	DUI With BAC < .08 –	A04Y
112	R/D	Driving Under The Influence-	A20Y
113	D	DUI Refusal –	A12Y
114	R/D	DUI – Controlled Substance –	A22Y
115	D	Leaving Scene Of Accident –	B05Y
116	R/D	Felony With (Non-Drug)	U03Y
117	R/D	Felony With (Drug-Related)	A50Y
118	5 (S)	Excessive Speed In	S15Y
119	3 (S non-MCSIA)	Passing Violation-	M70Y
120	6 (S)	Reckless Driving –	M84Y
121	3 (S)	Improper Lane Change –	M42Y
122	2 (S)	Following Too Closely –	M34Y
123	0 (S)	Violation Involving Fatal Acc –	U31Y
124	R/D (S)	Improper Class/Endorsement –	B91Y
125	R	Operating While Disq/Susp/Rev	B24 Y
126	R/D	Operating While Susp/Revoked	B26Y
127	D	Out Of Service Order Violation	B27Y
*128		(Replaced By 221)	
129	0	Haz Mat Violation	E53Y
*130		(Replaced By 220)	
*131		(Replaced By 223)	
*132		(Replaced By 224)	
*133		(Replaced By 225)	
*134		(Replaced By 226)	
*135		(Replaced By 227)	
136	D	OOS Vio-16+ Pass Or Hazmat	B19Y
137	R/D	Operating While Susp/Rev/Disq	B26Y
138	0	Admin Per Se .04-	A94Y
139	0	Admin Per Se .10 /CDL	A90
140	0	Admin DUI-Contr Subst /CDL	A22
141	3	Failure To Obey RR Restr	M09Y
142	D	Failure To Obey RR Cntl Dev	M10Y
143	D	Failure To Obey RR Not slow-	M20Y
144	D	Failure To Obey RR Not stop-	M21Y
145	D	Failure To Obey RR Drive-	M22Y
146	D	Failure To Obey RR Space-	M23Y
147	D	Failure To Obey RR Clearance-	M24Y
148	R/D	Negligent Homicide-	U09Y
149	D	Fatality Thru Negligent Oper-	U10Y
150	0	Not Used	
151	0	Crt Over Weight/No Permit	
152	0	Crt Over Weight/Exceed Permit	
153	0	Crt Overweight/Permit Suspended	
154	0	Crt Falsified Permit	

WV Code	PTs/Action	Conviction Description	ACD
155	0	Crt Forged Permit	
156	0	Crt Speeding 1-4	S01Y
157	0	Crt Aiding And/Or Abetting	
158	2	Crt Speeding 5-9	S92Y
159	3	Crt Speeding 10-14	S92Y
160	5 (S)	Crt Excessive Speeding In	S15Y
161	2 (S)	No CDL In Possession	B57
162	0(S)	Texting While Operating a CMV	M85
163	0	Using a Hand-held mobile phone/Driving	M86
164		Expired CDL License	B51
165-197		*Not used*	

End CMV Convictions

WV Code	PTs/Action	Conviction Description	ACD
198	0	Texting While Driving	M85
199	0	Using a Hand-Held Mobile Phone When Driving	M86
200	2	Impeding Traffic	F34
201	0	Improper/Unsecured Load	
202	0	Violating Road/Bridge/Tunnel Limits	
203	0	Motorcycle Safety/Helmet Violation	F03
204	2	Expired/No Operators	B51
205	0	Multiple Dl's/Failure To Surrender	D07
206	2	Improper Class/Endors/Restr-Non CDL	B91
207	0	False Swearing/Misrepresentation	D02
208	0	Handicapped Parking Violation	
209	0	Violate Child Support Order	D51
210		*Not Used*	
211		*Not Used*	
212	2	Improper Stop/Start	N83
213	2	Joyriding	
214	0	No/Improper Seatbelt	F04
215	0	Speeding 1-4 Mph Over Limit	S01
216	0	ATV Helmet Violation	
217	0	No/Improper ATV Training Certificate	
218	0	Improper Road Use – ATV	
219	0	ATV Passenger Violation	
220	0	GDL Cell Phone Violation	D29
221	0	FMCSR Violation	
222	0	IFTA Violation	
223	0	Weigh/Inspection Station Violation	
224	0	Violate Veh Permit Restriction/	
225	0	IRP Violation	
226	0	Log Book Violation	
227	0	School Bus Equip/Safety Violation	E56Y
228	R	Driving While Revoked-DUI	B26
229	R	Driving While Suspended-Misc	B26
230	0	Aggravated DUI (.15 Or >)	A20
231	0	DUI < .15	A20
232	D	ADM Per Se .051-.079 DMV CDL	A91
233		CDL Indicator N or Unknown DUI	A20

Point System Summary

Points range from 2 to 8. If a driver accumulates 12 or more points, there is a mandatory suspension. The DMV may deduct 3 points for drivers who complete an approve Defensive Driving Course. Licensees are not eligible who have taken the course within the last 2 years. Points are automatically removed from the record 2 years after conviction date.

Wisconsin

Administration	Important Telephone and Web Contacts

Donna Brown-Martin, Director
Bureau Driver Services
Division of Motor Vehicles
PO Box 7983, Madison 5370-7983
608-266-9890
www.dot.wisconsin.gov/drivers/
 	
Mitch Warren, Director
Bureau of Vehicle Services
Division of Motor Vehicles
PO Box 7949, Madison 53707
608-267-5121
www.dot.wisconsin.gov/drivers/vehicles/index.htm
	Driver Licensing 608-266-2353
	Driver Information Section 608-261-2261
	SR-22 & Financial Responsibility......................608-266-2261
	Commercial Driver License 608-264-7049
	Accident Records 608-266-8753
	Vehicle Record Information...............................608-266-1466
	State Department of Insurance 608-266-3585
	WI State Patrol..608-266-3212
	
	General Email for DL records.dmv@dot.wi.gov
	General Email for Vehicles: vehiclequestions@dot.wi.gov
	Motor Vehicle Laws at:
	   www.dot.wisconsin.gov/drivers/lawbook.htm
	Transportation Laws at:
	   www.dot.wisconsin.gov/library/research/law/index.htm

Driver's License Format, Issuance and Renewal

License Classes, Restrictions and Endorsements Appear After the Driving Record Content Section

License Format

Format is one letter followed by thirteen numbers. The coding of driver license numbers is as follows: License Number "A5364683945805"

A	=	First letter of last name
536	=	Coded from last name
468	=	Coded from first name and middle initial
39	=	Birth year
458	=	Coded month and day of birth, sex
05	=	Tie-breaker, check-digit

Document Appearance

Current Document – **The current** Wisconsin style driver licenses and ID cards began issuance in early 2012.

Security Characteristics: Teslin cards with laser engraving and an overlay featuring tri-color optically-variable device (OVD) with ultraviolet (UV) ink. Front laminate features images of the state seal, "Wisconsin" and "1848". Background security design line work features images of the Wisconsin State Capitol, sugar maple leaves and prairie wheat. Front of the card also contains overlapping ghost images (one color, one laser engraved) and a printed organ donor symbol or space for sticker placement after printing. The backside of the card contains a laser-engraved tactile date of birth. The 2-D bar code includes printed data from front of card and 1-D bar code includes an inventory control number. The back of the card also allows a writable surface for anatomical gift statement. License types are coded by using different colored fonts for the words DRIVER LICENSE and the type of license; Instruction Permit (purple), Probationary (red), Regular (blue) and Occupational (black).

Position of Photo: Upper left.

Minor Driver Locator: Vertical in format and indicates below the photo the date in which the holder turns 18 and/or 21 years of age. "Instruction Permit" indicated in purple and "Probationary Driver License" indicated in red.

CDL Indicator: CDL noted on current license by "Commercial Driver License" (green)

Legal Presence Indicator: Credential issued to those who are not a United States Citizen or Permanent Resident will be marked with "Limited Term".

Previous Documents (This style of driver licenses and ID cards began issuance in 2005.)

Security Characteristics: Cards are covered with a special security overlay to prevent tampering and alterations. The hologram design pre-printed into the overlay includes the word WISCONSIN and the coat of arms. Capturing new digital images enables DMV to compare customer images on file with the new ones to reduce the potential for identify theft. Also, vital information such as the license number, date of birth and name are in an increased font size, making the new card easier to read. The new driver license has a pink hue and the ID card has a green hue. The image background is light blue. Images that were captured before September 20, 2005 have a gray background. License types are color coded by using different colored fonts for the words DRIVER LICENSE and the type of license; occupational (black); commercial (green); regular (blue); probationary (red).

Position of Photo: Upper left.

Minor Driver Locator: Card is printed in a vertical format. "Turns 21 on (date)" appears under the photo in white lettering on a red background. "Turns 18 on (date)" appears under "Turns 21..." and is printed with black letters on a yellow background. The date of birth is printed in red.

CDL Indicator: Red (if under 21) or green (if over 21) letters on upper left - label "Commercial."

Legal Presence Indicator: "Temporary" will appear in blue on lower right corner if subject is not U.S. citizen or permanent resident.

Issuance

Location of Requirements for Proof of Identity:
Visit www.dot.wisconsin.gov/drivers/drivers/apply/doc/index.htm

Age Requirements

With the Graduated Driver Licensing Program, the Instruction Permit minimum age is 15 ½. One must pass the knowledge test, be enrolled in Driver Education, have a parent or legal guardian adult sponsor and pass the vision and hearing screenings. Also, one must hold an Instruction Permit for at least 6 months, and cannot have been convicted of any moving traffic violations for the 6 months prior to applying for Probationary License, and pass a skills test. For a Probationary License and if under 18, one must complete Driver Education, have an adult sponsor, and accumulate 30 hours of supervised driving experience. Ten of the 30 hours of driving must be during hours of darkness.

Also issued is an **Occupational License** which is a restricted driver license. Driving is limited to and from work, school, or other places indicated on the license for only specific times of the day. Operation for recreation or pleasure is not allowed for an Occupational License. Total driving time must be no more than 12 hours for any one day and no more than 60 hours for the entire week. Those eligible to obtain an Occupational License include drivers whose operating privilege was revoked or suspended under the following circumstances: under the general provision statute; a drug conviction under S.961.50 (except juveniles); nonpayment of child support under S.767.303; and a Habitual Traffic Offender (HTO) under Ch. 351. An Occupational License is not permitted for commercial use.

Residency
Drivers with a CDL are required to apply for a Wisconsin driver license within 30 days. Other drivers new to Wisconsin are required to apply for a Wisconsin driver license within 60 days of establishing residency.

The home state license of a non-resident age 16 or over is on a reciprocal basis.

Renewal
Licenses expire in the birth month of the eighth year. Renewal is not available online, except for renewals of non-driving ID Cards. Driver keeps same number when renewing, unless there is a name, DOB, or gender change.

Military personnel stationed out-of-state are not required to renew, but an out-of-state renewal is recommended. The renewal requires a vision test from another state DMV or authorized visual examiner. For more information, write to Qualifications & Issuance Section, PO Box 7995, Madison, WI 53707-7995 or call 608-264-7049.

Elderly-Related Restrictions
None indicated.

Vehicle Insurance, Title and Registration Facts

Registration Renewal
Renewal is annual and can be done in-person, by mail or online. Non-CDL vehicles can renew online if operator received an RRN number and the correct, current address is on file.

New Residents
When becoming a Wisconsin resident, one must obtain Wisconsin registration (license plates) for a vehicle within two days of moving here. To legally operate a vehicle one must display Wisconsin license plates within 2 business days of establishing residency.

Inspections and Emissions Testing
Wisconsin has no mandatory safety inspection requirement. However an emissions test is required for vehicles kept in certain southeast counties – Kenosha, Milwaukee, Ozaukee, Racine, Sheboygan, Washington and Waukesha. This emissions inspection is required every other year at the time of license plate renewal, beginning in the third year following the vehicle's model year. Vehicles under this requirement include cars and trucks with a manufacturer's gross vehicle weight rating under 8,501 pounds. Exceptions are vehicles produced prior to the 1996 model year and motorcycles.. Vehicles also exempt from emission requirements include model year 2006 and older vehicles that are powered by diesel fuel, vehicles with a GVWR over 14,000 pounds, motorcycles, dedicated farm vehicles, electric powered,

motorcycles and mopeds, school buses and human service vehicles with seating capacity of 16 or more. Note that hybrid vehicles are not exempt. Additionally, vehicles more than 5 model years old are required to be tested at the time of change of ownership

Passenger Plate Facts
There two plates with two decals (MO) (YR) on the rear plate. The state indicates there is no code sequence designating the county of issuance.

When sold the plates remain with seller for passenger vehicles, light trucks, motorcycles, and low-speed vehicles.

Insurance and Financial Responsibility
Wisconsin has a mandatory liability insurance requirement. Minimum insurance liability limits are $25,000/50,000/10,000. Drivers and owners of motor vehicles are required to show proof of insurance at traffic stops/accidents if requested by law enforcement. Proof is not necessary for trailers or semi-trailers. Proof of insurance is also required after certain suspensions and revocations. There is no proof of insurance requirement when obtaining a driver license or are registering a vehicle, unless that information is requested by DMV. Proof is a requirement before reinstatement of a driver license after a suspension or revocation. SR-22 forms are used.

Withdrawal Sanctions, and Alcohol and Drug Testing

Alcohol and Chemical Testing Limits
Wisconsin's illegal intoxication level is .08 percent and above for first, second and third offenses, and .02 percent and above for fourth and subsequent offenses. The intoxication level for persons driving a CMV is .04 percent and the level for persons under the age of 21 is .00 percent. Urine, blood, and breath testing are authorized. Wisconsin has both an implied-consent violation and a provision for an administrative suspension.

Suspensions and Revocations
The 2009 Wisconsin Act 28, effective January 1, 2010, placed Wisconsin in compliance with the provisions of the Motor Carrier Safety Improvement Act (MCSIA). See the Appendix for more information about these mandatory CDL disqualification sanctions.

Regular License - Point Accumulation During Twelve-Month Period and Length of Suspension

Twelve to Sixteen Points	Two months.
Seventeen to Twenty-two Points	Four months.
Twenty-three to Thirty Points	Six months.
Thirty-one or More Points	One year.

Probationary License Point Accumulation

Twelve to Thirty Point Accumulation.	Six months.
Thirty-one or More Points	One year.

Refusal to Submit to Chemical Test

First Offense	One-year revocation.
Second Offense	Two-year revocation.
Third or Subsequent Offense	Three-year revocation.

Administrative Suspension (Violation of Alcohol
Content) Based on Arrest...Six-month suspension.
   Operating While Intoxicated
First Offense...Six- to nine-month revocation.
Second Offense .... Twelve- to eighteen-month revocation.
Third or Subsequent Offense... Two- to three-year revocation.
   (Fourth Offense will be treated as a felony if it occurs within 5 years of an earlier offense)

Ignition Interlock Devices (IIDs)

Ignition Interlock Devices (IIDs) are mandatory for every vehicle owned by or registered to the offender, unless the vehicle is specifically exempted by the court, for the following convictions:

All repeat OWIs

All refusals

All 1st offense OWI with an alcohol concentration of 0.15 or higher

Wisconsin takes action on any out-of-state convictions for which Wisconsin statutes require a mandatory suspension or revocation of the operating privilege. Those convictions include

- Attempting to elude an officer
- Death of another
- Failure to stop and render aid after an accident resulting in:
- Great bodily harm resulting from the operation of a motor vehicle while under the influence
- Great bodily harm to another
- Homicide resulting from the operation of a motor vehicle while under the influence
- Injury by negligent operation of a motor vehicle while under the influence
- Operating while under the influence or with a prohibited alcohol concentration
- Perjury or making a false affidavit or statement to the department
- Personal injury to another
- Reckless driving
- Serious property damage (if specified by the court)
- Vehicle used in the commission of a felony

Reinstatement Requirements

Suspension $60.00 fee or $200.00 for alcohol related offenses; proof of financial responsibility required if suspension was due to violation of safety responsibility or damage judgment laws; re-examination may be required. An additional $50 reinstatement fee is required for all damage judgments and for safety responsibility suspensions if vehicle registration were also suspended.

Revocation $60.00 fee or $200.00 for alcohol related offenses; proof of financial responsibility may be required for revocations (EXCEPT for a first offense of operating while intoxicated or non-compliance with court-ordered alcohol assessments or driver safety plans); re-examination may be required

Disqualification $60.00 fee. (Disqualification Only)

Record Access: Laws, Rules, and Forms

Note: This Section Applies to Both Driver and Vehicle Records.

Governing Statutes and Rules

Motor Vehicle Laws at:
   www.dot.wisconsin.gov/drivers/lawbook.htm
Transportation Laws at:
   www.dot.wisconsin.gov/library/research/law/index.htm
Wisconsin statute does not specifically enumerate the federal exceptions. Federal Title 18 USC Section 2721-2725, WI S.19.36 (1), Statute S.S. 341.17 Trans. 19.31, 19.39, 19.62-19.80 all govern Wisconsin's provisions on release of records. The "exceptions" are provided for on Form MV 2896.

Policy Statement Regarding Permissible Uses

Wisconsin does not have specific provisions for DPPA exemptions (11), (12), and (14). Wisconsin added the following exceptions:
4. A federal, state, circuit, local, or tribal court, or employed by such, for the purpose of the court to carry out its functions.
5. A Wisconsin or out-of-state law enforcement agency, or employed by such, for the purpose of the law enforcement agency to carry out its functions.

Request and Consent Forms

Use of *Form MV2896* is required for all driving record or vehicle record requests other than Law Enforcement Teletype requests. Ongoing service providers must establish an account with the state. For requesters with non-permissible use, consent is required to receive a record with personal information and *Form MV2896* must be used. Written authorization by the subject must be attached to the form, the signature does not need to be notarized. The form is found at www.dot.wisconsin.gov/drivers/forms/mv2896.pdf.

Vendor and Third Party Access Policy

Approved online vendors can access records for other vendors (who are not online, etc.) who may sell to an end-user, as long as DPPA requirements are met by all vendors and the end-user.

Non-permissible Use Requests

Without consent or permissible use, full records are not released as well as any in-depth records without personal information. Casual use requesters must submit *Request Form MV2896* (see above). Note there are a number of free "status" type checks though.

Access to Driver-Related Records

Driving Records

General Information and Fees

Division of Motor Vehicles, Driver Records, PO Box 7995, Madison WI 53707-7995, 608-266-2353, records.dmv@dot.wi.gov.

The fee is $7.00 per written record request, add $5.00 for certification. Online fees are different, see below. The DMV charges for "no record found" reports. The driver's full name, sex, date of birth, or license number is needed when ordering.

In-Person – Counter service is not offered for driving record requests, including all Field Offices.

Mail – Mail-in requests are normally processed within 5 business days.

Electronic – Wisconsin offers interactive online inquiry for ongoing, approved requestors. The **PARS Program** enables the requester to have instant access to view a PDF image document of the driving record. See www.dot.wisconsin.gov/drivers/drivers/pars/introduction.htm.

A $5.00 fee per record applies; there is no annual fee or monthly minimum ordering requirements. For more information or to register, call 608-266-0928 or email to pars@dot.wi.gov. Note that users of PARS with direct access to DMV data are required to have a criminal background check performed by the requesting agency or business.

Email – Approved out-of-state requesters that are exempt from fees (law enforcement, courts, etc.) may request certified driving records by e-mailing wi.drivercerts@dot.wi.gov.

Bulk – The DMV makes available the complete driver record file for sale, as long as provisions of DPPA are followed by the requester. The file contains name, DOB, address, gender, license type and number for each record for those holding a valid license to operate a motor vehicle. It does not contain actions such as convictions accidents or license withdrawals. The fee is $250.00. For more information, contact the Qualification & Issuance Section at PO Box 7995, Rm 809A, Madison, WI 53707-7995, or call 608-264-7049.

By Person of Record – WI drivers may order by mail or online at www.dot.wisconsin.gov/drivers/drivers/request-record.htm. The fee is $5.50 per record, use of a credit card is required. The driver must submit full name, DOB, the DL# and the last four digits of the SSN. The abstract can be saved or printed. If an address change is need, this must be completed before ordering the record.

Driver's License Status

Check the current status of a driver's license; both automated systems are open 24 hours a day. These services are free.

By Telephone – Call 608-264-7133. Enter the driver's Social Security Number and date of birth or WI driver license number to access this information.

Online – See www.dot.wisconsin.gov/drivers/online.htm. Enter the WI driver license number, or SSN/DOB, or name/sex/DOB.

Notification/Monitoring Program

Employers of commercial and non-commercial motor vehicle drivers may enroll in the Employer Notification Program operated by PARS as described above. Employers may enroll any employee whose employment responsibilities include the operation of any motor vehicle. Participants create and maintain their own roster of employed drivers in PARS. Employers may obtain driving records of the enrolled employees when they are notified of activity on the record. The fee is $5.00 per record; there is no fee to enroll drivers. For more information or to register, call 608-266-0928 or email pars@dot.wi.gov.

Accident Reports

Reporting – Accidents involving death, injury, or property damage of $1,000.00 or more to one person's property, or over $200.00 damages to government property other than vehicles must be reported immediately to the nearest law enforcement authority.

If the police do not file a copy of the accident investigation with the Department of Transportation, the motorists involved must complete a *Wisconsin Driver Report of Accident Form MV4002* found at www.dot.wisconsin.gov/drivers/forms/mv4002.pdf. Reports should be sent to: Department of Transportation, Qualifications and Issuance, PO Box 7919, Madison 53707-7919. There are no special filing requirements for commercial drivers.

Record Access – Copies of accident reports can be obtained from the investigating law enforcement agency or from the Accident Records Unit of the Division of Motor Vehicles, 608-266-8753. The request should include the driver license number and/or by accident report number and date of accident. The fee for mailed copies of reports is $6.00 per report; prepayment is required if ordering more than one report. Records are available on average 2-3 weeks after receipt of the accident report and for the previous 4 years to present. Requests should be sent to the DMV, Qualifications and Issuance, Accident Records Unit, PO Box 7919, Madison, WI 53707-7919, 608-266-8753. Information involving juvenile citations is not released.

Access to Vehicle-Related Records

General Information

Department of Transportation, Vehicle Records Section, PO Box 8070, Madison WI 53708-8070, 608-266-1466. Email questions to vehiclequestions@dot.wi.gov.

The DOT maintains the database for vehicle titles, registrations, and liens. Boat and ATV information is with the Department of Natural Resources. Records are stored five years to present. The title or registration holder's address is provided on the record. Effective 2000, the titling of mobile homes over 45 feet in length was moved to the Department of Commerce. Note that counter service for record access has been discontinued.

Mail – All casual or occasional requesters must submit *Request Form MV2896*. The fee for VIN, lien and registration checks is $5.00 per record plus $.25 per photocopy. An additional $5.00 is charged for certification. Requests are available by-mail at the address listed above, and should contain as much of the following information as possible:

- License plate number and type of vehicle
- Vehicle identification number
- Title number

- Owner name and address
- Vehicle description (make and year) with owner's name

The fee must accompany the request, and payment should be made payable to "Registration Fee Trust." Any costs over the fee submitted will be billed. Vehicle history information is not available over the phone. Records are available for 5 years to present.

Electronic Commercial - Wisconsin offers interactive online inquiry for ongoing, approved requestors via the PARS program - www.dot.wisconsin.gov/drivers/drivers/pars/introduction.htm#vehicle. Requesters have access to vehicle abstract records including name and address of titled owners or lessees, plate info, vehicle information, and lien data. The system may or may not display address and DOB depending on how the data was input. Certain license plate records are not available through PARS, such as tribal, apportioned and dealer plates. You must obtain a Login Account to request access to PARS.

Electronic Free – Wisconsin offers several free data look-ups at www.dot.wisconsin.gov/drivers/online.htm. Available look-ups include a **free license plate check**, a **free lien look-up** and a **free title inquiry** (Where's My Title?) at the same web page. The title inquiry display the date of a completed transaction, providing the VIN and owner identifier data submitted match what the state has on The plate inquiry will display plate registration information including expiration date, vehicle year, vehicle make and the registration renewal number needed for online renewals.

There is also a free check to see if a driver has any restrictions (incidents) that would restrict the driver from obtaining a driver or vehicle product (such as a title, registration, etc.). The site is at *www.dot.wisconsin.gov/drivers/vehicles/incidents.htm*.

Electronic by Person of Record – WI drivers may order their own driver or vehicle record abstract online. The fee is $5.50 per record,

use of a credit card is required. The driver must submit VIN, full name, DOB, the DL# and the last four digits of the SSN. The abstract can be saved or printed.

See www.dot.wisconsin.gov/drivers/vehicles/request-record.htm.

Bulk – Only users with permissible purposes are permitted to purchase in bulk format. Each request is looked at on an individual basis. For more information contact the Bureau of Vehicle Services 608-266-1466. All DPPA restrictions apply. FTP input inquiry for specific records is available only to law enforcement agencies or their agents.

Access to Vessel-Related Records

General Information, Access and Fees

Department of Natural Resources, 101 S. Webster, Madison WI, 53703, 608-267-7246, fax: 608-264-6130

http://dnr.wi.gov/permits/registrationandtitling.html

This agency registers boats, ATVs, UTVs, and snowmobiles. All motorized or sail boats 16 ft and over must be titled and registered. All motorized or sail boats under 16 ft must be registered. Lien information appears on the title record. Record information can be requested by the

owner name or boat registration information number. There is no fee if under 10 records. Credit cards are accepted. Turnaround time is 10 days. One can request information over the telephone, or by fax. The office is open 7AM-10PM seven days a week.

10 records or more is considered a bulk records request and fees follow the Electronic Records Instructions, which will place fees at a $200 level. View or download the *Electronic Records Order Form* at http://dnr.wi.gov/org/caer/cs/apps/9400571.pdf.

Driving Record Content and Reciprocity

What's On or Not On the Driving Record

- The driver's address is provided on the record.
- Identification card information, juvenile record entries, arrests and medical information are confidential.
- Truck over weights are the only violations not listed on the driving record.
- The length of time moving violation convictions and suspensions/revocations are shown on the record is: five years from date of conviction.
- Alcohol-related or serious offenses, disqualifying convictions are shown for fifty-five years.
- Revocation based on damage judgment is shown for twenty years.
- Convictions for Operating While Intoxicated with violation dates on or after January 1, 1989, and certain commercial driving convictions are retained on the Wisconsin driving record for life (defined as 55 years).
- All accidents resulting in the injury or death of a person or resulting in more than $1,000.00 in property damage are reported for four years from date of accident. Also, any accidents resulting in $200.00 or more in damage to government property must be reported. Fault is not indicated.
- The state does not permit driver school attendance in lieu of conviction; however, once every three years three points can be removed for attending an approved traffic safety course.

Data Retention

Most traffic convictions are retained on Wisconsin's database for five years before being purged. Otherwise the table above is followed unless the conviction can trigger an extended withdrawal if there is a repeat offense. For CDL records, Wisconsin follows the timetable per federal regulations, see the Appendix.

Court to Repository

There are 3 ways citations can be sent to the WI DOT. Circuit courts send a daily batch file electronically. Some municipal courts send electronic data immediately after adjudication. Convictions not reported electronically are forwarded on paper documents and entered manually into the citation data base. The courts must report these convictions within five days; the information is entered by the Department within ten days of receipt from the court.

State Reciprocity for Non-CDL Drivers

- Will not suspend license of driver for unpaid out-of-state convictions.
- Record of new incoming driver is shown on MVR.
- Out-of-state convictions are shown on MVR.
- Out-of-state accidents are not shown on MVR.
- Convictions of out-of-state drivers are sent to home state.
- Record is forwarded to new state upon surrender of license.

License Classes, Types, Restrictions, and Endorsements

License Classes

Wisconsin began issuing the CDL on October 28, 1991.

Class A	Any combination of commercial motor vehicles weighing over 26,000 pounds. In addition, the towed unit must weigh more than 10,000 pounds.
Class B	A single commercial motor vehicle weighing over 26,000 pounds. In addition, any towed trailers must weigh less than 10,000 pounds.
Class C	Any vehicles that do not meet the definitions of Classes A and B. In addition, these vehicles must carry sixteen or more passengers (including the driver) or transport hazardous materials. Please note: You cannot drive this class of vehicle without the endorsement for passengers or hazardous materials.
Class D	Non-commercial vehicles other than motorcycles; includes regular passenger cars, light trucks, and mopeds.
Class M	Motorcycles.

License Types

REGI	Class D Instruction Permit
RGLR	Regular Commercial or Non-Commercial
PROB	Probationary (points double on second and subsequent violations)
SPRR	Special Restricted License
JUVP	Juvenile Restricted License
CYCI	Cycle Instruction Permit
JUVI	Juvenile Instruction Permit
MPDI	Moped/Motor Bicycle Instruction Permit

Restrictions

99	Special Restrictions Card(s)		L	Vehicles Without Air-Brakes
ALB	Artificial Limb(s)		LOM	Left Outside Mirror
ATR	Automatic Transmission		NFH	No Freeway or Interstate Highway
ATS	Automatic Turn Signals		PBC	"P" Endorsement on Classes B and C Only
CIO	No Operation in Interstate Commerce		PEC	"P" Endorsement on Class C Only
DAY	Daylight Driving Only		OTH	All Other Restrictions (spelled out on driving record)
FIN	Financial Responsibility		ROM	Right Outside Mirror
GLS	Corrective Lenses		SED	"S" Endorsement on Class D Only
HCT	Complete Hand-Controls			

Endorsements

T	Double-/Triple-Trailers		F	Farm Service Industry CMV
N	Tank Vehicles		S	School Bus
H	Hazardous Materials		P	Passengers

Abbreviations of Importance Found on Driving Record

AKA	Also known as
APL	Appealed - The conviction has been appealed to a higher court. Do not consider when counting priors.
BKP	Bankruptcy - Will appear in the comments field of a Damage Judgment revocation when a person has filed a bankruptcy with the court.
CAD/HAD	Commercial Alcohol causing Death
CAH/HAH	Commercial Alcohol causing Great Bodily Harm
CIAG	Court ordered or bankruptcy installment agreement
CR	Case Released
DED	Deceased
DI	Driver Interview
DIS	Dismissed
F	Fatal Accident
GBH/CBH/HBH	OWI causing Great Bodily Harm (always count)
IC/CIC/HIC	Implied Consent - Refusal
MOS	Moved out of state (to...)
NFI	Non-fatal injury accident
NHI/CHI/HHI	Negligent Homicide Intoxicated (always count)
OCS/CCS/HCS	OWI - Controlled Substance
OII/CII/HII	OWI causing Injury
OTH	If the status shows "OTH," this means the license type has been replaced with another license type and is no longer valid
OWI/PAC/CWI/HWI	Operating While Intoxicated
PIAG	Private Installment Agreement - Will appear in the comments field of a Damage Judgment withdrawal when a person has filed an agreement with the person/company that initiated the judgment in court.
PC	Permanent correspondence
PD	Property damage accident
PRS	Point reduction school (maximum 3 point reduction)
PTS REDSCH	Point Reduction School - The person has completed an approved traffic safety class and requested point reduction. Total point accumulation within the previous year will be reduced by 3.
RLI	Reinstated license issued
STM	Suspension terminated
TSS	Traffic safety school
VAC	Vacated
VTS	Voluntary temporary surrender
WS	Withdrawal of sponsorship

Conviction Table with Charge Code, ACD, Points and Description

Both tables are alphabetized by the **Code column,** which appears on the driving record. Obsolete convictions and entries that may show on older driving records are denoted with an asterisk * in front.

Code	ACD	Charge	Pts	Description
ACF	U31	004		Accident conviction fatal
ADL	D10	005	0	Altering driver license or ID card
AEO	U01	021	6-0	Attempting to elude officer
AFA	D02	211	0	Appear for an exam for another
BAC	A98	121	0	Blood Alcohol Content
BI	N82	007	2	Backing illegally
CA	A04	130	0	Commercial alcohol
CAC	A98	131	0	Commercial blood alcohol content
CAD	A21	132	0	Commercial alcohol; causing death
CAH	A21	133	0	Commercial alcohol; causing great bodily harm
CAI	A21	134	6	Commercial alcohol; causing injury
CBH	A21	135	0	Commercial OWI; causing great bodily harm
CCD	M81	136	0	Commercial careless driving (out-of-state only)
CCF	A50	137	0	Commercial controlled-substance felony
CCS	A22	138	6	Commercial OWI; controlled substance
CD	M81	010	0	Careless driving (out-of-state only)
CDL	M42	139	4	Commercial deviating from lane of traffic
CDS	B08	190	0	Commercial failure to stop after an accident causing property damage
CFA	D45	332	0	Commercial failure to appear
CFC	M34	140	3	Commercial following too closely
CFH	M56	009	2	Crossing/driving over fire-hose
CFI		339	0	Forge or alter proof of insurance
CFP	D53	336	0	Commercial failure to pay
CFR	B61	141	0	Commercial failure to report accident
CFS	B01	142	6	Commercial failure to stop after accident
CFU	B05	185	6	Commercial failure to stop after accident causing damage to unattended vehicle
CHI	U07	143	0	Commercial negligent homicide while intoxicated
CIC	A12	144	0	Commercial implied-consent, failure to take test to determine intoxication
CII	A21	145	6	Commercial OWI causing injury
CIN	A12	146	0	Commercial implied-consent, failure to take test to determine intoxication
CIS	S94	147	4	Commercial imprudent speed
CNC	D56	337	0	Commercial failure to comply
CNI	D36	115	0	Compulsory insurance – no insurance
CNP	B74	201	0	Compulsory insurance – no proof of insurance
COO	A26	148	0	Commercial absolute sobriety
CPB	A31	149	3	Commercial possession of intoxicating beverage
CPI	M70	150	3	Commercial passing illegally
CRD	M84	151	6	Commercial reckless driving
CSE	S92	152	6	Commercial speeding driving 20 or more mph over
CSI	S92	153	4	Commercial speeding driving 15-19 mph over
CSR	F02	106	0	Failure to use child safety restraint
CTF	S94	154	4	Commercial driving too fast for conditions
CUL	B56	155	3	Commercial unlawful operation
CVF	U03	156	0	Commercial vehicle used in commission of felony
CWI	A21	157	6	Commercial operating while intoxicated
D	A33	188	0	Drug conviction, see ch. 961 - 17 years or older on violation date
DAT	M14	015	3	Driving against traffic - one way street
DDH	M02	261	0	Driving on divided highway in space or barrier except through an opening, etc.
DLT	M42	013	4	Deviating from lane of traffic
DOF		272	0	Deface or obstruct official sign
DOW	M58	014	2	Driving over a walk
DS		081	2	Defective speedometer
DSP	B08	189	0	Failure to stop after an accident causing property damage (Duty upon striking property)
DWS	N72	016	4	Driving on wrong side of highway
FA	D02	094	0	Falsified application for driver license or ID card or registration
FAR		017	0	Falsified accident report

Code	ACD	Charge	Pts	Description
FAV	D02	273	0	Fraudulent application
FD		018	0	Found delinquent
FDL	E54	019	3	Failure to dim lights
FEM	M32	264	0	Following emergency vehicle
FFS	F04	114	0	Failure to fasten seat-belt
FGS	N40	020	3	Failure to give proper signal
FNC		258	0	Failure to notify DMV of address or name change
FOS	M14	022	6	Failure to obey traffic sign or signal - railroad
FOS	M14	022	0-3	Failure to obey traffic sign or signal
FRA	B61	024	0	Failure to report accident
FRA	B61	024	6	Failure to report accident - operator
FSA	B01	025	6	Failure to stop after accident - attended vehicle
FSB	M75	026	4	Failure to stop for school bus
FSB	M75	026	0	Failure to stop for school bus - owner
FSU	B01	184	6	Failure to stop after accident causing damage to unattended vehicle
FTC	M34	027	3	Following too closely
FTT		028	0	Failure to transfer title
FVC	N84	029	4	Failure to keep vehicle under control
FYL	M18	262	0	Flashing yellow (caution signal) violation
FYR	N01	033	4	Failure to yield right-of-way
FYR	N01	033	0	Failure to yield right-of-way - owner
GBH	A21	086	0	Great bodily harm
GCV	D29	202	3	Graduated driver license curfew violation
GPV	D29	203	3	Graduated driver license passenger violation
HAC	A98	158	0	Hazardous Commercial blood alcohol content
HAD	A21	159	0	Hazardous Commercial alcohol; causing death
HAH	A21	160	0	Hazardous Commercial alcohol; causing great bodily harm
HAI	A21	161	6	Hazardous Commercial alcohol; causing injury
HBH	A21	162	0	Hazardous Commercial OWI; causing great bodily harm
HCA	A04	163	0	Hazardous Commercial alcohol
HCF	A50	164	0	Hazardous Commercial controlled-substance felony
HCS	A22	165	6	Hazardous Commercial OWI-controlled substance
HDS	B08	191	0	Hazardous Commercial failure to stop after accident causing property damage
HFR	B61	166	0	Hazardous Commercial failure to report accident
HFS	B01	167	6	Hazardous Commercial failure to stop after accident
HFU	B05	186	6	Hazardous Commercial failure to stop after accident to unattended vehicle
HHI	U07	168	0	Hazardous Commercial negligent homicide while intoxicated causing death
HIC	A12	169	0	Hazardous Commercial implied-consent, failure to take test
HII	A21	170	6	Hazardous Commercial OWI causing injury
HIN	A12	171	0	Hazardous Commercial implied-consent, failure to take test
HVF	U03	172	0	Hazardous Commercial vehicle used in commission of felony
HWI	A21	173	6	Hazardous Commercial operating while intoxicated
IB	E31	031	3	Improper brakes
IC	A12	091	0	Implied consent - failure to take test to determine intoxication
ICU	A12	109	0	Implied-consent - failure to take test for intoxication
ID	M82	032	4	Inattentive driving
IDT	A41	187	0	Ignition/immobilization device; tampering
IE	E70	030	0/2	Improper equipment - horns, mirror, windshield wipers, fenders, mudguards, trailer hitch, no flag or lamp on load or vehicle train
IIV	A31	034	0	Intoxicant in vehicle while carrying underage person
IL	E55	035	3/0	No or improper lights
IM		036	0	Improper muffler
IP		037	0	Improper plates
IR	F06	038	2	Illegal riding (if passenger 0 points)
IS	S94	039	4	Imprudent speed
IT	N50	077	3	Illegal turn
IUC	M24	291	0	Insufficient undercarriage clearance
IUL	D16	041	0	Illegal use of operator's license
IVO	A35	112	0	Intoxicant in vehicle; operator
IVP	A35	113	0	Intoxicant in vehicle; passenger
JA		103	0	Juvenile alcohol

Code	ACD	Charge	Pts	Description
JCS	A33	178	0	Juvenile controlled substances
JID	B41	111	0	Improper use of juvenile identification
LNP	B57/B 78	079	0	License not on person when operating vehicle
LOL	D16	043	0	Loaning of driver license
MDO		204	0	Miscellaneous driving offenses - graduated driver license
MSC		040	0	Miscellaneous
NH	U07	045	0	Negligent homicide
NHI	U07	120	0	Negligent homicide; intoxicated
NSW		268	0	No siren on bicycle or motorbike
OAR	B25	044	3	Operating after revocation
OCS	A22	174	6	Operating while intoxicated - controlled substance
OII	A21	107	6	Operating while intoxicated, causing injury
OML	D07	175	3	Operating with multiple licenses
ORS		209	0	Operating vehicle while registration suspended
OSB	B91	048	3	Operating without school bus license endorsement
OSO	B27	331	3	Operating while out of service
OT	F34	049	2	Obstructing traffic
OV	D70	050	2	Obstructed view or control
*OWC				Operating without chauffer license
OWD	B24	183	3	Operating while disqualified
*OWE			3	Operating without cycle endorsement/license (Obsolete - now coded OWL)
*OWH				Aggravated OWI
OWI	A21	055	6	Operating under influence of intoxicant or controlled substance
OWL	B51	053	3	Operating without driver license
*OWO			0	Operating without owner's consent
OWS	B26	052	3	Operating while suspended
P	D78	056	0	Perjury
PAC	A21	212	6	Prohibited alcohol concentration
PI	M70	088	3	Passing illegally
PLS		266	0	Projecting loads on side of vehicle
POH		059	2/0	Parking on highway - zero points if 346.51(1)
PUP		061	0	Permitting unauthorized person to operate
R	S95	062	6	Racing
RD	M84	063	6	Reckless driving
RPS		263	0	Restrictions on parking & stopping
RRF	M22	290	3	Railroad – failure to stop
RRG	M23	289	6	Railroad grade violation – fail to stop
RRG	M23	289	3	Railroad grade violation – insufficient space
RRP		257	0	Reproducing evidence of registration prohibited
RRS	M20	288	6	Railroad sign violation
RVL		271	0	Roadway violation [346..29(2)]
S	S92	066	3	Speeding (1-10 mph over limit)
SE	S92	065	6	Speeding excess (20 mph or more over limit)
SI	S92	068	4	Speeding intermediate (11-19 mph over limit)
SLL		267	0	Special limitations on loads
SVL	E50	269	0	Signal violation
T		122	0	Truancy
TCC	F05	265	0	Transporting children in cargo areas of motor vehicle
TFC	S94	067	4	Driving too fast for conditions
TPV	N84	069	2	Transporting person or vehicle illegally
TWD	M85	340	4	Texting while driving
UA	S97	060	4	Unnecessary acceleration (spinning doughnuts, exhibition of power, squealing tires)
UAL		207	0	Underage alcohol violation
UAO	A60	108	0	Underage alcohol operation
UCD		210	0	Failure by juvenile to comply with a court ordered consent decree
UID	B41	208	0	Underage ID
UN		100	0	Unnecessary noise
UTD	M86	342	4	Use telephone while driving with probationary/instruction permit
UTR		256	0	Unlawful transfer of evidence of registration
UV		072	0	Unregistered vehicle

Code	ACD	Charge	Pts	Description
VOO	D29	073	6	Violation of occupational license
VOR	D29	074	3	Violation of driver license restriction
VUF	U03	075	0	Vehicle used in commission of felony

Withdrawal Table with Charge Code, ACD, Statute and Description

Note: Obsolete withdrawals and entries that may show on older driving records are denoted with an asterisk * in front.

Code	ACD	Charge	Statute	Description
3AR	W20	318	TR 107.08910c, 343.06(109e)	Three arrests for operating while intoxicated within 12-month period
AFU	W20	195		Chemical dependency level prohibits licensing
ALC	W20	198	TR 107.08	Alcohol related incident cancellation
BAC	A98	121		Blood alcohol content over the legal limit and/or a detectable amount of a restricted controlled substance
CAC	A98	131		Commercial administrative suspension
CFA	D56	332		Commercial failure to appear
CLA		320	343.265(1m)	Voluntary surrender – specific to one or more class and endorsement
DCI	D39	275	344.27	Failure to maintain payments on a court-ordered installment agreement
DCO	D39	279	344.27	Failure to maintain payments on a court-ordered installment agreement
DJB	D39	277	344.25	Dismissal of bankruptcy which included an unpaid judgment
DJN		012	344.25	Damage judgment - negligent operation
DJO	D39	278	344.25	Damage judgment non-individual - negligent operation
DPI	D39	276	344.25	Failure to maintain payments on a private installment agreement
DPO	D39	280	344.27	Failure to maintain payments on a private installment agreement
DQ2	W60	292	343.315(2)(j)	Disqualification – two railroad grade crossing violations within 2 years
DQ3	W61	293	343.315(2)(j)	Disqualification – three railroad grade crossing violations within 3 years
DQ4	W40	325	343.315	Disqualification – accumulation of 2 or more major offenses
DQ5	W41	326	343.315	Disqualification - additional major offense after reinstatement
DQ6	W50	327	343.315	Disqualification – accumulation of 2 out-of-service orders within 10 years
DQ7	W51	328	343.315	Disqualification – accumulation of out-of-service orders with passenger of hazmat endorsement
DQ8	W52	329	343.315	Disqualification – accumulation of 3 out-of-service orders within 10 years
DQ9	W70	330	343.315	Imminent hazard
DQF	W30	182	343.315	Disqualification (2 violations in 3 years)
DQF	W30	182	343.315	Disqualification (3 violations in 3 years)
DR	W01	011		Too many points in one-year period
EDT		321	343.265(1m)	Voluntary surrender – specific to one or more endorsements
F		003		Fatal Accident
FAE	D20	095		Failure to comply with prior consent (i.e. to appear for examination or to file requested medical report)
FAK	W20	294	343.25(4)	Failure to apply for a driver license or ID card using correct name
FAP		*295	343.25(7), 343.16(5)(b)	Failure to schedule appointment after failing a written or road test
FCC	W00	343	343.25(7), 343.16(5)(b)	Failure to complete course
FKS	W20	296	343.25(7), 343.16(5)(b)	Failure to take knowledge and sign recognition test
FOL		297	343.25(7)	Fraudulently obtained license
FPD	W00	206		Failure to pay driver improvement surcharge
FPF	D53	023	343.45(1)(b)	Failure to pay forfeiture
FPJ	D53	087	938.17(2)(d), 938.34(8), 938.343(2)	Failure to pay forfeiture or comply with a court order as a juvenile
FPN	D53	123	800.09(1)(c), 800.095(4)(b)4	Failure to pay forfeiture or non-traffic fine
FPS	D51	205	767, 769, 948.22(7)	Failure to pay family or child support
FRE	W20	298	343.25(7), 343.16(5)(b)	Failure to take complete re-examination of driving ability
FRI	W20	299	343.25(7), 343.16(5)(b)	Failure to submit required information
FRT	W20	300	343.25(7), 343.16(5)(b)	Failure to take road test
FSH	W09	214		Failed to surrender HAZMAT endorsement
HAC	A98	158		Operating a CMV carrying HAZMAT, with a prohibited alcohol concentration and/or detectible amount of a restricted controlled substance
HTO	W01	082		Habitual traffic offender
IH	W70	215		Imminent hazard
IID		338		No Ignition Interlock Device (IID) as required
INC	D36	199		Cancellation of insurance
INF		200		Insurance fraud

Code	ACD	Charge	Statute	Description
INS		322	343.265(1m)	Voluntary temporary surrender – specific to insurance reasons
LBA	W00	301	343.25(4)	No longer enrolled in basic motorcycle rider course
LBC	W00	303	343.25(4)	Check returned unpaid
LBR	W00	302	343.25(4)	No longer enrolled in basic motorcycle rider course
LED	W00	304	343.25(4)	No longer enrolled in approved driver's education course
LGL	W00	305	343.25(4)	Not 6 months of violation free driving prior to obtaining a probationary license
LHE	W09	306	343.25(4)	Law prohibits H endorsement
LID	W00	307	343.25(4)	Sponsor deceased
LIE	W00	308	343.25(4)	License issued in error
LIP	W00	309	343.06(1)(h), 343.25(4), 343.16(5)(b), TR 112.10(3)(c)(1)	License issuance prohibited
LIS	W13	310	343.25(4)	Improper sponsorship
LMR	W00	311	343.25(4)	Misrepresentation of Identity
LPI	W00	093		Law prohibits issue of driver license
LPO	W00	312	343.30(3)	Occupational license withdrawn by court order
LPS	W00	313	343.25(4)	Conviction prohibits endorsement
LSE	W00	314	343.25(4)	S endorsement prohibited because of felony conviction
MC		99		Medical correspondence
NC1	W20	319	TR 107.08(1)(h), 343.06(1)(f)	Failure to comply with the Driver Safety plan within 1 year of the assessment
NCA		194	343.06(1)(e)	Noncompliance with assessment fee
NCE	W20	197	343.30(1q)(d)	Non-compliance - failure to pay driver safety plan education fee
NCF	W20	101		Non-compliance with assessment fee
NCI	W20	102		Non-compliance - failure to complete mandatory assessment interview
NCP	W20	100		Non-compliance - failure to complete Driver Safety Plan recommendations
NCT	D20	196	343.30(1q)(d)	Non-compliance - failure to complete Driver Safety Plan treatment fee
NLP	W00	333		No legal presence - acceptable proof of U.S. citizenship not provided
OCR		104		Occupational-court ordered revocation
OSJ	D39	281	344.25	Out-of-state judgment from an out of state accident
OSO	W50	331	346(7)(a)1,2,3	Out of service order
OSS	D35	286	344.19(3)	Uninsured out-of-state motor vehicle accident
RHT	W01	213	351	Repeat habitual traffic defender
RLP		323	343.265(1m)	Voluntary temporary surrender specific to medical reasons
SDD	D35	284	344.18(3)	Safety responsibility - driver/owner default (can be failure to maintain installment payments for a motor vehicle accident)
SLR		260		Surrender of License and Registration Upon Revocation or Suspension
SOD	D35	283	344.18(3)	Safety Responsibility - Owner - Failure to maintain installment payments for a motor vehicle accident
SOL		259		Surrender of Licenses upon Cancellation, Revocation or Suspension
SR	D35	192	-	Uninsured motor vehicle accident, safety responsibility suspension
SRD	D35	285	344.18(3)	Failure to maintain installment payments for a motor vehicle accident
SRO		282		Uninsured motor vehicle accident, Safety Responsibility Suspension - Owner
SRR	D35	193	344.14	Uninsured motor vehicle accident
STM		092		Suspension terminated
SVO	D27	105	343.31(2u)	Serious violation while operating with a occupational license
TSS		090		Traffic Safety School
UE	W20	097		Unsuccessful driving examination
UEK	W20	317	343.16(5)(b), 343.25(4)	Unsuccessful examination - knowledge
UER	W20	315	TR 12.14, 343.16(5)(b), 343.25(4)	Unsuccessful examination – road test
UES	W20	316	343.16(5)(b), 343.25(4)	Unsuccessful examination – sign test
UKS	W20	295	343.16(5)(b), 343.25(4), 343.16(6)(a), TR 104.07	Unsuccessful examination - knowledge and sign test
VS	W10	098		Voluntary surrender of driver license

Point System Summary

Points range from 2 to 6. Accumulation of 12 points in a 12-month period can result in a suspension. Individuals holding probationary licenses are assessed double points on second and subsequent offenses.

With completion of an approved Traffic Safety course, one can request a 3-point reduction of demerit point total. One can also request a 3-point reduction upon completion of a motorcycle rider course for violations and convictions incurred while operating a motorcycle. Courses can be taken often; however, there is only one point reduction every 3 years.

The Transportation Chapter 101 (http://legis.wisconsin.gov/rsb/code/trans/trans101.pdf) presents a text list of points and assessments.

Wyoming

Administration	Important Telephone and Web Contacts
John Cox, Director Department of Transportation 307-777-4484 Tom Loftin, Support Services Div. Admin. 307-777-4484 Don Edington, Driver Services Program Manager 307-777-4802 Debbie Lopez, Motor Vehicle Srvs Manager 307-777-4851 5300 Bishop Boulevard Cheyenne, WY 82009-3340 www.dot.state.wy.us/wydot	Driver Licensing...307-777-4800 Vehicle License/Title................... 307-777-4851 or 4709 Financial Responsibility/SR-22....................307-777-4800 Commercial Driver License.........................307-777-4800 Vehicle Information.................... 307-777-4709 or 4825 State Department of Insurance ....307-777-7401 Highway Patrol..307-777-4301 Wyoming Statutes Title 31 – Motor Vehicles: http://legisweb.state.wy.us/statutes/compress/title31.doc Email Contact List at www.dot.state.wy.us/ContactWYDOT/

Driver's License Format, Issuance and Renewal

License Classes, Restrictions and Endorsements Appear After the Driving Record Content Section

License Format

The driver's license is nine numbers (six numbers, hyphen, three numbers; i.e., 101565-142). Numbers are computer-generated with a "check digit." An ID Card is composed of two numbers, hyphen, then seven numbers.

Document Appearance

License is a tamper proof laminate.

Security Characteristics: Signature of director appears vertically overlaying photographs. The background of both the driver license and ID card is the Grand Tetons mirrored lake image. The driver license has brown lettering "Driver License" at the top with matching brown bucking horse symbol. The ID Card has green lettering "IDENTIFICATION CARD" at top with matching green bucking horse symbol. Instruction permit has red lettering "INSTRUCTION PERMIT" at top with matching red bucking horse symbol.

Position of Photo: Left side.

Minor Age Driver Locator: Photo on left side, vertical layout of license, with red bar above signature at the bottom. Bar contains the 18th and 21st birthdays.

CDL Indicator: "COMMERCIAL DRIVER LICENSE" in blue lettering at top with matching blue bucking horse.

Issuance

Location of Requirements for Proof of Identity:
Visit www.dot.state.wy.us/wydot/driver_license_records, then click on "List of Required Documents"

Age Requirements
To obtain a WY license with full driving privileges a person must be at least 17 years of age; unless the person is 16 ½ years of age, has held a graduated driver's license for at least 6 months, and completed/passed an approved driver's education course. To obtain a commercial license for interstate driving, a person must be at least 21 years of age. A commercial license can be issued to a person under the age of 21; however, this person will be restricted to driving in Wyoming only (intrastate). To obtain a learner's permit, a person must be at least 15 years of age. To obtain a restricted license a person must be between the ages of 14 and 16 years of age. A person applying for the restricted class C license must first apply and receive a restricted instruction permit. New security requirements of obtaining a new driver license were recently instituted in 2011.

Residency
Home-state licenses of non-residents (if over sixteen years of age) are honored. One must apply for a Wyoming driver license within one year from the time residency is established, providing license currently held is NOT issued by one of the following states: Georgia, Massachusetts, Michigan, Tennessee or Wisconsin. These states are not part of the Driver's License Compact. If a license is held from one of these states, the driver must apply for a Wyoming license when residency is established. Those holding a CDL must transfer their driver license within 30 days.

Renewal
Renewal is birth date of fourth year. Driver keeps same number when renewing. Renewal is not available online, but licenses can be extended by mail. Military personnel stationed out-of-state are required to renew every four years, unless restriction has been issued stating "Expiration waived when accompanied by active military duty Identification Card."

Elderly-Related Restrictions
None indicated.

Vehicle Insurance, Title and Registration Facts

Insurance and Financial Responsibility

Minimum responsibility limits are $25,000/50,000/20,000. No owner may operate a motor vehicle without liability insurance. Wyoming does not have a no-fault insurance provision. Proof is required after conviction of an offense that carries mandatory suspension/revocation (DUI, reckless, etc.), uninsured accident suspension and compulsory insurance violation. SR-22 forms are used.

Registration Renewal
Renewal is annual. There is no statewide system for online renewal, but several counties offer this service.

New Residents
New residents must register vehicles upon accepting employment or establishing residency.

Inspections and Emissions Testing
Wyoming has no provisions for emission testing or safety inspection for gasoline and diesel motored vehicles.

Passenger Plate Facts
There are two plates with one decal (MO & YR) on each plate. The numbers 1 to 23 preceding the Bucking Horse image designate the county of issuance. The county codes for these 23 numbers are as follows: 1-Natrona; 2-Laramie; 3-Sheridan; 4-Sweetwater; 5-Albany; 6-Carbon; 7-Goshen; 8-Platte; 9-Big Horn; 10-Fremont; 11-Park; 12-Lincoln; 13-Converse; 14-Niobrara; 15-Hot Springs; 16-Johnson; 17-Campbell; 18-Crook; 19-Uinta; 20-Washakie; 21-Weston; 22-Teton; and 23-Sublette. Specialty plates (firefighter, EMT, etc.) do not have a county prefix. The symbol (firefighter, etc.) is printed in place of the county prefix. Apportioned and transporter plates do not have the county prefix and are number "A1-A99999" and "T1-T99999" respectively.

When a vehicle is sold the plates remain with seller

Withdrawal Sanctions, and Alcohol and Drug Testing

Alcohol and Chemical Testing
Wyoming's illegal intoxication level is .08 percent and above, .02 percent and above for youthful offenders, and .04 percent and above for CDL drivers. Urine, blood, and breath testing are authorized. Wyoming has provisions for an implied-consent violation and administrative suspension. Wyoming's provision for a refusal suspension was repealed July 1, 2011. Operating a boat under the influence is also considered illegal. Operating a horse or bicycle is not illegal under state law, but there may be some city ordinances that make it illegal.

Suspensions and Revocations
The Wyoming DMV is in compliance with the provisions of the Motor Carrier Safety Improvement Act (MCSIA). See the Appendix for more information about these mandatory CDL disqualification sanctions.

The difference between a suspension and a revocation is that after a suspension is completed one can get the old driver's license back if it is still valid. A revocation cancels the driver's license, and the driver must go through an investigation to be re-licensed once the revocation is over. Offenses that will cause a revocation are: 1) 3rd or subsequent DWUI; 2) leaving the scene of an injury accident; 3) homicide by vehicle; 4) felony that is a direct result of the manner of driving; 5) third or subsequent reckless driving conviction.

Below is a list of typical suspensions and revocations. Note that Wyoming's provision for a refusal suspension was repealed July 1, 2011.

Admin Per Se (over .08%)............Ninety-day suspension.
Admin Per Se Youthful offenders (.02 up to .08%)
  First Offense............Ninety-day suspension.
  Second Offense............Six-month suspension.
  Third or Subsequent Offense............Six-month revocation.
Any Four Moving Violations in Twelve-Month Period............Ninety-day suspension.
DWUI (If event occurred PRIOR to July 1, 2010)
  First Conviction in Five Years............Ninety-day suspension.
  Second Conviction in Five Years............One-year suspension.
  Third or Subsequent Conviction in Five Years............Mandatory three-year revocation.
  Fourth or Subsequent Conviction in Five Years, Felony............Mandatory three-year revocation.
DWUI (If event occurred AFTER July 1, 2010)
  First Conviction in Ten Years............Ninety-day suspension.
  Second Conviction in Ten Years............One-year suspension.
  Third or Subsequent Conviction in Ten Years............Mandatory three-year revocation.
  Fourth or Subsequent Conviction in Ten Years, Felony............Mandatory three-year revocation.
First Citation (moving violation) on Restricted License............Ninety-day suspension.
Each Consecutive Violation on Restricted License............Additional one-year suspension.
Leaving Scene of an Injury Accident............One-year revocation.
Felony Which is a Direct Result of Manner of Driving............One-year revocation.
Refusal of Chemical Test First Conviction............Six-month suspension.
Homicide by Vehicle............One-year revocation.
No Liability Insurance............Indefinite suspension.
Reckless Driving
  First Conviction in Five Years............Ninety-day suspension.
  Second Conviction in Five Years............Six-month suspension.
  Third or Subsequent Conviction in Five Years............One-year revocation.
Transporting Liquor to a Minor............One-year suspension.
Youthful Driver with Alcohol
  First Conviction............Ninety-day suspension.
  Second Conviction or Subsequent Conviction within Two Years............Six-month suspension.

Other Types of Suspensions
Child Support
Compulsory Insurance
Theft of Fuel
Multiple Moving Violations - Driver allowed up to 3 moving violations within a 12-month period. On the 4th moving violation, driving privilege will be suspended for 90 days. Each additional moving violation received within a 12-month period of last 3 moving violations, will cause an additional 90-day suspension. If driver has a restricted class (RC) license, driving privilege will be suspended for 90 days for 1st moving violation conviction, and 1 year for 2nd moving violation.

Non Resident Violator Compact - Suspension remains until requirements for reinstatement are met.

Uninsured Accident - Suspension remains until requirements for reinstatement are met.

Ignition Interlock - An Ignition Interlock Law relating to drivers suspended for DUI related offenses became effective July 1, 2006. In 2009, additional legislation created mandatory use of Ignition Interlock for certain time periods regarding alcohol-related offenses. Any person who has been convicted with a BAC of .15% or greater or for 2nd or subsequent conviction of a DUI or a refusal must have a vehicle equipped with the Ignition Interlock. An extensive list of the time periods is found at the home page. There is restricted driver's license (IIR) available to eligible drivers. In 2011, additional legislation authorized new administrative actions.

Reinstatement Requirements

Suspension $50.00 Reinstatement fee; any applicable fines; proof of financial responsibility.

Revocation $50.00 Reinstatement fee; conditions placed on license; proof of insurance for three years; alcohol evaluation if required; investigation conducted by the Division.

Note: Suspension for nonpayment of child support is a $5.00 fee.

Record Access: Laws, Rules, and Forms

Note: **This Section Applies to Both Driver and Vehicle Records.**

Governing Statutes and Rules

Title 31 – **Motor Vehicles** can be accessed at:
http://legisweb.state.wy.us/statutes/compress/title31.doc.
Per the Wyoming Department of Transportation Rule and Regulation, the state adopted the provisions of DPPA without exception.

Although the Rule and Regulation did not adopt DPPA permissible uses (11) and (13), per administrative rule, they are enforced. The state mandates that ongoing requesters sign documentation attesting to compliance with DPPA.

Request and Consent Forms

Driving Records: Commercial accounts and ongoing requesters must sign: 1) *Privacy Disclosure Agreement for Personal Information* which specifies the purpose of ongoing requests and must be accompanied by a client list. This form prohibits further sale or disclosure to third parties on the Internet or any other means, except those identified on the client list. *Form DSFR-11C* attests to permissible use and is required with each request made through the mail or in person for non-commercial accounts.

If the requester does not have a permissible use, *Form DSFR-11E* must be used; it requires signed consent and the signature of the requester.

See www.dot.state.wy.us/wydot/site/wydot/driving_records for both forms.

Vehicle Records: Requests must be in writing explaining purpose of request, with signature of requester (unless the request is from a law enforcement agency). Use of the *Vehicle Record & Privacy Disclosure Release* is suggested, it may be downloaded at www.dot.state.wy.us/wydot/titles_plates_registration/title_search. The form forbids sales to a third party

Vendor and Third Party Access Policy

Driving Records: The state allows disclosure to 3rd parties only when identified on an approved 3rd party list. An Agreement & Contract must be on file with WYDOT to resale or re-disclose information received to third party users. All authorized vendors must maintain records on such information for five years.

Vehicle Records: The contract user is restricted from further use or resale as defined in DPPA and Departmental Rules and Regulations.

Records Ordered For Non-permissible Uses

Without consent or signed authorization, requesters cannot obtain records, even records without personal information.

Access to Driver-Related Records

Driving Records

General Information and Fees

WY Department of Transportation, Driver Services, 5300 Bishop Boulevard, Cheyenne WY 82009-3340, 307-777-4800 or 4810.

The current fee is $5.00 per record, regardless of access method. The record can be ordered as a three to five-year record (for insurance purposes), or as a ten-year record (for commercial employers). Both records are available for commercial drivers. Add $2.50 fee if a credit card is used. The state charges for "no record found" reports.

In-Person – Counter requests are processed while you wait. Field offices will provide driving records to the subjects themselves, with proper identification. The driver's license number, or name and date of birth are needed when ordering.

Mail – Requests mailed to the state are processed in three to five business days. The driver's name and DOB and either license number or SSN are needed when ordering

Fax – Fax requests are accepted. A credit card can be used, but an additional $2.50 service fee is charged per record. Electronic checks are also accepted. Records are processed in 3 to 5 business days.

Electronic – Wyoming supports web service for the access of driving record requests for approved vendors and permissible users. The fee is $5.00 per record (the fee increased from $3.00 to $5.00 on January 1, 2012). To learn more about establishing an account, call Marianne Zivkovich, Driver Services at 307-777-4830.

Bulk – The entire state file with name, address and operator number is available electronically for $2,500, with bi-monthly updates for an additional fee. This service is only offered to approved vendors with a permissible use. A contract must be signed. For more information, write or call Marianne Zivkovich, Driver Services, at 307-777-4830.

By Person of Record – Wyoming drivers may order record on themselves as by either the mail or walk-in methods described above. At this time there is no online ordering available. Use of the *DSFR-11E Form* is suggested.

Notification/Monitoring Program

By utilizing the *Bulk* services described above, insurance or trucking companies, or driving record vendors may establish a monitoring system or notification program to track incidents of associated drivers.

Accident Reports

Reporting – For involvement in an accident in which there is an injury or property damage to an apparent extent of $1,000, all drivers must file an Operator's or Owner's Traffic Accident Report within 1 days. This is regardless who is at fault. The form is found at www.dot.state.wy.us/wydot/dot_safety/crash_report. The Wyoming Insurance Certificate (SR21) at the bottom of the accident report must also be completed even if insurance information was given to the investigating officer at the accident scene. Accident reports should sent to the Department of Transportation, Accident Records Section 5300 Bishop Blvd, Cheyenne, WY 82009-3340, 307-777-4450.

Record Access – Copies of accident reports can be obtained by writing to the Department of Transportation, Accident Records Section, 5300 Bishop Blvd, Cheyenne WY 82009, 307-777-4450. The date of the accident, location (county), and driver's name should be included with the request, along with $5.00 per request for a certified record or $3.00 for a non-certified record. Records are available for the past 10 years. Normal turnaround time is 2 to 3 days after payment received. Limited information is released by phone for no fee, no copies are sent until payment received. One must contact the investigating agency if photos or a CD is requested. An order form is not available online.

Access to Vehicle-Related Records

General Information and Fees

Department of Transportation, Motor Vehicle Services, Licensing and Titling Section, 5300 Bishop Blvd, Cheyenne WY 82009-3340, 307-777-4883

As of 01/01/2010, watercraft title records are also available from this agency. In Wyoming, regular county license plates and vehicle registrations are issued by the local county treasurers' offices in the county seat of the county of residence. Wyoming titles and lien filings are processed by the local county clerks' offices in the county seat of the county of residence. The DOT maintains the record database for vehicles and vessel titles, but not vessel registrations (see below). Records are searchable for 40 years for title records and up to 8 years for registration records; however a complete title or registration history is not available. Be sure to state if you wish to access data that is dated, otherwise only current data is provided.

The fee for Certificate of Title Search or for a License Plate Registration Search is $5.00 per search. Record requesters may use credit card for an additional $2.50 fee.

Lien records on vehicles and watercraft are not available from the DOT and must be obtained from the Wyoming County Clerk Offices.

In-Person, Mail – A reason for the record requests must be presented. Turnaround time is usually 1 week. The state requires submission of a special form with these requests. If by mail, include a copy of picture ID of the requester. Mail to the above address or present in person.

Fax – Approved, ongoing requester may order records via fax, a credit card may be used for payment.

Electronic – Wyoming does not offer online inquiry at this time.

Bulk – The cost for purchasing the statewide file on electronic format is $3,500.00. The file will have the registrant's name and address, license plate number, vehicle year, make and model, VIN, and the issue date. A form letter is sent to interested parties, which gives space for several questions pertaining to principal uses and other routine uses that will be made of the information. Inquiries can be sent to the address above or by phone to the Motor Vehicle Services at 307-777-4714.

Access to Vessel-Related Records

Access to Vessel Title Records

Department of Transportation, Motor Vehicle Services, Licensing and Titling Section, 5300 Bishop Blvd, Cheyenne WY 82009-3340, 307-777-4883

Effective 01/01/2010 titles must be issued for watercraft, light trailers (weighing 1,000 pounds), and snowmobiles. Records are managed by the same Motor Vehicle Services agency that manages vehicle titles. All existing watercraft, light trailers and snowmobiles were "grandfathered in" meaning that they do not need to have a title unless desired by the owner. Technically, as the law is written, all watercraft must be titled including canoes and rubber boats. However, since the Wyoming Game and Fish only issues registrations to motorized watercraft and a boat must be registered to be titled, only motorized watercraft will be able to be titled. As described above, titles will be issued at the local county agency, but the central database of record will be kept by the **Department of Transportation**. It will take up to 3 days for the title information to be forwarded on and placed on the centralized computer. Liens will not be found on the centralized computer and must be searched at the county level or state level if filed as a UCC.

Access to Vessel Registration Records

Wyoming Game and Fish Department, Watercraft Section, 5400 Bishop Blvd, Cheyenne WY 82006, 307-777-4638, fax 307-777-4610. http://wgfd.wyo.gov/

All motorized boats must be registered. There is no fee to do a registration record verification by fax or phone, but the agency prefers that long lists be mailed. They can search by name, hull # or registration #. Name searches and list requests must be in writing and submitted to the Director's Office as a Public Information Request. Fees are based on agency time involved. Call for further details. Records are indexed on computer for 2 years plus present years, and archived on paper for 3 years prior to those on computer. Turnaround time is 2 to 3 days. Liens are recorded at the county level.

Driving Record Content and Reciprocity

What's On or Not On the Driving Record

- All convictions are listed on the driving record except non-CDL drivers who speeding 5 or less MPH over the limit on highways with a 55 or greater posted limit UNLESS is construction or school zone.
- If a driver of a commercial vehicle is speeding 4 over or less in a 75 MPH zone, or 14 over or less in a 65 MPH zone, the speeding ticket will show on the record, but not count towards disqualification.
- The standard driving record includes:
  - 3 years of history for moving violations, uninsured accidents, compulsory insurance violations, administrative per se & refusals, nonresident violator compact violations, and proof of financial responsibility withdrawals...AND...
  - 5 years of history for driving under the influence, reckless driving, accident judgments, vehicular homicide, leaving the scene of an injury accident, a felony which is a result of manner of driving, and transporting liquor to a minor convictions and withdrawals.
- If the requester wants a 10-year record, this must be specified in the request.
- Since July 1, 1989, accidents are only reported if the driver has no insurance.
- The driver's address is provided as part of the driving record for permissible users or if a casual requester presents a signed released (by subject).
- There are no "cloaked" or redacted records released.
- The SSN is required on all driver license applications, unless the applicant signs an affidavit stating they do not have an SSN. However, the SSN does not appear on the driver license.
- The state does not permit driver school attendance in lieu of conviction.

Data Retention

In general, records are purged per guidelines above. An automatic record purge is run monthly. CDL driver records are purged based on the timetable per federal regulations (see the Appendix). Surrendered licenses to another jurisdiction are cancelled, but remain on database.

Court to Repository

Convictions sent by the District and Municipal Courts to the state are on paper and are key entered. Circuit Courts send convictions electronically. Courts try to meet a 10 day timeframe for transferring this conviction data. When a charge is entered, the purge date is calculated and captured in a separate field.

State Reciprocity for Non-CDL Drivers

- Will suspend license of driver for unpaid out-of-state convictions per NRVC.
- Record of new incoming driver is shown on MVR.
- Out-of-state convictions are shown on MVR.
- Out-of-state accidents are not shown on MVR.
- Convictions of out-of-state drivers are sent to home state.
- Record is forwarded to new state upon surrender of license.

Important Abbreviations

License Classes— Commercial

Wyoming began issuing the CDL in December of 1990.

Class A	Any combination of vehicles with a GCWR of 26,001 pounds or more—provided the GVWR of the vehicle or vehicles being towed is in excess of 10,000 pounds, including all vehicles under Class C (except motorcycles).
Class B	Any single vehicle with a GVWR of 26,001 or more pounds, or any such vehicle towing a vehicle which does not have a GVWR in excess of 10,000 pounds, including all vehicles under Class C (except motorcycles).
Class C	Any single vehicle or combination of vehicles that does not meet the definition of a Class A or B, but that either is designed to transport sixteen (16) or more passengers including driver or is placarded for transportation of hazardous materials.
Note:	Wyoming also offers a CDP (Commercial Driving Permit) which entitles a driver to operate a commercial vehicle only when accompanied by a person who possesses a commercial driver's license (CDL) for the vehicle being operated.

License Classes— Non-Commercial

Class A	Used for exempt persons (farmers/ranchers, firefighters, military for class & type of vehicle operated.
Class B	Used for exempt persons (farmers/ranchers, firefighters, military for class & type of vehicle operated.
Class C	For cars and pickups. Any single vehicle or combination of vehicles (except motorcycles) with a GVWR less than 26,001 pounds, or any such vehicle towing a vehicle which does not have a GVWR in excess of 10,000 pounds.
Class I	Instruction Permit for drivers who have applied for a Class C License or a restricted Class C License.
Class I2	May operate a non-commercial Class "C" and/or exempt commercial Class "B" vehicle within the following restrictions: (1) May drive only between the hours of 5 a.m. and 11 p.m., (2) cannot transport more than 1 passenger under the age of 18 years who is not an immediate family member, and (3) the licensee must ensure that all occupants in the vehicle are wearing seat belts.
Class M	Motorcycles or all terrain vehicles; may be added to license valid for other Classes, or may be issued as only class if the applicant is not licensed for other classification. No passengers allowed for Temporary, I2 or Restricted type M Licenses. If under 18, must wear a helmet.
Class RC	Restricted Class C - authorizes the holder, aged 14-16 years, to operate a motor vehicle (Class C type) between the hours of 5 am and 8 pm within a 50 mile radius of domicile. If **RC-M**, then included are motorcycles and 3-wheel trikes.
Class RM	Restricted Class M

Restrictions

B	Corrective Lenses	L	Vehicle Without Air Brakes (CDL only)
C	Mechanical Aid	M	Except Class A Bus (CDL only)
D	Prosthetic Aid	N	Except Class A and B Bus (CDL only)
E	Automatic Transmission	O	Except Tractor/Trailer (CDL only)
F	Outside Mirrors	R	Recreational Vehicle Only
G	Daylight Driving Only	V	Variance (CDL only)
H	Limit to Employment	Y	Annual Vision
I	Limited Other (shown on back of license)	Z	Annual Medical
J	Valid Without Photo (other)		
K	CDL Intrastate Only		

Endorsements

T	Double-/Triple-Trailers (presumably would only apply to Class A)	S	School Bus
H	Hazardous Material	P	Passenger; required for transportation of 16 or more passengers (including driver). Normally restricted to drivers 18 years or older; may be issued to licensed drivers between 16 and 18 who meet certain other criteria (school)
N	Tank		
X	Combines H and N		

Conviction Table with ACD, Statutes, and Actions

- In the Public column "Y" means this conviction will show on the driving record used by public – i.e. insurance, trucking, employment entities, etc. An "N" means this conviction is only shown to law enforcement and to other state motor vehicle agencies. Also, "N" usually signifies this is not a moving violation.
- In the Action column, "MV" means that this conviction is a moving violation may or could result in a suspension.
- The Code column may or may not reflect the ACD.
- In the Statute column, the law generally is found Under Title 31 – Traffic Law (http://legisweb.state.wy.us/statutes/compress/title31.doc)
- ** Signifies an Obsolete code. Do not use for out-of-state violations; Use for WY violations, unless crossed out.

Code	Description	Public	Action	Statute
A25	Ability Impaired	Y	MV	
A61	ADMIN PERSE (.02 BAC OR GREATER)	N	Susp	5-234; 6-108; 7-128hiA (susp) (Youthful Offender- BAC .02 or greater-1st)
A61-2	ADMIN PERSE (.02 BAC OR GREATER)	N	Susp	5-234; 6-108 (Youthful Offender- BAC .02 or greater-2nd)
A61-S	ADMIN PERSE (.02 BAC OR GREATER)	N	Susp	5-234; 6-108: 7-128hiC (susp) (Youthful Offender- BAC .02 or greater- 3rd)
A98	Admin PerSe w/Bac .08 or greater	Y	Susp	6-102e
A91	Administrative Per Se	Y	N	(out-of-state record)
A94	Administrative Per Se for .04 BAC	Y	Disq	7-307
A90	Administrative Perse	Y	Susp	6-102e (prior to 07/01/02)
A90CV	Administrative Perse	Y	Disq & Susp	6-102e (susp); 7-305aii (disq) (prior to 07/01/02)
E71	Brakes used improperly	N	N	
M81	Careless Driving	Y	MV	5-236 (new law –effective 7/09)
F05	Carrying unsecured pass. in open area of veh.	Y	MV	5-119c
F02	Child or youth restraint not used properly	N	N	5-1303a
**N81	Clinging to vehicles	N	N	5-119a
N80	Coasting (operating with rears disengaged)	Y	MV	5-230a&b
D35	Compulsory Insurance Violation	Y	Poss Susp- SR22	4-103a (Statute only)
D35A	Compulsory Insurance Violation	Y	SR22 (on file)	4-103a (Statute only) (SR22 with effective date after offense date already on file)
E31	Defective Brakes	N	N	5-950a&b, -951c
**E30	Defective equipment	N	N	5-952a
E33	Defective HAZMAT safety devices	N	N	
E34	Defective light	N	N	
**E35	Defective or noisy exhaust system or muffler	N	N	5-953a,b&c
E36	Defective school bus equipment	N	N	
E37	Defective tires	N	N	5-956a&f
**D73	Display unauthorized signs on traffic signs	N	N	5-406a&b
A26	Drinking alcohol while operating a vehicle	Y	MV	7-306a (CMV- Out of Service)
D70	Driver=s view obstructed	Y	MV	5-115c & -116a
D70A	Driver=s view obstructed	N	N	5-115d,-116b, & 955a
**A27	Driving after drinking- level not known	Y	MV	7-306a (now use A26) (CMV- Out of Service)
B57	Driving CMV w/o CDL in possession	Y	Poss Disq	(Serious traffic violation)
N70	Driving on wrong side	Y	MV	
N71	Driving on wrong side of divided highway	Y	MV	
N72	Driving on wrong side of undivided street or road	Y	MV	
S94	Driving too fast for conditions	Y	MV	5-301a
A23	Driving under the influence of alcohol and drugs	Y	Susp or Rev SR22	5-233biiC (offense); 7-127aii (rev) or- 128c (susp)
A20CP	Driving Under the Influence w/Child Passenger	Y	Susp or Rev SR22	5-233mi (offense); 7-127aii (rev) 128c (susp) -305ai (disq)
A20CP2	Driving Under the Influence w/Child Passenger – (2nd offense)	Y	Rev SR22	5-233mii (offense); 7-127aii (rev) 128c (susp) -305ai (disq)
B21	Driving while license barred	Y	Disq (if CMV)	
B22	Driving while license cancelled	Y	Disq (if CMV)	
B23	Driving while license denied	Y	Disq (if CMV	
B24	Driving while license disqualified	Y	Disq (if CMV)	
B25	Driving while license revoked	Y	Disq (if CMV)	
B20	Driving while susp, revoked, cancelled	Y	Disq (if CMV)	7-134a
B26	Driving while susp, revoked, cancelled	Y	Disq (if CMV)	
B26Y	Driving while susp, revoked, cancelled (youthful offense)	Y	Susp	7-134d
A11	Driving While Under the Influence	Y	N	(out-of-state record)
A20	Driving While Under the Influence	Y	Susp or Rev SR22	
A20F	Driving While Under the Influence	Y	Rev SR22	(4th DI -Felony)

Code	Description	Public	Action	Statute
A20PS	Driving While Under the Influence	Y	Susp SR22	(1st offense w/Admin Per Se)
A21PS	Driving While Under the Influence	Y	Susp SR22	(1st offense w/Admin Per Se)
A22PS	Driving While Under the Influence	Y	Susp SR22	(1st offense w/Admin Per Se)
A23PS	Driving While Under the Influence (1st offense w/Administrative Per Se)	Y	Susp SR22	(1st offense w/Admin Per Se)
A20CV*	Driving While Under the Influence (Commercial offense) (* can use A20 & mark CMV)	Y	Disq & Susp or Rev SR22	5-233 (offense); 7-127aii (rev) 128c (susp) -305ai (disq)
A20Y	Driving While Under the Influence (Youthful)	Y	Susp SR22	(used to give credit when A61 also on record)
A21	Driving While Under the Influence of Alcohol	Y	Susp or Rev SR22	5-233bi,biiA (offense); 7-127aii (rev) or- 128c (susp)
A22	Driving While Under the Influence of Drugs	Y	Susp or Rev SR22	5-233biiB (offense); 7-127aii (rev) or- 128c (susp)
A20R	Driving While Under the Influence w/Bodily Injury	Y	Rev SR22	5-233hi & hii
A21R	Driving While Under the Influence w/Bodily Injury	Y	Rev SR22	5-233hi & hii
A04	Driving with BAC of .04 or greater (conviction)	Y	Disq	7-305aii
A08	Driving with BAC of .08 or greater	Y	N	(out-of-state record)
N60	Driving wrong way			
N61	Driving wrong way at rotary intersection	Y	MV	5-208c
N63	Driving wrong way on one way street or road	Y	MV	5-208a&b
A10	DUI With BAC .10 or greater	Y	N	(out-of-state record)
A20D	DWUI deferral	Y	Disq	
A21D	DWUI deferral	Y	Disq	
A22D	DWUI deferral	Y	Disq	
A23D	DWUI deferral	Y	Disq	
E70	Equipment used improperly or obstructed	N	N	5-115n, & -932a
M42	Erratic (unsafe) lane changes	Y	MV & Poss Disq	209ai (Serious traffic violation)
**F16	Exceed or violate weight limits road/bridge/tunnel	N	N	18-802avG
**F12	Exceeding or violating size limits of vehicle/trk	N	N	18-802ai,aii,aiii,aivA, & aivB
**F13	Exceeding or violating weight limit of vehicle/trk	N	N	18-802avB-F, HI, HII, HIII avii, aviii
**F11	Exceeding passenger/cargo limit of vehicle	N	N	
S95	Exhibition Driving	Y	MV	18-705a; 24-1-110a&b
B51	Exp/No DL or permit	N	N	7-106a & -119a
B56	Expired or no commercial driver license	Y	Poss Disq	(Serious traffic violation)
**B53	Expired or no license plates or decal/sticker	N	N	4-101aii
**B54	Expired or no registration or title	N	N	4-101ai
**B13	Fail duties-damaging unattended veh or animal	Y	MV	5-1104 B
E01)	Fail to have or improperly installed signals	N	N	5-218b
M31	Fail to leave sufficient distance to overtake veh	Y	MV	5-210b&c
**B90	Fail to provide/submit title transfer documents	N	N	2-507b; 4-101d
**B72	Fail to show commercial driver license	Y	Poss Disq	use B51 (Serious traffic violation)
B74	Fail to show insurance certification	N	N	4-103b
**E52	Fail to use disabled vehicle warning devices	N	N	5-957ai&aii, -958a-e, 958f&h
B61	Failed to file accident report	N	N	5-1105, 1106a & 1107c
**B62	Failed to file change of address or name	N	N	7-137b&c
**B60	Failed to file document or report as required	N	N	7-301a
B64	Failed to file insurance certification	N	N	
B65	Failed to file med cert/disability info	N	N	
**B70	Failed to show driver license	N	N	7-116 (formerly B72)
**B80	Failed to surrender driver license	N	N	7-133aiv
D45	Failure to appear for trial or court appearance	N	N	5-1206a
D56	Failure to comply with terms of citation	N	N	
M23	Failure to have space to drive thru railroad crossing	Y	MV Disq	7-305hiv
M41	Failure to keep in proper lane	Y	MV	5-201c,-205aii&iii
D36	Failure to maintain required liability insurance	N	N	
D51	Failure to make payment of child support	Y		
D53	Failure to make required payment of fine & costs			
**M02	Failure to obey barrier	N	N	
M03	Failure to obey const or maint zone markers	N	N	
M05	Failure to obey lane markings or signal	Y	MV	5-209aiv
**M06	Failure to obey motor carrier rules/regulations	N	N	5-959a; 7-310; 18-304a,b,&d, -701a, -808c
M08	Failure to obey police or peace officer	Y	MV	5-104
M09	Failure to obey railroad crossing restrictions	Y	MV	5-511a; 18-605ai,aiii,aiv, &av
M09A	Failure to obey railroad crossing restrictions	N	N	18-602b&c
M10	Failure to obey railroad gates, signs, or signals	Y	MV & Disq (if	5-510a&b; 18-605aii 7-305hiv, hv

Code	Description	Public	Action (CMV)	Statute
M10A	Failure to obey railroad gates, signs, or signals	N	N	18-602d
M11	Failure to obey restricted lane	Y	MV	
M12	Failure to obey safety zone	Y	MV	5-224ai,aii; -608
M13	Failure to obey school crossing guard	Y	MV	
M14	Failure to obey sign or traffic control device	Y	MV	5-209aiii, -213b, -214b & -402a; 18-703, 24-1-109
M15	Failure to obey stop sign	Y	MV	5-222b
M17	Failure to obey traffic sign	Y	MV	
M16	Failure to obey traffic signal or light	Y	MV	5-403aiA&B, aiiA, aiiiA&B, -405ai & aii
M18	Failure to obey warning light or flasher			
M19	Failure to obey yield sign	Y	MV	5-222c
WDR	Failure to obtain WY DL within one year	N		
**D66	Failure to remove harmful substance from traffic	N	N	5-117b
B14	Failure to Reveal ID after Fatal or Injury Acc	N	N	
N42	Failure to signal intention to pass	Y	MV	
N43	Failure to signal lane change or turn	Y	MV	5-217a&b, -218a
M20	Failure to slow and check at railroad crossing	Y	MV Disq	7-305hi
M25	Failure to stop - unsigned intersection	Y	MV	5-506
B01	Failure to stop and render aid	Y	MV & Disq	5-1103
M22	Failure to stop at railroad-highway crossing	Y	MV Disq	7-305hiii
M21	Failure to stop; Tracks not clear at RR crossing	Y	MV Disq	7-305hii
E51	Failure to use brakes	N	N	
E50	Failure to use equipment as required	N	N	
E53	Failure to use HAZMAT safety devices as required	N	N	5-957b
E54	Failure to use headlight dimmer as required	Y	MV	5-924ai&aii
E54A	Failure to use headlight dimmer as required	N	N	5-920d
E55	Failure to use lights as required	Y	MV	5-115p & -910 , -911
E55A	Failure to use lights as required	N	N	5-920c,-922, -927, -928a, -931a&b
N40	Failure to use or improper signal	Y	MV	5-217c&d
E56	Failure to use school bus safety equip as required	N	N	5-929b
E57	Failure to use snow tires or chains as required	N	N	5-956e
**F20	Failure to weigh vehicle or stop at weigh station	N	N	18-301c, -805a & c
N01	Failure to yield right of way	Y	MV	5-801aii
SNW	Failure to yield right of way on snowmobile			
N31	Failure to yield right of way when turning	Y	MV	
**B84	False report of accident	Y	MV	5-1108e
U10	Fatality Caused by Negligent Operation of CMV	Y	Rev & Disq SR22	
U03	Felony	Y	Rev SR22	7-127ai (rev)
A50	Felony involving drugs	Y	Rev / Disq SR22	
U01	Fleeing or evading police or roadblock	Y	MV	5-225a
M33	Following fire equipment unlawfully	Y	MV	5-231
M30	Following Improperly	Y	MV	
M34	Following too closely	Y	MV & Poss Disq	5-210a (Serious traffic violation)
D02	Fraud on driver=s license application	Y	Can / Den	7-133av
N20	FTY ROW at crosswalk	Y	MV	5-602a&b
N22	FTY ROW at stop sign	Y	MV	
N23	FTY ROW at traffic sign	Y	MV	
N24	FTY ROW at traffic signal	Y	MV	5-403aiiiC
N25	FTY ROW at unsigned intersection	Y	MV	5-220a&b
N26	FTY ROW at unsigned intersection	Y	MV	
N04	FTY ROW to emergency vehicle	Y	MV	5-224a
N05	FTY ROW to funeral, procession or parade	Y	MV	5-123ai & b
N06	FTY ROW to other vehicle	Y	MV	5-221 & -223
N07	FTY ROW to overtaking vehicle	Y	MV	5-203aii
N08	FTY ROW to pedestrian	Y	MV	5-403aiC, -404ai, -609, & -611
U04FT	Fuel Theft	Y	Susp	6-3-402f
N44	Giving wrong signal	Y	MV	
U07	Homicide by vehicle	Y	Rev & Disq SR22	6-2-106a, bi & bii, -106c (rev)
A31	Illegal possession of alcohol	N	N	(out-of-state record)
A33	Illegal possession of drugs	N	N	
F34	Impeding Traffic	Y	MV	5-304a; 18-705b
A12	Implied Consent	Y	Susp	6-102d (offense) 1
A12CV	Implied Consent (commercial offense)	Y	Disq	7-305av & -307
A12Y	Implied Consent (youthful offender)	N	Susp	6-108bi (Youthful Offender Refusal) repealed 2011
N82	Improper backing	Y	MV	5-226a&b

Code	Description	Public	Action	Statute
B91A	Improper certification on driver license	N	N	
B91	Improper classification or endorsement on d.l.	Y	Poss Disq	(Serious traffic violation) 7-133avii
M40	Improper lane or location	Y	MV	5-123aii,-227
M48	Improper lane or location - in occupied lane	Y	MV	5-115e,f,g&j
M51	Improper lane or location - median	Y	MV	5-211
M56	Improper lane or location - on fire hose	Y	MV	5-232
M60	Improper lane or location - slower vehicle lane	Y	MV	5-201aiii&b
M49	Improper lane or location- in HOV/restricted lane	Y	MV	
**M54	Improper lane/location - not on truck route	Y	MV	
M57	Improper lane/location - oncoming traffic lane	Y	MV	5-201aiv & -205ai
M46	Improper lane/location - ramp	Y	MV	
M58	Improper lane/location - shoulder, ditch, sidewalk	Y	MV	5-120
M61	Improper lane/location - straddling center line	Y	MV	5-201aii
M62	Improper lane/location - traveling in turn lane	Y	MV	5-209aii, -214aiiiB
M50	Improper lane/location- limited access hwy	Y	MV	5-212
M44	Improper Lane: Crossover	Y	MV	
N51	Improper method of turning	Y	MV	5-217e
F06	Improper operation of or riding on a motorcycle	Y	MV	5-115a,b&k
M70	Improper passing	Y	MV	5-206b,-602e
N52	Improper position for turning	Y	MV	5-214aiiiA
N83	Improper starting	Y	MV	5-216
N55	Improper Turnaround (not U turn)	Y	MV	
N50	Improper Turning	Y	MV	
**F40	Improper vehicle used on roadway	N	N	5-124 & -801ai
M32	Improperly following an emergency vehicle	Y	MV	
D72	Inability to control vehicle	N	N	
M82	Inattentive Driving	Y	MV	Use for 'Improper Lookout'
M80	Inattentive, careless, or negligent driving	Y	MV	
M24	Insufficient undercarriage clearance: RR crossing	Y	MV Disq	7-305hvi
B04	Leaving accident scene before police arrive	Y	MV & Disq	
B05	Leaving accident scene before police arrive	Y	MV & Disq	5-1102
B08	Leaving accident scene before police arrive	Y	MV & Disq	
B03	Leaving the Scene of a Injury Accident	Y	Rev & Disq	5-1101a (offense); 7-127aiv (rev)
B07	Leaving the Scene of an Injury Accident	Y	Rev & Disq	
B02	Leaving the Scene of an Injury Accident (fatal)	Y	Rev & Disq	
B06	Leaving the Scene of an Injury Accident (fatal)	Y	Rev & Disq	
**F63	Leaving vehicle unattended with engine running	N	N	5-509
**D67	Littering from a motor vehicle	N	N	5-117a
**B92A	Loan Driver=s License	N	N	(formerly B92)
N53	Making improper left turn	Y	MV	5-214aii
N54	Making improper right turn	Y	MV	5-214ai
N56	Making improper U turn	Y	MV	5-215a&b
**D04	Misrep of identity/facts on app for regis/title	N	N	2-507a; 4-102a
D02A	Misrep of identity/facts on driver license app	N	N	7-119d
**B43	Missing, defaced, or obscured license plates	N	N	4-101aiii
F03	Motorcycle safety equip not used properly	Y	MV	5-115o
F03A	Motorcycle safety equip not used properly	N	N	5-115m
M83	Negligent Driving	Y	MV	
U09	Negligent Homicide While Operating a CMV	Y	Rev & Disq SR22	
**F21	No or improper trip permit	N	N	18-201s,t,u,w&y, -301b, -403a,b,e,h & j, -804 & e
M85	No Texting	Y	MV	5-237
**F22	No warning for projecting load	N	N	5-919; 18-802aiiiA&B
**F32	Non emergency stop	N	N	
D75	Not physically or mentally qualified to drive	Y		
**F64	Opening door into traffic or w/ vehicle in motion	N	N	5-121
**F41	Operated vehicle where prohibited	N	N	
S97	Operating at Erratic or Suddenly Changing Speeds	Y	MV	
D74	Operating vehicle improperly because of drowsiness	Y		
E04	Operating w/o HAZMAT placards/markings as required	N	N	5-959b
E06	Operating w/o school bus equip, as required	Y	MV	5-507b
E02	Operating without brakes as required by law	N	N	
E01	Operating without equipment as required by law	N	N	5-914, -954a&b, -955b&c; 18-802avA
E03	Operating without HAZMAT safety equip as	N	N	5-959c

Code	Description	Public	Action	Statute
	required			
E05	Operating without lights as required by law	N	N	5-912,-913,915,-917, -920a, -923b&c, & -932c
B19	Out of Service involving hazmat and/or 16(+) passengers	Y	Disq	7-305giv Formerly B27H
B27	Out of Service Order Violation	Y	Disq	7-305g
**F33	Parking in a handicap zone	N	N	5-501c
M72	Passing - violate opposite direction restriction	Y	MV	5-202
M71	Passing - violate posted sign/pavement mark	Y	MV	5-207a & b
M74	Passing on hill or curve	Y	MV	
M73	Passing on wrong side	Y	MV	5-201ai,206ai-ii
M75	Passing school bus displaying no pass warning	Y	MV	5-507a
M76	Passing where prohibited	Y	MV	
M77	Passing with insufficient distance or visibility	Y	MV	5-203ai, -204
D78	Perjury relating to operation of motor vehicle	Y	Rev	
**B92	Permit unlawful use of driver's license	Y	Susp	7-133aiii, avi
**B30	Permit unlicensed person to drive	N	N	7-135
D07	Possess multiple driver licenses	N	N	7-106c
B41	Possess or provide counterfeit/altered DL,CDL,ID	N		
**B40	Possess or provide counterfeit/altered document	N		
**B42	Possess or provide counterfeit/altered regis/title	N	N	4-102b , 4-101b
A35	Possession of open alcohol container	N	N	5-235 & b
M43	Ran off road	Y	MV	
M84	Reckless Driving	Y	Susp or Rev & Poss Disq SR22	5-229 (offense); 7-127aiii (rev) or -128a (susp) (Serious traffic violation)
**B09	Refusal to reveal identity after accident	N	N	5-1103 (formerly B01)
**U24	Removal, falsification, or unauth use of VIN/regis	N	N	11-103ai
F04	Seat belt not used properly	N	N	5-1402a
**D15	Show or use improperly-Doc/Item not specified	N	N	2-213k (Handicap placard)
D16	Show or use improperly-driver license	N	N	7-132 ; 7-133ai
S96	Speed less than minimum	Y	MV	5-304b
S51	Speeding	Y	MV	
**S61	Speeding	Y	MV	
S92	Speeding (speeds required)	Y	MV	5-301b , bii, biii, biv, & c, -305a
S93	Speeding (speeds unknown)	Y	MV	should be used only for violations in a commercial vehicle
S01	Speeding 01-05 mph above speed limit			
S14	Speeding 11-14 mph above speed limit	Y	MV	
**S11	Speeding 11-15 mph above speed limit	Y	MV	
S15	Speeding 15 mph or more above speed limit	Y	MV & Poss Disq	5-305f (disq) (Serious traffic violation)
S92S	Speeding 15 mph or more above speed limit			used for violations that should be S15 from other states
S16	Speeding 16-20 mph above speed limit	Y	MV & Poss Disq	(Serious traffic violation)
S21	Speeding 21-25 mph above speed limit	Y	MV & Poss Disq	(Serious traffic violation)
S71	Speeding 21-30 mph above speed limit	Y	MV	(Serious traffic violation)
S26	Speeding 26-30 mph above speed limit	Y	MV & Poss Disq	(Serious traffic violation)
S31	Speeding 31-35 mph above speed limit	Y	MV & Poss Disq	(Serious traffic violation)
S81	Speeding 31-40 mph above speed limit	Y	MV & Poss Disq	(Serious traffic violation)
S36	Speeding 36-40 mph above speed limit	Y	MV & Poss Disq	(Serious traffic violation)
S41	Speeding 41 mph or more above speed limit	Y	MV & Poss Disq	(Serious traffic violation)
S91	Speeding 41 mph or more above speed limit	Y	MV & Poss Disq	(Serious traffic violation)
S06	Speeding 6-10 mph above speed limit	Y	MV	
**S50	Speeding in a school zone	Y	MV	5-301bi
**S99	Speeding in a school zone			
S98	Speeding on freeway ("wasting fuel")			
S92C	Speeding/Construction zone ** must show >construction= zone on ticket= - if just shows >superintendent= zone - use S92	Y	MV	31-5-301c **
**F23	Spilling, dragging, unsecured, or unsafe load	N	N	5-228; 18-603
F34A	Stopping, standing or parking; obstructing traffic	N	N	5-504aiA,C,F&G, aiiA
**F35	Stopping, standing, or parking where prohibited	N	N	504aiB,D,E,H,J,K&M aiiB,C,D&E, aiiiA&B,b,-505a, -512a&b ; 5-512d
M85	Texting While Driving	Y	MV	5-237 (new law –effective 7/10) (was TXT prior to creation of ACD)
**F65	Towing or pushing vehicle improperly	N	N	18-802aivC, -803ai-av, -808bi-iii,d

Code	Description	Public	Action	Statute
**A52	Transporting Liquor to a Minor	Y	Susp	12-6-102a (Statute only)
**U25	Unauthorized use of vehicle or taking w/o consent	N	N	11-102
A60	Underage conviction: driving w/BAC .02% or greater	N	Susp	5-234 (conviction)
A60-2	Underage conviction: driving w/BAC .02% or greater (2ND or subsequent conviction)	N	Susp	5-234 (conviction)
F66	Unsafe condition of vehicle	N	N	5-901 & a, -970
N84	Unsafe operation	Y	MV	5-607
N84A	Unsafe operation	N	N	5-122, -1203
W09	USA Patriot Act: Hazmat Withd	Y		
**D25	Use another=s driver=s license	N	N	7-133aiii
**D20	Use improperly: Registration/plates or decals	N	N	31-4-101e
**E21	Use of colored lights or siren prohibited by law	N	N	5-928b&f, -952d
**E22	Use of emergency veh markings prohibited by law	N	N	5-928d
**E20	Use of equipment prohibited by law	N	N	5-952b,-956b&c,-961; 12-101a; 18-606 ; 962k
E23	Use of radar, laser detector prohibited	N	N	
**E24	Use of vehicle lights prohibited by law	N	N	5-928c
U05	Using a motor vehicle to aid and abet a felon	Y	MV	
M86	Using Hand-held Mobile Telephone While Driving	Y	MV	No Statute # - only ordinances (was CELL prior to creation of ACD)
U08	Vehicular manslaughter	Y	Rev & Disq SR22	
D27I*	Violate Intermediate Permit Conditions (I2C)	Y	Y	
D27A*	Violate limited license conditions	N	N	
D27*	Violate limited license conditions (RC license)	Y	Susp	7-117e
D29A	Violate restriction on driver license	N	N	
D29	Violation of a restriction on the driver license	Y	MV	Can use for any restriction except on RC – then use D27
A41	Violation of Ignition Interlock Device	Y		
**U30	Violation resulting in accident	Y	MV	
U31	Violation resulting in fatal accident	Y	Rev & Poss Disq	(Any violation that results in fatality) (Serious traffic violation)

Canadian Provinces and U.S. Territories

Canada

What You Need to Know

Many Canadian Provinces refer to driving records as **driver abstracts**. The driving record for commercial drivers is often called a **National Safety Code (NSC) abstract**. Addresses and web links to each Province are provided below along with the available access methods and fees.

In general, a signed release is required to obtain a driving record or vehicle-related record, especially if the record contains personal information. Many Provinces license or authorize third parties to provide record access. For example, these authorized agencies are called Registries in Alberta. In Ontario, sanitized driving and vehicle records may be obtained from kiosks and mall kiosks.

With the exception of lien records, vehicle related record searches in Canada are not available to the public. If you need a record, we suggest to call one of the Province phone numbers below for details on access and restrictions. Be prepared to submit a signed release.

About Vehicle Liens

Check out the Personal Property Registry System found at https://pprs.acol.ca/lc/index.do. This private site is a good resource countrywide for checking liens on vehicles. You should NOT use Lien Check to search for personal property other than a motor vehicle, trailer, mobile home, airplane, boat or outboard motor. Registration required and fees are $5.00 to $10.00 per search.

All the fees shown below are in Canadian dollars.

Alberta

Motor Vehicle Division, Alberta Registries, 10365 97th Street, 3rd Fl. Edmonton, Alberta T5J 3W7, 780-427-7013, fax: 780-423-0285.
www.servicealberta.gov.ab.ca/Drivers_MotorVehicles.cfm
In Alberta, the release of personal driving and motor vehicle information is governed by specific privacy legislation, the Access to Motor Vehicle Information Regulation (AMVIR). All forms are found at www.servicealberta.gov.ab.ca/1229.cfm.
Alberta provides both a regular Driver Abstract (SDA) and a Commercial Driver Abstract (CDA). Both records may be accessed from authorized local Registry Offices located throughout the Province. The CDA adds information related to instances of Commercial Vehicle Safety Alliance (CVSA) inspections to information from an individual's driving record that is normally embedded in the Driver Abstract. However, unlike the Driver Abstract, the CDA does not include driver's height, weight, sex, and date of birth information.
Printed Driver abstracts can be issued for a 3, 5 or 10 year period. An electronic 3-year electronic report is available to the insurance industry through CGI ("Conseillers en gestion et informatique"). The fee for an Abstract of Driving Record is $15.00 plus a Registry service fee, which will vary from location to location. Processing time is same day. The name, DOB, license number, reason for request, and a signed release from subject are required for a search. Records may be searched by mail or in person. Many Registries offer payment by credit card. Visit the web page for a list of Registries as well as a request form.

British Columbia

Licensing: ICBC, Driver Testing & Vehicle Information, 151 West Esplanade, Rm 154, North Vancouver, B.C., Canada V7M 3H9, 250-978-8300, fax: 250-978-8001. www.icbc.com/licensing/
Records: ICBC Licensing Support Services Box 3750 910 Government Street Victoria, BC Canada V8W 3Y5, 250-414-7732, Fax: 250-978-8012
The cost of a record search is $5.00, but there is no fee if the request is made by the subject of the search. Processing time is 2 to 3 days. The name, DOB, license number, and a signed release from the subject are required for a search.
To request a record on a commercial driver use the *National Safety Code Abstract Form* found at www.icbc.com/driver-licensing/driving-record/nsc-abstract.pdf. The record reports five years of activity. Records may be ordered by phone (only by the subject), in-person or mail. The agency will return the record by fax or email the abstract when asked. Credit cards are accepted. Information is not available online at this time.

Manitoba

Manitoba Public Insurance, Driver and Vehicle Licensing, Driver Records and Suspensions, Box 6300, Winnipeg, MB R3C 4A4, 204-985-0980, driver fax: 204-945-5357, vehicle fax-204-945-7366. www.mpi.mb.ca/english/english.html

Non-commercial driver records may be ordered from this office or any Driver and Vehicle Licensing Service Outlet in the province. Traffic convictions and accidents are reported for five years, criminal code convictions for ten years. The commercial driver abstract is a five-year driver record used by commercial drivers for employment purposes. The record conayins the information found on the regular abstract plus all convictions related to commercial driving laws. These records are available by mail, or fax or in-person, but only at the address listed above. An abstract is issued only to the driver or to someone with written permission from the driver to obtain this information. Accident reports are also available form this agency.

The fee of any of the above records is $10.00. Prepayment is required, VISA, MasterCard, checks or money orders to be made out to Manitoba Public Insurance. The processing time is 1 to 2 days. The name, DOB, license # and a signed release from subject are required for a search. MasterCard and Visa accepted.

New Brunswick

New Brunswick Department of Public Safety, Licensing & Records Branch, Driver (or Vehicle) Records, PO Box 6000, Fredericton, New Brunswick E3B 5H1, 506-453-2410, fax-506-457-6913.

www2.gnb.ca/content/gnb/en/departments/public_safety/drivers_vehicles.html email: DPS-MSP.information@gnb.ca

Driver Record Abstract and Carrier (commercial driver) Abstract is $20.00, an Accident Report Search is $8.00. Fees exclude the harmonized sales tax (HST).

The license number or the name and date of birth of the driver are required for a search. Records may be requested by mail, in person or online and can be returned by fax. The processing time is same day.

Abstracts may be obtained in person at SNB (Service New Brunswick) offices located at various locations throughout the Province or by telephone using a credit card at SNB Teleservice at 1-888-762-8600. An online, interactive system is available from a designated vendor. VISA and MasterCard are accepted. Make checks or money orders payable to Minister of Finance.

Newfoundland

Motor Vehicle Registration, Driver Records Section, PO Box 8710, St Johns, Newfoundland A1B 4J5, 709-729-0331, driver fax: 709-729-7616, vehicle fax: 709 729-6955.

www.gs.gov.nl.ca/drivers/DriversandVehicles/driverlicensing/abstract.html Email: driverrecords@gov.nl.ca

The cost of a driving record search is $10.00. Any person requesting a driver's record for another individual must have written permission in order for the record to be processed. The record may be obtained from any Motor Registry Office in the province. The processing time is less than a week. The name and either DOB or license number, and the signature of the requester are required for a search. Records may be requested by mail, fax, or in-person. Check or money order made payable to the NewFoundland Exchequer. VISA, MasterCard and debit cards are accepted. Send Postal address or fax number (with area code) where you would like the driver's abstract returned.

Records returned by fax incur an additional $5.00 fee. Email questions to driverrecords@gov.nl.ca.

Northwest Territories

Department of Transportation, Motor Vehicle Division, Yellow Knife Registries, Box 1320, (5003 – 49th Street), Yellow Knife, NW Territories X1A 2L9, 867-873-7487 or 873-7406, fax: 867-669-9094.

www.dot.gov.nt.ca/_live/pages/wpPages/home.aspx

A driver record may be obtained from any issuing agency in the Northwest Territories. The driver record will list all violations, suspensions or prohibitions issued within a three-year period. The driver abstract request form is found at www.dot.gov.nt.ca/_live/documents/content/Driver%20Abstract%20Request%20-%20Client.pdf

The cost of a Drivers Abstract, Accident Report, or certified copy of any document or report is $17.25. If a search of records is required, there is an additional $17.85 fee imposed. Major credit and debit cards are accepted. The name, DOB, license number, and a signed release from subject are required for a search. Records may be searched by mail, fax or in person. Processing time is 1 to 2 days. Information is not available online at this time. Email inquires to rls.inquiries@gov.nt.ca.

All inquires relating to Driver Records, Driver Medicals, Program Policy, Research and Road Safety issues should be directed to Road Licensing and Safety Division HQ at 867-873-7406. Or send email to: DVLicensing@gov.nt.ca.

Nova Scotia

Services of Nova Scotia, Driver Records Section, PO Box 1652, Halifax, Nova Scotia B3J 2Z3, 902-424-5851, fax: 902-424-0720. www.gov.ns.ca/snsmr/rmv

www.gov.ns.ca/snsmr/rmv/licence/abstracts.asp

Driver Abstracts contain a five-year history of collision and MVA conviction events, Criminal Code Convictions, departmental postings and processes, and a ten-year history of alcohol related convictions and revocations

Note that any accident resulting in death or involving damages in excess of $1000.00 and / or personal injury are also posted to the driving record.

The fee for a driver abstract is $17.13; a certified letter regarding specific information on a driver abstract is $12.10. Make checks payable to Registry of Motor Vehicles. VISA, MasterCard and debit cards are accepted. Records may be searched by mail, in person, or fax (credit card required). Online is not available. The processing time is 1 to 2 weeks by mail, immediate if in person, and same day for fax. There are 20 service centers that process walk-in requests. The name, DOB, and a signed release from subject are required for a search, the license number is helpful. A request form is found online.

Accidents reports are available from this office for $10.00 per report. An online, interactive system is available from a designated vendor, fees involved. For more information about an account call 888-624-2265 or fax 902-422-1675.

Ontario

Ministry of Transportation, Licensing Administration Office, Data Access Unit, 2680 Keele, Building A, Room 16

(Vehicle Records at Special Inquiry Unit, Rm 178), Downsview, Ontario M3M 3E6, 416-235-2999, fax: 416-235-4414.

www.mto.gov.on.ca/english/dandv/driver/record.shtml

The fee for a driver's license history search for a 5-year statement of driving record is $12.00, $18.00 if certified. A 10-year or completed record is $48.00 or $54 if certified. A copy of an accident report is $12.00, add $6.00 for certification. A Driver Confirmation Letter is $6.00, if certified then $12.00. A Driver License Validation is $2.00. Records can be ordered by mail or at a ServiceOntario Centre. The name, DOB and license number are required for a search. The 5-year driver's record and the accident report can be ordered online. Credit cards and debit cards are accepted.

For a list of online services, prices and links to order forms see: www.mto.gov.on.ca/english/dandv/catalogue_certified.shtml.

Prince Edward Island

Highway Safety Division, Driving Records Section, 33 Riverside Dr, PO Box 2000, Charlottetown, Prince Edward Island C1A 7N8, 902-368-5210, fax: 902-368-5236. Registrar of Vehicles in same building at 902-368-5200, 902-368-6847, fax: 902-569-7560.

www.gov.pe.ca/tpw/index.php3?number=1002493&lang=E

The driving record abstract can be requested by mail or in-person but by only the license holder, as it contains personal information. However, the insurance industry can request and receive records electronically. The cost of a driver abstract is $25.00.. Processing time is 1 to 2 days for mail requests. Insurance company requests can be returned electronically. The name, DOB, license number, and a signed release from subject are required for a search.   Credit cards are accepted. See www.gov.pe.ca/photos/original/tpw_dr_abstract.pdf for a request form.

Quebec

Société de l'assurance automobile du Québec (SAAQ), Driving Records Division, 333 Boulevard Jean-LeSage, PO Box 19600, Quebec, QC G1K 8J6, 418-643-7620, 800-361-7620

Address vehicle inquiries to Service De la Diffusion et De la Liaison Avec les Corps Policiers.

www.saaq.gouv.qc.ca/en/index.php

Note that Commercial vehicles are refereed to as heavy vehicles.

Records may be ordered over the phone or at Service Centers throughout the province. The cost of a driving record or vehicle is $11.25, for an accident report is $14.50. An automated verification of a driver's license or the right to register a vehicle is $1.60. These fees reflect a recent fee increase in 2013.

Records may be searched by mail or in person or one may order their own record at no charge. This is available online at www.saaq.gouv.qc.ca/saaqclic/en/public/drivingrecord/index.php. Record is mailed to the address listed on the license. Processing time is 2 to 3 days. The full name, DOB, license number (or most recent vehicle registration certificate), requester's phone number, and a signed release from subject are required for a search.   A release form is found at www.saaq.gouv.qc.ca/en/e_forms/index.php.

Saskatchewan

Driver Abstracts, Saskatchewan Government Insurance, 2260 11th Ave, Regina, Saskatchewan S4P 2N7, 306-775-6198, 306-751-1249, fax: 306-775-6681

www.sgi.sk.ca/individuals/licensing/driverabstract.html

The cost of a driver abstract with a plate record is $10.00, Major credit cards are accepted. Records go back 5 years with an option to go back to 1995. Records may be ordered by mail, fax, in person, or online. The abstract will be processed within 24 hours. The name, DOB, license number, and a signed release from subject are required for a search. Forms are at www.sgi.sk.ca/individuals/licensing/driverabstract.html

One may request their own abstract online through MySGI, record is mailed to the address on file with SGI.

Yukon

Department of Motor Vehicles, Yukon Territory, PO Box 2703 (C-22), Whitehorse, Yukon Y1A 2C6. The physical address is 308 Steele Street, Lynn Building in Whitehorse. Main Floor 867-667-5315, fax: 867-393-6220.

www.hpw.gov.yk.ca/mv/index.html

The cost of a driving record or an accident report is $10.00, MasterCard and VISA are accepted. Records requests can be processed at this office or at one of the eleven Territorial Offices (shown on web). Processing time is normally same day. The name, DOB, license number, and a signed release from subject are required for a search. Records may be searched by mail or fax. Information is not available online at this time. Direct questions to motor.vehicles@gov.yk.ca.

Selected U.S. Territories

Guam

There are two resources. Traffic records should be obtained from the Traffic Violations Bureau. A license status and vehicle record data can be obtained from the Motor Vehicle Division.

Department of Revenue & Taxation, Vehicle Records, PO Box 23607, GMF, Barrigada, Guam 96921, 671-635-7652. https://www.guamtax.com/about/mvd.html

The Motor Vehicle Division is comprised of three branches: Motor Carrier, Vehicle Registration, and Driver's License Examination Branch.

A certification substantiating status and validity of the Guam driver's license is $10.00. A copy of registration is $10.00. A copy of ownership is $20.00. A certification substantiating the validity of the ownership of the vehicle is $10.00. Fees have not increased since 2007. Note that vehicle records are not considered public records. You must have a court order and then submit request on their form.

Superior Court, Traffic Violations Bureau, 120 W. O'Brien Hagatna, Guam 96910, 671 475-3274, fax- 671 472-2856 fax www.Justice.Gov.Gu/superior.html (click on Traffic Court)

Records are public. To request by mail, email or fax, submit name, DOB and SSN. Include a self-addressed, stamped envelope. Email to traffic@mail.justice.gov.gu. In person requests are permitted. There is a $4.00 fee to search records or files. A Superior Court Clearance fee is $10.00, a Traffic Clearance Fee is $5.00. Certifictaion is $4.00, or $6.00 for a microfilm document. Make checks payable to Superior Court of Guam. They will not fax back documents.

Puerto Rico

Department of Transportation, Services Division, DISCO/Driver Services, PO Box 41243, San Juan, PR 00940-1240. 787-722-2929, 787-296-0290, 787-296-0289, 787-296-0294, or 787-296-0291

www.dtop.gov.pr/servicios/index.asp

The request must include full name as it appears on the Puerto Rico driver's license, Social Security Number, date of birth, license number, reason for request, address where the record should be mailed, and a daytime telephone number. Requester should also include a photocopy of a valid photo identification, and a money order in the amount of $1.50 per record made out to: Secretary of Treasury. Personal checks are not acceptable. Turnaround time is 10-14 days. Note records are never faxed.

Virgin Islands

Driving Records: Criminal Justice Complex, Records Bureau St. Thomas, Virgin Islands 00802, 340-715-5523 or 5529 or 5594; in St. Croix 340-712-6044 or 6059 or 6024; in St. John 340-693-8880.
www.vipd.gov.vi/Departments/Office_of_the_Police_Commissioner/Records_Bureau.aspx

A Police Traffic Record Check search request form is at www.vipd.gov.vi/Forms.aspx. The fee is $7.00 in certified funds made payable to the Government of the Virgin Islands. If not the license holder, a record request must have a signed released. Submit a photocopy of the driver's license and a self-addressed, stamped envelope. Also the Records Bureau requests to send a copy of the license holder's passport and SSN. Turnaround time is normally 1-2 days.

Vehicle Records: Virgin Island Police Department, C/O Motor Vehicle Bureau, Sub Base, St. Thomas, Virgin Islands 00801, 340-774-5765.

They will verify information over the phone, including lien information. To do a record request, submit a license plate number or VIN, $20.00 in certified funds, and a self-addressed, stamped envelope. Make check payable to the Government of the Virgin Islands.

The AAMVA Code Dictionary (ACD)

The ACD Table: a Key Component to Understanding Driving Records

As shown in this book, each state has unique conviction reporting language and codes inherent to their motor vehicle statutes and specific violations. Per federal regulations, there are requirements and set procedures states must use when communicating (about commercial drivers, problem drivers, out-of-state actions, and license disqualifications) with one another or with a centralized index. The question is then — *How do states know what the conviction codes from other states mean and how do they translate this information into their own language and code set?*

The answer is the states utilize the AAMVA Code Dictionary (ACD) as a translation table. The primary function of the ACD is to enable the state to use the Commercial Driver's License Information System (CDLIS) to exchange convictions and withdrawals. Other applications, such as the Problem Driver Pointer System (PDPS), use these codes as well.

So in practice, the ACD System is used to exchange conviction and withdrawal information between the states' driver licensing authorities. As a result, states will often display an ACD on driving records to indicate out-of-state convictions. Some states even have incorporated the three-character ACD Codes within their own conviction and action tables as a primary code set. For example, the conviction table reflects the ACD Code system as their primary conviction code table. Therefore, the knowledge of what a specific ACD Code means can be a very helpful indication when deciphering the meaning of a conviction or withdrawal action.

An ACD code is a three-character code composed of an alphabetic character and two numeric characters (e.g., "S15" is the code for "Speeding 15 or more mph above the speed limit"). The type of conviction or reason for the withdrawal is qualified by the Conviction Offense Detail field; the Withdrawal Reason ACD Detail Field; and the CMV, Hazmat, and Citation CDL Holder Indicators.

The American Association of Motor Vehicle Administrators

The balance of this chapter is copyrighted material from *The AAMVA Code Dictionary (ACD Manual), Release 4.0.0.* Note that Release 4.0.0 contains 141 pages. The selected pages from this Release reproduced herein include the following sections:
- Portions of Section 1 Introduction
- Appendix A - ACD Codes, Descriptions, And Abbreviations, pages A1 through A11.

Users of driving records should expect there will be changes made to the ACD annually, including this coming year. The web version of this book will include these changes if and when the new version is officially released.

1. INTRODUCTION

The American Association of Motor Vehicle Administrators (AAMVA) is the publisher of this AAMVA Code Dictionary (ACD) (Release 4.0.0) Manual, which is a set of ACD Codes used nation-wide to identify either (1) the type of conviction or (2) the reason for a withdrawal in messages sent over the AAMVAnet, AAMVA's proprietary, secure computer network that connects to each State Driver Licensing Agency (SDLA) of the 50 U.S. States and the District of Columbia (the jurisdictions).

1.1 PURPOSE AND SCOPE OF THE ACD (RELEASE 4.0.0) MANUAL

The purpose of the ACD (Release 4.0.0) Manual is to provide information on the business rules regarding the use of the ACD code set in the Commercial Driver's License Information System (CDLIS) (a U.S.-wide system about CDL holders and their driver histories) and in the Problem Driver Pointer Systems (PDPS) (the U.S.-wide system identifying drivers who have been convicted and/or withdrawn for federally specified offenses).

The scope of this AAMVA Code Dictionary (ACD) (Release 4.0.0) Manual includes a listing of the ACD codes with corresponding descriptions and abbreviations, as approved by AAMVA and implemented by each State Driver Licensing Agency (SDLA) in the jurisdictions. The major changes in this ACD (Release 4.0.0) Manual are the following

- Additions
    - B57 (Driving a CMV without a CDL in the driver's possession) to satisfy the requirement in 49 CFR §383.51(c)(7); the B51 (Expired or no driver license) was incorrectly mapped to 49 CFR §383.51(c)(7) in Appendix C
    - M85 (Texting While Driving) to satisfy the requirement in 49 CFR §383.51(c)(9)
    - M86 (Using a Hand-held Mobile Telephone While Driving)
    - Usage rules for both the M85 (Texting While Driving) and M86 (Using a Hand-held Mobile Telephone While Driving) added to section 3.2.6.6
- Revisions
    - Added 'distracted' to the definitions of M80 (Inattentive/distracted, careless, or negligent driving) and M82 (Inattentive/distracted driving)
    - Removed guidance for applying penalties for B19 (Driving while out of service order is in effect and operating a vehicle designed to transport 16 or more passengers, including the driver and/or transporting hazardous materials that require a placard) and B27 (Driving while an out of service order is in effect (for violations not covered by B19) from section 3.2.6.1; reference to Appendix C
    - Consolidated Appendices D and E; the Federal Regulation(s) and Uniform Vehicle Code Model Law(s) were added to Appendix E; the ACD Detail field was removed from Appendix E (reference made in introductory comments to section 2.2); Appendix D is still present (with a note that the data is in Appendix E) rather than removing Appendix D and re-designating the remaining appendices.
    - Removed references to Appendix D from the Index; changes are not shown
    - Updated references to Appendix E in the Index; changes are not shown
    - Removed E06, E36, and E56 from Table 3
    - Added data retention requirements for the SOC and SOW for out-of-state driver convictions and withdrawals in section 3.2.5
    - Added new Appendix F to show examples of ACD Code usage; Glossary now Appendix G
- Clarifications
    - Added note in Appendix C for violations of Out-of-Service Orders to indicate the usage of the Hazmat Indicator and ACD code
    - In section 2.4, clarified that the CMV indicator is set to '1' ('Yes') if the vehicle meets the definition of a commercial motor vehicle in 49 CFR §383.5
- Updates
    - Makes references to the CDLIS System Specifications and State Procedures Manual generic (no release number) to preclude having to update the ACD Manual every time CDLIS documentation is released.
- Errata from previous release
    - Corrects mapping for A20 (Driving under the influence of alcohol or drugs) to 49 CFR §383.51(b)(1) and (2).
    - Corrects the omission of 'S06' (06-10 > Speed limit (detail optional)) from Table 2 in section 2.2
    - Corrects the information in Appendix C for violations of Out-of-Service Orders
    - Corrects the definition of the B19 throughout – '...operating a vehicle designed to transport 16 or more passengers...' vs. '...operating a vehicle transporting 16 or more passengers...'
    - Adds the reference to the FMCSRs for the U31 (Violation resulting in a fatal accident) in Appendix D

Changes incorporated in this document will be effective August 1, 2011.

This document includes an explanation of the ACD codes, rules for specifying the type of conviction or reason for the withdrawal, validation rules, use of specific ACD codes, and retention periods as well as a complete description of the ACD codes and a mapping to the federal regulations, the Uniform Vehicle Code (UVC), and the ANSI D-20 Codes to assist jurisdictions in mapping the ACD codes to their jurisdiction statutes.

If you have any questions about this document, please feel free to contact the AAMVA Operations Department via telephone (888-AAMVA80) or e-mail Operations Help Desk Mailbox helpdesk@aamva.org.

1.2 HISTORY OF THE ACD CODE SET

The Commercial Motor Vehicle Safety Act (CMVSA) of 1986 mandated that a driver who has been disqualified from operating a Commercial Motor Vehicle (CMV) by the State of Record (SOR) must not be able to obtain a Commercial Driver's License (CDL) in any other jurisdiction. The CMVSA also mandated the creation of the Commercial Driver's License Information System to enable an SOR to maintain and electronically report a complete driver history record of each CDL holder and to enable a State of Conviction (SOC) to electronically report a conviction of an out-of-state driver to the driver's SOR. In support of the CMVSA and CDLIS, AAMVA and the jurisdictions developed the American National Standards Institute (ANSI) D-20 Code set, which enables driver-licensing authorities to communicate commercial driver's convictions and withdrawals between jurisdictions. In 1996, because of identified inadequacies of the ANSI D-20 Code set and the long time-frames involved with addressing the inadequacies, AAMVA and the jurisdictions developed and implemented the ACD code set as a replacement for the ANSI D20 code set. The following table highlights the changes to the ACD code set with the release number and date.

Table 1. History of Changes to the ACD Code Set

Release Date Release	Number	Major Changes
April 1997	1.1.0	A few corrections and additions were made
January 2002	1.2.0	Added and revised a few codes to support the federal regulations requiring disqualifications for specified Railroad Highway-Grade Crossing (RRGC) violations, as mandated by the Interstate Commerce Commission Termination Act (ICCTA) of 1995
April 2005	2.1.0 (known as the "revised code set")	Removed ACD codes that did not map to traffic safety violations or federal mandates. The revised code set also included the changes required to implement the Motor Carrier Safety Improvement Act (MCSIA) of 1999 and the Driver License Agreement (DLA)
September 2007	2.2.0	Addressed jurisdictions' questions raised since the release of the ACD Manual (Release 2.1.0). This release incorporated the answers to over 30 Frequently Asked Questions (FAQs) which provided clarifications by FMCSA to federal regulations and AAMVA documents.
June 2008	3.0.0	Incorporated two new ACD codes (W45 [Withdrawal for driving a CMV while disqualified for previous violations in a CMV] and W72 [Suspended pending final disposition]), clarified the usage of the B20-B26 [Driving while license withdrawn, barred, *etc.*], provided a table of conviction ACD codes where the CMV indicator must be '1' with acceptable values for the HAZMAT indicator, added retention periods for three categories (Falsify, Imminent Hazard, and the USA PATRIOT Act), and eliminated some redundant material found in other documentation. Changes were effective November 10, 2008.
May 2009	3.1.0	Added five new codes • S14 [11-14 > Speed limit (detail optional)] • U27 [Vehicular feticide (1st degree)] • U28 [Vehicular feticide (2nd degree)] • W80 [Failed employer-directed drug test] • W81 [Refusal to submit to an employer-directed drug test]

		Revised the definition of four codes: • M80 [Inattentive, careless, or negligent driving] • N21 [FTY ROW at rotary/roundabout/circular intersection] • N61 [Driving wrong way at rotary/roundabout/circular intersection] • N83 [Improper start from parked position] Added various clarifications and corrected errata from previous releases Changes were effective November 9, 2009
June 2010	3.2.0	Added • A91 [Administrative Per Se for BAC at _ _ (detail field required)'to mirror the existing A11] • definition of a CDL holder Revised • definition of A11 [Driving under the influence of alcohol with BAC at _ _ (detail field required)] to indicate it is the exact BAC reported • definitions of alcohol-related codes A04 and A94 to include the specific BAC ranges
August	3.2.1	Clarification • Revised the previously-provided guidance on Admin Per Se convictions and withdrawals (those based solely on an administrative action) must be reported with the A90, A91, A94, and A98 codes; A04 – A26 must be used for convictions and withdrawals based on court-adjudicated offenses; further discussions with the ACD Working Group's Legal Services liaison revised this: Admin Per Se convictions and withdrawals (those based solely on an administrative action based on a breath, blood, or urine test) must be reported with the A90, A91, A94, and A98 codes; A04, A08, A10, and A11 must not be used for admin per se convictions and withdrawals; codes A12 – A26 can have whatever withdrawal basis is deemed correct by the SOW Corrected errata from previous releases

APPENDIX A - ACD CODES, DESCRIPTIONS, AND ABBREVIATIONS

Listed below are all the ACD codes used to communicate convictions and withdrawals over AAMVAnet. The list is in alphabetic order by ACD code and is grouped by category of violations and group of violations. Each ACD code is followed by its ACD description and abbreviation. The abbreviations are a short form of the description of the ACD codes. The abbreviations are not sent in any messages, but are used in manual tasks, such as maintaining the equivalency tables.

ALCOHOL AND DRUG (CONTROLLED SUBSTANCES) VIOLATIONS

This category includes the codes that begin with an "A". The codes in this category have been defined to permit jurisdictions to report convictions for violations of exceeding a specific Blood Alcohol Concentration (BAC) level (A04, A08, and A10), exceeding a BAC level identified in the conviction detail field (A11), the more general type of convictions (A12, A20-A26), and other alcohol or drug related convictions (A31-A98).

ACD	Description	Abbreviation
Driving Under the Influence over Specified BAC levels (BAC Group)		
A04	Driving under the influence of alcohol with BAC of at least .04 but not greater than .079	DUI04BACPLI
A08	Driving under the influence of alcohol with BAC at or over .08	DUI>08BACPLI
A10	Driving under the influence of alcohol with BAC at or over .10	DUI>10BACPLI
A11	Driving under the influence of alcohol with BAC at __ (detail field required)	DUI>BAC PLI:
A12	Refused to submit to test for alcohol - Implied Consent Law	REFUSED TEST
General Driving Under the Influence (DUI Group)		
A20	Driving under the influence of alcohol or drugs	DUI ALC/DRUG
A21	Driving under the influence of alcohol	DUI ALCOHOL*
A22	Driving under the influence of drugs	DUI OF DRUGS
A23	Driving under the influence of alcohol and drugs	DUI ALC&DRUG
A24	Driving under the influence of medication not intended to intoxicate	DUI MEDICATN
A25	Driving while impaired	DRV IMPAIRED
A26	Drinking alcohol while operating a vehicle	DRNK WH OPER
Possession Offenses (POS Group)		
A31	Illegal possession of alcohol	POSS ALCOHOL
A33	Illegal possession of drugs (controlled substances)	POSSESS DRUG
A35	Possession of open alcohol container	OPEN CONTAIN
Ignition Interlock Devices (IID Group)		
A41	Driver violation of ignition interlock or immobilization device	NTRLOCK VIOL
Transporting a Controlled Substance (TCS Group)		
A50	Motor vehicle used in the commission of a felony involving the manufacturing, distributing, or dispensing a controlled substance	VEH : CNTR SUB
Underage Drinking Group (UDG Group)		
A60	Underage Convicted of Drinking and Driving at .02 or higher BAC	UNAGE D*DCOV
A61	Underage Administrative Per Se - Drinking and Driving at .02 or higher BAC	UNAGE D*DADM
Administrative Per Se		
A90	Administrative Per Se for BAC at or over .10	DUI@10ADMIN*
A91	Administrative Per Se for BAC at __ (detail field required)	DUI@--ADMIN*
A94	Administrative Per Se for BAC of at least .04 but not greater than .079	DUI@04ADMIN*
A98	Administrative Per Se for BAC at or over .08	DUI@08ADMIN*

DUTIES FAILED - REQUIREMENTS NOT MET - IMPROPER BEHAVIOR

This category includes the codes that begin with a "B" or a "D".

Hit & Run; Behaviors after Accidents (HRB Group)

B01	Hit and run - failure to stop and render aid after accident	H&R AFTR ACC
B02	Hit and run - failure to stop and render aid after accident - Fatal accident	H&R: FAT ACC
B03	Hit and run - failure to stop and render aid after accident - Personal injury accident	H&R: INJ ACC
B04	Hit and run - failure to stop and render aid after accident - Property damage accident	H&R: PDO ACC
B05	Leaving accident scene before police arrive	LVSC AFT ACC
B06	Leaving accident scene before police arrive - Fatal accident	LVSC: FAT ACC
B07	Leaving accident scene before police arrive - Personal injury accident	LVSC: INJ ACC
B08	Leaving accident scene before police arrive - Property damage accident	LVSC: PDO ACC
B14	Failure to reveal identity after fatal or personal injury accident	FL RV ID ACC

Driving After Withdrawal (DAW Group)

B19	Driving while out of service order is in effect and operating a vehicle designed to transport 16 or more passengers, including the driver and/or transporting hazardous materials that require a placard.	D W LIC OOSL
B20	Driving while license withdrawn	D W LIC WITH
B21	Driving while license barred	D W LIC BARR
B22	Driving while license canceled	D W LIC CANC
B23	Driving while license denied	D W LIC DENI
B24	Driving while license disqualified	D W LIC DISQ
B25	Driving while license revoked	D W LIC REVK
B26	Driving while license suspended	D W LIC SUSP
B27	General driving while out of service order is in effect (for violations not covered by B19)	D W LIC OOSO

Driver License/Vehicle Reg. & Title, Miscellaneous Duties (DRM Group)

B41	Possess or provide counterfeit or altered driver license (includes DL, CDL, and Instruction Permit) or ID	ALT/CFT DLID
B51	Expired or no driver license (includes DL, CDL, and Instruction Permit)	EXP/NO DL/ID
B56	Driving a CMV without obtaining a CDL	CMV NO CDL**
B57	Driving a CMV without a CDL in the Driver's possession	CMV NO CDL P
B61	Failed to file accident report	FL FILE ACCR
B63	Failed to file future proof of financial responsibility	FL FILE FUTP
B64	Failed to file insurance certification	FL FILE INSR
B65	Failed to file medical certification/disability information	FL FILE MEDC
B74	Failed to show insurance certification	FL SHOW INS
B78	Failed to show non-commercial driver license (includes Instruction Permit)	FL SHOW ID
B91	Improper classification or endorsement on driver license (includes DL, CDL, and Instruction Permit)	IMP CLS/NDOR

Misrepresentations (MIS Group)

D02	Misrepresentation of identity or other facts on application for driver license (includes DL, CDL, and Instruction Permit)	MISREP ID DL
D06	Misrepresentation of identity or other facts to obtain alcohol	MISRP ID ALC
D07	Possess multiple driver licenses (includes DL, CDL, and Instruction Permit)	MULTIPLE DLS
D10	Manufacture or make false driver license (includes DL, CDL, and Instruction Permit)	MAKE FAKE DL
D16	Show or use improperly - Driver license (includes DL, CDL, and Instruction Permit)	USE IMP DLID
D27	Violate limited license conditions	VIO LTD LICN
D29	Violate restrictions of driver license (includes DL, CDL, and Instruction Permit)	VIO RESTRICT

Financial Responsibility and Insurance Other than Filing (FRI Group)

D35	Failure to comply with financial responsibility law	FINANCL RESP

D36	Failure to maintain required liability insurance	NO LIABL INS
D37	Failure to pay for damages or make installment payment	FTP DAM/INST
D38	Failure to post security or obtain release from liability	NO SECUR/REL
D39	Unsatisfied judgment	UNSATIS JUDG

Failure to Appear or Pay (FTAP Group)

D45	Failure to appear for trial or court appearance (detail sometimes required)	FTA: TRIL/CT
D51	Failure to make required payment of child support	FTP: CH SUPT
D53	Failure to make required payment of fine and costs (detail sometimes required)	FTP: FINE***
D56	Failure to answer a citation, pay fines, penalties and/or costs related to the original violation (detail sometimes required)	FTA: FOR ORG

Miscellaneous Duty Failure (MDF Group)

D70	Drivers view obstructed	VIEW OBSTRUC
D72	Inability to control vehicle	NO CONTR VEH
D74	Operating a motor vehicle improperly because of drowsiness	OPER: DROWSY
D75	Operating a motor vehicle improperly due to physical or mental disability	OPER W DISAB
D78	Perjury about the operation of a motor vehicle	PERJURY VEHL

EQUIPMENT/VEHICLES - REGULATIONS, DEFECTS, AND MISUSE

This category includes the codes that begin with an "E" or an "F".

Equipment Required by Law (RBL Group)

E01	Operating without equipment as required by law	OMIT EQUPMNT
E02	Operating without brakes as required by law	OMIT BRAKES*
E03	Operating without HAZMAT safety equipment as required by law	OMIT HZM SAF
E04	Operating without HAZMAT placards/markings as required by law	OMIT HZM MRK
E05	Operating without lights as required by law	OMIT LIGHTS*
E06	Operating without school bus equipment as required by law	OMIT S B EQP

Equipment Prohibited by Law (PBL Group)

E23	Use of radar or laser detector prohibited by law	PROH RADAR/L

Defective Equipment (DE Group)

E31	Defective brakes	DFCT BRAKES*
E33	Defective HAZMAT safety devices	DFCT HZM SAF
E34	Defective lights	DFCT LIGHTS*
E36	Defective school bus equipment	DFCT S B EQP
E37	Defective tires	DFCT TIRES**

Failure to Use Equipment (FTU Group)

E50	Failure to use equipment as required	NUSE EQUPMNT
E51	Failure to use brakes	NUSE BRAKES*
E53	Failure to use HAZMAT safety devices as required	NUSE HZM SAF
E54	Failure to use headlight dimmer as required	FT DIM LIGHT
E55	Failure to use lights as required	NUSE LIGHTS*
E56	Failure to use school bus safety equipment as required	NUSE S B EQP
E57	Failure to use snow tires or chains as required	NUSE SNO T/C

Improper Equipment Use (IEU Group)

E70	Equipment used improperly or obstructed	MPRP EQUPMNT
E71	Brakes used improperly	MPRP BRAKES*

Restraints and Protective Equipment (RPE Group)

F02	Child or youth restraint not used properly as required	C/Y NOT USED
F03	Motorcycle safety equipment not used properly as required	M/C EQ N USD

F04	Seat belt not used properly as required	S B NOT USED
F05	Carrying unsecured passengers in open area of vehicle	PASS N OPN V
F06	Improper operation of or riding on a motorcycle	IMP OP/RD MC

Stopping, Standing & Parking (SSP Group)

| F34 | Stopping, standing, or parking: obstructing or impeding traffic | OBSTR TRAFFC |

Miscellaneous Equipment Violations (MEV Group)

| F66 | Unsafe condition of vehicle (no specified component) | VEHIC UNSAFE |

MANEUVERS - ILLEGAL OR IMPROPER

This category includes the codes that begin with an "M" or an "N".

Failure to Obey (FTO Group)

M02	Failure to obey barrier	FTO BARRIER*
M03	Failure to obey construction or maintenance zone markers	FTO CNST/MNT
M04	Failure to obey flagger	FTO FLAGGER*
M05	Failure to obey lane markings or signal	FTO LANE MRK
M08	Failure to obey police or peace officer	FTO OFFICER*
M09	For all drivers, failure to obey railroad-highway grade crossing restrictions not specifically noted in other railroad-highway grade crossing related codes	FTO RR RESTR
M10	For all drivers, failure to obey a traffic control device or the directions of an enforcement official at a railroad-highway grade crossing.	FTO RR GAT/S
M11	Failure to obey restricted lane	FTO RST LANE
M12	Failure to obey safety zone	FTO SAF ZONE
M13	Failure to obey school crossing guard	FTO SCH XING
M14	Failure to obey sign or traffic control device	FTO SIGN/TCD
M15	Failure to obey stop sign	FTO STP SIGN
M16	Failure to obey traffic signal or light	FTO TRF SGNL
M17	Failure to obey traffic sign	FTO TRF SIGN
M18	Failure to obey warning light or flasher	FTO WARN LIT
M19	Failure to obey yield sign	FTO YLD SIGN
M20	For drivers who are not required to always stop, failure to slow down at a railroad-highway grade crossing and check that tracks are clear of approaching train.	FTO RR NSLOW
M21	For drivers who are not required to always stop, failure to stop before reaching tracks at a railroad-highway grade crossing when the tracks are not clear.	FTO RR NSTOP
M22	For drivers who are always required to stop, failure to stop as required before driving onto railroad-highway grade crossing.	FTO RR DRIVE
M23	For all drivers, failing to have sufficient space to drive completely through the railroad-highway grade crossing without stopping.	FTO RR SPACE
M24	For all drivers, failing to negotiate a railroad-highway grade crossing because of insufficient undercarriage clearance.	FTO RR CLRNC
M25	Failure to stop - basic rule at unsigned intersection or when entering roadway from private driveway, alley, etc.	FAIL TO STOP

Following Improperly (FOL Group)

M30	Following improperly	FOL IMPROPER
M31	Failure to leave sufficient distance for overtaking by other vehicles	NSF DIST PAS
M32	Following emergency vehicle unlawfully	FOL EMER VEH
M33	Following fire equipment unlawfully	FOL FIRE EQU
M34	Following too closely	FOL TOO CLOS

Improper Lane or Location (ILL Group)

M40	Improper lane or location	IMPROPR LOCA
M41	Failure to keep in proper lane	STRAY FRM LN
M42	Improper or erratic (unsafe) lane changes	IMPR LANE CH

M43	Ran off road	RAN OFF ROAD
M44	Improper lane or location - crossover	IMP LOC XOVR
M45	Improper lane or location - crosswalk	IMP LOC XWLK
M46	Improper lane or location - entrance/exit ramp or way	IMP LOC RAMP
M47	Improper lane or location - in bicycle lane	IMP LOC BIKE
M48	Improper lane or location - in occupied lane	IMP LOC OCCL
M49	Improper lane or location - in HOV or restricted lane	IMP LOC HOVL
M50	Improper lane or location - limited access highway	IMP LOC LTAC
M51	Improper lane or location - median	IMP LOC MEDN
M55	Improper lane or location - on rail or streetcar tracks	IMP LOC TRAK
M56	Improper lane or location - on fire hose	IMP LOC FHOS
M57	Improper lane or location - oncoming traffic lane	IMP LOC ONCM
M58	Improper lane or location - road shoulder, ditch or sidewalk	IMP LOC SHLD
M60	Improper lane or location - slower vehicle lane	IMP LOC SLOV
M61	Improper lane or location - straddling center line(s)	IMP LOC CNTR
M62	Improper lane or location - traveling in turn (or center) lane	IMP LOC TURN

Passing (PAS Group)

M70	Improper passing	IMPROPR PASS
M71	Passing in violation of posted sign or pavement marking	PAS PST SIGN
M72	Passing in violation of opposite directions restriction	PAS OP DIREC
M73	Passing on wrong side	PAS WRNG SID
M74	Passing on hill or curve	PASS HIL/CRV
M75	Passing school bus displaying warning not to pass	PASS SCH BUS
M76	Passing where prohibited	PASS WH PROH
M77	Passing with insufficient distance or visibility	PAS NSF DIST

Reckless, Careless, or Negligent Driving (RCN Group)

M80	Inattentive/distracted, careless, or negligent driving	IN/CAREL/NEG
M81	Careless driving	CARELESS DRI
M82	Inattentive/distracted driving	INATTENT DRI
M83	Negligent driving	NEGLIGENT DR
M84	Reckless driving	RECKLESS DRI
M85	Texting While Driving	TEXT WH DRIV
M86	Using a Hand-held Mobile Telephone While Driving	HHMT WH DRIV

Failure to Yield (FTY Group)

N01	Failure to yield right of way (FTY ROW)	FT YLD R O W
N02	FTY ROW to animal rider or animal-drawn vehicle	FY 2 AN/RIDR
N03	FTY ROW to cyclist	FY 2 CYCLIST
N04	FTY ROW to emergency vehicle (i.e. ambulance, fire equipment, police, etc.)	FY 2 EMR VEH
N05	FTY ROW to funeral procession, procession or parade	FY 2 FUNERAL
N06	FTY ROW to other vehicle	FY 2 OTH VEH
N07	FTY ROW to overtaking vehicle	FY 2 OVT VEH
N08	FTY ROW to pedestrian (includes handicapped or blind)	FY 2 PEDESTR
N09	FTY ROW to school bus	FY 2 SCH BUS
N20	FTY ROW at crosswalk	FTY ROW@XWLK
N21	FTY ROW at rotary/roundabout/circular intersection	FTY ROW@ROTR
N22	FTY ROW at stop sign	FTY ROW@STOP
N23	FTY ROW at traffic sign	FTY ROW@T SN
N24	FTY ROW at traffic signal	FTY ROW@T SG
N25	FTY ROW at unsigned intersection	FTY ROW@UNSN
N26	FTY ROW at yield sign	FTY ROW@YLDS
N30	FTY ROW when warning displayed on other vehicle	FTY ROWWWARN
N31	FTY ROW when turning	FTY ROWWTURN

Failure to Signal (FTS Group)

N40	Failure to use or improper signal	IMPROPER SIG
N41	Failure to cancel directional signals	FT CANC SGNL
N42	Failure to signal intention to pass	FTS: PASSING
N43	Failure to signal lane change or turn	FTS CHNG/TRN
N44	Giving wrong signal	WRONG SIGNAL

Improper Turns (IMT Group)

N50	Improper turn	IMPROPR TURN
N51	Improper method of turning	IMP TRN METH
N52	Improper position for turning	IMP TRN PSTN
N53	Making improper left turn	IMP LEFT TRN
N54	Making improper right turn	IMP RGHT TRN
N55	Making improper turn around (not U turn)	IM TRN ROUND
N56	Making improper U turn	IMPROP U TRN

Wrong Way or Side (WWS Group)

N60	Driving wrong way	DR WRONG WAY
N61	Driving wrong way at rotary/roundabout/circular intersection	WW AT ROTARY
N62	Driving wrong way on divided highway	WW ON DIV HW
N63	Driving wrong way on one way street or road	WW ON ONEWAY
N70	Driving on wrong side	DR WRONG SID
N71	Driving on wrong side of divided highway	WS ON DIV HW
N72	Driving on wrong side of undivided street or road	WS ON UNDIVD

Miscellaneous Maneuvers (MMV Group)

N80	Coasting (operating with gears disengaged)	COASTING ***
N82	Improper backing	IMPROP BACKN
N83	Improper start from parked position	IMPROP START
N84	Unsafe operation	UNSAFE OPERA

SPEEDING

This category includes the codes that begin with an "S". Speeding (S**) was made a separate category in order to provide a set of codes which would enable all jurisdictions to report speeding convictions with the level of detail which they possess. AAMVA recommends a jurisdiction should report speeding with the speed limit and actual speed, however, it is recognized that not all jurisdictions have this data available to them and codes have been provided below in 5 mph and 10 mph ranges with optional use of the conviction detail field to indicate the speed limit, if known. When available the speed limit and actual speed are held in the Conviction Offense Detail field.

Speeding Excess in miles per hour (SPE Group)

	(5-mile range increments)	
S01	01-05 > Speed limit (detail optional)	SP XS: 01-05
S06	06-10 > Speed limit (detail optional)	SP XS: 06-10
S14	11-14 > Speed limit (detail optional)	SP XS: 11-14
S15	Speeding 15 mph or more above speed limit (detail optional)	SP XS: 15&GR
S16	16-20 > Speed limit (detail optional)	SP XS: 16-20
S21	21-25 > Speed limit (detail optional)	SP XS: 21-25
S26	26-30 > Speed limit (detail optional)	SP XS: 26-30
S31	31-35 > Speed limit (detail optional)	SP XS: 31-35
S36	36-40 > Speed limit (detail optional)	SP XS: 36-40
S41	41+ > Speed limit (detail optional)	SP XS: 41&GR
	(10-mile range increments)	
S51	01-10 > Speed limit (detail optional)	S51 SP XS:
S71	21-30 > Speed limit (detail optional)	SP XS

S81	31-40 > Speed limit (detail optional)	SP XS
S91	41+ > Speed limit (detail optional)	SP XS
S92	Speeding - Speed limit and actual speed (detail required)	SPEED DTAIL

Speeding (SPD Group)

S93	Speeding	SPEEDING****
S94	*Prima Facie* speed violation or driving too fast for conditions	PRIMA FACIE*
S95	Speed contest (racing) on road open to traffic	RACE CONTEST
S96	Speed less than minimum	INSUFF SPEED
S97	Operating at erratic or suddenly changing speeds	ERRATC SPEED
S98	Speeding on freeway ("wasting fuel")	WASTING FUEL

UNCLASSIFIED OFFENSES

This category includes codes that begin with a "U".

Vehicle Use in Prohibited Actions (VUP group)

U01	Fleeing or evading police or roadblock	EVADING/FLEE
U02	Resisting arrest	RESIST ARRST
U03	Using a motor vehicle in connection with a felony (not traffic offense)	VEH IN FELNY
U04	Using a motor vehicle in connection with a misdemeanor (not traffic offense)	VEH IN MSDEM
U05	Using a motor vehicle to aid and abet a felon	AID./ABET FEL
U06	Vehicular assault	VEH ASSAULT*
U07	Vehicular homicide	VEH HOMICIDE
U08	Vehicular manslaughter	V MANSLAUGTR
U09	Negligent homicide while operating a CMV	CMV HOMICIDE
U10	Causing a fatality through the negligent operation of a CMV	CMV FATALITY
U21	Illegal operation of emergency vehicle	IL OP EMRG V
U27	Vehicular feticide (1st degree)	VEH FETIC 1
U28	Vehicular feticide (2nd degree)	VEH FETIC 2

Unspecified Violations Causing Accidents (VCA Group)

U31	Violation resulting in fatal accident	VIO: FAT ACC

WITHDRAWALS

This category includes those codes from the other categories when a single conviction results in a withdrawal and the codes that begin with a "W". The codes used in the Withdrawal Category require information besides the ACD code to fully describe the withdrawal. This information is held in the Withdrawal Type Detail field. A description of the Withdrawal Type Detail is given, following the ACD codes below.

A number of withdrawals are federally mandated and have minimum disqualification periods. See the Federally Mandated Disqualifications section of this document for details.

Withdrawal Reasons for Specific Convictions (WRS Group)

	Withdrawal resulting from one designated conviction	
W45	Withdrawal for driving a CMV while disqualified for previous violations in a CMV	PR DISQ CMV

Withdrawals by Jurisdiction Law (WJL Group)

W00	Withdrawal, Non-ACD violation	NON-ACD*****
W01	Accumulation of convictions (including point systems and/or being judged a habitual offender or violator)	ACCUM/HABVIO
W72	Suspended pending final disposition	PEND FINAL
W80	Failed employer-directed drug test	FAIL DRUG
W81	Refusal to submit to an employer-directed drug test	REFUSE DRUG

Ineligibility Withdrawals (WIW Group)

W09	Failure to surrender HAZMAT endorsement as required by the USA PATRIOT Act	FTS HME
W13	Parental consent withdrawn	PARNT CONSNT
W14	Physical or mental disability	PHYS DISABLE
W15	Physicians' or specialists' report recommended	PHYSICN REPT
W20	Unable to pass DL test(s) or meet qualifications	FAILED QUAL*

Accumulated Federally-Mandated Commercial Violations (WSC Group)

W30	Two convictions for serious violations within three years	ACCUM2VIOL**
W31	Three convictions for serious violations within three years	ACCUM3VIO1**
W40	The accumulation of two or more convictions for major offenses	ACCUM2 MAJOR
W41	An additional convictions for a major offense after reinstatement	ACCUM+ MAJOR
W50	The accumulation of two convictions for out-of-service order general violations (violations not covered by W51) within 10 years	ACCUM2 OOSO*
W51	The accumulation of two out-of-service order violations within 10 years where the second is while operating a vehicle designed to transport 16 or more passengers, including the driver and/or transporting hazardous materials that require a placard	ACCUM2 OOSOL
W52	The accumulation of three or more convictions for out-of-service order violations within 10 years	ACCUM3 OOSO*
W60	The accumulation of two convictions for RRGC violations within 3 years	RRGC 2 AVIOL
W61	The accumulation of three or more convictions for RRGC violations within 3 years	RRGC 3 AVIOL

Imminent Hazard (WIH Group)

W70	Imminent hazard	IMINT HAZAR

SMS Motor Carrier Data and Violation Tables

CSA and the Motor Carrier Safety Measurement System (SMS)

Late in 2010, the Federal Motor Carrier Safety Administration (FMCSA) launched a new Compliance, Safety Accountability Program (CSA) which included a new Motor Carrier Safety Measurement System (SMS). The initiative is designed to improve large truck and bus safety and to reduce crashes, injuries, and fatalities that are related to commercial motor vehicles. See http://ai.fmcsa.dot.gov/sms/Default.aspx.

Simply stated, the Safety Measurement System assigns **safety assessments** to motor carriers. SMS is an automated system that quantifies the on-road safety performance of motor carriers so that FMCSA can identify unsafe carriers, prioritize them for intervention, and monitor if a motor carrier's safety and compliance problem is improving.

The SMS has three major components:

1. Measurement
2. Evaluation
3. Intervention

The Federal Motor Carrier Safety Administration uses the SMS to:

- Identify motor carriers for interventions, such as warning letters, investigations, or roadside inspections.
- Determine the specific safety problems of the carrier to focus on during an intervention.
- Monitor motor carrier noncompliance issues over time.

The Significance of the Program

Motor Carriers are Assessed and Rated Based on Driver Assessments

What is notable about this new program is the calculation of the safety assessment of a motor carrier is based on driver assessments. The driver criteria include roadside inspection violations, accidents, and tickets.

Motor Carrier Assessments are Open to the Public

Also significant is the fact that the safety assessments are open to the public. Using the carrier's assigned USDOT Number or Motor Carrier Pin Number, one can look-up the SMS monthly results of a motor carrier at http://ai.fmcsa.dot.gov/sms/. The resulting report also provides a complete profile of the carrier including registration information such as the number of drivers, vehicle miles, if interstate, if hazmat, etc.

December 2012 Changes and Enhancements to SMS

FMCSA designed the SMS expecting that changes would be made as new data, and additional analysis became available. After a preview and comment period, in March 2012 the Agency announced in the Federal Register a proposed set of SMS modifications. After another preview and comments period, FMSCA announced a finalized package of SMS enhancements in December 2012.

The modifications updated the June 2012 version of the foundational document and reflects SMS Methodology version 3.0. It is expected that further changes and improvements to the SMS will take place periodically.

Per the FMSCA web page, the December 2012 enhancements include these features:

1. Strengthening the Vehicle Maintenance Behavior Analysis and Safety Improvement Category (BASIC) by incorporating cargo/load securement violations from the Cargo-Related BASIC.

2. Changing the Cargo-Related BASIC to the Hazardous Materials (HM) Compliance BASIC to better identify HM-related safety and compliance problems.

3. Better aligning the SMS with Intermodal Equipment Provider (IEP) regulations.

4. Aligning violations that are included in the SMS with Commercial Vehicle Safety Alliance (CVSA) inspection levels by eliminating vehicle violations derived from driver-only inspections and driver violations from vehicle-only inspections.

5. More accurately identifying carriers that transport significant quantities of HM.

6.   More accurately identifying carriers involved in transporting passengers.

7.   Modifying the SMS display to: 1). Change current terminology, "inconclusive" and "insufficient data," to fact-based descriptions. 2). Separate crashes with injuries from crashes with fatalities.

8.   Removing 1 to 5 mph speeding violations.

9.   Lowering the severity weight for speeding violations that do not designate the mph range above the speed limit.

10. Aligning the severity weight of paper and electronic logbook violations. With these changes, all violations related to not having a logbook, electronic or paper, now have a severity weight of 5.

11. Changing the name of the Fatigued Driving (Hours-of-Service (HOS)) BASIC to the HOS Compliance BASIC.

How the SMS Assessment Measurements Work

SMS uses a motor carrier's data from roadside inspections, including all safety-based violations, state-reported crashes, and the Federal motor carrier census to quantify performance in Behavior Analysis and Safety Improvement Categories (**BASICs**).

SMS is organized into seven BASICs based on statistical analysis on key components that quantify the associations between violations and crash risks.

The BASICs are defined as follows:

1.   **Unsafe Driving** — Operation of commercial motor vehicles (CMVs) by drivers in a dangerous or careless manner. Example Violations: Speeding, reckless driving, improper lane change, and inattention. (FMCSR Parts 392 and 397)

2.   **Hours-of-Service (HOS) Compliance** — Operation of CMVs by drivers who are ill, fatigued, or in noncompliance with the HOS regulations. This BASIC includes violations of regulations pertaining to logbooks as they relate to HOS requirements and the management of CMV driver fatigue. Example Violations: HOS, logbook, and operating a CMV while ill or fatigued. (FMCSR Parts 392 and 395)

3.   **Driver Fitness** — Operation of CMVs by drivers who are unfit to operate a CMV due to lack of training, experience, or medical qualifications. Example Violations: Failure to have a valid and appropriate commercial driver's license and being medically unqualified to operate a CMV. (FMCSR Parts 383 and 391)

4.   **Controlled Substances/Alcohol** — Operation of CMVs by drivers who are impaired due to alcohol, illegal drugs, and misuse of prescription or over-the-counter medications. Example Violations: Use or possession of controlled substances/alcohol. (FMCSR Parts 382 and 392)

5.   **Vehicle Maintenance** — Failure to properly maintain a CMV and prevent shifting loads. Example Violations: Brakes, lights, and other mechanical defects, improper load securement, and failure to make required repairs. (FMCSR Parts 392, 393, and 396)

6.   **Hazardous Materials (HM) Compliance** — Unsafe handling of hazardous materials (HM) on a CMV. Example violations: leaking containers, improper placarding, improperly packaged HM. (FMCSR Part 397 and U.S. DOT HM Regulations Parts 171, 172, 173, 177, 178, 179 & 180)

7.   **Crash Indicator** — Histories or patterns of high crash involvement, including frequency and severity. It is based on information from State-reported crashes.

The Calculation

There are four principal steps are used to assess a carrier's performance in each BASIC and for the Crash Indicator.

1.   First, relevant inspection, violation, and crash data obtained from MCMIS are attributed to a carrier to create a safety event history for the carrier.

2.   Then each carrier's violations are classified into a BASIC.

3.   Then each violation is time weighted, severity weighted, and normalized to form a quantifiable measure for a carrier in each BASIC. There is a violation table for each BASIC, except for the Crash Indictor.

4.   Finally, based on a comparison of each carrier's BASIC measure to other carriers with a similar number of safety events, a rank and percentile are assigned.

After a measurement is determined, the carrier is then placed in a peer group of other carriers with similar numbers of inspections. Percentiles from 0 to 100 are then determined by comparing the BASIC measurements of the carrier to the measurements of other carriers within the peer group. A percentile of 100 indicates the worst performance.

An excellent presentation of these calculations is found in the Safety Measurement System (SMS) Methodology a http://csa.fmcsa.dot.gov/documents/SMSMethodology.pdf.

The next portion of this chapter presents the December 2012 BASICs Violation Code Tables.

The CSA Violation Code Tables

Six tables are presented – one table per each of the first six BASICs ratings as listed above. There is no table for Crashes. Each table has five columns; two have six columns as indicated.

1. The **Section Column** is the corresponding regulatory part per the Code of Federal Regulations (www.fmcsa.dot.gov/rules-regulations/rules-regulations.htm).

2. The **Description Column** is the violation description shown on Driver/Vehicle Examination Report given to CMV driver after a roadside inspection.

3. The **Group Column** identifies the violation group to which each violation is assigned. Each violation within a violation group is assigned the same severity weight.

4. Each violation is assigned a **Severity Weight** that reflects its relevance to crash risk using a scale from 1 to 10, where 1 represents the lowest crash risk and 10 represents the highest crash risk relative to the other violations in the BASIC. Crash risk is defined as the risk of crashes occurring and the consequences of the crash after it occurs.

5. The **DSMS Column** in these tables specifies whether or not each violation is also included in the Driver Safety Measurement System (DSMS). Eventually drivers also will receive an individual rating score, but at this time only carriers receive this rating score.

Notes for all Tables

- The tables are sorted first by the Severity rating column and then by Description column.
- In cases where a violation results in an out-of-service order as defined in 49 CFR 390.5, an additional weight of 2 is added to arrive at a total severity weight for the violation.
- Violation severity weights reflect the relative importance of each violation solely within each BASIC Table. These weights cannot be compared or added meaningfully across the other BASICs Tables.

Table 1: Unsafe Driving Violations

Section	Description	Group	Severity	DSMS
177.804B	Failure to comply with 49 CFR 392.80 - Texting while Oper a CMV - Placardable HM	Texting	10	Y
177.804C	Fail to comply with 392.82 - Using Mobile Phone while Oper a CMV - HM	Phone Call	10	Y
390.17DT	Operating a CMV while texting	Texting	10	Y
392.2R	Reckless driving	Reckless Driving	10	Y
392.2-SLLS4	State/Local Laws - Speeding 15 or more miles per hour over the speed limit	Speeding 4	10	Y
392.2-SLLSWZ	State/Local Laws - Speeding work/construction zone	Speeding 4	10	Y
392.2-SLLT	State/Local Laws - Operating a CMV while texting	Texting	10	Y
392.80(a)	Driving a commercial motor vehicle while Texting	Texting	10	Y
392.82(a)(1)	Using a hand-held mobile telephone while operating a CMV	Phone Call	10	Y
392.82(a)(2)	Allowing or requiring driver to use a hand-held mobile tel while operating a CMV	Phone Call	10	Y
392.16	Failing to use seat belt while operating CMV	Seat Belt	7	Y
392.2-SLLS3	State/Local Laws - Speeding 11-14 miles per hour over the speed limit	Speeding 3	7	Y
392.10(a)(1)	Failing to stop at railroad crossing—bus	Dangerous Driving	5	Y
392.10(a)(2)	Failing to stop at railroad crossing—chlorine	Dangerous Driving	5	Y
392.10(a)(3)	Failing to stop at railroad crossing—placard	Dangerous Driving	5	Y
392.10(a)(4)	Failing to stop at railroad crossing—HM cargo	Dangerous Driving	5	Y
392.14	Failed to use caution for hazardous condition	Dangerous Driving	5	Y
392.2C	Failure to obey traffic control device	Dangerous Driving	5	Y
392.2FC	Following too close	Dangerous Driving	5	Y
392.2LC	Improper lane change	Dangerous Driving	5	Y
392.2P	Improper passing	Dangerous Driving	5	Y
392.2RR	Railroad Grade Crossing violation	Dangerous Driving	5	Y
392.2T	Improper turns	Dangerous Driving	5	Y
392.2Y	Failure to yield right of way	Dangerous Driving	5	Y
392.6	Scheduling run to necessitate speeding	Speeding Related	5	N
392.71(a)	Using or equipping a CMV with radar detector	Speeding Related	5	Y
392.2-SLLS2	State/Local Laws - Speeding 6-10 miles per hour over the speed limit	Speeding 2	4	Y
392.2DH	Headlamps - Failing to dim when required	Misc Violations	3	Y
392.2LV	Lane Restriction violation	Misc Violations	3	Y

Section	Description	Group	Severity	DSMS
177.800(d)	Unnecessary delay in HM transportation to destination	HM Related	1	Y
390.2	Failing to properly secure parked vehicle	Other Driver Violations	1	Y
392.22(a)	Failing to use hazard warning flashers	Other Driver Violations	1	Y
392.2PK	Unlawfully parking and/or leaving vehicle in the roadway	Other Driver Violations	1	Y
392.2S	Speeding	Speeding Related	1	Y
392.60(a)	Unauthorized passenger on board CMV	Other Driver Violations	1	Y
392.62	Unsafe bus operations	Other Driver Violations	1	Y
392.62(a)	Bus—Standees forward of the standee line	Other Driver Violations	1	Y
397.13	Smoking within 25 feet of HM vehicle	HM Related	1	Y
397.3	State/local laws ordinances regulations	HM Related	1	Y
398.4	Driving of vehicle—migrant workers	Other Driver Violations	1	Y

Table 2: Hours-of-Service (HOS) Compliance Violations

Section	Description	Group	Severity	DSMS
392.3	Operating a CMV while ill/fatigued	Jumping OOS/Driving Fatigued	10	Y
392.3-FPASS	Fatigue - Operate a passenger-carrying CMV while impaired by fatigue.	Jumping OOS/Driving Fatigued	10	Y
392.3-FPROP	Fatigue - Operate a property-carrying CMV while impaired by fatigue.	Jumping OOS/Driving Fatigued	10	Y
392.3-I	Illness - Operate a CMV while impaired by illness or other cause.	Jumping OOS/Driving Fatigued	10	Y
395.13(d)	Driving after being declared out-of-service	Jumping OOS/Driving Fatigued	10	Y
392.2H	State/Local Hours-of-Service (HOS)	Hours	7	Y
395.1(h)(1)	15, 20, 70/80 HOS violations (Alaska-Property)	Hours	7	Y
395.1(h)(2)	15, 20, 70/80 HOS violations (Alaska-Passenger)	Hours	7	Y
395.1(h)(3)	Adverse driving conditions violations (Alaska)	Hours	7	Y
395.1(o)	16 hour rule violation (Property)	Hours	7	Y
395.3(a)(1)	Requiring or permitting driver to drive more than 11 hours	Hours	7	Y
395.3(a)(2)	Requiring or permitting driver to drive after 14 hours on duty	Hours	7	Y
395.3(b)	60/70 - hour rule violation	Hours	7	Y
395.3(c)	34 -hour restart violation (Property)	Hours	7	Y
395.3A1R	11 hour rule violation (Property)	Hours	7	Y
395.3A2-PROP	Driving beyond 14 hour duty period (Property carrying vehicle)	Hours	7	Y
395.3A2R	14 hour rule violation (Property)	Hours	7	Y
395.3A3-PROP	Driving beyond 11 hour driving limit in a 14 hour period. (Property Carrying Vehicle)	Hours	7	Y
395.3B1-PROP	Driving after 60 hours on duty in a 7 day period. (Property carrying vehicle)	Hours	7	Y
395.3B2	Driving after 70 hours on duty in a 8 day period. (Property carrying vehicle)	Hours	7	Y
395.3BR	60/70 - hour rule violation (Property)	Hours	7	Y
395.5(a)(1)	10 - hour rule violation (Passenger)	Hours	7	Y
395.5(a)(2)	15 - hour rule violation (Passenger)	Hours	7	Y
395.5(b)	60/70 - hour rule violation (Passenger)	Hours	7	Y
395.5A1-PASS	Driving after 10 hour driving limit (Passenger carrying vehicle)	Hours	7	Y
395.5A2-PASS	Driving after 15 hours on duty (Passenger carrying vehicle)	Hours	7	Y
395.5B1-PASS	Driving after 60 hours on duty in a 7 day period. (Passenger carrying vehicle)	Hours	7	Y
395.5B2-PASS	Driving after 70 hours on duty in a 8 day period. (Passenger carrying vehicle)	Hours	7	Y
395.8(e)	False report of driver's record of duty status	False Log	7	Y
398.6	Violation of hours of service regulations—migrant workers	Hours	7	Y
395.15(b)	Onboard recording device information requirements not met	Incomplete/Wrong Log	5	Y
395.15(f)	Onboard recording device failure and driver failure to reconstruct duty status	Incomplete/Wrong Log	5	Y
395.8(a)	No driver's record of duty status	Incomplete/Wrong Log	5	Y
395.8(f)(1)	Driver's record of duty status not current	Incomplete/Wrong Log	5	Y
395.8(k)(2)	Driver failing to retain previous 7 days' logs	Incomplete/Wrong Log	5	Y

Section	Description	Group	Severity	DSMS
395.15(c)	Onboard recording device improper form and manner	Other Log/Form & Manner	1	Y
395.15(g)	On-board recording device information not available	EOBR Related	1	Y
395.15(i)(5)	Onboard recording device does not display required information	Other Log/Form & Manner	1	N
395.8	Log violation (general/form and manner)	Other Log/Form & Manner	1	Y

Table 3. Driver Fitness Violations

Section	Description	Group	Severity	DSMS
386.72(b)	Failing to comply with Imminent Hazard OOS Order	Fitness/ Jumping OOS	10	Y
383.93(b)(5)	No school bus endorsement on CDL	License-related: High	8	Y
383.93(b)(4)	No hazardous materials endorsement on CDL	License-related: High	8	Y
383.93(b)(3)	No tank vehicle endorsement on CDL	License-related: High	8	Y
383.23(a)(2)	Operating a CMV without a CDL	License-related: High	8	Y
383.23(c)(2)	Operating on learner's permit without valid driver's license	License-related: High	8	Y
383.93(b)(2)	No passenger vehicle endorsement on CDL	License-related: High	8	Y
383.23(c)(1)	Operating on learner's permit without CDL holder	License-related: High	8	Y
383.93(b)(1)	No double/triple trailer endorsement on CDL	License-related: High	8	Y
383.21	Operating a CMV with more than one driver's license	License-related: High	8	Y
383.21(a)	Operating a CMV with more than one driver's license†	License-related: High	8	Y
383.23(c)	Operating on learner's permit without CDL holder	License-related: High	8	Y
383.51(a)	Driving a CMV (CDL) while disqualified	License-related: High	8	Y
383.51A-SIN	Driving a CMV while CDL is suspended for a safety-related or unknown reason and in the state of driver's license issuance.	License-related: High	8	Y
383.91(a)	Operating a CMV with improper CDL group	License-related: High	8	Y
383.93B5LCDL	License (CDL) - Operating a school bus without a school bus endorsement as described in 383.93(b)(5)	License-related: High	8	Y
383.95(a)	Violating airbrake restriction	License-related: High	8	Y
391.11(b)(7)	Driver disqualified from operating CMV	License-related: High	8	Y
391.11(b)(5)	Driver lacking valid license for type vehicle being operated	License-related: High	8	Y
391.11	Unqualified driver	License-related: High	8	Y
391.11B5-DEN	Driver operating a CMV without proper endorsements or in violation of restrictions.	License-related: High	8	Y
391.11B5-DNL	Driver does not have a valid operator's license for the CMV being operated.	License-related: High	8	Y
391.15(a)	Driving a CMV while disqualified	License-related: High	8	Y
391.15A-SIN	Driving a CMV while disqualified. Suspended for safety-related or unknown reason and in the state of driver's license issuance.	License-related: High	8	Y
383.51A-NSIN	Driving a CMV while CDL is suspended for a non-safety-related reason and in the state of driver's license issuance.	License-related: Medium	5	Y
383.51A-SOUT	Driving a CMV while CDL is suspended for safety-related or unknown reason and outside the driver's license state of issuance.	License-related: Medium	5	Y
391.15A-NSIN	Driving a CMV while disqualified. Suspended for non-safety-related reason and in the state of driver's license issuance.	License-related: Medium	5	Y
391.15A-SOUT	Driving a CMV while disqualified. Suspended for a safety-related or unknown reason and outside the driver's license state of issuance.	License-related: Medium	5	Y
177.816	Driver training requirements	General Driver Qualification	4	N
391.11(b)(2)	Non-English speaking driver	General Driver Qualification	4	Y
391.11(b)(1)	Interstate driver under 21 years of age	General Driver Qualification	4	Y
391.11B2S	Driver must be able to understand highway traffic signs and signals in the English language	General Driver Qualification	4	Y
391.11(b)(4)	Driver lacking physical qualification(s)	Physical	2	Y
398.3(b)	Driver not physically qualified	Physical	2	Y
383.51A-NSOUT	Driving a CMV while CDL is suspended for a non-safety-related reason and outside the state of driver's license issuance.	License-related: Low	1	Y
398.3(b)(8)	No doctor's certificate in possession	Medical Certificate	1	Y

Section	Description	Group	Severity	DSMS
391.15A-NSOUT	Driving a CMV while disqualified. Suspended for a non-safety-related reason and outside the state of driver's license issuance.	License-related: Low	1	Y
391.41(a)	Driver not in possession of medical certificate	Medical Certificate	1	Y
391.41A-F	Operating a property-carrying vehicle without possessing a valid medical certificate.	Medical Certificate	1	Y
391.41A-FPC	Operating a property-carrying vehicle without possessing a valid medical certificate. Previously Cited	Medical Certificate	1	Y
391.41A-P	Operating a passenger-carrying vehicle without possessing a valid medical certificate.	Medical Certificate	1	Y
391.43(h)	Improper medical examiner's certificate form	Medical Certificate	1	Y
391.45(b)	Expired medical examiner's certificate	Medical Certificate	1	Y
391.49(j)	No valid medical waiver in driver's possession	Medical Certificate	1	Y

Table 4. Controlled Substances/Alcohol Violations

Section	Description	Group	Severity	DSMS
392.4(a)	Driver uses or is in possession of drugs	Drugs	10	Y
392.5(c)(2)	Violating OOS order pursuant to 392.5(a)/(b)	Alcohol Jumping OOS	10	Y
392.5(a)	Possession/use/under influence alcohol-4hrs prior to duty	Alcohol	5	Y

Table 5. Vehicle Maintenance Violations

Note:　The **Prior Sev** column indicates the previous Severity Rating when the violation was previously listed in the former (pre-December 2012) Cargo-Related BASIC

Section	Description	Group	Severity	Prior Sev	DSMS
392.63	Pushing/towing a loaded bus	Towing Loaded Bus	10		Y
396.9(c)(2)	Operating an OOS vehicle	Vehicle Jumping OOS	10		Y
393.75	Tires/tubes (general)	Tires	8		Y
393.75(a)	Flat tire or fabric exposed	Tires	8		Y
393.75(a)(1)	Tire — ply or belt material exposed	Tires	8		Y
393.75(a)(2)	Tire — tread and/or sidewall separation	Tires	8		Y
393.75(a)(3)	Tire — flat and/or audible air leak	Tires	8		Y
393.75(a)(4)	Tire — cut exposing ply and/or belt material	Tires	8		Y
393.75(b)	Tire — front tread depth less than 4/32 of inch	Tires	8		Y
393.75(c)	Tire — other tread depth less than 2/32 of inch	Tires	8		Y
393.75(d)	Tire — bus regrooved/recap on front wheel	Tires	8		Y
396.3A1T	Tires (general)	Tires	8		Y
393.100(b)	Leaking/spilling/blowing/falling cargo	Improper Load Securement	7	10	Y
393.102(c)	No equivalent means of securement	Improper Load Securement	7	10	Y
393.116(d)(1)	Short, over 1/3 length past structure	Improper Load Securement	7	10	Y
393.116(d)(2)	Short, insufficient/no tiedowns	Improper Load Securement	7	10	Y
393.116(d)(3)	Short, tiedowns improperly positioned	Improper Load Securement	7	10	Y
393.116(d)(4)	Short, no center stakes/high log not secured	Improper Load Securement	7	10	Y
393.116(e)	Short, length; improper securement	Improper Load Securement	7	10	Y
393.118(b)	Improper placement of bundles	Improper Load Securement	7	10	Y
393.120(b)(1)	Coil/vertical improper securement	Improper Load Securement	7	10	Y
393.120(b)(2)	Coils, rows, eyes vertical - improper securement	Improper Load Securement	7	10	Y
393.120(c)(1)	Coil/eye crosswise improper securement	Improper Load Securement	7	10	Y
393.120(c)(2)	X-pattern on coil(s) with eyes crosswise	Improper Load Securement	7	10	Y
393.120(d)(1)	Coil with eye lengthwise-improper securement	Improper Load Securement	7	10	Y
393.120(d)(4)	Coils, rows, eyes length - improper securement.	Improper Load Securement	7	10	Y
393.122(b)	Rolls vertical - improper securement	Improper Load Securement	7	10	Y
393.122(c)	Rolls vertical /split - improper securement	Improper Load Securement	7	10	Y
393.122(d)	Rolls vertical /stacked - improper securement	Improper Load Securement	7	10	Y
393.122(e)	Rolls crosswise - improper securement	Improper Load Securement	7	10	Y
393.122(f)	Rolls crosswise/stacked load - improperly secured	Improper Load Securement	7	10	Y
393.122(g)	Rolls length - improper securement	Improper Load Securement	7	10	Y
393.122(h)	Rolls lengthwise/stacked - improper securement	Improper Load Securement	7	10	Y
393.122(i)	Improper securement - rolls on flatbed/curtain-sided vehicle	Improper Load Securement	7	10	Y
393.124(c)	Improper blocking of concrete pipe	Improper Load Securement	7	10	Y
393.124(d)	Improper arrangement of concrete pipe	Improper Load Securement	7	10	Y
393.124(e)	Improper securement, up to 45 in. diameter	Improper Load Securement	7	10	Y

Section	Description	Group	Severity	Prior Sev	DSMS
393.124(f)	Improper securement, greater than 45 inch diameter	Improper Load Securement	7	10	Y
393.126(c)(2)	All corners of chassis not secured	Improper Load Securement	7	10	Y
393.126(c)(3)	Front and rear of container not secured independently	Improper Load Securement	7	10	Y
393.126(d)(1)	Empty container not properly positioned	Improper Load Securement	7	10	Y
393.126(d)(2)	Empty container, more than 5 foot overhang	Improper Load Securement	7	10	Y
393.126(d)(4)	Empty container - not properly secured	Improper Load Securement	7	10	Y
393.128(b)(1)	Vehicle not secured - front and rear	Improper Load Securement	7	10	Y
393.128(b)(2)	Tiedown(s) not affixed to mounting points.	Improper Load Securement	7	10	Y
393.128(b)(3)	Tiedown(s) not over/around wheels.	Improper Load Securement	7	10	Y
393.130(b)	Item not properly prepared for transport	Improper Load Securement	7	10	Y
393.130(c)	Improper restraint/securement of item	Improper Load Securement	7	10	Y
393.132(c)(5)	Insufficient means to retain loose parts	Improper Load Securement	7	10	Y
393.134(b)(2)	Container not secured to front of vehicle	Improper Load Securement	7	10	Y
393.134(b)(3)	Rear of container not properly secured	Improper Load Securement	7	10	Y
393.136(b)	Improper placement/positioning of boulder	Improper Load Securement	7	10	Y
393.136(c)(1)	Boulder not secured with chain	Improper Load Securement	7	10	Y
393.136(d)	Improper securement - cubic boulder	Improper Load Securement	7	10	Y
393.136(e)	Improper securement - non-cubic boulder with stable base	Improper Load Securement	7	10	Y
393.136(f)	Improper securement - non-cubic boulder with unstable base	Improper Load Securement	7	10	Y
393.207(a)	Axle positioning parts defective/missing	Suspension	7		Y
393.207(b)	Adjustable axle locking pin missing/disengaged	Suspension	7		Y
393.207(c)	Leaf spring assembly defective/missing	Suspension	7		Y
393.207(d)	Coil spring cracked and/or broken	Suspension	7		Y
393.207(e)	Torsion bar cracked and/or broken	Suspension	7		Y
393.207(f)	Air suspension pressure loss	Suspension	7		Y
393.207(g)	No/defective air suspension exhaust control	Suspension	7		N
392.33	Operating CMV with lamps/reflectors obscured	Lighting	6		Y
393.17	No/defective lamp/reflector-tow-away operation	Lighting	6		Y
393.17(a)	No/defective lamps-towing unit-tow-away operation	Lighting	6		Y
393.17(b)	No/defective tow-away lamps on rear unit	Lighting	6		Y
393.19	Inoperative/defective hazard warning lamp	Lighting	6		Y
393.209(a)	Steering wheel not secured/broken	Steering Mechanism	6		Y
393.209(b)	Excessive steering wheel lash	Steering Mechanism	6		Y
393.209(c)	Loose steering column	Steering Mechanism	6		Y
393.209(d)	Steering system components worn/welded/missing	Steering Mechanism	6		Y
393.209(e)	Power steering violations	Steering Mechanism	6		Y
393.24(a)	Noncompliance with headlamp requirements	Lighting	6		Y
393.24(b)	Noncompliant fog/driving lamps	Lighting	6		Y
393.24(c)	Improper headlamp mounting	Lighting	6		N
393.24(d)	Improper head / auxiliary / fog lamp aiming	Lighting	6		Y
393.24BR	Noncompliant fog or driving lamps	Lighting	6		N
393.25(a)	Improper lamp mounting	Lighting	6		Y
393.25(b)	Lamps are not visible as required	Lighting	6		Y
393.25(e)	Lamp not steady burning	Lighting	6		Y
393.25(f)	Stop lamp violations	Lighting	6		Y
393.9H	Inoperative head lamps	Lighting	6		Y
393.9T	Inoperative tail lamp	Lighting	6		Y
393.9TS	Inoperative turn signal	Lighting	6		Y
385.103(c)	Fail to display current CVSA decal - Provisional Authority	Inspection Reports	4		N
392.7	No pre-trip inspection	Inspection Reports	4		Y
392.7(a)	Driver failing to conduct pre-trip inspection	Inspection Reports	4		Y
392.7(b)	Driver failing to conduct a pre-trip inspection of intermodal equipment	Inspection Reports	4		Y
393.40	Inadequate brake system on a CMV	Brakes, All Others	4		Y
393.41	No or defective parking brake system on CMV	Brakes, All Others	4		Y
393.42	No brakes as required	Brakes, All Others	4		Y
393.42A-BM	Brake - Missing required brake.	Brakes, All Others	4		Y
393.42A-BMAW	Brake - All wheels not equipped with brakes as required.	Brakes, All Others	4		Y
393.42A-BM-TSA	Brake - Missing on a trailer steering axle.	Brakes, All Others	4		Y

Section	Description	Group	Severity	Prior Sev	DSMS
393.43	No/improper breakaway or emergency braking	Brakes, All Others	4		Y
393.43(a)	No/improper tractor protection valve	Brakes, All Others	4		Y
393.43(d)	No or defective automatic trailer brake	Brakes, All Others	4		Y
393.44	No/defective bus front brake line protection	Brakes, All Others	4		Y
393.45	Brake tubing and hose adequacy	Brakes, All Others	4		N
393.45(a)(4)	Failing to secure brake hose/tubing against mechanical damage	Brakes, All Others	4		N
393.45(b)(2)	Failing to secure brake hose/tubing against mechanical damage	Brakes, All Others	4		Y
393.45(b)(3)	Failing to secure brake hose/tubing against high temperatures	Brakes, All Others	4		N
393.45(d)	Brake connections with leaks/constrictions	Brakes, All Others	4		N
393.45B2PC	Brake Hose or Tubing Chafing and/or Kinking - Connection to Power Unit	Brakes, All Others	4		Y
393.45B2UV	Brake Hose or Tubing Chafing and/or Kinking Under Vehicle	Brakes, All Others	4		N
393.45DCPC	Brake Connections with Constrictions - Connection to Power Unit	Brakes, All Others	4		Y
393.45DCUV	Brake Connections with Constrictions Under Vehicle	Brakes, All Others	4		N
393.45DLPC	Brake Connections with Leaks - Connection to Power Unit	Brakes, All Others	4		Y
393.45DLUV	Brake Connections with Leaks Under Vehicle	Brakes, All Others	4		Y
393.45PC	Brake Tubing and Hose Adequacy - Connections to Power Unit	Brakes, All Others	4		N
393.45UV	Brake Tubing and Hose Adequacy Under Vehicle	Brakes, All Others	4		N
393.47	Inadequate/contaminated brake linings	Brakes, All Others	4		Y
393.47(a)	Inadequate brakes for safe stopping	Brakes, All Others	4		Y
393.47(b)	Mismatched brake chambers on same axle	Brakes, All Others	4		Y
393.47(c)	Mismatched slack adjuster effective length	Brakes, All Others	4		Y
393.47(d)	Insufficient brake linings	Brakes, All Others	4		Y
393.47(e)	Clamp/Roto-Chamber type brake(s) out of adjustment	Brakes Out of Adjustment	4		Y
393.47(f)	Wedge type brake(s) out of adjustment	Brakes Out of Adjustment	4		Y
393.47(g)	Insufficient drum/rotor thickness	Brakes, All Others	4		Y
393.48(a)	Inoperative/defective brakes	Brakes, All Others	4		Y
393.48(b)(1)	Defective brake limiting device	Brakes, All Others	4		Y
393.48A-BCM	Brakes - Hydraulic Brake Caliper movement exceeds 1/8" (0.125") (3.175 mm)	Brakes, All Others	4		N
393.48A-BMBC	Brakes - Missing or Broken Components	Brakes, All Others	4		N
393.48A-BRMMC	Brakes - Rotor (disc) metal-to-metal contact	Brakes, All Others	4		N
393.48A-BSRFS	Brakes - Severe rusting of brake rotor (disc)	Brakes, All Others	4		N
393.50	Inadequate reservoir for air/vacuum brakes	Brakes, All Others	4		N
393.50(a)	Failing to have sufficient air/vacuum reserve	Brakes, All Others	4		N
393.50(b)	Failing to equip vehicle - prevent reservoir air/vacuum leak	Brakes, All Others	4		N
393.50(c)	No means to ensure operable check valve	Brakes, All Others	4		N
393.50(d)	No or defective air reservoir drain valve	Brakes, All Others	4		Y
393.51	No or defective brake warning device	Brakes, All Others	4		Y
393.52(a)(1)	Insufficient braking force as percent of GVW or GCW	Brakes, All Others	4		Y
393.53(a)	Automatic brake adjuster CMV manufactured on or after 10/20/1993 - hydraulic brake	Brakes, All Others	4		Y
393.53(b)	Automatic brake adjuster CMV manufactured on or after 10/20/1994 - air brake	Brakes, All Others	4		Y
393.53(c)	Brake adjustment indicator CMV manufactured on or after 10/20/1994 - external automatic adjustment	Brakes, All Others	4		Y
393.55(a)	ABS - all CMVs manufactured on or after 3/1/1999 with hydraulic brakes	Brakes, All Others	4		N
393.55(b)	ABS - malfunction indicators for hydraulic brake system	Brakes, All Others	4		N
393.55(c)(1)	ABS - all tractors manufactured on or after 3/1/1997 air brake system	Brakes, All Others	4		N
393.55(c)(2)	ABS - all other CMVs manufactured on or after 3/1/1998 air brake system	Brakes, All Others	4		N

Section	Description	Group	Severity	Prior Sev	DSMS
393.55(d)(1)	ABS - malfunctioning circuit/signal - truck tractor manufactured on or after 3/1/1997, single-unit CMV manufactured on or after 3/1/1998	Brakes, All Others	4		N
393.55(d)(2)	ABS - malfunctioning indicator to cab of towing CMV manufactured on or after 3/1/2001	Brakes, All Others	4		N
393.55(d)(3)	No or Defective ABS Malfunction Indicator for towed vehicles on vehicles manufactured after February 2001	Brakes, All Others	4		N
393.55(e)	ABS - malfunctioning lamps towed CMV manufactured on or after 3/1/1998, manufactured before 3/1/2009	Brakes, All Others	4		Y
396.1	Must have knowledge of and comply with regulations	Inspection Reports	4		Y
396.11	No or inadequate driver vehicle inspection report	Inspection Reports	4		Y
396.13(c)	No reviewing driver's signature on Driver Vehicle Inspection Report (DVIR)	Inspection Reports	4		Y
396.17(c)	Operating a CMV without periodic inspection	Inspection Reports	4		N
396.3A1B	Brakes (general)	Brakes, All Others	4		Y
396.3A1BA	Brake out of adjustment	Brakes Out of Adjustment	4		N
396.3A1BC	Brake-air compressor violation	Brakes, All Others	4		N
396.3A1BD	Brake-defective brake drum	Brakes, All Others	4		N
396.3A1BL	Brake-reserve system pressure loss	Brakes, All Others	4		N
396.9(d)(2)	Failure to correct defects noted on inspection report	Inspection Reports	4		N
398.7	Inspect/maintain motor vehicle - migrant workers	Inspection Reports	4		N
393.102(a)	Improper securement system (tiedown assemblies)	Tiedown	3	8	Y
393.102(a)(1)	Insufficient means to prevent forward movement	Failure to Prevent Movement	3	8	Y
393.102(a)(1)(i)	Insufficient means to prevent forward movement	Failure to Prevent Movement	3	8	Y
393.102(a)(1)(ii)	Insufficient means to prevent rearward movement	Failure to Prevent Movement	3	8	Y
393.102(a)(1)(iii)	Insufficient means to prevent lateral movement	Failure to Prevent Movement	3	8	Y
393.102(a)(2)	Tiedown assembly with inadequate working load limit	Tiedown	3	8	Y
393.102(a)(3)	Insufficient means to prevent lateral movement	Failure to Prevent Movement	3	8	Y
393.102(b)	Insufficient means to prevent vertical movement	Failure to Prevent Movement	3	8	Y
393.104(f)(1)	Knotted tiedown	Tiedown	3	8	Y
393.104(f)(2)	Use of tiedown with improper repair.	Tiedown	3	8	Y
393.104(f)(3)	Loose/unfastened tiedown.	Tiedown	3	8	Y
393.104(f)(4)	No edge protection for tiedowns	Tiedown	3	8	Y
393.104(f)(5)	No edge protection for tiedowns	Tiedown	3	8	Y
393.104F4R	No edge protection for tiedowns	Tiedown	3	8	Y
393.106(b)	Cargo not immobilized or secured	Failure to Prevent Movement	3	8	Y
393.106(c)(1)	No means to prevent cargo from rolling	Failure to Prevent Movement	3	8	Y
393.106(c)(2)	Cargo without direct contact/prevention from shifting	Failure to Prevent Movement	3	8	Y
393.106(d)	Insufficient aggregate working load limit	Tiedown	3	8	Y
393.11	No/defective lighting devices/reflective devices/projected	Reflective Sheeting	3		Y
393.110(b)	Insufficient tiedowns; without headerboard/blocking	Tiedown	3	8	Y
393.110(c)	Insufficient tiedowns; with headerboard/blocking	Tiedown	3	8	Y
393.110(d)	Large/odd-shaped cargo not adequately secured	Failure to Prevent Movement	3	8	Y
393.118(d)	Insufficient protection against lateral movement	Failure to Prevent Movement	3	8	Y
393.118(d)(3)	Insufficient/improper arrangement of tiedowns	Tiedown	3	8	Y
393.11LR	Lower retroreflective sheeting/reflex reflectors - Trailer manufactured on or after 12/1/1993	Reflective Sheeting	3		Y
393.11N	No retroreflective sheeting/reflex reflectors - Trailer manufactured on or after 12/1/1993	Reflective Sheeting	3		Y
393.11RT	Retroreflective sheeting not affixed as required - Trailer manufactured on or after 12/1/1993	Reflective Sheeting	3		Y
393.11S	No side retroreflective sheeting/reflex reflectors - Trailer manufactured on or after 12/1/1993	Reflective Sheeting	3		Y
393.11TL	No retro reflective sheeting or reflex reflectors on mud flaps - Truck Tractor manufactured on or after 7/1/1997	Reflective Sheeting	3		Y
93.11TT	No retroreflective sheeting/reflex reflectors - Truck Tractor manufactured on or after 7/1/1997	Reflective Sheeting	3		Y

Section	Description	Group	Severity	Prior Sev	DSMS
393.11TU	No upper body corners retroreflective sheeting/reflex reflectors - Truck Tractor manufactured on or after 7/1/1997	Reflective Sheeting	3		Y
393.11UR	No upper reflex reflectors retroreflective sheeting/reflex reflectors - Trailer manufactured on or after 12/1/1993	Reflective Sheeting	3		Y
393.120(e)	No protection against shifting/tipping	Failure to Prevent Movement	3	8	Y
393.124(b)	Insufficient working load limit - concrete pipes	Tiedown	3	8	Y
393.13(a)	Retroreflective tape not affixed as required for Trailers manufactured after 12/1/1993	Reflective Sheeting	3		Y
393.13(b)	No retroreflective sheeting or reflex reflective material as required for vehicles manufactured on or after 12/1/1993	Reflective Sheeting	3		Y
393.13(c)(1)	No side retroreflective sheeting or reflex reflective material as required for vehicles manufactored manufactured before 12/1/1993	Reflective Sheeting	3		Y
393.13(c)(2)	No lower rear retroreflective sheeting or reflex reflective material as required for vehicles manufactured before 12/1/1993	Reflective Sheeting	3		Y
393.13(c)(3)	No upper rear retroreflective sheeting or reflex reflective material as required for vehicles manufactured before 12/1/1993	Reflective Sheeting	3		Y
393.13(d)(1)	Improper side placement of retroreflective sheeting or reflex reflective material as required for vehicles manufactured on or after 12/1/1993	Reflective Sheeting	3		Y
393.13(d)(2)	Improper lower rear placement of retroreflective sheeting or reflex reflective material requirements for vehicles manufactured before 12/1/1993	Reflective Sheeting	3		Y
393.13(d)(3)	Upper rear retroreflective sheeting or reflex reflective material as required for vehicles manufactured on or after 12/1/1993	Reflective Sheeting	3		Y
393.132(c)	Insufficient tiedowns per stack cars	Tiedown	3	8	Y
393.134(b)(1)	No blocking against forward movement	Failure to Prevent Movement	3	8	Y
393.26	Requirements for reflectors	Reflective Sheeting	3		Y
393.28	Improper or no wiring protection as required	Other Vehicle Defect	3		Y
393.30	Improper battery installation	Other Vehicle Defect	3		Y
393.68	Compressed natural gas (CNG) fuel container does not conform to regulations	Other Vehicle Defect	3		Y
393.70	Fifth wheel	Coupling Devices	3		N
393.70(a)	Defective coupling device — improper tracking	Coupling Devices	3		N
393.70(b)	Defective/improper fifth wheel assemblies	Coupling Devices	3		Y
393.70(b)(2)	Defective fifth wheel locking mechanism	Coupling Devices	3		Y
393.70(c)	Defective coupling devices for full trailer	Coupling Devices	3		Y
393.70(d)	No/improper safety chains/cables for full trailer	Coupling Devices	3		Y
393.70(d)(8)	Improper safety chain attachment	Coupling Devices	3		Y
393.70B1II	Defective / Improper fifth wheel assembly upper half	Coupling Devices	3		Y
393.71	Improper coupling driveaway/tow-away operation	Coupling Devices	3		Y
393.71(g)	Prohibited towing connection / device	Coupling Devices	3		Y
393.71(h)	Towbar requirement violations	Coupling Devices	3		Y
393.71(h)(10)	No/improper safety chains/cables for towbar	Coupling Devices	3		Y
393.75(e)	Tire — regrooved on front wheel of truck/truck-tractor	Tire vs. Load	3		Y
393.75(f)	Tire — load weight rating/under inflated	Tire vs. Load	3		Y
393.75(f)(1)	Weight carried exceeds tire load limit	Tire vs. Load	3		Y
393.75(f)(2)	Tire underinflated	Tire vs. Load	3		Y
393.75(h)	Tire underinflated	Tire vs. Load	3		Y
393.76	Sleeper berth requirement violations	Other Vehicle Defect	3		Y
393.77	Defective and/or prohibited heaters	Other Vehicle Defect	3		Y
393.77(b)(11)	Bus heater fuel tank location	Other Vehicle Defect	3		Y
393.77(b)(5)	Protection of operating controls from tampering	Other Vehicle Defect	3		Y
393.80	Failing to equip vehicle with two rear vision mirrors	Other Vehicle Defect	3		Y
393.81	Horn inoperative	Other Vehicle Defect	3		Y
393.82	Speedometer inoperative / inadequate	Other Vehicle Defect	3		Y
396.5	Excessive oil leaks	Other Vehicle Defect	3		N

Section	Description	Group	Severity	Prior Sev	DSMS
396.5(a)	Failing to ensure that vehicle is properly lubricated	Other Vehicle Defect	3		N
396.5(b)	Oil and/or grease leak	Other Vehicle Defect	3		N
396.7	Unsafe operations forbidden	Other Vehicle Defect	3		Y
398.5	Parts/access - migrant workers	Other Vehicle Defect	3		Y
392.22(b)	Failing/improper placement of warning devices	Cab, Body, Frame	2		Y
392.8	Failing to inspect/use emergency equipment	Emergency Equipment	2		Y
393.201(a)	Frame cracked / loose / sagging / broken	Cab, Body, Frame	2		Y
393.201(b)	Bolts securing cab broken/loose/missing	Cab, Body, Frame	2		N
393.201(c)	Frame rail flange improperly bent/cut/notched	Cab, Body, Frame	2		N
393.201(d)	Frame accessories improperly attached	Cab, Body, Frame	2		N
393.201(e)	Prohibited holes drilled in frame rail flange	Cab, Body, Frame	2		N
393.203	Cab/body parts requirements violations	Cab, Body, Frame	2		Y
393.203(a)	Cab door missing/broken	Cab, Body, Frame	2		Y
393.203(b)	Cab/body improperly secured to frame	Cab, Body, Frame	2		Y
393.203(c)	Hood not securely fastened	Cab, Body, Frame	2		Y
393.203(d)	Cab seats not securely mounted	Cab, Body, Frame	2		Y
393.203(e)	Cab front bumper missing/ unsecured/protruding	Cab, Body, Frame	2		Y
393.205(a)	Wheel/rim cracked or broken	Wheels, Studs, Clamps, Etc.	2		Y
393.205(b)	Stud/bolt holes elongated on wheels	Wheels, Studs, Clamps, Etc.	2		Y
393.205(c)	Wheel fasteners loose and/or missing	Wheels, Studs, Clamps, Etc.	2		Y
393.23	Required lamp not powered by vehicle electricity	Clearance Identification Lamps/Other	2		Y
393.84	Inadequate floor condition	Cab, Body, Frame	2		Y
393.86	No or improper rearend protection	Cab, Body, Frame	2		Y
393.86(a)(1)	Rear impact guards - all trailers/semitrailers manufactured on or after 1/26/98	Cab, Body, Frame	2		N
393.86(a)(2)	Impact guard width - all trailers/semitrailers manufactured on or after 1/26/98	Cab, Body, Frame	2		N
393.86(a)(3)	Impact guard height - all trailers/semitrailers manufactured on or after 1/26/98	Cab, Body, Frame	2		N
393.86(a)(4)	Impact guard rear - all trailers/semitrailers manufactured on or after 1/26/98	Cab, Body, Frame	2		N
393.86(a)(5)	Cross-sectional vertical height - all trailers/semitrailers manufactured on or after 1/26/98	Cab, Body, Frame	2		N
393.86(b)(1)	Rear Impact Guards - motor vehicles manufactured after 12/31/52, see exceptions	Cab, Body, Frame	2		Y
393.88	Improperly located television receiver	Cab, Body, Frame	2		Y
393.89	Bus driveshaft not properly protected	Cab, Body, Frame	2		Y
393.9	Inoperative required lamps	Clearance Identification Lamps/Other	2		Y
393.9(a)	Inoperative required lamps	Clearance Identification Lamps/Other	2		Y
393.90	Bus - no or obscure standee line	Cab, Body, Frame	2		Y
393.91	Bus - improper aisle seats	Cab, Body, Frame	2		Y
393.93(a)	Bus - not equipped with seatbelt	Cab, Body, Frame	2		Y
393.93(a)(3)	Seats not secured in conformance with FMVSS	Cab, Body, Frame	2		N
393.93(b)	Truck not equipped with seatbelt	Cab, Body, Frame	2		Y
393.95(a)	No/discharged/unsecured fire extinguisher	Emergency Equipment	2		Y
393.95(a)(1)(i)	No/discharged/unsecured fire extinguisher	Emergency Equipment	2		Y
393.95(b)	No spare fuses as required	Emergency Equipment	2		Y
393.95(c)	No spare fuses as required	Emergency Equipment	2		Y
393.95(f)	No / insufficient warning devices	Emergency Equipment	2		Y
393.95(g)	HM - restricted emergency warning device	Emergency Equipment	2		Y
396.3(a)(1)	Inspection/repair and maintenance parts and accessories	Wheels, Studs, Clamps, Etc.	2		Y
396.5A-HNLIW	Hubs - No visible or measurable lubricant showing in the hub - inner wheel	Wheels, Studs, Clamps, Etc.	2		N
396.5A-HNLOW	Hubs - No visible or measurable lubricant showing in the hub - outer wheel	Wheels, Studs, Clamps, Etc.	2		Y
396.5B-HLIW	Hubs - Oil and/or Grease Leaking from hub - inner wheel	Wheels, Studs, Clamps, Etc.	2		N
396.5B-HLOW	Hubs - oil and/or Grease Leaking from hub - outer wheel	Wheels, Studs, Clamps, Etc.	2		Y
396.5B-HWSLIW	Hubs - Wheel seal leaking - inner wheel	Wheels, Studs, Clamps, Etc.	2		N
396.5B-HWSLOW	Hubs - Wheel seal leaking - outer wheel	Wheels, Studs, Clamps, Etc.	2		Y
399.207	Vehicle access requirements violations	Cab, Body, Frame	2		N
399.211	Inadequate maintenance of driver access	Cab, Body, Frame	2		N
92.2WC	Wheel (Mud) Flaps missing or defective	Windshield/ Glass/ Markings	1		Y

Section	Description	Group	Severity	Prior Sev	DSMS
392.62(c)(1)	Bus - baggage/freight restricts driver operation	General Securement	1	7	Y
392.62(c)(2)	Bus - Exit(s) obstructed by baggage/freight	General Securement	1	7	Y
392.62(c)(3)	Passengers not protected from falling baggage	General Securement	1	7	Y
392.9	Failing to secure load	General Securement	1	7	Y
392.9(a)	Failing to secure load	General Securement	1	7	Y
392.9(a)(1)	Failing to secure cargo	General Securement	1	7	Y
392.9(a)(2)	Failing to secure vehicle equipment	General Securement	1	7	Y
392.9(a)(3)	Driver's view/movement is obstructed	General Securement	1	7	Y
393.100	Failure to prevent cargo shifting	General Securement	1	7	Y
393.100(a)	Failure to prevent cargo shifting	General Securement	1	7	Y
393.100(c)	Failure to prevent cargo shifting	General Securement	1	7	Y
393.104(a)	Inadequate/damaged securement device/system	Securement Device	1	7	Y
393.104(b)	Damaged securement system/tiedowns	Securement Device	1	7	Y
393.104(c)	Damaged vehicle structures/anchor points	Securement Device	1	7	Y
393.104(d)	Damaged dunnage/bars/blocking-bracing	Securement Device	1	7	Y
393.106(a)	No/improper front end structure/headerboard	Securement Device	1	7	Y
393.110	Failing to meet minimum tiedown requirements	General Securement	1	7	Y
393.112	Tiedown not adjustable by driver	Securement Device	1	7	Y
393.114	No/improper front end structure	General Securement	1	7	Y
393.114(b)(1)	Insufficient height for front-end structure	Securement Device	1	7	Y
393.114(b)(2)	Insufficient width for front-end structure	Securement Device	1	7	Y
393.114(d)	Front-end structure with large opening(s)	Securement Device	1	7	Y
393.116	No/improper securement of logs	General Securement	1	7	Y
393.118	No/improper lumber/building materials. securement	General Securement	1	7	Y
393.120	No/improper securement of metal coils	General Securement	1	7	Y
393.122	No/improper securement of paper rolls	General Securement	1	7	Y
393.124	No/improper securement of concrete pipe	General Securement	1	7	Y
393.126	Fail to ensure intermodal container secured	General Securement	1	7	Y
393.126(b)	Damaged/missing tiedown/securement device	Securement Device	1	7	Y
393.126(c)(1)	Lower corners of container not on vehicle/structure	Securement Device	1	7	Y
393.128	No/improper securement of vehicles	General Securement	1	7	Y
393.130	No/improper heavy vehicle/machinery securement	General Securement	1	7	Y
393.132	No/improper securement of crushed vehicles	General Securement	1	7	Y
393.132(b)	Prohibited use of synthetic webbing.	Securement Device	1	7	Y
393.134	No/improper securement of roll/hook container	General Securement	1	7	Y
393.136	No/improper securement of large boulders	General Securement	1	7	Y
393.60(b)	Windshields required	Windshield/ Glass/ Markings	1		Y
393.60(c)	Damaged or discolored windshield	Windshield/ Glass/ Markings	1		Y
393.60(d)	Glazing permits less than 70 percent of light	Windshield/ Glass/ Markings	1		Y
393.60EWS	Windshield - Obstructed	Windshield/ Glass/ Markings	1		Y
393.61	Inadequate or missing truck side windows	Windshield/ Glass/ Markings	1		Y
393.61(a)	Inadequate or missing truck side windows	Windshield/ Glass/ Markings	1		Y
393.61(b)(2)	Emergency exit window handle broken	Windshield/ Glass/ Markings	1		Y
393.62(a)	No or defective bus emergency exits - Bus manufactured on or after 9/1/1994	Windshield/ Glass/ Markings	1		Y
393.62(b)	No or defective bus emergency exits - Bus manufactured on or after 9/1/1973 but before 9/1/1994	Windshield/ Glass/ Markings	1		Y
393.62(c)	No or defective bus emergency exit windows - Bus manufactured before 9/1/1973	Windshield/ Glass/ Markings	1		Y
393.62(d)	No / defective Safety glass/push-out window - Bus manufactured before 9/1/1973	Windshield/ Glass/ Markings	1		Y
393.62(e)	No or inadequate bus emergency exit marking - Bus manufactured on or after 9/1/1973	Windshield/ Glass/ Markings	1		Y
393.65	Fuel system requirements	Fuel Systems	1		N
393.65(b)	Improper location of fuel system	Fuel Systems	1		Y
393.65(c)	Improper securement of fuel tank	Fuel Systems	1		Y
393.65(f)	Improper fuel line protection	Fuel Systems	1		Y
393.67	Fuel tank requirement violations	Fuel Systems	1		N
393.67(c)(7)	Fuel tank fill pipe cap missing	Fuel Systems	1		Y
393.67(c)(8)	Improper fuel tank safety vent	Fuel Systems	1		N
393.78	Windshield wipers inoperative/defective	Windshield/ Glass/ Markings	1		Y
393.79	Defroster / Defogger inoperative	Windshield/ Glass/ Markings	1		Y
393.83(a)	Exhaust system location	Exhaust Discharge	1		Y

Section	Description	Group	Severity	Prior Sev	DSMS
393.83(b)	Exhaust discharge fuel tank/filler tube	Exhaust Discharge	1		Y
393.83(c)	Improper exhaust - bus (gasoline)	Exhaust Discharge	1		Y
393.83(d)	Improper exhaust - bus (diesel)	Exhaust Discharge	1		Y
393.83(e)	Improper exhaust discharge (not rear of cab)	Exhaust Discharge	1		Y
393.83(f)	Improper exhaust system repair (patch/wrap)	Exhaust Discharge	1		Y
393.83(g)	Exhaust leak under truck cab and/or sleeper	Exhaust Discharge	1		Y
393.83(h)	Exhaust system not securely fastened	Exhaust Discharge	1		Y
393.87	Warning flag required on projecting load	Warning Flags	1	3	Y
393.87(a)	Warning flag required on projecting load	Warning Flags	1	3	Y
393.87(b)	Improper warning flag placement	Warning Flags	1	3	Y

Table 6: Hazardous Materials (HM) Compliance Violations

Note: The **New** column indicates new violations added in December 2012.

Section	Description	Group	Severity	New	DSMS
173.24((b))(1)	Release of HM from package	Load Securement - HM	10	N	N
173.24(b)	Failed to meet general package requirements	Load Securement - HM	10	Y	N
173.24(b)(a)	Bulk package outage or filling limit requirements	Load Securement - HM	10	Y	N
173.24(b)(d)(2)	Exceed max weight of rating on spec plate	Load Securement - HM	10	Y	N
173.24(c)	Unauthorized packaging	Load Securement - HM	10	Y	N
173.24(f)(1)	Closures for packagings must not be open or leaking	Load Securement - HM	10	Y	N
173.315(a)	Cargo or portable tank class 2 exceeds maximum filling density	Load Securement - HM	10	Y	N
173.33	Cargo tanks (general)	Load Securement - HM	10	Y	N
173.35(d)	Liquid filled IBC with Ullage over 98%	Load Securement - HM	10	Y	N
173.35(f)(2)	Intermediate bulk container (IBC) not secured to or within vehicle	Load Securement - HM	10	N	Y
173.431	Exceeded activity limits Type A or Type B package	Load Securement - HM	10	Y	N
173.441(b)	Exceeding radiation level allowed for transport of RAM under exclusive use provisions	Load Securement - HM	10	Y	N
173.443(a)	Radioactive contamination exceeds limits	Load Securement - HM	10	Y	N
177.834(a)	Package not secure in vehicle	Load Securement - HM	10	N	Y
177.834(f)	Using a tool likely to cause damage to the closure of any package or container	Load Securement - HM	10	N	Y
177.870(b)	Transporting unauthorized HM in a passenger-carrying vehicle	Load Securement - HM	10	Y	Y
177.870(c)	Prohibited Hazardous Materials on passenger carrying vehicle	Load Securement - HM	10	Y	Y
171.2(f)	Transporting HM not in accordance with this part	Package Integrity - HM	8	N	Y
171.2(g)	Cargo tank does not comply with HM Regulations	Package Integrity - HM	8	N	N
173.318(b)(10)	Fail to mark inlet, outlet, pressure relief device, or pressure control valve of cryogenic tanks	Package Integrity - HM	8	Y	N
173.35(a)	Intermediate bulk container requirements	Package Integrity - HM	8	N	Y
173.412	General Type A package failing to meet additional design requirements	Package Integrity - HM	8	Y	N
178.245-4	DOT51 integrity and securement	Package Integrity - HM	8	N	N
178.245-5	DOT51 valve protection	Package Integrity - HM	8	N	N
178.245-6(a)	DOT51 name plate Markings - HM	Package Integrity - HM	8	N	N
178.245-6(b)	Tank outlets not marked	Package Integrity - HM	8	N	N
178.251-4	DOT 56/57 integrity and securement	Package Integrity - HM	8	N	N
178.251-7(b)	DOT 56/57 spec Markings - HM	Package Integrity - HM	8	N	N
178.255-14	DOT 60 ID plate	Package Integrity - HM	8	N	N
178.255-4	DOT 60 manhole	Package Integrity - HM	8	N	N
178.255-7	DOT 60 valve protection	Package Integrity - HM	8	N	N
178.270-1	IM101/102 general design	Package Integrity - HM	8	N	N
178.270-11(d)(1)	IM101/102 pressure relief	Package Integrity - HM	8	N	N
178.270-14	IM101/102 spec plate	Package Integrity - HM	8	N	N
178.270-4	Structural integrity	Package Integrity - HM	8	N	N
178.270-6	IM 101/102 frames	Package Integrity - HM	8	N	N
178.270-8	IM101/102 valve protection	Package Integrity - HM	8	N	N
178.270-9	IM101/102 manholes	Package Integrity - HM	8	N	N
178.336-1	Protecting of fittings MC330	Package Integrity - HM	8	N	N
178.336-13	Anchoring of tank MC330	Package Integrity - HM	8	N	N
178.336-17	Metal ID plate marking MC330	Package Integrity - HM	8	N	N
178.336-17(a)	Certification plate MC330	Package Integrity - HM	8	N	N

Section	Description	Group	Severity	New	DSMS
178.336-9(a)	Safety relief devices MC330	Package Integrity - HM	8	N	N
178.336-9(c)	Marking of inlets/outlets MC330	Package Integrity - HM	8	N	N
178.337-10(a)	Protection of fittings MC331	Package Integrity - HM	8	N	N
178.337-11(a)(2)	Internal valve MC331	Package Integrity - HM	8	Y	N
178.337-13	MC331 supports and anchoring	Package Integrity - HM	8	N	N
178.337-17(a)	Metal ID plate missing MC331	Package Integrity - HM	8	N	N
178.337-8(a)	Outlets general requirements MC331	Package Integrity - HM	8	N	N
178.337-8(a)(2)	Outlets MC331	Package Integrity - HM	8	N	N
178.337-8(a)(3)	Internal or back flow valve MC331	Package Integrity - HM	8	N	N
178.337-8(a)(4)(i)	Remote closure device greater than 3500 gallons MC331	Package Integrity - HM	8	N	Y
178.337-8(a)(4)(ii)	Remote closure device less than 3500 gallons MC331	Package Integrity - HM	8	N	Y
178.337-9	Pressure relief devices MC331	Package Integrity - HM	8	Y	N
178.337-9(c)	Marking inlets/outlets MC331	Package Integrity - HM	8	N	N
178.338-10(a)	Protection of fittings MC338	Package Integrity - HM	8	N	N
178.338-10(c)	Rear end protection MC338	Package Integrity - HM	8	N	N
178.338-11(b)	Manual shutoff valve MC338	Package Integrity - HM	8	N	Y
178.338-12	Shear section MC338	Package Integrity - HM	8	N	N
178.338-13	Supports and anchoring MC338	Package Integrity - HM	8	N	N
178.338-18(a)	Name plate/Specification plate missing MC338	Package Integrity - HM	8	N	N
178.338-18(b)	Specification plate missing MC338	Package Integrity - HM	8	N	N
178.338-6	Manhole MC338	Package Integrity - HM	8	N	N
178.338-8	Pressure relief devices MC338	Package Integrity - HM	8	N	N
178.340-10(b)	MC306/307/312 metal certification plate missing	Package Integrity - HM	8	N	N
178.340-6	MC306/307/312 supports and anchoring	Package Integrity - HM	8	N	N
178.340-7(a)	MC306/307/312 ring stiffeners	Package Integrity - HM	8	N	N
178.340-7(c)	MC306/307/312 double bulkhead drain	Package Integrity - HM	8	N	N
178.340-7(d)(2)	MC306/307/312 ring stiffener drain hole	Package Integrity - HM	8	N	N
178.340-8(a)	MC306/307/312 appurtenances attachment	Package Integrity - HM	8	N	N
178.340-8(b)	MC306/307/312 rearend protection	Package Integrity - HM	8	N	N
178.340-8(c)	MC306/307/312 overturn protection	Package Integrity - HM	8	N	N
178.340-8(d)	MC306/307/312 piping protection	Package Integrity - HM	8	N	N
178.340-8(d)(1)	MC306/307/312 piping protection	Package Integrity - HM	8	N	N
178.340-8(d)(2)	MC306/307/312 minimum road clearance	Package Integrity - HM	8	N	N
178.341-3(a)	MC306 no manhole closure	Package Integrity - HM	8	N	N
178.341-4	MC306 venting	Package Integrity - HM	8	N	N
178.341-4(d)(1)	MC306 inadequate emergency venting	Package Integrity - HM	8	N	N
178.341-4(d)(2)	MC306 pressure activated vents	Package Integrity - HM	8	N	N
178.341-4(d)(3)	MC306 no fusible venting	Package Integrity - HM	8	N	N
178.341-5(a)	MC306 internal valves	Package Integrity - HM	8	N	N
178.341-5(a)(1)	MC306 heat actuated safety	Package Integrity - HM	8	N	N
178.341-5(a)(2)	MC306 remote control shutoff	Package Integrity - HM	8	N	Y
178.342-3	MC307 manhole closure	Package Integrity - HM	8	N	Y
178.342-4	MC307 venting	Package Integrity - HM	8	N	N
178.342-4(b)	Inadequate venting capacity	Package Integrity - HM	8	N	N
178.342-5(a)	MC307 internal valve	Package Integrity - HM	8	N	N
178.342-5(a)(1)	MC307 heat actuated safety	Package Integrity - HM	8	N	N
178.342-5(a)(2)	MC307 remote control shutoff	Package Integrity - HM	8	N	Y
178.343-3	Manhole closure MC312	Package Integrity - HM	8	N	N
178.343-4	Venting MC312 (show calculations)	Package Integrity - HM	8	N	N
178.343-5(a)	MC312 top outlet and valve	Package Integrity - HM	8	N	N
178.343-5(b)(1)	MC312 bottom valve/piping protection	Package Integrity - HM	8	N	N
178.345-1	DOT406/407/412 pressure relief	Package Integrity - HM	8	N	N
178.345-1(h)(i)(2)	DOT 406, 407, 412 Obstructed double bulkhead drain/vent	Package Integrity - HM	8	Y	N
178.345-1(i)(2)	DOT 406, 407, 412 Obstructed double bulkhead drain/vent	Package Integrity - HM	8	N	N
178.345-11(b)	DOT406/407/412 tank valves	Package Integrity - HM	8	N	N
178.345-11(b)(1)	DOT406/407/412 remote control	Package Integrity - HM	8	N	Y
178.345-11(b)(1)(i)	DOT406/407/412 remote control	Package Integrity - HM	8	N	Y
178.345-14(b)	DOT406/407/412 name plate	Package Integrity - HM	8	N	N
178.345-14(c)	DOT406/407/412 specification plate	Package Integrity - HM	8	N	N
178.345-5(d)	DOT406/407/412 manhole securement	Package Integrity - HM	8	N	N
178.345-5(e)	DOT406/407/412 manhole marking	Package Integrity - HM	8	N	N
178.345-6	DOT406/407/412 supports and anchoring	Package Integrity - HM	8	N	N

Section	Description	Group	Severity	New	DSMS
178.345-7(d)(4)	DOT406/407/412 ring stiffener drain	Package Integrity - HM	8	N	N
178.345-8(a)	DOT406/407/412 accident protection	Package Integrity - HM	8	N	N
178.345-8(a)(5)	DOT406/407/412 minimum road clearance	Package Integrity - HM	8	N	N
178.345-8(b)	DOT406/407/412 bottom damage protection	Package Integrity - HM	8	N	N
178.345-8(c)	DOT406/407/412 rollover damage protection	Package Integrity - HM	8	N	N
178.345-8(d)	DOT406/407/412 rear end protection	Package Integrity - HM	8	N	N
178.703(a)	Intermediate bulk container (IBC) manufacturer Markings - HM	Package Integrity - HM	8	N	N
178.703(b)	Intermediate bulk container additional Markings - HM	Package Integrity - HM	8	N	N
178.704(e)	Intermediate bulk container bottom discharge valve protection	Package Integrity - HM	8	N	N
179.300-12	DOT106/110aw protection of fittings	Package Integrity - HM	8	Y	N
179.300-13	DOT106/110aw venting and valves	Package Integrity - HM	8	Y	N
179.300-15	DOT106/110aw safety relief devices	Package Integrity - HM	8	Y	N
179.300-18	DOT106/110aw stamping of tanks	Package Integrity - HM	8	Y	N
180.205(c)	Periodic re-qualification of cylinders	Package Testing - HM	7	N	N
180.213(d)	Re-qualification Markings - HM	Package Testing - HM	7	N	N
180.352(b)	Intermediate bulk container retest or inspection	Package Testing - HM	7	N	N
180.352(d)	IBC retest date marking	Package Testing - HM	7	Y	N
180.352(e)	IBC retest date marking	Package Testing - HM	7	Y	N
180.405(b)	Cargo tank specifications	Package Testing - HM	7	N	N
180.405(j)	Certification withdrawal (failed to remove/cover/obliterate spec plate)	Package Testing - HM	7	N	N
180.407(a)(1)	Cargo tank periodic test and inspection	Package Testing - HM	7	N	N
180.407(c)	Failing to periodically test and inspect cargo tank	Package Testing - HM	7	N	N
180.415(b)	Cargo tank test or inspection Markings - HM	Package Testing - HM	7	N	N
180.605	Periodic testing of portable tanks	Package Testing - HM	7	Y	N
180.605(k)	Test date marking	Package Testing - HM	7	N	N
173.315(j)(3)	Residential gas tank not secure in transport	Fire Hazard - HM	6	N	Y
173.315(j)(4)	Liquefied Petroleum Gas (LPG) storage tank overfilled for transport	Fire Hazard - HM	6	N	N
173.32(h)(3)	IM101/102 bottom outlets prohibited	Fire Hazard - HM	6	Y	N
173.32(h)(3)(i)	IM101/102 bottom outlets authorized	Fire Hazard - HM	6	Y	N
173.54	Forbidden explosives, offering or transporting	Fire Hazard - HM	6	N	N
177.834	Load securement of different HM packages	Fire Hazard - HM	6	Y	N
177.834(c)	Smoking while loading or unloading	Fire Hazard - HM	6	N	Y
177.834(n)	Improper loading-specification 56, 57, IM101 and IM102	Fire Hazard - HM	6	N	N
177.835	Improper transportation of explosives (Class 1)	Fire Hazard - HM	6	Y	Y
177.835(a)	Loading/Unloading Class 1 with engine running	Fire Hazard - HM	6	N	Y
177.835(c)	Transporting Class 1 in combination vehicles	Fire Hazard - HM	6	N	N
177.835(j)	Transfer of Class 1 materials en route	Fire Hazard - HM	6	N	Y
177.837	Improper transporting of Class 3 hazardous materials	Fire Hazard - HM	6	Y	Y
177.838	Improper transport of class 4, 5 or division 4.2	Fire Hazard - HM	6	N	N
177.840	Improper transportation of Class 2 hazardous materials	Fire Hazard - HM	6	N	N
77.841	Improper transportation of Division 6.1 or Division 2.3 hazardous materials	Fire Hazard - HM	6	Y	Y
77.848(d)	Prohibited load/transport/storage combination	Fire Hazard - HM	6	N	N
97.11(a)	HM vehicle operated near open fire	Fire Hazard - HM	6	N	Y
97.11(b)	HM vehicle parked within 300 feet of fire	Fire Hazard - HM	6	N	Y
97.15	HM vehicle fueling violation	Fire Hazard - HM	6	N	Y
97.5(a)	Unattended explosives 1.1/1.2/1.3	Fire Hazard - HM	6	Y	Y
97.7(a)	Improperly parked explosives vehicle	Fire Hazard - HM	6	N	Y
97.7(b)	Improperly parked HM vehicle	Fire Hazard - HM	6	N	Y
71.2(c)	Representing a package./container for HM not meeting specs	Markings - HM	5	N	N
71.2(k)	Representing vehicle with HM, none present	Markings - HM	5	N	Y
72.300	Failing to comply with marking requirements	Markings - HM	5	Y	N
72.301	Non-bulk package marking - general	Markings - HM	5	Y	N
72.301(a)	No ID number on side/ends of non-bulk package - large quantity of single HM	Markings - HM	5	N	N
2.301(a)(1)	No proper shipping name and/or ID# marking on non-bulk	Markings - HM	5	N	N

Section	Description	Group	Severity	New	DSMS
172.302	Marking requirements bulk packagings	Markings - HM	5	Y	N
172.302(a)	No ID number (portable and cargo tank)	Markings - HM	5	N	Y
172.302(b)	Bulk package marking incorrect size	Markings - HM	5	N	N
172.303(a)	Prohibited HM marking on package	Markings - HM	5	N	N
172.304(a)(1)	Package marking not durable, English, or print	Markings - HM	5	N	N
172.304(a)(2)	Marking not on sharply contrasting color	Markings - HM	5	N	N
172.304(a)(3)	Marking obscured by label or attachments	Markings - HM	5	N	N
172.304(a)(4)	Marking not away from other marking	Markings - HM	5	N	N
172.308(a)	Package marked with unauthorized abbreviation	Markings - HM	5	Y	N
172.310(a)	No gross weight on radioactive materials package greater than 50 KG	Markings - HM	5	N	N
172.310(b)	Radioactive materials package not marked "Type A or B"	Markings - HM	5	N	N
172.313(a)	No "inhalation hazard" on package	Markings - HM	5	N	N
172.313(b)	No "poison" on non-bulk plastic package	Markings - HM	5	N	N
172.316(a)	Other regulated material non-bulk package not marked	Markings - HM	5	N	N
172.320(a)	Class 1 package not marked with ex-number	Markings - HM	5	N	N
172.322(b)	No marine pollutant marking on bulk packaging	Markings - HM	5	N	N
172.324	Non-bulk hazardous substance not marked	Markings - HM	5	N	N
172.325	No "hot" marking for bulk elevated temperature	Markings - HM	5	Y	N
172.325(a)	Elevated temperature not marked "Hot"	Markings - HM	5	N	N
172.325(b)	Improperly marked molten aluminum/sulphur	Markings - HM	5	N	N
172.326(a)	Portable tank not marked with proper shipping name or ID#	Markings - HM	5	Y	N
172.326(b)	No portable tank owner or lessee marking	Markings - HM	5	N	N
172.326(c)(1)	No ID number marking on vehicle carrying portable tank	Markings - HM	5	N	N
172.326(c)(2)	Shipper failed to provide ID number to carrier	Markings - HM	5	N	N
172.328	No ID number displayed on a cargo tank	Markings - HM	5	Y	N
172.328(a)	Shipper failed to provide or affix ID number for cargo tank	Markings - HM	5	N	N
172.328(b)	Cargo tank not marked for class 2	Markings - HM	5	N	N
172.328(c)	No quenched and tempered steel (QT)/other than quenched and tempered steel (NQT) marked on cargo tank (MC 330/331)	Markings - HM	5	N	N
172.328(d)	Fail to mark manual remote shutoff device	Markings - HM	5	N	N
172.330(a)(2)	Tank car tank (non cylinder) not marked as required	Markings - HM	5	N	N
172.330(b)	Motor vehicle with tank not marked	Markings - HM	5	N	N
172.331	Markings for other bulk packages	Markings - HM	5	Y	N
172.332	Required ID markings displayed	Markings - HM	5	N	N
172.334	Prohibited ID number marking	Markings - HM	5	N	N
172.334(a)	ID # displayed on Class 7/Class 1/Dangerous or Subsidiary placard	Markings - HM	5	N	N
172.336(b)	ID numbers not properly displayed	Markings - HM	5	N	N
172.336(c)(1)	Failing to display ID numbers on compartment cargo tank in sequence	Markings - HM	5	N	N
172.338	Carrier failed to replace missing ID number	Markings - HM	5	N	N
172.400	Labeling requirements	Markings - HM	5	Y	N
172.400(a)	Package/containment not labeled as required	Markings - HM	5	N	Y
172.401	Prohibited labeling	Markings - HM	5	N	N
172.402	Failing to affix additional labels when required	Markings - HM	5	Y	N
172.402(a)	No label for subsidiary hazard	Markings - HM	5	N	N
172.402(b)	Display of class number on label	Markings - HM	5	N	N
172.402(d)	Subsidiary labeling for radioactive materials	Markings - HM	5	N	N
172.402(e)	Subsidiary labeling for class 1 (explosive) materials	Markings - HM	5	N	N
172.403(a)	Radioactive material label requirement	Markings - HM	5	N	N
172.403(f)	Radioactive material package-2 labels on opposite sides	Markings - HM	5	N	N
172.403(g)	Failed to label radioactive material properly	Markings - HM	5	N	N
172.403(g)(2)	Class 7 label - no activity/activity not in SI units	Markings - HM	5	N	N
172.404(a)	Mixed package not properly labeled	Markings - HM	5	N	N
172.404(b)	Failed to properly label consolidated package	Markings - HM	5	N	N
172.406(a)(1)	Label placement not as required	Markings - HM	5	N	N
172.406(c)	Multiple label placement not as required	Markings - HM	5	N	N
172.406(d)	Label not on contrasting background or no border	Markings - HM	5	N	N

Section	Description	Group	Severity	New	DSMS
172.406(e)	Failed to display duplicate label as required	Markings - HM	5	N	N
172.406(f)	Label obscured by marking or attachment	Markings - HM	5	N	N
172.502(a)(1)	Prohibited placarding	Markings - HM	5	Y	N
172.502(a)(2)	Sign or device could be confused with HM placard	Markings - HM	5	Y	N
172.504	Placards not in table 1 or 2	Markings - HM	5	Y	N
172.504(a)	Vehicle not placarded as required	Markings - HM	5	N	Y
172.504(b)	Dangerous placard violation	Markings - HM	5	Y	N
172.505(a)	No placard for poison inhalation hazard	Markings - HM	5	Y	N
172.505(b)	Not placarded for RAM and Corrosive when required	Markings - HM	5	Y	N
172.505(c)	Placard for subsidiary dangerous when wet	Markings - HM	5	Y	N
172.506(a)	Failed to provide placards shipper	Markings - HM	5	Y	N
172.506(a)(1)	Placards not affixed to vehicle	Markings - HM	5	N	Y
172.507	Not placardarded for RAM highway route controlled quantity	Markings - HM	5	Y	N
172.512(a)	Freight container not placarded	Markings - HM	5	Y	N
172.514	Cargo tank placards	Markings - HM	5	Y	N
172.514(a)	Bulk package offered without placard	Markings - HM	5	Y	N
172.514(b)	Bulk package with residue of HM not properly placarded	Markings - HM	5	Y	N
172.516(a)	Placard not visible from direction it faces	Markings - HM	5	N	Y
172.516(c)(1)	Placard not securely affixed or attached	Markings - HM	5	N	Y
172.516(c)(2)	Placard not clear of appurtenance	Markings - HM	5	N	Y
172.516(c)(4)	Placard improper location	Markings - HM	5	N	Y
172.516(c)(5)	Placard not reading horizontally	Markings - HM	5	N	Y
172.516(c)(6)	Placard damaged, deteriorated, or obscured	Markings - HM	5	N	Y
172.516(c)(7)	Placard not on contrasting background or border	Markings - HM	5	N	Y
172.519	Placard does not meet specifications	Markings - HM	5	Y	N
173.25(a)	Failed to meet overpack conditions	Markings - HM	5	Y	N
173.25(c)	Failure to label and package poison properly, when transported with edible material	Markings - HM	5	N	Y
173.318(g)	No or Improper One Way Travel Time (OWTT) marking on cryogenic cargo tank	Markings - HM	5	Y	N
173.427(a)(6)(vi)	Exclusive use low specific activity (LSA) radioactive material not marked "Radioactive-LSA"	Markings - HM	5	N	Y
173.427(a)(vi)	Exclusive use low specific activity (LSA) radioactive material not marked "Radioactive-LSA"	Markings - HM	5	N	Y
177.823(a)	No placards/markings when required	Markings - HM	5	N	N
172.312(a)	No package orientation arrows	Cargo Protection - HM	4	N	N
172.312(a)(2)	No package orientation arrows	Cargo Protection - HM	4	N	N
172.312(b)	Prohibited use of orientation arrows	Cargo Protection - HM	4	N	N
173.24(a)(c)	Non-bulk package mixed contents requirements	Cargo Protection - HM	4	Y	N
173.29(a)	Empty package improper transportation	Cargo Protection - HM	4	N	N
173.30	Loading/unloading transport vehicles	Cargo Protection - HM	4	N	Y
173.33(a)	Cargo tank general requirements	Cargo Protection - HM	4	N	Y
173.33(b)	HM in cargo tank which had dangerous reaction with cargo tank	Cargo Protection - HM	4	N	Y
173.33(c)(2)	Cargo tank not marked with design or maximum allowable working pressure (MAWP)	Cargo Protection - HM	4	N	N
173.421(a)	Transporting limited quantity-radioactive material exceeds 0.5 millirem/hour	Cargo Protection - HM	4	N	N
173.427(a)(6)(iv)	No instructions for exclusive use packaging-low specific activity	Cargo Protection - HM	4	N	Y
173.427(a)(iv)	No instructions for exclusive use packaging-low specific activity	Cargo Protection - HM	4	N	Y
73.441(a)	Exceeding radiation level limitations allowed for transport	Cargo Protection - HM	4	N	N
73.442(b)(1)	External temperature of package exceeds 50 degrees Celcius (122 degrees F)	Cargo Protection - HM	4	Y	N
73.442(b)(2)	External temperature of package exceeds 85 degrees Celcius (185 degress F)	Cargo Protection - HM	4	Y	N
73.447	RAM transport storage violation	Cargo Protection - HM	4	Y	N
73.448	General RAM transport requirements	Cargo Protection - HM	4	Y	N
77.834(b)	Package not loaded according to orientation marks	Cargo Protection - HM	4	Y	N
77.834(i)	Attendance of cargo tank- (load or unload)	Cargo Protection - HM	4	N	Y
77.834(j)	Manholes and valves not closed or leak free	Cargo Protection - HM	4	N	Y

Section	Description	Group	Severity	New	DSMS
177.834(m)(1)	Securing specification 106a or 110a tanks	Cargo Protection - HM	4	N	N
177.837(c)	Cargo tanks not properly bonded/grounded	Cargo Protection - HM	4	N	N
177.837(d)	Improper unloading of combustible liquids	Cargo Protection - HM	4	N	N
177.839	Improper transportation of Class 8 hazardous materials	Cargo Protection - HM	4	Y	Y
177.840(g)	Discharge valve not closed in transit class 2	Cargo Protection - HM	4	N	Y
177.840(o)	Fail to test off-truck remote shutoff device	Cargo Protection - HM	4	N	Y
177.840(s)	Fail to possess remote shutoff when unloading	Cargo Protection - HM	4	N	Y
397.5(c)	Unattended hazmat vehicle	Cargo Protection - HM	4	Y	Y
172.200(a)	No shipping paper provided by offeror	Documentation - HM	3	Y	N
172.201(a)(1)	Hazrdous Materials not distinguished from non-Hazardous Materials	Documentation - HM	3	Y	N
172.201(a)(2)	Hazardous Materials description not printed legibly in English	Documentation - HM	3	Y	N
172.201(a)(3)	Hazardous Materials description contains abbreviation or code	Documentation - HM	3	Y	N
172.201(a)(4)	Additional information not after Hazardous Materials basic description	Documentation - HM	3	Y	N
172.201(c)	Failure to list page number of pages	Documentation - HM	3	Y	N
172.201(d)	ER phone number not listed	Documentation - HM	3	Y	N
172.202(a)(1)	Improper shipping name	Documentation - HM	3	Y	N
172.202(a)(2)	Improper hazard class	Documentation - HM	3	Y	N
172.202(a)(3)	Wrong or no ID number	Documentation - HM	3	Y	N
172.202(a)(4)	No packing group listed	Documentation - HM	3	Y	N
172.202(a)(5)	Total quantity not listed	Documentation - HM	3	Y	N
172.202(b)	Basic description not in proper sequence	Documentation - HM	3	Y	N
172.202(c)	Total quantity improper location	Documentation - HM	3	Y	N
172.202(e)	Non Hazardous Material entered with class or ID#	Documentation - HM	3	Y	N
172.203(a)	Exemption number not listed	Documentation - HM	3	Y	N
172.203(b)	Limited quantity not shown	Documentation - HM	3	Y	N
172.203(c)(1)	Hazardous substance entry missing	Documentation - HM	3	Y	N
172.203(c)(2)	RQ not on shipping paper	Documentation - HM	3	Y	N
172.203(d)(1)	Radionuclide name not on shipping paper	Documentation - HM	3	Y	N
172.203(d)(10)	No indication for Highway Route Controlled Quantity of Class 7 "HRCQ" on shipping paper	Documentation - HM	3	Y	N
172.203(d)(2)	No RAM physical or chemical form	Documentation - HM	3	Y	N
172.203(d)(3)	No RAM activity	Documentation - HM	3	Y	N
172.203(d)(4)	No RAM label category	Documentation - HM	3	Y	N
172.203(d)(5)	No RAM transport index	Documentation - HM	3	Y	N
172.203(d)(6)	No fissile radioactive entry	Documentation - HM	3	Y	N
172.203(d)(7)	No DOE/NRC package approval notation	Documentation - HM	3	Y	N
172.203(d)(8)	Export package or foreign made package not marked with IAEA Certificate	Documentation - HM	3	Y	N
172.203(d)(9)	No Exclusive Use notation	Documentation - HM	3	Y	N
172.203(e)	No empty packaging noted	Documentation - HM	3	Y	N
172.203(h)(1)	No qt/nqt for anhydrous ammonia	Documentation - HM	3	Y	N
172.203(h)(2)	No notation for QT / NQT for Liquified Petroleum Gas	Documentation - HM	3	Y	N
172.203(k)	No technical name for nos entry	Documentation - HM	3	Y	N
172.203(m)	No Poison Inhalation Hazard and / or Hazard Zone	Documentation - HM	3	Y	N
172.203(n)	No "hot" on shipping paper	Documentation - HM	3	Y	N
172.203(o)	No temperature controls noted for Class 4.1 or Class 5.2	Documentation - HM	3	Y	N
172.205	Hazardous waste manifest not as required	Documentation - HM	3	Y	N
172.301(b)	No technical name on non-bulk	Documentation - HM	3	N	N
172.301(c)	No special permit number on non-bulk package	Documentation - HM	3	N	N
172.301(d)	No consignee/consignor on non-bulk	Documentation - HM	3	N	N
172.302(c)	No special permit number on bulk package	Documentation - HM	3	N	N
172.600(c)	Emergency Response (ER) information not available	Documentation - HM	3	N	Y
172.602(a)	Emergency response information missing	Documentation - HM	3	N	Y
172.602(b)	Form and manner of emergency response information	Documentation - HM	3	N	Y
172.602(c)(1)	Maintenance/accessibility of emergency response information	Documentation - HM	3	N	Y
172.604(a)	Failing to provide an emergency response phone	Documentation - HM	3	Y	N

Section	Description	Group	Severity	New	DSMS
	number				
177.817	Shipping papers required	Documentation - HM	3	Y	N
177.817(a)	No shipping papers (carrier)	Documentation - HM	3	N	Y
177.817(b)	Shipper certification missing (when required)	Documentation - HM	3	N	N
177.817(e)	Shipping paper accessibility	Documentation - HM	3	N	Y
385.403	No HM Safety Permit	Documentation - HM	3	N	N
397.19	No instructions/documents when transporting Division 1.1/1.2/1.3 (explosive) materials	Documentation - HM	3	N	Y
397.19(c)	Required documents not in possession-explosive materials	Documentation - HM	3	N	Y
171.2(a)	Failure to comply with HM regulations	HM Other	2	N	Y
171.2(b)	Failure to comply with the requirements for HM transportation (including labeling and handling)	HM Other	2	N	Y
173.40	Small quantities for highway and rail	HM Other	2	Y	N
173.60	Materials of trade exemption	HM Other	2	Y	N
177.801	Accepting/transporting HM not prepared properly	HM Other	2	N	N
177.804	Failure to comply with FMCSR 49 CFR part 383 and 49 CFR parts 390 through 397	HM Other	2	Y	Y
177.841(e)	Poison label loaded with foodstuffs	HM Other	2	N	Y
177.842(a)	Total transport index exceeds 50- non-exclusive use	HM Other	2	N	N
177.842(b)	Distance from package to person-radioactive material	HM Other	2	N	N
177.842(d)	Blocking and bracing of radioactive material packages	HM Other	2	N	Y
177.848(f)	Class 1 load separation or segregation	HM Other	2	N	N
397.1(a)	Driver/carrier must obey part 397	HM Other	2	N	Y
397.1(b)	Failing to require employees to know/obey part 397	HM Other	2	N	Y
397.17	No tire examination on HM vehicle	HM Other	2	N	Y
397.2	Must comply with rules in parts 390-397- transporting HM	HM Other	2	N	Y
397.101(b)	Radioactive materials vehicle not on preferred route	HM Route	1	N	Y
397.101(d)	No or incomplete route plan-radioactive materials	HM Route	1	N	Y
397.101(e)(2)	Driver not in possession of training certificate	HM Route	1	N	Y
397.101(e)(3)	Driver not in possession of written route plan	HM Route	1	N	Y
397.67	HM vehicle routing violation (non-radioactive materials)	HM Route	1	N	N

Crash Indictor

The Crash Indicator is based on the histories or patterns of high crash involvement, including frequency and severity, based on information from state-reported crash reports. A crash is reported to FMCSA if it involves the following:

- A fatality: any person(s) killed in or outside of any vehicle (truck, bus, car, etc.) involved in the crash or who dies within 30 days of the crash as a result of an injury sustained in the crash; OR
- An injury: any person(s) injured as a result of the crash who immediately receives medical treatment away from the crash scene; OR
- A tow-away: any motor vehicle (truck, bus, car, etc.) disabled as a result of the crash and transported away from the scene by a tow truck or other vehicle.

The crash history used by the Crash Indicator is not specifically a behavior; rather, it is the consequence of behavior and may indicate a problem that warrants attention. Per the FMCSA:

"The CSMS assesses the Crash Indicator using relevant state-reported crash data reported in MCMIS. Individual carriers' Crash Indicator measures also incorporate carrier size in terms of PUs and annual VMT. These measures are used to generate percentile ranks that reflect each carrier's safety posture relative to carriers in the same segment with similar numbers of crashes. The Crash Indicator measure is calculated as the sum of severity and time weighted crashes divided by carrier average PUs multiplied by a Utilization Factor..."

Note for 2013: Per the December 2012 changes and enhancements to SMS, the Crashes Category will be broken out from the current "crashes with fatalities and injuries" into two separate categories:
1. crashes with fatalities
2. crashes with injuries

Appendix

The Appendix has 5 Sections

Appendix 1

CDL and Federal Regulations

The Two Key Components

The foundation of CDL federal requirements and standards is based on two rather significant cornerstones:

Title 49 of the Code of Federal Regulations (CFR)

The Code of Federal Regulations (CFR) is an official and complete text of federal agency regulations by the executive departments and agencies of the Federal Government. The annual codification of these general and permanent rules is published in the Federal Register.

The CFR is divided into 50 titles representing fairly broad areas subject to Federal regulation. Title 49 relates to Transportation. Part 383 of Title 49 (commonly shown as 49 CFR § 383) is the portion of the regulation on commercial driver's license standards; requirements and penalties. To see all the regulatory parts, visit www.fmcsa.dot.gov/rules-regulations/rules-regulations.htm.

The Federal Motor Carrier Safety Administration (FMCSA)

Within the Department of Transportation, the Federal Motor Carrier Safety Administration (FMCSA) is the regulatory agency that oversees commercial driver license (CDL) standards, testing, requirements, disqualifications, and penalties. Drivers are required to obtain and hold a CDL when they operate in interstate, intrastate, or foreign commerce and if they drive a vehicle that meets any of the classifications of a comme4rcial motor vehicle (CMV).

The home page for FMCSA is www.fmcsa.dot.gov. If the regulation of commercial drivers and vehicles is important to you or your company, bookmark this page. The FMSCA web page is a great resource for extensive information and guidance on regulatory compliance, research. FMSCA provides alerts and detailed information on forthcoming changes.

While of course there are laws passed annually that modify parts of 49 CFR, two laws of special significance should be mentioned.

Drivers are required to obtain and hold a CDL when they operate in interstate, intrastate, or foreign commerce and if they drive a vehicle that meets any of the classifications of a CMV described below.

Significant Past Legislation

While of course there are laws passed annually that modify parts of 49 CFR, two older laws of special significance should be mentioned.

Commercial Motor Vehicle Safety Act of 1986 (CMVSA)

A very significant piece of Federal legislation which influenced 49 CFR § 383 is the Commercial Motor Vehicle Safety Act of 1986 (CMVSA). The primary purposes of the Act were to improve highway safety by regulating Commercial Motor Vehicles (CMVs) and regulate the issuance of Commercial Driver Licenses. CMVSA retained the states' right to issue a CDL, but established minimum national standards for licensing CDL drivers. Since April 1, 1992, drivers have been required to have a CDL in order to drive a commercial motor vehicle.

The Motor Carrier Safety Improvement Act of 1999 (MCSIA)

The Motor Carrier Safety Improvement Act (MCSIA), aimed at improving commercial driver safety, brought about perhaps the most sweeping changes impacting commercial drivers since 1990. The law, which went into effect September 30, 2005, modified the CDL licensing process. It also standardized the CDL disqualification process outlining specific violations with a table of specified disqualification (shown later in this Appendix section). In addition, MCSIA requires states to disqualify CDL drivers who have high risk traffic offenses in their personal vehicles.

MCSIA also established The Federal Motor Carrier Safety Administration (FMCSA).

Current Legislation and Rule Changes

The Military Commercial Driver's License Act of 2012

The Military Commercial Driver's License Act of 2012 (S.3624) modifies the requirements regarding an individual who operates (or will operate) a CMV while a member of the military.

The act amends 49 USC 31311(a)(12):

- (A) ...the state may issue a commercial driver's license only to an individual who operates or will operate a commercial motor vehicle and is domiciled in the State.

- (B) ...the State may issue a CDL to an individual who operates or will operate a commercial motor vehicle and is not domiciled in a State that issues CDLs.
- (C) ...The State may issue a CDL to an individual who
  - operates or will operate a CMV
  - is a member of the active duty military, military reserves, National Guard, active duty United States Coast Guard, or Coast Guard Auxiliary and is not domiciled in the State
  - is not Domiciled in the State, but whose temporary or permanent duty station is located in the State.

Hours of Service (HOS) Final Rule

After a series of public listening sessions, the FMCSA's new Hours of Service (HOS) Final Rule that changes some of the working time regulations placed on commercial truckers. Some of the highlights of the new regulations include:

- Reduction by 12 hours the maximum number of hours a truck driver can work within a week. Under the old rule, truck drivers could work on average up to 82 hours within a seven-day period. The new HOS final rule limits a driver's work week to 70 hours.
- Truck drivers cannot drive after working eight hours without first taking a break of at least 30 minutes. Drivers can take the 30-minute break whenever they need rest during the eight-hour window.
- The rule requires truck drivers who maximize their weekly work hours to take at least two nights' rest when their 24-hour body clock demands sleep the most - from 1:00 a.m. to 5:00 a.m. This rest requirement is part of the rule's "34-hour restart" provision that allows drivers to restart the clock on their work week by taking at least 34 consecutive hours off-duty. The final rule allows drivers to use the restart provision only once during a seven-day period.

The final rule retains the current 11-hour daily driving limit. Commercial truck drivers and companies must comply with the HOS final rule by July 1, 2013.

See a copy of the rule at www.fmcsa.dot.gov/rules-regulations/topics/hos/index.htm.

December 2012 Changes and Enhancements to SMS

Late in 2010, the Federal Motor Carrier Safety Administration (FMCSA) launched a new Compliance, Safety Accountability Program (CSA) which included CSA's new Motor Carrier Safety Measurement System (SMS).

In March 2012, the Agency announced a proposed set of SMS modifications. After a preview and comments period, FMSCA announced a finalized package of SMS enhancements in December 2012. The modifications updated the June 2012 version of the foundational document and reflects SMS Methodology version 3.0.

See the Motor Carrier Safety Measurement System (SMS) chapter starting on page 755 for details on the complete program and the changes.

Homeland Security December 2012 Announcement: REAL ID Act Update

The REAL ID Act of 2005, signed by President George W. Bush as part of Public Law No: 109-13, is meant to improve the security state-issued driver licenses and identification cards. The Act prohibits the federal government from accepting state-issued driver's licenses or identification cards for any federal purpose (e.g. accessing federal facilities, boarding federally regulated commercial aircraft, etc.) unless the state-issued document meets standards developed by the Department of Homeland Security (DHS). The Act calls for non-compliant licenses and IDs to be clearly identified as such.

The Act is the result of recommendations coming from the 9/11 Commission regarding the need for tighter security standards. A copy of the Act can be found at http://thomas.loc.gov/home/thomas.php.

Although the Real ID Act does not directly affect motor vehicle record keeping or record access, it does play a critical role with state-issued driver licenses and non-driver identification cards. The Act established new, strict national standards for state-issued driver licenses and non-driver identification cards. Provisions include what data must be included on the card and what documentation must be presented before a card can be issued. For example, before a card can be issued, the applicant must provide the following:

- A photo ID or a non-photo ID that includes full legal name and birthdate.
- Documentation of birthdate.
- Documentation of legal status and Social Security number
- Documentation showing name and principal residence address.

A great many organizations and a number of states are strongly opposed to the Act. One reason is cost. The amount of money th states must spend to implement the REAL ID Act goes well beyond what Congress has appropriated to assist the states. Anothe reason is privacy. Many groups feel that the act is, in effect, creating a National ID that will lead to even more ID theft, as oppose to thwarting ID theft.

Portions of the Real ID Act were originally scheduled to take effect on May 11, 2008, but the deadline has been extended. Belo are portions of text taken from a Press Release issued by the Department of Homeland Security on December 20, 2012.

December 20, 2102 Press Release

(See www.dhs.gov/news/2012/12/20/dhs-determines-13-states-meet-real-id-standards)

"On December 20, 2012, the Department of Homeland Security (DHS) determined that thirteen states have met the standards of the REAL ID Act of 2005 ("Act") for driver's licenses and identification cards and has granted a temporary deferment for all other states and territories.

Currently, DHS has determined that Colorado, Connecticut, Delaware, Georgia, Iowa, Indiana, Maryland, Ohio, South Dakota, Tennessee, West Virginia, Wisconsin, and Wyoming have met the Act's requirements.

...Beginning January 15, 2013, those states not found to meet the standards will receive a temporary deferment that will allow Federal agencies to continue to accept their licenses and identification cards for boarding commercial aircraft and other official purposes."

For more information, DHS has posted frequently asked questions on its website at www.dhs.gov/secure-drivers-licenses.

New Medical Certification Requirements for Commercial Driver's License (CDL) Holders

This is covered in detail below - see pages 778-779.

The next portions of Appendix 1 present separate overviews of the regulations affecting **CDL License and Issuance**, **Testing**, **Record Keeping and Retention**, and **Disqualifications**.

Regulations on License and Issuance

Drivers are required to obtain and hold a CDL when they operate in interstate, intrastate, or foreign commerce and if they drive a vehicle that meets any of the classifications of a CMV described below.

Classes of License Standards

The Federal standard requires states to issue a CDL to drivers according to the following license classifications:

Class A   Any combination of vehicles with a GCWR of 26,001 or more pounds provided the GVWR of the vehicle(s) being towed is in excess of 10,000 pounds.

Class B   Any single vehicle with a GVWR of 26,001 or more pounds, or any such vehicle towing a vehicle not in excess of 10,000 pounds GVWR.

Class C   Any single vehicle, or combination of vehicles, that does not meet the definition of Class A or Class B, but is either designed to transport 16 or more passengers, including the driver, or is transporting material that has been designated as hazardous under 49 U.S.C. 5103 and is required to be placarded under subpart F of 49 CFR Part 172 or is transporting any quantity of a material listed as a select agent or toxin in 42 CFR Part 73.

The Commercial Driver's License Document

While FMCSA sets the minimum standards that States must meet regarding administration of the CDL program , the issuance of the license itself still remains the exclusive function of the States. States determine the application process, license fee, license renewal cycle, renewal procedures, and reinstatement requirements after a disqualification – provided that the Federal standards and criteria are met. States may exceed the Federal requirements for certain criteria, such as medical, fitness, and other driver qualifications.

Per Federal regulations, all CDL documents must contain the following information:

- The words "Commercial Driver's License" or "CDL;"
- The driver's full name, signature, and mailing address;
- The driver's date of birth, sex, and height;
- Color photograph;
- The driver's State license number;
- The name of the issuing State;
- The date of issuance and the date of the expiration of the license;
- The class(es) of vehicle that the driver is authorized to drive;
- Notation of the "air brake" restriction, if issued;
- The endorsement(s) for which the driver has qualified;

Note: The Social Security Number must be provided on the application, but does not need to be printed on the CDL.

States may issue Learner's Permits for purposes of behind-the-wheel training on public highways as long as the Learner's Permit holder is required to be accompanied by someone with a valid CDL appropriate for the class and type of vehicle being operated. Further, the Learner's Permits can only be issued for limited time periods. The permit holder cannot operate a commercial motor vehicle transporting hazardous materials as defined in §383.5. The permit holder must have a valid operators (non-CDL) driver's license, or have passed such vision, sign/symbol, and knowledge tests as the State issuing the learner's permit ordinarily administers to applicants for operator (non-CDL) drivers' licenses.

Nonresident Commercial Driver's License

In certain circumstances, States are permitted to issue a CDL to an individual who is not domiciled within its jurisdiction. If doing so, the word "Nonresident" must be prominently displayed on the CDL, but does not have to be contiguous with "Commercial Driver's License" or "CDL". As stated earlier, a Social Security Number is not required to be displayed on the license.

Nonresident CDL means a CDL issued by a State under either of the following two conditions:

1. To an individual domiciled in a foreign country, other than Mexico and Canada, if the person obtained the license from a State which complies with the testing and licensing standards required for CDL drivers.

2. To an individual domiciled in another State while that State is prohibited from issuing CDLs, if the person obtained the license from any State which elected to issue nonresident CDLs and which complies with the testing and licensing standards required for CDL drivers.

Exemptions

A State may, at its discretion, exempt firefighters, emergency response vehicle drivers, farmers and drivers removing snow and ice in small communities from the CDL requirements, subject to certain conditions. The use of this waiver is limited to the driver's home State unless there is a reciprocity agreement with adjoining States.

In addition, a State may issue a restricted license and waive the CDL knowledge and skills testing requirements for seasonal drivers in farm-related service industries and may waive certain knowledge and skills testing requirements for drivers in remote areas of Alaska. A State can also waive the CDL hazardous materials endorsement test requirements for part-time drivers working for the pyrotechnics industry, subject to certain conditions.

Until recently (per the Military Commercial Driver's License Act of 2012), each State must exempt from the requirements of 49 CFR 383 individuals who operate CMVs for military purposes. Now, per this Act, states may issue a commercial driver's license to drivers stationed in the state but not domiciled there. (See appropriate text earlier in this section).

Endorsements and Restrictions Standards

Drivers who operate special types of CMVs are required to pass additional tests in order to obtain any of the endorsements on their CDL. At a minimum, each state must use these endorsements as outlined.

T	Double/Triple Trailers (Knowledge test only)
P	Passenger (Knowledge and Skills Tests)
N	Tank Vehicle (Knowledge Test only)
H	Hazardous Materials (Knowledge Test and TSA Threat Assessment)
X	Combination of Tank Vehicle and Hazardous Materials
S	School Bus (Knowledge and Skills Tests)

Also, if a driver either fails the **air brake** component of the general knowledge test or performs the skills test in a vehicle not equipped with air brakes, the driver is issued an air brake restriction, restricting the driver from operating a CMV equipped with air brakes.

A driver must take the skills test in a motor vehicle which represents the type of motor vehicle that a driver applicant operates or expects to operate as defined by the vehicle classifications described above. While these classifications are general for the class of vehicle, additional requirements exist for the passenger and school bus endorsements. To obtain a passenger endorsement, the driver must test in a passenger vehicle. To obtain a school bus endorsement, the driver must test in a passenger vehicle equipped with school bus features (lights, signs, etc). If a driver possesses a Class A CDL, but obtains a passenger or school bus endorsement in a Class B vehicle the State must place a M restriction indicating that the driver can only operate Class B and C passenger vehicle or school buses. If a driver possesses a Class B CDL, but obtains a passenger or school bus endorsement in a Class C vehicle, the State must place an N restriction indicating that the driver can only operate Class C passenger vehicle or school buses.

New Medical Certification Requirements

Starting January 30, 2012 and no later than January 30, 2014, all CDL holders must provide information to their state drive licensing agency (SDLA) regarding the type of commercial motor vehicle operation they drive in or expect to drive in with their CDL. Drivers operating in certain types of commerce (see below) are required to submit a current medical examiner's certificate to their SDLA to obtain a "certified" medical status as part of their driving record.

CDL holders required to have a "certified" medical status who fail to provide and keep up-to-date their medical examiner's certificate with their SDLA will become "not-certified" and may lose their CDL.

All CDL drivers who are renewing, correcting or applying for an original Commercial Driver License (CDL) must self-certify which type of commercial motor vehicle (CMV) operation they will perform. The four types are:

*   NON-EXCEPTED INTERSTATE (NI) - The CDL holder is qualified to drive a commercial motor vehicle across state lines in accordance with 49 CFR Part 391 of the Federal Motor Carrier Safety Regulation (FMCSR).

*   NON-EXCEPTED INTRASTATE (NA) - The CDL holder is qualified to drive a commercial vehicle **ONLY** within the SDLA and to have an approved CDL Medical Waiver.

- EXCEPTED INTERSTATE (EI) - The CDL holder drives a commercial motor vehicle across state lines **ONLY** for specific excepted activities, such as to transport school children or staff, sick or injured persons, corpses, etc., in accordance with 49 CFR Part 391 of the Federal Motor Carrier Safety Regulations (FMCSR).
- EXCEPTED INTRASTATE (EA) - The CDL holder drives a commercial motor vehicle **ONLY** within the SDLA. Although exempt from the qualification requirements under 49 CFR Part 391 of the Federal Motor Carrier Safety Regulations (FMCSR) based on the type of driving performed, the CDL holder must meet all other state requirements without a CDL Medical Waiver.

The non-excepted CDL holders are required to submit a current medical examiner's certificate to their SDLA to obtain a "certified" medical status as part of their driving record. The status is called the "Medically Certified" status. The driver's physical qualification requirements are not changing. The medical certification status and the information on the medical examiner's certificate now is part of the Commercial Driver's License System (CDLIS) record.

If the DOT Medical Certificate is valid then the individual will have a Medically Certified status of "Certified" and the CDL holder can legally drive a CMV. The CDL holders required to have a "certified" medical status who fail to provide and keep up-to-date their medical examiner's certificate with their SDLA will become "not-certified" and they may lose their CDL.

For more information about this Federal regulation see www.fmcsa.dot.gov/registration-licensing/cdl/cdl-general-info.aspx.

Regulations on Testing

Driver Knowledge and Skills Tests

States may develop their own tests which must meet the minimum Federal standards provided for in Subpart G and H of 49 CFR § 383. Model driver and examiner manuals and tests are available to States to use, if they wish.

- Each basic knowledge test, i.e., the test covering the areas referred to in 49 CFR 383.111 for the applicable vehicle group, shall contain at least 30 items, exclusive of the number of items testing air brake knowledge.
- To pass the knowledge tests (general and endorsement), applicants must correctly answer at least 80 percent of the questions.
- To pass the skills test, applicants must successfully perform all the required skills (listed in 49 CFR 383.113 through 49 CFR 383.123). The skills test must be taken in a vehicle representative of the type of vehicle that the applicant operates or expects to operate. Depending on the type of passenger vehicle used in the skills test, the following restrictions must be added to the license: except Class A bus or except Class A and Class B bus.
- Require the driver applicant to surrender his/her driver's license issued by another State, if he/she has moved from another State.

Third Party Skills Testing

A State may authorize a person (such as another State, an employer, a private driver training facility or other private institution, or a department, agency or instrumentality of a local government) to administer the skills tests, if the following conditions are met:

- Tests must be the same as those given by the State.
- The third party has an agreement with the State containing, at a minimum, provisions that:
  - Allow the FMCSA, or its representative, and the State to conduct random examinations, inspections, and audits without prior notice.
  - Require the State to conduct on-site inspection at least yearly.
  - Require that all third party examiners meet the same qualification and training standards as State examiners.
- At least annually, State employees must evaluate the programs by taking third party tests as if they were test applicants, or by testing a sample of drivers tested by the third party and then comparing pass/fail rates.
- Reserve unto the State the right to take prompt and appropriate remedial action against the third-party testers in the event that the third-party fails to comply with State or Federal standards for the CDL testing program, or with any other terms of the third-party contract.

Exemption of Skills Testing Requirements

States have the option to exempt certain individuals with good driving records from the skills testing requirement (commonly referred to as "grandfathering"). The State shall impose conditions and limitations to restrict the applicants from whom a State may accept alternative requirements for the skills test described in 49 CFR 383.113. Such conditions must require at least the following:

- Driver has a current license at time of application; and Driver has a good driving record and previously passed an acceptable skills test; or driver has a **Good Driving Record** in combination with certain **Driving Experience**.

"Good Driving Record" Means:

A driver can certify that, during the 2-year period immediately prior to applying for a CDL he/she:

- Has not had more than one license;
- Has not had any license suspended, revoked, or canceled;
- Has not had any convictions in any type of motor vehicle for a major disqualifying offense defined in 49 CFR 383.51(b);

- Has not had more than one conviction for any type of motor vehicle for a serious traffic violation defined in 49 CFR 383.51(c);
- Has not had any violation of State or local law relating to motor vehicle traffic control arising in connection with any traffic accident, and has no record of an accident in which he/she was at fault.

"Driving Experience" Means:

A driver can certify and provide evidence that:

- He/she is regularly employed in a job requiring operation of CMV, and that either:
- He/she has previously taken and passed a skills test given by a State with a classified licensing and testing system, and that the test was behind-the-wheel in a representative vehicle for that applicant's driver's license classification; or
- He/she has operated a representative vehicle for at least 2 years immediately preceding application for a CDL.

Regulations on Record Keeping and Retention

State Standards for Certifications and Record Checks

When an individual applies for a CDL, or attempts to renew or update a CDL, the State must perform a check of:

- Its own records database
- The Commercial Driver's License Information System (CDLIS) (see Appendix 3)
- The National Driver Register (NDR) (see Appendix 3)

These checks are performed to ensure the driver is not disqualified and does not possess a license from more than one jurisdiction. If the driver possesses a license from another jurisdiction, the State must require the driver applicant to surrender his/her driver's license issued by that State before issuing a new license.

The State must request the complete driving record of the applicant from all jurisdictions where the driver was previously licensed in the past 10 years. This is held by the **State of Record** (SOR) for currently licensed drivers.

Record Data Retention

Record keeping for the records of commercial drivers or drivers who are operating a commercial vehicle is much different than record keeping for non-commercial drivers.

Per The Code of Federal Regulations 49 CFR §383.51 states must follow minimum standards that spell out how long certain convictions and withdrawals must be maintained and the reporting requirements for the Commercial Driver License Information System (CDLIS). These minimum retention periods apply to convictions and withdrawals incurred by a driver operating a CMV, and by CDL holders operating any motor vehicle. State jurisdictions may longer choose retention periods; in fact some states have never purged their database. Both the CMVSA and MCSIA (reviewed in Appendix 2) played a significant role in defining the regulations within 49 CFR §383.51.

A key factor is that the records of convictions and withdrawals must be kept by the state where the most recent license was issued. Thus, when a driver moves from one state to another, the driver's new state of record (SOR) will receive and maintain any records sent from the previous state. It is important that the SOR maintain the retention period for two reasons: 1) if the conviction data determines the length of a disqualification; 2) if accumulated convictions over time could lead to a disqualification.

The categories below indicate the minimum time a conviction or withdrawal must be retained from the conviction date for CDL or CMV-related convictions. Refer to the lists of the specific convictions considered **Major** or **Serious** as presented later in this Appendix.

CDL Data Retention Table

- **Major Convictions** ....55 years
  - An exception to this rule applies to a second conviction for the "Use of a commercial motor vehicle in the commission of a felony involving manufacturing, distributing, or dispensing a controlled substance." This conviction must be kept on the record for life.

- **Serious Convictions** ....4 years
- **Railroad Grade Crossing Convictions** ....4 years
- **Out-of-Service Convictions** ....15 years
- **All Other Convictions** ....3 year minimum
- **Withdrawal Actions** ....The length of time conviction is kept as specified in the tables above

Regulations on CDL Disqualifications

Per the Code of Federal Regulations 49 CFR §383.51, jurisdictions are required to impose a disqualification on CDL holder and persons required to have a CDL who have been convicted of certain offenses. This summary of these rules are categorized in alphabetical order as follows—

1. Failing to Surrender the HAZMAT Endorsement
2. Falsify Offense
3. Imminent Hazard Disqualification
4. Major Offenses
5. Railroad-Highway Grade Crossing Offenses
6. Serious Offenses
7. Violating of Out-of-Service Orders

Each of the seven categories table indicates the specific offenses, the disqualifications, and the ACD code(s) involved.

Major Offenses Table

Keep in mind that some of the offenses apply to any driver operating a CMV, some to a CDL holder operating any motor vehicle, and some specific to a CDL holder operating a CMV.

Major Offenses	Disqualifications
1. Driving a motor vehicle while under the influence of alcohol as prescribed by state law (A08, A10, A11[Where BAC $\geq$.08], A20, A21, A23, A90, A91 [Where BAC $\geq$.08], and A98) 2. Driving a motor vehicle while under the influence of a controlled substance (A20, A22, A23) 3. Driving a commercial motor vehicle while the person's blood alcohol concentration is 0.04% or more (A04, A11[When BAC >.04 but<.08], A91[When BAC >.04 but<.08], and A94) 4. Refusing to take an alcohol or drug test as required by a State or jurisdiction under its implied consent laws or regulations as defined in § 383.72 (after operating a motor vehicle) (A12) 5. Leaving the scene of an accident (driving a motor vehicle) (B01, B02, B03, B04, B05, B06, B07, and B08) 6. A felony involving the use of a motor vehicle, other than as described in #9 in this table. (U03) 7. Driving a commercial motor vehicle when as a result of prior violations committed operating a CMV, the driver's CDL is revoked, suspended, or canceled, or the driver is disqualified from operating a CMV (B20, B21, B22, B23, B24, B25, and B26 [see section 3.2.96.2] — the CMV Indicator must equal '1') 8. Causing a fatality through the negligent operation of a commercial motor vehicle, including but not limited to the crimes of motor vehicle manslaughter, homicide by motor vehicle, and negligent homicide (U07, U08, U09, and U10 — the CMV Indicator must equal '1') 9. Use of a motor vehicle in the commission of a felony involving manufacturing, distributing, or dispensing a controlled substance (A50)	**For 1st Major Offense:** • 1 year Disqualification - if the vehicle <u>was not</u> transporting hazardous materials required to be placarded • 3 years Disqualification - if the vehicle was transporting hazardous materials required to be placarded **2nd and separate incident of any major offense:** • Lifetime disqualification, but eligible for 10 year reinstatement (W40) **Incident after reinstatement** • Lifetime disqualification, not eligible for reinstatement (W41) **For Conviction Group 9** • Lifetime disqualification, not eligible for 10 year reinstatement (A50)

Serious Offenses Table

The following offenses are classified as "serious" and carry a different set of disqualification mandates.

Serious Offenses	Disqualifications
1. Speeds excessively, involving any speed of 15 mph or more above the posted speed limit (S15, S16, S21, S26, S36, S41, S71, S81, S91, S92 [if detail on S92 shows >15 over limit] 2. Drives recklessly, as defined by State or local law or regulation, including but not limited to offenses of driving a motor vehicle in willful or wanton disregard for the safety of persons or property (M84) 3. Makes improper or erratic traffic lane changes (M42)	**For 1st Conviction:** • No disqualification **2nd and separate incident of any offense in this table, during a 3 year period:** • 60 days disqualification (W30)

4. Follows the vehicle ahead too closely (M34) 5. Violates State or local law relating to motor vehicle traffic control arising in connection with a fatal accident (U31) 6. Driving a CMV without obtaining a CDL (B56) 7. Driving a CMV without a current CDL in the driver's possession (B51) 8. Driving a CMV without the proper class of CDL and/or endorsements for the specific vehicle group being operated or for the passengers or type of cargo being transported (B91)	**3rd or subsequent conviction of any incident of any offense in this table, during a 3 year period:** • 120 days disqualification (W31)

Imminent Hazard Disqualification Table

FMCSA has the authority to remove a CDL holder's driving privileges by determining the driver is an imminent hazard, which it defines as "the existence of a condition that presents a substantial likelihood that death, serious illness, severe personal injury, or a substantial endangerment to health, property, or the environment may occur before the completion date of a formal proceeding begun to lessen the risk of that death, illness, injury or endangerment" (49 CFR §382.52).

The imminent hazard rule in 49 CFR §383.52 specifies the periods for which a driver may be disqualified.

Imminent Hazard Disqualification	Disqualifications
Allowing the driver to continue to operate a commercial motor vehicle would create an imminent hazard (*W70*).	Emergency disqualification because driver posed an imminent hazard (W70) – up to 1 year disqualification

Railroad-Highway Grade Crossing Offenses Table

These offenses receive their own classification.

Railroad-Highway Grade Crossing Offenses	Disqualifications
If the driver operates a commercial motor vehicle in violation of a federal, state or local law and: 1. The driver is not required to always stop, but fails to slow down and check that tracks are clear of an approaching train (M20) 2. The driver is not required to always stop, but fails to stop before reaching the crossing, if the tracks are not clear (M21) 3. The driver is always required to stop, but fails to stop before driving onto the crossing (M22) 4. The driver fails to have sufficient space to drive completely through the crossing without stopping (M23) 5. The driver fails to obey a traffic control device or the directions of an enforcement official at the crossing (M10) 6. The driver fails to negotiate a crossing because of insufficient under-carriage clearance (M24)	For 1st Conviction: • No less than 60 days For 2nd Conviction of any offense in this table in a separate incident within a 3-year period: • No less than 120 days CMV disqualification (W60) 3rd or subsequent conviction of any offense in this table in a separate incident within a 3-year period: • No less than 1 year CMV disqualification (W61) **Note:** An employer who is convicted of a violation of a Federal, State, or local law or regulation, pertaining to railroad-highway grade crossings must be subject to a civil penalty of not more than $10,000.

Violating Out-of-Service Orders Table

These offenses receive their own classification.

Violating Out of Service Orders	Disqualifications
1. Driving while out of service order is in effect and transporting 16 or more passengers, including the driver and/or transporting hazardous materials that require a placard (B19) 2. General driving while out of service order is in effect (for violations not covered by B19) (B27)	For 1st Conviction in a HAZMAT CMV and/or a Passenger CMV (B19): • 180 days to 2 year disqualification (B19) For 1st Conviction in a CMV that was not a Passenger CMV or a HAZMAT CMV (B27) • 180 days to 2 year disqualification (B19)

Other Penalties:	For 2nd Conviction of a separate incident of an offense in this table, during a 10 year period in a HAZMAT CMV and/or a Passenger CMV (B19):
A driver who is convicted of violating an out-of-service order shall be subject to a civil penalty of not less than $2,500 for a first conviction and not less than $5,000 for a second or subsequent conviction, in addition to disqualification under §383.51(e). An employer who is convicted of a violation of an out-of-service order shall be subject to a civil penalty of not less than $2,750 nor more than $25,000.	• 3 year to five disqualification (W51) For 2nd Conviction of a separate incident of an offense in this table, during a 10 year period in a CMV that was not a Passenger CMV or a HAZMAT CMV (B27) • 2 year to five disqualification (W50) For 3rd Conviction of a separate incident of an offense in this table, during a 10 year period • 3 to 5 year disqualification (W52)

Falsify Offense Table

The rule in 49 CFR §383.73(g) specifies the period for which a driver must be disqualified for a conviction of a falsify offense.

False Offense	Disqualifications
Misrepresentation of identity or other facts on application for driver license (includes DL, CDL, and Instruction Permit) (D02)	60 days disqualification (D02)

Failing to Surrender the HAZMAT Endorsement Table

The rule in 49 CFR §383.141(c) specifies that a driver who does not successfully complete the Transportation Security Administration security threat assessment process may not be issued a hazardous materials endorsement.

Failing to Surrender the HAZMAT Endorsement	Disqualifications
Failure to surrender HAZMAT endorsement as required by the USA PATRIOT Act (W09)	Indefinite disqualification until CDL with HAZMAT endorsement is surrendered (W09)

Other Requirements of Note

States must also meet other requirements related to commercial driver's license holders and motor carriers.

BAC Standards

The FMCSA has established 0.04% as the blood alcohol concentration (BAC) level at or above which a CDL commercial motor vehicle operator who is required to have a CDL is deemed to be driving under the influence of alcohol and subject to the disqualification sanctions in the Federal regulations. Most States have established a BAC level of .08% as the level at or above which a person operating a non-commercial motor vehicle is deemed to be driving under the influence of alcohol.

Employer Notifications

Within 30 days of a conviction for any traffic violation, except parking, a driver must notify his/her employer, regardless of the nature of the violation or the type of vehicle which was driven at the time.

If a driver's license is suspended, revoked, canceled, or if he/she is disqualified from driving, his/her employer must be notified. The notification must be made by the end of the next business day following receipt of the notice of the suspension, revocation, cancellation, lost privilege or disqualification.

Employers may not knowingly use a driver who has more than one license or whose license is suspended, revoked or canceled, or is disqualified from driving. Violation of this requirement may result in civil or criminal penalties.

Notification of Previous Employment

All employers shall request and all person's applying for employment as a commercial motor vehicle operator shall provide, employment history information for the 10 years preceding the date the application is submitted. The request shall be made at the time of application for employment.

The Driver's Privacy Protection Act (DPPA)

The Driver's Privacy Protection Act (DPPA), named for Title XXXI "Protection of Privacy of Information in State Motor Vehicle Records," was signed into law by President Clinton in 1994. The intent of this law is to protect the personal privacy of persons licensed to drive.

DPPA prohibits disclosure of personal information from state driver history, vehicle registration and title files, EXCEPT for 14 specific **Permissible Uses**. The Act also defines *Personal Information* and *Highly Restricted Personal Information*. In general, the Permissible Use list permits ongoing, legitimate businesses and individuals to obtain full record data on their promise to follow compliance procedures.

States may choose not to adopt all 14 Permissible Uses listed in the DPPA, or may choose to adopt even more stringent policies. Each state chapter within this book indicates which of the 14 permissible uses that a particular state has adopted or not adopted. Also indicated is if the state has stricter rulemaking.

Keep in mind DPPA does not limit who can or cannot access motor vehicle records. Instead it dictates or limits who can access records containing personal information. A state may choose to sell driving records without personal information to a requester with a non-permissible use, or a state may not release any information to a casual requester unless the subject's signed release is presented as consent.

A 2000 amendment (Public Law 106-60, AKA the FY 2000 DOT Appropriations Act) to DPPA modified Section 350 of the DPPA. The amendment replaced the "opt-out" provision with and an "opt-in" policy, and defined sensitive personal information.

Below is the Driver's Privacy Protection Act, including the permissible uses, as modified by Public Law 106-69.

The Driver's Privacy Protection Act:

§2721 Prohibition on release and use of certain personal information from State motor vehicle records

(a) In General. - A State department of motor vehicles, and any officer, employee, or contractor thereof, shall not knowingly disclose or otherwise make available to any person or entity:

   (1) personal information, as defined in 18 U.S.C. 2725 (3), about any individual obtained by the department in connection with a motor vehicle record, except as provided in subsection (b) of this section; or

   (2) highly restricted personal information, as defined in 18 U.S.C. 2725 (4), about any individual obtained by the department in connection with a motor vehicle record, without the express consent of the person to whom such information applies, except uses permitted in subsections (b)(1), (b)(4), (b)(6), and (b)(9): Provided, That subsection (a)(2) shall not in any way affect the use of organ donation information on an individual's driver's license or affect the administration of organ donation initiatives in the States.

(b) Permissible Uses. - Personal information referred to in subsection (a) shall be disclosed for use in connection with matters of motor vehicle or driver safety and theft, motor vehicle emissions, motor vehicle product alterations, recalls, or advisories, performance monitoring of motor vehicles and dealers by motor vehicle manufacturers, and removal of non-owner records from the original owner records of motor vehicle manufacturers to carry out the purposes of titles I and IV of the Anti Car Theft Act of 1992, the Automobile Information Disclosure Act (15 U.S.C. 1231 et seq.), the Clean Air Act (42 U.S.C. 7401 et seq.), and chapters 301, 305, and 321-331 of title 49, and, subject to subsection (a)(2), may be disclosed as follows:

   (1) For use by any government agency, including any court or law enforcement agency, in carrying out its functions, or any private person or entity acting on behalf of a Federal, State, or local agency in carrying out its functions.

   (2) For use in connection with matters of motor vehicle or driver safety and theft; motor vehicle emissions; motor vehicle product alterations, recalls, or advisories; performance monitoring of motor vehicles, motor vehicle parts and dealers; motor vehicle market research activities, including survey research; and removal of non-owner records from the original owner records of motor vehicle manufacturers.

(3) For use in the normal course of business by a legitimate business or its agents, employees, or contractors, but only-

    (A) to verify the accuracy of personal information submitted by the individual to the business or its agents, employees, or contractors; and

    (B) if such information as so submitted is not correct or is no longer correct, to obtain the correct information, but only for the purposes of preventing fraud by, pursuing legal remedies against, or recovering on a debt or security interest against, the individual.

(4) For use in connection with any civil, criminal, administrative, or arbitral proceeding in any Federal, State, or local court or agency or before any self-regulatory body, including the service of process, investigation in anticipation of litigation, and the execution or enforcement of judgments and orders, or pursuant to an order of a Federal, State, or local court.

(5) For use in research activities, and for use in producing statistical reports, so long as the personal information is not published, redisclosed, or used to contact individuals.

(6) For use by any insurer or insurance support organization, or by a self-insured entity, or its agents, employees, or contractors, in connection with claims investigation activities, antifraud activities, rating or underwriting.

(7) For use in providing notice to the owners of towed or impounded vehicles.

(8) For use by any licensed private investigative agency or licensed security service for any purpose permitted under this subsection.

(9) For use by an employer or its agent or insurer to obtain or verify information relating to a holder of a commercial driver's license that is required under chapter 313 of title 49.

(10) For use in connection with the operation of private toll transportation facilities.

(11) For any other use in response to requests for individual motor vehicle records if the State has obtained the express consent of the person to whom such personal information pertains.

(12) For bulk distribution for surveys, marketing or solicitations if the State has obtained the express consent of the person to whom such personal information pertains.

(13) For use by any requester, if the requester demonstrates it has obtained the written consent of the individual to whom the information pertains.

(14) For any other use specifically authorized under the law of the State that holds the record, if such use is related to the operation of a motor vehicle or public safety.

(c) Resale or Redisclosure. - An authorized recipient of personal information (except a recipient under subsection (b)(11) or (12)) may resell or redisclose the information only for a use permitted under subsection (b) (but not for uses under subsection (b)(11) or (12)). An authorized recipient under subsection (b)(11) may resell or redisclose personal information for any purpose. An authorized recipient under subsection (b)(12) may resell or redisclose personal information pursuant to subsection (b)(12). Any authorized recipient (except a recipient under subsection (b)(11)) that resells or rediscloses personal information covered by this chapter must keep for a period of 5 years records identifying each person or entity that receives information and the permitted purpose for which the information will be used and must make such records available to the motor vehicle department upon request.

(d) Waiver Procedures. - A State motor vehicle department may establish and carry out procedures under which the department or its agents, upon receiving a request for personal information that does not fall within one of the exceptions in subsection (b), may mail a copy of the request to the individual about whom the information was requested, informing such individual of the request, together with a statement to the effect that the information will not be released unless the individual waives such individual's right to privacy under this section.

(e) Prohibition on Conditions. - No State may condition or burden in any way the issuance of an individual's motor vehicle record as defined in 18 U.S.C. 2725 (1) to obtain express consent. Nothing in this paragraph shall be construed to prohibit a State from charging an administrative fee for issuance of a motor vehicle record.

§ 2722 Additional unlawful acts

(a) Procurement for Unlawful Purpose. - It shall be unlawful for any person knowingly to obtain or disclose personal information, from a motor vehicle record, for any use not permitted under section 2721 (b) of this title.

(b) False Representation. - It shall be unlawful for any person to make false representation to obtain any personal information from an individual's motor vehicle record.

§ 2723 Penalties

(a) Criminal Fine.- A person who knowingly violates this chapter shall be fined under this title.

(b) Violations by State Department of Motor Vehicles.- Any State department of motor vehicles that has a policy or practice of substantial noncompliance with this chapter shall be subject to a civil penalty imposed by the Attorney General of not more than $5,000 a day for each day of substantial noncompliance.

§ 2724 Civil action

(a) Cause of Action. - A person who knowingly obtains, discloses or uses personal information, from a motor vehicle record, for a purpose not permitted under this chapter shall be liable to the individual to whom the information pertains, who may bring a civil action in a United States district court.

(b) Remedies.- The court may award-

(1) actual damages, but not less than liquidated damages in the amount of $2,500;

(2) punitive damages upon proof of willful or reckless disregard of the law;

(3) reasonable attorneys' fees and other litigation costs reasonably incurred; and

(4) such other preliminary and equitable relief as the court determines to be appropriate.

§ 2725 Definitions - In this chapter-

(1) "motor vehicle record" means any record that pertains to a motor vehicle operator's permit, motor vehicle title, motor vehicle registration, or identification card issued by a department of motor vehicles;

(2) "person" means an individual, organization or entity, but does not include a State or agency thereof;

(3) "personal information" means information that identifies an individual, including an individual's photograph, social security number, driver identification number, name, address (but not the 5-digit zip code), telephone number, and medical or disability information, but does not include information on vehicular accidents, driving violations, and driver's status;

(4) "highly restricted personal information" means an individual's photograph or image, social security number, medical or disability information; and

(5) "express consent" means consent in writing, including consent conveyed electronically that bears an electronic signature as defined in section 106(5) of Public Law 106-229.

Key Agencies, Agreements and Programs

The following are reviewed herein—

- The American Association of Motor Vehicle Administrators (AAMVA)
- The National Driver Register (NDR)
- Other Agencies of Note are Listed
- Commercial Driver License Information System (CDLIS)
- Driver License Agreement (DLA)
- Driver License Compact (DLC)
- Electronic Lien and Title (ELT)
- International Registration Plan (IRP)
- National Motor Vehicle Title Information System (NMVTIS)
- Non-Resident Violator Compact (NRVC)
- Pre-Employment Screening Program (PSP)
- Problem Driver Pointer System (PDPS)

Agencies

Editor's Note: Of course the U.S. Department of Transportation and the Federal Motor Carrier Safety Administration (FMCSA) play a significant role regarding motor vehicle records. See information about FMCSA in Appendix 1.

The American Association of Motor Vehicle Administrators (AAMVA)

The American Association of Motor Vehicle Administrators (AAMVA) is the non-profit organization that develops and coordinates model programs in the administration motor vehicle matters, law enforcement and highway safety. Founded in 1933, AAMVA members are administrators and public service executives who are responsible for motor vehicle administration, driver licensing issues, and the enforcement of state and national laws that govern the safe use of vehicles in the United States and Canada. Members also include corporate partners and representatives from other associations.

AAMVA is recognized as the **leading authority** on driver license, vehicle title, motor carrier, highway safety, security, identification and enforcement practice issues. AAMVA plays a very important role in helping the states implement the changes demanded by Congressional legislation that affect the motor vehicle industry. Examples include the Driver's Privacy Protection Act (DPPA), the Commercial Motor Vehicle Safety Act of 1986 (CMVSA), and the Motor Carrier Safety Improvement Act of 1999 (MCSIA).

The programs and agreements profiled later in this section are administered to a large degree by AAMVA.

AAMVA can be reached at 4310 Wilson Blvd #400, Arlington, VA 22203, 703-522-4200, www.aamva.org.

The National Driver Register (NDR)

The National Driver Register (NDR) is a national repository for information on problem drivers. NDR functions under the control of the National Highway Traffic Safety Administration, an agency of the U.S. Department of Transportation.

One purpose of NDR is to prevent the issuance of a driver's license to drivers whose licenses have been withdrawn or denied. State motor vehicle agencies provide NDR with names of individuals who have lost their driving privilege or who have been convicted of a serious traffic offense. When a person applies for a driver's license, a state will first check to see if subject name is on the NDR file. This will determine if the applicant has revocations, suspensions, denials or cancellations in other states. This system is called the Problem Driver Pointer System (PDPS). PDPS is reviewed on later pages,

Access to the NDR is not limited to state motor vehicle agencies. There are 7 named groups who can obtain information, plus the license holder. For example, an individual may request a NDR file check per the provisions of the U.S. Privacy Act.

While an employer make check the NDR file on a current or prospective employee, the employer must go to the local motor vehicle agency and ask for an NDR file check. The NDR web page provides the Current or Prospective Employee Form which can be downloaded and then completed by the employee. This form should be submitted to the State in which the employee is licensed. Any information on the NDR file that was reported by the states during the past 3 years will be disclosed. Any information received from the NDR should also be made available to the employee.

The National Driver Register can be reached at USDOT/NHTSA West Bldg, NVS-422, 1200 New Jersey Avenue, SE Washington, DC 20590, 202-366-4800 or 888-851-0436. www.nhtsa.gov/Data/National+Driver+Register+(NDR)

Other Selected Agencies of Note

There are many private organizations and non-for-profits involved with motor vehicle records. The six organizations listed below are very influential in motor vehicle matters and/or use driving records to a large degree. Collectively their members represent the majority of all entities in the private sector using driving records.

- **The American Trucking Associations - ATA -** www.truckline.com
- **The American Insurance Association - AIA -** www.aiadc.org
- **Property and Casualty Insurers Association of America (PCI) -** www.pciaa.net
- **National Association of Mutual Insurance Companies (NAMIC) -** www.namic.org
- **The Insurance Institute for Highway Safety (IIHS) -** www.iihs.org
- **National Association of Professional Background Screeners (NAPBS) -** www.napbs.com

Agreements and Programs

Commercial Driver License Information System (CDLIS)

The Commercial Motor Vehicle Safety Act of 1986 (CMVSA) established a Commercial Driver License Information System (CDLIS) to serve as a cooperative clearinghouse of information related to all U.S. commercial drivers.

CDLIS supports the issuance of commercial driver licenses by determining if a license applicant holds a commercial license (and history) elsewhere and to determine if withdrawals, denials, suspensions, etc., exist in other states.

CDLIS is actually an index or pointer file – not a complete database with historical records. A central site holds and index with basic identification information about each licensed commercial driver. This data includes the name, DOB, SSN, state driver license number, and AKA information, and the current State of Record (SOR).

When a state queries CDLIS to obtain information about an applicant prior to issuing a CDL, the CDLIS Central Site compares data provided by the State of Inquiry (SOI) against all records in CDLIS. If one or more matches are returned, then the CDLIS Central Site "points" the SOI to the State of Records (SOR). The SOR can then provide the detailed information about the driver's commercial driving history.

According to a recent estimate, the CDLIS index contains at least 14.1 million records.

The communications network that links the states to the CDLIS index and to the NDR is managed by AAMVA. All states use the AAMVA Code Dictionary (ACD) as the means to exchange and translate information among one another and with NDR.

See www.nationaldriverregister-forms.org/ndr/information/commercial_driver_s_license_information_system_cdlis.html or www.fmcsa.dot.gov/registration-licensing/cdl/cdl.htm.

Driver License Agreement (DLA)

At present, the DLC and NRVC Compacts are being revised and combined into a new Driver License Agreement (DLA). In an effort to truly establish a one driver one record license system, the new DLA will be a more efficient and effective agreement for the jurisdictions to share and transmit driver and conviction information.

In 2002, the Connecticut legislature enabled Connecticut to become a member of DLA. Also, Nevada passed a administrative rule to become a member. Although the DLA will take effect once two jurisdictions officially join, this new Agreement will not become reality until the states resolve issues associated with funding and the REAL ID ACT. It will probably take a number of years before all issues are resolved and all jurisdictions become members. During this transition period, the DLC and NRVC will remain in effect.

Driver License Compact (DLC)

The DLC, developed in 1961, gives states the means for a cooperative method to control problem drivers through the use of consistent reporting devices and the exchange of information contained in driver records. The Compact procedures include the reporting of convictions for major moving violations to a driver's home state and requiring the surrender of all other states' driver licenses before the issuance of a new license.

Thus, the major objective is to promote the one driver license and one record concept. The DLC members use PDPS (run by NDR), which serves as a national index of problem drivers. Member states voluntarily contribute information concerning driver license suspensions and revocations to the NDR. Then the NDR will, in turn, transmit data, upon request, to other states. 46 U.S. jurisdictions are members of the DLC. Non-members are Georgia, Massachusetts, Michigan, Tennessee, and Wisconsin. Note that non-members of the Compact may still comply with the procedures.

Electronic Lien and Title (ELT)

Electronic Lien and Title (ELT) is the paperless means that lien holders and state motor vehicle agencies use to exchange motor vehicle lien and title information. AAMVA developed the standards for exchanging motor vehicle information which ELT uses to simplify lien information exchanges between participating lien holders and motor vehicle agencies. Instead of printing a title and forwarding it to the lien holder, the state sends an electronic lien message. The lien holder stores the message electronically instead of filing the paper title. If there is an error, the lien holder will be able to notify the motor vehicle agency immediately. When the lien is satisfied, the lien holder sends a message to the state to release the lien. The state prints the title and sends it to the vehicle owner.

International Registration Plan (IRP)

The International Registration Plan (IRP) is a registration reciprocity agreement for licensing fees for commercial motor vehicles among U.S. states and provinces of Canada. The IRP, an organized entity belonging to AAMVA, acts as an agreement among the license-issuing jurisdictions. The IRP provides for payment of license fees on the basis of fleet miles operated in various jurisdictions.

The Plan authorizes proportional registration of commercial vehicles and for the recognition of such registrations in the participating jurisdictions. A carrier registers in a single "base jurisdiction." Fees for the vehicles are then calculated for each IRP jurisdiction according to the jurisdiction's unique fee requirements, then apportioned based on the percentage of total miles declared in that jurisdiction. For each vehicle, a carrier receives one license plate and one cab card listing each jurisdiction where the vehicle is registered. All IRP members are bound to recognize these documents as authorization for vehicles to operate in the jurisdictions specified. The base jurisdiction is responsible for collecting and distributing the fees.

The agreement affects all apportionable vehicles which "are any vehicles except for recreational vehicles, vehicles displaying restricted plates, city pick up and delivery vehicles, buses used in transportation of chartered parties, and government-owned vehicles, used or intended for use in two or more member jurisdictions that allocate or proportionally register vehicles and is used for the transportation of persons for hire or designed, used or maintained primarily for the transportation of property and:

1. is a power unit having two axles and a gross vehicle weight or registered gross vehicle weight in excess of 26,000 pounds or 11,793.401 kilograms; or
2. is a power unit having three or more axles, regardless of weight; or
3. is used in combination, when the weight of such combination exceeds 26,000 pounds or 11,793.401 kilograms gross vehicle weight.

Trucks and truck tractors, and combinations of vehicles having a gross vehicle weight of 26,000 pounds or 11,793.401 kilograms or less and buses used in transportation of chartered parties may be proportionally registered at the option of the registrant."

For more information about IRP visit www.irponline.org/.

National Motor Vehicle Title Information System (NMVTIS)

The Anti Car Theft Act of 1992 (Public Law 102-519, H.R. 4542) established a model for the National Motor Vehicle Title Information System (NMVTIS). The NMVTIS provides information to the states, law enforcement, prospective purchasers, and insurance carriers in order to reliably verify information on a vehicle prior to issuing a new title. NMVTIS is designed to protect consumers from fraud and unsafe vehicles and to keep stolen vehicles from being resold. NMVTIS is a DOJ program and DOJ is fully responsible for NMVTIS policy and operations. The American Association of Motor Vehicle Administrators (AAMVA) has acted as the third-party operator since inception and operates the system today.

Per the NMVTIS web page, 33 states participate, 8 states provide data only and 10 are in development. Currently 88% of DMV data is in NMVTIS system. NMVTIS records provide:

- current and previous state of title data

- title issue date
- latest odometer data
- theft history data (if any)
- any brand assigned to a vehicle and date applied
- salvage history, including designations as a "total loss" (if any)

Consumers can request vehicle history information through NMVTIS by selecting an approved service provider. Current fees range from approximately $2 to $7 per report. See www.vehiclehistory.gov or www.nmvtis.gov

Non-Resident Violator Compact (NRVC)

The purpose of the NRVC is to standardize methods used by a state to process non-resident violators receiving citations, and the violators' failure to appear or comply with an outstanding traffic summons.

The NRVC enables a participating jurisdiction (state) to inform another when a driver is cited out-of-state and has not complied with the terms of the citation. If the terms of the citation are not met (such as failure to pay traffic ticket), then the home state of the violator may suspend the licensee. Thus, the out-of-state citations affected include not only major violations, but also moving traffic violations that do not necessarily carry an automatic suspension or revocation.

The exchange of information governed by this Compact applies to citations for traffic offenses issued to all drivers. NRVC should not be confused with the exchange that occurs in the CDLIS (Commercial Drivers License Information System). 45 U.S. jurisdictions are members. Non-members are Alaska, California, Michigan, Montana, Oregon, and Wisconsin. Some of the non-member states will participate in the exchange of information for specific circumstances.

Pre-Employment Screening Program (PSP)

The Pre-Employment Screening Program (PSP), administered by the Federal Motor Carrier Safety Administration, helps motor carriers make more informed hiring decisions by providing electronic access to a driver's crash and inspection history from the FMCSA Motor Carrier Management Information System (MCMIS). Driver Information Resource records purchased through PSP contain the most recent 5 years of crash data and 3 years of roadside inspection data from the MCMIS system.

Records are available for 24 hours a day via the Web. NIC is the designated third party that manages the program, including the online access and retrieval of records. Through NIC, motor carriers may request driver information proving the driver has given written consent. Individual drivers may request their own driver information record at any time. The fee for this service is $10.00 for each requested driver history. There is an annual subscription fee of $100.00but carriers with fewer than 100 power units qualify for a discounted annual fee of $25.00 per year. Individuals can request a personal driving history for the same $10.00 fee; no subscription is necessary for individual drivers.

For more information, visit www.psp.fmcsa.dot.gov.

Problem Driver Pointer System (PDPS)

The Problem Driver Pointer System (PDPS) is used to search the National Driver Register index. Based on the search of identification data on problem drivers, the PDPS "points" to the state of record(s) (SOR) where an individual's driver status and history information is stored. Based on the information received from the SOR, the issuing state will decide if the applicant is eligible to receive a new or renew his driver license.

States report within 31 days to the NDR any individual—

1. Who is denied a motor vehicle driver's license for cause;
2. Whose motor vehicle driver's license is canceled, revoked, or suspended for cause;
3. Who is convicted of the following motor vehicle related or comparable offenses:
   a. Operation of a motor vehicle under the influence of, or impaired by, alcohol or a controlled substance;
   b. A traffic violation arising in connection with a fatal traffic crash, reckless driving, or racing on the highways;
   c. Failure to render aid or provide identification when involved in a crash which results in a fatality or personal injury;
   d. Perjury or the knowingly making of a false affidavit or statement to officials in connection with activities governed by a law or regulation relating to the operation of a motor vehicle.

Although states may submit an inquiry on any license applicant, they are required to query the PDPS each first-time, above minimum age driver license applicant before issuing a license to the applicant. States are required to submit inquires on behalf of entities authorized to access the NDR.

State Driver License Format and Driving Record Fees

Three Important Facts...

1. Additional fees are often charged for an online subscription accounts. These sign-up and/or annual fees usually range from $35 to $100 per year, but they can be higher. For example, in California there can be a one-time fee of $10,000.

2. Several states charge different fees if a licensee is obtaining his or her own driving record.

3. *SSN = Per federal law, the SSN has been phased out as a driver license number. However, some states may still have a few of the older DL documents with an SSN in circulation, as indicated.

State	License Format	Electronic Fee	Mail-in Fee	Walk-in Fee
Alabama	7#'s	7.75	5.75	5.75
Alaska	7#'s	10.00 (some vendors sell for 5.00)	10.00	10.00
Arizona	1 Let+8#'s or SSN*	5.00/ 6.00 - 39 month 6.00/8.00 - 5 year	3.00 - 39 month 5.00 - 5 year	3.00 - 39 month 5.00 - 5 year
Arkansas	9#'s or SSN*	8.50 - 3 year 11.50 - CDL	7.00 - 3 year 10.00 - CDL	7.00 - 3 year 10.00 - CDL
California	1 Let + 7#'s	2.00	5.00	n/a
Colorado	9#'s	2.00	2.20 / 2.70 cert	2.20 / 2.70 cert
Connecticut	9#'s	15.00	20.00	n/a except to person of record
Delaware	1-7#'s	15.00	15.00/20.00 cert	15.00/20.00 cert
District of Columbia	7#'s	13.00 - 10 yr only	7.00 - 3 year 13.00 - 10 year	7.00 - 3 year 13.00 -10 year
Florida	1 Let + 12#'s	8.00 - 3 year 10.00 - 7 year	8.00 - 3 year 10.00 -7 year or full	8.00 - 3 year 10.00 -7 year or full
Georgia	9#'s or SSN*	6.00 - 3 year 8.00 - 7 year	6.00 - 3 year 8.00 - 7 year	6.00 - 3 year 8.00 - 7 year
Hawaii	H + 8# or SSN*	23.00	20.00 / 9.00 if CDL	20.00 / 9.00 if CDL
Idaho	2 Let + 6 #s + 1 Let	9.00	7.00/21.00 cert	n/a
Illinois	1 Let + 11#'s	12.00	12.00	12.00
Indiana	10#'s	7.50	4.00 / 8.00 if complete	n/a
Iowa	9 digits or SSN or 3#-2Let-4#	8.50	5.50	5.50
Kansas	"K" + 8#'s	6.00 batch 6.60 interactive	10.00	10.00
Kentucky	1 Let + 8#s	5.00	3.00	3.00
Louisiana	0 + 8#'s	6.00	15.00	15.00
Maine	7#'s	7.00 - 3 year 12.00 - 12 year	5.00 - 3 year 10.00 - 10 year	5.00 - 3 year 10 - 10 year

State	License Format	Electronic Fee	Mail-in Fee	Walk-in Fee
Maryland	1 Let + 12#'s	12.00	9.00/12.00 cert	9.00/12.00 cert
Massachusetts	1 Let (usually S) + 8#'s	8.00	6.00/20.00 cert	6.00/20.00 cert
Michigan	1 Let + 12#'s	7.00	7.00/8.00 cert	n/a except to person of record
Minnesota	1 Let + 12#s	5.00	9.50/10.50 cert plus $1.00 per printed page	9.50/10.50 cert plus $1.00 per printed page
Mississippi	9 #'s or SSN*	14.00	11.00	11.00
Missouri	1 Let + 5-9#'s or 9#s or SSN*	No set fee per record. bulk purchase only	5.88	5.88 cert
Montana	13#'s or 9 digits or SSN*	7.25	4.00/10.00 cert	4.00/10.00 cert
Nebraska	1 Let + 3 to 8#'s	3.00	3.00	3.00
Nevada	10#s	7.00	7.00/11.00 cert	7.00/11.00 cert
New Hampshire	2#'s +3 Let +5#'s	12.00	15.00	15.00
New Jersey	1 Let + 14#'s	12.00	15.00	15.00
New Mexico	9#'s	6.50	No charge	No charge
New York	9#'s	7.00	10.00	10.00
North Carolina	1 to 12#'s	8.00	8.00/11.00 cert	8.00/11.00 cert
North Dakota	3 let + 6#'s or 9#'s or SSN*	3.00	3.00	3.00
Ohio	2 let + 6#'s	5.00	5.00	5.00/8.50
Oklahoma	One alpha+9#'s or SSN*	27.50	25.00/28.00 cert	25.00/28.00 cert
Oregon	Usually 7#'s can be 1-7#'s	9.68	1.50 3 year non-empl 2.00 3 year empl 3.00 court	Only at field offices, fee may vary.
Pennsylvania	8#'s	5.00	5.00/10.00 cert	5.00/10.00/cert
Rhode Island	7#'s or "V" + 6#'s	20.00	17.50	17.50
South Carolina	11#'s	7.25	6.00	6.00
South Dakota	8#'s or SSN or some old 6#'s	5.00	5.00	5.00
Tennessee	9#'s or 7-8 #'s (old)	7.00	5.00	5.00
Texas	8#'s	6.50/12.00 cert	6.00/10.00 or 20.00 cert	n/a
Utah	9#'s, can be 4-10#'s	9.00	6.00/10.75 cert	6.00/10.75 cert
Vermont	8#'s or 7#'s + "A"	15.00	13.00 3-year 16.00 complete/cert	13.00 3-year 16.00 complete/cert
Virginia	1 Let + 8#'s or SSN	7.00	8.00/13.00 cert	8.00/13.00 cert
Washington	5Let + 3# + 2Let or 2#	13.00	13.00	13.00
West Virginia	7 digits (1-2 let +5-6#'s)	9.00	5.00 / 6.00 cert (if DL not given add 1.00)	5.00 / 6.00 cert (if DL not given add 1.00)
Wisconsin	1 Let + 13#'s	5.00	7.00/12.00 cert	N/A
Wyoming	9#'s	5.00	5.00	5.00

1. Additional fees are often charged for an online subscription accounts. These sign-up and/or annual fees usually range fro~ $35 to $100 per year, but they can be higher. For example, in California there can be a one-time fee of $10,000.

2. Several states charge different fees if a licensee is obtaining his or her own driving record.

3. *SSN = Per federal law, the SSN has been phased out as a driver license number. However, some states may still have a fe~ of the older DL documents with an SSN, as indicated.

State Reciprocity of Conviction Information for Non-CDL Drivers

Note: There is true reciprocity between the states for drivers with a commercial driver's license (CDL)

State	Suspend Driver License for Unpaid Out-of-State Convictions?	Record of New Incoming Driver Shown on MVR?	Out-of-State Convictions Shown on MVR?	Conviction of Out-of-State Drivers Sent to Home State?	Record Forwarded to New State Upon Surrender of License?
Alabama	Yes	No	Yes	Yes	Not automatically
Alaska	No, but will cancel	Only majors	Yes	Only majors	Upon request
Arizona	Yes	No	Yes	Yes	Yes
Arkansas	Yes	Yes	Yes	Yes	Yes
California	No, but will not issue renewal	Yes	Yes	Yes	Yes
Colorado	Yes	No	Only majors	Yes	Not automatically
Connecticut	Yes, if FTA	No	Yes, if NRVC	Yes	Upon request
Delaware	Yes	Yes	Yes	Yes	If suspended, revoked, or if requested
District of Columbia	Yes	Yes	Yes	Yes	If suspended or revoked
Florida	Yes	Yes	Yes	Yes	Yes
Georgia	Yes	No	Yes	Yes	If requested
Hawaii	Yes	Yes	Yes	Yes	Yes
Idaho	Yes	No	Yes	Yes	Yes
Illinois	Yes, if NRVC state	No	Yes	Yes	Only if suspended or revoked or cancelled
Indiana	Yes	No	Yes	Yes	Upon request
Iowa	Yes	Yes	Yes	Yes	Yes
Kansas	Moving violations to NRVC states	Only Moving violations	Yes	Yes	Yes
Kentucky	Yes	No	Yes, except non-CDL speed violations	Yes	Yes
Louisiana	Yes	No	Yes	Yes	Upon request
Maine	Yes	Yes	Yes, if NRVC	Yes	Yes
Maryland	Yes	Yes	Yes	Yes	Upon request
Massachusetts	Yes, if NRVC state	Yes	Yes	Upon request	Upon request
Michigan	Yes	Yes	Yes	Yes	Yes
Minnesota	Yes	Yes	Yes	Yes	Yes

State	Suspend Driver License for Unpaid Out-of-State Convictions?	Record of New Incoming Driver Shown on MVR?	Out-of-State Convictions Shown on MVR?	Conviction of Out-of-State Drivers Sent to Home State?	Record Forwarded to New State Upon Surrender of License?
Mississippi	Yes	No	Yes	Yes	Upon Request
Missouri	May, it depends	No	Yes	Yes	Upon Request
Montana	No	Yes	Yes	Yes	Upon Request
Nebraska	Yes	No	Yes	Yes	Upon Request
Nevada	Yes	No	Yes, if moving violation	Yes	Upon Request
New Hampshire	Yes, if NRVC state	Yes	Yes	Yes	Upon Request
New Jersey	Yes	No	Moving violations only	Yes	Upon request
New Mexico	Yes	No	Yes	Yes	Upon request
New York	Yes in NRVC state	No	Only drug-, alcohol-, or fatality-related	Yes	Upon request
North Carolina	Yes	No	Yes	Yes	Upon request
North Dakota	Yes, if NRVC state	Only majors	Yes	Yes	Yes
Ohio	Yes	No	Certain majors or if unpaid	Yes	No, but will send to NDR
Oklahoma	Yes	Yes	Yes	Only moving violations	Yes
Oregon	Washington Only	Only majors	Yes	Only majors	Upon request
Pennsylvania	Yes, if NRVC state	No	Only Majors	Yes	Upon request
Rhode Island	Yes	Yes	Only Majors	Yes	Yes
South Carolina	Yes	Yes	Yes	Yes	Yes
South Dakota	Yes, if NRVC state	No	Yes, except speed	Yes	Yes
Tennessee	Yes	No	Yes	Yes	Upon request
Texas	Yes	No	Yes	Yes	Upon request
Utah	Yes, if NRVC state	Yes	Yes	Yes	Upon request
Vermont	Yes	Only Majors	Only Majors	If criminal suspension notice	Yes
Virginia	Yes, if NRVC state	Yes	Yes	Yes	Upon request
Washington	Yes	Only Certain Majors	Yes	Yes	Yes
West Virginia	Yes	Yes	Yes	Yes	Yes
Wisconsin	No	Yes	Yes	Yes	Yes
Wyoming	Yes, if NRVC state	Yes	Yes	Yes	Yes

About the Author

Michael Sankey has compiled and published this book annually since 1989. He has authored or edited over 75 publications and has more than 35 years of experience involving public record research and government record access.

Michael is the founder and CEO of BRB Publications, Inc. and he is also the Director of the Public Record Retriever Network (PRRN).

In the 1980's Michael was President of Rapid Info Services, a nationwide driving record provider.

Michael was part of the Steering Committee that founded the National Association of Professional Background Screeners (NAPBS). He was also elected to the first NAPBS Board of Directors in 2004 and served two years.

In the 1980's Michael was owner and President of Rapid Info Services, a nationwide driving record provider.

He is regarding as a leading industry expert in public records, criminal record access, state motor vehicle record policies and procedures, as well as knowing who's who in the commercial arena of public information vendors. His company web pages include www.brbpublications.com, www.prrn.us, www.CRAHelpDesk.com,and www.mvrdecoder.com.

Michael and his wife reside in Tempe, AZ and have two children in college. He can be reached at mike@brbpublications.com.